CONTEMPORARY
POETS

Contemporary Writers of the English Language

Contemporary Poets
Contemporary Novelists
  (including short story writers)
Contemporary Dramatists
Contemporary Literary Critics

CONTEMPORARY POETS

FOURTH EDITION

PREFACE TO THE FIRST EDITION
C. DAY LEWIS

PREFACE TO THE THIRD EDITION
MARJORIE PERLOFF

EDITORS
JAMES VINSON AND D.L. KIRKPATRICK

St J

ST. JAMES PRESS
LONDON AND CHICAGO

© St. James Press, 1985
All rights reserved. For information, write:
St. James Press, 3 Percy Street, London W1P 9FA
Printed at The Bath Press, Avon
First published in the U.K. in 1985
Reprinted 1988

ISBN 0-912289-30-9

CONTENTS

PREFACE
to the first edition

I have been asked to say something, by way of a preface, about what the writing and reading of poetry have meant to me in my own life. Writing it, which I did copiously from 14 or 15, must presently become either a way of life or a pleasant occasional pastime. For me it became the former: in my teens I wanted nothing so much as to be a Poet, and I firmly believed that I would never be capable of doing anything but write poetry: this is a good start, since it concentrates any powers one may have and sets up a strong initial momentum. Art cannot be a substitute for religion; but the habit of poetry has something in common with the habit of prayer—through it we search the unknown and search our own heart, to praise and to understand; we submit ourselves to a discipline which is partly a discipline of meditation and partly one of craft, of making language adapt itself to the conveying of states of mind incommunicable in any other way. The meditation and the craft are interfused, for his craft is the poet's mode of meditation.

Since words are what he works in, the young poet should always be extending his knowledge of them and of the way other poets have used them. He should read a page or two of the dictionary every day, as a priest reads his breviary. I wish I had done so myself. The colour, configuration, connotations of a single word may be the seed of a poem. Equally, he will read the work of poets living and dead, to learn what poetry is and gradually to understand how difficult it is to write a good poem. At school I read poetry because I wanted to be different, a one-man élite—it was a kind of social protest—Swinburne, Masefield, the early Yeats, and I was also attracted to Virgil, Wordsworth, Keats and Tennyson. What drew me—a raw, dreamy, provincial boy—was the sound of words, the shapes of lyric writing, the sense that I was on the brink of a glorious mystery, and my own feeling for nature reflected back and as it were justified by the poems of other men.

Just as in early manhood one makes the most lasting friendships, so one receives the strongest impressions from poetry: though I have admired many poets since my Oxford days, it is the ones I read there to whom I most often return: the later Yeats, Owen, Frost, Emily Dickinson, Hardy, the Meredith of *Modern Love*, Pope, the Metaphysicals. I was fortunate in getting to know a number of coaevals who wrote poetry. I was no less fortunate in being susceptible to their enthusiasms but not overwhelmed by them: Donne and Eliot were two of these; but, making nothing of them at first, I put them aside and was able to return to them later when I was ripe for them.

Most poets' reading is a desultory affair, not a diligent and orderly course of "required reading." The books he requires are those of poets who, at any given stage of his life, can offer him encouragement, new ways of approaching poetry and new technical possibilities which present both a challenge and a way in to some new phase of his own work. This is the meaning of tradition, the right use of influences. A mediating power.

I was also lucky to be one of a group (it was never consciously a "movement") of young men who came from not dissimilar environments and responded keenly to one another's work and to the weather of the times. A considerable momentum is set up when a group of poets is pulling in roughly the same direction: but the degree of the momentum cannot be gauged until each of the group has cast off from the others and is pursuing an individual course. That course is unpredictable. With certain poets—I am not one of them—hindsight reveals a continuity of development: my own work, though I can see its obsessive and recurrent themes, appears to me a hand-to-mouth affair—a seizing upon any subject which comes my way and trying to make something of it. "Making Something" of a subject means the deepening of its implications: but if one carries the deepening beyond what the subject will allow, the poem gets out of its depth and becomes an incoherent, echoing void filled with empty poeticisms.

One thing I have begun to learn from the reading and writing of poetry is level—the level at which a given poem should work. If we take such dissimilar objects as the writings of the Caroline poets and Clough's *Amours de Voyage*, we see how delicately these poets have adjusted their treatment to the weight of theme their verse can bear, never tempted into profundities where their subject would go astray and be lost. As we do not always want to be reading Shakespeare or Dante, so we should not always be pining to write the great poem. When I was young, I wished to write a better poem than Auden; later, I wanted each poem I was writing to be my best; now, I want to write another poem.

In the writing, I have always been so captivated by the charms and possibilities of more-or-less strict verse form that I very seldom have attempted the larger liberties of "free verse." It is as difficult to handle as the Protestant conscience—only a few poets in England and America have produced a first-class body of work in this medium. It may be that the poetry of the future will more and more be written in this formless form: we are told it enables the poem to be truly "organic"—whatever that may mean. But for me the endless fascination of verse, of organising a poem in metre and rhyme, outweighs any advantage that could be gained from the free way of writing. Form is not something a poet imposes on a poem: it is worked out by him in collaboration with the growing poem—its needs and nuances—as the meaning of that poem little by little becomes clear to him. I believe every artist is required to make coherent patterns out of chaos, not to reproduce it.

Nevertheless, one cannot have read poetry for fifty years, even in the specialised way poets read, without knowing that time and again the value of the great technical innovators has gone unrecognised by their contemporaries. The innovation of free verse as we know it, dating only from Whitman, is still resisted—if only by reactionary poets like myself. But so long as its practitioners can communicate in a memorable as well as a novel way, their work will justify itself: new forms will be seen to have emerged from behind the apparent formlessness, and the core of the poetic tradition be felt beneath a multiplicity of seemingly heterodox and even anarchic poems.

The present volume, which contains material about some thousand living poets from all over the world who write in English, is more than a handbook of information, less than a definitive roll of honour. We cannot tell how many of these names will survive through their work even beyond their own lifetime: 10%? 1%? Nevertheless, the book does honour to poetry, and provides a mass of information. It offers the serious reader a conspectus of representative writers from many countries, and so encourages him to extend his curiosity and broaden his reading. More important still, the book is a witness to the remarkable diversity of talents, the vigour and the inventiveness which poetry can command, even in a bitter, bewildering age when its sources are muddied or obstructed, "under conditions that seem unpropitious."

C. DAY LEWIS

PREFACE
to the third edition

Reading poetry in 1980, one often has the uneasy feeling that the revolution known as Modernism never occurred, that Ezra Pound never talked of "Direct treatment of the 'thing,' " or the "VORTEX" as "a radiant node or cluster ... from which, and through which, and into which, ideas are constantly rushing"; that Eliot never referred to "the law that poetry must not stray too far from the ordinary everyday language which we use and hear," or talked about the "intensity of the poetic process" and the need for "clear visual images." Consider the following poem:

At Claybank

Your parents lie buried
Under emblems of waves.
Cold surges of granite
Secure the ancient graves.

After pain and blindness,
With clouds closing in,
Summer lightning and rain,
We bring you to your kin.

What you asked is done.
You lie in their pure flood.
The rain washes the clay
Above it, dark as blood.

This little lyric has all the hallmarks of *fin de siècle*: the orderly quatrains of iambic trimeter, the semantically neutral rhymes ("waves"/"graves"; "flood"/"blood"), the use of abstract nouns, the vaguely mournful theme presented by means of ominous but unspecified nature images, the absence of what Yeats, himself a survivor of *fin de siècle*, called "dramatic tension" or the rhythm of "passionate, normal speech." But "At Claybank" was written neither by John Davidson nor by W.E. Henley. Its author is a very contemporary John Finlay, and it appeared in a 1979 issue of *Poetry Nation Review*.

Hard to believe? Here is a related example, this time from Anthony Hecht's *The Venetian Vespers*, which was extravagantly praised by Christopher Ricks on the front page of the *New York Times Book Review* (2 December 1979) and has been nominated for the annual Book Critics Circle Award:

Still Life

Sleep-walking vapor, like a visitant ghost,
    Hovers about a lake
Of Tennysonian calm just before dawn.
Inverted trees and boulders waver and coast
In polished darkness. Glints of silver break
Among the liquid leafage, and then are gone....

Like Rimbaud's "Le Dormeur du Val," this is a nature poem with a surprise ending: the idyllic setting is deceptive, for, as we learn in the last stanza, "I stand beneath a pine-tree in the cold,/Just before dawn, somewhere in Germany,/A cold, wet, Garand rifle in my hands." But unlike Rimbaud's poem, in which every image is functional, Hecht's is mostly window-dressing; it recalls such Georgian poets as Edward Thomas and J.C. Squire, poets who were the targets of such well-known Poundian dicta as "Don't chop your stuff into separate IAMBS": "A rhyme must have in it some slight element of surprise if it is to give pleasure": "Use no superfluous word, no adjective which does not reveal something. Don't use such an expression as 'dim lands of *peace*'. It dulls the image." Hecht's "Tennysonian calm" is made up of just such "expression(s) as 'dim lands of *peace*' ": for example, "Sleep-walking vapor," "visitant ghost," "Glints of silver," "polished darkness," "liquid leafage." And neither the rhymes—"ghost"/"coast"; "lake"/"break"—nor the conventionalized iambic pentameter can be said to create any particular "surprise."

The nostalgia for the peaceful decades before the First World War is everywhere with us. An apt emblem of that nostalgia is the recent BBC serialization of the life of Lily Langtry, the most celebrated of Edward VII's mistresses. The film *Lily* juxtaposes Whistler interiors in which Oscar Wilde is engaged in witty repartee with fellow poets and painters, to such idealized Edwardian images as the Garden Party, the Tryst in the Hunting Lodge, the Morning Ride in Hyde Park, the Presentation to the Queen. Furthermore, there is the ubiquitous presence of the servants, those humble, supportive, and charming folk who people the "upstairs and downstairs" of the Victorian and Edwardian celluloid world. Just so, in Anthony Hecht's "The Grapes," the speaker is a chambermaid who suddenly discovers, as she contemplates the light on the grapes in a bowl, that "There was nothing left for me now, nothing but years."

But nostalgia, no matter how strong, never reproduces the original. Despite the current conservatism of our literary quarterlies and publishing houses, despite the seeming preference for the safe, the orderly—the "cooked," as Philip Rahv called it—to the experimental, the messy, the "raw," there continues to be exciting experimentation in the poetry of our own *fin de siècle*, a poetry that is post-modern rather than neo-Victorian or Edwardian.

Consider, in the first place, the transformation of the long poem. Late Modernist long poems were almost invariably sequences: Robert Lowell's *Life Studies* (1959) and *Notebook* (1970), Charles Olson's *Maximus* (1960-68), Galway Kinnell's *The Book of Nightmares* (1971), Ted Hughes's *Crow* (1971), A.R. Ammons's *Sphere: The Form of a Motion* (1974). "The modern sequence," writes M.L. Rosenthal in *Contemporary Literature* (Summer 1977), "is a grouping of mainly lyric poems and passages, rarely uniform in pattern, tending to interact as an organic whole. It usually includes narrative and dramatic elements ... but its ordering is finally lyrical, a succession of *affects*." It is just such a "succession of *affects*" that poets are now questioning. John Cage puts it very cunningly in an essay called "The Future of Music" (1974):

We will continue to "wrestle with the Daimonic" .... But more and more this concern with personal feelings of individuals, even the enlightenment of individuals, will be seen in the larger context of society. We know how to suffer or control our own emotions. If not, advice is available. There is a cure for tragedy. The path to self-knowledge has been mapped out by psychiatry, by oriental philosophy, mythology, occult thought, anthroposophy, and astrology. We know all we need to know about Oedipus, Prometheus, and Hamlet. What we are learning is how to be convivial. "Here Comes Everybody."

Tongue-in-cheek as these remarks are, there is an important truth behind them. If self-knowledge and self-projection seem less important than they did to poets in the past, it is not because there is, in fact, "a cure for tragedy" (Cage knows better), but because, given the context of experience in the late 20th century, individual tragedy no longer seems quite plausible or real: we can, after all, turn on the television and watch the same things that trouble us happening to everyone else. "Learning how to be convivial" thus becomes a central element, and "Here Comes Everybody" involves narrative.

Thus James Merrill's celebrated "Book of Ephraim" (*Divine Comedies*, 1975) and its sequel *Mirabell: Book of Numbers* (1978) renounce the lyric sequence in favor of old-fashioned plot and a list of "Dramatis Personae" that include "Auden, W(ystan) H(ugh), 1907-/73, the celebrated poet," and "Deren, Eleonora ('Maya'),/1917-61, doyenne of our/American experimental film." At the opening of "Ephraim," the poet begins by disarming the reader's possible objections to a long narrative poem, full of events, information, and obscure references to the supernatural:

> Admittedly I err by undertaking
> This in its present form. The baldest prose
> Reportage was called for, that would reach
> The widest public in the shortest time.

And from here we move quickly to the scene: JM (Merrill) and DJ (his friend David Jackson) seated at the Ouija Board, calling up the spirit of Ephraim, a Greek Jew born in A.D. 8 and a favorite of the Emperor Tiberius, a character who proceeds to instruct the two protagonists on the meaning of history, philosophy, and especially the modern science of biology. Merrill's is a poetry that subordinates the Romantic image to the play of ideas, and so, in Aristotelian terms, it marks a return to the precedence of Mythos over Ethos, and of Dianoia over Melopoiea. "Ephraim" has brilliant buried rhymes and a panoply of clever verbal devices, but it is certainly not a musical or lyric poem.

The same turn from lyric to narrative can be found in other poems quite different from the elegant "Ephraim" and *Mirabell*. Contemporary narrative poems range from Ted Hughes's allegorical treatment of evil in *Gaudete* (1977), a violent and, I think, ultimately pretentious tale about an Anglican clergyman replaced by a changeling who seduces, one by one, all the good ladies of the parish until their men seek revenge and restore the "real" Reverend Lumb; to Ed Dorn's brilliant assemblage of cowboy epic, science fiction, drug culture *argot*, and Wittgensteinian logic in *Gunslinger* (1975); to the "exemplary narratives" embedded in the extraordinary "talk poems" of David Antin (*Talking at the Boundaries* [1976] and *Tuning* [1980]). A recent circular issued by the Poetry Project at St. Mark's-in-the-Bowery announced a reading by Howard A. Norman, "translator of *The Wishing Bone Cycle, Narrative Poems of the Swampy Cree Indians*":

> *The Wishing Bone Cycle* takes its name from the remarkable series of poem-stores that begin this book. Howard A. Norman, a young Canadian poet, first learned these poems about a wishing bone—capable of changing itself into various characters, objects and circumstances—from the venerable Swampy Cree Indian Jacob Slowstream. In addition to the thirty poems of this cycle, Norman has included a series of name-origin poems, a long animal-origin prose tale, and a group of songs and lullabies.

I cite this circular because it designates so clearly a kind of event that is taking place in our poetry world, a world that no longer worries much about the boundaries between poetry and prose, lyric and narrative. Howard A. Norman is a practitioner of a lively new discipline called *ethnopoetics*, which involves the transcription, translation, and discussion of the spoken and chanted word, especially the oral tradition of tribal peoples. The journal *Alcheringa: Ethnopoetics* publishes the work of Gary Snyder, Robert Kelly, Nathaniel Tarn, and Jerome Rothenberg, who is its leading spokesman. Rothenberg's own long poems—*Poland/1931* and *Seneca Journal*—as well as his distinctive anthologies—*Revolution of the Word, Technicians of the Sacred, America a Prophecy*—have made a great impact on younger poets. Indeed, Rothenberg's own collage-anthology *The Big Jewish Book* can be regarded as an intriguing postmodern narrative in its own right.

John Ashbery's latest collection, *As We Know* (1979), contains what I take to be the finest narrative poem of recent years, the 68-page "Litany." Written in double columns (which can be read both "across" and "down"), containing stories that fade in and out, overlap, mirror one another, or, on the contrary, cancel out each other's meanings, "Litany" beautifully exemplifies what Ashbery himself has called, in his *Three Poems* (1972), "an open field of narrative possibilities." We may, for example, read in the left-hand column:

> Just as everything seemed about to go wrong
> The music began; later on, the missing
> Refreshments would be found and served,
> The road turned caramel just as the first stars
> Were putting in a timid appearance, like snowdrops.

while the right-hand column presents a parody lecture on the sorrows of contemporary criticism:

> *Just one minute of contemporary existence*
> *Has so much to offer, but who*
> *Can evaluate it, formulate*
> *The appropriate apothegm, show us*
> *In a few well-chosen words of wisdom*
> *Exactly what is taking place all about us?*
> *Not critics, certainly, though that is precisely*
> *What they are supposed to be doing....*

Even these short passages will indicate to the reader that the narrative contained in "Litany" is fragmented and enigmatic. As Ashbery says of Gertrude Stein (in *Poetry*, July 1957):

> *Stanzas in Meditation* gives one the feeling of time passing, of things happening, of a "plot," though it would be difficult to say precisely what is going on. Sometimes the story has the logic of a dream..... But it is usually not events which interest Miss Stein. Rather it is their "way of happening," and the story of *Stanzas in Meditation* is a general, all-purpose model which each reader can adapt to fit his own set of particulars.

I cite these remarks at some length because they bring me to a related point about the poetry of the present. If narrative is, as I have been positing, once again central to poetry, this is not to say that it is the narrative of a William Morris or an Edwin Arlington Robinson. Postmodern narrative poetry is characterized by its peculiar indeterminacy, what Tzvetan Todorov has called its "undecidability" and other critics its "suspensiveness." Surely it is no coincidence that Ashbery's "Litany" appeared just a few years after Derrida's *Glas* (a critical commentary that has more in common with poetic discourse than with philosophy, and which is also written in double columns, the two voices ostensibly being those of Hegel and Genet), for Derrida's treatment of the absence of the signifier, if not applicable to poetry in general, is curiously applicable to the contemporary situation. In the enigma poetry of John Ashbery, a signal seems to be emitted, but the receiver's connection with the transmitter would seem to be on a faulty line. The poem is thus poised between sense and nonsense; it simultaneously discloses and conceals its meaning. This revelation/reveiling paradigm can be discovered not only in the word of Ashbery and his followers, but also in the Surrealist poetry of J.H. Prynne and Tom Raworth, the "Objectivist" lyric of Louis Zukofsky and George Oppen, and the performance art of John Cage and

David Antin. The poetry of indeterminacy can be traced back, as I suggest in my new book on the subject, to the verbal constructions of Beckett, and before him of Pound, Stein, and their French precursors both in poetry and in painting. I call this particular mode Rimbaldian because its first exemplar was the Rimbaud of the *Illuminations*.

"An open field of narrative possibilities," indeterminacy, the free play of ideas that refuses to harden into "statement"—this refusal to create the dense Symbolist network of High Modernist poetry is what I find especially exhilarating in the most interesting poetry of our own time. And here some related developments deserve discussion.

In "The ABC of Contemporary Reading" (*Esthetics Contemporary*, 1978), Richard Kostelanetz remarks: "The major esthetic innovations of recent art extend from three generative principles: minimalism, overload, and intermedia." Let me expand on some of Kostelanetz's suggestive generalizations.

Minimalism, "the principle of reducing the amount of surface content in a work—painting with only one color, say, or sculpture with smooth rectangular shapes, or fictions with very few words, or poems with a severely limited vocabulary"—is perhaps most obviously exemplified by the poetry of Robert Creeley, whose newest book, *Later* (1979), contains such lyrics as "Speech":

> Simple things
> one wants to say
> like, what's the day
> like, out there –
> who am I
> and where.

Such reductiveness is dangerous: the poem all but melts away. A very different minimalism is that of Geoffrey Hill in "The Pentecost Castle" (*Tenebrae*, 1978):

> shadows warned him
> not to go
> not to go
> along that road

or of George Oppen in "Of Being Numerous" (*Collected Poems*, 1974):

> It is the air of atrocity,
> An event as ordinary
> As a President.
>
> A plume of smoke, visible at a distance
> In which people burn.

And in the avant-garde journal $L = A = N = G = U = A = G = E$, a group of poets, most of whom are still too young and too little known to be represented in this volume—Charles Bernstein, Ray di Palma, Steve McCaffrey, Douglas Messerli, Michael Lally—as well as some more familiar ones like Larry Eigner, Tom Clark, Michael Brownstein, and Jackson Mac Low—are performing experiments with the decomposition of language, the dismantling of normal syntax and word usage so as to create a new language field. The $L = A = N = G = U = A = G = E$ poets look both to Gertrude Stein and to William Carlos Williams as their models, but perhaps the greatest Minimalist of all is the Beckett of "Ping," "Imagination Dead Imagine," "Fizzles," or "Lessness"—works that students of poetry (as opposed to drama and fiction) have oddly ignored.

"The contrary motive of overload," writes Kostelanetz, "informs such serial compositions as Milton Babbitt's *Relata 1* (1964), which presents an awesomely large number of discrete musical events in remarkably few minutes, or James Joyce's *Finnegans Wake*, where several stories, in several languages, are rendered on a single page." Overload is, in other words, simply the reverse side of minimalism.

Gunslinger, mentioned earlier, is a prime example, but so are the "novels" and parodic poems of the New York School: for example, James Schuyler's *The Home Book* (1977), Barbara Guest's *Seeking Air* (1978), and the recent prose poems of Kathleen Fraser. John Ashbery's cut-up poem "Europe," dismissed by certain critics as excessively disorderly and pointless, is a fine example of overload.

Intermedia, to my mind the most significant of Kostelanetz's "three generative principles," refers to "the new art forms that were invented by marrying the materials and/or concepts of one traditional genre with another (or others), or by integrating art itself with something previously considered nonartistic." Concrete Poetry was, of course, an early manifestation of the belief that the typography and lay-out of poetic texts creates its own range of meanings, a doctrine that can be traced back to Dada. But in the past decade, the more extreme forms of Concretism (as in the poetry of Ian Hamilton Finlay, bp Nichol, Aram Saroyan, and Mary Ellen Solt) have given way to a broader interest in what is now called Visible Language, a phenomenon not at all restricted to Minimalist forms. The publication of Zukofsky's *"A"* in the year of the poet's death in 1978, will undoubtedly lead to some interesting studies of Visible Language, and the $L = A = N = G = U = A = G = E$ group discussed above is, as its very name indicates, committed to the verbal-visual conjunction.

The relation of word to image is also found in the genre called "the artist's book," a genre that again can be traced back to Dada and Surrealism. Charles Tomlinson's collage-drawings in *In Black and White* are closely related to his sequence of prose poems called "Processes," although they are not printed in the same volume. Richard Howard's *Misgivings* (1979) contains a series of dramatic addresses to famous 19th-century figures photographed by Nadar, each poem being placed on the facing page of the Nadar photograph in question. Or again, in the delightful *Mobile Homes* (1980), Rudy Burkhardt takes portfolios of his own earlier photographs and juxtaposes them to pieces of a journal, prose sketches, poems, and playlets. Ron Padgett's *Tulsa Kid* (1980) creates a similar collage using cartoons rather than photographs. The artist's book will surely become an important genre in the years to come.

Meanwhile, intermedia involving word and music has given us what is now known as Sound Poetry. The father of Sound Poetry is surely John Cage; such performances as *Empty Words*, made up of sentences, phrases, words, and syllables taken from the journals of Thoreau, is at once musical and "poetic"—the verbal configurations, ever shifting and continually surprising in their variousness, are sometimes mimetic, sometimes abstract; they employ such "musical" devices as intervals and scales. In England, Michael Horovitz has worked with sound poetry, and there are now regular sound poetry festivals in many parts of the world, for example, "The Four Horsemen" in Toronto.

This brings me to a larger question: the role of *free verse* in late 20th-century poetry. Most theorists agree, I believe, that free verse is no longer a mode of defamiliarization, that it has become, on the contrary, the tedious norm. We are now as accustomed to free-verse poems, relating a particular personal experience in Imagist terms, as the Elizabethans were to the Petrarchan sonnet. To innovate in 1980 means, accordingly, to go beyond the free verse aesthetic of the 1960's: the breathless, end-stopped lines of Robert Bly or James Wright. One way to get around the "free verse problem" is to play off the linear base against the overriding syntax of the sentence and paragraph, much as earlier poets played off the speech rhythms of free verse against the iambic pentameter norm. A poem like Robert Hass's "Meditation at Lagunitas" calls attention to itself as a single, coherent paragraph, whose elements are always in tension with the line. Other poets, as diverse as Russell Edson, W.S. Merwin, Michael Benedikt, and Larry Eigner, have turned to the prose poem as a way out of the free verse impasse. Again, a "talk poet" like David Antin will utilize what Northrop Frye calls the "associative rhythm," his norm being not the sentence or verse line but the short fragmentary unit of ordinary speech, placed in the repetitive patterns of seemingly natural (but actually formalized in subtle ways) discourse. Still other poets—Donald Davie, Geoffrey Hill, Thom Gunn, Seamus Heaney—are returning to traditional metres and stanza forms: the ballad, the villanelle, the sestina, even the sonnet. At its best, as in Davie's "Three for Watermusic," a set of subtle and intricate meditations on our capacity to create myths and to believe in them, such recreation of fixed forms (here, heroic couplets, five-line trimeter stanzas rhyming abcb, and so on) is surely an example of Making It New.

Such consideration of traditionalism brings me back full circle to the point where I began: the neo-Edwardian or neo-Victorian lyric of a John Finlay or an Anthony Hecht. By now it will, I hope, be evident that the poetry of 1980 can only be "traditional" with a difference. To write a quatrain poem today involves a self-consciousness quite uncharacteristic of even the more mannered *fin-de-siècle* poets; its use requires the special tact of a Davie or a Hill. In the context of composition by field and fragmented narrative, of indeterminacy and suspensiveness, of visible language, sound poetry, performance art, of prose compositions that insist on being read as "poetry" and of ethnopoetics, the "traditional" poems currently most fashionable begin to remind one of the "Gothic" facades of Viollet-le-Duc. Behind those impressively intricate towers and turrets, the language of poetry is being recharged. For the Arthur Rackham fairy-tale castle we long for in our more nostalgic moments is, as John Ashbery puts it in "Valentine," "a house of cards.... and it is also built on/Shifting sands."

MARJORIE PERLOFF

EDITORS' NOTE

The selection of poets included in this book is based on the recommendations of the advisers listed on page xvii, many of whom have helped with all four editions.

The entry for each poet consists of a biography, a complete list of separately published books, and a signed essay. In addition, entrants were invited to comment on their work.

Original British and United States editions of all books have been listed; other editions are listed only if they are first editions. As a rule all books written about the entrant are listed in the Critical Studies section; the reviews and essays listed have been recommended by the entrant.

An appendix of entries has been included for some 14 poets who have died since 1960 but whose reputations are essentially contemporary.

We would like to thank the entrants and contributors for their patience and cooperation in helping us compile this book.

ADVISERS

Donald Allen
James Bertram
Earle Birney
Edward Kamau Brathwaite
Hayden Carruth
John Robert Colombo
John Cotton
James A. Emanuel
G.S. Fraser
Donald Hall
Daniel Halpern
Thomas Kinsella
Maurice Lindsay
Edward Lucie-Smith
Roland Mathias
Ralph J. Mills, Jr.

John Montague
Blake Morrison
Marjorie Perloff
William Plomer
Arthur Ravenscroft
Michael Schmidt
Howard Sergeant
Martin Seymour-Smith
Thomas W. Shapcott
A.J.M. Smith
C.K. Stead
Douglas Stewart
Allen Tate
Anthony Thwaite
Robert Vas Dias

CONTRIBUTORS

Duane Ackerson
Fleur Adcock
James Aitchison
Peter Alcock
Michael André
David Astle
Jane Augustine
Houston A. Baker, Jr.
Jonathan Barker
Bruce Beaver
Bernard Bergonzi
James Bertram
Jennifer Birkett
Harold Bloom
Carl Bode
Walter Bode
Elmer Borklund
Corrine E. Bostic
Robert Boyers
Gaynor F. Bradish
Edward Kamau Brathwaite
Lloyd W. Brown
Stewart Brown
Alan Brownjohn
George Bruce
Joseph Bruchac
Jim Burns
George F. Butterick
Don Byrd
Edward Callan
Rivers Carew
Hayden Carruth
D.D.C. Chambers
Ann Charters
Samuel Charters
Paul Christensen
Richard Church
Alan Clark
Austin Clarke
Anne Cluysenaar

Arthur A. Cohen
John Robert Colombo
William Cookson
John R. Cooley
Seamus Cooney
Neil Corcoran
John Cotton
Patricia Craig
Tony Curtis
Richard Damashek
Michael Davidson
Cynthia Day
R.H.W. Dillard
Dale Doepke
Max Dorsinville
David C. Dougherty
David Dowling
Charles Doyle
Louis Dudek
Jim Elledge
Gavin Ewart
Ian Fletcher
G.S. Fraser
Norman Friedman
Robin Fulton
Sally M. Gall
Norman T. Gates
Edward B. Germain
S.R. Gilbert
Dana Gioia
Michael Gnarowski
Lois Gordon
Alvin Greenberg
Thom Gunn
Ralph Gustafson
Rodney Hall
Ruth Harnett
David M. Heaton
Michael Heller
Geof Hewitt

William Heyen
Douglas Hill
John Hinchey
Philip Hobsbaum
Daniel Hoffman
Jan Hokenson
Janis Butler Holm
Eric Homberger
Theodore R. Hudson
Charles L. James
Elizabeth Jennings
Eldred D. Jones
Susan Kaplan
Nancy Keesing
Burton Kendle
Brendan Kennelly
Bruce King
James Korges
Richard Kostelanetz
Norbert Krapf
B.T. Kugler
Joan Hutton Landis
Estella Lauter
Geoffrey Lehmann
Stanley W. Lindberg
Carl Lindner
Maurice Lindsay
Edward Lucie-Smith
Glenna Luschei
Dennis Lynch
Norman MacCaig
Roy Macnab
Wes Magee
Roland Mathias
William Matthews
John Matthias
E.L. Mayo
George McElroy
Martin McGovern
David Meltzer
Ralph J. Mills, Jr.
Robert Miola
Shankar Mokashi-Punekar
John Mole
Charles Molesworth
John Montague
Edwin Morgan
Meenakshi Mukherjee
S. Nagarajan
Rudolph L. Nelson
John Newlove
Robert Nye
William Oxley
Jerry Paris
Joseph Parisi
Derek Parker
Jay S. Paul
E. Pereira
Marjorie Perloff
Kirsten Holst Petersen
Peter Porter
John Press
Glyn Pursglove
David Ray
John M. Reilly

Colin Rickards
James K. Robinson
Alan Roddick
Judith Rodriguez
Lawrence Russ
Anna Rutherford
Geoff Sadler
Carol Lee Saffioti
Andreas Schroeder
Alexander Scott
Peter Scupham
Fred Sedgwick
Howard Sergeant
Martin Seymour-Smith
Thomas W. Shapcott
David Shapiro
J.N. Sharma
Robert Sheppard
William David Sherman
Alan R. Shucard
Jon Silkin
A.J.M. Smith
Stan Smith
Kendrick Smithyman
Geoffrey Soar
Radcliffe Squires
William Stafford
Donald Barlow Stauffer
C.K. Stead
Timothy Steele
Carol Simpson Stern
Joan Stevens
Anne Stevenson
Douglas Stewart
Jennifer Strauss
Lucien Stryk
Rosemary Sullivan
Fraser Sutherland
William Sylvester
Julian Symons
John Taggart
Henry Taylor
Myron Taylor
Arthur Terry
Anthony Thwaite
Saundra Towns
John Tripp
Michael True
James Tulip
Robert Vas Dias
K. Venkatachari
Linda W. Wagner
Diane Wakoski
William Walsh
R.J.C. Watt
Eliot Weinberger
Nigel Wheale
John Stuart Williams
Margaret Willy
Joseph Wilson
George Woodcock
Judith Wright
Leopoldo Y. Yabes
Steven Young

CONTEMPORARY
POETS

Dannie Abse
Chinua Achebe
Diane Ackerman
Milton Acorn
Helen Adam
Léonie Adams
Perseus Adams
Robert Adamson
Fleur Adcock
A. Alvarez
Kingsley Amis
A.R. Ammons
Michael Anania
Jon Anderson
Maya Angelou
David Antin
John Ash
John Ashbery
Margaret Atwood
Alvin Aubert
Margaret Avison
Kofi Awoonor

Howard Baker
Gavin Bantock
Amiri Baraka
Douglas Barbour
George Barker
Coleman Barks
Taner Baybars
Bruce Beaver
Samuel Beckett
Patricia Beer
Henry Beissel
Ben Belitt
Marvin Bell
Michael Benedikt
Louise Bennett
Asa Benveniste
Anne Beresford
Stephen Berg
Carol Bergé
Bill Berkson
Charles Bernstein
Daniel Berrigan
Francis Berry
Wendell Berry
James Bertolino
Earle Birney
Bill Bissett
David Black
Robin Blaser
John Blight
Robert Bly
Charles Boer
Alan Bold
Martin Booth
Philip Booth
Keith Bosley
Ronald Bottrall
George Bowering
Marilyn Bowering
Edgar Bowers
Kay Boyle
John Brandi
Edward Kamau Brathwaite

Richard Emil Braun
Richard Brautigan
Ray Bremser
Kwesi Brew
Elizabeth Brewster
Robert Bringhurst
John Malcolm Brinnin
Edwin Brock
David Bromige
William Bronk
Gwendolyn Brooks
James Broughton
George Mackay Brown
Sterling A. Brown
Michael Dennis Browne
Alan Brownjohn
Michael Brownstein
George Bruce
Dennis Brutus
Tom Buchan
George Buchanan
Vincent Buckley
David Budbill
Charles Bukowski
Michael Bullock
Basil Bunting
William Burford
Kenneth Burke
Jim Burns
Stanley Burnshaw
Guy Butler

Alistair Campbell
Donald Campbell
George Campbell
Paul Carroll
Hayden Carruth
Martin Carter
Charles Causley
Syl Cheyney-Coker
John Ciardi
Amy Clampitt
John Pepper Clark
Tom Clark
Gillian Clarke
Jack Clemo
Lucille Clifton
Anne Cluysenaar
Bob Cobbing
Fred Cogswell
Leonard Cohen
Barry Cole
John Robert Colombo
Alex Comfort
Stewart Conn
Tony Connor
Robert Conquest
Anthony Conran
Stanley Cook
Clark Coolidge
Jane Cooper
Cid Corman
Alfred Corn
Sam Cornish
Gregory Corso
John Cotton

Jeni Couzyn
Malcolm Cowley
Louis Coxe
Robert Creeley
Judson Crews
Kevin Crossley-Holland
Andrew Crozier
Victor Hernández Cruz
Marcus Cumberlege
J.V. Cunningham
Allen Curnow
R.N. Currey

Philip Dacey
Peter Dale
Ruth Dallas
Robert Dana
D.K. Das
Kamala Das
Frank Davey
Michael Davidson
Donald Davie
Dick Davis
Peter Davison
Bruce Dawe
Anthony Delius
Ricaredo Demetillo
James Dickey
William Dickey
Patric Dickinson
R.H.W. Dillard
Diane di Prima
Rosemary Dobson
Stephen Dobyns
Ed Dorn
Basil Dowling
Freda Downie
Charles Doyle
Norman Dubie
Louis Dudek
Alan Dugan
Robert Duncan
Douglas Dunn
Stephen Dunn
Lawrence Durrell
Geoffrey Dutton
Bob Dylan

Charles Edward Eaton
Richard Eberhart
Michael Echeruo
George Economou
Lauris Edmond
Russell Edson
Larry Eigner
Alistair Elliot
Kenward Elmslie
James A. Emanuel
John Engels
Paul Engle
D.J. Enright
Theodore Enslin
Clayton Eshleman
Federico Espino
Mari Evans
Ronald Everson

William Everson
Peter Everwine
Gavin Ewart
Nissim Ezekiel

Ruth Fainlight
John Fairfax
Colin Falck
U.A. Fanthorpe
Elaine Feinstein
Irving Feldman
James Fenton
Lawrence Ferlinghetti
Edward Field
John Figueroa
Robert Finch
Donald Finkel
Ian Hamilton Finlay
Joan Finnigan
Allen Fisher
Roy Fisher
Robert Fitzgerald
Robert D. FitzGerald
Ian Fletcher
John Forbes
Carolyn Forché
Charles Henri Ford
R.A.D. Ford
Gene Fowler
Janet Frame
Robert Francis
Kathleen Fraser
Christopher Fry
John Fuller
Roy Fuller
Robin Fulton

Tess Gallagher
Brendan Galvin
Roger Garfitt
Raymond Garlick
George Garrett
David Gascoyne
Greg Gatenby
Gary Geddes
Karen Gershon
Brewster Ghiselin
Zulfikar Ghose
Monk Gibbon
Ruth Gilbert
Gary Gildner
David Gill
Valerie Gillies
Allen Ginsberg
Nikki Giovanni
Robert Gittings
Duncan Glen
Louise Glück
Denis Goacher
Patricia Goedicke
Albert Goldbarth
Phyllis Gotlieb
Henry Graham
Jorie Graham
W.S. Graham
Robert Graves

Robert Gray
Jonathan Greene
Arthur Gregor
Eldon Grier
Jonathan Griffin
Bryn Griffiths
Geoffrey Grigson
Barbara Guest
Harry Guest
Charles Gullans
Thom Gunn
Ralph Gustafson
Don Gutteridge

Marilyn Hacker
John Haines
Donald Hall
J.C. Hall
Rodney Hall
Daniel Halpern
Michael Hamburger
Ian Hamilton
Kenneth O. Hanson
Pauline Hanson
Michael S. Harper
Wilson Harris
Jim Harrison
Keith Harrison
Tony Harrison
David Harsent
Kevin Hart
William Hart-Smith
Michael Hartnett
Gwen Harwood
Lee Harwood
Robert Hass
Samuel Hazo
Seamus Heaney
John Heath-Stubbs
Anthony Hecht
Lyn Hejinian
Michael Heller
David Helwig
Hamish Henderson
A.L. Hendriks
Adrian Henri
Calvin C. Hernton
Phoebe Hesketh
Dorothy Hewett
Geof Hewitt
John Hewitt
William Heyen
Charles Higham
Geoffrey Hill
Daryl Hine
Jack Hirschman
George Hitchcock
Philip Hobsbaum
Sandra Hochman
Daniel Hoffman
Michael Hofmann
David Holbrook
John Hollander
Anselm Hollo
Geoffrey Holloway
John Holloway

Edwin Honig
Jeremy Hooker
A.D. Hope
Michael Horovitz
Dom Sylvester Houédard
Richard Howard
Anthony Howell
Barbara Howes
Andrew Hoyem
Alejandrino G. Hufana
Robert Huff
Glyn Hughes
Ted Hughes
Sam Hunt
Pearse Hutchinson

David Ignatow
Kenneth Irby
Kevin Ireland

Alan Jackson
Paul Jacob
Josephine Jacobsen
David Jaffin
Peter Jay
Elizabeth Jennings
Judson Jerome
Louis Johnson
Ronald Johnson
George Johnston
Brian Jones
D.G. Jones
Evan Jones
Glyn Jones
Erica Jong
June Jordan
Jenny Joseph
Donald Justice

Lenore Kandel
P.J. Kavanagh
Lionel Kearns
Richard Kell
Robert Kelly
X.J. Kennedy
Brendan Kennelly
Milton Kessler
Keorapetse Kgositsile
Galway Kinnell
Thomas Kinsella
James Kirkup
Carolyn Kizer
Etheridge Knight
John Knoepfle
Bill Knott
Kenneth Koch
Arun Kolatkar
James Koller
Ted Kooser
Bernard Kops
Richard Kostelanetz
Shiv K. Kumar
Maxine Kumin
Stanley Kunitz
Joanne Kyger

P. Lal
Philip Lamantia
Patrick Lane
Joseph Langland
Philip Larkin
James Laughlin
Irving Layton
Dennis Lee
Don L. Lee
Laurie Lee
Geoffrey Lehmann
John Lehmann
Tom Leonard
Douglas LePan
Laurence Lerner
Christopher Levenson
Denise Levertov
Peter Levi
Philip Levine
Larry Levis
John L'Heureux
Laurence Lieberman
Lyn Lifshin
Maurice Lindsay
Lou Lipsitz
Dorothy Livesay
Douglas Livingstone
Taban lo Liyong
Liz Lochhead
Ron Loewinsohn
John Logan
Christopher Logue
Michael Longley
Audre Lorde
Edward Lowbury
Edward Lucie-Smith

Lewis MacAdams
George MacBeth
Norman MacCaig
Gwendolyn MacEwen
Alastair Mackie
Alasdair Maclean
Jackson Mac Low
Roy Macnab
Jay Macpherson
Barry MacSweeney
Charles Madge
Wes Magee
Jayanta Mahapatra
Derek Mahon
Clarence Major
David Malouf
Eli Mandel
Bill Manhire
John Manifold
Chris Mann
Daphne Marlatt
Jack Marshall
Sid Marty
Harold Massingham
William H. Matchett
Roland Mathias
William Matthews
John Matthias
Gerda Mayer

Seymour Mayne
James J. McAuley
Michael McClure
Roger McDonald
David McFadden
Roy McFadden
Roger McGough
Thomas McGrath
Medbh McGuckian
Heather McHugh
Tom McKeown
Florence McNeil
Anthony McNeill
Sandra McPherson
George McWhirter
Matthew Mead
Arvind Krishna Mehrotra
Peter Meinke
David Meltzer
William Meredith
James Merrill
W.S. Merwin
Robert Mezey
James Michie
Christopher Middleton
Josephine Miles
Vassar Miller
Eric Millward
Ewart Milne
Robert Minhinnick
Adrian Mitchell
David Mitchell
John Moat
Judith Moffett
Shankar Mokashi-Punekar
John Mole
John Montague
Nicholas Moore
Dom Moraes
Edwin Morgan
Frederick Morgan
Pete Morgan
Robert Morgan
Howard Moss
Stanley Moss
Andrew Motion
Oswald Mtshali
Paul Muldoon
Richard Murphy
Les A. Murray
Rona Murray
Susan Musgrave

Pritish Nandy
Leonard Nathan
Howard Nemerov
John Newlove
Barrie Phillip Nichol
Norman Nicholson
John Frederick Nims
Leslie Norris
Harold Norse
Alice Notley
Kathleen Nott
Jeff Nuttall
Robert Nye

Philip Oakes
Ned O'Gorman
Desmond O'Grady
John Okai
Gabriel Okara
Mary Oliver
Elder Olson
Toby Olson
Michael Ondaatje
Joel Oppenheimer
John Ormond
Frank Ormsby
Gregory Orr
Simon J. Ortiz
Vincent O'Sullivan
Rochelle Owens
William Oxley

Robert Pack
Ron Padgett
Geoff Page
P.K. Page
Michael Palmer
Thomas Parkinson
R. Parthasarathy
Betty Parvin
Linda Pastan
Alistair Paterson
Brian Patten
Raymond R. Patterson
Tom Paulin
John Peck
Grace Perry
William Peskett
Lenrie Peters
Donald Petersen
Paul Petrie
W.H. Petty
Tom Pickard
Marge Piercy
William Pillin
Christopher Pilling
Robert Pinsky
Kenneth Pitchford
Ruth Pitter
Allen Planz
Stanley Plumly
Ralph Pomeroy
Peter Porter
A. Poulin, Jr.
Craig Powell
Neil Powell
F.T. Prince
Frederic Prokosch
J.H. Prynne
A.G. Prys-Jones
Sally Purcell
Al Purdy
Rodney Pybus

Craig Raine
Kathleen Raine
Carl Rakosi
A.K. Ramanujan
Paul Ramsey
Dudley Randall

Julia Randall
Margaret Randall
Tom Raworth
David Ray
James Reaney
Peter Redgrove
Henry Reed
Ishmael Reed
F.D. Reeve
Alastair Reid
Christopher Reid
Adrienne Rich
Laura Riding
Anne Ridler
Philip Roberts
Roland Robinson
Paul Roche
Alan Roddick
Stephen Rodefer
Carolyn M. Rodgers
Edouard Roditi
Judith Rodriguez
Alan Rook
William Pitt Root
Joe Rosenblatt
M.L. Rosenthal
Alan Ross
Jerome Rothenberg
David Rowbotham
J.R. Rowland
A.L. Rowse
Anthony Rudolf
Carol Rumens
Peter Russell
Vern Rutsala

Lawrence Sail
Bruce St. John
Sonia Sanchez
Ed Sanders
Stephen Sandy
Reg Saner
Aram Saroyan
May Sarton
Teo Savory
Vernon Scannell
James Schevill
Michael Schmidt
Dennis Schmitz
Andreas Schroeder
James Schuyler
Armand Schwerner
Alexander Scott
F.R. Scott
Tom Scott
E.J. Scovell
James Scully
Peter Scupham
Frederick Seidel
Hugh Seidman
Howard Sergeant
A.J. Seymour
Martin Seymour-Smith
Thomas W. Shapcott
David Shapiro
Harvey Shapiro

Karl Shapiro
Richard Shelton
Judith Johnson Sherwin
Penelope Shuttle
Jon Silkin
Leslie Silko
Alan Sillitoe
Charles Simic
James Simmons
Louis Simpson
R.A. Simpson
Keith Sinclair
C.H. Sisson
Sacheverell Sitwell
Robin Skelton
Knute Skinner
David Slavitt
Dave Smith
Iain Crichton Smith
John Smith
Ken Smith
Vivian Smith
William Jay Smith
Elizabeth Smither
Kendrick Smithyman
W.D. Snodgrass
Gary Snyder
Mary Ellen Solt
Gilbert Sorrentino
Gary Soto
Raymond Souster
Wole Soyinka
Barry Spacks
Muriel Spark
Francis Sparshott
Stephen Spender
Radcliffe Squires
William Stafford
Jon Stallworthy
Ann Stanford
George Starbuck
C.K. Stead
Stephen Stepanchev
Alan Stephens
Meic Stephens
Gerald Stern
Peter Stevens
Anne Stevenson
Douglas Stewart
Harold Stewart
Randolph Stow
Mark Strand
Lucien Stryk
Dabney Stuart
Andrew Suknaski, Jr.
Hollis Summers
Robert Sward
David Sweetman
May Swenson
Julian Symons
George Szirtes

John Tagliabue
Nathaniel Tarn
James Tate
Andrew Taylor

D.M. Thomas
R.S. Thomas
Anthony Thwaite
Terence Tiller
Richard Tillinghast
Charles Tomlinson
Rosemary Tonks
John Tranter
Sydney Tremayne
John Tripp
Constantine Trypanis
Lewis Turco
Gael Turnbull
Hone Tuwhare

John Updike
Constance Urdang

Jean Valentine
Mona Van Duyn
Monika Varma
Robert Vas Dias
Peter Viereck
José Garcia Villa

Miriam Waddington
David Wagoner
John Wain
Jeffrey Wainwright
Diane Wakoski
Derek Walcott
Anne Waldman
Margaret Walker
Ted Walker
Chris Wallace-Crabbe
Chad Walsh
Francis Warner
Rex Warner
Robert Penn Warren
Lewis Warsh
Andrew Waterman
Robert Watson
Roderick Watson
Tom Wayman
Harri Webb
Phyllis Webb
Ian Wedde
Theodore Weiss
Daniel Weissbort
James Welch
Robert Wells
David Wevill
Philip Whalen
Peter Whigham
Laurence Whistler
Ivan White
Kenneth White
James Whitehead
Ruth Whitman
Reed Whittemore
John Wieners
Richard Wilbur
Peter Wild
Nancy Willard
C.K. Williams
Emmett Williams

Gwyn Williams
Hugo Williams
John Stuart Williams
Jonathan Williams
Miller Williams
Clive Wilmer
Keith Wilson
Sheila Wingfield
Hubert Witheford
George Woodcock
John Woods
Charles Wright
David Wright

Judith Wright
Kit Wright

J. Michael Yates
John Yau
Al Young
David Young
Ian Young

Robert Zend
Paul Zimmer
Harriet Zinnes

APPENDIX

James K. Baxter
John Berryman
Paul Blackburn
Jean Garrigue
Randall Jarrell
Robert Lowell
Frank O'Hara

Charles Olson
Sylvia Plath
Theodore Roethke
Anne Sexton
Jack Spicer
James Wright
Louis Zukofsky

ABSE, Dannie. Welsh. Born in Cardiff, Glamorgan, 22 September 1923. Educated at St. Illtyd's College, Cardiff; University of South Wales and Monmouthsire, Cardiff; King's College, London; Westminster Hospital, London; qualified as physician 1950, M.R.C.S., L.R.C.P. Served in the Royal Air Force, 1951-54: Squadron Leader. Married Joan Mercer in 1951; one son and two daughters. Since 1954, Specialist in charge of the chest clinic, Central London Medical Establishment. Senior Fellow in Humanities, Princeton University, New Jersey, 1973-74. Since 1978, President, Poetry Society. Recipient: Foyle Award, 1960; Welsh Arts Council award, for verse, 1971, for play, 1980. Agent: Anthony Sheil Associates Ltd., 2-3 Morwell Street, London WC1B 3AR. Address: 85 Hodford Road, London N.W. 11, England; or, Green Hollows, Craig-yr-Eos Road, Ogmore-by-Sea, Glamorgan, Wales.

PUBLICATIONS

Verse

After Every Green Thing. London, Hutchinson, 1949.
Walking under Water. London, Hutchinson, 1952.
Tenants of the House. London, Hutchinson, 1957; New York, Criterion, 1958.
Poems, Golders Green. London, Hutchinson, 1962.
Dannie Abse: A Selection. London, Studio Vista, 1963.
A Small Desperation. London, Hutchinson, 1968.
Demo. Frensham, Surrey, Sceptre Press, 1969.
Selected Poems. London, Hutchinson, and New York, Oxford University Press, 1970.
Funland: A Poem in Nine Parts. Portland, Oregon, Portland University Press, 1971.
Corgi Modern Poets in Focus 4, with others, edited by Jeremy Robson. London, Corgi, 1972.
Funland and Other Poems. London, Hutchinson, and New York, Oxford University Press, 1973.
Lunchtime. London, Poem-of-the-Month Club, 1974.
Penguin Modern Poets 26, with D.J. Enright and Michael Longley. London, Penguin, 1975.
Collected Poems 1948-1976. London, Hutchinson, and Pittsburgh, University of Pittsburgh Press, 1977.
Way Out in the Centre. London, Hutchinson, 1981; as *One-Legged on Ice,* Athens, University of Georgia Press, 1981.

Recordings: *Poets of Wales,* Argo, 1972; *The Poetry of Dannie Abse,* McGraw Hill, n.d.; *Dannie Abse,* Canto, 1984.

Plays

Fire in Heaven (produced London, 1948). London, Hutchinson, 1956; revised version, as *Is the House Shut?* (produced London, 1964); revised version, as *In the Cage,* in *Three Questor Plays,* 1967.
Hands Around the Wall (produced London, 1950).
House of Cowards (produced London, 1960). Included in *Three Questor Plays,* 1967; in *Twelve Great Plays,* edited by Leonard F. Dean, New York, Harcourt Brace, 1970.
The Eccentric (produced London, 1961). London, Evans, 1961.
Gone (produced London, 1962). Included in *Three Questor Plays,* 1967.
The Courting of Essie Glass (as *The Joker,* produced London, 1962; revised version, as *The Courting of Essie Glass,* broadcast, 1975). Included in *Miscellany One,* 1981.
Three Questor Plays (includes *House of Cowards, Gone, In the Cage).* Lowestoft, Suffolk, Scorpion Press, 1967.
The Dogs of Pavlov (produced London, 1969; New York, 1974). London, Vallentine Mitchell, 1973.
Funland (produced London, 1975).
Pythagoras (produced Birmingham, 1976; London, 1980). London, Hutchinson, 1979.
Gone in January (produced London, 1978). Published in *Madog* (Pontypridd, Glamorgan), 1981.

Radio Plays: *Conform or Die,* 1957; *No Telegrams, No Thunder,* 1962; *You Can't Say Hello to Anybody,* 1964; *A Small Explosion,* 1964; *The Courting of Essie Glass,* 1975.

Novels

Ash on a Young Man's Sleeve. London, Hutchinson, 1954; New York, Criterion, 1955.
Some Corner of an English Field. London, Hutchinson, 1956; New York, Criterion, 1957.
O. Jones, O. Jones. London, Hutchinson, 1970.

Other

Medicine on Trial. London, Aldus, 1968; New York, Crown, 1969.
A Poet in the Family (autobiography). London, Hutchinson, 1974.
Three Poets, Two Children, with Leonard Clark and Vernon Scannell, edited by Desmond Badham-Thornhill. Gloucester, Thornhill Press, 1975.
Miscellany One. Bridgend, Glamorgan, Poetry Wales Press, 1981.
A Strong Dose of Myself. London, Hutchinson, 1983.

Editor, with Elizabeth Jennings and Stephen Spender, *New Poems 1956.* London, Joseph, 1956.
Editor, with Howard Sergeant, *Mavericks.* London, Editions Poetry and Poverty, 1957.
Editor, *European Verse.* London, Studio Vista, 1964.
Editor, *Corgi Modern Poets in Focus 1, 3, 5.* London, Corgi, 1971-73.
Editor, *Thirteen Poets.* London, Poetry Book Society, 1973.
Editor, *Poetry Dimension 2-5: The Best of the Poetry Year.* London, Robson, 1974-78; New York, St. Martin's Press, 1976-79; *The Best of the Poetry Year 6-7,* Robson, and Totowa, New Jersey, Rowman and Littlefield, 1979-80.
Editor, *Poetry Supplement, Christmas 1975.* London, Poetry Book Society, 1975.
Editor, *My Medical School.* London, Robson, 1978.
Editor, *Wales in Verse.* London, Secker and Warburg, 1983.
Editor, *Doctors and Patients.* Oxford, Oxford University Press, 1984.

*

Critical Studies: interviews in *Jewish Quarterly* (London), Winter 1962-63, *Flame* (Wivenhoe, Essex), March 1967, *Anglo-Welsh Review* (Tenby), Spring 1975, *The Guardian* (London), 31 January 1978, *Good Housekeeping* (London), May 1981, *The Times* (London), 28 February 1983, and *Sunday Times Magazine* (London), 22 May 1983; by Jeremy Robson, in *Corgi Modern Poets in Focus 4,* 1972; "Poet on Poet" by Fleur Adcock, in *Ambit 70* (London), 1977; "The Poetry of Dannie Abse" by Howard Sergeant, in *Books and Bookmen* (London), July 1977; by John Pikoulis and John Tripp, in *Poetry Wales* (Bridgend), October 1977; by David Punter, in *Straight Lines 2* (Norwich),

1979; by Renée Winegarten, in *Jewish Chronicle Literary Supplement* (London), 24 December 1982; *The Poetry of Dannie Abse: Critical Essays and Reminiscences* edited by Joseph Cohen, London, Robson, 1983; "Science Poetry: Approaches to Redgrove, Abse, and Ammons" by J.P. Ward, in *Poesis* (Bryn Mawr, Pennsylvania), Fall 1984.

*   *   *

After Every Green Thing, Dannie Abse's first book of poems, was declamatory, full of an eloquence natural to his gifted Jewish family background. His elder brother Leo, for many years M.P. for Pontypool and Torfaen, often spoke from a soap-box in Llandaff Fields and Dannie himself, a combative Socialist in a Catholic school, saw poetry as a generalised exposition of ideals and experiences, in which repetition and rhetoric were dominant features. When he became a medical student, first at Cardiff and then in London, the back pages of his notebooks were always "noisy with poems." This first work, notwithstanding its eloquent verbosity and the "publicness" of its poetic attitude (extended by Dannie's early practice in reading poetry to an audience), is attractive even when flawed, and his second book, *Walking under Water*, with its rejection of naivete and its much greater formal control, is at first sight a disappointment. But behind the new discipline, in which a variable refrain is often used to indicate the steps of the poetic argument and in which symbols as well as words are rigorously organised, the successes of the future were being prepared.

With *Tenants of the House* Dannie Abse emerged as a poet of undoubted significance. In this volume his hortatory intention is provided with a satisfactory vehicle and an understood destination. Briefly, an extended symbolic concept, itself the main or entire structure of the individual poem, uses the existing knowledge of the reader to make the narrative line or the poetic argument absolutely clear, enabling even the uninitiate among readers to "get at" the second level of meaning. Thus "Social Revolution in England" overtly presents a picture of a bewildered aristocratic household emptied by the bailiffs. His fondness for refrain, too, brought Abse at this stage to the discovery of a rhythmic structure which would carry the message of the poem just as well as an understood "picture." The nursery-rhyme basis of "The Trial"—"I'll sum up, the severe Judge moans/ showing the white of his knucklebones"—provides an area of unconscious suggestion in which the "meaning" is far more easily grasped.

Always remarkable for the sensitivity and honesty of his search for poetic experience, Dannie Abse, in his next volume, *Poems, Golders Green*, moved back to quieter and more personal country. This collection was perhaps less uniformly successful than its predecessor, but it contains some halfdozen very fine poems, amongst which "Return to Cardiff" (most of all for the scrupulousness of its "point") is outstanding:

> Unable to define anything I can hardly speak
> and still I love the place for what I wanted it to be
> as much as for what it unashamedly is
> now for me, a city of strangers, alien and bleak.

In *A Small Desperation* he made more obvious both the width of his interest and the variety of formal treatment he was prepared to give to poetry. The original eloquence entirely "gritted down," he brought his vocational knowledge of medicine into greater play, and his self-criticism, amused as well as searching, gave him an approach to "the condition of man" which is as little limited as are his moods. *Funland and Other Poems*, while making use of the title sequence to return to the extended allegory, an irreverent and surrealist picture of modern substitutes for faith, also went back to Wales more often. In this volume are to be found some of Dannie Abse's most memorable short poems (like "A New Diary" and "An Old Commitment") and the few additions to *Collected Poems* confirm that his costive publication (no more than five or six poems a year) is making less and less fallible the amalgam of irony, wit, and irreducible sentiment which the imagination he applies to simple and colloquial language so marvellously shapes. That he takes risks and pulls them off "Cousin Sidney" (with its repeated "silly ass") admirably illustrates, and his dream of Nell Gwynn in "The Test" points his success in keeping both preciousness and portentousness out of his writing. Dannie Abse's poetry is humane without being predictable, sensitive without seeking to screw the language tight on the reader's thumb. In all that he writes he is his own man, an important voice out of the midst of a confused generation.

—Roland Mathias

ACHEBE, Chinua. Nigerian.   Born Albert Chinualumogu in Ogidi, 16 November 1930. Educated at Government College, Umuahia, 1944-47; University College, Ibadan, 1948-53, B.A. (London) 1953. Married Christiana Okoli in 1961; two sons and two daughters. Talks Producer, Lagos, 1954-57, Controller, Enugu, 1958-61, and Director, Lagos, 1961-66, Nigerian Broadcasting Corporation; Chairman, Citadel Books Ltd., Enugu, 1967; Senior Research Fellow, 1967-73, and Professor of English, 1973-81, University of Nigeria, Nsukka. Visiting Professor, University of Massachusetts, Amherst, 1972-75, and University of Connecticut, Storrs, 1975-76. Since 1962, Founding Editor, Heinemann African Writers series, and since 1970, Director, Heinemann Educational Books (Nigeria) Ltd., and Nwankwo-Ifejika Ltd., later Nwamife, publishers, Enugu; since 1971, Editor, *Okike*, an African journal of new writing. Member, University of Lagos Council, 1966; Chairman, Society of Nigerian Authors, 1966, and since 1982 Chairman, Association of Nigerian Authors. Recipient: Margaret Wrong Memorial Prize, 1959; Nigerian National Trophy, 1960; Rockefeller Fellowship, 1960; Unesco Fellowship, 1963; Jock Campbell Award (*New Statesman*), 1965; Commonwealth Poetry Prize, 1973; Neil Gunn International Fellowship, 1974; Nigerian National Merit Award, 1979. D. Litt.: Dartmouth College, Hanover, New Hampshire, 1972; University of Southampton, 1975; University of Ife, 1978; University of Nigeria, 1981; University of Kent, Canterbury, 1982; D. Univ.: University of Stirling, 1975; LL.D.: University of Prince Edward Island, Charlottetown, 1976; D.H.L.: University of Massachusetts, 1977. Honorary Fellow, Modern Language Association of America, 1974; Member, Order of the Federal Republic of Nigeria, 1979; Honorary Member, American Academy, 1982. Address: P.O. Box 53, University of Nigeria, Nsukka, Nigeria.

PUBLICATIONS

Verse

Beware, Soul-Brother and Other Poems.   Enugu, Nwankwo-Ifejika, 1971; revised edition, Enugu, Nwamife, and London, Heinemann, 1972.
Christmas in Biafra and Other Poems.   New York, Doubleday, 1973.

Novels

Things Fall Apart. London, Heinemann, 1958; New York, McDowell Obolensky, 1959.
No Longer at Ease. London, Heinemann, 1960; New York, Obolensky, 1961.
Arrow of God. London, Heinemann, 1964; New York, Day, 1967.
A Man of the People. London, Heinemann, and New York, Day, 1966.

Short Stories

The Sacrificial Egg and Other Stories. Onitsha, Etudo, 1962.
Girls at War. London, Heinemann, and New York, Doubleday, 1972.

Other (for children)

Chike and the River. London and New York, Cambridge University Press, 1966.
How the Leopard Got His Claws, with John Iroaganachi. Enugu, Nwamife, 1972; New York, Third Press, 1973.
The Flute. Enugu, Fourth Dimension, 1977.
The Drum. Enugu, Fourth Dimension, 1977.

Other

African Aesthetics. Enugu, Nwamife, 1973.
Morning Yet on Creation Day: Essays. London, Heinemann, and New York, Doubleday, 1975.
In Person: Achebe, Awoonor, and Soyinka at the University of Washington. Seattle, University of Washington African Studies Program, 1975.
Literature and Society: An African View. Enugu, Fourth Dimension, 1980.
The Trouble with Nigeria. Enugu, Fourth Dimension, 1983; London, Heinemann, 1984.

Editor, *The Insider: Stories of War and Peace from Nigeria*. Enugu, Nwankwo-Ifejika, and Chatham, New Jersey, Chatham Booksellers, 1971.
Editor, with Dubem Okafor, *Don't Let Him Die: An Anthology of Memorial Poems for Christopher Okigbo*. Enugu, Fourth Dimension, 1978.
Editor, with C.L. Innes, *African Short Stories*. London, Heinemann, 1984.

*

Bibliography: in *Africana Library Journal* (New York), Spring 1970.

Critical Studies: *Chinua Achebe* by Arthur Ravenscroft, London, Longman, 1969, revised edition, 1977; *Chinua Achebe* by David Carroll, New York, Twayne, 1970, revised edition, London, Macmillan, 1980; *Critical Perspectives on Chinua Achebe* edited by Bernth Lindfors and C.L. Innes, London, Heinemann, and Washington, D.C., Three Continents, 1978.

*   *   *

With the publication of *Christmas in Biafra*, Chinua Achebe showed the kind of mature and sensitive voice which might make his book the kind of landmark in African writing which his first novel, *Things Fall Apart*, was fourteen years earlier.

Coming out of the incredible tragedy of a civil war, the poems show remarkable restraint, their language simple and careful, yet never lacking in depth. Their imagery, as in the first few lines of "After a War," is exact and intense: "After a war life catches/ desperately at passing/ hints of normalcy like/ vines entwining a hollow/ twig...." Many of the poems make use of biting irony, as in "Christmas in Biafra" where the seasonal music broadcast over the radio bears messages of "pure transcendental hate" and the starving mothers and children stare mutely at a manger where Jesus lies "plump-looking and rose-cheeked."

Not all of the poems are about the Biafran conflict, for Achebe ranges from personal statements to far-reaching satirical comments on Western foreign policy as in "He Loves Me; He Loves Me Not": "Harold Wilson he loves/ me he gave me/ a gun in my time/ of need to shoot/ my rebellious brother...." But Achebe's subject matter, as in his other writings, is rooted in the confused landscape of post-colonial Africa, where rotten politics and international deals affect the lives of people who still follow traditional paths. One of his best poems, "Beware, Soul Brother," which begins

> We are the men of soul
> men of song we measure out
> our joys and agonies
> too, our long, long passion week
> in paces of the dance

is a reminder to the African reader of his connection with the earth and warns against those "lying in wait leaden-footed, tone deaf/ passionate only for the deep entrails/ of our soil...," yet it is also a poem for all human beings who remember

> where a man's
> foot must return whatever beauties
> it may weave in air, where
> it must return for safety
> and renewal of strength....

—Joseph Bruchac

ACKERMAN, Diane. American. Born in Waukegan, Illinois, 7 October 1948. Educated at Boston University, 1966-67; Pennsylvania State University, University Park, 1967-70, B.A. 1970; Cornell University, Ithaca, New York (Academy of American Poets prize, Corson French Prize, Heermans-McCalmon Playwriting Prize, Corson Bishop Prize, Rockefeller fellow), M.F.A. 1973, M.A. 1976, Ph.D. 1978. Social worker, New York, 1967; government researcher, University Park, Pennsylvania, 1968; editorial assistant, *Library Journal*, New York, 1970; Lecturer, Cornell University, 1978-79; Assistant Professor, University of Pittsburgh, 1980-84. Writer-in-Residence, Spring 1984, and since 1984, Director of Writers Program and Writer-in-Residence, Washington University, St. Louis. Poet-in-Residence, College of William and Mary, Williamsburg, Virginia, 1982-83; Visiting Writer, Ohio University, Athens, Fall 1983. Associate Editor, *Epoch*, Ithaca, New York, 1971-77. Recipient: National Endowment for the Arts fellowship, 1976; Creative Artists Public Service fellowship, 1980. Agent: Elaine Markson Agency, 44 Greenwich Avenue, New York, New York 10011. Address: Department of English, Washington University, St. Louis, Missouri 63130, U.S.A.

PUBLICATIONS

Verse

The Planets: A Cosmic Pastoral. New York, Morrow, 1976.
Wife of Light. New York, Morrow, 1978.
Lady Faustus. New York, Morrow, 1983.

Plays

All Seasons Are Weather, in *Texas Arts Journal* (Dallas), Fall
    1979.
Reverse Thunder (produced New Brunswick, New Jersey,
    1982). Sections published in *American Poetry Review* (Phil-
    adelphia), July-August 1980, and *Denver Quarterly*, Winter
    1984.

Other

Twilight of the Tenderfoot: A Western Memoir. New York,
    Morrow, 1980.
On Extended Wings. New York, Atheneum, 1985.

*

Manuscript Collection: Boston University.

Critical Studies: "The Experience of the Idea" by Samuel Hazo,
in *Hudson Review* (New York), 1978; Frederick Busch in *Ade-
lina* (New York), May 1980; *Publishers Weekly* (New York), 29
July 1983; Patricia Bosworth in *Working Woman* (New York),
March 1984.

Diane Ackerman comments:
    People sometimes ask me about all of the Science in my work,
thinking it odd that I should wish to combine Science and Art,
and assuming that I must have some inner pledge or outer
maxim I follow. But the hardest job for me is trying to keep
Science out of my poetry. We live in a world where amino acids,
viruses, airfoils, and such are common ingredients in our daily
sense of Nature. Not to write about Nature in its widest sense,
because quasars or corpuscles are not "the proper realm of
poetry," as a critic once said to me, is not only irresponsible and
philistine, it bankrupts the experience of living, it ignores much
of life's fascination and variety. I'm a great fan of the Universe,
which I take literally: as One. All of it interests me, and it
interests me in detail.
    It must seem odd, then, that I also write books which have
little or no Science in them. I have no explanation for this, except
to say that the world fascinates me in various ways at various
times of my life. Poetry is my form of celebration and prayer, but
it is also the way in which I enquire about the world. I seem to be
driven by an intense, nomadic curiosity; my feeling of ignorance
is often overwhelming. As a result, prompted by unconscious
obbligatos, I frequently find myself in a state of complete rapture
about a discipline or field, and rapidly coming down with a
book. For as little as six months, perhaps, or as long as three
years, I will be so obsessed with aviation, or astronomy, or the
Old West, or horses, or the oceans, or the life of Sor Juana Inés
de la Cruz (17th-century Mexican nun, natural scientist, and
poet), that I'll become a pocket authority, learning everything
that we can know about the field. Any raw facts I might acquire
about the workings of Nature, fuel for my creative work, are
both secondary to my rage to learn about the human condition,
which I don't think can be seen whole from any one vantage
point. If I hadn't spent a year as a soccer journalist, to get

atmosphere for a novel set in the soccer world which I was
writing, I would never have learned as much as I did about the
history of play, and certainly never written the four soccer poems
at the end of *Lady Faustus*, which have nothing at all to do with
soccer, but are really about the rhythm of the mind, and what it
means to *know* something.
    I suppose the key to my work is that it is never about what
occasions it, or what it pretends to be about. I give myself
passionately, totally to whatever I'm observing, with as much
affectionate curiosity as I can muster, but only as a means to
release in me thoughts about what being human means, and
what it was like to have once been alive on the planet, how it felt
in one's senses, passions, and contemplations. I appear to be a
descriptive poet, a naturalist, perhaps; but I mainly think of
myself as a philosophical poet, or as a Nature poet, if what we
mean by Nature is, as I said earlier, the full sum of Creation.

*   *   *

    Diane Ackerman's first book, *The Planets: A Cosmic Pas-
toral*, gave her the reputation not, as is usually the case with a
young poet, as a "promising" poet, but rather as a prodigiously
gifted poet in full control of her craft and far from sullen art. The
book, a set of poetic explorations and meditations on the planets
in our solar system, Cape Canaveral, the asteroids, and even the
blurry disappointment of Comet Kohoutek, ranges in form and
content widely and well—its science up to date and accurate, and
its poetry a display of dazzling wit. It roused the astronomer Carl
Sagan to say that it demonstrates "how closely compatible planetary exploration and poetry, science and art really are." It bridges
the Two Cultures with a vigor and success not witnessed in
English and American poetry since the 18th century when Newton's *Opticks* and its implications excited poets and shaped their
poems.
    At the end of *The Planets*, Ackerman returns to Earth "like a
woman who, / waking too early each day, / finds it dark yet /
and all the world asleep." This situation also sums up her
dilemma as a poet, having pressed poetry to a service far beyond
that of most of the poems of her contemporaries and now being
faced by a choice of whether to join that sleeping world or return
to planetary exploration. In the poem, she concludes, "But how
could my clamorous heart / lie abed, knowing all of Creation /
has been up for hours?" In the poems which have followed her
cosmic pastoral, she has followed her clamorous heart, not back
out to the planets, but all around and into the lives and experiences of this planet home which we all share.
    In her second book, *Wife of Light*, she does explore the moon,
as "bull-headed / white cyst, you salty old mote / on the night's
backside," as namesake, as lover, as husband of "your wife of
light," but she also becomes of the earth earthy, playing a bluesy
"Menstrual Rag" or singing the true joy of sex with a metaphysical force. Appropriately enough, in one poem she speaks in the
voice of Anne Donne, calling her husband Jack to bed with a wit
he would certainly have admired had he the chance to read the
poem—the lament of "an offput woman on a night growing
bleaker, / and night was never longer, or woman weaker." Her
intellect is matched by the energy and exuberance of her verse;
she thinks fast, and her lines crackle in the mind like a string of
firecrackers. In "Ode to the Alien" she speaks of thought as "an
abstract fever," and her poems are certainly feverish with
thought.
    The title of her third collection, *Lady Faustus*, defines her
poetic stance. As she puts it in the title poem:

> I itch all over. I rage to know
> what beings like me, stymied by death

and leached by wonder, hug those campfires
    night allows,
    aching to know the fate of us all,
wallflowers in a waltz of stars.

And in the poems in the book, she continues her itchy explorations, diving under the sea, flying an airplane, brooding over rivers and bridges. Her wit in this book, as in the earlier ones, runs a full range, exhibiting mind, memory, sense, sanity, ingenuity, acumen, real thought, witty banter, and persiflage. Her enthusiasm carries her forward, but never beyond the bounds of genuine feeling and serious understanding. Ackerman takes off again and again in her poems, but she always returns to our shared darkness, our shared love that leads to the coming dawn. *The Planets* showed her to be a unique figure in modern American poetry. In her two later collections, she has maintained her distinctive voice and way of viewing things even as she has turned to more (literally) mundane topics. Hers is an exciting poetry, and the future work of this Lady Faustus should be more exciting yet.

—R.H.W. Dillard

ACORN, Milton. Canadian. Born in Charlottetown, Prince Edward Island, 30 March 1923. Educated in Charlottetown. Served in the Canadian Armoured Corps, 1939-43. Married Gwendolyn MacEwen, *q.v.* (divorced). Worked as fireman, shipper, freight handler, longshoreman, and carpenter; Editor, *Moment* magazine, Montreal, 1960-62. Recipient: Canadian Poets award, 1970; Governor-General's award, 1975. Address: c/o McClelland and Stewart Ltd., 25 Hollinger Road, Toronto, Ontario M4B 3G2, Canada.

PUBLICATIONS

Verse

In Love and Anger. Privately printed, 1956.
The Brain's the Target. Toronto, Ryerson Press, 1960.
Against a League of Liars. Toronto, Hawkshead Press, 1960.
Jawbreakers. Toronto, Contact Press, 1963.
I've Tasted My Blood: Poems 1956 to 1968, edited by Al Purdy. Toronto, Ryerson Press, 1969.
I Shout Love; On Shaving Off His Beard. Toronto, Village Book Store Press, 1971.
More Poems for People. Toronto, NC Press, 1972.
Jackpine Sonnets. Toronto, Steel Rail, 1977.
Captain MacDougal and the Naked Goddess. Charlottetown, Prince Edward Island, Ragweed, 1982.
Dig Up My Heart: Selected Poems 1952-1983. Toronto, McClelland and Stewart, 1983.

Recording: *Will I Ever Get to Heaven?*, Will o' Wind, 1977(?).

Play

The Road to Charlottetown, with Cedric Smith (produced Toronto, 1977). Included in *The Island Means Minago*, 1975.

Other

The Island Means Minago (miscellany). Toronto, NC Press, 1975.

*   *   *

Milton Acorn, after serving in the Canadian armed forces in World War II, gravitated to Montreal where he settled in the 1950's. Here, he published his first book, and, with two other writers, the poet Al Purdy and the poet/novelist Gwen MacEwen (whom he later married) he edited the little magazine, *Moment* (1960-1962). Acorn moved to Toronto in the early 1960's, and established himself as a figure of some prominence in the freer and less "established" sectors of that city's literary life. One of the first "public" poets and readers on the coffee house poetry reading scene in Canada in the 1950's, Acorn used to frequent and was variously associated with some of the great coffee houses of the period: *viz.* L'Echourie, El Cortijo, The Place, The Bohemian Embassy. He was honoured in a dramatic but genuine gesture by Canadian poets who presented him with the first Canadian Poets' Award in May of 1970 as an act of defiance and reproach aimed at the Governor General's Awards Committee which, with an American academic on its panel, had given the annual award to George Bowering and Gwendolyn MacEwen.

Milton Acorn is a poet of realistic statement and strong political feelings. A carpenter by training, he sees himself as a workingman's poet, and has taken a strong left-wing and nationalist stance. He says: "I have called myself many things; but I guess the one that sticks best is 'revolutionary poet'—that is 'revolutionary' in the political sense, not the poetic sense." From the outset, Acorn has written a poetry of direct, almost commonplace rhetoric, relying on hard, driving rhythms, and a near-palpable physicality of image. In scanning his own performance, Acorn has suggested that: "My own poetry, from 1956 on, has been built around the voice. I originally patterned the voice rhythm of my poems around that of the most intelligent (because the best-travelled and the best-read) of workers at that time—the merchant seamen."

Acorn's full range extends appreciably beyond the poetry of social and socialist concerns. He has a fine sense of locale which is revealed in his better poems which have to do with Maritime Canada; a certain lyrical bent which slides easily into his own peculiar kind of introspectiveness and poetic home-spun. Cragginess, a cragginess of mind and spirit, is Acorn's best quality:

Since I'm Island-born home's as precise
as if a mumbly old carpenter,
shoulder-straps crossed wrong,
laid it out,
refigured to the last three-eighths of a shingle.

—Michael Gnarowski

ADAM, Helen (Douglas). American. Born in Glasgow, Scotland, 2 December 1909. Educated at Seymour Lodge; Navin Academy; University of Ediinburgh for two years. Journalist in Edinburgh and London during the 1930's; moved to the United States in 1939, and worked at various office jobs in New York until 1949, then lived in California: naturalized, 1977. Address: 223 East 82nd Street, New York, New York 10028, U.S.A.

PUBLICATIONS

Verse

The Elfin Pedlar and Tales Told by Pixy Pool. London, Hodder and Stoughton, 1923; New York, Putnam, 1924.
Charms and Dreams from the Elfin Pedlar's Pack. London, Hodder and Stoughton, 1924.
Shadow of the Moon. London, Hodder and Stoughton, 1929.
The Queen o' Crow Castle. San Francisco, White Rabbit Press, 1958.
Ballads. New York, Acadia Press, 1964.
Counting-Out Rhyme. New York, Interim, 1972.
Selected Poems and Ballads. New York, Helikon Press, 1974.
Turn Again to Me and Other Poems. New York, Kulchur, 1977.
Gone Sailing. West Branch, Iowa, Toothpaste Press, 1980.
Songs with Music. San Francisco, Aleph Press, 1982.
The Bells of Dis. West Branch, Iowa, Toothpaste Press, 1984.
Stone Cold Gothic. New York, Kulchur, 1984.

Play

San Francisco's Burning, with Pat Adam (produced New York, 1966). Berkeley, California, Oannes, 1963.

Short Stories

Ghosts and Grinning Shadows: Two Witch Stories. New York, Hanging Loose Press, 1979.

*   *   *

Helen Adam was 30 before she emigrated from Scotland with her mother and sister. Born in Glasgow, she grew up in the coastal farming region of upper north Scotland, in Nairnshire, on Moray Firth, with its Neolithic ruins, its low-lying ground, and large private forests, the imagery and landscape of most of her poems. She worked as a journalist in Edinburgh and London before emigrating, and finally settled in San Francisco in 1953, where a poetic renaissance was in full flower. Her work gradually drew the attention of other poets, especially the appreciation of Robert Duncan, who has frequently praised her curious themes and ideas as a singular expression of the inner life. Indeed, she is without parallel in recent poetry in her recreation of medieval balladry and narrative—she writes in a patois of old Scots dialect and modern English, sounding very much like a transliteration of the old literature. But in fact her ballads and songs are entirely of her own composing and constitute a new extension of ballad tradition.

Her primary theme is love and the curious sort of underworld of spirits, demons, and allegorical monsters that inhabit the unconscious mind of any lover. Her landscapes are the forests and dark caves of medieval romance, the realm of unicorns, angels, mysterious gardens, all described with skillful allegorical awareness. In her *Selected Poems and Ballads* Adam chose poems that concentrate exclusively on the terror and grief of love—the havoc of jealousy, the desolation of stranded women, the powers of lust, the awesome and ghoulish revenge of the unrequited and jilted, the primal urgings of incest and cannibalism. All of these elements come together in a brief poem, "A Tale Best Forgotten," which narrates the awful fate of a male lover (most victims of her verse are males) who comes between a father and his daughter:

In the garden, in the garden, while the river slowly ran,
Walked the daughter, and her lover, and the dog-headed
man.
The daughter, and her lover, and the dog-headed man!
It's a tale best forgotten, but before the tale began
His daughter, by the river that reflected as it ran,
Fed the bones of her lover to the dog-headed man.

Most of her narratives end in the death of either one or both lovers, who then go on restlessly haunting the living or, as in "I Love My Love," pull the living into their graves. "I Love My Love" is especially gruesome as a tale of unrequited desire, in which a man slays his wife and buries her, and is then swept to his death by the tangle of her still-growing hair. "Doll Song" is the most stunning performance of *Selected Poems and Ballads*, in which a young girl models two dolls from clay and calls them Love and Hate. They grow into demons when the girl falls in love and become her ruthless guardians thereafter. The tale allegorizes the real emotions of a young girl maturing, who then lives in the exile of adulthood with these immense emotions to rule and torment her. The magical landscape glitters with psychological mystery throughout the poem, and the narrator widens the incident to universality by closing with images of other youths innocently making their own small dolls for their pillows.

Adam is an uncanny magician of the romantic and supernatural, but her purposes are grounded in a real earth of psychological facts. Her archaisms and dialect, her ancient landscapes and quaint plots, are all meant to heighten and illustrate themes that could be treated in other ways, of course, but not with the same poignancy and startling power as her damp, desolate Scottish moors create. Adam is a very modern poet in her perceptions of irrational processes, and in her sophisticated grasp of instinct and primal urge. But she is especially timely in her depiction of very powerful females and beautiful, but somehow vague, male suitors, a perspective of many contemporary women poets—who are exploring the mythos of their sex as the privileges and powers of gender in society shift base.

—Paul Christensen

————————

ADAMS, Léonie (Fuller). American. Born in Brooklyn, New York, 9 December 1899. Educated at Girls' High School; Barnard College, New York, B.A. (magna cum laude) 1922 (Phi Beta Kappa). Married the writer William Troy in 1933 (died, 1961). Bookshop assistant, Best and Company, New York, 1922-23; research secretary, Yale University Law School, New Haven, Connecticut, 1923-24; Editorial Assistant, Wilson Publishing Company, New York, 1924; Editor, *Measure,* New York, 1924-25; English teacher, Hamilton Institute for Girls, New York, 1925; Editorial Assistant, Metropolitan Museum of Art, New York, 1926-28; Instructor, Washington Square College, New York, 1930-32, Sarah Lawrence College, Bronxville, New York, 1933-34, and Bennington College, Vermont, 1935-37, 1941-45; Lecturer, New Jersey College for Women, New Brunswick, 1946-48, and Columbia University, New York, 1947-68; Consultant in Poetry, 1948-49, and Fellow in American Letters, 1949-55, Library of Congress, Washington, D.C.; Lecturer, New School for Social Research, New York, 1952-53; Fulbright Professor, France, 1955-56; Visiting Professor, Trinity College, Hartford, Connecticut, Summer 1960, University of Washington, Seattle, 1960, 1968-69, and Purdue University, Lafayette, Indiana, 1971-72. Recipient: Guggenheim Fellowship, 1928, 1929; American Academy grant, 1949; Harriet Monroe Poetry Award, 1954; Shelley Memorial Award, 1955; Bollingen Prize, 1955; Academy of American Poets Fellowship, 1959; National Endowment for the Arts grant, 1966; Brandeis University Creative Arts Award, 1968. D.Litt.: New Jersey College for Women, 1950. Secretary, National Institute of Arts and Letters, 1959-61. Address: CVCC, 30 Park Lane East, New Milford, Connecticut 06776, U.S.A.

PUBLICATIONS

Verse

Those Not Elect.   New York, McBride, 1925.
Midsummer.   Privately printed, 1929.
High Falcon and Other Poems.   New York, Day, 1929.
This Measure.   New York, Knopf, 1933.
Poems: A Selection.   New York, Funk and Wagnalls, 1954.

Other

Editor, and translator with others, *Lyrics of François Villon.* Croton Falls, New York, Limited Editions Club, 1933.

                              *

Manuscript Collection: Beinecke Library, Yale University, New Haven, Connecticut.

Critical Studies: by Eda Low Walton, in *The Nation* (New York), 1930; "Three Younger Poets" by Louis Untermeyer, in *The English Journal* (Champaign, Illinois), 1932; *Poetry in Our Time* by Babette Deutsch, New York, Holt, 1952, revised edition, New York, Doubleday, 1963.

Léonie Adams comments:
   Lyric poetry, in largely traditional forms. At formative period influenced by Elizabethan, early Romantic and, through Yeats largely, Symbolist poetry.
   My work has been decribed sometimes as "metaphysical" and sometimes as "romantic." It is perhaps some sort of fusion. Though its images are largely from nature (and tradition of Nature), I have tended in my better work toward a contemplative lyric articulated by some sort of speech music. To find my "figurative language" in the natural scene was less a literary habit I think than one absorbed from my mother, in whom the traditional American experience of nature remained unbroken by her translation from rural Maryland to the city. It was only thus I could catch and keep the tune. As for the other and larger modes I could admire, and (hopefully) possess, their use by others.

                    *   *   *

   The poetry of Léonie Adams is very traditional: the poet's imagery derives from careful observations of beauty in nature. Her diction is strongly reminiscent of the Romantics: possibly to accommodate rhyme, normal sentence structure is often ignored ("Those not Elect"):

>   Never, being damned, see paradise.
>   The heart will sweeten at its look;
>   Nor hell was known, till paradise
>   Our senses shook.

At times, this device is bothersome, and combined with the heavy emphasis on traditional, romantic subjects, results in archaic textures ("Words for the Raker of Leaves"):

>   Birds are of passage now,
>   Else-wending; where
>   (Songless, soon gone of late)
>   They night among us,
>   No tone now upon grass
>   Downcast from hedge or grove
>   With goldening day invites.

In counterpoint, the best of Adams's work incorporates traditional concerns with a contemporary vision. The reader has been lulled by her lyrics (which are varied enough rhythmically that their lulling is accomplished by subject, not tedious sing-song). "Ghost Tree" begins as a typically romantic ode: "Oh beech, unbind your yellow leaf, for deep/The honeyed time lies sleeping, and lead shade/Seals up the eyelids of its golden sleep." Suddenly, the poet abandons the multi-syllabic adjectives and allows the scene to describe its own potential:

>   And here is only the cold scream of the fox,
>   Only the huntsman following on the hound;
>   While your quaint-plumaged,
>   The bird that your green summer boughs lapped round,
>   Bends south its soft bright breast.

These poems are meticulously crafted. Nowhere does the reader feel that the poet has abandoned her poem in favor of a digressive second look at the subject. This single-mindedness sometimes results in an almost too-predictable unity to Adams's work, but the energy with which she welds her vision to her art provides an oasis for those who thirst after a time when the poem was a song of life, neither contradictory nor simple.

                                        —Geof Hewitt

                        _____

ADAMS, Perseus.   Pseudonym for Peter Robert Charles Adams.   South African.   Born in Cape Town, 11 March 1933. Educated at Cambridge, East London, and Sea Town high schools, Cape Town; University of Cape Town, B.A. in psychology and English 1952, Cert. Ed. 1962. Has worked as a journalist, psychologist, clerk, and English teacher in seven countries. Recipient: South African Poetry Prize, 1965. Address: 7 New End, Hampstead, London N.W.3, England.

PUBLICATIONS

Verse

The Land at My Door.   Cape Town, Human and Rousseau, 1965.
Grass for the Unicorn.   Cape Town, Juta, 1975.

                              *

Perseus Adams comments:
   (1970) Major themes: 1) subjects where the life-death, light-dark juxtaposition is sharply counterpointed; 2) creatures, people or animals, who have been robbed by life; 3) a metaphysical probing to discover our rightful place in the universe.
   I employ a free verse with powerful resonant rhythms and complex tones. My style can be harshly decisive or gently lyrical—depending on the subject matter or mood. I have been

called my country's "foremost lyricist," but this is not a title I care for.

* * *

Perseus Adams is essentially a lyric poet and even where he has grouped his poems under objective, thematic headings, the personal and subjective element comes through in the rhythms, texture, and structure of his verse. The mood varies from a Hopkinsian delight in nature and the joyful spontaneity of youth, to a more introspective frame of mind in which the lessons of experience are mulled over. If this results at times in too explicitly didactic a strain, the poet's seriousness of purpose and lyrical intensity rescue his work from the commonplace or trivial. His first volume, *The Land at My Door*, with its division of poems into "Morning" and "Afternoon," reflects the two contrasting moods postulated above—a grouping reminiscent of Blake's "Songs of Innocence and of Experience," though with none of the latter's conscious parallelism and antithesis. The mood of the "Morning" poems is closer to a Wordsworthian sense of awe, as in the closing section of the sonnet "Dawn on Table Mountain":

Nor has there ever been a presence of air to match
That tumult of impending absence that is
An African sky, and blue, so blue you feel
You are gazing at innocence and sacredness blended.
Now under that dome of an incandescent eye, three play
Their parts on this altar above the world: Grass, dew and sun
While joy shivers a watching bush-dove with supernal lightning.

The poems of this first volume are characterized by a somewhat indiscriminate abundance and variety of images which give, at times, an impression of contrived ingenuity. The sentiment, too, can be forced and stilted, imposed on rather than issuing from the poetic experience: this is true particularly of the closing lines of "Widow" and the self-consciously didactic "A Sky's Blue Innocence." It is worth noting that these failures of tone and technique occur mainly in poems whose subject-matter lies outside the writer's range of experience: the clichés and ritual gestures of "The War Veteran," for instance, reveal a sensibility not fully engaged by its subject. Against these, one can place poems such as "Crying Baby in a Grocer Shop," where the apparently commonplace is experienced in a way that invests it with a humane profundity, or "My Grandmother," where the closing stanzas present a beautifully sustained and entirely convincing vision of age advancing towards death and decay.

In *Grass for the Unicorn*, published ten years later, the verbal profusion of the earlier volume has given way to a markedly sparer style and a more austere, controlled expression of feeling. An empathic mode of perception is one of Adams's strengths as a poet; this is finely realized in "Mountain Protea," which illustrates also his flexible but highly functional command of form:

If—as I'm inclined to believe —
empathy is the art that comes
most naturally to the deeply quiet
                              spiralling out —

this sun pyx has it: high on Devil's Peak
with watch-fire head, all ears pricked
                              it unfolds
to enter into leopard and hawk
accenting their speed, a fleck in their sight
its tense repose, its dovetailing jet
theirs when they hunt....

Many of Adams's poems are inspired by his native Cape Town, its environs and peoples. He observes keenly but with a sense of humility and awe, as in the fine (and Frost-like) lines of "Bird Shrine," where the teacher-pupil roles are reversed as the normally backward class truant is transfigured by the "feathered glory" of his pigeons. Satire and protest are foreign to Adams's genius and when, as in "Indigenous" and "Woltemade" he resorts to overt social or political comment, he reduces the force and expansiveness of his lyrical gift. Similarly, though his metrical virtuosity is amply illustrated in *Grass for the Unicorn*, his experiments with typography and visual effect are extrinsic to his essentially metaphoric style and have little but novelty to commend them. The precision, force, and clarity encapsulated in a poem such as "Sea Scalpel" point to one salient aspect of Adams's poetry—his craftsmanship—and explain why he selected as motto for his second volume the remark by the Argentinian poet, Arturo Aquino, that he preferred poetry to prose because "poetry drops like an eagle and stabs before you know." The other major feature of Adams's poetry is his humanistic vision: he never forgets the Wordsworthian admonition that the poet is a man speaking to men. It is this probing but sympathetic awareness that informs his most successful efforts, as in the poignant "Elegy for the Pure Act," and gives an earnest of his still-developing powers.

—E. Pereira

ADAMSON, Robert. Australian. Born in Sydney, New South Wales, 17 May 1943. Married Cheryl Adamson in 1973. Worked as a pastry cook, fisherman, and journalist in the 1960's; Associate Editor, 1968-70, Editor, 1970-75, and Assistant Editor, 1975-77, *New Poetry* magazine, Sydney; Editor and Director, Prism Books, Sydney, 1970-77. Since 1979, Founding Editor and Director, with Dorothy Hewett, Big Smoke Books, Sydney. Designer for Prism Books and *New Poetry* magazine since 1970, and since 1979, Designer for Big Smoke Books. Recipient: Australia Council Fellowship, 1976, 1977; Grace Leven Prize, 1977. Address: Big Smoke Books, 1/2 Billyard Avenue, Elizabeth Bay, New South Wales 2011, Australia.

PUBLICATIONS

Verse

Canticles on the Skin.   Sydney, Illumination Press, 1970.
The Rumour.   Sydney, New Poetry, 1971.
Swamp Riddles.   Sydney, Island Press, 1974.
Theatre I-XIX.   Sydney, Pluralist Press, 1976.
Cross the Border.   Sydney, New Poetry, 1977.
Selected Poems.   Sydney, Angus and Robertson, 1977.
Where I Come From.   Sydney, Big Smoke, 1979.
The Law at Heart's Desire.   Sydney, Prism, 1982.

Novel

Zimmer's Essay, with Bruce Hanford.   Sydney, Wild and Woolley, 1974.

*

Manuscript Collection: Australian National Library, Canberra.

Critical Studies: by Dorothy Hewett in *New Poetry 27* (Sydney), no. 1; interview with John Tranter in *Makar 1* (Brisbane), 1979.

*   *   *

With five major collections (plus a *Selected Poems*) published since 1970, Robert Adamson has claimed for himself a central position among Australian poets of his generation—a generation that, in 1968, accomplished a remarkable revitalisation of poetic energies in this country. His work over this period has balanced an overt need to surprise or challenge (or even shock) the reader, with an ongoing discovery of sources of creative nourishment from personal experience and from his Hawkesbury River regional background. Adamson is not, however, a regional or a confessional poet. His 1979 volume, *Where I Come From*, would seem to be a collection of autobiographical pieces about parents, childhood, and a delinquent adolescence, related with a sort of deadpan selectivity. It is a carefully contrived game, exploring ways of approaching the self (and themes already uncovered in earlier volumes) that imply a complex relationship not only with the reader, but with the possibility of ever realising a state beyond "the lie" of the conscious artist. In all his verse Adamson has sought to transcend the easily ironic stance (or the glibly petulant). His poetry constantly undercuts its own pretentions, but the effect is lacerating, not denigratory. Its surface may range from the artful *simpliste* chronicler of *Where I Come From* to the arty fabulist of "The Grail Poems" but the masks are worn with a wholehearted willingness, a risk-taking, that drags us into the exploration—and the search. Adamson's work is, in the best sense, self-conscious. It is also consistent in its deeply felt need to seek out (if not to find) some transforming quality from the rawness of observed data and experience.

His first book, *Canticles on the Skin*, established all the ongoing concerns he has subsequently followed: poems of prison experience (notably the opening sequence, pointedly titled "The Imitator" and bearing an inscription from St. Paul that still illuminates Adamson's approach to art: "For though I be free from all men, yet have I made myself servant unto all, that I might gain the more"); poems of literary homage; poems of landscape homage; and those nervous drug/car/energy poems that were probably his most immediate successes. It was followed by *The Rumour* in 1971, with its long title centrepiece, pivotal poems of the early 1970's in Australia (the other two being John Tranter's "Red Movie" and Martin Johnston's "The Blood Aquarium"). Though its derivations are clear, "The Rumour" reveals a sense of intense purpose and a drive that carries it into areas almost unexplored in Australian verse. *Swamp Riddles*, though diffuse, prints the first outstanding group of Hawkesbury poems, and a much acclaimed set of elegies for his contemporary, Michael Dransfield. *Cross the Border*, ambitious and uneven, attempts a large synthesis, but survives through individual achievements. *Where I Come From* is a deliberate turning away from this aesthetic experiment in a (self-claimed) "New Romanticism." It is immediately gripping, and seemingly accessible. It is also a progress report.

As editor of the magazine *New Poetry* in Sydney, Robert Adamson has been intensely involved in the politics of poetry; his personal influence has been considerable. But it is the capacity to transform his own restless energy to lyrical and celebrative experiments that has given Adamson's own work a depth and overriding intensity unique among poets of his generation in Australia.

—Thomas W. Shapcott

ADCOCK, Fleur. British. Born in Papakura, New Zealand, 10 February 1934; emigrated to the United Kingdom in 1963. Educated in England, 1939-47; Wellington Girls' College and Victoria University of Ellington, New Zealand, M.A. (honours) in classics. Married Alistair Campbell, *q.v.*, in 1952 (divorced, 1957); two sons. Temporary Assistant Lecturer in Classics, University of Otago, Dunedin, 1958. Held library posts at the University of Otago, 1959-61, and at Turnbull Library, Wellington, 1962; Assistant Librarian, Foreign and Commonwealth Office Library, London, 1963-79. Arts Council Creative Writing Fellow, Charlotte Mason College of Education, Ambleside, Cumbria, 1977-78; Northern Arts Fellow, universities of Newcastle upon Tyne and Durham, 1979-81; Eastern Arts Fellow, University of East Anglia, Norwich, 1984. Recipient: Festival of Wellington Prize, 1961; New Zealand State Literary Fund Award, 1964; Buckland Award, 1967; Jessie MacKay Award, 1968, 1972; Cholmondeley Award, 1976; New Zealand Book Award, 1984. Address: 14 Lincoln Road, London N2 9DL, England.

PUBLICATIONS

Verse

The Eye of the Hurricane. Wellington, Reed, 1964.
Tigers. London, Oxford University Press, 1967.
High Tide in the Garden. London, Oxford University Press, 1971.
Corgi Modern Poets in Focus 5, with others, edited by Dannie Abse. London, Corgi, 1973.
The Scenic Route. London, Oxford University Press, 1974.
A Morden Tower Reading 5, with Gavin Ewart. Newcastle upon Tyne, Morden Tower, 1977.
In Focus. London, Poem-of-the-Month Club, 1977.
The Inner Harbour. London, Oxford University Press, 1979; New York, Oxford University Press, 1980.
Below Loughrigg. Newcastle upon Tyne, Bloodaxe, 1979.
Selected Poems. Oxford, Oxford University Press, 1983.
The Virgin and the Nightingale: Medieval Latin Poems. Newcastle upon Tyne, Bloodaxe, 1983.

Other

Editor, with Anthony Thwaite, *New Poetry 4.* London, Hutchinson, 1978.
Editor, *The Oxford Book of Contemporary New Zealand Poetry.* Auckland and Oxford, Oxford University Press, 1982.

*

Critical Study: introduction by Dannie Abse to *Corgi Modern Poets in Focus 5*, 1973.

Fleur Adcock comments:
I can't give a code of my poetic practice or a set of rules by which I have operated; I can only point to certain tendencies and outline an attitude. Poetry is a search for ways of communication; it must be conducted with openness, flexibility, and a constant readiness to listen. The content of my poems derives largely from those parts of my life which are directly experienced: relationships with people or places; images and insights which have presented themselves sharply from whatever source, conscious or subconscious; ideas triggered off by language itself. In recent years I have tended increasingly to use poetry as a method of writing fiction: the narratives of my poems (seldom ever

merely autobiographical) often now tell invented stories.

My verse forms are relatively traditional (traditions alter). In general they have moved away from strict classical patterns in the direction of greater freedom—as is usual with most artists learning a trade. It takes courage, however, to leave all props behind, to cast oneself, like Matisse, upon pure space. I still await that confidence. In the meantime I continue to learn; and sometimes find it fruitful to return to a rigid metrical form as a discipline and for a different kind of exploration.

I write primarily for the printed page, not for performance (regarding poetry readings as the trailer, not the movie). But because the sound of words is central to the experiencing of a poem I read my work aloud as it develops and try to remove anything which is clumsy or unacceptable to the ear. As for the eye, the patterns of lines in type don't particularly interest me; words, not their shape on the page, are what matter. If one is fortunate their destination, like their origin, will be as voices speaking in the mind.

*   *   *

Fleur Adcock generally writes within a tradition of English poetry which is distinguished by its clarity, fastidiousness, and sharp observation of scenes and events. A kind of emotional toughness and an innate reticence underlie the surface candour, and the combination is often extremely effective. It's the ironical aspect of personal relations that interests her, along with its proper mode of expression, pointed understatement. She is by turns amused, expectant, and self-effacing, but always composed and vigorous—if she assumes, for example, a posture of wilful bafflement it is probably because she's in a sceptical humour: "I do not understand your arrangements." The last line of this ("Hauntings"), "You needn't think I am here to stay," reads like a warning issued by someone who is very much in control; this is a characteristic stance.

One of the protective measures which places distance between the poet and the grotesque or threatening image is a certain jauntiness of tone ("Grandma"); another is the kind of salutary ruthlessness conveyed in "Think Before You Shoot": "They've eaten all the squirrels. They want you,/ And it's no excuse to say you're only children./ No one is on your side. What will you do?" If the central metaphor occasionally seems a little too contrived or expected, the poet is apt, with grace, to acknowledge this herself in the last verse—"Gardens are rife with sermon-fodder"—a trick which indicates self-awareness at the very least. More often, however, the comparison makes a deft summing-up of the theme and adds an oblique comment on it: in "Against Coupling," for example, "Pyramus and Thisbe are dead, but/ The hole in the wall can still be troublesome."

Fleur Adcock nearly always writes well about New Zealand, and about Ulster, another starting point for the ex-patriot's concern with origins, settled principles, and continuity. She distinguishes, however, between the backward look which is essentially disabused, and the retrogressive tendency which implies nostalgia. In "Please Identify Yourself," a remarkably economical and satisfactory poem, she is making fun of the civilized person exposed to bigotry, who can do nothing but align herself with the other side—"I scrawl incredulous notes under my hymnbook/ And burn with Catholicism." In a 1979 pamphlet, *Below Loughrigg*, the scene has moved to the Lake District where the poet is lucky enough to overhear a deep voice bellowing "Wordsworth"—an incident sufficiently odd and felicitous to work its own effect. But it is the more formal, intricate and condensed "Ex-Queen among the Astronomers" (in *The Inner Harbour*) that seems to me her most impressive work to date; this

shows how a near-metaphysical conceit may be presented without laboriousness or affectation.

—Patricia Craig

———

ALVAREZ, A(lfred).   British.   Born in London, 5 August 1929. Educated at Oundle School, Northamptonshire; Corpus Christi College, Oxford (Senior Research Scholar and Research Scholar of Goldsmiths' Company; 1952-53, 1954-55), B.A. 1952, M.A. 1956; Princeton University, New Jersey (Procter Visiting Fellow, 1953-54). Married 1) Ursula Barr in 1956 (marriage dissolved, 1961), one son; 2) Anne Adams, 1966, one son and one daughter. Gauss Lecturer, Princeton University, 1957-58; Visiting Professor, Brandeis University, Waltham, Massachusetts, 1960, and State University of New York, Buffalo, 1966. Advisory Poetry Editor, *The Observer*, London, 1956-66; Editor, *Journal of Education*, 1957; Drama Critic, *New Statesman*, London, 1958-60; Advisory Editor, Penguin Modern European Poets in Translation, 1965-75; Presenter, *Voices* programme, Channel 4 television, 1982. Recipient: Rockefeller Fellowship, 1955, 1958; D.H. Lawrence Fellowship, 1958; Vachel Lindsay Prize (*Poetry*, Chicago), 1961. Agent: Deborah Rogers Ltd., 49 Blenheim Crescent, London W11 2EF; or, Candida Donadio and Associates, 111 West 57th Street, New York, New York 10019, U.S.A. Address: c/o The Observer, 8 St. Andrew's Hill, London EC4V 5JA, England.

PUBLICATIONS

Verse

(Poems).   Oxford, Fantasy Press, 1952.
The End of It.   Privately printed, 1958.
Twelve Poems.   London, The Review, 1968.
Lost.   London, Turret, 1968.
Penguin Modern Poets 18, with Roy Fuller and Anthony Thwaite.   London, Penguin, 1970.
Apparition.   Brisbane, University of Queensland Press, 1971.
The Legacy.   London, Poem-of-the-Month Club, 1972.
Autumn to Autumn and Selected Poems 1953-1976.   London, Macmillan, 1978.

Play

Screenplay: *The Anarchist*, 1969.

Novels

Hers.   London, Weidenfeld and Nicolson,1974; New York, Random House, 1975.
Hunt.   London, Macmillan, 1978; New York, Simon and Schuster, 1979.

Other

The Shaping Spirit: Studies in Modern English and American Poets.   London, Chatto and Windus, 1958; as *Stewards of Excellence: Studies in Modern English and American Poets*, New York, Scribner, 1958.
The School of Donne.   London, Chatto and Windus, 1961; New York, Pantheon, 1962.

Under Pressure: The Artist and Society: Eastern Europe and the U.S.A.   London, Penguin, 1965.
Beyond All This Fiddle: Essays 1955-1967.   London, Allen Lane, 1968; New York, Random House, 1969.
The Savage God: A Study of Suicide.   London, Weidenfeld and Nicolson, 1971; New York, Random House, 1972.
Beckett.   London, Fontana, and New York, Viking Press, 1973.
Life after Marriage: Scenes from Divorce.   London, Macmillan, 1982; as *Life after Marriage: Love in an Age of Divorce*, New York, Simon and Schuster, 1982.
The Biggest Game in Town (on gambling).   London, Deutsch, and Boston, Houghton Mifflin, 1983.

Editor, *The New Poetry: An Anthology.*   London, Penguin, 1962; revised edition, 1966.

*

Critical Study: interview with Ian Hamilton, in *New Review* (London), March 1978.

*   *   *

The published poetry of A. Alvarez is slight indeed in volume, but rich in its economy. *Autumn to Autumn and Selected Poems* contained 37 poems, 16 published for the first time. Of the new poems, only eight were written since 1974, seven of them comprising the section called "Autumn to Autumn."

It is a shame that Alvarez, who has done so much to cultivate a climate receptive to the confessional poetry of Lowell, Berryman, and Plath—even though his essay on Plath in *The Savage God* could be criticized for feeding the public's nearly insatiable appetite to feast upon a poet's life to understand her art—and whose writings on Donne and Eliot have done much to clarify their place in the history of contemporary poetry, should be so restrained in his practice of poetry. Perhaps he is too wary of rendering a poetry in the style of the Movement which he so aptly described in his essay, "The New Poetry; or, Beyond the Gentility Principle." Does he fear that he cannot heed his own warning and remain "immune" to gentility? He complained of the nine poets who formed the Movement that their "academic-administrative verse, polite, knowledgeable, efficient, polished, and, in its quiet way, even intelligent," practiced its own pieties and strove too hard to make the poet appear like the man next door. Alvarez has found his own, colloquial, modern voice and a hard-to-find originality in his novel, *Hers*, but in his poetry he clings to a compression of style and formality of verse that seem ultimately to inhibit him. Perhaps the standard he sets in the close of the above-mentioned essay is too high. There he asks that contemporary poetry be like "Coleridge's Imagination," that it "reconcile a 'more than usual state of emotion' with more than usual order."

Alvarez's new poems continue the strain and form of the poems in *Lost*. They are poems of ephemera. Briefly an emotion is isolated, felt, and wafted away, leaving the persona with a sense of perplexity and regret. Often he depicts mates inhabiting their "grey untender rooms" divided by fears and dreams. In "He Said, She Said" from *Autumn to Autumn*, a scent and a presence pass through the bedroom as two autumnal lovers lie together. He names the smell "hawthorn" and says it beckons, "Come"; she scoffs and says it said "Gone." Alvarez closes the poem characteristically with a note of mild irony:

A flicker of gold, a smile, a far voice calling
Confusedly, "Come," "Gone," "Come." The jumbled scents

of Spring on the autumn night. "Our last chance," he said
And she answered, "You take it without me."

More than a decade earlier, in another poem of dialogue, "Autumn Marriage," the wife's words were equally matter-of-fact and loveless. Alvarez's range continues to be narrow. This volume, containing poetry of two decades, reflects his admiration for Eliot, Frost, and Donne, and for Plath and Hughes. Several of the poems written in the late 1950's and early 1960's recall Plath's stridency and savage treatment of love's anger. "Sunstruck" is such a poem, "Anger" another. "Operation," "Back," and "The Nativity in New Mexico" recall Plath's "Tulips" or "Cut." They shed a harsh, clinical light on a grinning midwife and thighs sticky with afterbirth. Others use an economy of words to call up ordinary scenes, closing time in a park, a sleeper awakening, the coming of old age. His preoccupation with dreams, restlessness, and disintegration mark his modernity; his verse forms and gift for understatement recall the traditional British poetry of the early 20th century.

—Carol Simpson Stern

AMIS, Kingsley (William).   British. Born in London, 16 April 1922. Educated at City of London School; St. John's College, Oxford, M.A. Served in the Royal Corps of Signals, 1942-45. Married 1) Hilary Ann Bardwell in 1948 (marriage dissolved, 1965), two sons, including the writer Martin Amis, and one daughter; 2) the writer Elizabeth Jane Howard in 1965 (divorced, 1983). Lecturer in English, University College, Swansea, Wales, 1949-61; Fellow in English, Peterhouse, Cambridge, 1961-63. Visiting Fellow in Creative Writing, Princeton University, New Jersey, 1958-59; Visiting Professor, Vanderbilt University, Nashville, Tennessee, 1967. Recipient: Maugham Award, 1955; *Yorkshire Post* award for fiction, 1974; Campbell Memorial Award, for fiction, 1977. Honorary Fellow, St. John's College, 1976. C.B.E. (Commander, Order of the British Empire), 1981. Agent: Jonathan Clowes Ltd., 22 Prince Albert Road, London NW1 7ST, England.

PUBLICATIONS

Verse

Bright November.   London, Fortune Press, 1947.
A Frame of Mind.   Reading, Berkshire, University of Reading School of Art, 1953.
(Poems).   Oxford, Fantasy Press, 1954.
A Case of Samples: Poems 1946-1956.   London, Gollancz, 1956; New York, Harcourt Brace, 1957.
The Evans Country.   Oxford, Fantasy Press, 1962.
Penguin Modern Poets 2, with Dom Moraes and Peter Porter. London, Penguin, 1962.
A Look round the Estate: Poems 1957-1967.   London, Cape, 1967; New York, Harcourt Brace, 1968.
Wasted, Kipling at Bateman's.   London, Poem-of-the-Month Club, 1973.
Collected Poems 1944-1979.   London, Hutchinson, 1979; New York, Viking Press, 1980.

Recordings: *Kingsley Amis Reading His Own Poems*, Listen, 1962; *Poems*, with Thomas Blackburn, Jupiter, 1962.

Plays

Radio Plays: *Something Strange*, 1962; *The Riverside Villas Murder*, from his own novel, 1976.

Television Plays: *A Question about Hell*, 1964; *The Importance of Being Harry*, 1971; *Dr. Watson and the Darkwater Hall Mystery*, 1974; *See What You've Done* (*Softly, Softly* series), 1974; *We Are All Guilty* (*Against the Crowd* series), 1975; *Break In*, 1975.

Novels

Lucky Jim. London, Gollancz, and New York, Doubleday, 1954.
That Uncertain Feeling. London, Gollancz, 1955; New York, Harcourt Brace, 1956.
I Like It Here. London, Gollancz, and New York, Harcourt Brace, 1958.
Take a Girl Like You. London, Gollancz, 1960; New York, Harcourt Brace, 1961.
One Fat Englishman. London, Gollancz, 1963; New York, Harcourt Brace, 1964.
The Egyptologists, with Robert Conquest. London, Cape, 1965; New York, Random House, 1966.
The Anti-Death League. London, Gollancz, and New York, Harcourt Brace, 1966.
Colonel Sun: A James Bond Adventure (as Robert Markham). London, Cape, and New York, Harper, 1968.
I Want It Now. London, Cape, 1968; New York, Harcourt Brace, 1969.
The Green Man. London, Cape, 1969; New York, Harcourt Brace, 1970.
Girl, 20. London, Cape, 1971.
The Riverside Villas Murder. London, Cape, and New York, Harcourt Brace, 1973.
Ending Up. London, Cape, and New York, Harcourt Brace, 1974.
The Alteration. London, Cape, 1976; New York, Viking Press, 1977.
Jake's Thing. London, Hutchinson, 1978; New York, Viking Press, 1979.
Russian Hide-and-Seek: A Melodrama. London, Hutchinson, 1980.
Stanley and the Women. London, Hutchinson, 1984.

Short Stories

My Enemy's Enemy. London, Gollancz, 1962; New York, Harcourt Brace, 1963.
Penguin Modern Stories 11, with others. London, Penguin, 1972.
Dear Illusion. London, Covent Garden Press, 1972.
The Darkwater Hall Mystery. Edinburgh, Tragara Press, 1978.
Collected Short Stories. London, Hutchinson, 1980.

Other

Socialism and the Intellectuals. London, Fabian Society, 1957.
New Maps of Hell: A Survey of Science Fiction. New York, Harcourt Brace, 1960; London, Gollancz, 1961.
The James Bond Dossier. London, Cape, and New York, New American Library, 1965.
Lucky Jim's Politics. London, Conservative Political Centre, 1968.

What Became of Jane Austen? and Other Questions. London, Cape, 1970; New York, Harcourt Brace, 1971.
On Drink. London, Cape, 1972; New York, Harcourt Brace, 1973.
Rudyard Kipling and His World. London, Thames and Hudson, 1975; New York, Scribner, 1976.
An Arts Policy? London, Centre for Policy Studies, 1979.
Every Day Drinking. London, Hutchinson, 1983.
How's Your Glass? London, Weidenfeld and Nicolson, 1984.

Editor, with James Michie, *Oxford Poetry 1949*. Oxford, Blackwell, 1949.
Editor, with Robert Conquest, *Spectrum [1-5]: A Science Fiction Anthology*. London, Gollancz, 5 vols., 1961-65; New York, Harcourt Brace, 5 vols., 1962-67.
Editor, *Selected Short Stories of G.K. Chesterton*. London, Faber, 1972.
Editor, *Tennyson*. London, Penguin, 1973.
Editor, *Harold's Years: Impressions from the New Statesman and the Spectator*. London, Quartet, 1977.
Editor, *The New Oxford Book of Light Verse*. London and New York, Oxford University Press, 1978.
Editor, *The Faber Popular Reciter*. London, Faber, 1978.
Editor, *The Golden Age of Science Fiction*. London, Hutchinson, 1981.

*

Bibliography: *Kingsley Amis: A Checklist* by Jack Benoit Gohn, Kent, Ohio, Kent State University Press, 1976; *Kingsley Amis: A Reference Guide* by Dale Salwak, Boston, Hall, and London, Prior, 1978.

Manuscript Collection (verse): State University of New York, Buffalo.

Critical Study: *Kingsley Amis* by Philip Gardner, Boston, Twayne, 1981.

Kingsley Amis comments:
I used to be lumped into the "Movement" of the 1950's. No doubt I have, or had, something in common with some of the other poets lumped into it.

*   *   *

Although Kingsley Amis's most celebrated work is his fiction, he began as a poet, continued to write and publish poems, and is unambiguously convinced that poetry is a higher form of art. His first book (*Bright November*) was decent but quite unremarkable, though it included one poem —"Beowulf"— which he has reprinted and which sits happily enough with his later work. The first clearly Amisian poems appeared in *A Frame of Mind*, most of the contents of which were collected in *A Case of Samples: Poems 1946-1956*. There is a good deal of variety here, both in form and content, and some evidence of well-learned and well-digested influence from Auden, Graves, and Amis's own admired contemporary, Phillip Larkin. The plain-man stance is apparent, with a distrust of extremes and reliance on disabused common-sense; but this is managed with more gravity, more mutedly, than in the novels. "Against Romanticism" sets the tone well, in its steady-eyed wish for a landscape

not parched or soured by frantic suns
Doubling the commands of a rout of gods,

Nor trampled by the havering unicorn;
  Let the sky be clean of officious birds
Punctiliously flying on the left;
  Let there be a path leading out of sight,
And at its other end a temperate zone:
  Woods devoid of beasts, roads that please the foot.

The novelist of *Lucky Jim* and its successors is more recognizable in *A Look round the Estate: Poems 1957-1967*, particularly in the sequence of coarse and comical vignettes, "The Evans Country," with its sly and almost admiring delineation of Dai Evans, South Walian hypocrite and lecher. "What about you?" —the question with which both the opening and closing poems end—is clear invitation not to cast the first stone at Dai before having a good look at oneself.

The love poems are less individual, and in fact the hand of Graves is too obvious in them. In general, though, the later poems seem intelligent, witty, concentrated, and essentially light by-products of the impulse that has made the Amis novels. They compare favourably with Larkin's rather similar lighter poems (such as "Naturally the Foundation Will Bear Your Expenses"), but with one early exception (the poem "Masters," which was first published in 1949), Amis has never approached the measured grandeur of Larkin's best work.

—Anthony Thwaite

AMMONS, A(rchie) R(andolph). American. Born in Whiteville, North Carolina, 18 February 1926. Educated at Wake Forest College, North Carolina, B.S. 1949; University of California, Berkeley, 1950-52. Served in the United States Naval Reserve, 1944-46. Married Phyllis Plumbo in 1949; one son. Principal, Hatteras Elementary School, North Carolina, 1949-50. Executive Vice-President, Friedrich and Dimmock, Inc., Millville, New Jersey, 1952-62. Assistant Professor, 1964-68, Associate Professor, 1969-71, since 1971, Professor of English, and since 1973, Goldwin Smith Professor of English, Cornell University, Ithaca, New York. Visiting Professor, Wake Forest University, 1974-75. Poetry Editor, *Nation*, New York, 1963. Recipient: Bread Loaf Writers Conference scholarship, 1961; Guggenheim Fellowship, 1966; American Academy Travelling Fellowship, 1967, and award, 1977; Levinson Prize (*Poetry*, Chicago), 1970; National Book Award, 1973; Bollingen Prize, 1975; MacArthur Fellowship, 1981; National Book Critics Circle Award, 1982. D.Litt.: Wake Forest University, 1972; University of North Carolina, Chapel Hill, 1973. Fellow, American Academy of Arts and Sciences, 1982. Address: Department of English, Cornell University, Ithaca, New York 14850, U.S.A.

PUBLICATIONS

Verse

Ommateum, with Doxology. Philadelphia, Dorrance, 1955.
Expressions of Sea Level. Columbus, Ohio State University Press, 1964.
Corsons Inlet. Ithaca, New York, Cornell University Press, 1965.
Tape for the Turn of the Year. Ithaca, New York, Cornell University Press, 1965.

Northfield Poems. Ithaca, New York, Cornell University Press, 1966.
Selected Poems. Ithaca, New York, Cornell University Press, 1968.
Uplands. New York, Norton, 1970.
Briefings: Poems Small and Easy. New York, Norton, 1971.
Collected Poems 1951-1971. New York, Norton, 1972.
Sphere: The Form of a Motion. New York, Norton, 1974.
Diversifications. New York, Norton, 1975.
The Snow Poems. New York, Norton, 1977.
The Selected Poems 1951-1977. New York, Norton, 1977.
Highgate Road. Ithaca, New York, Inkling Press, 1977.
For Doyle Fosco. Winston-Salem, North Carolina, Press for Privacy, 1977.
Poem. Winston-Salem, North Carolina, Press for Privacy, 1977(?).
Six-Piece Suite. Ithaca, New York, Palaemon Press, 1979.
Selected Longer Poems. New York, Norton, 1980.
A Coast of Trees. New York, Norton, 1981.
Worldly Hopes. New York, Norton, 1982.
Lake Effect Country. New York, Norton, 1983.

*

Bibliography: *A.R.Ammons: A Bibliography 1954-1979* by Stuart Wright, Wake Forest, North Carolina, Wake Forest University Press, 1980.

Critical Studies: "A Poem Is a Walk" by the author, in *Epoch* (Ithaca, New York), Fall 1968; "A.R. Ammons: When You Consider the Radiance" by Harold Bloom, in *The Ringers in the Tower*, Chicago, University of Chicago Press, 1971; "A.R. Ammons Issue" of *Diacritics* (Ithaca, New York), 1974; *A.R. Ammons* by Alan Holder, Boston, Twayne, 1978.

*   *   *

A.R. Ammons is an American Romantic in the tradition of Emerson and Whitman. He is committed to free and open forms, to the amassing of the exact details experience provides rather than the extrusion therefrom of any *a priori* order. His favorite subject is the relation of a man to nature as perceived by a solitary wanderer along the beaches and rural fields of New Jersey, where Ammons grew up. Because of the cumulative nature of his technique, Ammons's work shows to best advantage in poems of some magnitude. Perhaps the best, and best known, of these is the title poem from *Corsons Inlet*, in which, describing a walk along a tidal stream, he says,

I was released from forms,
from the perpendiculars,
straight lines, blocks, boxes, binds
of thought
into the hues, shadings, rises, flowing bends and blends of
    sight....

Ammons here as elsewhere accepts only what is possible to a sensibility attuned to the immediacy of experience, for he admits that "Scope eludes my grasp, that there is no finality of vision,/ that I have perceived nothing completely,/ that tomorrow a new walk is a new walk."

Another kind of poem characteristic of Ammons is the brief metaphysical fable, in which there are surprising colloquies between an interlocutor and mountains, winds, or trees, as in "Mansion":

So it came time
for me to cede myself
and I chose
the wind
to be delivered to.
The wind was glad
and said it needed all
the body
it could get
to show its motions with....

The philosophical implications in these poems are explicit in "What This Mode of Motion Said," a meditation upon permanence and change phrased as a cadenza on Emerson's poem "Brahma."

Ammons's *Collected Poems* was chosen for the National Book Award in 1973. Not included in this compendious volume is his book-length *Tape for the Turn of the Year*, a free-flowing imaginative journal composed in very short lines, written on a roll of adding-machine tape. The combination here of memory, introspection and observation rendered in ever-changing musical phrasing is impressive. Such expansiveness is Ammons's métier. *Sphere: The Form of a Motion* is a long poem in 155 12-line stanzas which comprise one unbroken sentence. Taking Whitman and Stevens as his models, Ammons combines the all-inclusive sensibility of the one with the meditative philosophical discourse of the other, as these excerpts may suggest:

...the identifying oneness of populations, peoples: I
know my own—the thrown peripheries, the stragglers,
  the cheated,
maimed, afflicted (I know their eyes, pain's melting
  amazement),

the weak, disoriented, the sick, hurt, the castaways, the
needful needless: I know them: I love them, I am theirs...

the purpose of the motion of a poem is to bring the
  focused,
awakened mind to no-motion, to a still contemplation of
  the
whole motion, all the motions, of the poem...

...by intensifying the alertness

of the conscious mind even while it permits itself to sink,
to be lowered down the ladder of structured motions to
  the
refreshing energies of the deeper self...
the non-verbal
energy at that moment released, transformed back through
  the
verbal, the sayable poem...

Ammons's work is consistent in its experimentation with open forms and its celebration of living processes and the identity of man with nature.

—Daniel Hoffman

———

ANANIA, Michael. American. Born in Omaha, Nebraska, 5 August 1939. Educated at the University of Nebraska, at Lincoln, 1957-58, at Omaha, B.A. 1961; State University of New York, Buffalo, Ph.D. 1969. Married Joanne Oliver in 1960. Bibliographer, Lockwood Library, State University of New York, Buffalo, 1963-64; Instructor in English, State University of New York, Fredonia, 1964-65, and Northwestern University, Evanston, Illinois, 1965-68. Instructor, 1968-70, and since 1970, Assistant Professor of English, University of Illinois, Chicago. Poetry Editor, *Audit*, 1963-64, and Co-Editor, *Audit/Poetry*, 1963-67, Buffalo. Since 1968, Literary Editor, Swallow Press, Chicago; since 1971, Member, Board of Directors, and since 1972, Member, Executive Committee, Coordinating Council of Literary Magazines. Recipient: Swallow Press New Poetry Series Award, 1970. Address: Department of English, University of Illinois at Chicago Circle, Box 4348, Chicago, Illinois 60680, U.S.A.

PUBLICATIONS

Verse

The Color of Dust. Chicago, Swallow Press, 1970.
Set/Sorts. Chicago, Wine Press, 1974.
Riversongs. Urbana, University of Illinois Press, 1978.

Novel

The Red Menace. New York, Thunder's Mouth Press, 1984.

Other

Editor, *New Poetry Anthology 1-2.* Chicago, Swallow Press, 1969-72.

*   *   *

In *The Color of Dust*, Michael Anania traces his passage from the timeless to the contemporary, from small-town life by the Missouri River to a state of mind questioning national myths and the consequences of war. By evoking a sense of the land and people, and by recognizing the permanence and the regenerative powers of the river, he demonstrates how identity stems from the knitting together of person and place ("We are not confused,/we do not lose our place"). But self-definition may be accomplished only one moment at a time and periods of doubt inevitably occur ("Am I a songster or a dealer?"). So, too, in his calling, the poet attempts to capture and maintain, thereby creating his own dilemma; the writing of a poem means the wresting of something from its organic context. But it is the nature of the creator to utter his vision and, in doing so, to preserve what he perceives. Time and again the poet must confront the realization that all things change; in Robert Creeley's words, "Everything is water/if you look long enough." Anania's attempts to preserve the interrelatedness of experience may be seen metaphorically in "The Fall" and dramatically in his war pieces. In the latter, he presents the survivors—those men with fragments of mind and those who suffer physical decay. Here Anania successfully weaves a living tapestry as he reveals the tragic operation of causality in human lives. Time goes on and man improves—his weapons; he progresses from shrapnel to napalm. The American hero, manifestation of national power, propagated by the media, wears "the satin cape/the big red S/meaning, after all, better than." Superman's cool efficiency and superior strength symbolize the power of a machine-driven culture.

In *Riversongs* the meaning and metaphor of the river is extended to encompass a sense of the historical past, the passage of time to the present, and the inevitable flow toward death. "The Riversongs of Arion," the ten-poem sequence which gives the book its name, recounts a recent attempt to retrace the Lewis and Clark journey; incorporated are excerpts drawn from Lewis's *Journals*. The river of historical time flows into now and becomes one with the mind of the persona. After all, the first rule—of river and mind—is motion. "...In time/the river side-winds its banks./Never the same soil...." Elements of the historical past, of the struggle to settle the frontier, clarify how human experience is continuous and intertwined as it flows into contemporary America; Lewis's words mingle with references to Billy the Kid, John Wesley Hardin, Wild Bill Hickok, Sacajawea, and Huck Finn. The poem's movement resembles the outward rippling caused by a stone dropped in water and, simultaneously, a deepening, for every journey is a life quest, individual, uncertain—

> each night I read my Journals
> like a novel, seeking some
> inevitability of plot, a hint
> of form pointing toward an end

The river of memory floats the persona back to the dead fathers of his family ("Reeving") and forward to time-present ("News Notes, 1970").

Poetry is music that moves like a river, a liquid music flowing and changing. In the play of liquid and light, illuminations sparkle like sunlight on wave-tips. In *Riversongs*, the best of Anania's poems embody the endurance of water wedded to the delicacy of light—things come in waves, they stream past the beholding eye, and they are gone. In the river's continuity and the light playing on its surface, Anania captures and preserves "Those shafts of light/the soul is mirror to."

—*Carl Lindner*

ANDERSON, Jon (Victor).   American.   Born in Somerville, Massachusetts, 4 July 1940. Educated at Northeastern University, Boston, B.S. 1964; University of Iowa, Iowa City, M.F.A. in creative writing 1968. Married 1) Nancy Garland in 1964 (marriage dissolved); 2) Linda Baker in 1967 (marriage dissolved); 3) Barbara Hershkowitz in 1971. Instructor, later Assistant Professor of Creative Writing, University of Portland, Oregon, 1968-72; Assistant Professor of Creative Writing, Ohio University, Athens, 1972-73, University of Pittsburgh, 1973-76, and University of Iowa, from 1976. Currently, Associate Professor of English, University of Arizona, Tucson. Recipient: Borestone Mountain Award, 1964; Oscar Blumenthal Prize (*Poetry*, Chicago), 1970; Guggenheim Fellowship, 1976; Shelley Memorial Award, 1983. Address: Department of English, University of Arizona, Tucson, Arizona 85721, U.S.A.

PUBLICATIONS

Verse

Looking for Jonathan.   Pittsburgh, University of Pittsburgh Press, 1968.
Death and Friends.   Pittsburgh, University of Pittsburgh Press, 1970.

In Sepia.   Pittsburgh, University of Pittsburgh Press, 1974.
Counting the Days.   Lisbon, Iowa, Penumbra Press, 1974.
Cypresses.   Port Townsend, Washington, Graywolf Press, 1981.
The Milky Way: Poems 1967-1982.   New York, Ecco Press, 1983.

*   *   *

Jon Anderson's *Looking for Jonathan* is principally a search for identity, both the poet's and our own. The formal, the christened, name seems to signify the essential person. The work belies that easy idea, however, by discovering that change is the human condition. Finally, being and becoming are identified, but this poetry elaborates the moribund nature of human metamorphosis. Images of light and metaphors of dark drive the poems, just as Anderson sees us forging through experience from illusion to disillusion.

"It is Morning; the Animals" opens the collection wonderfully. The paradisaical beasts are characterized by a uniquely tainted innocence which is the blessing of undeluded animality. The lion is central, as is the lamb, Christ, in the title poem of the second section, "The Summer Deaths." In a blazing sun the lion ironically, but gently, explains a sleeping man:

> *This is my peaceable son;*
> *my fond intention, dreaming,*
> *even unto death.*

Man's ignorance of his animal endowment forces him forever to dream (especially the illusion of his benignity). His dreaming may even be suicidal. Yet the poem concludes with a brilliant ambiguity that also allows us to see ourselves as the lion's progenitor:

> The man disappears, as though
> he was not ever in that house at all,
> but was invisible, or asleep
> deep in the lion's dark belly,
> or was the lion, dreaming of him.

Man's animality and spirituality are dreams of each other; yet the verse arrangement and syntax leave no doubt that both dreams are possible, in reality.

The second group mainly traces various vanishings, of experiences, relationships, whole persons. All drop into the wake of the speaker's progress, which is leading to "The New World," both a hope and a poem, which adroitly prefigures the book's finale. The third and last section is dominated by movement in deep shadow, erosion, and barren resignation. These poems culminate in the piece which gives the volume its title, a work prepared for by the psychological "clarity" of a self now borne "with...indifference." Seeing himself, the poet perceives not a "new world" but a weary America and his own industrially stained home town. Once-fecund religious myths yield here to a more difficult vision:

> When I saw America, she had danced all night,
> she was chalk-white,
> leaning on her husband's arm.
>
> I could see
> the orange home town, coming.
> I leaned honestly
> into my own reflection.
> I had no more stories of God.

In *Death and Friends* Anderson finds himself immersed in and then nearly drowned by myriad deaths. In the ragged separateness of all things he locates the veritable model of Donne's "pictures" of death. Not only does the grave take our friends, but Death's compatriots, like the "Angel of Departures" in *Looking for Jonathan*, are at work dissolving all connections, human and temporal. Personal and cosmic discontinuity merge. The poet sees the always travelling "Trucker" with a history of years

> ...like the stars
> he watched from the speeding cab,
> spaced unevenly...
> so many particular events.

The individual is no less fractured than the past. But now Anderson sometimes discovers that while the disconnected phases of our years and our own disparate personalities are unknowable to our friends, they are "friends" to each other and a source of that strange human unity Montaigne discerned in our constant inconsistency. This line of feeling is initiated in the first poem, "The Parachutist," and brought to fruition in "The Photograph of Myself," a poem at least as good as Adrienne Rich's "The Evil Eye." Addressing the image of his childhood self with wit, irony and a touch of Wordsworth's "the child is father of the man," the speaker allows that: "Good friend, believe me,/here I am, perhaps your best intention."

Anderson's third book, *In Sepia*, is a retrospect, a work of and for the memory. Reflection (the philosophic cast of mind, light upon surfaces, the mirror's image) is of the essence. The absolute terminus of life looms, especially as engulfing water or blackening forest. And across darkness, fragments of light (headlights on bridges, moon glimmerings in branches) pulse messages of life's ephemerality. But the poet now fraternizes with time and struggles to make his losses a "progress from judgment to compassion." The yellow-brown, autumnal stain is cast on the mind's memories of all seasons, but with a paradoxical ardor: "We who have changed, & have/No hope of change, must now love/The passage of time." The "Years" and one's friends are so many "Stories," but:

> ...the stories they lived
> Were not the same,
> Many were distracted into love,
> Slept, & woke alone, awhile serene.

Wordsworth has it that "Our birth is but a sleep and a forgetting." Anderson sees that, but he wants to know the dream of that sleep and its strange final memory, not before we are transported back into an eternal day, but as we sink into true darkness.

—David M. Heaton

———

ANGELOU, Maya (Marguerita Angelou, née Johnson). American. Born in St. Louis, Missouri, 4 April 1928. Educated at schools in Arkansas and California; studied music privately, dance with Martha Graham, Pearl Primus, and Ann Halprin, and drama with Frank Silvera and Gene Frankel. Married Paul De Feu in 1973; one son. Actress and singer. Associate Editor, *Arab Observer*, Cairo, 1961-62; assistant administrator, School of Music and Drama, University of Ghana Institute of African Studies, Legon and Accra, 1963-66; free-lance writer for *Ghanaian Times* and Ghanaian Broadcasting Corporation, both Accra,

1963-65; feature editor, *African Review*, Accra, 1964-66; lecturer, University of California, Los Angeles, 1966; Writer-in-Residence or Visiting Professor, University of Kansas, Lawrence, 1970, Wake Forest University, Winston-Salem, North Carolina, 1974, Wichita State University, Kansas, 1974, and California State University, Sacramento, 1974. Also television host and interviewer, and composer. Northern Coordinator, Southern Christian Leadership Conference, 1959-60; Member, American Revolution Bicentennial Council, 1975-76; Member of the Advisory Board, Women's Prison Association. Since 1975, Member of the Board of Trustees, American Film Institute. Recipient: Yale University Fellowship, 1970; Rockefeller grant, 1975; *Ladies Home Journal* award, 1976. Honorary degrees: Smith College, Northampton, Massachusetts, 1975; Mills College, Oakland, California, 1975; Lawrence University, Appleton, Wisconsin, 1976. Agent: Lordly and Dame Inc., 51 Church Street, Boston, Massachusetts 02116, U.S.A.

PUBLICATIONS

Verse

Just Give Me a Cool Drink of Water 'fore I Diiie. New York, Random House, 1971.
Oh Pray My Wings Are Gonna Fit Me Well. New York, Random House, 1975.
Poems. New York, Bantam, 1981.

Recordings: *Miss Calypso*, Liberty, 1957; *The Poetry of Maya Angelou*, GWP, 1969.

Plays

Cabaret for Freedom (revue), with Godfrey Cambridge (produced New York, 1960).
The Least of These (produced Los Angeles, 1966).
Ajax, from the play by Sophocles (produced Los Angeles, 1974).
And Still I Rise (also director: produced Oakland, California, 1976). New York, Random House, 1978.

Screenplays: *Georgia, Georgia*, 1972; *All Day Long*, 1974.

Television Documentaries: *Blacks, Blues, Black*, 1968; *Assignment America*, 1975; *The Legacy*, 1976; *The Inheritors*, 1976.

Other

I Know Why the Caged Bird Sings. New York, Random House, 1970.
Gather Together in My Name. New York, Random House, 1974.
Singin' and Swingin' and Gettin' Merry Like Christmas. New York, Random House, 1976.
The Heart of a Woman. New York, Random House, 1981.

*

Theatrical Activities:
Director: **Play**—*And Still I Rise*, Oakland, California, 1976; **Film**—*All Day Long*, 1974.
Actress: **Plays**—in *Porgy and Bess* by Gershwin, tour, 1954-55; *Calypso Heatwave*, New York, 1957; *The Blacks* by Genet, New York, 1960; *Cabaret for Freedom*, New York, 1960; *Mother Courage* by Brecht, Accra, Ghana, 1964; *Meda*, Hollywood, 1966; *Look Away*, New York, 1973.

*   *   *

William Shakespeare was Maya Angelou's "first white love," but her poems must be heard against a background of black rhythms. She has an uncanny ability to capture the sound of a voice on a page: *Just Give Me a Cool Drink of Water 'fore I Diiie*: vocal, oral, and written aspects blend in her poetry.

Ironically her own triumphs have drawn attention from the uniqueness of her poetry: she was named by Dr. Martin Luther King to be Northern Coordinator for his Southern Christian Fellowship, and by President Carter to be a member of the Commission for the International Women's Year. She has adapted Sophocle's *Ajax*, written for stage, TV, and films; she appeared in Genet's *The Blacks*, and had a highly successful career as a dancer. Her books have sold in the millions, but her poetry has received little serious critical attention.

In one sense of the word, however, her poetry is not "serious." As she herself puts it in the title poem of her volume *And Still I Rise*—"sassy." The word, however, has a powerful meaning: "Sassy" implies—we should assume from her own words—that "the impudent child was detested by God, and a shame to its parents and could bring destruction to its house...." This use of litotes is congenial with a peculiar sort of "coding" as in the kenning. "God's candle bright" is more of a token for the "sun" than a metaphor. So too, the title of her autobiography, *I Know Why the Caged Bird Sings*, is not a sentimental metaphor, but a litotes for humiliation. In her poetry, understatement is a style for presenting a shared experience, in its inconsistency and its energy without judging it and the "coding" can reinforce the anger implied by the "humor" as in "Sepia Fashion Show":

Their hair, pomaded, faces jaded
bones protruding, hip-wise,
The models strutted, backed and butted,
Then stuck their mouths out, lip-wise.

They'd nasty manners, held like banners,
while they looked down their nose-wise,
I'd see 'em in hell, before they'd sell
me one thing they're wearing, clothes-wise.

The Black Bourgeois, who all say "yah"
When yeah is what they're meaning
Should look around, both up and down
before they set out preening.

"Indeed" they swear, "that's what I'll wear
When I go country-clubbing,"
I'd remind them please, look at those knees
you got a Miss Ann's scrubbing.

The last line strikes the ear as "comic," and we share that sense of it, but then we react, and remember that black women literally had to show their knees to prove how hard they had cleaned. That change—the hearing, and then the reaction—is central to her poetry. We read the understated "nothing happens" in "Letter to an Aspiring Junkie," and then realize that it is a smashing litotes for "violence is everywhere":

Let me hip you to the streets,
Jim,
Ain't nothing happening.
Maybe some tomorrows gone up in smoke,
raggedy preachers, telling a joke
to lonely, son-less old ladies' maids.

Nothing happening,
Nothing shakin', Jim.
A slough of young cats riding that
cold, white horse,
a grey old monkey on their back, of course
does rodeo tricks.

No haps, man.
No haps.
A worn-out pimp, with a space-age conk,
setting up some fool for a game of tonk,
or poker or
get 'em dead and alive.

The streets?
Climb into the streets man, like you climb
into the ass end of a lion.
Then it's fine.
It's a bug-a-loo and a shing-a-ling,
African dreams on a buck-and-a-wing and a prayer.
That's the streets man,
Nothing happening.

The experience is particular: the word "conk" means a hair-do (rather like Little Richard's, for example) but the energy comes from the astonishing rhythms, and perhaps more accurately from the changes of rhythm.

She has composed poetry from the particulars and the rhythms she knows, and the changes of rhythm become a rhythm, the upsets and restarts in an unsteady state of soul which every life has experienced in some place or other.

When we read Maya Angelou's poetry, we share the sense of it but then we have a reaction from the energy, and have to reassess it, so that ultimately, when we hear her poetry, we listen to ourselves.

—William Sylvester

ANTIN, David.   American.   Born in Brooklyn, New York, 1 February 1932. Educated at City College, New York, B.A. 1955; New York University (Lehman Fellow), 1964-66, M.A. in linguistics 1966. Married Eleanor Fineman in 1960; one son. Freelance editor and translator, 1956-57; Chief Editor and Scientific Director, Research Information Service, New York, 1958-60; free-lance editor and consultant, Dover Press, New York, 1959-64; Curator, Institute of Contemporary Art, Boston, 1967. Director of the University Art Gallery and Assistant Professor of Visual Arts, 1968-72, and since 1972, Professor of Visual Arts, University of California, San Diego. Former Editor, with Jerome Rothenberg, *Some/Thing*, New York; Contributing Editor, *Alcheringa*, New York, 1972-80. Since 1979, Member of the Editorial Board, *New Wilderness*. Recipient: Longview Award, 1960; University of California Creative Arts award, 1972; Guggenheim Fellowship, 1976; National Endowment for the Arts fellowship, 1983. Address: P.O. Box 1147, Del Mar, California 92014, U.S.A.

PUBLICATIONS

Verse

Definitions.   New York, Caterpillar Press, 1967.
Autobiography.   New York, Something Else Press, 1967.

Code of Flag Behavior. Los Angeles, Black Sparrow Press, 1968.
Meditations. Los Angeles, Black Sparrow Press, 1971.
Talking. New York, Kulchur, 1972.
After the War (A Long Novel with Few Words). Los Angeles, Black Sparrow Press, 1973.
Talking at the Boundaries. New York, New Directions, 1976.
Who's Listening Out There? College Park, Maryland, Sun and Moon Press, 1980.
Tuning. New York, New Directions, 1984.

Other

Translator, *100 Great Problems of Elementary Mathematics: Their History and Solution,* by Heinrich Doerrie. New York, Dover, 1965.
Translator, *The Physics of Modern Electronics,* by W.A. Guenther. New York, Dover, 1967.

*

Critical Studies: "John Cage, Buckminster Fuller, and David Antin" by Barry Alpert, "Some Notes Toward a Discussion of the New Oral Poetry" by George Economou, and "A Correspondence Between the Editors Robert Kroetsch and William Spanos and David Antin," all in *Boundary 2* (Binghamton, New York), Spring 1975; interview with Barry Alpert, and articles by Gilbert Sorrentino, Hugh Kenner, Toby Olson, and David Bromige, in *Vort* (Silver Spring, Maryland), Winter 1975; *The Poetics of Indeterminacy* by Marjorie Perloff, Princeton, New Jersey, Princeton University Press, 1982; *So to Speak: Rereading David Antin* by Sherman Paul, London, Binnacle, 1982; "David Antin and the Oral Poetics Movement" by Henry Sayre, in *Contemporary Literature* (Madison, Wisconsin), Fall 1982; *The Poet's Prose* by Stephen Fredman, Cambridge, University Press, 1983.

*   *   *

Classical poetic theory regularly distinguished between the three terms *poeta* (the maker), *poesis* (the process of making), and *poema* (the thing which has been made). Modern theory, whether New Critical, Structuralist, or Post-Structuralist, is narrowly concerned with the third of these three terms: the poem as *text.* Further, because most discussion of contemporary poetry is still narrowly Romantic, it is taken for granted that a poem is a text expressing personal feelings, "emotion recollected in tranquillity." Turn the pages of any poetry magazine and you will quickly come upon the now-formulaic lyric poem in which an "I," standing in a wheat-field or crossing a brook or suddenly meeting someone loved long ago, ruminates on his or her personal experience and has an appropriate epiphany.

In such a context, it is not surprising that David Antin's extraordinary improvisations—he calls them "talk pieces" or "talk poems"—have been greeted with some hostility in establishment quarters. For the talk poems are improvised for particular occasions in particular places, recorded on tape, and only later transcribed on the typewriter. The written texts, collected in *Talking at the Boundaries* and elsewhere, are described by Antin as "the notations of scores of oral poems with margins consequently unjustified." As scores of actual talks, these texts obviously lack verse form: they do away not only with meter, but even with that last stronghold of free verse—lineation. To make matters worse, Antin has expressed a "distrust of ideas of interiority and the whole rhetorical ensemble of notions about 'feelings and emotions.' " Rather, he regards the "art of talking" as essentially the *language* art, and he is less interested in *ethos* or

pathos than in *dianoia,* which Aristotle defines as "all the thought that is expressed or effected by the words," or again, as "the ability to say what is possible and appropriate."

Is an Antin composition, then, written in "normal" prose? Not at all. "Prose," says Antin, "is an image of the authority of 'right thinking,' conveyed primarily through right printing—justified margins, conventional punctuation, and regularized spelling." The distinction between Antin's "talking" and "prose" was established in the early 1960's by Northrop Frye (in *The Well-Tempered Critic*):

> One can see in ordinary speech...a unit of rhythm peculiar to it, a short phrase that contains the central word or idea aimed at, but is largely innocent of syntax. It is much more repetitive than prose, as it is in the process of working out an idea, and the repetitions are largely rhythmical filler.

This "associative rhythm" as Frye calls the rhythm of speech, may be conventionalized in two ways:

> One way is to impose a pattern of recurrence on it; the other is to impose the logical and semantic pattern of the sentence. We have verse when the arrangement of words is dominated by recurrent rhythm and sound, prose when it is dominated by the syntactical relation of subject and predicate.

All three of these "primary rhythms of verbal expression" belong to *poesis* though not, of course, to *poema.* The interchange between the three provides the combinations which give literature its variety and complexity. When, for example, the "associative rhythm" is influenced, but not quite organized by, the sentence, we get what Frye calls "free prose," a form that develops much earlier than free verse: witness the associative monologue found in the personal letter, the diary, in Swift's *Journal to Stella,* and in *Tristram Shandy.* Beckett's *The Unnamable* is an important modern example.

There is thus a sense in which David Antin is a perfectly traditional poet; it is just that his tradition is no longer that of Romanticism and its Symbolist offshoots. The talk poems bypass Romanticism and return to a more classical notion of *poesis* as *making.* Frye remarks that "the associative rhythm represents the process of bringing ideas into articulation in contrast to prose or verse, which normally represent a finished product." Just so, Antin's "poetry," even his earlier, more conventionally lineated poems, like the elegy "Definitions for Mendy," is a process-oriented art.

How does it work in practice? Pieces like "is this the right place?" or "what am i doing here?" are, I think, governed by certain implicit rules:
(1) Just as there are no margins, so there are no complete sentences, the trick being to "keep it moving," in Charles Olson's words. Consider the following passage about cross-country jet travel:

> when i got on the plane i had the feeling i started out early in the day it was about 12 oclock to be on a plane 12 oclock on a plane is in some ways the worst possible time to get on a plane because what happens is you start out in the daylight and you wind up in the night and there never was any day and its odd you feel that youre travelling into the past

Notice that the first "when" clause is never completed by a main clause, for the speaker immediately interests himself in what it was like *when* he got on. Again, the proposition "it was about 12 oclock" leads, not to the expected account of what happened at twelve o'clock, but to a comic sequence about the peculiar feelings attendant upon boarding an East-bound flight at noon. And so it goes with rapid-fire shifts from one image or idea to another. The text is a transcription, not of a character's speech as one might find it in, say, a novel, but of David Antin's *talk*.

But if it's just "talk," what makes it *art*? Here three other rules come in.

(2) The talk poem incorporates as many different threads as can allow it to retain its improvisatory quality, yet those threads are all relational. The analogy is to a juggling act: as we watch Antin juggle the balls, we gradually realize that they will—or at least should—all be caught. So, in "Real Estate," the inquiry into the meaning of the words "real estate" and "currency" seems to get lost as we are given a series of comic narratives about various Antin relatives who did or did not own real estate. These "stories" are fun in themselves but, in considering in what sense, if any, a little hotel in the Catskills, bought by his eccentric uncle, is a "real" estate, Antin leads us right back to the possible meanings of his title.

Such three-ring performance is not easy. At one extreme, the talk may be too linear, too concerned with the exposition of a particular theme. At the other, the diverse materials—childhood memories, anecdotes about art shows, speculations on Homeric narrative, and so on—may fail to generate the necessary cross-references. So the successful talk poem is one that maintains a balance between leaving-out and putting-in.

(3) Closely related to (2): narrative (but not fiction) is an integral part of the talk poem. Pure exposition, rumination, meditation—these undercut the poet's emphasis on *poesis*, on the ongoing process of discovery in which one creates the self. Antin's narratives function as parodic examples; they prove the points the speaker is making but only because he wants them to, not because they have any sort of objective validity.

(4) The generation of a particular *voice* is one fictional element Antin allows himself. If, for example, one were to become ill while visiting San Diego and phoned David Antin for advice and help, he would undoubtedly be able to furnish some useful medical information. In a talk poem, however, a "medical center" is decomposed. Here is Antin's account of what happened when he and his family first arrived in Southern California and found that his little boy was sick:

> and i said to somebody in a shoestore "what do you do if somebody gets sick during lunch?"   and they said "theres a medical center right up the hill"   and i drove to the medical center   and there was a medical center   in california a medical center is unlike anything youve ever seen   unless youre a californian   medical centers depend on redwood trees   because theyre made out of redwood trees and ice plant   because what they do is level off an area   whatever was there they take a bulldozer and level it off   if there were eucalyptus trees they knock them down they push things out of the way   and then what they dont cover with redwood and blacktop they cover with iceplant   wherever you go theres iceplant

This is a good example of what the Russian Formalists called *defamiliarization*. Who else would define a medical center as a place made of redwood and iceplant? It has nothing to do with informational content but everything to do with the poet's first impressions of the strange new world which is Southern California.

The voice of the talk poems can describe persons, places, and events in the most minute detail, but a detail that would never do

for, say, a newspaper article. We don't *know* Dick Berlinger or the Uncle from Argentina or even the poet's wife "elly" (or "ely"); we merely witness certain fragmented gestures, words, or actions that provide a matrix for the speaker's talking. The mode here is synecdochic but the parts refer to no whole. Behind the manic behavior of "Dick," at the wheel of the 53 Chrysler or Candy's rejection of her would-be lover because of his cherry tattoo, there is an absent totality.

The refusal to claim knowledge either of himself or of his characters has suggested to some readers that Antin is unfeeling, that he refuses to take life "seriously." This is to misunderstand the nature of the talk poems completely. In adopting the stance of puzzled observer, of the unhabituated eye that sees persons and places as if for the first time, Antin can convey to us how the mind actually does experience the outside world. He can, moreover, embed such general questions as he does wish to raise—for example, is the photograph a true reproduction of visual reality?—in a set of images or narrative contexts so that the audience shares his own process of discovery. Antin's *dianoia* thus becomes ours. As he says: "now if you freeze life   its like frozen food," but "when you translate something it changes."

—Marjorie Perloff

ASH, John. British. Born 29 June 1948. Primary school teacher, 1970-71; research assistant 1971-75. Address: c/o Carcanet Press Ltd., 208 Corn Exchange Buildings, Manchester M4 3BQ, England.

PUBLICATIONS

Verse

Casino. London, Oasis, 1978.
The Bed and Other Poems. London, Oasis, 1981.
The Goodbyes. Manchester, Carcanet, 1982.
The Branching Stairs. Manchester, Carcanet, 1984.

*   *   *

With the publication of *The Branching Stairs*, John Ash firmly established himself as Britain's foremost younger innovative poet—an impressive achievement considering that his first published work had appeared only six years previously. That first work, the pamphlet *Casino*, which Ash called "a kind of homage to Symbolism and the Decadence," used a somewhat bizarre setting on the Riviera in winter for a series of imaginary portraits based on real figures—Laforgue, Baudelaire, Robert de Montesquiou, etc. The poems are unified by the theme of decadence, dissipation, and by a nostalgic vision of a sybaritic way of life and aesthetic that prefigures concerns in later books. Most of the poems express the point of view of one who is a contemporary of that group; the use of such a persona to gain dramatic immediacy as well as imaginative involvement is common in many of Ash's poems.

The second part of *The Branching Stairs* and Ash's second book, *The Bed*, are where his talent frees itself from a restricted and, some would say, hothouse theme and its derivative aesthetic to lay claim to an original poetic. Ash's poetry calls for more than its share of negative capability on the part of the reader, but the rewards in pure pleasure are munificent. He has a large imagination which he uses to full and varied effect. His is primarily a poetry of ambience and association in which the images, expressed most often in prose speech rhythms, flow thick and fast. The poems' constucts are frequently based on music, film, painting, or architecture. His English-language influences are undoubtedly American, and include Wallace Stevens in his use of the exotic and W.C. Williams's use of the glancing yet indelible image; the poems' nostalgic tone, the "urban pastoral," and the use of dialogue and such devices as rhetorical questions, image-clusters, and the extended, associative meditation, can be seen in the work of Frank O'Hara and John Ashbery. Certainly, too, Auden has been a crucial writer for Ash, particularly the former's elegance, versatility, wit, and sense of the social anomalies and absurdities of modern life.

Ash is one of Britain's very few "natural" poets; that is, whatever the work that may have gone into it, the poem appears as an immediate, autonomous, effortless construct which works by constantly developing imagistic materials—"variations with the 'theme' well concealed," in Ash's phrase—to build up a feeling-sense of place, persona, style, and event. This is the technique of surrealism; and many poems are surreal, though possessing "a 'sense of reality' that deepens/when realism is abandoned." The method leads to a characteristic unwillingness to ascribe too literal a motive for actions or responses and instead emphasizes appearance, uncertainty, and multiple responses to the same event. "It has been said," Ash has pointed out in an interview, "that poetry is not for offering solutions but for properly articulating the questions." In "Snow: A Romance," a prose poem in which the persona journeys to the south with a muse-like figure, Ash writes: "He sees resemblances everywhere. It is his trade, his survival technique." Much of the poetry is concerned with a style and way of life that represents the Midlands Englishman's yearning for the warmth and exoticism of the south, that is, the Mediterranean. At the same time, Ash, like Auden, expresses a sense of foreboding, an undefined loss, and a threat by the new, the barbarian or those in authority, and his is exceedingly conscious of the ruin of civilizations associated with that region. This awareness of decay extends of course to language: "O memoirs, documentaries, mountainous journal!/the text is always and in all places/irretrievably corrupted. Did you think/you could just pick up the language and use it...."

This approach to poetry demands a lot from the reader: he has to use his own imagination to fill the gaps, as it were, and sometimes the use of multiple personae, dislocated imagery, and surreal and dream images (Ash seems to me a poet who is very much in touch with the self as expressed in dreams and the subconscious) strains attention and sometimes leads to impatience. In this respect, *The Goodbyes* is more demanding than *The Branching Stairs*; the former seems less assured, more frenetic.

Unlike most contemporary British poets, John Ash is cosmopolitan and internationalist in outlook. The culture is primarily European and the methods American post-modernist. Though he can look backward both to childhood memories and in time to a late 19th-century process of dissolution and subsequent rebuilding (it's striking how many of his poems do concern the building of structures), the idea of deconstruction is ever-present, often expressed in paradoxical images and deliberately archaic words: "As tourists climb, in funiculars, to the apex of the arch, a deck of luxury apartments vanishes far off and silently, in an explosion like a burst of talc." The image is forever "there," in the subconscious, as a city (Beirut?) is deconstructed before our TV tourists' eyes.

—Robert Vas Dias

ASHBERY, John (Lawrence). American. Born in Rochester, New York, 28 July 1927. Educated at Deerfield Academy, Massachusetts; Harvard University, Cambridge, Massachusetts (Member of the Editorial Board, *The Harvard Advocate*), B.A. in English 1949; Columbia University, New York, M.A. in English 1951; New York University, 1957-58. Copywriter, Oxford University Press, New York, 1951-54, and McGraw-Hill Book Company, New York, 1954-55; Co-Editor, *One Fourteen*, New York, 1952-53; Art Critic, European Edition of *New York Herald Tribune*, Paris, 1960-65, and *Art International*, Lugano, Switzerland, 1961-64; Editor, *Locus Solus* magazine, Lans-en-Vercors, France, 1960-62; Editor, *Art and Literature*, Paris, 1963-66; Paris Correspondent, 1964-65, and Executive Editor, 1965-72, *Art News*, New York. Since 1974, Professor of English, Brooklyn College. Poetry Editor, *Partisan Review*, 1976-80; Art Critic, *New York* magazine, 1978-80. Since 1980, Art Critic, *Newsweek*, New York. Recipient: Fulbright Fellowship, 1955, 1956; Yale Series of Younger Poets Award, 1956; Poets Foundation grant, 1960, 1964; Ingram Merrill Foundation grant, 1962, 1972; Harriet Monroe Memorial Prize, 1963, Union League Civic and Arts Foundation Prize, 1966, and Levinson Prize, 1977 (*Poetry*, Chicago); Guggenheim Fellowship, 1967, 1973; National Endowment for the Arts grant, 1968, 1969; American Academy award, 1969; Shelley Memorial Award, 1973; Frank O'Hara Prize, 1974; Harriet Monroe Poetry Award, 1975; National Book Critic Circle Award, 1976; Pulitzer Prize, 1976; National Book Award, 1976; Rockefeller grant, for playwriting, 1978; English Speaking Union Prize, 1979; Bard College Charles Flint Kellogg Award, 1983; Academy of American Poets Fellowship, 1983. D.Litt.: Long Island University, Southampton, New York, 1979. Member, American Academy, 1980; American Academy of Arts and Sciences, 1983. Agent: Georges Borchardt Inc., 136 East 57th Street, New York, New York 10022, U.S.A.

PUBLICATIONS

Verse

Turandot and Other Poems. New York, Tibor de Nagy, 1953.
Some Trees. New Haven, Connecticut, Yale University Press, and London, Oxford University Press, 1956.
The Poems. New York, Tiber Press, 1961(?).
The Tennis Court Oath. Middletown, Connecticut, Wesleyan University Press, 1962.
Rivers and Mountains. New York, Holt Rinehart, 1966.
Selected Poems. London, Cape, 1967.
Three Madrigals. New York, Poet's Press, 1968.
Sunrise in Suburbia. New York, Phoenix Book Shop, 1968.
Fragment. Los Angeles, Black Sparrow Press, 1969.
Evening in the Country. San Francisco, Spanish Main Press, 1970.
The Double Dream of Spring. New York, Dutton, 1970.
The New Spirit. New York, Adventures in Poetry, 1970.
Penguin Modern Poets 19, with Lee Harwood and Tom Raworth. London, Penguin, 1971.
Three Poems. New York, Viking Press, 1972; London, Penguin, 1977.
The Vermont Notebook. Los Angeles, Black Sparrow Press, 1975.
The Serious Doll. Privately printed, 1975.
Self-Portrait in a Convex Mirror. New York, Viking Press, 1975.
Houseboat Days. New York, Viking Press, 1977.
As We Know. New York, Viking Press, 1979; Manchester, Carcanet, 1981.

Shadow Train. New York, Viking Press, 1981; Manchester, Carcanet, 1982.
A Wave. New York, Viking Press, and Manchester, Carcanet, 1984.

Plays

The Heroes (produced New York, 1952; London, 1982). Included in *Three Plays*, 1978.
The Compromise (produced Cambridge, Massachusetts, 1956). Included in *Three Plays*, 1978.
Three Plays (includes *The Heroes, The Compromise, The Philosopher*). Calais, Vermont, Z Press, 1978.
The Philosopher (produced London, 1982). Included in *Three Plays*, 1978.

Novel

A Nest of Ninnies, with James Schuyler. New York, Dutton, 1969.

Other

John Ashbery and Kenneth Koch (A Conversation). Tucson, Interview Press, 1965 (?).
R.B. Kitaj: Paintings, Drawings, Pastels, with others. Washington, D.C., Smithsonian Institution, 1981; London, Thames and Hudson, 1983.
Fairfield Porter: Realist Painter in an Age of Abstraction. Boston, New York Graphic Society, 1983.

Editor, *Penguin Modern Poets 24.* London, Penguin, 1973.
Editor, *Muck Arbour*, by Bruce Marcus. Chicago, O'Hara, 1975.
Editor, *The Funny Place*, by Richard F. Snow. Chicago, O'Hara, 1975.

Translator (as Jonas Berry), with Lawrence G. Blochman, *Murder in Montmartre*, by Noël Vexin. New York, Dell, 1960.
Translator, *Melville*, by Jean-Jacques Mayoux. New York, Grove Press, 1960.
Translator (as Jonas Berry), with Lawrence G. Blochman, *The Deadlier Sex*, by Geneviève Manceron. New York, Dell, 1961.
Translator, *Alberto Giacometti*, by Jacques Dupin. Paris, Maeght, 1963 (?).

*

Bibliography: *John Ashbery: A Comprehensive Bibliography* by David K. Kermani, New York, Garland, 1976.

Critical Studies: *John Ashbery: An Introduction to the Poetry* by David Shapiro, New York, Columbia University Press, 1979; *Beyond Amazement: New Essays on John Ashbery* edited by David Lehman, Ithaca, New York, Cornell University Press, 1980.

*   *   *

John Ashbery, who is now emerging as the outstanding poet of his generation, is still suspect in the eyes of those who long nostalgically for a poetry of statement. In a long review for the *Times Literary Supplement* (1978), Robert Boyers observed: "If we take meaning to refer to the possibility of shared discourse in which speaker and auditor may participate more or less equally," then Ashbery is "an instance of a poet who, through much of his career, eliminates meaning without achieving any special intensity. . . . Meaning is often left out of an Ashbery poem...to ensure the continuity of a quest for which ends are necessarily threatening." This is to regard *meaning* as some sort of fixed quantity that the poet as speaker can either "leave out" or proffer to the expectant auditor with whom he is engaged in "shared discourse." But what if there are other ways of "meaning"? Ashbury's penchant for *trompe l'oeil*, for "shifting sands," for rooms whose "fourth wall is invariably missing," is born of a conviction that, as he puts it in *Three Poems*, "the magic world really does exist," that to escape "the familiar interior which has always been there...is impossible outside the frost of a dream, and it is just this major enchantment that gave us life to begin with." But, he adds in the next breath, "Life holds us, and is unknowable."

Dream is thus regarded as the source of our energy, our élan, of life itself, and yet that life remains curiously "unknowable." This paradox is at the heart of Ashbery's poetry and accounts for his preoccupation with dream structure rather than dream content. Not *what* one dreams but *how*—this is the domain of Ashbery, whose stories "tell only of themselves," presenting the reader with "an open field of narrative possibilities." Again and again in Ashbery's poems, the "I" (or "you" or "we" or "he," for Ashbery tends to use these pronouns interchangeably) moves in and out of dream; his are visions that are, in the words of a recent title, "Lost and Found and Lost Again." Indeed, in a new 50 page poem called "Litany," each page has two columns of verse (the prayer and response form of the genre), and although each column is to be read independently, as one moves from page to page, it is often possible to move from left to right (or right to left), creating alternate plots or thought processes, each equally tantalizing and equally possible.

Such indeterminacy has no real precedent in Anglo-American poetry. Wallace Stevens is regularly cited as Ashbery's central precursor, and the early poetry does have the phrasing and accent of the late Stevens, but the two poets have very different sensibilities. A closer model is the Auden of the "Bucolics" and "In Praise of Limestone"—"Rivers and Mountains," for example, echoes Auden's "Mountains"—but Ashbery's landscape is like a comic-strip version of Auden's. In his introduction to the *Collected Poems* of Frank O'Hara, Ashbery describes the New York climate of the early 1960's, in which O'Hara came of age, as "Picasso and French poetry, de Kooning and Guston, Cage and Feldman. . . ." This was also Ashbery's own artistic climate: Cage, for instance, is surely a source for the two-column strategy of "Litany." Having lived in Paris for a decade (1955-65), Ashbery cast a cold eye on the Neo-Symbolism of his American contemporaries, their mania for what he called "over-interpretation" or "objective correlativitis." In an essay written in French for the special Reverdy issue of the *Mercure de France* (1962), he argued that, whereas Eliot and his followers insisted on endowing each word or phrase with symbolic significance, Reverdy's images existed in their own right as "living phenomena," their main characteristic being "transparency." Again, the quirky texts of Raymond Roussel are praised for their "mysteries of construction." Roussel's language, says Ashbery, "seems always on the point of revealing its secret, of pointing the way back to the 'republic of dreams' whose insignia blazed on his forehead."

Language on the point of revealing its secret without ever actually doing so—this is what we find in Ashbery's own enigma texts. Symbolist poetry, we know, is difficult, but it is not impossible to decode: behind the intricate collage of, say, *The Waste Land*, there is, after all, a coherent core of relational meanings. Ashbery takes poetry a step further. When we read a poem like "On the Towpath" (in *Houseboat Days*), we are confronted by a series of arresting, palpable images that seem to coalesce for a moment, about to disclose a hidden meaning. But here the ambiguity is not of the Empsonian kind; it is, rather, irreducible. As Ashbery puts it, in talking of Gertrude Stein's *Stanzas in Meditation*:

> *Stanzas in Meditation* gives one the feeling of time passing, of things happening, of a "plot," though it would be difficult to say precisely what is going on. Sometimes the story has the logic of a dream...at other times it becomes startlingly clear for a moment, as though a change in wind had suddenly enabled us to hear a conversation that was taking place some distance away. . . . But it is usually not events which interest Miss Stein, rather it is their "way of happening," and the story of *Stanzas in Meditation* is a general, all-purpose model which each reader can adapt to fit his own set of particulars. The poem is a hymn to possibility.

To create such "hymns to possibility" is by no means easy, as anyone who has read the countless imitations of Ashbery currently breaking into print knows. Too much disclosure produces contrivance; too much concealment, unintelligibility and boredom. Spell out the *content* of the dream and it loses its strangeness; conceal all clues, on the other hand, and you may lose your reader. In *The Tennis Court Oath* (1962), concealment is sometimes excessive. In such cut-up poems as "America" or "Europe," for example, even the "way of happening" becomes obscure. But, from the time of "These Lacustrine Cities" (1966), perhaps his first great "dream song," Ashbery creates a verbal landscape that reminds one of the Proustian magic-lantern show that enchants the child of *Swann's Way*. In the more recent *Houseboat Days* Ashbery's landscapes of desire are increasingly presented in the guise of what O'Hara called "charming artifice." Medieval romance, Elizabethan pageant, comic books, Arthur Rackham fairy-tale, Disney World T-shirts, flowered wallpaper, frosted wedding cakes, stage machinery, "grisaille shepherdesses," "terrorist chorales"—all these coalesce in the dream theater of *Houseboat Days*.

Not surprisingly, one of the finest poems in the book is called "Pyrography"; the process of burning designs on wood and leather with a heated tool here becomes the process of imprinting burning traces of memory and vision on a consciousness so fluid and amorphous that the "heated tool" is likely to slip on its surface. The scene of the poem is "Cottage Grove" (Chicago), the heart of the nation ("This is America calling"), but curiously it is also a fairy-tale world in which "The carriages/Are drawn forward under a sky of fumed oak." This contrast of old and new is nicely reflected in the stanza's rhythm which oscillates between the formality of "In service stairs the sweet corruption thrives," a perfect iambic pentameter line with inverted word order and heavy alliteration, and the prosaic inflection of "The page of dusk turns like a creaking revolving stage in Warren, Ohio."

In the second stanza, the "we" who are also "they" set out on a journey across the great American continent, first by boxcar through the "gyrating fans of suburbs" and "the darkness of cities," and then the scene suddenly dissolves and the travellers are moving up the Pacific coast to Bolinas, where "The houses doze and seem to wonder why." Along the way, they meet, in an echo of Baudelaire's "Le Voyage," the "disappointed, returning ones," but "the headlong night" beckons and it is too late to take warning and turn back. Indeed, as the journey continues, one proceeds, not westward or north to Canada, but into an imaginary world. A city has evidently been erected, "built...Partly over with fake ruins in the image of ourselves:/ An arch that

terminates in mid-keystone a crumbling stone pier/For laundresses, an open-air theater, never completed/And only partially designed." Where are we? Like Rimbaud's "Villes," or Ashbery's own "lacustrine cities," these cities cannot be specified; they emerge as part of a theater decor upon which the curtain may fall any minute. So the poet asks:

> How are we to inhabit
> This space from which the fourth wall is invariably missing,
> As in a stage-set or dollhouse, except by staying as we are,
> In lost profile, facing the stars. . . .

This question has haunted Ashbery from the beginning. He has known, all along, that "Everything has a schedule, if you can find out what it is," the difficulty being that you can't find out. Just so, the question posed in "Pyrography" is rhetorical, for the poet knows that the only way to inhabit a "space from which the fourth wall is invariably missing" is to accept it as the "stage-set or dollhouse" it really is, to realize that, in Yeats's words, "Man can embody truth but he cannot know it."

—Marjorie Perloff

ATWOOD, Margaret (Eleanor). Canadian. Born in Ottawa, Ontario, 18 November 1939. Educated at Victoria College, University of Toronto, B.A. 1961; Radcliffe College, Cambridge, Massachusetts, A.M. 1962; Harvard University, Cambridge, Massachusetts 1962-63, 1965-67. Divorced; one son. Lecturer in English, University of British Columbia, Vancouver, 1964-65; Instructor in English, Sir George Williams University, Montreal, 1967-68; Assistant Professor of English, York University, Toronto, 1971-72. Writer-in-Residence, University of Toronto, 1972-73. Recipient: E.J. Pratt Medal, 1961; President's Medal, University of Western Ontario, 1965; Governor-General's Award, 1966; Centennial Commission prize, 1967; Union League Civic and Arts Foundation Prize, 1969, and Bess Hokin Prize, 1974 (*Poetry*, Chicago); St. Lawrence Award, 1977; Radcliffe Medal, 1980; Molson Award, 1981; Welsh Arts Council International Writers Prize, 1982. D.Litt.: Trent University, Peterborough, Ontario, 1973; LL.D.: Queen's University, Kingston, Ontario, 1974. Agent: Phoebe Larmore, 2814 Third Street, Santa Monica, California 90405, U.S.A. Address: c/o Oxford University Press, 70 Wynford Drive, Don Mills, Ontario M3C 1J9, Canada.

PUBLICATIONS

Verse

Double Persephone. Toronto, Hawkshead Press, 1961.
The Circle Game (single poem). Bloomfield Hills, Michigan, Cranbrook Academy of Art, 1964.
Talismans for Children. Bloomfield Hills, Michigan, Cranbrook Academy of Art, 1965.
Kaleidoscopes: Baroque. Bloomfield Hills, Michigan, Cranbrook Academy of Art, 1965.
Speeches for Doctor Frankenstein. Bloomfield Hills, Michigan, Cranbrook Academy of Art, 1966.
The Circle Game (collection). Toronto, Contact Press, 1966.
Expeditions. Bloomfield Hills, Michigan, Cranbrook Academy of Art, 1966.
Who Was in the Garden. Santa Barbara, California, Unicorn, 1969.

The Animals in That County.   Boston, Little Brown, 1969.
Five Modern Canadian Poets, with others, edited by Eli Mandel.   Toronto, Holt Rinehart, 1970.
The Journals of Susanna Moodie.   Toronto, Oxford University Press, 1970.
Procedures for Underground.   Boston, Little Brown, 1970.
Power Politics.   Toronto, Anansi, 1971; New York, Harper, 1973.
You Are Happy.   New York, Harper, 1974.
Selected Poems.   Toronto, Oxford University Press, 1976; New York, Simon and Schuster, 1978.
Marsh, Hawk.   Toronto, Dreadnaught, 1977.
Two-Headed Poems.   Toronto, Oxford University Press, 1978; New York, Simon and Schuster, 1980.
True Stories.   Toronto, Oxford University Press, 1981; New York, Simon and Schuster, and London, Cape, 1982.
Notes Towards a Poem That Can Never Be Written.   Toronto, Salamander Press, 1981.
Snake Poems.   Toronto, Salamander Press, 1983.
Interlunar.   Toronto, Oxford University Press, 1984.

Recording: *The Poetry and Voice of Margaret Atwood*, Caedmon, 1977.

Plays

Television Plays: *The Servant Girl*, 1974; *Snowbird*, 1981.

Novels

The Edible Woman.   Toronto, McClelland and Stewart, London, Deutsch, and Boston, Little Brown, 1969.
Surfacing.   Toronto, McClelland and Stewart, 1972; London, Deutsch, and New York, Simon and Schuster, 1973.
Lady Oracle.   Toronto, McClelland and Stewart, and New York, Simon and Schuster, 1976; London, Deutsch, 1977.
Life Before Man.   Toronto, McClelland and Stewart, 1979; New York, Simon and Schuster, and London, Cape, 1980.
Bodily Harm.   Toronto, McClelland and Stewart, 1981; New York, Simon and Schuster, and London, Cape, 1982.

Short Stories

Dancing Girls and Other Stories.   Toronto, McClelland and Stewart, 1977; New York, Simon and Schuster, and London, Cape, 1982.
Murder in the Dark: Short Fictions and Prose Poems.   Toronto, Coach House Press, 1983; London, Cape, 1984.
Bluebeard's Egg.   Toronto, McClelland and Stewart, 1983.

Other

Survival: A Thematic Guide to Canadian Literature.   Toronto, Anansi, 1972.
Days of the Rebels 1815-1840.   Toronto, Natural Science of Canada, 1977.
Up in the Tree (juvenile).   Toronto, McClelland and Stewart, 1978.
Anna's Pet (juvenile), with Joyce Barkhouse.   Toronto, Lorimer, 1980.
Second Words: Selected Critical Prose.   Toronto, Anansi, 1982; Boston, Beacon Press, 1984.
Unearthing Suite.   Toronto, Grand Union Press, 1983.

Editor, *The New Oxford Book of Canadian Verse in English.*   Toronto, New York, and Oxford, Oxford University Press, 1983.

*

Bibliography: "Margaret Atwood: An Annotated Bibliography (Prose)" and "(Verse)" by Alan J. Horne, in *The Annotated Bibliography of Canada's Major Authors 1-2*, edited by Robert Lecker and Jack David, Downsview, Ontario, ECW Press, 2 vols., 1979-80.

Manuscript Collection: Fisher Library, University of Toronto.

Critical Studies: *Margaret Atwood: A Symposium* edited by Linda Sandler, Victoria, British Columbia, University of Victoria, 1977; *A Violent Duality* by Sherril Grace, Montreal, Véhicule Press, 1979; *The Art of Margaret Atwood: Essays in Criticism* edited by Arnold E. and Cathy N. Davidson, Toronto, Anansi, 1981; *Margaret Atwood* by Jerome H. Rosenberg, Boston, Twayne, 1984.

Margaret Atwood comments:
I feel that the task of criticizing my poetry is best left to others (i.e., critics) and would much rather have it take place after I am dead. If at all.

*   *   *

Margaret Atwood has justly been described as "the most discussed and widely read writer in Canada." She has distinguished herself as a poet, novelist, and critic, and has emerged not only as a best-selling author but also as a spokeswoman for both Canadian literature and feminist conerns. Her accomplishment is all the more surprising in that the outlook of her work could best be described as umpromising and uncompromising—ironic, detached, suggestive, intellectual, essentially poetic. Who would have believed the public was prepared for such a private person? The 125 poems in Atwood's *Selected Poems* reveal no thematic development but they do display a stylistic movement in the direction of poetry that is even more spare and economic, even delphic in deft indirection. Her recent *Two Headed Poems* may be read as being about personal relationships, but also as about the continual dialogue between French-speaking Quebec and the rest of English-speaking Canada:

> Your language hangs around your neck,
> a noose, a heavy necklace;
> each word is empire,
> each word is vampire and mother.
>
> As for the sun, there are as many
> suns as there are words for sun;
>
> true or false?

The dialogue breaks down into a monologue and then comes together again as "a duet": "This is not a debate/but a duet/with two deaf singers." The conceptions of the two countries or communities within Canada may not be new, but the intensity with which a writer is defining them and the wide currency they are receiving are new. The poems go beyond the political and the social analogue into the psychological and metaphysical realm of duality, for one poem, "The Right Hand Fights the Left," concludes: "The right hand holds the knife,/the left hand dances."

—John Robert Colombo

AUBERT, Alvin. American. Born in Lutcher, Louisiana, 12 March 1930. Educated at Southern University, Baton Rouge, Louisiana, B.A. 1959; University of Michigan, Ann Arbor (Woodrow Wilson Fellow), A.M. 1960; University of Illinois, Urbana, 1963-64, 1966-67. Married 1) Olga Alexis (divorced), one daughter; 2) Bernadine Tenant in 1959, two daughters. Instructor, 1960-62, Assistant Professor, 1962-65, and Associate Professor of English, 1965-70, Southern University; Visiting Professor of English, University of Oregon, Eugene, Summer 1970; Associate Professor of English, State University of New York, Fredonia, after 1970. Editor, *Obsidian* magazine, and Advisory Editor, *Drama and Theatre*, both Fredonia, New York. Recipient: Bread Loaf Writers Conference Fellowship, 1968; National Endowment for the Arts grant, 1973; Coordinating Council of Literary Magazines grant, 1979. Address: c/o Broadside Press, 74 Glendale Avenue, Highland Park, Michigan 48203, U.S.A.

PUBLICATIONS

Verse

Against the Blues. Detroit, Broadside Press, 1972.
Feeling Through. Greenfield Center, New York, Greenfield Review Press, 1975.

*

Critical Studies: by J.B., in *Kliatt* (West Newton, Massachusetts), November 1972; James Shokoff, in the *Buffalo Courier-Express*, 8 June 1973; Herbert W. Martin, in *Three Rivers Poetry Journal* (Pittsburgh), November 1978.

Alvin Aubert comments:

A poem is a verification (in every sense of the word) of experience in thought and feeling, but mostly the latter, for feeling is the means by which essential experience is transmitted. If the feeling is "right" the intellectual content is "right" also, which is to say that in the poem that works there takes place a mutual verification of thought by feeling, feeling by thought. From another perspective, a successful poem embodies an ordering of external data (experience), a forming of it to facilitate a significant connection of externals and internals, the data out there and the data within. I am an Afro-American, one who is very much aware of his roots in that somewhat unique region of the U.S., south Louisiana, with its French influence. But I am above all an Afro-American of African descent, and the two terms constitute a reality far beyond their sum. Thus, there is no question as to the source of that experience which verifies, as well as finds its verification in, a poem of mine. As for my thematic concerns, I concur in James Shokoff's assessment: "His themes are death, the shapes of the past, the terror of existence, and the pain of endurance, yet [hopefully] the poems are neither depressing nor pessimistic."

*   *   *

The title of Alvin Aubert's first book of poetry, *Against the Blues*, directs us to read his verse against a background of recalled popular sources. For example, "Whispers in a Country Church" simulates an exchange of worldly gossip among the, no

doubt, pious; "De Profundis" relates the practical plea of a drinker for some sign, less miraculous than a burning bush, to move him to sobriety. These stock comic figures are matched in a pair of poems, opening the book, that invoke Bessie Smith in an allusion to the muse and announce the news of the dispensation of the blues. None of the poems is long. All have the apparent simplicity of direct statement. And except for the references to Bessie Smith and, in another poem, Nat Turner, the immediate subjects are personal experiences. Just like the blues! The singer/ poet presents first-person experiences in ways that will make them typical.

As both singer and poet know, it is not so much the experience itself, though that is surely familiar, as the form in which it is rendered that makes the song and poem typical. Thus, Aubert typifies his poems through the patterns of language. The characters of Zenobia in "Photo Album" or "Uncle Bill" and "Granny Dean" are familiar not only because we may know people like them, but because the poet's lines about his characters approximate the habits of speech. Often a use of negatives or identical rhymes echoes the oral games of Black English. Sometimes, as in "Garden Scene," the verse nearly assumes the form of anecdotal *exemplum*. Yet, of course, it is not to imitate, even the patterns of spoken language, that Aubert writes. The typicality provided by linguistic patterns acknowledged by poet and reader serves as subject for creative imagination.

Aubert opens his second book of poetry with "Black Aesthetic," a poem that proposes to reverse Duchamp's *Nude Descending a Staricase* so that it would portray a black man going up, not down. And out. "Feeling Through," the title poem of the second book, illustrates Aubert's point, pulling experience up into reflective consciousness and setting it out as the new experience of a poem. With a characteristic syntactic economy, now become almost elliptical, Aubert establishes a situation. He, or his persona, sits on a porch swing, looking through a window at the reflection in a mirror of a carnival photograph. A partial dialogue is overheard but quickly displaced, so that wonder about the old photograph is transformed into soliloquy on the problem of recapturing the past. The scene and events of "Feeling Through" are the material of a family story. Narrative, however, remains inchoate as the poetic voice plays feelings held in the foreground of mind over the background of anecdote. The poem is, thus, both a gloss on the latent tale of the photograph and the expression of a newly defined experience.

Increasingly Aubert attaches subjective significance to his imagery. In poems such as "Economics" from the first volume or "The Opposite of Green" from the second details explain the mundane appearance of racism, but "Nightmare" and "Levitation," both in the second book, have highly personal references. Still, the tactics of language are consistent throughout Aubert's work. The texts of his poems maintain a continuity with Afro-American tradition by simulation and innovation that become a commentary on the richness of his sources and evidence of authentic re-creation.

—John M. Reilly

———

AVISON, Margaret (Kirkland). Canadian. Born in Galt, Ontario, 23 April 1918. Educated at the University of Toronto, B.A. 1940. Recipient: Guggenheim Fellowship, 1956; Governor-General's Award, 1961. Address: 17 Lascelles Boulevard, Apartment 108, Toronto, Ontario M4V 2B6, Canada.

PUBLICATIONS

Verse

Winter Sun. Toronto, University of Toronto Press, and London, Routledge, 1960.
The Dumbfounding. New York, Norton, 1966.
Sunblue. Hantsport, Nova Scotia, Lancelot Press, 1978.

Other

The Research Compendium, with Albert Rose. Toronto, University of Toronto Press, 1964.

*

Critical Study: *Margaret Avison* by E.H. Redekop, Toronto, Copp Clark, 1970.

*   *   *

Although her poems have been appearing in literary magazines and anthologies since the early 1940's, Margaret Avison did not publish a volume until 1960, when *Winter Sun* appeared, to be followed in 1966 by *The Dumbfounding*. With these, the reputation she had already acquired among a small group of critical readers as an original and significant modern poet was confirmed by an almost universal sanction.

Avison's originality lies partly in the stylistic and organizational boldness with which she gives expression to an extraordinary sensibility. This is first and most strikingly a visual one. Her poetry "begins (and often ends)," wrote the critic Milton Wilson, "with the perceptive eye." Problems of focus, structure, and design—intellectual, emotional, and moral—are everywhere at the heart of her early poems and persist with an added congruence into the later. Such titles as "Geometaphysics," "Perspective," and "Meeting Together of Poles and Latitudes" are indicative of this preoccupation. Her perceptive eye, however, is also a contemplative eye, metaphysical as well as physical, and it is not the eye alone that is made the instrument of critical awareness but the organs of the more intimate senses of smell, taste, and touch as well.

There are some literary affinities here perhaps, a hint occasionally of Wallace Stevens or Marianne Moore, of Herbert or Hopkins, but they are of little significance when set against the gnarled syntax and conglomerate diction she has forged out for herself. No single adjective is adequate to describe her diction: it is erudite, complex, archaic, simple, modern—an amalgam of the scientific and philosophical with the familiar and the new, a high style and a low, pillaged and put to work. Her poems come to terms with a reality that is heterogeneous and explosive. They set up a constant tension between a grainy local foreground and an eternal circumambiance of space and time.

In her second book Avison goes beyond perception and philosophy into a pure Christian poetry that brings something of the grace and humility of George Herbert easily and naturally into the modern world and into her own personal experience. "The Word," "The Dumbfounding," "Person, or a Hymn on and to the Holy Ghost," "Searching and Sounding," and the remarkable dramatic dialogue "A Story" are acts of submission and worship as well as poems. They are the result of a precisely dated mystical experience. I believe they have a validity as firm as the religious poetry of Hopkins or Eliot.

—A.J.M. Smith

AWOONOR, Kofi. Ghanaian. Born in Wheta, 13 March 1935. Educated at the University of Ghana, Accra, B.A. 1960; University of London (Longmans Fellow, 1967-68), M.A. 1968. Married; five children. Research Fellow, Institute of African Studies, Legon, 1960-64; Director, Ghana Ministry of Information Film Corporation, 1964-67. Poet-in-Residence, State University of New York, Stony Brook, 1968; Visiting Professor, University of Texas, Austin, 1972-73. Past Editor, *Okyeame*, Accra, and Past Co-Editor, *Black Orpheus*, Ibadan. Detained on suspicion of treason, Ghana, 1975-76. Professor of Literature, and Dean of the Faculty of Arts, University of Cape Coast, Ghana, 1977-82. Since 1984, Ghana Ambassador to Brazil. Recipient: Gurrey Prize, 1959. Address: Embassy of Ghana, Brasilia, Brazil.

PUBLICATIONS

Verse

Rediscovery and Other Poems. Ibadan, Mbari, and Evanston, Illinois, Northwestern University Press, 1964.
Night of My Blood. New York, Doubleday, 1971.
Ride Me, Memory. Greenfield Center, New York, Greenfield Review Press, 1973.
The House by the Sea. Greenfield Center, New York, Greenfield Review Press, 1978.

Plays

Ancestral Power, and *Lament*, in *Short African Plays*, edited by Cosmo Pieterse. London, Heinemann, 1972.

Novel

This Earth, My Brother: An Allegorical Tale of Africa. London, Heinemann, 1970; New York, Doubleday, 1971.

Other

In Person: Achebe, Awoonor, and Soyinka at the University of Washington. Seattle, University of Washington African Studies Program, 1975.
The Breast of the Earth: A Survey of the History, Culture, and Literature of Africa South of the Sahara. New York, Doubleday, 1975.
The Ghana Revolution. New York, Oasis, 1984.

Editor, with Geormbey Adali-Mortty, *Messages: Poems from Ghana*. London, Heinemann, 1970; New York, Humanities Press, 1971.
Editor, *Guardians of the Sacred Word: Ewe Poetry*. New York, Nok, 1974.
Editor, *Fire in the Valley: Ewe Folktales*. Enugu, Nigeria, Nok, 1981.

Translator, *When Sorrow-Song Descends on You*, by Vinoko Akpalu. Merrick, New York, Cross Cultural, 1981.

*

Kofi Awoonor comments:
Traditional oral poetry of the Ewes with its emphasis on lyricism, the chant, repetition of lines, symbolism and imagery transfused into English through the secondary influence of Pound, Dylan Thomas, etc.

*   *   *

Educated almost exclusively in Africa, Kofi Awoonor has been less influenced by the poetic traditions of Britain and America than many of his African contemporaries, though his work makes it obvious that he has read widely and he does not hesitate to use biblical references and echoes where he deems it necessary to his purpose. From the beginning of his poetic career, Awoonor made it his aim to write poetry in which genuine African experiences are communicated, in a language which owes something to the African vernaculars, even when writing in English (and he also writes in Ewe, his native tongue). So that when he says "In our beginnings lies our journey's end" ("Salvation"), the phrase is appropriate to the poem and the reader appreciates that the thought has not been taken over from Eliot, but derived from the actual experience of the Ghanaian poet; he has arrived at the same destination as Eliot from a completely different direction. He has, in fact, perceived the significance and value—both for his own writing as well as that of other poets—of the rich oral and folk traditions of Africa, and has experimented, not always successfully, with them in his poetry. Where other poets, and especially those educated in Britain and America, have felt alienated and have experienced an acute sense of conflict between the imposed values of western society and those of Africa, so that it became incumbent on them to emphasise their "African-ness," Awoonor has been able to be his natural self, without shouting the odds about Africa, to go on writing quite unperturbed by the conflicts around him (or so it might seem from his work). The title of his volume *Rediscovery* has implications at two levels—firstly, it celebrates the need to rediscover the African traditions of thought and way of life, which entails a knowledge of both the past and the present; secondly, it expresses the urge of the poet himself towards self-identification in terms of his own environment. At both levels he draws freely upon ideas and imagery from African rituals and ceremonies—sacrificial offerings, altars, bitter herbs, drums, purification rites, etc., abound in his work, to merge occasionally with specifically Christian images (as in "That Which Flesh Is Heir to")—and by a technique he describes as "transliteration of thoughts" introduces literally translated vernacular expressions and coinages into his English, which adds both freshness and meaning to his work. Although several of the poems in *Rediscovery* have been much anthologised, Awoonor has made rapid progress in the development of an individual style since the publication of his first volume. Amongst later poems are "Songs of Sorrow," based on an Anlo dirge, "The Sea Eats the Land at Home" and, one of his most ambitious and best-sustained efforts to date, the long poem entitled "I Heard a Bird Cry."

—Howard Sergeant

BAKER, Howard (Wilson). American. Born in Philadelphia, Pennsylvania, 5 April 1905. Educated at Whittier College, California, B.A. 1927; Stanford University, California, M.A. 1929; the Sorbonne, Paris, 1929-31; University of California, Berkeley (Phelan Fellowship, 1933-35), Ph.D. 1937 (Phi Beta Kappa). Married 1) the novelist Dorothy Dodds in 1931 (died, 1968), two daughters; 2) Virginia De Camp Beattie, 1969. Briggs-Copeland Instructor, Harvard University, Cambridge, Massachusetts, 1937-43; Visiting Professor, University of California, Berkeley, 1958-59, Davis, 1963-66. Editor, with Yvor Winters and Janet Lewis, *Gyroscope*, Palo Alto, California, 1929-30.

Founding Member, The Barn Theatre, Porterville, California. Olive and orange grower: Director, Lindsay Ripe Olive Company, Lindsay, California, 1956-57; President of the Board of Directors, Grand View Heights Citrus Association, 1962-73, and Tulare-Kern Citrus Exchange, 1969-73; Member, Citrus Advisory Board of California. Recipient: Guggenheim Fellowship, 1944. Agent: Lucille Sullivan, R.R.2, Box 171, West Brattleboro, Vermont 05301. Address: 24292 Avenue 108, Terra Bella, California 93270, U.S.A.

PUBLICATIONS

Verse

A Letter from the Country and Other Poems. New York, New Directions, 1941.
Ode to the Sea and Other Poems. Denver, Swallow, 1966.

Recording: *Ode to the Sea,* Library of Congress, 1949.

Plays

Trio, with Dorothy Baker (produced New York, 1944; as *Two Loves I Have,* produced London, 1952).
The Ninth Day, with Dorothy Baker (televised, 1957; produced Dublin, 1962). Dixon, California, Proscenium Press, 1967.

Television Play: *The Ninth Day,* 1957.

Novel

Orange Valley. New York, Coward McCann, 1931.

Other

Induction to Tragedy: A Study in the Development of Form in Gorboduc, The Spanish Tragedy, and Titus Andronicus. Baton Rouge, Louisiana State University Press, 1939.
Persephone's Cave: Cultural Accumulations of the Early Greeks. Athens, University of Georgia Press, 1979.

*

Critical Study: by William Van O'Connor, in *Poetry* (Chicago), January 1967.

Howard Baker comments:

Since our poetry begins with Homer, if you are going to be a poet, the best place to begin, ideally, is in the Epics and the Hymns. For me, living in the country in California, though the ideal was always present, the fulfillment was far beyond my capacities. But this was for the best, possibly, because, with a little digging into the poetry of Homer, the farm and the farm workshop, the seasons for hunting and fishing, and the astonishing sights that were to be met in the mountains and on the beaches, and in the crowded places where men congregate, became more freshly Homeric, I think, than the unvaried application to the Homeric text could have made them. The natural unavoidable impact of the past on the present and the present on the past, with no forced applications of the one on the other, is good for poets, and I would imagine for everyone. The ideal to be strived for is the scope of the Renaissance Man; and of the pre-Renaissance, pre-Socratic viewer of many races and many cities.

May I restate all this by quoting from the title poem in *A Letter from the Country*?

> Be much hedged in. Rehearse the ancient ways
> Till to your strong windbreak on wholesome days,
>   Timid, to fright still uninured,
>   Comes Amaryllis, reassured;
>
> Comes softly, briar-scratched, with tangled hair
> Leading those others who wait and shyly stare—
>   Masters who fled the savage wave,
>   Returned unkempt from their high cave.
>
> Then lean your head to their slow syllables:
> Whispering deep seas beneath the fleeting gulls:
>   The torch of Hecuba, the birth,
>   Ruined Ilium fading into earth. . . .

*   *   *

Among the pungent footnotes to Yvor Winters's important essay, "Problems for the Modern Critic of Literature," is the famous second, referring to one of Winters's best students, a poet and scholar who, after teaching at Harvard for three years became disgusted with academic politics and wastefulness of Departmental Life. The unnamed talented poet withdrew from the Academy, having decided there is more profit (and more intellectual honesty) in raising olives and oranges in a California valley. The unnamed subject of that footnote was Howard Baker. Baker has occasionally agreed to leave his orchards, giving a few lectures at a California university. He has also published some essays on classical subjects, essays which are stimulating as well as being learned. Since he does not have to "publish or perish," he publishes only what he thinks worthy of print. His standards tend to be higher than those of the academic marketplace.

Baker's "Advice to a Man Who Lost a Dog" (in a difficult stanza form) may remind readers of Winters's celebrated "Elegy on a Young Airedale Bitch Lost Some Years Since in the Salt-Marsh." Unfortunately Baker's poem is almost unknown; here is one of the seven stanzas:

> Think, when you hunt him on the windy brow
> Where the lean settler led his shaggy cow
> And questioning yielded to the tranquil plow,
>   That that fine poise bequeathed alone
>   A cellar overgrown.

And of course, neither poem is about a dead dog at all. The sonnet "Dr. Johnson" is one of Baker's best poems, tragically concluding: "We are all Boswells harkening the worms." The intelligence and the prosodic brilliance which inform his best poems make them models of their kind. At times, in the lesser poems, the irony may be easy; but there is scarcely a fault in "Pont Neuf." That poems about response to a public statue have become almost "set piece" now should not dull our response to Baker's poem, an almost perfect example of the kind. Other poems one wishes more people knew are "Quiet Folk," "The Passing Generation," and, despite Winters's objections to its associational technique, the long "Ode to the Sea":

> Conserving sea! To what auroral plains
> Have you consigned the meaning of the names
>   Augustine, Abelard,
>   Aquinas, Bede, Bernard?

Permanent, Lossless, undiminished Sea,
Change is the law of your stability!

Although Baker's poems tend to be passed over by anthologists who favor more showy pieces, his poems will remain a delight and an instruction to discriminating readers.

—James Korges

BANTOCK, Gavin (Marcus August).   British.   Born in Barnt Green, near Birmingham, Warwickshire, 4 July 1939. Educated at King's Norton Grammar School; New College, Oxford, M.A. (honours) in English language and literature 1964. Head of English department in various private secondary schools in England. Since 1969, Lecturer in English, Reitaku University, Kashiwa-shi, Chiba-ken, Japan. Recipient: Richard Hillary Memorial Prize, 1964; Alice Hunt Bartlett Prize, 1966; Eric Gregory Award, 1969. Agent: Peter Jay, 69 King George Street, London SE10 8PX, England.

PUBLICATIONS

Verse

Christ: A Poem in Twenty-Six Parts.   Oxford, Donald Parsons, 1965.
Juggernaut.   London, Anvil Press Poetry, 1968.
A New Thing Breathing.   London, Anvil Press Poetry, 1969.
Anhaga.   London, Anvil Press Poetry, 1970.
Gleeman.   Cardiff, Second Aeon, 1972.
Eirenikon.   London, Anvil Press Poetry, 1972.
Isles.   Feltham, Middlesex, Quarto Press, 1974.
Dragons.   London, Anvil Press Poetry, 1979.

Play

The Last of the Kings: Frederick the Great (produced Edinburgh, 1969).

Other

Land of the Setting Sun.   Tokyo, Kinseido, 1973.
Disunited Kingdom.   Tokyo, Kinseido, 1974.
Twenty Eggs in One Basket.   Tokyo, Kinseido, 1975.
Nobler in the Mind.   Tokyo, Kinseido, 1976.
Ten-Year Gaijin.   Tokyo, Kinseido, 1979.
Pioneers of English Poetry.   Tokyo, Kinseido, 1979.

*

Gavin Bantock comments:
   Themes and subjects: In *Christ*—Jesus as a man suffering human emotions and human love—a tragic, yet optimistic, interpretation of the Gospel Christ.
   In middle-length poems, "Hiroshima," "Juggernaut," "Ichor," and "Person"—examination of the human predicament, in a world of intense suffering where there is no God, except violence and destruction, and where life is lived only in the present with no possible planned future. Condemnation of narrow-minded and blindly orthodox people.
   Eirenikon is an attack on all those crying for peace, and on this

rotten western, capitalistic society—of which the U.S.A. is the chief culprit. Most evils of modern society originate in the U.S.A.

Dragons is a collection of poems, some with Japanese background, emphasizing the unknown behind the known, deepening one's concepts of seemingly ordinary things.

Verse forms etc.: Usually disciplined free verse, based on somewhat elevated speech rhythms; perhaps too much rhetorical usage; trying to eliminate this. (Much early practice in iambic English verse forms.)

Main sources and influences: Anglo-Saxon (I've made numerous translations), The Bible, Ezra Pound, Dylan Thomas, Ted Hughes. *Other strong interests*: Beethoven, Einstein, Astronomy, Dictators, Pipe-organs, Japanese archery, gardening, Shakespeare production.

My chief aims are to expose the short-comings of people who live narrow lives, who are unconscious of the strength of simplicity and of the practical wisdom of the much-damned attitude of loving-kindness. My attitude to such people is ruthless when they will not listen and sympathetic when they cannot listen. I have great admiration for people with strong wills and powers of endurance; I despise idleness and escapism and irresponsible action in human affairs.

Artistically, I hope to help maintain modern poetry steady in strength and efficiency of words used, in logical forms and order and in importance of subject. Too much poetry today is formless, trivial, arbitrary, small-minded, and does not make use of words or images designed to *develop* the language—too much of the language of modern poetry is dead and dull.

I believe writing poetry is a skilled craft, and must be learned. Too many people write lines of verse without ever making poetry, or make "poetic" utterances without knowing a thing about versification.

I am trying to make a distinction between the versifying of hippies and layabouts and the making of good poetry by dedicated poets. The public seem to be confused about the values of both.

*   *   *

"A bard of the old world living beyond his era"—this quotation, from his own poem "Seer," might not unfairly be applied to Gavin Bantock himself. The man as revealed in his writings seems totally out of sympathy with the present-day world he inhabits, rejecting our money-dominated society where happiness is translated as the accumulation of consumer goods, in favour of a return to older and more austere virtues. His long work *Eirenikon*, in particular, betrays a bitter hatred of all things American, at times becoming a diatribe against the plastic transatlantic pseudo-culture that spreads itself like an alien growth over so much of the world. Bantock turns his back on what he regards as a false set of values which have placed arbitrary limits on human growth, seeking his answers in ancient, neglected forms and value-systems. Like Crossley-Holland, he has a keen interest in Old English poetry—*Anhaga* contains many translations from original Saxon writings—and his moral world-view owes much to Biblical and Dark Age beliefs. In common with the early English masters, Bantock respects the disciplined ordering of words, regarding poetry as a hard-learned craft whose practice serves further to develop the language and its meaning. There is no room in his scheme of things for those modern poets who rely on a spontaneous outpouring of thoughts and images. Triviality, and its embodiment in the "Americanised" contemporary lifestyle, is anathema to him, and is ruthlessly condemned in a number of his poems.

Basically moralistic in outlook, Bantock's efforts are frequently on a heroic scale—his epic poem *Christ* is an example—

where sometimes the combination of a preaching tone and the packed solidity of his lines daunt the reader by sheer length and weight. Occasionally one feels that the poet is not unduly concerned whether or not his message is understood by the mass of his fellows. Intent as he is upon mining the potential of his own poetic experience, mankind tends to come second best. Certainly such works as *Gleeman* and *A New Thing Breathing* present him as a latterday wandering minstrel, travelling the world from one hall to the next, unsure of his reception but compelled by inner force to sing whatever the response. The central figure of his poems has the same love of wild, uninhabited places as Crossley-Holland has in his writings, seeking out the bleak terrain of mountains, or coasts where high seas break on the edge of the land. Bantock, it appears, communes most easily with the elements, finding hard, uncompromising truths in a wilderness bare of all other life: "my voice alone shattered the clear air/my breath alone clouded the ringing pinnacles//And no man heard me/so far was I removed from the world of men."

In place of our current gospel which despoils the earth in pursuit of money, power, and possessions, Bantock offers the ideals of self-knowledge and loving-kindness. These are worthy aims, but one feels they are presented in a singularly aggressive manner. Bantock's writing has a rugged force, and an often bitter edge, that sits ill with most Sunday School Christians, having more in common with the Old Testament and the Saxon blood-feud. From his Old English models he has refined his language to a strong, honed style that cuts and shapes his poems, the simplicity of utterance serving to emphasize the depths beneath. It is often in his simplest work that Bantock is most effective, as in this account of the poet's craft: "I have ways of singing worked for every deed/that has in it song somewhere/and every deed has." His writing echoes his Saxon forebears in its frequent use of alliteration, its word-juggling and wrestling with language. Images persist of the journeying singer, exiled and weeping at the sea's edge, returning to find the hall empty and only the ghost of a song to answer him. The sea itself dominates much of his verse, seen as a force for creation and growth, accepted despite its cruelty and destructive power as an integral part of the poet himself, the source of his being. To this, recurring symbol of his beloved wilderness, Bantock returns continually for his own strength and creativity to be renewed: "O my music-maker   when can I be with you again/and become   even from the most sunless places/as a new thing breathing on the shining face of the world."

—Geoff Sadler

BARAKA, Amiri. American. Born Everett LeRoi Jones in Newark, New Jersey, 7 October 1934. Educated at the Central Avenue School, and Barringer High School, Newark; Howard University, Washington, D.C. Served in the United States Air Force, 1954-56. Married 1) Hettie Cohen in 1958 (divorced, 1965), two daughters; 2) Sylvia Robinson in 1966, five children, two step-daughters, and one other daughter. Taught at the New School for Social Research, New York, 1961-64, and summers, 1977-79; State University of New York, Buffalo, Summer 1964; Columbia University, New York, 1964 and Spring 1980; Visiting Professor, San Francisco State College, 1966-67, Yale University, New Haven, Connecticut, 1977-78, and George Washington University, Washington, D.C. 1978-79. Since 1980, Assistant Professor of African Studies, State University of New York, Stony Brook. Founder, *Yugen* magazine and Totem Press, New

York, 1958; Editor, with Diane di Prima, *Floating Bear* magazine, New York, 1961-63; Founding Director, Black Arts Repertory Theatre, Harlem, New York, 1964-66. Since 1966, Founding director, Spirit House, Newark. Involved in Newark politics: Member of the United Brothers, 1967, and Committee for Unified Newark, 1969-75; Chairman, Congress of Afrikan People, 1972-75. Recipient: Whitney Fellowship, 1961; Obie Award, for drama, 1964; Guggenheim Fellowship, 1965; Dakar Festival Prize, 1966; Rockefeller grant, 1981. D.H.L.: Malcolm X University, Chicago, 1972. Member, Black Academy of Arts and Letters. Address: 808 South 10th Street, Newark, New Jersey 07108, U.S.A.

PUBLICATIONS (earlier works as LeRoi Jones)

Verse

Spring and Soforth. New Haven, Connecticut, Penny Poems, 1960.
Preface to a Twenty Volume Suicide Note. New York, Totem-Corinth, 1961.
The Dead Lecturer. New York, Grove Press, 1964.
Black Art. Newark, Jihad, 1966.
A Poem for Black Hearts. Detroit, Broadside Press, 1967.
Black Magic: Poetry 1961-1967. Indianapolis, Bobbs Merrill, 1969.
It's Nation Time. Chicago, Third World Press, 1970.
In Our Terribleness: Some Elements and Meaning in Black Style, with Fundi (Billy Abernathy). Indianapolis, Bobbs Merrill, 1970.
Spirit Reach. Newark, Jihad, 1972.
Afrikan Revolution. Newark, Jihad, 1973.
Hard Facts. Newark, Peoples War, 1976.
Selected Poetry. New York, Morrow, 1979.
AM/TRAK. New York, Phoenix Bookshop, 1979.
Reggae or Not! Bowling Green, New York, Contact Two, 1982.

Plays

A Good Girl Is Hard to Find (produced Montclair, New Jersey, 1958).
Dante (produced New York, 1961; as *The 8th Ditch*, produced New York, 1964). Included in *The System of Dante's Hell*, 1965.
The Toilet (produced New York, 1962). Included in *The Baptism, and The Toilet*, 1967.
Dutchman (produced New York, 1964; London, 1967). Included in *Dutchman, and The Slave*, 1964.
The Slave (produced New York, 1964; London, 1972). Included in *Dutchman, and The Slave*, 1964.
Dutchman, and The Slave. New York, Morrow, 1964; London, Faber, 1965.
The Baptism (produced New York, 1964; London, 1971). Included in *The Baptism, and The Toilet*, 1967.
Jello (produced New York, 1965). Chicago, Third World Press, 1970.
Experimental Death Unit No. 1 (also director: produced New York, 1965). Included in *Four Black Revolutionary Plays*, 1969.
A Black Mass (also director: produced Newark, 1966). Included in *Four Black Revolutionary Plays*, 1969.
The Baptism, and The Toilet. New York, Grove Press, 1967.
Arm Yrself or Harm Yrself (produced Newark, 1967). Newark, Jihad, 1967.

Slave Ship: A Historical Pageant (produced Newark, 1967; New York, 1969). Newark, Jihad, 1967.
Madheart (also director: produced San Francisco, 1967). Included in *Four Black Revolutionary Plays*, 1969.
Great Goodness of Life (A Coon Show) (also director: produced Newark, 1967; New York, 1969). Included in *Four Black Revolutionary Plays*, 1969.
Home on the Range (produced Newark and New York, 1968). Published in *Drama Review* (New York), Summer 1968.
Police, in *Drama Review* (New York), Summer 1968.
The Death of Malcolm X, in *New Plays from the Black Theatre*, edited by Ed Bullins. New York, Bantam, 1969.
Four Black Revolutionary Plays (includes *Experimental Death No. 1*, *A Black Mass*, *Great Goodness of Life (A Coon Show)*, *Madheart*). Indianapolis, Bobbs Merrill, 1969; London, Calder and Boyars, 1971.
Insurrection (produced New York, 1969).
Junkies are Full of (SHHH...), and Bloodrites (produced Newark, 1970). Published in *Black Drama Anthology*, edited by Woodie King and Ron Milner, New York, New American Library, 1971.
BA-RA-KA, in *Spontaneous Combustion: Eight New American Plays*, edited by Rochelle Owens. New York, Winter House, 1972.
Columbia the Gem of the Ocean (produced Washington, D.C., 1973).
A Recent Killing (produced New York, 1973).
The New Ark's a Moverin (produced Newark, 1974).
The Sidnee Poet Heroical (also director: produced New York, 1975). New York, Reed, 1979.
S-1 (also director: produced New York, 1976). Included in *The Motion of History and Other Plays*, 1978.
The Motion of History (also director: produced New York, 1977). Included in *The Motion of History and Other Plays*, 1978.
The Motion of History and Other Plays (includes *S-1* and *Slave Ship*). New York, Morrow, 1978.
What Was the Relationship of the Lone Ranger to the Means of Production? (produced New York, 1979).
At the Dim'crackr Convention (produced New York, 1980).
Boy and Tarzan Appear in a Clearing (produced New York, 1981).
Weimar 2 (produced New York, 1981).

Screenplays: *Dutchman*, 1967; *A Fable*, 1971.

Novel

The System of Dante's Hell. New York, Grove Press, 1965; London, MacGibbon and Kee, 1966.

Short Stories

Tales. New York, Grove Press, 1967; London, MacGibbon and Kee, 1969.

Other

Cuba Libre. New York, Fair Play for Cuba Committee, 1961.
Blues People: Negro Music in White America. New York, Morrow, 1963; London, MacGibbon and Kee, 1965.
Home: Social Essays. New York, Morrow, 1966; London, MacGibbon and Kee, 1968.
Black Music. New York, Morrow, 1968; London, MacGibbon and Kee, 1969.
Trippin': A Need for Change, with Larry Neal and A.B. Spell-

man.   Newark, Cricket, 1969 (?).

A Black Value System.   Newark, Jihad, 1970.

Gary and Miami: Before and After.   Newark, Jihad, n.d.

Raise Race Rays Raze: Essays since 1965.   New York, Random House, 1971.

Strategy and Tactics of a Pan African Nationalist Party.   Newark, National Involvement, 1971.

Beginning of National Movement.   Newark, Jihad, 1972.

Kawaida Studies: The New Nationalism.   Chicago, Third World Press, 1972.

National Liberation and Politics.   Newark, Congress of Afrikan People, 1974.

Crisis in Boston!!!!   Newark, Vita Wa Watu-People's War Publishing, 1974.

Afrikan Free School.   Newark, Jihad, 1974.

Toward Ideological Clarity.   Newark, Congress of Afrikan People, 1974.

The Creation of the New Ark.   Washington, D.C., Howard University Press, 1975.

Selected Plays and Prose.   New York, Morrow, 1979.

Spring Song.   Privately printed, 1979.

Daggers and Javelins: Essays 1974-1979.   New York, Morrow, 1984.

The Autobiography of Le Roi Jones.   New York, Freundlich, 1984.

Editor, *Four Young Lady Poets.*   New York, Totem-Corinth, 1962.

Editor, *The Moderns: New Fiction in America.*   New York, Corinth, 1963; London, MacGibbon and Kee, 1965.

Editor, with Larry Neal, *Black Fire: An Anthology of Afro-American Writing.*   New York, Morrow, 1968.

Editor, *African Congress: A Documentary of the First Modern Pan-African Congress.*   New York, Morrow, 1972.

Editor, with Diane di Prima, *The Floating Bear: A Newsletter, Numbers 1-37.*   La Jolla, California, Laurence McGilvery, 1974.

Editor, with Amini Baraka, *Confirmation: An Anthology of African American Women.*   New York, Morrow, 1983.·

*

Bibliography: *Le Roi Jones (Imamu Amiri Baraka): A Checklist of Works by and about Him* by Letitia Dace, London, Nether Press, 1971.

Critical Studies: *From Le Roi Jones to Amiri Baraka: The Literary Works* by Theodore Hudson, Durham, North Carolina, Duke University Press, 1973; *Baraka: The Renegade and the Mask* by Kimberly W. Benston, New Haven, Connecticut, Yale University Press, 1976, and *Imamu Amiri Baraka (Le Roi Jones): A Collection of Critical Essays* edited by Benston, Englewood Cliffs, New Jersey, Prentice Hall, 1978; *Amiri Baraka/ Le Roi Jones: The Quest for a "Populist Modernism"* by Werner Sollors, New York, Columbia University Press, 1978; *Amiri Baraka* by Lloyd W. Brown, Boston, Twayne, 1980; *To Raise, Destroy, and Create: The Poetry, Drama, and Fiction of Imamu Amiri Baraka (Le Roi Jones)* by Henry C. Lacey, Troy, New York, Whitston, 1981.

Amiri Baraka comments:

(1970) I identify with the "Black" school.
My major theme? The evolution of man.
(1974) The first step is Socialist Revolution.

*   *   *

Amiri Baraka (LeRoi Jones) is the leading revolutionary poet in America. Change is his consistent belief, progress his preoccupation. Every one of his books embodies such development. In *Home*, it is a matter of growing "blacker" during the very course of the essays, before our eyes; in *The Dead Lecturer* the turning points are the poems "An Agony. As Now," which catalogues the personal disease ending in a scream, and "Black Dada Nihilismus," which finds the West "a grey hideous space." There was much talk of death in the early poems, until it was realized—first in "Black Dada Nihilismus," then throughout *Black Magic* ("THE LONE RANGER/IS DEAD./THE SHADOW/IS DEAD./ALL YOUR HEROES ARE DYING. J. EDGAR HOOVER WILL/SOON BE DEAD. . . .")—that it was a culture that was dying, not the poet himself. Recognizing this, Baraka has been committed to re-creating himself in successive stages, and the world, the geo-political, socio-economic, hard-facts world, likewise.

His writing has gone through three obvious stages, and even more changes can be expected—revisions, advances. His first collections of poems reflect his commitment to the cultural avant-garde, with its generally "bohemian," decidedly anti-bourgeois stance shared by Olson, Creeley, Dorn, Ginsberg, Snyder, the post-modern Americans he published among and himself published. This was followed by his rebirth as a black man, the new identity exemplified by the new name, as the old associations, summarized in "The New World" early in *Black Magic*, were left behind:

Wasted lyricists, and men
who have seen their dreams come true, only
seconds after they knew those dreams to be horrible conceits
and plastic fantasies of gesture and extension,
shoulders, hair and tongues distributing misinformation
about the nature of understanding. . . .
Beatniks, like Bohemians, go calmly out of style.

The last lingering ties in "The Burning General" give way to "Black Art": "We want 'poems that kill.'/ Assassin poems, Poems that shoot/guns. Poems that wrestle cops into alleys/and take their weapons leaving them dead. . . ." The new black aesthetic makes possible the construction of a new nation, beginning with the poet's own community of Newark, a New Ark to sail out the destruction of the West. It seeks simultaneously to rouse and direct—raze and raise—toward a cooperative society of value and justice, so that, in his most recent work, cultural nationalism expands to a Marxist-Maoist socialism. The jihad of *Black Magic* and *It's Nation Time* gives way to the internationalism of *Hard Facts*, with no loss of fierceness. The address is to all the oppressed: "the fist of/the mighty is the whole fist."

Other poets have addressed political issues, to be sure, but what makes Baraka exceptional is that his language is equal to both his thought and his feelings. His poetry has the flexibility of syntax and deftness of diction, including vernacular richness, to deliver the message, with wit, irony, all the devices of effective language, at the same time upholding the nobility of its concerns. Every line in such an overt appeal as "The Nation Is Like Ourselves" is unpredictable invention. The oral empowers the dialectic line to move at speeds beyond dull demagoguery. Tireless, of sufficient complexity, with every trick of improvisation and typography allowable, every reach of vocabulary and ethnic association (even the direst), language is his special genius, his uniqueness (which is not the same as individualism, egocentricity). It is a poetry of strategy, exhortatory in the classic ways, propelled by urgency and belief. It is equally a poetry of feeling, though feeling controlled by a whip-like mind. "In the fact of feeling," he writes in *Raise Race Rays Raze*, "is the testing of the soul and the future evolution of men." Its language takes responsibility for itself, does not give itself up compulsively to either its own beauty or its thought. It is not self-hugging, narcissistic. His poetry, in its various developments, is an encouragement that liberation only *begins* with oneself. It is, above all, one of the few poetries today that is responsible to more than itself. Its lines are of lasting readiness. "Every breath must be a bullet, every step an attack," he writes in *Kawaida Studies*. The twist is on the words as they emerge from the bore.

—George F. Butterick

BARBOUR, Douglas. Canadian. Born in Winnipeg, Manitoba, 21 March 1940. Educated at Acadia University, Wolfville, Nova Scotia, B.A. in English 1962; Dalhousie University, Halifax, Nova Scotia, M.A. in English 1964; Queen's University, Kingston, Ontario (Canada Council Doctoral grant, 1967-68), Ph.D. in English 1976. Married Sharon Nicoll in 1966. Assistant Professor, 1969-76, Associate Professor, 1977-81, and since 1982, Professor of English, University of Alberta, Edmonton. Editor, *Quarry*, Kingston, for three years; Member of the Editorial Board, *White Pelican*, Edmonton, 1971-76; Poetry Editor, *Canadian Forum*, Toronto, 1978-80. Since 1978, Member of the Editorial Board, NeWest Press, Edmonton; since 1979, Member of the Editorial Board, Longspoon Press, Edmonton. Address: 10808-75th Avenue, Edmonton, Alberta T6E 1K2, Canada.

PUBLICATIONS

Verse

Land Fall. Montreal, Delta Canada, 1971.
A Poem As Long As the Highway. Kingston, Ontario, Quarry Press, 1971.
White. Fredericton, New Brunswick, Fiddlehead, 1972.
Songbook. Vancouver, Talonbooks, 1973.
He.&.She.&. Ottawa, Golden Dog Press, 1974.
Visions of My Grandfather. Ottawa, Golden Dog Press, 1977.
Shore Lines. Winnipeg, Turnstone Press, 1979.
Vision/Sounding. Toronto, League of Canadian Poets, 1980.
The Pirates of Pen's Chance: Homolinguistic Translations, with Stephen Scobie. Toronto, Coach House Press, 1981.
The Harbingers. Kingston, Ontario, Quarry Press, 1984.
Visible Visions: The Selected Poems of Douglas Barbour, edited by Smaro Kamboureli and Robert Kroetsch. Edmonton, NeWest Press, 1984.

Other

Worlds Out of Words: The SF Novels of Samuel R. Delany. Frome, Somerset, Bran's Head, 1979.

Editor, *The Story So Far Five.* Toronto, Coach House Press, 1978.
Editor, with Stephen Scobie, *The Maple Laugh Forever: An Anthology of Canadian Comic Poetry.* Edmonton, Hurtig, 1981.
Editor, with Marni Stanley, *Writing Right: Poetry by Canadian Women.* Edmonton, Longspoon Press, 1982.

Editor, *Three Times Five: Short Stories by Harris, Sawai, Stenson.* Edmonton, NeWest Press, 1983.
Editor, *Selected and New Poems*, by Richard Sommer. Montreal, Véhicule Press, 1984.

*

Critical Studies: "Douglas Barbour: The Land Was Ours Before We Were the Land's" by Wayne Tefs, in *Essays on Canadian Writing* (Downsview, Ontario), Summer-Fall 1980; "Shore Lines" by Andrew Brooks, in *Writers News Manitoba* (Winnipeg), December 1982.

Douglas Barbour comments:

To entertain possibility in the process of writing the poem: that is my desire. My early poems tended to begin in a clear perception of the outer world: that landscape, that event, that encounter; and I was trying to say something of what I had seen and felt. By the mid-1970's I had, in what I feel are my best works, moved to a more direct encounter with language. If I could listen carefully enough, I'd hear something interesting and perhaps be able to transcribe it.

I try to write poems from a poetic stance which proposes that language is alive and not simply a "tool" to be "used" or "manipulated" for some ulterior purpose. I can only discover purpose in the process of writing if I am sufficiently open to what language speaks through me. Which is not to say that poems don't mean, but that in their wholly grounded being (when I am lucky enough to write a good one) they mean more complexly than ordinary discourse or any conscious ideas I might wish to purvey. It's always more interesting to follow the line of a poem's thought as it leads me on to new discoveries. One of the great arguments of such a poetry discovered and heard in openness is the value of such human openness before the world. This is an ideal, one I try in my writing to live up to.

*   *   *

Douglas Barbour is one of the younger generation of poets who emerged in the later 1960's, and whose work is distinguished by open if intensely self-contained forms, and a new eclecticism as far as related or absorbed influences are concerned. Not directly descended from any one of the three major movements in contemporary Canadian poetry, he has combined an awareness of the speaking voice in the poem with a somewhat more tenacious reliance on form, albeit open form, which in its turn is more disciplined than the compositional openness of the "field" theorists. In his first slim collection, *Land Fall*, Barbour moved between examples of prefigured concreteness and what one reviewer described as his "mindscapes." In his second volume the process of the poem became dependent on the physical tracings of a cross-country journey in which geography buttressed perception, and the act of travelling issued its summons to the imagination. *Songbook*, Barbour's fourth book, is a collection of lyrical jottings which, by virtue of being part impression and part reminiscence, strikes one as somewhat less imaginatively secure, although it has fine moments in which the sensuous and the personal are challenged by the unpunctuated austerities of lowercase statement, and the lonely sharpness of mind-images.

—Michael Gnarowski

BARKER, George (Granville). British. Born in Loughton, Essex, 26 February 1913. Educated at Marlborough Road School, Chelsea, London; Regent Street Polytechnic, London. Married Elspeth Langlands in 1964; several children. Professor of English Literature, Imperial Tohoku University, Sendai, Japan, 1939-41; lived in Rome, 1960-65; Visiting Professor, State University of New York, Buffalo. 1965-66; Arts Fellow, York University, 1966-67; Visiting Professor, University of Wisconsin, Madison, 1971-72, and Florida International University, Miami, 1974. Patron of the Poetry Society, Oxford University, 1953. Recipient: Royal Society of Literature bursary, 1950; Guinness Prize, 1962; Levinson Prize (*Poetry*, Chicago), 1965; Borestone Mountain Poetry Prize, 1967; Arts Council bursary, 1968; Cholmondeley Award, 1980. Agent: John Johnson Ltd., 45-47 Clerkenwell Green, London EC1R 0HT. Address: Bintry House, Itteringham, Aylsham, Norfolk, England.

PUBLICATIONS

Verse

Thirty Preliminary Poems.   London, Parton Press, 1933.
Poems.   London, Faber, 1935.
Calamiterror.   London, Faber, 1937.
Elegy on Spain.   London, Parton Press, 1939.
Lament and Triumph: London, Faber, 1940.
Selected Poems.   New York, Macmillan, 1941.
Sacred and Secular Elegies.   New York, New Directions, 1943.
Eros in Dogma.   London, Faber, 1944.
Love Poems.   New York, Dial Press, 1947.
The True Confession of George Barker.   London, Fore, 1950; augmented edition, New York, New American Library, 1964; London, MacGibbon and Kee, 1965.
News of the World.   London, Faber, 1950.
A Vision of Beasts and Gods.   London, Faber, 1954.
Collected Poems 1930-1955.   London, Faber, 1957; New York, Criterion, 1958.
The View from a Blind I.   London, Faber, 1962.
Penguin Modern Poets 3, with Charles Causley and Martin Bell.   London, Penguin, 1962.
Collected Poems 1930-1965.   New York, October House, 1965.
Dreams of a Summer Night.   London, Faber, 1966.
The Golden Chains.   London, Faber, 1968.
At Thurgarton Church.   London, Trigram Press, 1969.
Runes and Rhymes and Tunes and Chimes (for children).   London, Faber, 1969.
What Is Mercy and a Voice.   London, Poem-of-the-Month Club, 1970.
To Aylsham Fair (for children).   London, Faber, 1970.
The Alphabetical Zoo (for children).   London, Faber, 1970.
Poems of Places and People.   London, Faber, 1971.
III Hallucination Poems.   New York, Helikon Press, 1972.
In Memory of David Archer.   London, Faber, 1973.
Dialogues etc.   London, Faber, 1976.
Seven Poems.   Warwick, Greville Press, 1977.
Villa Stellar.   London, Faber, 1978.
Anno Domini.   London, Faber, 1983.

Plays

Two Plays (*The Seraphina* and *In the Shade of the Old Apple Tree*).   London, Faber, 1958.

Radio Plays: *The Seraphina*, 1956; *Oriel O'Hanlon* (published as *In the Shade of the Old Apple Tree*), 1957.

Novels

Alanna Autumnal.   London, Wishart, 1933.
Janus (two novellena).   London, Faber, 1935.
The Dead Seagull.   London, Lehmann, 1950; New York, Farrar Straus, 1951.

Other

Essays.   London, MacGibbon and Kee, 1970.

Editor, *Idylls of the King and a Selection of Poems*, by Alfred, Lord Tennyson.   New York, Doubleday, 1961.

*

Manuscript Collections: University of Texas, Austin; Lockwood Memorial Library, State University of New York, Buffalo; Berg Collection, New York Public Library.

Critical Studies: "A Prolegomena to George Barker" by Patrick W. Swift, in *X* (London), 1960; *George Barker* by Martha Fodaski, New York, Twayne, 1969; *English Poetry 1900-1950* by C.H. Sisson, London, Hart Davis, 1971, revised edition, Manchester, Carcanet, and New York, Methuen, 1981; *Homage to George Barker on His 60th Birthday* edited by John Heath-Stubbs and Martin Green, London, Martin Brian and O'Keeffe, 1973.

*   *   *

During his poetic career, George Barker's reputation has perhaps suffered on two counts. First, he emerged as a poet at the same time as Dylan Thomas, and at almost exactly the same age. From the beginning they were often linked by critics as being in some sense "romantic," as poets of personal concern and extravagant gesture, somehow seen in opposition to the supposedly more social concerns of Auden, Spender, and MacNeice. And though the essays in Francis Scarfe's *Auden and After* (a book which gives a fair picture of critical orthodoxies in the early 1940's) give equal prominence to Barker and Thomas, Thomas's later reputation, particularly after his death, seems to have obscured Barker's. Second, the anti-romantic tide in the mid-1950's turned against Barker, making him seem a period figure and wrongly lumping him indiscriminately with the New Apocalyptics and the wholly inflated tone which was taken to be the mark of the bad old wartime days.

In fact Barker's development has been much more interesting than this. There is an awkward Miltonic grandeur about some of the early work in *Thirty Preliminary Poems* and *Poems*, expressed in flowing and serpentine syntax, and a heady rhetoric which was given a more extended outing in his long poem *Calamiterror.* But the first fully achieved books are *Lament and Triumph* and *Eros in Dogma*, particularly in those poems (such as "Allegory of the Adolescent and the Adult," "Resolution of Dependence," and the much-anthologised "To My Mother") which show an effort of concentration on some external object or narrative.

With *News of the World*, there begins a relaxation of tone and a greater linguistic simplicity which Barker has continued through his later books. His themes were by this time established: elegies, both particular and general; the furies and betrayals of love; celebration and disgust. All reached their most concentrated, ambitious and notorious expression in *The True Confession of George Barker*, a long poem in which Barker seemed to take a baleful delight in trying on the various masks (Villon and

Baudelaire, for example) of a damned, despairing but nevertheless jaunty creature:

> I know only that the heart
> Doubting every real thing else
> Does not doubt the voice that tells
> Us that we suffer. The hard part
> At the dead centre of the soul
> Is an age of frozen grief
> No vernal equinox of relief
> Can mitigate, and no love console.

The View from a Blind I shows two more recent manners, in his sardonic or satirical ballads (such as "The Ballad of Yucca Flats" and "Scottish Bards and an English Reviewer"), and in the limpid and sometimes even conversational "Roman Poems." The heavy rhetorical tread of the early poems has been replaced by something much more spontaneous and lyrical, though equally copious—and sometimes, even now, prolix, as in parts of the recent loosely-connected sequence of quatrains in *The Golden Chains*. Barker's faults of verbal absurdity and self-indulgence are plain for all to see, but the compensations of energy and eloquence have not sufficiently been noticed.

(1980) In *Poems of Places and People, In Memory of David Archer, Dialogues,* and *Villa Stellar,* George Barker has continued to follow chiefly the "limpid and sometimes even conversational" style noted above in *The View from a Blind I.* The tone is often one of puzzled plain questioning, of the past and of past mistakes, of human frailty and absurdity, relieved with something more sardonic and ironical. Interleaved with such poems are elegies for dead friends and artists, meditations on death, and some purely lyrical poems of a kind one can recognise in much earlier Barker books. The recent work is sometimes self-lacerating and self-puncturing, sometimes bewildered and humble in a way that is certainly quite different from the jauntily aggressive persona he once donned; the danger is that some of it sounds like prosaic muttering. But at his best Barker is still producing effects which are astonishingly direct and exaltedly eloquent: one might note particularly, from *Villa Stellar,* the poem numbered 44, which begins "To all appearances the life serene."

Barker is still as prolific as ever, after over 45 years of production, and perhaps because of this copiousness his reputation is still uncertain: for some time, it has probably been higher in the United States than in Britain. But even if only as a type-case, perhaps the last survivor of the romantic, bohemian, self-condemned and yet dedicated poet, he has a unique position in poetry written in English.

—Anthony Thwaite

———————

BARKS, Coleman (Bryan). American. Born in Chattanooga, Tennessee, 23 April 1937. Educated at the University of North Carolina, Chapel Hill, 1955-59, B.A. in English 1959; University of California, Berkeley, 1959-61, M.A. in English 1961; University of North Carolina, 1961-65, Ph.D. in English 1968. Married Susan Kathleen Greenwood in 1962 (divorced, 1974); two sons. Instructor, University of Southern California, Los Angeles, 1965-67. Assistant Professor, 1967-72, and since 1972, Associate Professor of English, University of Georgia, Athens. Writer-in-Residence, University of Michigan, Ann Arbor, 1974. Recipient:

National Endowment for the Arts grant, 1979; Guy Owen Poetry Award (*Southern Poetry Review*), 1983. Address: 196 Westview Drive, Athens, Georgia 30606, U.S.A.

PUBLICATIONS

Verse

The Juice. New York, Harper, 1972.
New Words. Austell, Georgia, Sweetwater Press, 1976.
We're Laughing at the Damage. Davidson, North Carolina, Briarpatch Press, 1977.

Other

Translator, with Robert Bly, *Night and Sleep,* by Rumi. Cambridge, Massachusetts, Yellow Moon Press, 1981.
Translator, with John Moyne, *Open Secret,* by Rumi. Putney, Vermont, Threshold, 1984.

*   *   *

Coleman Barks's *The Juice* sported, for a first book of such vitality and achievement, a suitable jaunty title. That Barks could be grave the book shows in several poems, but its prevailing tone is the exhilarated pleasure of the skillful maker. The short "Body Poems" that begin the book are quick sketches, maxims, wisecracks, psychological definitions of the physical.

> the one chance
> I will ever have
> to go to Finland
>
> is a long lake
> frozen to my leg
>
> —"Scar"
>
> that time
> private as blood
> comes to light
> on my face
>
> like a pocket
> pulled inside out
>
> —"Blush"

Barks's next two books, both published in limited editions, exhibit more somber tones, and the earlier one, *New Words,* is dedicated to the poet's parents (both of whom died in 1971 after work on the manuscript for *The Juice* has been completed). The 10-page title poem is about words that are in fact old words, long fallen from common usage but new to the poet, who is the poem's central character. It begins like this:

> like *goaf* that Galway Kinnell
> revives in *The Book of Nightmares*
> for a storage bin in a barn
> or in a mine the dark place
> the ore's been taken from.
>
> A name
> for my yearlong trance,

Where's Coleman.
He's back up in the goaf somewhere.

So Barks's investigation of old words is a sort of mining expedition into memory of the language, and there the poet needs to find whatever will make it possible for him to return to daily life from the trance caused by the rupture of his family history.

Some words we have no record of.
Some get written down
and last for centuries
before they lose their limits
and come to mean almost anything,
nonsense words.

The best is sense and nonsense both,
child and parent,
earth and sky.

Thus linked again with his parents by language, the poet imagines himself in an attic (the student, the searcher of lost words) and also in the streets of common life again.

Close the book
and listen.

There's a man shouting
in the middle of the street.

Get up,
for what it means.

If it's a dance,
you must dance.
If it's death,
you must die.

In *We're Laughing at the Damage*, a sequence of untitled poems about spiritual restlessness, a marriage under terminal strain, and the poet's struggle to accept the violence and waste of life, we find him still working with the language itself, not only as raw material but also as a source of knowledge.

Do you know the etymology of *desire*?
Con sideris, consider, to be with

the stars,
de sideris,
to be cut off, down
from them
overcast.
This night
is between the two,
consider and desire.

Since those books Barks has been working on collaborative translations with John Moynes from the mystical Sufi poet Rumi (1207-73). Moynes translates from the original Persian, and then Barks works from Moynes's versions. The results appear in *Night and Sleep*, a book shared with Robert Bly's versions of Rumi, and in *Open Secret*. The poems are reports—sometimes joyful, sometimes frightening, often both—from a kind of life in which the most ordinary certainties of definition are challenged or ignored.

The clear bead at the center changes everything.
There are no edges to my loving now.

I've heard it said there's a window that opens
from one mind to another,

but if there's no wall, there's no need
for fitting the window, or the latch.

Another example:

When I die, lay out the corpse.
You may want to kiss my lips,
just beginning to decay. Don't be frightened
if I open my eyes.

And Barks has been working on a new book or poems, now nearly complete in manuscript, which will include the poem "New Words" but in which most of the work is much more recent. Those poems combine the poet's humor, brooding sensitivity to language and emotional nuance, and the mystical proclivities manifested in his work on Rumi. If these have sometimes seemed disparate impulses and modes in his work to date, they have all been responses to the poet's confrontation with his and everyone's mortality, and the new poems braiding these elements together marks the maturity of an already accomplished and widely known poet.

—William Matthews

BAYBARS, Taner. British. Born in Nicosia, Cyprus, 18 June 1936. Educated privately, and at the Turkish Lycée, Nicosia. Served in the Royal Air Force, 1954-55. Married Kristin Hughes-Stanton in 1959 (divorced, 1977); one daughter. Books assistant, 1956-66, book exhibition assistant, 1966-67, periodicals assistant, 1967-72, head of overseas reviews scheme, 1972-81, in design production and publishing department, 1981-82, and since 1983, book promotion officer, British Council, London. Address: 69 Onslow Gardens, London N10 3JY, England.

PUBLICATIONS

Verse

Mendilin Ucundakiler (Corners of a Handkerchief).   Nicosia, Çardak Yayinevi, 1953.
To Catch a Falling Man.   Lowestoft, Suffolk, Scorpion Press, 1963.
Susila in the Autumn Woods.   Rushden, Northamptonshire, Sceptre Press, 1974.
Narcissus in a Dry Pool.   London, Sidgwick and Jackson, 1978.
Pregnant Shadows.   London, Sidgwick and Jackson, 1981.

Novel

A Trap for the Burglar.   London, Owen, 1965.

Other

Plucked in a Far-Off Land: Images in Self Biography.   London, Gollancz, 1970.

Editor, with Osman Türkay, *Modern Turkish Poetry.* London, Modern Poetry in Translation, 1971.

Translator, *Selected Poems of Nazim Hikmet.* London, Cape, 1967; New York, Humanities Press, 1968.
Translator, *The Moscow Symphony and Other Poems*, by Nazim Hikmet. London, Rapp and Whiting, 1970; Chicago, Swallow Press, 1971.
Translator, *The Day Before Tomorrow*, Nazim Hikmet. Oxford, Carcanet, 1972.
Translator, *The Snowy Day/Karli bir gün*, by Ezra Jack Keats. London, Bodley Head, 1980.
Translator, *Peter's Chair/Peter'in sandalyasi*, by Ezra Jack Keats. London, Bodley Head, 1980.

*

Critical Studies: "Voice Production" by Frederick Grubb, in *Poetry Review* (London), 1964; "Bigger Than Both of Us" by Bernard Share, in *Irish Times* (Dublin), 12 June 1965; *The Poet Speaks* by Peter Orr, London, Routledge, 1966; "Plucked Untimely" by Raymond Gardner, in *The Guardian* (London), 19 May 1970; "Flame by Flame" by Peter Lewis, in *Times Literary Supplement* (London), 3 October 1978.

Taner Baybars comments:
   In my view, a poem is the culmination of an intense experience which could not be expressed in any other form. If it could, then it would cease to be a poem although it might retain the *shape* of a poem. Also, because of its intense nature, a poem is essentially short: only an exceptionally great poet is able to sustain such intensity on a longer scale. There is an obvious difference between poetry and verse, but that difference, nowadays, is almost always ignored.

*   *   *

   Taner Baybars is a Cypriot whose first book of poems, written in Turkish, was published in Nicosia in 1953. Coming to England 12 years later with the expressed intention of studying Law (he soon gave up that idea), he decided to stay in London and has adopted English as his literary language with quite remarkable effect. If he experienced any difficulties in writing his poems in a second language, he has enjoyed an advantage over his British contemporaries in that he has remained free of group pressures and influences, and has never shown the slightest inclination to follow prevailing fashions in diction or style. His poems, successful, or otherwise, have always been quite unlike anyone else's.
   The poems in his *To Catch a Falling Man* are arranged in chronological order so that it is possible to trace his development as a poet throughout the volume. The collection begins with the description of a cycle journey through the English countryside and these early pieces reflect a simplicity or clarity of vision allied to an unusually sophisticated and well-informed outlook, reinforced by a creative mind that enables him to evoke the scene in such phrases as "the coquettish wind perambulating in the wheels" or "the waves unkiss the cliff." Though his themes are quotidian—the demolition of an old house, taking barbitone for sleep, the end of a musical concert, spelling out his name, chopping down a tree, or even the sound of a key turning in the lock—he somehow contrives to surround them with a sinister atmosphere, as in his poem about a computer, "The Oracle":

We are much honoured; we hold conferences and
discuss what the most fitting question should be;

when we find it we march and surround the machine;

the problem is fed in, the drone irregularly
distends, no answer is laid. We grow old and visit
every day the clean, compact brain and wait.

   In his later work the simplicity of his earlier style gives way to a search for the unexpected, for what goes on below the surface of human relationships, for the motives beneath the conversation, for the realities underlying appearances. "Demolishing a House" demonstrates Baybars's skill at piling detail upon detail without overwhelming the poem:

Yet while I ate and poised the fork in the air,
the noise of a drill shivered the glass facade,
the fake plants shook, too, a little afraid.
I had to open my mouth to let the noise out.
Then I heard the crash of another falling wall.

Narcissus in a Dry Pool begins where *To Catch a Falling Man* concludes, stylistically. The individual nature of Baybars's enquiry into the phenomena of existence and his odd and sometimes bizarre approach to his subject lends a sort of piquancy to his poetry. For a single volume there is a wide range of styles and types of writing, from the three-line haiku, to a series of love poems, "Explorations," to "The Loneliness of Columbus," a dramatic monologue. The description of a boy's "Circumcision Just Before Puberty" leaves nothing to the imagination, but is nevertheless handled with extraordinary delicacy and understanding. The group of poems "for Susila Jane," his daughter, manifest a new preoccupation, that of observing his daughter's gradual introduction to the external world and her development through touch, taste, sight and smell:

Seeing your own reflection on a doorknob
you begin to utter your name, then stop
in that conflux of brass stained by my hand.
Who? I hold you against the windowglass.

You exclaim: Dark! I put you down. You live
in a galaxy of sounds absorbed by your tongue
and keeping your name a secret to your tongue
and grow in full awareness of others.

What seems to impress him most in this exploration of infancy and childhood is the paradox of innocence combining with an almost frightening kind of inner certainty arising from the need for self-fulfilment.
   Perhaps most interesting of all are the poems devoted to the relationship between man and woman, the man always being Baybars himself and the woman a particular woman drawn from his private circle; they are, of course, love poems in every sense of the word, yet for Baybars the love relationship is complicated, for his partners are not merely women or lovers, but each, willingly or unwillingly, acquires a symbolistic quality which takes its idiosyncratic scope from some aspect of Baybars's experience—his native country, his childhood, his family, his adolescence, etc.—and which, inevitably defines the relationship for him.

—Howard Sergeant

BEAVER, Bruce (Victor). Australian. Born in Sydney, New South Wales, 14 February 1928. Educated at Manly Public School and Sydney Boys' High School. Married to Brenda Beaver. Lived in New Zealand, 1958-62. Free-lance writer. Recipient: *Poetry Magazine* Award, Sydney, 1963; Commonwealth Literary Fellowship, 1967; Captain Cook Bi-Centenary Prize, 1970; Grace Leven Prize, 1970; Poetry Society of Australia Award, 1970; Patrick White Award, 1982. Address: 14 Malvern Avenue, Manly, New South Wales 2095, Australia.

PUBLICATIONS

Verse

Under the Bridge. Sydney, Beaujon Press, 1961.
Seawall and Shoreline. Sydney, South Head Press, 1964.
Open at Random. Sydney, South Head Press, 1967.
Letters to Live Poets. Sydney, South Head Press, 1969.
Lauds and Plaints: Poems (1968-1972). Sydney, South Head Press, 1974.
Odes and Days. Sydney, South Head Press, 1975.
Death's Directives. Sydney, New Poetry, 1978.
As It Was. Brisbane, University of Queensland Press, 1979.
Selected Poems. Sydney, Angus and Robertson, 1979.

Novels

The Hot Spring. Sydney, Horvitz, 1965.
You Can't Come Back. Adelaide, Rigby, 1966.

*

Critical Studies: *New Impulses in Australian Poetry,* edited by Thomas W. Shapcott and Rodney Hall, Brisbane, University of Queensland Press, 1968; "Gift-Bearing Hands: The Poetry of Bruce Beaver" by Craig Powell, in *Quadrant* (Sydney), XII, 5, 1968; "Bruce Beaver's Poetry" by Robert D. FitzGerald in *Meanjin* (Melbourne), September 1969; "New Australian Poetry" by James Tulip, in *Southerly* (Sydney), 1970; *Poets on Record 7,* Brisbane, University of Queensland Press, 1972; "The 'Livres composés' of Bruce Beaver" by J. and R.M. Beston, in *WLWE* (Perth), April 1975.

*   *   *

Something of a maverick among Australian poets, Bruce Beaver is an original and idiosyncratic writer whose reputation has grown with the appearance of each book. A first collection of poems, *Under the Bridge,* was published in 1961 to some critical acclaim and not a little grumbling. Though his work was said to be colourful and lively in its descriptions of landscapes and regional settings, the human element touched on throughout was vaguely eccentric and even in part perverse; it certainly does not have the dryly humorous to openly heroic characterisation that appeals to so many Australian poets.

In his second book he consolidated the thematic development of 20th century man in and sometimes versus a landscape. In "A View from the Bridge-rail" and "Letters from Sydney" he stressed the relative brevity and existential pressures of human life, setting these against a Heraclitean background of flux and fusion in the book's title poem "Seawall and Shoreline." An impressive sequence entitled "Harbour Sonnets" describes with a lyrical fervour the landscape near his home at Manly, N.S.W.

The same attachment, almost obsessional, to an intimate landscape is seen in the opening pages of his third book, some-

what diffidently entitled *Open at Random,* in poems such as "Excursion" and "Remembering." Again the critics were divided in their estimates of this non-conforming talent. Some found the characterisation too splenetic, others remarked on the apparent opacity of some of the verses, yet the book has had its share of praise and an elder poet of stature, R.D. FitzGerald, has stated that he considers one of the poems, "The Killers," as among the best poems written in Australia.

—Staff of *Poetry Australia*

BECKETT, Samuel (Barclay). Irish. Born near Dublin, 13 April 1906. Educated at Portora Royal School, County Fermanagh; Trinity College, Dublin, B.A. in French and Italian 1927, M.A. 1931. Worked at the Irish Red Cross Hospital, St. Lô, France, 1945. Married Suzanne Deschevaux-Dumesnil in 1961. French teacher, Campbell College, Belfast, 1928; Lecturer in English, Ecole Normale Supérieure, Paris, 1928-30; Lecturer in French, Trinity College, Dublin, 1930-31. Closely associated with James Joyce in Paris in the late 1920's and 1930's. Settled in Paris in 1937 and has written chiefly in French since 1945; translates his own work into English. Recipient: *Evening Standard* award, for drama, 1955; Obie award, for drama, 1958, 1960, 1962, 1964; Italia Prize, 1959; International Publishers Prize, 1961; Prix Filmcritice, 1965; Tours Film Prize, 1966; Nobel Prize for Literature, 1969; National Grand Prize for Theatre (France), 1975. D.Litt.: Dublin University, 1959. Member, German Academy of Art; Companion of Literature, Royal Society of Literature. Address: c/o Editions de Minuit, 7 rue Bernard-Palissy, Paris 75006, France.

PUBLICATIONS

Verse

Whoroscope. Paris, Hours Press, 1930.
Echo's Bones and Other Precipitates. Paris, Europa Press, 1935.
Gedichte (collected poems in English and French, with German translations). Wiesbaden, Limes, 1959.
Poems in English. London, Calder, 1961; New York, Grove Press, 1963.
Collected Poems in English and French. London, Calder, and New York, Grove Press, 1977; revised edition, as *Collected Poems 1930-1978,* Calder, 1984.

Plays

Le Kid, with Georges Pelorson (produced Dublin, 1931).
En Attendant Godot (produced Paris, 1953). Paris, Minuit, 1952; translated by the author as *Waiting for Godot: Tragicomedy* (produced London, 1955; Miami and New York, 1956), New York, Grove Press, 1954; London, Faber, 1956.
Fin de Partie: Suivi de Acte sans Paroles (produced London, 1957). Paris, Minuit, 1957; translated by the author as *Endgame: A Play in One Act; Followed by Act Without Words: A Mime for One Player* (*Endgame,* produced New York and London, 1958; *Act Without Words,* produced New York, 1960), New York, Grove Press, and London, Faber, 1958.
All That Fall (broadcast, 1957). New York, Grove Press, and London, Faber, 1957.

Krapp's Last Tape (produced London, 1958; New York, 1960).   Included in *Krapp's Last Tape and Embers*, 1959; in *Krapp's Last Tape and Other Dramatic Pieces*, 1960.

Embers (broadcast, 1959).   Included in *Krapp's Last Tape and Embers*, 1959; in *Krapp's Last Tape and Other Dramatic Pieces*, 1960.

Krapp's Last Tape and Embers.   London, Faber, 1959.

Act Without Words II (produced New York, 1959; London, 1960).   Included in *Krapp's Last Tape and Other Dramatic Pieces*, 1960; in *Eh Joe and Other Writings*, 1967.

Krapp's Last Tape and Other Dramatic Pieces (includes *All That Fall, Embers, Act Without Words I* and *II*).   New York, Grove Press, 1960.

Happy Days (produced New York, 1961; London, 1962).   New York, Grove Press, 1961; London, Faber, 1962; bilingual edition, edited by James Knowlson, Faber, 1978.

Words and Music, music by John Beckett (broadcast, 1962).   Included in *Play and Two Short Pieces for Radio*, 1964; in *Cascando and Other Short Dramatic Pieces*, 1968.

Cascando (broadcast, in French, 1963).   Paris, Minuit, 1963; translated by the author as *Cascando: A Radio Piece for Music and Voice* (broadcast, 1964; in *Beckett 3*, produced London, 1970; produced New York, 1976), included in *Play and Two Short Pieces for Radio*, 1964; in *Cascando and Other Short Dramatic Pieces*, 1968.

Play (produced Ulm-Donau, 1963; New York and London, 1964).   Included in *Play and Two Short Pieces for Radio*, 1964; in *Cascando and Other Short Dramatic Pieces*, 1968.

Play and Two Short Pieces for Radio (includes *Words and Music* and *Cascando*).   London, Faber, 1964.

Eh Joe (televised, 1966; produced New York, 1978).   Included in *Eh Joe and Other Writings*, 1967; in *Cascando and Other Short Dramatic Pieces*, 1968.

Come and Go: Dramaticule (produced Paris, 1966; Dublin, 1968; London, 1970; New York, 1974).   London, Calder and Boyars, 1967; in *Cascando and Other Short Dramatic Pieces*, 1968.

Eh Joe and Other Writings (includes *Act Without Words II* and *Film*).   London, Faber, 1967.

Cascando and Other Short Dramatic Pieces (includes *Words and Music, Eh Joe, Play, Come and Go, Film*).   New York, Grove Press, 1968.

Film.   New York, Grove Press, 1969; London, Faber, 1972.

Breath (part of *Oh! Calcutta!*; produced New York, Glasgow, and London, 1970).   Included in *Breath and Other Shorts*, 1971.

Breath and Other Shorts (includes *Come and Go, Act Without Words I* and *II*, and the prose piece *From an Abandoned Work*).   London, Faber, 1971.

Not I (produced New York, 1972; London, 1973).   London, Faber, 1973; in *First Love and Other Shorts*, 1974.

Tryst (televised, 1976).   Included in *Ends and Odds*, 1976.

That Time (produced London and Washington, D.C., 1976; New York, 1977).   London, Faber, 1976; in *Ends and Odds*, 1976.

Footfalls (also director: produced London and Washington, D.C., 1976; New York, 1977).   London, Faber, 1976; in *Ends and Odds*, 1976.

Ends and Odds: Dramatic Pieces (includes *That Time, Footfalls, Tryst, Not I*).   New York, Grove Press, 1976; as *Ends and Odds: Plays and Sketches* (includes *Not I, That Time, Footfalls, Ghost Trio, ...but the clouds..., Theatre I* and *II, Radio I* and *II*), London, Faber, 1977.

Rough for Radio (broadcast, 1976).   As *Radio II*, included in *Ends and Odds*, 1977.

Shades (televised, 1977).   Included in *Ends and Odds*, 1977.

A Piece of Monologue (produced New York, 1980).   Included in *Three Occasional Pieces*, 1982.

Rockaby (produced Buffalo, New York, and New York City, 1981; London, 1982).   Included in *Rockaby and Other Works*, 1981; in *Three Occasional Pieces*, 1982.

Rockaby and Other Works.   New York, Grove Press, 1981.

The Ohio Impromptu (produced Columbus, Ohio, 1981; New York, 1983; Edinburgh and London, 1984).   Included in *Three Occasional Pieces*, 1982; in *Ohio Impromptu, Catastrophe, and What Where*, 1984.

Three Occasional Pieces.   London, Faber, 1982.

Quad (televised, 1982).   Included in *Collected Shorter Plays*, 1984.

Catastrophe (produced Avignon, 1982; New York, 1983; Edinburgh and London, 1984).   Included in *Collected Shorter Plays*, 1984.

Nacht und Traume (televised, 1983).   Included in *Collected Shorter Plays*, 1984.

What Where (produced in German, Graz, 1983; in English, New York, 1983; Edinburgh and London, 1984).   Included in *Collected Shorter Plays*, 1984.

Collected Shorter Plays.   London, Faber, and New York, Grove Press, 1984.

Ohio Impromptu, Catastrophe, and What Where.   New York, Grove Press, 1984.

Screenplay: *Film*, 1965.

Radio Plays: *All That Fall*, 1957; *Embers*, 1959; *Words and Music*, 1962; *Cascando*, 1963; *Rough for Radio*, 1976.

Television Plays: *Eh Joe*, 1966; *Tryst*, 1976; *Shades* (*Ghost Trio, Not I, ...but the clouds...*), 1977; *Quad*, 1982; *Nacht und Traume*, 1983.

Novels

Murphy.   London, Routledge, 1938; New York, Grove Press, 1957.

Molloy.   Paris, Minuit, 1951; translated by the author and Patrick Bowles, Paris, Olympia Press, and New York, Grove Press, 1955; London, Calder, 1959.

Malone meurt.   Paris, Minuit, 1951; translated by the author as *Malone Dies*, New York, Grove Press, 1956; London, Calder, 1958.

L'Innommable.   Paris, Minuit, 1953; translated by the author as *The Unnamable*, New York, Grove Press, 1958; London, Calder, 1959.

Watt (written in English).   Paris, Olympia Press, 1953; New York, Grove Press, 1959; London, Calder, 1963.

Comment C'Est.   Paris, Minuit, 1961; translated by the author as *How It Is*, New York, Grove Press, and London, Calder, 1964.

Mercier et Camier.   Paris, Minuit, 1970; translated by the author as *Mercier and Camier*, London, Calder and Boyars, 1974; New York, Grove Press, 1975.

Compagnie.   Paris, Minuit, 1980; translated by the author as *Company*, London, Calder, and New York, Grove Press, 1980.

Short Stories and Texts

More Pricks Than Kicks.   London, Chatto and Windus, 1934; New York, Grove Press, 1970.

Nouvelles et Textes pour Rien.   Paris, Minuit, 1955; translated by the author and Richard Seaver as *Stories and Texts for Nothing*, New York, Grove Press, 1967; in *No's Knife:*

Selected Shorter Prose, 1945-1966, 1967.
From an Abandoned Work.   London, Faber, 1958.
Imagination morte imaginez.   Paris, Minuit, 1965; translated by the author as *Imagination Dead Imagine*, London, Calder and Boyars, 1965.
Assez.   Paris, Minuit, 1966; translated by the author as *Enough*, in *No's Knife*, 1967.
Bing.   Paris, Minuit, 1966; translated by the author as *Ping*, in *No's Knife*, 1967.
Têtes-Mortes (includes *D'Un Ouvrage Abandonné, Assez, Bing, Imagination morte imaginez*).   Paris, Minuit, 1967; translated by the author, in *No's Knife*, 1967.
No's Knife: Selected Shorter Prose, 1945-1966 (includes *Stories and Texts for Nothing, From an Abandoned Work, Imagination Dead Imagine, Enough, Ping*).   London, Calder and Boyars, 1967.
L'Issue.   Paris, Georges Visat, 1968.
Sans.   Paris, Minuit, 1969; translated by the author as *Lessness*, London, Calder and Boyars, 1971.
Séjour.   Paris, Georges Richar, 1970.
Premier Amour.   Paris, Minuit, 1970; translated by the author as *First Love*, London, Calder and Boyars, 1973.
Le Dépeupleur.   Paris, Minuit, 1971; translated by the author as *The Lost Ones*, London, Calder and Boyars, and New York Grove Press, 1972.
The North.   London, Enitharmon Press, 1972.
First Love and Other Shorts.   New York, Grove Press, 1974.
Fizzles.   New York, Grove Press, 1976.
For to End Yet Again and Other Fizzles.   London, Calder, 1976.
All Strange Away.   New York, Gotham Book Mart, 1976; London, Calder, 1979.
Four Novellas (*The Expelled, The Calmative, The End, First Love*).   London, Calder, 1977; as *The Expelled and Other Novellas*, London, Penguin, 1980.
Six Residua.   London, Calder, 1978.
Mal vu mal dit.   Paris, Minuit, 1981; translated by the author as *Ill Seen Ill Said*, London, Calder, and New York, Grove Press, 1982.
Worstword Ho.   London, Calder, and New York, Grove Press, 1983.

Other

"Dante...Bruno. Vico..Joyce," in *Our Exagmination round His Factification for Incamination of Work in Progress*.   Paris, Shakespeare and Company, 1929; London, Faber, 1936; New York, New Directions, 1939.
Proust.   London, Chatto and Windus, 1931; New York, Grove Press, 1957; with *Three Dialogues with Georges Duthuit*, London, Calder, 1965.
Bram von Welde, with others.   Paris, Georges Fall, 1958; translated by the author and Olive Classe, New York, Grove Press, 1960.
A Samuel Beckett Reader.   London, Calder and Boyars, 1967.
I Can't Go On: A Selection from the Work of Samuel Beckett, edited by Richard Seaver.   New York, Grove Press, 1976.
Disjecta: Miscellaneous Writings and a Dramatic Fragment, edited by Ruby Cohn.   London, Calder, 1983; New York, Grove Press, 1984.
Collected Shorter Prose 1945-1980.   London, Calder, 1984.

Translator, *Anthology of Mexican Poetry*, edited by Octavio Paz.   Bloomington, Indiana University Press, 1958; London, Thames and Hudson, 1959.
Translator, *The Old Tune*, by Robert Pinget.   Paris, Minuit,

1960; in *Plays 1*, by Pinget, London, Calder, 1963; in *Three Plays*, by Pinget, New York, Hill and Wang, 1966.
Translator, *Zone*, by Guillaume Apollinaire.   Dublin and London, Dolmen Press-Calder and Boyars, 1960.
Translator, *Drunken Boat*, by Arthur Rimbaud, edited by James Knowlson and Felix Leakey.   Reading, Whiteknights Press, 1977.

*

Bibliography: *Samuel Beckett: His Work and His Critics: An Essay in Bibliography* by Raymond Federman and John Fletcher, Berkeley, University of California Press, 1970 (through 1966).

Manuscript Collections: University of Texas, Austin; Ohio State University, Columbus; Washington University, St. Louis, Missouri; Dartmouth College, Hanover, New Hampshire; Reading University, England.

Critical Studies (selection): *Samuel Beckett: A Critical Study*, New York, Grove Press, and London, Calder, 1962, revised dition, Berkeley, University of California Press, 1968, and *A Reader's Guide to Samuel Beckett*, New York, Farrar Straus, and London, Thames and Hudson, 1973, both by Hugh Kenner; *Samuel Beckett: The Comic Gamut*, New Brunswick, New Jersey, Rutgers University Press, 1962, and *Back to Beckett*, Princeton, New Jersey, Princeton University Press, 1974, both by Ruby Cohn; *Samuel Beckett* by William York Tindall, New York, Columbia University Press, 1964; *Samuel Beckett* by Richard N. Coe, New York, Grove Press, 1964; *Samuel Beckett: A Collection of Critical Essays* edited by Martin Esslin, Englewood Cliffs, New Jersey, Prentice Hall, 1965; *Beckett at 60: A Festschrift* edited by John Calder, London, Calder and Boyars, 1967; *Samuel Beckett* by Ronald Hayman, London, Heinemann, 1968, New York, Ungar, 1974; *Samuel Beckett Now: Critical Approaches to His Novels, Poetry and Plays* edited by Melvin J. Friedman, Chicago, University of Chicago Press, 1970; *Samuel Beckett's Whoroscope: A Linguistic-Literary Interpretation* by Johannes Hedberg, Saltsjö-Duvnäs, Sweden, Moderna Språk, 1972; *Samuel Beckett* by John Pilling, London, Routledge, 1976; *Beckett/Beckett* by Vivian Mercier, New York, Oxford University Press, 1977, London, Oxford University Press, 1979; *Samuel Beckett: A Biography* by Deirdre Bair, New York, Harcourt Brace, and London, Cape, 1978; *Samuel Beckett: The Critical Heritage* edited by Raymond Federman and Lawrence Graver, London, Routledge, 1979; *The Samuel Beckett Manuscripts: A Critical Study* by Richard L. Admussen, London, Prior, 1979; *Samuel Beckett* by Charles Lyons, New York, Grove Press, 1983.

Theatrical Activities:
Director: **Plays**—*Come and Go*, Paris, 1966; *Endgame*, Berlin, 1967; *Krapp's Last Tape*, Berlin, 1969; *Krapp's Last Tape* and *Act Without Words*, Paris, 1970; *Krapp's Last Tape* and *Endgame*, London, 1971; *Happy Days*, Berlin, 1971, London, 1979; *Waiting for Godot*, Berlin, 1975, New York, 1977, London, 1984; *Krapp's Last Tape* and *Not I*, Paris, 1975; *Footfalls*, London, 1976; *Krapp's Last Tape*, Berlin, 1977, and London, 1978. **Television**—*Eh Joe*, 1966 (Germany).

*   *   *

Samuel Beckett published two very short volumes of verse in his youth, each with minority presses, *Whoroscope* and *Echo's Bones*. They attracted no critical attention at all and in 1961, when he was a very famous writer indeed, and John Calder brought out the bulk of these early poems as *Poems in English*, so far as I know I was the only reviewer to write about them, and that briefly and anonymously. They are, indeed, minor poems as Joyce's are but, like Joyce's poems at their best (and like those plays of Beckett's, *All That Fall* and *Embers*, for instance, which were not translated from Beckett's French but written directly in English—Irish English—for radio), they express the author's intimate feelings with a certain concentration and they have a rooted feeling, a local lovingness, and offer some intimate clues to Beckett's bitterness. It is impossible for anybody to be as chillingly negative in verse, consistently, as Beckett is in prose. He is a great master of prose and, like Joyce, only a rather small and precious master in verse, and very much in the Irish tradition of the glumps, or melodious subjective gloom. In verse, unlike prose, the writer has to expose, or give away, the intimate hurts of the inner heart. And these, for Beckett as for most people, are the hurts of lost or rejected love, and the self-disgust, or the self-despisal, that goes with rejection:

> the churn of stale words in the heart again
> love love love thud of the old plunger
> pestling the unalterable
> whey of words

The metaphor is from butter-making and one seems to smell the stale milk smells of a dairy. The Anglo-Irish aspirate *w* where the English do not and in standard English "whey of words" becomes "way of words." *Plunger* and *pestling* and *unalterable*, like *churn*, suggest a mechanical, desperate, barren sexuality. But the most moving short poem in the book is one of a set on Dieppe, written first in French, and then in very traditional Irish English, echoing Synge and Lady Gregory, in Kiltartan or *Playboy of the Western World* language, one might say:

> I would like my love to die
> and the rain to be falling on the graveyard
> and on me walking the streets
> mourning the first and last to love me.

These four lines have lasted in my memory with a hurting poignancy. I spoke of them, when I wrote my too brief review, as expressing "the quiet persistence of loving self-hurt, the innocent, exorbitant, childish bitterness preserved and hardened in manhood and used to claw down the world."

—G.S. Fraser

BEER, Patricia. British. Born in Exmouth, Devon, 4 November 1924. Educated at Exmouth Grammar School; Exeter University, B.A. (honours) in English (London); St. Hugh's College, Oxford, B.Litt. Married to Damien Parsons. Lecturer in English, University of Padua, 1946-48, British Institute, Rome, 1948, and Ministero Aeronautica, Rome, 1950-53; Senior Lecturer in English, Goldsmiths' College, London, 1962-68. Address: c/o Hutchinson Publishing Group Ltd., 17-21 Conway Street, London W1P 6JD, England.

PUBLICATIONS

Verse

Loss of the Magyar and Other Poems. London, Longman, 1959.
The Survivors. London, Longman, 1963.
Just Like the Resurrection. London, Macmillan, 1967.
The Estuary. London, Macmillan, 1971.
Spanish Balcony. London, Poem-of-the-Month Club, 1973.
Driving West. London, Gollancz, 1975.
Selected Poems. London, Hutchinson, 1979.
The Lie of the Land. London, Hutchinson, 1983.

Plays

The Enterprise of England (produced Upottery, Devon, 1979).

Radio Play: *Pride, Prejudice, and the Woman Question*, 1975.

Novel

Moon's Ottery. London, Hutchinson, 1978.

Other

Mrs. Beer's House (autobiography). London, Macmillan, 1968.
An Introduction to the Metaphysical Poets. London, Macmillan, and Totowa, New Jersey, Rowman and Littlefield, 1972.
Reader: I Married Him. London, Macmillan, and New York, Barnes and Noble, 1974.
Patricia Beer's Devon. London, Hutchinson, 1984.

Editor, with Ted Hughes and Vernon Scannell, *New Poems 1962.* London, Hutchinson, 1962.
Editor, *New Poems 1975.* London, Hutchinson, 1975.
Editor, with Kevin Crossley-Holland, *New Poetry 2.* London, Arts Council, 1976.
Editor, *Poetry Supplement.* London, Poetry Book Society, 1978.

*

Patricia Beer comments:

(1970) In my opinion my verse has changed radically since the publication of *Loss of the Magyar* in 1959. I do not repudiate my early work but I am now aiming at something quite different. I am trying to break away from the limitations imposed by traditional metres and have been turning increasingly to free verse and syllabics. I am also aiming at using less obvious metaphor.

The writing of my autobiography has influenced my work in two ways: the intensive use of prose has made me try for greater precision in my poetry; and since the publication of the autobiography I have felt able to deal poetically with subjects of a more overtly personal nature. I am not speaking in terms of confessional poetry because that is a mode which, though I respect it, is not for me. But I find I have less need to present my themes objectively by the use of, for example, legend.

The poets whom, currently, I most admire are Yeats, Robert Lowell, Ted Hughes.

*   *   *

Patricia Beer's work has a solid, dependable feel that the poetry reader finds reassuring. The lay-out of the poem on the page, the unforced and straightforward method of using narrative, the subject matter recognisable and comprehensible: all these factors go to make well-wrought poems whose place is thoroughly mainstream. And always, working away underneath, is a wry, chuckling sense of West Country humour. Yet beyond the everyday nature of the poems' subjects (a postcard, a branch railway line, a scratch) there are intimations of darker possibilities, real threats. With a nudge here and a wink there the reader is led by the hand to a grimmer awareness, as in "Concert at Long Melford Church":

> They spread all over the churchyard. They scan
> The crowd, recognise, smile and shake hands.
> By each tombstone a well-dressed person stands.
> It looks just like the Resurrection.

In many respects—its economy, its social observations, that oblique glance—this quotation is typical work from Beer. Even though she has moved, in recent collections, to a freer line and developed an interest in syllabics the style remains. The input of a sense of semi-surprise gives her work an element of charm.

The poems strike an independent note, not noticeably feminist or strident but singularly determined to stand their ground. A toughness inhabits a number of pieces but any tendency to over-statement is usually put down by that unfailing ability to control the material, as in "Christmas Eve":

> As it gets dark a drunk
> Comes tacking up the road
> In a white macintosh
> Charming as a yacht

While the vast majority of the poems fit comfortably on a single page, "The Loss of the Magyar" is a sequence comprising eight sections. Generally, though, the narratives and anecdotes run their course and are confined to the single page with economy and a highly readable flow. The casual look of the stanzas is not easy to catch, and therein lies the poet's skill. She handles her material without strain.

Death makes its presence felt in many of the pieces. Not gloomily or in mordant vein but with a measure of respect. That wry humour also alleviates what could be painful, as in "Head of a snowdrop":

> Anti-vivisectionists show men
> Keeping dogs' heads alive, yapping even.
> Schoolboys studying the Stuarts laugh
> About Charles talking with his head off.

and 'Arms':

> ....He put his arms
> Round his son and there he stood,
> Protector, up to his knees
> In death, and that was the last
> That anyone saw of him.

Beer often makes mention of family and her childhood experiences. She sets her roots firmly and so offers the reader something to latch on to; her other life—the academic pursuits—also pops up now and then. But this isn't cloistered, wind-bag, posing poetry, more an ordered and considered communication with people. Patricia Beer's poems don't offer many answers or profundities, but they are a consolation in their humanity and elegance and for that reason deserve the widest possible readership.

—Wes Magee

BEISSEL, Henry (Eric). Canadian. Born in Cologne, Germany, 12 April 1929; emigrated to Canada in 1951; naturalized, 1956. Educated at the University of Cologne, 1948-50; University College, London, 1950-51; University of Toronto (Epstein Award, 1958; Davidson Prize, 1959), 1957-60, B.A. 1958, M.A. 1960. Packer, salesman, and clerk, in Canada, 1951-54; freelance writer and film-maker, Canadian Broadcasting Corporation, 1954-58; Lecturer, University of Munich, 1960-62, University of Alberta, Edmonton, 1962-64, and University of the West Indies, Trinidad, 1964-66. Assistant Professor, 1966-68, Associate Professor, 1968-76, and since ·1976, Professor of English, Sir George Williams University, now Concordia University, Montreal. Editor, *Edge* magazine, Montreal, 1963-69. Recipient: Canada Council grant, 1967, 1968, 1969, 1971, 1973, 1974 (2 grants). Address: Department of English, Concordia University, 1455 de Maisonneuve Boulevard West, Montreal, Quebec H3G 1M8, Canada.

PUBLICATIONS

Verse

Witness the Heart. Toronto, Green Willow Press, 1963.
New Wings for Icarus: A Poem in Four Parts. Toronto, Coach House Press, 1966.
The World Is a Rainbow (for children), music by W. Bottenberg. Toronto, Canadian Music Centre, 1969.
Face on the Dark. Toronto, New Press, 1970.
Quays of Sadness. Montreal, Delta Press, 1973.
The Salt I Taste. Montreal, DC Books, 1975.
Three Poems. Toronto, League of Canadian Poets, 1980.
Cantos North. Alexandria, Ontario, Ayorama, 1980.

Plays

The Curve, adaptation of a play by Tankred Dorst (produced Edmonton, 1963). Included in *Three Plays,* 1976.
A Trumpet for Nap, adaptation of a play by Tankred Dorst (produced London, 1968). Toronto, Playwrights, 1973.
Skinflint: A Marionette Play (produced Montreal, 1969; London, 1971).
Inook and the Sun (produced Stratford, Ontario, 1973; London, 1974). Toronto, Playwrights, 1974.
Three Plays (*The Curve, A Trumpet for Nap, Grand Tirade at the Town-Wall*), by Tankred Dorst. Toronto, Playwrights, 1976.
Goya (produced Montreal, 1976; Dallas, 1981). Toronto, Playwrights, 1978.
For Crying Out Loud, in *Cues and Entrances,* edited by Beissel. Toronto, Gage, 1977.
Under Coyote's Eye: A Play about Ishi (produced Chicago, 1978). Toronto, Playwrights, 1979.
Are You Afraid of Thieves, adaptation of a play by Louis-Dominique Lavigne. Toronto, Simon and Pierre, 1978.
Waiting for Gaudreault, with Arlette Francière, adaptation of a play by André Simard. Toronto, Simon and Pierre, 1978.
The Emigrants, adaptation of a play by Slawomir Mrozek (produced Montreal, 1981). New York, French, 1984.
Hedda Gabler, adaptation of the play by Ibsen. Toronto, Playwrights, 1983.

Other

Introduction to Spain (filmstrip and text). London, Common Ground, 1955.

Editor, *Cues and Entrances: 10 Canadian One-Act Plays.* Toronto, Gage, 1977.

Translator, *The Price of Morning: Selected Poems*, by Walter Bauer. Vancouver, Prism International Press, 1968.
Translator, *A Different Sun*, by Walter Bauer. Ottawa, Oberon Press, 1976.

*   *   *

Henry Beissel is a poet whose considerable interest in drama is readily apparent in his work. He is immensely conscious of the poet's role, both in the practice of his art and in relation to the society in which he finds himself. This consciousness has found expression in various acts of protest or strong social comment which should be linked to Beissel's views on poetry which he has made known at poetry readings and in his editorial in *Edge 7* (Winter 1967-68). He has summarised his own and the poet's function in the following excerpt: "On the other hand the poet as myth-maker: all art, as Yeats said, is founded upon personal vision, and myth is the embodiment of man's vision of himself and his world. It is this vision that distinguishes man from all other forms of being. And here too, in a time like ours determined to pervert the individual and to obscure all true vision, the poet's task is of especial magnitude." Beissel's first noteworthy statement is contained in *New Wings for Icarus*, a book-length poem in four parts in which his personal vision works to telescope time and experience in what is, on occasion, a critical but generally affirming comment on the human process: "...to render us human/for the one night in which we bloom." *Face on the Dark* is a more personal and more intimately considered collection of poems. Again, there is something of the conscious poetic *persona* operating in the verse, and there is a good deal of drawing on travel as an ordering experience. Social comment crops up in one or two rather tense poems. Otherwise, the line has become longer, the poems, structurally more complex.

As a more recent development, Beissel has shifted his energy into drama. His translation of the German poems of Walter Bauer was widely and favourably reviewed.

—Michael Gnarowski

BELITT, Ben. American. Born in New York City, 2 May 1911. Educated at the University of Virginia, Charlottesville, B.A. 1932 (Phi Beta Kappa), M.A. 1934, 1934-36. Served in the United States Army Infantry, 1942-44; Editor-Scenarist, Signal Corps Photographic Center Combat Film Section, 1945-46. Assistant Literary Editor, *The Nation*, New York, 1937-38. Since 1938, Member of the English Department, and currently Professor of literature and languages, Bennington College, Vermont. Taught at Mills College, Oakland, California, 1939, and Connecticut College, New London, 1948-49. Recipient: Shelley Memorial Award, 1937; Guggenheim Fellowship, 1945; Oscar Blumenthal Award, 1957, and Union League Civic and Arts Foundation prize, 1960 (*Poetry*, Chicago); Brandeis University Creative Arts Award, 1962; American Academy award, 1965, and Russell Loines Award, 1981; National Endowment for the Arts grant, 1967. Address: Department of English, Bennington College, Bennington, Vermont 05201, U.S.A.

PUBLICATIONS

Verse

The Five-Fold Mesh. New York, Knopf, 1938.
Wilderness Stair. New York, Grove Press, 1955.
The Enemy Joy: New and Selected Poems. Chicago, University of Chicago Press, 1964.
Nowhere But Light: Poems 1964-1969. Chicago, University of Chicago Press, 1970.
The Double Witness: Poems 1970-1976. Princeton, New Jersey, Princeton University Press, 1977.
Possessions: New and Selected Poems. Boston, Godine, 1985.

Other

Adam's Dream: A Preface to Translation. New York, Grove Press, 1978.

Editor and Translator, *Poet in New York: Federico García Lorca.* New York, Grove Press, 1955; London, Thames and Hudson, 1956.
Editor and Translator, *Selected Poems of Pablo Neruda.* New York, Grove Press, 1961.
Editor and Translator, *Juan de Mairena and Poems from the Apocryphal Songbooks.* Berkeley, University of California Press, 1963.
Editor and Translator, *Selected Poems of Rafael Alberti.* Berkeley, University of California Press, 1966.
Editor, and Translator with Alastair Reid, *A New Decade: Poems 1958-67*, by Pablo Neruda. New York, Grove Press, 1969.
Editor and Translator, *Splendor and Death of Joaquin Murieta*, by Pablo Neruda. New York, Farrar Straus, 1972; London, Alcove Press, 1973.
Editor and Translator, *New Poems 1968-1970*, by Pablo Neruda. New York, Grove Press, 1973.
Editor and Translator, *Five Decades: Poems 1925-1970*, by Pablo Neruda. New York, Grove Press, 1974.

Translator, *Four Poems by Rimbaud: The Problem of Translation.* Denver, Swallow, 1947; London, Sylvan Press, 1948.
Translator, with others, *Cántico: Selections*, by Jorge Guillén. Boston, Little Brown, 1965.
Translator, *Poems from Canto General*, by Pablo Neruda. New York, Racolin Press, 1968.
Translator, with others, *Selected Poems 1923-1967*, by Jorge Luis Borges. New York, Delacorte Press, 1972.
Translator, *A la pintura*, by Rafael Alberti. West Islip, New York, Universal Art Editions, 1972.

*

Bibliography: "Ben Belitt Issue" of *Voyages* (Washington, D.C.), Fall 1967, and of *Modern Poetry Studies* (Buffalo), 1976.

Manuscript Collections: University of Virginia Library, Charlottesville; State University of New York Library, Buffalo; Mugar Memorial Library, Boston University.

Critical Studies: "In Search of the American Scene" by the author, in *Poets on Poetry*, edited by Howard Nemerov, New York, Basic Books, 1966; "The Fascination of What's Difficult" by Howard Nemerov, in *Reflexions on Poetry and Poetics*, New Brunswick, New Jersey, Rutgers University Press, 1972; "Antipodal Man: An Interview with Ben Belitt," in *Quadrille* (Bennington, Vermont), Spring 1973, and "A Wild Severity: The Poetry of Ben Belitt," in *Salmagundi* (Saratoga Springs, New York), April 1973, both by Joan Hutton; "Confronting Nullity: The Poetry of Ben Belitt" by Robert Boyers, in *Sewanee Review* (Tennessee), Fall 1973.

*   *   *

Ben Belitt's poetry is especially difficult. As preface to his first volume, he made these *apparently* simple remarks: "...it has been my hope to suggest a discipline of integration, rather than a series of isolated poetic comments. . . . What has been sought is an effect of sequence..., beginning with simple responses to the natural world, [moving] on to an awareness of the personal identity, and [attempting] finally to establish usable relationships between the personal and contemporary world." Clear enough, but in each of Belitt's books the "sequence" is not just evolutionary. Something elliptical in an early poem renders it opaque; but when one discovers a key to it, perhaps in a poem very far into the collection, he must care with cryptogrammic enthusiasm to backtrack and get things clarified. Without that effort, individual poems *and* the "sequence" evade comprehension. This feature is what Howard Nemerov treats in his essay on Belitt, "The Fascination of What's Difficult." He cites particularly the reciprocal bond between the first and penultimate poems of *The Enemy Joy*. His effort to champion this facet of Belitt's approach is compelling, but his truth is not easily enforced on the battleground.

A similar problematical characteristic is Belitt's allusiveness. When he speaks, as above, of the "personal [world]," he has no casual autobiographical self in mind. He has digested an enormous portion of Western culture; his easy frame of reference is as broad as Eliot's, surely. Those who know Belitt as critic and translator must respect both his enormous knowledge and intimate literary acquaintance. But this scholarly plus can be a limitation in his verse, as when cultural and biographical paraphernalia overburden, even choke off the emotional impact of a poem. Early in his career, what he calls the "contemporary world" seemed to be subsumed by his learning. But increasingly since *The Enemy Joy* he has let his vision of the contemporary world control his learning, which has made his poetry *and* his erudition ever more salutary. Moreover, this weakness has always been sporadic, though the demand which his erudition makes has been pretty steady. In "The Gorge" (*Nowhere But Light*) we had best know Cuernevaca somehow on our own, because Belitt renders it via not only Dante's "Inferno" but Doré's illustrations, and (in a brief span) there are Rahab, Quetzalcoatl, Grendel, Zochiphili, Timon, and Lear into the bargain. In "Veteran's Hospital" (same collection) we begin decisively with Agamemnon, in fairly fine detail, as a way of moving to the "expendables of Metz.../the guerillas of Bien-Hoa and Korea." In the first case, we can't stop scanning our brains, as though amidst litter—and the finale is a whimper; in the second, Agamemnon serves well—in our own epoch, for our own grief.

Belitt also offers up one of the most exacting vocabularies in modern poetry. Some will find it finicky or eccentric, certainly overdemanding. But patience can prove it functional. In any setting, Belitt wants all objects first absolutely present, then absolutely differentiated. Finally, however, Belitt is kin to Stevens, and these extraordinarily presented things exist mysteriously, as though at a point between themselves and the mind of the perceiver. For each phase of such a project, the *mot juste* is a constant demand. It is thus that we observe the turtle, as "tourist," in the third poem of "Departures" (*Wilderness Stair*). The turtle is "iron over pith," "a marble saddle." He exists "where the ebb gives phosphor, and begins/Its tender overturn/A fathom's depth in shale,/Under the mica gardens and the fins." But the setting expands, upward, for turtle and (human) tourist, because we are also "Under the sidelong quibble of the gull." Nothing here is a mere thing in itself and the ultimate image includes turtle and human as "a green sojourn," toward the sea itself, to "strike a strenuous sweetness out of brine."

Belitt has struggled to locate life "in the spirit," a quality of and balance between all living things and the human being alone. This ephemeral, but plausible, ideal has on occasion led to excessive paradoxical convolutions. But when Belitt gets it right, as in "The Orange Tree" (*Nowhere But Light*), his strength is like Yeats's, as in the "great-rooted blosssomer" figure of "Among School Children":

> To be
> intact and unseen
> like the orange's scent
> in the orange tree. . . .

Belitt goes on to identify the "sunburst of white in the leaves" with "the odor's epiphany," a condition likened to "the karat/in the void of the jeweler's glass." This plenitude in vacuity, this presence in absence, is "life in the spirit," wonderfully realized. It dwells in the orange and the man alike, and in what passes between.

—David M. Heaton

BELL, Marvin (Hartley). American. Born in New York City, 3 August 1937. Educated at Alfred University, New York, B.A. 1958; Syracuse University, New York, 1958; University of Chicago, M.A. 1961; University of Iowa, Iowa City, M.F.A. 1963. Served as a Foreign Military Training Officer in the United States Army 1964-65. Married 1) Mary Mammosser in 1958; 2) Dorothy Murphy in 1961; two sons. Visiting Lecturer, 1965, Assistant Professor, 1966-69, Associate Professor, 1969-75, and since 1975, Professor of English, University of Iowa. Visiting Professor, Oregon State University, Corvallis, Summer 1969, Goddard College, Plainfield, Vermont, Summer 1972, and University of Hawaii, Honolulu, 1981; Fulbright Scholar, in Yugoslavia, 1983. Editor, *Statements* magazine, 1959-64; Poetry Editor, *North American Review*, Mount Vernon, Iowa, 1964-69, and *Iowa Review*, 1969-71. Since 1975, Columnist ("Homage to the Runner"), *American Poetry Review*, Philadelphia. Recipient: Lamont Poetry Selection Award, 1969; Bess Hokin Prize (*Poetry*, Chicago), 1969; Emily Clark Balch Prize (*Virginia Quarterly Review*), 1970; Guggenheim Fellowship, 1975; National Endowment for the Arts grant, 1978, 1984; *American Poetry Review* prize, 1982. Address: Writers Workshop, University of Iowa, Iowa City, Iowa 52242, U.S.A.

PUBLICATIONS

Verse

Two Poems. Iowa City, Hundred Pound Press, 1965.
Things We Dreamt We Died For. Iowa City, Stone Wall Press, 1966.
Poems for Nathan and Saul. Mount Vernon, Iowa, Hillside Press, 1966.
A Probable Volume of Dreams. New York, Atheneum, 1969.

The Escape into You: A Sequence.   New York, Atheneum, 1971.

Woo Havoc.   Somerville, Massachusetts, Barn Dream Press, 1971.

Residue of Song.   New York, Atheneum, 1974.

Stars Which See, Stars Which Do Not See.   New York, Atheneum, 1977.

These Green-Going-to-Yellow.   New York, Atheneum, 1981.

Segues: A Correspondence in Poetry, with William Stafford. Boston, Godine, 1983.

Drawn by Stones, By Earth, By Things That Have Been in the Fire.   New York, Atheneum, 1984.

Recording: *The Self and the Mulberry Tree*, Watershed, 1977.

Other

Old Snow Just Melting: Essays and Interviews.   Ann Arbor, University of Michigan Press, 1983.

Editor, *Iowa Workshop Poets 1963.*   Iowa City, Statements-Midwest Magazine, 1963.

*

Critical Studies: "The Poetry of Marvin Bell" by Peter Elfed Lewis, in *Stand* (Newcastle upon Tyne), xiii, 4, 1972; "Marvin Bell: 'Time's Determinant/Once, I Knew You' " by Arthur Oberg, in *American Poetry Review* (Philadelphia), May-June 1976.

*   *   *

Marvin Bell's work satisfies a need for every kind of laugh and reminds us that comedy is at least as tough as tragedy. From the outset, however, he has been modulating the balance of amusement and profundity in his poetry. Early on his wit was, by turns, clever and probing, tending at one moment to trivialize his work, at another to deepen it. But over the long haul, he has exerted mature control.

His method stresses spontaneity. Verse sections are rarely linked by any kind of discursive rhetoric, often by semi-conscious associations arising from imagery and diction. He will organically combine a cliché, an aphoristic biblical phrase and a straightforward ethical assertion. Trusting his subconscious, Bell doesn't finally patch his work together with accessible generalizations. He has said that he prefers to go on finding the meaning of a poem *after* he has finished it. But he has devised structures for his poems which render them both artfully finished and in progress. At worst, and infrequently, a poem is dubiously cryptic, maybe even a willful conundrum, as with "The Giving In" (*A Probable Volume of Dreams*). At best, a poem unselfconsciously but overtly relates the visceral experience behind itself to the semantic form it has taken, as with "Life" (*These Green-Going-to-Yellow*). Bell is also not afraid of social comment, though not as a mentor. In this province he is never as wonderfully nasty as Alan Dugan, but his range of feeling is greater.

The title *A Probable Volume of Dreams* is from "Treetops," wherein Bell dreams his dead father alive. The collection is largely about the roots of identity. Overarching, perhaps, is the paradox that we can and can't perpetuate the dead—bodily and in imagination. The dead include, especially, the father and the ancestral line, significantly but not parochially Jewish. Nonetheless, as in "The Delicate Bird Who Is Flying Up Our Asses," Bell is often the wiseacre.

With *The Escape into You* Bell came to the love sequence,

regulating the stanza throughout. So much for tradition. Divorce, amorous fatigue, and marital boredom take their place with the faithful heart. The verbal fabric whimsically includes every piece of sexual slang and the belly laugh abounds: "We sold the chairs.../then the squeaking sagged-/in-the-center four-poster baby farm..." ("The Auction"). By the end, however, bawdy merely shares the stage with eroticism and tender heartedness.

In *Residue of Song* something like mid-life encroaches. Thirteen pieces are for the abiding father, proved "in the distance of a wrist." This sequence affectingly moves between the past in Long Island and Russia. Romantic love is other residue. Songs here traverse a line from outrageous wisecracking ("Impotence") through nearly self-aware adolescent yearning ("Set in Hollywood Hills") to awakening after great loss ("Dissolution").

The title poem of *Stars Which See* comments remarkably on Seurat's "Grande Jatte." It catches a poignant relation between our natural yearning and decorum. Animals and trees dominate this elegantly simple collection, freer of prosodic experimentation than earlier volumes. The beautiful "The Self and the Mulberry" is approximately Taoist. The final piece, "Gemwood," connects a son's loss of his lab "rat" to the parent's projection of losses to come. The authentic sadness and the poet's real attention to children are why this poem isn't merely adroit, as are so many of its ilk.

The gingko's dying leaves supply *These Green-Going-to-Yellow* its title. The book traces the moribund passage of everything toward autumn. Yet Bell avoids morbidity with frequently uplifting notes of resistance. A doctor's in "Benny Hooper" and his own in the exactingly bleak landscape of "At the Airport" are notable. Trees are meant to dominate, but machines may. The analogies underlying the final two poems, which humanize the willow and the gingko, strain credibility. But the machinery of the grittier "At the Airport" and "The Motor" is perfectly successful, however grim.

Collected over two years, *Segues* is a poem-by-poem exchange with William Stafford. Its forte is the revelation of one poem's discourse generating another's. But this verges on what is also problematical. Here it is more difficult even than in an ordinary volume for any piece to stand alone. And the reader may sense an excess of literature, over experience, as the wellspring of these poems. Additionally, Stafford's probes (for good or ill) have elicited much undiluted autobiography in Bell's *reactions*.

Drawn by Stones is about the habit, beyond childhood, of non-wonderment, a death within life: "I was Taps," in a "youthful half stupor." But Bell has been saved, as the last line of the book contends paradoxically: "it killed me—and almost cost me a life." This is why he can wrap up "To Be" by saying that "still a child appears/in the guise of a grownup...at story-time." This poem sits next to the wonderful "In Those Days," wherein Bell discovers the "mortar in the bloodstream" which enables one to see that "Phosphor in the paint on the ceiling/gave constellations their shine. . . ."

—David M. Heaton

BENEDIKT, Michael.   American.   Born in New York City, 26 May 1935. Educated at New York University, B.A. in English 1956; Columbia University, New York, M.A. in comparative literature 1961. Served in the United States Army, 1958-59. Associate Editor, Horizon Press, publishers, New York, 1959-61; New York correspondent, *Art International*, Lugano, 1965-67; Associate Editor, *Art News* magazine, New York, 1963-72;

Instructor in Language and Literature, Bennington College, Vermont, 1968-69; Poet in Residence, Sarah Lawrence College, Bronxville, New York, 1969-73; Associate Professor of Arts and Humanities, Hampshire College, Amherst, Massachusetts, 1973-75; Saxton Professor of Poetry, 1975, and Visiting Professor, 1977-79, Boston University; Associate Professor, Vassar College, Poughkeepsie, New York, 1976-77. Poetry Editor, *Paris Review*, 1973-78. Since 1973, Contributing Editor, *American Poetry Review*, Philadelphia. Recipient: Bess Hokin Prize (*Poetry*, Chicago), 1968; Guggenheim Fellowship, 1969; National Endowment for the Arts prize, 1970, and fellowship, 1979; Creative Artists Public Service grant, 1975. Agent: Georges Borchardt Inc., 136 East 57th Street, New York, New York 10022. Address: 315 West 98th Street, New York, New York 10025, U.S.A.

PUBLICATIONS

Verse

Serenade in Six Pieces.   Privately printed, 1958.
Changes.   Detroit, New Fresco, 1961.
8 Poems.   Privately printed, 1966.
The Body.   Middletown, Connecticut, Wesleyan University Press, 1968.
Sky.   Middletown, Connecticut, Wesleyan University Press, 1970.
Mole Notes.   Middletown, Connecticut, Wesleyan University Press, 1971.
Night Cries.   Middletown, Connecticut, Wesleyan University Press, 1976.
The Badminton of Great Barrington; or, Gustav Mahler and the Chattanooga Choo-Choo.   Pittsburgh, University of Pittsburgh Press, 1980.

Recording: *Today's Poets 5*, Folkways, 1968.

Plays

The Vaseline Photographer (playlet; produced New York, 1965).
The Orgy Bureau, in *Chelsea* (New York), 1968.
Box (multi-media event, with others; produced New York, 1970).

Other

Editor, with George E. Wellwarth, *Modern French Theatre: The Avant-Garde, Dada and Surrealism.*   New York, Dutton, 1964; as *Modern French Plays: An Anthology from Jarry to Ionesco*, London, Faber, 1965.
Editor, with George E. Wellwarth, *Postwar German Theatre: An Anthology of Plays.*   New York, Dutton, 1967; London, Macmillan, 1968.
Editor and Translator, *Ring Around the World: The Selected Poems of Jean L'Anselme.*   London, Rapp and Whiting, 1967; Denver, Swallow, 1968.
Editor, *Theatre Experiment: New American Plays.*   New York, Doubleday, 1967.
Editor, with George E. Wellwarth, *Modern Spanish Theatre: An Anthology of Plays.*   New York, Dutton, 1968.
Editor, *22 Poems of Robert Desnos.*   Santa Cruz, California, Kayak, 1971.
Editor, *The Poetry of Surrealism: An Anthology.*   Boston, Little Brown, 1974.
Editor, *The Prose Poem: An International Anthology.*   New York, Dell, 1976.

*

Manuscript Collection: Humanities Research Center, University of Texas, Austin.

Critical Studies: *Benedikt: A Profile*, Tucson, Grilled Flowers Press, 1978.

Michael Benedikt comments:

(1970) Major theme is probably the relationship of matter and spirit; sometimes the sensual and the "pure." General sources and influences: the French Symbolists and Surrealists until about 1968; most recently, the English romantic poets. Stylistically, I am interested in the treatment of "difficult" subjects with clarity, since their reality *is* very clear (at least to me). I am probably as much influenced by contemporary painting, film, and theatre as I am by any movement in poetry. I have become interested in the possibilities of the poem in prose as well as verse.

(1985) Newer work is largely in verse, concerned with the incorporation in the above contexts of more "realistic" materials. Titles of work-in-progress: *Family Blessings, Family Curses* (narrative poems, descriptive of the difficulties of a person undergoing a divorce, and the new life and travels that can await him [her]); *Dear Alice/Kate* (one long narrative poem, on the subject of two cats who were/are pets). Also an as-yet-untitled ms. of shorter poems on the joys and sorrows of living in a capitalist system of economics.

*   *   *

There are many ways to imagine The Poet: warbling his native woodnotes wild, legislating unknown to the rest of us, speaking in the language that men do know, giving to airy nothing a local habitation and a name, making things that are palpable and mute. Michael Benedikt typifies the poet as the eternal outsider, the poet against the world. And what a world it is, filled with "traditional poets," "collegiate English instructors" "Women of the Earth" (who use their snatches "to snatch at people with"), "Power People" (who shout through loudspeakers "Get up off your asses and make a revolution!"), guests at garden parties in Scarsdale, "X" (whose lovers are dull: "so that others glimpsing them, and after conversation, would remark: 'Agh! phooey! you wouldn't catch us talking to them at even the dullest cocktail party ever thrown!'...["For Love or Money"]). So many cocktail parties, so many references to the upper west side of New York; a whole poem devoted to sneering at Troy, New York, which all New York poets know is Nowheresville. I sense in this work a life dedicated to chastising opponents of true culture, true art, true life, whatever *that* is. In his book *Mole Notes* there is one passage that for me sums up Benedikt's work, expresses the stance he takes toward the world: "Also, at this very moment, there is someone in a Civilian Submarine at the bottom of the Gulf of Mexico whose actions affect us all with their secluded elegance, their secret grandeur, grace, and repose" ("Molar Advent in Retrospect"). In poem after poem Benedikt takes the position of the commander of that submarine, alternately raving about his enemy the world, or lamenting its abysmal ignorance, or pitying its failure to be sensitive, graceful, grand, or elegant. Submarines keep appearing throughout his work, always as out-moded vehicles of transport, "civilian" or "pleasure" submarines, the very latest model for the year 1915. These and other images and objects in the work give it a dated air, reminding me of those Surrealist collages that juxtapose steam engines and harpies, corset ads and patent velocipedes.

Benedikt has translated a great deal of Surrealist poetry, and edited *The Poetry of Surrealism*. It would be surprising if this interest weren't reflected in his own poetry. But what does it mean to be writing Surrealist poetry in the 1970's, to be guided by an avant-garde esthetic now a half a century old? The very objects in many of these poems recall the interiors of early 20th-century Europe: umbrella stands, mirrors, bowler hats, decolletage. I don't mean to say that Benedikt is a kind of verbal Edward Gorey, camping out among the Edwardiana, for many of his poems are set firmly in the present. It's just that he hasn't always been able to resist using the same *things* that are familiar to us from that earlier work, and so his poems necessarily partake of that earlier poetry's peculiar historical "feel."

Some of his poems read like exercises in Surrealism. "The European Shoe," for example, consists of 15 short sections, each having The European Shoe as its subject: "Tears fall from the eye of the European Shoe as it waves goodbye to us/ from the back balcony of the speeding train" (*The Body*). The use of the same incongruous object in a repetitive pattern; the animation of the inanimate (or the other way around); these are devices made familiar to us by the Surrealists, and to find them in a contemporary poem is to be reminded of the poet's forebears, and also to perceive the poem as a crafted thing, a consciously made artifact. Hence my difficulty with this and other poems in *The Body* and *Sky*, for the Surrealists despised the idea of art as craftsmanship. We are confronted here with something that seems very much like the anti-Surrealist Surrealist poem. This destruction of what one wishes to celebrate must necessarily come along with the use of Surrealism as a style. In "A Beloved Head," Benedikt employs the Surrealist device of turning something organic into something mechanical: here Surrealism exists only at the surface of the poem, decorating the straightforward idea that some men manipulate women as if they were machines. André Breton would not have approved.

Mole Notes, an elegantly printed volume of short prose pieces, seems a logical development in Benedikt's work. In *The Body* and *Sky* there is a gradual but noticeable drift toward the long line, a growing sense of paragraphs rather than stanzas, or stanza-like forms. But the tone of *Mole Notes* remains consistent with the earlier work, the sense of a series of collisions, of unexpected juxtapositions. In some of the pieces the comic and the serious can work beautifully together ("The Bewitched Lover"):

> And whenever you carry me away, it is as if you
> were bringing me something! O come to me, true
> beloved, so that you can go away in a hurry again!

Here there is a kind of fusion, or better, an alternating current that expresses exactly the attraction and repulsion cycle of love. But the common problem of poets who turn to short prose works appears here as well, the sense that in writing prose the poet can be unbuttoned, casual, and kick over the traces of form. Many of these mole notes seem loose to the point of carelessness. "The Secret of Scotch" and "The Pain Alarm" strike me as being very good stand-up comic routines, and no doubt they lay them in the aisles at readings, but they disappoint the reader.

—Steven Young

BENNETT, (Simone) Louise. Jamaican. Born in Kingston, 7 September 1919. Educated at primary and secondary schools in Jamaica; Royal Academy of Dramatic Art, London (British Council Scholarship). Married to Eric Coverley. Worked with the BBC (West Indies Section) as resident artist, 1945-46 and 1950-53, and with repertory companies in Coventry, Huddersfield, and Amersham. Returned to Jamaica, 1955. Drama Specialist with the Jamaica Social Welfare Commission, 1955-60; Lecturer in drama and Jamaican folklore, Extra-Mural Department, University of the West Indies, Kingston, 1959-61. Lecturer and radio and television commentator. Represented Jamaica at the Royal Commonwealth Arts Festival in Britain, 1965. Recipient: Silver Musgrave Medal of the Institute of Jamaica; Norman Manley Award of Excellence. D.Lit.: University of the West Indies, 1982. M.B.E. (Member, Order of the British Empire); Order of Jamaica. Address: Enfield House, Gordon Town, St. Andrew, Jamaica.

PUBLICATIONS

Verse

Dialect Verses.   Kingston, Gleaner, 1940.
Jamaican Dialect Verses.   Kingston, Gleaner, 1942; expanded version, Kingston, Pioneer Press, 1951.
Jamaican Humour in Dialect.   Kingston, Gleaner, 1943.
Miss Lulu Sez.   Kingston, Gleaner, 1948.
Anancy Stories and Dialect Verse, with others.   Kingston, Pioneer Press, 1950.
Laugh with Louise: A Potpourri of Jamaican Folklore, Stories, Songs, Verses.   Kingston, Bennett City Printery, 1960.
Jamaica Labrish.   Kingston, Sangster, 1966.
Anancy and Miss Lou.   Kingston, Sangster, 1979.

Recordings: *Jamaican Folk Songs*, Folkways, 1954; *Jamaican Singing Games*, Folkways, 1954; *West Indies Festival of Arts*, Cook, 1958; *Miss Lou's Views*, Federal, 1967; *Listen to Louise*, Federal, 1968; *The Honourable Miss Lou*, 1981; *Miss Lou Live*, 1983.

*

Critical Study: introduction by Rex Nettlefold, to *Jamaica Labrish*, 1966.

Louise Bennett comments:
I have been described as a "poet of utterance performing multiple roles as entertainer, as a valid literary figure and as a documenter of aspects of Jamaican life, thought, and feeling." I would not disagree with this.

*   *   *

Louise Bennett is to Jamaica what the calypsonian The Mighty Sparrow is to Trinidad and Tobago: an articulate voice of the people, a political commentator, a satirist, and, in many ways, a social historian. The difference between them is the difference between the traditional Trinidadian calypso and the traditional Jamaican mento. The calypso, however, when set down in the cold light of print, loses its sparkle and its inflections and becomes dull and often meaningless, because it has lost its music. The mento, on the other hand, can be understood and enjoyed merely from the printed page.

The "West Indian English" which is in common use, and in which Miss Bennett works, is gradually being recognised by anthropologists and linguistic specialists as a language with its own grammar, syntax and rules, rather than as a mere dialect. "English," the Barbadian poet and novelist George Lamming has said, "is a West Indian language." "West Indian English"—called Creole in some islands, Patois in others (especially those which have been, for periods in their history, French)—has enabled Louise Bennett to get many points across in pithy phrases which would have taken a whole paragraph to say in dictionary terms. It has the kind of racy flavour which suits her style, and she has been quick to use, too, some of the words and phrases in common daily use which go back to the standard English of Elizabethan and Cromwellian times.

Louise Bennett's researches have rescued from oblivion, often from extinction, a number of the island's folk songs, stories and sayings, and her stage productions have put Jamaican vernacular before large audiences.

There is a mass of her writing scattered about, very largely in Jamaica's newspapers and magazines over the years, and much of it was collected into a book entitled *Jamaica Labrish* (a dialect word meaning chatter or gossip) in 1966.

No subject has been too sacred for her fancy and biting wit. She has tackled the changing city, the war, Jamaican history, politics, middle-class attitudes, immigration and many other things, and no poet in Jamaica has a better understanding of the island and its people.

—Colin Rickards

BENVENISTE, Asa. British. Born in New York City, 25 August 1925; emigrated to England in 1950; became British citizen in 1965. Educated at James Monroe High School, New York; New School for Social Research, New York, B.A. 1948; the Sorbonne, Paris, 1950. Served as a radio operator in the United States Army Infantry, 1943-46. Married Pip Walker in 1949; three stepsons. Researcher, Jewish News Agency, New York, 1947; Co-Editor, *Zero Quarterly*, Paris, Tangier, and London, 1948-56; correspondent, *Nugget Magazine*, London, 1956-57; copy editor, Doubleday and Company, publishers, New York, 1957-58; Senior Art Editor, Paul Hamlyn Ltd., publishers, London, 1959-61; Senior Editor, Studio Vista Ltd., publishers, London, 1961-63. Publisher, Trigram Press Ltd., London. Address: c/o Anvil Press Poetry, 69 King George Street, London SE10 8PX, England.

PUBLICATIONS

Verse

Poems of the Mouth. London, Trigram Press, 1966.
A Word in Your Season: A Portfolio of Six Seriagraphs, with Jack Hirschman. London, Trigram Press, 1967.
Count Three. Berkeley, California, Maya, 1969.
The Atoz Formula. London, Trigram Press, 1969.
Free Semantic No. 2. London, Wallrich, 1970.
Umbrella. London, Wallrich, 1972.
Time Being, with Ray Di Palma and Tom Raworth. London, Trigram Press, 1972.
Blockmakers Black. London, Steam Press, 1973.
Certainly Metaphysics. London, Trigram Press, 1973.
It's the Same Old Feeling Again. London, Trigram Press, 1973.
Edge. London, Joe DiMaggio Press, 1974.

Dense Lens, with Brian Marley. London, Trigram Press, 1975.
A Part Apart. Middlesex, White Dog Press, 1975.
Listen. Bowling Green, Ohio, Doones Press, 1975.
Poems. London, Joe DiMaggio Press, 1976.
Loose Use. Newcastle upon Tyne, Pig Press, 1977.
Colour Theory. London, Trigram Press, 1977.
Throw Out the Life Line, Lay Out the Corse: Poems 1965-1985. London, Anvil Press Poetry, 1983.

Plays

Radio Plays: *Tangier for the Traveller*, 1956; *Piano Forte*, 1957.

Other

An Introduction to Brothers and Sisters, a Novel by Ivy Compton-Burnett. New York, Zero Press, 1956.
Autotypography: A Book of Design Priorities. London, Latimer New Dimensions, 1974.

*

Manuscript Collection: Washington University, St. Louis.

Critical Study: "Great Rejoicing" by Anselm Hollo, in *Ambit 41* (London), 1969.

Asa Benveniste comments:
Environmentalists will agree: describe the situation and you describe yourself. It's become clearer that poets mainly function within two areas: description or language. Most English poets fall within the former range ("Breakfast in the morning, then how do I compare with everyone else's corn flakes"). I can see how this might have a narrowing effect on the employment of language—and usually does, all around us. You can tell from the first line what the last line will read like. It's that prelude to tedium: To Thine Own Self Be True. Good enough for my aunt, good enough for me. Housman, Tennyson, after all, *are* good poets.

The second kind of work verges on the hysterical. Logic, clarity, description, narration, connecting links, have to make it as best they can, so long as they don't interfere with the *other* exercise, the possibility of hitting psychic accuracy and the sheer pleasure of two words coming together for the first time ever, and miraculously. For example: Robert Fludd, John Clare, Blake, Novalis, Zukofsky. Language for itself, and then its by-products like meaning, truth, perspicacity, play, pleasure, secret rejoicing. But it's dense material to work with and anyone who argues publicly in favor of it is bound to lose.

*   *   *

Asa Benveniste writes with light. Illuminates poems. Clear, subtle, lucid. I often imagine that even his punctuation marks become prisms on the page.

He is able to verify the mystical vision and tradition in poems often as simple as breath and that's the essence of their power and immediacy. He is able to give added dimension to the real and enhance commonplace objects with mystery. Conversely he makes real and accessible the remote symbols of the Kabbalah and gives them face and form.

Tradition tells us that the great secrets and mysteries exist beyond the book and can only be exchanged from teacher to disciple through speech. Much of the available literature demonstrates the difficulty of verbalizing the inner journey and its unfolding, and of balancing the visible with the invisible and delineating the continual interplay between these two realities.

Therefore, Benveniste's books of poetry must be considered as valuable guides to the creative use of the process. They are sparks and must be cherished for their clarity.

Each volume develops possibilities inherent in a given mystical realm. *Poems of the Mouth* expands a proposition in the *Sefer Yetsira*, a primary Kabbalist textbook. *The Atoz Formula* explores the Hebrew Alphabet and the metaphorical/meta-actual progression of symbols enclosed within the cards of the Tarot.

It must also be noted that Asa Benveniste is an imaginative and elegant printer. The books he has issued from the Trigram Press are of consistently high quality.

—David Meltzer

BERESFORD, Anne (Ellen). British. Born in Redhill, Surrey, 10 September 1929. Educated privately, and at Central School of Speech Training and Dramatic Art, London. Married Michael Hamburger, *q.v.*, in 1951 (divorced, 1970, and remarried, 1974), one son and two daughters. Stage actress, 1948-70, and broadcaster, BBC, 1960-70; drama teacher, Wimbledon High School, 1969-73, and Arts Educational School, London, 1973-76; teacher at the Poetry Workshop, Cockpit Theatre, London, 1971-73. Member of the General Council, Poetry Society, 1976-79. Address: Marsh Acres, Middleton, Saxmundham, Suffolk IP17 3NH, England.

PUBLICATIONS

Verse

Walking Without Moving. London, Turret, 1967.
The Lair. London, Rapp and Whiting, 1968.
Footsteps in Snow. London, Agenda, 1972.
Modern Fairy Tale. Rushden, Northamptonshire, Sceptre Press, 1972.
The Courtship. Brighton, Unicorn Bookshop, 1972.
The Curving Shore. London, Agenda, 1975.
Words, with Michael Hamburger. East Bramley, Surrey, Words Press, 1977.
Unholy Giving. Knotting, Bedfordshire, Sceptre Press, 1977.
The Songs of Almut from God's Country. Yoxford, Suffolk, Yoxford Publications, 1980.
Songs a Thracian Taught Me. London, Boyars, 1980.

Plays

Radio Plays: *Struck by Apollo*, with Michael Hamburger, 1965; *The Villa*, 1968.

Other

Translator, *Alexandros: Selected Poems*, by Vera Lungu. London, Agenda, 1974.

*

Manuscript Collection: Humanities Research Center, University of Texas, Austin.

Critical Studies: review by Christopher Levenson, in *Queen's Quarterly* (Kingston, Ontario), September 1971; review in *Times Literary Supplement* (London), 13 October 1972.

*   *   *

Ezra Pound wrote: "Our life is, in so far as it is worth living, made up in great part of things indefinite, impalpable; and it is precisely because the arts present us these things that we—humanity—cannot get on without the arts" (*Selected Prose*, London, Faber, 1973, p.33). Much of the subtlety of Anne Beresford's poetry stems from her attempts to define moments and states of mind of this nature—those aspects of consciousness and daily life which are most impatient of words. Beresford's "Heimweh" is short enough to give in its entirety:

> a thrush sings
> every evening
> in the ash tree
>
> it has been singing
> for as long
> as I can remember
> only then
> the tree was probably
> an oak
>
> the song
> aches and aches
> in the green light
> if I knew
> where it was
> I would go
> home

Beresford seldom overstates, but is reticent and elliptical. This gives her work an impersonal quality which is rare. At its best her writing expresses an imagination (*not* fancy) unlike that of any other contemporary poet. This is connected, in a strange way, with humour and satire. Her irony succeeds because it is not obvious.

A fault present in some poems is a tenuousness of rhythm, where the emotions don't seem strong enough to generate sufficient rhythmic energy. But this is sometimes offset by a clarity and simplicity of imagery which evoke much, particularly if these poems are lived with rather than read quickly: "outside, high on the mountains/is the great plain with wild flowers/wild flowers and air so fresh/one's head goes light." ("Eurydice"). At times the imagery is menacing: "You have come to a tower of slate/crumbling into grey sky./Don't climb, not there..." ("Half-Way"). This is not poetry which strives for immediate effect; hence a first reading often misses how much meaning her usually very simple words contain.

Beresford uses dream and myth to express states of mind which are real, never as ornament or literary device. Her recent work makes use of dramatic monologue and shows an historical consciousness which raises her poetry above that of contemporary writers of the short poem who seem to be incapable of embodying subjects other than the personal and the incidentals of everyday life. I shall close these notes by quoting "Nicodemus" in full:

> Keeping a sense of proportion
> lip service to what is considered correct
> I have brought what is needed to bury the dead.
> Once again I come to you by night.

This time to take away all visible proof of my understanding.
In secret I have applied myself
to seek out wisdom
to know what is before my face—
the inside and the outside are reversed
that which is
has become that which is not—
displaced, troubled
I live naked in a house that is not my own
and the five trees of Paradise evade me.

—William Cookson

BERG, Stephen (Walter). American. Born in Philadelphia, Pennsylvania, 2 August 1934. Educated at the University of Pennsylvania, Philadelphia; Boston University; University of Iowa, Iowa City, B.A. 1959; University of Indiana, Bloomington. Married Millie Lane in 1959; two daughters. Formerly, Instructor in English, Temple University, Philadelphia; also taught at Princeton University, New Jersey, and Haverford College, Pennsylvania. Currently, Professor, Philadelphia College of Art. Poetry Editor, *Saturday Evening Post*, Philadelphia, 1961-62. Since 1972, Founding Editor, with Stephen Parker and Rhoda Schwartz, *American Poetry Review*, Philadelphia. Recipient: Rockefeller-Centro Mexicano de Escritores grant, 1959-61; National Translation Center grant, 1969; Frank O'Hara Prize (*Poetry*, Chicago), 1970; Guggenheim Fellowship, 1974; National Endowment for the Arts grant, 1976; Columbia University Translation Center award, 1976. Address: American Poetry Review, 1616 Walnut Street, Philadelphia, Pennsylvania 19103, U.S.A.

PUBLICATIONS

Verse

Berg Goodman Mezey. Philadelphia, New Ventures Press, 1957.
Bearing Weapons. Iowa City, Cummington Press, 1963.
The Queen's Triangle: A Romance. West Branch, Iowa, Cummington Press, 1970.
The Daughters. Indianapolis, Bobbs Merrill, 1971.
Nothing in the Word: Versions of Aztec Poetry. New York, Grossman, 1972.
Grief: Poems and Versions of Poems. New York, Grossman, 1975.
With Akmatova at the Black Gates: Variations. Urbana, University of Illinois Press, 1981.
In It. Urbana, University of Illinois Press, 1985.

Other

Editor, with Robert Mezey, *Naked Poetry: Recent American Poetry in Open Forms*. Indianapolis, Bobbs Merrill, 1969.
Editor, with S.J. Marks, *Between People*. Chicago, Scott Foresman, 1972.
Editor, with S.J. Marks, *About Women*. New York, Fawcett, 1973.
Editor, with Robert Mezey, *The New Naked Poetry*. Indianapolis, Bobbs Merrill, 1976.
Editor, *In Praise of What Persists*. New York, Harper, 1983.

Editor, *Singular Voices: Poems and Essays on Poetry*. New York, Avon, 1985.

Translator, with Steven Polgar and S.J. Marks, *Clouded Sky*, by Miklos Radnoti. New York, Harper, 1972.
Translator, with Diskin Clay, *Oedipus the King*, by Sophocles. New York and London, Oxford University Press, 1978.

*

Stephen Berg comments:
All comments on my work—such as the introductions to *Nothing in the Word, Clouded Sky*, and *Grief*—are random and apply to the particular books and poems in question.

*   *   *

Many of the poems in Stephen Berg's large collection *The Daughters* break forth with an almost breathless fury of speech, the expression of an agonized, compassionate mind and sensibility confronting the bitter realities of modern existence:

We, the dooms, your future, the bloody fire
between places, dancers on the corpses of who,
we eat what there is. Are you
sitting at a table? Is there food? Us,
the zero washing itself, bones entering the floor,
leaves zigzagging down through silt, through farms
in the lone face of a mirror.

Berg appears to write with the example of such poets as Neruda, Vallejo, Patchen, among others, behind him. Like them he strives for a language and imagery that will encompass the irony, fatality, and suffering of a life everywhere overshadowed by mortality, a life unredeemed and unaccounted for either by reason or by any known God. In this endeavor Berg often stretches words and syntax to their extreme limits; frequently his means of progression—more evident, naturally, in his longer pieces, where there are greater space and freedom—are elliptical and associative rather than logical or merely sequential. Sometimes his poems surge and lash out seemingly uncontrollably; yet this is never the case, I think, for a strong, inventive imagination operates constantly, drawing together disparate details, linking objects and bodies, love and death, pain and anger, until the reader feels himself inside a poetic universe which lights up his own sense of the world with sudden, vivid and terrible lightning strokes of vision. To be sure, Berg's poetry has at times its lapses, excesses, and repetitions, but these are minor in comparison with the ambitiousness and force of what he attempts, and recent, as yet uncollected poems, show a calmer, more reflective side to his writing. Berg is an energetic and highly talented poet, translator, and editor of whom considerable accomplishment may be expected. "I can go anywhere, I can let go forever/and live in the middle of fire, in silence...."

—Ralph J. Mills, Jr.

BERGÉ, Carol (née Peppis). American. Born in New York City, 4 October 1928. Educated at New York University, 1946-52; New School for Social Research, New York, 1952-54. Married Jack Bergé in 1955; one son. Editorial assistant, Syndicate Publications, Simon and Schuster, publishers, *Forbes* magazine, and Hart Publishing Company, New York, 1950-54; Assistant to the President, Pendray Public Relations, New York, 1955. Member of the Board of Directors, COSMEP, 1971-73; lecturer at Thomas Jefferson College, Allendale, Michigan, 1975-76, Goddard College, Plainfield, Vermont, 1976, University of California, Berkeley, 1976-77, Indiana University, Bloomington, 1977, University of Southern Mississippi, Hattiesburg, 1977-78, University of New Mexico, Albuquerque, 1978-79, Wright State University, Dayton, Ohio, 1979, and State University of New York, Albany, 1981. Editor, *Center* magazine, Santa Barbara, California, 1971-81, *Mississippi Review*, Hattiesburg, 1977-78, and *Paper Branches*, Albuquerque, 1978-79; Contributing Editor, *Woodstock Poetry Review*, New York, 1977-79. Since 1980, Editor, *Shearsman*. Recipient: MacDowell Fellowship (four times); New York State Council on the Arts grant, for editing, 1971, for fiction, 1974; National Endowment for the Arts grant, 1979. Agent: Rhoda Weyr, William Morris Agency, 1350 Avenue of the Americas, New York, New York 10019, U.S.A.

PUBLICATIONS

Verse

Four Young Lady Poets, with others, edited by LeRoi Jones. New York, Totem-Corinth, 1962.
The Vulnerable Island. Cleveland, Renegade Press, 1964.
Lumina. Cleveland, 7 Flower Press, 1965.
Poems Made of Skin. Toronto, Weed/Flower Press, 1968.
Circles, As in the Eye. Santa Fe, Desert Review Press, 1969.
An American Romance. Los Angeles, Black Sparrow Press, 1969.
The Chambers. Aylesford Priory, Kent, Aylesford Review Press, 1969.
From a Soft Angle: Poems about Women. Indianapolis, Bobbs Merrill, 1972.
The Unexpected. Milwaukee, Membrane Press, 1976.
Rituals and Gargoyles. Bowling Green, Ohio, Newedi Press, 1976.
A Song, A Chant. Albuquerque, Amalgamated Sensitivity Publications, 1978.
Alba Genesis. Woodstock, New York, Aesopus Press, 1979.
Alba Nemesis: The China Poems. Albuquerque, Amalgamated Sensitivity Publications, 1979.

Novel

Act of Love: An American Novel. Indianapolis, Bobbs Merrill, 1973.

Short Stories

The Unfolding. New York, Theo Press, 1969.
A Couple Called Moebius. Indianapolis, Bobbs Merrill, 1972.
Timepieces. Union City, California, Fault, 1977.
The Doppler Effect. Berkeley, California, Effie's Press, 1979.
Remembrance of Things to Come. New York, Theo Press, 1979.
Fierce Metronome: The One-Page Novel and Other Short Fiction. Mount Kisco, New York, Window, 1981.

Other

The Vancouver Report: A Report and Discussion of the Poetry Seminar at the University of British Columbia. New York,

Peace Eye, 1964.
A Chronograph of the Poets: A History of the "Deux Mégots Poets" from 1959-65. New York, Island Press, 1965.

Editor, with Dale Boyer, *The Clock of Moss*, by Judson Crews. Boise, Idaho, Ahsahta Press, 1983.

*

Manuscript Collection: Humanities Research Center, University of Texas, Austin.

Critical Studies: by Hayden Carruth, in *Hudson Review* (New York), 1969; Howard McCord, in *Measure* (Pullman, Washington), 1970; Ishmael Reed, in Washington, D.C., *Post*, 1973.

Carol Bergé comments:
   I worked in poetry through 1968 and had been moving more and more into prose as the big challenge since 1965. With the publication of the 190-page collection, *From a Soft Angle*, in 1972, a book that encompasses work from 1959 through 1971, I feel the work in that field is wrapped up, and am working almost solely in prose now. The book of stories *A Couple Called Moebius* has been well-received and reviewed and I'm content to be represented by the stories therein. The novel *Acts of Love* is as well-made as I can achieve at this time: it operates on at least three levels: that of a sociological/historical novel, that of a description of contemporary life, and that of an interesting and occasionally amusing fiction. It was a joy to write. I am now working on a third novel (the first novel, unpublished, needs revision); this one is concerned with the alternatives offered to Singles, a subdivision of which I have been a part for a long time. I hope to be as good a writer as Isak Dinesen, as Kobo Abe, as Jacov Lind, as Margaret Mitchell, as Lady Murasaki. There is no separating the life from the work. These days, I will write perhaps one poem every two months or so; therefore, I no longer feel I can be classified as a poet, but as a novelist.

*   *   *

   Female intensities, of wit, of lust, tenderness, the intelligence of the body, its groping, the ravage and despair, and all in language as varied as the weather, formalities of basic talk, spontaneous yet out of much reading, responding, looking: this is Carol Bergé's poetry. But foremost and always female, in her own voice or in dozens of personae, the terrible endlessness of sexual need, loving, hating, fighting, forgiving:

   The women breast to breast across empty
   across lava-strewn bitter plains
   facing lidless eyes of the majestic surgeons
   who demand they empty their wombs
   of the quintuplet dolls shaped like "husband"
   Women offering full teats to
   men with infant faces who drink with mouths
   the violet of sleep or of healed circumcision

And so on and on, the hurt imagination putting out, but not sloganizing or attitudinizing—at least not much. And then the nuances of observances of self:

        these days
        when you draw back
        as I reach for you
        it is an old wound you rip
        open...

Bergé can be, and often is talkative. Her poems sometimes seem put together from random images, broken by unlikely shifts of tone and texture, with little attempt at lyric unity. But her talk is intelligent, tough, urbane, and original, which is more than can be asked for a good deal of poetry. And when she breaks through her talk into genuine poems of her own, they are moving and lucid, and they show a degree of maturity that most writing by other self-conscious female poets today cannot approach.

—Hayden Carruth

BERKSON, Bill. American. Born in New York City, 30 August 1939. Educated at Brown University, Providence, Rhode Island, 1957-59; New School for Social Research, New York (Dylan Thomas Memorial Award, 1959); Columbia University, New York, 1959-60; New York University Institute of Fine Arts. Editorial Associate, *Portfolio and Art News Annual*, New York, 1960-63; Associate Producer, *Art-New York* series, WNDT-TV, New York, 1964-65; taught at the New School for Social Research, 1964-69; Guest Editor, Museum of Modern Art, New York, 1965-69; Editor, *Best & Company* magazine, 1969; Teaching Fellow, Ezra Stiles College, Yale University, New Haven, Connecticut, 1969-70; Editor, *Big Sky* magazine and Big Sky Books, Bolinas, California, 1971-78. Since 1976, teacher, California Poets in the Schools Program. Teacher, Naropa Institute, Boulder, Colorado, 1977, New College of California, 1977, 1983, Southampton College, 1980, California College of Arts and Crafts, 1983-84, and San Francisco Art Institute, 1984-85. Recipient: Poets Foundation grant, 1968; Yaddo fellowship, 1968; Coordinating Council of Literary Magazines grants, 1973-77; National Endowment for the Arts grant, 1979; Briarcombe Fellowship, 1983. Address: Box 389, Bolinas, California 94924, U.S.A.

PUBLICATIONS

Verse

Saturday Night: Poems 1960-61. New York, Tibor de Nagy, 1961.
Shining Leaves. New York, Angel Hair, 1969.
Two Serious Poems and One Other, with Larry Fagin. Bolinas, California, Big Sky, 1972.
Recent Visitors. New York, Angel Hair, 1973.
Ants. Berkeley, California, Arif Press, 1974.
Hymns of St. Bridget, with Frank O'Hara. New York, Adventures in Poetry, 1974.
100 Women. Chicago, Simon and Schuchat, 1974.
Enigma Variations. Bolinas, California, Big Sky, 1975.
Blue Is the Hero: Poems 1960-1975. Kensington, California, L Publications, 1976.
Red Devil. Bolinas, California, Smithereens Press, 1983.
Start Over. Bolinas, California, Tombouctou, 1984.
Lush Life. Calais, Vermont, Z Press, 1984.

Other

Editor, *In Memory of My Feelings*, by Frank O'Hara. New York, Museum of Modern Art, 1967.

Editor, with Irving Sandler, *Alex Katz.* New York, Praeger, 1971.
Editor, with Joe LeSueur, *Homage to Frank O'Hara.* Bolinas, California, Big Sky, 1978.

*

Manuscript Collection: University of Connecticut, Storrs.

*   *   *

Bill Berkson is a late arrival to the New York Ferment that produced such poets as Frank O'Hara, Kenneth Koch, John Ashbery, and James Schuyler in the 1950's, when abstract expressionism released new energies of awareness for poets as well as painters. Jackson Pollock and Willem de Kooning were giants at the center of this creative apocalypse and their projections through paint of various states of conscious (and unconscious) experience liberated art from its old logical categories. Suddenly free and fluid forms of self-expression became the norm of such art, and by the mid-1950's poets applied to syntax and diction the same release and invented a fresh discourse. Frank O'Hara is the reigning figure of this revolution in poetics, who, as associate curator of the Museum of Modern Art, served as liaison between painting and writing.

Berkson is from the next generation, but his credentials were good: born in New York to upper-class parents, private-school education, writer for *Art News*, occasional work with the Museum of Modern Art. In addition, Berkson edited a book of O'Hara's poems, *In Memory of My Feelings*, and collaborated with him on a second, *Hymns of St. Bridget*. Details of a life, but they add up to a sophisticated apprenticeship to writing a certain style of poetry, one that requires considerable daring and finesse, since much of it is calculated to swing into and well out of ordinary sense. There is about the New York style a punning sense of reality, that objects and events are only tenuously situated in fixity, and that the whole texture of one's certainty is as easily disturbed as a creek bed. A delicate, sometimes foolish humor overtakes such lyric, but behind it is a philosophical impetus—a gnawing frustration with the usual and the vague, a repressed but squirming vitality beneath the mundane and the actual, as in "Leave Cancelled":

What we need is a great big vegetable farm!
Every vegetable to stand up and be counted,
and all the farmers to love one another
in their solid, lazy dreams.

Then this would be all knowledge,
all hygiene, and the plants we feel,
and it comes down to Boy and Dad and kind
balloons of sight. The sky's neat sweep,

the irrational, would be this butterfly dish
where lovely woman stacks her arms....

Berkson only narrowly skirts sense in his own work, now collected in *Blue Is the Hero*, and this sets up an interesting tension in reading him. Although the language often seems to be a runaway *logopoeia*—words ordered by sounds alone—with a little scrutiny the thread of a reasoning process is discernible, as in this typical passage:

Are you different from that shelter you
Built for knives? On the side walk, sapphires.
On the fifth floor, fungus was relaxing. I have put on

The crimson face of awareness you gave me.
What is the heart-shaped object that thaws your fingers?
It is a glove and in it a fist.

Sometimes Berkson's experiments break through to a new level of metaphor that ties extraordinary words together ("In the Mean"):

Running water—
it makes you think of all you didn't do
but not regret it, no: *de ma jeunesse.*
You didn't know I was the President
of a great cloud of falling bricks, did you?
Zoom. Bent. The bare stalk of the corn tree plant
of October thirty-one, of November one, November two....

In such work, however, the strain for novelty can become an effort, and there is much dogged flippancy in Berkson:

What am I indicting that heads off gardenia?
green green stove-pipe
arm around me stalk wherein pegged a relax bus
globule of often-candelabra in the cake
of soap...

and so on. The intention, we might suppose, is to draw attention to the maker, to the process of mind that gives rise to words, or even more precisely, the compromising nature of words as indications of a consciousness words can only guess at. The intellection of lines such as these would suggest more than one process is at work although words themselves track a single linear reasoning. But then the poetic itself has only found the fault of language, not its virtues and possibilities. Taken far enough, this kind of experiment produces a stingy nonsense, and Berkson mercifully backs off and pursues more often a lyric of genuine feeling.

—Paul Christensen

BERNSTEIN, Charles.   American.   Born in New York City, 4 April 1950. Educated at Harvard University, Cambridge, Massachusetts, 1968-72, A.B. in philosophy 1972 (Phi Beta Kappa); Simon Fraser University, Burnaby, British Colombia (King Fellow, 1973-74). Married Susan Bee Laufer in 1977. Writer on medical and health topics; also arts administrator and health clinic coordinator. Editor, with Bruce Andrews, *L=A=N=G=U=A=G=E,* New York, 1978-81. Recipient: National Endowment for the Arts fellowship, 1980. Address: 464 Amsterdam Avenue, New York, New York 10024, U.S.A.

PUBLICATIONS

Verse

Parsing.   New York, Asylum's Press, 1976.
Shade.   College Park, Maryland, Sun and Moon Press, 1978.
Poetic Justice.   Baltimore, Pod, 1979.
Senses of Responsibility.   Berkeley, California, Tuumba Press, 1979.
Legend, with others.   New York, Segue, 1980.
Controlling Interests.   New York, Roof, 1980.

Disfrutes.   Needham, Massachusetts, Potes and Poets Press, 1981.
The Occurrence of Time, photographs by Susan Bee Laufer. New York, Segue, 1981.
Stigma.   Barrytown, New York, Station Hill Press, 1981.
Islets/Irritations.   New York, Jordan Davies, 1983.
Resistance.   Windsor, Vermont, Awede Press, 1983.

Other

Content's Dream: Essays 1975-1984.   College Park, Maryland, Sun and Moon Press, 1985.

Editor, with Bruce Andrews, *The L=A=N=G=U=A=G=E Book.* Carbondale, Southern Illinois University Press, 1984.

*

Critical Studies: "Charles Bernstein Issue" of *Difficulties* (Kent, Ohio), ii, 1, 1982; "L=A=N=G=U=A=G=E Poetry in the Eighties" by Marjorie Perloff in *American Poetry Review* (Philadelphia), May-June 1984.

Charles Bernstein comments:
    The sense of music in poetry: the music of *meaning*—emerging, fogging, contrasting, etc. Tune attunement in understanding—the meaning sounds. It's impossible to separate prosody from the structure of the poem. You can talk about strategies of meaning generation, shape, the kinds of sounds accented, the varieties of measurement (of scale, of number, of line length, of syllable order, of word length, of phrase length, of punctuation). But no one has primacy—the music is the orchestrating these into poems, the angles one plays against another, the shading.
    My interest in not conceptualizing the field of the poem as a unitary plane: that any prior principle of composition violates the priority I want to give to the inherence of surface, to the total necessity in the durational space of the poem for every moment to *count.* Writing as a process of pushing whatever way, or making the piece cohere as far as can: stretching my mind—to where I know it makes sense but not quite why—suspecting relations that I understand, that make the sense of the ready—to hand, i.e. pushing the composition to the very limits of sense, meaning, to that razor's edge where judgment/aethetic sense is all I can go on (knowhow).

*   *   *

    Lyn Hejinian published Bernstein's book *Senses of Responsibility,* indeed printed and designed it, on her Tuumba Press in 1979. It is written in a style that could only stike Hejinian as in accord with her own suspended style of discourse, a language intended never quite to touch earth or to assemble in a final pattern of unified meanings. Instead, Bernstein, like Hejinian and vintage John Ashbery, particularly his double monolog "As You Know," tends to make poetry stand still, accumulate sound, not expository sense. The juxtapositions of sound phrases owe their invention to Gertrude Stein, who stood poetry on its ear in 1914 with publication of her teasing book *Tender Buttons.*
    But there is a doleful, somnolent quality to Bernstein's long lyrics. They seem rooted in American symbolist meditations, the sort T.S. Eliot wrote in the 1910's, including "The Love Song of J. Alfred Prufrock," "Preludes," and "Portrait of a Lady." The poetry tends to explore the discord of a speaker's mind, the ravaged emotions and confused thinking breought on by some unnamed crisis or impending disaster.

Bernstein is less insistent on disasters in his own poems, but clearly seems intent on making speech raise up airy indeterminate structures without explicit connection to experience. He tracks a twilit state of mind in many of his poems, preferring settings that suggest asylums, prison cells, waiting rooms, confinements where the immobile, frustrated speaker is bereft of all possessions and is let loose within his own agitated interiors.

There is, at midcentury, a crossroads of intentions among various writers of America and England—writing that John Barth once called "the literature of exhaustion." In such work, one finds spent characters unable to act, only to utter rushes of thought that express their deadened willpower to change situations or to take hold of circumstances. Robert Creeley's poetry has long plumbed the subtleties of inert characters, whose world has become their own minds. He has expressed his pleasure in the similar excursions of Bernstein, whose characters seem all the more pinned to chairs as they wait out some fate unmentioned in their monologs. Their speech all but escapes the representational function of language, as crabbed syntax unfolds layers of linguistically refracted awareness:

> That's the trouble around here
> through which, asking as it does
> a different kind of space, who
>
> much like any other, relives
> what's noise, a better shoe, plants
> its own destination, shooting up
>
> at a vacant—which is forever
> unreconstituted—wedding party,
> rituals in which, acting out of
>
> a synonymous disclosure that
> "here" loses all transference falling
> back to, in, what selfsame
>
> dwelling is otherwise unaccounted for.

Many of his speakers are at peace in their enclosures, able to discern qualities within that are too concealed or delicate to be dissected by active, working citizens. Immobility has ironically freed such characters to dwell on themselves, relieved of routine responsibility and care. In that way, Bernstein is refreshing, an inevitable recoil to the work-centered culture of society, where life is rushed and formulated to the point of unthinking monotony.

Poetic Justice, published by Pod Books in 1977, bears fingerprints on its cover to suggest the booking of a prisoner. It is another of Bernstein's prose sequences of a waiting man, whose resources of language allow him to delicately dissect his every sensation and turn of thought.

> Listen. I can feel it. Specifically and intentionally.
> It does hurt. I like it. Ringing like this. The hum.
> Words peeling. The one thing. Not so much
> limited as conditioned. Here. In this. Spurting. It
> tastes good. Clogs. Thick with shape. I carry it
> with me where ever I go. I like it like this. Smears.

In *Parsing*, self-published in 1976, the final 15 pages are a list of familiar objects each beginning with "my." The list is preceded by a quote from Swami Sachnananda, "Count the number of things you call mine. This is the distance between you and enlightenment." Bernstein's poetry clearly suggests the disinclination to possess of his speakers is pointing toward a purging or

purification of spirit, where the disclosures, now wrapped in verbiage, distorted, inflated language, may one day come clean and limpid. His flourishes of language in lyric may be a way of satirizing the confused materialistic culture of contemporary America.

Like Hejinian and Ashbery, Bernstein frequently borrows dated language and discarded forms of eloquence to fill out his poetry; it is craftily achieved and often moving for its unusual powers of music, its haunting qualities of memory and distant association:

> There is an emptiness that fills
> Our lives as we meet
> On the boulevards and oases
> Of a convenient attachment. Boats
> In undertone drift into
> Incomplete misapprehension, get
> All fired up inside.

Bernstein edited a bimonthly journal of poetics and poetry, *L=A=N=G=U=A=G=E*, which brought together poets and prose writers attracted to semantic and linguistic experiment. The journal has initiated a movement of sorts among many interested in turning a reader's concentration onto the medium of words instead of the meanings to be abstracted from them. Writers of the journal together seem to agree that the language of art has been too well appropriated by others for political and commercial ends, and only by distorting and experimenting with its syntax and grammar can it be renewed for artistic purposes.

—Paul Christensen

BERRIGAN, Daniel J., S.J. American. Born in Virginia, Minnesota, 9 May 1921. Educated at Woodstock College, 1943-46; Weston (Jesuit) Seminary, Massachusetts: ordained Roman Catholic priest, 1952. Teacher, St. Peter's Preparatory School, Jersey City, New Jersey, 1945-49; auxiliary military chaplain, 1954; taught French and philosophy, Brooklyn Preparatory School, 1954-57; teacher of New Testament Studies, LeMoyne College, Syracuse, New York, 1957-63; Director of United Christian Work, Cornell University, Ithaca, New York, 1967-68; jailed for anti-war activities, 1968; Visiting Lecturer, University of Manitoba, Winnipeg, 1973, University of Detroit, 1975, University of California, Berkeley, 1976, and Yale University, New Haven, Connecticut, 1977. Recipient: Lamont Poetry Selection Award, 1957; Thomas More Association Medal, 1970; Melcher Book Award, 1971. Address: 220 West 98th Street, New York, New York 10025, U.S.A.

PUBLICATIONS

Verse

Time Without Number. New York, Macmillan, 1957.
Encounters. Cleveland, World, 1960.
The World for Wedding Ring: Poems. New York, Macmillan, 1962.
No One Walks Waters. New York, Macmillan, 1966.
False Gods, Real Men: New Poems. New York, Macmillan, 1966.
Love, Love at the End: Parables, Prayers, and Meditations. New York, Macmillan, 1968.

Night Flight to Hanoi: War Diary with 11 Poems. New York,
Macmillan, 1968.
Crime Trial. Boston, Impressions Workshop, 1970.
Trial Poems. Boston, Beacon Press, 1970.
Selected and New Poems. New York, Doubleday, 1973.
Prison Poems. Greensboro, North Carolina, Unicorn Press,
1973.
Prison Poems. New York, Viking Press, 1974.
May All Creatures Live. N.p., Berliner, 1983.
Journey to Black Island. Greensboro, North Carolina, Uni-
corn Press, 1984.

Recording: *Not Letting Me Not Let Blood: Prison Poems,*
National Catholic Reporter, 1976.

Play

The Trial of the Catonsville Nine (produced Los Angeles, 1970;
New York and London, 1971). Boston, Beacon Press, 1970.

Other

The Bride: Essays in the Church. New York, Macmillan, 1959.
The Bow in the Clouds: Man's Covenant with God. New York,
Coward McCann, and London, Burns Oates, 1961.
They Call Us Dead Men: Reflections on Life and Conscience.
New York, Macmillan, 1966.
Consequences: Truth and.... New York, Macmillan, and Lon-
don, Collier Macmillan, 1967.
Go from Here: A Prison Diary (includes verse). San Francisco,
Open Space, 1968.
No Bars to Manhood. New York, Doubleday, 1970.
The Dark Night of Resistance. New York, Doubleday, 1971.
*The Geography of Faith: Conversations Between Daniel Berri-
gan, When Underground, and Robert Coles.* Boston, Bea-
con Press, 1971.
*Absurd Convictions, Modest Hopes: Conversations after Prison
with Lee Lockwood.* New York, Random House, 1972.
America Is Hard to Find. New York, Doubleday, 1972; Lon-
don, SPCK, 1973.
Jesus Christ. New York, Doubleday, 1973.
Vietnamese Letter. New York, Hoa Binh Press, 1973 (?).
Lights On in the House of the Dead: A Prison Diary. New
York, Doubleday, 1974.
*The Raft Is Not the Shore: Conversations Toward a Bud-
dhist/Christian Awareness,* with Thich Nhat Hanh. Boston,
Beacon Press, 1975.
A Book of Parables. New York, Seabury Press, 1977.
Uncommon Prayer: A Book of Psalms. New York, Seabury
Press, 1978.
The Words Our Savior Gave Us. Springfield, Illinois, Temple-
gate, 1978.
Beside the Sea of Grass: The Song of the Lamb. New York,
Seabury Press, 1978.
*The Discipline of the Mountain: Dante's Purgatorio in a Nuclear
World.* New York, Seabury Press, 1979.
We Die Before We Live: Conversations with the Very Ill. New
York, Seabury Press, 1980.
Ten Commandments for the Long Haul. New York, Seabury
Press, 1981.
Portraits of Those I Love. New York, Crossroad, 1982.
The Nightmare of God. Portland, Sunburst, 1983.

*

Bibliography: *The Berrigans: A Bibliography of Published
Works by Daniel, Philip, and Elizabeth McAlister Berrigan* by
Anne Klejment, New York, Garland, 1980.

Critical Study: *Apologies, Good Friends...: An Interim Biography of Daniel Berrigan* by John Deedy, Chicago, Fides Clare-
tian, 1981.

*   *   *

In spite of his Jesuit training there is little in Daniel Berrigan's
poetry to remind us of so conspicuously available a model as
Gerard Manley Hopkins. Reading the *Imprimaturs* and the *Nihil
Obstats* on the early volumes is surprising to the reader who has
come to Berrigan from his later work where such marks of
orthodoxy are so conspicuously absent, perhaps even unavail-
able. Hopkins was probably too abstractly theological to be a
model for Dan Berrigan's taste. Berrigan's early poems have
more the feel of 17th-century English devotional verse. His references to Simone Weil suggest an indebtedness to her favorite
poet among the English writers—George Herbert. The early
volumes brought quick success to Berrigan as a poet:

Style
envelops a flower like its odor;
bestows on radiant air
the spontaneous word that greets and makes a king.

An early poem addressed to Wallace Stevens interestingly
accepts the techniques but repudiates the metaphysics that was a
part of the Stevens aesthetic:

Awakening
When I grew appalled by love
and promised nothing, but stood, a sick man
first time on feeble knees
peering at walls and weather
like the feeble minded—
the strange outdoors, the house of strangers—
there, there was a beginning.

But even the early poems were dedicated to Dorothy Day, the
quiet figure so central to the life of radical Catholicism in
America—*beata pauperes spiritu* and *beata pacifici* they intone
in their dedications, and Berrigan was to take the words
seriously.
His opposition to the Vietnam War led him to found Clergy
and Laymen Concerned about Vietnam when he returned to the
U.S. This ecumenical action so enraged Cardinal Spellman that
he exiled Berrigan to South America, a move that proved so
unpopular that the Cardinal was quickly forced to rescind the
action. But the tour through South America—the response to the
appalling poverty he saw there—brought him back to the U.S. a
convinced religious radical. *Consequences: Truth and...*is the
record of his spiritual and political development during that
period.
A post as professor of religion and poetry at Cornell University did not dampen his growing involvement with his brother
Philip in active opposition to the war. Pouring blood on draft
files led on to the burning of draft files in Catonsville, Maryland.
As he turned increasingly to direct action, he also turned to
prose. His poetry was used to focus his personal reaction to the
events he experienced. In *Night Flight to Hanoi* he wrote of
holding one child saved from bombing:

Children in the Shelter
Imagine; three of them.

As though survival
were a rat's word,
and a rat's end
waited there at the end
And I must have
in the century's boneyard
heft of flesh and bone in my arms
I picked up the littlest
a boy, his face
breaded with rice (his sister calmly feeding him
as we climbed down)
In my arms fathered
in a moment's grace, the messiah
of all my tears. I bore, reborn
a Hiroshima child from hell.

The Trial of the Catonsville Nine brought Berrigan to world-wide attention, and his prison journals were among the eloquent publications of the last years of the 1960's. *The Dark Night of Resistance,* published in that period, illustrated the growing influence on Berrigan of St. John of the Cross. Read in the 1950's by poets influenced by the religious revival of that period, one has a sense that Berrigan came to understand him in the late 1960's. He found St. John of the Cross in his prison experience a model to be lived rather than a style to be imitated.

Berrigan remains a Roman Catholic and a Jesuit. He is less active in writing poetry now, and more active in building a society that can be honestly celebrated in poetry. Despite the serious moral and political issues he forced through his personal involvement, there remains throughout his poetry a sustained joyousness—a marked characteristic of all his work.

—Myron Taylor

BERRY, Francis. British. Born in Ipoh, Malaya, 23 March 1915. Educated at Hereford Cathedral School; Dean Close School; University College, Exeter, 1937, 1946; University of London, B.A. 1947; University of Exeter, M.A. 1960. Served in the British Army, 1939-46. Married 1) Nancy Melloney Graham in 1947 (died, 1965), one son and one daughter; 2) Patricia Thomson in 1970 (marriage dissolved, 1975); 3) Eileen Lear in 1979. Lecturer, then Professor of English, University of Sheffield, 1947-70; Professor of English, Royal Holloway College, University of London, Egham, Surrey, 1970-80, now Emeritus. Visiting Lecturer, Carleton College, Northfield, Minnesota, 1951-52, and University of the West Indies, Jamaica, 1957; British Council Lecturer in India, 1966-67; W.P. Ker Lecturer, University of Glasgow, 1979; Visiting Fellow, Australian National University, Canberra, 1979; Visiting Professor, University of Malawi, 1980-81; British Council Lecturer in Japan, 1983. Fellow, Royal Society of Literature, 1968. Address: 33 Lyndhurst Avenue, Sunbury on Thames, Middlesex TW16 6QZ, England.

PUBLICATIONS

Verse

Gospel of Fire. London, Mathews and Marrot, 1933.
Snake in the Moon. London, Williams and Norgate, 1936.
The Iron Christ: A Poem. London, Williams and Norgate, 1938.

Fall of a Tower and Other Poems. London, Fortune Press, 1943.
Murdock and Other Poems. London, Dakers, 1947.
The Galloping Centaur: Poems 1933-1951. London, Methuen, 1952.
Morant Bay and Other Poems. London, Routledge, 1961.
Ghosts of Greenland. London, Routledge, 1966.
From the Red Fort. Bristol, Redcliffe, 1984.

Plays

Radio Plays: *Illnesses and Ghosts at the West Settlement,* 1965; *The Sirens,* 1966; *The Near Singing Dome,* 1971; *Eyre Remembers,* 1982.

Novel

I Tell of Greenland. London, Routledge, 1977.

Other

Herbert Read. London, Longman, 1953; revised edition, 1961.
Poets' Grammar: Person, Time and Mood in Poetry. London, Routledge, 1958; Westport, Connecticut, Greenwood Press, 1974.
Poetry and the Physical Voice. London, Routledge, and New York, Oxford University Press, 1962.
The Shakespeare Inset: Word and Picture. London, Routledge, 1965; New York, Theatre Arts, 1966; revised edition, Carbondale, Southern Illinois University Press, 1971.
John Masefield: The Narrative Poet (lecture). Sheffield, University of Sheffield, 1968.
Thoughts on Poetic Time (lecture). Abingdon-on-Thames, Berkshire, Abbey Press, 1972.

Editor, *Essays and Studies 22.* London, Murray, 1969.

*

Manuscript Collections: Lockwood Memorial Library, State University of New York, Buffalo; Sheffield Public Library; Brotherton Collection, Leeds University Library.

Critical Studies: "Francis Berry" by G. Wilson Knight, in *Neglected Powers,* London, Routledge, and New York, Barnes and Noble, 1971; *Tradition and Experiment in English Poetry* by Philip Hobsbaum, London, Macmillan, and Totowa, New Jersey, Rowman and Littlefield, 1979.

Francis Berry comments:

Have been deeply enchanted by geography—the Mediterranean, the West Indies, Greenland—for the settings it supplies for human actions. Strongest emotion used to be fear in its varieties, especially around sunset or in the night. But even strong noon-tide sunlight provoked anxiety. Cruelty figures in early poems because I am frightened of cruelty. Have felt responsive to other times as well as other places: so history and myths are also poetic preoccupations. I believe the dead might still care, and would not hurt them. It is a gratification to have written any poem that I think is good enough, but the long poem, narrative or dramatic, of lively structure, compact, of varied rhythm, and vivid images, is what I would most delight in making: its making would sustain the maker day after day during its making and render tolerable the return of first consciousness each morning.

*   *   *

Francis Berry is a master of the long poem, and his finest work is in that genre. Because of this, he has been under-represented in magazines and anthologies and his reputation has yet to match the opinion which such critics as G. Wilson Knight and Donald Davie have formed of his work.

The Iron Christ tells of a statue made from the guns of the frontier fortresses of Chile and Argentina and the attempt to erect this on the highest point of the Andes as a symbol of peace. The struggle up the mountain is rendered graphically:

>   The driver turns his face, his arm to throttle
>   Levering steam, but, with a cursing, spin
>   The driving-wheels, skidding upon raw rails,
>   Circuiting vainly, then grab, heel over rods,
>   Pistons pant, valves hiss, wheels grip, groan, grab...

Fall of a Tower shows a town dominated and overshadowed by a church, and the attempt of a man, Edmund, to blow that church up:

>   Struts straddle; West Front
>   Walks apart, begins ungainly waddle,
>   Collapses on its face; brick and mortar
>   Flee yelling from their stocks...

Murdock chronicles the unending affray of two ghostly brothers:

>   We of this Village know our heavy Wood
>   Haunted by Brothers in their furious Mood.
>   Two Brothers, locked and pledged to nightly Duel,
>   Fight under Trees, hidden at fullest moon.
>   Though dumb, their Blows do toss upon the Gale;
>   Their Groans disturb us at our Murdock fires;
>   Their sobs are heard through Falls of Autumn Rain...

Morant Bay deals with a negro uprising in Jamaica, put down ruthlessly by Governor Eyre in 1865. The exotic coloration is instantly compelling:

>   ...On the other side of the ravine
>   Rises the opposing flank of another spur,
>   Its sandstone swooned from the blurs of that sun,
>   Dotted with thorned scrub, roots bedded in stone,
>   On which the red spider darts or the lizard waits
>   Before his next scurry with a sobbing throat...

Equally compelling are the different voices that interweave the narration. One thinks of the diatribe which emanates from the black Deacon Bogle. He denounces the governor and is echoed by the impassioned responses of his congregation:

>   "Der he be
>   In dat King's House, an' he eat"—
>   *In dat King's House, an' he eat.*
>   "He eat fishes an' he eat meat,"
>   *He eat fishes an' he eat meat,*
>   *War-o, heavy war-o...*

Because he uses the voices of his protagonists, Berry is able to enter into their characters and see all sides of this question—Eyre, courageous but bigoted; the coloured Gordon, intelligent and envious; Deacon Bogle, personification of the superstitious blacks. What is so impressive about this poem upon a vexed subject—race hatred—is that it does not take sides. Instead, it seeks to understand the difficulty of a situation. In many ways, *Morant Bay* is a great Catholic poem. It sees the massacre at Morant Bay in terms of original sin, an obeah "Whose magic undergoes all manner of transfer/But cannot be cast out."

In *Illnesses and Ghosts at the West Settlement*, Berry's recreation of voices takes a further step and enters a new terrain. This is the Greenland colonized at the end of the first millennium A.D. by Erik the Red. Plague strikes down the little settlement, smashing the sanctions that govern even this primitive society. The remnant of people staying there becomes demoralized. The whole poem is couched in terms of a recollection by the various ghosts hovering above the colony where they suffered so dreadfully a thousand years ago. Erik's daughter-in-law, Gudrid, is the central character. Her voice comes across the centuries in characteristically tentative metres, recreating a woman's agony in the face of male intransigence:

>   Illnesses and ghosts.
>   You founded Greenland, I've seen enough of your Greenland
>   And I want the sun for a while, husband or no husband.
>   I want the sun because I am so cold, you know I am so cold,
>   That I could hear that particular sound again
>   Oh, I am so old
>   Before I am hardly girl. Dear Father, Father-in-law, help me...

It is questionable whether any contemporary poet can show so great a range of technique and subject-matter. And the characteristically exotic settings are a means of staging a penetration into the motives behind human affection and human action. The story doesn't end with Greenland, however. Francis Berry's most recent major work, not yet published, was broadcast in the summer of 1971. It concerns Shah Jehan who built the Taj Mahal in memory of his wife. Here is the voice of another woman: the dead Mumtaz accusing her husband of wishing her dead in order to erect his immemorial dome:

>   I died because you wanted me to die.
>   Or thought you did...Sometimes. For I could read
>   That silent thought in the way you looked
>   At me...sometimes. It made me sad—for you,
>   Because I surmised you would be desolate
>   And helpless...I gone. And that you would regret
>   That thought you had allowed me to discern...
>   Sometimes...though you should have not...

This is a sparser, more austere verse than we are used to from Berry. And indeed *The Near Singing Dome* may still be part of a work in progress. The reputation of the man who wrote this, and *Illnesses and Ghosts*, *Morant Bay*, *Murdock*, *Fall of a Tower* and *The Iron Christ*, may continue to grow slowly, as great reputations will. But the admirers of Francis Berry believe that his work will certainly endure.

Postscript. Since the remarks above were set up in type, an interesting selected poems, *From the Red Fort*, has been issued. It reprints the title-poem of *Murdock* and puts *The Near Singing Dome*, now *The Singing Dome*, into print in a revised version. Among the new poems are "Mbona" and "The Banana Plant," both in a setting based on Malawi. The former relates a battle between an old rainmaker and a young one. "The Banana Plant" tells of the rivalry between two wives married to the same man. The exotic setting does not distract the reader from the human quality of the story; rather, that quality is enhanced. The favoured wife, Magépo, dies and comes back as a banana plant, tended by the husband. The less favoured wife destroys the plant. The poems ends:

The stump withers,
Would not renew with tears, but still the husband
Remembers it green, and Magépo alive
And loving, for then how surely he had been
The most favoured of men.

The spaced-out stress pattern and quiet internal rhymes are only two elements of a verse that secures attention and sympathy. Nothing is more extraordinary in Berry's work than his ability to use geographical and cultural distance as a means of getting a situation intimately under his reader's guard. "This happened to me" or "I recognize that" are responses that compel themselves to utterance as we peruse rivalries in a Nyasa village or the bereavement of a Mogul emperor or a riot in mid-Victorian Jamaica. None of this poignancy would be possible without the author's command over language, the experience that his range of travel has given him, and his power to evoke highly specific atmosphere for those not sharing that command or that experience. The more recent poems in this remarkable collection show that over half a century of storytelling has not blunted the sensibility and skill of this most distinguished narrative poet.

—Philip Hobsbaum

BERRY, Wendell (Erdman). American. Born in Henry County, Kentucky, 5 August 1934. Educated at the University of Kentucky, Lexington, A.B. 1956, M.A. 1957; Stanford University, California (Stegner Fellow), 1958-59. Married Tanya Amyx in 1957; one daughter and one son. Taught at Stanford University, 1959-60, and New York University; Member of the English Department, University of Kentucky, 1964-77. Since 1977, staff member, Rodale Press, Emmaus, Pennsylvania. Recipient: Guggenheim Fellowship, 1951; Rockefeller Fellowship, 1965; Bess Hokin Prize (*Poetry*, Chicago), 1967; National Endowment for the Arts grant, 1969. Address: Port Royal, Kentucky 40058, U.S.A.

PUBLICATIONS

Verse

November Twenty-Six, Nineteen Hundred Sixty-Three. New York, Braziller, 1964.
The Broken Ground. New York, Harcourt Brace, 1964; London, Cape, 1966.
Openings. New York, Harcourt Brace, 1969.
Findings. Iowa City, Prairie Press, 1969.
Farming: A Hand Book. New York, Harcourt Brace, 1970.
The Country of Marriage. New York, Harcourt Brace, 1973.
An Eastward Look. Berkeley, California, Sand Dollar, 1974.
To What Listens. Crete, Nebraska, Best Cellar Press, 1975.
Horses. Monterrey, Kentucky, Larkspur Press, 1975.
Sayings and Doings. Lexington, Kentucky, Gnomon, 1975.
The Kentucky River: Two Poems. Monterrey, Kentucky, Larkspur Press, 1976.
There Is Singing Around Me. Austin, Texas, Cold Mountain Press, 1976.
Three Memorial Poems. Berkeley, California, Sand Dollar, 1977.

Clearing. New York, Harcourt Brace, 1977.
A Part. Berkeley, California, North Point Press, 1980.
The Wheel. Berkeley, California, North Point Press, 1982.

Novels

Nathan Coulter. Boston, Houghton Mifflin, 1960.
A Place on Earth. New York, Harcourt Brace, 1967; revised edition, Berkeley, California, North Point Press, 1982.
The Memory of Old Jack. New York, Harcourt Brace, 1974.

Other

The Rise. N.p., Graves Press, 1968.
The Long-Legged House. New York, Harcourt Brace, 1969.
The Hidden Wound. Boston, Houghton Mifflin, 1970.
The Unforeseen Wilderness: An Essay on Kentucky's Red River Gorge, photographs by Eugene Meatyard. Lexington, University Press of Kentucky, 1971.
A Continuous Harmony: Essays Cultural and Agricultural. New York, Harcourt Brace, 1972.
The Unsettling of America: Culture and Agriculture. San Francisco, Sierra Club, 1977.
Recollected Essays 1965-1980. Berkeley, California, North Point Press, 1981.
The Gift of Good Land: Further Essays Cultural and Agricultural. Berkeley, California, North Point Press, 1981.
Standing by Words: Essays. Berkeley, California, North Point Press, 1983.

*   *   *

The most important fact about Wendell Berry is that, except for brief periods of study and teaching, he has stayed close to his own place on earth, in Kentucky, on the Kentucky River not far from where it flows into the Ohio. Berry's poetic world is largely the physical and social world of his native region. Berry is a regionalist, not a provincialist. A deep sense of his native place animates all his works, the poetry, the essays, the novels. He knows the land literally at first hand, for he farms it. He understands the cycle of the seasons, planting, tending, harvesting, animal husbandry, country people. Because his ancestors have been in his region for two centuries, he has a strong feeling for ancestral inheritance. He enunciates the familial bond in "The Gathering" (*The Country of Marriage*):

At my age my father
held me on his arm
like a hooded bird,
and his father held him so....
          My son
will know me in himself
when his son sits hooded on
his arm and I have grown
to be brother to all
my fathers, memory
speaking to knowledge
finally, in my bones.

Like Edwin Muir, whose poetry and prose Berry has publicly praised, Berry conveys the story of his life in the context of a fable of a family: faithful watchers guard the traditional day.

Berry's seriousness about small farming is informed and passionate. He is the first real farmer-poet of stature in American history. He sees clearly and tells us forthrightly how Kentucky land has been overworked and ruined by greedy men and is now being dehumanized by agribusinessmen forcing crops and polluting soil and air with chemical fertilizers and huge machines.

Berry's central subjects are central subjects: love and death. There is no contemporary American poet more inclined to, or successful with, the elegy. Berry first attracted national notice with *November Twenty-Six, Nineteen Hundred Sixty-Three*, the only successful elegy, in this writer's opinion, prompted by the death of President Kennedy. There have followed at least three other important elegies: "Elegy: Pryor Thomas Berry" (*The Broken Ground*), "In Memory: Stuart Egnol" (*Openings*), and "Elegy" (on Owen Flood), the first section of *Three Memorial Poems*. Poems on love are numerous, many deeply serious, some light and witty, like "The Mad Farmer's Love Song" (*The Country of Marriage*), here quoted in full:

> O when the world's at peace
> and every man is free
> then will I go down to my love
>
> O and I may go down
> several times before that.

Berry's style is deceptively simple. Though his language is not actually the language of Kentuckians, it sounds authentic. It would hardly be mistaken, say, for that of a New Englander or a Westerner. His prosody is mainly open form or "naked," though occasionally, especially in more recent work, there are rhymes and meter. The characteristic mode is didactic. Berry goes behind the nature of things to assert the causes of things. His poetry has not changed markedly in theme, style or intention since he began publishing. But it has grown in sureness, in power, in passionate directness.

—James K. Robinson

BERTOLINO, James. American. Born in Hurley, Wisconsin, 4 October 1942. Educated at the University of Wisconsin, Stevens Point, Madison, and Oshkosh, B.S. in English and art, 1970; Washington State University, Pullman, 1970-71; Cornell University, Ithaca, New York, 1971-73, M.F.A. 1973. Married the artist Lois Behling in 1966. Teaching Assistant, Washington State University, 1970-71; Teaching Assistant, 1971-73, and Lecturer in Creative Writing, 1973-74, Cornell University; Assistant Professor, 1974-77, and Associate Professor of English, 1977-84, University of Cincinnati. Visiting Professor, Western Washington University, Bellingham, Winter 1984. Editor, *Abraxas* magazine and Abraxas Press, Madison, Wisconsin, and Ithaca, New York, 1968-72; Editor, Stone Marrow Press, Ithaca, New York, 1970-72; Assistant Editor, *Epoch* magazine, Ithaca, New York, 1971-73; Founding Editor, *Cincinnati Poetry Review*, 1975-82; Poetry Editor, *Eureka Review*, New Canaan, Connecticut, 1975-81. Founder, Elliston Book Award, for small press poetry books, 1977. Recipient: Hart Crane Memorial Foundation award, 1969; Book-of-the-Month Club Award, 1970; YM-YWHA Poetry Center Discovery Award, 1972; National Endowment for the Arts grant, 1974; Ohio Arts Council grant, 1979; Betty Colladay Award (*Quarterly Review of Literature*), 1984. Address: P.O. Box 1157, Anacortes, Washington 98221, U.S.A.

PUBLICATIONS

Verse

Day of Change. Milwaukee, Gunrunner Press, 1968.
Drool. Madison, Wisconsin, Quixote Press, 1968.
Mr. Nobody. Marshall, Minnesota, Ox Head Press, 1969.
Ceremony: A Poem. Milwaukee, Morgan Press, 1969.
Maize: A Poem. Madison, Wisconsin, Abraxas Press, 1969.
Stone Marrow. Madison, Wisconsin, Anachoreta Press—Abraxas Press, 1969.
Becoming Human. Oshkosh, Wisconsin, Road Runner Press, 1970.
The Interim Handout. Privately printed, 1972.
Employed. Ithaca, New York, Ithaca House, 1972.
Edging Through. Berkeley, California, Serendipity, 1972.
Soft Rock. Tacoma, Washington, Charas Press, 1973.
Making Space for Our Living. Port Townsend, Washington, Copper Canyon Press, 1975.
Terminal Placebos. New York, New Rivers Press, 1975.
The Gestures. Providence, Rhode Island, Bonewhistle Press, 1975.
The Alleged Conception. Southampton, New York, Granite, 1976.
New and Selected Poems. Pittsburgh, Carnegie Mellon University Press, 1978.
Are You Tough Enough for the Eighties? New York, New Rivers Press, 1979.
Precinct Kali, and The Gertrude Spicer Story. St. Paul, New Rivers Press, 1982.

Other

Editor, *Quixote: Northwest Poets.* Madison, Wisconsin, Quixote Press, 1968.
Editor, *Provisions*, by Anselm Parlatore. Berkeley, California, Serendipity, 1971.
Editor, *The Abraxas/5 Anthology.* Ithaca, New York, Abraxas Press, 1972.

*

Manuscript Collections: Murphy Library, University of Wisconsin, La Crosse; Ohio University Library, Athens.

Critical Studies: "Three Good Prospects" by James Naiden, in *Granite* (Hanover, New Hampshire), August 1972; "Observations on a Book of Poetry" by Steven Granger, in *Seizure* (Eugene, Oregon), Fall-Winter 1972; "Employed" by Ripley Schemm, in *Bartleby's Review 2* (Machias, Maine), 1973; "Facing the Eighties with James Bertolino" by Jane Somerville, in *Bluefish* (Southampton, New York), Autumn 1983; "James Bertolino: An Overview" by Edward Butscher, in *Poet Lore* (Boston), Summer 1984.

James Bertolino comments:
  I think my poetry has gone through stages which conform to William Blake's three stages of personal evolution: Innocence, Experience, and Radical Innocence. I like to feel that my work has entered the third stage.

*   *   *

Despite many collections to his credit, James Bertolino is a young poet whose work exhibits a variety of directions which are continually developing, expanding, and even, at times, doubling back onto themselves. His poetry may be divided into three distinct "types" which are very loosely chronological but which, more importantly, may be based on subject, theme, and technique.

The subject and viewpoint of Bertolino's earliest work are often decidedly midwestern and are marked by a flatness of language and a matter-of-factness of tone—a homespun-ness all round. Regardless of the regional focus they display, their themes are universal: sexual awakening ("I Had a Packard"), love ("Storms"), maturation ("Changes"), loneliness ("Mom & Sally"), and death ("Sálmon Fishing, Boundary Bay"). The poems of this group are solid, quiet, finely honed observations that, as often as not, owe their success to Bertolino's ability to imply his meaning effortlessly, or so it seems, and to his remembering to eschew the overt statement, as in the conclusion to "Elegy," in which a "green Mack truck" has run over "a preoccupied / wren"

> & before the feathers
> had settled
> three sparrows &
> the rest
> of the wrens
> were singing again.

Bertolino's socio-political poetry, the second division of his work, has appeared chiefly, but not exclusively, since the mid-1970's, and owes no allegiance to any specific political cadre and supports no particular group or strata of society over another. Rather, Bertolino's motivation and chief theme are his concern over the individual's—and, indeed, humankind's—ability to survive the various forces which threaten him. Particularly strong examples of this work include "Killer Chemicals," a found poem; the disturbing, strangely brutal sequence "Modern Lives"; and "The Nice Guy," whose conclusion is shocking. A bitterness that rivals that in Weldon Kees's poetry underlies many of the poems of this group, even those in which Bertolino assumes the persona of the malefactor, such as in "The Library," which begins chillingly: "I am Harry Truman / & have hurt you more than / you can know."

Finally, Bertolino's more recent work often takes on a mystical surrealism characteristic of much of the poetry of the 1960's such as "The Institute." In such poems, he makes a conscious effort to accept—even to embrace whole-heartedly and, at times, blindly—the odd, the quirky, or the bizarre. In "The Eleventh Hour Poem" he offers a reason for this facet of his work: "Logic / is the formal accident we / will have no part in." The language of his recent poems is their most striking characteristic, running the full gamut from a wacky playfulness ("Oh Avis it Hertz!" in "Ontological Pornography"), which is evident even in the "serious" work of this period, to a hi-tech diction ("fear is the black chute, / the nanosecond that never ends" in "St. Irwin, the Martyr"), which contrasts sharply with and, ultimately, satisfies less than the more lyrical, early work.

—Jim Elledge

BIRNEY, (Alfred) Earle. Canadian. Born in Calgary, North West Territories (now Alberta), 13 May 1904. Educated at the University of British Columbia, Vancouver, 1922-26, B.A. (honours) in English 1926; University of Toronto (Leonard Fellow), M.A. 1927, Ph.D. 1936; University of California, Berkeley, 1927-30; Queen Mary College, London (Royal Society of Canada Fellow), 1934-35. Served in the Canadian Army, in the reserves, 1940-41, and on active duty, 1942-45: Major-in-Charge, Personnel Selection, Belgium and Holland, 1944-45. Married 1) Sylvia Johnstone in 1933 (marriage annulled, 1936); 2) Esther Bull in 1940 (divorced, 1977), one son. Summer school lecturer, University of British Columbia, 1927-37; Instructor in English, University of Utah, Salt Lake City, 1930-34; Lecturer, 1936-40, and Assistant Professor of English, 1940-42, University of Toronto; Supervisor, European Foreign Language Broadcasts, Radio Canada, Montreal, 1945-46; Professor of Medieval English Literature, 1946-63, and Professor and Chairman of the Department of Creative Writing, 1963-65, University of British Columbia. Visiting Professor, University of Oregon, Eugene, 1961; Writer-in-Residence, University of Toronto, 1965-67, and University of Waterloo, Ontario, 1967-68; Regents Professor in Creative Writing, University of California, Irvine, 1968; Writer-in-Residence, University of Western Ontario, London, 1981-82, and University of Alaska, Fairbanks, 1984. Since 1968, freelance writer and lecturer. Literary Editor, *Canadian Forum*, Toronto, 1936-40; Editor, *Canadian Poetry Magazine*, Vancouver, 1946-48; Editor, *Prism International*, Vancouver, 1964-65; Advisory Editor, *New: American and Canadian Poetry*, Trumansburg, New York, 1966-70. Recipient: Governor-General's Award, for verse, 1943, 1946; Stephen Leacock Medal, 1950; Borestone Mountain Poetry Award, 1951; Canadian Government Overseas Fellowship, 1953, and Service Medal, 1970; Lorne Pierce Medal, 1953; President's Medal, University of Western Ontario, 1954; Nuffield Fellowship, 1958; Canada Council Senior Arts Fellowship, 1962, 1974, Medal, 1968, Special Fellowship, 1968, 1978, and Travel Award, 1971, 1974. LL.D.: University of Alberta, Calgary, 1965; D.Litt.: McGill University, Montreal, 1980; University of Western Ontario, 1984. Fellow, Royal Society of Canada, 1954; Officer, Order of Canada, 1970. Lives in Toronto. Address: c/o McClelland and Stewart, 25 Hollinger Road, Toronto, Ontario M4B 3G2, Canada.

PUBLICATIONS

Verse

David and Other Poems. Toronto, Ryerson Press, 1942.
Now Is Time. Toronto, Ryerson Press, 1945.
The Strait of Anian: Selected Poems. Toronto, Ryerson Press, 1948.
Trial of a City and Other Verse. Toronto, Ryerson Press, 1952.
Ice Cod Bell or Stone. Toronto, McClelland and Stewart, 1962.
Near False Creek Mouth. Toronto, McClelland and Stewart, 1964.
Selected Poems 1940-1966. Toronto, McClelland and Stewart, 1966.
Memory No Servant. Trumansburg, New York, New Books, 1968.
The Poems of Earle Birney. Toronto, McClelland and Stewart, 1969.
Pnomes, Jukollages and Other Stunzas, edited by B.P. Nichol. Toronto, Ganglia Press, 1969.
Rag and Bone Shop. Toronto, McClelland and Stewart, 1971.
Four Parts Sand: Concrete Poems, with others. Ottawa, Oberon Press, 1972.
The Bear on the Delhi Road: Selected Poems. London, Chatto and Windus, 1973.
What's So Big about Green? Toronto, McClelland and Stewart, 1973.

The Collected Poems, edited by John Newlove.   Toronto,
McClelland and Stewart, 2 vols., 1975.
*The Rugging and the Moving Times: Poems New and Uncol-
lected 1976.*   Coatsworth, Ontario, Black Moss Press, 1976.
Alphabeings and Other Seasyours, edited by Jamie Hamilton.
London, Ontario, Pikadilly Press, 1976.
Ghost in the Wheels: Selected Poems 1920-1976.   Toronto,
McClelland and Stewart, 1977.
Fall by Fury and Other Makings.   Toronto, McClelland and
Stewart, 1978.
The Mammoth Corridors.   Okemos, Michigan, Stone Press,
1980.

Recordings: *David*, 1964; *Earle Birney Reads His Poems*,
Barnet, 1970; *Birney*, Ontario Institute for Studies in Education,
1971; *Nexus and Earle Birney*, Nexus, 3 albums, 1984.

Plays

The Damnation of Vancouver: A Comedy in Seven Episodes
(broadcast, 1952).   Included in *Trial of a City*, 1952; revised
version (produced Seattle, 1957; Vancouver, 1978), in *Selected
Poems*, 1966.
Words on Waves (radio plays), edited by Howard Fink.   Montreal, Véhicule Press, 1984.

Radio Play: *The Damnation of Vancouver*, 1952.

Novels

Turvey: A Military Picaresque.   Toronto, McClelland and
Stewart, 1949; London and New York, Abelard Schuman,
1959; as *The Kootenay Highlander*, London, Four Square,
1960; revised edition, McClelland and Stewart, 1976.
Down the Long Table.   Toronto, McClelland and Stewart,
1955; London, Abelard Schuman, 1959.

Short Stories

Big Bird in the Bush: Selected Stories and Sketches.   Oakville,
Ontario, Mosaic Press, 1978.

Other

Canada Calling.   Montreal, CBC, 1946.
The Creative Writer.   Toronto, CBC, 1966.
*The Cow Jumped over the Moon: The Writing and Reading of
Poetry.*   Toronto, Holt Rinehart, 1972.
*Spreading Time: Remarks on Canadian Writing and Writers 1:
1926-1949.*   Montreal, Véhicule Press, 1980.

Editor, *20th Century Canadian Poetry.*   Toronto, Ryerson
Press, 1953.
Editor, *Record of Service in the Second World War.*   Van-
couver, University of British Columbia, 1955.
Editor, with others, *New Voices.*   Toronto, Dent, 1956.
Editor, with Margerie Lowry, *Selected Poems of Malcolm Lowry.*
San Francisco, City Lights, 1962.
Editor, with Margerie Lowry, *Lunar Caustic*, by Malcolm Lowry.
New York, Grossman, 1963; London, Cape, 1968.

*

Bibliography: by Peter Noel-Bentley, in *The Annotated Bibliography of Canada's Major Authors 4*, edited by Robert Lecker
and Jack David, Downsview, Ontario, ECW Press, 1983.

Manuscript Collections: Fisher Library, University of Toronto;
Queen's University, Kingston, Ontario; University of British
Columbia, Vancouver.

Critical Studies: *Earle Birney* by Frank Davey, Toronto, Copp
Clark, 1971; *Earle Birney* by Richard Robillard, Toronto,
McClelland and Stewart, 1971; "Maker of Order, Prisoner of
Dreams: The Poetry of Earle Birney" by W.H. New, in *Articulat-
ing West*, Toronto, New Press, 1973; *Earle Birney* edited by
Bruce Nesbitt, Toronto, McGraw Hill Ryerson, 1974; "A Stub-
born Master: The Poetry of Earle Birney" by William Walsh, in
Lugano Review (Switzerland), 1975; "Visual Poetry in Canada:
Birney, Bissett, and bp" by Jack David, in *Studies in Canadian
Literature* (Fredericton), Summer 1977; "Poet on Poet" by
Kevin Crossley-Holland, in *Ambit 74* (London), 1978; "Birney's
Makings" by George Woodcock, in *Ontario Review* (Windsor),
Fall-Winter 1978-79; *Earle Birney* by Peter Aichinger, Boston,
Twayne, 1979; *Perspectives on Earle Birney* edited by Jack
David, Downsview, Ontario, ECW Press, 1981; "Earle Birney
Issue" of *Essays on Canadian Writing* (Toronto), Spring 1981;
Earle Birney: Portrait of a Poet (documentary), National Film
Board of Canada, 1981.

Earle Birney comments:
   In the last 30 years I have been successively influenced by Beat,
Projectivist, Concretist, and Sound poetry, and I hope to remain
responsive—but eclectic—in relation to contemporary change
and experimentation. I believe that poetry is both an oral entertainment and a visual notation.
   I write out of compulsion to talk to another man within me, an
intermittent madman who finds unpredictable emblems of the
Whole in the trivia of my experience, and haunts me with them
until I have found a spell of words and rhythms to exorcise these
ghosts and, for the moment, appease him. For me, the hauntings
and the exorcizings are happenings so intense as to be beyond
pleasure or pain—ends in themselves. But I go on to publish
some of the result because I believe that my poems are the best
proof I can print of my Humanness, signals out of the loneliness
into which all of us are born, and in which we die, affirmations of
kinship with all the other wayfarers.
   I have tried to develop an ability to read my own poetry
effectively, and I have sought audiences wherever there was a
knowledge of the English language. In Canada I have many times
toured the universities and colleges from Vancouver Island to
Newfoundland, and have also read to students in high schools,
and to audiences in art galleries and public libraries. With the
help of Canada Council grants I have sounded my work and that
of other living Canadians in most of the universities of Australia
and New Zealand, Chile, Peru, Mexico, the West Indies, and
about 30 universities in the U.S.A. I have also read in Japan,
Hong Kong, Singapore, Malaya, Sri Lanka, India, Tanzania,
Uganda, Egypt, Kenya, Nigeria, Ghana, Sierra Leone, Gambia,
and at the University of Bordeaux. I have given readings in
Dublin and in the chief cities of England and Scotland, especially
to working class groups and in public houses. Recently I have
been performing sound-poems in company with a percussion
group and dancers and participating in the making of films based
on my poems and my life.

*   *   *

   The earliest of the poems which Earle Birney included in his
most recent selection from a life's work, *Ghost in the Wheels*, was
written, at least in first draft, in his teens, but his first book of

verse, *David*, was not published until 1942, when he was already 38. He came into prominence as one of the generation of the 1940's, following on the pioneer work of Smith, Scott, and Pratt, yet one of the influences that permanently affected his writing was the political radicalism of the 1930's. His academic speciality, Old and Middle English, also deeply influenced his choice of form and language—even now one observes in kennings and alliterations the lingering debt he owes to the Anglo-Saxon scops. Finally, an acute consciousness of the physical environment, bred in a childhood lived in the Rockies, has given a peculiarly topographical nature to a great deal of his poetry.

This characteristic has been intensified by Birney's love of travel, and by the way in which each phase of wandering seemed to mark a period of his writing. He himself divided his *Collected Poems* according to region, and the arrangement throws into highlight the remarkable poems—among the best he ever wrote—that came out of travel in Asia and Latin America during the late 1950's and early 1960's, poems like "A Walk in Kyoto," "Cartagena de Indias," and the splendid "Bear on the Delhi Road," observing Kashmiri hunters trying to teach a bear they have captured to dance:

> It is no more joyous for them
> in this hot dust to prance
> out of reach of the praying claws
> sharpened to paw for ants
> in the shadows of deodars
> It is not easy to free
> myth from reality
> or rear this fellow up
> to lurch, lurch with them
> in the tranced dancing of men

In these travel poems Birney develops a characteristic stance, that of the observer who appears as a character in the poem and so emphasizes the strangeness of the bridges by which two cultures meet.

One is aware, all the time, of a man observing and reflecting on his world, on other worlds, on himself, and one of the most striking features of the process is the way the voices and manner change according to the situation. When he writes poems about America and Americans, his voice often takes on an emphatic jerkiness, often spasmodic, which affects the visual shape of the poem as well as its sound when read. In other poems, particularly those he wrote during the 1960's, the voice slows down, broadening its flow, taking a narrative pace in the travel poems, and assuming an eloquent loping rhythm in that magnificent meditation on human destiny, "November Walk near False Creek Mouth," with its notable ending:

> But still on the highest shelf of ever
> washed by the curve of timeless returnings
> lies the unreached unreachable nothing
> whose winds wash down to the human shores
> and slip   showing
>
> into each thought nudging my footsteps now
> as I turn to my brief night's ledge
>
> *in the last of warmth*
> *and the fading of brightness*
> *on the sliding edge of the beating sea*

One characteristic of Birney as a poet is his disinclination to be definite and final. This means that when he republishes his poems, from collection to collection, they are often radically revised, so that the version we finally have may have been 20 years in the writing, though the best of his poems—the fine travel poems—have usually been written in a force of feeling that refuses revision. Related to his desire to change and improve is his restless urge to experiment in form and language. From Joycean experiments in the 1940's he came to dabblings in concrete poetry in the 1960's, and his recent book *Fall by Fury* is a strange combination of typographical patterns and the vulnerable love poems of old age:

> Loving you is beyond wings
> is to sway with primal weed
> is to dance with fins
> in a joy too salt
> for sounding

Both these types of later poems exemplify and perhaps intensify the element of playfulness that quite early on became an essential factor in Birney's poetry, and which continues in the verse that, since the publication of his last important volume, Birney has been publishing in periodicals and brochures. Yet at the same time one finds a darker process of philosophic change at work in his more recent poetry. As the Canadian critic Frank Davey has justly remarked, the "humanistic themes" of his earlier volumes are repudiated "to envision a vast, indifferent cosmos in whose 'mammoth corridors' human energy is little more than a glorious absurdity." The heroic vision of "David" is replaced by the comic but anti-heroic vision of the poet surviving by evasion and chance, a vision curiously anticipated in Birney's Schweikian novel, *Turvey* (1949).

—George Woodcock

BISSETT, Bill (William Frederick Bissett). Canadian. Born in Halifax, Nova Scotia, 23 November 1939. Since 1962, Editor and Printer, Blewointmentpress, Vancouver. Artist: Individual Shows—Vancouver Art Gallery, 1972, and Western Front Gallery, Vancouver, 1977. Recipient: Canada Council grant, 1967, 1968, 1972, 1975, 1977, bursary and travel grant, 1971, 1977. Address: c/o Talon Books, 201-1019 East Cordova, Vancouver V6A 1M8, Canada.

PUBLICATIONS

Verse

Th jinx ship nd othr trips: pomes-drawings-collage.   Vancouver, Very Stone House, 1966.
we sleep inside each other all (with drawings).   Toronto, Ganglia Press, 1966.
Fires in th Tempul (with drawings).   Vancouver, Very Stone House, 1967.
where is miss florence riddle.   Toronto, Luv Press, 1967.
what poetiks.   Vancouver, Blewointmentpress, 1967.
(th) Gossamer Bed Pan.   Vancouver, Blewointmentpress, 1967.
Lebanon Voices.   Toronto, Weed/Flower Press, 1967.
Of th Land/Divine Service Poems.   Toronto, Weed/Flower Press, 1968.
Awake in the Red Desert!   Vancouver, Talonbooks, 1968.
Killer Whale.   Vancouver, See Hear Productions, 1969.
Sunday Work?   Vancouver, Blewointmentpress-Intermedia Press, 1969.

Liberating Skies. Vancouver, Blewointmentpress, 1969.
The Lost Angel Mining Co. Vancouver, Blewointmentpress, 1969.
A Marvellous Experience. Vancouver, Blewointmentpress, 1969(?).
S th Story I to. Vancouver, Blewointmentpress, 1970.
Th Outlaw. Vancouver, Blewointmentpress, 1970.
blew trewz. Vancouver, Blewointmentpress, 1970.
Nobody Owns th Earth. Toronto, Anansi, 1971.
air 6. Vancouver, Air, 1971.
Tuff Shit Love Pomes. Windsor, Ontario, Bandit/Black Moss Press, 1971.
dragon fly. Toronto, Weed/Flower Press, 1971.
what fukin thery. Vancouver, Blewointmentpress, 1971.
drifting into war. Vancouver, Talonbooks, 1971.
Four Parts Sand: Concrete Poems, with others. Ottawa, Oberon Press, 1972.
th Ice bag. Vancouver, Blewointmentpress, 1972.
pomes for yoshi. Vancouver, Blewointmentpress, 1972.
air 10—11—12. Vancouver, Air, 1972.
Polar Bear Hunt. Vancouver, Blewointmentpress, 1972.
Pass th Food, Release th Spirit Book. Vancouver, Talonbooks, 1973.
th first sufi line. Vancouver, Blewointmentpress, 1973.
Vancouver Mainland Ice & Cold Storage. London, Writers Forum, 1973.
what. Vancouver, Blewointmentpress, 1974.
drawings. Vancouver, Blewointmentpress, 1974.
Medicine my mouths on fire. Ottawa, Oberon Press, 1974.
space travl. Vancouver, Air, 1974.
yu can eat it at th opening. Vancouver, Blewointmentpress, 1974.
Living with the Vishyun. Vancouver, New Star, 1974.
IBM. Vancouver, Blewointmentpress, n.d.
Th fifth sun. Vancouver, Blewointmentpress, 1975.
Image being. Vancouver, Blewointmentpress, 1975.
stardust. Vancouver, Blewointmentpress, 1975.
Venus. Vancouver, Blewointmentpress, 1975.
th wind up tongue. Vancouver, Blewointmentpress, 1976.
Plutonium Missing. Vancouver, Intermedia, 1976.
An Allusyun to Macbeth. Coatsworth, Ontario, Black Moss Press, 1976.
sailor. Vancouver, Talonbooks, 1978.
Five Ways, with Bob Cobbing. Toronto, Writers Forum, 1978.
Sa n th monkey. Vancouver, Blewointmentpress, 1980.
Selected Poems: Beyond Even Faithful Legends. Vancouver, Talonbooks, 1980.
Northern Birds in Colour. Vancouver, Talonbooks, 1981.
Sa n his crystal ball. Vancouver, Blewointmentpress, 1982.
Seagull on Yonge Street. Vancouver, Talonbooks, 1982.

Plays

Television Documentaries: *In search of innocence*, 1963; *Strange grey day this*, 1964; *Poets of the 60's*, 1967.

*

Critical Study: "The Typography of bill bissett" by bpNichol, in *we sleep inside each other all*, 1966.

Bill Bissett comments:
    poet and painter: abt equal time nd involvment, been merging th fields for sum time now, since abt '62 nd previous with con-crete poetry, which i early got into with lance farrell, allowing th words to act visually on th page, was aware of such effects before i cud accept th use of say grammatical thot in writing as such appeard too limiting to th singularly amazing development of th person.
    spelling—mainly phonetic
    syntax—mainly expressive or musical rather than grammatic
    visual form—apprehension of th spirit shape of th pome rather than stanzaic nd rectangular
    major theme—search for harmony within th communal self thru sharing (dig Robin Hood), end to war thereby—good luck
    characteristic stylistic device—elipse
    favorite poet—mick jagger
    general source—there is only one, nd th variation that spawnd th fingrs of night woven grace issue (romanticism or elevation, i don't feel th I, i.e. ME writes but that i transcribe indications of flow mused spheres sound), from a hoop

*   *   *

    I like Bill Bissett's poetry when it's most woolly. He admits he can't spell or write right: "the way is clear, the free hard path, no correct spelling, no grammar rules." Puns seem to replace meter: "hes closin in all the doors then iul open them yer all stond." Drugs seem to replace vision. The language is dialect, what's known around here as the Southwestern Ontario Rock 'n Roll Accent. Stupidity, almost, is faked, as in Chaucer, adding a little, as in Chaucer, to the difficulty of the dialect of speeding speech:

    did yu blow cock eat cunt make a good
    business deal and still relate were yu are
    yu happy were yu good just once did yu today
    have an existential moment in no time were yu
    normal today did yu screw society but found
    sum innocent outlets like no one knew or evry
    one knew did yu buy sum orange pop sticks green
    ones did yu have a treat and were clean were yu
    a dirty outlet for a while managin at th same
    time to find pleasure in nature and read a thot
    conditionin book by a provocative author did. ...

Bissett asks a lot of questions. His monologues are unpunctuated but best when interrogatory. It's exuberant. It's genuinely written by someone who is outside himself, making rapid connections. Perhaps calling popsicles pop sticks is a trifle cutesy. Bissett draws, writes narrative, political and concrete poetry and chants. But there is sadness, still interrogatory:

    why just when my body nd souls startin to fit
    sum they rip it all up mother i was happy
    in sum of those open spaces why hard times
    again did yu catch me foolin with th images
    now how can i carry any once cross this

    swamp ium sinkin in th deep mud myself

Hopkins? There is a religious aspect, drugs seem a mere polite excuse for vision. Analogously, Warhol's starting to look like Burroughs, and gets sadder, and sadder, and lines form. It's not poetry, those lines. Bissett wears a mask in his poetry; the art in a man's face, the lines, are not fictive, which is why I wish I knew Bissett personally. Still, Burroughs and Warhol are distant from Bissett. Bissett's *Nobody Owns th Earth* values the earth, love and country. Did I say cliché? Not really, just downhome talk. Smart people, like Chaucer, know the difference between cliché and proverb; Canadians are a young people like Chaucer's English were. Nevertheless, I prefer New Yorkers, and wonder if it is precisely the provinciality of Canada that pushes Bissett beyond sadness into heavy hopelessness:

> there is
> nothing
> to hope
>
> th candul
> yu lit it
> is going
>
> there is
> nothing
> to hope
>
> shut out
> the wind
> flame
>
> there is
> nothing
> to hope
>
> a sea of
> skulls in
> th harbor

These lines are from a chant in which Bissett turns from a benign "mother" to give some orders to "flame." Bissett's assertive mood is heavy. When he stops asking and hoping, he starts hinting at an apocalypse. Of course, that hinting is itself a hoping, the hope for an end.

—Michael André

BLACK, David (Macleod).   Scottish.   Born in Cape Town, South Africa, 8 November 1941. Educated at Edinburgh University, M.A. in philosophy 1966; University of Lancaster, M.A. in religious studies. Recipient: Scottish Arts Council prize, 1968, and publication award, 1969; Arts Council of Great Britain bursary, 1968. Address: 5/33 Eton Avenue, London N.W.3, England.

PUBLICATIONS

Verse

Rocklestrakes.   London, Outposts, 1960.
From the Mountains.   London, Outposts, 1963.
Theory of Diet.   London, Turret, 1966.
With Decorum.   Lowestoft, Suffolk, Scorpion Press, 1967.
A Dozen Short Poems.   London, Turret, 1968.
Penguin Modern Poets 11, with Peter Redgrove and D.M. Thomas.   London, Penguin, 1968.
The Educators: Poems.   London, Barrie and Rockliff-Cresset Press, 1969.
The Old Hag.   Preston, Lancashire, Akros, 1972.
The Happy Crow.   Edinburgh, M.Macdonald, 1974.
Gravitations.   Edinburgh, M.Macdonald, 1979.

*

Critical Studies: "The World of D.M. Black" by John Herdman, in *Scottish International 13* (Edinburgh), February 1971; *Contemporary Scottish Poetry* by Robin Fulton, Edinburgh, M.Macdonald, 1974; Andrew Greig, in *Akros 46* (Nottingham), April 1981; *Science and Psychodrama: The Poetry of Edwin Morgan and David Black* by Robin Hamilton, Frome, Somerset, Bran's Head, 1982.

David Black comments:
   Looking back over four book-length collections, and several pamphlets and other things, it's clear that amid all the inconsistencies there's been a consistency: a preoccupation with narrative poetry, and a tendency from great formal freedom to a much more disciplined style. I would claim originality for my use of the hendecasyllabic line in the long narrative poems in *Gravitations*, which mark the culmination of these trends so far. Scottish poets seem both more passionate and more intellectual than poets in England, and in that sense I would also claim an affinity with my nation. As for the future—it is open.

*   *   *

   The 1960's saw a revived interest in surrealism, and no doubt David Black's earlier poetry reflected this, but it was a surrealism of a modified type, laced by side-shrieks from George MacBeth's poetry of cruelty, tinged by science-fiction and mythmaking, and peppered by the place-names of a hallucinatory Edinburgh. The heady mixture was poured into a flat, deadpan, jerkily enjambed free verse which at moments of stress could take off into lyrical humours and mild, almost pop horror. Long exotic narratives like "Theory of Diet," "Without Equipment," and "The Rite of Spring," which refuse to come into clear focus, present nightmare explorations of cannibal islands, dwarfs speaking dwarf language, a prince whose mother is devoured by ants. Among the shorter poems, violent and extraordinary fantasies are more successfully related to a ruling idea: in "My Species" it is artificial insemination, in "The Educators" it is the generation gap, in "The Fury Was on Me" it is the transforming power of anger, in "The Eighth Day" it is the revenge of fruitfulness on asceticism. In some of the most attractive poems, fantasy shades off towards reality: "Leith Docks" and "The Red Judge" with their evocation of the dramatic northernness and Calvinist tensions of Edinburgh, "With Decorum" celebrating the mysterious sense of renewal in death like a 28-line *Finnegans Wake*, "Clarity" turning a track-suited lout into a dancer:

> Open the
> windows, Jock! My
> beauties, my
> noble horses—yoked in
> pairs, white horses, drawing my great
> hearse, galloping and
> frolicking over the cropped turf.

In his later work he has made rather a specialty of the long poem, with a clarifying of style and a leaning towards myth, romance, and fairy-tale. In *The Happy Crow*, "Peter MacCrae Attempts the Active Life" deals with an incestuous brother-sister relationship, and "Melusine," in a variant of a medieval French legend, tells the story of the Count's wife who periodically turns into a fish. In *Gravitations*, other long poems start off from Grimm's fairy-tales and the Sumerian Gilgamesh cycle, or give the tormented Browningesque confessions of a monk. These are poems of psychological and metaphysical search; their unusualness can sometimes make them seem to promise more than they actually deliver; but the attempt to revive narrative poetry is to be applauded. Black continues to develop. He refreshingly, if at times unaccommodatingly, goes his own way.

—Edwin Morgan

BLASER, Robin (Francis). Canadian. Born in Denver, Colorado, United States, 18 May 1925; naturalized Canadian citizen, 1972. Educated at Northwestern University, Evanston, Illinois, 1943; College of Idaho, Caldwell, 1943-44; University of California, Berkeley, B.A. 1952, M.A. 1954, M.L.S. 1955. Librarian, Harvard University Library, Cambridge, Massachusetts, 1955-59; Assistant Curator, California Historical Society, 1960-61; Librarian, San Francisco State College Library, 1961-65. Lecturer, 1966-70, since 1970, Professor of English, and since 1981, Professor, Centre for the Arts, Simon Fraser University, Burnaby, British Columbia. Co-Founder, *Measure*, Boston, 1957; Editor, *Pacific Nation*, Vancouver, 1967-69. Recipient: Poetry Society Award, 1965; National Endowment for the Arts grant, 1968; Canada Council award, 1970. Address: Department of English, Simon Fraser University, Burnaby, British Columbia V5A 1S6, Canada.

PUBLICATIONS

Verse

The Moth Poem.   San Francisco, Open Space, 1964.
Les Chimères (versions of Gérard de Nerval).   San Francisco, Open Space, 1965.
Cups.   San Francisco, Four Seasons, 1968.
The Holy Forest Section.   New York, Caterpillar, 1970.
Image-nations 1-12, and The Stadium of the Mirror.   London, Ferry Press 1974.
Image-nations 13-14.   Vancouver, Cobblestone Press, 1975.
Suddenly.   Vancouver, Cobblestone Press, 1976.
Syntax.   Vancouver, Talonbooks, 1983.

Other

Editor, *The Collected Books of Jack Spicer.*   Los Angeles, Black Sparrow Press, 1975.
Editor, *Particular Accidents*, by George Bowering.   Vancouver, Talonbooks, 1980.

*

Robin Blaser comments:
  I have had two great companions in poetry, Jack Spicer and Robert Duncan. And there is a real debt to Charles Olson.
  I have insisted in my work upon a poetry which in its imagery is cosmological. I have tried to include, take in, and bring over in the content of that work images of those worlds to which one is given the possibility of entrance.
  I am interested in a particular kind of narrative—what Jack Spicer and I agreed to call in our own work the serial poem—this is a narrative which refuses to adopt an imposed story line, and completes itself only in the sequence of poems, if, in fact, a reader insists upon a definition of completion which is separate from the poems themselves. The poem tends to act as a sequence of energies which run out when so much of a tale is told. I like to describe this in Ovidian terms, as a *carmen perpetuum*, a continuous song, in which the fragmented subject matter is only apparently disconnected. I believe a poet must reveal a mythology which is as elemental as air, earth, fire, and water; and that the authors who count take responsibility for a map of those worlds that is addressed to companions of the earth, the world, and the spirit.

*   *   *

  Literature misses a lot of things. Of course, people miss a lot of literature. They missed Robin Blaser. He's an unknown classic—some of the people in this book are classic unknowns, so that's a small and utter difference.
  But literature does miss a lot of things. Robin Blaser, besides an audience, missed the future. I'm talking about his style, about:

above

This poem is doubtless something archaic, something free versey, and something symbolic, not something "avant-garde." I have not yet looked at the poem you have looked at, above. This poem was selected at random by pointing my finger at a passage in a random Blaser book.
  Dear Mr. Blaser, Why don't you answer your mail? Here you see an example of the truth of the aleatory mode. Are you at all familiar with this? I am a great fan of yours. I worry, though, that you imagine you write perfectly—but perfect writing is not marred by insensitive attitudes, and is more adventurous than yours.
  Still, Blaser has written some superb poems. Here is the beginning of Poem 8 from *Cups*:

There is no salutation. The
harvesters with gunny sacks
bend picking up jade stones

(Sure that Amor would appear
in sleep. Director. Guide.)

Secret borrowings fit into their hands.

Cold on the tongue
White flecks on the water.

These jade pebbles are true green
when wet.

On the seventh night, the branches parted.
            The other replied,
How photographic. Amor doesn't appear
or demand. He's more like a snake skin.
If he fits, he lets you in
or sheds your body against the rocks.

—Michael André

BLIGHT, John.   Australian.   Born in Unley, South Australia, 30 July 1913. Educated at Brisbane State High School, qualified in accountancy. Married Madeline D'Arcy Irvine in 1942; two daughters. Worked as clerk, orchardist, swagman, and public servant; cost accountant, 1951-57; retired as secretary to a sawmilling company, 1968. Member, Timber Inquiry Commission, 1949-50. Recipient: Myer Award, 1965; Australia Council Writers Senior Fellowship, 1973-75, 1976-79; National Book Council Award, 1976; Patrick White Prize, 1976; Grace Leven Prize, 1977; Christopher Brennan Award, 1981. Address: 34 Greenway Street, Grange Heights, Queensland 4051, Australia.

PUBLICATIONS

Verse

The Old Pianist.   Sydney, Dymock's Book Arcade, 1945.
The Two Suns Met: Poems.   Sydney, Edwards and Shaw, 1954.
A Beachcomber's Diary: Ninety Sea Sonnets.   Sydney, Angus and Robertson, 1964.
My Beachcombing Days: Ninety Sea Sonnets.   Sydney, Angus and Robertson, 1968.
Hart.   Melbourne, Nelson, 1974.
Selected Poems 1939-1975.   Melbourne, Nelson, 1976.
Pageantry for a Lost Empire.   Melbourne, Nelson, 1977.
The New City Poems.   Sydney, Angus and Robertson, 1980.

*

Critical Studies: *Preoccupations in Australian Poetry* by Judith Wright, Melbourne and London, Oxford University Press, 1965; "John Blight: An Elder Practising Poet's Point of View," in *Southerly* (Sydney), 1974; "Two Views of the Poetry of John Blight" by Bruce Beaver and David Malouf, in *Southerly* (Sydney), 1976.

John Blight comments:

I have written published poetry for over 40 years. In that time I have written as I would speak, with the difference that when I write a poem my vision is naturally heightened by aftersight, and my speech, therefore, becomes more intense. The poem pronounces with certitude upon an aspect of life. The success of the poem is relative to the acuteness of the vision.

Goethe comes closest for me in his definition of poetry—a criticism of life. If you are looking for theme in my poetry, take heed of Goethe's definition. I like to examine closely this quality of matter—life. It is simple then to become intense and excited about it—to become poetical.

In the past I have deliberately chosen the sonnet as the vehicle for my poetry. I have adapted it to suit my purpose, not deeming it relevant to conform to Elizabethan or Wordsworthian patterns. I have striven to use it allegorically rather than lyrically.

It has benefited my work by avoidance of the abstract, in concentrating illumination of the subject, holding it before one for a brief space of time like life itself.

*   *   *

In the early 1970's, nearly 30 years after his first book, John Blight's poetic career seemed established and well-understood. His was one-topic, regional, and on both counts minor poetry—poetry of the Queensland sea-coast. Distinguished contemporaries—Judith Wright and Douglas Stewart—appreciated the scope Blight found in his subject, and the vivid plainness of his talk. Still, "Becalmed," chosen by Stewart for a 1964 anthology,

shows Blight's kinship with ten-year-old work by Wright, say, and even Hope, rather than his individual touch. It goes through the motions of reasoning, to approach a dreamily-imaged metaphysical puzzle:

> "Which of us now is you, is me?"
> Everything double under the sun;
> And doubly doubled to prove which one
> Is under which, which sun above.
> "God, if the counterpart would move."
> But movement there or here is none.

For a majority of readers Blight was a one-poem poet; "Death of a Whale" was repeatedly anthologized and "set," and attempts were made in a thousand schoolrooms to beg the conclusion, for children to whom Hitler's ways with Jews were the latest but also the last example of genocide, amply bewept: "—Sorry we are, too when a child dies;/But at the immolation of a race, who cries?"

By 1968 (*My Beachcombing Days*) Blight was confirmed as Australia's most obstinate sonneteer. His were felt to be rough-hewn attempts. The sonnet in those years was well-behaved, and mostly in the hands of second-rate writers, though a much younger Queensland writer of note, Thomas Shapcott, persisted in using it. Not till six years later did Les Murray publish his notable couplet-rhymed "spiral of sonnets" on the University ("Sidere Mens Eadem Mutato"); it was another four years before John Tranter, another cult-leader, published a book of one hundred sonnets. By then, Blight had moved on. His sonnets always kept in touch with actual language and living.

Blight a decade later—a new poet! With talk in Sydney and Melbourne about "the New Poetry" it is a dangerous term, for Blight made course with no-one. Only Brisbane-based *Makar*, among "New" periodicals, published any of the poems in *Hart*. Yet with *Hart*, and his *Selected Poems* a year later, Blight broke the strait-jacket of generalizations about him. "It finished their writing when we dirtied the surf" Blight begins an unrhymed fourteen lines entitled "His Best Poems Are about the Sea." The new subject matter is personal, but also open-eyed, social, even polemic:

> I am too old to advantage myself of its beauty
> which I find now synthetic with the purchase
> of sand for its far-famed beaches, at approximately
> a dollar a grain...and those kids constantly
> riding the surf—the surfies off the headlands
> where the great grey-nurses paraded and even
> seasonal whales.
>   ...Blue, pure and beautiful!
> Blue skies of the tourist brochure, I am beginning
> to loathe that colour with its aura of beauty contests;
> seeing the winners, knowing their fuck is not far away.

Once his new work was seen in quantity, there was recognition for the strength of Blight's ambling, sometimes Frostian observations about the world's habits and happenings. Any game people play, and anything, is fit for comment—an idiomatic phrase, ship's rubbish spewed into the sea, bubbles growing and breaking, modesty, the bomb, old furniture, a plane-flight, racial prejudice, people unknown...clearly, Blight's collected poems will need an index of topics.

For Blight, his new-found poetic life has been exhilarating. All but one poem in *Pageantry for a Lost Empire* were written in one year. It is hard to say what outside factors have contributed—he is no disciple. Blight has had ready for today's Australia a habit of mind it relishes; but this is not to say he has stood still. He has emerged into freer forms; he is ready to hop, skip, and jump, to play or plod, according to the proper impulse of the poem. Blight engages large issues, often challenging the evaluation of a topic as "large" or "small"; and, caring little for the poet's dignity, he cares greatly for poetry's ("Anthology," "Burnt Poems," "The Poet at Work").

In his gusto, and the fruitful wedding of features of prose and poetry, Blight knowingly runs the risks of triviality and looseness. But his best is worth risks ("The Gold Watch"):

> I touch it
> knowing it will always last, although
> the silly little trickling minutes which coursed
> through it have passed. What-ho for Uncle! I
> remember him now. Could I beg such a monument?

or "Old Man and Tree":

> This, I gave courage as the seedling;
> now there sits a song for me on
> every bough; and longer as
> I live, companionship, shade, and
> comfort on the hottest day....

Among senior Australian poets, only David Campbell rivals Blight in his openness to life.

—Judith Rodriguez

BLY, Robert (Elwood).   American.   Born in Madison, Minnesota, 23 December 1926. Educated at St. Olaf College, Northfield, Minnesota, 1946-47; Harvard University, Cambridge, Massachusetts, B.A. (magna cum laude) 1950; University of Iowa, Iowa City, M.A. 1956. Served in the United States Naval Reserve, 1944-46. Married 1) Carolyn McLean in 1955 (divorced, 1980), four children; 2) Ruth Counsell Ray in 1981. Founding Editor, since 1958, *The Fifties* magazine (later *The Sixties* and *The Seventies*), and the Fifties Press (later The Sixties and The Seventies Press), Madison, Minnesota. Recipient: Fulbright Fellowship, 1956; Amy Lowell Traveling Fellowship, 1964; Guggenheim Fellowship, 1964, 1972; American Academy grant, 1965; Rockefeller Fellowship, 1967; National Book Award, 1968. Address: 308 First Street, Moose Lake, Minnesota 55767, U.S.A.

PUBLICATIONS

Verse

The Lion's Tail and Eyes: Poems Written Out of Laziness and Silence, with James Wright and William Duffy.   Madison, Minnesota, Sixties Press, 1962.
Silence in the Snowy Fields.   Middletown, Connecticut, Wesleyan University Press, 1962; London, Cape, 1967.
The Light Around the Body.   New York, Harper, 1967; London, Rapp and Whiting, 1968.
Chrysanthemums.   Menomenie, Wisconsin, Ox Head Press, 1967.
Ducks.   Menomenie, Wisconsin, Ox Head Press, 1968.
The Morning Glory: Another Thing That Will Never Be My Friend: Twelve Prose Poems.   San Francisco, Kayak, 1969;

revised edition, 1970; complete version, New York, Harper, 1975.
The Teeth Mother Naked at Last.   San Francisco, City Lights, 1970.
Poems for Tennessee, with William Stafford and William Matthews.   Martin, Tennessee Poetry Press, 1971.
Water under the Earth.   Rushden, Northamptonshire, Sceptre Press, 1972.
Christmas Eve Service at Midnight at St. Michael's.   Rushden, Northamptonshire, Sceptre Press, 1972.
Jumping Out of Bed.   Barre, Massachusetts, Barre, 1973.
Sleepers Joining Hands.   New York, Harper, 1973.
The Dead Seal near McClure's Beach.   Rushden, Northamptonshire, Sceptre Press, 1973.
The Hockey Poem.   Duluth, Minnesota, Knife River Press, 1974.
Point Reyes Poems.   San Francisco, Mudra, 1974.
Grass from Two Years, Let's Leave.   Denver, Ally Press, 1975.
Old Man Rubbing His Eyes.   Greensboro, North Carolina, Unicorn Press, 1975.
The Loon.   Marshall, Minnesota, Ox Head Press, 1977.
This Body Is Made of Camphor and Gopherwood: Prose Poems.   New York, Harper, 1977.
This Tree Will Be Here for a Thousand Years.   New York, Harper, 1979.
Visiting Emily Dickinson's Grave and Other Poems.   Madison, Wisconsin, Red Ozier Press, 1979.
The Man in the Black Coat Turns.   New York, Dial Press, 1981.
Finding an Old Ant Mansion.   Bedford, Martin Booth, 1981.
The Eight Stages of Translation.   Boston, Rowan Tree, 1983.
Four Ramages.   Daleville, Indiana, Barnwood Press, 1983.
Out of the Rolling Ocean.   New York, Dial Press, 1984.

Recording: *Today's Poets 5*, with others, Folkways.

Other

A Broadsheet Against the New York Times Book Review.   Madison, Minnesota, Sixties Press, 1961.
Talking All Morning: Collected Conversations and Interviews.   Ann Arbor, University of Michigan Press, 1979.

Editor, with David Ray, *A Poetry Reading Against the Vietnam War.*   Madison, Minnesota, American Writers Against the Vietnam War, 1966.
Editor, *The Sea and the Honeycomb: A Book of Poems.*   Madison, Minnesota, Sixties Press, 1966.
Editor, *Forty Poems Touching on Recent American History.*   Boston, Beacon Press, 1970.
Editor, *Leaping Poetry: An Idea with Poems and Translations.*   Boston, Beacon Press, 1975.
Editor, *Selected Poems*, by David Ignatow.   Middletown, Connecticut, Wesleyan University Press, 1975.
Editor, *News of the Universe: Poems of Twofold Consciousness.*   San Francisco, Sierra Club, 1980.

Translator, *The Illustrated Book about Reptiles and Amphibians of the World*, by Hans Hvass.   New York, Grosset and Dunlap, 1960.
Translator, with James Wright, *Twenty Poems of Georg Trakl.*   Madison, Minnesota, Sixties Press, 1961.
Translator, *The Story of Gösta Berling*, by Selma Lagerlöf.   New York, New American Library, 1962.
Translator, with James Wright and John Knoepfle, *Twenty*

Poems of César Vallejo. Madison, Minnesota, Sixties Press, 1962.

Translator, with Eric Sellin and Thomas Buckman, *Three Poems*, by Tomas Tranströmer. Lawrence, Kansas, T. Williams, 1966.

Translator, *Hunger*, by Knut Hamsun. New York, Farrar Straus, 1967; London, Duckworth, 1974.

Translator, with Christina Paulston, *I Do Best Alone at Night*, by Gunnar Ekelöf. Washington, D.C., Charioteer Press, 1967.

Translator, with Christina Paulston, *Late Arrival on Earth: Selected Poems of Gunnar Ekelöf.* London, Rapp and Carroll, 1967.

Translator, with others, *Selected Poems*, by Yvan Goll. San Francisco, Kayak, 1968.

Translator, with James Wright, *Twenty Poems of Pablo Neruda.* Madison, Minnesota, Sixties Press, and London, Rapp and Whiting, 1968.

Translator, *Forty Poems of Juan Ramón Jiménez.* Madison, Minnesota, Sixties Press, 1969.

Translator, *Ten Poems*, by Issa Kobayashi. Privately printed, 1969.

Translator, with James Wright and John Knoepfle, *Neruda and Vallejo: Selected Poems.* Boston, Beacon Press, 1971.

Translator, *Twenty Poems of Tomas Tranströmer. Madison, Minnesota, Seventies Press, 1971.*

Translator, The Fish in the Sea Is Not Thirsty: Versions of Kabir. Itahaca, New York, Lillabulero Press, 1971.

Translator, *Night Vision*, by Tomas Tranströmer. Ithaca, New York, Lillabulero Press, 1971; London, London Magazine Editions, 1972.

Translator, *Ten Sonnets to Orpheus*, by Rainer Maria Rilke. San Francisco, Sephyrus Image, 1972.

Translator, *Lorca and Jiménez: Selected Poems.* Boston, Beacon Press, 1973.

Translator, *Elegy, Some October Notes*, by Tomas Tranströmer. Rushden, Northamptonshire, Sceptre Press, 1973.

Translator, *Basho.* San Francisco, Mudra, 1974.

Translator, *Friends, You Drank Some Darkness: Three Swedish Poets, Henry Martinson, Gunnar Ekelöf, Tomas Tranströmer.* Boston, Beacon Press, 1975.

Translator, *Grass from Two Years*, by Kabir. Denver, Ally Press, 1975.

Translator, *Twenty-Eight Poems*, by Kabir. New York, Siddha Yoga Dham, 1975.

Translator, *Try to Live to See This! Versions of Kabir.* Rushden, Northamptonshire, Sceptre Press, and Denver, Ally Press, 1976.

Translator, *The Kabir Book.* Boston, Beacon Press, 1977.

Translator, *The Voices*, by Rainer Maria Rilke. Knotting, Bedfordshire, Sceptre Press, and Denver, Ally Press, 1977.

Translator, with Lewis Hyde, *Twenty Poems of Vicente Aleixandre.* Madison, Minnesota, Seventies Press, 1977.

Translator, *Twenty Poems of Rolf Jacobson.* Madison, Minnesota, Seventies Press, 1977.

Translator, *Mirabai Versions.* New York, Red Ozier Press, 1980.

Translator, *I Am Too Alone in the World*, by Rainer Maria Rilke. New York, Silver Hands Press, 1980.

Translator, *Canciones*, by Antonio Machado. West Branch, Iowa, Toothpaste Press, 1980.

Translator, *Truth Barriers*, by Tomas Tranströmer. San Francisco, Sierra Club, 1980.

Translator, *Selected Poems*, by Rainer Maria Rilke. New York, Harper, 1981.

Translator, with Coleman Barks, *Night and Sleep*, by Rumi.

Cambridge, Massachusetts, Yellow Moon Press, 1981.

Translator, with Will Kirkland, *Selected Poems and Prose*, by Antonio Machado. Buffalo, White Pine Press, 1983.

Translator, *Times Alone: Selected Poems of Antonio Machado.* Middletown, Connecticut, Wesleyan University Press, 1983.

*

Bibliography: "Robert Bly Checklist" by Sandy Dorbin, in *Schist 1* (Willimantic, Connecticut), Fall 1973.

Critical Studies: *Alone with America* by Richard Howard, New York, Atheneum, 1969, London, Thames and Hudson, 1970, revised edition, Atheneum, 1980; *The Inner War: Forms and Themes in Recent American Poetry* by Paul A. Lacey, Philadelphia, Fortress Press, 1972; "Robert Bly Alive in Darkness" by Anthony Libby, in *Iowa Review* (Iowa City), Summer 1972; "Robert Bly: Radical Poet" by Michael True, in *Win* (Rifton, New York), 15 January 1973; *Four Poets and the Emotive Imagination* by Ronald Moran and George Lensing, Baton Rouge, Louisiana State University Press, 1976; *Moving Inward: A Study of Robert Bly's Poetry* by Ingegerd Friberg, Gothenburg, Gothenburg Studies in English, 1977; Charles Molesworth, in *Ohio Review* (Athens), Fall 1978; *Of Solitude and Silence: Writings on Robert Bly* edited by Kate Daniels and Richard Jones, Boston, Beacon Press, 1982; *Robert Bly: An Introduction to the Poetry* by Howard Nelson, New York, Columbia University Press, 1984; "In Search of an American Muse" by the author, in *The New York Times Book Review*, 22 January 1984.

*   *   *

Robert Bly emerged from the early 1960's as one of the more stubbornly independent and critical poets of his generation, boldly stating positions against war and corporate monopoly, broadening federal powers, crassness in literature wherever forums were open to him. He was a dominating spokesman for anti-war groups during the Vietnam War, staging readings around the United States and compiling (with David Ray) extraordinary poetic protests in the anthology *A Poetry Reading Against the Vietnam War.* Throughout his career, he has been a cranky but refreshing influence on American thought and culture, as much for the grandeur of his positions as for the force of his artistic individuality.

Although Bly's output has been relatively small in an era of prolific poets, his books follow a deliberate course of deepening conviction and broader conceptions. *Silence in the Snowy Fields*, his first book, is a slender collection of polished, mildly surreal evocations of his life in Minnesota and of the northwestern landscape, with its harsh winters and huddled townships. Bly's brief poems impute to nature a secret, willful life-force, as in this final stanza from "Snowfall in the Afternoon":

> The barn is full of corn, and moving toward us now,
> Like a hulk blown toward us in a storm at sea:
> All the sailors on deck have been blind for many years.

Silence in the Snowy Fields has an immediacy of the poet's personal life that reflects the inward shift of poetry during the late 1950's and early 1960's, a direction that Bly then actively retreated from, claiming poetry deserved a larger frame of experience than the poet's own circumstances and private dilemmas.

The Light Around the Body moves into the political and social arena with poems against corporate power and profiteering, presidential politics, and the Vietnam War. These poems are more boldly imaginative and take reckless leaps into a surreal mode of discourse. The poems fuse together the banal and the bizarre: "Accountants hover over the earth like helicopters,/ Dropping bits of paper engraved with Hegel's name" ("A Dream of Suffocation") and "Filaments of death grow out./The sheriff cuts off his black legs/and nails them to a tree" ("War and Silence").

To explain his poetic and to give it context, Bly edited an interesting volume of poems entitled *Leaping Poetry* where he argued that consciousness had now expanded to a new faculty of the brain where spiritual and supralogical awareness is stored. His commentary is wonderfully speculative and vivid, but bluffly assertive of its premise. A subsequent elaboration of this thesis appears in the essay, "I Came Out of the Mother Naked," included in the book of poems *Sleepers Joining Hands*, where he suggests that society is now returning to a matriarchal order, in which sensuous awareness and synthetic reason will replace the old patriarchal emphasis on rationality and analysis. *The Kabir Book*, Bly's translations of the 15th-century Indian mystic, are, in Lowell's sense, imitations of the work of a poet who "leaps" in his poetry and manifests the androgynous sensibility Bly has championed recently.

In the prose poems of *This Body Is Made of Camphor and Gopherwood* Bly has become a master of his own sensuous self-awareness, creating in a dreamy language states of consciousness that unite self and nature, mind and viscera. The illustrations of Gendron Jensen show a snail shell progressively turning through a single revolution, just as the poems appear to turn round for us the human inner life through a revolution of emotions. Bly seems to have found a means of linking primal thought to contemporary verse, and the resulting lyric is profoundly moving.

Bly continues to read poetry on the university circuit and to translate Scandinavian literature as his livelihood, but even in these facets of his life he has rooted his new convictions. His readings are now made dramatic with primitive masks, chanting, and extemporaneous lectures on the new mind he feels is remaking the culture of the West.

—Paul Christensen

BOER, Charles. American. Born in Cleveland, Ohio, 25 June 1939. Educated at Western Reserve University, Cleveland, 1957-61, A.B. 1961; University of Florence (Fulbright Fellow), 1961-62; Harvard University, Cambridge, Massachusetts (Woodrow Wilson Fellow, 1962-63); State University of New York, Buffalo, 1963-66, Ph.D. in comparative literature 1967. Assistant Professor, 1966-70, Associate Professor, 1970-75, and since 1975, Professor of English, University of Connecticut, Storrs. Recipient: Swallow Press New Poetry Series Award, 1969. Address: Box 69, Pomfret Center, Connecticut 06258, U.S.A.

PUBLICATIONS

Verse

The Odes. Chicago, Swallow Press, 1969.
Varmint Q.: An Epic Poem on the Life of William Clarke Quantrill. Chicago, Swallow Press, 1972.

Other

Charles Olson in Connecticut (biography). Chicago, Swallow Press, 1975.

Editor, with George F. Butterick, *The Maximus Poems of Charles Olson, Volume Three.* New York, Grossman, 1975.

Translator, *The Homeric Hymns.* Chicago, Swallow Press, 1971; revised edition, Dallas, Spring, 1979.
Translator, *The Bacchae of Euripides*, in *An Anthology of Greek Tragedy*. Indianapolis, Bobbs Merrill, 1972.
Translator, *The Book of Life*, by Marsilio Ficino. Dallas, Spring, 1980.

*   *   *

Classicist Charles Boer puts the ancient forms of ode and epic, now largely fallen into disuse, in the service of perennial themes of war, love, and loss, but with a contemporary mood. Predominantly serious in tone, his score of irregular odes follow English tradition in variety but favor fragmentary colloquialism in grammatical structure. In apostrophes to sea nymphs, movie stars, a Wagnerian soprano, in scenes of wartime Europe and a nameless French river, classical allusions resonate within the matrix of the modern idiom. Unhampered by frequent punctuation, run-on lines drive a sometimes breathless lyric, while ambiguity and repetition give phrase and verse an oracular air, though at the price of dissipating force by frequently choppy caesurae and by strained and jerky syntax. Eschewing the confessional mode, Boer's lines lack the precision and polish of Allen Tate's and the charm of Frank O'Hara's. Individual images—petals and the four elements, especially fiery sun and timeless ocean, are his favorites—strike vividly, but the impression is often blunted by a nebulous context or a too-sudden shift of subject. Classical metaphor can control by maintaining distance, but it can also mask the personal. When the difficult or obscure is avoided, and the poet speaks directly, as in "The Water Ode," his voice is more affecting.

Varmint Q., "an epic poem on the life of William Clarke Quantrill," mocks epic conventions with wry humor but fits more comfortably with picaresque fiction. The history and myth of Q., alias Charley Hart, alias Capt. Quantrill, of the "peculiar eyes" are told through poetry interlarded with the sometimes semi-literate narratives and letters of his accomplices and antagonists, forming a novelistic composite of contrasting points-of-view. Boer sets the ironic tone with "An Invocation to John Greenleaf Whittier As an Aside" and with a genealogy of Q.'s fraudulent, forging kin (incidentally having Mary Quantrill snatch from the "old gray head" of Barbara Frietchie, Whittier's heroine, the honor of saving the flag at Frederick). In contrast to Whittier's high-toned narratives, Boer portrays the violent career of a juvenile delinquent whose sadistic tendencies held him in good stead as Indian-fighter, Civil War guerilla, and tutor of Cole Younger and the James Boys. Q.'s own letters to his mother reveal a poetic sensibility, unfortunately belied by ox-theft, gambling, attempted and successful murder, among other things. Having fun with folklore, Boer plays ironic counterpoint throughout by recounting conflicting reports of Q.'s treacherous exploits (for example, he helps the Underground Railroad steal slaves to freedom then sells them back, after setting up the massacre of the Abolitionists) and by adding a descant of asides and rhetorical questions. Spurred on by his adulterous muse, Annie Walker (invoked under her other name, A. Slaughter), Q.'s odyssey surveys the deadly life of the Western underworld, in which the scoundrel-hero can and does take both sides. Even the epic "game" is disreputable, a horse race in which Q.'s filthy steed wins by a mile, and a ruse. In his final madness, Q. offers as a hecatomb the massacre and burning of Lawrence, Kansas, and he dreams of assassinating Lincoln. Ill-omened and too late for that, he dies ingloriously, but not without the poet's reflections on the demise of the wild West by urbanization and on the making of an American myth.

—Joseph Parisi

BOLD, Alan (Norman). Scottish. Born in Edinburgh, 20 April 1943. Educated at Broughton Secondary School, Edinburgh; Edinburgh University (travelling scholarship in fine art, 1964), 1961-65. Married Alice Howell in 1963; one daughter. Editor, *Gambit*, 1963, 1965, and *Rocket*, 1965-66, Edinburgh; member of the editorial staff, *Times Educational Supplement*, London, 1966-67. Recipient: Scottish Arts Council bursary, 1967, 1974, 1979. Address: Balbirnie Burns East Cottage, near Markinch, Fife KY7 6NE, Scotland.

PUBLICATIONS

Verse

Society Inebrious. Edinburgh, Mowat Hamilton, 1965.
The Voyage, adaptation of a poem by Baudelaire. Edinburgh, M. Macdonald, 1966.
To Find the New. London, Chatto and Windus-Hogarth Press, 1967; Middletown, Connecticut, Wesleyan University Press, 1968.
A Perpetual Motion Machine. London, Chatto and Windus-Hogarth Press, and Middletown, Connecticut, Wesleyan University Press, 1969.
Penguin Modern Poets 15, with Edward Kamau Brathwaite and Edwin Morgan. London, Penguin, 1969.
The State of the Nation. London, Chatto and Windus-Hogarth Press, and Middletown, Connecticut, Wesleyan University Press, 1969.
He Will Be Greatly Missed: A Poem. London, Turret, 1971.
The Auld Symie (as Jake Flower). Preston, Lancashire, Akros, 1971.
A Century of People. London, Academy, 1971.
A Pint of Bitter. London, Chatto and Windus, and Middletown, Connecticut, Wesleyan University Press, 1971.
A Lunar Event: A Poem and a Drawing. Richmond, Surrey, Keepsake Press, 1973.
Scotland, Yes: World Cup Football Poems. Edinburgh, Paul Harris, 1978.
This Fine Day. Dunfermline, Fife, Borderline Press, 1979.
A Celtic Quintet, with John Bellany. Balbirnie, Fife, Balbirnie Editions, 1983.
In This Corner: Selected Poems 1963-1983. Edinburgh, M. Macdonald, 1983.
Haven, with John Bellany. Balbirnie, Fife, Balbirnie Editions, 1984.
Summoned by Knox. Paisley, Wilfion, 1984.

Short Stories

Hammer and Thistle, with David Morrison. Wick, Caithness Books, 1974.

The Edge of the Wood. Barr, Ayrshire, Luath Press, 1984.

Other

Art and Action (lecture). London, Peter Moran, 1965.
Bonnie Prince Charlie. London, Pitkin Pictorials, 1973.
Robert Burns. London, Pitkin Pictorials, 1973.
Scottish Clans. London, Pitkin Pictorials, 1973.
Thom Gunn and Ted Hughes. Edinburgh, Oliver and Boyd, 1976.
Mary Queen of Scots. Hove, Sussex, Wayland, 1977.
Scottish Tartans. London, Pitkin Pictorials, 1978.
Robert the Bruce. London, Pitkin Pictorials, 1978.
George Mackay Brown. Edinburgh, Oliver and Boyd, and Totowa, New Jersey, Barnes and Noble, 1978.
The Ballad. London, Methuen, 1979.
Scotland's Kings and Queens. London, Pitkin Pictorials, 1980.
The Palace of Holyroodhouse. London, Pitkin Pictorials, 1980.
The Sensual Scot. Edinburgh, Paul Harris, 1982.
MacDiarmid: The Terrible Crystal. London, Routledge, 1983.
Modern Scottish Literature. London, Longman, 1983.
True Characters, with Robert Giddings. London, Longman, 1983.
The Book of Rotters, with Robert Giddings. Edinburgh, Mainstream, 1984.

Editor, *The Penguin Book of Socialist Verse.* London, Penguin, 1970.
Editor, *Cambridge Book of English Verse 1939-1975.* Cambridge, University Press, 1976.
Editor, *The Martial Muse: Seven Centuries of War Poetry.* Exeter, Wheaton, 1976.
Editor, *Making Love: The Picador Book of Erotic Verse.* London, Pan, 1978.
Editor, *The Bawdy Beautiful: The Sphere Book of Improper Verse.* London, Sphere, 1979.
Editor, *Mounts of Venus: The Picador Book of Erotic Verse.* London, Pan, 1980.
Editor, *Drink to Me Only: The Prose (and Cons) of Drinking.* London, Robin Clark, 1982.
Editor, *Smollett: Author of the First Dimension.* London, Vision Press, 1982; Totowa, New Jersey, Barnes and Noble, 1983.
Editor, *The Sexual Dimension in Literature.* London, Vision Press, 1982.
Editor, *A Scottish Poetry Book* (and *Second* book). Oxford, Oxford University Press, 2 vols., 1983-84.
Editor, *Sir Walter Scott: The Long-Forgotten Melody.* London, Vision Press, and Totowa, New Jersey, Barnes and Noble, 1983.
Editor, *Byron: Wrath and Rhyme.* London, Vision Press, and Totowa, New Jersey, Barnes and Noble, 1983.
Editor, *The Thistle Rises: A MacDiarmid Miscellany.* London, Hamish Hamilton, 1984.
Editor, *MacDiarmid: Aesthetics in Scotland.* Edinburgh, Mainstream, 1984.
Editor, *The Letters of Hugh MacDiarmid.* London, Hamish Hamilton, 1984.
Editor, *The Poetry of Motion.* Edinburgh, Mainstream, 1984.
Editor, *Muriel Spark: An Odd Capacity for Vision.* London, Vision Press, and Totowa, New Jersey, Barnes and Noble, 1984.
Editor, *Harold Pinter: You Never Heard Such Silence.* London, Vision Press, and Totowa, New Jersey, Barnes and Noble, 1984.

*

Manuscript Collection: National Library of Scotland, Edinburgh; Edinburgh University Library.

Critical Studies: "Poet in Search of a Public" by Philip Oakes, in *Sunday Times* (London), 8 February 1970; "Labours of a Prodigious Wordsmith" by Harry Reid, in *Glasgow Herald*, 8 August 1983; *Companion to Scottish Literature* by Trevor Royle, London, Macmillan, 1983.

Alan Bold comments:

(1970) I am mainly concerned in my poems to explore the insights made available to modern man through scientific research and political change. However, I do not limit myself to one type of poem such as the discursive epic or the short satirical poem. I believe that modern poetry should be judged by the same rigorous standards we apply to the literature of the past and consequently I have made it my business to equip myself with the full range of poetic forms. In this way I am able to emphasise thematic unity by the use of formal variety. Most modern poetry is timid, pretentious, incompetent, and inadequate. I would like to see instead of the present fashions—confessional verse, concrete poetry, etc.—a poetry of precision which tested the authenticity of its emotion against the observable world of fact. I want poetry to be more ambitious than the novel and the play and to win a new mass audience. And I would like to contribute to this process.

(1974) When I look at my statement in the 1970 edition it seems to suggest that poetry is simply a mechanical process of perfecting a technique and then applying it to all and sundry subjects. I now see that technical expertise is but a beginning and that it can never be fully attained, as each *real* poem demands its own particular technical as well as emotional solution. Thus my poetry has become more experimental (using the word in its scientific sense as the exploration of possibilities, not its lit. crit. sense) and more personal as I feel less inclined to pontificate on the world and more sure of my own feelings. Not that I intend to produce a self-pitying form of versified pessimism but I am now more likely to create a poem in and through personally meaningful language whereas before I would think of something to say and then execute it in poetry. I still feel contemporary English poetry (and that includes Scottish poetry in English, of course) is inadequate: a safety-first response to life in timid and academically acceptable phraseology. I want to write poems that have a life of their own and that reflect life in general and not books or other men's styles. Probably the most significant recent development in my books has been my entry into the visual field. In 1972 I had six exhibitions: of etchings, drawings, paintings, and Illuminated Poems. These Illuminated Poems are a combination of original manuscript and watercolour illustration.

(1980) Since making the above statements (which ring together with the absolutist chime of a final Credo) I have discarded my urban environment and come to terms with rural life in a cottage in a Dantean wood in Fife. The impact of this change has been vital; giving me a new lease of creative life. Coming to live in Balbirnie was, in many ways, a revolutionary experience for me. Before that, like most urban poets from Baudelaire downwards, I was expected to produce work that was personal to the point of solipsism—the city as mere backdrop to the historic and omnipotent "I"—and deracinated to the point of vacuity. Now I feel a part of (not apart from) a total process of growth and natural creativity. As a result my poetry is no longer a matter of factual statement but a question of suggestion. Altogether more sensuous, more integrated, more joyous. I still regard poetry as the most *memorable* form of literature; an artistic idiom that gives full scope to inventive ingenuity, inspirational insights, and technical expertise. But in the past I was conscious of a desire to display the structural complexity of a poem whereas now my priority is the achievement of a natural fluency so that the poems, at their best, speak eloquently for themselves.

(1985) The more one writes poetry—and on reflection I've been producing poems for about 20 years—the more one realises that no single statement can define the poetic aspirations of any individual. Whatever the poet says is liable to be a rationalisation and the poetry will, thankfully, speak for itself. So I recognise the mood of different moments in my previous statements and know they take little account of the sense of mystery I acknowledge in my creative work. For example, I end my poem "Natural" on an enigmatic tercet:

> Suddenly rain falls and the landscape is drenched,
> Suddenly a million possibilities are launched:
> I look at my hands, my fists are clenched.

Critically, I still have strong opinions about the nature of verse. I deplore spurious fashions in poetry, especially when these reinforce a school of poets who concentrate on being as prosaic as possible. Poetry depends on being an extraordinary verbal creation so it should always be ostentatiously exceptional, should rise majestically to every occasion. Poetry needs to shine with a lyrical lustre but it also needs an informative foundation so the reader can relate to intellectual as well as emotional aspects of the poet. The best poetry—at least the poetry I like best—avoids fragmentation into different modes such as lyrical, descriptive, confessional, narrative, and so on. It is technically adroit and reaches out from the isolation of the individual to embrace, theoretically, the whole of humanity. Too many poets are content to moan about a personal predicament and are unable, or unwilling, to make individual variations on a major theme—which is what poets should accept as a creative priority. I now feel that all my poems are essentially part of a lifelong sequence affirming the continuity of the creative life. Which is why, in my poem "Markinch Hill," I say:

> And though the earth
> Is older than it was
> And though the birdsong now
> Competes with the passing train
> I know this moment is forever,
> I know it will come round again.

*   *   *

Alan Bold was brought up in a "typically anti-social, anti-cultural working class environment," as he described it, which he categorises as "an oppressive prison." His resistance to this condition is the basic motivation of his poetry. The title of his first collection of poetry, *Society Inebrious*, describes the characteristic response of the "prisoners" to their social condition. At the age of 22 Bold had embarked on creating a poetry of social protest. In his second book, *To Find the New*, he wrote: "Damn it!/Our voices are not made for singing now/But for straight talking." There were good precedents for a declaratory poetry in the Scottish literary tradition from Dunbar to MacDiarmid, the vitality of the tradition being ensured by the Scots tongue, a more communal vehicle than English. Bold's poetry of protest, however, has been made in English, which has put his large utterances at risk. Such lines as

> When
> Was the world more in need of poetry?
> Real poetry—the kind that sings
> The facts and yells the truth

presume an effect which their rhetoric fails to carry, while there is the presumption of youth in the didacticism of "I come with a message on the state of the nation/on the definition of our moment," which begins Bold's book-long poem *The State of the Nation*. The blurb for the poem claims: "An enormous variety of moods, verse-techniques and subjects are interwoven and sustained to re-create for the reader an impression of the epic potential of a world increasingly perceived as a single nation." This focuses attention on an effect which is not achieved, but several passages witness to a vigorous intelligence which has already absorbed a wide range of literary experience—a mind impatiently seeking out a rationale which will take account of the cruelties and distortions to life of which Bold is acutely conscious. When that mind moves from the hortatory to deal with given, particular experience, in some cases painful experience, it has the necessary detachment, and poetic technique. I have in mind the admirable tragic poem "A Memory of Death," a narrative of the death of his father. The death is seen through several perspectives. The poet begins by placing it in a historical perspective: "Nineteen fifty six was a momentous year,/The year of Suez and Hungary and the death/Of my father. I was thirteen. He was forty-nine." Here are firmness, courage, and compassion—the right words in the right place. As impressive as the straight telling is the shifting context provided by voices off in the form of interpolations in prose, one officially recording the death, others being passages from letters of sympathy.

There are other achievements in the area of portrayal, such as "Old Neil," the ironic, competent "Portrait of Norbert," and "That's Life" about the death of a tramp in Princes Street, Edinburgh, in which the suppressed rage of the writer against the indifference of society comes through. It is a poem after the style of MacDiarmid, though Bold has made it his own. These three poems appear in *To Find the New*. Even so the tendency to use a spent idiom in the presence of the "great event" has not been eradicated by 1969, in which year a fine poem, "1 June at Buchenwald" (in *A Perpetual Motion Machine*), was flawed by such lines as, "We are not helpless/Creatures crashing onwards irresistibly to doom." But the range of experience under control by this date has widened. "A Memory of Death" is in this collection, and also a charming "Dedicatory Poem, For my daughter, Valentina," which has these lines:

> The earth turns round and tells that our
>   Precarious point in space
> Is not forever—but these sour
> Predictions vanish every hour
>   We chatter face to face.

Once Bold has used a form—and the variety is wide—it will return with variants. In a little anthology, *Poets and Peasants* (1978), there is this stanza in Bold's poem "Poverty":

> Poverty is a dank and darkened room
> Situated almost anywhere;
> There is a stench in the gloom
> And you can taste despair.

Social concern remains the prime consideration, but the approaches to it run from tender feeling for the disadvantaged to comic portrayals. He puts himself at the centre of a comic, ironic fantasy in "The Day I Committed..." (suicide) (in *A Pint of Bitter*). The flow and rhyming of the poem are exhilarating, but a serious attack is being made on a society which will not support real values. Bold's comic creation of the town councillor—"He will be greatly missed"—whose bigotry extends to the football team he supports, who "Whistles green whistles, shouts green shouts," exhibits a characteristic form of Scottish, myopic mindlessness. To create poetry from such roughage is no small achievement—and Bold feels for and against this society. To judge by Bold's statements, he may not have cast himself in the role of an interpreter of character and a creator of characters, but his main contribution to literature may be along these lines.

Yet since 1978 a different poetic persona has developed. He has responded to the natural beauty of his home in the Fife countryside, to which he had moved from Edinburgh, with a sensuous, delicate poetry. In this setting he places his wife:

> And you sat beside me near the lake
> you walked with me by the little pond
> together we drifted among the teaming leaves.

This is far removed from the propagandist writer. The character of a more reflective verse is evident in the new poems of Bold's collection, *In This Corner: Selected Poems 1963-1983*. He looks out from Markinch Hill:

> I stand on the hill
> That stands on delicate sand
> And stones smoothed by rain
> And think of how, in Autumn,
> Agricola's soldiers watched the earth
> Covering up in cones
> And sweet chestnut seeds;
> Saw leaves from the oak,
> From the beech, from the sycamore,
> Fall from the trees
> To glide and tumble down
> Six Roman terraces;
> Six levels made homely
> By tramping Roman feet.

The direct, simple speech, without any reaching after effects, indicates the presence of a concerned, sometimes passionate, mind, which in other recent poems continues to evaluate social issues.

—George Bruce

BOOTH, Martin. British. Born near Longridge, Lancashire, 7 September 1944. Educated at King George V School, Hong Kong; Trent Park College of Education (now Enfield Polytechnic), Barnet, Hertfordshire, Cert. Ed. 1968. Married Helen Barber in 1968; one son and one daughter. Taught in secondary schools, 1968-84. Schoolmaster Fellow, St. Peter's College, Oxford, 1971-74; Visiting Writer, University of Nebraska, Lincoln, 1978, and University of New Hampshire, Durham, 1979; Fellow Commoner, Corpus Christi College, Cambridge, 1981; Visiting Writer, University of Miami, Coral Gables, Florida, 1982. Founder, 1968, and since 1983, Managing Editor, Sceptre Press Ltd., Frensham, Surrey, later Rushden, Northamptonshire, and Knotting, Bedfordshire. Former Editor, Fuller d'Arch Smith Ltd. and Omphalos Press, London. Critic and reviewer, *Tribune* and *British Book News*, London, and *Pacific Quarterly*. Secretary, Poets Workshop, London, 1967-72; Member of the Executive and General councils, Poetry Society, London, 1968-74. Recipient: Guinness Award, 1970; Eric Gregory Award, 1971; Greenwood Prize, 1971. Fellow, Royal Society of Literature, 1980. Agent: A.M. Heath, 40-42 William IV Street, London WC2N 4DD, England.

PUBLICATIONS

Verse

Paper Pennies and Other Poems.   Privately printed, 1967.
Supplication to the Himalayas.   Frensham, Surrey, Sceptre Press, 1968.
In the Yenan Caves.   Frensham, Surrey, Sceptre Press, 1969.
The Borrowed Gull; After Virginia Woolf.   Frensham, Surrey, Sceptre Press, 1970.
A Winnowing of Silence.   Richmond, Surrey, Keepsake Press, 1971.
The Crying Embers.   London, Fuller d'Arch Smith, 1971.
Pilgrims and Petitions.   Birmingham, Aquila, 1972.
On the Death of Archbishop Broix.   Cardiff, Second Aeon, 1972.
Nature Study.   St. Ives, Cornwall, Poetry St. Ives, 1972.
Teller.   London, Poet and Printer, 1972.
Coronis.   St. Brelade, Jersey, Channel Islands, Andium Press, 1973.
In Her Hands.   Rushden, Northamptonshire, Sceptre Press, 1973.
Spawning the Os.   Feltham, Middlesex, Quarto, 1974.
Yogh.   Denver, Ally Press, 1974.
Brevities.   New Rochelle, New York, Elizabeth Press, 1974.
Snath.   London, Oasis, 1975.
Two Boys and a Girl, Playing in the Churchyard.   Hitchin, Hertfordshire, Mandeville Press, 1975.
Hands Twining Grasses.   Godalming, Surrey, Words Press, 1975.
Stalks of Jade.   London, Menard Press, 1976.
Rider and Horse.   Richmond, Surrey, Keepsake Press, 1976.
The Knotting Sequence.   New Rochelle, New York, Elizabeth Press, 1977.
The Dying: In Memoriam A.L.P.   Knotting, Bedfordshire, Sceptre Press, 1978.
Extending upon the Kingdom.   London, Poets Yearbook, 1978.
The Earth Man Dreams of a Turned Sod.   Higham Ferrers, Northamptonshire, Greylag Press, 1978.
The Cnot Dialogues.   New Rochelle, New York, Elizabeth Press, 1979.
Winter's Night, Knotting.   Knotting, Bedfordshire, Sceptre Press, 1979.
Devils' Wine.   Gerrards Cross, Buckinghamshire, Colin Smythe, 1980.
Meeting the Snowy North Again.   London, Fuller d'Arch Smith, 1982.
Missile Summer.   Bradford, Rivelin Press, 1982.
Looking for the Rainbow: Poems of America.   Newcastle upon Tyne, Bloodaxe, 1983.
Killing the Moscs.   Durham, Taxus Press, 1984.

Plays

Television Scripts (juvenile): *John of Badsaddle, Mary Mad, The Claw of Mammon, Beth and the Hand of Glory, The Winter Warrior,* 1976-78; *The Dolphin Touch,* 1982.

Novels

The Carrier.   London, W.H. Allen, 1978.
The Bad Track.   London, Collins, 1980.

Other

White Bat (juvenile).   London, Macmillan, 1974.
Travelling Through the Senses: A Critical Study of the Poetry of George MacBeth.   Portree, Isle of Skye, Aquila, 1984.
Driving Through the Barricades: British Poetry 1964-1984.   London, Routledge, 1985.

Editor, *Unpublished Poems and Drafts of James Elroy Flecker.*   Richmond, Surrey, Keepsake Press, 1971.
Editor, with George MacBeth, *The Book of Cats.*   London, Secker and Warburg, 1976; New York, Morrow, 1977.
Editor, *Decadal: Ten Years of Sceptre Press.*   Knotting, Bedfordshire, Sceptre Press, 1979.
Editor, *Contemporary British and North American Verse: An Introductory Anthology.*   Oxford, Oxford University Press, 1981.

*

Manuscript Collections: National Manuscript Collection, University of Birmingham; University of New Hampshire, Durham.

Critical Studies: in *Palantir* (Preston, Lancashire), March 1977, May 1978.

*   *   *

From the start of his literary career Martin Booth had a fine command of language and an ear for rhythm and music. In many of his early poems his style was very compressed and elliptic. He was inclined to leave too much to the reader. Despite his remarkable descriptive and lyrical gifts, many of the separate pieces seemed like extracts from a longer sequence, so that, read in isolation, they failed to make the impact they might otherwise have had. One must obviously exclude from this generalisation such admirable poems as "Cathedral Starlings," "Hunt," "The Black Cranes" and "Dismissal at the Building of the Tower of Babel."

With the publication of *The Crying Embers* his intentions became a good deal clearer and it is possible to discern the unity of his work, which draws substantially on dream imagery. The best thing in this volume is "Orbis Picture," a series of emblem poems based upon woodcuts from Comenius's pedagogical work published in Nuremberg in 1658. Although largely descriptive, the significant details have been selected to recreate the atmosphere of the printshop; each section is as stark and clearly defined as the woodcut concerned and the language is perfectly controlled.

Coronis, divided into three sections and containing the ambitious long poem "On the Death of Archdeacon Broix," shows the distance Booth has travelled and confirms the promise of his early work. His best poems written between 1971 and 1973 are included.

Individual poems appear in magazines and anthologies which have not yet been collected in more permanent form. "Letter from the Gone Before" (for Robin Skelton) provides a new aspect of his work: "take my hand/for I bear no dull messages/ see in me/no pity or exactitude/of love/I am not here to blind you/or to crack your double joints...."

The Knotting Sequence is paradoxically concerned with the Bedfordshire hamlet of Knotting, where Martin Booth lives. To draw closer to the land and its history, Booth recreates the persona of Cnot, the Anglo-Saxon founder of the hamlet. From Chenotinga to Knotting "they have called/this the/Place of/the Sons/of Cnot." As if to imply the tenuous relationship between the poet and the Anglo-Saxon forerunner, and the effort required in communication with a spirit from the past, the language is sparse and fragmented, almost like echoes at times. The longest piece, "Noises from the Wold," is reminiscent of Ted Hughes's "Crow's Account of the Battle" and depicts a skirmish between the local Belgae and the Roman invaders. Needless to say, Cnot seems to show the same instinct for survival as Crow—although

> "the local
> tribe were resoundingly
> defeated
>
> I remember *that*
> Cnot says
>
> I didn't go
> to help
>
> no sense in drawing
> them over here
>
> he counted his
> wives again and
> a new
> moaning washed
> across the evening"

Gradually Cnot gives way to the poet, who secures his rights of possession through his feelings for the landscape and its inhabitants.

Extending upon the Kingdom, together with *The Knotting Sequence*, marks a clear stage in the poet's development. "Replicas" and "Shooting a Fox" in this volume are keenly observed and demonstrate the new power of Booth's writing.

—Howard Sergeant

BOOTH, Philip. American. Born in Hanover, New Hampshire, 8 October 1925. Educated at Dartmouth College, Hanover, A.B. 1948 (Phi Beta Kappa); Columbia University, New York, M.A. 1949. Served in the United States Army Air Force, 1944-45. Married Margaret Tillman in 1946; three daughters. Instructor, Bowdoin College, Maine, 1949-50; Assistant to the Director of Admissions, 1950-51, and Instructor, 1954, Dartmouth College; Assistant Professor, Wellesley College, Massachusetts, 1954-61. Associate Professor, 1961-65, and since 1965, Professor of English and Poet-in-Residence, Syracuse University, New York. Taught at the University of New Hampshire Writers Conference, Durham, 1955; Spencer Memorial Lecturer, Bryn Mawr College, Pennsylvania, 1959; taught at Tufts University Poetry Workshop, Medford, Massachusetts, 1960,

1961. Phi Beta Kappa Poet, Columbia University, 1962. Recipient: Bess Hokin Prize (*Poetry*, Chicago), 1955; Lamont Poetry Selection Award, 1956; *Saturday Review* prize, 1957; Guggenheim Fellowship, 1958, 1965; Emily Clark Balch Prize (*Virginia Quarterly Review*), 1964; American Academy award 1967; Rockefeller Fellowship, 1968; Theodore Roethke Prize (*Poetry Northwest*), 1970; National Endowment for the Arts Fellowship, 1980; Academy of American Poets Fellowship, 1983. Litt.D.: Colby College, Waterville, Maine, 1968. Address: Main Street, Castine, Maine 04421, U.S.A.

PUBLICATIONS

Verse

Letter from a Distant Land.   New York, Viking Press, 1957.
The Islanders.   New York, Viking Press, 1961.
North by East.   Boston, Impressions Workshop, 1966.
Weathers and Edges.   New York, Viking Press, 1966.
Margins: A Sequence of New and Selected Poems.   New York, Viking Press, 1970.
Available Light.   New York, Viking Press, 1976.
Before Sleep.   New York, Viking Press, 1980.

Recording: *Today's Poets 4*, with others, Folkways.

Other

Editor, *The Dark Island.*   Lunenberg, Vermont, Stinehour Press, 1960.
Editor, *Syracuse Poems 1965* (and *1970, 1973, 1978*, and *Syracuse Stories and Poems*).   Syracuse, New York, Syracuse University Department of English, 5 vols., 1965-83.

*

Manuscript Collections: State University of New York, Buffalo; University of Texas, Austin; Dartmouth College, Hanover, New Hampshire.

Critical Study: *Three Contemporary Poets of New England* by Guy Rotella, Boston, Twayne, 1983.

*   *   *

The poetry of Philip Booth spans three decades and represents a mighty effort to push through the limits of language into the reality of things. Ever on the edge of reality, clinging to surfaces, he struggles with an intractable world which, though it yields itself to his manipulation, will not allow him to possess it. Frustrated by this condition, Booth hones words to form a bridge across the abyss he feels separates him from true being. The process wears him out. In his early work, *Letter from a Distant Land, The Islanders*, and *Weathers and Edges*, he forges some of the most disciplined poems of his generation. His poems are eloquent testimonials to the world he knows he must reach, but which ever eludes him. Indeed, in an age where so many others are challenging society and plumbing the depths of the neurotic self, Booth is seeking metaphysical affirmation, an ontological relationship with the world. Hard disciplined forms, short lines, and cool images carry the weight of his determined search. Booth's poems remind one of the best of the Imagists in their cool detachment in fixing nature in an image, and at the same time the best of personal poetry in our age. To paraphrase T.S. Eliot,

Booth's poems are not an escape from personality, but a means of establishing it.

Booth found his medium early in *Letter from a Distant Land*, and then worked it and reworked it for nearly three decades. Each poem is a search for an ineffable reality, a dimly grasped world of being beyond being, a sunlit world of real shapes and truth. But finding the key to that illusive world was like searching for the impossible dream: the dream behind the dream, the dream we call life but which fades to darkness and becomes nothing. All the sunlit beaches, the light filtering through the trees, the hard-rock Maine coast, the muted ancestors whose ghost-like presence could be felt in the earth and in the Booth ancestral home, all merge into a kaliedoscope of images that tumble from the poet's fertile imagination in a lifetime of search for meaning and existence.

In his more recent work, *Margins*, *Available Light*, and *Before Sleep*, the struggle begins to wear the poet out. Progressively more hard put to maintain the struggle, Booth seems to retreat to more and more confined space, literally his ancestral home where in one room he assesses his struggle and seeks aid and comfort from the generations of his family that have inhabited this home. As the light dims and must be sought with a fierce intensity, the desire to sleep after a life-time of effort seems to become an ever-growing preoccupation. The entire last volume, *Before Sleep*, carries strong indications of a fatigue that has become so pervasive as to threaten the poet's life. Even the body has worn out. Images of death and decay vie with moments of quickening, of life suddenly revealed, a truth hammered home in a silent revelation. Darkness and nothingness creep in like fog and the poet finds himself adrift, rudderless, alone and lost, as in "Fog":

> I'm rowing
>
> where measure is lost, I'm barely moving,
> in a circle of translucence that moves with me
> without compass
>
> I can't see out or up into;
> I sit facing backwards,
> pulling myself slowly
> toward the life I'm still trying to get at.

More dangerous still is the condition of the man who "sits all day/on the edge of nothing,/after a while he gets numb and falls in" ("Narrative").

It is difficult to see where Booth can go from here, unless he is able to pull himself back from the abyss and find some way to affirm himself in the midst of the irrevocable and unremitting decay of body and mind. But whether he is able to rescue himself or not, he has already given us a treasure of poems that speak powerfully and honestly of the modern condition.

—Richard Damashek

BOSLEY, Keith.   British.   Born in Bourne End, Buckinghamshire, 16 September 1937.   Educated at Borlase School, Marlow, Buckinghamshire, 1949-56; University of Reading, B.A. (honours) in French 1960; also attended the universities of Paris and Caen. Married 1) Helen Sava in 1962, one son; 2) Satu Salo in 1982, one son. Since 1961, staff member, BBC External Services. Recipient (for translations): Finnish State Prize, 1978; English Goethe Society prize, 1982; British Comparative Literature Association prize, 1982. Address: 108 Upton Road, Slough, Berkshire SL1 2AW, England.

PUBLICATIONS

Verse

The Possibility of Angels.   London, Macmillan, 1969.
Dark Summer.   London, Menard Press, and Berkeley, California, Serendipity, 1976.
The Three Houses.   Knotting, Bedfordshire, Sceptre Press, 1976.
Stations.   London, Anvil Press Poetry, 1979.

Play

The Last Temptations, adaptation of an opera by Joonas Kokkonen (produced Savonlinna, Finland, 1977).

Other

Tales from the Long Lakes: Finnish Legends from the Kalevala (juvenile).   London, Gollancz, 1966; as *The Devil's Horse: Tales from the Kalevala*, New York, Pantheon, 1971.
And I Dance: Poems Original and Translated (juvenile).   London, Angus and Robertson, 1972.

Editor and Translator, with Matti Kuusi and Michael Branch, *Finnish Folk Poetry: Epic*.   Helsinki, Finnish Literature Society, and London, Hurst, 1977.
Editor, *The Elek Book of Oriental Verse*.   London, Elek, 1979; as *Poetry of Asia*, New York, Weatherhill, 1979.

Translator, *Russia's Other Poets*.   London, Longman, 1968; as *Russia's Underground Poets*, New York, Praeger, 1969.
Translator, *An Idiom of Night*, by Pierre Jean Jouve.   London, Rapp and Whiting, 1969.
Translator, *The War Wife: Vietnamese Poetry*.   London, Allison and Busby, 1972.
Translator, *The Song of Aino: From the Kalevala*.   High Wycombe, Buckinghamshire, Moonbird, 1973.
Translator, *The Song of Songs*.   Andoversford, Gloucestershire, Whittington Press, 1976.
Translator, *The Poems*, by Stephane Mallarmé.   London, Penguin, 1977.
Translator, *A Round O: Eighteen Poems*, by André Frénaud.   Egham, Surrey, Interim Press, 1977.
Translator, *Whitsongs*, by Eino Leino.   London, Menard Press, and Berkeley, California, Serendipity, 1978.
Translator, *A Reading of Ashes*, by Jerzy Ficowski.   London, Menard Press, 1981.
Translator, *From the Theorems of Master Jean de la Ceppède: LXX Sonnets*.   Ashington and Manchester, MidNAG-Carcanet, 1983.

*

Critical Study: "Keith Bosley: A Poet on the Problems of Translation: Interview by Erkki Toivanen," in *Books from Finland* (Helsinki), 1979.

*   *   *

Keith Bosley is a poet of considerable charm and much technical ability. At his best, he achieves a tender lyricism rare in this violent age ("The Smoke"): "Summer persists./The smoke/from that squat chimney climbs/into a perfect sky/this still October, trees/hang yellow against blue/longing for leaf fall...." Again, at his best Bosley can manage a clear plot-line better than many of his contemporaries. This is true of "The Unknown Language" where the speaker mysteriously picks up on the 16-metre band of his radio the tongue of the ancient Incas. It is true also of "Haunted"—a poem about a mad grandmother sniped at by soldiers who are imaginary and who go away after her death—which is real.

Very strikingly, the argument commands attention in"Wind at Midnight":

> The night I was away you said the wind
> vaulted the horizon, tore overland
> snatched at the trees and stole their dark green sleep
> fingered the river and set it gasping
>
> and then walked to our house, quite quietly
> to where you lay alone....

The wind behaves like an interloper, howling to get in, sighing when excluded, going away as disappointed as a man. Then

> Tonight we are together. Listen: your
> horizon, land, trees, river move. I stand
> shut in my tomb or kennel at the door
> real and whimpering as any wind.

In a more recent work, *Dark Summer*, Bosley voices characteristic themes of disillusion, loneliness, despair. This is a sequence drawing quite explicitly upon poets of other tongues—Jouve, Montale, Hölderlin, Stefan George, and, most notably of all, Dante. The fact that he tends to assimilate all their idioms to the same hushed minor key does not diminish the candour and authenticity of the verse:

> Sorry it's been so long in coming back—
> the note is not signed, but the hand is hers.
> Forgotten books, forgotten borrowers:
> a parcel, a replacing on the rack...

This is moving enough, with its quiet play upon words. But it also acts as a kind of footnote to the story of Paolo and Francesca who in Dante first kiss over a book which itself tells of a guilty love.

It seems that Bosley's original work has learned a good deal from his translations. There are a good many of them—this, from Ransetsu, for example, "The house is locked up:/around a paper lantern/the bats are dancing." Bosley shows considerable felicity in his verse renderings of Ransetsu, and Ransetsu's master, Bashō. He is equally at home with that very European elegist, Lorca, and with the ellipses of Mallarmé. We owe him a particular debt for his versions of less familiar material, for example, the Vietnamese translations in *The War Wife*. In our age of disruption and violence Keith Bosley is not only a technically adept poet but a distinguished practitioner of the civilised art of translation.

—Philip Hobsbaum

BOTTRALL, (Francis James) Ronald. British. Born in Camborne, Cornwall, 2 September 1906. Educated at Redruth County School; Pembroke College, Cambridge (Foundress' Scholar; Charles Oldham Shakespeare Scholar, 1927), M.A. (honours); Princeton University, New Jersey (Commonwealth Fund Fellowship, 1931-33). Served with the Air Ministry, 1940-41. Married 1) Margaret Florence Saumarez Smith in 1934 (marriage dissolved, 1954), one son; 2) Margot Pamela Samuel in 1954. Lector in English, University of Helsingfors, Finland, 1929-31; Johore Professor of English Language and Literature, Raffles College, Singapore, 1933-37; Assistant Director and Professor of English, British Institute, Florence, 1937-38; Secretary, School of Oriental and African Studies, University of London, 1939-45. British Council Representative in Sweden, 1941; Italy, 1945; Brazil, 1954; Greece, 1957; Japan (and Cultural Counsellor, Tokyo), 1959-61. Chief, Fellowships and Training Branch, Food and Agricultural Organization of the United Nations, Rome, 1963-65. Reviewer, *Times Literary Supplement*, London, 1965-74. Recipient: Coronation Medal, 1953; Syracuse International Poetry Prize, 1954. Fellow, Royal Society of Literature, 1955. Grand Officer of the Order of Merit, Italy, 1973. C.B.E. (Commander, Order of the British Empire), 1949. Knight Commander, Order of St. John of Jerusalem, 1977. Address: 17 Clarence Gate Gardens, London NW1 6AY, England.

PUBLICATIONS

Verse

The Loosening and Other Poems. Cambridge, Gordon Fraser, 1931.
Festivals of Fire. London, Faber, 1934.
The Turning Path. London, Barker, 1939.
Farewell and Welcome. London, Editions Poetry London, 1945.
Selected Poems. London, Editions Poetry London, 1946.
The Palisades of Fear. London, Editions Poetry London, 1949.
Adam Unparadised. London, Verschoyle, 1954.
The Collected Poems of Ronald Bottrall. London, Sidgwick and Jackson, 1961.
Day and Night. London, London Magazine Editions, 1973.
Poems 1955-1973. London, Anvil Press Poetry, 1974.
Reflections on the Nile. London, London Magazine Editions, 1980.
Against a Setting Sun: Poems 1974-1983. London, Allison and Busby, 1984.

Other

Rome. London, Joseph, and Cleveland, World, 1968.

Editor, with Gunnar Ekelöf, *Dikter*, by T.S. Eliot. Stockholm, Bonniers, 1942.
Editor, with Margaret Bottrall, *The Zephyr Book of English Verse.* Stockholm, Zephyr, 1945.
Editor, with Margaret Bottrall, *Collected English Verse.* London, Sidgwick and Jackson, 1946.

*

Manuscript Collections: State University of New York, Buffalo; University of Texas, Austin; British Library, London.

Critical Studies: preface by Edith Sitwell to *Selected Poems*, 1946; *The Modern Writer and His World* by G.S Fraser, London, Verschoyle, 1953, New York, Criterion, 1955, revised edition, London, Deutsch, 1964, New York, Praeger, 1965; *The Present Age: After 1920* by David Daiches, London, Cresset Press, 1958, as *The Present Age in British Literature*, Bloomington, Indiana University Press, 1958; introduction by Charles Tomlinson to *The Collected Poems*, 1961; *Guide to Modern World Literature* by Martin Seymour-Smith, London, Wolfe, 1973.

Ronald Bottrall comments:

At the beginning one has plenty of thematic material but only after trial and error can one use it effectively. In mid-career things coalesce and clarify and when situations present themselves one has the technique and experience to deal with them to the best of one's ability. In later years the technical skill is still there, but the situations are harder to grasp and transmute into poetry. My imagery derives from my early years in Cornwall in the country and by the sea. Later from my extensive travels. The greatest influence on my early poetry was Ezra Pound's *Hugh Selwyn Mauberley*. In the course of my work I have used a great many metrical forms, including, from 1946, syllabic verse. An ability to make use of metrical forms is most important for a poet.

*   *   *

Ronald Bottrall is a figure whose considerable stature as a poet still seems to be generally underestimated, despite the advocacy of many whose voices might have been expected to exert an influence in such matters. At different times his admirers have included F.R. Leavis, Edith Sitwell, Anthony Burgess, Robert Graves, Charles Tomlinson, and Eugenio Montale. In the very diversity of the names in that list there perhaps exists an important clue. It is not to be imagined that, say, Edith Sitwell and Charles Tomlinson (not to mention F.R Leavis) are critics of identical tastes. Each of these (and other) admirers of Bottrall's work has, more often than not, been pointing with approbation towards a different aspect, even a different phase, of his output.

Bottrall has always been a verse-writer of extraordinary competence and fluency. He is one of the modern masters of versification. At times this very fluency has led him into the over-facile imitation of the manners of other poets. It is almost frightening to see the ease with which he can take on the voices of other poets—in, for example, "Dead Ends (Homage to T.S. Eliot)," "The Sea: For Dylan Dead," "Weep not for Dylan Thomas," or the ultra-Poundean "Un Bel Homme du Temps Jadis." He has been, at various times, the author of graceful sestinas (e.g., "Peregrinations," "Sestina: Ritornello," "Sestina: For Our Time," "Dream Is Reality: For Peter Jay"), Villanelles ("Poeta Loquitur"), Rondeaux ("To Edith Sitwell"), and Ballades ("Ballade to Joseph Needham," "Ballade for F.T. Prince"), as well as of formally casual light verse ("Letter to a Politician," "Fibi pronounced Phoebe," or "Cosmetics"). He has been the author of anecdotal narratives like "Copacabana 1955" or "Bruckner at the Royal Albert Hall," as well as of highly wrought dramatic monologues like *Adam Unparadised*. This last is magniloquent and wide-ranging in its study of dispossession, loneliness, and guilt, and contrasts greatly with Bottrall's most recent verse.

Where many of the later poems are largely informal in manner, frequently records of experience wittily transformed in the perception and the telling, *Adam Unparadised* is a work in the grand manner. On the one hand are poems characterised by the spontaneity and vivacity of the sketch (some of the poems in *Day and Night* were compositions over which Bottrall reports himself to have had little conscious control; one, he tells us, was six minutes in the writing), on the other a full-scale Baroque canvas. He has produced poems of his Cornish family and background ("Terns and Cormorants," "One Cornishman to Another—Peace Alfred Wallis," "Cornish Sea," "Talking to the Ceiling," "Auntie Mabel") and poems which are cosmopolitan in setting and international in manner. He is a master of the sonnet ("The Minotaur," "Proserpine at Enna," "Hazardous Approaches") and has displayed his abilities in the Skeltonics of "Aubade." His poems of the 1940's (*The Palisades of Fear*) are frequently knotted in expression and densely allusive; songs like "Nightlight" or "Summer Song" are models of lucidity. He is, indeed, a poet of extraordinary contrast and diversity.

No reader is likely to place an equal value on the diverse areas of his work. Indeed there is reason to think that many have been put off by the difficulty of getting a sense of the poet "whole," as it were. It may, of course, be suggested that this is a failure on the part of readers and critics and that Bottrall is not to be blamed for their inadequacies. Yet the suspicion remains that too often manner has been overvalued; that too rarely has a line of thought been pursued consistently. Bottrall may well be the kind of poet whose works will need the winnowing process of time before their full value can be discerned. What must, though, be affirmed is that his already considerable output is capable of affording pleasure to most readers, and ought to be regarded as a central body of work in modern English poetry.

—Glyn Pursglove

BOWERING, George (Henry). Canadian. Born in Keremeos, British Columbia, 1 December 1938. Educated at South Okanagan High School, Oliver, British Columbia; Victoria College, British Columbia, 1953-54; University of British Columbia, Vancouver, B.A. 1960, M.A. 1963; University of Western Ontario, London. Served in the Royal Canadian Air Force, 1954-57. Married Angela Luoma in 1962; one daughter. Has worked for the British Columbia Forest Service and for the Federal Department of Agriculture. Assistant Professor, University of Calgary, Alberta, 1963-66; Writer-in-Residence, 1967-68, and Assistant Professor of English, 1968-72, Sir George Williams University, Montreal. Since 1972, Associate Professor, then Professor of English, Simon Fraser University, Burnaby, British Columbia. Editor, *Tish*, Vancouver, 1961-63, and *Imago*, 1964-74. Since 1966, Editor, Beaver Kosmos Folios. Recipient: Canada Council grant, 1968, 1971; Governor-General's Award, for verse, 1969, and for fiction, 1981. Agent: Linda McCartney, 104 Lyndhurst Avenue, Toronto, Ontario M5R 2Z1. Address: 2499 West 37th Avenue, Vancouver, British Columbia V6M 1P4, Canada.

PUBLICATIONS

Verse

Sticks and Stones. Vancouver, Tishbooks, 1963.
Points on the Grid. Toronto, Contact Press, 1964.
The Man in Yellow Boots. Mexico City, El Corno Emplumado, 1965.
Sitting in Mexico. Calgary, Imago, 1965.
The Silver Wire. Kingston, Ontario, Quarry Press, 1966.

Baseball. Toronto, Coach House Press, 1967.
Two Police Poems. Vancouver, Talonbooks, 1968.
Rocky Mountain Foot: A Lyric, A Memoir. Toronto, McClelland and Stewart, 1968.
The Gangs of Kosmos. Toronto, Anansi, 1969.
George, Vancouver: A Discovery Poem. Toronto, Weed/Flower Press, 1970.
Genève. Toronto, Coach House Press, 1971.
Touch: Selected Poems 1960-1970. Toronto, McClelland and Stewart, 1971.
The Sensible. Toronto, Massasauga, 1972.
Autobiology. Vancouver, New Star, 1972.
Layers 1-13. Toronto, Weed/Flower Press, 1973.
Curious. Toronto, Coach House Press, 1973.
At War with the U.S. Vancouver, Talonbooks, 1974.
In the Flesh. Toronto, McClelland and Stewart, 1974.
Allophanes. Toronto, Coach House Press, 1976.
Poem and Other Baseballs. Coatsworth, Ontario, Black Moss Press, 1976.
The Catch. Toronto, McClelland and Stewart, 1976.
My Lips Are Red. Vancouver, Cobblestone Press, 1976.
The Concrete Island: Montreal Poems 1967-1971. Quebec, Véhicule Press, 1977.
Another Mouth. Toronto, McClelland and Stewart, 1979.
Uncle Louis. Toronto, Coach House Press, 1980.
Particular Accidents: Selected Poems, edited by Robin Blaser. Vancouver, Talonbooks, 1980.
Ear Reach. Vancouver, Alcuin, 1982.
West Window. Toronto, General, 1982.
Smoking Mirror. Edmonton, Longspoon Press, 1982.
Kerrisdale Elegies. Toronto, Coach House Press, 1984.

Plays

A Home for Heroes, in *Prism International* (Vancouver), 1962; in *Ten Canadian Short Plays*, edited by Peter Stevens, New York, Dell, 1975.

Television Play: *What Does Eddi Williams Want?*, 1965.

Novels

Mirror on the Floor. Toronto, McClelland and Stewart, 1967.
A Short Sad Book. Vancouver, Talonbooks, 1977.
Burning Water. Toronto, General, and New York, Beaufort, 1980.
En Eaux Troubles. Montreal, Quinze, 1982.

Short Stories

Flycatcher. Ottawa, Oberon Press, 1974.
Concentric Circles. Coatsworth, Ontario, Black Moss Press, 1977.
Protective Footwear. Toronto, McClelland and Stewart, 1978.
A Place to Die. Ottawa, Oberon Press, 1983.

Other

How I Hear "Howl". Montreal, Sir George Williams University, 1968.
Al Purdy. Toronto, Copp Clarke, 1970.
Three Vancouver Writers. Toronto, Coach House Press, 1979.
A Way with Words. Ottawa, Oberon Press, 1982.
The Mask in Place. Winnipeg, Turnstone Press, 1982.

Editor, *Vibrations: Poems of Youth.* Toronto, Gage, 1970.

Editor, *The Story So Far.* Toronto, Coach House Press, 1971.
Editor, *Imago (Twenty) 1964-1974.* Vancouver, Talonbooks, 1974.
Editor, *Great Canadian Sports Stories.* Ottawa, Oberon Press, 1979.
Editor, *Fiction of Contemporary Canada.* Toronto, Coach House Press, 1980.
Editor, *Loki Is Buried at Smoky Creek: Selected Poems*, by Fred Wah. Vancouver, Talonbooks, 1980.
Editor, *My Body Was Eaten by Dogs: Selected Poems*, by David McFadden. Toronto, McClelland and Stewart, and Flushing, New York, Cross Country, 1981.
Editor, *The Contemporary Canadian Poem Anthology.* Toronto, Coach House Press, 4 vols., 1983.
Editor, *Sheila Watson: The Poet and Her Critics.* Ottawa, Golden Dog, 1984.

*

Manuscript Collection: Douglas Library, Queen's University, Kingston, Ontario.

Critical Study: introduction by the author to *Touch: Selected Poems*, 1971.

George Bowering comments:
(1974) I don't think that I will make a "personal statement introducing my work" because I don't write personal poetry. In fact when personal poetry gets to be confessional poetry I turn it off & reach for the baseball scores. I'll share with you what I wrote as notes 2 days ago: The snowball appears in hell every morning at seven. Dr Babel contends about the world's form, striking its prepared strings endlessly, a pleasure moving rings outward thru the universe. All sentences are to be served. You've tried it & tried it & it cant be done, you cannot close your ear—i.e. literature must be thought, now. Your knee oh class equal poet will like use a simile because he hates ambiguity. The snowball says it: all sentences are imperative.

*   *   *

"I was all those things that other poets always are on the dust jackets before they became poets." George Bowering's boast must be true, for his work is immensely various and the poet himself seems at times a powder-keg of energy. Wondering what Bowering will publish next is almost a pastime in Canadian poetry circles.

Bowering's work is terribly uneven, however, and irritatingly bad when it is poor. The virtues and vices are both found in *Touch: Selected Poems 1960-1970*, which includes poems from his earlier books, including *Rocky Mountain Foot* for which he received the Governor-General's Award in 1969. This last book is the first that groups poems thematically rather than chronologically, for as he explained, "Now nearly all I work on are books themselves."

A few of the vices include his misspelled words; his endless egotism; his philistinism; his ultra-radical chic. Some of his virtues are a vivid sense of space and time; a lyricism that is capable of sprouting wings; a happy-go-lucky sensibility (when not radicalized); an instant sympathy for the oppressed. It could be said his work has more tone than taste.

"Emphasis is on voice," Bowering wrote, and his poetry does have a decided cadence, a nonchalance of its own, and a quickness that is characteristic and enjoyable. Perhaps the spirit of his work can best be caught in a poem like "Grandfather" which begins:

Grandfather
                    Jabez Harry Bowering
strode across the Canadian prairie
hacking down trees
                              & building churches
delivering personal baptist sermons in them
leading Holy holy holy lord god almighty songs in them.

The poem does not conclude so much as end: "Till he died the day before his eighty fifth birthday/in a Catholic hospital of sheets white as his hair." The need to create a personal mythology is here, as it is in Whitman's verse, and Bowering's poems all seem interconnected in some vast Life of the Western Canadian Poet.

Perhaps Hugh MacCallum best summed up Bowering's work when he wrote: "The speaker in these poems achieves at times an almost bardic simplicity of manner that allows him to revel in the ordinary, the commonplace, the self-evident. But there is also a kind of wonder at the fullness and assertiveness of phenomena. Energy is the thing that arouses the poet's imagination—energy in landscape, man, or woman."

—John Robert Colombo

BOWERING, Marilyn (Ruthe). Canadian. Born in Winnipeg, Manitoba, 13 April 1949. Educated at the University of British Columbia, Vancouver, 1968-69; University of Victoria, British Columbia, B.A. 1971, M.A. 1973; University of New Brunswick, Fredericton, 1975. Married Michael S. Elcock in 1982. School teacher, Masset, British Columbia, 1974-75; editor and writer, Gregson Graham Marketing, Victoria, 1978-82; sessional lecturer, 1982-83, and visiting lecturer, 1983-84, University of Victoria. Recipient: Canada Council award, 1973, 1981, 1984. Address: Manzer Road, R.R.1, Sooke, British Columbia V0S 1N0, Canada.

PUBLICATIONS

Verse

The Liberation of Newfoundland. Fredericton, New Brunswick, Fiddlehead, 1973.
One Who Became Lost. Fredericton, New Brunswick, Fiddlehead, 1976.
The Killing Room. Victoria, British Columbia, Sono Nis Press, 1977.
Third Child; Zian. Knotting, Bedfordshire, Sceptre Press, 1978.
The Book of Glass. Knotting, Bedfordshire, Sceptre Press, 1978.
Sleeping with Lambs. Victoria, British Columbia, Press Porcépic, 1980.
Giving Back Diamonds. Victoria, British Columbia, Press Porcépic, 1982.
The Sunday Before Winter. Toronto, General, 1984.

Novel

The Visitors Have All Returned. Erin, Ontario, Press Porcépic, 1979.

Plays

Radio Plays: *Grandfather Was a Soldier*, 1983; *Marilyn Monroe: Anyone Can See I Love You*, 1984.

Other

Editor, with David A. Day, *Many Voices: An Anthology of Contemporary Canadian Indian Poetry.* Vancouver, Douglas, 1977.
Editor, *Guide to the Labour Code of British Columbia.* Victoria, Government of British Columbia, 1980.

*

Critical Studies: "The Hidden Dreamer's Cry: Natural Force as Point of View" by M. Travis Lane, in *Fiddlehead* (Fredericton, New Brunswick), Winter 1977; "Verse into Poetry" by George Woodcock, in *Canadian Literature* (Vancouver), Autumn 1983.

Marilyn Bowering comments:

My poems, I'm told, are full of surprises: the juxtaposition of the metaphysical with the sensuous and the everyday. Not that I'm after surprise, but that in speculating about the large things I can only use what I know. Serious in intent, certainly, but also with some irony, especially when considering men and women, and relatives.

Death remains a favourite topic.

Poetry is always an attempt to make sense and order and is a conjunction of the emotional and physical life with something that "cannot be said." In that sense it attempts to go beyond words, yet keeps the pleasure and shock of words as reward and impetus for the journey. My early work was (as is so often the case) much concerned with the natural world and the past: the links of history and mythology that give the illusion of substance (and order) to the process of being alive. Later I became much more interested in exploring consciousnesses other (if that's possible) than my own. In the two verse radio works, *Grandfather Was a Soldier* and *Marilyn Monroe: Anyone Can See I Love You*, especially.

I admire poems that suggest story and this has led me to write more fiction. Most of all I like the dissatisfaction that the best poems encourage, as if there is something just out of reach beyond the edge of perception and with the right risks taken it can be held in the hands.

*   *   *

A prolific writer, Marilyn Bowering has begun to turn her energies to prose. But she is best known as a poet. A line in her first book, *The Liberation of Newfoundland*, "all things are full of gods," sums up her poetic predilections. As well, the aqueous imagery found in this book recurs in much of her work since, as does an obsession with islands, caves, cliffs, dreams, bones, and killing. An early poem, "Thera" in *One Who Became Lost*, sets forth this skeletal vision:

The island hills
arch grey spines
from the sea.
Facing them—
white jagged ribs of the land.

Bonemakers

Although in other poems she frequently derives her diction from the surrealists, Bowering does not cast their wide net of content. Indeed, her preoccupations appear private, centred— even in their projection into natural forms of sea and land—on personal agonies. As if to exorcise the latter, she is attracted to fairy tales and often resorts to charms, incantations, spells, and curses as mediums of expression. In her early work, such as *One Who Became Lost*, a certain montonousness of perception tends to make one poem blur into another; more recent books like *Sleeping with Lambs* evidence greater variety and grasp of shape. Into the title poem of *Giving Back Diamonds* she adroitly weaves the lines:

> I love you forever
> there's no one like you
> I'd do anything for you
> I want you just as you are
> goodbye forever, goodbye

The repetitive emphasis of this ironic refrain is given extra point by the book's epigraph from Zsa Zsa Gabor: "I never hated a man enough to give diamonds back." Perhaps a title in the "Giving Back Diamonds" section of *The Sunday Before Winter* best describes Bowering's attitude to her materials: "Well, it ain't no sin to take off your skin and dance around in your bones."

—Fraser Sutherland

BOWERS, Edgar. American. Born in Rome, Georgia, 2 March 1924. Educated at the University of North Carolina, Chapel Hill, B.A. 1947; Stanford University, California, M.A. 1949, Ph.D. 1953. Served in the United States Army, 1943-46. Instructor, Duke University, Durham, North Carolina, 1952-55; Assistant Professor, Harpur College, Binghamton, New York, 1955-58. Since 1958, Member of the English Department, and currently Professor of English, University of California, Santa Barbara. Recipient: Fulbright Fellowship, 1950; Swallow Press New Poetry Series Award, 1955; Guggenheim Fellowship, 1958, 1969; *Sewanee Review* Fellowship; Edward F. Jones Foundation Fellowship; University of California Institute of Creative Arts Fellowship; Ingram Merrill award, 1974; Brandeis University Creative Arts Medal, 1978. Address: 1502 Miramar Beach, Santa Barbara, California 93108, U.S.A.

PUBLICATIONS

Verse

The Form of Loss. Denver, Swallow, 1956.
Five American Poets, with others, edited by Ted Hughes and
   Thom Gunn. London, Faber, 1963.
The Astronomers. Denver, Swallow, 1965.
Living Together: New and Selected Poems. Boston, Godine,
   1973; Manchester, Carcanet, 1977.
Witnesses. Los Angeles, Symposium Press, 1981.

*

Critical Studies: *Forms of Discovery* by Yvor Winters, Denver, Swallow, 1967; *Alone with America* by Richard Howard, New York, Atheneum. 1969, London, Thames and Hudson, 1970,

revised edition. Atheneum, 1980; "The Theme of Loss in the Earlier Poems of Catherine Davis and Edgar Bowers," in *Southern Review 9* (Baton Rouge, Louisiana), and "Contexts for 'Being,' 'Divinity,' and 'Self' in Valéry and Edgar Bowers," in *Southern Review 13*, both by Helen A. Trimpi.

*   *   *

Sometimes a major poet may be ignored by the majority of readers, so that he must content himself with fit audience, though few. Sometimes a major poet may seem less "important" than more public figures, for instance, poets who disturb political conventions or march on the Pentagon, or who titillate the public with confessional songs and sonnets. No matter how worthy their causes or how honest their confessions, poets must be judged by their poems, not their activities or biographies. Edgar Bowers has not sought publicity, nor has he achieved notoriety. He has not written in the modish confessional manner of divorce, madness, and self-advertisement. He has simply written some of the great poems of our time. One needs to read his work slowly and carefully; his poems are worth taking the time to understand.

Bowers's powerful treatment of themes of deception and honesty, of shadow and lucidity, of loss and form can be found in his earliest poems; but his depth and range have grown, with no diminution of his prosodic mastery. A chief characteristic of his poems, as Yvor Winters pointed out, is that "sensory perception and its significance are simultaneous." This is especially true of "Autumn Shade," a sequence of ten poems that ends *The Astronomers* and that Winters mistakenly slighted. The sequence begins with a sense of destiny which amounts almost to predestination, a sense that appears in other poems by Bowers:

> Now, toward his destined passion there, the strong,
> Vivid young man, reluctant, may return
> From suffering in his own experience
> To lie down in the darkness.

The young man wakes, he works, he sleeps again; but the first poem ends with a chilling image: "The snake/Does as it must, and sinks into the cold." In another poem the young man lights a fire as the night grows cold:

>   Gently
> A dead soprano sings Mozart and Bach.
> I drink bourbon, then go to bed, and sleep
> In the Promethean heat of summer's essence.

This is pentameter so subtle in modulation that one may miss a good deal of the technical virtuosity which makes the apparently colloquial notation of actions possible. So much is packed into the subdued, suggestive style that one may overlook the complexity of life and of emotional response to sensations being presented: perception and significance are simultaneous, statement and meaning coincide. The young man of the sequence is aware that the things "I have desired/Evade me, and the lucid majesty/That warmed the dull barbarian to life./So I lie here, left with self-consciousness." One of Winters' mistakes in reading the sequence seems to have been a confusion of "self-consciousness" with solipsism. Within the sequence, the young man's books, his old neighbor who drives through rain and snow, the recollection of Hercules (though the young man does not try for the great task), and of his own father (a form of loss), and his view out the window of a Cherokee trail ("I see it, when I look up from the page"), all indicate the reality of the external world. The density of reference suggests the presence of the past, and the complexity of a man's perceptions. The young man is trying in this dark night, during these seasons of the soul, to understand his own past and thus his present. His old neighbor's driving in snow recalls to him his own driving in war:

> Was this our wisdom, simply, in a chance
> In danger, to be mastered by a task,
> Like groping round a chair, through a door, to bed?

Not many poets in the language could have written those lines. The verbal precision evokes deep resonance of response. His firm control, his stylistic brilliance permit Bowers a potentially dangerous ending for the sequence: it would be trite, after this night of darkness and cold to have the sunlight transform the room, so that even shadows become "substantial light." But like all masters, Bowers takes the potentially trite and makes it hugely moving. The man of the sequence survives: "I stay/Almost as I have been, intact, aware,/Alive, though proud and cautious, even afraid." This ending is indicative of one of Bowers's strengths, as man and as poet: his refusal to be deceived, his almost desperate honesty.

The dramatic monologue "The Prince" is a major examination of what we term "German war guilt"; in it, familial relations become the vehicle for a poetic rendering of moral relations:

> My son, who was the heir
> To every hope and trust, grew out of caring
> Into the form of loss as I had done,
> And then betrayed me who betrayed him first.

Likewise, in another fine poem, "From J. Haydn to Constanze Mozart (1791)," a verse letter expressing grief becomes a meditation on the rare fusion of mind and body, sense and reason that Mozart's music embodies: "Aslant at his clavier, with careful ease,/To bring one last enigma to the norm,/Intelligence perfecting the mute keys." These poems, along with "Amor vincit omnia" (the greatest poem on the theme of the Magi since Yeats's), "The Mountain Cemetery," and "The Astronomers of Mont Blanc" are part of the enduring body of work that distinguishes Edgar Bowers's books. One can return to these poems as one returns to Campion, Donne, or Landor: to clear one's sense of language. For in Bowers we have a poet at once exact and exciting in his use of language. The word always fits the sense; and the sense never exceeds what language is capable of doing: "Whereof we cannot speak, thereof we must be silent."

—James Korges

BOYLE, Kay. American. Born in St. Paul, Minnesota, 19 February 1902. Educated at the Cincinnati Conservatory of Music; Ohio Mechanics Institute, 1917-19. Married 1) Richard Brault in 1922 (divorced); 2) Laurence Vail in 1931 (divorced), five daughters and one son; 3) Baron Joseph von Franckenstein in 1943 (died, 1963). Lived in Europe for 30 years. Foreign correspondent, *The New Yorker* magazine, 1946-53. Professor of English, San Francisco State University, 1963-80; since 1980 Professor Emerita. Lecturer, New School for Social Research, New York, 1962; Fellow, Wesleyan University, Middletown, Connecticut, 1963; Director, New York Writers Conference, Wagner College, New York, 1964; Fellow, Radcliffe Institute for Independent Study, Cambridge, Massachusetts, 1964-65; Writer-in-Residence, University of Massachusetts, Amherst, 1967, Hollins College, Virginia, 1970-71, and Eastern Washington Univer-

sity, Cheney, 1984. Recipient: Guggenheim Fellowship, 1934, 1961; O. Henry Award, for short story, 1935, 1941; San Francisco Art Commission award, 1978; National Endowment for the Arts grant, 1980; Before Columbus Foundation award, 1983; Celtic Foundation award, 1984. D.Litt: Columbia College, Chicago, 1971; Southern Illinois University, Carbondale, 1982; D.H.L.: Skidmore College, Saratoga Springs, New York, 1977. Member, American Academy, 1979. Agent: Watkins Loomis Agency, 150 East 35th Street, New York, New York 10016, U.S.A.

PUBLICATIONS

Verse

A Statement.   New York, Modern Editions Press, 1932.
A Glad Day.   New York, New Directions, 1938.
American Citizen: Naturalized in Leadville, Colorado.   New York, Simon and Schuster, 1944.
Collected Poems.   New York, Knopf, 1962.
Testament for My Students and Other Poems.   New York, Doubleday, 1970.
This Is Not a Letter.   College Park, Maryland, Sun and Moon Press, 1985.

Novels

Plagued by the Nightingale.   New York, Cape and Smith, and London, Cape, 1931.
Year Before Last.   New York, Smith, and London, Faber, 1932.
Gentlemen, I Address You Privately.   New York, Smith, 1933; London, Faber, 1934.
My Next Bride.   New York, Harcourt Brace, 1934; London, Faber, 1935.
Death of a Man.   New York, Harcourt Brace, and London, Faber, 1936.
Monday Night.   New York, Harcourt Brace, and London, Faber, 1938.
Primer for Combat.   New York, Simon and Schuster, 1942; London, Faber, 1943.
Avalanche.   New York, Simon and Schuster, and London, Faber, 1944.
A Frenchman Must Die.   New York, Simon and Schuster, and London, Faber, 1946.
1939.   New York, Simon and Schuster, and London, Faber, 1948.
His Human Majesty.   New York, McGraw Hill, 1949; London, Faber, 1950.
The Seagull on the Step.   New York, Knopf, and London, Faber, 1955.
Generation Without Farewell.   New York, Knopf, 1960.
The Underground Woman.   New York, Doubleday, 1975.

Short Stories

Short Stories.   Paris, Black Sun Press, 1929.
Wedding Day and Other Stories.   New York, Cape and Smith, 1930; London, Pharos, 1932.
The First Lover and Other Stories.   New York, Smith and Haas, 1933; London, Faber, 1937.
The White Horses of Vienna and Other Stories.   New York, Harcourt Brace, 1936; London, Faber, 1937.
The Crazy Hunter: Three Short Novels.   New York, Harcourt Brace, 1940; as *The Crazy Hunter and Other Stories*, London, Faber, 1940.

Thirty Stories.   New York, Simon and Schuster, 1946; London, Faber, 1948.

The Smoking Mountain: Stories of Post War Germany.   New York, McGraw Hill, 1951; London, Faber, 1952.

Three Short Novels.   Boston, Beacon Press, 1958.

Nothing Ever Breaks Except the Heart.   New York, Doubleday, 1966.

Fifty Stories.   New York, Doubleday, 1980; London, Penguin, 1981.

Other

The Youngest Camel (juvenile).   Boston, Little Brown, and London, Faber, 1939; revised edition, New York, Harper, 1959; Faber, 1960.

Breaking the Silence: Why a Mother Tells Her Son about the Nazi Era.   New York, Institute of Human Relations Press-American Jewish Committee, 1962.

Pinky, The Cat Who Liked to Sleep (juvenile).   New York, Crowell Collier, 1966.

Pinky in Persia (juvenile).   New York, Crowell Collier, 1968.

Being Geniuses Together 1920-1930, with Robert McAlmon.   New York, Doubleday, 1968; London, Joseph, 1970.

The Long Walk at San Francisco State and Other Essays.   New York, Grove Press, 1970.

Four Visions of America, with others.   Santa Barbara, California, Capra Press, 1977.

Editor, with Laurence Vail and Nina Conarain, *365 Days.*   New York, Harcourt Brace, and London, Cape, 1936.

Editor, *The Autobiography of Emanuel Carnevali.*   New York, Horizon Press, 1967.

Editor, with Justine Van Gundy, *Enough of Dying! An Anthology of Peace Writings.*   New York, Dell, 1972.

Translator, *Don Juan*, by Joseph Delteil.   New York, Cape and Smith, 1931.

Translator, *Mr. Knife, Miss Fork*, by René Crevel.   Paris, Black Sun Press, 1931.

Translator, *The Devil in the Flesh*, by Raymond Radiguet.   New York, Smith, 1932; London, Grey Walls Press, 1949.

Translator, *Babylon*, by René Crevel.   San Francisco, North Point Press, 1985.

Ghost-writer for the books *Relations and Complications, Being the Recollections of H.H. the Dayang Muda of Sarawak*, by Gladys Palmer Brooke, London, Lane, 1929, and *Yellow Dusk*, by Bettina Bedwell, London, Hurst and Blackett, 1937.

*

Manuscript Collection: Morris Library, Southern Illinois University, Carbondale.

Kay Boyle comments:

Although I have published over twenty books of short stories and novels, I consider myself primarily a poet.

[My poetry] is extremely personal in motivation and deals in the main with social and political problems. I have been influenced by William Carlos Williams, D.H. Lawrence, James Joyce, and Padraic Colum.

*   *   *

Kay Boyle has been an important novelist, short story writer,

and poet since the expatriate generation of the 1920's, and her fiction and poetry have enriched one another. Perhaps the distinguishing formal characteristic of her poetry has been her emphasis upon the implied narrative occasion of most lyric poems. In her work this narrative framework, which incites the lyric response, has been handled in contrasting ways. In certain poems, and these extend throughout her career, the story-telling elements are deliberately made obvious to the point that the poems contain passages of both prose and verse, with the prose usually presenting more factual material and the verse intensifying it to poetic significance. The complex, macabre, and splendid "A Complaint for Mary and Marcel" is an arresting variation of this technique. The opposite method is also used. In these poems the narrative or plot elements are withheld but assumed, and the poems have the mysterious immediacy of overheard conversation. The poems, also characteristic of her work throughout, give an up-to-date, "coded" quality to her writing and seem to anticipate the work of such recent poets as James Merrill.

In content Boyle's poems, taken as a whole, expand the personal emotion of private relationships toward a strong communal and political consciousness, with an accompanying stress upon the social role of the artist. Over the years she has focused her sensibilities and quiet outrage upon political injustice, from the victims of the Fascists to the problems of American students in the 1960's. But her point of view was and remains positive. There is a strong emphasis upon youth and death in her poetry, but her frequent use of images of nature, and the importance of spring and renewal in her work, point to a kind of informed Shelleyan optimism and place her in the mainstream of American romanticism. If her poetry is sometimes more effusive than current taste prefers, Kay Boyle represents nevertheless the testament of a committed artist to an active belief in the possibilities of a heightened human identity, which has been after all the great and underlying theme of poetry since its beginning.

—Gaynor F. Bradish

<hr>

BRANDI, John.   American.   Born in Los Angeles, California, 5 November 1943.   Educated at California State College, Northridge, B.F.A. 1965.   Married Gioia Tama de Brandi in 1968; two children.   Member, Peace Corps, South America, 1965-68.   Artist and bookmaker: has exhibited paintings in the United States and Mexico.   Recipient: *Portland State Review Prize*, for prose, 1971; National Endowment for the Arts fellowship, 1980; Witter Bynner translation grant, 1984.   Address: Star Route, Box 760, Corrales, New Mexico 87048, U.S.A.

PUBLICATIONS

Verse

Poem Afternoon in a Square of Guadalajara.   San Francisco, Maya, 1970.

Emptylots: Poems from Venice and LA.   Bolinas, California, Nail Press, 1971.

San Francisco Lastday Homebound Hangover Highway Blues.   Bolinas, California, Nail Press, 1973.

A Partial Exploration of Palo Flechado Canyon.   Bolinas, California, Nail Press, 1973.

The Phoenix Gas Slam.   Bolinas, California, Nail Press, 1974.

Firebook.   Virgin River, Utah, Smoky the Bear Press, 1974.

In a December Storm. Bowling Green, Ohio, Tribal Press, 1975.
Looking for Minerals. Cherry Valley, New York, Cherry Valley Editions, 1975.
Smudgepots: For Jack Kerouac. Guadalupita, New Mexico, Nail Press, 1975.
Poems from Four Corners. Fort Kent, Maine, Great Raven, 1978.
Andean Town Circa 1980. Guadalupita, New Mexico, Tooth of Time, 1978.
Rite for the Beautification of All Beings. West Branch, Iowa, Toothpaste Press, 1983.
That Back Road In: Poems from the American Southwest 1972-1983. Berkeley, California, Wingbow Press, 1984.
Poems at the Edge of Day. Buffalo, White Pine Press, 1984.
That Crow That Visited Was Flying Backwards. Santa Fe, Tooth of Time, 1984.

Short Stories

The Cowboy from Phantom Banks. Point Reyes, California, Floating Island, 1983.

Other

Desde Alla. Santa Barbara, California, Christopher's Press, 1971.
One Week of Mornings at Dry Creek. Santa Barbara, California, Christopher's Press, 1971.
Towards a Happy Solstice: Mine, Yours, Everybody. Santa Barbara, California, Christopher's Press, 1971.
Y Aun Hay Mas: Dreams and Explorations: New and Old Mexico. Santa Barbara, California, Christopher's Press, 1972.
Narrowgauge to Riobamba. Santa Barbara, California, Christopher's Press, 1975.
Memorandum from a Caribbean Isle. Brunswick, Maine, Blackberry, 1977.
Diary from Baja California. Santa Barbara, California, Christopher's Press, 1978.
Diary from a Journey to the Middle of the World. Berkeley, California, Figures, 1979.

Editor, *Chimborazo: Life on the Haciendas of Highland Ecuador.* Rooseveltown, New York, Akwesasne Notes, 1976.
Editor, with Larry Goodell, *The Noose: A Retrospective: Four Decades*, by Judson Crews. Oakland, California, Duende Press, 1980.

*

Manuscript Collection: University of California, Davis.

John Brandi comments:
Desde Alla and *Narrowgauge to Riobamba* are two books akin to two separately painted panels translating the one-same diorama, that of isolated hamlets in the inter-mountain basins of the remote Andes where I spent a few years living with Quechua-speaking peasants.
Whenever I journey, I travel in two separate vehicles. One over the physical landscape, the other within the meta-physical. My writing and painting link the two spheres, migrating back and forth between inner and outer geographies.
That's what my books are about. They're geography books. Earth primers.

*   *   *

John Brandi is a prolific and energetic writer/artist. He has filled journal after journal with writings, poems, drawings, collages. His work seeks source and renewal in new geographies and in the act of travel with its inevitable encounters, mysteries, and misunderstandings. He's a spy of sorts who looks, listens, takes notes, sketches interesting sights with a flair. Because he is an accomplished graphic artist, Brandi is able to describe the jungles of Ecuador or the mesas of New Mexico or Alaska's endless night with rich visual attention to physical detail. There are both a naivety and a shrewd persona present in his writing. Sometimes it reads like a curious union of *Candide* and Céline. Not unlike many writers born in post-World War II urban sprawl, Brandi attempts self-geography which sometimes gets in the way of his text and diminishes the nuances of his writing.
Brandi's work exemplifies the impressionistic postcard travel-writing style established by Jack Kerouac. The surfaces are often extremely attractive, and poverty and suffering are dealt with in near-romantic detail. Depth is often absent in visceral celebrations of place. As strangers, we bring expectations to a place and its people which, as artists, we hope to translate into myth. Travel writing, in many cases, becomes an elusive form of colonialism, though in Brandi's case his books of travel remain essentially the record of a search, a quest. He is the artist-wanderer (or fool-monk) on the road to enlightenment which, as it is rumoured, is being totally awake in the present—no matter where one is. Despite his often finely stated descriptions of place, Brandi makes clear that these books of travel are a continuing inward journey, portraits of the artist as a young man, filled with self-revelation, examination, self-doubt, dreams, and theories.
His verse is not as sure as his prose. There is a confusion as to where the prose ends and the poem begins. His eye and ear seem tuned to the rhythms of prose. Up to 1976 his poems were mainly long-lined Ginsbergian chants of dissatisfaction with the U.S.A. and of journeys taken to Ecuador, Alaska, Mexico, and of his home environment of Los Angeles. Generally the tone of these poems remains similar to that of his prose. It's as if he merely chopped prose into poetic lines to highlight the content of a piece.
Since that time his lines have shortened into compact lyrics, sometimes terse and direct, dealing with love, landscape, domestic realities, social occasions. Though they fail to project the music of poetry, they do demonstrate Brandi's development as a poet and do bear indications of a growing lyric simplicity, and an emerging sureness of style and verbal sensitivity.

—David Meltzer

BRATHWAITE, Edward Kamau. Barbadian. Born in Bridgetown, Barbados, 11 May 1930. Educated at Harrison College, Barbados; Pembroke College, Cambridge (Barbados Scholar), 1950-54, B.A. (honours) in history 1953, Cert.Ed. 1954; University of Sussex, Falmer, 1965-68, D.Phil. 1968. Married Doris Monica Welcome in 1960; one son. Education Officer, Ministry of Education, Ghana, 1955-62; Tutor, University of the West Indies Extra Mural Department, St. Lucia, 1962-63. Lecturer, 1963-76, Reader, 1976-83, and since 1983, Professor of Social and Cultural History, University of the West Indies, Kingston. Plebiscite Officer in the Trans-Volta Togoland, United Nations, 1956-57. Founding Secretary, 1966, Caribbean Artists Movement. Since 1970, Editor, *Savacou* magazine, Mona.

Recipient: Arts Council of Great Britain bursary, 1967; Camden Arts Festival prize, London, 1967; Cholmondeley Award, 1970; Guggenheim Fellowship, 1972; City of Nairobi Fellowship, 1972; Bussa Award, 1973; Casa de las Americas Prize, 1976; Fulbright Fellowship, 1983; Institute of Jamaica Musgrave Medal, 1983. Address: Department of History, University of the West Indies, Mona, Kingston 7, Jamaica.

PUBLICATIONS

Verse

The Arrivants: A New World Trilogy.   London and New York, Oxford University Press, 1973.
  Rights of Passage.   London, Oxford University Press, 1967.
  Masks.   London, Oxford University Press, 1968.
  Islands.   London, Oxford University Press, 1969.
Penguin Modern Poets 15, with Alan Bold and Edwin Morgan. London, Penguin, 1969.
Panda No. 349.   London, Royal Institute for the Blind, 1969.
Days and Nights.   Mona, Jamaica, Caldwell Press, 1975.
Other Exiles.   London and New York, Oxford University Press, 1975.
Black + Blues.   Havana, Casa de las Americas, 1976.
Mother Poem.   London, Oxford University Press, 1977.
Soweto.   Mona, Jamaica, Savacou Cooperative, 1979.
Word Making Man: A Poem for Nicólas Guillèn.   Mona, Jamaica, Savacou Cooperative, 1979.
Sun Poem.   Oxford and New York, Oxford University Press, 1982.
Third World Poems.   London, Longman, 1983.

Recordings: *The Poet Speaks 10,* Argo, 1968; *Rights of Passage,* Argo, 1969; *Masks,* Argo, 1972; *Islands,* Argo, 1973; *The Poetry of Edward Kamau Brathwaite,* Casa de las Americas, 1976.

Plays

Four Plays for Schools (produced Saltpond, Ghana, 1961-62).   London, Longman, 1964.
Odale's Choice (produced Saltpond, Ghana, 1962).   London, Evans, 1967.

Other

The People Who Came 1-3 (textbooks).   London, Longman, 1968-72.
Folk Culture of the Slaves in Jamaica.   London, New Beacon, 1970.
The Development of Creole Society in Jamaica 1770-1820.   Oxford, Clarendon Press, 1971.
Caribbean Man in Space and Time.   Mona, Jamaica, Savacou, 1974.
Contradictory Omens: Cultural Diversity and Integration in the Caribbean.   Mona, Jamaica, Savacou, 1974.
Our Ancestral Heritage: A Bibliography of the Roots of Culture in the English-Speaking Caribbean.   Kingston, Carifesta, 1976.
Wars of Respect: Nanny, Sam Sharpe, and the Struggle for People's Liberation.   Kingston, API, 1977.
Jamaica Poetry: A Checklist 1686-1978.   Kingston, Jamaica Library Service, 1979.
Barbados Poetry: A Checklist, Slavery to the Present.   Mona, Jamaica, Savacou, 1979.
The Colonial Encounter: Language.   Mysore, University of

Mysore, 1984.
History of the Voice: The Development of Nation Language in Anglophone Caribbean Poetry.   London, New Beacon, 1984.

Editor, *Iouanaloa: Recent Writing from St. Lucia.*   Castries, University of the West Indies Department of Extra-Mural Studies, 1963.

*

Critical Studies: "The Poetry of Edward Brathwaite" by Jean D'Costa, in *Jamaica Journal* (Kingston), September, 1968; *The Chosen Tongue* by Gerald Moore, London, Longman, 1969; "Brathwaite's Song of Dispossession" by K.E. Senanu, in *Universitas* (Accra), March 1969; "The Poetry of Edward Brathwaite" by Damian Grant, in *Critical Quarterly* (London), Summer 1970; "Dimensions of Song" by Anne Walmsley, in *Bim 51* (Bridgetown, Barbados), July-December 1970; "Three Caribbean Poets" by Maria K. Mootry, in *Pan-Africanist,* ii, 1, 1971; "This Broken Ground" by Mervyn Morris, in *New World Quarterly* (Kingston), v, 3, 1971; "Islands," in *Caribbean Studies* (Rio Piedras, Puerto Rico), January 1971, "Songs of the Skeleton: A Poetry of Fission," in *Trinidad and Tobago Review* (Port of Spain), 1980-81, and *Pathfinder: Black Awakening in "The Arrivants" of Edward Kamau Brathwaite,* Port of Spain, 1981, all by Gordon Rohlehr; "Walcott Versus Brathwaite" by Patricia Ismond, in *Caribbean Quarterly 17* (Kingston), September-December 1971; "A Study of Some Ancestral Elements in Brathwaite's Trilogy" by Samuel Asein, in *African Studies Association of the West Indies Bulletin 4* (Mona, Jamaica), December 1971; "Edward Brathwaite y el neoafricanismo antillano" by G.R. Coulthard, in *Cuadernos Americanos* (Mexico City), September-October 1972; "Odomankoma Kyerema se: A Study of *Masks*" by Maureen Warner, in *Caribbean Quarterly* (Kingston), June 1973; "E. Brathwaite y su poesia antillana" by Nancy Morejon, in *Bohemia 22* (Havana), 3 June 1977; "The Cyclical Vision of Edward Kamau Brathwaite" by Lloyd W. Brown, in *West Indian Poetry,* Boston, Twayne, 1978, revised edition, London, Heinemann, 1984; "Edward Brathwaite" by J. Michael Dash, in *West Indian Literature* edited by Bruce King, London, Macmillan, 1979; " Brathwaite and Walcott Issue" of *Caribbean Quarterly 26* (Mona, Jamaica), nos. 1-2, 1980; Robert Bensen, in *Critical Survey of Poetry* edited by Frank N. Magill, Englewood Cliffs, New Jersey, Salem Press, 1983.

Edward Kamau Brathwaite comments:
what caused the death of the amerindians: the holocaust of slavery: the birth of tom and caliban
in terms of my weltanschauung: my culture-view: it all began with the fall of the roman empire: this imperial achievement had created an equilibrium of material/spirit: metropole/province: law/chaos: which made possible a definition of values with the decline and fall of rome: flux appeared: movements of magic into the metropole: custom replaced statute: gargoyle replaced statue
the vikings moved in from the north: the goths, huns, magyars came on from the east; the crescent of islam curved north; african and aztec civilizations began to prophesy disaster christianity (the holy roman empire) attempted to restore/retain the equilibrium but it was impossible: there were too many alternatives: there was mohamet: there were magi: there was the new science of copernicus, the natural philosophers, the medical school at salerno, there was a choice: galilee or galileo: emperor or pope: priest or politician
and then money became the centre of this shattered universe: market, bourg, bourse: commerce, ship, merchant, bank: middle

class, taxes, nations, mercantilism: travel to new lands: control of
new markets: the shift of authority outwards: supported by bullet
and bible: but no prayer: but purse: not custom anymore, but
curse
marco polo overland to china; the portuguese by stepping stone
to africa; columbus to san salvador
moctezuma collapsed: chichen itza defeated: geronimo doomed:
saskatchewa: mohican: esquimo and ewe whale-worshippers:
timbucto, kumasi, ile-ife, benin city, zimbabwe caribs moving
towards malaria and syphilis; cherokees moving towards the
horse, the weston rifle, the waggon train; ibo and naga to slave
ships; zulus towards the locomotive tank; masai towards the
jumbo jet, caliban to new york, paris, london town, so that here
in the caribbean we have people without (apparent) root: values
of whip, of bomb, of bottle: the culture of materialism, not
equilibrium
food, flesh, house, harbour: not stone, demon, wilderness, space:
extermination of the arawaks
first 10, then 20
first 20, then 200
first 200 then 200,000 africans: slaves, lukumi, tears
200,000: 300,000: 400,000: a million: tears, tears, lukumi
1 million: 2 million: 3 Million: 4 Million: materialism buildings
    hotels, plantation houses
10 million: 20 million: lukumi: lukumi: tears
30 million: 40 million: 50 million: we could go on counting: men:
    money: materialism:
tears: tears: lukumi
the spaniards drained the lake of mexico away: the modern city
    sited in the dust bowl
where are the bison of the prairies: leviathan of the pacific
    indians
where are those 50 million africans: without tongue, without
    mother, without god *can you*
expect us to establish houses here?
to build a nation here? where
will the old men feed their flocks?
where will we make our markets? (*Masks*, p. 21)
the history of catastrophe requires such a literature to hold a
    broken mirror up to broken
nature.

*   *   *

Edward Kamau Brathwaite's solid reputation as a major West
Indian poet rests largely on the well-known trilogy *Rights of
Passage, Masks,* and *Islands*—reprinted in one volume as *The
Arrivants.* But since the publication of the trilogy two other
important volumes of poetry have appeared—*Other Exiles* and
Mother Poem—together with a Spanish translation of selected
poems, published in Cuba as *Black + Blues.*

Of these five major collections *Other Exiles* spans a considerable period of Brathwaite's activity as a poet, 25 years to be exact,
prior to its actual publication. In these circumstances it is not
surprising that it is a rather varied collection, reflecting that
diversity of interests and techniques which is characteristic of
Brathwaite's work as a whole, but which is often obscured by a
prevailing tendency to see him, on the basis of *The Arrivants,* as
the monolithic, collective voice of the "Black Diaspora." The
collection actually ranges from the exile's intense sense of personal isolation in Europe ("The Day the First Snow Fell") to the
satirically detached portrait of the growth of an archetypal
young colonial ("Journeys"). In "Conqueror" the personal voice
shifts from that of the colonial governor in the Caribbean to the
collective consciousness of an emerging Caribbean nationalism,

one that has emerged with the West Indian's step from "slave to
certain owner."

The collection is also Brathwaite's most uneven work, a reflection, perhaps, of the degree to which it spans his development
from inexperienced writer to mature artist. The precisely drawn
portrait of the colonial psyche in "Journeys" is therefore far
superior to the self-indulgence and flabbiness of language which
mar the word pictures of jazz artists in "Blues." Similarly "Conqueror" demonstrates an acute ear for the discriminating and the
effectively appropriate use of language, a quality that is lacking
in rather sentimental pieces like "At the Death of a Young Poet's
Wife" and "Schooner." On the whole *Other Exiles* is significant
in that it reflects, at its best, those qualities which have become
the hallmarks of Brathwaite's mature poetry—the enormous
suppleness of language which facilitates a deceptive ease of transition from one viewpoint to the other ("Conqueror"), the complex sense of personality which allows the poet to develop his
persona both as a distinctive individual and as the archetype of a
collective experience ("Journeys"), the imaginative handling of
folk language as the expression of a distinctive West Indian
culture, and, even in the badly flawed "Blues," a crucial interest
in the expressive significance of music in the history and culture
of Blacks inside and outside the Caribbean.

These are all the qualities that underlie the success of the
trilogy. The ambiguity of Brathwaite's poetic "I" (as both private
individual and collective archetype) is perfectly adapted to the
poet's exploration of the Caribbean experience in both its private
dimension and in its significance to an inclusive West Indian
culture. And in turn that ambiguity pinpoints the role of the poet
himself—voicing his vision in personal terms that are analogous
to and comparable with those of musicians and other artists. And
at the same time the terms of that personal vision symbolize a
group experience in which the creative energies of the culture—
like the poetic imagination itself—represent and celebrate the
vitality that has persisted in spite of slavery and colonialism.

Rights of Passage, the first section of the trilogy, concentrates
on Blacks in the Americas, moving from the West Indies to
North America and back. In the process the poet discovers
affinities between the songs, dances, and language forms through
which Blacks have responded to a common history, not only in
the New World but also in Africa. The exploration of these
connections in *Rights of Passage* amounts to a prelude of sorts to
the themes of *Masks* where the poet reverses the historical Middle Passage of slavery by returning from the New World to
Africa.

Africa is the source of much that has been explored in *Rights
of Passage,* and here in *Masks* the poet expands upon that sense
of a common source. The continent is simultaneously the historical root and the contemporary essence of a global Black presence. The sense of affinities is not only geographical but temporal: the New World Black's return to West Africa is therefore
described in terms which recall the forcible departure of the
visitor's ancestors into New World slavery, and the sights and
sounds of pre-colonial Africa are at times indistinguishable from
those of both contemporary Africa and the modern Caribbean.
The past and the present also co-exist in *Islands* where the poet
returns to the contemporary West Indies after symbolically
retracing the original voyages of enslavement. Here the images of
slavery and colonialism are juxtaposed, for the purposes of
dramatic contrast, with symbols of the new West Indian
nationalism.

Finally, the self-conscious use of a variety of language forms
(West Indian and Black American as well as West African) is
fundamental to Brathwaite's themes throughout the trilogy. The
very variety of language enforces the poet's vision of West Indian
culture as the diverse product of several sources—Africa,

Europe, Asia, and the New World itself. In a similar vein the journey themes which dominate the narrative design of the trilogy reinforce a sense of cultural and historical continuities as we move with the poet, through space and time, from one point of the Black diaspora to another. And this impression of continuous movement also dramatizes that cultural and psychic progression which gradually culminates, in the trilogy, in the emergence of a national consciousness that displaces traditional self-hatred and entrenched colonial values.

Mother Poem is actually an intensified and detailed continuation of the themes of *The Arrivants*, for here the progression from a destructive past to a future of creative possibilities is concentrated in Barbados. The mother image that dominates the work (a long continuous poem) is a dual one: it connotes a personal mother and it reflects the perception of Barbados itself as a mother country, as a cultural source of the poet's perception of self and society. This duality intensifies the vision of growth and change: the progression is simultaneously cultural in a broad social sense and deeply personal. And in turn this sustained duality attests to the persistence of one of Brathwaite's most important assets as poet—his ability to integrate the personal and public voices into a complex poetic language which allows each voice to remain distinctive.

—Lloyd W. Brown

BRAUN, Richard Emil. American. Born in Detroit, Michigan, 22 November 1934. Educated at the University of Michigan, Ann Arbor, 1952-59, A.B. 1956, A.M. 1957; University of Texas, Austin, 1960-62, 1968, Ph.D. 1969. Lecturer, 1962-64, Assistant Professor, 1964-69, Associate Professor, 1969-76, and since 1976, Professor of Classics, University of Alberta, Edmonton. Recipient: President's Medal, University of Western Ontario, London, 1965; Bread Loaf Writers Conference Robert Frost Fellowship, 1968; Canada Council bursary, 1969. Agent: Joan Daves, 59 East 54th Street, New York, New York, 10022, U.S.A. Address: Department of Classics, University of Alberta, Edmonton, Alberta T6G 2E5, Canada.

PUBLICATIONS

Verse

Companions to Your Doom. Detroit, New Fresco, 1961.
Children Passing. Austin, University of Texas Press, 1962.
Bad Land. Penland, North Carolina, Jargon, 1971.
The Foreclosure. Urbana, University of Illinois Press, 1972.

Plays

Antigone, adaptation of the play by Sophocles (produced Stellenbosch, 1979; Washington, D.C., 1983). New York, Oxford University Press, 1973; London, Oxford University Press, 1974.
Rhesos, adaptation of the play by Euripides (produced London, 1980). New York, Oxford University Press, 1978; London, Oxford University Press, 1979.

Other

Editor, *Satires,* by Juvenal, translated by Jerome Mazzaro. Ann Arbor, University of Michigan Press, 1965.

Translator, *Satires,* by Persius. Lawrence, Kansas, Coronado Press, 1983.

*

Bibliography: *Journal of Modern Literature 6* (Philadelphia), no. 4, 1977.

Manuscript Collection: Humanities Research Center, University of Texas, Austin.

Critical Studies: "Putting It Together: The Poetry of Richard Emil Braun" by Jerome Mazzaro in *Modern Poetry Studies 5* (Buffalo), Winter 1974; "Deceptive Symmetry: Classical Echoes in the Poetry of Richard Emil Braun" by Roy Arthur Swanson, in *Modern Poetry Studies 7* (Buffalo), Winter 1976; *The Art of the Real* by Eric Homberger, London, Dent, 1977.

Richard Emil Braun comments:

(1980) 1) I suggest that a reader go through my books from front to back, since I mean them to be read that way. *Bad Land* has been called a "verse novel." *Children Passing* and *The Foreclosure* are selections (*not* collections) of poems placed in a formal order.

2) My "ethical" aims may, in great part, be learned from Richard Ellmann's introduction to his *Selected Writings of Henri Michaux.* Ellmann says, "With dreams and nightmares to corroborate him, he [Michaux] has seemed to suggest that if any formula can be elicited from experience, it is that the unexpected happens to the unready." He reports a remark of Gide's that Michaux makes us feel "both the strangeness of natural things and the naturalness of strange things." And last: "His *saeva indignatio...*is usually concealed, and he is less explicit than Swift or Voltaire in describing what man might be.... But his standards are, like theirs, medicinal; good and evil fall into place."

3) My manner of writing is the opposite of Michaux's, however. Michaux rejects construction and tradition. In my view, disorders of experience demand methodical exposition. I think that non-conformity may best operate through parody, or willful misuse, of traditional forms and notions; that is, by tactics of subversion.

I aim at progressively tighter integration of larger and more varied mixtures of subject matter, and at fast-linked schemes of metaphor and image; and aim to eliminate local metaphors and merely illustrative comparisons.

The tradition I parody and abuse is that of naturalism. Thus I employ what seems to be informative or atmospheric description; but my "details" are symbolic emblems or poetic images which work with others, never singly. Discursive, dramatic, and narrative structures are really camouflaged juxtapositions which have metaphoric force, or act as imagistic or symbolic arrangements. Therefore, argumentation may be cogent or illogical, dialogue either true or stilted, and any real-life plot may be interrupted by fantasy, according to the needs of the large scheme or of emotional tensions which pervade it. Even when I approximate fiction, the characters and their stories belong more to the world of dream (and of vaudeville) than to that of the realistic novel.

Finally, the verses themselves. Most are composed in authentic verse-modes, where sounds are counted predictably; but the style often mocks some conventional pattern (a pentameter that is not iambic, or a ballad bared of rhyme). At all times—even (or especially) when the subject matter is humorous, grotesque, or downright horrible—the lyricist's phonemic blendings and the dramatist's rhythmic periods abound.

(1985) In paragraph (3), I am in error. Michaux did not reject tradition in writing, but constructed in modes such as the Traveller's Tale and the Memoir. Also, I ought to have said "patterned," instead of "methodical" exposition.

On the paragraph beginning "I aim," I should note that "larger and more varied mixtures" have led me to write ever longer and more complicated poems. Also, I must acknowledge that since 1971 or 2 I have gained strength and freshness from F.O. Copley's essay "Aristotle to Gertrude Stein: the Arts of Poetry," *Mosaic*, vol. 5, no. 4. To the final paragraph, I should add that since 1976 I have composed much accentual verse, seeking to define and obey rules compatible with modern phoneticians' descriptions of present-day English stress.

*   *   *

Richard Emil Braun writes a massive, highly sculptured poetry, moulded equally by classical forms and philosophy (he is a professor of classics at the University of Alberta) and those of modern prose, and their echoes in the surrealism of Henri Michaux and the classicism of John Crowe Ransom and Robert Frost. The delicate balance thus achieved makes great demands on the reader, who would do well to bear in mind the opening lines of "Against Nature":

To combat
nature, not man,
is what men do which is most concordant
with nature.

In Braun's poetry, the accidental coincidences and anonymous consequences of nature (i.e., everything that is not self, as with Rilke) require the action of a mind watching them, and the structure of a poetic "conscience of identities" to record them.

To engage this combat with nature, Braun turns most frequently to the epic form of narration and episode, told through interior monologue. The narrator's highly specific point of view watches, records, and transforms:

Now I am old you'll look to me for beauty;
you'll want a metric close, a final turn
to ground suspended cadences. I warn
you, though: clear statement isn't clarity.

he says in "Late Promenades," one of his earliest published poems. In this coupled, doubled vision of the poem and the narrator, the events of reality begin to shimmer and dissolve, allowing us to peer dimly through them, to "actively invert to core/that is the real external."

In close conjunction with the multiple points of view, the poems themselves reorganize reality, by means of both their overall shape and their specific detail. *Bad Land* is an epyllion, or epic lyric, seven long, interconnected poems that recount forty years in the lives of John Greer and John Harlan and their wives and families, travelling to and from two cities "in the geometrical center of the United States." The classical balance and formal organization of this sequence has been explicated by Roy Arthur Swanson and Jerome Mazzaro in its rich internal symmetries, and echoes of the *Iliad*. Such links of places and ages are not irrelevant to Braun's poetry: as John Greer meditates, "What God once was, we are now./Whatever God today is, we will one day be."

The formal organization of *Bad Land* resonates in detail throughout Braun's work. Ellie H., Harlan's daughter and Greer's wife, reappears, like a musical theme, in "Listening," the opening poem of *The Foreclosure*. Here, she squats, nearly

immobile, unblinking, "listening for the possibilities of sight." The narrator, "to spare you pain," warns her of the distortions of funhouse mirrors, but seeing her,

as I brag
("You'll never see some of yourself,
Louella, as so
fine as reflected in my eyes")

he realizes that her tears "are for me,/for my, my pain."

These recurrences enlarge the breadth of the poems, just as Braun's poetry provides a musical background for his themes and variations. In the ambiguous rhyme scheme of "Late Promenades," the *abba* scheme in the four lines quoted above becomes so elusive later that it can be read as a different, harmonic scheme. In "Listening," the assonances and consonances of "yourself/Louella," "as so," and "fine...my eyes" hint at the detailed craftsmanship of his work. Throughout his work, Braun presents a unique and deeply considered way of seeing, describing the shapes of essences, until (as in "Ties That Bind") "The arcs join,/mend a circle. We are upon it./The circle, like us, has a memory."

—Walter Bode

———————

BRAUTIGAN, Richard. American. Born in Tacoma, Washington, 30 January 1933. Married Virginia Dionne Adler in 1957 (divorced); one daughter. Poet-in-Residence, California Institute of Technology, Pasadena, 1967. Recipient: National Endowment for the Arts grant, 1968. *Died (suicide) in September 1984.*

<small>PUBLICATIONS</small>

Verse

The Return of the Rivers. San Francisco, Inferno Press, 1957.
The Galilee Hitch-Hiker. San Francisco, White Rabbit Press, 1958.
Lay the Marble Tea: Twenty-Four Poems. San Francisco, Carp Press, 1959.
The Octopus Frontier. San Francisco, Carp Press, 1960.
All Watched Over by Machines of Loving Grace. San Francisco, Communication, 1967.
Please Plant This Book. San Francisco, Mackintosh, 1968.
The Pill Versus the Springhill Mine Disaster (Poems 1957-1968). San Francisco, Four Seasons, 1968; London, Cape, 1970.
Rommel Drives On Deep into Egypt. New York, Delacorte Press, 1970; London, Pan, 1973.
Five Poems. Berkeley, California, Serendipity, 1971.
Loading Mercury with a Pitchfork. New York, Simon and Schuster, 1976.
June 30th, June 30th. New York, Delacorte Press, 1978.

Recording: *Listening to Richard Brautigan*, Harvest, 1970.

Novels

A Confederate General from Big Sur. New York, Grove Press, 1965; London, Cape, 1971.

Trout Fishing in America.   San Francisco, Four Seasons, 1967;
London, Cape, 1970.
In Watermelon Sugar.   San Francisco, Four Seasons, 1968;
London, Cape, 1970.
The Abortion: An Historical Romance 1966.   New York,
Simon and Schuster, 1971; London, Cape, 1973.
The Hawkline Monster: A Gothic Western.   New York, Simon
and Schuster, 1974; London, Cape, 1975.
Willard and His Bowling Trophies: A Perverse Mystery.   New
York, Simon and Schuster, 1975; London, Cape, 1976.
Sombrero Fallout: A Japanese Novel.   New York, Simon and
Schuster, 1976; London, Cape, 1977.
Dreaming of Babylon: A Private Eye Novel 1942.   New York,
Delacorte Press, 1977; London, Cape, 1978.
The Tokyo-Montana Express.   New York, Delacorte Press,
1980; London, Cape, 1981.
So the Wind Won't Blow It All Away.   New York, Delacorte
Press, 1982; London, Cape, 1983.

Short Stories

Revenge of the Lawn: Stories 1962-1970.   New York, Simon
and Schuster, 1971; London, Cape, 1972.

*

Bibliography: by Stephen R. Jones, in *Bulletin of Bibliography*
(Boston), January 1976.

Critical Studies: *Richard Brautigan* by Terence Malley, New
York, Warner, 1972; *Richard Brautigan* by Marc Chénetier,
London, Methuen, 1983; *Richard Brautigan* by Edward H. Fos-
ter, Boston, Twayne, 1983.

*   *   *

"I'm a minor poet," writes Richard Brautigan in "The Literary
Life in California/1964," and few would argue that his volumes
of verse are as uniformly and richly satisfying as his remarkable
collection of novels. While there is seldom a false note struck in
his prose fiction, his poetry at its worst can sound embarrassingly
flat. Brautigan's early work especially suffers from the notion
that almost any random thought can make a poem, as in "Xerox
Candy Bar":

> Ah,
> you're just a copy
> of all the candy bars
> I've ever eaten.

Yet in his attempt to find poetry in unusual places and topics,
Brautigan shows a willingness to take chances with his craft, and
when the gamble pays off (as it does in such oft-anthologized
poems as "San Francisco" and "Romeo and Juliet," two works
set in a laundromat), the results are wondrous, and though the
younger Brautigan sometimes pushes a joke too far (four poems
in his second volume consist merely of a title, including "A
48-Year-Old Burglar from San Diego"), more often he is able to
make us laugh, as in "Attila at the Gates of the Telephone
Company." With his ironic and self-deprecating glimpses of life
in our times, Brautigan makes us feel "surrounded by general
goofiness."

Few of Brautigan's poems are more than a few lines long; thus,
each must stand or fall on a single image—or a single joke.
Brautigan's short poems work best as part of a longer sequence,
as in *The Galilee Hitch-Hiker* (which has Baudelaire visiting

America, opening a flowerburger stand, and going to baseball
games) or in the "Group Portrait," "Montana," and "Captain
Martin" poems in *Loading Mercury with a Pitchfork*. His short
poems also work well when they deal with themes that merit
attention and can show Brautigan's sensitivity and compassion
at their finest: touching elegies like "Death Is a Beautiful Car
Parked Only," exquisite love lyrics like "Catfish Friend" and "In
Her Sweetness She Folds My Wounds," and simple poems to
nature like "Yes, the Fish Music."

To do the seemingly impossible and to make it appear easy—
to load mercury with a pitchfork—is the poet's craft, Brautigan's
writings suggest, and often we see him master this feat. His most
deeply affecting volume is *June 30th, June 30th,* a poetic diary of
a trip to Japan. In the introduction to this work, Brautigan says
of Basho and Issa, "I liked the way they used language concentrating emotion, detail and image until they arrived at a form of
dew-like steel," and then he proceeds to give us poems of dew-like
steel, sharp and clean as any haiku. Here Brautigan's technique is
happily wedded to his topic, and each individual poem fits neatly
into the pattern of the book. Moreover, the journey to Japan
becomes a metaphor of the author's journey into himself: "All
the possibilities of life,/all roads led here." *June 30th, June 30th*
is a quietly haunting, fully realized work. Interestingly, one of its
major themes was presaged in "Karma Repair Kit: Items 1-4" in
his first volume:

> 1. Get enough to eat,
>   and eat it.
> 2. Find a place to sleep where it is quiet,
>   and sleep there.
> 3. Reduce intellectual and emotional noise
>   until you arrive at the silence of yourself,
>   and listen to it.
> 4.

In this poem and in many others, Brautigan cuts through the
intellectual and emotional noise to touch us all.

—Dennis Lynch

BREMSER, Ray.   American.   Born in Jersey City, New Jersey, 22 February 1934. Served in the United States Air Force,
1951. Married Bonnie Frazer in 1959, two daughters; lived with
Judy Johnson, 1976-79, one son. Served prison terms for armed
robbery, 1952-58 and 1961-65, parole violation, 1959-60, and
bail jumping. Lives in Utica, New York. Address: c/o Cherry
Valley Editions, 2314 Georgian Woods Place, Wheaton, Maryland 20902, U.S.A.

PUBLICATIONS

Verse

Poems of Madness.   New York, Paper Book Gallery, 1965.
*Angel: The Work of One Night in the Dark, Solitary Confine-
ment, New Jersey State Prison, Trenton.*   New York, Tomp-
kins Square Press, 1967.
*Drive Suite: An Essay on Composition, Materials, Reference,
Etc.*   San Francisco, Nova Broadcast Press, 1968.
Black Is Black Blues.   Buffalo, New York, Intrepid Press, 1971.

Blowing Mouth: The Jazz Poems 1958-1970.   Cherry Valley, New York, Cherry Valley Editions, 1978.

*   *   *

The best of Ray Bremser's poetry is a celebration of life as it is lived by some of the denizens of our 20th-century cities, a wild, swinging (in the jazz sense) discourse on the ups and downs, and the joys and sorrows, of the streets and apartments and prisons which—in Bremser's case, at least—form such an integral part of the total experience. And it's fitting that the language of the poems is often as chaotic and colourful as the subject-matter, as varied and sometimes shocking as Bremser's own activities.

It is language which is the key factor in the poems, and it can move within a single stanza from a knowing patter redolent of street corners and jazz cellars and prison cells to an articulate imagery which displays a highly-developed awareness of the impact of the pure sound of words. And it is always rhythmic. It would not be absurd to suggest that Bremser's work is best read to a background of fast-moving jazz records.

In suggesting that his main attribute is a penchant for lively language one doesn't wish to play down his knowledge, unpolished and fragmentary though it may often be. He was once described as an "American primitive," and it is an accurate summing-up of his general position. One sees him as wandering through the city, occasionally involved in its quick pleasures, and then again capable of grassroots flashes of insight which highlight the pain and corruption also to be found there.

True, Bremser has certain basic faults. He can be tasteless, and his verbal trickiness can lead to passages which, rhythmic though they are, have little of substance in them. One accepts them in the context of the poems, just as one accepts tawdry advertisements found in parts of a city, but there is nothing to be learned from them. They are, to be fair, a part of the whole scene, but one moves on to more profitable things. Bremser's lapses should be ignored, if possible, and his less-frenetic expressions studied with care. When he succeeds he offers a personal view of life which, despite its limitations, is often more accurate and honest than that proposed by poets with seemingly-superior techniques.

—Jim Burns

BREW, O.H. Kwesi.   Ghanaian.   Born in Cape Coast, Ghana, in 1928.   Educated at schools in Cape Coast, Kumasi, Tamale and Accra; University College of the Gold Coast (now the University of Ghana), Legon.,Entered the Administrative Service in 1953; Government Agent at Keta for nearly two years, then Assistant Secretary in the Public Service Commission. Now in the Ghana Foreign Service: has been Ambassador for Ghana to Britain, France, India, Germany, the U.S.S.R., Mexico, and Senegal. Recipient: British Council Prize. Lives in Accra, Ghana. Address: c/o Greenfield Review Press, P.O. Box 80, Greenfield Center, New York 12833, U.S.A.

PUBLICATIONS

Verse

The Shadows of Laughter.   London, Longman, 1968.
Pergamon Poets 2: Poetry from Africa, with others, edited by Howard Sergeant.   Oxford, Pergamon Press, 1968.

African Panorama.   Greenfield Center, New York, Greenfield Review Press, 1981.

Play

Screenplay: *The Harvest.*

*   *   *

Kwesi Brew has a much wider range, both of subject and style, than most of his African contemporaries, and over the years he has developed a voice inherently his own. He has written poems about childbirth ("Gamelli's Arm Has Broken into Buds"), childhood memories, youthful indiscretions, and middle-age reflections ("The Middle of the River"), as well as some of the most tender love poems to come out of Africa ("Flower and Fragrance," "The Two Finds," "The Mesh," etc.). Ghanaian folk song and customs are intricately woven into the tapestry of his poetry and since Brew has exceptional descriptive gifts the Ghanaian landscape and idiom come suddenly to life for non-African readers when he makes use of them, as he frequently does as a background element. If he has written about such specifically traditional subjects as ancestor-worship ("Ancestral Faces") and the passing of the fighting tribes ("Questions of Our Time"), he has not hesitated to deal with a recent event of great significance for his country—the downfall of President Nkrumah—in a poem entitled "A Sandal on the Head." In this fascinating poem, which appeared in *Outposts* shortly after the event it celebrates, Brew maintained a careful distance from his subject by employing an objective correlative appropriate to the situation in the Ghanaian custom of touching the head of a chief with one of his own sandals to declare him "de-stooled." "Ghost Dance," "The Master of the Common Crowd," "The Secrets of the Tribe," "A Plea for Mercy," "The Harvest of Our Life," and many other poems draw strongly upon the African way of life and present the conflict between old and new, between tribal instinct and national aspiration, and between the regional and the universal.

—Howard Sergeant

BREWSTER, Elizabeth (Winifred).   Canadian.   Born in Chipman, New Brunswick, 26 August 1922.   Educated at the University of New Brunswick, Fredericton, B.A. 1946; Radcliffe College, Cambridge, Massachusetts, A.M. 1947; King's College, London, 1949-50; University of Toronto (Pratt Gold Medal and Prize, 1953), B.L.S. 1953; Indiana University, Bloomington, Ph.D. 1962. Cataloguer, Carleton University Library, Ottawa, 1953-57, and Indiana University Library, 1957-58; Member of the English Department, Victoria University, British Columbia, 1960-61; Reference Librarian, Mount Allison University Library, Sackville, New Brunswick, 1961-65; Cataloguer, New Brunswick Legislative Library, Fredericton, 1965-68, and University of Alberta Library, Edmonton, 1968-72; Visiting Assistant Professor of English, University of Alberta, 1970-71. Assistant Professor, 1972-75, Associate Professor, 1975-80, and since 1980, Professor of English, University of Saskatchewan, Saskatoon. Recipient: Canada Council award, 1971, 1976, 1978; President's Medal, University of Western Ontario, 1980. Litt.D.: University of New Brunswick, 1982. Address: Department of English, University of Saskatchewan, Saskatoon, Saskatchewan S7N 0W0, Canada.

PUBLICATIONS

Verse

East Coast. • Toronto, Ryerson Press, 1951.
Lillooet. Toronto, Ryerson Press, 1954.
Roads and Other Poems. Toronto, Ryerson Press, 1957.
Five New Brunswick Poets, with others, edited by Fred Cogs-
    well. Fredericton, New Brunswick, Fiddlehead, 1962.
Passage of Summer: Selected Poems. Toronto, Ryerson Press,
    1969.
Sunrise North. Toronto, Clarke Irwin, 1972.
In Search of Eros. Toronto, Clarke Irwin, 1974.
Sometimes I Think of Moving. Ottawa, Oberon Press, 1977.
The Way Home. Ottawa, Oberon Press, 1982.
Digging In. Ottawa, Oberon Press, 1982.

Novels

The Sisters. Ottawa, Oberon Press, 1974.
Junction. Windsor, Ontario, Black Moss Press, 1982.

Short Stories

It's Easy to Fall on the Ice. Ottawa, Oberon Press, 1977.
A House Full of Women. Ottawa, Oberon Press, 1983.

*

Critical Studies: "The Poetry of Elizabeth Brewster" by Des-
mond Pacey, in *Ariel* (Calgary, Alberta), July 1973; "Speeding
Towards Strange Destinations: A Conversation with Elizabeth
Brewster" by Paul Denham, in *Essays on Canadian Writing*
(Downsview, Ontario), Summer-Fall 1980.

*   *   *

"I have written poems principally to come to a better understanding of myself, my world, and other people," Elizabeth
Brewster has explained. Her work does dramatize (again in her
own words) "the struggle to lead a human rational life in a world
which is increasingly inhuman and irrational."

This credo applies particularly to *Passage of Summer: Selected
Poems*, which brings together the best poems of the New
Brunswick-born writer's earlier collections. These poems are
sometimes slight and always sentimental, celebrating as they do
life in "one of its gentler moods" (as Miss Brewster wrote on one
occasion). The poet's early memories are brought to life and
given an overall structure in "Lillooet," a poem about a Maritime
village written in twenty pages of rhyming couplets. The poem
concludes: "No matter where I live, my neighbour still/Will be
Miss Ruby Mullins or Peter Hill." It is a moving experience to
read "Lillooet," but it is not a particularly memorable work.

The poems of Miss Brewster's more recent book, *Sunrise
North*, are less concerned with the past and more focused on the
present and the future. They display to advantage a new facet of
the poet's personality: a delightful, rather pixie-like, sense of
humour. There is a poem called "Munchausen in Alberta" which
ends: "That's the only time/I was ever a fire-eater." And in "Gold
Man" she concludes: "Next time I am born/I intend to come/
from a different country."

The forms of the new poems are all free and flowing, rather in
the manner of Raymond Souster. They are Souster-ish, too, in
that the lyric spirit takes off imaginatively from an anecdote or
an incongruity observed by the poet. The poems are quiet but
somewhat fanciful, as if the author has been freed to some extent

from her earlier credo ("human *rational* life") and may now
explore less rational realms of desire and imagination.

One does not expect Miss Brewster to turn into a Confessional
poet, but she has become a truly contemporary poet. She is
beginning to write more out of her personality, and it is interesting to note the last line of "Advice to the Fearful Self": "If
necessary, scream." One wonders whether or not she will.

—John Robert Colombo

———————

BRINGHURST, Robert. Canadian. Born in Los Angeles,
California, 16 October 1946; grew up in the United States, Mex-
ico, and Canada. Educated at Massachusetts Institute of
Technology, Cambridge, 1963-64, 1970-71; University of Utah,
Salt Lake City, 1964-65; Indiana University, Bloomington, 1971-
73, B.A. in comparative literature 1973; University of British
Columbia, Vancouver, M.F.A. 1975. Served in the United States
Army, in California, Israel, and Panama Canal Zone, 1966-69.
Married Miki Cannon Sheffield in 1974 (divorced, 1981); one
daughter. Visiting Lecturer in Creative Writing, 1975-77, and
Lecturer in English, 1979-80, University of British Columbia;
lecturer in typographical history, Simon Fraser University, Burn-
aby, British Columbia, 1983-84; Poet-in-Residence, Banff Centre School of Fine Arts, Alberta, 1983. Guest Editor, *Contem-
porary Literature in Translation*, Vancouver, 1974, 1976.
Recipient: Ontario Arts Council grant, 1982. Address: 3253
Point Grey Road, Vancouver, British Columbia V6K 1B3; or,
c/o Writers Union of Canada, 24 Ryerson Avenue, Toronto,
Ontario M5T 2P3, Canada.

PUBLICATIONS

Verse

The Shipwright's Log. Bloomington, Indiana, Kanchenjunga
    Press, 1972.
Cadastre. Bloomington, Indiana, Kanchenjunga Press, 1973.
Deuteronomy. Delta, British Columbia, Sono Nis Press, 1974.
Pythagoras. Vancouver, Kanchenjunga Press, 1974.
Eight Objects. Vancouver, Kanchenjunga Press, 1975.
Bergschrund. Delta, British Columbia, Sono Nis Press, 1975.
Jacob Singing. Vancouver, Kanchenjunga Press, 1977.
Death by Water. Vancouver, University of British Columbia
    Library, 1977.
The Stonecutter's Horses. Vancouver, Standard Editions, 1979.
The Knife in the Measure. Steelhead, British Columbia, Bar-
    barian Press, 1980.
Song of the Summit. Toronto, Dreadnaught Press, 1982.
The Salute by Tasting. Vancouver, Slug Press, 1982.
Tzuhalem's Mountain. Lantzville, British Columbia, Oolichan
    Press, 1982.
The Beauty of the Weapons: Selected Poems 1972-82. Toronto,
    McClelland and Stewart, 1982.
Saraha. Lexington, Kentucky, King Library Press, 1984.

Other

The Raven Steals the Light: Stories, with Bill Reid. Van-
    couver, Douglas and McIntyre, and Seattle, University of
    Washington Press, 1984.
Ocean/Paper/Stone. Vancouver, William Hoffer, 1984.

Editor, with others, *Visions: Contemporary Art in Canada.* Vancouver, Douglas and McIntyre, 1983.

*

Critical Studies: William Meads, in *Kayak* (Santa Cruz, California), February 1977; Jane Munro, in *CV 2* (Winnipeg), Winter 1980-81; Wayne Holder, in *Vancouver Literary News*, April 1983; Sam Hamill, in *Western American Literature* (Logan, Utah), Fall 1983; Robert Fulford, in *Saturday Night* (Toronto), March 1984.

*   *   *

The poems of Robert Bringhurst seem almost to contradict the statement of method and intentions he makes in the "Prefatory Note" to *The Beauty of the Weapons*, a collection which gathers much of his work published by small presses: "Most of the poems are products more of oral composition than of writing, and have survived into this selection only with repeated performance as a test...they exist in the voice, to which the page, though we enshrine it, is in the right order of things a subservient medium." Yet in their formal beauty, resembling that of runes and hieroglyphics, Bringhurst's poems almost seem expressly designed for the page and deserving of thick paper and elegant typography. For all his allegiance to air, breath, music (one of the book's valuable notes says that a poem, "Hachadura," is intended "as music, not as cartography. For listening; not, like a map or a roadsign, for reading"), Bringhurst adores indelible materials. Even air becomes substantial ("the chipped air" and "black blades of the wind" in "Three Deaths") and he observes "the stricture/of uncut, utterly/uncluttered light" ("Poem about Crystal"). Erudite, hard-edged, Bringhurst is a philosophical materialist, praising the presocratics (in a note for the section "The Old in Their Knowing") who "knew no distinction between physicist, philosopher, biologist and poet."

For Bringhurst, mind becomes visible, as in "Pherekydes":

There remains of the mind of Pherekydes
the esker and the glacial milk,
the high spring runoff in the gorge,

and the waterfalls hammered out of cloud
against the mid cliff,
vanishing in the hungry Himalayan air

Although the poet may sometimes be guilty of imagistic over-reaching ("quiet as butterflies' bones" in "Four Glyphs") he composes work of carved shapeliness, as "A Quadratic Equation":

Voice: the breath's tooth.
Thought: the brain's bone.
Birdsong: an extension
of the beak of speech:
the antler of the mind.

Using a variety of voices (Francesco Petrarca; an old Coast Salish Indian) and locales (the Old Testament wilderness; El Salvador) Bringhurst consistently meditates on the fundamental, primary, elemental, whether it be the Pentateuch or Aztec mythology or love itself ("Hic Amor, Haec Patria"):

All knowledge is carnal.
Knowledge is meat,
knowledge is muscle.
Old woman, old woman,

what is this hunger
grown hard as a bone?

In Gaston Bachelard's system, Bringhurst would be termed a poet whose element is earth. Certainly—in more senses than one—he is a poet of substance.

—Fraser Sutherland

———————

BRINNIN, John Malcolm. American. Born in Halifax, Nova Scotia, Canada, 13 September 1916. Educated at the University of Michigan, Ann Arbor, B.A. 1941; Harvard University, Cambridge, Massachusetts, 1941-42. Associate Editor, Dodd Mead, publishers, New York, 1942-47, and at the University of Connecticut, Storrs, 1951-62. Director, YM-YWHA Poetry Center, New York, 1949-56. State Department Lecturer and Delegate in Europe in 1954, 1956 and 1961. Professor of English, Boston University, 1961-78, now Emeritus. Recipient: Levinson Prize (*Poetry*, Chicago), 1943; Poetry Society of America Gold Medal, 1955; American Academy grant, 1968. Member, American Academy. Address: King Caesar Road, Duxbury, Massachusetts 02332, U.S.A.

PUBLICATIONS

Verse

The Garden Is Political. New York, Macmillan, 1942.
The Lincoln Lyrics. New York, New Directions, 1942.
No Arch, No Triumph. New York, Knopf, 1945.
The Sorrows of Cold Stone: Poems 1940-1950. New York, Dodd Mead, 1951.
The Selected Poems of John Malcolm Brinnin. Boston, Little Brown, and London, Weidenfeld and Nicolson, 1963.
Skin Diving in the Virgins and Other Poems. New York, Delacorte Press, 1970; London, Macmillan, 1974.

Recording: *The Poetry of John Malcolm Brinnin*, McGraw Hill, n.d.

Other

Dylan Thomas in America; An Intimate Journal. Boston, Little Brown, 1955; London, Dent, 1956.
The Third Rose: Gertrude Stein and Her World. Boston, Little Brown, 1959; London, Weidenfeld and Nicolson, 1960.
William Carlos Williams: A Critical Study. Minneapolis, University of Minnesota Press, 1961.
Arthur: The Dolphin Who Didn't See Venice (for children). Boston, Little Brown, 1961.
William Carlos Williams. Minneapolis, University of Minnesota Press, 1963.
The Sway of the Grand Saloon: A Social History of the North Atlantic. New York, Delacorte Press, 1971; London, Macmillan, 1972.
Sextet: T.S. Eliot and Truman Capote and Others. New York, Delacorte Press, 1981; London, Deutsch, 1982.
Beau Voyage: Life Aboard the Last Great Ships. New York, Congdon and Lattès, 1981; London, Thames and Hudson, 1982.

Editor, with Kimon Friar, *Modern Poetry: American and British*.
New York, Appleton Century Crofts, 1951.
Editor, *A Casebook on Dylan Thomas*. New York, Crowell,
1960.
Editor, *Poems*, by Emily Dickinson. New York, Dell, 1960.
Editor, with Bill Read, *Modern Poets: An American-British
Anthology*. New York, McGraw Hill, 1963; revised edition,
1970.
Editor, *Selected Operas and Plays of Gertrude Stein*. Pitts-
burgh, University of Pittsburgh Press, 1970.
Editor, with Bill Read, *Twentieth Century Poetry, American and
British (1900-1970): An American-British Anthology*. New
York, McGraw Hill, 1971.

*

Critical Study: by the author, in *Poets on Poetry*, edited by
Howard Nemerov, New York, Basic Books, 1966.

*   *   *

It is obvious enough that the surface of John Malcolm Brinnin's verse has caught something of the tone of both Dylan
Thomas and of Theodore Roethke; but this has tended to mis-
lead readers—especially at that level of discussion which, while it
doesn't reach print, makes or mars reputations—from his own
qualities. I doubt if he is a poet much actually read except in
anthologies; and this is unjust. For, unlike Thomas (who was not
an intellectual at all), and in a manner totally different from
Roethke's, Brinnin works very hard, and with persistent intelligence, to control his verbally excited surface. This amounts to a
method—not to an excess—and it is a method that is instructive.
Whether it is entirely successful is another matter; but poetry, at
much cost to the individual poet, thrives on failure. Brinnin is
consistently interesting and serious: his poetry deserves to be
better known than his famous *Dylan Thomas in America*, and
this is not the case.

Brinnin is infinitely better educated than Thomas (which does
sometimes add an unnecessary dimension of literary rhetoric to
his work, but also gives it greater coherence) and less violently
self-centred than Roethke. A better clue to the nature of his
work, however, is to be found in his admiration of, and fine
translation from, the poetry of the gifted Ecuadorian Jorge
Carrera Andrade—who was one of the favourite poets of William Carlos Williams, on whom Brinnin has written a book.
Andrade, who employed surrealism but was not a surrealist,
learned much from the early poetry of Francis Jammes, and one
of Brinnin's qualities is the possession of a Jammesian gentleness
and melancholy. He thus has two distinct styles (his capacity for
pastiche is a third that is avowedly less serious): the Bardic-
religious, with overtones of Thomas, of which "The Worm in the
Whirling Cross" is the most representative example, and a more
pellucid, direct and humorous manner. There is no doubt that
the latter comes more naturally to him; but the former is (and
understandably) more ambitious. Thus, the language of "The
Worm in the Whirling Cross" cannot quite match up to its highly
complex content, and even falls back on Hopkins (a surprising
fault in a poet already mature):

No further, fathering logos, withering son,
Shall I my sense for want of grace confess,
But vouch this matter of decaying green
That with a shark's-tooth grin
Hinges the rooftree of my dwelling place....

He is more effective, and in fact as profound, when he is less
ambitious, as in "Architect, Logician," the little poem about a
snail: "Architect, logician, how well the snail/ Narrates his tenuous predicament!/.... Each hauls his house; the trick's to live in
it."

Brinnin's ultimate problem as a poet is the introduction of
himself—as any kind of entity other than a literary one—into the
work: he seems not to exist in his poems, to evade the quality of
his own feeling. This strategy sometimes does, of course, reveal
the poetic personality, and one may point to him as a composer
of very superior literary artifacts. But poetry requires something
more, and here Brinnin (so far) has only shown himself in a few,
and too widely dispersed, lines.

—Martin Seymour-Smith

—————

BROCK, Edwin. British. Born in London, 19 October
1927. Educated at state primary and grammar schools. Served
in the Royal Navy, 1945-47. Married 1) Patricia Brock in 1959
(marriage dissolved, 1964); 2) Elizabeth Brock in 1964; three
children. Editorial Assistant, Stonhill and Gillis, London, 1947-
51; Police Constable, Metropolitan Police, London, 1951-59;
advertising writer, Mather and Crowther, 1959-63, J. Walter
Thompson, 1963-64, and Masius Wynne-Williams, 1964, all
London; creative group head, S.H. Benson, London, 1964-72.
Since 1972, free-lance writer, Ogilvy Benson and Mather, London. Since 1960, Poetry Editor, *Ambit* magazine, London.
Agent: David Higham Associates Ltd., 5-8 Lower John Street,
London W1R 4HA. Address: The Granary, Lower Tharston,
Norfolk NR15 2YN, England.

PUBLICATIONS

Verse

An Attempt at Exorcism. London, Scorpion Press, 1959.
A Family Affair: Two Sonnet Sequences. London, Scorpion
Press, 1960.
With Love from Judas. Lowestoft, Suffolk, Scorpion Press,
1963.
Penguin Modern Poets 8, with Geoffrey Hill and Stevie Smith.
London, Penguin, 1966.
Fred's Primer: A Little Girl's Guide to the World Around Her.
London, Macmillan, 1969.
A Cold Day at the Zoo. London, Rapp and Whiting, 1970.
Invisibility Is the Art of Survival: Selected Poems. New York,
New Directions, 1972.
The Portraits and the Poses. London, Secker and Warburg,
and New York, New Directions, 1973.
I Never Saw It Lit. Santa Barbara, California, Capra Press,
1974.
Paroxisms: A Guide to the ISMS. New York, New Directions,
1974.
The Blocked Heart. London, Secker and Warburg, 1975; New
York, New Directions, 1976.
Song of the Battery Hen: Selected Poems 1959-1975. London,
Secker and Warburg, 1977.
The River and the Train. London, Secker and Warburg, and
New York, New Directions, 1979.

Plays

Radio Play: *Night Duty on Eleven Beat*, 1960.

Television Play: *The Little White God*, 1964.

Novel

The Little White God.   London, Hutchinson, 1962.

Other

Here. Now. Always (autobiography).   London, Secker and
Warburg, and New York, New Directions, 1977.

*

Manuscript Collection: State University of New York, Buffalo.

Critical Studies: *The New Poets* by M.L. Rosenthal, New York
and London, Oxford University Press, 1967; introduction by
Alan Pryce-Jones to *Invisibility Is the Art of Survival*, 1972.

Edwin Brock comments:
   (1974) One of the more embarrassing chores foisted by publishers upon their writers is that of writing the autobiographical
note for the book's jacket; writing an introduction to one's work
runs it a very close second. On one such jacket-note I said
recently that I have spent the years since 1927 waiting for something to happen, and that poetry is the nearest thing to an activity
I have yet found. This statement was not as flip as it sounds: I
believe that most activity is an attempt to define oneself in one
way or another: for me poetry, and only poetry, has provided this
self-defining act. With such an attitude, it was inevitable that my
early poetry would be autobiographical; and, indeed, there is still
an autobiographical core to most of my writing. But self-
examination is an open-ended process: there comes a point at
which if one is to "make" or define oneself, one has first to make
or define a Maker. It is this which provided the content of most of
my recent work. "Consequently I rejoice, having to construct
something/ Upon which to rejoice," said the maestro, and this
seems, to me, to be a role of the artist. If this sounds a self-
centred, non-communicating attitude for a writer, I would add
that it is only when the process of defining/ making/ constructing
results in something which has an objective "shareable" reality
that it becomes exciting—both for the writer and the reader.
   So far, critics have traced the following influences in my work:
Dylan Thomas, Robert Graves, Philip Larkin, Edmund Blunden,
Ted Hughes, Thomas Hardy, and William Blake. To find a
common factor in that lot, you have to be...another critic!

*   *   *

   It might be said that all Edwin Brock's poetry is concerned
with the vital question of personal identity, and most of the
poems in his first two books, *An Attempt at Exorcism* and *A
Family Affair*, are directly autobiographical. In an attempt to
define his own identity he writes about his relationships with his
grandparents, about growing up with a working-class background in South London, about his brother in a military prison,
about his wife and children, and falling in and out of love—but
always there is sense of guilt present in greater or less degree.
Perhaps he had still to come to terms with the mother symbol:

                              I have loved
     all mothers from time to time: mother
     Church, mother Hubbard and poor old
     mother Brock, yet I will never understand
     why every woman taking my dumb hand
     between her own remains so true to type:
     many-mouthed, loudly critical, alone,
     declaring that the best is always past
     and swearing that each mouthful is my last.

He evinces the same preoccupations in *With Love from Judas*,
and, despite so many poems in which he denies the reality of God
("An Ordered Sabbath"), he constantly reverts to God: "Dear
God, accepting that you cannot win/without my intervention,
can't we, as/fathers, settle for a non-aggression pact?" In the title
poem, again as a result of conflicts with his children, we have:

                              I watch tears
     run from my daughter's side, showing her
     no mercy. Repentance later will decide
     but, for this moment, Christ is dead

and in the group of poems on the break-up of his marriage, he
simply cannot keep God out of it, though even there he is
forcefully insisting that his wife carries her dead god to church
"like a decayed foetus" and links it with the death of love. But
With Love from Judas marks an important stage in Brock's
development, not only because he has found a natural and less
formal mode of expression, but because, in a poem entitled "Five
Ways to Kill a Man" (a poem much-anthologized) he turns
outward from his private obsessions to a public theme and shows
how admirably he can deal with it:

     These are, as I began, cumbersome ways
     to kill a man. Simpler, direct, and much more neat
     is to see that he is living somewhere in the middle
     of the twentieth century, and leave him there.

An even better poem on a subject particularly appropriate to our
age is his "Song of the Battery Hen":

     You can tell me: if you come by
     the North Door, I am in the twelfth pen
     on the left-hand side of the third row
     from the floor; and in that pen
     I am usually the middle one of three.
     But even without directions, you'd
     discover me. I have the same orange-
     red comb, yellow beak and auburn
     feathers; but as the door opens and you
     hear above the electric fan a kind of
     one-word wail, I am the one
     who sounds loudest in my head....
     God made us all quite differently,
     and blessed us with this expensive home.

Although disposed of in earlier books, god is much in evidence
in *The Portraits and the Poses* and the poet tells us that he
abandoned God for "bicycles, filmstars, Glenn Miller/and my
penis", yet paradoxically, in "Five Exposures" admits later that
"superstitiously/I touch prayer/to make/a photograph/for
God/to love." If in *The Portraits and the Poses* Brock is still
trying to find himself and claim an identity in his own inner
world, in *The Blocked Heart* he attempts to explore the external
world with the same objectives. Since he is an advertising executive (he was a policeman when he first started to write), it is

hardly surprising that he turns, with some disquiet, to the adman's sphere of marketing, products, market research and techniques, commodities and consumers: "and inasmuch as you/will climb to heaven/on a neighbour's neck/I will sell you spiked climbing boots."

Brock has undoubtedly been more influenced by American poetry than almost any other British poet, both in the confessional style of writing and in the adoption of very short lines—what Peter Porter has described as "extraordinarily pure, almost abstract language." His latest book, *The River and the Train*, is more assurd and more compassionate in the poet's acceptance of his place by the river (East Anglia), in the train on his regular visits to London, in his daily occupations, and more important, in relation to at least one other person:

> "My love, it is no longer dialogue but
> myself entering home again and again
> to make this beginning which is this
> becoming which is this continuous end."

Now that Brock seems to have found himself and his own place in the scheme of things, perhaps we can look forward to the major work of which he is capable and for which he has acquired, by a painful process, the understanding, the language and the skill.

—Howard Sergeant

BROMIGE, David (Mansfield). Canadian. Born in London, England, 22 October 1935. Educated at Haberdashers' Aske's School for Boys, London; University of British Columbia, Vancouver, B.A. 1962; University of California, Berkeley (Woodrow Wilson Fellow, 1962-63; Poet Laureate Competition prize, 1964; Phelan Award, 1968), M.A. 1964. Married 1) Ann Livingston in 1957 (divorced, 1961); 2) Joan Peacock in 1961 (divorced, 1970), one son; 3) Sherril Jaffe in 1970. Dairy farm worker, 1950-53; mental hospital attendant, 1954-55; elementary school teacher, in England, 1957-58, and in British Columbia, 1959-62; freelance reviewer, Canadian Broadcasting Corporation, 1960-62; Insructor in English, University of British Columbia, Summer 1964; Teaching Assistant, 1965-69, and Instructor in English, 1969-70, University of California, Berkeley. Since 1970, Assistant Professor of English, Sonoma State University, California. Editor, *Raven* magazine, 1960-62; Poetry Editor, *Northwest Review*, Eugene, Oregon, 1963-64; Editor, *R.C. Lion*, Berkeley, 1966-67. Recipient: Canadian Broadcasting Corporation prize, 1961; KVOS-TV prize, for play, 1962; Canada Council grant, 1965, 1966, and bursary, 1971; National Endowment for the Arts grant, 1969. Address: Department of English, Sonoma State University, 1801 East Cotati Avenue, Rohnert Park, California 94928, U.S.A.

PUBLICATIONS

Verse

The Gathering. Buffalo, Sumbooks, 1965.
Please, Like Me. Los Angeles, Black Sparrow Press, 1968.
The Ends of the Earth. Los Angeles, Black Sparrow Press, 1968.

The Quivering Roadway. Berkeley, California, Archangel Press, 1969.
In His Image. Berkeley, California, Twybyl Press, 1970.
Threads. Los Angeles, Black Sparrow Press, 1970.
The Fact So of Itself. Los Angeles, Black Sparrow Press, 1971.
They Are Eyes. San Francisco, Panjundrum Press, 1972.
Birds of the West. Toronto, Coach House Press, 1973.
Tight Corners and What's Around Them. Los Angeles, Black Sparrow Press, 1974.
Spells and Blessings. Vancouver, Talonbooks, 1974.
Out of My Hands. Los Angeles, Black Sparrow Press, 1974.
Ten Years in the Making: Selected Poems, Songs, and Stories 1961-1970. Vancouver, New Star, 1974.
Credences of Winter. Santa Barbara, California, Black Sparrow Press, 1976.

Plays

Radio and Television Plays: *Palace of Laments*, 1957; *The Medals*, 1959; *The Cobalt Poet*, 1960; *Save What You Can*, 1961.

Short Stories

Three Stories. Los Angeles, Black Sparrow Press, 1973.

*

David Bromige comments:

(1970) Primary among my associations in the field of poetry is the work of Robert Creeley, Charles Olson, and Robert Duncan—particularly Duncan—and therefore those poets they draw on, and those who share certain terms of the poem with the three named. But I use whatever I can, I can see, wherever.

I would sooner not state what, to my mind, are my major themes, preferring to leave that up to the reader. Again, he will be the best judge of my so-called stylistic devices—though I would draw attention to the note at the end of my book *The Ends of the Earth*. I have no usual verse forms, although no doubt patterns are apparent; certainly I love rime as passionately as I deplore (unless that *is* the concern of the specific poem) a mindless regularity of meter.

I am not interested in poetry as vehicle for ideas but rather as speech arising from dumb desire and passion and arousing further word clusters until constellations emerge I had previously no knowledge were within me. Nor, in a sense, were they: speaking, we enter a Speech, and though we may think we sit each in his aloneness, yet the words which then enter bear news of others; I was not born with that vocabulary, nor were those who, reading my poems, make of them something more than I could ever plan to give. In the instant when I had assumed I had understood certain linguistic and philosophical arguments intended to destroy faith in language—"we must all be talking about a different place," one recent poet put it—I found their flaw. Seekers after "the truth" who, in order to keep clear their minds, would dismiss much that is imagination's creation, choose not to see the prior acts of their own imaginations which have created so singular a notion of the truth.

I believe a poet is one both by birth and nurture; I don't believe that everyone can be a poet; nor can I see why anyone should *want* to be. There are obsessions which weigh less heavily and constantly upon a life. This is no request for gratitude. One is what one is and is used accordingly. However, there are poets who, because they wrote, and published, have enabled me to go on living; that is enough for me.

*   *   *

David Bromige's work comes out of Black Mountain via the Vancouver nexus of poets around the magazine *Tish*. His dissertation was on Duncan and Creeley, but even before that, in his first book, *The Gathering*, he had written some of the best Creeley criticism I know—criticism in the form of poems which elucidate Creeley's techniques by intelligent adaptation. There was more to the book than this, of course—among other things the first workings in an area of subject matter he has continued to mine, personal erotic-psychological experience, and long narrative-based poems which have also continued. Less elusively than many of Creeley's, Bromige's poems too, even when they do subsume a narrative element, always locate their action on the page, not in some anterior "real" world. Always, too, they have more than one kind of interest: feeling, tone, music, logopoeia, and (a particular strength of his) a rapidly eliding muscular syntax which keeps pace with the mind's play rather than imposing too neat an order on a linguistic end-product. The results are invigorating and delightful. I wish I could quote several poems to show his range—from *The Gathering*: "She Rose Up Singing" for its lovely music, "We Could Get a Drink" for its energetic use of an Olson-like open structure, and "The Sign" for its humor; from *The Ends of the Earth*: "A Call" and "Forgets Five" as short and long examples of his convincing dream poems, and "A Kind Numbness" for its tender and traditional imagery (interestingly—and oddly—comparable to Larkin's "At Grass"); and from *Threads*: "For—" with its erotic tribute to the muse-goddess. And many others. Space being limited, here is one short piece to give a glimpse of his wit:

> "I can see arguments for both sides"
> how impressive this intelligence
> where will its weight be placed—
> in this scale here
> in that scale here...

—Seamus Cooney

BRONK, William. American. Born in Fort Edward, New York, 17 February 1918. Educated at Dartmouth College, Hanover, New Hampshire, A.B. 1938. Served in the United States Army, 1941-45: Lieutenant. Owns and manages a lumber business, Hudson Falls, New York. Recipient: American Book Award, 1982. Address: 57 Pearl Street, Hudson Falls, New York 12839, U.S.A.

PUBLICATIONS

Verse

Light and Dark. Ashland, Massachusetts, Origin Press, 1956.
The World, The Worldless. New York and San Francisco, New Directions—San Francisco Review Press, 1964.
The Empty Hands. New Rochelle, New York, Elizabeth Press, 1969.
That Tantalus. New Rochelle, New York, Elizabeth Press, 1971.
To Praise the Music. New Rochelle, New York, Elizabeth Press, 1972.
Utterances. Providence, Rhode Island, Burning Deck, 1972.

Looking at It. Rushden, Northamptonshire, Sceptre Press, 1973.
Silence and Metaphor. New Rochelle, New York, Elizabeth Press, 1975.
The Stance. Port Townsend, Washington, Graywolf Press, 1975.
My Father Photographed with Friends and Other Pictures. New Rochelle, New York, Elizabeth Press, 1976.
The Meantime. New Rochelle, New York, Elizabeth Press, 1976.
Finding Losses. New Rochelle, New York, Elizabeth Press, 1976.
Twelve Losses Found. Lincoln, Grosseteste Press, 1976.
That Beauty Still. Providence, Rhode Island, Burning Deck, 1978.
The Force of Desire. New Rochelle, New York, Elizabeth Press, 1979.
Life Supports: New and Collected Poems. New Rochelle, New York, Elizabeth Press, 1981.
Light in a Dark Sky. Concord, New Hampshire, William B. Ewert, 1982.

Other

A Partial Glossary: Two Essays. New Rochelle, New York, Elizabeth Press, 1974.
The New World (essays). New Rochelle, New York, Elizabeth Press, 1974.
The Brother in Elysium. New Rochelle, New York, Elizabeth Press, 1980.
Vectors and Smoothable Curves: Collected Essays. Berkeley, California, North Point Press, 1983.

*

Critical Studies: in *Grosseteste Review 5* (Pensnett, Staffordshire), Spring 1972; interview with Robert Bertholf, in *Credences 3* (Kent, Ohio), 1976; *William Bronk: An Essay* by Cid Corman, Carrboro, North Carolina, Truck Press, 1976; Felix Stefanile, in *Parnassus 5* (New York), Spring-Summer 1977; Norman Finklestein, in *Contemporary Literature 23* (Madison, Wisconsin), no. 4, 1982.

*   *   *

William Bronk has lived most of his life in Hudson Falls, a small town in upstate New York, where he has owned and operated a lumber yard. His sophisticated, intelligent, pessimistic poems seem to be moments of crisis in an on-going monologue. It doesn't occur to the reader to ask whom he is talking to; it is so obviously himself.

In his work Bronk shares little with his contemporaries. Of a generation for which Pound's dictum, "Go in fear of abstraction," was law, he uses the poem as a register of thought. Of a generation obsessively concerned with poetic form, Bronk sees forms as a practical matter. Staying for the most part with a line which at least suggests pentameter, he writes poems which are tight, neatly crafted, and logical. He is not a formal experimenter or innovator. Although his early work shows clear signs of Wallace Stevens's influence, the voice which emerged in the late 1950's was distinctively his own. In his more recent work, he has pared his most characteristic moves down to the barest essentials. "Spring Storm" is typical of his attempts to get down to the minims of both his style and his themes:

I heard two claps of thunder this afternoon.
I didn't see the lightning. Well, we hear
—sometimes we see, which doesn't say there is
a world or we are. But something is.

Bronk is a transcendentalist, of sorts, but the contact between the lived world and the real one is extremely tenuous. He is a 20th-century version of Carlyle rather than of Emerson. In a short essay, "Costume as Metaphor," he writes, "Clothing as metaphor not to dress ourselves nor to say what the world is if we knew but to praise that world however it might be." There is much contemporary poetry in which metaphor seems nothing but decoration to sentiments which carry no conviction as mere statement. The crucial difference between Bronk's poetry and the merely decorative is that Bronk is decorative with a vengeance. In "Corals and Shells," for example, a nine-line poem, there are only four concrete nouns. The poem's statement is complete and meaningful without the phrase from which it takes its title. The poem concludes: "Alive, we couldn't endure it; we die to endure,/endure to die. It kills us. We are glad it does/Corals and shells. Shall we ever cover a land?" The corals and shells are in one sense mere decoration. They are not, in fact, invoked by the organic demands of the poem. In another sense, however, they provide the terms of the dissonance which is most characteristic of Bronk's work. Many of Bronk's poems end with a shudder which results from the sudden recognition that the concrete world is *only* decoration. It has a structure which is vaguely rational, it is a place in which it is possible to create certain fictions, but at every turn the rationality and the fiction collapse, leaving us in precisely the most frightening and desirable place: confronting the unspeakable reality, with the full realization that *no* fiction or logic is supreme.

Bronk is a poet who deserves more attention than he has received. His is a chilling vision, but it is his assumption that we must somehow snatch a life out of the awe-fullest possibilities.

—Don Byrd

BROOKS, Gwendolyn. American. Born in Topeka, Kansas, 7 June 1917. Educated at Wilson Junior College, Chicago, graduated 1936. Married Henry L. Blakely in 1939 (divorced); one son and one daughter. Publicity Director, NAACP Youth Council, Chicago, in the 1930's. Taught at Northeastern Illinois State College, Chicago, Columbia College, Chicago, Elmhurst College, Illinois, and University of Wisconsin, Madison; Distinguished Professor of the Arts, City College, City University of New York, 1971. Editor, *Black Position* magazine. Recipient: Guggenheim Fellowship, 1946; American Academy grant, 1946; Eunice Tietjens Memorial Prize (*Poetry*, Chicago), 1949; Pulitzer Prize, 1950; Anisfield-Wolf Award, 1968; Shelley Memorial Award, 1976. L.H.D.: Columbia College, 1964; D.Litt.: Lake Forest College, Chicago, 1965; Brown University, Providence, Rhode Island, 1974. Poet Laureate of Illinois, 1969. Address: 7428 South Evans Avenue, Chicago, Illinois 60619, U.S.A.

PUBLICATIONS

Verse

A Street in Bronzeville. New York, Harper, 1945.
Annie Allen. New York, Harper, 1949.

Bronzeville Boys and Girls (for children). New York, Harper, 1956.
The Bean Eaters (for children). New York, Harper, 1960.
Selected Poems. New York, Harper, 1963.
In the Time of Detachment, In the Time of Cold. Springfield, Illinois, Civil War Centennial Commission of Illinois, 1965.
In the Mecca. New York, Harper, 1968.
For Illinois 1968: A Sesquicentennial Poem. Chicago, Illinois Sesquicentennial Commission, 1968.
Riot. Detroit, Broadside Press, 1970.
The Wall. Detroit, Broadside Press, n.d.
Family Pictures. Detroit, Broadside Press, 1970.
Aloneness. Detroit, Broadside Press, 1971.
Aurora. Detroit, Broadside Press, 1972.
Beckonings. Detroit, Broadside Press, 1975.
To Disembark. Chicago, Third World Press, 1981.

Novel

Maud Martha. New York, Harper, 1953.

Other

A Portion of That Field, with others. Urbana, University of Illinois Press, 1967.
The World of Gwendolyn Brooks (miscellany). New York, Harper, 1971.
Report from Part One: An Autobiography. Detroit, Broadside Press, 1972.
The Tiger Who Wore White Gloves; or, What You Are You Are (for children). Chicago, Third World Press, 1974.
A Capsule Course in Black Poetry Writing, with Don L. Lee, Keorapetse Kgositsile, and Dudley Randall. Detroit, Broadside Press, 1975.
Young Poets' Primer. Chicago, Brooks Press, 1981.
Very Young Poets. Chicago, Brooks Press, 1983.

Editor, *A Broadside Treasury*. Detroit, Broadside Press, 1971.
Editor, *Jump Bad: A New Chicago Anthology*. Detroit, Broadside Press, 1971.

*

Bibliography: *Langston Hughes and Gwendolyn Brooks: A Reference Guide* by R. Baxter Miller, Boston, Hall, and London, Prior, 1978.

*   *   *

In what has now become a well-known episode, Gwendolyn Brooks describes an auspicious turning point in her career, a turning point that came in 1967 when she attended the Second Black Writers' Conference at Fisk University in Nashville. The Pulitzer-Prize winning poet was stunned and intrigued by the energy and electricity generated by LeRoi Jones (Amiri Baraka) and Ron Milner, among others, on that predominantly black campus. The excitement was at once surprising and stirring and contagious, and Brooks admits that from that moment she entered a "new consciousness." What had occurred in fact is that Brooks discovered a "new" audience: young people full of a new spirit and ready, as she characterized them, to take on the challenges. The sturdy ideas that she earlier held were no longer valid in this "new world" and several years later she would untendentiously remark: "I am trying to weave the coat that I shall wear."

The older coat that Brooks doffed is made of the material for which she is best known: such vignettes of ghetto people in

Chicago as "The Anniad," "The Sundays of Satin-Legs Smith," "The Bean Eaters," or "We Real Cool," for example. They are works of a poet who brings a patrician mind to a plebeian language; a poet always in search for the stirring, unusual coloration of words; the poet in whom Addison Gayle, Jr., has noted what he calls "a tendency towards obscurity and abstraction" and "a child-like fascination for words." But like Emily Dickinson, Brooks was in constant search for fresh sounds and imagery produced by word clusters that startled rather than obscured:

> Let it be stairways, and a splintery box
> Where you have thrown me, scraped me with your kiss,
> Have honed me, have released me after this
> Cavern kindness, smiled away our shocks.

Most of her poems written before 1967, before the Fisk conference, are her "front yard songs," poems whose making reflects the self-consciousness of a poet whose audience seeks lessons in a lyric that ostensibly transcends race. They are solid, highly imaginative poems, and if they suggest comparisons with Wallace Stevens, as several critics have noted, they also recall for this eye Emily Dickinson's ingenuity with language, her ironic ambiguities:

> A light and diplomatic bird
> Is lenient in my window tree.
> A quick dilemma of the leaves
> Discloses twist and tact to me.

They recall as well the "grotesques" who habituate the fictional world of Sherwood Anderson's *Winesburg, Ohio*:

> True, there is silver under
> The veils of the darkness,
> But few care to dig in the night
> For the possible treasure of stars.

But above all, there is the unmistakable rhythmic shifting—"My hand is stuffed with mode, design, device./But I lack access to my proper stone"—and the haunting incongruities—"Believe that even in my deliberateness I was not deliberate."

The startling Fisk conference, however, may be metaphorically viewed as Brooks's peek at "the back yard" ("Where it's rough and untended and hungry weed grows"), the escape, as George Kent says, from the highly ordered and somewhat devitalized life of her "front yard training." The backyard offers a new vitality, a new consciousness. Brooks, beyond age 50, strikes up a dialogue in free verse with the subjects of her earlier poetry. The distances narrow and the angles flatten: "we are each other's/harvest:/we are each other's/business:/we are each other's magnitude and bond."

The angles of vision have changed to suit what Brooks describes as "my newish voice": "[It] will not be an imitation of the contemporary young black voice, which I so admire, but an extending adaptation of today's G.B. [sic] voice." So there is something of a near elegiac tone in Brooks's "transcendence" of her poetic past; but it is elegy without regrets, for she has moved from a place of "knowledgeable unknowing" to a place of "Know-now" preachments:

> I tell you
> I love You
> and I trust You.
> Take my Faith.
> Make of my Faith an engine.
> Make of my Faith
> a Black Star. I am Beckoning.

—Charles L. James

BROUGHTON, James (Richard). American. Born in Modesto, California, 10 November 1913. Educated at Stanford University, California, B.A. 1936; New School for Social Research, New York. Married Suzanna Hart in 1962 (divorced, 1978); two children. Worked in the merchant marine, and as a printer, waiter, and ghost-writer; book reviewer, New York *Herald-Tribune*; resident playwright, San Francisco Playhouse, 1958-64; Lecturer, San Francisco State University, 1966-76; Lecturer, San Francisco Art Institute, 1968-81. Since 1948, Director, Farallone Films. Recipient: Phelan Award, 1948; Avon Foundation grant, 1968; Guggenheim Fellowship, 1970, 1973; National Endowment for the Arts grant, 1976, 1982; City of San Francisco Award of Honor, 1983; film awards in Edinburgh, 1953, Cannes, 1954, and Oberhausen, 1968, and from *Film Culture Magazine*, 1975. D.F.A.: San Francisco Art Institute, 1984. Address: P.O. Box 183, Mill Valley, California 94941, U.S.A.

PUBLICATIONS

Verse

Songs for Certain Children. San Francisco, Adrian Wilson, 1947.
The Playground. San Francisco, Centaur Press, 1949.
The Ballad of Mad Jenny. San Francisco, Centaur Press, 1950.
Musical Chairs: A Songbook for Anxious Children. San Francisco, Centaur Press, 1950.
An Almanac for Amorists. Paris, Olympia Press, 1954; New York, Grove Press, 1955.
True and False Unicorn. New York, Grove Press, 1957.
Wedding Song. Mendocino, California, Panpipe Press, 1962.
The Water Circle: A Poem of Celebration. San Francisco, Pterodactyl Press, 1965.
Tidings. San Francisco, Pterodactyl Press, 1967.
Look In Look Out. Eugene, Oregon, Toad Press, 1968.
High Kukus. Highlands, North Carolina, Jargon, 1969.
A Long Undressing: Collected Poems 1949-1969. Highlands, North Carolina, Jargon, 1971.
Going Through Customs. San Francisco, Arion Press, 1976.
Erogeny. San Francisco, ManRoot, 1977.
Odes for Odd Occasions. San Francisco, ManRoot, 1977.
Song of the Godbody. San Francisco, ManRoot, 1978.
Hymns to Hermes. San Francisco, ManRoot, 1979.
Shaman Psalm. Mill Valley, California, Syzygy Press, 1981.
Graffiti for the Johns of Heaven. Mill Valley, California, Syzygy Press, 1982.
Ecstasies. Mill Valley, California, Syzygy Press, 1983.

Recording: *The Bard and the Harper*, MEA, 1965.

Plays

A Love for Lionel (produced New York, 1944).
Summer Fury (produced Palo Alto, California, 1945). Published in *The Best One-Act Plays of 1945*, edited by Margaret Mayorga, New York, Dodd Mead, 1946.
Burning Questions (produced San Francisco, 1958).
The Last Word. Boston, Baker, 1958.
The Rites of Women (produced San Francisco, 1959).
How Pleasant It Is to Have Money (produced San Francisco, 1964).
Bedlam; or, America the Beautiful Mother (produced Waterford, Connecticut, 1969).

Films: *The Potted Psalm*, 1946; *Mother's Day*, 1948; *Adventures of Jimmy*, 1950; *Four in the Afernoon*, 1951; *Loony Tom the Happy Lover*, 1951; *The Pleasure Garden*, 1953; *The Bed*, 1968; *Nuptiae*, 1969; *The Golden Positions*, 1970; *This Is It*, 1971; *Dreamwood*, 1972; *High Kukus*, 1973; *Testament*, 1974; *The Water Circle*, 1975; *Erogeny*, 1976; *Together*, 1976; *Windowmobile*, 1977; *Song of the Godbody*, 1978; *Hermes Bird*, 1979; *The Gardener of Eden*, 1981; *Shaman Psalm*, 1981; *Devotions*, 1983.

Novel

The Androgyne Journal. Oakland, California, Scrimshaw Press, 1977.

Other

The Right Playmate. London, Hart Davis, and New York, Farrar Straus, 1952; revised edition, San Francisco, Pterodactyl Press, 1964.
Something Just for You. San Francisco, Pisani Press, 1966.
Seeing the Light. San Francisco, City Lights, 1977.

*

Manuscript Collection: Special Collections, Kent State University, Ohio.

Critical Studies: *Visionary Film* by P. Adams Sitney, New York, Oxford University Press, 1974; "James Broughton Issue" of *Film Culture 61* (New York), 1975; "Celebration" by Terry Sheehy, in *Film Quarterly* (Berkeley), Summer 1976; "Quest for the Ecstatic" by Robert Lipman, in *Credences* (Kent, Ohio), March 1978.

James Broughton comments:
   Although I have done as much work in theatre and cinema forms as I have in pure verse, I consider myself first and foremost a poet, for all my work is motivated by a poet's view and attitude. I have been associated with various San Francisco groups since 1949, but I do not belong to any school of poetry.
   The greatest influences upon my poetry: Bach, Blake, Mother Goose, Shakespeare, Stravinsky, Yeats, Joyce, Firbank, Stein, and folk song.
   Fellow poets who have personally taught me the most: Auden, Cummings, Robert Duncan, Dylan Thomas.
   Poetry is a search for essence, becomes an essence, remains an essential.
   The poet has to allow everything to happen to him, or he can make nothing happen. The poet has to let go in order to hold on.
   A poet is in the service of something larger than his personal life, his craft, or his published works. Poetry is an act of love, it asks no rewards.

To live poetically is more important than to write good poems.
   Poetry may be a criticism of life, as Arnold said, but life triumphs over all criticism.
   Poetry is a quest for liberation. But it must be limited in order to be liberated. A poem is a uniqueness defined by its limitations.
   A poem is a stone, a wind, a glass of water, a fire on the plain.
   Writing the poem is not difficult except that the poet must know and must not know what he is doing. Poets are both more irrational and more conscious than other human beings.
   Without joy there is no wonder, and without wonder there is no magic, and without magic there is no poem.
   A book of poems is a seed catalogue, a tarot pack, a package of dynamite, a menu for gourmets, a field of stars, a map of the sea floor.
   A poem can be about anything if it is not about anything but itself.
   Poetry is always both sense and nonsense: the sense in nonsense, and the nonsense of sense.
   There is an enormous difference between art and self-expression.
   Poetry is a confessional, but it also an altar. It is vessel of transformation, it is the host and the communion cup. But it is also the fly on the windowpane.
   Poetry is impersonal about the personal, personal about the non-personal, and personably transpersonal.
   A poem is, was, and will be. It is of the present only if it is connected to the past and to the future. A contemporary poem needs some fragrance of the ancient, an echo of the primordial, a taste of the everlasting: otherwise it has no parents nor progeny.
   A poem can be what it always is when it can become what it already was. "Attain the inevitable!"
   Poets are defined by businessmen, as everything is defined by its opposite. And opposites always need each other, else there is no wholeness nor texture.
   In school time learn, in love time sing, in wisdom ripen. Allness is ripe.

Do you ever hear it?
Do You know
      what your voice is
      always singing?
Listen!
      It sings
      (like everything)
as if no song
      were ever sung before like
      this
It
      is the song you have been singing
      all your life.

*   *   *

James Broughton has always been considered a San Francisco poet, though as he says himself he has ranged over the world both as traveler and as artist. In the years after the second World War—during what was called the San Francisco poetry renaissance—he and, among many others, Kenneth Rexroth and Weldon Kees, were at the center of San Francisco's creative life, and his plays and films were as widely known as his poetry. He approaches life with a sensitive, often outraged humanism that expresses itself in poems that are sometimes angry and hard, dense and difficult, but with a surface simplicity that leads the eye into the poem, even when there is no sureness as to where it's being led. He is brought up against the cruel reality of the modern world time and time again. "Did you every try embacing a hangman?" he asks in one poem. At best he allows himself a bare, dangerous optimism. You can almost feel him walking a grim, trembling tight rope when he lets himself hope:

> I stopped where I stepped, sleep I dared not,
> I waited awake—then was banged overside
> by shepherd that grew utter beast on a cord.

Often his imagery centers on innocent animals, as often on the death and corruption of the body and the flesh. It is poetry of emotional thrusts and hard questioning, that always comes back again to his anger at the ferocity of the world around him, because it is love that he wants to return to. Wherever he begins, whatever he forces himself, and us, to look at, he returns again and again to the place he has described as "where the birth and the death and the life are one/and the last word I speak is Love."

—Samuel Charters

BROWN, George Mackay. British. Born in Stromness, Orkney, Scotland, 17 October 1921. Educated at Stromness Academy, 1926-40; Newbattle Abbey College, Dalkieth, Midlothian, 1951-52, 1956; Edinburgh University, 1956-60, 1962-64, B.A. (honours) in English 1960. Recipient: Arts Council Award, 1965; Society of Authors Travel Award, 1968; Scottish Arts Council Literature Prize, 1969; Katherine Mansfield Menton Prize, 1971. M.A.: Open University, 1976; LL.D.: University of Dundee, 1977. Fellow, Royal Society of Literature, 1977. O.B.E. (Officer, Order of the British Empire), 1974. Address: 3 Mayburn Court, Stromness, Orkney KW16 3DH, Scotland.

PUBLICATIONS

Verse

The Storm.   Kirkwall, Orkney Herald Press, 1954.
Loaves and Fishes.   London, Hogarth Press, 1959.
The Year of the Whale.   London, Hogarth Press, 1965.
The Five Voyages of Arnor.   Falkland, Fife, K.D. Duval, 1966.
Twelve Poems.   Belfast, Festival, 1968.
Fishermen with Ploughs: A Poem Cycle.   London, Hogarth Press, 1971.
Poems New and Selected.   London, Hogarth Press, 1971; New York, Harcourt Brace, 1973.
Lifeboat and Other Poems.   Crediton, Devon, Gilbertson, 1971.
Penguin Modern Poets 21, with Iain Crichton Smith and Norman MacCaig.   London, Penguin, 1972.
Winterfold.   London, Hogarth Press, 1976.
Selected Poems.   London, Hogarth Press, 1977.
Voyages.   London, Chatto and Windus, 1983.

Recording: *George Mackay Brown,* Claddagh, 1977.

Plays

Witch (produced Edinburgh, 1969).   Included in *A Calendar of Love,* 1967.
A Spell for Green Corn (broadcast, 1967; produced Edinburgh, 1970).   London, Hogarth Press, 1970.
The Loom of Light (produced Kirkwall, 1972).   Included in

Three Plays, 1984.
The Storm Watchers (produced Edinburgh, 1976).
The Martyrdom of St. Magnus (opera libretto), music by Peter Maxwell Davies, adaptation of the novel *Magnus* by Brown (produced Kirkwall and London, 1977; Santa Fe, 1979). London, Boosey and Hawkes, 1977.
The Two Fiddlers (opera libretto), music by Peter Maxwell Davies, adaptation of the story by Brown (produced London, 1978).   London, Boosey and Hawkes, 1978.
The Voyage of Saint Brandon (broadcast, 1984).   Included in *Three Plays,* 1984.
Three Plays (includes *The Loom of Light, The Well, The Voyage of Saint Brandon*).   London, Chatto and Windus, 1984.

Radio Plays: *A Spell for Green Corn,* 1967; *The Voyage of Saint Brandon,* 1984.

Television Plays: three stories from *A Time to Keep,* 1969; *Orkney,* 1971; *Miss Barraclough,* 1977; *Four Orkney Plays for Schools,* 1978; *Andrina,* 1984.

Novels

Greenvoe.   London, Hogarth Press, and New York, Harcourt Brace, 1972.
Magnus.   London, Hogarth Press, 1973.
Time in a Red Coat.   London, Chatto and Windus, 1984.

Short Stories

A Calendar of Love.   London, Hogarth Press, 1967; New York, Harcourt Brace, 1968.
A Time to Keep.   London, Hogarth Press, 1969; New York, Harcourt Brace, 1970.
Hawkfall and Other Stories.   London, Hogarth Press, 1974.
The Sun's Net.   London, Hogarth Press, 1976.
Witch and Other Stories.   London, Longman, 1977.
Andrina and Other Stories.   London, Chatto and Windus, 1983.

Other

Let's See the Orkney Islands.   Fort William, Inverness, Thomson, 1948.
Stromness Official Guide.   London, Burrow, 1956.
An Orkney Tapestry.   London, Gollancz, 1969.
The Two Fiddlers (juvenile).   London, Chatto and Windus, 1974.
Letters from Hamnavoe (essays).   Edinburgh, Wright, 1975.
Edwin Muir: A Brief Memoir.   West Linton, Peeblesshire, Castlelaw Press, 1975.
Pictures in the Cave (juvenile).   London, Chatto and Windus, 1977.
Under Brinkie's Brae.   Edinburgh, Wright, 1979.
Six Lives of Fankle the Cat (juvenile).   London, Chatto and Windus, 1980.
Portrait of Orkney, photographs by Werner Forman.   London, Hogarth Press, 1981.

*

Manuscript Collections: Scottish National Library, Edinburgh; Edinburgh University.

Critical Study: *George Mackay Brown* by Alan Bold, Edinburgh, Oliver and Boyd, and New York, Barnes and Noble, 1978.

George Mackay Brown comments:

Themes: mainly religious (birth, love, death, resurrection, ceremonies of fishing and agriculture). Verse forms: traditional stanza forms, sonnets, ballads, *vers libre*, prose poems, runes, choruses, etc. Sources and influences: Norse sagas, Catholic rituals and ceremonies, island lore.

*   *   *

In the preface to *Winterfold*, George Mackay Brown insists that "It should not be obligatory for poets to celebrate, as best they can, only the greyness of contemporary life. Some of the poems in this book are swatches cut from here and there in one weave of time." This seems to me very precisely to suggest both the scope of his achievement and its severe limitations. In his best work he does, indeed, produce a dramatic, historically dense poetry feeding off legend, saga, and myth which remind us of our origins in a pre-sophisticated, homogeneous, rural culture imaginatively expressing itself in religion, rune, and ritual. But there is always the nagging doubt that he is too ready to presume the "greyness" of the contemporary, too little willing to search out what sustenance there is in the life of his own time, and, as a result, capable not exactly of romanticising the past, but of being too resolutely *intended* about it. The actual poetry itself sometimes seems too thin to cope with the obvious richness of the imaginative conception behind it. The schematic push is more recognisable than the realised form.

This "schematic push," in which Brown self-consciously attempts to recreate something of the ancient bardic function of the poet, focuses most intensely on the history and legends of the Orkney islands, the community of fishermen and farmers into which he was born and in which he has chosen to continue to live; and on the tradition of Roman Catholicism, the religion he chose to enter in 1961. He creates, in his work, a composite "mythology" of a place he calls "Hamnavoe" in which man is situated in his most essential, elemental condition—working the difficult, resistant ground and the treacherous sea for his food; praying to the gods for comfort; enacting the processes of generation; succumbing to decay and death.

In the long poem-cycle *Fishermen with Ploughs* this "mythologising" extends from the first settlements on Orkney in the 9th century, through its present depopulation, to an imagined resettlement after a nuclear holocaust. The visionary poetic energy of the section of the poem dealing with this post-nuclear world is intense, and is by far the best thing in the book; it suggests, perhaps, that Brown's imagination is most at home when most unhampered by the need to deal with ordinary social contingency. When it does have to respond to this need, there is often something static and tableau-like about his presentation of historical moments, and something perfunctory about his characterisation, that make for a certain lack of vitality in his verse. For all its obsession with elemental man, situated "between crib and coffin," there is little of that tension and pain which other mythologising and historicising poets such as Geoffrey Hill, Seamus Heaney, and David Jones have found in their material and embodied in their language. To be too certain of the "greyness" of the contemporary is to miss the opportunity for real richness in one's own work, which must, of necessity, be written out of contemporary experience, however much it attempts to disguise the fact.

But at his best Brown is a poet extraordinarily full of reverence and tenderness for animal and human life, and for the processes of ritual and religion. This tenderness is particularly apparent in the many poems he addresses to the Virgin Mary, and, indeed, in his whole feeling for women. The prayer to Saint Lucy, called "Lighting Candles in Midwinter," in his most recent volume,

Voyages, makes this clear, and suggests also the quiet, meditative rhythm at the heart of Brown's work—while it also, perhaps, for all its beauty and delicacy, suggests that this poet, this man fixed in the task of the "interrogation of silence," as he calls the poet's work, is not altogether a fully *contemporary* poet:

> Saint Lucy, see
> Seven bright leaves in the winter tree
>
> Seven diamonds shine
> In the deepest darkest mine
>
> Seven fish go, a glimmering shoal
> Under the ice of the North Pole
>
> Sweet St. Lucy, be kind
> To us poor and wretched and blind.

—Neil Corcoran

BROWN, Sterling A(llen).   American.   Born in Washington, D.C., 1 May 1901.   Educated at public schools in Washington, D.C.; Williams College, Williamstown, Massachusetts, A.B. 1922 (Phi Beta Kappa); Harvard University, Cambridge, Massachusetts, A.M. 1923. Married Daisy Turnbull in 1927. Teacher at Virginia Seminary and College, Lynchburg, 1923-26, Lincoln University, Jefferson City, Missouri, 1926-28, and Fisk University, Nashville, Tennessee, 1929. Since 1929, Professor of English, Howard University, Washington, D.C. Visiting Professor, New York University, New School for Social Research, New York, Vassar College, Poughkeepsie, New York, and University of Minnesota, Minneapolis. Literary Editor, *Opportunity* magazine, Washington, D.C., in the 1930's; Editor of *Negro Affairs* for the Federal Writers' Project, 1936-39; staff member, *American Dilemma*. Recipient: Guggenheim Fellowship, 1937; Lenore Marshall Prize, 1981. Honorary degrees: Atlanta University; Boston University; Brown University, Providence, Rhode Island; Harvard University; Howard University; Lewis and Clark College, Portland, Oregon; Lincoln University, Pennsylvania; University of Maryland, College Park; University of Massachusetts, Amherst; Northwestern University, Evanston, Illinois; University of Pennsylvania, Philadelphia; Williams College; Yale University, New Haven, Connecticut. Poet Laureate of the District of Columbia, 1984. Address: 1222 Kearny Street N.E., Washington D.C. 20017, U.S.A.

PUBLICATIONS

Verse

Southern Road.   New York, Harcourt Brace, 1932.
The Last Ride of Wild Bill and Eleven Narrative Poems.   Detroit, Broadside Press, 1975.
The Collected Poems of Sterling A. Brown, edited by Michael S. Harper.   New York, Harper, 1980.

Recording: *16 Poems*, Folkways, 1973.

Other

Outline for the Study of the Poetry of American Negroes (study

guide for James Weldon Johnson's *The Book of American Negro Poetry*).   New York, Harcourt Brace, 1931.
The Negro in American Fiction.   Washington, D.C., Associates in Negro Folk Education, 1937.
Negro Poetry and Drama.   Washington, D.C., Associates in Negro Folk Education, 1937.
James Weldon Johnson, with A.B. Spingarn and Carl Van Vechten.   Nashville, Fisk University Department of Publicity, 1941 (?).
The Negro in Washington, with *Negro Newcomers in Detroit*, by George Edmund Haynes.   New York, Arno Press, 1969.

Editor, with Arthur P. Davis and Ulysses Lee, *The Negro Caravan: Writings by American Negroes*.   New York, Dryden Press, 2 vols., 1941.

                    *   *   *

Essentially a traditional song-maker and story teller, Sterling Brown has witnessed cross-currents of American literature, and chooses in his poetry to depict blacks and the clash of their roles with those of whites in the variegated society of the American South, particularly in the time caught between two world wars.
His poetry has been collected in anthologies as early as James Weldon Johnson's *The Book of American Negro Poetry* (1922), and, like Johnson himself and Langston Hughes, he set about disrupting the patently false and banal image of the docile American Negro with his charming *patois*, artificially stylized and mimicked by the whites in the minstrel shows still popular in the 1920's and 1930's. Johnson says in his preface of Hughes and Brown that they "*do* use a dialect, but it is not the dialect of the comic minstrel tradition or the sentimental plantation tradition: it is the common, racy, living, authentic speech of the Negro in certain phases of real life."
Brown uses original Afro-American ballads such as "Casey Jones," "John Henry," and "Staggolee" as counterpoint for his modern ones, but the portent of his ironic wit should not be underestimated, for it is actually a tool to shape an ironic, infernal vision of American life as Hades: "The Place was Dixie I took for Hell," says Slim in "Slim in Hell." The American Negro is heralded not as Black Orpheus but a modern tragic hero Mose, a leader of *all* people while futilely attempting to save his own: "A soft song, filled with a misery/Older than Mose will be." In "Sharecropper" he is broken as Christ was broken; his landlord "shot him in the side" to put him out of his misery; he is lost and wild as Odysseus in "Odyssey of a Big Boy"; and found again:

> Man wanta live
> Man want find himself
> Man gotta learn
> How to go it alone.

Though minimal in quantity, Brown's poetry is epic in conception; his ballad, blues, and jazz forms are the vehicles for creative insight into themes of American life.

                                                    —Carol Lee Saffioti

                    _____

BROWNE, Michael Dennis.   American.   Born in Walton-on-Thames, Surrey, England, 28 May 1940; moved to the United States, 1965; naturalized citizen, 1978.   Educated at St. George's College, Weybridge, Surrey; Hull University 1958-62, B.A.

(honours) in French and Swedish 1962; Oxford University, 1962-63, Cert. Ed. 1963; University of Iowa, Iowa City (Fulbright Scholar, 1965), 1965-67, M.A. in English 1967. Visiting Lecturer in Creative Writing, University of Iowa, 1967-68; Adjunct Assistant Professor, Columbia University, New York, 1968-69; member of the English Department, Bennington College, Vermont, 1969-71. Since 1971 Member of the Department, and since 1983 Professor of English, University of Minnesota, Minneapolis. Recipient: Hallmark Prize, 1967; National Endowment for the Arts grant, 1977, 1978; Bush Foundation Fellowship, 1981. Address: Department of English, University of Minnesota, Lind Hall, 207 Church Street S.E., Minneapolis, Minnesota 55455, U.S.A.

PUBLICATIONS

Verse

The Wife of Winter.   London, Rapp and Whiting, 1970; revised edition, New York, Scribner, 1970.
Fox.   Duluth, Minnesota, Knife River Press, 1974.
Sun Exercises.   Loretto, Minnesota, Red Studio Press, 1976.
The Sun Fetcher.   Pittsburgh, Carnegie Mellon University Press, 1978.
Smoke from the Fires.   Pittsburgh, Carnegie Mellon University Press, 1984.

Recording: *The Poetry of Michael Dennis Browne*, McGraw Hill, n.d.

Plays

How the Stars Were Made (cantata for children), music by David Lord (produced Farnham, Surrey, 1967).   London, Chester, 1967.
The Wife of Winter (song cycle), music by David Lord (produced Aldeburgh, Suffolk, 1968).   London, Universal, 1968.
The Sea Journey (cantata for children), music by David Lord (produced Farnham, Surrey, 1969).   London, Universal, 1969.
Nonsongs, music by David Lord.   London, Universal, 1973.
Carol of the Candle, music by Stephen Paulus.   N.p., AMSI, 1977.
Carol of the Hill, music by Stephen Paulus.   N.p., Hinshaw, 1977.
The Village Singer, music by Stephen Paulus, adaptation of a story by Mary Wilkins Freeman (produced St. Louis, 1979).

                              *

Michael Dennis Browne comments:
    (1974) Since my first book, I have become very interested in material very dangerous and pretentious, and maybe also essential, for a young writer to approach. Writers like Jung (always), Erich Neumann, Joseph Campbell. I am finally reading *The Golden Bough*.... I come to this material by way of my dreams, which have presented me with images of such power I have had to follow them out into contexts much larger than my own individual life. I hope that I will always write poems which are lyrical, vivid, and happy; I want also to find forms, find the music, for the deeper motions I find beginning to move in myself. I hope, as does any poet who plans to grow, to be able to make larger and more visionary discoveries and statements in my work. But I love clarity in poetry and hope to keep my work, in the best sense, *clear*. I am also beginning to write fables, children's stories,

where there are few rhetorical comforts, and all that is required of the writer is invention!

Finally, I am excited by the landscapes I am beginning to see. Whether or not I can reach them, I do not know.

(1980) This last year I have been on sabbatical and have been building a house in the north woods of Minnesota. This activity and landscape have given me a great many things to write about and I hope that my new work, to be in my third book, will have at least some of the vividness of this exceptional territory.

*   *   *

Michael Dennis Browne is a poet of hard, surprising images. The clarity and suddenness of imagery make real the dreams that fill *The Wife of Winter*: the order of reality is successfully inverted and the crazy world of the dream is the real, the normal, and not at all nightmarish.

Browne's voice affirms with a kind of joy—although there is a sardonic edge to the war poems and the Michael Morley sequence; he dreams and sings in face and spite of some nameless, abstract things which underlie the world of the poems:

And you can forget the poems
that have run away from you in horror
like headless birds in the dark
you have not quite killed,

because in this house and place
there are good fresh ghosts,
there are small & near ones here.

The poems are not preoccupied with traditional "themes" and grand ideas ("The Terrible Christmas"), but focus on the naming of things to create his world. He praises a woman, because "When the king of ideas advanced through the wood/you fed him an image and he went away." Another woman, the speaker of the excellent title sequence, the "Wife of Winter," finds that waking and the morning are

Dark. A new dark. I am dropped
from the high claw of a dream. Fox

retrieves me, wolf waits.
Who is the owl with wings of snow?
And where is my eagle now?
He is not here, my lady they cry.

Browne leaps past prose with recurring, angry eagles, apples, Fox, snow, images which may attain the symbolic in much the same way that Roethke—one of Browne's strongest influences—created symbols. Browne has learned much from Roethke. It is readily apparent in his rhythms and the song-like quality of many of his poems, even in an occasional image, but Browne's own voice remains clear.

More recently, for example in *The Sun Fetcher*, the energy has remained clear even while Browne has developed other touchstones of his prosody. The narrative, which was submerged or only suggested in *The Wife of Winter*, is strong in such poems as "Fox" and "Uncle Frank." This change in voice diminishes the dream which was at the center of the earlier poems so that, now, it flickers like a moment's aberration or insight, or an occasional interruption of justifiable paranoia. While some of the images of Browne's poems in the 1970's seem momentary, and too topical, the technical experimentation and development of his craft advances. A continuation of the Morley character in a sequence, for example, results in a giddy intensification of abrupt, dream-

like humor which results in high anxiety. There is an ironic sense of celebration to "Paranoia," and the poet is at great pains to reach for vitality, and even, at times, peace, through his work.

Happier, happier are we not
both now?
O painful, painful we people are,
but once again dancing!

—Joseph Wilson

———

BROWNJOHN, Alan (Charles). British. Born in Catford, London, 28 July 1931. Educated at Brownhill Road School, London; Brockley County School, London; Merton College, Oxford, 1950-53, B.A. 1953, M.A. 1961. Married 1) the writer Shirley Toulson in 1960 (divorced, 1969), one son; 2) Sandra Willingham in 1972. Wandsworth Borough Councillor, London, 1963-65; Labour Party Parliamentary Candidate, Richmond, Surrey, 1964. Senior Lecturer in English, Battersea College of Education, now Polytechnic of the South Bank, London, 1965-79; Tutor in Poetry, Polytechnic of North London, 1981-83. Poetry Critic, *New Statesman*, London, 1968-76. Member of the Arts Council Literature Panel, 1967-72; Chairman of the Greater London Arts Association Literature Panel, 1973-77. Deputy Chairman, 1979-82, and since 1982, Chairman, Poetry Society. Recipient: Cholmondeley Award, 1979. Address: 2 Belsize Park, London N.W. 3, England.

PUBLICATIONS

Verse

Travellers Alone. Liverpool, Heron Press, 1954.
The Railings. London, Digby Press, 1961.
The Lions' Mouths. London, Macmillan, and Chester Springs, Pennsylvania, Dufour, 1967.
Oswin's Word (libretto for children). London, BBC, 1967.
Woman Reading Aloud. Oxford, Sycamore Press, 1969.
Being a Garoon. Frensham, Surrey, Sceptre Press, 1969.
Sandgrains on a Tray. London, Macmillan, and Chester Springs, Pennsylvania, Dufour, 1969.
Penguin Modern Poets 14, with Michael Hamburger and Charles Tomlinson. London, Penguin, 1969.
A Day by Indirections. Frensham, Surrey, Sceptre Press, 1969.
Brownjohn's Beasts (for children). London, Macmillan, and New York, Scribner, 1970.
Synopsis. Frensham, Surrey, Sceptre Press, 1970.
Frateretto Calling. Frensham, Surrey, Sceptre Press, 1970.
Transformation Scene. London, Poem-of-the-Month Club, 1971.
An Equivalent. Rushden, Northamptonshire, Sceptre Press, 1971.
Warrior's Career. London, Macmillan, 1972.
She Made of It. Rushden, Northamptonshire, Sceptre Press, 1974.
A Song of Good Life. London, Secker and Warburg, 1975.
A Night in the Gazebo. London, Secker and Warburg, 1980.
Collected Poems 1952-1983. London, Secker and Warburg, 1983.

Other

To Clear the River (novel for children; as John Berrington).
London, Heinemann, 1964.
The Little Red Bus Book.   London, Inter-Action, 1972.
Philip Larkin.   London, Longman, 1975.

Editor, *First I Say This: A Selection of Poems for Reading
Aloud*.   London, Hutchinson, 1969.
Editor, with Seamus Heaney and Jon Stallworthy, *New Poems
1970-1971*.   London, Hutchinson, 1971.
Editor, with Maureen Duffy, *New Poetry 3*.   London, Arts
Council, 1977.
Editor, *New Year Poetry Supplement*.   London, Poetry Book
Society, 1982.

Translator, *Torquato Tasso*, by Goethe.   London, Angel, 1985.

*

Manuscript Collection: Manor House Library (Lewisham Public Library), London.

Critical Studies: review by Peter Porter, in *London Magazine*,
October 1969; *The Society of the Poem* by Jonathan Raban,
London, Harrap, 1971; Roger Garfitt, in *British Poetry since
1960* edited by Michael Schmidt and Grevel Lindop, Oxford,
Carcanet, 1972; Barbara Everett in *London Review of Books*,
May 1981; Claud Rawson, in *Poetry Review* (London), April
1984.

Alan Brownjohn comments:
   In consulting with Peter Digby Smith, the publisher of my first
hardback volume of verse, *The Railings*, I evolved for the dust-
jacket the simple statement "Poems concerned with love, politics, culture, time."
   I think this still defines the themes of my verse, with one or
other of these four dominant at different moments. But they all,
of course, intersect and interrelate: states of politics or culture
affect the values of love; love and time constantly stare at one
another, amused, shame-faced or fatalistic; time watches politics
rise to honourable humane achievement, or decline into vanity.
   I've come to some recent conclusions about the language, tone
and temperament of my poetry which critics might confirm; or
contradict. Although I am quietly, but very seriously, atheist,
socialist and internationalist, it's the English-ness of what I write
that strikes me most as I look back at it—the use of language, the
attitudes rehearsed, the codes of honour and styles of reticence
employed. I don't feel like making apology for this, because I
greatly admire certain English puritan values and feel that English rationalism, democracy and humanity would be our best
post-imperial contribution to the world at large; the vehicle for
transmission of these values being the English language.
   Every poet would like to feel he was writing for, communicating to, the world; and if I ever succeed in doing that, in any thing
at all, I'd like to feel it was in the above terms, and transmitting
the above values. But of course we should, and do, receive values
from other literatures; and I am aware, more and more as I grow
older, of unconscious debts in my own verse to European poetry,
e.g., that of France, Germany, and the Eastern European
countries.

*   *   *

   With the publication of his *Collected Poems* Alan Brownjohn
can now be clearly seen as one of the major talents of present-day
British poetry, a poet much of his time and the best of our social
poets. For though the subject matter of Brownjohn's poetry
ranges widely, taking in such traditional themes as love and
childhood, it is his expression of his concern for social issues that
marks his poetry out as specially his own. His poem "Knights-
bridge Display Window" ends "Sometime we'll get perhaps/ A
commonwealth of sense, and not with guns" which is in line with
his statement that the poem aims "at a kind of cheerful democratic puritanism." An ideal not without a degree of paradox; but
that may well be in the nature of most ideals. In his first collection, *The Railings*, Brownjohn's concern can be seen from the
beginning as very much a poet's concern:

> Don't look for hunger and disease before
> You blame a country. Stop and listen, now,
> For the unquestioned currency of talk
> Its people handle.

This is a standpoint from which a society is to be judged by the
quality of life it engenders. In *The Lions' Mouths* this concern is
pursued, and we find that while it is compassionate it is, nevertheless, allied to an uncompromising critical stance. "Why shouldn't
they do as they like?" asks the "Fool-libertarian voice" in the
poem "A Hairdressers." "No," the poet replies, "I can't wish I
were as liberal as that." Here is the puritan speaking, a voice
which persists, and which we find in his more recent collection, *A
Song of Good Life*, where he writes sadly, even harshly, of
modern development and New Towns "In Hertfordshire":

> It has fangs of reinforced concrete and triple glazing,
> Its eyes are huge stacks of strip-light in Industrial Areas
> Refining precisions to blur life, imprinting so tidy on
> Clicking cards the specific patterns of your death.

Yet the human spirit is more robust than that, as in the same
collection his group of poems on the wiles and adventures of the
Old Fox would suggest.
   In all Brownjohn's poetry there is the same sharp mind probing and enquiring. The poem "For a Journey" explores the
significance of what at first seems an unlikely subject, the naming
of country fields—"Topfield," "Third field," and the like—to
conclude: "Who knows what could become of you where/ No one
has understood the place with names?" This need for Brownjohn
to analyse is reflected in the language he uses. On occasions it can
become as complex as the line of thought he pursues.

> It is with metaphor
> We can assuage, abolish and
> Create. I will apologise
> With metaphors

he writes in "Apology for Blasphemy," and the tendency is for
such poetry to become abstract in both content and form. Yet in
Sandgrains on a Tray we find him successfully combating this,
and developing a clarity and directness which give added
strength and purpose to his work, as does his deliberate avoidance of decoration or embellishment. The words are made to
work in their own right, consistent again with his cheerful
puritanism.
   In his collection *Warrior's Career*, poems such as "Ode to
Centre Point" and "A Politician" see him making his points
much more directly, and a new, more personal element is to be
observed emerging in the section of love poems. Meanwhile the
thread of social concern continues in the group of poems in *A
Song of Good Life* which presents a picture of life in the 1970's
through their observation of modern habits and fashions. In a

more recent collection, *A Night in the Gazebo*, the narrative aspect of Brownjohn's poetry comes more to the fore, and via the observations of character and attitude explored in these fictions the oblique questionings and probings of society emerge: "There are too many evils, they race too fast, you loose/ Much more than a point if you don't continue to intercept them."

A *Collected Poems* is often seen as a seal on a poet's work and, of course, it is; nevertheless, Alan Brownjohn is still a poet who is developing, exploring new forms and ideas. We haven't, by a long chalk, heard the end of him.

—John Cotton

BROWNSTEIN, Michael. American. Born in Philadelphia, Pennsylvania, 25 August 1943. Educated at Antioch College, Yellow Springs, Ohio; New School for Social Research, New York. Taught creative writing, University of Colorado and Naropa Institute, Boulder, 1976-77. Recipient: Poets' Foundation Grant, 1966; Fulbright Scholarship, 1967; Frank O'Hara Award, 1969. Address: c/o Sun and Moon Press, 4330 Hartwick Road, College Park, Maryland 20740, U.S.A.

PUBLICATIONS

Verse

Behind the Wheel. New York, "C" Press, 1967.
Highway to the Sky. New York, Columbia University Press, 1969.
Three American Tantrums. New York, Angel Hair, 1970.
30 Pictures. Stinson Beach, California, Grape Press, 1972.
Strange Days Ahead. Calais, Vermont, Z Press, 1975.
Oracle Night: A Love Poem. College Park, Maryland, Sun and Moon Press, 1982.

Novel

Country Cousins. New York, Braziller, 1974.

Short Stories

Brainstorms. Indianapolis, Bobbs Merrill, 1971.

Other

Editor, *The Dice Cup: Selected Prose Poems*, by Max Jacob. New York, Sun, 1980.

*   *   *

Highway to the Sky, Michael Brownstein's first collection, is cryptic, elliptical, ironic, witty, occasionally symbolic or surreal; it's also inbred and a bit smartassed. "Genius," he says, is "to eat and mumble in peace." His poems about poetry are not the usual jejune praise:

Life is Beautiful.   However

The only truly human, American expressions
        of its staggering rich moments
    (two baby bulldogs in open window, 3:17 a.m.)
Aren't really forms of expression like language, but

The only truly human, American expressions
        of its staggering rich moments
    (two baby tomatoes in open window, 3:17 a.m.)
Aren't really forms of expression like language, but

Parallels manifesting themselves right alongside
Those moments, like music.

Brownstein is at his most brilliant when he concentrates on what something represents or, that horrid word, "symbolizes." "The method must be purest meat, and no symbolic dressing," Ginsberg says, speaking for many of his generation. In his usual weird tone, Brownstein deadpans agreement with this Beat and Black Mountain formula:

A naturalist witnessing the scene begins to weep
for joy. A small child of either sex joins him:
        it's a tableau, simple and real.
No "symbols," no straining after a meaning
that wasn't there in the beginning, obvious to all,
        before the first walrus appeared...

His assent is mitigated by that last line and the gratuitously bizarre and generalized "small child of either sex." Brownstein's second book, in fact, consists of prose poems of mythic, symbolic and even (cf. Empson) ambiguous import. "The Overcoat," for instance, contrasts the political and sexual implications of a preference for overcoats over t-shirts. In "Who Knows Where the Time Goes" a mythy figure of magic asks the persona of the poem more and more curious questions till finally the persona wearily indicates he's merely a Bowery bum giving a good rap for his dime. The stone outlaw seems tougher and more impassive than the other outlaws in his gang till it transpires, finally, that he is a literal statue. Brownstein's recent work in fiction suggests that though he struck a tone in poetry, for its blossoming he needs the larger forms of prose.

—Michael André

BRUCE, George. British. Born in Fraserburgh, Aberdeenshire, Scotland, 10 March 1909. Educated at Fraserburgh Academy; Aberdeen University, M.A. (honours) in English. Married Elizabeth Duncan in 1935; one son and one daughter. Taught English and history, Dundee High School, 1933-46. General Programmes Producer, Aberdeen, 1946-56, and since 1956, Documentary Talks Producer, BBC, Edinburgh. Fellow in Creative Writing, Glasgow University, 1971-73; Visiting Professor, Union Theological Seminary, Richmond, Virginia, 1974; Writer-in-Residence, Prescott College, Arizona, 1974; Visiting Professor of English, College of Wooster, Ohio, 1976-77. Recipient: Scottish Arts Council award, 1968, 1971; Scottish Australian Writing Fellowship, 1982. Litt.D.: College of Wooster, 1977. O.B.E. (Officer, Order of the British Empire), 1984. Address: 25 Warriston Crescent, Edinburgh EH3 5LB, Scotland.

PUBLICATIONS

Verse

Sea Talk. Glasgow, Maclellan, 1944.
Selected Poems. Edinburgh, Oliver and Boyd, 1947.
Landscapes and Figures: A Selection of Poems. Preston, Lancashire, Akros, 1967.
The Collected Poems of George Bruce. Edinburgh, Edinburgh University Press, 1970.

Plays

To Scotland, With Rhubarb (produced Edinburgh, 1965).

Radio Play: *Tonight Mrs. Morrison*, music by David Dorward, 1968.

Other

Scottish Sculpture, with T.S. Halliday. Dundee, Findlay, 1946.
Neil M. Gunn. Edinburgh, National Library of Scotland, 1971.
Anne Redpath. Edinburgh, Edinburgh University Press, 1974.
The City of Edinburgh: A Historical Guide. London, Pitkin Pictorials, 1974; revised edition, 1977.
Festival in the North: The Story of the Edinburgh Festival. London, Hale, 1975.
Some Practical Good: The Cockburn Association 1875-1975. Edinburgh, Cockburn Association, 1975.
William Soutar 1898-1943: The Man and the Poet. Edinburgh, National Library of Scotland, 1978.

Editor, *The Exiled Heart: Poems 1941-1956*, by Maurice Lindsay. London, Hale, 1957.
Editor, with Edwin Morgan and Maurice Lindsay, *Scottish Poetry One* to *Six*. Edinburgh, Edinburgh University Press, 1966-72.
Editor, *The Scottish Literary Revival: An Anthology of Twentieth Century Poetry*. London, Collier Macmillan, and New York, Macmillan, 1968.

*

Manuscript Collections: State University of New York, Buffalo; National Library of Scotland, Edinburgh.

Critical Studies: *The Scottish Tradition in Literature* by Kurt Wittig, Edinburgh, Oliver and Boyd, 1958; *The Scots Literary Tradition* by John Spiers, London, Faber, 1962; "Myth-Maker: The Poetry of George Bruce" by Alexander Scott, in *Akros* (Preston, Lancashire), December 1975.

George Bruce comments:
  (1970) I belong, I suppose, to the current Scottish Literary Revival, though I believe I owe nothing in style to any of my Scottish contemporaries. I have learned the craft of verse especially from Ezra Pound.
  From about 1941 to 1953 the main subject-matter was life in a sea town and the environment of that life. The approach was definitive rather than descriptive: I was concerned to establish the extraordinary nature of the case, that people continued to believe in life and to make a particular thing of it in circumstances that might have warranted despair; but then should one not despair in any case of human life which is, *ipso facto*, precariously placed between light and dark.

  I came to this subject when the war seemed to confirm by its explicit outrage on human dignity the evidence of Eliot's *The Waste Land*. In these circumstances I found myself—for I did not seek to do so—making a statement in verse about the establishing of life on a minimal basis. I noted the fishermen whose lives were almost continuously threatened by the life giving and killing element from which they drew their livelihood. To their adaptation to, and acceptance of, their situation they added an apparently unreasonable belief in a personal God. I could not identify myself with their attitudes, nor with them. But in looking with particularity at them the sense of a separate existence came home at a time when the word "object" was almost meaningless to me. I had found an "objective correlative."
  I proceeded to apply a craft of verse that I had learned from Ezra Pound, particularly from *Mauberley*, with, as far as I could, clinical exactness. Just as much of my country was mere rock so my language should be, so the rhythms short and vigorous. When I applied my ear to what I had written I found the tone and accent an articulation of the words and sentences related more closely to the manner of speech of the community in which I had been brought up (and to some extent continued about me, for I believe there is a tendency in educated Scottish speech, in English, to certain general characteristics) than to the implied accent of Pound or to the speech of Southern England. A strong emphasis on consonants and a high articulation is characteristic. In my more successful poems of this period I think these elements are present. This was a point of beginning. All my poems were in English.
  Then I became increasingly interested in the idea of order. That aspect of nature I knew best, and the irregular characteristics of growth itself threatened order. My poem about St. Andrews, "A Gateway to the Sea," is written as an exposition on the order of a mediaeval town which embodies theological concepts of order in its structure, an order that is threatened by men and by the ravages of the sea. This interest is subordinated in several poems to a rejoicing in the irregularity and variety of creation. It is easy enough to accept that variety as one looks back in history, it is more difficult to accept when the force of life expresses itself in what appears to be brashness and vulgarity. This is the main concern of my poem *Landscapes and Figures*.
  (1980) In the 1970's there have been two new developments in my poetry. The one is the use of contemporary events, social and political, as material, on which I have made generally satiric comment; the other is the writing of poetry in Scots, which medium I have also applied to the current social scene. This led Alexander Scott to comment on my having "an uproarious sense of sardonic humour."
  (1985) As my poetic interests widened I came to use a longer line but to incorporate short lines for incantatory or dramatic purposes. Then I included Scots in my poems as the voice of a *persona*, using the same brief rhythms as I had done in English, the abruptness of the Scots reflecting the utterances of the fishermen under duress. More recently I have written poems in Scots as ironic commentaries on the social scene, but where I have felt most intensely the casual cruelties and injustices of our time, I have made my comment in poems in English, these frequently provoking as counterbalance personal love poems.

*   *   *

The term "regional poet" can either mean a minor writer who celebrates his locality with a certain amount of enthusiasm and charm, or a writer who uses the sights and smells and sounds of his native district as imaginative material for containing problems and predicaments that are humanity's. It is in this second, good sense, that George Bruce is the poet of the North East of

Scotland, with its cold farm-lands, its rugged cliffscapes, and its dour and tenacious fishermen.

That tenacity, that necessary continuing belief in life at its basic food-winning level during the early years of the second World War, inspired some of the poems in Bruce's first book, *Sea Talk*. His technique he learned to some extent from Eliot, though principally from Pound, especially *Mauberley*. But the tone and timbre of the application of the technique are very much his own, relating to those durable qualities among which he had been brought up. "Just as much of my country was mere rock," the poet has explained, "so my language should be, so the rhythms short and vigorous." Comparing the graciousness which allowed Gothic spires to florish in wind-swept Balbec and Finistère with the granite knuckle-thrust where the Buchan fisherman has his being, Bruce exclaims:

> To defend life thus and so to grace it
> What art! but you, my friend, know nothing of this,
> Merely the fog, more often the east wind
> That scours the sand from the shore,
> Bequeathing it to the sheep pasture,
> Whipping the dust from fields,
> Disclosing the stone ribs of earth—
> The frame that for ever presses back the roots of corn
> In the shallow soil. This wind,
> Driving over your roof,
> Twists the sycamore's branches
> Till its dwarf fingers shoot west,
> Outspread on bare country, lying wide.
> Erect against the element
> House and kirk and your flint face.

Just as the relentless action of wind and waves has shaped his coastline, so past generations have moulded his North East character:

> This which I write now
> Was written years ago
> Before my birth
> In the features of my father.
>
> It was stamped
> In the rock formations
> West of my hometown.
> Not I write
>
> But perhaps, William Bruce,
> Cooper....

The poet's words become "the paint/Smeared upon/The inarticulate."

Against this backcloth of the elements, Bruce sets the hero, determinedly going about his business, doing what needs to be done: "The short man waves his hand,/Half turns, and then makes off./He is going to the country...."

Such experiences, as Kurt Wittig has remarked, spring from specific moments of the poet's personal life, and are "explained in very personal symbols (such as the curtain half way up the stairs) and seen in flashes of very personal and momentary observation."

Perhaps because of the role of impresario to other poets which Bruce's post as a BBC Producer has imposed on him, he has published all too little. Twenty-three years lie between *Sea Talk* and *Landscapes and Figures*. By the second collection, the range and power of the verse have deepened. There is still the hero, "a man of inconsequent build," his "Odyssey the trains between/Two ends of telephone...." He is still

> ...the small man
> With broad pale brow lined deep as if the pen
> Held tight in hand had pressed its ink
> In strokes.

There are also clear, objective recollections of the details of childhood, as in the much-praised "Tom." In one part of this sequence, "Tom on the Beach," the poet asks himself:

> How many years since with sure heart
> And prophecy of success
> Warmed in it
> Did I look with delight on the little fish,
>
> Start with happiness, the warm sun on me?
> Now the waters spread horizonwards,
> Great skies meet them,
> I brood upon uncompleted tasks.

Now Bruce occasionally uses Scots, though usually only for special colloquial effects in the counterpoint of his verse's rugged music. Henry Moore's sculpture, the impact of distant wars through the television screen and the experience of an Italian sojourn have given him new thematic material. When eventually a fuller collection of Bruce's work is published, though there will undoubtedly be surprises and fresh riches discovered, I doubt if anything will surpass "A Gateway to the Sea," his elegy for the changelessness of change. The "gateway" leads to ruined St. Andrew's Cathedral, where once there was living gossip:

> ...Caesar's politics.
> And he who was drunk last night;
> Rings, diamants, snuff boxes, warships,
> Also the less worthy garments of worthy men!

Here once:

> The European sun knew these streets
> O Jesu parvule; Christus Victus: Christus Victor.
> The bells singing from their towers, the waters
> Whispering to the waters, the air tolling
> To the air—the faith, the faith, the faith.

But "All that was long ago. The lights/Are out, the town is sunk in sleep...." And yet:

> Under the touch the guardian stone remains
> Holding memory, reproving desire, securing hope
> In the stop of water, in the lull of night.
> Before dawn kindles a new day.

I know of no other "regional" poet whose treatment of the oldest and most Universal theme of all is as powerfully affecting as Bruce's in this poem. The voice is Scottish, but the words are warmed into poetry by a European mind.

—Maurice Lindsay

BRUTUS, Dennis (Vincent). British (South African). Born in Salisbury, Rhodesia, 28 November 1924. Educated in South Africa at Paterson High School; Fort Hare University, Alice, B.A. in English 1947; Witwatersrand University, Johannesburg,

1963-64. Married May Jaggers in 1950; eight children. High school teacher and journalist for 14 years. Served 18 months in Robben Island Prison, for opposition to apartheid, 1964-65. Left South Africa in 1966. Director, Campaign for Release of South African Political Prisoners, London, 1966-71; Staff Member, International Defence and Aid Fund, London, 1966-71. Visiting Professor, University of Denver, 1970. Since 1971, Professor of English, Northwestern University, Evanston, Illinois. Visiting Professor, University of Texas, Austin, 1974-75, Amherst College, Massachusetts, 1982-83, and Northeastern University, Boston, 1984. Founder-Director, Troubadour Press, Del Valle, Texas, 1971. Since 1959, Secretary, South African Sports Association; since 1963, President, South African Non-Racial Olympic Committee; since 1972, Chairman, International Campaign Against Racism in Sport; since 1976, Member of the Editorial Board, *Africa Today*, Denver; since 1984, Chairman, Africa Network. Recipient: Mbari Prize, 1962. D.H.L.: Worcester State College, Massachusetts, 1982. Address: 18 Hilton Avenue, London N. 12, England; or, 624 Clark Street, Evanston, Illinois 60201, U.S.A.

PUBLICATIONS

Verse

Sirens, Knuckles, Boots.   Ibadan, Mbari, 1963; Evanston, Illinois, Northwestern University Press, 1964.
Letters to Martha and Other Poems from a South African Prison.   London, Heinemann, 1968.
Poems from Algiers.   Austin, University of Texas, 1970.
Thoughts Abroad (as John Bruin).   Del Valle, Texas, Troubadour Press, 1971.
A Simple Lust: Selected Poems.   London, Heinemann, and New York, Hill and Wang, 1973.
China Poems.   Austin, University of Texas, 1975.
Strains, edited by Wayne Kamin and Chip Dameron.   Austin, Texas, Troubadour Press, 1975.
Stubborn Hope.   London, Heinemann, and Washington, D.C., Three Continents Press, 1977.
Salutes and Censures.   Enugu, Nigeria, Fourth Dimension, and Trenton, New Jersey, Africa World Press, 1982.

*

Manuscript Collection: Northwestern University Library, Evanston, Illinois.

Critical Studies: *Introduction to African Literature* by Ulli Beier, Evanston, Illinois, Northwestern University Press, 1967; *Who's Who in African Literature* by Janheinz Jahn, Tübingen, Germany, Erdman, 1972; *African Authors* by Donald Herdeck, Washington, D.C., Black Orpheus Press, 1973; *The Black Mind* by O.R. Dathorne, Minneapolis, University of Minnesota Press, 1974, abridged edition as *African Literature in the 20th Century*, London, Heinemann, 1976.

Dennis Brutus comments:
   (1970) A lyrical poet: "protest" elements are only incidental, as features of the South African scene obtrude. Favourite poets: John Donne, Browning, Hopkins.
   (1985) My concerns have widened to embrace larger social issues, especially nuclear annihilation and the problems of the Third World.

*   *   *

   Dennis Brutus is one whose life has always been deeply connected to both commitment and controversy. Largely responsible, as President of the South African Non-Racial Olympic Committee, for the exclusion of South Africa from international sports competitions, Brutus began his crusade against apartheid while teaching in South Africa. It resulted in his being banned from teaching, writing, and publishing. In 1963, the same year which saw the publication of his first book of poetry, he was arrested, imprisoned for eighteen months, and eventually exiled. His most recent battle took place in 1983 when he fought deportation from the United States, where he had been teaching for more than a decade, and was finally granted political asylum after a lengthy struggle during which hundreds of Americans (both other writers and those who share his opposition to racial injustice) rallied to his defence.
   However, despite his deep political involvement, Brutus's voice as a poet has been marked, from his earliest published work, by a tone of maturity and restraint. This can be seen most clearly, perhaps, in the book he wrote following his imprisonment, *Letters to Martha*—a title which reflects the fact that he was banned from writing anything of a publishable nature and had to disguise his poems as letters to his sister-in-law. There his deft understatement, while presenting the harsh reality of life as a political prisoner, makes the message all the more powerful:

> And sometimes one mistook
> the weary tramp of feet
> as the men came shuffling from the quarry
> white-dust-filmed and shambling
> for the rain
> that came and drummed and marched away.

   Although Brutus has experienced personal suffering (which has ranged from the physical suffering of imprisonment on the infamous Robben Island—where he was shot in the back while attempting escape—to the spiritual suffering caused by his own exile and the continuing atrocities of apartheid), there is never a tone of self-pity. He has even found it possible to write gentle love poems (though even there the hard truths of recent history may still intrude). In fact, the powerful last lines of an often-quoted poem from his first collection, *Sirens, Knuckles, Boots*, might be taken as the philosophy the poet has lived by:

> Patrols uncoil over the asphalt dark
> hissing their menace to our lives,
>
> most cruel, all our land is scarred with terror,
> rendered unlovely and unlovable;
> sundered are we and all our passionate surrender
>
> but somehow tenderness survives.

   This is not to say that there is not a great deal of anger and even bitterness. Frustration, rage, and great sorrow can be found in Brutus, but that possibility of redemption, a "splendid Gethsemane," always exists. The world he opposes himself to may be brutal, but his opposition, while strong, is also a celebration of the value of human sensitivity and individual human lives. His vocabulary is that of a highly educated man but one who has not lost touch with the basic reality of ordinary human lives. Thus his tone is both elevated and basic, both passionate and restrained. His literary language is not polite or indirect, however, and he never hesitates to broaden his concerns to include contemporary issues. "We all live on a Three Mile Island/in a sea/which can transmogrify mankind," he says in a recent poem.

His newest poetry, as seen in the volumes *Stubborn Hope* and *Salutes and Censures*, shows a wider concern for the third world, linking Chile, Nicaragua, and other areas of national struggle with the problems of Africa, and specifically South Africa. His poem "No Matter for History" takes its title from a statement of Pablo Neruda's. Typical of the form of much of Brutus's poetry, free verse marked by cadence and repetition, these lines also embody his views of the inevitability of social democracy and the power of the poet, a power which comes from the people:

> in death
> the generals festered over him
> like blowflies
>
> his voice
> sings on,
> sings men to resistance,
> to hope, to life;
>
> Neruda is dead
> no matter.

Dennis Brutus has led many lives, worked continuously for social justice, visited many lands. His work reflects that diversity of experience and that continuity of commitment. His poems of imprisonment are not merely an indictment of the continuing injustice of apartheid, but also a statement of the enduring power of the human spirit against adversity. His poems of exile, a long and often painful exile which has taken him to almost every part of the world, are charged with hope. Throughout, he has remained a poet of the highest social commitment, yet one who has seldom sacrificed poetry for polemic.

—Joseph Bruchac

BUCHAN, Tom (Thomas Buchanan Buchan). Scottish. Born in Glasgow, 19 June 1931. Educated at Jordanhill College School; Balfron High School; Aberdeen Grammar School; University of Glasgow, 1947-53, M.A. (honours) in English 1953. Married Emma Chapman in 1962; three children. Teacher, Denny High School, Stirlingshire, 1953-56; Lecturer in English, University of Madras, India, 1957-58; warden, Community House, Glasgow, 1958-59; teacher, Irvine Royal Academy, 1963-65; Senior Lecturer in English and Drama, Clydebank Technical College, Glasgow, 1967-70. Co-Director, Kalachaitanya Madras, a touring repertory company, in the 1950's, and Director of the Craigmillar and Dumbarton festivals in the 1970's; Editor, *Scottish International*, Edinburgh, in the 1970's; member of the Rajneesh Ashram, Poona, in the 1970's. Agent: Barbara Hargeaves, Mains of Faillie, Daviot, Inverness-shire. Address: Scoraig, Dundonnell, Wester Ross IV23 2RE, Scotland.

PUBLICATIONS

Verse

Ikons. Madras, Tambaram Press, 1958.
Dolphins at Cochin. London, Barrie and Rockliff-Cresset Press, and New York, Hill and Wang, 1969.

Exorcism. Glasgow, Midnight Press, 1972.
Poems 1969-1972. Edinburgh, Poni Press, 1972.
Forwards. Glasgow, Glasgow Print Studio Press, 1978.

Plays

Tell Charlie Thanks for the Truss (produced Edinburgh, 1972).
The Great Northern Welly Boot Show, lyrics by Billy Connolly (produced Glasgow and London, 1972).
Knox and Mary (produced Edinburgh, 1972).
Over the Top (produced Edinburgh, 1979).
Bunker (produced Findhorn, Moray, 1980).

Novel

Makes You Feel Great. Edinburgh, Poni Press, 1971.

Other

Editor, with Nora Smith and John Forsyth, *Genie: Short Stories.* Edinburgh, Edinburgh University Press, 1974.

*

Manuscript Collection: Mitchell Library, Glasgow.

*   *   *

Tom Buchan's poetry shows a distinctive and consistent development from his first collection, *Dolphins at Cochin*, to his most recent *Poems 1969-1972*. His distinction, in the first instance, is in his making a true aesthetic response to machine imagery of the twentieth century. He in no way indulges this response, but it provides the cutting edge to his satire. Thus he depicts "The White Hunter" in *Dolphin at Cochin*:

> The white hunter in his newly laundered outfit
> emerges from the acacias hung about with guns,
> compasses, bandoliers, belts, charms, binoculars,
> Polaroid sun-specs, cameras and a shockproof watch.

The more vividly the equipment displays itself the greater the doubt cast on the reality of the person encased in it. Buchan's effects are immediate; their impact is decisive. "The Everlasting Astronauts" begins:

> These dead astronauts cannot decay—
> they bounce on the quilted walls of their tin grave
> and very gently collide with polythene balloons
> full of used mouthwash, excrements and foodscraps.

The hallucinatory effect of the floating bodies is captured, but the emphasis is on doubt as to the values of the achievement of modern man. The nausea suggested in the last line of the quatrain becomes in Buchan's second collection a more important factor in a book which exhibits passionate indignation, disgust and contempt at the hypocrisy and callousness of officials in power in modern society. The achievement is in the creation of a nightmare world inhabited by politicians who seem to be caricatures of actual persons. These creations induce belief. They are seen as we know them projected on screens of the cinema and television. He presents "Mister Nixon President" thus:

announces the U.S. invasion of Cambodia
(Cambodia) on TV and sincerely his sincere right eye
fixes the poor old silent US majority
with Operation Total Myopic Solemnity.

The observation is cruel, comic and with some truth in it.
Buchan's stated "subversive" intention does not limit him to
satirising capitalist politicians. In the same poem he hits off
Brezhnev:

> meanwhile dateline moss-cow Comrade Leonid
> Nebuchadnezzar Brezhnev in a weird soft hat
> reviews the latest lumpen May Day
> parade with a stiff diminutive wave
> reminiscent of our own dear Queen....

The poet undermines the reader's sense of the truth of the
observation by injecting into his text such references as CUT and
CAM 2, reminding him that for him these are shadows on a
screen. He uses the idea of our seeing the object through a
camera lens to a more subtle and profound purpose in his very
fine poem, "The Flaming Man," in which we seem to witness the
death of a man by burning napalm in slow motion.

Indignation in this poem gives way to compassion. This is
Buchan at his best. Occasionally he resorts to political campaigning and to an indulgence in nausea, which characteristics
manifest themselves in a strident rhetoric. But for the greater
part Buchan's rhetoric gives a sinewy strength to his verse.

—George Bruce

BUCHANAN, George (Henry Perrott). British. Born in
Kilwaughter, County Antrim, Northern Ireland, 9 January
1904. Educated at Campbell College and Queen's University,
Belfast. Served in the Royal Air Force Coastal Command, 1940-
45: Operations Officer. Married 1) Mary Corn in 1938 (marriage
dissolved, 1945); 2) Noel Ritter in 1949 (died, 1951); 3) Janet
Margesson in 1952 (died, 1968), two daughters; 4) Sandra
McCloy in 1974. Reviewer for the Times Literary Supplement,
London, 1928-40; on the editorial staff, The Times, London,
1930-35; columnist and drama critic, News Chronicle, London,
1935-38. Chairman, Town and Country Development Committee, Northern Ireland, 1949-53; Member of the Executive Council of the European Society of Culture, Venice, 1954-80. Address:
27 Ashley Gardens, London S.W. 1, England.

PUBLICATIONS

Verse

Bodily Responses. London, Gaberbocchus, 1958.
Conversation with Strangers. London, Gaberbocchus, 1961.
Annotations. Oxford, Carcanet, 1970.
Minute-Book of a City. Oxford, Carcanet, 1972.
Inside Traffic. Manchester, Carcanet, 1976.
Possible Being. Manchester, Carcanet, 1980.
Adjacent Columns. London and Manchester, Menard Press-
Carcanet, 1984.

Plays

Dance Night (produced London, 1934). London, French,
1935.
A Trip to the Castle (produced London, 1960).
Tresper Revolution (produced London, 1961).
War Song (produced London, 1965).

Novels

A London Story. London, Constable, 1935; New York, Dut-
ton, 1936.
Rose Forbes: The Biography of an Unknown Woman (part
1). London, Constable, 1937.
Entanglement. London, Constable, 1938; New York, Appleton
Century, 1939.
The Soldier and the Girl. London, Heinemann, 1940.
Rose Forbes (parts 1 and 2). London, Faber, 1950.
A Place to Live. London, Faber, 1952.
Naked Reason. New York, Holt Rinehart, 1971.

Other

Passage Through the Present: Chiefly Notes from a Journal.
London, Constable, 1932; New York, Dutton, 1933.
Words for Tonight: A Notebook. London, Constable, 1936.
Serious Pleasures: The Intelligent Person's Guide to London.
London, London Transport, 1938.
Green Seacoast (autobiography). London, Gaberbocchus, 1959;
New York, Red Dust, 1968.
Morning Papers (autobiography). London, Gaberbocchus,
1965.
The Politics of Culture. London, Menard Press, 1977.

*

Critical Studies: "George Buchanan Special Supplement" of
Honest Ulsterman 59 (Belfast), 1978.

George Buchanan comments:

The book titles suggest preoccupations: passage through the
present, bodily responses, conversation with strangers—mainly
to do with the role of the imagination in submerged mass-life in a
city ("I am in the poem, not the poem in me"). Which implies also
a permanent intention. ("Perhaps poetry is/our desires expressed
as laws./ We desire what is absolutely necessary./...The next line
may be the next line.")

The Russian Formalists saw that writers often took a subliterary genre and turned it to literature (e.g., Pushkin and the *vers de
société*). We may take the subliterary genre of intelligent conversation and turn it, if we can, to poetic speech.

*   *   *

George Buchanan is a quirky, eccentric poet: a man with
something quite specifically different to say, and with a different
way of saying it. In his earlier small volumes, such as *Bodily
Responses* and *Conversation with Strangers*, the footnotes are
larger and better (in the sense of being epigramatically provocative) than the poems, which are both lightweight and themselves
prosy. This is partly because he tended towards the use of a line
whose length he was not adept at handling: the genuinely epigrammatic effect of his footnotes is lost in arhythmic drag:

Sneering at the sheer number of others is a drug for
   self-cultivators
Who are also (they won't believe it) particles of the mass.
All of us are; and are filled with that million-made blaze.

The footnotes are those of a very odd-man-out indeed: a man
whose intelligence is refreshingly angled to the stream of fashion.
Much more of this emerges in the recent poetry of *Minute-Book
of a City* (no footnotes), in the poems of which form plays an
important part in the creation of tension, leading to a sharper
and more effective wit—as in "Anger":

> Cut out feeling (they say) yet often
> policy is the expression of a bad temper:
> when feeling's excluded, anger is the exception.
> We're at the mercy of official tempers.
> Irritable statesmen set the tone.
> Would well-intentioned villagers
> form a milder Cabinet,
> or would their rural eyes flash
> in ultra defiance even more animal?

—Martin Seymour-Smith

BUCKLEY, Vincent (Thomas). Australian. Born in Rom-
sey, Victoria, 8 July 1925. Educated at St. Patrick's (Jesuit)
College, East Melbourne; University of Melbourne, B.A. 1950,
M.A. 1954; Cambridge University, 1955-57. Served in the Australian Air Force. Married Penelope Curtis in 1976 (second
marriage); four children. Lockie Fellow, 1958-60, Reader, 1960-
67, and since 1967 Professor of English, University of Melbourne. Formerly, Member of the Editorial Board, *Prospect*
magazine. Recipient: Australian Literature Society Gold Medal,
1959; Myer award, 1967. Address: Department of English, University of Melbourne, Parkville, Victoria 3052, Australia.

PUBLICATIONS

Verse

The World's Flesh. Melbourne, Cheshire, 1954.
Masters in Israel. Sydney, Angus and Robertson, 1961.
Arcady and Other Places. Melbourne, Melbourne University
   Press, and London, Cambridge University Press, 1966.
Golden Builders and Other Poems. Sydney, Angus and
   Robertson, 1976.
Late-Winter Child. Melbourne, Oxford University Press, 1979;
   Atlantic Highlands, New Jersey, Humanities Press, 1980.
The Pattern. Melbourne, Oxford University Press, and Atlan-
   tic Highlands, New Jersey, Humanities Press, 1979.
Selected Poems. Sydney, Angus and Robertson, 1981.

Other

Essays in Poetry, Mainly Australian. Melbourne, Melbourne
   University Press, 1957.
*Poetry and Morality: Studies on the Criticism of Matthew
   Arnold, T.S. Eliot, and F.R. Leavis.* London, Chatto and
   Windus, 1959.
Henry Handel Richardson. Melbourne, Lansdowne Press,
   1961.

Poetry and the Sacred. London, Chatto and Windus, and New
   York, Barnes and Noble, 1968.
*Between Two Worlds: "Loss of Faith" and Late Nineteenth
   Century Australian Literature.* Sydney, Wentworth Press,
   1979.

Editor, *The Incarnation in the University: Studies in the University Apostolate.* Melbourne, University Catholic Federation of Australia, 1955; London, International Movement of
   Catholic Students, and Chicago, Young Christian Students,
   1957.
Editor, *Australian Poetry 1958.* Sydney, Angus and Robertson, 1958.
Editor, *The Campion Paintings,* by Leonard French. Melbourne, Gayflower Press, 1962.
Editor, *Eight by Eight.* Brisbane, Jacaranda Press, 1963.

*   *   *

Of the many Australian poets who work as teachers of literature, Vincent Buckley has been perhaps the most successful in
performing the functions of both professions. A respected
teacher, he has broken new ground—always by way of self-
preparation—in his published criticism, beginning, bravely for
the time, with the field of Australian poetry. Hindsight and their
later work would qualify his judgment of contemporaries, but
his affirmation of, for instance, the visionary value of C.J.
Brennan's poetry illuminated both Brennan criticism and Buckley's large preoccupations. The holder, like Brennan, of a personal chair at his university, Buckley has written searchingly of
culture in Australia and has scathing epigrams upon the pretensions which attend it ("Margins").

The early books of poems declared force, wit, and craftsmanship. They owed a debt to the English poets of the 1930's, witness
their firm diction, controlled forms, and the intensifying interaction of social comment and personal obsession ("Secret
Policeman"):

> Pledge me: I had the hangman for a father
> And for my mother the immortal State;
> My playground was the yard beside the lime-pit,
> My play-songs the after-cries of hate...
>
> The dead eyes point the way I go,
> The dead hands presage me in air.
> I run on shifting pavements, by fired walls
> Falling, and weighted lamp-posts everywhere.

But, also in *Arcady and Other Places,* the first considerable
achievement was the sequence "Stroke." Here Buckley found his
own voice, precisely in confronting his father's death and the
heritage of a native place, a temperament, and mortality.

> Every clod reveals an ancestor.
> They, the spirit hot in their bodies,
> Burned to ash in their own thoughts; could not
> Find enough water; rode in a straight line
> Twenty miles across country
> For hatred jumping every wire fence...
> Remembering always, when I think of death,
> The grandfather, small, loveless, sinister,
>   ["The most terrible man I ever seen,"
>   Said Joe, who died thin as rice paper]

Horse-breaker, heart-breaker, whose foot scorches,
Fifty years after, the green earth of Kilmore.
It's his heat that lifts my father's frame
Crazily from the wheel-chair, fumbles knots,
Twists in the bed at night,
Considers every help a cruelty.

This voice, humane and precise, speaks still in "Golden Builders," whose 27 sections, in forms varying from Blakean quatrains to very free verse, first appeared in *Poetry Australia* in 1972, in the same issue as Murray's "Walking to the Cattle Place." It was an impressive juxtaposition: large utterances both, Buckley's strictly urbane, keeping in the whole Christian-European experience, asking after the City of God from the streets of Carlton in inner Melbourne. This, the precinct of the University of Melbourne, in years of unrest pointed by disgust with the Vietnam war participation, was a heavily migrant-populated district of rooming-houses, cafés and billiard-rooms, where personal crisis the more easily seen as social emergency, both figured for Buckley in the barking of the dogs kept for experiments in biology. Not only in the epigraph and the poem called "Blake in the Body," Buckley walks by the London prophet.

This great poem, so various that quotation must be unjust, is of that kind that gives literary and visionary existence to a place and its people, by invoking wider relevance. An important poem in the same book is "Ghosts, Places, Stories, Questions," which talks of belief and "the few poems/that are the holy spaces of my life"; and in several shorter poems about horses and riders, weather and travel, Buckley strikes out, in extraordinary lines and half-lines, peculiar kinetic presence:

and the horse at dawn
breathing and stamping   touching
       the cold air with his whole body
       hair swinging like rain

the whistling weight of leather, children
darkening by the roadside,
cars barbed with sun, the shimmering
late odour of traffic

Since this book, Buckley's interest has steered back beyond his Australian forbears to his background in Ireland, where he plans an extended stay, and of which he writes as a homeland. He plans a book on Metaphor ("It won't be an academic book"). These are fresh directions but consistent, striking deeper; there is a mild irony in the arrival of Buckley, a pioneer in the serious criticism of Australian poetry, at this point just as the academic generality turns to Aust-Lit conferencing. Buckley's movement, however, is a controlled progression, no mere trendiness.

Buckley's output has been comparatively small. His qualities are an authority which is not unacademic, a native force that bulges the utterance, and occasionally a deftly placed, uplifting sweetness. The possibility of his surprising us with new work on a large scale should not be discounted.

—Judith Rodriguez

BUDBILL, David.   American.   Born in Cleveland, Ohio, 13 June 1940.   Educated at Muskingum College, New Concord, Ohio; Columbia University, New York; Union Theological Seminary, New York, M.Div. Married to Lois Budbill; one son and one daughter. Has worked as cook, gardener, road repairer, coffee house manager, researcher, carpenter's apprentice, forester, and English teacher; now a full-time writer. Lives in Wolcott, Vermont. Address: c/o Countryman Press, Box 175, Woodstock, Vermont 05091, U.S.A.

PUBLICATIONS

Verse

Barking Dog.   Cochranville, Pennsylvania, Barking Dog Press, 1968.
The Chain Saw Dance.   Johnson, Vermont, Crow's Mark Press, 1977.
Pulp Cutters Nativity.   Woodstock, Vermont, Countryman Press, 1981.
From Down to the Village.   New York, Ark, 1981.

Plays

Mannequins' Demise.   Boston, Baker, 1964.
Knucklehead Rides Again (produced New York, 1966).
Judevine: A Vermont Anthology (produced Princeton, New Jersey, 1984).

Novel

The Bones on Black Spruce Mountain.   New York, Dial Press, 1978.

Other

Christmas Tree Farm (for children).   New York, Macmillan, 1974.
Snowshoe Trek to Otter River (for children).   New York, Dial Press, 1976.

*

Critical Study: "Simply Survival: David Budbill and Joel Oppenheimer" by David W. Landrey, in *Credences* (Buffalo), Fall-Winter 1981-82.

*   *   *

"I don't know when I've come across a book so straightforwardly 'unpoetic,'" says the poet Tom McGrath on the back of David Budbill's book, *The Chain Saw Dance*, and his remark is as good a place as any to start a short review of Budbill's work.

Budbill's poetry is free-form, more than free-form; it *seems* to operate without any control whatever: without particular attention to line endings, without regular stanzas or meters, without heightened language. Lines like the following from a poem called "Forrest" are typical:

Forrest died five years ago.
I never knew him.
But I saw him, almost daily, winter and summer,
flapping down the Dunn Hill road to the family graves
up where Hermie used to live.

The careful reader, however, will soon discover that these remarkable poems have a rhythm of their own, a rhythm that originates in the poet's feeling for his subject and in the subject's own demands and needs. A natural and therefore powerful music occurs as Budbill enters the lives of the people he loves:

> Guy Desjardins, trucker of logs and lumber
> who just this morning while loading the biggest butt-log beech
> he ever saw in his life, snapped the boom.

If Budbill's style then is unpoetic, so too is his subject, or life in Northern Vermont, in Judevine, the town he has created as Faulkner created Yoknapatawpha County. Most of the titles in his books are the names of people who live in Judevine, such as Antoine, the French Canadian Christmas tree farm laborer, and Granny, the old widow in perpetual mourning for her husband, and Roy McInnes, the passionate welder. As the poems progress, these lives spill over and reflect each other. The citizens of Judevine share the beautiful and rugged landscape, a common poverty, and the ancient values of farmers and country people everywhere. They are a people who face extinction, whose small farms and stores have been overwhelmed by big government and technology. In spite of this they go on believing in an honest day's work and life's simple pleasures. Some, when they lose their farms or when their skills become useless, go mad or take to drink, and Budbill's compassion for both their pride and their fall is great; perhaps nowhere greater than in his poem about a farm couple who have been together fifty years, "Raymond and Ann" (*From Down to the Village*):

> Ann was slim and quick, full breasts and hips,
> and although her face was plain, she was to me
> unspeakably beautiful. She wore her white hair
> and wrinkled skin the way a summer flower wears its bloom.
> And in her eyes, even at the age of seventy, burnt a fire
> so bright and fierce, a passion so intense,
> it made me feel old and worn. In her presence
> I was sick at the slackness of my life.

Budbill's ear for dialect is good, and perhaps nowhere does he capture the spirit of the north country better than in the voices of the people themselves. Let Antoine speak then in indirect praise of the poet:

> Graoun's a bullin', David. Time ta plant da seed.
> Yew got tew make yer wedder. Got tew du it naow.
> Jes' da right time. It's mudder nature. Like a wimens.
> You be like me las' year, cabbage an' tomato
> gone ta hell but ah get a sidehill a patada
> an' a baby girl. Did year Poppa gonna plow
> da whole goddamn state for his gardin.

—Cynthia Day

BUKOWSKI, Charles. American. Born in Andernach, Germany, 16 August 1920; emigrated to the United States in 1922. Attended Los Angeles City College, 1939-41. Divorced; one child. Formerly, Editor, *Harlequin*, Wheeler, Texas, then Los Angeles, and *Laugh Literary* and *Man the Humping Guns*, both in Los Angeles. Columnist ("Notes of a Dirty Old Man"), *Open City*, Los Angeles, then Los Angeles *Free Press*. Recipient: Loujon Press award; National Endowment for the Arts grant, 1974. Address: P.O. Box 132, San Pedro, California 90731, U.S.A.

PUBLICATIONS

Verse

Flower, Fist and Bestial Wail. Eureka, California, Hearse Press, 1959.
Longshot Poems for Broke Players. New York, 7 Poets Press, 1961.
Run with the Hunted. Chicago, Midwest, 1962.
Poems and Drawings. Crescent City, Florida, Epos, 1962.
It Catches My Heart in Its Hands: New and Selected Poems, 1955-1963. New Orleans, Loujon Press, 1963.
Grip the Walls. Storrs, Connecticut, Wormwood Review Press, 1964.
Cold Dogs in the Courtyard. Chicago, Chicago Literary Times, 1965.
Crucifix in a Deathhand: New Poems, 1963-65. New Orleans, Loujon Press, 1965.
The Genius of the Crowd. Cleveland, 7 Flowers Press, 1966.
True Story. Los Angeles, Black Sparrow Press, 1966.
On Going Out to Get the Mail. Los Angeles, Black Sparrow Press, 1966.
To Kiss the Worms Goodnight. Los Angeles, Black Sparrow Press, 1966.
The Girls. Los Angeles, Black Sparrow Press, 1966.
The Flower Lover. Los Angeles, Black Sparrow Press, 1966.
Night's Work. Storrs, Connecticut, Wormwood Review Press, 1966.
2 by Bukowski. Los Angeles, Black Sparrow Press, 1967.
The Curtains Are Waving. Los Angeles, Black Sparrow Press, 1967.
At Terror Street and Agony Way. Los Angeles, Black Sparrow Press, 1968.
Poems Written Before Jumping Out of an 8-Story Window. Berkeley, California, Litmus, 1968.
If We Take.... Los Angeles, Black Sparrow Press, 1969.
The Days Run Away Like Wild Horses over the Hills. Los Angeles, Black Sparrow Press, 1969.
Penguin Modern Poets 13, with Philip Lamantia and Harold Norse. London, Penguin, 1969.
Another Academy. Los Angeles, Black Sparrow Press, 1970.
Fire Station. Santa Barbara, California, Capricorn Press, 1970.
Mockingbird Wish Me Luck. Los Angeles, Black Sparrow Press, 1972.
Me and Your Sometimes Love Poems. Los Angeles, Kisskill Press, 1972.
While the Music Played. Los Angeles, Black Sparrow Press, 1973.
Love Poems to Marina. Los Angeles, Black Sparrow Press, 1973.
Burning in Water, Drowning in Flame: Selected Poems 1955-1973. Los Angeles, Black Sparrow Press, 1974.
Africa, Paris, Greece. Los Angeles, Black Sparrow Press, 1975.
Weather Report. North Cambridge, Massachusetts, Pomegranate Press, 1975.
Winter. Evanston, Illinois, No Mountain, 1975.
Tough Company, with *The Last Poem*, by Diane Wakoski. Santa Barbara, California, Black Sparrow Press, 1976.
Scarlet. Santa Barbara, California, Black Sparrow Press, 1976.
Maybe Tomorrow. Santa Barbara, California, Black Sparrow Press, 1977.
Love Is a Dog from Hell: Poems 1974-1977. Santa Barbara, California, Black Sparrow Press, 1977.

Legs, Hips, and Behind. Los Angeles, Wormwood Review Press, 1979.

Play the Piano Drunk Like a Percussion Instrument until the Fingers Begin to Bleed a Bit. Santa Barbara, California, Black Sparrow Press, 1979.

A Love Poem. Santa Barbara, California, Black Sparrow Press, 1979.

Dangling in the Tournefortia. Santa Barbara, California, Black Sparrow Press, 1981.

War All the Time. Santa Barbara, California, Black Sparrow Press, 1984.

Novels

Post Office. Los Angeles, Black Sparrow Press, 1971; London, London Magazine Editions, 1974.

Factotum. Los Angeles, Black Sparrow Press, 1975; London, W.H. Allen, 1981.

Women. Santa Barbara, California, Black Sparrow Press, 1978; London, W.H. Allen, 1981.

Ham on Rye. Santa Barbara, California, Black Sparrow Press, 1982; London, Airlift, 1983.

Short Stories

Notes of a Dirty Old Man. North Hollywood, California, Essex House, 1969.

Erections, Ejaculations, Exhibitions and General Tales of Ordinary Madness. San Francisco, City Lights, 1972; abridged edition, as *Life and Death in the Charity Ward*, London, London Magazine Editions, 1974.

South of No North. Los Angeles, Black Sparrow Press, 1973.

Bring Me Your Love. Santa Barbara, California, Black Sparrow Press, and London, Airlift, 1983.

Hot Water Music. Santa Barbara, California, Black Sparrow Press, and London, Airlift, 1983.

There's No Business. Santa Barbara, California, Black Sparrow Press, and London, Airlift, 1984.

Other

Confessions of a Man Insane Enough to Live with Beasts. Bensenville, Illinois, Mimeo Press, 1965.

All the Assholes in the World and Mine. Bensenville, Illinois, Open Skull Press, 1966.

A Bukowski Sampler, edited by Douglas Blazek. Madison, Wisconsin, Quixote Press, 1969.

Art. Santa Barbara, California, Black Sparrow Press, 1977.

What They Want. Santa Barbara, California, Neville, 1977.

We'll Take Them. Santa Barbara, California, Black Sparrow Press, 1978.

You Kissed Lilly. Santa Barbara, California, Black Sparrow Press, 1978.

Shakespeare Never Did This. San Francisco, City Lights, 1979.

Editor, with Neeli Cherry and Paul Vangelisti, *Anthology of L.A. Poets.* Los Angeles, Laugh Literary, 1972.

*

Bibliography: *A Bibliography of Charles Bukowski* by Sanford Dorbin, Los Angeles, Black Sparrow Press, 1969.

Manuscript Collection: University of California, Santa Barbara.

Critical Studies: *Charles Bukowski: A Biographical Study* by Hugh Fox, Somerville, Massachusetts, Abyss, 1968; *Bukowski: Friendship, Fame, and Bestial Myth* by Jory Sherman, Augusta, Georgia, Blue Horse Press, 1982.

*   *   *

It is instructive to look at the way attitudes towards Charles Bukowski's poetry have evolved. In 1974, he is described by the editors of a reference work, *Contemporary Authors*, as a poet "who tends toward hysterical and ferocious verse." Two years later, in 1976, this description has been refined into "a poet of rough-hewn ferocity." By 1978, the editors give him a whole paragraph of description, including this sentence, "A strength of his work is his ability to record and define his life-style, without self-pity, in direct and affecting language." And about this time, his work actually gets reviewed in the Sunday *New York Times Book Review* (August 8) by Richard Elman, who says, in a highly favorable review of Bukowski's novel *Factotum*, "not since Orwell has the condition of being down and out been so well recorded in the first person."

It is Bukowski's fiction which has made him a best-seller in Germany and Sweden, and made his work so widely known in general. But he uses the persona of the dirty old man, which was developed in his poems, as a kind of Dionysian way of showing that our stereotypes of drunkards, womanizers, gamblers, and people not blessed with much formal education are not always correct. His work has satirized the "niceness" required by the American dream, as a form of weakness rather than virtue. The zest and humor and fire of this satirization have caught the imagination of many readers, including the very academics and aesthetes he debunks.

In spite of his popularity, however, Bukowski has not yet penetrated the American literary establishment sufficiently to have won any major prizes or grants or to have much serious criticism written about his work; but then this tends to be true of most poets working in the Dionysian rather than the Apollonian mode of poetry. Americans, ironically, honor truth, the poor man who works his way to the top, the person who chooses integrity rather than success, and most of all honesty; yet we seem to find these virtues more easily in someone who has gone to Harvard than someone who never went to college, someone who writes about difficult things in beautiful terms rather than someone who really tells it like it is.

Bukowski is a master of satire, and many of his poems are organized like a stand-up comedian's jokes. He tells a story, often filled with details that almost seem designed to represent the grosser side of life. Then he suddenly turns the tables on the reader. In his poem "On the Hustle" (*Dangling in the Tournefortia*), he's on a college campus for a poetry reading, has walked out of a classroom in disgust, and is looking at the pretty coeds,

> suddenly I braced myself
> against a tree and began
> pukin...
>
> "Look at that old
> man," a sweet birdie with
> brown eyes said to a sweet
> birdie with pale green eyes,
> "he's really
> *fucked-up...*"
>
> the truth, at
> last.

It's those one-liners which make Bukowski's fans shout and cheer. Suddenly we are faced with the reality that not only does Bukowski see himself clearly (and without self-pity) but also he sees himself as others see him, clearly and, even more astoundingly, without self-pity. One never gets the feeling that Bukowski recapitulates or regrets or feels apologetic or remorseful about himself, no matter how clearly he sees the figure of the dirty old man. But what makes this interesting is that we are forced to realize he is satirizing everyone: himself, the society he criticizes and abuses, and finally any vision that might be foolishly called "the truth." What Bukowski knows so well is that there *is* no truth, only points of view. And we can each one see holes in others' points of view.

Almost all of Bukowski's work has been published in the United States by John Martin of Black Sparrow Press. There is a close working relationship between poet and publisher, rare in publishing. Perhaps having an editor-publisher who has had such faith in his work has given Bukowski the greater possibilities of writing his controversial poems and fictions without ever feeling that he has to capitulate or renounce even a jot of that singular vision, one which allows him to represent, for many Europeans, a very clear and true picture of American life.

—Diane Wakoski

BULLOCK, Michael (Hale). British. Born in London, 19 April 1918. Educated at Stowe School, Buckinghamshire; Hornsey College of Art, London. Married Charlotte Schneller in 1941 (died); one daughter and one son. Chairman, Translators Association, London, 1964-67. McGuffey Visiting Professor of English, Ohio University, Athens, 1968; Professor of Creative Writing, University of British Columbia, Vancouver, 1969-83, now Emeritus. Founding Editor, *Expression* magazine, London; Member of the Editorial Board, *Canadian Fiction Magazine*, Vancouver. Recipient: Schlegel-Tieck Translation Prize, 1966; Canada Council fellowship, 1968, and translation award, 1979; Social Sciences and Humanities Research Council fellowship, 1981. Agent: International Copyright Bureau, 26 Charing Cross Road, London W.C.2, England; or, Joan Daves, 59 East 54th Street, New York, New York 10022, U.S.A. Address: 3836 West 18th Avenue, Vancouver, British Columbia V6S 1B5, Canada.

PUBLICATIONS

Verse

Transmutations (as Michael Hale). London, Favil Press, 1938.
Sunday Is a Day of Incest. London and New York, Abelard Schuman, 1961.
World Without Beginning, Amen! London, Favil Press, 1963.
Zwei Stimmen in Meinem Mund (bilingual edition, translated by Hedwig Rohde). Andernach, Germany, Atelier, 1967.
A Savage Darkness. Vancouver, Sono Nis Press, 1969.
Black Wings, White Dead. Fredericton, New Brunswick, Fiddlehead, 1978.
Lines in the Dark Wood. London, Ontario, Third Eye, 1981.
Prisoner of the Rain: Poems in Prose. London, Ontario, Third Eye, 1983.
Brambled Heart. London, Ontario, Third Eye, 1984.
Quadriga for Judy. London, Ontario, Third Eye, 1984.

Plays

The Raspberry Picker, adaptation of a play by Fritz Hochwälder (produced London, 1967).
Not to Hong Kong (produced London, 1972). Published in *Dialogue and Dialectic*, Guelph, Ontario, Alive Press, 1973.
The Island Abode of Bliss (produced Vancouver, 1972).
The Coats (produced London, Ontario, 1975).
Biography: A Game, adaptation of a play by Max Frisch (produced New York, 1979).

Novels

Randolph Cranstone and the Glass Thimble. London, Boyars, 1977.
The Story of Noire. London, Ontario, Third Eye, 1984.

Short Stories

Sixteen Stories as They Happened. Vancouver, Sono Nis Press, 1969.
Green Beginning Black Ending. Vancouver, Sono Nis Press, 1971.
Randolph Cranstone and the Pursuing River. Vancouver, Rainbird Press, 1975.
The Man with Flowers Through His Hands. London, Ontario, Third Eye, 1984.

Other

Translator, with Jerome Ch'ên, *Poems of Solitude.* London and New York, Abelard Schuman, 1961.
Translator, *The Tales of Hoffmann.* London, New English Library, 1962; New York, Ungar, 1963.
Translator, with Jerome Ch'ên, *Mao and the Chinese Revolution, With 37 Poems by Mao Tse-tung.* London, Oxford University Press, 1965.
Translator, *The Stage and Creative Arts.* Greenwich, Connecticut, New York Graphic Society, 1969.
Translator, *Foreign Bodies*, by Karl Krolow. Athens, Ohio University Press, 1969.
Translator, *Invisible Hands*, by Karl Krolow. London, Cape Goliard Press, and New York, Grossman, 1969.
Translator, with Jagna Boraks, *Astrologer in the Underground*, by Andrzej Busza. Athens, Ohio University Press, 1971.
Translator, *Stories for Late Night Drinkers*, by Michel Tremblay. Vancouver, Intermedia, 1977.

Other translations include novels and plays by Max Frisch and over 130 other French and German books.

*

Critical Studies: by John Ditsky, in *Canadian Forum* (Toronto), February 1971; Richard Hopkins, in *British Columbia Library Quarterly* (Victoria), January 1972; "Light on a Dark Wood" by John Reid, in *Canadian Literature* (Vancouver), Autumn 1972; interview with Richard Hopkins, in *British Columbia Library Quarterly* (Victoria), June 1973.

Michael Bullock comments:
I consider myself a surrealist, or at least a neo-surrealist, in that I base my work upon the free play of the imagination without, however, sacrificing clarity of expression. I seek to use vivid and striking imagery to convey states of mind and emotion

and to create an autonomous world freed from the restrictions and limitations of everyday existence. This world and the means I use to give it form remain the same whether I am writing verse, prose or drama. I believe that my writing in all three genres can with almost equal right be described as poetry. All of it is a vehement rejection of realism. I like to hope that there is some truth in the comment of a reviewer who wrote that my fables "bear witness to one of the most wildly imaginative minds ever to reach the printed page" and in Anaïs Nin's description of my work as "a liberating expansion of what is reality." The two remarks together sum up what I am trying to do.

*   *   *

In the poem "Escape" (*A Savage Darkness*), which might easily stand as his personal manifesto, Michael Bullock explains:

> The real surrounds me
> with its barbed wire entanglements
> Leaping upwards I clutch at a cloud
> and stuff it into my head
>
> In a blue haze
> figures emerge
> and drift
> in an endless floating dance
>
> Women with streaming hair
> fall downwards
> holding burning flowers
> Flocks of eyes fly around gazing
> and flapping their lids
>
> Stretched out
> on the cloud in my mind
> I wait for the approach
> of the ultimate dream...

The poem continues, but the most important catch-phrase has occurred: "the ultimate dream." For Michael Bullock is a Surrealist, almost an orthodox one in fact, and both his poetry and his prose insist entirely on the freedom, the total possibility which is the dream—both as a source and as mode. Bullock's poems are associative, fantastical, alogical; they leap and swirl to the arabesques of the imagination like a free-form dance. Through his writings Bullock re-enacts creation according to his own laws, according to a triumphantly lyrical, non-lineal progression both in time and space:

> Out of the air I draw the memory of a bird.
> Out of the earth I draw the memory of a tree.
> From the memory of the bird
> and the memory of the tree
> I make the memory of a poem
> that weighs lighter than air
> and floats away without wind...

The result is that Bullock's poetry almost always departs from unexpected places and arrives at unfamiliar destinations. And the means by which it gets there is, needless to say, no less unpredictable.

—Andreas Schroeder

———————

BUNTING, Basil.   British.   Born in Scotswood on Tyne, Northumberland, 1 March 1900. Educated at Ackworth School; Leighton Park School; London School of Economics, 1919-22. Jailed as a conscientious objector during World War I. Married 1) Marian Culver in 1930, two daughters and one son (deceased); 2) Sima Alladadian in 1948, one son and one daughter. Assistant Editor, *Transatlantic Review*, Paris, in the 1920's; music critic, *The Outlook*, London; lived in Italy and the United States in the 1930's; Persian correspondent for *The Times*, London, after World War II; Sub-Editor, Newcastle *Chronicle*, for 12 years. Taught at the University of California, Santa Barbara; Poetry Fellow, universities of Durham and Newcastle, 1968-70; taught at the universities of British Columbia, Vancouver, Binghamton, New York, and Victoria, British Columbia. President, Poetry Society, London, 1972-76, and Northern Arts, 1974-78; Honorary Life Visiting Professor, University of Newcastle upon Tyne. Recipient: Levinson Prize (*Poetry*, Chicago), 1966; Arts Council bursaries; Cholmondeley Award, 1982. D.Litt.: University of Newcastle upon Tyne, 1971. Fellow, Royal Society of Literature. Address: c/o Oxford University Press, Walton Street, Oxford OX2 6DP, England.

PUBLICATIONS

Verse

Redimiculum Matellarum.   Milan, Grafica Moderna, 1930.
Poems 1950.   Galveston, Texas, Cleaners' Press, 1950.
First Book of Odes.   London, Fulcrum Press, 1965.
Loquitur.   London, Fulcrum Press, 1965.
The Spoils: A Poem.   Newcastle upon Tyne, Morden Tower, 1965.
Ode II/2.   London, Fulcrum Press, 1965.
Briggflatts.   London, Fulcrum Press, 1966.
Two Poems.   Santa Barbara, California, Unicorn Press, 1967.
What the Chairman Told Tom.   Cambridge, Massachusetts, Pym Randall Press, 1967.
Collected Poems.   London, Fulcrum Press, 1968; revised edition, London and New York, Oxford University Press, 1978.
Version of Horace.   London, Holborn, 1972.

Other

Descant on Rawthey's Madrigal (*Conversations with Jonathan Williams*).   Lexington, Kentucky, Gnomon Press, 1968.

Editor, *Selected Poems*, by Ford Madox Ford.   Cambridge, Massachusetts, Pym Randall Press, 1971.
Editor, *Selected Poems*, by Joseph Skipsey.   Sunderland, Ceolfrith Press, 1976.

*

Bibliography: *Basil Bunting: A Bibliography of Works and Criticism* by Roger Guedalla, Norwood, Pennsylvania, Norwood Editions, 1973.

Critical Studies: in *Agenda 4* (London), 1966; "Basil Bunting Issue" of *Poetry Information 19* (London), 1978, and *Agenda* (London), Spring 1978.

Basil Bunting comments:
    Minor poet, not conspicuously dishonest.

* * *

"With sleights learned from others and an ear open to melodic analogies I have set down words as a musician pricks his score, not to be read in silence, but to trace in the air a pattern of sound that may sometimes, I hope, be pleasing." Thus Basil Bunting defines his purpose in the Preface to his *Collected Poems*, adding, characteristically, "Unabashed boys and girls may enjoy them. This book is theirs." Bunting has learnt from many others, and he is generous in his acknowledgments; but it is from Ezra Pound and the "sterner, stonier" Louis Zukofsky that he derived this essentially Renaissance pre-occupation with an art which delights by the sheer candour of its cadence and contour. Bunting describes his major poem, *Briggflatts*, as "an autobiography, but not a record of fact.... The truth of the poem is of another kind"; and indeed, it is the articulation of image and theme in a "Flexible, unrepetitive line/...laying the tune on the air,/nimble and easy as a lizard" that brings together the poet, his Northumbrian landscape, and the history that lies behind them. Speaking in the persona of the Japanese poet Chomei in another poem, Bunting defines the distinctive combination of parochial and universal (so much larger than the cosmopolitan) which characterizes *Briggflatts*:

> Neither closed in one landscape
> nor in one season
> the mind moving in illimitable
> recollection.

Briggflatts opens with the stonemason's inscription of a name on a tombstone: "the stone spells a name/naming none,/a man abolished." By the end of the poem, it is clear that this is not just the poet's own literal epitaph but also an analogy for that literary death-in-life by which a man is translated into language, into words that inscribe not only his labour but that of all the hands that go to make a finished book. In a lambent metaphor, the traces which record our disappearance are compared to the light from a star which, taking 50 years to reach us, compacts time, as, throughout the poem, the brutal Anglo-Saxon world of Eric Bloodaxe and the Celtic lament for the slain of Aneurin pervade the personal present and mingle with the poet's regrets for a lost love:

> Then is Now. The star you steer by is gone...
>   Light from the zenith
> spun when the slowworm lay in her lap
> fifty years ago.
> The sheets are gathered and bound,
> the volume indexed and shelved,
> dust on its marbled leaves.

The slowworm, with its obvious phallic imagery, in its blind relentless progress through the poem, makes another correlation, between sexuality and artistic creation. *Briggflatts* returns repeatedly to a kind of poetic *tristitia post coitum* in which the poet laments the "flawed fragments" of his labours, never able to consummate the perfect match of form and content: "He lies with one to long for another.../obstinate, mating/beauty with squalor to beget lines still-born." Yet this struggle with the intractable is the highest task of the artist. Like Schoenberg rather than Monteverdi, the poet tells us, his task is to "entune a bogged orchard,/its blossom gone,/fruit unformed, where hunger and/damp hush the hive. "Throughout *Briggflatts* there is a powerful counterpoint of the demotic and the aesthetic, the monosyllabic beat of Anglo-Saxon noun and verb in tight-packed proximity and a heavy alliterative metre with a larger, more elaborate vocabulary, syntax, and rhythm. Stylistically this reinforces the urgency with which, in the image of the sweating Pasiphaë mounted by the bull-god, a major theme is presented: the holiness of the bestial, that sordid material being which is the groundbass of all our finer tones.

Bunting's progress from his earliest poems, the odes he wrote in the 1920's, has indeed been a retreat from an orotund latinity, excessively adjectival in style, to the tangible, concrete immediacy of his latest work. The odes written during the 1930's suggest that it was not only the tradition of Modernism, mediated by Pound, Eliot, and Auden, but also the actual social experience of the period which effected this change. These 1930's poems are full of a sense of the human locked in effort, struggle, hard material labour, "resigned to/anything except your own numb toil, the/seasonal plod to spoil the land alone" (*"O ubi campi!"*). But the obverse of this is solidarity between poet and *menu peuple* which is expressed in sexual terms in "The Orotava Road," which speaks of his encounter with young peasant girls on donkeys:

> You can guess their balanced nakedness
> under the cotton gown and thin shift....
> They say "Adios!" shyly but look back
> more than once, knowing our thoughts
>   and sharing our
> desires and lack of faith in desire.

This last note is characteristic: like Chomei, in Bunting's own words, he has an "urbane, sceptical and ironical temper" which prevents him from ever "preaching the simple life." Unequivocally rooted, Buntings's poetry is nevertheless, like Hugh MacDiarmid's, heir to world literature, as his translations ("Overdrafts" he calls them, thereby signalling an ironic relationship to his inheritance) and his complex allusiveness within the body of his poems to Oriental, Persian, Classical, and Renaissance literature all indicate. An irony that can transcend archness or cynicism is rare in modern poetry, but Bunting's is finally rich and affirmative, as is revealed most succinctly perhaps, in the short and apparently simple lyric which opens his *Odes II/2* where the last line invites us to re-view the lines which precede it, offering a balanced comment on the poetic and the human vocations:

> A thrush in the syringa sings.
>
> "Hunger ruffles my wings, fear,
> lust, familiar things.
>
> Death thrusts hard. My sons
> by hawk's beak, by stones,
> trusting weak wings
> by cat and weasel, die.
>
> Thunder smothers the sky.
> From a shaken bush I
> list familiar things,
> fear, hunger, lust."
>
> O gay thrush!

—Stan Smith

BURFORD, William (Skelly). American. Born in Shreveport, Louisiana, 20 February 1927. Educated at Amherst College, Massachusetts (Glasscock Memorial Award, Mount Holy-oke College, 1949), B.A. (magna cum laude) 1949 (Phi Beta Kappa); the Sorbonne, Paris, 1950-52 (Fulbright Scholar); Johns Hopkins University, Baltimore, M.A. 1956, Ph.D. 1966. Served in the United States Army, 1945. Married Lolah Egan in 1956; three daughters. Assistant to the President, Richardson Refining Company, Texas City, 1949-50; Instructor in English, Southern Methodist University, Dallas, 1950-51, 1952-54, and Johns Hopkins University, 1955-58; Assistant Professor, 1958-64, and Associate Professor of English, 1964-65, University of Texas, Austin; Associate Professor of Humanities, University of Montana, Missoula, 1966-68; Professor of English, Texas Christian University, Fort Worth, Texas, 1968-72. Since 1972, teacher in the National Endowment for the Arts Poetry-in-the-Schools Program. Poet-in-Residence, Evergreen State College, Olympia, Washington, 1974; Fellow, Dallas Institute of Humanities, 1980. Recipient: Walt Whitman Memorial Award, 1962. Address: 3000 West Gambrell, Fort Worth, Texas 76133, U.S.A.

PUBLICATIONS

Verse

Man Now.   Dallas, Southern Methodist University Press, 1954.
Faccia Della Terra/Face of the Earth (bilingual edition).   Bolo-gna, Libreria Antiquaria Palmaverde, 1960.
A World.   Austin, University of Texas Press, 1962.
A Beginning.   New York, Norton, 1966.
Gymnos: Uncollected Poems.   Olympia, Washington, Four Mountains Press, 1973.

Other

The Art of Anaïs Nin, with *On Writing*, by Nin.   Yonkers, New York, Baradinsky, 1947.

Editor and Translator, with Christopher Middleton. *The Poet's Vocation: Selections from the Letters of Hölderlin, Rimbaud, and Hart Crane*, Austin, University of Texas Press, 1967.
Editor and Translator, with Jean Autret, *On Reading*, by Proust. New York, Macmillan, and London, Souvenir Press, 1972.

*

Manuscript Collection: Lockwood Library, State University of New York, Buffalo.

Critical Study: review by David Ignatow, in *The New York Times*, 6 January 1967.

William Burford comments:
   Poetry, at least as I have learned to want to write it, is a way of giving reality and even courage to the life a man senses within himself, and which he knows, by living among other men, is their chief possession also. The poetry which seems to me the most admirable is characterized by a certain firm delicacy, a style which at once both moves and instructs the sense of life in us. If a man writes poems for any length of time, he learns how much experience of both life and art is required to achieve this style, how few men have been masters of it, and these few seemingly by some grace of nature or intelligence or artistic perception, that cannot be willed by himself into his own possession but only perhaps gradually approached if he has a view of the goal.

*   *   *

In scenes of childhood innocence, in cities of youthful pleasure lurk recurring forms of terror, loneliness, and melancholy. A childish game destroys a harmless life. A boy, frightened by his nurse's disfigured face, marks his fate with clocks ticking the hours of a father's absence. A father bids his son remove annoy-ing sparrows which return in nightmare as birds of prey. In sunlit Paris the youth denies the phantom of himself. He finds Venice "sunk to a sewer." In Amsterdam an old man tells him: "To live is to persist." The poet sees with the eyes of the painter; indeed, paintings become subjects for some of his strongest lines. The once-benevolent surgeon's scapel stabs the brain that was a world. The sensuous face to the sexless monk mocks the artist. Stones arranged like human bones spell out station-names in fields lying in ashes. Images of frost, marble waves, slivers of glass quickly etch vignettes made even more poignant by the poet's delicate, controlling hand. Yet William Burford's incisive, sombre scenes do not depress but comfort and enlighten; for usually a calm instilled by oblique and muted Christian symbo-lism pervades and promises hope, which in later poems finds fruition in the loving presence of a sleeping wife and awkward grace of an adolescent son.
   Burford seeks to capture "that moment fatal in our lives" by asking: "Where does one go for love these days?" This probing for the fundamental gives his poetry a continuity of theme and purpose (and several early poems reappear, revised, in later volumes); he traces the private world of child and youth as it opens to the social consciousness of maturity. But early he learned that passion is "aged to a patience." He cried, "My name is man, and I am dumb from pain." "In an ironic age," he discovers, "reasonable men" are hospitable to the Devil they do not believe in; judges behind their tinted glass are still "hypnotiz-ing existence." Solipsistic man thinks his body is the world, "And so a final philosophy." The perfect young dancer thinks himself immortal, though destruction waits in the wings. The poet, too, has "measureless privacy," but he turns his penetrating eye upon the ephemeral and finds the "self is strong, unisolated,/ And from its birth forms bonds throughout all." Unlike the windy, undisci-plined, but fashionable voices decrying a fractured world in despair, Burford depicts in short, polished verse a destructive universe still capable of meaning through humanity and faith.

—Joseph Parisi

BURKE, Kenneth (Duva).   American.   Born in Pittsburgh, Pennsylvania, 5 May 1897. Educated at Peabody High School, Pittsburgh; Ohio State University, Columbus, 1916-17; Colum-bia University, New York, 1917-18. Married 1) Lily Mary Bat-terham in 1919 (divorced), three daughters; 2) Elizabeth Batter-ham in 1933, two sons. Research worker, Laura Spelman Rockefeller Memorial, New York, 1926-27. Music critic, *Dial*, New York, 1927-29, and *The Nation*, New York, 1934-35; Edi-tor, Bureau of Social Hygiene, New York, 1928-29. Lecturer, New School for Social Research, New York, 1937; University of Chicago, 1938, 1949-50; Bennington College, Vermont, 1943-61; Princeton University, New Jersey, 1949, 1975; Kenyon College, Gambier, Ohio, 1950; Indiana University, Bloomington, 1953, 1958; Drew University, Madison, New Jersey, 1962, 1964; Penn-sylvania State University, University Park, 1963; Regents Pro-fessor, University of California, Santa Barbara, 1964-65; Lec-turer, Central Washington State University, Ellensburg, 1966; Harvard University, Cambridge, Massachusetts, 1967-68; Washington University, St. Louis, 1970-71; Wesleyan University, Middletown, Connecticut, 1972; University of Pittsburgh, 1972; University of Washington, Seattle, 1976; University of Nevada, Reno, 1976. Recipient: *Dial* Award, 1928; Guggenhein Fellowship, 1935; American Academy grant, 1946, and Gold Medal, 1975; Princeton Institute for Advanced Study Fellowship, 1949; Stanford University Center for Advanced Study in Behavioral Sciences Fellowship, 1957; Rockefeller grant, 1966; Brandeis University Creative Arts Award, 1967; National Endowment for the Arts Award, 1968; New School for Social Research Horace Gregory Award, 1970; Ingram Merrill Foundation Award, 1970; American Academy of Arts and Sciences Award, 1977; National Medal for Literature, 1981; Bobst Award, 1983; D.Litt: Bennington College, 1966; Rutgers University, New Brunswick, New Jersey, 1968; Dartmouth College, Hanover, New Hamsphire, 1969; Fairfield University, Connecticut, 1970; Northwestern University, Evanston, Illinois, 1972; University of Rochester, New York, 1972; Indiana State University, Terre Haute, 1976; Kenyon College, 1979. Member, American Academy; American Academy of Arts and Sciences; Honorary Fellow, Modern Language Association. Address: R.D. 2, Andover, New Jersey 07921, U.S.A.

PUBLICATIONS

Verse

Book of Moments: Poems 1915-1954. Los Altos, California, Hermes, 1955.
Collected Poems 1915-1967. Berkeley, University of California Press, and London, Cambridge University Press, 1968.

Novel

Towards a Better Life, Being a Series of Epistles or Declamations. New York, Harcourt Brace, 1932; revised edition, Berkeley, University of California Press, and London, Cambridge University Press, 1966.

Short Stories

The White Oxen and Other Stories. New York, Boni, 1924.
The Complete White Oxen: Collected Shorter Fiction. Berkeley, University of California Press, 1968.

Other

Counter-Statement. New York, Harcourt Brace, 1931; revised edition, Berkeley, University of California Press, and London, Cambridge University Press, 1968.
Permanence and Change: An Anatomy of Purpose. New York, New Republic, 1935; revised edition, Los Altos, California, Hermes, 1954.
Attitudes Towards History. New York, New Republic, 2 vols., 1937; revised edition, Los Altos, California, Hermes, 1959.
The Philosophy of Literary Form: Studies in Symbolic Action. Baton Rouge, Louisiana State University Press, 1941; revised edition, New York, Random House, 1957; London, Peter Smith, 1959.
A Grammar of Motives. New York, Prentice Hall, 1945; London, Dobson, 1947.
A Rhetoric of Motives. New York, Prentice Hall, 1950; London, Bailey Brothers and Swinfen, 1955.
The Rhetoric of Religion: Studies in Logology. Boston, Bea-

con Press, 1961.
Perspectives by Incongruity, edited by Stanley Edgar Hyman. Bloomington, Indiana University Press, 1964.
Language as Symbolic Action: Essays on Life, Literature and Method. Berkeley, University of California Press, and London, Cambridge University Press, 1966.
Dramatism and Development. Worcester, Massachusetts, Clark University Press, 1972.
Ideas for Environment [Reading and Writing, Science, Spelling and Phonics, Sports, American History, Americans—All, Consumer Education, Men and Women of the World, World History], with Julie Kranhold. Belmont, California, Lear Siegler Fearon, 10 vols., 1973-74.
William Carlos Williams (lectures), with Emily H. Wallace. East Brunswick, New Jersey, Fairleigh Dickinson University Press, 1974.

Translator, *Death in Venice,* by Thomas Mann. New York, Knopf, 1925; revised edition, New York, Modern Library, 1970.
Translator, *Genius and Character,* by Emil Ludwig. New York, Harcourt Brace, 1927; London, Cape, 1930.
Translator, *Saint Paul,* by Emile Baumann. New York, Harcourt Brace, 1929.

*

Critical Studies: *Kenneth Burke and the Drama of Human Relations* by William H. Rueckert, Minneapolis, University of Minnesota Press, 1963, revised edition, Berkeley, University of California Press, 1982, and *Critical Responses to Kenneth Burke 1924-1966* edited by Rueckert, University of Minnesota Press, 1969 (includes checklist by Armin and Mechtchild Frank); *Kenneth Burke* by Armin Frank, New York, Twayne, 1969; *Kenneth Burke* by Merle E. Brown, Minneapolis, University of Minnesota Press, 1969; *Representing Kenneth Burke* edited by Hayden White and Margaret Brose, Baltimore, Johns Hopkins University Press, 1983.

Kenneth Burke comments:
    In calling my theory of language as symbolic action "Dramatistic" (as contrasted with "Scientistic") I have in mind a distanction that boils down to this: A "Scientistic" approval centers in "It is/it is not"; a "Dramatistic" approach centers in "Do/don't." My aim is to develop a theory of language in general, with emphasis upon its application to specific texts.

*   *   *

    My favorite among Kenneth Burke's *Collected Poems 1915-1967* is a 17-page poem in 5 parts entitled "Tossing on Floodtides of Sinkership: A Diaristic Fragment." Driving across the country, the speaker floats on a turbulent sea of memories, reflections, and feelings—the dangers of traffic, the power of the machine, pollution, reactions to America's face and fate, politics, Vietnam, his own inner conflicts—but concludes with the stubborn persistence of spring and of the sunrise. Now Burke writes most frequently about our public life, but what I find distinctive in this poem is the way in which the public is seen in terms of the personal, for not only do the larger issues arise naturally and dramatically out of the particular situation, but they are also seen *in relation* to the speaker and his own turmoil. He sees the destructiveness of highspeed autos in political terms—the easy manipulation of such vicarious power may tend to make us docile citizens—and he feels the fascination of his own suicidal urge to spin off the road as well. He sees the deterioration of the land, and he senses a connection with his own desolation: "half experimental animal,/half control group./I am mine own disease." And when he comes to the Vietnam issue, he not only vents his indignation—"Cook them with napalm in the name of freedom/tear up their way of life"—he also confronts his own hesitation—"Gad! I couldn't tell them that!"—and concludes this section (IV) with the wry admission that "To be safe in striking at the powerful/make sure that your blows are powerless."

It is not, alas, always thus. Too often his poems are simply public statements without either tension or intensity. Excellent critic that he is, Burke offers a Foreword and various explanatory prose excursions, whose gist is that, contrary to our common assumptions, prose is more subtle, conditional, and qualified than lyric poetry. Criticism, he says in "Extraduction from What?," is "moderate in tone and at least theoretically charitable.... The very attempt to be circumspect in criticism could make one, by rebound, at least *wish* for *some* verse in the style of a news broadcast blasting forth pellets...." And therein lies the problem, for the very life of the lyric depends upon its stemming from and embodying a sense of personal urgency, it seems to me, and if you would write the unqualified sort, as E.E. Cummings does, for example, your sense of self must be intense, accepting, intuitive, passionate, and transcendent, so that when it confronts the troublesome public world it will do so on the basis of inner confidence. Yet, in "Extraduction," he speaks of "my morbid Selph, lost among the monsters of machinery and politics." And in his admiring elegy on Cummings, he takes pleasure in opining that Cummings had more brains than he admitted to—"you secretly, like the scholastics' God,/an intellectual"—as if to say that Cummings' mysticism was less than whole-hearted.

An instructive contrast to the Vietnam section of "Tossing" is found in another, shorter poem on the same subject, "The Great Debate," which is in this "news broadcast" style, and which concludes:

> But time is running out.
> Where we but increase our forces
> the enemy escalates.
>
> Give us an honorable peace
> And we'll stop
> Our dishonorable war.
>
> (There's shouting in the streets—and I wanna go home)

There is irony here, of course, but it is still, as is the rest of the poem, rather flat, and the final line is an ineffectual attempt to supply a dramatic base, for it is a deliberately forlorn gesture and is simply stuck on at the end—quite different in function and effect from the similar conclusion of Cummings' "pity this busy monster, manunkind": "listen: there's a hell/of a good universe next door; let's go."

One would think, then, that Burke would be more at home in writing the qualified sort of lyric, as in "Tossing," in which the sense of personal urgency arises from tension, conflict, intelligence, consideration, and self-confrontation, and one recalls Yeats's sobering remark that we make rhetoric out of our quarrel with others, but poetry out of our quarrel with ourselves. But Burke's poetic self is just as tenuous when confronting itself as the public world, betraying its uncertainties and avoidances in a wobbly style which skitters from the melodic to the prosaic, and touches doggerel, slang, nonsense, and puns along the way. And self-knowledge rarely gets in touch either with the possibility that the public is an extension of ourselves or that it becomes internalized and sticks within as a part of ourselves.

It is this awareness which surfaces but seldom in Burke's poetry, and when it does it finds its acknowledged symptom in insomnia. Nevertheless, in six successive lyrics entitled "On a Photo of Himself," "Self-Portrait," "Know Thyself," "Now I Lay Me," "On the Reflexive," and "Personality Problem," the speaker presents himself with gentleness, wit, and frankness as sleepless and aging:

> One-third insomnia
> One-third art
> One-third The Man
> With the Cardiac Heart....
>
> I'm flunking my Required Course
> In Advanced Burkology.

This is less powerful than "half experimental animal, etc.," but it is effective in its own way. And he can on occasion combine self-study with social criticism, as in "Photo," which concludes:

> *Bring on your bombs, your bugs, and the trick chemicals.*
> *Get this damned business done*
>
> *But in the interim*
> *Curse me for a not-yet-housebroken cur*
> *And rub my nose in filthy lucre.*

And "L'Auberge" is a lovely counterpart, in its depiction of a respite at an inn while traveling, to the similar concluding section of Part I of "Tossing," but it drives even deeper into the recesses of the self. Here and throughout he appears as an engaged and engaging poet indeed, more moderate and charitable than he seems to think he is. I could only wish that he did not feel his poetry represented an escape from his more brilliant and arduous critical work.

—Norman Friedman

BURNS, Jim. British. Born in Preston, Lancashire, 19 February 1936. Educated at local schools and Bolton Institute of Technology, Lancashire, B.A. (honours) 1980. Served in the British Army, 1954-57. Married in 1958 (divorced, 1973); two sons. Worked in mills, offices, and factories, 1952-64. Editor, *Move* magazine, Preston, 1964-68. Since 1964, regular contributor, *Tribune*. London; since 1978, Editor, *Palantir*, Preston.

PUBLICATIONS

Verse

Some Poems. New York, Crank, 1965.
Some More Poems. Cambridge, R Books, 1966.
My Sad Story and Other Poems. Chatham, Kent, New Voice, 1967.
The Store of Things. Manchester, Phoenix Pamphlet Poets Press, 1969.
A Single Flower. St. Brelade, Jersey, Channel Islands, Andium Press, 1972.
Leben in Preston. Cologne, Palmenpresse, 1973.
Easter in Stockport. Sheffield, Rivelin Press, 1975.
Fred Engels in Woolworths. London, Oasis, 1975.

Playing It Cool. Swansea, Galloping Dog Press, 1976.
The Goldfish Speaks from Beyond the Grave. London, Salamander Imprint, 1976.

Other

Cells: Prose Pieces. Lincoln, Grosseteste Press, 1967.
Saloon Bar: 3 Jim Burns Stories. London, Ferry Press, 1967.
Types: Prose Pieces and Poems. Cardiff, Second Aeon, 1970.

*

Critical Studies: "The American Influence" by the author, in *New Society* (London), 7 December 1967; "Exit to Preston" by Raymond Gardner, in *The Guardian* (London), 10 August 1972; "A Poet in His Northern Corner" by Bel Mooney, in *Daily Telegraph Magazine* (London), 2 March 1973; "Jim Burns' Poems" by John Freeman, in *Cambridge Quarterly*, 1975; "Mit Poesie Kannst Du Kein Auto Fahren" by Michael Buselmeir, in *Frankfurter Rundschau*, 8 April 1978.

Jim Burns comments:

(1970) I suppose my main subject-matter tends towards the "domestic," i.e., that which I know best and experience personally. Brevity and wit are attributes I admire in a poet and I think (or hope) that some of this comes in some of my own work.

My main influences have been contemporary American and English poets, and some translations from the Chinese and Japanese. I like the directness in these latter. If asked to single out one poet whose work I particularly like and find stimulating I would name Kenneth Rexroth.

I have a deep feeling that the most significant ideas can be expressed in direct and clear language, and that the unusual and significant are in the obvious.

The reader may also get an idea of my leanings from the opinions expressed in the articles I have contributed (since 1964) to *Tribune* on little-magazines and related publications.

(1974) In the past three or four years, my poetry has, I think, tended to diversify, both in form and content. I still like brevity and wit, but have found that, in order to deal with matters outside the domestic concerns my poems once related to, I've had to become perhaps more discursive. In a sense, as the subject-matter widens, so do the forms I use. The lines tend to be longer, the rhythm less precise. Interestingly enough, however, I find that when I do revert to "domestic" concerns the form tightens again.

*   *   *

If one had to find a single word to describe Jim Burns's poems it would be "anecdotal." Each poem tells a story and the tone adopted is that of the raconteur where the impetus relies more on the narrative flow and the ultimate making of a point than on language or rhythm as such. What informs each story is the persona adopted, that of the wryly candid man who, though beguiled by the romantic, is never taken in by it; whether it be romantic love—"Better to make love in bed, turn/your back afterwards. Sleep easy" ("The Way It Is")—or the pretentiousness of romantic politics ("Meanwhile"):

> The left wing intellectuals
> had fought the Paris Commune, the
> General Strike, the Spartacist uprising
> and the Spanish Civil War all over
> again and would have sung the Red Flag

> had they known the words or tune.
> Instead, they ordered another round
> and the landlord rubbed his hands
> and then called time. For everyone

Indeed, it seems to be Burns's mission to deflate gently the phoney and the ostentatious; gently because he too knows the temptations and has some sympathy with those who succumb. For this reason the language used avoids the "high flown" to the point of flatness; Burns's sense of rhythm and the narrative flow carrying the poems on. Nevertheless, the truth must out. "Is a man any less a poet/because he stays at home/with his wife and children" he asks in "A Single Flower." Poetry stands or falls by what is on the page; it is irrelevant if the author washes himself, sleeps with his sister or has two heads, if he is an arch bishop or an arch-Villon:

> I once slept out all night
> with the homeless, and although
> it taught me pity
> it did not teach me poetry.

And he is right; though there are some who will not forgive him for that! But self-depreciatory, honest and always caring as he is, one cannot help liking the man behind the poems.

—John Cotton

———

BURNSHAW, Stanley. American. Born in New York City, 20 June 1906. Educated at Columbia University, New York, 1924; University of Pittsburgh, B.A. 1925; University of Poitiers, 1927; University of Paris, 1927-28; Cornell University, Ithaca, New York, M.A. 1933. Married 1) Madeline Burnshaw in 1934 (divorced); 2) Lydia Powsner in 1942; one daughter and two stepchildren. Advertising Assistant, Blaw-Knox Company, Blawnox, Pennsylvania, 1925-27; Advertising Manager, The Hecht Company, New York, 1928-32; Co-Editor and drama critic, *The New Masses*, New York, 1934-36; Editor-in-Chief, The Cordon Company, publishers, New York, 1937-39; President and Editor-in-Chief, Dryden Press, New York, 1939-58; Vice-President, 1958-66, and Consultant to the President, 1966-68, Holt, Rinehart and Winston Inc., publishers, New York. Lecturer, New York University, 1958-62; Visiting Regents Lecturer, University of California, Davis, 1980. Founding Editor (and hand setter), *Poetry Folio* magazine, and Folio Press, Pittsburgh, 1926-29. Contributing Editor, *Modern Quarterly*, 1932-33, and *Theatre Workshop* magazine, 1935-38. Director, American Institute of Graphic Arts, 1960-61. Recipient: American Academy award, 1971. D.H.L.: Hebrew Union College, Cincinnati, 1983. Address: Lamberts Cove, Martha's Vineyard, Massachusetts 02568, U.S.A.

PUBLICATIONS

Verse

Poems. Pittsburgh, Folio Press, 1927.
The Great Dark Love. Privately printed, 1932.
The Iron Land: A Narrative. Philadelphia, Centaur Press, 1936.

The Revolt of the Cats in Paradise: A Children's Book for
    Adults.   Gaylordsville, Connecticut, Crow Hill Press, 1945.
Early and Late Testament.   New York, Dial Press, 1952.
Caged in an Animal's Mind.   New York, Holt Rinehart, 1963.
The Hero of Silence.   Privately printed, 1965.
In the Terrified Radiance.   New York, Braziller, 1972.
Mirages: Travel Notes in the Promised Land: A Public Poem.
    New York, Doubleday, 1977.

Play

The Bridge (in verse).   New York, Dryden Press, 1945.

Novels

The Sunless Sea.   London, Davies, 1948; New York, Dial Press,
    1949.
The Refusers: An Epic of the Jews.   New York, Horizon Press,
    1981.

Other

A Short History of the Wheel Age.   Pittsburgh, Folio Press,
    1928.
André Spire and His Poetry: Two Essays and Forty Translations.
    Philadelphia, Centaur Press, 1933.
The Seamless Web: Language-Thinking, Creature-Knowledge,
    Art-Experience.   New York, Braziller, and London, Allen
    Lane, 1970.

Editor, *Two New Yorkers* (Kruse lithographs and Kreymborg
    poems).   New York, Bruce Humphries, 1938.
Editor, with others, *The Poem Itself: 45 Modern Poets in a New*
    Presentation.   New York, Holt Rinehart, 1960; London,
    Penguin, 1964.
Editor, *Varieties of Literary Experience: Eighteen Essays in*
    World Literature.   New York, New York University Press,
    1962; London, Owen, 1963.
Editor, with T. Carmi and Ezra Spicehandler, *The Modern*
    Hebrew Poem Itself, From the Beginnings to the Present:
    Sixty-Nine Poems in a New Presentation.   New York, Holt
    Rinehart, 1965.

*

Critical Studies: "The Great Dark Love" by André Spire, in
Mercure de France (Paris), 1 December 1933; "The Poem Itself"
by Lionel Trilling, in *The Mid-Century* (New York), August
1960; "On Translating Poetry" by Herbert Read, in *Poetry* (Chicago), April 1961; "The Poet Is Always Present" by Germaine
Brée, in *The American Scholar* (Washington, D.C.), Summer
1970; "In the Terrified Radiance" by James Dickey, in *New York
Times Book Review,* 24 September 1972; "Stanley Burnshaw
Issue" of *Agenda* (London), Winter-Spring 1983-84.

Stanley Burnshaw comments:
   Poetry is the expression of the creator's total organism—or, as
I say at the beginning of *The Seamless Web*:

   Poetry begins with the body and ends with the body. Even
   Mallarmé's symbols of abstract essence lead back to the
   bones, flesh, and nerves. My approach, then is "physiological," yet it issues from a vantage point different from
   Vico's when he said that all words originated in the eyes,
   the arms, and the other organs from which they were

grown into analogies. My concern is rather with the type
of creature-mind developed by the evolutionary shock
which gave birth to what we have named self-consciousness. So far as we know, such biological change failed to
arise in any other living creature. So far as we can tell, no
other species, dead or alive, produced or produces the
language-think of poetry. We are engaged, then, with a
unique phenomenon issuing from a unique physiology
which seems to function no differently from that of other
animals—in a life-sustaining activity based on continuous
interchange between organism and environment.

Poetry begins with the body and ends with the body—*The Seamless Web* pursues and confronts the implications of this statement from three different vantage points: 1) Language-Thinking,
2) Creature-Knowledge, 3) Art-Experience. The Third (Art-
Experience) offers the clearest introduction to my poetry, especially for the reader who has at hand a copy of my *Caged in an
Animal's Mind*; there are numerous references to the pages in
that volume of my poems.

*   *   *

   Writing of man's struggle through science and technology to
master Nature, and the culmination of that struggle in the discovery and use of atomic power, Stanley Burnshaw says: "The
war against Nature had been confidently waged and won; and we
post-moderns, of 1945-and-after, breathe the spirit of a different
epoch, and we have a different terror on our minds: Now that
man is victorious, how shall he stay alive?"
   This question is a recurring one in his poems, as death, love,
and life wage unceasing war, observed by a coal-hard intellect
striving relentlessly to illuminate the world, "this eden," through
a sense of its kinship with the world of nature. In his sixty-year-
long poetry-writing career, Burnshaw has remained contemporary, and in his view of the urgency of confronting man's imminent self-annihilation through the destruction of nature he is in
agreement with many poets younger than himself. His latest
collection, *In the Terrified Radiance*, gives us those parts of his
earlier work he wants us to remember, and his *oeuvre* is made to
seem remarkably of a piece. From the beginning, he has filled his
lyrics with stones, flames, wind, trees, singing, and blood—an
imagery suggestive at times of Robinson Jeffers and at others of
Theodore Roethke; in all of them, however, Burnshaw is distinctively (if somewhat monotonously and humorlessly) himself.
   In his dense, hard-surfaced poems one encounters a harsh,
relentless, and totally committed intelligence confronting with
mind and senses the inexorable facts of death and life. The effect
is a seamless web (to borrow the title of his book about the
physiological origins of the creative act) of images of storm, fire,
growth, destruction, and the nourishment of creativity by the
forces that destroy. These are not simply poems about the "good
that comes from evil" or of the cyclical quality of nature; there is
something much more elemental in their feeling of primordial
unity. Burnshaw, in a paradox of cerebral style and physiological
message—what he refers to as creature-knowledge—seems a
solemn shaman preserving his intellectual detachment whilst in
an ecstasy of sympathy with the tides of being.

—Donald Barlow Stauffer

BUTLER, (Frederick) Guy. South African. Born in Cradock, Cape Province, 21 January 1918. Educated at local high school; Rhodes University, Grahamstown, M.A. 1939; Brasenose College, Oxford, M.A. 1947. Served in the South African Army in the Middle East, Italy, and the United Kingdom, 1940-45. Married Jean Murray Satchwell in 1942; three sons and one daughter. Lecturer in English, University of Witwatersrand, Johannesburg, 1948-50. Since 1952, Professor of English, Rhodes University. D.Litt.: University of Natal, Durban, 1970; University of Witwatersrand, 1984. Recipient: CNA Award, 1976. Address: Department of English, Rhodes University, Grahamstown 6140, South Africa.

PUBLICATIONS

Verse

Stranger to Europe: Poems 1939-1949. Cape Town, Balkema, 1952; augmented edition, 1960.
South of the Zambezi: Poems from South Africa. London, Abelard Schuman, 1966.
On First Seeing Florence. Grahamstown, South Africa, New Coin-Rhodes University, 1968.
Selected Poems. Johannesburg, Donker, 1975.
Songs and Ballads. Cape Town, David Philip, 1978.

Plays

The Dam (produced Cape Town, 1953). Cape Town, Balkema, 1953.
The Dove Returns (produced Cape Town, 1956). Cape Town, Balkema, and London, Fortune Press, 1956.
Take Root or Die (produced Grahamstown, 1966). Cape Town, Balkema, 1970.
Cape Charade (produced Cape Town, 1968). Cape Town, Balkema, 1968.
Richard Gush of Salem. Cape Town, Maskew Miller, 1982.

Other

An Aspect of Tragedy. Grahamstown, Rhodes University, 1953.
The Republic of the Arts. Johannesburg, Witwatersrand University Press, 1964.
Karoo Morning: An Autobiography 1918-35. Cape Town, David Philip, 1977; Totowa, New Jersey, Rowman and Littlefield, 1978.
Bursting World: An Autobiography 1936-45. Cape Town, David Philip, 1983.

Editor, *A Book of South African Verse.* London, Oxford University Press, 1959.
Editor, *When Boys Were Men.* Cape Town, Oxford University Press, 1969.
Editor, with Tim Peacock, *Plays from Near and Far: Twelve One-Act Plays.* Cape Town, Maskew Miller, 1973 (?).
Editor, *The 1820 Settlers: An Illustrated Commentary.* Cape Town, Human and Rousseau, 1974.
Editor, with Christopher Mann, *A New Book of South African Verse in English.* Cape Town, Oxford University Press, 1979; Oxford, Oxford University Press, 1980.

*

Bibliography: in *Olive Schreiner and After: Essays on South*

African Literature in Honour of Guy Butler edited by Malvern van Wyk Smith and Don Maclennan, Cape Town, David Philip, 1983.

Manuscript Collection: Thomas Pringle Collection for English in Africa, Rhodes University, Grahamstown.

Guy Butler comments:
Much of my poetry—but by no means all—is generated by the European-African encounter as experienced by someone of European descent, who feels himself to belong to Africa. I am, I think, a product of the old, almost forgotten Eastern Cape Frontier tradition, with its strong liberal and missionary admixture. The nature of the frontier has changed and spread, until all articulate men, but particularly artists, are frontiersmen and/or interpreters. English, as the chosen language of literature of millions of Blacks, has a great and exciting future in Africa; and I've made it my life's business to encourage its creative use in this corner of the world.

*   *   *

Guy Butler's work is a sustained endeavour to distinguish and reconcile the two strains of Europe and Africa—chiefly, but not merely, the southern part of the continent; to record and interpret the local scene; to find appropriate media—vocabulary, imagery, forms—through which to discover and express something of the African essence and primitive consciousness; to establish an African mythology and archetypes (Livingstone, Camoens, the last Trekker); to acclimatize as far as possible "the Grecian and Mediaeval dream." Orpheus has an "African incarnation" ("Myths"), Apollo must come to "cross the tangled scrub, the uncouth ways" ("Home Thoughts") and join the Dionysian dance.

Africa almost becomes an image for a state of mind in which the poet's imagination tries to find dwelling and the human being strives to come to terms with himself, a testing ground for his beliefs and values. The inescapable preoccupation of the modern artist, to find his place in his world, is, for the English poet in Africa, sensitive to European history, art and thought, perhaps more dramatically evident than for his British counterpart. The struggle to articulate, clarify, harmonize and balance contending forces, and be true to experience, informs Butler's poetry with tension and some anguish, and lifts it above trivialities. Circumstances tempt the South African writer to exploit rather than explore his material, to be self-conscious or self-pitying, to address too limited a home audience, to slide into fashionable political or literary cant. Butler rarely succumbs.

T.S. Eliot observes of the genuine poet that "his strict duty is to his *language*, first to preserve, and second to extend and improve." Butler's responsible and experimental use of language is grounded in such an awareness of literary tradition. This leads him to genres other than the ubiquitous meditative lyric—ballad, song, sonnet, elegy, narrative, metaphysical debate, in a variety of measures; and particularly the long poem where he shows a not inconsiderable architectonic skill. Besides verse drama, there is the seemingly casual free verse anecdote ("Sweet-Water") and the formal symphonic poem in fairly elaborate stanzas ("Bronze Heads"). With an understanding of neoclassic decorum, he uses a range of styles, language prismatic or transparent, speaking voice or singing robes. Sometimes regarded as an old-fashioned versifier playing safe, he is in fact often taking risks, with rhyme, intricate verse and image patterns, colloquialisms, cliché, plain statement or rhetorically splendid utterance. The long poem "On First Seeing Florence" is a complex structure of varied styles, rhythms and images which eloquently presents a moment of vision.

Because of this readiness to undertake the hazardous and difficult, this range, breadth, and technical skill, and because he has something to say, Butler is possibly the most considerable poet now writing in South Africa. Others may reach greater heights in individual poems; few can present a body of work which has such a wholeness, complexity, variety and approachableness. Nor is his appeal merely local, though certain poems will have a particular poignancy for his countrymen. A lyric like "Stranger to Europe," a meditation like "Myths," will be read wherever poetry is recognized.

—Ruth Harnett

———————

CAMPBELL, Alistair (Te Ariki). New Zealander. Born in Rarotonga, Cook Islands, 25 June 1925; emigrated to New Zealand in 1933. Educated at Anderson's Bay School, 1933-39; Otago Boys' High School, Dunedin, 1940-43; University of Otago, 1944; Victoria University, Wellington, 1945-47, 1951-52, B.A. in Latin and English; Wellington Teachers College, degree. Married 1) Fleur Adcock, *q.v.*, in 1952 (divorced 1957), two sons; 2) Meg Andersen in 1958, one son and two daughters. Staff member, Health Department Records Office, Wellington, 1944; gardener, Mowai Red Cross Hospital, Wellington, 1948-49; Editor, Department of Education School Publications Branch, Wellington, 1955-72. Since 1972, Senior Editor, New Zealand Council for Educational Research, Wellington. President, P.E.N. New Zealand Centre, 1976-79. Recipient: La Spezia Film Festival Gold Medal, 1974; New Zealand Book Award, 1982. Address: 4 Rawhiti Road, Pukerua Bay, Wellington, New Zealand.

PUBLICATIONS

Verse

Mine Eyes Dazzle: Poems 1947-49. Christchurch, Pegasus Press, 1950; revised edition, 1951, 1956.
Wild Honey. London, Oxford University Press, 1964.
Blue Rain. Wellington, Wai-te-ata Press, 1967.
Drinking Horn. Paremata, Bottle Press, 1970.
Walk the Black Path. Paremata, Bottle Press, 1971.
Kapiti: Selected Poems 1947-71. Christchurch, Pegasus Press, 1972.
Dreams, Yellow Lions. Waiura, Alister Taylor, 1975.
The Dark Lord of Savaiki. Pukerua Bay, Te Kotare Press, 1980.
Collected Poems. Martinborough, Alister Taylor, 1982.

Recording: *The Return and Elegy*, Kiwi.

Plays

Sanctuary of Spirits (broadcast, 1963). Wellington, Victoria University-Wai-te-ata Press, 1963.
The Suicide (broadcast, 1965). Published in *Landfall 112* (Christchurch), 1974.
When the Bough Breaks (produced Wellington, 1970). Published in *Contemporary New Zealand Plays*, edited by Howard McNaughton, Wellington, Oxford University Press, 1974.

Radio Plays: *Sanctuary of Spirits*, 1963; *The Homecoming*, 1964; *The Proprietor*, 1964; *The Suicide*, 1965; *Death of the Colonel*, 1966; *The Wairau Incident*, 1967.

Television Documentaries: *Island of Spirits*, 1973; *Like You I'm Trapped*, 1975.

Other

The Fruit Farm (for children). Wellington, School Publications Branch, 1953.
The Happy Summer (for children). Christchurch, Whitcombe and Tombs, 1961.
New Zealand: A Book for Children. Wellington, School Publications Branch, 1967.
Maori Legends. Wellington, Seven Seas, 1969.
Island to Island (memoirs). Christchurch, Whitcoulls, 1984.

*

Manuscript Collection: University of Canterbury, Christchurch.

Critical Studies: by James Bertram, in *Comment* (Wellington), January-February 1965; "Alistair Campbell's *Mine Eyes Dazzle:* An Anatomy of Success" by David Gunby, in *Landfall* (Christchurch), March 1969; "Alistair Campbell's *Sanctuary of Spirits:* The Historical and Cultural Context" by F.M. McKay, in *Landfall* (Christchurch), June 1978; *Introducing Alistair Campbell* by Peter Smart, Auckland, Longman Paul, 1982.

Alistair Campbell comments:

Primarily a lyric poet. My early verse, written in a variety of mainly regular verse forms, shows the influence of such poets as Tennyson, Yeats, Pound, and Edward Thomas. More recently, Latin-American and Spanish poets, among others, have shown me how to write with a new freedom and spontaneity, while Maori history has provided me with new themes.

*   *   *

Alistair Campbell was born in Rarotonga of Scottish sailor father and a Polynesian mother of chiefly rank. The early deaths of both parents led to his upbringing as orphan and exile in New Zealand. Such radical uprooting, joined with the failure of his first marriage to Fleur Adcock (subsequently a talented poet in her own right), as well as major problems of mental health for both partners of his subsequent marriage, have left conspicuous traces through his poetry. These have been movingly presented, as to his parentage in four "Personal Sonnets" and, in respect of marriage, notably in his play *When the Bough Breaks* (based on his earlier *The Homecoming*) and in a number of poems of which some are incorporated in that play (e.g., "Why Don't You Talk to Me?"). Campbell's other radio drama deals with schizophrenia (*The Suicide*), marital breakdown based on Greek myth in absurdist style (*The Proprietor*) and Maori-European clash (*The Wairau Incident*). His hillside coastal home presents a commanding view of the island of Kapiti, now a bird sanctuary, once the island citadel of Maori warrior chief ("the Maori Napoleon") Te Rauparaha. Both island and chief are potent entities in several poems, notably the sequence *Sanctuary of Spirits* with its terrifying ending:

The wind rises,
        lifts the lid off my brain—

Madman, leave me alone!

This biographical clearing of the ground seems necessary preparation for entry into a world musical, often hedonist, of brief and
personal, often haunted, lyrics of love, of nature and, increasingly in recent years, of traditional Maori culture.

Campbell's first volume—brief, rich, formal, ultra-Romantic,
or late Victorian lyrics—was somewhat of a *succès d'estime*. It
was notable for "Elegy" (on a friend killed climbing)—a highly
animistic lyric sequence—and his mysterious and atavistic "The
Return" that presents below "the long pouring headland" and
"on the surf-loud beach" both "men...moving between the fires"
and "Their heads finely shrunken to a skull, small/ And delicate,
with small black rounded beaks/...rain-jewelled, leaf green/ Bodies...Plant gods, tree gods,"together with "Face downward/
And in a small creek mouth all unperceived;/ The drowned Dio-
nysus...." Crisis and transition characterize *Sanctuary of Spirits*.
Commissioned for radio, this book (like the related television
documentary a decade later) is "more a series of images than a
documentary" and culminates in "Against Te Rauparaha" which
Campbell himself calls "an exorcism." Frank McKay, however,
doubts its efficacy and, more positively, suggests "that subcon-
sciously at least desire to belong to a tribe lies behind these
poems." Certainly from here on the Georgian formalism of
Campbell's earlier work, though never abandoned, is definitively
transcended and his approximation to Maori and Polynesian
oratory may be thought to have both psychologically freed his
style and enabled him more fully to use both Polynesian content
and, presumably, attitudes. Examples include "Reflections on
Some Great Chiefs," "Waiting for the Pakeha," and most
recently the plangent "Friend":

        This is the dearest of my wishes,
        The last leaf shaken from the tree—
        Sow the South Wind with my ashes
        To fall in tears on Kapiti.

In general the more brooding personal lyrics of the 1960's seem
left behind in recent poetry that, along with the nihilism of, say,
"Walk the Black Path," embraces also the (very Maori) fantasy
cowboy myth in "The Gunfighter," surrealist abreaction of "The
Manner Is to Be Deplored," humane rebuke of "Memo to Mr.
Auden"—"Mr. Auden...You are the delicate/Expensive ship
that sees something amazing, perhaps/ Even tragic—a boy falling out of the sky,/ But you have a poem to finish and sail calmly
on"—and his unfailing gift for nature lyric in "Flowering Apple,"
and sensitively mature personal reaction in "The Australian
Girl." His neighbour, the younger poet Sam Hunt, has spoken
usefully of Campbell's gifts for natural imagery, for "the whimsical and earthy," and adds: "something which is rarely mentioned
in such discussion—and, along with some other critics, we
believe it to be the key to Campbell's best work—is the *duende* of
the poems.... The Spanish poet Lorca described that power as
being 'the spirit of the earth.' " Campbell's total poetic output is
slender; his uncomplex prosody, early and late, runs largely to
short lines and quatrains; *Sanctuary of Spirits*, happy coincidence
of radio needs and oral inheritance, has "freed" much of his later
work; "the earthy" in his work never for long precludes the
somewhat dandiacal aesthete. A recent substantial sequence,
The Dark Lord of Savaiki, is set in Tongareva (Penrhyn, Cook

Islands) and records ancestral echoes resulting from a voyage
there.

—Peter Alcock

CAMPBELL, Donald. Scottish. Born in Wick, Caithness,
25 February 1940. Educated at Boroughmuir Senior Secondary School, Edinburgh. Married Jean Fairgrieve in 1966; one
son. Writer-in-Residence, Edinburgh Education Department,
1974-75. Recipient: Scottish Arts Council bursary, 1973. Agent:
Joanna Marston, Rosica Colin Ltd., 1 Clareville Grove Mews,
London SW7 5AH, England. Address: 85 Spottiswoode Street,
Edinburgh EH9 1BZ, Scotland.

PUBLICATIONS

Verse

Poems. Preston, Lancashire, Akros, 1971.
Rhymes 'n Reasons. Edinburgh, Reprographia, 1972.
Murals: Poems in Scots. Edinburgh, Lothlorien, 1975.
Blether: A Collection of Poems. Nottingham, Akros, 1979.

Plays

The Jesuit (produced Edinburgh, 1976). Edinburgh, Harris,
     1976.
Somerville the Soldier (produced Edinburgh, 1978). Edin-
     burgh, Harris, 1978.
The Widows of Clyth (produced Edinburgh, 1979). Edin-
     burgh, Harris, 1979.
Blackfriars Wynd (produced Edinburgh, 1980).
Till All the Seas Run Dry (produced Musselburgh, Midlothian,
     1981).
Sun Circle (produced Stirling, 1981).

Radio Plays: *The Last Viking*, 1981; *Servants*, 1983.

Television Play: *The Old Master*, 1984.

Other

A Brighter Sunshine (history of Royal Lyceum Theatre, Edin-
     burgh). Edinburgh, Polygon, 1983.

                                    *

Manuscript Collection: Scottish National Library, Edinburgh.

Critical Studies: "The Progress of Scots" by John Herdman, in
Akros (Preston, Lancashire), 1972; "The MacDiarmid Makars"
by Alexander Scott, in *Akros* (Preston, Lancashire), 1972; *Two
Younger Poets: Duncan Glen and Donald Campbell: A Study of
Their Scots Poetry* by Leonard Mason, Preston, Lancashire,
Akros, 1976.

Donald Campbell comments:
     The bulk of my work is written in Scots—that is to say, in the
language which is, to a greater or lesser extent, the language of
the greater part of the Scottish people. Now, this in itself proba-

bly requires a great deal of explanation—but, without going into a mass of detail, I will be as brief as possible. Most people who know little of Scots poetry appear to assume that Scots is a language (like English or Spanish) which died out years ago and that the work of the Modern Scots poets is no more than a sentimental attempt to revive or re-create it. This is not the case. Scots has never been subject to formal documentation like most other modern languages and survives for two reasons (a) its proximity to English (most English speakers can, with little difficulty, learn to read and understand Scots) and (b) because it has been sustained for over seven centuries by its own distinctive literary tradition. It is within this tradition that I appear to work. The advantages for a poet who is working in Scots (and who can work in Scots) are that he is not restricted by so many "rules of langauge" and that, although there is a great deal of poetry in our tradition, there are vast uncharted areas of poetic possibility that have never been explored. For instance, although we have had many poets who have written what you might call poems of "direct statement," not much work has been done with the use of images in Scots. We have had many great formal craftsmen (Dunbar, Henrysoun, Fergusson, etc.) but very few who can handle free verse.

My work as a poet does not start and end with Scots however. That is only the tool. I have no concise aims (poets should never have aims) but what I am against *as a man* is the erection of barriers among men. This may seem paradoxical unless you realise that Standard English is a great barrier in Scotland. The inability to speak "correct" English often prevents our people from realising their full potential—and I am naturally against that not simply because they are Scottish but because they are human beings. I want to help exorcise the shame of having for your most natural speech a language which is not only recognised as an official language but is, as often as not, not recognised as a language at all. I think all this shows in my poems.

My influences have been mostly foreign—the main ones being the Russian Mayakovsky, the Frenchman Jacques Prévert, and the English poet Gerard Manley Hopkins. Scots poets who have influenced me have been Hugh MacDiarmid, Sydney Goodsir Smith, Robert Garioch, and, most important of all both the Alexander Scotts—the medieval love poet from Dalkeith and the modern poet an dramatist from Aberdeen. I am also a great admirer of the artistry and language of Norman MacCaig.

*   *   *

In Donald Campbell's first pamphlet, *Poems*, all the verse was in Scots, and its energy and contemporary concern suggested better work to come when those qualities were combined with greater self-criticism and technical care. This combination has been achieved in a majority of the poems in *Rhymes 'n Reasons*. The characteristic Scottish expression of tenderness through the medium of a darkly-ironical apparent callousness is a difficult mode to master, but Campbell brings it off with fine panache in "Vietnam on My Mind," while in another political—or anti-political—poem, "Bangla Desh," he accomplishes the even trickier feat of expressing sympathy through its seeming denial. This command of ambiguity finds a subject in itself in "Ye Say 'Glass,' "and enables a love-poem. "You're the Warst,' to end a series of amusing paradoxes by becoming a savage hate-poem too. Yet Campbell is also capable of restraint, and the quietness of "At a Party" is fairly appropriate to its desolate theme of two lovers failing to meet. His few poems in English, sharing the human sympathy expressed in such Scots work as "Keelie" and "Communion at Dunkirk," have a nice delicacy of under-emphasis.

Although *Murals* contains only 14 poems, these still range widely in content, mood and style. An ironical beast-fable, "Jist Shows Ye!," on the theme of the early bird and the worm, combines comedy and pathos in its quaint reversal of the customary moral; a satirical dramatic monologue, "Hauf-roads up Schiehallion," demonstrates an impeccable ear for the nuances of contemporary Scots speech as well as insight into the tragicomic complexities of adolescent passion; "Betrayal in Morninside" makes effective—and unusual—use of the reductive idiom in order to reduce the stature of the writer himself; and "In the Tenement of My Mind" dares to employ the actualities of tenement existence in singing a lament for "the long littleness of life." Other verses display a kind of brash rhetoric lacking the sensitivity to evoke a poetic response, but when Campbell eschews exclamation and allows his subjects to speak for themselves he achieves a striking interplay between the imaginative and the real.

—Alexander Scott

———————

CAMPBELL, George. Jamaican. Born in Panama, 26 December 1916. Educated at St. George's College, Kingston, Jamaica; New School for Social Research, New York. Married Odilia Crane in 1948; four daughters. Journalist, *Jamaica Daily Gleaner*, Kingston, and an editor in the Jamaican welfare department; secretary with the little theatre movement, Jamaica; Program Director. Jewish centers, New York, for 30 years. Currently, Publications Consultant, Institute of Jamaica, Kingston. Address: Institute of Jamaica, 12-16 East Street, Kingston, Jamaica.

PUBLICATIONS

Verse

First Poems. Privately printed, 1945; revised edition, New York, Garland, 1981.

Play

A Play Without Scenery (produced Kingston, 1947). Published in *Focus* magazine (Kingston).

*

George Campbell comments:

Much of my early poetry is identified by critics with the struggle for Jamaican independence, a struggle that lasted from the late 1930's until separation from British colonial rule in 1962. The publication of *First Poems* was considered something of a "landmark"; it was recognised as a break away from Victorian poetry and as a valid usage of free verse. It influenced Jamaican and other Caribbean poets (one of the poems, "Litany," was used as a symbol for the first "Carifesta," held in Guyana in 1972). The themes of my poems vary: as Louis Simpson wrote in *Air with Armed Men*, they deal with the beauty of people, protest, and love. The more recent poetry is philosophical, and about nature and love.

*   *   *

George Campbell is one of the most important figures in the transition from colonial apprenticeship to a sense of the autochthonous and its expression. His work dominated Edna Manley's *Focus*, one of the four locally based West Indian journals which provided a forum for the emerging Caribbean writers of the 1930's and early 1940's (the others were the *Beacon* in Trinidad, *Bim* in Barbados and *Kyk-over-al* in Guyana).

As with most West Indian poets, especially those of the transitional period (1900-50), nature appears as the first inspiration for Campbell's poetry, with, as with M.G. Smith, E.M. Roach, and H.M. Telemaque, a strong sense of the pantheistic about it (see "Litany," "Essential," "Infinity," "Hymm to Being," among others). Love, a certain social optimism, and a feeling for the League of Nations of all peoples, leading to a kind of Christian Socialism—even his patriotism within a multi-racial plural society—all stem from this vision of original nature. The pity is that Campbell (again, like most poets of this period) hardly ever found the sustained language to move the body of his poetry out of the post-Victorian into the modern Caribbean. Although there is a certain arresting Imagism, it is strongly coloured, as with McKay's Jamaican poems, with romanticism: "These people with their scarlet heads/ Bear baskets of their golden fruit/ Down blue streets/ Into market beds/ Of leaf green heaps/ And crimson blaze,/ They stoop before their golden fruit," At his best, Campbell transcended these limitations through developing a sense of form (in "Litany," "Last Queries," and "History Makers") where word/sound combine with social criticism and vision to create:

> Women stone breakers
> Hammers and rocks
> Tired child makers
> Haphazard frocks.
>
> Strong thigh
> Rigid head
> Bent nigh
> Hard white piles
> Of stone
> Under hot sky
> In the gully bed.
>
> No smiles
> No sigh
> No moan.
>
> Women child bearers
> Pregnant frocks
> Wilful toil sharers
> Destiny shapers
> History makers
> Hammers and rocks.

But even this is not his finest achievement. Campbell may have started as an Imagist, and developed, given his place and time, an acute and important social criticism; but more than any other poet of the 1930's he was also involved in the struggle for and articulation of political autonomy for the Caribbean. The popular uprisings throughout the archipelago led to the formation of militant nationalist parties and the promise, wrenched from the Mother Country, of self-rule and eventual Independence. It was at this juncture that Campbell's talents responded most securely to the movement of his time, calling out of himself an enduring eloquence he had not known before ("On This Night"):

> On this momentous night O God help us.
> With faith we now challenge our destiny.
> Tonight masses of men will shape, will hope,
> Will dream, with us; so many years hang on

> Acceptance. Who is that knocking against
> The door? Isle of Jamaica is it you
> Looking for destiny, or is it
> Noise of the storm?...
> Wind where cometh the fine technique
> Of rule passing through me? My hands wet with
> The soil and I knowing my world.

—Edward Kamau Brathwaite

CARROLL, Paul (Donnelly Michael). American. Born in Chicago, Illinois, 15 July 1927. Educated at the University of Chicago, M.A. in English 1952. Served in the United States Naval Reserve, 1945-46. Married 1) Inara Birnbaum in 1964 (divorced, 1973), one son; 2) Maryrose Finnegan Groth in 1977. Poetry Editor, *Chicago Review*, 1957-59; Editor, *Big Table Magazine*, Chicago, 1959-61; Editor, Big Table Books, Follett Publishing Company, Chicago, 1966-71. Visiting Professor of Poetry, University of Iowa, Iowa City, 1966-67. Since 1968, Professor of English and Chairman of the Program for Writers, University of Illinois, Chicago. Poet-in-Residence, Branford College, Yale University, New Haven, Connecticut, Spring 1969. Founding President, The Poetry Center, Chicago, 1973-74; Host, *The Name and Nature of Poetry* program, WFMT radio, Chicago, 1972-82. Address: 1682 North Ada Street, Chicago, Illinois 60622, U.S.A.

Publications

Verse

Odes. Chicago, Follett, 1968.
The Luke Poems. Chicago, Follett, 1971.
New and Selected Poems. Chicago, Yellow Press, 1979.

Other

The Poem in Its Skin. Chicago, Follett, 1968.

Editor, *The Edward Dahlberg Reader.* New York, New Directions, 1967.
Editor, *The Young American Poets.* Chicago, Follett, 1968.
Editor, *The Earthquake on Ada Street.* Lake Bluff, Illinois, Jupiter Press, 1979.

*

Paul Carroll comments:
I can't imagine life without poetry.

*   *   *

Paul Carroll's esthetic understanding abruptly flowered in three volumes of 1968-69. *The Poem in Its Skin* analyzed ten poems by, to Carroll's eyes, the ten leading American poets. *The Young American Poets*, an anthology of 54 poets, encouraged and further directed young poets. *Odes*, Carroll's own selected poems, promulgates in verse the same sensibility and fashions as the essays and anthology.

In the essay on James Wright in *The Poem in Its Skin*, Carroll characterizes Wright's poem as a hip or "impure" homage to Po

Chu-i. Similar homage is a motive in Carroll's own odes, though Carroll offers homage not to past poets like Trakl or Po Chu-i but to leading contemporaries like Dickey, Ginsberg, Logan, Wright, and, especially, Neruda. *Odes* owes its title and certain techniques to Neruda's *Odas Elementales*; Carroll acknowledges this explicitly by offering an "Ode to Neruda." "Ode on My 40th Birthday," the opening poem, rewords the theme of Dickey's "Heaven of Animals," a poem Carroll analyzed in *The Poem in Its Skin*. Dickey typically divides life between predator and prey, and reconciles them in a "ritual" hunt. Carroll, spiritually a Catholic, finds a Saint Francis who succumbs less to ritual than "role," becoming, briefly, the glint-toothed, priestly predator:

> Francis free finally to be
> the timber wolf he's feared in dreams
> because its teeth and fur are yours
> slaughters the lamb for the feast reciting
> the prayer at the top of his voice.

Some lines later Carroll dextrously invokes Dickey's antithesis, the Buddish Allen Ginsberg:

> Do you dance
> on your own body throughout eternity
> as your new lover Allen Ginsberg says?

Carroll's earliest poems depend, significantly, on the literally Catholic and allusive manner of Lowell's *Lord Weary's Castle*. An "Ode to Claes Oldenburg" alerts us that the "impure poem"— a poem, celebrated in Carroll's criticism, which is markedly contemporaneous—derives from Pop art. Carroll's musical odes appeal to the kindly, well-dressed mandarin-about-town.

—Michael André

CARRUTH, Hayden. American. Born in Waterbury, Connecticut, 3 August 1921. Educated at the University of North Carolina, Chapel Hill, B.A. 1943; University of Chicago, M.A. 1947. Served in the United States Army Air Corps during World War II. Married 1) Sara Anderson in 1943, one daughter; 2) Eleanore Ray in 1952; 3) Rose Marie Dorn in 1961, one son. Editor, *Poetry*, Chicago, 1949-50; Associate Editor, University of Chicago Press, 1950-51, and Intercultural Publications Inc., New York, 1952-53. Visiting Professor, Johnson State College, Vermont, 1972-74, University of Vermont, Burlington, 1975-78, and St. Michael's College, Winooski, Vermont. Since 1979, Professor of English, Syracuse University, New York. Poetry Editor, *Harper's*, New York, 1977-82. Since 1976, Member of the Editorial Board, *Hudson Review*, New York. Recipient: Bess Hopkin Prize, 1954; Vachel Lindsay Prize, 1956; Levinson Prize, Eunice Tietjens Memorial Prize, and Morton Dauwen Zabel Prize, 1968 (*Poetry*, Chicago); Harriet Monroe Award, 1960; Bollingen Fellowship, 1963; Carl Sandburg Prize, 1963; Emily Clark Balch Prize (*Virginia Quarterly Review*), 1964; Guggenheim Fellowship, 1965, 1979; National Endowment for the Arts grant, 1966, 1968, 1974, 1984; Shelley Memorial Award, 1979; Lenore Marshall Prize, 1979. Address: 158 Edgehill Road, Syracuse, New York 13224, U.S.A.

PUBLICATIONS

Verse

The Crow and the Heart, 1946-1959. New York, Macmillan, 1959.
In Memoriam: G.V.C. Privately printed, 1960.
Journey to a Known Place. New York, New Directions, 1961.
The Norfolk Poems, 1 June to 1 September 1961. Iowa City, Prairie Press, 1962.
North Winter. Iowa City, Prairie Press, 1964.
Nothing for Tigers: Poems 1959-64. New York, Macmillan, 1965.
Contra Mortem. Johnson, Vermont, Crow's Mark Press, 1967.
For You. New York, New Directions, 1970; London, Chatto and Windus, 1972.
The Clay Hill Anthology. Iowa City, Prairie Press, 1970.
From Snow and Rock, From Chaos: Poems 1965-1972. New York, New Directions, and London, Chatto and Windus, 1973.
Dark World. Santa Cruz, California, Kayak, 1974.
The Bloomingdale Papers. Athens, University of Georgia Press, 1974.
Loneliness: An Outburst of Hexasyllables. West Burke, Vermont, Janus Press, 1976.
Aura. West Burke, Vermont, Janus Press, 1977.
Brothers, I Loved You All. New York, Sheep Meadow Press, 1978.
Almanach du Printemps Vivarois. New York, Nadja, 1979.
The Sleeping Beauty. New York, Harper, 1982.
The Mythology of Dark and Light. Syracuse, New York. Tamarack, 1982.
If You Call This Cry a Song. Woodstock, Vermont, Countryman Press, 1983.

Novel

Appendix A. New York, Macmillan, 1963.

Other

After "The Stranger": Imaginary Dialogues with Camus. New York, Macmillan, 1965.
Working Papers: Selected Essays and Reviews, edited by Judith Weissman. Athens, University of Georgia Press, 1982.
Effluences from the Sacred Caves: More Selected Essays and Reviews. Ann Arbor, University of Michigan Press, 1983.

Editor, with James Laughlin, *A New Directions Reader.* New York, New Directions, 1964.
Editor, *The Voice That Is Great Within Us: American Poetry of the Twentieth Century.* New York, Bantam, 1970.
Editor, *The Bird/Poem Book: Poems on the Wild Birds of North America.* New York, McCall, 1970.

*

Manuscript Collection: Guy W. Bailey Library, University of Vermont, Burlington.

Critical Studies: "The Real and Only Sanity" by Geoffrey Gardner, in *American Poetry Review* (Philadelphia), January-February 1981; "The Odyssey of Hayden Carruth" by R.W. Flint, in *Parnassus* (New York), Summer 1984.

*   *   *

At this point in his poetic career we can begin to see the emerging shape of Hayden Carruth's work. At the center of his first book, *The Crow and the Heart*, is his important long poem "The Asylum" which establishes one of the central themes and concerns of his poetry: the interplay between (so-called) madness and sanity. Like most of his early work, "The Asylum" is tightly controlled verse dominated by iambic lines and rhymed couplets. He describes a long winter spent in a mental institution. Like Roethke, Carruth struggles through nightmare and chaos; "how hard the search here for the self at last!" He comes to the painful conclusion that, if nothing else is possible, "*Save thou thyself.*" The poem slowly enlarges to encompass America in her own illness ("This land once was asylum when we came..."). But madness and decay now grow throughout the land. Leaving the asylum, he rebuilds his life "on a windy knoll," held in check now by labor and the land. He discovers that in this "house of pain" called life, we each have "our particular hells" to endure. On this foundation of pain and understanding he rebuilds: "we lie all nailed and living, love's long gain." "The Asylum," even in its later, revised form, is not, I think, so good as Roethke's "The Lost Son," but it is comparable. Certainly Carruth's windswept Vermont farm country is as important to his restoration and vision as was the greenhouse to Roethke. This poem is also central to our engagement with his later work, for it establishes Carruth's crucial and complex interplay between chaos and order, between the nightmare of the asylum and the relative control that comes from farm labor and the cycle of the seasons.

Throughout his work Carruth has returned, again and again, to the form of the long poem, ususally containing many parts and often many voices. It is a form which serves him admirably, allowing sufficient room for the loose, imagistic form in which he excels. *For You* is his richest exploration of the long poem form. It opens with a revised and extended version of "The Asylum," containing the essential core of the earlier poem, but ending with the unsettling, but perhaps more honest lines, "here am I, drowned, living, loving, and insane." "North Winter" is the central poem of this volume; its unleashed, icy blasts seem to chill all that surround it. "North" and "winter" are many things to Carruth, but above all they are states of mind. "North is a horror from which a horror grows...." Later we find that, in addition to horror, "north is the aurora north is/ deliverance emancipation.../ north is...nothing...." With *For You* Carruth's poetry begins to extend strongly beyond the self and the region, speaking to issues both national and human. As Adrienne Rich expressed it, "his poetry is radical in its need for roots, and its hatred of the rootless shifting opportunism and greed and dishonor which are wasting our country..."

From Snow and Rock, From Chaos is a collection of Carruth's shorter poems. We learn a landscape of Vermont place-names and farm labors, and meet more than one "tough minded Yankee." Carruth manages, despite the omipresence of Robert Frost, to make the familiar topics of farming fresh with life, and with a voice quite his own. His poems here are like fragments wrested, torn from tree, rock, and earth, and forced into poems—like a leaf torn in two, "one leaf/ torn to give you half/ showing...love's complexity in an act...." In many of these poems we witness pain being endured through suffering and waiting, until the release that brings wider vision and moments of intense love.

Brothers, I Loved You All contains some of Carruth's finest work yet. He captures here, as in many earlier poems, sharply etched images of momentary events. Some of these, notably the long poems, "Vermont," and several that follow it, are very Frostian in theme. The volume ends with "Paragraphs," a 28-part poem in improvisational style, which honors Carruth's favorite musicians. But his subject is best expressed by the line, "RAVAGE, DEVASTATE, SACK." With shock and rage, he sees even the pastoral hills of Vermont ravaged and devastated by the greedy and shortsighted. He reproaches his nieghbors, by name, for selling their farms to make way for stores and trailer parks, and "for a hot pocketful of dollars." Through them he accuses all America: "your *best* is what you gave them/ o my friends—/your lives, your farms." With this poem a much more direct and forceful public voice emerges, one we need identify with Gary Snyder and most particularly with Wendell Berry, as poets crying forcefully againt the environmental destructiveness of our culture. Thus we see Hayden Carruth not only as a survivor of chaos, but also as a revolutionary poet who sees "all dark ahead and behind, his fate/a need without hope: *the will to resist.*"

—John R. Cooley

CARTER, Martin (Wylde). Guyanan. Born in Georgetown, British Guiana, now Guyana, in 1927. Educated at Queen's College, Georgetown. Worked as a clerk in the Civil Service for four years: forced to resign as a result of his political activities. Formerly, representative for Guyana at the United Nations.

PUBLICATIONS

Verse

The Hill of Fire Glows Red. Georgetown, Miniature Poets, 1951.
To a Dead Slave. Privately printed, 1951.
The Kind Eagle. Privately printed, 1952.
The Hidden Man. Privately printed, 1952.
Poems of Resistance from British Guiana. London, Lawrence and Wishart, 1954.
Poems of Succession. London, New Beacon, 1977.
Poems of Affinity 1978-1980. Georgetown, Release, 1980.

Other

Man and Making—Victim and Vehicle (lecture). Georgetown, National History and Art Council, 1971.
Creation: Works of Art. N.p., Carinna, 1977.

*   *   *

Apart from contributions in the now defunct Guyanese journal, *Kyk-over-al*, the main significant body of Martin Carter's work is to be found in *Poems of Resistance* (1954) and "Jail Me Quickly," five poems first published in 1964 by the *New World Fortnightly.*

Carter's specific concern is with politics, political revolution, and colonial oppression. *Poems of Resistance* was written when the poet was placed in detention for his political views in 1953. "Jail Me Quickly" is a direct response to the political crisis in Guyana in 1962, when the Guyanese Constitution, under Dr. Cheddi Jagan, was suspended by the British Government and British troops were moved in to uphold "law and order" in the country ("Black Friday 1962"):

were some who ran one way.
were some who ran another way.
were some who did not run at all.
were some who will not run again.
and I was with them all,
when the sun and streets exploded,
and a city of clerks
turned a city of men!

This is Carter's hope—that the individual man may become an aware and fully rounded person, despite the horrors and failures of his colonial past ("I Come from the Nigger Yard"):

I come from the nigger yard of yesterday
leaping from the oppressor's hate
and the scorn of myself;
from the agony of the dark hut in the shadow
and the hurt of things...

But Carter's poetry reveals little *substantial* awareness of the past. He asserts that he will "turn to the histories of men and the lives of the peoples"; but unlike his older contemporary, A.J. Seymour, he has produced no work of reconstruction. Because of this shallow soil of heritage, Carter, poet of the revolution, has really only himself and the revolution and a hope for the future to sustain his vision ("The Knife of Dawn"):

The sharp knife of dawn glitters in my hand
but how bare is everything—tall tall tree
infinite air, the unrelaxing tension of the world
and only hope, hope only, the kind eagle soars and
                                                wheels in flight.

What is more fully realized in his poetry is an apprehension of terror (here he reminds us of Yeats), of hopelessness and futility: "And I have seen some creatures rise from holes, / and claw a triumph like a citizen, / and reign until the tide!" ("Black Friday").
But this hopelessness and terror and futility are transformed through Martin Carter's energy of image and metaphor into a triumph of the writer's art; the elevation of a single mind against the world ("University of Hunger"):

The long streets of night move up and down
baring the thighs of a woman
and the cavern of generation.
The beating drum returns and dies away
the bearded men fall down and go to sleep
the cocks of dawn stand up and crow like bugles.

And again ("I Come from the Nigger Yard"):

O it was the heart like this tiny star near to the sorrows
straining against the whole world and the long twilight
spark of man's dream conquering the night
moving in darkness stubborn and fierce
till leaves of sunset change from green to blue
and shadows grow like giants everywhere.

—Edward Kamau Brathwaite

CAUSLEY, Charles (Stanley). British. Born in Launceston, Cornwall, 24 August 1917. Educated at Launceston National School; Horwell Grammar School; Launceston College; Peterborough Training College. Served in the Royal Navy, 1940-46. Taught in Cornwall, 1947-76. Honorary Visiting Fellow in Poetry, University of Exeter, 1973-74. Literary Editor of BBC radio magazines *Apollo in the West* and *Signature*, 1953-56. Member of the Arts Council Poetry (later Literature) Panel, 1962-66. Vice-President, West Country Writers Association; Vice-President, Poetry Society, London. Recipient: Society of Authors travelling scholarship, 1954, 1966; Queen's Gold Medal for Poetry, 1967; Cholmondeley Award, 1971. Fellow, Royal Society of Literature, 1958. D.Litt.: University of Exeter, 1977; M.A.: Open University, 1982. Agent: David Higham Associates Ltd., 5-8 Lower John Street, London W1R 4HA. Address: 2 Cyprus Well, Launceston, Cornwall PL15 8BT, England.

PUBLICATIONS

Verse

Farewell, Aggie Weston.   Aldington, Kent, Hand and Flower Press, 1951.
Survivor's Leave.   Aldington, Kent, Hand and Flower Press, 1953.
Union Street.   London, Hart Davis, 1957; Boston, Houghton Miffin, 1958.
The Ballad of Charlotte Dymond.   Privately printed, 1958.
Johnny Alleluia.   London, Hart Davis, 1961.
Penguin Modern Poets 3, with George Barker and Martin Bell. London, Penguin, 1962.
Ballad of the Bread Man.   London, Macmillan, 1968.
Underneath the Water.   London, Macmillan, 1968.
Pergamon Poets 10, with Laurie Lee, edited by Evan Owen. Oxford, Pergamon Press, 1970.
Timothy Winters, music by Wallace Southam.   London, Turret, 1970.
Six Women.   Richmond, Surrey, Keepsake Press, 1974.
Collected Poems 1951-1975.   London, Macmillan, and Boston, Godine, 1975.
St. Martha and the Dragon, music by Phyllis Tate.   London, Oxford University Press, 1978.
Hymn.   North Tawton, Devon, Morrigu Press, 1983.
Secret Destinations.   London, Macmillan, 1984.

Recordings: *Here Today 1*, Jupiter; *The Poet Speaks 8*, Argo; British Council tapes, 1960, 1966, 1968; *Causley Reads Causley*, Sentinel, 1975; *Pushing the Business On*, Plant Life, 1977.

Published Songs: *Shore Leave*, music by Michael Hurd; *Round the Town*, music by Michael Hurd; *Cowboy Song*, music by William Bowie; *The Sheep on Blackening Fields*, music by William Bowie; *Three Masts*, music by William Bowie; *Nursery Rhyme of Innocence and Experience*, music by Betty Rice; *Daystar in Winter*, music by Geoffrey Bush; *Mary, Mary Magdalene*, music by Phyllis Tate.

Verse (for children)

Figure of 8: Narrative Poems.   London, Macmillan, 1969.
Figgie Hobbin: Poems for Children.   London, Macmillan, 1970; New York, Walker, 1973.
The Tail of the Trinosaur.   Leicester, Brockhampton Press, 1973.

As I Went Down Zig Zag. London and New York, Warne,
1974.
Here We Go Round the Round House. Leicester, New Broom
Press, 1976.
The Hill of the Fairy Calf. London, Hodder and Stoughton,
1976.
The Animals' Carol. London, Macmillan, 1978.

Plays

Runaway. London, Curwen, 1936.
The Conquering Hero. London, Curwen, and New York,
Schirmer, 1937.
Benedict. London, Muller, 1938.
How Pleasant to Know Mrs. Lear. London, Muller, 1948.
The Gift of a Lamb (for children), music by Vera Gray. Lon-
don, Robson, 1978.
The Ballad of Aucassin and Nicolette, music by Stephen McNeff
(produced London, 1978). London, Kestrel, 1981.

Short Stories

Hands to Dance. London, Carroll and Nicholson, 1951; augmented edition, as *Hands to Dance, and Skylark,* London,
Robson, 1979.

Other (for children)

When Dad Felt Bad. London, Macmillan, 1975.
Dick Whittington. London, Penguin, 1976.
Three Heads Made of Gold. London, Robson, 1978.
The Last King of Cornwall. London, Hodder and Stoughton,
1978.

Editor, *Dawn and Dusk: Poems of Our Time.* Leicester,
Brockhampton Press, 1962; New York, Watts, 1963.
Editor, *Rising Early: Story Poems and Ballads of the 20th
Century.* Leicester, Brockhampton Press, 1964; as *Modern
Ballads and Story Poems,* New York, Watts, 1965.
Editor, *In the Music I Hear: Poems by Children.* Gillingham,
Kent, Arc, 1970.
Editor, *Oats and Beans and Barley: Poems by Children.* Gil-
lingham, Kent, Arc, 1971.
Editor, *The Puffin Book of Magic Verse.* London, Penguin,
1974.
Editor, *The Puffin Book of Salt-Sea Verse.* London, Kestrel,
1978.
Editor, The Batsford Book of Stories in Verse for Children.
London, Batsford, and New York, Hippocrene, 1979.
Editor, *The Sun, Dancing: Christian Verse.* London, Kestrel,
1982.

Translator, *Schondilie.* Leicester, New Broom Press, 1982.

Other

Editor, *Peninsula: An Anthology of Verse from the West-
Country.* London, Macdonald, 1957.
Editor, *An Octave,* by Siegfried Sassoon. London, Arts Coun-
cil, 1966.
Editor, *Modern Folk Ballads.* London, Studio Vista, 1966.
Editor, *Selected Poems,* by Frances Bellerby. London, Eni-
tharmon Press, 1971.

Translator, *Twenty-five Poems,* by Hamdija Demirović. Richmond, Surrey, Keepsake Press, 1980.

Manuscript Collections: State University of New York, Buffalo;
University of Exeter Library, Devon.

Critical Studies: *Poetry Today 1957-60* by Elizabeth Jennings,
London, Longman, 1961; "Of Tigers and Trees" by John Pett, in
The Guardian (London), 15 January 1965; *Poets of the 1939-
1945 War* by R.N. Currey, London, Longman, 1967; "Charles
Causley Talks to Peter Orr", on British Council Tape Recording
1390, 1968; "Haiku in the Park" by Norman Hidden, in *The
Times Educational Supplement* (London), 17 November 1972;
Poetry Today 1960-1973 by Anthony Thwaite, London, Long-
man, 1973; "The Poetry of Charles Causley" by Edward Levy, in
PN Review (London), v, 2, 1978; *An Introduction to Fifty Mod-
ern British Poets* by Michael Schmidt, London, Pan, 1979, as *A
Reader's Guide to Fifty Modern British Poets,* London, Heine-
mann, 1979, New York, Barnes and Noble, 1982; Dana Gioia, in
Poets of Great Britain and Ireland 1945-1960 edited by Vincent
B. Sherry, Jr., Detroit, Gale, 1984.

                    *   *   *

Charles Causley's poems are not the sort of work that would
readily attract the adjective "pioneer": most of them are, or seem
to be, utterly traditional. Yet Causley's handling of ballad and
lyrical forms, and his jaunty, vivid, humorous way with language, seem—in a way not often acknowledged—to lie behind
much of the "pop" poetry of the late 1960's: a poetry intended to
be spoken aloud, to be grasped immediately and cheerfully by a
mass audience.

Causley was writing such poems before many of his debtors
were born. *Farewell, Aggie Weston* and *Survivor's Leave* contain work which could easily fit into his later book, *Underneath
the Water*; and their simple ballad rhythms, their hyperbolic
images and their spry blending of old and new imagery could sit
comfortably in such a collection as *Love Love Love*—though
they are considerably better written and more intelligent:

> I saw a shot-down angel in the park
> His marble blood sluicing the dyke of death,
> A sailing tree firing its brown sea-mark
> Where he now wintered for his wounded breath.

These early poems also remind one sometimes of Roy Campbell, but they lack the often oppressive (and aggresive) personality of Campbell. In fact, a legitimate charge against much of
Causley's work up until *Underneath the Water* would be that it is
too blandly and automatically anonymous, a voice without a
man behind it: an attractive but rather irrelevant voice. There
was also a feeling that sombre and complex subjects were being
prettified and over-simplified, as in "Recruiting Drive":

> Down in the enemy country
>   Under the enemy tree
> There lies a lad whose heart has gone bad
>   Waiting for me, for me.

All these are justifiable objections, but they do not take in the
whole of Causley, by any means. From the beginning, he could
break away from lilting measures and gaudy diction when it
suited him, as in "Chief Petty Officer," which is an excellent
comic sketch in free verse, and—in a more traditional mode—he
could be weighty, as in "I Am the Great Sun." More impressively, *Underneath the Water* contains poems drawing more
closely from the personal and the circumstantial, with the old

lyrical sweetness but with new depths: for example, "Conducting a Children's Choir":

> I bait the snapping breath, curled claw, the deep
> And delicate tongue that lends no man its aid.
> The children their unsmiling kingdoms keep,
> And I walk with them, and I am afraid.

Causley's wartime experiences in the Navy, the mundane stuff of his childhood and present life as a teacher, are handled with a brisk attention to real detail. Yet the "folk" properties and the oral narrative characteristics are still there as plainly and successfully as ever, in "By St. Thomas Water," "Reservoir Street," "In Coventry," "Lord Sycamore" and "Ballad of the Bread Man." These poems are not artless: what Roy Campbell wrote of Causley several years ago is still true: "The poems have an apparent freshness and spontaneity about them which, with their fine finish, could never have been attained without the most careful work and subtle refinement." His work has an initial availability (often to children as well as to adults) which, unlike that of some more recent popular poets, bears rehearing and re-reading: the rhythms and images work their way into the memory, and earn their keep there.

—Anthony Thwaite

CHEYNEY-COKER, Syl. Sierra Leonean. Born in Freetown, 28 June 1945. Educated at the University of Oregon, Eugene, 1967-70; University of California, Los Angeles, 1970; University of Wisconsin, Madison, 1971-72. Worked as drummer and as factory and dock worker; journalist, Eugene *Register Guard*, Oregon, 1968-69, teaching assistant, University of Wisconsin, 1971; Head of Cultural Affairs, Radio Sierra Leone, 1972-73; free-lance writer, 1973-75; Visiting Professor of English, University of the Philippines, Quezon City, 1975-77. Lecturer, 1977-79, and since 1979 Senior Lecturer, University of Maiduguri, Nigeria. Recipient: Ford Foundation grant, 1970. Address: Department of English, University of Maiduguri, P.M.B. 1069, Maiduguri, Nigeria.

PUBLICATIONS

Verse

Concerto for an Exile. New York, Africana, 1972; London, Heinemann, 1973.
The Graveyard Also Has Teeth. London, New Beacon, 1974.

*

Syl Cheyney-Coker comments:
(1974) I hold the terrible distinction of being the only poet from my country who has published a sizeable volume of poems. I say terrible not in the pejorative sense but from a feeling of painful awareness that before my appearance, my country was a ghetto of silence.
A popular awareness of self and the creation of different modes of expression of our social and cultural needs seem to me to be the immediate task of the Sierra Leonean writer. We are a strange people; our history, language and culture are not to be confused with those of other English-speaking Africans.

The admixture of English philanthropy and African exotica that has produced and shaped the Sierra Leonean Creole is for me the makeup of any genuine Sierra Leonean Literature.
My "Afro-Saxon" heritage has meant a lot for me as I summarize my passion and I hope it will convey something of the strangeness of my people to the reader.

*   *   *

The question of ancestry is a central concern in the writing of many Third World poets. In the poems of Syl Cheyney-Coker, especially those collected in his book *Concerto for an Exile*, this concern becomes a fixation, his

> ...Creole ancestry
> which gave me my negralised head
> all my polluted streams

providing the impulse for poems which, in the extravagance and precise violence of their imagery, match some of the best writing of Vallejo and U'Tamsi, two poets whom Cheyney-Coker acknowledges as influences.
There are also definite echoes of the Negritude school and the poems of David Diop. The "Africa, my Africa" of Diop's poems has, however, been narrowed down to a specific nation, Sierra Leone, the land of freed slaves where a patois language, Creole and a Western influenced capital, Freetown, are ironic heritages of the colonial era:

> In my country the Creoles drink only
> Black and White with long sorrows
> hanging from their colonial faces...

Cheyney-Coker's poems are cries of bitter agony and bright illumination at one and the same time. They present the picture—as in "Agony of the Dark Child" or in "Misery of the Convert" with its lines:

> I was a king before they nailed you on the cross
> converted I read ten lies in your silly commandments
> to honour you my Christ
> when you have deprived me of my race...

—of a nation and a poet tortured by a culture and a religion imposed upon them, a nation and a poet who may find salvation through defiance.
Painful is a word which can be readily applied to much of Syl Cheyney-Coker's writing, just as another word—truthful—can also be applied to the same poems. He attempts, through a wrenching examination of personal and national histories, to create a new vision, a more honest world. In his poem "Guinea," written on the unsuccessful invasion of that nation by Portuguese mercenaries, he defines his role:

> I am not the renegade
> who has forsaken your shores
> I am not the vampire
> gnawing at your heart
> to feed capitalist banks
> I am your poet
> writing No to the world.

—Joseph Bruchac

CIARDI, John (Anthony). American. Born in Boston, Massachusetts, 24 June 1916. Educated at Bates College, Lewiston, Maine, 1934-36; Tufts College, Medford, Massachusetts, B.A. (magna cum laude) 1938 (Phi Beta Kappa); University of Michigan, Ann Arbor (Hopwood Award, 1939), A.M. 1939. Served in the United States Army Air Corps, 1942-45: Air Medal, Oak Leaf Cluster. Married Myra Judith Hostetter in 1946; one daughter and two sons. Instructor, University of Kansas City, Missouri, 1940-42, 1946; Briggs Copeland Instructor in English, 1946-48, and Assistant Professor, 1948-53, Harvard University, Cambridge, Massachusetts; Lecturer, 1953-54, Associate Professor, 1954-56, and Professor of English, 1956-61, Rutgers University, New Brunswick, New Jersey; Lecturer, 1947-73, and Director, 1956-72, Bread Loaf Writers Conference, Vermont. Editor, Twayne Publishers, New York, 1949; lecturer, Salzburg Seminar in American Studies, 1951; poetry editor, *Saturday Review*, New York, 1956-73, and contributing editor, 1973-80; host, *Accent* program, CBS-TV, 1961-62; contributing editor, *World Magazine*, New York, 1972-73. Director, 1955-57, and President, 1958-59, National College English Association. Recipient: Oscar Blumenthal Prize, 1943, Eunice Tietjens Memorial Prize, 1944, Levinson Prize, 1946, and Harriet Monroe Memorial Prize, 1955 (*Poetry*, Chicago); New England Poetry Club Golden Rose, 1948; American Academy in Rome Fellowship, 1956; Boys' Clubs of America award, 1962; National Council of Teachers of English award, 1982. D.Litt.: Tufts College, 1960; Ohio Wesleyan University, Delaware, 1971; Washington University, St. Louis, 1971; Hum.D.: Wayne University, Detroit, 1963; LL.D.: Ursinus College, Collegeville, Pennsylvania, 1964; D.L.H.: Kalamazoo College, Michigan, 1964; Bates College, 1970; Honorary Doctorate: Kean College, Union, New Jersey, 1977. Member, American Academy, and American Academy of Arts and Sciences. Address: 359 Middlesex Avenue, Metuchen, New Jersey 08840, U.S.A.

PUBLICATIONS

Verse

Homeward to America. New York, Holt, 1940.
Other Skies. Boston, Little Brown, 1947.
Live Another Day. New York, Twayne, 1949.
From Time to Time. New York, Twayne, 1951.
As If: Poems New and Selected. New Brunswick, New Jersey, Rutgers University Press, 1955.
I Marry You: A Sheaf of Love Poems. New Brunswick, New Jersey, Rutgers University Press, 1958.
39 Poems. New Brunswick, New Jersey, Rutgers University Press, 1959.
In the Stoneworks. New Brunswick, New Jersey, Rutgers University Press, 1961.
In Fact. New Brunswick, New Jersey, Rutgers University Press, 1962.
Person to Person. New Brunswick, New Jersey, Rutgers University Press, 1964.
This Strangest Everything. New Brunswick, New Jersey, Rutgers University Press, 1966.
An Alphabestiary: Twenty-Six Poems. Philadelphia, Lippincott, 1967.
A Genesis: 15 Poems. New York, Touchstone, 1967.
The Achievement of John Ciardi: A Comprehensive Selection of His Poems with a Critical Introduction, edited by Miller Williams. Chicago, Scott Foresman, 1969.
Lives of X. New Brunswick, New Jersey, Rutgers University Press, 1971.

The Little That Is All. New Brunswick, New Jersey, Rutgers University Press, 1974.
Limericks: Too Gross, with Isaac Asimov. New York, Norton, 1978.
For Instance. New York, Norton, 1979.
A Grossery of Limericks, with Isaac Asimov. New York, Norton, 1981.
Selected Poems Fayetteville, University of Arkansas Press, 1984.

Recordings: *As If,* Folkways; *John Ciardi,* Everett Edwards, 1972.

Verse (for children)

The Reason for the Pelican. Philadelphia, Lippincott, 1959.
Scrappy the Pup. Philadelphia, Lippincott, 1960.
I Met a Man. Boston, Houghton Mifflin, 1961.
The Man Who Sang the Sillies. Philadelphia, Lippincott, 1961.
You Read to Me, I'll Read to You. Philadelphia, Lippincott, 1962.
John J. Plenty and the Fiddler Dan: A New Fable of the Grasshopper and the Ant. Philadelphia, Lippincott, 1963.
You Know Who. Philadelphia, Lippincott, 1964.
The King Who Saved Himself from Being Saved. Philadelphia, Lippincott, 1965.
The Monster Den; or, Look What Happened at My House— and to It. Philadelphia, Lippincott, 1966.
Someone Could Win a Polar Bear. Philadelphia, Lippincott, 1970.
Fast and Slow: Poems for Advanced Children and Beginning Parents. Boston, Houghton Mifflin, 1975.

Other

The Wish-Tree (for children). New York, Crowell Collier, 1962.
Dialogue with an Audience. Philadelphia, Lippincott, 1963.
Dante Alighieri: Three Lectures, with J.C. Mathews and Francis Fergusson. Washington, D.C., Library of Congress, 1965.
On Poetry and the Poetic Process, with Joseph B. Roberts, Jr. Troy, Alabama, Troy State University Press, 1972.
Manner of Speaking (Saturday Review columns). New Brunswick, New Jersey, Rutgers University Press, 1972.
A Browser's Dictionary and Native's Guide to the Unknown American Language. New York, Harper, 1980; *A Second Browser's Dictionary,* 1983.
Plain English in a Complex Society, with Laurence Urdang and Frederick Dickerson. Bloomington, Indiana University Poynter Center, 1980.

Editor, *Mid-Century American Poets.* New York, Twayne, 1950.
Editor, *How Does a Poem Mean?* Boston, Houghton Mifflin, 1960; revised edition, with Miller Williams, 1975.
Editor, with James M. Reid and Laurence Perrine, *Poetry: A Closer Look.* New York, Harcourt Brace, 1963.

Translator, *The Divine Comedy,* by Dante. New York, Norton, 1977.
　　The Inferno. New Brunswick, New Jersey, Rutgers University Press, 1954.
　　The Purgatorio. New York, New American Library, 1961.
　　The Paradiso. New York, New American Library, 1970.

*

Bibliography: *John Ciardi: A Bibliography* by William White, Detroit, Wayne State University Press, 1959.

Manuscript Collections: Wayne State University, Detroit; Library of Congress, Washington, D.C.

Critical Study: *John Ciardi* by Edward Krickel, Boston, Twayne, 1980.

John Ciardi comments:

Poetry, for me, finds voices, but the aim should not be an idiosyncratic single voice immediately recognizable as the voice of a given man (style as signature). Something of that sort is bound to happen as a man learns to write into himself; there will be some of the lubdub of his own heart if the writing lives at all. I take that personalization to be essential and inevitable but secondary. The ideal accomplishment of a poem may be put as *homo fecit*. A man did it, and any man may say it of himself as one of the voices of his humanity, of his humanity quickened to itself.

*   *   *

Poet, teacher, acerbic commentator on contemporary life, John Ciardi has created one of the major careers in modern American poetry. His importance does not depend upon the significance of individual poems nor is it marred by the occasional redundancy of others. The frequent, short volumes of his poetry compose an unannounced but inevitably accumulating journal of a sensitive everyman who, in the tradition of Wordsworth and Whitman, but in a different age and in a highly individual voice, links the personal to the universal, the present imperfect to the ideal, and by "what light there is" seeks to discern from the fragments of closely observed experience some certitude in a larger design.

Ciardi's poetic method, with its continuing and controlling metaphors combining the personally important and timely with the generally significant and timeless, is evident in the opening lines of his early collection *Other Skies*: "Delicatessen and Carnival, the beach / Slopes under the continental shelf" ("Record Crowds at Beaches"). Here and throughout the poem a contemporary genre scene and its present participants ironically expand into the reaches of an evolutionary landscape and a distant, mythic reality. Subsequently, expanding settings and characters are usually more directly autobiographical. Recollections of growing up ("A Knothole in Spent Time"), his marriage ("Men Marry What They Need. I Marry You"), war service ("Death of a Bomber"), children ("Two Poems for Benn"), death of family and friends ("Aunt Mary," "Elegy, for Kurt Porjescz, Missing in Action, 1 April 1945"), all the commonplaces of everyday life, are constantly placed in larger contexts and examined by the comparison.

But these commonplaces of everyday life that are so persistently the points of departure for his poems' encompassing metaphors nevertheless represent, in the constant presence of the ideal they prefigure, imperfection. It is Ciardi's acceptance of this imperfection of present experience that gives to his work its most characteristic tension and that helps to define as well his concept of the poet. The disparities between the flawed and the sought-after perfection are presented somewhat abstractly in the figures of the Damaged Angel and the Improved Ape in "A Dialogue in

the Shade" and in the modern debate of Body and Soul in "Tenzone." But in his portraits of his father and his "friend and teacher, John Holmes" ("The Poet's Words") he offers both a more personal version and one that centers upon acceptance. He acknowledges "My father died imperfect as a man" and in the significantly titled latter poem concludes that "The best of a man / is what he thought of and could not be." And it is here that he suggests as well the complementary and paradoxical role of the imperfect poet. Although "Language ends in the tongue's clay pit," it is this same "Language" that must be "the wind / that brings all thought to mind."

If Ciardi's own poems move inevitably toward a larger coalescence, his concerns with the universal and the ideal move as well toward order and certitude, a tendency not emphasized but not unexpected in so distinguished a translator of Dante. The design his poems sketch out by allusion is not the orthodox one of Dante's time, however, but a less secure modern order based on his references to evolution, to myth, to the cosmic regularity of tides, seasons, day and night. A splendid example is provided in lines from one of his finest poems, "Poem for My Twenty-Ninth Birthday," in the eerie and lovely double image of death plane and sun rising:

We take our places while a switch is pressed,
And sun and engines rise from the hillside—
A single motion and a single fire
To burn, return, and live upon desire.

—Gaynor F. Bradish

CLAMPITT, Amy. American. Born in New Providence, Iowa, 15 June 1920. Educated at Grinnell College, Iowa, B.A. (honors) in English 1941 (Phi Beta Kappa); Columbia University, New York, 1941-42. Secretary and promotion director, Oxford University Press, New York, 1943-51; Reference Librarian, National Audubon Society, New York, 1952-59; free-lance editor and researcher, New York, 1960-77; Editor, E.P. Dutton, publishers, New York, 1977-82. Writer-in-Residence, College of William and Mary, Williamsburg, Virginia, 1984-85. Recipient: Guggenheim Fellowship, 1982; American Academy award, 1984. D.H.L.: Grinnell College, 1984. Address: 160 East 65th Street, Apartment 4-F, New York, New York 10021, U.S.A.

PUBLICATIONS

Verse

Multitudes, Multitudes. New York, Washington Street Press, 1974.
The Isthmus. New York, Coalition of Publishers for Employment, 1982.
The Kingfisher. New York, Knopf, 1983; London, Faber, 1984.
The Summer Solstice. New York, Sarabande Press, 1983.
A Homage to John Keats. New York, Sarabande Press, 1984.
What the Light Was Like. New York, Knopf, 1985.

*

Critical Studies: "On the Thread of Language" by Helen Vendler, in *New York Review of Books*, 3 March 1983; Joel

Conarroe, in *Washington Post Book World*, 3 April 1983; "The Hazardous Definition of Structures" by Richard Howard, in *Parnassus* (New York), Spring-Summer 1983; "Nature, Fantasy, Art" by Richard Tillinghast, in *New York Times Book Review*, 7 August 1983; J.D. McClatchy, in *Poetry* (Chicago), December 1983.

*   *   *

Amy Clampitt's debt to Gerard Manley Hopkins is clear in *The Kingfisher*, her first book of poetry. The book's epigraph and title poem come from his own famous lines, "As kingfishers catch fire, dragonflies draw flame." Although in Clampitt's "The Kingfisher," a poem about mutability and loss, she does not echo Hopkins's faith, his "just man justices, keeps grace," her language and her rhythms are similar to his:

> through the long evening
> of a dazzled pub crawl, the halcyon color, portholed
> by those eye-spots' stunning tapestry, unsettled
> the pastoral nightfall with amazements opening.

Indeed, for lovers of language, of sheer sound in poetry, Clampitt is reminiscent not only of Hopkins, but more recently of Dylan Thomas whose death she notes in "The Kingfisher." She is alliterative. She uses adjectives galore. She packs her lines with vowel sounds, with hard consonants, with unusual or difficult words. And she often rhymes. Here are some typical examples of Clampitt's style: "chain-gang archangels that in their prismatic / frenzy fall, gall and gash the daylight" ("The Outer Bar"); "crossed by young gusts' / vaporous fripperies, liquid / footprints flying, lacewing / leaf-shade brightening / and fading" ("The Edge of the Hurricane"); "in winter / whisking its wolfish spittle to a froth / that turned whole townships into / white wallow." ("The Woodlot").

What Clampitt's poems have to say is sometimes obscured by this show of technique, and often they are more glittery than meaningful. When her meaning is clear, however, when her verbal gifts do not overwhelm the occasion, she communicates a reverence for the natural world. In nature she finds miracle and mystery enough. In the sea mouse, for example, or in articles washed up by the sea, in the killdeer's camouflaged nest, nature appears to have knowledge far surpassing that of man, as in "Camouflage":

> In her bones, in her genes, in
> the secret code of her behavior,
> she already knew more than all our
> bumbling daydreams, our palaver
> about safeguards

When Clampitt approaches a deer, she does so with great care, aware of her inadequacy. Her approach is an act of worship, as in "Slow Motion":

> One ear
> shifted its ponderous
> velour to winnow
> what my own bare
> tympanum merely spilled
> and scattered like
> a gust of lost pollen.

Apart from nature poems, however, there are poems in *The Kingfisher* about the poet's father, art, the midwest, Europe—all

of them distinguished by Clampitt's singular voice. *The Kingfisher* is a remarkably mature and skillful volume.

—Cynthia Day

CLARK, John Pepper. Nigerian. Born in Kiagbodo, 6 April 1935. Educated at Warri Government College, Ughelli, 1948-54; Ibadan University, 1955-60, B.A. (honours) in English 1960; Princeton University, New Jersey (Parvin Fellowship), 1962-63; Ibadan Unversity (Institute of African Studies Research Fellowship, 1963-64). Married; three daughters and one son. Nigerian Government Information Officer, 1960-61; Head of Features and Editorial Writer, *Daily Express*, Lagos, 1961-62. Founding-Editor, *The Horn* magazine, Ibadan; former Co-Editor, *Black Orpheus* magazine, Lagos. Since 1965, Member of the English Department, and currently Professor of English, University of Lagos. Founding Member, Society of Nigerian Authors. Address: Department of English, University of Lagos, Lagos, Nigeria.

PUBLICATIONS

Verse

Poems. Ibadan, Mbari, 1962.
A Reed in the Tide: A Selection of Poems. London, Longman, 1965; New York, Humanities Press, 1970.
Casualties: Poems 1966-68. London, Longman, and New York, Africana, 1970.
Urhobo Poetry. Ibadan, Ibadan University Press, 1980.
A Decade of Tongues: Selected Poems 1958-1968. London, Longman, 1981.

Plays

Song of a Goat (produced Ibadan, 1961; London, 1965). Ibadan, Mbari, 1961; in *Three Plays*, 1964.
Three Plays: Song of a Goat, The Raft, The Masquerade. London, Oxford University Press, 1964.
The Masquerade (produced London, 1965). Included in *Three Plays*, 1964.
The Raft (broadcast, 1966; produced New York, 1978). Included in *Three Plays*, 1964.
Ozidi. Ibadan, London, and New York, Oxford University Press, 1966.

Screenplay: *The Ozidi of Atazi.*

Radio Play: *The Raft*, 1966.

Other

America, Their America. London, Deutsch-Heinemann, 1964; New York, Africana, 1969.
The Example of Shakespeare: Critical Essays on African Literature. London, Longman, and Evanston, Illinois, Northwestern University Press, 1970.
The Ozidi Saga. Ibadan, Ibadan University Press, 1975.
The Hero as a Villain. Lagos, University of Lagos Press, 1978.

*

Critical Studies: *Three Nigerian Poets: A Critical Study of the Poetry of Soyinka, Clark, and Okigbo* by Nyong J. Udoeyop, Ibadan, Ibadan University Press, 1973; *A Critical View on John Pepper Clark's Selected Poems* by Kirsten Holst Petersen, London, Collings, 1981.

*   *   *

John Pepper Clark is a dramatist as well as a poet, but whereas his drama production is held together by a certain unity of theme and style, his poetry is not. *A Reed in the Tide* is a collection of occasional poems. Each poem seems to be inspired by an actual occurrence in the poet's life such as watching Fulani cattle, seeing a girl bathing in a stream, or flying across America. The incident takes on a symbolic and sometimes a moral value, and this is worked out in the poem, partly through description and partly through explicit commentary; "Agbor Dancer" is a good example of this. Seeing a girl dance the traditional Agbor dance, Clark describes the event. "See her caught in the throb of a drum...entangled in the magic maze of music....," and this leads him to a feeling of loss because he can no longer do the dance, i.e., he is alienated from tribal life. This in turn leads to a wish for reintegration. "Could I, early sequester'd from my tribe, / Free a lead-tether'd scribe / I should answer her communal call...." The theme of cultural integration which runs through some of the poems is supported by the poems dealing with traditional African themes like "Abiku" and also by the poems which evoke Clark's native Nigerian town and landscape; this last section contains the most successful poems of the collection. Both the Ezra Pound-inspired poem about Ibadan and the very sensitive evocation of the wet tropical Niger delta in "Night Rain" are excellent visual descriptions which gain much from not having any philosophy tagged onto them. The poems dealing with modern American life provide a logical contrast to the loving concern with traditional life. Here Clark dwells on the alienating effect of technology like the slot-machine ("Service") and the underground train ("Cave Call").

Clark's next collection, *Casualties*, deals with the Biafran War and can thus be said to have a unified theme. Clark took a personal part in the war, intervening on behalf of a friend, and he also was personally acquainted with several of the most important leaders in the conflict. An intimate knowledge of the details of the war is necessary for an understanding of the poetry which is mainly narrative / argumentative, and Clark has felt obliged to provide footnotes to most of the poems, to explain, for instance, that the crocodile in "The Reign of the Crocodile" is Major-General Ironsi who carried a stuffed crocodile as a swagger-stick. The collection suffers badly from this concern with the actual details of the war. One can only agree with Clark when he writes in the Preface to Notes that "I sometimes wish I had written in prose this personal account...." Some of the poems, however, are transfused with a sadness which transcends the details and brings across not just the misery of war, but the particular misery of civil war where friendships and family ties are tested and broken.

—Kirsten Holst Petersen

CLARK, Tom (Thomas Willard Clark). American. Born in Chicago, Illinois, 1 March 1941. Educated at the University of Michigan, Ann Arbor (Hopwood Prize, 1963), B.A. 1963; Cambridge University (Fulbright Fellow, 1963-65), 1963-65; University of Essex, Wivenhoe, 1965-67. Married Angelica Heinegg in 1968; one daughter. Poetry Editor, *Paris Review*, 1963-73; Instructor in American Poetry, University of Essex, 1966-67. Since 1978, Senior Writer, *Boulder Monthly*, Colorado. Recipient: Bess Hokin Prize, 1966, and George Dillon Memorial Prize, 1968 (*Poetry*, Chicago); Poets Foundation Award, 1967; Rockefeller Fellowship, 1968; Guggenheim Fellowship, 1970. Address: c/o Harcourt Brace Jovanovich Inc., 757 Third Avenue, New York, New York 10017, U.S.A.

PUBLICATIONS

Verse

Airplanes. Brightlingsea, Essex, Once Press, 1966.
The Sand Burg: Poems. London, Ferry Press, 1966.
Bun, with Ron Padgett. New York, Angel Hair, 1968.
Stones. New York, Harper, 1969.
Air. New York, Harper, 1970.
The No Book. Wivenhoe Park, Essex, Ant's Forefoot, 1971.
Green. Los Angeles, Black Sparrow Press, 1971.
John's Heart. London, Cape Goliard Press, and New York, Grossman, 1972.
Back in Boston Again, with Ted Berrigan and Ron Padgett. Philadelphia, Telegraph, 1972.
Smack. Los Angeles, Black Sparrow Press, 1972.
Blue. Los Angeles, Black Sparrow Press, 1974.
Suite. Los Angeles, Black Sparrow Press, 1974.
Chicago. Los Angeles, Black Sparrow Press, 1974.
At Malibu. New York, Kulchur, 1975.
Baseball. Berkeley, California, Figures, 1976.
Fan Poems. Plainfield, Vermont, North Atlantic, 1976.
An Arthur Felgenheimer Sachet. Privately printed, 1977.
35. Berkeley, California, Poltroon Press, 1977.
How I Broke In / Six Modern Masters. Bolinas, California, Tombouctou, 1978.
When Things Get Tough on Easy Street: Selected Poems 1963-1978. Santa Barbara, California, Black Sparrow Press, 1978.
Nine Songs. Isla Vista, California, Turkey Press, 1981.
A Short Guide to the High Plains. Santa Barbara, California, Cadmus, 1981.
Heartbreak Hotel. West Branch, Iowa, Toothpaste Press, 1981.
Under the Fortune Palms. Isla Vista, California, Turkey Press, 1982.

Play

The Emperor of the Animals. London, Goliard Press, 1967.

Novels

Who Is Sylvia? Eugene, Oregon, Blue Wind Press, 1979.
The Master. Markesan, Wisconsin, Pentagram, 1979.

Short Stories

The Last Gas Station and Other Stories. Santa Barbara, California, Black Sparrow Press, 1980.

Other

Neil Young. Toronto, Coach House Press, 1971.
Champagne and Baloney: The Rise and Fall of Finley's A's. New York, Harper, 1976.

No Big Deal, with Mark Fidrych. Philadelphia, Lippincott, 1977.
The World of Damon Runyon. New York, Harper, 1978.
A Conversation with Hitler. Santa Barbara, California, Black Sparrow Press, 1978.
The Mutabilitie of the Englishe Lyrick (parodies). Berkeley, California, E Typographeo Poltroniano, 1978.
One Last Round for the Shuffler: A Blacklisted Ball Player's Story. St. Paul, Minnesota, Truck, 1979.
The Great Naropa Poetry Wars. Santa Barbara, California, Cadmus, 1980.
Jack Kerouac. New York, Harcourt Brace, 1984.

*

Manuscript Collection: University of Connecticut, Storrs.

*   *   *

Tom Clark's poetry published in the 1960's can give the impression of the man who got on his horse and rode off in all directions at once. The "look" of the poems is frequently reassuring, the lines of more-or-less equivalent length grouped into equivalent units on the page, promising a rational structure. But within these units chaos can sometimes reign. The thin, or non-existent punctuation often creates syntactical confusions. There is also a certain fondness for quirky modifiers, as though the poet were a computer choosing at random from a bank of nouns and a bank of adjectives combining the result. To place a "secretive tambourine" and a "sober dog" back-to-back in the poem "Comanche" from *Stones* suggests an interest more in the way words can collide than in their potentiality for pleasing combinations. This fondness for playing with words also surfaces in some poems in the form of a jingly sound effects. Also, Clark seems fond of the chain poem where repetition of a single word or phrase in each section ties the whole together, as in his brash parody of Wallace Stevens's famous Blackbird poem, "Eleven Ways of Looking at a Shit Bird" (*Stones*).

The poems published during the 1970's move away from the scattergun effects I've described. This work seems clearer, cleaner, though with the same drive and energy, the general feeling that Clark is perpetually *en route*. Also, the range of subjects widens here, the introspection of the earlier work giving way to concern with things and people in the world. One of my favorites is "To Kissinger" (*When Things Get Tough on Easy Street*), a wacky series of insults that makes a forceful political point with humor. There are a number of poems about running in the same collection, some short, throwaway pieces, others, such as "Morning Leaves Me Speechless," expressing beautifully the euphoria that can appear on the other side of physical exertion.

In a number of books published during this time Clark seems overly fond of the tiny poem. *Green* and *Blue* contain a number of poems that consist of one sentence, or even less; *Smack* is made up entirely of single sentences arranged vertically on the page. These efforts at minimal art via the word aren't always successful; they give the impression of notebook jottings, casual ideas that might grow into poems. There is a throwaway streak in Clark's work, a willingness to let things go, to gallop on to the next poem, to get on down the road. While this tendency may undermine the shorter poems, in the longer ones where there is room for discursive, casual, or colloquial effects, it can produce exciting poetry. A good example of this is "Chicago" (*When Things Get Tough on Easy Street*), an extended recollection of the poet's youthful experiences as an usher at various stadiums, ball-parks, and convention halls in the Chicago area that ends up by evoking an entire era—that strange period of American History known as "the fifties." There is an interesting and unexpected idea implied in this poem, that poets and ushers have something in common. Both are employed spectators, in it for more than entertainment.

Clark is a world-class spectator, his work a grand record of his passionate looking-on. In many of his sports poems, especially those dealing with baseball, he tries to invest the game with meaning far beyond its position in American society as an entertainment. Clark is a *Fan*; he doesn't write about baseball, he celebrates it. These poems belong to the tradition of the encomium, and the names of the players ring through them like a Homeric roll-call: Orestes Minoso, Catfish Hunter, Vida Blue, Bert Campaneris, Bill Lee. The poem on Bill Lee is perhaps the best of these, a long, warm appreciation of that player's eccentric intelligence.

In his most recent poems, Clark seems to have abandoned baseball as a subject, perhaps because he has been able to celebrate the sport in prose in a number of books and articles, but his fondness for the encomium persists in a group of poems about artists—two on Reverdy, one each on Ungaretti, Vuillard, Kafka, and Lenny Bruce. But this recent work isn't all hero worship; in "How I Broke In," the poem sequence that concludes *When Things Get Tough on Easy Street*, Clark shuffles and reshuffles a number of images, allusions, individual lines, upping the ante in each section, increasing the pressure until I began to wonder how he could sustain it and keep going. To read this sequence is to confront something powerful, even dangerous, barely held in control. The experience is exhilarating.

—Steven Young

CLARKE, Gillian (née Williams). Welsh. Born in Cardiff, Glamorgan, 8 June 1937. Educated at St. Clare's Convent, Porthcawl, Glamorgan; University College, Cardiff, B.A. in English 1958. News researcher, BBC, London, 1958-60. Since 1960, broadcaster: regular presenter of *Time for Verse*, Radio 4, and *Poetry Now*, Radio 3. Lecturer in Art History, Gwent College of Art and Design, Newport, 1975-84; Welsh Arts Council Writing Fellow, St. David's University College, Lampeter, Dyfed, 1984-85. Editor, *Anglo-Welsh Review*, Cardiff, 1976-84. Recipient: Welsh Arts Council prize, 1979. Address: 1 Cyncoed Avenue, Cyncoed, Cardiff, Wales.

PUBLICATIONS

Verse

Snow on the Mountain. Swansea, Christopher Davies, 1971.
The Sundial. Llandysul, Dyfed, Gomer, 1978.
Letter from a Far Country. Manchester, Carcanet, 1982.

Plays

Radio Poems: *Talking in the Dark*, 1975; *Letter from a Far Country*, 1979.

*   *   *

Making her first appearance in print in 1970, Gillian Clarke has now a firm reputation in literary Wales. She has written two successful short verse plays for radio but continues to publish poetry infrequently. *The Sundial* brings together 39 poems and, as in the work of Dylan Thomas, the basic properties of stone, sea, sun, survival, growth, and fertility abound. Gillian Clarke goes too for the big ending, an epiphany or, at least "significance," and so occasionally risks the reader's sympathy: "Neatly, slowly I folded / Clothes, and survived ("Lines"). And again: "its stone / Profile of an ancient priest / Preaches continually / In the face of turning tides" ("St. Augustine's Penarth"). But at her best, and that means in at least half of the poems in this collection, the conception is underpinned by a force of language that is fulfilling and, at times, astonishing, as in "Harvest at Mynachlog":

> We talk
> Of other harvests. They remember
> How a boy, flying his plane so low
> Over the cut fields that his father
>
> Straightened from his work to wave his hat
> At the boasting sky, died minutes later
> On an English cliff, in such a year
> As this, the barns brimming gold.
>
> We are quiet again, holding our cups
> In turn for the tilting milk, sad, hearing
> The sun roar like a rush of grain
> Engulfing all winged things that live
> One moment in the eclipsing light.

The transference of the grain's fruitful rush back to the heat of the sun is an exciting use of language, and allows one to forget the excesses of "boasting sky" and "tilting milk." Here is a real talent. The extent to which that gift blossoms would appear to be in Gillian Clarke's own hands.

—Tony Curtis

CLEMO, Jack (Reginald John Clemo). British. Born in St. Austell, Cornwall, 11 March 1916. Educated at Trethosa Village School. Married Ruth Grace Peaty in 1968. Recipient: Atlantic Award, Birmingham University, 1948; Arts Council Festival Prize, 1951; Civil List pension, 1961, supplemented in 1966 and 1969. D.Litt.: University of Exeter, 1981. Address: Goonamarris, St. Stephen's, St. Austell, Cornwall; or, 24 Southlands Road, Rodwell, Weymouth, Dorset DT4 9LQ, England.

PUBLICATIONS

Verse

The Clay Verge. London, Chatto and Windus, 1951.
The Map of Clay. London, Methuen, 1961; Richmond, Virginia, John Knox Press, 1968.
Penguin Modern Poets 6, with Edward Lucie-Smith and George MacBeth. London, Penguin, 1964.
Cactus on Carmel: Poems. London, Methuen, 1967.
The Echoing Tip. London, Methuen, 1971.
Broad Autumn. London, Eyre Methuen, 1975.

Novels

Wilding Graft. London, Chatto and Windus, and New York, Macmillan, 1948.

Other

Confession of a Rebel (autobiography). London, Chatto and Windus, 1949.
The Invading Gospel (theology). London, Bles, 1958; revised edition, London, Morgan Marshall and Scott, 1972; Old Tappan, New Jersey, Revell, 1973.
The Marriage of a Rebel: A Mystical Erotic Quest. London, Gollancz, 1980.
The Bouncing Hills: Dialect Talks and Light Verse. Redruth, Cornwall, Truran, 1983.

*

Manuscript Collection: Exeter University Research Library.

Critical Studies: *Rule and Energy* by John Press, London, Oxford University Press, 1963; *Religious Trends in English Poetry,* vol. 6, by Hoxie N. Fairchild, New York, Columbia University Press, 1968; *The Ironic Harvest* by Geoffrey Thurley, London, Arnold, 1974; *Dissentient Voice* by Donald Davie, Notre Dame, Indiana, University of Notre Dame Press, 1980.

Jack Clemo comments:

(1970) I intended to be chiefly a prose writer, but the loss of my sight in 1955 forced me to restrict myself to composing verse.

Apart from a few poems describing the Cornish clay district, my poetry reflects various phases of Christianity as an experience of personal conversion. Its main themes are the Christian view of "fallen nature," the sacrament of marriage, and the place of suffering in the achievement of true happiness. There are also some fierce Barthian structures on religious humanism, and a realistic Evangelical optimism akin to Browning's. My first two collections of verse were chiefly odes in the Francis Thompson vein, though grimmer and bleaker because I used the imagery of clay-mining. In my later work, I have developed a more modern imagist technique with sprung rhythm and a minimum of rhyme; the symbols are more frequently drawn from nature, and I show a deep affinity with primitive Catholic visionaries like Bernadette. This, however, does not involve any discarding of my earlier creed or my taste for stark aesthetic patterns. I write entirely on spiritual inspiration and do not consciously choose either the subject or the style of my poems. My erotic mysticism, though it answers D.H. Lawrence, was spontaneously evolved under the pressure of my emotional crisis. Incidents from my own life are often depicted in my verse, and the range is widened by dramatic monologues and tributes to various writers, saints and preachers. I think that my four collections make a fairly complete statement of my philosophy, but the physical handicaps of my mature years have restricted my output and are too often dragged in by critics to explain my beliefs and attitudes which I had already adopted while unhandicapped.

*   *   *

Jack Clemo is a Cornish poet whose early faith appears to have been nourished in all the paraphernalia of the local clay-pits—the dumps, cinder heaps, the snow-covered quarries—rather than the natural beauty of his native countryside; there has always been a sense of conflict between his attitude to nature and his concept of divine grace. That is because his early spiritual struggles were conducted against such a background. In his prose volume, *The Invading Gospel*, which might be described as his testament of faith, he tells us that he had "to fight among the clay-kilns and refuse-barrows of mid-Cornwall the same sort of battle as D.H. Lawrence fought among the headstocks and slagheaps of the Derbyshire collieries." It is a kind of landscape which seems to reflect in some ways the personal experience of a poet who has been stone-deaf for most of his life, and who, after spells of blindness during his schooldays, has suffered from blindness since 1955.

In his first book of poems, *The Clay Verge*, he has little to say in favour of nature and he will have nothing to do with the God of nature-worshippers. His Calvinistic creed and the almost savage mythology expressed in this volume are likely to antagonize those who have been conditioned to respond in a particular way whenever the "mysteries of Nature" are mentioned. But the puritanical strength and the intensity of vision underlying these poems, and the organic unity and content, can hardly be ignored. It is a poetry not merely of renunciation, but of vilification of the natural world. Here and there the technical influences of both Hardy and Lawrence can be discerned, but they are not obtrusive. It is precisely because of his own sensitivity to sense impressions and fears that his spiritual life may be imperilled by undue attachment to "Nature's teeming perfidies" that he reacts so violently. This over-emphasis upon isolated points of belief, together with the harsh symbolism of the clay-pits tended to distort the ideas he was trying to present, yet his concept of Christianity as a "redemptive invasion of nature by the divine grace which is outside nature" would probably be acceptable to most Christians.

There is a strong sexual element in all Clemo's poetry, whether he is referring to human relationships or not. In his earliest poems he was inclined to equate sexual feeling with the corruption to be found in nature, and this set up a sense of conflict since it involved his own instincts as well as his religious concepts. In "The Plundered Fuchsias," where the conflict is most clearly marked, he finds a grim satisfaction in the destruction of the flowers by his lady companion, apparently without appreciating the sensual symbolism of the act itself, and then proceeds to indulge his own nature:

> She married the rhythm of soil,
>   She checked fertility
> And then, the last flower trampled on,
>   She turned more naughtily
> And gave her lips to me.

Clemo's second collection traces his development, step by step, from the isolationist position he had taken up after his conversion to the more enlightened state in which he recognized the need for solidarity with other Christians. In "The Broadening Winter" he compares the experience of C. H. Spurgeon with that of his own—Clemo's views on predestination approach those of Barth and Spurgeon, whom he has studied to some effect. Clemo's most revitalizing influences, however, have been visiting American evangelists, Renee Martz, the child evangelist, and Billy Graham, in particular. In *The Map of Clay* a new "jazz" phraseology begins to replace that previously drawn from the Cornish clayworks—"God's jazzdrums seemed to thunder..." or "Hot ragtime stains the austere track..."—to match the new mood of pentecostal gaiety.

Most of the poems in *The Echoing Tip* were written after his marriage in 1968, and it is noticeable that the sexual element has been subdued and almost replaced by a preoccupation with "objective portraiture" (there are reflective poems on Beethoven, Helen Keller, Simone Weil, and "The Death of Karl Barth"). The

clay-pit symbolism has disappeared altogether and there is a revealing poem, "Wedding Eve," in celebration of his forthcoming marriage: "And I feel in your flushed curves, / In your kiss, the world-renouncing nun."

In *Broad Autumn* he refers to his own pilgrimage in the title poem, and his resolution of his personal conflicts allows him to turn outwards to the problems and experiences of others— Gerard Manley Hopkins, John Clare, Kagawa, Joseph Hocking, John Wesley, Donne, and Mary Slessor. It can now be said that as a religious poet, and as a landscape poet, Jack Clemo has few challengers. It remains to be seen how his work will develop in the future.

—Howard Sergeant

CLIFTON, Lucille (Thelma, née Sayles).   American.   Born in Depew, New York, 27 June 1936. Educated at Howard University, Washington, D.C., 1953-55; Fredonia State Teachers College, New York, 1955. Married Fred J. Clifton in 1958; six children. Claims clerk, New York State Division of Employment, Buffalo, 1958-60; Literature Assistant, U.S. Office of Education, Washington, D.C., 1969-71. Visiting Writer, Columbia University School of the Arts; Poet-in-Residence, Coppin State College, Baltimore, 1971-74. Recipient: YM-YWHA Poetry Center Discovery Award, 1969; National Endowment for the Arts grant, 1969; Juniper Prize, 1980. Agent: Marilyn Marlow, Curtis Brown Ltd., 575 Madison Avenue, New York, New York 10022. Address: 2605 Talbot Road, Baltimore, Maryland 21216, U.S.A.

PUBLICATIONS

Verse

Good Times.   New York, Random House, 1969.
Good News about the Earth.   New York, Random House, 1972.
An Ordinary Woman.   New York, Random House, 1974.
Two-Headed Woman.   Amherst, University of Massachusetts Press, 1980.

Novel

Generations of Americans: A Memoir.   New York, Random House, 1976.

Other (for children)

The Black BC's.   New York, Dutton, 1970.
Some of the Days of Everett Anderson.   New York, Holt Rinehart, 1970.
Everett Anderson's Christmas Coming [*Year, Friend, 1—2—3, Nine Month Long, Goodbye*].   New York, Holt Rinehart, 6 vols., 1971-83.
Good, Says Jerome.   New York, Dutton, 1973.
All Us Come Cross the Water.   New York, Holt Rinehart, 1973.
Don't You Remember: New York, Dutton, 1973.
The Boy Who Didn't Believe in Spring.   New York, Dutton, 1973.
The Times They Used to Be.   New York, Holt Rinehart, 1974.
My Brother Fine with Me.   New York, Holt Rinehart, 1975.

Three Wishes. New York, Viking Press, 1976.
Amifika. New York, Dutton, 1977.
The Lucky Stone. New York, Delacorte Press, 1979.
My Friend Jacob. New York, Dutton, 1980.
Sonora Beautiful. New York, Dutton, 1981.

*

Lucille Clifton comments:
     I am a black woman poet, and I sound like one.

*   *   *

Lucille Clifton creates a poetry of ideas in which the ordinary is revealed to be extraordinary, in which the indigenously commonplace yields universal truth. Two realities influence the mode and substance of this poetry: she is black and she is a woman.

Over a decade ago, in "after Kent State," she wrote "white ways are / the ways of death / come into the / Black / and live"; in a relatively recent volume, in a poem addressed "To Ms. Ann" (a historically ubiquitous title and name applied derisively to white "ladies") she writes, "you have never called me sister / and it has only been forever and / i will have to forget your face." Thus, she turns away from whiteness to affirm and to celebrate blackness.

The optimism that pervades Clifton's poetry is rooted in her ethnic heritage and milieu. She teaches that black life is, indeed, fraught with danger and adversity: "i went into my mother as / some souls go into a church /...listen, eavesdroppers, there is no such thing / as a bed without affliction; / the bodies all may open wide but / you enter at your own risk." Still, one must take the risks: "i'm trying for the lone one mama, / running like hell and if i fall / i fall." The result:

                    i survive
                         survive
                    survive.

One must see the beauties and lessons in the lives of forerunners; one must see the beauties and possibilities in one's own life. In "Last Note to My Girls" Clifton says, "i command you to be / good runners / to go with grace."

In an autobiographical prose work, *Generations,* Clifton asserts, "Things don't fall apart. Things hold. Lines connect in thin ways that last and last and lines become generations made out of pictures and words just kept." This heritage-inspired, almost mystical, faith and motivation are common in her poetry, as in the lines "someone calling itself Light / has opened my inside. / i am flooded with brilliance / mother, / / someone of it is answering to / your name."

Clifton's sense of extended black family is especially strong in poems written from her feminine point of view. Her feminism does not manifest itself in a strident voice of protest for equality of the sexes; neither does it manifest itself in depictions of fragile daintiness, shielded vision, protective seclusion, or cloying sentimentality. Hers is a dignified, active, poised, self-assured, insightful, and sensitive woman-ness. Poems such as "the lost baby poem," about an abortion, and "Conversation with My Grandson, Waiting to Be Conceived" obviously were written by such a woman.

The settings and situations that inform Clifton's poetry are those in which "little" people endure and function admirably, even heroically. The heroes that inspire or populate her poetry are public black heroes such as Angela Davis and, more important, the unexpected and unsung heroes such as "Miss Rosie," a "wet brown bag of a woman."

That religion is a source of her optimism is evident in Clifton's poems. A number of them are built upon metaphorical constructs derived from the Bible. In one poem, immediately after confessing that "i am not equal to the faith required," she reports that although "i try to run from such surprising presence; / the angels stream before me / like a torch." Clifton's God, it might be said, is a God that can be perceived by black people. In one poem the biblical Mary speaks with syntax and grammar identified with Afro-Americans, and in "Palm Sunday" the people lay "turnips / for the mule to walk on / waving beets / and collards in the air." And in keeping with Afro-American religious traditions, theirs is a beatific faith.

Clifton's poems are short, graceful, incisive. They continue to open as the reader contemplates or re-experiences them. Their understated yet insistent, and occasionally wryly humorous, endings often surprise. The best generic term to characterize their form and technique is "free verse." Her lines are sinewy, lithe, rather matter-of-fact; her diction is clear, precise, often in the idioms of ordinary Afro-Americans. She is not given to elaborate conceits or metaphors or to florid figurative language; when she does employ such devices, they work well for poetic effect, as in "To a Dark Moses": "you are the one / i am lit for. / come with your rod / that twists / and is a serpent. / i am the bush. / i am burning. / i am not consumed."

Critical appraisals of Lucille Clifton's poetry are generally very commendatory. The New York *Times* selected her *Good Times* as one of the ten best books of 1969. The State of Maryland has named her its official Poet Laureate. In addition to poetry, Clifton writes fiction and children's literature that has won critical praise.

—Theodore R. Hudson

———————

CLUYSENAAR, Anne (Alice Andrée). Irish. Born in Brussels, Belgium, 15 March 1936. Educated at Trinity College, Dublin (Vice-Chancellor's Prize, 1956), B.A. (honours) in English and French 1957; University of Edinburgh, diploma in general linguistics 1963. Married Walter Freeman Jackson in 1976; three stepchildren. Reader to the writer Percy Lubbock for one year; Assistant Lecturer, Manchester University, 1957-58, and King's College, Aberdeen University, 1963-65; Lecturer in General Linguistics, Lancaster University, 1965-71; Senior Lecturer in Language and Literature, Huddersfield Polytechnic, Yorkshire, 1972-73; Lecturer in Linguistics, Birmingham University, 1973-76. Senior Lecturer, and currently Principal Lecturer in English Studies, Sheffield City Polytechnic. Chair, Verbal Arts Association, 1983; active in National Poetry Society Poets-in-Schools workshops. General Editor, *Sheaf*; regular poetry reviewer, *Stand*, Newcastle upon Tyne. Address: Woodend Farm, Joan Royd Road, Pennistone, Sheffield, South Yorkshire S30 6AW, England.

PUBLICATIONS

Verse

A Fan of Shadows. Manchester, David Findley Press, 1967.
Nodes. Dublin, Dolmen Press, 1969.
Double Helix, with Sybil Hewat. Manchester, Carcanet, 1982.

Other

Introduction to Literary Stylistics: A Discussion of Dominant Structures in Verse and Prose. London, Batsford, 1976; as *Aspects of Literary Stylistics,* New York, St. Martin's Press, 1976.
Verbal Arts: The Missing Subject. London, Methuen, 1985.

Editor, *Selected Poems,* by Burns Singer. Manchester, Carcanet, 1977.

*

Anne Cluysenaar comments:

I consider *Double Helix* the best I have done so far. In a review of *Double Helix* in *Writing Women* Linda Anderson caught exactly what I had hoped would be the effect of the book. In particular, she sees my mother's memoirs, together with other family documents, letters and photographs, as providing "an eloquent record of family history reaching back over three generations." My poems seek to interpret this record in terms of "the boundaries of self and others." They are "meditations...on precisely those gaps and silences where lives meet and separate, where writing begins and ends." In writing the book, I was attempting to set down only what appeared to me to be literally true and to find poetry in such reality. Without, of course, believing that this is the only way in which poetry can be written, I felt the need to assure myself that "poetry" is not so much a sophisticated fiction as a simple, everyday experience shared by everyone if not always recognised for what it is. I hoped *Double Helix* would be receivable as this reviewer received it: "What the reader experiences is the repeated sense of overlapping subjectivities—not just what can be created and told of another life but also where that understanding ends. The gaps, absences, differences between the various texts create space for the reader and necessitate a kind of collaborative reading experience, the meeting of our own subjectivity with that evidenced by the text"; so that the reader's realities come to enrich those whose traces survive on the written page.

*   *   *

Anne Cluysenaar's earlier poetry belongs to the school of Valéry and Beckett. Her poems evoke formally what it is to "be" human—the perceiving centre, constantly changing, of a universe itself in a constant state of flux. *Fan of Shadows* is a collection of models of the human condition, explained in appended notes as figures of "continuous creation," or "radiations from an occasionally moving centre." In "Figures," the image of Derwentwater is "love's point of balance" between opposites—stillness and movement, presence and absence, love and solitude, liquid and solid:

> The variant self awakes
> To hills, fields, open water,
> Newly aware of their stillness.
>
> Between a kiss and the stillness
> Of lonely thought, water
> Off balance on a stony shore.

In "Sea," the stillness of mid-ocean is complemented by the moving tides; in "Petrarch," the "still pool" is speechless, and only knows itself in its overflow, "river-song." The sameness of experience is underlined by the accumulation of archetypes of desire—Orpheus, Laura, Balder—and by a repetition of words,

phrases, and whole verses which in several poems dictates the entire structure. The love-lyric "Sea" falls into two near-mirror halves; "Epithalamium" opens as "The rings of the sun rise" to close on an echo: "The rings of a winter sunrise." The details of the difference are what makes the present moment, which Cluysenaar seeks to flesh out, charting, in the words of the more recent "La Belle Otero," what she calls "The strangely similar gaze in two chance moments."

The changes in the quality of her perceptions of the present are what distinguish her development—and progress—as a poet. In her earlier work, she doesn't always successfully cross the divide between eternal verity and dead cliché. Her landscapes remain abstract, shot through by mind rather than sensuous matter. A poem like "Figures" can in its separate moment pinpoint an interesting and self-defining interpenetration of thinker and perceived world:

> A slim wave's shadow
> Sinks into the hammered gold
> Of dry stone creased with water.
>
> Fish become concentrations
> Of light, on which waves wind
> Tongue-rolls of clear water.

But the vein it works is limited, and the strain of avoiding the twin evils of banality and preciosity constantly shows through. In later works, there is more warmth, and a personal voice finally makes itself heard. "Maker" recognises the poet's problem—the distance between the vivid colour of the real world and the abstractly arid version on the dead paper before him. "The May Fox" solves it; a surprise confrontation with death (the narrow escape of a fox, caught in the car's headlights) turns into love, a moment of shared human and animal warmth which dramatically re-enacts the exchange of meaning between man, nature, and the ideas and objects of man's creation.

Double Helix is a blend of letters, photographs, family documents and poems which raises all human experience to the level of lyric. The voice of "the unnecessary poet" ("In Time-lapse") blends with others, past and present, in a celebration of human community where "I" is no more nor less than the individual inflection of the "universal experiences," the "natural signs," of all daily life. To be human is to recreate from the abstract flow the sensuous detail of reality: "the stream/whose tiny, illegal trout/ come to fingers patient with memories" ("Resting the Ladder"). "The Line on the Map," in the poem of that title, "has become hills, trees/A place not a direction." This place is not circumscribed; its expanding ripples reach out to include whole literary traditions (Milosz, Housman), cross the frontiers of class, nation, and politics, and abolish all limits, even those of death. Where private possession is abolished by community, there is no loss ("Resting the Ladder"):

> Watching, this first year, the swallow
> change to a silent icicle
> over the stable door,
> and knowing this will be the view
> of my old age, I warn myself
> we shall never own this place outright.

Cluysenaar's poetry reserves its anger for the merchants of loss and destruction, the authors of the concentration camps, the atom bomb, unemployment, repression, against whom her closing pages rise to a dignified rage that twists syntax but not sense, linking indissolubly poetic, personal, and political value ("7 September—Ready to Leave"):

What duty can we meantime fulfil
other than that which has always been ours?
To grow with such persistent angry will
that what is to be killed is worth dying for?

Whereas *Double Helix* draws on the strength of past lives, Cluysenaar's most recent poems, experiments in sonnet form, look to the future. The mirror of a new "Double," the child, reveals the real terrors concealed by the familiar language and rituals of everyday life. "In the Midst," its mirror-pattern rhyme schemes constraining writhing, broken rhythms, points the destructive nature of abstract and abstracted adult language, "the lip nice/on shattering syllables," for which the sole remedy is the baby's primitive scream: "It cries, and their mimed fear/Is as nothing to the real, modern horror./It cries, we laugh. We catch our breath."

—Jennifer Birkett

COBBING, Bob. British. Born in Enfield, Middlesex, 30 July 1920. Educated at Enfield Grammar School; Bognor Training College, teaching certificate 1949. Married Jennifer Pike in 1963; three sons and two daughters from previous marriages. Civil servant, 1937-41; farmer, 1942-43; teacher in Swindon, Wiltshire, 1944-47, and London, 1949-64; manager, Better Books Poetry Bookshop, London, 1964-67. Since 1967, freelance writer and performer. Since 1954, Editor, with John Rowan, *And*; since 1963, Publisher, Writers Forum, London; since 1971, Editor, with Dom Sylvester Houédard and Peter Mayer, *Kroklok*; since 1980, Editor, with Peter Hodgkiss, 1980-83, and since 1983 with Gilbert Adair, *Poetry and Little Press Information.* Performer with abAna group and Australian Dancers, both now inactive, and with Konkrete Canticle, Oral Complex, and Random Access. Founding Member, Vice-President, and Chairman, Association of Little Presses. Recipient: C. Day Lewis Fellowship, Goldsmiths' College, 1973. Address: 89A Petherton Road, London N5 2QT, England.

PUBLICATIONS

Verse

Massacre of the Innocents, with John Rowan. London, Writers Forum, 1963.
Sound Poems: An ABC in Sound. London, Writers Forum, 1965.
Eyearun. London, Writers Forum, 1966.
Chamber Music. Stuttgart, Hansjörg Mayer, 1967.
Kurrirrurriri. London, Writers Forum, 1967.
SO: Six Sound Poems. London, Writers Forum, 1968.
Octo: Visual Poems. London, Writers Forum, 1969.
Whisper Piece. London, Writers Forum, 1969.
Why Shiva Has Ten Arms. London, Writers Forum, 1969.
Whississippi. London, Writers Forum, 1969.
Etcetera: A New Collection of Found and Sound Poems. Cardiff, Vertigo, 1970.
Kwatz. Gillingham, Kent, Arc, 1970.
Sonic Icons. London, Writers Forum, 1970.
Triptych One: Are Your Children Safely in the Sea [*Two: Undum Eidola*; *Six: Variations on a Theme*]. London, Writers Forum, 3 vols., 1970-81.

Kris Kringles Kesmes Korals. Cardiff and London, Vertigo-Writers Forum, 1970.
Three Poems for Voice and Movement. London, Writers Forum, 1971.
Konkrete Canticle. London, Covent Garden Press, 1971.
Beethoven Today. London, Covent Garden Press, 1971.
Spearhead. London, Writers Forum, 1971.
Five Visual Poems. London, Writers Forum, 1971.
The Judith Poem. London, Writers Forum, 1971.
Poster No. 2. Brighton, Judith Walker Posters, 1971.
Songsignals. Cardiff, Second Aeon, 1972.
Tomatomato. Kettering, Northamptonshire, All-In, 1972.
15 Shakespeare-Kaku. London, Writers Forum, 1972.
Trigram. London, Writers Forum, 1972.
E colony. London, Writers Forum, 1973.
Circa 73-74. London, Writers Forum, 1973.
Alphapitasuite. London, Writers Forum, 1973.
In Any Language. London, Writers Forum, 1973.
The Five Vowels. London, Writers Forum, 1974.
Picture Sheet One. London, Good Elf, 1974.
A Winter Poem. London, Writers Forum, 1974.
Five Performance Pieces. London, Writers Forum, 1975.
Yedo Keta Waro. London, Writers Forum, 1975.
Hydrangea. London, Writers Forum, 1975.
Kyoto to Tokyo. London, Good Elf, 1975.
A Round Dance. Stockholm, Writers Forum, 1976.
Poems for the North West Territories. London, Writers Forum, 1976.
Bill Jubobe: selected texts 1942-1975. Toronto, Coach House Press, 1976.
Jade-Sound Poems. London, Writers Forum, 1976.
Furst Fruts Uv 1977, with Lawrence Upton. London, Good Elf—Writers Forum, 1977.
Title: Of the Work. London, Writers Forum, 1977.
Number Structures. Stockholm, Writers Forum, 1977.
Tu To Ratu: Earth Best. London, Writers Forum, 1977.
Cygnet Ring: collected poems 1. London, Tapocketa Press, 1977.
And Avocado. London, Writers Forum, 1977.
Bob Cob's Rag Bag. London, Writers Forum, 1977.
Anan An' Nan. London, Writers Forum, 1977.
Scorch Scores. London, Writers Forum, 1977.
Citycisms. London, Writers Forum, 1977.
Windwound. London, Writers Forum, 1977.
Voice Prints. London, Writers Forum, 1977.
Janus. London, Writers Forum, 1977.
Fingrams. London, Writers Forum, 1977.
Fracted. London, Writers Forum, 1977.
Cuba. London, Writers Forum, 1977.
Visual Poems, with *Towards the City, Fragments I-VII*, by Jeremy Adler. London, Writers Forum, 1977.
Five Ways, with Bill Bissett. Toronto, Writers Forum, 1978.
NiagarA. London, Writers Forum, 1978.
A Movie Book. London, Writers Forum, 1978.
Two Leaf Book. London, Writers Forum, 1978.
Found: Sound. London, Tapocketa Press, 1978.
Principles of Movement. London, Writers Forum, 1978.
Meet Bournemouth. London, Writers Forum, 1978.
Fugitive Poem No. X. London, Writers Forum, 1978.
Game and Set. London, Writers Forum, 1978.
Ginetics. London, Writers Forum, 1978.
A B C/Wan Do Tree: collected poems 2. London, El Uel Uel U, 1978.
Sensations of the Retina. Toronto, Gronk, 1978.
A Peal in Air: collected poems 3. Toronto, AnonbeyondgrOnkontaktewild Presses, 1978.

Grin. London, Writers Forum, 1979.
A Short History of London, with Jeremy Adler. London, Writers Forum, 1979.
The Kollekted Kris Kringle (collected poems 4). London, Anarcho Press, 1979.
Pattern of Performance. London, Writers Forum, 1979.
Notes from the Correspondence, with Jeremy Adler. London, Writers Forum, 1980.
Voicings. London, Writers Forum, 1980.
The Sacred Mushroom. London, Writers Forum, 1980.
Statue of Liberty Suite. Leamington Spa, Other Branch Readings, 1980.
(Soma) Light Song. London, Writers Forum, 1981.
Serial Ten (Portraits). London, Writers Forum, 1981.
Four Letter Poems. London, Writers Forum, 2 vols., 1981.
Fencott and Cobbing in Miami [*Baltimore, New York, Buffalo, Toronto, at Bay, San Diego; Clyde Dunkob in Vancouver*]. Miami, Balitimore, New York, Buffalo, Toronto, San Francisco, San Diego, and Vancouver, El Uel Uel U-Writers Forum, 8 vols., 1982.
In Line. London, Writers Forum, 1982.
Sound of Jade. London, Writers Forum, 1982.
Baker's Dozen. London, Writers Forum, 1982.
Processual: One [*Two, 3, Four, Quintet, Spin-Off, Novation; Processual (Almost) Random Snippets from Works in Progress; A Processual Notation*]. London, Writers Forum, 9 vols., 1982-84.
Lightsong Two. London, Writers Forum, 1983.
Prosexual. Milan, Writers Forum, 1984.

Recordings: *An ABC in Sound*, with Ernst Jandl, Writers Forum, 1965; *Chamber Music*, Swedish Radio-Fylkingen, 1968; *Whississippi*, Swedish Radio-Fylkingen, 1969; *Marvo Moves Natter* and *Spontaneous Appealinair contemprate Apollinaire*, Ou, 1969; *Variations on a Theme of Tan*, Stedelijk Museum, Amsterdam, 1970; *As Easy*, Swedish Radio-Fylkingen, 1971; *Ga(il s)o(ng)*, *Suesequence, Poem for Voice and Mandoline and Poem for Gillian, Hymn to the Sacred Mushroom*, Arts Council, 1971; *Khrajrej*, Opus Magazine, 1973; *E colony*, Typewriter Magazine, 1973; *Hymn to the Sacred Mushroom*, CBS/Sugar, 1975; *Portrait of Robin Crozier*, Fylkingen, 1977; *15 Shakespeare-kaku*, with Laurence Casserley, Cramps, 1978; *Vive Rabelais*, with Henri Chopin, Pipe, 1980; on cassette: *Bob Cobbing and abAna*, Polytechnic of Central London, 1975; *Slowly Slowly the Tongue Unrolls*, Balsam Flex, 1979; *Trigram*, Balsom Flex, 1979; *An ABC in Sound*, Balsam Flex, 1980; *Cobbing at Orpington, and at King's College*, Herne Tapes, 1981; *abAna*, Writers Forum, 1982; *Scrambles*, with Clive Fencott, Writers Forum, 1982; *Various Throats*, with Steve Smith and Keith Musgrove, Underwhich, 1982; *Oral Complex at the October Gallery* [*at L.M.C.*], Writers Forum, 1982-83.

Other

Three Manifestos. London, Writers Forum, 1970.
Concrete Sound Poetry. London, Writers Forum, 1974.
Some Myths of Concrete Poetry, with Peter Mayer. London, Writers Forum, 1976.
Some Statements on Concrete Sound Poetry. London, Writers Forum, 1978.
Concerning Concrete Poetry (omnibus), with Peter Mayer. London, Writers Forum, 1978.

Editor, *Pamphlet One*. London, Writers Forum, 1968.
Editor, *A Typographical Problem*. London, Writers Forum, 1969.

Editor, *Free Form Poetry I* and *II*. London, Writers Forum, 2 vols., 1970-71.
Editor, *Samples of Concrete Poetry*. London, Writers Forum, 1970.
Editor, *British Modernism: Fact or Fiction?* London, Writers Forum, 1971.
Editor, with Peter Mayer, *International Concrete Poetry*. London, Writers Forum, 1971.
Editor, *Group and Woup: A Folio of Concrete Poetry*. Todmorden, Lancashire, Arc, 1974.

*

Manuscript Collections: State University of New York, Buffalo; Ruth and Marvin Sackner Archive of Concrete and Visual Poetry, Miami.

Critical Studies: by Dom Sylvester Houédard, in "Bob Cobbing Issue" of *Extra Verse 17* (London), 1966; Eric Mottram, in *Second Aeon 16-17* (Cardiff), 1973; *Bob Cobbing and "Writers Forum"* edited by Peter Mayer, Sunderland, Ceolfrith Press, 1974.

Bob Cobbing comments:

(1975) My earlier poems "might seem to be conventionally linear; but their urge is towards stabilized diagram, itemised pieces of information in a spatial lay-out which is, in fact, the syntax" (Eric Mottram). In later poems, the dance of letters, half-letters, syllables and words on the page is score for "a ballet of the speech organs" (Victor Shklovsky). In still later poems, the scores are for instrumental as well as vocal poetry; for a ballet of the whole body and not just the voice.

I have been described as "a lettriste, thirty years out of date" (François Dufrêne), and it is true that I value lettriste principles, but not solely. My work derives equally from Joyce, Stein and the Kerouac of "Old Angel Midnight"; from François Dufrêne's post-lettriste cri-rythmes and the vocal micro-particles of Henri Chopin. This leads Dom Sylvester Houédard to note the range of my personal scale (a) from eye to ear, (b) from most to least abstract.

At present I am working on single-voice poems; multi-voiced poems; poems based on words; poems not using words or even letters; poems for electronic treatment on tape; poems for "voice as instrument and instruments as speaking voices" (*Time Out* magazine, concerning the group abAna with which I perform); poems as scores for dance or drama, invitations to act out an event in space, sound and choreography.

"History points to an origin that poetry and music share in the dance that seems to be a part of the make-up of homo sapiens and needs no more justification or conscious control than breathing" (Basil Bunting). This attitude is worth exploring again and means both a going back and a going forward.

(1985) Increasingly, I find myself performing with musicians, jazz, improvising, electronic and contemporary classical, and also with dancers.

*   *   *

Bob Cobbing is one of the major exponents of the international concrete poetry movement in Great Britain. What is immediately impressive about his work, in comparison with that of other poets in the field, is its range: the published texts (free-standing visual poems) are also "scores" for vocal performance as sound poems. Two of Cobbing's titles, *Songsignals* and *Sonic*

Icons, stress the interdependence of the two sides of his work; his division of labour between self-publishing and performance ensures the unity of a creative project of considerable importance.

Cobbing seems to have been a visual artist before he became a poet; his earliest duplicator print of 1942 presages his later work and his interest in the mechanics and accidents of printing. But it was not until 1964, with the completion of *ABC in Sound*, that Cobbing came to maturity with an alliterative sequence of great cham. Perhaps the best known poem from this work is "Tan Tandinanan," a complex series of mantric variations for chanting, which begins:

> tan tandinanan tandinane
> tanan tandina tandinane
> tanare tandita tandinane
> tantarata tandina tandita....

About this time, he began to make "visualisations" of earlier, often conventional, poems, utilising the ink duplicator as a medium: thus the mimetic crawling superimposition of "WORM" (1964) is based upon a 1954 linear original. He used letters as elements in a visual design, but although Cobbing used his artistic skills, his materials remained anchored to language. Accepting these "signs" as if they were hieroglyphs of a forgotten language, they could be freely interpreted as sound. As texts became less lexical, and more like black and white abstracts, suggestive landscapes of sound, so the emphasis was away from phonetics toward the use of "vocal mico-particles": anything from a whisper to a bellow. The lip-prints used for "U" from *The Five Vowels* might be considered as the most direct and primitive of linguistic signs. The semantic element, slenderly present in "WORM," for example, rarely surfaces in later work: interpretation is no longer a matter of literary hermeneutics, but of performance. Rather than a series of works, Cobbing's poetry is a continuing acitivity.

Cobbing performs in various ensembles, sometimes with improvising musicians, but often with other sound poets. As with any form of improvised art, rapport between performers is essential to the fluency and unity of the work. A group can develop techniques and procedures, and possibly even conventions of translating marks on the page into sound, but the surprises of spontaneous improvisation are still the joys of such work. However much the sound poetry approaches contemporary music, the emphasis is always more linguistic than musical, even in works where the voice is modified by electronics or accompanied by musical instruments. In one of the "Three Variations on a Theme of *Tan*" paralinguistic, but non-musical, sounds, such as grunting, panting, and coughing, take over the rhythm of the poem. Whenever professional singers perform the piece they tend to regulate the pitch, harmony, articulation, and timbre according to musical criteria, whereas Cobbing is most interested in the full potentialities of the human voice.

This exploratory work, extending towards other art-forms, can be usefully considered as one of the enduring (and most pleasurable) forms of intermedia and performance-art from the 1960's and 1970's. Yet Cobbing has frequently asserted that his work belongs to a centuries-long tradition of phonological and graphological invention *within* the mainstream of literature. His work can therefore be seen as the result of experiments in foregrounding one or more of the conventional units of poetic structure (such as rhyme and alliteration, or line and lay-out), allied to a concentration upon the materiality of language as sound or sign. While he makes sophisticated use of the technologies of printing and electronics, Cobbing believes his work to be essentially primitive, a direct mode of communication verging, at times, on the pre-linguistic. He insists that poetry belongs, not

just to the vocal chords, but to the whole body and, in works such as *Three Poems for Voice and Movement*, he has scored for dancing as well. In work of the late 1970's and early 1980's, particularly in a series of variations entitles *Processual*, he has used non-linguistic marks (sometimes natural forms) as though they were significant linguistic signs, as elements in his texts. While no major theoretical shift has occurred, it is almost as if the world itself as a visual configuration or "impression" is being given a voice.

—Robert Sheppard

COGSWELL, Fred(erick William). Canadian. Born in East Centreville, New Brunswick, 8 November 1917. Educated at the University of New Brunswick, Fredericton (Carman Medal, 1946, 1947), B.A. 1949, M.A. 1950; University of Edinburgh, Ph.D. 1952. Served in the Canadian Army, 1940-45. Married Margaret Hynes in 1944; two daughters. Assistant Professor, 1952-57, Associate Professor, 1957-61, and Professor of English, 1961-83, now Emeritus, University of New Brunswick. Editor, *Fiddlehead* magazine, 1952-66, Fiddlehead Poetry Books, 1960-82, and *Humanities Association Bulletin*, 1967-72, all in Fredericton. Recipient: Nuffield Fellowship, 1959; Canada Council Fellowship, 1966; Canadian-Scottish Writing Fellowship, 1983. LL.D.: St. Francis University, Antigonish, Nova Scotia, 1983. Officer, Order of Canada, 1981. Address: 769 Reid Street, Fredericton, New Brunswick E3B 3V8, Canada.

PUBLICATIONS

Verse

The Stunted Strong. Fredericton, New Brunswick, Fiddlehead, 1954.
The Haloed Tree. Toronto, Ryerson Press, 1956.
Descent from Eden. Toronto, Ryerson Press, 1959.
Lost Dimension. London, Outposts, 1960.
Five New Brunswick Poets, with others, edited by Cogswell. Fredericton, New Brunswick, Fiddlehead, 1962.
Star-People. Fredericton, New Brunswick, Fiddlehead, 1968.
Immortal Plowman. Fredericton, New Brunswick, Fiddlehead, 1969.
In Praise of Chastity. Fredericton, New Brunswick, Chapbooks, 1970.
The Chains of Liliput. Fredericton, New Brunswick, Fiddlehead, 1971.
The House Without a Door. Fredericton, New Brunswick, Fiddlehead, 1973.
Light Bird of Life: Selected Poems. Fredericton, New Brunswick, Fiddlehead, 1974.
Against Perspective. Fredericton, New Brunswick, Fiddlehead, 1977.
Scroll. Wolfville, Nova Scotia, Wombat Press, 1980.
A Long Apprenticeship: Collected Poems. Fredericton, New Brunswick, Fiddlehead, 1980.
Our Stubborn Strength. Toronto, League of Canadian Poets, 1980.
Selected Poems. Montreal, Guernica, 1983.
Pearls. Charlottetown, Prince Edward Island, Ragweed Press, 1983.

Other

Editor, *A Canadian Anthology*. Fredericton, New Brunswick, Fiddlehead, 1960.
Editor, *Five New Brunswick Poets*. Fredericton, New Brunswick, Fiddlehead, 1962.
Editor, with Robert Tweedie and S.W. MacNutt, and contributor, *The Arts in New Brunswick*. Fredericton, University of New Brunswick, 1966.
Editor, with Thelma Reid Lower, *The Enchanted Land: Canadian Poetry for Young Readers*. Toronto, Gage, 1967.
Editor, *The Home Place*, by Marion McLellan. Charlottetown, Prince Edward Island, 1973 Centennial Commission, 1973.
Editor and Translator, *The Poetry of Modern Quebec*. Montreal, Harvest, 1975.
Editor, with Kay Smith and Constance Soulikias, *Mysterious Special Sauce*. Ottawa, Canadian Council of Teachers of English, 1982.
Editor and Translator, *The Complete Poems of Emile Nelligan*. Montreal, Harvest, 1983.
Editor, *The Atlantic Anthology: Poems and Prose, Past and Present*. Charlottetown, Prince Edward Island, Ragweed Press, 1983.

Translator, *The Testament of Cresseid*, by Robert Henryson. Toronto, Ryerson Press, 1957.
Translator, *One Hundred* [and *A Second Hundred*] *Poems of Modern Quebec*. Fredericton, New Brunswick, Fiddlehead, 1970-71.
Translator, *Confrontation*, by G. Lapointe. Fredericton, New Brunswick, Fiddlehead, 1973.

*

Fred Cogswell comments:
My poetry is a response, as a rule, to direct personal experience. It finds its own form instinctively out of the various forms which I have encountered either traditional or modern. It is marked by directness, economy, sincerity, and the avoidance of long words.

*   *   *

"It is marked by directness, economy, sincerity, and avoidance of long words." This is not a critic dissecting Fred Cogswell's verse, but the poet himself discussing his own work. The statement displays all the characteristic self-deprecation of the poet. For many years Cogswell has tirelessly served the interests of fellow writers, as a teacher of English, as the publisher of *The Fiddlehead*, the best magazine of poetry in the Maritimes, and as the publisher of Fiddlehead Poetry Books, a seemingly endless stream of chapbooks devoted in the main to the work of new young poets.

All along Cogswell has been publishing a rivulet, if not a stream, of booklets of brief poems. His first publication, *The Stunted Strong*, is a series of arresting vignettes dramatizing the negative aspects of life in the small communitites that make up Atlantic Canada; the collection had a decided influence on the early work of Alden Nowlan and was widely read across the country. The early phase of biographical and autobiographical poems ended in the publication of *Descent from Eden*, a kind of selected poems. Since then the poems have been elliptical and epigrammatic as well as lyric, as two more recent publications, *The Chains of Liliput* and *The House Without a Door*, demonstrate.

"It was the chains of Liliput/Taught Gulliver he was a giant," Cogswell explains. The poet cannot resist a too-easy parody called "Spiv's Innisfree" which begins: "I will arise and go to a pub in Piccadilly/And six quick ones will I down there, of Scotch and soda made." His strengths are shown in this verse from "Unhappy Clown":

> I smile and I sing,
> And I laugh like a king
> For the same reason as you,
> To be part of the show.

One is always aware, reading a Cogswell poem, that the poet is aware of writing it. Sometimes the poet is able to make this work to his—and the reader's—advantage, as it does in this sincere poem "In Defence of Rosaries":

> and God whose stillness
> speaks as loud as noise
> will understand
> my private prayer

—John Robert Colombo

COHEN, Leonard (Norman). Canadian. Born in Montreal, Quebec, 21 September 1934. Educated at McGill University, Montreal, B.A. 1955; Columbia University, New York. Composer and singer: has given concerts in Canada, the United States, and Europe. Artist-in-Residence, University of Alberta, Edmonton, 1975-76. Recipient: McGill University Literary Award, 1956; Canada Council Award, 1960; Quebec Literary Award, 1964. D.L.: Dalhousie University, Halifax, Nova Scotia, 1971. Lives in Montreal and Greece. Address: c/o McClelland and Stewart Ltd., 25 Hollinger Road, Toronto, Ontario M4B 3G2, Canada.

PUBLICATIONS

Verse

Let Us Compare Mythologies. Montreal, Contact Press, 1956.
The Spice-Box of Earth. Toronto, McClelland and Stewart, 1961; New York, Viking Press, 1965; London, Cape, 1971.
Flowers for Hitler. Toronto, McClelland and Stewart, 1964; London, Cape, 1973.
Parasites of Heaven. Toronto, McClelland and Stewart, 1966.
Selected Poems 1956-1968. New York, Viking Press, 1968; London, Cape, 1969.
Leonard Cohen's Song Book. New York, Collier, 1969.
Five Modern Canadian Poets, with others, edited by Eli Mandel. Toronto, Holt Rinehart, 1970.
The Energy of Slaves. London, Cape, 1972; New York, Viking Press, 1973.
Two Views. Toronto, Madison Gallery, 1980.
Book of Mercy. London, Cape, and New York, Villard, 1984.

Recordings: *The Songs of Leonard Cohen*, Columbia, 1968; *Songs from a Room*, Columbia, 1969; *Songs of Love and Hate*, Columbia, 1971; *Live Songs*, Columbia, 1973; *New Skin for the Old Ceremony*, Columbia, 1974; *The Best of Leonard Cohen*,

Columbia, 1975; *Death of a Lady's Man*, Warner Brothers, 1977; *Recent Songs*, CBS, 1979.

Plays

The New Step (produced Ottawa and London, 1972). Included in *Flowers for Hitler*, 1964; in *Selected Poems*, 1968.
Sisters of Mercy: A Journey into the Words and Music of Leonard Cohen (produced Niagara-on-the-Lake, Ontario, and New York, 1973).
A Man Was Killed, with Irving Layton, in *Canadian Theatre Review* (Downsview, Ontario), Spring 1977.

Novels

The Favorite Game.   New York, Viking Press, and London, Secker and Warburg, 1963.
Beautiful Losers.   Toronto, McClelland and Stewart, and New York, Viking Press, 1966; London, Cape, 1970.

Other

Death of a Lady's Man.   Toronto, McClelland and Stewart, 1978; London, Deutsch, and New York, Viking Press, 1979.

*

Bibliography: by Bruce Whiteman, in *The Annotated Bibliography of Canada's Major Authors 2*, edited by Robert Lecker and Jack David, Downsview, Ontario, ECW Press, 1980.

Manuscript Collection: University of Toronto.

Critical Studies: *Leonard Cohen* by Michael Ondaatje, Toronto, McClelland and Stewart, 1970; *The Immoral Moralists: Hugh MacLennan and Leonard Cohen* by Patricia Morley, Toronto, Clarke Irwin, 1972; *Leonard Cohen: The Artist and His Critics* edited by Michael Gnarowski, Toronto, McGraw Hill Ryerson, 1976; *Leonard Cohen* by Stephen Scobie, Vancouver, Douglas and McIntyre, 1978.

*   *   *

The figures of Leonard Cohen's poems rise like figures in Chagall, transformed from the ordinary, surprised into a world of visionary experience. Out of the junk of the everyday—"the garbage and the flowers"—the magical world of the imaginative is created. There is a strong sense in which his poetry is a prodigious search of experience for the exit from the ordinary. But it is not always violently so. Some of the earlier lyrics—"Go by Brooks," for instance—have a simple lyricism that is also intense. Occasionally, it slopes off into a wry humour that is characteristic of him; more often its apparent Emily Dickinson simplicities conceal a toughness and a danger for which only the ballad form is adequate. And it is in the ballad that his greatest strength lies. The concentration of the imagery and the force of the rhyme give a telling intensity to the surrealist experiences of his imagination—an intensity that becomes at times almost gnomic:

> History is a needle
> for putting men asleep
> anointed with the poison
> of all they want to keep.

Certain themes continue to pre-occupy Cohen as certain images haunt his imagination. His search is for the sensual heaven of "The Sisters of Mercy," not the skeletal world of the ideal, the astringent dead world of "I Have Not Lingered in European Monasteries." Indeed, his religion is the rejection of the suffering ascetic—"I disdain God's suffering. / Men command sufficient pain"—for a priapic world in which the liturgical celebrations are the extreme of physical—a "constant love / and passion without flesh"—that is not a bloodless mysticism but the apogee of the physical, almost like "high." But even in the physical world his fear of entrapment by the deadly females of such poems as "The Unicorn Tapestries" or "I Long to Hold Some Lady" is strong. They become in his poetic fabric the creatures—associated with doctors, rabbis, and priests—of the liturgy of death. "The Story of Isaac" lurks behind the sacrificial metaphors to which he recurs. What is most telling in this balladic pre-occupation with the undefined horror is Cohen's recognition of it not as external to himself, but part of his own psyche. Dachau is everyday Montreal; the amatory is also the murderous "tasting blood on your tongue / does not shock me." So the poetry (of *Flowers for Hitler* especially) is exculpatory, and the desire to escape from the "ape with angel glands" the more intense.

In his later poetry there is a sense of imminence. The partisan's retreat is more embattled even than "the small oasis where we lie" of his earlier love poems. His concern with freedom, his feeling of the "incomparable sense of loss" to which he refers in "Queen Victoria and Me," is more than nostalgia for a lost land of freedom and the spirit. It is a matter of skirmishes in the hills "on the side of the ghost and the king," a matter of escaping from the horrific city whose terrors are also the terrors of "the armies marching still" towards the war that must surely come.

A mode like Ferlinghetti's saves such poems as "The killers that run other countries" from sentimentalism. And Cohen's "Song for My Assassin" (another ballad) has the same wryness as his love songs—a wryness that recognizes that the pretty fictions (even his women) are in large measure self-amusements. Occasionally he slips from his customary Horatian tone to a heavy-handed Juvenalian, and when feeling is too close to be contained the poem can be very flat indeed. But even in the ostensible absence of the muse Cohen can write a fine poem, of which "The poems don't love us anymore" (in *The Energy of Slaves*) is a good example.

Cohen's voice is most sympathetic and most telling, not in his escapes from the horror and the junk into the fashionable "pot" world of despair, but in his celebrations of the poet's capacity not only to hold out against the faceless butchers but to make acclaim of "orange peels, / cans, discarded guts." The gaiety of vision is also his *seigneur*, and the surrealism, that is so much a part of the Canadian sensibility provides him with a new way of seeing the ordinary transformed: "One of the lizards / was blowing bubbles / as it did pushups on the carpet." The conclusion to that poem is "I believe the mystics are right / when they say we are all One." The Prophets and *The Song of Songs* inform this voice. Its celebration is a beauty, entirely human, that prevails over "the clubfoot crowds." Its affirmation is that not only all poets but "all men will be sailors."

—D. D. C. Chambers

COLE, Barry.   British.   Born in Woking, Surrey, 13 November 1936. Served in the Royal Air Force for two years. Married Rita

Linihan in 1958; three daughters. Worked in the Central Office of Information, London, 1965-70. Northern Arts Fellow in Literature, universities of Newcastle upon Tyne and Durham, 1970-72. Address: 68 Myddelton Square, London EC1R 1XP, England.

PUBLICATIONS

Verse

Blood Ties. London, Turret, 1967.
Ulysses in the Town of Coloured Glass. London, Turret, 1968.
Moonsearch. London, Methuen, 1968.
The Visitors. London, Methuen, 1970.
Vanessa in the City. London, Trigram Press, 1971.
Pathetic Fallacies. London, Eyre Methuen, 1973.
The Rehousing of Scaffardi. Richmond, Surrey, Keepsake Press, 1976.
Dedications. Nottingham, Byron Press, 1977.

Novels

A Run Across the Island. London, Methuen, 1968.
Joseph Winter's Patronage. London, Methuen, 1969.
The Search for Rita. London, Methuen, 1970.
The Giver. London, Methuen, 1971.
Doctor Fielder's Common Sense. London, Methuen, 1972.

*

Barry Cole comments:

The subjects of my poems are myself, love, my wife; the world I know I see and the world I think I see. My verse forms are neither traditional nor *avant garde*, but of my own time at any given moment. Sometimes they rhyme, sometimes they don't, but I try for precision, brevity and clarity. The poems aim at wit and intelligence, though they may hit none or any of these. Their sources are my own felt and thought experiences and those of sympathetic antecedents and contemporaries. Influences are few and unrecognizable.

*   *   *

Barry Cole is both a poet and a novelist. The novels have an instantly recognisable atmosphere—one of strangeness rooted in the ordinary, as if a different order, with totally different rules, subsumed the mundane world we see, and manifested itself unexpectedly at moments of crisis. The atmosphere in Cole's most interesting poems is exactly the same as that which we discover in the novels—they are, in fact, capsule versions of the, stories he tells in prose. The thing that counts is the total image; not the individual line. Quoted in fragments, the poetry often seems flat. It is only when we read the poem through as a narrative that we see what the poet's purpose is.

—Edward Lucie-Smith

COLOMBO, John Robert. Canadian. Born in Kitchener, Ontario, 24 March 1936. Educated at Waterloo College, Ontario, 1956-57; University College, University of Toronto, 1959-60, B.A. (honours) 1959. Married Ruth Brown in 1959; one daughter

and two sons. Editorial Assistant, University of Toronto Press, 1957-60; Assistant Editor, Ryerson Press, 1960-63; Senior Advisory Editor, McClelland and Stewart, Toronto, 1964-70. Former Editor, *The Montrealer*, *Exchange*, and *Tamarack Review*, Toronto; occasional instructor, York University, Toronto, 1963-66; Writer-in-Residence, Mohawk College, Hamilton, Ontario, 1978; Host, *Colombo's Quotes* television series, 1978. Member, Canada Council Arts Advisory Panel, 1968-70. Recipient: Canada Council grant, 1967, 1971; Centennial Medal, 1967. Address: 42 Dell Park Avenue, Toronto, Ontario M6B 2T6, Canada.

PUBLICATIONS

Verse

Fragments. Privately printed, 1957.
Variations. Kitchener, Ontario, Hawkshead Press, 1958.
This Citadel in Time. Kitchener, Ontario, Hawkshead Press, 1958.
This Studied Self. Kitchener, Ontario, Hawkshead Press, 1958.
In the Streets (as Ruta Ginsberg). Toronto, Hawkshead Press, 1959 (?).
Poems and Other Poems. Toronto, Hawkshead Press, 1959.
Two Poems. Toronto, Hawkshead Press, 1959.
This Is the Work Entitled Canada. Toronto, Purple Partridge Press, 1959.
Fire Escape, Fire Esc, Fire. Toronto, Hawkshead Press, 1959.
The Impression of Beauty. Toronto, Hawkshead Press, 1959.
Poems to Be Sold for Bread. Toronto, Hawkshead Press, 1959.
Lines for the Last Day. Toronto, Hawkshead Press, 1960.
The Mackenzie Poems. Toronto, Swan, 1965.
The Great Wall of China: An Entertainment. Montreal, Delta Canada, 1966.
Abracadabra. Toronto, McClelland and Stewart, 1967.
Miraculous Montages. Toronto, Heine, 1967.
John Toronto: New Poems by Dr. Strachan, Found by John Robert Colombo. Ottawa, Oberon Press, 1969.
Neo Poems. Vancouver, Sono Nis Press, 1970.
The Great San Francisco Earthquake and Fire. Fredericton, New Brunswick, Fiddlehead, 1971.
Praise Poems and Leonardo's Lists. Toronto, Weed/Flower Press, 1972.
Translations from the English. Toronto, Peter Martin, 1974.
The Sad Truths. Toronto, Peter Martin, 1974.
The Great Collage. Privately printed, 1974.
Proverbial Play. Toronto, Missing Link Press, 1975.
Mostly Monsters. Toronto, Hounslow Press, 1977.
Variable Cloudiness. Toronto, Hounslow Press, 1977.
Private Parts. Toronto, Hounslow Press, 1978.
The Great Cities of Antiquity. Toronto, Hounslow Press, 1979.
Recent Poems. Toronto, League of Canadian Poets, 1980.
Selected Poems. Windsor, Ontario, Black Moss Press, 1982.
Selected Translations. Windsor, Ontario, Black Moss Press, 1982.

Other

CDN SF & F: A Bibliography of Canadian Science Fiction and Fantasy. Toronto, Hounslow Press, 1979.
Blackwood's Books: A Bibliography Devoted to Algernon Blackwood. Toronto, Hounslow Press, 1981.
Canadian Literary Landmarks. Toronto, Hounslow Press, 1984.

Great Moments in Canadian History. Toronto, Hounslow Press, 1984.

Editor, *Rubato: New Poems by Young Canadian Poets.* Toronto, Purple Partridge Press, 1958.

Editor, *The Varsity Chapbook.* Toronto, Ryerson Press, 1959.

Editor, with Jacques Godbout, *Poésie 64 / Poetry 64.* Toronto and Montreal, Ryerson Press-Editions du Jour, 1963.

Editor, with Raymond Souster, *Shapes and Sounds: Poems of W.W.E. Ross.* Toronto, Longman, 1968.

Editor, *How Do I Love Thee: Sixty Poems of Canada (and Quebec)....* Edmonton, Hurtig, 1970.

Editor, *New Direction in Canadian Poetry.* Toronto, Holt Rinehart, 1970.

Editor, *Rhymes and Reasons: Nine Canadian Poets Discuss Their Work.* Toronto, Holt Rinehart, 1971.

Editor, *An Alphabet of Annotations.* Montreal, Gheerbrant, 1972.

Editor, *Colombo's Canadian Quotations.* Edmonton, Hurtig, 1974; *Concise Canadian Quotations,* 1976.

Editor, *Colombo's Little Book of Canadian Proverbs, Graffiti, Limericks, and Other Vital Matters.* Edmonton, Hurtig, 1975.

Editor, *Colombo's Canadian References.* Toronto, Oxford University Press, 1976; London and New York, Oxford University Press, 1977.

Editor and Translator, with Nikola Roussanoff, *The Balkan Range: A Bulgarian Reader.* Toronto, Hounslow Press, 1976.

Editor, *East and West: Selected Poems,* by George Faludy.- Toronto, Hounslow Press, 1978.

Editor, *The Poets of Canada.* Edmonton, Hurtig, 1978.

Editor, *Colombo's Book of Canada.* Edmonton, Hurtig, 1978.

Editor, *Colombo's Names and Nicknames.* Toronto, NC Press, 1978.

Editor, *Colombo's Book of Marvels.* Toronto, NC Press, 1979.

Editor, *Other Canadas: An Anthology of Science Fiction and Fantasy.* Toronto, McGraw Hill Ryerson, 1979.

Editor, *Dark Times,* by Waclaw Iwaniuk, translated by Jagna Boraks. Toronto, Hounslow Press, 1979.

Editor, *Colombo's Hollywood.* Toronto, Collins, 1979; as *Wit and Wisdom of the Moviemakers,* London, Hamlyn, 1979; as *Popcorn in Paradise,* New York, Holt Rinehart, 1980.

Editor, *The Canada Colouring Book.* Toronto, Hounslow Press, 1980.

Editor, *222 Canadian Jokes.* Cobalt, Ontario, Highway Book Shop, 1981.

Editor, *Far from You: Poems,* by Pavel Javor, translated by Rom Banerjee. Toronto, Hounslow Press, 1981.

Editor, *Friendly Aliens.* Toronto, Hounslow Press, 1981.

Editor, *Poems of the Inuit.* Ottawa, Oberon Press, 1981.

Editor, with Michael Richardson, *Not to Be Taken at Night: Classic Canadian Tales of Mystery and the Supernatural.* Toronto, Lester and Orpen Dennys, 1981.

Editor, *Years of Light: A Celebration of Leslie A. Croutch.* Toronto, Hounslow Press, 1982.

Editor, *Colombo's Last Words.* Cobalt, Ontario, Highway Book Shop, 1982.

Editor, *Colombo's Laws.* Cobalt, Ontario, Highway Book Shop, 1982.

Editor, *Colombo's Canadiana Quiz Book.* Saskatoon, Saskachewan, Western Producer, 1983.

Editor, *Windigo: An Anthology of Fact and Fantastic Fiction.* Saskatoon, Saskatchewan, Western Producer, and Lincoln, University of Nebraska Press, 1983.

Editor, *Colombo's 101 Canadian Places.* Toronto, Hounslow Press, 1983.

Editor, *René Lévesque Buys Canada Savings Bonds and Other Great Canadian Graffiti.* Edmonton, Hurtig, 1983.

Editor, *Songs of the Indians.* Ottawa, Oberon Press, 2 vols., 1983.

Editor, *The Toronto Puzzle Book.* Toronto, McClelland and Stewart, 1984.

Translator, with Robert Zend, *From Zero to One,* by Zend. Vancouver, Sono Nis Press, 1973.

Translator, with Nikola Roussanoff, *Under the Eaves of a Forgotten Village: Sixty Poems from Contemporary Bulgaria.* Toronto, Hounslow Press, 1975.

Translator, with Nikola Roussanoff, *The Left-Handed One,* by Lyubomir Levchev. Toronto, Hounslow Press, 1977.

Translator, with Nikola Roussanoff, *Remember Me Well,* by Andrei Germanov. Toronto, Hounslow Press, 1978.

Translator, with Nikola Roussanoff, *Depths,* by Dora Gabe. Toronto, Hounslow Press, 1978.

Translator, with Waclaw Iwaniuk, *Such Times: Selected Poems,* by Ewa Lipska. Toronto, Hounslow Press, 1981.

Translator, with Robert Zend, *Beyond Labels,* by Zend. Toronto, Hounslow Press, 1982.

Translator, with Petronela Negosanu, *Symmetries,* by Marin Sorescu. Toronto, Hounslow Press, 1982.

Translator, with George Faludy, *Learn This Poem of Mine by Heart,* by Faludy. Toronto, Hounslow Press, 1983.

*

Manuscript Collection: Mills Memorial Library, McMaster University, Hamilton, Ontario.

Critical Studies: by Northrop Frye, in *University of Toronto Review,* July 1959; Al Purdy, in *Toronto Globe and Mail,* 4 June 1966; George Woodcock, in *Canadian Literature* (Vancouver), Summer 1966; Louis Dudek, in *Montreal Gazette,* 22 October 1966; Miriam Waddington, in *Toronto Globe and Mail,* 18 March 1967; Hugh MacCallum, in *University of Toronto Review,* July 1967 and July 1968.

*   *   *

The appearance of John Robert Colombo's *Abracadabra* in 1967 marked a welcome return by him to a poetry whose resonances were familiar and whose values were less stridently asserted—closer to the central human experience. To use his own lines: "What is immensely important here is life itself: man/feeding on the world." It is that affirmation that one finds celebrated in the *Abracadabra* volume—the more than cerebral apprehension of terror in "There Is No Way Out," for instance.

Not all his celebrations are as fortunate, however. "The hot wells of your flowing kidneys" must surely be classed among the great lines of "unredeemed poetry." And the preciosity incumbent upon a sustained attention to works of art bespeaks, and is exacerbated by, the leaden "relevances" of a naive and isolated provincialism often present in his work.

This feeling of the provincially claustrophobic is present in *The Mackenzie Poems.* There is a sense in which these pieces of "found poetry" or "redeemed prose" are made to assume the mantle of a Canadian Gettysburg, and they (even as prose) will not stand the strain. If there is something sympathetic and attractive in the firebrand character of Mackenzie's life it is not an attractiveness that his prose conveys. Ultimately the factiousness becomes tedious, and, worse, the limitations of Mackenzie's imagination ("System is everything") work at variance to the larger mundo of poetry.

Coleridge said that the power of poetry "reveals itself in the balance or reconciliation of opposite or discordant qualities;...a more than usual state of emotion, with more than usual order." The emotion in these poems, unfortunately, is scarcely ever above the pedestrian. This is not the politically visionary stuff of Blake or Milton, or even Pope. At its best it is Felix Holt. And when the order is "more than usual" it is so because the prose itself has a rhetorical (e.g. Ciceronian) structure that encourages the transformation into poetry.

No such structure underlies the private and public letters of Bishop Strachan—the raw material of Colombo's next volume *New Poems by Dr. Strachan*. Strachan and Mackenzie were adversaries in the early polity of Upper Canada—Strachan as resolutely Church of England establishment as Mackenzie was non-conformist radical. *New Poems* was announced as a book that "tells the other half of the story," but one wonders, remembering Arnold's observations on the turgid flatulence of Victorian Toronto society, whether "the story" was worth the candle—let alone two volumes of poetry.

Something of the deadness of Strachan's position (let alone the issues) is conveyed in the "poem" "Universal Corruption": "I am still the same Tory/that you knew me to be/forty years ago." This is a man who can refer to the magnificent wilderness, still unspoiled, as "a dismal wood." Even Mr. Casaubon in all his dullness was not arrayed so drably as this. Minds as lapidary as Strachan's are not creative of great prose, let alone poetry. Even in his private reflections we have the sense of a man dead at the centre—the complacent (and complaisant) voice of orotund establishment, feeding its piety with goose dinners and Addisonian maxims, assured that the business of religion is in dispensing the unquestionable intellectual and moral superiority of the British nation.

The reader has a similar sense of weighty indigestion in *The Great Wall of China* but there the weariness comes from a weight of accumulated statistic and observation, lightened only occasionally by such magical poems as "The Legendary Mound of Ch'in." For there the felicities are of the realm of the lyrical imagination as the pleasures of "Arabesque" (another poem in the sequence, taken from Maugham) are the rhetorical enchantments of a high order of descriptive prose.

In *Neo Poems* again one has the sense of a notebook full of possible poems, never quite realised. Many if not most are collections of para-Haiku, at their best finely descriptive: "the sea drifts into France" or "The mind has/a tongue in both its cheeks." But Colombo is not alone among Canadian poets in allowing the gnomic to become merely the cute. "I want to scribble passionate marginalia all through the Book of Life" is too close to Rod McKuen for comfort of mind.

Part of Colombo's problem here is a distinctively Canadian one—a rather adolescent stridency that tends to a chauvinism that is both personal and national. (Often they tend to become confused.) Quoting with approval Symons's "it is not natural to be what is called 'natural' any longer," the poet assumes the role of exile-in-one's-own-country and exalts the sententious and truistic to the level of the profound. We are offered "In all literature, the traditional must expose the actual" as if that statement (piece of poetry?) meant something.

This is a pity, for Colombo is a good poet and a fine wit—a poet who has yet to find a medium appropriate to his sensibility. For ultimately it is not his "found poetry" but his "made poetry" that has the greater stature. And it is in this mode that (as he says of Wyeth) "a detail becomes a dimension" because the imaginative life that sustains it is not fortuitous or ideologically strident but integral and creative, and affirmative of life at its highest pitch.

—D.D.C. Chambers

COMFORT, Alex(ander). British. Born in London, 10 February 1920. Educated at Highgate School, London, 1932-36; Trinity College, Cambridge (Styring Scholar; Senior Scholar), 1938-40, M.B., B.Ch. 1944, M.A. 1945; London Hospital (Scholar), M.R.C.S. and L.R.C.P., 1944, D.C.H. 1945, Ph.D. (biochemistry) 1949, D.Sc. (gerontology) 1963. Married 1) Ruth Muriel Harris in 1943 (marriage dissolved, 1973), one son; 2) Jane Tristram Henderson in 1973. House Physician, London Hospital, 1944; Resident Medical Officer, Royal Waterloo Hospital, London, 1944-45; Lecturer in Physiology, 1945-51; Honorary Research Associate, Department of Zoology, 1951-73, and Director of Research on the Biology of Ageing, 1966-73, University College, London; Professor of Pathology, University of California School of Medicine, Irvine, 1976-78. Since 1974, Lecturer in Psychiatry, Stanford University, California; since 1975, Senior Fellow, Institute for Higher Studies, Santa Barbara, California; since 1978, Consultant Psychiatrist, Brentwood Hospital, Los Angeles; since 1980, Adjunct Professor, Neuropsychiatric Institute, University of California, Los Angeles. Editor, with Peter Wells, Poetry Folios, Barnet, Hertfordshire, 1942-46. President, British Society for Research on Ageing, 1967. Recipient: Nuffield Research Fellowship, 1952; Ciba Foundation Prize, 1958; Borestone Mountain Poetry award, 1962; Karger Memorial Prize in Gerontology, 1969. Address: 683 Oak Grove Drive, Santa Barbara, California 93108, U.S.A.

PUBLICATIONS

Verse

France and Other Poems. London, Favil Press, 1941.
Three New Poets, with Roy McFadden and Ian Serraillier. Billericay, Essex, Grey Walls Press, 1942.
A Wreath for the Living. London, Routledge, 1942.
Elegies. London, Routledge, 1944.
The Song of Lazarus. Barnet, Hertfordshire, Poetry Folios, and New York, Viking Press, 1945.
The Signal to Engage. London, Routledge, 1947.
And All But He Departed. London, Routledge, 1951.
Haste to the Wedding. London, Eyre and Spottiswoode, 1962; Chester Springs, Pennsylvania, Dufour, 1964.
All But a Rib: Poems Chiefly of Women. London, Mitchell Beazley, 1973; as *Coming Together: Poems Chiefly about Women,* New York, Crown, 1975.
Poems for Jane. London, Mitchell Beazley, and New York, Crown, 1979.

Plays

Into Egypt: A Miracle Play. Billericay, Essex, Grey Walls Press, 1942.
Cities of the Plain: A Democratic Melodrama. London, Grey Walls Press, 1943.

Television Play: *The Great Agrippa,* 1968.

Novels

The Silver River, Being the Diary of a Schoolboy in the South Atlantic, 1936.   London, Chapman and Hall, 1938.
No Such Liberty.   London, Chapman and Hall, 1941.
The Almond Tree: A Legend.   London, Chapman and Hall, 1942.
The Power House.   London, Routledge, 1944; New York, Viking Press, 1945.
On This Side Nothing.   London, Routledge, and New York, Viking Press, 1949.
A Giant's Strength.   London, Routledge, 1952.
Come Out to Play.   London, Eyre and Spottiswoode, 1961; New York, Crown, 1975.
Tetrarch.   Boulder, Colorado, Shambhala, 1980; London, Wildwood House, 1981.

Short Stories

Letters from an Outpost.   London, Routledge, 1947.

Other

Peace and Disobedience.   London, Peace News, 1946.
Art and Social Responsibility: Lectures on the Ideology of Romanticism.   London, Falcon Press, 1946.
The Novel and Our Time.   Letchworth, Hertfordshire, Phoenix House, and Denver, Swallow, 1948.
Barbarism and Sexual Freedom: Six Lectures on the Sociology of Sex from the Standpoint of Anarchism.   London, Freedom Press, 1948.
First-Year Physiological Techniques.   London, Staples Press, 1948.
The Pattern of the Future.   London, Routledge, and New York, Macmillan, 1949.
The Right Thing to Do, Together with the Wrong Thing to Do.   London, Peace News, 1949.
Authority and Delinquency in the Modern State: A Criminological Approach to the Problem of Power.   London, Routledge, 1950; revised edition, as *Authority and Delinquency*, London, Sphere, 1970.
Sexual Behaviour in Society.   London, Duckworth, and New York, Viking Press, 1950; revised edition, as *Sex in Society*, Duckworth, 1963; New York, Citadel Press, 1966.
Delinquency (lecture).   London, Freedom Press, 1951.
Social Responsibility in Science and Art.   London, Peace News, 1952.
The Biology of Senescence.   London, Routledge, and New York, Rinehart, 1956; revised edition, as *Ageing: The Biology of Senescence*, 1964; revised edition, as *The Biology of Senescence*, Edinburgh, Churchill Livingston, and New York, Elsevier, 1979.
Darwin and the Naked Lady: Discursive Essays on Biology and Art.   London, Routledge, 1961; New York, Braziller, 1962.
The Process of Ageing.   New York, New American Library, 1964; London, Weidenfeld and Nicolson, 1965.
The Nature of Human Nature.   New York, Harper, 1965; as *Nature and Human Nature*, London, Weidenfeld and Nicolson, 1966.
The Anxiety Makers: Some Curious Preoccupations of the Medical Profession.   London, Nelson, 1967.
What Rough Beast? and What Is a Doctor? (lectures).   Vancouver, Pendejo Press, 1971.
The Joy of Sex: A Gourmet's Guide to Love Making.   New York, Crown, 1972; London, Quartet, 1973.
More Joy: A Sequel to "The Joy of Sex."   London, Mitchell Beazley, 1973; New York, Crown, 1974.
A Good Age.   New York, Crown, 1976; London, Mitchell Beazley, 1977.
The Facts of Love: Living, Loving, and Growing Up (juvenile), with Jane Comfort.   New York, Crown, 1979; London, Mitchell Beazley, 1980.
I and That: Notes on the Biology of Religion.   London, Mitchell Beazley, and New York, Crown, 1979.
The Education of a Doctor.   New York, Van Nostrand Reinhold, 1980.
What Is a Doctor? Essays on Medicine and Human Natural History.   Philadelphia, Stickley, 1980.
Practice of Geriatric Psychiatry.   New York, Elsevier, 1980.

Editor, with Robert Greacen, *Lyra: An Anthology of New Lyric.* Billericay, Essex, Grey Walls Press, 1942.
Editor, with John Bayliss, *New Road 1943* and *1944: New Directions in European Art and Letters.*   London, Grey Walls Press, 2 vols., 1943-44.
Editor, *History of Erotic Art, I.*   London, Weidenfeld and Nicolson, and New York, Putnam, 1969.
Editor, *Sexual Consequences of Disability.*   Philadelphia, Stickley, 1978.

Translator, with Allan Ross Macdougall, *The Triumph of Death*, by C.F. Ramuz.   London, Routledge, 1946.
Translator, *The Koko Shastra.*   London, Allen and Unwin, 1964; New York, Stein and Day, 1965.

*

Bibliography: "Alexander Comfort: A Bibliography in Progress" by D. Callaghan, in *West Coast Review* (Burnaby, British Columbia), 1969.

Critical Studies: *The Freedom of Poetry* by Derek Stanford, London, Falcon Press, 1947; "The Scientific Humanism of Alex Comfort" by Wayne Burns, in *The Humanist 11* (London), November-December 1951; "The Anarchism of Alex Comfort" by John Ellerby, "Sex, Kicks and Comfort" by Charles Radcliffe, and "Alex Comfort's Art and Scope" by Harold Drasdo, all in *Anarchy 33* (London), November 1963; *Alex Comfort* by Arthur E. Salmon, Boston, Twayne, 1978.

*   *   *

Alex Comfort's best known poems are concerned with sexual love—with a sometimes tender, sometimes bawdy exploration of the sexual impulse in man and woman. If other poets have occasionally explored this area, Dr. Comfort is (apart from his contemporary, Gavin Ewart) the only poet who is known almost exclusively for it—partly no doubt because of his extrapoetic writing, often about sexual psychology and physiology, and partly through the continual anthologisation of his fine poem "For Ruth" ("There is a white mare that my love keeps/ unridden in a hillside meadow...").

Comfort's earlier poems, owing much (as whose did not?) to Eliot, consisted often of meditations on death—not only on violent death in war (as in *Elegies*), but death seen lurking in the natural world of landscape: "The condemned cell of the woods lies round our doors,/ the trees are bars, and barbs the bramble carries...." His later war poems (in *The Signal to Engage*) were as bitter as those of Siegfried Sassoon, a generation earlier, who sometimes seems indeed to have been a direct influence (cf."Song for the Heroes").

But it was later, in the 1960's, that Dr. Comfort found the theme and the style, sometimes extrovert, sometimes interior, which was to enable him to write the poems in which he is seen at his most amusing, accomplished and wise. His range, within that theme, is considerable, from the lyrical to the epigrammatic ("Babies' and lovers' toes express/ecstasies of wantonness.-/That's a language which we lose/with the trick of wearing shoes").

Comfort's technical range is not great, yet he does command a technique which enables him to make his points in a sinewy and terse language which only occasionally is marred by sentimentality. His anecdotes, often telling a short story which might have appealed to Maupassant (cf. "The Charmer"), are succinct, and if he turns his hand to a purpose-made piece, as in the epithalamion *Haste to the Wedding*, the note is never false and invariably lively.

His attitude to love, now increasingly shared by his younger readers, is celebrated in poetry like none that has been written since the Restoration: direct and uncompromising, a note of wholehearted enjoyment: he is tired of "the best pentameters," of "eloquence overdone": "That first act of our own/is still the best act left. Let's go to bed." Of course this means there are limitations: Dr. Comfort has never perhaps wholly recaptured the tenderness of "For Ruth." But many other poets have written single poems of considerable beauty; not so many have written, for instance, a complaining elegy on bed-manufacturers: "Surely the trade has one Stradivarius?/If not, I know why in Neolithic days/the Goddess was steatopygic./For the meantime let us unroll the rug."

His later love poems succeed perhaps *because* they lack the painful intensity of longing that pierces the verse of poets both less happy as lovers and more intent on their poetry. Comfort's verse celebrates, not mourns nor yearns. His words "serve to fill the space/between meeting and meeting—/this is the eloquent thing/that they are celebrating/and nothing that we write/myself or any other/matches the fine content/of what we do together."

—Derek Parker

CONN, Stewart. British. Born in Glasgow, Scotland, 5 November 1936. Educated at Kilmarnock Academy and Glasgow University. National Service: Royal Air Force. Married Judith Clarke in 1963; two sons. Since 1962, radio drama producer, currently Head of Drama (Radio), BBC, Glasgow. Literary Adviser, Edinburgh Royal Lyceum Theatre, 1973-75. Recipient: Eric Gregory Award, 1963; Scottish Arts Council Poetry Prize and Publication Award, 1968, award, 1979; *The Scotsman* prize, 1981. Lives in Edinburgh. Agent: Nina Froud, Harvey Unna and Stephen Durbridge Ltd., 24-32 Pottery Lane, London W11 4LZ, England.

PUBLICATIONS

Verse

Thunder in the Air. Preston, Lancashire, Akros, 1967.
The Chinese Tower. Edinburgh, M. Macdonald, 1967.
Stoats in the Sunlight. London, Hutchinson, 1968; as *Ambush and Other Poems*, New York, Macmillan, 1970.

Corgi Modern Poets in Focus 3, with others, edited by Dannie Abse. London, Corgi, 1971.
An Ear to the Ground. London, Hutchinson, 1972.
Under the Ice. London, Hutchinson, 1978.

Plays

Break-Down (produced Glasgow, 1961).
Birds in a Wilderness (produced Edinburgh, 1964).
I Didn't Always Live Here (produced Glasgow, 1967). Included in *The Aquarium, The Man in the Green Muffler, I Didn't Always Live Here,* 1976.
The King (produced Edinburgh, 1967; London, 1972). Published in *New English Dramatists 14,* London, Penguin, 1970.
Broche (produced Exeter, 1968).
Fancy Seeing You, Then (produced London, 1974). Published in *Playbill Two,* edited by Alan Durband, London, Hutchinson, 1969.
Victims (includes *The Sword, In Transit,* and *The Man in the Green Muffler*) (produced Edinburgh, 1970). *In Transit,* published New York, Breakthrough Press, 1972; *The Man in the Green Muffler* included in *The Aquarium, The Man in the Green Muffler, I Didn't Always Live Here,* 1976.
The Burning (produced Edinburgh, 1971). London, Calder and Boyars, 1973.
A Slight Touch of the Sun (produced Edinburgh, 1972).
The Aquarium (produced Edinburgh, 1973). Included in *The Aquarium, The Man in the Green Muffler, I Didn't Always Live Here,* 1976.
Thistlewood (produced Edinburgh, 1975). Todmorden, Lancashire, Woodhouse, 1979.
Count Your Blessings (produced Pitlochry, Perthshire, 1975).
The Aquarium, The Man in the Green Muffler, I Didn't Always Live Here. London, Calder, 1976.
Play Donkey (produced Edinburgh, 1977). Todmorden, Lancashire, Woodhouse, 1980.
Billy Budd, with Stephen Macdonald, adaptation of the novel by Melville (produced Edinburgh, 1978).
Hecuba (produced Edinburgh, 1979).
Herman (produced Edinburgh, 1981).

Radio Plays: *Any Following Spring,* 1962; *Cadenza for Real,* 1963; *Song of the Clyde,* 1964; *The Canary Cage,* 1967; *Too Late the Phalarope,* from the novel by Alan Paton, 1984.

Television Plays: *Wally Dugs Go in Pairs,* 1973; *The Kite,* 1979.

Other

Editor, *New Poems 1973-74.* London, Hutchinson, 1974.

*

Manuscript Collection: Scottish National Library, Edinburgh.

Critical Studies: interviews with James Aitchison in *Scottish Theatre* (Edinburgh), March 1969, Allen Wright in *The Scotsman* (Edinburgh), 30 October 1971, and Joyce McMillan in *Scottish Theatre News* (Glasgow), August 1981; introduction by Dannie Abse to *Corgi Modern Poets in Focus 3,* 1971.

Theatrical Activities:
Director: **Radio**—many plays, including *Armstrong's Last Goodnight* by John Arden, 1964; *The Anatomist* by James Bridie, 1965; *My Friend Mr. Leakey* by J.B.S. Haldane, 1967; *Mr. Gillie* by James Bridie, 1967; *Happy Days Are Here Again* by

Cecil P. Taylor, 1967; *Wedderburn's Slave* by Douglas Dunn, 1980.

*   *   *

At the age of 26 Stewart Conn wrote "Todd," a characterization of an uncle of his father who had a passionate love for horses. In its effect of concentrated intensity it is a remarkable poem. It begins:

> My father's white uncle became
> Arthritic and testamental in
> Lyrical stages...

The "white uncle," at once legendary in its suggestion, becomes almost immediately suffering actuality in "arthritic," before turning Old Testament prophet in "testamental," but this prophet's fires burn in his passion for horses; yet the horses themselves are "a primal extension of rock and soil," though equally they have "cracked hooves" and are fed on "bowls of porridge." The world of the stable is activated in sounds—"thundered nail"—and in smells—"his own horsey breath"—the uncle's breath, as horse and he are one. The words are charged with meaning as they flow to-fro between the actual and the mythical. The people from Conn's childhood, purposeful and vigorous, become vividly alive in the poems:

> From the byre, smack on time
> Old Martha comes clattering out,
> With buttered bannocks and milk in a pail.

About the same time as Conn was writing poems bred from his community, he wrote dramatic, laconic poems dealing with barbarities evoking in the reader repulsion and nausea. These historical or quasi-historical episodes I frequently found contrived, but they were a genuine endeavour to accept alienation into Conn's oeuvre, a necessary move if his poetry was to respond to contemporary conditions. In any case his domestic themes increasingly committed Conn to deal with suffering. The poem "crippled Aunt" ends with the poet observing the aunt, who is paralysed from the waist down, in church:

> Watching them wheel you down the aisle, I am humble.
> I, who would curse the fate
>   That was twisted you into what
> You are, shudder to hear you say life's ample
> For your needs, Christian by such example.

But this situation still belongs to Conn's past. His finest achievement, as in his collection *Under the Ice*, uses, for the most part, domestic situations of the present, as a means of contemplating contemporary distresses and perplexities. When the horror story is told now, as in "Reawakening," it is no longer an attempt to create a cruel past; it relates to the frightening, unguided missile in which we travel through space and time. The only answer which proposes itself to the poet is to be found in love between two people, but no sooner is the idea proposed, as in "Arrivals," than it is questioned:

> The plane meets
> its reflection on the wet
> runway, then crosses
> to where I wait
> behind plate glass.

> I watch
> with a mixture
> of longing and despair
> as you re-enter
> the real world.

The poet's beloved returns to him, who is at a remove behind glass. She returns to the "real world" but we are left wondering where that is. Conn can now put a fine edge on daily experiences, guiding the reader to recognize the strangeness of existence, but not allowing a refuge in simple statements. The ambiguities and perplexities remain, but refined into poetry.

—George Bruce

CONNOR, Tony (John Anthony Augustus Connor). British. Born in Manchester, Lancashire, 16 March 1930. Left school at 14. Served as a tank driver in the 5th Royal Inniskilling Dragoon Guards, 1948-50. Married Frances Foad in 1961; three children. Textile Designer, Manchester, 1944-60. Assistant in Liberal Studies, Bolton Technical College, 1961-64; Visiting Poet, Amherst College, Massachusetts, 1967-68. Visiting Poet and Lecturer, 1968-69, and since 1971, Professor of English, Wesleyan University, Middletown, Connecticut. Visiting Playwright, Oxford Playhouse, England, 1974-75. M.A.: Manchester University, 1968; Wesleyan University, 1971. Fellow, Royal Society of Literature. Address: 44 Brainerd Avenue, Middletown, Connecticut 06457, U.S.A.

PUBLICATIONS

Verse

With Love Somehow. London, Oxford University Press, 1962.
Poems: A Selection, with Austin Clarke and Charles Tomlinson. London and New York, Oxford University Press, 1964.
Lodgers. London, Oxford University Press, 1965.
12 Secret Poems. Manchester, MICA, 1965.
Kon in Springtime. London, Oxford University Press, 1968.
In the Happy Valley. London, Oxford University Press, 1971.
The Memoirs of Uncle Harry. London, Oxford University Press, 1974.
Seven Last Poems from the Memoirs of Uncle Harry. Newcastle upon Tyne, Northern House, 1974.
To a Friend, Who Asked for a Poem. Knotting, Bedfordshire, Sceptre Press, 1975.
Twelve Villanelles. Derry, Pennsylvania, Rook Press, 1977.
A Foreign Bird in Winter. Edinburgh, Exiles Press, 1980.
New and Selected Poems. London, Anvil Press Poetry, and Athens, University of Georgia Press, 1982.

Recording: *Poems*, with Norman Nicholson, Argo, 1974.

Plays

Billy's Wonderful Kettle (produced Manchester, 1971).
I Am Real and So Are You, A Visit from the Family, and *Crewe Station at 2 A.M.* (produced London, 1971).
The Last of the Feinsteins (produced London, 1972).
A Couple with a Cat (produced London, 1972).

Otto's Interview (produced London, 1973).
Dr. Crankenheim's Mixed-Up Monster (produced Oxford, 1974). London, Dobson, 1975.
David's Violin, adaptation of a Yiddish play (produced New York, 1976).

Other

Translator, with George Gömöri, *Love of the Scorching Wind*, by Laszlo Nagy. London, Oxford University Press, 1973.

*

Tony Connor comments:

(1970) There are no critical studies of Tony Connor's work, which has received scant and condescending attention from English reviewers. In the U.S.A., however, he is considered "one of the poets now bringing new life to English verse" (M.L. Rosenthal, *Saturday Review*, 1968) and "undoubtedly one of the best and most authentic of recent British poets" (*Poetry*, January 1969).

His poetry is unacademic, independent and original and uses domestic themes and imagery in a free-flowng, at times surrealstic, manner. The moral ambiguity of Mr. Connor's apparent simplicities reminds one of Frost more than of any modern English poet, and this, perhaps, helps to explain the fact that his reputation stands higher in the United States than in his own country.

*   *   *

Love, childhood, family and family life, old age, memory, death—such topics, universal in their appeal but unique in the hands of Tony Connor, run more-or-less regularly through his solid, subtle, deeply felt, yet never sentimental work. Throughout his productive career, he has eschewed the razzle-dazzle with which many of his third-rate contemporaries attempt to camouflage their lack of talent for a poetry of quiet, exacting observations—often tinged with humor—in which the narrative plays as important a role as the lyrical.

Connor's lyrical touch is precise; his vision sharp. He is poet and wizard simultaneously. Heaven and earth are instantaneously, magically bridged in the first stanza of "Names on Stones":

> In old graveyards
> I could wonder what mattered.
> All those particular names
> affect me like a starry sky.

In "New Place," two persons making love as "headlights sweep [their] room" first "are two thrashing / ghosts" in the passing traffic's lights, then, at rest, they simply "appear / disappear, appear as the night cools." The focus of "In New York City" shifts from a panorama of urban life to lonely lives within the city:

> in silent, scented bedrooms,
> young women fresh from showers
> examine the ferny vein-
> patterns on their inner thighs.

Connor's special brand of, and ease with, narrative can be seen in many of his poems. "Sunday Afternoon: Heaton Hall" contains one strange tableaux after another of stuffed cats dressed as human beings and posed as if taking part in human activities.

Mrs. Cohen in "Desertion, Doom, and Mistaken Identity" is the bride of a soldier serving on foreign shores during WWI. Her death—"she was / / burned to death when her nightgown / went up in flames"—may or may not have been an accident. "The Attack," whose conclusion is wonderfully open—

> Something has won something,
> for what it is worth. Your strong
> being prowls through the house.
> The moon is anonymous.

—employs a submerged, or implied, narrative combined with bursts of lyricism. Even in "Mrs. Root," an earlier poem about a busybody who is as helpful to, and needed by, her neighbors as she is off-putting but whom

> ...nobody thanked.... Why doesn't
> she mind her own business? they said—
> who'd leant upon her. Crude and peasant-like
> her interest in brides and the dead

and with whom the poet has discovered a kinship—his "secret poems were like her actions: both / pried into love and savoured death"—also combines the lyric and narrative seamlessly.

Throughout his career, Connor has also written many strong poems about poetry. These fall into one of two groups: those in which poetry is discussed outright and those in which poetry is briefly mentioned in passing. In the former group, Connor steers clear of the *arts poetica* variety of such verse, attempting instead to define poetry's relationship to his life. "A Photograph of My Mother with Her Favourite Lodger" reveals the past to be a viable source of inspiration and personal mythology. "Middle Age" investigates the poet's "responsibility" to his art, "a settled habit." In poems of the latter group—such as "Morning Song" and "*Stud, Hustler, Penthouse, et al.*"—Connor's references to poetry are as organic as the trees a landscape painter includes in a forest scene. Consequently, his art is shown to be an everyday occurrence, one as ordinary, and special, as a heart beating.

Connor is one of a handful of contemporaries who is equally at home, and successful, in rhymed verse. His is in no way stodgy; the opposite is the case. "In the Locker Room" delightfully combines contemporary theme and subject with an effective, unobtrusive rhyme—

> Between the locker rows
> heaps of abandoned clothes
> lie like a beaten race
> crumpled in its disgrace

—one which enhances the poem's witty conclusion—

> I rub my itching balls:
> the seed of criminals
> and maniacs waits
> in those hanging fruits.

The confessional "A Short Account at Fifty" is saved from the mode of, say, an Anne Sexton by its rhyme:

> Look for me on a barstool,
> or in some kind woman's bed,
> talking hard, and undismayed
> by folks who think me a fool.

Humor and, with it, an acceptance of this world on its own terms underlie Tony Connor's work—a rare and, for his readers, a gratifying feat.

—Jim Elledge

CONQUEST, (George) Robert (Acworth).   British.   Born in Great Malvern, Worcester, 15 July 1917. Educated at Winchester College; Magdalen College, Oxford, B.A. 1939; University of Grenoble. Served in the Oxfordshire and Buckinghamshire Light Infantry, 1939-46. Married 1) Joan Watkins in 1942 (divorced, 1948), two sons; 2) Tatiana Mihailova in 1948 (divorced, 1962); 3) Caroleen Macfarlane in 1964 (divorced, 1978); 4) Elizabeth Neece in 1979. Member of the U.K. Diplomatic Service, 1946-56; Fellow, London School of Economics, 1956-58; Lecturer in English, University of Buffalo, 1959-60; Literary Editor, *The Spectator*, London, 1962-63; Senior Fellow, Columbia University, New York, 1964-65; Fellow, Woodrow Wilson Center, Washington, D.C., 1976-77; Visiting Scholar, Heritage Foundation, Washington, D.C., 1980-81; Research Associate, Ukrainian Research Institute, Cambridge, Massachusetts, 1981. Senior Research Fellow, Hoover Institution, Stanford, California, 1977-79, and since 1981. Editor, *Soviet Analyst*, London, 1971-73. Recipient: P.E.N. prize, 1945; Festival of Britain prize, 1951. M.A. 1972, and D.Litt. 1974: Oxford University. Fellow, Royal Society of Literature, 1972. O.B.E. (Officer, Order of the British Empire), 1955. Address: c/o Brown Shipley and Company, Founder's Court, Lothbury, London E.C. 2, England.

PUBLICATIONS

Verse

Poems.   London, Macmillan, and New York, St. Martin's Press, 1955.
Between Mars and Venus.   London, Hutchinson, and New York, St. Martin's Press, 1962.
Arias from a Love Opera.   London, Macmillan, and New York, Macmillan, 1969.
Casualty Ward.   London, Poem-of-the-Month Club, 1974.
Coming Across.   Menlo Park, California, Buckabest, 1978.
Forays.   London, Chatto and Windus, 1979.

Novels

A World of Difference.   London, Ward Lock, 1955; New York, Ballantine, 1964.
The Egyptologists, with Kingsley Amis.   London, Cape, 1965; New York, Random House, 1966.

Other

Where Do Marxists Go from Here? (as J.E.M. Arden).   London, Phoenix House, 1958.
The Soviet Deportation of Nationalities.   London, Macmillan, and New York, St. Martin's Press, 1960.
Common Sense about Russia.   London, Gollancz, and New York, Macmillan, 1960.
Courage of Genius: The Pasternak Affair.   London, Collins-Harvill Press, and Philadelphia, Lippincott, 1961.

Power and Policy in the U.S.S.R.   London, Macmillan, and New York St. Martin's Press, 1962.
The Last Empire.   London, Ampersand, 1962.
Marxism Today.   London, Ampersand, 1964.
Russia after Khrushchev.   London, Pall Mall Press, and New York, Praeger, 1965.
The Great Terror: Stalin's Purge of the Thirties.   London, Macmillan, and New York, Macmillan, 1968; revised edition, 1973.
The Nations Killers: The Soviet Deportation of Minorities.   London, Macmillan, and New York, St. Martin's Press, 1970.
Where Marx Went Wrong.   London, Stacey, 1970.
Lenin.   London, Fontana, and New York, Viking Press, 1972.
Kolyma: The Arctic Death Camps.   London, Macmillan, and New York, Viking Press, 1978.
Present Danger: Towards a Foreign Policy.   Oxford, Blackwell, and Stanford, California, Hoover Institution, 1979.
The Abomination of Moab.   London, Temple Smith, 1979.
We and They: Civic and Despotic Cultures.   London, Temple Smith, 1980.
What to Do When the Russians Come: A Survivor's Guide, with Jon Manchip White.   New York, Stein and Day, 1984.

Editor, *New Lines 1-2*.   London, Macmillan, 2 vols., 1956-63.
Editor, *Back to Life* (anthology).   London, Hutchinson, and New York, St. Martin's Press, 1958.
Editor, with Kingsley Amis, *Spectum [1-5]: A Science Fiction Anthology*.   London, Gollancz, 5 vols., 1961-65; New York, Harcourt Brace, 5 vols., 1962-67.
Editor, *Soviet Studies Series*.   London, Bodley Head, 8 vols., 1967-68; New York, Praeger, 8 vols., 1968-69.
Editor, *Pyotr Yakir*.   London, Macmillan, 1972; New York, Coward McCann, 1973.
Editor, *The Robert Sheckley Omnibus*.   London, Gollancz, 1973.
Editor, *The Russian Tradition*, by Tibor Szamuely.   London, Secker and Warburg, 1974; New York, McGraw Hill, 1975.

Translator, *Prussian Nights*, by Alexander Solzhenitsyn.   London, Collins-Harvill Press, 1977; New York, Farrar Straus, 1978.

*

Critical Studies: in *Times Literary Supplement* (London), 30 May 1955; by D.J. Enright, in *The Month* (London), May 1956; John Holloway, in *Hudson Review* (New York), xiv, 4, 1961; Thom Gunn, in *The Spectator* (London), 4 May 1962.

Robert Conquest comments:
   I suppose my main theme is the poet's relationship to the phenomenal universe—in particular to landscape, women, art and war. Forms usually, though not always, traditional. Sometimes straight lyric, more often with development of a train of thought: an attempt to master, or transmit, a presented reality in intellectual and emotive terms simultaneously. The vocabulary often runs to words—not specialist ones—drawn from the technical, scientific and philosophical spheres, and mediatised into the ordinary language.
   Since all this is in principle a complex and difficult process, a strong effort goes into keeping it as comprehensible as possible, avoidance of forced obscurities, and provision of a rigorous guidance of sound and structure.

* * *

Although as a very young man in the late thirties Robert Conquest had contributed some Audenesque exercises to *Twentieth Century Verse*, he did not emerge as a mature poet until his first collection, *Poems*, came out in 1955. A year later Conquest edited *New Lines*, an anthology of the poets of the so-called "Movement," and his own poetry exhibited the favoured qualities of that school: exactness of form, intellectual structure, emphasis on empiricism and common-sense values, and a certain preoccupation with the nature of the poetic process. But Conquest was distinguished from the other contributors to *New Lines* by the greater range of his subject matter. He wrote love poems and poems about Eastern Europe and the Mediterranean, and philosophical reflections on the nature of perception. And in "The Landing in Deucalion" Conquest wrote the first of several poems inspired by his abiding interest in science fiction. *Poems* was an enjoyable, even distinguished first collection. It presented the reader with an urbane and civilized mind, widely read and widely travelled, sympathetically curious about most forms of human activity. The poetic influences were from Auden and Robert Graves, but they were well assimilated, and Conquest's voice was highly personal, however much he employed the general idiom of the Movement. Formal precision was combined with delicacy of response, and though feeling was controlled it was unmistakably present. The qualities of Conquest's best poetry can be seen in his sonnet, "Guided Missiles Experimental Range," where he responds to a modern, technological subject with a precisely deployed classical reference. Here is the sestet:

> Stronger than lives, by empty purpose blinded,
> The only thought their circuits can endure is
> The target-hunting rigour of their flight;
>
> And by that loveless haste I am reminded
> Of Aeschylus' description of the Furies:
> "*O barren daughters of the fruitful night.*"

If most of the poems in the book are in traditional metres and rhyme schemes, one of the finest, "Near Jakobslev," is in free verse, a beautifully rendered account of a sub-arctic landscape in summer.

Conquest's later poetry continues the subjects of his first book: love, landscapes, science fiction, poetry itself. But it is generally less rewarding; the precision of the verse has become a little mechanical, and the pressure of feeling to be contained is less immediate. There is a heavy reliance on certain recurring key words—"love," "poem," "girl"—and an air of self-imitation. Even so, the craftsmanship remains admirable at a time when the formal virtues that Conquest argued for and exhibited in the mid-fifties have been disregarded by many younger poets. And he remains capable of formidable feats of skill, as in his completion of two fragments of verse from a Housman manuscript, turning them into finished poems in the form and metre of Housman's drafts ("Two Housman Torsos," *Times Literary Supplement*, 19 October 1973). One regrets, though, that so gifted a poet has remained content with his own gifts, and developed them so little.

—Bernard Bergonzi

CONRAN, Anthony. British. Born in Kharghpur, India, 7 April 1931. Educated at University College of North Wales, Bangor, B.A. (honours) in English and philosophy, M.A. in English. Since 1957, Research Fellow and Tutor, University College of North Wales. Recipient: Welsh Arts Council award, 1960, and bursary, 1968. Address: 1 Frondirion, Glanrafon, Bangor, Gwynedd, Wales.

PUBLICATIONS

Verse

Formal Poems. Llandybie, Carmarthenshire, Christopher Davies, 1960.
Metamorphoses. Pembroke Dock, Pembrokeshire, Dock Leaves Press, 1961; revised edition, Market Drayton, Shropshire, Tern Press, 1979.
Icons. Privately printed, 1963.
Asymptotes. Privately printed, 1963.
A String o Blethers. Privately printed, 1963.
Sequence of the Blue Flower. Privately printed, 1963.
The Mountain. Privately printed, 1963.
For the Marriage of Gerard and Linda. Privately printed, 1963.
Stelae and Other Poems. Oxford, Clive Allison, 1965.
Guernica. Denbigh, Gee, 1966.
Collected Poems. Oxford, Clive Allison, 1 vol., 1966; Denbigh, Gee, 3 vols., 1966-68.
Claim, Claim, Claim. Guildford, Surrey, Circle Press, 1969.
Spirit Level and Other Poems. Llandybie, Carmarthenshire, Christopher Davies, 1974.
Poems 1951-67. Bangor, Deiniol Press, 1974.
Life Fund. Llandysul, Dyfed, Gomer, 1979.

Other

The Cost of Strangeness: Essays on the English Poets of Wales. Llandysul, Dyfed, Gomer, 1982.

Editor and Translator, *The Penguin Book of Welsh Verse*. London, Penguin, 1967.

Translator, *Eighteen Poems of Dante Alighieri*. Market Drayton, Shropshire, Tern Press, 1975.

*

Critical Studies: by Gwyn Thomas, in *Poetry Wales* (Cardiff), Spring 1967; Jeremy Hooker, in *Anglo-Welsh Review* (Tenby), Spring 1975.

Anthony Conran comments:

I regard myself as a poet of Wales, though I write in English. Behind me are Anglo-Welsh poets like Hopkins, Idris Davies, Dylan Thomas, and R.S. Thomas; but also I have felt the groundswell of the age-old Welsh tradition, from Taliesin in the 6th century to Bobi Jones in the 20th.

I write poems when people seem to want them. The demands of what they want form the co-ordinates of my poems.

* * *

Anthony Conran is one of the foremost translators of Welsh poetry and has edited the *Penguin Book of Welsh Verse*, doing valuable work in bringing a number of masterpieces before a wider audience.

His own collected poems, *Spirit Level*, cover the years 1956-68, including a section of experiments in strict metre from Chinese, Japanese, Provençal, and Celtic, which are certainly different and partly successful. He also includes his "gift-poems"—pieces of praise, and celebrations of other people's marriages (given as presents on wedding-days) and the births of their children. Conran dedicates many of his poems to friends and writers, alive and dead. He says that the giving and receiving of gifts and odes formed the "central arch of Welsh civilisation," and he should know, because he is steeped in it. There are plenty of these poems in his volumes, following a groove of sentimentality, and leaving a slightly syrupy taste in the mouth.

Conran favours custom and ceremony, ritual, elegy, tradition, and the formal language-splash of Dylan Thomas, to whose memory he dedicated an earlier poem in which he employs Thomas compounds, like "womblight," "dreamdank," "outwombward," "chapeldownunder" (which sounds a reference to an Australian church), "gift of gab devil" and "steepled town." Elsewhere, although originally a stranger and outsider to Wales who sank eagerly into its culture, he writes of his "Lineage":

> My lineage is kingly. Once, my fathers ruled
> The broad acres of an island sweet with grass
> And climbed the volcanic hills, through dingle
> Of birch and pinetree, scrubland where wild deer
> Picked out their path to the bald peak:
> There the visiting gods conversed, who came
> As friends to friends with the kings my fathers....

And these lines to a Welsh potter:

> And the racks in your front-room shop
> No longer fill
> Quietly, quietly, with the cups and jugs
> Of your fingers' skill;
>
> And because now, though the potter's gone
> And the clay dries dead
> We are glad that the love of a bride
> Has graced your bed—

Of Conran's erudition, stockpiled classical allusions, intermittent elegance and varied technical skill, one has no doubt, but these frequently run into the sand, or explode in trivial puffs of smoke which soon drift away. All that scholarly brilliance still has a whiff of the midnight-candle about it, as if plotted from an ivory-tower above a quadrangle. A measure of fustian also inhabits his work, loading some thin subject-matter that simply cannot carry the weight.

As a critic, he has a reputation for severity, often using a sledgehammer to crack a nut by bringing the considerable weapons of his armoury to bear on marginal work. He interpolates rare and precious words of praise into devastating, remorseless hatchet-jobs, which are often massacres disguised as reviews. He also has a weakness for fashionable psychology-based criticism, which occasionally leads him into a weird area of precipitate assumption, odd parallels and comparisons, and manufactured mysteries where none exist. It is a perilous area, which temptingly invites hasty surmise in the absence of evidence, and dramatic overstatement, as well as the inaccurate analysis of sexual imagery.

Conran's premier accomplishment as a translator ranges from Taliesin (late 6th century) to the excellent moderns, such as R. Williams Parry, Saunders Lewis, Gwenallt Jones, Euros Bowen, and Waldo Williams. He is adept at assessing what some mistakenly consider to be a minor and ancillary literature, about which no general opinion has previously been built up. His main purpose has been to make poetic sense, in English, of sometimes very difficult poems, and to this end he has stated that he often departed further from the literal meaning than would easily be justifiable were his purpose purely scholarly—though he has always attempted to be literal. In his extremely knowledgeable introduction to the Penguin selection, he also makes it clear that the special relationship which the Welsh-language "bard" has with his public is very different from the English poet's connection with his minority audience. The Welshman is something of a leader within his own community, often a national figure who appears at public functions and is constantly asked to give opinions on poetry, political matters, and even international affairs, knowing that many "influential" people are going to listen. As Anthony Conran adds: "No English poet has been able to do this since Tennyson."

—John Tripp

COOK, Stanley. British. Born in Austerfield, Yorkshire, 12 April 1922. Educated at Doncaster Grammar School, 1933-40; Christ Chruch, Oxford, 1940-44, B.A. in English language and literature 1943, M.A. 1948. Married Kathleen Mary Daly in 1947; two daughters and one son. Assistant Master, Barrow-in-Furness Grammar School, 1944-48; Sixth Form English Master, Bury Grammar School, 1948-55; Senior English Master, Firth Park School, Sheffield, 1955-68; Lecturer, 1969-78, and Senior Lecturer in English, 1978-81, Huddersfield Polytechnic. Since 1981, Editor, *Poetry Nottingham*. Recipient: Hull Arts Centre-BBC Competition Prize, 1969; Cheltenham Festival Competition Prize, 1972. Address: 600 Barnsley Road, Sheffield, South Yorkshire S5 6UA, England.

PUBLICATIONS

Verse

Form Photograph. Stockport, Cheshire, Harry Chambers, 1971.
Signs of Life. Manchester, E.J. Morten, 1972.
Staff Photograph. Stockport, Cheshire, Harry Chambers, 1976.
Alphabet. Stockport, Cheshire, Harry Chambers, 1976.
Woods Beyond a Cornfield. Richmond, Surrey, Keepsake Press, 1979.
Woods Beyond a Cornfield and Other Poems. Bradford, Rivelin Press, 1981.

Other

Seeing Your Meaning: Concrete Poetry in Language and Education. Huddersfield, The Polytechnic, 1975.
Come Along: Poems for Younger Children. Privately printed, 1978.
Word Houses: Poems for Juniors. Privately printed, 1979.
Come Again: More Poems for Younger Children. Huddersfield, Kirklees and Calderdale Branch of the National Association for the Teaching of English, 1982.

*

Critical Studies: by Robert Nye, in *The Times* (London), 10 February 1972; *Critical Quarterly* (Manchester), Spring 1972; *The Teacher* (London), 3 March 1972; Colin Bulman, in *The Teacher* (London), 27 October 1972; "Signs of Life" in *The Times* (London), 14 December 1972; *Times Literary Supplement* (London), 17 August 1973.

Stanley Cook comments:

My attitude to my poetry is expressed in the Introduction to *Form Photograph:*

You live with your subject matter for years; one day something puts it into your head to write about it. After that it is simply a case of stating accurately what you have observed. Of course you have observed inaccurately and the accurate recording of the distinctive inaccuracies of which you are unaware is the theme of your poems. There ought to be more in a poem than you are conscious of expressing and more than your reader is conscious of receiving.

As far as style is concerned, I hope the steelworker and his wife next door would never need a dictionary to read my poems. I like to feel, too, that I have been as practical and unsentimental with a poem as if I had farmed, smithed or carpentered it—that the rest of the family would think I had done some "real work" and had not let them down.

Assuming I have written that kind of poem in the past, I have kept on writing it. If my work has developed, I hope this has been not by altering but by adding. I am now very interested in the visual impact of printed literature on the reader's unconscious, largely destroyed by the utilitarian format of paperbacks. My concrete poems aim to test-drill for such impacts.

I have come to realise that the Augustans were roughly right: Dryden to Crabbe is the greatest period of our poetry. One can't lecture on it without learning from it; and until one is learning from it one can't lecture on it.

Still suffering from provincial isolation, I have had to publish *Come Along* and *Word Houses* myself. I can see that eventually most of the poems in "Come Along" will have been anthologised by various publishers, none of whom was willing to publish the collection. The all-or-nothing reaction of the children for whom they were written is refreshingly different.

*   *   *

For many years Stanley Cook was a schoolmaster in Sheffeld. His two main themes are Yorkshire and education. The metre he characteristically uses is a roughened blank verse. This is conducive to the description of exact minutiae that make up his world. It has taken some years for his work to gain a hearing, for his qualities are not the obvious ones. His tone is subdued, his day overcast, his walks through depressed areas and neglected parks. Cook is at his best when his landscapes are equipped with figures. The murderer, Charles Peace, gives him a cue for black comedy; so does his mother's landlord. That other Sheffield poet, James Montgomery, merits only satire for his lack of an eye to the world about him—that Sheffield world of rain and railings which Cook observes with acquaintance and insight. The most moving poems are those about the author's family, especially those who had to endure the hungry thirties. The one about his father is, in middle age, also about himself:

My body is buried, when I used to be my father,
In the overspill from the village churchyard
Into a field, where a single electrified wire
Keeps back the cows but not the grass or flowers.
Now he is I he waits for a worthwhile task
In which to succeed, better than the water towers
And colliery washers bulky as beer-drinkers
He built as foreman. Pity everyone
Who had, like him, to swim for it in the Thirties,
Fully clothed in the nation's economy.
Those days when he sat in his chair with nothing to smoke
And dressed in his best suit weekly to draw the dole
Pared people down to their character...

Read on. The verse is never as simple as it seems. Cook's voice inflects and turns with the independence of its native speech. Glamour, romance and melodrama are not his stock in trade: his power is in his redoubtable honesty. No critic can sum up Cook as well as he can himself: "I promised myself this walk in a minor key / Along the old canal dismissed from its trade...."

—Philip Hobsbaum

COOLIDGE, Clark. American. Born in Providence, Rhode Island, 26 February 1939. Attended Brown University, Providence, 1956-58. Married to Susan Hopkins; one daughter. Editor, *Joglars* magazine, Providence, 1964-66. Recipient: National Endowment for the Arts grant, 1966; New York Poets Foundation Award, 1968. Lives in Hancock, Massachusetts. Address: c/o Tombouctou Books, P.O. Box 265, Bolinas, California 94924, U.S.A.

PUBLICATIONS

Verse

Flag Flutter and U.S. Electric. New York, Lines, 1966.
(Poems). New York, Lines, 1967.
Ing. New York, Angel Hair, 1969.
Space. New York, Harper, 1970.
The So. New York, Boke, 1971.
Moroccan Variations. Bolinas, California, Big Sky, 1971.
Suite V. New York, Boke, 1973.
The Maintains. San Francisco, This Press, 1974.
Polaroid. New York, Boke, 1975.
Quartz Hearts. San Francisco, This Press, 1978.
Own Face. Lenox, Massachusetts, Angel Hair, 1978.
Smithsonian Depositions, and Subject to a Film. New York, Vehicle, 1980.
American Ones. Bolinas, California, Tombouctou, 1981.
Research. Berkeley, California, Tuumba Press, 1982.

Play

To Obtain the Value of the Cake Measure from Zero, with Tom Veitch. San Francisco, Pants Press, 1970.

*

Critical Studies: "Clark Coolidge Issue" of *Big Sky 3* (Bolinas, California), 1972; interview, in *This 4* (San Francisco), Spring

1973; *The End of Intelligent Writing* by Richard Kostelanetz, New York, Sheed and Ward, 1974; "A Symposium on Clark Coolidge," in *Stations 5* (Milwaukee), Winter 1978.

Clark Coolidge comments:

The context of my works is the Tonality of Language (seen, heard, spoken, thought) itself, a tonality that centers itself in the constant flowage from meaning to meaning, and that sideslippage between meanings. All the books we shall perhaps never read again form a constant background of reference points. We are free now to delight in the Surface of Language, a surface as deep as the distance between (for instance) a noun (in the mind) (in a dictionary) and its object somewhere in the universe.

*   *   *

None of the young experimental poets in America has been as various, intelligent and prolific as Clark Coolidge, who also edited one of the few genuinely avant-garde literary magazines of the sixties, *Joglars*. His opening book, *Flag Flutter and U.S. Electric*, collected his early forays into post-Ashberyan acoherence, where the poet tries to realize the semblance of literary coherence without resorting to such traditional organizing devices as meter, metaphor, exposition, symbolism, consistent allusion, declarative statements or autobiographical reference. (The key Ashbery work in this vein is "Europe," 1960, collected in *The Tennis Court Oath*, 1962.) In a theoretical statement contributed to Paul Carroll's anthology of *The Young American Poets* (1968), Coolidge wrote that "Words have a universe of qualities other than those of descriptive relation: Hardness, Density, Sound-Shape, Vector-Force, & Degrees of Transparency/Opacity," and his earlier poems revealed rather exceptional linguistic sensitivities, especially regarding the selection and placement of words. The intelligence informing his creative processes is radically poetic, precisely because it is *not* prosaic.

In his subsequent work Coolidge pursued not just varieties of acoherence, but reductionism, joining Kenneth Gangemi and Robert Lax among America's superior minimal poets. In the back sections of Coolidge's fullest retrospective, *Space*, are several especially severe examples, such as the untitled poem, beginning "by a I" which contains individually isolated words, none more than two letters long, that are scattered across the space of a single page (which has so far been Coolidge's primary compositional unit). These words are nonetheless related to each other—not only in terms of diction and corresponding length (both visually and verbally), but by spatial proximity; for if the individual words were arranged in another way, both the poem and the reading experience would be different. It should also be noted that Coolidge's work extends radically the Olsonian traditions both of "composition by field," as opposed to lines, and of emphasizing syllable, rather than rhyme and meter.

Like all genuinely experimental artists, Coolidge accepted the challenge of an inevitable next step, extending his delicate reductionist technique into two of the most remarkable long poems of the 1960's: "AD," originally published in *Ing* and then reprinted in *Space*; and *Suite V*, which appeared as a booklet in 1973, although it was initially composed several years before. "AD" begins in the familiar Coolidgean way, with stanzas of superficially unrelated lines, but the poetic material is progressively reduced over twenty pages (thereby recapitulating Coolidge's own poetic development, in a kind of formalist autobiography) until the poem's final pages contain just vertically ordered fragments of words. *Suite V* is yet more outrageously spartan, containing nothing more than pairs of three-letter words in their

plural forms, with one four-letter word at the top and the other at the bottom of otherwise blank pages.

Coolidge has scattered his writings through numerous periodicals and anthologies, as well as small-press booklets, and much of his work remains unpublished. The best introduction to his excellences is not *Space*, which also suffers from ineptly tiny typography, but the third issue of *Big Sky*, a periodical edited by Bill Berkson. The poetry collected there is far more various and, for that reason, more indicative of Coolidge's experimental temper. It is my considered opinion that he is the most extraordinary American poet of our mutual generation.

—Richard Kostelanetz

COOPER, Jane (Marvel). American. Born in Atlantic City, New Jersey, 9 October 1924. Educated at Vassar College, Poughkeepsie, New York, 1942-44; University of Wisconsin, Madison, B.A. 1946 (Phi Beta Kappa); University of Iowa, Iowa City, M.A. 1954. Since 1950, Member of the Department of English, Sarah Lawrence College, Bronxville, New York. Recipient: Yaddo grant, 1958, 1967, 1968; Guggenheim Fellowship, 1960; MacDowell Colony grant, 1965; Lamont Poetry Selection Award, 1968; National Endowment for the Arts grant, 1969; Ingram Merrill Foundation grant, 1971; Creative Artists Public Service grant, 1974; Shelley Memorial Award, 1978. Address: Department of English, Sarah Lawrence College, Bronxville, New York 10708, U.S.A.

PUBLICATIONS

Verse

The Weather of Six Mornings. New York, Macmillan, 1969.
Maps and Windows. New York, Macmillan, 1974.
Calling Me from Sleep: New and Selected Poems 1961-1973. Bronxville, New York, Sarah Lawrence College, 1974.
Threads: Rosa Luxemburg from Prison. New York, Flamingo Press, 1979.
Scaffolding: New and Selected Poems. London, Anvil Press Poetry, 1984.

Other

Editor, with others, *Extended Outlooks: The "Iowa Review" Collection of Contemporary Women Writers.* New York, Macmillan, 1982.

*

Jane Cooper comments:

My earliest poems (largely unpublished) were heavily metrical. I thought of writing a book of war poems from the point of view of a woman, a non-combatant. What concerned me was what could survive in the way of an individual feeling, or moral life, in a world at war. There is no longer a specific war in most of the poems I write now, but there is the same conviction that we live in a very stripped-down landscape. At the same time joy, if not happiness, is important. Many of my poems have to do with deaths; others with love, the life of the physical world in and around us, and above all with the possibility of writing, of speaking out.

Poetry is a kind of non-abstract musical composition. In my latest work, I am interested in a more open American speech line and in the activity that goes on between lines and even words of a poem, almost more than in what is "said." Pasternak is an influence, in his emphasis on the poem happening *now*. The long poem has always been a challenge. I like trying sequences of shorter poems, almost apparently unrelated; what is their effect on one another? I want to get more fluidity into single pieces now; the self is variable, places change and disappear. I should like to write city poems—another version of life fragmented as if by war.

*   *   *

Jane Cooper's first volume of poems represents her creative efforts over a period exceeding ten years. Although she has no radical experiments in form, her poems demonstrate a versatility ranging from highly patterned to spare, free verse. And though her images are seldom vivid or startling, she employs them, most notably images of weather, with precision and appropriateness.

Most of her poems, and her best, are drawn from the intimate reserves of her own experience: memories of her childhood, of her mother, her loves, her encounters with death, and most effectively her moments of loss, regret, and loneliness. Cooper's poems seldom function as a single, unambiguous perception of an experience. Her poems, as she says in "A Letter for Philo Buck," leave "the tongue unraveling sweets from sours." Many poems seem balanced between emotional polarities of release and joy (the ecstasy of "Morning on the St. John's") and restraint and resignation (the advice in "A Little Vesper" to "bed with what we are"). A poem recalling the childhood rapture of collecting butterflies is entitled "Practising for Death"; and one of her most successful poems, "Obligations," images the speaker and her lover "wrapped in the afternoon/As in a chrysalis of silken light" awaking reluctantly to "the long war, and shared reality,/And death and all we came here to evade."

The inescapable reality of time and change and memory seems increasingly to concern Jane Cooper. "Once you leave the landing," she says in "Leaving Water Hyacinths," "Your whole life will be sailing back."

—Dale Doepke

CORMAN, Cid (Sidney Corman). American. Born in Boston, Massachusetts, 29 June 1924. Educated at Boston Latin School; Tufts College, Medford, Massachusetts, A.B. 1945 (Phi Beta Kappa); University of Michigan, Ann Arbor (Hopwood Award, 1947), 1946-47; University of North Carolina, Chapel Hill, 1947; the Sorbonne, Paris (Fulbright Fellow), 1954-55. Married Shizumi Konishi in 1965. Poetry broadcaster, WMEX, Boston, 1949-51; teacher in Italy, 1956-67, and at Kyoto Joshidai, Japan, 1958-60, Ryukoku University, Kyoto, 1962-64, and Doshisha University, Kyoto, 1965-66. Since 1951 Editor, *Origin* magazine and Origin Press, Ashland, Massachusetts, and Kyoto. Owner, Cid Corman's Dessert Shop, Kyoto, 1974-79, and Sister City Tea Shop, Boston, since 1981. Recipient: Chapelbrook Foundation grant, 1967-69; Co-ordinating Council of Little Magazines grant, 1970, 1978; National Endowment for the Arts grant, 1974; Lenore Marshall Memorial Prize, 1975. Address: c/o Black Sparrow Press, Box 3993, Santa Barbara, California 93130, U.S.A.

PUBLICATIONS

Verse

subluna (juvenilia). Privately printed, 1945.
Night Claims (song), music by Hugo Calderón. New York, Schirmer, 1950.
A Thanksgiving Eclogue from Theocritus. New York, Sparrow Press, 1954.
Ferrini and Others, with others. Berlin, Gerhardt, 1955.
The Precisions. New York, Sparrow Press, 1955.
The Responses. Ashland, Massachusetts, Origin Press, 1956.
Stances and Distances. Ashland, Massachusetts, Origin Press, 1957.
The Marches. Ashland, Massachusetts, Origin Press, 1957.
Clocked Stone. Ashland, Massachusetts, Origin Press, 1959.
A Table in Provence. Kyoto, Origin Press, 1959.
The Descent from Daimonji. Kyoto, Origin Press, 1959.
For Sure. Kyoto, Origin Press, 1960.
Sun Rock Man. Kyoto, Origin Press, 1962; New York, New Directions, 1970.
For Instance. Kyoto, Origin Press, 1962.
In No Time. Privately printed, 1963.
In Good Time. Kyoto, Origin Press, 1964.
For Good. Kyoto, Origin Press, 1964.
All in All. Kyoto, Origin Press, 1964.
Nonce. New Rochelle, New York, Elizabeth Press, 1965.
For You. Kyoto, Origin Press, 1966.
Stead. New Rochelle, New York, Elizabeth Press, 1966.
For Granted. New Rochelle, New York, Elizabeth Press, 1967.
Words for Each Other. London, Rapp and Carroll, 1967.
& Without End. New Rochelle, New York, Elizabeth Press, and London, Villiers, 1968.
No Less. New Rochelle, New York, Elizabeth Press, 1968.
Hearth. Kyoto, Origin Press, 1968.
The World as University. Kyoto, Origin Press, 1968.
No More. New Rochelle, New York, Elizabeth Press, 1969.
Plight. New Rochelle, New York, Elizabeth Press, 1969.
Nigh. New Rochelle, New York, Elizabeth Press, 1970.
Livingdying. New York, New Directions, 1970.
Of the Breath of. Berkeley, California, Maya, 1970.
For Keeps. Kyoto, Origin Press, 1970.
For Now. Kyoto, Origin Press, 1971.
Cicadas. Amherst, New York, Slow Loris Press, 1971.
Out and Out. New Rochelle, New York, Elizabeth Press, 1972.
Be Quest. New Rochelle, New York, Elizabeth Press, 1972.
A Language Without Words. Saffron Walden, Essex, Byways, 1973.
So Far. New Rochelle, New York, Elizabeth Press, 1973.
Poems: Thanks to Zuckerkandl. Rushden, Northamptonshire, Sceptre Press, 1973.
Breathings. Tokyo, Mushinsha, 1973.
Three Poems. Rushden, Northamptonshire, Sceptre Press, 1973.
Yet. New Rochelle, New York, Elizabeth Press, 1974.
RSVP. Knotting, Bedfordshire, Sceptre Press, 1974.
O/I. New Rochelle, New York, Elizabeth Press, 1974.
For Dear Life. Los Angeles, Black Sparrow Press, 1975.
Once and for All: Poems for William Bronk. New Rochelle, New York, Elizabeth Press, 1975.
Not Now. N.p., Moschatel Press, 1975.
Unless. Kyoto, Origin Press, 1975.
'S. New Rochelle, New York, Elizabeth Press, 1976.
For the Asking. Santa Barbara, California, Black Sparrow Press, 1976.
Any How. Nagoya, Kisetsusha, 1976.

Leda and the Swan.   Paris, Hocguard, 1976.
Antics.   Boston, Origin Press, 1977.
Gratis.   Boston, Origin Press, 1977.
Auspices.   Milwaukee, Pentagram Press, 1978.
Of Course.   Boston, Origin Press, 1978.
So.   Boston, Origin Press, 1978.
At Their Word.   Santa Barbara, California, Black Sparrow
Press, 1978.
In the Event.   Bangor, Maine, Theodore Press, 1979.
Tabernacle.   Boston, Origin Press, 1980.
Manna.   West Branch, Iowa, Toothpaste Press, 1981.
At Least (2).   Iowa City, Corycian Press, 1981.
Tu.   West Branch, Iowa, Toothpaste Press, 1983.
Aegis: Selected Poems 1970-1980.   Barrytown, New York, Station Hill Press, 1984.

Other

At: Bottom.   Bloomington, Indiana, Caterpillar, 1966.
William Bronk: An Essay.   Carrboro, North Carolina, Truck
Press, 1976.
The Act of Poetry and Two Other Essays.   Santa Barbara,
California, Black Sparrow Press, 1976.
Word for Word: Essays on the Art of Language.   Santa Barbara, California, Black Sparrow Press, 1977.

Editor, *The Gist of "Origin": An Anthology.*   New York,
Grossman, 1975.

Translator, *Cool Melon*, by Basho.   Ashland, Massachusetts,
Origin Press, 1959.
Translator, *Cool Gong.*   Ashland, Massachusetts, Origin Press,
1959.
Translator, with Susumu Kamaike, *Selected Frogs*, by Shimpei
Kusano.   Kyoto, Origin Press, 1963.
Translator, *Back Roads to Far Towns*, by Basho.   Tokyo,
Mushinsha, 1967; New York, Grossman, 1971.
Translator, with Susumu Kamaike, *Frogs and Others: Poems*,
by Shimpei Kusano.   Tokyo, Mushinsha, 1968; New York,
Grossman, 1969.
Translator, *Things*, by Francis Ponge.   Tokyo, Mushinsha,
and New York, Grossman, 1971.
Translator, *Leaves of Hypnos*, by René Char.   Tokyo, Mushinsha, and New York, Grossman, 1973.
Translator, *Breathings*, by Philippe Jaccottet.   New York,
Grossman, 1974.
Translator, with William Alexander and Richard Burns, *Roberto
Sanesi: A Selection.*   Pensnett, Staffordshire, Grosseteste,
1975.
Translator, with Susumu Kamaike, *Asking Myself / Answering
Myself*, by Shimpei Kusano.   New York, New Directions,
1984.
Translator, *One Man's Moon* (versions of haiku).   Frankfort,
Kentucky, Gnomon Press, 1984.

*

Manuscript Collections: University of Texas, Austin; Kent State
University, Ohio; Indiana University, Bloomington; New York
University; State University of New York, Buffalo.

Critical Study: "Cid Corman Issue" of *Madrona* (Seattle),
December 1975.

Cid Corman comments:
   My work has developed from the pioneer poetry of Pound-
Williams-Stevens, but much also from contact with French poetry. No forms, but a strict sense of the sounded meaning of words,
pauses, verses, etc., and the felt thought that poetry is. Brevity,
immediacy, clarity. A poetry that makes the role of the critic
pointless, needless. The ideal, always, to join that most human
society of poets whose work is published under the title of
ANON.
   Poetry calls for anonymity. It appeals, in short, to the each in
all and the all in each. Its particularity must become yours.
Autobiography is implicit in anyone's work and may be taken
for granted, but what has been realized and so set out as to be
shared loses itself in the self that is found extended without end
in song.
   As the author has elsewhere put it: *If I have nothing to offer
you in the face of death—in its stead—the ache behind every
ache, the instant man knows, I have no claim as poet. My song
must sing into you a little moment, stay in you what presence can
muster—of sense more than meaning, of love more than sense,
of giving the life given one with the same fulness that brought
each forth, each to each from each, nothing left but the life that is
going on.*

                    *   *   *

   Cid Corman's poems are tight, reticent, and resonant. He has
learned (from the Japanese principally, one assumes) how evocative the minimal registration of specifics can be, and he has
combined with this his own life-long concern for the sound of
poetry, syllable by syllable (Zukofsky is for him, as for Creeley, a
measure of such possibilities). The result, both in the longer
more discursive poems of *Sun Rock Man* or *& Without End* and
in the short haiku-like poems of such books as *Nonce*, *Stead*,
and *Nigh*, is a poetry of considerable grace and strength.
   As one reads the early poems now, they seem to cry out for the
compression of the later style. "First Farm North" from *The
Precisions* begins: "I stood above at the bathroom window" and
goes on, in leisurely anecdotal style, to evoke a mood by careful
accumulation of detail, ending:

> The mirror was thawed into the scene
> and the brightness of the morning
> pressed a cool handful of water
> into my eyes and my pulse raced song.

Corman is already free of iambic regularity while retaining a
sense of measure in these lines, but the poem, though charming,
is diffuse. In other poems one notices 1950's elegance ("Leaves
discuss the wind") consorting somewhat uneasily with touches of
what has come to seem Corman's characteristic sensibility ("It
takes all my time, and my father's, / to let life go").
   Between such early work and the development seen in *Sun
Rock Man* there intervenes the first stay in Japan and the
translations from Bashō and others published in *Cool Gong* and
Cool Melon. A gain in expressive means—shorter lines, barer
statement, more fluid syntax—is seen throughout the 1962
book. Here is "The Gift":

> First night in a
> strange town to
> be going home
>
> passing a
> strange girl saying
> goodnight to me

how night is
when she says so
suddenly good

The line breaks are like Creeley's, the syntax with its dangling participles and the canny deployment which gets the clinching phrase at the end owes something to Williams (cp. "Poem": "As the cat/climbed over...") and the syllabic grid (4—3—4; 3—4—4; 3—4—4) suggests Marianne Moore. But the poem is, in its feelings, wholly Corman's. And the entire book, its sum exceeding its parts as a tribute to a place and people—the Italian town where the poet spent a year teaching English—marks the emergence of Corman's mature voice.

In the next book, *For Instance*, one finds more specific oriental influences in content, tone, and technique. Number 7 reads:

gong gone
odor of cherry tolling
eventide

Though a haiku translation, the juxtaposed verbless phrases evoking that mood of contemplative harmony with natural surroundings that one associates with Japanese poetry, this is nevertheless a western poem in its reliance on metaphor, assonance, and connotative language (who'd have thought it possible to rescue "eventide" for a modern poem?).

Corman's work has continued along the lines of the two books just mentioned. It cannot be denied that his emotional range is narrow and that his tone can verge on too easy a plangency, too self-indulgent an acquiescence in the drift towards dissolution. "The Mystery," for instance, from *In Good Time*, ends (speaking of swallows): "How each/pursued/ /each,/pursued/by a green sky/as the sun settles,/ /desperate/to let themselves/go, O/against night." Unfair, of course, to crowd it like that, but it may be agreed that the melodramatic "desperate" and the moaning "o" sounds produce too facile a pathos and distract attention from the things seen to the emoting observer. Contrast the restraint of a successful poem on roughly the same thing:

Someone will
sweep the fallen
petals away

away. I know,
I know. Weight of
red shadows.

Here the talking voice is never swamped and the tone plays against and makes more convincing the feelings that weigh on the speaker. Even more fully impersonal is the following, also from *Nonce*:

The leaf that moved with the wind
moves
with the stream.

The energy is released by so simple a means as a change in tense. And the emotional effect is complex—transience is recognized but also cyclical renewal—and all is made to inhere in the thing seen, not worked up by the sensibility of the poet. When he writes like this, and he does it often enough for every book to be rewarding, Corman's is a voice that earns our careful attention.

—Seamus Cooney

———

CORN, Alfred. American. Born in Bainbridge, Georgia, 14 August 1943. Educated at Emory University, Atlanta, 1961-65, B.A. in French 1965; Columbia University, New York (Woodrow Wilson Fellow; Faculty Fellow), 1965-67, M.A. 1967; Fulbright Fellow, Paris, 1967-68. Married Ann Jones in 1967 (divorced, 1971). Preceptor, Columbia University, 1968-70; Associate Editor, *University Review*, New York, 1970; staff writer, DaCapo Press, New York, 1971-72; Assistant Professor, 1978, and Visiting Lecturer, 1980-81, Connecticut College, New London; Visiting Lecturer, Yale University, New Haven, Connecticut, 1977, 1978, 1979, Columbia University, 1983, 1985, and City University of New York, 1983, 1985. Recipient: Ingram Merrill fellowship, 1974; George Dillon Prize, 1975, Oscar Blumenthal Prize, 1977, and Levinson Prize, 1982 (*Poetry*, Chicago); Davidson prize, 1982; American Academy award, 1983. Address: 54 West 16th Street, New York, New York 10011, U.S.A.

PUBLICATIONS

Verse

All Roads at Once. New York, Viking Press, 1976.
A Call in the Midst of the Crowd. New York, Viking Press, 1978.
The Various Light. New York, Viking Press, 1980.
Notes from a Child of Paradise. New York, Viking Press, 1984.

*

Critical Studies: "Alfred Corn's Speaking Gift" by George Kearns, in *Canto* (Andover, Massachusetts), Fall 1978; "In the Place of Time" by G.E. Murray, in *Parnassus* (New York), Spring-Summer 1983.

Alfred Corn comments:

My poems have often been compared to those of Elizabeth Bishop, John Ashbery, and James Merrill; but perhaps just as useful a comparison could be made with the trio that figured importantly in their own development—Marianne Moore, Stevens, Auden. Subject matter favored: human relationships, especially love; landscape and cityscape; the arts; the difficult fitting between poetry and truth; the poet's vocation; the search for response in an inanimate world with no (at least denominational) religious dimension; suffering and death; social injustice; historical events and persons; childhood; imagination and introspective life.

In my first book I tried several tones of voice, still hewing fairly close to the ideal of speechly sound, middle diction, and the avoidance of syllable-stress meter. These tendencies continue in the second volume, which, in addition to an opening suite of lyrics, includes the long seasonally arranged title poem (with historical prose extracts interpolated) on New York City. (A precedent, on a somewhat smaller scale, was the sequence, "Pages from a Voyage," in the first book, a meditation on Darwin's round-the-world expedition, contemporary civilization, and personal fate.) In my third book, landscape came to replace cityscape in importance; and syllable-stress meter and rhyme are frequently used. Many of the poems might be described as late-Symbolist or simply introspective, notably, the 200-line (roughly) "Lacrimae Rerum," a meditation on sensory, and impalpable, reality.

Notes from a Child of Paradise I see as completing the sequence beginning with *A Call in the Midst of the Crowd* and *The Various Light*. A 3000-line autobiographical and meditative poem, it takes part of its structure from the *Commedia* of Dante but is finally concerned with finding a place in an American tradition defined by Emerson and the author of "Song of Myself" and "A Passage to India." At the factual level, it recounts the life of its subject from the years 1964 to 1969, the marriage and separation of two graduate students active in the antiwar movement.

*   *   *

"Getting Past the Past" is both a title and a leitmotif in Alfred Corn's impressive first book, *All Roads at Once*. Both in style and subject matter, past is present—or, as he puts it, "the past is a project/To be continued"—viewed and revised by a keenly individual sensibility: "We invent/The world and a wide cup to catch it in." Whether remembering childhood reading of and identification with fairy tales or traveling in Italy, France, and the Caribbean, the poet is caught by an evanescent past beyond recapture, if not recall, by the gift of imagination: "Yet somehow it's lost./The instinct to save, to fix in words,/Drains color, excitement dying to be/Art for others, from which you withdraw,/Victim of an imagination." Thus the artist's awareness of his vocation, and his ambivalence about it, joy and inevitable disappointment, and meanwhile the hope in this "double life, to be read and dreamed/Until the secret order appears."

Creating "poems across the trenches/of time" is one way to impose an order on "the curve of history," while waiting for the indefinite future. And already Corn demonstrates master craftsmanship in the traditional poetic forms. If in his sophistication he sometimes sounds too world-weary, even languid, the sharpness of his observations and apercus, his wit and word-play (often twisting clichés and turning puns into newer and neater truisms) prevent these poems from being merely facile, though not always from being mannered. Corn's verbal ability and technical virtuosity are reminiscent of James Merrill, as his gift for evoking associative meaning through catalogue and astute juxtaposition owe more than a little to John Ashbery. The weights of tradition, however, like those of his own past, are not so much burdens as influences transformed into a distinctive identity. Thus, Hart Crane's *The Bridge* helps Corn make his own philosophical and spiritual connections; while "Passages from a Voyage," the brilliantly sustained long poem which concludes the volume, uses Darwin's account of his journey as a base for personal, poetic explorations of the duality of man's life, the ambiguity of consciousness and the body's "ignorant optimism," and mutability and its terrors, the whole becoming an "experience arranged in a splendid contraption."

With *A Call in the Midst of the Crowd*, Corn continues to develop his themes of love and loss, but here self-assuredness replaces the self-consciousness of his earlier work. Again we find the subtle allusions to illustrious predecessors, the bright phrases and descriptive catalogues; but now the abstract and concrete combine in lyrics capable of capturing even the most elusive mood—or the immensity and diversity of a great city. Once again, too, travel is a subject, the dislocation provoking unease as "thoughts come stunned/And out of order." But the very disarray proves a creative stimulus. Though the "world of objects perpetually/Closes in," Corn has many a "rare moment when seeing comes of age," particularly in the long title poem on New York City which makes up most of the book. The four-part poem is itself half made up of astutely selected and cleverly arranged quotations from Crane, Henry James, Poe, Melville, Whitman, de Tocqueville, Wallace Stevens, whose comments play counterpoint to Corn's own observations about the city, its effect on the individual adventurer (or exile) there, and the course of a broken then mended romance. As the poem progresses, often ironically, through the seasons of love, it reveals the infinite possibilities, for achievement and failure, the chaos, distractions, and sheer abundance that make the excitement and danger of the city. As long urban history merges with the individual present with oblique significance, we are told "Our births choose us; then our lives; then our deaths." But, for all that, the city grants freedom to the poet, for here he is "Free once more to stroll where I'm drawn, hero/Of my own story." The promise Corn finds in the city is the same this book holds for its author: "The speaking gift that falls to one who hears/A word shine through the white noise of the world."

—Joseph Parisi

CORNISH Sam(uel James). American. Born in Baltimore, Maryland, 22 December 1935. Educated at Booker T. Washington High School, Baltimore. Military service, 1958-60. Married Jean Faxon in 1967. Former Editor of the Enoch Pratt Library publication *Chicory*, Baltimore. Currently, Editor, *Mimeo* magazine. Consultant in elementary-school teaching, Central Atlantic Regional Educational Laboratories Humanities Program. Recipient: National Endowment for the Arts grant, 1967, 1969. Address: c/o Bookstore Press, Box 191, R.F.D. 1, Freeport, Maine 04032, U.S.A.

PUBLICATIONS

Verse

In This Corner: Sam Cornish and Verses. Baltimore, Fleming McAllister, 1961.
People Beneath the Window. Baltimore, Sacco, 1962.
Generations. Baltimore, Beanbag Press, 1964.
Angles. Baltimore, Beanbag Press, 1965.
Winters. Cambridge, Massachusetts, Sans Souci Press, 1968.
Short Beers. Cambridge, Massachusetts, Beanbag Press, 1969 (?).
Generations: Poems. Boston, Beacon Press, 1971.
Streets. Chicago, Third World Press, 1973.
Sometimes: Ten Poems. Cambridge, Massachusetts, Pym Randall Press, 1973.
Sam's World. Washington, D.C., Decatur House, 1978.

Other

Your Hand in Mine. New York, Harcourt Brace, 1970.
Grandmother's Pictures (for children). Lenox, Massachusetts, Bookstore Press, 1974.
Walking the Street with Mississippi John Hurt (for children). Scarsdale, New York, Bradbury Press, 1978.

Editor, with Lucian W. Dixon, *Chicory: Young Voices from the Black Ghetto.* New York, Association Press, 1969.
Editor, with Hugh Fox, *The Living Underground: An Anthology of Contemporary American Poetry.* East Lansing, Michigan, Ghost Dance Press, 1969.

*

Critical Study: introduction by Ron Schreiber to *Winters*, 1968.

Sam Cornish comments:

Most of my major themes are of urban life, the negro predicament here in the cities and my own family. I try to use a
minimum of words to express the intended thought or feeling,
with the effect of being starkly frank at times. Main verse form is
unrhymed, free. Main influences—Lowell, T.S. Eliot, LeRoi
Jones.

*   *   *

Sam Cornish's inclusion in nearly all major anthologies of
new black poetry, including the one edited by Clarence Major,
indicates his rapidly growing stature among contemporary
Black American poets and points to richer future achievement.
Cornish feels that T.S. Eliot, Robert Lowell, and LeRoi Jones
have influenced him and this influence is evident in his affinity
with Jones in his themes and the subtle irony of his poetry, a
quality so significant in Eliot and Lowell. The three dominant
themes in his poetry are urban life, the situation of the Negro,
and his own family. In form, his poetry is strikingly concise, even
terse, and his verse unrhymed. The short poem "Sam's World" is
a representative sample of the poet's sharp consciousness of the
Blacks' plight and, simultaneously, his perception of the identity
and dignity possible even in that plight:

sam's mother has
grey combed hair

she will never touch
it with a hot iron

she leaves it
the way the lord
intended

she wears it proudly
a black and grey
round head of hair

In his comments on his well-known "Generations 1," Cornish
says that he "walked to the east side of Baltimore trying to find
and remember the boys that grew up with me and were still living
on the streets: laughing, talking and thinking about the streets,
the playgrounds that had turned into parking lots, or weeded
places after the riots. The poem grew out of those meetings and
remembering what it was like to grow up alone, how I felt about
women, the church, what I wanted to do with my life." Remembered, re-lived, and reflected-upon events provide a major basis
for his poetry. But the unrecognizable and beautiful transformations of these events into poetry will be obvious to anyone
reading "Generations 1." Specific details about the familiar figures of everyday life become highly generalised and evocative in
such lines as these:

he would come into her cold apartment
wondering if he had the special knowledge
that women wanted from men
endured the pain she moaned
the odor between her breasts

and wanted god to remember
he was young
and in much trouble

with himself

Cornish's poetry shows an intense awareness of what it means
to be human and, especially, to be black in contemporary America. It fuses in a complex way a tender awareness of intimate
man-woman relations, close family ties, and a sympathy and
understanding for fellow blacks. As a black poet, Cornish suffers
the anguish of his people and writes about it in a way that
combines the immediacy of one sharing the experience and the
control of the detached observer. It is this tone of wistfulness and
this control that make his poetry deeply moving without being
shriekingly militant.

—J.N. Sharma

———

CORSO, (Nunzio) Gregory. American. Born in New York
City, 26 March 1930. Married 1) Sally November in 1963
(divorced), one daughter; 2) Belle Carpenter in 1968, one daughter and one son; 3) Jocelyn Stern, one son. Manual laborer,
1950-51; Reporter, Los Angeles *Examiner*, 1951-52; merchant
seaman, 1952-53. Member of the Department of English, State
University of New York, Buffalo, 1965-70. Recipient: Longview
Foundation Award; Poetry Foundation Award. Address: c/o
New Directions, 80 Eighth Avenue, New York, New York
10011, U.S.A.

PUBLICATIONS

Verse

The Vestal Lady on Brattle and Other Poems. Cambridge,
Massachusetts, Richard Brukenfeld, 1955.
Gasoline. San Francisco, City Lights, 1958.
Bomb. San Francisco, City Lights, 1958.
A Pulp Magazine for the Dead Generation: Poems, with Henk
Marsman. Paris, Dead Language, 1959.
The Happy Birthday of Death. New York, New Directions,
1960.
Minutes to Go, with others. Paris, Two Cities, 1960.
Selected Poems. London, Eyre and Spottiswoode, 1962.
Long Live Man. New York, New Directions, 1962.
Penguin Modern Poets 5, with Lawrence Ferlinghetti and Allen
Ginsberg. London, Penguin, 1963.
The Mutation of the Spirit: A Shuffle Poem. New York, Death
Press, 1964.
*There Is Yet Time to Run Through Life and Expiate All That's
Been Sadly Done.* New York, New Directions, 1965.
*The Geometric Poem: A Long Experimental Poem, Composite
of Many Lines and Angles Selective.* Milan, privately
printed, 1966.
10 Times a Poem. New York, Poets Press, 1967.
Elegiac Feelings American. New York, New Directions, 1970.
Egyptian Cross. New York, Phoenix Book Shop, 1971.
Ankh. New York, Phoenix Book Shop, 1971.
(Poems). New York, Phoenix Book Shop, 1971.
The Night Last Night Was at Its Nightest. New York, Phoenix
Book Shop, 1972.
Earth Egg. New York, Unmuzzled Ox, 1974.
Herald of the Autochthonic Spirit. New York, New Direc-
tions, 1981.

Plays

In This Hung-Up Age (produced Cambridge, Massachusetts, 1955). Published in *New Directions 18*, edited by James Laughlin, New York, New Directions, 1964.
Standing on a Streetcorner, in *Evergreen Review 6* (New York), March-April 1962.
That Little Black Door on the Left, in *Pardon Me Sir, But Is My Eye Hurting Your Elbow?*, edited by Bob Booker and George Foster. New York, Geis, 1968.
Way Out: A Poem in Discord. Kathmandu, Nepal, Bardo Matrix, 1974.

Novel

The American Express. Paris, Olympia Press, 1961.

Other

The Minicab War (parodies), with Anselm Hollo and Tom Raworth. London, Matrix Press, 1961.

Editor, with Walter Höllerer, *Junge Amerikanische Lyrik*. Munich, Hanser, 1961.

*

Bibliography: *A Bibliography of the Works of Gregory Corso 1954-1965* by Robert A. Wilson, New York, Phoenix Book Shop, 1966.

Manuscript Collections: Columbia University, New York; University of Texas, Austin; State University of New York, Buffalo; University of Kansas, Lawrence.

Critical Study: *Riverside Interviews 3* edited by Gavin Selerie, London, Binnacle Press, 1982.

Gregory Corso comments:
   [I am a] mental explorer, un-Faustian.
   [My verse is] hopeful—naive—strange—sweet—soon smart—why not.

*   *   *

To say that Gregory Corso is a member of the Beat Generation might be thought to say it all. But even though he was one of its most ardent apologists, he is no more typical than any of the others: Ginsberg, Ferlinghetti, Kerouac, Snyder. Still, they all shared that anti-social, apocalyptic, love-centered, freedom-loving mystique that has become so familiar to us. With Ginsberg and Kerouac, Corso was part of a kind of Beat triumvirate, each encouraging and supporting the other and his work. If Kerouac was the father-figure and Ginsberg the rabbi-figure, Corso was the child-figure and the clown.

Born into a poor immigrant family in Manhattan, Corso grew up as an underprivileged kid and became a juvenile delinquent who before he was 20 spent three years in prison for attempted robbery. He read widely and voraciously in prison, and after his release eventually found his way to the Harvard Library, where he continued his self-education and was taken up by local students and writers, who subsidized and saw through the press his first book of poems, *The Vestal Lady on Brattle*. It was at this point that Ginsberg and Kerouac "discovered" him.

Corso's poems are a mixture of powerful statement and bombast. He can be funny, maudlin, original, hackneyed, outrageous, sentimental—sometimes all in one poem. His stance is that of the sophisticated child, looking about him at a world gone mad and wondering why he is here. But madness is also a virtue, in the Blakean sense, since it is a response to and release from the sanity and conformity of the suburban fifties against which the Beats were reacting. As Corso puts it, "Man is great and mad, he was born mad and wonder of wonders the sanity of evolution knoweth not what to do."

Corso thinks of himself rather self-consciously as a poet, which leads him into excesses of language, archaisms, "poetic" phrasing, and unusual words. As one might expect of an autodidact, he wears his learning rather heavily, scattering literary and mythological allusions through his work. He likes to use words like "swipple," "precocial," "spatchcock," and the like; he can use a word like "writ" without apparent irony, and he seems to want such lines as "Life has meaning and I do not know the meaning" to be taken at face value. We can see the strong influence of Kerouac at work here, with his belief in letting it all hang out and writing without revision. This hit-or-miss technique of composition sometimes results in powerfully expressed feelings and ideas, but they often fall wide of the mark. He is not afraid to take chances, and there is something both endearing and annoying about the mixture of prosy language and verbal excess. Here is a typical piece of fustian taken at random:

> O walking crucifixes hooded and bowed
> treking catacombic apothecaries
> Grains drams and ounces of aphasia
> Etherized Popes their desperado nods
> raise welts of confessional memories on my lips

His subjects include large ones, like the plight of man and American society, Zen Buddhism, Egyptian religion, and Art, and smaller ones, like travel in Europe and Africa, his childhood, and the literary life. His most frequently anthologized poem is his best: that funny-sad meditation called "Marriage." The famous "Bomb" poem, printed in the shape of a mushroom cloud, shows a richness of invention which is one of his hallmarks, and an obsession with death, which is another. The title of one of his collections is *The Happy Birthday of Death*, a title ostensibly chosen at random from among a long list of such possibilities as Fried Shoes, Gargoyle Liver, The Rumpled Backyard, Radiator Soup, etc. Other good poems include "Giant Turtle," which describes a turtle laying eggs, "Hair," another repetitious but inventive poem, and "Seed Journey." Two long efforts in *Elegiac Feelings American* should be noted. The title poem, inscribed "for the dear memory of John Kerouac," is an attack on America and its destruction of Kerouac, rather incoherent in its excesses and logical inconsistencies. "The Geometric Poem" is a facsimile reproduction of a long handwritten manuscript complete with cartoon-like illustrations and hieroglyphics drawn by the poet; it is an elaborate and not wholly successful evocation of Egyptian culture and religion.

It is difficult not to like Corso as a person seen through his poetry: he is the perennial bad boy, jack-off (a recurrent but minor theme), hipster, clown, rebel, and misty-eyed romantic. Already, though, much of his poetry seems rather dated and quaint, and one wonders whether this 55-year-old child will be able to continue mining the same vein and whether the poems themselves will survive the era in which they were written.

—Donald Barlow Stauffer

COTTON, John. British. Born in London, 7 March 1925. Educated at London University, B.A. (honours). Served as an officer in the Royal Naval Command in the Far East during World War II. Married Peggy Cotton in 1948; two sons. Since 1947, teacher, and headmaster of a comprehensive school, Hertfordshire, 1963-84. Founder, with Ted Walker, and Editor, 1962-72, *Priapus* magazine; Editor, *The Private Library*, 1969-79. Since 1975, Publisher, Priapus Press. Chairman, The Poetry Society, 1972-74, 1977, London. Recipient: Arts Council award, 1971. Address: 37 Lombardy Drive, Berkhamsted, Hertfordshire HP4 2LQ, England.

PUBLICATIONS

Verse

Fourteen Poems. Berkhamsted, Hertfordshire, Priapus, 1967.
Outside the Gates of Eden and Other Poems. Bushey Heath, Hertfordshire, Taurus Press, 1969.
Ampurias. Berkhamsted, Hertfordshire, Priapus, 1969.
Old Movies and Other Poems. London, Chatto and Windus-Hogarth Press, 1971.
The Wilderness. Berkhamsted, Hertfordshire, Priapus, 1971.
Columbus on St. Dominica. Rushden, Northamptonshire, Sceptre Press, 1972.
A Sycamore Press Broadsheet. Oxford, Sycamore Press, 1973.
Preludes: San Martin. Rushden, Northamptonshire, Sceptre Press, 1973.
Roman Wall. Richmond, Surrey, Keepsake Press, 1973.
Casablanca. Berkhamsted, Hertfordshire, Priapus, 1973.
Kilroy Was Here: Poems 1970-74. London, Chatto and Windus-Hogarth Press, 1975.
Places. Berkhamsted, Hertfordshire, Priapus, 1976.
Fragments 11, 12, and 13. Knotting, Bedfordshire, Sceptre Press, 1976.
Powers. Berkhamsted, Hertfordshire, Priapus, 1977.
A Berkhamsted Three, with Fred Sedgwick and Freda Downie. Berkhamsted, Hertfordshire, Priapus, 1978.
Piers. Leicester, New Broom Press, 1979.
Torches. Berkhamsted, Hertfordshire, Priapus, 1979.
A Letter for a Wedding. Berkhamsted, Hertfordshire, Priapus, 1980.
Somme Man. Berkhamsted, Hertfordshire, Priapus, 1980.
Wishful Thinking. Leicester, New Broom Press, 1980.
Poems for a Course, with Wes Magee. Berkhamsted, Hertfordshire, Priapus, 1980.
The Totleigh Riddles. Berkhamsted, Hertfordshire, Priapus, 1981.
Day Book. Privately printed, 1981.
Catullus at Sirmio. Berkhamsted, Hertfordshire, Priapus, 1982.
Day Book Continued. Leicester, New Broom Press, 1982.
The Highfield Write-a-Poem, with Bevis Cotton. Berkhamsted, Hertfordshire, Priapus, 1982.
Day Book. Berkhamsted, Hertfordshire, Priapus, 1983.
The Storyville Portraits. West Kirby, Merseyside, Headland, 1984.
The Crystal Zoo. Oxford, Oxford University Press, 1984.

Other

British Poetry since 1965. London, National Book League, 1973.

*

Critical Studies: in *Poetry Book Society Bulletin 69* and *84* (London), 1971, 1975; by Anne Cluysenaar, in *Stand* (Newcastle upon Tyne), xiv, 1, 1972; by Fred Sedgwick, in *Hertfordshire Countryside* (Hitchin), December 1979; interview with Moira Andrew, in *School's Poetry Review*, 1984.

John Cotton comments:

Overstatement is the obvious and inherent peril in writing a piece of this kind. Yet if it sounds pretentious to say that my pursuit of the art basically constitutes an exploration of that area between our wish to make it last forever and our consciousness that it never can, I can plead that it is the nearest I can get to an explanation of what I attempt to do. Having gone thus far, I may as well compound things by saying that with Aristotle I look upon one of the purposes of our fictions as a means of bringing order to the plethora of disparate experiences to which we are subjected. In mitigation I would add that while I take the art seriously, I do not take myself so.

*   *   *

John Cotton's work strikes one as utterly English; the poems seem rooted in the attributes of decency and compassion, and there is evidence of a square-shouldered stance in the face of the inevitable enemy. English, yes, even though Cotton ranges far for his subject matter—outer space (in "Report Back"), New Orleans (in *The Story-ville Portraits*), or Spain (in *Kilroy Was Here*). Despite this wanderlust Cotton remains the careful, considerate and deliberate poet with feet firmly planted on the English landscape.

He prefers a "natural" line length which can look untidy and unformed but which reads well. A resonant tone echoes through the poems whatever the length of the piece; he is adept with the brief landscape sketch ("Moorland Signals") and the extended sequence as instanced in *Day Book*, 32 "fragments." While reluctant to let himself go on the page, there is nevertheless occasion for humour, for the belly-laugh, for the sensual, as in "Old Movies":

> And their apartments,
> vast as temples,
> full of unused furniture,
> the sideboards bending with booze,
> and all those acres of bed!
> She, in attendance, wearing
> diaphanous, but never quite
> diaphanous enough, nightwear.

At times he can be clumsily poetic ("Did the grey climacteric beast have to choose") but instances of such over-writing are rare. More common is a clear diction, a feeling that each poem knows exactly where it is going. Recent work has darkened; human situations are presented without camouflage, as in the moving "The Night Ward." Here, Cotton spells out without stridency or blather the dread experienced by those being stalked by death. The observations are sharp, the compassion palpable:

> The drip measures it
> As it feeds down into the arm,
> Spelling out its fractions
> By the bobbing of a small plastic ball.
> Listen. You might just hear it.
> God help the heart that is as quiet.
> We wait for dawn from the trenches of our beds.

Cotton not only moves but entertains the reader. He is not one to stick with gloom; past experiences in the cinema, and poems such as "The Westerners" are packed with incident and good lines. Like the washing on the line in "Moorland Signals" Cotton's poems are "a bright bunting/of challenge to the grey power...."

—Wes Magee

COUZYN, Jeni. Canadian. Born in South Africa, 26 July 1942; became Canadian citizen, 1975. Educated at the University of Natal, B.A. 1962, B.A. (honours) 1963. Drama teacher, Rhodesia, 1964; producer, African Music and Drama Association, Johannesburg, 1965; teacher, Special School, London, 1966; poetry organiser and gallery attendant, Camden Arts Centre, London, 1967. Since 1968, freelance poet, lecturer, and broadcaster. Writer-in-Residence, University of Victoria, British Columbia, 1976. Recipient: Arts Council grant, 1971, 1974; Canada Council grant, 1977, 1984. Address: c/o Bloodaxe Books, P.O. Box 1SN, Newcastle upon Tyne NE99 1SN, England.

PUBLICATIONS

Verse

Flying. London, Workshop Press, 1970.
Monkeys' Wedding. London, Cape, 1972; revised edition, Vancouver, Douglas and McIntyre, and London, Heinemann, 1978.
Christmas in Africa. London, Heinemann, 1975.
House of Changes. London, Heinemann, 1978.
The Happiness Bird. Victoria, British Columbia, Sono Nis Press, 1978.
A Time to Be Born. London, Heinemann, 1981.
Life by Drowning: Selected Poems. Toronto, Anansi, 1983; expanded edition, Newcastle upon Tyne, Bloodaxe, 1984.

Other

Editor, *Twelve to Twelve: Poems Commissioned for Poetry D-Day, Camden Arts Festival 1970.* London, Poets' Trust, 1970.
Editor, *The Bloodaxe Book of Contemporary Women Poets.* Newcastle upon Tyne, Bloodaxe, 1984.

*

Jeni Couzyn comments:
I am interested in using symbol rather than image, and tend to write with as much clarity as I can. I am at times monosyllabic, and look for the shortest and simplest words I can find. I believe poetry should be "true" at the deepest possible level, and dislike the kind of poetry that appears to be complex on the surface, crammed with learned references and tricky images, but which finally has little to say.

I write in free verse, using rhythm and stress to underline meaning and to counterpoint the sense whenever I can. Similarly I use rhyme for surprise and emphasis rather than in any metrical pattern. I am particularly fond of imperfect rhymes, especially where the rhyming syllable falls on the unstressed part of the word.

I believe that poetry should be spoken, and read on the page only as a kind of specialised reference—as music is written to be played and listened to. Reviewers at this time in the history of poetry use the words "poetry circuit" as a dirty word, as though it were some kind of big roundabout that only the common and the simple people climbed aboard. The simply expressed but profound truth of a poem like Robert Frost's "Nothing Gold Can Stay" is what I most admire in poetry and most seek for. The criteria I use to judge my own work are: is it interesting; is it relevant to other people's lives; is it music; is it true in the deepest sense—in a lasting way. To the extent that these criteria are approached, I am pleased or displeased with a poem.

In sound I have been most influenced by Dylan Thomas—not so much in his technique as in his courage in defying the dry tradition of poetry he was born into.

That I am a poet in an age where the "unintellectual" (i.e., almost everybody) think of poetry as something they didn't like when they were at school, and the intellectual think it something the masses should be excluded from, is sad for me. This age has too much reverence for poetry, and too little respect—for by the same token it is very difficult indeed to earn a living from poetry. Nor are poets considered valid members of the community—you will never see a panel set up to discuss drug usage, for example, or terrorism in Ireland, with a poet among the psychiatrists, students, businessmen, clergy and housewives being asked to give their view.

For me being a poet is a job rather than an activity. I feel I have a function in society, neither more nor less meaningful than any other simple job. I feel it is part of my work to make poetry more accessible to people who have had their rights withdrawn from them. Standing in the way of this are the poetry watchdogs who bark in the Sunday reviews, trying to preserve their sterile territory. Also it is necessary to overcome the apathy and ignorance of a whole society with a totally untrained ear and a profoundly sluggish imagination.

*   *   *

Jeni Couzyn's first book, *Flying,* came as a surprise even to readers who thought themselves sophisticated. Few of the poems contained in it had reached the usual magazines and anthologies, though Couzyn was known for her appearances on the recital circuits. *Flying* consisted, among other things, of reflections upon her South African background, descriptions of London's grey suburbia, dramatisations of love relationships, and revelations of mental stress. These last were at their best when the author expressed her internal conflicts by way of her flow of exotic imagery. For example, "The Farm" deals with what looks like a depressive illness, but it does so in terms almost of a child's holiday.

> On the farm there are two
> cows.
> And there are a lot of
> trees. They change their leaves
> whenever they like. When they change their leaves you
> know
> that it is autumn. The two cows have a calf and then you
> know
> that it is spring.
> You can take your cat with you to the farm or whatever
> you like. You can take your
> bicycle
> or your
> typewriter
> or all your books
> you can take whatever you like with you to the farm...

These patient monosyllables ratify a childish acceptance of what becomes more abnormal the further the poem proceeds. The resultant conflict, between the innocent and the sinister, sets up an uneasy tension, too, in the reader. Couzyn, when she projects a parable of the mind's cliffs of fall, is a distinguished poet.

But her second book, *Monkeys' Wedding*, suffers from over-explicitness. Many of the attitudes are straight out of Women's Lib. The collection contains some powerful work; perhaps most notably "The Babies," a painful poem about contraception and abortion: "On the table the baby lay / pulped like a water-melon, a few / soft bits of skull protruding from the mush...." One may feel here, however, that the skin of fiction is stretched too thin over the agony. We are more conscious of outcry than of experience. Emotion of this sort demands an objective correlative if it is not to seem shrill.

Such a correlative is sought for in *Christmas in Africa*. Couzyn makes considerable use of science fiction, notably the work of Brian Aldiss: "I am your priest and your prophet. / May the long journey end / may the ship come home...." But this would be obscure to a reader who did not know *Non-Stop*. And the reader who does know that remarkable book may wonder why he has need of Couzyn's poem. More striking are what seem to be reminiscences of Couzyn's childhood in South Africa, e.g., "In the House of the Father":

The snakes were the price. In their hundreds they inhabited
our world at Christmas. They were the hazard
in the garden. And they were everywhere
tangled in undergrowth, slithering over your feet in the
                                                    pathway
stretched across doorways in the sun
lurking under the banana plant and nesting in the luckybean
    tree....

But, sharp though these details are, they don't have the pressure of implication that we find in the African imagery of *Flying*. Nor are they contained within a sufficiently decisive form: the verse is discursive.

In *House of Changes* we are, for the most part, deprived even of sharp details. Imagery gives way to incantation: "Leprechaun take back thy curse / Leprechaun take back thy curse...." This seems to be wrenched from a context, but no adequate context is given to us in the book. There are more science fiction poems, but they are even more dependent upon Philip K. Dick than the earlier ones were upon Brian Aldiss. Only occasionally do the two interrelate—

Insatiable one, I'm exhausted with eating
I'm a bag of stones, I am all stomach. Bloated
I lie here unable to move in my sea of flesh.
My thighs and breasts flow without shape
my head sags in a heap of chins
I lie here defiled in a mound of
self-disgust, in a pool of half digested fluids
yet you hunger and hunger in me.
I was a woman once....

This is from a poem called "I and Wolverine" which I take to be a dialogue between an exhausted woman and the unappeasable sexuality that devours her. It suggests that Couzyn is by no means at the end of her poetic range. Yet one is conscious, in all her books, of a gap between potentiality and achievement. Though she has touched notes beyond the set register of her early work, Couzyn cannot really be said to have improved her tessitura. No fiction has quite replaced her early formalism as a correlative for incipient violence and hysteria. The science fic-

tion analogues and the incantations alike show that she is still in search of a form that will also be a plot. Her many admirers will follow her future explorations in the hope of sharing in a fresh sense of discovery.

—Philip Hobsbaum

COWLEY, Malcolm. American. Born in Belsano, Pennsylvania, 24 August 1898. Educated at Peabody High School, Pittsburgh; Harvard University, Cambridge, Massachusetts (Editor, *The Advocate*, 1919), A.B. (cum laude) 1920 (Phi Beta Kappa); University of Montpellier, France, 1921-22, diploma 1922. Served in the American Ambulance Service in France, 1917, and the United States Army, 1918; with Office of Facts and Figures, Washington, D.C., 1942. Married 1) Marguerite Frances Baird in 1919 (divorced, 1932); 2) Muriel Maurer in 1932; one son. Writer, *Sweet's Architectural Catalogue*, New York, 1920-21 and 1923-24; Associate Editor, *Broom* magazine, New York, 1923; free-lance writer and translator, 1925-29; Literary Editor, *New Republic*, New York, 1929-44. Visiting Professor: University of Washington, Seattle, 1950; Stanford University, California, 1956, 1959, 1960-61, 1965; University of Michigan, Ann Arbor, 1957; University of California, Berkeley, 1962; Cornell University, Ithaca, New York, 1964; University of Minnesota, Minneapolis, 1971; University of Warwick, Coventry, England, 1973. Since 1948, Literary Adviser, Viking Press, New York. Director of the Yaddo Corporation. Recipient: Levinson Prize, 1927, and Harriet Monroe Memorial Prize, 1939 (*Poetry*, Chicago); American Academy grant, 1946, and Gold Medal, 1981; National Endowment for the Arts grant, 1967; Signet Medal, 1976; Modern Language Association Medal, 1979; Who's Who in America Achievement award, 1984. Litt.D.: Franklin and Marshall College, Lancaster, Pennsylvania, 1961; Colby College, Waterville, Maine, 1962; University of Warwick, 1975; University of New Haven, Connecticut, 1976; Monmouth College, West Long Branch, New Jersey, 1978; University of Connecticut, Storrs, 1983. President, National Institute of Arts and Letters, 1956-59, 1962-65; Chancellor, American Academy, 1967-76. Address: Church Road, Sherman, Connecticut 06784, U.S.A.

PUBLICATIONS

Verse

Blue Juniata. New York, Cape and Smith, 1929.
The Dry Season. New York, New Directions, 1941.
Blue Juniata: Collected Poems. New York, Viking Press, 1968.

Other

Racine. Paris, privately printed, 1923.
Exile's Return: A Narrative of Ideas. New York, Norton, 1934; London, Cape, 1935; revised edition, as *Exile's Return: A Literary Odyssey of the 1920's*, New York, Viking Press, 1951; London, Bodley Head, 1961.
The Literary Situation. New York, Viking Press, 1954.
Black Cargoes: A History of the Atlantic Slave Trade 1518-1865, with Daniel P. Mannix. New York, Viking Press, 1962; London, Longman, 1963.

The Faulkner-Cowley File: Letters and Memories 1944-1962,
with William Faulkner.   New York, Viking Press, 1966;
London, Chatto and Windus, 1967.
Think Back on Us: A Contemporary Chronicle of the 1930's,
edited by Henry Dan Piper.   Carbondale, Southern Illinois
University Press, 1967.
*A Many-Windowed House: Collected Essays on American Wri-
ters and American Writing*, edited by Henry Dan Piper.
Carbondale, Southern Illinois University Press, 1970.
A Second Flowering: Works and Days of the Lost Generation.
New York, Viking Press, and London, Deutsch, 1973.
*—And I Worked at the Writer's Trade: Chapters of Literary
History 1918-1978*.   New York, Viking Press, 1978.
The Dream of the Golden Mountains: Remembering the 1930's.
New York, Viking Press, 1980.
The View from 80.   New York, Viking Press, 1980.
The Flower and the Leaf, edited by Donald Faulkner.   New
York, Viking Press, 1985.

Editor, *Adventures of an African Slaver, Being a True Account
of the Life of Captain Theodore Canot*, by Brantz Mayer.
New York, Boni, and London, Routledge, 1928.
Editor, *After the Genteel Tradition: American Writers since
1910*.   New York, Norton, 1937; revised edition, Carbondale,
Southern Illinois University Press, 1964.
Editor, with Bernard Smith, *Books That Changed Our Minds*.
New York, Doubleday, 1939.
Editor, *The Portable Hemingway*.   New York, Viking Press,
1944.
Editor, with Hannah Josephson, *Aragon, Poet of the French
Resistance*.   New York, Duell, 1945; as *Aragon, Poet of Res-
urgent France*, London, Pilot Press, 1946.
Editor, *The Portable Faulkner*.   New York, Viking Press, 1946;
revised edition, Viking Press, and London, Chatto and Win-
dus, 1967.
Editor, *The Portable Hawthorne*.   New York, Viking Press,
1948; revised edition, Viking Press, and London, Penguin,
1969; as *Nathaniel Hawthorne: Selected Works*, London,
Chatto and Windus, 1971.
Editor, *The Complete Poetry and Prose of Walt Whitman*.
New York, Pellegrini and Cudahy, 1948; as *The Works of
Walt Whitman*, New York, Funk and Wagnalls, 2 vols., 1968.
Editor, *Stories*, by F. Scott Fitzgerald.   New York, Scribner,
1951.
Editor, *Tender Is the Night*, by F. Scott Fitzgerald.   New York,
Scribner, 1951.
Editor, with Edmund Wilson, *Three Novels of F. Scott Fitzge-
rald*.   New York, Scribner, 1953.
Editor, *Writers at Work: The "Paris Review" Interviews*.   New
York, Viking Press, and London, Secker and Warburg, 1958.
Editor, *Leaves of Grass, The First (1855) Edition*, by Walt
Whitman.   New York, Viking Press, 1959; London, Secker
and Warburg, 1960.
Editor, *The Bodley Head Scott Fitzgerald 5-6*.   London, Bod-
ley Head, 2 vols., 1963.
Editor, with Robert Cowley, *Fitzgerald and the Jazz Age*.   New
York, Scribner, 1966.
Editor, with Howard E. Hugo, *The Lessons of the Masters: An
Anthology of the Novel from Cervantes to Hemingway*.
New York, Scribner, 1971.
Editor, *Walt Whitman* (revised edition), edited by Mark Van
Doren.   New York, Viking Press, 1974; as *The Portable Walt
Whitman*, London, Penguin, 1977.
Editor, with Carl Bode, *The Portable Emerson*.   New York and
London, Penguin, 1981.

Translator, *On Board the Morning Star*, by Pierre MacOrlan.
New York, Boni, 1924.
Translator, *Joan of Arc*, by Joseph Delteil.   New York, Minton
Balch, 1926.
Translator, *Variety*, by Paul Valéry.   New York, Harcourt
Brace, 1927.
Translator, *Catherine-Paris*, by Marthe Lucie Bibesco.   New
York, Harcourt Brace, 1928.
Translator, *The Green Parrot*, by Marthe Lucie Bibesco.   New
York, Harcourt Brace, 1929.
Translator, *The Sacred Hill*, by Maurice Barrès.   New York,
Macaulay, 1929.
Translator, *The Count's Ball*, by Raymond Radiguet.   New
York, Norton, 1929.
Translator, *Imaginary Interviews*, by André Gide.   New York,
Knopf, 1944.
Translator, with James R. Lawler, *Leonardo Poe Mallarmé*, by
Paul Valéry.   Princeton, New Jersey, Princeton University
Press, and London, Routledge, 1972.

*

Bibliography: *Malcolm Cowley: A Checklist of His Writings
1916-1973*, by Diane U. Eisenberg, Carbondale, Southern Illinois University Press, 1975.

Manuscript Collection: Newberry Library, Chicago.

Critical Studies: introduction by Henry Dan Piper to *A Many-
Windowed House*, 1970; by Lewis P. Simpson, in *Sewanee
Review* (Tennessee), Autumn 1974; *The Early Career of Malcolm Cowley: A Humanist among the Moderns* by James M.
Kempf, Baton Rouge, Louisiana State University Press, 1984;
introduction by Donald Faulkner to *The Flower and the Leaf*,
1985.

*   *   *

Malcolm Cowley's output as a poet has never been copious.
Throughout a long and distinguished literary career he has been
known primarily as a critic and historian of American literature
rather than a poet. Nevertheless, *Blue Juniata*, the 1968 volume
of collected poems, shows that Cowley's talents as a poet are real
and unforced, however infrequently he may have exercised them.
He sees his poems as expressions and illustrations of his personal
and intellectual history, beginning in a Pennsylvania childhood
in the opening year of this century; an attachment to country life
and the natural world is a recurring theme in his poetry. But as
well as its personal dimension, Cowley's poetry also documents
and crystallizes crucial moments in modern American history.
Thus, "Chateau de Soupir: 1917" is a sharp recollection of the
First World War; "Ezra Pound at the Hotel Jacob" recalls the
expatriate Parisian literary life of the 1920's; "Tomorrow Morning" reflects the political passions of the 1920's and the impact of
the Spanish Civil War. Most recently, "Here with the Long Grass
Rippling" looks in passing at the Vietnam war.
    Cowley's poetry is not dramatic or particularly vivid in its
language. But it possesses the solid virtues of craftsmanship,
urbanity, controlled lyricism, and exact observation of the physical world.

—Bernard Bergonzi

COXE, Louis (Osborne). American. Born in Manchester, New Hampshire, 15 April 1918. Educated at St. Paul's School, Concord, New Hampshire, graduated 1936; Princeton University, New Jersey, A.B. 1940. Served in the United States Naval Reserve, 1942-46. Married Edith Winsor in 1946; three sons and one daughter. Instructor, Princeton University, 1946; Briggs-Copeland Fellow, Harvard University, Cambridge, Massachusetts, 1948-49; Assistant Professor, then Associate Professor, University of Minnesota, Minneapolis, 1949-55. Professor of English, 1955-56, and since 1956, Pierce Professor of English, Bowdoin College, Brunswick, Maine. Fulbright Lecturer, Trinity College, Dublin, 1959-60, and University of Aix-Marseilles, 1971-72. Recipient: Donaldson Award, for drama, 1952; *Sewanee Review* Fellowship, 1956; Brandeis University Creative Arts Award, 1960; National Endowment for the Arts award, 1977; Academy of American Poets Prize, 1977. Address: Department of English, Bowdoin College, Brunswick, Maine 04011, U.S.A.

PUBLICATIONS

Verse

The Sea Faring and Other Poems. New York, Holt, 1947.
The Second Man and Other Poems. Minneapolis, University of Minnesota Press, 1955.
The Wilderness and Other Poems. Minneapolis, University of Minnesota Press, 1958.
The Middle Passage. Chicago, University of Chicago Press, 1960.
The Last Hero and Other Poems. Nashville, Tennessee, Vanderbilt University Press, 1965.
Nikal Seyn, Decoration Day: A Poem and a Play. Nashville, Tennessee, Vanderbilt University Press, 1966.
Passage: Selected Poems 1943-1978. Columbia, University of Missouri Press, 1979.

Plays

Billy Budd, with Robert Chapman, adaptation of the story by Melville (as *Uniform of Flesh,* produced New York, 1949; revised version, as *Billy Budd,* produced New York, 1951). Princeton, New Jersey, Princeton University Press, 1951; as *The Good Sailor* (produced London, 1956), London, Heinemann, 1966.
The General (produced Cambridge, Massachusetts, 1954).
The Witchfinders (produced Rochester, Minnesota, 1955; New York, 1958).

Other

Christianity and Education. Brunswick, Maine, St. Paul's Episcopal Church, 1958.
Edwin Arlington Robinson. Minneapolis, University of Minnesota Press, 1962.
Edwin Arlington Robinson: The Life of Poetry. New York, Pegasus, 1969.
Enabling Acts: Selected Essays in Criticism. Columbia, University of Missouri Press, 1976.

Editor, *Chaucer.* New York, Dell, 1963.

*   *   *

The Sea Faring, the title of his first book, is also Louis Coxe's favorite theme. The sea acts not only as a setting for individual displays of courage and villainy but also as a powerful metaphor for the universal struggles endured in man's precarious moral voyages. The poet frames his astute observations with skilful verse forms, but several early and some later works suffer from a hypercerebral tone, overly technical terminology, and complex and constricting syntax; what might be music is muffled by a heavy academic pall, which also gives the impression of greater profundity than actually lies beneath the convoluted surface. Even here, however, the search for fundamentals, for the eternal designs behind the ephemeral, gives Coxe's lines their particular strength. The persona asks, "How shall he tell you: Mac, the war/Was rugged?" and answers through descriptions of strategic maneuvers and vignettes of warship personnel, for brief and vivid abstracts best convey the fearful order in the larger strife. Later, in the panoramic treatment of a disastrous naval battle, "The Strait," he commemorates the "Thousands who burned or drowned died to no end...far from imagined loves" at Pearl Harbor and in the South Pacific, and reveals the deadly artistry behind apparent chaos.

Coxe's sense of history—as a cyclic, usually violent, seldom redemptive process—underlines and unifies the several strands in his work. The harsh Colonial past is peopled by the likes of Hannah Dustin, who castrates and scalps her Indian rapist with his own knife; by Samuel Sewall, late witch-burner now obsessed with guilt and possessed by the Devil; by Thomas Jefferson, imposing his classical designs upon the treacherous wilderness that is the young country—and the heart of man. Salem and Boston send forth handsome sailing ships, whose "wrecks grow timber out of shale." The greed, destructiveness, and sexual perversion behind the Puritan facade of salty self-reliance is most brilliantly revealed in the long blank-verse narrative, *The Middle Passage.* A shrewd but seemingly innocent nineteen-year-old, Canot, soon commandeers *The Happy Delivery,* a slaveship disguised as a whaler, half outwits its crafty Yankee owners, but experiences a sea-change; the filthy but lucrative business exacts its toll, 300 blacks drowned and the loss of Canot's soul in an orgy of sadistic lust, drink, and drugs, culminating in grand theft and murder: "New Englanders don't damn/The easy way...." But all is part of the pattern. The sins of the Forefathers breed the current misery of the cities: "We are strangers on the earth,/To one another, and lament a private loss." We are left with "separate lives inside, grown separate hells." "Progress" is merely repetition of original sin, a myth amounting to a moral stand-still.

Despite the seriousness of most of Coxe's verse, its effect is not gloomy. He has a gift for dramatic exposition. Even when the perhaps inexplicable motivations of the "Heroes" of *The Middle Passage* and *Nikal Seyn* remain murky, we share the fascination of the limited and unreliable narrators with their flamboyant adventures. Poems celebrating nature, particularly flights of birds, rise with lyrical power. Several portraits strip historical personages to the core: Dean Swift, "Who studied hate lest pity turn him mad"; Ambrose Bierce, of whom Coxe asks, "Yet how can sworn enemy/of corruption rot/embalmed by hate?" Often poignant and witty, especially in "personal" poems dedicated to family and friends, Coxe's best lines give the satisfaction that comes when problems and paradoxes are subtly restated and elegantly shaped by art.

—Joseph Parisi

CREELEY, Robert (White). American. Born in Arlington, Massachusetts, 21 May 1926. Educated at Holderness School,

Plymouth, New Hampshire; Harvard University, Cambridge, Massachusetts, 1943-44, 1945-47; Black Mountain College, North Carolina, B.A. 1956; University of New Mexico, Albuquerque, M.A. 1960. Served with the American Field Service in India and Burma, 1944-45. Married 1) Ann MacKinnon in 1946 (divorced, 1955), two sons and one daughter; 2) Bobbie Louise Hall in 1957 (divorced, 1976), three daughters; 3) Penelope Highton in 1977, one son and one daughter. Farmer near Littleton, New Hampshire, 1948-51; lived in France, 1951-52, and Mallorca, 1952-53; Instructor, Black Mountain College, Spring 1954, Fall 1955; taught in a boys school, Albuquerque, 1956-59, and on a finca in Guatemala, 1959-61; Visiting Lecturer, 1961-62, and Visiting Professor, 1963-66, 1968-69, 1978-80, University of New Mexico; Lecturer, University of British Columbia, Vancouver, 1962-63. Visiting Professor, 1966-67, Professor 1967-78, and since 1978, Gray Professor of Poetry and Letters, State University of New York, Buffalo. Visiting Professor, San Francisco State College, 1970-71. Operated the Divers Press, Palma de Mallorca, 1953-55. Editor, *Black Mountain Review*, North Carolina, 1954-57, and associated with *Wake*, *Golden Goose*, *Origin*, *Fragmente*, *Vou*, *Contact*, *CIV/n*, and *Merlin* magazines in the early 1950's, and other magazines subsequently. Recipient: Levinson Prize, 1960, Oscar Blumenthal Prize, 1964, and Union League Civic and Arts Foundation Prize, 1967 (*Poetry*, Chicago); D.H. Lawrence Fellowship, 1960; Guggenheim Fellowship, 1964, 1971; Rockefeller grant, 1965; Shelley Memorial Award, 1981; National Endowment for the Arts grant, 1982; DAAD Fellowship, 1983. Lives in Waldoboro, Maine. Address: Department of English, State University of New York, Buffalo, New York 14260, U.S.A.

PUBLICATIONS

Verse

Le Fou.   Columbus, Ohio, Golden Goose Press, 1952.
The Kind of Act of.   Palma, Mallorca, Divers Press, 1953.
The Immoral Proposition.   Karlisruhe-Surlach, Germany, Jonathan Williams, 1953.
A Snarling Garland of Xmas Verses.   Palma, Mallorca, Divers Press, 1954.
All That Is Lovely in Men.   Asheville, North Carolina, Jonathan Williams, 1955.
Ferrini and Others, with others.   Berlin, Gerhardt, 1955.
If You.   San Francisco, Porpoise Bookshop, 1956; London, Lion and Unicorn Press, 1968.
The Whip.   Worcester, Migrant Press, and Highlands, North Carolina, Jonathan Williams, 1957.
A Form of Woman.   New York, Jargon-Corinth, 1959.
For Love: Poems 1950-1960.   New York, Scribner, 1962.
Distance.   Lawrence, Kansas, Terrence Williams, 1964.
Two Poems.   San Francisco, Oyez, 1964.
Hi There!   Urbana, Illinois, Finial Press, 1965.
Words.   Rochester, Minnesota, Perishable Press, 1965.
About Women.   Los Angeles, Gemini, 1966.
Poems 1950-1965.   London, Calder and Boyars, 1966.
For Joel.   Madison, Wisconsin, Perishable Press, 1966.
A Sight.   London, Cape Goliard Press, 1967.
Words.   New York, Scribner, 1967.
Robert Creeley Reads (with recording).   London, Turret-Calder and Boyars, 1967.
The Finger.   Los Angeles, Black Sparrow Press, 1968.
5 Numbers.   New York, Poets Press, 1968.
The Charm: Early and Uncollected Poems.   Mount Horeb,

Wisconsin, Perishable Press, 1968; London, Calder and Boyars, 1971.
The Boy.   Buffalo, Gallery Upstairs Press, 1968.
Numbers.   Stuttgart and Dusseldorf, Domberger-Galerie Schmela, 1968.
Divisions and Other Early Poems.   Mount Horeb, Wisconsin, Perishable Press, 1968.
Pieces.   Los Angeles, Black Sparrow Press, 1968.
Hero.   New York, Indianakatz, 1969.
A Wall.   New York and Stuttgart, Bouwerie-Domberger, 1969.
Mazatlan: Sea.   San Francisco, Poets Press, 1969.
Mary's Fancy.   New York, Bouwerie, 1970.
In London.   Bolinas, California, Angel Hair, 1970.
The Finger: Poems 1966-1969.   London, Calder and Boyars, 1970.
For Betsy and Tom.   Detroit, Alternative Press, 1970.
For Benny and Sabina.   New York, Samuel Charters, 1970.
As Now It Would Be Snow.   Los Angeles, Black Sparrow Press, 1970.
America.   Miami, Press of the Black Flag, 1970.
Christmas: May 10, 1970.   Buffalo, Lockwood Memorial Library, 1970.
St. Martin's.   Los Angeles, Black Sparrow Press, 1971.
Sea.   San Francisco, Cranium Press, 1971.
1.2.3.4.5.6.7.8.9.0.   Berkeley, California, and San Francisco, Shambala-Mudra, 1971.
For the Graduation.   San Francisco, Cranium Press, 1971.
Change.   San Francisco, Hermes Free Press, 1972.
One Day after Another.   Detroit, Alternative Press, 1972.
A Day Book (includes prose).   New York, Scribner, 1972.
For My Mother.   Rushden, Northamptonshire, Sceptre Press, 1973.
Kitchen.   Chicago, Wine Press, 1973.
His Idea.   Toronto, Coach House Press, 1973.
Sitting Here.   Storrs, University of Connecticut Library, 1974.
Thirty Things.   Los Angeles, Black Sparrow Press, 1974.
Backwards.   Knotting, Bedfordshire, Sceptre Press, 1975.
Away.   Santa Barbara, California, Black Sparrow Press, and Solihull, Warwickshire, Aquila, 1976.
Selected Poems.   New York, Scribner, 1976.
Myself.   Knotting, Bedfordshire, Sceptre Press, 1977.
Thanks.   Deerfield, Massachusetts, Deerfield Press, 1977.
The Children.   St. Paul, Truck Press, 1978.
Hello: A Journal, February 23—May 3, 1976.   New York, New Directions, and London, Boyars, 1978.
Later.   West Branch, Iowa, Toothpaste Press, 1978.
Desultory Days.   Knotting, Bedfordshire, Sceptre Press, 1978.
Later: New Poems.   New York, New Directions, 1979; London, Boyars, 1980.
Corn Close.   Knotting, Bedfordshire, Sceptre Press, 1980.
The Collected Poems of Robert Creeley 1945-1975.   Berkeley, University of California Press, 1982; London, Boyars, 1983.
Echoes.   West Branch, Iowa, Toothpaste Press, 1982.
A Calendar.   West Branch, Iowa, Toothpaste Press, 1983.
Mirrors.   New York, New Directions, 1983; London, Boyars, 1984.
Memories.   Durham, Pig Press, 1984.

Recordings: *Today's Poets 3*, with others, Folkways; *Robert Creeley Reads*, Turret-Calder and Boyars, 1967.

Play

Listen (produced London, 1972).   Los Angeles, Black Sparrow Press, 1972.

Novel

The Island.   New York, Scribner, 1963; London, Calder, 1964.

Short Stories

The Gold Diggers.   Palma, Mallorca, Divers Press, 1954.
Mister Blue.   Frankfurt, Insel, 1964.
The Gold Diggers and Other Stories.   London, Calder, and
   New York, Scribner, 1965.

Other

An American Sense (essay).   London, Sigma, 1965 (?).
Contexts of Poetry.   Buffalo, Audit, 1968.
A Quick Graph: Collected Notes and Essays.   San Francisco,
   Four Seasons, 1970.
A Day Book.   Berlin, Graphis, 1970.
Notebook.   New York, Bouwerie, 1972.
A Sense of Measure (essays).   London, Calder and Boyars,
   1972.
The Creative.   Los Angeles, Black Sparrow Press, 1973.
Contexts of Poetry: Interviews 1961-1971, edited by Donald
   Allen.   Bolinas, California, Four Seasons, 1973.
Inside Out: Notes on the Autobiographical Mode.   Los Angeles,
   Black Sparrow Press, 1973.
Presences: A Text for Marisol.   New York, Scribner, 1976.
Mabel: A Story, and Other Prose.   London, Boyars, 1976.
Was That a Real Poem or Did You Just Make It Up Yourself.
   Santa Barbara, California, Black Sparrow Press, 1976.
Was That a Real Poem and Other Essays, edited by Donald
   Allen.   Bolinas, California, Four Seasons, 1979.
*Charles Olson and Robert Creeley: The Complete Correspon-
   dence,* edited by George F. Butterick.   Santa Barbara, Cali-
   fornia, Black Sparrow Press, 5 vols., 1980-83.
The Collected Prose of Robert Creeley.   New York, Scribner,
   and London, Boyars, 1984.

Editor, *Mayan Letters,* by Charles Olson.   Palma, Mallorca,
   Divers Press, 1953; London, Cape, and New York, Grossman,
   1968.
Editor, with Donald Allen, *New American Story.*   New York,
   Grove Press, 1965.
Editor, *Selected Writings,* by Charles Olson.   New York, New
   Directions, 1966.
Editor, with Donald Allen, *The New Writing in the U.S.A.*
   London, Penguin, 1967.
Editor, *Whitman.*   London, Penguin, 1973.

*

Bibliography: *Robert Creeley: An Inventory 1945-1970* by Mary
Novik, Montreal, McGill-Queen's University Press, 1973.

Manuscript Collection: Washington University, St. Louis.

Critical Studies: review by Robert Duncan, in *New Mexico
Quarterly* (Albuquerque), Autumn-Winter 1962-63; "Introduction to Robert Creeley" in *Human Universe and Other Essays* by
Charles Olson, San Francisco, Auerhahn Press, 1965; "Address
and Posture in the Poetry of Robert Creeley" by Kenneth Cox,
in *Cambridge Quarterly,* Summer 1969; Louis B. Martz, in *Yale
Review* (New Haven, Connecticut), Winter 1970; *Three Essays
on Creeley* by Warren Tallman, Toronto, Coach House Press,
1973; "Robert Creeley's *For Love: Poems 1950-1960*" in *Additional Prose* by Charles Olson, Bolinas, California, Four Sea-

sons, 1974; *Measures: Robert Creeley's Poetry* by Ann Mandel,
Toronto, Coach House Press, 1974; "Robert Creeley Issue" of
Boundary 2 (Binghamton, New York), Spring-Fall 1978; *Robert
Creeley's Poetry: A Critical Introduction* by Cynthia Edelberg,
Albuquerque, University of New Mexico Press, 1978; *Robert
Creeley* by Arthur L. Ford, Boston, Twayne, 1978; *The Lost
America of Love: Rereading Robert Creeley, Edward Dorn, and
Robert Duncan* by Sherman Paul, Baton Rouge, Louisiana
State University Press, 1981; *Poet's Prose: The Crisis in Ameri-
can Verse* by Stephen Fredman, Cambridge, Cambridge Univer-
sity Press, 1983.

Robert Creeley comments:
   I write to realize the world as one has come to live in it, thus to
give testament. I write to move in *words,* a human delight. I write
when no other act is possible.

*   *   *

   Rarely has a living poet enjoyed the wide critical attention
Robert Creeley now receives. Book-length critical studies are
beginning to appear, and essays analyzing all aspects of his
writing abound in current literary journals. He has been interviewed with wearying frequency, but through it all Creeley has
responded with unusual charm and freshness. Clearly Creeley
has touched a nerve of life in such a way as to provoke this
intensity of response. That nerve may be his own inner life,
which Creeley has plumbed with rare precision and thoroughness. His language is a delicate x-ray of the emotions under the
stress and near madness of marriages gone wrong. This lyric
self-analysis has exposed the masculine uncertainty rife in the
age, and has also called into question the very substance of
reality lying beyond and around self. His canon seems a clearing
house of issues that have troubled literature since the close of
World War II—dilemmas of identity and relationship to others.
Hence the critical furor to pinpoint the work to certain formu-
lable ideas which its processual nature has so far eluded.
   Creeley's early poems, collected in *For Love: Poems 1950-
1960,* are intensely formal in their compactness and closure.
Many tend toward epigram in their brevity and pithy advice. A
typical instance is "The Warning":

> For love—I would
> split open your head and put
> a candle in
> behind the eyes,
>
> Love is dead in us
> if we forget
> the virtue of an amulet
> and quick surprise.

   The best of the short poems define the self from an oblique but
penetrating angle of insight, as in the three couplets of "The
End":

> When I know what people think of me
> I am plunged into my loneliness. The grey
>
> hat bought earlier sickens.
> I have no purpose no longer distinguishable.

A feeling like being choked
enters my throat.

Creeley's marital theme is expressed in the majority of poems in *For Love*, but "The Whip," "A Form of Women," "The Way," "A Marriage," and "Ballad of the Despairing Husband" capture its dilemmas with great clarity. Other poems in this large collection depict the female as more than sexual partner, but as a force or element necessary to sustain male consciousness. "The Door," among the longest and most ambitious of these poems, explores the female in her divine and archetypal aspect.

Recently, Creeley has dissolved the formalisms of his verse in order to create verse fields in book-length serial compositions, in the manner of Charles Olson and Robert Duncan. He has abandoned the structural neatness of his earlier verse, and the more fluid compositions of *Words*, *Pieces*, and *A Day Book* tend to scrutinize the fine filaments of consciousness in tiny fragments of lyric. A 1976 book, *Away*, marks a regretful close to his second marriage and may signal an end to this long preoccupation with marriage crises. A brief pamphlet of poems in sequence entitled *Later* shows steps of this departure with its reminiscences on childhood.

His prose work, the short fiction collected in *The Gold Diggers*, a novel *The Island*, the first half of *A Day Book*, and *Presences*, a long commentary on the sculptor Marisol, all follow the themes of his verse. The novel closely recounts the last year of marriage to his first wife. Creeley's prose is unique in modern fiction: his use of detail is extraordinarily delicate and precise, producing an uncanny perceptiveness in his narrators. Self-absorption in *The Island* is all the more compelling as the narrator dismantles his own thinking process to inspect the deterioration jealousy causes in him. Although a highly provocative writer of prose, his poetry has had more pervasive influence on younger writers.

In his criticism, *A Quick Graph*, and in interviews, collected in *Contexts of Poetry*, he has proved an astute chronicler of modern poetry, particularly on the work and influence of Charles Olson, with whom he launched the movement now known as Black Mountain poetry.

With the recent publication from University of California Press of his collected poems, Creeley's stature as a major poet is secure. One realizes for the first time in glancing over this immense volume of poems that his life has been a steady outpouring of subtle, dissecting verses, few of which err in monotonous imitation of his previous style or attempt more than the modest but inimitable aims of his brief lyrics. Among America's contemporary writers, few possess Creeley's philosophical resourcefulness and sophistication—his poems have leapt into the curious opening created by the philosophical speculations about the body's interference with thought in the writings of Heidegger, Merleau-Ponty, and Wittgenstein. His surest lyrics have been compared to the subtle precisions of Samuel Beckett. But unlike Beckett, there is little or no pessimism in Creeley--he has denied his critics' claims that the void is negative in his work. The void is in fact a clearing space, as it is in Buddhist thought, and his has argued in recent interviews that his radical simplicity is nothing more than the appreciation of a mental distraction and mere verbiage.

Creeley's career has rounded a cycle in his most recent poems. He began writing imagist poems in youth, parsed them into fragments and syllables in mid-career, and in the last few years has begun to write more fully again of his emotions, in poems that flesh out their concerns with lusher arrangements of imagery. Even this turn away from former practice is welcomed and unusual—he approaches lyric articulation with great care and understatement, and when imagery does appear, it stuns the reader by its intensity and accuracy. Of the original postmodernists of the mid-century, Creeley has lasted and is now indisputably the final flowering of its enormous energies and innovations.

—Paul Christensen

CREWS, Judson (Campbell). American. Born in Waco, Texas, 30 June 1917. Educated at La Vega High School, Waco; Baylor University, Waco, A.B. 1941, M.A. in sociology and psychology 1944, graduate work in art, 1946; Kinzinger Field School of Art, Taos, New Mexico, 1947. Served in the United States Army Medical Corps, 1942-44. Married Mildred Tolbert in 1947 (divorced, 1980); two daughters. Graduate Assistant in Sociology, Baylor University, 1941-42; publisher, Motive Press, Waco, and Este Es Press, Taos, 1946-66; consumer market researcher, Stewart Dougal and Associates, New York, 1948; job-printer, Taos *Star*, *El Crepusculo*, and Taos *News*, 1948-66; caseworker, El Paso County Child Welfare Unit, Texas; Instructor in Sociology and Psychology, Wharton County Junior College, Texas, 1967-70; Counselor, Community Mental Health Center, Gallup, New Mexico, 1970-71; Lecturer in Sociology, University of New Mexico Branch College, Gallup, 1971-72; director of intensive care unit, State Training School for Girls, Chillicothe, Missouri, 1973; Lecturer in Social Development Studies, University of Zambia, Lusaka. During the 1930's, 1940's, and 1950's, Editor, *Vers Libre*, *Motive*, *Flying Fish*, *Suck-Egg Mule*, *Taos*, *Deer and Dachshund*, *Poetry Taos*, and *Naked Ear* magazines. Address: c/o Ahsahta Press, Department of English, Boise State University, Boise, Idaho 83725, U.S.A.

PUBLICATIONS

Verse

Psalms for a Late Season.   New Orleans, Iconograph Press, 1942.
No Is the Night.   Privately printed, 1949.
A Poet's Breath.   Privately printed, 1950 (?).
Come Curse to the Moon.   Privately printed, 1952 (?).
The Anatomy of Proserpine.   Privately printed, 1955.
The Wrath Wrenched Splendor of Love.   Privately printed, 1956.
The Heart in Naked Hunger.   Ranches of Taos, New Mexico, Motive Book Shop, 1958.
To Wed Beneath the Sun.   Privately printed, 1958 (?).
A Sheaf of Christmas Verse.   Washington, D.C., Three Hands, n.d.
The Ogres Who Were His Henchmen.   Eureka, California, Hearse Press, 1958.
Inwade to Briney Garth.   Taos, New Mexico, Este Es Press, 1960.
The Feel of Sun and Air upon Her Body.   Eureka, California, Hearse Press, 1960.
A Unicorn When Needs Be.   Taos, New Mexico, Este Es Press, 1963.
Hermes Past the Hour.   Taos, New Mexico, Este Es Press, 1963.
Selected Poems.   Cleveland, Renegade Press, 1964.
You, Mark Antony, Navigator upon the Nile.   Privately printed, 1964.

Angels Fall, They Are Towers. Taos, New Mexico, Este Es Press, 1965.
Three on a Match, with Wendell B. Anderson and Cerise Farallon. Privately printed, 1966.
The Stones of Konarak. Santa Fe, New Mexico, American Poets Press, 1966.
Nations and Peoples. Cherry Valley, New York, Cherry Valley Editions, 1976.
Nolo Contendere, edited by J. Whitebird. Houston, Wings Press, 1978.
Never Will Dan Cause No One to. Albuquerque, Holy Terrible Editions, n.d.
Modern Onions and Sociology. Taos, New Mexico, St. Valentine's Press, 1978.
Selected Poems. Berkeley, California, Thorpe Springs Press, 1979.
Roma a Fat At. Albuquerque, Instantaneous Centipede, 1979.
Gluons, Q. Albuquerque, Namaste Press, 1979.
The Noose: A Retrospective: Four Decades, edited by Larry Goodell and John Brandi. Oakland, California, Duende Press, 1980.
If I. Stockton, California, Wormwood Review Press, 1981.
The Clock of Moss, edited by Carol Bergé and Dale Boyer. Boise, Idaho, Ahsahta Press, 1983.

Other

The Southern Temper. Waco, Texas, Motive Book Shop, 1946.
Patocinio Barela: Taos Wood Carver, with Mildred Crews and Wendell B. Anderson. Taos, New Mexico, Taos Recordings and Publications, 1955; revised edition, 1962.

Editor, with A. Thomas Trusky, *Songs*, by Charley John Greaseybear. Boise, Idaho, Ahsahta Press, 1979.

*

Manuscript Collections: University of Texas, Austin; University of California, Los Angeles; Yale University, New Haven, Connecticut.

Critical Study: *A Critical Analysis of Poems by a Contemporary Poet of the Avant-Garde: Judson Crews*, by Wendell B. Anderson, Rindge, New Hampshire, Franklin Pierce College, unpublished thesis, 1969.

*   *   *

In the poetry of Judson Crews, the imagination of a man of the Southwestern United States comes into contact with the poetic innovations of Pound, Williams, Charles Olson and Wallace Stevens. Crews's response to these innovations is original and idiosyncratic. He is something of a primitive poet, doggedly pursuing his own way. Mostly short lyrics, his poems range from simple songs to abstract meditations. Verbal experiment is used both for its own sake and as a kind of exploration into the sources of creative life.

Often Crews begins a poem with a striking, sometimes strange phrase ("No wail it went the gladsome son"), and pursues its meanings through the use of language generated by similarity of sound or by a kind of verbal inventiveness ("he sought the wicked in the middle heart/night was lonelier than a restless wing"). Many poems are brief, often zany fables that reach towards mythic realities, towards dimly grasped terrors and possibilities of courage. Language is pushed to hyperbole, even

to nonsense, for the sheer sake of celebration. It is true that at times the language is too "poetic" and that the poems at times move with rhythmical monotony and a kind of glibness. The lyric extravagance allows the inclusion of much that is banal. But beyond the affectation and excess are a rambunctious kind of humor and an eager open sense of wonder.

This humor and this wonder seem rooted in the man himself and in his region. The young Crews, wrote Henry Miller, "reminded one, because of his shaggy beard and manner of speech, of a latter-day prophet." And there is something larger than ordinary life in the energy and constant power of invention present in Crews's poetic career. Certainly his imagination is indiscriminate; but it is also prolific. And he writes with a gusto that is rare in contemporary American poetry.

—Jerry Paris

———————

CROSSLEY-HOLLAND, Kevin (John William). British. Born in Mursley, Buckinghamshire, 7 February 1941. Educated at Bryanston School; St. Edmund Hall, Oxford, B.A. (honours) in English language and literature. Married to Gillian Cook; two sons and one daughter. Editor, Macmillan, publishers, London, 1962-71; Gregory Fellow, University of Leeds, 1969-71; talks producer, BBC, London, 1972; Editorial Director, Victor Gollancz, Ltd., publishers, London, 1972-77; English Lecturer, University of Regensburg, 1978-80. Since 1975, General Editor, Mirror of Britain series, André Deutsch Ltd., publishers, London. Recipient: Arts Council award, 1968, 1977, 1978. Agent: Deborah Rogers Ltd., 49 Blenheim Crescent, London W11 2EF, England.

PUBLICATIONS

Verse

On Approval. London, Outposts, 1961.
My Son. London, Turret, 1966.
Alderney: The Nunnery. London, Turret, 1968.
Confessional. Frensham, Surrey, Sceptre Press, 1969.
Norfolk Poems. London, Academy, 1970.
A Dream of a Meeting. Frensham, Surrey, Sceptre Press, 1970.
More Than I Am. London, Steam Press, 1971.
The Wake. Richmond, Surrey, Keepsake Press, 1972.
The Rain-Giver. London, Deutsch, 1972.
Petal and Stone. Knotting, Bedfordshire, Sceptre Press, 1975.
The Dream-House. London, Deutsch, 1976.
Between My Father and My Son. Minneapolis, Black Willow Press, 1982.
Time's Oriel. London, Hutchinson, 1983.

Other (for children)

Havelok the Dane. London, Macmillan, 1964; New York, Dutton, 1965.
King Horn. London, Macmillan, 1965; New York, Dutton, 1966.
The Green Children. London, Macmillan, 1966; New York, Seabury Press, 1968.
The Callow Pit Coffer. London, Macmillan, 1968; New York, Seabury Press, 1969.

Wordhoard: Anglo-Saxon Stories, with Jill Paton Walsh. London, Macmillan, and New York, Farrar Straus, 1969.
The Pedlar of Swaffham. London, Macmillan, 1971; New York, Seabury Press, 1972.
The Sea-Stranger. London, Heinemann, 1973; New York, Seabury Press, 1974.
The Fire-Brother. London, Heinemann, and New York, Seabury Press, 1975.
Green Blades Rising: The Anglo-Saxons. London, Deutsch, 1975; New York, Seabury Press, 1976.
The Earth-Father. London, Heinemann, 1976.
The Wildman. London, Deutsch, 1976.
The Dead Moon and Other Tales from East Anglia and the Fen Country. London, Deutsch, 1982.
Beowulf. Oxford, Oxford University Press, 1982.
Tales from the Mabinogion, with Gwyn Thomas. London, Gollancz, 1984.
Axe-Man, Wolf-Age: A Selection for Children from the Norse Myths. London, Deutsch, 1985.
Storm. London, Heinemann, 1985.

Other

Pieces of Land: Journeys to Eight Islands. London, Gollancz, 1972.
The Norse Myths: A Retelling. London, Deutsch, and New York, Pantheon, 1980.

Editor, *Running to Paradise: An Introductory Selection of the Poems of W.B. Yeats*. London, Macmillan, 1967; New York, Macmillan, 1968.
Editor, *Winter's Tales for Children 3*. London, Macmillan, 1967.
Editor, *Winter's Tales 14*. London, Macmillan, 1968.
Editor, with Patricia Beer, *New Poetry 2*. London, Arts Council, 1976.
Editor, *The Faber Book of Northern Legends [Northern Folktales]* (for children). London, Faber, 2 vols., 1977-80.
Editor, *The Riddle Book* (for children). London, Macmillan, 1982.
Editor, *Folk-Tales of the British Isles*. London, Folio Society, 1985.

Translator, *The Battle of Maldon and Other Old English Poems*, edited by Bruce Mitchell. London, Macmillan, and New York, St. Martin's Press, 1965.
Translator, *Beowulf*. London, Macmillan, and New York, Farrar Straus, 1968.
Translator, *Storm and Other Old English Riddles* (for children). London, Macmillan, and New York, Farrar Straus, 1970.
Translator, *The Exeter Riddle Book*. London, Folio Society, 1978; as *The Exeter Book of Riddles*, London, Penguin, 1979.
Translator, *The Anglo-Saxon World*. Woodbridge, Suffolk, Boydell Press, 1982.

*

Kevin Crossley-Holland comments:

(1974) If the society reflected in Old English poetry now seems alien, many of its moods are wholly familiar, essentially English: an out-and-out heroism, a dogged refusal to surrender, a love of the sea, an enjoyment of melancholy, nostalgia. In translating it, my staple diet has been a non-syllabic four-stress line, controlled by light alliteration. There are plenty of cases, though, where I have not conformed to this pattern; my concern has been to echo rather than slavishly to imitate the originals. My diction inclines

to the formal, though it certainly is less formal than that of the Anglo-Saxon poets; it seemed to me important at this time to achieve truly accessible versions of these poems, that eschewed the use of archaisms, inverted word orders, and all "poetic" language. I have not gone out of my way to avoid words that spring from Latin roots, but the emphasis has fallen naturally on words derived from Old English. My translations are, I believe, faithful by and large to the letter of the originals, but it is the mood I have been after. And if I have not caught anything of it, then I have not succeeded in my purpose.

*   *   *

In Kevin Crossley-Holland one encounters a poet whose vision covers a wide sweep of history, one to whom remote past and immediate present reveal themselves as a continuous, related process. He is an accomplished translator of Old English literature, and his work demonstrates a definite kinship with the Anglo-Saxon poets, and an admiration for the traditional virtues embodied in their writing. The qualities of rugged individualism, stoical endurance, loyalty, and truthfulness appear constantly in his poems, celebrated in a hard, laconic style pruned of all superfluities. Crossley-Holland has a storyteller's gifts, and such works as "Dead Moon," a retelling of East Anglian folktales, or his superb version of *Beowulf* for younger readers, are proof of his ability. As a poet, his language is at once spare and richly descriptive, the inspired use of alliteration rendered effective in contemporary as well as historical contexts. In common with earlier writers, he is aware of the unyielding strength of the earth, and of those bleak landscapes where man must either adapt, or struggle to survive. Poems like "Hills" and "Fortification" emphasize the harshness of nature, its intractability to man and his efforts to change it: "No little people come out of that hill./It is a gaunt grey whale,/Taking light, killing it, offering nothing." Yet for all their grimness, Crossley-Holland sees these forbidding regions as places of magic and is irresistibly drawn to them, regarding them as in some way essential to his own fulfilment and growth: "Yet I come. Here alone I cannot sham./The place insists that I know who I am."

Practical and physical in his approach, an amateur archaeologist collecting history's evidence, Crossley-Holland has an outward toughness countered by his sensitivity when dealing with human relationships, the tenderness towards loved ones shown in such poems as "Rapids" or "A Wreath." He loves riddles, and humour surfaces occasionally in his work, as instanced in his wry appraisal of three pretty archaeology students in "A Small Ritual." Able to portray the acts of heroes when required, he is also wary of hymning their glories. "At Mycenae," with its evocation of shepherds and flocks untroubled by the strife of gods or kings, reaffirms his commitment to more common lives. His writing concentrates on the universal themes of love and death, loneliness and exile—whether that of the Saxon "Wanderer", or the ageing survivor of the British Raj in "Postcards from Kodai." Crossley-Holland's poems appear to compose themselves from a mass of fragments, the sharply observed images coalescing to form a distinctive whole. With equal assurance he presents visions of bare hillsides and remote marshlands, the reflections of a monk in pursuit of salvation, the terror of an old woman faced by death. In "Neenie" the random, disconnected utterances of his dying grandmother are made to take on the nature of a revelation: "I listen and think you are telling something/Greater than its parts, a breath and sum/of life itself, the ego dispossessed."

Alternately tough and tender, earthy and lyrical, Crossley-Holland remains a seeker after his individual vision. Mournful over the lost magic of his youth, he refuses to give up the search for those half-remembered secret places: "Time's wind bristles.

But what/is left in its wake is stubborn/and persistent: emblems/ of an undying enchantment./Only keep your head well down/ alert for the telltale signs."

—Geoff Sadler

CROZIER, Andrew. British. Born in 1943. Educated at Cambridge University, M.A.; University of Essex, Wivenhoe, Ph.D. Lecturer in English, University of Sussex, Brighton. Address: Arts B, University of Sussex, Brighton, Sussex BN1 9RH, England.

PUBLICATIONS

Verse

Loved Litter of Time Spent. Buffalo, Sumbooks, 1967.
Train Rides: Poems from '63 and '64. Pampisford, Cambridgeshire, R., 1968.
Walking on Grass. London, Ferry Press, 1969.
In One Side and Out the Other, with John James and Tom Phillips. London, Ferry Press, 1970.
Neglected Information. Sidcup, Kent, Blacksuede Boot Press, 1973.
The Veil Poem. Providence, Rhode Island, Burning Deck, 1974.
Printed Circuit. Cambridge, Street, 1974.
Seven Contemporary Sun Dials, with Ian Potts. Brighton, Ian Potts, 1975.
Pleats. Bishops Stortford, Hertfordshire, Great Works, 1975.
Duets. Guildford, Surrey, Circle Press, 1976.
Residing. Belper, Derbyshire, Aggie Weston's, 1976.
High Zero. Cambridge, Street, 1978.
Were There. London, Many Press, 1978.
Utamaro Variations. London, Tetrad, 1982.
Majority. London, Agneau 2, 1985.

*   *   *

As an editor and as a collaborator, Andrew Crozier has provided occasions for poetry by others, and generosity informs his own poetry. In many collections over the past two decades his poems move from the "I" outward, to bestow a sense of sharing.

What do I know? I know that I perceive, and the process of perception moves from the "I" to the outer world. The process is complex, as the poem "Marriage" demonstrates, with a beautifully strange ironic sheen. More directly, perhaps, there is

> More to be learnt
> looking from the window of a train
> riding through north London into the fields
> than from prolonged scrutiny of the
> others in the buffet car.

Velocity is a derivative of space with respect to time, or the motion of space itself involves time: "The Shores of Romney Marsh/have probably been there since the sea/withdrew...." The perception of motion involves the perception of space, and space involves the past, and perceiving the past brings us back to the present or, in the words of Charles Olson, "The chain of

memory is resurrection." From the past, the present shore, the slope was

> ...sheltering me as I walked
> along its contour to enter Rye
> across the sluice
>   from the other side.

How can I tell what I know? *What* I know belongs to *how* I know, and *how* involves the act of telling, which changes through time:

> Yes that's true very good
>   more beautiful
> and no less true
>   than ever before.
>
>   Say it again
> You cannot say it again

The "I" implies "everybody." Listening, and seeing recreate the outer world, as in "Grand Hotel":

> The three old men are silent
> listening to the sound of laughter
> happy voices rise from lighted windows
> the murmered song of the sea
> blends with the gramophone.

Many of Crozier's collections are beautifully printed, and in particular *Utamaro Variations*, in 18 point Baskerville, on Somerset Cream paper, where a strict orthogonality of lines in Ian Tyson's art creates an interesting dialogue of inner spaces and outer space. These poems move in an unexpected *terza rima*, recalling the poet of light and of moving light:

> The colours break out and float
> In the appearance of a world
> Reflecting the shadows of a boat
>
> As though an inner life unfurled
> Like waves and eddying water
> In a photograph its edges curled
>
> With age...

The "inner life" has to move out, has to be "unfurled." Perception moves, and awareness of motion is perception, the motion of "curled" from age.

The End of a Row of Conjectural Units

> Formerly the pure element Of itself, it might last forever
> and seem as indistinct as the glare of the sun on a white wall
> before the thought of shadows has fallen across it; as if the
> flood of natural light surfacing the bricks, the cement and
> paintwork had absorbed them all in unimpeded descent and
> could keep on going: absolute space.

In 1967, Stephen Rodefer (a poet whose "inner life unfurled" has continued to give birth to poems) noticed what Andrew Crozier essentially shares with the reader:

What you see is not what you know. And what you know you may not, you probably do not, understand. But you do know it. You have it. You carry it with you. It is what is yours most dearly.

—William Sylvester

CRUZ, Victor Hernández. Puerto Rican. Born in Aguas Buenas, 6 February 1949; emigrated to the United States in 1954. Educated in public schools in New York City. Married; one son. Formerly, Editor, *Umbra* magazine, New York, Instructor, San Francisco State University, lecturer, University of California, Berkeley, and employed by San Francisco Art Commission. Address: c/o Momo's Press, 45 Sheridan Street, San Francisco, California 94103, U.S.A.

PUBLICATIONS

Verse

Papo Got His Gun. New York, Calle Once, 1966.
Snaps. New York, Random House, 1969.
Mainland. New York, Random House, 1973.
Doing Poetry. Berkeley, California, Other Ways, n.d.
Tropicalization. Berkeley, California, Reed Cannon and Johnson, 1976.
By Lingual Wholes. San Francisco, Momo's Press, 1982.

Other

Editor, with Herbert Kohl, *Stuff: A Collection of Poems, Visions and Imaginative Happenings from Young Writers in Schools—Opened and Closed.* Cleveland, World, 1970.

*

Victor Hernández Cruz comments:
   I sit on a fence between two languages, thus I write in three simultaneously: Spanish as base, English as usage, and Bilingual when the occasion merits. From the mixture a totally new language emerges, an intense collision, not just of words but of attitudes. My situation is that of the emigrant which in a way is the story of our time, migration, escape from choking conditions into the cosmopolity—but always with a strange nostalgia for the original beans. Hispano-America is the result of years and years of racial and cultural mixture; my mind is creole and can fuse many unlikely things together: outer variety, inner unity; we are an experiment in communications; I am now moving towards writing more in Spanish and translation.

*   *   *

   Some of Victor Hernández Cruz's poems exhibit the urgency of the new world poets to write stirring and highly motivated work. Others seem vehicles of the poetic-political meld to be read silently, or aloud, throughout the Third and transcending worlds. Such poetry demands validation of older and new world ideals:

when they stop poems
in the mail & clap
their hands or dance to
them
when women become pregnant
by the side of poems
the strangest sounds making
the river go along.

   Cruz was born in Puerto Rico. However, he grew up in New York City, and much of his work reflects a bilingual ease: "thoughts in Spanish run through/the mind/the buildings seem broken English." With a combination Latin/Anglo imagery he creates a tense warm lyricism:

Que Pasa?
Y los palos
do not feel a home anymore La luna
goes round the star dotted cielo? Let's watch
in this part of Mexico
Se habla inglish

   The poetry of Cruz is filled with humorous, angry, brilliant imagery that makes him one of America's finest young poets.

—Corrine E. Bostic

CUMBERLEGE, Marcus (Crossley). British. Born in Antibes, France, 23 December 1938. Educated at Sherborne School, Dorset; St. John's College, Oxford, B.A. 1961. Married 1) Ava Nicole Paranjoti in 1965 (divorced, 1972), one daughter; 2) Maria Lefever in 1973. Worked for the British Council in Lima, Peru, 1957-58, 1962-63; advertising executive, Ogilvy and Mather, London, 1964-67; advertising assistant, British Travel Authority, London, 1967-68; taught at the Lycée International, St. Germain-en-Laye, 1968-70. Since 1978, visiting lecturer in poetry and oriental studies, International University of Lugano, Hilversum, and University of Limburg. Editor, with Scott Rollins, *Dremples,* Amsterdam, 1977. Also a translator. Recipient: Eric Gregory Award, 1967. Address: Westmeers 84, 8000 Bruges, Belgium.

PUBLICATIONS

Verse

Oases. London, Anvil Press Poetry, 1968.
Poems for Quena and Tabla. Oxford, Carcanet, 1970.
Running Towards a New Life. London, Anvil Press Poetry, 1972.
Firelines. London, Anvil Press Poetry, 1977.
The Poetry Millionaire. Swanage, Dorset, Dollar of Soul Press, 1977.
La Nuit Noire. Bruges, Manufaktuur, 1977.
XX Vriendelijke Vragen. Bruges, Ganzespel, 1977.
Bruges/Brugge, with Owen Davis. Bruges, Orion, 1978.
Northern Lights. Bruges, Manufaktuur, 1981.
Life Is a Flower. Bruges, Drukkerij Setola, 1981.
Sweet Poor Hobo. Bruges, Manufaktuur & Babel, 1984.

*

Marcus Cumberlege comments:

(1980) Major influences: César Vallejo, the French Symbolists, Lorca, Blake, Rilke, Eliot, Yeats. Later influences: Gautier, Pessoa, Van Ostaijen and Flemish Expressionism; Basho, Wang Wei, Rumi; Mellie Uyldert and Henri van Praag.

Earlier themes: (1) survival of "human beings" in urban society, compassion for the former while satirizing shortcomings of the latter; (2) automatic poetry attempting to situate the poet geographically and define his role as interpreter of mysteries; (3) original poetry in Spanish, French, and Dutch; translation from contemporary Latin American poets. Recent themes: Connemara and West Flanders: haiku; he remains an experimentalist in practice and his poetry is concerned with changing the quality of life at an environmental level, partly through direct co-operation with musicians and graphic artists. He is conscious of poetry's educational function, and although he treats writing as an act of personal spiritual discipline, he regards his books as an extended physical manifestation of his own personality, seeking through publication to serve, delight, and ultimately enlighten others.

(1985) More recently I begin to make free use of Dutch, French, Spanish, and Irish in my original work, with a return to automatic writing.

*   *   *

Marcus Cumberlege had been writing poems for about ten years before the publication of his first major collection, *Running Towards a New Life*, though his smaller collections, *Oases* and *Poems for Quena and Tabla*, had introduced his work to the public. During that period it seemed that he was working towards the development of an individual style, experimenting with styles, ideas, forms, and the use of language to obtain different effects. The result was that *Running Towards a New Life*, covering the whole of that period, gives the impression that his work was a great deal more uneven than it had become by the time of publication.

Sometimes the influences are a little too obvious in the earlier poems—one can identify the Auden style and the Brian Patten manner, for instance—but there is a calm assurance about the latest poems in the book, which has a roughly chronological sequence. Nevertheless, whatever the style or tone, Cumberlege has always written civilised verse, work that is witty, sophisticated, and rooted in European poetry, demonstrating a wide reading of classical and modern poetry. The polished couplets of "Mural for the Country Residence of a Latin American President," with its deliberate connection with Eliot's "Prufrock" at the beginning, is still one of the best things he has done. His knowledge of technique is remarkable, but his most striking characteristic is a capacity for finding the startlingly apt image or metaphor; when he manages to combine these qualities with a driving theme he can be quite superb. In "There Are Days" he shows his real potentiality.

Having worked his way systematically through the relatively long process of experimentation, Cumberlege appears to be reaping the benefit, if one can judge from his second major collection, *Firelines*. The volume is divided into five sections—"The Sun-Dial," "The Ram," "Harmonia's Necklace," "The Murmuring Branches," and "Errisberg"—each with its dedication, epigraph, and poetic style. He exerts a firmer control over his material, manipulates language in a more effective manner, and gives more attention to precision of statement, while demonstrating his versatility in a range of styles. The first section is more structured than the rest and more traditionally lyrical—

No South or North. I turn.
Sun breathes, warm as a dog

Chasing sheep into rock. The moon
Thrusts its slane into the bog

—but one might hazard a guess that these poems are from an earlier phase. "Oasis" and "Lord Dunsany" were, in fact, included in *Oases*, published nine years earlier. Certainly one can imagine that Cumberlege would not now be content with the following stanza from "Hesperides":

Sun dips a brush in darkness.
The paintbox in the west
Closing, one drop of scarlet
Splashes the robin's breast.

Still, there are some attractive pieces in which the rhyming or half-rhyming pattern lends deceptive simplicity ("Eclipse"):

The river clambers to its source,
Apples awaken as they fall.
Ghosts of the famine stalked our house
And whispered through a moonlit wall.

"The Ram" section, which links astrological symbols, Tarot concepts, with "fierced-eyed Mrs. Mop," "the Connaught moon," the "Moorish dreams of Potocki," "the Western Buddha," "The House of Opposites," and St. John, has striking phraseology here and there, but with its slightly surrealistic use of imagery is likely to be inaccessible to many readers. The most outstanding poems are all collected in the "Harmonia's Necklace" section— "The Connemara Cradle," "A Hot Chestnut," "Questions for Goldilocks," "The Perfect Man," and "Coole Park and Ballylee, Winter."

Cumberlege lived part of his childhood in Ireland and later spent some time on the West Coast of Ireland. It is not surprising, then, that this experience seems to have made a strong impact upon his poetry. "The Murmuring Branches" section contains his fine translations from the Spanish of Lorca (including "The Faithless Wife") and Carlos Bousoño, the Flemish of Herman Leys, and the French of Jacques Prévert.

—Howard Sergeant

CUNNINGHAM, J(ames) V(incent). American. Born in Cumberland, Maryland, 23 August 1911. Educated at St. Mary's College, Kansas, 1928; Stanford University, California, A.B. 1934, Ph.D. 1945. Married 1) Barbara Gibbs in 1937 (divorced, 1942), one daughter; 2) Dolora Gallagher in 1945 (divorced, 1949); 3) Jessie MacGregor Campbell in 1950. Instructor, Stanford University, 1937-45; Assistant Professor, University of Hawaii, Honolulu, 1945-46, University of Chicago, 1946-52, and University of Virginia, Charlottesville, 1952-53. Professor of English, 1953-76, University Professor, 1976-80, and since 1980, Professor Emeritus, Brandeis University, Waltham, Massachusetts. Visiting Professor, Harvard University, Cambridge, Massachusetts, 1952, University of Washington, Seattle, 1956, Indiana University, Bloomington, 1961, University of California, Santa Barbara, 1963, and Washington University, St. Louis, 1976. Recipient: Guggenheim Fellowship, 1959, 1967; American Academy grant, 1965; National Endowment for the Arts grant, 1966; Academy of American Poets Fellowship, 1976. Lives in Sudbury, Massachusetts. Address: Department of English, Brandeis University, Waltham, Massachusetts 02154, U.S.A.

PUBLICATIONS

Verse

The Helmsman. San Francisco, Colt Press, 1942.
The Judge Is Fury. New York, Swallow Press-Morrow, 1947.
Doctor Drink. Cummington, Massachusetts, Cummington Press, 1950.
Trivial, Vulgar, and Exalted: Epigrams. San Francisco, Poems in Folio, 1957.
The Exclusions of a Rhyme: Poems and Epigrams. Denver, Swallow, 1960.
To What Strangers, What Welcome: A Sequence of Short Poems. Denver, Swallow, 1964.
Some Salt: Poems and Epigrams.... Madison, Wisconsin, Perishable Press, 1967.
The Collected Poems and Epigrams of J. V. Cunningham. Chicago, Swallow Press, and London, Faber, 1971.
Selected Poems. Mount Horeb, Wisconsin, Perishable Press, 1971.

Recording: *J. V. Cunningham Reading at Stanford*, Stanford University, 1974.

Other

The Quest of the Opal: A Commentary on "The Helmsman." Denver, Swallow, 1950.
Woe or Wonder: The Emotional Effect of Shakespearean Tragedy. Denver, University of Denver Press, 1951.
Tradition and Poetic Structure: Essays in Literary History and Criticism. Denver, Swallow, 1960.
The Journal of John Cardan: Together with The Quest of the Opal and The Problem of Form. Denver, Swallow, 1964.
The Collected Essays of J. V. Cunningham. Chicago, Swallow Press, 1976.

Editor, *The Renaissance in England*. New York, Harcourt Brace, 1966.
Editor, *The Problem of Style*. New York, Fawcett, 1966.
Editor, *In Shakespeare's Day*. New York, Fawcett, 1970.

*

Bibliography: *A Bibliography of the Published Writings of J. V. Cunningham* by Charles Gullans, Los Angeles, University of California Library, 1973.

Critical Studies: *The Poetry of J. V. Cunningham* by Yvor Winters, Denver, Swallow, 1961; *Connoisseurs of Chaos* by Denis Donoghue, New York, Macmillan, 1965, London, Faber, 1966; "The Poetry of J.V. Cunningham" by Patrick Cosgrave, in *Spectator* (London) 23 October 1971; "The Collected Poems and Epigrams" by John Hollander, in *New York Times Book Review*, 21 November 1971; "A Location of J.V. Cunningham" by Hayden Carruth, in *Michigan Quarterly Review* (Ann Arbor), Spring 1972; "The Collected Essays" by Denis Donoghue, in *New York Times Book Review*, 7 August 1977; "The Poetry of J.V. Cunningham" by Robert Pinsky, in *New Republic* (Washington, D.C.), 28 January 1978; "Far Lamps at Night: The Poetry of J.V. Cunningham" by Adam Shapiro, in *Critical Inquiry* (Chicago), March 1983; "The Example of J.V. Cunningham" by Henry Taylor, in *Hollins Critic* (Virginia), October 1983.

J.V. Cunningham comments:
I have a prejudice for brevity.

*   *   *

In *The Quest of the Opal* J.V. Cunningham comments that the later poems in his first book, *The Helmsman*, "were direct statements of something he had to say, given form and definitiveness by the technique of verse." Throughout his career, especially when he is writing in a less serious vein, he achieves a finely chiseled definitiveness—indeed a lapidary style—that reminds us that light verse need not be lightweight. Cunningham writes effectively in the tradition of the Greek Anthology or of the Latin and Renaissance epigrammatists. Take, for example, his exuberant portrayal of a young man's sexual awakening: "*Arms and the man I sing*, and sing for joy,/ Who was last year all elbows and a boy." This ear-pleasing heroic couplet—Pope has few things finer—represents the poet at his epigrammatic best: two perfectly crafted decasyllables, the opening trochaic reversal stressing the key word "arms," the masterful handling of stress and pause in the second highlighting the antithetical "elbows." Also, the witty epic allusion suggests the consuming subjective importance of a first love experience, and at the same time slyly hints that to the rest of the world it may not be of quite such heroic proportions. Note too how the obvious enjoyment of linguistic manipulation for its own sake serves as an additional device for projecting the new sophistication of a boy recently become a man.

In his other 99 or so epigrams Cunningham is generally more cynical, sardonic, satirical, or scurrilous than in "*Arms and the man*": "Mistress of scenes, good-by. Your maidenhead/ Was fitter for the couch than for the bed," or "I married in my youth a wife./ She was my own, my very first./ She gave the best years of her life./ I hope nobody gets the worst." But counter this blast at domestic bliss with his delightfully complimentary lyric to his wife, "The Metaphysical Amorist."

Actually, Cunningham's lyric impulse has something of the compression of the epigram, so that one or two lines—especially the first—frequently capsulize the lyric heart of a poem. He may wander thereafter into the aridity that sometimes accompanies an overemphasis on statement in poetry, or into unearned desolation, or into a hard-boiled stance that is finally too limited to engage our full sympathy. But back to first lines: "I drive Westward. Tumble and loco weed/ Persist," "On either side of the white line," "In a few days now when two memories meet," "You have here no otherness,/ Unadressed [sic] correspondent," "The soft lights, the companionship, the beers." These are from the first five poems of his most ambitious venture, the sequence *To What Strangers, What Welcome*. Cunningham's collected poems and epigrams run to only 142 pages, and his venture into the genre of the modern lyric sequence is correspondingly minimal— 15 short poems. (Compare *The Waste Land* or Yeats's Irish civil war sequences, much less *Song of Myself* or *The Cantos*.) At the heart of this little tale of love recaptured and lost by the Pacific is a bleakness familiar from the earlier "Montana Pastoral," where the poet finds "no images of pastoral will,/ But fear, thirst, hunger, and this huddled chill," and "Horoscope," where he sees "Neither Venus nor Mars" in his heaven. In *To What Strangers* a humiliated and lonely sensibility is presented more nakedly:

> We neither give nor receive:
> The unfinishable drink
> Left on the table, the sleep
> Alcoholic and final
> In the mute exile of time.

On the other hand, the sequence also projects moments of considerably higher morale—"Innocent to innocent,/One asked, What is perfect love," "Hemming a summer dress as the tide/ Turns at the right time"—and a cool, defining clarity: "Good is what we can do with evil," "A premise of identity/Where the lost hurries to be lost." Such evocative and incisive lines, together with his consistently high craftsmanship and sharp wit, are the hallmark of Cunningham's best work.

—Sally M. Gall

CURNOW, Allen. New Zealander. Born in Timuru, 17 June 1911. Educated at Christchurch Boys' High School, 1924-28; University of Canterbury, Christchurch, 1929-30; University of Auckland, 1931-33, B.A. 1938; St. John's College (Anglican theological), Auckland, 1931-33. Married 1) Elizabeth J. LeCren in 1936 (divorced, 1965), three children; 2) Jenifer Mary Tole in 1965. Cadet journalist, Christchurch *Sun*, 1929-30; reporter and sub-editor, 1935-48, and dramatic critic, 1945-47, *The Press*, Christchurch; reporter and sub-editor, *News Chronicle*, London, 1949. Lecturer in English, 1951-66, and Associate Professor of English, 1967-76, University of Auckland. Recipient: New Zealand Literary Fund travel award, 1949; British Council grant, 1949; Carnegie grant, 1950; New Zealand University Research Committee grant, 1957, 1966; Jessie Mackay Poetry Award, 1958, 1963; Fulbright grant, 1961; Institute of Contemporary Arts Fellowship, Washington, D.C., 1961; Library of Congress Whittall Fund award, 1966, 1974; New Zealand Book Award, 1975, 1980; Katherine Mansfield Memorial fellowship, 1983. Litt.D.: University of Auckland, 1966; University of Canterbury, 1975. Agent: Curtis Brown (Australia) Pty. Ltd., 86 William Street, Paddington, New South Wales 2021, Australia. Address: 62 Tohunga Crescent, Parnell, Auckland 1, New Zealand.

PUBLICATIONS

Verse

Valley of Decision. Auckland, University College Press, 1933.
Three Poems. Christchurch, Caxton Press, 1935.
Another Argo, with Denis Glover and A.R.D. Fairburn. Christchurch, Caxton Press, 1935.
Enemies: Poems 1934-36. Christchurch, Caxton Press, 1937.
Not in Narrow Seas. Christchurch, Caxton Press, 1939.
A Present for Hitler and Other Verses (as Whim-Wham). Christchurch, Caxton Press, 1940.
Recent Poems, with others. Christchurch, Caxton Press, 1941.
Island and Time. Christchurch, Caxton Press, 1941.
Verses, 1941-42 (as Whim-Wham). Christchurch, Caxton Press, 1942.
Verses 1943 (as Whim-Wham). Wellington, Progressive, 1943 (?).
Sailing or Drowning. Wellington, Progressive, 1943.
Jack Without Magic. Christchurch, Caxton Press, 1946.
At Dead Low Water, and Sonnets. Christchurch, Caxton Press, 1949.
Poems 1949-57. Wellington, Mermaid Press, 1957.
The Hucksters and the University. Auckland, Pilgrim Press, 1957.
Mr. Huckster of 1958. Auckland, Pilgrim Press, 1958.

The Best of Whim-Wham. Hamilton, Paul's Book Arcade, 1959.
A Small Room with Large Windows: Selected Poems. Wellington and London, Oxford University Press, 1962.
Trees, Effigies, Moving Objects: A Sequence of Poems. Wellington, Catspaw Press, 1972.
An Abominable Temper and Other Poems. Wellington, Catspaw Press, 1973.
Collected Poems 1933-73. Wellington, Reed, 1974.
An Incorrigible Music: A Sequence of Poems. Auckland, Auckland University Press-Oxford University Press, 1979; Oxford, Oxford University Press, 1980.
You Will Know When You Get There: Poems 1979-81. Auckland, Auckland University Press-Oxford University Press, 1982.
Selected Poems. Auckland, Penguin, 1982.

Plays

The Axe: A Verse Tragedy (produced Christchurch, 1948). Christchurch, Caxton Press, 1949.
Moon Section (produced Auckland, 1959).
The Overseas Expert (broadcast, 1961). Included in *Four Plays,* 1972.
Doctor Pom (produced Auckland, 1964).
The Duke's Miracle (broadcast, 1967). Included in *Four Plays,* 1972.
Resident of Nowhere (broadcast, 1969). Included in *Four Plays,* 1972.
Four Plays (includes *The Axe, The Overseas Expert, The Duke's Miracle,* and *Resident of Nowhere*). Wellington, Reed, 1972.

Radio Plays: *The Overseas Expert,* 1961; *The Duke's Miracle,* 1967; *Resident of Nowhere,* 1969.

Other

New Zealand Through the Arts, with Sir Tosswill Woollaston and Witi Ihimaera. Wellington, Friends of the Turnbull Library, 1982.

Editor, *A Book of New Zealand Verse 1923-45.* Christchurch, Caxton Press, 1945; revised edition, 1951.
Editor, *The Penguin Book of New Zealand Verse.* London, Penguin, 1960.

*

Manuscript Collection: Turnbull Library, Wellington.

Critical Studies: "Allen Curnow's Poetry (Notes Towards a Criticism)" by C.K. Stead, in *Landfall* (Christchurch), March 1963; "Conversation with Allen Curnow: Interview by MacDonald P. Jackson," in *Islands* (Auckland), Winter 1973; "Allen Curnow: Forty Years of Poems" by Terry Sturm, in *Islands* (Auckland), Autumn 1975; *Allen Curnow* by Alan Roddick, Wellington, Oxford University Press, 1980, Oxford, Oxford University Press, 1981.

Allen Curnow comments:
I don't know of any school I would care to belong to. New Zealand is difficult enough for me.
I don't know anything about "themes," "subjects," etc., only that "occasions" for poems or plays crop up, as one feels a need

(intermittently) to touch something, to check on its existence or one's own.

I don't know about influences either, but sometimes think of Yeats's dictum, "All that is personal soon rots; it must be packed in ice or salt. Ancient salt is best packing." This is bound to be misinterpreted. I would like to be a poet writing verse so radically old that it looks radically new. I would have to be a much better poet than I am.

Forty years ago I wrote a good few poems "about" New Zealand, as much to find out what I was, as what it was. Worry about one's country is one of the major human worries; of course, one can think of "universality" and worry about that instead, but it's an arid ground for poetry. One learns to live with the oddity of one's country, like Byron's lame foot or Wallace Stevens's insurance company, and these "universal" poems record the learning-process. Poetry won't bear too much accidental stuff, but must have some. Warning: do not exceed the stated dose.

*   *   *

Allen Curnow is a central figure in modern New Zealand poetry. His *A Book of New Zealand Verse 1923-1945*, a selection of poems supported by an impressive introduction, made apparent for the first time that New Zealand's modern poets had produced the beginnings of a distinct tradition. The period of colonial literature was over—this was Curnow's point, demonstrated by the fact that the poets were no longer romanticising their environment with an eye to, or with the eyes of, English readers, but coming to terms with it as it was. Curnow's argument was further supported by an enlargement of his anthology in 1951, and extended in his 1960 *Penguin Book of New Zealand Verse*.

The critical writing went hand in hand with the writing of his poetry, contributing to the development of his subject matter, which had always, however personal its origins, reached towards public statement. In the 1930's, while still finding his voice, he wrote political and social satire. But his characteristic middle style as he found it in the 1940's, was one of ironic perplexity, brooding over one or another distinctly New Zealand scene or historical event, making its detail sharply present to the senses, yet working at it verbally until its particulars rendered up some broader significance. A sonnet in memory of a cousin killed in North Africa begins: "Weeping for bones in Africa, I turn/Our youth over like a dead bird in my hand." By the end, the dead soldier has assumed, not heroic, but national proportions:

But O if your blood's tongued it must recite

South Island feats, those tall, snow-country tales
Among incredulous Tunisian hills.

A recording of a Beethoven quartet becomes "Your 'innermost Beethoven' in the uttermost isles." The skeleton of the extinct moa "on iron crutches" in a museum suggests a vision of the New Zealand poet: "Not I, some child, born in a marvellous year/Will learn the trick of standing upright here." Even in his more difficult poems Curnow's gift for dazzling phrase arrests and holds attention. His lines have the ring of major statement: "Small gods in shawls of bark, blind, numb and deaf,/But buoyant, eastward, in the blaze of surf."

In poems written, most of them, in the mid-1950's, very different occasions or "subjects" seem to have led Curnow consistently to the same preoccupation, weighing objective against subjective, real against ideal. In the real—the present time and place—and in that alone, our salvation, or more simply our satisfaction,

lies. It is the pursuit of the ideal that will damn us. The self is discovered and defined only as it confronts what exists *out there*:

A kingfisher's naked arc alight
Upon a dead stick in the mud
A scarlet geranium wild on a wet bank
A man stepping it out in the distance
With a dog and a bag.

In the 1950's Curnow's anthologies brought him into conflict with a younger generation of poets. Then (the two facts are not necessarily connected) for fifteen years from 1957, he published almost no new poems. In 1972 (the year of James K. Baxter's death) came Curnow's sequence *Trees, Effigies, Moving Objects*, which put him right back into the centre of new developments in New Zealand poetry. This was followed by a less striking collection, *An Abominable Temper*, in 1973; and in 1979 by the extraordinary and powerful sequence, *An Incorrigible Music*. In this latter book Curnow juxtaposes images of coastal New Zealand with modern urban Italy, and a Borgia murder with that (exactly 500 years later) of the Italian statesman Aldo Moro. The mind and the poetic skills are cast out wide to bring together these various realities, each of them a means of confronting death in a new way. Curnow has never written better.

—C.K. Stead

———————

CURREY, R(alph) N(ixon).   British.   Born in Mafeking, South Africa, 14 December 1907. Educated in South Africa; Kingswood School, Bath; Wadham College, Oxford, 1927-30. M.A. (honours) in modern history 1930. Served in the British Army, 1941-46: Commissioned with the Royal Artillery, Staff Major after 1945, writing and editing Army Bureau of Current Affairs publications. Married Stella Martin in 1932; two sons. Senior English Master, 1946-72, and Senior Master for Arts Subjects, 1964-72, Royal Grammar School, Colchester, Essex. President of the Suffolk Poetry Society, Ipswich, 1967-79. Recipient: Viceroy's Prize, 1945; South African Poetry Prize, 1959. Fellow, Royal Society of Literature, 1970. Address: 3 Beverley Road, Colchester, Essex CO3 3NG, England.

PUBLICATIONS

Verse

Tiresias and Other Poems.   London, Oxford University Press, 1940.
This Other Planet.   London, Routledge, 1945.
Indian Landscape: A Book of Descriptive Poems.   London, Routledge, 1947.
The Africa We Knew.   Cape Town, David Philip, 1973.

Plays

Radio Plays: *Between Two Worlds*, 1948; *Early Morning in Vaaldorp*, 1961.

Other

Poets of the 1939-1945 War.   London, Longman, 1960; revised edition, 1967.

Editor, with R.V. Gibson, *Poems from India by Members of the Forces.* Bombay, Oxford University Press, 1945; London, Oxford University Press, 1946.

Editor, *Letters and Other Writings of a Natal Sheriff: Thomas Phipson 1815-1876.* Cape Town and London, Oxford University Press, 1968.

Translator, *Formal Spring: French Renaissance Poems of Charles d'Orléans and Others.* London, Oxford University Press, 1950.

*

Critical Studies: *A Critical Survey of South African Poetry in English* by G.M. Miller and Howard Sergeant, Cape Town, Balkema, 1957; by W.G. Saunders, in *South African Poetry: A Critical Anthology*, edited by D.R. Beeton and W.D. Maxwell-Mahon, Pretoria, University of South Africa Press, 1966.

R.N. Currey comments:

(1980) It takes a lifetime to discover what kind of poet one is. I appear to be an occasional poet, having written much more at some periods of my life than at others.

In the war I found myself placed, quite unprepared by any previous technical training, in a highly technical branch of warfare, in which destruction was carried out impersonally at a distance. I received from this experience an intense impression of what I take to be the likely warfare of the future, in which it will require a strong effort of imagination on the part of the killer to realize what he is doing. I wrote of this in *This Other Planet* and in *Between Two Worlds*, and am intrigued to find out that some of the poems in which I tried to express my response to this are now being anthologized more often than the conventional war poems that found more favour at the time.

When I was posted to India, I found there, still going on, the Middle Ages I had read about when studying History at Oxford. Indians still went on pilgrimage, as people did in the England of Chaucer's time, and my anti-aircraft gunners, who had the same names as the gods in the Indian temples, belonged to the same pre-industrial world. The excitement of this theme is still with me, and I hope to write about it again. Translating French poems, of the Renaissance and Middle Ages, has also given me an entry into those pre-industrial times; and I am glad to find that these poems, too, have the vitality that gets them reprinted many years after first being published.

I have written other topographical poems about places of special importance to me. South Africa, where I spent my boyhood, and where I have a long family connexion, has underlined contrasts and aroused tensions of the sort that produce poetry. *The Africa We Knew* is a book of South African poems, most of which have been printed and broadcast both in England and in South Africa. I recently edited the letters of a great-grandfather who went to South Africa in 1849, and found much that called for a poetical rather than a historical treatment. This I hope to give it at some time. Meanwhile I have completed a biographical study of a pioneer, Thomas Vinnicombe (1854-1932) who kept a *verse* account of a lifetime spent in many of the places where South African history was made; he found verse (for mnemonic reasons) more suitable to a life often spent on horseback and in covered waggons where writing was often impracticable.

I find that I have to go to a new country to discover the one in which I live, to move for a while into a different period in order to come to terms with the present. Both North Africa and the Western United States have given me new viewpoints from which to see the imperial world in which I grew up.

I have published poems, at different times in my life, in different countries, mainly in England, but also in the United States, India, South Africa and Ireland. For many years I have done my writing and broadcasting alongside teaching English and running an English Department at a grammar school, but have now retired to do more writing. There is a great deal that I want to do.

*   *   *

T.S. Eliot said of R.N. Currey that he was the best war-poet, in the precise sense of the word, that World War II produced. This was high praise since between 1939 and 1945 some very distinguished verse appeared in the little reviews and the numerous anthologies of the period. But the war poems, collected in his volume *This Other Planet*, reconsidered after forty years, seem still to hold the essence of their period, in what was felt and thought by those who were the *dramatis personae* of "this damned unnatural sort of war," where so much was remote and impersonal. Like the enemy pilot:

> To us he is no more than a machine
> Shown on an instrument; what can he mean
> In human terms?—a man, somebody's son,
> Proud of his skill; compact of flesh and bone,
> Fragile as Icarus—and our desire
> To see that damned machine come down on fire.

It was as a war poet that Currey really established his reputation, and it is significant that he was chosen by the British Council to write their publication *Poets of the 1939-1945 War*. Nevertheless, it is largely as a South African poet that he has developed, finding his themes in, and feeding his imagination on, the physical Africa that he knew as a boy and on the history of men and things in that complicated but fascinating Eur-African world with its odd duality: "Eating our Christmas pudding beneath the grace/Of feminine willows on the vivid grass" or "My father, all that tawny homeward run,/Remembering snow as I remember sun."

Although Currey has lived most of his adult life in Britain, he goes home from time to time, and his long work, *Early Morning in Vaaldorp*, successfully broadcast by the BBC, is in a sense a tribute to his South African *oeuvres*, "which could not have been written if I had not come from a long South African tradition and spent most of my impressionable years there." North Africa, particularly Morocco, has been responsible for other impressive poems by Currey, who claims to be able to see the Southern Cross from both ends of the Dark Continent, a kind of unifying light in his work. India, too, where much of his war was spent, makes a further link in this chain of poetic topography.

Some of his most memorable poems, of love particularly, have a lyric poignancy that, devoid of any particular context of time or place, achieves a universality of appeal. Such is his beautifully constructed "Song," revealing how truth emerges only from the tug-of-war of contrasts:

> There is no joy in water apart from the sun,
> There is no beauty not emphasized by death,
> No meaning in home if exile were unknown;
> A man who lives in a thermostat lives beneath
> A bell of glass alone with the smell of death.

In such poems as these, Currey reveals himself as a poet of considerable artistry, taking infinite pains with his verse-making

to derive the maximum impact from word or image, an observer
of life or landscape with very particular vision.

—Roy Macnab

DACEY, Philip. American. Born in St. Louis, Missouri, 9
May 1939. Educated at St. Louis University, B.A. 1961; Stanford
University, California, M.A. 1967; University of Iowa, Iowa
City, M.F.A. 1970. Married Florence Chard in 1963; three children. United States Peace Corps volunteer in Eastern Nigeria,
1963-65; Instructor in English, University of Missouri, St. Louis,
1967-68. Since 1970, Member of the Department, now Professor
of English, Southwest State University, Marshall, Minnesota.
Recipient: New York YM—YWHA Discovery Award, 1974;
National Endowment for the Arts fellowship, 1975, 1980; Minnesota State Arts Board fellowship, 1975, 1983; Bush Foundation fellowship, 1977; Loft-McKnight fellowship, 1984. Address:
Box 346, Cottonwood, Minnesota, 56229, U.S.A.

PUBLICATIONS

Verse

The Beast with Two Backs. Milwaukee, Gunrunner Press,
1969.
Fist, Sweet Giraffe, The Lion, Snake, and Owl. Poquoson,
Virginia, Back Door Press, 1970.
Four Nudes. Milwaukee, Morgan Press, 1971.
How I Escaped from the Labyrinth and Other Poems. Pitts-
burgh, Carnegie Mellon University Press, 1977.
The Boy under the Bed. Baltimore, Johns Hopkins University
Press, 1979.
The Condom Poems. Marshall, Minnesota, Ox Head Press,
1979.
*Gerard Manley Hopkins Meets Walt Whitman in Heaven and
Other Poems.* Great Barrington, Massachusetts, Penmaen
Press, 1982.
Fives. Peoria, Illinois, Spoon River Poetry Press, 1984.

Other

Editor, with Gerald M. Knoll, *I Love You All Day: It Is That
Simple.* St. Meinrad, Indiana, Abbey Press, 1970.
Editor, with David Jauss, *Strong Measures: Contemporary
American Poetry in Traditional Forms.* New York, Harper,
1985.

*

Critical Studies: by Dabney Stuart, in *Shenandoah* (Lexington,
Virginia), Winter 1971; David Jauss, in *Great River Review*
(Minneapolis), Fall 1977; Vernon Young, in *Hudson Review*
(New York), December 1977; Leonard Nathan, in *Parnassus*
(New York), Fall-Winter 1978; Joseph B. Wagner, in *Tar River
Poetry* (Greenville, North Carolina), Spring 1979; interview, in
Voices (Marshall, Minnesota), April-May 1979; Philip Jason, in
Poet Lore (Boston), Fall 1979 and Winter 1981-82; Bob Fauteux,
in *Minnesota Daily* (Minneapolis), 16 June 1981; Barton Sutter,
in *Minneapolis Tribune*, 8 May 1983.

*   *   *

Philip Dacey's three substantial collections provide a compendium of poetic delights: wit, wisdom, and the full spectrum of
feeling. He is equally at home in the natural world and in the
realm of meditation. His language may consist of spare, flat
diction or rich, flowing imagery, but it is always *right*, always
evocative of a sensibility and a moment.

How I Escaped from the Labyrinth and Other Poems is too
accomplished to be labeled a first volume. Dacey's poems have a
way of lingering. They haunt with their gentleness, lift with their
lightness. How much he packs into his one-line poem, "Thumb"
("The odd, friendless boy raised by four aunts"). How imaginatively he fashions, then exploits, the metaphor of pornography in
"Porno Love" to explore the elements of artistic and personal
risk: "I've been exposing my genitals/in poems for a long time
now,/at least when they're good." It is by risking that the artist
(the lover) declares "I trust you." So we see "how certain private
parts/made vulnerable/give greatest pleasure/in a consumma-
tion/of good will." In "Learning to Swim in Mid-Life" the
speaker is able at last to give himself to water (to woman, to
others, ultimately to himself): "So I enter you/and you keep me
up,/longer than I have/ever expected." The swimmer now feels
"For once it would be easy/to carry myself./With no strain,/I
could give myself/to others./I would say, Here,/take me. It
would be that simple." By themselves, his hands "are taking/
what they need/to pull me forward." At last "I am wet/with your
wetness."

The Boy under the Bed considers a group of themes which are
personal and universal: the tension between self-preservation
and one's need for others; the struggle to maintain love against
the onslaught of time; the revelation of freedom deriving from
one's ability to have faith. "The Door Prohibited" dramatizes life
as a series of doors and rooms. If one is tempted to open doors,
there is also the need to keep at least one door closed. "The Orgy"
masterfully conveys sexual innuendo in simple diction as it
underscores the not-so-simple questions of whether and when to
risk a new experience: "What would we do/without the line/that
runs between/your piece and mine?" With regret the speaker
declines the invitation ("Better stay home/in certain nooks");
however, his sense of lost opportunity is offset by the arrival of
another invitation. Life is rich in possibilities.

"Watching a Movie in a Foreign Language Without Subtitles"
captures the speaker's sense of displacement, alienation, and
failed communication. The poem opens "For years now, you
have starred/In your own foreign movie." A family man, the "I"
sadly realizes that he now comprehends strangers better than his
own wife and children. In "The Last Straw" the speaker's marriage has collapsed: "One minute the camel was standing there,/
then it was not. I said it was her/straw that did it, she said it was
mine./The fact is, if any one/of all those previous straws had
been withheld,/the camel would not now be dead./So who can
assign responsibility?" Thus, Dacey breathes life into cliché
through a combination of bold, exact metaphor and colloquial
connotative language.

Not only does Dacey craft poems which breathe free of artifice, but they buoy the spirit as the dramatize how faith and
self-trust are ultimately the same. In "Levitation" the speaker is
in love with the magician's assistant and her "faith in air." After
she tells him "You have nothing to rely on," she instructs him to
"Go higher/higher." Dacey does just that. As "The Runner" he
becomes thinner, refines himself; his bones surface, "Coming
foward to meet/the eye. Or slowly developing like/a picture in a
darkroom or the features/of a darkened room to a would-be
sleeper./The flesh was all a lie. The bones were true/and now
were rising as he ran." So death and speaker run together,

partners, "The two of them. The one he'd come to meet/beside him. That shadow, scything the flowers/and leaving them intact." And as he hears the surprising off-rhyme of "health and death," the shadow becomes finally "A lover. And he/had come to rendezvous." Poems like "Proofreading" and "The Way It Happens" develop and reinforce this willingness to trust, this giving over which makes possible the acts of transcendence and transformation.

Gerard Manley Hopkins Meets Walt Whitman in Heaven and Other Poems consists of a sequence based on the historical and imagined life of the British poet. Dacey is marvelous in (re)creating moments and circumstances relating to Hopkins's life. Employing Hopkins's own vocabulary and sprung rhythm, he succeeds not only in making accessible, but resurrecting, Hopkins's sensibility for the reader. The title poem—a combination painting and stage play—depicts heaven as a swimming hole where the two poets meet, grapple, and join at last to strike an appropriately Whitmanesque (and Manley) pose. In his "Author's Note" Dacey hopes "that the spirit of the Fr. Hopkins who lived from 1844 to 1889 can get comfortable between the lines of these poems, if not in them." Hopkins can. Dacey has seen to that.

—Carl Lindner

DALE, Peter (John). British. Born in Addlestone, Surrey, 21 August 1938. Educated at Strode's School, Egham, Surrey; St. Peter's College, Oxford, 1960-63, B.A. (honours) in English 1963. Married Pauline Strouvelle in 1963; two children. English Master, 1965-71, and Head of English, 1971-72, Glastonbury High School, Sutton, Surrey. Since 1972, Head of English, Hinchley Wood School, Esher, Surrey. Associate Editor, 1971-82, and since 1982 co-Editor, *Agenda* magazine, London. Recipient: Arts Council bursary, 1969. Address: 10 Selwood Road, Sutton, Surrey, England.

PUBLICATIONS

Verse

Nerve. Privately printed, 1959.
Walk from the House. Oxford, Fantasy Press, 1962.
The Storms. London, Macmillan, and Chester Springs, Pennsylvania, Dufour, 1968.
Mortal Fire. London, Macmillan, and Chester Springs, Pennsylvania, Dufour, 1970; revised edition, London, Agenda, and Athens, Ohio University Press, 1976.
Cross Channel. Sutton, Surrey, Hippopotamus Press, 1977.
One Another: A Sonnet Sequence. London, Agenda, 1978.
Too Much of Water: Poems 1976-82. London, Agenda, 1984.

Other

Translator, *The Legacy and Other Poems of François Villon.* London, Agenda, 1971; revised edition, as *The Legacy, The Testament, and Other Poems*, London, Macmillan, and New York, St. Martin's Press, 1973.
Translator, *The Seasons of Cankam.* London, Agenda, 1974.
Translator, *Selected Poems of Villon.* London, Penguin, 1978.

*

Critical Studies: "Notes on the Poetry of Peter Dale" by William Cookson, in *Agenda* (London), viii, 3—4, 1970; "The Poetry of Peter Dale" by Terry Eagleton, in *Agenda* (London), xiii, 3, 1975; "Father's Story" by Donald Davie, in *The Listener* (London), October 1976; "The Poetry of Ordinariness," in *Agenda* (London), xiv, 4—xv, 1, 1977, and "Fathers and Sons: Peter Dale's *Mortal Fire*," in *Southern Review* (Baton Rouge, Louisiana), Winter 1979, both by William Bedford; "Reciprocals: Peter Dale and Timothy Steele" by Wyatt Prunty, in *Southern Review* (Baton Rouge, Louisiana), July 1981.

Peter Dale comments:

Reason tells one when a phase of the work is finished; the publishing history of my work shows how often reason has reckoned wrong—as would the variorum of Auden or Lowell's work. So I cannot really make about my work any statement which would be much use. I have no confidence that I should agree with it fully by the time this volume is published. It would not be wise to try to guess what one's skills and learnings were, and hazardous to listen too intently to what critics may assert. It is therefore foolish to prognosticate. Skills one has mastered are no longer necessarily relevant to the making of new poems and to rationalise about them and make them self-conscious could hinder and ossify one's approach and progress. Yet I would not like to imply that poetry is entirely intuitive or instinctive. Coleridge's set of paired opposites best describes it; the creative and critical faculties are concurrent in composition. The poems will have to speak for themselves.

*   *   *

Peter Dale took as epigraph to his first hardback collection, *The Storms*, a line of William Blake, "the most sublime act is to set another before you." He is obsessed with two things in his poetry: the problem of suffering and the problem of "knowing" another person. The first is worked out in various poems based on jobs in hospitals; the second in love poems and friendship poems. His early booklet, *Walk from the House*, criticizes the Christian view: "I would erect suffering into a belief...." This idealisation is rejected and other poems in that book and *The Storms* set suffering sometimes savagely in its animal/human context. "Just Visiting" represents the human difficulties in attending the sick:

> And some of them have indolent golden hair.
> Over there a woman is dying, the line
> of used laughter hung in bands on the lean
> bones. And what you say I cannot hear.

In this context, the poetry is more and more concerned with the uselessness of compassion to alleviate pain, to "know" another's suffering. "Passing the Gates" and "Patient in a Ward" are two poems that analyse this.

The problem of knowing another person runs through the same books and is perhaps best summed up in "The Storms" that deals with a painter and writer who tried to "record" the same tree and their troubled friendship. The theme occurs more fully in "Having No Alternative" (*Mortal Fire*), where drug addiction strains a friendship to breaking point. The final poem in the sequence, "Thinking of Writing a Letter," ends with a sense of loneliness, distances, and desolation which is deeply moving.

Old themes, but what is fresh is the obsessive power of the poems, their direct yet subtle unfolding of the situations. Peter

Dale is a realist and portrays the world, recognisable and tragic. There are a hardness and honesty about his poetry which preclude sentimentality. Work which is rootedly personal and yet never runs the risk of embarrassing the reader is rare. What T.S. Eliot has called "private experience at its greatest intensity becoming universal" seems an appropriate description. Much of this power comes from the quiet, concealed control of technique. The central prosodic quality of these poems is freedom within form. The forms range from traditional stanzas through experiments with various rhyme techniques to a free verse which owes little to Pound, Eliot, or Williams. And always there is the individual tone of a voice talking quietly with a great force of controlled emotion behind the words, as in "Unaddressed Letter":

> Now it is autumn...And rain...Big drops you can trace.
> I notice how one drop's enough to tear
> an amber leaf out of the brittle trees.
> I suppose much the same happened last year,
> but it is now I notice watching a caricature
> of your face talking to myself as I stare
> out of the window where the puddles stir.

Along with the range of forms goes a range of approach and tone. Dale can manage dramatic monologue with great variety: there is the detached irony of "Afternoon Operating List"—early version in *Walk from the House*—and the powerful involvement of "It Is Finished" (*Mortal Fire*). There are the humorous "Obtainable at All Good Herbalists," the quiet gratitude of "Dedication," and the Imagist concision of "Last Respects."

The directness of the finest of Peter Dale's poems often veils a more subtle undercurrent to the feeling and the thought. They stand the acid tests that, once read, they remain in the mind, and, reread, they do not bore, but gain strength. The blurb of *The Storms* suggests that while the poems are haunting, there are no memorable lines. This is partly due to method; the shifting caesuras and constant overrunning of lines prevent this. But what is memorable is the clarity and delicacy of the imagery: "and underwings extend wood-ember white," or "Across the playing fields the amber leaves/shine oldgold through the frost," or "Your presence, love,/like underlight of trees/within a wood."

The revised and much improved 1976 edition of *Mortal Fire*, which is really a selected poems, contains a powerful sequence of love poems, "The Going," which further explores, in a highly rhythmic and controlled free verse, the problem of knowing another person I've already referred to. Spare and uncluttered by rhetoric, these lyrics are informed by a new richness of metaphor: "Scotch fir, the trunk/staked in the still pools of its boughs/on the old hill." "The Going" has a simplicity akin to Dale's version from the Tamil, *The Seasons of Cankam*, a beautiful little book, which has qualities in common with Pound's translations from the Chinese.

Since *Mortal Fire* Dale has further widened his scope by translating almost the complete works of François Villon. This is a strict metrical translation which faithfully reproduces the rhyme schemes of the original—an incredibly difficult task in English. By this method, Dale has recreated the spirit of Villon with sometimes electric energy. He has written, in my opinion, the finest English Villon we are likely to get—certainly no other version has expressed with such power the humour, word-play, and swift changes of tone of the French together with its elegiac lyricism. The difference between Dale's Villon and his own poetry is a good measure of the breadth and versatility of his writing.

One Another is a sequence of 62 sonnets. Tracing the relationship of a man and woman through many years, these are poems to be lived with and experienced slowly: the images interweave and shed light on each other in a complex pattern, so that each rereading gives a sense of discovery. Possessing the truth of the imagination, the most moving sonnets are the final group, which express the man's memories and responses to the woman's death: "Now, love, you are the north/my memory steers from, late, so very late."

Peter Dale has probably produced a greater variety and extent of work which will endure than other poets of his generation. Undeflected by fashions and influences, his poetry is instantly recognisable. The loudest voices soon grow hoarse.

—William Cookson

DALLAS, Ruth. Pseudonym for Ruth Mumford. New Zealander. Born in Invercargill, 29 September 1919. Recipient: New Zealand Literary Fund Achievement Award, 1963; Robert Burns Fellowship, University of Otago, 1968; New Zealand Book Award, 1977; Buckland Literary Award, 1977. Litt.D.: University of Otago, Dunedin, 1978. Address: 448 Leith Street, Dunedin, New Zealand.

PUBLICATIONS

Verse

Country Road and Other Poems 1947-1952. Christchurch, Caxton Press, 1953.
The Turning Wheel. Christchurch, Caxton Press, 1961.
Experiment in Form. Dunedin, Otago University Bibliography Room, 1964.
Day Book: Poems of a Year. Christchurch, Caxton Press, 1966.
Shadow Show. Christchurch, Caxton Press, 1968.
Song for a Guitar and Other Songs, edited by Charles Brasch. Dunedin, University of Otago Press, 1976.
Walking on the Snow. Christchurch, Caxton Press, 1976.
Steps of the Sun. Christchurch, Caxton Press, 1979.

Other (for children)

Sawmilling Yesterday. Wellington, Department of Education, 1958.
The Children in the Bush. London, Methuen, 1969.
Ragamuffin Scarecrow. Dunedin, Otago University Bibliography Room, 1969.
A Dog Called Wig. London, Methuen, 1970.
The Wild Boy in the Bush. London, Methuen, 1971.
The Big Flood in the Bush. London, Methuen, 1972; New York, Scholastic, 1974.
The House on the Cliffs. London, Methuen, 1975.
Shining Rivers. London, Methuen, 1979.
Holiday Time in the Bush. London, Methuen, 1983.

*

Manuscript Collection: Hocken Library, University of Otago, Dunedin, New Zealand.

Critical Studies: by James Bertram, in *Landfall 29* and *62* (Christchurch), March 1954, and June 1962; introduction by Charles Brasch to *Song for a Guitar*, 1976; "The Rhythm of

Change: Comments on the Work of Ruth Dallas" by John Gibb, in *Pilgrims 3* (Dunedin), nos. 1-2, 1978; Basil Dowling, in *Landfall* (Christchurch), December 1980.

Ruth Dallas comments:

I am sometimes rather frowningly called a "nature poet"; but I have never lived in a large city and been separated from the life of the earth and the coming up and going down of the sun in unpolluted skies; so I take my imagery where I find it. I have tried to keep in the forefront of my mind my position in space and time; I want never to forget that I am on a remote small planet in space, and never to forget that I am on it at present and must soon leave. And who is to say that I am to write 20th-century poetry, or any other kind of poetry? It is chance that I was born in the 20th century and not the 10th, and chance that I was born in New Zealand and not Scandinavia or China. I care nothing for fashion in poetry and think a poem should be as free as one of the far-ranging seabirds I have watched by the hour flying in storm and calm about the coasts of New Zealand. A bird is not always flying; when it is still it is very still; but you know what it can do. Perhaps for this reason I have been attracted to the ancient meditative poems of the Chinese and Japanese, who used words with as much thought as they used the brush-strokes from which their poems are hardly separable. I, too, like to use words sparingly, and to make them carry as many overtones as possible, but all should seem spontaneous. A poem is a human utterance, like dance and song, or an involuntary cry. What would please me most would be to find that my poems appeared effortless, however hard I work on them. But if I fail, it is difficult to believe that it matters. Poetry runs in our veins, and over the centuries will flower now here, now there. If it does not come from my pen it will come from another's.

Steps of the Sun shows less Chinese influence and more exploration of the possibilities of the imagination.

*   *   *

Ruth Dallas first became known as a regional poet, a meditative recorder of rural life and incident in Southland, the lonely province at the bottom of New Zealand that looks inland to small farms, mountain lakes, and brooding beech-forests, and south to Antarctica. This is hard country (Central Otago concentrates wilderness, fruitlands, and climatic extremes), and a girl growing up in intellectual isolation, threatened with blindness and with an ailing mother to care for, had to develop her own inner discipline and self-reliance. The result was a lyrical poetry of plain statement and diction, responsive to the play of natural and historical forces on human lives: *Country Road* has several poems ("Milking Before Dawn," "Grandmother and Child," "The World's Centre") that soon became stock New Zealand anthology pieces, and Ruth Dallas was conveniently typed as a nature poet with a limited range.

Eight years later, however, *The Turning Wheel* revealed a more restless and capacious mind. The title-sequence is still concerned with seasonal growth and change, but the "Letter to a Chinese Poet" (Po Chü-I) is a much more ambitious sequence in which local and personal material is assimilated into a cultural and metaphysical synthesis of real power and intensity. An autobiographical essay, "Beginnings" (*Landfall*, December 1965), describes the independent reading which led to a new interest in Buddhist influences in Indian, Chinese, and Japanese literature: "Through my lack of formal, dogmatic education, there were no walls to break down, and I was able to pass as freely into one culture as into another." Ruth Dallas's first writing in Invercargill had been encouraged by the critic and editor M.H. Holcroft;

when she moved to Dunedin she began a long association with the poet Charles Brasch in the editing of *Landfall* which is clearly traceable in the development of her thought. It would be misleading to describe her as a philosophical poet; she is no system-maker, her best work remains concentrated in short lyrical forms. But like Ruth Pitter, perhaps, Ruth Dallas has produced a considerable body of lyrical work, often experimental in shape and texture and apparently purely decorative or musical, which carries a gravity of thought and perception quite disproportionate to its limited compass.

During the 1970's, Ruth Dallas had some international success with her stories for children, and must now be considered a creative prose-writer as well as a poet. Yet her verse volume *Walking in the Snow* won the New Zealand Book Award for Poetry in 1977, and there is evidence of a steadily widening appreciation of her distinctive lyrical achievement. She is one of the most independent and unfashionable of New Zealand writers; but her purity of diction and clear singing note seem likely to preserve her work when more aggressively modern verse is forgotten. She has no doubts about what she is striving for—the unassuming mastery of a Japanese jar glimpsed in a pottery film: "The jar was uneven, casual, easy, nonchalant; it seemed almost accidental, but was not. That's how I should like my finished work to appear."

—James Bertram

———————

DANA, Robert (Patrick). American. Born in Allston, Massachusetts, 2 June 1929. Educated at Drake University, Des Moines, Iowa, B.A. 1951; University of Iowa, Iowa City, M.A. 1953. Served as a radioman in the United States Navy, 1946-48. Married 1) Mary Kowalke in 1951, two daughters and one son; 2) Peg Sellen. Instructor, 1954-58, Assistant Professor, 1958-62, Associate Professor, 1962-68, and Professor of English, 1968-85, Cornell College, Mount Vernon, Iowa. Editor, Hillside Press, 1957-67, and *The North American Review*, 1964-68, both Mount Vernon. Recipient: Danforth grant, 1959; Rinehart Foundation Fellowship, 1960; Ford-ACM grant, 1966; Rainer Maria Rilke Prize, 1984. Address: Department of English, Cornell College, Mount Vernon, Iowa 52314, U.S.A.

PUBLICATIONS

Verse

My Glass Brother and Other Poems. Iowa City, Constance Press, 1957.
The Dark Flags of Waking. Iowa City, Qara Press, 1964.
Journeys from the Skin: A Poem in Two Parts. Iowa City, Hundred Pound Press, 1966.
Some Versions of Silence: Poems. New York, Norton, 1967.
The Power of the Visible. Chicago, Swallow Press, 1971.
The Watergate Elegy. Chicago, Wine Press, 1973.
Tryptych. Chicago, Wine Press, 1974.
Winter Poems, with Debora Greger and George O'Connell. Lisbon, Iowa, Penumbra, 1977.
In a Fugitive Season. Athens, Swallow Press-Ohio University Press, 1980.
On a View of Paradise Ridge from a Rented House. Kendrick, Idaho, Two Magpies Press, 1980.

Keats in Detroit to Byron in California.   Privately printed,
1982.
What the Stones Know.   Iowa City, Seamark Press, 1984.

*

Bibliography: *Voyages to the Inland Sea 3* edited by John Judson, La Crosse, University of Wisconsin Press, 1973.

Critical Study: "A World That Comes Apart like a Surprise" by
Anselm Hollo, in *New Letters* (Kansas City, Missouri), Summer
1973.

Robert Dana comments:

I see myself as a poet—I don't believe in poets as prophets, or
priests, or even as people of superior intelligence and feeling.
Though I'm sure I once did and once in a while still do. Ultimately, I think, I believe what Auden and Cunningham have
believed before me—that the poet's only magic is with words. He
begins life with a natural gift for handling them and hearing
them. He loves them for their sounds, their taste, their soft or
their steel feel. And for their enduring strangeness. Each word
has, for him, its own perfect story.

Much later, when the poet begins to develop a style, he comes
to recognize that style is not just a way of saying things but a way
of seeing things. And seeing them with the whole being at once.
Poetry is felt thought, Eliot once said. And so it is. But being both
at once, it is neither. A poem is an experience of a total kind in
which the transitory in our existence passes into permanence.

*   *   *

Robert Dana crafts in irony the perishing world as it becomes
part of his inner-life, charting his country's taste for concrete in
images "Unlikely as Chicago," the American view of nature:
"Pigs blister the hillside.../ Morning may strike us anywhere."

Separate, but not separated from that, as in a never-consum-
mated divorce, Dana looks for balance in another direction,
towards the T'ang poets he translates or to

> The grace of simple food...
> ...the table wooden as the loneliness of plain fact
>
> And bread for the moon
> the heart's small loaf.

Sometimes the tension between these worlds is manifest in his
silences, sometimes it's in the "zag zag zag of sodium lamps/blue
across the causeways," sometimes it's in the precision of an
elegant image. His technical skill carries it through a range of
modern poetic strategies.

In Pound's terms, Robert Dana is a master rather than an
inventor, moving through a variety of techniques and images,
frequently using them better than their originators. His first
book contains a tense world, sparse, attenuated details of vivid
intensity, controlled word-by-word, his technique at its best
nearly equal to Creeley's at *his* best. Dana works primarily with
resonances, articulate matter accusing itself across silences.

In his second book, the poetry becomes metamorphic, turns
toward dreams:

> And I am driving into my own sleep
> of white chickens
> past barnyard harvests of junked cars
> the wind slumps through the empty eyes of cows.

The landscape begins to flash surrealistically, Los Angeles
slumps into the ocean after nine days rain, Kennedy is assassinated again, "razors could not cut the rain from the glass."
Without reveling in vatic zeal or surreal petulance, however, the
poet "whistles under the true sky of his troubles/walking slow-
ly/inside himself," realizing that regardless of the emotions that
flood him, he gains only a measured wisdom:

> I see that I am what I always was
> that ordinary man on his front steps
> bewildered under the bright mess of the heavens
> by the fierce indecipherable language of its stars.

It is this balance, or candidness, that more and more characterizes Dana's recent poetry, with its growing breadth of concern, its
remarkable sureness of technique: one learns to have confidence
in this voice.

—Edward B. Germain

———————

DAS, D(eb) K(umar).   Indian.   Born in Calcutta, 22 December
1935. Educated at St. Xavier's College, Calcutta University
(Quinlan Medalist, 1955; Tata Fellowship, 1955), B.A. (honours)
1955; Queens' College, Cambridge, B.A. 1958, M.A. 1962.
Member of the management staff, I.C.I., Calcutta, 1959-61;
Teaching Assistant, University of Washington, Seattle, 1961-63;
Instructor, then Superintendent, S.O.I.C., Seattle, 1967-70;
Deputy Director, then Director of Research and Planning, State
Board for Community College Education, Seattle, 1970-72.
Since 1972, director and evaluator of federal projects in educa-
tion and community development, Seattle. Broadcaster, View-
point radio program, for 2 years. Paintings exhibited in India
and the United States. Agent: P. Lal, Writers Workshop, 162-92
Lake Gardens, Calcutta, 700 045, India.

PUBLICATIONS

Verse

The Night Before Us.   Calcutta, Writers Workshop, 1960.
Through a Glass Darkly.   Calcutta, Writers Workshop, 1965.
The Eyes of Autumn: An Experiment in Poetry.   Calcutta,
   Writers Workshop, 1968.
The Four Labyrinths.   Calcutta, Writers Workshop, 1969.
The Fire Canto.   Calcutta, Writers Workshop, 1971.
The Winterbird Walks.   Calcutta, Writers Workshop, 1976.
Always Once Was: Experiments in Metapoetics.   Calcutta,
   Writers Workshop, 1977.

Other

Navbharat Papers: A Political Programme for a New India.
   Seattle, San Vito Press, 1968.
Freedom and Reality, Parts I to VI.   Privately printed, 1968.
The First Philosopher: Yājñavalka.   Seattle, San Vito Press,
   1971.
The Agony of Arjun and Other Essays.   Privately printed, 1971.
*Svatvavāda: Towards a Theory of Property 2000 B.C.—1800
   A.D.: An Essay in Three Parts.*   Privately printed, 1972.
State Planning for the Disadvantaged, with Dennis Carlson.

Seattle, Washington Board for Community College Planning, 1972.

An Essay on the Forms of Individualism. Seattle, SFSC Press, 1973.

What Final Frontier? or, The Future of Man in Space. Seattle, SFSC Press, 1973.

Beginnings of Human Thought: The Rig Vedas. Seattle, SFSC Press, 1973.

Translator, *Sankarāchārya: A Discourse on the Real Nature of Self.* Calcutta, Writers Workshop, 1970.

Translator, *The Iśa and Kena Upanishads.* Calcutta, Writers Workshop, 1971.

Translator, *Jabala and Paingala Upanisads.* Calcutta, Writers Workshop, 1979.

*

D.K. Das comments:

My interest is divided about equally between *writing* (in all forms), *painting* (have had several one-man exhibitions in India and U.S.A.), and *research/teaching* in mathematics/economics.

Conflict is a basic theme in my poetry; that between past and future, order and anarchy, passion and reason—with war as an extension of this contemporary human condition. My presuppositions are those of the *Bhagavad Gita*; by image as well as reference, I have tried to translate into contemporary terms its message that centrality, being, even meaning, can be found in the *heart* of conflict; the "eye of the storm," its still centre. Space exploration and technological images/themes appear frequently in my poetry, because of my search for modern metaphors, and a contemporary frame of reference. Other than Indian philosophy (especially Vedanta), the strongest influences on my work were undoubtedly T.S. Eliot and W.H. Auden; my mathematical training also influenced my language and "poetic logic"; Albert Camus' *Myth of Sisyphus* also entered many of my poetic intuitions. I am also experimenting with poetic form, trying to create small and large poetic formats capable of carrying poetic *as well as* metaphysical meaning.

*   *   *

Writer, poet, and economist, D.K. Das, in 1958, helped found Calcutta's Writers Workshop whose purpose was to discuss, encourage and publish Indo-English writing. Exceptionally, he often uses traditional verse-forms—most successfully, blank verse, though rhyme sometimes adds irony or piquancy.

He acknowledges influences from Eliot, Auden, and Camus, but more basically the Bhagavat-Gita and Vedanta classics (he has translated upanisads and Sankarāchārya's *A Discourse on the Real Nature of Self*). He uses his logical-mathematical training to organize poems as penetrations from conflicts and paradoxes into cores of central meaning—the "still point" at the heart of every storm. This may be sardonic—to improve the army computer, which, one factor missing, fire-bombs its own unit then duly notifies next-of-kin, he suggests creating "a special digit/for machine error's contradiction.../a voice that click-clacked error, to the last." More seriously, in "Descartes' God" God's "death" might logically prove Descartes did not exist—or was he wrong, for the wrong reasons, and so logically, right: "Man's mind was a parasite/In symbiosis with a word called God."

Words, like God, are matters of faith. Poets coin names to keep events whole, lest historians simplify them—yet in saying they "mean" feelings or facts, "we are only/crossing our

fingers—/Praying that those three blind/movings/(words, feelings, facts)/Are moving Together, finitely."

The Fire Canto, Das's most successful attempt at combining "poetic...[and] metaphysical meaning," finds Fire the primal substance, man's mind the "Fire of this forever universe," whose burning, "we being merely Fire-bearers must affirm; in order to be and to become Ourselves."

Das found it increasingly hard to so affirm in India's "clock-work existence"; it had "too many anxious excuses for everything/Except the freedom of the firefly's search/...Truth repeated two hundred thousand times/until its words were only incantations." In 1968 he went to Seattle to teach economics and math to ghetto children. He continued to send to Writers Workshop poems, stories and translations, but—no doubt for this desertion—Pritish Nandy pointedly omitted him from his 1972 anthology of Indo-English poetry.

—George McElroy

DAS, Kamala (née Nair). Indian. Born in Malabar, South India, 31 March 1934. Educated privately. Married K. Madhava Das in 1949; three sons. Poetry Editor, *Illustrated Weekly of India*, Bombay, 1971-72, 1978-79; Editor, *Pamparam*, Trivandrum, Kerala; Director, Book Point, Bombay. President, Jyotsha Art and Education Academy, Bombay. Recipient: P.E.N. Prize, 1964; Kerala Sahitya Academy Award, for fiction, 1969; Chaiman Lal Award, for journalism, 1971. Address: Nalapat House, Punnayurkulam, Kerala, India.

PUBLICATIONS

Verse

Summer in Calcutta: Fifty Poems. Delhi, Everest Press, 1965.
The Descendants. Calcutta, Writers Workshop, 1967.
The Old Playhouse and Other Poems. Madras, Longman, 1973.
Tonight This Savage Rite: The Love Poetry of Kamala Das and Pritish Nandy. New Delhi, Arnold-Heinemann, 1979.

Novel

Alphabet of Lust. New Delhi, Orient, 1977.

Short Stories

Pathu Kathakal (Ten Stories), *Tharisunilam* (Fallow Fields), *Narachirukal Parakkumbol* (When the Bats Fly), *Ente Snehita Aruna* (My Friend Aruna), *Chuvanna Pavada* (The Red Skirt), *Thanuppu* (Cold), *Rajavinte Premabajanam* (The King's Beloved), *Premathinte Vilapa Kavyam* (Requiem for a Love), *Mathilukal* (Walls). Trichur, Kerala, Current Books, 1953-72.
A Doll for the Child Prostitute. New Delhi, India Paperbacks, 1977.

Other

Driksakshi Panna (Eyewitness) (juvenile). Madras, Longman, 1973.
My Story. New Delhi, Sterling, 1976; London, Quartet 1978.

*

Critical Studies: *Kamala Das* by Devindra Kohli, New Delhi, Arnold-Heinemann, 1975; *Expressive Form in the Poetry of Kamala Das* by Anisur Rahman, New Delhi, Abhinav, 1981; *Kamala Das and Her Poetry* by A.N. Dwivedi, New Delhi, Doaba, 1983.

Kamala Das comments:

(1970) I began to write poetry with the ignoble aim of wooing a man. There is therefore a lot of love in my poems. I feel forced to be honest in my poetry. I have read very little poetry. I do not think that I have been influenced by any poet. I have liked to read Kalidasa. When I compose poetry, whispering the words to myself, my ear helps to discipline the verse. Afterwards, I count the syllables. I like poetry to be tidy and disciplined.

(1974) My grand-uncle is Nalapat Narayana Menon, the well-known poet-philosopher of Malabar. My mother is the well-known poetess Nalapat Balamani Amma. I belong to the ma-triarchal community of Nayars. Our ancestral house (Nalapat House) is more than 400 years old and contains valuable palm-leaf manuscripts like the *Varahasamhita, Susrutha Samhita*, and books of mantras.

As I have no degree to add to my name, my readers considered me in the beginning like a cripple. My writing was like the paintings done by "foot and mouth" painters or like the baskets made by the blind. I received some admiration, but the critics, well-known academicians, tore my writing to shreds. This only made my readers love me more. All I have wanted to do is to be real and honest to my readers.

*   *   *

Kamala Das is an intensely, and consciously, subjective poet. Her own experience—a rich, love-filled childhood, a marriage that failed to provide emotional fulfilment and autonomy and growth to her "self," and her restless longing for a fulfilling relationship—is the dominant subject-matter of her poetry. As she says in "The Old Playhouse," a barely veiled address to her own man,

> It was not to gather knowledge
> Of yet another man that I came to you but to learn
> What I was, and by learning, to learn to grow, but every
> Lesson you gave was about yourself.

This ardent yearning for a love complete with sexual fulfilment but offering more is expressed in "The Freaks," one of her best poems, where the man can only excite physical passion, none too strongly; whose "Nimble finger-tips unleash/ Nothing more alive than the/ Skin's lazy hungers?"; who fails to evoke or match the woman's "Flamboyant lust," which is the poet's ideal of love between man and woman.

Kamala Das's almost pathological obsession with her own feelings, urges, and frustrations makes her poetry thematically narrow and repetitious not in the poems' concerns alone but in the phrases and metaphors as well. At the same time, this obses-sion makes her poetry disturbingly spontaneous and gives her metaphors and images a striking vitality and freshness. Early critics were quick to note the unstrained candour of her sexual views—shocking for an upper-class married woman—and this candour gives authenticity and power to her poetry. Though her movingly fierce emotionalism is the force behind her poems, they are not, as many critics think they are, crude in form. Many of them conceal a subtle craftsmanship, a care in achieving com-

pression and vividness without diluting the strength of the emotion.

Juxtaposed with present yearnings and frustrations in her poetry is a nostalgia for a time and place that fill life with beauty, excitement, and love—the ancestral house in Kerala and the fond grandmother, who understood the child's needs and lavished tender care on her: the "house now far away where once/I received love.... That woman died,/The house withdrew into, silence...." And the house where, she asks the reader if he would believe, "I lived...and/Was proud, and loved.... I who have lost/ My way and beg now at strangers' doors to/ Receive love, at least in small change?"

At its best Kamala Das's language is not recognizably Indian English; and yet occasionally her phrases and lines have an Indian flavour that need not bother either the poet or the reader, for it only enhances the authenticity of the expression of an Indian sensibility whose responses to the world around as well as within have established their universal interest. Her prose fiction is chiefly an extension, barely competent, of themes which her poetry has already treated much more beautifully. Her interest and power as a writer remain essentially in her intense personal-ity, as brought out in her poetry and in her exceptionally frank, sometimes over-sentimental, over-dramatic, autobiography, *My Story*.

—J.N. Sharma

———————

DAVEY, Frank(land Wilmot). Canadian. Born in Vancouver, British Columbia, 19 April 1940. Educated at the University of British Columbia, Vancouver, 1957-63, B.A. 1961, M.A. 1963; University of Southern California, Los Angeles (Canada Coun-cil Fellow), 1965-68, Ph.D. 1968. Married 1) Helen Simmons in 1962 (divorced, 1969); 2) Linda McCartney in 1969; one son and one daughter. Teaching Assistant, University of British Colum-bia, 1961-63; Lecturer, 1963-66, and Assistant Professor, 1967-69, Royal Roads Military College, Victoria, British Columbia; Writer-in-Residence, Sir George Williams University, Montreal, 1969-70. Assistant Professor, 1970-72, Associate Professor, 1972-79, Coordinator of the Creative Writing Program, 1976-79, and since 1980 Professor of English, York University, Toronto. Visiting Professor, Shastri Indo-Canadian Institute, Karnatak University, India, 1982. Founding Editor, *Tish* magazine, Van-couver, 1961-63. Since 1965, Founding Editor, *Open Letter*, Toronto; since 1973, General Editor, Quebec Translations series, and since 1975, Member of the Editorial Board, Coach House Press, Toronto; since 1977, General Editor, New Canadian Criti-cism series, Talonbooks, Vancouver; since 1984, Director, *Swift Current* literary database and magazine project. Recipient: Humanities Research Council of Canada grant, 1974, 1981; Canada Council travel grant, 1971, 1973, and Fellowship, 1974; Canadian Federation for the Humanities grant, 1979. Address: Department of English, York University, 4700 Keele Street Downsview, Ontario M3J 1P3, Canada.

PUBLICATIONS

Verse

D-Day and After. Vancouver, Tishbooks, 1962.
City of the Gulls and Sea. Privately printed, 1964.
Bridge Force. Toronto, Contact Press, 1965.

The Scarred Hull. Calgary, Imago, 1966.
Four Myths for Sam Perry. Vancouver, Talonbooks, 1970.
Weeds. Toronto, Coach House Press, 1970.
Griffon. Toronto, Massasauga, 1972.
King of Swords. Vancouver, Talonbooks, 1972.
L'An Trentiesme: Selected Poems 1961-1970. Vancouver, Community Press, 1972.
Arcana. Toronto, Coach House Press, 1973.
The Clallam; or, Old Glory in Juan de Fuca. Vancouver, Talonbooks, 1973.
War Poems. Toronto, Coach House Press, 1979.
The Arches: Selected Poems, edited by B.P. Nichol. Vancouver, Talonbooks, 1980.
Capitalistic Affection! Toronto, Coach House Press, 1982.
Edward and Patricia. Toronto, Coach House Press, 1983.

Other

Five Readings of Olson's "Maximus." Montreal, Beaver Kosmos, 1970.
Earle Birney. Toronto, Copp Clark, 1971.
From There to Here: A Guide to English-Canadian Literature since 1960. Erin, Ontario, Press Porcépic, 1974.
Louis Dudek and Raymond Souster. Vancouver, Douglas and McIntyre, 1980; Seattle, University of Washington Press, 1981.
Surviving the Paraphrase. Winnipeg, Turnstone Press, 1983.
Margaret Atwood: A Feminist Poetics. Vancouver, Talonbooks, 1984.

Editor, *Tish 1—19.* Vancouver, Talonbooks, 1975.
Editor, *Mrs. Dukes' Million,* by Wyndham Lewis. Toronto, Coach House Press, 1977.
Editor, *The Browser's Opal L. Nations.* Toronto, Coach House Press, 1981.

*

Manuscript Collection: Simon Fraser University, Burnaby, British Columbia.

Critical Studies: interviews with Elizabeth Komisar in *White Pelican* (Edmonton, Alberta), 1975, and with George Bowering in *Open Letter 4* (Toronto), Spring 1979; "Frank Davey: Finding Your Voice to Say What Must Be Said" by Douglas Barbour, in *Brave New Wave* edited by Jack David, Windsor, Ontario, Black Moss Press, 1978.

Frank Davey comments:

Since 1964 my poetry has been written mostly in sequences of from ten to eighty pages. I've been especially interested in the abrupt shifts of tone and diction that are possible between the sections of a serial poem, and in the writing of European (*King of Swords, Weeds*) or United States (*The Clallam, Capitalistic Affection!*) mythology from a Canadian perspective. All of it is concerned with the decentralization of literary mythologies, and the enabling and creation of alternative texts.

*   *   *

Frank Davey is best known for his espousal of Black Mountain poets in Canada, introduced through the monthly mimeographed newsletter *Tish,* continued through the triannual *Open Letter* (from 1965), and embodied in his own teaching and in articles, reviews, and the pages of *From There to Here,* a useful though opinionated handbook. Davey's own poetry, judged by *L'An Trentiesme: Selected Poems* and *Arcana,* is not at all doctrinaire, but light and lyrical (contrary to what George Bowering is quoted as saying in *There to Here*): "description/is a bird who comes down/all too easy." This comes from "out &/on," a poem from the "Bridge Force" part of the selected poems. The other volume includes occasional poems plus meditations on the Tarot cards. It could be argued that Davey is basically an occasional poet. He has written semi-documentary, semi-lyrical poems on a number of marine disasters, culminating in *The Clallam,* a long poem that recreates very successfully the sinking of a ship. Perhaps his credo is best summed up in "The Mirror XIV" from Arcana:

> I write these words
> that someone, will remember me,
> or at least finding me here
> poisd, burnd, loved, unloved, will see words
> moving.

—John Robert Colombo

DAVIDSON, Michael. American. Born in Oakland, California, 18 December 1944. Educated at San Francisco State University, 1963-67, B.A. 1967; State University of New York, Buffalo, 1967-71, Ph.D. 1971; post-doctoral fellow, University of California, Berkeley, 1974-75. Married Carol Wikarska in 1970 (divorced, 1974). Visiting Lecturer, San Diego State University, 1973-76. Since 1975, Director of Archive for New Poetry, Assistant Professor, 1977-81, and since 1981, Associate Professor of English, University of California, San Diego. Advisory Editor, *Fiction International,* Canton, New York; Assistant Editor, *Credences,* Buffalo; Editor, *The Archive Newsletter* and *Documents for New Poetry,* both in La Jolla, California. Recipient: National Endowment for the Arts grant, 1976. Address: 1220 Hygeia, Leucadia, California 92024, U.S.A.

PUBLICATIONS

Verse

Exchanges. Los Angeles, Prose and Verses Press, 1972.
Two Views of Pears. Berkeley, California, Sand Dollar, 1973.
The Mutabilities, and The Foul Papers. Berkeley, California, Sand Dollar, 1976.
Summer Letters. Santa Barbara, California, Black Sparrow Press, 1976.
Grillwork. Montreal, M.B.M. Monographs, 1980.
Discovering Motion. Berkeley, California, Little Dinosaur Press, 1980.
The Prose of Fact. Berkeley, California, Figures, 1981.

Other

The San Francisco Renaissance and Postmodern Poetics. Cambridge, Cambridge University Press, 1983.

*

Critical Studies: reviews by Robert Bertholf in *Credences 5—6* (Kent, Ohio), and Jed Rasula in *Open Letter 8* (Toronto), Spring 1978.

Michael Davidson comments:

My first encounters with poetry occurred, as they did for most of my generation, via Brooks and Warren's *Understanding Poetry*. As I remember, "classic" poems were presented followed by four or five seminal questions which, once answered by the bright literature student, would solve the curious riddle hidden (intentionally, no doubt) in the poem. Such an approach to poetry was pretty intimidating for a young writer; after all, the poet presumably had thought these strategies out before sitting down to write, and my early practice simply involved writing "toward" some vaguely formed idea. The Brooks and Warren method of literary analysis was accompanied in Creative Writing workshops by stern lectures on what was then called the "craft" of poetry—that is, the poet's ability to exert his will to power over form. The supreme poet, then, was one who could channel the multifarious happenings of daily life into a series of discrete, oblique figures, usually involving some part of the poet's inner organs or perhaps his ancestral origins. This rather inhospitable atmosphere was an important formulating experience for my own work but, under the salutary influence of the poetry renaissance of the late 1950's and early 1960's in San Francisco, I resumed the practice of writing "toward" some vaguely formed idea.

I would like to think of my work as an interrogation or exploration of its own processes—not for the sake of formalist exercise but in order to test the thresholds of meaning. In this sense, poetry is a profoundly human activity since it refuses to take the world for granted while believing utterly in its multi-faceted character. The most difficult task for the poet, as Jack Spicer pointed out, is avoiding what YOU want to say since this invariably results in a trivializing of that initial charge that drove you to write in the first place. And oddly enough, the result is something extremely personal if only because the writing embodies the wandering, desultory quality of one's thoughts. At times this "tracing" involves areas of interruption and semantic breakdown since it is often where language fails to provide necessary information (or where it provides the unwanted figure, slip of tongue or typo) that it most reveals. How, then, to capture that quality? At the simplest level, by being open to the qualities and textures and confusions of one's own language as it struggles with difficult material, and alternately by avoiding the lure of an imperializing rhetoric which yearns to "temper" that experience by subordinating its semantic plurality. This may not be a practical solution, but it is at least the atmosphere in which the various solutions offered in my writing have been nurtured.

*   *   *

"To 'do' one's art," Michael Davidson writes, "means to solve problems in a language which the art establishes as it is being created. Its grammar and lexicon emerge less as a result of a commitment to prior forms and more as a response to immediate necessity." The locus of interest in Davidson's *The Mutabilities* is precisely in watching the response to immediate necessity unfold. The poems are, as it were, live performances.

The epigraph to the volume is from *Tristram Shandy*, and the pervading tone is Shandean. Davidson's poetry turns on a sense of language as a persistent but unreliable medium. Above all, "I"—that sign which traditionally holds a privileged place in language, as the center of control—is very slippery and unstable. It would not be an oversimplification to say that Davidson's work is an investigation of language in which the "I" becomes as much a matter of conjecture as everything else:

> Marking this way
> as a direction one comes to know

> one is known,
> hence you are still you
> and I
> am not so sure.

Lacking a dependable ordering ego, the poems are variations on unstated (and unstatable) themes, or, as in "Often he felt uncomfortable," on a theme which is itself mutable. The idiomatic phrase, "to come out," is loaded with ambiguities, and in this poem Davidson uses it in a half-dozen or more different senses. The central matter of conjecture, however, is how *words* come out. Of all things their coming out is most mysterious: "and the vipers and bats and lizards come out of nowhere / which is a word out of which other words come out." The origins of language are completely concealed by the fact that whatever they might be can only be stated in language:

> in the beginning was the word and when it was out
> there was a space projected like a little star
> out of which all the light we have ever seen came pouring
> one word at a time.

There is nothing occult, nothing hidden, in Davidson's poetry. It is, like the poetry of Michael Palmer, a poetry of surfaces.

"The Foul Papers" (*The Mutabilities*) are prose poems, but their strategies are fundamentally like those found in Davidson's other work. In the title piece of this section, for example, there are seven paragraphs about some unnamed "he" who is, however, "close to," if not identical with, the "I" who gives the account. Although the paragraphs are very loosely organized, they do have centers of concerns: the first is about his loss of virginity, the second a concert by the Coasters, the third his "47 Plymouth with blue Satin seat covers," the fourth the cat odors in his house, the fifth is a list of things which he has to do on some relatively uneventful day, the sixth is about a love affair (perhaps with the woman with whom he speaks in the second), and the last about a conversation with another woman. Although it is possible to trace several lines of connection through the piece, one of the primary conjectural centers has to do with smell. The piece concludes: "so their conversation draws on into empty night, the prospect emptying itself into their conversation until only smells remain and which, in time, take on the unexpected pressure of beauty." It is just that "unexpected pressure of beauty," issuing from what seems rather unpromising material, which is the dominant effect of Davidson's work.

—Don Byrd

DAVIE, Donald (Alfred). British. Born in Barnsley, Yorkshire, 17 July 1922. Educated at Barnsley Holgate Grammar School; St. Catharine's College, Cambridge, B.A. 1947, M.A. 1949, Ph.D. 1951. Served in the Royal Naval Volunteer Reserve, 1941-46: Sub-Lieutenant. Married Doreen John in 1945; two sons and one daughter. Lecturer in English, 1950-57, and Fellow of Trinity College, 1954-57, University of Dublin; Lecturer in English, 1958-64, and Fellow of Gonville and Caius College, 1959-64, Cambridge University; Professor of English, 1964-68, and Pro-Vice-Chancellor, 1965-68, University of Essex, Wivenhoe; Professor of English, 1968-74, and Palmer Professor in Humanities, 1974-78, Stanford University, California. Since 1978, Andrew W. Mellon Professor of Humanities, Vanderbilt University, Nashville. Visiting Professor, University of California, Santa Barbara, 1957-58; British Council Lecturer, Budapest, 1961; Elliston Lecturer, University of Cincinnati, 1963; Clark Lecturer, Cambridge University, 1976. Recipient: Guggenheim Fellowship, 1973. D.Litt.: University of Southern California, Los Angeles, 1978. Honorary Fellow, St. Catharine's College, 1973; Fellow, American Academy of Arts and Sciences, 1973; Honorary Fellow, Trinity College, Dublin, 1978. Address: 4400 Belmont Park Terrace, Nashville, Tennessee 37215, U.S.A.; or, 4 High Street, Silverton, Exeter, Devon, England.

PUBLICATIONS

Verse

(Poems).   Oxford, Fantasy Press, 1954.
Brides of Reason.   Oxford, Fantasy Press, 1955.
A Winter Talent and Other Poems.   London, Routledge, 1957.
The Forests of Lithuania, adapted from a poem by Adam Mick-
    iewicz.   Hessle, Yorkshire, Marvell Press, 1959.
A Sequence for Francis Parkman.   Hessle, Yorkshire, Marvell
    Press, 1961.
New and Selected Poems.   Middletown, Connecticut, Wes-
    leyan University Press, 1961.
Events and Wisdoms: Poems 1957-1963.   London, Routledge,
    1964; Middletown, Connecticut, Wesleyan University Press,
    1965.
Poems.   London, Turret, 1969.
Essex Poems 1963-1967.   London, Routledge, 1969.
Six Epistles to Eva Hesse.   London, London Magazine Edi-
    tions, 1970.
Collected Poems 1950-1970.   London, Routledge, and New
    York, Oxford University Press, 1972.
Orpheus.   London, Poem-of-the-Month Club, 1974.
The Shires.   London, Routledge, 1974; New York, Oxford
    University Press, 1975.
In the Stopping Train and Other Poems.   Manchester, Car-
    canet, 1977; New York, Oxford University Press, 1980.
Three for Water-Music, and The Shires.   Manchester, Car-
    canet, 1981.
Collected Poems 1970-1983.   Manchester, Carcanet, 1983.

Recording: *Donald Davie Reading at Stanford,* Stanford University, 1974.

Other

Purity of Diction in English Verse.   London, Chatto and Win-
    dus, 1952; New York, Oxford University Press, 1953.
Articulate Energy: An Enquiry into the Syntax of English Poetry.
    London, Routledge, 1955; New York, Harcourt Brace, 1958.
The Heyday of Sir Walter Scott.   London, Routledge, and New
    York, Barnes and Noble, 1961.
*The Language of Science and the Language of Literature 1700-
    1740.*   London and New York, Sheed and Ward, 1963.
Ezra Pound: Poet as Sculptor.   London, Routledge, and New
    York, Oxford University Press, 1964.
Thomas Hardy and British Poetry.   New York, Oxford Univer-
    sity Press, 1972; London, Routledge, 1973.
Poetry in Translation.   Milton Keynes, Buckinghamshire, Open
    University, 1975.
Pound.   London, Fontana, 1975; New York, Viking Press,
    1976.
The Poet in the Imaginary Museum: Essays of Two Decades,
    edited by Barry Alpert.   Manchester, Carcanet, and New
    York, Persea Press, 1977.

*A Gathered Church: The Literature of the English Dissenting
    Interest 1700-1930.*   London, Routledge, and New York,
    Oxford University Press, 1978.
Trying to Explain.   Ann Arbor, University of Michigan Press,
    1979; Manchester, Carcanet, 1980.
English Hymnology in the Eighteenth Century (lecture), with
    Robert Stevenson.   Los Angeles, William Andrews Clark
    Memorial Library, 1980.
Kenneth Allott and the Thirties (lecture).   Liverpool, Univer-
    sity of Liverpool, 1980.
Dissentient Voice: The Ward-Phillips Lectures for 1980.   Notre
    Dame, Indiana, University of Notre Dame Press, 1980.
These the Companions: Recollections.   Cambridge, Cambridge
    University Press, 1982.

Editor, *The Late Augustans: Longer Poems of the Later Eigh-
    teenth Century.*   London, Heinemann, and New York,
    Macmillan, 1958.
Editor, *Poems: Poetry Supplement.*   London, Poetry Book
    Society, 1960.
Editor, *Poetics Poetyka.*   Warsaw, Panstwowe Wydawn, 1961.
Editor, *Selected Poems of Wordsworth.*   London, Harrap,
    1962.
Editor, *Russian Literature and Modern English Fiction: A Col-
    lection of Critical Essays.*   Chicago, University of Chicago
    Press, 1965.
Editor, with Angela Livingstone, *Pasternak.*   London, Macmil-
    lan, 1969.
Editor, "Thomas Hardy Issue" of *Agenda* (London), Spring-
    Summer 1972.
Editor, *Augustan Lyric.*   London, Heinemann, 1974.
Editor, *The Collected Poems of Elizabeth Daryush.*   Manches-
    ter, Carcanet, 1975.
Editor, *Collected Poems,* by Yvor Winters.   Manchester, Car-
    canet, 1978.
Editor, *The New Oxford Book of Christian Verse.*   Oxford,
    Oxford University Press, 1981; New York, Oxford University
    Press, 1982.

Translator, *The Poems of Doctor Zhivago,* by Boris Pasternak.
    Manchester, Manchester University Press, and New York,
    Barnes and Noble, 1965.

*

Manuscript Collection: University of Essex, Wivenhoe.

Critical Studies: by Calvin Bedient, in *Iowa Review* (Iowa City),
1971; "A Breakthrough into Spaciousness" by Donald Greene, in
Queen's Quarterly (Kingston, Ontario), 1973; "Donald Davie
Issue" of *Agenda* (London), Summer 1976; *Donald Davie and
the Responsibilities of Literature* edited by George Dekker,
Manchester, Carcanet, 1984.

*   *   *

The poet comments: "A good poem is necessarily a response to
a human situation. To make poetry out of moral commonplaces,
a poet has to make it clear that he speaks not in his own voice...
but as the spokesman of a social tradition." One associates
formal elegance, an urbane wit, meticulous syntax, restraint, and
plain diction—the Neo-Augustan—with Donald Davie. He is
dedicated to a chaste and austere poetry; he treats the contemporary need for personal moderation and restraint in forms that
reflect his vision. The word itself—indeed language—requires
purification; if the poet can purify the dialectic of the tribe,

perhaps the values of propriety and control, those moral values that inspire integrity and courage, may return to the decadent modern world. Man may then better understand his personal and perhaps even metaphysical place in the scheme of things.

In his earliest work Davie was associated with the *New Lines* anthology and the 1950's "the Movement." His name was often linked with Wain, Amis, Larkin, Gunn, Conquest, Enright, and the other "reactionary" poets who stood against the romantic excesses of the British poets of the 1940's, e.g., Dylan Thomas, and the early Anglo-American moderns. *Brides of Reason*, basically in traditional meter, appeals to the "logic" in man: "So poets may astonish you/With what is not, but should be, true,/And shackle on a moral shape." The poet's social function is clear: "The practice of...[my] art/is to connect all terms/into the terms of art" ("Hypochondriac logic").

Influenced especially by the Augustans Johnson, Cowper, and Goldsmith, as well as by Pound, Pasternak, and Yvor Winters, Davie evolved a poetry often compared to Charles Tomlinson's, in his insistence upon the connection between form and morality. Davie stood fast against his fashionable contemporaries—the confessional Roethke, Plath, Lowell—and even the great myth-makers of the century, Yeats and Eliot. Although Davie's aims have not been unlike theirs—to inspire action and change in a philistine contemporary world (for Davie, post-imperial Britain)—he would accomplish these through poetic example, rather than through the lessons universalized in myth; he would, through his verse, inspire conscious control. Through Davie's example of proper rhyme, meter, and syntax, for example, one might feel himself affirming the proper values of the more stable and civilized past. In "Vying," he writes: "I, the sexton, battle/Earth that will overturn/Headstones, and rifle tombs,/and spill the tilted urn."

Although he has also worked with a shorter, brisker line in a less obscure poetry (with an increasing emotional involvement with landscapes, and history), his abhorrence of a poetry consumed with the poet's "messy ego" has remained. Language is at the root of England's moral decay; he will not follow current usage: "the stumbling, the moving voices," "the Beat and post-Beat poets,/the illiterate apostles" ("Pentecost"). What is always needed is reasonableness, "common values" ("The Garden Party"), and "a neutral tone" ("Remembering the Thirties").

Six Epistles to Eva Hesse, Pound's translator, is a sort of "Essay on Criticism" ("Heroic comedy, I suggest,/Fits American history best"), in which he again utilizes the verse epistle form. Typically, Davie goes back in history to contemplate old and new values:

> Confound it, history...[sic] We transcend it
> Not when we agree to bend it
> To this cat's cradle or that theme
> But when, I take it, we redeem
> This man or that one, La Pérouse
> Lives when he's no longer news.

One associates most of Davie's subjects with England, and the *Collected Poems 1950-1970* contains his statement of "faith that there are still distinctively English—rather than Anglo-American or 'international'—ways of responding imaginatively to the terms of life in the twentieth century." Many of his poems compare the Mediterranean and Northern worlds, yet Davie has as well composed "The Forests of Lithuania," based on Mickiewicz's *Pan Tadeusz*, about Lithuania during its Russian Occupation in 1811-12. "A Sequence for Francis Parker" deals with Davie's response to North America. His *tour de force*, entirely about England, is *The Shires*, which consists of 40 poems, one for each county (arranged in alphabetical order, from Bedfordshire

to Yorkshire). It contains autobiographical information and reminiscences about the English landscape, culture, and history itself. At times he is serious and even bitter about the problems of his world; at other times, he is wry and witty. In "Suffolk" he writes: "My education gave me this bad habit/Of reading history for a hidden plot/And finding it; invariably the same one,/Its fraudulent title always, 'Something Gone.' " The poems are filled with historical figures—Bunyan, Calvin, Drake, Hawkins, and literary figures, Hamburger, Housman, Auden, Blake, Smart, John Fowles. Man is described in terms of his relationship with his past: "We run through a maze of tunnels for our meat/As rats might.../Drake, This is the freedom that you sailed from sure/To save us for?"

The extraordinary "Trevenen" is a verse biography, a narrative tragedy, of the late 18th-century Cornish naval officer who, after a heroic career, was used, abused, and driven mad by those he served. Trevenen lived in "an age much like our own;/As lax, as vulgar, as confused/.../Where that which was and that which seemed/Were priced the same;/where men were duped/And knew they were." Davie's portrayal of Trevenen's heroic life, basic naivety, and final death are among his most moving lines:

> Aware man's born to err,
> Inclined to bear and forbear.
> Pretense to more is vain.
> Chastened have they been.
> Hope was the tempter, hope.
> Ambition has its scope
> (Vast: the world's esteem);
> Hope is a sickly dream.

Davie's most recent work, including several new pieces in *Collected Poems 1970-1983*, reaffirms his commitment to pure language and syntax, less now, however, for the purposes of strengthening social and moral law than as an instrument to clarify and come to terms with the personal self, "the man going mad inside me." In "In the Stopping Train," the poet boards a slow train which allows him time for personal reflection. Writing in the third person and not entirely unlike the confessional poets, he indicts himself: "Torment him with his hatreds...with his false loves." The poem's future is "a slow/and stopping train through places/Whose names used to have virtue." In "To Thom Gunn" Davie admits the joys and terrors of the poet-exile, and he admits of the fear that accompanies the search for meaning: "What am I doing, I who am scared of edges?"

Poetry will always remain the means of approaching the inscrutable, of carving out one's space in the vast unknowable, although, finally, "Most poems, or the best/Describe their own birth, and this/is what they are—a space/Cleared to walk around in." *Three for Water-Music* is reminiscent of Eliot's *Four Quartets* in its use of multiple allusion and in its formal divisions which treat specific places, dates, personal concerns, and philosophical matters. Its images are more sensuous and highly colored than those in *The Shires*.

—Lois Gordon

DAVIS, Dick. British. Born in Portsmouth, Hampshire, 18 April 1945. Educated at King's College, Cambridge. Married Afkham Darbandi in 1974. Teacher in Greece and Italy, and in Iran, 1970-78. Lives in Norfolk. Recipient: Royal Society of

Literature Heinemann Award, 1981. Address: c/o Anvil Press Poetry, 69 King George Street, London SE10 8PX, England.

PUBLICATIONS

Verse

Shade Mariners, with Clive Wilmer and Robert Wells. Cambridge, Gregory Spiro, 1970.
In the Distance. London, Anvil Press Poetry, 1975.
Seeing the World. London, Anvil Press Poetry, 1980.
The Covenant. London, Anvil Press Poetry, 1984.

Other

Wisdom and Wilderness: The Achievement of Yvor Winters. Athens, University of Georgia Press, 1983.

Editor, *The Selected Writings of Thomas Traherne*. Manchester, Carcanet, 1980.

Translator, with Afkham Darbandi, *The Conference of the Birds*, by Attar. London, Penguin, 1984.

*   *   *

It is too soon to give more than the most provisional account of the poetry of Dick Davis whose first full-length collection, *In the Distance*, was published only in 1975. Nonetheless, certain distinctive features are apparent in that volume and in his next, *Seeing the World*. Initially, in poems like "The Diver" or "A Mycenean Broach" one could see his early work as definitely inheriting the mantle of the so-called "tight-lipped" school of the late 1960's, plus that movement's inevitable tendency towards a minimalist art, exemplified in such pieces of Davis's as "Service," "Desire," or the positively paltry "An Affair...." A number of the poems of *In the Distance* are marred by a vagueness derived from either too much abstraction or an over-anxiety for precision leading to a gnomic and static utterance; with sometimes, too, a carelessness of syntax as in "The Shore": "he rolls/Aside to watch the deep/Thought may not sound," or in "Old Man Seated Before a Landscape": "each separate/Discrete particular, an animate/Uncertain will claiming attention: no." In or out of context those lines verge on syntactical nonsense.

On the other hand, several of the poems in that initial volume of Davis's are fully achieved pieces. Particularly accomplished is the mythologically dreamlike "Diana and Actaeon," "Odysseus in Ithaca," and "A Memory"—the last showing a lyrical propensity. While in "Love In Another Language" the lines: "The meaning crammed/Through unfamiliar channels, in new tones,/With a choked force" are excellent summary of both Davis's craft-problem and that of modern poets in general.

Persisting, however, with his intolerable wrestle with words and form, Davis advanced considerably with his second volume. There is more inevitability and less academic forcing about the poems. His gift for discovering the fine line, the meaningful and memorable utterance, is further developed—only now he is able, in poem after poem, to find a perfectly supportive context for his insights. "Marriage As a Problem of Universals" is quite brilliant: a poem on large abstractions that works on the practical level, the "form" being turned and tuned in masterly fashion. In "Desert Stop at Noon" thought and compassionate feeling are communicated readily to the reader; and "Baucis and Philemon" and "Semele" further re-inforce the sense of a sensitive and maturing talent, one informed by a serious authority.

If one may be permitted to generalize, there are several identifiable thematic strands in Davis's work, several distinct *personae*, as it were. There is the academic persona of "Art Historian" or "The Epic Scholar"—one "desolate with love" of his subject and with the past, one who would willingly "rest here and fantasize the willing past." Then, too, there is something of the philosopher in Davis. Indeed, there had to be to enable him to write "Marriage As a Problem of Universals." Though the success of that particular poem also required the poet to be celebrant: to be a man in love with not just the nuptial state (as a moralist or a philosopher might be), but with a real live woman too. Then the man who early perceived the limits of irony ("Irony does not save") is clearly on the way to some sort of religious awareness. And I think there are pointers towards that end in many of the poems. Not just because of the occasional religious poem such as "The Virgin Mary" or "St. Christopher," but because of the more subtle evidence of a growing "wisdom" in the poet; and wisdom always uncovers the divine in things. A yet further persona of Davis is concerned with classical myth; and even poems that make no reference to the Graeco-Roman world—e.g., "Scavenging after a Battle" or "Touring a Past"—strongly suggest a poet who has wandered, like Keats, much in the golden realms of Homer et al.

Consequently, in Dick Davis we encounter a varied talent and one which, combining "imaginative ambitiousness with technical honesty" (to borrow the words of the *Times Literary Supplement* about his first volume), suggests a sound poetic future. And, provided Davis can still find things to say, it seems a future that is assured. For, clearly, his is a soundly based and intelligent talent. To borrow Michael Robert's famous pointer of genuine poetry, there is a certain "elegance" about Dick Davis's writing.

—William Oxley

———————

DAVISON, Peter (Hubert). American. Born in New York City, 27 June 1928. Educated at the Fountain Valley School, Colorado Springs; Harvard University, Cambridge, Massachusetts, A.B. (magna cum laude) 1949 (Phi Beta Kappa); St. John's College, Cambridge (Fulbright Scholar), 1949-50. Served in the United States Army, 1951-53. Married 1) Jane Truslow in 1959 (died, 1981), one son and one daughter; 2) Joan E. Goody in 1984. Page in the United States Senate, 1944. Editorial Assistant, 1950-51, and Assistant Editor, 1953-55, Harcourt Brace, publishers, New York; Assistant to the Director, Harvard University Press, 1955-56. Associate Editor, Executive Editor, 1959-64, Director, 1964-79, and since 1979, Senior Editor, Atlantic Monthly Press, Boston. Since 1972, Poetry Editor, *Atlantic Monthly*, Boston. Recipient: Yale Series of Younger Poets Award, 1964; American Academy award, 1972. Address: 70 River Street, Boston, Massachusetts 02108, U.S.A.

PUBLICATIONS

Verse

The Breaking of the Day and Other Poems. New Haven, Connecticut, Yale University Press, 1964.
The City and the Island. New York, Atheneum, 1966.
Pretending to Be Asleep. New York, Atheneum, 1970.
Dark Houses. Cambridge, Massachusetts, Halty Ferguson, 1971.

Walking the Boundaries: Poems 1957-1974. New York, Atheneum, and London, Secker and Warburg, 1974.
A Voice in the Mountain. New York, Atheneum, 1977.
Barn Fever and Other Poems. New York, Atheneum, 1981; London, Secker and Warburg, 1982.
Praying Wrong: New and Selected Poems 1957-1984. New York, Atheneum, 1984.

Other

Half Remembered: A Personal History. New York, Harper, 1973; London, Heinemann, 1974.

Editor, *Hello Darkness: The Collected Poems of L.E. Sissman.* Boston, Little Brown, and London, Secker and Warburg, 1978.
Editor, *The World of Farley Mowat: A Selection from His Works.* Toronto, McClelland and Stewart, and Boston, Little Brown, 1980.

*

Manuscript Collection: Beinecke Library, Yale University, New Haven, Connecticut.

Critical Studies: Foreword by Dudley Fitts to *The Breaking of the Day and Other Poems*, 1964; *Three Contemporary Poets of New England* by Guy Rotella, Boston, Twayne, 1983.

*   *   *

Most of Peter Davison's poetry has an even, gem-like quality that typifies intelligent, academic verse. Davison's work, generously laden with mythical allusions, is often rhymed and carefully metered. At its best, the poetry illuminates a moment or an observation from the poet's life without straining towards an undeserved depth. In "Lunch at the Coq D'Or," Davison portrays a fancy restaurant where "Each noon at table tycoons crow/ And flap their wings around each other's shoulders." He is waiting for an associate, Purdy, who eventually "is seated with his alibis":

> I know my man. Purdy's a hard-nosed man.
> Another round for us. It's good to work
> With such a man. "Purdy," I hear myself,
> "It's good to work with you." I raise
> My arm, feathery in the dimlight, and extend
> Until the end of it brushes his padded shoulder.
> "Purdy, how are you? How you doodle do?"

Here, Davison has included himself among the blamed by repeating the feather-wing imagery of the tycoons and then his own arm of luncheon goodwill. The humor of his concluding line emphasizes the nonsense encountered in daily business intercourse.
   Too often, Davison lacks this detachment; he becomes merely a clever man with a pen, rhyming when he should be working his guts in ink. His position is ambiguous: surely, "Conviction Means Loss of License" deals with a serious subject, but Davison seems only to consider the fatal car crash of three brothers an opportunity to exercise his wit. And worse, he preaches in the sardonic manner of a radar cop:

> For they were faithful to the plan
> That nature must make way for man

> And fed their faith in this great cause
> By putting speed above the laws
> Designed to neither help nor hurt.

> Inertia rendered them inert.

In other poems, particularly "Intacta," (where he tells the familiar story of a seemingly virginal, but permissive girl) and "Winter Fear," which ends, "The weather tells of famine and defeat,/ Of lying leaves and how we were betrayed/ By spring. But winter never yet has won," he seems too pat. How, after all, does he know that the girl of "Intacta" is loose unless he's been in her pants? And, although it's true that winter "never yet has won," neither has any season (or condition of mind, the poem suggests to me) triumphed over winter. In short, Davison refuses to confess his own possible guilt or confusion.
   These comments are perhaps unfairly negative, for there is much to admire in the body of Davison's work. "The Breaking of the Day," title poem of his first collection, is a perfect refutation of the criticisms I levy against the least successful poetry. Here, the poet takes the risk of baring himself to the reader, acknowledging his doubts: "I shall never know myself/ Enough to know what things I half believe/ And, half believing, only half deny." In a poem such as this, the fusion of craft and insight is fully realized, and Davison proves himself the poet of skill his reputation holds him to be.
   Dark Houses is a seven-part retrospective in verse on the life of his father, poet Edward Davison, whose presence is fully documented in Peter Davison's *Half Remembered*, an autobiography. *Dark Houses* is a very fine poem, crafted with a precision less and less evident among contemporary poets:

> And now his thirsty body
> Is part of the land at last, land of his children,
> Where the grey ungiving stone can always stand
> For fathers, thrusting up above the fields
> Not ever his own, though dearer than the land
> That gave him birth but never knew his name.

—Geof Hewitt

DAWE, (Donald) Bruce. Australian. Born in Geelong, Victoria, 15 February 1930. Educated at Northcote High School; Melbourne University; Queensland University, Brisbane, B.A., M.A., Ph.D.; University of New England, Armidale, New South Wales, Litt.B. 1973. Served in the Royal Australian Air Force for 9 years. Married Gloria Desley; four children. Worked as labourer, gardener, postman. Currently, Senior Lecturer in Literature, Darling Downs Institute of Advanced Education, Darling Heights, Toowoomba, Queensland. Recipient: Myer Prize, 1966, 1969; Ampol Arts Award, 1967; Mary Gilmore Medal, 1973; Grace Leven Prize, 1979; Patrick White Literary Award, 1981; Christopher Brennan Award, 1984. Address: 30 Cumming Street, Toowoomba, Queensland, Australia.

PUBLICATIONS

Verse

No Fixed Address. Melbourne, Cheshire, 1962.
A Need of Similar Name. Melbourne, Cheshire, 1965.

An Eye for a Tooth. Melbourne, Cheshire, 1968.
Beyond the Subdivision. Melbourne, Cheshire, 1969.
Heat-Wave. Melbourne, Sweeney Reed, 1970.
Condolences of the Season. Melbourne, Cheshire, 1971.
Just a Dugong at Twilight: Mainly Light Verse. Melbourne, Cheshire, 1975.
Sometimes Gladness: Collected Poems 1954-1978. Melbourne, Longman Cheshire, 1978; revised edition, 1982.

Short Stories

Over Here, Harv! and Other Stories. Melbourne, Penguin, 1983.

Other

Five Modern Comic Writers. Toowoomba, Queensland, Darling Downs Institute of Advanced Studies, 1981.

Editor, *Dimensions.* Sydney, McGraw Hill, 1975.

*

Manuscript Collection: Fryer Library, University of Queensland, Brisbane.

Critical Studies: *The Man down the Street,* edited by Ian V. Hansen, Melbourne, V.A.T.E., 1972; *Times and Seasons: An Introduction to Bruce Dawe* by Basil Shaw, Melbourne, Cheshire, 1974.

Bruce Dawe comments:
    The themes I deal with are the common ones of modern civilization, loneliness, old age, death, dictatorship, love. I like the dramatic monologue form, and use it in free, blank and rhymed verse-forms, attempting at the same time to capture something of the evanescence of contemporary idiom, which is far richer and more allusive than the stereotyped stone-the-crows popular concept of Australian speech would have people believe.

*   *   *

    Bruce Dawe was certainly the most central and pivotal poet in Australia during the decade of the 1960's. His work first appeared in Melbourne in the late 1950's and broke through to a wide audience with *No Fixed Address,* his first collection. *No Fixed Address* displayed a freshness and gaiety quite unusual in Australian literature at the time, and, more importantly, demonstrated a highly developed sense of local speech cadence and inflection. Bruce Dawe has always been concerned with the celebration of the maligned denizens of the great sprawl of outer suburbs that surround our cities. He views them with affection, sympathy and wit, and an ear attuned to natural speech rhythms that is more precise and more immediately convincing than that of any other poet. This perceptiveness is coupled with a brilliant feeling of language and, particularly, of image.
    Dawe broke through to a whole new generation of Australian readers, and his popularity has been gained without any loss of integrity or style; indeed, because of the genuineness of his essential attitudes, such popularity is a natural aspect of his poetic justification. Over recent years, and in his later volumes, Bruce Dawe has been concerned with developing his initial vision and perceptions. He has been one of the few Australian poets who has found a convincing method of dealing with current political events and issues without loss of poetic validity. This is an area

where Australian poetry has always been backward and undeveloped. In 1971 a selected volume *Condolences of the Season* offered readers a summary of Dawe's work. His later poems tend to employ a more elegiac cadence, but though the subject matter is often eclectic and wide flung, it would seem, still, that his contribution related primarily to the admission into the corpus of Australian poetry of an area of suburban reality and liveliness that had only been approached in the most awkward and uncomfortable way by his predecessors.

—Thomas W. Shapcott

————

DELIUS, Anthony (Ronald St. Martin). South African. Born in Simonstown, 11 June 1916. Educated at St. Aidan's College, Grahamstown; Rhodes University, Grahamstown, B.A. 1938. Served in the South African Intelligence Corps, 1940-45. Married in 1941; two chldren. Staff Member, Port Elizabeth *Evening Post,* 1947-50; Parliamentary Correspondent, *Cape Times,* Cape Town, 1951-54, 1958-67. Banned from the South Africa House of Assembly for his *Cape Times* political commentary. Writer, BBC Africa Service, London, 1968-77. Since 1977 free-lance writer. Former Co-Editor, *Standpunte,* Cape Town. Since 1962, Member of the Editorial Board, *Contrast* magazine, Cape Town. Recipient: CNA Literary Award, 1977. Address: 30 Graemesdyke Avenue, London SW14 7BJ, England.

PUBLICATIONS

Verse

An Unknown Border. Cape Town, Balkema, 1954.
The Last Division. Cape Town, Human and Rousseau, 1959.
A Corner of the World: Thirty-Four Poems. Cape Town, Human and Rousseau, 1962.
Black South-Easter. Grahamstown, New Coin, 1966.

Play

The Fall: A Play about Rhodes. Cape Town, Human and Rousseau, 1957.

Novels

The Day Natal Took Off: A Satire. Cape Town, Human and Rousseau, and London, Pall Mall Press, 1963.
Border. Cape Town, David Philip, 1976.

Other

The Young Traveller in South Africa. London, Phoenix House, 1947; revised edition, 1959.
The Long Way Round (travel in Africa). Cape Town, Timmins, 1956.
Upsurge in Africa. Toronto, Canadian Institute of International Affairs, 1960.

*

Manuscript Collection: Rhodes University, Grahamstown.

*   *   *

Anthony Delius has described himself as one of the most indoctrinated of South Africans, a misleading description, since it would imply an acceptance of current socio-political attitudes in his country which would be the opposite of the truth. What one can properly infer, however, is that of the poets of his country writing in English he is probably the most consciously South African. It is an identification with *A Corner of the World*—the title of his 1962 collection—that is his own but it is more than a country, rather the African continent as a whole, many of his poems reflecting his travels there. From his early poems, including the long impressive "Time in Africa" written during the Second World War, Delius has shown himself fascinated by what living in Africa has accumulated over the centuries, seeing history as a continuous process working on his own contemporary experience and on into the future like a prophecy.

In "Black South-Easter," probably the best long poem produced by a South African in a generation, Delius, twenty years after "Time in Africa," succeeded in using history as a poet should, taking imagination as catalyst to produce a recipe for the making of myth. The poet, struggling through the windy Cape night, is confronted by historical ghosts, by symbolical figures of contemporary values, the millionaire and the actress and by his own many-sidedness, his own "Indian file of selves," while his mind and memory are swept dramatically on a course of their own through a wider and deeper disorder of time and circumstance—for instance, seeing the Fifteenth Century navigator Diaz thus:

> His niche was the stern
> Of a torpedoed tanker, cliff-hung
> Like an opera box.

Here is a tremendously ambitious poem; that it succeeds is the measure of the poet's power to use language to control a variety of influences working on the imagination at the same time. If Delius has proved his staying power in attempting the long distances (since *The Lusiads*, the Cape presents a surviving challenge to South African poets to go for the big theme), yet his enduring reputation may well lie among some of his short poems, such as the exquisite "The Gamblers," about Cape Coloured fishermen, a popular anthology piece since it first appeared in *The New Yorker*:

> Day flips a golden coin—but they mock it.
> With calloused, careless hands they reach
> Deep down into the sea's capacious pocket
> And pile their silver counters on the beach.

"Deaf and Dumb School" is another poem beautifully conceived to express the poet's compassion: "Silence like a shadow shows the room/ Of minds that make their signs and mouth their cries."

There is another kind of compassion, perhaps of the best kind, that which comes after very clear vision has stripped away from situations and people what humbug, false myth and sloth have accumulated about them. In this process satire acts like a paint-stripper, and Delius, as satirist, has long been active in the South African context. Though echoes of Roy Campbell sometimes interrupt originality, there are parts of *The Last Division* whose humour will preserve it long after the lampooned figures of politics have been forgotten.

—Roy Macnab

DEMETILLO, Ricaredo. Filipino.   Born in Dumangas, Iloilo, 2 June 1920. Educated at Silliman University, Dumaguete City, A.B. in English 1947; University of Iowa, Iowa City, M.F.A. in English and creative writing 1952. Married Angelita Delariarte in 1944; four children. Assistant Professor, 1959-70, Chairman of the Department of Humanities, 1961-62, Associate Professor, 1970-75, and since 1975, Professor of Humanities, University of the Philippines, Diliman, Quezon City. Recipient: Rockefeller Fellowship, 1952; Rigal award, 1963; University of the Philippines Golden Jubilee Award; Philippines Republic Cultural Heritage Award, 1968; Palanca award, for play, 1975. Address: 38 Bulacan Street, West Avenue, Quezon City, Philippines.

PUBLICATIONS

Verse

No Certain Weather.   Quezon City, Guinhalinan Press, 1956.
La Via: A Spiritual Journey.   Quezon City, Diliman Review, 1958.
Daedalus and Other Poems.   Quezon City, Guinhalinan Press, 1961.
Barter in Panay.   Quezon City, University of the Philippines Office of Research Coordination, 1961.
Masks and Signature.   Quezon City, University of the Philippines Press, 1968.
The Scare-Crow Christ.   Quezon City, Diliman Review, 1973.
The City and the Thread of Light and Other Poems.   Quezon City, Diliman Review, 1974.
Lazarus, Troubadour.   Quezon City, New Day, 1974.
Sun, Silhouettes, and Shadow, photographs by B. David Williams, Jr.   Quezon City, New Day, 1975.

Play

The Heart of Emptiness Is Black (produced Quezon City, 1973).   Quezon City, University of the Philippines Press, 1975.

Novel

The Genesis of a Troubled Vision.   Quezon City, University of the Philippines Press, 1976.

Other

The Authentic Voice of Poetry.   Quezon City, University of the Philippines Office of Research Coordination, 1962.
My Sumakwelan Works in the Context of Philippine Culture.   Quezon City, University of the Philippines Press, 1976.

*

Critical Studies: "The Wounded Diamond," in *Bookmark* (Manila), 1964 and article in *Solidarity Magazine* (Manila), 1968, both by Leonard Casper.

Ricaredo Demetillo comments:
(1970) My poetry has been much influenced by the New Criticism in America, but I don't belong to any "school."
My poetry has been concerned with the following major themes: the rebellion of the young against the conventional values of an overly repressive society; the modern journey of the individual from lostness to wholeness and fullest creativity; the

rise and fall of civilization using the myth of Daedalus in ancient Crete to objectify and evoke the human condition; and the important position of the artists as the bearers and the creators of volumes necessary to the renewal of society. To project all these themes, I have used the lyric, the elegiac, the poetic essay, the epic, etc., with relatively good success. Always, I have been concerned with the human condition and also celebrated the hierarchy of light. Strongest influences: Homer, Dante, Baudelaire, Dylan Thomas, W.B. Yeats and Auden, not to mention myths of all sorts, including the Filipino ones.

(1974) My recent book, *The Scare-Crow Christ*, was written mostly during the troubled period of student activism in Manila and contains poems objectifying the poverty and the spiritual confusion of the time. One poem speaks of the indifference of the average man to the welfare of the "diminished, unfulfilled" man and asks: "Are you not Judas to his scare-crow Christ?"; still another one pays "tall tribute to the hardihood of man" that is able to survive the horrors of war (in Vietnam and elsewhere).

But these new poems are evocations, not propagandistic statements.

My verse drama, *The Heart of Emptiness Is Black*, really a sort of sequel to *Barter in Panay*, deals centrally with the conflict between tribalism and emergent individualism; which may have relevance to the present situation of the Philippines under martial law. I chose the drama as a form so that I can be heard by the public, for poetry locally is mostly unheard and unread, if not dead.

The City and Other Poems objectifies or evokes the lostness of man in the modern city and the poet's search for any available meaning in the human condition today.

*   *   *

Ricaredo Demetillo's poetry, fiction, and criticism belong to a tradition that is both East and West, and are being recognized, though a bit slowly, as a distinct part of the world cultural heritage, a blending of Oriental and Occidental values. His writings should offer a rich mine for the student of culture, or the science of culture.

He deals with a variety of themes: the revolt of youth against oppressive society, the rise and fall of civilizations, the spiritual bankruptcy of language which presages political violence and economic distress, the poet's Dantean/Faustian journey through the morass of living to the higher life. An important work, the poet himself says, "evokes and proclaims the life-forwarding sacrifices of the artists, the 'unstable men,' who are the harbinger of the truths—and values—that invigorate and renew society during critical epochs." Another critic has observed that an earlier work, *La Via*, is the most sustained argument in verse in any language by a Filipino.

What many students consider Demetillo's most ambitious work is the literary epic sequence which he adapted from the ethno-linguistic legend popularly know as *Maragtas*. He has rewritten the story in three parts (the third part not yet published), each complete in itself. *Barter in Panay*, the first of the three, concerns the pseudo-historical settlement of the island of Panay, in central Philippines, by a few boatlands of people from Borneo not through armed conquest but peacefully through friendly barter (gold for land) with an earlier group of settlers. This story is transformed into a serious literary epic with the intention to project, not crudely tribal values, but national, even international, ideals about justice, liberty, racial harmony, democratic government, and interrelationships of a people whose leaders act only with the consent of the governed. The principles of freedom and democracy brought out in the traditional story of *Barter in Panay* are applicable even today.

In the second part of the sequence, *The Heart of Emptiness is Black*, Demetillo dramatizes the tragic conflict between Kapinanga and Guronggurong, a pair of tragic lovers, on the one hand, and the oppressive authority of the leader of the expedition, Datu Sumakwel, and the priest Bangutbanwa, on the other. Kapinanga's adultery with Guronggurong leads to his death and her exile, decreed by her husband, Sumakwel. In the third part, both Kapinanga and Sumakwel have become chastened by their individual experience, and this leads to reconciliation. What started out as a bucolic narrative and continued as high tragedy winds up as romantic melodrama.

One may discern in the lifework of Demetillo an eloquent argument for the integrity of the artist as both individual human being and as social person. Jose Garcia Villa, the other major Philippine poet of the 20th century, may feel patronizing about Demetillo's social commitments, about which Demetillo feels proud while recognizing the superior quality Villa's personal lyricism. While both Villa and Demetillo accept the centrality of the formal or aesthetic values in a work of art, Villa stops there, but Demetillo moves on, looking for peripheral values which may enhance the beauty and significance of human life. As a poet, Ricaredo Demetillo has attained a stature that in Philippine literature is hard to erode and is difficult to surpass.

—Leopoldo Y. Yabes

DICKEY, James (Lafayette). American. Born in Atlanta, Georgia, 2 February 1923. Educated at Clemson College, South Carolina, 1942; Vanderbilt University, Nashville, Tennessee, B.A. (magna cum laude) 1949 (Phi Beta Kappa), M.A. 1950. Served in the United States Army Air Force during World War II and in the Air Force during the Korean War. Married 1) Maxine Syerson in 1948 (died, 1976), two sons; 2) Deborah Dodson in 1976, one daughter. Taught at Rice University, Houston, 1950, 1952-54, and the University of Florida, Gainesville, 1955-56; Poet-in-Residence, Reed College, Portland, Oregon, 1962-64, San Fernando Valley State College, Northridge, California, 1964-66, and the University of Wisconsin, Madison, 1966. Consultant in Poetry, Library of Congress, Washington, D.C., 1967-69. Since 1969, Professor of English and Writer-in-Residence, University of South Carolina, Columbia. Recipient: *Sewanee Review* Fellowship, 1954; Union League Civic and Arts Foundation Prize (*Poetry*, Chicago), 1958; Vachel Lindsay Prize, 1959; Longview Foundation Award, 1960; Guggenheim Fellowship, 1961; Melville Cane Award, 1966; National Book Award, 1966; American Academy grant, 1966; Prix Médicis, for novel, 1971. Member, American Academy. Address: 4620 Lelia's Court, Lake Katherine, Columbia, South Carolina 29206, U.S.A.

PUBLICATIONS

Verse

Into the Stone and Other Poems. New York, Scribner, 1960.
Drowning with Others. Middletown, Connecticut, Wesleyan University Press, 1962; selection, as *The Owl King*, New York, Red Angel Press, 1977.
Helmets. Middletown, Connecticut, Wesleyan University Press, and London, Longman, 1964.

Two Poems of the Air.   Portland, Oregon, Centicore Press, 1964.

Buckdancer's Choice.   Middletown, Connecticut, Wesleyan University Press, 1965.

Poems 1957-1967.   Middletown, Connecticut, Wesleyan University Press, and London, Rapp and Carroll, 1967.

The Achievement of James Dickey: A Comprehensive Selection of His Poems, with a Critical Introduction, edited by Laurence Lieberman.   Chicago, Scott Foresman, 1968.

The Eye-Beaters, Blood, Victory, Madness, Buckhead and Mercy.   New York, Doubleday, and London, Hamish Hamilton, 1970.

The Zodiac.   Bloomfield Hills, Michigan, Bruccoli Clark, 1976; revised edition, New York, Doubleday, 1976; London, Hamish Hamilton, 1977.

The Strength of Fields.   Bloomfield Hills, Michigan, Bruccoli Clark, 1977; revised edition, New York, Doubleday, 1979.

Veteran Birth: The Gadfly Poems 1947-1949.   Winston-Salem, North Carolina, Palaemon Press, 1978.

Head-Deep in Strange Sounds: Free-Flight Improvisations from the UnEnglish.   Winston-Salem, North Carolina, Palaemon Press, 1979.

Falling, May Day Sermon, and Other Poems.   Middletown, Connecticut, Wesleyan University Press, 1981.

The Early Motion.   Middletown, Connecticut, Wesleyan University Press, 1981.

Puella.   New York, Doubleday, 1982.

The Central Motion: Poems 1968-1979.   Middletown, Connecticut, Wesleyan University Press, 1983.

Recordings: *Poems*, Spoken Arts, 1967; *James Dickey Reads His Poetry*, Caedmon, 1971.

Plays

Deliverance: A Screenplay, edited by Matthew J. Bruccoli. Carbondale, Southern Illinois University Press, 1981.

Screenplay: *Deliverance*, 1972.

Television Play: *The Call of the Wild*, from the novel by Jack London, 1976.

Novel

Deliverance.   Boston, Houghton Mifflin, and London, Hamish Hamilton, 1970.

Other

The Suspect in Poetry.   Madison, Minnesota, Sixties Press, 1964.

A Private Brinksmanship (address).   Claremont, California, Pitzer College, 1965.

Spinning the Crystal Ball: Some Guesses at the Future of American Poetry.   Washington, D.C., Library of Congress, 1967.

Metaphor as Pure Adventure (lecture).   Washington, D.C., Library of Congress, 1968.

Babel to Byzantium: Poets and Poetry Now.   New York, Farrar Straus, 1968.

Self-Interviews, edited by Barbara and James Reiss.   New York, Doubleday, 1970.

Sorties (essays).   New York, Doubleday, 1971.

Exchanges ...: Being in the Form of a Dialogue with Joseph Trumbull Stickney.   Bloomfield Hills, Michigan, Bruccoli Clark, 1971.

Jericho: The South Beheld, paintings by Hubert Shuptrine.   Birmingham, Alabama, Oxmoor House, 1974.

God's Images: The Bible: A New Vision, illustrated by Marvin Hayes.   Birmingham, Alabama, Oxmoor House, 1977.

Tucky the Hunter (for children).   New York, Crown, 1978; London, Macmillan, 1979.

The Enemy from Eden.   Northridge, California, Lord John Press, 1978.

In Pursuit of the Grey Soul (on fishing).   Columbia, South Carolina, Bruccoli Clark, 1979.

The Water-Bug's Mittens: Ezra Pound, What We Can Use (lecture).   Moscow, University of Idaho, 1979.

The Starry Place Between the Antlers: Why I Live in South Carolina.   Columbia, South Carolina, Bruccoli Clark, 1981.

The Eagle's Mile.   Columbia, South Carolina, Bruccoli Clark, 1981.

False Youth: Four Seasons.   Dallas, Pressworks, 1982.

The Poet Turns on Himself.   Portree, Isle of Skye, Aquila, 1982.

For a Time and Place.   Columbia, South Carolina, Bruccoli Clark, 1983.

Night Hurdling: Poems, Essays, Conversations, Commencements, and Afterwords.   Columbia, South Carolina, Bruccoli Clark, 1983.

Sorties.   Baton Rouge, Louisiana State University Press, 1984.

Translator, *Stolen Apples*, by Yevgeny Yevtushenko.   New York, Doubleday, 1971; London, W.H. Allen, 1972.

*

Bibliography: *James Dickey: A Bibliography 1947-1974* by Jim Elledge, Metuchen, New Jersey, Scarecrow Press, 1979; *James Dickey: A Bibliography* by Stuart Wright, Dallas, Pressworks, 1982.

Manuscript Collection: Olin Library, Washington University, St. Louis.

Critical Studies: Introduction by Laurence Lieberman to *The Achievement of James Dickey*, 1968; *James Dickey: The Expansive Imagination: A Collection of Critical Essays* edited by Richard J. Calhoun, Deland, Florida, Everett Edwards, 1973, and *James Dickey* by Calhoun and Robert W. Hill, Boston, Twayne, 1983; "James Dickey Issue" of *South Carolina Review* (Columbia), April 1978; *James Dickey: Splintered Sunlight* edited by Patricia De La Fuente, Edinburgh, Texas, Pan American University School of Humanities, 1979; *The Imagination as Glory: Essays on the Poetry of James Dickey* edited by Bruce Weigl and T.R. Hummer, Urbana, University of Illinois Press, 1984.

Theatrical Activities:
    Actor: **Film**—*Deliverance*, 1972.

James Dickey comments:
    I like to think the major theme, if there is one, is continuity between the self and the world, and the various attempts by men to destroy this (wars, and so on: heavy industry and finance and the volume-turnover system). I try to say something about the individual's way, or ways, of protecting this sense of continuity in himself, or of his attempts to restore it. Much of my work deals with rivers, mountains, changes of weather, seas and the air. I am lately trying to move into a kind of poetry in which the exchanges between people—rather than between one person and, say, the landscape—will have more part.

*   *   *

James Dickey has wanted "to give each cluster of words its own fierce integrity," and to achieve with "the balance of the poem on the page" a balance analogous to that "given to the trunk of a tree by its limbs, or by the twigs to the stem." He has been experimental, in moving from work to work, in ways not apparent to readers who have not sensed the frustrations of a talent expressing a deep and obsessive concern with form. Dickey is an authentic artist and technician of words, and his restless search through various forms has confused those who prefer the comforts of typecasting. In his preface to *Falling, May Day Sermon, and Other Poems* in 1981, Dickey spoke of his desire to create poetry "almost three-dimensionally real...the shape of a solid bank, an on-end block or wall of words, solid or almost solid, black with massed ink, through which a little light from behind would come at intermittent places. Gradually I began to construct such a wall outside myself, at first with words typed and then cut out with scissors and placed in various combinations on a piece of cardboard from a shirt come back from the laundry. The shape of the cardboard was the shape of the poem, and I moved the words around as in a game of metaphysical Scrabble, with the payoff coming in images and new directions of thought from lucky conbinations."

I have cited this passage at length, rather than discuss Dickey's best-known poems (such discussions are easily available) because the passage is very revealing. It is boyish, intense, confessedly naïve, indifferent to fashion or to hardly any concern other than self-expression and the success of the expressive enterprise. The activity he describes is tactile and playful, and is neither abstract nor merely intellectual. He is creating a wall, with chinks left for insights and aperçus. He is hunting for meanings, and bringing back those he has found, as a hunter would bring back his prey; Dickey is known to hunt with bow and arrow. There is also a desperation about the enterprise. The poet who was lionized in *Life* magazine in 1966, given the National Book Award for *Buckdancer's Choice* in 1966, made Poetry Consultant to the Library of Congress, celebrated as author of a bestselling novel, *Deliverance*, in 1970 (the movie version appeared in 1972), has hardly grown self-satisfied and content with his laurels. The restless and tactile creativity of a boy, a boy perhaps with certain identity problems that make him fascinated with the old stuff of myth—transmogrified identities, violence inherent in love, exchanges between the living and the spirit world and between man and animals—still operates within an ever-hungry quest for meaning and fable-making.

Dickey has dared more than most of our poets. He has tried always for an epic quality, and has tried to drive extensive dramatic landscapes that might well have become novels and dramas into poems. *The Zodiac*, for example, could easily have been written as a novel, and in fact the work shared Melville's penchant for citing astrology, the Bible, and the great philosophers. His hero's concern with learning through suffering and the author's insistence on posing major metaphysical questions also remind some readers of Melville. Dickey's concern, he states, is for "*our* images of God's *Images*," which may be Melville's pasteboard masks theme restated.

Dickey's love of narrative and drama has protected him from charges of the trivial. He has been controversial, and has drawn the fire of critics who see in his poems of violence a love of violence. He has been passionately scorned and widely loved, but he has not met with indifference or the charge that his work has no power. Regardless of the validity or not of the analyses that have been made, regarding the internal ethics of his work, I'd credit him for the courage to raise such issues by his boldness and the sheer verve of his talent. Certainly a poet who once professed

fascination with "the creative possibilities of the lie" should be granted some capacity for subtlety and irony. I choose to believe that the ugliness apparent in some of his personae (e.g., in "The Fiend," "The Firebombing," and "Slave Quarter") is presented with irony and an invitation to scrutiny and criticism; some readers have taken that invitation all too literally.

In "A Folk Singer of the Thirties," a poem of powerful lyricism, Dickey speaks eloquently of his American themes:

> I said to myself that the poor
> Would always be poor until
> The towers I knew of should rise
> And the oil be tapped:
> That I had literally sung
> My sick country up from its deathbed,
> But nothing would do.
> No logical right holds the truth.
> In the sealed rooms I think of this,
> Recording the nursery songs
> In a checkered and tailored shirt
> As a guest on TV shows
> And in my apartment now:
> This is all a thing I began
> To believe, to change, and to sell
> When I opened my mouth to the rich.

To the sensitive, Dickey seems to say, there are never true riches or true successes when poverty is widespread and despair inherent in sanctified inequality.

—David Ray

DICKEY, William (Hobart). American. Born in Bellingham, Washington, 15 December 1928. Educated at Reed College, Portland, Oregon, B.A. 1951 (Phi Beta Kappa); Harvard University, Cambridge, Massachusetts, M.A. 1955; University of Iowa, Iowa City, M.F.A. 1956; Jesus College, Oxford (Fulbright Scholar), 1959-60. Married Shirley Ann Marn in 1959 (divorced, 1972). Instructor, Cornell University, Ithaca, New York, 1956-59; Assistant Professor, Denison University, Granville, Ohio, 1960-62. Assistant Professor, 1962-65, Associate Professor, 1966-69, and since 1970, Professor of English, San Francisco State University. Visiting Professor, University of Hawaii, Honolulu, Spring 1973. Formerly, Managing Editor, *Western Review*, Silver City, New Mexico, and Editorial Assistant, *Civil War History*. Recipient: Yale Series of Younger Poets Award, 1959; Union League Civic and Arts Foundation Prize (*Poetry*, Chicago), 1962; National Endowment for the Arts fellowship, 1977; University of Massachusetts Press Juniper Prize, 1978; American Academy award, 1980. Address: 486 Chenery Street, San Francisco, California 94131, U.S.A.

PUBLICATIONS

Verse

Of the Festivity. New Haven, Connecticut, Yale University Press, 1959.
Interpreter's House. Columbus, Ohio State University Press, 1963.

Rivers of the Pacific Northwest. San Francisco, Twowindows Press, 1969.
More under Saturn. Middletown, Connecticut, Wesleyan University Press, 1971.
The Rainbow Grocery. Amherst, University of Massachusetts Press, 1978.
The Sacrifice Consenting. San Francisco, Pterodactyl Press, 1981.
Six Philosophical Songs. Cumberland, Iowa, Pterodactyl Press, 1983.
Joy. Cumberland, Iowa, Pterodactyl Press, 1983.

*

William Dickey comments:
I am closest to various poets who studied at the Writers Workshop of the University of Iowa in the 1950's; but I don't know that it would be recognized as a school.

*   *   *

William Dickey's first book was W.H. Auden's last selection as the editor of the Yale Younger Poets, and the older poet was clearly one of the chief influences on the then neophyte:

> And through the morns the ample ladies gather
> The ribbons of their lives and press them dear.
> They are intrinsic selves and need no other
> Posture to arrive and interfere.

Dickey's book overflows with the posturings of several selves, and often the several postures of the individual divided against himself. But such division is always controlled, always measured. The title poem of this volume is elaborately rhymed with simple words and concerns the speaker's inanition, his fear of the potential disruption of love, but it also reveals an awe of communication mingled with doubt of its efficacy ("And all the words my mouth has ever said / Will fail to tell us whether we live or die"). The poems are learned, but not to a fault, though too often they form a commentary on experience rather than a presentation of it. As such, the book stood at the end of a decade whose poetic idiom, replete with irony and balanced wit, it substantially epitomized.
More under Saturn differs radically: an aesthetic of openness, of imaginative suddenness, has replaced the earlier, formalistic decorum. Now we have Macy's department store instead of Caesar's Gallic Wars, an almost surreal jangle of images in place of the structured rhetoric, and a coarse colloquial ear keeping measure, rather than the polished flow of iambs. Here is a poem, complete, called "The Instructor Has Not Followed the Lesson Plan Very Carefully":

> The motor grinds & won't catch.
> Nowhere worth going to: so the car thinks.
>
> And I think. Once there was punctuation
> worth listening to. I was used to that & I said:
>
> Here are all the commas you will use up in a normal life.
> The students bit at my wrists & ankles &
>
> A wild deer burst into the office & bled to death
> Kicking the files to mush.

The irony is still there, but now instead of bringing things into focus, it's employed to break open the closures of the poems, to

celebrate madness rather than to contain neurotic stasis. The ampersand and the colon have replaced the comma, and, instead of assured articulation, we are offered, almost threatened with, insistent juxtapositions.
Dickey's startling development, or devolution if looked at from another angle, is symptomatic of changes in American poetry throughout the 1960's. As the Eliotic-Audenesque hegemony broke apart, the dominant idiom splintered, and many poets, certainly Dickey among them, were set adrift. His career is too heterogeneous to judge easily, and his main strengths at this point are his quiet responsiveness and his continued responsibility to use langauge to sharpen the contours of his experience. This may require release as well as concision for the moment. He is a poet in mid-stride, though obviously very capable of energetic movement.

—Charles Molesworth

DICKINSON, Patric (Thomas). British. Born in Nasirabad, India, 26 December 1914. Educated at St. Catharine's College, Cambridge (Crabtree Exhibitioner), B.A. (honours) in English and classics 1936. Served with the Artists' Rifles, 1939-40. Married Sheila Shannon in 1946; one son and one daughter. Schoolmaster, 1936-39; Producer, 1942-45, and Acting Poetry Editor, 1945-48, BBC, London: originator and compiler, *Time for Verse,* 1945-77. Since 1948, free-lance writer and broadcaster. Gresham Professor of Rhetoric, City University, London, 1964-67. Recipient: Atlantic Award, 1948; Cholmondeley Award, 1973. Address: 38 Church Square, Rye, Sussex, England.

<small>PUBLICATIONS</small>

Verse

The Seven Days of Jericho. London, Dakers, 1944.
Theseus and the Minotaur, and Poems. London, Cape, 1946.
Stone in the Midst and Poems. London, Methuen, 1948.
The Sailing Race and Other Poems. London, Chatto and Windus, 1952.
The Scale of Things. London, Chatto and Windus, 1955.
The World I See. London, Chatto and Windus-Hogarth Press, 1960.
This Cold Universe. London, Chatto and Windus-Hogarth Press, 1964.
Selected Poems. London, Chatto and Windus, 1968.
More Than Time. London, Chatto and Windus-Hogarth Press, 1970.
A Wintering Tree. London, Chatto and Windus-Hogarth Press, 1973.
The Bearing Beast. London, Chatto and Windus-Hogarth Press, 1976.
Our Living John and Other Poems. London, Chatto and Windus-Hogarth Press, 1979.
Winter Hostages. Hitchin, Hertfordshire, Mandeville Press, 1980.
Poems from Rye. Rye, Sussex, Martello Bookshop, 1980.
A Rift in Time. London, Chatto and Windus, 1982.

Plays

Theseus and the Minotaur (broadcast, 1945). Included in *Theseus and the Minotaur, and Poems,* 1946.

Stone in the Midst (produced London, 1949). Included in *Stone in the Midst and Poems*, 1948.

Robinson, adaptation of a play by Jules Supervielle (produced London, 1953).

The Golden Touch (produced Wolverhampton, Staffordshire, 1959; London, 1960).

A Durable Fire (produced Canterbury, 1962; London, 1963). London, Chatto and Windus, 1962.

Pseudolus, adaptation of the play by Plautus (produced Stoke on Trent, 1966).

Ode to St. Catharine, music by Bernard Rose (produced Cambridge, 1973).

Creation, music by Alan Ridout (produced Ely, 1973).

The Miller's Secret, music by Stephen Dodgson (produced Cookham, Berkshire, 1973).

The Return of Odysseus, music by Malcolm Arnold (produced London, 1975). London, Faber, 1976.

Good King Wenceslas, music by Alan Ridout (produced Wells, Somerset, 1979).

The Business Man, adaptation of a play by Plautus (produced Stoke on Trent, 1983).

Radio Plays and Documentaries (selection): *Theseus and the Minotaur*, 1945; *The First Family*, 1960; *Wilfred Owen*, 1970; *The Pensive Prisoner*, 1970; *Phaeton*, music by Alan Ridout, 1977.

Television Play: *Lysistrata*, from the play by Aristophanes, 1964.

Other

A Round of Golf Courses: A Round of the Best Eighteen. London, Evans, 1951.

The Good Minute: An Autobiographical Study. London, Gollancz, 1965.

Editor, *Soldiers' Verse.* London, Muller, 1945.

Editor, *Byron: Poems.* London, Grey Walls Press, 1949.

Editor, with Erica Marx and J.C. Hall, *New Poems 1955.* London, Joseph, 1955.

Editor, *Poetry Supplement.* London, Poetry Book Society, 1958.

Editor, with Sheila Shannon, *Poems to Remember* (for children). London, Harvill Press, 1958.

Editor, with Sheila Shannon, *Poets' Choice: An Anthology of English Poetry from Spenser to the Present Day.* London, Evans, 1967.

Editor, *C. Day Lewis: Selections from His Poetry.* London, Chatto and Windus, 1967.

Editor, *The Selected Poems of Henry Newbolt.* London, Hodder and Stoughton, 1981.

Translator, *Aristophanes Against War: Three Plays.* London, Oxford University Press, 1957.

Translator, *The Aeneid of Virgil.* New York, New American Library, 1961.

Translator, *The Complete Plays of Aristophanes.* London, Oxford University Press, 2 vols., 1971.

*

Manuscript Collection: British Library, London; Birmingham University; Humanities Research Center, University of Texas, Austin.

Patric Dickinson comments:

Bias towards country subjects since I live in the country. No "usual" verse forms: a tendency to invention. General sources: English poetry from 1500. Influences in youth: Yeats, Frost, Edward Thomas, in particular. Stylistic devices: a continual attempt at greater honesty, clarity, and conciseness.

*   *   *

The essential Patric Dickinson is a stubborn lyricist who thrives on paradox. He seems endlessly surprised by emblematic landscapes, refining them into "a particular / Sharp agony of atmosphere," and his most successful poems are (to borrow from a title) passionate, graceful distillations of Outsight to Insight. Their impact derives from the tension between fear and affirmation, loss and gratitude, a cold impersonal universe and the intimacy of "our sweet immediate life." Some of the early work gestures too largely; the influence of Yeats is conspicuous and there are strong echoes of late-1930's Auden: "Against you all I set up love / And cry it in your teeth." Here it is the *poetry* that is set up, a willed confrontation in the grand manner of romantic stoicism sharpened by contemporary reference, but Dickinson worked this need to posture out of his system quickly, and by the time he published his excellent 1948 collection, *Stone in the Midst*, he had become altogether more subtle. In one of this book's best poems, "The Ammonite," he considers "how we / Are riddled with creation," and in that challenging pun lies the ambiguity which remains at the centre of his subsequent achievement; to live is to suffer, and suffering gives the edge to love. The riddle is the actual pain and the illusive mystery. Here is a complete, and characteristic, short poem, "Winter Sun" (*The Scale of Things*):

> Out of the sea the sun
> Rose into cloudlessness.
> All that the heart could tell
> Of certainty was there
> In the pure blessing air.
> No need for poetry, peace
> Between symbol and real was signed
> By the thrush in the bare tree
> And the mind in its life-cell.
>
> But the grief-divining ray
> Aware of its nakedness
> Wove round itself a cloud—
> That tribute of small tears
> No day is day nor love
> Is daily love without.

Time and again, Dickinson insists upon "how lonely all men are" among the bewildering generosities of nature, how this loneliness both intensifies our awareness of beauty (he's a poet who is neither afraid of that word nor uses it sentimentally) and agitates us towards destruction: "all nature's / A prisoner on parole / To our violence." Above all, though, despite the grim recesses of the human condition, he never turns away towards an easier, more diffuse light or indulges in melancholy: it is "The dark sea bed of the soul where move / All the creative impulses of love," and, as he remarks in "A Wintering Tree," it is "The condition of being rooted / That gives a creature worth." This strong sense of particularity is what gives his finest poems their resonant firmness and a memorable context for their weightier generalisations. A stanza may begin "Walking together through time," courting the portentousness of abstraction, but on that journey "every cobblestone snaps down / A lid as a foot falls," giving an immediacy to the experience which is simply (though not easily achieved) the hallmark of true poetry.

If Dickinson's work is characterised by the thematic tensions noted at the beginning, it must in the end be emphasised that what gives so many of the poems their force is the precision and accuracy of their notation. There have been patches of meandering dullness in several of the books, but these are outnumbered by the elegant, moving lyrics in which an individual, lovingly troubled voice is clearly heard:

> But if a secret is born of a secret
> And kept to the very death
> Of itself and you within and without,
> It is indeed the proof
> In mortal man
> Of divinity enough.

—John Mole

DILLARD, R(ichard) H(enry) W(ilde). American. Born in Roanoke, Virginia, 11 October 1937. Educated at Roanoke College, Salem, Virginia, 1955-58, B.A. 1958 (Phi Beta Kappa); University of Virginia, Charlottesville (Woodrow Willson Fellow, 1958-59; DuPont Fellow, 1959-61), M.A. 1959, Ph.D. 1965. Married Cathy Hankla (second marriage) in 1979. Instructor in English, Roanoke College, Summer 1961, and University of Virginia, 1961-64. Assistant Professor, 1964-68, Associate Professor, 1968-74, since 1971, Chairman of the Graduate Program in Contemporary Literature and Creative Writing, and since 1974, Professor of English, Hollins College, Virginia. Since 1973, Vice-President, *Film Journal*, New York. Contributing Editor, *Hollins Critic*, Hollins College, Virginia, 1966-77. Recipient: Academy of American Poets Prize, 1961; Ford grant, 1972. Agent: Blanche C. Gregory, 2 Tudor City Place, New York, New York 10017. Address: Box 9671, Hollins College, Virginia, 24020, U.S.A.

PUBLICATIONS

Verse

The Day I Stopped Dreaming about Barbara Steele and Other Poems. Chapel Hill, University of North Carolina Press, 1966.
News of the Nile. Chapel Hill, University of North Carolina Press, 1971.
After Borges. Baton Rouge, Louisiana State University Press, 1972.
The Greeting: New and Selected Poems. Salt Lake City, University of Utah Press, 1981.

Play

Screenplay: *Frankenstein Meets the Space Monster*, with George Garrett and John Rodenbeck, 1966.

Novels

The Book of Changes. New York, Doubleday, 1974.
The First Man on the Sun. Baton Rouge, Louisiana State University Press, 1983.

Other

Horror Films. New York, Monarch Press, 1976.

Editor, with Louis D. Rubin, Jr., *The Experience of America: A Book of Readings.* New York, Macmillan, and London, Collier Macmillan, 1969.
Editor, with George Garrett and John Rees Moore, *The Sounder Few: Essays from "The Hollins Critic."* Athens, University of Georgia Press, 1971.

*

R.H.W. Dillard comments:

Although I have thought a good deal about what I am doing in my poems, I don't know that I really am able to express the results of that thinking very clearly, except (I hope) in the poems themselves. Allow me, then, to offer in place of an introductory statement about my poetry, excerpts from three poems which might do the job.

The first, from the poem "News of the Nile," is just a description of the source of my poems—experience in the broadest sense: "All these things I have read and remembered,/ Witnessed, imagined, thought and written down...."

The second, from the poem "Construction," may be a bit more helpful, for it is as close as I've come to an explicit esthetic statement, and it also makes explicit my central concern with the vital involvement of seeing and saying, of action and belief:

> To say as you see. To see as by stop-action,
> Clouds coil overhead, the passage of days,
>
> Trees bend by the side of the road
> Like tires on a curve, plants uncurl,
>
> How the world dissolves in the water of the eye:
> The illusion speed produces. The reality of speed.
>
> A result: to see as you say,
> As gravity may bend a ray of light.
>
> To say the earth's center is of fire:
> Life leaps from the soil like sun flares.
>
> To see the world made true,
> An art of rocks and stones and trees,
>
> Real materials in real space,
> *L'esthétique de la vitesse.*

The third, from the long poem *January: A Screenplay*, is a prayer which states briefly the faith and the humility which I hope is at the heart of everything I do:

> For my sorrow in this depth of joy,
> Gift beyond reward, I'm sorry.
> For the joy I feel in this broken world,
> This sorrow, this woe, I thank you,
> I thank you.

*   *   *

Each of R.H.W. Dillard's volumes is an important contribution to American poetry. The first, *The Day I Stopped Dreaming about Barbara Steele*, despite its echoes of Williams, Auden, Stevens, Ransom and Tate, is a highly sophisticated, humorous and unique representation of experience. The most traditionally formal of the three volumes, it is most impressive in its sardonic rendering of a wide range of "things." Dillard, fascinated by the power of his imagination, transforms into objects of beauty things—objects, emotions, experiences—that might otherwise be ephemeral or unnoticed. The wit in this volume does not diminish the sense of tragedy but as in Williams's "Pictures from Brueghel: Landscape with the Fall of Icarus," enlarges it by placing it in a comic context. At the same time it should be emphasized that the "thinginess" is definitely not that of the empiricist, realist or naturalist, but more that of the esthete.

News of the Nile, his second volume, is a further development of a distinctive voice. The See-er of visions of the imagination, intellectualized and witty, becomes autobiographical, personal, subjective, troubled. The models shift to Lowell and Roethke. Perhaps too much influenced by his study of horror movies, Dillard examines the perverse in human nature and experience— blood lust, cannibalism, the macabre. Poems such as "Night of the Living Dead," "Event; A Gathering; Vastation," "Act of Detection," studies of the predatory and bestial nature of man, revel in visions of horror. Other poems, much lighter, struggle in the poet's soul to deal honestly with the substance of his own time and place and his relationship to it.

Dillard's third volume, *After Borges*, represents a mature achievement. The title signals a profound experience with the work of the Argentine writer, Jorge Luis Borges. The shock of a recent discovery of evil of too many of the poems in *News of the Nile* has given way to the good humor and wit of the first volume. Poems such as "Round Ruby," "What Can You Say to Shoes," "Sweet Strawberries," and "Wings" express a new found and authentic joy in life, its triviality, absurdity, beauty and pathos. Others, such as "Limits," "The Other Tiger," "Argumentum Ornithologicum," and "Epilogue" which purport to be "after the Spanish of Jorge Luis Borges," are more serious and complex. At the base of these poems is an extreme solipsism. Thus "Epilogue" tells us of the poet who sets "out to shape a world," and finds at the end of his work a "face, wearing/ And worn, warm as worn stone,/ A face you know: your own." The tension in this and other poems is based on the conflict of ego struggling to see through, beyond, or around itself, its face, to another self or world which seems inaccessible. Perhaps most important about the direction of these latest poems is that, if his work is becoming more psychological and personal, it is also more conscious of the psyche in history. Dillard's discovery of Borges's labyrinth helped him to see himself in a deeper and richer, if more difficult, context.

—Richard Damashek

---

di PRIMA, Diane. American. Born in New York City, 6 August 1934. Attended Swarthmore College, Pennsylvania, 1951-53. Married 1) Alan S. Marlowe in 1962 (divorced); 2) Grant Fisher in 1972 (divorced); five children. Contributing Editor, *Kulchur* magazine, New York, 1960-61; Co-Editor, with LeRoi Jones, 1961-63, and Editor, 1963-69, *Floating Bear* magazine, New York; also associated with *Yugen, Signal, Guerilla,* San Francisco *Sunday Paper,* and *Rallying Point.* Publisher, Poets Press, 1964-69, and since 1974, Eidolon Editions, San Francisco. Founder, with Alan Marlowe, New York Poets Theatre, 1961-65. Teacher in the Poetry-in-the-Schools program, 1971-75; visiting faculty member, Naropa Institute, Boulder, Colorado; Artist-in-Residence, Napa State Hospital, 1976-77.

Since 1980, Member of the Core Faculty, New College of California, San Francisco. Recipient: National Endowment for the Arts grant, 1966, 1973; Coordinating Council of Little Magazines grant, 1967, 1970. Address: Box 15068, Suite 103, San Francisco, California 94115, U.S.A.

PUBLICATIONS

Verse

This Kind of Bird Flies Backward. New York, Totem Press, 1958.
The Monster. New Haven, Connecticut, Penny Poems, 1961.
The New Handbook of Heaven. San Francisco, Auerhahn Press, 1963.
Unless You Clock In. Palo Alto, California, Patchen Cards, 1963.
Combination Theatre Poem and Birthday Poem for Ten People. New York, Brownstone Press, 1965.
Poems for Freddie. New York, Poets Press, 1966; as *Freddie Poems,* Point Reyes, California, Eidolon, 1974.
Haiku. Topanga, California, Love Press, 1967.
Earthsong: Poems 1957-59, edited by Alan S. Marlowe. New York, Poets Press, 1968.
Hotel Albert. New York, Poets Press, 1968.
New Mexico Poem, June-July 1967. New York, Roodenko, 1968.
The Star, The Child, The Light. Privately printed, 1968.
L.A. Odyssey. New York, Poets Press, 1969.
New As.... Privately printed, 1969.
Revolutionary Letters. San Francisco, City Lights, 1970.
The Book of Hours. San Francisco, Brownstone Press, 1970.
Kerhonkson Journal 1966. Berkeley, California, Oyez, 1971.
Prayer to the Mothers. Privately printed, 1971.
So Fine. Santa Barbara, California, Yes Press, 1971.
XV Dedications. Santa Barbara, California, Unicorn Press, 1971.
The Calculus of Letters. Privately printed, 1972.
Loba, Part 1. Santa Barbara, California, Capra Press, 1973.
North Country Medicine. Privately printed, 1974.
Brass Furnace Going Out: Song, After an Abortion. Syracuse, New York, Pulpartforms-Intrepid Press, 1975.
Selected Poems 1956-1975. Plainfield, Vermont, North Atlantic, 1975; revised edition, 1977.
Loba as Eve. New York, Phoenix Book Shop, 1975.
Loba, Part 2. Point Reyes, California, Eidolon, 1976.
Loba, Parts 1-8. Berkeley, California, Wingbow Press, 1978.

Plays

Paideuma (produced New York, 1960).
The Discontentment of the Russian Prince (produced New York, 1961).
Murder Cake (produced New York, 1963).
Like (produced New York, 1964).
Poets Vaudeville, music by John Herbert McDowell (produced New York, 1964). New York, Feed Folly Press, 1964.
Monuments (produced New York, 1968).
The Discovery of America (produced New York, 1972).
Whale Honey (produced San Francisco, 1975; New York, 1976).

Novels

The Calculus of Variation. New York, Poets Press, 1966.
Spring and Autumn Annals. San Francisco, Frontier Press, 1966.

Love on a Trampoline, with Sybah Darrich.   New York, Olympia Press, 1968.
Of Sheep and Girls, with Robert M. Duffy.   New York, Olympia Press, 1968.
Memoirs of a Beatnik.   New York, Olympia Press, 1969.

Short Stories

Dinners and Nightmares.   New York, Corinth, 1961; revised edition, 1974.

Other

Notes on the Summer Solstice.   Privately printed, 1969.

Editor, *Various Fables from Various Places*.   New York, Putnam, 1960.
Editor, *War Poems*.   New York, Poets Press, 1968.
Editor, with LeRoi Jones, *The Floating Bear: A Newsletter, Numbers 1-37*.   La Jolla, California, Laurence McGilvery, 1974.

Translator, with others, *The Man Condemned to Death*, by Jean Genet.   New York, Poets Press, 1963.
Translator, *Seven Love Poems from the Middle Latin*.   New York, Poets Press, 1965.

*

Manuscript Collection: Southern Illinois University, Carbondale.

*   *   *

The publication of Diane di Prima's *Selected Poems* and *Loba, Parts 1-8* provided us with the opportunity to see the full form of her work to date. In all its progressions and occasional regressions, what is visible remains a consistent and inventive level of excellence.

Di Prima's work is an uncompromising history of herself as woman, mother, citizen, artist, and mythmaker. From the early works in *This Kind of Bird Flies Backwards* and *Earthsong* and their refinement in *Freddie Poems*, to the in-progress (or in-process) exploration of a feminine archetype, *Loba*, her work retains clarity and unity of purpose. Though the work is diverse, there are no contradictions as to its totality. The magical poems in *The New Handbook of Heaven* in no way betray the straightforward practical polemics of *Revolutionary Letters*; the exact and lyric *Kerhonkson Journal* complements the erotic vaudevilles in *Memoirs of a Beatnik*. There remains in all of her work a forthright, tender, and emotional honesty which continues to develop as the power of her art does.

Loba is a culmination of the works preceding it and enters more deeply into the realms of mystery. In this case, the mystery is the feminine, the myths embodied in the wolf Loba, Lilith, the vengeful first bride of Adam, Eve, Persephone, Iseult. Di Prima's poetic language affirms and expands the strength and spirit of the feminine without exploiting them. She restores the mythmaking powers of the feminine by often using literary and mythic examples from a past created for the most part by males in male-dominated cultures. She presents these myths from the center of the feminine and reveals the realms of woman's spiritual reality active in the mysteries and the realities. Whether in childbirth, or blessing a daughter's entry into womanhood, or as succubus or divine beloved, woman remains complete within her domain. *Loba* is deeply rendered and richly annotated work.

—David Meltzer

———————

DOBSON, Rosemary (de Brissac).   Australian.   Born in Sydney, New South Wales, 18 June 1920. Educated at Frensham, Mittagong, New South Wales; Sydney University. Married A.T. Bolton in 1951; one daughter and two sons. Recipient: *Sydney Morning Herald* prize, 1946; Myer Award, 1966; Robert Frost Award, 1979; Australia Council fellowship, 1980. Address: 61 Stonehaven Crescent, Deakin, Canberra, ACT 2600, Australia.

PUBLICATIONS

Verse

Poems.   Mittagong, New South Wales, Frensham Press, 1937.
In a Convex Mirror.   Sydney, Dymock's Book Arcade, 1944.
The Ship of Ice and Other Poems.   Sydney, Angus and Robertson, 1948.
Child with a Cockatoo and Other Poems.   Sydney, Angus and Robertson, 1955.
(Poems), selected and introduced by the author.   Sydney, Angus and Robertson, 1963.
Cock Crow: Poems.   Sydney, Angus and Robertson, 1965.
Rosemary Dobson Reads from Her Own Work (with recording).   Brisbane, University of Queensland Press, 1970.
Three Poems on Water-Springs.   Canberra, Brindabella Press, 1973.
Selected Poems.   Sydney, Angus and Robertson, 1973; revised edition, 1980.
Greek Coins: A Sequence of Poems.   Canberra, Brindabella Press, 1977.
Over the Frontier.   Sydney, Angus and Robertson, 1978.
The Three Fates and Other Poems.   Sydney, Hale and Iremonger, 1984.

Other

Focus on Ray Crooke.   Brisbane, University of Queensland Press, 1971.
A World of Difference: Australian Poetry and Painting in the 1940's (lecture).   Sydney, Wentworth Press, 1973.

Editor, *Australia, Land of Colour, Through the Eyes of Australian Painters*.   Sydney, Ure Smith, 1962.
Editor, *Songs for All Seasons: 100 Poems for Young People*.   Sydney, Angus and Robertson, 1967.
Editor, *Australian Voices: Poetry and Prose of the 1970's*.   Canberra, Australian National University Press, 1975.
Editor, *Sisters Poets 1*.   Carlton, Victoria, Sisters, 1979.

Translator, with David Campbell, *Moscow Trefoil*.   Canberra, Australian National University Press, 1975.
Translator, with David Campbell, *Seven Russian Poets*.   Brisbane, University of Queensland Press, 1979.

*

Manuscript Collections: National Library of Australia, Canberra; Fryer Memorial Library, University of Queensland, Brisbane.

Critical Studies: "Rosemary Dobson: A Portrait in a Mirror" by A.D. Hope, in *Quadrant* (Sydney), July-August 1972; "The Poetry of Rosemary Dobson" by James McAuley, in *Australian Literary Studies* (Hobart, Tasmania), May 1973.

*   *   *

Rosemary Dobson wrote, designed, and printed her first collection of poems in 1937, while she was still at school. They are juvenilia, but already apparent is a sense of purpose, and also a quiet elegance: it is a beautifully designed small volume. *In a Convex Mirror* is to a large extent made up of poems originally published in the Sydney *Bulletin*, and which had attracted considerable interest by their vivacity and concern with an immediately experienced world without loss of lyric poise. The title poem, which takes as its starting-point a famous Vermeer interior, is significant also for its preoccupation with time, a subject that became of overriding concern for a number of poets in this period of dramatic upheaval. For Rosemary Dobson, time was most fully explored in the long title poem of her next collection, *The Ship of Ice*, which begins: "Time is a thief at the end of a road, is a river," and maintains a fine balance between wit and tension. This book also contains the vivacious sequence "The Devil and the Angel" which broke new ground in Australian writing of that period, with its joyful irony and alert conversational tone. But it was in her next volume, *Child with a Cockatoo*, that Rosemary Dobson fully explored what has become her most admired achievement, the "Poems from Paintings." Art had always played an important part in her concerns, and its particular capacity to exist, as it were, outside time provides the essential frisson behind these witty and perceptive poems. The underlying sensibility remains elegant and alert, though perhaps the poems in monologue form most sharply retain that particular freshness which made their first appearance so notable.

It was to be ten years before Rosemary Dobson's next publication, *Cock Crow*. There is a considerable deepening of feeling in the opening poems, "Child of Our Time" and "Out of Winter," poems of personal apprehension reminiscent perhaps of the work of Judith Wright. Rosemary Dobson has always been careful about intruding the naked personality into her poems, and the first section of *Cock Crow* represents, through its very attempts at overcoming a natural reticence, a moving testament to the poet's inner agony. The second section of the book is more playful, especially in the poems that translate figures from classical mythology into thoroughly Australian settings.

Another long period of silence intervened before the publication of *Selected Poems*. This contained 26 new poems, some written in England and some from Greece and Crete. Their firm lyrical tone and occasional moments of witty observation place them securely in the characteristic Dobson style. *Over the Frontier* is her most recent collection. Its most engaging quality is still that carefully modified informality, as in "Callers at the House" or "Oracles for a Childhood Journey," as well as the more overtly lyrical "Canberra Morning" or poems that explore classical, literary, and even scientific themes. Her translation, with David Campbell, of contemporary Russian poets, *Moscow Trefoil*, has added a subtle flavour and tension to the best of the recent work (and most notably in the title poem of this collection), though the centrepiece is the sequence "Poems from Pausanias." Attracted by the immediate vividness of Pausanias's

Guide to Greece she has utilised her own response to re-negotiate its immediacy; thus the theme of time, always essential to her vision, becomes a subtly recurring third theme explored here. The reader becomes part of an ongoing chain of recognition and discovery.

—Thomas W. Shapcott

DOBYNS, Stephen. American. Born in Orange, New Jersey, 19 February 1941. Educated at Shimer College, Mount Carroll, Illinois, 1959-60; Wayne State University, Detroit, B.A. 1964; University of Iowa, Iowa City, M.F.A. 1967. Instructor in English, State University of New York College, Brockport, 1968-69; reporter, Detroit *News*, 1969-71; Visiting Lecturer, University of New Hampshire, Durham, 1973-75, University of Iowa, 1977-78, and Boston University, 1978-79. Since 1978, Member of the Department of Creative Writing, Goddard College, Plainfield, Vermont. Recipient: Lamont Poetry Selection award, 1971; MacDowell Colony Fellowship, 1972, 1976; Yaddo fellowship, 1972, 1973, 1977; National Endowment for the Arts grant, 1974. Address: Department of Creative Writing, Goddard College, Plainfield, Vermont 05667, U.S.A.

PUBLICATIONS

Verse

Concurring Beasts.   New York, Atheneum, 1972.
Griffon.   New York, Atheneum, 1976.
Heat Death.   New York, Atheneum, 1980.
The Balthus Poems.   New York, Atheneum, 1982.

Novels

A Man of Little Evils.   New York, Atheneum, 1973; London, Davies, 1974.
Saratoga Longshot.   New York, Atheneum, 1976; London, Hale, 1978.
Saratoga Swimmer.   New York, Atheneum, 1981.
Dancer with One Leg.   New York, Dutton, 1983.

*   *   *

In his books *Concurring Beasts, Griffon*, and *Heat Death* Stephen Dobyns continues to write the same poem, rarely varying from his free-form yet controlled, solid, somewhat prosey stanzas. This is not a criticism in the least; rather this dry, almost matter-of-fact style effectively conveys this poet's sense of irony and horror in a violent world.

While Dobyns shows the influence of Latin American and Spanish poets such as Neruda, Alberti, and Cortázar in both form and content, he applies their surrealism to his own distinctly American imagination and experience. In a voice that remains steady and dispassionate, through direct statements that accrue rapidly and forcefully, his speaker, his "I," reveals a world both absurd and highly dangerous:

Four walls open to the sky: you are
in a small prison. There is no door.
You are here for hatred, theft; it doesn't
matter. You might have been here all your life.

The prison in "Song for Putting Aside Anger" is the one in which Everyman, the "you" to whom so many poems are addressed, exists. Dobyns's landscape is Kafkaesque, and his men and women are trapped. They cannot name where they are. They cannot understand what has happened to them. They are passive before the violence and disorder of life. They are "getting through to the end" as the title of one of his poems puts it:

> We have been brought here,
> through the name on the wall
> we have finally read,
> past the man in the burning chair
> who has spoken at last.
> We have earned this.
> We have seen through the eyes of the blind.
> We have listened to the music of the deaf.
> We have been brought here.

In such a world almost anything can happen. Dobyns is not without humor, however bleak. A man fashions a woman out of his morning's oatmeal. A creative writing teacher and his students eat Pablo Neruda. The poem itself comes to life, and the poet sees it "fighting it out with knives in the front yard," sitting on a bench at the train station, becoming food and shelter:

> You are lost and without shelter. People
> avoid you, storms seek you out. Take this poem.
> It is a tent to put around you.

"Grimoire," the fifth section of his book *Griffon*, is perhaps Dobyns's poetry at its best. Here the deadly sins and the black emotions such as fear, gluttony, and anger are allowed to speak for themselves. In a language that is plain and highly compressed, these states of mind reveal their essences and force us to recognize our own worst feelings. Says Vanity accusingly, "I write this,/you read this." Says Fear, "You forget what you were looking for when you/reached into this corner and touched me." Acute perceptions such as these show Dobyns to have a fine understanding of the dark side of human nature.

—Cynthia Day

DORN, Ed(ward Merton). American. Born in Villa Grove, Illinois, 2 April 1929. Educated at the University of Illinois, Urbana, 1949-50; Black Mountain College, North Carolina, 1950, 1954. Married to Jennifer Dunbar. Taught at Idaho State University, Pocatello, 1961-65; Visiting Professor of American Literature (Fulbright Lecturer, 1965-66, 1966-67), University of Essex, Wivenhoe, England, 1965-68, 1974-75; Visiting Poet, University of Kansas, Lawrence, 1968-69; Regents Lecturer, University of California, Riverside, 1973-74; Writer-in-Residence, University of California at San Diego, La Jolla, 1976, Northeastern Illinois State College, Chicago, and University of Colorado, Boulder, 1977-80. Editor, *Wild Dog* magazine, Salt Lake City, 1964-65. Recipient: National Endowment for the Arts grant, 1966, 1968; D.H. Lawrence Fellowship, 1969. Address: c/o Four Seasons Foundation, P.O Box 31190, San Francisco, California 94131, U.S.A.

PUBLICATIONS

Verse

Paterson Society. Privately printed, 1960.
The Newly Fallen. New York, Totem Press, 1961.
From Gloucester Out. London, Matrix Press, 1964.
Hands Up! New York, Totem-Corinth, 1964.
Idaho Out. London, Fulcrum Press, 1965.
Geography. London, Fulcrum Press, 1965; revised edition, 1968.
The North Atlantic Turbine. London, Fulcrum Press, 1967.
Song. Newcastle upon Tyne, Northern Arts, 1968.
Gunslinger, Book I. Los Angeles, Black Sparrow Press, 1968.
The Midwest Is That Space Between the Buffalo Statler and the Lawrence Eldridge. Lawrence, Kansas, Terrence Williams, 1968.
Gunslinger, Book II. Los Angeles, Black Sparrow Press, 1969.
Gunslinger 1 and 2. London, Fulcrum Press, 1969.
Twenty-Four Love Songs. San Francisco, Frontier Press, 1969.
The Cosmology of Finding Your Spot. Lawrence, Kansas, Cottonwood, 1969.
Ed Dorn Sportcasts Colonialism. Privately printed, 1969 (?).
Songs: Set Two, A Short Count. West Newbury, Massachusetts, Frontier Press, 1970.
Spectrum Breakdown: A Microbook. LeRoy, New York, Athanor, 1971.
A Poem Called Alexander Hamilton. Lawrence, Kansas, Tansy-Peg Leg Press, 1971.
The Cycle. West Newbury, Massachusetts, Frontier Press, 1971.
The Kultchural Exchange. Seattle, Wiater, 1971.
Old New Yorkers Really Get My Head. Lawrence, Kansas, Cottonwood, 1972.
The Hamadryas Baboon at the Lincoln Park Zoo. Chicago, Wine Press, 1972.
Gunslinger, Book III: The Winterbook Prologue to the Great Book IIII Kornerstone. West Newbury, Massachusetts, Frontier Press, 1972.
Recollections of Gran Apacheria. San Francisco, Turtle Island, 1974.
Gunslinger, Books I, II, III, IV. Berkeley, California, Wingbow Press, 1975.
The Collected Poems 1956-1974. Bolinas, California, Four Seasons, 1975.
Manchester Square, with Jennifer Dunbar. London, Permanent Press, 1975.
Slinger. Berkeley, California, Wingbow Press, 1975.
Hello La Jolla. Berkeley, California, Wingbow Press, 1978.
Selected Poems, edited by Donald Allen. Bolinas, California, Grey Fox Press, 1978.
Yellow Lola: Formerly Titled Japanese Neon (Hello, La Jolla, Book II). Santa Barbara, California, Cadmus, 1981.

Recording: *Edward Dorn Reads from "The North Atlantic Turbine,"* Livingdiscs, 1967.

Short Stories

Some Business Recently Transacted in the White World. West Newbury, Massachusetts, Frontier Press, 1971.

Other

What I See in the Maximus Poems. Ventura, California, and

Worcester, Migrant Press, 1960.

Prose 1, with Michael Rumaker and Warren Tallman. San Francisco, Four Seasons, 1964.

The Rites of Passage: A Brief History. Buffalo, New York, Frontier Press, 1965; revised edition, as *By the Sound*, Mount Vernon, Washington, Frontier Press, 1972.

The Shoshoneans: The People of the Basin-Plateau. New York, Morrow, 1967.

The Poet, The People, The Spirit, edited by Bob Rose. Vancouver, Talonbooks, 1976.

Roadtesting the Language: An Interview, with Stephen Fredman. San Diego, University of California Archive for New Poetry, 1978.

Views, Interviews, edited by Donald Allen. Bolinas, California, Four Seasons, 2 vols., 1980.

Translator, with Gordon Brotherston, *Our Word: Guerrilla Poems from Latin America*. London, Cape Goliard Press, and New York, Grossman, 1968.

Translator, with Gordon Brotherston, *Tree Between Two Walls*, by José Emilio Pacheco. Los Angeles, Black Sparrow Press, 1969.

Translator, with Gordon Brotherston, *Selected Poems*, by César Vallejo. London, Penguin, 1976.

Translator, *Image of the New World: The American Continent Portrayed in Native Texts*, edited by Gordon Brotherston. London, Thames and Hudson, 1979.

*

Bibliography: *A Bibliography of Ed Dorn* by David Streeter, New York, Phoenix Book Shop, 1973.

Manuscript Collection: Northwestern University, Evanston, Illinois.

Critical Studies: "An Interview with Ed Dorn," in *Contemporary Literature* (Madison, Wisconsin), 15, 3; *The Lost America of Love: Rereading Robert Creeley, Edward Dorn, and Robert Duncan* by Sherman Paul, Baton Rouge, Louisiana State University Press, 1981; *Internal Resistances: The Poetry of Ed Dorn* by Donald Wesling, Berkeley, University of California Press, 1985.

*   *   *

Ed Dorn's work has been widely praised in both England and America. Russell Banks, writing in *Lillabulero*, has compared him, not invidiously, with Olson, Williams, and Pound. In England, A. Alvarez decided that Dorn has produced "a handful of beautifully pure and unaffected love-songs, and an intriguing long poem about a drive, 'Idaho Out,' in which cultural worry loses out to a kind of anarchic, footloose vitality and a feeling for the vast, frozen emptiness of the American West." Dorn's work reminds Alvarez of Hemingway, and it is true that Dorn is concerned with capturing idiomatic speech accurately; but he also indulges a kind of jam-pack jumbling of observations that is more the poetic counterpart of exuberant and excited writers like Thomas Wolfe. Dorn's recall of childhood, his feeling for places and writers, his political convictions, his tourism, all find their way, in cascades of energy, into his loose, straying verse—though it is only fair to say that there is, supposedly, some underlying structure based more or less on "projective verse" sympathies.

Dorn's reactions to England, where he lived for some time, are particularly sensitive:

As we go
through Sussex, hills are round
bellies are the downs
pregnantly lovely
the rounds of them, no towns
the train passes
shaking along the groove
of the countryside.

He purports "to love/that, and retain an ear for/the atrocities of my own hemisphere," critizing, with simplistic pessimism, almost everything about America:

The thorn however
remains, in the desert
of american life, the thorn
in the throat of our national hypocrisy.

And yet he is also sentimental at will about his land: "And yes Fort Benton is lovely/and quiet, I would gladly give it as a gift/to a friend/...." Indeed, at his best, Dorn is a sentimentalist for the America he denounces:

Bitterly cold were the nights.
The journeymen slept in the lots of filling stations
and there were the interrupting lights
of semis all night long as those beasts
crept past or drew up to rest their motors
or roared on.

And his *Gunslinger* must be built on these strong native feelings; it is an effort at building a comic epic on the Western, for Dorn finds there the archetypal characters and enthusiasms that reveal America. For painting and wit, the commendable:

And why do you have a female horse
Gunslinger? I asked. Don't move
he replied
the sun rests deliberately
on the rim of the sierra.

This work also moves away from the Ego as center, which was getting to be a problem in long poems in which Dorn spoke as a seer; it is only to be hoped that he does not lose other qualities of his earlier work—exuberance, puritanical anger, authority about his enthusiasms.

—David Ray

———————

DOWLING, Basil (Cairns). British. Born in Southbridge, Canterbury, New Zealand, 29 April 1910. Educated at St. Andrew's College; Canterbury University College, Christchurch, M.A. 1932; Otago University, Dunedin, 1933-35; Cambridge University, 1936-37; New Zealand Library School, Wellington, diploma 1946. Married Margaret Wilson in 1938; one son and two daughters. Librarian, Otago University, 1947-52; Assistant Master, Downside School, Surrey, 1952-54; Assistant Master, 1954-65, and Head of the Department of English, 1965-75, Raine's Foundation Grammar School, London. Since 1975, free-lance writer. Recipient: Jessie Mackay Memorial Prize (New Zealand), 1961. Address: 12 Mill Road, Rye, East Sussex, TN31 7NN, England.

PUBLICATIONS

Verse

A Day's Journey.   Christchurch, Caxton Press, 1941.
Signs and Wonders: Poems.   Christchurch, Caxton Press, 1944.
Canterbury and Other Poems.   Christchurch, Caxton Press, 1949.
Hatherley: Recollective Lyrics.   Dunedin, University of Otago Bibliography Room, 1968.
A Little Gallery of Characters.   Christchurch, Nag's Head Press, 1971.
Bedlam: A Mid-Century Satire.   Christchurch, Nag's Head Press, 1972.
The Unreturning Native.   Christchurch, Nag's Head Press, 1973.
The Stream.   Christchurch, Nag's Head Press, 1979.
Windfalls.   Christchurch, Nag's Head Press, 1983.

*

Manuscript Collections: State University of New York, Buffalo; Hocken Library, Otago University, Dunedin, New Zealand; Alexander Turnbull Library, Wellington, New Zealand.

Critical Studies: *Recent Trends in New Zealand Poetry* by James K. Baxter, Christchurch, Caxton Press, 1951; "Unreturning Native: The Poetic Achievement of Basil Dowling" by David Dowling, in *Landfall* (Christchurch), March 1979.

Basil Dowling comments:
   [My poetry] has been said to be at its best when descriptive of the New Zealand landscape, more particularly that of Canterbury. Certainly, landscape, both for its own sake and as a background to human life and history, has been a main preoccupation, but many of my poems have had philosophical overtones, and perhaps something reminiscent of the English metaphysical poets of the seventeenth century. I have been influenced most, I should say, by Hardy, Edward Thomas, Robert Frost and Andrew Young, and to some extent by Wilfred Owen and Siegfried Sassoon. As for method and manner, I like metrical variety, lightness of touch, however serious the subject, and, most of all, precision and economy of statement.

*   *   *

   Basil Dowling's poems are traditional in form, technically neat, and somewhat Georgian in their general flavour. The prevailing mode is New Zealand pastoral—contemplative description lit with verbal felicities—although there is an epigrammatic wryness in some of his shorter lyrics and his range extends also to the deservedly much-anthologized ballad "The Early Days."
   Dowling was prolific in the 1940's, coming into his full powers in *Canterbury and Other Poems*, but he has published relatively little since; he appears to have suffered a poetic amputation when he cut himself off from the South Island environment which so profoundly permeated his most vigorous work. His poems about the Canterbury landscape are full of crisp, accurate visual details, beautiful and often exultant descriptions of scenes and weathers, gentle pictures of birds, animals, trees. He is compassionate when he writes (more rarely) of people, and calm when he writes (even less frequently) about his personal life; but there is a deep pessimism underlying all but the most sunfilled of his poems. This becomes most intense in *Bedlam: A Mid-Century Satire*,

written in 1958, in which the Christian philosophy of his earlier work has given way to gloomy fatalism.
   In *A Little Gallery of Characters*, he returns to his "holy land of childhood," a peopled place this time, to portray sympathetically or with half-wistful humour the more memorable acquaintances of his early youth.

—Fleur Adcock

———————

DOWNIE, Freda (Christina).   British.   Born in London, 20 October 1929. Educated at schools in England and Australia. Married David Turner in 1957. Has worked for music publishers and art agents, and at a bookshop, all in London. Recipient: Stroud Festival prize, 1970; Arts Council prize, 1977. Address: 32 Kings Road, Berkhamsted, Hertfordshire HP4 3BD, England.

PUBLICATIONS

Verse

Night Music.   Hitchin, Hertfordshire, Mandeville Press, 1974.
A Sensation.   Hitchin, Hertfordshire, Cellar Press, 1975.
Night Sucks Me In.   Berkhamsted, Hertfordshire, Priapus, 1976.
A Stranger Here.   London, Secker and Warburg, 1977.
A Berkhamsted Three, with Fred Sedgwick and John Cotton. Berkhamsted, Hertfordshire, Priapus, 1978.
Man Dancing with the Moon.   Hitchin, Hertfordshire, Mandeville Press, 1979.
Plainsong.   London, Secker and Warburg, 1981.

*   *   *

   Though Freda Downie was born in 1929, her poems have appeared sparingly, gathered in the last few years into pamphlets and one substantial collection: their number is relatively small, the possibility of seeing a changing, developing talent in those which have been published is slight. These poems, though, veil and reveal an intelligence and sensitivity of remarkable quality. She is a formalist, an apparent mandarin, a writer whose syntax is easy and conversational, but whose vocabulary shows a refinement of epithet and habit of exactitude which ensure that her work rarely falls below a level where the reader must keep alert and supple. She creates a world of nuance; there are always a grace and play about the poems which rarely fall into preciosity or fine writing. The interplay between the precisions of her aesthetic sense and the dark, indifferent spaces of the world is central to her craft:

> And that tiny boat there is not rocking on an
> Armful of jewels, but proceeds with audacity
> Across the cold arena like a butterfly
> Moving over the green gravel of a formal grave.

   The dark spaces are stitched together, in part, by the sufficient worlds of music and painting. Their enigmatic consolations are real, their effects ambiguous. When the running thread of music closes "The empty bandstand still wears its steady crown/Prolonging a silent music/And the damp grass bends its perfume." These arts have been a part of Freda Downie's life—she has worked for a music publisher and art agent—and the poems frequently move between a posed landscape, a fiction which shimmers, dissolves, and reforms, and the rough unfocused directions of life. Her poems may suggest a glass perfection—worlds proper to Chagall, Corot, Oriental silk painting, the Douanier—but the key word is "suggest." The artists do not remove her from life; they transfigure and clarify life for her, as "Meister Bertram 1345-1415," where Christ appears

> Then red robed again, on a shrewd ass,
> Sadly entering Jerusalem
> And adored by devout gentlemen,
> While others hurrah Him with wrong leaves,
> Or show stylish legs in smart blue hose
> From a good view in intricate trees.
>
> These exquisite errors find Him.
> All mine, less bright, leave me where I am.

Freda Downie's world, cleansed and lit by art, is a personal world: a world of properly human pleasures and pains. Life is celebrated with an adroit and witty affection; she has a clear-sighted admiration for codes of stoical behaviour and for those strategies of style by which life is given a substantial meaning. Her father and a swan mirror each other in an old photograph, "And my father has one hand in his pocket/As though he, too, were unacquainted with base emotion/And incapable of sudden flight." Always in her work there is a bed-rock knowledge that under that agreeable armful of jewels life is a rough passage, whatever the possibilities of redemption, through halls of loss and indifference,

> While the occupants of that tiny boat cast out
> Their hopes, and knowing the balm of occupation,
> Drag abundant sustenance from the wet charnel
> Of lives and voyages lost in dark inundation.

—Peter Scupham

DOYLE, Charles (Desmond). Pseudonym: **Mike Doyle.** British/Canadian. Born in Birmingham, Warwickshire, 18 October 1928. Educated at Wellington Teachers College, New Zealand, Dip. Teach. 1956; Victoria University College, University of New Zealand (Macmillan Brown Prize, 1956), B.A. 1956, M.A. 1958; University of Auckland, Ph.D. Served in the Royal Navy. Married Doran Ross Smithells in 1959 (second marriage); three sons and one daughter. Taught at the University of Auckland; Visiting Fellow, Yale University, New Haven, Connecticut (American Council of Learned Societies Fellowship), 1967-68. Currently, Professor of English, University of Victoria, British Columbia. Editor, *Tuatara* magazine. Recipient: Jessie Mackay Memorial Prize, 1955; Unesco Creative Artists Fellowship, 1958. Address: Department of English, University of Victoria, Victoria, British Columbia V8W 2Y2, Canada.

PUBLICATIONS

Verse

A Splinter of Glass: Poems 1951-55. Christchurch, Pegasus Press, 1956.
The Night Shift: Poems on Aspects of Love, with others. Wellington, Capricorn Press, 1957.

Distances: Poems 1956-61. Auckland, Paul's Book Arcade, 1963. '
Messages for Herod. Auckland, Collins, 1965.
A Sense of Place. Wellington, Wai-te-ata Press, 1965.
Earth Meditations: 2. Auckland, Aldritt, 1968.
Noah, with *Quorum,* by Robert Sward. Vancouver, Soft Press, 1970.
Earth Meditations. Toronto, Coach House Press, 1971.
Abandoned Sofa. Victoria, British Columbia, Soft Press, 1971.
Earthshot. Exeter, Exeter Books, 1972.
Preparing for the Ark. Toronto, Weed/Flower Press, 1973.
Planes. Toronto, Seripress, 1975.
Stonedancer. Auckland, Auckland University Press—Oxford University Press, 1976.
A Month Away from Home. Victoria, British Columbia, Tuatara, 1980.
A Steady Hand. Erin, Ontario, Porcupine's Quill, 1982.

Other

Small Prophets and Quick Returns: Reflections on New Zealand Poetry. Auckland, New Zealand Publishing Society, 1966.
R.A.K. Mason. New York, Twayne, 1970.
James K. Baxter. Boston, Twayne, 1976.
William Carlos Williams and the American Poem. London, Macmillan, and New York, St. Martin's Press, 1982.

Editor, *Recent Poetry in New Zealand.* Auckland, Collins, 1965.
Editor, *William Carlos Williams: The Critical Heritage.* London, Routledge, 1980.

*

Manuscript Collection: Hocken Library, Otago University, Dunedin, New Zealand.

Critical Studies: *Aspects of New Zealand Poetry* by James K. Baxter, Christchurch, Caxton Press, 1967; "Earth Meditations One to Five" in *Quarry* (Kingston, Ontario), Summer 1972; "Le Longue Voyage de Mike Doyle" by John Greene, in *Ellipse* (Quebec), 1977; "Quiet Islands," in *Anthos* (Ottawa), Winter 1978; "Poetic Journeys," in *Canadian Literature 79* (Vancouver), 1979; "Mike Doyle and the Poet's Progress" by David Dowling, in *West Coast Review* (Vancouver), Winter 1981.

*   *   *

Because of his residence in Britain, New Zealand, America, and Canada, and his occupation as academic, critic, and editor, Charles Doyle's poetic career might well be described in the words of an acknowledged master, W.C. Williams, as the attempt to "find a local speech." The sense of geographical displacement in the 1950's is exchanged for a sense of intellectual displacement in the 1960's, while in the 1970's the search for poetic form dominated. His best poetry is when a balance between inventive form, philosophical reflection, and deeply felt personal experience is achieved.

His earlier lyrics contrast Europe ("our derelict hearts abandoned in distant places") with New Zealand (he wonders why "in a green country / where the cricket sings / there is such heartache / at the heart of things"). When he does attempt to verbalise the here and now, the real says "I am a thing, and that / Defeats you utterly." In *Messages for Herod* Doyle is vividly capable of evoking the present in dramatic lyrics, like the one when the clear smile of a hitchhiker is glimpsed from a car window. But the title poem shows the poet's dread of the personal as the parochial: Herod slaughters the children because one of them denies that Auckland is the centre of the universe.

Doyle seeks a solution in a Yeatsian Byzantium — "To make is to discover." *Earth Meditations* is a sustained intellectual mosaic, like *The Waste Land* welding together disparate fragments of form—concrete, imagist, lyric—and aesthetic idea— Magritte ("woid voice us imidge"), Joyce, Spinoza, Butler—in a search for meaning. For all it linguistic inventiveness, the sequence affirms the real in theory ("Could you have made / that same daub / without the dame?" the poet asks Magritte) and in practice, in autobiography (life in New Zealand as sitting on "a cairn / of sheep currants").

More arid experimentation is found in *Earthshot* and *Noah*, another long sequence which betrays Doyle's occasional mawkish naivety ("all that water?" and "Perhaps paradise / is always / what is lost?"). Yet even here there are those superb moments when emotion is crisply captured: when lamenting separation from his love "arms in my head / grow long three thousand miles," or in *Noah*, "Even the windowpanes / wept."

All these volumes may be seen as a long apprenticeship for the flowering of *Stonedancer*. In a remarkable variety of forms, these poems are wedded to occasional as well as more profound meditations with the sculptural simplicity, grace, and rightness of the Gaudier-Brzeska work of the title. A comparison of the title poem of Doyle's first volume—

I have shed an abstruse skin, and my bone's necrosis
Leaves Love's uncomplicated land to rediscover
Simple as still water or a moving tree

—with the last poem of *Stonedancer*, "The Journey of Meng Chiao"—

I must leave you here by the pinewoods under the sky.
I must go now. What do I hope to find when I arrive?
If I am lucky, the pinewoods under the sky

—shows Doyle's advance in philosophy and technique. An oriental simplicity of form and acceptance of emotion pervade the volume, as in "Shen Kua's Specifications for Travel" or the bliss of fulfilled love: "And on the hill slope, look / at the beautiful skiers. / See them go, see them go / over the frozen snow."

So much of this volume achieves Doyle's new ideal of the "poem as breathing" ("I dig those small / thin poems" he says) but also as "Dionysiac ravings." Fortunately Doyle escapes mystic platitudes by retaining that vigorous engagement with the world which has always marked his poetry. There is a superb poem about the torture of an innocent African, for example, which ends: "It was nobody's fault / that, as far as life is concerned, by the end of it / he knew everything else there was to know."

The volume suggests that Doyle "may have saved / the fullest wine until / gross appetite's discarded / its first, careless edge"; his speech is local to each poem, like a unique bouquet. Such versatility in thought, feeling, and technique as Doyle shows is rare among modern poets. For all his academic fluency, he can always be relied upon to give us in each poem Williams's ideal— "a new world that is always 'real.' "

Doyle's latest volume, *A Steady Hand*, belies its title in a restless variety of forms and themes. The poet is best when looking at the "simple history" of the natural world, evoking it through the aesthetic theory of a Klee ("*I am possessed by colour*"), or polishing set pieces like "The Journey of Meng

Chiao" or the powerful political protest of "The Inquisitor". But along with this mastery of form and tone go many uninspired lyrics including a long separation sequence, suggesting a restless talent still uncommitted, unfulfilled.

—David Dowling

DUBIE, Norman (Evans, Jr.). American. Born in Barre, Vermont, 10 April 1945. Educated at Goddard College, Plainfield, Vermont, 1964-69, B.A. 1969; University of Iowa, Iowa City, 1969-71, M.F.A. 1971. Married 1) Francesca Stafford in 1969 (divorced, 1973), one daughter; 2) Pamela Stewart in 1974 (divorced, 1979); 3) Jeannine Savard in 1981. Teaching Assistant, 1969-71, and Lecturer in Creative Writing, 1971-74, University of Iowa; Assistant Professor, Ohio University, Athens, 1974-75. Writer-in-Residence, 1975-76, Director of the Graduate Writing Program, 1976-77, Associate Professor, 1978-82, and since 1982, Professor of English, Arizona State University, Tempe. Poetry Director, Prison Writers and Artists Workshop, Iowa City, 1973-74. Recipient: Bess Hokin Prize (*Poetry*, Chicago), 1976; Guggenheim grant, 1977. Address: Department of English, Arizona State University, Tempe, Arizona 85281, U.S.A.

PUBLICATIONS

Verse

The Horsehair Sofa. Plainfield, Vermont, Goddard Journal, 1969.
Alehouse Sonnets. Pittsburgh, University of Pittsburgh Press, 1971.
Indian Summer. Iowa City, Elizabeth Press, 1974.
The Prayers of the North American Martyrs. New York, Penumbra Press, 1975.
Popham of the New Song and Other Poems. Port Townsend, Washington, Graywolf Press, 1975.
In the Dead of the Night. Pittsburgh, University of Pittsburgh Press, 1975.
The Illustrations. New York, Braziller, 1977.
A Thousand Little Things and Other Poems. Omaha, Cummington Press, 1978.
Odalisque in White. Seattle, Porch, 1978.
The City of the Olesha Fruit. New York, Doubleday, 1979.
The Everlastings. New York, Doubleday, 1980.
The Window in the Field. Copenhagen, Razorback Press, 1981.
Selected and New Poems. New York, Norton, 1983.

*

Manuscript Collection: University of Iowa Special Collections, Iowa City.

Critical Study: interview in *American Poetry Review* (Philadelphia), July-August 1978.

*   *   *

Norman Dubie writes a rich, evocative poetry that is sensuous and intricate. Each poem creates a world both complete and vastly larger than itself. Dubie recreates places, events, and people with an ear and eye that are remarkably deft and skillful. He works with remote times and places much as Borges does in his fiction. Yet these little worlds and brief lives, that seem so exotic and foreign to our own, are not so, and bear up the endless commonality of human situations. Dubie's individuals struggle for freedom and further understanding, and despite their frequent failures he treats them with compassion and understanding. The poems have appropriately been called "realizations of history." His voice is so convincing there is little doubt he has visited Hedda Gabler, gotten drunk with William Hazlitt, traveled with runaway slaves. His poems are convincing moments in the amber of time, so brightly illuminated they are their own reason for being.

Alehouse Sonnets is a series of related poems circling the life and circumstances of English critic William Hazlitt. At times the poet is Hazlitt's drinking partner; occasionally the voice is Hazlitt's interior monologue; at times we hear a contemporary voice explaining our world to the Englishman ("And, yes, we have new weapons; / tanks, flame-throwers, bomb squadrons, / choking gas with the odor of horseradish, the H-bomb..."). This is an impressive first book, both in its sustained use of the sonnet, and in its re-creation of a historical figure. One is driven forward, as if reading a novel, and rewarded with memorable images, such as "my wife comes spilling from the pond / fresh buckets of water for our bath." Still, I found myself tiring of the drunken revelries of Dubie and Hazlitt, and of the inevitable aftermath: "Hazlitt, we'll spend the night curled / up in a sheep's head like two fat / round worms."

In the Dead of the Night presents a much wider range of lives and voices. Dubie transports us, with equal ease to a Pennsylvania battlefield in 1774, or to "Genoa where sailboats smell of barns." He gives us here a remarkably wide range of voices that might have been far away and long ago, but that speak timelessly and remind us of our commonality ("it is another century; things are / not better or worse..."). Dubie's voice if often omniscient and editorial, as in "I didn't tell you the blind soldier had shot *himself*." His re-creation of historical moments reminds me in subject, but not in style, of Robert Lowell's strong historicity. A further and fundamental quality of his poetry is his philosophy of correspondences. Dubie gives us great insight into the parallels and interrelationships of living things. (As a priest walks home at night, "he picks up his robes, they leave / a figure in the snow / like when a rabbit is grabbed by a snare....") History often intrudes upon us in these poems with unexpected violence, or tenderness: "A giant with black hair has kicked through the double doors; / with a machine gun sprays you back and forth. And then tosses / a flower onto the floor."

The Illustrations contains Dubie's finest work yet. His poems are longer and more memorable; his voice has greater authority and control. His poems affirm life, even in its most terrible moments. To live is to struggle, these poems so often say, but the struggle also has its brief rewards, its moments of pleasure, its illuminations. His poetry does not give us the unity of a single place and time, but it gives a unity nonetheless. From separate, seemingly disparate images, he presents a unifying tableau of humanity, from its tragic to its humorous guises. ("The bald heads of two priests can be seen / like the white buttocks of the lovers fleeing into the trees.") One of Dubie's personae comments, "I want to know what is going / to happen to everyone"— a statement that is close to the heart of Norman Dubie's imaginative brilliance.

—John R. Cooley

DUDEK, Louis. Canadián. Born in Montreal, Quebec, 6 February 1918. Educated at Montreal High School; McGill University, Montreal, B.A. 1939; Columbia University, New York, M.A. in history 1946, Ph.D. in English and comparative literature 1955. Married 1) Stephanie Zuperko in 1943 (divorced, 1965); 2) Aileen Collins in 1970; one son. Instructor in English, City College of New York, 1946-51. Since 1951, Member of the Department of English, and since 1969, Greenshields Professor of English, McGill University. Associated with *First Statement* magazine, Montreal, 1941-43; Editor, McGill Poetry Series, 1956-66, and *Delta*, Montreal, 1957-66; former Publisher, Contact Press, Toronto, and Delta Canada Press, Montreal. Currently, Publisher, DC Books, Montreal. Director-at-Large, Canadian Council of Teachers of English; Member, Humanities Research Council of Canada. Recipient: Quebec Literary Award, 1968. Address: 5 Ingleside Avenue, Montreal, Quebec H3Z 1N4 Canada.

PUBLICATIONS

Verse

Unit of Five, with others, edited by Ronald Hambleton.   Toronto, Ryerson Press, 1944.
East of the City.   Toronto, Ryerson Press, 1946.
The Searching Image.   Toronto, Ryerson Press, 1952.
Cerberus, with Irving Layton and Raymond Souster.   Toronto, Contact Press, 1952.
Twenty-Four Poems.   Toronto, Contact Press, 1952.
Europe.   Toronto, Laocoon Press, 1954.
The Transparent Sea.   Toronto, Contact Press, 1956.
En México.   Toronto, Contact Press, 1958.
Laughing Stalks.   Toronto, Contact Press, 1958.
Atlantis.   Montreal, Delta Canada, 1967.
Collected Poetry.   Montreal, Delta Canada, 1971.
Epigrams.   Montreal, DC, 1975.
Selected Poems.   Ottawa, Golden Dog Press, 1975.
Cross-Section: Poems 1940-1980.   Toronto, Coach House Press, 1980.
Poems from Atlantis.   Ottawa, Golden Dog Press, 1980.
Continuation 1.   Montreal, Véhicule Press, 1981.

Recording: *The Green Beyond*, CBC, 1973.

Other

Literature and the Press: A History of Printing, Printed Media, and Their Relation to Literature.   Toronto, Ryerson Press-Contact Press, 1960.
The First Person in Literature.   Toronto, CBC Publications, 1967.
DK: Some Letters of Ezra Pound.   Montreal, DC, 1974.
Selected Essays and Criticism.   Ottawa, Tecumseh Press, 1978.
Technology and Culture.   Ottawa, Golden Dog Press, 1979.
Ideas for Poetry.   Montreal, Véhicule Press, 1983.

Editor, with Irving Layton, *Canadian Poems 1850-1952*.   Toronto, Contact Press, 1952; revised edition, 1953.
Editor, *Selected Poems*, by Raymond Souster.   Toronto, Contact Press, 1956.
Editor, *Montréal, Paris d'Amérique / Paris of America*, photographs by Michel Régnier.   Montreal, Editions du Jour, 1961.
Editor, *Poetry of Our Time: An Introduction to Twentieth-*

Century Poetry, Including Modern Canadian Poetry. Toronto, Macmillan, 1965.
Editor, with Michael Gnarowski, *The Making of Modern Poetry in Canada: Essential Articles on Contemporary Canadian Poetry in English*. Toronto, Ryerson Press, 1967.
Editor, *All Kinds of Everything: Worlds of Poetry*. Toronto, Clarke Irwin, 1973.

*

Bibliography: *Louis Dudek: A Check-list* by Karol W.J. Wenek, Ottawa, Golden Dog Press, 1975.

Critical Studies: "A Critic of Life: Louis Dudek as Man of Letters" by Wynne Francis, in *Canadian Literature* (Vancouver), Autumn 1964; "Louis Dudek Issue" of *Yes 14* (Montreal), September 1965; *The Oxford Anthology of Canadian Literature* edited by Robert Weaver and William Toye, Toronto, Oxford University Press, 1973; *Louis Dudek and Raymond Souster* by Frank Davey, Vancouver, Douglas and McIntyre, 1980, Seattle, University of Washington Press, 1981; "Louis Dudek: Texts and Essays" edited by B.P. Nichol and Frank Davey, in *Open Letter* (Toronto), Summer 1981.

*   *   *

> I hate travel
> but all the poetry I've ever written
> seems to be about travel.

Louis Dudek was born in Montreal; lives in Montreal; always returns to the harbour of his birthright and local knowledge. And with all this adherence to place, to the environment which formed him and the context which identifies him, he is constant voyager. He is the true Balboa of Canada; eternally discovering his Pacifics with courage and resourcefulness and accumulation of stubborn wonder.

His outer life is witness to this. He is the instigator to farther horizons. He brings back his horizons to where he lives with others; teaching the young, instituting vehicles of expression, implementing starting-points. He is a professor of European literature and modern poetry at McGill University; he set up in type and launched ten years of excitement in his magazine *Delta*; helped found and keep alive for new books of poetry Contact Press, and his present Delta Press. His energy is witnessed in a hundred places.

His poetry is witness. The energy and driving aesthetic are put into his books for anyone to have; shaped, committing, intellectual and passionate. Fourteen volumes, starting way back over forty years ago. He was written off by the pundits on his seventh, 25 years ago. What did they know? What does anyone know about a poet's timing? His genius is to stop the clocks. Dudek has always stopped clocks. He stops them always at the present. In *Atlantis* we have the accumulated wisdom and resolutions of the eternal voyager, this Canadian of regional placement shaping in poetry his Pacific. Cosmic regionalism the university tailors of literature call it, stitching on their labels. Dudek takes a trip and comes up with a contemporary epic; goes to Naples, Rome, Paris and London, and brings them back to Montreal. A Ulysses and his Ithaca. He is after what is worth of the past for the illumination of the present. Others have poetically descended from Ezra Pound but none has practised Pound with more affinity and cogency than Dudek.

What is Dudek's City of Dioce whose walls are seven of seven colours? First, and a first which makes the others of little matter, first: all-encompassing love, Walt Whitman's love, love that is human compassion—and love not left romantic. Dudek has sufficient knowledge of the negative that is everywhere, alas:

> The price is suffering,
>   it doesn't matter.
> "We've had it, Chiquita."
>   (The waste if frightening.)
> What does matter is the dawn,
> The nimbus, the brief light of love.
> Try standing in the sun for a minute once a day.

And there Dudek does stand, his minute in the sun, before the horrendous world innocent so that he can have wonder.

Wonder crowds his mind; a broken stick, a newly patched farmhouse in Way's Mills—his corner of the Eastern Townships in Quebec far enough away from the halls of McGill's academia in Montreal for him to enter into new wonders—all of this made to trip up old habit and thus stimulate wondrous recovery. There is danger in a continual intellectual business of assessing the newly found: passion gives way to lucubration, statement humiliates exhibition—concurrently and inevitably rhythm becomes unstructured and music is disinherited. His record of poetic moments being explored in his series called *Continuations* becomes, he himself says, "a poetic gurgle."

But the danger is self-imposed. He escapes. We are left with what we are always left with, reading Dudek: illuminations.

He has the answer, this poet of Canada:

> Always everywhere
>   to treat everyone as a person
> worthy and serious, and vulnerable to love.

—Ralph Gustafson

———————

DUGAN, Alan. American. Born in Brooklyn, New York, 12 February 1923. Educated at Queens College, New York; Olivet College, Michigan; Mexico City College, B.A. 1951. Served in the United States Army Air Force during World War II. Married to Judith Shahn. Worked in advertising, publishing and for a medical supply company; taught at Sarah Lawrence College, Bronxville, New York, 1967-71. Since 1971, Staff Member for Poetry, Fine Arts Work Center, Provincetown, Massachusetts. Recipient: Yale Series of Younger Poets Award, 1961; Pulitzer Prize, 1962; National Book Award, 1962; American Academy in Rome Fellowship, 1962; Guggenheim Fellowship, 1963, 1972; Rockefeller Fellowship, 1966; Levinson Prize (*Poetry*, Chicago), 1967; Shelley Memorial Award, 1982. Address: c/o Ecco Press, 1 West 30th Street, New York, New York 10001, U.S.A.

PUBLICATIONS

Verse

General Prothalamion in Populous Times. Privately printed, 1961.
Poems. New Haven, Connecticut, Yale University Press, 1961.
Poems 2. New Haven, Connecticut, Yale University Press, 1963.
Poems 3. New Haven, Connecticut, Yale University Press, 1967.

Collected Poems. New Haven, Connecticut, Yale University Press, 1969; London, Faber, 1970.
Poems 4. Boston, Little Brown, 1974.
Sequence. Cambridge, Massachusetts, Dolphin, 1976.
New and Collected Poems 1961-1983. New York, Ecco Press, 1983.

*   *   *

Alan Dugan is a fine poet who has created a significant body of work while cultivating a confining style and exercising his caustic intelligence on a relatively narrow range of subjects. One does not get terribly excited about his work, but one nevertheless returns to it with increasing regularity, for it successfully inhabits that middle ground of experience which our best poets today seem to loathe to admit. In Dugan, at least, if one is able to hope at all, he hopes to endure rather than to triumph. If one feels trapped, he will strive not for ultimate freedom and total indepedence, but for the sensation of freedom, temporary, imperfect, illusory. Dugan's spirit is best expressed in the conditional, which is to say that nothing he feels or thinks is very far removed from regret for what might have been. It has been generally accepted that Dugan is something of a moralist, and I suppose it is possible to go along with such a view if we understand a moralist to be someone who experiences convulsive fits of nausea from time to time, whenever he remembers what he is and to what he has given his approval if only by means of undisturbed acquiescence. Dugan's is an intensely private, almost a claustrophobic vision, and his poems usually communicate small perceptions appropriate to the lives of small people, so that we listen not because of any glittering eye, but because we feel we should. The voice that apprehends us is as earnest as any we might hope to encounter, and the combination of brittle surfaces and an underlying warmth is relentlessly imposing.

Dugan's poems have variety, but they might all be drawn together as a single long poem. The same alert but static sensibility is operant in all of them, and the speaker rarely indulges the sort of emotional extremism which might distinguish his more inspired from his more characteristically quotidian utterences. Particulars in the work are easily reducible to an elementary abstraction in which polarities are anxiously opposed until, under the wry focus of Dugan's imagination, they somehow coalesce. Alternatives become merely matters of perspective, and the wise man gradually learns that as between one choice and another, we had best avoid choices altogether.

The predictable, low-keyed humor, so often remarked upon by others, does little to mitigate the stinging venom of self-contempt that courses through so much of Dugan's work. His is a bitter eloquence. If the cadence is austere, it is rarely impoverished, and the muscular flow of his terse diction is rarely purchased at the expense of complexity. Dugan invites us to witness with him, without any redemptive qualification, the sordid spectacle of our common humiliation. It is a strangely unimpassioned witnessing, but the amusement of ironic detachment has much to recommend it, or so it would seem. What Dugan fears most is that neutrality which predicts the death of the spirit, but more and more it appears to him that this is indeed his most authentic reality.

—Robert Boyers

DUNCAN, Robert (Edward). American. Born Edward Howard Duncan in Oakland, California, 7 January 1919; adopted in 1920 and given name Robert Edward Symmes. Educated at the University of California, Berkeley, 1936-38, 1948-50. Editor, *Experimental Review,* 1938-40, *Phoenix,* and *Berkeley Miscellany,* 1948-49, all in Berkeley. Lived in Mallorca, 1955-56. Taught at Black Mountain College, North Carolina, 1956; Assistant Director of the Poetry Center (Ford grant), 1956-57, and Lecturer in the Poetry Workshop, 1965, San Francisco State College; Lecturer, University of British Columbia, Vancouver, 1963. Recipient: Union League Civic and Arts Foundation Prize, 1957, Harriet Monroe Memorial Prize 1960, Levinson Prize, 1964, and Eunice Tietjens Memorial Prize 1967 (*Poetry,* Chicago); Guggenheim Fellowship, 1963; National Endowment for the Arts grant, 1966 (two grants). Address: c/o New Directions, 80 Eighth Avenue, New York, New York 10011, U.S.A.

PUBLICATIONS

Verse

Heavenly City, Earthly City. Berkeley, California, Bern Porter, 1947.
Poems 1948-1949. Berkeley, California, Berkeley Miscellany, 1950.
Medieval Scenes. San Francisco, Centaur Press, 1950.
The Song of the Border-Guard. Black Mountain, North Carolina, Black Mountain College, 1952.
Fragments of a Disordered Devotion. Privately printed, 1952.
Caesar's Gate: Poems 1949-1950. Palma, Mallorca, Divers Press, 1955.
Letters. Highlands, North Carolina, Jargon, 1958.
Selected Poems. San Francisco, City Lights, 1959.
The Opening of the Field. New York, Grove Press, 1960; London, Cape, 1969.
Roots and Branches. New York, Scribner, 1964; London, Cape, 1970.
Writing, Writing: A Composition Book of Madison 1953, Stein Imitations. Albuquerque, New Mexico, Sumbooks, 1964.
Wine. Berkeley, California, Oyez, 1964.
Uprising. Berkeley, California, Oyez, 1965.
A Book of Resemblances: Poems 1950-1953. New Haven, Connecticut, Henry Wenning, 1966.
Of the War: Passages 22-27. Berkeley, California, Oyez, 1966.
The Years As Catches: First Poems 1939-1946. Berkeley, California, Oyez, 1966.
Boob. Privately printed, 1966.
Epilogos. Los Angeles, Black Sparrow Press, 1967.
The Cat and the Blackbird. San Francisco, White Rabbit Press, 1967.
Christmas Present, Christmas Presence! Los Angeles, Black Sparrow Press, 1967.
Bending the Bow. New York, New Directions, 1968; London, Cape, 1971.
My Mother Would Be a Falconess. Berkeley, California, Oyez, 1968.
Names of People. Los Angeles, Black Sparrow Press, 1968.
The First Decade: Selected Poems 1940-1950. London, Fulcrum Press, 1968.
Derivations: Selected Poems 1950-1956. London, Fulcrum Press, 1968.
Play Time, Pseudo Stein. New York, Poets Press, 1969.
Achilles' Song. New York, Phoenix Book Shop, 1969.
Poetic Disturbances. San Francisco, Maya, 1970.

Bring It Up from the Dark. Berkeley, California, Cody's Books, 1970.

Tribunals: Passages 31-35. Los Angeles, Black Sparrow Press, 1970.

In Memoriam Wallace Stevens. Storrs, University of Connecticut, 1972.

Poems from the Margins of Thom Gunn's Moly. Privately printed, 1972.

A Seventeenth Century Suite. Privately printed, 1973.

An Ode and Arcadia, with Jack Spicer. Berkeley, California, Ark Press, 1974.

Dante. Canton, New York, Institute of Further Studies, 1974.

The Venice Poem. Sydney, Prism, 1975; Burlington, Vermont, Poets' Mimeo, 1978.

Veil, Turbine, Cord, and Bird. New York, Jordan Davies, 1979.

The Five Songs. San Diego, California, Friends of the USCD Library, 1981.

Ground Work: Before the War. New York, New Directions, 1984.

Recording: *Letters,* Stream.

Plays

Faust Foutu (produced San Francisco, 1955; New York, 1959-60). Published as *Faust Foutu: Act One of Four Acts: A Comic Mask,* San Francisco, White Rabbit Press, 1958; complete edition, as *Faust Foutu: An Entertainment in Four Parts,* Stinson Beach, California, Enkidu Surrogate, 1960.

Medea at Kolchis: The Maiden Head (produced Black Mountain, North Carolina, 1956). Berkeley, California, Oyez, 1965.

Other

The Artist's View. Privately printed, 1952.

On Poetry (radio interview with Eugene Vance). New Haven, Connecticut, Yale University, 1964.

As Testimony: The Poem and the Scene. San Francisco, White Rabbit Press, 1964.

The Sweetness and Greatness of Dante's "Divine Comedy," 1265-1965. San Francisco, Open Space, 1965.

Six Prose Pieces. Rochester, Michigan, Perishable Press, 1966.

The Truth and Life of Myth: An Essay in Essential Autobiography. New York, House of Books, 1968.

65 Drawings: A Selection of 65 Drawings from One Drawing-Book: 1952-1956. Los Angeles, Black Sparrow Press, 1970.

Notes on Grossinger's "Solar Journal: Oecological Sections." Los Angeles, Black Sparrow Press, 1970.

An Interview with George Bowering and Robert Hogg, April 19, 1969. Toronto, Coach House Press, 1971.

Fictive Certainties: Five Essays in Essential Autobiography. New York, New Directions, 1979.

Towards an Open Universe. Portree, Isle of Skye, Aquila, 1982.

*

Manuscript Collection: Bancroft Poetry Archive, University of California, Berkeley.

Critical Studies: "Robert Duncan Issue"of *Origin* (Kyoto), June 1963, *Audit 4* (Buffalo), 1967, and *Maps 6,* 1974; *Godawful Streets of Man* by Warren Tallman, Toronto, Coach House Press, 1976; *The Lost America of Love: Rereading Robert Creeley, Edward Dorn, and Robert Duncan* by Sherman Paul, Baton Rouge, Louisiana State University Press, 1981.

* * *

Following 25 years of intense activity in the life of poetry, relatively little was heard from Robert Duncan in the 1970's, seemingly because of a private decision to publish little for a long period (15 years, it has been said). Duncan retreated to "Ground Work," to what he called, in an unpublished piece, "speculations and appreciations, associations, rantings if need be, phantasies, lectures, nocturnes and mind soul and spirit dances and inventions." Much of this locates both the nature, and the problems, of his work, most of the best of which is in three volumes, *The Opening of the Field, Roots and Branches* and *Bending the Bow,* all collections first published in the 1960's, when the Black Mountain poets, among whom Duncan is a leading figure, were at the height of their energy and influence.

A desire for privacy, an obliqueness, which is a central feature even of his technique, has always been part of Duncan's enigmatic "presence" as a writer. In *The Years as Catches,* which gathers work from his earlier career (1939-46), he says: "From the beginning I had sought not the poem as a discipline or paradigm of my thought and feeling but as a source of feeling and thought, following the movement of an inner impulse and tension rising in the flow of returning vowel sounds and in measuring stresses that formed phrases of a music for me, having to do with mounting waves of feeling and yet incorporating an inner opposition of reproof of such feeling." He speaks of poetry as "at once a dramatic projection and...a magic ritual," of himself as a poet of "many derivations" and as one whose faith is in "the process of poetry itself."

Curiously, when seen in the long perspective of his work, Duncan's first book, *Heavenly City, Earthly City,* was influenced by the British poet George Barker, a romantic *poète maudit,* of whose verse he said later that it "agreed with Freud's concept of the underlying disturbed and disturbing bisexuality of man's nature." Equally, however, Duncan was influenced by the musical metrics of the Tudor poets Wyatt and Surrey. Both influences fed his own early-formed sense of the poem as manipulative magic.

The important influence of Ezra Pound was also present in Duncan's work from very early, combining with that of a little-known poet, Sanders Russell, to develop in Duncan an aesthetic, almost a mystique, of awareness. Pound's middle cantos (LII-LXXI) helped strengthen Duncan's already acute musical sense, as is manifest in the early "Persephone":

memory: farfields of morning,
   maimd winter, wheel & hoofhammerd weeds,
bare patches of earth. We heard rumor of the rape
among the women who wait at the wells with dry urns,
talk among leaves and among the old men
who sift tincans and seashells searching for driftwood
to make fires on cold hearthstones.

(The spelling here, the elided "e," is a convention adopted later.) Duncan makes a related point, made earlier by Eliot and Valéry: "When a rhythm began in my writing it would career me on into a dimension in which fantasy, the glow and fusion of images... would take over." Later, stating his aesthetic for Donald Allen's *The New American Poetry 1945-60,* Duncan showed that his position was fundamentally the same—poetry as ritual emerging from a deeper, perhaps divine, level. Meantime he had been saved from total introversion by perceiving his own life as part of a larger human life and in opposition to American capitalism and world *realpolitik*. An early reading of Lorca, and particularly "Ode to the King of Harlem," helped merge in Duncan's psyche the realms of fantasy and reality.

Duncan sees poems as "intentions" towards the one great poem. A certain literariness, derivativeness from other poems or works of art, is paradoxically part of his openness and spontaneity. A further paradox is that he sees art as an alternative reality, a "made" reality (this is explored in the sequence "The Structure of Rime") and yet as part of the process which is the universal whole. In "Rites of Participation" he consents to the insight of Paracelsus, that "the key to man's nature is contained in the larger nature," and his best work gradually enriches and amplifies this insight.

Duncan once cited with approval Gertrude Stein's remark in *Composition as Explanation* that, "The composition is the thing seen by everyone living in the living they are doing." Duncan has shared this sense of process with Charles Olson and Robert Creeley, and like them he is concerned with open form, though the texture of his poetry has the air, at least, of being more traditional. Like Olson, he derives from Edward Sapir the idea that a shared language is a shared experience, so (in a sense) no experience is purely individual and experience has a kind of flowing quality *through* individuals. Duncan's sense of himself as poet is of one joining in a participation mystique (here he is influenced by Geza Roheim's work on the Australian aborigines). In the autobiographical essay "Towards an Open Universe," he has said: "Our consciousness and the poem as a supreme effort of consciousness comes in a dancing organization between personal and cosmic identity." He is fond of using the dance of the bees as a relevant figure. Following Erwin Schrödinger's *What Is Life?* he sees life as interaction between matter and environment, an orderly disequilibrium, which "to the poet means that by its nature life is orderly and that the poem might follow the primary processes of thought and feeling, the immediate impulse of psychic life."

The sheer music of Duncan's best work, combined with what M.L. Rosenthal rightly terms "mystical directness," is exemplified in "Often I Am Permitted to Return to a Meadow," and in the musical qualities especially in, say, "Food for Fire, Food for Thought" and the well-known "A Poem Beginning with a Line by Pindar." Duncan is a flowing, musing poet, the impact of whose work is in its totality rather than in set pieces. Partly this is because he is less interested in statement and meaning than in evocation and incantation. Yet, in the greatest poetry, the two are not inevitably separated. Certainly, "one may lose sight of the target in order to gain insight of the target," as Duncan once observed in a piece on Olson's Maximus, but this is somewhat like his preference for intuition over wisdom. Need one choose?

Stating these perceived limitations is uncomfortable, for (especially to those engaged in the life of poetry) Duncan's work and example are enormously engaging. There is a kind of modesty, as well as pride, in the way he has presented himself and his work over the years. Among American poets of the last 30 years he is one of the most naturally gifted, and it would be against the grain of those gifts to expect from him a larger quota of "finished" poems, or gilt-edged anthology pieces. Despite a certain lack of imagistic presence, *The Opening of the Field* and *Roots and Branches* are among the richest books of their period in poetic fibre.

—Charles Doyle

DUNN, Douglas (Eaglesham). British. Born in Inchinnan, Renfrewshire, 23 October 1942. Educated at Renfrew High School; Camphill School, Paisley; Scottish School of Librarianship; University of Hull, 1966-69, B.A. in English 1969. Married Lesley Balfour Wallace in 1964 (died, 1981). Library Assistant, Renfrew County Library, Paisley, 1959-62, and Andersonian Library, Glasgow, 1962-64; Assistant Librarian, Akron Public Library, Ohio, 1964-66; Librarian, Chemistry Department Library, University of Glasgow, 1966; Assistant Librarian, Brynmor Jones Library, 1969-71, and Fellow in Creative Writing, 1974-75, University of Hull; Fellow in Creative Writing, University of Dundee, 1981-82; Writer-in-Residence, University of New England, Armidale, New South Wales, and Scottish Arts Council-Australia Council Exchange Fellow, 1984. Poetry Reviewer, *Encounter* magazine, London, 1971-78. Recipient: Eric Gregory Award, 1966; Scottish Arts Council award, 1970; Maugham Award, 1972; Faber Memorial Prize, 1976; Hawthornden Prize, 1982; Society of Authors Travelling Scholarship, 1982. Fellow, Royal Society of Literature, 1981. Agent: A.D. Peters, 10 Buckingham Street, London WC2N 6BU. Address: c/o Faber and Faber Ltd., 3 Queen Square, London WC1N 3AU, England.

PUBLICATIONS

Verse

Terry Street. London, Faber, 1969; New York, Chilmark Press, 1973.
Corgi Modern Poets in Focus 1, with others, edited by Dannie Abse. London, Corgi, 1971.
Backwaters. London, The Review, 1971.
Night. London, Poem-of-the-Month Club, 1971.
The Happier Life. London, Faber, and New York, Chilmark Press, 1972.
Love or Nothing. London, Faber, 1974.
Barbarians. London, Faber, 1979.
St. Kilda's Parliament. London, Faber, 1981.
Europa's Lover. Newcastle upon Tyne, Bloodaxe, 1982.
Elegies. London, Faber, 1985.

Plays

Screenplays (verse commentaries): *Early Every Morning*, 1975; *Running*, 1977.

Radio Plays: *Scotsmen by Moonlight*, 1977; *Wedderburn's Slave*, 1980.

Television Play: *Ploughman's Share*, 1979.

Other

Editor, *New Poems 1972-73*. London, Hutchinson, 1973.
Editor, "British Poetry Issue" of *Antaeus 12* (New York), 1973.
Editor, *A Choice of Byron's Verse*. London, Faber, 1974.
Editor, *Two Decades of Irish Writing*. Manchester, Carcanet, and Philadelphia, Dufour, 1975.
Editor, *What Is to Be Given: Selected Poems of Delmore Schwartz*. Manchester, Carcanet, 1976.
Editor, *The Poetry of Scotland*. London, Batsford, 1979.
Editor, *Poetry Supplement 1979*. London, Poetry Book Society, 1979.
Editor, *A Rumoured City: New Poets from Hull*. Newcastle upon Tyne, Bloodaxe, 1982.

Editor, *To Build a Bridge: A Celebration of Verse in Humber-side*. Lincoln, Lincolnshire and Humberside Arts, 1982.

*

Manuscript Collection: Brynmor Jones Library, University of Hull.

*   *   *

Douglas Dunn's first book, *Terry Street*, became famous almost before publication for its deft evocation of life in a working-class suburb of Hull. Bikes, dogshit, perms, cheap perfumes, "old men's long underwear/(Dripping) from sagging clotheslines"—these poems, fulls of lists, dour and unrhymed, filled corners of pages in the *TLS*, *New Statesman*, *London Magazine* in the late 1960's. They seemed to inhabit the same country that was part of Larkin's terrain.

Dunn, however, right from the start, had a way of lifting the end of a poem with an utterly surprising symbol that made the epithet "realist" inappropriate. The second part of the book confirmed that he would not be trapped in a post-Movement stance. Notice, for example, the daring rightness of the first two lines of "Love Poem," and the telling glance at time in the last line:

> I live in you, you live in me;
> We are two gardens haunted by each other.
> Sometimes I cannot find you there,
> There is only the swing creaking, that you have just left,
> Or your favourite book beside the sundial.

The first line echoes with disturbing effect the Book of Common Prayer's prayer of humble access: "that we may evermore dwell in him, and he in us." The whole piece set up a world of implication and nuance that was way beyond the minimalist post-Movementeers of the time.

Terry Street had an unusually loyal readership, and much of that readership must have been disappointed by the second and third books. *The Happier Life* contained some moving lyrics: one, "Billie 'n' Me," tinily but significantly weakened by an alteration from its first publication in *The New Statesman*, a meandering piece about being a poet of Faber's list (that "made it seem like hell," wrote James Fenton), and some flattish rhyming couplets in the Roger Woddis vein. *Love or Nothing* tried the patience of many reviewers with its multi-syllabic obscurity—even the most satisfying poems had a searching, unsatisfying feel. Perhaps Dunn had fallen prey, someone wondered, to that Yeatsian will to *develop*.

But *Barbarians* confirmed that he is one of the very best poets we have. An elegant, technically highly achieved verse is concerned with obscure people—like the inhabitants of Terry Street, but who have dragged themselves out of their "holes in the ground somewhere" to wave their "quaint and terrible grudges" at their masters. A quasi-Marxist presence haunts many of these poems—"Gardeners," for example, with its angry ending, "The Student," and "An artist waiting in a country house." "Transcendance" has this presence, but echoes *Terry Street* in more than one way:

> Fish-smelling bedroom of the gutted heart;
> A port town built for departures, dockside bars—
> Flat town, that's warm and sleazy, here's your art:
> A climb on excrement to reach the stars.

St. Kilda's Parliament also looks at the problems of the obscure—"That absinthe drinker and his sober wife"—but more often than before through the eyes of art. Dunn's vision of the ordinary man has matured, the rhythms have tightened, taking our attention from the first lines of the opening poem ("on either side of a rock-paved lane,/Two files of men are standing bare-foot,/Bearded, waistcoated...") to the last poem, a half-self-mocking, sensuous meditation on Ratatouille, love, and the terrible danger implicit for us all in modern politics.

Dunn has published several long poems since *St. Kilda's Parliament* exclusively concerned with bereavement. They are by their nature difficult to comment on, but they are very moving and technically brilliant. Dunn has always been interested in images of clothes. "All that time," he wrote in *Terry Street*, "I had been in love with a coat," and later he observes himself infatuated with Billie Holiday and impersonating a sophisticate "in my white tuxedo." Now his poems centre on "Empty, perfumed wardrobes" where "...once hung the silks and prints of 'If/Only,' and the clothes she gave to her friends."

Dunn is one of the more important poets of our time: resolutely honest, going deeper than glossy surfaces.

—Fred Sedgwick

DUNN, Stephen. American. Born in New York City, 24 June 1939. Educated at Hofstra University, Hempstead, New York, 1958-62, B.A. in history 1962; New School for Social Research, New York, 1964-66; Syracuse University, New York, 1968-70, M.A. in creative writing 1970. Served in the United States Army. Married Lois Kelly in 1964; two daughters. Professional basketball player for the Williamsport Billies, Pennsylvania, 1962-63; copywriter, National Biscuit Company, New York, 1963-66; Assistant Editor, Ziff-Davis, publishers, New York, 1967-68; Assistant Professor of Creative Writing, Southwest Minnesota State College, Marshall, 1970-73. Since 1974, Associate Professor, then Professor, Stockton State College, New Jersey. Visiting Poet, Syracuse University, 1973-74, and University of Washington, Seattle, Winter 1979. Recipient: Academy of American Poets prize, 1970; National Endowment for the Arts Fellowship, 1973, 1982; Bread Loaf Writers Conference Robert Frost Fellowship, 1975; Theodore Roethke Prize (*Poetry Northwest*), 1977; New Jersey Arts Council fellowship, 1979, 1983; Guggenheim Fellowship, 1984. Address: 445 Chestnut Neck Road, Port Republic, New Jersey 08241, U.S.A.

PUBLICATIONS

Verse

Five Impersonations. Marshall, Minnesota, Ox Head Press, 1971.
Looking for Holes in the Ceiling. Amherst, University of Massachusetts Press, 1974.
Full of Lust and Good Usage. Pittsburgh, Carnegie Mellon University Press, 1976.
A Circus of Needs. Pittsburgh, Carnegie Mellon University Press, 1978.
Work and Love. Pittsburgh, Carnegie Mellon University Press, 1981.
Not Dancing. Pittsburgh, Carnegie Mellon University Press, 1984.

Other

Editor, *A Cat of Wind, An Alibi of Gifts* (anthology of children's poetry). Trenton, New Jersey State Council on the Arts, 1977.
Editor, *Silence Has a Rough, Crazy Weather* (poems by deaf children). Trenton, New Jersey State Council on the Arts, 1979.

*

Stephen Dunn comments:

I write what I discover to be true or effective or moving in the act of writing. Then I rewrite for coherence and, ideally, beauty. Certain obsessions emerge. I have a vague idea what they are, but I don't wish to know them too consciously. I want the poem to emerge from my own imperatives and reach out to the reader, naturally, clearly, as if I had cut through all the sanctioned lies, and was simply speaking.

*   *   *

The voice of Stephen Dunn's poems is sure, lyric, and comic, with just the proper mixture of love and of distance from those nearest him. There is also a persistent note of joy in his work, even as he struggles to feel at home in an occasionally inhospitable world. In "Truck Stop: Minnesota," for example, "The waitress looks at my face as if it were a small tip," the customer says, trying to win a friendly response from a woman treated familiarly by regular customers, the truckers, who call her "Sweetheart,... Honey. Doll." "She is the America I would like to love," the speaker admits, warily. "I'm full of lust and good usage, lost here."

It is Dunn's lust for life that makes him ill-at-ease, when he insists upon saying hello to everyone on Main Street in "Small Town: The Friendly" and in wanting to know, as he stalks the beach, in "A Private Man Confronts His Vulgarities at Dawn," "how/to cherish all of this, and just how many debts/a body is allowed." Not surprisingly, he feels most at home among salesmen and degenerates, "men with raincoats/on their laps, who chew their sleeves," as they watch a pornographic film, in "Visiting the City Again":

> We are comrades in a way; alone, embarrassed
> when the lights go on.
> I step into the men's room to pee and wash up.
> There are four feet in one stall, their owners
> have heard me and are still.
> I do what I came for, quickly,
> and walk out into the cold Minneapolis air,
> inexplicably pleased.

The joy of Dunn's poems grows out of their insistence on the "this-ness" of the body, a refusal to ignore its pleasures, in the midst of awkwardness and pain. The speaker wants to wear his body naturally and pleasantly, but someone or something reminds him continually that it just won't do. In "Modern Dance Class," for example, "the instructor looks at me/the way gas station attendants/look at tires whose treads are gone." And the dancer, who knows "grace/is what occurs after technique/has been loved a long while/and then forgotten," tries hard to pull himself together. The reader's enjoyment of such poems is a direct result of the poet's successful rendering of his and of our difficulty in doing so.

Stephen Dunn has accurately described the speaker in his poems as "the normal man, gone public," the person whose "private little efforts/to fulfill himself/are/not unlike yours, or anyone's." And there is something approaching perfection in the way his work combines appreciation and satire, with its simplicity of language and intelligence of style. His poems of love and recollection, including "Those of Us Who Think We Know" and "The Visitant," are as beautiful, in their rightness, as the comic poems.

—Michael True

DURRELL, Lawrence (George). British. Born in Julundur, India, 27 February 1912. Educated at the College of St. Joseph, Darjeeling, India; St. Edmund's School, Canterbury, Kent. Married 1) Nancy Myers in 1935 (divorced, 1947); 2) Eve Cohen in 1947 (divorced); 3) Claude Durrell in 1961 (died, 1967); 4) Ghislaine de Boysson in 1973 (divorced, 1979); two daughters. Has had many jobs, including jazz pianist (Blue Peter nightclub, London), automobile racer, and real estate agent. Lived in Corfu, 1934-40. Editor, with Henry Miller and Alfred Perlès, *The Booster* (later *Delta*), Paris, 1937-39; Columnist, *Egyptian Gazette*, Cairo, 1941; Editor, with Robin Fedden and Bernard Spencer, *Personal Landscape*, Cairo, 1942-45; Special Correspondent in Cyprus for *The Economist*, London, 1953-55; Editor, *Cyprus Review*, Nicosia, 1954-55. Taught at the British Institute, Kalamata, Greece, 1940. Foreign Service Press Officer, British Information Office, Cairo, 1941-44; Press Attaché, British Information Office, Alexandria, 1944-45; Director of Public Relations for the Dodecanese Islands, Greece, 1946-47; Director of the British Council Institute, Cordoba, Argentina, 1947-48; Press Attaché, British Legation, Belgrade, 1949-52; Director of Public Relations for the British Government in Cyprus, 1954-56. Andrew Mellon Visiting Professor of Humanities, California Institute of Technology, Pasadena, 1974. Has lived in France since 1957. Recipient: Duff Cooper Memorial Prize, 1957; Foreign Book Prize (France), 1959. Fellow, Royal Society of Literature, 1954. Address: c/o Grindlay's Bank, 13 St. James's Square, London S.W.1, England.

PUBLICATIONS

Verse

Quaint Fragment: Poems Written Between the Ages of Sixteen and Nineteen. London, Cecil Press, 1931.
Ten Poems. London, Caduceus Press, 1932.
Ballade of Slow Decay. Privately printed, 1932.
Bromo Bombastes: A Fragment from a Laconic Drama by Gaffer Peeslake. London, Caduceus Press, 1933.
Transition. London, Caduceus Press, 1934.
Mass for the Old Year. Privately printed, 1935.
Proems: An Anthology of Poems, with others. London, Fortune Press, 1938.
A Private Country. London, Faber, 1943.
The Parthenon: For T.S. Eliot. Privately printed, 1945 (?).
Cities, Plains, and People. London, Faber, 1946.
On Seeming to Presume. London, Faber, 1948.
A Landmark Gone. Privately printed, 1949.
Deus Loci. Ischia, Italy, Di Mato Vito, 1950.
Private Drafts. Nicosia, Cyprus, Proodos Press, 1955.
The Tree of Idleness and Other Poems. London, Faber, 1955.

Selected Poems. London, Faber, and New York, Grove Press, 1956.
Collected Poems. London, Faber, and New York, Dutton, 1960; revised edition, 1968.
Penguin Modern Poets 1, with Elizabeth Jennings and R.S. Thomas. London, Penguin, 1962.
Poetry. New York, Dutton, 1962.
Beccaffico Le Becfigue (English, with French translation by F.-J. Temple). Montpellier, France, La Licorne, 1963.
A Persian Lady. Edinburgh, Tragara Press, 1963.
Selected Poems 1935-1963. London, Faber, 1964.
The Ikons and Other Poems. London, Faber, 1966; New York, Dutton, 1967.
The Red Limbo Lingo: A Poetry Notebook for 1968-1970. London, Faber, and New York, Dutton, 1971.
On the Suchness of the Old Boy. London, Turret, 1972.
Vega and Other Poems. London, Faber, 1973.
Lifelines. Edinburgh, Tragara Press, 1974.
Selected Poems, edited by Alan Ross. London, Faber, 1977.
Collected Poems 1931-1974, edited by James A. Brigham. London, Faber, and New York, Viking Press, 1980.

Plays

Sappho: A Play in Verse (produced Hamburg, 1959; Edinburgh, 1961; Evanston, Illinois, 1964). London, Faber, 1950; New York, Dutton, 1958.
Acte (produced Hamburg, 1961). London, Faber, and New York, Dutton, 1965.
An Irish Faustus: A Morality in Nine Scenes (produced Sommerhausen, Germany, 1966). London, Faber, 1963; New York, Dutton, 1964.
Judith (shortened version of screenplay), in *Woman's Own* (London), 26 February-2 April 1966.

Screenplays: *Cleopatra*, with others, 1963; *Judith*, with others, 1966.

Radio Script: *Greek Peasant Superstitions*, 1947.

Television Scripts: *The Lonely Roads*, with Diane Deriaz, 1970; *The Search for Ulysses* (USA); *Lawrence Durrell's Greece*; *Lawrence Durrell's Egypt.*

Recording: *Ulysses Come Back: Sketch for a Musical* (story, music, and lyrics by Durrell), 1971.

Novels

Pied Piper of Lovers. London, Cassell, 1935.
Panic Spring (as Charles Norden). London, Faber, and New York, Covici Friede, 1937.
The Black Book: An Agon. Paris, Obelisk Press, 1938; New York, Dutton, 1960; London, Faber, 1973.
Cefalû. London, Editions Poetry London, 1947; as *The Dark Labyrinth*, London, Ace, 1958; New York, Dutton, 1962.
The Alexandria Quartet. London, Faber, and New York, Dutton, 1962.
  Justine. London, Faber, and New York, Dutton, 1957.
  Balthazar. London, Faber, and New York, Dutton, 1958.
  Mountolive. London, Faber, 1958; New York, Dutton, 1959.
  Clea. London, Faber, and New York, Dutton, 1960.
White Eagles over Serbia. London, Faber, and New York, Criterion, 1957.
The Revolt of Aphrodite. London, Faber, 1974.

Tunc. London, Faber, and New York, Dutton, 1968.
Nunquam. London, Faber, and New York, Dutton, 1970.
Monsieur; or, The Prince of Darkness. London, Faber, 1974; New York, Viking Press, 1975.
Livia; or, Buried Alive. London, Faber, 1978; New York, Viking Press, 1979.
Constance; or, Solitary Practices. London, Faber, and New York, Viking Press, 1982.
Sebastian; or, Ruling Passions. London, Faber, 1983; New York, Viking Press, 1984.

Short Stories

Zero, and Asylum in the Snow. Privately printed, 1946; as *Two Excursions into Reality*, Berkeley, California, Circle, 1947.
Esprit de Corps: Sketches from Diplomatic Life. London, Faber, 1957; New York, Dutton, 1958.
Stiff Upper Lip: Life among the Diplomats. London, Faber, 1958; New York, Dutton, 1959.
Sauve Qui Peut. London, Faber, 1966; New York, Dutton, 1967.
The Best of Antrobus. London, Faber, 1974.

Other

Prospero's Cell: A Guide to the Landscape and Manners of the Island of Corcyra. London, Faber, 1945; with *Reflections on a Marine Venus*, New York, Dutton, 1960.
Key to Modern Poetry. London, Peter Nevill, 1952; as *A Key to Modern British Poetry*, Norman, University of Oklahoma Press, 1952.
Reflections on a Marine Venus: A Companion to the Landscape of Rhodes. London, Faber, 1953; with *Prospero's Cell*, New York, Dutton, 1960.
Bitter Lemons (on Cyprus). London, Faber, 1957; New York, Dutton, 1958.
Art and Outrage: A Correspondence about Henry Miller Between Alfred Perlès and Lawrence Durrell, with an Intermission by Henry Miller. London, Putnam, 1959; New York, Dutton, 1960.
Groddeck (on Georg Walther Groddeck). Wiesbaden, Limes, 1961.
Briefwechsel über "Actis", with Gustaf Gründgens. Hamburg, Rowohlt, 1961.
Lawrence Durrell and Henry Miller: A Private Correspondence, edited by George Wickes. New York, Dutton, and London, Faber, 1963.
La Descente du Styx (English, with French translations by F.-J. Temple). Montpellier, France, La Murène, 1964; as *Down the Styx*, Santa Barbara, California, Capricorn Press, 1971.
Spirit of Place: Letters and Essays on Travel, edited by Alan G. Thomas. London, Faber, and New York, Dutton, 1969.
Le Grand Suppositoire (interview with Marc Alyn). Paris, Belfond, 1972; as *The Big Supposer*, London, Abelard Schuman, and New York, Grove Press, 1973.
The Happy Rock (on Henry Miller). London, Village Press, 1973; Belfast, Maine, Bern Porter, 1982.
The Plant-Magic Man. Santa Barbara, California, Capra Press, 1973.
Blue Thirst. Santa Barbara, California, Capra Press, 1975.
Sicilian Carousel. London, Faber, and New York, Viking Press, 1977.
The Greek Islands. London, Faber, and New York, Viking Press, 1978.

A Smile in the Mind's Eye. London, Wildwood House, 1980;
New York, Universe, 1982.
*Literary Lifelines: The Richard Aldington-Lawrence Durrell
Correspondence*, edited by Harry T. Moore and Ian S. Mac-
Niven. New York, Viking Press, and London, Faber, 1981.

Editor, with others, *Personal Landscape: An Anthology of Exile.*
London, Editions Poetry London, 1945.
Editor, *A Henry Miller Reader.* New York, New Directions,
1959; as *The Best of Henry Miller*, London, Heinemann,
1960.
Editor, *New Poems 1963*. London, Hutchinson, 1963.
Editor, *Lear's Corfu: An Anthology Drawn from the Painter's
Letters*. Corfu, Corfu Travel, 1965.
Editor, *Wordsworth*. London, Penguin, 1973.

Translator, *Six Poems from the Greek of Sikelianos and Seferis.*
Privately printed, 1946.
Translator, with Bernard Spencer and Nanos Valaoritis, *The
King of Asine and Other Poems*, by George Seferis. Lon-
don, Lehmann, 1948.
Translator, *The Curious History of Pope Joan*, by Emmanuel
Royidis. London, Verschoyle, 1954; revised edition, as
Pope Joan: A Romantic Biography, London, Deutsch, 1960;
New York, Dutton, 1961.

*

Bibliography: *Lawrence Durrell: An Illustrated Checklist* by
Alan G. Thomas and James A. Brigham, Carbondale, Southern
Illinois University Press, 1983.

Manuscript Collections: University of California, Los Angeles;
University of Illinois, Urbana.

Critical Studies: *The World of Lawrence Durrell* edited by
Harry T. Moore, Carbondale, Southern Illinois University
Press, 1962; *Lawrence Durrell* by John Unterecker, New York,
Columbia University Press, 1964; *Lawrence Durrell* by John A.
Weigel, New York, Twayne, 1966; *Lawrence Durrell: A Critical
Study*, London, Faber, 1968, New York, Dutton, 1969, and
Lawrence Durrell, London, Longman, 1970, both by G.S.
Fraser; *Lawrence Durrell Newsletter* (Kelowna, British Colum-
bia).

*   *   *

Lawrence Durrell's world fame is based on his series of novels
of the 1950's, *The Alexandria Quartet*, but critics like Francis
Hope, who dislike these and also the subterranean novel of the
late 1930's, published in Paris, *The Black Book*, see his real
achievement in his poems and in his three travel books, which
have much of the quality of his poems, about Corfu before the
Second World War, Rhodes during its post-war Allied occupation, and Cyprus during the troubles of the early 1950's. Those
who feel that as a novelist Durrell is over-rated would probably
say that in *The Alexandria Quartet* the set scenes, the landscapes, the evocations of local atmosphere are the work of a poet
but that the handling of incident and character is excessively
romantic, in a "story-book" sense. It is oddly true that the tone
and diction of the poems are quieter, more subdued, much less
boldly coloured than much of the prose of *The Alexandria
Quartet* and *Tunc*: Durrell does not seem to be trying so hard,
straining his resources so much, and it may be therefore that as a
poet he is at his most convincing.

There is not much development in the poetry, and in his
collected and selected poems Durrell rightly arranges the poems
according to affinities of kind, tone, or subject-matter rather
than in chronological order. Though he is very obviously a
"modern" poet, he owes a great deal of two of his favourite poets
of the nineteenth century, Landor and Browning. In short lyrics
like "Water Music" he aims at, and often achieves, a Landorian
perfection of form. Longer poems about characters or places
have deliberately a certain Browningesque looseness or roughness of texture, and resemble Browning's dramatic monologues
in setting great figures of the past, Byron, Horace, Rochefou-
cauld, in a perspective of ambiguous self-questioning; but more
obviously than Browning, influenced perhaps by Browning's
disciple Ezra Pound, Durrell is using such figures to express or
sometimes to reject aspects of his own nature.
Poems about places, like the effective "Alexandria," written in
war-time, similarly use a place and sometimes friends and enemies in a place to concretise a creative mood. The place becomes,
as in the good little poem about the cold chaste beauty of the
English West Country, "Bere Regis," a symbol for a whole
complex of attitudes to be savoured, appreciated, perhaps
finally to be relegated to the large category of attitudes which,
for Durrell, are not finally adequate. Durrell is not an objective
poet of landscape like his friend, that fine, neglected poet, Bernard Spencer, but a poet of what may be called moodscape.
A third category of poems is what Robert Graves calls "satires
and grotesques": humorous and fantastic poems, but always in
the end affectionate rather than sharply satirical, like "Unce-
bunke" or "The Ballad of the Good Lord Nelson." There are
some poems like the early "Sonnet of Hamlet" or the later short
"Nemea" where the main interest seems to be in the poetry of
vocabulary, in surprising collocations or strange and beautiful
echoings of words: such poems are perhaps the equivalent of
what T.S. Eliot called "five-finger exercises."
The total impression that one derives from Durrell's poems is
of a benign quietism, something like that of a humorous Chinese
sage gazing on waterfalls from a hut on a mountain. Born in
India, Durrell has always been deeply interested in Eastern
thought, in what he calls the "expurgation" of the self, in the
achievement of states of calm contemplation. This spiritual bent
is expressed, however, in scene or anecdote, strange joke, or
hushed and gentle lyric rather than in abstract or dogmatic
terms. The sage is strangely married, also, to the literary dandy.
Durrell's kind of poetry is today distinctly unfashionable; it is
not confessional, it is not socially committed, its language and
attitudes may seem excessively "literary." It never clamours for
attention. Yet it has always pleased good critics and it will last.

—G.S. Fraser

———————

DUTTON, Geoffrey (Piers Henry). Australian. Born in An-
laby, South Australia, 2 August 1922. Educated at Geelong
Grammar School, Victoria, 1932-39; University of Adelaide,
1940-41; Magdalen College, Oxford, 1946-49, B.A. 1949. Served
in the Royal Australian Air Force, 1941-45: Flight Lieutenant.
Married Ninette Trott in 1944; two sons and one daughter.
Senior Lecturer in English, University of Adelaide, 1954-62;
Commonwealth Fellow in Australian Literature, University of
Leeds, 1960; Visiting Professor, Kansas State University, Man-
hattan, 1962. Editor, Penguin Australia, Melbourne, 1961-65.
Since 1965, Editorial Director of Sun Books Pty. Ltd., Mel-
bourne; since 1980, Editor, *Bulletin Literary Supplement*, Syd-

ney. Co-Founder, *Australian Letters*, Adelaide, 1957, and *Australian Book Review*, Kensington Park, 1962. Member, Australian Council for the Arts, 1968-70, Commonwealth Literary Fund Advisory Board, 1972-73, and Australian Literature Board, 1973-78. Recipient: Grace Leven Prize, 1959. Officer, Order of Australia, 1976. Address: Piers Hill, Williamstown, South Australia 5351, Australia.

PUBLICATIONS

Verse

Night Flight.   Melbourne, Reed and Harris, 1944.
Antipodes in Shoes.   Sydney, Edwards and Shaw, 1955.
Flowers and Fury.   Melbourne, Cheshire, 1963.
On My Island: Poems for Children.   Melbourne, Cheshire, 1967.
Poems Soft and Loud.   Melbourne, Cheshire, 1968.
Findings and Keepings: Selected Poems 1940-1970.   Adelaide, Australian Letters, 1970.
New Poems to 1972.   Adelaide, Australian Letters, 1972.
A Body of Words.   Sydney, Edwards and Shaw, 1977.

Novels

The Mortal and the Marble.   London, Chapman and Hall, 1950.
Andy.   Sydney and London, Collins, 1968.
Tamara.   Sydney and London, Collins, 1970.
Queen Emma of the South Seas.   Melbourne and London, Macmillan, 1976; New York, St. Martin's Press, 1978.
The Prowler.   Sydney, Collins, 1982.
The Eye-Opener.   Brisbane, University of Queensland Press, 1982.

Short Stories

The Wedge-Tailed Eagle.   Melbourne, Macmillan, 1980.

Other

A Long Way South (travel).   London, Chapman and Hall, 1953.
Africa in Black and White.   London, Chapman and Hall, 1956.
States of the Union (travel).   London, Chapman and Hall, 1958.
Founder of a City: The Life of William Light.   Melbourne, Cheshire, and London, Chapman and Hall, 1960.
Patrick White.   Melbourne, Lansdowne Press, 1961; revised edition, London and New York, Oxford University Press, 1971.
Walt Whitman.   Edinburgh, Oliver and Boyd, and New York, Grove Press, 1961.
Paintings of S.T. Gill.   Adelaide, Rigby, 1962.
Russell Drysdale (art criticism).   London, Thames and Hudson, 1962; revised edition, Sydney and London, Angus and Robertson, 1981.
Tisi and the Yabby (juvenile).   Sydney and London, Collins, 1965.
Seal Bay (juvenile).   Sydney and London, Collins, 1966.
The Hero as Murderer: The Life of Edward John Eyre, Australian Explorer and Governor of Jamaica, 1815-1901.   Melbourne, Cheshire, and London, Collins, 1967.
Tisi and the Pageant (juvenile).   Adelaide, Rigby, 1968.
Australia's Last Explorer: Ernest Giles.   London, Faber, 1970.

Australia since the Camera: From Federation to War 1901-14.   Melbourne, Cheshire, 1972.
White on Black: The Australian Aborigine Portrayed in Art.   Melbourne, Macmillan, 1974.
A Taste of History: Geoffrey Dutton's South Australia.   Adelaide, Rigby, 1978.
Patterns of Australia, photographs by Harri Peccinotti.   Melbourne, Macmillan, 1980; London, Macmillan, 1981.
Impressions of Singapore, photographs by Harri Peccinotti.   Melbourne and London, Macmillan, 1981.
S.T. Gill's Australia.   Melbourne, Macmillan, 1981.
The Australian Heroes.   Sydney, Angus and Robertson, 1981; London, Angus and Robertson, 1982.
Country Life in Old Australia.   South Yarra, Victoria, O'Neill, 1982.
In Search of Edward John Eyre.   Melbourne, Macmillan, 1982.

Editor, *The Literature of Australia.*   Melbourne, Penguin, 1964; revised edition, 1976.
Editor, *Modern Australian Writing.*   London, Fontana, 1966.
Editor, *Australia and the Monarchy: A Symposium.*   Melbourne, Sun, 1966.
Editor, with Max Harris, *The Vital Decade: 10 Years of Australian Art and Letters.*   Melbourne, Sun, 1968.
Editor, with Max Harris, *Sir Henry Bjelke, Don Baby, and Friends.*   Melbourne, Sun, 1971.
Editor, *Republican Australia?*   Melbourne, Sun, 1977.

Translator, with Igor Mezhakoff-Koriakin, *Bratsk Station*, by Yevgeny Yevtushenko.   Melbourne, Sun, 1966; New York, Doubleday, 1967; London, Hart Davis, 1968.
Translator, with Igor Mezhakoff-Koriakin, *Fever and Other New Poems*, by Bella Akhmadulina.   Melbourne, Sun, 1968; New York, Morrow, 1969; London, Peter Owen, 1970.
Translator, with Igor Mezhakoff-Koriakin, *Little Woods: Recent Poems*, by Andrei Voznesensky.   Melbourne, Sun, 1972.
Translator, *Kazan University and Other New Poems*, by Yevgeny Yevtushenko.   Melbourne, Sun, 1973.

*

Geoffrey Dutton comments:

My poetry began in the turmoil of war, and the *Angry Penguins* period of modernism in Australia; my poetic thinking was heavily influenced by modern French and German as well as the English and American poetry. I was fortunate enough to be in close contact with a remarkable group of poets in Adelaide in the 1940's, which included Donald Kerr, Max Harris, and Paul Pfeiffer; both Kerr and Pfeiffer were killed in the R.A.A.F. during the war. In Melbourne in 1944 I shared my ideas with the poet Alister Kershaw and the painters Arthur Boyd and Sidney Nolan.

Six years in Oxford, London and France after the war, and friendship with Roy Campbell and Richard Aldington, made me work towards a greater clarity and technical control. My wandering life and return to Australia were reflected in my poems.

In the early 1960's I was much influenced towards attempting a more complex human response to my own country by studying Walt Whitman. In the late 1960's I met and travelled in Russia with the poet Yevgeny Yevtushenko, having with Igor Mezhakoff-Koriakin translated a large number of his poems; with Igor Mezhakoff-Koriakin I also translated Bella Akhmadulina's new poems, and met her on my visits to Russia in 1966 and 1967. In these visits I discovered the vast field of modern Russian poetry, and have learnt a great deal from the modern Russian poets about the relation between poetry and the modern world on both sides of the so-called iron curtain. Also the importance of rhyme and rhythm in Russian has helped shore up my technical beliefs in them at a time when regular rhyme and rhythm have been unpopular.

I think many of the poems which are nearest to what I had hoped they might be are to do with love; it is difficult to write anything about these.

I welcome what has been called the new nationalism in Australia, not for narrow pseudo-patriotic reasons, but because it may help give Australian poets confidence in welcoming the nourishment most good poets draw from the soil in which they grew.

*   *   *

Remarkable for its intrinsic light-heartedness, the poetry of Geoffrey Dutton has tended to be under-rated by most critics while a growing audience of appreciative readers testifies to its inherent qualities.

Despite the light-heartedness, this poet is capable of extended lyrical meditations of a uniquely beautiful nature. His best work to be found in poems such as "Abandoned Airstrip, Northern Territory" in which he recapitulates his memories as a flyer in the Second World War; "Night Fishing," a long nocturne celebrating the shared lives and joys of an Australian couple in love and experiencing the primal mateship of hunters alone in an eternally providing world; and "The Smallest Sprout," a poem written in memory of his mother in which his natural lyricism is enriched by elegiacal overtones.

His recent work has been spread evenly among suites and individual pieces descriptive of his travels in Russia—elsewhere his versions of Yevtushenko are noteworthy—and America, equally appreciative of the most positive as well as the negative aspects of both countries and the inhabitants, and in tart and pungent satires criticising and ridiculing the tasteless and the chauvinistic in modern Australia. His comments in verse on the Vietnamese war show him to be capable of clear-headed and compellingly written poems of protest, but it is in the longer autobiographical poem imbued with lyrical insights and quiet humour that this fine poet's best work is found.

—Bruce Beaver

DYLAN, Bob. American. Born Robert Zimmerman in Duluth, Minnesota, 24 May 1941. Attended the University of Minnesota, Minneapolis, 1960. Composer and performer: concert appearances in the United States, 1961-66, 1971, 1974, 1978, Europe, 1964-66, 1978, 1984, and Australia, 1964-66. Recipient: Emergency Civil Liberties Committee Tom Paine Award, 1963. D.Mus.: Princeton University, New Jersey, 1970. Address: P.O. Box 870, Cooper Station, New York, New York 10276, U.S.A.

PUBLICATIONS

Verse

Tarantula. New York, Macmillan, 1966.
Approximately Complete Works. Amsterdam, De Bezige Bij-Thomas Rap, 1970.
Poem to Joanie. London, Aloes Press, 1972.
Words. London, Cape, 1973.

Writings and Drawings. New York, Knopf, and London, Cape, 1973.
The Songs of Bob Dylan 1966-1975. New York, Knopf, 1976.
XI Outlined Epitaphs, and Off the Top of My Head. London, Aloes Seola, 1981 (?).

Scores: *The Bob Dylan Songbook,* New York, Witmark, 1963; *Songs for Voice and Guitar,* New York, Witmark, 2 vols., 1968; *Bob Dylan's Songs for Harmonica,* New York, Witmark, 1968; *Song Book,* Witmark, 1970.

Recordings: *Bob Dylan Himself,* Columbia, 1962; *The Freewheelin' Bob Dylan,* Columbia, 1963; *The Times They Are A-Changin',* Columbia, 1963; *Another Side of Bob Dylan,* Columbia, 1964; *Bringing It All Back Home,* Columbia, 1965; *Highway 61 Revisited,* Columbia, 1965; *Blonde on Blonde,* Columbia, 1966; *Bob Dylan's Greatest Hits,* Columbia, 1967; *John Wesley Harding,* Columbia, 1968; *Nashville Skyline,* Columbia, 1969; *Self Portrait,* Columbia, 1970; *New Morning,* Columbia, 1970; *Bob Dylan's Greatest Hits, vol. 2,* Columbia, 1971; *Dylan,* Columbia, 1974; *Planet Waves,* Island, 1974; *Before the Flood,* Asylum, 1974; *Blood on the Tracks,* Columbia, 1975; *The Basement Tapes,* CBS, 1975; *Desire,* Columbia, 1976; *Hard Rain,* CBS, 1976; *Street Legal,* CBS, 1978; *Bob Dylan at Budokan,* 1979; *Slow Train Coming,* 1979; *Saved,* 1980; *Shot of Love,* 1981; incidental music for the film *Pat Garrett and Billy the Kid,* 1972.

Other

Bob Dylan in His Own Words, compiled by Miles, edited by Pearce Marchbank. London, Omnibus Press, and New York, Quick Fox, 1978.

*

Critical Studies: *Bob Dylan: A Retrospective* edited by Craig McGregor, New York, Morrow, 1972, revised edition, London, Angus and Robertson, 1980; *Bob Dylan* by Anthony Scaduto, New York, New American Library, 1973; *Rolling Thunder Logbook* by Sam Shepard, New York, Viking Press, 1977, London, Penguin, 1978; *Bob Dylan: An Illustrated History* by Robert Alexander, London, Elm Tree, 1978; *Bob Dylan: His Unreleased Works* by Paul Cable, London, Scorpion-Dark Star, 1978, New York, Associated Music, 1980; *The Art of Bob Dylan, Song and Dance Man* by Michael Gray, London, Hamlyn, and New York, St. Martin's Press, 1981; *Twenty Years of Recording: The Bob Dylan Reference Book* by Michael Korgsgaard, Copenhagen, Scandinavian Institute for Rock Research, 1981; *Bob Dylan: From a Hard Rain to a Slow Train* by Tim Dowley, Tunbridge Wells, Kent, Midas, 1982; *Voice Without Restraint: A Study of Bob Dylan's Lyrics and Their Background* by John Herdman, Edinburgh, Harris, and New York, Delilah, 1982; *Performed Literature: Words and Music by Bob Dylan* by Betsy Bowden, Bloomington, Indiana University Press, 1982; *No Direction Home: The Lives and Times of Bob Dylan* by Robert Shelton, London, New English Library, 1983; *Blood on the Tracks: The Story of Bob Dylan* by Chris Rowley, New York, Proteus, 1983; *A Darker Shade of Pale: A Backdrop to Bob Dylan* by Wilfrid Mellers, London, Faber, 1984.

Theatrical Activites:
Actor: **Films**—*Don't Look Back,* 1965; *Eat the Document,* 1966; *Pat Garrett and Billy the Kid,* 1972; *Renaldo and Clara,* 1978.

*   *   *

Bob Dylan's lyrics spring from two regions of the mind—the Minnesota "North Country" that stands still in time and New York City, the magnification of change. And to Dylan in the late 1950's, constancy seemed oppressive. He went to New York, taking along rhythms and motifs absorbed from folk songs and blues. He wrote of Minnesota and events of the City, but compared to his later verse, these songs were tame. For three reasons: the subjects were not widely known, the person sounded too vulnerable and was prone to melodrama, and Dylan had not learned to integrate images from various sources into a single poem.

He pitched his young voice toward the Byronic, becoming old beyond his years, "an arch criminal who'd done no wrong." Singing like one of the changing instilled confidence:

My road it might be rocky,
The stones might cut my face.
But as some folks ain't got not road at all,
They gotta stand in the same old place.
Hey, hey, so I guess I'm doin' fine.

Satire and protest allowed him to speak vehemently without revealing himself. Encountering bizarre individuals ("I Shall Be Free") or atomic holocaust ("Talking World War III Blues"), he played a victim as irrepressible as Chaplin:

Well, I rung the fallout shelter bell
And I leaned my head and I gave a yell,
"Give me a string bean, I'm a hungry man."
A shotgun fired and away I ran.
I don't blame him too much, though,
He didn't know me.

"I don't like to be stuck in print," he admitted in "11 Outlined Epitaphs." He preferred to watch the night "unwind" because "there's no end t' it / and it's so big." The songs became "nothin' but the unwindin' of / my happiness."

By his fifth album, *Bringing It All Back Home*, Dylan was comfortable with the rhetoric of existentialism. "i accept chaos," he wrote for the liner notes; "i am not sure whether it accepts me." "The / Great Books've been written"; art had to be change, action. This urgency required dynamic language, lucid, rapidly shifting images. The results ranged from the frenetic "Subterranean Homesick Blues" ("Get sick, get well / Hang around the ink well") to "Mr. Tambourine Man" and (perhaps the tightest poem) "Love Minus Zero / No Limit":

The bridge at midnight trembles,
The country doctor rambles.
Bankers' nieces seek perfection,
Expecting all the gifts that wise men bring.
The wind howls like a hammer,
The night blows cold and rainy.
My love she's like some raven
At my window with a broken wing.

Then *Highway 61 Revisited* intensified his achievement. "Like a Rolling Stone" raised pointlessness one power to invisibility. The iconoclast verged on insanity ("Tombstone Blues"). Riding the mailtrain, the wanderer wearily mused, "I went to tell everybody, / But I could not get across." Dylan called the songs "exercises in tonal breath control...the subject matter—though meaningless as it is—has something to do with the beautiful strangers." Indeed, with "Desolation Row" and "Highway 61 Revisited" his early efforts culminated in a visionary intensity.

Most of Dylan's recent lyrics are not compelling poetry. He is more interested, these days, in performance—experimenting with instrumentation, singing *to* an audience rather than protesting *at* them. The elusiveness is gone, the mystique of the seer. When, as in "Lily, Rosemary, and the Jack of Hearts" (*Blood on the Tracks*), he articulates a vision, it is one of compassion. The fast-talking irreverence has given way to a quiet, even grieving voice.

The only sustained handling of this theme of compassion remains *John Wesley Harding* (1968). With parable and heroic folk song for antecedents, Dylan sings his empathy for the oppressed rather than implying it, as before, through attacks on the oppressors. In "I Pity the Poor Immigrant" he creates an outcast who spends himself without assurance of comfort. The suffering figure in "I Dreamed I Saw St. Augustine" moves the singer to tears. "All Along the Watchtower" acknowledges that all is far from well, but insists on affirmation: "There are many here among us who feel that life is but a joke," Dylan advises, harkening to his theme of absurdity; "But you and I, we've been through that, and this is not our fate." Even though there is a sense of foreboding, the watchers are patient, not angry or jeering.

On such occasions, Dylan finds his way back to the North Country, singing griefs that are timeless instead of the grievances that belong to the moment.

—Jay S. Paul

EATON, Charles Edward. American. Born in Winston-Salem, North Carolina, 25 June 1916. Educated at Duke University, Durham, North Carolina, 1932-33; University of North Carolina, Chapel Hill, 1933-36, B.A. 1936 (Phi Beta Kappa); Princeton University, New Jersey, 1936-37; Harvard University Cambridge, Massachusetts, 1938-40, M.A. in English 1940. Married Isabel Patterson in 1950. Instructor, Ruiz Gandia School, Poncé, Puerto Rico, 1937-38; Instructor in Creative Writing, University of Missouri, Columbia, 1940-42; Vice Consul, American Embassy, Rio de Janeiro, Brazil, 1942-46; Professor of Creative Writing, University of North Carolina, 1946-51. Free-lance writer and art critic, and organizer of art shows. Recipient: Bread Loaf Writers Conference Robert Frost fellowship, 1941; Boulder, Colorado, Writers Conference fellowship, 1942; Ridgely Torrence Memorial Award, 1951; Gertrude Boatwright Harris award, 1954; *Arizona Quarterly* award, 1956, 1977, 1979, 1982; New England Poetry Club Golden Rose, 1972; O. Henry award, for fiction, 1972; Alice Fay di Castagnola award, 1974; Arvon Foundation award, 1981; *Hollins Critic* award, 1983. Member, American Academy of Poets. Address: 808 Greenwood Road, Chapel Hill, North Carolina 27514, U.S.A.

PUBLICATIONS

Verse

The Bright Plain. Chapel Hill, University of North Carolina Press, 1942.
The Shadow of the Swimmer. New York, Fine Editions Press, 1951.

The Greenhouse in the Garden. New York, Twayne, 1955.
Countermoves. New York and London, Abelard Schuman, 1962.
On the Edge of the Knife. New York and London, Abelard Schuman, 1969.
The Man in the Green Chair. South Brunswick, New Jersey, A.S. Barnes, and London, Yoseloff, 1977.
Colophon of the Rover. South Brunswick, New Jersey, A.S. Barnes, 1980.
The Thing King. East Brunswick, New Jersey, Cornwall, 1982.

Play

Sea Psalm (produced Chapel Hill, North Carolina, 1933). Published in *North Carolina Drama*, Richmond, Virginia, Garrett and Massie, 1956.

Novel

A Lady of Pleasure. Lunenburg, Vermont, North Country, 1972.

Short Stories

Write Me from Rio. Winston-Salem, North Carolina, John F. Blair, 1959.
The Girl from Ipanema. Lunenburg, Vermont, North Country, 1972.
The Case of the Missing Photographs. South Brunswick, New Jersey, A.S. Barnes, 1978.

Other

Charles and Isabel Eaton Collection of America Paintings. Chapel Hill, University of North Carolina Art Department, 1970.
Karl Knaths. Washington, Connecticut, Shiver Mountain Press, 1971.
Karl Knaths: Five Decades of Painting. Washington, D.C., International Exhibitions Foundation, 1973.
Robert Broderson: Paintings and Graphics. Washington, Connecticut, Shiver Mountain Press, 1975.

*

Manuscript Collections: (verse) Southern Historical Collection, University of North Carolina, Chapel Hill; (prose) Mugar Memorial Library, Boston University.

Critical Studies: by Louise Untermeyer, in *Yale Review* (New Haven, Connecticut), Winter 1944; Robert Hillyer, in *New York Times Book Review*, 22 July 1951; "The Poetry of Charles Edward Eaton" by W.W. Davidson, in *Georgia Review* (Athens), Spring 1956; Gerard P. Meyer, in *Saturday Review* (New York), 31 March 1956; in *Booklist* (Chicago), 1 May 1956; May Swenson, in *Poetry* (Chicago), March 1957; "The Greenhouse in the Garden" by William Carlos Williams, in *Arizona Quarterly* (Tucson), Spring 1957; Wallace Fowlie, in *New York Times Book Review*, 12 May 1963; John Engels in *Poetry* (Chicago), September 1963; F.C. Flint, in *Virginia Quarterly Review* (Charlottesville), Autumn 1963; "Betwixt Tradition and Innovation" by Robert D. Spector, in *Saturday Review* (New York), 26 December 1970; "The Crisis of Regular Forms" by John T. Irwin, in *Sewanee Review* (Tennessee), Winter 1973; "The Shining Figure: Poetry and Prose of Charles Edward Eaton" by Dave Smith, in *Meanjin* (Melbourne), Summer 1974; Robert Miola,

in *Commonweal* (New York), 18 August 1978; M.L. Hester, in *Southern Humanities Review* (Auburn, Alabama), Fall 1979 and Fall 1981; John Hollander, in *Yale Review* (New Haven, Connecticut), Autumn 1983.

Charles Edward Eaton comments:

Though I am resistant in general to definitions of poetry and poets as too limiting, if pressed, I might admit to being a modern formalist, but I should insist on the importance of the qualifying adjective. I compose in a number of verse forms, and write lyrical as well as dramatic poetry, but I do not lean on any poet of the past or present for technical inspiration. I believe that each poet must develop his own organic sense of form and adapt even the most conventional meter to his personal rhythm. For example, a number of my poems are written in triptychs, their long lines rhyming every other line, modulated in an entirely individual way. William Carlos Williams, in a study of my work, called this three line stanza an Americanization of *terza rima*. Perhaps he felt it was very American in its love of freedom and yet somewhat European in its formal allegiance. There is no doubt that I like poetry that is both vigorous and controlled.

In his respect, I think the best short statement about my work has been made by Robert D. Spector in *The Saturday Review*: "Charles Edward Eaton may not belong at all in the category of unconventional poets, and yet, it seems to me, his use of conventions becomes a very personal thing that removes him from tradition.... If Eaton's poetry, with its use of rhymed stanzas, appears superficially to belong to a formal tradition, his long, free lines and sometimes brutal imagery and diction, pushing his feelings to their limit, suggest otherwise. *On the Edge of the Knife* combines conventional and unconventional in such a way that it is finally the poet's own work. Perhaps, after all, that is the way of poetry. Whether bound to tradition or not, its value rests on the peculiar virtues of the poet."

I am in emphatic accord with any statement about my work which indicates that I believe in working powerfully and freely on one's own terms within the entire range of poetry. I am in no sense a reductionist, but have confidence in the fundamental richness of poetry and the surprise lurking in its possibilities. Form should be an energetic expression of the poet's own psychology not an artificial imposition, and the poem should convey some sense of the struggle which went into the formal achievement:

I have a powerful nature in pursuit of pleasure,
Peace, good will, and I do not share
My time's contempt for passion balanced by strict measure.

An extension of what is involved in this position is given at the conclusion of "The Turkey":

So the bird I know is like a gaudy catafalque.
If you should carry a secret hump upon your back,
You, too, would have a burdened and uncertain walk.

This is what it is to spread an image in the sun—
This is how we teach thick, precarious balance as if the land moved like a ship
And one set sail heavily, slowly, encumbered with imagination.

As to my subject matter, it is greatly influenced by where I am living and what I am doing at any given time. In this sense, it is always around me, and it moves forward with me as I go along. Almost every poem, hidden though it may be to the reader, has its *donnée* from some aspect of experience. Landscape wherever I have lived (North Carolina, Puerto Rico, Brazil, Connecticut, etc.) comes strongly into my work, but I do not consider myself a nature poet. Animals and flowers are continuous with and contiguous to my interest in human beings, and are a constant motif in my work, but I am not interested in fauna or flora *per se*, and am in no sense a botanical or zoological poet. All of my subjects are finally a way of talking about people in the expanding enclave of interest and experience I have chosen to explore. I have been amused by one magazine editor's recognition of my predilection for "all things, great and small" in welcoming a new submission as another poet from "the Garden of Eaton."

Painting has been another seminal influence, and I have long enjoyed what John Singleton Copley called "the luxury of seeing." This interest is the specific motivation in such poems as "The Gallery," "The Museum," "Homage to the Infanta," and "Nocturne for Douanier Rousseau," among others, but it is a constantly underlying, energizing source. "Five Etudes for the Artist" (*Art International*, November 1972) is an extended statement of this pictorial dedication which has been noted by numerous artists, including the New England painter Karl Knaths who has commented at length on the "vital imaginative reality" of the visual qualities of the poems.

The intellectual content of my poetry and its final outlook and credo has been greatly strengthened by the study of philosophy. Writing in the *New York Times* about *Countermoves*, Wallace Fowlie recognized this influence when he said: "Charles Eaton demonstrates an admirable technical control over the effects he wishes to make, and a clear awareness of at least one major function of poetry. This would be the art of questioning everything, and of questioning in particular the power of poetry."

Fowlie's acknowledgment of the power of sentiment as balancing the intellectual in the poetry is reflected in a line from my long poem, "Robert E. Lee: An Ode": "I believe in the world seen through a temperament." I am certain that it is always the task of the writer to give us his personal vision of reality. This means an uncommon dedication, a determination to keep the fine arts fine, a perpetual sense of renewal and reaffirmation. One must constantly ask oneself in times of discouragement: Who will do my particular kind of writing if I don't? Who will take care of my dreams when I am gone? In our dispersive time, it is not easy to keep a sense of personality and purpose, and, as a consequence, attention to the disciplines of character is equally important with ability. Probably more writers fail through lack of character than of ability. Morale is one of the essential fibres of a meaningful life. Cézanne reminded himself every morning to be "*Sur le motif!*" So must the poet.

*   *   *

The poetry of Charles Edward Eaton ranges from the quiet, reflective, and calmly precise to the colorful, daring, gripping, and raw. The best of his work provides the reader with a delightful though sometimes disturbing experience: he advances confidently, secure in the carefully controlled rhythms, the superbly disciplined energies of syntax, until of a sudden he loses his balance. Upon recovering it the reader discovers that he has been walking on a tightrope, stretched precariously between the world as he usually sees it and the world as it really is.

Eaton is a poet who allows his mind and heart to play upon experience. He sings of ordinary things: the amber light of the sun, the fading fragrance of purple lilacs, the red fire of October, the bodies of swimmers, golden and hard muscled, a day in spring, "...like a bell / Rung suddenly in many tones of green, / Sprung full and clear-toned well / Into the rounded air...." He sings also of extraordinary things: the Giggler, Voyeur, Centaur, Eunuch, Cowboy, Woman with a Scar, and Madame Midget, "Her tiny heart, loaded with feeling close as a plum is to its

stone." Repeatedly, through skillful use of conventional form and variations, the poet demonstrates how tenuous and fluctuating is the distinction between the two. For Eaton all experience, the ordinary as well as the extraordinary, the painful as well as the pleasant, is matter for poetry to assimilate and rearrange. "From bee-sting, spider-bite, thorn-prick, hammer-bruise," no less than from "lip-brush" and "hand-grasp," the flesh learns and "grows wise."

On the Edge of the Knife and *The Man in the Green Chair* explore with increasing boldness and vigor the abnormality of the normal. They reveal the bestial power of Eros and they descend into the primitive darkness deep within each of us. The verse, like the song of the Tree Frog, is often "raw with harsh and heartfelt music," a music which reverberates through the intelligent verse paragraphs, the chiselled quatrains, the unorthodox, long-lined triptychs. Such rawness never chafes or offends. For the mastery of form, achieved by years of experience and adopted to the distinctive sound of the poet's individual voice, finally teaches the heart the lesson it learns in "Della Robbia in August," not only to grieve, but to rise "in a brilliant form of care."

—Robert Miola

EBERHART, Richard (Ghormley). American. Born in Austin, Minnesota, 5 April 1904. Educated at the University of Minnesota, Minneapolis, 1922-23; Dartmouth College, Hanover, New Hampshire, B.A. 1926; St. John's College, Cambridge, B.A. 1929, M.A. 1933; Harvard University, Cambridge, Massachusetts, 1932-33. Served in the United States Naval Reserve, 1942-46: Lieutenant Commander. Married Helen Butcher in 1941; two children. Tutor to the son of King Prajadhipok of Siam, 1930-31. English teacher, St. Mark's School, Southboro, Massachusetts, 1933-41, and Cambridge School Kendal Green, Massachusetts, 1941-42. Assistant Manager to Vice-President, Butcher Polish Company, Boston, 1946-52; now honorary Vice-President and Member of the Board of Directors. Visiting Professor, University of Washington, Seattle, 1952-53, 1967, 1972; Professor of English, University of Connecticut, Storrs, 1953-54; Visiting Professor, Wheaton College, Norton, Massachusetts, 1954-55; Resident Fellow and Gauss Lecturer, Princeton University, New Jersey, 1955-56. Professor of English and Poet-in-Residence, 1956-68, Class of 1925 Professor, 1968-70, and since 1970, Professor Emeritus, Dartmouth College. Elliston Lecturer, University of Cincinnati, 1961; Visiting Professor, Columbia University, New York, 1975, University of California, Davis, 1975, and University of Florida, Gainesville, winter term, 1974-82; Wallace Stevens Fellow, Timothy Dwight College, Yale University, New Haven, Connecticut, 1976. Founder, 1950, and First President, Poets' Theatre, Cambridge, Massachusetts; Member, 1955, and since 1964, Director, Yaddo Corporation. Consultant in Poetry, 1959-61, and Honorary Consultant in American Letters, 1963-69, Library of Congress, Washington, D.C. Recipient: Guarantor's Prize, 1946, and Harriet Monroe Memorial Prize, 1950 (*Poetry*, Chicago); New England Poetry Club Golden Rose, 1950; Shelley Memorial Award, 1952; Harriet Monroe Poetry Award, 1955; American Academy grant, 1955; Bollingen prize, 1962; Pulitzer prize, 1966; Academy of American Poets fellowship, 1969; National Book Award, 1977; President's Medallion, University of Florida, 1977; Sarah Josepha Hale Award, 1982. D.Litt: Dartmouth College, 1954; Skidmore College, Saratoga, New York, 1966; College of Wooster, Ohio, 1969; Colgate University, Hamilton, New York, 1974; D.H.L.: Franklin Pierce College, Rindge, New Hampshire, 1978. Poet Laureate of New Hampshire, 1979. Since 1972, Honorary President, Poetry Society of America. Member, American Academy, 1960, and American Academy of Arts and Sciences, 1967. Address: 5 Webster Terrace, Hanover, New Hampshire 03755, U.S.A.

PUBLICATIONS

Verse

A Bravery of Earth. London, Cape, 1930; New York, Cape and Smith, 1931.
Reading the Spirit. London, Chatto and Windus, 1936; New York, Oxford University Press, 1937.
Song and Idea. London, Chatto and Windus, 1940; New York, Oxford University Press, 1942.
A World-View. Medford, Massachusetts, Tufts College Press, 1941.
Poems, New and Selected. New York, New Directions, 1944.
Rumination. Hanover, New Hampshire, Wayzgoose Press, 1947.
Burr Oaks. New York, Oxford University Press, and London, Chatto and Windus, 1947.
Brotherhood of Men. Pawlet, Vermont, Banyan Press, 1949.
An Herb Basket. Cummington, Massachusetts, Cummington Press, 1950.
Selected Poems. New York, Oxford University Press, and London, Chatto and Windus, 1951.
Undercliff: Poems 1946-1953. London, Chatto and Windus, 1953; New York, Oxford University Press, 1954.
Great Praises. New York, Oxford University Press, and London, Chatto and Windus, 1957.
The Oak: A Poem. Hanover, New Hampshire, Pine Tree Press, 1957.
Collected Poems 1930-60, Including 51 New Poems. New York, Oxford University Press, and London, Chatto and Windus, 1960.
The Quarry: New Poems. New York, Oxford University Press, and London, Chatto and Windus, 1964.
The Vastness and Indifference of the World. Milford, New Hampshire, Ferguson Press, 1965.
Fishing for Snakes. Privately printed, 1965.
Selected Poems 1930-1965. New York, New Directions, 1965.
Thirty One Sonnets. New York, Eakins Press, 1967.
Shifts of Being. New York, Oxford University Press, and London, Chatto and Windus, 1968.
The Achievement of Richard Eberhart: A Comprehensive Selection of His Poems, edited by Bernard F. Engle. Chicago, Scott Foresman, 1968.
Three Poems. Cambridge, Massachusets, Pym Randall Press, 1968.
Fields of Grace. New York, Oxford University Press, and London, Chatto and Windus, 1972.
Two Poems. West Chester, Pennsylvania, Aralia Press, 1975.
Collected Poems 1930-1976, Including 43 New Poems. New York, Oxford University Press, and London, Chatto and Windus, 1976.
Poems to Poets. Lincoln, Massachusetts, Penmaen Press, 1976.
Hour, Gnats. Davis, California, Putah Creek Press, 1977.
Survivors. Brockport, New York, Boa, 1979.
Ways of Light: Poems 1972-1980. New York, Oxford University Press, and London, Chatto and Windus, 1980.

New Hampshire: Nine Poems. Roslindale, Massachusetts, Pym Randall Press, 1980.
Four Poems. Winston-Salem, North Carolina, Palaemon Press, 1980.
Florida Poems. Gulfport, Florida, Konglomerati, 1981.
The Long Reach: New and Uncollected Poems 1948-1983. New York, New Directions, 1984.
Snowy Owl. Winston-Salem, North Carolina, Palaemon Press, 1984.
Throwing Yourself Away. Roslyn, New York, Stone House Press, 1984.

Recording: *Richard Eberhart Reading His Own Poems,* Caedmon, 1966.

Plays

The Apparition (produced Cambridge, Massachusetts, 1951). Included in *Collected Verse Plays,* 1962.
The Visionary Farms (produced Cambridge, Massachusetts, 1952). Included in *Collected Verse Plays,* 1962.
Triptych (produced Chicago, 1955). Included in *Collected Verse Plays,* 1962.
The Mad Musician, and Devils and Angels (produced Cambridge, Massachusetts, 1962). Included in *Collected Verse Plays,* 1962.
Collected Verse Plays (includes *Triptych, The Visionary Farms, The Apparition, The Mad Musician, Devils and Angels, Preamble I and II*). Chapel Hill, University of North Carolina Press, 1962.
The Bride from Mantua, adaptation of a play by Lope de Vega (produced Hanover, New Hampshire, 1964).
Chocurua. New York, Nadja Press, 1981.

Other

Poetry as a Creative Principle (lecture). Norton, Massachusetts, Wheaton College, 1952.
Of Poetry and Poets. Urbana, University of Illinois Press, 1979.

Editor, with others, *Free Gunner's Handbook,* revised edition. Norfolk, Virginia, Naval Air Station, 1944.
Editor, with Selden Rodman, *War and the Poet: An Anthology of Poetry Expressing Man's Attitude to War from Ancient Times to the Present.* New York, Devin Adair, 1945.
Editor, *...Dartmouth Poems.* Hanover, New Hampshire, Dartmouth Publications-Butcher Fund, 12 vols., 1958-59, 1962-71.

*

Manuscript Collection: Dartmouth College Library, Hanover, New Hampshire.

Critical Studies: "Richard Eberhart" by Ralph J. Mills, Jr., in *Contemporary American Poetry,* New York, Random House, 1960; *Richard Eberhart* by Ralph J. Mills, Jr., Minneapolis, University of Minnesota Press, 1966; introduction to *The Achievement of Richard Eberhart,* 1968, and *Richard Eberhart,* New York, Twayne, 1972, both by Bernard F. Engle; "The Cultivation of Paradox: The War Poetry of Richard Eberhart" by Richard J. Fein, in *Forum* (Muncie, Indiana), Spring 1969; *Richard Eberhart: The Progress of an American Poet* by Joel Roache, New York, Oxford University Press, 1971; *Richard Eberhart* (film), directed by Samuel Mandelbaum, New York,

Tri-Pix, 1972; *Richard Eberhart* (film), directed by Irving Broughton, Seattle, University of Washington, 1974; *Richard Eberhart: A Celebration*, edited by Sydney Lea and others, n.p., Kenyon Hill, 1980.

Richard Eberhart comments:

My poetry celebrates life, which does not last long, and mankind, which is temporal as well, through understanding and perception of my times, insofar as I am able to create poems which may communicate values and meanings I can know.

*   *   *

The poet comments: "Divisive man can know unity only at death (or so he can speculate), and he cannot know what kind of unity that is. He lives in continuous struggle with his imperfection and the imperfection of life. If one were only conscious of harmony, there would be no need to write."

Throughout the 50 years of his career Richard Eberhart has been consumed with the extremes of Romantic vision—wonder, ecstasy, emptiness, isolation, and despair. Often, the poet sings of a radiance in nature, and exultant joy, as he feels a harmony with all living things and Spirit. Through the splendid imagination, he writes, "You breathe in maybe God," and then write "with a whole clarity." Hence he writes in "This Fevers Me":

> This fevers me, this sun on green,
> On grass glowing, this young spring.
> The secret hallowing is come,
> Regenerate sudden incarnation,
> Mystery made visible
> In growth...

In "The Groundhog," observing the groundhog's disintegration and absorption into nature, the poet experiences a deep sense of man's "naked frailty," which arouses a "passion of the blood," a "fever," which transforms into "a flame/...Immense energy in the sun." He simultaneously identifies with "Alexander," "Montaigne," and "Saint Theresa," who similarly suffered vision, through imaginative realization of man's mortality.

Witnessing the wild "Ospreys in Cry," Eberhart again identifies in the birds his own mortality, while proclaiming his inspired role:

> I felt a staggering sense
> Of the victor and.of the doomed,
> Of being one and the other,
> Of being both at one time,
> I was the seer
> And I was revealed.

What moves the spirit is the fusion of imagination with a "divine" force emanating from nature: "our wills are with hers [nature] fused/And we would impregnate her with our shape"; in the "great moments of being, something/Beyond our wills, is the prime Mover" ("Necessity").

Although death may be the moment of revelation, of "wordless ecstasy/Of mystery" ("The Soul Longs to Return Whence It Came"), there are moments when the transcendent joy and sense of unity desert Eberhart, when the poet laments that understanding, and perhaps vision itself, is impossible, and in these often blunt portraits of man's mortality and the finality of all things, resound the moving strains of man's weary and lonely old age, and his ultimate loneliness and despair in the face of an indifferent universe. "A name may be glorious but death is death,"writes the poet ("I Walked over the Grave of Henry James"). When intellect rules spirit, "the hard intellectual light/That kills all delight/...brings the solemn, inward pain/Of truth into the heart again" ("In a Hard Intellectual Light"). Thus, Eberhart may yearn for "the incomparable light," "Where everything is as it was in my childhood," and he may ask: "Oh where/Has gone that madness wild?" In "Flux" he says: "There is a somber, imponderable fate./Enigma rules, and the heart has no certainty."

Eberhart acknowledges man's fallen state, the cruelty he is capable of enduring and imposing. In "The Fury of Aerial Bombardment" he asks: "Was man made stupid to see his own stupidity?" But because he would wish humanity to embrace love—to Eberhart human love "concrete, [and] specific" is the primary human experience—his work is filled with the rhetorical "Am I My Brother's Keeper?" Love is "discoverable here/Difficult, dangerous, pure, clear,/The truth of the positive hour/Composing all of human power" ("The Goal of Intellectual Man").

The *Collected Poems 1930-1976* contains 43 new poems, many of which again concern the poet's visionary powers and yet his sense of limited selfhood, his joy and fear in the presence of a beautiful but indifferent world. In "Trying to Hold It All Together," a poem on Auden's death he writes:

> We are faced with the hard facts of time,
> Beyond any man...
> We cannot hold it all together, the depth,
> We cannot trick it out with word embroidery,
> Time is the master of man, and we know it.

In "Usurper" he speaks of being captured in nature and how "art momentarily" controls "myths of consciousness"; he cries:

> Not to be supine! Not to lie
> On the face of the earth dreaming
> As a boy as you used to be,
> Your eyes full of sensual hope,
> But to stand up to nature,
> To stand up to time, and say
> I seize your power, I am.

"Mind and Nature" celebrates both the immutability of nature and the mortality and transcendent imagination of man:

> I can imagine anything I can imagine,
> Nature is not my lover, I am the lover of nature,
> I kick the boulder with the foot of Hercules,
> The boulder sits, but I can walk around it.

"Big Rock" contains the simple, direct language we associate with the great Eberhart, as he transforms keenly felt experience through its very language into larger, more metaphysical, even mystical, experience. The poet, Eberhart has said, "makes the world anew; something grows out of the old, which he locks in words."

Man is chosen, however; all men are chosen, for

> In the secret heart all are free
> Each has a secret heart of pure imagination.
> Each man struggles with reality.

—Lois Gordon

ECHERUO, Michael (Joseph Chukwudalu). Nigerian. Born in Umunumo, Mbano Division, 14 March 1937. Educated at Stella Maris College, Port Harcourt, 1950-54; University College, Ibadan, 1955-60, B.A. (honours) 1960; Cornell University, Ithaca, New York (Phi Beta Kappa), 1962-65, M.A. 1963, Ph.D. 1965. Married Rose N. Ikwueke in 1968; five children. Lecturer, Nigerian College of Arts and Technology, Enugu, 1960-61. Lecturer, 1961-70, Senior Lecturer, 1970-73, and Professor, 1973-74, University of Nigeria, Nsukka; Professor of English, 1974-80, and Dean of the Postgraduate School, 1978-80, University of Ibadan. Since 1981, Vice-Chancellor, Imo State University, Owerri. Since 1977, Founding President, Nigerian Association for African and Comparative Literature. Recipient: All-Africa Poetry Competition prize, 1963. Address: Vice-Chancellor's Office, Imo State University, Owerri, Nigeria.

PUBLICATIONS

Verse

Mortality. London, Longman, 1968.
Distanced: New Poems. Enugu, I.K., 1975.

Other

Joyce Cary and the Novel of Africa. London, Longman, and New York, Africana, 1973.
Victorian Lagos: Aspects of Nineteenth-Century Lagos Life. London, Macmillan, 1977; New York, Holmes and Meier, 1978.
Poets, Prophets, and Professors. Ibadan, Ibadan University Press, 1977.
The Conditioned Imagination from Shakespeare to Conrad: Studies in the Exo-Cultural Stereotype. London, Macmillan, and New York, Holmes and Meier, 1978.
Joyce Cary and the Dimensions of Order. London, Macmillan, and New York, Barnes and Noble, 1979.

Editor, *Igbo Traditional Life, Literature, and Culture.* Austin, Texas, Conch, 1972.
Editor, *The Tempest,* by Shakespeare. London, Longman, 1980.

*   *   *

Michael Echeruo, like his late countryman Christopher Okigbo, has forged, from the crossroads experience of an African heritage and a "European" education, poetry which is wide-ranging, deceptively simple and highly individual. Although the poems in his first volume *Mortality* often come out of his experiences as an M.A. and doctoral student in the United States, they are still like trees with their roots deep in African soil, no matter how high their branches reach into a foreign sky. The return to Africa, whether physically or metaphorically, is implicit, as in the first poem in the book, "Debut":

> Have we not looked the whole world out,
>   searched the whole hearth out
>   till we saw the palm-nuts again
> by which we were to live?

It is, therefore, no accident that an entire section of his book is titled "Defections" and that he says in the poem "Harvest Time": "Village maidens/are the bearers of my harvest...."

Wit and irony also figure strongly in Echeruo's poetry, along with a sense of what it is to be an African poet in a foreign land:

> ... like an unfeathered bird
> in their spring—
> white and spruce and clean—
> ... like an unclassified gift
> to their museums
> where they spin out fine tall tales
> all day long
> amid the blistering flurries
> of their bleak December days.

Though his Nigeria figures strongly in his verse, Echeruo also ranges, capably, throughout Western literature, bringing in such diverse sources as the Bible, D.H. Lawrence, Joyce and St. John of the Cross. His poem "The Signature," which revolves around the figure of O'Brien (who seems to be an Irish priest like the Flannagan of Chris Okigbo's "Limits"), draws a picture of African ceremonies in conjunction with Catholic rites and draws the conclusion that "The priests and elders of my past/would love to see O'Brien's paradise."

There is one last quality about Echeruo's poetry which should be taken note of. Whether ironic or celebratory, whether a poem of love or a poem of satire, there is a current of lyricism which runs through all of Echeruo's verse, a lyricism which can be felt in these lines from his poem "Wedding," lines which speak of birth and stress again his ties to the soil:

> Tap roots beneath the giant
> speak like the gods
> and life comes
> like a spasm of light....

—Joseph Bruchac

———————

ECONOMOU, George. American. Born in Great Falls, Montana, 24 September 1934. Educated at Colgate University, Hamilton, New York, A.B. 1956; Columbia University, New York, M.A. 1957, Ph.D. 1967. Married Rochelle Owens, *q.v.,* in 1962. Lecturer, Wagner College, New York, 1958-60; Member of the Department of English Long Island University, Brooklyn, 1961-83. Since 1983, Professor of English, University of Oklahoma, Norman. Editor, *Chelsea Review,* New York, 1958-60; Editor, *Trobar,* New York, 1960-64. Field Editor for Old and Middle English, Twayne English Authors. Recipient: American Council of Learned Societies fellowship, 1975; Creative Artists Public Service fellowship, 1976. Addres: 606 West 116th Street, New York, New York 10027, U.S.A.

PUBLICATIONS

Verse

The Georgics. Los Angeles, Black Sparrow Press, 1968.
Landed Natures. Los Angeles, Black Sparrow Press, 1969.
Poems for Self-Therapy. Mount Horeb, Wisconsin, Perishable Press, 1972.
Ameriki: Book One and Selected Earlier Poems. New York, Sun, 1977.

Other

The Goddess Natura in Medieval Literature. Cambridge, Massachusetts, Harvard University Press, 1972.

Editor, with Joan M. Ferrante, *In Pursuit of Perfection: Courtly Love in Medieval Literature.* Port Washington, New York, Kennikat Press, 1975.
Editor, *Geoffrey Chaucer: A Collection of Criticism.* New York, McGraw Hill, 1975.
Editor, *Proensa: An Anthology of Troubadour Poetry Selected and Translated by Paul Blackburn.* Berkeley, University of California Press, 1978.

Translator, *Philodemos, His Twenty-Nine Extant Poems.* Mount Horeb, Wisconsin, Perishable Press, 1983.

*

Manuscript Collection: Butler Library, Columbia University, New York.

Critical Studies: reviews by Harry Lewis, in *Mulch* (Amherst, Massachusetts), Spring 1972, and in *San Francisco Review of Books*, 1978; by Gerald Dorset, in *Northeast Rising Sun* (Cherry Valley, New York), Fall 1978.

George Economou comments:
   (1970) Major themes—Nature, the great one we live in and the small ones that are myself and those I love.
   (1980) I want to explore the landscapes of America and Americans in my poems. Their forms are determined by my responses to their discovered topographical and psychological models.

*   *   *

George Economou is most closely associated with poetry of the "deep image," and for a time co-edited, along with Robert and Joan Kelly, *Trobar*, the "deep image" poetry journal. Robert Kelly defined "deep image" as poetry filled with "intensity and immediacy," and "containing the primal gestures of language." First referred to in Jerome Rothenberg's *Poems from the Floating World*, the "deep image" comes from dream, from the invisible pull and tug of life. It is a poetry charged with the rough, raw energy transmitted by direct and primal human actions. Most of these qualities are present in George Economou's poetry. His poems contain the facts and rituals of life close to the earth; earth rhythms and surprises animate it.
   Economou's *The Goddess Natura in Medieval Literature* illuminates his frequent poetic reference to his muse and patron, the goddess Natura. She is the allegorical personification of nature in classic and medieval literature, and also an intermediary between man and God. Like Chaucer's "Nature" in *The Parliament of Fowls*, Economou's goddess presides over a harmonious landscape, and fruitfulness in love and romance. In "Prayer of a Natural Man" he asks Natura to set his heart high, to let him "be the sure handler/of every bird and snake it finds...." Economou's poems are informal and conversational— the words of a poet who walks for his health, talks to himself, invokes muses and animal spirits. The poet's "secret life" in nature is everywhere present: "I am a magnificent animal..."; "I become wolf/I become wolf man...." The first portion of *Landed Natures* is composed of eight "Georgics," and even though the landscape is the American West there are thematic connections

with Virgil's *Georgics.* Economou, as earth husband, consoles the "poor earth we live off/nobody here loves you...." He advises the shepherd in us to love our flock:

> caress them daily and be
> kind as you can,
> enter their dumb world
> without a word or thought.

There are qualities here reminiscent of the earth poems of Gary Snyder, and, to a lesser degree, of Galway Kinnell and James Dickey, but Economou is not at this point up to the calibre of such poets. Yet there is a compelling directness in these conversations between poet and reader. Earth guide, mystic traveler, George Economou speaks as one who has been to the territory and who, given a chance, will reveal some of nature's finest mysteries.

—John R. Cooley

———

EDMOND, Lauris (Dorothy). New Zealander. Born 2 April 1924. Educated at Napier Girls High School, 1937-41; University of Waikato, B.A. 1968; Victoria University, Wellington, M.A. 1972. Married Trevor Edmond in 1945; five daughters and one son. Teacher, Huntly College, 1968-69, and Heretaunga College, Wellington, 1970-72; Editor, Post-Primary Teachers Association, Wellington, 1973-80. Since 1980, Off-Campus Tutor and Lecturer, Massey University, Palmerston North. Recipient: New Zealand P.E.N. award, 1975; Katherine Mansfield-Menton fellowship, 1981. Address: 22 Grass Street, Oriental Bay, Wellington, New Zealand.

PUBLICATIONS

Verse

In Middle Air. Christchurch, Pegasus Press, 1975.
The Pear Tree and Other Poems. Christchurch, Pegasus Press, 1977.
Salt from the North. Wellington, Oxford University Press, 1980.
Seven. Wellington, Wayzgoose Press, 1980.
Wellington Letter. Wellington, Mallinson Rendel, 1980.
Catching It. Wellington, Oxford University Press, 1983.
Selected Poems. Wellington, Oxford University Press, 1984.

Plays

Between Night and Morning (produced Wellington, 1980).

Radio Plays: *The Mountain* (cycle of 4 plays), 1980-81.

Other

Editor, *Dancing to My Tune: Verse and Prose,* by Denis Glover. Wellington, Catspaw Press, 1974.
Editor, *Young Writing.* Wellington, P.E.N. New Zealand Centre, 1979.
Editor, *A Remedial Persiflage,* by Chris Ward. Wellington, Post-Primary Teachers Association, 1980.

Editor, *The Letters of A.R.D. Fairburn*.   Wellington, Oxford University Press, 1981.

*

Critical Studies: in *New Zealand Listener* (Wellington), 11 June 1983; *Landfall* (Christchurch), September 1983.

Lauris Edmond comments:

I came to poetry publishing late—though I had always written some, even during the busiest years when I lived in country towns and brought up my six children. In 1974 I first sent poems to an editor (of *Islands*, a N.Z. literary journal); they were accepted, and I began seriously to work on half-finished drafts and notes. By 1975 I had a MS ready for publication, and I have published five further volumes since then, with a *Selected Poems* this year.

The chief effect of this pattern of living my life first, as it were, and becoming a committed writer second, is that all my work is filled with a sense of relationship. This is sometimes with people, but also with events, experiences, the natural world; I don't think I write anything without this sense of being a part of a larger experience, and in relationship with it, being expressed in some way.

This quality is reflected in the process of writing by my awareness that the creation of a poem is as much a matter of listening as speaking; the experience which lies at the centre of the poem has from the moment of inception its own life, to which I as poet respond. Since I have an abiding sense of the living quality in the natural environment, and the psychological environment in which I live, it seems natural to me to find this relationship again and again, even in the smallest details of existence, each of which has its own uniqueness.

I wrote my first novel because I was awarded the Writer's Fellowship which sends a New Zealand writer to the south of France for a year, to live in Menton. I do not believe that poetry can be written according to any kind of organised programme, so I wrote a novel, and having done so I intend to write others. I found an immediate parallel between the vitality of the "world of the poem" and that of the fictional world of my novel, though many of the details of the writing process were different.

Beginning late has some obvious advantages (though I didn't do it by conscious choice). The main one is that the maturity that one hopes has been learned in 30 years of adult life forms the basic outlook or point of view in everything I write. Some kinds of apprenticeship, it seems, do not have to be passed through. There is also a considerable sense of urgency, which I think may give pace and energy to my writing. The volume of *Selected Poems* shows rather less variation between early and later poems than a poet who began writing in youth would display. And I could never regret my children!

*   *   *

Lauris Edmond has published six volumes of poetry in eight years, with a selected poems in 1984. This outpouring comes comparatively late in a life devoted initially to a large family in a small New Zealand town. While recognising in her *Landfall* interview that she has "the powerful enthusiasm of the late starter," Edmond is pleased to have been able to experience a "personal life" and then a career. With her many poetry readings, tours, and editing jobs, she is now at the height of that career.

Her first volume, *In Middle Air*, sounds recurrent themes: the brutality of rural living (of a sensitive boy it is sneered, "He'll

roughen up"), the cold alien-ness of the physical environment, the ravages of time, the necessity for love ("We starve alone") and for putting observation into words. There is, however, a strain of high romantic lyricism which is at odds with the more supple, intimate dramatic sense which was slowly to emerge as the poet's distinctive voice; and an uncertainty of line. In *The Pear Tree* the line fits more naturally a more forthright voice, often addressing friends (male or female) as "you," and arguing for philosophical positions such as the importance of the here and now. A series of portraits of older women forms a minor theme in Edmond's writing, like "At Mary's House," which typically draws analogies between body, spirit and the natural landscape ("nobody/has weeded here for a long time").

In *Wellington Letter* the poet criticises her people—"we cultivate mind's middle distances." Instead, Edmond tries to move up close to experience, or to stand back and make a crisp generalisation, such as that the great poets had "unshakeable courage." The dangers of bald poetic philosophising are obvious, and the poet's recent development has wisely been towards the quotidian—"it was not anything achieved;/the art was just to let it happen." So the first half of *Salt from the North* shows a surer focus, sense of line, and an unforced completeness in each poem. Unfortunately in the second half of that and her most accomplished volume, *Catching It*, the moralising does creep in, effective only when proceeding from a vivid personal setting, e.g., "Latter Day Lysistrata," an anti-war poem where the poet in her garden protests male folly:

> Let us show them the vulnerable
> earth, the transparent light that slips
> through slender birches falling over
> small birds that sense in the miniscule
> threads of their veins...

Many of Edmond's poems are about trees, their rootedness and memories. The Mansfield Fellowship in Menton in 1981 gave her roots and a perspective elsewhere, to revitalise her poetry. In *Catching It* the lines are often shorter, surer, the moment or performance brought off more often. Whether she is gazing back home ("I am the child of exiles who dreamt/of the lost garden") or at Frenchmen sitting in a town square, she "catches it." Her dominant sense of transience and death finds strong dramatic form in the poem "At Delphi" where she imagines the sacrifice of an older woman.

Less varied in her tone and subject matter than her countrywoman Fleur Adcock, less philosophically inclined than Judith Wright, Lauris Edmond also sometimes lacks the metrical variety of each of these poets; but this is the distinguished company in which she now belongs. She has built up a commanding body of work in a short time, and her voice has always been crisp, clear, and articulate. Her poems often touch obliquely, gently, themes of New Zealand life and the stages of womanhood that are too often elsewhere ponderously exposed. Nowhere does she do this better than in her early poem "Sunday Morning" which catches smalltown New Zealand forever:

> and the boys, off-hand and matey,
> eyes on the weather, ready
> to roll up the day, stow in
> the boot, nothing doing
> around here, get what's left
> of Saturday's grog bugger off
> leave boredom behind.
>
> And they go—cars hot,
> sliding past polished like buns

straight out of summer's oven;
where is it, the sun-drumming
dazzle they're after? Who knows—
not us—it's anywhere but here.

—David Dowling

EDSON, Russell. American. Born 9 April 1935. Educated at the Art Students League, New York; New School for Social Research, New York; Columbia University, New York; Black Mountain College, North Carolina. Married to Frances Edson. Recipient: Guggenheim Fellowship, 1974; National Endowment for the Arts grant, 1976, fellowship, 1982. Agent: Georges Borchardt Inc., 136 East 57th Street, New York, New York 10022. Address: 149 Weed Avenue, Stamford, Connecticut 06902, U.S.A.

PUBLICATIONS

Verse

Appearances: Fables and Drawings. Stamford, Connecticut, Thing Press, 1961.
A Stone Is Nobody's: Fables and Drawings. Stamford, Connecticut, Thing Press, 1961.
The Boundry (sic). Stamford, Connecticut, Thing Press, 1964.
The Very Thing That Happens: Fables and Drawings. New York, New Directions, 1964.
The Brain Kitchen: Writings and Woodcuts. Stamford, Connecticut, Thing Press, 1965.
What a Man Can See. Highlands, North Carolina, Jargon, 1969.
The Childhood of an Equestrian. New York, Harper, 1973.
The Clam Theatre. Middletown, Connecticut, Wesleyan University Press, 1973.
A Roof with Some Clouds Behind It. Hartford, Connecticut, Bartholomew's Cobble, 1975.
The Intuitive Journey and Other Works. New York, Harper, 1976.
The Reason Why the Closet-Man Is Never Sad. Middletown, Connecticut, Wesleyan University Press, 1977.
Edson's Mentality. Chicago, Oink Press, 1977.
The Traffic. Madison, Wisconsin, Red Ozier Press, 1978.
The Wounded Breakfast: Ten Poems. Madison, Wisconsin, Red Ozier Press, 1978.
With Sincerest Regrets. Providence, Rhode Island, Burning Deck, 1981.
Gulping's Recital. Rhinebeck, New York, Guignol, 1984.

Plays

The Falling Sickness: A Book of Plays. New York, New Directions, 1975.

*

Critical Studies: *A Prose Poem Anthology,* edited by Duane Ackerson, Pocatello, Idaho, Dragonfly Press, 1970; "Prose Poems" by William Matthews, in *New: American and Canadian Poetry 15* (Trumansburg, New York), 1971; "I Am Sure Happiness Is Not Too Far Away" by Thomas Meyer, in *Parnassus* (New York), ii, 1, 1974; "On Russell Edson's Genius" by Donald Hall, in *American Poetry Review 6* (Philadelphia), no. 5, 1977; "The Essential Russell Edson: A Surrealist Reading" by Larry Smith, in *Stardancer 7* (New York), 1983.

Russell Edson comments:

I write short prose pieces which are neither fiction nor reportage. Perhaps the currently popular term in America (although we certainly didn't originate it), *prose poem,* is vague enough to describe the blurred borders of my gross generality. But, as soon as I say this I want to shout that I refuse to write prose poems, that I want to write the work that is always in search of itself, in a form that is always building itself from the inside out.

In that I am more at home in my work than in describing it, I offer an example below, "A Chair":

A chair has waited such a long time to be with its person. Through shadow and fly buzz and the floating dust it has waited such a long time to be with its person.

What it remembers of the forest it forgets, and dreams of a room where it waits—Of the cup and the ceiling—Of the animate one.

* * *

In an introduction to his first major book, *The Very Thing That Happens,* Denise Levertov says this of Russell Edson: "Russell Edson is one of those originals who appear out of the loneliness of a vast, thronged country to create a peculiar and defined world." Several books later, this impression of Edson's eccentric genius (as perhaps all true genius appears eccentric) remains as strong as ever. His is the world seen from all the frightening, and funny, perspectives adults so often forget to see, or choose to forget: worlds seen through the wrong end of the spyglass, or through the looking glass, where everything pursues a strange, relentless logic of its own. His soap bubble worlds refuse to pop, returning us, like the knowledge we have had a dream, to the reassuring; instead, the world they reflect comes apart in the face of a dream logic. A man's hand is a white spider, and, driven by the necessity of such metamorphoses, suspends the man eventually from the ceiling by the spider webs it has woven. Edson's prose poetry is more carefully wedded to metaphor, and the pursuit of metaphor to its sometimes ludicrous, sometimes lovely ends, than most verse, as in "Antimatter," where Edson manages a fine blend of both:

On the other side of a mirror there's an inverse world, where the insane go sane; where bones climb out of the earth and recede to the first slime of love.

And in the evening the sun is just rising.

Lovers cry because they are a day younger, and soon childhood robs them of their pleasure.

In such a world there is much sadness which, of course, is joy....

Edson is also a playwright, and the earlier poems of *What a Man Can See* and *The Very Thing That Happens* are like miniature theatre-of-the-absurd plays, vignettes of family life in which everyone converses in shouts and parents pass on parental wisdom untouched by human thought. Though the humor touches on cartoons (Edson's father was a famous cartoonist) and the black humor of the absurd, there is an undercurrent of pathos reminiscent of Chekhov and O'Neill; these prose poems and fables constitute *A Long Day's Journey into Night* without the tedium.

Edson's range is considerable, from these exchanges to still-life portraits like "A Chair" ("A chair has waited such a long time to be / with its person...") or beast fables tinged with melancholy, like "How a Cow Comes to Live with Long Eared Ones," in which an over-inquisitive cow is kidnapped by a rabid rabbit. Edson pulls such antics off, and creates a real slapstick tragedy, the sort of thing other American artists like Chaplin have been drawn to attempt. Sometimes, the moral explicitness we might expect from the traditional fable is there (though more often, as in "A Journey by Water," Edson creates a sort of anti-fable that satirizes didacticism), as in "A Lovely Man":

A man is such a lovely man; he really is if you'll only look past him into the flower garden.

Wait, shall he move so that you can look more fully into the garden?

Shall he die and be put under the flower garden to nourish beauty and never to be in the way of it again?

The prevailing mood of many of these poems is melancholy, but it's a darkness defined by quick lightning streaks of humor, like a figure in a cubistic woodcut (which Edson's drawings in his various collections resemble) cracking a grin. Edson's prose poems tend to attack the false security and self satisfaction by which we too often live, to dismantle our umbrellas and let us see the storm that is always raging. They throw off just enough light to let us see that black sky overhead again.

—Duane Ackerson

EIGNER, Larry (Lawrence Joel Eigner). American. Born in Lynn, Massachusetts, 7 August 1927. Educated at home; Massachusetts Hospital School, Canton, 2 years; correspondence courses from University of Chicago. Palsied from birth. Address: 2338 McGee Avenue, Berkeley, California 94703, U.S.A.

PUBLICATIONS

Verse

From the Sustaining Air. Palma, Mallorca, Divers Press, 1953; augmented edition, Eugene, Oregon, Toad Press, 1967.
Look at the Park. Privately printed, 1958.
On My Eyes. Highlands, North Carolina, Jargon, 1960.
The Music, The Rooms. Albuquerque, New Mexico, Desert Review Press, 1965.
The Memory of Yeats, Blake, DHL. London, Circle Press, 1965.
Six Poems. Portland, Oregon, Wine Press, 1967.
Another Time in Fragments. London, Fulcrum Press, 1967.
The-/Towards Autumn. Los Angeles, Black Sparrow Press, 1967.
Air the Trees. Los Angeles, Black Sparrow Press, 1967.
The Breath of Once Live Things, In the Field with Poe. Los Angeles, Black Sparrow Press, 1968.
A Line That May Be Cut. London, Circle Press, 1968.
Valleys, Branches. London, Big Venus, 1969.

Flat and Round. New York, Pierrepont Press, 1969.
Over and Over, Ends, As the Wind May Sound. Cambridge, Massachusetts, Restau Press, 1970.
Poem Nov. 1968. London, Tetrad Press, 1970.
Circuits: "A Microbook, A Microbook." LeRoy, New York, Athanor Press, 1971.
Looks Like Nothing, The Shadow Through Air. Guildford, Surrey, Circle Press, 1972.
Earth Ship No. 8. Privately printed, 1972.
What You Hear. London, Edible Magazine, 1972.
Selected Poems, edited by Samuel Charters and Andrea Wyatt. Berkeley, California, Oyez, 1972.
Words Touching Ground Under. Belmont, Massachusetts, Hellric, 1972.
Shape Shadow Elements Move. Los Angeles, Black Sparrow Press, 1973.
Things Stirring Together or Far Away. Los Angeles, Black Sparrow Press, 1974.
Anything on Its Side. New Rochelle, New York, Elizabeth Press, 1974.
No Radio. Boulder, Colorado, Lodestar Press, 1974.
My God the Proverbial. Kensington, California, L, 1975.
Suddenly It Gets Light and Dark in the Streets: Poems 1961-74. Winchester, Green Horse Press, 1975.
The Ear Is A Wheatfield No. 15. Privately printed, 1975.
Tottel's No. 15. Privately printed, 1975.
The Music Variety. Newton, Massachusetts, Roxbury, 1976.
The World and Its Streets, Places. Santa Barbara, California, Black Sparrow Press, 1977.
Watching How or Why. New Rochelle, New York, Elizabeth Press, 1977.
Cloud, Invisible Air. Rhinebeck, New York, Station Hill Press, 1978.
Flagpole Riding. Alverstoke, Hampshire, Stingy Artist, 1978.
Running Around. Providence, Rhode Island, Burning Deck, 1978.
Heat Simmers Cold. Malakoff, France, Orange Export, 1978.
Time Details of a Tree. New Rochelle, New York, Elizabeth Press, 1979.
Lined Up Bulk Senses. Providence, Rhode Island, Burning Deck, 1979.
Earth Birds: Forty Six Poems Written Between May 1964 and June 1972. Guildford, Surrey, Circle Press, 1981.
Now There's a Morning Enormous Hulk of the Sky. New Rochelle, New York, Elizabeth Press, 1981.
Water, Places, A Time. Santa Barbara, California, Black Sparrow Press, 1981.

Play

Murder Talk: The Reception: Suggestions for a Play; Five Poems, Bed Never Self Made. Placitas, New Mexico, Duende, 1964.

Short Stories

Clouding. New York, Samuel Charters, 1968.
Farther North. New York, Samuel Charters, 1969.

Other

Country Harbor Quiet Act Around: Selected Prose, edited by Garrett Whatten. San Francisco, This Press, 1978.

*

Bibliography: *A Bibliography of Works by Larry Eigner, 1937-1969* by Andrea Wyatt, Berkeley, California, Oyez, 1970.

Manuscript Collection: Kenneth Spencer Research Library, University of Kansas, Lawrence.

Critical Studies: *Some Poems / Poets* by Samuel Charters, Berkeley, California, Oyez, 1969; by Cid Corman, in *Essays on the Art of Language 2*, Santa Barbara, California, Black Sparrow Press, 1978; "Eigner's Style" by Benjamin Friedlander, in *Jimmy & Lucy's House of "K"* (Berkeley, California), May 1984; Tom Clark, in *San Francisco Chronicle / Examiner*, 9 September 1984; "Larry Eigner Notes" by Clark Coolidge, in *The L=A=N=G=U=A=G=E Book* edited by Bruce Andrews and Charles Bernstein, Carbondale, Southern Illinois University Press, 1984.

Larry Eigner comments:

Maybe the most that you can do with verse is assess things come to or arrived at, the line (/) or stanza (//) break providing the emphasis, mostly anyway, this being a potential when there are no natural stresses to obscure, interfere with it (there's lacuna, indent, and whatever else, typography can't be ignored much as long as you have writing on paper)—or, since there's no ranking, to realize (the weight or import of) things. You'd think more than two or three things have to be together enough to make a whole, for there to be a weighing, but a poem can stop at any point, after a few words. While a prose piece has to be of some length, has to be continuous. Prose is fairly indeterminate, unbounded, informal; it's the way people run on.

*   *   *

For Larry Eigner the circumstances of his life have given a form and a shape to his poetry. He is a spastic, and most of his life has been spent in a glassed-in front porch of a frame house on a side street of a small Massachusetts town (he now lives in California). Through the windows—and through the window of his bedroom—he follows the world of the seasons, the sky, the birds, the trees. There has been some travel—to visit his brothers in San Francisco and Missouri—and smaller trips into Boston or further along Cape Ann to see other poets. And despite the limits of his physical world he is part of the community of American poets through a wide and open correspondence, and continued reading of the books and magazines that pile up on his desk. He has always thought of himself as close to the poets who broke from the Anglo-American tradition, and there are clear elements of style from Williams, Olson, and Creeley in his poetry—though he doesn't work in the larger forms that characterize the work of Olson—or of Pound, another poet Eigner thinks of as a source. His prose pieces, which tie closely to the poetry and have their own distinct presence, have some correspondences to the Gertrude Stein of the *Autobiography*. The intense use of the immediate image is at the center of his work, and in poem after poem he has framed the physical world he sees through his windows. He can write a poem complete within a few words, so total is his glimpse of this world: "the wind masses such birds / green inside the tree." There is excitement in the poetry about his surroundings—fire engines go by, cars pass in the night, storms grip the trees, birds come, children play loudly—but a dominating theme in his evocation of this scene is a nostalgia at the impermanence of it,

two big pigeons on the new roof
below which he grew corn
          ten years back, one year

a nostalgia that becomes sad, musing: "But I grow old / because I was too much a child." And even though much of his published work was written while he was still in his twenties and thirties he has had to spend too many hours in hospitals, and he is deeply conscious of the presence of death: "once a man is born he has to die / and that is time." A poem that is often quoted:

the knowledge of death, and now
     the knowledge of the stars

     there is one end

               and the endless
Room at the center
     passage / in no time
a rail thickets hills grass

But as often as the mood is subdued the poems more often have an open, direct optimism. They have also a lightness, a deftness, but with such care in their detail that he can make sudden emphases, sudden shifts of meaning with only a few words. He does not insist on his own presence in the work—there is an essential modesty in the poetry, as well as a large intelligence that he uses only to keep the elements of the poem in easy balance with each other. There is much of Eigner's work published, all of it with his distinctive voice and style. The longer poems of a few years ago have given way to short, almost haiku-like poems of recent collections, but this has not been an intentional shift in direction, only an intuitive strengthening and purifying of his line. The work will continue, and the new direction could as well be back to the longer poem. It is this strength of his response—the persistence of it—that will go on in the poetry. As he says:

The fountain of youth is a poetry
and whether we are one minute older
the present always arrives.

—Samuel Charters

ELLIOT, Alistair. British. Born in Liverpool, Lancashire, 13 October 1932. Educated at schools in Wigan, Hoylake, and the United States, 1941-45; Fettes College, Edinburgh; Christ Church, Oxford, B.A. 1955, M.A. 1958. Married Barbara Demaine in 1956; two sons. Actor and stage manager, English Children's Theatre, London, 1957-59; Assistant Librarian, Kensington, London, 1959-61; Cataloguer, Keele University Library, 1961-65; Accessions Librarian, Pahlavi University Library, Shiraz, Iran, 1965-67; Special Collections Librarian, Newcastle upon Tyne University Library, 1967-82. Since 1983, free-lance writer. Recipient: Arts Council grant, 1979; Prudence Farmer Award (*New Statesman*), 1983; Ingram Merrill Foundation fellowship, 1983; Djerassi Foundation fellowship, 1984. Address: 27 Hawthorn Road, Newcastle upon Tyne NE3, 4DE England.

PUBLICATIONS

Verse

Air in the Wrong Place. Newcastle upon Tyne, Eagle Press, 1968.
Contentions. Sunderland, Ceolfrith Press, 1977.
Kisses. Sunderland, Ceolfrith Press, 1978.
Talking to Bede. Ashington, Mid-Northumberland Arts Group, 1982.
Talking Back. London, Secker and Warburg, 1982.
On the Appian Way. London, Secker and Warburg, 1984.

Other

Editor, *Poems by James I and Others*. Newcastle upon Tyne, Eagle Press, 1970.
Editor, *Lines on the Jordan*. Newcastle upon Tyne, Eagle Press, 1971.
Editor, *The Georgics with John Dryden's Translation*, by Virgil. Ashington, Mid-Northumberland Arts Group, 1981.

Translator, *Alcestis*, by Euripides. San Francisco, Chandler, 1965.
Translator, *Peace*, by Aristophanes, in *Greek Comedy*. New York, Dell, 1965.
Translator, *Femmes/Hombres, Women/Men*, by Verlaine. London, Anvil Press Poetry, 1979; New York, Sheep Meadow Press, 1984.
Translator, *The Lazarus Poems*, by Heinrich Heine. Ashington, Mid-Northumberland Arts Group, 1979.

*

Manuscript Collection: Literary and Philosophical Society, Newcastle upon Tyne.

Critical Studies: by Alan Hollinghurst, in *Times Literary Supplement* (London), 30 September 1983; Peter Jones, in *The Times* (London), 18 July 1984; Peter Porter, in *The Observer* (London), 29 July 1984.

Alistair Elliot comments:

My poems are usually in traditional forms (and either with full or half-rhymes) because I think I perform better on a frame than when just jumping about.

Their contents are fairly varied: for example, a modern party explained to a long-dead poet; walking (instead of driving) to work; meeting someone who has the exact voice of someone I once loved; a blanket spun and woven by my grandmother; clipping toenails (as an activity common to all human cultures and times); and most recently a journey from Rome to Brindisi (a book-length poem).

I don't think there are limits on what one can write "about"— lately I have begun to feel that perhaps when I die I can take with me anything I have mentioned in a poem, so I think about furnishing my after-life. On the other hand, the insurable contents of a poem are not it seems entirely in the poet's control. I used to see it as a matter of pulling a poem from its hiding-place by the tail, knowing it can shed the tail and get away. Now it seems more as if I am trying to mind-read the Muse, who has seen the unwritten poem somewhere in a Book of the Future.

I try hard to make my work clear and comprehensible; at least the gist of a poem should come across when read aloud to an audience. But I think that should make the audience feel eager to meet the poem itself, that is, the poem on the page, the real whole

poem as opposed to one of its sonic shadows. I don't see this audience, these creatures feeding round the pool of general knowledge, in very definite terms—I just expect they will be like me, members of a species that on the whole delights in language, in stories about itself, in nifty problems, in imagined and described things. Some poets try to use verse to change or fortify their readers' point of view. I don't seem to be interested in that, in general, but I have written the odd argumentative poem.

*   *   *

First published with, among others, Craig Raine and George Szirtes in Faber's *Poetry Introduction* (1978), Alistair Elliot, in the first book of his own, *Contentions*, hardly prepared his readers for the extraordinary accomplishment of his second, *Talking Back*. Elliot's talent needed time to come into its own.

At first sight the poems in *Talking Back* might perhaps appear bookish or over-scholarly (titles such as "Talking to Bede" or "The Aegean: Summer 493 B.C." hardly help dispel this image); but, once read with care and a feeling intelligence, they begin to reveal their depths as well. Elliot is a poet who sees nothing wrong in writing intelligent poems which sometimes presuppose a degree of knowledge in a shared literary tradition from the reader. Of the 24 pages of *Talking to Bede* 3 consist of a chronology of useful dates from 547-1370 A.D., and 6 are notes on the poem! What is surprising given these facts is the essential liveliness of idiom and tone in the poem which literally does *talk* with Bede and the reader:

> You think historians must be keen to see
> What followed their escape from history?
> You think we can't find out? I'd rather hear
> The earth described. Remind us of the Wear,
> The creatures, plants and light where I began
> To look around the domicile of man

Thus, Elliot gives Bede a local habitation in his poem. This is the very best use of scholarship in poetry. In the poem learning is never on display to impress, but rather always born of an enthusiasm for bringing history to life in the now. This side of Elliot is counterbalanced by his ability (perhaps already independently achieved by his contemporary Tony Harrison) to write plainly about matters of his own family history. His poem on his grandfather, "John Elliot," throughout its length maintains a correlation between events in history contemporaneous with events in the personal history, from birth to death, of his grandfather, linking the private life with public events. It ends with a stark image:

> Still never losing your temper,
> you grew old in the long beard,
> and died, before my parents met.
> Years later, my father recognised your arm-bone
> held out in the grave
> at his mother's funeral:
> I'd have seen you—if I'd gone.

The care which has gone into making this poem and its truthfulness to a family memory allow the image a most sensitive delicacy of emotion, as the grandfather joins his wife in a grave. The dead are allowed dignity without a trace of sentimentality. Those who say that Elliot's imagination is most forcefully fuelled by Virgil, Horace, Livy, and other classics should bear poems such as "John Elliot," or the as-yet-uncollected and equally moving "Bless the Bed That I Lie On" for his grandmother Marion Elliot, in mind. The latter poem, through the image of a blanket made by his grandmother, records another instance of the loving-kindness which binds together husband and wife in life and death. Elliot's virtuosity with language controls and shapes personal emotion in these poems.

Elliot is also an extremely distinguished translator, with English versions of Heinrich Heine's *The Lazarus Poems* and Paul Verlaine's *Femmes/Hombres* to his credit. These translations, scholarly, metrically adept, and lively, celebrate life alternately in its sombre and erotic aspects with equal relish.

On the Appian Way, a book-length poem, traces Elliot's journey in Italy along the route taken from Rome by the Latin poet Horace in 37 B.C. The poem combines Elliot's usual liveliness of narration with an effortless and urbane artistry. Elliot celebrates everyday things, such as, for instance, breakfast in a bar, while also including enough allusions to Horace's poem on the same journey to fill 10 pages of notes at the back of a poem which the author claims "is as unobscure and impersonal as I could make it." The poem, divided into 15 sections, each marking one day and the places seen, is in heroic couplets: the tone, to me perhaps reminiscent of Arthur Hugh Clough's masterpiece "Amours de Voyage," allows Elliot to be both formal and relaxed:

These are the hardest hours to justify,
Not envied by the dead—the hours I pass
Gaping at their possessions behind glass,
Windowshopping like Tantalus, an ape
That, hands in pockets, comprehends pure shape
Vacuously.

Elliot's poems, his first book aside, are of a consistently high quality, both as literate entertainment and as art. His reputation has grown over the past few years and can only increase in the years to come among those who really care for poetry.

—Jonathan Barker

ELMSLIE, Kenward (Gray). American. Born in New York City, 27 April 1929. Educated at Harvard University, Cambridge, Massachusetts, B.A. 1950. Worked with the Karamu Inter-Racial Theatre, Cleveland. Art Critic, *Art News*, New York, 1966-67. Since 1972, Editor, Z Press, Calais, Vermont. Recipient: Ford grant, 1964; National Endowment for the Arts grant, 1966, 1978; Frank O'Hara Award, 1971. Address: Poets Corner, Calais, Vermont 05648, U.S.A.

PUBLICATIONS

Verse

Pavilions. New York, Tibor de Nagy, 1961.
The Power Plant Poems. New York, "C" Press, 1967.
The Champ. Los Angeles, Black Sparrow Press, 1968.
Album. New York, Kulchur, 1969.
Circus Nerves. Los Angeles, Black Sparrow Press, 1971.
Motor Disturbance. New York, Columbia University Press, 1971.
Girl Machine. New York, Angel Hair, 1971.
Penguin Modern Poets 24, with Kenneth Koch and James Schuyler. London, Penguin, 1973.
Tropicalism. Calais, Vermont, Z Press, 1975.

Communications Equipment. Providence, Rhode Island, Burning Deck, 1979.
Moving Right Along. Calais, Vermont, Z Press, 1980.

Plays

Unpacking the Black Trunk with James Schuyler (produced New York, 1965).
Lizzie Borden, music by Jack Beeson (produced New York, 1965). New York, Boosey and Hawkes, 1965.
Miss Julie, music by Ned Rorem (produced New York, 1965). New York, Boosey and Hawkes, 1965.
The Sweet Bye and Bye, music by Jack Beeson (produced Kansas City, 1973). New York, Boosey and Hawkes, 1966.
The Grass Harp, music by Claibe Richardson, adaptation of the novel by Truman Capote (produced New York, 1971). New York, French, 1971.
City Junket (produced New York, 1974). New York, Boke, 1972.
The Seagull, music by Thomas Pasatieri, adaptation of the play by Chekhov (produced Houston, 1974). Melville, New York, Belwin Mills, 1974.
Washington Square, music by Thomas Pasatieri, adaptation of the novel by Henry James (produced Detroit, 1976). Melville, New York, Belwin Mills, 1976.
Lola, music by Claibe Richardson (produced New York, 1982).

Novel

The Orchid Stories. New York, Doubleday, 1973.

Other

The Baby Book. New York, Boke, 1965.
The 1967 Gamebook Calendar. New York, Boke, 1967.
Shiny Ride. New York, Boke, 1972.
The Alphabet Work. Washington, D.C., Titanic Press, 1978.
Palais Bimbo Snapshots. Grindstone City, Michigan, Alternative Press, 1982.
Bimbo Dirt. Calais, Vermont, Z Press, 1982.

Editor, *Miltie Is a Hackie: A Libretto*, by Edwin Denby. Calais, Vermont, Z Press, 1973.
Editor, *Mobile Homes*, by Rudy Burckhardt. Calais, Vermont, Z Press, 1979.

*

Critical Studies: "Poetry and Public Experience" by Stephen Donadio, in *Commentary* (New York), February 1973; "Figure in the Carport" by John Ashbery, in *Parnassus* (New York), Summer 1976; "A Tribute to Kenward Elmslie" by Michael Silverblatt, in *Blarney* (Los Angeles), Spring 1984.

Kenward Elmslie comments:
Since about 1961, I've considered myself primarily a poet; before that I thought of myself, and *was*, primarily a writer of lyrics for theatre songs. I have continued to write for the theatre, have ventured into fiction, but I feel most centred (as a writer) when working on a poem. I enjoy collaborating with composers and visual artists, and, increasingly, I've begun singing poem-songs, set to music I've made up. I am sometimes listed as a member of the New York School of Poets, an outgrowth of friendship with the founders—Kenneth Koch, John Ashbery, James Schuyler, and the late Frank O'Hara, but it makes me

uneasy to think of my work thus conjoined, partly because of the range of influences that have been of use: Wallace Stevens, John Latouche, Bert Brecht, Ron Padgett, Jane Bowles, John Ashbery, Frank O'Hara, Kenneth Koch, Evelyn Waugh, Lorenz Hart, Ira Gershwin, Alex Katz, Red Grooms, Joe Brainard, Ken Tisa, Donna Dennis, and the films of Jacques Tati.

*   *   *

Poet, librettist and novelist, Kenward Elmslie has affinities with the New York school, with O'Hara and Ashbery, or perhaps Ted Berrigan and Joe Brainard. His poems and prose-poems (the opera libretti are rather different) are characterised by the juxtaposition of precise, and yet bizarre, sensory observations, as in "Tropicalism":

> Ate orange.
> Legs stained...stains turn into fur patches...
> fur patches turn into puma hide...palaver re
> escape route...boy's lips...chicken feather along
> outer perimeter of lower redder one, with
> up-and-down wrinkles fly is negotiating...
> too much pursing...spooky profiles peer
> sideways on high-rise balconies....

Elmslie is a poet of transformation and metamorphosis; things flow into things with an almost delirious momentum. Experience has no order which might allow the observer to stand at a discreet distance from the observed, as in "Olden Scrapple Sonnet":

> Wept at the way they gave of theirselves,
> the flasher's midriff entangled in cobwebs,
> the way Thebes, roped off, mazurka-polka'd,
> sex nuances forgotten for glitz of vernal equinox.
> Then by bad roads out of the sad mountains,
> lit-up arrows arching into stage-shows,
> Bijou: self-acting clogs in orphanage orangerie,
> Palace: abandoned. Lugged myself to primal hut.

Elmslie writes of the "maelstrom of remembered sights and sounds" ("Long Haul"), and at times there emerges from the seeming modernity of his linguistic usage an atmosphere of whimsy and nostalgia which can verge on the sentimentally lyrical. Poetic structure is a problem; at times syntax is abandoned while other poems retain a more or less orthodox syntactical organisation. One interesting development has been the use, in poems such as "Regret space not include" and "One Hundred I Remembers" of a formal device whereby each "verse" begins with the same verbal formula, rather in the manner of, say, Christopher Smart's *Jubilate Agno*. It is here, perhaps, that many readers will find Elmslie most accessible. His confrontation with life's particularities is described in "Black Froth":

> Disjointed a necessary mode of life ill-prepared for.
> Eager for the seamlessness underneath.

The search for the "seamlessness" produces challenging verbal constructions which occasionally exclude the reader. At his best, however, Elmslie's energy and invention combine to create records of a very individual sensibility.

—Glyn Pursglove

EMANUEL, James A(ndrew, Sr.). American. Born in Alliance, Nebraska, 15 June 1921. Educated at Alliance High School, 1935-39; Howard University, Washington, D.C., 1946-50, B.A. (summa cum laude) 1950; Northwestern University, Evanston, Illinois, 1950-53, M.A. 1953; Columbia University, New York, 1953-62, Ph.D. 1962. Served in the 93rd Infantry Division, United States Army, 1944-46: Army Commendation Ribbon. Married Mattie Johnson in 1950; one son. Canteen steward, Civilian Conservation Corps, Wellington, Kansas, 1939-40; elevator operator, Des Moines, Iowa, 1940-41; weighmaster, Rock Island, Illinois, 1941-42; confidential secretary, Office of the Inspector General, United States War Department, Washington, D.C. 1942-44; civilian chief, Pre-Induction Section, Army and Air Force Induction Station, Chicago, 1951-53; instructor, Harlem YWCA Business School, New York, 1954-56; instructor, 1957-62, Assistant Professor, 1962-70, Associate Professor, 1970-72, and Professor of English, 1972-84, City College of New York. Fulbright Professor of American Literature, University of Grenoble, 1968-69, and University of Warsaw, 1975-76; Visiting Professor of American Literature, University of Toulouse, 1971-73, 1979-81. General Editor, Broadside Press "Critics Series," Detroit. Recipient: John Hay Whitney fellowship, 1952; Saxton Memorial Fellowship, 1965. Address: Department of English, City College of New York, Convent Avenue, New York, New York 10031, U.S.A.

PUBLICATIONS

Verse

The Treehouse and Other Poems. Detroit, Broadside Press, 1968.
At Bay. Detroit, Broadside Press, 1969.
Panther Man. Detroit, Broadside Press, 1970.
Black Man Abroad: The Toulouse Poems. Detroit, Lotus Press, 1978.
A Chisel in the Dark: Poems, Selected and New. Detroit, Lotus Press, 1980.
A Poet's Mind. New York, Regents, 1983.
The Broken Bowl: New and Uncollected Poems. Detroit, Lotus Press, 1983.

Other

Langston Hughes. New York, Twayne, 1967.
How I Write 2, with MacKinlay Kantor and Lawrence Osgood. New York, Harcourt Brace, 1972.

Editor, with Theodore L. Gross, *Dark Symphony: Negro Literature in America.* New York, Free Press, 1968.

*

Manuscript Collection: Jay B. Hubbell Center, Perkins Library, Duke University, Durham, North Carolina.

Critical Studies: in *Road Apple Review* (Oshkosh, Wisconsin), Winter 1971-72; "James A. Emanuel: The Perilous Stairs," in *Caliban*, n.s. xii, 1976, and "Black Man Abroad: James A. Emanuel," in *Black American Literature Forum* (Terre Haute, Indiana), Fall 1979, both by Marvin Holdt; *Black American Poetry: A Critical Commentary* by Ann Semel and Kathleen Mullen, New York, Monarch Press, 1977.

James A. Emanuel comments:

(1974) Some of the personal history, and many of the ideas, reflected in my poetry can be found in my contribution to the book *How I Write 2*. By now, writing poetry is my principal method of finding and expressing what life means. From the time that I began to write poetry steadily, in the late 1950's, the exacting labor and the large mysteries of that activity—usually carried on late at night—have centered upon vital, everyday matters. The categories into which my poems can be divided describe areas of experience and thought with which ordinary men are well acquainted (and I have wanted my poetry to be fundamentally clear to the largest possible audience): recurrent subjects are youth (centrally my son, James) and miscellaneous Black experience; other subjects include writers, anti-Semitism, blues, war, etc.; the lyrics continue philosophical, descriptive, and personal themes; the tone is usually serious, sometimes satirical, once in a while humorous; the form varies from strict sonnets to free verse that attempts to catch nuances of Black American speech patterns that might be heard on a Harlem street. My poetry runs roughly parallel to my life: a movement from the reflective traditional to the compressed tensions of the 1970's, with inevitably special emphasis on racism, but also with constantly interspersed lyrics that have little to do with our perilous decades. Thus I hope that my poetry, in its unplanned evolution and variety, attests the crucial, dual role of the Black poet: to struggle as embroiled man, but to reflect as clear Mind; to denude and expose as destroyer, yet to clothe and grace as creator; to live as Black and therefore made for the wide world, yet American and therefore made for the narrow cauldron that our nation has become.

My latest work, especially "The Toulouse Poems" and generally those written in and after 1972, might well suggest that three loves develop in my work: parental, racial, and romantic. These common passions are the staple of my poetry. Trying to fathom them and to transform them into art. I am content to be judged by that mass of readers who feel as strongly as they think and who are drawn to what I want increasingly to keep in my poetry: the bite and song of reality.

(1980) Reviewing my poems written recently in London and Paris, I find experiments with anti-realism coming into my work—perhaps as an intensification of my grappling with such subjects as tyranny, art, and time.

*   *   *

James A. Emanuel's sympathies are clear even without his statement in *Panther Man* that young people are "the only people whom I tend to respect as a group." Poems like "A Clown at Ten," "The Young Ones, Flip Side," "Fourteen," "Sixteen, Yeah," and "Fisherman" celebrate with an understanding smile the passion and energy of youth while they steer clear of Housmanian idolatry and pathos. Young adulthood is pain, punching, and confusion for the poet, the hopeful stage through which the world passes to confrontation. Behind it stretches the pre-lapsarian vista of childhood. The poet captures the antics of the bathtub sailor in "The Voyage of Jimmy Poo," a time of sterling memory in "I Wish I Had a Red Balloon," and the joy of answering children's questions in "For the 4th Grade, Prospect School: How I Became a Poet."

Manhood brings a different order: understanding, rebellion, militancy, anguish, and death. "Emmett Till," "Where Will Their Names Go Down," and "For Malcolm, U.S.A." pay tribute to the victims, while "Panther Man," "Animal Tricks," "Crossover: for RFK," and "Black Man, 13th Floor" speak in strident (sometimes black, idiomatic) tones of the growth of a generation of men who are rising to take control.

Surrounding and undergirding all stages, however, is the essential romantic humanism of the poet. "Nightmare" and "Christ, One Morning" let us know that all is in the hands of man; there is no God who can be trusted. And ceaselessly, Emanuel reaffirms the power of the imaginative intellect to scale the heights of its own treehouse and dream ("A Negro Author" and "The Treehouse"), or to bring the authoritarian assumptions of the world down with a wince ("Black Poet on the Firing Range"). The poems from Toulouse show a sweep and maturity that combine this essential vision with a firm formal mastery.

—Houston A. Baker, Jr.

———————

ENGELS, John (David). American. Born in South Bend, Indiana, 19 January 1931. Educated at the University of Notre Dame, Indiana, A.B. 1952; University College, Dublin, 1955; University of Iowa, Iowa City, M.F.A. 1957. Served in the United States Navy, 1952-55: Lieutenant. Married Gail Jochimsen in 1957; two daughters and four sons (one deceased). Instructor in English, Norbert College, West De Pere, Wisconsin, 1957-62. Assistant Professor, 1962-70, and since 1970, Professor of English, St. Michael's College, Winooski Park, Vermont. Visiting Lecturer, University of Vermont, Burlington, 1974, 1975, 1976; Slaughter Lecturer, Sweet Briar College, Virginia, 1976. Secretary, 1971-72, and Trustee, 1971-75, Vermont Council on the Arts. Recipient: Bread Loaf Writers Conference scholarship, 1960, and Robert Frost fellowship, 1976; Guggenheim fellowship, 1979. Address: Department of English, St. Michael's College, Winooski Park, Vermont 05404, U.S.A.

PUBLICATIONS

Verse

The Homer Mitchell Place. Pittsburgh, University of Pittsburgh Press, 1968.
Signals from the Safety Coffin. Pittsburgh, University of Pittsburgh Press, 1975.
Vivaldi in Early Fall. Burlington, Vermont, Bittersweet Press, 1977.
Blood Mountain. Pittsburgh, University of Pittsburgh Press, 1977.
Vivaldi in Early Fall (collection). Athens, University of Georgia Press, 1981.
The Seasons in Vermont. Syracuse, Tamarack, 1982.
Weather-Fear: New and Selected Poems 1958-1982. Athens, University of Georgia Press, 1983.

Other

Writing Techniques, with Norbert Engels. New York, McKay, 1962.
Experience and Imagination, with Norbert Engels. New York, McKay, 1965.

Editor, *The Merrill Guide to William Carlos Williams.* Columbus, Ohio, Merrill, 1969.
Editor, *The Merrill Checklist of William Carlos Williams.* Columbus, Ohio, Merrill, 1969.
Editor, *The Merrill Studies in Paterson.* Columbus, Ohio, Merrill, 1971.

Through five full volumes—the fifth a selection spanning a quarter of a century's work—John Engels's poems reveal themselves to be parts of one long, complex, and intense meditation on the struggle of mind with matter, of earth with air, of death with love. These poems, varied in particular subject and manner, never arrive at easy answers, but rather pause at soul's leap into air or recoil at earth's deadly bull's eye or end in a terrible balance between brute fact and injured thought.

The poems all center in the consciousness of a man living for many years in a single house in Vermont, aware always of the stagnant water seeping into his cellar and up into his living air, wary and worried by winter's deadly encroachments, wounded beyond solace by the death of his baby son, and yet still able to count over the names of his living family, wife and children, still able to make the act of love which consists of his continuing attempts to name the world, to give it words by which to live. The scope of his poetry is, then, small—this house, these people, these doubts and concerns; its range and depth are enormous as Engels worries these simple subjects into a poetry as disciplined and intense and deeply meaningful as that of any modern poet.

Engels is never content with the results of his words' wrestle with matter: from his first book, *The Homer Mitchell Place*, to his most recent, *Weather-Fear*, he has returned to the same subjects, the same themes, the same images, reshaping them, restating them, reassessing them, always pressing them deeper and deeper toward a continually elusive meaning. In *Weather-Fear* he has reworked and relined poems, compressing them on the page, holding back the flow of their rich rhythms, aware always that they still do not say enough of what they must say if they are to push away from earth's grave downpulling into soul's freed flight. This dissatisfaction, which is at the heart of his poetry's dynamic tension, emerges explicitly in the long and central poem, "Interlachen," with which he ends his selected poems:

> I tend to speak, though lacking
> clarity, not knowing
> the names, not having in need
> the language, given to interminable
> revision of the text. And this is where
> the true anger locates itself,
> that I have no ability or hope
> that I may speak to the ordinary with much
> in the way of truth or generosity.
> And it must seem I make these rituals
> as if they were sole judge of the truth,
> not merely sanctimonies of procedure, noble
> appearances of moral care
> by reason of which the names refuse themselves,
> and it all ends
> in such unsatisfactory obliquities as this.

Engels's speaking to the ordinary has, despite and perhaps because of his sense of inadequacy in the face of that overwhelming task (as he described Mozart's music), "seized in the real and made to flash forth/the mute transparencies/of matter." His is a major voice in American poetry, one not given proper credit at a time when simple anecdote or surreal political statement are accorded lavish critical attention. And yet his sure growth from the controlled metrical force of his early poems through the mythic break-through of the poems in *Blood Mountain* to the sustained musical visions of the later poems in *Vivaldi in Early Fall* and the grand reassessments of *Weather-Fear* is that of a serious craftsman and a genuinely visionary artist. Like those other artists of whom he has written—Mozart and Vivaldi, Mahler and Van Gogh—he has produced a body of work in which change and sustained vision are in total harmony, in which we dare name our darkness, know the shock of our fall that made the whole earth shake, and feel the bruise that congeals at the very root of our being.

What he finally gives us is our most basic fear made tangible, grounded in a language of weight and substantial gravity, and, from that ground, he forces us aloft, lifts our gaze from the sealed grave and the gaping cellar hole to a vision earned in all that painful darkness, a moment (as he puts it in "The Disconnections")

> in the dazzling, translucid sea-light, union of
>   particles
> beyond all series, never so light as then, the earth
> closed on itself and centered, gravid
> with bodies, trembling to give birth.

—R.H.W. Dillard

ENGLE, Paul (Hamilton). American. Born in Cedar Rapids, Iowa, 12 October 1908. Educated at Coe College, Cedar Rapids, B.A. 1931 (Phi Beta Kappa); University of Iowa, Iowa City, M.A. 1932; Columbia University, New York, 1932-33; Merton College, Oxford (Rhodes Scholar); B.A. 1936, M.A. 1939. Married 1) Mary Nissen in 1936, two daughters; 2) Hualing Nieh in 1971. Director of the Creative Writing Program, 1937-65, Professor of English, 1946-77, and Director of the International Writing Program, 1966-77, University of Iowa. Member of the Advisory Commission on the Arts, and the National Council on the Arts. Recipient: Yale Series of Younger Poets award, 1932; Guggenheim fellowship, 1953; Lamont Poetry Selection Award, 1962; Rockefeller fellowship; Ford fellowship. D.Litt.: Coe College, 1946; LL.D.: Monmouth College, Illinois, 1949; L.H.D.: Iowa Wesleyan College, Mount Pleasant, 1956; University of Dubuque, 1981; University of Colorado, Boulder, 1981. Agent: William Morris Agency Inc., 1350 Avenue of the Americas, New York, New York 10019. Address: 1104 North Dubuque Street, Iowa City, Iowa 52240, U.S.A.

PUBLICATIONS

Verse

Worn Earth. New Haven, Connecticut, Yale University Press, 1932.
American Song. New York, Doubleday, 1934; London, Cape, 1935.
Break the Heart's Anger. New York, Doubleday, and London, Cape, 1936.
Corn. New York, Doubleday, 1939.
New Englanders. Muscatine, Iowa, Prairie Press, 1940.
West of Midnight. New York, Random House, 1941.
American Child. Privately printed, 1944.
American Child: A Sonnet Sequence. New York, Random House, 1945; revised edition, as *American Child: Sonnets for My Daughter, with Thirty Six New Poems*, New York, Dial Press, 1956.
The Word of Love. New York, Random House, 1951.

Book and Child: Three Sonnets. Iowa City, Cummington Press, 1956.
Poems in Praise. New York, Random House, 1959.
Christmas Poems. Privately printed, 1962.
A Woman Unashamed and Other Poems. New York, Random House, 1965.
Embrace: Selected Love Poems. New York, Random House, 1969.
Images of China: Poems Written in China, April-June 1980. Beijing, New World Press, 1981.

Plays

For the Iowa Dead, music by Philip Bezanson. Iowa City, State University of Iowa, 1956.
Golden Child, music by Philip Bezanson (televised, 1960). New York, Doubleday, 1962.

Novels

Always the Land. New York, Random House, 1941.
Golden Child. New York, Dutton, 1962.

Other

Robert Frost. Iowa City, State University of Iowa Library, 1959.
A Prairie Christmas. New York, Longman, 1960.
Who's Afraid? (for children). New York, Crowell Collier, 1963.
An Old-Fashioned Christmas. New York, Dial Press, 1964.
Portrait of Iowa, photographs by John Zielinski. Minneapolis, Adams Press, 1976.
Women in the American Revolution. Chicago, Follett, 1976.

Editor, with Harold Cooper, *West of the Great Water: An Iowa Anthology.* Iowa City, Athens Press, 1931.
Editor, *Ozark Anthology,* by G.F. Newburger. Cedar Rapids, Iowa, Torch Press, 1938.
Editor, *Prize Stories 1954* [to *1959*]: *The O. Henry Awards.* New York, Doubleday, 6 vols., 1954-59.
Editor, with Warren Carrier, *Reading Modern Poetry.* Chicago, Scott Foresman, 1955; revised edition, 1968.
Editor, *Homage to Baudelaire, on the Centennial of "Les Fleurs du Mal," from the Poets at the State University of Iowa.* Iowa City, Cummington Press, 1957.
Editor, with Henri Coulette and Donald Justice, *Midland.* New York, Random House, 1961.
Editor, with Joseph Langland, *Poet's Choice.* New York, Dial Press, 1962.
Editor, *On Creative Writing.* New York, Dutton, 1964.
Editor, *Midland 2.* New York, Random House, 1970.
Editor, with others, *Writing from the World.* Iowa City, University of Iowa, 1976.

Translator, with Hualing Nieh, *Poems of Mao Tse-tung.* New York, Dell, 1972; as *The Poetry of Mao Tse-tung,* London, Wildwood House, 1973.

*

Manuscript Collection: University of Iowa Library, Iowa City.

Paul Engle comments:

My poetry tries to find the most concentrated human feeling in the fewest words. It was a sprawling effort in the early years and has tightened up in the later years. The poems about Edmund Blunden at Oxford University represent the struggle to absorb direct experience into direct language. Emotion without sentimentality, images containing the emotion as object. Rilke and Yeats the greatest influences.

*   *   *

Paul Engle has been a major figure in American poetry for 40 years and more. As a principal in the founding and development of the famous Writers Workshop at the University of Iowa, as a teacher and editor, he has been an important and encouraging influence for many young poets: several are important contemporary voices. Engle's current efforts are largely directed toward the development of a Translation Workshop, also at the University of Iowa.

As a poet, Engle's reputation is based on more than ten volumes published since 1932. It is perhaps not surprising to note that these contain consistently energetic poems of affirmation. It is an optimistic verse which frequently states its opposition to the modern voice of despair and makes use of so-called "American themes": *Corn, A Prairie Christmas,* "Coney Island," "American Harvest." It is a verse which, like his titles, and even in the later volumes which reach outside of America for some subject matter, is direct and uncomplicated:

> Her spine curves like a C,
> But does it therefore beg
> For pity and despair
> Like Lautrec's crooked leg?
>
> No! For the food she grows
> That Tokyo may eat,
> Comes from determination
> Perfect and complete.

A poet of Engle's ability and temperament has apparently had to answer some hard questions: How is one to affirm in a world where despair is more obvious and cynicism seems safer? How do we have a popular poetry, of good taste, in a nation where the real has so often been merely vulgar?

Engle has proclaimed and praised with control and clear speech in each of his volumes. His subjects and attitudes are occasionally close to Whitman or Sandburg or Lindsay, but it would be wrong to say Engle sings or celebrates. The tone of his early poems is reminiscent of the Georgians and, in later volumes, several reviewers have noted that the poems are nostalgic although occasionally "worn" or "repetitive."

He is at his best when his verse is simplest:

> That was a shocking day
> When we watched, lying prone,
> The two trout sidle under
> The underwater stone...

And in "Pair":

> Nothing can live alone,
> Two are behind each birth.
> Every fallen stone
> Lies on the rock of earth.

Never a single thing
Has the whole power to be.
Always the wind must bring
Pollen from tree to tree.

A man is how he stands,
Thrust of foot in shoe.
I am my own long hands
And their live touch of you.

But in the eagerness to attack despair, too often there are lines which are prosaic or merely sentimental:

There is a primitive old strength of heart
Men have called courage and that we call guts,
It bore the Crucifix and warped the wagons
Of Boone's men westward through the frozen ruts...(1939)

or "Abruptly in her black and grateful eyes/The red firecrackers of her heart explode (1965).

One of the excellences of contemporary poetry has been its recognition that there are moments of special emotion when the poet should be struck speechless, and his poem communicate that "silence between the words." It is the essayist or teacher who explains, or over-explains, and too often explains away, but the essayist or teacher is seeking a different, and predominantly intellectual, credibility.

Engle's technique has been markedly influenced by several poets: Shelley in the early volumes, Donne's use of paradox and metaphor, Eliot in several poems (e.g., "Harlem Airshaft"), Auden's Christmas oratorio, Frost, and his former teacher at Oxford, Edmund Blunden. Like Blunden he keeps a distance from the physical—and from his subjects—which is often as aristocratic as aesthetic. Engle's best poems for the contemporary ear are lyric and personal, avoiding strong masculine rhymes, similes, and deliberate iambics. "Kaarlo in Finland" is a sensitive sequence of "letters" around the "Russo-Finnish" war. The title sequence of *A Woman Unashamed* and "In a Bar near Shibuya Station, Tokyo" are good examples of his best work in which there is a striking delicacy: "As if on a summer day, in the dazzle of noon,/One snowflake fell on my astonished hand."

—Joseph Wilson

ENRIGHT, D(ennis) J(oseph). British. Born in Leamington, Warwickshire, 11 March 1920. Educated at Leamington College; Downing College, Cambridge, B.A. (honours) in English 1944, M.A. 1946; University of Alexandria, Egypt, D.Litt. 1949. Married Madeleine Harders in 1949; one daughter. Lecturer in English, University of Alexandria, 1947-50; Organising Tutor, Extra-Mural Department, Birmingham University, 1950-53; Visiting Professor, Konan University, Kobe, Japan, 1953-56; Gastdozent, Free University, West Berlin, 1956-57; British Council Professor of English, Chulalongkorn University, Bangkok, 1957-59; Professor of English, University of Singapore, 1960-70; Temporary Lecturer in English, University of Leeds, Yorkshire, 1970-71; Honorary Professor of English, University of Warwick, Coventry, 1975-80. Co-Editor, *Encounter* magazine, London, 1970-72; Editorial Adviser, 1971-73 and Member of the Board of Directors, 1973-82, Chatto and Windus, publishers, London. Recipient: Cholmondeley Award,

1974; Society of Authors travelling scholarship, 1981; Queen's Gold Medal for Poetry, 1981. D.Litt.: University of Warwick, 1982. Fellow, Royal Society of Literature, 1961. Agent: Watson Little Ltd., Suite 8, 26 Charing Cross Road, London WC2H ODG. Address: 35-A Viewfield Road, London SW18 5TD, England.

PUBLICATIONS

Verse

Season Ticket.   Alexandria, Editions du Scarabee, 1948.
The Laughing Hyena and Other Poems.   London, Routledge, 1953.
The Year of the Monkey.   Privately printed, 1956.
Bread Rather Than Blossoms.   London, Secker and Warburg, 1956.
Some Men Are Brothers.   London, Chatto and Windus, 1960.
Addictions.   London, Chatto and Windus, 1962.
The Old Adam.   London, Chatto and Windus, 1965.
Unlawful Assembly.   London, Chatto and Windus, and Middletown, Connecticut, Wesleyan University Press, 1968.
Selected Poems.   London, Chatto and Windus, 1969.
The Typewriter Revolution and Other Poems.   New York, Library Press, 1971.
In the Basilica of the Annunciation.   London, Poem-of-the-Month Club, 1971.
Daughters of Earth.   London, Chatto and Windus, 1972.
Foreign Devils.   London, Covent Garden Press, 1972.
The Terrible Shears: Scenes from a Twenties Childhood.   London, Chatto and Windus, 1973; Middletown, Connecticut, Wesleyan University Press, 1974.
Rhyme Times Rhyme (for children).   London, Chatto and Windus, 1974.
Sad Ires and Others.   London, Chatto and Windus, 1975.
Penguin Modern Poets 26, with Dannie Abse and Michael Longley.   London, Penguin, 1975.
Paradise Illustrated.   London, Chatto and Windus, 1978.
A Faust Book.   London, Oxford University Press, 1979.
Walking in the Harz Mountains, Faust Senses the Presence of God.   Richmond, Surrey, Keepsake Press, 1979.
Collected Poems.   Oxford and New York, Oxford University Press, 1981.
Instant Chronicles.   Oxford and New York, Oxford University Press, 1985.

Novels

Academic Year.   London, Secker and Warburg, 1955.
Heaven Knows Where.   London, Secker and Warburg, 1957.
Insufficient Poppy.   London, Chatto and Windus, 1960.
Figures of Speech.   London, Heinemann, 1965.

Other

A Commentary on Goethe's "Faust."   New York, New Directions, 1949.
The World of Dew: Aspects of Living Japan.   London, Secker and Warburg, 1955; Chester Springs, Pennsylvania, Dufour, 1959.
Literature for Man's Sake: Critical Essays.   Tokyo, Kenkyusha, 1955; Philadelphia, West, 1976.
The Apothecary's Shop.   London, Secker and Warburg, 1957; Chester Springs, Pennsylvania, Dufour, 1959.

Robert Graves and the Decline of Modernism (address).   Singapore, Craftsman Press, 1960.

Conspirators and Poets.   London, Chatto and Windus, and Chester Springs, Pennsylvania, Dufour, 1966.

Memoirs of a Mendicant Professor.   London, Chatto and Windus, 1969.

Shakespeare and the Students.   London, Chatto and Windus, 1970; New York, Schocken, 1971.

Man Is an Onion: Essays and Reviews.   London, Chatto and Windus, 1972; LaSalle, Illinois, Library Press, 1973.

A Kidnapped Child of Heaven: The Poetry of Arthur Hugh Clough (lecture).   Nottingham, University of Nottingham, 1972.

The Joke Shop (for children).   London, Chatto and Windus, and New York, McKay, 1976.

Wild Ghost Chase (for children).   London, Chatto and Windus, 1978.

Beyond Land's End (for children).   London, Chatto and Windus, 1979.

A Mania for Sentences.   London, Chatto and Windus, 1983; Boston, Godine, 1985.

Editor, *Poets of the 1950's: An Anthology of New English Verse.*   Tokyo, Kenkyusha, 1955.

Editor, with Takamichi Ninomiya, *The Poetry of Living Japan.* London, Murray, and New York, Grove Press, 1957.

Editor, with Ernst de Chickera, *English Critical Texts: 16th Century to 20th Century.*   London and New York, Oxford University Press, 1962.

Editor, *A Choice of Milton's Verse.*   London, Faber, 1975.

Editor, *Rasselas*, by Samuel Johnson.   London, Penguin, 1976.

Editor, *The Oxford Book of Contemporary Verse 1945-1980.* Oxford, Oxford University Press, 1980.

Editor, *The Oxford Book of Death.*   Oxford and New York, Oxford University Press, 1983.

Editor, *Fair of Speech: The Uses of Euphemism.*   Oxford and New York, Oxford University Press, 1985.

Translator, with Madeleine Enright, *Nature Alive*, by Colette Portal.   London, Chatto and Windus, 1980.

*

Critical Studies: *D.J. Enright: Poet of Humanism* by William Walsh, London, Cambridge University Press, 1974; "No Easy Answer: The Poetry of D.J. Enright" by Shirley Chew, in *New Lugano Review* (Lugano, Switzerland), vol. 3, no. 1-2, 1977; Anthony John Harding, in *Poets of Great Britain and Ireland 1945-1960* edited by Vincent B. Sherry, Jr., Detroit, Gale, 1984.

*   *   *

The chief stimulus for the highly individual talent of D.J. Enright has been the landscape and people of the countries, mainly in the Far East, where he has spent most of his working life. Some characteristic attitudes were, however, already apparent in early poems about his native Black Country (in, for example, his pointing the incongruity between the idyllic name and dreary reality of Swan Village); and have persisted in later work like the disenchanted cameos of commuter London in *Sad Ires* or of the contemporary English scene satirized in *Paradise Illustrated.*

But it is through his pictures of life abroad that his sense of ironic contrast is most memorably communicated, as in "The Beach at Abousir" between holidaymakers and those "pointed shapes, like trees in winter—/Aged men and ancient children" patiently waiting their chance to pilfer from the prosperous. In Japan the cherry "comes to its immaculate birth" amidst poverty, hunger, and disease. A beautiful peasant girl is found a perfect subject by film-makers "except for the dropsy/Which comes from unpolished rice" (the grim word-play of the title, "A Polished Performance," is typical). Ragged subway sleepers, tensely "hectic rice-winners" commuting on the underground, the ragman who "picks his comfort" in the gentle beauty of the Kyoto autumn, make their silent but uncompromising comment on a society of extremes. In "A Pleasant Walk," contrasting the rows of banks lining "a noble promenade...paved in gold from every nation" with "the brutal village sunk in slush," Enright bitterly observes: "High commerce civilizes, there's no doubt of that." The banker of "Happy New Year," bemoaning the falling yen as he shows off his opulent house and art treasures, is relentlessly juxtaposed with the empty-pocketed "masters of their fourpenny kites/That soar in the open market of the sky"; the "moderate ambitions" of princes and generals for an air-conditioned palace, a smarter G.H.Q., with the refugees of "Brush-Fire" in flight from their burning shacks, pushing bicycles piled with small bundles. The controlled anger of "The Monuments of Hiroshima" is matched by the deadly fairy-tale idiom employed to recount a bombing error in "The Pied Piper of Akashi."

To Enright's acute, compassionate eye, the great enemy is indifference to suffering, whether in the anonymous multitude or the individual tragedy like that of the 13-year-old suicide who found rat poison cheaper than aspirin. In his dry, amused relish of the ludicrous he can often be very funny; but it is a humour, as in the caustic comment of "Public Address System" on the grotesqueries of excessive official politeness, from which the biting edge is seldom absent. "Simply, he was human, did no harm, and suffered for it" is his epitaph for the poor and oppressed; his sense of the common sadness of the human condition is most poignantly crystallized in the diffident, fragile nocturnal melody, at once elegiac and celebrating survival, of "The Noodle-Vendor's Flute."

The shock of large-scale misery and squalor to a caring Western sensibility is frequently registered through the accent of deliberate, almost casual understatement which allows the recorded fact to speak for itself; and this powerful restraint serves to intensify by contrast the impassioned force of the writer's pity and indignation. In common with his fellows of the "Movement," Enright has resolutely refused to sentimentalize the apparently picturesque—rejecting "Epochs of parakeets, of peacocks, and paradisaic birds" for unembellished "images that merely were." This is reflected in his astringent advice in "Changing the Subject," and the wry self-mockery of an acknowledged poetic temptation in "Displaced Person Looks at a Cage-Bird"; while both "Nature Poetry" and the enchanting "Blue Umbrellas" survey our distortions of reality by "the dishonesty of names."

Slyly quizzical, irreverent, socially inconvenient in his impatience of humbug, Enright directs the same remorseless wit towards his own shortcomings (in "The Fairies," "The Ageing Poet," and "A Commuter's Tale") as barbs his scrutiny of the human sham from minister of state to theorizing anarchist or romanticizing poet. A sceptical inner voice prompts him to question whether his own persistent choice of exotic backgrounds might not represent an escapist "rest from meaning." the answer is provided by his characteristic affirmation that "Nothing is exotic, if you understand,/If you stick your neck out for an hour or two." The special tone of this civilized, ironic, unostentatious voice is invoked in "Elegy in a Country Suburb":

Wholly truthful, intimate
And utterly unsparing,
A man communing with himself.

—Margaret Willy

ENSLIN, Theodore (Vernon). American. Born in Chester, Pennsylvania, 25 March 1925. Educated in public and private schools; studied composition with Nadia Boulanger, 1943-44. Married 1) Mildred Marie Stout in 1945 (divorced, 1961), one daughter and one son; 2) Alison Jane Jose in 1969, one son. Columnist ("Six Miles Square"), *The Cape Codder*, Orleans, Massachusetts, 1949-56. Recipient: Nieman Award, for journalism, 1955; National Endowment for the Arts grant, 1976. Address: R.F.D. Box 289, Kansas Road, Milbridge, Maine 04658, U.S.A.

PUBLICATIONS

Verse

The Work Proposed. Ashland, Massachusetts, Origin Press, 1958.
New Sharon's Prospect. Kyoto, Japan, Origin Press, 1962.
The Place Where I Am Standing. New Rochelle, New York, Elizabeth Press, 1964.
This Do (and The Talents). Mexico City, El Corno Emplumado, 1966.
New Sharon's Prospect and Journals. San Francisco, Coyote's Journal, 1966.
To Come To Have Become. New Rochelle, New York, Elizabeth Press, 1966.
The Four Temperaments. Privately printed, 1966.
Characters in Certain Places. Portland, Oregon, Prensa da Lagar-Wine Press, 1967.
The Diabelli Variations and Other Poems. Annandale-on-Hudson, New York, Matter, 1967.
2/30—6/31: Poems 1967. Cabot, Vermont, Stoveside Press, 1967.
Agreement and Back: Sequences. New Rochelle, New York, Elizabeth Press, 1969.
The Poems. New Rochelle, New York, Elizabeth Press, 1970.
Forms. New Rochelle, New York, Elizabeth Press, 5 vols., 1970-74.
Views 1—7. Berkeley, California, Maya, 1970.
The Country of Our Consciousness. Berkeley, California, Sand Dollar, 1971.
Etudes. New Rochelle, New York, Elizabeth Press, 1972.
Views. New Rochelle, New York, Elizabeth Press, 1973.
Sitio. Hanover, New Hampshire, Granite, 1973.
In the Keepers House. Dennis, Massachusetts, Salt Works Press, 1973.
With Light Reflected. Fremont, Michigan, Sumac Press, 1973.
The Swamp Fox. Dennis, Massachusetts, Salt Works Press, 1973.
The Mornings. Berkeley, California, Shaman/Drum, 1974.
Fever Poems. Brunswick, Maine, Blackberry, 1974.
The Last Days of October. Dennis, Massachusetts, Salt Works Press, 1974.

The Median Flow: Poems 1943-73. Los Angeles, Black Sparrow Press, 1974.
Synthesis 1—24. Plainfield, Vermont, North Atlantic, 1975.
Ländler. New Rochelle, New York, Elizabeth Press, 1975.
Some Pastorals. Dennis, Massachusetts, Salt Works Press, 1975.
Papers. New Rochelle, New York, Elizabeth Press, 1976.
Carmina. Dennis, Massachusetts, Salt Works Press, 1976.
The July Book. Berkeley, California, Sand Dollar, 1976.
The Further Regions. Milwaukee, Pentagram Press, 1977.
Ascensions. Santa Barbara, California, Black Sparrow Press, 1977.
Circles. Lewiston, Maine, Great Raven Press, 1977.
Concentrations. Dennis, Massachusetts, Salt Works Press, 1977.
Ranger CXXII and CXXVIII. Rhinebeck, New York, Station Hill Press, 1977.
Tailings. Milwaukee, Pentagram Press, 1978.
16 Blossoms in February. Brunswick, Maine, Blackberry, 1978.
Ranger, Ranger 2. Richmond, California, North Atlantic, 2 vols., 1979-80.
May Fault. Lewiston, Maine, Great Raven Press, 1979.
Opus 31, No. 3. Milwaukee, Membrane Press, 1979.
The Flare of Beginning Is in November. New York, Jordan Davies, 1980.
The Fifth Direction. Milwaukee, Pentagram Press, 1980.
Star Anise. Milwaukee, Pentagram Press, 1980.
Two Geese. Milwaukee, Pentagram Press, 1980.
In Duo Concertante. Milwaukee, Pentagram Press, 1981.
Markings. Milwaukee, Membrane Press, 1981.
Opus O. Milwaukee, Membrane Press, 1981.
Processionals. Dennis, Massachusetts, Salt Works Press, 1981.
Fragments/Epigrammata. Dennis, Massachusetts, Salt Works Press, 1982.
Axes 52. Willimantic, Connecticut, Ziesing Brothers, 1982.
A Man in Stir. Milwaukee, Pentagram Press, 1983.

Play

Barometric Pressure 29.83 and Steady (produced New York, 1965).

Short Stories

2 + 12. Dennis, Massachusetts, Salt Works Press, 1979.

Other

Mahler. Los Angeles, Black Sparrow Press, 1975.

Editor, *The Selected Poems of Howard McCord 1961-1971.* Trumansburg, New York, Crossing Press, 1975.
Editor, *F.P.* Willimantic, Connecticut, Ziesing Brothers, 1982.

*

Manuscript Collection: Fales Collection, New York University Libraries.

Critical Studies: "The Frozen State" by the author, in *Elizabeth* (New Rochelle, New York), 1965; "Theodore Enslin Issue" of *Truck 20* (St. Paul), 1978.

Theodore Enslin comments:

I suppose I would classify as a "non-academic," and have been allied with those who broke with the "New Criticism" in the early fifties.

Perhaps, as Cid Corman once said, I write more "you" poems than anyone else now alive. My "themes" are what I find around me, and since I live in the country, this has sometimes led to thinking that I am in some way a "Nature poet." I heartily disavow this. My poems are intensely introspective from which I attempt to produce the impersonality/personality which I feel necessary to any valid work of art. My formal structure is based on sound, and I feel that my musical training has shaped this more than anything else. The line breaks/stresses are indicated as a type of notation, something which concerns me, since I believe we have no adequate notation for poetry, and I conceive of any poem as requiring a performance. It should be read aloud. In ways, some important to me, and some to the work itself, I would say that Rilke, W.C. Williams, Thoreau, and latterly Louis Zukofsky, were influences. The rest must be said in the poems themselves.

*   *   *

Theodore Enslin's work became known in the pages of *Origin*, the seminal magazine edited by Cid Corman, who also published Enslin's first book. It's not surprising, then, to find a continuity between the work of the two men. Both write spare, quiet, post-Williams poems grounded in a shared respect for the otherness and autonomy of natural things and a distrust of the romantic ego. A basic premise is that sufficiently careful naming of phenomena can by itself energize attention. But Enslin is more diffuse than Corman. Many of his poems, read quickly, seem merely flat, no more than prose jottings. Reread, however, with due attention to the lineation and sound, the best of them take on a pondered weight and become meditations rather than mere statements. His method of condensing daily experience and observation into poems can be seen in the charming *New Sharon's Prospect*, which gives both the prose anecdotes and sketches and the poems which crystallize out of them. Enslin's work is filled with the places, people, and things of rural New England, where he lives. If at times it reminds you of a Frost landscape, it is free of Frost's often intrusive "personality." Others of his poems are more abstract notations of emotion or of the problematic relations of observer and external reality; this one is from *The Place Where I Am Standing*:

I turned once to the window
and once
to you
    not here.
I would have shown you
a world I see there,
but it would not have been your world.
It is better this way.
In absence, you come to the window,
look out on just those things
I have shown you.

The five volumes of *Forms*, a long open-structure poem, are the product of "sixteen years of experiment and discovery" which he describes as "my apperception of art, of history, of experience, whatever any of it may have been worth, and no matter how limited." First acquaintance suggests that it is less rewarding than the short poems, but the interest of the latter is

grounds enough for thinking the long work will deserve frequentation.

—Seamus Cooney

———

ESHLEMAN, Clayton. American. Born in Indianapolis, Indiana, 1 June 1935. Educated at Indiana University, Bloomington, 1953-61, B.A. in philosophy 1958, M.A. in English 1961. Married Barbara Novak in 1961 (divorced, 1967), one son; 2) Caryl Reiter in 1969. Instructor, University of Maryland Eastern Overseas Division, Japan, 1961-62; Instructor in English, Matsushita Electric Corporation, Osaka, Japan, 1962-64; lived in Peru, 1965; Instructor, New York University American Language Institute, 1966-68; Member of the School of Critical Studies, California Institute of the Arts, Valencia, 1970-72; taught at University of California, Los Angeles, 1975-77; taught in a black ghetto high school in Los Angeles (California Arts Council grant), 1977-78; Lecturer, University of California, San Diego and Riverside, 1979-80; Dreyfuss Poet-in-Residence, and Lecturer, California Institute of Technology, Pasadena, 1979-84. Publisher, Caterpillar Books, 1966-67, and Editor, *Caterpillar* magazine, New York, 1967-70, and Sherman Oaks, California, 1970-73; reviewer, *Los Angeles Times Book Review*, 1979-84; Editor, *Sulfur*, Pasadena, 1980-84. Recipient: National Translation Center award, 1967, 1968; Union League Civic and Arts Foundation Prize (*Poetry*, Chicago), 1968; National Endowment for the Arts grant, 1969, and fellowship, 1979, 1981; Coordinating Council of Literary Magazines grant, 1969, 1970, 1971, 1975; P.E.N. award, for translation, 1977; Guggenheim Fellowship, 1978; National Book Award, for translation, 1979. Address: 852 South Bedford Street, Los Angeles, California 90035, U.S.A.

PUBLICATIONS

Verse

Mexico and North. Privately printed, 1962.
The Chavin Illumination. Lima, Peru, La Rama Florida, 1965.
Lachrymae Mateo: 3 Poems for Christmas 1966. New York, Caterpillar, 1966.
Walks. New York, Caterpillar, 1967.
The Crocus Bud. Reno, Nevada, Camels Coming, 1967.
Brother Stones. New York, Caterpillar, 1968.
Cantaloups and Splendour. Los Angeles, Black Sparrow Press, 1968.
T'ai. Cambridge, Massachusetts, Sans Souci Press, 1969.
The House of Okumura. Toronto, Weed/Flower Press, 1969.
Indiana. Los Angeles, Black Sparrow Press, 1969.
The House of Ibuki: A Poem, New York City, 14 March—30 Sept. 1967. Fremont, Michigan, Sumac Press, 1969.
Yellow River Record. London, Big Venus, 1969.
A Pitchblende. San Francisco, Maya, 1969.
Mad Windows. Privately printed, 1969.
The Wand. Santa Barbara, California, Capricorn Press, 1971.
Bearings. Santa Barbara, California, Capricorn Press, 1971.
Altars. Los Angeles, Black Sparrow Press, 1971.
The Sanjo Bridge. Los Angeles, Black Sparrow Press, 1972.
Coils. Los Angeles, Black Sparrow Press, 1973.
Human Wedding. Los Angeles, Black Sparrow Press, 1973.

The Last Judgment: For Caryl Her Thirty-First Birthday, The End of Her Pain. Los Angeles, Plantin Press, 1973.
Aux Morts. Los Angeles, Black Sparrow Press, 1974.
Realignment. Providence, Rhode Island, Treacle Press, 1974.
Portrait of Francis Bacon. Sheffield, Rivelin Press, 1975.
The Gull Wall: Poems and Essays. Los Angeles, Black Sparrow Press, 1975.
Cogollo. Newton, Massachusetts, Roxbury, 1976.
The Woman Who Saw Through Paradise. Lawrence, Kansas, Tansy Press, 1976.
Grotesca. London, New London Pride, 1977.
On Mules Sent from Chavin: A Journal and Poems 1965-66. Swansea, Galloping Dog Press, 1977.
Core Meander. Santa Barbara, California, Black Sparrow Press, 1977.
The Gospel of Celine Arnauld. Willits, California, Tuumba Press, 1978.
The Name Encanyoned River. New Paltz, New York, Treacle Press, 1978.
What She Means. Santa Barbara, California, Black Sparrow Press, 1978.
A Note on Apprenticeship. Chicago, Two Hands Press, 1979.
The Lich Gate. Barrytown, New York, Station Hill Press, 1980.
Nights We Put the Rock Together. Santa Barbara, California, Cadmus, 1980.
Our Lady of the Three-Pronged Devil. New York, Red Ozier Press, 1981.
Hades in Manganese. Santa Barbara, California, Black Sparrow Press, 1981.
Foetus Graffiti. East Haven, Connecticut, Pharos Press, 1981.
Fracture. Santa Barbara, California, Black Sparrow Press, 1983.
Visions of the Fathers of Lascaux. Los Angeles, Panjandrum, 1983.

Other

Editor, *A Caterpillar Anthology: A Selection of Poetry and Prose from Caterpillar Magazine.* New York, Doubleday, 1971.

Translator, *Residence on Earth,* by Pablo Neruda. San Francisco, Amber House, 1962.
Translator, with Denis Kelly, *State of the Union,* by Aimé Césaire. Bloomington, Indiana, Caterpillar, 1966.
Translator, *Seven Poems,* by César Vallejo. Reno, Nevada, Quark, 1967.
Translator, *Poémas Humanos/Human Poems,* by César Vallejo. New York, Grove Press, 1968; London, Cape, 1969.
Translator, with José Rubia Barcia, *Spain, Take This Cup from Me,* by César Vallejo. New York, Grove Press, 1974.
Translator, *Letter to André Breton,* by Antonin Artaud. Los Angeles, Black Sparrow Press, 1974.
Translator, with Norman Glass, *To Have Done with the Judgement of God,* by Antonin Artaud. Los Angeles, Black Sparrow Press, 1975.
Translator, with Norman Glass, *Artaud the Momo,* by Antonin Artaud. Santa Barbara, California, Black Sparrow Press, 1976.
Translator, with José Rubia Barcia, *Battles in Spain,* by César Vallejo. Santa Barbara, California, Black Sparrow Press, 1978.
Translator, with José Rubia Barcia, *The Complete Posthumous Poetry,* by César Vallejo. Berkeley, University of California Press, 1978.

Translator, with Annette Smith, *Notebook of a Return to the Native Land,* by Aimé Césaire. New York, Montemora, 1979.
Translator, with Norman Glass, *Four Texts,* by Antonin Artaud. Los Angeles, Panjandrum, 1982.
Translator, with Annette Smith, *The Collected Poetry,* by Aimé Césaire. Berekely, University of California Press, 1983.
Translator, *Sea-Urchin Harakiri,* by Bernard Bador. Los Angeles, Panjandrum, 1984.
Translator, *Given Giving: Selected Poems of Michel Deguy.* Berkeley, University of California Press, 1985.

*

Manuscript Collection: Lilly Library, Indiana University, Bloomington; Fales Collection, New York University; University of California, San Diego.

Critical Studies: by Hayden Carruth, in *New York Times Book Review,* 13 February 1972; introduction by the author to *Coils,* 1973; Robert Peters, in *Margin 24-26* (Milwaukee); Eric Mottram, in *Margins 27* (Milwaukee); Diane Wakoski, in *Iowa Review* (Iowa City), Winter 1975; Paul Zweig, in *New York Times Book Review,* 1 February 1976; "Clayton Eshleman Issue" of *Oasis 19* (London), 1977; Alan Williamson, in *Parnassus* (New York), Spring 1979; by Walter Freed, in *American Poets since World War II* edited by Donald J. Greiner, Detroit, Gale, 1980; A. James Arnold, in *Virginia Quarterly Review* (Charlottesville), Winter 1983.

Clayton Eshleman comments:
    As species disappear, the paleolithic grows on us; as living animals disappear, the first outlines become more dear, not as reflections of a day world, but as the primal contours of psyche, the shaping of the underworld, at the point Hades was an animal. The new wilderness is thus the spectral realm created by the going out of animal life and the coming in of these primary outlines. Our tragedy is to search further and further back for a common non-racial trunk in which the animal is not separated out of the human while we destroy the turf on which we actually stand.

*   *   *

    For any reader interested in a poet's processes of self-discovery, Clayton Eshleman must be a primary figure. Since 1962, when he published his first chapbook of poems, Eshleman has been searching in private ways through Reichian therapy and scientology, and literary ways through translating the works of César Vallejo and Aimé Césaire, and critical ways through editing his magazines *Caterpillar* and *Sulfur,* and historical ways through his researches into the paleolithic caves in France, for means to throw off the swaddled bourgeois midwestern American identity he was born with and emerge as a completely self-created new man. A new man who understands and values women enough to be called a feminist, one who values the exotic and fights isolationist American ideas, one who writes in a language and voice which are uniquely his own.
    In speaking of his literary origins and practices in the *New York Times* (3 February 1972), Hayden Carruth wrote, with great accuracy:

    his verbal practice, based on the isolated phrase, with many elisions and enjambments, a free cadence, strange juxtapositions, and extremes of diction, places him pretty squarely in our native Black Mountain tradition. Unlike some other Black Mountain poets, however, such as Robert Duncan, Denise Levertov or Robert Kelly, Eshleman aims less for verbal felicity or musicality than for conceptual discrimination. Sometimes this leads to mere fussiness, sometimes to genuine analytical elegance. But always his tone is tough, involuted and dense with separate movements of feeling characteristically sustained over rather long passages.

One problem with locating Eshleman in the Black Mountain tradition is that so many different ideas grow out of that concept, and in fact what seems most significant about Eshleman's work at present is that the dense textured langauge which he uses is an attempt at some primal use of speech, psychologically, rather than linguistically. And all Black Mountain theory leads to linguistics. When Olson bids us to go back to pre-Socratic times and relearn the possibilities of poetry, he really means to relearn the possibilities of poetic speech. But Eshleman is exploring those paleolithic drawings and cave paintings, psychologically, to find a sense of self and where the self begins in creative terms. Consequently, Eshleman's language is often infantile (scatological, for instance, or using baby talk) and tries for descriptions of the feelings using body terminology, so that he can attempt a visceral language, one that goes back to the stirrings in man's consciousness that began to allow language, culture, finally art. Psycho-language, rather than poesis. In his poem, "Winding Windows," Eshleman creates a kind of manifesto:

> Poetry's function is racemose,
> not to bloom from the urge of its stem,
> poems are not cymose
>
> but lead into secondary axes,
> ox pulls in the genetic tick of grandfather
> odor, a rattle to chkachk a bit of gravel
>
> into the plate the sound in
> poetry has become, gravel;
> gravy and gravel, either too mammal or
>
> too human.

It is this attempt to find the fusion between the human and the animal, neither gravy nor gravel, that now dominates Eshleman's work and his continuing exploration of self, creation of self, making of a poetry which is an attempt to define (and perhaps save?) humanity. In meditating on Cro-Magnon man in his poem "The Decanting," he concludes by saying,

> O wounded animal of complaint,
> even though you have no hands, use your hooves,
> pack back into yourself the intestinal
> topology you have, with my incision,
> draped about the world.

This theme of the coiled serpent of the intestines and of the phallus strangling the world is one that recurs often in Eshleman's work, as he sees clearly the troubles of our masculine, male-dominated civilization, taking the hunter's and killer's power to rule the world. There is nothing narcissistic or self-involved in Eshleman's obsessive searches for self-discovery. His poetry, this act of self-discovery, is an attempt to see and discover human civilization and its powers for self-destruction in the macrocosm of himself.

—Diane Wakoski

ESPINO, Federico (Licsi, Jr.). Filipino. Born in Pasig, Rizal, 10 April 1939. Educated at the University of Santo Tomas, Manila, Litt.B. in journalism 1959. Feature writer, 1960-63, and assistant editor, 1964-71, *Mirror Magazine*, Manila. Since 1972, free-lance writer. Recipient: Asia Foundation Silliman University Fellowship, 1966; Palanca Memorial Award, 1967, 1969, 1972; *Free Press* Short Story prize, 1972; *Graphic* Short Story prize, 1972; Basterra prize (Spain), 1977; Guerrero award, 1978; Zobel prize, 1979. Address: 178 M.H. del Pilar, Pasig, Metro Manila, Philippines.

PUBLICATIONS

Verse

In Three Tongues: A Folio of Poems in Tagalog, English, and Spanish. Quezon City, Bustamante Press, 1963.
Apocalypse in Ward 19 and Other Poems. Quezon City, Journal Press, 1965.
The Shuddering Clavier. Quezon City, Journal Press, 1965.
Sa Paanan ng parnaso. Quezon City, Journal Press, 1965.
Toreng Bato, Kastilyong Pawid. Quezon City, Journal Press, 1966.
Balalayka ni Pasternak at iba pang tula (in Tagalog and English). Manila, Pioneer Press, 1967.
A Rapture of Distress. Manila, Pioneer Press, 1968.
Alak na buhay, hinog na abo, phoenix na papel (in Tagalog and English). Manila, Pioneer Press, 1968.
Dark Sutra. Quezon City, Pioneer Press, 1969.
Burnt Alphabets: Poems in English, Tagalog, and Spanish. Manila, Pioneer Press, 1969.
Dawn and Downsitting. Quezon City, Pioneer Press, 1969.
Counterclockwise: Poems 1965-69. Quezon City, Bustamante Press, 1969.
A Manner of Seeing: A Folio of Poems. Privately printed, 1970.
Caras y Caretas de Amor. Quezon City, Bustamante Press, 1970.
The Winnowing Rhythm. Quezon City, Bustamante Press, 1970.
Makinilya at lira, tuluyan at tula. Manila, Pioneer Press, 1970.
From Mactan to Mandiola: A Poem of Protest, and Others. Quezon City, Manlapaz, 1971.
Twinkling: A Sheaf of Poems. Privately printed, 1972.
Letters and Nocturnes: Poems 1972-73. Manila, Pioneer Press, 1973.
Puente del Diablo: A Poem in Three Movements. Manila, Pioneer Press, 1973.
Makabagong panulaan. Quezon City, Manlapaz, 1974.
Circumference of Being. Privately printed, 1975(?).
In the Very Torrent. Privately printed, 1975.
Opus 27. Manila, Pioneer Press, 1976.
Tambor de Sangre. Bilbao, Ayala, 1977.
Ritmo ng lingkaw. Manila, Solidaridad, 1978.

Dalitan at tuksuhan: Mga tula. Manila, A. Placido Press, 1979.
Lightning-Rods, Pararrayos. Quezon City, Soller, 1980.
Siddhartha in Saigon, Christ in Manila: New Poems. Quezon City, Martinez, 1983.
Rhapsody on Themes of Brecht, Recto, and Others. Quezon City, Soller, 1983.

Short Stories

The Country of Sleep. Quezon City, Bustamante Press, 1969.
Percussive Blood: Selected Stories. Manila, Pioneer Press, 1972.

Other

English-Filipino Thesaurus. Quezon City, Soller, 1980.
The Woman Who Had Many Birthdays and Other Works (miscellany). Quezon City, Martinez, 1983.

*

Critical Study: "Philippine Poetry in English: Some Notes for Exploration" by Cirilo Bautista, in *Solidarity Magazine* (Manila), December 1970.

Federico Espino comments:
    I have been compared to the French Symbolists though the affinity I have with them is only a matter of subject matter, not of form. I do not, however, believe in a Rimbaudian derangement of the senses or in the Baudelairean theory of correspondences and I eschew the celebration of neurosis, though in my stories I write about neurotic people. The psychological minorities interest me only in relation to a Catholic frame of reference.

*   *   *

    Federico Espino is not only an English language poet: he has the distinction of being the leading Filipino writer in Tagalog, which is the language of Manila and its environs, and which forms the basis of the artificial national language. Nothing that he has done in English verse is as good as the short stories collected in *The Country of Sleep*; but he shows signs of development. His English poetry is often too obviously derivative and self-consciously experimental, and he seems to have been over-influenced by his important compatriot José Garcia Villa (although Villa, strangely, is generally much disliked in his native country): various sorts of technical effects, often well-executed, tend to swallow up or diminish the content of his poems. He is at his best when his subject is the actual problem of poetic procedure, with which he is honestly and unpretentiously concerned. His use of Lowell and Stevens has been unproductive: but Guillén, with his sonorous, nostalgic toughness, has been a valuable influence. His difficulties may originate in his bilingualism: there is not really a large or appreciative audience for Tagalog writing, and it is natural enough that an author with a perfect command of English should turn to the latter language. The decision has been successful in the realm of short fiction; but one is bound to wonder if Espino's Tagalog poetry is not better than his English: more authentically his own.

—Martin Seymour-Smith

─────────

EVANS, Mari. American. Born in Toledo, Ohio. Attended the University of Toledo. Writer-in-Residence, Indiana University-Purdue University, Indianapolis, 1969-70; Assistant Professor, Indiana University, Bloomington, 1970-78, and Purdue University, West Lafayette, Indiana, 1978-80. Writer-in-Residence, Northwestern University, Evanston, Illinois, 1972-73; Visiting Professor, Washington University, St. Louis, 1980, and Cornell University, Ithaca, New York, 1981-82. Producer, writer, and director, The Black Experience television program, Indianapolis, 1968-73. Recipient: John Hay Whitney fellowship, 1965; Woodrow Wilson Foundation grant, 1968; Black Academy of Arts and Letters award, 1971; MacDowell fellowship, 1975; Copeland fellowship, 1980; National Endowment for the Arts award, 1981; Yaddo fellowship, 1984. L.H.D.: Marion College, Indianapolis, 1975. Address: P.O. Box 483, Indianapolis, Indiana 46206, U.S.A.

<small>PUBLICATIONS</small>

Verse

Where Is All the Music? London, Paul Breman, 1968.
I Am a Black Woman. New York, Morrow, 1970.
Whisper. Los Angeles, Center for Afro-American Studies, 1979.
Nightstar. Los Angeles, Center for Afro-American Studies, 1981.

Plays

River of My Song (also director: produced Indianapolis, 1977).
Eyes (produced, Cleveland).

Other

JD (for children). New York, Doubleday, 1973.
I Look at Me. Chicago, Third World Press, 1973.
Singing Black. Indianapolis, Reed, 1976.
Jim Flying High (for children). New York, Doubleday, 1979.

Editor, *Black Women Writers 1950-1980: A Critical Perspective.* New York, Doubleday, 1984.

*   *   *

    Though she was born during the Harlem Renaissance, Mari Evans' poetry reveals little of the inclination toward compromise with white values and forms that was cherished by most black intellectuals of that period. Quite the contrary, her work is informed by the uncompromising black pride that burgeoned in the 1960's, and she stands tall with Don Lee, Nikki Giovanni, Sonia Sanchez, and the resuscitated Gwendolyn Brooks as a powerful poetic proclaimer of the new black awareness.
    That she is conscious of the change in black stance is demonstrated by the deliberate contrast she achieves between Countée Cullen's famous plaint of the mid-1920's "Yet Do I Marvel" and her "Who Can Be Born Black." Where Cullen constructs a Shakespearian sonnet replete with classical allusions to express his wonder at God's great capacity to create horror, the most amazing example of which is "To make a poet black, and bid him sing," she responds briefly and without apparent artifice:

               Who
               can be born black

and not
sing
the wonder of it
the joy
the
challenge

Who
can be born black
and not exult!

Mari Evans, like the best of the new black poets, usually keeps close to the bone of black experience and frequently works through the rhythms of its speech and music. Hopefully a non-black will find that experience, as filtered through her poetry, a paradigm of the human condition, but it is clear that she is unconcerned about the feelings of those who are too opaque to find it so.

—Alan R. Shucard

EVERSON, Ronald (Gilmour). Canadian. Born in Oshawa, Ontario, 18 November 1903. Educated at the University of Toronto, 1923-27, B.A. 1927; Upper Canada Law Society, 1927-30: called to the Ontario Bar 1930. Served with British Security Co-ordination, 1940-45. Married Lorna Jean Austin in 1931. Managing Director, 1936-47, and President, 1947-63, Johnston, Everson and Charlesworth Ltd, Toronto. Chairman, Communications-6 Inc., Montreal, 1964-66. Co-founding Director, Delta Canada Books, Montreal, 1960-63; Director, Ryerson Press, Toronto, 1960-65; Co-founder, League of Canadian Poets, 1966. Address: 4855 ch. Côte St.-Luc, Montreal, Quebec H3W 2H5, Canada.

PUBLICATIONS

Verse

Three Dozen Poems. Montreal, Cambridge Press, 1927.
A Lattice for Momos. Toronto, Contact Press, 1958.
Blind Man's Holiday. Toronto, Ryerson Press, 1963.
Four Poems. Norwich, Vermont, American Letters Press, 1963.
Wrestle with an Angel. Montreal, Delta Canada, 1965.
Incident on Côte des Neiges. Amherst, Massachusetts, Green Knight Press, 1966.
Raby Head and Other Poems. Amherst, Massachusetts, Green Knight Press, 1967.
The Dark Is Not So Dark. Montreal and Santa Barbara, California, Delta Canada-Unicorn, 1969.
Selected Poems 1920-70. Montreal, Delta Canada, 1970.
Indian Summer. Ottawa, Oberon Press, 1976.
Carnival. Ottawa, Oberon Press, 1978.
Everson at Eighty. Ottawa, Oberon Press 1983.

Other

Of This and That, with J. G. Johnston and J. L. Charlesworth. Privately printed, 1940.

*

Bibliography: in Salt (Moose Jaw, Saskatchewan), Summer 1973.

Critical Studies: by Magaret Avison in Poetry (Chicago), June 1959; James Dickey, in Sewanee Review (Tennessee), Autumn 1960, and in Poetry (Chicago), February 1964; Munro Beattie, in Literary History of Canada, Toronto, University of Toronto Press, 1965; M. J. Sidnell, in Canadian Forum (Toronto), January 1966; Robert Gibbs, in Fiddlehead (Fredericton, New Brunswick), April 1970; Al Purdy in Quarry (Kingston, Ontario), Spring 1970; Ralph Gustafson, in Canadian Literature (Vancouver), Summer 1971; William Dickey, in Hudson Review (New York), April 1971; Charles Molesworth, in Poetry (Chicago), May 1972.

*   *   *

"I admire poetry that risks going out beyond the end of thinking," Ronald Everson has written. Everson published his first book in 1927; his second appeared over thirty years later when he was fifty-four years old. But the Montreal poet has made up for lost time, for since then the former public-relations consultant has gained the admiration of James Dickey who perceptively noted that Everson "thinks of practicality as one of the greatest of the artistic virtues, and as underlying all real imagination."

After a reading of his Selected Poems 1920-1970, it is difficult not to see Everson as the perfect embodiment of his United Empire Loyalist ancestors. He is his own man, like the New England farmer. A true "U.E.L.," he retains a realistic approach to life without requiring the consolations of compromise or moral superiority. He seems to be an agnostic, but not an atheist, for he can write: "I do not know where we are/ None knows where we are."

Everson is knowledgeable without being pedantic, shrewd without being cutting, worldly-wise without being sophisticated. He is a great traveller, yet his poems about the places he has been are neither anecdotal nor picturesque, and hence escape the label "travel poetry." Instead they are splendid and precise evocations, in the imagistic manner, of the associations that a modest and reasonable man would have in the presence of the unyielding world.

Everson's particular stamping ground is the Maritimes and rural Ontario, although he has written about other parts of Canada as well. In "Love Poem," he writes about having "given up on the salvation of mankind." Perhaps this accounts for his mellow outlook. In another poem, he meditates on "a field of Ontario Quaker graves." The poem comes to a magnificent conclusion:

No new graves
Congregation gone
Religion gone
They entered underground to lie unknown
on their own plan
I stare at the chance-taking dead.

—John Robert Colombo

EVERSON, William (Oliver). American. Born in Sacramento, California, 10 September 1912. Educated at Fresno State College, California, 1931, 1934-35. Conscientious objector during World War II: with the Civilian Public Service, 1943-46. Married 1) Edna Poulson in 1938 (divorced, 1948); 2) Mary Fabilli in 1948 (divorced, 1960); 3) Susanna Rickson in 1969, one step-son. Worked for the Civilian Conservation Corps, 1933-34; Co-Founder, Untide Press, Waldport, Oregon; staff member, University of California Press, Berkeley, 1947-49; member of the Catholic Worker Movement, 1950-51; Dominican lay brother (Brother Antoninus), 1951-69; Poet-in-Residence, Kresge College, University of California, Santa Cruz, 1971-82. Recipient: Guggenheim Fellowship, 1949; Shelley Memorial Award, 1978; National Endowment for the Arts grant, 1982. Address: 312 Swanton Road, Davenport, California 95017, U.S.A.

PUBLICATIONS

Verse (as William Everson)

These Are the Ravens. San Leandro, California, Greater West, 1935.
San Joaquin. Los Angeles, Ward Ritchie Press, 1939.
The Masculine Dead: Poems 1938-1940. Prairie City, Illinois, James A. Decker, 1942.
X War Elegies. Waldport, Oregon, Untide Press, 1943.
Waldport Poems. Waldport, Oregon, Untide Press, 1944.
War Elegies. Waldport, Oregon, Untide Press, 1944
The Residual Years: Poems 1940-1941. Waldport, Oregon, Untide Press, 1945.
Poems MCMXLII. Waldport, Oregon, Untide Press, 1945.
The Residual Years. New York, New Directions, 1948.
A Privacy of Speech: Ten Poems in Sequence. Berkeley, California, Equinox Press, 1949.
Triptych for the Living. Oakland, California, Seraphim Press, 1951.
There Will Be Harvest. Berkeley, California, Albion Press, 1960.
The Year's Declension. Berkeley, California, Albion Press, 1961.
The Blowing of the Seed. New Haven, Connecticut, Henry W. Wenning, 1966.
Single Source: The Early Poems of William Everson 1934-1940. Berkeley, California, Oyez, 1966.
In the Fictive Wish. Berkeley, California, Oyez, 1967.
The Springing of the Blade. Reno, Nevada, Black Rock Press, 1968.
The Residual Years: Poems 1934-1948. New York, New Directions, 1968.
Gale at Dawn. Santa Cruz, California, Lime Kiln Press, 1972.
Tendril in the Mesh. Aromas, California, Cayucos, 1973.
Black Hills. San Francisco, Didymus Press, 1973.
Man-Fate: The Swan Song of Brother Antoninus. New York, New Directions, 1974.
River-Root: A Syzygy for the Bicentennial of These States. Berkeley, California, Oyez, 1976.
Missa Defunctorum. Santa Cruz, California, Lime Kiln Press, 1976.
The Mate-Flight of Eagles. Newcastle, California, Blue Oak Press, 1977.
Blackbird Sundown. Northridge, California, Lord John Press, 1978.
Rattlesnake August. Northridge, California, Santa Susana Press, 1978.
The Veritable Years: Poems 1949-1966. Santa Barbara, California, Black Sparrow Press, 1978.
Cutting the Firebreak. Swanton, California, Kingfisher Press, 1978.
Blame It on the Jet Stream! Santa Cruz, California, Lime Kiln Press, 1978.
The Masks of Drought. Santa Barbara, California, Blak Sparrow Press, 1980.
Eastward the Armies: Selected Poems 1935-1942 That Present the Poet's Pacifist Position Through the Second World War, edited by Les Ferriss. Torrance, California, Labyrinth, 1980.
Renegade Christmas. Northridge, California, Lord John Press, 1984.
In Medias Res. San Francisco, Adrian Wilson Press, 1984.

Verse (as Brother Antoninus)

At the Edge. Privately printed, 1952.
A Fragment for the Birth of God. Oakland, California, Albertus Magnus, 1958.
An Age Insurgent. San Francisco, Blackfriars, 1959.
The Crooked Lines of God: Poems 1949-1954. Detroit, University of Detroit Press, 1959.
The Hazards of Holiness: Poems 1957-1960. New York, Doubleday, 1962.
The Poet Is Dead: A Memorial for Robinson Jeffers. San Francisco, Auerhahn Press, 1964.
The Rose of Solitude. Berkeley, California, Oyez, 1964.
The Vision of Felicity. Cambridge, Massachusetts, Lowell House, 1966.
The Rose of Solitude (collection). New York, Doubleday, 1967.
The Achievement of Brother Antoninus: A Comprehensive Selection of His Poems with a Critical Introduction, by William Stafford. Chicago, Scott Foresman, 1967.
A Canticle to the Waterbirds. Berkeley, California, Eizo, 1968.
The City Does Not Die. Berkeley, California, Oyez, 1969.
The Last Crusade. Berkeley, California, Oyez, 1969.
Who Is She That Looketh Forth as the Morning. Santa Barbara, California, Capricorn Press, 1972.

Recording: *Savagery of Love,* Caedmon, 1968.

Other

The Dominican Brother: Province of the West. Privately printed, 1967.
Robinson Jeffers: Fragments of an Older Fury. Berkeley, California, Oyez, 1968.
If I Speak Truth: An Inter View-ing, with Jerry Burns. San Francisco, Goliards Press, 1968.
Earth Poetry. Berkeley, California, Oyez, 1971.
Archetype West: The Pacific Coast as a Literary Region. Berkeley, California, Oyez, 1976.
Earth Poetry: Essays and Interviews. Berkeley, California, Oyez, 1980.
Birth of a Poet: The Santa Cruz Meditations, edited by Lee Bartlett. Santa Barbara, California, Black Sparrow Press, 1982.

Editor, *The Alpine Christ,* by Robinson Jeffers. Aromas, California, Cayucos, 1973.
Editor, *Brides of the South Wind: Poems 1917-1922,* by Robinson Jeffers. Aromas, California, Cayucos, 1974.
Editor, *Granite and Cypress,* by Robinson Jeffers. Santa Cruz, California, Lime Kiln Press, 1975.

Editor, *The Double Axe and Other Poems*, by Robinson Jeffers. New York, Liveright, 1977.

Editor, *American Bard, by Walt Whitman, Being the Preface to the First Edition of Leaves of Grass, Now Restored to Its Native Verse Rhythms and Presented as a Living Poem*. Santa Cruz, California, Lime Kiln Press, 1981; as *American Bard, Walt Whitman*, New York, Viking Press, 1982.

*

Bibliography: *William Everson: A Descriptive Bibliography 1934-1976* by Lee Bartlett and Allan Campo, Metuchen, New Jersey, Scarecrow Press, 1977.

Manuscript Collections: (earlier work) William Andrews Clark Library, University of California, Los Angeles; (middle period) Bancroft Library, University of California, Berkeley.

Critical Studies: *William Everson: Poet from the San Joaquin* by Allan Campo, D.A. Carpenter, and Bill Hotchkiss, Newcastle, California, Blue Oak Press, 1978; *Benchmark and Blaze: The Emergence of William Everson* edited by Lee Bartlett, Metuchen, New Jersey, Scarecrow Press, 1979, and "God's Crooked Lines: William Everson and C.G. Jung," in *Centennial Review 27* (Lansing, Michigan), no. 4, 1983, and "Creating the Autochthon: Kenneth Rexroth, William Everson, and *The Residual Years*," in *Sagetrieb 2* (Orono, Maine), no. 3, 1983, both by Bartlett; "William Everson: Peacemaker with Himself" by D.A. Carpenter, in *Concerning Poetry 13* (Bellingham, Washington), 1980; "Where We Might Meet Each Other" by Joe Marusiak, in *Literary Review 24* (Rutherford, New Jersey), 1981; "Waiting for Jacob's Angel" by Benilde Montgomery, in *Renascence* (Milwaukee), Summer 1981; "Landscape of the Psyche" by Albert Gelpi, in *New Boston Review*, November-December 1982; James A. Powell, in *The Beats: Literary Bohemians in Postwar America* edited by Ann Charters, Detroit, Gale, 1983; "Neglected Poets 2: William Everson and Bad Taste" by Diane Wakoski, in *American Poetry 2* (Albuquerque), no. 1, 1984.

William Everson comments:

(1970) I was born William Oliver Everson, the son of Louis Waldemar Everson, an immigrant Norwegian musician and composer, and Francelia Maria Herber, a Minnesota farm girl of German-Irish extraction who was twenty years his junior. With an older sister and younger brother I grew up in the little town of Selma, California, where our father was bandmaster. My mother had been born a Catholic, but left that faith to marry my father; we children were brought up as Christian Scientists. In adolescence I became an agnostic, but at Fresno State College, I encountered the verse of Robinson Jeffers, whose mystical pantheism opened my soul to the constitutive religious reality sustaining the cosmos, and I dropped out of college to go back to the land and become a poet in my own right, to plant a vineyard, commune with nature, and marry my highschool sweetheart.

In World War II I was drafted as a conscientious objector and spent three and a half years in the work camps of Oregon. At Waldport I headed a Fine Arts Program and helped establish the Untide Press, one of the few experimental presses of the war period. After release I migrated to San Francisco, joining the group of anarchists and poets around Kenneth Rexroth. I remarried, this time to the writer Mary Fabilli. Through her hands I encountered Catholicism, and we separated to enter the Roman Catholic Church in 1949. There followed a year on a Guggenheim Fellowship, and another year of troubled interior search; I served with the Catholic Worker movement in the Oakland slums, and resolved to leave the world to find my

vocation as a monk, just as I had once left college to find my vocation as a poet.

Thus I became a Dominican lay brother in 1951, receiving the name of Brother Antoninus and for seven years of monastic withdrawal disappeared from the literary scene. I re-emerged with the San Francisco Renaissance in the late fifties, identifying with the Beat Generation because it proclaimed against a triumphant American pragmatism the necessity for mystical vision, and because as a literary movement it launched dionysian revolt against that pretentious highbrow formalism which, owing to the disassociation between the American poet and the American people, is always able to pass itself off as genuine tradition. Resuming publication, I used the detached freedom possible in monastic life to spend long periods on the poetry reading circuits, developing my own platform style based on oracular Beat intensity as befitting the prophetic mission of the poet, but embodying my own sense of the encounter which has, since Isaiah, constituted the archetype of religious awareness whenever a poet and his people confront.

I began as a nature poet with religious overtones but upon embracing Catholicism began to write a poetry of emphatic religious content etched against the immense backdrop of the American West. It is not surprising, then, that stylistically I favor a more rhetorical idiom than is currently fashionable. Rhetoric is the vehicle of consequence. That it can be faked does not dispense us from its essential use, for life is consequential, existence is infinitely consequential. The area of deepest consequence I believe to be the sexual exaltation and travail between man and woman, insofar as this encounter is the analogue of the exaltation and travail between man and God. I believe that the solution to the problem of violence is found only in the Cross, but I also believe that the poet alone can accommodate the violence of his age to the Cross. This for me constitutes his archetypal role as prophet to his time. It is his failure, and it is awesome, that sends the best minds of his generation in search of solutions where none can ever be found.

(1974) In 1969 I left the Dominican Order to marry Susanna Rickson, and spent two years with her and her infant son Jude at Stinson Beach, north of San Francisco. In 1971 I became Poet in Residence at Kresge College, University of California, Santa Cruz. My preoccupation with the Cross as solution to the mystery of violence, noted above, has not abated, but in the ecological crisis has shifted to the numen subsistent in Nature, as totem, or metaphor, in the encounter between man and God. Rational European theological speculation exhausted the human and divine aspects of the Incarnation. It remains now to recover the atavistic implications inherent in the flesh of Christ. Thus in the final phase of my life now opening I look for aboriginal modes of response to the fact of existence on this continent, and in my work will seek to recover the pertinence of Wilderness as purifier to the corrupt civilized dream.

(1980) The publication of *The Veritable Years* in 1978 finally placed before the public the shape of my overall endeavor, the lifetime trilogy I have chosen to call *The Crooked Lines of God*. Composed of three related volumes, *The Residual Years*, *The Veritable Years: Poems 1949-1966*, and *The Integral Years: Poems 1966—*, it constitutes a sort of Hegelian triad in its accent of thesis, antithesis, and synthesis. Thus, the primal preoccupation with Nature in *The Residual Years* was followed by a corresponding preoccupation with God in *The Veritable Years*, emerging as a consequent preoccupation with God-in-Nature in *The Integral Years*, as indicated in my 1974 statement above.

Just as the first two volumes were composed of private printings, booklets and broadsides issued as I went along, so with *The Integral Years*, now in progress. Its chief components so far are the collections *Man-Fate* and *The Masks of Drought*, but the individual poems *Tendril in the Mesh, The City Does Not Die,* and *Blame It on the Jet Stream!* will all take their place within it. For across the whole span of *Crooked Lines* the thematic disposition is markedly chronological. And this in turn is because the abiding force is confessional, whether as thesis, antithesis, or synthesis. It is this confessional attitude that meets the issue of relevance to the central concern of contemporary poetry. As M. L. Rosenthal has written, "To build a great poem out of the predicament and horror of the lost Self has been the recurrent effort of the most ambitious poetry of the last century." Hence it is the attitude of existential confrontation, whether with Man or God or Nature, that both shapes the trilogy in its thrust towards wholeness and denotes its relevance to its time.

(1985) Upon my turning seventy in 1982 a National Endowment of the Arts grant enabled me to retire from the University. The cycle of poems begun with *The Masks of Drought* (1980) was continued, but a diminishing emphasis may be seen in its sequel, *Renegade Christmas* (1984), verse as closely crafted but more predictable, a clear sign that the cycle has run its course. Instead, preoccupation with biography and the past precipitated an autobiographical epic—not surprising, given retirement, but unforeseen in my purview of *The Integral Years* above. Called *Dust Shall Be the Serpent's Food*, issued canto by canto as written; the first, *In Medias Res*, already constitutes my most recently published work. This project has all the earmarks of the Great Works Archetype, my lifelong nemesis, leaving my wake littered with the wreckage of many august productions, all valiantly begun but eventually unsustainable. From the detritus I have salvaged only my poems, and not by any personal prescience either, but simply because my grand schemes have involved my ego, permitting my muse the freedom to work undistracted behind the scenes, the unconscious evolution that is the permanent bestowal of what I have done. Equally unforeseen was the onset of Parkinson's disease, curtailing action, sapping energy, rendering problematical all creativity, but chastening the mind. I will continue to write poetry as long as breath lasts, but not desperately, for though much remains to be said, my intuition tells me that *The Crooked Lines of God* is basically achieved. More varied verse could flesh it out, and perhaps it will; but if I die tonight the circle is joined, the Old Lizard bites his tail.

*   *   *

Slowly, from various outposts he found during the 1940's, William Everson began to send out his own kind of direct, emphatic poems of social judgment. Though he listed no church affiliation when he was held as a conscientious objector in work camps in Oregon and California during World War II, his writings—like those of Robinson Jeffers, who influenced him greatly—were always moral and principled, and serious; and by the time those poems came into general notice in the early 1950's William Everson had become Brother Antoninus, a Dominican lay brother, and one of the early and influential participants in the "San Francisco Group" of "Beat Poets."

In his career since that early seasoning, when he actually had to live outside American society and look at it long, Brother Antoninus has continued his measured assessment, in many periodicals and many books and many public readings. His language has taken on religious tonality but in a way to make ritual violently confront jagged experience. His progression has not been so much toward leaving the Robinson Jeffers non-human stance as it has been toward combining the brute world and the church. He hammers the language of religion into statements that create shock: bleak juxtapositions, stern assertions. In his most characteristic works, the landscapes and the creature-scapes of a rugged coastal region get yoked into a chant of judgment, as in *A Canticle to the Waterbirds*:

Clack your beaks you cormorants and kittiwakes,
North on those rock-croppings finger-jutted into the rough
    Pacific surge...
Break wide your harsh and salt-encrusted beaks unmade for
    song
And say a praise up to the Lord.

—William Stafford

EVERWINE, Peter (Paul). American. Born in Detroit, Michigan, 14 February 1930. Educated at Northwestern University, Evanston, Illinois, B.S. 1952; Stanford University, California, 1958-59; University of Iowa, Iowa City, Ph.D. 1959. Served in the United States Army, 1952-54. Divorced; two children. Instructor in English, University of Iowa, 1959-62. Since 1962, Professor of English, California State University, Fresno. Recipient: Lamont Poetry Selection Award, 1972; Guggenheim Fellowship, 1976. Address: Department of English, California State University, Fresno, California 93710, U.S.A.

PUBLICATIONS

Verse

The Broken Frieze.   Mt. Vernon, Iowa, Hillside Press, 1958.
In the House of Light: Thirty Aztec Poems.   Iowa City, Stone
    Wall Press, 1970.
Collecting the Animals.   New York, Atheneum, 1973.
Keeping the Night.   New York, Atheneum, 1977.

Other

Editor and Translator, with Shulamit Yasny-Starkman, *The
    Static Element: Selected Poems of Natan Zach.*   New York,
    Atheneum, 1982.

*   *   *

The quantity of Peter Everwine's poetry is slight; the quality is gem-like. Some of the poems in *Keeping the Night* were collected earlier in *The New Naked Poetry*; "nude" would have been a more fitting adjective to describe his art. His poetry is neither raw, nor bare. It is subtler—precise, but unadorned; palpable and dumb. It achieves its effect slowly. It wants to be read over and over. It unfolds in silence and in empty spaces. "Night" from *Keeping the Night* is typical of Everwine's manner; it is quite like Haiku:

In the lamplight falling
on the white tablecloth
my plate
my shining loaf of quietness.

I sit down.
Through the open door
all the absent I love enter
and we eat.

At its best, Everwine's poetry is deceptively simple. Largely monosyllabic, invariably brief, his poems mold speech to express unspoken, deeply-felt truths found in moments selected from ordinary life, either his own or that of his kin.

The earlier volume *In the House of Light* is comprised of his translations of Spanish transcriptions of poems of the Nahuatl Indians in Mexico. Everwine observed that one of the words used to mean poet in Nahuatl is "tlamatine: one who knows something," and in his verse translations he offers "an attempt to locate that ancient presence in my own speech" (*Collecting the Animals*). He succeeds excellently.

The seeming simplicity of his poetry establishes an aura of trust and candor rarely found in contemporary poetry. His poetry is unmarred by self-consciousness. There are no stridency, no verbal fireworks, no exhibitionism. Nor is there any hint of sentimentality in the many memories he evokes. In "Drinking Cold Water" (*Collecting the Animals*) his recreation of his tough-spirited grandmother who "lay down in the shale hills of Pennsylvania" 20 years ago is completely authentic:

> all I can think of is your house—
> the pump at the sink
> spilling a trough of clear
> cold water from the well—
> and you, old love,
> sleeping in your dark dress
> like a hard, white root.

His Italian grandfather who emigrated to the United States and spat in the wind, quit his job, and returned to Italy every time his bosses maddened him is depicted with equal vividness in "Paolo Castelnuova" (from *Keeping the Night*) which ends with the grandson, the persona, penning the will the old man did not leave:

> I, Paolo, give my stone to the priests.
> Tell them to make it bread.
>
> Water I give to those loving how money sweats.
>
> Fire I leave to my children
>
> As for air,
> give it to the buzzard who is the first
> and last of kings.

The other portraits in *Keeping the Night* and *Collecting the Animals*, of Dorothy, "her ass rubbed raw through half the fields in Armstrong County," of his emigrant mother who was never really American until grass closed over her gravestone, of his sons, are equally precise and real.

Whether Everwine searches for a language to hold night's secrets, or childhood recollections, or the paradoxical condition of a man who eats dinner talking with his guests of the past dead and never looking at "the axe lying in the courtyard, a crust of blood and feathers on its edge" ("The Dinner," *Keeping the Night*), he catches exactly the experience he knows. He has learned his experience and his craft "hand over hand," as he says in another poem in a slightly different context.

—Carol Simpson Stern

EWART, Gavin (Buchanan). British. Born in London, 4 February 1916. Educated at Wellington College; Christ's College, Cambridge (Exhibitioner), B.A. (honours) in English 1937, M.A. 1942. Served in the Royal Artillery, 1940-46: Captain. Married Margaret Adelaide Bennett in 1956; one son and one daughter. Salesman, Contemporary Lithographs, 1938; Production Manager, Editions Poetry London, 1946; worked for the British Council, 1946-52; advertising copywriter, 1952-71. Since 1971, free-lance writer. Chairman, Poetry Society, 1978-79. Recipient: Cholmondeley Award, 1971; Eric Gregory traveling scholarship, 1977. Fellow, Royal Society of Literature, 1981. Address: 57 Kenilworth Court, Lower Richmond Road, London SW15 1EN, England.

PUBLICATIONS

Verse

Poems and Songs. London, Fortune Press, 1939.
Londoners. London, Heinemann, 1964.
Throwaway Lines. Richmond, Surrey, Keepsake Press, 1964.
Two Children. Richmond, Surrey, Keepsake Press, 1966.
Pleasures of the Flesh. London, Alan Ross, 1966.
The Deceptive Grin of the Gravel Porters. London, Alan Ross, 1968.
Twelve Apostles. Belfast, Ulsterman, 1970.
Folio, with others. Frensham, Surrey, Sceptre Press, 1971.
The Gavin Ewart Show. London, Trigram Press, 1971.
Venus. London, Poem-of-the-Month Club, 1972.
The Select Party. Richmond, Surrey, Keepsake Press, 1972.
Alphabet Soup. Oxford, Sycamore Press, 1972.
Penguin Modern Poets 25, with B.S. Johnson and Zulfikar Ghose. London, Penguin, 1974.
Be My Guest! London, Trigram Press, 1975.
A Question Partly Answered. Knotting, Bedfordshire, Sceptre Press, 1976.
No Fool Like an Old Fool. London, Gollancz, 1976.
A Morden Tower Reading 5, with Fleur Adcock. Newcastle upon Tyne, Morden Tower, 1977.
Or Where a Young Penguin Lies Screaming. London, Gollancz, 1977.
The First Eleven. London, Poet and Printer, 1977.
All My Little Ones: The Shortest Poems of Gavin Ewart. London, Anvil Press Poetry, 1978.
The Collected Ewart 1933-1980. London, Hutchinson, 1980.
The New Ewart: Poems 1980-1982. London, Hutchinson, 1982.
More Little Ones: Short Poems. London, Anvil Press Poetry, 1982.
Capital Letters. Oxford, Sycamore Press, 1983.
The Ewart Quarto. London, Hutchinson, 1984.

Play

Tobermory, music by John Gardner, adaptation of the story by Saki (produced London, 1977).

Other

Editor, *Forty Years On: An Anthology of School Songs.* London, Sidgwick and Jackson, 1964.
Editor, *The Batsford Book of Children's Verse.* London, Batsford, 1976.
Editor, *New Poems 1977-78.* London, Hutchinson, 1977.

Editor, *The Batsford Book of Light Verse for Children*.   London, Batsford, 1978.
Editor, *The Penguin Book of Light Verse*.   London, Allen Lane, 1980.
Editor, *Other People's Clerihews*.   Oxford, Oxford University Press, 1983.

*

Manuscript Collection: National Library of Scotland, Edinburgh; Humanities Research Center, University of Texas, Austin; Brynmor Jones Library, University of Hull.

Critical Study: by David Montrose, in *Honest Ulsterman* (Belfast), Spring 1978.

*   *   *

Gavin Ewart began precociously early. In 1933, at the age of seventeen, he was contributing assured and witty poems to Geoffrey Grigson's *New Verse*. They included "Phallus in Wonderland," a set of epigrams and short poems written in skilful pastiche of Pound, Eliot, Auden and other contemporaries, an "Audenesque for an Initiation," which showed Ewart to be an early if critical admirer of the dominating English poet of the thirties. As a young poet in the pre-war years Ewart exhibited the social and political concerns of the age, though in a wryly individual voice. What is striking about his subsequent career is that some fifty years later Ewart is still writing in much the same way about similar subjects: the occasional splendours and frequent absurdities of sex; himself, as *l'homme moyen sensuel*; and the kaleidoscope surface of modern urban life. From the beginning Ewart has been the master of a kind of writing that is poised between amusing light verse and an authentic poetry of serious social comment or personal reflection. When the poise fails he is inclined to fall into slack triviality on the one hand or neat sentimentalities on the other. He has a good ear and can write memorable lines and elegant lyrics. At the same time, he is rather complacently attached to his favourite stylistic devices; having found that "kisses" makes an effective rhyme for "cissies" in a poem published in 1937 he was still using the same rhymes in *The Gavin Ewart Show* in 1971.

Thematically, too, there is variation rather than great development. In his earliest poems Ewart treated sexual subjects with the characteristic bravado and anxiety of adolescence. "Young Blondes: A Religious Poem" is a crisp and poignant instance from the forties. In the sixties and seventies similar themes are presented with the more urgent anxiety of middle-age, often rather tastelessly. If there is a new element in Ewart's poetry it is a greater compassion that undercuts his characteristic tone of cool ironic comment on human folly. A striking example of this quality is "The Gentle Sex" (1974), a horrified and horrifying account of an atrocity in Northern Ireland. Increasingly his greatest irony is directed at himself, as in "The Ewart Organization" or the delightful "2001: The Tennyson/Hardy Poem" which looks forward to a time when the poet will have outlived all his contemporaries. Here Ewart once more displays his skill as a writer of pastiche, this time of Thomas Hardy:

> Soon comes the day when the stream runs dry
> And the boat runs back as the tide is turning,
> The voice once strong no more than a sigh
> By the hearth where the fire is scarcely burning.
> Stiff in my chair like a children's guy,

> Simply because I have no seniors
> The literati will raise the cry:
>   Ewart's a genius!

Ewart preserves in a remarkably pure form the positive qualities of the poetry of the thirties: the wit, the formal skill, the willingness to combine comic means and serious ends, and, at his best, an attractive intellectual gaiety.

—Bernard Bergonzi

EZEKIEL, Nissim. Indian.   Born in Bombay, 16 December 1924. Educated at the University of Bombay (Lagu prize, 1947), 1941-47, M.A. 1947. Married Daisy Jacob in 1952; two daughters and one son. Lecturer, Khalsa College, Bombay, 1947-48; Professor of English and Vice-Principal, Mithibai College, Bombay, 1961-72. Since 1972, Reader in American Literature, University of Bombay. Visiting Professor, University of Leeds, 1964, and University of Chicago, 1967. Editor, *Quest* magazine, 1955-57; Associate Editor, *Imprint* magazine, 1961-67; art critic, *The Times of India*, Bombay, 1964-67. Lived in London, 1948-52. Recipient: Farfield Foundation travel grant, 1957. Address: Department of English, University of Bombay, University Road, Bombay 400 032, India.

PUBLICATIONS

Verse

A Time to Change and Other Poems.   London, Fortune Press, 1952.
Sixty Poems.   Bombay, Strand Bookshop, 1953.
The Third.   Bombay, Strand Bookshop, 1958.
The Unfinished Man: Poems Written in 1959.   Calcutta, Writers Workshop, 1960.
The Exact Name: Poems 1960-1964.   Calcutta, Writers Workshop, 1965.
Pergamon Poets 9, with others, edited by Howard Sergeant. Oxford, Pergamon Press, 1970.
Hymns in Darkness.   New Delhi and London, Oxford University Press, 1976.

Plays

Three Plays (includes *Nalini, Marriage Poem, The Sleepwalkers*) (produced Bombay, 1969).   Calcutta, Writers Workshop, 1969.

Other

The Actor: A Sad and Funny Story for Children of Most Ages. Bombay, India Book House, 1974.
Latter-Day Psalms.   New Delhi, Oxford University Press, 1982.
Our Cultural Dilemmas: Tagore Memorial Lectures 1981-82. Ahmedabad, Gujarat University, n.d.

Editor, *A New Look at Communism*.   Bombay, Indian Committee for Cultural Freedom, 1963.
Editor, *Indian Writers in Conference*.   Mysore, P.E.N. All India Writers Conference, 1964.

Editor, *Writing in India*. Lucknow, P.E.N. All India Writers Conference, 1965.

Editor, *An Emerson Reader*. Bombay, Popular Prakashan, 1965.

Editor, *A Martin Luther King Reader*. Bombay, Popular Prakashan, 1969.

Editor, *All My Sons*, by Arthur Miller. Madras, Oxford University Press, 1972.

*

Critical Studies: *The Poetry of Nissim Ezekiel* by Meena Belliapa and Rajeev Taranath, Calcutta, Writers Workshop, 1966, and article by Taranath, in *Quest 74* (Bombay), January-Febuary, 1972; *Nissim Ezekiel: A Study* by Chetan Karnani, New Delhi, Arnold-Heinemann, 1974; "Nissim Ezekiel Issue" of *Journal of South Asian Literature* (Rochester, Michigan), September-December 1974; *The Poetry of Encounter: Three Indo-Anglian Poets* by Emmanuel Narendra Lall, New Delhi, Sterling, 1983.

Nissim Ezekiel comments:

(1974) I do not identify myself with any particular school of poetry. Labelled "Indo-Anglian" or "Indo-English," i.e., an Indian poet writing in English, I accept the label. I am satisfied at present to be included among the poets of the Commonwealth, but hope to be better known in the U.K. and U.S.A. as an *Indian* poet. I consider myself a modernist but not avant-garde.

I have written in the traditional verse forms as well as in free verse. Major influences: Pound, Eliot, Auden, MacNeice, Spender, Yeats and modern English and American poetry in general. My latest poetry, 1966-73, is beyond all influences. Some of my recent poems are in Indian English. I have written "found" poems on scientific subjects and several on newspaper reports and personal letters. Major themes: love, personal integration, the Indian contemporary scene, modern urban life, spiritual values. I aim at clarity above all, claim never to have written an obscure poem. I like to make controlled, meaningful statements, avoiding extremes of thought and expression.

*   *   *

In the foreword to *Sixty Poems*, Nissim Ezekiel confesses that his main reason for publishing the poems is that he has not the courage to destroy them. "There is in each line or phrase, an idea or image which helps me to maintain some sort of continuity in my life. If I could transcend the personal importance of these poems, I would not publish them....[The present collection] does not claim to be poetry, but it reveals a few small discoveries in the pursuit of poetry." What makes Ezekiel worthy of the respect of students of contemporary Indian poetry is this dedication. His scrupulousness is both aesthetic and moral. He is deeply concerned with the craftsmenship of his poems and with self-understanding. While there is much in his early volumes that is crude in thought, feeling and expression, with *The Exact Name* Ezekiel achieved a fine combination of freedom and discipline, of alertness and relaxation: "To Force the pace and never to be still/Is not the way of those who study birds/Or women." (The poem from which this quotation comes, "Poet, Lover, Bird-watcher," is itself a fine example of this development.) There is still an occasional line or two in this collection that does not quite fit in—for example, the line "Exactly as described in books on Indian birds" in the otherwise excellent poem "Paradise Flycatcher." Ezekiel's latest collection *Hymns in Darkness* bears ample testimony to the steady development of his poetic personality: a fine sense of rhythm; an exact diction, sparing of adjec-

tives; utter clarity; a clear eye both for the external world and the internal; and a genuinely sincere self-appraisal which is different in kind from the attitudinizing of some of his contemporaries with whom such self-introspection is a mode of hedging their bets. Many of the poems in this collection delicately etch a scene or character in such a way that the "comment on experience" is both unobtrusive and irresistible ("Ganga").

Ezekiel is an Indian Jew, and a certain measure of cultural isolation is perhaps unavoidable in the circumstances. While this isolation has sharpened his powers of observation and inclined him towards rationalism and humanism, several of the poems express an unfulfilled desire to discover religious values also. He is aware that he has been clinging "too long to the same static vision" ("The Room"). He is aware that his prayers have been those of an egoist. The "Hymns" end with the declaration: "Belief will not save you,/nor unbelief.//All you have/is the sense of unreality,/unfathomable/as it yields its secrets/slowly /one/by/one." The connexion between belief and a sense of reality is left unexplored. It is also not clear whether reality simply "is," or whether it has "secrets" that have to be wrested; and how reality differs from the romantic ego's perceptions of the external world and of itself. These dilemmas confront every sensitive poet who is unable to acquire a sense of tradition.

—S. Nagarajan

FAINLIGHT, Ruth (Esther). American. Born in New York City, 2 May 1931. Educated at schools in America and England, and at Birmingham and Brighton colleges of art. Married Alan Sillitoe, *q.v.*, in 1959; one son and one adopted daughter. Address: 14 Ladbroke Terrace, London W11 3PG, England.

PUBLICATIONS

Verse

A Forecast, A Fable. London, Outposts, 1958.
Cages. London, Macmillan, 1966; Chester Springs, Pennsylvania, Dufour, 1967.
18 Poems from 1966. London, Turret, 1967.
To See the Matter Clearly and Other Poems. London, Macmillan, 1968; Chester Springs, Pennsylvania, Dufour, 1969.
Poems, with Alan Sillitoe and Ted Hughes. London, Rainbow Press, 1971.
The Region's Violence. London, Hutchinson, 1973.
21 Poems. London, Turret, 1973.
Another Full Moon. London, Hutchinson, 1976.
Two Fire Poems. Knotting, Bedfordshire, Sceptre Press, 1977.
The Function of Tears. Knotting, Bedfordshire, Sceptre Press, 1979.
Sibyls and Others. London, Hutchinson, 1980.
Two Wind Poems. Knotting, Bedfordshire, Martin Booth, 1980.
Climates. Newcastle upon Tyne, Bloodaxe, 1983.
Fifteen to Infinity. London, Hutchinson, 1983.

Play

All Citizens Are Soldiers, with Alan Sillitoe, adaptation of a play by Lope de Vega (produced London, 1967). London, Macmillan, and Chester Springs, Pennsylvania, Dufour, 1969.

Short Stories

Penguin Modern Stories 9, with others. London, Penguin, 1971.
Daylife and Nightlife. London, Deutsch, 1971.

Other

Translator, *Coral*, by Sophia de Mello Breyner Andresen. Manchester, Carcanet, 1982.
Translator, *Navigacions*, by Sophia de Mello Breyner Andresen. Lisbon, Casa da Moeda, 1983.

*   *   *

The poetry of Ruth Fainlight reflects a systematic mining of personal experience. Central to her work are the interwoven themes of the poet's role in "normal" life, and that of a woman in a world whose standards are still defined by men. Both of these concerns are explored directly, the woman/poet giving evidence of their effect upon her. As a writer, Fainlight is conscious of herself as being in possession of a gift that to some extent distances her from the ordinary world, a mixed blessing whose compulsive urge for expression devours her own existence as its raw material. Force of this need within her, and the paralysing frustration in those arid periods when she is unable to write, are keenly observed in a number of poems, not least the hospital convalescence of "Late Afternoon." Warring with the poetic urge is the harder, more practical side of Fainlight's nature, what she refers to as "My Stone-Age Self," its earth-bound cynicism denying all spiritual values, insisting that "nothing/but the body's pleasure,/use, and comfort, matters." Such works as "Passenger" indicate that on more than one occasion the poet has found herself wondering if creativity is worth the trouble, if it would not if fact be better were she a "normal" non-poetic person, unravaged by these debilitating forces that cannibalize the self.

The roles of woman and pet interlock once more in Fainlight's relationship with her mother, presented in several of her poems. This is seen as ambivalent, varying somewhere between love and resentment, and in some ways equates with her attitude towards poetry itself—significantly, Fainlight regards the Muse as a mother-figure, whose status she is not always willing to acknowledge. Similarly in the case of love, while responding to that other compulsive urge, she is aware of the threat it poses, the gradual absorption of the self into family life. "Here" presents domesticity as at once a prison and a dangerous lure, the attractions of which compel her to accept against her better judgment. The male-female confrontation, its conflict and resolution, is tracked by Fainlight back into the looming shadow of myth and fairytale, imaged in Adam's Fall, or the story of Beauty and the Beast. At once a wife and mother, and an individual, she balances the warring opposites with a clear, unjaundiced vision, setting them down in measured polarities in her verse.

More than second-class citizenship or lack of inspiration, death is the final restriction, the limit placed on all created things. Robbed of her loved brother, a fellow-poet who died young, Fainlight is aware of death as a constantly lurking threat, reminders of its presence appearing when least expected, in a chance sighting of the moon in the night sky, or the coming of another spring. In her account of her brother's funeral, the sudden breaking of a storm matches her grief, his death the crucial event that convinces her of the fearful end to everything: "I shall not meet my dead again/as I remember them/alive, except in dreams or poems./Your death was the final proof/I needed to accept that knowledge."

Meanwhile she observes and records what she sees, whether descriptive travel sketches of India or the Sinai desert, her impressions of paintings, or reflections on Greek mythology and her own dreams. Throughout, hers is a voice that urges commitment. Fainlight despises those studied neutrals who balance both sides of a question, intellectualising a problem rather than stirring themselves to act. Though herself torn often between freedom and obligation, she manages in "Box and Sampler" to unite the two in a memorable image. A man carving while his wife stitches, their separate acts somehow bring them closer in a shared ritual, seeking "through craftsmanship and piety" to earn favour from the household gods. Fainlight sees clearly, and is conscious of the past and its continuity, shown in "Red Message" as a kind of programming passed on to successive generations through the sacrifice of their ancestors, those "lives gone into the earth like water." The poems she writes are a mirror of her own complex personality, and the more immediate the experience the stronger is her message. Whether viewing London derelicts, or her grown son taking photographs, pondering death's onset or resenting the "using up" of her life in writing, the vision is faithfully conveyed, and the voice remains unmistakably her own.

—Geoff Sadler

FAIRFAX, John. British. Born in London, 9 November 1930. Educated at public school in Plymouth, and privately. Married Esther Berk in 1952; two sons. Editor of *Nimbus* magazine in the early 1950's. School teacher, 1955-62. British Editor, *Panache* magazine, New York; Poetry Editor, *Resurgence* magazine. Since 1967, Director, Phoenix Press, Newbury, Berkshire. Since 1968, Co-Founding Director, Arvon Foundation, Devon. Recipient: Eric Gregory Award, 1960, 1969; Society of Authors award; Arts Council award, 1973. Agent: A.D. Peters, 10 Buckingham Street, London WC2N 6BU. Address: The Thatched Cottage, Hermitage, Newbury, Berkshire, England.

<small>PUBLICATIONS</small>

Verse

This I Say: Twelve Poems. Newbury, Berkshire, Phoenix Press, 1967.
The 5th Horseman of the Apocalypse. Newbury, Berkshire, Phoenix Press, 1969.
Double Image, with Michael Baldwin and Brian Patten. London, Longman, 1972.
Adrift on the Star Brow of Taliesin. Newbury, Berkshire, Phoenix Press, 1975.
Bone Harvest Done. London, Sidgwick and Jackson, 1980.

Other

The Way to Write, with John Moat. London, Elm Tree, and New York, St. Martin's Press, 1981.

Editor, *Listen to This: A Contemporary Anthology*. London, Longman, 1967.
Editor, *Stop and Listen: An Anthology of Thirteen Living Poets*. London, Longman, 1969.

Editor, *Frontier of Going: An Anthology of Space Poetry.*
    London, Panther, 1969.
Editor, *Horizons.*   London, Arnold, 1971.

*

Critical Studies: by Graham Fawcett, in *Southern Arts Review*
(Winchester, Hampshire), March and May 1970; Roger Garfitt,
in *London Magazine*, August-September 1975.

John Fairfax comments:
    My style has been called "analogical." I go along with this.
Form tending to be traditional. I write for the ear and voice as
well as for the reading eye. Rhythm is very important. I like my
work to be read aloud. I am concerned with a magical and
spell-casting quality in poetry—with the power to encompass
myth and mystery.

*   *   *

    John Fairfax appears to hold no particular brief for or alle-
giance to any particular group or school. He goes his own way, a
somewhat remote and unworldly figure if we are to believe his
writings.
    He has attempted, with some considerable success, the long
poem (*The 5th Horseman of the Apocalypse*) and the poem-
sequence (*Adrift on the Star Brow of Taliesin*). Both rely heavily
on myth/legend, and, try hard as he does in both pieces, Fairfax
falls short of a top-class end-product. The sequence becomes a
sub-species of Hughes's "Crow" poems and relies too much on
repetition. Read aloud it *sounds* right, but on the page seems
thin, limp. *The 5th Horseman of the Apocalypse* employs short
lines and at times lists items when economy of word usage would
perhaps have made for a tighter poem:

> He is alone.
> Is seen alone.
> He is in the teeth
> Of cornered rat,
> In the raving of insanity,
> The unseeing eye of fear,
> The ripped nails of unutterable
> Anguish.

    The natural world is never far away, in spite of the Fairfax
wish to break new ground. Even in his "space poems" with their
attention to technology the work is firmly rooted in an imagination fed by known landscapes. While the "space poems" are
readable and interesting, the "I," the "my," and the "we" appear
with distracting regularity. One's belief was suspended:

> The sinews tighten as my head tilts back
> To look at the sky; in particular the moon.
> My eyes travel through the peels of space
> To those ancient bodies that might still be.

One notes, also, certain received poeticisms making their presence felt. The language remains down-to-earth.
    Time and again the theme of regeneration crops up. An
impression is left that here we have an idiosyncratic and individualistic poet who has not quite found an adequate subject matter. The work is readable and considered, yet it remains at arm's
length; the poems fail fully to involve or move the reader.

—Wes Magee

FALCK, Colin.   British.   Born in London, 14 July 1934. Educated at Christ's Hospital; Magdalen College, Oxford, B.A. in
philosophy, politics and economics 1957, B.A. in philosophy,
psychology and physiology 1959. Served in the British Army,
1952-54. Lecturer in Sociology, London School of Economics,
1961-62; part-time lecturer in literature, London and Hertfordshire, 1962-64. Since 1964, Lecturer in Humanities, Chelsea College, London. Associate Editor, *The Review*, Oxford and London, 1962-72; Poetry Editor, *The New Review*, 1974-78. Address:
20 Thurlow Road, London NW3 5PP, England.

PUBLICATIONS

Verse

The Garden in the Evening, adaptations of poems by Antonio
    Machado.   Oxford, The Review, 1964.
Promises.   London, The Review, 1969.
Backwards into the Smoke.   Cheadle, Cheshire, Carcanet,
    1973.
In This Dark Light.   London, TNR, 1978.

Other

Editor, with Ian Hamilton, *Poems since 1900: An Anthology of
    British and American Verse in the Twentieth Century.*   Lon-
    don, Macdonald and Jane's, 1975.

*

Colin Falck comments:
    Writing a poem means persuading the semi-verbal impulses
which start up at the back of one's mind under the pressure of
some insistent emotion to arrange themselves poetically on the
page. By doing this one discovers more about what the emotion
was. The only test I can find for a poem's validity is that it should
be moving—should generate the distinctive feeling or *frisson* (cf.
Housman and others) which signals the presence of poetry. For
me this has a lot to do with rhythm and sound-texture—but no
analysis seems to take one very near to understanding what is
really going on.
    The poems I have written so far are quite short. I could wish
they were longer, but the writing of short poems has been—for
me—a bottleneck that has to be gone through. I would like to be
able to get through it and to move on from poems of straightforward mood and atmosphere to poems which handle larger
amounts of material and more public themes—but which handle
them poetically, rather than merely versifying attitudes and opinions or stringing out a lot of images on one long idea (this may be
some kind of reaction to the poetry which was prevalent in
Britain during the 1950's). *Backwards into the Smoke* is a mood-
sequence, to do with learning to accept life, learning where one's
more negative and irrational impulses can lead, hoping to accept
such impulses and remain dedicated to life and humanity. I
would like, before very long, to be able to write poems which
look more obviously adequate to such heavyweight preoccupations, and have perhaps begun to do so in one or two poems
included in the pamphlet *In This Dark Light.*
    Since about 1977 I have been studying and writing philosophy,
but I hope and intend to get back to poetry very soon.

*   *   *

    Colin Falck is one of a group of poets and critics associated
during the 1960's with the English magazine, *The Review*, who

made a deliberate attempt to revive Imagism as a poetic discipline and a mode of imaginative apprehension. Falck is an explicit theorist in criticism and he has argued that Imagism continues the essential insights of Romanticism: a poem, whatever else it does, must articulate the emotion of a particular moment as truthfully as possible. Falck's own poems present Imagist notations of encounters and places. They are calculatedly small-scale and, in a sense, insubstantial; sometimes they remain merely frail and even trivial, but at other times they achieve a haunting resonance with a very few words. In his love poems Falck is courageously vulnerable; where they succeed they are tremulously beautiful and where they fail they tumble into bathos. He is literally on firmer ground in his poems based on places, such as "Central Ohio," "End of the Summer Term at Christ's Hospital," "Box Hill" and "Lyme Regis Station." He is considerably influenced by modern Spanish poetry, and has published a set of exquisite translations of poems by Antonio Machado.

—Bernard Bergonzi

FANTHORPE, U(rsula) A(skham). British. Born in Lee Green, London, 29 July 1929. Educated at St. Anne's College, Oxford, 1949-53, B.A. 1953, M.A. 1958; University of London Institute of Education, 1953-54, Dip. Ed. 1954; University College, Swansea, diploma in school counselling 1971. Assistant English teacher, 1954-62, and Head of English, 1962-70, Cheltenham Ladies' College, Gloucestershire; clerk in various businesses in Bristol, 1972-74; hospital clerk and receptionist, Bristol, 1974-83. Arts Council Creative Writing Fellow, St. Martin's College, Launceton, 1983-85. Recipient: Society of Authors travelling scholarship, 1984. Address: Culverhay House, Wotton under Edge, Gloucestershire, England.

PUBLICATIONS

Verse

Side Effects. Liskeard, Cornwall, Harry Chambers/Peterloo Poets, 1978.
Four Dogs. Liskeard, Cornwall, Treovis Press, 1980.
Standing To. Liskeard, Cornwall, Harry Chambers/Peterloo Poets, 1982.
Voices Off. Liskeard, Cornwall, Harry Chambers/Peterloo Poets, 1984.

*   *   *

U.A. Fanthorpe had an Oxford education and went on to teach at a prestigious school. She gave this up to become, after various temporary jobs, a clerical worker at a hospital. Such a biography may sound like that of an English eccentric. But there is nothing eccentric about Fanthorpe's verse. It is true that she gives more than a passing nod to Betjeman and is clearly aware of the more comedic aspects of Auden. These affinities, however, are as much a matter of rivalry as of imitation. Her most obvious literary relationship seems to be with a phase of poetry, colloquial and not infrequently acidulous, which began in Britain soon after the Second World War. Fanthorpe by that time was already a young adult, but she had many years to go before she published a book of her own. Further, behind any of the more

palpable analogues are the poets preserved for Fanthorpe's generation in the Oxford Editions of Standard Authors.

Fanthorpe's verse does not in every respect relate to the classics. This is a result of her subject-matter. Socially speaking, it is rather down the hill. Wordsworth had some odd encounters, and so had Coleridge, but they never met Julie the encephalitic or Alison with the damaged brain. Tennyson wrote of sickbeds, it is true, but not quite like Fanthorpe—"The smashed voice roars inside the ruined throat/Behind the mangled face...." Yet we have not lost the Standard Authors entirely. Further on, the poem, ironically entitled "Linguist," modulates into a style that Tennyson would have recognized—"A silent clock that speaks/The solemn language of the sun...." All this goes to show how genuinely inclusive the English tradition is.

Even her subject-matter, that which would seem to set Fanthorpe apart, is not quite what it seems. There is always a positive note somewhere, though occasionally it is deceptive: "rain falls in every life,/But rainbows, bluebirds, spring, babies or God/Lift up our hearts...." This is, of course, a special effect. Fanthorpe has donned, for purposes of parody, the singing-robes of Patience Strong and wears them with a flourish that even the bard of *Woman's Own* never knew. Such nonce-style is, moreover, a clue as to how much of this poetry works. Fanthorpe tends to infiltrate her quarry, using his own tactics to bring him down. In her poem "Sir John," "dear distractions" and "dreary inner eye," phrases which Betjeman himself might have coined, served to indicate a sense of the void beneath the somewhat chintzy cheeriness of that great man.

Fanthorpe's world, though fraught with wit, is not a cosy one. The functionaries in her poems deal with sickness and death at close quarters. The hospital secretary requires a sense of order in typing out her fatal lists, and the clerk needs a strong back to tote her files. Moreover, all of this takes place in a busily social atmosphere. Almost the best of these poems is "Lament for the Patients." Here, a startling use is made of interpolated statement:

> To me came the news of their dying:
> From the police (*Was this individual*
> *A patient of yours?*); from ambulance
> Control (*Our team report this patient*
> *You sent us to fetch is deceased already*);
> From tight-lipped telephoning widowers
> (*My wife died in her sleep last night...*)

These interpolations are not so prosaic as they might seem out of context. An ironic effect is gained through the way in which natural language is displaced by official language, causing some odd ambiguities. The word necessarily used by the police, "individual," fortuitously drains its referent of identity. The "deceased" is no longer a patient but has, precipitately, become a corpse. All this, moreover, is contrasted with the central persona who has to cope with these incoming calls, succinctly and with a degree of alliterative skill. This produces a rhythmic momentum that may remind us of the break-through in the early 1950's, when James Kirkup inaugurated a new mood in poetry with "A Correct Compassion" and D.J. Enright sent back his wry dispatches from Egypt and Japan.

Much that Fanthorpe writes about seems as drab and basic as the topics chosen by those poets. Characteristically, however, each subject is irradiated by an enlivening gleam. What Fanthorpe says of the winter adventurers in her poem "Hang-gliders in January" is true of her own verse also—"Like all miracles, it has a rational/Explanation...." Here, as elsewhere, it is the naturalistic detail that seems to carry the romantic charge—"We saw the aground flyers, their casques and belts/And defenceless legs...." This gives the immediately preceding statement, "It was all quite simple, really," an ironic turn. We are tempted to follow the poem beyond its literal meaning. The skill and perception of U.A. Fanthorpe make her appear, among the gyrations of so many latter-day imagists in our own time, "Like a bird at home in the sky."

—Philip Hobsbaum

FEINSTEIN, Elaine.   British.   Born in Bootle, Lancashire, 24 October 1930. Educated at Wyggeston Grammar School, Leicester; Newnham College, Cambridge. Married Dr. Arnold Feinstein in 1956; three sons. Editorial staff member, Cambridge University Press, 1960-62; Lecturer in English, Bishop's Stortford Training College, Hertfordshire, 1963-66; Assistant Lecturer in Literature, University of Essex, Wivenhoe, 1967-70. Recipient: Arts Council grant, 1970, 1979, 1981; Daisy Miller Award, for fiction, 1971; Kelus Prize, 1978. Fellow, Royal Society of Literature, 1980. Agent: (verse) Olwyn Hughes, 38 Stratford Villas, London NW1 9SG; (fiction) Gill Coleridge, Anthony Sheil Associates Ltd., 2-3 Morwell Street, London WC1B 3AR; (plays and film) Phil Kelvin, Goodwin Associates, 19 London Street, London W2 1HL. Address: c/o Hutchinson Publishing Group Ltd., 17-21 Conway Street, London W1P 6JD, England.

PUBLICATIONS

Verse

In a Green Eye.   London, Goliard Press, 1966.
The Magic Apple Tree.   London, Hutchinson, 1971.
At the Edge.   Rushden, Northamptonshire, Sceptre Press, 1972.
The Celebrants and Other Poems.   London, Hutchinson, 1973.
Some Unease and Angels: Selected Poems.   London, Hutchinson, and University Center, Michigan, Green River Press, 1977.
The Feast of Euridice.   London, Faber, 1980.

Plays

Radio Plays: *Echoes*, 1980; *A Late Spring*, 1982; *A Captive Lion*, 1984; *A Day Off*, 1985.

Television Plays: *Breath*, 1975; *Lunch*, 1982; *Country Diary of an Edwardian Lady* series, from work by Edith Holden, 1984; *A Brave Face*, 1985.

Novels

The Circle.   London, Hutchinson, 1970.
The Amberstone Exit.   London, Hutchinson, 1972.
The Glass Alembic.   London, Hutchinson, 1973; as *The Crystal Garden*, New York, Dutton, 1974.
Children of the Rose.   London, Hutchinson, 1975.
The Ecstasy of Dr. Miriam Garner.   London, Hutchinson, 1976.
The Shadow Master.   London, Hutchinson, 1978; New York, Simon and Schuster, 1979.
The Survivors.   London, Hutchinson, 1982.
The Border.   London, Hutchinson, 1984.

Short Stories

Matters of Chance.   London, Covent Garden Press, 1980.
The Silent Areas.   London, Hutchinson, 1980.

Other

Editor, *Selected Poems of John Clare.*   London, University Tutorial Press, 1968.
Editor, with Fay Weldon, *New Stories 4.*   London, Hutchinson, 1979.

Translator, *The Selected Poems of Marina Tsvetayeva.*   London, Oxford University Press, 1971; revised edition, Oxford and New York, Oxford University Press, 1981.
Translator, *Three Russian Poets: Margarita Aliger, Yunna Moritz, Bella Akhmadulina.*   Manchester, Carcanet, 1979.

*

Manuscript Collection: Cambridge University.

Critical Studies: "Modes of Realism: Roy Fisher and Elaine Feinstein" by Deborah Mitchell, in *British Poetry since 1970* edited by Michael Schmidt and Peter Jones, Manchester, Carcanet, and New York, Persea, 1980; Peter Conradi, in *British Novelists since 1960* edited by Jay L. Halio, Detroit, Gale, 1983.

Elaine Feinstein comments:
     When I began writing in the early sixties I felt the influence of the Americans (Stevens and perhaps even Emily Dickinson as much as W.C. Williams); and I suppose the turning point in finding a voice of my own arose, paradoxically, from working on the translations of Marina Tsvetayeva and other modern Russian poets. And perhaps also from writing prose, which began at first as an extension of the poetic impulse, but (after several novels) works as a channel for the exploration of my humanist concerns, and leaves me freer now to take greater risks with language when I choose to write lyric poetry. Perhaps both experiences have encouraged me to write longer poems (such as the title poem of *The Celebrants* and more recently "New Poems for Dido and Aeneas"), and to find longer lines and new rhythms, as well as richer subject matter.

*   *   *

     "Anniversary," which opens the collection *The Magic Apple Tree*, makes the act of faith in humanity on which all Elaine Feinstein's poetry is posited:

          Listen, I shall have to whisper it
          into your heart directly: we are all
          supernatural/every day
          we rise new creatures/cannot be predicted.

Confronting the banal, flat surfaces of modern existence, symbolised by the mud, mists and rain of the East Anglian fens, "our brackish waters" ("The Magic Apple Tree"), she acknowledges the limitations set to the human by "the tyranny of landscape" ("Moon") and by our rooting in a particular and all-pervasive present: "How do you change the weather in the blood?" ("I Have Seen Worse Days Turn"). The techniques of poetry are the "alembic," the alchemist's vessel which effects a transformation which is not the transcendence but a sharpening of the real, the celebration of "what in the landscape of cities/has to be prized" ("Some Thoughts on Where"). Feinstein shares with the reader the liberating power of new perceptions: "We have broken some magic barrier" to become "open to the surprises of the season" ("Renaissance February 7"). She delights in the surprises of imagery, colour, syntax, tone, and rhythms which set "your own East Anglian children/...dancing. To an alien drum" ("Moon"). "Our Vegetable Love Shall Grow" develops the surrealist quality of Marvell's image, in the mock-horror of a vampire crocus, grotesquely yoking the energies of nature and the city to drain away the lesser vitality of the human. Black humour is the vehicle for modern man—and woman—to reassert dominance of a reality that threatens to overwhelm. The invocation of Buster Keaton ("Out") ·is no accident; nor is the marvellous, punning cynicism of "West," whose hesitating and stabbing rhythms embrace exactly the bitterly revealing twists of Mae West's comedy.

Beyond the struggle, the creative effort for freedom, what is sought is a sense of repose—"to live freely in silver light/here a visitor" ("Some Local Resistance"), experiencing "the peculiar joy of abandoning restlessness" which is generated by the icon, or by the "infantine" vision of Samuel Palmer's painting ("The Magic Apple Tree"). Feinstein moves incessantly between the turmoil and the sense of peace, carrying the poet's burden of personal responsibility for the remaking of harmony and unity out of a torn, disjointed world. The broken utterances of "Marriage" catch the pain of human separateness on an intensely personal note:

> tender whenever we touch   what
> else we share   this flesh   we
> bring together   it hurts to
> think of dying as we lie close

In the realm of private loves, Feinstein can convey the kind of raw emotion she found in Tsvetayeva, whom she praised in the introduction to her translations for the "wholeness of her self-exposure." She also, however, goes beyond the purely personal. *At the Edge* evokes the new understanding reached through the "lyric daze" of carnal passion but makes it clear that the knowledge gained at these frontiers can only be kept through the interpretative but distancing medium of poetic language: "We were washed in salt on the same pillow together/and we watched the walls change level gently as water...."

The title poem of *The Celebrants* recounts the perpetual struggle for meaning through love, science, art, and religion, seeking to evade the limits of death and corruption bounding the world of the body, waiting for the gratuitous moment of poetic surprise "to free us from the/black drama/of the magician." The other poems in this volume have a darker tone than earlier work, a deeper and richer seriousness, and a more biting and bitter humour. But still the abiding note struck is one of an optimism which finds in given reality not only its torment but its reassurance: "the earth has another language, we have been/given complexities of the soil against the taste of the grave" ("A Ritual Turning," dedicated to Octavio Paz). *Some Unease and Angels*, essentially a well-chosen retrospect with some new poems, confirms her determination to create through language a new balance of man, woman, and their world with nature and its warring elements, as in "Watersmeet":

> everywhere plant flesh
> and rich ores had eaten into each other, so that
> peat, rain, green leaves and August fused
> even the two of us together; we took
> a new balance from the two defenceless
> kingdoms bonded in hidden warfare underfoot.

In Feinstein's most recent work—*The Feast of Euridice* and the "Nine Songs for Dido and Aeneas"—the perspective of myth and legend throws that balance back into question. Virgil's epic celebration of empire is brilliantly turned to a denunciation of the devouring lust for power and possession that drives the imperialist hero, "stony-eyed," "cruel," bringer of death, ash and sterility, with whom no bonds are possible. Dido's ancient, orderly kingdom, freely offering its nurturing affections to exorcise Aeneas's ghosts, is laid waste by his ambitions. But at the end, it is Dido who wins immortality, not by any witch's magic but by natural powers of endurance and love, the true incarnation of the piety and virtue that the lying Aeneas claims as his own: "...when my bones lie/between white stones at last/and fine white dust/rises over all, no one who/survives among the dead/will scorn my ghost."

—Jennifer Birkett

FELDMAN, Irving (Mordecai). American. Born in Brooklyn, New York, 22 September 1928. Educated at the City College of New York, B.S. 1950; Columbia University, New York, M.A. 1953. Married Carmen Alvarez in 1955; one son. Taught at the University of Puerto Rico, Rio Piedras, 1954-56, University of Lyons, France, 1957-58, and Kenyon College, Gambier, Ohio, 1958-64. Since 1964, Professor of English, State University of New York, Buffalo. Recipient: Jewish Book Council of America Kovner Award, 1962; Ingram Merrill Foundation grant, 1963; American Academy grant, 1973; Guggenheim Fellowship, 1973; Creative Artists Public Service grant, 1980. Address: 349 Berryman Drive, Buffalo, New York 14226, U.S.A.

PUBLICATIONS

Verse

Work and Days and Other Poems. Boston, Little Brown, and London, Deutsch, 1961.
The Pripet Marshes and Other Poems. New York, Viking Press, 1965.
Magic Papers and Other Poems. New York, Harper, 1970.
Lost Originals. New York, Holt Rinehart, 1972.
Leaping Clear. New York, Viking Press, 1976.
New and Selected Poems. New York, Viking Press, 1979.
Teach Me, Dear Sister, and Other Poems. New York, Viking Press, 1983.

*   *   *

Irving Feldman's poetry strives, as one critic has said, "to infuse the tangible word with numinous significance." While such an attempt at transcendence is more or less doomed to failure—as Feldman himself seems aware—he has pursued it with wit, humility, and a refreshingly varied and agile poetry. "Life is unhappy, life is sweet!" concludes his newly born Gingerbread Man, ecstatic at the "thrilling absolute of original breath" ("As Fast As You Can," *Lost Originals*) and Feldman's work is inspired throughout by this sense of tragic optimism.

The tragic heroes of his first book, *Works and Days*, are figures like Cato and Prometheus, overwhelmed by their fate, and yet ultimately revenged—in the latter's case, by humor: "the rictus of cosmic spite./Then nothing really mattered—as his mirth bubbled off in a mist.//O come to the mountain and see a suit of clothes on a nail" ("Non-being," *Works and Days*). Feldman examines the fates of heroes of all types, from the mythic Prometheus and the Gingerbread Man, to Charles Olson and the passengers of the *Titanic*, to the fictional Antonio, the inept Spanish *botones*, or bell-boy (of "Antonio, *Botones*" in *Leaping Clear*), who becomes a paradigm of innocence and humanity passed over by progress.

Family and friends, Jewish society and customs, politics, religion, painting, and philosophy all take equal weight in Feldman's work, and as frustrating as this puckish diversity can sometimes be, it is welded together by his search for a transcendent knowledge, or at least a transcendent joy in the continuity and identity of life's faceted brilliance. As he says of the fat, balding athletes in "Handball Players at Brighton Beach,"

> So what! the sun does not snub,
> does not overlook them, shines,
>
> and the fair day flares,
> the blue universe booms and blooms.

Amid life's corruscating reality, there looms always a brighter Ideal.

Like his subject matter, Feldman's technique is highly varied and his forms diverse. Although he often adopts or adapts the ballad, elegy, or other established forms, his writing has frequently turned to the vernacular line, and many of his latest works are set in paragraphs. Even earlier, for instance in the title poem of *The Pripet Marshes*, he is beginning to use prose stanzas:

> Often I think of my Jewish friends and seize them as they are
> and transport them in my mind to the *shtetlach* and ghettos,
>
> And set them walking the streets, visiting, praying in *shul*,
> feasting and dancing. The men I set to arguing, because I
> love dialectic and song....

"Dialectic and song" is an ensign of Feldman's diversity, and while many influences are present in his work, from the classical references of *Works and Days* to Whitmanesque songs or a bit of Olson's Objectism, Feldman has rarely rested in a single one, and his real poetic kin are meditative poets like John Ashbery and Richard Howard.

Transmuting personal and intellectual experience in his very dense, thoughtful poetry, Feldman clearly identifies the writing of poetry itself (in "Colloquy") with the project of transcendence, as even the titles *Magic Papers* and *Lost Originals* indicate.

> I have long wanted to confess
> but do not know to whom
> I must speak, and cannot
> spend a life on my knees.
> Nonetheless, I have always
> wanted to save the world.

Through his dialectic and song, Feldman tries to save the world not only in the political and religious senses, but also in the sense of reclamation. "We wake to poetry from a deeper dream, a purer meditation—expanse of light in water pressing unquenched on our eyes" (second elegy in "New Poems," *New and Selected Poems*) and Feldman rejoices in the writing of poetry itself for its revivifying of the senses, its assertion of time's ineluctable continuity, and its appreciation of a moment's glorious effulgence:

> And the light
>   (everywhere
> off ridge, rock, window, deep
> drop) says,
>   I leap clear.

—Walter Bode

FENTON, James (Martin). British. Born in Lincoln, 25 April 1949. Educated at Durham Choristers School; Repton School; Magdalen College, Oxford (Newdigate Prize, 1968), B.A. 1970, M.A. Assistant Literary Editor, 1971, Editorial Assistant, 1972, and political columnist, 1976-78, *New Statesman*, London; free-lance journalist, Indo-China, 1973-75; German correspondent, *Guardian*, London, 1978-79; Theatre Critic, *Sunday Times*, London, 1979-84. Since 1984, Chief Literary Critic, *The Times*, London. Recipient: Eric Gregory Award, 1969; Geoffrey Faber Memorial Prize, 1984. Fellow, Royal Society of Literature, 1983. Agent: A.D. Peters, 10 Buckingham Street, London WC2N 6BU. Address: 1 Bartlemas Road, Oxford OX4 1XU, England.

PUBLICATIONS

Verse

Our Western Furniture. Oxford, Sycamore Press, 1968.
Put Thou Thy Tears into My Bottle. Oxford, Sycamore Press, 1969.
Terminal Moraine. London, Secker and Warburg, 1972.
A Vacant Possesion. London, TNR, 1978.
Dead Soldiers. Oxford, Sycamore Press, 1981.
A German Requiem. Edinburgh, Salamander Press, 1981.
The Memory of War. Edinburgh, Salamander Press, 1982.
Children in Exile. Edinburgh, Salamander Press, 1983.
The Memory of War and Children in Exile: Poems 1968-83. London, Penguin, 1983; as *Children in Exile*, New York, Random House, 1984.

Plays

Rigoletto, adaptation of a libretto by F.M. Piave from a play by Hugo, music by Verdi (produced London, 1982; New York, 1984). London, Calder, 1982.

Television Documentary: *Burton: A Portrait of a Superstar*, 1983.

Other

You Were Marvellous (theatre reviews). London, Cape, 1983.

*   *   *

James Fenton is quite the opposite of a prolific poet; he publishes rarely, and collects his work infrequently into exceptionally slim volumes. "A parsimonious brilliance," John Mole has said of Fenton, "is its own reward"; and certainly the brilliance of his individual poems, which seem to surround themselves with an exceptional silence, to create a very generous space for themselves in the crowded world of contemporary poetry, has earned Fenton a commensurate critical acclaim. This parsimony, however, is clearly not the result of a planned strategy of self-publicity. On the contrary, his poems—which differ so markedly one from another as to seem the products of several distinct kinds of imagination—convey a powerful sense of the single thing uniquely done, of the single matter and the single form uniquely exhausted. The individual Fenton poem embodies within itself a sense of how boring it would be to have anything like it done again. Fenton himself is certainly not going to be the bore to do it.

In briefly characterising Fenton's work, then, it is difficult to say much that will prove generally true; but, despite being his own man, his poems do have their influences and analogues. Of the former, Auden is certainly the strongest. Auden acts for Fenton as a model for a varied formal inventiveness and ingenuity; for a sense of how apparently stubbornly recalcitrant material, of a factual kind, can be embraced by poems (can, indeed, prompt and release poems); and for an indication of how the impersonal, objective play of an art is also heavily, if obliquely, implicated in a morality. Of Fenton's analogues, the clearest are the new English "narrative" poets—the conception of the poem as a compressed fiction is central to some of his work—and the "Martian" school (which Fenton actually named). Only rarely does Fenton employ the Martians' extravagant visual simile and metaphor, and sometimes I suspect it's in a rather tongue-in-cheek way: "The winter vines shimmered like chromosomes"; "the fireflies' brilliant use of the hyphen." But he does share with them a feeling for the strangeness and alienness of the apparently "ordinary" world.

It is in these various ways of denying the poem any authentic, recognisable lyric voice that something vitally sustaining can be discovered in Fenton. The impression his poems most profoundly convey is that what can be learned about the world is infinitely more important than what can be learned about the self; and the "world," in Fenton's case, means rather more of it than is the case with many contemporary English poets. His work as a journalist took him to Vietnam and to Germany during the 1970's, and these experiences, however obliquely, inform—or "undermine," perhaps—a great deal of his work. Fenton's objectivity—his penchant for the "found" poem, his desire for the poem in which the reader might notice *only* the subject matter—might perhaps be regarded as the reticence of a man appalled before some of the facts of his own experience. If the reticence began as an aesthetic choice, it has continued as a moral necessity.

To write directly of some of his subjects—Cambodia in "Cambodia," "In A Notebook," and "Dead Soldiers"; the Third Reich in "A German Requiem"; nuclear holocaust (probably) in "Wind"—would be to risk banality or sentimentality. He does perhaps run this risk in the poem in which he most clearly articulates his own feelings, "Children in Exile," about Cambodian refugees coming to terms with a new life in Italy. But even here, I think, the personal feeling is less important than the creation of a tone in which it is possible for this very reticent poet to solicit, or cajole, the feelings of the reader. The apparent naivety of the poem's palpable design upon us is an earnest of the significance of the subject:

> From five years of punishment for an offence
>   It took America five years to commit
> These victim-children have been released on parole.
>   They will remember all of it.

Elsewhere in Fenton's poems, the self-effacement is more complete, and the absence of sententiousness is the clear reward in poems which address themselves to the largest modern themes. In "A German Requiem," for instance, the eerie final section creates an unforgettable muted image for the huge suffering, and, in explicitly stating the poem's theme of the implicit and the unstated, suggests the way Fenton's own reticent imagination has here found its most impressive expression to date. It is surely not without point that the image here owes something, at some level, not to Auden but to the master of the eerie, the sinister, and the inexplicit, T.S. Eliot:

> His wife nods, and a secret smile,
> Like a breeze with enough strength to carry one dry leaf
> Over two pavingstones, passes from chair to chair.
> Even the enquirer is charmed.
> He forgets to pursue the point.
> It is not what he wants to know.
> It is what he wants not to know.
> It is not what they say.
> It is what they do not say.

—Neil Corcoran

FERLINGHETTI, Lawrence (Mendes-Monsanto). American. Born in Yonkers, New York, 24 March 1919; lived in France, 1920-24. Educated at Riverside Country School, 1927-28, and Bronxville Public School, 1929-33, both New York; Mount Hermon School, Greenfield, Massachusetts, 1933-37; University of North Carolina, Chapel Hill, B.A. in journalism 1941; Columbia University, New York, 1947-48, M.A. 1948; the Sorbonne, Paris, 1948-49, Doctorat de L'Université 1949. Served in the United States Naval Reserve, 1941-45: Lieutenant Commander. Married Selden Kirby-Smith in 1951 (divorced, 1976); one daughter and one son. Worked for *Time* magazine, New York, 1945-46; French teacher, San Francisco, 1951-53. Co-Founder, 1952, with Peter L. Martin, and since 1955, Owner, City Lights Bookstore, and Editor-in-Chief, City Lights Books, San Francisco. Delegate, Pan American Cultural Conference, Concepción, Chile, 1960. Recipient: Etna-Taormina Prize (Italy), 1968. Address: City Lights Books, 261 Columbus Avenue, San Francisco, California 94133, U.S.A.

PUBLICATIONS

Verse

Pictures of the Gone World. San Francisco, City Lights, 1955.
A Coney Island of the Mind. New York, New Directions, 1958.
Tentative Description of a Dinner Given to Promote the Impeachment of President Eisenhower. San Francisco, Golden Mountain Press, 1958.
One Thousand Fearful Words for Fidel Castro. San Francisco, City Lights, 1961.
Berlin. San Francisco, Golden Mountain Press, 1961.
Starting from San Francisco. New York, New Directions, 1961; revised edition, 1967.
Penguin Modern Poets 5, with Allen Ginsberg and Gregory Corso. London, Penguin, 1963.
Where Is Vietnam? San Francisco, City Lights, 1965.
To Fuck Is to Love Again; Kyrie Eleison Kerista; or, The Situation in the West; Followed by a Holy Proposal. New York, Fuck You Press, 1965.

Christ Climbed Down. Syracuse, New York, Syracuse University, 1965.

An Eye on the World: Selected Poems. London, MacGibbon and Kee, 1967.

After the Cries of the Birds. San Francisco, Dave Haselwood, 1967.

Moscow in the Wilderness, Segovia in the Snow. San Francisco, Beach Books, 1967.

Repeat After Me. Boston, Impressions Workshop, 1967(?).

Reverie Smoking Grass. Milan, East 128, 1968.

The Secret Meaning of Things. New York, New Directions, 1968.

Fuclock. London, Fire, 1968.

Tyrannus Nix? New York, New Directions, 1969; revised edition, 1973.

Back Roads to Far Towns after Basho. Privately printed, 1970.

Sometime During Eternity. Conshohocken, Pennsylvania, Poster Prints, 1970(?).

The World Is a Beautiful Place. Conshohocken, Pennsylvania, Poster Prints, 1970(?).

The Illustrated Wilfred Funk. San Francisco, City Lights, 1971.

A World Awash with Fascism and Fear. San Francisco, Cranium Press, 1971.

Back Roads to Far Places. New York, New Directions, 1971.

Love Is No Stone on the Moon: Automatic Poem. Berkeley, California, Arif Press, 1971.

Open Eye, with *Open Head,* by Allen Ginsberg. Melbourne, Sun, 1972; published separately, Cambridge, Massachusetts, Pomegranate Press, 1973.

Constantly Risking Absurdity. Brockport, New York, State University College, 1973.

Open Eye, Open Heart. New York, New Directions, 1973.

Populist Manifesto. San Francisco, Cranium Press, 1975; revised edition, San Francisco, City Lights, n.d.

Soon It Will Be Night. Privately printed, 1975(?).

The Jack of Hearts. San Francisco, City Lights, 1975(?).

Director of Alienation. San Francisco, City Lights, 1975(?).

The Old Italians Dying. San Francisco, City Lights, 1976.

Who Are We Now? New York, New Directions, 1976.

White on White. San Francisco, City Lights, 1977.

Adieu à Charlot. San Francisco, City Lights, 1978.

Northwest Ecolog. San Francisco, City Lights, 1978.

The Sea and Ourselves at Cape Ann. Madison, Wisconsin, Red Ozier Press, 1979.

Landscapes of Living and Dying. New York, New Directions, 1979.

The Love Nut. Lincoln, Massachusetts, Penmaen Press, 1979.

Mule Mountain Dreams. Bisbee, Arizona, Bisbee Press Collective, 1980.

A Trip to Italy and France. New York, New Directions, 1981.

The Populist Manifestos, Plus an Interview with Jean-Jacques Lebel. San Francisco, Grey Fox Press, 1981.

Endless Life: The Selected Poems. New York, New Directions, 1981.

Over All the Obscene Boundaries: European Poems and Transitions. New York, New Directions, 1984.

Recordings: *Poetry Readings in "The Cellar,"* with Kenneth Rexroth, Fantasy, 1958; *Tentative Description of a Dinner to Impeach President Eisenhower and Other Poems,* Fantasy, 1959; *Tyrannus Nix? and Assassination Raga,* Fantasy, 1971; *The World's Greatest Poets 1,* with Allen Ginsberg and Gregory Corso, CMS, 1971; *Lawrence Ferlinghetti,* Everett-Edwards, 1972.

Plays

The Alligation (produced San Francisco, 1962; New York, 1970). Included in *Unfair Arguments with Existence,* 1963.

Unfair Arguments with Existence: Seven Plays for a New Theatre (includes *The Soldiers of No Country, Three Thousand Red Ants, The Alligation, The Victims of Amnesia, Motherlode, The Customs Collector in Baggy Pants, The Nose of Sisyphus*). New York, New Directions, 1963.

The Customs Collector in Baggy Pants (produced New York, 1964). Included in *Unfair Arguments with Existence,* 1963.

The Soldiers of No Country (produced London, 1969). Included in *Unfair Arguments with Existence,* 1963.

3 by Ferlinghetti: Three Thousand Red Ants, The Alligation, The Victims of Amnesia (produced New York, 1970). Included in *Unfair Arguments with Existence,* 1963.

Routines (includes 13 short pieces). New York, New Directions, 1964.

Novel

Her. New York, New Directions, 1960; London, MacGibbon and Kee, 1967.

Other

Dear Ferlinghetti/Dear Jack: The Spicer-Ferlinghetti Correspondence. San Francisco, White Rabbit Press, 1962(?).

The Mexican Night: Travel Journal. New York, New Directions, 1970.

A Political Pamphlet. San Francisco, Anarchist Resistance Press, 1975.

Literary San Francisco: A Pictorial History from Its Beginnings to the Present Day, with Nancy J. Peters. San Francisco, City Lights, 1980.

Leaves of Life: Fifty Drawings from the Model. San Francisco, City Lights, 1984.

Editor, *Beatitude Anthology.* San Francisco, City Lights, 1960.

Editor, with Michael McClure and David Meltzer, *Journal for the Protection of All Beings 1* and *3.* San Francisco, City Lights, 2 vols., 1961-69.

Editor, *City Lights Journal.* San Francisco, City Lights, 4 vols., 1963-78.

Editor, *Panic Grass,* by Charles Upton. San Francisco, City Lights, 1969.

Editor, *The First Third,* by Neal Cassady. San Francisco, City Lights, 1971.

Editor, *City Lights Anthology.* San Francisco, City Lights, 1974.

Translator, *Selections from Paroles by Jacques Prévert.* San Francisco, City Lights, 1958; London, Penguin, 1963.

Translator, with Anthony Kahn, *Flowers and Bullets, and Freedom to Kill,* by Yevtushenko. San Francisco, City Lights, 1970.

Translator, with Richard Lettau, *Love Poems,* by Karl Marx. San Francisco, City Lights, 1977.

*

Bibliography: *Lawrence Ferlinghetti: A Comprehensive Bibliography to 1980* by Bill Morgan, New York, Garland, 1982.

Manuscript Collection: Bancroft Library, University of California, Berkeley.

Critical Studies: *Ferlinghetti: A Biography* by Neeli Cherkovsky, New York, Doubleday, 1979; *Lawrence Ferlinghetti: Poet-at-Large* by Larry Smith, Carbondale, Southern Illinois University Press, 1983.

*   *   *

Lawrence Ferlinghetti is a writer whose work remains as exciting today as it was in the 1950's when he was one of the founders and the chief impresario of the Beat group of poets. While most of the other Beats have died or have gradually drifted away from the literary world, Ferlinghetti remains a powerful force on the poetic scene, not only as an author, but also as an editor who has encouraged and published numerous young authors, and as the proprietor of the City Lights Bookstore.

Like Walt Whitman, Ferlinghetti believes that the poet should be an agitator whose message should reach the great masses of people too often ignored by more traditional poets; like Whitman, Ferlinghetti has had great success at this. Ferlinghetti's *A Coney Island of the Mind* remains one of the all-time bestsellers for a volume of poetry. Part of its success was no doubt due to its experimental technique (which owed much to E.E. Cummings) and to its use of some shocking (for the time of publication) words. Published during a time of great conventionality, Ferlinghetti's book provided a rousingly vigorous alternative view of life. The book celebrates love, sex, and freedom and attacks the crass materialism which, as these lines "Christ Climbed Down" indicate, controls society:

> Christ climbed down
> from His bare Tree
> this year
> and ran away to where
> no intrepid Bible salesmen
> covered the territory
> in two-tone Cadillacs

This godless society is the frequent target of Ferlinghetti's satiric attacks. "Beat is the soul of beatific," Jack Kerouac said, and all the Beats had a strong concern for the spiritual side of man. Ferlinghetti's poetry stems from his intense moral concern about where "the Bosch-like world" is heading.

"When the guns are roaring the Muses have no right to be silent," writes Ferlinghetti, and during the violence-filled 1960's he continued to make his voice heard. His poetry took on a surrealistic edge, in part because of the surreal rush of events in the decade. "Some days I'm afflicted/with Observation Fever/omnivorous perception of phenomena" begins "Buckford's Buddha," and in the world of "death TV" sensory overload ensues. About this time some of Ferlinghetti's poems were written under the influence of LSD, a drug the poet took not because of hedonism but instead, in the words of one volume's title, to find "the secret meaning of things." The poems of this period are more fragmented than his earlier work, but their message, as expressed in "Assassination Raga," a powerful elegy for the Kennedys, remains the same: "There is no god but Life...love love and hate hate."

In the 1970's Ferlinghetti's technical experiments involved working with the prose poem and creating Indian chants and mantras in English. He continued to keep an "open eye, open heart" on his society and to condemn "a world awash with fascism and fear." For Ferlinghetti there was no middle-aged

mellowing or watering-down of his ideals. A few lines from "Overheard Conversation" indicate how little his concept of poetry changed in two decades: "And still the whole idea of poetry being/to take control of life/out of the hands of/the Terrible People." On rare occasions the Terrible People Ferlinghetti attacks are hackneyed subjects, as in the long poem "Vegas Tilt" which exposes the materialism of Las Vegas, hardly a novel or challenging concept; but more frequently his adversaries are well chosen. With Whitman, Vachel Lindsay, and Carl Sandburg, Ferlinghetti stands in the great line of American poets who have been gadflies, yea-sayers to humanity, naysayers to the forces of repression. One of his finest and most recent poems, "Populist Manifesto," expresses Ferlinghetti's ideas about and hopes for poetry. It is a clarion call: "Poets, come out of your closets.../You have been holed-up too long/in your closed world" It continues by stating that poetry has become too stifling. Ironically echoing his friend Allen Ginsberg, Ferlinghetti writes, "We have seen the best minds of our generation/destroyed by boredom at poetry readings," and after a Whitman-like catalogue of all the various schools of poetry flourishing today, Ferlinghetti exhorts other writers, crying

> Poets, descend
> to the street of the world once more
> And open your minds and eyes
> with the old visual delight
> Clear your throat and speak up,
> Poetry is dead, long live poetry
> with terrible eyes and buffalo strength.

Lawrence Ferlinghetti practices what he preaches. One only wishes that more poets would write with his immediacy, power, and passion.

—Dennis Lynch

FIELD, Edward. American. Born in Brooklyn, New York, 7 June 1924. Attended New York University. Served in the United States Army Air Force, 1942-45. Lecturer, YM-YWHA Poetry Center, New York. Recipient: Lamont Poetry Selection Award, 1962; Guggenheim Fellowship, 1963; Shelley Memorial Award, 1975; American Academy in Rome Fellowship, 1981. Address: 463 West Street, New York, New York 10014, U.S.A.

PUBLICATIONS

Verse

Stand Up, Friend, With Me. New York, Grove Press, 1963.
Variety Photoplays. New York, Grove Press, 1967.
Sweet Gwendolyn and the Countess. Gulfport, Florida, Konglomerati Press, 1977.
A Full Heart. New York, Sheep Meadow Press, 1977.
Stars in My Eyes. New York, Sheep Meadow Press, 1977.

Novel

Village (as Bruce Elliot, with Neil Derrick). New York, Avon, 1982.

Other

Editor and Translator, *Eskimo Songs and Stories, Collected by Knud Rasmussen on the Fifth Thule Expedition.* New York, Delacorte Press, 1973.
Editor, *A Geography of Poets: An Anthology of New Poetry.* New York, Bantam, 1979.

* ·

Critical Studies: review by Robert Mazzocco, in *New York Review of Books*, 1967; *Alone with America* by Richard Howard, New York, Atheneum, 1969, London, Thames and Hudson, 1970, revised edition, Atheneum, 1980.

*   *   *

Edward Field writes poems for which the reader is honestly grateful. They are heart-felt. Straightforward and unadorned, they have little or no figurative language, but are conversational and colloquial. The speaker may be humble, sad, funny (ribald, witty, wry), and self-deprecating. And there is unabashed sentimentality. At the same time Field manages to control and distance intensely personal material. He understates, he responds, he perceives. And, finally, he joins, brings together. As he expresses those feelings of shame and frustration which characterized his childhood years, he opens the door to his private hell—"the terror and guilt/and self-loathing" he felt in his father's house.

Field's hopes for himself and the world are centered in the triumph of love, the gifts of affection and sexuality. The freedom to feel, to be natural and uninhibited—the freedom to be—these are his concerns. And so he attempts to bring people together, to overcome distances, to bring down barriers. By inviting the reader to share intimacies, by embracing the reader, Field resembles a Jewish Walt Whitman. In his emphasis on companionship and sexuality, on love above all, he is most Whitmanesque.

Gentle, yearning, believing that "all men and women are my brothers and sisters now" ("Visiting Home"), Field writes confessional poetry. Because it is personal, it cannot help but be. It is a poetry of skepticism, of cautious hope, of the sorrow of estrangement and alienation, of the search for one's say in the world. One must be one's own guru: "you have to trust to your heart/-Which often needs more than one lifetime to make a man" ("Union City").

The courage of the heart is what Field's poetry is most about. He is not afraid to be himself, to reveal his weaknesses, his fears, his humiliations ("Unwanted"):

His aliases tell his history: Dumbbell, Good-for-nothing
Jewboy, Fieldinsky, Skinny, Fierce Face, Greaseball, Sissy.

Warning: This man is not dangerous, answers to any name
Responds to love, don't call him or he will come.

Through his unassuming honesty, he touches the reader with prose-poetry. Field's humor is effective and genuinely funny. Laughter—as device and response—enables him to avoid falling into the slough of selfpity. Laughter is a great leveler; not surprisingly, Field's bawdiness serves a democratic function. It reminds us that we all eat, excrete, copulate: "As the smile is to the face/the hard-on is to the body" ("Chopped Meat").

In *Variety Photoplays*, he uses humor to offset maudlin sentiment as he discovers in old movies the familiar and universal themes—frustrated love, alienation, loneliness, prejudice, force of circumstance. His three Frankenstein poems are especially admirable. "He is pursued by the ignorant villagers,/Who think he is evil and dangerous because he is ugly and makes ugly noises." Finally the majority—the real beast—succeeds in creating a monster worse than the Baron: "He was out to pay them back/to throw the lie of brotherly love/in their white Christian teeth." The poem arrives at a moment of triumph:

So he set out on his new career
his previous one being the victim,
the good man who suffers.

Now no longer the hunted by the hunter
he was in charge of his destiny.

Cinema creates and shapes the fairy-tales of American culture. The gothic motifs, the soap opera, the happily-ever-after quality which deceives the audience and often the actors—all are treated by Field with wry clarity and sad-eyed humor. If there is nostalgia, a sharp realization of the brevity of youth and fame ("Whatever Happened to May Caspar"), there is also the poet's unique parable, *Sweet Gwendolyn and the Countess*. This poem depicts the victimization of innocence and beauty by power and aggression; Field implies that as long as "innocence" refuses to see and participate in the real world, refuses to be active rather than passive, it will not only continue to be victimized but actually be contributing to its own subjugation and demise.

A Full Heart has clear moments of joy, of exuberance. The book is more genuinely happy for there are the fulfillment of love and the quickening of life that accompanies it. No longer the outsider, Field has been invited to the party. And when love is lost, he can console himself for his having had it. Field begins this collection by celebrating "New York"—"I live in a beautiful place, a city/...this is a people paradise." Nothing is too little or ugly to praise: "Thank God for dogs, cats, sparrows, and roaches."

A Full Heart shows how Field goes forward and how sometimes this requires a going backward first. In "Pasternak: In Memoriam" Field stresses personal fulfillment as opposed to heroism:

You were right:
This real person in my arms
is who I want
not the moment of passion on the barricades
not the dream of the ideal
love in a perfect world.

Survive in this world
love as you can
and go on with your work.

This is what the poet has come to learn. And in such poems as "Both My Grandmothers" and "Visiting Home" he deals with the need for roots, for a sense of origin. His Jewishness—tradition and culture more than a particularized system of belief—helps him to realize his identity in a shifting and arbitrary world. If, in the second of these poems, he acknowledges the severe difficulties visited upon him by his father, he can also say "thank God I am my mother's son too/for what she gave me/is what I survived by." Suffering and love—the two are wedded in this world and in Field's. He is poet whose heart is "full" and, in sharing, he fills the reader's heart as well.

—Carl Lindner

FIGUEROA, John (Joseph Maria). Jamaican. Born in Kingston, 4 August 1920. Educated at St. George's College, Kingston, 1931-37; College of the Holy Cross, Worcester, Massachusetts, 1938-42, A.B. (cum laude) in English and philosophy 1942; University of London Institute of Education (British Council Fellow, 1946-47), 1946-50, teacher's diploma 1947, M.A. in education 1950; University of Indiana, Bloomington (PILEI Fellow, 1964), 1964. Married Dorothy Grace Murray Alexander; four sons and three daughters. Clerk, Water Commission, Kingston, 1937-38; teacher in secondary schools in Jamaica, 1942-46, and London, 1946-48; Lecturer in English and Philosophy, University of London Institute of Education, 1948-53; Professor of Education, 1957-73, and Dean of the Faculty of Education for 4 years, University College of the West Indies, Kingston; Professor of English and Consultant to the President of the University, University of Puerto Rico, Rio Piedras and Cayey, 1971-73; Professor of Humanities and Consultant in Community Education, El Centro Caribeno de Estudios Postgraduados, Puerto Rico, 1973-76; Professor of Education and Acting Dean, University of Jos, Nigeria, 1976-79; Visiting Professor and Consultant in Multicultural Education, Bradford College, Yorkshire, 1979-80; member of the Third World Studies course team, Open University, Milton Keynes, Buckinghamshire, 1980-83. Since 1984, Adviser on multi-cultural studies and West Indian language and literature, Manchester Education Authority. Since 1946, broadcaster and sports reporter for the BBC, London. Recipient: Carnegie Fellowship, 1960; Guggenheim Fellowship, 1964; Lilly Foundation grant, 1973; Institute of Jamaica Medal, 1980. L.H.D.: College of the Holy Cross, 1960. Address: 77 Station Road, Woburn Sands, Buckinghamshire MK17 8SH, England.

PUBLICATIONS

Verse

Blue Mountain Peak. Kingston, Gleaner, 1944.
Love Leaps Here. Liverpool, Tinling, 1962.
Ignoring Hurts. Washington, D.C., Three Continents Press, 1976.

Other

Staffing and Examinations in Secondary Schools in the British Caribbean. London, Evans, 1963.
Society, .Schools and Progress in the West Indies. Oxford, Pergamon Press, 1971.

Editor, *Caribbean Voices: An Anthology of West Indian Poetry*. London, Evans, 2 vols., 1966-70, revised edition of vol. 1, 1982; Washington, D.C., Luce, 1 vol., 1973.
Editor, with others, *Caribbean Writers*. Washington, D.C., Three Continents Press, 1979.
Editor, *An Anthology of African and Caribbean Writing in English*. London, Heinemann, 1982.
Editor, *Carribbean Sampler*. Milton Keynes, Buckinghamshire, Open University Press, 1983.

*

Critical Studies: by Derek Walcott, in *Trinidad Guardian*, 1962; Cecil Gray, in *Bim 55* (Bridgetown, Barbados), July-December 1972; in *Caribbean Writers* edited by Figueroa and others, 1979; Alan MacLeod, in *Bim* (Bridgetown, Barbados), June 1983.

John Figueroa comments:

I hope that [my verse] is influenced by Horace and Virgil and Sappho as well as by our Jamaican speech rhythms and Trinidadian calypsoes. But I'm hardly the one to say. Once in the early days a well-known critic excused himself from commenting (in a broadcast) on the verse, on the grounds that it was "very religious." Perhaps he was being tactful. On the other hand, I have been called "basically a love poet."

Alan MacLeod has no doubt been too kind in saying, "John Figueroa has acted as a bellwether of Jamaican poetry for the past half century...he has moved to increasingly personal statements on art, love, religion, pointing out the antitheses they involve, the pain they create, and the ends that they serve...." But in the midst of "la lucha" it is good to hear such things.

* * *

John Figueroa is well-known throughout the Caribbean as poet, editor, critic and educationalist. However, his poetry is not as widely known outside the West Indies as it ought to be. Figueroa is certainly an original poet at his best and quite unlike any other West Indian poet. He is acutely aware of the physical world and responds to contrasts of colour, and even contrasts in modes of living. He constantly seems to be relating one thing to another, the known to the unfamiliar, darkness to light, and rough to smooth.

An eminent scholar, Figueroa has obviously read widely. His influences might be said to be partly environmental (i.e., Jamaican speech rhythms, Trinidadian calypsoes, etc.) and partly classical (Virgil, Sappho, and particularly Horace, a good deal of whose verse he has translated). Indeed, in his poetry there seems to be some kind of conflict between the two, so that the struggle to achieve a balance between the urge to express his own individual experience and the need for technical control, is not easily resolved. At times, the academic pressures seem to prevent him from speaking in his own voice.

John Figueroa has a wide range of styles and subjects, but his work falls into five broad categories: 1) reflective poems, 2) poems with a religious theme or insight, 3) poems arising out of experiences in other countries, 4) personal and anecdotal poems, and 5) translations. His greatest strength, however, lies in his reflective and philosophical poetry. In such poems as "On Hearing Dvorak's 'New World' Symphony," "Other Spheres," "Green Is the Colour of Hope," "The Three Epiphanies," "From the Caribbean with Love," and "Columbus Lost," one finds significant utterance combined with unusual craftsmanship.

—Howard Sergeant

FINCH, Robert (Duer Claydon). Canadian. Born in Freeport, Long Island, New York, United States, 14 May 1900. Educated at the University of Toronto (Jardine Memorial Prize, 1924), B.A. 1925; the Sorbonne, Paris, 1928; studied music with Alberto Guerrero and Wanda Landowska. Lecturer, 1928-30, Assistant Professor, 1931-42, Associate Professor, 1942-51, and Professor of French, 1952-68, now Emeritus, University College, University of Toronto. Painter: 13 individual shows, in Toronto, Paris, New York, and elsewhere. Recipient: Governor-General's Award, 1947, 1962; Lorne Pierce Medal, 1968. LL.D.: University of Toronto, 1973; York University, Toronto, 1976; University of Winnipeg, 1984. Agent: Sybil Hutchinson, 409

Ramsden Place, 50 Hillsboro Avenue, Toronto, Ontario M5R 1S8. Address: Massey College, 4 Devonshire Place, Toronto, Ontario M5S 2E1, Canada.

PUBLICATIONS

Verse

Poems. Toronto, Oxford University Press, 1946.
The Strength of the Hills. Toronto, McClelland and Stewart, 1948.
Acis in Oxford and Other Poems. Oxford, privately printed, 1959; Toronto, University of Toronto Press, 1961.
Dover Beach Revisited and Other Poems. Toronto, Macmillan, 1961.
Silverthorn Bush and Other Poems. Toronto, Macmillan, 1966.
Variations and Theme. Erin, Ontario, Porcupine's Quill, 1980.
Has and Is. Erin, Ontario, Porcupine's Quill, 1981.
Twelve for Christmas. Erin, Ontario, Porcupine's Quill, 1982.
The Grand Duke of Moscow's Favourite Solo. Erin, Ontario, Porcupine's Quill, 1983.
Double Tuning. Erin, Ontario, Porcupine's Quill, 1984.

Play

A Century Has Roots (produced Toronto, 1953). Toronto, University of Toronto Press, 1953.

Other

The Sixth Sense: Individualism in French Poetry 1686-1760. Toronto, University of Toronto Press, 1966.

Editor, with C.R. Parsons, *René*, by Chateaubriand. Toronto, University of Toronto Press, 1957.
Editor, with Eugène Joliat, *French Individualist Poetry 1686-1760: An Anthology.* Toronto, University of Toronto Press, 1971.
Editor, with Eugène Joliat, *Sir Politick Would-Be*, by Saint-Evremond. Geneva, Droz, 1978.
Editor, with Eugène Joliat, *Les Opéra*, by Saint-Evremond. Geneva, Droz, 1979.

*   *   *

Literary verse is infrequently attempted presently in Canada, that area of verse-making where the form commands the content, where the thought is sophisticate, the metaphor more cogent than daring. It is an area out of fashion, an area dangerous and difficult to achieve success in—dangerous since to fail is to leave the literary rather than the vital effect; difficult, for it demands that the formality become necessary to the communication.

Robert Finch dares the hazards of this kind of poetry and proves them surmountable. Amid the turbulence of the world, he dares to write sonnets; his adherence to grace of thought demands his formality. It is a poetry of pensive mood and sensitive craftsmanship. To read his books is to have walked, aware of the melancholy world outside, in a garden of Le Nostre.

Finch first found assertion long ago in that watershed of an anthology, *New Provinces.* His presentation then was as an Imagist when Imagism and the French Symbolists might not have existed as far as Canadian awareness was concerned: "Lacks a blue buck bearing vermilion horns/led by a groom in

tightest daffodil?" Finch soon established himself with a poetry of precision and form and accurate detailed sensuousness. The definition is not surprising. Finch is a skilled musician, painter—and professor of French in Toronto. His eye is that of the painter:

> The dark green truck on the cement platform
> is explicit as a paradigm
> Its wheels are four black cast-iron starfish...
> The truck holds eleven cakes of ice,
> each cake a different size and shape.
> Some look as though a weight had hit them.
> One, solid glass, has a core of sugar.
> They lean, a transitory Icehenge.

This imagist stasis is deceived into movement. The movement proceeds by paradox; the logic, by metaphor. He is as fond of variations as a musician. His book *Dover Beach Revisited and Other Poems* contains eleven variations on the theme of Matthew Arnold's poem. It witnesses the quality of his mind, a quiet perception of tides and time in a verse of intellectual lyricism. The passage of the seasons is everywhere evident. Reliance on the variations in weather to express mood and emotion is to admit the usual conventional dangers. Finch startles in his best poems of this kind by concurrent, spare intellectualism, a sophistication of taste and perception. The happy wind, the pensive trees

> have all gone and we are far away
> Where every season is a winter's day
> That comes and goes and always is the same
>
> Except that we, more than its atmosphere,
> Still know and feel and see and breathe and hear
> That wind, that grass, those trees, that eager stream.

Finch's poetry is a poetry of personality, seasoned, spare yet sensuous, astringent yet warm with humility and compassion. Its effect is that of a resolution in music, inevitable and "Building with Euclidean grace."

—Ralph Gustafson

FINKEL, Donald. American. Born in New York City, 21 October 1929. Educated at Columbia University, New York, B.S. in philosophy 1952 (Phi Beta Kappa), M.A. in literature 1953. Married Constance Urdang, *q.v.*, in 1956; two daughters and one son. Instructor, University of Iowa, Iowa City, 1957-58, and Bard College, Annandale-on-Hudson, New York, 1958-60. Since 1960, member of the Department of English, and since 1965, Poet-in-Residence, Washington University, St. Louis. Visiting Lecturer, Bennington College, Vermont, 1966-67, and Princeton University, New Jersey, Spring 1985. Visited Antarctica, 1969-70, at invitation of National Science Foundation. Recipient: Helen Bullis Prize (*Poetry Northwest*), 1964; Guggenheim Fellowship, 1967; National Endowment for the Arts grant, 1969, 1973; Ingram Merrill Foundation grant, 1972; Theodore Roethke Memorial Prize, 1974; American Academy Morton Dauwen Zabel Award, 1980. Address: 6943 Columbia Place, St. Louis, Missouri 63130, U.S.A.

PUBLICATIONS

Verse

The Clothing's New Emperor and Other Poems.   New York,
   Scribner, 1959.
Simeon: Poems.   New York, Atheneum, 1964.
A Joyful Noise.   New York, Atheneum, 1966.
Answer Back.   New York, Atheneum, 1968.
The Garbage Wars.   New York, Atheneum, 1970.
Adequate Earth.   New York, Atheneum, 1972.
A Mote in Heaven's Eye.   New York, Atheneum, 1975.
Going Under, and Endurance: An Arctic Idyll: Two Poems.
   New York, Atheneum, 1978.
What Manner of Beast.   New York, Atheneum, 1981.
The Detachable Man.   New York, Atheneum, 1984.

Play

The Jar (produced Boston, 1961).

*

Manuscript Collection: Washington University Library, St.
Louis.

Critical Study: *Alone with America*, by Richard Howard, New
York, Atheneum, 1969, London, Thames and Hudson, 1970,
revised edition, Atheneum, 1980.

*   *   *

   "Plain speech is out of place in the pulpit,/poetry is out of
place in the square," writes Donald Finkel, who in his works has
attempted to combine prose and poetry, and the religious and
the secular worlds. As an early poem like "Hands" indicates,
Finkel is a strong believer in the power of poetry, even though he
is not totally happy with its present condition:

   The poem makes truth a little more disturbing
   like a good bra, lifts it and holds it out
   in both hands. (In some of the flashier stores
   there's a model with the hands stitched on, in red or black.)

   Lately the world you wed, for want of such hands,
   sags in the bed beside you like a tired wife.
   For want of such hands, the face of the moon is bored,
   the tree does not stretch and yearn, nor the groin tighten.

   Devious or frank, in any case,
   the poem is calculated to arouse.
   Lean back and let its hands play freely on you:
   there comes a moment, lifted and aroused,
   when the two of you are equally beautiful.

The struggle to make poetry once again a force capable of
arousing and disturbing us has led Finkel in his later work to
increased experimentation. This began with the use of the collage technique in his long sequence "Three for Robert Rauschenberg" (*A Joyful Noise*), but this innovation seems pale next
to what Finkel attempts in his later books. In these amazing
volumes Finkel manages to develop a voice and a technique
uniquely his own.
   Answer Back is an astonishing book arranged around the

metaphor of cave exploration. It has six sections, each of which
is named after a particular part of Mammoth Cave. Speleology,
though, is only one of Finkel's concerns here: his other topics
include Vietnam, the relation of the sexes, the nature of religion,
the function of poetry, the origins of the universe, and much
more. His voice modulates from biblical tones to satiric ones,
and his verse ranges from lyrics to doggerel. Interspersed
between the bits of poetry are passages of prose, about two per
page, from such varied sources as Lenny Bruce, Admiral Byrd,
Camus, Heraclitus, Hoyle, the *I Ching*, Jesus, Kafka, the *Kama
Sutra*, the Missouri State Penitentiary, *Playboy*, Pound, and
Lord Raglan. Needless to say, the whole effect is rather staggering. While one is impressed with Finkel's erudition and is often
amused by the clever juxtaposition he creates, one also feels that
the poet has been too unrestrained and has produced a poem too
fragmented.
   Like *Answer Back* the long poem "Water Music" in *The
Garbage Wars* has a controlling metaphor (experimentation on
dolphins) and it, too, uses many prose borrowings. Yet here
Finkel has refined his technique and uses it more subtly. His next
book, *Adequate Earth*, is his masterpiece. Once again Finkel is
daring in his choice of subject, for this book is a series of seven
long poems about Antarctica. Finkel spent a month on that
continent in 1969 and his experiences form the basis of some of
the sections. Other parts have as a narrative frame the explorations of Amundsen, Byrd, and others. As usual Finkel interpolates prose passages from various authors, but here it is more
tightly focused than previously. And, as usual, Finkel tries to
bring everything into his poetry, from science to theology to
politics to psychology. Here, though, he has finally chosen a
subject which can stand all this weight and at the same time offer
great narrative potentiality. As a result, *Adequate Earth* is one of
the few fine contemporary epic poems. It has a vast sweep: part
of it is myth-making, as Finkel "takes the liberty of quoting at
length throughout from the gospels of the Emperor Penguins," a
remarkably allegorical document; part of it is devastating satire,
such as the section "Pole Business," which is a bitter attack on
the commercialism encroaching on our planet's last wilderness;
part of it is tragedy in its accounts of ill-fated attempts to explore
the polar regions; and all of it is a tribute to man's ability to
endure in even the harshest of worlds:

   We'll get used to that bite in the air
   soon enough; we'll get used to
   everything. It's what we do:
   the adaptable animal, whelped in the time
   of ice, we adapt to anything.

Full justice cannot be done to Finkel's work by brief quotations
from it; like a collage its power comes not from any one part
alone but from the interaction of all its parts. Finkel's collages
are daring attempts to bring unity to the world's chaos through
art. At his worst he can be obscure and pedantic; at his best he
can produce works of startling resonance.
   Interestingly, Finkel returns to the metaphors of exploring
caves and Antarctica in his 1978 book(s) *Going Under* and
Endurance, a volume which is literally two books in one. Finkel,
who has constantly confounded expectations about the proper
subjects for poetry, here confounds expectations about the very
way a book is printed and presented. The result is a bibliographer's nightmare but a reader's delight. Fortunately, these
poems give the reader none of the disappointment one often feels
in reading sequels. Indeed, each work is in some way superior to
its predecessor because each has a much sharper narrative focus;
Going Under centers on the strange lives of two Mammoth Cave
explorers, *Endurance* on one doomed polar expedition. It is no

surprise that Don Finkel is so intrigued by the stories of adventurers; few writers are as ambitious and daring as he.

—Dennis Lynch

FINLAY, Ian Hamilton. Scottish. Born in Nassau, Bahamas, 28 October 1925. Left school at 13. Married to Susan Finlay; two children. Concrete Poetry exhibited at Axiom Gallery, London, 1968, Scottish National Gallery of Modern Art, Edinburgh, 1972, National Maritime Museum, Greenwich, 1973, Southampton Art Gallery, 1976, Graeme Murray Gallery, Edinburgh, 1976, Kettle's Yard, Cambridge, 1977, Serpentine Gallery, London, 1977; Sundials: University of Kent, Canterbury, in Biggar, Lanarkshire, Royal Botanic Garden, Edinburgh; Poems designed for Max Planck Institute, Stuttgart. Editor, *Poor. Old. Tired. Horse*, Dunsyre, Lanarkshire, 1962-67; Publisher, with Sue Finlay, Wild Hawthorn Press, Edinburgh, 1961-66, Easter Ross, 1966, and since 1969, Dunsyre, Lanarkshire. Recipient: Scottish Arts Council bursary, 1966, 1967, 1968; Atlantic-Richfield Award (USA), 1968. Address: Stonypath, Dunsyre, Lanarkshire, Scotland.

PUBLICATIONS

Verse

Books and booklets (all published by Wild Hawthorn Press unless otherwise noted): *The Dancers Inherit the Party*, Worcester, Migrant Press, 1960; *Glasgow Beasts, an a Burd*, 1961; *Concertina*, 1962; *Rapel*, 1963; *Canal Stripe Series 3 and 4*, 1964; *Telegrams from My Windmill*, 1964; *Ocean Stripe Series 2 to 5*, 1965-67; *Cythera*, 1965; *Autumn Poem*, 1966; *6 Small Pears for Eugen Gomringer*, 1966; *6 Small Songs in 3's*, 1966; *Tea-Leaves and Fishes*, 1966; *4 Sails*, 1966; *Headlines Eavelines*, Corsham, Wiltshire, Openings Press, 1967; *Stonechats*, 1967; *Canal Game*, London, Fulcrum Press, 1967; *The Collected Coaltown of Callange Tri-kai*, Newport, Monmouthshire, Screwpacket Press, 1968; *Air Letters*, Nottingham, Tarasque Press, 1968; *The Blue and The Brown Poems*, New York, Atlantic Richfield-Jargon Press, 1968; *After the Russian*, Corsham, Wiltshire, Openings Press, 1969; *3/3's*, 1969; *A Boatyard*, 1969; *Lanes*, 1969; *Wave*, 1969; *Rhymes for Lemons*, 1970; *"Fishing News" News*, 1970; *30 Signatures to Silver Catches*, Nottingham, Tarasque Press, 1971; *Poems to Hear and see*, New York, Macmillan, 1971; *A Sailor's Calendar*, New York, Something Else Press, 1971; *The Olsen Excerpts*, Göttingen, Verlag Udo Breger, 1971; *A Memory of Summer*, 1971; *From "An Inland Garden,"* 1971; *Evening/Sail 2*, 1971; *The Weed Boat Masters Ticket, Preliminary Text (Part Two)*, 1971; *Sail/Sundial*, 1972; *Jibs*, 1972; *Honey by the Water*, Los Angeles, Black Sparrow Press, 1973; *Butterflies*, 1973; *A Family*, 1973; *Straiks*, 1973; *Homage to Robert Lax*, 1974; *A Pretty Kettle of Fish*, 1974; *Silhouettes*, 1974; *Exercise X*, 1974; *So You Want to Be a Panzer Leader*, 1975; *Airs Waters Graces*, 1975; *The Wild Hawthorn Wonder Book of Boats*, 1975; *A Mast of Hankies*, 1975; *The Axis*, 1975; *Trombone Carrier*, 1975; *Homage to Watteau*, 1975; *Three Sundials*, Exeter, Rougemont Press, 1975; *Imitations, Variations, Reflections, Copies*, 1976; *The Wild Hawthorn Art Test*, 1977; *Heroic Emblems*, Calais, Vermont, Z Press, 1977; *The Boy's Alphabet Book*, Toronto, Coach House

Press, 1977; *The Wartime Garden*, 1977; *Trailblazers*, 1978; *Homage to Poussin*, 1978; *Peterhead Fragments*, 1979; *"SS"*, 1979; *Dzaezl*, 1979; *Woods and Seas*, 1979; *Two Billows*, 1979; *Romances, Emblems, Enigmas*, 1981; *3 Developments*, 1982.

Some 200 cards, folding cards, and poem/prints published by Wild Hawthorn Press.

Short Stories

The Sea-Bed and Other Stories. Edinburgh, Alna Press, 1958.

*

Manuscript Collection: Lilly Library, University of Indiana, Bloomington.

Critical Studies: "Ian Hamilton Finlay Issue" of *Extra Verse 15* (London), Spring 1965; Bryan Robertson, in *Spectator* (London), 6 September 1968; *Ian Hamilton Finlay* by Francis Edeline, Paris, Atelier de l'Agneau, 1978; exhibition catalogues by Stephen Bann, Scottish National Gallery of Modern Art, Edinburgh, 1972, Stephen Scobie, Southampton Art Gallery, 1976, Stephen Bann and others, Kettle's Yard, Cambridge, 1977, and Stephen Bann, Serpentine Gallery, London, 1977.

Ian Hamilton Finlay comments:

(1970) As a "concrete" poet I am interested in poetry as "the best words, in the best possible order"...*in the best materials*, i.e., such as glass or stone for interiors or gardens. I have been described as "the leading concrete poet now writing in English." But "concrete" has no meaning nowadays. What is concrete?

My verse is not a *single* thing since it has changed over the years. On the other hand, I have usually tried for the same ends—lucidity, clarity, a resolved complexity. I have used many forms, from traditional rhymed verse to poems designed as entire gardens (such as the poem I prepared for the American architect John Johansen). I consider that the seasons, nature, inland waterways, and oceans are proper themes for poetry. I do not expect poems to solve my problems. I do not believe in "the new man." Possibly A. Alvarez is the stupidest writer I have ever come across. I admire the poems of George Herbert. In the context of this time, it is not the job of poetry to "expand consciousness" but to offer a modest example of a decent sort of order.

(1980) The subject of my work is culture, without any undemocratic distinction between past and present. Besides, though one "knows" the past is past one may *experience* it as present, as Nietzsche (for example) did when he was writing on the Greek Pre-Socratics. Recently I have taken to publishing the bibliographies of my seemingly "graphic" works, in part to "categorise" them as "poetry," in part to alert the viewer (reader?) to the subject beyond the object—to Plutarch in the case of the "E" (aircraft carrier) series, or to the European emblem tradition (see Praz, *Studies in Seventeenth Century Imagery*), in such reliefs as "Woodland Is Pleasing to the Muses" (see my *Heroic Emblems*). It is relevant to note that the old emblematists used bibliography less as a particular illumination than as a means of "splicing" the emblem to a concept of classical culture as a whole.—1977.

To my original list of "proper themes" for poetry I should now add *culture* (not excluding warships, aircraft carriers, and warplanes). Increasingly, as our culture abandons its own traditional perspectives, the idea of a poet's "statement" (of his intentions?) becomes a perplexing one. To whom is such a statement actually addressed? To the public—as was peremptorily demanded of me by the Scottish Arts Council—though even in 1800 Friedrich Schlegel was unable to believe in a "public" except as an "idea"? (Today the "public" would be 50,000 "ideas.") Or is one expected to "communicate" with our secularising Arts Council art-bureaucrats, public art gallery "keepers," and publishers, as if they had some essential (actual) concern with culture, history, and truth? "Only through the relationship to the infinite do content and utility arise"—Schlegel once again. Where truth has ceased to be an aspiration and has become a synonym for The Convenient (as "nice" for "pure," "depression" for "despair," and so on), statements become a matter of dramatic allegory: the life is not the work but it is the only possible commentary *on* the work; the commentary "neither uttered nor hidden" is revealed by biography—event as "Event."—1979.

*　　*　　*

Ian Hamilton Finlay's poetry has undergone a considerable evolution, but the movements in that evolution are not random or (in the wrong sense) "experimental." The main driving-force behind his work may be called classical, if classicism implies a deliberate search for order, form, and economy, yet his classicism is accompanied by obviously romantic and playful elements. He indicated something of this in sub-titling his collection *Rapel* "10 fauve and suprematist poems." The fauve element preserves his work from frigidity, as the suprematist element preserves it from clutter and indulgence.

His first book, *The Dancers Inherit the Party*, contained short poems of much charm and humour, in traditional rhyming verse, about love, people, fishing, Orkney. The brevity of many of these poems was taken a step farther in his next two productions, *Glasgow Beasts* and *Concertina*, both of which had illustrations closely tied to the text. As well as the enhanced visual presentation, there was again a strong infusion of humour in both books.

The visual element, and the movement towards verbal economy, both predisposed Finlay to react with enthusiasm to the international development known as concrete poetry, which he learned about in 1962. Most of his work from *Rapel* (1963) onwards has been received and discussed under the "concrete" label, unsatisfactory and amorphous as that term has now become. Essentially it should signify (to quote the Brazilian Poets' "Pilot-Plan for Concrete Poetry" of 1958) a poetry that "begins by being aware of graphic space as structural agent" and is "against a poetry of expression, subjective and hedonistic." To Finlay, it was a poetry that would link back to the purity and harmony of artists like Malevich and Mondrian, and in general to those Constructivist ideals of half a century ago which had been sterilized by a new wave of expressionism. Painter as well as poet, he found no difficulty in seeing and accepting this formal extension of a verbal art into a visual domain; that many people do find it difficult he has had to admit. But whether his work is to be called "poetry" or something else, it will win over most unprejudiced eyes by its beauty and complete integrity.

"Little Calendar" could be quoted as representing his concrete approach at its most transparent:

april	light	light	light	light
may	light	trees	light	trees
june	trees	light	trees	light
july	trees	trees	trees	trees
august	trees'	light	trees'	light
september	lights	trees	lights	trees

But from this basis, which is still that of the poem printed on the page, Finlay evolved a range of ancillary conceptions of the poem: standing poems (printed on specially folded cards), poster poems, "kinetic" poems which release a serial meaning through the act of turning over the pages of a book, and three-dimensional poem-objects and poem-environments involving the use of metal or stone or glass and produced in cooperation with craftsmen in these materials. These meticulously designed and striking objects (especially successful are *Autumn Poem* and *Ocean Stripe 5* among the "kinetic" books, and "Wave/Rock" and Seas/Ease" among the three-dimensional poems) have a characteristic distinction of using the simplest of means, and often a very Scottish and homely simplicity—rocks and water, boats and fishing-nets, canals and tugs, stars and potato-fields—to bring out patterns, harmonies, analogies, and meanings that transcend their strongly local and native roots.

Much of his effort has gone into making his own home environment at Stonypath a garden of emblems and symbols. Trees and water, plants and flowers, are brought into intimate relationship with inscribed slabs, benches, sundials, and other objects in such a way as to suggest new perspectives, and to restore old echoes, of the relation between man and nature. A slab inscribed with Albrecht Dürer's monogram is placed in a setting reminiscent of an actual Dürer water-colour; an aircraft-carrier carved out of stone and set on a plinth becomes a bird-bath, with real birds as imaginary aeroplanes; the slate conning-tower of a nuclear submarine stands black and sinister at the edge of a pond; the network of lines on a stone sundial suggests fishermen's nets on the sea. The recurrent use he makes in some of these works, and in other works of the 1970's, of formalized and emblematic military images, generally from the Second World War, raises questions of response, about which much remains to be written. But whatever questions his work gives rise to, it continues to exert its own distinctive fascination.

—Edwin Morgan

FINNIGAN, Joan. Canadian. Born in Ottawa, Ontario, 25 November 1925. Educated at Carleton University, Ottawa; Queen's University, Kingston, Ontario. B.A. Married Charles Grant MacKenzie (died, 1965); three children. Formerly, school teacher, and reporter for the Ottawa *Journal*. Since 1965, free-lance writer, for the National Film Board of Canada and the Canadian Broadcasting Corporation, Toronto. Recipient: Borestone Mountain Poetry Prize, 1959, 1961, 1963; Canada Council grant, 1965, 1967, 1968, 1969, 1973; Centennial prize, 1967; President's Medal, University of Western Ontario, 1968; Etrog award, for screenplay, 1969. Address: Moore Farm, Hambly Lake, Hartington, Ontario K0H 1W0, Canada.

PUBLICATIONS

Verse

Through the Glass, Darkly. Toronto, Ryerson Press, 1957.
A Dream of Lilies. Fredericton, New Brunswick, Fiddlehead, 1965.
Entrance to the Green-house. Toronto, Ryerson Press, 1968.
It Was Warm and Sunny When We Set Out. Toronto, Ryerson Press, 1970.

In the Brown Cottage on Loughborough Lake.   Toronto, CBC
Learning Systems, 1970.
Living Together.   Fredericton, New Brunswick, Fiddlehead,
1976.
A Reminder of Familiar Faces.   Toronto, NC Press, 1978.
This Series Has Been Discontinued.   Fredericton, New Bruns-
wick, Fiddlehead, 1981.

Plays

Up the Vallee (produced Ottawa, 1978).

Screenplay: *The Best Damn Fiddler from Calabogie to Kaladar*,
1969.

Other

Canada in Bed (as Michelle Bedard).   Toronto, Pagurian
Press, 1967.
Kingston: Celebrate This City.   Toronto, McClelland and Stew-
art, 1976.
I Come from the Valley.   Toronto, NC Press, 1976.
Canadian Colonial Cooking.   Toronto, NC Press, 1976.
Canada, Country of the Giants.   Burnstown, Ontario, General
Store, 1981.
Giants of Canada's Ottawa Valley.   Burnstone, Ontario, Gen-
eral Store, 1981.
Some of the Stories I Told You Were True.   Ottawa, Deneau,
1981.
Look! The Land Is Growing Giants: A Very Canadian Legend
(for children).   Montreal, Tundra, 1983.
Laughing All the Way Home.   Ottawa, Deneau, 1984.

*

Manuscript Collections: Queen's University, Kingston, Ontario;
Public Archives of Canada, Ottawa.

Joan Finnigan comments:
   Since I was seven I have been writing poetry. At forty I came
to creative film-scripts and so began to write long poems. My
poetry always veered towards the dramatic and my film-scripts
are strongly poetic. The reason a creative film-script, done with
integrity, is like a long poem is that both are condensations of
intensity, a boiling down to the quintessence, a search for ultimate essence. I had matured enough to move from the short
form—the poem—to the one requiring greater sustaining
power—the screenplay—when the National Film Board of Canada began commissioning me to work for them.

*   *   *

   That "poetry is not a turning loose of emotion but an escape
from emotion" has become axiomatic in the criticism and the
writing of modern poetry. Such a statement finds support in the
general scientific and philosophic evolution of the age, and it
informs the modern poetical canon's scepticism towards the
perception of Nature as a paradigm for benevolent humanism or
the articulation of traditional themes (love, birth, death, marriage) through the filter of sensibility removed from the conditioning factors of man-made environment. In Canada, this consciousness is central to the work of an E.J. Pratt and the poets of
The McGill Movement, and it is emblematized in the wilderness-
garden mythos of the Frye school of poets from D.G. Jones to
Margaret Atwood. The rejection of facile romanticism at the
core of Eliot's pronouncement was germane to the poetics
initiated in the Twenties in Canada as a reaction against the
nineteenth century Confederation Poets. At any rate, it is a
commonplace now that the eternal verities can be improved by
being expressed in diction and vision attuned to the age.
   With these considerations in mind, it is no small surprise to
encounter the poetry of Joan Finnigan celebrating a domestic
world revolving around family life, the family cottage, the family
friends, love and nature rendered in language free from sophistication. An openness toward self and others characterizes an
outlook whose subjective correlative is the operations of benevolent Nature. The world is Edenic and pristine in her first three
books, dominated by radiant colors and cheerful sounds controlled by the key symbol of the sun shining at the height of
summer. There exudes a feeling of oneness with the elements
culminating in transcendental intimations of immortality, no
doubt sincerely felt by the poetess. Eve-like, but unlike Eve since
her boundless innocence cannot precipitate any Fall of Man, she
celebrates a garden whose paradisiacal emoluments she has no
reason to suspect. To be sure, a few queries are raised ("Oh, who
in all of heathendom./Is half so sad as I?"), but they pose no
threat of disruption to this Arcadia where no vital concerns are
entertained.
   Miss Finnigan's two favorite themes—love and nature—recur
in her last books. The related feelings of nostalgia, flight of time,
urbanophobia conveying an undercurrent of sweet melancholy
are now accentuated with the intrusion of death. In *It Was
Warm and Sunny When We Set Out*, the theme is, at first,
embarrassingly stated—"And I think perpetually now of your
dead HEART (for no one could get directions to that place, not
even yourself)..."—in the not surprising ingenuous confessional
style—"Who, who could ever believe our private murders or the
possibility of this revenge?"—which the poetess delights in. It
finds a more felicitous expression, however, in the contrasting
use of symbols. The sun that hitherto glowed on a bountiful
world presently reflects the destruction of the Covenant: it is
blinding, bleeding, mocking, scorching. Though the diction
falters—"If people really love one another,/snow, why do they
die?"—one finds interesting, nonetheless, the substitution of the
symbolic winter grip for the vision of warmth generated by
summer. The intensity of personal suffering finally yields
through visceral apprehension a sober consciousness structured
by a lucid polarization of the universals in Miss Finnigan's 1970
book, *In the Brown Cottage on Loughborough Lake*. In a book
markedly contrasting with her early work, the weaving of alternating polarities (light and dark, summer and autumn, outer life
and inner life, life and death, happiness and sorrow) germinates
in the mature expression of pain endured, challenged and possibly conquered. Her beloved Nature is still there, as anthropo-
morphic as ever, the language is still mined with clichés, the
world as restricted as usual. But this elegy, which can all too
easily be assigned to the Wordsworthian canon, is quite moving
in its expression of emotions barely recovering from the trauma
of exposure to the existence of pain and cruelty. Even fraction-
ally the poetess has been able to master and contain pain and
bear witness to this control over emotion by finding a structure
of objective correlatives, making this her best work to date.
Maybe Eliot was not wrong after all.

—Max Dorsinville

FISHER, Allen. British. Born in Norbury, London, 1 November 1944. Attended Battersea Grammar School; Open University; Goldsmiths' College, University of London, 1983-84. Married Elaine Fisher in 1969 (died, 1981). Clerk, warehouseman, sales representative, manager, and buyer in lead and solder, plastics, and copper manufacturing, 1962-83. Co-publisher, New London Pride, 1975-81. Since 1972, Co-publisher, Aloes Books, and since 1974, Publisher, Spanner, both London. Recipient: Alice Hunt Bartlett Prize, 1974. Address: 64 Lanercost Road, London SW2 3DN, England.

PUBLICATIONS

Verse

Thomas Net's Tree-Birst. London, Edible Magazine, 1971.
Before Ideas, Ideas. London, Edible Magazine, 1971.
Spaces for Winter Solstice (Blueprint). Cullompton, Devon, Beau Geste Press, 1972.
Sicily. London, Aloes, 1973.
Place. London, Aloes, 1974; Carrboro, North Carolina, Truck, 1976.
Long Shout to Kernewek. London, New London Pride, 1975.
5 Plages 'shun. N.p., Prison Clothes Press, 1975.
Paxton's Beacon. Todmorden, Lancashire, Arc, 1976.
Gripping the Rail. Newcastle upon Tyne, Pig Press, 1976.
"Der Verolene" Operation. London, Mugshots, 1976.
Stane. London, Aloes, 1977.
Fire-Place, with *Hearth-Work,* by Pierre Joris. Hebden Bridge, Yorkshire, Hatch, 1977.
Self-Portraits, Pink 149. London, Good Elf, 1977.
Doing. Maidstone, Kent, Twisted Wrist, 1977.
Samuel Matthews. Privately printed, 1977.
Docking. Bishops Stortford, Hertfordshire, Great Works, 1978.
London Blight. London, Tapocketa, 1978.
Convergences, in Place, of the Play. London, Spanner, 1978.
Becoming. London, Aloes, 1978.
The Apocalyptic Sonnets. Newcastle upon Tyne, Pig Press, 1978.
Intermediate Spirit Receiver. London, Zune Heft, 1980.
Hooks (Taken Out of Place 32). Baltimore, pod, 1980.
Eros, Father, Pattern. Warehorne, Kent, Secret, 1980.
Imbrications. Cambridge, Lobby Press, 1981.
Unpolished Mirrors. London, Spanner, 1981.
The Art of Flight VI-IX. London, Writers Forum, 1982.
Poetry for Schools, Including Black Light, Shooting-Out, and Other Poems. London, Aloes, 1982.
Bending Windows. London, Spanner, 1982.
Defamiliarising—*. London, Spanner, 1983.
African Boog. London, Ta' wil, 1983.
Banda. London, Spanner-Open Field, 1983.

Other Texts

Bavuska. London, Big Venus, 1969.
My Bijou, with Dick Miller. London, IB Held, 1971.
All Horses Have Feathers, with Dick Miller. London, IB Held, 1971.
Shitwell Bernado, with Dick Miller. London, IB Held, 1971.
Fields. London, Mail Shots, 1972.
Milk in Bottles. London, Edible Magazine, 1972.
Ffacece. London, Aloes, 1972.
Circles Lines Wheelbarrows. Oldenburg, Germany, International Art Co-operative, 1973.

Creek in the Ceiling Beam. London, Aloes, 1973.
Five for Grahams'. London, Aloes, 1973.
Prosyncel. Penfield, New York, Strange Faeces, 1975.
The Leer. London, Branch Redd, 1976.
The Preparation, with David Miller. London, X Press, 1977.
Atherapy Studies Q. London, Writers Forum, 1978.
Sssspeech. London, Writers Forum, 1978.
Reich. London, Spanner, 1978.
Combs. London, Spanner, 1979.
Kessingland Studies. London, Spanner, 1979.
South Thames Studios. London, Spanner, 1980.
Blood Bone Brain. London, Spanner, 7 vols., 1981-82.
Careful Absence. New Malden, Surrey, Figlet, 1982.
Ideas on the Culture Dreamed Of. London, Spanner, 1983.

*

Allen Fisher comments:

Surveying a bibliography of over 80 items is clearly difficult, so as comment that may "be useful to the general reader" (a phrase I find highly suspect) I have chosen to simply suggest introductory approaches to the work/s.

I have been a poet since 1961 and have at various times since then been a performance artist, a mail artist, a printer/painter, a publisher and book maker. Introducing myself, therefore, as a poet, for me seriously limits any reader's engagement with my work. Having said that, however, it is quite obviously possible to simply pick up one or two books and read them as the work of a poet in ignorance of other activities the poet links them to.

So: as a starter, I suggest thinking of the works as grouped into four broad approaches (without forgetting that they overlap and impinge on each other). The four broad groups could be (i) the *Place* project; (ii) *The Art of Flight* and other constructivist works; (iii) works such as the *Blood Bone Brain* project which include performance documentation as well as poetry and graphic/printer/painter material; and (iv) books of poetry separate (in the main) from those groups mentioned. (i) The *Place* project can be approached by reading four main books, they are: *Place, Stane, Becoming,* and *Unpolished Mirrors.* The work starts in 1971 and is "completed" in 1981. These books will lead interested readers, where they want to, into other parts of the work. (ii) A selection from *The Art of Flight* was published as *Paxton's Beacon.* With this book I would suggest readers look also at *Defamiliarising—** and at *Convergences, in place, of the play.* (iii) The 9 microfiches adequately cover a variety of concerns for this group to which I would suggest readers add one or more of the specifically painter/printer books such as *Careful Absence* or *South Thames Studios.* (iv) One of the concerns in my work has been with the use of different vocabularies: as introductions I suggest *Pam Burnel's Political Speeches* (in *Rawz,* 1979) and the book *Imbrications.* Another concern may be discerned from the books *Poetry for Schools* and *Apocalyptic Sonnets.* I am at present engaged on a new project titled *Gravity as a consequence of shape;* an example of this may be the chapbook *Banda. Unpolished Mirrors,* mentioned in (i) may be a useful introduction to some of the concern-complexes of this group-variety.

*   *   *

The English poet Allen Fisher was born in 1944 in a part of Surrey which is now London. Uprooted, then, not by choice, but by what he calls, in Book III of *Place,* "The great wen," Fisher embarked on his life as a poet and a small-press publisher of other poets in the late 1960's.

With his late wife, Elaine, he founded New London Pride Editions, and in that series, published a book titled *Long Shout to Kernewek*, the tone of whose explorations allied Fisher to the 20th-century American tradition of Pound, Williams, and Olson.

However, the leitmotifs of irony and romantic lyricism made his early work distinctive rather than imitative. The originality of his voice and his vision was authenticated by his major work to date, *Place*, a long series of sequential, interlocking, but non-linear poems. It was a ten-year project, and the completed work a major achievement.

By the close of the 1970's, Fisher's interests in science, and in painting and art history, had deepened to the point where his work as a visual artist began to emerge from the background, and his work as a poet and a publisher incorporated structures, ideas, and energies from post-modern experimentations in music and in other areas outside of the tradition of the written and the spoken word. For about five years after the completion of *Place*, Fisher struggled with a variety of forms, including the hermetic and collective project known as *Clothes*, in order to find new points of departure.

In his Spanner Editions series, he published *Defamiliarising* and *Ideas on the Culture Dreamed Of*, two books of a proposed six book series. Because of his attempts to find a language equal to his vision, disclosing, rather than describing or descriptive, and committed to a sense of the universe as a metrical field, an open field, Fisher's work demands enormous input from the reader, an act of initiatory participation. His newer work develops a side of his poetry different from that of *Place*. *Thomas Net's Tree-Birst*, *Prosyncel*, and *The Leer* are all examples of a combination of found poems, *poésie concrète*, and experiments in *logopoeia*, as Pound named it in *How to Read*. In the latest published work, *Banda*, the convolutions and recombinations begin again to turn outward.

Fisher's work as a publisher and as a visual artist have kept him in the active vanguard of British movements. His international reputation among radically experimental poets as the author of *Place*, clearly his masterwork to date, has earned Fisher prominence not only on the poetry-reading circuit of his own country, but in the U.S. and France.

Place is still unquestionably the work on which his reputation has depended. A long, rambling, prolix but precise and highly intense visionary series or sets of poems, *Place* is perhaps the most decentered long poem (or series of poems) in the entire history of English verse. This is despite the fact that its unfolding of multiplicities of realities usually occurs, geographically, in London, a city as central to Fisher's vision as it was to Blake's.

—William David Sherman

FISHER, Roy. British. Born in Handsworth, Birmingham, Warwickshire, 11 June 1930. Educated at Wattville Road Elementary School; Handsworth Grammar School; Birmingham University, B.A., M.A. Married Barbara Venables in 1953; two sons. Pianist with jazz groups since 1946. School and college teacher, 1953-63; Principal Lecturer and Head of the Department of English and Drama, Bordesley College of Education, Birmingham, 1963-71; Member of the Department of American Studies, University of Keele, 1972-82. Since 1982 free-lance writer and musician. Recipient: Kelus Prize, 1970; Cholmondeley Award, 1981. Address: Eleven Steps, Upper Hulme, near Leek, Staffordshire ST13 8UG, England.

PUBLICATIONS

Verse

City. Worcester, Migrant Press, 1961.
Ten Interiors with Various Figures. Nottingham, Tarasque Press, 1967.
The Memorial Fountain. Newcastle upon Tyne, Northern House, 1967.
Collected Poems 1968: The Ghost of a Paper Bag. London, Fulcrum Press, 1969.
Correspondence. London, Tetrad Press, 1970.
Matrix. London, Fulcrum Press, 1971.
Three Early Pieces. London, Transgravity Advertiser, 1971.
Also There. London, Tetrad Press, 1972.
Bluebeard's Castle. Guildford, Surrey, Circle Press, 1972.
Cultures. London, Tetrad Press, 1975.
Neighbours! Guildford, Surrey, Circle Press, 1976.
Nineteen Poems and an Interview. Pensnett, Staffordshire, Grosseteste, 1976.
Four Poems. Newcastle upon Tyne, Pig Press, 1976.
Widening Circles: Five Black Country Poets, with others, edited by Edward Lowbury. Stafford, West Midland Arts, 1976.
Barnardine's Reply. Knotting, Bedfordshire, Sceptre Press, 1977.
Scenes from the Alphabet. Guildford, Surrey, Circle Press, 1978.
The Thing about Joe Sullivan: Poems 1971-1977. Manchester, Carcanet, 1978.
Comedies. Newcastle upon Tyne, Pig Press, 1979.
Poems 1955-1980. Oxford, Oxford University Press, 1980.
Talks for Words. Cardiff, Blackweir, 1980.
Consolidated Comedies. Durham, Pig Press, 1981.

Other

Then Hallucinations: City 2. Worcester, Migrant Press, 1962.
The Ship's Orchestra (prose poem). London, Fulcrum Press, 1966.
Titles. Nottingham, Tarasque Press, 1969.
Metamorphoses (prose poems). London, Tetrad Press, 1971.
The Cut Pages (prose poems). London, Fulcrum Press, 1971.
The Half-Year Letters: An Alphabet Book, with Ronald King. Guildford, Surrey, Circle Press, 1983.

*

Critical Studies: "Resonances and Speculations upon Reading Roy Fisher's *City*" by Gael Turnbull, in *Kulchur 7* (New York), 1962; Stuart Mills and Simon Cutts, in *Tarasque 5* (Nottingham), 1967; "Roy Fisher's Work" by Eric Mottram, in *Stand* (Newcastle upon Tyne), xi, 1, 1969; "Roy Fisher: An Appreciation" in *Thomas Hardy and British Poetry* by Donald Davie, New York, Oxford University Press, 1972, London, Routledge, 1973; Preface by Jon Silkin to *Poetry of the Committed Individual*, London, Gollancz-Penguin, 1973; "Metal or Stone" by David Punter in *Delta 62* (Ely), 1981; "A City of the Mind" by Philip Gardner, in *Times Literary Supplement* (London), 20 March 1981; *The British Dissonance* by A. Kingsley Weatherhead, Columbia, University of Missouri Press, 1983.

*   *   *

In a poem about Joe Sullivan, Roy Fisher evokes the pleasure which a listener experiences as his own perceptions, following Joe Sullivan's "through figures that sound obvious / find corners everywhere, / marks of invention, wakefulness; / the rapid and perverse / tracks that ordinary feelings / make when they are driven / hard enough against time." The reader, following through Roy Fisher's poems "the dry track of half a voice," finds that this poet preserves visual details of life with such accuracy—the winter afternoon sunlight on a slope "clear and pale like a redcurrant"—than an absolute confidence is built up as to the eventual emergence of significance, even when this is elusive: the poems are a triumph of conveying without saying. One could say that there are three movements in reading Fisher: first, intensely objective "language," verbal and perceptual; second, intensely subjective awareness of a state of mind, the "meaning" of the riddle; last, a joyful, objective recognition of the meeting of separate minds, vouched for by the emergence of that awareness. Two classicisms on either side of a romanticism.

Perhaps it is always true of a good poem that it is, at some level, a riddle whose meaning has to be incarnated in the reader but eludes paraphrase. With Fisher, though, the matching of awareness through the medium of art seems to occupy the philosophical centre. Although he is not a poet who is often explicit about his intentions—"What kind of man / comes in a message?"—there are passages throughout his work which indicate this clearly. True responses, *true* in the fullest sense, are for him both problematic and vitally important. The source of joy in art is precisely that, following the "dry track" left by the artist, we become aware, simultaneously, of his and our own struggle for clean, attentive life, issuing in the success of the work as direct experience.

The core of Fisher's writing, whether in prose or verse, is in this sense positive, though never brashly optimistic. There is sadness, even bitterness, concerning the attitudes our culture induces: "What's now only disproved / was once imagined." But "a genuine poet," as Goethe said, "always feels a call to fill himself with the glory of the world," and in *City* Fisher wrote: "Once I wanted to prove the world was sick. Now I want to prove it healthy." Tempted, one guesses, to "go mad after the things which are not," and yet determined not to be "able to feel only vertically, like a blind wall, or thickly, like the tyres of a bus," Fisher inhabits a ground of perceptual precisions made taut by a heart-rending, though quiet, sense of inexplicable significance beyond. The more one reads him, the more one wants to read, tantalised as by one's own immediate experience. "If you take a poem / you must take another / and another / till you have a poet," he has written. As one does so, one's moral and aesthetic response is increasingly to a man, an approach to living, rather than to isolated utterances.

Fisher's fineness lies in the extraordinary intimate communication he achieves, through the medium of a sophisticated, well-mannered art whose illusory coldness is the sign of a real respect for his own and his reader's individuality.

—Anne Cluysenaar

FITZGERALD, Robert (Stuart). American. Born in Geneva, New York, 12 October 1910. Educated at Springfield High School, Illinois; Choate School, Wallingford, Connecticut, graduated 1929; Harvard University, Cambridge, Massachusetts, 1929-31, 1932-33, A.B. 1933; Trinity College, Cambridge, 1931-32. Served in the United States Naval Reserve, 1943-46: Lieutenant. Married 1) Sarah Morgan in 1947 (marriage dissolved), four sons and two daughters; 2) Penelope Laurans in 1982. Reporter, New York *Herald-Tribune*, 1933-35; staff wri-

ter, *Time* magazine, 1936-40, 1941-43, 1946-49. Instructor, Sarah Lawrence College, Bronxville, New York, 1946-53, and Princeton University, New Jersey, 1950-52; poetry reviewer, *New Republic*, Washington, D.C., 1948-52. Lived in Italy, 1953-64. Visiting Professor, Notre Dame University, Indiana, 1957, University of Washington, Seattle, 1961, and Mount Holyoke College, South Hadley, Massachusetts, 1964. Boylston Professor of Rhetoric, Harvard University, 1965-81, emeritus from 1981. From 1951, Fellow, Indiana University School of Letters, Bloomington. Recipient: Midland Author's Prize (*Poetry*, Chicago), 1931; Guggenheim Fellowship, 1952, 1971; Shelley Memorial Award, 1956; American Academy grant, 1957; Ford grant, 1959; Bollingen Award, for translation, 1961; Bollingen Fellowship, 1965; National Endowment for the Arts grant, 1969, 1972; Ingram Merrill Foundation grant, 1973, and award, 1978; Landon Translation Award, 1976, 1983; New England Poetry Club Golden Rose, 1976. D.Litt.: College of the Holy Cross, Worcester, Massachusetts, 1967; Rosary College, Rochester, New York, 1976; Loyala University, Chicago, 1976. Member American Academy 1961; Member, American Academy of Arts and Sciences, 1962. Chancellor, Academy of American Poets, 1968. *Died 16 January 1985.*

PUBLICATIONS

Verse

Poems.   New York, Arrow, 1935.
A Wreath for the Sea.   New York, Arrow, 1943.
In the Rose of Time: Poems 1931-1956.   New York, New Directions, 1956.
Ombra di Primavera (bilingual edition).   Milan, Ediziòni del Triangolo, 1959.
Spring Shade: Poems 1931-1970.   New York, New Directions, 1971.
Willow Words.   Milwaukee, Shelters Press, n.d.

Other

Editor, *The Aeneid of Virgil, Translated by John Dryden.* New York, Macmillan, 1965.
Editor, *The Collected Poems of James Agee.*   Boston, Houghton Mifflin, 1968.
Editor, *The Collected Short Prose of James Agee.*   Boston, Houghton Mifflin, 1968; London, Calder and Boyars, 1972.
Editor, with Sally Fitzgerald, *Mystery and Manners: Occasional Prose,* by Flannery O'Connor.   New York, Farrar Straus, 1969.
Editor, *In Another Country: Poems 1935-1975,* by James Laughlin.   San Francisco, City Lights, 1978.

Translator, with Dudley Fitts, *Alcestis,* by Euripides.   New York, Harcourt Brace, 1936.
Translator, with Dudley Fitts, *Antigone,* by Sophocles.   New York, Harcourt Brace, 1939.
Translator, *Oedipus at Colonus,* by Sophocles.   New York, Harcourt Brace, 1941; London, Faber, 1957.
Translator, with Dudley Fitts, *Oedipus Rex,* by Sophocles.   New York, Harcourt Brace, 1949; London, Faber, 1950.
Translator, with Dudley Fitts, *The Oedipus Cycle.*   New York, Harcourt Brace, 1958.
Translator, *Amphion, Semiramis,* and *The Narcissus Cantata,* in *Plays,* by Paul Valéry.   New York, Pantheon, and London, Routledge, 1960.

Translator, The Odyssey, by Homer. New York, Doubleday, 1961; London, Heinemann, 1962.
Translator, Chronique, by St. John Perse. New York, Pantheon, 1961.
Translator, Birds, by St. John Perse. New York, Pantheon, 1965.
Translator, Dante, in *Two Addresses*, by St. John Perse. New York, Pantheon, 1966.
Translator, Deathwatch on the Southside, by Jorge Luis Borges. Cambridge, Massachusetts, Grolier Book Shop, 1968.
Translator, The Little Passion: 37 Wood-cuts by Albrecht Dürer...with the Latin Poems of Benedictus Chelidonius... Verona, Italy, Officina Bodoni, 1971.
Translator, The Iliad, by Homer. New York, Doubleday, 1974.
Translator, The Aeneid, by Virgil. New York, Random House, 1983; London, Harvill Press, 1984.

*

Manuscript Collection: Houghton Library, Harvard University, Cambridge, Massachusetts; Berg Collection, New York Public Library.

Robert Fitzgerald comments:
I have been independent and trustful of my own powers. Poetry can be at least an elegance, at most a revelation, and I have worked as opportunity offered between these limits. Eliot was and remains a great touchstone and irritant. The Greek Masters have been before me often, and more lately so has Dante. I hold by constructive beauty, energy of language, depth of life.

*   *   *

Robert Fitzgerald's original poetry has probably not had the attention it deserves because (ironically) of his great distinction as a teacher and as a translator. Furthermore, as Donald Davidson wrote in reviewing his first book—one of, he claimed, "major" accent—Fitzgerald's "subject and form are minor."

As befits one of this century's finest translators of Greek in the English language, Fitzgerald's sense of form—best described as pliant rather than free—is highly developed. From the beginning his poems, whatever their scope, were word perfect, rhythmically impeccable. In an early poem "In This House," the enjambements already display a practised and craftsmanlike poet:

> In this house of the untidy lamp, a
> man is leafing lexicons, his
> Limpid fingers in forgotten
> Brains....
>
> Who dreamt he bedded with a whore
> 's face, body of a child....

There is here already, too, a somewhat over-bookish, though never dry, quality, which has characterized all Fitzgerald's poetry. He is nothing if not a literary poet. However, and again in poetry of the first half of the Thirties, he anticipated many aspects of post-war poetry—aspects that were not to be confined to English poetry. Sometimes he is merely mannered ("...Keenly / Clenching the eye push into bone wisp, see / How thick the shadow is, teems, is prodigious, / Stored with time...") but at others he is genuinely concerned with the interior of the mind—in a manner somewhat akin to that of the Swedish poet Ekelöf in his immediately post-surreal "suicidal" phase of the mid-Thirties. Thus he could produce, before 1935, a line such as

"Between dinner and death the crowds shadow the loom of steel"—and that this is "Park Avenue" (the title) does not diminish, but rather reinforces, the inner resonances.

Fitzgerald's post-war poetry became more rhetorical, more cultural (in the "American-in-Europe" sense), a little simpler: the poems are not perhaps as suggestive as the earlier, but the ear has remained as sure, and one is always in the presence of an elegant and educated sensibility. "The Painter" thus packs in much comment on its subject, and is as intellectually calculated as it is eloquent, as its opening stanza shows:

> On bluish inlets bristling
> Black in the tall north,
> Like violet ghosts risen
> The great fish swam forth,
> And hoary blooms and submarine
> Lightning in the cradling west
> Lent summer her vivid sheen
> For the deep eye's interest.

—Martin Seymour-Smith

FitzGERALD, Robert D(avid). Australian. Born in Hunters Hill, New South Wales, 22 February 1902. Educated at Sydney Grammar School; Sydney University, 1920-21; Fellow, Institution of Surveyors. Married Marjorie-Claire Harris in 1931; four children. Surveyor, FitzGerald and Blair, 1926-30; Native Lands Commission Surveyor, Fiji, 1931-36; Municipal Surveyor, 1936-39; Surveyor, Australian Department of the Interior, 1939-66, now retired. Visiting Lecturer, University of Texas, Austin, 1963. Recipient: Australian Sesqui-Centenary Poetry Prize, 1938; Australian Literature Society Gold Medal, 1938; Grace Leven Prize, 1953, 1960, 1963; Fulbright grant, 1963; Encyclopaedia Britannica Award, 1965; Robert Frost Medallion, 1974. O.B.E. (Officer, Order of the British Empire), 1951; Member, Order of Australia, 1982. Address: 4 Prince Edward Parade, Hunters Hill, New South Wales 2110, Australia.

PUBLICATIONS

Verse

The Greater Apollo. Privately printed, 1927.
To Meet the Sun. Sydney, Angus and Robertson, 1929.
Moonlight Acre. Melbourne, Melbourne University Press, 1938.
Heemskerck Shoals. Melbourne, Mountainside Press, 1949.
Between Two Tides. Sydney, Angus and Robertson, 1952.
This Night's Orbit: Verses. Melbourne, Melbourne University Press, 1953.
The Wind at Your Door: A Poem. Sydney, Talkarra Press, 1959.
Southmost Twelve. Sydney, Angus and Robertson, 1962.
Of Some Country: 27 Poems. Austin, University of Texas, 1963.
(Poems), selected and introduced by the author. Sydney, Angus and Robertson, 1963.
Forty Years' Poems. Sydney, Angus and Robertson, 1965.
Product. Sydney, Angus and Robertson, 1978.

Other

The Elements of Poetry. Brisbane, University of Queensland
Press, 1963.
Of Places and Poetry. Brisbane, University of Queensland
Press, 1976.

Editor, *Australian Poetry 1942.* Sydney, Angus and Robert-
son, 1942.
Editor, *Selected Verse,* by Mary Gilmore. Sydney and Lon-
don, Angus and Robertson, 1948; revised edition, 1969.
Editor, *The Letters of Hugh McCrae.* Sydney, Angus and
Robertson, 1970.

*

Critical Studies: *Six Australian Poets* by T. Inglis Moore, Melbourne, Robertson and Mullen, 1942; *Literature of Australia*
edited by Geoffrey Dutton, Melbourne, Penguin, 1964, revised
edition, 1976; *Preoccupations in Australian Poetry* by Judith
Wright, Melbourne and London, Oxford University Press,
1965; *Robert D. FitzGerald* by A. Grove Day, New York,
Twayne, 1973; *R.D. FitzGerald* by G.A. Wilkes, Melbourne,
Oxford University Press, 1981.

*   *   *

The outstanding characteristics of Robert D. FitzGerald's
poetry are his command of technique and, in Matthew Arnold's
term, his "high seriousness." His verse is plain, bare without
ornament and almost without adjectives, taking its life from his
vigorous individual speech rhythm and the controlled emotional
intensity of his thought; and his thought is concerned with
Australia's national destiny in this place "which lay, unleased, /
beneath its empty centuries and stars turning, /...waking under
his love"; with the aspiration that has taken mankind into far
places and far thought and achievements:

> the necessity in men, deep down, close cramped,
> not seen in their own hearts, for some attempt
> at being more than ordinary men,
> rising above themselves;

and ultimately, because both national destiny and worthwhile
achievement depend upon it, with human integrity:

> Attitude matters: bearing. Action in the end
> goes down the stream as motion, merges as such
> with the whole of life and time; but islands stand:
> dignity and distinction that attach
> to the inmost being of us each.
> It matters for man's private respect that still
> face differs from face and will from will.

> It is important how men looked and were.
> Infirm, staggering a little as Hastings was,
> his voice was steady as his eyes. Kneeling at the bar
> (ruler but late of millions) had steeled his poise;
> he fronted inescapable loss
> and thrown, stinking malice and disrepute,
> calmly, a plain man in a plain suit.

Though he has written many admirable short poems, from his
early lyrical reflections on life and landscape set in Fiji (where he
spent some years as a surveyor) to the more recent profound
meditations of *Product,* his reputation rests chiefly on a number
of medium-length and long poems. Among these, "The Hidden
Bole" is a curious exploration of the banyan tree for the "hidden
bole," the central principle hidden in the complexity of existence. "Essay on Memory," which won the poetry prize in the
Australian sesqui-centenary competition, deals with the influence of the past in human history upon the present. "The Face of
the Waters," unusually fluid in technique, is an extraordinary
vision of the creation and perpetual recreation of the universe.
Between Two Tides, a poem of book length, is an epic of tribal
war in Tonga, by implication a commentary on power politics
and corruption by power. And "Heemskerck Shoals" (about the
navigator Abel Janszoon Tasman), "Fifth Day" (about the shorthand writer who recorded the trial of Warren Hastings), and
"The Wind at Your Door" (about the convicts and their masters
who were the first settlers of Australia) are poems of that middle
length in which his powers of sustained thought and construction and the portrayal of character in action have reached their
most impressive combination.

—Douglas Stewart

———————

FLETCHER, Ian. British. Born in London, 22 August 1920.
Educated at Dulwich College, London; Goldsmiths' College,
University of London; University of Reading, Berkshire, Ph.D.
1965. Served in the Middle East in the Ministry of Information
and Forces Broadcasting, 1942-46. Married Loraine Hollyman
in 1965; two children. Chidren's Librarian, Lewisham Borough
Council, 1946-55. Reader, 1965-78, and Professor of English
Literature, 1978-82, now Emeritus, University of Reading. Since
1982, Professor of English, Arizona State University, Tempe.
Address: Department of English, Arizona State University,
Tempe, Arizona 85281, U.S.A.

PUBLICATIONS

Verse

An Homily to Kenneth Topley. Privately printed, 1945.
Orisons, Picaresque and Metaphysical. London, Editions
Poetry London, 1947.
*The Lover's Martyrdom: Translations from the Italian of Dante,
Guarini, Tasso, and Marino with Original Texts.* Oxford,
Fantasy Press, 1957.
Motets: Twenty One Poems. Reading, University of Reading,
1962.
*The Milesian Intrusion: A Restoration Comedy Version of Iliad
XIV.* Nottingham, Byron Press, 1968.
Lauds: Four Poems. London, Stevens, 1980.

Plays

A Passion Play. Khartoum, Sudan Bookstore, 1943.
Get Up What Stairs?, with Peter Myers (produced London,
1948).
Dead End (produced London, 1981).

Other

Partheneia Sacra. Aldington, Kent, Hand and Flower Press,
1950.
Walter Pater. London, Longman, 1959; revised edition, 1971.

A Catalogue of the Imagist Poets, with Wallace Martin.   New York, J.H. Woolmer, 1966.
Beaumont and Fletcher. London, Longman, 1967.
Swinburne. London, Longman, 1973.

Editor, with G. S. Fraser, *Springtime: An Anthology of Young Poets and Writers.* London, Peter Owen, 1953.
Editor, *The Complete Poems of Lionel Johnson.* London, Unicorn Press, 1953; revised edition, as *The Collected Poems*, New York, Garland, 1982.
Editor, *Romantic Mythologies.* London, Routledge, and New York, Barnes and Noble, 1967.
Editor, *Meredith Now.* London, Routledge, and New York, Barnes and Noble, 1971.
Editor, *Selections from British Fiction 1880-1900.* New York, New American Library, 1972.
Editor, *Poems of Victor Plarr.* London, Stevens, 1974.
Editor, *Collected Poems of John Gray.* London, Cecil Woolf, 1974.
Editor, with John Pilling, *The Group.* Reading, University of Reading Library, 1974.
Editor, *Fifty Renascence Love Poems,* translated by Edwin Morgan. Reading, Whiteknights Press, 1975.
Editor, with John Stokes, *The Decadent Consciousness: A Hidden Archive of Late Victorian Literature.* New York, Garland, 1977.
Editor, *Decadence and the Eighteen-Nineties.* London, Arnold, 1979; New York, Holmes and Meier, 1980.
Editor, *A Letter to Edgar Jepson,* by Lionel Johnson. London, Stevens, 1979.
Editor, with others, *Return to Oasis.* London, Shepheard Walwyn, 1980.
Editor, with John Lucas, *Poems of G.S. Fraser.* Leicester, Leicester University Press, 1981.
Editor, *Six Sonnets,* by John Barlas. London, Stevens, 1981.
Editor, *The Paying Guest,* by George Gissing. Brighton, Harvester, 1982.
Editor, with others, *From Oasis to Italy.* London, Shepheard Walwyn, 1983.
Editor, *The Kiss,* by Theodore de Banville, translated by John Gray. Edinburgh, Tragara Press, 1983.

*

Manuscript Collections: State University of New York, Buffalo; University of Kansas, Lawrence; University of Reading, Berkshire.

Ian Fletcher comments:
    Dualism; topographical and architectural topics; moderately strict verse forms. Influence, Yeats; I like trying my hand at free translation. Syllabics need not apply.

*   *   *

    Ian Fletcher was one of the most interesting poets to reach maturity during the Forties, and some critics have expressed regret that he seems to have half-abandoned his career—whether this is so or not, he has certainly published much less in recent years. But some of this strongly-thewed and energetic later work shows signs of a development towards a greater directness and increase in purely descriptive power. His early poems were highly involute, well-made, reflecting an intelligence engaged with problems of culture, often expressed in terms of the past, and with the significance of religious change. *The Maenad under the Cross,* the title of a projected volume that never appeared,

aptly sums up his position. His best-known poem, "Adolescents in the Dusk," is the apogee of his earlier manner, and well illustrates his technical control, subtle use of metaphor, and the metaphysicality that underlies his pictorial imagination:

About this time when dusk falls like a shutter
Upon the decomposition of the time
Eliding eye and day and surfaces and shapes,
Whitening of faces like stoles in the twilight...
When the gardens between the houses are rose-
Encumbered with sidereal roses
And the roads like gorges grey in the tired light of falling....

The new poems are less involute, more confident, stronger in thrust—but they do not sacrifice the old subtlety. Fletcher was once a leading poet of his generation, and a serious one; it is to be hoped that current fashions will not obscure his earlier or his later achievement, and that he will be encouraged to put himself forward, once again, as the owner of a distinctive voice and manner.

—Martin Seymour-Smith

———————

FORBES, John.   Australian.   Born in Melbourne, Victoria, 1 September 1950; grew up in New Guinea, North Queensland, and Malaya. Educated at University of Sydney, B.A. (honours) 1973. Editor, *Surfer's Paradise,* 1974-83. Recipient: *New Poetry* prize, 1972; Australia Council Literature Board grant, 1973, 1975, 1982; *Southerly* prize, 1976. Address: C/74 Corruna Road, Stanmore, New South Wales 2048, Australia.

PUBLICATIONS

Verse

Tropical Skiing.   Sydney, Angus and Robertson, 1976.
On the Beach.   Sydney, Sea-Cruise, 1977.
Drugs.   N.p., Black Lamb Press, 1980.
Stalin's Holidays.   Sydney, Transit Press, 1981.

*

John Forbes comments:
    I can't really "introduce" my work because the poems are all there is to it. On the other hand, I have a few ideas about poetry: that it should be pleasurable; that if it is expression then it's only a matter of crafting what's already been recognized, i.e., if you can't find a partner, don't whisper sweet nothings to your wooden chair; that the current collapse into naturalism is misdirected and that this state of affairs is not going to continue much longer, at least, not here.

*   *   *

    "He begins to consider Meaning as it actually is, decentred and contingent, and shows up our structured images of it (in this case Memory) for the icons they are....Writers like X treat language as a window onto the world, unaware, or not wanting to know, that it's a mirror." Steaming into battle in a 1984 *Meanjin* review, John Forbes lets fly with the canons of post-Modernism. The heavy fire is to do with language, although there is a good deal of *peripheral* modernity in his poetry: ampersands, slashes and lower case titles, drug poems, the extension of self-referentiality to in-group references to places and people—references which irritate some readers by their arbitrariness and randomness, qualities which proceed, however, predictably enough from the refusal to give such names the centred Meaning of typicality. Types would be only a step from universals, and if these cannot be abolished entirely by passing "A SENTENCE ON HUMANISM" ("Am I a Door / Six Poems Say Yes"), they can be debunked with a larrikin energy:

> Tho' this poem has universals in it
> shittiness, fuck—
> upedness etc.
> in the tradition of Shelley, et cetera

Not being too respectful to literary icons is one way of throwing off what John Tranter defines as one of the crosses born by the new poetry, "the quasi-religious rhetoric of University English departments." Nonetheless, literary allusion is central to some of Forbes's best poems. In "The Photograph" when "this mass seizure into marble/left no one holding their breath for years," the Keatsian reference is only a flourish on the poem's preoccupation with "cool blurred process," a phrase that might well describe the linear structure, blurring between verse and prose. Elsewhere, in "Four Heads & How To Do Them," a cool precise process (along with a preoccupation with the act of perceiving as the act of creating) has tempted readers to thoughts of Wallace Stevens, but it is to his rival William Carlos Williams that allegiance seems offered in "A Bad Day":

> "Everything depends on the context"
> I consoled the revolutionary
> dying behind
> the red wheelbarrow section
> of our barricade.

The rather cryptic title "jacobean," in offering a complex allusion to a literature that has informed our death sensibility, adds an extended dimension to a poem that, in its interwoven metaphors, triumphantly overrides the apparent dualism of learning—experiencing and being told—posited by the poem's conclusion:

> .... these things you only learn
> by drowning, the souvenir
> of going home.
> That, or the guide tells you.

The flat unsatisfactoriness of being told returns us to Forbes's view of language as the essential and most interesting aspect of his modernism. "Four Heads & How To Do Them" remains his most extended and stylishly witty demonstration of language in the process of creating fictions, the reality of literature, not of the world; so, in "The Conceptual Head":

> 1) The breeze moves
>   the branches as sleep moves the old man's head:
>   neither moves the poem.

> 4) Yet the head is not a word
>   & the word means "head"
>   only inside the head or its gesture,
>   the mouth.
>   So the poem can't escape,
>   trapped inside its subject

> & longing to be a piece of flesh & blood
> as
>   Ten Pounds of Ugly Fat
>   versus
>   The Immortal Taperecorder
> forever.

From this dilemma, in Forbes's argument, it is metaphor rather than truth that delivers.

—Jennifer Strauss

FORCHÉ, Carolyn (Louise). American. Born in Detroit, Michigan, 28 April 1950. Educated at Michigan State University, East Lansing, B.A. in international relations and creative writing 1972; Bowling Green State University, Ohio, M.F.A. 1975. Visiting Lecturer, Michigan State University, 1974; Visiting Lecturer, 1975, and Assistant Professor, 1976-78, San Diego State University; Visiting Lecturer, University of Virginia, Charlottesville, 1979, 1982-83; Assistant Professor, 1980, and Associate Professor, 1981, University of Arkansas, Fayetteville; Visiting Lecturer, New York University, 1983, Vassar College, Poughkeepsie, New York, 1984, and Columbia University, New York, 1984-85. Poetry Editor, *New Virginia Review*, Norfolk, 1981; Editor, *Tendril*, Green Harbor, Massachusetts. Journalist for Amnesty International in El Salvador, and Beirut Correspondent, "All Things Considered" radio program, 1983. Recipient: Yale Series of Younger Poets award, 1975; *Chicago Review* award, 1975; Devine Memorial Prize, 1975; Bread Loaf Writers Conference Tennessee Williams fellowship, 1976; National Endowment for the Arts fellowship, 1977, 1984; Guggenheim Fellowship, 1978; Emily Clark Balch Prize (*Virginia Quarterly Review*), 1979; Lamont Poetry Selection Award, 1981; Poetry Society of America Alice Fay di Castagnola Award, 1981. Address: 430 Greenwich Street, New York, New York 10013, U.S.A.

PUBLICATIONS

Verse

Gathering the Tribes. New Haven, Connecticut, Yale University Press, 1976.
The Country Between Us. Port Townsend, Washington, Copper Canyon Press, 1981; London, Cape, 1983.

Other

Women in American Labor History 1825-1935: An Annotated Bibliography, with Martha Jane Soltow. East Lansing, Michigan State University School of Labor and Industrial Relations, 1972.
El Salvador: The Work of Thirty Photographers, edited by Harry Mattison, Susan Meiselas, and Fae Rubenstein. New York and London, Writers and Readers, 1983.

Translator, *Flowers from the Volcano*, by Claribel Alegria. Pittsburgh, University of Pittsburgh Press, 1982.

*

Critical Study: by Terrence Diggory, in *Salmagundi* (Saratoga Springs, New York), Spring 1984.

*   *   *

Since the publication of Carolyn Forché's second collection of poems, *The Country Between Us*, she has become visible as a "political" poet, as well as a poet of consummate craft. (The latter is attested to in that her first book won the Yale Younger Poets award; the second, the Lamont.) But there are dangers in all such categorizations: to call Forché "political" is to deny the excellence of all her poems, not only those that deal with life in El Salvador or the political concerns of both America and the world. Forché is political in the broadest, healthiest possible sense: in that her poems grow from the genuine, intense concerns of the poet as living person. They bespeak her age, her craft, her education, her origins, her sex, and her intellectual persuasions. They also reflect the fact that she spent several years living in El Salvador, becoming a translator of several poets, a friend of many others, and a keen observer of life in that country. But her Salvadoran experience is no more important to her development as a poet than was her experience in the southwest desert or in the midwest. Forché is a poet who uses whatever she has experienced, transmuting her material regardless of its source into sharply defined images that reach far past the "personal" or "local."

Her roots are clearly in the Williams and Roethke schools of American poetry, but she has moved past their sometimes academic limitations to a free expression of all her concerns. She is an impassioned poet, whether she writes about a girlhood friend she has lost track of, or a dying idealist, or a brutal military man. Whatever subject Forché chooses, the shape and movement of the poem evokes the appropriate mood.

Forché is a poet of great versatility. What unifies poems in a collection is not style, but rather the repetition of images. Images of loss, absence, muted or stilled voices, broken lives, the simple and often tawdry objects of poverty, and—in contrast—of touch appear in poems that range from stark external description to implicit dramatic monologue to letter to confession.

When she writes in "The Visitor," a short, image-centered poem, "In Spanish he whispers there is no time left," she establishes the pattern of language forestalled, forbidden. That whisper is amplified in other of the Salvador poems. "The Memory of Elena" gives us apparent language ("We find a table, ask for *paella*.... As she talks, the hollow/clopping of a horse, the sound/of bones touched together") but the central image, of the dark tongues of bells, ends in perversion. "The Island" also recreates language, a dialogue between the poet persona and the worn Salvadoran woman, who insistently demands "Carolina, do you know how long it takes/any one voice to reach another?" "San Onofre, California" sets up another ironic dialogue between the living and the missing. Ironically, the only successful communication in *The Country Between Us* occurs in "The Colonel," when the military figure pours a sackful of human ears on the dinner table where the poet has been dining. Speech has been realized, but instead of saving, it desecrates everything human. *The Country Between Us* becomes Forché's "epistemology of loss," just as *Gathering the Tribes* was her more positive statement of human endurance. As she writes in "Message," where voices are "sprayed over the walls/dry to the touch of morning" and patriots are sent off to be killed as the poet pledges,

I will live
and living cry out until my voice is gone
to its hollow of earth, where with our
hands and by the lives we have chosen
we will dig deep into our deaths.

For all the variety of Forché's forms, for all the somber stain of her Salvadoran experience, for all the poignance of her personal fabric of recollection, *The Country Between Us* succeeds in creating some sense of joy. "Because One Is Always Forgotten," "Poem for Maya," "Ourselves or Nothing," "For the Stranger"— each poem embodies images, and tones, of hope: "all things human take time"; "We have, each of us, nothing./ We will give it to each other."

Forché's poems are meditative and lyric, narrative and song-like. They draw from dream and myth, both directly and subtly. They escape categorization as they lace together images of terrain and language, touch and separation, brutality and love that are so closely related as to fuse, through metaphor. The unity of both Forché's collections is achieved through a singleness of vision, a finely expressed, various vision, delightful in its chameleon-like trappings, despite the seriousness of its intention. She is already a major poet.

—Linda W. Wagner

FORD, Charles Henri. American. Born in Hazlehurst, Mississippi, 10 February 1913. Lived in Paris in the 1930's. Editor, *Blues*, Columbus, Mississippi, 1929-30; *View*, New York, 1940-47. Photographer and painter: individual shows—Institute of Contemporary Arts, London, 1955; Galerie Marforen, Paris, 1956; Galerie du Dragon, Paris, 1957, 1958; Cordier and Ekstrom Gallery, New York, 1965; New York Cultural Center, 1975; Carlton Gallery, New York, 1975. Address: 1 West 72nd Street, New York, New York 10023, U.S.A.

PUBLICATIONS

Verse

A Pamphlet of Sonnets. Mallorca, Caravel Press, 1936.
The Garden of Disorder and Other Poems. New York, New Directions, and London, Europa, 1938.
ABC's. Prairie City, Illinois, James A. Decker, 1940.
The Overturned Lake. Cincinnati, Little Man Press, 1941.
Poems for Painters. New York, View, 1945.
The Half-Thoughts, The Distances of Pain. New York, Gotham Bookmart, 1947.
Sleep in a Nest of Flames. New York, New Directions, 1949.
Spare Parts. New York, New View, 1966.
Silver Flower Coo. New York, Kulchur, 1968.
Flag of Ecstasy: Selected Poems, edited by Edward B. Germain. Los Angeles, Black Sparrow Press, 1972.
7 Poems. Kathmandu, Bardo Matrix, 1974.
Om Krishna. Cherry Valley, New York, Cherry Valley Editions, 1979.
Om Krishna II. Cherry Valley, New York, Cherry Valley Editions, 1981.
Om Krishna III. New York, Red Ozier Press, 1982.

Play

Screenplay: *Johnny Minotaur*, 1971.

Novel

The Young and Evil, with Parker Tyler.   Paris, Obelisk Press,
   1933; New York, Arno Press, 1973.

Other

Editor and Translator, *The Mirror of Baudelaire*.   New York,
   New Directions, 1942.
Editor, *A Night with Jupiter and Other Fantastic Stories*.   New
   York, View, 1945; London, Dobson, 1947.

*

Manuscript Collection: University of Texas, Austin.

Critical Studies: Introduction by William Carlos Williams to
The Garden of Disorder and Other Poems, 1938; Introduction
by Edith Sitwell to *Sleep in a Nest of Flames*, 1949.

*   *   *

   When he began publishing in 1929, Charles Henri Ford was
unique: America's surrealist poet. In retrospect, he is seminal.
His first two books create American surrealism. *Garden of
Disorder* welds together radio jazz and iambic pentameter, surrealist conceits and the sonnet form. *The Overturned Lake*
shows Ford as influenced by Whitman, Poe, and Mother Goose
as by Breton, Reverdy, and Eluard, employing a freer line and
lyric forms. It demonstrates Ford's forte: the surrealist image. In
one poem, Ford transforms the day from a poem into a horse.
He turns the sky into an arm, a mouth, a man, a thief, and then
into an enormous face. The sun, he makes into a wound, a jewel,
an equation, an eye, a tear. Night is a ditch. All in eight lines,
with obvious ease, and clarity.
   The "New York School" centered around Frank O'Hara and
John Ashbery owes something to these early surrealist lyrics.
During World War II, Ford encouraged young poets, like Philip
Lamantia, in the pages of his influential surrealist magazine,
View—the first literary magazine to publish Allen Ginsberg.
Ford himself began writing longer poems at this time, typically
part dream or ghost-story, part amoral allegory, filled with
convulsive imagery and sexual themes. Often parts of these
poems are greater than their whole. The self-conscious mannerism implicit in many of them surfaces in Ford's next two books,
Spare Parts and *Silver Flower Coo*, collage poems which are
exercises in gratuitous eroticism. Another, far more interesting
series, written but not published during this period, are Ford's
prose-poems and found-poetry, represented in the "Drawings"
section of his selected poems.
   Ford's best work lies predominantly with the rather narrow
lyric form in his early books. Some of these poems, "Plaint" for
example, are among the most evocative and moving short lyrics
of our century. In most, Ford creates wonder, wit, and a sensuous beauty free from the predictable tropes and rapacious glibness of much surrealist-influenced poetry of the 1960's and
1970's.

—Edward B. Germain

FORD, R(obert) A(rthur) D(ouglass).   Canadian.   Born in
Ottawa, Ontario, 8 January 1915. Educated at the University of
Western Ontario, London, B.A. 1937; Cornell University,
Ithaca, New York, M.A. 1940. Married Maria Thereza Gomes
in 1946. Member of the Department of History, Cornell Univer-
sity, 1938-40. Joined the Canadian Department of External
Affairs, 1940; served in Rio de Janeiro, Moscow, and London,
1940-51; Head of the European Division, Ottawa, 1954-57;
Ambassador to Colombia, 1957-58, to Yugoslavia, 1959-61, to
Egypt, 1961-63, and to the Soviet Union, 1964-80. Since 1980,
Special Adviser on East-West Relations. Member of the Palme
Commission on Disarmament; Founding Member, Interna-
tional Institute of Geopolitics. Recipient: Governor-General's
Medal, 1957. D.Litt.: University of Western Ontario, 1965.
Companion of Order of Canada, 1971. Address: Château de la
Poivrière, Saint Sylvestre Pragoulin, 63310 Puy de Dôme,
France.

PUBLICATIONS

Verse

A Window on the North.   Toronto, Ryerson Press, 1956.
The Solitary City.   Toronto, McClelland and Stewart, 1969.
Holes in Space.   Toronto, Hounslow Press, 1979.
Needle in the Eye.   Toronto, Mosaic Press, 1983.

Other

Editor and Translator, *Russian Poetry: A Personal Anthology*.
   Toronto, Mosaic Press, 1984.

*   *   *

   The poetic canon of R.A.D. Ford is relatively small, but one
clear voice emerges. These are quiet, serious poems, lyric rather
than dramatic, but always restrained. They explore around the
edges of emotion, seldom taking risks. They offer little irony, less
of the comic, very few surprises. And yet they are nearly all
worth reading—consistently competent, sincere, quietly rewarding.
   A sense of isolation pervades Ford's poems, whether in the
loneliness of open spaces or the equally barren "landscape of the
past." Also regularly present—especially in *A Window on the
North*—is an oppressive sense of the Cold, silently "smothering
the world," pressing into rooms and lives, invading

   The sanctity of man propped lone on
   The plain edge of winter, not
   Day but the dull half white dawn
   Of the never-ending snow night....

   For the most part Ford's poetry is marked by clear statement
and traditional meters. He sometimes employs rhyme effectively
(as in "Avoiding Greece"), but usually when rhyme is present,
too much else appears sacrificed to it. This intrusion of technique is, somewhat surprisingly, more common in *The Solitary
City* than in his first book. Fortunately, he avoids rhyme in most
of his poems, and the best of his later work demonstrates a
growing freedom from form and a more successful, more believably earned realization of experience (as in "The Thieves of
Love" and "How Doth the Solitary City Stand").
   Ford's translations deserve special note, for they demonstrate
both fidelity to the spirit of the originals and a view of Ford's
abilities that remain hidden behind self-imposed restraints in

much of his own poetry. The quality of the translations and adaptations appears consistently high, and the range of his interests (from the Russian of Pasternak, Akhmatova, Yessenin, and others, to Brazilian Portuguese, French, and Serbo-Croatian) is in itself impressive. Together they reinforce the impression one has from Ford's own poems, that the deeply quiet, unpretentious voice of R.A.D. Ford is one worth hearing.

—Stanley W. Lindberg

FOWLER, Gene. American. Born in Oakland, California, 5 October 1931. Attended Oakland High School, graduated 1949. Served in the United States Army, 1950-53. Married April Corioso in 1981; one step-daughter. Served prison sentence for armed robbery, San Quentin Prison, 1954-59. Clerk and semi-official computer programmer, University of California, Berkeley, 1959-63; Poet-in-Residence, University of Wisconsin, Milwaukee, Summer 1970. Founder, The Re-Geniusing Project, Berkeley, 1981. Recipient: National Endowment for the Arts grant, 1970. Address: 1432 Spruce Street, Berkeley, California, 94709, U.S.A.

PUBLICATIONS

Verse

Field Studies. El Cerrito, California, Dustbooks, 1965.
Quarter Tones. Grande Ronde, Oregon, GRR Press, 1966.
Shaman Songs. El Cerrito, California, Dustbooks, 1967.
Her Majesty's Ship. Sacramento, California, Grande Ronde Press, 1969.
Fires. Berkeley, California, Thorp Springs Press, 1971.
Vivisection. Berkeley, California, Thorp Springs Press, 1974.
Felon's Journal. San Francisco, Second Coming Press, 1975.
Fires: Selected Poems 1963-1976. Berkeley, California, Thorp Springs Press, 1975.
Return of the Shaman. San Francisco, Second Coming Press, 1981.
The Quiet Poems. Chapel Hill, North Carolina, Wren Press, 1982.

Other

Waking the Poet. Berkeley, California, Re-Geniusing Project, 1981.

*

Critical Study: by James K. Bell, in *Eikon* (Ogunquit, Maine), i, 1, 1967.

Gene Fowler comments:

(1980) There are no "positions" for non-academic poets. Officially, I am illiterate. Not qualified to teach the use of language, existing literature or other such.

I am not and have never been a member of a school of poetry—though reviewers have tried to stuff me into one or another. I battle against such entities.

Whitman wrote critical analysis of his own work—but under other names. I've done what amounts to c. a. in letters. But, here, I'll say only what I believe I'm up to. I want to write poems that when recalled are confused with the reader's own experiences, not recalled—at first—as "something read" but as "something that happened." Fighting against myth perpetuated by both outlaws and academics that craft is the same thing as academic tone. I take the Orphic myth literally. Believe words can induce and manipulate perceptions. Intend, in my poems, to prove this.

(1985) Beyond entertaining, informing, or even transforming the listener or reader with the shaped contents of poems, it's possible, in the making of the poem in the recipient's awareness, to rouse the experience-making faculties, the poet, in that listener or reader. And by guiding that poet through the shaping of my poem, to stir it to life, to "waken" it. While I teach this "waking" in seminar-workshops and in my "seminar in a book," *Waking the Poet,* the main work in my poems, too, is this "waking" of the active or working poet in my listener...or listening reader.

*   *   *

Gene Fowler is a contemporary symbolist, a maker of surprising equations. In poems like "The Lover," these equations develop dramatically, become revelations; the body of the beloved is the earth. "The Words" is a little allegory about writing:

> I carry boulders across the day
> From the field to the ridge,
> And my back grows tired...
> I take a drop of sweat
> Onto my thumb,
> Watch the wind furrow its surface,
> Dream of a morning
> When my furrows will shape this field,
> When these rocks will form my house.
> Alone, with heavy arms,
> I listen through the night to older farms.

Unlike Creeley, who has a collection titled *Words,* Fowler finds writing a heavy labor. His rhythms, in poems like "Venus Returns to the Sea," are heavy (though that is not a literal deduction from a symbolic equation). What happens to words transmuted into poems? They grow hot, like coals or fires: "i come upon stones/in the wind shoved grasses/ /they wait/ tensed/curled in on themselves/ /i reach out to touch/sun warmed quiet and flame/jumps to scorch my fingers."

Fowler's first major collection is called *Fires.* The symbols are systematically deployed. "Shaman Songs," collected in *Fires* (though mangled by the publisher), compares society to an Indian tribe and the poet to a neglected shaman. The songs rise above symbol and allegory to ritual and magic, as in "on taking coal from the fire in naked fingers": "The word/is in the hand./ Under the moon/in the hand./At the head of the valley/in the hand./It glows in the hand./Here!/Look here/in the hand./ Look at the word/in the hand./It glows./A great translucence/in the hand./Go thru the translucence/in the hand./Into the world/in the hand."

—Michael André

FRAME, Janet. New Zealander. Born in Dunedin, 28 August 1924. Educated at Oamaru North School; Waitaki Girls' High School; Otago University Teachers Training College, Dunedin. Recipient: Hubert Church Prose Award, 1952, 1964, 1974; New Zealand Literary Fund Award, 1960; New Zealand Scholarship in Letters, 1964, and Award for Achievement, 1969; Otago University Robert Burns Fellowship, 1965; Buckland Literary Award, 1967; James Wattie Award, 1983. D.Litt.: Otago University, 1978. C.B.E. (Commander, Order of the British Empire), 1983. Lives in Auckland. Agent: Brandt and Brandt, 1501 Broadway, New York, New York 10036, U.S.A.

PUBLICATIONS

Verse

The Pocket Mirror. New York, Braziller, and London, W.H. Allen, 1967.

Novels

Owls Do Cry. Christchurch, Pegasus Press, 1957; New York, Braziller, 1960; London, W.H. Allen, 1961.
Faces in the Water. Christchurch, Pegasus Press, and New York, Braziller, 1961; London, W.H. Allen, 1962.
The Edge of the Alphabet. Christchurch, Pegasus Press, New York, Braziller, and London, W.H. Allen, 1962.
Scented Gardens for the Blind. Christchurch, Pegasus Press, and London, W.H. Allen, 1963; New York, Braziller, 1964.
The Adaptable Man. Christchurch, Pegasus Press, New York, Braziller, and London, W.H. Allen, 1965.
A State of Siege. New York, Braziller, 1966; London, W.H. Allen, 1967.
The Rainbirds. London, W.H. Allen, 1968; as *Yellow Flowers in the Antipodean Room,* New York, Braziller, 1969.
Intensive Care. New York, Braziller, 1970; London, W.H. Allen, 1971.
Daughter Buffalo. New York, Braziller, 1972; London, W.H. Allen, 1973.
Living in the Maniototo. New York, Braziller, 1979; London, Women's Press, 1981.

Short Stories

The Lagoon: Stories. Christchurch, Caxton Press, 1952; revised edition, as *The Lagoon and Other Stories,* 1961.
The Reservoir: Stories and Sketches. New York, Braziller, 1963.
Snowman, Snowman: Fables and Fantasies. New York, Braziller, 1963.
The Reservoir and Other Stories. Christchurch, Pegasus Press, and London, W.H. Allen, 1966.
You Are Now Entering the Human Heart. London, Women's Press, 1984.

Other

Mona Minim and the Smell of the Sun (for children). New York, Braziller, 1969.
An Autobiography:
 1. *To the Is-Land.* New York, Braziller, 1982; London, Women's Press, 1983.
 2. *An Angel at My Table.* New York, Braziller, and London, Women's Press, 1984.

*

Bibliography: by John Beston, in *World Literature Written in English* (Arlington, Texas), November 1978.

Critical Study: *Janet Frame* by Patrick Evans, Boston, Twayne, 1977.

*   *   *

Janet Frame is best known as a novelist. She has published only one collection of poems—*The Pocket Mirror.* It has the appearance, not of a nervous slim volume of carefully selected, carefully worked samples of the writer's best, but of a file of poems, each hastily written and quickly forgotten, taken up and sent to the publisher without revision, perhaps to be rid of them. All their strengths and limitations depend on the casual indifference with which they have been written. Janet Frame is not indifferent to her subject matter but to the art of poetry itself. She is also immensely talented, endlessly inventive, fluent, and has a good ear. Her natural mode of thinking is not abstract but in images. So her poems are mostly "thoughts," "ideas," put down in the form of free verse. Their weakness is often that they are neither fish nor fowl—too abstract for the images to seem solid, hard, irreducible reality; and not rigorous enough to seem more than whimsical when considered as ideas. They are also a kind of verbal conjuring, the images conjured into being as an illustration of her thought rather than convincingly confronted in nature. Thus Miss Frame has primacy over Nature, which seems the wrong way about.

But Miss Frame has the enviable freedom of a talented writer not wholly committed to poetry. To compare her with another New Zealand woman poet, Fleur Adcock, is instructive. There can be no doubt that Miss Adcock's poems are better made—yet her work can seem crabbed and cramped when set alongside the novelist's casual fluency, which can afford so many misses and still score enough remarkable hits to make her presence as a poet felt.

—C.K. Stead

FRANCIS, Robert (Churchill). American. Born in Upland, Pennsylvania, 12 August 1901. Educated at Harvard University, Cambridge, Massachusetts, A.B. 1923, Ed.M. 1926. Phi Beta Kappa Poet, Tufts University, Medford, Massachusetts, 1955, and Harvard University, 1960. Recipient: Fémina Prize, 1934; Shelley Memorial Award, 1939; New England Poetry Club Golden Rose, 1942; American Academy in Rome Fellowship, 1957; Jennie Tane Award (*Massachusetts Review*), 1962; Amy Lowell Traveling Scholarship, 1967; Brandeis University Creative Arts Award, 1974; Academy of American Poets Fellowship, 1984. L.H.D.: University of Massachusetts, Amherst, 1970. Address: Fort Juniper, 170 Market Hill Road, Amherst, Massachusetts 01002, U.S.A.

PUBLICATIONS

Verse

Stand with Me Here. New York, Macmillan, 1936.
Valhalla and Other Poems. New York, Macmillan, 1938.

The Sound I Listened For.   New York, Macmillan, 1944.
The Face Against the Glass.   Privately printed, 1950.
The Orb Weaver: Poems.   Middletown, Connecticut, Wesleyan University Press, 1960.
Come Out into the Sun: Poems New and Selected.   Amherst, University of Massachusetts Press, 1965.
Six Poems.   Montague, Massachusetts, Sawmill Press, 1970.
Like Ghosts of Eagles: Poems 1966-1974.   Amherst, University of Massachusetts Press, 1974.
Collected Poems 1936-1976.   Amherst, University of Massachusetts Press, 1976.
Butter Hill and Other Poems.   N.p., Paul Carman, 1984.

Recordings: *Today's Poets 1*, with others, Folkways, 1967; *Robert Francis Reads His Poems*, Folkways, 1975.

Novel

We Fly Away.   New York, Swallow Press, 1948.

Other

Rome Without Camera (lecture).   Amherst, Massachusetts, Jones Library, 1958.
The Satirical Rogue on Poetry (essays).   Amherst, University of Massachusetts Press, 1968.
The Trouble with Francis: An Autobiography.   Amherst, University of Massachusetts Press, 1971.
A Certain Distance.   Woods Hole, Massachusetts, Pourboire Press, 1976.
Pot Shots at Poetry.   Ann Arbor, University of Michigan Press, 1980.

Editor, *A Time to Talk: Conversations and Indiscretions*, by Robert Frost.   Amherst, University of Massachusetts Press, 1972; London, Robson, 1973.

*

Critical Studies: "Constants Carried Forward: Naturalness in the Poetry of Robert Francis" by John Holmes, in *Massachusetts Review* (Amherst), Summer 1960; Albert Stewart, in *Masterplots: 1967 Annual*, New York, Salem Press, 1967.

Robert Francis comments:

Neither avant-garde nor traditional. Less and less dependence on accepted forms while stressing form itself, the forming of the poem. Early poems, quiet and brooding; later poems, more active and colorful. During the 60's some poems in a new technique I call "word-count." Still more recently poems that explore surface fragmentation to intensify impact of total poem.

*   *   *

Robert Francis is a balanced poet, both in art and sensibility. Although his rhythms are variable, his rhyming flexible, his language fresh, and his world is an out-of-doors and immediate universe, his poems are carefully structured, often too carefully structured. And, although his outlook is mature and in some ways profound, it is more placid and complacent than intense and compelling. Each poem represents a serene process of unfolding rather than a shocking flash of revelation, suffering from a kind of overdevelopment caused by excessive explicitness in dealing with the material and drawing out its meaning. And this in turn, paradoxically, seems to be the effect of a certain limitation of insight, as if over-explicitness were a compensation for deficiency of vision and passionate involvement.

The first section of *The Orb Weaver*, for example, deals largely with skill and the analogies the poet sees between various bodily skills and those of art. He writes about boys riding horses, baseball players, wrestlers, divers, swimmers, and so on. And his interest lies in the tension of balance that such skills must sustain between opposing forces. And yet, as in "Two Wrestlers," all is too perfectly balanced and worked out; he at once says too much and implies too little. The second section is mainly about Nature—her fruits, seasons, mountains, creatures, and so on. These are good poems, and they speak movingly of fulness. "Waxwings," for example, depends more for its effect on imagery and less on explanation than usual: "Four Tao philosophers as cedar waxwings/chat on a February berrybush/in sun, and I am one." Section III is primarily concerned with the relation of people to Nature. "The Revellers" is one of the most effective, portraying crowds joyously enthralled by summer, and so is reminiscent of Stevens' "Sunday Morning" and "Credences of Summer" but it is, alas, almost entirely without the greater poet's depth and intensity. The fourth section gets darker, dwelling more on the side of night and winter, and the stanza-patterns become more regular, perhaps as a sign of the need to control a threatening mood. "Three Darks Come Down Together" is quite good. The fifth and final section is darker still, dealing with death, winter, and loss. Robert Frost is a strong influence, and this becomes most specific in the title poem, "The Orb Weaver," which is about a ghastly spider much like the one in Frost's "Design." A reading of Francis' conclusion, however, will not sustain the comparison: "I have no quarrel with the spider/But with the mind or mood that made her/To thrive in nature and in man's nature." "Two Bums Walk Out of Eden," though, is interesting, and "Cold," which describes a freeze, is excellent:

> Under the glaring and sardonic sun,
> Behind the icicles and double glass
> I huddle, hoard, hold out, hold on, hold on.

Collected Poems 1936-1976 contains *The Orb Weaver*, all of his previous volumes, plus his most recent ones, *Come Out into the Sun* and *Like Ghosts of Eagles*. His development, as he says in his Preface, is becoming "bolder and livelier," and it is true that his recent work shows significant signs of diversification in mood, style, and structure. He is experimenting with word count, fragmented surface, and fused syntax. And yet he remains by and large objective and impersonal, not in the modernist sense of integrating the intensely subjective into the controlling structure of the poem, but rather in the sense of being simply an observer—acute, perceptive, witty, but with neither an anguished self that must wrestle with experience nor an ability to blend with and dramatize the anguish of others. Too much of his autobiography is kept from his poems; indeed, much of it is rather low-keyed in *The Trouble with Francis*, his autobiography, itself.

—Norman Friedman

FRASER, Kathleen.   American.   Born in Tulsa, Oklahoma, 22 March 1937. Educated at Occidental College, Los Angeles, B.A. in English 1959; Columbia University and New School for Social Research, both New York, 1960-61; San Francisco State University, 1976-77, Doctoral Equivalency in creative writing.

Married Jack Marshall, *q.v.*, in 1961 (divorced, 1970); one son. Visiting Professor, Writers Workshop, University of Iowa, Iowa City, 1969-71; Writer-in-Residence, Reed College, Portland, Oregon, 1971-72. Director of the Poetry Center, 1972-75, and since 1975, Associate Professor of Creative Writing, San Francisco State University. Recipient: YM-YWHA Discovery Award, 1964; National Endowment for the Arts grant, 1969, and Fellowship, 1978. Address: Department of English, San Francisco State University, 1600 Holloway Avenue, San Francisco, California 94132, U.S.A.

PUBLICATIONS

Verse

Change of Address and Other Poems.   San Francisco, Kayak, 1966.
In Defiance of the Rains.   Santa Cruz, California, Kayak, 1969.
Little Notes to You from Lucas Street.   Iowa City, Penumbra Press, 1972.
What I Want.   New York, Harper, 1974.
Magritte Series.   Willits, California, Tuumba Press, 1978.
New Shoes.   New York, Harper, 1978.

Recording: *The Poetry of Kathleen Fraser*, McGraw Hill, n.d.

Other (for children)

Stilts, Somersaults, and Headstands: Game Poems Based on a Painting by Peter Breughel.   New York, Atheneum, 1968.
Adam's World: San Francisco, with Miriam F. Levy.   Chicago, Whitman, 1971.

*

Kathleen Fraser comments:

My poetry has moved from girlish, Plath-fed lyrics, first published in the mid-1960's, towards a recognition—inside the poem—of life as a more undecided and precarious process. Language is, for me, exploratory—the fluid and changing record of daily risk-taking. I use my writing to locate myself in particulars, to catch the multiplicity, the layering of thoughts, feelings, visual impressions experienced simultaneously. Writing is, in a sense, taking a reading on what has thus far transpired and what my attitude toward it is...there is, hopefully, a movement back and forth. I use my poetry as my most serious way of paying attention to the world outside of my own interior struggle. The poems begin as acts of attention and try to allow in whatever is there waiting to make itself heard. And seen. I regard the ability to write as a gift which must be honored with the utmost seriousness. My great permission-giver, in learning to use that gift, was Frank O'Hara. He still appears in my dreams as a guide and friend. I am also deeply indebted to Virginia Woolf and Gertrude Stein, for complexity. American jazz (particulary Eddie Jefferson's lyrics and Betty Carter's scat) has made a much greater range of tonalities and movements available to me. Painting has always been important and often provides paths to unconscious material which I bring into the poetry. Surely my father's early chanting of limericks and lyrics from *Alice* and *Through the Looking-Glass* will always be there as playful resonance in my work. And my mother's singing. To catch the exact angle of light as two planes shift. To catch the unbroken moment between two people and speak it.

*   *   *

Kathleen Fraser's subjects are those of many of the women poets of her generation: sexual love, marriage, divorce, motherhood—the business of day-to-day survival in a busy and confusing world. The special distinction Fraser brings to these subjects is one of *tone*; an unusual attentiveness coupled with a nice comic detachment, a buoyancy and warmth that make the most ordinary incidents seem special.

Fraser's command of the ethical argument had to be learned; her early poems do not always avoid a self-conscious Sylvia Plath note: "Feelings stick to me like expensive glue," or, in a poem about pregnancy, "Is it you? Are you there, / thief I can't see...New mystery floating up my left arm, clinging to the curtain." Such metaphors are merely clever, and Fraser soon turned from the elaboration of metaphysical conceits to the surrealistic image, the boundary between what really happens and what one imagines dissolving:

> But over here, where it's dark out,
>   I'm just me
>   feeling uneasy in these nights
> cold and black.
>   I turn the heat up
>   higher
>   thinking other people's lives
> are warmer....

The playful self-mockery of this passage recalls Frank O'Hara as well as Kenneth Koch with whom Kathleen Fraser studied. From both these poets, she learned, in the words of Charles Olson's "Projective Verse," how to "keep it moving." In "Because You Aren't Here to Be What I Can't Think Of," for instance, Fraser invents a dazzling inventory, reminiscent of Koch's "Sleeping with Women" or O'Hara's "Having a Coke with You." In this catalogue poem, the speaker blithely tries to convince herself that she is *not* going to care about her lover's involvement with someone else, all the while doing everything in her power to conjure up his presence. The distance between the lovers takes on fantastic proportions: "Because the moon's another streetlight and your lights are off, and on in someone else's," or "Because there's a saxophone playing between our telephones but you can't pick it up." Yet, injured party that she is, the speaker wryly and wisely concludes that, life being what it is, things could be worse: "because I'm not on a dancefloor with you, but here, / hanging out with my shadow over a city of windows, / lit-up, imagining another kind of life almost like this one." The lover's absence is irritating but not, finally, tragic. The same rueful comedy is found in "The Fault," in which the poet watches another woman make the wrong moves to a man she herself has not hitherto paid much notice, but whom she now suddenly finds an attractive challenge:

> I felt myself in love with him watching his tongue run over
>   his lips
> and remembered Fredericka
>
>   always keeping the tube of vaseline in her purse
> always gliding it over her mouth should there be someone
>   to kiss
>
> and thought how I liked space and long unending lines,
>   how my life
> was that way, without visible connections or obvious
>   explanations

                                           how I was glad
I'd washed my hair

This is a witty analysis of a woman's momentary self-satisfaction, of the pleasure that fortuitous circumstances sometimes bring. Other poems in her recent book *New Shoes*, most notably the "Magritte Series," give this kind of material more complex treatment. The Magritte poems are not "about" the paintings that give them their titles; rather, Fraser uses a given Magritte as a stimulus for psychological exploration. Take "L'Invention Collective / Collective Invention," which is based on Magritte's grotesque and haunting image of a sort of reverse-mermaid: a fish with human legs, slender and feminine, and pubic hair. In Magritte's painting, the fish-woman is oddly erotic and repulsive; the single blank fish eye confronts the beholder, whose eye is drawn downward to her (its?) lower parts. She lies on the edge of the beach, the white-caps of a silly blue ocean beating pointlessly behind her. Fraser invents a narrative that can incorporate this image: her story is of a tacky, domestic heroine, part comic-book, part fairy-tale, whose role in life is to keep things "neat and tidy," so that she is quite unable to "see / her seducers in a line and shaking their fingers." Only in her dreams does she see herself lying "at the edge of the waters," the sand scratching her body, and watches herself turn into a fish: "a face cut deep with gills and the sad eyes panting / and the absolute quiet of something about to arrive." What this something is we don't know but it is frightening, in the poem as well as in the Magritte painting. The pose of the figure invites rape, but what would that mean in this context? Fraser is playing with notions of smugness and self-deception, exploring the fantasy life of the little woman who wanted life for herself and her little boy to be "as fresh as Watermelon slice."

In her recent prose poems—for example, "Green and Blue Piece for Francie Swimming, in Which Grace Enters"—Fraser is moving further in the direction of the "painterly" poem, the text as elaborate word-system in which a fixed number of items, here the colors "blue" and "green," the "body swimming," the words of Grace and the paint strokes of Francie, undergo a series of permutations until nothing remains what it once was. If "Green and Blue Piece" is less jaunty than Fraser's previous work, it has a new explanatory quality, probing behind the surfaces of personal relationships. As she puts it in one of the Magritte poems, "The secrets between men and women are of peculiar fascination."

—Marjorie Perloff

FRY, Christopher. British. Born Christopher Fry Harris in Bristol, 18 December 1907. Educated at Bedford Modern School, 1918-26. Served in the Non-Combatant Corps, 1940-44. Married Phyllis Marjorie Hart in 1936; one son. Teacher, Bedford Froebel Kindergarten, 1926-27; actor and office worker, Citizen House, Bath, 1927; schoolmaster, Hazelwood School, Limpsfield, Surrey, 1928-31; secretary to H. Rodney Bennett, 1931-32; Founding Director, Tunbridge Wells Repertory Players, 1932-35; lecturer and editor of schools magazine, Dr. Barnardo's Homes, 1934-39; Director, 1939-40, and Visiting Director, 1945-46, Oxford Playhouse; Visiting Director, 1946, and Staff Dramatist, 1947, Arts Theatre Club, London. Also composer. Recipient: Shaw Prize Fund Award, 1948; Foyle Poetry Prize, 1951; New York Drama Critics Circle Award, 1951, 1952, 1956; Queen's Gold Medal for Poetry, 1962; Heinemann Award, 1962. Fellow, Royal Society of Literature. Agent: ACTAC Ltd.,

16 Cadogan Lane, London S.W.1. Address: The Toft, East Dean, near Chichester, West Sussex PO18 0JA, England.

PUBLICATIONS

Verse

Root and Sky: Poetry from the Plays of Christopher Fry, edited by Charles E. and Jean G. Wadsworth. Cambridge, Rampant Lions Press, and Boston, Godine, 1975.

Plays

Youth and the Peregrines (produced Tunbridge Wells, Kent, 1934).
She Shall Have Music (lyrics only, with Ronald Frankau), book by Frank Eyton, music by Fry and Monte Crick (produced London, 1934).
To Sea in a Sieve (as Christopher Harris) (revue: produced Reading, 1935).
Open Door (produced London, 1936). Goldings, Hertfordshire, Printed by the Boys at the Press of Dr. Barnardo's Homes, n.d.
The Boy with a Cart: Cuthman, Saint of Sussex (produced Coleman's Hatch, Sussex, 1938; London, 1950; New York, 1953). London, Oxford University Press, 1939; New York, Oxford University Press, 1951.
The Tower (pageant; produced Tewkesbury, Gloucestershire, 1939).
Thursday's Child: A Pageant, music by Martin Shaw (produced London, 1939). London, Girls' Friendly Society, 1939.
A Phoenix Too Frequent (produced London, 1946; Cambridge, Massachusetts, 1948; New York, 1950). London, Hollis and Carter, 1946; New York, Oxford University Press, 1949.
The Firstborn (broadcast, 1947; produced Edinburgh, 1948). Cambridge, University Press, 1946; New York, Oxford University Press, 1950; revised version (produced London, 1952; New York, 1958), London and New York, Oxford University Press, 1952, 1958.
The Lady's Not for Burning (produced London, 1948; New York, 1950). London and New York, Oxford University Press, 1949; revised version, 1950, 1958.
Thor, With Angels (produced Canterbury, 1948; Washington, D.C., 1950; London, 1951). Canterbury, H.J. Goulden, 1948; New York, Oxford University Press, 1949.
Venus Observed (produced London, 1950; New York, 1952). London and New York, Oxford University Press, 1950.
Ring round the Moon: A Charade with Music, adaptation of a play by Jean Anouilh (produced London and New York, 1950). London and New York, Oxford University Press, 1950.
A Sleep of Prisoners (produced Oxford, London and New York, 1951). London and New York, Oxford University Press, 1951.
The Dark Is Light Enough: A Winter Comedy (produced Edinburgh and London, 1954; New York, 1955). London and New York, Oxford University Press, 1954.
The Lark, adaptation of a play by Jean Anouilh (produced London, 1955). London, Methuen, 1955; New York, Oxford University Press, 1956.
Tiger at the Gates, adaptation of a play by Jean Giraudoux (produced London and New York, 1955). London, Methuen, 1955; New York, Oxford University Press, 1956; as *The Trojan War Will Not Take Place* (produced London, 1983), Methuen, 1983.

Duel of Angels, adaptation of a play by Jean Giraudoux (produced London, 1958; New York, 1960).   London, Methuen, 1958; New York, Oxford University Press, 1959.

Curtmantle (produced Tilburg, Holland, 1961; London, 1962).   London and New York, Oxford University Press, 1961.

Judith, adaptation of a play by Jean Giraudoux (produced London, 1962).   London, Methuen, 1962.

The Bible: Original Screenplay, assisted by Jonathan Griffin.   New York, Pocket Books, 1966.

Peer Gynt, adaptation of the play by Ibsen (produced Chichester, 1970).   London and New York, Oxford University Press, 1970.

A Yard of Sun: A Summer Comedy (produced Nottingham and London, 1970; Cleveland, 1972).   London and New York, Oxford University Press, 1970.

The Brontës of Haworth (televised, 1973).   London, Davis Poynter, 2 vols., 1974.

Cyrano de Bergerac, adaptation of the play by Edmond Rostand (produced Chichester, 1975).   London and New York, Oxford University Press, 1975.

Paradise Lost, music by Penderecki, adaptation of the poem by Milton (produced Chicago, 1978).   London, Schott, 1978.ty

Screenplays: *The Beggar's Opera*, with Denis Cannan, 1953; *The Queen Is Crowned* (documentary), 1953; *Ben Hur*, 1959; *Barabbas*, 1962; *The Bible: In the Beginning*, 1966.

Radio Plays: for *Children's Hour* series, 1939-40; *The Firstborn*, 1947; *Rhineland Journey*, 1948.

Television Plays: *The Canary*, 1950; *The Tenant of Wildfell Hall*, 1968; *The Brontës of Haworth* (four plays), 1973; *The Best of Enemies*, 1976; *Sister Dora*, from the book by Jo Manton, 1977.

Other

An Experience of Critics, with *The Approach to Dramatic Criticism* by W.A. Darlington and others, edited by Kaye Webb.   London, Perpetua Press, 1952; New York, Oxford University Press, 1953.

The Boat That Mooed (for children).   New York, Macmillan, 1966.

Can You Find Me: A Family History.   London, Oxford University Press, 1978; New York, Oxford University Press, 1979.

Death Is a Kind of Love (lecture).   Cranberry Isles, Maine, Tidal Press, 1979.

Translator, *The Boy and the Magic*, by Colette.   London, Dobson, 1964.

Incidental Music: *A Winter's Tale*, London, 1951; recorded by Cáedmon.

                                        *

Bibliography: "A Bibliography on Fry" by B.L. Schear and E.G. Prater, in *Tulane Drama Review 4* (New Orleans), March 1960.

Critical Studies: *Christopher Fry: An Appreciation*, London, Nevill, 1950, and *Christopher Fry*, London, Longman, 1954, revised edition, 1962, both by Derek Stanford; *The Drama of Comedy: Victim and Victor* by Nelson Vos, Richmond, Virginia, John Knox Press, 1965; *Creed and Drama* by W.M. Merchant, London, SPCK, 1965; *The Christian Tradition in Modern British Verse Drama* by William V. Spanos, New Brunswick,

New Jersey, Rutgers University Press, 1967; *Christopher Fry* by Emil Roy, Carbondale, Southern Illinois University Press, 1968: *Chrisopher Fry: A Critical Essay*, Grand Rapids, Michigan, Eerdmans, 1970, and *More Than the Ear Discovers: God in the Plays of Christopher Fry*, Chicago, Loyola University Press, 1983, both by Stanley M. Wiersma.

Theatrical Activities:
Director: **Plays**—*How-Do, Princess?* by Ivor Novello, toured, 1936; *The Circle of Chalk* by James Laver, London, 1945; *The School for Scandal* by Sheridan, London, 1946; *A Phoenix Too Frequent*, Brighton, 1950; *The Lady's Not for Burning*, toured, 1971; and others.

Actor: **Plays**—in repertory, Bath, 1937.

Christopher Fry comments:

Influences are difficult to pin-point. Certainly, as it must be with anyone of my generation, T.S. Eliot was a releasing factor. In the plays I have tried to work towards an end which I broadly expressed in a lecture: "No event is understandable in a prose sense alone. Its ultimate meaning (that is to say, the complete life of the event, seen in its eternal context) is a poetic meaning." I have tried to shape a verse form (a metrical system) which could contain both the "theatrical" elements (rhetoric, broad colours, etc.) and the rhythms and tone of the colloquial, which would work for the "artificial comedy," or the historical, or the conversation of the present time.

                        *   *   *

It was Christopher Fry (and, later, T.S. Eliot) who led the short revival of interest in the poetic drama during the decade or so after the second world war—an interest which now seems completely dead. *A Phoenix Too Frequent*, an imperfect sentimental farce, attracted some attention in 1946; and with *The Lady's Not for Burning* Fry captured the imagination of the critics, and of a potentially large audience. The most obviously brilliant of Fry's plays, it was fortunate in an impeccable production by John Gielgud, and a fine cast, headed by Pamela Brown, Claire Bloom, Richard Burton and Gielgud himself. Its amusing plot and the natural yet highly decorated language, finely characterised and surpemely dramatic (Fry himself wås for some time an actor), were a revelation after the dryness and aridity of the language of wartime drama. Over-succulent on the page, the verse (especially when delivered in the romantic style of acting still predominant in the late 1940's) seemed irresistible in performance.

But as Fry's technical assurance grew, so critical and public interest waned. *Venus Observed*, written for Laurence Olivier, was a critical and to some extent public failure; a graver comedy of autumn, its language was more disciplined and restrained, still often witty, but quieter and without the obvious verbal fireworks of its predecessor. In *A Sleep of Prisoners*, perhaps his most entirely successful piece, Fry turned to wholly serious matters, and most obviously to his perennial theme of "the growth of vision: the increased perception of what makes for life and what makes for death." Prisoners-of-war penned up in a Church explore each other's personalities in their dreams. It is a moving and totally realised poetic drama. *The Dark Is Light Enough*, a winter play based on Fabre's parable of the butterfly making its way through storm and profound darkness to arrive brightly inviolate at its destination, was written for Edith Evans and staged in 1954. It was disliked both by critics and by the public. Since its production Fry has concentrated for the most part on translation (from Anouilh and Giraudoux, for instance) and film scripting. He has, however, written a play which completes the quartet of plays of the seasons—a comedy of high summer.

His place in the theatre is perhaps ephemeral; he has been compared, damagingly, to the Victorian poetic dramatist Stephen Phillips, whose *Paolo and Francesca* seemed at the turn of the century to be a masterpiece, but is now almost totally forgotten. The comparison seems unfair; Fry is more accomplished both as poet and dramatist than Phillips. His language is, on the page, overblown, and seems lacking in muscle and discipline. But in performance it is always amusing and dramatically viable; and its sentiment is at worst harmlessly touching. It is strange now to remember that many critics found Fry "difficult" in the 1940's and 50's. Whatever he is, he is not that. Accused of over-writing ("Too many words!") Fry replied (in *An Experience of Critics*, 1952): "It means, I think, that I don't use the same words often enough; or else, or as well, that the words are an ornament on the meaning and not the meaning itself. That is certainly sometimes—perhaps often—true in the comedies, though almost as often I have meant the ornament to be, dramatically or comedically, an essential part of the meaning; and in my more sanguine moments I think the words are as exact to my purpose as I could make them at the time of writing."

Posterity may find this claim to be true. It is unlikely that he is in any sense a major writer, but within his own set limits Fry is a craftsman of considerable accomplishment, and where he is most successful, he is memorable.

—Derek Parker

FULLER, John (Leopold). British. Born in Ashford, Kent, 1 January 1937; son of Roy Fuller, *q.v.* Educated at St. Paul's School; New College, Oxford (Newdigate Prize, 1960), B.A. 1960, M.A. 1964, B. Litt. 1965. Married Cicely Prudence Martin in 1960; three daughters. Visiting Lecturer, State University of New York, Buffalo, 1962-63; Assistant Lecturer, Manchester University, 1963-66. Since 1966, Fellow of Magdalen College, Oxford. Publisher, Sycamore Press, Oxford. Recipient: Richard Hillary Memorial Prize, 1961; Eric Gregory Award, 1965; Faber Memorial Prize, 1974; Prudence Farmer Prize (*New Statesman*), 1975; Southern Arts prize, 1980; Cholmondeley Award, 1983; Whitbread Award, 1983. Address: 4 Benson Place. Oxford, England.

PUBLICATIONS

Verse

Fairground Music. London, Chatto and Windus-Hogarth Press, 1961.
The Tree That Walked. London, Chatto and Windus-Hogarth Press, 1967.
The Art of Love. Oxford, The Review, 1968.
The Labours of Hercules: A Sonnet Sequence. Manchester, Manchester Institute of Contemporary Arts, 1969.
Three London Songs, music by Bryan Kelly. London, Novello, 1969.
Annotations of Giant's Town. London, Poem-of-the-Month Club, 1970.
The Wreck. London, Turret, 1970.
Cannibals and Missionaries. London, Secker and Warburg, 1972.

Boys in a Pie. London, Steam Press, 1972.
Hut Groups. Hitchin, Hertfordshire, Cellar Press, 1973.
Penguin Modern Poets 22, with Adrian Mitchell and Peter Levi. London, Penguin, 1973.
Epistles to Several Persons. London, Secker and Warburg, 1973.
Poems and Epistles. Boston, Godine, 1974.
Squeaking Crust (for children). London, Chatto and Windus, 1974.
A Bestiary. Oxford, Sycamore Press, 1974.
The Mountain in the Sea. London, Secker and Warburg, 1975.
Bel and the Dragon. Oxford, Sycamore Press, 1977.
The Wilderness. Buffalo, Lockwood Memorial Library, 1977.
Lies and Secrets. London, Secker and Warburg, 1979.
The Illusionists: A Tale. London, Secker and Warburg, 1980.
The January Divan. Hitchin, Hertfordshire, Mandeville Press, 1980.
The Ship of Sounds. Sidcot, Somerset, Gruffyground, 1981.
Waiting for the Music. Edinburgh, Salamander Press, 1982.
The Beautiful Inventions. London, Secker and Warburg, 1983.
Come Aboard and Sail Away (for children). Edinburgh, Salamander Press, 1983.

Plays

Herod Do Your Worst, music by Bryan Kelly (produced Thame, Oxfordshire, 1967). London, Novello, 1968.
Half a Fortnight, music by Bryan Kelly (produced Leicester, 1970). London, Novello, 1973.
The Spider Monkey Uncle King, music by Bryan Kelly (produced Cookham, Berkshire, 1971). London, Novello, 1975.
Fox-Trot, music by Bryan Kelly (produced Leicester, 1972).
The Queen in the Golden Tree, music by Bryan Kelly (produced Edinburgh, 1974).
How Did You Get Here, Jonno?, music by Bryan Kelly (produced Wolverhampton, 1975).
The Ship of Sounds, music by Bryan Kelly (produced Leicester, 1975).
Adam's Apple, music by Bryan Kelly (produced Abingdon, Oxfordshire, 1975).
Linda, music by Bryan Kelly (produced Reading, 1975).
St. Francis of Assisi, music by Bryan Kelly (produced London, 1981).

Novel

Flying to Nowhere. Edinburgh, Salamander Press, 1983; New York, Braziller, 1984.

Other

A Reader's Guide to W.H. Auden. London, Thames and Hudson, and New York, Farrar Straus, 1970.
The Sonnet. London, Methuen, 1972.
The Last Bid (for children). London, Deutsch, 1975.
Carving Trifles: William King's Imitation of Horace (lecture). London, Oxford University Press, 1976.
The Extraordinary Wool Mill and Other Stories (for children). London, Deutsch, 1980.

Editor, with others, *Light Blue Dark Blue: An Anthology of Recent Writings from Oxford and Cambridge Universities.* London, Macdonald, 1960.
Editor, *Oxford Poetry 1960.* Oxford, Fantasy Press, 1960.
Editor, *Poetry Supplement.* London, Poetry Book Society, 1962.

Editor, with Harold Pinter and Peter Redgrove, *New Poems 1967*. London, Hutchinson, 1968.
Editor, *Poetry Supplement*. London, Poetry Book Society, 1970.
Editor, *Nemo's Almanac*. Oxford, Sycamore Press, 1971.
Editor, *New Poetry 8*. London, Hutchinson, 1982.
Editor, *Dramatic Works*, by John Gay. Oxford, Clarendon Press, 2 vols., 1983.
Editor, with Howard Sergeant, *The Gregory Poets 1983-84*. Edinburgh, Salamander Press, 1984.

*

Critical Study: "The Poetry of John Fuller" by Edward Mendelson, in *New Republic* (Washington, D.C.), 28 May 1977.

*   *   *

Though appreciating John Fuller's technical control, skilled craftsmanship, and intelligence, reviewers have also noted "a seriousness lacking at the heart of his work," "the impression of a rooted reticence," and a "sense of uneasiness." This versatile and intellectual poet ranges from entertaining light verse (such as "An Exchange Between the Fingers and the Toes" in *The Tree That Walked* and "Sorrel" or "Valentine" in *The Beautiful Inventions*) to discerning and provocative explorations of doubts, deceptions, and dissemblings—indeed, often showing "a massive concentration on the things we find uncertain" ("Sonata" in *Waiting for the Music*). At times, as in *The Illusionists*, the comic and the serious are ingeniously and inextricably combined.

Despite this diversity, all his poems are accomplished, elegant, and technically sophisticated. His control of language and of form—concern with technique, structure and order, and the manipulation of words—produces a detachment that moderates the immediate impact of the ideas expressed by the poems (rather than the poet) but makes them no less powerful. Indeed, the power of the poetry lies in the artfulness with which meanings are implied rather than directly stated whether through jokes, riddles, and word-games (as in *Lies and Secrets* or *The Illusionists*) or through the astonishing, unexpected imagery that he frequently employs as in the sea associations of "Girl with Coffee Tray" (*Fairground Music*), the speaking hedges in "Hedge Tutor" (*The Tree That Walked*), or the little boy with the toy tank in "Galata Bridge" (*The Beautiful Inventions*).

In *The Illusionists* Fuller comments that "similes should make you see / What otherwise is just asserted," and insists that,

> ...the poet retails
> Only the goods he wants to stock.
> Go to life's warehouse to unlock
> That gloomy inventory of details
> You need to validate the truth:
> Put down the book and hire a sleuth.

Earlier, in "A Dialogue Between Caliban and Ariel" (*Fairground Music*), he notes the limitations of language in contemplating, mirroring, or determining truth or reality. "For all their declaration / And complexity, / Words cannot see..." and are mere tokens ("Words are but counters in a childish game...") rather than agents or effective tools ("Words would not help the channeled sea to prove / It was not ocean-free, nor pine no fuel...").

The similarities often seen between Fuller's and Auden's poetry make the above noted "rooted reticence" less a criticism, perhaps, than a reminder of Auden's lines: "truth in any serious sense, / Like orthodoxy, is a reticence" ("The Truest Poetry Is the Most Feigning"), while the "sense of uneasiness" might arise from Fuller's overriding dependence on the order and structure of a poem rather than on the words themselves. There are limits to what can be articulated or directly stated in poetry and, for Auden, the success of a poem is achieved by the "luck of verbal playing"—at which John Fuller is unquestionably very clever indeed—rather than by assertion or declaration.

—B.T. Kugler

FULLER, Roy (Broadbent). British. Born in Failsworth, Lancashire, 11 February 1912. Educated at Blackpool High School, Lancashire; qualified as a solicitor, 1934. Served in the Royal Navy, 1941-46; Lieutenant, Royal Naval Volunteer Reserve. Married Kathleen Smith in 1936; one son, John Fuller, *q.v.* Assistant Solicitor, 1938-58, Solicitor, 1958-69, and since 1969, Director, Woolwich Equitable Building Society, London. Chairman of the Legal Advisory Panel, 1958-69, and since 1969, a Vice-President, Building Societies Association. Professor of Poetry, Oxford University, 1968-73. Chairman, Poetry Book Society, London, 1960-68; Governor, BBC, 1972-79; Member, Arts Council of Great Britian, and Chairman of the Literature Panel, 1976-77 (resigned). Recipient: Arts Council Poetry Award, 1959; Duff Cooper Memorial Prize, 1968; Queen's Gold Medal for Poetry, 1970; Cholmondeley Award, 1980. M.A.: Oxford University. Fellow, Royal Society of Literature, 1958. C.B.E. (Commander, Order of the British Empire), 1970. Address: 37 Langton Way, Blackheath, London S.E.3, England.

PUBLICATIONS

Verse

Poems. London, Fortune Press, 1940.
The Middle of a War. London, Hogarth Press, 1942.
A Lost Season. London, Hogarth Press, 1944.
Epitaphs and Occasions. London, Lehmann, 1949.
Counterparts. London, Vershoyle, 1954.
Brutus's Orchard. London, Deutsch, 1957; New York, Macmillan, 1958.
Collected Poems 1936-1961. London, Deutsch, 1962.
Buff. London, Deutsch, 1965.
New Poems. London, Deutsch, 1968.
Pergamon Poets 1, with R.S. Thomas, edited by Evan Owen. Oxford, Pergamon Press, 1968.
Off Course. London, Turret, 1969.
Penguin Modern Poets 18, with A. Alvarez and Anthony Thwaite. London, Penguin, 1970.
To an Unknown Reader. London, Poem-of-the-Month Club, 1970.
Song Cycle from a Record Sleeve. Oxford, Sycamore Press, 1972.
Tiny Tears. London, Deutsch, 1973.
An Old War. Edinburgh, Tragara Press, 1974.
Waiting for the Barbarians: A Poem. Richmond, Surrey, Keepsake Press, 1974.
From the Joke Shop. London, Deutsch, 1975.
The Joke Shop Annexe. Edinburgh, Tragara Press, 1975.
An Ill-Governed Coast. Sunderland, Ceolfrith Press, 1976.
Re-treads. Edinburgh, Tragara Press, 1979.

The Reign of Sparrows.   London, London Magazine Editions, 1980.
The Individual and His Times: A Selection of the Poetry of Roy Fuller, edited by V.J. Lee.   London, Athlone Press, 1982.
House and Shop.   Edinburgh, Tragara Press, 1982.
As from the Thirties.   Edinburgh, Tragara Press, 1983.
Mianserin Sonnets.   Edinburgh, Tragara Press, 1984.

Novels

The Second Curtain.   London, Verschoyle, 1953; New York, Macmillan, 1956.
Fantasy and Fugue.   London, Verschoyle, 1954; New York, Macmillan, 1956.
Image of a Society.   London, Deutsch, 1956; New York, Macmillan, 1957.
The Ruined Boys.   London, Deutsch, 1959; as *That Distant Afternoon,* New York, Macmillan, 1959.
The Father's Comedy.   London, Deutsch, 1961.
The Perfect Fool.   London, Deutsch, 1963.
My Child, My Sister.   London, Deutsch, 1965.
The Carnal Island.   London, Deutsch, 1970.

Other (for children)

Savage Gold   London, Lehmann, 1946.
With My Little Eye.   London, Lehmann, 1948; New York, Macmillan, 1957.
Catspaw.   London, Alan Ross, 1966.
Seen Grandpa Lately?   London, Deutsch, 1972.
Poor Roy.   London, Deutsch, 1977.
The Other Planet and Three Other Fables.   Richmond, Surrey, Keepsake Press, 1979.
More about Tompkins and Other Light Verse.   Edinburgh, Tragara Press, 1981.
Upright, Downfall, with Barbara Giles and Adrian Rumble.   Oxford, Oxford University Press, 1983.

Other

Owls and Artificers: Oxford Lectures on Poetry.   London, Deutsch, and New York, Library Press, 1971.
Professors and Gods: Last Oxford Lectures on Poetry.   London, Deutsch, 1973; New York, St. Martin's Press, 1974.
Souvenirs (memoirs).   London, London Magazine Editions, 1980.
Vamp Till Ready: Further Memoirs.   London, London Magazine Editions, 1982.
Home and Dry: Memoirs 3.   London, London Magazine Editions, 1984.

Editor, *Byron for Today.*   London, Porcupine Press, 1948.
Editor, with Clifford Dyment and Montagu Slater, *New Poems 1952.*   London, Joseph, 1952.
Editor, *The Building Societies Acts 1874-1960: Great Britain and Northern Ireland,* 5th edition.   London, Franey, 1961.
Editor, *Supplement of New Poetry.*   London, Poetry Book Society, 1964.
Editor, *Fellow Mortals: An Anthology of Animal Verse.*   Plymouth, Macdonald and Evans, 1981.

*

Manuscript Collections: State University of New York, Buffalo; British Library, London; Brotherton Collection, Leeds University.

Critical Studies: "Private Images of Public Ills: The Poetry of Roy Fuller" by George Woodcock, in *Wascana Review 4* (Regina, Saskatchewan), 1969; *Roy Fuller* by Allan E. Austin, Boston, Twayne, 1979; "Deane Me Today" by Neil Powell, in *PN Review 21* (Manchester), 1981.

*   *   *

The themes of Roy Fuller's earliest poetry, which was very much influenced by poets of the 1930's, are largely social and political, though they do not describe particular events or issues. His style, too, was markedly Audenesque, as in, for instance, "August 1938" with its references to "the sexy lighthouse" beneath "the usual sky" and "the pleasure towns where most / Have come to live or die." Some of these verbal mannerisms and social themes persist for some time after the war, but increasingly the poems are about personal fears and anxieties. Indeed the principal subject of the war poems is the worries, the boredom, the sense of loneliness of servicemen separated by the War from loved ones. As the war closes one poem ("During a Bombardment by V-Weapons") notes the return of the "real" world:

> And love I see your pallor bears
> A far more pointed threat than steel
> Now all the permanent and real
> Furies are settling in upstairs.

A persistent theme, however, of his poetry since the war has been his sense of the imminence of world disaster ("Doom, total of the human race," "Obituary of R. Fuller"). "The Lake" envisages a later Gibbon by Lake Geneva translating "Our frightful end to ornamental prose." He is continually aware of the frailty of life and the nightmare of possible human disaster. There is some consolation to be found in nature's capacity for survival ("The Lawn, Spring and Summer"). But even this hope is tentative—life is so frail, and, in any case, man's successor may prove even more of an oppressor: "Though who's to say the formic city less / Unjust than ours, and that the dove, evolved / Wouldn't impose tyrannical modes of love?" ("Elephant, Ants, Doves"). The images used in connection with this theme are often autumnal or of disease, and a parallel is frequently drawn between our world and the last days of the Roman Empire threatened by barbarian invasion.

Another major theme running throughout Fuller's poetry is art. Many of the poems draw their subjects from the worlds of art, literature, and music, and are preoccupied with the creative process, the function of art, and particularly the relation of art to life. Poetry tries to be exact and truthful but inevitably it falsifies the reality it seeks to portray. The successful image pleases but distorts in the very process of producing art: "words alone / ...are, like all art, condemned / To failure in the sense that they succeed" ("Expostulation and Inadequate Reply"). All the artist can do is attempt to be as truthful as possible.

In "Dedicatory Epistle" (*Collected Poems*) Fuller describes his style as "a muted, sparse accompaniment" to the times we live in, and certainly his poetry does not contain many vivid and sensuous phrases. The tone is generally thoughtful, sometimes self-mocking and sardonic. Frequently his technique is to begin a poem with a minute and particular description of an object, a landscape, a bird or animal, and to use this as a starting-point for his thoughts on some general aspect of human behaviour and emotion. So in "Ambiguities" he notes a blackbird suffering from "some malignancy" catch a caterpillar, and this begins a contemplation of the "Ambiguities of pain and greed." A number of subjects are often woven together and the similarities and differences are juxtaposed for the purposes of comparison and contrast. A good example of his technique in "On Reading *The Bostonians* in Algeciras Bay" in which his thoughts on James's novel, memories of the Spanish Civil War, and observation of an old man sitting near him are threaded together with his thoughts and feelings about society and change. This is also his first use of syllabic verse. He has always used a wide variety of forms in his poetry, but the 11 or 13 syllabic line, he feels, has allowed him greater freedom in his use of subject-matter, while at the same time imposing a rigorous and disciplined pattern on his poetry.

Fuller has always insisted on the importance of discipline, order, and coherence in poetry, and has criticised in his Oxford lectures the lack of this in contemporary "so-called" poetry. Certainly care and intellect are characteristics of both his poetry and novels.

—David Astle

FULTON, Robin. Scottish. Born on the Isle of Arran, Scotland, 6 May 1937. Educated at Edinburgh University, M.A. 1959, Ph.D. 1972. Editor, *Lines Review*, Edinburgh, 1967-76. Recipient: Eric Gregory Award, 1966; Edinburgh University Writer's Fellowship, 1969-71; Arts Council bursary, 1972; Swedish Authors' Fund bursary, 1973, 1976; Artur Lundkvist Award, for translation, 1977; Swedish Academy Award, for translation, 1978. Lives in Scandinavia. Address: c/o Macdonald Publishers, Edgefield Road, Loanhead, Midlothian EH20 9ST, Scotland.

PUBLICATIONS

Verse

A Matter of Definition. Edinburgh, Giles Gordon, 1963.
Instances. Edinburgh, Macdonald, 1967.
Inventories. Thurso, Caithness Books, 1969.
The Spaces Between the Stones. New York, New Rivers Press, 1971.
Quarters. West Linton, Peeblesshire, Castlelaw Press, 1971.
The Man with the Surbahar. Edinburgh, Macdonald, 1971.
Tree-Lines. New York, New Rivers Press, 1974.
Music and Flight. Knotting, Bedfordshire, Sceptre Press, 1975.
Between Flights: Eighteen Poems. Egham, Surrey, Interim Press, 1976.
Places to Stay In. Knotting, Bedfordshire, Sceptre Press, 1978.
Following a Mirror. London, Oasis, 1980.
Selected Poems 1963-1978. Edinburgh, Macdonald, 1980.
Fields of Focus. London, Anvil Press Poetry, 1982.

Other

Contemporary Scottish Poetry: Individuals and Context. Edinburgh, Macdonald, 1974.

Editor, *Trio: New Poets from Edinburgh.* New York, New Rivers Press, 1971.
Editor, *Selected Poems 1955-1980,* by Iain Crichton Smith. Edinburgh, Macdonald, 1982.
Editor, *Complete Poetical Works,* by Robert Garioch. Edinburgh, Macdonald, 1983.

Editor, *A Garioch Miscellany: Selected Prose and Letters,* by Robert Garioch. Edinburgh, Macdonald, 1983.

Translator, *An Italian Quartet: Versions after Saba, Ungaretti, Montale, Quasimodo.* London, Alan Ross, 1966.
Translator, *Blok's Twelve.* Preston, Lancashire, Akros, 1968.
Translator, *Selected Poems,* by Lars Gustafsson. New York, New Rivers Press, 1972.
Translator, *Selected Poems,* by Gunnar Harding. London, London Magazine Editions, 1973.
Translator, *Selected Poems* by Tomas Tranströmer. London, Penguin, 1974; augmented edition, Ann Arbor, Michigan, Ardis, 1980.
Translator, *Citoyens,* by Tomas Tranströmer. Rushden, Northamptonshire, Sceptre Press, 1974.
Translator, *The Hidden Music and Other Poems,* by Östen Sjöstrand. Cambridge, Oleander Press, 1975.
Translator, *Selected Poems,* by Werner Aspenström. London, Oasis, 1976.
Translator, *Mary Poppins and Myth,* by Staffan Bergsten. Stockhom, Almqvist & Wiksell, 1978.
Translator, *How the Late Autumn Night Novel Begins,* by Tomas Tranströmer. Knotting, Bedfordshire, Sceptre Press, 1980.
Translator, *Baltics,* by Tomas Tranströmer. London, Oasis, 1980.
Translator, *Family Tree: Thirteen Prose Poems,* by Johannes Edfelt. London, Oasis, 1981.
Translator, *The Blue Whale and Other Prose Pieces,* by Werner Aspenström. London, Oasis, 1981.
Translator, *Starnberger See,* by Gunnar Harding. London, Oasis, 1983.

*   *   *

Robin Fulton was a fastidious craftsman early in his profession as poet, the craftsmanship showing itself, not in conventional verse forms, but in the controlled response to the exacting objectives of his art. In "A Lifework" he writes:

> to say what you mean is hazardous
> to sort out and plainly describe
> one mere subdivision
> of a minor species takes more
> than a home made poet with a simple lens.

At his simplest he is, as he entitles the poem, "A Meticulous Observer," in which he writes:

> he watched the boys with almost pre-
> hensile feet on high walls
> where they risked their short lives
> for reasons no-one else would appreciate
>
> he watched girls with newly-shaped
> bodies advertising themselves
> without guile in the summery light
> and without needing a reason to guide them

The reader is not permitted to participate in the physical sensations of these just and sensitive recordings of physiological facts. To Fulton all is seen in the mind's eye. In the progression of his poetry he uses the "meticulous observations" as means of going beyond them, much as he can use a light, witty touch as an entry to the area of humane concern, as in "Forecast for a Quiet Night":

By dawn too a generation of mice
will have been sniped by a night-shift of owls
working separately and almost in silence

and the mild local disturbance behind the eyes
of the invalid
will have been noted by the next of kin.

The detached, inquisitorial mind allows Fulton to make a critical scrutiny of events which generally have evoked passionate rhetoric from poets. He reports the Vietnam war as seen on the television screen:

the images are true because the actors are bad
the president knows how to raise an eyebrow and smile
but his victim burns clumsily unconvincingly

Fulton observes the reversal of natural expectation, and leaves the reader with the questions—where is truth and where is reality? The danger of the clinical approach is that the natural free response to the actual is inhibited, but Fulton's detachment does not go as far as aloofness, for in his verse he puts his own self under inspection, and on his settling in Sweden his poetry reflected the change in the symbolic statements which the landscape made to him. In "In Memoriam Antonius Blok," which is charged with memories of Bergman's *The Seventh Seal*, the Swedish scene is threatening and beautiful:

Perched like ornaments on dim shelves
owls wait for the bewildering sky to darken
and from the wood's edge you can see the birches
silver and standing at ease before the shadowy
straight ranks....

The wood is also identified as Dante's, and like Dante at the beginning of the *Inferno*, Fulton is in middle age:

It has taken you half a lifetime to reach
an understanding with the black shadow of the pine.
In the middle of life the dark wood darkens.

Increasingly Fulton's poetry takes account of the human dilemma of being tied to the here and now, and yet in imagination free. He does so by occupying the doubtful ground between the actual and the metaphysical. Already his achievement is impressive.

—George Bruce

GALLAGHER, Tess (née Bond). American. Born in Port Angeles, Washington, 21 July 1932. Educated at the University of Washington, Seattle, B.A. 1963, M.A. 1970; University of Iowa, Iowa City, M.F.A. 1974. Married 1) Lawrence Gallagher in 1963 (divorced, 1968); 2) Michael Burkard in 1973 (divorced, 1977); since 1978, has lived with the writer Raymond Carver. Instructor, St. Lawrence University, Canton, New York, 1974-75; Assistant Professor, Kirkland College, Clinton, New York, 1975-77; Visiting Lecturer, University of Montana, Missoula, 1977-78; Assistant Professor, University of Arizona, Tucson, 1978-80. Since 1980, Associate Professor of English, Syracuse University, New York. Visiting Fellow, Willamette University, Salem, Oregon, 1981. Recipient: Creative Artists Public Service grant, 1976; Elliston Award, 1976; National Endowment for the Arts grant, 1977, 1981; Guggenheim Fellowship, 1978; *American Poetry Review* award, 1981. Address: Department of English, Syracuse University, Syracuse, New York 13210, U.S.A.

PUBLICATIONS

Verse

Stepping Outside.   Lisbon, Iowa, Penumbra Press, 1974.
Instructions to the Double.   Port Townsend, Washington, Graywolf Press, 1976.
Under Stars.   Port Townsend, Washington, Graywolf Press, 1978.
Portable Kisses.   Seattle, Sea Pen Press, 1978.
On Your Own.   Port Townsend, Washington, Graywolf Press, 1978.
Willingly.   Port Townsend, Washington, Graywolf Press, 1984.

Plays

Screenplay: *The Night Belongs to the Police*, 1982.

Television Play: *The Wheel*, 1970.

*

Critical Studies: reviews by Hayden Carruth in *Harper's* (New York), April 1979, and Peter Davison, in *Atlantic Monthly* (New York), May 1979; interview in *Ironwood* (Tucson), October 1979.

Tess Gallagher comments:
    When I was a young girl salmon fishing with my father in the Straits of Juan de Fuca in Washington State I used to lean out over the water and try to look past my own face, past the reflection of the boat, past the sun and the darkness, down to where the fish were surely swimming. I made up charm songs and word-hopes to tempt the fish, to cause them to mean biting my hook. I believed they would do it, if I asked them well and patiently enough, and with the right hope. I am writing my poems like this. I have used the fabric and the people of my life as the bait. More and more I have learned how to speak for the others, the ones who do not speak in poetry, though their lives are of it. What do I write about? The murder of my uncle by thieves in the night, the psychic death of my husband in the Viet Nam war, walking through Belfast in 1976, a horse with snow on its back circling a house where the dancers have fallen to the floor by daybreak. I have wanted the words to go deep. I have wanted music and passion and human tenderness in the poems. Intelligence and loss. Only in the language I have made for myself in the poems am I in touch with all the past, present, and future moments of my consciousness and unconsciousness. The poem is the moment of all possibilities where I try to speak in a concert of tenses. I don't want to disappear into the present tense, the awful NOW. I want to survive it and take others with me. I am more concerned about the kind of writing that allows WITH than I was in the beginning. Not just TO or FOR or AT. The Irish have no word for "mine" or for "wife"... only "he or she who goes along with me." *My* poetry. I can't say that. Only "that which goes along with me."

*   *   *

Born in the Pacific Northwest, the oldest of five children of a logger turned longshoreman, Tess Gallagher was a member of the last class taught by Theodore Roethke at the University of Washington, and also a student there of David Wagoner. That is not to say her work bears theirs much resemblance beyond great vitality and an obsessive desire to make words count.

Instructions to the Double is full of doubles, doubles of two kinds: persons with whom the speaker closely identifies—father, mother, uncle, husband—and likenesses—reflections in a mirror, water, or eyes, resemblances, shadows, ghosts, photographs. Whichever the kind, the poems which disappoint are those whose subjects remain generalized. The most successful are concrete, rooted in intimate and intimately felt family experience: "Two Stories," about an uncle murdered by thieves, "Coming Home," "The Woman Who Raised Goats," "Black Money," and "Time Lapse with Tulips." This last is one of Gallagher's best; it brilliantly considers and rejects illusion and fixes on a passionate reality. The wedding photograph which is the occasion for the poem is illusory in at least two senses: a photographic image is an illusion, and the particular image "preserves/a symmetry of doubt with us/at the center." The poem has its own symmetry of statement. The first stanza retrospectively denies the impact of a marital kiss and the prospects of living in connubial bliss into old age. The second stanza denies the assumptions of tulips that they will be accepted by the bride, the third the uncertainties of the wedding guests, the "symmetry of doubt." The turn suggested in stanza two ("But they are wrong") is declared at the beginning of stanza four: "Whatever the picture says, it is wrong." The real picture is something else, something not doubtful. Instead of what the photograph portrays, passion suppressed, is passion ready to be released, passion comprehending love and death:

> Inside, the rare bone of my hand and that harp
> seen through a window suddenly so tempting
>
> you must rush into that closed room, you must
> tear your fingers across it.

Symmetry and harmony are about to be achieved.

After *Instructions to the Double, Under Stars* is a letdown. The first half of the book, "The Ireland Poems," derives from Gallagher's travels in Ireland in 1976. A traveller's impressions, even those of a sensitive poet with ethnic affinities for the land visited, almost inevitably disappoint. After reading Seamus Heaney, say, with his profoundly apprehended vision of the Irelands, one is tempted to characterize Gallagher's poems, especially such ones as "Disappearances in the Guarded Sector" and "The Ballad of Ballymote," with their eternal notes of sadness, as simply more news from that unhappy land. The second half of the book, "Start Again Somewhere," is not so much a second start as a return to subjects explored in *Instructions to the Double*; for instance, there are such poems as "3 A.M. Kitchen: My Father Talking" and "My Mother Remembers That She Was Beautiful." Yet even in these less successful poems Gallagher is clearly a strong young poet: passionate, elegant, painstaking.

—James K. Robinson

GALVIN, Brendan. American. Born in Everett, Massachusetts, 20 October 1938. Educated at Malden Catholic High School; Boston College, 1956-60, B.S. in natural sciences 1960; Northeastern University, Boston, 1962-64, M.A. in English 1964; University of Massachusetts, Amherst, 1965-70, M.F.A. 1967, Ph.D. in English 1970. Married Ellen Baer in 1968; one son and one daughter. Instructor in English, Northeastern University, 1964-65; Assistant Professor of English, Slippery Rock State College, Pennsylvania, 1968-69. Since 1969, member of the faculty, now Professor of English, Central Connecticut State University, New Britain. Visiting Professor, Connecticut College, New London, 1975-76. Since 1981, Editor, with George Garrett, *Poultry: A Magazine of Voice*, Truro, Massachusetts. Recipient: Fine Arts Work Center fellowship, 1971; National Endowment for the Arts fellowship, 1974; Artists' Foundation grant, 1978; Connecticut Commission on the Arts fellowship, 1981. Address: P.O. Box 54, Durham, Connecticut 06422, U.S.A.

PUBLICATIONS

Verse

The Narrow Land. Boston, Northeastern University Press, 1971.
The Salt Farm. Fredericton, New Brunswick, Fiddlehead, 1972.
No Time for Good Reasons. Pittsburgh, University of Pittsburgh Press, 1974.
The Minutes No One Owns. Pittsburgh, University of Pittsburgh Press, 1977.
Atlantic Flyway. Athens, University of Georgia Press, 1980.
Winter Oysters. Athens, University of Georgia Press, 1983.
A Birder's Dozen. Bristol, Rhode Island, Ampersand Press, 1984.

Play

Screenplay: *Massachusetts Story*, 1978.

*

Critical Studies: article in *American Poets Since World War II* edited by Donald J. Greiner, Detroit, Gale, 1980, and "This Business of Getting the World Right: The Poetry of Brendan Galvin," in *Three Rivers Poetry Journal 19-20* (Pittsburgh), 1982, both by George Garrett; Philip Jason, in *Critical Survey of Poetry* edited by Frank N. Magill, Englewood Cliffs, New Jersey, Salem Press, 1982.

Brendan Galvin comments:

Critics have noted a rural-urban conflict in my work, where Cape Cod and its austere landscape, and particularly its bird life, are seen in positive terms, and cities are seen as destructive to the possibility of community. Where rural and urban themes overlap, the poems sometimes point up how development and "city values" corrupt the environment. I have also been identified as having a quick sense of the comic, of having my attention always on the rhythm of the experience at hand, of having language and imagery always organically functional in the immediate scene and emotion. For better or worse, my poems are often compared with those of Theodore Roethke, D.H. Lawrence, Frost, William Stafford, James Dickey, and James Wright. The main thrust of my work is topical, and I tend to use catalogues, reveal my subjects immediately, and try to leave plenty of clues that will admit the reader without straining his credibility. Clarity is a key word here, and I abhor much of the recent neo-surrealist verse. Trained in the natural sciences originally, I have tried to maintain accurate scientific description as much as possible, and the psychic center of my work continues to be Cape Cod, where I live part of each year, and which is the "natural bed" out of which my poems grow. The journey motif is also strong in much of my work, and recently I have been experimenting with voices other than my own in narrative poems, trying to extend my range into longer poems.

*   *   *

In the poem "Mockingbird" in his recent collection of poems *Winter Oysters*, Brendan Galvin seems to be making an aesthetic statement about his own poetry. The mockingbird tries to recall his own song, but he is instead filled with all of the songs around him. "This business of getting/the world right," Galvin goes on to say, "isn't for dilettantes; when/the voices fill you,/you must say nothing wrong." A poet like Galvin, for whom clarity and accuracy of vision and speech are paramount, must, like the mockingbird, "bring it all back/alive as the repertoire/of your inner ear."

His early training as a biologist has been apparent from his earliest poems through his most recent; he pays close and detailed attention to the world around him, and he works hard at "getting the world right." Although his background is Irish and quite unlike that of his 19th-century New England literary forebears, he has the same sharp eye and the same ability to draw significance out of things seen that makes the work of Henry Thoreau so valuable and distinctive. When Galvin writes a poem about a natural landscape or an animal, he *expresses* his subject in the fullest sense. His bats are, for example, the frightening creatures of legend, but also the oddly formed real creatures looking "like something crucified/to a busted umbrella," and as well the beautiful inhabitants of a bat tree—"hundreds folded upside down/pealing their single bell-notes through the dark."

In each of his four major collections, he writes of nature with that skilled eye and ear, but he does not limit himself to the owls and pitch pines, marsh and shore scenes of the world around him. He also speaks with great feeling and force of the human world of work and family, of shared experience and hurtful inequality. His poem "Tar," in *The Minutes No One Owns*, applies his scientist's eye to the lives of highway asphalt workers, "those true fly-by-nights/who sprayed earth/with the nether world's hot fossils." He observes them accurately and without sentimentality, but also without condescension—from within their experience rather than from above or even alongside. He speaks often in the voices of those who have been injured or trapped by an indifferent modern world; the speaker of "The Hitchhiker" lives in a moving environment of distrust and fear:

My God, I would sit for hours
in somebody's Volkswagen,
with a Doberman cocked like a .45
at the base of my only skull—

just to be moving
out of these everyday lives.

He can be hard-eyed and tough-minded, but he can also express the tenderness in these everyday lives, and he can also find the humor. His misfit character, Bear, figures large in the first two books; other comic moments of vision continue to occur in the later work. And in his poems directly about his family Galvin shows his ability to handle personal subjects of

great delicacy and complexity with the same discipline and craft that he brings to his more "objective" poems.

The poems from book to book are recognizably his, but he expands the range of his interests and subjects even as he develops his control of language and form. In *Atlantic Flyway* he moved into history with his powerful long poem, "1847," about the great Irish famine, and in that same volume he moved more directly to place his immediate world into wider contexts of both time and space. This growing sense of connection is one of the most interesting and engaging things about his later verse. Like ripples moving out from a tossed stone in Thoreau's pond, Galvin's poems enlarge steadily into new experience and new expression. A projected *New and Selected Poems* should make clear to even more readers and critics what the readers of his separate volumes have been seeing all along: that Brendan Galvin is a poet to be reckoned with, both for his considerable achievement and for the great promise which his future work holds.

—R.H.W. Dillard

GARFITT, Roger.   British.   Born in Melksham, Wiltshire, 12 April 1944. Educated at Tiffin School, Kingston upon Thames, Surrey, 1955-62; Merton College, Oxford, 1963-68, B.A. (honours) 1968. Secretary, Oxford Community Workshop, 1969-70; English teacher, Ousedale School, Newport Pagnell, Buckinghamshire, 1970-71, and Bicester School, Oxfordshire, 1971-72; Arts Council Creative Writing Fellow, University College of North Wales, Bangor, 1975-77; Writer-in-Residence, Sunderland Polytechnic, Tyne and Wear, 1978-80; Northern Arts Writer, Durham County Library, 1980; Welsh Arts Council Poet-in-Residence, Ebbw Vale, 1983. Poetry critic, *London Magazine*, 1973-76; Editor, *Poetry Review*, London, 1978-81. Recipient: Guinness Award, 1973; Eric Gregory Award, 1974; Arts Council bursary, 1983. Address: c/o Carcanet Press, 208-212 Corn Exchange Buildings, Manchester M4 3BQ, England.

PUBLICATIONS

Verse

Caught on Blue.   Oxford, Carcanet, 1970.
West of Elm.   Cheadle, Cheshire, Carcanet, 1974.
Unwritten Histories.   Manchester, Carcanet, 1980.
Wall, with others, edited by Noel Connor.   Brampton, Cumbria, LYC Press, 1981.
Rowlstone Haiku, with Frances Horovitz and Alan Halsey. Madley, Herefordshire, Five Seasons Press, 1982.
The Broken Road.   Newcastle upon Tyne, Northern House, 1982.

*

Roger Garfitt comments:
   My early poems began as a direct response to landscape, and especially to the play of light on a landscape. I tried to recreate in language the quality and intensity of that light. Recently I have become more interested in the landscapes as a register of the lives lived there and in particular the unacknowledged lives of the majority of us. History, as it has generally been written, is the business of kings and ministers, of manufacturers and mer-

chants: if we look instead at the unwritten histories, at the lives of the working people, our perspective is completely changed. To write those unwritten histories is to unwrite the official histories.

*   *   *

It would be too easy to slip Roger Garfitt's poetry into place somewhere in the long tradition of English pastoral poetry and leave it at that. He can certainly write skilfully and feelingly of the countryside, of the world of cattle in "Spring Grazing"— "The bullocks back and churn in a mill by the gate/Their breath hangs in snarls in the unravelling mist./They balk at the open field"—and he has a fine eye for the landscape of agriculture— "The harvest field shelved away, a bare shelf/set with a trap: white-rimmed stumps, pebbles and cracked soil" ("Out of a Clear Blue Sky")—or for the dunes and the sea—"Sand gathers grass. Mud grows samphire./The seven silences of water/turn to the one silence of earth" ("Titchwell").

But the urban poems, "Equinox," "Born 1940," "The Hitch-Hiker," and the group of poems written for Shelter, are all equally as well observed and as sensitively written. Can these two aspects of Roger Garfitt's works be reconciled? Is there a common factor besides that of authorship? Indeed, there is and it is that most English of preoccupations, the seasons. That aspect of external nature which affects the lives of country and town dwellers alike. The shorter of the poems written for Shelter, "Spring Greens," illustrates this clearly where the climate is related to the keenest of urban images:

> Whiskers on the moss. Rust
> burns beneath the overflow. In the tenements
> the damp is changing seasons.
> And all the tins in Tesco's sharpen their colours

Here the movement of the seasons is as essential to the town dweller as to the cattle in "Spring Grazing." There is winter in the city: "Dropping over the roofs a husk of twilight/caught neatly up by magnesium fans/into circle and black," or summer at Bablock Hyth: "Out of hours, the road is warm stone/a basking place beside the stream." The titles too reveal this essential pivot on which the world of Garfitt's poetry turns: "Winter Economy," "September Morning," "Trees in City Winter," as well as the others already mentioned. It is the element in which we are all caught and involved, the climatic environment that shapes our lives, our moods, and our outlook.

Roger Garfitt's poetry is quietly voiced. It eschews verbal fireworks, but is the more effective for that, working gently as it does towards atmosphere and significance.

—John Cotton

GARLICK, Raymond. Welsh. Born in London, 21 September 1926. Educated at the University College of North Wales, Bangor, 1944-48, B.A. 1948. Married Elin Jane Hughes in 1948; one son and one daughter. Taught in Wales, 1948-59, and the Netherlands, 1960-67. Senior Lecturer in English, 1967-72, and since 1972, Director of Welsh Studies and Principal Lecturer, Trinity College, Carmarthen. Founding Editor, *Dock Leaves*, later *The Anglo-Welsh Review*, Pembroke Dock, 1949-60. Recipient: Welsh Arts Council prize, 1969, 1973, 1977. Member of the Welsh Academy. Fellow, Royal Society of Arts.

Address: 30 Glannant House, College Road, Carmarthen SA31 3EF, Wales.

PUBLICATIONS

Verse

Poems from the Mountain-House. London, Fortune Press, 1950.
Requiem for a Poet. Pembroke Dock, Dock Leaves Press, 1954.
Poems from Pembrokeshire. Pembroke Dock, Dock Leaves Press, 1954.
The Welsh-Speaking Sea. Pembroke Dock, Dock Leaves Press, 1954.
Blaenau Observed. Pembroke Dock, Dock Leaves Press, 1957.
Landscapes and Figures: Selected Poems 1949-63. London, Merrythought Press, 1964.
A Sense of Europe: Collected Poems 1954-1968. Llandysul, Dyfed, Gomer, 1968.
A Sense of Time: Poems and Antipoems 1969-1972. Llandysul, Dyfed, Gomer, 1972.
Incense: Poems 1972-1975. Llandysul, Dyfed, Gomer, 1976.

Recording: *Poets of Wales* series, Argo.

Other

An Introduction to Anglo-Welsh Literature. Cardiff, University of Wales Press, 1970; revised edition, 1972.
Anglo-Welsh Literature. Port Talbot, Alum, 1979.

Editor, *Poetry from Wales.* Brooklyn, Poetry Book Magazine, 1954.
Editor, with Roland Mathias, *Anglo-Welsh Poetry 1480-1980.* Bridgend, Glamorgan, Poetry Wales Press, 1984.

*

Bibliography: in *A Bibliography of Anglo-Welsh Literature, 1900-1965* by Brynmor Jones, Swansea, Library Association, 1970.

Manuscript Collection: National Library of Wales, Aberystwyth.

Critical Studies: "The Poetry of Raymond Garlick" by John Hill, in *The Anglo-Welsh Review* (Pembroke Dock), Summer 1972; statement by the author, in *Artists in Wales 2*, edited by Meic Stephens, Llandysul, Dyfed, Gomer, 1973; Anthony Conran, in *Poetry Wales* (Swansea), Winter 1977, and *The Cost of Strangeness* by Conran, Llandysul, Dyfed, Gomer, 1982; Tony Bianchi, in *Planet* (Llangeitho, Dyfed), November 1977.

Raymond Garlick comments:
    Major themes: Wales and Europe, landscapes and figures, justice and non-violence, art and time. Preoccupation with English as a language of Wales, clarity of communication, poetry as structure and shape. General influence: Anglo-Welsh poetry from the late fifteenth century onwards.

*   *   *

Raymond Garlick is a central figure in Anglo-Welsh literature in that he founded, in 1949, *Dock Leaves*, later *The Anglo-*

Welsh Review, a magazine that was to present the best writing from Wales. He is totally committed to the concept of Anglo-Welsh literature, and through his editorship and other critical writings was a major contributor to the growth of interest and debate about the tradition of writing in English from Wales. His *Introduction to Anglo-Welsh Literature* is a useful survey of the tradition.

His *Collected Poems 1954-1968* carries the title *A Sense of Europe*, and the book emphasises both the poet's seven years' teaching in Holland and his continuing commitment to Europe as a real entity, expressing real values and underlying unities. That said, for Garlick his adopted country Wales is the focus of his ideas and their expression in poetry. He has learned Welsh and lives in the Welsh-speaking town of Carmarthen. Also, his has been one of the strongest literary voices in promoting Welsh nationalism. He castigates the old enemy England at every opportunity, as in "Waterloo":

> I didn't know before
> that any Dutch were near the place.
> I'd always thought it was
> just French and Prussians face to face—
> and the English of course,
> that other violent race.

As he says at the end of *A Sense of Europe*, "My poems/are speeches,/clumsy speeches for Wales" ("Clues"). The implications of that self-proclamation are profound: the political poet is invariably more political than poet. Certainly, there are "poems and anti-poems" in *A Sense of Europe* that fail as pieces of writing because the poetic structure and invention are swamped by the anger of the politics. In one such poem, "Passion 72," the Welsh Language Society protestors are spoken of in terms of Christ: "The police/are always with us,/Roman, Dyfed-Powys,/and the Passion/unfolds before us/in unchanging fashion." Many readers would find that extremity in the writing to be ludicrous. How much more controlled and effective are poems such as "View from Llansteffan" and "Agincourt." This is the dilemma facing the politically committed writer, and one hopes that Raymond Garlick moves towards a resolution in his future work. Certainly, recent magazine publications indicate a more personal subject-matter, moving towards the confessional stance. Whether or not one is carried along by his anger, Garlick is clearly to be viewed as one of the most interesting of poets at present active in Wales.

—Tony Curtis

GARRETT, George (Palmer, Jr.). American. Born in Orlando, Florida, 11 June 1929. Educated at Sewanee Military Academy; The Hill School, graduated 1947; Princeton University, New Jersey, 1947-48, 1949-52, B.A. 1952, M.A. 1956; Columbia University, New York, 1948-49. Served in the United States Army Field Artillery, 1952-55. Married Susan Parrish Jackson in 1952; two sons and one daughter. Assistant Professor, Wesleyan University, Middletown, Connecticut, 1957-60; Visiting Lecturer, Rice University, Houston, 1961-62; Associate Professor, University of Virginia, Charlottesville, 1962-67; Writer-in-Residence, Princeton University, 1964-65; Professor of English, Hollins College, Virginia, 1967-71; Professor of English and Writer-in-Residence, University of South Carolina, Columbia, 1971-73; Senior Fellow, Council of the Humanities, Princeton University 1974-77; Adjunct Professor, Columbia University, 1977-78; Writer-in-Residence, Bennington College, Vermont, 1979, and University of Michigan, Ann Arbor, 1979-84. Since 1984, Hoyns Professor of English, University of Virginia, Charlottesville. President of Associated Writing Programs, 1971-73. United States Poetry Editor, *Transatlantic Review*, Rome (later London), 1958-71; Contemporary Poetry Series Editor, University of North Carolina Press, Chapel Hill, 1962-68; Co-Editor, *Hollins Critic*, Virginia, 1965-71. Since 1970, Contributing Editor, *Contempora*, Atlanta; since 1971, Assistant Editor, *Film Journal*, Hollins College, Virginia; since 1972, Co-Editor, *Worksheet*, Columbia, South Carolina; since 1981, Editor, with Brendan Galvin, *Poultry: A Magazine of Voice*, Truro, Massachusetts. Recipient: *Sewanee Review* fellowship, 1958; American Academy in Rome fellowship, 1958; Ford grant, for drama, 1960; National Endowment for the Arts grant, 1967; *Contempora* award, 1971; Guggenheim fellowship, for fiction, 1974. Agent: Perry Knowlton, Curtis Brown Ltd., 575 Madison Avenue, New York, New York 10022. Address: 1853 Fendall Avenue, Charlottesville, Virginia 22903, U.S.A.

PUBLICATIONS

Verse

The Reverend Ghost. New York, Scribner, 1957.
The Sleeping Gypsy and Other Poems. Austin, University of Texas Press, 1958.
Abraham's Knife and Other Poems. Chapel Hill, University of North Carolina Press, 1961.
For a Bitter Season: New and Selected Poems. Columbia, University of Missouri Press, 1967.
Welcome to the Medicine Show: Postcards, Flashcards, Snapshots. Winston-Salem, North Carolina, Palaemon Press, 1978.
Love's Shining Child: A Miscellany of Poems and Verses. Winston-Salem, North Carolina, Palaemon Press, 1981.
The Collected Poems of George Garrett. Fayetteville, University of Arkansas Press, 1984.

Plays

Sir Slob and the Princess: A Play for Children. New York, French, 1962.
Garden Spot, U.S.A. (produced Houston, 1962).

Screenplays: *The Young Lovers*, 1964; *The Playground*, 1965; *Frankenstein Meets the Space Monster*, with R.H.W. Dillard and John Rodenbeck, 1966.

Novels

The Finished Man. New York, Scribner, 1959; London, Eyre and Spottiswoode, 1960.
Which Ones Are the Enemy? Boston, Little Brown, 1961; London, W.H. Allen, 1962.
Do, Lord, Remember Me. New York, Doubleday, and London, Chapman and Hall, 1965.
Death of the Fox. New York, Doubleday, 1971; London, Barrie and Jenkins, 1972.
The Succession: A Novel of Elizabeth and James. New York, Doubleday, 1983.

Short Stories

King of the Mountain.   New York, Scribner, 1958; London, Eyre and Spottiswoode, 1959.
In the Briar Patch.   Austin, University of Texas Press, 1961.
Cold Ground Was My Bed Last Night.   Columbia, University of Missouri Press, 1964.
A Wreath for Garibaldi and Other Stories.   London, Hart Davis, 1969.
The Magic Striptease.   New York, Doubleday, 1973.
To Recollect a Cloud of Ghosts: Christmas in England.   Winston-Salem, North Carolina, Palaemon Press, 1979.

Other

James Jones.   New York, Harcourt Brace, 1984.

Editor, *New Writing from Virginia*.   Charlottesville, Virginia, New Writing Associates, 1963.
Editor, *The Girl in the Black Raincoat*.   New York, Duell, 1966.
Editor, with W.R. Robinson, *Man and the Movies*.   Baton Rouge, Louisiana State University Press, 1967.
Editor, with R.H.W. Dillard and John Moore, *The Sounder Few: Essays from "The Hollins Critic."*   Athens, University of Georgia Press, 1971.
Editor, with O.B. Hardison, Jr., and Jane Gelfman, *Film Scripts 1-4*.   New York, Appleton Century Crofts, 4 vols., 1971-72.
Editor, with William Peden, *New Writing in South Carolina*.   Columbia, University of South Carolina Press, 1971.
Editor, with John Graham, *Craft So Hard to Learn*.   New York, Morrow, 1972.
Editor, with John Graham, *The Writer's Voice*.   New York, Morrow, 1973.
Editor, with Walton Beacham, *Intro 5*.   Charlottesville, University Press of Virginia, 1974.
Editor, with Katherine Garrison Biddle, *The Botteghe Oscure Reader*.   Middletown, Connecticut, Wesleyan University Press, 1974.
Editor, *Intro 6: Life As We Know It*.   New York, Doubleday, 1974.
Editor, *Intro 7: All of Us and None of You*.   New York, Doubleday, 1975.
Editor, *Intro 8: The Liar's Craft*.   New York, Doubleday, 1977.
Editor, with Michael Mewshaw, *Intro 9*.   Austin, Texas, Hendel and Reinke, 1979.

*

Bibliography: in *Seven Princeton Poets*, Princeton, New Jersey, Princeton University Library, 1963; "George Garrett: A Checklist of His Writings" by R.H.W. Dillard, in *Mill Mountain Review* (Roanoke, Virginia), Summer 1971; "George Garrett: A Bibliographical Chronicle 1947-1980" by Stuart Wright, in *Bulletin of Bibliography* (Boston), January-March 1981.

Manuscript Collection: University of Virginia, Charlottesville; Stuart Wright, Winston-Salem, North Carolina.

Critical Studies: by James B. Meriwether, in *The Princeton University Library Chronicle 25* (New Jersey), 1, 1963; "The Poetry of George Garrett" by Henry Taylor, in *Latitudes 2* (Houston), 2, 1968; "The Poetry of Garrett" by R.H.W. Dillard, in *Masterpieces of World Literature 6*, New York, Salem Press, 1968; "The Poetry of George Garrett" by Richard Moore, in *Mill Mountain Review* (Roanoke, Virginia), Summer 1971.

George Garrett comments:
    All of my work in all forms, including the verse, is part and parcel of the same voice. I make no distinction in the voice only the forms.

*   *   *

George Garrett's poetry shares much of the character of his fiction. His language is free and colloquial, but always strictly under control and serving the larger ends of his thought and feeling. He is personal without being confessional, and his vision is Christian without being pietistic. His work is composed upon a framework of contradictions, of polarities. The sinner who is a saint, the wounding truth that finds its only anodyne in a lie, the spirit trapped in the cage of flesh which discovers moral freedom in physical action, the cruel and painful joy (and mystery) of love—these are some of the enigmas upon which Garrett builds the lively textures of his poems.

The world of George Garrett's seeing and saying is a fallen one, a world of clenched fists and dark bruises where we all still suffer the consequences of Adam's fall in bone and flesh, and where we act out that fall again and again each passing day. His Salome describes that world in the important poem that bears her name:

> A bad marriage from the beginning,
> you say, a complete mismatch.
> Flesh and spirit wrestle
> and we call it love.
>
> We couple like dogs in heat.
> We shudder and are sundered.
> We pursue ourselves,
> sniffing, nose to tail
> a comic parade of appetites.
>
> That is the truth,
> but not the whole truth.
> Do me a little justice.
> I had a dream of purity
> and I have lived in the desert ever since.

In the desert, one holds to what he has (and what he had), learning like Adam and Eve after they were cast out of the garden "to lie a little and to live together." That learning is not always serious, and Garrett is capable of writing comic poems, some of which satirize our vice and folly and others of which celebrate our vital foolishness (particularly as it expresses itself in the relationships between men and women). But the tone and substance of his poetry are perhaps best expressed by the closing stanza of "For My Sons," a poem which figures importantly in the novel *Death of the Fox*:

> Nothing of earned wisdom I can give you,
> nothing save the old words like rock candy
> to kill the taste of dust on the tongue.
> Nothing stings like the serpent, no pain greater.
> Bear it. If a bush should burn and cry out,
> bow down. If a stranger wrestles, learn his name.
> And if after long tossing and sickness you find
> a continent, plant your flags, send forth a dove.
> Rarely the fruit you reach for returns your love.

—R.H.W. Dillard

GASCOYNE, David (Emery). British. Born in Harrow, Middlesex, 10 October 1916. Educated at Salisbury Cathedral Choir School; Regent Street Polytechnic, London. Married Judy Tyler in 1975. Lived in France, 1937-39, 1954-65. Recipient: Rockefeller-Atlantic Award, 1949; Biella European Poetry prize, 1983. Fellow, Royal Society of Literature, 1951. Agent: Alan Clodd, 22 Huntingdon Road, London N2 9DU. Address: 48 Oxford Street, Northwood, Cowes, Isle of Wight PO31 8PT, England.

PUBLICATIONS

Verse

Roman Balcony and Other Poems. London, Lincoln Williams, 1932.
Man's Life Is This Meat. London, Parton Press, 1936.
Hölderlin's Madness. London, Dent, 1938.
Poems 1937-1942. London, Editions Poetry London, 1943.
A Vagrant and Other Poems. London, Lehmann, 1950.
Night Thoughts. London, Deutsch, and New York, Grove Press, 1956.
Collected Poems, edited by Robin Skelton. London, Oxford University Press-Deutsch, 1965.
Penguin Modern Poets 17, with Kathleen Raine and W.S. Graham. London, Penguin, 1970.
The Sun at Midnight: Notes on the Story of Civilisation Seen as the History of the Great Experimental Work of the Supreme Scientist. London, Enitharmon Press, 1970.
Collected Verse Translations, edited by Robin Skelton and Alan Clodd. London, Oxford University Press-Deutsch, 1970.
Three Poems. London, Enitharmon Press, 1976.
Early Poems. Warwick, Greville Press, 1980.

Play

The Hole in the Fourth Wall; or, Talk, Talk, Talk (produced London, 1950).

Novel

Opening Day. London, Cobden Sanderson, 1933.

Other

A Short Survey of Surrealism. London, Cobden Sanderson, 1935; San Francisco, City Lights, 1982.
Thomas Carlyle. London, Longman, 1952.
Knights (for children). Oxford, Blackwell, 1977.
Paris Journal 1937-1939. London, Enitharmon Press, 1978.
Journal 1936-37. London, Enitharmon Press, 1980.

Editor, *Outlaw of the Lowest Planet,* by Kenneth Patchen. London, Grey Walls Press, 1946.

Translator, *Conquest of the Irrational,* by Salvador Dali. New York, Levy, 1935.
Translator, with Humphrey Jennings, *A Bunch of Carrots: Twenty Poems,* by Benjamin Péret. London, Roger Roughton, 1936; revised edition, as *Remove Your Hat,* 1936.
Translator, *What is Surrealism?,* by André Breton. London, Faber, 1936.

*

Bibliography: "David Gascoyne: A Checklist" by A. Atkinson, in *Twentieth-Century Literature 6* (Los Angeles), 1961.

Manuscript Collection: British Library, London; University of Tulsa, Oklahoma; State University of New York, Buffalo; New York Public Library.

Critical Studies: by Edwin Muir, in *The Observer* (London), December 1950; "Poetry and Ideas II: David Gascoyne" by Anthony Cronin, in *London Magazine,* July 1957; "The Restoration of Symbols," in *Every Changing Shape* by Elizabeth Jennings, London, Deutsch, 1961; "A Voice from the Darkness" by Gavin Ewart, in *London Magazine,* November 1965; "David Gascoyne and the Prophetic Role," in *Defending Ancient Springs* by Kathleen Raine, London and New York, Oxford University Press, 1967; *David Gascoyne: The Evolution of the Ideas of a Surrealist Poet* by Michel Rémy, University of Nancy, unpublished thesis, 1968; *The Ironic Harvest* by Geoffrey Thurley, London, Arnold, 1974; *An Introduction to Fifty Modern British Poets* by Michael Schmidt, London, Pan, 1979, as *A Reader's Guide to Fifty Modern British Poets,* London, Heinemann, 1979, New York, Barnes and Noble, 1982.

*   *   *

David Gascoyne began his literary career precociously early. Whilst still in his teens he was an active propagandist for the Continental surrealist movement, and was one of the few English poets to produce work in the surrealist manner that still looked like genuine poetry. Gascoyne's surrealist apprenticeship gave him a feeling for the arresting image, and for the way in which unexpectedly juxtaposed images can produce a disturbing but memorable effect. In the late thirties and early forties Gascoyne produced the major phase of his work; the poems he wrote at the time were collected in his *Poems 1937-1942,* which remains one of the most distinguished collections of the decade. In these poems Gascoyne was preoccupied with several recurring themes: a sense of personal anguish expressed in the terms of existential philosophy, as in such poems as "Noctambules," "A War-Time Dawn" and "The Gravel-Pit Field"; an awareness of a world first threatened by war and then overwhelmed by it; and a deep interest in the central symbols of Christianity. Gascoyne used these very effectively in a sequence of poems called "Miserere," though his interest in the Christian religion was that of a poetic mythologizer rather than that of an orthodox believer. The opening of "Pieta" from this sequence shows Gascoyne's ability to express intense feeling in vivid images, in a verse that is mannered and yet at the same time highly controlled:

Stark in the pasture on the skull-shaped hill,
In swollen aura of disaster shrunken and
Unsheltered by the ruin of the sky,
Intensely concentrated in themselves the banded
Saints abandoned kneel.

Elsewhere, in "Snow in Europe," which is dated "Christmas, 1938," Gascoyne shows both his awareness of the pressures of history and his adroit handling of images:

The warring flags hang colourless a while;
Now midnight's icy zero feigns a truce
Between the signs and seasons, and fades out
All shots and cries. But when the great thaw comes,
How red shall be the melting snow, how loud the drums!

Gascoyne's post-war poetry is, by comparison, less intense and generally less interesting. *Night Thoughts*, a long semi-dramatic poem intended for radio, may have come across effectively in that medium, but is flat and diffuse on the page.

—Bernard Bergonzi

GATENBY, Greg. Canadian. Born in Toronto, Ontario, 5 May 1950. Educated at York University, Toronto, 1968-72. B.A. in English 1972. Editor, McClelland and Stewart, publishers, Toronto, 1973-75. Since 1975, Literary Coordinator, Habourfront, and since 1980, Artistic Director, Harbourfront International Festival of Authors, Toronto. Canadian Editor, *Kudos*. Recipient: Ontario Arts Council grants, 1975-84; Canada Council grant, 1975, 1977. Agent: Lucinda Vardey Agency, 228 Gerrard Street East, Toronto, Ontario M5A 2E8. Address: c/o Harbourfront Reading Series, 417 Queen's Quay West, Toronto, Ontario M5V 1A2, Canada.

PUBLICATIONS

Verse

Rondeaus for Erica. Toronto, Missing Link Press, 1976.
Adrienne's Blessing. Toronto, Missing Link Press, 1976.
The Brown Stealer. Oxford, Avalon, 1977.
The Salmon Country. Windsor, Ontario, Black Moss Press, 1978.
Growing Still. Windsor, Ontario, Black Moss Press, 1981.

Other

Editor, *52 Pickup.* Toronto, Dreadnaught Press, 1976.
Editor, *Whale Sound: An Anthology of Poems about Whales and Dolphins.* Toronto, Dreadnaught Press, 1977.
Editor, *Whales: A Celebration.* Toronto, Lester and Orpen Dennys, and Boston, Little Brown, 1983.

Translator, with Irving Layton and Francesca Valente, *Selected Poems,* by Giorgio Bassani. Toronto, Aya Press, 1980.

*

Critical Studies: reviews by John Bemrose, in *Globe and Mail* (Toronto), 20 February 1982; Chris Hume, in *Toronto Star,* 2 October 1983; in *New York Times Book Review,* 20 November 1983; Bernard Levin, in *The Observer* (London), 11 December 1983; *Maclean's* (Toronto), 12 December 1983; *The Weekend Australian* (Sydney), 3-4 March 1984.

Greg Gatenby comments:

I try to write poems which are accessible to anyone who cares to spend the few moments required to read my lyrics. That more poets do not write more satire continually surprises me, as this seems to be an age crying out for the pricks of poets to puncture the pretensions of the age. Perhaps the lucre of the academies has been too irresistible for too many poets in North America.

*   *   *

Greg Gatenby's activities as co-ordinator of Toronto's Harbourfront Reading Series and its International Authors' Festival have deflected attention away from his own poetic achievement. From the organizer of Canada's premier reading venue, one would expect wit and urbanity. Indeed, these are characteristics of the poems included in his two principal collections, *The Salmon Country* and *Growing Still*.

Wit is a weapon ever at the ready. It is directed against the act of writing in "Specs," which begins: "This poem is being written / with a Parler 804, silver, with a slip spring...." The poem continues: "Of course, for a lyric I use the Bic 29 Fine Point: / I believe it's the standard for all lyric poets." Wit is ever-present in Gatenby's best-known poem, "Academic Report on Literature III," which likens Canadian literature to a horse race: "Major U.S. indicators continue to outstrip Canadian futures... the interest rate in academia continued to decline..." etc.

Wit and urbanity are characteristics which combine in a poem like "the Sophisticates," with stanzas like the following:

> ...and outside I take a deep breath
> of the dirty smog of the city
> and note for the first time
> how much I need to enjoy it.

Gatenby is no stranger to modern cities but, like many cosmopolitans, he feels less at home in modern countries. The world of nature is more virtuous than the world of man in "The Salmon Country":

> May Sisyphus stay a European visitor;
> these stupid fish make a tale primeval
> are endemic to this land, this nation, us.

The natural world is meaced by the human world in "The Narwhal," which refers to Eskimo villages and their stock-in-trade, soapstone carvings:

> Each village of 300 kills a thousand
> and you can smell the extinction
> in every sculpture the city dwellers buy
> for the primitive art, for the natives,
> for nature.

Gatenby has written a slew of skillful poetic parodies of the works of poets like Leonard Cohen and Al Purdy. These read excellently on the platform, but perhaps Gatenby's real strength lies in his subtler love poems. "Ours" begins in this way:

> Soft as waits
> for feathers to fall
> rare as tusks
> of the white narwhal,
> your love.

"Reunion" presents love as "what once was intimate, / cedilla soft." That last phrase echoes throughout the poem, which ends: "Is now a furtive child, cynic hardened, lonely." Gatenby encountered his favourite movie star, the Quebec actress Carole Laure, in New York. Here is how he described the encounter in "Screen Siren: "I made her / hear my love for dolphins, talked of books still to come— / any nonsense to protract her presence, to let me / repose fluid kite tail dancing and happy."

In all, Gatenby has published a limited number of poems, but all of them are characteristically his own. His language, occasionally like that of elusive speech-patterns, is sometimes gritty and abrasive, sometimes light and lyrical. When it is gritty and abrasive, it conveys a restlessness and resistance to social norms and restrictions, as in "The Salmon Country," which concludes like this:

> In Ireland they would have crushed you with contempt,
> but this country will skewer you with its indifference.

It is difficult to be indifferent to Gatenby's poetry which is self-aware and not terribly forgiving of human foibles and failures.

—John Robert Colombo

GEDDES, Gary. Canadian. Born in Vancouver, British Columbia, 9 June 1940. Educated at the University of British Columbia, Vancouver, 1958-62, B.A. 1962; Reading University, Berkshire, 1963-64, Dip.Ed. 1964; University of Toronto, 1964-68, M.A. and Ph.D. Married Jan Geddes in 1973; three daughters. Visiting Assistant Professor, Trent University, Peterborough, Ontario, 1968-69; Lecturer, Carleton University, Ottawa, 1971-72, and University of Victoria, British Columbia, 1972-74; Writer-in-Residence, 1976-77, and Visiting Associate Professor, 1977-78, University of Alberta, Edmonton. Visiting Associate Professor, 1978-79, and since 1979, Associate Professor of English, Concordia University, Montreal. General Editor, Studies in Canadian Literature series, Douglas and McIntyre, publishers, Vancouver. Recipient: E.J. Pratt Medal, 1970; Canadian Authors Association prize, 1982. Address: Department of English, Concordia University, 1455 de Maisonneuve Boulevard West, Montreal, Quebec H3G 1M8, Canada.

PUBLICATIONS

Verse

Poems. Waterloo, Ontario, Waterloo Lutheran University, 1970.
Rivers Inlet. Vancouver, Talonbooks, 1972.
Snakeroot. Vancouver, Talonbooks, 1973.
Letter of the Master of Horse. Ottawa, Oberon Press, 1973.
War and Other Measures. Toronto, Anansi, 1976.
The Acid Test. Winnipeg, Turnstone Press, 1981.
The Terracotta Army. Ottawa, Oberon Press, 1984.

Play

Les Maudits Anglais, with the Theatre Passe Muraille (produced Montreal, 1978).

Other

Conrad's Later Novels. Montreal, McGill-Queen's University Press, 1980.

Editor, *20th-Century Poetry and Poetics.* Toronto, Oxford University Press, 1969.
Editor, with Phyllis Bruce, *15 Canadian Poets.* Toronto, Oxford University Press, 1970; revised edition, as *15 Canadian Poets Plus Five,* 1978.

Editor, *Skookum Wawa: Writings of the Canadian Northwest.* Toronto, Oxford University Press, 1975.
Editor, *Divided We Stand.* Toronto, Martin Associates, 1977.
Editor, *The Inner Ear: An Anthology of New Canadian Poets.* Montreal, Quadrant, 1983.

*

Gary Geddes comments:
(1980) My poetry begins as an effort to come to terms with the influence of family and place in my life. Eventually it broadens out to include history generally, moving from lyric to narrative in order to accommodate anecdote and story. Unformed historical fragments (the Spanish conquests, the fall of Hong Kong, a reported journey of Chinese Buddhists to North America centuries ago, etc.) seem to give my imagination all it needs to work on. At the moment I am moving back and forth between poetry and fiction, writing short stories and exploring the fruitful ground between the two genres in longer forms, trying perhaps to write an epic for our times. Robert Kroetsch has said of *War and Other Measures* that it "builds, incredibly builds, it's the kind of long poem poets are only supposed to be able to dream." The trick is to combine the intensity of the lyric with the comprehensiveness of the epic. The lyrics continue to come, though, the recent poem on the killings at Kent State, "Sandra Lee Scheuer," shows where my voice goes; Al Purdy has said of this poem that it is the kind of piece poets wait a lifetime for, and some never achieve.

*   *   *

Gary Geddes is one of those people for whom the world is not quite acceptable as it is. As an anthologist, he argues for regionalism in *Skookum Wawa* and for nationalism in *Divided We Stand,* straining to find the meeting—if not the breaking—point for these opposites, wherever that may be. In his poetry, especially in his longer poems, he takes pains to contrast the world's bright appearance with its grim reality. In *Letter of the Master of Horse* "bright plumes, scarlet tunics" are stripped away to reveal "yellow teeth, bloody gums," so that the poet may pose the rhetorical question in the back of his mind: "What is the shape of freedom/after all?" On 18 May 1966, one Paul Joseph Chartier tried to blow up the Parliament Building in Ottawa and succeeded only in killing himself. Out of this anarchistic act, Geddes has written *War and Other Measures,* an episodic long poem full of narrative and nuance: "It's all a matter/of roots, etymologies./Dynamite: from the Greek/*dynamos,* meaning power." Pondering the problem of the just and equitable use of power, Geddes finds in violent acts a *rationale* all their own—short on reason perhaps, but strong on emotion:

> Out of this blood another rose
> will burst, its fragrance
> confound the universe.
>
> History is being made,
> I am the materials.

So Geddes, as anthologist and poet, is both activist and analyst. The two passions come to an equipoise in his most successful poems.

—John Robert Colombo

GERSHON, Karen. British. Born in Bielefeld, Germany, 29 August 1923; emigrated to England in 1938, to Israel in 1969. Married; four children. Recipient: Arts Council bursary, 1967; *Jewish Chronicle* prize, 1967; President of Israel's grant, 1967; Pioneer Women Award, 1968. Address: The Coach House, Coach House Lane, St. Austell, Cornwall PL 25 5AD, England.

PUBLICATIONS

Verse

New Poets 1959, with Christopher Levenson and Iain Crichton Smith. London, Eyre and Spottiswoode, 1959.
Selected Poems. London, Gollancz, and New York, Harcourt Brace, 1966.
Legacies and Encounters: Poems 1966-1971. London, Gollancz, 1972.
First Meeting. Richmond, Surrey, Keepsake Press, 1974.
My Daughters, My Sisters and Other Poems. London, Gollancz, 1975.
Jephthah's Daughter. Knotting, Bedfordshire, Sceptre Press, 1978.
Coming Back from Babylon. London, Gollancz, 1979.

Novel

Burn Helen. Brighton, Harvester Press, 1980.

Other

Editor, *We Came as Children: A Collective Autobiography*. London, Gollancz, and New York, Harcourt Brace, 1966.
Editor, *Postscript: A Collective Account of the Lives of Jews in West Germany since the Second World War*. London, Gollancz, 1969.

Translator, *Obscene: The History of an Indignation*, by Ludwig Marcuse. London, MacGibbon and Kee, 1965.

*   *   *

Karen Gershon is the most personal of poets, one whose writing communicates the intensity and anguish of lived experience. Study of her work reveals an orphan's longing for family ties, the search of a refugee for a homeland. As a teenage girl she survived the Nazi holocaust, in which her parents died, and the ordeal has left its scars. Much of her early poetry recalls the catastrophe and its effect upon her. Even on those occasions when she does not speak of it directly, one cannot help but hear its echoes: "I think of children with sad eyes/the dead the living the unborn/coins that pay for human choice/whose mothers mourn." Gershon's factual works, *We Came as Children* and *Postscript*, describe respectively the experience of refugees from the Nazi terror, and Jews living in post-war West Germany. In subsequent poems she continues to assert her own Jewish identity, seeking cultural roots in Jerusalem while for many years making her home in England, in whose language her work is written. Gradually, she has moved away from the past and its shadow to the more universal ground of human relationships. Deprived early of her own family, the husband and children she has gained take on a more intense significance, reminders of mother, father and sisters. Gershon, it seems, needs the bonds of family, yet at the same time is conscious of it as a threat, a stifling of her individual nature and its desires. One senses in her poems an extreme possessiveness towards her sons, a wariness of the

girls they have chosen to replace her. Elsewhere, one finds a resentment that so much of her own life is used up in serving the needs of others, a yearning to break free. This feeling emerges clearly in her novel *Burn Helen*, whose middle-aged heroine, on learning that she is soon to die, questions the enclosed nature of her married life.

Touch, the warmth of contact, is prized by Gershon as essential to fulfilment. She recalls with sadness the loved sister, now dead, who while alive would never allow herself to be touched. For Gershon physical passion, the "burning" of flesh, is to be celebrated, a proof of love and vigour. In "Separation" she indicates its importance: "Children playing at statues/till they're released by touch/exploit a primary truth:/contact keeps the flesh warm./Your absence spreads a chill/from which no spell can guard me." Here, her obvious conclusion is that "to remain flesh, I must burn." As need drives her, so love brings fulfilment. Some of her most touching poems are devoted to the relationship with her husband, as in "Late Summer" or "Married Love," where, watching him hold up their child, she decides: "That was the moment I stopped being orphaned." With love and its touch, continuity is assured, that flowing together of generations which re-asserts the triumph of life over death and destruction: "All currents come together:/my daughters, sisters, mother,/in me meet each other."

Gershon's poetry can be monotonous, even awkward at times, and her honesty is often painful. Nevertheless, her work contains a number of basic truths. If these seem hard to some, it is necessary to remember the furnace in which she forged them, and pay tribute to her strength and endurance in continuing to say what she means.

—Geoff Sadler

GHISELIN, Brewster. American. Born in Webster Groves, Missouri, 13 June 1903. Educated at the University of California, Los Angeles, A.B. 1927, and Berkeley, M.A. 1928, 1931-33; Oxford University, 1928-29. Married Olive F. Franks in 1929; two sons. Instructor in English, University of Utah, Salt Lake City, 1929-31; Assistant in English, University of California, Berkeley, 1931-33. Instructor, 1934-38, Lecturer, 1938-39, Assistant Professor, 1939-46, Associate Professor, 1946-50, Director of the Writers' Conference, 1947-66, Professor of English, 1950-71, Distinguished Research Professor, 1967-68, and since 1971, Professor Emeritus, University of Utah. Poetry Editor, 1937-46, and Associate Editor, 1946-49, *Rocky Mountain Review*, later *Western Review*, Salt Lake City and Lawrence, Kansas. Recipient: Ford fellowship, 1952; Ben and Abby Grey Foundation Award, 1965; American Academy award, 1970; Oscar Blumenthal Prize, 1973, and Levinson Prize, 1978 (*Poetry*, Chicago); William Carlos Williams Award, 1981; Utah Arts Council Governor's Award, 1982. Address: Department of English, University of Utah, Salt Lake City, Utah 84112, U.S.A.

PUBLICATIONS

Verse

Against the Circle. New York, Dutton, 1946.
The Nets. New York, Dutton, 1955.

Images and Impressions, with Edward Lueders and Clarice
  Short. Salt Lake City, University of Utah Printmaking
  Department, 1969.
Country of the Minotaur. Salt Lake City, University of Utah
  Press, 1970.
Let There Be Light. Seattle, Mill Mountain Press, 1976.
Light. Omaha, Abattoir, 1978.
Windrose: Poems 1929-1979. Salt Lake City, University of
  Utah Press, 1980.
The Dreamers. Winston-Salem, North Carolina, Palaemon
  Press, 1981.

Other

Writing. Washington, D.C., American Association of University Women, 1959.

Editor, *The Creative Process: A Symposium*. Berkeley, University of California Press, 1952.

*

Manuscript Collection: Lockwood Memorial Library, State
University of New York, Buffalo.

Critical Studies: *Spinning the Crystal Ball* by James Dickey,
Washington, D.C., Library of Congress, 1967; "An Earthen
Vessel" by William Ralston, in *Sewanee Review* (Tennessee),
Summer 1969; Radcliffe Squires, in *Concerning Poetry* (Bel-
lingham, Washington), Fall 1970; Kathleen Raine, in *Sewanee
Review* (Tennessee), Spring 1971; Samuel French Morse, in
Michigan Quarterly Review (Ann Arbor), Fall 1971; Henry Tay-
lor, in *Masterplots: 1971 Annual* and *Magill's Literary Annual
1981*, New York, Salem Press, 1971, 1981; "The Long and Short
of It" by Robert B. Shaw, in *Poetry* (Chicago), March 1972; "The
Needle and the Garment" by X.J. Kennedy, in *Counter/Mea-
sures 3* (Bedford, Massachusetts), 1974; "Brewster Ghiselin
Issue" of *The Blue Hotel 1* (Lincoln, Nebraska), 1980; "The
Poetry of Brewster Ghiselin" by Dave Smith, in *Western
Humanities Review* (Salt Lake City), Summer 1981.

Brewster Ghiselin comments:
   Like almost every poet, I feel that my poetry can live only in
being heard—that it must be given the body of life, as sensation
of sound and of vibration and movement of the articulating
voice. Though I have used a great variety of forms and measures,
I have never written free verse. The measure I have most often
found right is *accentual*, a strongly stressed and syllabically
various flow that I first heard clearly when I read *Beowulf* in Old
English, and turned to my own freer use, long before I read any of
Gerard Manley Hopkins.
   In my writing of poetry, all considerations of verse form arise
from the fact that the shaping of verse is the shaping of breath—
the breath of life in every sense. If a poet says that "The poetry
does not matter," as T.S. Eliot did in one context, meaning, I
suppose, that nothing matters except what has been called "the
ground of being," he simply reminds me of the vast importance
of poetry, which only through accord with that inexhaustible
attains whatever life it has. In the degree that poetry is realization and communion, it is false to say that it does not matter:

              The poetry matters:
              Whom the wind scatters
              Breath makes one again.

My central subject is men's struggle for breath, for being and
light. Under the universal necessity of change, which sweeps
away all form, man can have integrity and wholeness only
through ceaseless shaping and reshaping of himself and his
course and of those perspectives of vision that direct it. What
draws my interest most and gives me matter and theme is the
passion of living creatures to transcend the limits that choke
them, and to find and enjoy the limits that, each in changing
succession, are the freeing form of a moment of breath.

                    *   *   *

   Brewster Ghiselin's two early collections offered many poems
whose parts were so polished that it was difficult to grasp the
whole. The effect was that of Byzantine mosaics seen close, an
effect of brilliant yet disparate atomies rather than of anatomy.
Yet in his later collection, *Country of the Minotaur*, the opposite
is true. The parts are still burnished, but the confluence of a tidal
rhythm, an audacious language, and important themes distances
the poems, so that one sees their integrity and strength, as Yeats
saw the integrity and strength of the lofty mosaics at Ravenna.
This virtuous distance has come because Ghiselin has developed
into one of the few poets today whose faith rests in universals.
Because his quandaries are eternal they remain pure, for they
remain unresolved. Because his passions are conceived as parallels of the passions of vast energies, like sea and land, they remain
at peace; most at peace when most violent.
   Passion and peace define the boundaries of his poems, and the
field within the boundaries is that Nature which modern science
has made both more heartless and more mysteriously beautiful
than the Nature Wordsworth knew. It is a Nature that can only
be understood as a broad order which barely superintends random movement, fluctuation. Except for St.-John Perse I can
think of no one who is so majestically at home in this nomadic
drift-land. And in some ways Ghiselin is the better poet, for he
varies his focus, and Perse does not.

                                                —Radcliffe Squires

------

GHOSE, Zulfikar. British. Born in Sialkot, Pakistan, 13
March 1935. Educated at Keele University, England, B.A. in
English and philosophy 1959. Married in 1964. Cricket corres-
pondent for *The Observer*, London, 1960-65; teacher in London,
1963-69. Since 1969, Professor of English, University of Texas,
Austin. Recipient: Arts Council of Great Britain bursary, 1967.
Agent: Anthony Sheil Associates Ltd., 2-3 Morwell Street, Lon-
don WC1B 3AR, England. Address: Department of English,
University of Texas, Austin, Texas 78712, U.S.A.

PUBLICATIONS

Verse

The Loss of India. London, Routledge, 1964.
Jets from Orange. London, Macmillan, 1967.
The Violent West. London, Macmillan, 1972.
Penguin Modern Poets 25, with Gavin Ewart and B.S. Johnson.
  London, Penguin, 1974.

Novels

The Contradictions. London, Macmillan, 1966.
The Murder of Aziz Khan. London, Macmillan, 1967; New York, Day, 1969.
The Incredible Brazilian:
  The Native. London, Macmillan, and New York, Holt Rinehart, 1972.
  The Beautiful Empire. London, Macmillan, 1975; New York, Overlook Press, 1984.
  A Different World. London, Macmillan, 1978; New York, Overlook Press, 1985.
Crump's Terms. London, Macmillan, 1975.
Hulme's Investigations into the Bogart Script. Austin, Texas, Curbstone Press, 1981.
A New History of Torments. New York, Holt Rinehart, and London, Hutchinson, 1982.
Don Bueno. London, Hutchinson, 1983; New York, Holt Rinehart, 1984.

Short Stories

Statement Against Corpses, with B.S. Johnson. London, Constable, 1964.

Other

Confessions of a Native-Alien (autobiography). London, Routledge, 1965.
Hamlet, Prufrock, and Language. London, Macmillan, and New York, St. Martin's Press, 1978.
The Fiction of Reality. London, Macmillan, 1984.

*   *   *

Like several of his distinguished contemporaries from the Commonwealth, the Pakistani poet Zulfikar Ghose combines sophistication of technique with a sense of deracination. His gift for the rendering of minutiae is considerable, as in "Getting to Know Fish":

  Bombay's famous fish is called Bombay Duck.
  Slim and lazy-eyed like English haddock,
  it is a small fish, dried in the sun,
  hanging, hooked to string, among coconut trees.
  It stinks. When dry, it is boiled and eaten
  with rice; through the hollows of its eyes
  its bone-juice is pressed out, salted and spiced...

Such particularity has, for a Western reader, an attraction beyond its grip on circumstance. What is matter-of-fact for Ghose is, for his audience in West, exotic. Thus, in speaking realistically of his childhood, Ghose commands a colour and romance over and above his ostensible subject. It would be deprecating Ghose's intelligence to assume that he is unaware of the fascination of his subject matter. He appears himself in his careful verses as an alien presence; he calls attention to his crooked nose, his "morose-Ghose face." But the point about Ghose is that he is alien everywhere. He looks for his roots ("To My Ancestors"); he loses India ("The Loss of India"); he falls in love with England ("This Landscape, These People"). Yet he is not at home there: English tolerance permits an air of drought between himself and the natives ("The Alien"); he cries "I belong to this landscape but not to these people" ("Marriages"). Zulfikar Ghose is a poet, not of love, but of distance; not of belonging but of alienation.

This indicates the presence of a dichotomy deep down in the plasm of his verse. He has adopted a language so completely that he must be regarded as one of its modern masters. Yet his precision of detail is a pattern about a void. This is seen quite clearly when Ghose attempts a major theme, as in "War in India":

  In Delhi I saw this:
    a man, yes a man and not a reptile,
    crawl from the bank of the pavement to defile
  the streamlined river of traffic with his

  blood....

There is a disparity between the theme and its expression. The technique, adequate for tourist sketches and domestic settings, unintentionally reduces its subject matter. It is as though the eye, unsteadied by what it perceives, slides from the battle to the peripheries. A tank, immobilised, is seen as a crab upside down; the valleys, policed with air-strips, seem to Ghose like bowls scoured of ice. Restricted by sensibility or by technique, it seems that Ghose cannot rise far beyond the recording of minutiae.

All the poems quoted so far occur in Zulfikar Ghose's first collection, *The Loss of India.* It is a fine book, but it has the limitations of its fineness. Deracination seems to have set limits to Ghose's imaginative horizons. And the subsequent collections extend those horizons only nominally. *Jets from Orange* brings in France ("Choosing a Language," "Of Animate and Inanimate Matter") but in much the same externalising way as the first book brought in Britain. *The Violent West* evokes America, but it is an America of the yellow butterflies of Lake Travis, the brown earth of Texas. In both books there are Indian poems, and it is they that act as the real attraction. "The Attack on Sialkot," "The Kleptomaniac," "In the Desert" have something of the intensity and the nostalgia of the poems about India in the first collection. But, if the considerable distinction of Zulfikar Ghose is not to depend on one book only he will have to find ways of integrating his past with his present experience. Already he has done extraordinarily well in pitting an alien background against a metropolitan technique. His admirers will look forward to his future work in the hope of seeing him attain an even greater degree of wisdom, balance, and fusion.

—Philip Hobsbaum

GIBBON, (William) Monk. Irish. Born in Dublin, 15 December 1896. Educated at St. Columba's College, Rathfarnham; Keble College, Oxford (Open History Exhibitioner); Dublin University, Ph.D. Served as an Officer in the Royal Army Service Corps, 1914-18. Married Mabel Winifred Dingwall in 1928; two sons and four daughters. Taught at Chateau d'Oex, Switzerland; Clive House, Prestatyn; Oldfield School, Swanage, Dorset; Aravon School, Bray, County Wicklow; Brook House, Monkstown, County Dublin. Tredegar Lecturer, Royal Society of Literature, 1952; Tagore Centenary Lecturer, Abbey Theatre, 1961. Recipient: Tailteann Games Silver Medal, 1928. Fellow, Royal Society of Literature, 1950. Member, 1960, and Vice-President, 1967, Irish Academy of Letters. Address: 24 Sandycove Road, Sandycove, County Dublin, Ireland.

PUBLICATIONS

Verse

The Tremulous String: Poems in Prose.   Fair Oak, Hampshire,
    At the Sign of the Grayhound, 1926.
Wise Small Birds.   Dublin, Cuala Press, 1926.
The Branch of Hawthorn Tree.   London, Grayhound Press,
    1927.
Within a Little Field.   Dublin, Cuala Press, 1927.
For Daws to Peck At.   London, Gollancz, and New York,
    Dodd Mead, 1929.
A Ballad.   Winchester, Hampshire, Grayhound Press, 1930.
Now We'll Forget the Windy Hill.   Dublin, Cuala Press, 1931.
Seventeen Sonnets.   London, Joiner and Steele, 1932.
This Insubstantial Pageant: Collected Poems in Verse and Prose.
    London, Phoenix House, and New York, Devin Adair, 1951.
The Velvet Bow and Other Poems.   London, Hutchinson, 1972.

Other

The Seals (autobiography).   London, Cape, 1935.
The Stapleton Children in Jersey.   Privately printed, 1938.
Mount Ida (autobiography).   London, Cape, 1948.
The Red Shoes Ballet: A Critical Study.   London, Saturn Press,
    and New York, Auvergne, 1948.
Swiss Enchantment.   London, Evans, 1950.
The Tales of Hoffman: A Study of the Film.   London, Saturn
    Press, 1951; with *The Red Shoes Ballet*, New York, Garland,
    1977.
An Intruder at the Ballet.   London, Phoenix House, 1952.
Austria.   London, Batsford, 1953.
In Search of Winter Sport.   London, Evans, 1953.
Western Germany.   London, Batsford, 1955.
The Rhine and Its Castles.   London, Putnam, 1957; New York,
    Norton, 1958.
The Masterpiece and the Man: Yeats As I Knew Him.   London,
    Hart Davis, 1959; New York, Macmillan, 1960.
Netta (biography of Henrietta Franklin).   London, Routledge,
    1960.
The Climate of Love (autobiography).   London, Gollancz,
    1961.
Inglorious Soldier (autobiography).   London, Hutchinson, 1968.
The Brahms Waltz (autobiography).   London, Hutchinson,
    1970.
The Pupil: A Memory of Love.   Dublin, Wolfhound Press,
    1981.

Editor, *The Living Torch: An Anthology of Prose by AE, Prin-
    cipally Drawn from "Irish Statesman."*   London, Macmil-
    lan, 1937; New York, Macmillan, 1938.
Editor, *Poems from the Irish*, by Douglas Hyde.   Dublin, Allen
    Figgis, 1963.
Editor, *The Poems of Katherine Tynan.*   Dublin, Allen Figgis,
    1963.
Editor, *Thy Tears Might Cease*, by Michael Farrell.   London,
    Hutchinson, and New York, Knopf, 1964.

*

Bibliography: by Alan Denson, in *Dublin Magazine*, Autumn-
Winter 1966.

Manuscript Collection: Queen's University, Kingston, Ontario.

Critical Studies: "Metanoia" by Alan Denson, in *Irish Press*
(Dublin), 8 July 1972; "The Treason of Memory" by Eavan
Boland, in *Irish Times* (Dublin), 5 August 1972; "The Monk
Gibbon Papers" by Norman MacKenzie, in *Canadian Journal
of Irish Studies* (Vancouver), December 1983.

Monk Gibbon comments:

A poet can be lucky enough to be borne along upon the
contemporary tide, or it may happen to have set against him.
Herbert Palmer described me in a review as "one of the most
neglected of poets today whose work is of consequence." He
meant that I was not "with it." My own view is that a poem, even
when topical, should lie outside time. My earlier poetry is very
simple, my later a good deal more complex; but I have had a few
venerated readers who could take both sorts. It is hard not to be
influenced by fashion, but I think that readers should be completely above all poetic snobbery. I am lost in admiration for
Dylan Thomas's allusive "Fern Hill." But that doesn't prevent
me thinking Housman and W.H. Davies superb poets. Poetic
coteries fight hard for their own—which is laudable—and even
harder against their opposites—which is contemptible.

I try in my verse to crystallise certain moments of vision,
delight, or mere contemplation. I try quite often to embalm the
past: I try to give an inkling of how profoundly our emotions can
record, transmute or interpret the external world.

*   *   *

Compared to much present-day poetry Monk Gibbon's inevitably appears old-fashioned. Though he has experimented successfully with free verse, by far the greater part of his poetry has
been written in strict metrical forms. His diction and syntax
make few concessions to modern colloquial usage and his
subject-matter is rooted in an earlier tradition. The list of touchstones in "Ultimates" illustrates Monk Gibbon's traditional
approach to his craft:

> All else passes
> These remain
> Sun's warmth,
> Wind, rain;
>
> Grass underfoot
> Cloud overhead
> Birds in flight,
> Man's slow tread...

Throughout his career Monk Gibbon has remained detached
from the mainstream of modern poetry, concentrating on his
own exploration of traditional themes and on the preservation of
an individual and distinctive voice. The theme to which he
returns most often is the celebration of beauty, mainly as embodied in woman. It follows that a good deal of his output consists
of love poems. These are generally tender and reflective, poems
of admiration rather than of passionate involvement, though at
times passion breaks through. "The Black Heart" presents a
finely controlled statement of polarities in love:

> So all night long we spell
> Love's language slowly out,
> Who have forgotten that theft
> Ends always as great drouth.
>
> For theft is always loss—
> "Yet theft is ecstasy?"

This, at the mouth of hell,
My black heart says to me.

Monk Gibbon's pre-occupations are generally private rather than public, metaphysical rather than actual. Often there is a troubled awareness of the fragility of man's consciousness, floating for a while on a tide of sensation between dark and dark:

My life is like a dream:
I do not know
How it began, nor yet
How it will go.

Out of the night a bird
Has quickly flown
Across the lighted room
And now is gone

Into the dark again
From whence it came...

Monk Gibbon's poetry demonstrates only a modest degree of involvement with the Ireland of tradition or of the present day, although social and political comment does find a place in his later poetry. Some of the more recent poems and the collection of sonnets dating from 1932 show him technically at his most ambitious, but when he attempts to fill the larger or more difficult structures the inspiration is not always sufficient to meet the demands made upon it. He is generally most satisfying when writing economically and the finest of the simple lyrics from the earlier collections, *The Branch of the Hawthorn Tree* and *For Daws to Peck At* are still among his best.

—Rivers Carew

GILBERT, (Florence) Ruth.   New Zealander.   Born in Greytown, 26 March 1917. Educated at Hamilton High School; Otago School of Physiotherapy, Dunedin. Married to Dr. John Bennett Mackay; two daughters and two sons. Formerly, Physiotherapist, Otago School of Physiotherapy. Recipient: Jessie Mackay Poetry Award, 1948, 1949, 1967. Address: 83 Donald Street, Karori, Wellington, New Zealand.

PUBLICATIONS

Verse

Lazarus and Other Poems. Wellington, Reed, 1949.
The Sunlit Hour. London, Allen and Unwin, 1955.
The Luthier. Wellington, Reed, 1966.
Collected Poems. Wellington, Black Robin, 1984.

*

Manuscript Collection: Turnbull Library, Wellington.

Ruth Gilbert comments:
My chosen forms are the lyric and the quatrain, and my aim in writing: clarity, simplicity, economy. The brevity of the quatrain

appeals to me, while the lyric holds the music which my ear demands. Should my subject need more room I find the lyric sequence, which I use often, the perfect medium. Poetry is my only form of creative writing.

*   *   *

Ruth Gilbert's talent is for the straightforward evocation of brief moments of emotion, particularly those of the child or the woman, within the tradition of the romantic lyric. For her, the poetry seems to lie more in the words themselves than in the experiences; she is willing to take over poetic resonances established by others, reshuffling them for her own purposes:

How steeped in beauty these old names are:
Saffron, Sandalwood, Cinnibar...

This is a Georgian attitude, resulting in low-pressure poems of simple statement. If she has a poetic ancestor, it is Walter de la Mare, who is close at hand in "Phobia," "Legendary Lady" and "Portrait."

Some of these moments of emotion are as imagined in the lives of others, particularly within Bible stories, where such figures as Joseph, Rachel and Lazarus are sympathetically probed. Some are personal to the poet, as "Sanatorium" and, nearer to the bone, "Fall Out." Some are crystallised into small perfection, as in "Li Po," "Metamorphosis" and "The Trees of Corot."

Ruth Gilbert has made several attempts to increase her scale, by binding lyrics into a sequence. Of these the most successful is *The Luthier,* which, even if conventionally romantic in essence, has the merit of a more vigorous vocabulary, and more complex rhythms than she has commanded elsewhere.

At her best, she can set up quiet ripples—never disturbing ones—which take her meaning beyond the sensitive but unadventurous moment which she describes. Her later work, however, suggests a growing awareness of the forces to be tapped when the form has been hammered out by the pressure of the content and is not a mere relaxed rehandling of old words and shapes. There may therefore be different work ahead of her. But her natural place is with the Georgians.

—Joan Stevens

GILDNER, Gary.   American.   Born in West Branch, Michigan, 22 August 1938. Educated at Michigan State University, East Lansing, B.A. 1960, M.A. 1961. Married Judy McKibben in 1963; one daughter. Writer in university relations department, Wayne State University, Detroit, 1961-62; Instructor, Northern Michigan University, Marquette, 1963-65. Since 1966, Member of the Department, now Professor of English, Drake University, Des Moines, Iowa. Visiting Professor and Writer-in-Residence, Reed College, Portland, Oregon, 1983-85. Recipient: Bread Loaf Writers Conference Robert Frost Fellowship, 1970; National Endowment for the Arts fellowship, 1971, 1976; Yaddo fellowship, 1972, 1973, 1975, 1976, 1978; MacDowell Colony fellowship, 1974; Theodore Roethke Prize, 1976, and Helen Bullis Prize, 1979 (*Poetry Northwest*); William Carlos Williams Prize (*New Letters*), 1977. Agent: Nat Sobel Associates, 146 East 19th Street, New York, New York 10003. Address: 2915 School Street, Des Moines, Iowa 50311, U.S.A.

PUBLICATIONS

Verse

First Practice. Pittsburgh, University of Pittsburgh Press,
    1969.
Digging for Indians. Pittsburgh, University of Pittsburgh
    Press, 1971.
Eight Poems.   Denver, Bredahl, 1973.
Nails. Pittsburgh, University of Pittsburgh Press, 1975.
Letters from Vicksburg. Greensboro, North Carolina, Unicorn
    Press, 1976.
The Runner. Pittsburgh, University of Pittsburgh Press, 1978.
Jabón. Portland, Oregon, Breitenbush, 1981.
Blue Like the Heavens: New and Selected Poems.   Pittsburgh,
    University of Pittsburgh Press, 1984.

Short Stories

The Crush. New York, Ecco Press, 1983.

Other

Toads in the Greenhouse. Des Moines, Iowa, Perfection Form,
    1978.

Editor, with Judith Gildner, *Out of This World: Poems from the
    Hawkeye State*. Ames, Iowa State University Press, 1975.

                              *

Manuscript Collection: University of Pittsburgh.

Gary Gildner comments:

My poems are narrative, mainly. Little fictions. I am fond of
the persona, and have, among my characters, a Mexican innocent named Soap; a boy at his first football practice in a school
basement which doubles as a bomb shelter; a woman who has
lost part of her hand; a Civil War soldier writing cocky letters,
which become less so, home to his young wife; a German youth,
drafted by Napoleon to help him take Russia, who ends up,
warm at last, in Iowa; a former pro athlete speaking from his
wheelchair at a pig roast; an old man lost in a retirement home; a
young man in love with a goshawk in his attic; a man and his
daughter making angels in the snow...

Clarity, setting, story, engagement, promise, conflict, music
(gathering sound), mystery, resolution—I am fond of these elements as well. Nouns and verbs. Names. And respect for the line.

I started late. I was almost 28 when I wrote my first poem. I
wrote it out of frustration, I think, because the story I wanted to
write would not grow beyond the single sheet of paper it occupied. Thinking one page not enough for a short story, I decided
that the stubborn text wanted to be a poem. Not much is shorter,
is it?

I was not eager to try poetry. What did I know about it? The
first and last "poems" I'd written were in college, moonstruck
and stealing from Whitman, trying to win a stunning girl whose
legs were long and sleek and whose sea-green eyes troubled me
everywhere, in darkness and in light. (She later had her nose
bobbed and became a fashion model.)

But I played with those sentences anyway, working them into
lines I thought interesting. In truth, I had six short stories like
that, one-pagers, all of them facing me on a humid summer's day
in the middle of America when what I really wanted to be writing
was a novel—a man's work!—for which the six short story
notions were to be warmup exercises. (I had just abandoned a

novel I'd worked five years on; with every annual rewrite it got
better but it would never sing and I knew it.) I was almost 28. I
was in a hurry. I turned the six *short* stories into six poems and
sent them off, one each, to six magazines, mainly to be rid of
them, the bastards. But they were all accepted. And that changed
everything.

                   *   *   *

Gary Gildner has displayed since his earliest poems (*First
Practice*) a strong sense of narrative, character, voice, and situation; his poems are rich in prose virtues, and his ear is quick to
hear ways American speech rhythms can fruitfully play with the
rhythms of verse in English. In this regard he is, for a midwesterner, solidly in the poetic line of Emerson and Frost.

His earliest poems contain memorable snapshots of family life
and adolescence that reverberate in the reader's memory. Here's
"Geisha" from *Digging for Indians*:

> The boxer bitch is pregnant
> puffed up like an Oriental wrestler!
>
> The boys stand back,
> aloof, embarassed
> or unsure of their hands.
>
> But the girls, their cheeks aflame,
> are down on shiny knees
> praising all the nipples.

But the title of *Digging for Indians* and of Gildner's next book,
Nails, along with the resonances and depths of his earlier anecdotal poems, suggested a broadening concern, and in 1976
Gildner published *Letters from Vicksburg*. Working from actual
letters, he made a sonnet sequence of letters home from a Civil
War soldier to his wife. His continuing concern for family life
and domestic continuity were part of larger meditations on the
disruptions and recurring themes of American history.

The Vicksburg poems appear in *The Runner*, along with other
poems that begin in Gildner's recognizable voice but treat characters and situations new to his work. "In the blue winter of
1812/ Johann Gaertner, a bag of bones,/ followed Napoleon
home," one of them begins, and "When the Retarded Swim"
continues in its first lines the sentence begun by the title, "at the Y
on Fridays/ a lot of time is taken up/ with holding them, so they
do not drown." Another poem is a 133-line monologue by a
young athlete paralyzed from the waist down in a motorcycle
accident; yet another poem is spoken by a mad gardener who
brings into his greenhouse toads to control the ladybugs he
brought in to control the scale attacking his orchids, and who
winds up neglecting the plants to feed the toads, which desert him
at the onset of frost. There are also poems of marital despair. The
poems in *The Runner* are longer and more resourceful than
Gildner's earlier vignettes, as if they had sought and found abilities to include the rush of pain and confusion held somewhat at
bay by shorter forms, but which seem in this book to be struggling with the poet for the very dominion of the book.

In 1981 Gildner published *Jabón*. Jabón is a kind of wise fool,
a crazy Mexican who washes and blesses the taxis in a small
village and who, because he cannot understand in rational, adult
terms the life that swirls around him, comes to understand and
accept life in more immediate and intuitive terms. The character
of Jabón is remarkably unsentimentalized and is, buffeted
fiercely for not having conventional worldly skills, but by blessing taxis and the yellow pail in which he keeps the water to wash
them, he is in some way in tune with life rather than in desperate

contest with it. Late in the sequence Jabón joins forces with a precocious eight-year-old boy, and two American travelling opportunists are sitting over lunch and discussing philosophically the alliance between Jabón and the boy.

> ...You know what
> flashed in my head? It's some kind of cult.
> Fifty years from now, a hundred, they'll dance
> in the streets to those two, and put up a statue—
> and guys like us will be nowhere, eating the special.

Blue Like the Heavens: New and Selected Poems have an emotional equilibrium in sharp contrast to the tumults of *The Runner*, though the dark strains of that fine book are not missing. Memory, and thus by extension the imagination itself, is the central preoccupation in these poems. One begins with a lady salesman on the telephone trying to sell the speaker insulation, and ends like this:

> "Are your children safe? Your loved ones?" she said.
> Oh dear lady beyond these cold hands,
> nothing is safe in my presence. I am a small hog
> with a sore throat. A frog, the last egg
> from the nest of a swan, even the puny squeal
> of a porcupine—I will steal anything for a song.
> Even your timid voice, dear lady,
> lost at the other end for a way to make me warm.

Gildner's confrontation with nostalgia, memory, and his own imaginative impulses promises further interesting development from a poet who has consistently grown in skill and stature, proposing each step of the way more complex formal and imaginative tasks for himself. It may be that he is speaking to such possibilities in a new poem like "Always in Late Summer Now, in the City":

> I think of how the gulls hang
> lightly over the lake's edge,
> and how a small perch slips to the surface, tiger-striped,
> and how the white birch, in places, can look at you all day
> —and I think of pushing away
> from the dock, pulling forward into the farther dark,
> the line of pine and fir on the far shore black,
> a cut moon, a few stars to lighten my cupped hands,
> wondering what's under my heart
> that could take me deeper.

—William Matthews

GILL, David (Lawrence William). British. Born in Chislehurst, Kent, 3 July 1934. Educated at Chislehurst and Sidcup Grammar School; University College, London, B.A. (honours) in German 1955, B.A. (honours) in English 1970; Birmingham University, Cert.Ed. 1959. Served in the Royal Signals, 1955-57. Married Irene Zuntz in 1958; three children. Taught at Bedales School, Hampshire, 1960-62, Nyakasura School, Fort Portal, Uganda, 1962-64, and Magdalen College School, Oxford, 1965-71. Since 1971, Lecturer, Buckinghamshire College of Higher Education, High Wycombe. Recipient: Birmingham *Post* prize, 1959. Address: 32 Boyn Hill Road, Maidenhead, Berkshire, England.

PUBLICATIONS

Verse

Men Without Evenings.   London, Chatto and Windus-Hogarth Press, 1966; Middletown, Connecticut, Wesleyan•University Press, 1967.
The Pagoda and Other Poems.   London, Chatto and Windus-Hogarth Press, 1969; Middletown, Connecticut, Wesleyan University Press, 1970.
Peaches and Aperçus.   London, Poet and Peasant, 1974.
The Upkeep of the Castle.   Bakewell, Derbyshire, Hub, 1976.
One Potato, Two Potato, with Dorothy Clancy.   London, Macmillan, 1985.

Other

Editor and Translator, *In the Eye of the Storm: Fifty Years of Poetry*, by Ondra Lysohorsky.   Bakewell, Derbyshire, Hub, 1976.

*

David Gill comments:

(1970) I began writing verse as a schoolboy on chemistry labs, daffodils, gym masters, myself, love and other universal topics. A late developer, I wrote one good poem at university. The influences of my German reading—Rilke, Stefan George, as well as Welsh idols such as Dylan Thomas and Wilfred Owen—had a delayed action. Rilke's *Dinggedichte* plus a certain mistrust of the abstract brought home to me the importance of things at the centre of poems, visual things like roundabouts, pagodas, punch-and-judy shows, cartwheels, missiles.

In 1958 I became involved in the struggle against nuclear weapons, and, in poetry, in a parallel struggle to tame proud and angry feelings in a cage of words. At the same time (1959-62) I wanted to say quieter things about the Hampshire hangers and beech-forests near Selbourne, and became aware of the truth that poems are ways of stating the contrasts that bother the mind, the contrast of present and past ("On the Cathedral Floor"):

> Bunches of angels hang from exploding branches
> Watching the aisles. Six hundred years below
> My son makes progress on the gothic floor,
> Ant-explorer, crawling to and fro
> Between the massive trees.

Or the contrast of here and elsewhere in the world-village ("I Must Withdraw"):

> This day as every day my clock-shod mind
> Has tramped to crises in the Timbuctoos,
> Tibets and Thailands of the headlined news,
> But only at such frontiers to find
> The vultures knife-eyed; victims small and blind.

The shape of my verse has travelled from quatrains to more complex stanzas to a kind of free-verse, which at times goes near to prose. Preoccupations with people, politics, landscape, animals, dominate the collection of poems written in Uganda and entitled *Men Without Evenings*. Of these poems the *Guardian* critic Bernard Bergonzi wrote: "His poems are immersed in the colours, sounds, and smells of the country, but they have an intelligent moral dimension which makes them something more than touristic snapshot verse."

(1980) During the early 1970's I began to take part in public poetry readings, writing more for the straining ear, and with greater directness. The need to express feelings against my natural drift to elegy has led me to invest in disguises and dramatic monologues. In my latest book I vanish into a hunch-backed Archduke, the poet Edmund Waller, and the last unpolluted man on earth.

*   *   *

If David Gill's verse rarely quickens the pulse, it rarely embarrasses. The verse muses with a learned, occasionally pedantic, voice on ethical and political issues, the disciplines of artists as diverse as Beatrix Potter and Cezanne, the generations, and man's relation to the natural world and the cosmos. The earnestness and plausibility of this voice compensate for Gill's sentimentality, preachiness, and lapses of poetic tact.

In general, the longer, often iambic, lines of his first two volumes, *Men Without Evenings* and *The Pagoda*, suit his discursive talent more than the shorter lines that dominate his last two books. *Men Without Evenings* attempts to dramatize European wonder at the African world where "there's no time left for mixed emotions, " as well as a pukka liberal guilt over the white man's sins and stupidities ("Trial" reveals the futility of English justice and "Swamp" the pointlessness of transplanted technology). More interesting are the imagined African responses to European artifacts, though lines like "his hours of cockroach boredom" ("The Kaleidoscope") tend to produce a white man's burden of condescending compassion. Gill's apparently unintentional repetition of images weakens them: "they weave the rushmats of their low alluvial lives" ("Them") becomes "our neighbors weave the slow grass mats / of their dark green unfathomable lives" ("Them and Us"). These compound nouns and adjective-noun duads represent an unfortunate tendency in much of Gill's verse. Regular meter and predictable metaphors reinforce this mechanical effect: "the grass-fires of my crisp emotions burn" ("Dry Safari").

Yet some carefully observed passages magically transcend their realistic details, the loosening of the meter perhaps signalling the freeing of Gill's imagination, as when elephants "plod in solemn lines across / the highway picking up their feet like pieces of litter / distastefully, shambling on in their overall hides / three sizes too large" ("A Non-Elegy in a National Game Park"). And Gill's speaker sometimes engagingly invites the reader behind the facade of the finished verse: "dark baby of my sonnet without rhyme" ("Adoption"), or "pathetic fallacy to twist" ("Africán Night"). Whatever their ostensible subjects, such verses become partially dramatizations of the art of making poems. But the heavy ideological commitment of many of the poems in *The Pagoda*, however attractive the beliefs, subverts Gill's wit and freshness: "Mohandas Gandhi, the mahatma, raised the eyes / of the indigo-pickers of Champerei to the forgotten hills / of self-esteem..." ("Mohandas Gandhi and the Onion-Pickers").

Peaches and Aperçus, a title that invites criticism, abandons ideology to celebrate the natural world and female beauty in short-lined verse. The poems which attempt to develop single controlling images in place of the shifting figures of the earlier volumes are often blandly tentative. The best of several striking exceptions is "Moonthought," which subtly fuses sexual and seasonal rhythms: "The moon is o so Far away / Yet every year the same / the harvest, drunken / rises in ricks."

The twenty short poems of *The Upkeep of the Castle* demonstrate a reasonable level of competence. More than competent is the long-lined "Edmund Waller's Recessional," which presents the "real" Waller behind the Saccharissa poems, the man bitter

and passionately involved, the artist objectively aware of the artistic advantages of his frustration:

> Ironic-eyed and iron-hearted Saccharissa,
> Hard as the rocks at Tunbridge Wells.
> No salving waters, though. No springs to slake my thirst
> Must use that sometime in a verse.

Here the mask implies the actual personality absent from Gill's African disguises.

The delicacy and strength of some of Gill's effects, the sense of a curious mind and real feeling, however bookish in origin, stem from an authentic voice sometimes bound to ideological and formal rigidity. A passage from "Cutty Sark" is emblematic of Gill's special talent, minor but genuine, for conveying experience at several removes from the actual:

> Once on her tilting decks the sailor Conrad
> stood braced to record the cadence of her prose
> between the margins of two continents.
> Through him I have some feeling
> for this ship.

—Burton Kendle

GILLIES, Valerie (née Simmons). Scottish. Born in Edmonton, Alberta, Canada, 4 June 1948. Educated at Trinity Academy, Edinburgh, 1953-66; University of Edinburgh, 1966-70, 1972-74, M.A. 1970, M. Litt. 1974; University of Mysore, India, 1970-71. Married William Gillies in 1972; one son and one daughter. Writer-in-Residence, Boroughmuir School, Edinburgh, 1978-79. Recipient: Scottish Arts Council bursary, 1976; Eric Gregory Award, 1976. Address: c/o Canongate Publishing Ltd., 17 Jeffrey Street, Edinburgh EH1 1DR, Scotland.

PUBLICATIONS

Verse

Trio: New Poets from Edinburgh, with Roderick Watson and Paul Mills, edited by Robin Fulton. New York, New Rivers Press, 1971.
Each Bright Eye: Selected Poems. Edinburgh, Canongate, 1977.

Plays

Radio Plays: *Rabbits*, 1978; *Stories of the Mountains*, 1979; *The Ballad of Tam Lin*, 1979.

Other

Kim: Notes. London, Longman, 1981.

Editor, *Scottish Short Stories 1979* and *1980*. London, Collins, 2 vols., 1979-80.

*

Valerie Gillies comments:

I first began writing at about the age of 14. A poem would come into my head while I was out walking: I'd write it down when I got back, altering it here and there. This is my method of composition still. I like to fool around with words, to play with half-rhymes. I write in strict form and in freer verse too. About the time I went to India I was experimenting with the poetry of meditation. The denser poems in *Each Bright Eye* are a result of that kind of concentration. The love poem and the divine poem were my first preoccupations, and I have written enough animal poems to begin a bestiary. I am not afraid of ideas, and I like to make them strike sparks off one another in the old metaphysical way, but I am working towards a clearer, simpler voice in my poems today.

*   *   *

Canadian-born Valerie Gillies grew up and was educated in Scotland and at the University of Mysore. The influences both of India and the Scotland in which she has now married and settled are apparent in her verse. Unlike some women poets, she is capable of a keen objectivity that is matched by the lithe strength of her poetic structures. She favours *vers libre*, varied occasionally with a kind of lolloping casual rhyme of half-rhyme. Her best free-verse poems hold together, so to say, from the centre.

It is difficult for any poet other than a master of the first order to capture and convey the "feel" of an alien country. Gillies's poems with Indian subject-matter are thus, not surprisingly, her least successful, partly because the sense of someone "outside looking-in" results in a certain sense of verbal opacity, not helped by the now-and-then use of Indian terms or experiences unlikely to be understood by a non-Indian reader. When she is writing of people, whether of her grandfather, minded "to make a crook and staff," or Indians like "Mister B. Rajan, diamond buyer" in "Fellow Passenger," or, even more vividly, in "The Piano-Tuner," she captures, not just the pathos of the unsuccessful disguise of unadmitted personal limitation in her subject, but the lingering echoes of the vanished British Raj culture:

Two hundred miles, he had come
    to tune one piano, the last hereabouts.
Both of them were relics of imperial time:
    the Anglo-Indian and the old upright knockabout.

He peered, and peered again
    into its monsoon-warped bowels.
From the flats of dead sound he'd beckon
    a tune on the bones out to damp vowels.

His own sounds were pidgeon....

She has written both love poems and poems about birth. The former are seriously tender, concentrating on the nature of the association that binds lovers together rather than on anatomical detail; the latter, delicately original, as "For a Son's First Birthday": "Your first breath / blew you up so pink / you were ragged robin in the marshes./ / What I forget / is your first sound: / loud, brilliant and reedy." That double meaning of the word "reedy" binds the images together, aligns them to complement each other, like glasses in a telescope, and reveals the technique of a true poet.

Gillies's real strength, however, shows itself to strongest advantage in her animal poems. It is one of the received Eng. Lit. myths of our time that every poet who writes about animals must

in some way be under the influence of Ted Hughes: absurd, of course, since many older poets were well aware of what goes on in the forests of the night. Gillies's special concern is with animals in motion, as in "The Greyhound," "The Salmon-Loup" (in which the comparison between the salmon about to make "his curve of a fish-leap" and her lover, "newly arrived in fresh sight / A silverskin of atlantic littoral" is beautifully made), and in her picture of "Deerhounds": "Long dogs, you move with air / belling the vault of your ribcage. / You subdue the miles below your hocks.../ The bracken hurdles below your height, / the rushes make way for you; / your hard eye holds in sight the rapid hills...."

—Maurice Lindsay

GINSBERG, Allen. American. Born in Newark, New Jersey, 3 June 1926. Educated at Paterson High School, New Jersey; Columbia University, New York, B.A. 1948. Served in the Military Sea Transport Service. Book reviewer, *Newsweek*, 1950; market researcher, New York and San Francisco, 1951-53. Free-lance writer: participant in many poetry readings and demonstrations. Since 1971, Director, Committee on Poetry Foundation, New York; Director, Kerouac School of Poetics, Naropa Institute, Boulder, Colorado. Recipient: Guggenheim Fellowship, 1965; National Endowment for the Arts grant, 1966; American Academy grant, 1969; National Book Award, 1974; National Arts Club Gold Medal, 1979; Los Angeles *Times* award, 1982. Member, American Academy, 1973. Address: P.O. Box 582, Stuyvesant Station, New York, New York 10009, U.S.A.

PUBLICATIONS

Verse

Howl and Other Poems. San Francisco, City Lights, 1956; revised edition, San Francisco, Grabhorn Hoyem, 1971.
Siesta in Xbalba and Return to the States. Privately printed, 1956.
Empty Mirror: Early Poems. New York, Totem-Corinth, 1961.
Kaddish and Other Poems 1958-60. San Francisco, City Lights, 1961.
A Strange New Cottage in Berkeley. San Francisco, Grabhorn Press, 1963.
Reality Sandwiches 1953-60. San Francisco, City Lights, 1963.
Penguin Modern Poets 5, with Lawrence Ferlinghetti and Gregory Corso. London, Penguin, 1963.
The Change. London, Writers Forum, 1963.
Kral Majales. Berkeley, California, Oyez, 1965.
Prose Contribution to Cuban Revolution. Detroit, Artists' Workshop Press, 1966.
Wichita Vortex Sutra. London, Peace News Poetry, 1966.
T.V. Baby Poems. London, Cape Goliard Press, 1967; New York, Grossman, 1968.
Wales—A Visitation, July 29, 1967. London, Cape Goliard Press, 1968.
Scrap Leaves, Hasty Scribbles. New York, Poets Press, 1968.
Message II. Buffalo, Gallery Upstairs Press, and London, Ad Infinitum, 1968.
Planet News 1961-1967. San Francisco, City Lights, 1968.

Airplane Dreams: Compositions from Journals. Toronto, Anansi, 1968; San Francisco, City Lights, 1969.
Ankor Wat. London, Fulcrum Press, 1968.
The Moments Return. San Francisco, Grabhorn Hoyem, 1970.
Notes after an Evening with William Carlos Williams. New York, Charters, 1970.
Iron Horse. Toronto, Coach House Press, 1972; San Francisco, City Lights, 1974.
The Fall of America: Poems of These States 1965-1971. San Francisco, City Lights, 1972.
The Gates of Wrath: Rhymed Poems 1948-1952. Bolinas, California, Grey Fox Press, 1972.
Open Head, with *Open Eye,* by Lawrence Ferlinghetti. Melbourne, Sun, 1972.
New Year Blues. New York, Phoenix Book Shop, 1972.
Bixby Canyon Ocean Path Word Breeze. New York, Gotham Book Mart, 1972.
Sad Dust Glories. Berkeley, California, Workingman's Press, 1975.
First Blues: Rags, Ballads, and Harmonium Songs 1971-1974. New York, Full Court Press, 1975.
Mind Breaths: Poems 1972-1977. San Francisco, City Lights, 1978.
Poems All Over the Place: Mostly Seventies. Cherry Valley, New York, Cherry Valley Editions, 1978.
Mostly Sitting Haiku. Paterson, New Jersey, From Here Press, 1978; revised edition, 1979.
Careless Love: Two Rhymes. Madison, Wisconsin, Red Ozier Press, 1978.
Straight Hearts' Delight: Love Poems and Selected Letters 1947-1980, with Peter Orlovsky, edited by Winston Leyland. San Francisco, Gay Sunshine Press, 1980.
Plutonian Ode: Poems 1977-1980. San Francisco, City Lights, 1982.
Collected Poems 1947-1980. New York, Harper, 1984.

Recordings: *Howl and Other Poems,* Fantasy-Galaxy, 1959; *Kaddish,* Atlantic Verbum, 1966; *William Blake's Songs of Innocence and Experience Tuned by Allen Ginsberg,* 1969; *First Blues,* Folkways, 1982.

Plays

Don't Go Away Mad, in *Pardon Me, Sir, But Is My Eye Hurting Your Elbow?,* edited by Bob Booker and George Foster. New York, Geis, 1968.
Kaddish (produced New York, 1972).

Other

The Yage Letters, with William S. Burroughs. San Francisco, City Lights, 1963.
Notes on an Interview with Allen Ginsberg, by Edward Lucie-Smith. London, Turret, 1965.
Indian Journals: March 1962—May 1963: Notebooks, Diary, Blank Pages, Writings. San Francisco, Dave Haselwood, 1970.
Improvised Poetics, edited by Mark Robison. Buffalo, Anonym Press, 1971.
Declaration of Independence for Dr. Timothy Leary. San Francisco, Hermes Free Press, 1971.
Gay Sunshine Interview, with Allen Young. San Francisco, Grey Fox Press, 1974.
Allen Verbatim: Lectures on Poetry, Politics, Consciousness, edited by Gordon Ball. New York, McGraw Hill, 1974.

The Visions of the Great Rememberer (on Jack Kerouac). Amherst, Massachusetts, Mulch Press, 1974.
Chicago Trial Testimony. San Francisco, City Lights, 1975.
To Eberhart from Ginsberg. Lincoln, Massachusets, Penmaen Press, 1976.
As Ever: The Collected Correspondence of Allen Ginsberg and Neal Cassady, edited by Barry Gifford. Berkeley, California, Creative Arts, 1977.
Journals: Early Fifties—Early Sixties, edited by Gordon Ball. New York, Grove Press, 1977.
Composed on the Tongue: Literary Conversations 1967-1977, edited by Donald Allen. Bolinas, California, Grey Fox Press, 1980.

*

Bibliography: *A Bibliography of Works of Allen Ginsberg October 1943-July 1, 1967,* by George Dowden, San Francisco, City Lights, 1970; *Allen Ginsberg: An Annotated Bibliography 1969-1977* by Michelle P. Kraus, Metuchen, New Jersey, Scarecrow Press, 1980.

Manuscript Collections: Columbia University, New York; University of Texas, Austin.

Critical Studies: *Allen Ginsberg in America* by Jane Kramer, New York, Random House, 1968, as *Paterfamilias,* London, Gollancz, 1970; *Allen Ginsberg* by Thomas F. Merrill, New York, Twayne, 1969; *Scenes Along the Road,* edited by Ann Charters, New York, Gotham Book Mart, 1971; *Allen Ginsberg in the 60's* by Eric Mottram, Brighton, Sussex, Unicorn Bookshop, 1971; *The Visionary Poetics of Allen Ginsberg* by Paul Portugues, Santa Barbara, California, Ross-Erikson, 1978; *Cometh with Clouds (Memory: Allen Ginsberg)* by Dick McBride, Cherry Valley, New York, Cherry Valley Editions, 1983.

Theatrical Activities:
Actor: **Films**—*Pull My Daisy,* 1961; *Guns of the Trees, Wholly Communion,* 1965; *Chappaqua,* 1966; *Renaldo and Clara,* 1978; *Fried Shoes, Cooked Diamonds,* 1978; *This Is for You, Jack,* 1984.

Allen Ginsberg comments:
    (1970) Beat-Hip-Gnostic-Imagist.
    Major themes: transformation of consciousness to include visionary gleam of planet-light in Eternity before death. Characteristic subject: my own body or imagistic body of planet. Usual forms and sources: Bible and Kit Smart, parallelism and litany. Sources in Whitman, Rimbaud, Shakespeare, Blake above all, Pound, Jack Kerouac, and W.C. Williams. Influenced by "Black Mountain" poets, Olson, Creeley, Duncan. Travels and music of Orient leading into Mantra chanting reflect back on poesy as prophetic Shamanistic Chaunt. I have achieved the introduction of the word *fuck* into texts inevitably studied by schoolboys.
    (1974) A.D. 1973 studying poetics and meditation in the whispered transmission school of Mila Repa (12th century Tibetan Buddhist yogi-poet) with Rimpoche Chögyam Trungpa Lama, also a poet; tendency of my poetry practice last 2 years has been toward natural minded improvisation, taking for granted that "first thought is best thought," an attitude necessary for the realization of spontaneous flow of rhymed lines; presently in U.S. black Blues form and wedded to traditional triple-chord (CFG or GCD etc.) Western Blues. This is outgrowth of a decade's monochord practice mantra-chanting, followed by sev-

eral years tuning Blake's lyrics to actual song (restoring the words to song, so to speak).

The tradition of improvising poems on the spot in communal situation is I believe older than written tradition and perhaps more distinguished—as in the work of Homer or the much more ancient oral epic tradition of Australian Aborigine Song Men with whom I've had some brief contact Spring 1972. In any case it may be appropriate to restore facility in the bardic improvised manner in this over-civilized day and age when we are not sure that the supply of electric or paper will outlast the century, outlast our own lives. So as a conservation of viable poetries independent of material base (printed book) in case of, just in case of, historical necessity, and as outgrowth of Beat-hip-gnostic-imagistic spontaneous mind style, I am practicing improvised poetry.

*   *   *

Allen Ginsberg is perhaps the crucial figure in the revival of American poetry in the 1950's and 1960's. His intellectual contributions to the new American poetry are not as important as Charles Olson's; his technical contributions are not as important as Robert Duncan's; his work may not in the long-run be as satisfying as Edward Dorn's, John Ashbery's, Jack Spicer's or Robert Creeley's. It was, however, Ginsberg who created the public image of the poet for his generation. Seldom have previous generations been so fortunate, to be represented in the public eye by a poet of his abilities. It is difficult to sort out Ginsberg the phenomenon from Ginsberg the poet. He is, however, a genuine poet whose achievement cannot be doubted.

Post-Whitmanian poetry—and it is Whitman's tradition the poets of the 1950's renewed—is a poetry which recognizes the perpetual state of crisis in which language exists. That is, it appeals to precisely the fact which poetry has traditionally attempted to diminish by the ritualization of itself and of experience. The new American poetry, though it often has an important religious concern, is timely rather than eternal, political rather than religious, immediate rather than ritualized. The apparent ritual of a Ginsberg performance—the chanting and the priest-like presence of the poet himself—has a totally non-ritual meaning: the destiny of this poetry is to *discover* its destiny syllable by syllable and line by line. Ginsberg created this poetry for the popular audience, without compromising it. Never has such a dense, difficult, and learned poetry had such a vast appeal.

That Ginsberg is a learned poet is a point worth emphasizing. It is impossible to read through his work without being aware that he knows the literary tradition thoroughly. He is widely read in philosophy, eastern religion, and history. His knowledge of current politics is neither casual nor merely fashionable. When he speaks in *Howl* of the poets "who studied Plotinus Poe St. John of the Cross telepathy and bop kaballa because the cosmos instinctively vibrated at their feet in Kansas," he might have been speaking about Allen Ginsberg and Paterson, N.J. Ginsberg's strategy is to call both the private and the public crisis into the critical space of the poem. He insists that language register the flow and feel of consciousness which does not allow itself the comfort of ritualizing itself. The uncertainties and ambiguities of sexual identity, the possibilities for consciousness opened by drugs, the sense that religious and visionary experience is at most fleeting, and the overt, obvious dangers of political life are brought to bear on the immediate occasion of speech and perception. Although they may outrage traditional notions of poetic craftsmanship, Ginsberg's compositions on a tape recorder are no less demanding of attention and care than the most polished poems. He has an impeccable ear. Many poets who endlessly revise their work write more dull, lifeless lines than Ginsberg does.

In *Indian Journals*, Ginsberg writes, "We think in blocks of sensation & images. IF THE POET'S MIND IS SHAPELY HIS ART WILL BE SHAPELY. That is, the page will have an original but rhythmic shape—inevitable thought to inevitable thought, lines dropping inevitably in place on the page, making a subtle infinitely varied rhythmic SHAPE." The poem, in other words, cannot be dissociated from spiritual discipline as a whole, and Ginsberg's world-wide quest for spiritual guidance is a poetic quest. His work is one of the clearest records we have of the quest for a shapely mind.

Ginsberg is not a poet who should be read for great passages or anthology pieces. The most interesting fact of his work is that he has been able to *sustain* his energies. The Ginsbergian flow of speech is always available as an energy source.

—Don Byrd

GIOVANNI, Nikki (Yolande Cornelia Giovanni).   American. Born in Knoxville, Tennessee, 7 June 1943. Educated at Fisk University, Nashville, Tennessee, 1960-61, 1964-67, B.A. (honors) in history 1967; University of Pennsylvania School of Social Work, Philadelphia, 1967; Columbia University, New York, 1968. Has one son. Assistant Professor of Black Studies, Queens College, Flushing, New York, 1968; Associate Professor of English, Livingston College, Rutgers University, New Brunswick, New Jersey, 1968-70. Founder, Niktom Publishers, New York, 1970-74. Editorial Consultant, *Encore* magazine, Albuquerque, New Mexico. Recipient: Ford grant, 1968; National Endowment for the Arts grant, 1969. D.H.: Wilberforce University, Ohio, 1972; D.Litt.: University of Maryland, Princess Anne, 1974; Ripon University, Wisconsin, 1974; Smith College, Northampton, Massachusetts, 1975. Address: c/o William Morrow Inc., 105 Madison Avenue, New York, New York 10016, U.S.A.

PUBLICATIONS

Verse

Black Judgement.   Detroit, Broadside Press, 1968.
Black Feeling, Black Talk.   Privately printed, 1968.
Re: Creation.   Detroit, Broadside Press, 1970.
Black Feeling Black Talk / Black Judgment.   New York, Morrow, 1970.
Poem of Angela Yvonne Davis.   New York, TomNik, 1970.
My House.   New York, Morrow, 1972.
The Women and the Men.   New York, Morrow, 1975.
Cotton Candy on a Rainy Day.   New York, Morrow, 1978.
Those Who Ride the Night Winds.   New York, Morrow, 1983.

Recordings: *Truth Is on Its Way,* Right On, 1971; *Like a Ripple on a Pond,* Niktom, 1973; *The Way I Feel,* Niktom, 1975; *Legacies,* Folkways, 1976; *The Reason I Like Chocolate,* Folkways, 1976.

Verse (for children)

Spin a Soft Black Song.   New York, Hill and Wang, 1971.
Ego Tripping and Other Poems for Young Readers.   Westport, Connecticut, Lawrence Hill, 1973.
Vacation Time.   New York, Morrow, 1980.

Other

Gemini: An Extended Autobiographical Statement on My First Twenty-Five Years of Being a Black Poet. Indianapolis, Bobbs Merrill, 1971; London, Penguin, 1976.
A Dialogue: James Baldwin and Nikki Giovanni. Philadelphia, Lippincott, 1973.
A Poetic Equation: Conversations Between Nikki Giovanni and Margaret Walker. Washington, D.C. Howard University Press, 1974.

Editor, *Night Comes Softly: An Anthology of Black Female Voices.* New York, TomNik, 1970.

*

Manuscript Collection: Mugar Memorial Library, Boston University.

*   *   *

After awaking to "the possibility of / Blackness / and the inevitability of / Revolution"; after dispensing with refined language for colloquial talk ("Can a nigger kill the Man / Can you kill nigger / Huh?"); after using that power to deal with social issues and at the same time whispering a desire to do something "counterrevolutionary" like making love ("Seduction"); after committing herself to a life encounter, abandoning bourgeois ways to become "a for real Black person who must now feel / and inflict / pain," and admonishing all Blacks to do the same ("You must invent your own games," she advises in "Poem for Black Boys," "and teach us old ones / not how to play"); after celebrating Blackness in "Nikki-Rosa," "Beautiful Black Men" and "Ego Tripping"; Nikki Giovanni published an autobiography, *Gemini* and conducted a tour through *My House*, a place rich with family remembrance, distinctive personalities, and prevailing love, where

> the old man said my time is getting near
> the old man said my time
> is getting near
> he looked at his dusty cracked boots to say
> sister my time is getting near
> and when i'm gone remember i smiled
> when i'm gone remember
> i smiled
> i'm glad my time is getting near

and where if, "the revolution screeeeeeeeeeeching / to a halt," the dream was dead, there was "a free future"; if she was disappointed, she was going to live on lovingly. But the latest look into her private life, *Cotton Candy on a Rainy Day*, revealed discouragement and fatigue, Giovanni likening herself to "the unrealized dream of an idea unborn," thinking "I should write a poem / but there's almost nothing / that hasn't been said / and said and said," finally saying in "Being and Nothingness," "i don't want to exert anything."

In *The Women and the Men*, her richest collection of poems, the women can "sit and wait" for love, or resent one another, or keep their integrity into old age, or aspire to greatness, or be assertive to men. "The Women Gather" shows their effectuality. Preparing for a funeral, in a time when "we are no longer surprised / that the unfaithful pray loudest," the women leave off being selfish to be merciful and loving. Despite the tendency to forgive "because we have trespassed" and comfort "because we need comforting,"

> The women gather
> with cloth and ointment
> their busy hands bowing to laws that decree
> willows shall stand swaying but unbroken
> against even the determined wind of death.

"Because it is not unusual to know [a man] through those who love him," we judge, but by being merciful we make a more generous accounting of "dreams" and "deeds," of "intent" and "shortcomings." The women "sift/ through ashes/ and find an unburnt picture."

For Giovanni a poem, "pure energy/horizontally contained/ between the mind / of the poet and the ear of the reader," is vital for touching others and preparing the young for their lives. As Paula Giddings puts it, in her Introduction to *Cotton Candy*, Giovanni is "a witness," whose poems are "souvenirs extracted from the site of a precious moment" rather than "flawless gems." Power prevails in Giovanni's world, but she sustains the hope for love having effect. "i dream of black men and women walking/ together side by side into a new world."

—Jay S. Paul

GITTINGS, Robert (William Victor). British. Born in Portsmouth, Hampshire, 1 February 1911. Educated at St. Edward's School, Oxford; Jesus College, Cambridge (Chancellor's Medal, 1931), B.A. 1933, M.A. 1936. Married 1) Katharine Edith Cambell in 1934 (marriage dissolved), two sons; 2) Joan Grenville Manton in 1949, one daughter. Research Student and Research Fellow, 1933-38, and Supervisor in History, 1938-40, Jesus College, Cambridge. Producer and scriptwriter, BBC, 1940-63. Visiting Professor, Vanderbilt University, Nashville, Tennessee, Summer 1966, Boston University, 1970, and University of Washington, Seattle, 1972, 1974, 1977; Leslie Stephen Lecturer, Cambridge University, 1980. Recipient: Heinemann Award, for non-fiction, 1955, 1979; Phoenix Trust Award, 1963; Smith Award, for non-fiction, 1969; Christian Gauss Award, 1975; Black Memorial Prize, for non-fiction, 1979. Litt.D.: Cambridge University, 1970; University of Leeds, 1981. Honorary Fellow, Jesus College, Cambridge, 1979. Fellow, Royal Society of Literature. C.B.E. (Commander, Order of the British Empire), 1970. Address: The Stables, East Dean, Chichester, West Sussex, England.

PUBLICATIONS

Verse

The Roman Road and Other Poems. London, Oxford University Press, 1932.
The Story of Psyche. Cambridge, University Press, 1936.
Wentworth Place. London, Heinemann, 1950.
Famous Meeting: Poems, Narrative and Lyric. London, Heinemann, 1953.
This Tower My Prison and Other Poems. London, Heinemann, 1961.
Matters of Love and Death. London, Heinemann, 1968.
American Journey: Twenty-Five Sonnets. London, Heinemann, 1972.
Collected Poems. London, Heinemann, 1976.

Plays

The Seven Sleepers (produced London, 1950).
The Makers of Violence. London, Heinemann, 1951.
Through a Glass, Lightly. London, Heinemann, 1952.
Man's Estate: A Play of Saint Richard of Chichester, in *Two Saints Plays,* edited by Leo Lehman. London, Heinemann, 1954.
Out of This Wood: A Country Sequence of Five Plays (includes *The Brontë Sisters, Our Clouded Hills, Parson Herrick's Parishioners, Thomas Tusser's Wife, William Cowper's Muse*). London, Heinemann, 1955.
Love's A Gamble: A Ballad Opera, music by Doris Gould. London, Oxford University Press, 1961.
This Tower My Prison (produced London, 1961). Included in *This Tower My Prison and Other Poems,* 1961.
Conflict at Canterbury: An Entertainment in Sound and Light (produced Canterbury, 1970). London, Heinemann, 1970.

Son et Lumière scripts: *This Tower My Prison,* 1961; *St. Paul's,* 1968; *Conflict at Canterbury,* 1970.

Radio Writing: adaptations and features, 1939-63, including *Famous Meetings* series, 1948-51.

Other

The Peach Blossom Forest and Other Chinese Legends, with Jo Manton. London, Oxford University Press, 1951.
John Keats: The Living Year, 21 September 1818 to 21 September 1819. London, Heinemann, and Cambridge, Massachusetts, Harvard University Press, 1954.
The Mask of Keats: A Study of Problems. London, Heinemann, and Cambridge, Massachusetts, Harvard University Press, 1956.
Windows on History, with Jo Manton. London, Hulton, 4 vols., 1959-61.
Shakespeare's Rival: A Study in Three Parts. London, Heinemann, 1960; Westport, Connecticut, Greenwood Press, 1976.
The Story of John Keats (for children), with Jo Manton. London, Methuen, 1962; New York, Dutton, 1963.
The Keats Inheritance. London, Heinemann, 1964; New York, Barnes and Noble, 1965.
Makers of the Twentieth Century, with Jo Manton. London, Hulton, 1966.
John Keats. London, Heinemann, and Boston, Little Brown, 1968.
The Odes of Keats and Their Earliest Known Manuscripts in Facsimile. London, Heinemann, and Kent, Ohio, Kent State University Press, 1970.
Young Thomas Hardy. London, Heinemann, and Boston, Little Brown, 1975.
The Flying Horses: Tales from China (for children), with Jo Manton. London, Methuen, and New York, Holt Rinehart, 1977.
The Older Hardy. London, Heinemann, 1978; as *Hardy's Later Years,* Boston, Little Brown, 1978.
The Nature of Biography. London, Heinemann, and Seattle, University of Washington Press, 1978.
The Second Mrs. Hardy, with Jo Manton. London, Heinemann, and Seattle, University of Washington Press, 1979.

Editor, *The Living Shakespeare.* London, Heinemann, 1960; New York, Fawcett, 1961.
Editor, with Evelyn Hardy, *Some Recollections,* by Emma Hardy. London, Oxford University Press, 1961.

Editor, *Selected Poems and Letters of John Keats.* London, Heinemann, and New York, Barnes and Noble, 1966.
Editor, *Omniana; or, Horae otiosiores,* by Robert Southey and Samuel Taylor Coleridge. London, Centaur Press, 1969.
Editor, *Letters of John Keats: A New Selection.* London, Oxford University Press, 1970.
Editor, with James Reeves, *Selected Poems of Thomas Hardy.* London, Heinemann, 1981.

*

Robert Gittings comments:

I have tried to use, so far as one ever consciously does, the best, or what seems to me best, of what is old and what is new.

Major themes are probably indicated by the title of my book of verse, *Matters of Love and Death.*

I do not feel I have fully achieved this, but am still trying.

Technically, I am interested in the use of verse for dramatic and narrative purposes, have written verse-plays and verse-scripts for Son et Lumière productions and for broadcasting.

*   *   *

There can be little doubt that Robert Gittings's reputation as a critic and, in particular, his study of John Keats, has overshadowed his attributes as a poet in his own right. In his earliest work he tended to write in an unfashionably traditional mode, though at any other period his poems would have attracted attention. Since then, however, he has produced several volumes of poetry and developed a personal style and approach, and it is high time that his poetic talents were properly recognised. In his narrative vein he is quite unlike any other poet, for most of his contemporaries have found it extremely difficult to write convincing narrative verse. Robert Gittings can and does—with a quite extraordinary flair. This is probably best demonstrated in *Famous Meeting* which contains nine narrative poems on such diverse subjects as the meeting between Wellington and Nelson, Livingstone, Boswell's "London Journal," and a lost explorer in the Australian desert. His next volume, *This Tower My Prison,* takes its title from the dramatic monologue between Robert Carr, Earl of Somerset, and Frances Howard, on the murder of Sir Thomas Overbury and makes skillful use of the historic present.

Gittings's understanding of character and his dramatic gifts are to be discerned, once again, in the long poems included in his *Matters of Love and Death*: "Antony and Cleopatra," "The Secret Mistress," and "By the Lake" (a sequence on D.H. Lawrence and Frieda). Each of these volumes also contains a number of lyrics which, if assembled in a single collection, would be enough to establish a sound reputation for any poet. Amongst these are to be found such admirable poems as "The Guillemot's Egg," "Kilvert at Clyro," "A Breath of Air," "A Daughter," and "The Middle-Aged Man." *American Journey* is a collection of 25 sonnets, all competently executed, inspired by a winter journey by air to America.

—Howard Sergeant

GLEN, Duncan. Scottish. Born in Cambuslang, Lanarkshire, 11 January 1933. Educated at West Coats School, Cambuslang, 1938-46; Rutherglen Academy, 1946-49; Heriot-Watt

College, Edinburgh, 1950-53; Edinburgh College of Art, 1953-56. Served in the Royal Air Force, 1956-58. Married Margaret Eadie in 1957; one son and one daughter. Typographic designer, Her Majesty's Stationery Office, London, 1958-60; Lecturer in Typographic Design, Watford College of Technology, 1960-63; Editor, Robert Gibson and Sons Ltd., publishers, Glasgow, 1963-65; Lecturer in Graphic Design, Preston Polytechnic, Lancashire, 1965-78. Since 1978, Head of Department of Visual Communications, Trent Polytechnic, Nottingham. Owner, Akros Publications, and Editor, *Akros*, Preston, later Nottingham, 1965-83; Editor, *Knowe*, 1971, and *Graphic Lines*, 1975-78, both Preston. Since 1983, Editor, *Ayno*, Nottingham. Fellow, Society of Industrial Artists and Designers. Address: 25 Johns Road, Radcliffe on Trent, Nottingham NG12 2GW, England.

PUBLICATIONS

Verse

Stanes: A Twalsome of Poems (as Ronald Eadie Munro). Kinglassie, Fife, Duncan Glen, 1966.
Idols: When Alexander Our King Was Dead. Preston, Lancashire, Akros, 1967.
Kythings and Other Poems (as Ronald Eadie Munro). Thurso, Caithness Books, 1969.
Sunny Summer Sunday Afternoon in the Park? Preston, Lancashire, Akros, 1969.
Unnerneath the Bed. Preston, Lancashire, Akros, 1970.
In Appearances. Preston, Lancashire, Akros, 1971.
Clydesdale: A Sequence o Poems. Preston, Lancashire, Akros, 1971.
Feres. Preston, Lancashire, Akros, 1971.
A Journey Past: A Sequence o Poems. Preston, Lancashire, Akros, 1972.
A Cled Score. Preston, Lancashire, Akros, 1974.
Mr. and Mrs. J.L. Stoddart at Home. Preston, Lancashire, Akros, 1975.
Buits and Wellies; or, Sui Generis. Preston, Lancashire, Akros, 1975.
Follow! Follow! Follow! and Other Poems. Preston, Lancashire, Akros, 1976.
Spoiled for Choice. Preston, Lancashire, Akros, 1976.
Weddercock. Privately printed, 1976.
Gaitherings: Poems in Scots. Preston, Lancashire, Akros, 1977.
Traivellin Man. Preston, Lancashire, Harris Press, 1977.
In Place of Wark; or, Man of Art. Preston, Lancashire, Akros, 1977.
Of Philosophers and Tinks. Preston, Lancashire, Akros, 1977.
The Inextinguishable. Preston, Lancashire, Harris Press, 1977.
My Preston. Preston, Lancashire, Herbert, 1977.
Ten Sangs. Preston, Lancashire, Akros, 1978.
Ither Sangs. Preston, Lancashire, Akros, 1978.
Ten Bird Sangs. Preston, Lancashire, Akros, 1978.
Ten Sangs of Luve. Preston, Lancashire, Akros, 1978.
Poet at Wark. Nottingham, Bonington Press, 1979.
Realities Poems. Nottingham, Akros, 1980.
On Midsummer Evenin Merriest of Nichts? Nottingham, Akros, 1981.
Facts Are Chiels. Privately printed, 1983.
The State of Scotland. Nottingham, Duncan Glen, 1983.
Portraits. Nottingham, Trent Polytechnic, 1983.
The Stones of Time. Nottingham, Duncan Glen, 1984.

Other

Hugh MacDiarmid: Rebel Poet and Prophet, A Short Note on His Seventieth Birthday. Hemel Hempstead, Hertfordshire, Drumalban Press, 1962.
Hugh MacDiarmid and the Scottish Renaissance. Edinburgh, Chambers, 1964.
The Literary Masks of Hugh MacDiarmid. Glasgow, Drumalban Press, 1964.
Scottish Poetry Now. Preston, Lancashire, Akros, 1966.
An Afternoon with Hugh MacDiarmid. Privately printed, 1969.
A Small Press and Hugh MacDiarmid: With a Checklist of Akros Publications 1962-1970. Preston, Lancashire, Akros, 1970.
The MacDiarmids: A Conversation Between Hugh MacDiarmid and Duncan Glen with Valda Grieve and Arthur Thompson. Preston, Lancashire, Akros, 1970.
The Individual and the Twentieth Century Scottish Literary Tradition. Preston, Lancashire, Akros, 1971.
A Bibliography of Scottish Poets from Stevenson to 1974. Preston, Lancashire, Akros, 1974.
Preston's New Buildings, with John Brook. Preston, Lancashire, Harris Press, 1975.
Five Literati. Preston, Lancashire, Harris Press, 1976.
Forward from Hugh MacDiarmid; or, Mostly Out of Scotland, Being Fifteen Years of Duncan Glen/Akros Publications, with a Check-List of Publications August 1962-August 1977. Preston, Lancashire, Akros, 1977.
Hugh MacDiarmid: An Essay for 11th August 1977. Preston, Lancashire, Akros, 1977.
Have Pen Will Travel. Edinburgh, Ramsay Head Press, 1984.

Editor, *Poems Addressed to Hugh MacDiarmid and Presented to Him on His Seventy-Fifth Birthday.* Preston, Lancashire, Akros, 1967.
Editor, *Selected Essays of Hugh MacDiarmid.* London, Cape, 1969; Berkeley, University of California Press, 1970.
Editor, *The Akros Anthology of Scottish Poetry 1965-1970.* Preston, Lancashire, Akros, 1970.
Editor, *Whither Scotland? A Prejudiced Look at the Future of a Nation.* London, Gollancz, 1971.
Editor, *Hugh MacDiarmid: A Critical Survey.* Edinburgh, Scottish Academic Press, and New York, Barnes and Noble, 1972.
Editor, with Nat Scammacca, *La Nuova Poesia Scozzese.* Palermo, Celebes, 1976.
Editor, *Preston Polytechnic Poets.* Preston, Lancashire, Harris Press, 1977.
Editor, *Graphic Designers as Poets.* Preston, Lancashire, Harris Press, 1977.
Editor, *Typoems.* Preston, Lancashire, Harris Press, 1977.
Editor, *Akros Verse 1965-1982.* Nottingham, Akros, 1982.

*

Manuscript Collections: National Library of Scotland, Edinburgh; Edinburgh University Library.

Critical Studies: by Paul Duncan, in *Sou' Wester* (Carbondale, Illinois), Summer 1970; Sam Adams, in *Anglo-Welsh Review* (Pembroke Dock, Wales), Autumn 1970; John C. Weston, in *Akros* (Preston, Lancashire), April 1971; Anne Cluysenaar, in *Stand* (Newcastle upon Tyne), xii, 4, 1971; "Meaning and Self" by Walter Perrie, in *Chapman* (Hamilton, Lanarkshire), Spring, 1972; "The Progress of Scots" by John Herdman, in *Akros*

(Preston, Lancashire), December 1972; *Two Younger Poets: Duncan Glen and Donald Campbell: A Study of Their Scots Poetry*, by Leonard Mason, Preston, Lancashire, Akros, 1976; *Our Duncan, Who Art in Trent: A Festschrift for Duncan Glen* edited by Philip Pacey, Preston, Lancashire, Harris Press, 1978; *The Dialect Muse* by Ken Edward Smith, Wetherby, Ruined Cottage, 1979; George Bruce, in *Lines Review 74* (Edinburgh), September 1980.

                    *   *   *

Duncan Glen belongs to that important community of Scottish writers who have developed a style in Scots (or Lallans—the fashionable term) on a prose base. Glen, one feels, or his people, might speak with the same calculated understatement or with the not unkindly irony of his poetry. His idiom allows him to sketch the picture of his dead father in his poem, "My Faither," with a sense of truth, respect and manliness. The poem begins:

> Staunin noo aside his bress-haunled coffin
> I mind him fine aside the black shinin range
> In his grey strippit troosers, galluses and nae collar
> For the flannel shirt. My faither.

> (Standing now beside his brass handled coffin
> I remember him well beside the black shining range
> In his grey striped trousers, braces and no collar
> For the flannel shirt. My father.)

This honest, modest achievement is characteristic of a deal of the rather better writing in Scots, but Glen goes beyond this in his finer poems. In the last verse of "My Faither" the writer looks down on the body, "laid oot in the best/Black suitin...." This father ("My father")—he uses the English spelling—he does not know. The solid, known person becomes dramatically unknowable.

The domestic imagery in Scots is Glen's point of beginning. His poem "Progress" begins from naive statement, bouncing along like a nursery rhyme, but there is a remorseless logic in it. It proceeds thus: "Is not nature wonderful/We cam oot heid first—get a slap/and oor mither toungue." By the end one is aware Glen is applying a kind of Socratic dialogue to the argument. The bright tone darkens. He takes this development further in "Bacchae in Suburbia." Written in a homely Scots ("You are feart son?"), one hears, as it were, behind the words, the knock on the door that might mean death or torture, as it has done for many in Europe in our time.

Despite the success of the concentrated moments in Glen's short poems the idiom of colloquial Scots/English speech, which comes naturally from his pen, lends itself more readily to his reflective longer poems. These have frequently suffered from diffuseness and flatness of tone, but in 1980 the publication of *Realities Poems*, a book-long sequence, marked a new achievement. Much of the subject matter was, characteristically, domestic-autobiographical, but the enjoyment of family life—and how freshly and affectionately done are all these passages—is set within a wider framework, partly philosophic and partly drawn from aspects of existence today seen as a threat to the caring family and to the aspirations which stem from the confidence such living breeds. Glen achieves this presentation in poetic terms by setting one type of·experience against the other. On the one hand he tells of the happiness of, when young, chasing with Margaret, now his wife:

> My breath comin quick as yours,
> we race doun to the lochside house

> and warmth by the rug by the fire
> —and wunnerin what Mrs MacDonald thocht,

> as she served us our tea.

Against this human warmth is life in "The House at Half-Way Point," "the new seat/of civilisation" where the proprietors of the hotel control those who would climb to the mountain-top by experiment and daring:

> The routes hae built-in plastic railweys
> and guides in uniform like railwey
> porters walk the paths. There are
> cassettes to be hired
> gien a commentary on the set weys.

In such passages through particular experiences, couched in Glen's modest sceptical tongue, large issues are implicit. No writer in Scots has taken this way to these issues. Consequently it may be claimed that in doing this Duncan Glen has extended a Scots literary sensibility.

—George Bruce

GLÜCK, Louise (Elisabeth). American. Born in New York City, 22 April 1932. Attended Sarah Lawrence College, Bronxville, New York, 1962; Columbia University, New York, 1963-65. Married 1) Charles Hertz, Jr., in 1967 (divorced); 2) John Dranow in 1977; one son. Taught at Goddard College, Plainfield, Vermont, 1971-72, 1973-74, 1976-80, University of North Carolina, Greensboro, 1973, University of Iowa, Iowa City, University of Cincinnati, 1978, Columbia University, 1979, Warren Wilson College, Swannanoa, North Carolina, 1978-80, University of California at Berkeley, 1982, at Davis, 1983, at Irvine, 1984, and at Los Angeles, 1985, and Williams College, Williamstown, Massachusetts, 1983. Recipient: Academy of American Poets prize, 1966; Rockefeller Fellowship, 1967; National Endowment for the Arts grant, 1969, 1979; Eunice Tietjens Memorial Prize (*Poetry*, Chicago), 1971; Guggenheim Fellowship, 1975; American Academy award, 1981. Address: Creamery Road, Plainfield, Vermont 05667, U.S.A.

PUBLICATIONS

Verse

Firstborn. New York, New American Library, 1968; London, Anvil Press Poetry, 1969.
The House on Marshland. New York, Ecco Press, 1975; London, Anvil Press Poetry, 1976.
The Garden. New York, Antaeus, 1976.
Teh. New York, Antaeus, 1976.
Descending Figure. New York, Ecco Press, 1980.

                              *

Critical Studies: by Calvin Bedient, in *Sewanee Review* (Tennessee), Winter 1976, and in *Parnassus* (New York), Spring-Summer 1981; Joan Hutton Landis, in *Salmagundi* (Saratoga Springs, New York), Winter 1977; Helen Vendler in *New Republic* (Washington, D.C.), 17 June 1978.

*   *   *

Louise Glück's firstborn volume, *Firstborn*, does not lack for influences, as discerning critics have been quick to remark. Most obvious are the traces of Stanley Kunitz, with whom she studied at Columbia University, and of early Robert Lowell. There are also indications that she has gone to school to Plath and Sexton, Hart Crane, Jarrell, and Dugan. "My life Before Dawn," with its emphasis on sexual violence and on male mental cruelty, may well represent the first manner. The poem begins,

Sometimes at night I think of how we did
It, me nailed in her like steel, her
Over-eager on the striped contour
Sheet (I later burned it) and it makes me glad
I told her—in the kitchen cutting bread—
She always did too much—I told her Sorry baby you have had
Your share (I found her stain had dried into my hair.).

Here, already, is a subtle command of a basically five-beat line, of slant rhyme, of a *persona* sharply conceived and convincingly rendered.

The House on Marshland is decisively Glück's own. Its pervasive theme is loss. The obsessive feeling is pain experienced in relationships with men. The triumphant achievement is the balancing of an almost misogynist bitterness with an undeterrable hopefulness. Most of the poems are in the confessional tradition, though there is no reason to assume they are autobiographical. "The Letters," "The Apple Tree," and "School Children" are outstanding examples. Paradoxically, Glück, like Tennyson and many another before them, writes most powerfully when she turns away from presumably private or personally apprehended experience. The less personal the experience the more intense is the feeling with which its expression is charged. "All Hallows" seems to derive from a landscape painting; a scene of "barrenness/of harvest or pestilence" suggests a question to a wife leaning out of a window: amid all this barrenness, can she be fertile? "Brennende Liebe—1904" is a poetized love letter from an aristocratic lady in which the mood of love longing is elegantly conveyed. If the supposed writer was an ancestor, one can understand why Glück has retained her umlaut. The most psychologically penetrating and striking poem is "Abishag." The account in *I Kings* of the young woman brought to King David's bed is from David's perspective. So have been treatments by such poets as Rilke, the Hebrew Fichman, the French Spire. Glück offers Abishag's voice and perspective: recollection is dreamlike; only a colon impedes the flow of the opening stanza. The concluding stanza of the first section, however, is firmly end-stopped, staccato, bitter: "They took me as I was./Not one among the kinsmen touched me,/no one among the slaves./No one will touch me now." Abishag has a classical feminine oedipal fantasy. She rages at her father for letting her be taken by someone other than himself. The second and final section deserves quotation in full:

In the recurring dream my father
stands at the doorway in his black cassock
telling me to choose
among my suitors, each of whom
will speak my name once
until I lift my hand in signal.
On my father's arm I listen
for not three sounds: *Abishag.*
but two: *my love—*

I tell you if it is my own will
binding me I cannot be saved.
And yet in the dream, in the half-light
of the stone house, they looked
so much alike. Sometimes I think
the voices were themselves
identical, and that I raised my hand
chiefly in weariness. I hear my father saying
Choose, choose. But they were not alike
and to select death, O yes I can
believe that of my body.

Rage at father has become hatred of self for having imagined she has been used.

In *The Garden* Glück may be signalling a new phase. As she has written, "The impulse to write is usually spent in a brief lyric." "Abishag" is 49 lines long, by far the longest poem in *The House on Marshland. The Garden* is half again as long. Consisting of five almost independent lyrics about fear, *The Garden* is a coherent, powerful whole, perhaps Glück's highest achievement to date.

Glück has clearly begun what can no longer be called merely a promising career. Her command of voices, diction, rhythm is great. Command of a wider range of feeling and theme will doubtless follow.

—James K. Robinson

GOACHER, Denis. British. Born in London, 9 June 1925. Has four children. Address: Dioné House, Wembworthy, Chulmleigh, North Devon, England.

PUBLICATIONS

Verse

The Marriage Rite, with Peter Whigham. Ditchling, Sussex, Ditchling Press, 1960.
Logbook. Kingswinford, Staffordshire, Grosseteste, 1972.
Transversions. Kingswinford, Staffordshire, Grosseteste, 1973.
Night of the 12th, 13th. Rushden, Northamptonshire, Sceptre Press, 1973.
Three Songs from the Romany King of Wembworthy. Knotting, Bedfordshire, Sceptre Press, 1976.
To Romany. Kyoto, Origin Press, 1976.
If Hell, Hellas. Orono, Maine, National Poetry Foundation, 1980.

Other

Editor, *Soldier On*, by Colonel Sir Michael Ansell. London, Davies, 1973.
Editor, *Riding High*, by Colonel Sir Michael Ansell. London, Davies, 1974.
Editor, *Leopard*, by Colonel Sir Michael Ansell. Colchester, Essex, Quartilles, 1980.

Translator, *Inferno* (Cantos 29-31), by Dante. London, BBC, 1965.

*

Denis Goacher comments:

I cannot advise how a maker of poems should keep his nose clean—perhaps he shouldn't—let alone gain his bread, but he should try not to write anything else (save love letters—and all letters should be love letters), he should not want to be a *writer*, he should not want to tell anyone else what to do, he should run as fast as legs will allow from any body, any group, blundering mad and drunk on the contagious collective fumes of a CAUSE.

> O let me not destroy a city!
> If fortune, keep it small, my own,
> Let me escape the notice of rulers,
> No one's captive, to reap as I've sown.

—Aeschylus

*   *   *

Denis Goacher's poems have a sense of style, and contain some freshly perceptive and original lines. He is elliptical, and it is clearly a problem to him as to how to preserve the sound of his own voice and yet to maintain the communicability he seeks. In the first three lines of "Dead Friends"—"How many years?/ My capsule holds a smeary track/signals pass"—he succeeds because of the resonances set up by the evocative second line, and the rhythmical assuredness. Elsewhere he does preserve his own way of speaking (and hearing), but at the expense of failing to achieve coherence. But the praise he has received from Basil Bunting and Herbert Read has been deserved: this is a positive and entirely honest response, and a voice (as Bunting has pleaded) that is original:

> I touched a buttercup petal fell
> not far
> saw the shrew dead on her back
> then blessed one foxglove gave my finger
> luck
> and heart's ease....

—Martin Seymour-Smith

GOEDICKE, Patricia. American. Born in Boston, Massachusetts, 21 June 1931. Educated at Middlebury College, Vermont, B.A. 1953 (Phi Beta Kappa, 1952); Ohio University, Athens, M.A. 1963. Married Leonard Wallace Robinson in 1971. Editorial Assistant, Harcourt Brace and World, publishers, New York, 1953-54, and T.Y. Crowell, publishers, New York, 1955-56. Instructor in English, Ohio University, 1962-68, and Hunter College, New York, 1969-71; Instructor in Creative Writing, Instituto Allende, San Miguel de Allende, Mexico, 1972-79; Writer-in-Residence, Kalamazoo College, Michigan, 1977; member of the writing program, Sarah Lawrence College, Bronxville, New York, 1980-81. Poet-in-Residence, 1981-83, and since 1983, Associate Professor in Creative Writing, University of Montana, Missoula. Recipient: National Endowment for the Arts award, 1969, and grant, 1976; William Carlos Williams Award (*New Letters*), 1976; Duncan Frazier Prize (*Loon*), 1976; *Quarterly West* prize, 1977. Address: 310 McLeod Avenue, Missoula, Montana 59801, U.S.A.

PUBLICATIONS

Verse

Between Oceans.   New York, Harcourt Brace, 1968.
For the Four Corners.   Ithaca, New York, Ithaca House, 1976.
The Trail That Turns on Itself.   Ithaca, New York, Ithaca House, 1978.
The Dog That Was Barking Yesterday.   Amherst, Massachusetts, Lynx House Press, 1979.
Crossing the Same River.   Amherst, University of Massachusetts Press, 1980.
The King of Childhood.   Lewiston, Idaho, Confluence Press, 1984.
The Wind of Our Going.   Port Townsend, Washington, Copper Canyon Press, 1984.

*

Critical Studies: "The Fruit of Her Orchard" by Tom O'Grady and Shirley Bossert, in *New Letters* (Kansas City), Fall 1977; "A Bow to Women for Poetic Providing Wealth" by G.E. Murray, in *Sun-Times* (Chicago), 9 July 1978; "The Trail That Turns on Itself" by Peter Schjedahl, in *New York Times Book Review*, 17 December 1978; "The Desperate Tongue" by Ron Slate, in *Three Rivers Poetry Journal* (Pittsburgh), March 1979; Rochelle Ratner, in *Library Journal* (New York), March 1980; David Clothier, in *Los Angeles Times Book Review*, 27 April 1980; David Kirby, in *Times Literary Supplement* (London), 13 June 1980; *Virginia Quarterly Review* (Charlottesville), Summer 1980; Robert Phillips, in *New Letters* (Kansas City), Summer 1980; Hayden Carruth, in *Harper's* (New York), December 1980; Donald M. Hassler, in *Tar River Poetry* (Greenville, North Carolina), Spring 1981.

*   *   *

Patricia Goedicke's poetry was for many years neglected, and her 1968 volume, *Between Oceans*, out of print and missing from most libraries. In her first book she dealt with spasmodic power with the chief themes that have haunted her since—myth and dreams, childhood fantasies, the I-Thou relationship wherever it is found—be it in marriage, friendship, or the larger community—and the issue of paradise and hell in our experience. Most powerfully she has spoken of the experience of death. Her first book has a poem about a suicide ("Priscilla") and a loved one's death in hospital ("The Gift"), and a sense of death pervades poems like "The World Draped in White Sheets," which treats the miracle of childhood, when the capacity for perceiving even tragedy and accident as beautiful has not yet been lost:

> No one ever remembers how it rained when we were children.
> There may have been bucketfuls more than now
>   bigger
>   better
>   sluicing down over the hills
> Great wet gallons of it spilling down the streets
> but no, it is the snow, the snow we remember
>   the scabbed corpse covered up
>   the world draped in white sheets.

The poet moves with the eyes of the children who are inventing myth, learning to abstract the unacceptable into the acceptable, and continuing their survivors' duty to marvel:

The couple that smothered in the car
   and the cold, the cold
      the turnip-white fingers and toes
         the old feet stumbling, stumbling

In her later books Goedicke copes as bravely as any poet of our time with her own mortality; her poems might describe the fight against a life-threatening illness, and she uses all the resources of wit and metaphor to hold onto poetry's sustaining power and to the people whose love can be crucial—and yet she acknowledges the loneliness and alienation of her struggles:

     Slipping out of the sleeping bag of our love
     Only for a little, to try it
     In the warm bedroom, in the city

     I am astonished, at first
     The air is empty, I am naked
     None of your arms enfold me

     Nevertheless I must walk
     Once in awhile by myself

At every turn she reminds the beloved addressed and the reader (sometimes the reader *is* her beloved addressed) that it is essential, even a duty, to grasp the beauty of every moment. Yet "...the future is lying in wait/with sad eyes looking back/like a huge slaughtered mountain."

Goedicke is a romantic, and her love poems are always intense and willing to risk:

     I'm drinking nothing but rain these days
     Thinking how much I love you

     I still pour tears
     Even in brilliant sunshine,
     Even in snow.

She is alert to the need for change and social responsibility:

     Each day's a hot potato, let me see
     How to say it...
     Between the milk and the orange juice
     I think of the night before, the knife
     Edge of my own tongue—
     But the soldier never intended
     To murder the women and children—

Her poems often express a startled awareness of the I—Thou fellowship of those who have loved and suffered:

     What faces we hold out to each other! See
     We take off our glasses,
     At meetings our startled smiles

     Shine in the lamplight like such good children
     Nobody believes us, nobody
     Believes anybody

Her concern with what's wrong with our world pervades both personal grief and everyday mundanity:

While we're out there standing beside a general doing nothing,
Standing beside the latest rocket doing nothing,
While we're standing beside the cash registers doing nothing.

Clearly her search is for serenity: "For the shape of self pity is a real swamp, finally." And there is comfort in a relationship, even with the dead: "I put my arms around you/My last sight of you/For I am about to be killed, too." Goedicke has documented the familiar but unavoidable stages of grief and concluded: "In the courtyard of my ears/Everyone's death comes whispering." And yet she bravely, even wisely, asserts hope: "We must build more on less."

The neglect of Goedicke by critics might be to some extent due to her subject matter, for even her bold assertions of beauty and the miraculous are tested by the heavy weight of naturalism and grief. She loads the vines heavily, and the vines bear thorns. For those who turn to poetry for escape, Patricia Goedicke offers very little. For those who want to share a struggle through a threatened existence, she offers as much as any poet writing today.

                          —David Ray

GOLDBARTH, Albert. American. Born in Chicago, Illinois, 31 January 1948. Educated at University of Illinois, Chicago, B.A. 1969; University of Iowa, Iowa City, M.F.A. 1971; University of Utah, Salt Lake City, 1973-74. Instructor, Elgin Community College, Illinois, 1971-72, Central YMCA Community College, Chicago, 1971-73, and University of Utah, Salt Lake City, 1973-74; Assistant Professor, Cornell University, Ithaca, New York, 1974-76; Visiting Professor, Syracuse University, New York, 1976. Since 1977, Assistant Professor of Creative Writing, University of Texas, Austin. Advisory Editor, *Seneca Review*, Geneva, New York. Recipient: Theodore Roethke Prize (*Poetry Northwest*), 1972; *Ark River Review* prize, 1973, 1975; National Endowment for the Arts grant, 1974, 1979; Guggenheim Fellowship, 1983. Address: Department of English, University of Texas, Austin, Texas 78712, U.S.A.

PUBLICATIONS

Verse

Under Cover. Crete, Nebraska, Best Cellar Press, 1973.
Coprolites. New York, New Rivers Press, 1973.
Opticks: A Poem in Seven Sections. New York, Seven Woods Press, 1974.
Jan. 31. New York, Doubleday, 1974.
Keeping. Ithaca, New York, Ithaca House, 1975.
A Year of Happy. Raleigh, North Carolina Review Press, 1976.
Comings Back: A Sequence of Poems. New York, Doubleday, 1976.
Curve: Overlapping Narratives. New York, New Rivers Press, 1977.
Different Fleshes. Geneva, New York, Hobart and William Smith Colleges Press, 1979.
Eurekas. Memphis, St. Luke's Press, 1980.
Ink Blood Semen. Cleveland, Bits Press, 1980.
Smugglers Handbook. Wollaston, Massachusetts, Chowder Chapbooks, 1980.
Faith. New York, New Rivers Press, 1981.
Who Gathered and Whispered Behind Me. Seattle, L'Epervier Press, 1981.

Original Light: New and Selected Poems 1973-1983. Princeton,
New Jersey, Ontario Review Press, 1983.

Other

Editor, *Every Pleasure: The "Seneca Review" Long Poem
Anthology.* Geneva, New York, Seneca Review Press, 1979.

*

Critical Study: by the author, in *The Generation of 2000* edited
by William Heyen, Princeton, New Jersey, Ontario Review
Press, 1984.

Albert Goldbarth comments:

(1980) I don't much care to turn my poems over and study
their undersides: motives, influences, psychic needs filled. I'd
rather go on to a new poem instead. What can be said briefly,
and I think truly, is that my interest in the long poem and its
possibilities grows stronger. By this I don't mean to turn my back
on the shorter poem—*Comings Back*, though it included the
15-page "Letter to Tony," included a 6-line poem I like as well.
But the extended poem that includes narrative, or has scope
enough to play with large bodies of time, or that finds room for
dialogue or quoted source materials, that can build up litany or
weave motifs in and out with the huge sweep a suite has....
Different Fleshes, for instance, is a "novel/poem" and is one
book-length piece of alternating prose and poetry sections,
which is able—happily, I think—to allow moments of pure lyric
visionary intensity to take place within a novel-like framework:
plot, historic and invented characters, quoted conversation. My
hope is that some of its best moments have learned from, even
include, the concentration and connotation one expects from a
brief poem—but that those moments accumulate toward, and
then take place within, an even richer context. In any case, that's
the challenge I feel right now, and I suspect my next few efforts
will record how well or poorly I've faced it.

(1985) I grow, if anything, more wary of statements of poetics.
I believe my work asks to be self-sufficient: it is not a script,
requiring public performance; not a set of lyrics, requiring musical accompaniment; not an arcane puzzle, requiring for its fullest
understanding prose commentary—not even, perhaps not especially, my own. All my poetry asks for is a few people who will, in
solitude, care to enter the world of its pages.

*   *   *

Albert Goldbarth is bent on restoring some useful clutter to
American lyric—for years now the tendency has been to keep
stripping down language to some ultimate essence, some vital
center where all the truth may be put down in a phrase or a word.
Most lyric language since World War II has been as gaunt as
winter branches. Charles Olson stretched the line longer and
freighted it with more content, Robert Lowell crabbed syntax
and meter, and other poets have managed to spread language
more thickly along the line, but Goldbarth has about him a
certain genius to patter on indefinitely and keep it interesting.

His poems open any subject and become pretexts for labyrin-
thine monologues; his logic is a bramble bush of interconnections. Goldbarth's poetic, if one may hazard discerning it, is to
pull everything around him into the form at hand. In one way,
his mode is high parody of our universal lust to consume, to own,
to put it all into the shopping cart even if the money runs out.

The poem comes back to its premise eventually, but the means is
primary for a Goldbarth poem—the joy is in watching him
drown in chatter and float back up again with a point.

Jan. 31 departs somewhat from this florid verse style, but the
leaner lyric has some advantage for Goldbarth—he shows himself a moving tensely emotional observer of the cold weather of
Chicago, which he makes his vortex for a close commentary on
love, love-making, survival, friendship, urban squalor, isolation,
thinking, and finally hopefulness. Much of the book is written at
half his range, however, and as a journal of poetic notations and
some fully fledged poems, it lacks the delirious variety of his
more exuberant, free-form explosions.

Albert Goldbarth renews poetic discourse by dropping back
in time into the grandiloquent style of Elizabethan verse—
Shakespeare's and Jonson's—and he does it shamelessly, lavish-
ing on his verse all the naive punning and word play, sonorous
embellishment, exaggeration, polysyllabia that geysered up at
the birth of English dialect. Laid over this older baroque is
Goldbarth's sure touch with American slang, and the pastiche
works, as in "A Week on the Show":

CORRECT-O! The Lung is the Foot on the Breath-Stop!
  Gwendolyn
Halverstrom, clovequeen and fingerwhorls etched with spittle
turning Newark's alley-cobbles to delta with life electrode
  in you
as in cue-chalk, skewering, shewering, NOW
for the slats are down and the scent of muff of Gazelle,
  as the hand
prongs five is the fifth of the gift and Luck the gland
  the Lord forgot:
What astronomical body circles the earth and has phases?

But there is more to Goldbarth than mere verbal performance.
His poems are nearly desperate about language and the need to
keep talking, the need to explain the slightest facet of personal
history with all the terminological armament of science and
philosophy. His most fully conceived book, *Comings Back*, is
also the clearest instance of how Goldbarth intends his poetry to
be a point of convergence between the individual and the
immense culture heaped around him. Perhaps Goldbarth intends
us to see that we are again at a birth of language, a dawning of
new technological speech which he dares to use as his own
personal utterance. *Comings Back* is charged with scientific lore,
with facts of all sorts, with statistical junk, heaps of otherwise
useless information, all put to lyric use.

His persona is chameleon, dropping into other periods and
other voices at whim, and seems also to suggest how the poet
now may not have a culture to possess personally—he may
plunder its codes and some of its lesser secrets in swashbuckling
verse, but he too is a drifter in a much larger and increasingly
impersonal human realm. Unlike the vast majority of other
poets now writing, Goldbarth is not interested in staking out
some part of the human realm as his own—his attention wanders
from old lovers to friends, to the deep past, to fragments of
experience belonging to all of human experience.

A poetic vision more in-the-making than fully formed lies
below the verbal froth of his recent books—Goldbarth has been
doggedly pursuing a certainty that life is a Moebius strip. "History repeats itself," he blandly declares at one point of *Jan. 31*,
but that theme is pervasive in *Comings Back*, and is the whole
point of a 1977 chapbook, *Curve: Overlapping Narratives*. This
premise dominates contemporary thought and art, but Gold-

barth makes it his personal discovery in the range and depth of his own writing, with its seemingly inexhaustible energy to find new metaphors for capturing it.

—Paul Christensen

———————

GOTLIEB, Phyllis (Fay, née Bloom). Canadian. Born in Toronto, Ontario, 25 May 1926. Educated at public schools in Toronto; University of Toronto, B.A. in English 1948, M.A. 1950. Married Calvin Gotlieb in 1949; one son and two daughters. Agent: Virginia Kidd, Box 278, Milford, Pennsylvania 18337, U.S.A. Address: 29 Ridgevale Drive, Toronto, Ontario M6A 1K9, Canada.

PUBLICATIONS

Verse

Who Knows One? Toronto, Hawkshead Press, 1962.
Within the Zodiac. Toronto, McClelland and Stewart, 1964.
Ordinary, Moving. Toronto, Oxford University Press, 1969.
The Works: Collected Poems. Toronto, Calliope Press, 1978.

Plays

Doctor Umlaut's Earthly Kingdom (broadcast, 1970; produced Ontario, 1972). Toronto, Calliope Press, 1974.
Silent Movie Days (broadcast, 1971). Included in *The Works,* 1978.
Garden Varieties (broadcast, 1973; produced Ontario, 1973). Included in *The Works,* 1978.

Radio Plays: *Doctor Umlaut's Earthly Kingdom,* 1970; *Silent Movie Days,* 1971; *The Contract,* 1972; *Garden Varieties,* 1973; *God on Trial Before Rabbi Ovadia,* 1974.

Novels

Sunburst. New York, Fawcett, 1964; London, Coronet, 1966.
Why Should I Have All the Grief? Toronto, Macmillan, 1969.
O Master Caliban! New York, Harper, 1976; London, Corgi, 1979.
A Judgment of Dragons. New York, Berkley, 1980.
Emperor, Swords, Pentacles. New York, Ace, 1982.

Short Stories

Son of the Morning and Other Stories. New York, Ace, 1983.

*

Critical Studies: by Fred Cogswell, in *Canadian Literature* (Vancouver); Mary Keyes, in *Canadian Forum* (Toronto), January 1970; Michael Hornyansky, in *University of Toronto Quarterly,* July 1970; Louis Martz, in *Yale Review* (New Haven, Connecticut), Summer 1970; Daisy Alden, in *Poetry* (Chicago), April 1971; "A Cornucopia of Poems" by Douglas Barbour, in *Tamarack Review* (Toronto), Winter 1979.

Phyllis Gotlieb comments:
    My work, poetry or prose, makes use of any aspect of human culture and experience I can manage to find out about: family, childhood, growing up in Toronto; Jewish background, either learned or experienced, Talmud or Kabbala, rational or mystic; early interests in Greek and Roman cultures; folklore all over the world; enthusiasms for as much science as I can understand: biology, medicine, astronomy, anthropology; painting, sculpture. I'd like to call myself a universalist except that the abstract leaves me floundering. Humanity is my department.

*   *   *

    Phyllis Gotlieb writes in two seemingly disparate sub-genres: science fiction, and poems of a more esoteric focus. Yet the common theme which binds the two strains, and which is most easily seen in *Within the Zodiac,* is also appropriate to each. In all her work there is a preoccupation with the unity of all things in the universe and an exploration of the energy which binds them. In the latest collection, *The Works,* poems from a span of 15 years clearly demonstrate her persistent interest in the interrelationship of matter. Such a concern pertains naturally enough to the science-fiction stories and these need not be considered as more than largely well-written examples of the school. It is not, however, a theory which is so easily situated in literary forms which look away from the explicatory for their narrative or stylistic emphasis. And in dealing with her theory in such contexts, Gotlieb meets with varied success.
    In *Within the Zodiac,* for example, the early poems are marred by dry style and the essentially cerebral and yet curiously over-clear statements in which they attempt to objectify the myriad, incongruous aspects of the universe. These early poems lack any poetic rhythm and any personal response to the universe they so dispassionately detail. In the poem "Day Falcon," however, Gotlieb seeks in memory for congruity within this apparent confusion, developing her personal myth in brilliant, naturalistic description. And, as a result, the poem rises above the others. Like "Day Falcon," the later poems in the collection open the more personal avenues of memory ("A Bestiary of the Garden for Children Who Should Know Better") and the Jewish tradition ("Who Knows One"). The point-of-view to which these final *Zodiac* poems lean is more fully assumed in *Ordinary, Moving,* a vastly more successful collection of poems.
    In *Ordinary, Moving* Gotlieb becomes more intimate with her creation, while maintaining an intellectual reserve and without becoming sentimental. She still considers ideas that are metaphysical and catholic but now views them as weighted equally with skeletal parts, bricks and old telephone numbers. Indeed, by grounding her musings in homely objects, she simultaneously strengthens her myth of unity and avoids the aridity of the *Zodiac* poems. Here, the rhythms are actively present and if the musical patterns (as well as the sense of family memory) is Jewish in sensibility, it is nevertheless accessible to gentile readers. This is not to suggest that Gotlieb's characteristic economy of words, sparsity of figures, and avoidance of allusions have been altered. Nor does it suggest that she has totally escaped the sometimes obscure and often derivative stylistics of the earlier poems (and of some later ones). However, her personal myth has been expanded and made sufficiently comprehensible that it shines through the form. At last in *Ordinary, Moving* the reader not only understands what Gotlieb is saying, but feels he has himself experienced it before.
    The novel *Why Should I Have All the Grief?,* however, lies outside the experience of most readers. It cannot be denied that the suffering of the Jews fits into Gotlieb's spectrum of universality, but its expression in this novel is too strongly dependent on a response to Jewish sentiment to appeal to those who lack it. (This is unfortunate since Gotlieb can often elucidate foreign

territory with considerable success; in *O Master Caliban!*, for example, she brings alive a totally imaginary and futuristic world.) Moreover, Gotlieb worries over the plot with an attention bordering on hysteria and the denouement is very early given away. Unable to do his own thinking and stranger in an alien, Talmudic culture, the reader cannot identify as he does with the *souvenirs* of the *Ordinary, Moving* poems, cannot associate himself with the joys and sufferings of the fictional world presented or the larger universe assumed, and quickly loses interest.

That he is not disinterested in the *Ordinary, Moving* poems is a significant statement of the appeal of anchoring the suggested in the familiar. The collage of *Ordinary, Moving* demonstrates that Gotlieb did, indeed, "Like all writers [spend her youth] listening in buses, cars & cafes/trams & subways/streets & alleyways...." And furthermore, it celebrates the concentric energies by which all that she overheard is joined and in which the reader by the last line also becomes part of the unity and then "begin[s] again."

—S.R. Gilbert

GRAHAM, Henry. British. Born in Liverpool, Lancashire, 1 December 1930. Educated at Liverpool College of Art. Painter; exhibitions in London and Northern England; gave up painting for poetry at the age of 30. Since 1969, Lecturer in Art History, Liverpool Polytechnic. Poetry Editor, *Ambit* magazine, London. Recipient: *Ambit* prize, 1968; Arts Council award, 1969, 1971. Lives in Liverpool. Address: c/o Ambit, 17 Priory Gardens, London N.6, England.

PUBLICATIONS

Verse

Soup City Zoo, with Jim Mangnall. London, Anima Press, 1968.
Good Luck to You Kafka / You'll Need It Boss. London, Rapp and Whiting, 1969.
Passport to Earth. London, Rapp and Whiting-Deutsch, 1971.
Poker in Paradise Lost, with Jim Mangnall. Liverpool, Glasshouse Press, 1977.
Europe after Rain. West Kirby, Wirral, Headland Publications, 1981.

*

Critical Study: "A Quote and a Comment" by the author, in *Ambit 92* (London), 1983.

Henry Graham comments:
(1974) My early influences in writing were the modern American poets, Pound, Olson, Duncan, etc. But now the Englishness of all the English arts interests me more; Auden, for instance, is one of the poets I admire most. The arts, and especially poetry, are not an attempt on my part to communicate, but are a way of looking into myself and the universe. If, as sometimes seems to happen, others are interested in and find in me what lies outside themselves, good; if not, good.

(1985) Today my writing is concerned principally with an international philosophy of modernism, i.e., expressionism, surrealism, and abstraction, and not with any parochial literary stance.

*   *   *

Henry Graham deals in images. His work as a painter and art historian often informs both the subjects of his verse—Chirico, Magritte, Klee, Samuel Palmer are mentioned with affection—and its techniques, which are visual and painterly. His better poems combine with this a sense of the special resources of poetic language.

Much of Graham's smallish output dates from the late 1960's and early 1970's when jokiness and whimsical fantasy became a political duty and the grubby hustlings of businessman and politician were seen as emanations of death, enemies of the poet-dreamer. Though this scheme occasionally surfaces in his work, he keeps language, material, and attitudes under better control than some of the Liverpool poets, with whom his name has perhaps misleadingly been coupled. A sense of social justice helps rescue his verse from shallowness.

Recurrent in *Good Luck to You Kafka / You'll Need It Boss* are poems about discontent, loneliness, resentment, and the way everyday sights and events are altered by such emotions. Verse wryly recording the bathos of his own ordinary responses to living is more impressive for its humanity than for its tension or energy. His imaginative engagement is stronger when his subject is the already achieved work of art. Ten poems on paintings by Samuel Palmer derive their force from the same images as the paintings. But Palmer's distorted landscapes and figures, his monstrous moons, which show the kinship of all created things and reveal God and the spritual via the real, are reinterpreted here: Palmer's pastorals become nightmares, his symbols of fecundity threats. By contemplating symbols as pure images, Graham reveals them as exaggerated, grotesque, surreal.

Palmer's moons become Graham's own. In *Passport to Earth* he looks at "the pitted face of the moon / and think[s] of the bodies in the pits / at Belsen." This is the moon's public, "pitted" face, but it stands for personal horror too: "The huge million watt / bulb of the moon / crushes me against its face." Cold, bright, and unearthly, the moons illuminate, but in doing so they reveal the monstrosities which darkness would conceal. With these and other images Graham makes an interesting attempt to structure a book of verse by primarily visual means.

But language, too, is a mode of power, pointing away from the forlorn isolations of art and self, the sad prisoners of canvas and frame, towards the bigger world. The seven poems of *Poker in Paradise Lost*, written with Jim Mangnall, made by cut-up of photo-captions from *Time* magazine, offer surrealist glimpses of the U.S.A. Lacking in focus and structure, arbitrarily scattering effects, these pieces are nevertheless successful in coupling of occasional images: "a young Eisenhower after sophomore / year at San Quentin."

Graham's poetry succeeds when he gives play to his sense of the power of juxtaposed images mysteriously to conjure emotion, where the tiny formalised marks which are the artist's and the writer's stock-in-trade can gesture towards the greatest meanings:

> The sun a crescent moon
> a brown line; the cosmos. The tiny
> square and circle, peace.

—R.J.C. Watt

GRAHAM, Jorie.   American.   Born in New York City, 5 September 1951. Educated at the Sorbonne, Paris; New York University, B.A.; University of Iowa, Iowa City, M.F.A. 1978. Married James Galvin in 1983; one daughter. Taught at California State University, Humboldt, 1979-81, and Columbia University, New York, 1981-83. Since 1983, staff member, University of Iowa. Recipient: Ingram Merrill Foundation grant; Guggenheim Fellowship; Bunting Fellowship; National Endowment for the Arts grant. Address: 436 EPB, University of Iowa, Iowa City, Iowa 52242, U.S.A.

PUBLICATIONS

Verse

Hybrids of Plants and Ghosts.   Princeton, New Jersey, Princeton University Press, 1980.
Erosion.   Princeton, New Jersey, Princeton University Press, 1983.

*

Critical Studies: by Helen Vendler in *New York Times Book Review*, 17 July 1983; Peter Stitt, in *Georgia Review* (Athens), Spring 1984.

*   *   *

Here is the beginning of Jorie Graham's "Flooding," from *Hybrids of Plants and of Ghosts*:

Just rain for days and everywhere it goes it fits,
like a desire become too accurate
to be of use, the water
a skirt the world
is lifting and
lifting

like a debt ceiling....

For Graham the world is like a vast text deserted by its author late in the process of composition. One can almost read it fully. "The clues are everywhere," says one poem, and in another starlings make "a regular syntax on wings." In another: "Indeed the tulips / change tense / too quickly." She sees "small building materials / awaiting an idea." Here are two further tropes that embody her characteristic *explication du monde* (from "One in the Hand" and "The Mind"):

A bird re-entering a bush,
like an idea regaining
its intention, seeks
the missed discoveries
before attempting
flight again.

...The leaves,
pressed against the dark
window of November
soil, remain unwelcome
till transformed, parts
of a puzzle unsolvable
till the edges give a bit

and soften. See how
then the picture becomes clear,
the mind entering the ground
more easily in pieces,
and all the richer for it.

Notice that in the first passage above the world is not lifting its skirts to keep them above the rising water, but that the world's skirts *are* the rising water, and that, like a debt ceiling, they will likely go higher and higher, the way a desire rises of its own momentum when it isn't of use (though why accurate desires aren't of use is neither self-evident nor made clear by Graham's complex figure).

Her work is sustained by continuous associative activity; her poems seem almost to be woven, and into her raw material go ideas, visual images, abstract and very concrete nouns, and, again and again, figures for language itself. The play of perception over the waters of the perceivable world make a kind of continual reference to Genesis, and remind us what an important poet Wallace Stevens is for Graham. Occasionally, as in the passage from "Flooding" above, her associative urgency causes a skein to ravel, but her intellectual abilities and ambitions give her work gravity and free her from anecdote and occasion.

For *Erosion* Graham developed some new formal strategies. One is a short-line stanza, usually of six lines, with indentations, as in this one from "Love":

Here it's harvest. Dust
coarsens
the light. In the heat
in the distance
the men burn
their fields

to heal them...

Because the stanzas are almost never end-stopped, but swirl down the page in long, complex sentences, this stanza form resembles in its tumbling speed down the page the other stanza form Graham uses frequently in *Erosion*, a long single-strophed poem with all the lines printed flush left to the margin and the lines of carefully varied lengths. Thus "Mother of Vinegar" begins like this:

Because contained damage makes for beauty, it shines
like a brain at the bottom of each vat, the sand
in the shell,
a simple animal.

Graham has spent a lot of time in Italy, much of it looking at paintings. Pieces by Piero della Francesca, Luca Signorelli, Masaccio, Goya, and Gustav Klimt are central to poems in *Erosion*, and one poem from that book is called "Still Life with Window and Fish." By such means her poems refer not to a body of knowledge or connoisseurship, "art history," but to a live tradition, a palpable continuity in the present of the longer sense of history Italy gives than American landscape. Graham's sense that culture is an organism rather than an artifact distinguishes her work and keeps it free from cultural tourism.

The closing lines of "San Sepolcro" suggest the reach and amplitude her best poems attain.

...It is this girl
by Piero
della Francesca, unbuttoning
her blue dress,

her mantle of weather,
    to go into

labor. Come, we can go in.
    It is before
the birth of god. No-one
    has risen yet
to the museums, to the assembly
    line—bodies

and wings—to the open air
    market. This is
what the living do: go in.
    It's a long way.
And the dress keeps opening
    from eternity

to privacy, quickening.
    Inside, at the heart,
is tragedy, the present moment
    forever stillborn,
but going in, each breath
    is a button
coming undone, something terribly
    nimble-fingered
finding all the stops.

—William Matthews

GRAHAM, W(illiam) S(ydney). British. Born in Greenock, Renfrewshire, Scotland, 19 November 1918. Educated at Greenock High School; Workers Educational Association College, Newbattle Abbey, Edinburgh, 1 year. Married. Lecturer, New York University, 1947-48. Recipient: Atlantic Award, 1947. Address: 4 Mountview Cottages, Madron, Penzance, Cornwall, England.

PUBLICATIONS

Verse

Cage Without Grievance. Glasgow, Parton Press, 1942.
The Seven Journeys. Glasgow, Maclellan, 1944.
2nd Poems. London, Editions Poetry London, 1945.
The Voyages of Alfred Wallis. London, Anthony Froshaug, 1948.
The White Threshold. London, Faber, 1949; New York, Grove Press, 1952.
The Nightfishing. London, Faber, and New York, Grove Press, 1955.
Malcolm Mooney's Land. London, Faber, 1970.
Penguin Modern Poets 17, with David Gascoyne and Kathleen Raine. London, Penguin, 1970.
Implements in Their Places. London, Faber, 1977.
Collected Poems 1942-1977. London, Faber, 1979.
Selected Poems. New York, Ecco Press, 1980.

*

Manuscript Collection: National Library of Scotland, Edinburgh.

Critical Studies: "Notes on a Poetry of Release" by the author, in *Sewanee Review* (Tennessee), 1947; "W.S. Graham's Threshold" by Edwin Morgan, in *Nine 3* (London), Spring 1950; *Babel to Byzantium* by James Dickey, New York, Farrar Straus, 1968.

W.S. Graham comments:
    I do recognise a Scots timbre in my "voice" although I can't see myself, in any way, as characteristic of Scots poetry.
    Major themes: The difficulty of communication; the difficulty of speaking from a fluid identity; the lessons in physical phenomena; the mystery and adequacy of the aesthetic experience; the elation of being alive in the language.
    Although I love the ever-present metronome in verse, I am greedy for my rhythmic say. The gesture of speech often exists, moving seemingly counter to the abstract structure it is in. The three-accent line, not specially common in the body of English poetry, even a kind of strait-jacket, interested me enough for me to keep to it for a bit and try to ring the changes within.
    As far as I can discern, my verse is influenced by the prose of Joyce and Beckett and by the verse of Marianne Moore, Pound and Eliot. And the texture of my verse shows, I think, a fondness for Anglo-Saxon and Scandinavian roots, also for translations of early Jewish and Scottish Gaelic verse.

*   *   *

Probably because he was one of the most verbally gifted poets of his generation in Scotland, W.S. Graham had a struggle to clarify a personal style that first carried large acknowledgements of other wordsmiths like Dylan Thomas, Gerard Manley Hopkins, and James Joyce. His early volumes—*Cage Without Grievance, The Seven Journeys*, and *2nd Poems*—have a tendency to thrash around with adjectives and to produce obscurely exciting effects, yet his devotion to the *word*, and his sense of the poem as a voyage of discovery, were not perverse. In exploring the self, and the poet's relation to his living audience and the audience of all the dead, Graham was working within a network of image and reference that was anchored to his Clydeside upbringing—indeed all his poetry is haunted by sea and shipyards, and by place-names from the countryside around Glasgow. The best of the early poems shows a distinctive lyricism ("O Gentle Queen of the Afternoon") and a deepening sense of mortality ("Many Without Elegy").
    In *The White Threshold* and *The Nightfishing* Graham produced a very remarkable poetry, strong, musical, and intense, where the central sea imagery feeds a range of subtly related themes: his autobiography, wartime shipwrecks and drowning, fishing, and the metaphorical "white threshold" of all life and death which Herman Melville had tried to plumb before him. Apart from the two long title-pieces in these volumes, there are several shorter poems of great beauty and force: "Listen. Put on Morning," "Gigha," "Men Sign the Sea," "Night's Fall Unlocks the Dirge of the Sea," and "Letter VI." A growing lucidity humanizes the verse, but without removing its obsessional preoccupation with the endless dyings and metamorphoses of the self:

I bent to the lamp, I cupped
My hand to the glass chimney.
Yet it was a stranger's breath
From out of my mouth that
Shed the light.

After a 15-year silence, Graham published two new collections in the 1970's. Continuity with the earlier work, in both themes and technique, was clear, but to the younger generation of poets and critics, to whom his earlier poetry was perhaps little known, these two volumes came across with considerable impact and gave his reputation—for integrity, for craftsmanship—a new boost. Among poems on places and persons in Cornwall (where he had been living) and poems on the difficulty and necessity of communication (his most recurrent theme), there are some particularly fine poems of memory, or a mingling of memory and imagination, or memory and dream, in which he evokes his family and his childhood on Clydeside. "The Dark Dialogues," "Greenock at Night I Find You," and "To Alexander Graham" have a firm, reserved pathos which is very impressive:

> See, I am back. My father turned and I saw
> He had the stick he cut in Sheelhill Glen.
> Brigit was there and Hugh and double-breasted
> Sam and Malcolm Mooney and Alastair Graham.
> They all were there in the Cartsburn Vaults shining
> To meet me but I was only remembered.

—Edwin Morgan

GRAVES, Robert (von Ranke). British. Born in Wimbledon, London, 24 July 1895. Educated at King's College School and Rokeby School, Wimbledon; Copthorne School, Sussex; Charterhouse School, Surrey, 1907-14; St. John's College, Oxford (exhibitioner; Editor, *The Owl*, from 1919, and *Winter Owl*, 1923), 1919-25, B.Litt. 1925. Served in the Royal Welch Fusiliers, 1914-19: Captain; was refused admittance into the armed forces in World War II. Married 1) Nancy Nicholson in 1918 (divorced, 1949), two daughters (one deceased) and two sons (one deceased); 2) Beryl Pritchard in 1950 (lived with her from 1939), three sons and one daughter. Professor of English, Egyptian University, Cairo, 1926; with Laura Riding established the Seizin Press, 1928, and *Epilogue* magazine, 1935. Lived in Deyá, Mallorca, 1929-36, the United States, 1936, England, 1937-46, and Deyá since 1946. Clark Lecturer, Trinity College, Cambridge, 1954-55; Professor of Poetry, Oxford University, 1961-66; Arthur Dehon Little Memorial Lecturer, Massachusetts Institute of Technology, Cambridge, 1963. Recipient: Bronze Medal for Poetry, Olympic Games, Paris, 1924; Hawthornden Prize, for fiction, 1935; Black Memorial Prize, for fiction, 1935; Femina Vie Heureuse Prize, for fiction, 1939; Loines Award, 1958; National Poetry Society of America Gold Medal, 1960; Foyle Poetry prize, 1960; Arts Council award, 1962; Italia Prize, for radio play, 1965; Gold Medal for Poetry, Cultural Olympics, Mexico City, 1968; Queen's Gold Medal for Poetry, 1969. M.A.: Oxford University, 1961. Honorary Member, American Academy of Arts and Sciences, 1970; Honorary Fellow, St. John's College, 1971. Agent: A.P. Watt Ltd., 26-28 Bedford Row, London WC1R 4HL, England.

PUBLICATIONS

Verse

Over the Brazier. London, Poetry Bookshop, 1916; New York, St. Martin's Press, 1975.
Goliath and David. London, Chiswick Press, 1916.
Fairies and Fusiliers. London, Heinemann, 1917; New York, Knopf, 1918.

The Treasure Box. London, Chiswick Press, 1919.
Country Sentiment. London, Secker, and New York, Knopf, 1920.
The Pier-Glass. London, Secker, and New York, Knopf, 1921.
Whipperginny. London, Heinemann, and New York, Knopf, 1923.
The Feather Bed. Richmond, Surrey, Hogarth Press, 1923.
Mock Beggar Hall. London, Hogarth Press, 1924.
Welchman's Hose. London, The Fleuron, 1925.
(Poems). London, Benn, 1925.
The Marmosite's Miscellany (as John Doyle). London, Hogarth Press, 1925.
Poems (1914-1926). London, Heinemann, 1927; New York, Doubleday, 1929.
Poems (1914-1927). London, Heinemann, 1927.
Poems 1929. London, Seizin Press, 1929.
Ten Poems More. Paris, Hours Press, 1930.
Poems 1926-1930. London, Heinemann, 1931.
To Whom Else? Deyá, Mallorca, Seizin Press, 1931.
Poems 1930-1933. London, Barker, 1933.
Collected Poems. London, Cassell, and New York, Random House, 1938.
No More Ghosts: Selected Poems. London, Faber, 1940.
Work in Hand, with Alan Hodge and Norman Cameron. London, Hogarth Press, 1942.
(Poems). London, Eyre and Spottiswoode, 1943.
Poems 1938-1945. London, Cassell, 1945; New York, Creative Age Press, 1946.
Collected Poems (1914-1947). London, Cassell, 1948.
Poems and Satires 1951. London, Cassell, 1951.
Poems 1953. London, Cassell, 1953.
Collected Poems 1955. New York, Doubleday, 1955.
Poems Selected by Himself. London, Penguin, 1957; revised edition, 1961, 1966, 1972.
The Poems of Robert Graves. New York, Doubleday, 1958.
Collected Poems 1959. London, Cassell, 1959.
More Poems 1961. London, Cassell, 1961.
Collected Poems. New York, Doubleday, 1961.
New Poems 1962. London, Cassell, 1962; as *New Poems*, New York, Doubleday, 1963.
The More Deserving Cases: Eighteen Old Poems for Reconsideration. Marlborough, Wiltshire, Marlborough College Press, 1962.
Man Does, Woman Is 1964. London, Cassell, and New York, Doubleday, 1964.
Love Respelt. London, Cassell, 1965.
Collected Poems 1965. London, Cassell, 1965.
Seventeen Poems Missing from "Love Respelt." Privately printed, 1966.
Collected Poems 1966. New York, Doubleday, 1966.
Colophon to "Love Respelt." Privately printed, 1967.
(Poems), with D.H. Lawrence, edited by Leonard Clark. London, Longman, 1967.
Poems 1965-1968. London, Cassell, 1968; New York, Doubleday, 1969.
Poems about Love. London, Cassell, and New York, Doubleday, 1969.
Love Respelt Again. New York, Doubleday, 1969.
Beyond Giving. Privately printed, 1969.
Poems 1968-1970. London, Cassell, 1970.
Advice from a Mother. London, Poem-of-the-Month Club, 1970.
The Green-Sailed Vessel. Privately printed, 1971.
Corgi Modern Poets in Focus 3, with others, edited by Dannie Abse. London, Corgi, 1971.

Poems 1970-1972. London, Cassell, 1972; New York, Doubleday, 1973.
Deyá. London, Motif Editions, 1973.
Timeless Meeting. London, Rota, 1973.
At the Gate. London, Rota, 1974.
Collected Poems 1975. London, Cassell, 2 vols., 1975.
New Collected Poems. New York, Doubleday, 1977.

Recordings: *Robert Graves Reading His Own Poems*, Argo and Listen, 1960; *Robert Graves Reading His Own Poetry and The White Goddess*, Caedmon; *The Rubaiyat of Omar Khayyam*, Spoken Arts.

Plays

John Kemp's Wager: A Ballad Opera. Oxford, Blackwell, and New York, Edwards, 1925.
Nausicaa (opera libretto), adaptation of his novel *Homer's Daughter*, music by Peggy Glanville-Hicks (produced Athens, 1961).

Television Documentary: *Greece: The Inner World*, 1964 (USA).

Novels

My Head! My Head! London, Secker, and New York, Knopf, 1925.
No Decency Left (as Barbara Rich, with Laura Riding). London, Cape, 1932.
The Real David Copperfield. London, Barker, 1933; as *David Cooperfield by Charles Dickens, Condensed by Robert Graves*, edited by Merrill P. Paine, New York, Harcourt Brace, 1934.
I, Claudius.... London, Barker, and New York, Smith and Haas, 1934.
Claudius the God and His Wife Messalina.... London, Barker, 1934; New York, Smith and Haas, 1935.
Antigua, Penny, Puce. Deyá, Mallorca, Seizin Press, and London, Constable, 1936; as *The Antigua Stamp*, New York, Random House, 1937.
Count Belisarius. London, Cassell, and New York, Random House, 1938.
Sergeant Lamb of the Ninth. London, Methuen, 1940; as *Sergeant Lamb's America*, New York, Random House, 1940.
Proceed, Sergeant Lamb. London, Methuen, and New York, Random House, 1941.
The Story of Marie Powell: Wife to Mr. Milton. London, Cassell, 1943; as *Wife to Mr. Milton*, New York, Creative Age Press, 1944.
The Golden Fleece. London, Cassell, 1944; as *Hercules, My Shipmate*, New York, Creative Age Press, 1945.
King Jesus. New York, Creative Age Press, and London, Cassell, 1946.
Watch the North Wind Rise. New York, Creative Age Press, 1949; as *Seven Days in New Crete*, London, Cassell, 1949.
The Islands of Unwisdom. New York, Doubleday, 1949; as *The Isles of Unwisdom*, London, Cassell, 1950.
Homer's Daughter. London, Cassell, and New York, Doubleday, 1955.
They Hanged My Saintly Billy. London, Cassell, and New York, Doubleday, 1957.

Short Stories

The Shout. London, Mathews and Marrot, 1929.

¡Catacrok! Mostly Stories, Mostly Funny. London, Cassell, 1956.
Collected Short Stories. New York, Doubleday, 1964; London, Cassell, 1965; as *The Shout and Other Stories*, London, Penguin, 1978.

Other

On English Poetry. New York, Knopf, and London, Heinemann, 1922.
The Meaning of Dreams. London, Cecil Palmer, 1924; New York, Greenberg, 1925.
Poetic Unreason and Other Studies. London, Cecil Palmer, 1925.
Contemporary Techniques of Poetry: A Political Analogy. London, Hogarth Press, 1925.
Another Future of Poetry. London, Hogarth Press, 1926.
Impenetrability; or, The Proper Habit of English. London, Hogarth Press, 1926.
The English Ballad: A Short Critical Survey. London, Benn, 1927; revised edition, as *English and Scottish Ballads*, London, Heinemann, and New York, Macmillan, 1957.
Lars Porsena; or, The Future of Swearing and Improper Language. London, Kegan Paul Trench Trubner, and New York, Dutton, 1927; revised edition, as *The Future of Swearing and Improper Language*, Kegan Paul Trench Trubner, 1936.
A Survey of Modernist Poetry, with Laura Riding. London, Heinemann, 1927; New York, Doubleday, 1928.
Lawrence and the Arabs. London, Cape, 1927; as *Lawrence and the Arabian Adventure*, New York, Doubleday, 1928.
A Pamphlet Against Anthologies, with Laura Riding. London, Cape, 1928; as *Against Anthologies*, New York, Doubleday, 1928.
Mrs. Fisher; or, The Future of Humour. London, Kegan Paul Trench Trubner, 1928.
Goodbye to All That: An Autobiography. London, Cape, 1929; New York, Cape and Smith, 1930; revised edition, New York, Doubleday, and London, Cassell, 1957; London, Penguin, 1960.
But It Still Goes On: A Miscellany. London, Cape, and New York, Cape and Smith, 1930.
T. E. Lawrence to His Biographer Robert Graves. New York, Doubleday, 1938; London, Faber, 1939.
The Long Week-end: A Social History of Great Britain 1918-1939, with Alan Hodge. London, Faber, 1940; New York, Macmillan, 1941.
The Reader over Your Shoulder: A Handbook for Writers of English Prose, with Alan Hodge. London, Cape, 1943; New York, Macmillan, 1944.
The White Goddess: A Historical Grammar of Poetic Myth. London, Faber, and New York, Creative Age Press, 1948; revised edition, Faber, 1952, 1966; New York, Knopf, 1958.
The Common Asphodel: Collected Essays on Poetry 1922-1949. London, Hamish Hamilton, 1949.
Occupation: Writer (includes the play *Horses*). New York, Creative Age Press, 1950; London, Cassell, 1951.
The Nazarene Gospel Restored, with Joshua Podro. London, Cassell, 1953; New York, Doubleday, 1954.
The Crowning Privilege: The Clark Lectures 1954-1955; Also Various Essays on Poetry and Sixteen New Poems. London, Cassell, 1955; as *The Crowning Privilege: Collected Essays on Poetry*, New York, Doubleday, 1956.
Adam's Rib and Other Anomalous Elements in the Hebrew Creation Myth: A New View. London, Trianon Press, 1955; New York, Yoseloff, 1958.

The Greek Myths.   London and Baltimore, Penguin, 2 vols., 1955.

Jesus in Rome: A Historical Conjecture, with Joshua Podro. London, Cassell, 1957.

5 Pens in Hand.   New York, Doubleday, 1958.

Steps: Stories, Talks, Essays, Poems, Studies in History.   London, Cassell, 1958.

Food for Centaurs: Stories, Talks, Critical Studies, Poems.   New York, Doubleday, 1960.

The Penny Fiddle: Poems for Children.   London, Cassell, 1960; New York, Doubleday, 1961.

Greek Gods and Heroes (for children).   New York, Doubleday, 1960; as *Myths of Ancient Greece*, London, Cassell, 1961.

Selected Poetry and Prose, edited by James Reeves.   London, Hutchinson, 1961.

The Siege and Fall of Troy (for children).   London, Cassell, 1962; New York, Doubleday, 1963.

The Big Green Book.   New York, Crowell Collier, 1962; London, Penguin, 1978.

Oxford Addresses on Poetry.   London, Cassell, and New York, Doubleday, 1962.

Nine Hundred Iron Chariots: The Twelfth Arthur Dehon Little Memorial Lecture.   Cambridge, Massachusetts Institute of Technology, 1963.

The Hebrew Myths: The Book of Genesis, with Raphael Patai. New York, Doubleday, and London, Cassell, 1964.

Ann at Highwood Hall: Poems for Children.   London, Cassell, 1964.

Majorca Observed.   London, Cassell, and New York, Doubleday, 1965.

Mammon and the Black Goddess.   London, Cassell, and New York, Doubleday, 1965.

Two Wise Children (for children).   New York, Harlin Quist, 1966; London, W.H. Allen, 1967.

Poetic Craft and Principle.   London, Cassell, 1967.

The Poor Boy Who Followed His Star (for children).   London, Cassell, 1968; New York, Doubleday, 1969.

The Crane Bag and Other Disputed Subjects.   London, Cassell, 1969.

On Poetry: Collected Talks and Essays.   New York, Doubleday, 1969.

Poems: Abridged for Dolls and Princes (for children).   London, Cassell, and New York, Doubleday, 1971.

Difficult Questions, Easy Answers.   London, Cassell, 1972; New York, Doubleday, 1973.

An Ancient Castle (for children), edited by W.D. Thomas. London, Owen, 1980; New York, Kesend, 1982.

Selected Letters of Robert Graves, edited by Paul O'Prey:
  1. *In Broken Images: 1914-1946.*   London, Hutchinson, 1982.
  2. *Between Moon and Moon: 1946-1972.*   London, Hutchinson, 1984.

Editor, with Alan Porter and Richard Hughes, *Oxford Poetry 1921.*   Oxford, Blackwell, 1921.

Editor, *John Skelton (Laureate), 1460(?)-1529.*   London, Benn, 1927.

Editor, *The Less Familiar Nursery Rhymes.*   London, Benn, 1927.

Editor, *The Comedies of Terence.*   New York, Doubleday, 1962; London, Cassell, 1963.

Translator, with Laura Riding, *Almost Forgotten Germany*, by Georg Schwarz.   Deyá, Mallorca, Seizin Press, London, Constable, and New York, Random House, 1936.

Translator, *The Transformations of Lucius, Otherwise Known as The Golden Ass*, by Apuleius.   London, Penguin, 1950; New York, Farrar Straus, 1951.

Translator, *The Cross and the Sword*, by Manuel de Jésus Galván.   Bloomington, Indiana University Press, 1955; London, Gollancz, 1956.

Translator, *The Infant with the Globe*, by Pedro Antonio de Alarcón.   London, Trianon Press, 1955; New York, Yoseloff, 1958.

Translator, *Winter in Majorca*, by George Sand.   London, Cassell, 1956.

Translator, *Pharsalia: Dramatic Episodes of the Civil Wars*, by Lucan.   London, Penguín, 1956.

Translator, *The Twelve Caesars*, by Suetonius.   London, Penguin, 1957.

Translator, *The Anger of Achilles: Homer's Iliad.*   New York, Doubleday, 1959; London, Cassell, 1960.

Translator, with Omar Ali-Shah, *Rubaiyat of Omar Khayyam.*   London, Cassell, 1967; New York, Doubleday, 1968.

Translator, *The Song of Songs.*   New York, Potter, and London, Collins, 1973.

*

Bibliography: *A Bibliography of the Works of Robert Graves* by Fred H. Higginson, London, Vane, 1966; "Robert Graves: A Checklist of His Publications 1965-74" by A.S.G. Edwards and Diane Tolomeo, in *Malahat Review 35* (Burnaby, British Columbia), 1975.

Manuscript Collections: Lockwood Memorial Library, State University of New York at Buffalo; University of Victoria, British Columbia; New York City Public Library; University of Texas Library, Austin.

Critical Studies (selection): *Robert Graves*, London, Longman, 1956, revised edition, 1965, 1970, and *Robert Graves: His Life and Work*, London, Hutchinson, 1982, New York, Holt Rinehart, 1983, both by Martin Seymour-Smith; *Robert Graves* by J.M. Cohen, Edinburgh, Oliver and Boyd, 1960, New York, Barnes and Noble, 1965; *Swifter Than Reason: The Poetry and Criticism of Robert Graves* by Douglas Day, Chapel Hill, University of North Carolina Press, 1963, London, Oxford University Press, 1964; *Robert Graves* by George Stade, New York, Columbia University Press, 1967; *Barbarous Knowledge: Myth in the Poetry of Yeats, Graves, and Muir* by Daniel Hoffman, New York and London, Oxford University Press, 1967; *The Poetry of Robert Graves* by Michael Kirkham, New York, Oxford University Press, and London, Athlone Press, 1969; *Robert Graves, Peace-Weaver* by James S. Mehoke, The Hague, Mouton, 1975; *Robert Graves* by Katherine Snipes, New York, Ungar, 1979; *Robert Graves* by Robert H. Canary, Boston, Twayne, 1980; *A Wild Civility: Interactions in the Poetry and Thought of Robert Graves* by Patrick J. Keane, Columbia, University of Missouri Press, 1980.

*   *   *

The poetry of Robert Graves may, allowing for anticipations and regressions, be divided into four main phases: from his schoolboy beginnings in 1906 until his discovery of the poetry of the American poet Laura Riding (now Laura Jackson) in 1925; the duration of his literary and personal association with Miss Riding (1926-39); the period of his war-time sojourn in a South Devon farmhouse and of the first years of his return to Mallorca (1939-56); and what may be called the years in which he entered into world fame. The two main events in his poetic life have been the impact upon him of four years' trench warfare in World War I, and his response to the poetry and personality of Laura Riding. While the effect of Graves's war experiences has been adequately appreciated by his critics, the influence of Miss Riding has been very seriously underestimated, owing, one feels, to failure to understand her poetry. Whether the general verdict on this poetry will be reversed or not (one suspects that it may be, from the private interest that has been shown in it), it is certainly true to say that no one who will not make the effort to understand Miss Riding's poetry (she stopped writing it in 1939) can hope to understand Graves's. (That this is a statement he himself fully endorses does not prove it to be correct, but it is a fact not irrelevant for students of his poetry.)

As Graves has written in a note to the 1965 English edition of his *Collected Poems*, "...I always aimed at writing more or less as I still do." This is only another way of saying that his development has been less a matter of a series of fresh inventions, or successions of changed attitudes, than of a continuously expanding awareness of his purposes as a poet. His faith in the poem he has to write—although not attended by any careless arrogance about his capacities to write it—has been as great as that of any English poet, perhaps greater. In this sense the poem, for Graves, is a thing outside himself, a task of truth-telling—and not a thing to be invented or "composed." Poem-writing is a matter of absolute truthfulness to the emotional mood of self-revelation. Graves is not a craftsman who invents shapes in stone, to his own desires; but one who seeks, by means of intuition, to discover the exact shape in the middle of the stone, in which he has absolute faith.

If one of the signs of a major as distinct from a minor poet is development, then Graves is certainly a major poet. Yet his experiments have always been within the limits of tradition. As a schoolboy he worked on hosts of complicated rhyme-schemes and verse-forms, including the Welsh *englyn*, as well as with assonance and dissonance. For his subject-matter he drew on the world of chivalry, romance and nursery rhyme. Much of his technical facility and his capacity to use folk-themes without parodying them he owed to his father, Alfred Perceval Graves, who was a graceful minor Irish poet.

Graves was one of a group of war-poets which included Sassoon and Owen; but unlike theirs his poetry did not mature during the war, and he has rejected nearly all his war poetry. Much of his immediately post-war poetry, written under the twin (and opposing) influences of war-trauma and pastoral marriage, he has also rejected. It is technically accomplished, charming, and with an underlying complexity that is not as typically Georgian as is its surface. Graves was at this time working—under the influence of W.H.R. Rivers, the anthropologist—on the Freudian theory that poetry was therapeutic, a view he largely abandoned in the later Twenties.

Little of the poetry of Graves's first period has been preserved in his *Collected Poems*; but its main positive features—delight in nonsense, preoccupation with terror, the nature of his love for women—have survived into his later poetry. What was purged was softness and cloying over-sweetness. A poem (preserved) such as *The Pier-Glass* (1921) perfectly illustrates the qualities of the early poems and at the same time delineates the area that the later poems were to explore so meticulously and movingly. Written in the person of a lonely female ghost doomed to wander a lonely mansion, it conjures up a picture of utter lifelessness, so that the ghost cries to her "sullen pierglass, cracked from side to side" for "one token" that life exists, "So be it only this side Hope"; anything but "this phantasma." Graves was to explore the life "this side Hope," only to find it dangerous and phantasmagoric; but his poetry gained immensely in vitality and depth.

Laura Riding was on the fringes of the American Fugitive Group (which included John Crowe Ransom, Allen Tate and Robert Penn Warren) and it was in *The Fugitive* that Graves first encountered her work. What influenced him was not her procedures—which were, rhythmically, totally unlike his—but the content of her poems and the personality that went with this. The poems of his maturity are in no sense at all imitations of hers; but her remarkably complicated view of life (and therefore the work in which she expressed this) are relevant to them: he shared, or rather, attempted devotedly to learn, this view, and the material of the poems is his struggle to accommodate himself lovingly to it and to her. The process proved impossible in the end, as he foresaw in "Sick Love," written in the late Twenties: "O Love, be fed with apples while you may," this begins; and it ends: "Take your delight in momentariness,/Walk between dark and dark—a shining space/With the grave's narrowness, though not its peace." The poems Graves wrote in his second period record, with great directness and in a diction of deliberate hardness and strength, the nerve-strains of impossible love ("To the galleys, thief, and sweat your soul out" one begins) and his attempt to achieve an existence that accorded with the goodness that Graves and (at that time) Laura Riding saw as residing in poetry above every other human activity. These are therefore extremely "existential" poems, and to be understood they must be read in this way: they are at once an account of a condition of romanticized devotedness, of a search for perfection (always tempered with ironic realism and earthly masculine robustness) and of human failures. Poems such as "The Legs" describe the distractions that Graves saw as tempting him from the concentration his single-minded quest for poetic wisdom required. His "historical grammar of poetic myth," *The White Goddess*, is essentially a generalization from his experiences of these years of devoted struggle to serve a savagely demanding muse, whom in "On Portents" he has seen as a vast propeller, a "bladed mind" strongly pulling through the "ever-reluctant element" of Time. These poems, by which—together with those of the succeeding phase—Graves will probably be chiefly remembered, provide what will almost certainly become the classic latter-day record of romantic love; this is so not least because of their unsentimentality, their tough and unidealistic acceptance of the author's strong masculine recalcitrance. Thus, his mood changes from confidence, as in "End of Play"—

We tell no lies now, at last cannot be
The rogues we were—so evilly linked in sense
With what we scrutinized that lion or tiger
Could leap from every copse, strike and devour us.

—to zestful gloom, as in "The Succubus":

Yet why does she
Come never as longed-for beauty
Slender and cool, with limbs lovely to see...?

As he wrote in 1965, "My theme was always the practical impossibility, transcended only by miracle, of absolute love continuing between man and woman." It is the tension between "practical impossibility" and "miracle," a tension reflected in universal experience, that gives Graves's poetry its unique power.

The poems of Graves's third phase, written when he had abandoned his prodigious enterprise of creating—with Laura Riding—an existence in which poetry and what it represents would be a natural way of life (for more details of this, see Laura Riding's Introduction to her *Collected Poems*, 1938), reflect upon the meaning of his experience ("A Love Story"):

her image
Warped in the weather, turned beldamish.
Then back came winter on me at a bound,
The pallid sky heaved with a moon-quake.

Dangerous had it been with love-notes
To serenade Queen Famine....

They also discover new love, in some of the most beautiful love lyrics in English: "Have you not read/The words in my head,/And I made part/Of your own heart?" ("Despite and Still"). Finally they humorously state his position and accept that fame has caught up with him, as in "From the Embassy," where he refers to himself as "ambassador of Otherwhere/To the unfederated States of Here and There."

The poetry of Graves's most recent phase has continued to develop. More technically impeccable than ever, more consciously cunning in its artistry than anything that has gone before it, it lacks the tension of the earlier work—but never the convincing tone of a man in love. It owes a good deal to the Sufist ideas by which Graves has been influenced in recent years, and it discovers the peaceful figure of the Black Goddess who lies behind the crueller one of the White Goddess. Love, to Graves in these new poems, walks "on a knife-edge between two different fates": one fate is to consort with the White Goddess, and is physical; the other, more difficult yet more rewarding, to find peace in the domains of the Black Goddess. Frequently the poems are so lapidary as to remind the reader of Landor; but they reach a greater power than ever Landor achieved when they envisage the hell of a world made dead by a too great reliance upon physical passion. Of one who is trapped in this hell, who in departing too casually has said, "I will write," he says in a poem of the same title: "Long letters written and mailed in her own head—/There are no mails in a city of the dead." Graves's latest poems provide, in their explorations of the possibilities of a world purged of what he calls "the blood sports of desire," and of the agonies of alienation from such a world, a fitting sequel to those of his earlier years. He will be, perhaps, the last romantic poet to operate within wholly traditional limits—and his mastery of these is not in question.

—Martin Seymour-Smith

GRAY, Robert. Australian. Born 23 February 1945. Recipient: Literature Board of Australia Senior fellowships; Marten Bequest travelling scholarship, 1982. Address: c/o Angus and Robertson, P.O. Box 290, North Ryde, New South Wales, 2113, Australia.

PUBLICATIONS

Verse

Introspect, Retrospect. Normanhurst, New South Wales, Lyre-Bird Writers, 1970.
Creekwater Journal. Brisbane, University of Queensland Press, 1974.
Grass Script. Sydney, Angus and Robertson, 1978.
The Skylight. Sydney, Angus and Robertson, 1983.

Other

Editor, with Geoffrey Lehmann, *The Younger Australian Poets.* Sydney, Hale and Iremonger, 1983.

*   *   *

Robert Gray is among the most influential and highly regarded Australian poets writing now and is the model for a number of younger writers. His poetry is attractive and accessible to the common reader, but the "beauty"—such as it is—of his work is the result of internal, not external imperatives. He is fairly indifferent about publication of his work—particularly in magazines—and prefers to withhold a poem, often for years, revising it, before releasing it in book form.

The image is central to his poetic method. Sometimes the image exists in itself, unassisted by metaphor or simile as in this short poem: "The station master/looking across the wide, hot flats,/empties tea-leaves on the tracks." Frequently simile or metaphor intensifies the image, as in this poem from the same series: "This torch beam/I feel with, through the pouring night,/is smoke."

Implicit correspondences among images and the accurate transfer of physical and visual sensations into words become ends in themselves in many poems. Sometimes this concern becomes extreme and strains normal syntax and logic. The opening lines of "A Labourer" are an example:

He goes out early, before work, half asleep,
webs of frost on the grass; wading
paspalum to the wood-heap,
a bone-smooth axe handle pointing at him. It lifts the block
on a corner of beetled, black
earth. The logs are like rolled roasts,
they tear apart on red-fibred meat. The axe squeaks out.

The sceptical and this-worldly elements of Taoist and Buddhist philosophy, and also socialism, inform his poetry. In his volume *The Skylight* some of his arguably less successful poems are the political aphorisms. His political concerns express themselves more memorably when he writes about social underdogs.

His interest in eastern religions is embodied in poems written directly about historical figures such as "To the master Dogen Zenji," which opens with these lines: "Dogen came in and sat on the wood platform,/all the people had gathered/like birds upon the lake." The simplicity of this opening recalls Arthur Waley's translations from the Chinese. Other poems infuse Buddhism and Taoism into the Australian landscape. An example is the long poem "Dharma Vehicle" (*Grass Script*). In that poem episodes of landscape merge with quotations or incidents from the lives of sages. The statement that for the sage "there is nothing in the world that is greater/than the tip of a hair/that grows in spring" is also a manifesto of Gray's own poetic.

His subject matter ranges from country landscape to cityscape. Poems about family and lovers are important but less frequent. He uses mainly free verse forms. Each of his books has marked an advance in technique with the language becoming more complex and musical, the lines longer, the syntax more orchestral and less abrupt.

Humour and occasional informality and deliberate awkwardness are used to ensure intimacy of tone. There are a humanity and relaxed warmth in what he writes. Anecdote has become as important as imagery in some recent poems, perhaps as a raison d'être to support structures longer and more sustained than the pointillistic insights for which Gray has become known.

—Geoffrey Lehmann

GREENE, Jonathan (Edward). American. Born in New York City, 19 April 1943. Educated at Bard College, Annandale-on-Hudson, New York, B.A. Married; one daughter. Since 1965, Founding Editor, Gnomon Press, Lexington, later Frankfort, Kentucky. Apprentice printer, than assistant production manager, and production manager and designer, University Press of Kentucky, 1966-75. Recipient: National Endowment for the Arts grant, 1969, 1978. Address: P.O. Box 106, Frankfort, Kentucky 40602, U.S.A.

PUBLICATIONS

Verse

The Reckoning. Annandale-on-Hudson, New York, Matter, 1966.
Instance. Lexington, Kentucky, Buttonwood Press, 1968.
The Lapidary. Los Angeles, Black Sparrow Press, 1969.
A 17th Century Garner. Lexington, Kentucky, Buttonwood Press, 1969.
An Unspoken Complaint. Santa Barbara, California, Unicorn Press, 1970.
Scaling the Walls. Lexington, Kentucky, Gnomon Press, 1974.
Glossary of the Everyday. Toronto, Coach House Press, 1974.
Peripatetics. St. Paul, Minnesota, Truck Press, 1978.
Once a Kingdom Again. Berkeley, California, Sand Dollar, 1979.
Quiet Goods. Monterey, Kentucky, Larkspur Press, 1980.
Idylls. Emory, Virginia, Iron Mountain Press, 1983.
Small Change for the Long Haul. Barrytown, New York, Station Hill Press, 1984.
Trickster Tales. St. Paul, Minnesota, Coffee House Press, 1984.

Other

Editor, *Kentucky Renaissance: An Anthology of Contemporary Writings.* Frankfort, Kentucky, Gnomon Press, 1976.
Editor, *Fiftieth Brithday Celebration for Jonathan Williams.* Frankfort, Kentucky, Truck-Gnomon Press, 1979.

Translator, *The Poor in Church,* by Arthur Rimbuad. Lexington, Kentucky, Polyglot Press, 1973.

*

Jonathan Greene comments:
  (1970) Friendships early on with "deep image" poets important; close ties with Robert Kelly, Robert Duncan and Robin Blaser.
  No school, but a tradition involving individual poets felt strongly: Blake, Yeats and more recent incarnations.
  (1980) My recent work has delved into psychological / philosophical ruminations as well as being concerned with living in a rural setting.

*   *   *

Jonathan Greene may be placed among the group of writers affiliated (through shared concerns rather than "influence") with Robert Kelly. (Others include Charles Stein and Harvey Bialy and the prose writer Richard Grossinger.) Kelly published and wrote the introduction for Greene's first book and was his teacher and friend at Bard College. The hermetic tradition as mediated through such writers as Blake, H.D., and Robert Duncan is a major informing presence in Greene's work. One consequence is a frequently baffling abstractness and allusiveness, but even in the obscurest poems there is evident a care for the weight and sound of each syllable. Greene speaks of "the work, / which is / love / persistent" and of how "the *care-/takers* / portion out / their harvests, / the bounty." The bounty for us, in the most successful poems, is a delicate but tough lyricism—see, for example, "The Definition" from *The Lapidary.* Much influenced by Jung, Greene writes out of a sense of poetry as "given" from a source "beyond" and thus inevitably dealing in archetypal material. "A Palimpsest" opens:

> The old story keeps writing itself.
> Dark woods & the turn of the road
> again. I do not write it. A *turn
> of the road,* writes itself. *A
> changed life,* interpolates from
> an unknown source. Underneath,
> the writing still goes on.
> The true writing.

And a haiku-like poem from *Instance* puts it more imagistically: "the old tales are told, / migratory birds / come home to / the heart."
  It should be added that Greene's uncollected recent work shows a welcome inclusion of more directly personal subject matter, while retaining the qualities of ear and of access to depth evidenced in his earlier books.

—Seamus Cooney

GREGOR, Arthur. American. Born in Vienna, Austria, 18 November 1923; emigrated to the United States, 1939, naturalized, 1945. Educated at Newark College of Engineering, New Jersey, B.S. in electrical engineering 1945. Engineer, Electronic Transformer Corporation, New York, 1945-54; Editor, Whitney Publications, New York, 1955-61; Senior Editor, Macmillan Company, publishers, New York, 1962-70; Visiting Professor, California State University, Hayward, 1972-73. Since 1973, Professor and Director of the Creative Writing Center, Hofstra University, Hempstead, New York. Recipient: First Appearance Prize (*Poetry,* Chicago), 1948; Palmer Award, 1962. Address: 131 West 78th Street, New York, New York 10024, U.S.A.

PUBLICATIONS

Verse

Octavian Shooting Targets. New York, Dodd Mead, 1954.
Declensions of a Refrain. New York, Poetry London-New York Books, 1957.
Basic Movements. New York, Gyre Press, 1966.

Figure in the Door.   New York, Doubleday, 1968.
A Bed by the Sea.   New York, Doubleday, 1970.
Selected Poems.   New York, Doubleday, 1971.
The Past Now: New Poems.   New York, Doubleday, 1975.
Embodiment and Other Poems.   New York, Sheep Meadow
    Press, 1982.

Plays

Continued Departure (produced New York, 1968).   Published
    in *Accent* (Urbana, Illinois), 1951.
Fire (produced Urbana, Illinois, 1952).
The Door Is Open (produced New York, 1970).

Other (for children)

1 2 3 4 5.   Philadelphia, Lippincott, 1956.
The Little Elephant.   New York, Harper, 1956.
Animal Babies.   New York, Harper, 1959.
A Longing in the Land: Memoir of a Quest (for adults).   New
    York, Schocken, 1983.

                                    *

Manuscript Collection: Mugar Memorial Library, Boston University.

Critical Studies: reviews by Laurence Lieberman, in *Yale
Review* (New Haven, Connecticut), Spring 1968; Hayden Car-
ruth, in *Hudson Review* (New York), Spring 1968; Robert A.
Carter, in *Modern Poetry Studies* (Buffalo, New York), Autumn
1971; Thomas Lask, in *The New York Times*, 9 December 1971;
Christopher Collins, in *The Nation* (New York), 15 February
1972; F.D. Reeve, in *Poetry* (Chicago), January 1973; Josephine
Jacobsen, in *Nation* (New York), 9 October 1976; Grace Schul-
man, in *Twentieth Century Literature* (Hempstead, New York),
October 1977; James Finn Cotter, in *Hudson Review* (New
York), Spring 1978.

Arthur Gregor comments:

   I have tried to explore and to articulate what I consider the
poetic reality in myself—a reality which lies in all. My influences
have been art, nature, and those in whom throb powerfully the
magic, the mystery of life.

                    *   *   *

   During a time when the evolution of American poetry has
been defined by large movements with clearly directed aims,
Arthur Gregor has followed a decidedly independent, sometimes
contrary course. In part it is a question of his European origin.
He was born and raised in Vienna, and has traveled extensively
in the Old World; his poetry relies upon images and allusions
drawn from European history and culture. But the distinction is
more basic than this. If we agree that the great movement of
American poetry in the past 25 years has been away from the
symbolist tradition and the dominance of such poets as Eliot and
Yeats, and toward a poetry based not only on native themes and
idioms but on an objectivist view of reality (which does not
preclude mythic values), then Gregor has clearly stood against
the main stream with his insistence upon the continuing human
validity of symbolist modes of perception. It has not been an
argued insistence. Though Gregor has been a journalist and
editor, as well as an engineer, he has rarely resorted to theoretical
statements about his own work. But in his poetry his philosophical affinities are clear: they are with the great symbolists of the

European tradition, and particularly with such poets of the
richly colored, central European imagination as Rilke and
Hofmannsthal.
   It is easy to overemphasize the programmatic importance of
these distinctions, however. Gregor fits comfortably enough in
the present American literary scene. In tone and verbal texture
his verse resembles the contemporary free-form writing of most
American poets. In fact from his first poems in the 1940's Gregor
used a freer, more flexible line than the formalist conventions of
that period sanctioned. He could never have been classed with
the academics. On the other hand his early work did show an
ornateness of diction and figure which seemed very baroque at
the time, as if this European poet had taken the manner of
Wallace Stevens and converted it to foreign ends, though the
actual influence of Stevens, if it existed at all, was superficial.
From these beginnings Gregor moved toward quieter, gentler
poems that reached ever farther into his mystical view of experience. An evocation of unseen presences, a realization of history
or of the minds of ancestors, a glimpse of the "elsewhere" that
lies somehow within the defined particulars of each new place:
these and similar themes occupied him more and more. It is
difficult to say precisely what his religious orientation may be;
his poems are written always obliquely, as if alongside the standard forms of spiritual evolution, not within them. Allusions can
be detected to Hebrew, Christian, Gnostic, and Vedantic motifs,
but they are allusions of feeling, not form, of spirit, not substance. His vision is clearly his own. And in his poems about
people, though they are often richly erotic, it is the essential
mystery of the person toward which the vision aspires.
   The danger of Gregor's vision is that words will fail its myste-
riousness and turn into mere talk—talking about what cannot be
sufficiently embodied, the failure of symbolism. It is a danger
that Gregor has not always surmounted. But in his best poems—
some of those about his parents and his travels—his vision is
conveyed intact. It is a private vision, hence in some sense
exclusive or even elitist, at odds with the prevailing temper of the
age. Yet Gregor's work has a gentleness and seriousness which
have won it considerable popularity in recent years, especially
among young people, and his somewhat alien voice has become
a distinct and useful element in the American literary sensibility
of the time.

                                            —Hayden Carruth

GRIER, Eldon (Brockwill).   Canadian.   Born in London,
England, to Canadian parents, in 1917. Educated in Montreal,
Ottawa, and Toronto; studied painting in Mexico with Diego
Rivera after 1945. Married Sylvia Tait in 1953; two daughters
and one son. Painter: taught at the Montreal Museum of Art;
group show: Burnaby Gallery, British Columbia, 1978. Address:
6221 St. Georges Place, West Vancouver, British Columbia
V7W 1YC, Canada.

PUBLICATIONS

Verse

A Morning from Scraps.   Privately printed, 1955.
Poems.   Privately printed, 1956.
The Ring of Ice.   Montreal, Cambridge Press, 1957.
Manzanillo and Other Poems.   Privately printed, 1958.

A Friction of Lights. Toronto, Contact Press, 1963.
Pictures on the Skin. Montreal, Delta Canada, 1967.
Selected Poems 1955-1970. Montreal, Delta Canada, 1971.
The Assassination of Colour. Fredericton, New Brunswick,
Fiddlehead, 1978.

Play

Radio Play: *Fitzgerald and My Father,* 1976.

*   *   *

Eldon Grier came to poetry through painting. He studied
under John Lyman, the most influential early modernist painter
in Canada; he went on to Mexico and studied fresco under Diego
Rivera, for whom he worked as plasterer; he returned to Canada
and began to teach painting under Arthur Lismer in Montreal. It
was a life crisis in his middle thirties that started him writing
poetry. He developed tuberculosis, recovered from it, and
shortly afterwards married the painter Sylvia Tait. It was on
their long honeymoon in Spain that he wrote in 1955, when he
was 38, his first poems—"quite inexplicably," as he has remarked.
His life as a painter was ended, at least overtly, though through
his wife he retained his link with the visual arts, for she illustrated
at least two of his books of poems, while the fact of having once
been a painter has undoubtedly influenced his poetry, which is
sharply visual, and is often at its best when he is addressing some
painter or sculptor with whom he feels an affinity, such as
Morandi, Picasso, the Canadian Morrice, or Marino Marini: "It
is the portrait heads / that are sure to appeal to a writer...."

One could describe Eldon Grier as a verbal colourist, for he
has a remarkable power of evoking scenes that shine in the
mind's eye, and his language itself has a vividness that runs the
range from subtlety to gaudiness. Yet his poetry is not merely
sensual. It has a literary ancestry. Grier developed in a Montreal
setting where he came into contact with Canadian modernists
like F.R. Scott and Louis Dudek (who published his first books),
and in his early, rather declarative phase one cannot fail to
observe the diffused influence of Ezra Pound.

But there were other formative factors. Grier has always travelled widely, and some of his best poems are about Mexico,
where he has lived on and off for considerable periods: a good
example is "Mountain Town—Mexico":

Arms at my side like some inadequate sign,
I lie awake in a dark room in an alien country.
While plates of frost slide past my face, and needles
cluster in the crêpe-like air, my friend who has made
his adjustment, urinates into a bucket with a thunderous
    ring.

I must impress myself with certain things;
the honesty of mountain people, the lightheartedness
of a people never conquered by arms—and yet
the monster of the mines lies dead beneath their homes,
its scattered mouths decaying in a final spittle of stones....

I lie awake until the blackness burns to filaments
of tired red. A horse sparks up the cobblestones.
A voice speaks cleanly from the stage of cold beyond.
No spout of sunlight ever entered to my bed, but stealthily
an orange cat comes snaking through the door in search of
    food.

And there has always been a subtle French influence which

Grier has adeptly transmuted into English poetry. Guillaume
Apollinaire has always fascinated him:

I am almost asleep
with your poems on my chest,
Apollinaire,
I am almost asleep
but I feel the transfusion of fine little letters
dripping slantwise into my side.

Beyond Apollinaire, Grier has moved towards surrealism,
impelled largely by his sense of the necessarily irrational nature
of poetry:

Our poets must give themselves to a kind
Of unsensible madness;
They must hear music not meaning as they write.

Yet in his own way Eldon Grier is almost monumentally sensible, since he never loses sight of the meaning that is in the senses,
and this indeed is his special virtue which has led him, more than
once, to a rediscovery of the insights of imagism:

Under the lids of the roof
the sun comes in discreetly
white, whiter than milk in a porcelain cup.

And always in his work there is a strange hovering of feeling, a
regret for an art lost in the acquisition of another, so that in a
piece about painters he says: "Poems, I know by now, go out like
stars."

—George Woodcock

GRIFFIN, Jonathan. Pseudonym for Robert John Thurlow
Griffin. British. Born in Worthing, Sussex, in 1906. Edu-
cated at Radley School; New College, Oxford, B.A. Married 1)
Joan Scudamore Creyke (marriage dissolved); 2) Kathleen
Evelyn Willson. Director of European Intelligence, BBC, Lon-
don, 1940-44; Second Secretary, British Embassy, Paris, 1945-
51. Address: c/o Menard Press, 8 The Oaks, Woodside Avenue,
London N12 8AR, England.

PUBLICATIONS

Verse

The Rebirth of Pride. London, Secker and Warburg, 1957.
The Oath and Other Poems. London, Gordon, 1963.
In Time of Crowding: Selected Poems 1963-1974. London,
Brookside Press, 1975.
In This Transparent Forest. University Center, Michigan,
Green River Press, 1977.
Outsing the Howling: An Interlude. London, Permanent
Press, 1979.
The Fact of Music. London, Menard Press, 1980.
Commonsense of the Senses. London, Menard Press, 1982.

Plays

The Master of Santiago, and *Malatesta*, adaptations of plays by
   Henry de Montherlant (produced London, 1957).
   Included in *The Master of Santiago and Four Other Plays*,
   London, Routledge, and New York, Knopf, 1951.
The Hidden King: A Poem for the Stage in the Form of a Trilogy
   (produced Edinburgh, 1957). London, Secker and War-
   burg, 1955.
The Cardinal of Spain, adaptation of a play by Henry de
   Montherlant (produced Guildford, Surrey, 1969). Published
   in *Plays of the Year 37*, London, Elek, 1969.
The Prince of Homburg, adaptation of a play by Heinrich von
   Kleist (produced Manchester, 1976). Published in *Plays of
   the Year 36*, London, Elek, 1969.
Break of Noon, adaptation of a play by Paul Claudel (produced
   Ipswich, 1972).
The Deep Man, adaptation of a play by Hugo von Hofmanns-
   thal (produced Manchester, 1979).

Screenplay: *Diary of a Country Priest* (English version), 1950.

Other

Britain's Air Policy: Present and Future. London, Gollancz,
   1935.
Alternative to Re-armament. London, Macmillan, 1936.
Glass Houses and Modern War. London, Chatto and Windus,
   1938.
The Czechoslovak-German Frontier: Its Strategic Importance.
   London, Czechoslovak Broadsheets, 1938.
*Lost Liberty? The Ordeal of the Czechs and the Future of
   Freedom*, with Joan Griffin. London, Chatto and Windus,
   1939.

Translator, *The Hussar on the Roof*, by Jean Giono. London,
   Museum Press, 1953; as *The Horseman on the Roof*, New
   York, Knopf, 1954.
Translator, *Christ Recrucified*, by Nikos Kazantzakis. Ox-
   ford, Cassirer, 1954; as *The Greek Passion*, New York, Simon
   and Schuster, 1954.
Translator, *Freedom and Death*, by Nikos Kazantzakis. Ox-
   ford, Cassirer, 1956; as *Freedom or Death*, New York, Simon
   and Schuster, 1956.
Translator, *The Roots of Heaven*, by Romain Gary. London,
   Joseph, and New York, Simon and Schuster, 1958.
Translator, *Fernando Pessoa I-IV*. Oxford, Carcanet, 1971.
Translator, *Selected Poems*, by Fernando Pessoa. London,
   Penguin, 1974; revised edition, 1982.
Translator, *Memories for Tomorrow* (autobiography), by Jean-
   Louis Barrault. London, Thames and Hudson, 1975.
Translator, *Camões: Some Poems*. London, Menard Press,
   1976.
Translator, with Mary Ann Caws, *Poems of René Char*. Prince-
   ton, New Jersey, Princeton University Press, 1976.

Many other translations published.

*

Jonathan Griffin comments:
   If I write true poems, I learned it from Arthur Schnabel. I first
met him in (I think) 1931. I was not a good enough pianist to be a
pupil of his: he read my thoughts and invited me to his master
classes as a listener. What he taught, by speech and example, was

to find how the great music is made and what it says, combining
truthfulness and passion. So he lit every art.
   I still waited about 16 years—did not have enough to say. I
wanted to include and go beyond politics. The idea of *The
Hidden King* came as my liberation. The questions which most
people desperately want answered have no evident answer: if
there is a truth about these questions, a play may take us nearer
to it through clashes between imaginary living people. A similar
way may be to bring together poems that interact.
   Every true poem, however light, is committed; yet a distinction between politically committed and pure poems has been
found helpful. I am impelled to write poems of both kinds, and it
seems to me good, when publishing, to mix them.
   Though love poetry has a big part in *The Hidden King*, I have
written hardly any love poems. The things lovers say to each
other are mostly trite, discoveries to them: to make beautiful
poems of such words was customary, but by now they have been
that-much-more "done to death." Poems to a girl were a part of
courtship, now young men and girls hurry to the point. The great
love poems of recent times have tended (Williams, "O asphodel...";
George Oppen, "Anniversary Poem"; Basil Bunting, *Briggflatts*;
Peter Whigham, *The Ingathering of Love*) to be by older men
about a remembered love or a love which has endured until the
parting by natural death seems near.
   Details of my own life are rather rare in my poems: I live it
with zest but am short on the feeling that whatever has happened
to me must interest other people. Also, privacy is a precious
freedom—more threatened, in some places, than freedom of
speech. Yet my poems are mine and passionate—

> my pure joys yes
>   hardly won barely held
> faith   yes   not sins and glosses...
> In my art I evade my evasions
> I go away and rise above myself

Ambition: to sing truth. One must keep faith with doubt and, if a
grand poem which is honest comes, dare it.
   I am driven to write about my neighbour rather than myself,
my neighbour in the future as well as now. As I grow older I
become more firmly a modern poet: forward-looking. To waste
life on feelings of guilt about old wrongs is absurd and a parasitic
indulgence, since our guilt about the present is to be looked at,
and lessened. But the injuries being done to our successors and to
Earth are even greater—their (if possible) reversal more urgent.
(One instance: the continuing crime in Brazil, against the rain
forests and their soil, is Hitlerian, and international corpora-
tions are in it.) Shame makes me write love poems to Earth and
poems of solicitude for wronged posterity.

*   *   *

   The card catalogue of the New York Public library assumes
that there are three Jonathan Griffins: The English poet, the
1930's journalist and expert on military affairs, and the translator of a shelf-full of books from seven European languages. To
these we might add the "would-be" pianist who studied with
Schnabel in Berlin in the early 1930's, the director of BBC
European Intelligence during World War II, the diplomat in
Paris, the screenwriter in Rome, the playwright featured at the
Edinburgh Festival in 1957. But amidst this flock of public
Griffins, the poet—the one whose work will last—has scarcely
been visible. Until quite recently the poems rarely appeared in
magazines, and his books were published by the smallest of small
presses. Today Griffin is somewhat more visible—if one looks
hard enough—but there is still, as yet, no critical attention paid

him, other than a few short reviews. One poem was anthologized once; no survey of contemporary writing has hitherto mentioned his name. He is, in short, something of a secret treasure; few of his stature are so little known.

The voice is unique, and even at first glance a Griffin poem is unmistakable: titles which seem to come from nowhere, catching the reader off-guard ("You May Come Out"; "Ear to House—"; "3 Angels in Supernova"; "Into the Straight"; "At the Crucifixion of One's Heirs"; "The World Is Bugged"); rhymes that appear and disappear; neologisms (*breathprint, terracide, gravechill, brainstone*); rhythms like shattering glass; breath-pauses presented on the page through a system of indentation he has apparently invented. The music can be as dense as the later Bunting; the language as personal as that of David Jones (though, unlike Jones, Griffin never displays his erudition—the poems are entirely without literary reference). "The syntax," George Oppen has commented, "moves of its own force, moves in the force of the world, it restores light and space to poetry. It is what the poetry of England has lacked for—how long?"

He was first published in his (and the century's) fifties, and the work contains none of the indulgences of younger poets. There is wit but never cleverness, no fanciful speculation, no anecdote, few occasional pieces, and—other than some recent meditations on death—no autobiography, no confession. The "I" of the poem, when it appears, is linked only to verbs of thought, declaration, or perception. Griffin's nuclear words are *man, God, music, pride, humility*. There is always the sense that the poet has been impelled to speech.

This may be the first poetry to contemplate seriously the new vision of earth given us by the lunar missions. It is a poetry of planetary consciousness, but without the occultism and nostalgia for a Golden Age that has characterized more popular writing. Accordingly, given the times, the vision is double; the poet's response both ecstasy and rage. The intense lyrics in celebration of natural beauty—some of the loveliest in the language—are almost eclipsed by the bleak and apocalyptic meditations. Griffin is one of the few poets today who is confronting, *in the poem*, this earth of pesticide, radiation, holocaust, overpopulation, deforestation, chemical waste—the way we live now, in the first age to devastate the future. His is a voice at world's end: "We need no prophets We know what is coming/but can we live with it?"

Although the poems continue the English spiritual tradition (and indeed Griffin seems closer to Vaughan, Herbert and Traherne, Hopkins and Dixon, than to any poet of this century) the God of organized religion never enters these contemplations. Griffin's God is idiosyncratic and complex: a divine force which is either destructive or does not exist; a God that is the Goddess, planet earth; a God that "is men making music." One of his darkest lines simply states: "Entropy is God."

In the absence of a creator God, the poetry becomes spiritual in the broadest sense: the spirit of incantation, incantation meaning music, poetry, prayer ("I believe in prayer not in God.") In a world where "we voted with our feet a deadness to live in," Griffin's prayer is a grim one: "for/Earth to be saved from Man." He writes: "I believe in man but not much."

2000 years ago, Wei Hung stated: "The music of an age on the verge of ruin is mournful and thoughtful." Griffin's music is both, and yet, given his vision, strangely ecstatic. For Jonathan Griffin, the "fact of music"—that it is there, that we are capable of making it—may be, in the end all that matters:

> Is it too late? Before it is too late
> remember the great music. Because small
> mammals dreamed it, because it is at all,

preserve the world, continue Man. Let great
work, by the few unlikely, inseminate
silence—the private silences, the All
Silence—with new music: to the still, small
tune of Man the last waste reverberate.

—Eliot Weinberger

GRIFFITHS, Bryn(lyn David). Welsh. Born in Swansea, West Glamorgan, 7 February 1933. Educated at St. Thomas School, Swansea; Swansea Technical College, 1960-61; Coleg Harlech, Merioneth, 1961-62. Married; two children. Merchant seaman, 1951-58; carpenter, salesman, and building worker, 1958-62; free-lance writer, 1962-76; arts co-ordinator for industry, Trades and Labour Council of Western Australia, Perth, 1976-82. Writer-in-Residence, Western Australian College of Advanced Education, Perth, 1983. Since 1983, free-lance writer. Address: P.O. Box 23, Doubleview, Perth, Western Australia 6018, Australia; or, 65 Gwili Terrace, Mayhill, Swansea, Wales.

PUBLICATIONS

Verse

The Mask of Pity. Llandybie, Dyfed, Christopher Davies, 1966.
The Stones Remember. London, Dent, 1967.
Scars. London, Dent, 1969.
At the Airport. Frensham, Surrey, Sceptre Press, 1971.
The Survivors. London, Dent, 1971.
Beasthoods: Poems. London, Turret, 1972.
Starboard Green. Blackwood, Monmouthshire, Imble, 1973.
The Dark Convoys: Sea Poems. Breakish, Isle of Skye, Aquila, 1974.
Love Poems. Perth, Western Australia, Artlook, 1980.

Recording: *The Stones Remember*, with Bryan Walters, Argo, 1974.

Plays

King Arthur's Egg (for children; produced 1975).

Radio Plays: *The Sailor*, 1967; *The Dream of Arthur*, 1968; *The Undertaker*, 1970.

Other

Editor, *Welsh Voices: An Anthology of New Poetry from Wales.* London, Dent, 1967.

*

Manuscript Collection: National Library of Wales, Aberystwyth.

Bryn Griffiths comments:

I am primarily concerned with humanity and the relationship of mankind and other life on this planet. I am concerned with landscape, the environment, time, sensuality, love, the sea, and sadness, and our possible imminent oblivion. My sources are history, Celtic myth, the sea, my personal life, and everyday life.

                              *   *   *

After a somewhat mixed experience as a welder, painter, labourer, seaman and car-tester, Bryn Griffiths started his writing career at a time when, partially as a result of the activities of the "pop" poets, the general public was being persuaded to take an increasing interest in poetry readings—an interest which Griffiths has subsequently done a good deal to encourage and sustain. As his poetry is pithy, down-to-earth, and direct in impact, it is hardly surprising that, from the beginning, it has had a great appeal for listeners, as well as readers. In fact, his earliest work seems to reflect both the strength and weakness of the poet whose platform performance is almost equal to his technical skill—the ability to communicate a rich variety of thought and feelings to a wide audience, combined with an occasional tendency to content himself with superficial impressions.

With the publication of his second volume, *The Stones Remember*, it became apparent that Griffiths was undergoing a period of rapid development and exploring his own experience at great depth. He has always been preoccupied with the landscape, people and traditions of his native Wales, but with this volume, and *Scars*, which followed two years later, he produced clear evidence of having found an individual voice. *The Survivors* is largely concerned with his experiences on two trips to Australia, but even in that vast continent, impressed as he is by the strange grandeur of his new environment, he looks back to his native country: "I take you with me, Wales, wherever I go."

                                                    —Howard Sergeant

---

GRIGSON, Geoffrey (Edward Harvey). British. Born in Pelynt, Cornwall, 2 March 1905. Educated at St. Edmund Hall, Oxford. Married 1) Frances Galt (died, 1937), one daughter; 2) Berta Kunert (marriage dissolved), one son and one daughter; 3) Jane McIntire (i.e., the writer Jane Grigson), one daughter. Formerly, staff member, *Yorkshire Post*, Leeds, and Literary Editor, *Morning Post*, and BBC, London. Founding Editor, *New Verse*, London, 1933-39. Recipient: Duff Cooper Memorial Prize, 1971; Oscar Blumenthal Prize (*Poetry*, Chicago), 1971. Agent: David Higham Associates Ltd., 5-8 Lower John Street, London W1R 4HA. Address: Broad Town Farm, Broad Town, Swindon, Wiltshire, England.

PUBLICATIONS

Verse

Several Observations: Thirty Five Poems. London, Cresset Press, 1939.
Under the Cliff and Other Poems. London, Routledge, 1943.
The Isles of Scilly and Other Poems. London, Routledge, 1946.
Legenda Suecana: Twenty-Odd Poems. Privately printed, 1953.
The Collected Poems of Geoffrey Grigson 1924-1962. London, Phoenix House, 1963.
A Skull in Salop and Other Poems. London, Macmillan, and

Chester Springs, Pennsylvania, Dufour, 1967.
Ingestion of Ice-Cream and Other Poems. London, Macmillan, 1969.
Discoveries of Bones and Stones. London, Macmillan, 1971.
Penguin Modern Poets 23, with Edwin Muir and Adrian Stokes. London, Penguin, 1973.
Sad Grave of an Imperial Mongoose. London, Macmillan, 1973.
The First Folio. London, Poem-of-the-Month Club, 1973.
Angles and Circles and Other Poems. London, Gollancz, 1974.
The Fiesta and Other Poems. London, Secker and Warburg, 1978.
History of Him. London, Secker and Warburg, 1980.
Twists of the Way. Hitchin, Hertfordshire, Mandeville Press, 1980.
Collected Poems 1963-1980. London, Allison and Busby, 1982.
The Cornish Dancer and Other Poems. London, Secker and Warburg, 1982.
Montaigne's Tower. London, Secker and Warburg, 1984.

Other

Henry Moore. London, Penguin, 1943.
Wild Flowers in Britain. London, Collins, and New York, Hastings House, 1944.
Samuel Palmer: The Visionary Years. London, Kegan Paul, 1947.
The Harp of Aeolus and Other Essays on Art, Literature, and Nature. London, Routledge, 1948.
An English Farmhouse and Its Neighbourhood. London, Parrish, 1948.
The Scilly Isles. London, Elek, 1948; revised edition, London, Duckworth, 1977.
Places of the Mind. London, Routledge, 1949.
The Crest on the Silver: An Autobiography. London, Cresset Press, 1950.
Flowers of the Meadow. London, Penguin, 1950.
Wessex. London, Collins, 1951.
A Master of Our Time: A Study of Wyndham Lewis. London, Methuen, 1951; New York, Gordon Press, 1952.
Essays from the Air (broadcasts). London, Routledge, 1951.
West Country. London, Collins, 1951.
Gardenage; or, The Plants of Ninhursaga. London, Routledge, 1952.
The Female Form in Painting, with Jean Cassou. London, Thames and Hudson, and New York, Harcourt Brace, 1953.
Freedom of the Parish. London, Phoenix House, 1954.
Gerard Manley Hopkins. London, Longman, 1955; revised edition, 1962.
The Englishman's Flora. London, Phoenix House, 1955.
English Drawing from Samuel Cooper to Gwen John. London, Thames and Hudson, 1955.
The Shell Guide to Flowers of the Countryside [*Trees and Shrubs, Wild Life*]. London, Phoenix House, 3 vols., 1955-59; in *The Shell Nature Book,* 1964.
Corot. New York, Metropolitan Museum, 1956.
Painted Caves. London, Phoenix House, 1957.
England. London, Thames and Hudson, 1957; New York, Studio, 1958.
Fossils, Insects, and Reptiles. London, Phoenix House, 1957; in *The Shell Nature Book,* 1964.
Art Treasures of the British Museum. London, Thames and Hudson, and New York, Abrams, 1957.
The Wiltshire Book. London, Thames and Hudson, 1957.

The Three Kings. Bedford, Gordon Fraser, 1958.
English Villages in Colour. London, Batsford, 1958.
*Looking and Finding and Collecting and Reading and Investi-
gating and Much Else* (juvenile). London, Phoenix House,
1958; revised edition, London, Baker, 1970.
A Herbal of All Sorts. London, Phoenix House, and New
York, Macmillan, 1959.
English Excursions. London, Country Life, 1960.
Samuel Palmer's Valley of Vision. London, Phoenix House,
1960.
Christopher Smart. London, Longman, 1961.
The Shell Country Book. London, Phoenix House, 1962.
The Shell Book of Roads. London, Ebury Press, 1964.
Shapes and Stories: A Book about Pictures (for children), with
Jane Grigson. London, Baker, and New York, Vanguard
Press, 1964.
The Shell Nature Book. London, Phoenix House, and New
York, Basic Books, 1964.
The Shell Country Alphabet. London, Joseph, 1966; as *Geof-
frey Grigson's Countryside,* London, Ebury Press, 1982.
Shapes and Adventures (for children), with Jane Grigson.
London, Marshbank, 1967; as *More Shapes and Stories: A
Book about Pictures,* New York, Vanguard Press, 1967.
Shapes and People: A Book about Pictures (for children).
London, Baker, and New York, Vanguard Press, 1969.
Poems and Poets. London, Macmillan, and Chester Springs,
Pennsylvania, Dufour, 1969.
Notes from an Odd Country. London, Macmillan, 1970.
Shapes and Creatures (for children). London, Black, 1973.
The Contrary View: Glimpses of Fudge and Gold. London,
Macmillan, and Totowa, New Jersey, Rowman and Little-
field, 1974.
*A Dictionary of English Plant Names and Some Products of
Plants.* London, Allen Lane, 1974.
Britain Observed: The Landscape Through Artists' Eyes.
London, Phaidon, 1975.
*The Goddess of Love: The Birth, Triumph, Death, and Return
of Aphrodite.* London, Constable, 1976; New York, Stein
and Day, 1977.
Blessings, Kicks, and Curses: A Critical Collection. London,
Allison and Busby, 1982.
The Private Art: A Poetry Notebook. London, Allison and
Busby, 1982.
Recollections—Mainly of Writers and Artists. London,
Chatto and Windus, 1984.

Editor, with others, *The Year's Poetry.* London, Lane, 1934.
Editor, *The Arts Today.* London, Lane, 1935.
Editor, with Denys Kilham Roberts, *The Year's Poetry 1937-
38.* London, Lane, 1938.
Editor, *New Verse: An Anthology.* London, Faber, 1939.
Editor, *The Journals of George Sturt.* London, Cresset Press,
1941.
Editor, *The Romantics: An Anthology.* London, Routledge,
1942; Cleveland, World, 1962.
Editor, *Visionary Poems and Passages; or, The Poet's Eye.*
London, Muller, 1944.
Editor, *The Mint: A Miscellany of Literature, Art, and Criticism.*
London, Routledge, 2 vols., 1946-48.
Editor, *Before the Romantics: An Anthology of the Enlighten-
ment.* London, Routledge, 1946; Great Neck, New York,
Granger, 1978.
Editor, *Poems of John Clare's Madness.* London, Routledge,
1949.
Editor, *Poetry of the Present: An Anthology of the Thirties and
After.* London, Phoenix House, 1949.

Editor, *Selected Poems of William Barnes 1800-1866.* Lon-
don, Routledge, and Cambridge, Massachusetts, Harvard
University Press, 1950.
Editor, *Selected Poems,* by John Clare. London, Routledge,
1950.
Editor, *Selected Poems,* by John Dryden. London, Grey Walls
Press, 1950.
Editor, *Poems,* by George Crabbe. London, Grey Walls Press,
1950.
Editor, *The Victorians: An Anthology.* London, Routledge,
1950.
Editor, *Thornton's Temple of Flora,* by Robert John Thornton.
London, Collins, 1951.
Editor, *Poems,* by Samuel Taylor Coleridge. London, Grey
Walls Press, 1951.
Editor, *About Britain* series. London, Collins, 13 vols., 1951.
Editor, with Charles Harvard Gibbs-Smith, *People, Places and
Things.* London, Grosvenor Press, and New York, Haw-
thorn Press, 4 vols., 1954.
Editor, *The Three Kings: A Christmas Book of Carols, Poems,
and Pieces.* Bedford, Gordon Fraser, 1958.
Editor, *Country Poems.* London, Hulton, 1959.
Editor, *The Cherry Tree: A Collection of Poems* (for child-
ren). London, Phoenix House, and New York, Vanguard
Press, 1959.
Editor, *Poets in Their Pride* (for children). London, Phoenix
House, 1962; New York, Basic Books, 1964.
Editor, *The Concise Encyclopaedia of Modern World Litera-
ture.* London, Hutchinson, and New York, Hawthorn,
1963; revised edition, Hutchinson, 1970; Hawthorn, 1971.
Editor, *O Rare Mankind! A Short Collection of Great Prose*
(juvenile). London, Phoenix House, 1963.
Editor, *Poems,* by Walter Savage Landor. London, Centaur
Press, 1964; Carbondale, Southern Illinois University Press,
1965.
Editor, *The English Year: From Diaries and Letters.* London,
Oxford University Press, 1967.
Editor, *A Choice of William Morris's Verse.* London, Faber,
1969.
Editor, *A Choice of Thomas Hardy's Poems.* London, Mac-
millan, 1969.
Editor, *A Choice of Robert Southey's Verse.* London, Faber,
1970.
Editor, *Thirty-Eight Poems,* by Pennethorne Hughes. Lon-
don, Baker, 1970.
Editor, *Rainbows, Fleas, and Flowers* (for children). London,
Baker, 1971; New York, Vanguard Press, 1974.
Editor, *Unrespectable Verse.* London, Allen Lane, 1971; as
The Penguin Book of Unrespectable Verse, London, Pen-
guin, 1980.
Editor, *The Faber Book of Popular Verse.* London, Faber,
1971; as *The Gambit Book of Popular Verse,* Boston, Gambit,
1971.
Editor, *The Faber Book of Love Poems.* London, Faber, 1973;
as *The Gambit Book of Love Poems,* Boston, Gambit, 1975.
Editor, *Cotton.* London, Penguin, 1974.
Editor, *The Penguin Book of Ballads.* London, Penguin, 1975.
Editor, *The Faber Book of Epigrams and Epitaphs.* London,
Faber, 1977.
Editor, *The Faber Book of Nonsense Verse.* London, Faber,
1979.
Editor, *The Oxford Book of Satirical Verse.* Oxford and New
York, Oxford University Press, 1980.
Editor, *The Faber Book of Poems and Places.* London, Faber,
1980.
Editor, *The Faber Book of Reflective Verse.* London, Faber,

1984.

*

Manuscript Collections: British Library, London; Birmingham University Library.

Critical Study: in *Times Literary Supplement* (London), 31 July 1969.

Geoffrey Grigson comments:

I deduce from my poems that I write by this conviction: graces enter and exist in living; they start up, vanish, and are seen again in glimpses. It is sentimental treason to suppose that we can be anaesthetized or satisfied by these graces, but the grand treason, realizing the constancy of the bad and the worst, is not as well to admit and celebrate and be thankful for these consolatory graces, or viaticum.

*   *   *

Geoffrey Grigson is one of the most interesting of the so-called "Auden generation" of English poets who began writing in the 1930's; but his merits as a poet have always been overshadowed by his activities as an entrepreneur of letters. For several years in the thirties Grigson was editor of the influential magazine *New Verse*, and throughout his life he has been an active and polemical critic. His early poetry was marked by its precise, imagistic observations of the contemporary scene; Grigson was a believer in the brief snapshot of reality, presented without elaboration or comment, though the political preoccupations so evident in the poetry of Auden or Spender were often implicitly present in his verse. These early poems were redeemed from flatness by Grigson's delicate and very personal sense of rhythm. They can still be read with pleasure, although at the same time they are very much of their period, when poets were following up Eliot's fascination with urban landscape, and were actively interested in sociological enquiry: the 1930's movement called Mass Observation echoes the title of Grigson's book of poems *Several Observations*.

His later poetry, though still anchored to the discipline of exact description, is less austere and more overtly emotional. In addition to his original discipleship of Auden and the Imagists, Grigson developed a great admiration for John Clare, and much of his description of natural objects recalls the precise botanical observations of Ruskin or Hopkins. Although Grigson remains what he has always been, a writer of short poems, there are pieces in his *Collected Poems* that show he has occasionally been more ambitious, like the short verse play "The Islanders," and a rather impressive sequence of love poems called "Legenda." Yet a brief poem like "Elms under Cloud" remains most typical of Grigson's art:

>Elms, old-men with thinned-out hair,
>And mouths down-turned, express
>The oldness of the English scene:
>
>And up the hill a pale road reaches
>To a huge paleness browned with scattered,
>Irritated cloud....

A later poem, "Driving Through Dead Elms," provides a sad and ironic companion piece, in a response to the ravages of elm disease in the English countryside.

Grigson's second volume of collected poems does not show any surprising developments of form and feeling. It continues his characteristic vein of imagistic observation and sour, sometimes cryptic epigrams, though the passions and disappointments of a poet moving into old age bring a new sharpness to his small, precise notations of experience.

—Bernard Bergonzi

GUEST, Barbara. American. Born in Wilmington, North Carolina, 6 September 1920. Educated at the University of California, Berkeley, A.B. 1943. Married 1) Lord Stephen Haden-Guest in 1948 (divorced, 1954), one daughter; 2) Trumbull Higgins in 1954, one son. Editorial Associate, *Art News*, New York, 1951-54. Recipient: Yaddo fellowship, 1958; Longview Foundation award, 1960; National Endowment for the Arts grant, 1980. Address: 37 Pleasant Lane, Southampton, New York 11968, U.S.A.

PUBLICATIONS

Verse

The Location of Things.   New York, Tibor de Nagy, 1960.
Poems: The Location of Things, Archaics, The Open Skies. New York, Doubleday, 1962.
The Blue Stairs.   New York, Corinth, 1968.
I Ching: Poems and Lithographs, with Sheila Isham.   Paris, Mourlot, 1969.
Moscow Mansions.   New York, Viking Press, 1973.
The Countess from Minneapolis.   Providence, Rhode Island, Burning Deck, 1976.
The Türler Losses.   Montreal, Mansfield, 1979.
Biography.   Providence, Rhode Island, Burning Deck, 1980.
Quilts.   New York, Vehicle Press, 1981.

Plays

The Ladies Choice (produced New York, 1953).
The Office (produced New York, 1963).
Port (produced New York, 1965).

Novel

Seeking Air.   Santa Barbara, California, Black Sparrow Press, 1978.

Other

Robert Goodnough, with B. H. Friedmann.   Paris, G. Fall, 1962.
Herself Defined: The Poet H.D. and Her World.   New York, Doubleday, 1984; London, Collins, 1985.

*

Manuscript Collections: University of Kentucky, Lexington; Lockwood Memorial Library, State University of New York, Buffalo; New York University.

Critical Study: in *How(ever)* (San Francisco), vol. 1, no. 3.

Barbara Guest comments:

From Wallace Stevens's "finikin thing of air," the poem gathers itself (becomes embodied) the way a narrative diffuses and is sustained by movements, auditory and visual, transcending their own context as they echo and foreshadow other moments in the poem, deploying their own patterns and lyric arrangements.

*   *   *

The poems of Barbara Guest ignore almost every convention in metrics in English and American poetry—past and present; this fact can create difficulties for the reader and leaves one searching for analogies in painting, the art which she has been closely identified with as editor and commentator, in order to describe her work. Paintings are her subject in several poems, their effect reminiscent of the full bright canvasses of Matisse, without frames. In "Passage," for John Coltrane, she compares the two arts directly:

> Words
>   after all
> are syllables *just*
> and you put them
>   in their place
>   notes
>   sounds
> a painter using his stroke...
> slashed as it was with color
>   called "being"
>   or even "it"

A typical poem by Barbara Guest is a pastiche of colors, shapes, natural setting in which the objects create the mood. She constantly explores problems in aesthetics, how beauty makes itself felt, enjoying "the transformed colors and shapes that the imagination makes possible," as William Van O'Connor once said of Wallace Stevens' work. Her poems are a search for a definable form, as if she were discovering the shape of things for the first time. She tells the painter Robert Motherwell, for example in "All Elegies Are Black and White": "(How wise you are to understand / the use of orange with blue. / 'Never without the other.')" For all their distinctive charm, however, a reader may wonder how concretely the poems relate to this world, this time, and how as reader, viewer, audience, one can participate in the poet's original discovery, in the poetic excitement and awe and wonder that prompted her highly imaginative and impressionistic response. Many of the poems lack moral weight, a social or ethical grounding.

Guest writes as if the Imagist movement began yesterday, saying "no ideas but in things," moving persistently toward some revelation no one else has discovered. At its best, her poetry brings together the Imagist delight in objects, landscapes, and seascapes, and the uneasiness of a person attuned to suffering, anxiety, pain. At one point, she wonders "if this new reality is going to destroy me." But the dominant note, as in "Now," is one of joy and confidence in the lyrical beauty that surrounds her:

> It's Autumn
> It's Fall. A red cloth with
> Yellow leaves is chosen. And the
> Sophisticated color of mauve
> Burnt orange for the touch. To affect
> A change. Where the ripe dawn
> Hurries a red is.

—Michael True

GUEST, Harry (Henry Bayly Guest). British. Born in Penarth, Glamorganshire, Wales, 6 October 1932. Educated at Malvern College, Worcestershire, 1946-50; Trinity Hall, Cambridge, 1951-54, B.A. in modern languages 1954; the Sorbonne, Paris, 1954-55, D.E.S. 1955 (thesis on Mallarmé). Married Lynn Dunbar in 1963; one daughter and one son. Assistant Master, Felsted School, Essex, 1955-61; Head of Modern Languages Department, Lancing College, Sussex, 1961-66; Assistant Lecturer, Yokohama National University, Japan, 1966-72. Since 1972, Head of Modern Languages Department, Exeter School. Address: 1 Alexandra Terrace, Exeter, Devon EX4 6SY, England.

PUBLICATIONS

Verse

Private View. London, Outposts, 1962.
A Different Darkness. London, Outposts, 1964.
Arrangements. London, Anvil Press Poetry, 1968.
The Cutting-Room. London, Anvil Press Poetry, 1970.
Penguin Modern Poets 16, with Jack Beeching and Matthew Mead. London, Penguin, 1970.
The Place. Rushden, Northamptonshire, Sceptre Press, 1971.
Text and Fragment, The Inheritance, Miniatures. Southampton, Hampshire, Earth Ship 13, 1972.
The Achievements of Memory. Rushden, Northamptonshire, Sceptre Press, 1974.
The Enchanged Acres. Knotting, Bedfordshire, Sceptre Press, 1975.
Mountain Journal. Sheffield, Rivelin Press, 1975.
A House Against the Night. London, Anvil Press Poetry, 1976.
English Poems. London, Words Press, 1976.
Two Poems. Knotting, Bedfordshire, Sceptre Press, 1977.
The Hidden Change. Higham Ferrers, Northamptonshire, Greylag Press, 1978.
Zeami in Exile. Knotting, Bedfordshire, Sceptre Press, 1978.
Elegies. Durham, Pig Press, 1980.
Lost and Found: Poems 1975-1982. London, Anvil Press Poetry, 1983.
The Emperor of Outer Space. Durham, Pig Press, 1983.

Plays

The Inheritance (broadcast, 1973). Included in *Text and Fragment, The Inheritance, Miniatures*, 1972.

Radio Plays: *Beware of Pity*, from a play by Stefan Zweig, 1961; *Trial of Strength*, from a play by G.A. Golfar, 1964; *The Inheritance*, 1973; *The Emperor of Outer Space*, 1976.

Novel

Days. London, Anvil Press Poetry, 1978.

Other

Another Island Country (essays). Tokyo, Eikôsha, 1970.

Editor and Translator, with Lynn Guest and Kajima Shozo, *Post-War Japanese Poetry.* London, Penguin, 1972.
Editor, with others, *The Elek Book of Oriental Verse.* London, Elek, 1979.
Editor and Translator, *The Distance, The Shadows: Selected*

Poems, by Victor Hugo.   London, Anvil Press Poetry, 1981.

Harry Guest comments:

(1970) Lyrical analysis of personal relationships, bisexual love, landscapes, etc. Certain amount of intellectual demand: European rather than transatlantic: syllabics or stress-length lines: high premium on musicality.

I admire Klee, the early Godard, Debussy's piano music.

(1974) *Private View* is a poem in XIV sections dealing with the relationships between art and reality, imagination and love. "Matsushima" (1967) examines the shadow-line crossed when death is felt in the marrow as inevitable. "Metamorphoses" (1968) uses a highly condensed, elliptical language for its "Six Poems on Related Themes." *The Place* is 15 connected meditations about a holiday on the west coast of Japan, and *Miniatures* is 36 brief poems recording a visit with the poet's daughter to a volcanic island.

The short poems in various structural forms are primarily lyrical or narrative—love-poems like "The Summers of Nowhere" or "At Shoreham"; problems of perception like "Allegories," "Autumns," or "Nocturnes for the Dead of Winter"; or of art— "The Painter...," "Cinema."

The kind of poetry that most appeals to me has music and density, appeals to the senses as much as to the mind and spirit.

(1985) The six *Elegies* come as near as anything I have yet written to a statement of poetic faith—the role of memory, the mysterious commands of religion, the problem of meaning in the heart of language: this last reinforced by my experience in translating a selection of Victor Hugo's work.

English Poems celebrate a return to familiarity after six bewildered and thrilling years in Japan. The tantalising clues of prehistory inspired several poems about Avebury, sites in northern Arizona and Brittany.

The attempt is always to show the surprise latent in the everyday, as well as to display the relevance of the extraordinary.

*   *   *

Harry Guest was first introduced to the reading public with two booklet collections in the *Outposts Modern Poets Series—Private View* and *A Different Darkness. Private View* is a series of reflective poems arising out of a visit to an art exhibition, largely concerned with the relationship between the artist and his subject, as well as the part played by the artist himself:

If I could catch his eye, we'd bolt for the pub
And over Guinness alternate the old crude gags
With laments for oh the brevity of beauty,
The change within a year of the expression on flesh,
The slender moving to the coarse,
Metamorphoses of the delicate.

Though he treats his theme with respect his sense of humour does not allow him to become unduly earnest.

Like much of his poetry, *Private View* makes its impact by means of skilfully manipulated images and association of ideas. In *Arrangements* the poems are divided under such headings as "Problems," "Relationships," "Criticisms," "Narratives," and "Techniques," but this classification tends to obscure his real strengths and virtues as a poet. One might remark upon his skill and note the interest he displays in the techniques of other writers, reflected in such poems as "Statement," "About Baudelaire," and "Elegy for Jean Cocteau." "Sterility and regret are the only muse," he says in one of these poems, and this would seem to be true for Harry Guest, for he writes most effectively about

his regrets for lost opportunities, situations not grasped, failures of communication and response. Some critics have praised his "travel" poems, but he has a style all his own and rarely writes a simple descriptive piece. "Matsushima" and "A Bar in Lerici" demonstrate his use of the environment to effect new insights into the human situation:

We talk of love,
Balanced as always between the recollection—
The afternoon spent across the bay in sunlight—
And anticipation of the stars
Tending to disappoint.
    Darkness
After being born should be familiar
And natural as the scenery of the Milky Way.

Perhaps best of all are his poems celebrating the man-woman relationship, the marital relationship in particular, on which he can be lyrical and tender without losing control over his material.

In *The Cutting-Room*, written in Japan, Guest extended his range of subject and treatment, and produced his most ambitious work up to that time, the "Metamorphoses" sequence of six poems, but again the more personal references to lover, wife, and daughter show his capacity for dealing with intimate relationships. *A House Against the Night* collects the poems written between 1969 and 1973. It is perhaps most noticeable that, continuing his experiments with form and diction, Guest has adopted a much shorter line and exercises far tighter control of both diction and imagery, and, except in "Anniversary," seems deliberately to avoid the warmer aspects of human relationships. "I am a man for whom the external world exists," he said in an earlier poem, and he would appear to be exploring the external world at much greater depth than before in order to find himself and to define his own psychological limits, as in "Lacunae":

These distant images bring pain.
The tors stood out,
first greyness on the silence.
If there was laughter
the echoes carried isolation,
companionship
struck stone.

All this adds up to an unusual austerity reflected to a lesser extent in the later pamphlets.

—Howard Sergeant

GULLANS, Charles (Bennett).   American.   Born in Minneapolis, Minnesota, 5 May 1929. Educated at the University of Minnesota, Minneapolis, B.A. 1948, M.A. 1951; King's College, Durham (Fulbright Fellow, 1953-55); Stanford University, California (Fellow in Creative Writing, 1952), Ph.D. 1956. Taught at the University of Washington, Seattle, 1955-61. Since 1961, Member of the English Department, Associate Professor, 1965-72, and since 1972, Professor of English and Director of Creative Writing, University of California, Los Angeles. Recipient: University of California Institute of Creative Arts Fellowship, 1965. Address: 1620 Greenfield, Los Angeles, California 90025, U.S.A.

PUBLICATIONS

Verse

Moral Poems.   Palo Alto, California, John Hunter Thomas, 1957.
Arrivals and Departures.   Minneapolis, University of Minnesota Press, 1962.
Imperfect Correspondences.   Los Angeles, Symposium Press, 1978.
Many Houses.   Los Angeles, Symposium Press, 1981.
A Diatribe to Dr. Steele.   Los Angeles, Symposium Press, 1982.
The Bright Universe.   Omaha, Abattoir, 1983.
Under Red Skies.   Florence, Kentucky, R.L. Barth, 1983.

Other

The Decorative Designers, 1895-1931: An Essay.   Los Angeles, University of California Library, 1970.
A Bibliography of the Published Writings of J.V. Cunningham.   Los Angeles, University of California Library, 1973.

Editor, *The English and Latin Poems of Sir Robert Ayton.*   Edinburgh, Blackwood, 1963.
Editor, with John Espey, *A Checklist of Trade Bindings Designed by Margaret Armstrong.*   Los Angeles, University of California Library, 1968.

Translator, with Franz Schneider, *Last Letters from Stalingrad.*   New York, Morrow, 1962.

*

Manuscript Collection: University of California, Los Angeles.

Critical Studies: "A Study of the Poetry of Charles Gullans" by Mary Cecile Caestecker, in *Barat Faculty Review* (Lake Forest, Illinois), January 1966; "Of Pearls and Prices" by Turner Cassity, in *Parnassus* (New York), Fall-Winter 1981.

*   *   *

For 30 years Charles Gullans has been writing poems characterized by metrical dexterity, clear and acute diction, and an unmannered examination of human experience. These virtues are evident in Gullans's first full-scale collection, *Arrivals and Departures.* Much of the work in this book features exposition which is at once abstract and forceful, and in general the style somewhat recalls that of Renaissance masters like Ralegh and Jonson. Gullans's material, however, is thoroughly modern, and in poems such as "After Analysis" his skillful directness of statement achieves extraordinary power.

Gullans's later poems, while retaining the engaging precision of the early work, show a greater range of subject matter and surer circumstantiality. *Imperfect Correspondences* is a sharply observed group of poems about a failed romantic relationship; *Under Red Skies* contains several interesting poems which explore the difficulties of regulating one's existence with care and civility in an age when public violence and trauma intrude harshly and continually on private life; and *Diatribe to Dr. Steele* (of which the present writer must confess himself the dedicatee) amusingly anatomizes contemporary poetic practice. It may be appropriate here to cite Gullans's remarks on the staggering inflation of poets and poetry in recent years:

> An editor wrote me the other day,
> Who said he gives his magazine away
> To the—now count with me—six hundred best
> Poets in this America. The test?
> What is a man to say. There aren't that many
> In the *Oxford Book of English Verse.* Did any,
> Did all the greatest ages sport that number?
> Lord, what a load of literary lumber.

Gullans's single most impressive collection is *Many Houses.* The collection contains two of Gullans's best short poems, "Labuntur Anni" and "John Wilkes," and the most memorable of his longer poems, "Many Houses," a remarkable ten-poem sequence which deals with life and love in Los Angeles, where Gullans has lived for some twenty-odd years. The sequence, written in flexible but never lax blank verse, opens with a striking evocation of the city:

> I'm home and finding the Los Angeles
> Nobody loves where everybody lives,
> The concrete miles that crouch beneath Bel Air
> And Brentwood to the sea, if living is the word
> For bare accommodation in these rooms
> With nothing that we do not bring to them.
> In the impersonal we make some life
> With a few sticks and rags, a bed, a chair,
> Some pottery, some pictures, and the phone.
> No attics and no basements, thus, no past;
> No history, therefore no legacy.
> Transience is not symbolic, it is real
> In the unfurnished places of our lives.

The sequence moves through a suite of thoughtfully studied scenes of domestic life, in the course of which the poet tries to establish, by friendship and hospitality with others, the "legacy" and sense of community that the external circumstances of urban life appear overwhelmingly to deny. Ultimately, the legacy is secured and the poet reconciled to his surroundings; and if "Many Houses" is one of the best of Gullans's works, it is also, in its final statement, one of the sunniest.

The penultimate poem of the sequence acknowledges, however, that the sorts of love and labor which give meaning to existence come to us partly by chance and that not all people have the good luck to find affections and activities necessary to produce an ordered and satisfying life. At the end of this poem, Gullans speaks of the fact that "many have had nothing all their lives, / and many lives no time in which to love." These lines could well serve as the epigraph for Gullans's most recent collection, *The Bright Universe,* one of the central concerns of which is the plight of those outcast and adrift in contemporary society, those for whom the American Dream and the promise of the Good Life seem to have narrowed irrevocably to meagreness and bafflement. This concern finds poignant expression in "In a Queer Country (Hollywood)" and "The Local." In the latter, Gullans describes a tavern whose regular patrons gather nightly for what looks to be a warm fellowship of conversation and pretzels and beer. Yet midway through the poem, the mood abruptly changes, and, though the fellowship suggested earlier is not contradicted but asserted more firmly, it is seen from a different and deeper angle and is thereby transformed into a chilling and moving vision of loneliness:

> What boozy camaraderie it is,
> Or seems to be, until you look again,
> Until you see. It is the maimed who come here,
> Widowed, divorced, or unattached, the lost,

The lonely, the deserted. Time at the local
Is less a pleasure than a way of life,
Since this is where they live, where they belong,
Where they are known and welcomed every night.
Their needs have been refined to this, this bar,
This night, this recognition of their name.

Except for *Arrivals and Departures*, Gullans's collections
have appeared in fine-press or limited-edition publications. For
the last 20 years in the United States, the climate of literary
opinion has not been favorable to the aims and achievements of
Gullans's work. There are signs this situation may be changing.
In any event, what is needed now is a generous selection of
Gullans's later poems, published in a trade edition, to bring his
work to a wider audience. At the conclusion of his *Diatribe*,
Gullans remarks with humorous sadness:

> ...Let's drink
> Until we can forget that tides of ink
> Obliterate good poems we have found,
> One here, one there, upon our native ground.

It would be a shame indeed if the present tides of ink were
allowed to obliterate Gullans's poems. They are among the very
finest in contemporary verse.

—Timothy Steele

GUNN, Thom(son William). British. Born in Gravesend,
Kent, 29 August 1929. Educated at University College School,
London; Trinity College, Cambridge, B.A. 1953, M.A. 1958;
Stanford University, California, 1954-55, 1956-58. Served in the
British Army, 1948-50. Member of the English Department,
1958-66, and since 1975, Visiting Lecturer, University of Cali-
fornia, Berkeley. Poetry reviewer, *Yale Review*, New Haven,
Connecticut, 1958-64. Recipient: Levinson Prize (*Poetry*, Chi-
cago), 1955; Maugham Award, 1959; Arts Council of Great
Britain award, 1959; American Academy grant, 1964; Rocke-
feller award, 1966; Guggenheim Fellowship, 1971; W.H. Smith
Award, 1980. Address: 1216 Cole Street, San Francisco, California 94117, U.S.A.

PUBLICATIONS

Verse

(Poems). Oxford, Fantasy Press, 1953.
Fighting Terms. Oxford, Fantasy Press, 1954; revised edition,
    New York, Hawk's Well Press, 1958; London, Faber, 1962.
The Sense of Movement. London, Faber, 1957; Chicago, Uni-
    versity of Chicago Press, 1959.
My Sad Captains and Other Poems. London, Faber, and Chi-
    cago, University of Chicago Press, 1961.
Selected Poems, with Ted Hughes. London, Faber, 1962.
A Geography. Iowa City, Stone Wall Press, 1966.
Positives, photographs by Ander Gunn. London, Faber, 1966;
    Chicago, University of Chicago Press, 1967.
Touch. London, Faber, 1967; Chicago, University of Chicago
    Press, 1968.
The Garden of the Gods. Cambridge, Massachusetts, Pym
    Randall Press, 1968.

The Explorers. Crediton, Devon, Gilbertson, 1969.
The Fair in the Woods. Oxford, Sycamore Press, 1969.
Poems 1950-1966: A Selection. London, Faber, 1969.
Sunlight. New York, Albondocani Press, 1969.
Last Days at Teddington. London, Poem-of-the-Month Club,
    1971.
Moly. London, Faber, 1971.
Corgi Modern Poets in Focus 5, with others, edited by Dannie
    Abse. London, Corgi, 1971.
Poem after Chaucer. New York, Albondocani Press, 1971.
Moly, and My Sad Captains. New York, Farrar Straus, 1971.
Mandrakes. London, Rainbow Press, 1973.
Songbook. New York, Albondocani Press, 1973.
To the Air. Boston, Godine, 1974.
Jack Straw's Castle. New York, F. Hallman, 1975.
Jack Straw's Castle (collection). London, Faber, and New
    York, Farrar Straus, 1976.
The Missed Beat. Sidcot, Somerset, Gruffyground Press, and
    West Burke, Vermont, Janus Press, 1976.
Games of Chance. Omaha, Abattoir, 1979.
Selected Poems 1950-1975. London, Faber, and New York,
    Farrar Straus, 1979.
Bally Power Play. Toronto, Massey Press, 1979.
Talbot Road. New York, Helikon Press, 1981.
The Menace. San Francisco, ManRoot, 1982.
The Passages of Joy. London, Faber, 1982; New York, Farrar
    Straus, 1983.

Other

*The Occasions of Poetry: Essays in Criticism and Autobio-
    graphy*, edited by Clive Wilmer. London, Faber, and New
    York, Farrar Straus, 1982.

Editor, *Poetry from Cambridge 1951-52: A Selection of Verse by
    Members of the University.* London, Fortune Press, 1952.
Editor, with Ted Hughes, *Five American Poets.* London,
    Faber, 1963.
Editor, *Selected Poems of Fulke Greville.* London, Faber, and
    Chicago, University of Chicago Press, 1968.
Editor, *Ben Jonson.* London, Penguin, 1974.

*

Bibliography: *Thom Gunn: A Bibliography 1940-1978* by Jack
W.C. Hagstrom and George Bixby, London, Rota, 1979.

Manuscript Collections: University of Maryland, College Park;
Amherst College, Massachusetts.

Critical Studies: by Martin Dodsworth, in *The Survival of Poe-
try*, London, Faber, 1970; "The Stipulative Imagination of
Thom Gunn" by John Miller, and "A Critical Performance of
Thom Gunn's *Misanthropos*" by Merle E. Brown in *Iowa
Review* (Iowa City), Winter 1973; *Thom Gunn and Ted Hughes*
by Alan Bold, Edinburgh, Oliver and Boyd, 1976; "Uncertain
Violence" by Colin Falck, in *New Review* (London), 1977; by the
author, in *The Occasions of Poetry*, 1982.

*   *   *

In one of his early poems, Thom Gunn observes, famously,
that Elvis Presley "turns revolt into a style." Elaborating this in
the poem's final stanza, Gunn provides a peg on which we can, if
we like, hang the immense variety of his own work:

> Whether he poses or is real, no cat
> Bothers to say: the pose held is a stance,
> Which, generation of the very chance
> It wars on, may be posture for combat.

A "pose"—apparently superficial, a matter, possibly, of advertising, of presenting self for sale—solidifies into a "stance," a relation between the self and the world that has a more achieved and focused integrity; and this, as a "posture for combat," may embrace a political or philosophical relation.

The title of Thom Gunn's fifth collection, *Moly*, takes its name from the herb which Hermes offered Ulysses to keep him proof against transformation into one of Circe's pigs. And, while Gunn has not, of course, transformed himself into a pig, he has certainly never protected himself against the processes of metamorphosis. Geographically, he has moved from England to America, more specifically from 1950's Cambridge to 1960's San Francisco; metrically, he has moved from highly disciplined traditional forms, through syllabics to a very loose kind of free form; and thematically, he has made use of such widely varied influences as French existentialist thought and American lysergic acid. And, even emotionally and sexually, Gunn has moved from poems overtly addressed to women to openly frank homosexual poems. He is, altogether, a poet difficult to get clear and difficult to get whole.

There is also the further difficulty that, if one appreciates the strenuous energy under control, the formal stanzaic grandeur of poems like "On the Move" or "In Santa Maria del Popolo," it is difficult not to feel that the later work is often sentimental or downright silly. (The latter criticism seems almost mild against the poem, "Listening to Jefferson Airplane," which reads, in its entirety, "The music comes and goes on the wind,/Comes and goes on the brain.") But one can be generous even about these poems, perhaps, if one sees Gunn's whole enterprise as a series of "poses" creating a "stance" of combative self-definition in relation to society and to the world. The poems' "posturing" may then be seen as a kind of moral assertion. Gunn's ultimate "carnal knowledge," in the well-known poem of that title, is that "Even in bed I pose"; and knowledge—of oneself, as well as of others—is an infinitely recessive series ("You know I know you know I know you know," contained only by its pentameter bounds) in which one *is* what one presents oneself as. Gunn's poems are, as he has himself described some of them, "a debate between the passion for definition and the passion for flow."

Some of his more recent poems are an explicit examination of these processes and passions. The sequence "The Geysers," for instance, situates Gunn in a state between sleep and waking, between water and air, in the bath house of the geysers in Sonoma County, California. The poem mimics the processes occurring on the frontiers of consciousness:

> I am part of all
>   hands take
>   hands tear and twine
>
> I yielded
>   oh, the yield
>   what have I slept?
> my blood is yours the hands that take accept...
>
> torn from the self
>   in which I breathed and trod
> I am

> I am raw meat
>
> I am a god

Some of Gunn's best effects are achieved, as they are here, when language, still disciplined and restrained, spreads and spills to accommodate the phases of "definition and flow." In the act of love and in sleep these processes are at their most immediate: one is both defined in one's own being, and involved in the being of others. The act of love and the moment of sleep are returned to again and again in Tom Gunn's work, and they come together at the conclusion of the marvellous poem "Touch":

> What is more, the place is
> not found but seeps
> from our touch in
> continuous creation, dark
> enclosing cocoon round
> ourselves alone, dark
> wide realm where we
> walk with everyone.

In his most recent volume, *The Passages of Joy*, the clearest new note is that of nostalgia, as the poet growing older in America remembers his past in England. The sequence "Talbot Road" is that, and is also an elegy for his friend, Tony White. It crosses the experiences of childhood with a maturing sexuality, in a way that brings together again in Gunn's work these processes of definition and flow, of innocence and experience—as when, for instance, Hampstead Heath is viewed as both the theatre of childhood games and homosexual sex:

> In a Forest of Arden, in a summer night's dream
> I forgave everybody his teens.

—Neil Corcoran

GUSTAFSON, Ralph (Barker). Canadian. Born in Lime Ridge, Quebec, 16 August 1909. Educated at Bishop's University, Lennoxville, Quebec, B.A. 1929, M.A. 1930; Oxford University, B.A. 1933. Married Elisabeth Renninger in 1958. Taught at Bishop's College School, 1930, and St. Alban's School, Brockville, Ontario, 1934. Worked for the British Information Services, 1942-46. Since 1960, music critic, Canadian Broadcasting Corporation. Professor of English and Poet-in-Residence, Bishop's University, 1963-79. Recipient: Prix David, 1935; Canada Council Senior Fellowship, 1959, award, 1968, 1971, 1980; Governor-General's Award, 1974; A.J.M. Smith award, 1974; Queen's Silver Jubilee Medal, 1978. M.A.: Oxford University, 1963; D.Litt.: Mount Allison University, Sackville, New Brunswick, 1973; D.C.L.: Bishop's University, 1977. Address: P.O. Box 172, North Hatley, Quebec J0B 2C0, Canada.

PUBLICATIONS

Verse

The Golden Chalice. London, Nicholson and Watson, 1935.
Alfred the Great (verse play). London, Joseph, 1937.
Epithalamium in Time of War. Privately printed, 1941.
Lyrics Unromantic. Privately printed, 1942.
Flight into Darkness: Poems. New York, Pantheon, 1944.

Rivers among Rocks. Toronto, McClelland and Stewart, 1960.
Rocky Mountain Poems. Vancouver, Klanak Press, 1960.
Sift in an Hourglass. Toronto, McClelland and Stewart, 1966.
Ixion's Wheel: Poems. Toronto, McClelland and Stewart, 1969.
Theme and Variations for Sounding Brass. Sherbrooke, Quebec, Progressive, 1972.
Selected Poems. Toronto, McClelland and Stewart, 1972.
Fire on Stone. Toronto, McClelland and Stewart, 1974.
Corners in the Glass. Toronto, McClelland and Stewart, 1977.
Soviet Poems. Winnipeg, Turnstone Press, 1978.
Sequences. Windsor, Ontario, Black Moss Press, 1979.
Landscape with Rain. Toronto, McClelland and Stewart, 1980.
Conflicts of Spring. Toronto, McClelland and Stewart, 1981.
Gradations of Grandeur. Victoria, British Columbia, Sono Nis Press, 1982.
The Moment Is All: Selected Poems 1944-1983. Toronto, McClelland and Stewart, 1983.
Solidarnosc: Prelude. Sherbrooke, Quebec, Progressive, 1983.
At the Ocean's Verge. Redding Ridge, Connecticut, Black Swan, 1984.
Impromptus. Lantzville, British Columbia, Oolichan, 1984.
Manipulations on Greek Themes. Toronto, Roger Ascham Press, 1984.
Directives of Autumn. Toronto, McClelland and Stewart, 1984.

Short Stories

The Brazen Tower. Tillsonburg, Ontario, Roger Ascham Press, 1974.
The Vivid Air: Collected Stories. Victoria, British Columbia, Sono Nis Press, 1980.

Other

Poetry and Canada. Ottawa, Canadian Legion Educational Service, 1945.
A Literary Friendship: The Correspondence of Ralph Gustafson and W.W.E. Ross, edited by Bruce Whiteman. Toronto, ECW Press, 1984.

Editor, *Anthology of Canadian Poetry (English).* London, Penguin, 1942.
Editor, *A Little Anthology of Canadian Poets.* New York, New Directions, 1943.
Editor, *Canadian Accent: A Collection of Stories and Poems by Contemporary Writers from Canada.* London, Penguin, 1944.
Editor, *The Penguin Book of Canadian Verse.* London, Penguin, 1958; revised edition, 1967, 1975, 1984.

*

Bibliography: "Ralph Gustafson: A Bibliography in Progress" by L.M. Allison and Wendy Keitner, in *West Coast Review* (Burnaby, British Columbia), June 1974.

Manuscript Collections: State University of New York, Buffalo; Queen's University, Kingston, Ontario; University of Saskatchewan, Saskatoon.

Critical Studies: *Literary History of Canada,* Toronto, University of Toronto Press, 1966; *Oxford Companion to Canadian History and Literature,* Toronto, Oxford University Press, 1968; "Ralph Gustafson: A Review and Retrospect" by Robin Skelton, in *Mosaic* (Winnipeg, Manitoba), 1974; "Gustafson's Double Hook" by Wendy Keitner, in *Canadian Literature* (Vancouver), February 1979; *Ralph Gustafson* by Wendy Keitner, Boston, Twayne, 1979.

Ralph Gustafson comments:
  Those interested might see my "Foreword to the Revised Edition" of *The Penguin Book of Canadian Verse,* 1975, especially p. 36. Some aphorisms to my "Towards a Noticeable Notebook" run as follows:

> Poetry is not only a way of happening; it as a way of concluding.
> Poetry can't wind clocks—but it tells the time.
> Poetry is a verbal rite, if it is right.
> Science tries hard; poetry understands.
> Poetry is exalted pragmatism.
> Poetry faces truth without make-up.
> Present poets? Too much I am in their iamb.
> Ironic comedy is presently the only mode possible.

*   *   *

Ralph Gustafson is one of the most prolific, various and technically accomplished of contemporary Canadian poets. After a somewhat unpromising start with a volume of romantic lyrics and sonnets and a poetic play on the subject of King Alfred in the mid-thirties, Ralph Gustafson found an original style and an individual voice in the sardonic and tender poetry produced during and after World War II. *Flight into Darkness* assimilated, rather than shook off, influences of Hopkins and Donne and demonstrated the relevance of the metaphysical dialectic to the problem of preserving an individual integrity in the kaleidoscopic new world of the post-war breakdown.
  The poet's elliptical and intensely allusive style took on a new subtlety and his work a wider field of interest in three volumes published since 1960, *Rivers among Rocks, Rocky Mountain Poems* and *Sift in an Hourglass.* In these, travel across Canada, especially to the Rockies and the mountains of the north-west coast, and to Italy, Greece and Scandinavian countries, has provided the stimulus for a prolific outburst of poetry in which the themes of nature, art, history, love and sex are given a highly individual treatment. As Professor Earle Birney has written: "Ralph Gustafson has a way all his own of fusing music and passion with sophisticated feeling and graceful craft.... A stylist given to paradox and poetic wit, he is nonetheless serious, and his sensitive judgments rise from a warm heart."
  Mr. Gustafson has written also a number of prize-winning short stories and has edited three influential anthologies.

—A.J.M. Smith

GUTTERIDGE, Don(ald George). Canadian. Born in Point Edward, Ontario, 30 September 1937. Educated at the University of Western Ontario, London, 1956-60, 1962-63, B.A. (honours) 1960. Married Anne Barnett in 1961; one daughter and one son. English teacher, Elmira School Board, Ontario, 1960-62; Teaching Fellow, University of Western Ontario, 1962-63; Head of the Department of English, Ingersoll School Board,

Ontario, 1963-64, and London Board of Education, Ontario, 1964-68. Assistant Professor, 1968-74, Associate Professor, 1975-77, and since 1977, Professor of English, University of Western Ontario. Recipient: President's Medal, University of Western Ontario, 1971; Canada Council travel grant, 1973. Address: 114 Victoria Street, London, Ontario N6A 2B5, Canada.

PUBLICATIONS

Verse

The Brooding Sky. Privately printed, 1960.
New Poems 1964. Privately printed, 1965.
Other Woods: New Poems. Privately printed, 1966.
Intimations of Winter: Poems for the Latter Half of 1966. New York, Bitterroot Press, 1967.
Riel: A Poem for Voices. Fredericton, New Brunswick, Fiddlehead, 1968; revised edition, Toronto, Van Nostrand Reinhold, 1972.
The Village Within: Poems Toward a Biography. Fredericton, New Brunswick, Fiddlehead, 1970.
Death at Quebec and Other Poems. Fredericton, New Brunswick, Fiddlehead, 1971.
Perspectives. London, Ontario, Pennywise Press, 1971.
Saying Grace: An Elegy. Fredericton, New Brunswick, Fiddlehead, 1972.
Coppermine: The Quest for North. Ottawa, Oberon Press, 1973.
Borderlands. Ottawa, Oberon Press, and London, Dobson, 1975.
Tecumseh. Ottawa, Oberon Press, 1976.
A True History of Lambton County. Ottawa, Oberon Press, 1977; London, Dobson, 1978.
God's Geography. Ilderton, Ontario, Brick, 1982.

Novels

Bus-Ride. Nairn, Ontario, Nairn Publications, 1973.
All in Good Time. Windsor, Ontario, Black Moss Press, 1981.

Other

Language and Expression: A Modern Approach (textbook). Toronto, McClelland and Stewart, 1970.
Mountain and Plain. Toronto, McClelland and Stewart, 1978.
The Country of the Young. London, Ontario, University of Western Ontario, 1978.
Brave Season: Reading and the Language Arts in Grades Seven to Ten. London, Ontario, University of Western Ontario Faculty of Education, 1983.

*

Critical Studies: *Survival: Themes in Canadian Literature* by Margaret Atwood, Toronto, Anansi, 1971; "Rivering of Vision" by David Cavanagh, in *Alive* (Guelph, Ontario), August 1973; "*Tecumseh*" by D.H. Sullivan, in *West Coast Review* (Burnaby, British Columbia), January 1978; *A Native Heritage: Images of the Indian in English-Canadian Literature* by Leslie Monkman, Toronto, University of Toronto Press, 1981; "Don Gutteridge's Mythic Tetralogy" by Keith Garebian, in *Canadian Literature* (Vancouver), Winter 1981; interview with Dennis Cooley, in *CV 2* (Winnipeg), August 1982; "Places in Time: Poetry of Historical Roots" by Peter Baltensberger, in *CV 2* (Winnipeg), September 1983.

Don Gutteridge comments:

One of our poets has called Canada a "country without a mythology"; little wonder, then, that my work—like that of many Canadian writers—is concerned with the sense of place and the perspective of time, with roots into the past and what myths can be made in the face of such vast geography and empty stretches of history. My work takes two forms: personal poems about my childhood village and narrative poems on Canadian historical figures (real and imagined). Though quite different in content and form, these two types are related in that they share my concern for making something of my own past as well as that of my country, and my belief, however naive, that the two are somehow connected

*   *   *

"History is the biography of great men," Carlyle once said, and Don Gutteridge would probably agree with him, for to the teacher (who was born in an historic section of Ontario and teaches in the old city of London, Ontario) history and biography are very much a unity. So far he has published poems of two types: historical and autobiographical.

The historical poems are the more familiar, although to date these have not won him too many readers. His widest read work, *Riel: A Poem for Voices*, might at first glance seem an ideal script for a radio documentary about the leader of the two Métis uprisings on the Canadian prairies, for the long poem is constructed, as a mason would construct a wall, of bits and pieces—editorials, letters, lyrical interludes.

Gutteridge promises to tell "what Riel really was in Canadian terms," and the short lyric poems are always on the verge of revealing some psychological or universal truth:

> When my body
> swings like a
> dead tongue
> from the white-man's
> scaffolding,
> will there be
> an eloquence
> to tell....

Riel remains an enigma wrapped up in a mystery swinging from the white man's scaffolding. *Riel* is a labour of love, but essentially a pastiche, and as such unrevealing and undramatic.

The same might be said of *Death at Quebec and Other Poems* and *Coppermine: The Quest for North* which attempt to build dramatic monologues on the personalities of early missionaries and explorers as revealed through their writings. Gutteridge deserves credit for spotting the poetic possibilities in these figures from the past, but the language he uses is neither of the period nor particular to the person, and so seems inappropriate.

Although the historical poems are so far more adventurous than the autobiographical poems, it is perhaps in this latter area that Gutteridge may develop in the future. *Saying Grace: An Elegy* is a short, impressionistic poem written on the death of his mother. It includes these moving lines, somewhat quirky, yet moody and effective: "Death does not/'take us,' it/moves into the/waiting spaces//is welcome."

—John Robert Colombo

HACKER, Marilyn. American. Born in New York City, 27 November 1942. Educated at Bronx High School of Science, New York; Washington Square College, New York University, B.A. 1964; Art Students League, New York. Married the writer Samuel R. Delany in 1961 (divorced, 1980); one daughter. Worked as teacher, mail sorter, and editor of books, magazines, and trade journals; antiquarian bookseller, London, 1971-76; lecturer, George Washington University, Washington, D.C., 1976. Editor, *City Magazine*, 1967-70, *Quark*, 1969-70, and *Little Magazine*, 1977-80, all New York. Since 1982, Editor, *13th Moon*, New York. Recipient: YM-YWHA Discovery Award, 1973; Lamont Poetry Selection Award, 1973; National Endowment for the Arts grant, 1974; National Book Award, 1975; Guggenheim Fellowship, 1980; New York State Council on the Arts grant, 1980; Ingram Merrill Foundation Fellowship, 1984; Co-ordinating Council of Little Magazines Editor's Fellowship, 1984. Address: c/o Alfred A. Knopf Inc., 201 East 50th Street, New York, New York 10022, U.S.A.

PUBLICATIONS

Verse

The Terrible Children. Privately printed, 1967.
Highway Sandwiches, with Thomas M. Disch and Charles Platt. Privately printed, 1970.
Presentation Piece. New York, Viking Press, 1974.
Separations. New York, Knopf, 1976.
Taking Notice. New York, Knopf, 1980.
Assumptions. New York, Knopf, 1985.

Recording: *The Poetry and Voice of Marilyn Hacker*, Caedmon, 1976.

Other

Editor, with Samuel R. Delany, *Quark 1-4.* New York, Paperback Library, 4 vols., 1970-71.
Editor, *.Woman Poet: The East.* Reno, Nevada, Women in Literature, 1982.

*   *   *

Marilyn Hacker's poems combine the classical rhyming forms of sestina, sonnet, and villanelle with a blunt terse declarative sentence-structure to express the deranged black richness of contemporary experience. More than any other poet currently writing, Hacker has employed the sestina as vehicle for display of the lurid and quirky obsessions of contemporary minds. Her language is jewel-encrusted, reminiscent of Jacobean drama and the early Robert Lowell; it resonates thoroughly with the excesses of over-ripe technological backdrop and metaphor for a devastated inner world of difficult loving, tangled sexuality, and the cool torture generated by convoluted relationships. The act of converting these horrors into elegant rhymed poems appears to be the only consolation for this poet as she travels through the landscape of nightmare. Her intelligence refuses to overlook— indeed has some fascination for—terrifying situations: a *ménage à trois*, death of a young self-destructive lover, betrayals, loneliness, and the encroaching debris of junkies and lunatics on New York and San Francisco streets. Such self-exposure takes guts, and it cannot be labelled "confessional," because no guilt or self-pity muddies the poet's objective view of the way the world manifests, not as she designed it. Still it comprises the milieu she is committed to, and she directs her energy to it.

Fear, alienation, and rejection are hard stones for her sculptor's tools. Her poems therefore come to resemble great baroque jewels, blood-red or purple in craggy settings. She often uses semi-precious gems—onyx, amethyst, alexandrite—as metaphors for the hardness, mystery, and rich perverse intensity of experience. Lured by whatever is foreign and strange, Hacker invents vaguely Latin-American scenes of revolution and insurrection to reflect restless social chaos. She invents "imaginary translations" which allow her to play with exotic locales and overblown emotions. While these poems almost seem experiments, *tours de force*, they lead into the deepest, most essential employment of her craft and intellect, which is to elucidate her own intense passions, both sexual and moral. The realism of "The Callers" is a grotesque "translation" of the usual mother-child relationships, though it reads as a word-for-word tape recording of an interview with a madwoman. "Prism and Lens" has the detail and flavor of Hacker's personal experience, but these do not differ greatly from the "fiction" of such poems as "La Vie de Château" and "After the Revolution."

But since form is inseparable from function, the sequence entitled "Separations," written in sonnet form, de-emphasizes obsession and becomes a graceful, almost Shakespearean delineation of the aspects of love. If love always springs lively and ubiquitous in Hacker, despite difficulties, then death also surrounds her all-pervadingly. The intertwining of love and death is the note on which *Presentation Piece* opens. There she speaks of "the skull of the beloved" as a brooding nobleman in a Jacobean play addresses the skull of his dead mistress. Death is the gruesome smog we must all breath; Hacker enters its presence with the weapon of language even while knowing she can't win. The powerful ten-poem sequence "The Navigators" in *Presentation Piece* is prelude and foreshadowing to the heartbroken elegy "Geographer" in *Separations*, a poem which unites in formal sestina-like word repetition her continuing themes of death, cities, gems, language, obsession and painful but persisting love:

> I have held your death the way I hold my child,
> but is has no weight and no voice. The death
> of a red begonia from frost, the hibernal death
> of the Heath horse-chestnuts, colored, odored words
> pile up. But I have not found the words
> to thread the invisible waste of your death;
> the quicksilver veins threading the way of the city,
> till the lights all froze out, all over the city.

Hacker's poetry welds strong intellect to consummate language skill, and brave vision to humane commitment. She is able to draw on the rich resources of English literature as she explores the ambiguous gifts of contemporary life. Such a combination is extremely unusual and makes Marilyn Hacker an outstanding figure in American writing today.

—Jane Augustine

———————

HAINES, John (Meade). American. Born in Norfolk, Virginia, 29 June 1924. Educated at art schools in Washington, D.C., and New York. Served in the United States Navy, 1943-46. Married 1) Jo Ella Hussey in 1960; 2) Jane Everett in 1970; four step-children. Homesteaded in Alaska, 1947-69. Free-lance writer. Poet-in-Residence, University of Alaska, Anchorage, 1972-73, University of Washington, Seattle, 1974, and University of Montana, Missoula, 1975. Recipient: Corcoran Gallery Sculpture prize, 1948; Jennie Tane Award (*Massachusetts Review*), 1964; Guggenheim Fellowship, 1965; National Endowment for the Arts grant, 1967; Amy Lowell Traveling Scholarship, 1976. Address: c/o Wesleyan University Press, 110 Mount Vernon Street, Middletown, Connecticut 06457, U.S.A.

PUBLICATIONS

Verse

Winter News. Middletown, Connecticut, Wesleyan University Press, 1966.
Suite for the Pied Piper. Menomonie, Wisconsin, Ox Head Press, 1967.
The Legend of Paper Plates. Santa Barbara, California, Unicorn Press, 1970.
The Mirror. Santa Barbara, California, Unicorn Press, 1971.
The Stone Harp. Middletown, Connecticut, Wesleyan University Press, and London, Rapp and Whiting-Deutsch, 1971.
Twenty Poems. Santa Barbara, California, Unicorn Press, 1971.
Ryder, with Alan Brilliant. Santa Barbara, California, Unicorn Press, 1971 (?).
Leaves and Ashes. Santa Cruz, California, Kayak, 1974.
North by West, with William Stafford, edited by Karen and John Sollid. Seattle, Spring Rain Press, 1975.
In Five Years Time. Missoula, Montana, SmokeRoot Press, 1976.
The Sun on Your Shoulder. Privately printed, 1976.
Cicada. Middletown, Connecticut, Wesleyan University Press, 1977.
In a Dusty Light. Port Townsend, Washington, Graywolf Press, 1977.
Other Days. Port Townsend, Washington, Graywolf Press, 1981.
News from the Glacier: Selected Poems 1960-1980. Middletown, Connecticut, Wesleyan University Press, 1982.

Play

Television Documentary: *The River Is Wider Than It Seems*, 1979.

Other

The Writer as Alaskan. Tempe, Arizona, Porch, 1979.
Living Off the Country: Essays on Poetry and Place. Ann Arbor, University of Michigan Press, 1981.

Translator, *El Amor Ascendia*, by Miguel Hernández. Menomonie, Wisconsin, Ox Head Press, 1967.

*

Manuscript Collection: University of Alaska Library, Fairbanks.

Critical Studies: review by Paul Zweig, in *The Nation* (New York), 27 March 1967, and *Parnassus* (New York), Winter 1972-73; Ira Sadoff, in *Seneca Reivew* (Geneva, New York), April 1971; William Witherup, in *Kayak* (Santa Cruz, California), 1972; "John Haines Issue" of *Stinktree* (Memphis), November 1972; by the author, in *Cutbank 6*, Spring 1976; Sam Hamill in *Cutbank 10*, Winter 1979.

John Haines comments:

(1980) The early poems for which I am perhaps best known (*Winter News*) grew out of my experience in the Alaskan wilderness. It is a poetry of solitude—to say it oversimply—but a peopled solitude. The subject matter is drawn mainly from nature and its citizens—animals, birds, trees, ice and weather, and the occasional human traveler. These things had their counterpart in my imagination—the durable stuff of childhood fantasies of life in the great north woods—and that as much as anything else gives the poems what significance they may have. They can be read as part of a continuing interior monologue, but it seems to me that they contain plenty of actual sticks and stones to stumble on and be bruised by.

For a time in the late 1960's I was preoccupied with events in the outside world—politics, social conflict, all that absorbed so many of us at the time. I tried to deal with these things in my poems (*The Stone Harp*). In a few of them I think I was successful, but on the whole I was too far from the events themselves for them to dominate my poems as convincingly as the wilderness world had up until that time.

For a number of reasons I became dissatisfied with the isolation I have been living in, and made a decisive break with it in 1969. The poems I have published since then have ranged more widely in their materials. *Cicada* contained a number of poems addressed to or directly concerned with individuals. In some ways this book marks the close of a line of thought, or development, and appears to open the possibility of another. *In a Dusty Light* returns to something like the world of *Winter News*, but here the subject matter is drawn not only from Alaska, but from Montana and the Northwest, and from events generally.

Writing continues to be for me a necessary undertaking, a means by which I place myself in the world. I am still interested in the long poem, in its modern form as sequence. I write considerably more prose than I used to, and I'm preparing a book of essays for publication. I have also begun a long prose work, an account of my Alaska years, and which I hope will turn out to be a useful meditation on wilderness, as well as a book on life generally.

*   *   *

American literature has had its share of writers separating themselves from the safety of the known. Thoreau, of course, left Concord for the woods near Walden Pond, and Pound and Henry James set out for Europe. Although Thoreau went only a few miles from home, and Pound and James had as their self-professed goal, not finding a pastoral wilderness, but leaving a cultural one, they share a respect for place which one gains only by jostling the commonplace. John Haines also shares this respect and spent years homesteading in Alaska deepening it. One is tempted to speak of Haines as a writer of the "last frontier," but he warns against such a label himself, in *Living Off the Country*, when he points out that ideally "writing in Alaska, and of Alaska, would be a continuous attempt to identify this place, to give it range and substance beyond mere geography and the descriptions in travel brochures." The ability to identify that place comes, one might say, from his increased ability there "to pay attention, to learn in detail" what he had not known before. The ability to go "beyond mere geography" and cliché, however, results from more than the acquisition of new knowledge; it results from Haines's desire to "give this material a life in imagination, a vitality beyond mere appearance." This imaginative transformation is, for Haines, a transformation into poetry.

The style of Haines's first book, *Winter News*, illustrates that desire to identify and describe, then to transform. Perhaps most indicative of this process, in terms of style, is Haines's title poem:

They say the wells
are freezing
at Northway where
the cold begins.

Oil tins bang
as evening comes on,
and clouds of
steaming breath drift
in the street.

Men go out to feed
the stiffening dogs,

the voice of the snowman
calls the white-
haired children home.

Haines uses a straightforward free verse line, breaking the line for the most part at the level of phrase, to take the reader from pure description to a fusion of the natural and the human. The poem's movement resembles the movement of the haiku, the whiplash effect of the poem's end fulfilling the acute observations leading up to it.

In later books—*The Stone Harp*, *Cicada*, and *Twenty Poems* —the straight-forwardness of *Winter News* takes a not altogether fortunate turn toward the ornate. While the effort to enrich the poems by increasing the use of metaphor is admirable, some of the poems—"The Insect," to take one example—feel burdened by the number of metaphors and similes:

Maggots, wrinkled white men
building a temple of slime.

Green blaze of the blowfly
that lights the labor of corpses.

The carrion beetle awakening
in a tunnel of drying flesh
like a miner surprised by the sun....

In other poems from these collections, however, Haines trusts fewer and stronger images to carry the poems. "The Middle Ages" is a case in point:

Always on the point of falling asleep,
figures of men and beasts.

Faces deeply grained with dirt,
a soiled finger pointing inward.

Like Dürer's Knight, always haunted
by two companions:

the Devil, with a face like a matted hog,
dishevelled and split...

Haines allows a minimum of devices, the two similes in stanzas three and four, to do the work, the image of the devil-hog especially powerful in its delayed placement and its simplicity. The way in which the poems in these three books, and in *In a Dusty Light*, move from the plain style of Haines's early poems to an ornate use of imagery, then back to the plain style, finds a parallel in his description of settling in the wilderness: "I watched a tree no bigger than my wrist when I first built there, grow tenfold over the years, until I had to cut away its branches from the rain gutters of the house" (*Living Off the Country*).

Haines is not simply a nature poet. One of the "most important metaphors of our time," he writes, "is the journey out of wilderness into culture."

Like Thoreau, Haines returns to "civilization," and in poems such as "In the Middle of America" and "The Sweater of Vladimir Ussachevsky," he writes out of environments, Ohio and Manhattan, quite different from the Alaska he homesteaded. Yet the poems often only begin in these new settings; they end in a return to open land. Reaching the countryside after leaving a city, the poet writes, in "Driving through Oregon (Dec. 1973)," that this "is the country we knew / before the cities came, / lighted by sun, moon, and stars." Through his well-crafted poems and determined vision, John Haines has lighted his own corner in American writing.

—Martin McGovern

HALL, Donald (Andrew, Jr.). American. Born in New Haven, Connecticut, 20 September 1928. Educated at Phillips Exeter Academy, New Hampshire; Harvard University, Cambridge, Massachusetts (Garrison and Sergeant prizes, 1951), B.A. 1951; Oxford University (Henry Fellow; Newdigate Prize, 1952), B.Litt. 1953; Stanford University, California (Creative Writing Fellow), 1953-54. Married 1) Kirby Thompson in 1952 (divorced, 1969), one son and one daughter; 2) Jane Kenyon in 1972. Junior Fellow, Society of Fellows, Harvard University, 1954-57; Assistant Professor, 1957-61, Associate Professor, 1961-66, and Professor of English, 1966-75, University of Michigan, Ann Arbor. Poetry Editor, *Paris Review*, Paris and New York, 1953-62; Member of the Editorial Board for Poetry, Wesleyan University Press, 1958-64. Lived in England, 1959-60, 1963-64. Recipient: Lamont Poetry Selection Award, 1955; Edna St. Vincent Millay Memorial Prize, 1956; Longview Foundation award, 1960; Guggenheim Fellowship, 1963, 1972; Sarah Josepha Hale Award, 1983. Poet Laureate of New Hampshire, 1984. Agent: Gerard McCauley Agency Inc., 141 East 44th Street, New York, New York 10017. Address: Eagle Pond Farm, Danbury, New Hampshire 03230, U.S.A.

PUBLICATIONS

Verse

(Poems). Oxford, Fantasy Press, 1952.
Exile. Privately printed, 1952.
To the Loud Wind and Other Poems. Cambridge, Massachusetts, Harvard Advocate, 1955.
Exiles and Marriages. New York, Viking Press, 1955.
The Dark Houses. New York, Viking Press, 1958.
A Roof of Tiger Lilies. New York, Viking Press, and London, Deutsch, 1964.
The Alligator Bride. Menomonie, Wisconsin, Ox Head Press, 1968.
The Alligator Bride: Poems New and Selected. New York, Harper, 1969.
The Yellow Room Love Poems. New York, Harper, 1971.
A Blue Tit Tilts at the Edge of the Sea: Selected Poems 1964-1974. London, Secker and Warburg, 1975.
The Town of Hill. Boston, Godine, 1975.

Kicking the Leaves. Mount Horeb, Wisconsin, Perishable Press, 1975.
Kicking the Leaves (collection). New York, Harper, 1978; London, Secker and Warburg, 1979.
The Toy Bone. Brockport, New York, Boa, 1979.
The Twelve Seasons. Deerfield, Massachusetts, Deerfield Press, and Dublin, Gallery Press, 1983.
Brief Lives. Concord, New Hampshire, William B. Ewert, 1983.
Great Day in the Cows' House. Mt. Carmel, Connecticut, Ives Street Press, 1984.

Recording: *Today's Poets 1,* with others, Folkways, 1967.

Plays

An Evening's Frost (produced New York, 1965).
Bread and Roses (produced Ann Arbor, Michigan, 1975).
Ragged Mountain Elegies (produced Peterborough, New Hampshire, 1983).

Other

Andrew the Lion Farmer (for children). New York, Watts, 1959; London, Methuen, 1961.
String Too Short to Be Saved: Childhood Reminiscences. New York, Viking Press, 1961; London, Deutsch, 1962.
Henry Moore: The Life and Work of a Great Sculptor. New York, Harper, and London, Gollancz, 1966.
Marianne Moore: The Cage and the Animal. New York, Pegasus, 1970.
As the Eye Moves: A Sculpture by Henry Moore. New York, Abrams, 1970.
The Gentleman's Alphabet Book. New York, Dutton, 1972.
Writing Well. Boston, Little Brown, 1973; revised edition, 1976, 1979.
Dock Ellis in the Country of Baseball, with Dock Ellis. New York, Coward McCann, 1976.
Riddle Rat (for children). New York, Warne, 1977.
Remembering Poets: Reminiscences and Opinions—Dylan Thomas, Robert Frost, T.S. Eliot, Ezra Pound. New York, Harper, 1978.
Goatfoot Milktongue Twinbird: Interviews, Essays, and Notes on Poetry 1970-6. Ann Arbor, University of Michigan Press, 1978.
Ox-Cart Man (for children). New York, Viking Press, 1979; London, MacRae, 1980.
To Keep Moving. Geneva, New York, Seneca, 1980.
To Read Literature: Fiction, Poetry, Drama. New York, Holt Rinehart, 1981.
The Weather of Poetry: Essays, Reviews, and Notes on Poetry 1977-81. Ann Arbor, University of Michigan Press, 1982.
The Man Who Lived Alone (for children). Boston, Godine, 1984.
Fathers Playing Catch with Sons: Essays on Sport (Mostly Baseball). Berkeley, California, North Point Press, 1985.

Editor, *The Harvard Advocate Anthology.* New York, Twayne, 1950.
Editor, with Robert Pack and Louis Simpson, *New Poets of England and America.* Cleveland, Meridian, 1957; London, New English Library, 1974; *Second Selection,* with Pack, 1962.
Editor, *Whittier.* New York, Dell, 1961.
Editor, *Contemporary American Poetry.* London, Penguin, 1962; revised edition, 1971.

Editor, *A Poetry Sampler.* New York, Watts, 1962.
Editor, with Stephen Spender, *The Concise Encyclopedia of English and American Poets and Poetry.* London, Hutchinson, and New York, Hawthorn, 1963; revised edition, 1970.
Editor, with Warren Taylor, *Poetry in English.* New York, Macmillan, 1963; revised edition, 1970.
Editor, *The Faber Book of Modern Verse,* revised edition. London, Faber, 1965.
Editor, *A Choice of Whitman's Verse.* London, Faber, 1968.
Editor, *The Modern Stylists: Writers on the Art of Writing.* New York, Free Press, 1968.
Editor, *Man and Boy: An Anthology.* New York, Watts, 1968.
Editor, *American Poetry: An Introductory Anthology.* London, Faber, 1969.
Editor, *The Pleasures of Poetry.* New York, Harper, 1971.
Editor, with D.L. Emblen, *A Writer's Reader.* Boston, Little Brown, 1976; revised edition, 1979, 1982.
Editor, *The Oxford Book of American Literary Anecdotes.* New York and Oxford, Oxford University Press, 1981.
Editor, *The Contemporary Essay.* Boston, Bedford, 1983.
Editor, *The Oxford Book of Children's Verse in America.* New York, Oxford University Press, 1985.

*

Critical Studies: by Ralph J. Mills, Jr., in *Iowa Review* (Iowa City), Winter 1971; "Donald Hall Issue" of *Tennessee Poetry Journal* (Martin), Winter 1971.

*   *   *

Donald Hall lives with his wife, the poet Jane Kenyon, in his ancestral farm house in New Hampshire. Through the zero winters they burn wood in ancestral woodstoves—eight cords, cut, split, delivered in the fall. Don rises in the night to stoke the fires. In the summers Jane grows a garden. The farm grows hay, which others cut. The barn is dilapidated now, the old buggy still inside which Don's grandfather drove to church three-quarters of a century ago. In New England no one throws much away. Upstairs are spinning wheels, wedding dresses, a churn. The main floor is filled with books, hundreds of feet of bookshelves added in 1975 when Hall left a professorship at the University of Michigan to come to this place and live by writing.

He writes every day from 6 or so until noon: essays, reviews, short stories, plays, textbooks, and poems. He writes about the house, about the fathers who have lived there before. "Naming the Horses" eulogizes generations of horses that worked the farm. Other poems make eulogies to grandparents, their lives, the vanishing rural occupations, shearing sheep, making ox carts. He and Jane hunt through a grave yard for his grandfather's grave. They find it. They don't find it. Different poems.

He watches his dreams. His grandparents come back to the house "laughing with pleasure at our surprise." He wakes again "hearing a voice from sleep: 'The blow of the axe resides in the acorn,' " and he writes it down.

Hall is returned, fully mature, to a well-spring of themes and values. He is not sentimental and his poetry is not pastoral; it is tinged with the politically alert, ironic restlessness of an urban, sophisticated mind. He looks from a window at Boston lawyers' summer places "with swimming pools cunningly added to cowsheds," but he knows "we are all of us sheep, and death is our shepherd,/and we die as the animals die."

Hall has learned to build poems centrifugally from chance beginnings. This takes time—two years per poem on the average, lines breaking and reforming. He has become willing to give over everything written so far to the next shaping impulse, to the new image, to the dream-self if it surfaces in the poem. He discovers "meaning" last. "In recent years," Hall writes, "I have come to accept the beginning of a poem, or even a whole draft, without the slightest clue to the subject matter.... The process of writing a poem is a process of shaping the words which the poem begins with...." This process produces poetry of a complete pattern, at its best, as in "Naming the Horses," symphonic—layers of music: the last, elegiac line—"O Roger, Mackerel, Riley, Ned, Nellie, Chester, Lady Ghost"—names the horses, recapitulating and resolving the progressions of assonance that structure the poem. It is a powerful conclusion, with more than the spirits of the horses lingering in the last name.

Hall grew up in metrics. His grandfather recited set-pieces to him as they did chores in the summer—"Casey at the Bat," "Over the Hills to the Poor House." He grew up with his grandfather's New England morality, but aware of its limitations. His first book of poems reiterates one theme: whether posed by the witty and ironic voice of the student ("The Lone Ranger") or by the reflective, uncertain graduate ("Exiles"), the problem is how to reach one's deep selves, the anima, dreams; how even to begin to understand the inner "world that must remain unvisited" since "no man can knock his human fist upon/the door...." All of Hall's subsequent work has struggled with that problem.

Partly because of his education (Exeter, Harvard, Oxford), Hall stayed in "careful ignorance" of the Black Mountain poets and the Beats until the late 1950's. In his third book of poems, metrics alternate with open forms for 44 pages until a sequence of poems on the sculpture of Henry Moore. Here images, not ideas, predominate. Immediately, the functioning of the images changes.

In the next pages the assassination of John F. Kennedy becomes an image of how Hall had let the requirements of his daily, mechanical life kill off his dreams. He accepts this responsibility for the first time ("I squeeze slowly" on the trigger). Images show him a well of sexual fear; he climbs out. Crashed airplanes have recurred in his poems. Now the pilot's spirit revives in the "narrow cockpit/although his muscles are stiff." He starts his plane and flies "in a beam of the late sun" to join the souls of the human race.

Hereafter images become more accessible to latent (unconscious) information, especially in Hall's next book, *The Alligator Bride*, with its aura of surrealism. Puzzling over the change in his poetry, Hall produced a remarkable essay on the creative process, "The Vatic Voice," which concludes: "I truly think that to clear the passageway to the insides of ourselves, to allow the vatic voice to speak through us, is the *ultimate* goal to which men must address themselves. It is what to live for, it is what to live by." The vatic voice probably speaks inside every man. Keats heard it (negative capability); so did André Breton. By 1969, Hall heard it. It shaped his decision to return to the ancestral farm. It shaped his poems. But he was not and will not be a surrealist poet. His inward journey extends only to that point where we fear to lose our identity in the inner chaos of faces and animals and confused scenes. Of this area, this passageway, Hall is a precise mapmaker.

With the publication of *Kicking the Leaves*, Hall steps away from the direct influence of any movement, poet, or school. His poems are still concerned with self-revelation, but the Self is extended now. It reaches to Hall's youth and childhood and to the lives of others who have touched him. The mature voice speaks with compassion and humor. Its tone is typically elegiac (even to a mock-heroic elegy for cheeses) and full of the music of American speech. He has written again on creativity; "Milktongue, Goatfoot, Twinbird" finds the psychic origins of creativity in the baby-self and locates the experience of a poem in the mouth and body as well as in the mind. It is an essential primer on his own work and on art as "regression in the service of the ego."

Hall is becoming one of the best American poets. He is a superb reader. Summing up his work-to-date, he writes: "The poem is a vehicle for self discovery.... The premise is that if you discover something that is deep enough inside yourself, it's going to be a part of other people's insides, too, and reveal themselves to themselves."

—Edward B. Germain

HALL, J(ohn) C(live). British. Born in London, 12 September 1920. Educated at Leighton Park, Reading, Berkshire; Oriel College, Oxford. Has two children. Formerly, a book publisher. Since 1955, Member of the Staff, *Encounter* magazine, London. Address: 198 Blythe Road, London W14 0HH, England.

PUBLICATIONS

Verse

Selected Poems, with Keith Douglas and Norman Nicholson. London, Bale and Staples, 1943.
The Summer Dance and Other Poems. London, Lehmann, 1951.
The Burning Hare. London, Chatto and Windus-Hogarth Press, 1966.
A House of Voices. London, Chatto and Windus-Hogarth Press, 1973.
Selected and New Poems 1939-1984. London, Secker and Warburg, 1985.

Other

Edwin Muir. London, Longman, 1956.

Editor, *Collected Poems of Edwin Muir 1921-1951.* London, Faber, 1952; New York, Grove Press, 1957; revised edition, Faber, 1960; New York, Oxford University Press, 1965.
Editor, with Patric Dickinson and Erica Marx, *New Poems 1955.* London, Joseph, 1955.
Editor, with G.S. Fraser and John Waller, *The Collected Poems of Keith Douglas*, revised edition. London, Faber, 1966.
Editor, with G.S. Fraser and John Waller, *Alamein to Zem Zem*, by Keith Douglas. London, Faber, 1966; New York, Chilmark Press, 1967.

*   *   *

J.C. Hall's early poems, collected in *The Summer Dance*, though reflective and carefully formed, lack any strongly individual quality. As he himself acknowledged: "All these long years I've pondered how to make/A poetry I could truly call my own." In the next volume, *The Burning Hare*, the influence of Edwin Muir is all-pervasive. "Before This Journeying Began" and "The Double Span" are dedicated to him, and "The Island" reads like a pastiche of Muir. Hall is a conservative poet, conscious of his debt to literary tradition, and "The Playground by the Church," with its allusions to Valéry, is typical of his meditative poetry, which questions and explores the world of ideas and of philosophical apprehensions.

A House of Voices relies less than the previous collections on myth and symbol, although Hall remains aware of their potency. The tone of the verse is more relaxed, and the poems are more firmly rooted in the world of everyday experience. In "The Double" Hall ends on a note of metaphysical speculation, but the first three stanzas are more humorous and colloquial than anything in his earlier work:

> I often wonder what he was really like,
> That identical boy—whether he knew of me
> Taking the rap, riding round on my bike
> Secretly proud of the devil I dared not be.

Hall's patient search for a poetry truly his own appears finally to have been successful.

—John Press

HALL, Rodney. Australian. Born in Solihull, Warwickshire, England, 18 November 1935; emigrated to Australia during his childhood. Educated at City of Bath Boys' School; Brisbane Boys' College; University of Queensland, Brisbane, B.A. 1971. Married Maureen Elizabeth MacPhail in 1962; three daughters. Free-lance scriptwriter and actor, 1957-67, and film critic, 1966-67, Australian Broadcasting Commission, Brisbane. Tutor, New England University School of Music, Armidale, New South Wales, summers 1967-71 and 1977-80; Youth Officer, Australian Council for the Arts, 1971-73. Since 1979, Lecturer in Recorder, Canberra School of Music. Since 1962, Advisory Editor, *Overland* magazine, Melbourne; since 1967, Poetry Editor, *The Australian* daily newspaper, Sydney. Travelled in Europe, 1958-60, 1963-64, 1965, and the United States, 1974. Australian Department of Foreign Affairs Lecturer in India, 1970, and Malaysia, 1972 and 1980. Recipient: Australian National University Creative Arts fellowship, Canberra, 1968; Commonwealth Literary Fund fellowship, 1970; Literature Board fellowship, 1973; Grace Leven Prize, 1974. Address: c/o University of Queensland Press, P.O. Box 42, St. Lucia, Queensland 4067, Australia.

PUBLICATIONS

Verse

Penniless till Doomsday. London, Outposts, 1962.
Four Poets, with others. Melbourne, Cheshire, 1962.
Forty ·Beads on a Hangman's Rope: Fragments of Memory. Newnham, Tasmania, Wattle Grove Press, 1963.
Eyewitness. Sydney, South Head Press, 1967.
The Autobiography of a Gorgon. Melbourne, Cheshire, 1968.
The Law of Karma: A Progression of Poems. Canberra, Australian National University Press, 1968.
Heaven, In a Way. Brisbane, University of Queensland Press, 1970.
A Soapbox Omnibus. Brisbane, University of Queensland Press, 1973.
Selected Poems. Brisbane, University of Queensland Press, 1975.
Black Bagatelles. Brisbane, University of Queensland Press, 1978.
The Most Beautiful World: Fictions and Sermons. Brisbane, University of Queensland Press, 1981.

Recording: *Romulus and Remus,* University of Queensland Press, 1971.

Novels

The Ship on the Coin: A Fable of the Bourgeoisie. Brisbane, University of Queensland Press, 1972.
A Place among People. Brisbane, University of Queensland Press, 1976.
Just Relations. Ringwood, Victoria, Penguin, 1982; London, Allen Lane, and New York, Viking Press, 1983.

Other

Social Services and the Aborigines, with Shirley Andrews. Canberra, Federal Council for Aboriginal Advancement, 1963.
Focus on Andrew Sibley. Brisbane, University of Queensland Press, 1968.
J.S. Manifold: An Introduction to the Man and His Work. Brisbane, University of Queensland Press, 1978.
Australia, Image of a Nation, with David Moore. Sydney, Collins, 1983.

Editor, with Thomas W. Shapcott, *New Impulses in Australian Poetry.* Brisbane, University of Queensland Press, 1968.
Editor, *Australian Poetry 1970.* Sydney, Angus and Robertson, 1970.
Editor, *Poems from Prison.* Brisbane, University of Queensland Press, 1974.
Editor, *Australians Aware: Poems and Paintings.* Sydney, Ure Smith, 1975.
Editor, *Voyage into Solitude,* by Michael Dransfield. Brisbane, University of Queensland Press, 1978.
Editor, *The Second Month of Spring,* by Michael Dransfield. Brisbane, University of Queensland Press, 1980.
Editor, *The Collins Book of Australian Poetry.* Sydney, Collins, 1981; London, Collins, 1983.

*

Rodney Hall comments:

I suppose the only way I'd be prepared to describe my own work is to say that it is basically non-confessional. It is my hope that each poem may take on an independent life of its own. If this is possible the emotional experience, it would seem to me, becomes available to the reader in a far more pure and direct form than is generally possible with confessional poetry, where the poet as a person perpetually obtrudes and everything is limited to his vision of himself. My experiences are nearly always projected into imaginary situations—often in an attempt to relate them back to that skeleton of our world-view, legends and myths.

I have also concentrated on a special form, which I call a Progression. This consists of many short poems, each capable of standing alone, tightly inter-related so that they become something akin to a single long poem with all the peaks left in and the discursive passages cut. I have published five of these progressions so far. The average length is forty poems, the largest is sixty-six.

*   *   *

Of Australian poets who came to prominence in the early 1960's, only Rodney Hall and Bruce Beaver have achieved, to date, a fully creative integration in their work of the two very opposed cultural stress-points of the 1960's and the 1970's—and the work of Beaver, in the 1960's, is more peripheral to its period than is Hall's output of early maturity.

Penniless till Doomsday, published in England in 1962, aroused immediate attention in Hall's adopted country, Australia. Its qualities of wit, wry appraisal, and implicit social involvement were exactly what the new decade, in Australia, was seeking—a way out of the cultural impasse of tired regionalism and provincial introversion that was the thinning out of the important 1940's "new *Bulletin* school" energies into a 1950's caution and intellectual sloth. Rodney Hall was one of the contributors to *Four Poets* (1962), the collection that made an important claim for a new group of Brisbane poets at this time, when Sydney was also being challenged by Melbourne as the centre of Australian poetry. Hall's regional—Brisbane—associations were essentially peripheral to his real poetic concerns, which were ambitiously developed in his succeeding volumes. He has been a prolific writer, and these collections reveal a restless and sometimes strenuously alert intelligence preoccupied by the allure of invention. *Eyewitness* holds on to models of detachment and observation, and some of its individual poems still attack the reader with their terse exactitude and surprise. But the two extended sequences *The Autobiography of a Gorgon* and *The Law of Karma* present, in a very real way, the culmination of the 1960's in Australian poetry. *The Autobiography of a Gorgon*, shorter, encapsuled in a tight case of irony and deliberate self-regard, is, I contend, the masterpiece of its decade. *The Law of Karma* is a deliberate attempt at a schematic poem, and its self-conscious virtuosity in fact mitigates against its final effect, substituting the power to impress for the power to move. Yet it remains a minefield of expressive force. The 1970's emphasised the impromptu and the immediate in poetry; *The Law of Karma* is deliberate, terrifyingly insistent upon inexorable processes. In a sense it codifies the very order that was, in the year of its composition and publication, to be overthrown by a new generation.

It is interesting to note that Rodney Hall, as poetry editor for the national newspaper *The Australian*, was to become central in recognising the emerging forces of this succeeding generation of poets, and in making their work available. *The Law of Karma* is built upon a premise of social observation and indeed responsibility—something the oncoming "generation of 1968" (as it has, retrospectively, been termed) was to make central in their concerns, tightened by the Vietnam conscription commitment of the Australian government of the day. Hall's next two books, *Heaven, In a Way* and *A Soapbox Omnibus*, can be seen, now, as transition pieces, where the poet, acutely sensitive to the dynamics of life around him and bounded, finally, by his very virtuosity of technical accomplishment (many of the pieces here are almost rigid in their cleverness, many are acutely moving in their interplay of tensions), tries out various structures and forms to weld together his intellectual and his responsive abilities in confrontation with this turning point in the culture's history. "Folk Tales," the concluding sequence of *A Soapbox Omnibus*, points decisively to a pedal-point in Hall's work. *Selected Poems* is perhaps the most remarkable of its kind in Australian literary history, as it is nearly half given over to a long new sequence ("The Owner of My Face") that would seem almost entirely unprepared for in any of the earlier work. Hall had very early on developed what he called a "progression" of poems—*The Law of Karma* was the most fully extended of these. But "The Owner of My Face" broke radical new ground, in that it explored states of subjective being and intuitive response—almost a direct opposition to his prior command of authorial irony and interplay of controllled nuances ("walking the tightrope of passion and detachment" he once called it).

Black Bagatelles expands further this area of subjective vulnerability in Hall's work, but with important modifications: his sense of theatre, of event, is given free play (the work is a series of dialogues with Death), and his sense of irony is counterpointed (often brilliantly) with the very willingness to be "open" that is at the heart of the 1970's exploration. It is a work that allows Hall's brilliance, and deep humanity, full play, and interplay. It is also a work of deep pain, one of the high points of its decade in Australlian poetry.

—Thomas W. Shapcott

HALPERN, Daniel. American. Born in Syracuse, New York, 11 September 1945. Educated at San Francisco State College, 1963-64; California State University, Northridge, 1966-69, B.A. in psychology 1969; Columbia University, New York (Woolrich Fellow), 1970-72, M.F.A. 1972. Since 1969, Editor, *Antaeus* magazine, New York; since 1971, Editor-in-Chief, Ecco Press, New York; since 1978, Director, National Poetry Series, New York. Instructor, New School for Social Research, New York, 1971-76; Visiting Professor, Princeton University, New Jersey, 1975-76. Since 1976, Associate Professor, and since 1978, Chairman, Columbia University School of the Arts. Recipient: Rehder Award (*Southern Poetry Review*), 1971; YM-YWHA Discovery Award, 1971; National Endowment for the Arts fellowship, 1973, 1974; Bread Loaf Writers Conference Robert Frost Fellowship, 1974; Creative Artists Public Service grant, 1978. Address: 1 West 30th Street, New York, New York 10001, U.S.A.

PUBLICATIONS

Verse

Traveling on Credit. New York, Viking Press, 1972.
The Keeper of Height (as Angela McCabe) New York, Barlenmir House, 1974.
The Lady Knife-Thrower. Binghamton, New York, Bellevue Press, 1975.
Treble Poets 2, with Gerda Mayer and Florence Elon. London, Chatto and Windus, 1975.
Street Fire. New York, Viking Press, 1975.
Life among Others. New York, Viking Press, 1978.
Seasonal Rights. New York, Viking Press, 1982.

Other

Editor, with Norman Thomas di Giovanni and Frank MacShane, *Borges on Writing*. New York, Dutton, 1973; London, Allen Lane, 1974.
Editor, *The American Poetry Anthology*. Boulder, Colorado, Westview Press, 1975.

Translator, *Songs of Mririda, Courtesan of the High Atlas*, by Mririda n'Aït Attik. Greensboro, North Carolina, Unicorn Press, 1974.

*   *   *

Highly educated, moderately successful as an author, editor, and translator, Daniel Halpern is caught in the alienation, isolation, and yearning for spontaneous feeling that incites much contemporary poetry. "The Ethnic Life," the first poem in his first book of poetry, *Traveling on Credit*, begins "I've been after the exotic/For years" and ends "For years I've lived simply/Without luxury—/With the soundness of the backward/Where the senses can be heard." The headlong rush to identify ethnic and exotic with simple still leaves Halpern stopped, as he so often is, at the sense, stranded between objective sensations and subjective feelings.

Traveling on Credit and *Street Fire* are carefully arranged into sections by topic: places are seen with a fine precision of mood; the vagaries of affection between men and women rise up out of stillness; the small rituals of daily life and social gatherings ward off larger fears. The language of both books hews to a clear speech neither too idiomatic nor too elevated, set in lines of regular length. Throughout, Halpern aims at a middle road, oscillating between melancholy lyricism and bemused objectivity.

Wary of extremes in emotional life and of the norms of accepted tradition, Halpern concentrates on the seductive pull of the imagination. "Aubade" (*Life among Others*) modifies it traditional form by being neither particularly joyous, wholly of the morning, nor precisely of lovers parting. It begins at night with the lovers going to bed: "It is when I fall to dream in your arms/that I climb into the arms of another:/...until I am back again beside you/in the first light, the morning of the different day." The protagonist of Halpern's poems is a man to whom life, and especially women, has come easily, but this ease has spawned a restless investigation into the ambiguities and difficulties of communication.

Life among Others focuses more directly on the dimensions of these difficulties, addressing openly the isolation which was held at arm's length in his earlier work. The first section puts into service the delicate atmospheric descriptions of *Traveling on Credit* to present the loneliness of the traveler's rooms:

> I sit in front of my window, I tempt
> the solitary lights that go on and off
> on the water: lights of boats, cape lights,
> the lights across the water. They pile up
> in darkness here. It is a collection, a pastime.
> Now I have the chance to speak—not to explain
> but to return everything—your bright lives
> rooted to nothing more than a light seen at a distance
> that diminishes as it moves closer and closer.

The desire for speech comes in such moments, but its consummation escapes him. The others remain nameless and faceless. The poems of the second section spring from memories and images, moments of pain and loss when the protagonist tries to accept his isolation, or at least to understand it. The final four interconnected poems—"White Tent," "White Train," "White Contact," and "I Am a Dancer"—envelope his isolation in a series of images:

> White, the color of clarity
> where nothing has to live.
> It matches everything and can go
> anywhere. It fits in and is nothing.
> White contact in a house where nothing
> is said.

> The tent of dream
> is a privacy, the bird a way out,
> the train, power to keep on. I'm
> not really unpleasant, and there is no crime
> committed against others.

However, this neat summary belies the strength of the attempt, and the sentences are too coolly structured to give us the feeling of a break in the protagonist's intellectual reserve. Despite this, the book is a clear step forward. Halpern seems a patient poet, and his patience may yet be further rewarded.

—Walter Bode

HAMBURGER, Michael (Peter Leopold). British. Born in Berlin, 22 March 1924; emigrated to England in 1933. Educated at schools in Germany; George Watson's School, Edinburgh; The Hall, Hampstead, London; Westminster School, London; Christ Church, Oxford, B.A. in modern languages, M.A. 1948. Served as an infantryman, non-commissioned officer, and lieutenant, Royal Army Eduational Corps, 1943-47. Married Anne Beresford, *q.v.*, in 1951 (marriage dissolved, 1970; remarried 1974); three children. Assistant Lecturer in German, University College, London, 1952-55; Lecturer, then Reader in German, University of Reading, Berkshire, 1955-64; Florence Purington Lecturer, Mount Holyoke College, South Hadley, Massachusetts, 1966-67; Visiting Professor, State University of New York, Buffalo, 1969, and Stony Brook, 1970, Wesleyan University, Middletown, Connecticut, 1971, University of Connecticut, Storrs, 1972, University of California, San Diego, 1973, University of South Carolina, Columbia, 1973, Boston University, 1975, 1977, and University of Essex, Wivenhoe, 1978. Recipient: Bollingen Fellowship, 1959, 1965; German Academy Voss Prize, for translation, 1964; Schlegel-Tieck Prize, for translation, 1967, 1978, 1981; Arts Council translation prize, 1969; Levinson Prize (*Poetry*, Chicago), 1972; Institute of Linguists Gold Medal, 1977; Wilhelm-Heinse Prize, 1978. Fellow, Royal Society of Literature, 1972. Address: Marsh Acres, Middleton, Saxmundham, Suffolk, England.

PUBLICATIONS

Verse

Later Hogarth. London, Cope and Fenwick, 1945.
Flowering Cactus: Poems 1942-49. Aldington, Kent, Hand and Flower Press, 1950.
Poems 1950-1951. Aldington, Kent, Hand and Flower Press, 1952.
The Dual Site. New York, Poetry London-New York, 1957; London, Routledge, 1958.
Weather and Season: New Poems. London, Longman, and New York, Atheneum, 1963.
In Flashlight. Leeds, Northern House, 1965.
In Massachusetts. Menomonie, Wisconsin, Ox Head Press, 1967.
Feeding the Chickadees. London, Turret, 1968.
Travelling: Poems 1963-68. London, Fulcrum Press, 1969.
Penguin Modern Poets 14, with Alan Brownjohn and Charles Tomlinson. London, Penguin, 1969.
Home. Frensham, Surrey, Sceptre Press, 1969.
In Memoriam Friedrich Hölderlin. London, Menard Press, 1970.
Travelling I-V. London, Agenda, 1972.
Ownerless Earth: New and Selected Poems 1950-1972. Cheadle, Cheshire, Carcanet, and New York, Dutton, 1973.

Conversations with Charwomen. Rushden, Northamptonshire, Sceptre Press, 1973.
Babes in the Wood. Knotting, Bedfordshire, Sceptre Press, 1974.
Travelling VI. London, I.M., 1975.
Travelling VII. Luxembourg, Club 80, 1976.
Real Estate. London, Anvil Press Poetry, 1977.
Real Estate (collection). Manchester, Carcanet, 1977.
Palinode: A Poet's Progress. Knotting, Bedfordshire, Sceptre Press, 1977.
Moralities. Newcastle upon Tyne, Morden Tower, 1977.
Variations in Suffolk IV. Knotting, Bedforshire, Sceptre Press 1980.
Variations. Manchester, Carcanet, 1981; Redding Ridge, Connecticut, Black Swan, 1983.
In Suffolk. Madley, Herefordshire, Five Seasons Press, 1982.
Collected Poems 1941-1983. Manchester, Carcanet, 1984.

Plays

The Tower, adaptation of a play by Peter Weiss (produced New York, 1974).

Radio Play: *Struck by Apollo*, with Anne Beresford, 1965.

Other

Reason and Energy: Studies in German Literature. London, Routledge, and New York, Grove Press, 1957; revised edition, London, Weidenfeld and Nicolson, 1971; as *Contraries: Studies in German Literature*, New York, Dutton, 1971.
Hugo von Hofmannsthal: Zwei Studien. Göttingen, Sachse and Pohl, 1964; translated as *Hofmannsthal: Three Essays*, Princeton, New Jersey, Princeton University Press, 1970; Cheadle, Cheshire, Carcanet, 1974.
From Prophecy to Exorcism: The Premisses of Modern German Literature. London, Longman, 1965.
Zwischen den Sprachen: Essays und Gedichte. Frankfurt, Fischer, 1966.
The Truth of Poetry: Tensions in Modern Poetry from Baudelaire to the 1960's. London, Weidenfeld and Nicolson, 1969; New York, Harcourt Brace, 1970.
A Mug's Game: Intermittent Memoirs 1924-1954. Cheadle, Cheshire, Carcanet, 1973.
Art as Second Nature: Occasional Pieces 1950-1974. Manchester, Carcanet, 1975.
A Proliferation of Prophets: German Literature from Nietzsche to the Second World War. Manchester, Carcanet, and New York, St. Martin's Press, 1983.

Editor and Translator, *Beethoven: Letters, Journals, and Conversations.* London, Thames and Hudson, and New York, Pantheon, 1951; revised edition, London, Cape, 1966; revised edition, Thames and Hudson, 1984.
Editor, and Translator with others, *Poems and Verse Plays*, by Hugo von Hofmannsthal. New York, Pantheon, and London, Routledge, 1961.
Editor and Translator, with Christopher Middleton, *Modern German Poetry, 1910-1960: An Anthology with Verse Translations.* London, MacGibbon and Kee, and New York, Grove Press, 1962.
Editor, and Translator with others, *Selected Plays and Libretti*, by Hugo von Hofmannsthal. New York, Pantheon, and London, Routledge, 1963.
Editor, *Das Werk: Sonette, Lieder, Erzählungen*, by Jesse Thoor. Frankfurt, Europäische Verlagsanstalt, 1965.

Editor and Translator, *East German Poetry: An Anthology in German and English.* Oxford, Carcanet, and New York, Dutton, 1972.
Editor, *Selected Poems*, by Thomas Good. London, St. George's Press, 1973.

Translator, *Poems*, by Hölderlin. London, Nicholson and Watson, 1943; revised edition, as *Hölderlin: His Poems*, London, Harvill Press, 1952; New York, Pantheon, 1953; revised edition, as *Selected Verse*, London, Penguin, 1961; revised edition, as *Poems and Fragments*, London, Routledge, 1966; Ann Arbor, University of Michigan Press, 1967; revised edition, Cambridge, University Press, 1980.
Translator, *Twenty Prose Poems of Baudelaire.* London, Editions Poetry London, 1946; revised edition, London, Cape, 1968.
Translator, *Decline: 12 Poems*, by Georg Trakl. St. Ives, Cornwall, Latin Press, 1952.
Translator, *The Burnt Offering*, by Albrecht Goes. New York, Pantheon, and London, Gollancz, 1956.
Translator, *Egmont*, by Goethe, in *Classic Theatre 2*, edited by Eric Bentley. New York, Doubleday, 1959.
Translator, with Yvonne Kapp, *Tales from the Calendar*, by Bertolt Brecht. London, Methuen, 1961.
Translator, with Christopher Middleton, *Selected Poems*, by Günter Grass. London, Secker and Warburg, and New York, Harcourt Brace, 1966.
Translator, *Poems*, by Hans Magnus Enzensberger. Newcastle upon Tyne, Northern House, 1966.
Translator, *Lenz*, by Georg Büchner, with *Immensee* by Theodor Storm and *A Village Romeo and Juliet* by Gottfried Keller.- London, Calder and Boyars, 1966; in *Leonce and Lena, Lenz, Woyzeck*, 1972.
Translator, with others, *O the Chimneys*, by Nelly Sachs. New York, Farrar Straus, 1967; as *Selected Poems, Including the Verse Play "Eli,"* London, Cape, 1968.
Translator, with Jerome Rothenberg and the author, *Poems for People Who Don't Read Poems* by Hans Magnus Enzensberger. New York, Atheneum, and London, Secker and Warburg, 1968; as *Poems*, London, Penguin, 1968.
Translator, *And Really Frau Blum Would Very Much Like to Meet the Milkman: 21 Short Stories*, by Peter Bichsel. London, Calder and Boyars, 1968.
Translator, *Journeys: Two Radio Plays: The Rolling Sea at Setúbal, The Year Lacerta*, by Günter Eich. London, Cape, 1968.
Translator, with Christopher Middleton, *Poems*, by Günter Grass. London, Penguin, 1969.
Translator, with Matthew Mead, *The Seeker and Other Poems*, by Nelly Sachs. New York, Farrar Straus, 1970.
Translator, *Stories for Children*, by Peter Bichsel. London, Calder and Boyars, 1971.
Translator, with Christopher Middleton, *Selected Poems*, by Paul Celan. London, Penguin, 1972.
Translator, *Leonce and Lena, Lenz, Woyzeck*, by Georg Büchner. Chicago, University of Chicago Press, 1972.
Translator, *Selected Poems*, by Peter Huchel. Manchester, Carcanet, 1974.
Translator, *German Poetry 1910-1975.* New York, Urizen, 1976 (withdrawn); Manchester, Carcanet, 1977; New York, Persea, 1981.
Translator, with Christopher Middleton, *In the Egg and Other Poems*, by Günter Grass. New York Harcourt Brace, 1977; London, Secker and Warburg, 1978.
Translator, *Texts*, by Helmut Heissenbüttel. London, Boyars, 1977.

Translator, with André Lefevere, *Seedtime (La Semaison): Extracts from the Notebooks 1954-1967*, by Philippe Jaccottet. New York, New Directions, 1977.

Translator, *Poems*, by Franco Fortini. Todmorden, Lancashire, Art, 1978.

Translator, *Poems*, by Paul Celan. Manchester, Carcanet, and New York, Persea, 1980.

Translator, *An Unofficial Rilke: Poems 1912-1926*. London, Anvil Press Poetry, 1981; as *Poems 1912-1926*, Redding Ridge, Connecticut, Black Swan, 1983.

Translator, *Selected Poems*, by Marin Sorescu. Newcastle upon Tyne, Bloodaxe, 1982.

Translator, *Urworte Orphisch: Five Poems*, by Goethe. London, Klaus Meyer, 1982.

Translator, *Poems and Epigrams*, by Goethe. London, Anvil Press Poetry, 1983; as *Roman Elegies and Other Poems*, Redding Ridge, Connecticut, Black Swan, 1983.

Translator, *The Garden of Theophrastus and Other Poems*, by Peter Huchel. Manchester, Carcanet, 1983.

*

Manuscript Collections: University of Texas, Austin; Lockwood Memorial Library, State University of New York, Buffalo; University of Reading, Berkshire.

Critical Studies: "The Subject Beneath the Subject" by the author, in *Christian Science Monitor* (Boston), 31 January 1967; "Across Frontiers: Michael Hamburger as Poet and Critic" by Jon Glover, in *Stand* (Newcastle upon Tyne), 1970; "Rhythm" by the author, in *Agenda* (London), x, 4—xi, 1, 1972-1973; "More New Poetry" by Terry Eagleton, in *Stand* (Newcastle upon Tyne), 1973; "Forward, Ay, and Backward" by Martin Dodsworth, in *The Guardian* (London), 5 April 1973; "Ownerless Earth" by Donald Davie, in *New York Times Book Review*, 28 April 1974; "Travellers" by John Matthias, in *Poetry* (Chicago), April 1974.

*   *   *

Michael Hamburger's is a poetry of ideas made as sensuous as possible by being passed through images of nature, tinged very frequently with a decent uncloying melancholy. The turning point in his poetry is made in *Weather and Season* in which all the traditionally metrical and rhyming forms have almost entirely been disbanded because, as he stated in the reading he gave at the University of Iowa in 1969 (and I paraphrase) "in my previous books I used the traditional forms to protect myself from the pressure and intensity of my feelings; whereas I subsequently came to feel that, in writing the later poems, I no longer wished to evade or mask these feelings." This frank, direct criticism of an earlier stance, together with his decision to shuck off the encrustments of such forms, has brought rewards.

The poetry has two contexts. One is that of men socialized into a dilemma which may be resolved only by using the charged, moral conscience ("In a Cold Season"); the other context is nature, although as one critic has recently, and justly, pointed to some affinity with Edward Thomas, so I suggest that he is no more a nature poet than Thomas is. Leavis in *New Bearings* has indicated that for Thomas nature was used as the arena of delicate and scrupulous psychological re-enactment, and for Hamburger this is also valid. Many of the poems in his pamphlet *In Flashlight* cohere to form an exploration of the use and stamina of memory. A capacity for valuation, issuing directly from responsive memory which absorbs the two nodes of experience seen here as change through exploration and settled re-

currence, is examined in "Tides" and "The Road" (*Weather and Season*). In the latter, memory is the recognising faculty by which the conscious mind penetrates its unconscious, to find natural images built there into an ideal country—an absolute, alluring and unattainable—and which the teller does "not look for...when awake."

The question of identity, subsumed in the role of poet in "Man of the World" (*Weather and Season*), is more inclusively embodied in "The Search" (*Weather and Season*). In that search, "as commanded," the familiar country of the man's origins is discovered as alien, and when, through tracts of nature, he reaches the village, the symbolic ideal is released to him, to be discovered as actual, in its quality as "Why, Mors, need we tell you, mors, MORS." Expectedly enough this is the last poem of *Weather and Season*.

The extrapolation from biography into criticism is dubious, but I think it's relevant here to indicate that Hamburger is a Jew, of German birth, and that he with most of his family emigrated to England in the year of Hitler's rise to power, and averted for themselves the Nazi holocaust. Hamburger is acutely fitted to write such a poem as "The Search," with all its narrower, more defined implications. It is the Jewish component of this poet that hiddenly but with integrated power explores the landscape of nature and village and finds that the search discovers his origins and death to be identical. The same qualification permits him to write of the issues of conscience in relation to Eichmann.

Eliot has declared in another context that "Humankind cannot bear very much reality," but it is Hamburger's alert and intelligent contention that it is the burden of humanity as well as its necessary precondition for survival that it use language as searchingly as possible and with as faithful a rendering of the referents in experience, and interpretation of them, as can be. Mercy, honesty and perception are in this context integral: "Dare break one word and words may yet be whole." Hamburger's language is quiet and naturally spoken, even when speaking of violence. The intensity of the poetry is in the *un*extraordinary and seemingly nonmanipulative but exact use of ordinary language—"the sea, that basher of dumb rock"—and its unassumingly painful exploration of painful experience ("For a Family Album"). Metaphoric imagery is used rarely. The images are visually referential; or else the metaphors live in consideration of the metaphysical data as if the data was actual, or physically tangible. And these are fed through hovering, tentative but persistent rhythms fitted to their unrhymed, speech-moulded cadences.

Hamburger has shown a preference for the comforting rural (or even cultivated) natural phenomena of creature and plant. This desire for their presence as a sanitive has continued. It is this poet's matrix, on which everything else is sounded, and often judged. Perhaps such a preference accounts, in part, for the slow-moving rhythms of much of his verse.

A collection called *Travelling* contained a poem of that name, and this has been the seed of Hamburger's most interesting, ambitious, and sustained poem to date—with the possible exception of "In a Cold Season." In this early version, the poem is in two sections. In *Real Estate* the poem has a third section, and the whole has become the first of a suite of 11 poems under the same title. In the "Envoi" to *Travelling*, Hamburger wrote: "Goodbye, words..../ Go out and lose yourselves in a jabbering world, / Be less than nothing." The injunction is only half-true for Hamburger. The "jabbering world" of which he complains, has, in the full version of "Travelling," become more acutely judged—an earth committed to (human) acquisition and possession. It is a human world that must give up what it possesses in order to enter into what cannot be possessed either, although supremely desired—love given to and received from another: "The place that, holding you still, / Could fill and affirm your name." "Still" means both unmoving and a condition continuous in time. Travelling involves the need for a fixed point of return (the compasses image in Donee's "A Valediction: Forbidding Mourning"). At that point of return one realises that to be in that "place" is not to possess it ("Ownerless Earth"): "Last of my needs, you / I'll unlearn, reliquish / If that was love. Too late, / Let you go, return, stay / And move on."

The close-grained, almost possessed energy of Hamburger's earlier poems tends, in "Travelling," to become something other. There is an almost invariably direct syntax, and a greater rhythmical assurance both in line length and enjambments. Some of this assurance is obtained by a "likeable" repetition: there are pairs or triads of things—"sand, pebble, rock," "On cobbles, on brick, on slabs," or of verbs, such as "Propel, transmute; and create / again"; in this last example development is described (not enacted). This triadic formation also tends to occur in the rhythmic structure of a line, producing a wavering, wave-like movement, at once "tentative and persistent"; and therein lies Hamburger's enacted argument with himself. Linguistically, that argument tends to get dissolved in a resolute search for, and an achievement of, clarity. The clarity sometimes irons out, or expunges, what one senses as greater tensions or antagonisms beneath the surface. The achievement of "Travelling" (and its synonym *Real Estate*) is, nevertheless, high and consistent. The long poem (a risk these days) sustains itself round the go / stay, fixed / moving paradox where abnegation and love form the field of the drama. Even the determination to be plain and understandable has for the reader a moving vulnerability; it may not be a central part of the poem, but it is a bonus—surely not what the poet had meant us to observe: a struggling to "get it right."

—Jon Silkin

HAMILTON, (Robert) Ian. British. Born in King's Lynn, Norfolk, 24 March 1938. Educated at Darlington Grammar School; Keble College, Oxford (Editor, *Tomorrow*, 1959-60), B.A. (honours) 1962. Married 1) Gisela Dietzel in 1963, one son; 2) Ahdaf Soueif in 1981, one son. Editor, *Review*, 1962-72, and *New Review*, 1974-79, London; poetry reviewer, *London Magazine*, 1962-64, and *The Observer*, London, 1965-70; Poetry and Fiction Editor, *Times Literary Supplement*, London, 1965-73; Lecturer in Poetry, University of Hull, Yorkshire, 1972-73. Since 1984, Presenter, *Bookmark* programme, BBC Television. Recipient: Eric Gregory Award, 1963; Poetry Society of America Melville Cane Award, 1983. Address: 18 Dorset Square, London N.W. 1, England.

PUBLICATIONS

Verse

Pretending Not to Sleep. London, The Review, 1964.
The Visit: Poems. London, Faber, 1970.
Anniversary and Vigil. London, Poem-of-the-Month Club, 1971.

Other

A Poetry Chronicle: Essays and Reviews. London, Faber, and

New York, Barnes and Noble, 1973.
The Little Magazines: A Study of Six Editors. London, Weidenfeld and Nicolson, 1976.
Robert Lowell: A Biography. New York, Random House, 1982; London, Faber, 1983.

Editor, *The Poetry of War, 1939-45.* London, Alan Ross, 1965.
Editor, *Selected Poetry and Prose*, by Alun Lewis. London, Allen and Unwin, 1966.
Editor, *The Modern Poet: Essays from "The Review."* London, Macdonald, 1968; New York, Horizon Press, 1969.
Editor, *Eight Poets.* London, Poetry Book Society, 1968.
Editor, *Selected Poems*, by Robert Frost. London, Penguin, 1973.
Editor, with Colin Falck, *Poems since 1900: An Anthology of British and American Verse in the Twentieth Century.* London, Macdonald and Jane's, 1975.
Editor, *Yorkshire in Verse.* London, Secker and Warburg, 1984.

*   *   *

Response in our time to the problem of how to render intimate and profound emotion in poetry has been extremely varied; often confused. Some poets have preferred to keep off the terrain almost altogether, sublimating pure feeling while employing it as the driving-force for a poetry which makes general, impersonal statements of another kind. Some have taken masks to disguise it, expressing it obliquely or with ironic detachment. Others have adopted the very direct, confessional manner, holding nothing back, hoping that the raw, detailed truth of their utterances will validate the poetry which contains them. Ian Hamilton's achievement has been to establish an alternative different from any of these: an area where personal feeling can be expressed not only with vividness and fidelity to experience but also with a subtlety and a reticence which do not diminish its force. It is a very private, very individual mode of writing: but the emotions are recognizable and universal.

Hamilton's output has been small. His one volume, *The Visit*, contained some thirty poems only, written during seven years; and beyond it, there are so far only a few uncollected new poems printed in magazines, or as yet unpublished. All the poems are short, none exceeding twenty lines. They are most of them direct and simple; or simple once the situation—between father and son, poet and wife, poet and child—has been grasped. Dwelling on significant human moments has been a very deliberate choice. In a note in the *Bulletin* of the Poetry Book Society (Summer 1970), Hamilton defines his poems as "dramatic lyrics...the intense climactic moment of drama." The reader must supply "the prose part...the background data" from clues inside the brief statements the poems make. Yet reading Hamilton is never a matter of puzzling out a wilfully cryptic technique. The authenticity and strength—and the interest and relevance for the reader—of the emotions, are immediately apparent. Re-reading gradually uncovers the full situation, the exact intention, affording an increasing sense of the scrupulousness and delicacy with which he handles images and verbal effects.

Sorrow, alarm, tragedy are never far away in Hamilton's verse, but they are contained (in both senses) in small human gestures or minute, careful observations of objects: the movements of hands, or hair, or breath, the play of light in a room, a sudden scent. In "Trucks," the light from the vehicles at night "Slops in and spreads across the ceiling, / Gleams, and goes." The sick, or dreaming, loved one speaks suddenly: "You're taking off, you say, / And won't be back. / Your shadows soar." But her remoteness from him will turn again into a kind of closeness, if he can only wait: "Very soon / The trucks will be gone. Bitter, you will turn / Back again. We will join our cold hands together." An entire situation is caught in 13 very simple lines in which images of light and shadow, the gestures of hands, enact its "climactic moment"; sensitive judgment of punctuation and line-endings captures a speaking tone which movingly renders both the intimacy and the alarm. In "Father, Dying," petals from a rose suggest the dying flower, but act also, in words of quiet yet intense physical immediacy, as images for the dying man: "Trapped on your hand / They darken, cling in sweat, then curl / Dry out and drop away." The end of the poem, as the man's hand bleeds from the thorns on the bare stem, suggests effects in the poetry of Sylvia Plath: "'My hand's / In flower,' you say, 'My blood excites / This petal dross. I'll live.'" There is a certain debt here to a more florid confessional poetry; but the economy and precision, the avoidance of overt drama, are something only Hamilton achieves.

The poems towards the end of *The Visit* are no less moving and arresting, but tend even more towards the laconic; as if the poet feels he can suggest all the more by saying even less. Hamilton's immense skill (very much a personal technical skill) in writing short poems of great tenderness and resonance has tempted many imitators who lack his resource and judgment. As a poet who has helped to keep certain areas of personal sensitivity open at a time when crudity and rhetoric have invaded so much personal verse, his place is assured. But the difficulty of emulating him should be clearly demonstrated by the fine complexity and irony of "Friends," an uncollected poem in which even the plain-looking title contributes a dimension of bitter meaning:

"At one time we wanted nothing more
Than to wake up in each other's arms."
Old enemy,
You want to live forever
And I don't
Was the last pact we made
On our last afternoon together.

—Alan Brownjohn

HANSON, Kenneth O(stlin). American. Born in Shelley, Idaho, 24 February 1922. Educated at schools in Shelley; University of Idaho, Pocatello and Moscow, B.A. in English 1942; University of Washington, Seattle, 1946-54. Served in the United States Army, 1942-46. Instructor, 1954-58, Assistant Professor, 1958-60, Associate Professor, 1960-63, Professor, 1963-83, and since 1983, Kenan Professor of English, Reed College, Portland, Oregon. Delegate to the first Institute in Chinese Civilization, Formosa (Fulbright Fellowship), 1962. Recipient: Bollingen award, 1962; Rockefeller Award, 1966; Lamont Poetry Selection Award, 1966; Asia Society award, 1971; Amy Lowell Traveling Scholarship, 1973; National Endowment for the Arts grant, 1976, 1982. Address: Reed College, Portland, Oregon 97202, U.S.A.

PUBLICATIONS

Verse

8 Poems 1958. Privately printed, 1958.

Poems. Portland, Oregon, Portland Art Museum, 1959.
Five Poets of the Pacific Northwest, with others, edited by Robin Skelton. Seattle, University of Washington Press, 1964.
The Distance Anywhere. Seattle, University of Washington Press, 1967.
Saronikos and Other Poems. Portland, Oregon, Press-22, 1970.
The Uncorrected World. Middletown, Connecticut, Wesleyan University Press, 1973.
Portraits: Friends: Artists, prints by LaVerne Krause. Portland, Oregon, Press-22, 1978.
Lighting the Night Sky. Portland, Oregon, Breitenbush Press, 1983.

Other

Editor, *Clear Days: Poems by Palamás and Elytis, in Versions by Nikos Tselepides.* Portland, Oregon, Press-22, 1972.

Translator, *Growing Old Alive: Poems,* by Han Yü. Port Townsend, Washington, Copper Canyon Press, 1978.

*

Critical Study: "On Translation," interview with William Stafford, in *Madrona* (Seattle), Summer 1973.

Kenneth O. Hanson comments:
Chief influences on my work have been Pound, Williams, the Chinese language, the Greek landscape, Prévert, Cavafy, and my third-grade teacher Miss Warwas, who taught me how to pay attention.

*   *   *

The first poem in Kenneth O. Hanson's *The Distance Anywhere* describes a skin-diver who hangs "hours on the surface of one world / and stares into another." A frequent visitor to Greece and a serious student of classical Chinese culture, Hanson might in those lines be describing a central situation in his poems. As an observer he likes to be inconspicuous ("Beginning the day with ouzo / you're one jump ahead. / I stick to beer"), and reticent ("Sometimes / a thing can be made / too clear").

His rhetoric is colloquial, understated. His more formal tone, usually elegiac, is closer to Waley's and Rexroth's translations from Chinese poetry than to British or American models: "What is empty? What is full? Only / the four corners of the past stand pat."

Most of *The Uncorrected World* is set in Greece; a few poems at the book's end long for Greece and meditate on what it means to be a traveller, and to be back in America. Throughout the book age-old Greece and its current political situation collide:

This rocky
landscape Hesiod how could he
plow a straight furrow?
Three thousand years.
Sun. Moon. Stone. Sky.
Against the whitewashed wall.
Official pronouncements.

But the world is uncorrected, and Greek political life is a manifestation, rather than a cause, of that fact. Hanson in Greece is a shrewd version of the American innocent abroad, but Hanson even at home is a traveller, because we all are:

We like to seem importunate

before this world of change.
O plains o vasty deep o marge and void
etc. We move but not through distance

into time, as if the fatal toad
in time's thin stone still faintly ticked
somewhere beyond. Aficionados of the moon!

O distances we gaze into!

—William Matthews

HANSON, Pauline.   American.   Born in Massachusetts. Assistant to the Director, Yaddo, Saratoga Springs, New York, 1950-76. Recipient: Eunice Tietjens Memorial Prize (*Poetry*, Chicago), 1965; National Endowment for the Arts grant, 1972; American Academy award, 1972. Address: 219 Freeman Street, Brookline, Massachusetts 02146, U.S.A.

PUBLICATIONS

Verse

The Forever Young.   Denver, Swallow, 1948.
The Forever Young and Other Poems.   Denver, Swallow, 1957.
Across Countries of Anywhere.   New York, Knopf, 1971.

*

Critical Studies: by George P. Elliott, in *Choice 9*, 1975; Nancy Sullivan, in *Poetry Pilot* (New York), September 1980.

*   *   *

The landscape of Pauline Hanson's poetry is stark, vast, and abstract; seasons slip into seasons, years into centuries, one dead into many, the flesh into spirit—and all are unspecified. Frequently, the nameless persona stands before the altars of the night ("Like Anyone Who Waits Here" from *Across Countries of Anywhere* or "Poems for the Night" from *The Forever Young and Other Poems*) and struggles to think her way out of the silence and into a knowledge of death, love, and her place in the scheme of things. The roads she travels are time and space; the people she meets are spectres and shadows, as in "The Ways":

And once, beyond the words of it,
slowly then all suddenly,
imagined in the longest night
the way, the only way, was time...

When you touched me, when I touched you,
when your shadows, when my shadows,
shimmered into the sensuous flesh
of my body, of your body:
lust into lust we moved and then—
then dreamed from every secret self
of our remembering, it was
like lost...like found...like always love.

Whether Hanson practices a mental athleticism as she speculates on atomic theory, astrophysics and Hindu mysticism in "The Questions of the One Question," or whether in her less pretentious long poem, "The Forever Young and Never Free" (originally titled "The Forever Young"), she fashions her story in the form of arduous questionings, she characteristically leads her reader through tight paradoxes and tortured syntax unrelieved by conventional imagery to an understanding of life's mysteries.

In "The Forever Young" and many other of her poems, it is a particular death, the death of her lover, that lies behind all the deaths she probes and gives her verse its poignancy and power. This lover also figures in poems where the living and dead are fused in love and love transcends the bonds of time: "Love is to the farthest place—/love is to so far a place/from always its greater distances,/to see where death was, I look back" ("And I Am Old To Know"). Hanson's refusal to employ figurative language and her insistence on a limited vocabulary of familiar but haunting words used repetitively contribute to the ritualistic, hypnotic quality of her poetry: "Where the constant winter was,-/where stricken from myself I went/into the cold and colder sweep/of snow on snow already deep" ("The Ways"). At times her heavy dependence upon repetition coupled with her habit of leaving her pronouns without referents renders her verse unintelligible rather than ambiguous; but generally, her craft does not falter and the austere language is poetically effective. That she can evoke concrete images is illustrated in several of her poems. Eager to celebrate the living and contrast it to the unknown, she recalls a "small bird's crimson flight" ("The Forever Young"). In "So Beautiful Is the Tree of Night" the arched branches of the great tree are etched against the sky. In the grotesque lines of "We Meet," she appalls us with her piteous image of the hanging jew child:

*   *   *

....Of God who for these hours is to let him hang here—
  with his hands tied, with his feet tied—put here for others
     to look at—
  put up here as high as he has seen at home branches hang
     and
  he reached up his hand but could not touch the flowers on
     them,
  could not touch the shining apples on them.

But these images are rare. Generally, her poetry is one of questioning, examining life's paradoxes. Like Gerontion, she keeps reminding her reader and herself to "think now." Her setting is astral; the ways she travels take her beyond time; and her place is nowhere and anywhere as she tries to answer "Who I am?"

—Carol Simpson Stern

HARPER, Michael S(teven).   American.   Born in Brooklyn, New York, 18 March 1938. Educated at City College of Los Angeles, A.A. 1959; California State University, Los Angeles, B.A. 1961, M.A. in English 1963; University of Iowa, Iowa City, M.A. 1963; University of Illinois, Urbana, 1970-71. Married Shirley Ann Buffington in 1965; one daughter and two sons. Taught at Contra Costa College, San Pablo, California, 1964-68; Reed College and Lewis and Clark College, Portland,

Oregon, 1968-69; California State University, Hayward, 1970. Since 1971, Professor of English, and since 1983, Kapstein Professor, Brown University, Providence, Rhode Island. Recipient: American Academy award, 1972; Black Academy of Arts and Letters award, 1972; Guggenheim Fellowship, 1976; National Endowment for the Arts grant, 1977; Melville Cane Award, 1977. Address: Box 1852, Brown University, Providence, Rhode Island 02912, U.S.A.

PUBLICATIONS

Verse

Dear John, Dear Coltrane. Pittsburgh, University of Pittsburgh Press, 1970.
History Is Your Own Heartbeat. Urbana, University of Illinois Press, 1971.
Photographs: Negatives: History as Apple Tree. San Francisco, Scarab Press, 1972.
Song: I Want a Witness. Pittsburgh, University of Pittsburgh Press, 1972.
Debridement. New York, Doubleday, 1973.
Nightmare Begins Responsibility. Urbana, University of Illinois Press, 1974.
Images of Kin: New and Selected Poems. Urbana, University of Illinois Press, 1977.
Rhode Island: Eight Poems. Roslindale, Massachusetts, Pym Randall Press, 1981.
Healing Song for the Inner Ear. Urbana, University of Illinois Press, 1984.

Other

Editor, *Heartblow: Black Veils* (anthology). Urbana, University of Illinois Press, 1975.
Editor, with Robert B. Stepto, *Chant of Saints: A Gathering of Afro-American Literature, Art, and Scholarship.* Urbana, University of Illinois Press, 1979.
Editor, *The Collected Poems of Sterling A. Brown.* New York, Harper, 1980.

*

Critical Study: unpublished dissertation by Joseph Raffa, Columbia University, New York, 1984.

*   *   *

Michael S. Harper's collections reveal a broad diversity of themes and his disparate interests, ranging from music (jazz and blues), to nature (birth and death), to history and myth. But it is soon apparent that they are manifestations of a highly sensitized Black witness within whom all these themes coalesce and then are transposed into emotional and spiritual expressions. Harper states that "relationships between speech and body, between men, between men and cosmology are central to my poetry."

In certain respects his poetry defies characterization for it is controlled by intensely personal rhythms emanating from his deeply rooted jazz and blues impulses. (He tells us for example that "Billie Holiday played piano in my family's house when I was 12.") At the same time the scope of his writing is attuned to a historical sense of moment, something of what T.S. Eliot called a perception not only of the pastness of the past, but of its presence. Harper sets out to affirm his conviction that man must not allow himself to be dislocated from his historical continuum:

"When there is no history there is no metaphor." It is with such conviction that his poetry at once synthesizes and articulates this sensibility. And it is out of his own Blackness as well as his own humanness that Africa is viewed as the "potent ancestor" providing "a strong ancestral base that reflects the African spirit wherever it is located":

> And we go back to the well: Africa,
> the first mode, and man, modally,
> touched the land of the continent,
> modality: we are one; a man is another
> man's face, modality, in continuum,
> from man, to man, contact-high, to man....

It is out of this spiritual and historical consciousness as well that Michael Harper defines relationships between people and the cosmos, and generates metaphor:

> This suture is race
> as it is blood,
> long as the frozen
> lake building messages
> on typewritten paper,
> faces of my ancestors,
> warm in winter only
> as their long scars touch ours.

Conviction of course means responsibility; Harper's responsibility as poet is to take on "the very tenuous 'business' of operating on historical legacies," creating a "clinical imagery to draw attention, to shock a reader with a detailed, medical closeness and approximation." Thus, when surgeon is poet and flesh is landscape with its history, tradition and myth, debridement becomes metaphor and restoration becomes image. In this sense Michael Harper's poems may be perceived as "healing songs."

> Ragboned Bob Hayden, shingled in slime,
> reaches for his cereus ladder of midnight flight,
> his seismographic heartbeats
> sphinctered in rhiney polygraphs of light:
> Dee-troit born and half-blind
> in diction of arena and paradise,
> his ambient nightmare-dreams streak his tongue;
> mementos of his mother, of Erma, he image-makes
> peopling the human family of God's mirror,
> mingling realities, this creature of transcendence
> a love-filled shadow, congealed and clarified.

—Charles L. James

———

HARRIS, (Theodore) Wilson. British. Born in New Amsterdam, British Guiana, now Guyana, 24 March 1921. Educated at Queen's College, Georgetown. Married 1) Cecily Carew in 1945; 2) Margaret Whitaker in 1959. Government Surveyor in the 1940's, and Senior Surveyor, 1955-58, Government of British Guiana; moved to London in 1959. Visiting Lecturer, State University of New York, Buffalo, 1970; Writer-in-Residence, University of the West Indies, Kingston, Jamaica, and Scarborough College, University of Toronto, 1970; Commonwealth Fellow in Caribbean Literature, Leeds University, Yorkshire, 1971; Visiting Professor, University of Texas, Austin, 1972, and

1981-82, University of Mysore, 1978, Yale University, New Haven, Connecticut, 1979, and University of Newcastle, New South Wales, 1979; Regents Lecturer, University of California, Santa Cruz, 1983. Delegate to the National Identity Conference, Brisbane, 1968; to Unesco Symposium on Caribbean Literature, Cuba, 1968. Recipient: Arts Council grant, 1968, 1970; Guggenheim Fellowship, 1973; Henfield Writing Fellowship, 1974; Southern Arts Writing Fellowship, 1976. Address: c/o Faber and Faber Ltd., 3 Queen Square, London WC1N 3AU, England.

PUBLICATIONS

Verse

Fetish.   Privately printed, 1951.
The Well and the Land.   Georgetown, Magnet, 1952.
Eternity to Season.   Privately printed, 1954; revised edition, London, New Beacon, 1979.

Novels

The Guiana Quartet:
  Palace of the Peacock.   London, Faber, 1960.
  The Far Journey of Oudin.   London, Faber, 1961.
  The Whole Armour.   London, Faber, 1962.
  The Secret Ladder.   London, Faber, 1963.
Heartland.   London, Faber, 1964.
The Eye of the Scarecrow.   London, Faber, 1965.
The Waiting Room.   London, Faber, 1967.
Tumatumari.   London, Faber, 1968.
Ascent to Omai.   London, Faber, 1970.
Black Marsden: A Tabula Rasa Comedy.   London, Faber, 1972.
Companions of the Day and Night.   London, Faber, 1975.
Da Silva da Silva's Cultivated Wilderness, and Genesis of the Clowns.   London, Faber, 1977.
The Tree of the Sun.   London, Faber, 1978.
The Angel at the Gate.   London, Faber, 1982.
Carnival.   London, Faber, 1985.

Short Stories

The Sleepers of Roraima.   London, Faber, 1970.
The Age of the Rainmakers.   London, Faber, 1971.

Other

Tradition, The Writer, and Society: Critical Essays.   London, New Beacon, 1967.
History, Fable, and Myth in the Caribbean and Guianas.   Georgetown, National History and Arts Council, 1970.
Fossil and Psyche (lecture on Patrick White).   Austin, University of Texas, 1974.
Explorations: A Selection of Talks and Articles, edited by Hena Maes-Jelinek.   Aarhus, Denmark, Dangaroo Press, 1981.
The Womb of Space: The Cross-Cultural Imagination.   Westport, Connecticut, Greenwood Press, 1983.

*

Manuscript Collections: University of the West Indies, Mona, Kingston, Jamaica; University of Texas, Austin; University of Indiana, Bloomington; University of Guyana, Georgetown.

Critical Studies: "The Necessity of Poetry" by Louis James, and

"Kyk-over-Al and the Radicals" by Edward Brathwaite, in *New World* (Georgetown), 1966; *The Naked Design*, Aarhus, Denmark, Dangaroo Press, 1976, and *Wilson Harris*, Boston, Twayne, 1982, both by Hena Maes-Jelinek.

Wilson Harris comments:

(1970) *Fetish* and *Eternity to Season*, along with other miscellaneous poems of the early 1950's, stand at the beginning of an exploration which extends deeper and further at a later stage in my work in the novel over the 1960's. The development of the novels is foreshadowed, to some extent, in the earlier poems. Constant to that exploration within poem and novel is the use I continue to make of the brooding continental landscape of Guiana as a gateway to memory between races and cultures, Amerindian, European, African, Asian.

*   *   *

The poetry of Wilson Harris, like his contribution to the art of the novel since 1960 (he has published no poetry since this date), is outside the present mainstream of Caribbean writing in English. Like Martin Carter, also of Guyana, his metaphorical perception and expression are more akin to that of the Martiniquan poet Aimé Césaire and the Cuban writer Alejo Carpentier. One does not find in Harris's work the clear air of the anglophone islands' poets. His sensibility has been formed by the world of the Guyanese forest and its rivers, its complexities and contradictions ("Amazons"):

> The world-creating jungle
> travels eternity to season. Not an individual artifice
> this living movement
> this tide
> this paradoxical stream and stillness rousing reflection.

Harris's poetry is to be found in *Kyk-over-Al* and in the privately published *Eternity to Season*, which contain his most important poems. He does not concern himself with social conditions, individual problems, the "historical" colonial past, or a possible or impossible future. His themes are time (into which he subsumes history), creation, separation and unity. His burden is not the Faustian ego but the environmental collective. There is some evidence of the operation of a Hegelian/Marxist dialectic in his poems. When individuals appear in his poetry, they are gigantic mythologized figures like Hector "hero of time," Agamemnon, Achilles (the great runner) and Teiresias. Harris uses these figures, and simple material existences like rice, water and charcoal to initiate journeys both (and often simultaneously) into cosmic space and human time. Because of the nature of Harris's perception, some of his poetry is obscure (although most of it deposits its meaning after repeated reading) and sometimes (perhaps through the need to make meaning clear) Harris eschews metaphor for "prose" statement:

> But earth cannot simply be
> a cosmic and arbitrary discovery! what of its changing roots
> and purposive vitality? External and internal
> forces are separate illusions that move
> beyond the glitter and the gloom with a knife to cut inner and outer times from each other
> as they weave and interweave in the tapestry of life....

Earlier in this same poem, "Amazon," this *statement* had been already almost magically expressed as:

Branches against the sky smuggle to heaven the extreme
   beauty
of the world: the store-house of that very heaven
breaks walls to drop tall streams like falls.

The green islands of the world
and the bright leaves lift their tender blossom of sunrise
to offset arenas of sunset
and wear a wild rosette like blood.

This self same blossom burns the clouds....

Nor is Harris alone in this paradoxical riverain and arboreal
continuum. Two hundred years before his time, George Pinck-
ard, an English army doctor, travelling on Guyanese water,
received and recorded the same kind of environmental breakdown and unification that Harris has transmuted into poetry
(*Notes on the West Indies*, 1806, vol. 2, pages 470-71):

The watery medium made no impression upon the eye,
but the open azure expanse was seen the same, whether
we looked upwards or downwards. We seemed suspended in the centre of a hollow globe, having the same
concave arch above and below, with an inverted and an
upright forest on either hand. At one spot we met a huge
mass of earth resembling a small island, floating down
the silent river, with a variety of plants and shrubs growing upon it; and from the water being invisible, the perfect
reflection of this little plantation gave it the appearance
of a clump of young trees calmly moving in a wide
vacuum, with each plant growing perpendicularly upward
and downward, in precise resemblance. If we held out a
hand or an oar...the same was seen below, without discovering the limpid medium between them. In short we
seemed to move, like our globe itself, in ethereal space.

From this world, Harris has derived his sensibility. His achievement has been the creation of it into poetry. And at its best, this
poetry moves even beyond recreation into enactment; so that
often we are able to participate in the creation (out of elements of
space, time and material) of the poet's vision ("Vision at the
Well"):

Touched by vision
the light fingertips of rain pass softly
to change the stone and burden of her perfection
into rapt walls that house joy and pain and living
   imperfection.
Her cheeks are the dark glow of blood
beneath the frail temper of space and eternity, the history
of her flesh and blood is strange and new.

—Edward Kamau Brathwaite

HARRISON, Jim (James Thomas Harrison). American.
Born in Grayling, Michigan, 11 December 1937. Educated at
Michigan State University, East Lansing, B.A. 1960; M.A. in
comparative literature 1964. Married Linda King in 1960; two
daughters. Assistant Professor of English, State University of
New York, Stony Brook, 1965-66. Now lives on a farm in
Michigan. Recipient: National Endowment for the Arts grant,

1967, 1968, 1969; Guggenheim Fellowship, 1969. Agent: Robert
Datilla, 233 East 8th Street, New York, New York 10028.
Address: Box 120a, Lake Leelanau, Michigan 49653, U.S.A.

PUBLICATIONS

Verse

Plain Song. New York, Norton, 1965.
Locations. New York, Norton, 1968.
Walking. Cambridge, Massachusetts, Pym Randall Press, 1969.
Outlyer and Ghazals. New York, Simon and Schuster, 1971.
Letters to Yesenin. Fremont, Michigan, Sumac Press, 1973.
Returning to Earth. Ithaca, New York, Ithaca House, 1977.
Selected and New Poems 1961-1981. New York, Delacorte
   Press, 1982.

Novels

Wolf. New York, Simon and Schuster, 1971.
A Good Day to Die. New York, Simon and Schuster, 1973.
Farmer. New York, Viking Press, 1976.
Legends of the Fall (novellas). New York, Delacorte Press,
   1979; London, Collins, 1980.
Warlock. New York, Delacorte Press, and London, Collins,
   1981.
Sundog. New York, Dutton, 1984.

Other

Natural World, with Diana Guest. Barrytown, New York,
   Open Book, 1983.

*

Jim Harrison comments:
   I write "free verse" which is absurdly indefinite as a name for
what any poet writes. I consider myself an "internationalist" and
my main influences to be Neruda, Rilke, Yeats, Bunting, Lorca,
and, in my own country, Whitman, Hart Crane, Robert Duncan
and Ezra Pound. Not that this helps much other than to name
those I esteem, and, perhaps vacantly, wish to emulate. Most of
my poems seem rural, vaguely surrealistic though after the Spanish rather than the French. My sympathies run hotly to the
impure, the inclusive, as the realm of poetry. A poet, at best,
speaks in the "out loud speech of his tribe," deals in essences
whether political, social or personal. All of world literature is his
province though he sees it as a "guild" only to be learned from, as
he must speak in his own voice.

*   *   *

   The work of Jim Harrison is imbued with a deeply rooted
sense of place, and that place is in the middle of America in
northern Michigan, "the only locus I know." In "Ghazals" he
writes, "And I want to judge the poetry table at the County
Fair./A new form, poems stacked in pyramids like prize potatoes," and his volumes comprise a county fair of delights with
their stark, simple images of rural life. Poems such as "Young
Bull," "Lisle's River," and "Dead Deer" are Harrison's songs of
the plains.
   From the poet's sense of place comes an understanding of
nature's way. "I insist on a one-to-one relationship with nature,"
he says at one point, later adding, "I want to have my life/in
cloud shapes, water shapes, wind shapes,/crow call, marsh hawk

swooping over grass and weed tips." In poems such as "Cold August," "Natural World," and "February Swans," the shapes of nature are quietly celebrated. Consider "Dusk":

> Dusk over the lake,
> clouds floating
> heat lightning
> a nightmare behind branches;
> from the swamps
> the odor of cedar and fern,
> the long circular
> wail of the loon—
> the plump bird aches for fish
> for night to come down.
>
> Then it becomes so dark
> and still
> that I shatter the moon with an oar.

At the end of the sequence called "A Year's Changes," looking into a pool of black water the poet thinks,

> It appears bottomless,
> An oracle I should worship at; I want
> some part of me to be lost in it and return
> again from the darkness, changing the creature,
> or return to draw me back to a home.

In reflections of nature, Harrison looks into his own soul. His work is shallow, though, when nature is not there to provide a mirror or a muse. *Outlyer* is a disjointed and dispirited volume that includes poems praising whiskey and women "pliant as marshmellows." "All my poems are born dead," Harrison writes here. "I'm a bad poet." But he writes, "If I clean up my brain...the Sibyl well return as an undiscovered lover."

The Sibyl does indeed return with *Letters to Yesenin*, a profoundly powerful and affecting work. This long prose poem sequence is not only a homage to the Soviet poet Sergei Yesenin, but also a meditation on such topics as life, love, freedom, the poet's craft—and nature. This "suicide note to a suicide" is a "record of agony" in which Yesenin's sufferings in totalitarian Russia are juxtaposed with Harrison's pains in rural America. The self-pitying and egocentric tone of *Outlyer* is replaced here with compassion for all humanity. "A good poet is only a sorcerer bored with magic who has turned his attention elsewhere," Harrison writes, and here is a subject worthy of attention.

With this volume and with his following ones, Harrison has "returned to earth," has found the sure ground that is his proper subject. The example of Yesenin gives Harrison the power to shake off the suicidal musings of *Outlyer* and to choose life, with all of its elaborate sufferings and simple joys. Harrison closes his collected poems with "After Reading Takahasi" and closes that poem with a characteristic passage in which by looking at nature he is able to look past himself:

> I've been warned by a snowy night, an owl,
> the infinite black above and below me to look ·
> at all creatures and things with a billion eyes,
> not struggling with the single heartbeat
> that is my life.

—Dennis Lynch

HARRISON, Keith (Edward). Australian. Born in Melbourne, Victoria, 29 January 1932. Educated at Trinity Grammar School, Melbourne; Melbourne Teachers' College, 1951; University of Melbourne (Masefield Prize, 1954), 1952-54, B.A. in English and French 1954; University of Iowa, Iowa City, 1966-67, M.A. 1967. Married Inger Christina Götesdotter Haglund in 1965; two daughters: High school teacher, Victoria, 1954-57; lecturer, City Literary Institute, London, 1959-63; tutor, University of London Extra-Mural Department, 1963-65; Visiting Poet, University of Iowa, 1966; Lecturer in English, York University, Toronto, 1966-68. Assistant Professor, 1968-74, since 1974, Associate Professor of English, and since 1970, Director of the Arts Program, Carleton College, Northfield, Minnesota. Recipient: Canada Council grant, 1968; Department of Health, Education, and Welfare Seminar on South Asian Studies fellowship, 1969, 1970; Arts Council of Great Britain award, 1972. Address: Department of English, Carleton College, Northfield, Minnesota 55057, U.S.A.

PUBLICATIONS

Verse

Points in a Journey and Other Poems.   London, Macmillan, 1966; Chester Springs, Pennsylvania, Dufour, 1967.
Two Variations on a Ground.   London, Turret, 1968.
Songs from the Drifting House.   London, Macmillan, 1972.
The Basho Poems.   Iowa City, Cyathus Press, 1975.

Other

Translator, *Sir Gawain and the Green Knight.*   London, Folio Society, 1983.

*

Manuscript Collection: Carleton College Library, Northfield, Minnesota.

Critical Studies: reviews by Mingo Jones, in *Saturday Night* (Toronto), April 1967, Stan Fefferman, in *Toronto Telegram*, April 1967, and Carl Harrison-Ford, in *New Poetry* (Sydney), April 1973.

Keith Harrison comments:

(1974) Teaching still seems to me the best and worst job for a poet. Young people are so starved at their high schools for good literature—good art of any kind—that introducing them to poetry both at an interpretive and a creative level is an urgent necessity, as well as an exciting challenge. The trick is to find enough time for your own work—and no university poet whom I know has solved that one, except by becoming a public institution, an "instant personality."

To get to more substantial matters; I think there are stable mythic patterns. Chiefly: to grow, it would seem that artists, as well as everybody else, have to go through hell. Modern man is a neurotic mess and that is the ground we have to stand on. The evasive strategies of madness, suicide or incoherence simply won't do. The difficult thing, the damnably difficult thing, is to take one's private predicament and by imaginative heat to forge something hard and emblematic out of it. One hopes that on the other side of all that one will be able to write a poetry that is full of sunlight and broad humour (there is too little *pleasure* in contemporary poetry)—but there is no easy way out of hell. I have just finished a book of very dark poems and I hope the darkness is made acceptable by the validity and accuracy of the language. (I also hope it's the last dark thing that I ever do.)

Poetry readings are currently the dullest and most ill-organized form of entertainment we have. I would like, both as a writer and a reader to improve them to the level of, say, a concert given by a group of bright young musicians. The whole art of poetry—writing, understanding, reading aloud—is still in its infancy in this country, and in most others.

*   *   *

An Australian, Keith Harrison has lived and studied in both England and America for a considerable number of years. Like so many poets, he has found it necessary to work through the experiences of childhood before being able to experiment with new styles and ideas. His first book, *Points in a Journey*, records in an eight-part autobiographical poem, the discoveries he has made about himself, his family and his background. The second part of this book consists of a series of dramatic monologues of which the most outstanding is "Leichardt in the Desert" (Leichardt was a nineteenth-century German explorer who died while attempting to cross the Australian desert):

I did not choose to make this westward journey
Into the dry rock country of the dead
Where in the torpid light the lizards
Flick from our tracks into the mean rock shadows;
To slash that tunnel through the mountain forest,
Cross the grasslands, wade the inland rivers—
I did not choose; say rather I was called....

Other pieces of interest are "The Island Weather of the Newly Betrothed," "Wife Waiting" and "Dentist at Work." The third section contains more formal experiments, set in Spain and London, and these poems are not quite so successful as the rest.

In *Songs from the Drifting House*, Keith Harrison still persists in the role of ironic observer, commenting upon life as he sees it on his travels. "Swedish Vignettes" and "Midwestern Blues" make their point with due economy. The title of the book is taken from a series of lyrics which are pleasant enough but in no way outstanding. There are some competent translations from Ronsard, Baudelaire and Rimbaud, but overall one gains the impression of a poet lacking a real sense of direction. Harrison undoubtedly has talent, but so far his promise is greater than his achievement.

—Howard Sergeant

HARRISON, Tony. British. Born in Leeds, Yorkshire, 30 April 1937. Educated at Cross Flatts County Primary, Leeds, 1942-48; Leeds Grammar School, 1948-55; University of Leeds, 1955-60, B.A. in classics, postgraduate diploma in linguistics. Married Rosemarie Crossfield in 1962; one daughter and one son. Lecturer in English, Ahmadu Bello University, Zaria, Northern Nigeria, 1962-66, and Charles University, Prague, 1966-67; Editor, with Jon Silkin and Ken Smith, *Stand*, Newcastle upon Tyne, 1968-69; Resident Dramatist, National Theatre, London, 1977-78. Delegate, Conference on Colonialism and the

Arts, Dar-es-Salaam, Tanzania, July 1971. Recipient: Northern Arts fellowship, 1967, 1976; Cholmondeley Award, 1969; Unesco fellowship, 1969; Faber Memorial Award, 1972; Gregynog Fellowship, 1973; U.S. Bicentennial Fellowship, 1979; European Poetry Translation Prize, 1983. Address: 9 The Grove, Gosforth, Newcastle upon Tyne NE3 1NE, England.

PUBLICATIONS

Verse

Earthworks. Leeds, Northern House, 1964.
Newcastle Is Peru. Newcastle upon Tyne, Eagle Press, 1969.
The Loiners. London, London Magazine Editions, 1970.
Corgi Modern Poets in Focus 4, with others, edited by Jeremy Robson. London, Corgi, 1971.
Ten Poems from the School of Eloquence. London, Rex Collings, 1976.
The School of Eloquence and Other Poems. London, Rex Collings, 1978.
Looking Up, with Phillip Sharpe. West Malvern, Worcestershire, Migrant Press, 1979.
Continuous: 50 Sonnets from the School of Eloquence. London, Rex Collings, 1981.
A Kumquat for John Keats. Newcastle upon Tyne, Bloodaxe, 1981.
U.S. Martial. Newcastle upon Tyne, Bloodaxe, 1981.
Selected Poems. London, Viking Press, 1984.
The Fire-Gap. Newcastle upon Tyne, Bloodaxe, 1985.

Plays

Aikin Mata, with James Simmons, adaptation of *Lysistrata* by Aristophanes (produced Zaria, Nigeria, 1965). Ibadan, Oxford University Press, 1966.
The Misanthrope, adaptation of a play by Molière (produced London, 1973; Washington, D.C., and New York, 1975). London, Rex Collings, 1973; New York, Third Press, 1974.
Phaedra Britannica, adaptation of the play by Racine (produced London, 1975). London, Rex Collings, 1975.
Bow Down, music by Harrison Birtwistle (produced London, 1977). London, Rex Collings, 1977.
The Passion, from the York Mystery Plays (produced London, 1977). London, Rex Collings, 1977; Totowa, New Jersey, Rowman and Littlefield, 1978.
The Bartered Bride, adaptation of an opera by Sabina, music by Smetana (produced New York, 1978). New York, Schirmer, 1978; in *Dramatic Verse*, 1985.
The Oresteia, music by Harrison Birtwistle, adaptation of the plays by Aeschylus (produced London, 1981). London, Rex Collings, 1981; Totowa, New Jersey, Rowman and Littlefield, 1982.
The Big H, music by Dominic Muldowney (televised, 1984). Included in *Dramatic Verse*, 1985.
Dramatic Verse 1973-1985 (includes *The Misanthrope, The Bartered Bride, Phaedra Britannica, Bow Down, The Big H*). Newcastle upon Tyne, Bloodaxe, 1985.

Television Play: *The Big H*, music by Dominic Muldowney, 1984.

Other

Translator, *Poems*, by Palladas. London, Anvil Press Poetry, 1975.

*

Manuscript Collections: University of Newcastle upon Tyne; Newcastle Literary and Philosophical Society.

*   *   *

Tony Harrison is very much his own man in contemporary British poetry, having little in common with any recognisable school or movement. This detachment is reflected in the fact that he has usually been published by small or out-of-the-way presses; and it is reflected, more integrally, in his subject matter, which has consistently had to do with the tensions and pressures of having been born into the northern English working class, but having been educated away from it by a university degree in classics, that most deeply traditional and conservative of all English liberal educations. The desire to speak in poetry for those who have had no voice in literature for themselves informs a great deal of Harrison's work. He goes to sources in the history of Europe for exemplary instances of power and political and religious oppression, as in his terrifying poem—a monologue by Queen Isabella—on the Inquisition, "The Nuptial Torches." And he derives a kind of aesthetic, and certainly a rationale, from the way such things are central in his conception of his own family:

> How you became a poet's a mystery!
> Wherever did you get your talent from?
>
> I say, I had two uncles, Joe and Harry—
> one was a stammerer, the other dumb.

As this suggests, Harrison's material necessarily makes him profoundly self-conscious about his own role as a poet. He is, in fact, more public in his work than many poets, having worked on translations and versions for the National Theatre—notably his very controversial version of the Oresteia—and on libretti for international opera companies. The cosmopolitan glamour of the life such work gives him, when it features in poems juxtaposed with poems on his origins, has occasionally, I think, an element of the over-insistent: the tone in which he tells us, for instance, about receiving a gift of guavas—a fruit shaped like the female pudendum—from Jane Fonda is altogether uncertain and distasteful.

In general, however, Harrison is a highly intelligent poet very much in control of his effects. He is also, formally, highly ingenious: the most telling ironies in his work derive from form itself. His iambics, his couplets, his octosyllabics—when combined with Harrison's demotic and colloquial—subvert the aristocratic and bourgeois traditions which fostered them. His sixteen-line Meredithian sonnet sequence, The School of Eloquence—a sequence in progress and likely to be so, perhaps, for some time—makes this plain enough: in, for instance, "Turns":

> I thought it made me look more "working class"
> (as if a bit of chequered cloth could bridge that gap!)
> I did a turn in it before the glass.
> My mother said: It suits you, your dad's cap.
> (She preferred me to wear suits and part my hair:
> You're every bit as good as that lot are!)

> All the pension crew came out to stare.
> Dad was sprawled beside the postbox (still VR),
> his cap turned inside up beside his head,
> smudged H A H in purple Indian ink
> and Brylcreem slicks displayed so folk might think
> he wanted charity for dropping dead.
>
> He never begged. For nowt! Death's reticence
> Crowns his life's, and me, I'm opening my trap
> to busk the class that broke him for the pence
> that splash like brackish tears into our cap.

The plangency here, as in many poems in the sequence, runs the severe risk of mawkishness. Christopher Reid has suggested that the mawkishness may be deliberate: a sort of awkwardness of emotion to parallel the undoubted awkwardnesses of rhythm and metaphor in the sequence—both dedicated to revising the middle-class reader's notions of the poetically acceptable. This may be true: there is certainly the sense that the poem has earned its plangencies; the familiar tenderness is close to class despair, and it admits that anything subversive in Harrison must do battle with every poet's complicity, in some ways, with the owners of the language he uses. There remains, however, the awkward fact, an awkwardness presumably not intended, that not all of these poems are at all as effective on a second reading as they are on the first: there can, sometimes, seem an element of the factitious or the histrionic in them.

Perhaps the best of Tony Harrison will, in the end, turn out to be the work in which he achieves a greater measure of release for his wit and humour, his sensuousness, and his delighted eroticism—such as, for instance, the long poem in couplets, A Kumquat for John Keats. Despite my own reservations about the procedures of some poems in The School of Eloquence, there is no doubt that Harrison is one of the most important and challenging poets now writing in English: he is one of the few whose every new poem can be awaited with real expectation.

—Neil Corcoran

HARSENT, David.   British.   Born in Devonshire, 9 December 1942. Divorced; one daughter and two sons. Bookseller in Aylesbury; then worked for the publishers Eyre Methuen, Arrow Books, and Deutsch, all London; ran his own imprint, Enigma; fiction critic, Times Literary Supplement, London, 1965-73, and poetry critic, Spectator, London, 1970-73; now a full-time writer. Recipient: Eric Gregory Award, 1967; Cheltenham Festival prize, 1968; Arts Council bursary, 1969; Faber Memorial Award, 1978. Lives in London. Address: c/o Oxford University Press, Walton Street, Oxford OX2 6DP, England.

PUBLICATIONS

Verse

Tonight's Lover.   London, The Review, 1968.
A Violent Country.   London, Oxford University Press, 1969.
Ashridge.   Oxford, Sycamore Press, 1970.
After Dark.   London, Oxford University Press, 1973.
Truce.   Oxford, Sycamore Press, 1973.
Dreams of the Dead.   London, Oxford University Press, 1977.
Mister Punch.   Oxford, Oxford University Press, 1984.

Novel

From an Inland Sea.   London, Viking Press, 1985.

Other

Editor, *New Poetry 7.*   London, Hutchinson, 1981.

*   *   *

Pain, frustration, madness, and death are enduring themes in David Harsent's poetry. In *A Violent Country* he writes with raw intensity and directness, often relying heavily on descriptive detail and perhaps showing greater concern with the projection of experience than with the perfection of poetic form. Both in this collection and in *After Dark*, many of the poems gravitate to the "confessional," focusing on personal experience conveyed either by direct observation (as in "Going Back" or "The Visit" in *A Violent Country*) or through attempts to recover forgotten but formative childhood events (as in "Old Photographs" or "Homecoming" in *After Dark*).

For Harsent, "All we know of love / is pain and the response to pain" ("Fishbowl" in *Dreams of the Dead*), and tenderness is balanced with the harshness—if compassion—of his madness and death poems, sometimes by vivid juxtaposition. "A girl, I dreamt you as / a kind of fable: Keats, / Orlando, Abelard," for example, is set against the actuality of "a rutting beast, / mad cells, / a cup of blood" ("The Love-Match" in *A Violent Country*).

In the later poems of *After Dark* Harsent begins to use the physical world to achieve an emotional distancing which extends his range beyond his personal experience. "Figures in a Landscape," for example, ends:

> Too tired to sleep and knowing of no way
> to quieten you, I've walked to this cold bench.
>
> Above the fields
> mountains of purple cloud lumber through drizzle.
>
> Between your open window and this place
> the land is dark and wringing wet.

This anchoring of personal experience in landscape and places is extended to link series of images in the poem-sequences of *Dreams of the Dead*. The poetry becomes less static and more versatile with personal experience placed in a larger perspective and events in themselves becoming less important.

The first Punch poems in *Dreams of the Dead* mark a move to archetypal images—primitive, irrational, internalised images that form the mythological substratum to all human experience. Indeed, Punch himself "feels so old, something primordial..." ("Punch and the Judy") and Harsent's latest collection of poems, *Mister Punch*, introduces him as Trickster, a spirit of disorder that undermines and disrupts order and reality but reinstates a sense of proportion. From poem to poem, Punch progresses from his traditional dissipation, violence, and cunning ("He could taste blood / at the back of his throat— / a hound / led out for the chase"—"Punch in the Ancient World") to contemplation of "his sickness and sin" ("Punch the Anchorite") to penitence and pleas of "Virgin intercede" ("Punch at His Devotions").

Mister Punch opens with a quotation from C.G. Jung. Within this framework, portraying a general search for identity, Punch tries to reconcile *puer aeternus* aspects of the Trickster archetype—indulging in fantasies, living out experiences for their own sake and engaging in casual, promiscuous relationships—with

aspects of the *senex* such as the wisdom born of experience, the exercise of judgment, and a respect for tradition—a reconciliation which attempts to retain positive qualities of the *puer aeternus* such as energy, enthusiasm, and innovative skill. Certainly "Punch at His Devotions" addresses novel prayers to the Virgin:

> Loved One, Flawless Mirror,
> Tamer of Unicorns, Dove,
> Star of the Sea, I enter
> A plea of diminished laughter.

Harsent, while still retaining the incisive and powerful elements characteristic of his earlier poetry, has, in *Mister Punch*, considerably enlarged his vision.

—B.T. Kugler

———————

HART, Kevin.   Australian.   Born in London, England, 5 July 1954; moved to Australia in 1966. Educated at Australian National University, Canberra (Tillyard Award, 1976), 1973-76, B.A. (honours) 1977; Stanford University, California (Stegner Fellow), 1977-78; graduate study, University of Melbourne, since 1983. Co-ordinator, Department of Philosophy and Religious Studies, Geelong College, Victoria, 1979-83. Since 1979, part-time tutor, Humanities Faculty, Deakin University, Victoria; since 1984, part-time lecturer in philosophy, Melbourne University. Recipient: Neilson prize, 1976; Australian Literature Board Fellowship, 1977; Fulbright award, 1977; Harri Jones award, 1982. Address: 4 Calder Street, Manifold Heights, Victoria 3218, Australia.

PUBLICATIONS

Verse

Nebuchadnezzar.   Canberra, Open Door Press, 1976.
The Departure.   Brisbane, University of Queensland Press, 1978.
The Lines of the Hand: Poems 1976-1979.   Sydney, Angus and Robertson, 1981.
Your Shadow.   Sydney, Angus and Robertson, 1984.

*   *   *

Kevin Hart is an accomplished poet in a variety of forms, ranging from the prose poem to the sonnet and sestina. His early book *The Departure* perhaps leaned too heavily on an empty formalism deriving from the Movement poets of the 1950's and ultimately from the much richer formalism of Auden. This formalism produced a number of tired lines such as these: "Those years rise up and peel away. I see / I cannot exempt myself from history." But already in this book Hart was capable of the tough precision and brilliance of the sonnet "Lovers," which concludes:

> I stroke you slowly
> downwards, then kiss and sip the chalice
>
> between your thighs. I shift again,
> closer, and push into your body
> hard, until you close around me—

immediate, suffuse. Your eyes
are jammed open with joy and strain
as all about us darkness dies.

His next two books, *The Lines of the Hand* and *Your Shadow*, demonstrate an increasing emancipation of verse form which coincided with his conversion to the Anglican and later the Catholic Church. It seems likely that the formalized passion of Christianity provided a channel for the genuine religious emotion of these books, freeing language as well as feeling.

His devotional poems look back to the metaphysical poets of the 17th century, particularly George Herbert, for their inspiration. This affectionate pietism can be heard in the opening lines of "To Christ Our Lord":

My only friend,
whose face I could not recognize in a
    crowd,
whose voice would not make me turn,
forgive me for thinking such things important,
for trusting in only what I can touch.

But it is also a tone of voice which is typically 20th century European (as distinct from Anglo-Saxon) and abstract in its sensibility, employing symbols such as clocks, fields, the wind, trees as objects in a dream landscape having no reference to a particular time or place. Both volumes include a number of translations from modern European poets. Perhaps his most successful translation is "The Flies" from the Spanish of Antonio Machado.

Your Shadow presents itself as a spiritual *livre composé*, a pilgrimage from darkness into light. The volume contains a number of poems called "Your Shadow." These "shadow" poems with their invocation of "your body's very own black flower" tend to be too genteel and morbid in their introversion. The dualism and belief in original sin which permeate these poems are difficult for the non-Christian to appreciate, although Hart's poems of religious affirmation and celebration will be enjoyed by most readers. "Easter Psalm" is an affectionate and controlled poem with a classic simplicity and restraint. The book concludes with "Poem to the Sun," which is an exultation in Christ, and is equally fine.

These two later volumes include a different vein of poetry which is just as successful as the devotional poems. "The Members of the Orchestra" and "Nadia Comanechi" are successful this-worldly poems with great energy and control of language. These lines from "The Hammer" demonstrate equal power:

This is the sanctus, the pause for preparation, for

screwing the mind's energies tightly into muscle;
this is the archer's erasure of himself from his tense
matrix of forces, the moment of conditioned release

when the mind delights in its freedom to step outside
and adore the body, a perfected instrument of will.
And so the instant comes, intense and blurred, the head

strikes the nail through the knotted grain, jumping
back as though appalled by such precise violence and
for a moment containing the man's mind, pure energy.

—Geoffrey Lehmann

HART-SMITH, William. Australian. Born in Tunbridge Wells, Kent, England, 23 November 1911; emigrated to New Zealand in 1924, and to Australia in 1936; retired to New Zealand. Educated in Scotland; St. Clair, Walmer, Kent; Gunnersbury Preparatory School, London; Belmont Primary School, Auckland; Seddon Memorial Technical College, Auckland. Served in the Australian military forces, 1941-43. Married 1) M. Wynn in 1939 (marriage dissolved, 1949); 2) P.A. McBeath in 1949 (separated); four children. Clerk, New Zealand Shipping Company, Auckland, 1926-27; radio salesman and mechanic, Wisemans Ltd., Auckland, 1927-30; radio serviceman, Auckland, 1930-36, and Baden-Cameron company, Hobart, Tasmania, 1936-37; radio copywriter and announcer, Station 2CH, Sydney, 1937-44; free-lance writer, Sydney, 1944-47; tutor organizer, Adult Education Department, Canterbury, New Zealand, 1948-55; advertising copywriter, Jack Penny Ltd., Christchurch, 1956-60; manager, Christchurch Office, 1960-62, and advertising manager, Sydney, 1962-66, Charles Kidd and Company; radio technician, Amalgamated Wireless of Australasia, Sydney, 1966-70; clerk and part-time tutor, Western Australian Institute of Technology, Perth, 1972-78. President, Poetry Society of Australia, 1963-64. Recipient: Crouch Memorial Medal, 1959; Grace Leven Prize, 1967; three Australian Arts Council fellowships, 1973-78. Agent: Angus and Robertson Ltd., P.O. Box 290, North Ryde, New South Wales 2113, Australia. Address: 17 Raeben Avenue, Takapuna, Auckland, New Zealand.

PUBLICATIONS

Verse

Columbus Goes West. Adelaide, Economy Press, 1943.
Harvest. Melbourne, Georgian House, 1945.
The Unceasing Ground. Sydney, Angus and Robertson, 1946.
Christopher Columbus: A Sequence of Poems. Christchurch, Caxton Press, 1948.
On the Level: Mostly Canterbury Poems. Timaru, New Zealand, Timaru Herald, 1950.
Poems in Doggerel. Wellington, Handcraft Press, 1955.
Poems of Discovery. Sydney, Angus and Robertson, 1959.
The Talking Clothes. Sydney, Angus and Robertson, 1966.
Poetry from Australia: Pergamon Poets 6, with Judith Wright and Randolph Stow, edited by Howard Sergeant. Oxford, Pergamon Press, 1969.
Minipoems. Perth, Western Australian Institute of Technology, 1974.
Let Me Learn the Steps: Poems from a Psychiatric Ward, with Mary Morris. Privately printed, 1977.

*

Manuscript Collection: Fisher Library, University of Sydney.

Critical Studies: *Australian Literature* by E. Morris Miller and F.T. Macartney, revised edition, Sydney, Angus and Robertson, 1956; by Sister Veronica Brady, in *Westerly* (Perth), March 1976.

William Hart-Smith comments:
Began reading widely, age of 19. Shortly after 21st birthday made a definite decision to be a poet and stay with it at all costs, earning a living as best I could. Have travelled widely both in Australia and New Zealand, so that "landscape and spirit of place" are strongly in evidence. Was closely associated with an Australian nationalist movement, "Jindyworobak," early 1940's. Have experimented with form, style, and method a great deal.

Strongest early influences were from two New Zealand poets, Gloria Rawlinson and D'Arcy Cressswell; later, in Australia, matured suddenly, particularly because of the profound effect the Australian environment had on me. Main literary influences would be D. H. Lawrence, Ezra Pound, and modern American poetry in general which gave me carte blanche to experiment. Read much of the Imagists so that the main aim would appear to be to concentrate with an almost painterly eye on the concrete visual image. However prime intention is, using the Sufi approach, to let the image itself and the reader's enjoyment of it as an image per se, to disguise, or merely hint at, what the visual image is really trying to say, or stand in for. Many poems, therefore, are little parables, or poems using the device of parable. It's the only way I can find effectively to verbalise moments of insight and intuition. Another aim has been extreme compression, at the same time to listen to the verbal music the words make. The poems are never just dashed off as some may think: the original draft is only the starting point of an attempt to give even the shortest, Zen-like poem a strictly disciplined structure of interlocking rhyme and para-rhyme, assonance and dissonance. In other words, no matter how compressed the poem may be, how sparingly the words are used, the aim is to retain the poem's authenticity as a work of thorough craftsmanship and be a pleasure to the ear as well as the eye; or, act as a stimulus to the reader's *own* imagination, no matter what level of consciousness he can reach. Most of my poems record brief moments of extreme joy and delight. Insights, Discoveries, moments of Understanding.

*   *   *

Over the years since 1936, William Hart-Smith, who left England at the age of twelve, has consistently written of his adopted country, Australia, and sometimes of New Zealand where he has also lived some years. His spare economy of language, the simple, usually free, shapes of his poems and the lucidity and apparent casualness of their statements have kept his work from becoming fashionable, but also lent it strength. He seems to have found his way easily into both his new countries as providers of symbol and background, and his pithy conversational rhythms have much in common with their speech.

Few of his poems take much space to make their point. His one long poem, *Christopher Columbus*, consists of forty-three short poems, few of more than page-length, each devoted to some aspect of Columbus' story and each complete in itself. Comment is kept at a minimum; with Hart-Smith, it is selection that does the commenting; and he chooses his momentary glimpses of the voyages, or his quotations from the documents, much as a good documentary film-maker does, for their visual or human illuminations.

There is, indeed, something of document in many of his poems, directed as they are towards objects, events or persons. To write this kind of verse, into which the poet as person intrudes so minimally, is not easy, if the poet is to avoid a cool pedestrianism of vision. This danger for Hart-Smith's poetry is increased by the fact that though his vision is individual, ironic and continually interesting, it does not seem to be directed through any deep interior conviction or world-view. This apparent lack of thematic connection between separate poems is reinforced by the lack of much change or apparent poetic development over the years, though there has been a perceptible increase in tautness of manner, a sharpening of his use of language, and a lessening in his earlier more lyrical attack.

An important influence in his work was the "Jindyworobak" movement, through which a group of Australian poets attempted to work their way into a "native" attitude to Australian themes. Hart-Smith was one of the most distinguished of the poets in the movement, and his verse still displays some of their characteristic tenets. In a comment on the movement's achievement, he once wrote: "It is more than a few rather fanatical individuals trying to be exclusively and most Aboriginally Australian in the English language; it's a case of a number of creative writers pointing the way back to...the childhood of the human race, 'to a land that is common to us all.'" His poems, he says, are "poems of discovery," "attempts to record moments of understanding." Their concentration on objects and events of the outer world is motivated by this attempt to re-see them in a fresh light.

At his best, he does this with memorable individuality. Such poem-titles as "Boomerang," "Bathymeter," "A Snail," "Number," "Candles" indicate the directions in which he turns the searchlight of his verse.

Though he has published a number of books of verse, no complete collection has yet appeared. When this happens, it will be possible to see that, instead of a succession of descriptive and commentary verses, he has produced a gallery of portraits and still-lifes that illuminate the world from the viewpoint of an original and ironic mind.

—Judith Wright

HARTNETT, Michael. Gaelic name: Mícheál Ó hAirtnéide. Irish. Born in County Limerick, 18 September 1941. Educated at Newcastle West Secondary School; University College, Dublin; Trinity College, Dublin. Married; one daughter. Has worked as civil servant, dishwasher, postman, tea-boy, housepainter, telephonist; currently teacher, National College of Physical Education, Limerick. Contributor to *Irish Times*, Dublin, and Radio Eireann. Editor, with James Liddy and Liam O'Connor, *Arena*, Dublin, 1963-65. Recipient: Irish American Cultural Institute Award, 1975; Irish Arts Council Award, 1975. Address: c/o Gallery Press, 19 Oakdown Road, Dublin 14, Ireland.

PUBLICATIONS

Verse

Anatomy of a Cliché.   Dublin, Dolmen Press, 1968.
Selected Poems.   Dublin, New Writers Press, 1971.
Cúlúide, The Retreat of Ita Cagney (Gaelic and English).   Dublin, Goldsmith Press, 1975.
A Farewell to English and Other Poems.   Dublin, Gallery Press, 1975; revised edition, edited by Peter Fallon, 1978.
Poems in English.   Dublin, Dolmen Press, 1977.
Prisoners.   Deerfield, Massachusetts, Deerfield Press, 1978.
Adharca Broic (Gaelic).   Dublin, Gallery Press, 1978.
Daoine (Gaelic).   Dublin, Gallery Press, 1979.

Other

Editor, with Desmond Egan, *Choice: An Anthology of Irish Poetry.*   Dublin, Goldsmith Press, 1970; revised edition, 1979.

Translator, *The Hag of Beare: A Rendition of the Old Irish.* Dublin, New Writers Press, 1970.
Translator, *Gipsy Ballads*, by Lorca.   Dublin, Goldsmith Press, 1970.

Translator, *Tao: A Version of the Tao Te Ch'ing*.   Dublin, New Writers Press, 1972.

*

Critical Study: interview in *The Poet Speaks*, edited by Peter Orr, London, Routledge, and New York, Barnes and Noble, 1966.

Michael Hartnett comments:

Major themes: The woman as human being; deaths (not *Death*); "nature" in human terms.

Characteristic Subjects: Love Poems; the hunting of animals; wake poems.

Usual Verse Forms: Lyric, syllabic, assonantal, rhyme (sparingly), metric (rarely in the classical sense); developing more complex forms.

General Sources and Influences: Mainstream English poetry; Gaelic poetry.

Characteristic Stylistic Devices: Compound words; anglosaxon (*not* in the D.H. Lawrence sense) vocabulary; the animal as symbol.

*   *   *

Michael Hartnett's achievement as a poet so far has been distinguished by its emotional intensity, its scrupulous attention to the subtleties of craftsmanship, its thematic variety, and its essentially experimental and adventurous character. In his work, intelligence and music play equally important parts. There is no arid intellectualizing, no meaningless melody. Reading through his output so far, one has the sense of a dedicated artist who refuses to admit anything shabby or shoddy into his work. Some critics in fact say that Hartnett is fastidious to the point of being finicky, that his obsession with technique conceals very serious emotional limitations. This, to my mind, is a complete misreading of Hartnett's purpose and achievement. Hartnett, as far as I can see, has the full equipment for a poet of stature. He is well on his way to becoming a master of language, his *own* language; he has a keen ear for the subtlest rhythms; almost everything he writes haunts the reader for its cutting insight expressed in appropriate verbal music; and, above all, his poems at their best have that quiet authority which is the surest mark of confidence.

Take, for example, the last of "Four Sonnets," from *Selected Poems*:

> I saw magic on a green country road—
> That old woman, a bag of sticks her load,
>
> Blackly down to her thin feet a fringed shawl,
> A rosary of bone on her horned hand,
> A flight of curlews scribing by her head,
> And ashtrees combing with their frills her hair.
>
> Her eyes, wet sunken holes pierced by an awl,
> Must have deciphered her adoring land:
> And curlews, no longer lean birds, instead
> Become ten scarlet comets in the air.
>
> Some incantation from her canyoned mouth,
> Irish, English, blew frost along the ground,
> And even though the wind was from the South
> The ashleaves froze without an ashleaf sound.

The picture of that old woman is completely, yet concisely, imagined. The form is old enough for anyone's taste; but the diction is novel and energetic. This blend of the old and the new is reflected in the imagery of the poem: "curlews, no longer lean birds, instead / Become ten scarlet comets in the air."

In his vision of the past as a source of vitality and inspiration, Michael Hartnett has produced a moving, elegant version of the Chinese classic, the *Tao*, and a magnificent translation of the greatest of Old Irish poems, *The Hag of Beare*. This latter poem shows Hartnett's technical dexterity at its most brilliant. He makes a fine, sustained attempt to convey something of the rhythms of the original by interlocking assonance and by alliteration. Many Irish poets have tried to translate this marvellous lament for lost youth, this outcry against the ravages of time. I think that Michael Hartnett's is the best.

Very fine, too, are his translations of the *Gipsy Ballads* of García Lorca. It is obvious that no translator can fully capture Lorca's magic; all he can hope to do, at best, is to suggest something of its nature and effects. In his versions of Lorca's "The Flight," "San Miguel," "Gabriel," and "Ballad of the Black Sorrow," Michael Hartnett succeeds in making precisely that suggestion.

What have we then? We have a gifted and dedicated poet, as intensely interested in the cultures of other lands as in that of his own. Hartnett is one of the most accomplished and enterprising poets now writing in Ireland.

—Brendan Kennelly

HARWOOD, Gwen(doline Nessie, née Foster).   Australian. Born in Taringa, Queensland, 8 June 1920. Educated at Brisbane Girls' Grammar School. Married Frank William Harwood in 1945; three sons and one daughter. Formerly, organist, All Saints' Church, Brisbane; secretary to a consultant physician, Hobart, Tasmania, 1964-73. Recipient: *Meanjin* prize, 1958, 1959; Commonwealth Literary Fund grant, 1973; Grace Leven Prize, 1976; Robert Frost Award, 1977; Patrick White Award, 1978. Address: Halcyon, Kettering, Tasmania 7155, Australia.

PUBLICATIONS

Verse

Poems.   Sydney, Angus and Robertson, 1963.
Poems: Volume Two.   Sydney, Angus and Robertson, 1968.
Selected Poems.   Sydney, Angus and Robertson, 1975.
The Lion's Bride.   Sydney and London, Angus and Robertson, 1981.

Plays

The Fall of the House of Usher, music by Larry Sitsky (produced Hobart, 1965).
Commentaries on Living, music by James Penberthy (produced Perth, 1972).
Lenz, music by Larry Sitsky, adaptation of the story by Georg Büchner (produced Sydney, 1974).
Sea Changes, music by Ian Cugley (produced Hobart, 1974).
Fiery Tales, music by Larry Sitsky (produced Adelaide, 1976).

Radio Play: *Voices in Limbo*, music by Larry Sitsky, 1983.

*

Manuscript Collections: Australian National Library, Canberra; Fryer Memorial Library, University of Queensland, Brisbane.

Critical Studies: by David Moody, in *Meanjin* (Melbourne), no. 4, 1963; "The Poet as Döppelganger" by Dennis Douglas, in *Quadrant* (Sydney), April 1969; "Gwen Harwood and the Professors" by A.D. Hope, in *Australian Literary Studies* (Hobart), 1972, and a reply to Professor Hope by Dennis Douglas, May 1973; "Artists and Academics in the Poetry of Gwen Harwood" by John B. Beston, in *Quadrant* (Sydney), 1974; "Truth Beyond the Language Game: The Poetry of Gwen Harwood" by N. Talbot, in *Australian Literary Studies* (Brisbane), May 1976; "Worlds Beyond Words: Gwen Harwood's *Selected Poems*" by D. Dodwell, in *Westerly* (Perth), June 1977; "A Fire-Talented Tongue: Some Notes on the Poetry of Gwen Harwood" by R.F. Brissenden, in *Southerly* (Sydney), March 1978; "Die Kröte-Gedichte," in *Das Bild Suburbias in der modernen australischen Dichtung* by Beate Ursula Josephi, Frankfurt, Haag Herchen, 1979; "Toward the Heart's True Speech: Voice-Conflict in the Poetry of Gwen Harwood" by Elizabeth Lawson, in *Southerly 1* (Sydney), 1983.

Gwen Harwood comments:
My major themes are music and musicians; the celebration of love and friendship. I write in a number of styles but the qualities I value most in poetry are power and clarity. I want my poems "to shape joy from the flux of sense."

*   *   *

Although her output has not been prolific, since poetry has had to compete with libretto-writing in engrossing a diverse and complex talent, Gwen Harwood's reputation continues to stand high.

In *Selected Poems* and its predecessors, attention is probably first commanded by the dramatic poems. Energetic, combining delight in precisely detailed observations of human behavior with the power to imbue particularity with general significance, they startle by the contiguity of the satirical and the sacramental. Two "characters" stand out. The intellectual Professor Eisenbart prizes "his dry / indifference to love and luck," but flesh and spirit take revenge as experience intrudes, with comic humiliations ("Prize-Giving") or with an apocalyptic leap ("Painter and Peacock") not unlike that of the lion on his "bride" in the title poem of her 1981 volume. Here Eisenbart is gone, but the musician Kröte persists, an outsider in a not-altogether-barbarous world in which he is frustrated, depressed, exasperated until, as when a "crazy joke redeem(s) / the dismal day," he is allowed to modulate into the celebration of "Music, my joy, my full-scale God" ("A Scattering of Ashes").

So from the beginning the satirist co-existed with a poet whose lyricism is not merely grave with the "pure seriousness" she attributes to her admired Wittgenstein ("Some Thoughts in the 727"), but of a tenderness so open that its flouting of sentimentality cannot be adequately explained by sudden twists of wit or an angular tempering of its melodiousness. Her meditative lyrics, often attached to an autobiographical episode, a figure, a landscape, have a cluster of persistent preoccupations. One of these is art, to which she attributes a two-fold power: to voice the unknown, summoning "a world out of unmeasured darkness" ("New Music"), and to "sing this ordinary day" as in "Giorgio Morandi," where art re-validates the familiar, shaping, as she says she tries to do in poetry, "a sense of joy in the flux of time," a joy gained in the face of the terrors of mortal flesh destined for the "gross darkness" of death and of spirit vulnerable to another darkness, the wasting and betraying of the light of perception.

In "Nightfall: To the Memory of Vera Cottew," while death takes everything into the darkness of time and art and light are incarnational, it is memory that enables the mind to hold the two elements together, as life holds birth and death, pain and joy. The characteristic Harwoodian setting, on the shoreline between earth and sea, is especially appropriate to this poem, but for Harwood a poem itself seems something of a littoral region, since "the world is on one side of us, / and on the other hand / language, the mirror of the world" ("Wittgenstein and Engelmann"). The conclusion of that poem—"truth / whereof one cannot speak"—may sound old-fashioned compared to the sophistication of "Language is not a perfect game,/ and if it were, how could we play?" ("Thought Is Surrounded by a Halo"); however, in the fine poem "Scenic Lookout" she brings the two ideas together in showing that, even in times and places where "no language games survive," we must somehow, to be human, "find [a] tongue."

—Jennifer Strauss

HARWOOD, Lee. British. Born in Leicester, 6 June 1939. Educated at state schools; Queen Mary College, London, B.A. (honours) in English 1961. Married to Judith Walker (divorced); two sons and one daughter. Monumental mason's mate, 1961; library and museum assistant, 1962-64, 1965-66; packer, 1964; assistant, 1966-67, and manager of the poetry department, 1971, Better Books, London; bus conductor, Brighton, 1969; lived in the United States, 1970, 1972-73; Writer-in-Residence, Aegean School of Fine Arts, Paros, Greece, Summer 1971, 1972; post office worker, Brighton, 1973-77, 1979-83. Editor, *Night Scene* magazine, London, 1963; Co-Editor, *Night Train* magazine, London, 1963; Editor, with Johnny Byrne, *Horde* magazine, London, 1964; Editor, with Claude Royet-Journoud, *Soho* magazine, London and Paris, 1964; Editor, *Tzarad* magazine, London and Brighton, 1965-69; Co-Editor, *Boston Eagle*, 1973-74. Recipient: Poets Foundation Award (USA), 1966; Alice Hunt Bartlett Award, 1976. Address: c/o 9 Highfield Road, Chertsey, Surrey, England.

PUBLICATIONS

Verse

Title Illegible. London, Writers Forum, 1965.
The Man with Blue Eyes. New York, Angel Hair, 1966.
The White Room. London, Fulcrum Press, 1968.
The Beautiful Atlas. Brighton, Kavanagh, 1969.
Landscapes. London, Fulcrum Press, 1969.
The Sinking Colony. London, Fulcrum Press, 1970.
Penguin Modern Poets 19, with John Ashbery and Tom Raworth. London, Penguin, 1971.
The First Poem. Brighton, Unicorn Bookshop, 1971.
New Year. London, Wallrich, 1971.
Captain Harwood's Log of Stern Statements and Stout Sayings. London, Writers Forum, 1973.
Freighters. Newcastle upon Tyne, Pig Press, 1975.
H.M.S. Little Fox. London, Oasis, 1975.
Notes of a Post Office Clerk. Gloucester, Massachusetts, Bezoar, 1976.

Boston—Brighton. London, Oasis, 1977.
Old Bosham Bird Watch and Other Stories. Newcstle upon
    Tyne, Pig Press, 1977; revised edition, 1978.
Wish You Were Here, with Antony Lopez. Deal, Kent, Trans-
    gravity Press, 1979.
All the Wrong Notes. Durham, Pig Press, 1981.
Faded Ribbons. Leamington Spa, Warwickshire, Other Branch,
    1982.
Wine Tales (includes prose), with Richard Caddel. Newcastle
    upon Tyne, Galloping Dog Press, 1984.
Crossing the Frozen River: Selected Poems 1965-80. Bolinas,
    California, Tombouctou, 1984.

Recording: *Landscapes*, Stream, 1968.

Other

Tristan Tzara: A Bibliography. London, Aloes, 1974.

Translator, *A Poem Sequence*, by Tristan Tzara. Gillingham,
    Kent, Arc, 1969; revised edition, as *Cosmic Realities Vanilla
    Tobacco Dawnings*, 1975.
Translator, *Destroyed Days*, by Tristan Tzara. Colchester,
    Essex, Voiceprint, 1971.
Translator, *Selected Poems*, by Tristan Tzara. London, Tri-
    gram Press, 1975.

*

Critical Studies: in *Records and Recording* (London), April
1969; by Raymond Gardiner, in *The Gaurdian* (London), 8 July
1970; interview with Victor Bockris, in *Pennsylvania Review 1*
(Philadelphia), 1970; *The Ironic Harvest: English Poetry in the
20th Century* by Geoffrey Thurley, London, Arnold, 1974; interview with Eric Mottram, in *Poetry Information 14* (London),
Winter 1975-76; "The Illusions of Freedom: The Poetry of Lee
Harwood" by Paul Selby, in *Poetry Information 15* (London),
1976; *The British Dissonance: Essays on Ten Contemporary
Poets* by A.Kingsley Weatherhead, Columbia, University of
Missouri Press, 1983.

Lee Harwood comments:
    I like to think of my writing as a form of collage that tries to
present and create a balanced world, a four-dimensional whole.
My poems work with a mixture of fragments, of stories, direct
talk, suggestions and at times quotations from other artists. They
jump about, like most minds and imaginations do, and hope the
reader or listener is willing to make the effort to follow, to work a
bit and to collaborate in the making of the text. No writer wants
to be obscure or difficult, but one can't always talk in simplistic
terms. Sometimes the nature of a subject, if it's to be expressed
with any clarity and precision, must allow for complexity.

*   *   *

    "I just want to tell you the truth," says Lee Harwood's voice in
Boston—Brighton— not through self-conscious symbols, but
with "the small daily details." And if the reader objects: "There's
no pleasing some folks. / You pays your money / and you takes
your choice." Observing process is Harwood's forte. How seeing
"rows of white houses" evolves into a song title. How hearing the
song brings or does not bring the houses back into view. How we
compose a reality out of fragments, and within this "picture,"
how everyone goes or does not go about his own way—and the
"strange pleasures" we find "inside it all."
    He makes no statements about Fate or Meaning. Whereas,

say, Robert Frost sets an eternal, metaphysical watch at the
ocean's edge for people who can see "Neither Out Far Nor In
Deep," Harwood simply sets up what you might expect:

> a lone freighter
> silhouetted
> maybe three freighters
> with crews and cooks and captains
> are silhouetted
> are even clear out to sea
>
>   there
> I point in front of my face.

That awareness, an ordinary alertness "so that no thoughts are
[supernaturally] clear, and, therefore, obsessive" an accessible
curiosity. Postcards from Boston full of practical history; drawings of the earth's substrate supporting the Thames valley;
sketches of positions the River Adur has occupied since the 13th
century: this is part of what *Boston—Brighton* contains.
    This world has formed on the edge of the "ghost" world of the
past. Yet in it we become what we "choose" and face and "exciting...Progress" "out to the possible—no bounds...." What
interests Harwood most in this world of tempered optimism is
motion—motion between the past and present, between the
unconscious and conscious and back again. *H.M.S. Little Fox*
began charting that world, reckoning with ghosts (Rilke, de
Chirico, Stendhal) and their dreams that move through him
(choose him?). He seeks a clear representation of "the process /
to live on land the roots growing down / in one place   a
movement, yes / but a constant—that simplicity."
    Given our unconscious / ghost roots, poems happen when you
rub a pencil over grain you didn't know was there. Life itself is "a
bare canvas, but not empty—/ all there under the surface."
Harwood reveals this life by exposing movements; sometimes he
sees himself as a ship, or as a fox precariously crossing a river on
a log. It's as though we are all "passengers," "like accomplices in
the dream / we all know," yet as we move in any direction, we feel
the wind ruffle our hair.
    H.M.S. Little Fox acknowledges itself as an historical romance
integrating dream and fairy tales sparingly into its story of a love
affair. Not merely his lady's house, for example, but "the small
and isolated fortress / that lies to the north / where you are left."
Harwood creates a mutable reality here that changes as his mind
adjusts its focal length. We read backward into time and so see
the world become what it was. By section IV we are in 1969-70
where Harwood is using masks, inhabiting other voices (chance
overhearings, phrases in books), walking in a world that threatens to become a hieroglyph for himself, to become "a matter of
lists / that act as buttresses, even defenses" behind which he (we)
play at being ourselves.
    This world frequently achieves the intensity of myth, both
symbolically, through allusions to the Egyptian gods the lovers
imitate or that once stood as expressions of such a love, and
naively, when love integrates and focuses the world of the lovers
so that "a cool breeze comes up the river / and ruffles your hair."
But the "Image is the ultimate enemy," as Harwood has more
recently written: "pictures of ourselves distract / abstract us from
being ourselves. The final section of *H.M.S. Little Fox* shows a
sequence of returning heroes in ironic perspectives ("the returned
astronaut waves / a *hankerchief* from the capsule's door"). Each
is a different mask of the poet; each leaves "the prison of images
pursuing...the hero of the ritual." Elsewhere, Harwood has investigated that "prison." In *The Sinking Colony* and *Landscapes*,
for example, he finds in precise detail the connections between
the images in our eyes and the images coming from our minds.
Here, he moves away from this ritual obsession; it was "about

time / I woke up... and appreciated the possible / sincerity of...people and bodies." It was about time that he met his lady; she puts him in a "Dazzle" and threads together the poems of *H.M.S. Little Fox*. She is "REAL" and she helps him to see it is about time that he get an answer to a simple question: "I mean what is happening?—NOW!" She makes it possible for him to say, seven years later, "I just want to tell you the truth."

The question comes in the penultimate poem of *H.M.S. Little Fox*. The final poem is a sequence of satires on surrealism, from which Harwood appears to have turned away. The question may be a turning point for him; certainly it is a beginning for the reader. We have been reading backwards, into ghost roots. Now the question requires us to turn this all around, to put together going in the other direction—as Harwood did. This chronological strategy is unusual and successful: the poems come to life.

—Edward B. Germain

HASS, Robert. American. Born in San Francisco, California, 1 March 1941. Educated at St. Mary's College, Moraga, California, B.A. 1963; Stanford University, California (Woodrow Wilson Fellow; Danforth Fellow), 1964-67, M.A. 1965, Ph.D. 1976. Married Earlene Leif in 1962; three children. Has taught at the State University of New York, Buffalo, University of Virginia, Charlottesville, St. Mary's College, and Goddard College, Plainfield, Vermont; Poet-in-Residence, The Frost Place, Franconia, New Hampshire, 1978. Recipient: Yale Series of Younger Poets Award, 1972; US—UK Bicentennial Exchange Fellowship, 1976; Guggenheim Fellowship, 1979. Address: c/o Ecco Press, 1 West 30th Street, New York, New York 10001, U.S.A.

PUBLICATIONS

Verse

Field Guide. New Haven, Connecticut, Yale University Press, 1973.
Winter Morning in Charlottesville. Knotting, Bedfordshire, Sceptre Press, 1977.
Praise. New York, Ecco Press, 1979; Manchester, Carcanet, 1981.
Five American Poets, with others. Manchester, Carcanet, 1979.

Other

Twentieth Century Pleasures: Prose on Poetry. New York, Ecco Press, 1984.

Translator, with Robert Pinsky, *The Separate Notebooks*, by Czeslaw Milosz. New York, Ecco Press, 1984.

*   *   *

Robert Hass's poetry moves quietly through a landscape of natural life and rhythm, until it arrives in a world of personal feeling and intimate reflection. Hass reexamines some of the central problems of the Romantic imagination, using the unforced order of nature as a lens with which to focus on the effects of time

and death in man's life, and the inescapable division between consciousness and the pulse of the created world. In accepting this separation of the natural and imaginal worlds, Hass finds a potentially rich source of understanding. In *Field Guide* the poet is constantly outdoors, walking the California coast where he grew up, the upstate New York city where he taught, or even the landscape of literature—in the group of poems which form the central section of the volume. These last poems mark the crossroads of Hass's concerns, where (in "Measure") "Last light / rims the blue mountain / and I almost glimpse / what I was born to / not so much in the sunlight / or in the plum tree / as in the pulse / that forms these lines." While a great many of the poems in *Field Guide* recall Lowell in the attempt to situate the poet in historical time and place, Hass has none of Lowell's intense need for confrontation. More like Stevens or perhaps Roethke in tone, Hass attempts to integrate past and present as the two arms of a single balance.

Hass's painterly descriptions of the natural world flood the poems, and flow naturally into observations of how consciousness transforms that world. In "Songs to Survive the Summer," a gentle meditation on death's presence in life, he describes a summer that is both backdrop and reflecting mirror:

These are the dog days,
unvaried
except by accident,

mist rising from soaked lawns,
gone world, everything
rises and dissolves in air,

Whatever it is would
clear the air
dissolves in air and the knot

of days unties
invisibly like a shoelace.

Hass measures the shape and weight of feeling in its place, its season, temperature, and texture. The poems are a measure in themselves, and Hass's natural unit of writing is the thought. He uses typographical lines to divide, recombine, and link thoughts with their fellows. Rhythm provides another measure of the poem's activity, whether it is the short, steady pulse of the lines above, or the slow, solid pounding of the tides. With these simple cadences, Hass adjusts the speed of our association of words, allowing him to use a simple vocabulary divorced from its usual banality through line and rhythm.

Death

in the sweetness, in the bitter
and the sour, death
in the salt, your tears,

this summer ripe and overripe.
It is a taste in the mouth,
child.

"Songs to Survive the Summer" is Hass's longest published poem, and the longer form seems to allow him to relax more comfortably into his own particular atmosphere. The shorter poems frequently attempt to condense recognitions into a single word, resulting in an abrupt shift in the level of awareness that is little consonant with the general feeling of the poem. The longer poems have a greater fullness and body due to the more complete evolution of feeling in them.

In his work since *Field Guide*, Hass seems to be advancing more deeply into the seasons of the mind. While carrying with him the careful modulation of tone and atmosphere and the meticulous observation of the earlier poems, he is more concerned with imaginative objects rather than concrete ones. In "Heroic Simile" an Akira Kurosawa film calls up a vision of a poor woodsman and his uncle chopping at a monumental log: "They have stopped working / because they are tired and because / I have imagined no pack animal / or primitive wagon." Though the woodsmen are patient and the poet concerned, he concludes "There are limits to the imagination."

Yet Hass is not uncomfortable with limits. He acquiesces to them, even celebrates them with the gentle good humor and watchful restraint typical of his work. Above all, it is his sense of balance, whether on tiptoe or firmly on his feet, that gives Robert Hass's poetry the warmth of life.

—Walter Bode

HAZO, Samuel (John). American. Born in Pittsburgh, Pennsylvania, 19 July 1928. Educated at Notre Dame University, Indiana (Mitchell Award, 1948), B.A. (magna cum laude) 1948; Duquesne University, Pittsburgh, M.A. 1955; University of Pittsburgh, Ph.D. 1957. Served in the United States Marine Corps, 1950-53: Captain. Married Mary Anne Sarkis in 1955; one son. Instructor, Shady Side Academy, 1953-55. Instructor, 1955-58, Assistant Professor, 1958-60, Associate Professor, 1960-61, Associate Dean, 1961-66, and since 1964, Professor of English, Duquesne University. Visiting Professor, University of Detroit, 1968. Since 1966, Director, International Poetry Forum, Pittsburgh. Contributing Editor, *Mundus Artium* magazine, Athens, Ohio; Poetry Editor, *America*, Washington, D.C. United States State Department Lecturer in the Middle East and Greece, 1965, in Jamaica, 1966. Recipient: Pro Helvetia Foundation grant (Switzerland), 1971. D.Litt.: Seton Hill College, Greensburg, Pennsylvania, 1965; D.Hum.: Theil College, Greenville, Pennsylvania, 1981. Address: 785 Somerville Drive, Pittsburgh, Pennsylvania 15243, U.S.A.

PUBLICATIONS

Verse

Discovery and Other Poems. New York, Sheed and Ward, 1959.
The Quiet Wars. New York, Sheed and Ward, 1962.
Listen with the Eye, photographs by James P. Blair. Pittsburgh, University of Pittsburgh Press, 1964.
My Sons in God: Selected and New Poems. Pittsburgh, University of Pittsburgh Press, 1965.
Blood Rights. Pittsburgh, University of Pittsburgh Press, 1968.
The Blood of Adonis, with Adonis (Ali Ahmed Said). Pittsburgh, University of Pittsburgh Press, 1971.
Twelve Poems, with George Nama. Pittsburgh, Byblos Press, 1972.
Seascript: A Mediterranean Logbook. Pitttsburgh, Byblos Press, 1972.
Once for the Last Bandit: New and Previous Poems. Pittsburgh, University of Pittsburgh Press, 1972.

Quartered. Pittsburgh, University of Pittsburgh Press, 1974.
Inscripts. Athens, Ohio University Press, 1975.
Shuffle, Cut, and Look. Derry, Pennsylvania, Rook Press, 1977.
To Paris. New York, New Directions, 1981.
Thank a Bored Angel: Selected Poems. New York, New Directions, 1983.

Novels

The Very Fall of the Sun. New York, Popular Library, 1978.
The Wanton Summer Air. Berkeley, California, North Point Press, 1982.

Other

Hart Crane: An Introduction and Interpretation. New York, Barnes and Noble, 1963; revised edition, as *Smithereened Apart: A Critique of Hart Crane,* Athens, Ohio University Press, 1978.

Editor, *The Christian Intellectual: Studies in the Relation of Catholicism to the Human Sciences.* Pittsburgh, Duquesne University Press, 1963.
Editor, *A Selection of Contemporary Religious Poetry.* Glen Rock, New Jersey, Paulist Press, 1963.

Translator, with Beth Luey, *The Growl of Deep Waters: Essays,* by Denis de Rougemont. Pittsburgh, University of Pittsburgh Press, 1976.
Translator, *Transformation of the Lover,* by Adonis. Athens, Swallow Press-Ohio University Press, 1983.

*

Critical Study: "Swimming in Sharkwater: The Poetry of Samuel Hazo" by R.H.W. Dillard, in *Hollins Critic* (Hollins College, Virginia), February, 1969.

Samuel Hazo comments:

Suffice to say that I regard poetry as the best form of conversation with largely unknown readers or hearers whose answer is hopefully their attention and assent. The rest is for critics to discover and evaluate.

*   *   *

Samuel Hazo's first two collections, *Discovery* and *The Quiet Wars,* introduced a meditative Christian poet concerned with the tough and enduring realities of death and suffering. He displayed the technical mastery necessary to avoid portentousness and unearned statement; his style is at once traditional and colloquial—that of a thinking modern man's believable metrical utterance.

Listen with the Eye, a small collection of poems with accompanying photographs by James Blair, involves a technical departure of some importance; many of the poems are cast in a strongly iambic free verse. The result is not so much rhythmic freedom as it is a stronger sense of the weight of each line. This quality distinguishes the new poems of *My Sons in God,* a collection of new and selected earlier poems in which the union of style and theme marks the arrival of an important American poet. Among the new poems is a group of "transpositions" from the Arabic of Ali Ahmed Said, the contemporary Lebanese poet; here again this fresh technical influence brings to Hazo's own poems an additional firmness of line. A larger selection of Said's poems, *The Blood of Adonis*, appeared in 1971.

Once for the Last Bandit: New and Previous Poems hones down the selection of early poems which appeared in *My Sons in God*; it includes generous selections from that book and from *Blood Rights*. Nearly half of the book is given over to the title sequence, a group of poems having some qualities of a journal, or as Hazo calls it, "an almanac of a penman in transit." The sinuous, heavily iambic free verse is a genuine new direction for Hazo; while his themes of loss, God, and persistence are still central, a larger variety of starting points and tones had become available to this very resourceful, still vitally developing poet.

—Henry Taylor

HEANEY, Seamus (Justin). Irish. Born in Castledawson, County Derry, Northern Ireland, 13 April 1939. Educated at Anahorish School; St. Columb's College, Londonderry, 1951-57; Queen's University, Belfast, 1957-61, B.A. (honours) in English 1961. Married Marie Devlin in 1965; two sons and one daughter. Teacher, St. Thomas's Secondary School, Belfast, 1962-63; Lecturer, St. Joseph's College of Education, Belfast, 1963-66; Lecturer in English, Queen's University, 1966-72; Guest Lecturer, University of California, Berkeley, 1970-71; moved to County Wicklow, Republic of Ireland, 1972; did regular radio work, and teaching at American universities; Teacher, Carysfort Training College, Dublin, 1975-81; Allott Lecturer, University of Liverpool, 1978. Since 1982, Visiting Professor, Harvard University, Cambridge, Massachusetts. Recipient: Eric Gregory Award, 1966; Cholmondeley Award, 1967; Faber Memorial Prize, 1968; Maugham Award, 1968; Irish Academy of Letters award, 1971; Denis Devlin Memorial Award, 1973, 1980; American-Irish Foundation Award, 1975; American Academy E.M. Forster Award, 1975; Duff Cooper Memorial Award, 1976; Smith Literary Award, 1976; Bennett Award, 1982. Member, Irish Academy of Letters. Lives in Dublin. Address: c/o Faber and Faber Ltd., 3 Queen Square, London WCIN 3AU, England.

PUBLICATIONS

Verse

Eleven Poems. Belfast, Festival, 1965.
Death of a Naturalist. London, Faber, and New York, Oxford University Press, 1966.
Room to Rhyme, with Dairo Hammond and Michael Longley. Belfast, Arts Council of Northern Ireland, 1968.
A Lough Neagh Sequence. Manchester, Phoenix Pamphlet Poets Press, 1969.
Door into the Dark. London, Faber, and New York, Oxford University Press, 1969.
Night Drive: Poems. Credition, Devon, Gilbertson, 1970.
Boy Driving His Father to Confession. Frensham, Surrey, Sceptre Press, 1970.
Land. London, Poem-of-the-Month Club, 1971.
Wintering Out. London, Faber, 1972; New York, Oxford University Press, 1973.
North. London, Faber, and New York, Oxford University Press, 1975.
Bog Poems. London, Rainbow Press, 1975.
Stations. Belfast, Ulsterman, 1975.

After Summer. Old Deerfield, Massachusetts, Deerfield Press, 1978.
Hedge School (Sonnets from Glanmore). Newark, Vermont, Janus Press, 1979.
Field Work. London, Faber, and New York, Farrar Straus, 1979.
Ugolino. Dublin, Andrew Carpenter, 1979.
Selected Poems 1965-1975. London, Faber, 1980.
Poems 1965-1975. New York, Farrar Straus, 1980.
An Open Letter. Londonderry, Field Day Theatre Company, 1983.
Sweeney Astray: A Version from the Irish (includes prose). Londonderry, Field Day Theatre Company, 1983; London, Faber, and New York, Farrar Straus, 1984.
Station Island. London, Faber, and New York, Farrar Straus, 1984.

Other

The Fire i'the Flint: Reflections on the Poetry of Gerard Manley Hopkins (lecture). London, Oxford University Press, 1975.
Robert Lowell: A Memorial Lecture and an Eulogy. Privately printed, 1978.
The Making of a Music: Reflections on the Poetry of Wordsworth and Yeats. Liverpool, University of Liverpool Press, 1978.
Preoccupations: Selected Prose 1968-1978. London, Faber, and New York, Farrar Straus, 1980.

Editor, with Alan Brownjohn and Jon Stallworthy, *New Poems 1970-1971.* London, Hutchinson, 1971.
Editor, *Soundings 2.* Belfast, Blackstaff Press, 1974.
Editor, with Ted Hughes, *1980 Anthology: Arvon Foundation Poetry Competition.* Todmorden, Lancashire, Kilnhurst, 1982.
Editor, with Ted Hughes, *The Rattle Bag: An Anthology.* London, Faber, 1982.

*

Critical Studies: *Seamus Heaney* by Robert Buttel, Lewisburg, Pennsylvania, Bucknell University Press, 1975; *Seamus Heaney* by Blake Morrison, London, Methuen, 1982; *The Art of Seamus Heaney* edited by Tony Curtis, Bridgend, Poetry Wales Press, 1982.

*   *   *

As an Ulster Catholic, Seamus Heaney has always been aware of the complex and violent history that has gone to shape modern Ireland. In "Shoreline" (*Door into the Dark*) he hears in the tide, "rummaging in / At the foot of all fields," echoes of successive waves of invaders, Celts, Danes, Normans; in *North* he writes of "those fabulous raiders," the Vikings, "ocean-deafened voices / warning me, lifted again / in violence and epiphany." Elsewhere in the same volume "Ocean's Love to Ireland" recalls, in a sinister compounding of copulation and murder which is a recurring motif, the complicity of courtier-poet Ralegh in the Irish massacres; while "Bog Oak" (*Wintering Out*) with a cool obliqueness insinuates, into the "dreaming sunlight" of Edmund Spenser's pastoral, hints of the atrocities he supervised. "For the Commander of the 'Eliza' " and "At a Potato Digging" evoke the Great Hunger and the ruthless expediencies of British rule in 1845. "Docker," with a forced but urgent understanding, depicts the Northern Protestant not only to recall past bigotry but to offer, in 1966, prophetic anticipation of its renewal ("That fist would drop a hammer on a Catholic—/ Oh yes, that kind of thing could start again").

From his first volume onwards, Heaney has written extensively of the strenuous, unremitting life of rural labour in County Derry and beyond. Many of the poems celebrate the people, crafts, and skills which sustain communal life; others, such as "The Wool Trade" or "Traditions," explore the linguistic and commercial nexus that "beds us down into / the British isles." In many poems Heaney effects a remarkable transition between manual and mental labour, the currencies of material life and of language. In "Digging," the first poem of his first volume, this theme is already enunciated: the poet digs with his pen as father and grandfather dug with their spades the rich peat of Ireland. Violence is hinted at by the simile which adds a third implement to the human repertoire ("The squat pen rest; snug as a gun"). The title poem of *Death of a Naturalist* extends this menace, recalling the poet as a boy sickened by the pools of frogspawn which tell of a repulsive world beyond the human: "The great slime kings / Were gathered there for vengeance and I knew / That if I dipped my hand the spawn would clutch it." Throughout this volume the water-rat recurs as image of an alien yet terrifyingly familiar world, a world finally admitted, in "Personal Helicon," to be close to the poet's own creative springs, as, "pry[ing] into roots...finger[ing] slime," this "big-eyed Narcissus" is startled by a rat that "slapped across my reflection." Poetry itself is a "door into the dark" where we seek our own carnal origins, and "Bogland" and "Bann Clay" stress this symbolic digging for a lost, primordial centre of being: "Under the humus and roots / This smooth weight. I labour / towards it still. It holds and gluts." The very language in which Heaney writes partakes of this glutinous physical presence. There is a tactile, viscous quality to his words, speaking of "the sucking clabber" of water, the "soft gradient / of consonant, vowel-meadow," or "the tawny guttural water" which "spells itself." "Anahorish," "Toome," "Broagh" (*Wintering Out*) explore the very sounds of the old Irish words, stressing their status as material utterance, the muscular effort of a "guttural muse" whose "uvula grows / vestigial" ("Traditions"). In poems such as "Gifts of Rain" or "Oracle" the human organs of communication are in turn transferred to nature ("small mouth and ear / in a woody cleft, / lobe and larnyx / of the mossy places"). Throughout *North* language is equated with the rich, secretive loam of the Irish bog, which engulfs and preserves, but can be kindled over and over into meaning, as the title poem indicates: "Lie down / in the word-hoard, burrow / the coil and gleam / of your furrowed brain.// Compose in darkness." The whole volume is as much about the difficulty of poetic composition as about the fratricidal decomposition of Ireland: death and love, language, poetry and politics, converge in poem after poem. Several, developing the insight of "Tollund Man" (*Wintering Out*), draw upon P.V. Glob's book *The Bog People* for a potent imagery of atrocity. In Glob's photographs of those ancient human sacrifices, preserved by the "dark juices" of the Danish peat bog, Heaney finds an analogy to the role of the modern Irish poet, the "artful voyeur" who is both an accomplice and helpless witness to "the exact / and tribal, intimate revenge" spoken of in a poem such as "Punishment." Superficially much influenced by Ted Hughes, Heaney perhaps in this double understanding of complicity and betrayal, establishes his own distinctive moral and emotional stance. Unlike Hughes, he is finally concerned with the redemption, not the dismissal, of the human, its exhumation from a "mother ground /...sour with the blood / of her faithful."

Field Work skilfully balances the parochial and a larger world, as in "The Skunk" deliberately estranging, in a California setting, the traditional glamour of the love poem. But the prevailing mood of this volume is elegiac, speaking, in the title sequence, of

a world "stained / to perfection," making those local deaths of which it speaks elsewhere part of a universal loss and abandoning which is nevertheless the ground, the true field, within which human life is fulfilled. *Station Island*, with its title "sequence of dream encounters with familiar ghosts" set on the island in Lough Derg which is a traditional place of penitential pilgrimage, explores the guilt of such encounters with the dead, returning from a remove to make peace with that which has been abandoned. Exile of various kinds, and the loving fidelity of the emigré to that which is left behind, provides a motive force to the volume. This is a poetry of departures and returns, acknowledging that "you can't go home again" in the most bathetic figure of all, the lobster taken out of the tank in a restaurant, "the hampered one, out of water, / fortified and bewildered," like the poet himself who cannot clear his head of those lives still "in their element" ("Away from It All"). The threat of being devoured for someone else's enjoyment is an anxiety which pervades the poetic stance throughout. It explains the poet's identification in the third part with the 7th-century Irish king Sweeney, "transformed into a bird-man and exiled to the trees by the curse of St. Ronan," finding in madness a relief from misery. The identification is strong enough to have led Heaney to translate the medieval Irish poem *Buile Suibhne* in *Sweeney Astray*, a volume which, in combining his own inimitable style with fidelity to the original, provides an instance of the delicate relation between Heaney's aspirant talent and his native realm. "The First Gloss," which opens "Sweeney Redivivus," sums this relation up in miniature with its multiple puns: "Subscribe to the first step taken / from a justified line / into the margin." Heaney's Sweeney too finds himself, in "Sweeney Redivivus":

> incredible to myself,
> among people far too eager to believe me
> and my story, even if it happened to be true.

—Stan Smith

HEATH-STUBBS, John (Francis Alexander). British. Born in London, 9 July 1918. Educated at Bembridge School; Worcester College for the Blind; and privately; Queen's College, Oxford, B.A. (honours) in English 1942, M.A. 1972. English teacher, Hall School, Hampstead, London, 1944-45; Editorial Assistant, Hutchinson and Company, publishers, London, 1945-46. Gregory Fellow in Poetry, Leeds University, 1952-55; Visiting Professor of English, University of Alexandria, Egypt, 1955-58, and the University of Michigan, Ann Arbor, 1960-61. Lecturer in English, College of St. Mark and St. John, London, 1963-73. Recipient: Arts Council bursary, 1965; Queen's Gold Medal for Poetry, 1973; Oscar Williams-Gene Derwood Award, 1977. Fellow, Royal Society of Literature, 1953. Address: 35 Sutherland Place, London W.2, England.

PUBLICATIONS

Verse

Wounded Thammuz. London, Routledge, 1942.
Beauty and the Beast. London, Routledge, 1943.
The Divided Ways. London, Routledge, 1946.
The Charity of the Stars. New York, Sloane, 1949.

The Swarming of the Bees. London, Eyre and Spottiswoode, 1950.

A Charm Against the Toothache. London, Methuen, 1954.

The Triumph of the Muse and Other Poems. London, Oxford University Press, 1958.

The Blue-Fly in His Head. London, Oxford University Press, 1962.

Selected Poems. London, Oxford University Press, 1965.

Satires and Epigrams. London, Turret, 1968.

(Selected Poems), with Thomas Blackburn. London, Longman, 1969.

Artorius, Book I. Providence, Rhode Island, Burning Deck, 1970; London, Enitharmon Press, 1973.

Penguin Modern Poets 20, with F.T. Prince and Stephen Spender. London, Penguin, 1971.

Four Poems in Measure. New York, Helikon Press, 1973.

The Twelve Labours of Hercules. San Francisco, Arion Press, 1974.

A Parliament of Birds (juvenile). London, Chatto and Windus, 1975.

The Watchman's Flute: New Poems. Manchester, Carcanet, 1978.

The Mouse, The Bird, and The Sausage. Sunderland, Ceolfrith, 1978.

Birds Reconvened. London, Enitharmon Press, 1980.

Buzz Buzz: Ten Insect Poems. Sidcot, Avon, Gruffyground, 1981.

This Is Your Poem. London, Pisces Press, 1981.

Naming the Beasts. Manchester, Carcanet, 1982.

Plays

The Talking Ass (produced London, 1953). Included in *Helen in Egypt and Other Plays,* 1958.

Helen in Egypt and Other Plays (includes *The Talking Ass, The Harrowing of Hell*). London, Oxford University Press, 1958.

Other

The Darkling Plain: A Study of the Later Fortunes of Romanticism in English Poetry from George Darley to W. B Yeats. London, Eyre and Spottiswoode, 1950.

Charles Williams. London, Longman, 1955.

The Verse Satire. London, Oxford University Press, 1969.

The Ode. London, Oxford University Press, 1969.

The Pastoral. London, Oxford University Press, 1969.

Editor, *Selected Poems of Shelley.* London, Falcon Press, 1947.

Editor, *Selected Poems of Tennyson.* London, Falcon Press, 1947.

Editor, *Selected Poems of Swift.* London, Falcon Press, 1947.

Editor, with David Wright, *The Forsaken Garden: An Anthology of Poetry 1824-1909.* London, Lehmann, 1950.

Editor, *Mountains Beneath the Horizon: Selected Poems,* by William Bell. London, Faber, 1950.

Editor, *Images of Tomorrow: An Anthology of Recent Poetry.* London, SCM Press, 1953.

Editor, with David Wright, *The Faber Book of Twentieth Century Verse: An Anthology of Verse in Britain 1900-1950.* London, Faber, 1953; revised edition, 1965, 1975.

Editor, *Selected Poems of Alexander Pope.* London, Heinemann, 1964; New York, Barnes and Noble, 1966.

Editor, with Martin Green, *Homage to George Barker on His 60th Birthday.* London, Martin Brian and O'Keeffe, 1973.

Editor, *Selected Poems,* by Thomas Gray. Manchester, Carcanet, 1981.

Editor, with Phillips Salman, *Poems of Science.* London, Penguin, 1984.

Translator, *Poems from Giacomo Leopardi.* London, Lehmann, 1946.

Translator, *Aphrodite's Garland.* St. Ives, Latin Press, 1952.

Translator, with Peter Avery, *Thirty Poems of Hafiz of Shiraz.* London, Murray, 1952.

Translator, with Iris Origo, *Selected Poetry and Prose,* by Giacomo Leopardi. London, Oxford University Press, 1966; New York, New American Library, 1967.

Translator, *The Horn/Le Cor,* by Alfred de Vigny. Richmond, Surrey, Keepsake Press, 1969.

Translator, with Shafik Megally, *Dust and Carnations: Traditional Funeral Chants and Wedding Songs from Egypt.* London, TR Press, 1977.

Translator, with Peter Avery, *The Ruba'iyat of Omar Khayyam.* London, Allen Lane, 1979.

Translator, with Carol Whiteside, *Anyte.* Warwick, Greville Press, 1979.

*

Manuscript Collections: Humanities Research Center, University of Texas, Austin; Claude Colleer Abbott Memorial Library, State University of New York, Buffalo.

Critical Studies: *Poetry and Personal Responsibility* by George Every, London, SCM Press, 1948; "John Heath-Stubbs: A Poet in Alexandria" by Shafik Megally, in *Cairo Bulletin of English Studies,* 1959; *The Price of an Eye* by Thomas Blackburn, London, Longman, and New York, Morrow, 1961; *Rule and Energy* by John Press, London, Oxford University Press, 1963; "John Heath-Stubbs Issue" of *Aquarius 10* (London), 1978; "Triad from Great Britain" by Tony Stoneburner, in *The Poetics of Faith,* Missoula, Montana, Scholars Press, 1978.

John Heath-Stubbs comments:

Influenced at Oxford by teaching of C.S. Lewis and Charles Williams; also by friendship with fellow undergraduate poets Sidney Keyes, Drummond Allison, and William Bell.

*   *   *

A remarkable feel for words, a fine metrical ear, a highly perceptive and sound critical intellect, a profound and retentive memory, a good imagination, plus a sense of humour—such have been clear attributes of John Heath-Stubbs's poetic genius from the beginning. From the time of his contributions to Michael Meyer's *Eight Oxford Poets,* and his own first book of verse, *Wounded Thammuz,* right down to more recent works like *The Watchman's Flute* and that remarkable sub-epic *Artorius,* Heath-Stubbs has been an accomplished craftsman and all-round poet: an Augustan with more than a touch of the Elizabethan about him. Time has matured his writings so that, now, even the most trivial offering of his pen is in some measure a deft piece of poetic wisdom—or, perhaps, one should say of "poeticised wisdom." Certainly, there is both the feeling and the evidence that whatever piece of esoteric lore, mythological gleaning, or practical information is thrown up from the remarkably erudite mind of this particular poet—and there is an almost unrivalled quantum of such data there in Heath-Stubbs—it is touched, however lightly, by the magic of the Muse. And rightly so, for only two or three at most of poets since the last War in England have so consistently dedicated themselves to the service of Apollo's daughter.

Although he is in many respects a most neglected poet—and certainly one far outside the run of fashions and movements and academic acclaim in each successive decade since he began writing—those critics who have chosen to note Heath-Stubbs's work echo, in their different ways, Derek Stanford's description of the persona that the poems project: "The influence of his learning and the inborn dignity of his mind influenced me the more strongly because he himself made no effort to." And, indeed, as all who know Heath-Stubbs will appreciate: he is a diffident man; a solitary one even—despite all the company he keeps in Fitzrovia and elsewhere. Michael Meyer has written of him: "John Heath-Stubbs is the most uninstitutionable of men, one of those towering solitaries, like Doughty and Charles Williams...who go their own way, contemptuous of literary fashion"; and Michael Hamburger: "I see John Heath-Stubbs as a tragic figure—the insider, by conviction and allegiance, who 'was not preferred'...not preferred because the Establishment to which he has always been committed was shifting all the time, and he was not; and because it has little use for poets who are neither sychophants or clowns. He has borne that affliction with...courage and dignity...for me he has changed far less than anyone else I know." Again, Sean Hutton has written: "His sensibility is strongly marked by that tragic feeling, compounded with stoicism, which one associates with Greek lyric poetry." While the poet himself has stated his "policy," as it were, in verse: "I would emulate rather those / Who countered despair with elegance, / Emptiness with a grace," and has never ceased to recognize the primary objective or purpose of poetry: "...I would have you remember: / Your poetry is no good / Unless it move the heart," adding by way of stressing the point: "...And the human heart, / The heart which you must move, / Is corrupt, depraved and desperately wicked."

As a true servant of the Muse, then, Heath-Stubbs has opted—despite the knowledge of "corruption, depravity and wickedness—to celebrate, or if not to celebrate always, at least to counter "despair with elegance, emptiness with a grace." And what emerges from all these critical comments by the poet, or by others, is, a sense of authority. An authority which has grown gradually as a result of his having "borne" the "affliction with courage and dignity." It is an authority that exerts its influence according to Stanford through "inborn dignity of mind" and through "learning." The constant factor that all the critics, overtly or implicitly, recognize is this inborn dignity; as they also acknowledge a growth-element brought about by the constant expansion of the poet's eruditon: "He has brought erudition out of the libraries and given it roots and leaves," as Anne Stevenson says. As to why Michael Hamburger finds the poet so unchanging—indeed, he must have been tempted to say "timeless"—it is because, despite all the tragic vicissitudes of time, Heath-Stubbs has retained, nay, enhanced his human integrity. Hence the sense of authority in his poetry and why he has even been described as "magisterial."

But what kind of poetry is Heath-Stubbs's? Can it be reasonably summed up? Probably the most frequent and useful epithet that has been applied to it is "classical—romantic." In fact, in *The Darkling Plain*, a prose study of poetry, the poet himself wrote: "The Classical vision is the most complete, rounded, and perfected of which the human mind is capable....In a sense, we must all attempt to be Classicists, but have to be Romantics first of all, before we can achieve this, and few of us in this life can hope to pass that stage." An even clearer summing up of his *ars poetica* occurs in the poem entitled "The Blue-Fly In His Head" (1962): "The intellect shapes, the emotions feed the poem, / Whose roots are in the senses, whose flower is imagination." And

one other description of Heath-Stubbs's poetry that I cannot forbear quoting is by J. Van Domelen's: "There is a certain Byzantine quality in much of John Heath-Stubbs' poetry. An encyclopaedic knowledge of past cultures and a continual application of this knowledge that is reminiscent of Byzantium."

The one overriding quality of Heath-Stubbs's poetry, however, that insufficient stress has been laid upon (perhaps because it is so obvious) is that it is a poetry, linguistically speaking, "of as good blood as any in England" like the poet. That is to say: Heath-Stubbs's poetry is supremely English, in the way that Shakespeare's or the pristine Chaucer's was supremely English. It is an Anglo-Saxon language plasm imbued, even softened, by the rich Celtic Blood of the West (which was how "English" came to be: the Latin influence being formatively peripheral in comparison). To the Celtic element Heath-Stubbs owes his gift for mythological transformation of experience; to the English (or Anglo-Saxon as developed via Chaucer) the capacity to embrace ideas and subtler intellectual states than Celtic perversity and magic allows for. And to the English strain too he owes his humour: something which must be emphasised because he is the only *serious poet* writing in England today (with the exception of Dannie Abse) who also has a great sense of humour. In fact, he is both poet and wit, though he is one to whom I would rather apply the phrase "a visionary and humourist," in order to emphasise the somewhat unique character of his achievement.

It was Sebastian Barker who wrote of the "intelligent and fully conscious delight" that the reader "may expect from Heath-Stubbs' rhythms." In fact, this statement unintentionally directs at least one reader to the only real weakness to be found in Heath-Stubbs's poetry. Not infrequently there is an over-consciousness present in the poetry that leads to a diminution, even an absence, of rhythm. Now, rhythm is part of the essential life-blood of the true poem, and no amount of flexing of the poet's metrical muscles (something Heath-Stubbs is particularly good at) will guarantee this vital factor. Consequently, quite a few respectable and interesting items get knocked off his virtuoso anvil that are nothing more than cerebral artefacts expressed in cautious but always competent metres. Not shoddy goods, of course, but simply pieces that lack the lustre of life, lack a living vitality, lack, in short, rhythm. Such are not really inspired or Muse-given pieces at all, but either metrical exercises or just plain failed poems. Naturally, they do interest—as all Heath-Stubbs's work interests—but they do not delight, do not "move the heart" as Heath-Stubbs knows and says a true poem should. In a prolific poet of course—indeed, in any poet—such failures are to be expected; not even Shakespeare hit the right note, thought, and rhythm at the same time and every time. But these critical remarks must be understood as introduced simply to help "round the picture," as it were. For it remains generally true that the work of John Heath-Stubbs—culminating in his remarkable epic for voices *Artorius*—forms one of the major poetical *oeuvres* in modern times by any standards. True it is a corpus that has yet to be studied in the depth it deserves; but when it is, a major poet will have been firmly added to the somewhat exclusive canon of English literature.

—William Oxley

HECHT, Anthony (Evan).   American.   Born in New York City, 16 January 1923. Educated at Bard College, Annandale-on-Hudson, New York, B.A. 1944; Columbia University, New York, M.A. 1950. Served in the United States Army during

World War II. Married 1) Patricia Harris in 1954 (divorced, 1961); 2) Helen D'Alessandro in 1971; three sons. Taught at Kenyon College, Gambier, Ohio, 1947; University of Iowa, Iowa City, 1948; New York University, 1949; Smith College, Northampton, Massachusetts, 1956-59; Bard College, 1962-67. Since 1967, Member of the Department of English, Rochester University, New York. Hurst Professor, Washington University, St. Louis, 1971; Visiting Professor, Harvard University, Cambridge, Massachusetts, 1973, and Yale University, New Haven, Connecticut, 1977; member of the faculty, Salzburg Seminar in American Studies, 1977. Recipient: American Academy in Rome fellowship, 1951; Guggenheim Fellowship, 1954, 1959; *Hudson Review* fellowship, 1958; Ford fellowship, for drama, 1960, for verse, 1968; Brandeis University Creative Arts Award, 1964; Rockefeller fellowship, 1967; Loines Award, 1968; Pulitzer Prize, 1968; Academy of American Poets Fellowship, 1969; Bollingen Prize, 1983. D.Litt.: Bard College, 1970; L.H.D.: Georgetown University, Washington, D.C., 1981. Chancellor, Academy of American Poets, 1971. Member, American Academy, and American Academy of Arts and Sciences. Address: 19 East Boulevard, Rochester, New York 14610, U.S.A.

PUBLICATIONS

Verse

A Summoning of Stones.   New York, Macmillan, 1954.
The Seven Deadly Sins.   Northampton, Massachusetts, Gehenna Press, 1958.
Struwwelpeter.   Northampton, Massachusetts, Gehenna Press, 1958.
A Bestiary, illustrated by Aubrey Schwartz.   Los Angeles, Kanthos Press, 1962.
The Hard Hours.   New York, Atheneum, and London, Oxford University Press, 1967.
Aesopic: Twenty Four Couplets....   Northampton, Massachusetts, Gehenna Press, 1967.
Millions of Strange Shadows.   New York, Atheneum, and London, Oxford University Press, 1977.
The Venetian Vespers.   Boston, Godine, 1979; expanded version, New York, Atheneum, 1979; Oxford, Oxford University Press, 1980.

Other

Editor, with John Hollander, *Jiggery-Pokery: A Compendium of Double Dactyls.*   New York, Atheneum, 1967.

Translator, with Helen Bacon, *Seven Against Thebes*, by Aeschylus.   New York, Oxford University Press, 1973.
Translator, *Poem upon the Lisbon Disaster*, by Voltaire.   Great Barrington, Massachusetts, Penmaen, 1977.

*   *   *

Anthony Hecht is a gifted craftsman who blends image, rhythm, and idea into rich and subtle music. His work shows imperial command over the energies of word, line, and stanza. Hecht's talents are on full display in early poems like "La Condition Botanique" and "The Gardens of the Villa D'Este," intricate, witty *tours de force*, lavish of image and allusion, filled with striking turns of thought. Witness one stanza from the latter poem:

> The intricate mesh of trees,
> Sagging beneath a lavender snow
> Of wisteria, wired by creepers, perfectly knit
> A plot to capture alive the migrant, tourist soul
> In its corporeal home with all the deft control
> And artifice of an Hephaestus' net.
> Sunlight and branch rejoice to show
> Sudden interstices.

Here the verbal music and the profusion of sound and color perfectly convey the poet's manifold delight in the garden, in its primitive hypnotic power ordered by the formal esthetics of the artistic imagination. The allusion to Hephaestus' net, which trapped Ares and Aphrodite *in flagrante delicto*, gives mythological license to the garden as home of earthly pleasure and hints also at the paradox of incarnation. Such richness of texture is characteristic of Hecht, though in later works, notably in *The Hard Hours* and in *Millions of Strange Shadows*, he sometimes writes with simplicity and directness. Early and late, elegant seriousness often combines with colloquial jest to surprise and delight.

The poetry of Anthony Hecht achieves its distinctive weight and eloquence by frequently recalling Biblical and classical passages and motifs as well as many ancient and modern authors. Plato, Sophocles, Ronsard, Du Bellay, Milton, Swift, Baudelaire, Yeats, and Stevens, for example, contribute their voices to his polyphonous harmonies. Hecht writes in various metrical patterns and stanzaic forms—the double dactyl, sonnet, double sonnet, sestina, blank verse, to name just a few—and demonstrates time and again superb balance, discipline, and control, in a word, complete technical mastery.

Important subjects for Hecht's poetry include the love of men and women, of parents for children, the tense union of flesh and spirit; and the holocaust. On this last topic Hecht has written a number of profound and searching poems. "More Light! More Light!" portrays victims who betray each other thus extinguishing all hope for human dignity; "Rites and Ceremonies" meditates *de profundis* on human suffering and Biblical promise; "It Out-Herods Herod. Pray You, Avoid It." features a father's rueful reflection that, despite his children's admiration of him, "Half God, half Santa Claus," he "could not, at one time, / Have saved them from the gas"; "The Feast of Stephen" sharply perceives the relations between the cults of athleticism and Nazism. In lighter moments Hecht parodies Matthew Arnold in "The Dover Bitch," humorously considers the seduction of a young admirer in "The Ghost in the Martini," and regales the Guggenheim foundation with "Application for a Grant" (freely from Horace), which closes thus:

> As for me, the prize for poets, the simple gift
> For amphybrachs strewn by a kind Euterpe,
> With perhaps a laurel crown of the evergreen
> Imperishable of your fine endowment
> Would supply my modest wants, who dream of nothing
> But a pad on Eighth Street and your approbation.

The Venetian Vespers features several long poems and versions of Joseph Brodsky. The title poem is a lengthy monologue by an expatriate American on the decadent ruins of Venice. He meditates on the transformation of garbage into the "admirable and shatterable triumph" of Murano glassware. He ponders the processes of birth, death, and decay, the relationship between art and life, the movements of memory and aspiration. The corrupt and dirty city affords no pleasant garden to meditate in at eventide, no cure for "Something profoundly soiled, pointlessly hurt," no ablution or "impossible reprieve, / Unpurchased at a scaffold, free, bequeathed / As rain upon the just and unjust, / As in the fall of mercy, unconstrained, / Upon the poor, infected place beneath." Instead he finds the neighborhood Madonna, "Sister Mary Paregoric, Comforter," and the momentary refuge of a thunderstorm wherein "One takes no thought whatever of tomorrow, / The soul being drenched in fine particulars." As the poignant statement of a man, "Who was never even at one time a wise child," the poem brilliantly reflects modern confusion, neurosis, and despair. Along with Hecht's many other achievements, it promises much significant work to come.

—Robert Miola

HEJINIAN, Lyn.   American.   Born in San Francisco, California. Editor, Tuumba Press, and *Poetics Journal*, both Berkeley, California. Address: Tuumba Press, 2639 Russell Street, Berkeley, California 94705, U.S.A.

PUBLICATIONS

Verse

A Thought Is the Bride of What Thinking.   Willits, California, Tuumba Press, 1976.
A Mask of Motion.   Providence, Rhode Island, Burning Deck, 1977.
Writing Is an Aid to Memory.   Berkeley, California, The Figures, 1978.
Gesualdo.   Berkeley, California, Tuumba Press, 1978.

Novel

My Life.   Providence, Rhode Island, Burning Deck, 1980.

*   *   *

American practicality has always been a goad to poets to find some loophole in its philosophical plainness or to puncture it with ribald humor in an attempt to dismiss its deep rootedness in the American psyche. As long as it remains an essential norm of taste, it will make poems squirm to overcome it or to find humorous alternatives to it. Certainly New England's poets have troubled themselves deeply to unseat the prominence of this slightly disguised Puritan virtue. Robert Frost and Wallace Stevens both lavished much irony on the homely virtue; E.E. Cummings mocked it tirelessly in childlike nonsense poems and love lyrics.

Lyn Hejinian, like Frost, was born in San Francisco and educated in New England. At twenty-seven, she returned to the Bay Area and began writing a hauntingly ungraspable mode of lyric—in which a voice, disembodied but felt, unidentifable and yet familiar, whispers to the reader of things that never converge to argument, but evaporate as softly as they came. She too has waged war on practicality, on the utilitarian notion of the poem as message or advice.

And also like Frost, she seems undecided between two orders of things in the mind, or, between two narratives or subjects, neither of which gains her attention long enough to become belief. Instead, like a double helix unwinding from a spool, two possibilities simply travel together loosely in parallel as she teases and frustrates her readers with seemingly ordered speech, but which defied resolution or interpretation.

Gesualdo, a prose meditation, published by her own Tuumba Press in 1978, offers this curious, but typical observation on the doubleness of her poetry:

> The capacity of artists to manipulate for their own ends forms invented in a different spirit is one of the facts of life...was dying by artists whose passion and sensuousness essentially distinguished them...because they tremble, as it were, on the brink of one or the other commitment.

Gesulado is, one speculates, an older poet, mentor to the younger, who speaks and is copied down by his protégé with few intrusions. He has wisdom but none of it is abstractable from the rambles of his monolog. Guesualdo offers more admonitions than advice—but since little of it is removeable from the flow of his discourse, it hardly matters. But that admonitory stance is already the dominant tone of her work in a previous prose pamphlet, *A Thought Is the Bride of What Thinking*, also published by her Tuumba Press in 1976. More tentative than *Gesualdo*, it nonetheless reveals the intention of all her later work—experiments in tonality, in reordering syntax, in riddling her grammar with interjection and transposition. Her meditations draw heavily on older styles of eloquence, much of it coming from the Victorian and Edwardian era, giving her poems a mood like that of old films and photographs.

A Mask of Motion, her first open verse poems, was issued by Keith Waldrop's Burning Deck Press in 1977, and is a further extension of the suspended style of the other two prose books: "I'm confusing two different stories, she said; I know I'm mixing them up. But somehow, strange as it seems, completely unrelated events can intertwine in my memory and then I see they had something in common." This is as good an explanation of Hejinian's own method as will be found in her work. It indicates the nervous doubling of her thought, and speaks to her indecisiveness throughtout.

Her most recent writing is collected in *Writing Is an Aid to Memory*, published by the Figures in 1978. Her preface prepares the reader for what follows:

> I am always conscious of the disquieting runs of life slipping by, that the message remains undelivered, opposed to me. Memory cannot, though the future return, and proffer raw confusions. Knowledge is part of the whole, as hope is, from which love seeks to contrast knowledge with separation.

The book is a sequence of 42 passages, a relentlessly unpredictable discourse in monolog form that moves from one topic to another and from tone to tone without transition. But like a palimpsest the language reveals patterns and meanings buried in the flow of the text, submerged like the river stones or fish forms in a swiftly flowing river. There are enough such glimpses of actual things in the discourse, as in the tour of the caves at Dordogne in *A Mask of Motion*, to make the reader grasp at them, as the language moves along with its shimmering but intangible possibilities. Hejinian proves that language can do more than state explicit arguments; it can move a reader to different emotional states merely by the configurations of its words and tones, its subtle and unyielding mysteries.

—Paul Christensen

HELLER, Michael D. American. Born in New York City, 11 May 1937. Educated at Miami Beach Senior High School, graduated 1955; Rensselaer Polytechnic Institute, Troy, New York (Managing Editor, *Rensselaer Engineeer*, and Editor, *Bachelor* magazine), B.S. in management engineering 1959; City College, New York 1961-63; New School for Social Research, New York (Coffey Prize, 1964), 1963-64; New York University, 1970-71. Married 1) Doris C. Whytal in 1962 (divorced, 1978), one son; 2) the writer Jane Augustine in 1979. Chief Technical Writer, Norelco Corporation, New York, 1963-65; part-time teacher in Spain, 1965-66; free-lance industrial and advertising writer, 1966-67. Since 1967, Member of the Faculty, now Master Teacher, American Language Institute, New York University. Since 1970, teacher with New York State Poetry in the Schools program. Adjunct Lecturer in Developmental Skills, New York City Community College, 1973. Contributing Editor, *Montemora* magazine and staff member, Montemora Foundation, New York. United States Editor, *Origin* magazine. Recipient: Creative Artists Public Service grant, 1975; National Endowment for the Humanities grant, 1979; Poetry Society of America Alice Fay di Castagnola Award, 1980. Address: P.O. Box 981, Stuyvesant Station, New York, New York 10009, U.S.A.

PUBLICATIONS

Verse

Two Poems. Mount Horeb, Wisconsin, Perishable Press, 1970.
Accidental Center. Fremont, Michigan, Sumac Press, 1972.
Figures of Speaking. Mount Horeb, Wisconsin, Perishable Press, 1977.
Knowledge. New York, Sun Press, 1979.

Other

Conviction's Net of Branches: Essays on the Objectivist Poets and Poetry. Carbondale, Southern Illinois University Press, 1984.

*

Critical Studies: "Moving Heaven and Earth" by James Guimond, in *Parnassus* (New York), Winter 1972; "A Review of *Knowledge*" by Laszlo K. Gefin, in *Sagetrieb* (Orono, Maine), Spring 1984.

*   *   *

The publication in 1972 of *Accidental Center* announced an authentic, hard-edged, meditative poet of truly contemporary sensibility who worked in the Objectivist manner, a poet who exemplified Oppen's "sense of the poet's self among things" and Reznikoff's detailed, literal, compassionate witnessing of the modern city dweller, a poet who knew that

the words
are precipitates
—in themselves
precipitous
rare and expensive dust
desperately grasped
in the amalgam.

For Michael D. Heller, the words represent a process of distillation: they are hard-won, to be treasured and used sparingly. At the same time, there's a willingness to follow where the words lead, into darkness, mystery; this is a fundamental recognition, based on his awareness of physical principles, of "how each / word is a shift of matter."

Accidental Center was remarkable in that, unlike most first books, there was a complete absence of that "overwriting" which masks lack of assurance and control. The poems result from an intense concentration, a focusing on the objective, in Zukofsky's early formulation of Objectivist poetry. In fact, the photo-image is prevalent in the book—"the moment in the sense" caught and held—almost as if Objectivist principles were being given a technical underpinning. *Accidental Center* is a serious book that takes language seriously. The method of many of the poems is to proceed by means of simple, declarative constructs to form an image as proposition—a logic based on the "thingness of things," on exact observation. The poems are often based on the paradoxical image, provoking us to respond to the artifact as material for a contemporary mythology. Numerous references employing the terms of astrophysics, chemistry, and biology function almost as a traditional mythic or religious gloss, amplifying and expanding the particular emotive context ("Operation Cicero"):

writing of the great light of cities
...these are entropic times
and those bright clusters
in our lives
in their rot
are black bodies
and absorb it all
like a woman
on one's bed
who cannot bear the light

The paradoxical quality results also from the contrast between the precision of the scientific terms, economy of language, the short lines and spare style—and the genuine acceptance of a sort of negative capability: things, ideas, emotions—oneself in the world—are not rendered simplistically but exactly as a measure of their subtle relativity and mystery: what we know is a function of how we know.

Heller expresses throughout the poems of *Accidental Center* an explicit or implicit ontological concern, not in the form of abstract disquisition, but as speculation on the objects which relate to and define the self. The finest example of a poem given over wholly to this concern is the impressive "Meditation on the Coral," in which our existence as city-dwellers is explored in terms of the coral symbolizing in its cellular structure our dependent and communal way of life but also, in its origins in the sea, our atavistic urges, "and the warm saline / — as of the birth sac / still a dream."

Heller's second major collection, *Knowledge*, contains in addition to the speculative poetry which characterized the earlier book, poems which are more discursive, leisurely, descriptive—though no less formal in intent. Having settled into a style, he is now able to accommodate more immediate and personal concerns without, however, sacrificing intensity. Thus, events which mark the perception of both continuity and change in family relationships—with father, mother, wife, son—become occasions for poems in which the occasion makes its own space and pace. Literalness coexists with irony in a number of these poems, producing a gentle humor. "Bialystok Stanzas" recalls the incisiveness, objectivity, and compassion of Reznikoff's depictions of traditional Jewish life and the holocaust. But in even as occasional a poem as "On the Beach," Heller never relaxes his gaze; though the occasion may seem commonplace—"watching square yards of such flesh / Baste itself with oil"—nevertheless, "Even here, amid these minor increments / of peril, one is consoled. In this / Careless resort of life of beaches / Deceptions themselves are a kind of truth."

The energy which informs Heller's poems—and the reason he is so rewarding as a poet—derives from "the world already existing/without a name," in which the impulse is to question, to take nothing for granted, while perceiving what is there, in a very real sense, for all to know. The concluding section of "At Albert's Landing (with my son)" specifies the process of that special knowledge:

Different as the woods are
This is no paradise to enter or leave.
Just the real, and a wild nesting
Of hope in the real
Which does not know of hope.
Things lean and lean, and sometimes
Words find common centers in us
Resonating and filling speech.
Let me know a little of you.

—Robert Vas Dias

HELWIG, David (Gordon). Canadian. Born in Toronto, Ontario, 5 April 1938. Educated at Stamford Collegiate Institute; University of Toronto, B.A. 1960; University of Liverpool, M.A. 1962. Married Nancy Keeling in 1959; two daughters. Member of the Department of English, Queen's University, Kingston, Ontario, 1962-80. Address: 106 Montreal Street, Kingston, Ontario K7K 3E8, Canada.

PUBLICATIONS

Verse

Figures in a Landscape. Ottawa, Oberon Press, 1967.
The Sign of the Gunman. Ottawa, Oberon Press, 1969.
The Best Name of Silence. Ottawa, Oberon Press, 1972.
Atlantic Crossings. Ottawa, Oberon Press, 1974.
A Book of the Hours. Ottawa, Oberon Press, 1979.
The Rain Falls Like Rain. Ottawa, Oberon Press, 1982.
Catchpenny Poems. Ottawa, Oberon Press, 1983.

Play

A Time in Winter (produced Kingston, Ontario, 1967). Included in Figures in a Landscape, 1967.

Novels

The Day Before Tomorrow. Ottawa, Oberon Press, 1971; as Message from a Spy, Don Mills, Ontario, Paperjacks, 1975.
The Glass Knight. Ottawa, Oberon Press, 1976.
Jennifer. Ottawa, Oberon Press, 1979; New York, Beaufort, 1983.
The King's Evil. Ottawa, Oberon Press, 1981; New York, Beaufort, 1984.

It Is Always Summer. Toronto, Stoddart, and New York, Beaufort, 1982.
A Sound Like Laughter. Toronto, Stoddart, and New York, Beaufort, 1983.
The Only Son. Toronto, Stoddart, and New York, Beaufort, 1984.

Short Stories

The Streets of Summer. Ottawa, Oberon Press, 1969.

Other

A Book about Billie (documentary). Ottawa, Oberon Press, 1972; as Inside and Out, Don Mills, Ontario, Paperjacks, 1975.

Editor, with Tom Marshall, Fourteen Stories High: Best Canadian Stories of 71. Ottawa, Oberon Press, 1971.
Editor, with Joan Harcourt, 72, 73, 74 and 75: New Canadian Stories. Ottawa, Oberon Press, 4 vols., 1972-75.
Editor, Words from Inside. Kingston, Ontario, Prison Arts, 1972(?).
Editor, The Human Elements: Critical Essays (and Second Series). Ottawa, Oberon Press, 2 vols., 1978-81.
Editor, Love and Money: The Politics of Culture. Ottawa, Oberon Press, 1980.
Editor, with Sandra Martin, 83 and 84: Best Canadian Stories. Ottawa, Oberon Press, 2 vols., 1983-84.
Editor, with Sandra Martin, Coming Attractions 1983 and 1984. Ottawa, Oberon Press, 2 vols., 1983-84.

*

Critical Studies: "Spells Against Chaos" by Tom Marshall, in Quarry (Kingston, Ontario), Spring 1968; "David Helwig's New Timber," in Queen's Quarterly (Kingston, Ontario), Summer 1974.

*   *   *

David Helwig's recent muse is less violent and political than in some of his earlier poetry. In The Sign of the Gunman, for instance, there was a curious stridency and rhetorical pose that seemed artificial and laboured: "They are burning our cities / they are shooting at us with bullets." This is not good poetry and it goes hand in hand with occasional distasteful revelling in sutures and seared flesh that reminds one of nothing so much as the songs of Tom Lehrer: "Somewhere is a photograph / of a man in two pieces / burned until he is only / two pieces of a cooked man." When the violence is necessary to greatness, as it is in his "Apollo and Daphne," it is right, and felt as a conclusion to the poem. Helwig, however, does not escape the fashionable Canadian taste for Frye-esque mythology where Harlequin and the acrobat, like the Zeus of his "Metamorphosis," appear to stand for more than they are, gesturing for significance.

In Atlantic Crossings, however, the four poems that comprise the collection are not racked by symbol. The image of the louse, in the Columbus section, moving "off the edge of my swollen brain / into a new world" has an appropriately Donnean quality. It is indicative of what preserves this collection from mere indulgence in the horrific world of madness through which it travels.

The strength of Helwig's earliest poetry is present again in his more recent work—a strength that owes much to a fine-edged description. Helwig's admiration for Andrew Wyeth is evident in his "After Brueghel" where winter is a season "of sudden long white distances / that empty the mind." There is something of the Pacific North West School (William Stafford, for instance) in Helwig's "Still Life" or "Sunday Breakfast":

> Orange, one egg, tea in a cup
> of blue and white, composing silences
> against the hurt nerves fluttering.

Although some of the poems in *A Book of the Hours* come perilously close to McKuen, his affection for the familial and domestic is rarely sentimental. A classic of toughness is his poem "A Shaker Chair":

> I see in the Shaker rocking chair
> stillness turning, stillness moving,
> contemplation and silent standing,
> even the denial of the body.

Occasionally, too, one senses Helwig's debt to the impressionist transformation of simple painterly objects in to a larger life, a debt that gives us echoes of Stevens: "We swim before we walk. The tropic sea / within the caul is home." Certainly the inflexions are Stevens's, and they are congenial to an attractive toughness in the verse that saves Helwig's taste for darkness, secrecy, night, and their magic from being merely fantasy. Fantasy at its best, though, is present in his "Summer Landscapes" where "the house running away to the stars / on the feet of mice" has the quality of a Louis de Niverville painting.

Like many Canadian artists Helwig seemed to find his voice abroad. Liverpool nurtured him and in his best poems one hears not the Mersey sound or poets but the voices of "the old women / climbing Brownlow Hill / in the killing fog" that he celebrates in "Liverpool."

In the best of his poetry there is a fine sense of detachment. That is why his poems on Diefenbaker, the Orange Lodge, and American political issues are so weak. His spontaneous emotion is too close to their creation. The picture one retains of him is of a distant walker, a figure in his own landscape, above the world he deplores and celebrates—the world he describes in "Christmas, 1965," in which "Silence / had overwhelmed the noise of men" leaving only the poet's voice.

—D.D.C. Chambers

HENDERSON, Hamish. British. Born in Blairgowrie, Perthshire, Scotland, 11 November 1919. Educated at Blairgowrie High School; Dulwich College, London; Downing College, Cambridge, M.A. Served with the Highland Division during World War II. Married; two daughters. Since 1951, Senior Lecturer and Research Fellow, School of Scottish Studies, University of Edinburgh. Recipient: Maugham Award, 1949. LL.D.: University of Dundee. Address: School of Scottish Studies, University of Edinburgh, Old College, South Bridge, Edinburgh EH8 9YL, Scotland.

PUBLICATIONS

Verse

Elegies for the Dead in Cyrenaica. London, Lehmann, 1948.
Freedom Come-All-Ye, in *Chapbook* special issue (Aberdeen), iii, 6, 1967.

Other

Editor, and contributor, *Ballads of World War II Collected by Seumas Mor Maceanruig.* Glasgow, Caledonian Press, 1947.

*

Critical Study: *The Poet Speaks* edited by Peter Orr, London, Routledge, and New York, Barnes and Noble, 1966.

*   *   *

Hamish Henderson's one book of verse, *Elegies for the Dead in Cyrenaica,* was published as long ago as 1948, and was the product of the desert war which inspired so much of the best English poetry of World War II, including that of Keith Douglas. Appearing when it did, it tended to miss the tide of interest in "war poetry" which had been nourished by the conflict itself. The fact that the author has never produced another collection has also not aided his reputation. Yet Henderson has always had a small band of admirers, and re-reading his elegies it is easy to see why.

The book has two advantages—it can be read complete, as a whole, not just as a collection of poems written in different moods and on different occasions; and it has a comfortable relationship to the modernist tradition (something more likely to happen with Scottish poets than with English ones). Henderson was obviously much influenced by the Eliot of *Four Quartets*—it was difficult not to be, at that period; that is, if one hadn't succumbed to the influences of Dylan Thomas or Edith Sitwell. But one also hears within his work the voices of Europe—Goethe and Hölderlin, who supply him with epigraphs; and the Alexandrian Greek, Cavafy, whom he quotes. The poems are that comparatively rare thing in 20th-century English poetry—successful philosophical verse.

He combines this philosophical bent with a delicate naturalism, and a skilful control of tone, which means that these comparatively long poems can rise up into the "high" style and leave it again without difficulty, just as the author requires. Here is an example, from the beginning of the Second Elegy:

> At dawn, under the concise razor-edge
> of the escarpment, the laager sleeps. No petrol fires yet
> blow flame for brew-up. Up on the pass a sentry
> inhales his Nazionale. Horse-shoe-curve of the bay
> grows visible beneath him. He smokes and yawns.
> Ooo-augh,
>   and the limitless
> shabby lion-pelt of the desert completes and rounds
> his limitless ennui.

One suspects, at a distance of more than thirty-five years, that this is the kind of wartime verse most likely to last and be read by posterity.

—Edward Lucie-Smith

HENDRIKS, A(rthur) L(emière). Jamaican. Born in Kingston, 17 April 1922. Educated at Jamaica College; Ottershaw College, Surrey, England. Married to Jacqueline Elissa Cox; five daughters, two sons, and one stepson. Clerk, Arthur Hendriks Furniture Company, Jamaica, 1940-50; sales manager,

Radio Jamaica Ltd., 1950-60; general manager, Jamaica Broadcasting Corporation, 1961-64; Caribbean Director, Thomson Television Ltd., London, 1964-71. Since 1971, free-lance writer. Address: Box 265, Constant Spring, Kingston 8, Jamaica.

PUBLICATIONS

Verse

On This Mountain and Other Poems.   London, Deutsch, 1965.
These Green Islands and Other Poems.   Kingston, Bolivar Press, 1971.
Muet.   London, Outposts, 1971.
Madonna of the Unknown Nation.   London, Workshop Press, 1974.
The Islanders and Other Poems.   Kingston, Savacou, 1983.
The Naked Ghost and Other Poems.   London, Outposts, 1984.

Other

Archie and the Princess and the Everythingest Horse (for children).   Kingston, Gleaner, 1983.
Great Families of Jamaica.   Kingston, Gleaner, 1984.

Editor, with Cedric Lindo, *The Independence Anthology of Jamaican Literature.*   Kingston, Arts Celebration Committee of the Ministry of Development, 1962.

*

Critical Study: "He Will Write Again" by John Figueroa, in *New Poetry* (London), 1976.

A.L. Hendriks comments:
    To speak simply; for this grace I pray (George Seferis).
    Je vis un rêve permanent qui s'arrête in nuit in jour (Georges Enesco).

*   *   *

    A.L. Hendriks is one of perhaps a half dozen impressive contemporary West Indian poets. His poetry is less agitated by themes of race, alienation and identity than is much West Indian writing, and the impression his poems make on the reader is that they are the private meditations of a delicate soul. There is a certain sobriety in his idiom, a coolness in approach, and a feeling of control and tranquility. His tone is subdued, his voice without stridency or affectation; the rhythms are quiet and they engage the person or subject in a private way. Some of his best poems join sympathy for a particular place, a sense of its quality and particularity, with a capacity for attentive listening. The poetry seems to me to be a mode of intimate access to some truth of experience not yet articulated, not yet quite held:

    This thin and oval stone, cold upon the brown earth,
    is not dumb, nor is the grass, nor the curved stick
    lying smooth by the brook's edge; you may listen
    and through the unapparent sense learn from them
    a new music, secret, and played on no instrument.

    In some of his poems, for example "Song for My Brothers and Cousins" and "On This Mountain," Hendriks is troubled out of his secluded world and contemplative posture:

    We no longer belong to a private
    society and cannot hide
    private misdemeanours, we are
    one people in one house and cannot leave it.

The idea trembling on the edge in this stanza is never brought to the passionate explicitness that it would have in the verse of Edwárd Brathwaite, for example. Indeed, the feeling, even in his more public poems, is less torn and troubled. It has, on the other hand, an unaffected inward dignity, of the kind that is to be seen in his restrained but sensitive relish for the old in "An Old Jamaican Woman Thinks about the Hereafter":

    What would I do forever in a big place, who
    have lived all my life in a small island?
    The same parish holds the cottage I was born in, all
    my family, and the cool churchyard.

In all of Hendriks's poetry we find a sensibility which thrives on smallness, coolness, and a fine human simplicity.

                                                                    —William Walsh

————————

HENRI, Adrian (Maurice).   British.   Born in Birkenhead, Cheshire, 10 April 1932. Educated at St. Asaph Grammar School, North Wales, 1945-51; King's College, Newcastle, B.A. (honours) in fine arts 1955. Married Joyce Wilson in 1957 (separated). Lecturer, Manchester College of Art and Design, 1961-64, and Liverpool College of Art, 1964-68. Member of the Liverpool Scene, poetry-rock group, 1968-70, American tour, 1969. Painter: individual shows—Institute of Contemporary Arts, London, 1968; Art Net, London, 1975; retrospective, Wolverhampton, 1976; Demarco Gallery, Edinburgh, 1977. Since 1970, full-time writer, singer, and painter, with occasional work with Grimms, and Henri and Friends groups; Writer-in-Residence, Tattenhall Centre, Cheshire, 1980-82. President, Liverpool Academy of Arts, 1972-80, and Merseyside Arts Association, 1978-80. Recipient: Arts Council of Northern Ireland prize, for painting, 1964; John Moores Exhibition Prize, 1972. Agent: Deborah Rogers, 49 Blenheim Crescent, London W11 2EF. Address: 21 Mount Street, Liverpool L1 9HD, England.

PUBLICATIONS

Verse

The Mersey Sound: Penguin Modern Poets 10, with Roger McGough and Brian Patten.   London, Penguin, 1967; revised edition, 1974, 1983.
Tonight at Noon.   London, Rapp and Whiting, 1968; New York, McKay, 1969.
City.   London, Rapp and Whiting, 1969.
Talking after Christmas Blues, music by Wallace Southam.   London, Turret, 1969.
Poems for Wales and Six Landscapes for Susan.   Gillingham, Kent, ARC, 1970.
Autobiography.   London, Cape, 1971.
America.   London, Turret, 1972.
The Best of Henri: Selected Poems 1960-70.   London, Cape, 1975.
One Year.   Todmorden, Lancashire, ARC, 1976.

City Hedges: Poems 1970-76. London, Cape, 1977.
Words Without a Story. Liverpool, Glasshouse Press, 1979.
From the Loveless Motel: Poems 1976-1979. London, Cape, 1980.
Harbour. London, Ambit, 1982.
Penny Arcade: Poems 1978-1982. London, Cape, 1983.
New Volume, with Roger McGough and Brian Patten. London, Penguin, 1983.

Recordings: (with Liverpool Scene) *St. Adrian Co., Broadway and 3rd*, RCA, 1970; *Heirloon*, RCA, 1970; *Recollections*, Charisma, 1972; (solo) *Adrian Henri*, Canon, 1974; *British Poets of Our Times*, with Hugo Williams, Argo; *Gifted Wreckage*, with Roger McGough and Brian Patten, Talking Tape, 1984.

Plays

I Wonder: A Guillaume Apollinaire Show, with Michael Kustow (produced London, 1968).
I Want, with Nell Dunn, adaptation of their own novel (produced Liverpool, 1983).

Television Play: *Yesterday's Girl*, 1973.

Novel

I Want, with Nell Dunn. London, Cape 1972.

Other

Environments and Happenings. London, Thames and Hudson, 1974; as *Total Art: Environments, Happenings and Performances*, New York, Praeger, 1974.
Eric the Punk Cat (juvenile). London, Hodder and Stoughton, 1982.

*

Critical Studies: *Art in a City* by John Willett, London, Methuen, 1967; introduction by Edward Lucie-Smith to *The Liverpool Scene*, London, Rapp and Carroll, and New York, Doubleday, 1967; *The Society of the Poem* by Jonathan Raban, London, Harrap, 1971; "Bathos, Schmathos" by Michael Hulse, in *New Poetry 49* (London), 1980; "Penny Arcade" by Geoffrey Ward, in *Ambit 47* (London), 1984.

Adrian Henri comments:
(1970) I was trained as a painter and still paint and exhibit paintings. I make a living primarily by performing the works that I write, mostly with music. I think of myself as a maker, and presenter, of images in various media. "Pop Poet" is, I think, the most common label.
My major influences are T.S. Eliot, Apollinaire, Mallarmé, Ginsberg, Olson and recently Tennyson, Creeley and Hugh MacDiarmid; also the prose of Joyce and William Burroughs. I am an autobiographical poet: my poems are extensions of my own life, some fact, some fantasy. For this reason I write perhaps more love-poems than anything else. I am excited by new uses of language in the mass-media, like TV commercials or pop songs, and am only interested in "older" verse-forms (i.e. rhyme, etc.) as they survive in modern society, e.g. ballad and particularly Blues. I would like my poems to be read by as many people as possible, since I can't see any point either personally or politically in writing for an elite minority. I think by doing readings

and by working with the "Liverpool Scene" I am beginning to reach a bigger and largely "non-literary" audience.
(1974) Since a serious heart illness in 1970 my way of life, and to some extent my way of working, has changed somewhat. At the moment my poetry is perhaps quieter and more "traditional" in character. Since spending some time in Somerset and Shropshire I have become interested in the English landscape tradition, notably Wordsworth and Housman, and the Pre-Raphaelite painters. My work as a painter is similarly involved in an investigation into the possibilities of landscape.
(1980) I am still involved with landscape, but have recently extended this to "Debris" paintings, studies of urban wasteland. *City Hedges* perhaps reflects this. Current work includes a musical version of Jarry's *Ubu*. Economic problems have made musical collaborations less possible, but I still work with guitarist Andy Roberts, and others, when I can.
(1985) After a period of "retrenchment" in the 1970's, there seems to be a return to a greater freedom and wider range of idiom, and some of the concerns of the 1960's, in *From the Loveless Motel* and *Penny Arcade*. Touring in Germany, Canada, Norway, the U.S.A., etc., as well as round Britain, has generated a number of travel-poems, and I'm still interested in the long poem (as previously with *City, Autobiography, One Year*) and the problems (first articulated by Poe) of making it work at the same level of intensity as the lyric. I have been increasingly affected by the prose writings of Malcolm Lowry. In an increasingly fragmented and divisive society I still see my main problem as trying to reach as wide an audience as possible while still writing what I feel to be valid modern poetry.

*   *   *

Not a poet only, Adrian Henri is one of a number of contemporary artists who have forsaken their conventional roles for a more "total" concept that involves public performance. Henri has at various times been painter, novelist, critic, singer, and actor-out of his own poetic creations. There is in his work an affinity with the American artist Allan Kaprow, pioneer of the "environment" and the "happening." Henri has written on the subject, and significantly his collection of poems *Penny Arcade* shares its title with one of Kaprow's assemblages. The element of "action collage" is constant in his writing, evidenced early on with the barrage of images in "I Want to Paint Pictures" and the nightmare Bosch landscape of "The Triumph of Death," still present years later in "Death in the Suburbs" and "Annunciation."
An intensely serious writer, Henri at the same time displays a sly humour, and is capable of a deceptive simplicity. Some of his work in the 1960's is reminiscent of pop song lyrics, hardly surprising in one who has worked with rock musicians and once led his own group, Liverpool Scene. Thus the direct, childlike lines of "Batpoem," or the gentler "Love Is": "Love is feeling cold in the backs of vans/ Love is a fanclub with only two fans". Lyrics of this kind cannot disguise the verbal skill, the strong structural sense that underlies Henri's most freewheeling flights, akin to those of jazzmen like Parker or Coltrane. "Adrian Henri's Talking after Christmas Blues" and, more recently, "Talking Toxteth Blues" are examples both of a biting wit and a parodist's measure of the form. The same humour is found in "Red Card," with football imagery applied to seduction and its aftermath, and "Any Prince to Any Princess," where fairytale themes are hilariously revamped in governmental jargon. Aware of most poetic styles, Henri has throughout his career attempted various "homages" to bards of the past—some more serious than others—including Blake, Byron, and Housman. "Tonight at Noon" is his tribute to the jazz musician Charles Mingus, and

has in turn inspired a record album by the Jam, while in "New York City Blues" Henri mourns the passing of John Lennon.

As is inevitable with an artist whose poetry is drawn from his own experience, much of Henri's writing is devoted to love and its memories. More than most, he is able to fix in a handful of words the transitory nature of human relationships, the sense of desolation that loss of love so often brings: "The sea has carefully mislaid the beach/beyond our reach. It looks like rain/Over the boardwalk bridge we trace in vain/your lost shell earring— remembered image/of harbour, swans and rainbow—gone per- haps/back to its watery element."

Autobiography is his masterpiece, a self-portrait from birth to the year 1970. From the first vivid childhood recollections, through the loves and influences of youth, Henri captures super- bly the flavour of his time, its scents and colours. Darting from one clutch of memories to the next, seizing with what seems like total recall on the essence of each, he involves the reader in his past, bringing a vanished world alive. His personality pervades the work ("sad/boy-to-be-poet/head full of words/understood by no one"), lending its unique voice to what is throughout an individual testament. *Autobiography* marks the beginning of an increased preoccupation with landscapes in subsequent poems, whether idyllic country scenes or bleak inner cities and motor- ways. Though love remains, and humour flickers occasionally, the overall tone is sombre. Sad elegies to Housman and D.H. Lawrence, rather than the zany 1960's fantasy of "Mrs. Albion You've Got a Lovely Daughter," seem the order of the day. Yet whatever the prevailing mood, Henri remains himself, his gifts no less evident than in former days.

In common with most "performance" poets, Henri is perhaps read less often today. On reflection, this doesn't count for much. Poetic fashion is a continuing cycle which will in time come round to him again. The best of Henri is constant, too good to be missed. He offers a vision drawn direct from life, scattered like life into random insights lit by a poet's intense imagination: "I give you/fragments of broken dreams/bustickets/torn snap- shots.../...don't see only know/a landscape in your body/a river in my eyes."

—Geoff Sadler

HERNTON, Calvin C(oolidge). American. Born in Chatta- nooga, Tennessee, 28 April 1933. Educated at Howard High School, 1946-50; Talladega College, Alabama, 1950-54, B.A. 1954; Fisk University, Nashville, Tennessee, 1954-56, M.A. in sociology 1956; Columbia University, New York, 1961. Married Mildred Webster in 1959; one child. Social worker, Youth House, New York, 1956-57; Instructor in Sociology, Benedict College, Columbia, South Carolina, 1957-58, Alabama Agricul- tural and Mechanical College, Huntsville, 1958-59, Edward Waters College, Jacksonville, Florida, 1959-60, and Southern University, Baton Rouge, Louisiana, 1960-61; social investiga- tor, Department of Welfare, New York, 1961-62; Writer-in- Residence, Central State University, Wilberforce, Ohio, 1969. Faculty member since 1970, and currently Professor of Black Studies, Oberlin College, Ohio. Co-Founder, *Umbra* magazine, New York, 1963. Address: 35 North Prospect Street, Oberlin, Ohio 44074, U.S.A.

PUBLICATIONS

Verse

The Coming of Chronos to the House of Nightsong: An Epical Narrative of the South. New York, Interim, 1964.
Medicine Man: Collected Poems. Berkeley, California, Reed Cannon and Johnson, 1976.

Plays

Glad to Be Dead (produced Jacksonville, Florida, 1958).
Flame (produced Jacksonville, Florida, 1958).
The Place (produced Oberlin, Ohio, 1972).

Novel

Scarecrow. New York, Doubleday, 1974.

Other

Sex and Racism in America. New York, Doubleday, 1965; as *Sex and Racism,* London, Deutsch, 1969.
White Papers for White Americans. New York, Doubleday, 1966.
Coming Together: Black Power, White Hatred, and Sexual Hangups. New York, Random House, 1971.
The Cannabis Experience: An Interpretative Study of the Effects of Marijuana and Hashish, with Joseph Berke. Lon- don, Owen, 1974.

*

Manuscript Collection: Ohio University Library, Athens.

Critical Studies: "A Voice from a Tumultuous Time," in *Obsi- dian* (Fredonia, New York), Spring-Summer 1980, and "Umbra Poets 1980," in *Black American Literature Forum* (Terre Haute, Indiana), Fall 1980, both by Tom Dent; *Bounds Out of Bounds: A Compass for Recent American and British Poetry* by Roberta Berke, New York, Oxford University Press, 1981.

Calvin C. Hernton comments:

I used to make statements about what I wrote, how I wrote it, my method, my process, my poetics, and that stuff. But I don't do that anymore. My poetry is my statement. However, I will say this much. I write about anything, and from as many standpoints as possible. I've written poems about war, hatred, racism, racial violence, social and personal suffering and joy as well; poems about trees, making love, loss of love, the blues, being scared in an airplane, persons I've known such as musicians, painters, friends, lovers, enemies and people rushing along the streets with umbrellas open when it is no longer raining; poems about what- ever I happen to feel necessary at the time; poems for children, women, and poems for nobody but myself! I have noticed that one thing runs through all of my poems no matter what the subject, style or poetic level: and this is an almost too human concern for humanity.

*   *   *

Calvin C. Hernton's poetry is concerned with the plight of the black masses, the coming of age of the existential Negro, and the misconceptualization of race relations in the United States:

Laughter and scorn on the lips of Edsel automobiles
instructing the populace to love God, be kind to puppies
and the Chase Manhattan National Bank
Because of this there is no Fourth of July this year
No shouting, no popping of firecrackers, no celebrating,
    no parade
But the rage of a hopeless people
Jitterbugging
    in the streets.

He speaks of creative impersonalization:

> I am not a metaphor or symbol.
> This you hear is not the wind in the trees,
> Nor a cat being maimed in the street.
> I am being maimed in the street.
> It is I who weep, laugh, feel pain or joy.

And finally he symbolizes America spiritually replenished through organic changes in her total civilization:

> to see ALL Americans in freedom and passion for one
> another, lift ourselves above that lifeless thing (material-
> ism). What America needs most now is room, a kind of
> transcendent humanity, whereby all men and women can
> work, love and acquire self-esteem without having to
> maim one another in the struggle.

—Corrine E. Bostic

HESKETH, Phoebe (née Rayner).   British.   Born in Preston, Lancashire, 29 January 1909. Educated at Preston High School, 1914-16; Dagfield Birkdale School, 1918-24; Cheltenham Ladies' College, Gloucestershire, 1924-26. Married William Aubrey Martin Hesketh in 1931; two sons and one daughter. Woman's Page Editor, Bolton *Evening News*, 1942-45; Lecturer, Bolton Women's College, 1967-69; teacher of creative writing, Bolton School, 1976-78. Member, Arts Council Poets Reading Poems and Writers in the Schools panels. Recipient: Poetry Society Greenwood Prize, 1948, 1966; Arts Council grant, 1965. Fellow, Royal Society of Literature, 1971. Address: 10 The Green, Heath Charnock, Chorley, Lancashire PR6 9JH, England.

PUBLICATIONS

Verse

Poems.   Manchester, Sherratt and Hughes, 1939.
Lean Forward, Spring!   London, Sidgwick and Jackson, 1948.
No Time for Cowards.   London, Heinemann, 1952.
Out of the Dark: New Poems, edited by Richard Church. London, Heinemann, 1954.
Between Wheels and Stars.   London, Heinemann, 1956.
The Buttercup Children.   London, Hart Davis, 1958.
Prayer for Sun.   London, Hart Davis, 1966.
A Song of Sunlight (for children).   London, Chatto and Windus, 1974.
Preparing to Leave.   London, Enitharmon Press, 1977.
The Eighth Day: Selected Poems 1948-1978.   London, Enitharmon Press, 1980.

Plays

Radio: many documentaries, and the plays *One Pair of Eyes* and *What Can the Matter Be?*, 1979.

Other

My Aunt Edith (biography of Edith Rigby).   London, Davies, 1966.
Rivington: The Story of a Village.   London, Davies, 1972.

*

Manuscript Collection: Lockwood Memorial Library, State University of New York, Buffalo.

Phoebe Hesketh comments:

I've never belonged to any literary circle and was amazed when Sidgwick and Jackson's poetry reader said they'd like to publish a collection (1948). After the early influences of border ballads, R.L. Stevenson, and de la Mare, I fell, in my teens, under the spell of the Romantics, which undoubtedly coloured my first published work. Gradually, through rare strokes of fortune and the common blows of fate, I began to cast off the lyrical, romantic garments for sparser, bleaker material. Writing for me now is the process of stripping to the bone—with rare bursts of lyricism. I never seem able to write the poem I want to write: when I get the germ of an idea—as soon as it takes form—the poem gets hold of me and takes me where *it* wills, not where I will. I never know how a poem is to end. There are longer and longer periods between poems when I'm certain I'll never write again. I can't sustain a poem from "the top half of the brain"; it comes, unbidden, from a deeper level. It is the poem, not I, that achieves the initial creation. The hard labour comes in the next stages of actual composition and revision. I feel with Robert Frost: "A poem may be labored over once it is in being; it may not be labored into being."

*   *   *

Some of Phoebe Hesketh's most effective imagery springs from her native northern landscape of "heather-shouldered fells," "grey thin-fingered wind" and "stormy solitudes...where reluctant spring/Retards the leaf." As she says in "Northern Stone":

> Sap of the sullen moor is blood of my blood.
> The whale-back ridge and whiplash of the wind
> Stripping the branches in a rocking wood—
> All these are of my life-stream, scoured and thinned.

Her moors are Brontëan. So too is the visionary quest "to find the Unknown through the known" expressed in many other evocations of this stark and stubborn country, including "Bleasdale: on Fairsnape," "Mountain Top," and the symbolism of solitary search, bereft of consoling certainties, in "Winter Journey." Her depiction of nature is never merely descriptive: its moods and seasons serve always as metaphor to communicate the experience of the human spirit, and a pervasive apprehension of "what is hidden and yet near/And intimate as breath." Emily Brontë is again irresistibly recalled in poems like "Revelation," "In Praise of Darkness," and 'Vision': "The air grows luminous and light takes hold/Of darkness till my searching eyes are filled,/I see, beyond the Seen, new worlds unfold."

Yet this poet also delights in the world of sense: the "beer-bubble stream," the winter sun "muffled in a wool of sullen cloud," the autumn hill where the wind "with iron-fisted blows/ Hammers the colours bleeding to the ground." Like Edward Thomas she celebrates the everyday simplicities of rural sights and pursuits—ploughing or gathering sticks, coltsfoot on a slag-heap, midsummer smoke "pale blue as lupin spires." Animals and birds—the pent-up rage of the solitary bull, the melancholy chestnut mare "with drooping underlip.../ Tail-in to the wind," the alertly quivering fox "the colour of last year's beech-leaves"; the mallard and her brood surprised by a stoat, the heron "with elegiac wings"—are captured with sharp and vivid immediacy. The same loving precision informs her portraits of country people: village children tumbling out of school, their days "wide open as a daisy to the sun," the classroom dunce grown wise in his hedgerow truancies, an old man "withered as a gaunt sun-wrinkled tree." It is characteristic that several of these human cameos should explore the theme of spiritual riches implicit in physical deprivation. For the blind, not only the other senses but inward vision too is miraculously heightened; while the cripple's intuition of the intense life in flowers, rooted like himself, en-ables him "to travel though I may not rise and go." A similar paradox of liberation through captivity is expressed in "Rescue," in the image of the bird finally returning to the Falconer: "Thus chained and hooded, I am free at last."

Phoebe Hesketh's deeply felt conviction that modern man, his life "caged with steel" and "moulded into rods by the machine," has betrayed and desecrated his natural heritage is conveyed with telling impact through poems like "Born Between the Wheels," "The Invading Spring," "No Pause for Death," and her bleak vision of the future in "The Dark Side of the Moon." On all sides she sees "devastation in the unsacred name/ Of science mock the cratered human heart." Yet however fiercely "stoned with doubt," her faith always finally reasserts itself. Walking in the city, she discovers in "one weak spire" of grass in a broken paving-stone "strength enough to break/ The angled world of concrete."

Seldom unconscious of "The ache of living—beauty spiked with pain," or that "Even upon a peak of joy the flint comes piercing through," Phoebe Hesketh has continued to affirm her hard-won belief in the attainment of inward growth through such griefs as bereavement, love renounced, and loneliness; the spectacle of childhood's unsuspecting innocence overshadowed by the future, and the sadness of old age. As she declares in "Reflection"—"Through temporal loss of light we learn to find/ The substance of a Sun that makes no shadow." In recent work like the symbolically titled *Preparing to Leave*, she has largely forsaken her earlier lyrical cadences and romantic imag-ery for a spare austerity which echoes her prevailing mood of "wintering in the dark."

—Margaret Willy

HEWETT, Dorothy (Coade). Australian. Born in Perth, Western Australia, 21 May 1923. Educated at Perth College; University of Western Australia, Perth, 1941-42, 1959-63, B.A. 1961, M.A. 1963. Married Lloyd Davies in 1944 (marriage dis-solved, 1949); lived with Les Flood, 1950-59, three sons; married Merv Lilley in 1960, two daughters. Millworker, 1950-52; adver-tising copywriter, Sydney, 1956-58; Senior Tutor in English, University of Western Australia, 1964-73. Writer-in-Residence, Monash University, Melbourne, 1975, and University of New-

castle, New South Wales, 1977. Poetry Editor, *Westerly* maga-zine, Nedlands, Western Australia, 1972-73. Member of the Editorial Board, *Overland* magazine, Melbourne, since 1970, and *Sisters* magazine, Melbourne, since 1979; since 1979, Editor and Director, Big Smoke Books, and Review Editor, *New Poe-try*, both Sydney. Recipient: Australian Broadcasting Corpora-tion Prize, 1945, 1965; Australia Council grant, 1973, 1976, 1979; Australian Writers Guild award, 1974; International Women's Year grant, 1976. Agent: Howard Nicholson, 16 Tay-lor Street, Taylor's Square, Sydney, New South Wales. Address: 49 Jersey Road, Woollahra, New South Wales 2025, Australia.

PUBLICATIONS

Verse

What about the People, with Merv Lilley. Sydney, Realist Writers, 1962.
Windmill Country. Sydney, Edwards and Shaw, 1968.
The Hidden Journey. Newnham, Tasmania, Wattle Grove Press, 1969.
Late Night Bulletin. Newnham, Tasmania, Wattle Grove Press, !970.
Rapunzel in Suburbia. Sydney, New Poetry, 1975.
Greenhouse. Sydney, Big Smoke, 1979.

Plays

This Old Man Comes Rolling Home (produced Perth, 1966; revised version, produced Perth, 1968). Sydney, Currency Press, 1976.
Mrs. Porter and the Angel (produced Sydney, 1969).
The Chapel Perilous; or, The Perilous Adventures of Sally Ban-ner,music by Frank Arndt and Michael Leyden (produced Perth, 1971). Sydney, Currency Press, 1972; London, Eyre Methuen, 1974.
Bon-Bons and Roses for Dolly (produced Perth, 1972). Included in *Bon-Bons and Roses for Dally, and The Tatty Hollow Story*, 1976.
Catspaw (produced Perth, 1974).
Miss Hewett's Shenanigans (produced Canberra, 1975).
Joan (produced Canberra, 1975).
The Tatty Hollow Story (produced Sydney, 1976). Included in *Bon-Bons and Roses for Dolly, and The Tatty Hollow Story*, 1976.
Bon-Bons and Roses for Dolly, and The Tatty Hollow Story. Sydney, Currency Press, 1976.
The Beautiful Miss Portland, in *Theatre Australia* (Sydney), November-December and Christmas 1976.
The Golden Oldies (produced Melbourne, 1977; London, 1978). Included in *Susannah's Dreaming, and The Golden Oldies*, 1981.
Pandora's Box (produced Sydney, 1978). Published in *Theatre Australia* (Sydney), September-October 1978.
The Man from Mukinupin (produced Perth, 1979). Sydney, Currency Press, 1979.
Susannah's Dreaming, and The Golden Oldies. Sydney, Cur-rency Press, 1981.

Screenplays: *For the First Time*, with others, 1976; *Journey among Women*, with others, 1977.

Radio Plays: *Frost at Midnight*, 1973; *He Used to Notice Such Things*, 1974.

Novel

Bobbin Up. Sydney, Australasian Book Society, 1959.

Short Stories

The Australians Have a Word for It. Berlin, Seven Seas, 1964.

Other

Editor, *Sandgropers: A Western Australian Anthology.* Nedlands, University of Western Australia Press, 1973.

*

Manuscript Collections: Australian National Library, Canberra; Fisher Library, University of Sydney; Flinders University, Adelaide, South Australia.

Critical Studies: "Confession and Beyond" by Bruce Williams, in *Overland* (Sydney), 1977; interview with Jim Davidson, in *Meanjin* (Melbourne), 1979.

Dorothy Hewett comments:

(1980) My first collection, *Windmill Country,* was long delayed and therefore incorporated much that I had already outgrown. The locale of the book is firmly Western Australian, with consequent emphasis on landscape and ancestor-worship. There is also a strong strain of politicizing in the book, influenced by regionalism and the Australian poets of my own generation, particularly Judith Wright. The book is uneven, romantic, and didactic. *Rapunzel in Suburbia,* my second collection, covers my time as an academic. It is strongly confessional, obviously influenced by Lowell and Plath, and romantic in style and subject. Fantasy is a central element in the book; there is also an introverted imagination linked with a sense of the dramatic. *Greenhouse* is an even more radical departure. The book covers my last three years in Sydney and is influenced by the city and by younger Australian city poets. There are a wider range of experimentation, a firmer control, and more substantial intellectual content. The lyrical, the fantastic, and the analytical predominate.

*   *   *

Dorothy Hewett's career as a poet often seemed overshadowed by the much more public dimension of her obsessive plays, until a poem ("Uninvited Guest") in *Rapunzel in Suburbia,* brought to notice by a quotation in a review in the quarterly *Westerly,* became the target of legal action by her first husband. The notoriety of the resulting financial settlements has warned off booksellers in her native Western Australia and affected production prospects of plays, especially as they share with her poetry a scarcely masked autobiographical derivation. A reissue of the book substituted for the offending poem an "Envoi" patently addressed to her husband.

Hewett's birthdate surprises her reader by placing her in the same generation of Australian poets as Judith Wright, Rosemary Dobson, and Gwen Harwood. With only the last of these has she a strong affinity, declared indeed in her recent collection, by virtue of their frank statements about sexuality and their bold self-imaging. Her adventurous attitude to life and the freedom of her verse forms in fact outdo most of the generation born since 1945—she unites the publishing history of a "late starter" with an agelessly avant-garde élan.

It is her literary training and references that might perhaps "place" her. "In Pissing Alley" is a list of influences, but most notably she early absorbed the achievements of Yeats and T.S. Eliot, and writes with awareness of current United States work. She takes a contemporary view of her Australian writing association in "Creeley in Sydney."

Her formidable talent emerges clearly in her 1970's books. A noteworthy device in *Rapunzel in Suburbia* is a ransacking of a between-wars up-bringing and 1940's and 1950's living for catchwords and characteristic objects. In this book and *Greenhouse* the poet re-writes or takes up significant detail from legends, literature, and biographies in order to interpret female sexuality—stories of mermaids come ashore, the Lady of Shalott, Rapunzel, the Snow Queen, Madame Bovary, Anna Karenina, Hedda Gabler, Psyche, Sappho, as in "Grave Fairytale":

> Bald as a collaborator I sit walled in the thumb-nosed
>   tower,
> wound round three times with ropes of autumn leaves.
> And the witch...sometimes I idly kick
> a little heap of rags across the floor.
> I notice it gets smaller every year.

Alongside the fairly lengthy daring expositions of "Calling on Mother," "Underneath the Arches," "Blue Movie," and "Miss Hewett's Shenanigans" are short lyrics of affecting beauty—"In Moncur Street," "Forsaken Mermaid," "The Child":

> But since she came
> she passes by
> so often that we've grown hard;
> yet like a dust mote in the eye
> her beauty troubles us, her cry
> still shakes me: in the empty yard
> I tremble that all things must die
> and call and call her name.

Hewett's indignant refusal to bow to taboos confronts and contains guilt rather than exoricising it: her self-knowing energy intensely wills both fulfilment and despair. Hers is a celebration of desperate love, proof by its ephemeral magnificence and its visionary source against hostile forces ("Winter Solstice: 1 May):

> my mortal hand begins to play
> with leaves & grass & eerily
>   the child to say:
> *she does not live with you & me*
> the hoax   the joke   the booby prize!
> a porpoise tumbles in the bay,
> I twist the knife, I shake, I rise,
> past luminous mushrooms on the track
> the child is carried piggyback;
> I try this hairshirt on for size....

The final poems of her latest book come to the image of the labyrinth, in which the poet faces art, age, the world, and death. The charge of unevenness can be brought against Hewett; the charge of irrelevance never.

—Judith Rodriguez

———

HEWITT, Geof (George F. Hewitt). American. Born in Glen Ridge, New Jersey, 1 September 1943. Educated at Cornell University, Ithaca, New York (Academy of American Poets

Prize, 1966), 1962-66, B.A. 1966; Johns Hopkins University, Baltimore, 1966-67, M.A. 1967; University of Iowa, Iowa City, 1967-69, M.F.A. 1969. Married Janet Lind in 1971; two children. Assistant Editor, *Epoch Magazine*, 1964-66, and Editor-in-Chief, *Trojan Horse* magazine, 1965-66, both Ithaca. Gilman Teaching Fellow, Johns Hopkins University, 1966-67; Teaching Assistant, University of Iowa, 1967-69; Instructor, Coe College, Cedar Rapids, Iowa, 1969, and University of Hawaii, Honolulu, 1969-70. Contributing Editor, *Cornell Alumni News*, 1970-76, and *New Letters*, Kansas City, Missouri, 1971-76. Since 1966, Founding Editor, Kumquat Press, Montclair, New Jersey, later Enosburg, Vermont. Recipient: Coordinating Council of Literary Magazines grant, 1967, 1969; Vermont Council on the Arts grant, 1974. Address: Calais, Vermont 05648, U.S.A.

PUBLICATIONS

Verse

Poem and Other Poems. Montclair, New Jersey, Kumquat Press, 1966.
Waking Up Still Pickled. Aurora, New York, Lillabulero Press, 1967.
Stone Soup. Ithaca, New York, Ithaca House, 1974.
The Corn. Tucson, Arizona, Blue Moon Press, 1975.
I Think They'll Lay My Egg Tomorrow. Montpelier, Vermont Council on the Arts, 1976.

Other

Editor, *Quickly Aging Here: Some Poets of the 1970's.* New York, Doubleday, 1969.
Editor, *Selected Poems of Alfred Starr Hamilton.* Highlands, North Carolina, Jargon, 1969.
Editor, *Living in Whales: Stories and Poems from Vermont Public Schools.* Montpelier, Vermont Council on the Arts, 1972.

*

Critical Studies: reviews by Michael Benedikt, in *Poetry* (Chicago), December 1968, and by Thomas Lask, in *The New York Times*, 20 February 1970.

Geof Hewitt comments:
I write poetry when I can. There is a tension between the public and the private person, between ambition and sloth, between the joy of language and the sincerity of silence.
Poetry is not a "a career" for me, nor am I presumptuous enough to claim it as a way of life.
I write what I can whenever I can, sometimes call it "poetry," and am always grateful when it comes.

*   *   *

Geof Hewitt's poetry, even from such early poems as "The Gift" and "Laramie, 1851," both written about 1965, relies heavily on humor and word-play. These two poems, the former relatively serious, the latter more farcically playful, both announce and anticipate technique and tone to come; the former turns on two connotations of the word "fail," while the latter juggles word permutations like a slap-happy acrobat ("mugs," "smug," and "gums," all within four lines), while both exhibit a sense of humor, whether about himself or others. While many of Hewitt's poems stick close to his own experience and describe convin-

cingly real, if occasionally bizarre events ("The Couple Parking on the Motorcycle," for example, which could be subtitled, "love in gear"), Hewitt sometimes makes a leap into science fiction-related poetry, and some of his s.f. poetry is among the more interesting poetry of this sort. "The Frozen Man" is about a man, quick frozen, who wakes up in the future to find himself merely another t.v. dinner; "My Martian Girl Friend" describes the attributes of an extraterrestrial dream girl, and "At One with the Blue Night" manages to be at once both a metaphysical journey in the vein of *2001* and a highly lyrical love poem.

Hewitt's poetry displays the exuberance of someone excited, rather than intimidated, by the possibilities of language, a poet not afraid to use its full resources: connotation, anagrams, punning, or outrageous internal rhymes we're more accustomed to encountering in nonsense poetry: "men too cool to coo through glass" (from "November 23, 1971"). It takes daring, an admirable penchant for risk-taking which Hewitt has in abundance, to attempt being funny about a serious subject in as slapstick a way as Hewitt is in these lines from "Shudder":

For months there were hints she was disenchanted:
the banana peel in the bathtub, a roller
skate balanced on the ladder rung
while you repaired the roof of your now-empty

—Duane Ackerson

HEWITT, John (Harold). British. Born in Belfast, Northern Ireland, 28 October 1907. Educated at Methodist College, Belfast, Queen's University, Belfast, B.A. 1930, M.A. 1951. Married Roberta Black in 1934. Art Assistant, then Deputy Director, Belfast Museum and Art Gallery, 1930-57; Art Director, Herbert Art Gallery and Museum, Coventry, 1957-72, now retired. Writer-in-Residence, Queen's University, 1976-79. Associate Editor, *Lagan* magazine, Lisburn, County Antrim, 1945-46; Poetry Editor, *Threshold* magazine, Belfast, 1957-61. Fellow, Museums Association. Recipient: Irish-American Cultural Institute Prize, 1983. D.Litt.: New University of Ulster, Coleraine, 1974; Queen's University, 1983. Member, Irish Academy of Letters, 1960. Freeman, City of Belfast, 1983. Address: 11 Stockman's Lane, Belfast BT9 7JA, Northern Ireland.

PUBLICATIONS

Verse

Conacre. Privately printed, 1943.
No Rebel Word. London, Muller, 1948.
Tesserae. Belfast, Festival, 1967.
Collected Poems 1932-1967. London, MacGibbon and Kee, 1968.
The Day of the Corncrake: Poems of the Nine Glens. Belfast, Glens of Antrim Historical Society, 1969.
The Planter and the Gael, with John Montague. Belfast, Arts Council of Northern Ireland, 1970.
An Ulster Reckoning. Privately printed, 1971.
Out of My Time: Poems 1967-1974. Belfast, Blackstaff Press, 1974.
Time Enough: Poems New and Revised. Belfast, Blackstaff Press, 1976.

The Rain Dance: Poems New and Revised. Belfast, Blackstaff Press, 1978.

Kites in Spring: A Belfast Boyhood. Belfast, Blackstaff Press, 1980.

The Selected John Hewitt, edited by Alan Warner. Belfast, Blackstaff Press, 1981.

Mosaic. Belfast, Blackstaff Press, 1981.

Loose Ends. Belfast, Blackstaff Press, 1983.

Play

The Bloody Brae (produced Belfast, 1957). Published in *Threshold* (Belfast), Autumn 1957.

Other

Coventry: The Tradition of Change and Continuity. Coventry, Coventry Corporation, 1966.

Arts in Ulster 1: Paintings, Drawings, Prints, and Sculpture. Belfast, Blackstaff Press, 1977.

John Luke (1906-1975). Belfast, Arts Council of Northern Ireland, 1978.

Editor, with Sam H. Bell and Nesca A. Robb, *The Arts in Ulster: A Symposium.* London, Harrap, 1951.

Editor, *Poems of William Allingham.* Dublin, Dolmen Press, 1967.

Editor, *Rhyming Weavers and Other Country Poets of Antrim and Down.* Belfast, Blackstaff Press, 1974.

*

Critical Studies: "Regionalism into Reconciliation: The Poetry of John Hewitt" by John Montague, in *Poetry Ireland* (Dublin), Spring 1964; "The Poetry of John Hewitt" by Seamus Heaney, in *Threshold* (Belfast), Summer 1969; "John Hewitt; Land and People" by Terence Brown, in *Northern Voices,* Dublin, Gill and Macmillan, 1975; "The Poetry of John Hewitt" by Alan Warner and "John Hewitt, Ulsterman of Planter Stock" by Britte Blinder, both in *Studies in Anglo-Irish Literature* edited by Heinz Kosok, Bonn, Bouvier, 1983.

John Hewitt comments:

My poetry is a quest for identity as an individual, as an Irishman of settler stock, as a twentieth-century man.

In imagery, for evocation of mood, I seek accuracy of sensory experience. My verse is low-charged, conversational in tone. I normally use regular forms, largely iambic; now free verse tends to replace blank verse, but with renewed interest in sonnet.

Influences: Wordsworth, Frost, Yeats, Pound, Edward Thomas.

*   *   *

John Hewitt, Ulster's senior poet, presents the paradox of largely rural inspiration, and an urban (Belfast) background. As he says in "The Lonely Heart":

My father was a city schoolmaster
for forty years acclimatised to air
stale with hot breath, wet jerseys, chalk and crumbs,
in a tall building islanded in slums.

He first began to publish in the socialist thirties, both nature lyrics like "The Leaf" or "The Little Lough," and others in which he asserted his identity as an Irishman of Planter stock: "Once

alien here my fathers built their house, / claimed, drained, and gave the land the shape of use..." ("Once Alien Here").

In the 1940's these two themes came together in a series of long poems, the best known being *Conacre.* Several others appeared in *Lagan,* the leading Ulster magazine of the period, grouped under the title of "Freehold"; as well as the private world of "The Lonely Heart" there was the more public: "To Ulster then, my region, now I turn, / new to sworn service, with so much to learn..." ("The Glittering Sod"). The poems of this period were part of a conscious attempt to foster Ulster Regionalism, as a companion to the Lallans movement in Scotland. In his extended essay, "Ulster Poets, 1800-1850," first read to the Belfast Literary Society (January, 1950) Hewitt sketched what he calls the "true Ulster tradition," ignoring the Gaelic writers of the province in favour of rural bards and rhyming weavers. But in his first English collection, *No Rebel Word,* he allowed himself to be presented (in the preface by Geoffrey Taylor) as part of the tradition of English nature poetry; a few poems apart, the only hint of defiance is in the title.

Something similar occurs in his *Collected Pomes* where, with a kind of retrospective modesty, Hewitt has tended to skimp the more controversial aspects of his career. But a careful reading will discover a development in his thinking about Ulster, especially in the parable poem, "The Colony," which compares the Protestant position to that of a Roman settlement in the declining Empire. There is a more detached note in the later poems, due to his leaving Belfast for an English gallery (cf. "An Irishman in Coventry"). But his affection for the landscape of Antrim remains a constant factor, as Donegal was for the nineteenth century fore-runner whose poems he edited for the Irish Arts Council, William Allingham.

—John Montague

HEYEN, William (Helmuth). American. Born in Brooklyn, New York, 1 November 1940. Educated at State University of New York, Brockport, 1957-61, B.S. 1961; Ohio University, Athens, 1961-67, M.A. 1963, Ph.D. 1967. Married Hannelore Greiner in 1962; one son and one daughter. English teacher, Springville High School, New York, 1961-62; Instructor in English, State University of New York, Cortland, 1963-65. Since 1967, Member of the Department of English, currently Professor, State University of New York, Brockport. Senior Fulbright-Hays Lecturer in American Literature, Germany, 1971-72; Visiting Professor, University of Hawaii, Honolulu, Spring 1985. Recipient: Borestone Mountain award, 1966; National Endowment for the Arts fellowship, 1974, 1984; Guggenheim Fellowship, 1977; *Ontario Review* award, 1977; Eunice Tietjens Memorial Prize (*Poetry,* Chicago), 1978; American Academy Witter Bynner Prize, 1982. Address: 142 Frazier Street, Brockport, New York 14420, U.S.A.

PUBLICATIONS

Verse

The Mower. Privately printed, 1970.

Depth of Field. Baton Rouge, Louisiana State University Press, 1970.

The Fireman Next Door. Buffalo, Slow Loris Press, 1971.

The Train. Rochester, New York, Valley Press, 1972.

The Trail Beside the River Platte. Rushden, Northampton-
shire, Sceptre Press, 1973.
The Pigeons. Mount Horeb, Wisconsin, Perishable Press,
1973.
Noise in the Trees: Poems and a Memoir. New York, Van-
guard Press, 1974.
Mermaid. Derry, Pennsylvania, Rook Press, 1975.
Cardinals. Derry, Pennsylvania, Rook Press, 1976.
Cardinals/The Cardinal. Derry, Pennsylvania, Rook Press,
1976.
The Pearl. Pittsburgh, Slow Loris Press, 1976.
Of Palestine: A Meditation. Omaha, Abattoir, 1976.
Pickerel. Derry, Pennsylvania, Rook Press, 1976.
Dusk. Derry, Pennsylvania, Rook Press, 1976.
Eighteen Poems and a Story. Derry, Pennsylvania, Rook
Press, 1976.
The Trench. Derry, Pennsylvania, Rook Press, 1976.
The Carrie White Auction at Brockport, May 1974. Derry,
Pennsylvania, Rook Society, 1976.
XVII Machines. Pittsburgh, Sisyphus, 1976.
Ars Poetica. Derry, Pennsylvania, Rook Press, 1976.
Mare. Derry, Pennsylvania, Rook Press, 1976.
Darkness. Derry, Pennsylvania, Rook Society, 1977.
The Swastika Poems. New York, Vanguard Press, 1977.
Fires. Athens, Ohio, Croissant, 1977.
The Elm's Home. Derry, Pennsylvania, Scrimshaw, 1977.
Son Dream/Daughter Dream. Ruffsdale, Pennsylvania, Rook
Press, 1978.
The Ash. Potsdam, New York, Banjo Press, 1978.
Witness. Madison, Wisconsin, Rara Avis Press, 1978.
Lord Dragonfly. Ruffsdale, Pennsylvania, Scrimshaw, 1978.
Brockport's Poems. Brockport, New York, Challenger Press,
1978.
The Children. Knotting, Bedfordshire, Sceptre Press, 1979.
Long Island Light: Poems and a Memoir. New York, Van-
guard Press, 1979.
The City Parables. Athens, Ohio, Croissant, 1979.
Evening Dawning. Concord, New Hampshire, William B.
Ewert, 1979.
The Snow Hen. Concord, New Hampshire, William B. Ewert,
1979.
Abortion. Ruffsdale, Pennsylvania, Stefanik, 1979.
Mantle. Concord, New Hampshire, William B. Ewert, 1979.
The Descent. Knotting, Bedfordshire, Sceptre Press, 1979.
The Shy Bird. Concord, New Hampshire, Rosemary Duggan,
1980.
Our Light. Syracuse, Tamarack, 1980.
My Holocaust Songs. Concord, New Hampshire, William B.
Ewert, 1980.
1829-1979: The Bells. Brockport, New York, Challenger Press,
1980.
December 31, 1979: The Candle. Knotting, Bedfordshire,
Sceptre Press, 1980.
The Ewe's Song. Concord, New Hampshire, William B.
Ewert, 1980.
Bean. Concord, New Hampshire, South Congregational
Church, 1981.
The Eternal Ash. Syracuse, Tamarack, 1981.
Lord Dragonfly: Five Sequences. New York, Vanguard Press,
1981.
The Bees. Syracuse, Tamarack, 1981.
The Trains. Worcester, Massachusetts, Metacom Press, 1981.
Blackberry Light. Concord, New Hampshire, William B.
Ewert, 1981.
The Berries. Concord, New Hampshire, William B. Ewert,
1982.

Jesus. Syracuse, Tamarack, 1983.
Along This Water. Syracuse, Tamarack, 1983.
Ram Time. Roslyn, New York, Stone House Press 1983.
Ensoulment. Concord, New Hampshire, William B. Ewert,
1983.
The Numinous. Salisbury, Maryland, Scarab Press, 1983.
Erika: Poems of the Holocaust. New York, Vanguard Press,
1984.
Wenzel/The Ghost. Concord, New Hampshire, William B.
Ewert, 1984.

Other

*From This Book of Praise: Poems and a Conversation with
William Heyen,* edited by Vince Clemente. Port Jefferson,
New York, Street Press, 1978.

Editor, *Profile of Theodore Roethke.* Columbus, Ohio,
Charles E. Merrill, 1971.
Editor, *American Poets in 1976.* Indianapolis, Bobbs Merrill,
1976.
Editor, *I Would Also Like to Mention Aluminum: A Conversa-
tion with William Stafford.* Pittsburgh, Slow Loris Press,
1976.
Editor, *The Generation of 2000: Contemporary American Poets.*-
Princeton, New Jersey, Ontario Review Press, 1984.

*

Bibliography: "Nothing We Do Is Ever Lost to the Light: William Heyen, A Preliminary Bibliography" by Ernest Stefanik, in
Bulletin of Bibliography (Boston), Summer 1979.

Manuscript Collections: Mugar Memorial Library, Boston
University; University of Rochester Library, New York.

Critical Studies: "*The Swastika Poems*" by Sandra McPherson,
November-December 1977, "Chapter and Verse" by Stanley
Plumly, January-February 1978, and "One Man's Music" by
Dave Smith, March-April 1980, all in *American Poetry Review*
(Philadelphia); "The Harvest of a Quiet Eye" by Michael
McFee, in *Parnassus* (New York), Spring-Summer 1982; John
Drury, in *Critical Survey of Poetry* edited by Frank N. Magill,
Englewood Cliffs, New Jersey, Salem Pess, 1983.

William Heyen comments:
    I'm glad to say that as the years have gone by I've found it
easier to write. I'm not sure of all the reasons for this, and don't
want to be too sure of them, but style is involved, the slow and
painful evolution of a voice; also involved, unfashionable as it
may be even to suggest this, is an evolving conception of the
central themes and purposes of poetry, and of the kinds of poetry
I most deeply believe in. During the act of writing, this is not a
conscious thing, of course (and this comment itself is a kind of
second-guessing, surely), but I may have come to feel, at last,
that I am doing some good, that my poems characteristically
create a consciousness engaged in finding its way through conflict to clarity, hoping for some kind of musical resolution that
means, that will, for now, suffice, until the next poem.

*   *   *

    When Heyen began to explore his Long Island past in *Noise in
the Trees,* he became a visionary poet. He balances his formal
control with emotional openness. It is as though he heard the

voice of the great Long Island poet Walt Whitman and begins his own version of the journey outlined in "Song of Myself." In the spirit of Thoreau, who "travelled much in Concord," Heyen stays at home and descends within himself into various layers of the past. The spirits of American literary forefathers, pre-eminently that of Whitman, accompany him. Ultimately Heyen ascends with fragments of his local, regional, and national heritage. He suffers pain over the loss of the land, which he dares to equate with the loss of young love, but he grows spiritually as a result.

The emotional openness of the collection is paralleled by an experiment in form. Between the two sequences of poems, Heyen places a prose memoir, "Noise in the Trees," which is a series of 25 vignettes from his youth, sketches, prose poems, dreams, fantasies, legends, excerpts from histories, journals, and even a geological dictionary. The poems and prose are fused together by the author's obsessive retrieval of what he calls his "island of the mind."

In *The Swastika Poems*, an obsession with family heritage drives Heyen into the darkness of the Holocaust. He had addressed poems to his Nazi uncles in his first collection. As revised for their new context, however, these poems more clearly emerge as part of Heyen's dialogue with the darker side of himself. When he tells his Nazi father-in-law, "I have a stake in this," he speaks for all moral beings. To paraphrase the epigraph from Sontag, the function of this urgent remembering is moral. Hansjörg Greiner is "another one I don't know how/to talk to, but have to."

From the opening poem about his father on the boat to America, to the concluding title poem where he recalls the same man scraping away swastikas drawn on their Brooklyn windows, Heyen engages us in his descent into the inferno of the Holocaust. As we emerge from the darkness at the end of the book-length sequence, we are left in silence and light, "our heart beat[ing] with it."

Long Island Light is an expansion and deepening of *Noise in the Trees*. Some 31 new poems and ten prose pieces, written with increased authority, intensify the return to origins, extend the search for heritage into the present, and clarify the timelessness of the vision. The new poems about his life as husband and father in his "second home," upstate Brockport, N.Y., add a maturity and a progression which suggest that Heyen may even have the resources to enlarge this ambitious collection.

Without exaggeration, Heyen's project may be compared to Whitman's ever-expanding *Leaves of Grass*. The depth of Heyen's emotional and spiritual commitment, the growth of his technical skills, and the intensification of his vision have already elevated the people and places of his Long Island past—the farmer Wenzel, Gibbs Pond, Lake Ronkonkoma, Short Beach, St. James Harbor, Nesconset, even the Jericho Turnpike—to the status of myth. In less than ten years, Heyen has indeed discovered "detail that deepens to fond symbol."

In the 1970's no American poet published stronger back-to-back collections than *The Swastika Poems* and *Long Island Light*. In his feeling for nature and people—in his reverence for life—Heyen is reminiscent of James Wright. No contemporary American poet has written better prose than the memoirs "Noise in the Trees" and "Erica" and the "Afterword" to the exquisite haiku-like sequence *Lord Dragonfly*. Heyen has become one of the major American poets of the post-World War II era.

—Norbert Krapf

HIGHAM, Charles. British. Born in London, 18 February 1931. Educated at St. Peter's School, Cranleigh, Clayesmore. Book critic, 1956-63, and film critic, 1968-69, Sydney *Morning Herald*; feature writer, Sydney *Daily Mirror*, 1956-63, and *Nation*, Sydney, 1960-62; Literary Editor, *The Bulletin*, Sydney, 1963-68; Australian correspondent, *Sight and Sound*, London, and *Hudson Review*, New York, 1961-69; Hollywood correspondent, 1971-80, and since 1980 regular contributor, New York *Times*. Visiting Regents Professor, University of California, Santa Cruz, 1969. Recipient: Poetry Society prize, London, 1949; Sydney *Morning Herald* prize, 1956; Académie Française Prix des Créateurs, 1978. Lives in Los Angeles. Agent: Barbara Lowenstein, 250 West 57th Street, New York, New York 10107, U.S.A.

PUBLICATIONS

Verse

A Distant Star. Aldington, Kent, Hand and Flower Press, 1951.
Spring and Death. Aldington, Kent, Hand and Flower Press, 1953.
The Earthbound and Other Poems. Sydney, Angus and Robertson, 1959.
Noonday Country: Poems 1954-1965. Sydney, Angus and Robertson, 1966.
The Voyage to Brindisi and Other Poems 1966-1969. Sydney, Angus and Robertson, 1970.

Other

The Celluloid Muse: Hollywood Directors Speak, with Joel Greenberg. London, Angus and Robertson, 1969; Chicago, Regnery, 1971.
Hollywood in the Forties, with Joel Greenberg. London, Zwemmer, and Cranbury, New Jersey, A.S. Barnes, 1969.
The Films of Orson Welles. Berkeley, University of California Press, 1970.
Hollywood Cameramen: Sources of Light. Bloomington, Indiana University Press, and London, Thames and Hudson, 1970.
Ziegfeld. Chicago, Regnery, 1972; London, W.H. Allen, 1973.
Hollywood at Sunset. New York, Saturday Review Press, 1972.
Cecil B. DeMille. New York, Scribner, 1973; London, W.H. Allen, 1974.
The Art of the American Film 1900-1971. New York, Doubleday, 1973.
Ava. New York, Delacorte Press, and London, W.H. Allen, 1974.
Warner Brothers. New York, Scribner, 1975.
Kate: The Life of Katharine Hepburn. New York, Norton, and London, W.H. Allen, 1975.
Charles Laughton: An Intimate Biography. New York, Doubleday, and London, W.H. Allen, 1976.
The Adventures of Conan Doyle: The Life of the Creator of Sherlock Holmes. New York, Norton, and London, Hamish Hamilton, 1976.
Marlene: The Life of Marlene Dietrich. New York, Norton, 1977; London, Granada, 1978.
Celebrity Circus (interviews). New York, Delacorte Press, 1979.
Errol Flynn: The Untold Story. New York, Doubleday, and London, Granada, 1980.

Star Maker: The Autobiography of Hal B. Wallis, with Wallis. New York, Macmillan, 1980.
Bette: The Life of Bette Davis. New York, Macmillan, and London, New English Library, 1981.
Trading with the Enemy: An Exposé of the Nazi-American Money Plot 1933-1949. New York, Delacorte Press, and London, Hale, 1983.
Princess Merle, with Roy Moseley. New York, Coward McCann, 1983; as *Merle: A Biography of Merle Oberon*, London, New English Library, 1983.
Sisters: The Story of Olivia de Havilland and Joan Fontaine. New York, Coward McCann, 1984; as *Olivia and Joan*, London, New English Library, 1984.
Audrey: The Life of Audrey Hepburn. New York, Macmillan, 1984.

Editor, with Alan Brissenden, *They Came to Australia: An Anthology.* Melbourne, Cheshire, 1961; London, Angus and Robertson, 1962.
Editor, with Michael Wilding, *Australians Abroad: An Anthology.* Melbourne, Cheshire, 1967.
Editor, *Australian Writing Today.* London, Penguin, 1968.

*

Manuscript Collections: Boston University; University of Southern California, Los Angeles; State University of New York, Buffalo.

Critical Study: in *Times Literary Supplement* (London), 23 September 1960.

Charles Higham comments:

(1970) My poems are written in a large variety of largely invented forms, and sometimes words; and their subject matter is equally various. The ocean—a dominating presence in the world I live in—swamps, jungles, strange towns, animals and birds all form the basis of what I believe is essentially a poetry of the senses, and of primitive nature. I try to strike through to the places that are still untouched by man's ruinings; hence my interest in Australia, the West Indies, above all Luzon in the Philippines and parts of Japan. If I were asked to set a landscape which my poems live in, I would say: a green sky, with a mid-day moon; palms slanting from a swamp from which rise strange wading and flying birds; a lonely figure digging for clams on a fringing beach beyond which lies the flat, metallic Pacific.

(1974) In the early part of 1974, after a long hiatus, I began writing a new series of poems based on Rilkean exotic themes.

(1980) Since that time, I have been writing poetry more frequently, all of it published in Australian literary periodicals.I have resumed my earlier formal modes, perhaps in response to the increasing disintegration of Western culture. I have written increasingly of American experience: two recent poems, "Salmon Fishing" and "Los Angeles Sequence," have been indicative of a return to the "Northern" atmosphere of my very earliest work in *A Distant Star* and *Spring and Death* but without my early Neo-Georgian "problems." I can now be described as a stateless poet, having lived in England, Australia, and now California, but I still think of myself as a British poet in exile both from the urban modes that have dominated British verse in my lifetime, and from (at this time) the more strongly regional elements in Australian poetry. I am still a poet of exotic experience.

(1985) Work on my first two political books, *Trading with the Enemy* and *American Swastika* (forthcoming), have drained away much energy since 1980—but I am now returning to verse. I have recently discovered the work of James Merrill and Amy Clampitt, and have found it inspiriting. I am engaged on poems about childhood, more exact and less romantic than my earlier work, and written in variations of sprung rhythm. Rilke's verse is also an influence.

*   *   *

Although he is an Englishman, Charles Higham has adapted to his Australian identity with remarkable intelligence. His best poems, most of which deal with Australian experience or history, present an interesting and revealing point of view that is, so to say, both involved and yet detached. This newer, Australian poetry is considerably superior to his earliest, English poetry, which was feebly derivative (even neo-Georgian), debilitated and lacking in self-confidence or purpose. He can still write too patly, without tension, relying too much on technical convention, as in these lines from "Rushcutter's Bay":

In winter, trapped by gloom, we long for this:
The body stripped, sex in blue trunks, the leap
Of water to be carved by pressing shoulders....

But in his powerful "The Kelly Show"—surely an extraordinary poem to have come from one who is not a native of Australia— the tight rhyming form (in which he usually chooses to write) is vitalized by a personal rhythm and a tragic urgency. His weaknesses—a tendency to cliché, a fondness for making trite or commonplace points, as well as others already mentioned—have vanished. The last stanza reads:

The curtain falls; she waves a final hand.
He quotes his jot of evidence; he treads
Into the proper place; his smile is bland.
Applause demands her curtsey into beds,
And so she lewdly nods her short assent.
He drops and twists: the watchers nod their heads
And write his name upon the continent.

—Martin Seymour-Smith

HILL, Geoffrey. British. Born in Bromsgrove, Worcestershire, 18 June 1932. Educated at Fairfield Junior School; County High School, Bromsgrove; Keble College, Oxford, B.A. Married Nancy Whittaker in 1956 (marriage dissolved), three sons and one daughter. Member of the Department of English from 1954, and Professor of English Literature, 1976-80, University of Leeds. Since 1981, University Lecturer in English, and Fellow of Emmanuel College, University of Cambridge. Visiting Lecturer, University of Michigan, Ann Arbor, 1959-60, and University of Ibadan, Nigeria, 1967; Churchill Fellow, University of Bristol, 1980. Recipient: Eric Gregory Award, 1961; Hawthornden Prize, 1969; Faber Memorial Prize, 1970; Whitbread Award, 1971; Alice Hunt Bartlett Award, 1971; Heinemann Award, 1972; Duff Cooper Memorial Prize, 1979; American Academy Russell Loines Award, 1983. Honorary Fellow, Keble College, 1981. Fellow, Royal Society of Literature, 1972. Address: Emmanuel College, Cambridge CB2 3AP, England.

PUBLICATIONS

Verse

(*Poems*).   Oxford, Fantasy Press, 1952.
For the Unfallen: Poems 1952-1958.   London, Deutsch, 1959;
   Chester Springs, Pennsylvania, Dufour, 1960.
Preghiere.   Leeds, Northern House, 1964.
Penguin Modern Poets 8, with Edwin Brock and Stevie Smith.
   London, Penguin, 1966.
King Log.   London, Deutsch, and Chester Springs, Pennsyl-
   vania, Dufour, 1968.
Mercian Hymns.   London, Deutsch, 1971.
Somewhere Is Such a Kingdom: Poems 1952-1971.   Boston,
   Houghton Mifflin, 1975.
Tenebrae.   London, Deutsch, 1978; Boston, Houghton Mif-
   flin, 1979.
The Mystery of the Charity of Charles Péguy.   London,
   Agenda, 1983; New York, Oxford University Press, 1984.

Recording: *The Poetry and Voice of Geoffrey Hill*, Caedmon,
1979.

Play

Brand, adaptation of the play by Ibsen (produced London,
   1978).   London, Heinemann, 1978; revised version, Minneapolis, University of Minnesota Press, 1981.

Other

The Lords of Limit: Essays on Literature and Ideas.   London,
   Deutsch, and New York, Oxford University Press, 1984.

*

Critical Studies: *Geoffrey Hill and "The Tongue's Atrocities"*,
Swansea, University College, 1978, and *The Force of Poetry*,
Oxford, Clarendon Press, 1984, both by Christopher Ricks; *An
Introduction to 50 Modern British Poets* by Michael Schmidt,
London, Pan, 1979, as *A Reader's Guide to Fifty Modern Brit-
ish Poets*, London, Heinemann, 1979, New York, Barnes and
Noble, 1982; *Double Lyric* by Merle E. Brown, London, Rout-
ledge, 1980; "The Poetry of Geoffrey Hill" by Andrew Water-
man, in *British Poetry since 1970* edited by Peter Jones and
Michael Schmidt, Manchester, Carcanet and New York, Persea,
1980; by the author, in *Viewpoints: Poets in Conversation with
John Haffenden*, London, Faber, 1981; *Geoffrey Hill: Essays on
His Work* (includes bibliography) edited by Peter Robinson,
Milton Keynes, Buckinghamshire, Open University Press, 1984.

*   *   *

Geoffrey Hill's poems are poems of extremity. Their thematic
poles are the extremes of sex and of death—the body's proxi-
mate cravings and terrors, and the body's remotest cravings and
terrors. Their manner of proceeding—costive, densely allusive,
highly polished—is the self-protective stylistic shield of a man
appalled before his experience, and by what he understands to be
the experience of his race in history. The poems ironically deflect
their subject matter through dramatic contexts and fictionalised
locations. "The Songbook of Sebastian Arrurruz," for instance,
is a poem "about" sexual despair; but the heart-rending poignancy of some of its moments is undermined by the elaborate
literary deceit of the poem's form. If there is personal utterance
behind the "Songbook," its tracks are well covered by the artifice

in which Hill creates a fictional poet—"Arrurruz" himself—and
then "translates" his work into English. The deliberated wit of
this is entirely characteristic, as is its modernist cult of
impersonality.

If such procedures have the effect, occasionally, of making
Hill's poetry hermetic to the point of a reader's despair, they are
also the signals of an intensely dramatic, historically empathetic
imagination. Hill's best poems attempt to dissolve the self into
history, legend, and myth, and to find a meeting-point between
personal and communal meaning. I am thinking especially of his
poem-sequences "Of Commerce and Society," "Funeral Music,"
Mercian Hymns, "An Apology for the Revival of Christian
Architecture in England," and *The Mystery of the Charity of
Charles Péguy*. In these poems, in very different ways, Hill's
essential "commerce" is with what he calls "the speechless dead,"
re-imagining the occasions of their suffering, and finding in it
paradigms for the ways in which we all, necessarily, live and die.

It will perhaps be obvious from this that Hill is a poet immensely self-conscious about language itself, and a poet whose
moral and political preoccupations deepen everywhere into
preoccupations which may properly be called religious. In the
sequences "The Pentecost Castle" and "Lachrimae" these themes
are focussed through an attempt to come to some kind of terms
with the figure of Christ as it has been presented by the mystical
tradition of European Christianity. They are sequences of dark
paradox which combine longing, rejection, self-abasement, and
a kind of grim hope—what Hill calls elsewhere "cries of rapture
and despair."

In *The Mystery of the Charity of Charles Péguy* the politico-
religious interest is newly concentrated into a lengthy meditation
on the figure of Péguy, whom Hill, in a note, describes as "one of
the great souls, one of the great prophetic intelligences of our
century." Péguy, it must be said, is, on the face of it, an unlikely
candidate for such celebration: a French Catholic nationalist
whose *Le Mystère de la Charité de Jeanne d'Arc* embodies a kind
of mystical patriotism.

Hill's ambition in the poem is to probe—as he probes also in
his essay "Our Word Is Our Bond"—some of those questions
about the relationship between poetic language and political
action which also fascinated Yeats, a poet clearly centrally
important to Hill. The poem's procedures, however, are oracular
and hermetic: Hill depends to a large degree on various kinds of
wordplay and pun, and on some use of the French language. As a
result, perhaps, there has been considerable disagreement over
what exactly is involved in Hill's conception of the "patria."
John Lucas has also found—as I find myself—something disconcertingly "schoolmasterly" about the poem's tone in places, a
tendency to "advertise its seriousness." But, although it is impossible yet to come to any final judgement on this worrying,
complicated, resonant poem, in one respect at least it clearly
brings to a climax something central to Geoffrey Hill's work: an
extreme sensuousness of evocation, in which the natural world
and human thought are seen to interpenetrate each other, in a
way reminiscent of some of Eliot's *Quartets*:

Yours is their dream of France, militant-pastoral:
musky red gillyvors, the wicker bark
of clematis braided across old brick
and the slow chain that cranks into the well

morning and evening. It is Domrémy
restored; the mystic strategy of Foch
and Bergson with its time-scent, dour panache
deserving of martyrdom. It is an army

of poets, converts, vine-dressers, men skilled
in wood or metal, peasants from the Beauce,
terse teachers of Latin and those unschooled
in all but the hard rudiments of grace.

—Neil Corcoran

HINE, (William) Daryl. Canadian. Born in Burnaby, British
Columbia, 24 February 1936. Educated at McGill University,
Montreal, 1954-58; University of Chicago, M.A. 1965, Ph.D. in
comparative literature 1967. Lived in Europe 1958-62. Assistant
Professor of English, University of Chicago, 1967-69. Editor,
Poetry, Chicago, 1968-78. Recipient: Canada Foundation-
Rockefeller Fellowship, 1958; Canada Council grant, 1959,
1979; Ingram Merrill grant, 1962, 1963, 1983; Guggenheim Fel-
lowship, 1980; American Academy Award, 1982. Address: 2740
Ridge Avenue, Evanston, Illinois 60201, U.S.A.

PUBLICATIONS

Verse

Five Poems 1954. Toronto, Emblem, 1954.
The Carnal and the Crane. Toronto, Contact Press, 1957.
The Devil's Picture Book. London and New York, Abelard
  Schuman, 1960.
Heroics: Five Poems. Fontainebleau, France, Gosswiller, 1961.
The Wooden Horse. New York, Atheneum, 1965.
Minutes: Poems. New York, Atheneum, 1968.
*The Homeric Hymns and The Battle of the Frogs and the
  Mice.* New York, Atheneum, 1972.
Resident Alien. New York, Atheneum, 1975.
In and Out: A Confessional Poem. Privately printed, 1975.
Daylight Saving. New York, Atheneum, 1978.
Selected Poems. Toronto, Oxford University Press, 1980; New
  York, Atheneum, 1981.

Plays

Defunctive Music (broadcast, 1961). Published in *Tamarack
  Review* (Toronto), Winter 1966.
The Death of Seneca (produced Chicago, 1968).

Radio Plays: *Defunctive Music*, 1961 (Canada); *A Mutual
Flame* (UK); *Alcestis*, 1972 (UK).

Novel

The Prince of Darkness & Co. London and New York, Abelard Schuman, 1961.

Other

Polish Subtitles: Impressions from a Journey. London and
  New York, Abelard Schuman, 1962.

Editor, with Joseph Parisi, *The "Poetry" Anthology 1912-
  1977.* Boston, Houghton Mifflin, 1978.

Translator, *Idylls and Epigrams*, by Theocritus. New York,
Atheneum, 1982.

*

Critical Studies: *Alone with America* by Richard Howard, New
York, Atheneum, 1969, London, Thames and Hudson, 1970,
revised edition, Atheneum, 1980; "Coming Full Circle" by
Robert Martin, in *Modern Poetry Studies 7* (New York), no. 1,
1977; "Fabulous Traveller" by John Hollander, in *Canto 3*
(Andover, Massachusetts), no. 1, 1979.

*   *   *

When *The Carnal and the Crane* appeared in 1957, Northrop
Frye described Daryl Hine's first book of poems as "a brilliant
series of phrases" moving "across a mysteriously dark background." Now, several books of poetry, a novel and a travel
book later, the phrases retain their brilliance and the background its mystery. Elegance is characteristic of all of Hine's
writing, which may be appreciated for its formal qualities if not
for its expressiveness. His work resembles nothing more than an
excellent, clear, but very dry wine.

The poet has called his first book "rhapsodic" and surreal in
imagery and structure. *The Carnal and the Crane* was followed
by *The Devil's Picture Book*, a more crafted work. *The Wooden
Horse*, which explored the possibilities of dramatic monologues,
led Hine to his most intimate book to date, *Minutes*. This gave
way to a technical *tour de force*, *The Homeric Hymns*, translations from once-oral Greek poems written anonymously in the
Homeric manner. With these noble-sounding praises, the worlds
of poetry and classical scholarship merge for Hine, as in the
dactylic hexameters of the first line of "To Apollo": "How
should I hymn you, Apollo, so handsomely sung of already?"

Hine's classical learning, far from being confined to *The
Homeric Hymns*, reverberates rather than echoes with Greek,
Roman, Christian and even Celtic references throughout all his
poetry. It is an attractive characteristic of his work that he can
capture an image with crystal clarity in a Symbolist fashion, as in
"Les Yeux de la Tête" from *Minutes*:

A tiny palace and a formal garden
In miniature, lawns, flowers, jewelled trees
By Fabergé, and in the midst a fountain
Whose precious drops like tear drops fill the eyes.

Hine's poems proceed from image to image, building on the
principle of polarity, finding in the irreconcilability of opposites
proof of the inability of people to merge, the impossibility of
history, in a world in which "all our wisdom is unwillingness."

—John Robert Colombo

HIRSCHMAN, Jack. American. Born in New York City,
13 December 1933. Educated at City College of New York,
1951-55, B.A. 1955; Indiana University, Bloomington, A.M.
1957, Ph.D. 1961. Married Ruth Epstein in 1954; one son and
one daughter. Instructor, Dartmouth College, Hanover, New
Hampshire, 1959-61; Assistant Professor, University of California, Los Angeles, 1961-66. Painter and collage-maker: exhibitions in Venice, California, 1972, and Los Angeles, 1972. Associated with *Tree* magazine, Bolinas, California. Address: P.O.
Box 26517, San Francisco, California 94126, U.S.A.

PUBLICATIONS

Verse

Fragments. Privately printed, 1952.
A Correspondence of Americans. Bloomington, Indiana University Press, 1960.
Two, lithographs by Arnold Belkin. Los Angeles, Zora Gallery, 1963.
Interchange. Los Angeles, Zora Gallery, 1964.
Kline Sky. Privately printed, 1965.
Yod. London, Trigram Press, 1966.
London Seen Directly. London, Goliard Press, 1967.
Wasn't It Like This in the Woodcut. London, Cape Goliard Press, 1967.
William Blake. Topanga, California, Love Press, 1967.
A Word in Your Season, with Asa Benveniste. London, Trigram Press, 1967.
Ltd. Interchangeable in Eternity: Poems of Jackruthdavidcelia Hirschman. Privately printed, 1967.
Jerusalem: A Three Part Poem. Topanga, California, Love Press, 1968.
Aleph, Benoni and Zaddik. Los Angeles, Tenfingers Press, 1968.
Jerusalem, Ltd. London, Trigram Press, 1968.
Shekinah. Mill Valley, California, Maya, 1969.
Broadside Golem. Venice, California, Box Zero, 1969.
Black Alephs: Poems 1960-1968. New York, Phoenix Book Shop, and London, Trigram Press, 1969.
NHR. Goleta, California, Christopher's, 1970.
Scintilla. Bolinas, California, Tree, 1970.
Soledeth. Venice, California, Q Press, 1971.
DT. Santa Barbara, California, Yes Press, 1971.
The Burning of Los Angeles. Venice, California, J'Ose Press, 1971.
HNYC. Topanga, California, Skyline Press, 1971.
Les Vidanges. Venice, California, Beyond Baroque Press, 1972.
The R of the Ari's Raziel. Los Angeles, Press of the Pegacycle Lady, 1972.
Adamnan. Santa Barbara, California, Christopher's, 1972.
K'wai Sing: The Origin of the Dragon. Venice, California, Beyond Baroque Press, 1973.
Cantillations. Santa Barbara, California, Yes/Capra Press, 1973.
Aur Sea. Bolinas, California, Tree, 1974.
Djackson. Salt Lake City, Rainbow Resin Press, 1974.
Cockroach Street. San Francisco, Street, 1975.
The Cool Boyetz Cycle. San Francisco, Golden Mountain Press, 1975.
Kashtaniyah Segodnyah. San Francisco, Beatitude Press, 1976.
Lyripol. San Francisco, City Lights, 1976.
The Arcanes of Le Compte de St. Germain. San Francisco, Amerus Press, 1977.
The Jonestown Arcane. San Francisco, Poetry for the People, 1979.
The Cagliostro Arcane. San Francisco, Michael Hargreaves, 1981.
The David Arcane. San Francisco, Amerus Press, 1982.
Kallatumba. Fremont, California, Ruddy Duck Press, 1984.
The Necessary Is. San Francisco, Fishy Afoot Press, 1984.

Other

Editor, *Artaud Anthology.* San Francisco, City Lights, 1965.

Translator, with Victor Erlich, *Electric Iron*, by Vladimir Mayakovsky. Mill Valley, California, Maya, 1970.
Translator, *Love Is a Tree*, by Antonin Artaud. Fairfax, California, Red Hill Press, 1972.
Translator, *A Rainbow for the Christian West*, by René Depestre. Fairfax, California, Red Hill Press, 1972.
Translator, *The Exiled Angel*, by Luisa Pasamanik. Fairfax, California, Red Hill Press, 1973.
Translator, *Igitur*, by Stéphane Mallarmé. Los Angeles, Press of the Pegacycle Lady, 1973.
Translator, *Wail for the Arab Beggars of the Casbah*, by Ait Djafer. Los Angeles, Papa Bach, 1973.
Translator, *The Crucifixion*, by Jean Cocteau. Bethlehem, Pennsylvania, Quarter Press, 1975.
Translator, *The Book of Noah*, by Johann Maier. Berkeley, California, Tree, 1975.
Translator, with Alexander Altmann, *Three Tracts*, by Eleazer of Worms. San Francisco, Beatitude Press, 1976.
Translator, *Orange Voice*, by Alexander Kohav. San Francisco, Beatitude Press, 1976.
Translator, *Four Angels in Profile, Four Bears in Fullface*, by Alexander Kohav. San Francisco, Beatitude Press, 1976.
Translator, *Requiem*, by Robert Rodzhdestvensky. San Francisco, Beatitude Press, 1977.
Translator, *Hunger*, by Natasha Belyaeva. Mill Valley, California, D'Aurora Press, 1977.
Translator, *Emigroarium*, by Alexander Kohav. San Francisco, Amerus Press, 1977.
Translator, *Yossiph Shyryn*, by Santo Cali. Trapani, Sicily, Antigruppo, 1981.
Translator, *Jabixshak: Poems and Songs of Socialist Albania.* San Francisco, Amerus Press, 1982.
Translator, *Elegy*, by Pablo Neruda. San Francisco, David Books, 1983.
Translator, *Poems*, by Sarah Kirsch. Santa Cruz, California, Alcatraz Press, 1983.
Translator, *Three Clicks Left*, by Katerina Gogou. San Francisco, Night Horn, 1983.
Translator, *Communist*, by Agim Gjakora. San Francisco, Fishy Afoot Press, 1984.

*

Jack Hirschman comments:

(1970) Poetry is man at his most complete state of consciousness. As I write this, in March of 1969, I am conscious of whirling bodies of Vietnamese women and children in the long process of death; and aware that "poetry does nothing" is truth; I reject that truth for the poem I am now going to plunge into. Long live the creative act! May the overlords of the world learn the real meaning of death.

(1974) Putting my poems, my visual works, and my kabbalist interests together, my poetry may be seen more and more to reflect—through the amuletic/hieroglyphic tradition—a politically Left position which sees Hanoi as the extension of the idea of Blake's *Jerusalem*. Free to translate from many languages, and moreover to broadcast such works, as well as my own, on Pacifica Radio in Los Angeles, my works reveal all that is beautifully decayed in western capitalistic societies in the hope that the interchange between the West and the future Asia and Africa takes place, so to speak, across the arc of rainbows rather than the broken backs of those who still have not forfeited the earth to machinery.

(1980) For the past six years I've been living and writing in San Francisco, especially in North Beach, as a propagandist for communism as the poetic energy of revolution itself. I've learned how to translate and to write in Russian, and have worked with different cadres on the street, i.e., the Beatitude group and then the Amerus group. Poems are written in American and Russian and daily read. Since 1974 I have given away some 50,000 handmade poster-poems in the tradition of Mayakovsky—the genuine poet-painter of the Russian Revolution—and William Blake. Early Jewish Kabbalism has given way to the Kabbalistic Soviet, rooted in the Cyrillic language. This extension of work represents the foremost affirmation of my creative life and is an ongoing process. The latest development is the Union of Street Poets which provides hand-out texts of poems to the people of San Francisco. Long life to the revolutionary poets everywhere.

*   *   *

Introducing his first book, Karl Shapiro hailed Jack Hirschman exuberantly as "an inventor" who had "evolved his own particular version of the language" and who was "a kind of Hart Crane, without Crane's fatal humorlessness." Such praise is hard to live down, or up to. For years Hirschman's subsequent work appeared mainly in fugitive small editions—many of them experiments in format, such as *Interchange*, with its loose cards to be shuffled, or *Ltd.*, hand-calligraphed on paper strips—and until the 1969 London collection, *Black Alephs*, he seemed an isolated figure. Recently, however, he has worked in collaboration with David Meltzer and appears regularly in the latter's bi-annual of cabbalistic lore and poetry, *Tree*. In his writing, while the content has grown more esoteric, the emphasis on linguistic originality has continued. The early work owed much to a Dylan Thomas-like *Hwyl* and to the comic gusto of the Joyce of *Finnegans Wake*. But what is disarming in a first book can grow tiresome, and those who find the associated names of Crane, Thomas, and Joyce portentous in a depressing way will not read Hirschman's later work with much reward. Both in verse and in the "breath-style" prose-poems of recent years, the writing communicates more a generalized energy and afflatus than any very strictly definable meaning or emotion. The effect aimed at seems usually to be a hectic visionary intoxication and exaltation, as in these opening lines of "Drive":

> What a whine of a mouth in the engine of robot tit
> what an eye of blue chrome thorax my sweet
> necrophiliac my yackity rattling spit hiss my
> lilith leather slashwhip desire my voluptuous
> lynch

Still, when he cares to, Hirschman can write more quietly and convincingly, as in this poem, also from *Black Alephs*:

> I've had enough of love
> to know
> death a little
> way away is
> sleeping,
>
> her hand where she left it,
> on me, her hair
> tumbled over her mouth half
> open for
> more.

—Seamus Cooney

HITCHCOCK, George (Parks). American. Born in Hood River, Oregon, 2 June 1914. Educated at the University of Oregon, Eugene, B.A. (cum laude) 1935. Worked as laborer, shipfitter, smelter-man, mason, carpenter, and gardener; English teacher, San Francisco State College. Since 1969, Lecturer in Literature, University of California, Santa Cruz. Editor, *San Francisco Review*, 1958-63; Editor, and Publisher, *Kayak* magazine and Kayak Books, San Francisco, later Santa Cruz, 1964-84. Recipient: National Endowment for the Arts grant, 1968, 1969. Address: 325 Ocean View, Santa Cruz, California 95062, U.S.A.

PUBLICATIONS

Verse

Poems and Prints, with Mel Fowler. San Francisco, San Francisco Review, 1962.
Tactics of Survival and Other Poems. San Francisco, Bindweed Press, 1964.
The Dolphin with the Revolver in Its Teeth. Santa Barbara, California, Unicorn Press, 1967.
The One Whose Approach I Cannot Evade. Santa Barbara, California, Unicorn Press, 1967.
Two Poems. Santa Barbara, California, Unicorn Press, 1967.
A Ship of Bells: Poems. San Francisco, Kayak, 1968.
Twelve Stanzas in Praise of the Holy Chariot. San Francisco, Kayak, 1969.
The Rococo Eye. LaCrosse, Wisconsin, Juniper, 1970.
Notes of the Siege Year. Santa Cruz, California, Kayak, 1974.
Lessons in Alchemy. Reno, Nevada, West Coast Poetry Review, 1977.
The Piano Beneath the Skin. Port Townsend, Washington, Copper Canyon Press, 1979.
Mirror on Horseback. Berkeley, California, Cloud Marauder, 1979.
The Wounded Alphabet: Poems 1953-83. Santa Cruz, California, Jazz Press-Papa Bach, 1983.
Cloud Taxis. San Luis Obispo, California, Cafe Solo Press, 1984.

Plays

The Busy Martyr (produced Medford, Massachusetts, 1963). Included in *Five Plays*, 1981.
The Counterfeit Rose (produced Los Gatos, California, 1977). Santa Cruz, California, Kayak, 1977.
The Devil Comes to Wittenberg. Georgetown, California, Dragon's Teeth Press, 1980.
Five Plays (includes above plays and *Prometheus Found* and *The Housewarming*). Santa Cruz, California, Papa Bach, 1981.

Novel

Another Shore. Santa Cruz, California, Kayak, 1972.

Short Stories

October at the Lighthouse. Santa Cruz, California, Jazz Press, 1984.

Other

Editor, with Robert Peters, *Pioneers of Modern Poetry*. San

Francisco, Kayak, 1967.
Editor, *Losers Weepers: Poems Found Practically Anywhere*. San Francisco, Kayak, 1969.

*

Manuscript Collection: University of California, Santa Cruz.

*   *   *

George Hitchcock has mastered the technique of blending the surreal with the actual: his poems float, believably, from what appears to be subconscious impulse to the surface world that has demanded the poem. Unlike most of America's "surreal" poets, Hitchcock does not strain for his images; they emerge in spite of themselves, almost as if they've existed for all time, waiting to be discovered by a poet who would not elaborate them to death. Hitchcock observes without intellectual frippery; the observation, if fresh, is enough. Children, whose senses have not yet grown calloused, see this way ("The Ascension"):

Flotillas of leaves set sail in the birch trees.
They are answering the call of birds, their brothers;
they too would like to ascend like sonatas of glass
from pianos, but the twigs, the limbs, the roots
hold them back.

In such an April
we would all fly upward like sparks, but some emblem
in our shoes detains us.

The vocabulary is adult, but the vision is new.
Hitchcock's vision, however unstrained, goes *into* things, and it is here that the surreal blends with the actual. If we believe the statement, it is not surreal, whatever the nature of its texture. Hitchcock describes a sinking ship ("Portrait While Sinking"):

I watch her
dissolve into the arms of her
false twin caught in their watery hair
the plumes of terns
over their unknown name the keels
and sails of magic schooners

and, in "A Vogage": "Summer passes / The melon, / split / to the heart, / reveals / its secret / cargo / of mosquitoes." Notice that Hitchcock avoids the fashionable trap of bolstering his images with surprising adjectives: he is sure enough of his vision that the mosquitoes need not assume an unlikely color, or somehow become more human than they already are.
His work includes some of the best poetry that has been written about the war in Vietnam. After a while, most war poems sound the same, inspired as they are by the tragedy of hatred and the innocence of hatred's victims. But Hitchcock avoids revelling in useless rhetoric and his war poetry retains the best qualities of surrealism ("Scattering Flower"):

Freedom, a dancing girl,
lifts her petticoats of gasoline,
and on the hot sands of a deserted beach
a wild horse struggles, choking
in the noose of diplomacy.

Through his Kayak Press, Hitchcock has become an important force in the new American poetry: his magazine, *Kayak*, sometimes the most exciting of all the little magazines, has made available a variety of new forms, many of which Hitchcock has explored in his own work. These include found poetry, "cut-up," and collaborations.

—Geof Hewitt

HOBSBAUM, Philip (Dennis). British. Born in London, 29 June 1932. Educated at Belle Vue Grammar School, Bradford, Yorkshire; Downing College, Cambridge, 1952-55, B.A. 1955, M.A. 1961; Royal Academy of Music, London, licentiate 1956; University of Sheffield, 1959-62, Ph.D. 1968. Married 1) Hannah Kelly in 1957 (marriage dissolved, 1968); 2) Rosemary Singleton in 1976. Lecturer in English, Queen's University, Belfast, 1962-66. Lecturer, 1966-72, Senior Lecturer, 1972-79, and since 1979 Reader in English, University of Glasgow. Editor, *Delta*, Cambridge, 1954-55; Co-Editor, *Poetry from Sheffield*, 1959-61. Address: Department of English, The University, Glasgow G12 8QQ, Scotland.

PUBLICATIONS

Verse

The Place's Fault and Other Poems.   London, Macmillan, and New York, St. Martin's Press, 1964.
Snapshots.   Belfast, Festival, 1965.
In Retreat and Other Poems.   London, Macmillan, 1966; Chester Springs, Pennsylvania, Dufour, 1968.
Coming Out Fighting.   London, Macmillan, and Chester Springs, Pennsylvania, Dufour, 1969.
Some Lovely Glorious Nothing.   Frensham, Surrey, Sceptre Press, 1969.
Women and Animals.   London, Macmillan, 1972.

Plays

Radio Plays: *Children in the Woods*, 1974; *Round the Square*, music by Nick Bicât, 1976.

Other

A Theory of Communication: A Study of Value in Literature.   London, Macmillan, 1970; as *Theory of Criticism*, Bloomington, Indiana University Press, 1970.
A Reader's Guide to Charles Dickens.   London, Thames and Hudson, 1972; New York, Farrar Straus, 1973.
Tradition and Experiment in English Poetry.   London, Macmillan, and Totowa, New Jersey, Rowman and Littlefield, 1979.
A Reader's Guide to D.H. Lawrence.   London, Thames and Hudson, 1981.
Essentials of Literary Criticism.   London, Thames and Hudson, 1983.

Editor, with Edward Lucie-Smith, *A Group Anthology*.   London, Oxford University Press, 1963.
Editor, *Ten Elizabethan Poets....*   London, Longman, 1969.

*

Manuscript Collection: University of Texas, Austin.

Critical Studies: reviews by P.N. Furbank, in *The Listener* (London), May 1964, and by G.S. Fraser, in *The New York Review of Books*, 1964; *The Modern Writer and His World* by G.S. Fraser, London, Deutsch, 1964, New York, Praeger, 1965; *British Poetry since 1960* edited by Michael Schmidt and Grevel Lindop, Oxford, Carcanet Press, 1972; *The Group* edited by Ian Fletcher and John Pilling, Reading, University of Reading Library, 1974; "The Belfast Group" edited by Frank Ormsby, in *Honest Ulsterman* (Belfast), November-December 1976.

Philip Hobsbaum comments:

I have been associated, as founder of "The Group" in 1955, with Lucie-Smith, MacBeth, Porter, Bell, and Redgrove. But I must emphasize that this is a process of teaching creative writing, not a movement in verse. Other groups were started in Belfast in 1963 and in Glasgow in 1967. In recent years I have divided my time between writing a history of English poetry and a series of pieces, some of which have been broadcast, which I call *Poems for Several Voices*. I hope to collect these, to write a few plays and, eventually, to get down on paper a sequence of poems which has been long in my mind concerning autumnal and twilight themes.

*   *   *

Critics and criticism have exercised an enormous influence on the creative work of Philip Hobsbaum, and some might maintain that the impact has not always been supportive of his initial poetic impulse. At Cambridge he worked under F.R. Leavis and edited the magazine *Delta*, and founded "the Group," a group of poets who met regularly, first in Cambridge and later in London, for the purpose of critically examining each other's efforts. In 1959 Hobsbaum went to Sheffield University to do research under Professor Empson and his first volume, *The Place's Fault*, contains the poems written while he was at Sheffield, after a silence of several years. "Testimony" celebrates the return of his poetic gifts, using the analogy of Sarah's conception of a child in her period of barrenness—"Should I not rejoice / After these barren years being given a voice?"

If the title of his book and the epigraph from Philip Larkin ("waking at the fumes / And furnace-glares of Sheffield, where I changed...") acknowledge his debt to Larkin, and if there is a similarity in tone, Hobsbaum, unlike Larkin (who tends to observe human behaviour as if from a safe distance), is not afraid to commit himself to active participation; indeed most of his poems are about that involvement and its effects. In the title poem he says:

> We left (it was a temporary halt)
> The knots of ragged kids, the wired-off beach,
> Faces behind the blinds. I'll not return;
> There's nothing there I haven't had to learn,
> And I've learned nothing that I'd care to teach—
> Except that I know it was the place's fault.

But more often than not he is concerned with his own faults rather than those of the place or situation, and he is so anxious to be frank about himself, "warts and all," that he tends to lay undue emphasis upon physical defects in his wry, self-deprecating manner. He throws ridicule upon his fatness, his shortsightedness and decaying teeth (as in "A Journey round the Inside of My Mouth"). At times he can be very impressive as in "Household Gods," "Old Flame," and "Testimony," and even in his weakest poems he retains a craftsmanlike control over his materials. In the long "Man Without God," his most ambitious poem, he attempts to trace the development of his religious doubts from the superstitious rites of childhood to the intellectual questionings of maturity: but what comes across with greatest force is not so much his doubt in God as the strength of his belief in the invincibility of life.

A phrase from Larkin provides the keynote to *In Retreat*— "Lonely in Ireland, since it was not home." His loneliness (one suspects that he would be lonely anywhere) and the threat of losing his eyesight lends a plangent tone to the volume, yet if there is a certain amount of self-pity, there is something effectively human and communicative here, for in the present situation do not most poets experience this sense of exile and this groping in the half-light for certainties? Much of it is mock-serious, of course. He mocks himself as he remembers falling down the pub-stairs (due to his defective sight) or acting as "a balding, stout morose invigilator" and has a satirical touch in his "Interview with the Professor." But apart from such poems as "The Rock Pool" and "For a Young Nun," the best things in the collection, and those that indicate a new development for Hobsbaum, are the fine monologues on Chopin and Newman in which, turning his attention away from himself, he has a more balanced perspective and can define more clearly the predicament of others.

In *Coming Out Fighting* Hobsbaum concentrates largely upon the personal situation. Linked together, the poems describe a married man's unsatisfactory love affair with a younger girl, his pain and disillusionment, the break-up of his marriage, and his reflections upon the girl's own marriage later. Despite the energy, humour, and immediacy of these poems, the narrator seems able to write better when he can stand at a distance from the experience recorded, as in "The Ice Skaters":

> You
> Venture to catch them up, reach out, and
> Find yourself struggling in dirty water. Call,
>
> Ice in your mouth, spluttering blindly, down,
> Down into the mud, entangling with weed you go.
> Their laughter tinkles prettily over the ice.

Coming Out Fighting sets the scene for *Women and Animals* which studies "the nightmare of a divorce."

—Howard Sergeant

———

———

HOCHMAN, Sandra. American. Born in New York City, 11 September 1936. Educated at Bennington College, Vermont, B.A. 1957. Married 1) Ivry Gittis; 2) Harvey Leve in 1965 (divorced); one daughter. Actress. Poet-in-Residence, Fordham University, New York, 1965, and at City College, New York. Recipient: Yale Series of Younger Poets Award, 1963. Address: c/o Wyndham Books, Simon and Schuster, 1230 Avenue of the Americas, New York, New York 10020, U.S.A.

PUBLICATIONS

Verse

Voyage Home. Paris, Two Cities, 1960.

Manhattan Pastures. New Haven, Connecticut, Yale University Press, 1963.
The Vaudeville Marriage. New York, Viking Press, 1966.
Love Poems. Privately printed, 1966.
Love Letters from Asia. New York, Viking Press, 1968.
Earthworks: Poems 1960-1970. New York, Viking Press, 1971; London, Secker and Warburg, 1972.
Futures: New Poems. New York, Viking Press, 1974.

Plays

The World of Günter Grass (produced New York, 1966).
Explosion of Loneliness, music by Galt MacDermot (produced New York, 1977).

Screenplay: *Year of the Woman* (also director), 1973.

Novels

Walking Papers. New York, Viking Press, 1971.
Happiness Is Too Much Trouble. New York, Putnam, 1976.
Endangered Species. New York, Putnam, 1977.
Jogging. New York, Putnam, 1979.
Playing Tahoe. New York, Wyndham, 1981.

Other

The Magic Convention (for children). New York, Doubleday, 1971.
Satellite Spies: The Frightening Impact of a New Technology, with Sybil Wong. Indianapolis, Bobbs Merrill, 1976.
Streams: Life-Secrets for Writing Poems and Songs. Englewood Cliffs, New Jersey, Prentice Hall, 1978.

*

Manuscript Collection: Northwestern University, Evanston, Illinois.

Sandra Hochman comments:
  my written voice, my gift, is an instrument for memory,
love, praise & revelation; in my poems i swallow my pride and turn
  to the authentic teachers of the dreaming mind.
My work springs out of an inability to forget the loneliness of childhood and feeds upon all the metaphors of Nature & Revelation.

*   *   *

The flat, sometimes throwaway, delivery of Sandra Hochman's lines surprises the reader with unexpected, often ominous, echoes: "I scrape death from the black spots of a radish" ("I Live with Solomon"). This richness makes a carriage ride through Central Park subsume the great voyages of legend and history ("Hansoms") and supports the shock when "Old spring umbrellas / Bloom in the looking glass / As if in preparation for thunder" ("I Walk into the Pharmacy of Sleep"). "Poem for Alexandra," which might serve as Hochman's testament, traces this genesis of the miraculous:"...ridiculous stops / Are always turned to advantage—in improbable times / We discover whatever mystery we can." Though "The Love Singer" reduces a street bard to a "miracle-monger," art is the ultimate miracle, directing its force against both external and internal enemies: "David.../ Turned all songs to a stone / And overthrew the flesh" ("The Problem of David"). The poems about clowns and

magic in *The Vaudeville Marriage* root art in the commonplace it must ultimately transcend: "...I am / Aware of the tricks. They must be / What ugly feet are to the swan" ("The Magic Convention").

This immanence of wonder in the ordinary creates an appropriate landscape for Hochman's many poems about dreams that recreate the adult's vanished past, childhood dreams that persist, and dreams indistinguishable from the waking state. However frightening, however false, dreams shape the world: "She tries to construct / A small tower out of ivory and horn. / Dreams are nails..." ("Constructions: Upper East Side"). The travel poems of *Love Letters from Asia* celebrate a parallel world of waking miracles: "...How / Can this be all / And be so true? I / Breathe my whole life / In one morning.../ I tremble / All day / In a glass / Of water" ("Written at Vivian Court").

Poems in this volume and new poems in *Earthworks* dramatize this vulnerable but renascent selfhood through a fusion with the spirit of vegetation and, ultimately, in works like "The New Life," with the blossoming foetus within: "...Tonight / My marrow flowers into coral." Only lovers, whether in foreign landscapes or even beneath the sea in "The Couple," lack this regenerative power.

Hochman hymns her daughter's birth as compensation for the violently disrupted past, accessible only in dreams, of the earlier volumes: "...Then, in a white room, / A doctor behind a mask— perhaps a woman, / Perhaps a man—took out our childhood" ("How We Get Rid of Our Childhood"). Hochman's witty novel, *Walking Papers*, defines the ambiguous central incident of this poem as an abortion, but the literal treatment dissipates the force of the episode. Though the novel provides a scenario for many of the poems and often echoes their language, it tends to diminish their evocative power. That the poems generate as much force as they do is a tribute to Hochman's short, spare lines and often flat language, sometimes merely lists of objects. The poems make no attempt to seduce with sound effects, and generally the early poems use rhyme, usually in a final couplet. The casual tone, often self-deprecating, curbs excesses in paeans to vegetative and female fecundity. And Hochman can be directly, hilariously funny: "When a wheel broke, it was not the wheel of life, / Buddha's great wheel of birth and endless death, / It was the pierced flat tire of the car / Dying beneath the windows" ("About My Lie at That Time"). But ultimately Hochman succeeds with a rhythm that creates the shape of an image, the contours and the stuff of a mood, as in "The Spy":

If only there were a perfect word
I could give it to you—a word like some artichoke
That could sit on the table, dry, and become itself.

—Burton Kendle

HOFFMAN, Daniel (Gerard). American. Born in New York City, 3 April 1923. Educated at Columbia University, New York, A.B. 1947 (Phi Beta Kappa), M.A. 1949, Ph.D. 1956. Served in the United States Army Air Force, 1943-46: Legion of Merit. Married Elizabeth McFarland in 1948; two children. Instructor in English, Columbia University, 1952-56; Visiting Professor, University of Dijon, 1956-57; Assistant Professor, 1957-60, Associate Professor, 1960-65, and Professor of English, 1965-66, Swarthmore College, Pennsylvania. Since 1966, Professor of English, since 1978, Poet-in-Residence, and since 1983, Felix E. Schelling Professor of English, University of Pennsylvania, Philadelphia. Fellow of the School of Letters, Indiana University, 1959; Elliston Lecturer, University of Cincinnati, 1964; Lecturer, International School of Yeats Studies, Sligo, Ireland, 1965. Consultant in Poetry, 1973-74, and Honorary Consultant in American Letters, 1974-77, Library of Congress, Washington, D.C. Recipient: YMHA Introductions Award, 1951; Yale Series of Younger Poets Award, 1954; Ansley Prize, 1957; American Council of Learned Societies fellowship, 1962; Columbia University Medal for Excellence, 1964; American Academy grant, 1967; Ingram Merrill Foundation grant, 1971; National Endowment for the Arts fellowship, 1975; Hungarian P.E.N. Medal, 1980; Guggenheim Fellowship, 1983. Since 1972, Chancellor, Academy of American Poets. Address: Department of English, University of Pennsylvania, Philadelphia, Pennsylvania 19104, U.S.A.

PUBLICATIONS

Verse

An Armada of Thirty Whales. New Haven, Connecticut, Yale University Press, 1954.
A Little Geste and Other Poems. New York and London, Oxford University Press, 1960.
The City of Satisfactions. New York and London, Oxford University Press, 1963.
Striking the Stones. New York and London, Oxford University Press, 1968.
Broken Laws. New York and London, Oxford University Press, 1970.
Corgi Modern Poets in Focus 4, with others, edited by Jeremy Robson. London, Corgi, 1971.
The Center of Attention. New York, Random House, 1974.
Able Was I Ere I Saw Elba: Selected Poems 1954-1974. London, Hutchinson, 1977.
Brotherly Love. New York, Random House, 1981.

Other

Paul Bunyan: Last of the Frontier Demigods. Philadelphia, University of Pennsylvania Press—Temple University, 1952.
The Poetry of Stephen Crane. New York, Columbia University Press, 1957.
Form and Fable in American Fiction. New York and London, Oxford University Press, 1961.
Barbarous Knowledge: Myth in the Poetry of Yeats, Graves, and Muir. New York and London, Oxford University Press, 1967.
Poe Poe Poe Poe Poe Poe Poe. New York, Doubleday, 1972;. London, Robson Books, 1973.
"Poetry since 1945," in *Literary History of the United States,* revised edition, edited by R.E. Spiller and others. New York, Macmillan, 1974.
Others: Shock Troops of Stylistic Change (lecture). Philadelphia, University of Pennsylvania, 1975.
"Moonlight Dries No Mittens": Carl Sandburg Reconsidered. Washington, D.C., Library of Congress, 1979.

Editor, *The Red Badge of Courage and Other Stories,* by Stephen Crane. New York, Harper, 1957.
Editor, *American Poetry and Poetics: Poems and Critical Documents from the Puritans to Robert Frost.* New York, Doubleday, 1962.
Editor, with Samuel Hynes, *English Literary Criticism: Romantic and Victorian.* New York, Appleton Century Crofts,

1963; London, Owen, 1966.
Editor, *New Poets 1970.* Philadelphia, University of Pennsylvania, 1970.
Editor, *University and College Prizes 1967-72.* New York, Academy of American Poets, 1974.
Editor, *Harvard Guide to Contemporary American Writing.* Cambridge, Massachusetts, Harvard University Press, 1979.
Editor, *Ezra Pound and William Carlos Williams: The University of Pennsylvania Conference Papers.* Philadelphia, University of Pennsylvania Press, 1984.

*

Bibliography: *Daniel Hoffman: A Comprehensive Bibliography* by Michael Lowe, Norwood, Pennsylvania, Norwood Editions, 1973.

Critical Studies: *Alone with America* by Richard Howard, New York, Atheneum, 1969, London, Thames and Hudson, 1970, revised edition, Atheneum, 1980; "Daniel Hoffman's Poetry of Affection" by William Sylvester, in *Voyages* (Washington, D.C.), Winter 1970; "Daniel Hoffman" by Jeremy Robson, in *Corgi Modern Poets in Focus 4,* 1971; interview with W.B. Patrick, in *Daniel Hoffman: A Comprehensive Bibliography,* 1973; "A Major Poet," in *Southern Review* (Baton Rouge, Louisiana), Summer 1975, and "An American Epic," in *Washington Post Book World,* 3 May 1981, both by Monroe K. Spears; "Another Country: The Poetry of Daniel Hoffman" by John Alexander Allen, in *Hollins Critic* (Hollins College, Virginia), October 1978; interview with Edward Hirsch, in *Shenandoah 32* (Lexington, Virginia), no. 4, 1981; "Using the Long Form" by Paul Mariani, in *Parnassus* (New York), Spring-Summer 1981; "The Philadelphia Story" by James Finn Cotter, in *Hudson Review* (New York), Autumn 1981; Peter Stitt, in *Georgia Review* (Athens), Summer 1982.

Daniel Hoffman comments:
The titles of my books, I now see, mark out an unpremeditated design in my work thus far. The character of my early verse is fairly suggested by the title poem in *An Armada of Thirty Whales,* a sportive fable which both celebrates the natural order and suggests that man is limited by his place in it. The theme is elaborated and mythologized in *A Little Geste,* a sequence of eight poems which recreates a 14th century legend (of Robin Hood) as a fertility ritual and dramatizes the conflicts between natural freedom and the harsh restraints of social order. The title poem of my third book, *The City of Satisfactions,* is a free-verse obsessional nightmare enactment of The Great American Dream—a frantic derailed train trip westward in search of treasure, in endlessly receding images evoked by the perpetual recession of the land, the treasure, the satisfactions.
"Striking the stones to make them sing" is the line in my fourth book from which I take its title: an image of the poet's task. The stones may be the pavements that surround us, for my work has come to range between the sea and the city, to include the natural order and its instinctual joys and also the chaos and anguish exacted from us by the intricate disorder of our mechanistic and unmemoried society.
I make no manifestos, save: Keep imagination free to speak its revelations of the true.

*   *   *

Daniel Hoffman's scansion is modern insofar as he frequently resorts to a shifting visual pattern of spacing, a line of varying length for rhetorical purposes of either reinforcement or of counterpoint. He both demonstrates and denotes his practise in the conclusion of *The Center of Attention*:

> The Poem
>
> Arriving at last,
>
> It has stumbled across the harsh
> Stones, the black marshes.

The appearance on the page is modern, but actually evokes traditional rhythms. The first line has two unmistakably strong beats, and the isolation of the first line invites a pause, so that the first word of the next line cannot be slighted. The distinction between stressed and unstressed is sharp and consistent. Later on in the poem—"Carved on memory's staff/The legend is nearly decipherable"—one finds a line that echoes a trochaic and choriambic, followed by a line with three primary stresses and a secondary. His lines are like a steady shifting of traditional meters, but never move into the cadences of unmistakable prose. His diction is consistently generic; he prefers to evoke a sense of swerving rather than the precisely classificatory hyperbole. The "stones" and "marshes" do not indicate a world out there, to be photographed, but are emblematic of an inner struggle, the "harsh, black" struggle of writing. The legend, what is read, what is available to all, like a scroll or a saint's life, is "nearly decipherable," "Casting its message/In a sort of singing." "A sort of" in the sense of "approximate," but the phrase has also the decipherably older meaning of "a particular kind" as when Swift writes about "a sort of jabber." Hoffman's use of rhyme, however sparing and occasional, however attenuated semantically or prosodically, brings him close to a tradition which by-passes Whitman and which assumes a correlation between literary and social decorum. In "The Sonnet," he contrasts his memory of Louise Bogan's faith in the sacredness of form to the formlessness of bearded youths and rumpled girls.

His province is conservative, a poetry that indirectly evokes, without imitating them, the worlds of Yeats and Muir, a "sort of singing" to make older ways of feeling accessible today. He is less interested in discovering new perceptions than in finding new ways of expressing feelings common to people now and in the past. He is chary of assuming a common knowledge and is sparing in specific literary references. When he quotes Mallermé, "donner un sens plus pur aux mots de la tribu," the allusion to his own interest in Poe is decipherable, but the central meaning of the quotation expresses his own aim. (Actually his poetry should be seen as one aspect of his total literary production.)

With his concern for *bon sens*, his development has been a shift of emphasis rather than an experimentation with new assumptions. He has put successively rigorous restraints upon his lines. The title "City of Satisfactions" has ironic overtones; whereas the multiple meanings of "Broken Laws"—legal, or natural identity papers or

> The broken laws
> Almost deciphered on
> This air we breathe

—occurred in a collection that was considerably less ironic than the predecessors. Irony implies a commonly held set of social assumptions, and has, perhaps, inevitably hierarchical implications of shared values. In the increasing pluralism of assumptions, Hoffman has brought the center of his attention to what can be shared. Each line has a sharply delimited focus, so that overtones emerge from the sequence of lines, and from the sequence of poems.

Hoffman is capable of a wide range of tones. The meditative mood of the poem "Himself" in a recent *Hudson Review* ("The one most like himself is not this mirror's/Dishonest representation...") is sustained to the end:

> The blessing given him at last
>
> Across the alien years
> Is that he now may judge his actions
> By what that one most like himself would do
>
> Whose ease with the world shames his unease,
> Whose delight exceeds the joys he's known,
> Whose gifts are greater than his own.

He is also capable of a certain playfulness as the title of his 1977 book suggests: *Able Was I Ere I Saw Elba*. The last, intense words of this book deserve particular attention because in one way or another, Hoffman's poems move toward a coping with order/disorder, unease/delight, dishonest/blessing, barbarous/knowledge:

> It's our life that's burning.
> Is it ever too late to thrust
> Ourselves into the ruins,
> Into the tempering flame?

—William Sylvester

HOFMANN, Michael.   German.   Born in Freiburg in 1957; came to England in 1961. Educated at schools in Bristol, Edinburgh, and Winchester; Madgalene College, Cambridge, B.A. in English; graduate study at University of Regensburg and Trinity College, Cambridge. Since 1983, free-lance writer, London. Recipient: Cholmondeley Award, 1984. Address: c/o Faber and Faber, 3 Queen Street, London WC1N 3AU, England.

PUBLICATIONS

Verse

Nights in the Iron Hotel.   London, Faber, 1983.

*   *   *

Michael Hofmann is unusual, for a young poet who has so far published only one book, in sounding distinctly like himself. There are, occasionally, in isolated phrases and images, noticeable links with Craig Raine's "Martian" manner: "A hedgehog/lies rolled over on its side like a broken castor"; a vacuum cleaner is "Thin and snub-nosed, a gas-mask on a stick"; the poem "Shapes of Things," about a nuclear war, gives the Martianisms of its observation an entirely novel shudder and shiver. But otherwise he has created, very early, his own distinct style. It is a style in some ways, however, indebted to the later work of Robert Lowell, whom Hofmann has studied as a postgraduate student; and noticing what he inherits from Lowell, whom he never actually *sounds* like, is a way of establishing the kind of poet Hofmann is.

The look of the poems on the page sometimes almost disconcertingly recalls Lowell's *Notebook* and *History* poems. They are peppered with dots and dashes of omission, elision, and disjunction. These are the signs, in punctuation, of a certain looseness of grammar and syntax. Sentences without main verbs, phrasal and clausal constructions, consort sometimes with only a tenuous coherence, and almost always with a vaguely disconsolate air. This functioning of grammar, which is frequently allied to the most prosaically flat rhythms, makes the poems seem elliptical, disenchanted, and deadpan. Their "climaxes" or resolutions frequently come in a flirting with epigram, rather half-heartedly moved towards and veered away from: "The pioneers of aviation were never alone—/ they named their machines after their loved ones"; "What is love? Men are like flies. She has to eat."

The manner, which I have made sound rather dejected and jaded (it is), is intimately appropriate to Hofmann's themes and interests. He writes poems about sex which are bored and sometimes narcissistic ("We are fascinated by our own anaesthesia,/ our inability to function"), although it is difficult always to know how ironic these are being about their own poses and attitudes. He evokes modern Germany in many poems, and is particularly compelled by its border towns ("These strips of towns, with their troubled histories,/ they are lost in the woods like Hansel and Gretel"). Several poems offer ironic perspectives on German and English Romanticism and their heritages, and some poems also have a baffled sense of the continuities and discontinuities between modern German and English cultures: "The Expressionists were Rupert Brooke's generation," he notes in "Fates of the Expressionists"—but the irony here is a double-edged one, since Brooke too, like the expressionists catalogued in the poem, died young. Hofmann is also, in other poems, fascinated by lonely or oddball lives, and these are sometimes handled in poems which are entirely reported speech. It will perhaps be obvious how responsive Hofmann's dejected grammar and rhythms are to these areas of subject matter.

The danger in such poems is that things will fall too far apart, and become incapable of the reader's reconstruction. The great virtue, when they work well, is that the apparently unrelated can be combined or juxtaposed in ways that enforce some genuinely original perception of oblique relatedness. When this happens, Hofmann's poems crackle with a kind of electric energy and charge. This has something to do, often, with a nervous, highly strung sexual feeling; and in the poems specifically about sex, the weird connections and perspectives create an utterly unsentimental, but powerfully erotic, language of inter-relationship— as in "Body Heat," for instance:

This evening belongs to a warmer day—
separated clouds, birds, bits of green...
We wake late, naked, stuck to each other:
the greenhouse effect of windows and bedclothes.

Fifty years late, you finish *Love on the Dole*.
—Who knows, perhaps it can really be done?
The Boots hair setting-gel no longer works;
your pecker is down. The underdog's leather jacket

is here to stay, the stubborn lower lip
of the disconsolate punk...The poor hedgehogs,
they must help each other to pull off the leaves
that covered them while they were hibernating.

The assurance of this makes it clear that Michael Hofmann is a poet of precocious maturity whose future work can be anticipated with some eagerness.

—Neil Corcoran

HOLBROOK, David (Kenneth). British. Born in Norwich, Norfolk, 9 January 1923. Educated at Colman Road Primary School; City of Norwich School; Downing College, Cambridge (Exhibitioner), 1941-42, 1945-47, M.A. 1946. Served as a Tank Troop Officer, and Explosives and Intelligence Officer, in the East Riding of Yorkshire Yeomanry, 1942-45: Lieutenant. Married Margot Davies-Jones in 1949; two sons and two daughters. Assistant Editor, *Our Time* magazine, London, 1947-48; Assistant Editor, Bureau of Current Affairs, London, 1948-51; Tutor Organiser, Workers' Educational Association, 1952-53; school teacher, 1953-61: at Bassingbourn Village College, Cambridgeshire, 1954-61; Fellow, King's College, Cambridge, 1961-65; College Lecturer in English, Jesus College, Cambridge, 1968-70; Compton Poetry Lecturer, University of Hull, 1969 (resigned); Writer-in-Residence, Dartington Hall, Devon (Elmgrant Trust grant), 1970-72. Assistant Director of Studies, 1973-74, and since 1981, Fellow and Director of English Studies, Downing College, Cambridge. British Council Lecturer in Germany, 1969, and grantee in Australia, 1970; Hooker Visiting Professor, McMaster University, Hamilton, Ontario, 1984. Recipient: King's College and Cambridge University Press grant, 1961; Leverhulme Fellowship, 1964; Arts Council grant, 1970, 1976, 1979; World Education Fellowship Prize, 1976. Agent: David Bolt, Cedar House, High Street, Ripley, Surrey GU23 6AE. Address: Denmore Lodge, Brunswick Gardens, Cambridge CB5 8DQ, England.

PUBLICATIONS

Verse

Imaginings. London, Putnam, 1961.
Against the Cruel Frost. London, Putnam, 1963.
Penguin Modern Poets 4, with Christopher Middleton and David Wevill. London, Penguin, 1963.
Object Relations. London, Methuen, 1967.
Old World, New World. London, Rapp and Whiting, 1969.
Chance of a Lifetime. London, Anvil Press Poetry, 1978.
Moments in Italy: Poems and Sketches. Richmond, Surrey, Keepsake Press, 1978.
Selected Poems 1961-1978. London, Anvil Press Poetry, 1980.

Plays (operas for children)

The Borderline, music by Wilfrid Mellers (produced London, 1959).
The Quarry, music by John Joubert. London, Novello, 1967.
The Wild Swans, music by John Paynter (produced Cambridge, 1979).

Novels

Flesh Wounds. London, Methuen, 1966.
A Play of Passion. London, W.H. Allen, 1978.

Short Stories

Lights in the Sky Country. London, Putnam, 1962.

Other

Children's Games. Bedford, Gordon Fraser, 1957.
English for Maturity. London, Cambridge University Press, 1961.
Llareggub Revisited (on Dylan Thomas). London, Bowes and

Bowes, 1962; as *Dylan Thomas and Poetic Dissociation*, Carbondale, Southern Illinois University Press, 1964.

The Secret Places: Essays on Imaginative Work in English Teaching and on the Culture of the Child. London, Methuen, 1964.

English for the Rejected. London, Cambridge University Press, 1964.

The Quest for Love. London, Methuen, 1964.

The Flowers Shake Themselves Free (songs set by Wilfrid Mellers). London, Novello, 1966.

The Exploring Word. London, Cambridge University Press, 1967.

Children's Writing. London, Cambridge University Press, 1967.

Human Hope and the Death Instinct. Oxford, Pergamon Press, 1971.

The Masks of Hate in Art, Thought and Life in Our Time. Oxford, Pergamon Press, 1971.

Sex and Dehumanisation: The Problem of False Solutions in the Culture of an Acquisitive Society. London, Pitman, 1972.

Dylan Thomas and the Code of Night. London, Athlone Press, 1972.

The Pseudo-Revolution: A Critical Study of Extremist "Liberation" in Sex. London, Stacey, 1972.

English in Australia Now. London, Cambridge University Press, 1973.

Changing Attitudes to the Nature of Man: A Working Bibliography. Hatfield, Hertfordshire, Hertis, 1973.

Gustav Mahler and the Courage to Be. London, Vision Press, 1975; New York, Da Capo Press, 1982.

Sylvia Plath: Poetry and Existence. London, Athlone Press, 1976.

Lost Bearings in English Poetry. London, Vision Press, and New York, Barnes and Noble, 1977.

Education, Nihilism, and Survival. London, Darton Longman and Todd, 1977; Greenwood, South Carolina, Attic Press, 1978.

English for Meaning. Windsor, NFER, 1980.

Editor, *Iron Honey Gold* (anthology of verse). London, Cambridge University Press, 1961.

Editor, *People and Diamonds* (anthology of stories). London, Cambridge University Press, 1962.

Editor, *Thieves and Angels* (anthology of drama). London, Cambridge University Press, 1963.

Editor, *Visions of Life* (anthology of prose). London, Cambridge University Press, 1964.

Editor, with Elizabeth Poston, *The Cambridge Hymnal.* London, Cambridge University Press, 1967.

Editor, *Plucking the Rushes* (anthology of Chinese poetry). London, Heinemann, 1968.

Editor, *I've Got to Use Words* (course for less-abled children). London, Cambridge University Press, 1969.

Editor, *The Case Against Pornography.* London, Stacey, 1972.

Editor, *The Honey of Man.* Melbourne, Nelson, 1973.

*

Critical Studies: *Toward a Moral Approach to English: A Study of the Writings of F.R. Leavis and David Holbrook* by Gordon Pradl, unpublished dissertation, Harvard University, Cambridge, Massachusetts, 1971; "Philosophical Anthropology: Two Views of Recent Work by David Holbrook," in *Human World* (Swansea), May 1973; "David Holbrook's Humanities" by Roger Poole, in *Books and Bookmen* (London), September 1973; Martin Hayden and Duke Maskell, in *Haltwhistle Quarterly*, Spring 1979.

David Holbrook comments:

A few people have seen that all my work is of a piece—Dr. Gordon Pradl, for instance, in his dissertation at Harvard (1971). In my poetry and prose fiction I am trying to find what meaning there might be in normal, everyday existence—assuming that it should be possible, *there*, to find a sense of having existed to some point. I have kept deliberately to domestic, quotidian living, searching for transcendence in that, since I believe we are doomed if we cannot. In my books for teachers and my anthologies I have tried to encourage those in education to cherish creativity in children, in the sense of helping to explore their normal existence, through symbolism, to find meaning in it.

To this exploration of authenticity, searching for what Maslow calls "peak-moments" in ordinary life, the hollow postures of hate are the greatest enemy. I have therefore tried to diagnose the schizoid trends in contemporary culture to show that they are false, and a bluff, from "James Bond" myths, to the sex novel, and pornography. At the same time I have tried to show how genuine artists may be engaged with schizoid problems of identity, and of not knowing where to find a sense of the meaning in life—namely Dylan Thomas, Sylvia Plath, and Gustav Mahler. In doing so I have come to find the prevalent "model" of man unsatisfactory—the belief of those from Freud to Lorenz, who seem to think instincts of aggression and sex are primary. I believe that culture and symbolism are man's primary needs—and I am trying to apply this view in educational books, in criticism, and in my own writing. This revolution in thought about man I believe to be part of a widespread change—encompassing psychoanalysis, phenomenology, post-Kantian philosophy, and philosophical anthropology. I find more interest in this revolution in Europe and America—while at home in England the thinking minority have betrayed "the people" into a new barbarism which is destroying values and making a more creative future impossible. Intellectuals slavishly follow the Sunday papers, or the trendy fashions, or the trivialities of television—and proclaim their right to indulge in pornography and other vices. The onslaught of this new Barbarism will make all our efforts towards a more creative education, towards new and more visionary works of the imagination, and even towards good community life useless—unless there is a change of heart. And meanwhile, all one can do is to go on as best one can, with creative writing, and trying to warn of the dangers to survival in cultural nihilism.

*   *   *

The subject matter of David Holbrook's poetry is, for the most part, domestic, personal and everyday: it is of the "real world" of which he is an advocate in so much of his critical and educational writing. It is a world that is explored with feeling and compassion and from which morals are drawn or implied. If not directly didactic, there is usually an undertow of didacticism to be detected in his poetry. It can be personal to the point of being candid. Thus in the poem "To His Wife Going to Bed" (the title itself is point enough) it is gooseflesh which is exposed "drawing your petticoat off—showing your husband what he after clings to in bed." Mind you, it is gooseflesh transfigured by being "like wind-touched-on-water." Sometimes the poems are personal to the point of embarrassment when in "Fingers in the Door" his emotion on seeing the pain caused by closing his child's fingers in a door jamb makes him wish "myself dispersed in hundred thousand pieces" when it was "For her I cast seed into her mother's womb."

But it is this sympathy for the pain and distress of others, and the ability to express it, that informs his best poems. In "Unholy Marriage," a poem about the death of a young girl pillion passenger on a motor-cycle who lies "anointed only by the punctured oil" while her parents wait worrying because "she's late tonight," the simple unemphasised ending—"Some news? They hear the gate/ A man comes: not the best"—gives strength to the direct emotion of what has gone before.

The language employed in most of his poems is straightforward and unadorned: "This is the sort of evening on which to write a poem"—a reaction, one imagines, against the verbosity of the forties which he castigates in his critical works. Though sometimes, when combined with the long freely written lines he employs, it tends towards a looseness of form which can compromise the strength of the feelings expressed. If there is a weakness in Holbrook's verse it is this, and the influence of a romanticism deriving from what would seem an idiosyncratic interpretation of the work of D.H. Lawrence and other literary heroes. The strength of his verse is its obvious and direct honesty, despite the pitfalls of naivety into which it sometimes leads him.

—John Cotton

HOLLANDER, John. American. Born in New York City, 10 October 1929. Educated at Columbia University, New York, A.B. 1950 (Phi Beta Kappa), M.A. 1952; Indiana University, Bloomington, Ph.D. 1959. Married 1) Anne Loesser in 1953 (divorced, 1978), two daughters; 2) Natalie Charkow in 1981. Junior Fellow, Society of Fellows, Harvard University, Cambridge, Massachusetts, 1954-57; Lecturer, Connecticut College, New London, 1957-59; Instructor, 1959-61, Assistant Professor, 1961-63, and Associate Professor of English, 1963-66, Yale University, New Haven, Connecticut; Professor of English, Hunter College, City University of New York, 1966-77. Since 1977, Professor of English, Yale University. Gauss Lecturer, Princeton University, New Jersey, 1962; Visiting Professor, Indiana University, 1964; Lecturer, Salzburg Seminar in American Studies, 1965; Overseas Fellow, Churchill College, Cambridge, 1967-68. Member of the Poetry Board, Wesleyan University Press, 1959-62; Editorial Assistant for Poetry, *Partisan Review*, New Brunswick, New Jersey, 1959-66; Contributing Editor, *Harper's* magazine, New York, 1969-71. Recipient: Yale Series of Younger Poets Award, 1962; American Academy grant, 1963; National Endowment for the Arts fellowship, 1973; Levinson Prize (*Poetry*, Chicago), 1974; Guggenheim Fellowship, 1979; Modern Language Association Shaughnessy Medal, 1982; Bollingen Prize, 1983. Chancellor, Academy of American Poets. Member, American Academy, and American Academy of Arts and Sciences. Address: Department of English, Yale University, New Haven, Connecticut 06520-3545, U.S.A.

PUBLICATIONS

Verse

A Crackling of Thorns. New Haven, Connecticut, Yale University Press, 1958.

Movie-Going and Other Poems. New York, Atheneum, 1962.
A Beach Vision. Privately printed, 1962.
A Book of Various Owls (for children). New York, Norton, 1963.
Visions from the Ramble. New York, Atheneum, 1965.
The Quest of the Gole (for children). New York, Atheneum, 1966.
Philomel. London, Turret, 1968.
Types of Shape. New York, Atheneum, 1969.
The Night Mirror. New York, Atheneum, 1971.
Town and Country Matters: Erotica and Satirica. Boston, Godine, 1972.
Selected Poems. London, Secker and Warburg, 1972.
The Head of the Bed. Boston, Godine, 1974.
Tales Told of the Fathers. New York, Atheneum, 1975.
Reflections on Espionage: The Question of Cupcake. New York, Atheneum, 1976.
Spectral Emanations: New and Selected Poems. New York, Atheneum, 1978.
In Place. Omaha, Abattoir, 1978.
Powers of Thirteen. New York, Atheneum, 1983; London, Secker and Warburg, 1984.

Play

An Entertainment for Elizabeth, Being a Masque of the Seven Motions; or, Terpsichore Unchained (produced New York, 1969). Published in *English Renaissance Monographs 1* (Amherst, Massachusetts), 1972.

Other

The Untuning of the Sky: Ideas of Music in English Poetry, 1500-1700. Princeton, New Jersey, Princeton University Press, 1961.
Images of Voice: Music and Sound in Romantic Poetry. Cambridge, Heffer, and New York, Chelsea House, 1969.
The Immense Parade on Supererogation Day (for children). New York, Atheneum, 1972.
Vision and Resonance: Two Senses of Poetic Form. New York and London, Oxford University Press, 1975.
Rhyme's Reason: A Guide to English Verse. New Haven, Connecticut, Yale University Press, 1981.
The Figure of Echo: A Mode of Allusion in Milton and After. Berkeley, University of California Press, 1981.
Dal Vero, with Saul Steinberg. New York, Whitney Museum of Art, 1983.

Editor, *Selected Poems,* by Ben Jonson. New York, Dell, 1961.
Editor, with Harold Bloom, *The Wind and the Rain: An Anthology of Poems for Young People.* New York, Doubleday, 1961.
Editor, with Anthony Hecht, *Jiggery-Pokery: A Compendium of Double Dactyls.* New York, Atheneum, 1967.
Editor, *Poems of Our Moment.* New York, Pegasus, 1967.
Editor, *Modern Poetry: Essays in Criticism.* London, Oxford University Press, 1968.
Editor, *American Short Stories since 1945.* New York, Harper, 1968.
Editor, with others, *The Oxford Anthology of English Literature.* New York and London, Oxford University Press, 2 vols., 1973.
Editor, with Reuben Brower and Helen Vendler, *I.A. Richards: Essays in His Honor.* New York, Oxford University Press, 1973.

Editor, with Irving Howe and David Bromwich, *Literature as Experience*.   New York, Harcourt Brace, 1979.

*

Manuscript Collections: Beinecke Library, Yale University, New Haven, Connecticut; Lockwood Memorial Library, State University of New York, Buffalo.

Critical Studies: *Alone with America* by Richard Howard, New York, Atheneum, 1969, London, Thames and Hudson, 1970, revised edition, Atheneum, 1980; "The Poem as Silhouette: A Conversation with John Hollander" by Philip L. Gerber and Robert J. Gemmett, in *Michigan Quarterly Review* (Ann Arbor), vol. 9, 1970; "The Sorrows of American Jewish Poetry," in *Commentary* (New York), March 1972, *Figures of Capable Imagination*, New York, Seabury Press, 1976, and "The White Light of Trope," in *Kenyon Review* (Gambier, Ohio), new series 1, 1979, all by Harold Bloom; " 'I Carmina Figurata' di John Hollander" by Cristina Giorcelli, in *Scritti in Ricordo di Gabriele Baldini*, Rome, Edizione di Storia e Letteratura, 1972; "Some American Masks" by David Bromwich, in *Dissent* (New York), Winter 1973; interview with Richard Jackson, in *The Poetry Miscellany 8* (Chattanooga), 1978; "Speaking of Hollander" by J.D. McClatchy, in *American Poetry Review* (Philadelphia), September-October 1982; "Virtuosity and Virtue: A Profile of John Hollander" by David Lehman, in *Columbia College Today* (New York), Spring 1983.

*   *   *

John Hollander has been compared to Ben Jonson by Richard Howard, and the exuberant classicism of Jonson, the sense that art was *hard work*, does inform the whole of Hollander's poetic career. Yet Hollander is one of several American poets of his generation (I think of Ashbery, Merwin, Merrill as analogues) who started out in the Fifties largely under an alien guise, as though they were going to be wit-poets of the age of Eliot and Auden. There is in early Hollander (*A Crackling of Thorns*) a technical debt to Auden as to Jonson and Marvell, but deep poetic influence has nothing to do with overt structures, and Hollander's true precursors, creators of his stance and sensibility, provokers of his authentic poetic anxieties, came out of a very different Anglo-American tradition: the Romantic skepticism of Shelley; the Epicurean nihilism of Rossetti, Pater and Wilde; the American elegiac intensities of Stickney, aspects of Stevens, and of Hart Crane; and the equally American tormented pathos of the Yiddish poet Moshe Leib Halpern.

Movie-Going evidenced Hollander's rapid darkening into his own tradition of visionary skepticism and self-conscious yet essentially wild phantasmagoria. The climax of Hollander's first phase is in the long poem, *Visions from the Ramble*, an American Expressionist brief epic in the mode of Crane's *The Bridge*. The poem is stunningly ambitious, but possibly written too soon in the poet's life, and several of its parts are clearly much more successful than the poem as a whole, which, though coherent, is self-divided and even uneasy in its tone, despite the continuous exuberance of invention and the sustained technical mastery.

A middle phase of Hollander's poetry truly begins not with *Types of Shape*, an almost brilliantly despairing collection, but with *The Night Mirror*, a book of introspective lyrics of the poet's first full maturity, and one of the genuinely distinguished volumes of its generation. Themes of mortality, of the sense that no spring can follow past meridian, are expressed here with a directness of emotional power previously untouched by Hol-

lander. The satirical and erotic verse of *Town and Country Matters* gives ebullient release to Hollander's other side, the now energized and grotesque wit of an inharmonious skeptic whose scholarly obsession always has been harmony. With the long poem or quasi-Stevensian sequence, "The Head of the Bed," Hollander opens himself fully to American nostalgias and American nightmares, and achieves his masterpiece, at least to date, giving us a work comparable to the best we have had since the death of Stevens in 1955.

—Harold Bloom

HOLLO, Anselm (Paul Alexis).   United States Resident.   Born in Helsinki, Finland, 12 April 1934; son of the professor and translator J.A. Hollo. Educated at schools in Helsinki and Cedar Rapids, Iowa; Helsinki University; University of Tübingen, Germany, 1952-56. Married Josephine Wirkus in 1957 (separated, 1974), three children. Translator and book reviewer for German and Finnish periodicals, and secretary to his grandfather, Professor Paul Walden, 1955-58; Program Assistant and Co-Ordinator, BBC, London, 1958-66. Visiting Lecturer, State University of New York, Buffalo, summers 1967, 1969; Visiting Lecturer, 1968-69, Lecturer in English and Music, 1970-71, and Head of the Translation Workshop, 1971-72, University of Iowa, Iowa City; Visiting Professor and/or Poet, Bowling Green University, Ohio, 1972-73, Hobart and William Smith Colleges, Geneva, New York, 1973-74, Michigan State University, East Lansing, 1975, University of Maryland, Baltimore, 1975-77, and Southwest State University, Marshall, Minnesota, 1977-78, Sweet Briar College, Virginia, 1978-81, Naropa Institute, Boulder, Colorado, 1981, 1984. Since 1981, Lecturer, New College of California, San Francisco. Contributing Editor, *Modern Poetry in Translation*, London, and *New Letters*, Kansas City, Missouri; Poetry Editor, *Iowa Review*, Iowa City, 1971-72. Recipient: Creative Artists Public Service award, 1976; Yaddo fellowship, 1978. Address: c/o Blue Wind Press, Box 7175, Berkeley, California 94707, U.S.A.

PUBLICATIONS

Verse

Sateiden Valilla (Rainpause).   Helsinki, Otava, 1956.
St. Texts and Finnpoems.   Birmingham, Migrant Press, 1961.
Loverman.   New York, Dead Language Press, 1961.
We Just Wanted to Tell You.   London, Writers Forum, 1963.
And What Else Is New.   Chatham, Kent, New Voice, 1963.
History.   London, Matrix Press, 1964.
Trobar: Loytaa (Trobar: To Find).   Helsinki, Otava, 1964.
Here We Go.   Newcastle upon Tyne, Strangers Press, 1965.
And It Is a Song.   Birmingham, Migrant Press, 1965.
Faces and Forms.   London, Ambit, 1965.
The Claim.   London, Goliard Press, 1966.
For the Sea: Sons and Daughters We All Are.   Privately printed, 1966.
The Going-On Poem.   London, Writers Forum, 1966.
Poems/Runoja (bilingual edition).   Helsinki, Otava, 1967.
Isadora and Other Poems.   London, Writers Forum, 1967.
Leaf Times.   Exeter, Exeter Books, 1967.
Buffalo-Isle of Wight Power Cable.   Buffalo, State University of New York, 1967.

The Man in the Tree-Top Hat. London, Turret, 1968.

The Coherences. London, Trigram Press, 1968.

Tumbleweed. Toronto, Weed/Flower Press, 1968.

Haiku, with John Esam and Tom Raworth. London, Trigram Press, 1968.

Waiting for a Beautiful Bather: Ten Poems. Milwaukee, Morgan Press, 1969.

Maya: Works 1959-1969. London, Cape Goliard Press, and New York, Grossman, 1970.

America del Norte and Other Peace Herb Poems. Toronto, Weed/Flower Press, 1970.

Message. Santa Barbara, California, Unicorn Press, 1970.

Gee Apollinaire. Iowa City, Nomad Press, 1970.

Sensation 27. Canton, New York, Institute of Further Studies, 1972.

Alembic. London, Trigram Press, 1972.

Smoke Writing. Storrs, University of Connecticut Library, 1973.

Spring Cleaning Greens, from Notebooks 1967-1973. Bowling Green, Ohio, Doones Press, 1973.

Surviving with America, with Jack Marshall and Sam Hamod. Iowa City, Cedar Creek Press, 1974.

Some Worlds. New Rochelle, New York, Elizabeth Press, 1974.

Sojourner Microcosms: New and Selected Poems 1959-1977. Berkeley, California, Blue Wind Press, 1977.

Heavy Jars. West Branch, Iowa, Toothpaste Press, 1977.

Phantom Pod, with Joe Cardarelli and Kirby Malone. Baltimore, pod, n.d.

Lingering Tangos. Baltimore, Tropos Press, 1977.

Lunch in Fur. St. Paul, Minnesota, Aquila Rose, 1978.

Curious Data. Buffalo, White Pine Press, 1978.

With Ruth in Mind. Barrytown, New York, Station Hill Press, 1979.

Finite Continued: New Poems 1977-1980. Berkeley, California, Blue Wind Press, 1980.

No Complaints. West Branch, Iowa, Toothpaste Press, 1983.

Play

In the Jungle of Cities, adaptation of a play by Brecht (produced New York, 1977). New York, Grove Press, 1966.

Other

The Minicab War (parodies), with Gregory Corso and Tom Raworth. London, Matrix Press, 1961.

Editor and Translator, *Kaddisch,* by Allen Ginsberg. Wiesbaden, Limes, 1962.

Editor and Translator, *Red Cats: Selections from the Russian Poets.* San Francisco, City Lights, 1962.

Editor, *Jazz Poems.* London, Vista, 1963.

Editor and Translator, *In der Flüchtigen Hand der Zeit,* by Gregory Corso. Wiesbaden, Limes, 1963.

Editor and Translator, *Huuto ja Muita Runoja,* by Allen Ginsberg. Turku, Finland, Tajo, 1963.

Editor and Translator, *Kuolema van Goghin Korvalle,* by Allen Ginsberg. Turku, Finland, Tajo, 1963.

Editor, *Negro Verse.* London, Vista, 1964.

Editor and Translator, *Selected Poems,* by Andrei Voznesensky. New York, Grove Press, 1964.

Editor and Translator, *Word from the North: New Poetry from Finland.* Blackburn, Lancashire, Screeches Press, 1965.

Editor and Translator, *Helsinki: Selected Poems,* by Pentti Saarikoski. London, Rapp and Whiting, 1967.

Editor and Translator, *Selected Poems,* by Paavo Haavikko. London, Cape Goliard Press, and New York, Grossman, 1968.

Editor and Translator, *The Twelve and Other Poems,* by Aleksandr Blok. Lexington, Kentucky, Gnomon Press, 1971.

Editor and Translator, with Gunnar Harding, *Modern Swedish Poetry in Translation.* Minneapolis, University of Minnesota Press, 1979.

Translator, *Some Poems,* by Paul Klee. Lowestoft, Suffolk, Scorpion Press, 1962.

Translator, *Hispanjalainen Jakovainaa,* by John Lennon. Helsinki, Otava, 1966.

Translator, *In the Dark, Move Slowly: Poems,* by Tuomas Anhava. London, Cape Goliard Press, and New York, Grossman, 1969.

Translator, with Sidney Berger, *Thrymskvitha* (Icelandic Skald). Iowa City, Windhover Press, 1970.

Translator, with Josephine Clare, *Paterson,* by W.C. Williams. Stuttgart, Goverts Verlag, 1970.

Translator, with Elliott Anderson, *Turbines: Twenty One Poems,* by Tomaz Salamun. Iowa City, Windhover Press, 1973.

Translator, *The Railway Journey,* by Wolfgang Schivelbusch. New York, Urizen, 1980.

Translator, *August Strindberg,* by Olof Lagerkrantz. New York, Farrar Straus, and London, Faber, 1984.

Translator, *Poems 1958-1980,* by Pentti Saarikoski. West Branch, Iowa, Toothpaste Press, 1984.

Other translations from German, French, and Swedish published.

*

Anselm Hollo comments:

(1970) Poems are *given*: they are also "graphs of a mind moving" (Philip Whalen). Each poem, if and when it works, is a singular, at times even "unique" formal, emotional, intellectual entity, posing no problems to the poet beyond those contained in itself. The sources are in the poet's life—and that includes his reading, his given "place" at any given "time," his awareness of all animate and inanimate objects (and subjects) around him. When he is in love, he writes, "for love"; and writing, he is, stands, falls, gets up and walks again, *in love.* That is the "House of Light," the "portable state of grace," described in one of the world's greatest poems, the Cherokee Indian "Spell for the Attraction of Affections."

(1974) One way or another, most of us poets tend to aim for the "direct hit," that deeply satisfying *ouch!* of the inner gunfighter toppling over on the dusty little main street of the Reader's Heart.... The Temper of that "hit" is various; inflated reputations are proposed on what in another medium, say painting or sculpture, would be instantly recognized and rejected as miserable tear-jerkers. However, no poet ever was, is, or will ever be in total control of his or her radar installation. The Built-In Shit Detector (invented by the late Mr. Hemingway) is always liable to freak out and start regurgitating into the system the very substance it was supposed to eliminate. It may take a long time, perhaps years, perhaps forever, to discover such malfunction and its causes. However, one keeps on trying, and when the poem is there, one knows it, and you know it too.

*   *   *

The poetry of Anselm Hollo is fun. In his later verse, further-more, we come to expect the unexpected with every turn of the page, almost with every new line; and we are seldom disap-pointed. Of late years, too, his diction has become less "English" (meaning decorous) and more "American" (meaning slangy and colloquial). But his poetry always has been unadorned and keyed to the rhythms of common speech. He speaks, that is, as "one of us" not from a platform, and this is surprising in view of the years he spent as a program director on the BBC. Or perhaps in his diction he is compensating for the fact that his father was an eminent professor of philosophy and theory of education at the University of Helsinki.

Hollo's career as a translator began at the University of Hel-sinki also, where he translated many European classics into Finnish including Cervantes, Dostoievski, and Henry James. I mention this because Hollo is still better known as a translator (especially for his magnificent translations into English of Alex-ander Blok and Andrei Voznesensky) than he is as a poet. Another fact delaying such recognition may be that Hollo is primarily a *comic* poet. (What is he laughing at? people ask themselves uneasily. Himself? Me? The world? The nature of things? T.S. Eliot never behaved like that.) Can it be that people have been conditioned into expecting poets to be *serious* and are at a loss with one who has an overmastering sense of the ridicu-lous, the absurd?

One of the recurrent themes in *Sensation* is the science fiction dream, which, it turns out, is only the old romantic pursuit of the blue flower in disguise:

>Let me tell you, the captain knew
>exactly what he would do
>soon as he reached the destination
>he would fuse with her
>plumulous essence
>& they would become a fine furry plant
>later travelers would run their sensors over
>to hear it hum
>"call me up in dreamland"
>by the old minstrel known as "the van"
>ultimate consummation of long ethereal affair
>he knew he would miss
>certain small addictions
>acquired in the colonies
>visual images baloney sandwiches
>but those would be minor deprivations
>hardly bothersome in the vita nuova
>he was flying high
>he was almost there
>& that is where
>we leave him to go hurtling through the great warp
>& at our own ineffable goals

A second recurrent theme is the goddess Maya, who is, he explains, "the energy/put forth in producing/the performance of the world." It follows, of course, that Hollo himself is an aspect of this goddess. It bucks a man up when he is eating out alone to think of himself as part of the cosmic force which makes possible "the performances of the world." Like the science fic-tion theme, the maya theme is comic, cheerful, with romantic overtones.

On occasion Mr. Hollo pokes fun at a sombre romantic classic, here Verlaine's "Il Pleur dans Mon Coeur": "after Ver-laine/ right now/it is raining in Iowa City/but it ain't rainin in

my heart/nor on my head/because my head/it wears a big floppy heart, ha ha/it wears a big floppy heart." The tragic note enters his poetry rarely and usually in his translations, and even here, as in this brief poem from the Finnish ("Tumbleweeds"), with an element of comic surprise: "go to the lakeshore go/throw in a feather and a stone/the stone   floats/it is the day your son comes home." A quieter more intimate tone prevails in some of his earlier lyrics, as in "Webern":

>switch off the light
>the trees stand together
>
>easier then
>to be in our bodies
>
>growing quietly
>"dem tode entgegen"
>
>slow it is
>a slow business
>
>to grow a few words
>to say love.

A traveler through many countries and languages, Hollo has a slightly off-planet slant on human affairs. Like Puck, he is con-vinced of our absurdity, but like Oberon, beneficent. Of his diction, Peter Schjedahl has commented, "His slight verbal hes-itance succeeds in communicating the sense of a man anxious lest his words misrepresent his feelings." And it is very important to this poet that such misunderstandings never occur. Verbal finery and decoration might get in the way of the laughter, the cheerful-ness, the outgoing spirit.

—E.L. Mayo

———————

HOLLOWAY, (Percival) Geoffrey. British. Born in Bir-mingham, Warwickshire, 23 May 1918. Educated at Alsop High School, Liverpool; King Edward's Grammar School, Birming-ham; University of Southampton, 1946-48, certificate in social science 1948. Served in the Royal Army Medical Corps, 1939-46. Married 1) Joyce Mildred Holloway (died, 1974), two daugh-ters; 2) Patricia Holloway in 1977. Library Assistant, Salop County Council, Shrewsbury, 1935-39, 1946; social worker, Hatton Psychiatric Hospital, Warwick, 1946-48; officer, Prison-er's Aid Society, Lincoln, 1950-51; hospital porter, Lincoln San-atorium, 1950-53; mental health worker, Westmorland County Council, Kendal, 1953-74; social worker, Cumbria County Council, Kendal, 1974-83. Member of Brewery Poets. Address: 4 Gowan Crescent, Staveley, near Kendal, Cumbria LA8 9NF, England.

PUBLICATIONS

Verse

To Have Eyes. London, Anvil Press Poetry, 1972.
Rhine Jump. London, London Magazine, 1974.
All I Can Say. London, Anvil Press Poetry, 1978.
Salt, Roses, Vinegar. Bradford, Yorkshire, Rivelin Grapheme Press, 1985.

Other

Editor, *Trio 2*. Kendal, Cumbria Poetry Society, 1977.

*

Geoffrey Holloway comments:

Much of what I have writen comes out as "war comment." Not merely in its purist, technical sense (though that is treated in poem sequences like "Five Parachutists"), but war as a civil fact: the fight man has against age, environment, his own tyranny, his own captivating suicidal toys.

Perhaps because my profession was that of a social worker, perhaps because I live in the country, I have written often about isolates: outsiders, victims, the bereaved. Sometimes the isolate is human, sometimes animal. One may lead to the other.

So far as metrical forms are concerned, I like to try as many as possible—in the hope the finished thing comes out like a gymnast's asana. Too frequently of course what one gets is a contortionist's nightmare. But I believe it is important to update old forms (think of Empson and the villanelle—before his arrival merely frivolous). So I've recycled, as it were, cwydds and rhupunts—the old Welsh teasers—as well as attempting, among others, senryu, renga, caligramme.

I also think it important to weave poetry in with other arts. Not to oust the printed page, but to stimulate and complement it. Thus one should have, on the page, impressionist, cubist, fauve, maybe even pointilliste poems; and off it poems with jazz, dance, strobic improvisation, for example. Each as natural as the other—and together, still natural.

Multi-media may have its critics, but one thing it does do is redefine the social image of the poet. No longer is he a circus giraffe with a wooden leg, but what he should be: an engaging and acceptable native in a companionable zoo.

*   *   *

Geoffrey Holloway draws very much on personal experience for his poetry. *To Have Eyes* is an impressive first collection. He uses his eyes and ears and skill to quite remarkable effect in writing about the changing seasons, cricket, a fat woman, a calf born on a Sunday, and so on, and though he sets out with the determination "not to sentimentalize the view," he does not allow this to cloud the issues or obscure, in any way, the natural tenderness exhibited in the poems featuring members of his family. There is, for instance, a touching poem about his daughter, with the gull-slanted nickname, "Doing the Length":

> And this, cardinal: a cord of grace
> giving strange substance to the loined accident,
> tying one into acute paternity,
> baptizing in the name of father, love.
> Thirty yards, learning to swim, be...
> within the pooled corroborated heart.

He has a fine command of language, an ironic sense of humour which permeates every poem, and an understanding of organic rhythm, which is important since most of his work is in "free verse."

Rhine Jump, a choice of the Poetry Book Society, covers his wartime experiences and also his childhood in Liverpool and Shropshire. There is the typical Holloway concern for accurate observation and rhythm. His hare (in "Neighbours") "canters past, diagonal," and his toad (in "Deadpan") is a "Primrose-leaf-backed old gargoyle / in the wild Elizabethan court-shoes." There are the contradictory attitudes to sexual passion in "One Up on Circe" and "Woman of the Philistines":

> It was worth it, to feel again
> with hairy hands the pillars' cold integrity;
> able, in the roaring hall,
> the hard male voices he could understand,
>
> to fight directly, without humbling love.

But as Holloway points out, *Rhine Jump* "comes out mainly as 'war comment'. Not merely war in its purist, technical sense..., but war as a civil fact: the fight man has against age, environment, his own tyranny, his own captivating suicidal toys." However, the best poems in this collection are not the direct war poems, but "Ode to the River Severn," "The Recidivists," "Galatea," and "Prospecting the Reserves."

Holloway's third collection, *All I Can Say*, is divided into four sections, and the last of these, "Tears on the Wind," contains the most moving and rawly honest attempts to cope with the death of his wife (to whom the book is dedicated) after years of subjection of cancer, years in which the poet was involved in nursing the victim and compelled to witness her humiliations. In "Odalisque Extraordinary" he tries to present his dying wife's feelings—

> For no impressive reason this is me:
> a one-girl seraglio under house-arrest:
> pet, pride of that ghostly sadist
> the sultan, who by threatening castration
>
> (and for the holy kingdom of pain's sake)
> has my husband as acting eunuch,
> and me daily titivated
> by one or other of his handmaidens...

—and his own emotional response, carefully controlled, to her death. *All I Can Say* demonstrates the poet's craftsmanship in the use of form and language and if to some extent it is dominated by a preoccupation with death (not only that of his wife) there is sufficient variety in subject and treatment and in the range of human situations to establish Holloway as one of our most compassionate and accomplished poets.

—Howard Sergeant

—————

HOLLOWAY, (Christopher) John. British. Born in London, 1 August 1920. Educated at County School, Beckenham, Kent; New College, Oxford (Open History Scholar), M.A. 1945, D.Phil. 1947. Served in the British Army, 1941-45. Married 1) Audrey Gooding in 1946, one son and one daughter; 2) Joan Black in 1978. Temporary Lecturer in Philosophy, New College, 1945, Fellow, All Souls College, 1946-60, and John Locke Scholar, 1947, Oxford; University Lecturer in English, Aberdeen University, 1949-54; University Lecturer in English, 1954-66, Fellow of Queens' College, 1955, Reader in Modern English, 1966-72, and Professor of Modern English, 1972-82, Cambridge University. Byron Professor, University of Athens, 1961-63; Alexander White Professor, University of Chicago, 1965; Hinkley Professor, Johns Hopkins University, Baltimore, 1972; Virginia Lecturer, Charlottesville, 1979. D.Litt.: Aberdeen University, 1954; Litt.D.: Cambridge University, 1969. Fellow, Royal

Society of Literature, 1956; Life Fellow, Queens' College, 1982. Address: Queens' College, Cambridge CB3 9ET, England.

PUBLICATIONS

Verse

(Poems). Oxford, Fantasy Press, 1954.
The Minute and Longer Poems. Hessle, Yorkshire, Marvell Press, 1956.
The Fugue and Shorter Pieces. London, Routledge, 1960.
The Landfallers: A Poem in Twelve Parts. London, Routledge, 1962.
Wood and Windfall. London, Routledge, 1965.
New Poems. New York, Scribner, 1970.
Planet of Winds. London, Routledge, 1977.

Other

Language and Intelligence. London, Macmillan, 1951; Hamden, Connecticut, Archon, 1971.
The Victorian Sage: Studies in Argument. London, Macmillan, and New York, St. Martin's Press, 1953.
The Charted Mirror: Literary and Critical Essays. London, Routledge, 1960; New York, Horizon Press, 1962.
The Story of the Night: Studies in Shakespeare's Major Tragedies. London, Routledge, 1961; Lincoln, University of Nebraska Press, 1963.
The Colours of Clarity: Essays on Contemporary Literature and Education. London, Routledge, and Hamden, Connecticut, Archon, 1964.
The Lion Hunt: A Pursuit of Poetry and Reality. London, Routledge, and Hamden, Connecticut, Archon, 1964.
Widening Horizons in English Verse. London, Routledge, 1966; Evanston, Illinois, Northwestern University Press, 1967.
A London Childhood (autobiography). London, Routledge, 1966; New York, Scribner, 1968.
Blake: The Lyric Poetry. London, Arnold, 1968.
The Establishment of English (lecture). London, Cambridge University Press, 1972.
The Proud Knowledge: Poetry, Insight, and the Self 1620-1920. London, Routledge, 1977.
Narrative and Structure: Exploratory Essays. London and New York, Cambridge University Press, 1979.
The Slumber of Apollo; Reflections on Recent Art, Literature, Language, and the Individual Consciousness. London, Cambridge University Press, 1983.

Editor, *Poems of the Mid-Century.* London, Harrap, 1957.
Editor, *Selected Poems,* by Shelley. London, Heinemann, 1959; New York, Macmillan, 1960.
Editor, *Little Dorrit,* by Dickens. London, Penguin, 1967.
Editor, with Joan Black, *Later English Broadside Ballads.* London, Routledge, 2 vols., 1975-79.

*

Critical Study: John Ferns, in *Poets of Great Britain and Ireland 1945-1960* edited by Vincent B. Sherry, Jr., Detroit, Gale, 1984.

John Holloway comments:

(1970) A few guiding ideas would be: indifference to all modishness; constant study and innovation; concentration and density; refusal to compromise over difficulty; interest in folk, street ballad and popular poetry; interest in a "classic" style, strictly in Eliot's sense; interest in musical analogues and rhythmic or repetition problems in poetry.

(1985) I have recently completed a book-length poem of which the continuing major theme is Cambridge and East Anglia from earliest geological times down to the present or maybe future.

*   *   *

Although John Holloway has never been thought of primarily as a poet, he has published several volumes of verse during the course of an active career as critic, scholar and teacher. During the 1950's he was sometimes regarded as Movement poet, and it is true that he contributed to the Movement anthology, *New Lines,* in 1956. But apart from his attachment to fairly strict and traditional verse forms, Holloway had little in common with the other contributors. His characteristic tone was grave, even solemn, rather than ironic, and his poetry was directed to myth rather than social comment. Holloway did, however, resemble some of his contemporaries in being influenced by the terse, formal lyrics of Robert Graves, though in his case the reflective mythopoeic poetry of Edwin Muir was equally influential. In Holloway's first collection, *The Minute,* there were a number of memorable, well-realized poems, such as "Journey to the Captial," "Poem for Deep Winter" and "Warning to a Guest." But there was, equally, a pervasive sense that the will was too much involved in the production of Holloway's poetry; many of his poems were well-written and carefully structured, but somehow lacking in content or point. And this tendency has become more pronounced in his subsequent poetry, much of which is frankly dull. The dedication to the ideal of writing poetry remains strong and commands respect but the spirit seems lacking. A book-length poem like *The Landfallers* is serious and ambitious rather than convincing or enjoyable; Holloway's gifts are more apparent in his evocations of Greek landscape in *Wood and Windfall.*

—Bernard Bergonzi

HONIG, Edwin. American. Born in New York City, 3 September 1919. Educated in public schools, New York; University of Wisconsin, Madison, B.A. 1941, M.A. 1947. Served in the United States Army, 1943-46. Married 1) Charlotte Gilchrist in 1940 (died, 1963); 2) Margot S. Dennes in 1963 (divorced, 1978); two sons. Library Assistant, Library of Congress, Washington, D.C., 1941-42; Instructor in English, Purdue University, Lafayette, Indiana, 1942-43, New York University and Illinois Institute of Technology, Chicago, 1946-47, University of New Mexico, Albuquerque, 1947-49, and Claremont College, California, Summer 1949; Instructor, 1949-52, and Briggs Copeland Assistant Professor, 1952-57, Harvard University, Cambridge, Massachusetts. Associate Professor, 1957-60, since 1960, Professor of English, and since 1962, Professor of Comparative Literature, Brown University, Providence, Rhode Island. Visiting Professor, University of California, Davis, 1964-65; Mellon Professor, Boston University, 1977. Poetry Editor, *New Mexico Quarterly,* Albuquerque, 1948-52. Director, Rhode Island Poetry in the Schools Program, 1968-72. Recipient: Guggenheim Fellowship, 1948, 1962; *Saturday Review* prize, 1957; New England Poetry Club Golden Rose, 1961; Bollingen grant, for translation, 1962; American Academy grant, 1966; Amy Lowell Traveling Fellowship, 1968; National Endowment for the Arts grant, 1975, 1977. M.A.: Brown University, 1958. Address: Box 1852, Brown University, Providence, Rhode Island 02912, U.S.A.

PUBLICATIONS

Verse

The Moral Circus.   Baltimore, Contemporary Poetry, 1955.
The Gazabos: Forty-One Poems.   New York, Clarke and Way,
  1959; augmented edition, as *The Gazabos: Forty-One Poems,
  and The Widow*, 1961.
Poems for Charlotte.   Privately printed, 1963.
Survivals.   New York, October House, 1965.
Spring Journal.   Providence, Rhode Island, Hellcoal Press,
  1968.
Spring Journal: Poems.   Middletown, Connecticut, Wesleyan
  University Press, 1968.
Four Springs.   Chicago, Swallow Press, 1972.
Shake a Spear with Me, John Berryman: New Poems (includes
  the play *Orpheus Below*).   Providence, Rhode Island, Copper
  Beech Press, 1974; augmented edition, as *The Affinities of
  Orpheus*, 1976.
At Sixes.   Providence, Rhode Island, Burning Deck, 1974.
Selected Poems 1955-1976.   Dallas, Center for Writers Press,
  1979.
Interrupted Praise: New and Selected Poems.   Metuchen, New
  Jersey, Scarecrow Press, 1983.
Gifts of Light.   Isla Vista, California, Turkey Press, 1983.

Plays

The Widow (produced Chicago, 1953).   Included in *The Gaza-
  bos*, 1961.
The Phantom Lady, adaptation of a play by Calderón (produced
  Washington, D.C., 1965).   Included in *Calderón: Four Plays*,
  1961.
Calderón: Four Plays, adaptations by Honig.   New York, Hill
  and Wang, 1961.
Cervantes: Eight Interludes, adaptations by Honig.   New York,
  New American Library, 1964.
Calisto and Melibea (produced Stanford, California, 1966).
  Providence, Rhode Island, Hellcoal Press, 1972; opera ver-
  sion (produced Davis, California, 1979).
Life Is a Dream, adaptation of a play by Calderón (broadcast,
  1970; produced Providence, Rhode Island, 1971).   New
  York, Hill and Wang, 1970.
Ends of the World and Other Plays.   Providence, Rhode
  Island, Copper Beech Press, 1983.

Radio Play: *Life Is a Dream*, 1970 (UK).

Other

García Lorca.   New York, New Directions, 1944; London, Edi-
  tions Poetry London, 1945; revised edition, New Directions,
  1963; London, Cape, 1968; New York, Octagon, 1980.
Dark Conceit: The Making of Allegory.   Evanston, Illinois,
  Northwestern University Press, 1959; London, Faber, 1960;
  revised edition, New York, Oxford University Press, 1966;
  Providence, Rhode Island, Brown University Press, 1973.
Calderón and the Seizures of Honor.   Cambridge, Massachu-
  setts, Harvard University Press, 1972.
The Foibles and Fables of an Abstract Man.   Providence,
  Rhode Island, Copper Beech Press, 1979.
Selected Translations.   Daleville, Indiana, Barnwood Press,
  1983.

*The Poet's Other Voice: Conversations about Literary Transla-
  tion.*   Amherst, University of Massachusetts Press, 1985.

Editor, with Oscar Williams, *The Mentor Book of Major Amer-
  ican Poets.*   New York, New American Library, 1961.
Editor, with Oscar Williams, *The Major Metaphysical Poets.*
  New York, Washington Square Press, 1968.
Editor, *Spenser.*   New York, Dell, 1968.

Translator, *The Cave of Salamanca*, by Cervantes. Boston,
  Chrysalis, 1960.
Translator, *Selected Poems of Fernando Pessoa.*   Chicago,
  Swallow Press, 1971.
Translator, *Divan and Other Writings*, by García Lorca.   Prov-
  idence, Rhode Island, Bonewhistle Press, 1974.
Translator, with A.S. Trueblood, *La Dorotea*, by Lope de Vega.
  Cambridge, Massachusetts, Harvard University Press, 1985.
Translator, with S.M. Brown, *The Keeper of Sheep*, by Fer-
  nando Pessoa.   Middletown, Connecticut, Wesleyan Uni-
  versity Press, 1985.

*

Bibliography: in *Books and Articles by Members of the
Department: A Bibliography* by George K. Anderson, Providence, Rhode Island, Brown University Department of English,
1967.

Manuscript Collection: John Hay Library, Brown University,
Providence, Rhode Island.

Critical Studies: "The Voice of Edwin Honig" by John Hawkes,
in *Voices* (Vinalhaven, Maine), January—April 1961; "To Seize
Truth Assault Dogmas" by Robert Taylor, in *Providence Sunday Journal* (Rhode Island), 4 March 1962; " 'Spring' Breakthrough in the New Poetry" by James Schevill, in *San Francisco
Examiner-Chronicle*, 5 January 1969; "Double Exposure" by
L.Alan Goldstein, in *The Nation* (New York), 19 May 1969;
interviews with H.J. Cargas, in *Webster Review* (Webster
Groves, Missouri), Fall 1977, and with Richard Jackson, in
Poetry Miscellany 8 (Chattanooga), 1978; in *American Poets
since World War II* edited by Donald J. Greiner, Detroit, Gale,
1980.

Edwin Honig comments:
   Matters that may have influenced my becoming a writer
(though perhaps this is only a nice rationalization) were an early
sense of exclusion owing to my being blamed for my younger
brother's accidental death when I was five, and a severe, nearly
fatal bout with nephritis when I was nine. A positive influence
was my illiterate grandmother, who spoke Spanish, Arabic, and
Yiddish (but no English); I lived with her and my grandfather for
a few years after my parents were divorced when I was twelve.
Experiences of this sort urged certain necessities upon me: one
was to write instead of choking; another, to make sense of the
world around me—but sense that would not exclude my own
fantasy. Both my poetry and my criticism seem to rise out of such
a mixed need: the criticism that creates—Spain (Calderón and
García Lorca) as well as allegory—and the poetry that criticizes
persons and places I have loved and distrusted—the "moral
circuses" where the "gazabos" live.
   My best poems are either unfinished or still merely notes in a
notebook. Some poems got away (were printed) but have since
been excluded from my books because they did not seem sub-

stantial enough or true. In the same way I quarrel constantly with the poems written by contemporaries old and young. No poet writing in English in the last sixty years has mastered his art or has resisted the nervous need to keep changing his style; and so none has been able to write as a complete human being. Perhaps Rilke and Lorca succeeded in a few poems. (I find, now that I have written the penultimate sentence, that I am echoing an opinion of Gottfried Benn.) I have taken to translating and to writing plays out of impatience with poetry and criticism; but I go on writing poetry—to stop would be a self-betrayal.

(1974) (This was written in 1966, and might just as well stand for what I feel today, though I think the statement bleaker than need be. There are probably more than two poets, for instance, who have done a service to the language or their language in the last sixty years, and I am almost willing to admit that Pound is one.)

*   *   *

Edwin Honig points out that some literary critics, idealizing a golden age of the near or distant past, "speak and write about the poetry of the past hundred and fifty years like a keeper fleaing an underbred dog that is only half the dog its sire was." Not only does Honig disagree with that critical judgment but he has also made his own substantial contribution to the healthy state of contemporary American poetry through his work as poet, teacher, critic, anthologist, translator, and playwright. Like the modernist poetry of a previous generation, much of Honig's poetry makes rigorous demands on the reader and thus has to find its own audience gradually—limited in size but appreciative of the depth, range, and skill they discover in the poems. It is a poetry of careful craftsmanship, breadth, of learning, sharp perceptions, and deep authentic feeling.

In the earlier volumes, obviously influenced by Eliot and the prevailing standards of modernism, the feeling is often, though not always, insulated by technical virtuosity and layers of erudition. For a time Honig moved away from the poem as carefully constructed artifact to a looser, though by no means formless, open-ended poem (*Four Springs*). The new form did not diminish any of his technique or learning, nor did it suddenly transform him into a poet easily accessible to the casual reader, but it did more readily release depths of personal emotion ("One wants to tell / how the memory rushes hungrily back to the remembered / life of the dead / beloved, until at a touch, of themselves, the episodes / rush on unreeling, / speed up beyond one's grasping; imagined again, / retelling themselves, / great hunks of life that plead again to be real!").

A headnote to *Four Springs* observing that "in 1966 or so I began writing a poem that very soon went beyond my conception of when or where it would end" and that the book's three concluding sections "continue the story to the present date, my fiftieth birthday" gave some evidence of an intention to explore further potentiality in this new form. More recent volumes, however, are reminiscent of his earlier style, with a strong added interest in myth. With the conviction that "though we can't live without myths, we find it hard to re-define and adapt them to our experience," Honig has, in *The Affinities of Orpheus*, dramatically reworded the Orpheus-Eurydice myth and has also included two sections of poems which develop further the significant experiences, emotions, and issues raised by the myth.

Honig's critical study of García Lorca calls attention to "his problematical forcing of the door of the constant enemy, death." The comment sheds as much light on Honig himself as it does on Lorca. His book titles (*Survivals, Spring Journal, Four Springs*)—and indeed the poet's work as a whole—affirm life, but the affirmation is wrested, often fiercely and explicitly, from the omnipresent threat of death. "Death with its cup of hopeful-

ness / needs nourishment / but won't be fed by leftovers—/ tired grief, / bewilderment of life's exhaust." Honig is a fine exemplar of his own concept of the function of the poet: "that voice which celebrates the difficult, joyous, imaginative process by which the individual man discovers and enacts his selfhood."

—Rudolph L. Nelson

HOOKER, Jeremy. British. Born in Warsash, Hampshire, 23 March 1941. Educated at St. Peter's, Southbourne, 1954-59; University of Southampton, 1959-65, B.A. 1963, M.A. 1965. Married Susan Hope Gill in 1968 (divorced, 1984), one son and one daughter. Lecturer in English, University College of Wales, Aberystwyth, 1965-84; Arts Council Creative Writing Fellow, Winchester School of Art, 1981-83. Recipient: Eric Gregory Award, 1969; Welsh Arts Council Prize, 1975, and bursary, 1976. Address: c/o Hayford, Northover Road, Pennington, Lymington, Hampshire, England.

PUBLICATIONS

Verse

The Elements. Llandybie, Dyfed, Christopher Davies, 1972.
Soliloquies of a Chalk Giant. London, Enitharmon Press, 1974.
Solent Shore: New Poems. Manchester, Carcanet, 1978.
Landscape of the Daylight Moon. London, Enitharmon Press, 1978.
Englishman's Road. Manchester, Carcanet, 1980.
A View from the Source: Selected Poems. Manchester, Carcanet, 1982.
Itchen Water. Winchester, Winchester School of Art Press, 1982.

Other

John Cowper Powys. Cardiff, University of Wales Press, 1973.
David Jones: An Exploratory Study of the Writings. London, Enitharmon Press, 1975.
John Cowper Powys and David Jones: A Comparative Study. London, Enitharmon Press, 1979.
Poetry of Place: Essays and Reviews 1970-1981. Manchester, Carcanet, 1982.

Editor, with Gweno Lewis, *Selected Poems of Alun Lewis.* London, Allen and Unwin, 1981.

*

Critical Studies: by Donald Davie, in *Poetry Nation 9* (Manchester), March 1979; Dick Davis, in *Agenda* (London), Winter-Spring 1982; Brian Hinton, in *Poetry Wales 18* (Bridgend), no. 3, 1983; Wynn Thomas, in *Anglo-Welsh Review* (Tenby), no. 74, 1983; *David Jones and Other Wonder Voyagers* by Philip Pacey, Bridgend, Poetry Wales Press, 1982.

Jeremy Hooker comments:

So far I have written from a sense of strong personal attachment to southern localities familiar to me since childhood, but where the presence of history and prehistory and also of other writers, such as Hardy, the Powys brothers, Richard Jefferies and Edward Thomas, is palpable. Thus I have attempted to establish my own way of experiencing, and also that of my forebears who were predominately agricultural labourers, the life of places that have strong literary and historical associations—associations that work both with and against the individual experience I try to express. There is, in the south, an opposition between continuity and discontinuity, and often a sense that all the air has been breathed, so that the relationship, and sometimes the sturggle, between the living and the dead, the present and the past is one of my principal themes. Above all, I am moved to write by the physical nature of the landscape itself, by the coexistence of such phenomena as Stonehenge and Porton, the Cerne giant and the jets from Boscombe Down, and by a sense of family history that is inseparable from this landscape. Living in Wales has helped to bring these themes into focus by distancing me from their place of origin, but also by making me aware of the Welsh poet's relationship to his material, which is quite different from that of the majority of his English counterparts.

I suppose everything that is implied by "belonging" and "not belonging" can be said to be at the root of my work. My inclination is to write extended sequences and sequences of related lyrics rather than occasional poems.

*   *   *

Five of the eight poems by Jeremy Hooker in *Introduction One* (1969) included references to other poets—Hardy, Alun Lewis, Edward Thomas, and Dafydd ap Gwilym: it has always been clear that Hooker is a poet consciously rooting himself in traditions. He is acutely aware of the traditions of writing in the South of England, his birthplace, and his adopted home, Wales.

This poet's commitment is to an exploration of structure—historical and metaphorical. His pamphlet *The Elements* included the notable "Elegy for the Labouring Poor"—

> No man's lonelier than James Mould
> As he wakes with stubble-scored legs
> In a rat's refuge of wattle and daub....
> But James Mould seeing the ocean
> Sees only flint acres
> Fought inch by inch, chalkdust rising,
> And hears only his ghostly kin
> Telling their names in the stunned brain.

This was a clear indication of the method that Hooker was to employ in his subsequent collections: the power of imagination to inhabit another's mind over the centuries.

Soliloquies of a Chalk Giant is a sequence of 38 short poems dealing with the significance in myth and history of the Cerne Abbas phallic man. The cumulative effect is impressive: Hooker uses the persona of the mysterious chalk figure to explore pre-Christian and Christian psyches whilst creating a credible being: "And beneath me / I feel the grass rise / And fall, like the slow, / Deep breaths of a giantess." The implicit danger of such an extended work is that the poet is eventually drawn into poetic exercises. *Soliloquies of a Chalk Giant* stops short of that, but *Solent Shore* was not as exciting, not as tightly controlled, as one would have wished from this talented poet. The book focussed on the poet's personal archetypes and can be seen as a natural sequel to the previous collection.

Too often the poems in *Solent Shore* rest on images that are competent but not exciting. The poet's aim is, to be fair, ambitious: to relate his life, the person he has become, to his background, the landscape and seascape of his heritage. The book's second section, "The Witnesses," is powerful. These related

poems turn around the rich 16th-century history of the Solent Waters. This has the necessary force to hold the poet to the core of his theme: "The very last souls I seen / was that man's father / and that man's / / Drowned like rattens, / drowned like rattens" ("Mary Rose, 1545").

Jeremy Hooker is an accomplished writer and critic to whom one looks for a significant book over the next decade: his is a vision which can only intensify and come into a compelling focus: "Wires still buzz with messages / from the *Titanic*. / A seance breaks up / when a cabin-boy screams."

—Tony Curtis

HOPE, A(lec) D(erwent).   Australian.   Born in Cooma, New South Wales, 21 July 1907. Educated at Sydney University (Associate Editor, *Arts Journal*), 1925-28, B.A. 1928; Oxford University (Irrawang Travelling Scholarship), 1928-30, B.A. 1931. Married Penelope Robinson in 1938; one daughter and two sons. Teacher, Department of Education, 1932, vocational psychologist, Department of Labour and Industry, 1933-36, and school counsellor, Department of Education, 1936, all in New South Wales; Lecturer in Education, 1937, and Lecturer in English, 1938-44, Sydney Teachers' College; Senior Lecturer in English, University of Melbourne, 1945-50; Professor of English and Head of the Department, 1951-67, Dean of the Faculty of Arts, 1960, Library Fellow, Chifley Library, 1967-72, and Temporary Lecturer-in-Charge, Medieval Studies, 1975, all at Canberra University College, later Australian National University. Visiting Professor of Poetry, Sweet Briar College, Virginia, 1970-71. President, Australian Association of Teachers of English, 1964-67, and Australian Society of Authors, 1966-67; Deputy-Chairman, Australia Council for the Arts Literary Board, 1973-74. Recipient: Grace Leven prize, 1956; Arts Council of Great Britain award, 1965; Britannica-Australia award, 1965; Volkswagen award, 1966; Myer award, 1967; Australian Literature Society award, 1968; Levinson Prize (*Poetry*, Chicago), 1969; Ingram Merrill Foundation award, 1969; Robert Frost award, 1976; *The Age* Book of the Year award, 1976. D.Litt.: Australian National University, 1972; Monash University, Clayton, Victoria, 1976; University of Melbourne, 1976. Member, Australian Academy of the Humanities; O.B.E. (Officer, Order of the British Empire), 1972; Companion, Order of Australia, 1981. Agent: Tim Curnow, Curtis Brown (Australia) Pty. Ltd., 86 William Street, Paddington, New South Wales 2021. Address: 66 Arthur Circle, Forrest, A.C.T. 2603, Australia.

PUBLICATIONS

Verse

(*Poems*), with Garry Lyle and Harry Hooton.   Privately printed, 2 vols., 1943-44.
The Wandering Islands.   Sydney, Edwards and Shaw, 1955.
Poems.   Sydney, Angus and Robertson, and London, Hamish Hamilton, 1960; New York, Viking Press, 1961.
(*Poems*), edited by Douglas Stewart.   Sydney, Angus and Robertson, 1963.

Collected Poems 1930-1965.   Sydney, Angus and Robertson,
  London, Hamish Hamilton, and New York, Viking Press,
  1966.
New Poems 1965-1969.   Sydney, Angus and Robertson, 1969;
  New York, Viking Press, 1970.
Dunciad Minor: An Heroick Poem.   Melbourne, Melbourne
  University Press, 1970.
Collected Poems 1930-1970.   Sydney and London, Angus and
  Robertson, 1972.
Selected Poems.   Sydney and London, Angus and Robertson,
  1973.
The Damnation of Byron.   Stratford, Ontario, Pasdeloup
  Press, 1973.
A Late Picking: Poems 1965-1974.   Sydney, Angus and
  Robertson, 1975.
A Book of Answers.   Sydney, Angus and Robertson, 1978.
The Drifting Continent and Other Poems.   Canberra, Brinda-
  bella Press, 1979.
Antechinus: Poems 1975-1980.   London, Angus and Robert-
  son, 1981.
The Age of Reason.   Melbourne, Melbourne University Press,
  1984.

Recording: *A.D. Hope Reads from His Own Work.* University
of Queensland Press, 1972.

Other

The Structure of Verse and Prose.   Sydney, Australasian Med-
  ical Publishing, 1943.
The Study of English (lecture).   Canberra, Canberra University
  College, 1952.
Australian Literature 1950-1962.   Melbourne, Melbourne Uni-
  versity Press, 1963.
The Cave and the Spring: Essays on Poetry.   Adelaide, Rigby,
  and San Francisco, Tri-Ocean, 1965.
The Literary Influence of Academies (lecture).   Sydney, Aus-
  tralian Academy of the Humanities, 1970.
*A Midsummer Eve's Dream: Variations on a Theme by William
  Dunbar.*   Canberra, Australian National University, and
  New York, Viking Press, 1970; Edinburgh, Oliver and Boyd,
  1971.
Henry Kendall: A Dialogue with the Past.   Sydney, Wentworth
  Press, 1971.
*Native Companions: Essays and Comments on Australian
  Literature 1936-1966.*   Sydney, Angus and Robertson, 1974.
Judith Wright.   Melbourne and London, Oxford University
  Press, 1975.
The Pack of Autolycus.   Canberra, Australian National Uni-
  versity Press, 1979.
The New Cratylus: Notes on the Craft of Poetry.   Melbourne,
  Oxford University Press, 1979.
Poetry and the Art of Archery (lecture).   Hobart, University of
  Tasmania, 1980.

Editor, *Australian Poetry 1960.*   Sydney, Angus and Robertson, 1960.
Editor, with Leonie Kramer, (*Poems*), by Henry Kendall. Melbourne, Sun, 1976.
Editor, *The Tragical History of Dr. Faustus,* by Christopher
  Marlowe.   Canberra, Australian National University Press,
  1982.

*

Bibliography: *A.D. Hope* by Joy Hooton, Melbourne, Oxford
University Press, 1979.

Manuscript Collection: Australian National Library, Canberra.

Critical Study: *A.D. Hope* by Leonie Kramer, Melbourne,
Oxford University Press, 1979.

                    *   *   *

To say that A.D. Hope is, along with Judith Wright, one of the
most highly respected of contemporary Australian poets is not,
perhaps, to say very much, since contemporary Australian poetry is so little known outside the antipodes. While Hope does not
acknowledge in his poetry the problems of being an "Australian
poet" in any obvious or insistent way, his whole achievement—
which is, I think, a very large one—is made possible only by his
writing from well outside the Anglo-American culture and tradition in which the language he uses has achieved its greatest
fulfilment. The early poem, "Australia," is more or less explicit
on the point. The country itself is savaged for its spiritual
barrenness:

> They call her a young country, but they lie:
> She is the last of lands, the emptiest,
> A woman beyond her change of life, a breast
> Still tender but within the womb is dry.

Yet he hopes to find in this "Arabian desert of the human mind"
a prophetic inspiration barbed with satiric venom to rail against
other sorts of barrenness in European culture, "some spirit
which escapes/The learned doubt, the chatter of cultured apes/
Which is called civilization over there."
   So: although Hope's poems only very rarely evoke the Australian landscape, and although he never uses specifically Australian speech-patterns or rhythms, the vision informing his
work, and the forms he uses to embody it, depend on his status as
an outsider. No poet within the Anglo-American tradition could
afford to summon so insistently and so unselfconsciously, in his
own forms, the great European ghosts of Byron, Donne, Pope,
and Yeats. But Hope's Australian recklessness, while it runs the
risk of toppling into pastiche, often conveys magnificently the
sense of enormous energy, or tension, or terror, or lust, or even,
occasionally, just delightedly exuberant humour, being kept
barely in check by the elaborate formal artifice of traditional
metric. This is, perhaps, especially true of his erotic verse, of
which he has written a great deal, in which there is a Swiftian
alteration of celebration and disgust:

> Stockings and drawers I shall peel off
> From your lithe legs and lovely thighs,
> And think the rustling silks you slough
> The foam from which, new-born, you rise.
>
> Thus love in mime despoils this world:
> Fashions, beliefs and customs fall;
> In brutal, naked grace unfurled
> He shows the root and ground of all.

   The tenderness which he sometimes finds in Eros is the central
affirmation in a poetry more often devoted to lacerating satire or
elegiac lament. His work is often, indeed, in the title of a poem,
"A Commination," heaping disdainful invective on those he
calls, memorably, "small turds from the great arse of self-
esteem." But, in his later work, there is a wider variety of tone
and, perhaps, a larger ambition. The sonnet sequences, "The

Planctus" and "Sonnets to Baudelaire," and the long poems, "The Double Looking Glass" and "Vivaldi, Bird and Angel," are poems for which I would make very large claims indeed. The imagination at work in them seems to me a unique one uniquely fulfilling itself. The conclusion of "Vivaldi, Bird and Angel," a poem which imagines Vivaldi conducting a rehearsal of one of his flute concertos, *Il Cardellino*, with the young girls of the *Ospedale della Pietà* in 18th-century Venice, rises to an explicit statement of a religious vision on the other side of satire and elegy. The angel, watching over the rehearsal, speaks:

> Yet men in the Great Music, I surmise
> Must also share, for what in reveries,
> In separateness, in silence they create,
> They only play if they participate.
> These six girls and their master play as one
> Perfected creature; in that unison
> They touch, at least, the state in which we move:
> A mutual ecstasy of consenting love.

It is a measure of Hope's accomplishment that such things can be said in his work without sentimentality and without portentousness. He is a very good poet indeed.

—Neil Corcoran

HOROVITZ, Michael. British. Born in Frankfurt, Germany, 4 April 1935; emigrated to England at the age of 2. Educated at William Ellis School, London; Brasenose College, Oxford, B.A. in English, M.A. Married Frances Hooker (i.e., the poet Frances Horovitz) in 1964 (died, 1983); one son. Since 1959, Editor and Publisher, *New Departures* magazine; also painter, musician, and singer; director, New Departures road show, World's Best Jam arts circuses, and international Poetry Olympics. Recipient: Arts Council Translator's Award, 1964, and Writer's Award, 1978. Address: Piedmont, Bisley, Stroud, Gloucestershire GL6 7BU, England.

PUBLICATIONS

Verse

Declaration. London, New Departures, 1963.
Strangers. London, New Departures, 1965.
Nude Lines for Barking (in Present Night Soho). London, Goliard Press, 1965.
High Notes from When I Was Rolling in Moss. London, New Departures, 1966.
Poetry for the People: A Verse Essay in "Bop" Prosody. London, Latimer Press, 1966.
Bank Holiday: A New Testament for the Love Generation. London, Latimer Press, 1967.
The Wolverhampton Wanderer: An Epic of Britannia. London, Latimer Press, 1971.
Love Poems: Nineteen Poems of Love, Lust, and Spirit. London, New Departures, 1971.
A Contemplation (of High Art, Solemn Music, and Classical Culture). London, Calder, 1978.

Growing Up: Selected Poems and Pictures 1951-79. London, Allison and Busby, 1979.
Midsummer Morning Jog Log. Madley, Herefordshire, Five Seasons Press, 1985.

Other

Alan Davie. London, Methuen, 1963.

Editor, *Children of Albion: Poetry of the "Underground" in Britain.* London, Penguin, 1969.
Editor, *"Big Huge" Reunion Anthology.* Bisley, Gloucestershire, New Departures, 1975.
Editor, *Poetry Olympics.* Bisley, Gloucestershire, New Departures, 3 vols., 1980-83.

Translator, with Stefan Themerson, *Europa*, by Anatol Stern. London, Gabberbocchus, 1962.
Translator, *The Egghead Republic: A Short Novel from the Horse Latitudes*, by Arno Schmidt, edited by Ernst Krawelh and Marion Boyars. London, Boyars, 1979.

*

Critical Studies: "Of Relative Importance" by Barry Cole, in *Ambit 26* (London), 1966; Afterword to *Children of Albion*, 1969, "Blake and the Voice of the Bard in Our Time," in *Books* (London), Winter 1972, "The Need for the Non-Literary," in *Times Literary Supplement* (London), 29 December 1972, in *The Listener* (London), 3 May 1973, *Poetry Information* (London), Autumn 1973, *New Review* (London), March 1975, "Judaism, the Midcentury, and Me," in *Next Year in Jerusalem* edited by Douglas Villiers, New York, Viking Press, and London, Harrap, 1976, and *City Limits* (London), 8 October 1982, all by the author; Adrian Mitchell, in *The Listener* (London), 14 May 1970; "Vanessa's Hangups," in *Ambit 48* (London), 1971, and "Warning: Poems Can Damage Your Leisure," in *The Guardian* (London), 10 November 1979, both by Jeff Nuttall; Christopher Logue, in *The Times* (London), 21 May 1977; Susana Duncan, in *New York Magazine*, 15 May 1978; Brocard Sewell, in *The Tablet* (London), 27 October 1979; Jim Burns, in *The Tribune* (London), 2 November 1979; Herbert Lomas, in *Literary Review* (London), April 1980; Peter Clothier, in *Los Angeles Times*, 13 July 1980; "The Pursuit of Innocence: Populism and Intellect in the Poetry of Horovitz" by Eric Mottram, in *PS 5* (London), October-November 1980; interview with Eric Baizer and Rick Peabody, in *Gargoyle 14* (Washington, D.C.), 1980; Tina Morris, in *Resurgence* (Bideford, Devon), July-August 1981; Miles Kington, in *Cambridge Voice*, November-December 1981; David Timms, in *Critical Quarterly* (Manchester), 7 July 1982; Peter Gilbert, in *Jewish Quarterly* (London), Autumn-Winter 1982-83; John Walsh, in *Books and Bookmen* (London), May 1983; Val Hennessy, in *The Guardian* (London), 1 December 1983; Laurence Marks, in *The Observer* (London), 4 December 1983.

Michael Horovitz comments:
I'm often regarded as anarchic—a far far out, free-range or spontaneous bop troubadour; but I'm gratified when discerning auditors see that my innovations are rooted in the time-honoured shaping spirit, and my dreams in shared realities. I hope I bring together pre-Renaissance inspirations with contemporary facts, without abusing the essence of either.
My early exposure to the rhythms, musics and reintegrative pressures of being Jewish in the post-Nazi Diaspora inevitably

conditioned the nature and techniques of my poetic mission. As the youngest of ten children, of whom my four sisters tended to rebel against the more restrictive or unquestioning mores taken "as read," by and large, by my brothers, I came to assume the role of outspoken mouthpiece for the idealism of the sisters. This sowed some of the seeds which bore fruit years later, when I started dropping out from my postgraduate research on Blake and Joyce, in favour of fulfilling the less academic implications of the diverse kinds of poetry I'd been writing since childhood— and of performing it along with my peers in writing, singing, music and all the arts together. We mounted a multi-medic non-conformist arts circus, which travelled all over Britain throughout the decades since 1959. Reviving the word-of-mouth tradition doubtless appealed to the part of me that had been steeped in another style of "underground" oral convention during my Jewish upbringing.

The public poet-spokesman and the cantor-rabbi stand in a somewhat parallel relation to their following. Allen Ginsberg has declared "Poet is Priest," invoking Blake's Old Testament-prophetic "voice of the Bard/Who present, past and future sees"; the basis of spoken poetry remains what Langston Hughes described as "the common loneliness of the folk song that binds one heart to all the others—and all the others to the one who sings the song." The wheel is coming full circle these days, bringing the word in its various manifestations closer to its origins in lawmaking, religion, and musical-dramatic configurations. The classic pattern of call and response joints the bonds of Reader and Congregation—although the resultant dialogue and activities are liable to cut way across the prevalent civic and clerical canons.

Responding to my fellow poets and minstrels, and eliciting a voluble response myself from audiences that sprang up around us as spontaneously as we ourselves had sprung, I recalled how so long before, in *dovening* (congregational prayers), I'd sometimes caught more than a whiff of authentic catharsis, the tribal pull, toward the experience of being "members of one another." And, for all that it was a harking back, I came to recognise positive aspects of primitive forms, such as communal incantation or even the selfsame foot-stomping outcry against tribal enemies I'd shied away from in my rationalist teens. They functioned, for example, in the manner of wild Afric tomtoms or jazz horns in frenzied climactic choruses, to exorcise demons— purging the shared emotions of fear (if not always of pity), affirming solidarity (if not always absolute aesthetic or political unity).

Quite often in the midst of supra-national poetry events I find myself involuntarily imagining *yom tov* (a Jewish festival— literally "good day"), in the ghettos of Sholom Aleichem and Marc Chagall, or sensing that vaunted continuum that links forefathers and descendants—celebrants all, consigned to harmonise, preach, teach, sing, dance, clap hands, achieving a genuinely popular yet ecstatic communion. Our large-scale happenings and recitals, festivals and *Poetry Olympicses* at venues like London's Royal Albert Hall and Westminster Abbey have in fact seemed positively Biblic to some—and more suggestive of the fall of the Roman Empire to others. As far as most of the poets are concerned, we hold with Blake that "poetry is religion, religion is politics and politics is brotherhood;" and with Adrian Mitchell, that we "want poetry to bust down the walls of its museum-tomb and learn to survive in the corrosive real world. The walls are thick but a hundred Joshuas are on the job."

The voice of prophecy rarely provides conventional directives. When I'd managed to split away from the chrysalis in which "the Lord is One" was wound round my brain and arm several times a day, to spread my butterfly wings and discover the diversity of religious and pagan myths, I was almost stupefied, at first, by the

rich stores of nourishment available. But old Jewry continued to inform the imagery that burgeoned from the apparently infinite plantations of reference interpollenating. Even now my spirit reels daily with rhythms and tunes that ran through my youth: the echoes of ancestral lamentations, from fast days and evening prayers and Talmudic or Kabbalistic ravings; of signal variations of the liturgy—the portions of the Torah, the Psalms and the Apocrypha that kept Jews in touch from every outpost of exile through the ages; of the light-fantastical trips and melancholy of plangent pipes and timbrels and velveteen viol woof; of chutzpah and Chelm, the laughter inseparable from tears in Yiddish humour and play; of exalted Hebraic dirges, chants, and benedictions (*duchening*), reJoyceing and overlapping with the wordsounds of "Hie'brouw clans" in MacDiarmid's Scotland and Bloom's Dublin—tracking back from Bialik to Yehuda Halevi to the Piyyuth and Ecclesiastes and the marvellous world of surreal-real praises in which the mountains skip like rams and the hills like young sheep...

It's this sacramental tradition of Israel's tents understood as art and poetry that survives with the power to release our children from the nuclear fires of Moloch and the money-mad yoke of Mammon—the inhuman pitch of exploitation and oppression exerted for the sake of ephemeral (albeit "super"-)powermanic advantages. The rebirth from materialism is well illustrated by Blake's engraving of Elijah (or God) alighting from the fiery chariot—the prophet who gives his cloak of inspiration to Elisha (or Adam), symbolising the poet who grasps the eternal truth of the imagination, the divine presence in man and woman, and hands it on. Jerusalem-builders on both sides of the Atlantic are rejecting the lights and obscurantism of an unknowable God of superhuman energy —in favour of something closer to Blake's visions, than to Orwell's "fallen" state of *1984*. Of course police states even more heinously repressive than that fictitious one already operate, but there's also a concerted underground or grass-roots growth over against them—plus a pearl necklace of small communities well away from them, decentralised pockets of resistance and independence—loosely knit, it's true, but growing all the time—not least in the persistent strands of our poetic industry.

*   *   *

It is often difficult to separate Michael Horovitz's poetry from his public image. This is not said in a derogatory sense, but more in acceptance of the fact that his good-humoured and enthusiastic appearances at readings, and his commitment to an entertaining approach to the writing and presentation of poetry, are always reflected in his work. It is full of surprises, and jabs at the reader/listener with light, fast punches which occasionally have a fair amount of power behind them.

Horovitz's public activities have been maintained over the years, and his own writing has had a constant tone, one which, with its colour and vigour, overcomes certain limitations of depth and precision. The use of language is sometimes noted more for its liveliness than its accuracy, with words being sprayed at the reader/listener in a machine gun-like manner, i.e., not all of them hit the target but some do and have the desired effect. At a public reading the problems of this approach are not too noticeable, but on the printed page they become obvious, and the poems can seem slack or thin.

There are, it's only fair to say, Horovitz poems which do aim at a greater degree of control than is evident in some of his work, and these often have an appealing lyricism. One can perhaps point to the love poems in this connection. But his reputation rests primarily on the longer poems, in particular his magnum opus, *The Wolverhampton Wanderer*, in which the role of the football star as working-class hero—and so a symbol of the true energy in our society—is tied in with the role of the poet as a kind of wandering bard. If any one work of Horovitz's deserves to last it is this, and its racy, humorous style is remarkably effective. It is, of course, very much a 1960's poem in its tone and social sense, and there may be some significance in the fact that it was that decade which saw Horovitz at his best.

It seems doubtful, in fact, that Horovitz will develop much beyond the point he reached in the 1960's, whether as poet or performer, although one cannot write him off as having relevance only in that period. He could still have the energy and vision to create something which will offer a view of Britain beyond the merely superficial. And given a resurgence of public poetry he could come back into his own, being the kind of poet who seems to produce best under pressure. However, although one should not under-estimate his contribution to the literary scene of the 1960's and early 1970's, it would seem fair to suggest that his limitations as a poet have, in a sense, caught up with him. A radical change in style might enable him to go beyond them.

—Jim Burns

HOUÉDARD, Dom (Pierre-)Sylvester. British. Born in Guernsey, Channel Islands, 16 February 1924. Educated at Elizabeth College, Guernsey; Jesus College, Oxford, 1942-44, 1947-49; Benedictine University of Sant'Anselmo, Rome, 1951-55, Ph.L.; ordained as priest 1959. Served in British Army Intelligence in the Far East, 1944-47. Benedictine monk: since 1949 at Prinknash Abbey, Gloucester. Librarian, Farnborough Abbey, 1959-61; Literary Editor for the New Testament, and sub-editor for the Old Testament, Jerusalem Bible, 1961. Since 1965, Founding Member and Vice President, Association of Little Presses; since 1971, Editor, with Bob Cobbing and Peter Mayer, *Kroklok*. Visual Poetry exhibited: St. Catherine's College, Oxford, 1964; Galerie Riquelme, Paris, 1964; Galerie Bressy, Lyons, 1965; Galerie Denise-Davy, Paris, 1965; Kornblee Gallery, New York, 1965; ICA, London, 1965; Signals Gallery, London, 1965; Tyler School of Art, Philadelphia, 1966; Peacetower, Los Angeles, 1966; Midland Gallery, Nottingham, 1966; Galeria Universitaria Aristos, Mexico City, 1966; Galeria Juana Mordo, Madrid, 1966; Gallery 10, London, 1966; Kunstcentrum 'tvenster, Rotterdam, 1966; Arnolfini Gallery, Bristol, 1966; Galeria Barandiaran, San Sebastian, Spain, 1966; Castello del Valentino, Turin, 1966; Subscription Rooms, Stroud, Gloucestershire, 1966; Brighton Festival, 1967; Lisson Gallery, London, 1967; New Metropole Arts Centre, Folkestone, Kent, 1967; French Institute, London, 1967; Festival de Fort Boyard, Rochefort-sur-Mer, France, 1967; Studio 2-B, Bergamo, Italy, 1967; Festival of Spain, 1967; Absalon, Bath, 1968; Galerie nächst St. Stephan, Vienna, 1968; Totem-1 Gallery, Salford, Lancashire, 1968; Westfälischer Kunstverein, Münster, 1969; Fine Arts Gallery, Vancouver, 1969; Axis, Bristol, 1969; Ceolfrith Gallery, Sunderland, 1970; Stedelijk Museum, Amsterdam, 1970; Victoria and Albert Museum, London (and tour), 1970-72; Bear Lane Gallery, Oxford, 1971; Avelles Gallery, Vancouver, 1971; Art Centre, Bristol, 1971; Laing Gallery, Newcastle-upon-Tyne, 1971, 1972; Oval House, London, 1974; LYC Museum, Brampton, Cumberland, 1974. Vice-President, The Poetry Society, 1974. Address: Prinknash Abbey, Gloucester GL4 8EX, England.

PUBLICATIONS

Verse

Yes-No. Daneway, Gloucestershire, Daneway Press, 1963.
Thalamus-Sol. Maidstone, Kent, St. Albert's Press, 1964.
Rock Sand Tide. Woodchester, Gloucestershire, Daneway Press—Openings Press, 1964.
Frog-Pond-Plop. Woodchester, Gloucestershire, Openings Press, 1965.
Atom. Woodchester, Gloucestershire, Openings Press, 1965.
Kinkon. London, Writers Forum, 1965; revised edition, as *Op and Kinkon Poems and Some Non-Kinkon*, 1965.
Worm-Wood/Womb-Word. Daneway, Gloucestershire, Daneway Press, 1966.
A Book of Chakras (8 Yantrics): Studies Towards Mechanical Fingers by dsh for Inner Moon Pointing. Watford, Hertfordshire, Watford School of Art, 1966.
To Catch a Whiteman by His Manifesto. Corsham, Wiltshire, Openings Press, 1967.
Tantric Poems, Perhaps. London, Writers Forum, 1967.
Book of 12 Mudras. Corsham, Wiltshire, Openings Press, 1967.
Book of Mazes and Troytowns. Corsham, Wiltshire, Openings Press, 1967.
Easter Frog Toy for Pesach-Skipover. Corsham, Wiltshire, Openings Press, 1967.
Eros A-Gape. London, Lisson Delta, 1967.
Semaine Euclidienne. Sherborne, Dorset, South Street, 1968.
Poster for the Breakdown of Nations 4th-World Conference. London, Resurgence, 1968.
Deus-Snap. Corsham, Wiltshire, Openings Press, 1968.
Miniposters. Sherborne, Dorset, South Street, 1968.
The Sun-Cheese Wheel-Ode: A Double-Rolling-Gloster Memorial for Ken Cox. Sherborne, Dorset, South Street, 1969.
A Snow Mouse. Bristol, Axis Multiple, 1969.
En Trance. Bristol, Axis Multiple, 1969.
12 Nahuatl Dancepoems from the Cosmic Typewriter. Sherborne, Dorset, South Street, 1969.
Texts, edited by John Sharkey. London, Lorrimer, 1969.
Streets Go Both Crazy Ways at Once. Sherborne, Dorset, South Street, 1969.
Book of Battledores. Sherborne, Dorset, South Street, 1969.
Book of Onomastikons. Sherborne, Dorset, South Street, 1969.
Splendid Weeping. Corsham, Wiltshire, Openings Press, 1969.
Successful Cube Tranceplant in Honor of Chairman Mao. Corsham, Wiltshire, Openings Press, 1970.
Ode to the Colonels. Corsham, Wiltshire, Openings Press, 1970.
Grove Sings: Reflecting Poem for ihf. Sunderland, Ceolfrith, 1970.
Auto-de-Chakra-Struction. Oxford, Bear Lane Gallery, 1971.
The Sign. Worcester, Stanbrook Abbey Press, 1971.
Main Calm Line. London, National Poetry Centre, 1972.
Like Contemplation. London, Writers Forum, 1972.
(Poems), edited by Charles Verey. Sunderland, Ceolfrith, 1972.
Begin Again: A Book of Reflections and Reversals. Brampton, Cumbria, LYC, 1975.

Other

Translator, *Office of Our Lady* (the Encalcat Office). London, Darton Longman Todd, 1962.

*

Critical Studies: in *(Poems)* edited by Charles Verey, 1972 (includes bibliography).

Dom Sylvester Houédard comments:

inevitably i feel my own work as the continuation of the unbroken traditions of benedictine poets & artists—beginning with the monastic literati of the ancient west who *created* civilization & the european cultural revolution until the mimetic embourgeoisification of art as revivalism—with the neo-isms of *re*naissance thru *neo*gothic—even for part of this period tho not right up till napoleon III's salon des refusés there is a wu-wei quality of playing the stringless lute in benedictine baroque as contrasted with the jesuit—& poetmonks in the west have always cultivated what newman calls "the alliance of benedict & virgil." eg:

s-abbo s-adelhard agobard b-alcuin s-aldhelm (the concretist) s-angilbert s-bede s-bertharius (caedmon) s-dunstan (another concretist) florus fridoard gerbert (sylvester II) heiric hepidamn-the-newsallust herimann v-hildebert hincmar b-hrabanus-maurus (concrete) abbess hroswitha the ladycatullus playwright hucbald itier-de-vassy lawrence of durham lupus modoin notkerbalbulus s-odo otfrid s-pascasiusradbert peter-the-venerable sigebert-the-newovid theodulf & walafridstrabo-the-newvirgil—not to mention the preservers & copiers of not only the pagan latin poets including the erotica but also of pagan icelandic sagas & (tho the danes later destroyed these mss) the earlier british poets (& celtic monkpoets were as honoured as their nonmonk-poets)—for similar reasons sahagun & other friars preserved the nahuatl poetry of aztec & earlier mexico.

to the modern contemplative & poet it is hard not to see the sweep of so called avantgarde creativeness from eg the impressionists & thru dada cage concrete antimimesis autodestructive streetguerilla & authentic je-je communication-dialog structures as so many searches for innerpath social liberation & the creative poetic monastic transcendental experience & vision of seeing things change into what they are—but i feel too this equally strong empathy with the monkprophet poets of other cultures—tho particularly with the siberian shamans & the feathery flowerdrum heart-&-face-making nahuatl singers & the welsh englynion makers & the zen haiga/haiku makers—yinyang acceptance of yinyang tension is the unifying field of west scriptorium & east zenga—onepointed poetry as spiritual askesis.

*   *   *

"There are certain fundamental types of questioning abt language that shld have occurred in English poetry before it got withered by the fesival of britain." So dom Sylvester Houédard wrote in 1964, and his output since then has tried to supply this lack of questioning, sometimes within previously accepted parameters of how poetry works, but more often through a radical denudation of subjective and expressionist language elements, producing a cool flicker of mathematical permutations and/or of sound-effects and/or of visual patterns. The works by which he is best-known are his "typestracts"—typed designs of extraordinary ingenuity which increasingly came to be ikons for contemplation, topological tantric forms linked to language or "poetry" only by the lingering literary hookup anything typewritten still tends to retain, or by a title like "slipping sideways into god" which slips the typestract into both poetry and religion, however nonverbal the design in itself.

Western and oriental meditation join their influences in his work, whether in the "sun/bridesroom" (sol/thalamus) Christ-

mas poem or in his version of Basho's Zen-directed haiku "frog/pond/plop," both using the spatialist techniques of concrete poetry. His ecumenical inclusiveness has been held against him, and his "borderblurs" (to use his own term for the dissolving of art-categories) have been regarded with some suspicion as well as admiration. But in the history of the avant-garde in Britain he has a distinctive place.

—Edwin Morgan

HOWARD, Richard (Joseph). American. Born in Cleveland, Ohio, 13 October 1929. Educated at Shaker Heights High School, Ohio; Columbia University, New York (Editor, *Columbia Review*), B.A. 1951, M.A. 1952; the Sorbonne, Paris, 1952-53. Lexicographer, World Publishing Company, Cleveland, 1954-56, and in New York, 1956-58. Since 1958, free-lance literary and art critic, and translator. Poetry Editor, *American Review*, New York; Director, Braziller Poetry Series. Recipient: Guggenheim Fellowship, 1966; Harriet Monroe Memorial Prize, 1969, and Levinson Prize, 1973 (*Poetry*, Chicago); American Academy grant, 1970, and Award of Merit Medal, 1980; Pulitzer Prize, 1970; American Book Award, for translation, 1983. Fellow, Morse College, Yale University, New Haven, Connecticut. Member, American Academy, 1983. Address: c/o Atheneum Publishers, 597 Fifth Avenue, New York, New York 10017, U.S.A.

PUBLICATIONS

Verse

Quantities. Middletown, Connecticut, Wesleyan University Press, 1962.
The Damages. Middletown, Connecticut, Wesleyan University Press, 1967.
Untitled Subjects. New York, Atheneum, 1969.
Findings. New York, Atheneum, 1971.
Two-Part Inventions (includes radio play *The Lesson of the Master*). New York, Atheneum, 1974.
Fellow Feelings. New York, Atheneum, 1976.
Misgivings. New York, Atheneum, 1979.
Lining Up. New York, Atheneum, 1984.

Plays

The Automobile Graveyard, adaptation of a play by Fernando Arrabal (produced New York, 1961).
Wildflowers (produced New York, 1976).
Natures (produced New York, 1977).
Two-Part Inventions (produced Chicago, 1979).

Other

Alone with America: Essays on the Art of Poetry in the United States since 1950. New York, Atheneum, 1969; London, Thames and Hudson, 1970; revised edition, Atheneum, 1980.

Editor, *Preferences: 51 American Poets Choose Poems from Their Own Work and from the Past.* New York, Viking Press, 1974.

Translator, *The Voyeur*, by Alain Robbe-Grillet. New York, Grove Press, 1958; London, Calder, 1959.

Translator, *The Wind*, by Claude Simon. New York, Braziller, 1959.

Translator, *The Grass*, by Claude Simon. New York, Braziller, 1960; London, Cape, 1961.

Translator, *Two Novels* (*Jealousy* and *In the Labyrinth*), by Alain Robbe-Grillet. New York, Grove Press, 1960.

Translator, *Najda*, by André Breton. New York, Grove Press, 1961.

Translator, *Last Year at Marienbad*, by Alain Robbe-Grillet. New York, Grove Press, and London, Calder and Boyars, 1962.

Translator, *Mobile*, by Michel Butor. New York, Simon and Schuster, 1963.

Translator, *Manhood*, by Michel Leiris. New York, Grossman, 1963; London, Cape, 1968.

Translator, *Force of Circumstance*, by Simone de Beauvoir. New York, Simon and Schuster, 1963; London, Deutsch-Weidenfeld and Nicolson, 1965.

Translator, *Erasers*, by Alain Robbe-Grillet. New York, Grove Press, 1964; London, Calder and Boyars, 1966.

Translator, *For a New Novel: Essays on Fiction*, by Alain Robbe-Grillet. New York, Grove Press, 1966.

Translator, *The Poetics of Paul Valéry*, by Jean Hytier. New York, Doubleday, 1966.

Translator, *Natural Histories*, by Jules Renard. New York, Horizon Press, 1966.

Translator, *History of Surrealism*, by Maurice Nadeau. New York, Macmillan, 1967; London, Cape, 1968.

Translator, *Histoire*, by Claude Simon. New York, Braziller, 1968; London, Cape, 1969.

Translator, *The Immoralist*, by André Gide. New York, Knopf, 1970.

Translator, *May Day Speech*, by Jean Genet. San Francisco, City Lights, 1970.

Translator, *Professional Secrets: An Autobiography*, by Jean Cocteau. New York, Farrar Straus, 1970; London, Vision Press, 1972.

Translator, *The Fall into Time*, by E.M. Cioran. Chicago, Quadrangle, 1970.

Translator, *The Battle of Pharsalus*, by Claude Simon. New York, Braziller, and London, Cape, 1971.

Translator, *A Happy Death*, by Albert Camus. New York, Knopf, and London, Hamish Hamilton, 1972.

Translator, *Critical Essays*, by Roland Barthes. Evanston, Illinois, Northwestern University Press, 1972.

Translator, *Rosa*, by Maurice Pons. New York, Dial Press, 1972; London, New English Library, 1973.

Translator, *Project for a Revolution in New York*, by Alain Robbe-Grillet. New York, Grove Press, 1972; London, Calder and Boyars, 1973.

Translator, *The Fantastic*, by Tzvetan Todorov. Cleveland, Case Western Reserve University Press, 1973.

Translator, *Song for an Equinox*, by St. -John Perse. Princeton, New Jersey, Princeton University Press, 1977.

Translator, *A Lover's Discourse: Fragments*, by Roland Barthes. New York, Hill and Wang, 1978; London, Cape, 1979.

Translator, *The Eiffel Tower and Other Mythologies*, by Roland Barthes. New York, Hill and Wang, 1979.

Translator, *New Critical Essays*, by Roland Barthes. New York, Hill and Wang, 1980.

Translator, *Camera Lucida: Reflections on Photography*, by Roland Barthes. New York, Hill and Wang, 1981; London, Cape, 1982.

Translator, *Les Fleurs du Mal*, by Baudelaire. Boston, Godine, and Brighton, Sussex, Harvester Press, 1982.

Translator, *Empire of Signs*, by Roland Barthes. New York, Hill and Wang, 1982; London, Cape, 1983.

Translator, *Corydon*, by André Gide. New York, Farrar Straus, 1983.

Translator, *The Fashion System*, by Roland Barthes. New York, Hill and Wang, 1983.

Translator, *The Grain of His Voice 1962-1980* (inteviews), by Roland Barthes. New York, Hill and Wang, 1984.

Translator, *The Conquest of America*, by Tzetvan Todorov. New York, Harper, 1984.

Translator, *The Responsibility of Forms*, by Roland Barthes. New York, Hill and Wang, 1984.

More than 100 other translations of French works published.

*   *   *

In the somewhat than twenty years since the appearance of his first book, *Quantities*, Richard Howard has established himself firmly in a distinguished career as one of our most prolific poets, critics, editors, and translators. And the course of his poetic development seems to me to represent the difficult and treacherous job of surmounting and transforming his learning, sophistication, brilliance, and knowingness, instead of simply displaying them. As with Auden, for example, an acknowledged model for Howard, he is so good at writing interesting and skilful poems that he tends to be taken in by his own cleverness, writing poems that are merely skilful and interesting rather than compelling or passionate—poetry that arises inevitably out of the self's confrontation with itself and the world.

In *Quantities*, with variety of subject, flexibility and power of language and structure, and penetration of insight, Howard has much to say coupled with a virtuoso ability to say it. "The Return from Montauk," for example, presents a beautifully balanced moment in terms of a natural yet complex and ambiguous symbol. The speaker is riding a train at nightfall, and, looking to the east, he sees an image of the setting sun reflected in a window. The double perspective is completed when he turns toward the west and sees through the train window the actual setting sun—imagining, however, in line with the logic of his previously-established conception, that it is the rising sun. Thus, at the moment of sunset, he can envision, out of the literal structure of the perception itself, the sunrise, and at the moment of despair, the rebirth of hope. It is a clear and delicate poem, intricately wrought, suggesting implications that go far below its pellucid surface—a thematically central poem in the book as a whole, for Howard characteristically deals with the knife-edge upon which opposites are balanced, but his vision of the abyss which falls between them is neither deep nor powerful, and hence the tension in his poems is often not strong. There is too much of the dandified manner and not enough of the presence of a man. Order is best when it comes out of energy, not out of literature.

With *The Damages* we find an increased assurance and depth, coupled with an increasing prolixity and confirmation of his glib knowingness. In "For Hephaistos," we find the inevitable and moving confrontation with Auden, who "taught me, taught us all a way/To speak our minds," and the speaker's grateful sense of being free from his master: "only now, at last/Free of you, my old ventriloquist,/Have I suspected what I have to say/Without hearing you say it for me first." In "The Encounter," we find a marvelously erotic and mysterious confrontation between a nameless Hero and The Female, which rises convincingly to the level of myth. And there are, on the other hand, Jamesian and Proustian vignettes of childhood ("Seeing Cousin Phyllis Off," "Intimation of Mortality," "Private Drive"); poems of friends, literature, and travel ("Seferiades," "Even the Most Beautiful Sunset"); and the clever poems, such as "To Aegidius Cantor," "Eusebius to Florestan," and "Bonnard: A Novel," which continue his own line of literary ventriloquism and which anticipate the extended fascination Howard is to develop for the "dramatic monologue" in subsequent volumes.

Thus, *Untitled Subjects* (Pulitzer Prize) consists entirely of 15 such monologues (mostly in the form of letters), spoken by such 19th-century Worthies as Scott, Ruskin, Thackeray, and Mrs. William Morris, and arranged chronologically from 1801 to 1915. Howard alludes to Browning in his dedication, "the great poet of otherness," and quotes that poet's saying, "I'll tell my state as though 'twere none of mine." This clearly implies that Browning was writing about himself while pretending to be speaking in the voices of others, and I think this is true. But I do not think either that this makes him simply a poet of otherness or that Howard's dramatic monologues are very similar to his master's. What Howard's poems do, in fact, is "to bring history alive," as the jacket blurb for a historical novel or costume drama might say: they bring the past closer to us, first, by treating it as if it were present, and second, by making it personal and intimate—putting back in, as it were, what the official histories leave out, an intelligent piece of literary legerdemain.

Similar poems make up the first part of *Findings*, and this time Howard does not hesitate to write a 14-page poem, "November, 1889," spoken by Browning himself as he nears the moment of death. Revealingly, Howard puts these words into the master's mouth:

> what is dead or dying
> is more readily apprehended by us
> than what is part of life.
> Nothing in writing is
> easier than to raise the dead.

Perhaps this *is* more Howard than Browning, and so he moves on in the second part to more personal poems of love and friendship. These, however, as with the others, remain merely skilful and interesting.

This impression, alas, is only strengthened by Howard's latest volumes. *Two-Part Inventions* varies the form by expanding monologue to dialogue and by broadening his range of subjects to include Hölderlin, Wilde's visit to Whitman, Ibsen at Capri, Edith Wharton, Rodin, and Di Fiore. *Fellow Feelings* returns to the more usual lyric mode but deals, nevertheless, in its first section with Hart Crane, Randall Jarrell, Valéry Larbaud, Auden, and Goethe. Although the second section occupies more personal ground, poets, as Howard himself says, make "themselves public/without making themselves known." And in the third section he comes back compulsively to his beloved *objets d'art*—by Donatello, Simone Martini, Bellini, and so on. *Misgivings*, finally, contains commentaries on the subjects photographed by Nadar, poems about people from the renaissance to the present, and a series of love poems.

Howard is still so over-civilized, so full of grace, learning, polish, and elegance, as to seem the victim of his own gifts, keeping himself and his life—even when he does write about these things—at such a distance from the poems that they emerge as snowflakes under glass rather than the prowling animals they have every right to be. The libraries and museums await a lifetime of future poems, an endless abundance of stalking horses for the self to hide behind. The bravura technique becomes, in short, a technique of evasion; no poet need trifle, especially a poet such as Howard who has potentially much to say.

—Norman Friedman

HOWELL, Anthony. British. Born in London, 20 April 1945. Educated at Leighton Park School, Berkshire; Royal Ballet School, London; Centre de la Danse Classique, Cannes. Married Signe Lie in 1972. Dancer with the Royal Ballet, London, 1966. Lecturer in Creative Writing, Grenoble University, 1969-70. Editor of Softly Loudly Books, London. Founder, The Theatre of Mistakes, 1974. Address: c/o 11 Ascham Street, London NW5 2PB, England.

PUBLICATIONS

Verse

Sergei de Diaghileff (1929). London, Turret, 1968.
Inside the Castle: Poems. London, Barrie and Rockliff-Cresset Press, 1969.
Imruil: A Naturalized Version of His First Ode-Book (pre-Islamic Arabic). London, Barrie and Rockliff-Cresset Press, 1970.
Femina Deserta. London, Softly Loudly, 1971.
Oslo: A Tantric Ode. London, Calder and Boyars, 1975.
The Mekon. London, Many Press, 1976.
Notions of a Mirror: Poems Previously Uncollected 1964-1982. London, Anvil Press Poetry, 1983.

Other

Editor, *Erotic Lyrics.* London, Studio Vista, 1970.
Editor, with Fiona Templeton, *Elements of Performance Art.* London, Ting, 1976; revised edition, 1977.

*

Critical Studies: reviews by Peter Porter, in *London Magazine*, 1970, and Robert Nye, in *The Times* (London), 1975.

Anthony Howell comments:
I write poetry because I was brought up in Reading. You write poetry do you? He writes poetry because he was brought up in Slough. She writes poetry. It doesn't write poetry. We write poetry because we were brought up. They write poetry because they were brought up in blazers.

*   *   *

Anthony Howell's *Inside the Castle*, his first collection, was a crowded book, comparable with Keats's *Poems* of 1817 in that it marked the emergence of a young man of much talent unable or unwilling to refine a capacity for confusion when he saw that he could employ it to keep a poem going when inspiration failed. The book also contained three very good poems ("The Growing Family," "The Head," and "A Reason for Fidelity") where in each case one clear poetic impulse worked the whole way through, nothing sounded forced, and the only obvious debt was to John Crowe Ransom and the Fugitives generally.

Imruil: A Naturalized Version of His First Ode-Book takes a handful of footnotes in an academic crib to the Mu'Allaqat or "Seven Suspended Odes" of pre-Islamic Arabia, and uses them as "a metaphor-cluster" in the making of an original sequence. A comparison of these verses and the texts of the scholar R.S. Rattray, from whence they are derived, would make a useful exercise for students of literary mechanics. More importantly, this Borgesian game provides Howell with a mask in the shape of a well-fitting *persona* in front of his own feelings, the opacities of

Inside the Castle are refined, and a number of individual poems reach a high level of lyrical excellence:

> Inhaling the wind out of the East
> One can tell it has satisfied
> The camphor leaves. "Bring
> Me a gift with nothing in your hands..."

Later work in magazines and pamphlets has shown the influence of John Ashbery.

—Robert Nye

HOWES, Barbara. American. Born in New York City, 1 May 1914. Educated at Beaver Country Day School, Boston; Bennington College, Vermont, B.A. 1937. Married William Jay Smith, *q.v.*, in 1947 (divorced, 1965); two sons. Editor, *Chimera* magazine, New York, 1943-47. Lived in Florence for four years, and in Oxford, France, and Haiti. Recipient: Bess Hokin Prize, 1949, and Eunice Tietjens Prize, 1959 (*Poetry*, Chicago); Guggenheim Fellowship, 1955; Brandeis University Creative Arts Award, 1958; American Academy award, 1971; New England Poetry Club Golden Rose, 1973; Christopher Award, 1974; Bennington Award, 1980. Agent: John Schaffner Associates, 114 East 29th Street, Suite 402, New York, New York 10016. Address: Brook House, North Pownal, Vermont 05260, U.S.A.

PUBLICATIONS

Verse

The Undersea Farmer. Pawlet, Vermont, Banyan Press, 1948.
In the Cold Country. New York, Bonacio and Saul-Grove Press, 1954.
Light and Dark. Middletown, Connecticut, Wesleyan University Press, 1959.
Looking Up at Leaves. New York, Knopf, 1966.
The Blue Garden. Middletown, Connecticut, Wesleyan University Press, 1972.
A Private Signal: Poems New and Selected. Middletown, Connecticut, Wesleyan University Press, 1977.
Moving. Cold Spring Harbor, New York, Elysian Press, 1983.

Christmas Card Poems: *Lachrymae Christi and In the Cold Country,* with William Jay Smith, 1948; *Poems: The Homecoming and The Piazza,* with Smith, 1949; *Two French Poems: The Roses of Saadi and Five Minute Watercolor,* with Smith, 1950; *The Triumph Of Love,* 1953; *Turtle,* 1955; *Early Supper,* 1956; *Lignum Vitae,* 1958; *The Snow Hole,* 1960; *Two Poems: Landscape, Deer Season; Dream of a Good Day,* 1962; *Looking Up at Leaves,* 1963; *Gulls,* 1964; *Leaning into Light,* 1965; *Wild Geese Flying,* 1966; *Elm-Burning,* 1967; *Otis,* 1968; *Talking to Animals,* 1969; *Returning to Store Bay,* 1970; *Evening: Crown Point,* 1971; *Reginae Coeli,* 1972; *Entrance, Casuarinas,* with Gregory Jay Smith, 1973; *Entrance: GJS; Casuarinas: BH,* 1974; *A Parable,* 1975; *Man with Violin,* 1976; *A Point of View,* 1977; *"The Persistence of Memory,"* 1978; *Wonders,* 1979; *Sitting Around Traveling,* 1980; *The Field of the Cloth of Gold—for John Len-*

non, 1981; *Being Me,* 1982; *Among Shells,* 1983—all privately printed. Other Occasional Poems: *To W. H. Auden on His Fiftieth Birthday,* 1957; *An Epithalamium: For Petie and Frank Palmer,* 1964; *Hubert Walking: A Profile; For Mother: A Log: On Her Eightieth Birthday,* 1968; *A Liking for People and Animals,* 1968; *Millefleurs: For the Presentation of a Tapestry,* 1969; *For Helen and Bob Allen,* 1970; *Gold Beyond Gold,* 1970; *The Sixth Color of the Afternoon,* 1974—all privately printed.

Short Stories

The Road Commissioner and Other Stories. N.p., Stinehour Press, 1983.

Other

Editor, *23 Modern Stories.* New York, Knopf, 1963.
Editor, *From the Green Antilles: Writings of the Caribbean.* New York, Macmillan, 1966; London, Souvenir Press, 1967.
Editor, with Gregory Jay Smith, *The Sea-Green Horse: A Collection of Short Stories* (juvenile). New York, Macmillan, 1970.
Editor, *The Eye of the Heart: Short Stories from Latin America.* Indianapolis, Bobbs Merrill, 1973.

*

Manuscript Collection: Yale University Library, New Haven, Connecticut.

Critical Studies: *Selected Criticism* by Louise Bogan, New York, Noonday Press, 1955; *Modern American Poetry* edited by Louis Untermeyer, New York, Harcourt Brace, 1962; *Poets on Poetry* edited by Howard Nemerov, New York, Basic Books, 1966; interview, in *Bennington Review* (Vermont), December 1980; "A Public Hearing for *A Private Signal*" by Dana Gioia, in *Cumberland Poetry Review* (Nashville), Spring 1982.

Barbara Howes comments:

(1970) [I am] a poet, a woman, a wife, a mother: all these things go to make up one's outline.

I am interested in form, and also in what I call "creative form," the working out of a unique form for that one poem. Also interested in the possibilities of free verse. Basically, in what will happen to me and my work next.

I am not very good at discussing my own work. In the essay in *Poets on Poetry* (edited by Howard Nemerov, New York, Basic Books, 1966), I probably stated things as well as I could. As I suggested above, one never knows what one will do next, or, as W.H. Auden said much more eloquently, one never knows if one will write another poem till one has done it. I have been especially influenced perhaps by Emily Dickinson, Yeats, Frost, Hopkins; really, in some way, by about everyone I read. I am much interested in trying to adapt Old French and other forms to modern or contemporary subjects and emotions. Am also interested in the fascinations and complexities of translation.

Basically, I am trying to deal with my experience through my writing; this is how to a degree one can order what one sees and what happens.

(1974) I guess I'll stand by what I said before. All one can do is do the best you can, and keep at it; all the dress-ups of worrying about reviews and getting to know the "right" people are disaster for the serious poet. You just have to keep on at dealing with your experience, whatever it is.

As it turns out, I seem to write about things I see, my children, my friends, my house, my attachments, our animals, the view from any window, in no special order or arrangement. *Place* (physical, not social), which so affects one, comes into it. If you can be attached to people, to a place or places, to ideas, to trees, you will be less likely to fall into the trap of the snarling little ego, which so ranges abroad. Too many writers give in to violence and spite. It is more interesting, though, to be alive, to find what stimulates the imagination, to meet what is beyond one's powers: then a poem may be hatching.

*   *   *

Barbara Howes's *Light and Dark, Looking Up at Leaves*, and *The Blue Garden* represent a gradual smoothing out and cooling off. In the first, we find that she is an explorer of the abyss, the inner self, and the forbidden. In "City Afternoon," for example, after sensing the vibrations of an unseen subway, an escalator, a disposal unit, and the cooped-up people in a large apartment building, she concludes by hearing, in a lull, the Iron Maiden closing on its spikes. Or again, in "The Undersea Farmer," the poem comes to its end by taking us back up out of the water and toward the land, as Arnold's Forsaken Merman's wife did, but still urges that we keep hold of our "subaqueous lifeline," as Margaret did not. And, in "The Nuns Assist at Childbirth," she wonders what a nun can make of this "Rude life" pouring "From the volcano," "Tragic, regenerate, wild."

She is especially good with women, treating them in terms of genuine passion and sexuality. "Danae," for example, compassionately and frankly sees bed as their destiny, whether it supports agony or joy. And she does not avoid the personal, as in "Indian Summer," where she ponders the man asleep in her arms. Nor is she afraid of love, as in "The Balcony," which portrays a true interchange between human beings. And "The New Leda" is one of her best. Leda awaits the god's arrival; a nun awaits Christ: what will be their various destinies—lust, new life, or emptiness? The poem ends with a powerful appeal to the speaker's "Sister, wastrels," to give over "sacrifice and harm / And deprivation."

The next two books, however, reveal a somewhat more complacent pattern. Each is divided similarly into two parts, entitled variously "A Short Way by Air" and "Vermont Poems," and "Away" and "At Home," which seems generally to refer to her habit of dividing her time between the West Indies and New England. Thus the one section contains poems of warmth and lushness, while the other embodies a more wintry climate, with human relations being treated in both.

Thus, for example, the first section of *Leaves* deals with seascapes, seabirds, fish, swimming, and boating, but it also has a remarkable poem called "Flight," in which a Russian spaceman, a Goya picture, a boy murdered on a subway, and the speaker's reflections on "the outer space of the mind" revealed by such brutality, are effectively made into symbols of one another. In "My Dear, Listen:," she says: "An artist should keep / The pathway open / To his inward life...." The intensity of cold is felt in the second section, especially in "The Snow Hole," which tells of a trip to a cleft in the mountains in which can be seen never-melting snow, and which concludes: "Chilled through / By now, we touch the world." And in the title poem, as well as in "A Few Days Ago," the speaker experiences an almost mythic identification with trees.

And yet the overall impression left by this book is more placid and attenuated than that of *Light*. Howes is still very fine, bright, and resourceful, but less turbulent and anguished. She is rather the keen observer and compassionate commentator than the involved participant, and she has settled on a calm concision of style which tends to flatten the emotional power of her insights—

even in as painful a poem as "Flight," which concludes: "Realizing of him / That nothing is the same as one young man, one son, / One good bet, gone." This is well said, and there is a poignant urgency in the last three repetitive phrases and final verb, but it is still a bit too level in tone.

> From that old cow in the field
>   A calf was born;
> He struggles now to rise—
>   No, he cannot
> Yet, on his tapestry legs....

A Private Signal contains selections from these three volumes, plus an additional dozen "New Poems." It is unsafe to spot a trend on the basis of so small a sample, but there are signs here of a renewed tightness of language and intensity of mood. Although these poems are mostly concerned with clear objects existing in the real world—a pool seen from a second-story window, Rome's Pietà, a mirror, her son's house—they often are presented gnomically and end cryptically, as if touched by the hand of a latter-day Emily Dickinson. The one about the pool, for example, is entitled "A Parable," and begins with the speaker looking down and feeling drawn to it. Then she says: "Kindling of bone—/ words reveal us—our backbone./ They are our structure...." And the poem concludes by defining "parable" as "wandering," "a theory / of blueness," "It is the pool."

Barbara Howes wrote, in *Light and Dark*, that "the wild cannot rest with the tame," and "the strange / Wild frantic clear-eyed ones are gone" ("Lament"), and if her recent work is any sign, she may be right. Nevertheless, if she is less wild and frantic, she may be becoming more strange and clear-eyed. It is not for us to say which is the better bargain.

—Norman Friedman

———————

HOYEM, Andrew. American. Born in Sioux Falls, South Dakota, 1 December 1935. Educated at Pomona College, Claremont, California, B.A. 1957. Served in the United States Navy, 1957-60: Lieutenant. Married 1) Sally Cameron Heimann in 1961 (divorced, 1964); 2) Judith B. Laws in 1971. Partner, with Dave Haselwood, Auerhahn Press, San Francisco, 1961-64; Owner, Andrew Hoyem, printer, San Francisco, 1965-66; Partner, Grabhorn-Hoyem, publishers, San Francisco, 1966-73. Since 1973, Owner, Andrew Hoyem, printer, and since 1975, Arion Press. Address: 566 Commercial Street, San Francisco, California 94111, U.S.A.

PUBLICATIONS

Verse

The Wake. San Francisco, Auerhahn Press, 1963.
Lafayette Park Place. San Francisco, Auerhahn Press, 1964.
The Music Room. San Francisco, Dave Haselwood, 1965.
Stranger. San Francisco, San Francisco Arts Festival, 1965.
Happy Birthday. San Francisco, Andrew Hoyem, 1965.
Chimeras: Transformations of "Les Chimères" by Gérard de Nerval. San Francisco, Dave Haselwood, 1966.
A Romance. San Francisco, Andrew Hoyem, 1966.

The Pearl, with John Crawford, translation of the Middle Eng-
   lish poem.   San Francisco, Grabhorn Hoyem, 1967.
Vengeance.   San Francisco, Grabhorn Hoyem, 1967.
Articles: Poems 1960-1967.   London, Cape Goliard Press, and
   New York, Grossman, 1969.
Try.   San Francisco, Grabhorn Hoyem, 1971.
Aim.   San Francisco, Grabhorn Hoyem, 1972.
Still Life.   New York, Valenti Angelo, 1973.
Petit Mal.   San Francisco, Grabhorn Hoyem, 1973.
*Picture/Poems: An Illustrated Catalogue of Drawings and
   Related Writings 1961-1974*.   San Francisco, Arion Press,
   1975.
The First Poet Travels to the Moon.   San Francisco, Arion
   Press, 1975.

                              *

Critical Studies: review by Gilbert Sorrentino, in *Kulchur 12*
(New York), Winter 1963, and Robert B. Shaw, in *Poetry* (Chicago), March 1972.

                   *   *   *

Andrew Hoyem is a poet so highly eclectic and derivative in
style that one is forced to suspect that he has, as yet, failed to
discover his own inner voice—or that, if he has, he does not yet
know how to speak in it. When he is direct, as in the prose-poem
"The Korean Conflict," he is simply ineffective; but his more
recondite work, while it demonstrates an excellent grasp of its
sources, does not have enough individual quality to make it
memorable. "Birds. Moss. Pebbles. Frog./ Fade./ The five finger
fern" is good enough for a diary entry, but as pastiche of Japanese or Imagist verse it only reminds us of failures. "Spook
Sheep," his "transformation" of de Nerval's most famous
sonnet, only manages to be either literal or to change the French
into an English de-fused of poetry. He can glide easily enough
from satirical observation—"This bachelor deluding himself/
whose children play in the streets"—to an archaic "Old High
Poesy" manner for which it is hard to see the point:

      Fain should I barren Beauty's breast
                  such shameless to secrete
      faint praise, fame, and fortunes of war,
                  at issue from her teat.

It is all very well to point to irony, Pound, the Provençal; but this
lacks attack, appears debilitated by any strong sense of direction
besides simply wanting to write poetry. One can at present,
regretfully, point only to an evident intelligence and a certain
charm and delicacy as Hoyem's positive virtues. But if a poet
lacks energy and a personal rhythm then he needs very special
qualities indeed to spark him into life; the pleasant and pacific
impression that Hoyem's poetry gives, when read as a whole, is
not enough.

                                    —Martin Seymour-Smith

                   _____

HUFANA, Alejandrino G.   Filipino.   Born in San Fernando,
La Union, Philippines, 22 October 1926. Educated at the Uni-
versity of the Philippines, Quezon City, A.B. in English 1952,
M.A. in comparative literature 1961; University of California,
Berkeley (Rockfeller Fellowship, 1961-62), 1957-58, 1961-62;

Columbia University, New York (John D. Rockefeller III Fund
Fellowship, 1968-70), M.S. in library science 1969. Served with
the North Luzon guerrillas, 1944. Married Julita Quiming in
1957; four daughters. Secretary and English teacher, Cebu Chi-
nese High School, 1952-54. Research Assistant in Social Science,
1954-56, since 1956, Member of the Department, and since 1975,
Professor of English and Comparative Literature, and Associate
Director, 1979-82, and Director, 1982-85, Creative Writing Center, University of the Philippines. Since 1970, Director of the
Library, since 1971, Editor, *Pamana* magazine, and since 1979,
Lahi magazine, Cultural Center of the Philippines, Manila.
Co-Founding Editor, *Signatures* magazine, 1955, *Comment*
magazine, 1956-67, *Heritage* magazine, 1967-68, and *University
College Journal*, later *General Education Journal*, 1961-72; Edi-
tor, *Panorama* magazine, 1959-61. Managing Editor, University
of the Philippines Press, 1965-66. Artist: exhibitions in Elmira,
New York, 1957, and Manila, to 1978. Recipient: Republic
Cultural Heritage Award, 1965. Address: 22 Casanova Street, B.
Culiat, Tandang Sora Avenue, Quezon City, Philippines.

PUBLICATIONS

Verse

13 Kalisud.   Quezon City, Collegian New Review, 1955.
Sickle Season: Poems of a First Decade 1948-1958.   Quezon
   City, Kuwan, 1959.
Poro Point: An Anthology of Lives: Poems 1955-1960.   Quezon
   City, University of the Philippines, 1961.
The Wife of Lot and Other New Poems.   Quezon City, Diliman
   Review, 1971.
Sieg Heil: An Epic on the Third Reich.   Quezon City, Tala,
   1975.
Imelda Romualdez Marcos: A Tonal Epic.   Manila, Konsen-
   sus, 1975.
Obligations: Cheers of Conscience.   Quezon City, Diliman
   Review, 1975.

Plays

Man in the Moon (produced La Union, 1956, Manila, 1970;
   revised version, produced Quezon City, 1972).   Published in
   Panorama (Quezon City), December 1960.
Curtain-Raisers: First Five Plays (includes *Gull in the Wind,
   Honeymoon, Ivory Tower, Terra Firma, View from Origin*).
   Quezon City, University of the Philippines Social Science
   Research Council, 1964.
The Unicorn, in *Pamana 1* (Manila), June 1971.
Salidom-ay, in *Pamana 2* (Manila), September 1971.

Other

Mena Pecson Crisologo and Iloko Drama.   Quezon City, Diliman Review, 1963.
Notes on Poetry.   Quezon City, Diliman Review, 1973.

Editor, *Aspects of Philippine Literature*.   Quezon City, Uni-
   versity of the Philippines, 1967.
Editor, *A Philippine Cultural Miscellany, Parts I and II*.   Que-
   zon City, University of the Philippines, 1968-70.
Editor, with others, *Introduction to Literature*.   Quezon City,
   Alemar Phoenix, 1974.
Editor, *Philippine Writings: Short Stories, Essays, Poetry*.
   Manila, Regal, 1977.

*

Manuscript Collections: University of the Philippines Library, Quezon City; University of Syracuse Library, New York; University of California Library, Berkeley; Cultural Center of the Philippines Library, Manila.

Critical Studies: "The Poetry So Far of A.G. Hufana" by Jean Edwardson, in *Collegian New Review* (Quezon City), January 1954; "Mutineer, Sight Ascending" by Leonard Casper, in *The Wayward Horizon: Essays on Modern Philippine Literature*, Manila, Community Publishers, 1961; "Poet's Portrait Gallery" by Andres Cristobal Cruz, in *Sunday Times* (Manila), 26 November 1961; "Dive in a Hypnosis: The Poetry of Alejandrino G. Hufana" by Albert Casuga, in *Philippine Writing 2* (Manila), 1963; *New Writing from the Philippines: A Critique and Anthology* by Leonard Casper, Syracuse, New York, Syracuse University Press, 1966; "Hufana: Rebellious Poet" by Florentino S. Dauz, in *Graphic* (Manila), 8 September 1966; "A Poet's Romance with Art" by Jolico Cuadra, in *Chronicle Magazine* (Manila), 1 July 1967; *Poetry in the Plays of A.G. Hufana* by Bernardita Castillo, University of Bohol, unpublished thesis, 1973.

Alejandrino G. Hufana comments:

The pre-publication discipline of any poet should be like the pre-performance training of the athlete or prize-fighter. All flaws considered in public must as such turn the performer back to this grind. Only birds, or such creatures, are born to the grace of what they do, which also happens to excuse their plunder.

*   *   *

Alejandrino G. Hufana is a fascinating and highly original poet. Some of his plans sound somewhat formidably grandiose, but such schemes often result in curtailed versions of the original intention—which must, almost certainly, in the case of mere sections of a work extending to more than 1,000 typescript pages each, be a good thing. Hufana studied in America, and has absorbed much from American poetry—in particular from that neglected master of epigram, Edwin Arlington Robinson. Deeply rooted in the complex culture of his native country, Hufana employs an ambitiously idiosyncratic diction that some non-Filipino readers have taken as evincing a lack of mastery of the English language—

> Unclothing so the Zambul Bali Dag
> May for her dead infanta deep be soft
> The black she-parent grieving on the crag
> A lullaby invokes: "Arrow aloft
> Time for your sleep, piece-of-my-thigh,
> The fletcher is not false, time for your dream,
> Meat will be yours...."

—but this is a serious error. One of Hufana's main aims is to discover and to express what is authentically Filipino, and this, given so complicated and foreign-influenced a culture (there are Filipinos writing in the national language, which is an artifact, and Spanish, as well as in English) is bound to yield results that have an odd appearance to the outside world. Hufana has been called the most successful "anthropological" poet writing in the English language, and the lines quoted above may confidently be employed as evidence in support of such a view. It is high time that both a British and an American publisher put out a compre-

hensive selection of his poetry.

—Martin Seymour-Smith

———————

HUFF, Robert. American. Born in Evanston, Illinois, 3 April 1924. Educated at Wayne State University, Detroit, A.B. in English 1949, A.M. in humanities 1952. Served as an aerial gunner and bombardier in the Eighth Air Force, 1943-46. Married Sally Ann Sener in 1959 (divorced, 1973); two daughters and one son. Instructor, Wayne State University, 1950-52, 1957-58, University of Oregon, Eugene, 1952-53, Fresno State College, California, 1953-55, and Oregon State University, Corvallis, 1955-57, 1958-60; Poet-in-Residence and Assistant Professor, University of Delaware, Newark, 1960-64. Since 1964, Member of the Department, and currently Professor of English, Western Washington State College, Bellingham. Writer-in-Residence, University of Arkansas, Fayetteville, 1967. Since 1968, Poetry Editor, *Concerning Poetry*, Bellingham. Recipient: Indiana University School of Letters Fellowship, 1957; Bread Loaf Writers' Conference scholarship, 1961; MacDowell Colony fellowship, 1963; Virginia Commonwealth University prize, 1977. Address: 2820 Eldridge Street, Bellingham, Washington 98225, U.S.A.

PUBLICATIONS

Verse

Colonel Johnson's Ride and Other Poems.   Detroit, Wayne State University Press, 1959.
Poems.   Portland, Oregon, Portland Art Museum, 1959.
The Course: One, Two, Three, Now!   Detroit, Wayne State University Press, 1966.
The Ventriloquists.   Chicago, Swallow Press, 1975.
The Ventriloquist: New and Selected Poems.   Charlottesville, University Press of Virginia, 1977.

Recordings: *The Sound of Pacific Northwest Poetry* with others, Washington State Poetry Foundation, 1968; *Robert Huff Reading at the Poetry Center of New York*, McGraw Hill, 1970.

Other

Activism in the Secondary Schools: Analysis and Recommendations, with Kenneth Erickson and George Benson.   Eugene, University of Oregon Bureau of Educational Research, 1969.

*

Manuscript Collections: University of Kentucky, Lexington; Wayne State University, Detroit; Carnegie Library, Syracuse University, New York.

Critical Studies: reviews by John Haislip, in *Northwest Review* (Eugene, Oregon), Summer 1967, and William Heyen, in *Poetry* (Chicago), February, 1968.

*   *   *

Robert Huff is a poet who generally writes in traditional forms; his mentors, as he himself makes clear in *The Course*, are

Roethke, Frost and Yeats. His poetry in *The Course* is an autobiographical unfolding of his life from childhood through recent years; topics include finding his vocation as a poet, memories of relatives, enduring the personal and historical shocks life has to deal him. The book might be regarded, like Delmore Schwartz's great short story ("In Dreams Begin Responsibilities") from which it gets its subtitle ("One, Two, Three, Now!"), as a sort of autobiographical fiction in which the author, like the photographer of that story, tries to get a good fix, the proper artistic slant, on the fluid stuff of life. Like all of us, Huff is both involved and a spectator, human being and artist. Like the confessional poets, he is working close to the nerve ends, as in "Fixed":

> These days I'm really sure I'm tranquilized
> When any little signal says I'm ready,
> Like this sweet thing teasing my inner ear
> Into a dream of hearing rubber whisper
>
> Along the humped blacktop back to that boy
> Spoiled sick to death between one smart fool's ad
> And this mean pen at a dead end hanging tight
> Until the good pill works its trick of bells.

This is powerful poetry, as are other poems in *The Course*, including the title poem, "If It's an Owl," "How Not to Make a Model in a Bottle in a Bar in Ithaca," and especially "Getting Drunk with Daughter"; the last is surely one of the finest poems ever written by an American poet, as is "Rainbow" in Huff's earlier collection, *Colonel Johnson's Ride*. Huff's language is dense and heavily allusive; occasionally, as in "Previews," the allusions seem to come too fast and to be too personal to really work for the reader. On the whole, this isn't true.

Many of Huff's poems deal with loss, and the things, like drink and death, that accelerate our sense of loss. There is, however, a moving affirmation underlying this work, a suggestion of the spiritual gains that move in to fill the gaps. This is evident in "Rainbow" ("And I am glad / That I have wounded her, winged her heart, / And that she goes beyond my fathering"), and again in "Although I Remember the Sound":

> Although I remember the sound
> The young snag made when I felled it,
> It was not noise or music mattered then.
> Briefly, the tree was silent on the ground.
>
> Of what it was that mattered I recall
> Simply, among the chips and dust
> And keener near the center of the cut,
> The sweet, new smell which rose after the fall.

—Duane Ackerson

HUGHES, Glyn. British. Born in Middlewic[...] May 1935. Educated at Altrincham Grammar S[...] 1946-52; Regional College of Art, Mancheste[...] 59, National Diploma in Design, 1956, Art T[...] 1959. Married 1) Wendy Slater in 1959 (mar[...] son; 2) Roya Liakopoulos in 1974. Art [...] schools in Lancashire and Yorkshire, [...] Prison, Manchester, 1969-71; Extra-[...]

University of Manchester, 1971-73. Member of the Manchester Institute of Contemporary Arts Committee, 1966-69; Arts Council Fellow, Lincoln, 1979-81, and Southern Arts Fellow, Hampshire, 1982-84. Recipient: Welsh Arts Council Prize, 1969; Arts Council Bursary, 1970, 1973; *Guardian* Fiction Prize, 1982; David Higham Prize, for novel, 1982. Agent: Maggie Noach, 21 Redan Street, London W14 0AB. Address: 28 Lower Millbank, Sowerby Bridge, West Yorkshire HX6 3ED, England.

PUBLICATIONS

Verse

The Stanedge Bull and Other Poems.   Manchester, Manchester Institute of Contemporary Arts, 1966.
Almost-Love Poems.   Oxford, Sycamore Press, 1968.
Love on the Moor: Poems 1965-1968.   Manchester, Phoenix Pamphlet Poets Press, 1968.
Neighbours: Poems 1965-1969.   London, Macmillan, and Chester Springs, Pennsylvania, Dufour, 1970.
Presence.   London, Poem-of-the-Month Club, 1971.
Towards the Sun: Poems/ Photographs.   Manchester, Phoenix Pamphlet Poets Press, 1971.
Rest the Poor Struggler: Poems 1969-71.   London, Macmillan, 1972.
The Breast.   Richmond, Surrey, Keepsake Press, 1973.
Alibis and Convictions.   Sunderland, Ceolfrith, 1978.
Best of Neighbours: New and Selected Poems.   Sunderland, Ceolfrith, 1979.

Plays

Mary Hepton's Heaven (produced Oldham, 1984).

Radio Plays: *The Yorkshirewomen*, 1978; *Dreamers*, 1979.

Novels

Where I Used to Play on the Green.   London, Gollancz, 1982.
The Hawthorn Goddess.   London, Chatto and Windus, 1984.

Other

Millstone Grit (on Yorkshire and Lancash[...] lancz, 1975.
*Fair Prospects: Journeys in G[...]

Editor, *Selected [...]
Ceolfrith [...]

[text obscured by torn page corner]
[...] ed in
[...] rain he
[...] nse of values
[...] self. It is such an
[...] life are shaped and
[...] poetic ecology) which
[...] ve on the Moor and in his
Hughes said in his introduc-
ealism about how people ought

[vertical text fragments on torn corner:]
the United States;
her, and reader for
daughter and on[...]
se gardener, night
948-50. Mar[...]
politan[...]
[...]roke[...]
Arts;

to live is implicit in every poem." This has been maintained in his later collections.

The terrain of Glyn Hughes's poems is one of those harsh, unrelenting inbred bits of country-side that still endure in 20th-century England, as in "Rock Bottom":

> the last place of rickets and bow legs
> aching from their grip of iced roads.
> Where the stranger's stared-at smile is unreturned,
> the stranger's house is shunned.

Even the joys of Spring sunshine are hard won ("Toward the Sun"):

> The fractured land bursts into grass.
> A farmer, woken by the sun and us,
> yaps like a terrier at the field's edge
> to defend his growth. We laugh,
> point, joke. Old walls glow
> like unripe apples as we cross his field
> to see the coltsfoot flowers.

Hughes's approach is as equally uncompromising and well suited to his subject matter. Unsentimental, it is not without compassion, as illustrated in "Love on the Moor" where the farmer's wife, stirred for a moment by the smile of a visiting salesman—"What might/have been that trickle of light/to the cinders of her heart/stopped at a scowling grate"—calls her man who shambles out "From his kitchen doze/fly open, feet in oven—/not that he'd ever lied/he would be different." Hughes's ability to touch on just the right nuance of feeling, in situations where the slightness of its manifestation belies its depth, is quite remarkable.

The life described is harsh; but hashness is not indulged for the sake of it, rather it is allied to the quality of life portrayed ("Neighours"):

> We communicate
> in other ways: we poke the grate,
> and whether we rise early or rise late
> is boasted from the roof. Each broods alone
> with a false air of no-one at home.

It is life withdrawn, pulled into itself—like a snail into its shell—in order to render it bearable. It is Glyn Hughes's achievement not only to have described his terrain with economy and accuracy, but to have expressed the spirit of it with a sensitivity which is masterly.

—John Cotton

1957-59: taught at the University of Massachusetts, Amherst. Founding Editor, with Daniel Weissbort, *Modern Poetry in Translation* magazine, London, 1964-71. Recipient: New York Poetry Center First Publication Award, 1957; Guinness Award, 1958; Guggenheim Fellowship, 1959; Maugham Award, 1960; Hawthornden prize, 1961; City of Florence International Poetry prize, 1969; Etna-Taormina prize, 1973; Queen's Gold Medal for Poetry, 1974; *Signal* Poetry Award, 1979, 1982; Royal Society of Literature Heinemann Award, 1980. O.B.E. (Officer, Order of the British Empire), 1977. Poet Laureate, 1984. Lives in North Tawton, Devon. Address: c/o Faber and Faber Ltd., 3 Queen Square, London WC1N 3AU, England.

PUBLICATIONS

Verse

The Hawk in the Rain. London, Faber, and New York, Harper, 1957.
Pike. Northampton, Massachusetts, Gehenna Press, 1959.
Lupercal. London, Faber, and New York, Harper, 1960.
Selected Poems, with Thom Gunn. London, Faber, 1962.
The Burning of the Brothel. London, Turret, 1966.
Recklings. London, Turret, 1967.
Scapegoats and Rabies: A Poem in Five Parts. London, Poet and Printer, 1967.
Animal Poems. Crediton, Devon, Gilbertson, 1967.
Gravestones (6 broadsides), linocuts by Gavin Robbins. Exeter, Devon, Exeter College of Art, 1967; as *Poems*, 1 vol., 1968.
I Said Goodbye to Earth. London, Turret, 1969.
A Crow Hymn. Frensham, Surrey, Sceptre Press, 1970.
The Martyrdom of Bishop Farrar. Crediton, Devon, Gilbertson, 1970.
A Few Crows. Exeter, Devon, Rougemont Press, 1970.
Four Crow Poems. Privately printed, 1970.
Crow: From the Life and Songs of the Crow. London, Faber, 1970; New York, Harper, 1971; revised edition, Faber, 1972.
Fighting for Jerusalem. Ashington, Northumberland, Mid-NAG, 1970.
Amulet. Privately printed, 1970.
Corgi Modern Poets in Focus 1, with others, edited by Dannie Abse. London, Corgi, 1971.
Crow Wakes. Woodford Green, Essex, Poet and Printer, 1971.
Poems, with Ruth Fainlight and Alan Sillitoe. London, Rainbow Press, 1971.
In the Little Girl's Angel Gaze. London, Steam Press, 1972.
Selected Poems 1957-1967. London, Faber, 1972; New York, Harper, 1973.
Prometheus on HIs Crag: 21 Poems. London, Rainbow Press, 1973
The Interrogator: A Titled Vulturess. London, Scolar Press, 1975.
Cave Birds. London, Scolar Press, 1975; revised edition, as *Cave Birds: An Alchemical Cave Drama*, London, Faber, 1978; New York, Viking Press, 1979.
The New World, music by Gordon Crosse. London, Oxford University Press, 1975.
Eclipse. Knotting, Bedfordshire, Sceptre Press, 1976.
Gaudete. London, Faber, and New York, Harper, 1977.
Chiasmadon. Baltimore, Seluzicki, 1977.
Sunstruck. Knotting, Bedfordshire, Sceptre Press, 1977.
Solstice. Knotting, Bedfordshire, Sceptre Press, 1978.
London, Rainbow Press, 1978.

_____

*
). British. Born in
Educated at Mex-
College, Cam-
ogy 1954,
ied 1)

Moortown Elegies. London, Rainbow Press, 1978.

Adam and the Sacred Nine. London, Rainbow Press, 1979.

Remains of Elmet: A Pennine Sequence, photographs by Fay Godwin. London, Rainbow Press, 1979; revised edition, London, Faber, and New York, Harper, 1979.

Night-Arrival of Sea-Trout, The Iron Wolf, Puma, Brooktrout, Pan, Woodpecker, Wolverine, Eagle, Mosquito, Tapir's Saga (broadsides). North Tawton, Devon, Morrigu Press, 1979-80.

Four Tales Told by an Idiot. Knotting, Bedfordshire, Sceptre Press, 1979.

In the Black Chapel (poster). London, Victoria and Albert Museum, 1979.

Moortown. London, Faber, 1979; New York, Harper, 1980.

Sky-Furnace, painting by Roger Vick. North Tawton, Devon, Caricia Fine Arts, 1981.

Selected Poems 1957-1981. London, Faber, 1982; as *New Selected Poems*, New York, Harper, 1982.

River, photographs by Peter Keen. London, Faber, 1983; New York, Harper, 1984.

Recordings: *Poets Reading 5*, Jupiter, 1962; *The Poet Speaks 5*, Argo, 1965; *Crow*, Claddagh, 1973; *The Poetry and Voice of Ted Hughes*, Caedmon, 1977; *Selections from Crow and Wodwo*, Caedmon, 1979.

Verse (for children)

Meet My Folks! London, Faber, 1961; Indianapolis, Bobbs Merrill, 1973.

The Earth-Owl and Other Moon-People. London, Faber, 1963.

Nessie the Mannerless Monster. London, Faber, 1964; as *Nessie the Monster*, Indianapolis, Bobbs Merrill, 1974.

Five Autumn Songs for Children's Voices. Crediton, Devon, Gilbertson, 1969.

Autumn Song. Kettering, Northamptonshire, Steane, 1971.

Spring, Summer, Autumn, Winter. London, Rainbow Press, 1974; revised edition, as *Season Songs*, New York, Viking Press, 1975; London, Faber, 1976.

Earth-Moon, illustrated by the author. London, Rainbow Press, 1976.

Moon-Whales and Other Moon Poems. New York, Viking Press, 1976.

Moon-Bells and Other Poems. London, Chatto and Windus, 1978.

Under the North Star. London, Faber, and New York, Viking Press, 1981.

What Is the Truth? A Farmyard Fable. London, Faber, 1984.

Plays

The House of Aries (broadcast, 1960). Published in *Audience* (Cambridge, Massachusetts), Spring 1961.

The Calm (produced Boston, 1961).

The Wound (broadcast, 1962). Included in *Wodwo*, 1967; revised version (produced London, 1972).

Epithalamium (produced London, 1963).

The House of Donkeys (broadcast, 1965). Published in *Living Language*, Autumn 1974.

Seneca's Oedipus (produced London, 1968; Los Angeles, 1973; New York, 1977). London, Faber, 1969; New York, Doubleday, 1972.

Orghast (produced Persepolis, 1971). Excerpt published in *Performance* (New York), December 1971.

Eat Crow. London, Rainbow Press, 1971.

The Story of Vasco, music by Gordon Crosse, adaptation of a play by Georges Schehadé (produced London, 1974). London, Oxford University Press, 1974.

Radio Plays: *The House of Aries*, 1960; *A Houseful of Women*, 1961; *The Wound*, 1962; *Difficulties of a Bridegroom*, 1963; *Dogs*, 1964; *The House of Donkeys*, 1965.

Plays (for children)

The Coming of the Kings (broadcast, 1964; produced London, 1972). Included in *The Coming of the Kings and Other Plays*, 1970.

The Tiger's Bones (broadcast, 1965). Included in *The Coming of the Kings and Other Plays*, 1970.

Beauty and the Beast (broadcast, 1965; produced London, 1971). Included in *The Coming of the Kings and Other Plays*, 1970.

The Price of a Bride (broadcast, 1966). Excerpt published in *Here, Now and Beyond*, edited by Nancy Coniston Martin, London, Oxford University Press, 1968.

The Demon of Adachigahara, music by Gordon Crosse (cantata; produced Shrewsbury, 1968). London, Oxford University Press, 1969.

Sean, The Fool, The Devil and the Cats (broadcast, 1968; produced London, 1971). Included in *The Coming of the Kings and Other Plays*, 1970.

The Coming of the Kings and Other Plays (includes *The Tiger's Bones; Beauty and the Beast; Sean, The Fool, The Devil and The Cats*). London, Faber, 1970; augmented edition, as *The Tiger's Bones and Other Plays for Children* (includes *Orpheus*), New York, Viking Press, 1974.

Orpheus (broadcast, 1971). Chicago, Dramatic Publishing Company, 1973.

The Pig Organ; or, Pork with Perfect Pitch, music by Richard Blackford (produced London, 1980).

Radio Plays: *The Coming of the Kings*, 1964; *The Tiger's Bones*, 1965; *Beauty and the Beast*, 1965; *The Price of a Bride*, 1966; *The Head of Gold*, 1967; *Sean, The Fool, The Devil, and the Cats*, 1968; *Orpheus*, 1971.

Short Story

The Threshold. London, Steam Press, 1979.

Other

How the Whale Became (for children). London, Faber, 1963; New York, Atheneum, 1964.

Wodwo (miscellany). London, Faber, and New York, Harper, 1967.

Poetry in the Making: An Anthology of Poems and Programmes from "Listening and Writing" (for children). London, Faber, 1967; abridged edition, as *Poetry Is*, New York, Doubleday, 1970.

The Iron Man: A Story in Five Nights (for children). London, Faber, 1968; as *The Iron Giant*, New York, Harper, 1968.

Shakespeare's Poem (essay). London, Lexham Press, 1971.

Henry Williamson: A Tribute. London, Rainbow Press, 1979.

Editor, with Patricia Beer and Vernon Scannell, *New Poems 1962*. London, Hutchinson, 1962.

Editor, *Here Today*. London, Hutchinson, 1963.

Editor, with Thom Gunn, *Five American Poets*. London, Faber, 1963.

Editor, *Selected Poems*, by Keith Douglas. London, Faber,

1964; New York, Chilmark Press, 1965.

Editor, with Olwyn Hughes, *Ariel*, by Sylvia Plath.   London, Faber, 1965; New York, Harper, 1966.

Editor, *A Choice of Emily Dickinson's Verse*.   London, Faber, 1968.

Editor, *With Fairest Flowers While Summer Last: Poems from Shakespeare*.   New York, Doubleday, 1971; as *A Choice of Shakespeare's Verse*, London, Faber, 1971.

Editor, *Crossing the Water*, by Sylvia Plath.   London, Faber, and New York, Harper, 1971.

Editor, *Winter Trees*, by Sylvia Plath.   London, Faber, 1971; New York, Harper, 1972.

Editor, and Translator with János Csokits, *Selected Poems* by János Pilinszky.   Manchester, Carcanet, 1976.

Editor, and Translator with Yehuda Amichai, *Amen*, by Amichai.   New York, Harper, 1977; London, Oxford University Press, 1978.

Editor, *Johnny Panic and the Bible of Dreams, and Other Prose Writings*, by Sylvia Plath.   London, Faber, 1977; augmented edition, Faber, and New York, Harper, 1979.

Editor, *New Poetry 6*.   London, Hutchinson, 1980.

Editor, *The Collected Poems of Sylvia Plath*.   London, Faber, and New York, Harper, 1981.

Editor, with Frances McCullough, *The Journals of Sylvia Plath*.   New York, Dial Press, 1982.

Editor, with Seamus Heaney, *1980 Anthology: Arvon Foundation Poetry Competition*.   Todmorden, Lancashire, Kilnhurst, 1982.

Editor, with Seamus Heaney, *The Rattle Bag: An Anthology*.   London, Faber, 1982.

Editor, *Selected Poems*, by Sylvia Plath.   London, Faber, 1985.

Translator, with Assia Gutmann, *Selected Poems*, by Yehuda Amichai.   London, Cape Goliard Press, 1968; expanded edition, as *Poems*, New York, Harper, 1969; London, Penguin, 1971.

Translator, with Yehuda Amichai, *Time*, by Amichai.   New York, Harper, and London, Oxford University Press, 1979.

*

Bibliography: *Ted Hughes: A Bibliography 1946-1980* by Keith Sagar and Stephen Tabor, London, Mansell, 1983.

Critical Studies: *Ted Hughes*, London, Longman, 1972, and *The Art of Ted Hughes*, London, Cambridge University Press, 1975, revised edition, 1978, both by Keith Sagar, and *The Achievement of Ted Hughes* edited by Sagar, Manchester, Manchester University Press, and Athens, University of Georgia Press, 1983; *Thom Gunn and Ted Hughes* by Alan Bold, Edinburgh, Oliver and Boyd, 1976; *Ted Hughes' Gaudete* by Hugh Probyn, Preston, Lancashire, Harris Press, 1977; *Sylvia Plath and Ted Hughes* by Margaret Dickie Uroff, Urbana, University of Illinois Press, 1979; *Ted Hughes: The Unaccommodated Universe, with Selected Critical Writings by Ted Hughes and Two Interviews* by Ekbert Faas, Santa Barbara, California, Black Sparrow Press, 1980; *Ted Hughes: A Critical Study* by Terry Gifford and Neil Roberts, London, Faber, 1981; *The Poetry of Ted Hughes: A Guide to the Poems* by Stuart Hirschberg, Portmarnock, County Dublin, Wolfhound Press, 1981; *Ted Hughes* by Thomas West, London, Methuen, 1984.

*   *   *

Ted Hughes is a kind of 20th-century Aesop whose fables lack an explicit moral because it is precisely the unreflective sponta-

neity of his creatures, their "bullet and automatic/Purpose," which constitutes their primary lesson for man. Yet his animals are highly ambiguous. As with "The Jaguar," "hurrying enraged/Through prison darkness after the drills of his eyes/On a short fierce fuse," their instinct can be limiting, self-destructive. Dead, as in "View of a Pig," they are "Just so much/A poundage of lard and pork" without dignity or grace. They exist only in the vital and luminous present. Though they may have the nine lives we are denied, may "outwit...our nimblest wits" and hold us "in utter mock" ("Of Cats"), they lack that self-consciousness, that sense of "absence" and otherness which in poems such as "Gog" enable us to ponder our "origins" and, in "Cleopatra to the Asp," our end. Cleopatra, braving "the bright mirror" and "the devil in it," knows both herself and the death which defines her ("Now that I seek myself in a serpent/My smile is fatal"). In "Thrushes" man's exteriorizing of himself through work both excludes him from happiness ("Though he bends to be blent in the prayer," racked by "distracting devils") and guarantees the continuance of the human world:

> With a man it is otherwise. Heroisms on horseback,
> Outstripping his desk-diary at a broad desk,
> Carving at a tiny ivory ornament
> For years: his act worships itself.

The necessity of the diabolic, a Manichaean conviction that the "divine" has to be restored to its origins, humbled in the ecstasy of the brute, pervades Hughes's work. In "Logos" this is presented through a variation of Christian paradox—that God, as both Father and Son, can only conceive Himself through his own fleshly creature. Hughes gives this a sardonic twist, in a tone which is characteristic of his later poetry: "And within seconds the new-born baby is lamenting/That it ever lived—/God is a good fellow, but His mother's against Him."

In "Theology" and "Reveille" the serpent emerges as coeval with God, a parody sibling and demiurge who does the real work of creation by introducing all those negatives out of which "the ashes of the future," of the real world, are forged. These dark antinomies, hatred, fear, pain, greed, lust and death itself, are the terrain on which *Crow* constructs its creation myths. Atrocity, madness, rapine, are the very grounds of being for this grimly comic persona, who surveys a world torn by violence and entropy, where all hierarchies break down into destruction, and survival, sheer naked continuance in the knowledge of guilt and damnation, is the nearest one comes to hope:

> So the survivors stayed.
> And the earth and sky stayed.
> Everything took the blame.
>
> Not a leaf flinched, nobody smiled.

This outraged and defiant theology at times seems like a paganized version of the fire-and-brimstone puritanism Hughes writes of in his earlier poems. But now the apocalypse has already taken place. In the attempted film scenario, *Gaudete*, Hughes begins to salvage something from this wilderness. Drawing on an epigraph from Heraclitus which claims the dark underworld of Hades and the obscene songs and festivals of Dionysos as expressions of the same primeval force, the poem dramatises a cosmic dualism of man and nature, male and female, mind and body, self and other, in terms of a struggle between brothers who are of one flesh. Recreating ancient fertility myths, *Gaudete* has an Anglican clergyman abducted to "the other world" by elemental spirits who leave in his place a surrogate shaped from an oak log. This changeling "proceeds to interpret the job of ministering the

Gospel of love in his own log-like way" by organizing the women of the parish into a sexual coven on whom he is to father the Messiah. But it is at this point that the real significance of Hughes's myth emerges. "While he applies himself to this," the Argument tells us, "he begins to feel a nostalgia for independent, ordinary human life, free of his peculiar destiny," and this forces the spirits to "cancel him," in an elaborate, ritualized sequence which has all Hughes's customary sadistic and compelling vividness. This nostalgia for a lost ordinariness seems to some extent to have been satisfied in his 1979 volume, *Remains of Elmet*, which is a loving return to Hughes's first world, the Yorkshire Pennines of his childhood. Recovered now only on the other side of outrage, the arcadian dream lies at the heart of Hughes's poetry which speaks of a world that "can't care any more" but "Where I let in—/As if for the first time—/The untouched joy."

Hughes's most recent volume, *River*, shows a slackening of power and originality. The temptation held at bay in *Remains of Elmet*—of producing a coffee-table book in which poems take second-place to glossy nature-photography—has here been succumbed to. Hughes seems caught up in pastiche of himself, like the "Famous Poet" of an early poem, desperately trying to repeat "the old heroic bang" for an admiring public. *River* is full of images of exhaustion, depletion, drying up, which are compensated for in the flash and flare of a 'Baroque superabundance" of verbs that are all churning, thrashing, bleeding, bulging; "spasms" itself is used as a verb more than once, but these seem dying rather than orgasmic turbulences. Hughes himself seems to be aware of this, as in "Dee," where he notes that:

> The expenditure of swift purity
> Nevertheless goes on. But so thinly,
> So meanly, and from such stale cellars
> No fish will face it.

He seems even to proclaim his own poetic obituary in "October Salmon"—a far cry from the furious energy of "Pike": "What a death-in-life—/to be his own spectre!" Yet at times he rises to a tragic pathos, as in "Ophelia," with its trout that leaps from the stream only to drop back "Into this peculiar engine/That made it and keeps it going/And that works it to death." We can only hope Hughes is not being worked to death by his own copious talent.

—Stan Smith

HUNT, Sam. New Zealander. Born in New Zealand, 4 July 1946. Recipient: Young Poets award, 1971; Burns fellowship, 1976; New Zealand Literary Fund award, 1979. Agent: Ray Richards, Richards Literary Agency, P.O. Box 31240, Milford, Auckland. Address: c/o Paremata Post Office, New Zealand.

PUBLICATIONS

Verse

Between Islands.   Privately printed, 1964.
A Fat Flat Blues (When Morning Comes).   Wellington, Bottle Press, 1969.
Selected Poems 1965-1969.   Wellington, Wellington Training College, 1970.
A Song about Her.   Wellington, Bottle Press, 1970.
Postcard of a Cabbage Tree.   Wellington, Bottle Press, 1970.

Bracken Country.   Wellington, Glenburvie Press, 1971.
Letter to Jerusalem.   Wellington, Bottle Press, 1971.
Bottle Creek Blues.   Wellington, Bottle Press, 1971.
Bottle Creek.   Wellington, Alister Taylor, 1972.
Beware the Man.   Wellington, Triple P Press, 1972.
Birth on Bottle Creek.   Wellington, Triple P Press, 1972.
South into Winter.   Wellington, Alister Taylor, 1973.
Roadsong Paekakariki.   Wellington, Triple P Press, 1973.
Time to Ride.   Wellington, Alister Taylor, 1975.
Drunkard's Garden.   Wellington, Hampson Hunt, 1978.
Collected Poems 1963-1980.   Auckland, Penguin, 1980.
Running Scared.   Christchurch, Whitcoulls, 1982.

Recordings: *Beware the Man*, with Mammal; *Bottle to Battle to Death*, Jayrem, 1983.

*

Critical Study: *Introducing Sam Hunt* by Peter Smart, Auckland, Longman Paul, 1981.

Sam Hunt comments:
   Lyric tradition.

*   *   *

Setting out in his late teens to make a living from his poetry, Sam Hunt found the role of rebel Romantic a rewarding profession. In his late thirties now, he remains a thoroughgoing professional, a Romantic poet still, but one whose themes and style have only lately begun to keep pace with his years.

He became known first for poetry that celebrated hard drinking and hard loving; for poems reflecting his brief teaching career as "'the poem man,' showing the kids and teachers/games they can easily play with words": poems like "The shallow stream through the city floats," and "School Policy on Stickmen," as well as for some moving family poems ("Purple Balloon," "My Father Scything").

On the printed page many of his poems look flat and prosaic, and his syllabic lines lack the stressed delivery of the spoken voice. In fact of course they are written for performance, which explains why Sam Hunt has for almost 20 years been one of New Zealand's most popular performers of poetry, touring the country to read in schools, in jails, at Parliament, with rock-groups, on records, on radio, and on television.

Hunt's family poems now embrace his own family (Kristin, and their son Tom), and the larger gestures of his younger days have with this change lost some of their violence, if not their vigour. Writing less, perhaps, than before, he still continues to explore an increasing range of forms; as a poet who has always appealed to a youthful audience, he is coming now to deal with the passions of his middle years. I look forward to learning what he makes from this challenge.

—Alan Roddick

HUTCHINSON, (William Patrick Henry) Pearse. Irish. Born in Glasgow, Scotland, 16 February 1927. Educated at Christian Brothers School, Dublin; University College, Dublin; Salzburg Seminar in American Studies, 1952. Translator, International Labor Organization, Geneva, Switzerland, 1951-53; Drama Critic, Radio Eireann, 1957-61, and Telefis Eireann, 1968. Gregory Fellow, University of Leeds, 1971-73. Lived in Barcelona, 1954-57, 1961-67. Recipient: Butler Award, for Gaelic writing, 1969. Address: c/o Gallery Press, 19 Oakdown Road, Dublin 14, Ireland.

PUBLICATIONS

Verse

Tongue Without Hands.   Dublin, Dolmen Press, 1963.
Faoistin Bhacach (Imperfect Confession).   Dublin, Clóchomhar, 1968.
Expansions.   Dublin, Dolmen Press, 1969.
Watching the Morning Grow.   Dublin, Gallery Press, 1973.
The Frost Is All Over.   Dublin, Gallery Press, 1975.
Selected Poems.   Dublin, Gallery Press, 1982.

Other

Translator, *Poems*, by Josep Carner.   Oxford, Dolphin, 1962.
Translator, *Friend Songs: Medieval Love-Songs from Galaico-Portuguese.*   Dublin, New Writers Press, 1970.

*

Pearse Hutchinson comments:
   Themes: Growing-up. Near-madness. Near-despair. The colour bar. The horrors of puritanical Irish Catholicity. Xenophobia and Xenophilia. Travel (especially Spain). The built-in dangers (to truth) of all revolt. The difficulty, tenuous possibility, and utter necessity, of love. Friendship. Social injustice. God. Pity.
   Forms: Free verse and strictly rhyming metres.
   Influences: Hard to say—but I suppose Auden, Cavafy, the 17th century Gaelic poet Pierce Ferriter, and the contemporary Catalans Salvador Espriu (especially as to cadence) and Pere Quart.

*   *   *

   Pearse Hutchinson lived for many years in Spain and his first volume consisted of verse translations from the work of a Catalan poet, Josep Carner. The effect of his experiences abroad can be plainly seen in his first two collections of poems, *Tongue Without Hands*, and *Expansions*. His delight in Mediterranean colour is shown in "Málaga":

The scent of unseen jasmine on the warm night beach.

The tram along the sea road all the way from town
through its wide open sides drank unseen jasmine down.
Living was nothing all those nights but that strong flower.

Equally gay is the lyrical "Fireworks in Córdoba":

          Cocks and coins and golden lupins,
          parachutes and parasols and shawls,
          pamplinas, maltrantos, and glass lawyers,
          giant spermatozoa, dwarf giants,
          greengage palms, and flying goldfish....

Hutchinson is one of the few Irish poets of today who writes of political oppression and bad social conditions. In "Questions" he describes attempts to suppress the use of the Catalan language by imprisonment and violence in a province: "Where one fine day, the gun smiles, and everyone rumours a thaw,/but next

night, the gun kills, and all remember the law."
   Hutchinson writes in various measures, including free verse. The poems which he has written on Irish life, both in city and country, are brisk, satiric and ironic, as in "Men's Mission":

          Some Lenten evening sharp, at five to eight,
          pick a suburban road both long and straight
          and leading—which do not?—to a Catholic church:
          you'll see, whisked out through every creaking gate,
          men only, walking all at the same brisk rate.

"Fleadh Cheoil" (a popular musical festival) is a lively account of a country town *en fête*:

          each other door in a mean twisting main street,
          flute-player, fiddler and penny-whistler
          concentrating on one sense only
          such a wild elegance of energy gay and sad
          few clouds of lust or vanity could form:
          the·mind kept cool, the heart kept warm;
          therein the miracle, three days and nights
          so many dances played and so much drinking done,
          so many voices raised in singing but none
          in anger nor any fist in harm.

From the manufacturing centres of England and Scotland, exiles "in flashy ties and frumpish hats" return for a few days to hear "an ancient music." "Friday in a Branch Post-Office" tells of the weekly queue of septuagenarians waiting patiently for their meagre pension and ends with an ironic comment: "We don't need a statue of Cú Chulainn/in our Branch Post-Office." The reference reminds us of Yeats's tribute to the statue of the ancient Irish hero in the General Post Office in Dublin.

—Austin Clarke

IGNATOW, David.   American.   Born in Brooklyn, New York, 7 February 1914. Educated in Brooklyn public schools. Married Rose Graubart in 1938; one son and one daughter. Worked as salesman, public relations writer, editor, shipyard handyman, newspaperman, and treasurer and president of a bindery firm. Instructor, New School for Social Research, New York, 1964-65; Visiting Lecturer, University of Kentucky, Lexington, 1965-66; Lecturer, University of Kansas, Lawrence, 1966-67, and Vassar College, Poughkeepsie, New York, 1967-69; Adjunct Professor, Southampton College, Long Island University, 1967-68 and Columbia University, New York, 1969-76; Visiting Professor, New York University, 1985. Poet-in-Residence, now Professor Emeritus, York College, City University of New York. Associate Editor, *American Scene* magazine, 1935-37; Literary Arts Editor, *New York Analytic* magazine, 1937; Co-Editor, *Beloit Poetry Journal*, Wisconsin, 1950-59; Poetry Editor, *The Nation*, New York, 1962-63; Consulting Editor, *Chelsea* magazine, New York, 1969-71; Editor-at-Large, *American Poetry Review*, Philadelphia, 1972-76. Recipient: American Academy award, 1964; Guggenheim Fellowship, 1965, 1973; Shelley Memorial Award, 1966; Rockefeller Fellowship, 1968; National Endowment for the Arts grant, 1969; Creative Artists Public Service grant, 1976; Bollingen Prize, 1977; Wallace Stevens Fellowship, 1977. President, Poetry Society of America, 1981. Address: P.O. Box 1458, East Hampton, New York 11937, U.S.A.

PUBLICATIONS

Verse

Poems.   Prairie City, Illinois, Decker Press, 1948.
The Gentle Weight Lifter.   New York, Morris Gallery, 1955.
Say Pardon.   Middletown, Connecticut, Wesleyan University Press, 1961.
Figures of the Human.   Middletown, Connecticut, Wesleyan University Press, 1964.
Rescue the Dead.   Middletown, Connecticut, Wesleyan University Press, 1968.
Earth Hard: Selected Poems.   London, Rapp and Whiting, 1968.
Poems 1934-69.   Middletown, Connecticut, Wesleyan University Press, 1970.
Facing the Tree.   Chicago, Swallow Press, 1973.
The Notebooks of David Ignatow, edited by Ralph J. Mills, Jr.   Chicago, Swallow Press, 1973.
Facing the Tree: New Poems.   Boston, Little Brown, 1975.
Selected Poems, edited by Robert Bly.   Middletown, Connecticut, Wesleyan University Press, 1975.
The Animal in the Bush: Poems on Poetry.   Pittsburgh, Slow Loris Press, 1977.
Tread the Dark: New Poems.   Boston, Little Brown, 1978.
Sunlight: A Sequence for My Daughter.   Brockport, New York, BOA, 1979.
Conversations.   Oceanside, New York, Survivor's Manual, 1980.
Whisper to the Earth: New Poems.   Boston, Little Brown, 1981.
Leaving the Door Open.   New York, Sheep Meadow Press, 1984.

Recording: *Today's Poets 3,* with others, Folkways.

Other

Open Between Us, edited by Ralph J. Mills, Jr.   Ann Arbor, University of Michigan Press, 1980.

Editor, *Political Poetry.*   New York, Chelsea, 1960.
Editor, *Walt Whitman: A Centennial Celebration.*   Beloit, Wisconsin, Beloit College, 1963.
Editor, *William Carlos Williams: A Memorial Chapbook.*   Beloit, Wisconsin, Beloit College, 1963.

*

Bibliography: *A Checklist of Writings* by Robert A. Smith, Storrs, University of Connecticut Library, 1966; in *Tennessee Poetry Journal* (Martin), Winter 1970.

Manuscript Collections: Lockwood Memorial Library, State University of New York, Buffalo; Olin Library, Wesleyan University, Middletown, Connecticut.

Critical Studies: by Edwin Honig, in *New Mexico Quarterly* (Albuquerque), Spring 1951; James Wright, in *Chelsea 12* (New York), September 1962; Victor Contoski, in *University Review* (Kansas City), Spring 1968; Robert Bly in *New Leader* (New York), 22 May 1968; Paul Zweig, in *The Sixties* (Madison, Minnesota), Summer 1968, and *American Poetry Review* (Philadelphia), January-February 1976; *Sorties* by James Dickey, New York, Doubleday, 1971; "Earth Hard: The Poetry of David Ignatow" by Ralph J. Mills, Jr., in *North Shore Review* (Chicago), Winter 1973; "Circumscriptions: The Poetry of David Ignatow" by Jerome Mazzaro, in *Salmagundi* (New York), Spring 1973; "American Poetry in and out of the Cave" by James Moore, in *The Lamp in the Spine* (St. Paul, Minnesota), Spring 1973.

David Ignatow comments:

(1970) I suppose it may be said that my early poems originated in the William Carlos Williams school of hardcore realism, free of the conventional rhyme and/or rhythm patterns. After my second book I found myself deeply interested in the school of surrealism.

I am constantly aware of the absolute and imminent tragedy of men in and among themselves through every level of their existence, socially, politically, privately, in love, family, business affairs. I deal with the entire range of experience given to each man in his life, as I seek through this apprehension of tragedy the saving grace, the cause for living in the act of serving tragedy itself. I dance with Yeats and Williams on the graves of the dead, as I would wish it done to me, in pleasure and homage to the dead.

My form is usually very free, content and/or idea determining it, while I use every conceivable device traditional and new for the proper realization of the poem. My private life, lives of my friends, lives of important men and women, historical events, scientific developments, the works of mythologies, philosophical treatises, the poems and novels of friends and interesting writers, all feed me with materials for poems. But most particularly, it is often history as it is being enacted today from which I draw a sense of the life of the times, with frequent reference to my life in that context. I search for *now*, using the method of introspection and dream in tandem with objective events or things.

In my poetry I have tried especially to make my life a metaphor for existence in these times, to the extent that I experience it. Each poem ultimately is designed with the purpose in mind, no matter the subject. It is for this reason that more than several critics have noticed the metaphysical basis to my work, Randall Jarrell for example, in a brief review many years ago. While I seek for the meaning to the experience, at the same time I am allowing the poem as it takes shape also to contribute its understanding of the experience. Language plays a decisive role in my projection of the experience though never losing sight of the objective event itself.

However, frequently in recent years I have presented completely fictitious events, given them an objective reality so to speak, as I explore the possibilities of the surrealist poem through this device. I have been led to surrealism by internal as well as external events, in a search for absolute understanding of the nature of relationships among us. These have suggested the need for a surrealistic approach. I don't know though whether I wish to continue in that phase, as I discover in myself a delight in projecting a sort of dream quality in the poem, as if it were from here that we take our final shape.

After having written some of the most bitter, terrifying dead end poems, with no place else to go from there, I conceive of the necessity for re-establishing relationships with myself and with the world on still another level, while life goes on. To quote in full from a recent paragraph I submitted for a recording of my poems by Scholastic Records, Inc.: "To me, the act of writing is a gesture of independence. I write with the thought of gaining control over my materials and over myself. With this achieved, I feel free once more to return to the balance and poise I prefer in my life, providing the poem of that moment has released me from the pressure, to my satisfaction. That does not happen often or long enough, as I am continually examining and re-examining my relations with the world and with myself. The poems that get written are what they are, poems; but I suppose, put all together, serve as an index to my way of life. I am very glad that this life within and without is so restless and disturbing to me since I get so much pleasure in writing about it."

(1974) I would only add that much of my early and perhaps later poetry was in response to the pessimism and withdrawal in the poetry of T.S. Eliot. I took my cue in the manner with which to respond from William Carlos Williams, but this is to acknowledge that Eliot played a deeply important role in shaping much of my thinking on my life and the world around me. In other words, I found myself as a kind of mediator between Eliot and Williams, giving respect to the qualities of both and, out of the necessities in my life, shaping my own poems out of an identity with Eliot's own problems while seeking for a resolution in the energy and freedom manifest in Williams' work.

*   *   *

The view of David Ignatow's early poems is essentially tragic, and his later poems do not substantially alter that perspective. "There must be something wrong with me/wanting to keep going through/the endless griefs, as if I had iron/bowels and a stone head," is a characteristic beginning, in a remarkable recent volume, *Facing the Tree*. Accepting this fate has brought him, after a half-century of writing, to a kind of peace, a modicum of joy. And in "The Pleasure" he admits his enjoyment in watching himself growing older: "I am authentic, I say/I belong with the others."

Although the new poems since 1977, the year he won the Bollingen Prize, add little to his impressive canon, poems such as the following, from *Tread the Dark*, are resonant with this happier mood.

> I live admiring the sky
> and the mountains and loving
> the day and the night,
> I am brother to the tree,
> runner with the rabbit
> who twitches his ears in the silence.

This poem, set against an equally impressive prose poem, indicates the range of feeling available to Ignatow from the beginning: "I am dreaming of the funeral of the world, watching it go by carried in an urn, reduced to ashes, and followed by a horde of mourners, a million abreast, across the broadest lands and all changing together. We are dead, we have killed ourselves. We are beyond rescue."

In the midst of personal and political crises, "caught in an insane world," Ignatow, like Whitman, affirms the essential value of life. In "For John Berryman," a tribute to a fellow poet, a suicide, Ignatow says that he goes on living,

> half a suicide,
> the need defended by the other half
> that thinks to live in that knowledge
> is praiseworthy.

Contending with a half-mad world is obviously no easy task. It takes, as Ignatow's poems suggest, all the intelligence and humor one can muster, and calls forth a wide range of moods to accommodate the peculiar nature of everyday experience. So his lyrics range from tragedy to mad comedy, each conveyed with equal authority and skill. They made considerable demands on the reader, moving beyond the conscious mind to the splendid, mysterious unconscious region—the night life, the dream-and-shadow world frequently ignored by less ambitious and less talented writers.

Yet there is control, too. Unlike many so-called surrealist writers, Ignatow never lets the complicated and paradoxical vision overwhelm him. In poems such as "Say Pardon" and "Rescue the Dead," the sparse, colloquial language fulfills its primary responsibility: communicating thought and feeling as economically, precisely, and beautifully as possible. Ignatow belongs, as Robert Bly has said, to the "William Carlos Williams school, of hardcore realism, lyrically presented." These skills among others, have won him a special place among the principal voices of his generation.

—Michael True

IRBY, Kenneth. American. Born in Bowie, Texas, 18 November 1936. Educated at the University of Kansas, Lawrence, B.A. 1958; Harvard University, Cambridge, Massachusetts, M.A. 1960; University of California, Berkeley, M.L.S. 1968. Served in the United States Army, 1960-62. Taught in the Department of English, Tufts University, Medford, Massachusetts, 1971-73, 1974-75; Visiting Professor, University of Copenhagen English Institute, 1973-74. Contibuting Editor, *Conjunctions* magazine, New York. Address: N-311 Regency Place, Lawrence, Kansas 66044, U.S.A.

PUBLICATIONS

Verse

The Roadrunner. Placitas, New Mexico, Duende Press, 1964.
The Oregon Trail. Lawrence, Kansas, Dialogue Press, 1964.
Kansas-New Mexico. Lawrence, Kansas, Dialogue Press, 1965.
Movements/Sequences. Placitas, New Mexico, Duende Press, 1965.
The Flower of Having Passed Through Paradise in a Dream: Poems 1967. Annandale-on-Hudson, New York, Matter, 1968.
Relation: Poems 1965-1966. Los Angeles, Black Sparrow Press, 1970.
To Max Douglas. Lawrence, Kansas, Tansy Press-Peg Leg Press, 1971; revised edition, 1974.
Archipelago. Willits, California, Tuumba Press, 1976.
In Excelsis Borealis. Eagle Bridge, New York, White Creek Press, 1976.
For the Snow Queen. Lawrence, Kansas, Tansy Press, 1976.
Catalpa: Poems 1968-73. Lawrence, Kansas, Tansy Press, 1976.
From Some Etudes. Lawrence, Kansas, Tansy Press, 1978.
Orexis. Barrytown, New York, Station Hill Press, 1981.
Riding the Dog. Greensburg, Pennsylvania, Zelot Press, 1982.
A Set. Lawrence, Kansas, Tansy Press, 1983.

Other

Editor, with Robert Callahan, *Seventeenth Century North America*, by Carl O. Sauer. Berkeley, California, Turtle Island, 1980.

*

Bibliography: "Kenneth Irby: A Checklist" by Robert Bertholf, in *Credences* (Kent, Ohio), February 1979.

Critical Studies: "Kenneth Irby Issue" of *Vort* (Silver Spring, Maryland), Summer 1973, and *Credences* (Kent, Ohio), Febru-

Kenneth Irby comments:

In earlier editions of the present work I included the following statement:

> My concern *seems* to have been muchly with *pastoral* verse—that is, poetry that *feeds* us—drawing on a common Great Plains Mysticism in the face of the landscape, that the landscape, *especially*, demands of us. but the concern of *poetry* is not finally at all limited.

I would now only wish to *doubly* underline that last sentence, and further refer the reader to the notes, "In Place of a Preface," in *Catalpa*. And add, as motto, in Mary Butts' words: "now make it all up out of cross balances." My major attention currently is devoted to the editing and introducing of Mary Butts' poems (only a few published in magazines during her lifetime, and a few afterwards, none ever collected into a book, most still in manuscript).

*   *   *

Kenneth Irby's *Catalpa* sets his earlier work in clearer relief, and, though he still has few readers, he begins to emerge as a central American poet, as the collection of essays on his work in *Credences* eloquently testifies.

Irby is a poet of geography, and his work, from *Kansas-New Mexico* on, progressively maps the North American continent as a simultaneously literal and visionary space. He is perhaps our only pastoral poet. As he writes: "The pastoral, as a mode of poetry (out of eight Sir Philip Sidney lists), seemed to me particularly of two concerns: a calmness, a quietude of the whole being, derived from all attentions and awareness; and a feeling of great closeness with the vegetation lived among—an ecological calm—poetry that feeds us (*pascere*), not just that tends the sheep." The conviction of pastoral poetry, he goes on to say, is "that the landscape demands us, and reveals us."

To Max Douglas probably offers the new reader the easiest access to Irby's somewhat demanding work. As one might expect of a pastoral poet, his mood is frequently elegiac, and this is a sequence of poems addressed to a promising young poet who died of an overdose of heroin. In it, Irby draws the most important line of his map: the Missouri-Kansas border. It is the center of the spatial coordinates which appear more fully in *Catalpa*: there the Civil War began; there the culture based on corn and timber gives way to the culture based on wheat and steel. For Irby, who grew up in Ft. Scott, Kansas, it is the heartland, the center around which the continent turns. His tribute to a poet whose home was St. Joseph, Missouri, just on the *other* side of the border, calls the tension of the region into play.

Catalpa (etymologically, "head with wings") is the vision of the entire continent. Most of the individual poems are dense structures of minute bits of geographic, historic, and personal information, typical of the earlier work. The vision is largely a function of the book's collage-like structure. In "Jed Smith and the Way," he writes:

> You can never get there
> the same way twice, and you always
> *have* to get there, this is the way
> North and South
> the way East and West
> this is the Secret History
> of the Continent.

In the secret history, the East is associated with the ego and the superego, the accumulated past, parents, and a paradise lost (see "Tufts"). The West is the location of the unconscious, and, when western knowledge comes, it is powerful and social but frequently also disorganizing and dangerous (see "Berkeley"). The North, the province of the Snow Queen as she appears in the last section of *Catalpa*, is like the West, a place of vision, but northern knowledge is cold, clear, isolated and isolating. The artist of the North is associated with Tennyson's Lady of Shallot. The South, though it is not fully explored in *Catalpa*, is sensuality (Irby's most southerly poem is "Delius," in *To Max Douglas*). Only in the center, in the heartland and in the heart, is there some hope of bringing immediacy, clarity, sensuality, and ego into satisfying and useful balance.

A small collection of poems which Irby published in 1978, *Some Etudes*, suggests that his work is undergoing a significant change. These tiny elegant poems are articulations of possibilities suggested by the inherent qualities of words themselves. Irby's work deserves much more attention than it has received.

—Don Byrd

IRELAND, Kevin (Mark). New Zealander. Born in Auckland, 18 July 1933. Married. Founding Editor, *Mate* magazine, Auckland. Address: c/o Cicada Press, P.O. Box 64-009, Birkenhead South, Auckland 10, New Zealand.

PUBLICATIONS

Verse

Face to Face. Christchurch, Pegasus Press, 1963.
Educating the Body. Christchurch, Caxton Press, 1968.
A Letter from Amsterdam. London, Amphadesma Press, 1972.
Orchids Hummingbirds and Other Poems. Auckland, Auckland University Press-Oxford University Press, 1974; London, Oxford University Press, 1975.
A Grammar of Dreams. Wellington, Wai-te-ata Press, 1975.
Literary Cartoons. Auckland, Island-Hurricane Press, 1978.
The Dangers of Art: Poems 1975-1980. Auckland, Cicada Press, 1981.

Other

Translator, *Poems*, by Hristo Botev. Sofia, Bulgaria, Sofia Press, 1974.

*   *   *

"Thin men/write gaunt poems/and each word/sticks out/like a rib," wrote Kevin Ireland in "Deposition": an accurate picture of some of his work at that time. Whatever the shape of the poet, however, his poems have not always been so spare; indeed his latest work is often quite "plump."

Seeking a congenial form for his witty, whimsical conceits and explorations of metaphors, Ireland adopted, early on, a strict discipline of short lines of one to three feet, with complex rhyme-schemes and patterns of words or phrases recurring from stanza to stanza. After some ten years of such strictness he turned in *A Letter from Amsterdam* to a more open and relaxed style, which he has continued in the love-poems of *Orchids Hummingbirds*, with their wry and affectionate humour, their clear-sightedness ("A Guide to Perfection"):

> you complain of your body
> and make out a detailed list
> of what you can call your worst deformities
> you start at your toes and proceed
> to ankles knees bottom stomach
> breast lungs jaw eyes hair skin
>
> I reply that this is vanity...
> low self-esteem is not aware
> of how to turn this way and that
> to show ill-favours quite so prettily....

In *A Grammar of Dreams* Ireland gives rein to exuberantly inventive fantasy with nine poems that celebrate youth and love, yet with an acknowledgment of age and liking, as in "Caroline as Scientist":

> and then you smiled and waited
> until in his slow-thinking time at last
> he reached and turned you half around
> and kissed your throat
> where it had loosened up and aged
> like his: and demonstrated in one certain act
> not love as image or concoction
> but as an attestation of true person
> passion time: confirming his undying love
> by evidence of mortal flesh

—Alan Roddick

JACKSON, Alan. Scottish. Born in Liverpool, Lancashire, England, 6 September 1938. Educated in Edinburgh schools; Royal High School; Edinburgh University, 1956-59, 1964-65. Married Margaret Dickson in 1963; two sons. Laborer; trainee psychiatric nurse, 1959-60; secretary, Scottish Committee of 100, 1961-62. Since 1965, Founding Director, Kevin Press, Edinburgh; since 1967, Director, Live Readings, Scotland. Recipient: Scottish Arts Council bursary, 1967, 1978.

PUBLICATIONS

Verse

Under Water Wedding. Privately printed, 1961.
Sixpenny Poems. Privately printed, 1962.
Well Ye Ken Noo. Privately printed, 1963.
All Fall Down. Edinburgh, Kevin Press, 1965.
The Worstest Beast. Edinburgh, Kevin Press, 1967.
Penguin Modern Poets 12, with Jeff Nuttall and William Wantling. London, Penguin, 1968.
The Grim Wayfarer. London, Fulcrum Press, 1969.
Idiots Are Freelance. Dyce, Aberdeenshire, Rainbow, 1973.

*

Alan Jackson comments:
   I regard the poet as the Blakean "bard" who turns the eye in,

tries to bring the dark to light.
   Themes: family (particularly the mother), sex (particularly as against Christian morality and also searching my own perversities), death of religion and the absence of myth, man as a pernicious life-form.
   Verse forms: many, longer ones often rhyming, and always close to speech, but interest in longer unrhymed rhythms and eluding grammer increasing; dozens of very short unrhymed highly compressed poems. Poems often kept for over a year, then to be worked and reworked. Clarity desired but not immediate understanding.
   Main influence, Jung; can see few limits to his importance. Main admiration: Norman Mailer. Nietzsche somewhere between the two. I try not to be influenced by poets, though I try to absorb lessons about writing. Finally, a man should not know what is characteristic of him.

*   *   *

Alan Jackson's work has subtle sympathy, ironic wit, technical dexterity and satirical verve, although other pieces express a raucous violence shrieking in concert with the fashionable taste for what Robert Lowell has called "raw, huge, blood-dripping gobbets of unreasoned experience"—as in "Fraulein," where a "shocking" tale of rape followed by syphilis appears merely sensational because presented in complete isolation from the rest of the environment. When he resists the temptation to drop his pants in public, however, his verse shows that although he is still young he has already attained individual achievement as a symbolist-cum-satirist, with such bitter brevities as "Loss" where, using a thin Scots close to urban speech, he turns conventional flower imagery to most unconventional ends in revealing the all too frequent fate of beauty in the Scottish climate. Most often, however, he writes in English, and in at least one poem, "Was a Shame," the influence of Blake is as evident in style as in content, theme and feeling. But elsewhere his work reveals an original stylist with a highly personal voice, capable of a stimulating variety of themes and forms, from the epigrammatic wit of "Young Politician" ("What a lovely moon./ And it's in the constituency too") to the controlled passion of rage and sorrow in the couplets picturing man as "the worstest beast" and to the sensuous richness and strangeness of the poem called "3 l/g 4" (three little green quarters) which explores the mysteries of time and fate in terms of superstitions of science and science-fiction.

—Alexander Scott

JACKSON, Laura (Riding). *See* **RIDING, Laura.**

JACOB, Paul. Indian. Born in Kerala, 27 April 1940. Educated at St. Columba's School, New Delhi; Madras Christian College; St. Stephen's College, Delhi. Member of the staff, *The Century* magazine, New Delhi, 1963-65. Since 1966, member of the editorial staff, *Enact* magazine, Delhi. Lives in New Delhi. Address: c/o Enact, Paul's Press, E44-11 Okhla Industrial Area, Phase II, New Delhi 110 020, India.

PUBLICATIONS

Verse

Sonnets.   Calcutta, Writers Workshop, 1968.
Alter-Sonnets.   Calcutta, Writers Workshop, 1969.
Swedish Exercises.   Calcutta, Writers Workshop, 1973.

*   *   *

Paul Jacob's poetry seems to be a continuous search for the perfect form. His first two volumes consisted of exercises in sonnet form, written in a taut, controlled style. In his latest volume, *Swedish Exercises*, he experiments with the Italian sestina consisting of six six-line stanzas. He has tried his hand at limericks and English poems in the Urdu *ghazal* form.

This concern with form is a challenge Jacob sets for himself and it suits his oblique suggestive style. Though he never writes poetry of plain statement, his poems, rather than appearing obscure, give the impression of almost total communicability at a non-logical level:

Anywhere there are children is no flaw, but youth
Must come out of darkness, newspaperish tar,
Forever celluloid, soundtrack, should warm up
As you review gulmohar, amaltaz, summerspring to truth.

(Gulmohar and amaltaz are orange and yellow flowering trees that blossom in India in the late spring and summer.)

Jacob uses words skilfully and sensitively, but sometimes also a little self-consciously as in his favourite antithetical devices like "A lifelong sleep, a deathshort sleeplessness," or "My bed shall not make others, others shall make my bed." The central theme of all his poems is self-exploration, but the frame of reference ranges from love to religion: "May every true prayer be repetition/Vain like a baby. May prayer itself be whole/Over this weekend the earth shall burn for you."

—Meenakshi Mukherjee

JACOBSEN, Josephine (Winder, née Boylan).   American. Born in Coburg, Ontario, Canada, 19 August 1908. Educated privately, and at Roland Park Country School, Baltimore, graduated 1926. Married Eric Jacobsen in 1932; one son. Poetry Consultant, 1971-73, and since 1973, Honorary Consultant in American Letters, Library of Congress, Washington, D.C. Vice-President, Poetry Society of America, 1979. Recipient: Borestone Mountain award, 1961, 1964, 1968, 1972; MacDowell Colony grant, 1973, 1974, 1976, 1978, 1981, 1983; *Prairie Schooner* award, for fiction, 1974; Yaddo grant, 1975, 1977, 1980, 1982, 1984; American Academy award, 1982. L.H.D.: College of Notre Dame, Baltimore, 1974; Goucher College, Baltimore, 1974; Towson State University, Baltimore, 1983. Address: Mountain View Road, Whitefield, New Hampshire 03598, U.S.A.

PUBLICATIONS

Verse

Let Each Man Remember.   Dallas, Kaleidograph Press, 1940.
For the Unlost.   Baltimore, Contemporary Poetry, 1946.

The Human Climate: New Poems.   Baltimore, Contemporary Poetry, 1953.
The Animal Inside.   Athens, Ohio University Press, 1966.
The Shade-Seller: New and Selected Poems.   New York, Doubleday, 1974.
The Chinese Insomniacs.   Philadelphia, University of Pennsylvania Press, 1981.

Short Stories

A Walk with Raschid and Other Stories.   Winston-Salem, North Carolina, Jackpine Press, 1978.

Other

The Testament of Samuel Beckett, with William Randolph Mueller.   New York, Hill and Wang, 1964; London, Faber, 1966.
Ionesco and Genet: Playwrights of Silence, with William Randolph Mueller.   New York, Hill and Wang, 1968.
From Anne to Marianne: Some American Women Poets (lecture).   Washington, D.C., Library of Congress, 1973.
The Instant of Knowing (lecture).   Washington, D.C., Library of Congress, 1974.
One Poet's Poetry (lecture).   Decatur, Georgia, Agnes Scott College, 1975.

*

Manuscript Collection: Mugar Memorial Library, Boston University.

Critical Studies: "Poetry and Preaching" by Hugh Kerr, in *Theology Today* (Princeton, New Jersey), October 1964; Richard Ohmann, in *Wisconsin Studies in Contemporary Literature* (Madison), Autumn 1965; "The Matter and Manner of Beckett" by David Helsa, in *Christian Scholar* (New York), Winter 1965; "Enduring Saturday" by Anthony Burgess, in *Spectator* (London), 29 April 1966; "The Human Condition," in *Irish Press* (Dublin), 11 June 1966; "The Essential Q," in *Times Literary Supplement* (London), 30 June 1966; John Logan, in *Epoch* (Ithaca, New York), Autumn 1966; "Art in Transition" by Laurence Lieberman, in *Poetry* (Chicago), March 1967; Rosemary Dee, in *Commonweal* (New York), 20 December 1968; in *Library Journal* (New York), 16 October 1981; *Epoch 32* (Ithaca, New York), no. 1, 1982; *Commonweal* (New York), 24 September 1982; *Nation* (New York), 16 October 1982.

Josephine Jacobsen comments:

I don't really value very highly "statements" from a poet in regard to her work. I can perhaps best introduce my own poetry by saying what I have not done, rather than defining what I have done. I have not involved my work with any clique, school, or other group; I have tried not to force any poem into an overall concept of "how I write poetry" when it should be left to create organically its own individual style; I have not been content to repeat what I have already accomplished or to establish any stance which would limit the flexibility of discovery. I have not confused technical innovation, however desirable, with poetic originality or intensity. I have not utilized poetry as a social or political lever. I have not conceded that any subject matter, any vocabulary, any approach or any form is in itself necessarily unsuitable to the uses of poetry. I have not tried to establish a reputation as poet on any grounds but those of my poetry.

*   *   *

"Terrestrial, we learned the accurate measure/Of sharpness is the brevity of touch," wrote Josephine Jacobsen in her early volume, *For the Unlost*. Capturing the brief but significant moment which reveals the essence of a subject has remained her forte. "Precise in its very act," the dance is an apt and frequent metaphor in poems celebrating our fleeting, earthly pleasures; its ephemeral beauty a figure for the "art of our mortality." She sizes up the existence by striking to the core. There she finds the shining boy that preceded the greedy, frightened man and the integral marble which shadows the hypocritical monument. In "The Big Hotel Closed Yesterday for the Winter" short scenes depicting rich snobs and selfish, superannuated virgins veer toward the sentimental, only to be cut dead by a savage wit, worthy of Dorothy Parker, which strips away the veneer. In poems written in time of war, she speaks directly; ever clear-eyed, she has strength to view the horrors of the "ugly feast," though her voice catches at the poignancy of suffering and loss. *"At dreadful high noon"* she writes in "Lines to a Poet," *"You may speak only to our heart,/Our honor and our need."*

Continuing her explorations in *The Human Climate*, she discovers more darkness at the center, and here her lines give up their meaning less easily. Hunger for experience and "utter freedom" leads to momentary confusion: "The blinded eye will have all color." Urgency, even wildness, marks poems in which personae strive for release from "deadly limit." Lost souls are caught in psychological binds, playing games lovers play. The young man travels to the brink of suicide; the old man treads the customary path of penury and loneliness. Here, despite the vivid pointillism, the poet's design can be obscure: details are precise, but the outline remains blurred. In "Variations on Variety" the object is clearer, as the vaudeville show becomes a paradigm of our transitory nature. In "April Asylum" old ladies like "docile sentient dead" watch Technicolor films, sacraments which bring them "lonely and together" a blessing in the empty morning hours. Probing ever more inward, Jacobsen seeks in *The Animal Inside* the mysterious soul which cannot be caught or tamed, but which, "Seen, can be loved." Brilliant flashes of color, flickering images of shadows, water and fire entice the reader into the marvelous poetic world but often leave him in a cul-de-sac. She examines the dying revolutionary, the deaf-mutes isolated in a ball-park, the ancient lady exhumed with her curious case, but maintains dramatic distance from them; despite analysis they remain inscrutable. The persona views religious spectacles, a ritual Indian sacrifice, a haunting All Soul's Day litany, from an original perspective; the Son of Man is seen in the tropical swamp, and Peter is called "crucifixion's clown." The poet seems, however, more in sympathy with wildlife. She reads chaos in a dessicated starfish and finds identity in the awkward-ness and hurt of a fiddler crab. "Almost nothing concerns me but communication," she writes, and if here she sometimes meets with failure, the adventure of these poems is worth the risk.

—Joseph Parisi

JAFFIN, David. American. Born in New York City, 14 September 1937. Educated at the University of Michigan, Ann Arbor (Hopwood Award, 1956; Oreon E. Scott Award), 1955-56; New York University (Penfield Fellow), 1956-66, B.A. 1959 (Phi Beta Kappa), M.A. 1961, Ph.D. in history 1966. Married Rosemarie Jaffin in 1961; two sons. Graduate Assistant, New York University, 1961-62; Lecturer in European History, University of Maryland European Division, Germany, 1966-69. Studied theology at the University of Tübingen, 1971-74: Vicar, Tübingen, 1974-75; Minister, Magstadt, 1975-78. Since 1978, Minister, Malmsheim. Address: Merklinger Strasse 22, 7253 Renningen 2 (Malmsheim), Germany.

PUBLICATIONS

Verse

Conformed to Stone.   New York, Abelard Schuman, 1968; London, Abelard Schuman, 1970.
Emptied Spaces.   London, Abelard Schuman, 1972.
Opened.   Sheffield, Headlands, 1973.
Late March.   Rushden, Northamptonshire, Sceptre Press, 1973.
At the Gate.   New Zealand, Edge Press, 1974.
Of.   Knotting, Bedfordshire, Sceptre Press, 1974.
As One.   New Rochelle, New York, Elizabeth Press, 1975.
In the Glass of Winter.   London, Abelard Schuman, 1975.
Changes.   Godalming, Surrey, Words, 1975.
The Half of a Circle.   New Rochelle, New York, Elizabeth Press, 1977.
Space Of.   New Rochelle, New York, Elizabeth Press, 1978.
Perceptions.   New Rochelle, New York, Elizabeth Press, 1979.
The Density for Color.   Plymouth, Shearsman, 1982.
For the Finger's Want of Sound.   Plymouth, Shearsman, 1982.
Selected Poems (English and Hebrew).   Givatayim, Israel, Massada, 1982.

*

Critical Studies: in *Library Journal* (New York), 15 September 1968, and 1 September 1977; *Yorkshire Post* (Leeds), 9 September 1972; *Bristol Evening Post*, 9 November 1972; by Edward Lucie-Smith, in *Emptied Spaces*, 1972, and *In the Glass of Winter*, 1975; *Workshop New Poetry 18* (London), 1973; *Samphire* (Bromsgrove, Worcestershire), ii, 4, 1973; *Poet Lore* (Boston), Summer 1974; "David Jaffin: An Introduction" by Tony Frazer, in *Imprint 1* (Hong Kong), 1980; *Sewanee Review* (Tennessee), Fall 1980; interview, in *Sheasman 3* (Plymouth), 1981.

David Jaffin comments:

My art is one of intense compression, both of form and meaning. I seek to create a world at once visually alive, tangible/explicit and yet abstract, inward and restrained. I feel the poetic process as an intensification of consciousness. I break through/break down those words inspired in my mind (revising over and over again while I'm writing), to derive their intrinsic form and relation. Jacques Lipchitz told me that my poems were sculpted as from stone. There must never be a word too many, no decoration, ornament, rhetoric. The craft involves the unity of image, sound, sense, tone and idea. The poem itself is a state of being, not a theme to be developed with the "poetic trimming." The poem simply is, is not about. But craftsmanship itself is only the prerequisite for the spiritual process. A "state of being" means for me a personal and new definition of reality. All meaningful art must be this. I often describe this via tangible objects, thereby actualizing the senses. My aesthetic moves on two levels, the one being physically alive, so vivid as to be almost touched, and yet when these poems succeed they create an absolute stillness and control. I am told my poems gain by constant re-reading. I always present them at least twice at public readings.

*   *   *

David Jaffin's *Conformed to Stone* and *Emptied Spaces* have a sculptural quality; the poems are spare, chiselled down to the essentials. The title of each is appropriate; the first collection contains more people among its statuary: "Creatures of Stone," "The Idiot," "Woodcarver," "Self Portrait"; the second collection moves away from human models to still lifes more remote from human life, though the artistic (and particularly, the sculptural) motif remains. In the latter book, Jaffin seems to be hollowing out his previous forms, trying for a sort of negative space to complement the positive space the previous book occupied; things defined by their absence, as in "Door Partly Opened":

> You let the light
>   in,
> Angled-off,
>
> Your hands closed as a
> Shadow hanging there
>
> You let the light
>   in
> As far as your face
>   could allow.

Poems like this remind one of French poets like Valéry, with their sense of moments of time mysteriously arrested; the poet seems to be inviting us to study some scene closely and at the same time denying total entrance. The poems are restrained, dignified, pictorial, superficially simple, but turning frequently on the ambiguities inherent in language; reading them is bracing, like stepping through ice that was not as thick as we thought. The poem above, like a number of others, turns on such ambiguities, and on the suggestion, beneath the ice of the poem, of deeper, philosophical ambiguities. The observed person in this poem is the one who has opened the door and shed light on the speaker, and yet, the light becomes merely a mask for the observed, himself no more than a shadow silhouette. The last two lines suggest a deliberate act of will as well as physical obstruction of the light, and remind us of the different disguises we wear; that openness and shedding light on things, illuminating others, can be a mask too. Such subtleties make David Jaffin's poetry rewarding.

—Duane Ackerson

JAY, Peter (Anthony Charles). British. Born in Chester, Cheshire, 24 May 1945. Educated at Lancing College, Sussex; Lincoln College, Oxford (Exhibitioner; Newdigate Prize, 1965), B.A. 1967. Editor, with John Aczel, *New Measure* magazine, Oxford, 1965-69. Currently, free-lance writer, and Publisher, Anvil Press Poetry, London. Assistant Director of Poetry International, London, 1969; taught in the writing program, University of Iowa, Iowa City, 1975-76. Recipient: Rockefeller grant, 1968. Address: c/o Anvil Press Poetry, 69 King George Street, London SE10 8PX, England.

PUBLICATIONS

Verse

Lifelines. Edinburgh, Satis, 1977.
Shifting Frontiers: Poems 1962-1977. Manchester, Carcanet, 1980.

Other

Expostulations of Teddy Hogge, with *The Wooden Muse, Part One,* by W.G. Shepherd. London, Antidote Press, 1970.

Editor, *The Greek Anthology and Other Ancient Greek Epigrams.* London, Allen Lane, and New York, Oxford University Press, 1973; revised edition, London, Penguin, 1981.
Editor, *All for the Wolves: Selected Poems 1947-1975,* by Peter Russell. London, Anvil Press Poetry, 1982; Redding Ridge, Connecticut, Black Swan, 1983.

Translator, *Adonis and Venus.* Santa Barbara, California, Peter Whigham, 1968.
Translator, *The Song of Songs.* London, Anvil Press Poetry, 1975.
Translator, with Petru Popescu, *The Still Unborn about the Dead,* by Nichita Stanescu. London, Anvil Press Poetry, and Iowa City, International Writing Program, 1975.
Translator, with Peter Whigham, *The Poems of Meleager.* London, Anvil Press Poetry, 1975; Berkeley, University of California Press, 1976.
Translator, with Virgil Nemoianu, *Alibi,* by Stefan Aug. Doinas. London, Anvil Press Poetry, and Iowa City, International Writing Program, 1975.
Translator, with Anthony Rudolf and Petru Popescu, *Boxes, Stairs, and Whistle Time,* by Popescu. Knotting, Bedfordshire, Omphalos Press, 1975.
Translator, with Carol Telford and Petru Popescu, *Burial of the Vine,* by Popescu. London, Barrie and Jenkins, 1975.
Translator, *Crater: Poems 1974-1975,* by János Pilinszky. London, Anvil Press Poetry, 1978.
Translator, *Plumb/Lead,* by George Bacovia. Bucharest, Minerva, 1980.
Translator, *The Chimeras,* by Gérard de Nerval. London, Anvil Press Poetry, 1984.

*   *   *

Unnecessarily shy about publishing his own poetry, Peter Jay is the outstanding translator of his generation, and certainly the finest to emerge since Michael Hamburger. His versions of the Romanian poet George Bacovia are the most brilliant of all renderings into English since Hamburger's Hölderlin. Jay is also a brilliant parodist, exposing the weaknesses of his victims with deadly geniality (and very funnily indeed). He is an extremely serious, fastidious poet, and none of his original poetry is less than presentable, which is unusual in an age of low standards. His difficulty lies in discovering his own style, and some of the poems reflect too keenly on his awareness of and sensitivity to many differing manners (Italian, ancient Greek, German, Romanian). Pound, much admired by him, may not have been a useful influence: like that of so many poets who have been dazzled by Pound, Jay's natural manner in no way resembles his; this seems, as in other cases, to have worked as an inhibitory influence. Jay is very stylish, only occasionally lapsing (in earlier poems) into a kind of hermeticism that does not work in English poetry. So far he has said less than he has expressed; yet one feels that he wishes for greater explicitness. But his descriptions of his moods already have a distinction that marks him out as one of the few truly serious poets of his generation—as in "The Gallery":

> There are days when the mind grazes,
> circling itself like an answer
> lazily guessing its question.
> Slowly they assemble, one
> by one: some whose faces
> shine with the smile of certain
> gestures long recalled....

—Martin Seymour-Smith

JENNINGS, Elizabeth (Joan). British. Born in Boston, Lincolnshire, 18 July 1926. Educated at Oxford High School; St. Anne's College, Oxford, M.A. in English language and literature. Assistant, Oxford City Library, 1950-58; reader, Chatto and Windus Ltd., publishers, London, 1958-60. Since 1961, free-lance writer. Guildersleeve Lecturer, Barnard College, New York, 1974. Recipient: Arts Council award, 1953, bursary, 1965, 1968, 1981, grant, 1972; Maugham Award, 1956; Richard Hillary Memorial Prize, 1966. Agent: David Higham Associates Ltd., 5—8 Lower John Street, London W1R 4HA. Address: 11 Winchester Road, Oxford OX2 6NA, England.

PUBLICATIONS

Verse

(Poems). Oxford, Fantasy Press, 1953.
A Way of Looking. London, Deutsch, 1955; New York, Rinehart, 1956.
The Child and the Seashell. San Francisco, Poems in Folio, 1957.
A Sense of the World. London, Deutsch, 1958; New York, Rinehart, 1959.
Song for a Birth or a Death and Other Poems. London, Deutsch, 1961; Philadephia, Dufour, 1962.
Penguin Modern Poets 1, with Lawrence Durrell and R.S. Thomas. London, Penguin, 1962.
Recoveries. London, Deutsch, and Philadelphia, Dufour, 1964.
The Mind Has Mountains. London, Macmillan, and New York, St. Martin's Press, 1966.
The Secret Brother and Other Poems for Children. London, Macmillan, and New York, St. Martin's Press, 1966.
Collected Poems 1967. London, Macmillan, and Chester Springs, Pennsylvania, Dufour, 1967.
The Animals' Arrival. London, Macmillan, and Chester Springs, Pennsylvania, Dufour, 1969.
Lucidities. London, Macmillan, 1970.
Hurt. London, Poem-of-the-Month Club, 1970.
Folio, with others. Frensham, Surrey, Sceptre Press, 1971.
Relationships. London, Macmillan, 1972.
Growing-Points: New Poems. Manchester, Carcanet, 1975.
Consequently I Rejoice. Manchester, Carcanet, 1977.
After the Ark (for children). London, Oxford University Press, 1978.
Moments of Grace: New Poems. Manchester, Carcanet, 1979.
Selected Poems. Manchester, Carcanet, 1979.

Winter Wind. Sidcot, Somerset, Gruffyground Press, and Newark, Vermont, Janus Press, 1979.
A Dream of Spring. Stratford upon Avon, Celandine, 1980.
Celebrations and Elegies. Manchester, Carcanet, 1982.

Other

Let's Have Some Poetry. London, Museum Press, 1960.
Every Changing Shape (religion and poetry). London, Deutsch, 1961.
Poetry Today 1957-60. London, Longman, 1961.
Frost. Edinburgh, Oliver and Boyd, 1964; New York, Barnes and Noble, 1966.
Christianity and Poetry. London, Burns Oates, 1965; as *Christian Poetry,* New York, Hawthorn, 1965.
Seven Men of Vision: An Appreciation. London, Vision Press, and New York, Barnes and Noble, 1976.

Editor, with Dannie Abse and Stephen Spender, *New Poems 1956.* London, Joseph, 1956.
Editor, *The Batsford Book of Children's Verse.* London, Batsford, 1958.
Editor, *An Anthology of Modern Verse 1940-1960.* London, Methuen, 1961.
Editor, *A Choice of Christina Rossetti's Verse.* London, Faber, 1970.
Editor, *The Batsford Book of Religious Verse.* London, Batsford, 1981.
Editor, *In Praise of Our Lady.* London, Batsford, 1982.

Translator, *The Sonnets of Michelangelo.* London, Folio Society, 1961; revised edition, London, Allison and Busby, 1969; New York, Doubleday, 1970.

*

Manuscript Collections: Oxford City Library; University of Washington, Seattle.

Critical Study: by Margaret Byers, in *British Poetry since 1960* edited by Michael Schmidt and Grevel Lindop, Oxford, Carcanet, 1972.

Elizabeth Jennings comments:
I do not much care for writing about my own poems. The main reason for this is, I believe, that it makes one too self-conscious. However, I would like to say that I am always interested in what I am writing at present and hope to write in the future. I like to experiment with different poetic forms, and, at this time, I am constantly seeking for more and more clarity. I am working on a series of prose poems about paintings (painting is my second favourite art), and a series of poems, in various forms and from several viewpoints, on religious themes. I have also been writing poems about craftsmen and various aspects of nature, particularly skyscapes. For me, poetry is always a search for order. I started writing at the age of thirteen and wrote only one 4-line poem I now wish to preserve from childhood. My Roman Catholic religion and my poems are the most important things in my life.

*   *   *

Elizabeth Jennings was the only woman to be included in Robert Conquest's anthology *New Lines*; and she shares with the other so-called "Movement" poets a "coolness which is worked for"—to quote her own description of a Chinese painter—in her lucid diction, use of traditional metres, and the keen and subtle intelligence in her exploration of ideas.

Her absorption in the processes of "art with its largesse and its own restraint" has led to many poems which attempt to enter the experience of fellow-writers and artists in other media: the sculptor, the composer, the dancer, and painters ranging in time from Rembrandt to Rouault, Botticelli to Bonnard, Cézanne and—recurringly—van Gogh. Other conditions of life which especially interest her are childhood and age. Her portraits of children are based on personal recollections of a timeless peace and safety from adult ambiguities, but still more of the distresses which "built a compassion that I need to share"; and she writes about the feelings of the very old with a tender intuitive sympathy. Her insight into contemplative states of being has also resulted in various intense imaginative projections into the lives of such personalities as St. John of the Cross, St. Teresa of Avila, St. Catherine, and St. Augustine; of the Virgin in fine poems like "Annuciation" and "The Visitation," and even into the loneliness and human conflicts of Christ. These prose poems and dramatic monologues, with her translations of Michelangelo's sonnets and Rimbaud, her classical imitations in the manner of the Greek Anthology, and an increasingly adventurous freedom and flexibility in her rhythms and verse-patterns, demonstrate the versatility of her gifts.

Italy, where she has travelled extensively, is the background for the number of poems which epitomize her great difference from the rest of the "Movement" group. A profound religious conviction colours her vision of life and permeates all her work. As a foreigner at confession in an unknown tongue amid the gold and mosaics, at a Roman mass, or at Assisi "where silence is so wide you hear it," she communicates the quietism most vividly realized in the magnificent "San Paolo Fuori le Mura," where the cool stillness of stone engenders an interior calm which is "a kind of coming home." In "Song for a Birth or a Death" the mystic's apprehensions of reality are as eloquently articulated as anywhere in contemporary poetry. "Notes for a Book of Hours" conjures the raptness of the visionary and his struggle for the elusive language capable of expressing the numinous. "A World of Light" re-creates "A mood the senses cannot touch or damage,/ A sense of peace beyond the breathing word," which grows in "a dazzling dark" as reminiscent of Vaughan as later poems like "Winter Night" and "Let there be dark for us to comtemplate."

This poet is, however, equally and bitterly familiar with another kind of darkness—the non-fruitful one of doubt, desolation, and despair: the abysses of Hopkins's "winter world" implied in her title "The Mind Has Mountains." Recurrent breakdowns led to spells in mental hospital; the guilt, bewilderment, frustrations of unfulfilled love and "very absolute of fear" which culminated in a state "clothed in confusion" are conveyed with poignant directness in many poems of her middle period. Yet this agonized experience of "climates of terror," and compassionate, yet unself-pitying vulnerability to the sufferings of her fellow-patients which are so movingly recorded led to a recognition that "Perhaps to know no desert is a lack": of the necessity of "The painful breaking/ Which brings to birth."

The recovery chronicled in "Growing-Points" and "Consequently I Rejoice" shows a full repossession of her lost capacity for contemplative stillness and receptivity to moments of mystical revelation, and a greater maturity of acceptance. The notable broadening of range of her choice of subject, a more objective awareness of the contemporary world and problems and predicaments other than her own, are matched by a new assurance and virtuosity in the handling of language. Her words describing a disabled countryman apply with equal aptness to Elizabeth Jennings's own impressive testimony and courage and spiritual resilience: "gentleness/Concealing toughness," which takes "pain as birds take buffets from/ The wind, then gather strength and fly and fly."

—Margaret Willy

JEROME, Judson. American. Born in Tulsa, Oklahoma, 8 February 1927. Educated at the University of Oklahoma, Norman, 1943-45; University of Chicago, M.A. 1950; Ohio State University, Columbus, Ph.D. 1955. Served in the United States Air Force, 1945-47: Sergeant. Married Martha-Jane Pierce in 1948; one son and four daughters. Professor of Literature, Antioch College, Yellow Springs, Ohio, 1953-72; Chairman of Humanities Division, College of Virgin Islands, St. Thomas, 1963-65; Director of the Center for Documentary Arts, Antioch Columbia, Columbia, Maryland, 1969-70; Poetry Columnist, *Cedar Rock*, New Braunfels, Texas, 1976-83. Since 1961, Poetry Columnist, *Writer's Digest*, Cincinnati. Recipient: Huntington Hartford Fellowship, 1959; Amy Lowell Traveling Fellowship, 1960. Address: 917 Xenia Avenue, Yellow Springs, Ohio 45387, U.S.A.

PUBLICATIONS

Verse

Light in the West. Francestown, New Hampshire, Golden Quill Press, 1962.
The Ocean's Warning to the Skin Diver and Other Love Poems. Point Richmond, California, Crown Point Press, 1964.
Serenade. Point Richmond, California, Crown Point Press, 1968.
I Never Saw.... Chicago, Whitman Press, 1974.
The Village. Hancock, Maryland, Trunk Press, 1976.
Public Domain. Hancock, Maryland, Trunk Press, 1977.
Myrtle Whimple's Sampler. Hancock, Maryland, Trunk Press, 1978.
Thirty Years of Poetry: Collected Poems 1949-1979. New Braunfels, Texas, Cedar Rock Press, 1980.
Partita in Nothing Flat. Daleville, Indiana, Barnwood Press, 1983.

Plays

Winter in Eden (produced Yellow Springs, Ohio, 1955). Included in *Plays for an Imaginary Theatre,* 1970.
The Wandering Jew (produced Yellow Springs, Ohio, 1963).
Candle in the Straw (produced St. Paul, Minnesota, 1963). Included in *Plays for an Imaginary Theatre,* 1970.
The Glass Mountain (produced St. Thomas, Virgin Islands, 1964). Included in *Plays for an Imaginary Theatre,* 1970.
Plays for an Imaginary Theatre (includes *Winter in Eden, Candle in the Straw, The Glass Mountain, Drums*). Urbana, University of Illinois Press, 1970.

Novel

The Fell of Dark. Boston, Houghton Mifflin, 1966.

Other

The Poet and the Poem.   Cincinnati, Writer's Digest, 1963;
   revised edition, 1974, 1979.
Poetry: Premeditated Art.   Boston, Houghton Mifflin, 1968.
*Culture Out of Anarchy: The Reconstruction of American
   Higher Learning.*   New York, Herder, 1970.
Families of Eden: Communes and the New Anarchism.   New
   York, Seabury Press, 1974; London, Thames and Hudson,
   1975.
Publishing Poetry.   New Braunfels, Texas, Cedar Rock Press,
   1976.
The Poet's Handbook.   Cincinnati, Writer's Digest, 1980.
On Being a Poet.   Cincinnati, Writer's Digest, 1984.

*

Judson Jerome comments:
   I believe "modernism" has had a devastating effect on contemporary poetry. By the example of my own work and through
my continuing letter to the world in *Writer's Digest* I have
endeavored to restore the art of poetry to its position of central
cultural significance by emphasizing form, clarity, communication, and other modes than the subjective lyric—such as narrative, drama, satire, and discourse. I would like to see poetry
become more accessible—and more entertaining as well as
edifying—to a larger audience than the intellectually elite.

*   *   *

   In his poetry, fiction and essays, Judson Jerome has been
examining contemporary American life in a way intended to
define possibilities of cultural order. Poetry he has described as a
vital, liberating illusion: "It is less ecstasy or rebellion or confession than a steady voice that tells a lie so completely that hearts
are moved and people live by it." This conception of poetry has
moral and aesthetic roots. It involves acknowledgement of radical human fault: "Acting/is honest, the courage to accept/our
false condition." And it emphasizes the powers of traditional
poetic techniques. Jerome has located tradition in American
poetry in the writings of Emily Dickinson, E.A. Robinson and
Robert Frost; and his own attention to technique is part of his
attempt to clarify experience. In "Cages," for example, he works
against meter to convey the limits of human freedom: "dear child
with touching hands,/night, day, age, youth, our veins,/our very
ribs, are cage."
   This interest in technique and in the magical aspect of poetry is
behind his *Plays for an Imaginary Theatre*, a collection of
related plays, essays and lyrics. The mixed format is peculiarly
appropriate to Jerome's talents as poet and critic; and the plays
themselves are lyric extravaganzas, less plays of character than
plays of ideas, of the possibilities of reconciling a radical individualism and the competing claims of communal order.
   At times in the plays, as in the poetry, the verbal facility, the
deliberate sense of artifice, approaches a kind of self-indulgence.
At its best, however, Jerome's writings, with their enthusiasm
and discipline, provide humane, clarifying insight.

—Jerry Paris

JOHNSON, Louis (Albert).   New Zealander.   Born in Wellington, 27 September 1924. Educated at Wellington Teachers'

Training College. Has three children. School teacher, 1951-54;
Editor, *New Zealand Parent and Child* magazine, 1955-59;
Assistant Editor, Department of Education School Publications
Branch, Wellington, 1963-68; Officer in Charge, Department of
Information Bureau of Literature, Port Moresby, Papua New
Guinea, 1968-69. Founding Editor, *Numbers* magazine, Wel-
lington, 1954-60; Editor, New Zealand Broadcasting Corpora-
tion Poetry programme, 1964, and "Column Comment" televi-
sion programme, 1968. Since 1970, free-lance writer. Secretary,
New Zealand P.E.N., 1954-59. Recipient: New Zealand Literary
Fund grants; New Zealand Book Award, 1976. Address: c/o
Mallinson Rendel, P.O. Box 9409, Wellington 1, New Zealand.

PUBLICATIONS

Verse

Stanza and Scene.   Wellington, Handcraft Press, 1945.
The Sun among the Ruins.   Christchurch, Pegasus Press, 1951.
Roughshod among the Lilies.   Christchurch, Pegasus Press,
   1951.
Poems Unpleasant, with Anton Vogt and James K. Bax-
   ter.   Christchurch, Pegasus Press, 1952.
*Two Poems: News of Molly Bloom, The Passionate Man and
   the Casual Man.*   Christchurch, Pegasus Press, 1955.
The Dark Glass.   Wellington, Handcraft Press, 1955.
New Worlds for Old.   Wellington, Capricorn Press, 1957.
The Night Shift: Poems on Aspects of Love, with others.   Wel-
   lington, Capricorn Press, 1957.
Bread and a Pension: Selected Poems.   Christchurch, Pegasus
   Press, 1964.
Land Like a Lizard: New Guinea Poems.   Brisbane, Jacaranda
   Press, 1970.
Onion.   Dunedin, Caveman Press, 1972.
Selected Poems.   Bathurst, New South Wales, Mitchell Col-
   lege, 1972.
Fires and Patterns.   Brisbane, Jacaranda Press, 1975.
Coming and Going.   Wellington, Mallinson Rendel, 1982.

Other

Editor, *New Zealand Poetry Yearbook 1-11.*   Wellington,
   Reed, 3 vols., 1951-53; Christchurch, Pegasus Press, 8 vols.,
   1954-64.

*

Critical Studies: *A Way of Saying* by Kendrick Smithyman,
Auckland and London, Collins, 1965; *Aspects of Poetry in New
Zealand* by James K. Baxter, Christchurch, Caxton Press, 1967.

Louis Johnson comments:
   (1970) I'm a sort of personal-liberal-existentialist of an atheis-
tic inclination.
   When I was beginning to write verse, in the early 1940's, New
Zealand was just "coming of age" in the art through the works of
Mason, Curnow, Glover, Fairburn, etc., and it seemed to me that
their "nationalism" was rather overdone, limited, and parochial,
especially since my own earlier poetic interests were people like
Auden, Yeats, Pound, men whose vision appeared unlimited by
the back fence. But from the "broad view" I turned to personal
experience, the "known and felt" thing rather than the "New
Zealand thing" as prescribed by Curnow, probing the field of
human relationships—especially between men and women, the

way we live here and now—and became known as "the poet of subtopia."

I have been concerned, in my work, with the way in which people have grown up in, and been shaped by, our small, restricted community; a great deal of the work has been written on themes of childhood and growth, the nature of reality and the manner of our illusions; there is also a strong social strain, almost political at times, in some of it.

My work has gone through several different stages of method—from an overdressed abstractionism to, recently, a direct colloquial "language as she is spoke" approach. Suddenly, in middle-age, I have found my feet as a poet in the mysteries of love; of a new volume in the process of being put together, my friend and colleague James K. Baxter said: "I didn't think any Kiwi would write love poetry like it. It's the best we've got."

*   *   *

"At the centre of it there is always a mystery," Louis Johnson wrote of the act which is a poem. "Poetry is an act of faith," he insisted at another time. "To the poet, nothing is unbelievable." The central mystery to which he refers is the imagination much as Coleridge conceived of it; the faith is faith in the potential power of imagination, as it may be for a child to whom "possibility is actual." The nominally real must be illusion; conversely, a lot of living may be disillusioning. Life is often an offence to the man able to imagine. To be adult is to be deprived, given over to a reality which endorses the probable at the expense of the possible.

Although sometimes Johnson would seem to want to appear a social realist, opinions of the kind above are at the heart of his view. He rejected a popular doctrine of the poet's obligation to respect "the reality prior to the poem" because the reality foreseen was thought to be too narrowly understood. The common impression of Johnson's vigorous, copious, ostensibly worldly poems is of writing at odds with his announced principles. His most evident engagement is with the external (or even extrinsic) show of life in a cultural province, whether urban, suburban or rural, which implies an accentuating of what is contemporary and thus peculiar because particular. He has been freely and loudly criticized because his sense of contemporary and of what he has referred to as formalism persuades him into practices which strike readers as wilful or gratuitously *farouche*. At his best he is a formalist. Disillusioned, he is a disenchanted romantic. At his most effectively contemporary—in which role he came near to founding a School—he is highly persuasive. At such times he is closest to the tradition, whether he is being a propagandist, a persuader, or a polemicist.

In 1968 Louis Johnson quit New Zealand, first for Papua New Guinea, later for southeastern Australia, and for a new wife as well. *Land Like a Lizard*, his Papua New Guinea book, works around the new wife and the new life, the moment which domestically is all promise, which publicly is confirmed in "fruit of a season/But cannot be counted except in the presence of love." The idyllic is open to qualification. In reacting to colonialism in place of a cultural provincialism Johnson began to work out for himself his own understanding of "the reality prior to the poem," to examine the conflict of the reality of primitive people or primal emotions with their own pasts and with a present which many were willing to enter, at expense to their innocence. He found a travesty of suburbia, and quit the land like a lizard. The New Guinea poems of *Fires and Patterns* are postscripts to an increasing distaste, partly distaste for himself, "Chewing at my disease," postscripts to a staging point in a new life. The book also contains poems of the closing off of his life in New Zealand. The last of these is an elegy for James K. Baxter which at its end

talks of "that final terror and burden—yourself" which is in part a burden of capacity for love. "Love is my burden too" Johnson said when he first got to New Guinea. It is a theme which recurs. Sardonically, it is the part of the white man's burden, but it is also in part the burden of history, of Emma Bovary in a tradition of one kind and of Queen Emma Coe in another kind, of the primitives and of the colonials. It affords in complex and distinct ways evidence of Johnson's reconstituting "the reality prior to the poem" more successfully than the overt reflections on history to be found in his six pieces on Captain Cook's voyage of 1769.

In 1980 Johnson returned to New Zealand after his Australian years and some travelling in Europe. His poems since his return are largely urbane, even benign, increasingly domestic. Love is less a burden, more often a comfort, especially as he contemplates the young children of his fifties. It is a less exciting poetry than formerly, and also a less venturesome craft.

—Kendrick Smithyman

JOHNSON, Ronald. American. Born in Ashland, Kansas, 25 November 1935. Educated at Columbia University, New York, B.A. 1960. Served in the United States Army, 1954-56. Poet-in-Residence, University of Kentucky, Lexington, 1970-71, and University of Washington, Seattle, 1972. Recipient: Inez Boulton Award (*Poetry*, Chicago), 1964; National Endowment for the Arts grant, 1969, 1974. Address: 73 Elgin Park, San Francisco, California 94103, U.S.A.

PUBLICATIONS

Verse

A Line of Poetry, A Row of Trees. Highlands, North Carolina, Jargon, 1964.
Assorted Jungles: Rousseau. San Francisco, Auerhahn Press, 1966.
Gorse / Goose / Rose and Other Poems. Bloomington, Indiana University Fine Arts Department, 1966.
Sunflowers. Woodchester, Glouchestershire, John Furnival, 1966.
Io and the Ox-Eye Daisy. Dunsyre, Lanarkshire, Wild Hawthorn Press, 1966.
The Book of the Green Man. New York, Norton, and London, Longman, 1967.
The Round Earth on Flat Paper. Urbana, Illinois, Finial Press, 1968.
Reading 1 and 2. Urbana, Illinois, Finial Press, 2 vols., 1968.
Valley of the Many-Colored Grasses. New York, Norton, 1969.
Balloons for Moonless Nights. Urbana, Illinois, Finial Press, 1969.
The Spirit Walks, The Rocks Will Talk. Highlands, North Carolina, Jargon, 1969.
Songs of the Earth. San Francisco, Grabhorn Hoyem, 1970.
Maze / Mane / Wane. Cambridge, Massachusetts, Pomegranate Press, 1973.
Eyes and Objects. Highlands, North Carolina, Jargon, 1976.
RADI OS I-IV. San Francisco, Sand Dollar, 1977.
Ark: The Foundations 1-33. Berkeley, California, North Point Press, 1980.
Ark 50: Spires 34-50. New York, Dutton, 1984.

Other

The Aficionado's Southwestern Cooking. Albuquerque, University of New Mexico Press, 1968.
The American Table. New York, Morrow, 1984.
Southwestern Cooking, New and Old. Albuquerque, University of New Mexico Press, 1985.

Translator, *Sports and Divertissments*, by Erik Satie. Edinburgh, Wild Hawthorn Press, 1965; Urbana, Illinois, Finial Press, 1969.

*

Manuscript Collection: University of Kansas, Lawrence.

Critical Studies: in *Vort 9* (Bloomington, Indiana).

Ronald Johnson comments:
(1970) I have been primarily infuenced by the Black Mountain "school" of poetry—i.e., Charles Olson out of Ezra Pound, Louis Zukofsky and Williams.
     To see the world in a grain of sand, to see the *word* in a grain of sand, this is where the poem begins. Thoreau questioned: "Who placed us with eyes between a microscopic and a telescopic world?" All is built from this position—a solid construct in the apparently invisible, exact words illuminating the ineffable. A grain of sand if looked at long enough waxes first as glowing, then as large as a moon. The architects tell us that large and small are a matter of placement, and that galactic and atomic are simply humming-birds within humming-birds, etc. To write a poem is to begin with words, and is it not where word becomes wor(l)d the primal poem exists? And it is only an arc from there to *whirled* and "the push of numerous humming-birds from a superior bush."
     (1974) After ten years of writing and walking out there in the trees, I have found, as William Blake knew all along, that the trees are in the head.
     (1980) I am at present at work on a three-book work titled *Ark*.

*   *   *

     To encounter Ronald Johnson's work, whether for the first or the hundredth time, is to slam against the universe and fall back dazed and changed. Intelligence is its foundation, but mystery plays an equal role. Indeed, Johnson is at home with opposites, and striking one against another is his chief technique.
     Johnson's erudition, obvious throughout his work, especially so in the highly experimental *Ark* books, may occasionally intimidate; more often, however, it inspires awe. The opening of an earlier poem exemplifies his more accessible work:

                    The Different Musics
come simultaneously
across water,
accumulating fume, spray, the flex of ripple.

As fume, from the Latin *fumus*, Greek
thymos: spirit, mind. "See

DUST, THEISM: cf.
FEBRUARY, FURY, PERFUME, THYME."

(Cf. means "compare" &

"leads to useful, interesting, or related material that is not, however, essential to an understanding of the meaning.")

     Opposites abound here: lyricism and epistemology, list and sentence, concrete image and abstraction, word and abbreviation, poetry and prose.
     "Stereopticon" may serve as an *ars poetica* of sorts:

     What we wanted

     was both words and worlds
     you could put your foot through. To be

     eye-deep in air,

     and the inside of all things
     clear

     to the horizon. Clear

     to the core.

Johnson desires the abstract ("words") and the physical ("worlds") simultaneously and to be at once within "all things" at the farthest reach ("the horizon") and at the heart of the universe ("the core"). In essence, he wishes to become the point at which opposites are united into one, and he has achieved his wish. He is able, for example, to weld seamlessly the scientific to the poetic so that one becomes dependent upon, even invigorates, the other, as in "Four Orphic Poems and Song": "Newton / —it is said—did not show the cause of an apple falling, / only the similitude between the apple / & the stars."
     However, in Johnson's work, words and space are equally important. In *RADI OS*—based on *Paradise Lost*, from which Johnson "erased" most of Milton's first four books, leaving only the words suiting his vision—word and space (i.e., wordlessness) create tension *and* meaning. Johnson's title is Milton's with six letters "erased"—*radi os*—extracting the highly technological world ("radios") from the prelapsarian while juxtaposing them. All but 13 words of Milton's first 13 lines were erased, composing: "O / tree / into the World, / Man / the chosen / Rose out of Chaos: / song." *RADI OS* beguiles, making sense despite occasional odd syntax, capitalization, or punctuation, as in: "we / build up / dream, / this place / Beyond / highth or depth, still first and last / sit we then projecting / —another World, / called Man." The epic grandeur of *Paradise Lost* has been absorbed by *RADI OS* and continues in Johnson's *Ark* books.
     When, in "Beam 28," "Voices" tell Johnson "TO GO INTO THE WORDS TO EXPAND THEM," his *Ark* volumes seem less elusive. With *RADI OS*, and an unfinished fourth book, they form a whole entitled *Wor(l)ds* and present, collectively and individually, worlds composed of words, and vice versa—the physical composed of abstractions, and vice versa. Johnson seeks "TO EXPAND" worlds / words by his presence—physical and intellectual, real and imagined—to stretch them, to create a new entity and perspective.
     The lushness of earlier volumes is evident throughout the *Ark* collections and is often counterpointed by scientific, historical, or sociological data or by "found" materials which force readers to "expand" their imaginations, as in "Beam 1:"

Clouds loom below. Pocked moon fills half the sky.   Stars
                    comb out its lumen
                         horizon
               in a gone-to-seed dandelion
          as of snowflakes hitting dark water, time, and again,

then dot the plain
186, 282 cooped up angles tall as appletrees....

His wordplay also transforms the ordinary, often with humorous results: "*daimon* diamond Monad I / Adam Kadmon in the
sky" ("Beam 10"). Johnson even challenges our concept of poetry. "Ark 38" is not a word poem, but "just over six minutes
of...songs of...birds..." taped by Johnson and broadcast by a
radio station. What we read in *Ark 50* is only the section titles
Johnson has given the birds' songs.

Regardless of his experimentalism, erudition, reliance on—
even reverence of—other texts, Johnson's is a lyric voice, at once
unique and common, strange and familiar, whose subjects are as
old as "Adam Kadmon":

I sing
the one wherein
all colors of this whirling world begin
and end.

—Jim Elledge

JOHNSTON, George (Benson). Canadian. Born in Hamil-
ton, Ontario, 7 October 1913. Educated at the University of
Toronto, B.A. 1936, M.A. 1945. Served in the Royal Canadian
Air Force, four years: Lieutenant. Married Jeanne McRae in
1944; three sons and three daughters. Assistant Professor of
English, Mount Allison University, Sackville, New Brunswick,
1946-48; Member of the English Department, Carleton University, Ottawa, 1950-79, now retired. LL.D.: Queen's University,
Kingston, Ontario, 1971; Lit.D.: Carleton University, 1979.
Address: 2590 Cook's Line, R.R.1, Athelstan, Quebec J0S
1A0, Canada.

PUBLICATIONS

Verse

The Cruising Auk.   Toronto, Oxford University Press, 1959.
Home Free.   Toronto, Oxford University Press, 1966.
Happy Enough.   Toronto, Oxford University Press, 1972.
Between.   Haworth, Yorkshire, Haworth Press, 1976.
Taking a Grip.   Ottawa, Golden Dog Press, 1979.
Auk Redivivus: Selected Poems.   Ottawa, Golden Dog Press,
1981.

Other

Editor, *Rocky Shores: An Anthology of Faroese Poetry.*   Paisley, Renfrewshire, Wilfion, 1981.

Translator, *The Saga of Gisli.*   Toronto, University of Toronto
Press, and London, Dent, 1963.
Translator, *The Faroe Islanders' Saga.*   Ottawa, Oberon Press,
1975.
Translator, *The Greenlanders' Saga.*   Ottawa, Oberon Press,
1976.
Translator, *Wind over Romsdal: Selected Poems,* by Knut
Ødegård.   Moonbeam, Ontario, Penumbra Press, 1981.

*

Critical Studies: by George Whalley, Winter 1968, Lawrence W.
Jones, Spring 1971, and D.G. Jones, Winter 1974, all in *Canadian Literature* (Vancouver).

George Johnston comments:

(1970) First volume, *The Cruising Auk,* was considered light
verse in mainly conventional forms.

Second volume, *Home Free,* is part light verse, part serious,
also largely conventional in form.

(1985) *Happy Enough* was a collected volume with a number
of new poems. Since then there have been more frequent occasional poems written in modified Old Norse metres.

*   *   *

The poetry of George Johnston, that most engaging Canadian
poet, shows itself as distinctively individual and very much of a
piece, the characteristic tone and idiom having been established
almost from the beginning. Not that it isn't difficult to define the
tone of verse which on the one side hesitates on the edge of
pathos, and on the other leans back from the brink of farce.
Perhaps we could say of it that it blends in an inimitably individual way sentiment and daftness, or flippancy and a strong central
orthodoxy. Perhaps this is no more than to say, human experience being as enigmatically complex as it is, that the poet's eye
registers nuances which the ordinary person, or just the rest of
us, loses in a blur of emotional cliché and commonsense expectation. The technique by which Johnston establishes some shade
of feeling or being varies from point to point: sometimes it may
be a grave disparity between the solemn treatment and the
ridiculous subject, as in "Noctambule":

Mr. Murple's got a dog that's long
And underslung and sort of pointed wrong;
When daylight fades and the evening lights come out
He takes him round the neighbour lawns about
To ease himself and leak against the trees
The which he does in drops and by degrees
Leaving his hoarded fluid only where
Three-legged ceremonious hairy care
Has been before and made a solemn sign.

Or it may be, as in "Fields," by the use of a bent parallel, two
stanzas laid out side by side, with a small distorting explosive in
the second; or it may be by the adoption of a certain simplicity or
even simple-mindedness of attitude as many of the poems of *The
Cruising Auk*; or it may be a neatly modulating use of repetition,
a device he uses very frequently to achieve a strikingly discon-
certing effect, as in the last stanza of "Eating Fish."

Johnston's versification is skillful in a traditional way, and
indeed the normality of his rhythms and figuration makes even
more impressive the individuality of the approach. The central
characteristic of that approach is the sort of wit which sees at
once what is the discrepant in the situation or the character. The
wit in Johnston is merely clever or sharp but issues from some
fundamental sagacity and repose. It is conveyed in diction of an
almost Chinese precision and clarity and with a tone of calm and
moderate good sense which adds to its point and sharpness.

What makes him so fine a comic poet is that his wit operates
within a certain context of desperation, the humour is played out
against a background suggestive of anxiety and distress. Like his
own Mr. Goom, "he finds he needs a drink / Or else a Turkish
bath to chase / His apperception from the brink / Of darkness to
a brighter place." Not only Mr. Goom but all his characters have

this sense of treading on the brink of darkness: Mr. Murple, Mrs. Beleek, Mrs. Belaney, Mrs. McGonigle, Miss Knit, Poor Edward and Miss Decharmes. In the same way the fantastic, which is so strong an element in his vision, works itself out against an ordinary suburban life, in a tar-warm city where people put ingenious stuff around their gardens "to baffle bugs and coax the ground":

> The call of the dufuflu bird
> For which I have an ear
> Falls like the uncreating word,
> But only some can hear.
>
> And often at the droop of day
> When evening grumbles in
> The great dufuflu has his say
> Above the braffic's din...

Graceful, pointed, odd, George Johnston's is a poetry modest in its pretension, effective in its individuality, successfully conveying a valid human vision. His universe is wry and peculiar but wholly recognisable, crazy but within everybody's competence and recognition. His poetry, in its wit, urbanity and fantasy, adds a genuinely different note to the canon of modern Canadian work.

—William Walsh

JONES, Brian. British. Born in 1938. Married; two children. Recipient: Cholmondeley Award, 1967; Gregory Award, 1968. Address: c/o Carcanet Press, 208 Corn Exchange Buildings, Manchester M4 3BQ, England.

PUBLICATIONS

Verse

Poems. London, Alan Ross, 1966.
A Family Album. London, Alan Ross, 1968.
Interior. London, Alan Ross, 1969.
The Mantis Hand and Other Poems. Gillingham, Kent, Arc, 1970.
For Mad Mary. London, London Magazine Editions, 1974.
The Spitfire on the Northern Line (for children). London, Chatto and Windus, 1975.
The Island Normal. Manchester, Carcanet, 1980.

Play

Radio Play: *The Lady with a Little Dog,* from a story by Chekhov, 1962.

* * *

Brian Jones's poetry explores a world of remembered landscapes and family routines, of household tasks and passing seasons. History is traced directly through the writer's own ancestors, the drama of their humdrum lives, or culled from headstones in country villages and anonymous rustic plays. The colloquial style he adopts is a conscious achievement, veiling as it does a mastery of structure and an astute deployment of half-rhyme. Jones's early work recalls that of Edward Thomas in such poems as "The Unlikely Stubborn Patch" and "Stripping Walls" with its self-deprecating humour. He shares with Thomas a clear, unsentimental knowledge of country life, and a pleasure in simple manual tasks—his account of cutting grass in "The Garden of a London House" shares similarities with the older poet's "Digging."

Unlike some of his contemporaries, Jones is convinced of the narrative possibilities of poetry, which he feels have yet to be developed. Some of his most ambitious efforts in this form, like "The Courtenay Play," fail to satisfy completely. While one concedes the validity of his intentions, the result in this case seems fragmented and diverse, its images over-emphasized. Similarly, the unity of *The Island Normal,* his most dense and concentrated collection to date, is not immediately apparent to the reader. This said, Jones's insistence on the extended foray justifies itself in *A Family Album,* an impressive sequence of individual portraits, each of which casts fresh light on the others. Here his narrative skill blends with an acute insight into the characters of his relatives, the mass of frailties and contradictions that render a person unique. Aunt Emily is especially memorable, not only dominating *A Family Album* but pervading several other works, among them the long title-poem of *For Mad Mary.* The same power to compel striking portrayals from domestic life is evident in *The Spitfire on the Northern Line,* an excellent volume aimed at the younger reader. In *A Family Album* and a number of shorter poems which home in on a single central incident or image, Jones is at his best. Examples of the latter include "Chopping Wood," where the passing years are seen as leading to a momentarily focused act, and the later "Church," with its contemplation of a country graveyard: "Here is the cliff-face of arrest/where good and mild and profligate/founder to a name and date/The chill comes off the stone like breath and not the cross/or altar spread/white, or words declaimed and sung/engender awe like those who once/were human, and are simply dead."

Aware of the false glamour of the countryside, which often screens an inner desolation, Jones nevertheless deplores the advance of the urban wasteland. Poems like "End of Pier" and "Return to Wasteground" note bleakly a world where piers and fairgrounds have given way to Volvo showrooms and office blocks, while "Summer Slides" depicts a Britain reduced by tourism to something between a musuem and a zoo. Commercialisation, it seems, is universal, encountered equally in the French town of Arles: "Angling a quick kill, mayfly tourist shops/stock sunflower prints and Gauguin-labelled beers/and endless shelves of bonsai chaises Van Gogh./We half-search for a stall of plastic ears."

Art, Jones informs us, has always been under threat, whether from power of the purse or sword. In previous ages Vergil and Andrew Marvell faced the same dilemma and survived. Salvation is found in the continued struggle of the poet with his craft, and the perfecting of individual relationships, given that none of us may fully know the other. Thus, in "Andrew Marvell Awaits His Charge" the poet is shown as seeing future hope in the child he educates. Similarly, Jones himself finds time to wonder at the vulnerability of his sleeping daughter, the trust embodied in her undefended bedroom: "You scatter/dreams through the world and let them take their chance./You sleep now, with the bedside lamp still glaring,/knowing your dolls still read, your gold shoes dance."

In his clarity of utterance, his evocation of the ordinary, Jones draws continually from the past while speaking directly—and often bluntly—to the reader of today. His poems lend eloquence to a common speech. He explores the familiar, and makes it memorable.

—Geoff Sadler

JONES, D(ouglas) G(ordon). Canadian. Born in Bancroft, Ontario, 1 January 1929. Educated at Grove School, Lakefield, Ontario; McGill University, Montreal, B.A. 1952; Queen's University, Kingston, Ontario, M.A. 1954. Married Monique Baril in 1976; four children from previous marriage. Lecturer, Royal Military College, Kingston, Ontario, 1954-55, Guelph Agricultural College, Ontario, 1955-61, and Bishop's University, Lennoxville, Quebec, 1961-63. Since 1963, Professeur Titulaire, English Department, University of Sherbrooke, Quebec. Recipient: President's Medal, University of Western Ontario, 1976; Governor-General's Award, 1977; A.J.M. Smith Prize, 1978. D.Litt.: Guelph University, Ontario, 1982. Address: P.O. Box 356, North Hatley, Quebec JOB 2CO, Canada.

PUBLICATIONS

Verse

Frost on the Sun. Toronto, Contact Press, 1957.
The Sun Is Axeman. Toronto, University of Toronto Press, 1961.
Phrases from Orpheus. Toronto, Oxford University Press, 1967.
Under the Thunder the Flowers Light Up the Earth. Toronto, Coach House Press, 1977.
A Throw of Particles: Selected and New Poems. Toronto, General, 1983.

Other

Butterfly on Rock: A Study of Themes and Images in Canadian Literature. Toronto, University of Toronto Press, 1970.

Translator, *The Terror of the Snows*, by Paul-Marie Lapointe. Pittsburgh, University of Pittsburgh Press, 1976.
Translator, with Marc Plourde, *Embers and Earth*, by Gaston Miron. Montreal, Guernica, 1983.

*

Critical Studies: "D.G. Jones: Etre chez soi dans le monde" by George Bowering, in *Ellipse 13* (Sherbrooke, Quebec), 1973; "The Masks of D.G. Jones" by E.D. Blodgett, in *Canadian Literature 60* (Vancouver), Spring 1974.

D.G. Jones comments:
A lyric poetry, relying heavily on a visual imagination ("rhyme of images") and on phrasing (or relationship in rhythm and sound of words to each other and to overall curve of statement) to create a line or sequence with a sense of inevitability or authority. Finally metaphysical (rather than descriptive, social, etc.) in intention. Attempts to digest for own use major influences of 20th century poetry (imagist-symbolist-metaphysical) and to connect with native Canadian tradition of two generations.

*   *   *

Verbal clarity, economy, precision, and a purity of imagery characterize the poetry of D.G. Jones. These aesthetic qualities are related to a philosophical state of mind and a quality of emotion which give the poetry an unusual consistency of tone and meaning. The relation between an "emptiness" or "barrenness" perceived in nature, on the philosophical plane (recurrent images in Jones), and an aesthetic of purity in poetry is familiar, especially in Mallarmé, and Jones can be usefully compared to the French master. Jones derives more directly from the Imagists, however, from H.D., and from Ezra Pound as critical mentor; later affinities are with Wallace Stevens and Marianne Moore. He is authentic in himself, also, and does not resemble so much as parallel these poets in general ways.

His first book, *Frost on the Sun*, already showed the taint of philosophic disenchantment and affected the shine of purity. *The Sun Is Axeman* revealed a marked advance in control and assurance and a full development of these features. Themes of silence, alienation, and emptiness recur—"a string of notes/limned on the stillness of a void"..."skeletons of trees"..."And silence like a snow is everywhere." A number of poems, with their patina of perfection, dealing with lighter subject matter—"Clotheslines," "Schoolgirls"—remind one of Gautier, the father of the aesthetes. A cosmic pessimism—"the universe bleeds into darkness"—underlies these poems.

Phrases from Orpheus is marked by personal suffering not unlike that of W.D. Snodgrass in *Heart's Needle*, but there is no further resemblance. Jones is not confessional; his book gives expression to pain and passion through the indirections of poetry, through the myth of Orpheus, through images and the incantations of symbolism, and through irony. Here "stars are not polite, and/even plants are/violent"; there is comfort in "that relatively immortal blue gas/the sky...." The poetry transcends the personal, and at its best achieves a noble indifference or stoicism that touches on the heroic without rhetoric or mannerism.

Phrases from Orpheus is a deeply moving book and one of the most important to appear in Canada in its decade. It has, unfortunately, been neglected in the hubbub created by numerous young poets appearing on the scene and by the phenomenon of popularity affecting poetry; but the book will no doubt take its place as one of the finest to appear in the fifties and sixties.

—Louis Dudek

JONES, Evan (Lloyd). Australian. Born in Melbourne, Victoria, 20 November 1931. Educated at Melbourne High School; University of Melbourne (Services' Canteen Fund Scholar, 1954-55), B.A. 1953, M.A. in history 1957; Stanford University, California (Writing Fellow, 1958-60), M.A. in English 1959. Married 1) Judith Ann Jones in 1954; 2) Margot Jones in 1966; four children. Tutor, then Senior Tutor in History, University of Melbourne, 1955-58; Lecturer in English, Australian National University, Canberra, 1960-63. Lecturer, 1964, and since 1965, Senior Lecturer in English, University of Melbourne. Address: Department of English, University of Melbourne, Parkville, Victoria 3052, Australia.

PUBLICATIONS

Verse

Inside the Whale. Melbourne, Cheshire, 1960.
Understandings. Melbourne, Melbourne University Press, 1967.
Recognitions. Canberra, Australian National University Press, 1978.
Left at the Post. St. Lucia, University of Queensland Press, 1984.

Other

Kenneth Mackenzie. Melbourne, Oxford University Press, 1969.

Editor, with Geoffrey Little, *The Poems of Kenneth Mackenzie.* Sydney, Angus and Robertson, 1972.

*

Evan Jones comments:

My poetry is characteristically highly formal in structure, diverse in diction. Forms range from the sestina to unrhymed trimeter. Early influences were a multitude of English, American and Australian poets, but especially W.H. Auden. Most poems are concerned in one way or another with the problem of maintaining or achieving coherence and equanimity in the face (as the anonymous blurb of my second book put it, rather heavy-handedly) of loneliness, separation and death: in the face of being a thinking and sentient being here and now.

*   *   *

Evan Jones must be considered one of the influential poets of his period and place: Melbourne in the late 1950's and early 1960's. *Inside the Whale* is full of student work in the once fashionable vein of what A.D. Hope calls "the discursive mode." At times, in this volume, Evan Jones almost appears to be self-parodying, as he practices older English stanzaic forms and apostrophizes the Melbourne University. Other poems, however, such as the much anthologised "Noah's Song," became key demonstrations of "the habit of irony" that pervaded University literary circles in the 1950's.

His second collection abandons this youthful donnish guise and concerns itself with a closer approach to the characteristic early adult experiences: love, marriage, estrangement. In these later poems, Evan Jones, though no longer a determinedly donnish poet, demonstrates a considerable erudition and an even more considerable command of language and cadence in a way that is always unspectacular, but often brilliantly sharp and precise. He seems to have settled into a line of quiet, reflective verse. He is, however, the sort of poet one would not be surprised to find emerge suddenly with some long and large-ranging epic after a gestation period of several years. But Jones is assured of a place in the re-animation and re-direction of Australian poetry that occurred, in Melbourne, at the end of the 1950's.

—Thomas W. Shapcott

JONES, (Morgan) Glyn. Welsh. Born in Merthyr Tydfil, Glamorgan, 28 February 1905. Educated at Castle Grammar

School, Merthyr Tydfil; St. Paul's College, Cheltenham. Married Phyllis Doreen Jones in 1935. Formerly a schoolmaster in Glamorgan; now retired. Former Vice-President, Yr Academi Gymreig (English Section). Recipient: Welsh Arts Council Prize, for non-fiction, 1969, and Premier Award, 1972. D.Litt.: University of Wales, Cardiff, 1974. Agent: Laurence Pollinger Ltd., 18 Maddox Street, London W1R 0EU, England. Address: 158 Manor Way, Whitchurch, Cardiff CF4 1RN, Wales.

PUBLICATIONS

Verse

Poems. London, Fortune Press, 1939.
The Dream of Jake Hopkins. London, Fortune Press, 1954.
Selected Poems. Llandysul, Dyfed, Gomer, 1975.

Play

The Beach of Falesá (verse libretto), music by Alun Hoddinott (produced Cardiff, 1974). London, Oxford University Press, 1974.

Novels

The Valley, The City, The Village. London, Dent, 1956.
The Learning Lark. London, Dent, 1960.
The Island of Apples. London, Dent, and New York, Day, 1965.

Short Stories

The Blue Bed. London, Cape, 1937; New York, Dutton, 1938.
The Water Music. London, Routledge, 1944.
Selected Short Stories. London, Dent, 1971.
Welsh Heirs. Llandysul, Dyfed, Gomer, 1977.

Other

The Dragon Has Two Tongues: Essays on Anglo-Welsh Writers and Writing. London, Dent, 1968.
Profiles: A Visitor's Guide to Writing in Twentieth Century Wales, with John Rowlands. Llandysul, Dyfed, Gomer, 1980.
Setting Out: A Memoir of Literary Life in Wales. Cardiff, University College Department of Extra Mural Studies, 1982.
Random Entrances to Gwyn Thomas. Cardiff, University College Press, 1982.

Editor, *Poems '76.* Llandysul, Dyfed, Gomer, 1976.

Translator, with T.J. Morgan, *The Saga of Llywarch the Old.* London, Golden Cockerel Press, 1955.
Translator, *What Is Worship?,* by E. Stanley John. Swansea, Wales for Christ Movement, 1978.
Translator, *When the Rose-bush Brings Forth Apples* (Welsh folk poetry). Gregynog, Powys, Gregynog Press, 1980.
Translator, *Honeydew on the Wormwood* (Welsh folk poetry). Gregynog, Powys, Gregynog Press, 1984.

*

Bibliography: by John and Sylvia Harris, in *Poetry Wales 19* (Bridgend, Glamorgan), nos. 3-4, 1984.

Manuscript Collection: National Library of Wales, Aberystwyth.

Critical Studies: *Glyn Jones* by Leslie Norris, Cardiff, University of Wales Press, 1973, and article by Norris in *British Novelists 1930-1959* edited by Bernard Oldsey, Detroit, Gale, 1983.

Glyn Jones comments:

I began my literary career as a poet and I hope to end it in the same way.

I believe I am usually thought of as belonging to the Anglo-Welsh group of poets, poets who are Welsh but who write in English.

The poets who have meant most to me are G.M. Hopkins, D.H. Lawrence, Walt Whitman, Dylan Thomas, plus some of the poets of my own country—I mean writers of poems in the Welsh language. I admire poets who are word- and language-conscious; but that does not mean I am indifferent to what the poet says. Hopkins appeals to me so much because I am in sympathy with his agonising over language, and I also find acceptable his subject matter and what he has to say about it.

*   *   *

Better known as a short story writer and novelist, Glyn Jones began as a poet, his first poems appearing in *The Dublin Magazine* in 1931. His critical work, *The Dragon Has Two Tongues*, reveals that not till later did he become well acquainted with the intricate rhyme-schemes and density of texture of much of the poetry in the Welsh language: the concern for *words* rather than ideas which he showed from the beginning was therefore a Welsh instinct, a natural eloquence which decorated and "blew up" the narrative line, sounding off a country of echoes on either side. Admiration for the rich and sensuous imagery of D.H. Lawrence is reflected in his earliest poems, but, this impetus exhausted, he turned to a kind of proletarian poetry, inspired by the *hen benillion* of the peasant past. Although far from the "public school communism" of the contemporary English mode, the effect of this was not very different on occasion from the new-romanticisms of Auden. Out of this windy alley grew other poems, realist rather than proletarian, "poems built up solid out of concrete nouns," strongly consonantal (a painter's poems, perhaps, for Jones applied sounds to his poem much as he would apply blocks of colour to his canvas), as "Dock":

The sky tilts suddenly, its sleety herringbone
Of pouring rain spills thick across the dock,
Shags up the furry liner's side, its blurred
Black iron cliff immense above the dock-wall,
Pelts the sheety concrete, sprawls its gusty growth
Its hiss of cold grey grass across the tingling streets.

His reading of G.M. Hopkins reinforced this development, and meetings with Dylan Thomas from 1934 onwards strengthened his view that the craft was more important than the audience, that social implications were secondary. At its least successful, his new mode of writing had a glutinous quality that could slough the reader; at its best, a distinctive glory of words and images that illuminated the greys of the natural scene ("Gull"):

Blush-feathered, frocked, above the grey-bled sea
He bears my beating heart with rosy webs,
The fire-bird, the flame-silked through the grieving sea-
   rain, swift
On hot flushed petal-flesh his flashing wings.

After 1940 he wrote much less poetry, though his smaller output included the radio ode "The Dream of Jake Hopkins" and the well-known "Merthyr," both of which made use of a humour and irony which had so far appeared only in his short stories. Novels and translations from the Welsh absorbed him, and it was 1967 before he broke poetic silence again with "Images of Light and Darkness." Unmoved by fashion, he was writing still out of that *cwm-taf* of images, that echo-making mountain of words before which his house had long stood, and the lyrical impulse was now uppermost. In "Profile of Rose" with which he opened 1969, despite its narrative line and tragic symbolism, the lyrical note is still strong:

Hair-bowed Rose, deep in lush grass of the river
Bank, watched through the crystal unflawed block of
Afternoon, broad waters of her tenth birthday
Under sunglare, bottomless ebony
Sheeted with green and shine, and elms black
Along the far brink, and the gold field
Beyond, a shallow dishful of buttercup
Liquor.

There are many who look at this "shallow dishful" wistfully and ask only that Glyn Jones shall honour his declared intention to end, as he began, by writing poetry.

—Roland Mathias

JONES, LeRoi. *See* **BARAKA, Amiri.**

JONG, Erica (née Mann). American. Born in New York City, 26 March 1942. Educated at Barnard College, New York (George Weldwood Murray Fellow, 1963), 1959-63, B.A. 1963 (Phi Beta Kappa); Columbia University, New York (Woodrow Wilson Fellow, 1964), M.A. 1965; Columbia School of Fine Arts, 1969-70. Married 1) Michael Werthman; 2) Allan Jong in 1966 (divorced, 1975); 3) the writer Jonathan Fast in 1977 (divorced, 1983), one daughter. Lecturer in English, City College of New York, 1964-66, 1969-70, and University of Maryland European Division, Heidelberg, Germany, 1967-68; Instructor in English, Manhattan Community College, New York, 1969-70. Since 1971, Instructor in Poetry, YM—YWHA Poetry Center, New York. Recipient: Bess Hokin Prize (*Poetry*, Chicago), 1971; New York State Council on the Arts grant, 1971; Madeline Sadin Award (*New York Quarterly*), 1972; Alice Fay di Castagnola Award, 1972; National Endowment for the Arts grant, 1973. Agent: Morton Janklow Associates, 598 Madison Avenue, New York, New York 10022. Address: P.O. Box 1034, Weston, Connecticut 06883, U.S.A.

PUBLICATIONS

Verse

Fruits and Vegetables. New York, Holt Rinehart, 1971; London, Secker and Warburg, 1973.
Half-Lives. New York, Holt Rinehart, 1973; London, Secker and Warburg, 1974.

Here Comes and Other Poems. New York, New American
Library, 1975.
Loveroot. New York, Holt Rinehart, 1975; London, Secker
and Warburg, 1977.
The Poetry of Erica Jong. New York, Holt Rinehart, 1976.
Selected Poems 1-2. London, Panther, 2 vols., 1977-80.
At the Edge of the Body. New York, Holt Rinehart, 1979;
London, Granada, 1981.
Ordinary Miracles: New Poems. New York, New American
Library, 1983; London, Granada, 1984.

Novels

Fear of Flying. New York, Holt Rinehart, 1973; London,
Secker and Warburg, 1974.
How to Save Your Own Life. New York, Holt Rinehart, and
London, Secker and Warburg, 1977.
*Fanny, Being the True History of the Adventures of Fanny
Hackabout-Jones.* New York, New American Library, and
London, Granada, 1980.
Parachutes and Kisses. New York, New American Library,
and London, Granada, 1984.
Megan's Book of Divorce: A Kid's Book for Adults. New
York, New American Library, 1984.

Other

Four Visions of America, with others. Santa Barbara, Cali-
fornia, Capra Press, 1977.
Witches (miscellany). New York, Abrams, 1981; London,
Granada, 1982.

*

Critical Studies: interviews in *New York Quarterly 16,* 1974,
Playboy (Chicago), September 1975, and *Viva* (New York), September 1977; by Emily Toth, in *Twentieth-Century American-
Jewish Fiction Writers* edited by Daniel Walden, Detroit, Gale,
1984.

Erica Jong comments:

(1974) Though I have been writing since childhood, my first
formal training in poetry came at Barnard College, where I
studied from 1959-63. At that time I loved the poetry of Auden,
Yeats, Keats, Byron and Alexander Pope, cultivated the command of formal verse, and developed an abiding interest in satire.
My early university poems were mostly expert, satirical and
somewhat academic. I went on to do a thesis on Alexander Pope
in Columbia's graduate English department. In my early and
mid-twenties, however, I became much more interested in
French surrealist poetry and its South American derivatives. I
came to love the poetry of Neruda and Alberti, and I learned the
value of poetry which delved deep into the unconscious and
relied on the association of images. It seems to me that these two
influences—crisp satire and an abiding belief in the importance
of unconscious material—have shaped my voice as a poet. I
believe that poetry can be serious and comic at the same time,
formal yet free. I think I was also liberated to write out of a
frankly female persona by reading the work of such poets as
Anne Sexton, Sylvia Plath, Muriel Rukeyser, Carolyn Kizer,
Adrienne Rich. It has been very important to me—both in poetry
and fiction—to write freely about women and women's sexuality. Throughout much of history, women writers have capitu-
lated to male standards, and have paid too much heed to what
Virginia Woolf calls "the angel in the house." She is that little
ghost who sits on one's shoulder while one writes and whispers,

"Be nice, don't say anything that will embarrass the family, don't
say anything your man would disapprove of...." The "angel in the
house" castrates one's creativity because it deprives one of essential honesty, and many women writers have yet to win the freedom to be honest with themselves. But once the right to honesty
has been established, we can go on to write about anything that
interests us. We need not *only* write about childbirth, menstruation and other feminist topics. I resist the subject matter fallacy in
any of its forms. Writing should not be judged on the basis of its
subject, but on the artistry with which that subject is treated. It
seems to me that all three of my published books (*Fruits and
Vegetables, Half-Lives* and *Fear of Flying*) have certain themes
in common: the search for honesty within oneself, the difficulty
of resolving the conflicting needs for security and adventure, the
necessity of seeing the world both sensuously and intelligently at
the same time. Having said all that, I should add that my views
about my writing will probably be entirely different by the time
this is printed.

*   *   *

Erica Jong's poetry places her firmly with her contemporary
female poets Carolyn Kizer, Adrienne Rich, and Diane Wakoski,
all of whom wrote "naked poetry," much of it explicitly concerned with women and women's sexuality. They also set her
poetry in the confessional mode practiced by Robert Lowell,
Sylvia Plath, and Anne Sexton. After the publication of her
novel *Fear of Flying,* Jong was hailed as the 1970's female
counterpart to J.D. Salinger. In the poetic vein, her writings
have been admired for their form, but more for their frankly
irreverent treatment of men, sex, women, and eating.

Henry Miller and Walt Whitman are the spirits behind *Loveroot.* Whitman's "Calamus" poems, his exuberant, rocking
cadences, his parallel syntactic constructions, his left-branching
sentences, and his unashamed, celebratory "Song of Myself"
inform Jong's verse. She offers him her hymn of "the body
electric":

> you were "hankering, gross, mystical, nude."
> You astonished with the odor of your armpits.
> You cocked your hat as you chose;
> you cocked your cock—
> but you knew "the Me myself"....
> The loveroot will germinate.
> The crotch will be a trellis for the vine,
>   & our threads will all be intermingled silk.

Miller's chaotic, Pantagruelian word play, his ribald accounts of
sexual athleticism, and his defiant proclamations are all felt in
Jong's poetry.

Her first two volumes of poetry offer her modern version of
William Blake's "Marriage of Heaven and Hell." "Arse Poetica,"
"Seven," and "The Commandments" in *Fruits and Vegetables*
are her equivalent to Blake's fancies, parables, and commandments. "Seventeen Warnings in Search of a Feminist Poem" and
"The Cabala According to Thomas Alva Edison" in *Half-Lives*
continues in this vein. In *Loveroot,* her debt to Blake and Miller
is of a different sort. "The Parable of the Four-Poster" fits with
the earlier poems, but the others share with Blake's and Miller's
writings in their pithiness, candor, and iconoclasm. This volume
pays homage to Jong's other mentors, Neruda, Keats, Sexton,
Plath, and Donne. *Fruits and Vegetables* in formal, chiselled
verse built poems thematically based on James Joyce's words:
"know me, come eat with me." In *Loveroot,* the mouth and
genitals are kissing, and the form is looser. The volume contains
many poems derivative of Plath's, but Jong's poem on Plath (the

second she has written) reflects her maturity and freedom from Plath's spell. Jong has a quality her mentors lack—her exuberant, affectionate, frolicking humor.

—Carol Simpson Stern

JORDAN, June.   American.   Born in New York City, 9 July 1936. Educated at Midwood High School, Brooklyn, New York; Northfield School for Girls, 1950-53; Barnard College, New York, 1953-55, 1956-57; University of Chicago, 1955-56. Married Michael Meyer in 1955 (divorced, 1966); one son. Assistant producer with the filmmaker Frederick Wiseman, 1963-64; research associate, Mobilization for Youth Inc., New York, 1965-66; English teacher, Connecticut College, New London, 1967-69, City College of New York, 1968-69, 1975-76, Sarah Lawrence College, Bronxville, New York, 1969-70, and Yale University, New Haven, Connecticut, 1974-75. Since 1981, Professor of English, State University of New York, Stony Brook. Member of the Board of Directors, Teachers and Writers Collaborative, and, since 1978, Poets and Writers; since 1980, Member of the Executive Board, P.E.N. American Center; since 1981, Member of the Executive Committee, American Writers Congress; since 1984, Member of the Board of Directors, Center for Constitutional Rights. Recipient: Rockefeller grant, 1969; American Academy in Rome Environmental Design prize, 1970; National Endowment for the Arts grant, 1981. Address: Department of English, State University of New York, Stony Brook, New York 11790, U.S.A.

PUBLICATIONS

Verse

*Some Changes.*New York, Dutton, 1971.
Poem: On Moral Leadership as a Political Dilemma (Watergate, 1973).   Detroit, Broadside Press, 1973.
New Days: Poems of Exile and Return.   New York, Emerson Hall, 1974.
Things That I Do in the Dark: Selected Poetry.   New York, Random House, 1977; revised edition, Boston, Beacon Press, 1981.
Passion: New Poems 1977-80.   Boston, Beacon Press, 1980.

Recordings: *Things That I Do in the Dark and Other Poems,* Spoken Arts, 1978; *For Somebody to Start Singing,* with Bernice Reagon, Black Box-Watershed.

Other (for children)

Who Look at Me?   New York, Crowell, 1969.
His Own Where—.   New York, Crowell, 1971.
Dry Victories.   New York, Holt Rinehart, 1972.
Fannie Lou Hamer (biography).   New York, Crowell, 1972.
New Life, New Room.   ·New York, Crowell, 1975.
Kimako's Story.   Boston, Houghton Mifflin, 1981.
Civil Wars (essays; for adults).   Boston, Beacon Press, 1981.

Editor, with Terri Bush, *The Voice of the Children.*   New York, Holt Rinehart, 1970.
Editor, *Soulscript: Afro-American Poetry.*   New York, Doubleday, 1970.

*   *   *

Poet, essayist, and author of children's fiction, June Jordan is among the most varied and prolific of contemporary Black writers. Together her works chart the artistic concerns of a poet who successfully maintains a sense of spiritual wholeness and the vision of a shared humanity, while relentlessly engaging a brutal and often brutalizing reality. The resultant combination—of courage and vulnerability—is suggested by the poem "Things That I Do in the Dark," in which the poet describes herself as a "stranger/learning to worship the strangers/around me/whoever you are/whoever I may become."

Artistically, Jordan's work shows the influences of two radically different aesthetic criteria. She has clearly been influenced by the Black Arts movement, the cultural arm of the Black Power movement of the 1970's, whose tenets require the work of art to address itself to a Black audience, explore the complexities of Black life, and work towards the building of an autonomous, vital Black culture. In subject matter, theme, and idiom, many of Jordan's poems evidence these tendencies. In others, however, she seems at one with current trends in mainstream American poetry. These poems are intensely personal, syntactically experimental, thematically elusive.

The underlying unity of Jordan's work lies in its uncompromising humanism, eloquently expressed in the historically allusive chronicle, "Who Look at Me," in which the speaker, sometimes a single Black, sometimes Blacks as a group, characterizes the search of African-Americans for visibility as "the search to find/a fatherhood a mothering of mind/a multimillion multicolored mirror/of an honest humankind," and their militance as, ultimately, a rejection of "a carnival run by freaks/who take a life/and tie it terrible/behind my back." The poet's own militance does not end with the political and social struggles of Blacks. She is keenly aware of the dehumanizing effects of economic exploitation ("Nowadays the Heroes" and "47,000 Windows"), as well as of the abuses of power too easily committed by government ("To My Sister Ethel Ennis" and "Poem Against the State [Of Things]").

Feminist concerns are poignantly expressed in the lyrical "Getting Down to Get Over," which celebrates the unique and often solitary role of the Black woman, who is "A full/Black/glorious/a purple rose...a shell with the moanin/of ages inside her/a hungry one feedin the folk/what they need." In the anguished "From an Uprooted Condition," the speaker, in quiet frenzy, ponders "the right way the womanly expression/of the infinitive that fights/infinity/*to abort?*" And finally, the precarious position of all women—in a world dominated by men—is effectively portrayed in "On Declining Values."

Despite their profusion, there is an underlying pessimism to Jordan's love poems. The central problem is not the inherent transitoriness of romantic love, a fact which the poet quietly acknowledges in "On a New Year's Eve." Rather, she seems to suggest that love's true enemy is a harsh and merciless reality. Thus, in "The Wedding," "the early wed Tyrone/and his Dizzella" are doomed before their life together begins, for they are "brave enough/but only two." And in poems such as "Shortsong from My Heart," "West Coast Episode," and "On Your Love" relationships are deemed temporary havens, brief respites. Reality, in the form of an impersonal, troubling, often hostile world, always hovers in the background. It is that larger world which, inevitably, reclaims the individual, and perhaps this poet, as its own.

—Saundra Towns

JOSEPH, Jenny (Jenefer Ruth Joseph).   British.   Born in Birmingham, Warwickshire, 7 May 1932. Educated at St. Hilda's College, Oxford, 1950-53, B.A. 1953. Reporter, Westminster Press Provincial Newspapers, in mid-1950's; Lecturer in extramural and adult education departments. Recipient: Eric Gregory Award, 1962; Cholmondeley Award, 1975; Arts Council grant, 1976. Agent: John Johnson, 45-47 Clerkenwell Green, London EC1R OHT. Address: 25 Myrtle Road, London W3 6DY, England.

PUBLICATIONS

Verse

The Unlooked-For Season.   Northwood, Middlesex, Scorpion Press, 1960.
Rose in the Afternoon and Other Poems.   London, Dent, 1974.
The Thinking Heart.   London, Secker and Warburg, 1978.
Descartes.   London, Secker and Warburg, 1983.

Fiction

Persephone.   Newcastle upon Tyne, Bloodaxe, 1984.

Other (for children)

Nursery Series (*Boots, Wheels, Water, Wind, Tea, Sunday*).   London, Constable, 6 vols., 1966-68.

*

Jenny Joseph comments:
    It is usually easier for a writer to talk about what he or she is interested in doing "now" or "next" than about what has been done. Work already published is there for all to see, and off the writer's hands. However, I will try to put down some of the things that have interested me in other writers—not that I would claim to be like them.
    I am interested in the use of the speaking voice, not merely to provide a "realistic" character for dramatic monologues, but as material, recognizable straight away on one level to the reader, in the musical use of language.
    Poetry, it seems to me, is not a novel manqué or a play manqué or a piece of music manqué or a line of philosophic inquiry manqué, but it should be able to deal with the material that goes into all of these. What I think I am doing at the moment is trying to gain enough mastery over structure—mostly in longish poems—to be able to include a wide range of material and give it a unity of tone.
    A book I finished in the summer of 1979 which I had been considering for many years is written in prose and verse. The "story-line" goes through the verse passages, the "atmosphere" is in the prose pieces which are a collection of different voices; the tone of the particular literary style chosen is meant to reflect the personality of the voice and so be part of the meaning. The book, called *Persephone*, was published in 1984.
    I think my poetry is fairly full of references to the surfaces of the world and contains a certain amount of enquiry into the questions of reality. "Art" and "artificial" are words which to me are closely allied—art forms a separate world which to have any point must always feed through roots in non-art, just as language must depend on something that is not language for its life.

*   *   *

    After reading English at Oxford, Jenny Joseph went to South Africa for a couple of years, returning to London in 1959. If in her first pamphlet collection, *The Unlooked-For Season*, there are few poems commenting on her period of residence in South Africa, certainly the experience was not without its impact upon her:

> I do not go near
> The station at such times for there are too many
> People who go home.
> Usually it is the season before the storms
> And had I not, long since, lost all tears
> I could weep enough to bring on thunder.

This feeling of exile, of loss, permeates the whole collection—she dwells upon desertion, abandonment, and death, lost or ruined houses, lost landscapes, deserted seaside towns and abandoned beaches. "Burial" features the burying of a dead seabird by four children. When she explores myths she turns, as Orpheus turned, to the loss of Eurydice. Even when a gold wrist watch is "Recovered from the Sea," it is on the "unloved body" of a middle-aged woman cast up on the shore—"The dead machine survived her beating heart." The background season to most of these poems is Winter. Summer is conceived as the "unlooked-for season," as an "amnesty." Already in these early poems, though, Joseph demonstrated her exceptional descriptive gifts and her capacity to organize her material.
    Published 14 years later, *Rose in the Afternoon* is less structured and employs a more colloquial language which, in a curious way, is appropriate to her work, fusing thought and emotion; and the descriptive gifts are now directed to the people, situations, and incidents related to the urban scene and used to more effective purpose. It is as if she had turned her gaze from the distant perspective to focus upon the oddities of normal everyday life. The direct encounter with the subject and the honesty in expression are extremely satisfying. "Warning," which describes how eccentric she expects to become when she grows old, was selected for the *Oxford Book of Twentieth Century Verse*; but "Old Man Going," a complementary poem, is equally outstanding:

> I don't mind what you do with the bits when I'm dead
> When you take off this ruddy drip and fold up the tubes
> And wheel away the catheter, for the last time Thank God,
> And let my stinking body rot in its uraemia
> There will not be any of it I want honoured.

A somewhat different attitude to that expressed in *The Unlooked-For Season*. Indeed, even the attitude to the season itself has changed:

> Perhaps our happiness is like this summer
> Holding, corrupting, laying on the air
> A sweet narcotic, making the plums fall
> Squelchy, ripe, tasteless when they lie too long.

Admittedly this is taken from one of the love poems which, while revealing a new aspect of the poet's personality, lose nothing in novelty of approach. There are some quite exciting poems in this collection, among them "To Keep Each Other Warm," "Language Teaching: Naming," "Old Man Going," "Certain Weathers," and "No Map Available"; but "Thoughts on Oxford Street from Provence and Elsewhere" is Joseph's most ambitious poem so far.

Though it contains some fascinating poems, *The Thinking Heart*, with its paradoxical title, seems to denote a period of indecision. In some of the poems there is more intricate use of simile, metaphor, and allegory and yet, as if conscious of this development, there is also the "Life and Turgid Times of a Citizen" with its almost deliberate and provocative proem "Against Metaphor":

I am not going to talk to you about islands
Or about waving grasses...
Oh no, if I want to say louse, pig or bastard,
That people are bullies and likely to watch others fall
On these broken pavements, and never lend a hand
Except to keep themselves up, I should say their names.

Well, sometimes she does say their names, however indelicate, and sometimes she doesn't, depending on her mood and intention. Her title, for instance, is taken from "Centrepiece: St. Sebastian," clearly an allegorical poem. In some poems she is concerned with the philosophical problems which have a bearing upon personal behaviour ("Love and Justice," "Trying to Understand Violence") or ironies and paradoxes of the human predicament, and in others she is content merely to talk aloud to herself about the trivia of encounters with tradesmen or doing the family wash. This volume marks a turning point; it will be interesting to see where she goes from here.

—Howard Sergeant

JUSTICE, Donald (Rodney). American. Born in Miami, Florida, 12 August 1925. Educated at the University of Miami, B.A. 1945; University of North Carolina, Chapel Hill, M.A. 1947; Stanford University, California, 1947-48; University of Iowa, Iowa City (Rockefeller grant, 1954), Ph.D. 1954. Married Jean Ross in 1947; one son. Visiting Assistant Professor, University of Missouri, Columbia, 1955-56; Assistant Professor, Hamline University, St. Paul, Minnesota, 1956-57; Lecturer, 1957-59, Assistant Professor, 1959-63, and Associate Professor, 1963-66, University of Iowa; Associate Professor, and Professor, Syracuse University, New York, 1966-70; Visiting Professor, University of California, Irvine, 1970-71; Professor of English, University of Iowa, 1971-82. Since 1982, Professor of English, University of Florida, Gainesville. Poet-in-Residence, Reed College, Portland, Oregon, 1962; Bain-Swiggett Lecturer, Princeton University, New Jersey, 1976; Visiting Professor, University of Virginia, Charlottesville, 1980. Recipient: Rockefeller grant, 1954; Lamont Poetry Selection Award, 1959; Inez Boulton Prize, 1960, and Harriet Monroe Memorial Prize, 1965 (*Poetry*, Chicago); Ford Fellowship, in theatre, 1964; National Endowment for the Arts grant, 1967, 1973, 1980; American Academy award, 1974; Guggenheim Fellowship, 1976; Pulitzer Prize, 1980. Address: Department of English, University of Florida, Gainesville, Florida 32611, U.S.A.

PUBLICATIONS

Verse

The Summer Anniversaries. Middletown, Connecticut, Wesleyan University Press, 1960.
A Local Storm. Iowa City, Stone Wall Press, 1963.

Night Light. Middletown, Connecticut, Wesleyan University Press, 1967.
Four Poets, with others. Pella, Iowa, C.U.I. Press, 1967.
Sixteen Poems. Iowa City, Stone Wall Press, 1970.
From a Notebook. Iowa City, Seamark Press, 1972.
Departures. New York, Atheneum, 1973.
Selected Poems. New York, Atheneum, 1979; London, Anvil Press Poetry, 1980.

Other

Platonic Scripts. Ann Arbor, University of Michigan Press, 1984.

Editor, *The Collected Poems of Weldon Kees.* Iowa City, Stone Wall Press, 1960; revised edition, Lincoln, University of Nebraska Press, 1975.
Editor, with Paul Engle and Henri Coulette, *Midland.* New York, Random House, 1961.
Editor, with Alexander Aspel, *Contemporary French Poetry.* Ann Arbor, University of Michigan Press, 1965.
Editor, *Syracuse Poems 1968.* Syracuse, New York, Syracuse University Department of English, 1968.

Translator, *L'Homme qui se ferme/The Man Closing Up*, by Guillevic. Iowa City, Stone Wall Press, 1973.

*

Manuscript Collection: University of Delaware Library, Dover.

Critical Studies: *Alone with America* by Richard Howard, New York, Atheneum, 1969, London, Thames and Hudson, 1970, revised edition, Atheneum, 1980; "On Donald Justice" by Greg Simon, in *American Poetry Review* 5 (Philadelphia), no. 2, 1976.

*   *   *

Donald Justice's modest, almost cautious, output sets him apart from many of his contemporaries; it is also a conscious demonstration of the care and craft which go into the making of his elegant and masterly poems. His three books of original poems, *The Summer Anniversaries*, *Night Light*, and *Departures*, could at last be seen as the achievement they always were when his *Selected Poems* (which also included previously uncollected work) was published.

Justice is one of America's most subtle and sure poets. He can achieve effects few others have the imagination, nerve, or skill to bring off. Moreover, his emotional and technical range is far wider than his output would have us believe; and the chief tool with which he achieves what he does is a transparent technique of quite awesome comprehensiveness always at the service of thought and feeling. He is above all else an artist with a near faultless ear and understanding of the sensitive perceptions which may be captured in words. An example might be "Memory of a Porch" which accommodates the "thin, skeletal music" of a wind chime as well as the "sighing of ferns/Half asleep in their boxes."

In contrast to much of his work is the early celebrated "Counting the Mad," a bizarre parody on the children's nursery rhyme "This Little Piggy" transposed to a lunatic asylum:

This one was put in a jacket,
This one was sent home,
This one was given bread and meat

But would eat none,
And this one cried No No No No
All day long.

Justice's formal skill and an inherent lack of egotism combine and enable him to perform small masterpieces in complex stanza forms; as in his poem "Variations for Two Pianos" for the pianist Thomas Higgins, which is itself a variation on the villanelle:

There is no music now in all Arkansas.
Higgins is gone, taking both his pianos.

Movers dismantled the instruments, away
Sped the vans. The first detour untuned the strings.
There is no music now in all Arkansas.

Or there is his "Sestina: Here in Katmandu," a poem which, through the extended metaphor of ascending and descending a mountain, explores how we all desire the opposite of what we have.

Justice is a noted translator from the French and it may be that his work has been influenced by his acquaintance with French literature as well as that of his native American and shared British traditions.

Another poem, "Early Poems," ironically comments on the early poems of poets generally. The metaphor this time is of a small town seen as a poem:

How fashionably sad those early poems are!
On their clipped lawns and hedges the snows fall.
Rains beat against the tarpaulins of their porches,
Where, Sunday mornings, the bored children sprawl,
Reading the comics before their parents rise.
—The rhymes, the meters, how they paralyze.

It is characteristic that Justice, a poet of formidable skill (as demonstrated in the poem) should feel free to be self-deprecating when many a poet with half his talent would defend himself to the last. Perhaps his quiet confidence dispels any need to assume the self-conscious identity of "poet"; and this, allied to his lack of pretension, has allowed his gifts to develop and broaden. His riddling poem titled simply "Poem" might almost be addressed to himself as well as his readers:

This poem is not addressed to you.
You may come into it briefly,
But no one will find you here, no one.
You will have changed before the poem will.

Quite different again is "First Death," a sequence of poems on the death of a grandmother; far from indulging an emotion, they instead create the emotion in the reader through the objective correlative of a sensitive recording of specific memories at the time of the event. Justice writes extremely well on memory without forcing his personality on us. The sensuous collage of another poem, "Thinking about the Past," is moving precisely because the personal memories are recorded without elaboration or (again) self-indulgence; so they somehow exist as actual images of relevance to all of us as well:

Certain moments will never change, nor stop being—
My mother's face all smiles, all wrinkles soon;
The rock wall building, built, collapsed then, fallen;
Our upright loosening downward slowly out of tune—

When many a larger name of today has slipped permanently

from view we will still read Donald Justice who has produced the real thing all along quite unobrusively in our midst over the last 25 years.

—Jonathan Barker

KANDEL, Lenore. American. Born in New York City. Educated at Los Angeles City College; New School for Social Research, New York, 3 years. Since 1960 has lived in San Francisco. Recipient: Borestone Mountain Poetry Award, 1962.

PUBLICATIONS

Verse

A Passing Dragon. Studio City, California, Three Penny Press, 1959.
A Passing Dragon Seen Again. Studio City, California, Three Penny Press, 1959.
An Exquisite Navel. Studio City, California, Three Penny Press, 1959.
The Love Book. San Francisco, Stolen Paper Review Editions, 1966.
Word Alchemy. New York, Grove Press, 1967.

*

Lenore Kandel comments:
Major theme—awareness of it all. Awareness of same as characteristic subjects—the creature and the planet, the angel and the star. Forms—as the subject demands. Sources—as above. Influences—as above. Devices—clarity that flies.

*   *   *

Lenore Kandel is an amazing lady who seems to have vanished from the public world of literature at the height of her success. Her most noted work is *The Love Book*—a passionate and explicit work which in turn became a *cause célèbre*. Its strong erotic content was perhaps even more provocative to the prurient and blue-nose alike because it was written by a woman celebrating love-making in an active voice, the voice usually relegated to the male poet: "[*The Love Book*] deals with physical love and the invocation, recognition, and acceptance of the divinity in man through the medium of physical love. In other words, it feels good. It feels so good that you can step outside your private ego and share the grace of the universe. This simple and rather self-evident statement, enlarged and exampled poetically, raised a furor difficult to believe...." *The Love Book* is a marvelously balanced hymn of praise and ascension and remains her most fully-realized accomplishment. Like *Dark Brown* by Michael McClure, *The Love Book* attempts to create an erotic and positive physical love poetry unique in American literaure.

Her only other collection, *Word Alchemy*, is a selection of shorter poems written from 1960 to 1967. It is uneven in its voice and strength. The most satisfying poems are those which combine precision, wit and sensitivity. For instance, "Melody for Married Men":

I like to watch the young girls walk
swinging their hips and hair
swinging their hopes and dreams in magic circles
they never walk alone, but move in twos and threes
confiding audacities to each other
twitching their tails and giggling
while thirty year old men watch from their windows
drinking coffee with their wives and making fantasies
of Moslem heaven

or this excerpt from "Spring 61":

yesterday we went to the ocean and prised mussels
from low-tide rocks
cooked them with onion   carrots   celery seed
   (delicious)
cut fingers healed in sea water...

reflect her ability to translate material into forthright and clear language. Many other poems in the collection have the tendency to become strident and break into areas of prose and polemic and lose power because of a lessening of attention to transformative language.

—David Meltzer

KAVANAGH, P(atrick) J(oseph Gregory).   British.   Born in Worthing, Sussex, 6 January 1931. Educated at the Douai School; Lycée Jaccard, Lausanne; Merton College, Oxford, M.A. Married 1) Sally Philipps in 1957 (died, 1958); 2) Catherine Ward in 1965; two sons. Lecturer, University of Indonesia, Jakarta; staff member, British Council, 1957-59; actor, 1969-70. Recipient: Richard Hillary Memorial Prize, 1966; *Guardian* Fiction Prize, 1969. Address: Sparrowthorn, Elkstone, Cheltenham, Gloucestershire, England.

PUBLICATIONS

Verse

One and One.   London, Heinemann, 1959.
On the Way to the Depot.   London, Chatto and Windus-Hogarth Press, 1967.
About Time.   London, Chatto and Windus-Hogarth Press, 1970.
Edward Thomas in Heaven.   London, Chatto and Windus-Hogarth Press, 1974.
Life Before Death.   London, Chatto and Windus-Hogarth Press, 1979.
Real Sky.   Andoversford, Berkshire, Whittington Press, 1980.
Selected Poems.   London, Chatto and Windus, 1982.

Plays

Television Plays: *William Cowper Lived Here* (documentary), 1971; *Journey Through Summer* (documentary), 1973; *Paradise in a Dream* (documentary), 1981; *Scarf Jack,* from his own novel, 1981.

Novels

A Song and Dance.   London, Chatto and Windus, 1968.
A Happy Man.   London, Chatto and Windus, 1972.
People and Weather.   London, Calder, 1978; New York, Riverrun, 1980.
The Irish Captain.   New York, Doubleday, 1979.

Other

The Perfect Stranger (autobiography).   London, Chatto and Windus, 1966.
Scarf Jack (for children).   London, Bodley Head, 1978.
Rebel for Good (for children).   London, Bodley Head, 1980.

Editor, *Collected Poems of Ivor Gurney.*   Oxford, Oxford University Press, 1982; New York, Oxford University Press, 1983.
Editor, with James Michie, *The Oxford Book of Short Poems.* Oxford, Oxford University Press, 1985.

*   *   *

As a poet P.J. Kavanagh is a difficult case—which means that he is interesting. Although skilled in the use of free rhythms and thoroughly professional in his procedures, he has nothing like the robustness to be considered as a major poet, and the content of his work shows no development—but to be a good minor poet has always been an achievement. How good is he? His main fault, and it is a serious one, has been well stated by a critic: "...the final impression, despite [his] neat descriptiveness, is of someone being a little too breezy in his acceptance, with a slightly maddening optimism." Kavanagh is a television entertainer, a failed comedian and a whimsy-sentimental purveyor of middlebrow travelogues: this presumably pot-boiling aspect show up, which it should not, in his verse. And yet he loves nature and is exceedingly accurate in his descriptions of it. What he has learned from Edward Thomas, Andrew Young, Edmund Blunden and others has been well assimilated. But something happened between his admittedly immature early poetry and his later (if not perhaps, his latest) work: incompetently equipped to deal with suffering as a young poet, he was none the less prepared to confront it; now that he is competently equipped his poetry might actually be described as a series of exercises in how to avoid it. If no other way will do, he is prepared to be deliberately banal or sentimental.

Yet when all this has been said—and it has to be said—Kavanagh is imaginative, intelligent and has a fine sense of delicacy. Occasionally, too, he can be angry—and when he is, he is very effective. An example is his sharp satire on the simple-minded Bardic posturings of Ted Hughes in "The Famous Poet," who, while snarling "right in the teeth of Life's snarl" does not really manifest quite the same attitude towards

Two charabancs
Of Poetry Students in summery clothes necking and laughing.
In dove-light he watches them straighten their clothes and faces,
Thrilled, soon, to frown in the presence of Truth.

Furthermore, Kavanagh's poetry, though it shows no intellectual advance, has consistently improved: observation increasingly takes the place of sentimentality (the habit of giggling banality has not yet been shed), and the rhythms are stronger and more confident. "Commuter" (this, like "The Famous Poet," is from *Edward Thomas in Heaven*) may even be seen as an oblique attempt to avoid the fault of "maddening optimism":

what it observes is by no means "breezy" in that manner which has become too notoriously associated with this poet. Broad description of "an open station platform in the Dordogne" narrows to the sinister precision of:

the rest of us waited, standing beside our cases.
When it arrived she left him and climbed on the train
Her face like dawn because of their conversation.
She suddenly turned, grabbed his neck in the crook of her arm,
Gave him the bones of her head, the bones of her body, violently,
Then climbed on again alone. Her face hardened
In seconds as the train moved away from her island.
Tight lipped she looked around for a seat on the sea.

This clearly demonstrates that Kavanagh is not a person who does not understand or has not seen suffering; his problem is rather to "place" it in his poetry. It should not be implied that it is his duty to indulge it—rather that he should not pretend it away. His poetry shows some signs that he is concerned to purge away its false elements.

—Martin Seymour-Smith

KEARNS, Lionel (John). Canadian. Born in Nelson, British Columbia, 16 February 1937. Educated at the University of British Columbia, Vancouver, B.A. in English 1961, M.A. 1964; School of Oriental and African Studies, University of London, 1964-65. Married to Gerri Sinclair (second marriage); four children. Since 1966, Member of the Department, currently Professor of English, Simon Fraser University, Burnaby, British Columbia. Recipient: Canada Council fellowship, 1964, 1965, and grant, 1968, 1973. Address: 1616 Charles Street, Vancouver, British Columbia V5l 2T3, Canada.

PUBLICATIONS

Verse

Songs of Circumstance. Vancouver, Tish Press, 1963.
Listen George. Montreal, Imago Press, 1965.
Pointing. Toronto, Ryerson Press, 1967.
By the Light of the Silvery McLune: Media Parables, Poems, Signs, Gestures, and Other Assaults on the Interface. Vancouver, Daylight Press, 1969.
About Time. Prince George, British Columbia, Caladonia, 1974.
Two Poems for a Manitoulin Island Canada Day. Vancouver, Blewointmentpress, 1976.
Practicing Up to Be Human. Toronto, Coach House Press, 1978.
Ignoring the Bomb: New and Selected Poems. Lantzville, British Columbia, Oolichan, 1982; Flushing, New York, Cross Country Press, 1983.
Convergences. Toronto, Coach House Press, 1984.

Film-Poems, with Gordon Payne: *The Birth of God,* 1973; *Negotiating a New Canadian Constitution,* 1974.

*

Critical Study: "Metaphysic in Time: The Poetry of Lionel

Kearns," in *A Way with Words* by George Bowering, Ottawa, Oberon Press, 1982.

Lionel Kearns comments:
A poem is a piece of language designed to have particular effect. Like any piece of art, it is life sharpened into a point, and so capable of penetrating with its message right into your heart. Of course, some messages are more important than others.
I am currently studying the interconnections between poetry, computers, and consciousness.

*   *   *

"Poems represent a spontaneous projection of my own concern at any particular moment," Lionel Kearns wrote about the verse in his first large-scale book, *Pointing.* The poems are clever and sometimes private. "Recall," for instance, ends: "They will perceive only/an insignificant/hiss of words/in the wind." In "Poet as Salesman" he seems at odds with inner life. "Anguish," he writes, "want some?"

Kearns's other major book is *By the Light of the Silvery McLune,* and the pun on the name of the Toronto media pundit Marshal McLuhan is a clue to the kind of poems that are in the book. From a poet concerned with semantics and semiology, Kearns has become a poet concerned with performance and effect. In this book are shaggy-dog poems, essentially stand-up comic routines, like "Telephone," which begins: "After completing his call/Roderick discovered/the phone-booth had no door." It ends, many pages later, on this note: "so that today/no one knows whether Roderick/is living or dead."

Perhaps it is possible to see in Kearns's work—which has so far only touched the surface of an imaginative world of its own making—an intelligence at work that will radically alter the relationship of the reader and the writer. One direction he might move in is into a West Coast Surrealism. At present he remains what George Bowering has dubbed him: "Lionel Kearns, the linguistic poet."

—John Robert Colombo

KELL, Richard (Alexander). British. Born in Youghal, County Cork, Ireland, 1 November 1927. Educated at Methodist College, Belfast; Wesley College, Dublin, 1944-46; Trinity College, Dublin, B.A. (honours) in English and French literature 1952. Married Muriel Adelaide Nairn in 1953 (died, 1975); two sons and two daughters. Assistant Teacher, Kilkenny College, Ireland, and Whinney Bank School, Middlesborough, Lancashire; Assistant Librarian, Luton Public Library, Bedfordshire, 1954-56, and Brunel College of Technology, Uxbridge, Middlesex, 1956-59; Assistant Lecturer, 1960-65, and Lecturer in English, 1966-70, Isleworth Polytechnic, London; Senior Lecturer in English, Newcastle upon Tyne Polytechnic, 1970-83. Address: 18 Rectory Grove, Gosforth, Newcastle upon Tyne NE3 1AL, England.

PUBLICATIONS

Verse

(Poems). Oxford, Fantasy Press, 1957.

Control Tower. London, Chatto and Windus-Hogarth Press, 1962.
Six Irish Poets, with others, edited by Robin Skelton. London, Oxford University Press, 1962.
Differences. London, Chatto and Windus-Hogarth Press, 1969.
Humours. Sunderland, Ceolfrith, 1978.
Heartwood. Newcastle upon Tyne, Northern House, 1978.
The Broken Circle. Sunderland, Ceolfrith, 1981.
Wall, with others, edited by Noel Connor. Brampton, Cumbria, LYC Press, 1981.

*

Manuscript Collection: Literary and Philosophical Society Library, Newcastle upon Tyne.

Richard Kell comments:

(1970) The poems in *Control Tower*, largely reflective and descriptive, were written without any awareness of a predominant theme; in retrospect, however, it appears that one of my main concerns was the opposition between negative and positive states (restraint and freedom, deprivation and fulfillment, apathy and love, scepticism and faith, inner blindness and vision), often with a note of regret for the elusiveness of the second. Though some aspect of the theme itself was implied fairly frequently, the experiences that represented it were varied—ranging from the sight of some empty coal carts to a meditation focused on the image of a Buddhist goddess. In *Differences*, the same kind of dichotomy emerges, but with an emphasis on harmony and conflict as concomitants of diversity. As for technique, I like to combine fairly well-defined verse forms—of many types, and not necessarily traditional—with rhythmic flexibility. In the choice and syntactic ordering of words I aim at intelligibility as well as imaginative precision (which does not preclude double meanings when these are useful). In general my poetry tends to be quiet and controlled rather than effusive: I love freedom but am distrustful of excess.

(1980) The poems in *Humours*, written in 1964 and 1965, and printed with accompanying pictures by Dick Ward, are concerned with familiar human dispositions, states of mind, beliefs, practices. These are often presented symbolically, and the style is dry and witty (broadly speaking) rather than lyrical. By contrast, the poems in *Heartwood* express personal feeling in a fairly direct way. They were written in memory of my wife, who died in a swimming accident in 1975.

(1985) *The Broken Circle* contains several poems of disenchantment in which the "negative and positive states" referred to above are associated with religious themes. "The Dancers" explores the possibility that aesthetic experience and artistic creation may be more meaningful witnesses to the Logos than formal religion. This poem is in five parts (not four, as a printer's error suggests): the last part begins "May they rest in peace."

*   *   *

Richard Kell was a slow developer, for his first collection, *Control Tower*, did not appear until he was thirty-five. It suggested that Kell was a Movement poet with a slight Irish accent. The hint of Yeats's tower in the title might be fortuitous, but there is a stronger echo in "The Swan" (one of Kell's best poems) which recalls another favourite Yeatsian emblem: "Cumbrous wings whacking the startled air/ And terror swirls the surface of the lake." But Kell avoids an emphatic Yeatsian rhetoric, and a more immediate model is a quieter poet, Robert Graves, whose

influence is apparent in "Citadels." Kell's qualities, as revealed in *Control Tower*, were those of several other British poets of the 1950's: formal skill and a satisfying precision of statement, plus a tendency to comment on experience rather than to explore it from within, and a comparatively narrow emotional range. There was also a tendency, ultimately derived from Auden, to lean heavily on a highly charged abstraction such as "love": "Down the long approach/ Of love, to love's darkness." But Kell's most positive quality was his capacity to render experience in clear visual images and a firm draughtsmanlike line.

In *Differences* Kell extended his range to take in new and less immediate areas of experience, such as dreams and Homeric myths. There were slightly fewer poems of sharp visual observation, tied to particular places or occasions, though the pervasive intelligence and the technical accomplishment were still evident. Of Kell's later poetry, *Heartwood* is outstanding, a moving but carefully wrought sequence of lyrics in memory of the poet's dead wife.

—Bernard Bergonzi

KELLY, Robert. American. Born in Brooklyn, New York, 24 September 1935. Educated at the City College of New York, A.B. 1955; Columbia University, New York, 1955-58. Translator, Continental Translation Service, New York, 1956-58; Lecturer in English, Wagner College, New York, 1960-61. Instructor in German, 1961-62, Instructor in English, 1962-64, Assistant Professor, 1964-69, Associate Professor, 1969-74, since 1974, Professor of English and since 1981, Director of Poetry, Avery Graduate School of the Arts, Bard College, Annandale-on-Hudson, New York. Assistant Professor of English, State University of New York, Buffalo, Summer 1964; Visiting Lecturer, Tufts University, Medford, Massachusetts, 1966-67; Poet-in-Residence, California Institute of Technology, Pasadena, 1971-72, University of Kansas, Lawrence, 1975, and Dickinson College, Carlisle, Pennsylvania, 1976. Editor, *Chelsea Review*, New York, 1958-60; Founding Editor, with George Economou, *Trobar* magazine, 1960-64, and Trobar Books, 1962-64, New York; Contributing Editor, *Caterpillar*, New York, 1969-73; Editor, *Los 1*, 1977. Since 1963, Editor, *Matter* magazine and Matter publishing company, New York, later Annandale-on-Hudson, New York; Contributing Editor, *Alcheringa: Ethnopoetics*, New York, since 1977, and *Sulfur*, Pasadena, California, since 1981. Recipient: New York City Writers Conference Fellowship, 1967; Los Angeles *Times* Book Prize, 1980. Address: Department of English, Bard College, Annandale-on-Hudson, New York 12504, U.S.A.

PUBLICATIONS

Verse

Armed Descent. New York, Hawks Well Press, 1961.
Her Body Against Time (bilingual edition). Mexico City, El Corno Emplumado, 1963.
Round Dances. New York, Trobar, 1964.
Tabula. Lawrence, Kansas, Dialogue Press, 1964.
Enstasy. Annandale-on-Hudson, New York, Matter, 1964.
Matter/Fact/Sheet/1. Buffalo, New York, Matter, 1964.
Matter/Fact/ Sheet/2. Annandale-on-Hudson, New York, Matter, 1964.

Lunes, with *Sightings* by Jerome Rothenberg. New York, Hawks Well Press, 1964.

Lectiones. Placitas, New Mexico, Duende Press, 1965.

Words in Service. New Haven, Connecticut, Robert Lamberton, 1966.

Weeks. Mexico City, El Corno Emplumado, 1966.

Songs XXIV. Cambridge, Massachusetts, Pym Randall Press, 1967.

Twenty Poems. Annandale-on-Hudson, New York, Matter, 1967.

Devotions. Annandale-on-Hudson, New York, Salitter, 1967.

Axon Dendron Tree. Annandale-on-Hudson, New York, Matter, 1967.

Crooked Bridge Love Society. Annandale-on-Hudson, New York, Salitter, 1967.

A Joining: A Sequence for H.D. Los Angeles, Black Sparrow Press, 1967.

Alpha. Gambier, Ohio, Pothanger Press, 1968.

Finding the Measure. Los Angeles, Black Sparrow Press, 1968.

Songs I—XXX. Cambridge, Massachusetts, Pym Randall Press, 1968.

Sonnets. Los Angeles, Black Sparrow Press, 1968.

From the Common Shore, Book 5. Great Neck, New York, George Robert Minkoff, 1968.

We Are the Arbiters of Beast Desire. Berkeley, California, MBVL, 1969.

A California Journal. London, Big Venus, 1969.

The Common Shore, Books I—V: A Long Poem about America in Time. Los Angeles, Black Sparrow Press, 1969.

Kali Yuga. London, Cape Goliard Press, 1970; New York, Grossman, 1971.

Flesh: Dream: Book. Los Angeles, Black Sparrow Press, 1971.

Ralegh. Los Angeles, Black Sparrow Press, 1972.

The Pastorals. Los Angeles, Black Sparrow Press, 1972.

Reading Her Notes. Privately printed, 1972.

The Tears of Edmund Burke. Annandale-on-Hudson, New York, Printed by Helen, 1973.

Whaler Frigate Clippership. Lawrence, Kansas, Tansy, 1973.

The Mill of Particulars. Los Angeles, Black Sparrow Press, 1973.

The Belt. Storrs, University of Connecticut Library, 1974.

The Loom. Los Angeles, Black Sparrow Press, 1975.

Sixteen Odes. Santa Barbara, California, Black Sparrow Press, 1976.

The Lady of. Santa Barbara, California, Black Sparrow Press, 1977.

The Convections. Santa Barbara, California, Black Sparrow Press, 1978.

The Book of Persephone. New Paltz, New York, Treacle Press, 1978.

The Cruise of the Pnyx. Barrytown, New York, Station Hill Press, 1979.

Kill the Messenger Who Brings Bad News. Santa Barbara, California, Black Sparrow Press, 1979.

Sentence. Barrytown, New York, Station Hill Press, 1980.

The Alchemist to Mercury, edited by Jed Rasula. Richmond, California, North Atlantic, 1981.

Spiritual Exercises. Santa Barbara, California, Black Sparrow Press, 1981.

Recording: *Finding the Measure*, Black Sparrow Press, 1968.

Plays

The Well Wherein a Deer's Head Bleeds (produced New York, 1964). Published in *A Play and Two Poems*, with Diane Wakoski and Ron Loewinsohn, Los Angeles, Black Sparrow Press, 1968.

Eros and Psyche, music by Elie Yarden (produced New Paltz, New York, 1971). Privately printed, 1971.

Novels

The Scorpions. New York, Doubleday, 1967; London, Calder and Boyars, 1969.

Cities. West Newbury, Massachusetts, Frontier Press, 1971.

Short Story

Wheres. Santa Barbara, California, Black Sparrow Press, 1978.

Other

Statement. Los Angeles, Black Sparrow Press, 1968.

In Time (essays). West Newbury, Massachusetts, Frontier Press, 1971.

Sulphur. Privately printed, 1972.

A Line of Sight. Los Angeles, Black Sparrow Press, 1974.

Under Words. Santa Barbara, California, Black Sparrow Press, 1983.

Editor, with Paris Leary, *A Controversy of Poets: An Anthology of Contemporary American Poetry*. New York, Doubleday, 1965.

Editor, *The Journals*, by Paul Blackburn. Los Angeles, Black Sparrow Press, 1975.

*

Manuscript Collection: Kent State University, Ohio.

Critical Studies: by Paul Blackburn, in *Kulchur* (New York), 1962; *American Poetry from the Puritans to the Present*, by Hyatt Waggoner, Boston, Houghton Mifflin, 1968; review by Diane Wakoski, in *Poetry* (Chicago), 1972; "Robert Kelly Issue" of *Vort* (Bloomington, Indiana), 1974.

Robert Kelly comments:

What help can I give the reader who would come to my work? First, tell him it is not *my* work, only Work, itself, somehow arisen through (or in spite of) my instrumentality. My personality is its enemy, only distracts. But what is there for the reader who reads to find the man? He'll find the man. The man is always there, the stink of him, the hope and fear he confuses with himself, the beauty of him, struggle, dim intuitions of a glory that is not personal, but that only persons can inhabit and share. That we are human in the world, and share our thoughts.

And this sharing of thought, perception, is what becomes the world. The world is our shared thought.

But in language the unperceived or newly perceived can arise, to break the fabric of the ordinary consensus of our lives. News from nowhere, a new handle for an old day.

Invited to introduce my work to the general reader, never!, the *specific* reader, I rehearse for our mutual benefit two answers my work has given, and I here transcribe.

1967. Prefix to *Finding the Measure*:

> Finding the measure is finding the mantram,
> is finding the moon, as index of measure,
> is finding the moon's source;

                                    if that source
is Sun, finding the measure is finding
the natural articulation of ideas.
                                    The organism
of the macrocosm, the organism of language,
the organism of I combine in ceaseless naturing
to propagate a fourth,

                                    the poem,
                                    from their trinity.

Style is death. Finding the measure is finding
a freedom from that death, a way out, a movement
forward.
    Finding the measure is finding the
specific music of the hour,
    the synchronous
consequence of the motion of the whole world.

(Measure as distinct from meter, from any precompositional
grid or matrix super-imposed upon the fact of the poem's own
growth "under hand.")
1973. Prefix to *The Mill of Particulars:*

    Language is the only genetics.
        Field
    "in which a man is understood & understands"
        & becomes
        what he thinks,
    becomes what he says
                    following the argument.

When it is written that Hermes or Thoth invented language, it is
meant that language is itself the psychopomp, who leads the
Individuality out of Eternity into the conditioned world of Time,
a world that language makes by discussing it.

    So the hasty road
    & path of arrow
    must lead up
    from language again
                    & in language the work be done,
    work of light,
            beyond.

Through manipulation and derangement of ordinary language
(*parole*), the conditioned world is changed, weakened in its
associative links, its power to hold an unconscious world-view
(consensus) together. Eternity, which is always there, looms
beyond the grid of speech.

    I have spoken a little about my motives and my intentions. I
have not presumed to speak about the work itself, which must,
true to its name, do its own work, and try to lure the reader to
dance with it.

                    *   *   *

The work of Robert Kelly presents particular difficulties to
the reader. He is extraordinarily prolific: still under 50 he has
published more than 40 volumes, many of them fairly substantial. His work is densely allusive, frequently compressed in style
and expression. Yet it must be asserted that, more often than
not, his work rewards its reader's efforts—his reader's contribution, one might say. Naturally enough, in a poet so prolific there
are areas of weakness: *The Common Shore* fails to cohere poetically and is more patently derivative than his best work; among
recent volumes *The Book of Persephone* is somewhat disap-

pointing. Kelly has, however, also produced a series of volumes
which claim a central place in American poetry of the last
twenty-five years. My own selection would include *Finding the
Measure, Songs I-XXX, Axon Dendron Tree, The Loom, The
Mill of Particulars, The Alchemist to Mercury, Spiritual Exercises,* and *Under Words.*

    Many of his central concerns are set out in *In Time,* probably
the best point at which to begin an exploration of Kelly. For
Kelly the poet is "a scientist of holistic understanding / a scholar
/ ...to whom all data whatsoever are of use". His model poets are
Pound, Goethe, Coleridge. The poet is "the DISCOVERER OF
RELATION / redintigrator, / explorer of ultimate connection /
& connectedness in among & all." In this quest for "relation"
Kelly's major tools include the mental and symbolic processes of
Alchemy and the Hermetic tradition, geography, history and
etymology. Alchemy is a model of transformation and perception, as is the record of dream. Kelly's work is fired by a sense of
curiosity which is both intellectual and erotic. A declaration like
the following is not casual in its choice of symbols: "Since we are
men, in the human scale of time & space relationships, the
discovery is of ourselves through the visible, of the visible
through ourselves. The gateway is the visible; but we must go in."
That "entrance" is pursued through an enormously wide-
ranging examination of human culture and through a ruthlessly
honest process of self-analysis, the two being articulated (at his
best) in verse of flexible grace. This is work which constitutes a
particularly American extension of the Romantic poetry of the
Egotistical Sublime: "the subjective alone / has the value / of
transcending time. And by a paradox / of being utterly personal
/ it transcends the limitations / of cultural presupposition" (*The
Loom*). In the precision and fullness with which it records the
movements (and the ecstasies) of a particularly perceptive mind,
there resides the "utterly personal," yet transcending, quality of
Kelly's work.

                                    —Glyn Pursglove

KENNEDY, X.J. Pseudonym for Joseph Charles Kennedy.
American. Born in Dover, New Jersey, 21 August 1929. Educated at Seton Hall College, South Orange, New Jersey, B.Sc.
1950; Columbia University, New York, M.A. 1951; the Sorbonne, Paris, Cert. Litt. 1956. Served in the United States Navy,
1951-55. Married Dorothy Mintzlaff in 1962; one daughter and
four sons. Teaching Fellow, 1956-60, and Instructor, 1960-62,
University of Michigan, Ann Arbor; taught at the University of
North Carolina, Greensboro, 1962-63; Assistant Professor,
1963-67, Associate Professor, 1967-73, and Professor of English,
1973-79, Tufts University, Medford, Massachusetts. Visiting
Lecturer, Wellesley College, Massachusetts, 1964, and the University of California, Irvine, 1966-67; Bruern Fellow in American
Literature, University of Leeds, 1974-75. Poetry Editor, *Paris
Review,* Paris and New York, 1962-64. Editor, with Dorothy M.
Kennedy, *Counter/Measures* magazine, 1972-74. Recipient:
Hopwood Award, 1959; Bread Loaf Writers Conference Fellowship, 1960; Lamont Poetry Selection Award, 1961; Bess Hokin
Prize (*Poetry,* Chicago), 1961; National Endowment for the Arts
grant, 1967; Shelley Memorial Award, 1970; Guggenheim Fel-
lowship, 1973. Agent: Curtis Brown, 575 Madison Avenue, New
York, New York 10022. Address: 4 Fern Way, Bedford, Massa-
chusetts 01730, U.S.A.

PUBLICATIONS

Verse

Nude Descending a Staircase: Poems, Song, A Ballad. New York, Doubleday, 1961.
Growing into Love. New York, Doubleday, 1969.
Bulsh. Providence, Rhode Island, Burning Deck, 1970.
Breaking and Entering. London, Oxford University Press, 1972.
Emily Dickinson in Southern California. Boston, Godine, 1974.
Celebrations after the Death of John Brennan. Lincoln, Massachusetts, Penmaen Press, 1974.
Three Tenors, One Vehicle: A Book of Songs, with James E. Camp and Keith Waldrop. Columbia, Missouri, Open Places, 1975.
One Winter Night in August and Other Nonsense Jingles (for children). New York, Atheneum, 1975.
The Phantom Ice Cream Man: More Nonsense Jingles (for children). New York, Atheneum, 1979.
Did Adam Name the Vinegarroon? (for children). Boston, Godine, 1982.
French Leave: Translations. Florence, Kentucky, Robert L. Barth, 1983.
Hangover Mass. Cincinnati, Bits Press, 1984.
Cross Ties: Selected Poems. Athens, University of Georgia Press, 1985.
The Forgetful Wishing-Well (for children). New York, Atheneum, 1985.

Other

The Owlstone Crown (for children). New York, Atheneum, 1983.

Editor, with James E. Camp, *Mark Twain's Frontier.* New York, Holt Rinehart, 1963.
Editor, *An Introduction to Poetry* (textbook). Boston, Little Brown, 1966; revised edition, 1971, 1974, 1978, 1982.
Editor, with Keith Waldrop and James E. Camp, *Pegasus Descending: A Book of the Best Bad Verse.* New York, Macmillan, and London, Collier Macmillan, 1971.
Editor, *Messages: A Thematic Anthology of Poetry.* Boston, Little Brown, 1973.
Editor, *An Introduction to Fiction.* Boston, Little Brown, 1976; revised edition, 1979, 1983.
Editor, *Literature: An Introduction to Fiction, Poetry, and Drama.* Boston, Little Brown, 1976; revised edition, 1979, 1983.
Editor, *The Tygers of Wrath: Poems of Hate, Anger, and Invective.* Athens, University of Georgia Press, 1981.
Editor, with Dorothy M. Kennedy, *The Bedford Reader.* Boston, Bedford, 1982.
Editor, with Dorothy M. Kennedy, *Knock at a Star: A Child's Introduction to Poetry.* Boston, Little Brown, 1982.

*

Critical Studies: "Squibs" by Bernard Waldrop, in *Burning Deck 2* (Providence, Rhode Island), Spring 1963; "Recent Poetry: The End of an Era" by Louis L. Martz, in *Yale Review* (New Haven, Connecticut), Winter 1970; Stephen Tudor, in *Spirit* (South Orange, New Jersey), Spring 1970; Henry Taylor, in *Masterplots Annual,* New York, Salem Press, 1970; in *Times Literary Supplement* (London), 24 December 1971; M.L. Rosenthal, in *Shen-*andoah* (Lexington, Virginia), Fall 1972; David Shapiro, in *Poetry* (Chicago), July 1976; Jeffrey D. Hoeper, in *Critical Survey of Poetry* edited by Frank N. Magill, Englewood Cliffs, New Jersey, Salem Press, 1983.

X.J. Kennedy comments:
[I belong to] the Wolgamot School (group of young poets including Donald Hall, W.D. Snodgrass, and Keith Waldrop, centering around the literary historian John Barton Wolgamot, begun at the University of Michigan in the 1950's).
Nearly always write in rime and metre. Favor narratives, lyrics to be sung.

*   *   *

Nude Descending a Staircase remains one of the most remarkable first volumes of poetry written by a 20th-century author. In it X.J. Kennedy gives a *tour de force* performance, offering serious poems such as the elegy "On a Child Who Lived One Moment," lyrical poems such as the title piece about a "one woman waterfall," poems to be sung such as the clever "In a Prominent Bar in Secaucus One Day," and light verse like "King Tut." It is a book which inspired hope of even better things from Kennedy, but sadly this hope has not been borne out. Instead, Kennedy in his later work has turned to writing little but light verse, epigrams, and parodies. Of these he can be a master; for example, his "Saint Bulsh" series of couplets, about a hypocritical priest reminiscent of Yeats's Archbishop, is a triumph of bitterly acerbic hilarity. Yet too often Kennedy slips into mere cuteness and writes such lines as these: "Meter/ Is the thrust rests thrust of loins and peter/ and rime,/ to come at the same time"; and sometimes he errs in pushing a joke too far: "Emily Dickinson in Southern California" offers not one but nine parodies of Dickinson.

Kennedy's humorous work is similar to that of Auden's later verse and, like Auden, he writes tightly structured poems. In "Reading Trip" the poet is advised "*Screw prosody*" and is asked "*Why take pains/ Trimming it neat? Nobody gonna play/* That game no more.*" Kennedy, though, gladly and expertly plays the prosody game. Yet one wishes that Kennedy would take as much care in his selection of content as he does with technique. Frequently he does not, as when the delicate structure of the villanelle is wasted on the trivial thoughts of "Drivers of Diaper-Service Trucks Are Sad." Kennedy's own advice on poetry is offered in "Ars Poetica": "The goose that laid the golden egg/ Died looking up its crotch/ To find out how its sphincter worked./ Would you lay well? Don't watch." But one seldom gets any feeling of spontaneity in Kennedy's work; instead, the reader is constantly being made aware of the poet at work.

At his best, though, Kennedy can produce such a fine poem as the magnificent sonnet "Nothing in Heaven Functions as It Ought":

> Nothing in Heaven functions as it ought.
> Peter's bifocals, blindly sat on, crack;
> His gates lurch wide with the cackle of a cock,
> Not turn with a hush of gold as Milton had thought;
> Gangs of the slaughtered innocents keep huffing
> The nimbers off the Venerable Bede
> Like that of an old dandelion gone to seed;
> And the beatific choir keeps breaking up, coughing.
>
> But Hell, sleek Hell hath no freewheeling part:
> None takes his own sweet time, none quickens pace.

Ask anyone, *How come you here, poor heart?*—
And he will slot a quarter through his face
You'll hear an instant click, a tear will start
Imprinted with an abstract of his case.

Here wit and seriousness, as well as form and function, are all in harmony. In the metrical irregularity of the octet and the metrical perfection of the sestet, technique nicely mirrors theme. Kennedy's fine irony, often too rampant in his verse, is tightly controlled and quite effective here.

—Dennis Lynch

KENNELLY, (Timothy) Brendan. Irish. Born in Ballylongford, County Kerry; 17 April 1936. Educated at St. Ita's College, Tarbert, County Kerry; Trinity College, Dublin, Ph.D. 1967; Leeds University. Married Margaret O'Brien in 1969; one daughter. Junior Lecturer, 1963-66, Lecturer, 1966-69, Associate Professor, 1969-73, and since 1973, Professor of Modern Literature, Trinity College, Dublin. Guildersleeve Professor, Barnard College, New York, 1971; Cornell Professor of English Literature, Swarthmore College, Pennsylvania, 1971-72. Recipient: AE Memorial Award, 1967. Address: 19 St. Alban's Park, Sandymount, Dublin, Ireland.

PUBLICATIONS

Verse

Cast a Cold Eye, with Rudi Holzapfel. Dublin, Dolmen Press, 1959.
The Rain, The Moon, with Rudi Holzapfel. Dublin, Dolmen Press, 1961.
The Dark about Our Loves, with Rudi Holzapfel. Dublin, John Augustine, 1962.
Green Townlands, with Rudi Holzapfel. Leeds, Bibliographical Press, 1963.
Let Fall No Burning Leaf. Dublin, New Square, 1963.
My Dark Fathers. Dublin, New Square, 1964.
Up and At It. Dublin, New Square, 1965.
Collection One: Getting Up Early. Dublin, Allen Figgis, 1966.
Good Souls to Survive. Dublin, Allen Figgis, 1967.
Dream of a Black Fox. Dublin, Allen Figgis, 1968.
Selected Poems. Dublin, Allen Figgis, 1969; New York, Dutton, 1971.
A Drinking Cup: Poems from the Irish. Dublin, Allen Figgis, 1970.
Bread. Dublin, Tara Telephone, 1971.
Love-Cry. Dublin, Allen Figgis, 1972.
Salvation, The Stranger. Dublin, Tara Telephone, 1972.
The Voices: A Sequence of Poems. Dublin, Gallery Press, 1973.
Shelley in Dublin. Dublin, Dublin Magazine Press, 1974; revised edition, Dublin, Beaver Row Press, 1982.
A Kind of Trust. Dublin, Gallery Press, 1975.
New and Selected Poems, edited by Peter Fallon. Dublin, Gallery Press, 1976.
Islandman. Dublin, Profile Press, 1977.
The Visitor. Dublin, St. Beuno's Press, 1978.
A Small Light. Dublin, Gallery Press, 1979.
In Spite of the Wise. Dublin, Trinity Closet Press, 1979.

The Boats Are Home. Dublin, Gallery Press, 1980.
The House That Jack Didn't Build. Dublin, Beaver Row Press, 1982.
Cromwell. Dublin, Beaver Row Press, 1983.

Novels

The Crooked Cross. Dublin, Allen Figgis, 1963; Boston, Little Brown, 1964.
The Florentines. Dublin, Allen Figgis, 1967.

Other

Editor, *The Penguin Book of Irish Verse*. London, Penguin, 1970; revised edition, 1972, 1981.

*

Critical Studies: B.A. thesis by Antonella Ceoletta, University of Venice, 1973; M.Litt. thesis by Frances Gwynn, Trinity College, Dublin, 1974.

Brendan Kennelly comments:

I used to divide my poetry into rather facile categories, such as poems written about the countryside, poems written about the city, and poems that tried to express some sort of personal philosophy. I think now that such categories are false and I believe instead that I select appropriate images from aspects of my experience and try to use them in such a way that they express what goes on within. This involves a continued struggle to discover and develop a proper language, carefully selected from the words of the world in which I live. There is this continual battle between civilized sluggishness and sharp seeing, seeing-into. The poem is born the moment one sees into and through one's world, and when one expresses that seeing-into in a totally appropriate language. By totally appropriate I mean a language of complete alertness. As I try to write I know that I am involved in an activity which is a deliberate assertion of energy over indifference, of vitality over deadness, of excitement and ecstasy over dullness and cynicism. Yet the poem must take account of all these negatives. In fact, it must often use them as its raw material, but, by a sort of dynamic, inner alchemy of language, rhythm and image, transform those negatives into living forms.

*   *   *

Brendan Kennelly's work is characterised by a great assurance of voice, by a certainty of rhythmic form, and by a wide range of subject matter. His craftsmanship is impeccable. A poem such as "The Feeding Dark" is an object lesson in the creative counterpointing of sentence and stanza structures. "Six of One" and "Law and Order" demonstrate two very different, but equally accomplished, uses of the sonnet. "The Singing Girl Is Easy in Her Skill" shows him using the villanelle for effects of great beauty and poignancy, and, to very different effect, the same form is employed in "And Who Will Judge the Judges in Their Time." Elsewhere his free verse is vigorous and controlled.

Among his characteristic subjects one notes song itself (*In Spite of the Wise*), the inevitability and variety of human failure ("The Cherrytrees," *Shelley in Dublin*, "In Spite of the Wise"), his Irish childhood ("The Brightest of All," "The Kiss"), Irish rural landscape and life ("The Pig-killer," "Killybegs," "Carrig"), the energy of animal life ("Dream of a Black Fox," "The Feeding Dark," "Outside the Church"), and the nature of invasion and colonisation ("Six of One" and "The House That Jack Didn't Build"). *Shelley in Dublin* is not entirely successful as a public poem on (among other things) the relation of England and Ireland—it deals with Shelley's revolutionary mission to Dublin in 1812. Unusually for Kennelly there is some flatness of rhythm and a failure to vivify the personalities involved. "The House That Jack Didn't Build," on the other hand, is altogether more convincing. The two voices ("a man convinced of his own indisputable superiority and a man capable of being conquered, but also capable of resisting his conquerors") are dramatically alive, humorous and moving by turns:

> I changed all the rooms.
> This took me quite a while.
> Visitors comment on their style.
> It's simple. I do everything well,
> Not exactly, to be fair, in a spirit of love
> But with a genuine desire to improve
> Others, particularly.

and

> I have lost touch with my own language.
> Nothing is stranger to me than what is my own.
> I am an exile from myself.
> Words are stones in my mouth.
> The bones of my head are trampled on.

The capacity for the dramatic assumption of other voices, evidenced by the poems of "The House That Jack Didn't Build," lies behind the success of his "Moloney" poems and sequences such as *Islandman*. Kennelly has spoken of the use of persona as "a method of extending the self by driving out the demons of embarrassment and inhibition." Both by this means and in more purely "personal" poems, Kennelly has produced telling, and frequently very beautiful, analyses of both the specifically Irish and the universal human experience.

—Glyn Pursglove

* * *

KESSLER, Milton. American. Born in Brooklyn, New York, 9 May 1930. Educated at DeWitt Clinton High School, New York; Harvard University, Cambridge, Massachusetts; University of Buffalo, New York, B.A. (magna cum laude) 1957 (Phi Betta Kappa); University of Washington, Seattle, M.A. 1962; Ohio State University, Columbus, 1959-63. Married Sonia Berer in 1952; two sons and one daughter. Teaching Assistant, University of Washington, 1957-58; Instructor, Boston University, 1957-58, and Ohio State University, 1958-63; lecturer in English, Queens College, City University of New York, 1963-65. Associate Professor, 1965-74, Director of Creative Writing, 1973-75 and 1978-79, and since 1975, Professor of English, State University of New York, Binghamton. Visiting Professor or Lecturer, University of the Negev, Israel, 1971-72, Haifa University, Israel, Spring 1973 and Spring 1981, University of Hawaii, Honolulu, Fall 1975, Antioch International Writing Seminars, Oxford, England, summers 1977-78, Keio University, Tokyo, Spring 1978, and University of Antwerp, 1985. Co-Editor, *Choice: A Magazine of Poetry and Graphics*, Chicago and Buffalo, 1971-82. Recipient: Bread Loaf Writers Conference Robert Frost Fellowship, 1961; Yaddo grants, 1965-77; MacDowell fellowship, 1966, 1979; National Endowment for the Arts grant, 1968; State University of New York fellowship, 1969; Millay Colony

grant, 1979; Virginia Center for Creative Arts grant, 1982. Address: 25 Lincoln Avenue, Binghamton, New York 13905, U.S.A.

PUBLICATIONS

Verse

A Road Came Once. Columbus, Ohio State University Press, 1963.
Called Home. Vestal, New York, Black Bird Press, 1967.
Woodlawn North. Boston, Impressions Workshop, 1970.
Sailing Too Far. New York, Harper, 1973.
Finding Peace. Cambridge, New York, White Creek, 1975.
Sweet Dreams. Hamlin, New York, Black Bird Press, 1979.
Anniversary Gift. N.p., Aeraiocht, 1982.

Other

Translator, with Tateo Imamura, *The Random Talks of Deibutsu: The Sayings of Kosho Shimizu.* Japan, 1978.

*

Critical Study: "The Poetry of Milton Kessler" by Ralph J. Mills, Jr., in *Moons and Lion Tailes* (Minneapolis), Fall 1977.

Manuscript Collection: Lockwood Library, State University of New York, Buffalo.

Milton Kessler comments:

(1970) Poetry is my private, almost my secret life. My poetry is the home I return to or the home to which I turn.

In my poems each word is another room, sky, another voice, gesture, spiritual configuration, atmosphere, like the change in a face that experiences invisible changes in its spirit, or the changes in his body felt by an asthmatic like myself. The poem is written, is reaching, into spatial planes or densities: within my arms, across the alley, beyond the far mountain, memory or sound, into my side, on the other side of this table. All in one line. It neither follows the natural breath nor the metrical music. I dream of it as very slow, to be held forever like that revery of St. Joan's weeping face in Carl Dreyer's silent masterpiece. In the line "Grandmother/Celia/save/my/David" each word is another place, each word illuminates another surface of a globe from within, each word addresses another phase of life, even though the whole sentence seems to be a clear linear development. Of course, what I say here is a kind of fiction, the fiction I need to remember myself. I surrender myself to the poems: my impurity, my wrath, my tenderness, my confusion. Regardless of the specific situation, I want each poem to embody my whole life. The universe must and does remind me of itself as God reminded Job. I am overheard and seen through by those who are wiser. It is not a poetry of wisdom or defenses. I do not possess a returning hero's wisdom. I can't imagine telling anyone how to live his life or what poetry should be. I think of my poems as prayer. I write for a miracle; the hurt, stalled people of my poems pray for a miracle, and sometimes, in the poems, it comes to pass. I write often, perhaps too often, of my Jewish family as it moves so vulnerably through its ordinary days. I am often frightened. My poems reach for solace, for miracles, sometimes even for the comfort of acknowledged delusions.

> Now, somewhere, as if I were really holy,
> I know that my savior is lonely.

(1974) Now three or four years later there is a difference, of course. An operation on my thyroid, a year in Israel, many readings in the United States, England, and Israel, and the coming of age of my children, a change in energy and desire has formed through which I hope to be able to express the rest of my experience of life in poems. And I do now feel that I am old enough to tell people what I think, what I have learned. I want to take some action in this world that will help. I've been in correspondence with poets in prison. For my sake, for the sake of poetry, I want their work to be known. I have a title for my next book, an idea and just the first few poems so far, *American Experiments*, poems of the daily life of Americans, which is much of the life I live. I will be reflecting as well on my own past life, representative past life, especially the period of World War II. That does seem now a very long time ago, long enough to turn back to, and I do feel the pressure of the end of the century. Since 1969 four more years of war and news of war. The end of the century in sight but no end to the wars. Yet I think I am less frightened than I was then and more in touch with the flow of life.

(1980) We must try to say how things are. We must have a voice in the way things change, but we don't hear that voice until later and further when we have to wonder at what we said. My recent poems are aware of this bewildering situation, more aware.

(1985) American Poetry is not well, in part as the result of the spread of creative writing programs in American universities. Although I have had a new manuscript of poems ready for over two years I am not satisfied yet that this is the real work. Those thousands of student poems bred in creative writing workshops, written for grades and the approval of workshop participants, dim and drain the air and make me wary. I extremely admire poets like Bunting, Rakosi, and Oppen who knew when not to publish, not to write. I sense the right way for my work is longer, more inclusive poems like *Everyone Loves Children* (forthcoming), poems which capture by illusions. How wrong everything seems now. Everything we say is somehow wrong, inaccurate—even our honesty about that. Rebuke and self-rebuke. How to be honest about the doubt and confusion and yet not lose strength for facts and songs? I intend to share much new work within the next two years.

*   *   *

Milton Kessler is the kind of writer whose earnestness, whose sympathy for the people and things he writes about, wins the sympathy of his readers. If we take Jung's notion that each man orients himself primarily by one of four basic means—intellect, feeling, sensation, or intuition—it is clear that Kessler's primary mode is feeling. Most of the best poems in *A Road Came Once* are poems of strong feeling for family and for the sorrows and troubles of other people—poems like "The El-Painter's Daughter" and "The Clerk Retires." His tone is often reminiscent of a Jewish cantor's, an energetic wailing tone which conveys the feeling that any life, no matter how small it may seem, is a thing worthy of high drama.

One of the faults of Kessler's past work, however, is that sometimes his language is so lofty and dramatic that it becomes melodramatic or removed from the simple subject of the poem; it makes it seem as if he were so anxious to bring the subject to a "higher" level that the kernel, the basic incident, gets left behind on the ground. For instance, in "The Games" Kessler tries to build a father watching his football-playing son's injury into a kind of Homeric lament, but the language grows too self-consciously grand, melodramatic and obtrusive. In addition, Kessler's poems are sometimes simply obscure.

Since his first volume, Kessler has shown that he has done a great deal to overcome his difficulties with obscurity and grandiose diction. A particularly fine poem is "Songs for Paul Blackburn." His poetry also has become more fanciful on occasion, and more joyous.

—Lawrence Russ

KGOSITSILE, Keorapetse (William).   South African.   Born in Johannesburg, 19 September 1938. Educated at Madibane High School, Johannesburg, 1958; Lincoln University, Pennsylvania; University of New Hampshire, Durham; Columbia University, New York, M.A.; New School for Social Research, New York (African-American Institute Fellow). Married to Melba Kgositsile. Poet-in-Residence, North Carolina Agricultural and Technical State University, Greensboro, 1971; Lecturer in Literature, University of Nairobi, Kenya, and University of Dar es Salaam, Tanzania. African Editor-at-Large, *Black Dialogue*, San Francisco. Recipient: Conrad Kent Rivers Award, 1969; National Endowment for the Arts grant, 1969. Address: Department of Literature, University of Nairobi, P.O. Box 30197, Nairobi, Kenya.

PUBLICATIONS

Verse

Spirits Unchained.   Detroit, Broadside Press, 1969.
For Melba.   Chicago, Third World Press, 1970.
My Name Is Afrika.   New York, Doubleday, 1971.
The Present Is a Dangerous Place to Live.   Chicago, Third World Press, 1974.
Places and Bloodstains: Notes for Ipelang.   Oakland, California, Achebe, 1975.

Other

A Capsule Course in Black Poetry Writing, with others.   Detroit, Broadside Press, 1975.

Editor, *The Word Is Here: Poetry from Modern Africa.*   New York, Doubleday, 1973.

*   *   *

"Because finally things have come to this," wrotes Keorapetse Kgositsile, "White world gray grim cold turning me into a killer/ Because I love love." The lines are ironic and paradoxical. Yet, their underlying truth argues a radical and profound humanism—the key to understanding the revolutionary poetic vision of this South African-in-exile.

In Kgositsile's cosmology, love transcends Western definitions: it is not simply felt, or sung about, or sought after; nor is it an essentially individual experience. Rather, love finds its true definition in the commitment of the individual to both self and nation. For Blacks, nation is all Black people, wherever they may live; they are united by a bond forged outside of time: "Searching past the pretensions of knowledge/ We move to the meeting place/ The pulse of the beginning the end and the beginning." Thus, the subjects of his first volume of poetry, *Spirits Unchained*, are the Africans and African Americans who dedicated themselves to Black liberation. Among the most moving of the poems are the lyrical "Elegy to David Diop," and the strident "When Brown Is Black," whose hero, H. Rapp Brown, becomes the metaphor for the long awaited insurrection of the oppressed: "...Go on, brother, say it. Talk/the talk slaves are afraid to live."

Militancy softens in *For Melba*, the volume dedicated to his wife; but Kgositsile never loses sight of the larger vision. The intense anguish and joy of interpersonal love—beautiful in itself—are but stepping stones to a union whose strength and commitment will spawn the future Black nation. When, finally, in *My Name Is Afrika*, songs of celebration and love give way to exhortation, it is, again, in the interest of the long view: "Gut it is will move us from the gutter...to the rebirth of real men."

—Saundra Towns

KINNELL, Galway. American. Born in Providence, Rhode Island, 1 February 1927. Educated at Princeton University, New Jersey, A.B. 1948; University of Rochester, New York, M.A. 1949. Served in the United States Navy, 1945-46. Married to Inés Delgado de Torres; one daughter and one son. Teacher at some 20 colleges, including the University of Grenoble, Juniata College, Huntingdon, Pennsylvania, University of California, Irvine, and New York University. Field worker, Congress of Racial Equality, 1963. Recipient: Fulbright scholarship, 1955; Longview Foundation award, 1962; National Institute of Arts and Letters grant, 1962, and Medal of Merit, 1976; Guggenheim Fellowship, 1963, 1974; Bess Hokin Prize, 1965, and Eunice Tietjens Memorial Prize, 1966 (*Poetry*, Chicago); Rockefeller grant, 1967; Cecil Hemley Prize, 1968; Brandeis University Creative Arts Award, 1968; National Endowment for the Arts grant, 1969; Amy Lowell Traveling Fellowship, 1969; Shelley Memorial Award, 1972; Academy of American Poets Landon Translation Award, 1978; American Book Award, 1983; Pulitzer Prize, 1983. Member, American Academy, 1981. Address: Sheffield, Vermont 05866, U.S.A.

PUBLICATIONS

Verse

What a Kingdom It Was. Boston, Houghton Mifflin, 1960.
Flower Herding on Mount Monadnock. Boston, Houghton Mifflin, 1964.
Poems of Night. London, Rapp and Carroll, 1968.
Body Rags. Boston, Houghton Mifflin, 1968; London, Rapp and Whiting, 1969.
Far Behind Me on the Trail. New York, Profile Press, 1969.
The Hen Flower. Frensham, Surrey, Sceptre Press, 1970.
First Poems 1946-1954. Mount Horeb, Wisconsin, Perishable Press, 1970.
The Book of Nightmares. Boston, Houghton Mifflin, 1971; London, J. Jay, 1978.
The Shoes of Wandering. Mount Horeb, Wisconsin, Perishable Press, 1971.
The Avenue Bearing the Initial of Christ into the New World: Poems 1946-1964. Boston, Houghton Mifflin, 1974.
Three Poems. New York, Phoenix Book Shop, 1976.
Brother of My Heart. Canberra, Open Door Press, 1977.
Fergus Falling. Newark, Vermont, Janus Press, 1979.

There Are Things I Tell to No One. New York, Nadja, 1979.
Two Poems. Newark, Vermont, Janus Press, 1979.
Mortal Acts, Mortal Words. Boston, Houghton Mifflin, 1980.
The Last Hiding Places of Snow. New York, Red Ozier Press, 1980.
Angling, A Day, and Other Poems. Concord, New Hampshire, William B. Ewert, 1980.
Selected Poems. Boston, Houghton Mifflin, 1982; London, Secker and Warburg, 1984.
The Fundamental Project of Technology. Concord, New Hampshire, William B. Ewert, 1983.

Recordings: *Today's Poets 5*, with others, Folkways; *The Poetry and Voice of Galway Kinnell*, Caedmon, 1976.

Novel

Black Light. Boston, Houghton Mifflin, 1966; London, Hart Davis, 1967; revised edition, Berkeley, California, North Point Press, 1980.

Other

3 Self-Evaluations, with Anthony Ostroff and Winfield Townley Scott. Beloit, Wisconsin, Beloit Poetry Journal, 1953.
The Poetics of the Physical World. Fort Collins, Colorado State University, 1969.
Walking Down the Stairs: Selections from Interviews. Ann Arbor, University of Michigan Press, 1978.
How the Alligator Missed Breakfast (for children). Boston, Houghton Mifflin, 1982.
Thoughts Occasioned by the Most Insignificant of Human Events. Concord, New Hampshire, William B. Ewert, 1982.
Remarks on Accepting the American Book Award. Concord, New Hampshire, William B. Ewert, 1984.

Translator, *Bitter Victory*, by René Hardy. New York, Doubleday, and London, Hamish Hamilton, 1956.
Translator, *Pre-Columbian Ceramics*, by Henri Lehmann. London, Elek, 1962.
Translator, *The Poems of François Villon.* New York, New American Library, 1965.
Translator, *On the Motion and Immobility of Douve*, by Yves Bonnefoy. Athens, Ohio University Press, 1968.
Translator, *The Lackawanna Elegy*, by Yvan Goll. Fremont, Michigan, Sumac Press, 1970.
Translator, *The Poems of François Villon.* Boston, Houghton Mifflin, 1977.
Translator, *Poems*, by Villon. Hanover, New Hampshire, University Press of New England, 1982.

*

Bibliography: *Galway Kinnell: A Bibliography and Index of His Published Works and Criticism of Them*, Potsdam, New York, State University College Frederick W. Crumb Memorial Library, 1968; by William B. Ewert and Barbara A. White, in *American Book Collector* (Arlington Heights, Illinois), July-August 1984.

*   *   *

Galway Kinnell's poems attempt to strike a delicate and unique balance among the urge to express the emotions of the private self, the need to identify with the creatures of the natural world, the wish to take a stance on public issues, and the obligation to discover a means of understanding the mortality of all creatures. Kinnell has been able to maintain this balance by developing an idiom that is carefully controlled. Precise language and spare, exact imagery characterize his poems.

Like many of his contemporaries, Kinnell has attempted to develop the poetic explorations of Robert Lowell and Theodore Roethke in order to learn how the breakthroughs of these poets can form a basis for a poetry that serves the needs of the final third of the 20th century. His own innovations have led him to abandon the intricate, allusive, and sometimes dense structures that characterized the works of the school of Eliot and Pound. His poems have avoided studied ambiguity; he has risked directness of address, precision of imagery, and experiments with surrealistic situations and images.

The first two collections, *First Poems, 1946-1954* and *What a Kingdom It Was*, employed intricate, traditional rhyme schemes, a practice Kinnell has increasingly abandoned in subsequent works. Like most of the later poems, these exhibit a narrative impulse and a preference for simple, uncluttered diction. Two of the best early poems, "First Song" and "To Christ Our Lord," employ the objectivity of narrative enhanced by rhyme to brilliant effects. Both are initiation poems. "First Song" tells the story of an Illinois farm boy who, after a day's demeaning labor, hears the frogs sing in a nearby pond. Joined by two neighbors, the boy accompanies the frogs' song with a primitive, homemade instrument. The music they make, accompanying these natural creatures, becomes for the boy his first intimation of the connectedness of the human and the natural world, a theme Kinnell continues to explore in all is poetry:

And into the dark in spite of a shoulder's ache
A boy's hunched body loved out of a stalk
The first song of his happiness, and the song woke
His heart into the darkness and into the sadness of joy.

This awakening, presented simply and directly, initiates the youth into the ambiguity that, for Kinnell, characterizes the human condition. The darkness becomes symbolic of our being surrounded by death, and the joy the youth learns depends on its opposite, sadness. The paradox is elementary, but it promises the thematic richness Kinnell's poems will develop.

A more extended and rewarding treatment of this theme energizes "To Christ Our Lord." This brief narrative deals with the tension between a Christian and a Darwinian perception of the world, as experienced by a young boy. Obliged to kill a bird for the Christmas dinner, the boy cannot resolve his feeling of the sacredness of the life of the bird with his animal need to kill in order to live. The snow yields tracks of elk and wolves, so the message of nature is that we must kill in order to survive. After the bird has been cooked, his family approves his action: "Now the grace praised his wicked act." The boy cannot reconcile this praise from his family with the guilt he felt when he shot the creature:

He had not wanted to shoot. The sound
Of wings beating into the hushed air
Had stirred his love, and his fingers
Froze in his gloves, and he wondered,
Famishing, could he fire? Then he fired.

The poem ends on an ambivalent note. The boy goes out after dinner and experiences a vision, in which the constellation the Swan becomes an emblem for the bird he killed and the Saviour whose Birth the day celebrates: "Then the Swan spread her wings, cross of the cold north,/The pattern and mirror of the acts of earth." The boy feels the intuition of the spiritual presence

in creation, but this intuition does not cancel out the need to prey on the creatures so that man may survive.

Kinnell's work does not provide easy answers, because his work has led him to distrust simple answers to complex problems. He continues to write effective poems about animals in order to explore the complex relations we form with creation. Two of his frequently anthologized poems, "The Bear" and "The Porcupine," employ a flexible narrative form to deal with the same theme. About these animals, Kinnell told an interviewer, "I've wanted to see them in themselves and also to see their closeness to us." Each poem is organized around a movement from violence on the animal to identification with the animal as the victim of human cruelty. "The Porcupine" vividly describes the shooting of the creature and its painful, prolonged death. As the poem ends, the speaker experiences imaginative empathy with the porcupine's suffering and recognizes that it is a "Blank/template of myself."

"The Bear" treats even more directly the process by which the killer becomes empathic with his victim. The speaker, an Eskimo, tells of his deliberate and brutal strategy to kill a bear. He sharpened a wolf's rib and hid it in blubber; when the bear ate the blubber, it punctured the linings of its stomach; thus began a death that lasted seven days. The hunter follows the bear these seven days, "living by now on bear blood alone," finds the dead bear, and disembowels it. To protect himself against the cold, he crawls inside the carcass, where he has a dream of total identification with the sufferings of this bear—a predicament the speaker has himself created. Awakening, the Eskimo is changed by the experience of his cruelty to nature, and is therefore able to sympathize with the life cycle of man's victims.

Kinnell's longer poems address the problem of finding personal integrity in a world torn by secularism, war, and the loss of the ideal of human justice. These poems, beginning with "The Avenue Bearing the Initial of Christ into the New World," through the book-length *The Book of Nightmares*, employ a distinctive meditational structure composed of a variety of spatially or sequentially superimposed images. "The Avenue" contains 14 unequal sections, most of which are images and impressions of the despair of the old, the blacks, Puerto Ricans, Jews, bag ladies, and vendors who inhabit Avenue C in New York City. The background for these impressions is the Holocaust; the epigraph, in German, recalls the gas ovens, and section 11 contains a form letter mailed by the Commandant of one of the death camps. The point of this association of the death camps with Avenue C is that each represents the failed promise of human society. The camps were intentional violations of that promise, whereas Avenue C represents an accidental violation. The poor and despairing on Avenue C suffer and die because of neglect: "The promise was broken too freely/To them and their fathers, for them to care."

Effective imagery communicates directly the frustrations of these forgotten citizens, whose only deliverance is death. Even death is denied the metaphysical consolation it held for Walt Whitman, but the poem echoes "Out of the Cradle Endlessly Rocking" to remind us that in the comprehensive world Whitman loved, death was completion and deliverance:

Maybe it is as the poet said,
And the soul turns to thee
O vast and well-veiled Death
And the body gratefully nestles close to thee—

The consolation is less convincing than it was to Whitman, and for the victims of "This God-forsaken Avenue bearing the initial of Christ/Through the haste and carelessness of the ages," death is less a transcendence than an escape.

Mortality is also the concern of *The Book of Nightmares*, a book composed of ten related poems, each in turn containing seven sections. This carefully crafted poem addresses the poet's children, and constitutes an inspiring effort to explain human mortality to those we bring into this world of suffering and death. Echoing Wordsworth ironically, the poet explains his infant daughter's waking fears:

> And yet perhaps this is the reason you cry,
> this is the nightmare you wake from:
> being forever
> in the pre-trembling of a house that falls.

The child's intimations of mortality cannot be answered, and they actually intensify the poet's own anxiety. The dilemma of existence cannot be resolved, but the book is an effort to provide at least an alternative. Love is Kinnell's answer to mortality, but love means confronting the facts of physical existence directly and honestly. To his daughter he offers the legacy of honest modern parents: "And then [when she is reminded of her mortality]/you shall open/this book, even if it is the book of nightmares." The mortal, loving parent cannot offer answers. But he can leave behind a legacy of love and an attempt to explain the world as it is.

At his best, Kinnell is a poet who confronts the dilemma of mortality directly. His poetry communicates the urgency of love in the face of our mortality. As Kinnell says in the recent "Goodbye," a poem addressed to his dying mother, "It is written in our hearts, the emptiness is all./That is how we have learned, the embrace is all."

—David C. Dougherty

KINSELLA, Thomas. Irish. Born in Dublin, 4 May 1928. Educated at O'Connells, Dublin; University College, Dublin. Married Eleanor Walsh in 1955; two daughters and one son. Worked in the Irish Civil Service, 1946-65, retired from the Department of Finance as Assistant Principal Officer. Writer-in-Residence, 1965-67, and Professor of English, 1967-70, Southern Illinois University, Carbondale. Since 1970, Professor of English, Temple University, Philadelphia. Director, Dolmen Press, Dublin, and Cuala Press, Dublin; Founder, Peppercanister publishers, Dublin, 1972. Artistic Director, Lyric Players Theatre, Belfast. Recipient: Guinness Award, 1958; Irish Arts Council Award, 1961; Denis Devlin Memorial Award, 1967, 1970; Guggenheim Fellowship, 1968, 1971; Before Columbus Foundation award, 1983. D.Litt.: National University of Ireland, Dublin, 1984. Member, Irish Academy of Letters, 1965. Address: Department of English, Temple University, Philadelphia, Pennsylvania, 19122, U.S.A.; or, c/o Peppercanister, 47 Percy Place, Dublin 4, Ireland.

PUBLICATIONS

Verse

The Starlit Eye. Dublin, Dolmen Press, 1952.
Three Legendary Sonnets. Dublin, Dolmen Press, 1952.
The Death of a Queen. Dublin, Dolmen Press, 1956.
Poems. Dublin, Dolmen Press, 1956.

Another September. Dublin, Dolmen Press, and Philadelphia, Dufour, 1958; revised edition, Dolmen Press, and London, Oxford University Press, 1962.
Moralities. Dublin, Dolmen Press, 1960.
Poems and Translations. New York, Atheneum, 1961.
Downstream. Dublin, Dolmen Press, 1962.
Six Irish Poets, with others, edited by Robin Skelton. London and New York, Oxford University Press, 1962,
Wormwood. Dublin, Dolmen Press, 1966.
Nightwalker. Dublin, Dolmen Press, 1967.
Nightwalker and Other Poems. Dublin, Dolmen Press, London, Oxford University Press, and New York, Knopf, 1968.
Poems, with Douglas Livingstone and Anne Sexton. London and New York, Oxford University Press, 1968.
Tear. Cambridge, Massachusetts, Pym Randall Press, 1969.
Butcher's Dozen. Dublin, Peppercanister, 1972.
A Selected Life. Dublin, Peppercanister, 1972.
Finistere. Dublin, Dolmen Press, 1972.
Notes from the Land of the Dead and Other Poems. Dublin, Cuala Press, 1972; New York, Random House, 1973.
New Poems 1973. Dublin, Dolmen Press, 1973; London, Oxford University Press, 1976.
Selected Poems 1956-1968. Dublin, Dolmen Press, and London, Oxford University Press, 1973.
Vertical Man. Dublin, Peppercanister, 1973.
The Good Fight. Dublin, Peppercanister, 1973.
One. Dublin, Peppercanister, 1974.
A Technical Supplement. Dublin, Peppercanister, 1976.
Song of the Night and Other Poems. Dublin, Peppercanister, 1978.
The Messenger. Dublin, Peppercanister, 1978.
Fifteen Dead. Dublin, Dolmen Press, and London, Oxford University Press, 1979.
One and Other Poems. Dublin, Dolmen Press, and London, Oxford University Press, 1979.
Peppercanister Poems 1972-1978. Winston-Salem, North Carolina, Wake Forest University Press, 1979.
Poems 1956-1973. Winston-Salem, North Carolina, Wake Forest University Press, 1979.
One Fond Embrace. Dublin, Gallery Press, and Hatfield, Massachusetts, Deerfield Press, 1981.

Other

Davis, Mangan, Ferguson? Tradition and the Irish Writer, with W.B. Yeats. Dublin, Dolmen Press, 1970.

Editor, *Selected Poems of Austin Clarke*. Dublin, Dolmen Press, 1976.
Editor, *Our Musical Heritage*, by Seán Ó Riada. Dublin, Dolmen Press, 1982.

Translator, *The Breastplate of St. Patrick*. Dublin, Dolmen Press, 1954; as *Faeth Fiadha: The Breastplate of St. Patrick*, 1957.
Translator, *Longes mac n-Usnig, Being The Exile and Death of the Sons of Usnech*. Dublin, Dolmen Press, 1954.
Translator, *Thirty Three Triads, Translated from the XII Century Irish*. Dublin, Dolmen Press, 1955.
Translator, *The Tain*. Dublin, Dolmen Press, 1969; London and New York, Oxford University Press, 1970.
Translator, with Sean O Tuama, *An Duanaire: 1600-1900: Poems of the Dispossessed*. Dublin, Dolmen Press, and Philadelphia, University of Pennsylvania Press, 1981.

*

Bibliography: by Hensley Woodbridge, in *Eire-Ireland* (St. Paul, Minnesota), 1966.

Critical Studies: *The New Poets: American and British Poetry since World War II* by M.L. Rosenthal, New York and London, Oxford University Press, 1967; "Thomas Kinsella Issue" of *The Hollins Critic* (Hollins College, Virginia), iv, 4, 1968; "The Poetry of Thomas Kinsella" by Robin Skelton, in *Eire-Ireland* (St. Paul, Minnesota), iv, 1, 1968; *Eight Contemporary Poets* by Calvin Bedient, London and New York, Oxford University Press, 1974; *The Poetry of Thomas Kinsella* by Maurice Harmon, Dublin, Wolfhound Press, 1974, Atlantic Highlands, New Jersey, Humanities Press, 1975.

Thomas Kinsella comments:

It is my aim to elicit order from significant experience, with a view to acceptance on the basis of some kind of understanding. Major themes are love, death and the artistic act. Methods various and developing.

*   *   *

Early Thomas Kinsella might be described as an intellectual troubadour, his desire to sing increasingly crossed by a need to explain. In his first book, *Poems*, traditional love lyrics, like "Soft to Your Places" and "Midsummer," were balanced by others like "Ulysses," where a dense vocabulary was pressed into the service of a still emerging vision. It was the elegant world of Richard Wilbur, with a metaphysical twist and an Irish music.

Another September represented a more thorough cultivation of the same private garden. The romantic dandy is still in evidence ("Fifth Sunday after Easter") but his presence does not unduly impede Kinsella's clarification of his main theme: an obsession with time. Its expression varies from the conventional ballad stanzas of "In the Ringwood," based on the Irish *aisling* or vision poem,

> Dread, a grey devourer,
> Stalks in the shade of love.
> The dark that dogs our feet
> Eats what is sickened of.
> The End that stalks Beginning
> Hurries home its drove,

to the more analytic pose of "Baggot Street Deserta," with the poet, against his favourite backdrop of nocturnal Dublin, declaring that we must "endure and let the present punish."

The principal reproach that might be levelled against *Another September* is that the poems were not sufficiently anchored in time and place. But a less remote quality was evident towards the end of the collection, especially in the sombre "Thinking of Mr. D." And in his second major collection, Kinsella emerges clearly as a *persona* with the "pious clerkly" hand of "Priest and Emperor" now leading to the dejected face which gazes into "A Mirror in February":

> Now plainly in the mirror of my soul
> I read that I have looked my last on youth
> And little more; for they are not made whole
> That reach the age of Christ.

Downstream can be said to mark Kinsella's change of gear from lyric to meditative; as he says in "Time's Mischief": "He

must progress/Who fabricates a path, though all about/Death, Woman, Spring, repeat their first success." The most noticeable change is his determination to grapple with public themes, from the local history and politics of "A Country Walk" to the problem of Hiroshima in "Old Harry." Perhaps too deliberately, for in the latter poem Truman is dignified with a moral complexity alien to his character, while the most striking effects are lavished on the atom bomb's destruction of "the notorious cities of the plain."

The same determination flows over into *Nightwalker*, the title poem of which exposes the moral vacuum of modern Ireland. But the monologue technique and diction are still close to early Eliot, and like "Chrysalides" and "Dick King" in *Downstream*, only the more private poems catch Kinsella's distinctive quality. The sequence on marital love, "Wormwood," is heavy with portentousness, but contains at least one poem, "First Light," where despair is crystallised, drop by terrible drop. And there are some moving attempts to face the problem of physical suffering ("Our Mother"):

> The girl whimpers in bed, remote
> Under the anaesthetic still.
> She sleeps on her new knowledge, a bride
> With bowels burning and disarrayed.

This vision of life as ordeal is more fully enunciated in the magnificently romantic intimacies of the long poem, "Phoenix Park." As well as a celebration of married love, it is also a farewell to his native Dublin, and one waited to see how America would affect Kinsella's work. For with his seriousness of purpose, and strength of intellect, went a Parnassian quality which could only benefit from a more experimental poetic climate. His translation of the early Irish epic, *The Táin*, does not wholly succeed in "making it new," but "A Hand of Solo" and "Hen Woman," parts of a new poetic sequence, show a relaxing of technique which augured well. "Notes from the Land of the Dead" is incorporated in *New Poems 1973* which, with *Selected Poems 1956-1968*, amounted to a new definition of his career. But he also established a private press, for broadsides like *Butcher's Dozen* and his meditation on John F. Kennedy, *The Good Fight*. So his career presents the paradox of definitive achievement and increasing adventurousness, a strong combination. The private and public life, love and waste, these were the antimonies that engaged Kinsella's intensely serious gaze, but the way he has extended his territory again in *One* and *Fifteen Dead* makes later Kinsella one of the darkest, strongest, least accommodating poets around, with a rare integrity.

—John Montague

KIRKUP, James (Falconer). British. Born in South Shields, County Durham, 23 April 1923. Educated at South Shields High School; Durham University, B.A. 1941. Gregory Fellow in Poetry, Leeds University, 1950-52; Visiting Poet and Head of the Department of English, Bath Academy of Art, Corsham, Wiltshire, 1953-56; travelling lecturer, Swedish Ministry of Education, Stockholm, 1956-57; Professor of English, University of Salamanca, Spain, 1957-58, and Tohoku University, Sendai, Japan, 1959-61; Lecturer in English Literature, University of Malaya, Kuala Lumpur, 1961-62; Professor of English Literature, Nagoya University, Japan, 1969-72. Since 1963, Professor of English Literature, Japan Women's University, Tokyo. Professor of English Literature and Poet-in-Residence, Amherst College, Massachusetts, 1968; Arts Council Creative Writer, University of Sheffield, 1974-75; Morton Visiting Professor, Ohio University, Athens, 1975-76; Dramatist-in-Residence, Sherman Theatre, Cardiff, 1976-77. Since 1977, Professor of English Literature, Kyoto University of Foreign Studies. Literary Editor, *Orient/West Magazine*, Tokyo, 1963-64; Founder, *Poetry Nippon*, Nagoya, 1966. Recipient: Atlantic-Rockefeller Award, 1950; Japan P.E.N. Club International Literary prize, 1965; Batchelder Award, for translation, 1968; Keats Prize, 1974. Fellow, Royal Society of Literature, 1962. Address: BM-Box 2870, London WC1N 3XX, England; or, Tenjin Haitsu 2-502, 1-13 Hachijogaoka, Nagaokakyo-shi, Kyoto-Fu 617, Japan.

PUBLICATIONS

Verse

Indications, with John Ormond and John Bayliss. London, Grey Walls Press, 1942.
The Cosmic Shape: An Interpretation of Myth and Legend with Three Poems and Lyrics, with Ross Nichols. London, Forge Press, 1946.
The Drowned Sailor and Other Poems. London, Grey Walls Press, 1947.
The Submerged Village and Other Poems. London, Oxford University Press, 1951.
The Creation. Hull, Lotus Press, 1951.
A Correct Compassion and Other Poems. London, Oxford University Press, 1952.
A Spring Journey and Other Poems of 1952-1953. London, Oxford University Press, 1954.
The Descent into the Cave and Other Poems. London, Oxford University Press, 1957.
The Prodigal Son: Poems 1956-1959. London, Oxford University Press, 1959.
The Refusal to Conform: Last and First Poems. London, Oxford University Press, 1963.
Japan Marine. Tokyo, Japan P.E.N. Club, 1965.
Paper Windows: Poems from Japan. London, Dent, 1968.
Japan Physical: A Selection, with Japanese translations by Fumiko Miura. Tokyo, Kenkyusha, 1969.
White Shadows, Black Shadows: Poems of Peace and War. London, Dent, 1970.
The Body Servant: Poems of Exile. London, Dent, 1971.
Broad Daylight. Frensham, Surrey, Sceptre Press, 1971.
A Bewick Bestiary. Ashington, Northumberland, MidNAG, 1971.
Transmental Vibrations. London, Covent Garden Press, 1971.
Zen Garden. Guildford, Surrey, Circle Press, 1973.
Many-Lined Poem. Sheffield, Headland Poetry, 1973.
Enlightenment. Osaka, Kyoto Editions, 1978.
Scenes from Sesshu. London, Pimlico Press, 1978.
Prick Prints. Privately printed, 1978.
Steps to the Temple. Osaka, Kyoto Editions, 1979.
Zen Contemplations. Osaka, Kyoto Editions, 1979.
The Tao of Water, with Birgit Skiöld. Guildford, Surrey, Circle Press, 1980.
Cold Mountain Poems. Osaka, Kyoto Editions, 1980.
Dengonban Messages. Osaka, Kyoto Editions, 1981.
Ecce Homo—My Pasolini. Osaka, Kyoto Editions, 1981.
No More Hiroshimas. Osaka, Kyoto Editions, 1982.
To the Ancestral North: Poems for an Autobiography. Tokyo, Asahi, 1983.

Plays

Upon This Rock: A Dramatic Chronicle of Peterborough Cathedral (produced Peterborough, 1955). London, Oxford University Press, 1955.
Masque: The Triumph of Harmony (produced London, 1955).
The True Mistery of the Nativity (televised, 1960). London and New York, Oxford University Press, 1956.
The Prince of Homburg, adaptation of a play by Heinrich von Kleist (produced New York, 1976). Published in *Classic Theatre 2*, edited by Eric Bentley, New York, Doubleday, 1959.
The True Mistery of the Passion: Adapted and Translated from the French Medieval Mystery Cycle of Arnoul and Simon Grélan (televised, 1960; produced Bristol, 1960). London and New York, Oxford University Press, 1962.
The Physicists, adaptation of a play by Dürrenmatt (produced London and New York, 1963). London, Cape, and New York, Grove Press, 1964.
The Meteor, adaptation of a play by Dürrenmatt (produced London, 1966). London, Cape, 1973; New York, Grove Press, 1974.
Play Strindberg, adaptation of a play by Dürrenmatt (produced New York, 1971; London, 1973). Chicago, Dramatic Publishing Company, n.d.
Peer Gynt, adaptation of the play by Ibsen (produced Cardiff, 1973).
The Magic Drum (for children; produced Newcastle upon Tyne, 1974; London, 1977).
Cyrano de Bergerac, adaptation of the play by Rostand (produced Newcastle upon Tyne, 1975).
The Anabaptists, Period of Grace, and *Frank the Fifth*, adaptations of plays by Dürrenmatt (produced Cardiff, 1976).
An Actor's Revenge, music by Minoru Miki (produced London, 1978). London, Faber, 1979.
Friends in Arms (produced Cardiff, 1980).
The Damask Drum, music by Paavo Heininen (produced Helsinki, 1984). Helsinki, Pan, 1984.

Radio Play: *Ghost Mother*, 1978.

Television Plays: *The Peach Garden*, 1954; *Two Pigeons Flying High*, 1955; *The True Mistery of the Passion*, 1960; *The True Mistery of the Nativity*, 1960.

Novels

The Love of Others.   London, Collins, 1962.
The Bad Boy's Bedside Book of Do-It-Yourself Sex.   Privately printed, 1978.

Other

The Only Child: An Autobiography of Infancy.   London, Collins, 1957.
Sorrows, Passions, and Alarms: An Autobiography of Childhood.   London, Collins, 1959.
These Horned Islands: A Journal of Japan.   London, Collins, and New York, Macmillan, 1962.
Tropic Temper: A Memoir of Malaya.   London, Collins, 1963.
England, Now.   Tokyo, Seibido, 1964.
Japan Industrial: Some Impressions of Japanese Industries.   Osaka, PEP, 2 vols., 1964-65.
Japan Now.   Tokyo, Seibido, 1966.
Frankly Speaking.   Tokyo, Eichosha, 1966.
Tokyo.   London, Phoenix House, and South Brunswick, New

Jersey, A.S. Barnes, 1966.

Filipinescas: Travels Through the Philippine Islands. London, Phoenix House, 1968.

Bangkok. London, Phoenix House, and South Brunswick, New Jersey, A.S. Barnes, 1968.

One Man's Russia. London, Phoenix House, 1968.

Aspects of the Short Story: Six Modern Short Stories with Commentary. Tokyo, Kaibunsha, 1969.

Streets of Asia. London, Dent, 1969.

Hong Kong and Macao. London, Dent, and South Brunswick, New Jersey, A.S. Barnes, 1970.

Japan Behind the Fan. London, Dent, 1970.

Insect Summer (for children). New York, Knopf, 1971.

The Magic Drum (for children). New York, Knopf, 1973.

Nihon Bungaku Eiyaku No Yuga Na Gijutsu (The Elegant Art of Literary Translation from Japanese to English). Tokyo, Kenkyusha, 1973.

Heaven, Hell, and Hara-Kiri: The Rise and Fall of the Japanese Superstate. London, Angus and Robertson, 1974.

America Yesterday and Today. Tokyo, Seibido, 1977.

Mother Goose's Britain. Tokyo, Asahi, 1977.

The Britishness of the British. Tokyo, Seibido, 1978.

Eibungaku Saiken (Discovery of English Literature). Tokyo, Taishukan, 1980.

Scenes from Sutcliffe: Twelve Meditations upon Photographs by Frank Meadow Sutcliffe. Osaka, Kyoto Editions, 1981.

Folktales Japanesque. Tokyo, Kenkyusha, 1982.

I Am Count Dracula. Tokyo, Asahi, 1982.

I Am Frankenstein's Monster. Tokyo, Asahi 1983.

When I Was a Child: A Study of Nursery Rhymes. Tokyo, Taibundo, 1983.

Editor, *Shepherding Winds: An Anthology of Poetry from East and West.* London, Blackie, 1969.

Editor, *Songs and Dreams: An Anthology of Poetry from East and West.* London, Blackie, 1970.

Translator, with Leopold Sirombo, *The Vision and Other Poems,* by Todja Tartschoff. London, Newman and Harris, 1953.

Translator, *Ancestral Voices,* by Doan-Vinh-Thal. London, Collins, 1956.

Translator, *Memoirs of a Dutiful Daughter,* by Simone de Beauvoir. Cleveland, World, and London, Weidenfeld and Nicolson-Deutsch, 1959.

Translator, *Don Carlo,* by Schiller, in *Classic Theatre 2,* edited by Eric Bentley. New York, Doubleday, 1959.

Translator, *The Gates of Paradise,* by Jerzy Andrzejewski. London, Weidenfeld and Nicolson, 1962.

Translator, with Oliver Rice and Abdullah Majid, *Modern Malay Verse.* London, Oxford University Press, 1963.

Translator, *My Great-Grandfather and I,* by James Krüss. London, English Universities Press, 1964.

Translator, *Immensee,* by Theodor Storm. London, Blackie, 1965.

Translator, *Tales of Hoffmann.* London, Blackie, 1966.

Translator, *Michael Kohlhaas: From an Old Chronicle.* London, Blackie, 1967.

Translator, *The Eternal Virgin,* by Paul Valéry. Tokyo, Orient Editions, 1970.

Translator, *Brand,* by Ibsen, in *The Oxford Ibsen,* edited by James Walter McFarlane. London, Oxford University Press, 1972.

Translator, with Michio Nakano, *Selected Poems of Takagi Kyozo.* Cheadle, Cheshire, Carcanet Press, 1973.

Translator, *Modern Japanese Poetry.* Brisbane, University of Queensland Press, 1978; edited by A.R. Davis, Milton Keynes, Buckinghamshire, Open University, 1979.

Translator, *The Guardian of the Word,* by Camara Laye. London, Collins, 1980; New York, Random House, 1984.

Translator, *The Bush Toads.* London, Longman, 1982.

Translator, *To the Unknown God,* by Petru Dimitriu. London, Collins, and New York, Seabury Press, 1982.

Translator, *An African in Greenland,* by Tété-Michel Kpomassie. London, Secker and Warburg, and New York, Harcourt Brace, 1983.

Translator, *Miniature Masterpieces of Kawabata Yasunari.* Tokyo, Taishukan, 1983.

*

James Kirkup comments:

Characterized by a very wide variety of themes and verse forms, including many oriental subjects and techniques. Most deeply influenced by Japanese and Chinese poetry, as well as by French. No English or American influences. Major themes: the sea, loneliness, music, painting, photography, sport, travel, the Orient, peace and war, science and space exploration, UFO's, legend, people, psychical research, medicine, satire, social criticism.

In my poetry I have attempted always to express an essence both of myself and of experience, a crystallization of my personal awareness of this world and worlds beyond. I feel I am slowly developing, after nearly 45 years of writing poetry, a voice that is only my own, and illuminating areas of experience and technique untouched by other poets. I am original, so I do not strive for originality for its own sake, or experiment with form unless the subject demands it. My aim is to be perfectly lucid yet to provide my candour with serious and mysterious undertones of sound and meaning.

*   *   *

The blurb on the dust wrapper of James Kirkup's collection *The Body Servant* includes this statement by the American poet and novelist, James Dickey: "With Kirkup's work I don't feel that facility is the problem, as it is with many writers." Certainly Kirkup sometimes gives the impression of being able to knock off a passable poem at the drop of a hat. Subject matter is never lacking: his dustbin, photographs in a railway compartment, the New Year, a pet cat, have all suggested poems. Kirkup's first collection, *The Drowned Sailor,* was published in 1947 and was very much a collection of its time in its style and language. A determined poeticism may be the best way of describing it with its peppering of enormous abstractions such as "memory's mountain" or "the candelabra of the soul." The other poets of the time (vide Wrey Gardiner's *Poetry Quarterly*) were full of such stuff as if there was an urgency to plump out otherwise flat poems, a sort of poetic padded bra'; but Kirkup was too adept at this for his own good. It was in Kirkup's second collection, *The Submerged Village,* that something distinctive was to be observed. There were still oddly old-fashioned pieces ("The Ship," "Music at Night" and "Poem for a New Year") which read like those poems the leisured gentlemen of previous centuries were so adept at "turning" as they would put it—competent, agreeable, but strangely impersonal. But among these were poems such as the title poem itself, "The Submerged Village," where it was as if the poet had taken a cool hard look at his subject and determined to deny himself the indulgence of his particular facility:

Calm, the surrounding mountains look upon
the steeple's golden cross, that still
emerges from the centre of the rising lake.
Like a sinking raft's bare mast and spar
anchored to earth by chains of stone.

The facility is still there, of course; but used to the purpose of the poem and not as a merely decorative addition.

This progress towards an individual voice and style was to flower in the next collection, *A Correct Compassion*, in which the title poem can stand with the finest poems written since the war. Here, in a poem written after watching the performance of an operation at the General Infirmary, Leeds, Kirkup combines keenly observed detail—

The glistening theatre swarms with eyes, and hands, and eyes.
On green-clothed tables, ranks of instruments transmit a sterile
    gleam.
The masks are on, and no unnecessary smile betrays
A certain tension, true concomitant of calm.

—while using the whole as a prolonged and deftly handled metaphor:

    —For this is imagination's other place,
Where only necessary things are done, with the supreme the
    grave
Dexterity that ignores technique; with proper grace
Informing a correct compassion, that performs its love, and
    makes it live.

It is as if from the controlled skill of the surgeon Kirkup has, as the poem makes clear, not only learnt something concerning the nature of art, but has found a parallel for his own technique. Another poem in this collection, "Matthew Smith," begins: "Yours, brother, is a masculine art,/The business of doing what you see." And in a sense with *A Correct Compassion* Kirkup's, too, becomes a masculine art.

It is true that the old temptations remain and "Rhapsody on a Bead Curtain" sees the facility at work wringing out to the last drop the metaphor of a bead curtain as a shower. But firmness prevails almost to the point of harshness in "Medusa": "those frog-like legs/Seem barely able to support/That sad, amorphous bum," where Kirkup is in danger of overbalancing the other way. Poems such as "The Ventriloquist," "A Visit to Brontë Land," "Photographs in a Railway Compartment," and "Summertime in Leeds" reassure us, however, that Kirkup has found his true voice:

No idle toy would have tempted Branwell
From the "Bull," and brandy; or kept that sister
From her tragic poems. They knew they had nothing but the
    moor
And themselves. It is we, who want all, who are poor.

and that he will stick to it, though tempted, like Branwell, by the "bull" as he sometimes is.

James Kirkup has published numerous collections. Some have been serious volumes, some rather more playful like *The Body Servant* with its journey over the body's parts and old chestnuts such as the part without a bone. But if, as it should be, a poet is to be remembered by his best work, then a "selected poems" for Kirkup is long overdue, if only as a show case for some of the more pleasing poems to have been written in the past decades.

—John Cotton

KIZER, Carolyn (Ashley). American. Born in Spokane, Washington, 10 December 1925. Educated at Sarah Lawrence College, Bronxville, New York, B.A. 1945; Columbia University, New York, 1945-46; University of Washington, Seattle, 1946-47. Married 1) Charles Stimson Bullitt in 1948 (divorced, 1954), two daughters and one son; 2) John Marshall Woodbridge in 1975. Founding Editor, *Poetry Northwest*, Seattle, 1959-65; State Department Specialist in Pakistan, 1964-65; Director of Literary Programs, National Endowment for the Arts, 1966-70; lecturer or poet-in-residence, University of North Carolina, Chapel Hill, 1970-74, Washington University, St. Louis, 1971, Barnard College, New York, 1972, Ohio University, Athens, 1975, and University of Iowa, Iowa City, 1976. Lives in Washington, D.C. Address: c/o Copper Canyon Press, P.O. Box 271, Port Townsend, Washington 98368, U.S.A.

PUBLICATIONS

Verse

Poems. Portland, Oregon, Portland Art Museum, 1959.
The Ungrateful Garden. Bloomington, Indiana University Press, 1961.
Five Poets of the Pacific Northwest, with others, edited by Robin Skelton. Seattle, University of Washington Press, 1964.
Knock upon Silence. New York, Doubleday, 1965.
Midnight Was My Cry: New and Selected Poems. New York, Doubleday, 1971.
Mermaids in the Basement: Poems for Women. Port Townsend, Washington, Copper Canyon Press, 1984.

Other

Editor, with Elaine Dallman and Barbara Gelpi, *Woman Poet— The West.* Reno, Nevada, Women-in-Literature, 1980.

                        *   *   *

Carolyn Kizer works in terms of the twinned tensions of life, those central paradoxes so directly felt by women. She poses the problem of the woman poet boldly in her remarkable "A Muse of Water":

        We who must act as handmaidens
        To our own goddess, turn too fast,
        Trip on our hems, to glimpse the muse
        Gliding below her lake or sea,
        Are left, long-staring after her
        Narcissists by necessity...

Mother and Muse, she can write tenderly of her own mother, who taught her to love nature even at its most loathsome, "a whole, wild, lost, betrayed and secret life / Among its dens and burrows." And though she has a poem on "Not Writing Poetry about Children" they are everywhere in her work. So are cats, symbols of the female condition, as in "A Widow in Wintertime,"

            trying
        To live well enough alone, and not to dream
        Of grappling in the snow, claws plunged in fur,

        Or waken in a caterwaul of dying.

The daring and diffidence of womanhood are celebrated in

poems of companionship, like "For Jan, In Bar Maria." But her most constant, resonant theme is love and loss, analysed in detail in the sequence "A Month in Summer." This ends with a quotation from Basho, and it is in the fatalism of that ancient civilisation that Carolyn Kizer finds a refuge and an artistic remedy for her womanly woes: " 'O love long gone, it is raining in our room.' / So I memorize these lines, without salutation, without close." She must be one of the best woman poets around, profoundly committed to the process of life, however painful.

—John Montague

KNIGHT, Etheridge. American. Born in Corinth, Mississippi, 19 April 1931. Educated in public schools. Served in the United States Army, 1947-51. Married 1) Sonia Sanchez, *q.v.* (divorced); 2) Mary McAnally in 1970; two children. Inmate, Indiana State Prison, 1960-68; Poet-in-Residence, University of Pittsburgh, 1968, Hartford University, West Hartford, Connecticut, 1969-70, and Lincoln University, Jefferson City, Missouri, 1970-71. Poetry Editor, *Motive*, Nashville, 1970-71; Co-Editor, *Black Box*, Washington, D.C., 1971-72. Recipient: National Endowment for the Arts grant, 1972; Guggenheim Fellowship, 1974. Address: c/o Broadside Press, 74 Glendale Avenue, Highland Park, Michigan 48203, U.S.A.

PUBLICATIONS

Verse

Poems from Prison. Detroit, Broadside Press, 1968.
The Idea of Ancestry. Rome, 1968.
2 Poems for Black Relocation Centers. Detroit, Broadside Press, 1968.
For Black Poets Who Think of Suicide. Detroit, Broadside Press, 1972.
A Poem for Brother Man. Detroit, Broadside Press, 1972.
Belly Song and Other Poems. Detroit, Broadside Press, 1973.
Born of a Woman: New and Selected Poems. Boston, Houghton Mifflin, 1980.

Recordings: *Poems from Prison* (tape), Broadside; *Tough Poems for Tough People*, Caedmon.

Other

Editor, *Voce negre dal carcere.* Rome, Laterza, 1968; as *Black Voices from Prison*, New York, Pathfinder Press, 1970.

*   *   *

In 1960, Etheridge Knight was sentenced to serve twenty years in Indiana State Prison. He was to say later: "I died in 1960 from a prison sentence and poetry brought me back to life." His collection *Poems from Prison* was published during this time and shortly thereafter he was released from prison on parole. Even though he has not been as prolific as some other Black poets, Knight has proven to be an especially significant voice of the sixties and seventies. His poetry is an explication in verse of a Malcolm X theme defining a new frame of reference to the prison experience for poor Blacks and Whites.

Knight spells out a direct relationship between "men behind

prison walls and men behind the myriad walls that permeate [the American] society." His philosophy captures the themes of Malcolm X when he states that "crime, criminality, and alienation can be understood as being the by-product of a society / culture whose technology has far outstripped its humanism." In this respect, prison is viewed as "the ultimate oppression" of Black people in the larger prison outside. That philosophy is summed up simply and effectively in his "The Warden Said to Me the Other Day":

> The warden said to me the other day
> (innocently, I think), "Say, etheridge,
> why come the black boys don't run off
> like the white boys do?"
> I lowered my jaw and scratched my head
> and said (innocently, I think), "Well, suh,
> I ain't for sure, but I reckon its cause
> we ain't got no wheres to run to."

Knight's style is particularly suited to his ends. His poems are almost rigidly patterned (among his offerings is a brief series of Haiku poems), meticulously structured, tough in terminology, yet they never seem forced or restrained or without eloquence. He is sometimes as disarmingly simple as Langston Hughes; he is capable of shifting with piston smoothness from the concrete to the abstract:

> This year there is a gray stone wall damming my stream, and when
> the falling leaves stir my genes, I pace my cell or flop on my bunk
> and stare at 47 black faces across the space, I am all of them,
> they are all of me, I am me, they are thee, and I have no sons
> to float in the space between.

—Charles L. James

KNOEPFLE, John. American. Born in Cincinnati, Ohio, 4 February 1923. Educated at Xavier University, Cincinnati, Ph.B. 1949, M.A. 1951; St. Louis University, Ph.D. 1967. Served in the United States Navy, 1942-46: Purple Heart. Married Margaret Sower in 1956; one daughter and three sons. Producer-Director, WCET Educational Television, Cincinnati, 1953-55; Assistant Instructor, Ohio State University, Columbus, 1956-57; Instructor, Southern Illinois University, East St. Louis, 1957-61, St. Louis University High School, 1961-62, and Mark Twain Institute, Clayton, Missouri; summers 1962-64; Assistant Professor, Maryville College, St. Louis, 1962-66, and Washington University, St. Louis, 1963-66; Associate Professor, St. Louis University, 1966-72; consultant, Project Upward Bound, Washington, D.C., 1967-70. Since 1972, Professor of Literature, Sangamon State University, Springfield, Illinois. Recipient: Rockefeller Fellowship, 1967. Address: Department of English, Sangamon State University, Springfield, Illinois 62708, U.S.A.

PUBLICATIONS

Verse

Poets at the Gate, with others. St. Louis, Arts Festival of

Washington University, 1965.

Rivers into Islands. Chicago, University of Chicago Press, 1965.

Songs for Gail Guidry's Guitar. New York, New Rivers Press, 1969.

An Affair of Culture and Other Poems. La Crosse, Wisconsin, Northeast-Juniper, 1969.

After Gray Days and Other Poems. Prairie Villlage, Kansas, Crabgrass Press, 1970.

The Intricate Land. New York, New Rivers Press, 1970.

The Ten-Fifteen Community Poems. Poquoson, Virginia, Back Door Press, 1971.

Whetstone. Shawnee Mission, Kansas, BkMk Press, 1972.

Deep Winter Poems. Lincoln, Nebraska, Three Sheets, 1972.

Thinking of Offerings: Poems 1970-1973. La Crosse, Wisconsin, Juniper Press, 1975.

A Gathering of Voices. Ruffsdale, Pennsylvania, Rook Press, 1978.

Five Missouri Poets, with others, edited by Jim Barnes. Kirksville, Missouri, Chariton Review Press, 1979.

Poems for the Hours. Menomonie, Wisconsin, Uzzano, 1979.

A Box of Sandalwood: Love Poems. La Crosse, Wisconsin, Juniper Press, 1979.

Other

Voyages to the Inland Sea: Essays and Poems, with Lisel Mueller and David Etter. La Crosse, Wisconsin Center for Contemporary Poetry, 1971.

Dogs and Cats and Things Like That: A Book of Poems for Children. New York, McGraw Hill, 1971.

Our Street Feels Good: A Book of Poems for Children. New York, McGraw Hill, 1972.

Regional Perspectives: An Examination of America's Literary Heritage, with others, edited by John Gordon Burke. Chicago, American Library Association, 1973.

Editor, with Dan Jaffe, *Frontier Literature: Images of the American West.* New York, McGraw Hill, 1979.

Translator, with Robert Bly and James Wright, *Twenty Poems of César Vallejo.* Madison, Minnesota, Sixties Press, 1962.

Translator, with Robert Bly and James Wright, *Neruda and Vallejo: Selected Poems.* Boston, Beacon Press, 1971.

*   •

Critical Studies: "Masks of Self-Deception" by Lloyd Goldman, and "The Reflective Art of John Knoepfle" by Raymond Benoit, in *Minnesota Review 8* (St. Paul), 1968.

John Knoepfle comments:

(1970) I consider myself a poet of the American Middle West, but aware of the same cosmic problems that beset everyone anywhere.

Poems written since the publication of *Rivers into Islands* are less nostalgic. They show bias toward events—often surrealistic ones—that occur in such moments when public and private experience overlap. The poetry does not attempt to analyze the content of these two kinds of experience so much as it tries to reproduce the dynamics of their encounter. This has not been particularly intentional on my part; it is simply the way the poems have been moving, perhaps in an effort to get away from a propagandist / fatalist dilemma which seems at the moment largely irrelevent. The past in these poems and the midcontinent as place are there, then, not so much as subject matter outside of

the poet as they are a part of a community of experience which I feel deeply involved in.

(1974) I am more and more concerned with the nature of a voice that is adequate, that can articulate the overlapping of public and private experience, some voice that is neither totally egocentric nor totally masked speech: how to capture such a voice.

*   *   *

John Knoepfle's poetry moves between farcical humor and a serious search for spiritual illumination. A desire for communion with God informs much of the work in *Deep Winter Poems* and *The Ten-Fifteen Community Poems,* but this is also underscored, especially in the latter pamphlet, by desire for communion between people. In numerous poems, religious ritual, particularly that of Catholicism, plays its part, and sometimes, as in an hilarious poem in *An Affair of Culture* ("Tunnel Blaster on Bear and Brotherhood"), the farcical and religious strains blend into a ludicrous parody of the mass:

> he thought hed hunt bear with his brother
> but the bear ate his brother
> and he shot the bear
> he came back in here on the monday
> with a bearmeat sandwich
> wanted me to eat half of it
> see how a bearmeat sandwich tasted
> I told him Im damned the day
> I ate any mans brother
> but he said there wasnt nothing to it
> the bear didnt have time to digest his brother

This sort of outrageous humor takes risks, and Knoepfle, as in this poem, frequently succeeds; he has a good feeling for colloquial speech, and a good sense of his midwestern locales. He is less successful when he tries for the spareness and starkness of Creeley, in poems like "At Forty," and flatly expresses his spiritual needs:

> god look down
> on me look
> down on me
> look at my
> face and tell
> me something

Many of Knoepfle's poems are concerned with death, whether actual, as in the first poem quoted, or impending, as in the second poem. In his major collection, *Rivers into Islands,* "Evening Departure" pictures the deceased as leaving on a train waving goodbye; another, "Night of Stars and Flowers," apparently again pictures death, but merely as an electing to be somewhere else. "The White Mule" is about a ghostly mule abandoned down in the mines who feeds on lost men. Poems like these, and many of the others about trains and rivers and other Midwestern scenes, are very evocative. Knoepfle has a real talent for the short poem, a talent that is particularly apparent where the rivers of verse in the first two parts of *Rivers into Islands* break up into the islands of short poems in the last part. His short poems seem even shorter in the collections since this one, terser, more compressed, with a greater sense of pressure pushing at their seams. His humor and colloquial grace remain strong assets.

—Duane Ackerson

KNOTT, Bill (William Kilborn Knott). American. Born in Gratiot County, Michigan, 17 February 1940. Educated at Carson City High School, Michigan. Served in the United States Army. Poet-in-Residence, Emerson College, Boston, 1976. Recipient: National Endowment for the Arts grant, 1968. Address: c/o Random House, 201 East 50th Street, New York, New York 10022, U.S.A.

PUBLICATIONS

Verse

The Naomi Poems, Book One: Corpse and Beans. Chicago, Follett, 1968.
Aurealism: A Study. Syracuse, New York, Salt Mound Press, 1970.
Are You Ready Mary Baker Eddy?, with James Tate. San Francisco, Cloud Marauder Press, 1970.
Auto-Necrophilia: The Bill Knott Poems, Book 2. Chicago, Follett, 1971.
Nights of Naomi. Somerville, Massachusetts, Barn Dream Press, 1971.
Love Poems to Myself. Boston, Barn Dream Press, 1974.
Rome in Rome. New York, Release Press, 1976.
Selected and Collected Poems. New York, Sun, 1977.
For Anne and Other Poems. Waban, Massachusetts, Munich Editions from Shell, 1977.
Destinations. Walton-on-Thames, Surrey, Outposts, 1978.
Becos. New York, Random House, 1983.

Novel

Lucky Daryll, with James Tate. New York, Release Press, 1977.

*

Bill Knott comments:
I identify with the "Aurealist" School, or the group known as "Posthumous Poets."
Influences: Yvette Mimieux movies. John Logan's ideas and personal example of dedication.
Major theme is avoidance of major themes. Characteristic subjects are my death in 1966 and subsequent posthumous existence, and my virginity.
My usual verse form is iambic prose poems.

*   *   *

The poems of Bill Knott, who wrote as St. Geraud (1940-1966), are often very brief, deeply psychological lyrics, and he is a master of this form. "Hair Poem," two lines long, is characteristic:

Hair is heaven's water flowing eerily over us
Often a woman drifts off down her long hair and is lost

The sensuality of Knott's work imbues it with value beyond that of the Freudian level where most "Confessional" poets take their steambaths. Knott shares with his reader the possibility of an organic unity, a world where hair and heaven's water are the same elusive obtainables: his "death" may well suggest the view that life and death, equally permeated by identical organic elements, are also the same.
Knott's enormous success with the "deep image" arises from

his stance. He seems to live in a world where heaven's water is commonplace, and hair is not. His surrealism arises from what seems to be a surreal existence where the tables and perceptions are turned completely; metaphor, therefore, is reversed, and the world is seen through a crystal lens: "If bombing children is preserving peace, then / my fucking you is a war-crime" ("Nuremburg, USA"). At times the image is tied to nothing but itself and its effect relies simply on the suggested idea, as in "Cueballs have invented insomnia in an attempt to forget eyelids," from *Nights of Naomi*, a 32-page sequence where the surrealist jars the reader over and over: accept the metaphorical condition or don't bother to read any further. The poem begins, "Prefrontal lightningbolt too lazy to chew the sphinx's loudest eyelash....Only a maze can remember your hair of buttered blowguns."
It makes for thick reading, and the reader must indeed accommodate Knott's unusual stance in a world where "They squeezed your blood back into grapes." The reward is a trip through unvisited rooms of experience, with one of the finest poetic imaginations in print, "Years spent wandering in front of a stab."

—Geof Hewitt

———————

KOCH, Kenneth. American. Born in Cincinnati, Ohio, 27 February 1925. Educated at Harvard University, Cambridge, Massachusetts, A.B. 1948; Columbia University, New York, M.A. 1953, Ph.D. 1959. Served in the United States Army, 1943-46. Married Mary Janice Elwood in 1955; one daughter. Lecturer in English, Rutgers University, New Brunswick, New Jersey, 1953-54, 1955-56, 1957-58, and Brooklyn College, 1957-59; Director of the Poetry Workshop, New School for Social Research, New York, 1958-66. Lecturer, 1959-61, Assistant Professor, 1962-66, Associate Professor, 1966-71, and since 1971, Professor of English, Columbia University. Associated with the magazine *Locus Solus*, 1960-62. Recipient: Fulbright Fellowship, 1950, 1978; Guggenheim Fellowship, 1961; National Endowment for the Arts grant, 1966; Ingram Merrill Foundation Fellowship, 1969; Harbison Award, for teaching, 1970; Frank O'Hara Prize (*Poetry*, Chicago), 1973; American Academy award, 1976. Address: Department of English, 414 Hamilton Hall, Columbia University, New York, New York 10027, U.S.A.

PUBLICATIONS

Verse

Poems. New York, Tibor de Nagy, 1953.
Ko; or, A Season on Earth. New York, Grove Press, 1960.
Permanently. New York, Tiber Press, 1960.
Thank You and Other Poems. New York, Grove Press, 1962.
Poems from 1952 and 1953. Los Angeles, Black Sparrow Press, 1968.
When the Sun Tries to Go On. Los Angeles, Black Sparrow Press, 1969.
Sleeping with Women. Los Angeles, Black Sparrow Press, 1969.
The Pleasures of Peace and Other Poems. New York, Grove Press, 1969.
Penguin Modern Poets 24, with Kenward Elmslie and James Schuyler. London, Penguin, 1973.
The Art of Love. New York, Random House, 1975.

The Duplications. New York, Random House, 1977.
The Burning Mystery of Anna in 1951. New York, Random House, 1979.
From the Air. London, Taranman, 1979.
Days and Nights. New York, Random House, 1982.
Selected Poems. New York, Random House, 1985.

Plays

Bertha (produced New York, 1959). Included in *Bertha and Other Plays,* 1966.
The Election (also director: produced New York, 1960). Included in *A Change of Hearts,* 1973.
Pericles (produced New York, 1960). Included in *Bertha and Other Plays,* 1966.
George Washington Crossing the Delaware (produced New York, 1962; London, 1983). Included in *Bertha and Other Plays,* 1966.
The Construction of Boston (produced New York, 1962). Included in *Bertha and Other Plays,* 1966.
Guinevere; or, The Death of the Kangaroo (produced New York, 1964). Included in *Bertha and Other Plays,* 1966.
The Tinguely Machine Mystery; or, The Love Suicides at Kaluka (also co-director: produced New York, 1965). Included in *A Change of Hearts,* 1973.
Bertha and Others Plays (includes *Pericles, George Washington Crossing the Delaware, The Construction of Boston, Guinevere; or, The Death of the Kangaroo, The Gold Standard, The Return of Yellowmay, The Revolt of the Giant Animals, The Building of Florence, Angelica, The Merry Stones, The Academic Murders, Easter, The Lost Feed, Mexico, Coil Supreme*). New York, Grove Press, 1966.
The Gold Standard (produced New York, 1969). Included in *Bertha and Other Plays,* 1966
The Moon Balloon (produced New York, 1969). Included in *A Change of Hearts,* 1973.
The Artist, music by Paul Reif, adaptation of the poem "The Artist" by Kenneth Koch (produced New York, 1972). Poem included in *Thank You and Other Poems,* 1962.
A Little Light (produced Amagansett, New York, 1972).
A Change of Hearts: Plays, Films, and Other Dramatic Works 1951-1971 (includes the contents of *Bertha and Other Plays,* and *A Change of Hearts; E. Kology; The Moon Balloon; Without Kinship; Ten Films: Because, The Color Game, Mountains and Electricity, Sheep Harbor, Oval Gold, Moby Dick, L'Ecole Normale, The Cemetery, The Scotty Dog,* and *The Apple; Youth;* and *The Enchantment*). New York, Random House, 1973.
Rooster Redivivus (produced Garnerville, New York, 1975).
The Art of Love, adaptation of his own poem (produced Chicago, 1976).
The Red Robins, adaptation of his own novel (produced New York, 1978). New York, Performing Arts Journal Publications, 1979.
The New Diana (produced New York, 1984).

Screenplays: *The Scotty Dog,* 1967; *The Apple,* 1968.

Novel

The Red Robins. New York, Random House, 1975.

Short Stories

Interlocking Lives, with Alex Katz. New York, Kulchur Press, 1970.

Other

John Ashbery and Kenneth Koch (A Conversation). Tucson, Interview Press, 1965(?).
Wishes, Lies, and Dreams: Teaching Children to Write Poetry. New York, Random House, 1970.
Rose, Where Did You Get That Red? Teaching Great Poetry to Children. New York, Random House, 1973.
I Never Told Anybody: Teaching Poetry Writing in a Nursing Home. New York, Random House, 1977.

Editor, with Kate Farrell, *Sleeping on the Wing: An Anthology of Modern Poetry, with Essays on Reading and Writing.* New York, Random House, 1981.

*

Theatrical Activities:
Director: **Plays**—*The Election,* New York, 1960; *The Tinguely Machine Mystery* (co-director, with Remy Charlip), New York, 1965.

*   *   *

Kenneth Koch was one of the three principal poets of the "New York school" in the middle and late 1950's, a somewhat amorphous and short-lived group which also included John Ashbery and Frank O'Hara. The three had joined forces while students at Harvard before transferring their activities to New York, where they became associated with the painters who were then ascendant in the American art world, a group known as "abstract expressionists." To a certain extent the poets seemed to be bringing to verbal constructs the principles of abstract expressionism, i.e., they used words totally abstractly and evocatively. At the same time their prosodic practice was in revolt against the academic austerity of mid-century American poetry, and their use of syntax and measure resembled that of the contemporaneous Beat movement. What distinguished the two groups, if anything, was the New York poets' retention of an earlier idea of art as in some sense a puristic activity, not socially amenable, and of the art object as distinct from and perhaps superior to the objects of "ordinary reality." In addition Koch was, during a period of residence abroad, deeply influenced by current French poetry with its emphasis on psychological particularism.

These groupings and distinctions have long since broken down, of course. Koch's association with New York poetry was, in effect, his apprenticeship. Much of his early work was very far out indeed; some was frankly incomprehensible, even to the poet. Since then Koch has elevated his lyric view to another level, not in the least "realistic" but better organized and more simplified than his earlier view, with the result that some of his recent work has been extremely effective. The freedom of his earlier verbal technique has given him a felicity which occasionally still descends to surrealistic glibness but which at its best is remarkably inventive and accurate. At the same time, substantially fixed in his poems is a depth of metaphysical concern that gives them the drive and intensity of genuinely serious experiments.

One distinction of the New York poets was their devotion to the lyric theater. Their connection with "off-Broadway" and "off-off-Broadway" gave them opportunities for experiments with dramatic writing that were open to few poets elsewhere in the country, and some of Koch's best writing occurs in the several books of plays he has published, books which have been generally neglected, however, by American poetry-readers and critics.

—Hayden Carruth

KOLATKAR, Arun (Balkrishna).   Indian.   Born in Kolhapur, Bombay, 1 November 1932. Works as a graphic artist in an advertising agency, Bombay. Recipient: Commonwealth Poetry Award, 1977. Address: c/o Clearing House, Palm Springs, Cusse Parade, Bombay 400 005, India.

PUBLICATIONS

Verse

Jejuri.   Bombay, Clearing House, 1976.

*   *   *

A bilingual (Marathi and English) poet, Arun Kolatkar virtually burst upon the Indo-English poetic scene when he won the Commonwealth Poetry Award for 1977 with *Jejuri. Jejuri* is his first book although his poems have appeared since 1955 in poetry magazines and anthologies. Kolatkar does not show any solipsistic uneasiness as A. K. Ramanujan and R. Parthasarathy do in using a foreign linguistic medium. His poetic idiom being objectivist does not surrender to the pulls of the past—cultural or linguistic—and is, indeed, characterised by an engaging "alfresco individualism."

Jejuri, comprising thirty one titled sections, stands out as a personal epic like W. C. Williams's *Paterson.* It dramatizes a Jungian passage to contemporary Hinduism symbolised by the shrine at Jejuri, where one has only "to scratch a rock / and a legend springs." Ironically, the rational-minded and irreverent ("God is the word / and I know it backwards") protagonist, Manohar, who regards myth-making as characteristic of decadent Hinduism, himself succumbs to it as his "pilgrimage" nears its end: the train indicator appears as "a wooden saint in need of paint" to Manohar who in sheer desperation is prepared to "slaughter a goat before the clock / smash a cocoanut on the railway track.../ bathe the station master in milk.../ If only some one would tell.../ when the next rain is due." Indeed, his easy, informal, though laconic, tone suggestive of post-Romantic expressionism belies his capacity to transfigure his world with his iconoclastic cast of thought. His awareness of the shrine of Khandoba at Jejuri and its railway station being mythical correlatives of the postulates of a purgatory could alone, perhaps, redeem his "pilgrimage."

Kolatkar's subtle use of the montage technique in *Jejuri* (indeed, his first impulse was to do a movie) to achieve the effect of symbolist aesthetic is characteristic of modern poetry. So also is his avoidance of the mixing of "an abstraction with the concrete" (Ezra Pound's dictum). He uses images instinct with the criticism of the unfolding scene—a Wasteland one—which do not lessen the vibrance of the perceiving self: "he doesn't reply/...and happens to notice / a quick wink of a movement / in a scanty patch of scruffy dry grass / burnt brown in the sun / and says / look / there's a butterfly / there." *Jejuri*—a virtuoso performance—exemplifies a movement towards a freer form of verse; this is what is most promising in Kolatkar's poetry.

—K. Venkatachari

KOLLER, James.   American.   Born in Oak Park, Illinois, 30 May 1936. Educated at North Central College, Naperville, Illinois, B.A. 1958. Has four daughters and two sons. Since 1964, Editor, *Coyote Journal* and Coyote Books, San Francisco, then New Mexico and Maine. Recipient: National Endowment for the Arts grant, 1968, 1973. Address: c/o Coyote Books, P.O. Box 629, Brunswick, Maine 04011, U.S.A.

PUBLICATIONS

Verse

Two Hands: Poems 1959-1961.   Seattle, James B. Smith, 1965.
Brainard and Washington Street Poems.   Eugene, Oregon, Toad Press, 1965.
Some Cows: Poems of Civilization and Domestic Life.   San Francisco, Coyote, 1966.
The Dogs and Other Dark Woods.   San Francisco, Four Seasons, 1966.
I Went to See My True Love.   Buffalo, Audit East/West, 1967.
California Poems.   Los Angeles, Black Sparrow Press, 1971.
Messages.   Canton, New York, Institute of Further Studies, 1972.
Dark Woman, Who Lay with the Sun.   San Francisco, Tenth Muse, 1972.
Bureau Creek.   Brunswick, Maine, Blackberry, 1975.
Poems for the Blue Sky.   Santa Barbara, California, Black Sparrow Press, 1976.
Messages/Botschaften (bilingual edition).   Munich, Köhler, 1977.
Andiamo, with Franco Beltrametti and Harry Hoogstraten. Fort Kent, Maine, Great Raven Press, 1978.
O Didn't He Ramble (bilingual edition).   Schwetzingen, Germany, and Brunswick, Maine, Bussard-Coyote, 1980.
One Day at a Time.   Markesan, Wisconsin, Pentagram, 1981.
Back River.   Brunswick, Maine, Blackberry, 1981.
Great Things Are Happening (bilingual edition).   Schwetzingen, Germany, Bussard, 1984.

Novels

Shannon Who Was Lost Before.   Pensnett, Staffordshire, Grosseteste Review, 1974.
If You Don't Like Me You Can Leave Me Alone.   Pensnett, Staffordshire, Grosseteste Review, 1974; Brunswick, Maine, Blackberry, 1977.

Other

Editor, with others, *Coyote's Journal* (anthology).   Berkeley, California, Wingbow Press, 1982.

*

Manuscript Collections: University of Connecticut, Storrs; Simon Fraser University, Burnaby, British Columbia.

Critical Studies: "Eyes and 'I' " by Richard Duerden, in *Poetry* (Chicago), May 1966; "James Koller Issue" of *Savage 2* (Chicago), 1972; Paul Kahn, in *Montemora* (New York), Spring 1977, and *Poetry Information* (London), Winter 1979-80.

*   *   *

James Koller is an earthy poet; perhaps even "raunchy" would not be the wrong adjective to put to his work, which seeks out communion with nature and sex at a visceral level. Though his work calls to mind, with its spontaneous, collage-like technique, the Beat or Black Mountain poets, he is less cerebral, or mystical, in approach than a poet like Olson or Ginsberg; his poetry is direct, sensual, wrenched still steaming from the innards of the other life he encounters—when he speaks of stepping inside a bear's body, the intentions are by no means as metaphysical as in the poems of identification with animal life of, for instance, Kinnell or Dickey.

He is interested in the retreat to a more primitive relationship with nature, with ecstasy and the dangerous, slippery terrain around madness. He takes the sort of risks that can result in bad taste, but also in sudden gains, as in "I Get Crazy in the Full Moon" from *California Poems*:

        I crawled over the dark ground
        planting squash, an owl
        over my shoulder, the moon

        she throws back her head, stretches
        her arms hands, ripple of muscle
        skin, the moon

        clouds, shadows
        between us
        the ground mostly lighted

        the flower first, fruit
        full & rounded
        the softest curve, ripple, moon

        the laughter very soft

                                —Duane Ackerson

KOOSER, Ted (Theodore Kooser). American. Born in Ames, Iowa, 25 April 1939. Educated at Iowa State University, Ames, B.S. 1962; University of Nebraska, Lincoln, M.A. in English 1968. Married 1) Diana Tressler in 1962 (divorced, 1969), one son; 2) Kathleen Rutledge in 1977. High school teacher, Madrid, Iowa, 1962-63; Correspondent, 1964-65, and Underwriter, 1965-73, Bankers Life Nebraska, Lincoln. Senior Underwriter, 1973-80, and since 1980, 2nd Vice-President, Lincoln Benefit Life. Since 1970, part-time instructor in creative writing, University of Nebraska. Since 1967, publisher, Windflower Press. Recipient: Prairie Schooner Prize, 1975, 1978; National Endowment for the Arts fellowship, 1976, 1984. Address: Route 1, Box 10, Garland, Nebraska 68360, U.S.A.

PUBLICATIONS

Verse

Official Entry Blank. Lincoln, University of Nebraska Press, 1969.
Grass County. Lincoln, Nebraska, Windflower Press, 1971.
Twenty Poems. Crete, Nebraska, Best Cellar Press, 1973.
A Local Habitation, and A Name. San Luis Obispo, California, Solo Press, 1974.
Shooting a Farmhouse; So This Is Nebraska. Denver, Ally Press, 1975.

Not Coming to Be Barked At. Milwaukee, Pentagram Press, 1976.
Hatcher. Lincoln, Nebraska, Windflower Press, 1978.
Old Marriage and New. Austin, Texas, Cold Mountain Press, 1978.
Cottonwood County, with William Kloefkorn. Lincoln, Nebraska, Windflower Press, 1979.
Sure Signs: New and Selected Poems. Pittsburgh, University of Pittsburgh Press, 1980.
The Blizzard Voices. St. Paul, Bieler Press, 1985.
One World at a Time. Pittsburgh, University of Pittsburgh Press, 1985.

Other

Editor, *The Windflower Home Almanac of Poetry.* Lincoln, Nebraska, Windflower Press, 1980.

                          *

Critical Study: in *On Common Ground* by Dana Gioia, Springfield, Missouri, Mark Sanders, 1984.

Ted Kooser comments:
I have been writing poetry for 25 years. For the first 15 of those years I was trying to get through to myself, and for the last ten I have been trying to get through to my readers. Looking back over my poems of all those years, I can see my work becoming more and more accessible to a reader whose interests are more general than literary. I would like to be a popular poet without having to compromise my artistic standards to any degree, and that's a difficult task. I like nothing so much as to have letters of praise from people who ordinarily don't read poetry, and I'm also very pleased when my work gets included in anthologies for use in the public school classroom. I feel like a useful person when I can contribute something to the lives of people who may be otherwise intimidated by art and artists. My poems are very often centered about single figures of speech, conceits, and I like to provide people with these new ways of seeing the associations between things. Several years ago, after reading a poem of mine in which I describe a little family of mice moving their nest up out of a field at spring plowing time, someone wrote me to say that he would never again look at a freshly plowed field in the same way. That was the highest compliment I've ever been paid, and my goal as a poet is to offer those moments to others for as long as I'm able to.

                    *   *   *

Ted Koosaer is a genuinely popular poet. This is not to say that he commands a mass public. No contemporary poet does — at least in America. Kooser is popular in that unlike most of his peers he writes naturally for a non-literary public. His style is accomplished but extremely simple — his diction drawn from common speech, his syntax conversational. His subjects are chosen from the everyday world of the Great Plains, and his sensibility, though more subtle and articulate, is that of the average midwesterner. He never makes an allusion that an intelligent but unbookish reader will not immediately grasp. There is to my knowledge no poet of equal stature who writes so convincingly in a manner the average American can understand and appreciate.

But to describe Kooser merely as a poet who writes plainly about the ordinary world is misleading insofar as it makes his work sound dull. For here, too, the comparison with popular art holds true. Kooser's work is uncommonly entertaining. His poems are usually short and perfectly paced; his subjects relevant and engaging. Finishing one poem, the reader instinctively wants to proceed to another. It has been Kooser's particular genius to develop a genuine poetic style which accommodates the average reader and portrays a vision which provides unexpected moments of illuminations from the seemingly threadbare details of everyday life.

If Kooser's work is visionary, however, it is on a decidedly human scale. He offers no blinding flashes of inspiration, no mystic moments of transcendence. He creates no private mythologies or fantasy worlds. Instead he provides small but genuine insights into the world of everyday experience. His work strikes the difficult balance between profundity and accessibility just as his style manages to be distinctively personal without being idiosyncratic. It is simple without becoming shallow, striking without going to extremes. He has achieved the most difficult kind of originality. He has transformed the common idiom and experience into fresh and distinctive poetry.

Kooser does have some significant limitations as a poet. Looking across all his mature work, one sees a narrow range of technical means, an avoidance of stylistic or thematic complexity, little interest in ideas, and an unwillingness to work in longer forms. In his weaker poems one sometimes notices a tendency to sentimentalize his subjects and too strong a need to be liked by his readers, which often expresses itself in a self-deprecatory attitude towards himself and his poetry. In short, Kooser's major limitation is a deep-set conservatism that keeps him working in areas he knows he can both master and please his audience.

Significantly, however, Kooser's limitations derive directly from his strengths. His narrow technical range reflects his insistence on perfecting the forms he uses. If Kooser has concentrated on a few types of poems, he has made each of these forms unmistakeably his own. If he has avoided longer forms, what member of his generation has written so many unforgettable short poems? If he has avoided complexity in his work, he has also developed a distinctive and highly charged kind of simplicity. What his poems lack in intellectuality they more than make up for in concrete detail. If he occasionally lapses into sentimentality, it is because he invests his poems with real emotion. Even Kooser's self-deprecatory manner betrays a consistent concern for the communal role of the poet. He will not strike superior bardic poses to bully or impress his audience.

Kooser has written more perfect poems than any American poet of his generation. In a quiet way he is also one of its most original poets. His technical and intellectual interest may be narrow (indeed in terms of limited techniques he shares a common fault of his generation), but his work shows an impressive emotional range all handled in a distinctively personal way. Finally, his work does coalesce into an impressive whole. Read individually, his poems sparkle with insight. Read together, they provide one of the few broad and believable portraits of contemporary America in our poetry.

—Dana Gioia

KOPS, Bernard. British. Born in London, 28 November 1926. Educated in London elementary schools to age 13. Married Erica Gordon in 1956; four children. Has worked as a docker, chef, salesman, waiter, lift man, and barrow boy. Writer-in-Residence, London Borough of Hounslow, 1980-82; Lecturer in Drama, Spiro Institute, 1984-85. Recipient: Arts Council bursary 1957, 1975; C. Day Lewis Fellowship, 1980. Agent: David Higham Associates, 5-8 Lower John Street, London W1R 4HA. Address: Flat 1, 35 Canfield Gardens, London N.W.6, England.

PUBLICATIONS

Verse

Poems. London, Bell and Baker Press, 1955.
Poems and Songs. Northwood, Middlesex, Scorpion Press, 1958.
An Anemone for Antigone. Lowestoft, Suffolk, Scorpion Press, 1959.
Erica, I Want to Read You Something. Lowestoft, Suffolk, Scorpion Press, and New York, Walker, 1967.
For the Record. London, Secker and Warburg, 1971.

Plays

The Hamlet of Stepney Green (produced Oxford, 1957; London and New York, 1958). London, Evans, 1959.
Goodbye World (produced Guildford, Surrey, 1959).
Change for the Angel (produced London, 1960).
The Dream of Peter Mann (produced Edinburgh, 1960). London, Penguin, 1960.
Enter Solly Gold, music by Stanley Myers (produced Wellingborough, Northamptonshire, and Los Angeles, 1962; London, 1970). Published in *Satan, Socialites, and Solly Gold: Three New Plays from England,* New York, Coward McCann, 1961; in *Four Plays,* 1964.
Home Sweet Honeycomb (broadcast, 1962). Included in *Four Plays,* 1964.
The Lemmings (broadcast, 1963). Included in *Four Plays,* 1964.
Stray Cats and Empty Bottles (televised, 1964; produced London, 1967).
Four Plays (includes *The Hamlet of Stepney Green, Enter Solly Gold, Home Sweet Honeycomb, The Lemmings*). London, MacGibbon and Kee, 1964.
The Boy Who Wouldn't Play Jesus (juvenile; produced London, 1965). Published in *Eight Plays: Book 1,* edited by Malcolm Stuart Fellows, London, Cassell, 1965; Chicago, Dramatic Publishing Company, n.d.
David, It Is Getting Dark (produced Rennes, France, 1970). Paris, Gallimard, 1970.
It's a Lovely Day Tomorrow, with John Goldschmidt (televised, 1975; produced London, 1976).
More Out Than In (produced on tour and London, 1980).
Ezra (produced London, 1981).

Radio Plays: *Home Sweet Honeycomb,* 1962; *The Lemmings,* 1963; *Born in Israel,* 1963; *The Dark Ages,* 1964; *Israel: The Immigrant,* 1964; *Bournemouth Nights,* 1979; *I Grow Old, I Grow Old,* 1979; *Over the Rainbow,* 1980; *Simon at Midnight,* 1982; *Trotsky Was My Father,* 1984.

Television Plays: *I Want to Go Home,* 1963; *Stray Cats and Empty Bottles,* 1964; *The Lost Years of Brian Hooper,* 1967; *Alexander the Greatest,* 1971; *Just One Kid,* 1974; *Why the Geese Shrieked,* and *The Boy Philosopher,* from stories by Isaac Bashevis Singer, 1974; *It's a Lovely Day Tomorrow,* 1975; *Moss,*

1975; *Rocky Marciano Is Dead*, 1976; *Night Kids*, 1983; *A Hole in the Wall*, 1985.

Novels

Awake for Mourning.   London, MacGibbon and Kee, 1958.
Motorbike.   London, New English Library, 1962.
Yes from No-Man's Land.   London, MacGibbon and Kee, 1965; New York, Coward McCann, 1966.
The Dissent of Dominick Shapiro.   London, MacGibbon and Kee, 1966; New York, Coward McCann, 1967.
By the Waters of Whitechapel.   London, Bodley Head, 1969; New York, Norton, 1970.
The Passionate Past of Gloria Gaye.   London, Secker and Warburg, 1971; New York, Norton, 1972.
Settle Down Simon Katz.   London, Secker and Warburg, 1973.
Partners.   London, Secker and Warburg, 1975.
On Margate Sands.   London, Secker and Warburg, 1978.

Other

The World Is a Wedding (autobiography).   London, MacGibbon and Kee, 1963; New York, Coward McCann, 1964.
The Umbiblical Cord.   London, Robson, 1985.

Editor, *Poetry Hounslow*.   London, Hounslow Civic Centre, 1981.

*

Manuscript Collections: University of Texas, Austin; Indiana University, Bloomington.

Critical Studies: "Bernard Kops" by Colin MacInnes, in *Encounter* (London), May 1960; "The Kitchen Sink" by G. Wilson Knight, in *Encounter* (London), December 1963; "Deep Waters of Whitechapel" by Nina Sutton, in *The Guardian* (London), 6 September 1969.

Bernard Kops comments:

Kops creates specific relationships in order that they might relate universally. He writes compulsively, for himself, and even if his work is acceptable to others, this is a secondary process. Nevertheless, he is pleased that he can sell his work and be able to live by writing. Kops is obsessed by family themes; this runs throughout his work. The relationships are of people bound up together in an intense emotional and intellectual involvement. He believes that the great themes of Shakespeare, Racine, Sophocles, O'Neill have lasted and will last because they deal with themes common to every human being. *King Lear* and its dream and despair lives for us because it lives through us—it is US. We give it life and constantly renew it. Kops is also obsessed with death but only because he is obsessed with life: He believes motives are impossible to define ultimately, but actions are not subjective and one must judge a man by his actions. He likes ambiguity. But he also believes in strict discipline, and thinks that the writer must know exactly what he is doing even if he has shown the subjectivity and complexity of human relationships. He writes constantly about the backgrounds and the people and things he knows, or thinks he knows. The only things that he is really certain about are: the existence of love, the need for it and that "they" no longer exist. There are only US left on this earth. Kops writes about this.

*   *   *

Bernard Kops's reputation stands on his plays and novels, yet these very substantial writings can be said to arise from the wellsprings of a talent and an approach to literature which is entirely that of a poet.

And, further, it is that of a special sort of poet—the sort contained in the familiar quotation about "the poet's eye in a fine frenzy rolling." Kops's poems usually exhibit a tendency to the frenetic—a free-wheeling fantasy, an extravagance of language and gesture, an explosive celebration of the things that he loves or that excite him, and an apocalyptic rejection of things that he hates or that appall him. He draws a great deal of his poetry from his fervent Jewishness—but not merely in the form of his sense of racial difference, or his horror at the Nazi holocaust. Many of his most successful poems grow out of his family's presence in the foreground of his experience, from which he can create universalised images for what he sees as the sad, proud, lonely, laughable continuity of human life. "Somewhere upon these impossible stairs," he wrote in a poem entitled "Prayer at Forty," "we are attempting love."

Though his poetic output has never been large, his assertion in it of the need to go on "attempting love" has been unflagging—and has figured equally large throughout his considerable oeuvre of plays, novels and that splendid poet's autobiography, *The World Is a Wedding*. That determined assertion has been his poetry's source of power, and its most lasting quality.

—Douglas Hill

KOSTELANETZ, Richard (Cory).   American.   Born in New York City, 14 May 1940. Educated at Brown University, Providence, Rhode Island, A.B. 1962 (Phi Beta Kappa); Columbia University, New York, M.A. 1966; King's College, London (Fulbright Fellow, 1964-65). Program Associate, John Jay College, New York, 1972-73; Visiting Professor, University of Texas, Austin, 1977; artist-in-residence, Mishkenot Sha'ananim, Jerusalem, 1979, and DAAD Kunstlerprogramm, Berlin, 1981-83. Co-Founder, Assembling Press, 1970-82; contributing editor, *Lotta Poetica*, Villa Nuova, Italy, 1970-71, *Arts in Society*, Madison, Wisconsin, 1970-75, *The Humanist*, Buffalo, 1970-78, and *New York Arts Journal*, 1980-82. Since 1976, Proprietor, Future Press; since 1977, Co-Editor and Publisher, *Precisely*. Visual poetry and related language art exhibited at galleries and universities since 1975. Recipient: Pulitzer Fellowship, 1965; Guggenheim Fellowship, 1967; National Endowment for the Arts grant, 1976, 1978, 1979, 1980, 1981; Vogelstein Foundation Fellowship, 1980. Address: P.O. Box 444, Prince Street Station, New York, New York 10012, U.S.A.

PUBLICATIONS

Verse

Visual Language.   New York, Assembling Press, 1970.
I Articulations, with *Short Fictions*.   New York, Kulchur, 1974.
Portraits from Memory.   Ann Arbor, Ardis, 1975.
Word Prints.   Privately printed, 1975.
Rain Rains Rain.   New York, Assembling Press, 1976.
Numbers: Poems and Stories.   New York, Assembling Press, 1976.

Illuminations. Woodinville, Washington, and New York, Laughing Bear-Future Press, 1977.
Arenas Fields Pitches Turfs. Kansas City, Bk Mk-University of Missouri, 1982.

Novels

In the Beginning. Somerville, Massachusetts, Abyss, 1971.
One Night Stood. New York, Future Press, 1977.
Exhaustive Parallel Intervals. New York, Future Press, 1979.

Short Stories

Accounting. Brescia, Italy, Amodulo, 1972; Sacramento, California, Poetry Newsletter, 1973.
Ad Infinitum. Friedrichsfehn, Germany, International Artists' Cooperation, 1973.
Openings and Closings. New York, D'Arc, 1975.
Constructs. Reno, Nevada, West Coast Poetry Review, 1975.
Come Here. New York, Assembling Press, 1975.
Extrapolate. New York, Assembling Press, 1975.
Three Places in New Inkland, with others. New York, Zartscorp, 1977.
Constructs Two. Milwaukee, Membrane, 1978.
Foreshortenings and Other Stories. Willits, California, Tuumba Press, 1978.
Tabula Rasa. New York, RK Editions, 1978.
Inexistences. New York, RK Editions, 1978.
And So Forth. New York, Future Press, 1979.
More Short Fictions. New York, Assembling Press, 1980.
Reincarnations. New York, Future Press, 1981.

Other

The Theatre of Mixed-Means: An Introduction to Happenings, Kinetic Environments, and Other Mixed-Means Performances. New York, Dial Press, 1968; London, Pitman, 1970.
Master Minds: Portraits of Contemporary American Artists and Intellectuals. New York, Macmillan, 1969.
The End of Intelligent Writing: Literary Politics in America. New York, Sheed and Ward, 1974.
Recyclings: A Literary Autobiography. New York, Assembling Press, 1974; augmented edition, New York, Future Press, 1984.
Grants and the Future of Literature. New York, RK Editions, 1978.
Wordsand. Burnaby, British Columbia, Simon Fraser Gallery, 1978.
Twenties in the Sixties: Previously Uncollected Critical Essays. Westport, Connecticut, Greenwood Press, 1979.
"The End" Essentials, "The End" Appendix. Metuchen, New Jersey, Scarecrow Press, 1979.
Metamorphosis in the Arts. New York, Assembling Press, 1980.
Autobiographies. Santa Barbara, California, Mudborn, 1981.
The Old Poetics and the New. Ann Arbor, University of Michigan Press, 1981.

Editor, *On Contemporary Literature: An Anthology of Critical Essays on Major Movements and Writers of Contemporary Literature.* New York, Avon, 1964; revised edition, 1969.
Editor, *The New American Arts.* New York, Horizon Press, 1965.
Editor, *Twelve from the Sixties.* New York, Dell, 1967.
Editor, *The Young American Writers: Fiction, Poetry, Drama, and Criticism.* New York, Funk and Wagnalls, 1967.

Editor, *Beyond Left and Right: Radical Thought for Our Time.* New York, Morrow, 1968.
Editor, *Imaged Words and Worded Images.* New York, Outerbridge and Dienstfrey, 1970.
Editor, *Possibilities of Poetry: An Anthology of American Contemporaries.* New York, Dell, 1970.
Editor, *John Cage.* New York, Praeger, 1970; London, Allen Lane, 1971.
Editor, *Moholy-Nagy.* New York, Praeger, 1970; London, Allen Lane, 1972.
Editor, *Assembling,* and *Second* through *Eleventh Assembling.* New York, Assembling Press, 12 vols., 1970-81.
Editor, *Future's Fictions.* New York, Panache, 1971.
Editor, *Human Alternatives: Visions for Our Time.* New York, Morrow, 1971.
Editor, *Social Speculations: Visions for Us Now.* New York, Morrow, 1971.
Editor, *In Youth.* New York, Ballantine, 1972.
Editor, *Seeing Through Shuck.* New York, Ballantine, 1972.
Editor, *Breakthrough Fictioneers: An Anthology.* New York, Something Else Press, 1973.
Editor, *The Edge of Adaptation: Man and the Emerging Society.* Englewood Cliffs, New Jersey, Prentice Hall, 1973.
Editor, *Essaying Essays.* New York, OOLP, 1975.
Editor, *Language and Structure.* New York, Kensington Arts, 1975.
Editor, *Younger Critics of North America: Essays on Literature and the Arts.* Fair Water, Wisconsin, Margins, 1977.
Editor, *Esthetic Contemporary.* New York, Prometheus, 1977.
Editor, *Assembling Assembling.* New York, Assembling Press, 1978.
Editor, *Visual Literature Criticism: A New Collection.* Carbondale, Southern Illinois University Press, 1979.
Editor, *Text-Sound Texts.* New York, Morrow, 1980.
Editor, *The Yale Gertrude Stein* (selection). New Haven, Connecticut, Yale University Press, 1980.
Editor, *Scenarios.* New York, Assembling Press, 1980.
Editor, *Aural Literature Criticism.* New York, Precisely-RK Editions, 1981.
Editor, *The Avant-Garde Tradition in Literature.* Buffalo, Prometheus, 1982.

*

Critical Studies: *Once Again,* edited by Jean-François Bory, New York, New Directions 1968; "Poetry and Space" by Carolo Alberto Sitta, in *The Gazette* (Modena, Italy), 4 November 1970; "Figured Verse and Calligrams" by Massin, in *Letter and Image,* Paris, Gallimard, and New York, Van Nostrand, 1970; *Text-Bilder/Visuelle Poésie International,* edited by Klaus Peter Dencker, Cologne, DuMont Schauberg, 1972; L.J. Davis, in *New York Times Book Review,* 21 October 1973; "Richard Kostelanetz" by Hugh Fox, in *West Coast Poetry Review 12* (Reno, Nevada), Summer 1974; Thomas Powers in *Harper's* (New York), November 1974; John W. Aldridge, in *Michigan Quarterly Review* (Ann Arbor), Summer 1975; Michael Joseph Phillips, in *Small Press Review* (Paradise, California), June-July 1976; "Just Plain Video and Video-Plus" by Davidson Gigliotti, in *Soho Weekly News* (New York), 30 December 1976; "Richard Kostelanetz; ou, La Notion de littérature généralisée" by Jacques Donguy, in *Artistes,* July 1984.

*   *   *

The appropriate descriptive term for Richard Kostelanetz's creative work is "visual poetry," indicating a specialized genre within poetry, or an intermedium between poetry and painting. His visual poems are non-linear and non-syntactic, in contrast to those "shape poems" whose ancestry is traceable back through Apollinaire and George Herbert to the illuminated manuscript and Chinese ideogram. They are consciously counter-conventional poems, reflecting a comprehensive knowledge of contemporary literary practice and deliberate avoidance of it, although they employ such specifically literary devices as punning, wit, allusion, alliteration, parallelism and contrast. Constructivism and minimalism in the visual art tradition have also influenced Kostelanetz. His early poems in *Visual Language*, written around 1967, are usually mimetic, often employing only one letter or word, and often erotic in content. In his second collection, *I Articulations*, he creates more complex structures involving synonyms, multiple repetitions and more philosophical concerns, frequently about the nature of language itself.

His style is immediately recognizable, not only because he has published more visual poetry than any other American practitioner, but because of his distinctive technical means—a common letter-stencil and shamelessly amateur calligraphy which represent calculated avoidance of the polished finish of commercial design. Another recognizable aspect of his style is the strict limitation he places on himself. In these volumes he uses no visual material other than letters in non-syntactic formations. This methodology mirrors his aesthetic conviction that a radical formal constraint is essential to true creativity.

From this style and its ramifications, he has moved into fiction—"sequential forms that still eschew the prosaic form of expository sentences"—and his most recent poems and fictions consist entirely of numbers, thus emphasizing that formal pattern and relationship, rather than semantic content or extrinsic reference, is at the center of his art.

Although traditionalists may object to such expansion of the genre, Kostelanetz's work continually challenges more moderate notions of "new directions" in poetry. It incorporates the values which have governed his work as a critic, anthologist and proponent of the avant-garde movement in America. Visual enhancement of language, he says, is not an exclusive successor to the past, but "one propitious future for literature."

—Jane Augustine

KUMAR, Shiv K(umar). Indian. Born in Lahore, Punjab, 16 August 1921. Educated at Forman Christian College, Panjab University, Lahore, 1941-43, B.A. 1941, M.A. 1943; Fitzwilliam College, Cambridge, 1953-56, Ph.D. 1956. Married Madhu Kumar in 1967; two sons and two daughters. Lecturer, D.A.V. College, Lahore, 1945-47, and Hansraj College, Delhi, 1948-49; Programme Executive, All India Radio, Delhi, 1949; Broadcaster, BBC, 1951-53; Senior Lecturer and Chairman of the Department of English, Government College, Chandigarh, 1953-56; Reader in English, Panjab University, Hoshiarpur, 1956-59; Professor and Chairman of the Department of English, Osmania University, Hyderabad, 1959-76; Professor and Chairman of the Department of English, and Dean of the School of Humanities, 1976-79, and Acting Chancellor, 1979-80, University of Hyderabad. Visiting Professor, Elmira College, New York, 1965-67, Marshall University, Huntington, West Virginia, 1968, and University of Northern Iowa, Cedar Falls, 1969; Cultural Award Visitor, Australia, Summer 1971; Visiting Professor, Drake University, Des Moines, Iowa, 1971-72, Hofstra University, Hempstead, New York, 1972, University of Kent,

Canterbury, 1977-78, Oklahoma University, Norman, 1980-82, and Franklin and Marshall College, Lancaster, Pennsylvania, 1982-84. President, All India English Teachers Conference, 1975. Member, Advisory Board (English), Sahitya Akademy, 1978-83. Recipient: Smith-Mundt Fellowship, 1962. Fellow, Royal Society of Literature, 1978. Address: 2-F/Kakatiya Nagar, P.O. Jamia Osmania, Hyderabad 500 007, India.

PUBLICATIONS

Verse

Articulate Silences.   Calcutta, Writers Workshop, 1970.
Cobwebs in the Sun.   New Delhi, Tata-McGraw Hill, 1974.
Subterfuges.   New Delhi, Oxford University Press, 1976.
Woodpeckers.   London, Sidgwick and Jackson, 1979.

Play

The Last Wedding Anniversary (produced Hyderabad, 1974). New Delhi, Macmillan, 1975.

Novels

The Bone's Prayer.   New Delhi, Arnold-Heinemann, 1979.
Nude Before God.   New York, Vanguard Press, 1983.

Short Stories

Beyond Love and Other Stories.   New Delhi, Vikas, 1980.

Other

Virginia Woolf and Intuition.   Hoshiarpur, Vishveshvaranand, 1957.
Virginia Woolf and Bergson's Durée.   Hoshiarpur, Vishveshvaranand, 1957.
Bergson and the Stream of Consciousness Novel.   London, Blackie, 1962; New York, New York University Press, 1963.
Examine Your English, with M.M. Maison.   New Delhi, Orient Longman, 1964.

Editor, *Modern Short Stories*.   Madras, Macmillan, 1958.
Editor, *Leaves of Grass*, by Walt Whitman.   New Delhi, Eurasia, 1962.
Editor, *Apollo's Lyre*.   Madras, Macmillan, 1962.
Editor, *The Red Badge of Courage*, by Stephen Crane.   New Delhi, Eurasia, 1964.
Editor, *British Romantic Poets: Recent Revaluations*.   New York, New York University Press, and London, University of London Press, 1966.
Editor, with Keith McKean, *Critical Approaches to Fiction*.   New York, McGraw Hill, 1968.
Editor, *British Victorian Literature: Recent Revaluations*.   New York, New York University Press, and London, University of London Press, 1969.
Editor, *The Life, Adventures, and Pyracies of the Famous Captain Singleton*, by Daniel Defoe.   London, Oxford University Press, 1969.
Editor, *Indian Verse in English 1970*.   Calcutta, Writers Workshop, 1971.

*

Critical Studies: "An Essay on the Poems of Shiv K. Kumar" by

R.K. Kaul, in *Osmania Journal of English Studies 11* (Hyderabad), 1, 1974; "Beyond the Empiric Point" by M. Sivaramkrishna, in *World Literature Written in English* (Arlington, Texas), November 1975; "Towards an Idiom of Sincerity" by K. Venkatachari, in *Journal of Indian Writing in English* (Gulbarga, Mysore), July 1976; "Between Kali and Cordelia" by T.G. Vaidyanathan, in *Osmania Journal of English Studies 13* (Hyderabad), 1, 1977; "Resonant Bones" by J. Birje-Patil, in *World Literature Today* (Norman, Oklahoma), Autumn 1977.

Shiv K. Kumar comments:

Although I scribbled some verse during my undergraduate days, it was only at the age of 49 or so that I wrote my first serious poem. Since then poetry has been one of my most continual sources of joy.

A poem comes to me as a phrase or a line or a nebulous image which then gets crystallized into a cluster of words. An idea never starts it off—I seem to have an innate distrust of statement. I believe that a poem achieves its most effective articulation when it emerges from the intensity of a writer's lived experience. It may not be "a kind of locked trunk of confessions" (as Gabriel Pearson puts it), but it acquires its sharp identity from the poet as a private person.

Of course the poet must never forsake the artistic distance and control which mould the disparate elements of experience into a pattern. Nor should a poet allow any kind of intellectual discipline to ossify his sensibility. My dual role as critic and writer has made me particularly conscious of this dilemma, but I agree with Anthony Thwaite that one's activity may "fall into different compartments and that the one doesn't influence the other."

I don't think I have been influenced by any poet, though I greatly admire the work of Robert Lowell, Sylvia Plath, and Anne Sexton. Ultimately each poet has to work out his own credo of life and imagination—"we perish each alone."

Do I consider the use of a language I am not born to a serious impediment to my creativity? No. I feel that it is as much the language that chooses its writer as the writer who selects his medium. In any case, I have grown up with the English language, and cannot write in any other, so I have no alternative.

It has sometimes been remarked that one of the recurring themes in my poetry is cultural interaction, a preoccupation with the polarities of East and West. But this preoccupation must be unconscious. Maybe I have stayed too long in the West, and my Indian sensibility keeps assessing my western experience. Fundamentally, I guess, I am something of a "primitivist" who may never overcome his nostalgia for prelapsarian innocence and simplicity. What hurts me most is any kind of regimentation—political, social, intellectual, or religious. I feel that poetry is an impassioned testament to man's inner freedom. I have done other kinds of creative writing, but it is the poem that satisfies me most because it summons forth my imagination in its intensest form. In the beginning was the word, and that word was the poem—man's profoundest experience articulated through cadence and harmony.

*   *   *

Although it was only in 1970 that Shiv K. Kumar appeared on the Indian literary scene with his first collection of poems *Articulate Silences*, his subsequent work has established him as a major Indo-anglian poet. He shares with some of his contemporaries (Dom Moraes, A.K. Ramanujan, and Nissim Ezekiel) a crisis of personal identity, an agonising search for some *locus standi* between East and West, between an irrepressible nostalgia for prelapsarian innocence and the compulsions of contemporary civilisation.

Educated at Cambridge, and frequently invited as Visiting Professor of literature at various American and British universities, he has remained an exile as much in his native country as elsewhere. This tension between his two warring selves lends his poetry a rare ironical thrust. "There is," says Roger Iredale, "in his poetry, a pervasive, ironic humour that is missing from the work of other Indian poets" (*Quest*, November-December 1975). It is irony that he uses to expose the smug complacency of his native Hindu culture. In his sequence poem "Broken Columns," he describes his adolescence: "At dusk Father shuffles us all/about on the coir-mat to pray./ We spout chants from the *Gita*. 'Feed not thy desire on objects of sense./ But like a tortoise/folding up its limbs within the shell/withdraw into supreme wisdom.' " But "a puff of wind rustles through a girl's skirt/and two tender legs/gyrate the air into fuzzy yearnings." Again, he evokes the image of a Hindu crematorium, with a vulture cogitating "upon human avidity—flesh offered/to the flames, bones and ashes/to the Ganges. No leavings/for the living."

"It is assumed," observes Birje-Patil (in *World Literature Today*, Autumn 1977) "that Indian poetry in English is essentially a post-Independence phenomenon.... Today we seem to be poised for a break-through and something that may be truly Indian is being written." Kumar's distinctive achievement, he avers, lies in his ability to convey "the experience of being Indian instead of the experience of feeling like an Indian." Kumar is at his best in his crisp, tautly controlled short lyrics like "My Co-respondent," "My Son," "My Mother's Death Anniversary," and "To a Prostitute." All such poems quicken into meaning through a subtle inter-play of images (for instance, a young Mango-Vendor revealing "through the slits/of her patched blouse/one bare shoulder/two white moons/pulling all horses/off the track") and a juxtaposition of polarities (affirmation and denial, intuition and logic) in a language that is supple and evocatively cadenced.

A striking feature of his poetry is his preoccupation with physical experience: sex, indeed, is almost a mode of perception for him. Even his nature imagery (sea, sky, wind, sun, fish) often implies some kind of sexual play. "The preponderance of erotic images is explicable not only in terms of an uninhibited delight in all sensuous things, but also in terms of the primacy of 'the religion of the blood' " (M. Sivaramkrishna, in *World Literature Written in English*, November, 1975). Kumar's poetry, however, is marked by an intellectual distrust of pure emotion as though he were chary of giving himself away ("Cerebral Love").

—K. Venkatachari

KUMIN, Maxine (née Winokur). American. Born in Philadelphia, Pennsylvania, 6 June 1925. Educated at Radcliffe College, Cambridge, Massachusetts, A.B. 1946, M.A. 1948. Married Victor M. Kumin in 1946; two daughters and one son. Instructor, 1958-61, and Lecturer in English, 1965-68, Tufts University, Medford, Massachusetts; Lecturer, Newton College of the Sacred Heart, Massachusetts, 1971; Visiting Lecturer/ Professor/Writer, University of Massachusetts, Amherst, 1972, Columbia University, New York, Spring 1975, Brandeis University, Waltham, Massachusetts, Fall 1975, Princeton University, New Jersey, Spring 1977, 1979, 1982, Washington University, St. Louis, 1977, Randolph-Macon Women's College, Lynchburg,

Virginia, 1978, Bucknell University, Lewisburg, Pennsylvania,
1983, and Massachusetts Institute of Technology, Cambridge,
1984. Poetry Consultant, Library of Congress, 1981-82. Since
1979, Woodrow Wilson Visiting Fellow. Scholar, 1961-63, and
since 1972, Officer, Society of Fellows, Radcliffe Institute,
Cambridge, Massachusetts. Recipient: Lowell Mason Palmer
Award, 1960; National Endowment for the Arts grant, 1966;
William Marion Reedy Award, 1968; Eunice Tietjens Memorial
Prize (*Poetry*, Chicago), 1972; Pulitzer Prize, 1973; Radcliffe
College award, 1978; American Academy award, 1980. Honor-
ary degrees: Centre College, Danville, Kentucky, 1976; Davis
and Elkins College, Elkins, West Virginia, 1977; Regis College,
Weston, Massachusetts, 1979; New England College, Henniker,
New Hampshire, 1982; Claremont Graduate School, California,
1983; University of New Hampshire, Durham, 1984. Agent:
Curtis Brown, 575 Madison Avenue, New York, New York
10022. Address: Joppa Road, Warner, New Hampshire 03278,
U.S.A.

PUBLICATIONS

Verse

Halfway. New York, Holt Rinehart, 1961.
The Privilege. New York, Harper, 1965.
The Nightmare Factory. New York, Harper, 1970.
Up Country: Poems of New England, New and Selected. New York, Harper, 1972.
House, Bridge, Fountain, Gate. New York, Viking Press, 1975.
The Retrieval System. New York, Viking Press, 1978; London, Penguin, 1979.
Our Ground Time Here Will Be Brief. New York, Viking Press, 1982.
Closing the Ring. Lewisburg, Pennsylvania, Press of Appletree Alley, 1984.

Novels

Through Dooms of Love. New York, Harper, 1965; as *A Daughter and Her Loves*, London, Gollancz, 1965.
The Passions of Uxport. New York, Harper, 1968.
The Abduction. New York, Harper, 1971.
The Designated Heir. New York, Viking Press, 1974.

Short Stories

Why Can't We Live Together Like Civilized Human Beings? New York, Viking Press, 1982.

Other (for children)

Sebastian and the Dragon. New York, Putnam, 1960.
Spring Things. New York, Putnam, 1961.
Summer Story. New York, Putnam, 1961.
Follow the Fall. New York, Putnam, 1961.
A Winter Friend. New York, Putnam, 1961.
Mittens in May. New York, Putnam, 1962.
No One Writes a Letter to the Snail. New York, Putnam, 1962.
Archibald the Traveling Poodle. New York, Putnam, 1963.
Eggs of Things, with Anne Sexton. New York, Putnam, 1963.
More Eggs of Things, with Anne Sexton. New York, Putnam, 1964.
Speedy Digs Downside Up. New York, Putnam, 1964.
The Beach Before Breakfast. New York, Putnam, 1964.
Paul Bunyan. New York, Putnam, 1966.

Faraway Farm. New York, Norton, 1967.
The Wonderful Babies of 1809 and Other Years. New York, Putnam, 1968.
When Grandmother Was Young. New York, Putnam, 1969.
When Mother Was Young. New York, Putnam, 1970.
When Great Grandmother Was Young. New York, Putnam, 1971.
Joey and the Birthday Present, with Anne Sexton. New York, McGraw Hill, 1971.
The Wizard's Tears, with Anne Sexton. New York, McGraw Hill, 1975.
What Color Is Caesar? New York, McGraw Hill, 1978.
To Make a Prairie: Essays on Poets, Poetry, and Country Living (for adults). Ann Arbor, University of Michigan Press, 1979.
The Microscope. New York, Harper, 1984.

*

Manuscript Collection: Mugar Memorial Library, Boston University.

*   *   *

Maxine Kumin is a poet who has written well about many subjects, in several styles. In her first poems she recreated the substance of her early life and Jewish ancestry, subjects given or even prescribed by a history that continues to engage her attention. The precision of her language is evident in "The Sound of Night," from her first collection: "Now every voice of the hour— the known, the supposed, the strange, / the mindless, the witted, the never seen—/ sing, thrum, impinge, and rearrange / endlessly." In *House, Bridge, Fountain, Gate*, published shortly after she received the Pulitzer Prize in 1973, she returned to those early years, in "The Thirties Revisited" and "Sperm," about her grandfather's issue.

The poems of the middle years are spoken in the voice of a person at odds with her surroundings, concerned, rebellious at times, and resentful of unexpected change. In "At the End of the Affair," one of the best poems, the speaker prepares himself / herself for the inevitable disappointment: "That it should end in an Albert Pick hotel / with the air conditioner gasping like a carp / and the bathroom tap plucking its one-string harp / and the sourmash bond half-gone in the open bottle." The sorrowful song of the victim, in "The Masochist," describes a similar betrayal:

> Beware of blackeyed lovers. Some
> who tease to see you all undone,
> who taste and take you in the game
> will later trample on your spine
> as if they never called you *mine*,
> *mine, mine*.

In these and other poems of this period, such as "For My Son on the Highways of the Mind," Kumin writes a language that successfully appropriates the rhythms of contemporary speech to the forms of art.

In more recent poems, she turns a careful eye toward the circumscribed world of her New Hampshire farm, a weekend and summer residence, in the midst of geese, horses, pine groves, and watering troughs, trying to be "terribly specific about many things." In "The Retrieval System," the title poem of a collection, the barnyard animals have come to dominate her imagination and memory. "Uncannily when I'm alone these features / come up to link my lost people / with the patient domestic beasts of my life.../ Fact: it is people who fade, / it is animals that retrieve them." Kumin finds this life quite comfortable, and in poems such as "Hello, Hello Henry," "The Excrement Poem," and "The Archeology of Marriage," she continues to enjoy and celebrate a world that her suicidal friend, in "Progress Report," "wouldn't wait for." As a poet of nature and domestic life, Kumin is content to let the middle years fall peacefully about her, "petals that stick / in my hair like confetti / as I cut my way through clouds of gnats and butterflies in the woods."

—Michael True

KUNITZ, Stanley (Jasspon). American. Born in Worcester, Massachusetts, 29 July 1905. Educated at Harvard University, Cambridge, Massachusetts (Garrison Medal, 1926), A.B. (summa cum laude) 1926 (Phi Beta Kappa), A.M. 1927. Served in the United States Army, 1943-45. Married 1) Helen Pearce in 1930 (divorced, 1937); 2) Eleanor Evans in 1939 (divorced, 1958), one daughter; 3) Elise Asher in 1958. Editor, *Wilson Library Bulletin*, New York, 1928-43. Member of the Faculty, Bennington College, Vermont, 1946-49; Professor of English, Potsdam State Teachers College (now State University of New York), 1949-50, and summers, 1949-53; Lecturer, New School for Social Research, New York, 1950-57; Visiting Professor, University of Washington, Seattle, 1955-56, Queens College, Flushing, New York, 1956-57, Brandeis University, Waltham, Massachusetts, 1958-59, Yale University, New Haven, Connecticut, 1970-72, Rutgers University, Camden, New Jersey, 1974, Princeton University, New Jersey, 1978, and Vassar College, Poughkeepsie, New York, 1981. Director, YM-YWHA Poetry Workshop, New York, 1958-62. Danforth Visiting Lecturer, United States, 1961-63. Lecturer, 1963-67, and since 1967, Adjunct Professor of Writing, Columbia University, New York: Since 1968 associated with the Fine Arts Work Center, Provincetown, Massachusetts. Editor, Yale Series of Younger Poets, Yale University Press, New Haven, Connecticut, 1969-77. Consultant in Poetry, Library of Congress, Washington, D.C., 1974-76. Formerly, Cultural Exchange Lecturer, U.S.S.R., Poland, Senegal, Ghana, Israel, and Egypt. Senior Fellow in Humanities, Princeton University, 1978. Since 1969, Fellow, Yale University. Recipient: Oscar Blumenthal Prize, 1941, and Levinson Prize, 1956 (*Poetry*, Chicago); Guggenheim Fellowship, 1945; Amy Lowell Traveling Fellowship, 1953; Harriet Monroe Award, 1958; Pulitzer Prize, 1959; Ford grant, 1959; American Academy grant, 1959; Brandeis University Creative Arts Award, 1964; Academy of American Poets Fellowship, 1968; Lenore Marshall Award, 1980; National Endowment for the Arts Senior Fellowship, 1984. Litt.D.: Clark University, Worcester, Massachusetts, 1961; Anna Maria College, Paxton, Massachusetts, 1977; L.H.D.: Worcester State College, Massachusetts, 1980. Member, American Academy; Chancellor, Academy of American Poets, 1970. Address: 37 West 12th Street, New York, New York, 10011, U.S.A.

PUBLICATIONS

Verse

Intellectual Things. New York, Doubleday, 1930.
Passport to the War: A Selection of Poems. New York, Holt, 1944.

Selected Poems 1928-1958. Boston, Little Brown, 1958; London, Dent, 1959.
The Testing-Tree. Boston, Little Brown, 1971.
The Terrible Threshold: Selected Poems 1940-1970. London, Secker and Warburg, 1974.
The Coat Without a Seam: Sixty Poems 1930-1972. Northampton, Massachusetts, Gehenna Press, 1974.
The Lincoln Relics. Port Townsend, Washington, Graywolf Press, 1978.
The Poems of Stanley Kunitz 1928-1978. Boston, Little Brown, and London, Secker and Warburg, 1979.
The Wellfleet Whale and Companion Poems. New York, Sheep Meadow Press, 1983.

Other

Robert Lowell, Poet of Terribilità (lecture). New York, Pierpont Morgan Library, 1974.
A Kind of Order, A Kind of Folly: Essays and Conversations. Boston, Little Brown, 1975.
From Feathers to Iron (lecture). Washington, D.C., Library of Congress, 1976.

Editor (as Dilly Tante), *Living Authors: A Book of Biographies.* New York, Wilson, 1931.
Editor, with Howard Haycraft and Wilbur C. Hadden, *Authors Today and Yesterday: A Companion Volume to "Living Authors."* New York, Wilson, 1933.
Editor, with others, *The Junior Book of Authors.* New York, Wilson, 1934; revised edition, 1961.
Editor, with Howard Haycraft, *British Authors of the Nineteenth Century.* New York, Wilson, 1936.
Editor, with Howard Haycraft, *American Authors, 1600-1900: A Biographical Dictionary of American Literature.* New York, Wilson, 1938.
Editor, with Howard Haycraft, *Twentieth Century Authors: A Biographical Dictionary of Modern Literature.* New York, Wilson, 1942; *First Supplement*, with Vineta Colby, 1955.
Editor, with Howard Haycraft, *British Authors Before 1800: A Biographical Dictionary.* New York, Wilson, 1952.
Editor, *Poems*, by John Keats. New York, Crowell, 1964.
Editor, with Vineta Colby, *European Authors, 1000-1900: A Biographical Dictionary of European Literature.* New York, Wilson, 1967.
Editor and Translator, with Max Hayward, *Poems of Akhmatova.* Boston, Little Brown, 1973; London, Harvill Press, 1974.
Editor and Co-Translator, *Orchard Lamps*, by Ivan Drach. New York, Sheep Meadow Press, 1978.

Translator, with others, *Stolen Apples*, by Yevgeny Yevtushenko. New York, Doubleday, and London, W.H. Allen, 1972.
Translator, with others, *Story under Full Sail*, by Andrei Voznesensky. New York, Doubleday, 1974.

*

Critical Studies: "The Poetry of Stanley Kunitz" by James Hagstrum, in *Poets in Progress* edited by Edward Hungerford, Evanston, Illinois, Northwestern University Press, 1962; *The Contemporary Poet as Artist and Critic* edited by Anthony Ostroff, Boston, Little Brown, 1964; "Man with a Leaf in His Head," in *The Nation* (New York), 20 September 1971, and "The Darkness of the Self," in *Times Literary Supplement* (London), 30 May 1980, both by Stanley Moss; "Voznesensky and Kunitz on Poetry," in *The New York Times Book Review*, 16 April

1972; *The Craft of Poetry* edited by William Packard, New York, Doubleday, 1974; "Imagine Wrestling with an Angel," in *Contemporary Poetry in America* edited by Robert Boyers, New York, Schocken, 1975; "The Language That Saves" by Richard Vine, in *Salmagundi* (Saratoga Springs, New York), Winter 1977; *Stanley Kunitz* by Marie Hénault, Boston, Twayne, 1978; "Stanley Kunitz Issue" of *Antaeus* (New York), Spring 1980; interview with Chris Busa, in *Paris Review*, Spring 1982; *Stanley Kunitz: An Introduction to the Poetry* by Gregory Orr, New York, Columbia University Press, 1985.

Stanley Kunitz comments:

Since my *Selected Poems* I have been moving toward a more open style, based on natural speech rhythms. *The Testing-Tree* (1971) embodied my search for a transparency of language and vision. Maybe age itself compels me to embrace the great simplicities, as I struggle to free myself from the knots and complications, the hang-ups, of my youth. I keep trying to improve my controls over language, so that I won't have to tell lies. And I keep reading the masters, because they infect me with human possibility. I am no more reconciled than I ever was to the world's wrongs and the injustice of time. The poetry I admire most is innocent, luminous, and true.

*   *   *

The poems of Stanley Kunitz have always been carefully made, finely crafted, and attentive to the subtleties of sound and sense. Theodore Roethke, Robert Lowell, and Ralph Mills, among others, have spoken of Kunitz as one of the truly powerful and skilled poets of our time, and he rightly thinks of his work not as a career, but as a life. Kunitz has had the grace, also, to grow and change over the years, exploring the possibilities of new styles that have dominated American poetry since World War II, but never being merely imitative of them. Even in his mid-70's he can write, in "Layers," "I am not done with my changes."

Kunitz's early verses were often highly intellectual or what is called metaphysical in style. One hears in them echoes of several 17th-century English poets, especially John Donne and Andrew Marvell, as well as of their 20th-century American counterparts, T.S. Eliot and John Crowe Ransom. The work of his second collection resembled the first, in its formal style and modernist theme. "Postscript," for example, speaks of the conflict between intellect and feeling, which provides the tension and drama of much of Kunitz's work. In "Benediction" and "Grammar Lesson," in couplets and quatrains respectively, he exhibits the gift for rhyme that brought him early to poetry. He once described his change in poetic style, from the lean, hard, and reasoned approach of the early years, to the more natural, simpler style, since 1960: in his youth, he said, he rather willed himself into being somewhat closed to outside influences; but in later years, he has tried to make his work more open and accessible, "without sacrificing its more complex inner tissue."

Kunitz's poetry, retracing the myth of the lost father, is usually informed by a tragic vision. "The heart breaks and breaks / and lives by breaking," he writes in "The Testing-Tree." But he also speaks in other styles and moods as well. "The Magic Curtain," written in the early 1970's, is a bouyant, nostalgic love poem to his mother's former housekeeper, beautiful yellow-haired Frieda, who took him to afternoon movies, during his childhood in Worcester, Massachusetts. The two of them skipped school in order to live for a few hours among "The Perils of Pauline" or the antics of the Keystone Kops and Charlie Chaplin. In another recent poem—a witty parody of the traditional love lyric—one partner compares the other to Chairman Mao. "Loving you was

a kind of Chinese guerilla war," the lover complains in "After the Last Dynasty."

Through a devotion to craft and an insistence upon a high standard of performance, Stanley Kunitz has produced a body of work that increases in stature over the years. In *Poems 1928-1978*, he collects the best of these poems. The essays in *A Kind of Order, A Kind of Folly*, particularly "Poet and State," provide useful commentary on his way of maintaining a distinctive and disciplined vision, the basis of his achievement in poetry.

—Michael True

KYGER, Joanne. American. Born in Vallejo, California, 19 November 1934. Educated at Santa Barbara City College, California, 1952-56. Married 1) Gary Snyder, *q.v.*, in 1960 (divorced, 1965); 2) John Boyce in 1966 (died, 1972). Lived in Japan, 1960-64; performer and poet in experimental television project, 1967-68. Recipient: National Endowment for the Arts grant, 1968. Lives in Bolinas, California. Address: c/o Dutton Inc., 2 Park Avenue, New York, New York 10016, U.S.A.

PUBLICATIONS

Verse

The Tapestry and the Web. San Francisco, Four Seasons, 1965.
The Fool in April: A Poem. San Francisco, Coyote, 1966.
Places to Go. Los Angeles, Black Sparrow Press, 1970.
Joanne. New York, Angel Hair, 1970.
Desecheo Notebook. Berkeley, California, Arif Press, 1971.
Trip Out and Fall Back. Berkeley, California, Arif Press, 1974.
All This Every Day. Bolinas, California, Big Sky, 1975.
Up My Coast / Sulla mia costa. Melano, Switzerland, Caos Press, 1978; Point Reyes, California, Floating Island, 1981.
The Wonderful Focus of You. Calais, Vermont, Z Press, 1980.
Mexico Blondé. Bolinas, California, Evergreen Press, 1981.
Going On: Selected Poems 1958-1980. New York, Dutton, 1983.

Other

Japan and India Journal 1960-1964. Bolinas, California, Tombouctou, 1981.

*

Manuscript Collection: University of California, San Diego.

Joanne Kyger comments:

I myself am a West Coast poet, but I also feel an affinity for much of the work of the younger New York poets.

My vision of the poet changes so I can stay alive and the muse can stay alive. I report on my states of consciousness and the story I am telling.

*   *   *

Joanne Kyger is not Circe, but she has admired Circe. Her first book, *The Tapestry and the Web*, exhibits great mythic propensities. In it she reactivates the Odysseus myth; only, unlike

Pound and Joyce and Olson, she enlarges the feminine aspect of the *Odyssey*. She is not Penelope, either, waiting on a man (or anyone else) for her fate. *Her* Penelope is not domesticated patience; rather, she is the mother of Pan, by a clever etymological pun. Kyger's destiny as poet is her own responsibility, and she has borne it as Pan, free-spirited and ranging. Her "Web" is metaphoric of the poem itself, patterned freely and self-supporting—the isolate narrative strands which, when bound together, capture the reader, bringing meaning. Her gifts as narrator in foregrounding the old tales are extraordinary. In fact, it is this technique that characterizes almost all her poems— a pattern marked by sudden cuts of consciousness, the narrative abruptly shifting in flight, not relying on startling imagery to mark changes of direction. A significant-early poem is "The Maze," in which there are several entrances but only a single exit or resolution or alternative to bewilderment.

Her early poems deliberately hold personality back. They are populated by disembodied presences—an unmoored "he" or "she," various "figures"—engaged in vague but effective drama. Her "I" is a non-confessional, impersonal, automatic speaker— Jack Spicer's influence, perhaps. In the later 1960's and 1970's she kept a greater account of herself, reporting directly in such books as *Joanne* and *All This Every Day* that it is "Joanne" that is interesting, wonderful to behold making her sense out of the world. She has kept close to what she knows, absorbed by the day's, any day's, contents and contentments, while rejecting disposable, paper-plate America (as in "Don't Hope to Gain by What Has Preceded").

The turning point comes—it can almost be dated—with "August 18" in *Places to Go*, where a new personality arises in phases like a moon over the mesa. By the time of *All This Every Day*, the "I" becomes more obviously the poet's own personality, and steps out into quotidian daylight, where there are sharper outlines. Titles now become dates ("October 29, Wednesday," "October 31," etc.), poems are entries in imagination's almanac, records of the day as lived a little closer to understanding, a catalogue of motives, concordances, accords. The daily brings with it a new ambition for *samadhi*, total consciousness, like Little Neural Annie attains in "Soon," with what has become characteristic humor for the poet:

> Little Neural Annie was fined $65 in the Oakland
> Traffic Court this season for "driving while in
> a state of samadhi." California secular law requires
> that all drivers of motor vehicles remain firmly seated
> within their bodies while the vehicle is in motion.
> This applies to both greater vehicles and lesser
> vehicles.

Kyger puts the comic back in cosmic. Relationships, too, yield attainment, as in these lovely lines: "She makes / herself, decorative, agreeable, for him. They nod / inside a flower, a wonderful room." It is a leisurely, drifting poetry, stirring in the breeze, absorbing the occasional muffled chaos, a day's small panics. Only in such a relaxed state do the lines work so effectively, without the uneconomical expense of willful pressure.

Generally, her work is characterized by eagerness, even in the face of a disaster such as the plundering of a camp cabin by a bear. "Destruction" may well become her most famous poem—a great chuckle of a poem, although a more formal analysis might speak of its excellent dramatic device by which to inventory a society, as the speaker follows the bear's path of destruction, pad and pencil in hand, as if for a police report or insurance claim:

> He eats all the apples, limes, dates, bottled decaffeinated
> coffee, and 35 pounds of granola. The asparagus soup
> cans
> fall to the floor. Yum!...Rips open the water bed, eats
> the incense and
> drinks the perfume...Knocks *Shelter, Whole Earth Catalogue,*
> *Planet, Drum, Northern Mists, Truck Tracks,* and
> *Women's Sports* into the oozing water bed mess.
>
>   He goes
> down stairs and out the back wall. He keeps on going
> for a long way and finds a good cave to sleep it all off.
> Luckily he ate the whole medicine cabinet, including
> stash
> of LSD, Peyote, Psilocybin, Amanita, Benzedrine, Valium
> and aspirin.

Her images are few; puns not essential; devices, tricks, syncopations unintended; diction is comfortable. Her lines are biomorphic, ever-adjusting to what they seek to accomplish—not to hold the world at bay or shore up ruined traditions, but extending out to join the oncoming freshened world. The value of her work lies in its openness, its whimsy, the acceptance of daily change. Her poems are attentive to a spirit's needs, a deep-drawn aim within aimlessness. She has never been less than autonomous, and thus is beyond the futile eddies of taste. Always a free spirit, she has rarely spoken for any group larger than her thoughts. It amounts to a style, to which she has faithfully adhered.

—George F. Butterick

LAL, P. Indian. Born in Kapurthala, Punjab, 28 August 1929. Educated at St. Xavier's School, Calcutta, B.A. 1950; Calcutta University, M.A. in English literature 1952. Married Shyamasree Devi in 1955; one son and one daughter. Professor of English, St. Xavier's College, Calcutta, 1952-67; now Honorary Professor. Since 1967, Professor of English, University of Calcutta. Visiting Professor, Hofstra University, Hempstead, New York, 1962-63, University of Illinois, Urbana, 1968, Albion College, Michigan, Spring 1973, Ohio University, Athens, 1973-74, and Berea College, Kentucky, 1977. Since 1958, Founder and Secretary, Writers Workshop, publishers, and Editor, *Writers Workshop Miscellany*, Calcutta; Editor with Alfred Schenkman, *Orient Review and Literary Digest*, Calcutta, 1954-58. Delegate, P.E.N. Conference, New York, 1966. Recipient: Jawaharlal Nehru Fellowship, 1969. D.Litt: Western Maryland College, Westminster, 1977. Awarded the Padmashri title by Government of India, 1970. Address: 162/92 Lake Gardens, Calcutta 700 045, India.

PUBLICATIONS

Verse

The Parrot's Death and Other Poems. Calcutta, Writers Workshop, 1960.
Love's the First. Calcutta, Writers Workshop, 1962.
"Change!" They Said: New Poems. Calcutta, Writers Workshop, 1966.

Draupadi and Jayadratha and Other Poems. Calcutta, Writers Workshop, 1967.
Creations and Transcreations: Three Poems, Selections from the Subhasita-Ratna-Kosa, and The First 92 Slokas from the Mahabharata. Calcutta, Dialogue, 1968.
Yakshi from Didarganj. Calcutta, Writers Workshop, 1969.
The Man of Dharma and the Rasa of Silence. Calcutta, Writers Workshop, 1974.
Calcutta. Calcutta, Writers Workshop, 1977.
The Collected Poems of P. Lal. Calcutta, Writers Workshop, 1977.

Other

The Art of the Essay. Delhi, Atma Ram, 1951.
An Annotated Mahabharata Bibliography. Calcutta, Writers Workshop, 1967.
The Concept of an Indian Literature: Six Essays. Calcutta, Writers Workshop, 1968.
Transcreation: Two Essays. Calcutta, Writers Workshop, 1971.
The Lemon Tree of Modern Sex and Other Essays. Calcutta, Writers Workshop, 1974.
The Alien Insiders: Indian Writing in English. Calcutta, Writers Workshop, 1979.
Personalities: Meetings with Writers. Calcutta, Writers Workshop, 1979.

Editor, *The Merchant of Venice,* by William Shakespeare. Delhi, Atma Ram, 1952.
Editor, with K.R. Rao, *Modern Indo-Anglian Poetry.* New Delhi, Kavita, 1959.
Editor, *T.S. Eliot: Homage from India: A Commemoration Volume of 55 Essays and Elegies.* Calcutta, Writers Workshop, 1965.
Editor, *The First Workshop Story Anthology.* Calcutta, Writers Workshop, 1967.
Editor, *Modern Indian Poetry in English: The Writers Workshop Selection: An Anthology and a Credo.* Calcutta, Writers Workshop, 1969.
Editor, *Selected Poems: A Selection of Lyrics,* by Manmohan Ghose. Calcutta, Writers Workshop, 1969.
Editor, *The First* [and *Second*] *Writers Workshop Literary Reader.* Calcutta, Writers Workshop, 1970-73.
Editor, *New English Poetry by Indian Women.* Calcutta, Writers Workshop, 1977.

Translator, *Premchand: His Life and Work,* by Hans Raj Rahbar. Delhi, Atma Ram, 1957.
Translator, with Jai Ratan, *Godan,* by Premchand. Bombay, Jaico, 1957.
Translator, *Great Sanskrit Plays in New English Transcreations.* New York, New Directions, 1964.

Transcreator, *Sanskrit Love Lyrics.* Calcutta, Writers Workshop, 1965.
Transcreator, *The Bhagavad-Gita.* Calcutta, Writers Workshop, 1965.
Transcreator, *The Golden Womb of the Sun: Rig-vedic Songs.* Calcutta, Writers Workshop, 1965.
Transcreator, *The Dhammapada.* New York, Farrar Straus, 1967.
Transcreator, *The Jap-Ji: Fourteen Religious Songs.* Calcutta, Writers Workshop, 1967.
Transcreator, *The Isa-Upanisad.* Calcutta, Writers Workshop, 1967.
Transcreator, *Some Sanskrit Poems.* Calcutta, Writers Workshop, 1967.

Transcreator, *The Farce of the Drunk Monk,* by Raja Mehendra-varman. Calcutta, Writers Workshop, 1968.
Transcreator, *The Avyakta-Upanisad.* Calcutta, Writers Workshop, 1969.
Transcreator, *The Mahabharata.* Calcutta, Writers Workshop, 120 monthly vols., 1969-79; condensed version, as *The Mahabharata of Vyasa,* New Delhi, Vikas, 1980.
Transcreator, *More Songs from the Jap-Ji.* Calcutta, Writers Workshop, 1969.
Transcreator, *Ghalib's Love Poems.* Calcutta, Dialogue, 1970.
Transcreator, *The Mahanarayana Upanisad.* Calcutta, Writers Workshop, 1971.
Transcreator, with Shyamasree Devi, *Tagore's Last Poems.* Calcutta, Writers Workshop, 1972.
Transcreator, *The Brhadaranyaka Upanisad.* Calcutta, Writers Workshop, 1974.
Transcreator, with Shyamasree Devi, *Where To, Tarapada-babu?* Calcutta, Writers Workshop, 1974.
Transcreator, with Nandini Nopany, *Twenty-Four Stories,* by Premchand. New Delhi, Vikas, 1980.
Transcreator, *The Ramayana of Valmiki.* New Delhi, Vikas, 1981.

*

Critical Studies: "P. Lal's Poetry" by Nita Pillai, in *Poetry India* (Bombay), i,3, 1965; *P. Lal: An Appreciation* by Shankar Mokashi-Punekar, Calcutta, Writers Workshop, 1968; "P. Lal: A Major Indo-English Poet" by Subhas C. Saha, in *The Banasthali Patrika* (Banasthali), January 1969; "The Poetry of P. Lal" by Suresh Kohli, in *Thought* (Delhi), xx, 30, 1969; "P. Lal's Literary Endeavours" by M.P. Kohli, in *Sunday Standard* (Bombay), 14 January 1979; "Metaphor, Music, and Morality: P. Lal's Poetry" by Prema Nandakumar, in *Deccan Herald* (Bangalore), 21 January 1979; "Doyen of Indo-Anglian Poets" by Rajkumar, in *The Tribune* (Chandigarh), 10 February 1979.

*   *   *

P. Lal is a key figure in the landscape of Indo-English creative writing. He has played a multiple role with remarkable success. Poet, ideologist for Indo-English creativity, avant-garde publisher for markedly new writing, translator of classics, responsible orientalist, he has filled a varied bill, which, in return, has conditioned his own growth through sudden transitions and empirical intuitions. The movements he seemed to lead in the early post-Independence years rallied a good many competent rebels around him under the simple banner: Indians can create in English; but they must break with the past genre of the pompous and the amorphous! To that slogan no contenders are left, and the movement should have reached the more painful state of self-examination with the question: Is that enough? But Lal's pluralist approach has skilfully doctored the movement into a painless transition. In the process, not only Lal's organising ability but his poetic practice has played a role, not exactly by trend-setting but by ice-breaking. Lal's poetry cannot be isolated from the multiple role he has played; it forms a setting for his growth.

Lal's first four collections mark a development, in themes, in technique, even in objectives, though the corpus is too thin to reveal it from book to later book. Since 1960, he has been bringing out collections at regular intervals; but before that is a fifteen-year stretch of apprenticeship. An early poem like "Beside the Pipal," recording a delicately veined Indian pastorale, is an index of some early ambition to poetise on national themes, abandoned under the compulsion of international norms, but restored to a later collection (*"Change!" They Said*) under a renewed sense of national commitment. An oddly rhetorical piece like "On Transience" in an early collection (*The Parrot's Death*) is the token of competent kitten play, too good to be thrown away but too out of character to fit into a stabler manner cultivated later: "and when the winds howl, their raucous breath/convulses the green continence of earth." To make these rhetorical convulsions click is a sign of healthy apprenticeship and can prove a second string to the bow when social commitments demand a raucous breath, as in *"Change!" They Said*: Lal's most stable manner, however, was the green continence of earth.

A studied and taut delicacy which seldom lapses into aestheticism may well be the most fascinating undertone of Lal's verse. A painfully keen love of beauty in nature, in flowers, birds and trees, is ever rendered sturdy by a vigorous mancentredness. Lal's perceptions are delicate and firm; he sketches them in clean strokes: "A mustard of butterflies/Hovers round a lovely eye." Not just a poetic image that, but a perception. Lal shows the same delicacy in love, a theme that dominates his second collection, *Love's the First*. Fortunately for us, Lal is not ashamed of his cleverness and we get fine cavalier swashbuckling:

> Love, twin-fuselaged
> Sweeps serenely thus
> (Weather Report: Unfair)
> To passion's terminus.

Lal constantly returns to the manner of spare expression and self-control. And while he belongs to the avant-garde, he must have his roses, petals, leaves and bees to stand by him. Why? We get a clue in poems of another kind, what may be described as lyrics of human behaviour. Lal constantly returns to an adoration of civilized behaviour, a fine instance of which is "The Letter"—a poem written in a mood of agonized gratitude to a brother whose letter opens up old wounds again by its painful but civil talk. Lal's love for language is the greater for its being the index of a rooted civility which is its distinctive feature. The same quality illuminates his effort at self-control and often at self-accusation; and that returns us to Lal the organizer. The finest expression of this "culture" is seen in a really ripe poem like "The Leaf" (in *"Change!" They Said*) in which he accurately sums up the stages of his life: "Cupped in decrepit easy chair/Mellow gum in eyes." Lal's care for words is not a part of his technique but a part of his vision of life—its beauty and tautness. Words, for Lal, are the indices of summations inherent in humanity's past experience, and Lal constantly tries to connect: "Here meaning is in fragrances/And life is the careful delivery of leaf."

Such attitudes cannot but compel Lal to seek roots in an Indian tradition; two trends are already significant—Lal's growing impatience with the rootless highbrow, and with the monstrous outgrowths of India's hurried social transformation which has inspired some raucous social satire of late; and a growing orientalism, primarily for translation, but inspiring poems like *Draupadi and Jayadratha*, which reveal an altogether different Lal.

—Shankar Mokashi-Punekar

LAMANTIA, Philip. American. Born in San Francisco, California, 23 October 1927. Educated in San Francisco public schools. Assistant Editor, *View* magazine, New York, 1944. Address: c/o City Lights Books, 261 Columbus Avenue, San Francisco, California 94133, U.S.A.

PUBLICATIONS

Verse

Erotic Poems. Berkeley, Calfornia, Bern Porter, 1946.
Tower, with *Manifesto* by Max Finstein. San Francisco, Golden Mountain Press, 1958.
Ekstasis. San Francisco, Auerhahn Press, 1959.
Destroyed Works: Hypodermic Light, Mantic Notebook, Still Poems, Spansule. San Francisco, Auerhahn Press, 1962.
Touch of the Marvelous. Berkeley, California, Oyez, 1966.
Selected Poems 1943-1966. San Francisco, City Lights, 1967.
Penguin Modern Poets 13, with Charles Bukowski and Harold Norse. London, Penguin, 1969.
The Blood of the Air. San Francisco, Four Seasons, 1970.
Becoming Visible. San Francisco, City Lights, 1981.

Other

Narcotica, with Antonin Artaud. San Francisco, Auerhahn Press, 1959.

*

Critical Study: prefatory note by Parker Tyler to *Touch of the Marvelous*, 1966.

Philip Lamantia comments:

I consider myself essentially a surrealist, but as Breton qualified this, it is *not* a "school," but a way of life.

I understand the act of poetry as the maximum volatile expression of Imagination, a *central power*, relating all levels of conscious and unconscious thought and being. I believe in poetry as a means of unqualified individual liberation. I believe in the poetry of primal melody and the revelation of the mysteries of cosmic being.

*   *   *

Although Philip Lamantia's life has been one of change and travel the poetry has continued its function as a tightly controlled inner ritual, and the poem has been continually characterized by a highly burnished surface that seems to gleam with such stillness that if the poem was turned from side to side light would glance off it. It was as a Surrealist that he was published, at the age of fifteen, by Charles Henri Ford and Parker Tyler in their magazine *View*. André Breton, then living in the United States, called him "a voice that rises once in a hundred years." The shifting of image, the layering of association that is characteristic of surrealism has continued in his work, and his language has the hardness of a glimpse through a prism: "The mermaids have come to the desert/They are setting up a boudoir next to the camel/who lies at their feet of roses." But with his first book, *Erotic Poems*, he felt that he had broken with the surrealists, and it was a lyric physicality that gave the book its dominant mood. Though there was still a complex surface imagery in the poems it was, as he had titled it, a collection of erotic poems. The language often had a closeness of physical contact that was almost like a breath: "The crash of your heart/beating its way through a fever of fish/is heard in every crowd of that thirsty tomorrow/ and your trip ends in the mask of my candle-lit hair."

A consciousness of brutality has continued in his poetry, even though he is sometimes able to shake it off long enough to see it at a distance from himself. The poem sometimes becomes obsessive in its awareness of cruelty:

> Come my ritual wax and circles
> my rose spitting blood
> When the day is lit up by our magic candles
> and the hours yell their sadistic songs and suck hard
> into the night when the cats invade our skulls

A similar cruelty is apparent in this example of early work finally published in *Touch of the Marvelous*: "The hanged girl in my mirror watches with horror/as I exchange my eyes for yours/ But, too late/I pull the gun's trigger/and the mirror shatters." But his work shifted away from this obsessiveness, and he began to find another imagery in his experience, and he was able to write "From a window I see the world/As I would see love." It was after this affirmation that his wanderings began. Of the younger group of San Francisco poets, Lamantia was the first to begin experimenting with altered states of consciousness. He was initiated into the Washo Indian peyote rites in Nevada in 1953, and then spent three years in Mexico, living for some time with the Cora Indians of Nayarit. It was at the close of this period that he destroyed all of his earlier work, and it was not until the late 1950's that he began publishing again. The poems he had destroyed were eventually published in 1962. He spent much of the 1960's in Europe, continuing his search into the forces and the planes of the poem.

Lamantia's work, coming out of a forties dominated in the United States by Eliot and Frost, Stevens and Cummings, seemed to be an entirely new element, an entirely new structuring of the emotions of the poem. Despite the efforts of Ford and others there had not been any wide attention paid to the surrealists, and the first American writing in the idiom forced a belated recognition of the power of surrealist technique. This is not to say that Lamantia became a poet with any kind of popular following, but he was widely read by other poets. In any outline of the main currents of American poetry of the 1940's his name must be considered as one of the forces that led to the burst of surrealist poetry in the United States in the 1950's and 1960's.

—Samuel Charters

LANE, Patrick. Canadian. Born in Nelson, British Columbia, 26 March 1939. Attended Vernon High School, British Columbia. Married 1) Mary Hayden in 1958 (divorced, 1967), two sons and one daughter; 2) Carol Beale in 1973 (divorced, 1978), two sons; now living with Lorna Uher. Worked in sawmills and logging camps, as house builder and field worker. Since 1966, Editor, Very Stone House, later Very Stone House in Transit, Vancouver. Writer-in-Residence, University of Manitoba, Winnipeg, 1978-79, University of Ottawa, 1980, University of Alberta, Edmonton, 1981-82, Saskatoon Public Library, 1982-83, and Globe Theatre Company, Regina, Saskatchewan, 1984-85. Also an artist and illustrator. Recipient: Canada Council grant, 1973-74, 1976-78, 1983-84; Ontario Arts Council grant, 1975, 1978; Governor-General's Award, 1978; Manitoba Arts Council grant, 1979; Saskatchewan Arts Council grant, 1983. Address: c/o League of Canadian Poets, 24 Ryerson Avenue, Toronto, Ontario M5T 2P3, Canada.

PUBLICATIONS

Verse

Letters from the Savage Mind. Vancouver, Very Stone House, 1966.
For Rita—In Asylum. Vancouver, Very Stone House, 1969.
Calgary City Jail. Vancouver, Very Stone House, 1969.
Separations. Trumansburg, New York, Crossing Press, 1969.
Sunflower Seeds. Vancouver, Western Press, 1969.
On the Street. Vancouver, Very Stone House, 1970.
Mountain Oysters. Vancouver, Very Stone House, 1971.
Hiway 401 Rhapsody. Vancouver, Very Stone House, 1972.
The Sun Has Begun to Eat the Mountain. Montreal, Ingluvin, 1972.
Passing into Storm. Vernon, British Columbia, Traumerei, 1973.
Beware the Months of Fire. Toronto, Anansi, 1974.
Certs. Prince George, British Columbia, College of New Caledonia, 1974.
Unborn Things: South American Poems. Madeira Park, British Columbia, Harbour, 1975.
For Riel in That Gawdam Prison. White Rock, British Columbia, Blackfish Press, 1975.
Albino Pheasants. Madeira Park, British Columbia, Harbour, 1977.
If. Toronto, Dreadnaught Press, 1977.
Poems, New and Selected. Toronto, Oxford University Press, 1978; London, Oxford University Press, 1979; New York, Oxford University Press, 1980.
No Longer Two People, with Lorna Uher. Winnipeg, Turnstone Press, 1979.
There Are Still the Mountains. Vancouver, Very Stone House, 1979.
The Measure. Windsor, Ontario, Black Moss Press, 1980.
The Garden. Toronto, League of Canadian Poets, 1980.
Old Mother. Toronto, Oxford University Press, 1982.

Other

(*Drawings*). Whitehorse, Yukon, Tundra Graphics, 1981.

*

Manuscript Collections: McMaster University, Hamilton, Ontario; University of British Columbia, Vancouver.

Critical Study: "Pine Boughs and Apple Trees" by Marilyn Bowering, in *Malahat Review* (Victoria, British Columbia), January 1978.

*   *   *

Patrick Lane is a native of the interior of British Columbia. The essential center of his poetry is its consciousness of that landscape and mythology: "Because I never learned how/to be gentle and the country/I lived in was hard with dead/animals and men, I didn't question...." If, as Lawrence Durrell says, landscape is character, Lane is a kind of Proteus taking on the shapes of his place, at once fierce and uncompromising in response to its violence and terrible beauty. He writes of logging camps and forests, of bush farming, hunting, herding cattle, all of which he knows at first hand. Whatever the private complex out of which he writes, he understands violence. He writes of people who survive by manipulating violence—the loggers, hustlers, religious bigots, even his father; and of those who have been smashed by it—the derelicts, prostitutes, the murdered child. He speaks without judgement, knowing the cannibal impulse in himself, "that brutal anger that cannot be relieved except on things," and perhaps this is the most exciting aspect of his work because he can write without sentimentality about ordinary cruelty. He also understands the traps of victimization. His poem "What Does Not Change," a long poem about a hooker, is the frankest and yet most compassionate poem I know about that world. Its language is tough and colloquial and yet the literary allusions the poet has managed to weave into the anecdotes give the whole a large reference that makes it a remarkable piece. Lane has a fine gift for image and writes of the tragic not histrionically but in understatement, deflecting attention to some small detail that is made to carry the full horror of a situation. He has an empathy for all of life that is pained and vulnerable: for the young woman dead from an abortion in a dingy hotel room, for the boy who blows his mother's arm off with a bomb, for the old man who shoves pins into his dead arm cadging drinks.

Many Canadian poets, such as P.K. Page, Al Purdy, and Earle Birney, have proven gifted tourists. In 1975, Lane published a fine sequence of South American poems, called *Unborn Things*, illustrated by his own drawings. The poems catch the mythic surreality and the breathing violence of that culture:

> After the dog drowns in the arroyo
> and the old people stumble into the jungle
> muttering imprecations at the birds
> and the child draws circles in the dust
> for bits of glass to occupy
> like eyes staring out of earth
> and the woman lies on her hammock
> dreaming of the lover who will save her
> from the need to make bread again
> I will go into the field
> and be buried with the corn.

Some poems speak from the Inca past, others from the present to create a remarkable sequence of South American voices.

Poems, New and Selected shows him engaging in a careful study of poetics and enlarging the range of his subject matter; this book places him securely as one of Canada's best poets.

—Rosemary Sullivan

LANGLAND, Joseph (Thomas). American. Born in Spring Grove, Minnesota, 16 February 1917. Educated at Spring Grove High School; Santa Ana Junior College, California, A.A. 1936; University of Iowa, Iowa City, B.A. 1940, M.A. 1941, 1946-48. Served in the United States Army, 1942-46: Captain. Married the artist Judith Gail Wood in 1943; one daughter and two sons. Schoolteacher, Winneshiek County, Iowa, 1936-38; Instructor in English, Dana College, Blair, Nebraska, 1941-42; Assistant Professor, then Associate Professor of English, University of Wyoming, Laramie, 1948-59. Associate Professor, 1959-64, and Professor of English, 1964-79, University of Massachusetts,

Amherst; now emeritus. Visiting Professor of Poetry, University of British Columbia, Vancouver, 1960, San Francisco State College, 1961, University of Washington, Seattle, 1964, and the University of Oregon, Eugene, 1968, 1969. Poetry Editor, *Massachusetts Review*, Amherst, 1960-66. Recipient: Ford Fellowship, 1953; Fund for the Advancement of Education in the Humanities grant, 1953; Amy Lowell Traveling Fellowship, 1955; Melville Cane Award, 1964; National Endowment for the Arts grant, 1966. D.Litt.: Luther College, Decorah, Iowa, 1974. Address: 16 Morgan Circle, Amherst, Massachusetts 01002, U.S.A.

PUBLICATIONS

Verse

For Harold. Augsburg, Germany, 1945.
The Green Town. New York, Scribner, 1956.
A Little Homily. Northampton, Massachusetts, Apiary Press, 1960.
The Wheel of Summer. New York, Dial Press, 1963.
The Sacrifice Poems. Cedar Falls, University of Northern Iowa, 1975.
A Dream of Love. Amherst, Massachusetts, Blue Triangle Press, 1976.
In the Shell of the Ear and Other Poems. Northampton, Massachusetts, Hampshire Typothetae, 1977.
Any Body's Song. New York, Doubleday, 1980.

Recording: *Today's Poets 1*, with others, Folkways, 1967.

Other

Editor, with James B. Hall, *The Short Story.* New York, Macmillan, 1956.
Editor, with Paul Engle, *Poet's Choice.* New York, Dial Press, 1962.

Translator, with Tamas Aczel and Laszlo Tikos, *Poetry from the Russian Underground.* New York, Harper, 1973.

*

Critical Studies: in *Southern Review* (Baton Rouge, Louisiana), i, 4, 1965; *Tri-Quarterly 5* (Evanston, Illinois), 1966; *Georgia Review* (Athens), Fall 1980.

Joseph Langland comments:

(1970) I began writing in relative isolation. While I know many of the living poets and have corresponded with many, I have never espoused a special group or followed any central creed or statement in poetry.

I join colloquial American speech to the traditions. While much of my immediate subject material has come from the landscape and life of rural America, its true subject is usually the relationship of the individual to the world. Forms are various, sources numerous. I think I am my own man. Presently, I am deeply interested in exploring the chaotic condition of American (and likely world) culture. My orientation is oral rather than visual; in all I write I wish never to neglect the singing voice, even in the harshest poem. All subjects pursue some kind of form, either out of themselves or their situations.

(1985) In the mid-1980's there is no dominant poet or critic of poetry writing in English. There are no leaders generally acknowledged; consequently, we have a large number of interesting and competent writers, and we await some new invention, or consolidation, beyond the vast proliferation of egocentric free verse.

*　　*　　*

Joseph Langland's best poems occur when a personal vision of history unites with a song-like immediacy, when his particular emotional intensity and subtlety meet with craft and intellect unnoticed—as in the long poem ("An Open Letter") to Ralph Ellison, and in many of the "Sacrifice" poems of *The Wheel of Summer.*

There is no discordance in such poems, and an authority rings in the voice and diction of "A Hiroshima Lullaby." The same power and quality are in early poems ("War"); and in "Norwegian Rivers" or "Dandelion" a quiet appropriateness fills both vision and voice:

> You are both a small sun
> and a pale moon.
> When you come
> flowering through the daylight
> my blood smiles in its skin.

But Langland finds horror, too ("Buchenwald"), or an expansive and "moving" sadness, as in "Libertyville," one of the Stevenson sequence.

The sequence of "Sacrifice" poems in Langland's award-winning volume relates the different deaths a boy experiences on a Minnesota farm as he comes of age. These are the sacrifices the world makes, it seems, to the spiritual education and filling of a man, and lest this seem presumptuous, the wheel becomes a cycle of dyings—from all various causes and sources—which the maturing youth comes to participate in and even, finally, perpetrate. All nature is caught in this cycle of dying, and in the poems a consciousness remembers joining, becoming aware of the deaths surrounding it and whirling mysteriously away into the past; the consciousness forms and wakens so that finally the "wheel of summer" is natural, a cause and celebration as well as death. Not surprisingly, then, the poems often function as loving equations, metaphors, although much of the surprise inherent in the structure of individual poems dissipates when the poems are placed in sequence or when Langland's concern for "first principles" strikes against his contemporary feeling for the intrinsic holiness of separate things.

Even Langland's early poems suggested music. More recently, especially in *Any Body's Song*, he has begun to celebrate his love of music in topic, form, and rhythm. Poems dedicated to composers, musicians, and lovers of music abound, and he often parallels the structures and lilt of song forms. In the title poem he sings:

> Take me from these new alarms;
> be a lute upon my arms.
> Tell me, for the body's sake,
> song and lute and heart will break.
> Though it bring disaster soon,
> I would tremble in this tune
> till our bodies rise and fade
> downward to another shade.

Langland's prosody has become increasingly noticeable and conscious. He has focused on the development of craft and form, so that the themes and symbols of raw nature which were so prominent in *The Wheel of Summer* do not provide the principal energy of these later poems. Frequently, his subjects come from the figures of literature and art as well as music; more importantly, the form and craft of the poems is as significant as their themes and the life they depend upon. Often, in fact, theme is submerged in form. Langland, in a "postscript" to *Any Body's Song* explains that

> I hear the cry, "Be natural!" and then I walk out and examine rocks, leaves, grass, birds, animals, people, the flow of wind and fire and water. They all cry out, "Form!" Without it all reproductive things die out. The absence of form is unnatural.... I believe in a kind of inspiration, but it comes most often to those who work at it.... Most good poems are unbalanced in favor of the art of their own ideas. They do not want to be neutral, nor does the poet behind them.... It is both popular and easy to forsake art in favor of the propaganda of the "right" idea....

—Joseph Wilson

LARKIN, Philip (Arthur). British. Born in Coventry, Warwickshire, 9 August 1922. Educated at King Henry VIII School, Coventry, 1930-40; St. John's College, Oxford, 1940-43, B.A. 1943, M.A. 1947. Librarian, Wellington, Shropshire, 1943-45; Assistant Librarian, University College, Leicester, 1946-49; Sub-Librarian, Queen's University, Belfast, 1950-54. Since 1955, Librarian, Brynmor Jones Library, University of Hull. Jazz feature writer, *Daily Telegraph*, London, 1961-71. Visiting Fellow, All Souls College, Oxford, 1970-71. Chairman, National Manuscript Collection of Contemporary Writers Committee, 1972-79; Member, Arts Council Literature Panel, 1980-82. Since 1984, Member of the Board, British Library. Recipient: Arts Council Prize, 1965; Queen's Gold Medal, 1965; Cholmondeley Award, 1973; Loines Award, 1974; Benson Medal, 1975, and Companion of Literature, 1978, Royal Society of Literature; Shakespeare Prize (Hamburg), 1976; Coventry Award of Merit, 1978; W.H. Smith Award, 1984. D.Lit.: Queen's University, Belfast, 1969; New University of Ulster, Coleraine, 1983; Oxford University, 1984; D. Litt.: University of Leicester, 1970; University of Warwick, 1973; University of St. Andrews, 1974; University of Sussex, Brighton, 1974. Honorary Fellow, St. John's College, Oxford, 1973. Fellow, Royal Society of Literature, and Royal Society of Arts; Honorary Member, American Academy of Arts and Sciences, 1975. C.B.E. (Commander, Order of the British Empire), 1975. Address: Brynmor Jones Library, University of Hull, Hull HU6 7RX, England.

PUBLICATIONS

Verse

The North Ship.   London, Fortune Press, 1945; revised edition, London, Faber, 1966.
XX Poems.   Privately printed, 1951.
(Poems).   Oxford, Fantasy Press, 1954.
The Less Deceived.   Hessle, Yorkshire, Marvell Press, 1955; New York, St. Martin's Press, 1960.
The Whitsun Weddings.   London, Faber, and New York, Random House, 1964.
The Explosion.   London, Poem-of-the-Month Club, 1970.
Corgi Modern Poets in Focus 5, with others, edited by Jeremy Robson.   London, Corgi, 1971.

High Windows. London, Faber, and New York, Farrar Straus, 1974.
Femmes Damnées. Oxford, Sycamore Press, 1978.
Aubade. Salem, Oregon, Seluzicki, 1980.

Recordings: *Philip Larkin Reading "The Less Deceived,"* Listen, 1959; *Philip Larkin Reads and Comments on "The Whitsun Weddings,"* Listen, 1965.

Novels

Jill. London, Fortune Press, 1946; revised edition, London, Faber, and New York, St. Martin's Press, 1964.
A Girl in Winter. London, Faber, 1947; New York, St. Martin's Press, 1957.

Other

All What Jazz: A Record Diary 1961-68. London, Faber, and New York, St. Martin's Press, 1970.
Required Writing: Miscellaneous Pieces 1955-1982. London, Faber, 1983; New York, Farrar Straus, 1984.

Editor, with Bonamy Dobrée and Louis MacNiece, *New Poems 1958.* London, Joseph, 1958.
Editor, *The Oxford Book of Twentieth-Century English Verse.* Oxford, Clarendon Press, 1973.
Editor, *Poetry Supplement.* London, Poetry Book Society, 1974.

*

Bibliography: *Philip Larkin: A Bibliography 1933-1976* by B.C. Bloomfield, London, Faber, 1979.

Manuscript Collection: British Library, London.

Critical Studies: *Philip Larkin* by David Timms, Edinburgh, Oliver and Boyd, 1973, New York, Barnes and Noble, 1974; "Philip Larkin Issue" of *Phoenix 11-12* (Manchester), Autumn-Winter 1973-74; *An Uncommon Poet for the Common Man: A Study of Philip Larkin's Poetry* by Lolette Kuby, The Hague, Mouton, 1974; *Philip Larkin* by Alan Brownjohn, London, Longman, 1975; *Philip Larkin* by Bruce K. Martin, Boston, Twayne, 1978; *The Art of Philip Larkin* by Simon Petch, Sydney, Sydney University Press, 1981; *Philip Larkin* by Andrew Motion, London, Methuen, 1982; *Larkin at Sixty* edited by Anthony Thwaite, London, Faber, 1982; *Backing Horses: A Comparison Between Larkin's and Hughes' Poetry* by Jane Wilson, Portree, Isle of Skye, Aquila, 1982.

*   *   *

It would be difficult to guess from Philip Larkin's first volume, *The North Ship,* that here were the beginnings of a considerable poet. Certainly it attracted little attention on its first appearance in 1945. Looking back now; one can see what seem to be hints, in a few lines and cadences, of what was to come; but this may be hindsight. A wan Yeatsianism, a steely touch of Auden here and there—these are the book's characteristics, and remarkable only in that they show none of the influences one would expect from an Oxford poet in the 1940's: there is no studied literariness, and no flushed and verbose New Apocalypse rhetoric. These poems are careful, yearning and a little dim.
It was in 1946 that Larking wrote the first poems of his maturity: "Waiting for Breakfast" (which is attached as a "coda"

to the 1966 Faber reissue of *The North Ship*) and "Wedding-wind," chronologically the first piece in *The Less Deceived.* Without showing any overt influence of Hardy, they mark the liberation and sense of direction which reading Hardy's poems had given Larkin. In Larkin's own words, spoken in a radio programme: "When I came to Hardy it was with the sense of relief that I didn't have to try and jack myself up to a concept of poetry that lay outside my own life.... One could simply relapse back into one's own life and write from it." This did not mean that in some way he became anything like what more recently have been called "confessional" poets: the emotional content of Larkin's poems is strong, but the tone is reserved, wry, often resigned, and never self-indulgently revelatory. The "human shows" of Hardy's verse fitted congenially into Larkin's temperament, as did Hardy's unselfpitying pessimism.
After *The North Ship,* Larkin did not publish another book of poems (with the exception of two slim pamphlets) until *The Less Deceived* appeared from the Marvell Press in 1955. (His two novels, *Jill* and *A Girl in Winter,* came in the interim, but—though above average pieces of work—they have no place in this entry.) *The Less Deceived,* though coming from an obscure press and without any barrage of publicity such as a richer publisher might have laid down, was quite quickly received with enthusiasm. The appearance of Robert Conquest's anthology *New Lines* in 1956, and the journalistic conscription of Larkin into the so-called "Movement" because of his inclusion in that book, probably hindered the acceptance of Larkin's true merits as much as they helped, though it did not take keen critical eyes to see that he was more like, say, Kingsley Amis than Dylan Thomas or W.S. Graham. Yet neither does he share very much, in outlook or style, with such companions in *New Lines* as Elizabeth Jennings, D.J. Enright or Thom Gunn. As for the supposed "neutral tone" of what have been called the Faceless Fifties, Larkin's voice is far too individual to be docketed with that label.
It is a voice that commands a range from the light mockery of "I Remember, I Remember" to the wincing brutality of "Sunny Prestatyn," from the tenderness (joyously rapt in the first, gravely compassionate in the second) of "Wedding-wind" and "Love Songs in Age" to the spiritual bleakness of "Mr. Bleaney." Some of Larkin's poems have that lightness of tone without levity that Auden used to command so well: "Toads," "Toads Revisited," "Naturally the Foundation Will Bear Your Expenses." His two longest, most sustained poems—"Church Going" from *The Less Deceived* and "The Whitsun Weddings" from the 1964 book of that title—use combinations or progressions of several of these tones. "Church Going" moves, through seven carefully-patterned 9-line stanzas, from easy, colloquial, mockingly casual beginnings, through reflection and half-serious questioning, to a rhetorical solidity at the close which is of such weight and deliberation that some readers have mistakenly supposed that Christianity is thereby being endorsed, which in fact is what the poem sets out with great pains *not* to do. Rather, what is being acknowledged—as in several of Larkin's poems, such as "An Arundel Tomb"—is the strange power of inherited order and habit. Like so many leading poets of the century (Eliot and Yeats are examples), Larkin's attitudes are often conservative, even "reactionary": see, for instance, two more recent and uncollected poems— "Posterity" (*New Statesman,* London, 28 June 1968) and "Homage to a Government" (*Sunday Times,* London, 19 January 1969). But he is not really a "public" poet at all, though he reflects common experiences and common concerns. He has no easy answers, but he does not wallow in fashionable *angst* either. There is an agnostic stoicism in his work, which confronts change, diminution, death with sardonic resignation. Though he would not relish the description, there is nobility in this.
"The Whitsun Weddings," which proceeds through its eight

10-line stanzas with none of the subdued gear-crashing of "Church Going," is the finest example of Larkin's temper, tone and technique. Its level descriptive sweep, its amused human observation, its intelligent sense of the inexplicable, all move with complete inevitability to the mysterious closing lines as the train with its load of newly-married couples slows as it reaches its destination: "And as the tightened brakes took hold, there swelled/A sense of falling, like an arrow-shower/Sent out of sight somewhere becoming rain." The force of this is partly cumulative, but it has a lot to do with an unerring ear for individual cadences too: that "sense of falling" which one hears in "Love Songs in Age":

> So
> To pile them back, to cry,
> Was hard, without lamely admitting how
> It had not done so then, and could not know.

or in "Reference Back": "They show us what we have as it once was,/Blindingly undiminished, just as though/By acting differently we could have kept it so," or in "Dockery and Son":

> Life is first boredom, then fear.
> Whether or not we use it, it goes,
> And leaves what something hidden from us chose,
> And age, and then the only end of age.

Unlike any other important modern British poet (with the exception of the otherwise utterly different Dylan Thomas), Larkin has constructed no system into which his poems can fit: like Parolles in *All's Well*, he seems to say "simply the thing I am shall make me live." It is an individual achievement, and a memorable one.

   (1980) Since the above piece was written, Larkin has published *High Windows* and the controversial anthology, *The Oxford Book of Twentieth Century Egnlish Verse*. The 24 poems in *High Windows*, representing his total output since *The Whitsun Weddings*, included at least three which stand among Larkin's very best: "The Old Fools," "The Building," and "The Explosion." "The Building," in fact, is the major statement in this book, just as "Church Going" and "The Whitsun Weddings" were in its forerunners. In it, Larkin's habitual theme of the ebbing-away of life is most persistently, elaborately, and movingly worked out. The details of what is in fact a hospital are throughout presented at one remove; the "building" is not specifically called a hospital, as if naming it would be to court disaster—though, ironically, the daily arrival of disaster—death—is what the poem is "about." "The Old Fools" confronts the same theme in terms of senility, while "The Explosion" is a strangely dream-like presentation of disaster and death merging into resurrection—itself seen as a dream.

   High Windows contains its share of ostensibly "light" poems, and rather more of them than hitherto; but lightness, or coarseness, of tone in Larken tends to be accompanied by a sardonic leer rather than laughter. Parts of "Sympathy in White Major," "High Windows," "The Card-Players," "Posterity," "This Be the Verse," "Annus Mirabilis," "Vers de Société," and "Money" are all examples of Larkin deliberately using his low style to make points of high seriousness. As Clive James put it in a long review of *High Windows* in *Encounter* (June 1974): "The book is the peer of the previous two mature collections, and if they did not exist would be just as astonishing...Larkin is the poet of the void. The one affirmation his work offers is the possibility that when we have lost everything the problem of beauty will still remain. It's enough."

—Anthony Thwaite

LAUGHLIN, James. American. Born in Pittsburgh, Pennsylvania, 30 October 1914. Educated at Le Rosey, Switzerland; Choate School, Connecticut, 1930-32; Harvard University, Cambridge, Massachusetts, A.B. 1939. Married 1) Margaret Keyser in 1942 (divorced, 1952), one son and one daughter; 2) Ann Clark Resor in 1956, two sons. Since 1936, Founding Editor, New Directions Publishing Corporation, New York. Regents Professor, University of California, San Diego, 1974; Bean Visiting Professor, University of Iowa, Iowa City, 1981, 1982, 1984; Adjunct Professor of English, Brown University, Providence, Rhode Island, 1983. Director, Goethe Bicentennial Foundation, 1949, and Aspen Institute of the Humanities, 1950; Member, U.S. National Commission for Unesco, 1960-63; Trustee, Allen-Chase Foundation; Trustee, Rosenbach Foundation, resigned 1983. President, Intercultural Publications; since 1956, Chairman, Creative Writing Panel, Institute for International Education Conference on Arts Exchange; since 1969, Trustee, Thomas Merton Legacy Trust. Recipient: American Academy Distinguished Service Award, 1977; Carey-Thomas Prize, for publishing, 1978; P.E.N. Publisher's Citation, 1978; National Arts Club Medal of Honor, 1983; Harvard University Signet Society Medal, 1984. D.Litt.: Hamilton College, Clinton, New York, 1969; Colgate University, Hamilton, New York, 1978; H.H.D.: Duquesne University, Pittsburgh, 1980; D.H.L.: Yale University, New Haven, Connecticut, 1982. Member, American Academy of Arts and Sciences; Chevalier, Legion of Honor, France. Address: New Directions, 80 Eighth Avenue, New York, New York 10011; or, Meadow House, Norfolk, Connecticut 06058, U.S.A.

PUBLICATIONS

Verse

Some Natural Things. New York, New Directions, 1945.
Report on a Visit to Germany. Lausanne, Switzerland, Held, 1948.
A Small Book of Poems. Milan, Scheiwiller, and New York, New Directions, 1948.
The Wild Anemone and Other Poems. Verona, Valdonega, and New York, New Directions, 1957.
Confidential Report and Other Poems. London, Gaberbocchus, 1959; as *Selected Poems*, New York, New Directions, 1960.
Pulsatilla (bilingual edition), translated by Mary de Rachewiltz. Milan, Scheiwiller, 1961.
Die Haare auf Grossvaters Kopf (bilingual edition), translated by Eva Hesse. Zurich, Verlag der Arche, 1966.
Quel che la Matita Scrive (bilingual edition), translated by Mary de Rachewiltz. Rome, Guanda, 1970.
The Pig. Mount Horeb, Wisconsin, Perishable Press, 1970.
The Woodpecker. Santa Barbara, California, Yes Press, 1971.
In Another Country: Poems 1935-1975, edited by Robert Fitzgerald. San Francisco, City Lights, 1978.

Other

Skiing: East and West, with Helene Fischer. New York, Hastings House, 1947.

Editor, *New Directions in Prose and Poetry.* New York, New Directions, 48 vols., 1937-84.
Editor, *Poems from the Greenberg Manuscripts: A Selection from the Works of Samuel B. Greenberg.* New York, New Directions, 1939.

Editor, with Albert Hayes, *A Wreath of Christmas Poems.* New York, New Directions, 1942; London, Sheldon Press, 1972.

Editor, *Spearhead: Ten Years' Experimental Writing in America.* New York, New Directions, and London, Falcon Press, 1947.

Editor, with Hayden Carruth, *A New Directions Reader.* New York, New Directions, 1964.

Editor, with Naomi Burton and Patrick Hart, *The Asian Journal of Thomas Merton.* London, Sheldon Press, 1974.

*

James Laughlin comments:

My poems are written by someone I cannot identify in another sphere. At odd moments they come into my mind complete and all I do is type them out in my personal visual metric of couplets which are the same length.

*   *   *

James Laughlin is known to many as the publisher who has been a particular friend to avant-garde writers in America. His firm, New Directions, which he founded in 1936 to print works then seriously neglected—especially by Ezra Pound and William Carlos Williams—has expanded over the years and now is one of the foremost publishing houses in the world devoted to serious imaginative writing. But until recently Laughlin's own poetry was little known, partly because he wrote little but chiefly because it has been published reticently and distributed among friends and associates. Starting in the 1960's, however, his poems began to appear in many anthologies and have been translated into several other languages.

The poems are in colloquial diction, arranged according to what Laughlin calls "prosody of the eye": when typed on a typewriter each line of the poem must be no more than one space (occasionally two) longer or shorter than the opening line. The verbal tension arises from a contrast between this intentional artificiality of design and the freedom of the colloquial, sometimes singsongy aural cadence. Beyond this, the poems rely for effect on the directness and acuteness of the poet's insight, as in "A Modest Proposal":

> I think I can offer this
> simple remedy for a part
>
> at least of the world's
> ills and evil I suggest
>
> that everyone should be
> required to change his
>
> name every ten years I
> think this would put a
>
> stop to a whole lot of
> ambition compulsion ego
>
> and like breeders of dis-
> cord and wasted motion.

A stop, too, to biographical directories; and that, one feels, would probably be o.k. with Laughlin.

—Hayden Carruth

LAYTON, Irving. Canadian. Born Irving Peter Lazarovitch in Neamtz, Romania, 12 March 1912; emigrated to Canada in 1913. Educated at MacDonald College, Sainte Anne de Bellevue, Quebec, B.Sc. in agriculture 1939; McGill University, Montreal, M.A. 1946. Served in the Canadian Army, 1942-43. Married 1) Betty Francis Sutherland in 1946, one son and one daughter; second marriage; 3) the writer Aviva Cantor in 1961, one son; 4) Harriet Bernstein in 1978 (divorced, 1984), one daughter. Lecturer, Jewish Public Library, Montreal, 1943-59; high school teacher, Montreal, 1954-60; part-time lecturer, 1949-65, and Poet-in-Residence, 1965-66, Sir George Williams University, Montreal; Writer-in-Residence, University of Guelph, Ontario, 1968-69; Professor of English Literature, York University, Toronto, 1970-78; Poet-in-Residence, University of Ottawa, 1978, Concordia University, Montreal, 1978-81, and University of Toronto, 1981. Co-Founding Editor, *First Statement,* later *Northern Review,* Montreal, 1941-43; Associate Editor, *Contact,* Toronto, and *Black Mountain Review,* North Carolina. Recipient: Canadian Foundation Fellowship, 1957; Canada Council award, 1959, 1967, 1973, 1979; Governor-General's Award, 1959; President's Medal, University of Western Ontario, 1961. D.C.L.: Bishop's University, Lennoxville, Quebec, 1970; D.Litt.: Concordia University, 1976; York University, 1979. Officer, Order of Canada, 1976. Address: 6879 Monkland Avenue, Montreal, Quebec H4B 1J5, Canada.

PUBLICATIONS

Verse

Here and Now. Montreal, First Statement Press, 1945.

Now Is the Place: Poems and Stories. Montreal, First Statement Press, 1948.

The Black Huntsman. Privately printed, 1951.

Cerberus, with Raymond Souster and Louis Dudek. Toronto, Contact Press, 1952.

Love the Conqueror Worm. Toronto, Contact Press, 1953.

The Long Pea-Shooter. Montreal, Laocoön Press, 1954.

In the Midst of My Fever. Palma, Mallorca, Divers Press, 1954.

The Cold Green Element. Toronto, Contact Press, 1955.

The Blue Propeller. Toronto, Contact Press, 1955.

The Blue Calf and Other Poems. Toronto, Contact Press, 1956.

Music on a Kazoo. Toronto, Contact Press, 1956.

The Improved Binoculars: Selected Poems. Highlands, North Carolina, Jargon, 1956; augmented edition, 1957.

A Laughter in the Mind. Highlands, North Carolina, Jargon, 1958; augmented edition, Montreal, Editions d'Orphée, 1959.

A Red Carpet for the Sun: Collected Poems. Toronto, McClelland and Stewart, and Highlands, North Carolina, Jargon, 1959.

The Swinging Flesh (poems and stories). Toronto, McClelland and Stewart, 1961.

Balls for a One-Armed Juggler. Toronto, McClelland and Stewart, 1963.

The Laughing Rooster. Toronto, McClelland and Stewart, 1964.

Collected Poems. Toronto, McClelland and Stewart, 1965.

Periods of the Moon. Toronto, McClelland and Stewart, 1967.

The Shattered Plinths. Toronto, McClelland and Stewart, 1968.

The Whole Bloody Bird (obs, aphs, and pomes). Toronto, McClelland and Stewart, 1969.

Selected Poems, edited by Wynne Francis. Toronto, McClelland and Stewart, 1969.

Five Modern Canadian Poets, with others, edited by Eli Mandel. Toronto, Holt Rinehart, 1970.

Collected Poems. Toronto, McClelland and Stewart, 1971.

Nail Polish. Toronto, McClelland and Stewart, 1971.

Lovers and Lesser Men. Toronto, McClelland and Stewart, 1973.

The Pole-Vaulter. Toronto, McClelland and Stewart, 1974.

Seventy-Five Greek Poems 1951-1974. Athens, Hermias, 1974.

Selected Poems: The Darkening Fire 1945-1968, The Unwavering Eye 1969-1975. Toronto, McClelland and Stewart, 2 vols., 1975.

For My Brother Jesus. Toronto, McClelland and Stewart, 1976.

The Uncollected Poems 1936-1959. Oakville, Ontario, Mosaic Press, 1976.

The Poems of Irving Layton, edited by Eli Mandel. Toronto, McClelland and Stewart, 1977.

Selected Poems. New York, New Directions, 1977.

The Covenant. Toronto, McClelland and Stewart, 1977.

Selected Poems, edited by Wynne Francis. London, Charisma, 1977.

The Tightrope Dancer. Toronto, McClelland and Stewart, 1978.

The Love Poems. Toronto, Canadian Fine Editions, 1978.

Droppings from Heaven. Toronto, McClelland and Stewart, 1979.

There Were No Signs, illustrated by Sassu. Toronto, Madison Art Gallery, 1979.

For My Neighbours in Hell. Oakville, Ontario, Mosaic Press, 1980.

Europe and Other Bad News. Toronto, McClelland and Stewart, 1981.

A Wild Peculiar Joy: Selected Poems 1945-82. Toronto, McClelland and Stewart, 1982.

The Gucci Bag. Oakville, Ontario, Mosaic Press, 1983.

The Reverence and Delight: The Love Poems. Toronto, McClelland and Stewart, 1984.

A Spider Danced a Cozy Jig. Toronto, General Publishing, 1984.

Play

A Man Was Killed, with Leonard Cohen, in *Canadian Theatre Review 14* (Downsview, Ontario), Spring 1977.

Other

Engagements: The Prose of Irvng Layton, edited by Seymour Mayne. Toronto, McClelland and Stewart, 1972.

Taking Sides: The Collected Social and Political Writings, edited by Howard Aster. Oakville, Ontario, Mosaic Press, 1977.

An Unlikely Affair: The Irving Layton-Dorothy Rath Correspondence. Oakville, Ontario, Mosaic Press, 1979.

Editor, with Louis Dudek, *Canadian Poems 1850-1952.* Toronto, Contact Press, 1952; revised edition, 1953.

Editor, *Pan-ic: A Selection of Contemporary Canadian Poems.* New York, Alan Brilliant, 1958.

Editor, *Poems for 27 Cents.* Privately printed, 1961.

Editor, *Love Where the Nights Are Long: Canadian Love Poems.* Toronto, McClelland and Stewart, 1962.

Editor, *Anvil: A Selection of Workshop Poems.* Privately printed, 1966.

Editor, *Poems to Colour: A Selection of Workshop Poems.* Privately printed, 1970.

Editor, *Anvil Blood: A Selection of Workshop Poems.* Privately printed, 1973.

Editor, *Shark Tank.* Toronto, York Poetry Workshop, 1977.

Editor, *Handouts from the Mountain.* Toronto, York University Poetry, 1978.

Translator, with Greg Gatenby and Francesca Valente, *Selected Poems,* by Giorgio Bassani. Toronto, Aya Press, 1980.

*

Bibliography: *Irving Layton: A Bibliography 1935-1977* by Joy Bennett and James Polson. Montreal, Concordia University Libraries, 1979.

Manuscript Collections: University of Saskatchewan, Saskatoon; University of Toronto; Concordia University, Montreal; Brown University, Providence, Rhode Island; University of Texas, Austin.

Critical Studies: "Layton on the Carpet" by Louis Dudek, in *Delta 9* (Montreal), October-December 1959; "The Man Who Copyrighted Passion" by A. Ross, in *Macleans* (Toronto), 15 November 1965; "Personal Heresy" by Robin Skelton, in *Canadian Literature* (Vancouver), Winter 1965; "A Grab at Proteus: Notes on Irving Layton" by George Woodcock, in *Canadian Literature* (Vancouver), Spring 1966; "That Heaven-Sent Lively Ropewalker, Irving Layton" by Hayden Carruth, in *Tamarack Review* (Toronto), Spring 1966; "Satyric Layton" by K.A. Lund, in *Canadian Author and Bookman* (Toronto), Spring 1967; "The Occasions of Irving Layton" by Mike Doyle, in *Canadian Literature* (Vancouver), Autumn 1972; *Irving Layton: The Poet and His Critics* edited by Seymour Mayne, Toronto, McGraw Hill Ryerson, 1978; *The Poetry of Irving Layton* by Eli Mandel, Toronto, Coles, 1981.

Irving Layton comments:

I believe the poet, at his best, is a prophet and a descendant of prophets. Once he allows himself to forget that, he becomes a mere tinkerer. He ends up making pillows and pillow-cases for old fogies to go to sleep on. These love nothing better than ecstatically to snore out their veneration for beauty and order in the old rhythms they have learned so well. The poet's job is to disturb and discomfit. He's an iconoclast, a smasher of cruel idols, even when he accomplishes their destruction with the quietest of lyrics. He speaks to all men, not only to the cultivated and sensitive. Now, more than ever, he must strive to keep alive the spirit of rebellion and dissent. In a world that reveres facts and details, the poet must insist on a complex, imaginative awareness and remain the sworn enemy of all dogmas and dogmatists. Whatever else, poetry is freedom—freedom to experience, to live fully and vitally. For the doctrinaire pedant, as for the doctrinaire politician and ideologist, the poet will always have an abiding contempt. Nothing less than perfect freedom and joy will ever content him. But until that time arrives he will continue to look into the hearts of all and with the dark ambivalences he finds there move them through terror and beauty. As long as the poet is alive and flourishing mankind still has a future.

*   *   *

The most prolific of Canadian poets and certainly the most fluent since Bliss Carman, Irving Layton published 15 volumes of verse between *Here and Now* (1945) and the *Collected Poems* of 1965, and since then new collections have appeared regularly. A various and indeed an uneven poet, Layton has shown a steady advance in technical accomplishment and in emotional and intellectual maturity. The shrill and strident verses of the earliest volumes had some success in shocking the bourgeoisie with sexual frankness and an uninhibited vocabulary, but they seem rather old-fashioned today and in any case were overshadowed by the later poetry that began with the two volumes of 1954 and 1955, *In the Midst of My Fever* and *The Cold Green Element.* Reviewing the first of these, the critic Northrop Frye wrote: "The question of whether Mr. Layton is a real poet is settled.... An imaginative revolution is proclaimed all through this book: when he says that 'something has taught me severity, exactness of speech' or 'has given me a turn for sculptured stone,' we see a new excitement and intensity in the process of writing. At last it is possible to see what kind of poet Mr. Layton is, and he proves to be not a satirist at all but an erudite elegiac poet, whose technique turns on an aligning of the romantic and the ironic."

In spite of an unmistakably romantic conception of the poet as the voice of the earth and the sun iterating a gospel of the natural and the instinctive that is personal and emotional—and straight out of Blake, Whitman and Lawrence—Layton is in his handling of language, metre, and poetic technique a thoroughly classical poet, the best of whose love poems are quite genuinely in the tradition of Ovid and Catullus. The quality of his sensibility can be seen in the vividness and accuracy of his perceptions and can be illustrated in a line or two:

> The maples glisten with the season's rain;
> The day's porous, as October days are,
> And objects have more space about them.
>
> All field things seem weightless, abstract,
> As if they'd taken one step back
> To see themselves as they literally are
> After the dementia of summer.

The *Collected Poems* contains 385 titles, of which perhaps 50 or 60 must rank with the best lyrical and reflective poems of the mid-century in English. The rest consists of squibs, satires, casual jottings, mordant light verse and some often rather childish curses and polemics, but these (along with the strange glorification of military violence found in *The Shattered Plinths*) should not be allowed to obscure the significance of Layton's contribution to North American poetry.

—A. J. M. Smith

LEE, Dennis (Beynon). Canadian. Born in Toronto, Ontario, 31 August 1939. Educated at the University of Toronto, B.A. 1962, M.A. in English 1964. Divorced; two daughters. Full-time writer. Taught at Victoria College, Toronto, 1964-67, Rochdale College, Toronto, 1967-69, and at the University of Toronto, and York University, Toronto; Artist-in-Residence, Trent University, Peterborough, Ontario, 1975. Editor, House of Anansi Press, Toronto, 1967-73; Consulting Editor, Macmillan of Canada, publishers, Toronto, 1974-76. Since 1981, Director of the Poetry Programme, McClelland and Stewart, publishers, Toronto; since 1982, songwriter, *Fraggle Rock* television programme. Recipient: Governor-General's Award, 1973; Canadian Library

Association Book of the Year Medal, for children's book, 1975, 1978; Ruth Schwartz Award, 1977; Philips Prize, 1984. Address: c/o House of Anansi Press Ltd., 35 Britain Street, Toronto, Ontario M5A 1R7, Canada.

PUBLICATIONS

Verse

Kingdom of Absence. Toronto, Anansi, 1967.
Civil Elegies. Toronto, Anansi, 1968.
Civil Elegies and Other Poems. Toronto, Anansi, 1972.
Not Abstract Harmonies But. Vancouver and San Francisco, Kanchenjunga, 1974.
The Death of Harold Ladoo. Vancouver and San Francisco, Kanchenjunga, 1976.
Miscellany. Privately printed, 1976.
The Gods. Vancouver and San Francisco, Kanchenjunga, 1978.
The Gods (collection). Toronto, McClelland and Stewart, 1979.

Verse (for children)

Wiggle to the Laundromat. Toronto, New Press, 1970.
Alligator Pie. Toronto, Macmillan, 1974; Boston, Houghton Mifflin, 1975.
Nicholas Knock and Other People. Toronto, Macmillan, 1974; Boston, Houghton Mifflin, 1976.
Garbage Delight. Toronto, Macmillan, 1977; Boston, Houghton Mifflin, 1978.
Jelly Belly. Toronto, Macmillan, and London, Blackie, 1983.
Lizzie's Lion. Toronto, Stoddart, and London, Hodder and Stoughton, 1984.

Recordings: *Alligator Pie*, music by Don Heckman, Caedmon, 1978; *Fraggle Rock*, music by Philip Balsam, Muppet Music, 1984.

Other

Notes on Rochdale. Ottawa, Canadian Union of Students, 1967 (?).
Savage Fields: An Essay in Literature and Cosmology. Toronto, Anansi, 1977.
The Ordinary Bath (for children). Toronto, Magook, 1979.

Editor, with R.A. Charlesworth, *An Anthology of Verse.* Toronto, Oxford University Press, 1964.
Editor, with R.A. Charlesworth, *The Second Century Anthologies of Verse, Book 2.* Toronto, Oxford University Press, 1967.
Editor, with Howard Adelman, *The University Game.* Toronto, Anansi, 1968.
Editor, *T.O. Now: The Young Toronto Poets.* Toronto, Anansi, 1968.

*

Manuscript Collection: Fisher Rare Book Room, University of Toronto.

Critical Studies: "Dennis Lee Issue" of *Descant* (Toronto), Winter 1982.

*   *   *

"They are poets who write for real...they're accessible to people with a wide range of consciousness...reading them in one sitting is a self-contained pleasure." This is Dennis Lee discussing a group of contemporary poets in *Read Canadian: A Book about Canadian Books* (1972); needless to say, these are essential qualities of Lee's own work. His range of consciousness is wide enough to encompass the academy (he has taught at several universities), the market place (he was the first editor of House of Anansi Press), and the anti-establishment (he helped found Rochdale College, a free university that flourished in Toronto in the 1960's).

Lee's poetic reputation rests on a single volume, *Civil Elegies and Other Poems*, which establishes the poet as a concerned citizen of liberal-leftist persuasion, worried by world trends. "Sibelius Park," a ruminating poem about Toronto life, ends ominously: "There is nothing to be afraid of." Other poems celebrate the "excellent pleasures," which are ultimately found wanting, of bourgeois life.

It is not in the short poems but in the longish elegies that Lee makes his mark. The nine elegies are basically free verse (one is tempted to say, "free prose"), meditations on "the quality of Canadian civilization." The ruminations were inspired by George Grant the moral philosopher and author of the influential book *Lament for a Nation* (1965), who saw Canada as a conservative country on a liberal continent engulfed by modern technology. In "Elegy 6," Lee peers into the future: "Though I do not deny technopolis I can see only the bread and circuses to come." By turns ponderous and profound, the elegies are as much concerned with the past as they are with the future, and references to historical and literary figures abound. It is in "Elegy 2" that Lee presents the reader with his measure of the past and standard for the future:

Master and Lord, there was a
measure once.
There was a time when men could say
my life, my job, my home
and still feel clean.
The poets spoke of earth and heaven. There were no symbols.

—John Robert Colombo

LEE, Don L(uther). Pseudonym: Haki R. Madhubuti. American. Born in Little Rock, Arkansas, 23 February 1942. Educated at Dunbar Vocational High School, Chicago; Chicago City College, A.A. 1966; Roosevelt University, Chicago, 1966-67. Served in the United States Army, 1960-63. Apprentice curator, DuSable Museum of African American History, Chicago, 1963-67; stock department clerk, Montgomery Ward, Chicago, 1963-64; post office clerk, Chicago, 1964-65; junior executive, Spiegels, Chicago, 1965-66. Taught at Columbia College, Chicago, 1968; Writer-in-Residence, Cornell University, Ithaca, New York, 1968-69; Poet-in-Residence, Northeastern Illinois State College, Chicago, 1969-70; Lecturer, University of Illinois, Chicago, 1969-71; Writer-in-Residence, Morgan State College, Baltimore, 1972-73, and Howard University, Washington, D.C., 1970-75. Director, Institute of Positive Education, Chicago. Since 1967, Editor and Publisher, Third World Press, Chicago; since 1972, Editor, *Black Books Bulletin*, Chicago. Recipient: National Endowment for the Arts grant, 1969; Kuumba Work-

shop Black Liberation Award, 1973. Address: Third World Press, 7524 South Cottage Grove Avenue, Chicago, Illinois 60619, U.S.A.

PUBLICATIONS

Verse

Think Black. Detroit, Broadside Press, 1967; revised edition, 1968, 1969.
Black Pride. Detroit, Broadside Press, 1968.
Back Again, Home. Detroit, Broadside Press, 1968.
One Sided Shoot-Out. Detroit, Broadside Press, 1968.
For Black People (And Negroes Too). Chicago, Third World Press, 1968.
Don't Cry, Scream. Detroit, Broadside Press, 1969.
We Walk the Way of the New World. Detroit, Broadside Press, 1970.
Directionscore: Selected and New Poems. Detroit, Broadside Press, 1971.
Book of Life. Detroit, Broadside Press, 1973.

Recording: *Rappin' and Readin'*, Broadside Press, 1971.

Other

Dynamite Voices: Black Poets of the 1960's. Detroit, Broadside Press, 1971.
From Plan to Planet: Life Studies: The Need for Afrikan Minds and Institutions. Detroit, Broadside Press, 1973.
A Capsule Course in Black Poetry Writing (as Haki R. Madhubuti), with others. Detroit, Broadside Press, 1975.
Enemies: The Clash of Races. Chicago, Third World Press, 1978.

Editor, with Patricia L. Brown and Francis Ward, *To Gwen with Love.* Chicago, Johnson, 1971.

*

Critical Studies: "Black Poetry's Welcome Critic" by Hollie I. West, in *The Washington Post* (Washington, D.C.), 6 June 1971; "A Black Poet Faces Reality" by Vernon Jarrett, in *Chicago Tribune*, 23 July 1971; "The Relevancy of Don L. Lee as a Contemporary Black Poet" by Annette Sands, in *Black World* (Chicago), June 1972; "Some Black Thoughts on Don L. Lee's *Think Black:* Thanks by a Frustrated White Academic Thinker" by Eugene E. Miller, in *College English* (Champaign, Illinois), May 1973; *New Directions from Don L. Lee* by Marlene Mosher, Hicksville, New York, Exposition, 1975.

*   *   *

Of the strong young Black poets of the "Black arts movement" that began in the United States in the late 1960's, Don L. Lee is one of the most powerful and persuasive in content, one of the most creative and influential in technique.

His poetry, consciously utilitarian, is directed to a Black audience, with themes centering around self-identity and self-definition, self-determination, the humanness of Black people and the depravity of white people ("unpeople"), and self-help through collective and institutional efforts. Examples are "In the Interest of Black Salvation," which shows disillusionment with orthodox Euro-American religion; "Move Un-Noticed to Be Noticed," an exhortation for sincerity in Blacks; "The Wall," a celebration of Black pride; "Back Home Again," which depicts an excursion into an alien (white) "establishment" world and a subsequent return to Blackness; "But He Was Cool," a satire on vapid and showy life styles affected by some Blacks; and "Re-Act for Action," a cry for aggression against racial injustices.

Lee's poems convey spontaneity and emotional compulsion as well as ideological commitment. He prefers the speech of the Black urban masses. Much of his poetry seems intended for oral delivery. (He is in demand for readings of his poetry.) He frequently achieves desired aural effects through extra vowels or consonants, phonetic spellings, elisions. He is fond of playing with words, particularly syntactic reversals and the breaking of words into components—for irony, purposeful double meaning, emphasis of components of meaning, aural effects, and other reasons. He is partial to scattered spatial arrangements, broken words, unconventional syntax, and unconventional punctuation, favoring the ampersand and diagonal. His imagery is strong, concrete, and specific. Frequently he builds up a poem's tension incrementally, withholding its point or resolution until the end at which time the poem's logic or impact is made manifest.

—Theodore R. Hudson

* * *

LEE, Laurie. British. Born in Stroud, Gloucestershire, 26 June 1914. Educated at Slad Village School, Gloucestershire, and Stroud Central School. During World War II made documentary films for the General Post Office film unit, 1939-40, and the Crown Film Unit, 1941-43, and travelled as a scriptwriter to Cyprus and India; Publications Editor, Ministry of Information, 1944-46; member of the Green Park Film Unit, 1946-47. Married Catherine Francesca Polge in 1950; one daughter. Caption Writer-in-Chief, Festival of Britain, 1950-51. Recipient: Atlantic Award, 1944; Society of Authors Traveling Award, 1951; Foyle Award, 1956; Smith Literary Award, 1960. Fellow, Royal Society of Literature. Freeman, City of London, 1982. M.B.E. (Member, Order of the British Empire), 1952. Address: 9/40 Elm Park Gardens, London SW10 9NZ, England.

PUBLICATIONS

Verse

The Sun My Monument. London, Hogarth Press, 1944; New York, Doubleday, 1947.
The Bloom of Candles: Verse from a Poet's Year. London, Lehmann, 1947.
My Many-Coated Man. London, Deutsch, 1955; New York, Coward McCann, 1957.
(Poems). London, Vista, 1960.
Pergamon Poets 10, with Charles Causley, edited by Evan Owen. Oxford, Pergamon Press, 1970.
Selected Poems. London, Deutsch, 1983.

Recording: *Laurie Lee Reading His Own Poems,* with Christopher Logue, Jupiter, 1960.

Plays

The Voyage of Magellan: A Dramatic Chronicle for Radio

(broadcast, 1946). London, Lehmann, 1948.
Peasants' Priest (produced Canterbury, 1947). Canterbury, Goulden, 1947.

Screenplays: *Cyprus Is an Island,* 1946; *A Tale in a Teacup,* 1947.

Radio Play: *The Voyage of Magellan,* 1946.

Other

Land at War. London, His Majesty's Stationery Office, 1945.
We Made a Film in Cyprus, with Ralph Keene. London, Longman, 1947.
An Obstinate Exile. Privately printed, 1951.
A Rose for Winter: Travels in Andalusia. London, Hogarth Press, 1955; New York, Morrow, 1956.
Cider with Rosie (autobiography). London, Hogarth Press, 1959; as *The Edge of Day: A Boyhood in the West of England,* New York, Morrow, 1960.
Man Must Move: The Story of Transport (for children), with David Lambert. London, Rathbone, 1960; as *The Wonderful World of Transportation,* New York, Doubleday, 1960; revised edition, 1969; as *The Wonderful World of Transport,* London, Macdonald, 1969.
The Firstborn (essay on childhood). London, Hogarth Press, and New York, Morrow, 1964.
As I Walked Out One Midsummer Morning (autobiography). London, Deutsch, and New York, Atheneum, 1969.
I Can't Stay Long. London, Deutsch, 1975; New York, Atheneum, 1976.
Innocence in the Mirror, photographs by Angelo Cozzi. New York, Morrow, 1978.
Two Women, photographs by the author. London, Deutsch, 1983.

Editor, with Christopher Hassall and Rex Warner, *New Poems 1954.* London, Joseph, 1954.

Translator, *The Dead Village,* by Avigdor Dagan. London, Young Czechoslovakia, 1943.

* * *

A first encounter with Laurie Lee's poems immediately reveals that they are loaded with charm, and almost always in the best sense of that tricky word. Their furniture is traditionally "poetic"—seas, moons, flowers, stars, girls, animals—and their mode romantic, but a fine tact protects the poems from the dangerous slide into sentimentality. Laurie Lee is a fluent creator of images and odd correspondences: sometimes one fancies one hears, though not too loudly, the echoing voice of Lorca:

> You were adventure's web,
> the flag of fear I flew
> riding black stallions
> through the rocky streets.

And sometimes, in his exact observations of physical details, he reminds one of Andrew Young—"holessuck in their bees," and "The birdlike stars droop down and die,/The starlike birds catch fire." Indeed, the outside world fills him, as it does Andrew Young, with a sort of devout pleasure.

But these influences, if they are influences and not coincidences, only occasionally intrude. Overall a Laurie Lee poem is very much his and no one else's. His rhythms, verbal textures, visual aperçus are all his own.

It stops there, though. If there are some melancholy poems, they are always of a personal and introspective sort. He does not take account of the miseries, not to say atrocities, that are happening all around us. When he looks outward it is at the physical world, but not the suffering people in it, and when he celebrates he never pushes his thinking very far. A result of this is that, in spite of the numerous felicities, his final effect is one of slightness. You will find in his poems no exclamation marks—but no questions either. One wishes that a man with his sensibility and his technical adroitness might range farther afield, might explore more deeply the larger experiences whose absence makes, in the end, these poems miniatures. However, he has not done that.

This may account for the smallness of his output. And it says something for his critical judgment that he has not made the slightness seem more slight by printing too much.

—Norman MacCaig

LEHMANN, Geoffrey (John). Australian. Born in Sydney, New South Wales, 20 June 1940. Educated at Shore School, Sydney; University of Sydney, B.A. 1960, LL.B. 1963; qualified as solicitor 1963; masters in law 1982. Practising solicitor, Sydney, 1963-76. Currently, Lecturer in Law and Tax, Commerce Faculty, University of New South Wales, Kensington. Member, Australia Council Literature Board, 1981-84. Recipient: Grace Leven Prize, 1966, 1982. Address: 8 Highfield Road, Lindfield, New South Wales 2070, Australia.

PUBLICATIONS

Verse

The Ilex Tree, with Les A. Murray. Canberra, Australian National University Press, 1965.
A Voyage of Lions and Other Poems. Sydney, Angus and Robertson, 1968.
Conversation with a Rider. Sydney, Angus and Robertson, 1972.
From an Australian Country Sequence. London, Poem-of-the-Month Club, 1973.
Selected Poems. Sydney, Angus and Robertson, 1976.
Ross' Poems. Sydney, Angus and Robertson, 1978.
Nero's Poems: Translations of the Public and Private Poems of the Emperor Nero. Sydney, Angus and Robertson, 1981.

Novel

A Spring Day in Autumn. Melbourne, Nelson, 1974.

Other

Australian Primitive Painters. Brisbane, University of Queensland Press, 1977.

Editor, *Comic Australian Verse.* Sydney, Angus and Robertson, 1972.

Editor, with Robert Gray, *The Younger Australian Poets.* Sydney, Hale and Iremonger, 1983.

*

Critical Studies: "A Governor, A Farmer, An Emperor: Rome and Australia in Geoffrey Lehmann" by Michele Morgan, in *Australian Literary Studies* (Hobart, Tasmania), May 1983; "Geoffrey Lehmann's Nero Poems" by Michael Sharkey, in *Quadrant* (Sydney), June 1984.

Geoffrey Lehmann comments:

In some of my earlier poems I tried to come to terms with my family. In others I found the voice of a Roman governor of Africa a congenial vehicle to explore the inevitable failure of each of us to control our own minds, as well as the natural and political world we inhabit. In these poems dolphins and lions symbolize the other-world, the separate consciousness of other living creatures which continues to elude the romantic.

My two most recent books *Ross's Poems* (my own, but not my publisher's spelling) and *Nero's Poems* differ sharply in the voice of their narrator. *Ross's Poems* employs the first-person voice of a living person, Ross, an Australian farmer who lives near Cowra, and uses the incidents of his life as a vehicle for a view of life which is partly his and partly mine. Where possible actual names have been used, but some of the poems are transcribed out of my experience into Ross's life. Ross is the observer of limits, a lover of the surprises, the minutiae and largeness of life, a conservationist who is sceptical about his own conservationism.

Nero's Poems purports to be translations from the poems of the Roman Emperor and aims at historical and psychological accuracy. Nero rejects limits and conventional decency and is completely urban. A number of poems celebrate gardens, aqueducts, eating with friends and urban life as a counterweight to the corruption and moral disintegration of his world. I have tried to preserve the contradictions of his character and rescue him from the aristocrats who detested a populist emperor and wrote the history books.

Since *Nero's Poems*, I have written more poems through the voice of Ross, also personal, imagistic poems about single parenthood.

*   *   *

Among the Australian poets of his generation, Geoffrey Lehmann is possibly the most prolific as well as the most immediately approachable. His verse relies largely on conventional techniques, being for the most part unrhymed iambic pentameters or simple stanzaic patterns of alternative rhymes and half-rhymes.

A penchant for sequences of homely, familial anecdotes and episodes in the lives of his father and grandfather has lent a deceptively simple aura to his reputation. In reality he is a poet of genuine subtleties and complex affiliations with standards of moderation and saneness that seem out of place, even anachronistic, in the present age. This appears to have led him to identify his thought and poetic persona with the immediate and the distant past rather than to take an existential stance in the present.

His most effective work is to be found in the excellent sequence entitled "Monologues for Marcus Furius Camillus, Governor of Africa" that opens his second book. Adopting the guise of a provincial administrator during ancient Rome's decadence he narrates a series of episodes in the Roman's career that have caused him to review his life and allegiances. Meditating upon the carefree life of dolphins or the degradation of lions in the Roman arenas, the governor lives and moves through these poems, one of the eternal contemporaries of literature.

—Bruce Beaver

LEHMANN, (Rudolph) John (Frederick). British. Born in Bourne End, Buckinghamshire, 2 June 1907; brother of the actress Beatrix Lehmann, and the novelist Rosamond Lehmann. Educated at Eton College (King's Scholar); Trinity College, Cambridge, B.A. Journalist in Vienna for several years prior to 1938. General Manager, 1931-32, 1938-46, and Partner, 1940-46, Hogarth Press, London; Founder and Managing Director, John Lehmann Ltd., publishers, London, 1946-52. Founding Editor, *New Writing, Daylight, New Writing and Daylight,* and *Penguin New Writing,* London, 1936-50, and *The London Magazine,* 1954-61; Advisory Editor, *The Geographical Magazine,* London, 1940-45; Editor, New Soundings, BBC Third Programme, 1952. Visiting Professor, University of Texas, Austin, 1970-71, State University of California, San Diego, 1970-71, University of California, Berkeley, 1974, and Emory University, Atlanta, 1977. Chairman, British Council Editorial Advisory Panel, 1952-58; President, Alliance Française in Great Britain, 1955-64; Member, Anglo-Greek Mixed Commission, 1962-68. President, Royal Literary Fund, 1966-76. Recipient: Prix du Rayonnement Français, 1961; Foyle Prize, 1964; Queen's Silver Jubilee Medal, 1977. D.L.H.: University of Birmingham, 1980. Officer, 1954, and Commander, 1961, Order of King George of the Hellenes; Officer, Legion of Honor, France, 1958; Grand Officer, Etoile Noir, 1960; Officer, Order of Arts and Letters, France, 1965. Fellow, Royal Society of Literature. C.B.E. (Commander, Order of the British Empire), 1964. Agent: David Higham Associates, 5-8 Lower John Street, London W1R 4HA, England; or, A. Watkins Inc., 77 Park Avenue, New York, New York 10016, U.S.A. Address: 85 Cornwall Gardens, London S.W. 7, England.

PUBLICATIONS

Verse

The Bud, Burial, Dawn, Grey Days, The Lover, The Mountain, Ruin, The Gargoyles, Turn Not, Hesperides. Privately printed, 10 broadsheets, 1928.
A Garden Revisited and Other Poems. London, Hogarth Press, 1931.
The Noise of History. London, Hogarth Press, 1934.
Forty Poems. London, Hogarth Press, 1942.
The Sphere of Glass and Other Poems. London, Hogarth Press, 1944.
The Age of the Dragon: Poems 1930-1951. London, Longman, 1951; New York, Harcourt Brace, 1952.
The Secret Messages. Stamford, Connecticut, Overbrook Press, 1958.
Collected Poems 1930-1963. London, Eyre and Spottiswoode, 1963.
Christ the Hunter. London, Eyre and Spottiswoode, 1965.
Photograph. London, Poem-of-the-Month Club, 1971.
The Reader at Night and Other Poems. Toronto, Basilike, 1974.

Novels

Evil Was Abroad. London, Cresset Press, 1938.
In the Purely Pagan Sense. London, Blond and Briggs, 1976.

Other

Prometheus and the Bolsheviks. London, Cresset Press, 1937; New York, Knopf, 1938.
New Writing in England. New York, Critics Group Press, 1939.
Down River: A Danubian Study. London, Cresset Press, 1939.
New Writing in Europe. London, Penguin, 1940.
The Open Night (essays). London, Longman, and New York, Harcourt Brace, 1952.
Edith Sitwell. London, Longman, 1952; revised edition, 1970.
In My Own Time: Memoirs of a Literary Life. Boston, Little Brown, 1969.
  1. *The Whispering Gallery.* London, Longman, and New York, Harcourt Brace, 1955.
  2. *I Am My Brother.* London, Longman, and New York, Reynal, 1960.
  3. *The Ample Proposition.* London, Eyre and Spottiswoode, 1966.
Ancestors and Friends. London, Eyre and Spottiswoode, 1962.
A Nest of Tigers: Edith, Osbert, and Sacheverell Sitwell in Their Times. London, Macmillan, and Boston, Little Brown, 1968.
Holborn: An Historical Portrait of a London Borough. London, Macmillan, 1970.
Lewis Carroll and the Spirit of Nonsense (lecture). Nottingham, University of Nottingham, 1974.
Virginia Woolf and Her World. London, Thames and Hudson, 1975; New York, Harcourt Brace, 1976.
Edward Lear and His World. London, Thames and Hudson, and New York, Scribner, 1977.
Thrown to the Woolfs: Leonard and Virginia Woolf and the Hogarth Press. London, Weidenfeld and Nicolson, 1978; New York, Holt Rinehart, 1979.
Rupert Brooke: His Life and Legend. London, Weidenfeld and Nicolson, 1980; as *The Strange Destiny of Rupert Brooke,* New York, Holt Rinehart, 1981.
The English Poets of the First World War. London, Thames and Hudson, 1981.
Three Literary Friendships: Byron and Shelley, Rimbaud and Verlaine, Robert Frost and Edward Thomas. London, Quartet, 1983; New York, Holt Rinehart, 1984.

Editor, with Denys Kilham Roberts and Gerald Gould, *The Year's Poetry.* London, Lane, 3 vols., 1934-36.
Editor, *New Writing.* London, Bodley Head, 2 vols., Lawrence and Wishart, 3 vols., 1936-38; with Christopher Isherwood and Stephen Spender, London, Hogarth Press, 2 vols., 1938-39; Hogarth Press, 1 vol., 1939.
Editor, with C. Day Lewis and T.A. Jackson, *A Writer in Arms,* by Ralph Fox. London, International, 1937.
Editor, with Stephen Spender, *Poems for Spain.* London, Hogarth Press, 1939.
Editor, *Penguin New Writing 1-40.* London, Penguin, 1940-50.
Editor, *Folios of New Writing.* London, Hogarth Press, 4 vols., 1940-41.
Editor, *"New Writing" and "Daylight."* London, Hogarth Press, 5 vols., 1942-47; London, Lehmann, 1 vol., 1946.
Editor, *Poems from "New Writing," 1936-1946.* London, Lehmann, 1946.

Editor, *French Stories from "New Writing."* London, Lehmann, 1947; as *Modern French Stories*, New York, New Directions, 1948.

Editor, *Demetrios Capetanakis: A Greek Poet in England.* London, Lehmann, 1947; as *Shores of Darkness: Poems and Essays*, New York, Devin Adair, 1949.

Editor, *Shelley in Italy: An Anthology.* London, Lehmann, 1947.

Editor, *Orpheus: A Symposium of the Arts.* London, Lehmann, and New York, New Directions, 1948.

Editor, *English Stories from "New Writing."* London, Lehmann, 1951; as *Best Stories from "New Writing,"* New York, Harcourt Brace, 1951.

Editor, *Pleasures of "New Writing": An Anthology of Poems, Stories, and Other Prose Pieces from the Pages of "New Writing."* London, Lehmann, 1952.

Editor, *Mòdern French Stories.* London, Faber, 1956.

Editor, with C. Day Lewis, *The Chatto Book of Modern Poetry 1915-1955.* London, Chatto and Windus, 1956.

Editor, *The Craft of Letters in England: A Symposium.* London, Cresset Press, 1956; Boston, Houghton Mifflin, 1957.

Editor, *Coming to London.* London, Phoenix House, 1957.

Editor, *Italian Stories of Today.* London, Faber, 1959.

Editor, *Selected Poems*, by Edith Sitwell. London, Macmillan, 1965.

Editor, with Derek Parker, *Selected Letters of Edith Sitwell 1919-1964.* London, Macmillan, 1970.

*

Manuscript Collections: Humanities Research Center, University of Texas, Austin; British Library, London; Bancroft Library, University of California, Berkeley.

*   *   *

During the 1940's John Lehmann published a number of prose poems which came as near as has yet proved possible to making a success of that difficult form in the English language. Many of them ("Spring Light," for instance, and "After the Fire") remain a tribute to Lehmann's command of the language. But a continual preoccupation with form and language, while it led to an enviable ease, in some respects inhibited his development as a poet. "The Sphere of Glass," one of his best poems, demonstrates a wholeness and intactness of form which make it much more than a conventional autobiographical anecdote; elsewhere, however, his poems are marked by a certain predictability of "poetic" language which can weaken them. One or two of the poems of the 1940's reflect as well as any other war poems not only the "style" but the emotion of the time, and deserve a place in any anthology of the period. His more recent poems are more organic than the earlier ones; their sum is greater than their parts, and quotation does them less than justice. If a slackening of impetus is hinted at by the rarer appearances of his poems in print, the poems that have appeared since the 1960's have also shown a more sober apprehension of the relative places of technique and "inspiration" in the making of a poem. It is much to be hoped that this always interesting poet will turn a little from accomplished literary journalism, and from the writing of interesting autobiography, and publish more poetry.

—Derek Parker

LEONARD, Tom. British. Born in Glasgow, Lanarkshire, 22 August 1944. Educated at St. Monica's Primary School and Lourdes Secondary School, Glasgow; Glasgow University, M.A. in English and Scottish literature. Married in 1971; two children. Has worked in a variety of mainly clerical jobs; organised, with Joan Hughson, sound-poetry festivals Sound and Syntax, 1978, and Poetsound '84, both in Glasgow. Recipient: Scottish Arts Council bursary, 1971, 1978. Address: 56 Eldon Street, Glasgow G3 6NJ, Scotland.

PUBLICATIONS

Verse

Six Glasgow Poems. Glasgow, Midnight Press, 1969.
A Priest Came On at Merkland Street. Glasgow, Midnight Press, 1970.
Poems. Dublin, E. and T. O'Brien, 1973.
Bunnit Husslin. Glasgow, Third Eye Centre, 1975.
Three Glasgow Writers, with Alex Hamilton and James Kelman. Glasgow, Molendinar Press, 1976.
My Name Is Tom. London, Good Elf, 1978.
Ghostie Men. Newcastle upon Tyne, Galloping Dog Press, 1980.
Intimate Voices: Writing 1965-83. Newcastle upon Tyne, Galloping Dog Press, 1984.

Plays

If Only Bunty Was Here (radio play). Glasgow, Print Studio Press, 1979.
A Bunch of Fives, with Liz Lochhead and Sean Hardie (produced Glasgow, 1983).

*

Critical Studies: "A Scots Quartette" by Edwin Morgan, in *Eboracum* (York), Winter 1973; "Tom Leonard: Man with Two Heads" by Tom McGrath, in *Akros* (Preston, Lancashire), April 1974; "Noo Lissnty Mi Toknty Yi" by George Rosie, in *Radio Times* (Scottish edition), 12-18 February 1977; *Tom Leonard*, Glasgow, National Book League, 1978; *Poésie Sonore Internationale* by Henri Chopin, Paris, Jean-Michel Place, 1979; "Poetry for the People in Glasgow Patois" by Alasdair Gray, in *Glasgow Herald*, 17 March 1984.

*   *   *

Tom Leonard is one of the most interesting of the younger Scottish poets who emerged during the 1960's. His reputation in Scotland has tended to centre on his poems in Glasgow dialect, but in fact, as the publication of his first general collection, *Poems*, made clear, he is a man of many styles, a restless formal experimenter whose language is laid with surprises, traps, and ironies. There is a considerable element of humour, sometimes fantastic and sometimes moderately black, to attract the reader, and a recurring deadpan strangeness is characteristic. Some of the ironical effects are slight, joky, throwaway. But in the best poems, like "simile please/say cheese," the interlock of images and ideas forces the humour to work in unusual and meaningful ways. The Glasgow poems make use of local idiom and pronunciation for a range of effects, from the bold outspoken backchat of schoolgirls skipping their bus-fares ("A Scream") to the more sophisticated meshing of religion and football in "The Good Thief." These poems take the risk of being obscure to English readers (though the book provides a translation) for the sake of offering a tribute to the much-attacked Glasgow environment—not that the tribute is anything but unsentimental.

Language, religion, sex, and politics continue to be explored in *Bunnit Husslin* and *Ghostie Men*, in poems of great precision and compression (though sometimes of an outspokenness alarming to education authorities), and *Intimate Voices* offers a useful collection and survey of his work from 1965 to 1983. The "voice" of this title is crucial, not only in the sense that Leonard's very accurate ear allows him to make use of monologues, dialogues, parodies, casual remarks, and language-games with a minimum of overlay or working-up or pretension, but also since it helps to suggest his growing interest in performance and in the dramatic or the semi-dramatic. The dramatic monologue, applied particularly to political subjects — and his political commitment, always there, has become more prominent — is developed in the slashing prose pieces of *Satires and Profanities* (forthcoming), a centenary tribute to James (B.V.) Thomson's book of the same title. Leonard is an instantly communicative poet whose work, including its "bad language" (about which there will always be diverse views), nevertheless repays close attention on the printed page.

—Edwin Morgan

LePAN, Douglas (Valentine). Canadian. Born in Toronto, Ontario, 25 May 1914. Educated at University of Toronto Schools; University College, University of Toronto, B.A.; Merton College, Oxford, M.A. Served in Canadian Army, 1942-45. Married Sarah Katharine Chambers in 1948 (separated, 1971); two sons. Lecturer, University of Toronto, 1937-38; Instructor and Tutor in English Literature, Harvard University, Cambridge, Massachusetts, 1938-41. Joined Canadian Department of External Affairs, 1945: First Secretary on the Staff of the Canadian High Commissioner in London, 1945-48; various appointments in the Department of External Affairs, including that of Special Assistant to the Secretary of State, Ottawa, 1949-51; Counsellor and later Minister Counsellor at the Canadian Embassy, Washington, D.C., 1951-55; Secretary and Director of Research, Royal Commission on Canada's Economic Prospects (Gordon Commission), 1955-58; Assistant Under-Secretary of State for External Affairs, 1958-59. Professor of English Literature, Queen's University, Kingston, Ontario, 1959-64. Principal, University College, 1964-70, and University Professor, 1970-79, University of Toronto. Member, Canada Council, 1964-70. Recipient: Guggenheim Fellowship, 1948; Governor-General's Award, for poetry, 1954, for fiction, 1965; Oscar Blumenthal Prize (*Poetry*, Chicago), 1972. D.Litt.: University of Manitoba, Winnipeg, 1964; University of Ottawa, 1972; University of Waterloo, Ontario, 1973; LL.D.: Queen's University, Kingston, Ontario, 1969; York University, Toronto, 1976; Dalhousie University, Halifax, Nova Scotia, 1980. Fellow, Royal Society of Canada, 1968. Address: Massey College, 4 Devonshire Place, Toronto, Ontario M5S 2E1, Canada.

PUBLICATIONS

Verse

The Wounded Prince and Other Poems. Toronto, Clarke Irwin, and London, Chatto and Windus, 1948.

The Net and the Sword. Toronto, Clarke Irwin, and London, Chatto and Windus, 1953.
Something Still to Find: New Poems. Toronto, McClelland and Stewart, 1982.

Novel

The Deserter. Toronto, McClelland and Stewart, 1964.

Other

Bright Glass of Memory: A Set of Four Memoirs. Toronto, McGraw Hill Ryerson, 1979.

*   *   *

When a man of letters is also a man of affairs, his public life cannot but influence his writing. Douglas LePan, who holds degrees from the University of Toronto and Oxford, saw action in the Italian Campaign of World War II. He joined the Department of External Affairs and rose to become Assistant Under-Secretary of State. Then he left to become a professor of English and finally principal of University College, University of Toronto. His careers have influenced his poetry in interesting ways.

His first two books of poems are largely concerned with his war experiences. *The Wounded Prince* views the grim events ironically and paradoxically. *The Net and the Sword*, which received the Governor-General's Award, recreates the Italian Campaign and views man mercilessly pitted against the forces of destruction. Along with paintings by the War Artists in the National Gallery in Ottawa, these war poems are a valuable record of the achievements of Canadian soldiers overseas. Both books are mature works full of rich, intellectualized imagery.

Like a public man, LePan is very much concerned with the responsibility of man. He admires the muscular man, whether gladiator, soldier, or *coureur de bois*. In *The Net and the Sword*, he has a poem on the latter:

Thinking of you, I think of the *coureur de bois*,
Swarthy men grown almost to savage size
Who put their brown wrists through the arras of the woods
and were lost—sometimes for months.

But he is also concerned with the repercussions of action, not with those "whose care is how they fall, not why." This has led him to theorize about the Canadian experience. The title of a poem in *The Wounded Prince* has become a catch-phrase of the period: "A Country Without a Mythology."

His only novel, *The Deserter*, concerns social responsibility and was awarded a Governor-General's Award. It probes the meaning of war to a soldier who deserts—not before or during a campaign, but after the armistice. LePan has recently published a number of essays on social philosophy—further evidence of his concern for the roots of the Canadian community.

—John Robert Colombo

LERNER, Laurence (David). British. Born in Cape Town, South Africa, 12 December 1925. Educated at the University of Cape Town, B.A. 1944, M.A. 1945; Pembroke College, Cambridge, B.A. 1949. Married Natalie Winch in 1948; four children. Schoolmaster, St. George's Grammar School, Cape Town, 1946-47; Assistant Lecturer, then Lecturer in English, University College of the Gold Coast, Legon, Ghana, 1949-53; Extra-Mural Tutor, then Lecturer in English, Queen's University of Belfast, 1953-62. Lecturer, then Reader, 1962-70, and since 1970, Professor of English, University of Sussex, Brighton. Visiting Professor, Earlham College, Richmond, Indiana, and University of Connecticut, Storrs, 1960-61; University of Illinois, Urbana, 1964; University of Dijon, 1967; University of Munich, 1968-69, 1974-75; University of Paris III, 1982; University of Ottawa, 1983. Recipient: Prudence Farmer Prize (*New Statesman*), 1975; South-East Arts Prize, 1979. Address: 50 Compton Avenue, Brighton, Sussex BN1 3PS, England.

PUBLICATIONS

Verse

(Poems). Oxford, Fantasy Press, 1955.
Domestic Interior and Other Poems. London, Hutchinson, 1959.
The Directions of Memory: Poems 1958-1963. London, Chatto and Windus, 1963.
Selves. London, Routledge, 1969.
Folio, with others. Frensham, Surrey, Sceptre Press, 1971.
A.R.T.H.U.R.: The Life and Opinions of a Digital Computer. Hassocks, Sussex, Harvester Press, 1974; Amherst, University of Massachusetts Press, 1975.
The Man I Killed. London, Secker and Warburg, 1980.
A.R.T.H.U.R. & M.A.R.T.H.A.; or, The Loves of the Computers. London, Secker and Warburg, 1980.
A Dialogue. Oxford, Pisces Press, 1983.
Chapter and Verse: Bible Poems. London, Secker and Warburg, 1984.
Selected Poems. London, Secker and Warburg, 1984.

Play

The Experiment (produced Brighton, 1980).

Novels

The Englishmen. London, Hamish Hamilton, 1959.
A Free Man. London, Chatto and Windus, 1968.

Other

English Literature: An Interpretation for Students Abroad. London, Oxford University Press, 1954.
The Truest Poetry: An Essay on the Question: What is Literature? London, Hamish Hamilton, 1960; New York, Horizon Press, 1964.
The Truthtellers: Jane Austen, George Eliot, and D.H. Lawrence. London, Chatto and Windus, and New York, Schocken, 1967.
The Uses of Nostalgia: Studies in Pastoral Poetry. London, Chatto and Windus, and New York, Schocken, 1972.
Thomas Hardy's "The Mayor of Casterbridge": Tragedy or Social History? London, Chatto and Windus, 1975.
An Introduction to English Poetry: Fifteen Poems Discussed. London, Arnold, 1975.
Love and Marriage: Literature and Its Social Context. London, Arnold, 1979.
The Literary Imagination: Essays on Literature and Society.

Brighton, Harvester, and New York, Barnes and Noble, 1982.

Editor, *Poems,* by Milton. London, Penguin, 1953.
Editor, *Shakespeare's Tragedies: A Selection of Modern Criticism.* London, Penguin, 1963.
Editor, with John Holmstrom, *George Eliot and Her Readers: A Selection of Contemporary Reviews.* London, Bodley Head, 1966.
Editor, *Shakespeare's Comedies: A Selection of Modern Criticism.* London, Penguin, 1967.
Editor, with John Holmstrom, *Thomas Hardy and His Readers: A Selection of Contemporary Reviews.* London, Bodley Head, 1968.
Editor, *Poetry South East 2: An Anthology of New Poetry.* Tunbridge Wells, Kent, South East Arts Association, 1977.
Editor, *The Victorians.* London, Methuen, and New York, Holmes and Meier, 1978.
Editor, *Reconstructing Literature.* Oxford, Blackwell, 1983.

Translator, *Spleen,* by Baudelaire. Belfast, Festival, 1966.

*

Laurence Lerner comments:

My poems are comprehensible, sad, modern in subject-matter rather than form. Some are lyrical and personal, many are dramatic and represent the attempt to enter a variety of selves. In *Chapter and Verse* I tried to perform the perhaps incompatible tasks of introducing the Bible to the modern secular reader for whom it is no longer culturally central, and subverting the traditional stories by means of an unusual viewpoint or unorthodox judgement. If I could write half a dozen more poems as good as "The Merman" or "Raspberries" I'd be satisfied. I hope my next collection will deal largely with my family, past and present, and their role in the poet's emotional life.

*   *   *

Like the best of his criticism, Laurence Lerner's poetry is sensible, direct and aware of the complexities of human behaviour. Many of the poems in his first collection, *Domestic Interior*, are reactions to different environments; their strength lies not so much in description as in the way they establish a mental *rapport* with the external world, in which closely-observed incidentals find their place in a wider pattern of experience:

> While shaping eyes stare from the moving train:
> Or else a water-colour landscape glows
> Grey-green and tawny under a wash of rain,
> Or blue with blobs of cabbages in rows.

Most of these poems are "efficient" and well-argued, in a sense which reminds one of the best Thirties' poetry, though occasionally the argument only partly conceals a certain diffuseness of detail. In the more successful ones, however, like the title-poem and "Meditation on the Toothache" (in actual fact, a meditation on the imagination), a powerful social concern is firmly rooted in the trivia of the individual life, and in the means by which these may be absorbed into artistic creation. The dramatic sense is evident in "Domestic Interior" and "Mimesis"—both poems in which the subject is approached through a number of protagonists.

Lerner's second collection, *The Directions of Memory*, is more adventurous in technique, and shows a willingness to handle more difficult kinds of experience. Though one still occasionally feels that a poem has not found its ideal form, there is a more subtle sense of construction and a growing skill in the use of imagery. Several of the most striking poems dealt with sexual relationships, sometimes from the woman's point of view. These range from the aggression-dream ("Housewife as Judith") to the qualified celebration of "The Anatomy of Love" and the fine "Midnight Swim," a poem in which a profoundly disturbing situation is conveyed through a brilliantly-controlled central metaphor. The same could be said of the most moving poem in the volume, "Years Later," the monologue of an unborn Jewish child, the victim (with its mother) of a Nazi atrocity. These poems show a determination to face up to the more disturbing aspects of life with honesty, intelligence and, at times, with wit.

The same combination of qualities persists, with increasing verbal power, in *Selves*, as well as in his vigorous and resourceful versions of Baudelaire. The central section of *Selves* includes a group of monologues in which various victims of human cruelty—a laboratory rat, a monkey involved in a feeding experiment, a battery-reared cockerel—comment on their situations with grimly humorous logic. Though in one sense such poems are a natural extension of Lerner's interest in current psychological theory, their real originality comes from the skill with which they render essentially inarticulate suffering in terms of a recognizable human idiom. In other poems ("The Merman," "Adam Names the Creatures," "Information Theory"), the concern with communication extends to the nature of language itself. Here, the deliberate assumption of inarticulateness becomes a powerful device for exploring the gap between words and reality ("The Merman"):

When humans talk they split their say in bits
And bit by bit they step on what they feel.
They talk in bits, they never talk in all.

So live in wetness swimming they call "sea";
And stand on dry and watch the wet waves call
They still call "sea".
 Only their waves don't call.

Lerner's continued questioning of the basis of language and perception lies at the root of *A.R.T.H.U.R.* It would be wrong to dismiss this as a *jeu d'esprit*: certainly, the poems are ingenious, entertaining, and wittier than anything else he has written, though none of this should blind one to their underlying seriousness. As the introductory poem makes clear, the world of *A.R.T.H.U.R.* ("Automatic Record Tabulator but Heuristically Unreliable Reasoner") is divided between "metal people" and "movers"—in other words, computers and human beings. This leads to some unusual perspectives: "Movers are constantly bending and running/Through a world of edges and obstacles. Cunning/Their reflexes, but cannot eliminate mourning." From the human point of view, the effect is one of "Making strange," a process which is carried still further in those poems, like "Literary Criticism" and "Arthur takes a test for divergent thinking," which are concerned with the properties of language itself. Here, the game seems innocent enough; elsewhere, however, as in certain stories by Borges, there are hints of more frightening possibilities: the sense, for example, that new objects can be brought into existence by the mere fact that it is possible to name them. Hence the ending of "Arthur's reply," with its brilliant final pun: "We can try anything: just turn me on,/Feed me the facts, and wait for trial and terror."

The possibilities of such poems are extended in *A.R.T.H.U.R. & M.A.R.T.H.A. or the Loves of the Computers*—an equally engaging collection in which human sexual relationships are tested almost to destruction by the witty application of scientific metaphor. Both sequences are impressive evidence of Lerner's inventiveness in a mode which few British poets have attempted and which represents, in Edwin Morgan's phrase, "a natural extension of the imagination in an age of science."

Lerner's two most recent collections, *The Man I Killed* and *Chapter and Verse: Bible Poems*, mark a partial return to earlier allegiances, though the directness of the best poems may owe something to the pointed simplicity and sureness of rhythm he had been compelled to practise in the "scientific" poems. The former takes its title from "The Experiment," one of Lerner's most powerful poems, in which his earlier preoccupation with the scientific treatment of animals is brought to a head in the imagined victimization of man at his own hands. Here and elsewhere the tone varies between humour, irony, and the deliberately flat statement of the horrific, with notable gains in economy of language and skill in counterpointing conversational rhythms against carefully controlled patterns of repetition. Less spectacularly, though no less forcefully, the spaciousness and verbal richness of the earlier dramatic monologues give way, as in the two Rembrandt poems ("Saskia" and "Youthful Self-Portrait") to a greater incisiveness in which the heaviest burden falls on the simplest words ("then," "now," "selves"), carefully spaced out within a verse pattern created largely by natural phrasing and the skilful use of eye-rhymes and line breaks.

Though *The Man I Killed* is probably Lerner's strongest collection to date, *Chapter and Verse* (published at the same time as the excellent *Selected Poems*) brings together and intensifies many of his earlier preoccupations in the course of re-creating a series of Biblical episodes from Genesis to Apocalypse. Though occasionally the commentary becomes a little predictable, the general effect is shrewd, entertaining, and at times (as in the fine poem on Poussin's painting of St. Matthew) deeply moving. Again, in a poem like "Ishmael" one admires the economy with which scattered hints from Genesis are taken up and welded into a coherent discourse which compels the reader to enter the speaker's subversive mentality and to see things from what, in his own terms, is a legitimate point of view. The deepest irony is that, at certain crucial moments, this point of view is made to overlap with the reader's own: phrases like "God's first Jew" and "What does the future cost?," by opening a channel between the present time and that of the speaker, emphasize both the relevance of the Biblical narrative and its power to disturb.

Despite their apparent novelty, these and other recent poems seem to come from a firm and individual centre of experience which Lerner can by now take for granted. For some time past, he has given the impression of a poet who is working hard on himself, and whose sheer resourcefulness makes it difficult to predict his future work. What seems certain, however, is that he will continue to explore the paradoxes of language and human experience with his characteristic blend of compassion and ingenuity.

—Arthur Terry

LEVENSON, Christopher. Canadian. Born in London, England, 13 February 1934; naturalized Canadian citizen, 1973. Educated at Downing College, Cambridge, 1954-57, B.A. 1957; University of Iowa, Iowa City, M.A. 1970. Conscientious Objector: worked with the Friends Ambulance Unit International Service, 1952-

54. Married Ursula Frieda Lina Fischer in 1958 (divorced), four sons. Taught at the International Quaker School, Eerde, Holland, 1957-58; English Lektor, University of Munster, West Germany, 1958-61; taught at Rodway Technical High School, Magotsfield, Gloucestershire, 1962-64. Since 1968, Member of the department of English, currently Associate Professor, Carleton University, Ottawa. Editor, *Delta* magazine for two years. Recipient: Eric Gregory Award, 1960. Address: Department of English, Carleton University, Ottawa, Ontario K1S 5B6, Canada.

PUBLICATIONS

Verse

New Poets 1959, with Iain Crichton Smith and Karen Gershon. London, Eyre and Spottiswoode, 1959.
Cairns. London, Chatto and Windus-Hogarth Press, 1969.
Stills. London, Chatto and Windus-Hogarth Press, 1972.
Into the Open. Ottawa, Golden Dog Press, 1977.
No Journey Back and Other Poems. Windsor, Ontario, Sesame Press, 1978.
No-Man's-Land. Toronto, League of Canadian Poets, 1980.

Other

Editor, *Poetry from Cambridge.* London, Fortune Press, 1958.
Editor, *Light of the World: An Anthology of Seventeenth-Century Dutch Religious and Occasional Poetry.* Windsor, Ontario, Netherlandic Press, 1982.
Translator, *Van Gogh,* by Abraham M.W.J. Hammacher. London, Spring, 1961.
Translator, *The Leavetaking,* by Peter Weiss. New York, Harcourt Brace, 1962; with *Vanishing Point,* London, Calder and Boyars, 1966.
Translator, *The Golden Casket: Chinese Novellas of Two Millennia* (translation from the German version by Wolfgang Bauer). London, Allen and Unwin, 1965; Westport, Connecticut, Greenwood Press, 1978.

*   *   *

A considerable body of verse by Christopher Levenson was published in volume form as long ago as 1959. It may be found in Edwin Muir's compilation *New Poets.* Nobody took sufficient notice at the time. Yet a discerning reader should have felt that here was distinctive voice:

Exiled ambassadors of their heart's country, refugees
Carry their futures in one attache case...

In the distorting mirrors of my travels,
Where is tomorrow, now that yesterday
Is bartered for snapshots...?

Past the last city, on to the great plain,
The fevered air grows still, the lights behind us,
Thrown from a thousand scattered windows, blur:
We are alone....

It was no accident that the author called this early collection "In Transit." The word "transit" recurs through his work. The characteristic persona is that of an exile observing the scenes through which he passes:

They came here in transit, would not learn the language
Their children gabble, had not meant to stay,
But gradually drained of will, subsided into
The institutional gray....

This is a later poem — "Transit Camp" — and the rhymes, though rather insistent, seem an attempt to variegate the Audenism of Levenson's basic verse-structure.

There is, in other words, a characteristic cadence in these poems, and it is evoked mainly when the author considers the plight of the wanderer. That cadence is a genuine contribution to poetry today:

I stand, tenebral, gazing down on a city
lost under smoke but luminous, to overhear
its many baffled night sounds, catch its drift
of hasty farewells, and sift through memory
a half-heard language I no longer know
in a remote country....

This is a strain dominant in the later poetry of Christopher Levenson. *Into the Open,* a comparatively recent book, show the characteristic style, but it is quarrying a deeper vein. The central facts of topography are in process of being allegorized. "Domestic Flight" begins

From above, the imposed civility
of maps, undeflected straight lines
of concession roads, and farms'
Foursquare geometry excised from wilderness....

But the poem dilates on that wilderness — "great gashes of the wolfish dark,/snow-muzzled tundra...." The allegory continues through the book. A patient is wired to an encephalograph, and his dreams are explored — "the frenzied writing on the drum descends/to a scrawl of slow valleys...."

Most ambitious of all, "The Journey Back," in the book of that name, is a long poem of some twenty pages relating Bela Bartok, the Hungarian composer, to his native terrain. It is particularly moving on the subject of Bartok collecting folk-songs. An old woman refuses to sing to order:

but he was no soooner gone,
not yet out of earshot, than she started, the melodies
bubbling back like a salt flat spring that the tides had covered,
restored, woven from silence, for herself only....

Levenson does not forget the present regime, hostile to Bartok and, by implication, all art. The artist cannot sing to order, whether that order is issued by a collector or by the "dark-suited commissars/at the Ministry of Culture."

The poem is a more impressive performance than could have been predicted from the earlier work. In this union of geography, art, and compassion, Levenson has reached a greater linguistic richness and a surer understanding of human motivation in what has turned out to be his unexpectedly fertile middle age.

—Philip Hobsbaum

LEVERTOV, Denise. American. Born in Ilford, Essex, England, 24 October 1923; emigrated to the United States, 1948; naturalized, 1955. Educated privately. Served as a nurse in

World War II. Married the writer Mitchell Goodman in 1947 (divorced); one son. Worked in antique shop and bookshop, London, 1946; nurse at British Hospital, Paris, Spring 1947; taught at the YM-YWHA Poetry Center, New York, 1964, City College of New York, 1965, and Vassar College, Poughkeepsie, New York, 1966-67; Visiting Professor, Drew University, Madison, New Jersey, 1965, University of California, Berkeley, 1969, Massachusetts Institute of Technology, Cambridge, 1969-70, Kirkland College, Clinton, New York, 1970-71, University of Cincinnati, Spring 1973, and Tufts University, Medford, Massachusetts, 1973-79; Fannie Hurst Professor (Poet-in-Residence), Brandeis University, Waltham, Massachusetts, 1981-83. Since 1982, Professor of English, Stanford University, California. Poetry Editor, *The Nation*, New York, 1961, 1963-65, and *Mother Jones*, San Francisco, 1975-78. Honorary Scholar, Radcliffe Institute for Independent Study, Cambridge, Massachusetts, 1964-66. Recipient: Bess Hokin Prize, 1960, Harriet Monroe Memorial Prize, 1964, Inez Boulton Prize, 1964, and Morton Dauwen Zabel Prize, 1965 (*Poetry*, Chicago); Longview Award, 1961; Guggenheim Fellowship, 1962; American Academy grant, 1966, 1968; Lenore Marshall Prize, 1976; Bobst Award, 1983. D.Litt.: Colby College, Waterville, Maine, 1970; University of Cincinnati, 1973; Bates College, Lewiston, Maine, 1984; St. Lawrence University, Canton, New York, 1984. Member, American Academy, 1980; Corresponding Member, Mallarmé Academy, 1983. Address: c/o New Directions, 80 Eighth Avenue, New York, New York 10011, U.S.A.

Publications

Verse

The Double Image. London, Cresset Press, 1946.
Here and Now. San Francisco, City Lights, 1956.
Overland to the Islands. Highlands, North Carolina, Jargon, 1958.
5 Poems. San Francisco, White Rabbit Press, 1958.
With Eyes at the Back of Our Heads. New York, New Directions, 1960.
The Jacob's Ladder. New York, New Directions, 1961; London, Cape, 1965.
O Taste and See: New Poems. New York, New Directions, 1964.
City Psalm. Berkeley, California, Oyez, 1964.
Psalm Concerning the Castle. Madison, Wisconsin, Perishable Press, 1966.
The Sorrow Dance. New York, New Directions, 1967; London, Cape, 1968.
Penguin Modern Poets 9, with Kenneth Rexroth and William Carlos Williams. London, Penguin, 1967.
A Tree Telling of Orpheus. Los Angeles, Black Sparrow Press, 1968.
A Marigold from North Viet Nam. New York, Albondocani Press-Ampersand, 1968.
Three Poems. Mount Horeb, Wisconsin, Perishable Press, 1968.
The Cold Spring and Other Poems. New York, New Directions, 1969.
Embroideries. Los Angeles, Black Sparrow Press, 1969.
Relearning the Alphabet. New York, New Directions, and London, Cape, 1970.
Summer Poems 1969. Berkeley, California, Oyez, 1970.
A New Year's Garland for My Students, MIT 1969-1970. Mount Horeb, Wisconsin, Perishable Press, 1970.
To Stay Alive. New York, New Directions, 1971.

Footprints. New York, New Directions, 1972.
The Freeing of the Dust. New York, New Directions, 1975.
Chekhov on the West Heath. Andes, New York, Woolmer Brotherston, 1977.
Modulations for Solo Voice. San Francisco, Five Trees Press, 1977.
Life in the Forest. New York, New Directions, 1978.
Collected Earlier Poems 1940-1960. New York, New Directions, 1979.
Pig Dreams: Scenes from the Life of Sylvia. Woodstock, Vermont, Countryman Press, 1981.
Wanderer's Daysong. Port Townsend, Washington, Copper Canyon Press, 1981.
Candles in Babylon. New York, New Directions, 1982.
Poems 1960-1967. New York, New Directions, 1983.
Oblique Prayers: New Poems with 14 Translations from Jean Joubert. New York, New Directions, 1984.
El Salvador—Requiem and Invocation. Concord, New Hampshire, William B. Ewert, 1984.
The Menaced World. Concord, New Hampshire, William B. Ewert, 1984.

Recording: *Today's Poets 3*, with others, Folkways.

Short Story

In the Night. New York, Albondocani Press, 1968.

Other

The Poet in the World (essays). New York, New Directions, 1973.
Conversation in Moscow. Cambridge, Massachusetts, Hovey Street Press, 1973.
Denise Levertov: An Interview, with John K. Atchity. Dallas, New London Press, 1980.
Light Up the Cave (essays). New York, New Directions, 1981.

Editor, *Out of the War Shadow: An Anthology of Current Poetry.* New York, War Resisters League, 1967.
Editor and Translator, with Edward C. Dimock, Jr., *In Praise of Krishna: Songs from the Bengali.* New York, Doubleday, 1967; London, Cape, 1968.

Translator, *Selected Poems*, by Guillevic. New York, New Directions, 1969.

*

Bibliography: *A Bibliography of Denise Levertov* by Robert A. Wilson, New York, Phoenix Bookshop, 1972.

Manuscript Collections: Humanities Research Center, University of Texas, Austin; Washington University, St. Louis; Indiana University, Bloomington; Fales Library, New York University; Beinecke Library, Yale University, New Haven, Connecticut; Brown University, Providence, Rhode Island; University of Connecticut, Storrs; Columbia University, New York; State University of New York, Stony Brook.

Critical Studies: *Denise Levertov* by Linda Wagner, New York, Twayne, 1967, and *Denise Levertov: In Her Own Province*, edited by Wagner, New York, New Directions, 1979; *Out of the Vietnam Vortex* by James Mersmann, Lawrence, University Press of Kansas, 1974; Hayden Carruth, in *Hudson Review* (New York), 1974; *The Imagination's Tongue: Denise Lever-*

tov's Poetic by William Slaughter, Portree, Isle of Skye, Aquila, 1981; *From Modern to Contemporary American Poetry 1945-1965* by James E.B. Breslin, Chicago, University of Chicago Press, 1984.

*   *   *

Though Denise Levertov was born in England, grew up and was educated there, even published her first book of poems there in 1946, she has become a thoroughly American literary figure, one whose work represents the most original gestures, thought of as significantly American. In particular, the use of simple language and an autobiographical voice. In spite of her conservative beginnings, her poetry was immediately encouraged by Kenneth Rexroth, and other avant garde figures, when she came to this country, and over the years it has been published by New Directions, the press most associated with the Pound/Williams modernist and post-modernist ideals. Though many call her a Black Mountain poet, that is not a term she feels comfortable with. However, her ideas about poetry being an "organic" art are closely allied with the breath-line theories of poetics proposed by both Olson and Creeley.

In recent years, Levertov has become very active in liberal politics, publicly protesting the Vietnam war and now the use of nuclear power in the arms race. Much poetry has grown out of this involvement, but many of her fans and critics believe that the best of her work still reflects the personal concerns, not the political ones, and that as sincere as her wishes are for a peaceful new world, her poetic vision discloses a much more frightening reality.

In *Life in the Forest*, her best book, the prevailing myth of The Garden as the primal jungle which existed before human civilization began, haunts a beautiful sequence of poems called "Homage to Pavese" but centered on her 90-year-old mother's final years and death. In "Death in Mexico" she chronicles the rapid return to jungle of her mother's carefully tended 20-year-old Mexican garden after she falls and begins to die. In that return to its primal reality, Levertov sees all of civilization reverting to something which is more enduring than anything humanity has created.

> But to me the weeds, the flowerless rosebushes, broken
> stems of the canna lilies and amaryllis, all
> a lusterless jungle green, presented—
> even before her dying was over—
> an obdurate, blind, all-seeing gaze:
> I had seen it before in the museums,
> in stone masks of the gods and victims.
> A gaze that admits
> no regrets, nostalgia has no part in its cosmos,
> bitterness is irrelevant.
> If it holds a flower—and it does,
> a delicate brilliant silky flower that blooms only
> a single day—it holds it clenched
> between sharp teeth.

This vision of the inexorable fall of man and banishment from this primal garden cannot be touched by her desire for human communication and peace. In another poem in the book, "Wedding-Ring," she talks wistfully of a divorced woman's wish that her wedding ring which now "lies in a basket/as if at the bottom of a well" could be reforged with jewels into a friendship ring and be worn to symbolize all the good things which happened in the long years of marriage, instead of hidden to bury the memory of the bad ones. But the poem is realistic in knowing this can never be. Putting these poems together with Levertov's ever

optimistic political actions is interesting. Her poetry does not permit even a moment of unrealistic wistful belief that real peace, harmony, or preservation from the final primal jungle can be achieved.

In her recent book, *Candles in Babylon*, she indicates in the title that our art and concern can at most produce a bit of light in a doomed time. One of the most moving poems in the book was originally written as a speech and is called, "A Speech: For Antidraft Rally, D.C. March 22, 1980." In it she meditates on the fact that lack of information including an ignorance of history is what characterizes the young, and thus there can really be no hope that we can save ourselves from ultimate nuclear destruction. While she invokes her listeners to change this, the poignant lyrical beauty of Levertov's language is in the lament itself:

> No violence they've seen
> on the flickering living-room screen familiar since infancy
> or the movies of adolescent dates, the dark
> so much fuller of themselves, of each other's presence than of
> history (and the history anyway
> twisted—not that they have a way to know that)
>   the dark
>   vibrant with themselves, with warm breath,
>   half suppressed mirth, the wonder
>   of being alive, terrified, entranced
>   by sexual fragrance each gives off
>   among popcorn, clumsy
>   gestures, the weird
>   response of laughter when on that screen
>   death's happening. Wow, *unreal*, and people
>   suffer, or dream aloud...None of that spoon-fed
>   violence
> prepares them. The disgusting routine horror of war
> eludes them. They think
> they would die for something they call America,
> vague, as true dreams are not;

Levertov's poetry continues to present a personal voice, eloquently vocative and American about one's desires, needs, and wishes. Yet the myth she is working out, inexorably, in the poems is that no personal wish or desire will be left when the man-made garden must finally revert to the primal forest which is greater than humanity, more savage and more powerful than anything we can create in art or life.

—Diane Wakoski

———————

LEVI, Peter (Chad Tigar). British. Born in Ruislip, Middlesex, 16 May 1931. Educated at Beaumont College, Berkshire, 1946-48; Campion Hall, Oxford, M.A. 1961. Married Deirdre Craig in 1977. Member of the Society of Jesus, 1948-77: ordained priest, 1964; resigned priesthood, 1977. Tutor and Lecturer in Classics, Campion Hall, 1965-77; Lecturer in Classics, Christ Church, Oxford, 1979-82. Since 1977, Fellow, St. Catherine's College, Oxford; since 1984, Professor of Poetry, Oxford University. Student, British School of Archaeology, Athens, 1965-68; archaeology correspondent, *The Times*, London, 1977-78. Recipient: Southern Arts Literature Prize, 1984. Fellow, Society of Antiquaries. Address: Austin's Farm, Stonesfield, Oxford, England.

PUBLICATIONS

Verse

Earthly Paradise.   Privately printed, 1958.
The Gravel Ponds.   London, Deutsch, and New York, Macmillan, 1960.
Orpheus Head.   Privately printed, 1962.
Water, Rock, and Sand.   London, Deutsch, and Philadelphia, Dufour, 1962.
The Shearwaters.   Oxford, Allison, 1965.
Fresh Water, Sea Water.   Llandeilo, Carmarthen, and London, Black Raven Press-Deutsch, 1965.
Pancakes for the Queen of Babylon: Ten Poems for Nikos Gatsos.   London, Anvil Press Poetry, 1968.
Ruined Abbeys.   London, Anvil Press Poetry, 1968.
Life Is a Platform.   London, Anvil Press Poetry, 1971.
Death Is a Pulpit.   London, Anvil Press Poetry, 1971.
Penguin Modern Poets 22, with Adrian Mitchell and John Fuller.   London, Penguin, 1973.
Collected Poems 1955-1975.   London, Anvil Press Poetry, 1976.
Five Ages.   London, Anvil Press Poetry, 1978.
Private Ground.   London, Anvil Press Poetry, 1981.
The Echoing Green: Three Elegies.   London, Anvil Press Poetry, 1983.

Novel

The Head in the Soup.   London, Constable, 1979.

Other

Beaumont 1861-1961.   London, Deutsch, 1961.
The Light Garden of the Angel King: Journeys in Afghanistan.   London, Collins, and Indianapolis, Bobbs Merrill, 1972.
John Clare and Thomas Hardy (lecture).   London, Athlone Press, 1975.
In Memory of David Jones (sermon).   London, The Tablet, 1975.
The Noise Made by Poems.   London, Anvil Press Poetry, 1977.
Atlas of the Greek World.   Oxford, Phaidon Press, 1980; New York, Facts on File, 1981.
The Hill of Kronos.   London, Collins, 1980; New York, Dutton, 1981.
The Greek World, photographs by Eliot Porter.   New York, Dutton, 1980; London, Aurum Press, 1981.
The Flutes of Autumn.   London, Harvill Press, 1983.

Editor, *The English Bible 1534-1859.*   London, Constable, and Grand Rapids, Michigan, Eerdmans, 1974.
Editor, *Pope.*   London, Penguin, 1974.
Editor, *A Journey to the Western Isles of Scotland, and The Journal of a Tour to the Hebrides,* by Johnson and Boswell.   London, Penguin, 1984.

Translator, with Robin Milner-Gulland, *Selected Poems of Yevtushenko.*   London, Penguin, and New York, Dutton, 1962; as *Poems Chosen by the Author,* London, Collins-Harvill Press, 1966; New York, Hill and Wang, 1967.
Translator, *Guide to Greece,* by Pausanias.   London, Penguin, 2 vols., 1971.
Translator, *The Psalms.*   London, Penguin, 1977.
Translator, *The Cellar,* by George Pavlopoulos.   London, Anvil Press Poetry, 1977.
Translator, *Marko the Prince* (Serbo-Croat epic poetry).   London, Duckworth, 1983.
Translator, *The Murderess,* by Alexandros Papadiamantis.   London and New York, Writers and Readers, 1983.

*   *   *

Peter Levi's poetry—like that of Wallace Stevens, with which it sometimes enters into a kind of dialogue—is often concerned with its own procedures; and in the early poem "The Tractor in Spring" Levi establishes a connection between his language and his theme which he has maintained throughout his work:

> I want words whose existence is this,
> the rough soil and the root work in them,
> praising heaven I ever took for theme
> this planet, its unnatural wishes,
> common reason and human justice,
> and growth of life, the last increase of time.

The words he finds for the abstractions of "reason" and "justice" often create a complex kind of interior landscape in which a mood is evoked, a scene described, in order to prompt some defining relation between the human consciousness and its embracing contingencies of nature and of history. In establishing this "definition," Levi uses, most characteristically, the mode of elegy. His favoured landscapes are seen through rain, wind, mist; he imagines himself "counting the pigeons in the snow-cold air,/listening to small voices of the other birds,/walking in the wind that sweeps this poem bare." And his sense of history is darkened by a central awareness of what he calls "the class divisions built into the language," and by the certainty that the humanist values represented by that language are in decay, that "in our lives Europe is saying goodnight." The poems move, then, ambivalently but honestly, between lament and gestures of encouragement. The long poem *Canticum,* for instance, which is, I think, one of Levi's major achievements, oscillates between exactly these poles when it attempts to feel out, in language, what a world radically alternative to the one we must live in might be like:

> Not one by one but everyone breaks in,
> we shall come back with armfuls of lilac
> and the crooked trees behind our kitchens
> will blossom again. It is the future
> which says death to us and which we love.

The desire to discover alternatives in poetic language itself to what Levi sees as the debilitation of middle-class English has prompted experimentation with kinds of writing not normally handled nowadays by serious writers in the English tradition, and especially with a kind of gentle surrealism inherited largely from modern Greek poetry. Levi has described this element in the work of George Pavlopoulos, which he has translated, as "a glitter on the skin of his poems," and this might also be said of Levi himself: the surrealism of his poetic sequence *Pancakes for the Queen of Babylon* never entirely loses touch with the real and avoids the more obvious dottinesses of the tradition as it has previously manifested itself in English. This sequence, and several others, such as "Thirty Ways of Drowning in the Sea," "Rivers," and "Five Ages of a Poet," are, in a poetry that depends so much on the establishing of mood and tone, on the creation of *context,* among Levi's most important works.

The recent poetry displays, I think, a deepened strength and authority, a sureness in his own voice and strategies; but shows also a striking out in some interesting new directions. There is a collection of vignettes, like "Officers and Gentlemen," which set a particular social class in the ironic perspectives of history; there is a handful of finely achieved, tenderly dignified love poems; and there is an altogether new note struck in the grotesquerie of the "Pigs" sequence, which I find immensely seductive:

> Pigs refuse pork sausages
> coated in chocolate. They do sniff them.
> Sows murder piglets.
> What has some smell of incest
> is not sheer cold horror.
> Who write this, an old silver-bristle.
> I am brutish enough.
> They are brutish enough.

Peter Levi's is a unique voice in contemporary English poetry; there is absolutely no one remotely like him. His sadness, his humour, his preposterously resilient assertiveness ("An easy smell blowing about a hill/is the beginning of the truth about life," for instance) are intoxicating. His achievement is one to be glad about.

—Neil Corcoran

LEVINE, Philip. American. Born in Detroit, Michigan, 10 January 1928. Educated at Wayne State University, Detroit, B.A. 1950, M.A. 1955; University of Iowa, Iowa City, M.F.A. 1957; Stanford University, California (Fellowship in Poetry, 1957). Married Frances Artley in 1954; three sons. Since 1958, member of the faculty, and since 1969, Professor of English, California State University, Fresno; since 1981, has taught fall semester at Tufts University, Medford, Massachusetts. Elliston Professor of Poetry, University of Cincinnati, 1976; Poet-in-Residence, National University of Australia, Canberra, Summer 1978; Visiting Professor, Princeton University, New Jersey, 1978, Columbia University, New York, 1978, 1981, 1984, University of California, Berkeley, 1980, and Brown University, Providence, Rhode Island, 1984. Recipient: San Francisco Foundation Joseph Henry Jackson Award, 1961; Chapelbrook Award, 1968; National Endowment for the Arts grant, 1969, 1970 (refused), 1976, 1982; Frank O'Hara Prize, 1972, and Harriet Monroe Memorial Prize, 1976 (*Poetry*, Chicago); American Academy grant, 1973; Guggenheim Fellowship, 1973, 1980; Lenore Marshall Prize, 1976; National Book Critics Circle Award, 1980; American Book Award, 1980. Address: 4549 North Van Ness Avenue, Fresno, California 93704, U.S.A.

PUBLICATIONS

Verse

On the Edge. Iowa City, Stone Wall Press, 1963.
Silent in America: Vivas for Those Who Failed. Iowa City, Shaw Avenue Press, 1965.
Not This Pig. Middletown, Connecticut, Wesleyan University Press, 1968.
Five Detroits. Santa Barbara, California, Unicorn Press, 1970.
Thistles: A Poem Sequence. London, Turret, 1970.
Pili's Wall. Santa Barbara, California, Unicorn Press, 1971.
Red Dust. Santa Cruz, California, Kayak, 1971.
They Feed They Lion. New York, Atheneum, 1972.

1933. New York, Atheneum, 1974.
New Season. Port Townsend, Washington, Graywolf Press, 1975.
On the Edge and Over: Poems Old, Lost, and New. Oakland, Cloud Marauder Press, 1976.
The Names of the Lost. New York, Atheneum, 1976.
7 Years from Somewhere. New York, Atheneum, 1979.
Ashes: Poems New and Old. New York, Atheneum, 1979.
One for the Rose. New York, Atheneum, 1981.
Selected Poems. New York, Atheneum, and London, Secker and Warburg, 1984.

Recording: *The Poetry and Voice of Philip Levine,* Caedmon, 1976.

Other

Don't Ask (interviews). Ann Arbor, University of Michigan Press, 1981.

Editor, with Henri Coulette, *Character and Crisis: A Contemporary Reader.* New York, McGraw Hill, 1966.
Editor and Translator, with Ernesto Trejo, *Tarumba: The Selected Poems of Jaime Sabines.* San Francisco, Twin Peaks Press, 1979.
Editor and Translator, with Ada Long, *Off the Map: Selected Poems of Gloria Fuertes.* Middletown, Connecticut, Wesleyan University Press, 1984.

*

Critical Studies: by X. J. Kennedy, in *Poetry* (Chicago), 1964; Robert Dana, in *North American Review* (Mt. Vernon, Iowa), 1964; Hayden Carruth, in *Hudson Review* (New York), 1968; "Personally, I'd Rather Be in Fresno" by Stuart Peterfreund, in *New: American and Canadian Poetry 15* (Trumansburg, New York), May 1971; "Borges and Strand, Weak Henry, Philip Levine" by James McMichael, in *Southern Review* (Baton Rouge, Louisiana), Winter 1972; "Interview with Philip Levine," in *American Poetry Review* (Philadelphia), i, 1, 1972; " 'The True and Earthly Prayer': Philip Levine's Poetry" in *American Poetry Review* (Philadelphia), iii, 2, 1974, and "Back to This Life," in *New England Review* (Hanover, New Hampshire), Winter 1979-80, both by Ralph J. Mills, Jr.; "The Burned Essential Oil: The Poetry of Philip Levine" by Charles Molesworth, in *Hollins Critic* (Virginia), December 1975; "Philip Levine" by Calvin Bedient, in *Sewanee Review* (Tennessee), Spring 1976; "New Poems" by Jay Parini, in *Poetry* (Chicago), August 1977; "Bringing It Home" by Stephen Yenser, in *Parnassus* (New York), Fall—Winter 1977; "The Poetry of Anarchism" by Paul Bernard, in *Marxist Perspectives*, Summer 1979; "The Politics of Philip Levine" by Phoebe Pettingen, in *New Leader* (New York), 13 August 1979; "The Second Self" by Dave Smith, in *American Poetry Review* (Philadelphia), November-December 1979; William Matthews, in *Ohio Review* 26 (Athens), 1981.

*   *   *

The poetry of Philip Levine is somber, reflective, and honest. It is spare in form, taut in expression, simple in idiom. Levine has turned away from conventional metrical form and rhyme to write largely in blank or free verse, often in flexible three or four beat lines. He employs the image, hard, clean, and concrete, stripped of effusive sentiment, free from intellectual editorials. Levine protests against the evils of the modern world and searches for personal freedom and fulfillment. At its best his poetry, highly personal and nostalgic, is stark, restrained, and powerful.

Levine often indicts modern urban life, exposing its joyless futility and ugliness. Witness these lines from "Clouds":

> Morning is exhaustion, tranquilizers, gasoline,
> the screamings of frozen bearings,
> the failures of will, the TV talking to itself.
>
> The clouds go on eating oil, cigars,
> housewives, sighing letters,
> the breath of lies. In their great silent pockets
> they carry off all our dead.

For their silence and acquiescence the poet concludes that clouds "should be punished every morning, / they should be bitten and boiled like spoons." The anger here frequently modulates into lament over the eternally gray cityscapes, the meaningless motions, the endless Mondays, "shrill with the smells of garbage / and gasoline." The poet's struggle to find a place in such a world often provokes confrontation with the past, present, and future. Most things valuable and precious, he uneasily realizes, are subject to time, to the power that turns all to ash. "New Season" meditates on the poet's mother turning seventy and concludes with striking and direct imagery:

> the woman
> is 70 now—the willow is burning,
> the rhododendrons shrivel
> like paper under water, all
> the small secret mouths are feeding
> on the green heart of the plum.

"Starlight" recalls the lost embrace of the poet's father and the lost world of childhood. Evident here is Levine's preoccupation with domestic life. In his darker moments he articulates the disappointments and pains of family relations. In "Father" the poet hisses "Don't come back"; in "My Son and I" he portrays the huge and silent spaces between himself and his son.

And yet, despite sensitivity to the assault of civilized life and to the pang of existential isolation, Levine sometimes finds cause for hope and joy. On such occasions his poems are hard-won affirmations, not facile celebrations. The poet draws inspiration from the earth and elemental things. In "Holding On," for example, he observes "Green fingers / holding the hillside, / mustard whipping in / the sea winds, one blood-bright / poppy breathing in / and out" and declares, "40 miles from Málaga / half the world away / from home, I am home and / nowhere, a man who envies / grass." In "A Sleepless Night," after noticing plum blossoms, sycamore, lime, poppies, and a mockingbird, he concludes, "A man has every place to lay his head." Levine also finds pleasure in old friends and acquaintances, especially those who were colorful outcasts: there is Uncle Joe, rough and salacious, who tenderly held up the new-born poet so he could see the winter sun ("No One Remembers"); blind Tatum, who "can't hardly wait" to "see" Willie Mays ("On the Corner"); Cal, "short for Calla, the lily," who sleeps on the job, at peace in the rain ("Making It New"). The most serious affirmations are poignantly imperfect victories of love over loneliness. In "Lost and Found" "father and child / hand in hand, the living and / the dead" enter the world; In "The Rains" the poet promises that he and his wife, also "hand in hand," will one day transcend the world, "soured / with years of never / giving enough, darkened / with oils and fire" to go forward "while our clothes darken / and our faces stream / with the sweet waters / of heaven." As the poet says in his recent volume *One for the Rose*, we do have "Each other" ("Sources").

For the most part, Philip Levine is an introspective poet. His recent volumes, however, show serious concern with the Spanish Civil War, subject for several moving tributes to fallen soldiers ("On the Murder of Lieutenent José Del Castillo by the Falangist Bravo Martinez, July 12, 1936," "For the Fallen," "Montjuich"). Though limited in range and over-reliant on minor chords, Levine's music is distinctive and intelligently modern.

—Robert S. Miola

LEVIS, Larry (Patrick). American. Born in Fresno, California, 30 September 1946. Educated at Fresno State College (now California State University), 1964-68, B.A. 1968; Syracuse University, New York (Ward Fellow), 1968-70, M.A. 1970; University of Iowa, Iowa City (Teaching Fellow), 1972-74, Ph.D. 1974. Married Marcia Southwick in 1975; one son. Teaching Assistant, Syracuse University, 1969; Instructor, Fresno State College, 1970; Lecturer, California State University, Los Angeles, 1970-72; Visiting Lecturer, University of Iowa, 1972-74, 1980-82. Since 1974, Assistant Professor of English, University of Missouri, Columbia. Recipient: YM-YWHA Discovery Award, 1971; National Endowment for the Arts Fellowship, 1973; Lamont Poetry Selection Award, 1976. Address: Department of English, University of Missouri, Columbia, Missouri 65201, U.S.A.

Publications

Verse

Wrecking Crew. Pittsburgh, University of Pittsburgh Press, 1972.
The Rain's Witness. Iowa City, Southwick Press, 1975.
The Afterlife. Iowa City, University of Iowa Press, 1977.
The Dollmaker's Ghost. New York, Dutton, 1981.

*

Larry Levis comments:

Most of my poems are bound to specific objects, places, persons, or circumstances, and these are usually places (like Fresno) or people who are part of my experience. This is not to say that I rely only upon my life or the facts of life. The most important thing I have tried to learn as a poet is to follow and to trust my owm imagination. Poets who continue to influence my work: Garcia Lorca, Zbigniew Herbert, Philip Levine, and a number of poets in my own generation.

*   *   *

Bedizened as he is with prizes, Larry Levis skilfully—and predictably—represents the style of poetry currently being taught and valued in American universities, those new power centers of the literary establishment. It's a sort of diluted, passionless surrealism, derivative of South American originals. There's a characteristic voice in which this poetry gets read by its authors, rising and falling in a special "holy" register, something between a chant and a lilt, far removed at any rate from speech, whether casual or passionate. The syntax is predominantly paratactic, the rhythms enervated and limp, the diction carefully flat, the imagery dominated by similes, and the whole frequently (to my instinct) ersatz.

Levis shows little development between *Wrecking Crew* and *The Afterlife*. True, there's a "pop" imagery of violence (rape, blood, wounds, etc.) in the first book that drops away, and there's what an admirer might call a syntactic advance in the second. (It mainly consists in asking rhetorical questions, as here: "Is it raining on a lame mare / About to be shot? / The horse goes down quickly..." etc., where if you answer a reasonable "Probably not" to the question, the rest of the poem collapses.) In both books we get a similar range of poems. There's the imitation of Roethke at his most cloyingly *faux naif*: "Maybe the dead know the ant's troubles, / or the debts snails pay out with their bodies..."; "Is the snow / a birth? / How can a root / stand itself?" In both books we get lots of Robert Bly brand epiphanies, like "Driving East," which I quote in its entirety: "For miles, the snow is on all sides of me, / waiting. / / I feel like / a lot of empty cattle yards, / my hinges swing open to the wind." What is this but a pathetic fallacy plus the imposition of the poet's ego on the landscape? What for the reader but an invitation to indulge in vague and facile feelings?

If one turns to the poems about people for relief, one finds little enough reward in either book. Here he is on his home town:

> In the town of 20 pool cues....
> the men laughed,
> they stole cars and left them in ditches, smoldering.
> Their wives, spitting at irons, never looked up.
> They grew older.

The characteristic reliance on plurals to impart a factitious universality instead deprives the referents of any but an ad hoc existence: these men and women are invented (we feel) to provide feelings for writer and reader, they don't exist in their own right. Again, "This poem so like the hour / when...the calm / professor burns another book...." Who can believe in this professor, so clearly a construct of paradoxes contrived for the sake of a mere immediate frisson? Even when the person is singular and presumably as real as Levis is, the exoticism of the decor and the careful flatness of the would-be resonant statements produce what I can only read as self-parody.

Very little evaluative criticism of current poetry gets published in America. In the new poetic stakes, every contender wins. Secure with his awards and publications, Levis can surely withstand—and deserves—close inspection by non-members of the club. He is no worse than several dozen of his contemporaries, equally or more deeply entrenched. His career will bear watching, but on the evidence of these two books, it will tell us more about "lit biz" than about literature.

—Seamus Cooney

L'HEUREUX, John (Clarke). American. Born in South Hadley, Massachusetts, 26 October 1934. Educated at the National Academy of Theatre Arts, 1952; College of the Holy Cross, Worcester, Massachusetts, 1952-54; Weston College, Massachusetts, Ph.L. 1960; Boston College, M.A. in English, 1963; Woodstock College, Maryland, S.T.L. 1967; Harvard University, Cambridge, Massachusetts, 1967-68. Married Joan Polston in 1971. Entered the Society of Jesus, 1954; ordained a priest, 1966; requested laicisation, 1970, and married with Vati-

can approval, 1971. Visiting professor/writer, Georgetown University, Washington, D.C., 1964-65, Regis College, Weston, Massachusetts, 1969-70, Hamline University, St. Paul, 1971, Tufts University, Medford, Massachusetts, 1971-72, and Harvard University, 1973. Associate Professor, 1973-79, and since 1981, Professor of English, Stanford University, California. Staff Editor, and since 1970, Contributing Editor, *The Atlantic*, Boston. Address: Department of English, Stanford University, Stanford, California 94305, U.S.A.

PUBLICATIONS

Verse

Quick as Dandelions. New York, Doubleday, 1964.
Rubrics for a Revolution. New York, Macmillan, 1967.
One Eye and a Measuring Rod. New York, Macmillan, 1968.
No Place for Hiding: New Poems. New York, Doubleday, 1971.

Novels

Tight White Collar. New York, Doubleday, 1972.
The Clang Birds. New York, Macmillan, 1972.
Jessica Fayer. New York, Macmillan, 1976.

Short Stories

Family Affairs. New York, Doubleday, 1974.
Desires. New York, Holt Rinehart, 1981.

Other

Picnic in Babylon: A Jesuit Priest's Journal 1963-1967. New York, Macmillan, 1967.

*

Manuscript Collection: Boston University; Stanford University, California.

*   *   *

A remark that John L'Heureux made in *Picnic in Babylon: A Jesuit Priest's Journal, 1963-1967* gives some insight into what he wishes to do in poetry. Stressing the harm done to American poetry by Poe's jingles and Whitman's "over developed ego," he said that "with the singular exception of Emily Dickinson there is no American poetry until 1900."

What one finds in L'Heureux's poetry, in other words, is a sensibility compatible with the interior religious struggles described in Dickinson and in her admirers among twentieth-century poets. In a sequence called "The Problem of God," he expresses something of the impatience Dickinson felt toward divinity: "The trouble with Christ is / he always comes at the wrong time." Yet, as one might suspect, the quarrel between L'Heureux and God is merely temporary. In fact, in the early poems their relationship (in "Death of a Man" and "The Unlikely Prophet") and his familiarity with God's chosen (in "The Journey" and "Joseph") appear too comfortable to be believed.

He is essentially a poet of celebration and of reconciliation, as James Dickey has said, who goes "eagerly toward events and people, open-handed and open-hearted." The final section of

L'Heureux's poem, "The Death of Kings," an epitaph for John F. Kennedy, conveys his essential faith in the nature of things:

> The end is vision:
> stones roll back and wonder cracks
> like morning on a disbelieving world.
> No Lazarus standing gray and stupid
> in his linen bands, but we—harlequins
> and fools—stride the fired air
> with feet of bronze. Laughter
> is our music. Let the earth tremble.

L'Heureux's strength of feeling and wit as a lyric poet exhibit themselves most fully in his recent poems, as in "The Command" and "Narcissus," whose passion and self-knowledge indicate a much wider range of feeling than the earlier conventionally religious poems. And in "A Pleasing Fragrance," the best of the old and the new directions come together:

> He was crowing
> on the rooftop
> of his sanctity
> when the house burned
> down. Crazy old cock
> larger than death
>
> he thought
> before the conflagration.
>
> ...
>
> And so he's gone,
> poor roasted soul,
>
> in blazing glory
> He made, despite himself,
> a good holocaust.

In his latest books, both poetry and fiction, L'Heureux recounts his struggle with and ultimate decision to leave the Jesuits. But the religious pilgrimage continues, and in poems such as "Incarnation" and "Foolsgold" it remains as much of a preoccupation as ever.

—Michael True

LIEBERMAN, Laurence (James). American. Born in Detroit, Michigan, 16 February 1935. Educated at the University of Michigan, Ann Arbor (Hopwood Award, 1958), B.A. 1956, M.A. in English, 1958; University of California, Berkeley. Married Bernice Braun in 1956; one son and two daughters. Former Poetry Editor, *Orange County Illustrated* and *Orange County Sun*, California. Taught at Orange Coast College, Costa Mesa, California, 1960-64, and College of the Virgin Islands, St. Thomas, 1964-68. Associate Professor of English, 1968-70, and since 1970, Professor of English, University of Illinois, Urbana. Poetry reviewer, *Yale Review*, 1968-74. Since 1971, Poetry Editor, University of Illinois Press. Recipient: Yaddo Fellowship, 1963, 1967; Huntington Hartford Foundation Fellowship, 1964; National Endowment for the Arts grant, 1969; University of Illinois Center for Advanced Study grant, 1971, 1981; Illinois Arts Council Fellowship, 1982. Address: Department of English, University of Illinois, Urbana, Illinois 61801, U.S.A.

PUBLICATIONS

Verse

The Unblinding. New York, Macmillan, 1968..
The Osprey Suicides. New York, Macmillan, and London, Collier Macmillan, 1973.
God's Measurements. New York, Macmillan, 1980.
Eros at the World Kite Pageant: Poems 1979-1982. New York, Macmillan, 1983.
The Mural of Wakeful Sleep. New York, Macmillan, 1985.

Other

Unassigned Frequencies: American Poetry in Review 1964-77. Urbana, University of Illinois Press, 1977.

Editor, *The Achievement of James Dickey: A Comprehensive Selection of His Poems with a Critical Introduction.* Chicago, Scott Foresman, 1968.

*

Critical Studies: "Fool, Thou Poet" by Vernon Young, in *Hudson Review* (New York) Winter 1973-74; "Tough Scarskins" by John R. Cooley, in *Modern Poetry Studies* (Buffalo), Winter 1974; "All's a Mirroring" by James Ballowe, in *Mississippi Valley Review* (Macomb, Illinois), Spring 1974; "Generous Props," in *Counter / Measures 3*, 1974, and "Castles, Elephants, Buddhas....," in *American Poetry Review* (Philadelphia), May-June 1981, both by Dave Smith; "Actions Undone" by Richard Johnson, in *Parnassus* (New York), Fall-Winter 1974; "Poems and Pictures" by David Quemada, in *New Letters* (Kansas City), March 1975; "Bending and Unbending into Beatitudes" by Ronald Wallace, in *Chowder Review* (Amherst, Massachusetts), Summer 1980; Leonard Neufeldt, in *New England Review* (Hanover, New Hampshire), Summer 1980; "Radiance Beyond Measure" by Peter Mackuck, in *Tar River Poetry* (Greenville, North Carolina), Fall 1980; "Acts of Grace: About One of Laurence Lieberman's Poems," in *Chariton Review* (Kirksville, Missouri), Fall 1980, and "Convergences" in *Sewanee Review* (Tennessee), Summer 1984, both by Thom Swiss; "Dimensions of Reality" by Peter Stitt, in *Georgia Review* (Athens), Winter 1980-81; "Confessions of Travelers and Pilgrims" by Peter Serchuk, in *Sewanee Review* (Tennessee), Spring 1981; "Poets and Peddlers" by Harry Thomas, in *Michigan Quarterly Review* (Ann Arbor), Winter 1982; G.E. Murray, in *Quarterly West* (Salt Lake City), Fall-Winter 1982-83; Robert Hill, in *South Carolina Review* (Clemson), Fall 1983; "Gaijin's Measurements," in *Parnassus* (New York), Winter 1984-85.

Laurence Lieberman comments:
(1975) My first and second volumes of poetry, *The Unblinding* and *The Osprey Suicides*, dealt principally with the four years I spent in St. Thomas (1964-68), exploring life in the Caribbean and the underwater world of the coral reefs as their primary subject. The underwater cycle of poems spanned two books, much as I expect my cycle of poems in progress about Japan to span the next two books. *God's Measurements* was completed this year, and it contains roughly half of the poems I plan to write about Japan, where I spent a year on a traveling fellowship, 1971-2.

*   *   *

Laurence Lieberman is one of the most remarkable poets of

his generation. He is a wizard of words. His command of the language is unrivaled by any of his contemporaries and one has to think of an Eliot, a Pound, or a Stevens to locate such eloquence. Sometimes that eloquence is misapplied or overdone as trivial subjects are rendered in a brilliant effusion of words. But in Lieberman's best poems there is a kind of Baroque or Elizabethan profusion of language that elevates and effects a form of transformation of experience into a rarified and rarely seen form of poetic art. Lieberman's first volume, *The Unblinding*, reveals this attempt to find his subject and his medium. In a remarkable poem, "The Family Tree," he finds it. He discovers a relationship felt, not thought, between his life and the life of things. Indeed, they grow together as one. The development of Lieberman's poetry is a continual recreation of this fundamental oneness of inner and outer.

Lieberman somehow seems to be blessed with a facility rarely found among his contemporaries. Instead of having to search for his experience and define it against the corruption of modern life, or lament his inability to apprehend reality, he discovers a world that he can embrace and that secures him from the sickness of the age. In the title poem of this first volume, he speaks of the "tough, unknown, real images that burn his senses and mind," "incandescent moments that fall into his hands unsought, undeservedly given or lent...visions...that can—and do on occasion—sweep me off into their own orbits." No alienated poet here, but rather a voice, a vehicle through which the power of "incandescent moments" sing.

A good part of Lieberman's published work is based on experiences he has had traveling to Japan, Hawaii, and South America. In these places exotic environments and experiences provide him a locale and subject matter for this force that illuminates his imaginative life. In *The Unblinding* he had already discovered the stark and beautiful power of the sea as a medium for his poetic exploration. But in *The Osprey Suicides, God's Measurements*, and *Eros at the World Kite Pageant*, he reaches out to this world with the poise and dexterity of a poet who has found his voice and subject. So committed to this world is Lieberman that *The Osprey Suicides* might be subtitled "the underwater world of Laurence Lieberman." No poet before him has written so devotedly and with such knowledge of this world. In poem after poem he searches the depths of faraway oceans, tides, and bays seeking in the coral and sea creatures a vision of some ultimate truth. Lurking in underwater caverns, in subterranean darkness, strange life forms challenge his senses, confound his mind. These poems abound in special moments and, as they accumulate, his poems become like pearls. Lieberman is not merely a spectator in this underwater world, but often an intruder. He hunts with a spear gun and kills for sport. Although such a relationship with this world suggests a fundamental alienation, the events of the poems are much like a Faulkner or Hemingway encounter with nature. Not only is there the moment of self-discovery and affirmation in the act of the hunt, but an experience of ultimate power. The hunt becomes a search for God. In the final section of *The Osprey Suicides*, Lieberman describes the danger of the hunt: the predator may become victim, may in fact become his own death wish.

In *Eros at the World Kite Pageant* Lieberman breaks new metaphysical ground. The poem "Psychodrama: Tokyo Mime Film" pushes his quasi-mystical passion for relationship or quest for life to new heights. In this poem the poet provides us with a vision of a profound psychic energy that pushes outward into the vacancy of the non-self to embrace and incorporate it as part of the oneness that he has sought throughout his work. This oneness is like that of a Buber I-Thou relationship: being is achieved only through relationship which allows each partner to be both itself and affirmed. Such is Lieberman's relationship with the world. Sometimes fraught with violence, sometimes threatening to destroy the poet himself, this relationship is the hard fought battle to overcome the alienation of a century and to establish a renewed covenant with things. For this work, Lieberman deserves a great deal of credit and our profoundest respect.

—Richard Damashek

LIFSHIN, Lyn (Diane, née Lipman). American. Born in Burlington, Vermont, 12 July 1942. Educated at Syracuse University, New York, B.A. 1961; University of Vermont, Burlington, M.A. 1963; Brandeis University, Waltham, Massachusetts; State University of New York, Albany, 1964-66; Bread Loaf School of English, Vermont. Married Eric Lifshin in 1963. Teaching Fellow, State University of New York, Albany, 1964-66; educational television writer, Schenectady, New York, 1966; writing consultant, Mental Health Department, Albany, New York, 1967; Instructor, State University of New York, Cobleskill, 1968, 1970; writing consultant, Empire State College, Albany, 1973; Poet-in-Residence, Mansfield State College, Pennsylvania, 1974. Recipient: Yaddo Fellowship, 1970, 1971; MacDowell Fellowship, 1973; Creative Artists Public Service Award, 1976; Cherry Valley Editions Jack Kerouac Award, 1984. Address: 2142 Apple Tree Lane, Niskayuna, New York 12309, U.S.A.

PUBLICATIONS

Verse

Why Is the House Dissolving. San Francisco, Open Skull Press, 1968.
Femina 2. Oshkosh, Wisconsin, Abraxas Press, 1970.
Leaves and Night Things. West Lafayette, Indiana, Baby John Press, 1970.
Black Apples. Trumansburg, New York, Crossing Press, 1971; revised edition, 1973.
Tentacles, Leaves. Belmont, Massachusetts, Hellric Press, 1972.
Moving by Touch. Traverse City, Michigan, Cotyledon Press, 1972.
Lady Lyn. Milwaukee, Morgan Press, 1972.
Mercurochrome Sun Poems. Tacoma, Washington, Charis Press, 1972.
I'd Be Jeanne Moreau. Milwaukee, Morgan Press, 1972.
Love Poems. Durham, New Hampshire, Zahir Press, 1972.
Forty Days, Apple Nights. Milwaukee, Morgan Press, 1973.
Audley End Poems. Long Beach, California, Mag Press, 1973.
The First Week Poems. Plum Island, Massachusetts, Zahir Press, 1973.
Museum. Albany, New York, Conspiracy Press, 1973.
All the Women Poets I Ever Liked Didn't Hate Their Fathers. St. Petersburg, Florida, Konglomerati, 1973.
The Old House on the Croton. San Lorenzo, California, Shameless Hussy Press, 1973.
Poems. Minneapolis, Northstone, 1974.
Selected Poems. Trumansburg, New York, Crossing Press, 1974.
Upstate Madonna: Poems 1970-1974. Trumansburg, New York, Crossing Press, 1974.
Shaker House. Tannersville, New York, Tideline Press, 1974.

Blue Fingers. Milwaukee, Shelter Press, 1974.
Plymouth Women. Milwaukee, Morgan Press, 1974.
Shaker House Poems. Chatham, New York, Sagarin Press, 1974.
Old House Poems. Santa Barbara, California, Capra Press, 1975.
North Poems. Milwaukee, Morgan Press, 1976.
Naked Charm. N.p., Fireweed Press, 1976.
Paper Apples. Stockton, California, Wormwood, 1976.
Some Madonna Poems. Buffalo, White Pine Press, 1976.
More Waters. Cincinnati, Waters, 1977.
Offered by Owner. Cambridge, New York, Natalie Slohm, 1978.
Leaning South. New York, Red Dust, 1978.
Glass. Milwaukee, Morgan Press, 1978.
Early Plymouth Women. Milwaukee, Morgan Press, 1978.
Crazy Arms. Chicago, Ommation Press, 1978.
Doctors. Santa Barbara, California, Mudborn, 1979.
35 Sundays. Chicago, Ommation Press, 1979.
Lips on That Blue Rail. San Francisco, Lion's Breath, 1980.
Colors of Copper Black. Milwaukee, Morgan Press, 1981.
Leaving the Bough. New York, New World Press, 1982.
Blue Dust, New Mexico. Fredonia, New York, Basilisk Press, 1982.
Finger Prints. Stockton, California, Wormwood, 1982.
Madonna Who Shifts for Herself. Long Beach, California, Applezaba, 1983.
Naked Charm (collection). Los Angeles, Illuminati Press, 1984.

Recording: *Offered by Owner*, Slohm, 1978.

Other

Editor, *Tangled Vines: A Collection of Mother and Daughter Poems*. Boston, Beacon Press, 1978.
Editor, *Ariadne's Thread: A Collection of Contemporary Women's Journals*. New York, Harper, 1982.

*

Bibliography: by Marvin Malone, in *Wormwood Review* (Stockton, California), xii, 3, 1971.

Critical Studies: by Bill Katz, in *Library Journal* (New York), June 1971, and December 1972; Carol Rainey, in *Road Apple Review* (Albuquerque, New Mexico), Summer-Fall 1971; Victor Contoski, in *Northeast* (La Crosse, Wisconsin), Fall-Winter 1971-72; James Naiden, in *Minneapolis Star*, 18 April 1972; Dave Etter, in *December* (West Springs, Illinois), 1972; "Lyn Lifshin" by Jim Evans, in *Windless Orchard* (Fort Wayne, Indiana), Summer 1972; Eric Mottram, in *Little Magazine* (New York), Summer-Fall 1972; *New York Times Book Review*, 18 December 1978; "Lyn Lifshin Issue" of *Poetry Now* (Eureka, California), 1980, and *Greenfield Review* (Greenfield Center, New York), 1983.

Lyn Lifshin comments:
    I'm usually better at doing something than talking about how and why I do it. One time I spent days trying to say how I wanted the words to be connected to touch the reader's body. Somehow. Except that sounded strange and so I tore it up.... It seems to me that the poem has to be sensual (not necessarily sexual, tho that's ok too) before it can be anything else. So rhythm matters a lot to me, most, or at least first. Before images even. I want whoever looks at, whoever eats the poem to feel the way old ebony feels at

4 o'clock in a cold Van Cortlandt mansion, or the smell of lemons in a strange place, or skin.
    Words that I like to hear other people say the poems are are: strong, tight, real, startling, tough, tender, sexy, physical, controlled—that they celebrate (Carol Rainey), reflect joy in every aspect of being a woman (James Naiden).
    I always steal things I like from people: other poets, especially from blues, old black and country blues rhythms (after most readings, people come and ask how, where I started reading the way I do; another mystery, really). So I was glad to have Dave Etter say that *Black Apples* "comes on like a stack of Cannonball Adderley records, blowing cool, blowing hot, sometimes lyrical and sweet, sometimes hard bop, terse and tough."

*   *   *

    Perhaps no other contemporary American poet has been as widely published as Lyn Lifshin, whose prolific production has sometimes overshadowed the true range and significance of her work. From her early poems, written soon after her departure from the academic world (to which she has never returned, unlike many other poets), in which she presents with painful accuracy the shallowness and insincerity of that world where one may "fail to understand the requirements," to her more recent work, in which she enters the lives of such diverse humans as women in early Plymouth and Indians on exhibit in museums, and deals straightforwardly with her own family (especially the relationship between mother and daughter) she has been a risk-taker. That risk has been most obvious, perhaps, in her poems of sexuality in which both the emotional and the physical relationships between men and women are laid bare. One would be hard-pressed to find another writer who has done as thorough a job of evoking the despair of a woman caught in those traps which social restrictions and marriage create for American women. However, she is far more than a poet with only one subject, even though her voice is one which is always recognizable.
    Lifshin's poetry is characterized by a breathless quality, a voice reflected by the page of short lines, incomplete sentences, pauses and sudden revelations. Her poems can be disarmingly simple—until that moment of explosion. At times, her candor, especially about sex, is as hard and cold as the sound of feet on the pavement of a redlight district late at night. Few have written more bitingly or more tenderly about modern sexual mores—especially as reflected in the lives of women. At other times, her "Madonna poems," for example, she explores worlds where the line between physical experience and imagination blurs. Lifshin's many "Madonnas" are both modern and wildly archetypal as she presents us with a "Parachute Madonna," a "Shifting for Herself Madonna," and others both funny and sad.
    Although her poems are the result of an almost religious devotion to her craft, she seems to reach many of the final versions of her poems not so much by rewriting and reworking a single poem as by producing series of poems which gradually—or even cumulatively—reach the desired effect. The result is a body of work which is impressive in its size, almost epic·in proportion—an irony when one considers that few individual Lifshin poems are more than 30 lines in length. Her work might be seen, in fact, as a journey through her own life and through time, through the lives of other women (her work as an anthologist is an indication of her interest in the writing of women in general), creating what might be seen as a poetic collage of the latter part of this century, its optimism and its depressions. In the midst of it all she has placed herself, continually searching for meaning and identity—as woman, as poet, as one of Jewish heritage, as a threatened member of the human species in the

confusing landscape of history, personal liberty, and social reality.

Where the writers of classical times wrote long connected epics, Lyn Lifshin has ventured with her short lyrics. Her voice is that of a female Odysseus, sometimes confused, often innocent, but always tenacious, one whose journey takes us along and teaches us as we go.

—Joseph Bruchac

LINDSAY, (John) Maurice. Scottish. Born in Glasgow, 21 July 1918. Educated at Glasgow Academy, 1928-36; Scottish National Academy of Music, now the Royal Scottish Academy of Music, Glasgow, 1936-39. Served in the Cameronians (Scottish Rifles) at the Staff College, Camberley, Surrey, and in the War Office during World War II. Married Aileen Joyce Gordon in 1946; one son and three daughters. Drama Critic, *Scottish Daily Mail*, Edinburgh, 1946-47; Music Critic, *The Bulletin*, Glasgow, 1946-60; Editor, *Scots Review*, 1949-50. Programme Controller, 1961-62, Production Controller, 1962-64, and Features Executive and Chief Interviewer, 1964-67, Border Television, Carlisle. Director, 1967-83, and since 1983, Consultant, Scottish Civic Trust, Glasgow. Editor, with Douglas Young, Saltire Modern Poets series, 1964. Editor, 1976-80, and since 1980, Editor, with Alexander Scott, *Scottish Review*. Since 1983, Honorary Secretary-General, Europa Nostra. Recipient: Atlantic-Rockefeller Award, 1946. D.Litt.: University of Glasgow, 1982. C.B.E. (Commander, Order of the British Empire), 1979. Address: 7 Milton Hill, Milton, Dumbarton, Dunbartonshire, G82 2TS, Scotland.

PUBLICATIONS

Verse

The Advancing Day. Privately printed, 1940.
Perhaps To-morrow. Oxford, Blackwell, 1941.
Predicament. Oxford, Alden Press, 1942.
No Crown for Laughter. London, Fortune Press, 1943.
The Enemies of Love: Poems 1941-1945. Glasgow, Maclellan, 1946.
Selected Poems. Edinburgh, Oliver and Boyd, 1947.
Hurlygush: Poems in Scots. Edinburgh, Serif, 1948.
At the Wood's Edge. Edinburgh, Serif, 1950.
Ode for St. Andrews Night and Other Poems. Edinburgh, New Alliance, 1951.
The Exiled Heart: Poems 1941-1956, edited by George Bruce. London, Hale, 1957.
Snow Warning and Other Poems. Arundel, Sussex, Linden Press, 1962.
One Later Day and Other Poems. London, Brookside Press, 1964.
This Business of Living. Preston, Lancashire, Akros, 1971.
Comings and Goings. Preston, Lancashire, Akros, 1971.
Selected Poems 1942-1972. London, Hale, 1973.
The Run from Life: More Poems 1942-1972. Burford, Oxfordshire, Cygnet Press, 1975.
Walking Without an Overcoat: Poems 1972-76. London, Hale, 1977.
Collected Poems, edited by Alexander Scott. Edinburgh, Paul Harris, 1979.

A Net to Catch the Winds and Other Poems. London, Hale, 1981.

Plays

Fingal and Comala (produced Braemar, 1953; London, 1958).
The Abbot of Drimock, music by Thea Musgrave (produced London, 1958).
The Decision, music by Thea Musgrave (produced London, 1967). London, Chester, 1967.

Other

A Pocket Guide to Scottish Culture. Glasgow, Maclellan, 1947.
The Scottish Renaissance. Edinburgh, Serif, 1949.
The Lowlands of Scotland: Glasgow and the North, Edinburgh and the South. London, Hale, 2 vols., 1953-56; revised edition, 1973-77.
Robert Burns: The Man, His Work, The Legend. London, MacGibbon and Kee, 1954; revised edition, 1968, 1978; New York, St. Martin's Press, 1979.
Dunoon: The Gem of the Clyde Coast. Dunoon, Town Council of Dunoon, 1954.
Clyde Waters: Variations and Diversions on a Theme of Pleasure. London, Hale, 1958.
The Burns Encyclopaedia. London, Hutchinson, 1959; revised edition, 1970; London, Hale, and New York, St. Martin's Press, 1980.
Killochan Castle, with David Somervell. Derby, Pilgrim Press, 1960.
By Yon Bonnie Banks: A Gallimaufry. London, Hutchinson, 1961.
The Discovery of Scotland: Based on Accounts of Foreign Travellers from the Thirteenth to the Eighteenth Centuries. London, Hale, and New York, Roy, 1964.
Environment: A Basic Human Right. Glasgow, Scottish Civic Trust, 1968.
The Eye Is Delighted: Some Romantic Travellers in Scotland. London, Muller, 1970.
Portrait of Glasgow. London, Hale, 1972.
Robin Philipson. Edinburgh, Edinburgh University Press, 1976.
History of Scottish Literature. London, Hale, 1977.
Lowland Scottish Villages. London, Hale, 1980.
Francis George Scott and the Scottish Renaissance. Edinburgh, Paul Harris, 1980.
The Buildings of Edinburgh, with Anthony F. Kersting. London, Batsford, 1981.
Thank You for Having Me (autobiography). London, Hale, 1983.
Unknown Scotland, with Dennis Hardley. London, Batsford, 1984.

Editor, *Poetry Scotland One, Two, Three.* Glasgow, Maclellan, 1943-46.
Editor, *Sailing To-morrow's Seas: An Anthology of New Poems.* London, Fortune Press, 1944.
Editor, *Modern Scottish Poetry: An Anthology of the Scottish Renaissance, 1920-1945.* London, Faber, 1946; revised edition, 1966.
Editor, *Pocket Guide to Scottish Culture.* Glasgow, Maclellan, 1947.
Editor, with Fred Urquhart, *No Scottish Twilight: New Scottish Stories.* Glasgow, Maclellan, 1947.

Editor, *Selected Poems of Sir Alexander Gray*.   Glasgow, Mac-
   lellan, 1948.
Editor, *Poems*, by Sir David Lyndsay.   Edinburgh, Oliver and
   Boyd, 1948.
Editor, with Hugh MacDiarmid, *Poetry Scotland Four*.
   Edinburgh, Serif, 1949.
Editor, with Helen Cruickshank, *Selected Poems of Marion
   Angus*.   Edinburgh, Serif, 1950.
Editor, *John Davidson: A Selection of His Poems*.   London,
   Hutchinson, 1961.
Editor, with others, *Scottish Poetry One* to *Nine*.   Edinburgh,
   Edinburgh University Press, 6 vols., 1966-72; Glasgow, Uni-
   versity of Glasgow Press, 1 vol., 1974; Manchester, Carcanet,
   2 vols., 1975-76.
Editor, *A Book of Scottish Verse*, revised edition.   London,
   Oxford University Press, 1967.
Editor, *Scotland: An Anthology*.   London, Hale, 1974; New
   York, St. Martin's Press, 1975.
Editor, *Modern Scottish Poetry: An Anthology of the Scottish
   Renaissance 1925-1975*.   Manchester, Carcanet, 1976.
Editor, *As I Remember: Ten Scottish Authors Recall How
   Writing Began for Them*.   London, Hale, 1979.
Editor, *Scottish Comic Verse: An Anthology*.   London, Hale,
   1981.

*

Manuscript Collections: National Library of Scotland, Edinburgh; Edinburgh University Library.

Critical Studies: Alexander Scott, in *Whither Scotland?*, edited
by Duncan Glen, London, Gollancz, 1971; *Studies in Scottish
Literature 1971*, Columbia, University of South Carolina Press,
1973; "A Different Way of Being Right: The Poetry of Maurice
Lindsay" by Donald Campbell, in *Akros* (Preston, Lancashire),
April 1974; Christopher Rush, in *Scottish Literary Journal*
(Aberdeen), Summer 1980.

Maurice Lindsay comments:

   I began writing because, from an early age, I wanted to try to
retrieve some tangible aspects from my own experience of living:
in other words, to probe the nature of satisfaction, whatever is a
"reality." Most theories of poetry seem to me pompous, egotistical, and more or less irrelevant. I have therefore never worked to
any "programme."
   Born a Scot and brought up in Scotland, in spite of being
subjected to an anglified public school education, I became
fascinated with that part of my literary heritage written in Scots,
and for a number of years wrote enthusiastically in Lallans (as
Lowland Scots was called by the poets of the "second wind"
phase—the expression was Eric Linklater's—of the "Scottish
Renaissance" movement, instituted by Hugh MacDiarmid in the
1920's and so dubbed by Denis Saurat). By the early 1950's this
concentration on language for its own sake, particularly a language in decline spoken more thinly and by fewer people every
year, seemed to me to be forcing a wedge behind that modern
Scotland of which I was a part, and the language in which I, and
some others, were writing. I therefore turned my attention to
writing in the tongue I, and the majority of Scots, actually speak:
a kind of Scotticised English. I have been attacked for "betraying" Lallans. This is nonsense. A Scots writer may have a choice
of three languages in which to write. That choice depends upon
circumstances all valid in the contemporary context. There can
therefore be no "right" language and no "wrong." I am entirely in
favour of teaching Scots literature and language in Scottish
schools so that what exists already may continue to be enjoyed

and understood. But the pressures of the modern world cannot
be resisted. Compulsion is not saving Ireland's Erse. Not even an
independent Scottish Government could successfully decree the
survival of the Scots tongue as a fully spoken medium.
   My interest in people, which led me to become a radio and
television interviewer at one point, has provided a constant
theme for my later poetry. Early training as a musician perhaps
accounts for the fascination that rhyme and half-rhyme have
always exercised upon me. I have seen poetry as one way,
perhaps the best, of making sense out of life, and I have therefore
been less interested in free verse than in verse in more closely
ordered forms.
   I deplore the present British academic practice of collecting
young poets into groups—"The Beats," "The Movement," "The
Confessionals"—each of which reflects, at most, the fashion of
half a decade, and their underlying implication that only the
newest group's work is of interest or value. Poets can't and
shouldn't try to change their styles to keep up with every latest
teenage fashion. While a poet and his work must be of, and
reflect, the age in which he lives, a poet at fifty may take a
different, though no less valid, view of that age than a poet at
twenty. The notions that poets are expendable at twenty-five and
that each new fashion is an "advance" on the one before, are to
me as absurd as any other evolutionary interpretation of the
Arts. This poet, in his late sixties, having decided to laugh at,
rather than cry with, the follies of mankind, has taken to light
verse in his old age. Poetry, like the Heaven of the Christian
imagination, has, after all, many mansions!
   From all of this it may have become apparent that I believe the
poet's job is to develop his talents and get on with his art,
ignoring the cat-calls of the cliques and the compartmentalising
of the more fashion-conscious critics. What is, or is not, of
permanent value will be assessed by calmer standards long after
the outcome is of personal concern to the poet.

*   *   *

   The publication of Maurice Lindsay's *Collected Poems* in
1979 confirmed his position as one of the most consistently
satisfying and accomplished poets writing in Britain today. He
has an assured technique, with great vitality of language and
imagery and a confident control of rhythm and rhyme; he has an
eye for the sharply defined detail that can quicken a subject into
life and for the underlying tensions beneath the surface; the voice
is characteristically compassionate but with an astringency of
tone when commenting on follies and barbarities. Above all,
Lindsay is a master of the incidental lyric, the poem that recreates an experience in a moment of insight and affirmation.
   These qualities have been present in his work for over 40 years
since the publication of *The Enemies of Love*, poems written
during the second world war, but it is in the later collection, *The
Exiled Heart*, when the last traces of uncertainty have been
eliminated, that he begins to speak in his mature voice. Since
then Lindsay has been consistently good, and three volumes in
particular—*Snow Warning*, *One Later Day*, and *This Business
of Living*—are outstanding achievements. And yet despite this
Lindsay has failed to win the wider recognition he deserves.
   To an extent this is the fate of all poets, but a possible explanation for Lindsay's comparative neglect is that there is no single
area of experience that is distinctively his own territory. His
fellow Scots, Norman MacCaig, Iain Crichton Smith, and
George Mackay Brown, have drawn their distinctive maps
around areas of life, and at the same time there is a sense of
physical, almost regional landscape in their work. (This charting
of territory—and sometimes the superimposing of the same
chart on different territories—is at its most obvious in the

aggressive mythologising of Hughes or the ultimate melancholies of Sisson.) But Lindsay refuses to colonise experience, preferring instead to travel without maps so that each new experience demands a fresh, an original response from the poet. Lindsay's vision is no less penetrating than his contemporaries', but it is in a sense less selective; his voice is no less distinctive, but it is a quieter voice, and one that is impossible to parody.

Ironically, this wider vision and quieter voice, this concern to be true to the particularities of experience, may have prevented some readers from seeing the deeper tensions that underlie much of Lindsay's work. For example, in his poems on childhood such as "Small Boy Writing" and "Aged Four" the poet intensifies the sense of innocence by implying its inevitable loss and the consequent hurt and bewilderment that every child must suffer. And when his work is seen as a whole there is a profound tension between the order and serenity of poems such as "June Rain," "Picking Apples," "At the Mouth of the Ardyne," and the love poems, in contrast to the savagery of the city in "Attending a Football Match," "Glasgow Nocturne," and "Glasgow Orange Walk." This conflict between civilised values and barbarism is the main preoccupation in Lindsay's most recent work, notably the long autobiographical poem "A Net to Catch the Winds" and the prose autobiography *Thank You for Having Me.*

Any statement on Maurice Lindsay's work would be incomplete without a comment on his achievements as an editor. In editing over 20 anthologies of Scottish poetry and also the leading Scottish literary magazine, *The Scottish Review*, Lindsay has always resisted the petty tyrannies of fashion in order to give the widest encouragement and recognition to Scottish poets.

—James Aitchison

LIPSITZ, Lou. American. Born in Brooklyn, New York, 29 October 1938. Educated at the University of Chicago, B.A. 1957; Yale University, New Haven, Connecticut, M.A. 1959, Ph.D. in political science 1964. Married Joan Scheff in 1959 (divorced, 1973); one daughter and one son. Reporter, Celina *Daily Standard*, Ohio, 1957-58; Instructor, University of Connecticut, Storrs, 1961-64. Assistant Professor, 1964-67, Associate Professor, 1967-74, and since 1974, Professor of Political Science, University of North Carolina, Chapel Hill. Recipient: National Endowment for the Arts grant, 1967. Address: 168 Lake Ellen Drive, Chapel Hill, North Carolina 27514, U.S.A.

PUBLICATIONS

Verse

Cold Water. Middletown, Connecticut, Wesleyan University Press, 1967.
Reflections on Samson. Santa Cruz, California, Kayak, 1977.

Other

Editor, *American Government: Behavior and Controversy.* Boston, Allyn and Bacon, 1967.
Editor, *The Confused Eagle: Division and Dilemma in American Politics.* Boston, Allyn and Bacon, 1973.
Editor, *Essentials of American Government Today.* New York, Random House, 1975.

Editor, *American Government Today.* New York, Random House, 1980.

*   *   *

Lou Lipsitz, like so many other recent American poets was influenced by the great modern European and Latin American poets such as Neruda, Vallejo, and Voznesensky. But, whereas many other young poets have merely taken the grand style of surrealism and passion and turned it either flippant or blandly mechanical, Lipsitz shares the spirit that informs the originals.

He has written a genuine urban poetry which deals with the callousness and despair of the city but maintains its own concern and gentleness. His range of emotions is wide, and he has written marvelous poems of personal joy and tenderness ("Cold Water," "A Note"), of humor which is not strident but rather pervaded by an affection for the human spirit ("Pancho Villa," "Why I Left My Job"), and of the spiritual imagination ("Night Train," "The Pipes"); but the poems which are perhaps the most impressive are the ones in which he demonstrates the rare and important capacity to feel, to comprehend, the difficult life of another being.

He explores the desperation of prize fighters from the slums, the awkward strangeness of young boys entering manhood, the suffering of emotionally disturbed children, with a fully engaged perceptiveness, portraying them in lines whose accuracy and force are at least as much a proof of his empathy and love as they are of his talent or skill.

—Lawrence Russ

LIVESAY, Dorothy. Canadian. Born in Winnipeg, Manitoba, 12 October 1909. Educated at Trinity College, University of Toronto, 1927-31, B.A. 1931; The Sorbonne, Paris, Diploma, 1932; London Institute of Education, 1959; University of British Columbia, Vancouver, M.Ed. 1966. Married Duncan Macnair in 1937 (died); one son and one daughter. Social worker, Englewood, New Jersey, 1935-36, and Vancouver, 1936-39, 1953-55; correspondent, *Toronto Daily Star*, 1946-49; documentary scriptwriter, Canadian Broadcasting Corporation, 1950-55; Lecturer in Creative Writing, University of British Columbia, 1955-56, 1965-66; high school teacher, Vancouver, 1956-58; Unesco English specialist, Paris, 1958-60, and Zambia, 1960-63; Writer-in-Residence, University of New Brunswick, Fredericton, 1966-68; Associate Professor of English, University of Alberta, Edmonton, 1968-71; Visiting Lecturer, University of Victoria, British Columbia, 1974-75, University of Manitoba, Winnipeg, 1975-76, University of Ottawa, 1977, Simon Fraser University, Burnaby, British Columbia, 1979, and Massey College, Toronto, 1983. Regional Editor, *New Frontier*, Toronto, 1936-37, and *Northern Review*, Montreal, 1945-47; Editor, *White Pelican*, Edmonton, 1971-72, and *CV 2* (Winnipeg), 1975-77. Recipient: Governor-General's Award, 1945, 1948; Lorne Pierce Medal, 1947; President's Medal, University of Western Ontario, 1954; Canada Council grant, 1958, 1964, 1971, 1977. D.Litt.: University of Waterloo, Ontario, 1973; Athabasca University, Alberta, 1983. Honorary Fellow, St. John's College, Winnipeg, and Trinity College, Toronto. Address: R.R. 1, Galiano, British Columbia VON 1PO, Canada.

PUBLICATIONS

Verse

Green Pitcher.   Toronto, Macmillan, 1928.
Signpost.   Toronto, Macmillan, 1932.
Day and Night.   Boston, Humphries, 1944.
Poems for People.   Toronto, Ryerson Press, 1947.
New Poems, edited by Jay Macpherson.   Toronto, Emblem, 1955.
Selected Poems.   Toronto, Ryerson Press, 1957.
The Colour of God's Face.   Vancouver, Unitarian Service Committee, 1964.
The Unquiet Bed.   Toronto, Ryerson Press, 1967.
Poets Between the Wars, with others, edited by Milton T. Wilson.   Toronto, McClelland and Stewart, 1967.
The Documentaries: Selected Longer Poems.   Toronto, Ryerson Press, 1968.
Post-Operative Instructions.   Kingston, Ontario, Quarry, 1968.
Plainsongs.   Fredericton, New Brunswick, Fiddlehead, 1969; revised edition, 1971.
Disasters of the Sun.   Burnaby, British Columbia, Blackfish, 1971.
Collected Poems: The Two Seasons.   Toronto, McGraw Hill Ryerson, 1972.
Nine Poems of Farewell 1972-1973.   Windsor, Ontario, Black Moss Press, 1973.
Ice Age.   Erin, Ontario, Press Porcépic, 1975.
Winter Ascending.   Prince George, British Columbia, Caledonia, 1977 (?).
The Woman I Am.   Erin, Ontario, Press Porcépic, 1977.
The Phases of Love: Adolescence 1925-1928.   Toronto, League of Canadian Poets, 1980.
The Raw Edges: Voices from Our Time.   Winnipeg, Turnstone Press, 1981.
The Phases of Love.   Toronto, Coach House Press, 1983.

Plays

Joe Derry (produced on tour, 1933).   Published in *Eight Men Speak and Other Plays from the Canadian Workers' Theatre*, edited by Richard Wright and Robin Endres, Toronto, Hogtown, 1976.
Call My People Home (broadcast, 1949).   Toronto, Ryerson Press, 1950.

Radio Play: *Call My People Home*, 1949.

Short Stories

A Winnipeg Childhood.   Winnipeg, Peguis, 1973; as *Beginnings*, Toronto, New Press, 1975.

Other

Right Hand, Left Hand (miscellany), edited by David Arnason and Kim Todd.   Erin, Ontario, Press Porcépic, 1977.

Editor, with Seymour Mayne, *40 Women Poets of Canada.*   Montreal, Ingluvin, 1971.
Editor, *Woman's Eye: 12 B.C. Poets.*   Vancouver, Air, 1978.

*

Bibliography: by Alan Ricketts, in *The Annotated Bibliography of Canada's Major Authors 4*, edited by Robert Lecker and Jack David, Downsview, Ontario, ECW Press, 1983.

Manuscript Collections: University of Alberta, Edmonton; Queen's University, Kingston, Ontario; University of Manitoba, Winnipeg.

Critical Studies: "My New Found Land" by W.E. Collin, in *The White Savannahs*, Toronto, Macmillan, 1936; "Out of Silence and Across the Distance: The Poetry of Dorothy Livesay," in *Queen's Quarterly 4* (Kingston, Ontario), Winter 1969, and "Dorothy Livesay: The Love Poetry," in *Canadian Literature* (Vancouver), Winter 1971, both by P. Stevens; "Livesay's Two Seasons" by Robin Skelton, in *Canadian Literature* (Vancouver), Autumn 1973; *From Here to There* by Frank Davey, Erin, Ontario, Press Porcépic, 1974; Tom Marshall, in *Canadian Forum* (Toronto), February 1979; "Dorothy Livesay Issue" of *Room of One's Own 5* (Vancouver), nos. 1-2, 1979.

Dorothy Livesay comments:

(1970) Early lyrical and imagist poetry became social and documentary (30's and 40's) and reverted to personal statement (50's and 60's). Influenced recently by West Coast movement (projective verse).

Themes and subjects: love and personal psychological relationships between lovers, parents, children. Problems of individual relationships to the question of our age: achieving the just society, how to stop war, how to understand other races and peoples. Recently in *The Unquiet Bed* my theme has been the importance of oneness with another person. If this harmony is achieved, many other harmonies spring from it.

I like to experiment with new forms, to find the subtleties for music in English words and word-arrangements. Poetry is speech and communication and should be said aloud.

                    *   *   *

Dorothy Livesay is one of the pioneers of modernism in Canadian poetry. Her early work in *Green Pitcher*, published when she was nineteen, while showing the influence of Imagism current at that time, was also distinguished by its simple lyricism and a rare maturity of spirit.

A start in newspaper writing was followed by university studies in Toronto and in France, and led eventually to a career in social work. Coincident with Livesay's studies at the Sorbonne, 1931-32, was the publication of *Signpost* which is a personal document and consists, in the main, of poems conceived before the politicizing process which befell Western intellectuals in the early 1930's. The suggestion exists, though, in this second chapbook, that Livesay's concerns are going to become progressive, political and committed. The private and the lyrical give way to social awareness which is informed not only by personal involvement in the lives of the under-privileged, but also by the world struggle against fascism. Out of this ambience comes *Day and Night*, a volume of socially relevant and committed writing. The institutional quality of social zeal, and that sense of *movimento* typical of the time were muted and improved upon by new well-springs of humanist affirmation in *Poems for People*. *Call My People Home* and *New Poems* are two chapbooks with an interim note about them, but with indications of a return to a more private verse concerned with the experiences of love and the joyful and evocative liberation of art. Following the publication of Livesay's *Selected Poems 1926-1956*, the poet's work seemed to mark time briefly until the emergence of a re-enforced sense of the musical phrase and new rhythms. In *The Colour of*

God's Face, a chapbook inspired by work and residence in Zambia, the strength of Livesay's rhythms is noteworthy, as is her success in balancing the imagistic with the interpretative. Influences of the Canadian West Coast *Tish*-movement are also at work in her later poems as evidenced in *The Unquiet Bed*, a collection which, with its private intensities, relies on established spareness and discipline, but which is also rich in the rhythm and musicality of its statement.

The process of shifting literary and political orientation did not affect profoundly Livesay's basic style. She continued to write in simple and direct verse forms with variations in tone from the lyrical and subdued, through the emotional and political to the genuinely humane and passionate.

Livesay's 1968 collection, *The Documentaries*, is a selection of key poems like "The Outrider" and "Call My People Home" which have a particular value not only as significant statement, but as milestones in the career of Dorothy Livesay.

—Michael Gnarowski

LIVINGSTONE, Douglas (James). South African. Born in Kuala Lumpur, Malaya, 5 January 1932. Educated at schools in Malaya, Australia, and South Africa; Kearney College, Natal, South Africa; qualified in Pathogenic Bacteriology, Pasteur Institute, Salisbury, Rhodesia. Officer in Charge, Pathological Laboratory, Broken Hill (Kabwe) General Hospital, Zambia, 1959-63. Since 1964, Bacteriologist in charge of marine work, Natal. Recipient: Guinness Prize, 1965; Cholmondeley Award, 1970; Olive Schreiner Prize, 1975; English Association Prize, 1978. Address: c/o Council of Scientific and Industrial Research, P.O. Box 17001, Congella, 4013 Natal, South Africa.

PUBLICATIONS

Verse

The Skull in the Mud. London, Outposts, 1960.
Sjambok and Other Poems from Africa. London and New York, Oxford University Press, 1964.
Poems, with Thomas Kinsella and Anne Sexton. London and New York, Oxford University Press, 1968.
Eyes Closed Against the Sun. London and New York, Oxford University Press, 1970.
The Sea My Winding Sheet and Other Poems. Durban, Theatre Workshop, 1971.
A Rosary of Bone, edited by Jack Cope. Cape Town, David Philip, 1975; revised edition, 1983.
The Anvil's Undertone. Johannesburg, Donker, 1978.
Selected Poems. Johannesburg, Donker, 1984.

Plays

The Sea My Winding Sheet (broadcast, 1963; produced Durban, 1971). Included in *The Sea My Winding Sheet and Other Poems*, 1971.
A Rhino for the Boardroom (broadcast, 1974). Published in *Contemporary South African Plays*, edited by E. Pereira, Johannesburg, Ravan Press, 1977.
The Semblance of the Real (produced Durban, 1976).

Radio Plays: *The Sea My Winding Sheet*, 1963 (Rhodesia); *A*

Rhino for the Boardroom, 1974.

Television Play: *A Question of Guilt*, 1980.

Other

The Distribution and Occurrence of Coliforms and Pathogenic Indicators of Pollution Within the Surf-Zone and Near-Shore Waters of the Natal Coast, with J.W. de Goede and B.A. Warren-Hansen. Natal, Council of Scientific and Industrial Research, 1968.

*

Bibliography: *Douglas Livingstone: A Bibliography* by A.G. Ullyatt, Pretoria, University of South Africa, 1979.

Critical Studies: *Douglas Livingstone: A Critical Study of His Poetry*, Johannesburg, Donker, 1981, and "Douglas Livingstone," in *South African English Poetry: A Modern Perspective*, Johannesburg, Donker, 1984, both by Michael Chapman.

Douglas Livingstone comments:

Some African themes, especially animals: to reflect the nature of man. Happier with "form." Attempts to "shape" poem to subject. Influences unknown, but favorite poets: Chaucer, John Clare, Catullus, Shelley, Marvell, Donne, Cavafy, E.A. Robinson, Wilfred Owen and Sylvia Plath among the dead.

*   *   *

Douglas Livingstone might be described as a poet without roots in any particular country or environment, which makes him rather difficult to place for the reader who automatically thinks in terms of nationalities. Born in Kuala Lumpur of middle-class Scottish parents, Livingstone spent his early years in Malaya, Australia, Ceylon, Scotland, South Africa, Rhodesia and Zambia. In Rhodesia he studied and qualified in pathological bacteriology. As he himself observes somewhat ruefully: "I have been to more schools than I care to remember, in several continents, but which to call a capillary, let alone a tap-root, had me foxed."

His earliest work appeared in *Outposts* and his first small collection of poems, *The Skull in the Mud*, was published by Outposts Publications in 1960. Although uneven in quality, this collection already exhibited the characteristics which the critics welcomed on the appearance of his second volume, and had an extraordinary vitality which, surprisingly enough for any Rhodesian or South African poet, owed nothing at all to Roy Campbell. Indeed, though it was obvious that Livingstone had read widely, no strong literary influences were anywhere apparent. In *The Skull in the Mud* Livingstone refers to himself as a "muscoid Jonah" and takes up his position as "sentry in the shade," recording what he sees with scrupulous attention to detail, yet never quite maintaining the stance of detached observer. He is, in fact, deeply committed to what he sees and apprehends, without knowing why he is so affected by the scene. There are both movement and compassion in these poems, the best of which reflect local colour and conditions; but it is the title poem which most fittingly expresses his individuality and allows him scope for the satirical streak which he has since developed with success.

Livingstone had moved to South Africa by the time his second collection, *Sjambok*, appeared, though the poems were all written in Zambia. *Sjambok* commanded immediate attention for its energy and power, its vigorous employment of language, and its originality in describing animals and landscape. It is curious that no one seems to have noticed the connection between his choice of title (*sjambok* = whip of plaited leather) and that of the magazine founded by Roy Campbell and William Plomer in 1926 (*voorslag* = whiplash) in order to "sting with satire the mental hindquarters...of the bovine citizenry of the Union." Certainly Livingstone is concentrating more and more upon the satirical element, though the satire is directed at social evils in general rather than those of South Africa in particular. Despite the superficial qualities so highly praised by the critics—the descriptive skill, the evocative phraseology and precision of imagery—*Sjambok* shows that Livingstone is preoccupied with the disrupting effects of Western civilisation upon primitive peoples and traditions. The ambivalence to be detected in his attitudes owes something to the unsettled nature of his own life as well as that of the African continent; and when he extends his range and raises his sights, as in "Suicide Note" and "Johnny Twenty-Three," he can be exceptionally shrewd and perceptive.

—Howard Sergeant

LIYONG, Taban lo.   Ugandan.   Born in Uganda, in 1938. Educated at Gulu High School; Sir Samuel Baker School; Government Teacher Training College, Kyambogo; Knoxville College, Tennessee; University of North Carolina, Chapel Hill; Georgetown University, Washington, D.C.; Howard University, Washington, D.C., B.A. in literature and journalism 1966; University of Iowa, Iowa City, M.F.A. 1968. After 1968, Member of the Institute for Development Studies, Cultural Division, and Lecturer in English, University of Nairobi, Kenya. Editor, *Mila.* Address: c/o Heinemann Educational (Nigeria) Ltd., Ighodaro Road, Jericho, PMB 5205, Ibadan, Nigeria.

PUBLICATIONS

Verse

Eating Chiefs: Lwo Culture from Lolwe to Malkal.   London, Heinemann, 1970; New York, Humanities Press, 1971.
Frantz Fanon's Uneven Ribs: With Poems More and More. London, Heinemann, 1971.
Another Nigger Dead.   London, Heinemann, 1972.
Ballads of Underdevelopment: Poems and Thoughts.   Kampala, East African Literature Bureau, 1974.
To Still a Passion.   London, Longman, 1977.

Novel

Meditations in Limbo.   Nairobi, Equatorial, 1970.

Short Stories

Fixions and Other Stories.   London, Heinemann, 1969.
The Uniformed Man.   Nairobi, East African Publishing House, 1971.

Other

The Last Word: Cultural Synthesism.   Nairobi, East African Publishing House, 1969.

Popular Culture of East Africa: Oral Literature.   Nairobi, Longman, 1972.
Thirteen Offensives Against Our Enemies.   Nairobi, East African Literature Bureau, 1973.
Meditations.   London, Rex Collings, 1978.

Editor, *Sir Apolo Kagwa Discovers England,* by Ham Mukasa, translated by Ernest Millar.   London, Heinemann, 1975.

*   *   *

A wry and acerbic wit, a ready sense of humor, an equally ready sense of tragedy, and a staggeringly wide range of reference points are the most obvious qualities of the poetry of Taban lo Liyong. His poems indicate these dimensions by their titles alone, to say nothing of the cornucopia (Taban is certainly copious and also, at times, corny) of work the reader finds himself confronted with (or assaulted by) when he begins to read them. "Language/is a figure/of speech," begins the first poem in his first book. "Bless the african coups/tragedy now means a thing to us," begins the initial poem in his second volume.

More than those of almost any other African poet, Taban lo Liyong's poems reflect the odyssey of his life as African and poet ranging from facetiousness to seriousness and from pathos to intentional bathos. His subject matter one minute is the break up of a "modern" African marriage (in the poem which begins "i walked among men in america for a year...") and the next minute the development of modern poetry (in "The Best Poets," a marvellous ramble through the history of poetic theory).

Call Taban lo Liyong a prodigy, a genius, a freak or an apostate; he might well be pleased with any or all of those titles. If there is any one fault in his work, in fact, it is that there is so much in his volumes that a reader may be overwhelmed. His is not a poetry which one reads to while away an evening or calm one's nerves after a harrowing day. It is a poetry that demands as much from its reader as it gives in return—a high price for quality merchandise.

—Joseph Bruchac

LOCHHEAD, Liz.   Scottish.   Born in Motherwell, Lanarkshire, 26 December 1947. Educated at Dalziel High School, Motherwell, 1960-65; Glasgow School of Art, 1965-70, Diploma in Art. Art Teacher at Bishopbriggs High School, Glasgow, and other schools in Glasgow and Bristol. Recipient: BBC Scotland Prize, 1971; Scottish Arts Council Award, 1973, and fellowship, 1978. Address: c/o Salamander Press, 34 Shandwick Place, Edinburgh EH2 4RT, Scotland.

PUBLICATIONS

Verse

Memo for Spring.   Edinburgh, Reprographia, 1972.
The Grimm Sisters.   London, Next Editions, 1981.
Dreaming Frankenstein, and Collected Poems.   Edinburgh, Polygon, 1984.

Plays

Blood and Ice (produced Edinburgh, 1982; London, 1984).
Edinburgh, Salamander Press, 1982; New York, Methuen,
1983.
A Bunch of Fives, with Tom Leonard and Sean Hardie (pro-
duced Glasgow, 1983).
Silver Service. Edinburgh, Salamander Press, 1984.

Screenplay: *Now and Then*, 1972.

Television Play: *Sweet Nothings* (*End of the Line* series), 1984.

*

Critical Study: *Liz Lochhead*, Glasgow, National Book League,
1978.

Liz Lochhead comments:

I want my poems to be clear. They should make sense to my
landlady and the man in the corner shop. But be capable of being
pondered over by the academics round at the University if they
like to. Probably I'd hope they'd find a lot of controlled ambiguities, puns—a lot of puns—and word play and double-meanings.
I hope they'd find them funny, with a lot of irony, but I'm
growing as I get older to distrust irony, despise the way an ironic
stance can allow one both to say something and deny responsibility for it, hate the way this kind of cowardice has to hide
behind its mask. I like to set up what are, I suppose, essentially
dramatic situations within a poem. The poems are almost invariably about people and they tell stories. Above all, I want everything to become so visually alive that it's real, physical, palpable.
This I'm always trying for, and I suppose it is exactly what
almost every other writer tries to do too.

*   *   *

Liz Lochhead's *Memo for Spring* made an immediate impact
with its freshness and truth to experience. The appeal was direct,
and yet the writing used more verbal devices than might appear
at a glance or on a first hearing. An ability to talk about very
ordinary things—her young sister trying on her shoes, a trip
from Glasgow to Edinburgh, her grandmother knitting, the
clang of steelworks, a child carrying a jug of milk, the end of a
love-affair—is in a few poems flattened out towards triviality or
the prosaic, but for the most part the warmly observing eye and
ear are convincingly on target. The experience had a Glasgow
and Lanarkshire background, but one attractive poem, "Letter
from New England," where elements of ironical comment on
small-town life were entertainingly presented through the persona of a surprised visitor, showed an encouraging ability to
move into a wider world.

Her subsequent books have confirmed her promise and
extended her range. *The Grimm Sisters* took up themes from
ballad and fairy-tale and re-told the stories either from a new
angle or with a modern perspective. *Dreaming Frankenstein*, a
collection of her earlier volumes with a substantial and impressive addition of new poems, showed both a development of her
storytelling gift and a deepening of her psychological probing of
human relationships, especially as seen from a woman's point of
view. The extension of her work into the theatre, with plays on
the Frankenstein and Dracula stories and an interest in cabaret-
type monologues, has given further evidence of a productive and
confident talent. If there are moments when one feels she could

be critically harder on herself, there is no doubting the sparkle
and boldness and emotional charge of her work.

—Edwin Morgan

LOEWINSOHN, Ron(ald William). American. Born in
Iloilo, Philippines, 15 December 1937. Educated at San Francisco State College; University of California, Berkeley, A.B.
1967 (Phi Beta Kappa); Harvard University, Cambridge, Massachusetts (Woodrow Wilson Fellow, 1967-68; Danforth Fellow, 1967-70; Harvard University Graduate Prize Fellow, 1967-
70), M.A. 1969, Ph.D. 1971. Taught poetry workshops at San
Francisco State College, 1960-61, and the Center for Adult
Education, Cambridge, Massachusetts, 1968; Teaching Fellow,
Harvard University, 1968-70. Since 1970, Member of the English Department, University of California, Berkeley. Editor,
Change, 1963, *Sum*, 1964, and *R.C. Lion*, 1966-67, all in Berke-
ley; Contributing Editor, *W.C. Williams Newsletter*, Middle-
town, Pennsylvania. Recipient: Poets Foundation Award, 1963;
Academy of American Poets Irving Stone Award, 1966; National
Endowment for the Arts Fellowship, 1979; Bay Area Book
Reviewers Association award, for fiction, 1984. Address:
Department of English, University of California, Berkeley, Cali-
fornia 94720, U.S.A.

PUBLICATIONS

Verse

Watermelons. New York, Totem, 1959.
The World of the Lie. San Francisco, Change Press, 1963.
Against the Silences to Come. San Francisco, Four Seasons,
1965.
L'Autre. Los Angeles, Black Sparrow Press, 1967.
*Lying Together, Turning the Head and Shifting the Weight, The
Produce District and Other Places, Moving—A Spring Poem*.
Los Angeles, Black Sparrow Press, 1967.
Three Backyard Dramas with Mamas. Santa Barbara, Cali-
fornia, Unicorn Press, 1967.
The Sea, Around Us. Los Angeles, Black Sparrow Press, 1968.
The Step. Los Angeles, Black Sparrow Press, 1968.
These Worlds Have Always Moved in Harmony, in *A Play and
Two Poems*, with Diane Wakoski and Robert Kelly. Los
Angeles, Black Sparrow Press, 1968.
Meat Air: Poems 1957-1969. New York, Harcourt Brace,
1970.
The Leaves. Los Angeles, Black Sparrow Press, 1973.
Eight Fairy Tales. Los Angeles, Black Sparrow Press, 1975.
Goat Dances. Santa Barbara, California, Black Sparrow
Press, 1976.

Novel

Magnetic Field(s). New York, Knopf, 1983.

Other

Editor, *Embodiment of Knowledge*, by William Carlos Williams. New York, New Directions, 1974.

* * *

So many young American poets owe allegiance and inspiration to the work of William Carlos Williams that we might well, remembering the 17th century Jonsonians known as the Tribe of Ben, speak now of the tribe of Bill. Ron Loewinsohn's first book was one of the many bearing a prefatory commendation by Williams; it bore too an introduction by that senior Tribesman, Allen Ginsberg, acclaiming the younger man expansively as part of the "great wave of Poetry...breaking over America now." In the years since 1959, Loewinsohn has gone on unobtrusively working in the Williams mode, acknowledging his source with almost insistent modesty (he is currently writing a critical book on Williams and his selected poems, *Meat Air*, is dedicated to him as "informing spirit"), but adding too a note we might connect with Ginsberg—that of a greater sexual explicitness than Williams ever permitted himself (e.g., the poem title "The Romaunt of the Rose Fuck"), still however in the service of a poetry of love. If Loewinsohn's work shows perhaps less sophisticated agility of mind than that of the deceptively mild-seeming doctor of Rutherford, it brings no less gusto to the celebration of the local and the demotic, and to the inventing of beauty in the literal particulars of the common world. *Three Backyard Dramas with Mamas* gives a touching Californian incarnation to the Persephone myth. "The Distractions; The Music" moves effectively between the social world of work and glimpsed violence and the private world of love and beauty. Noteworthy in Loewinsohn is a genuinely sweet lyricism; it's relevant that a recurring motif in his work is the figure of Mozart, exemplar of a lucid, unforced, unegoistic beauty. Here is the end of a short poem called "K. 282":

> That door
> is open & he is playing at his ease.
> He is maybe 18, the beloved of
> God, & is in love himself. Beauty
> falls from him as easily as the sun
> falls thru the windows. His fingers
> follow the play of his mind, dancing
> over the keys as he waits. He is 18,
> it is late summer, he can wait easily
> all day. the door is open. forever.

—Seamus Cooney

LOGAN, John (Burton). American. Born in Red Oak, Iowa, 23 January 1923. Educated at Coe College, Cedar Rapids, Iowa, B.A. in zoology 1943; University of Iowa, Iowa City, M.A. in English 1949; Georgetown University, Washington, D.C. Married Mary Guenevere Minor in 1945 (divorced); six daughters and three sons. Tutor, St. John's College, Annapolis, Maryland, 1947-51; Associate Professor, The General Program, University of Notre Dame, Indiana, 1951-63; Visiting Professor of English, University of Washington, Seattle, 1965, and San Francisco State College, 1965-66; Fellow, Indiana School of Letters, summers 1965, 1969. Since 1966, Professor of English, State University of New York, Buffalo. Visiting Professor, University of Hawaii, Manoa, 1975-76. Editor, *Choice*, Chicago, in late 1960's. Recipient: National Endowment for the Arts grant, 1966, 1968, 1980; Miles Modern Poetry Award, 1967; Rockefeller

grant, 1968; Morton Dauwen Zabel Award (*Poetry*, Chicago), 1974; Guggenheim Fellowship, 1979; Lenore Marshall-*Nation* Poetry Prize, 1982; William Carlos Williams Award, 1982. Address: Department of English, State University of New York, 427 Clemens Hall, Buffalo, New York 14260, U.S.A.

PUBLICATIONS

Verse

Cycle for Mother Cabrini. New York, Grove Press, 1955.
Ghosts of the Heart: New Poems. Chicago, University of Chicago Press, 1960.
Spring of the Thief: Poems 1960-1962. New York, Knopf, 1963.
The Zig-Zag Walk: Poems 1963-1968. New York, Dutton, 1969.
The Anonymous Lover: New Poems. New York, Liveright, 1973.
Poem in Progress. San Francisco, Dryad Press, 1975.
Only the Dreamer Can Change the Dream (single poem). Honolulu, Petronium Press, 1975.
Poems, photographs by Aaron Siskind. Rochester, New York, Visual Studies Workshop, 1976.
The Bridge of Change. Brockport, New York, BOA, 1979.
Only the Dreamer Can Change the Dream (collection). New York, Ecco Press, 1981.
The Transformation: Poems January to March 1981. San Francisco, Pancake Press, 1983.

Recording: *Today's Poets 5*, with others, Folkways.

Play

Of Poems, Youth, and Spring. New York, French, 1962.

Novel

The House That Jack Built; or, A Portrait of the Artist as a Sad Sensualist. Omaha, Abattoir, 1974.

Other

Tom Savage: A Boy of Early Virginia (for children). Chicago, Encyclopaedia Britannica Press, 1962.
A Ballet for the Ear: Interviews, Essays, and Reviews, edited by A. Poulin, Jr. Ann Arbor, University of Michigan Press, 1983.

*

Critical Studies: by Robert Bly, in *The Sixties 5* (Madison, Minnesota), 1981; James Dickey, in *Babel to Byzantium*, New York, Farrar Straus, 1986; Jerome Mazzaro, in *Salmagundi 8* (Flushing, New York), 1986; Paul Carroll, in *The Poem in Its Skin*, Chicago, Follett, 1968.

John Logan comments:

I think of poetry as a reaching, an anonymous loving, which occasionally becomes personal when there are those present who care to listen. I began using stresses in my first book. Moved to syllabic writing in my second and third books, invented the thirteen syllable line for my "Monologues of the Son of Saul" in my third book and then moved toward a form which adapts slant rhyme to free verse couplets and triplets, which I used for my fourth book. I think of Ogden Nash as an influence in this "delayed rhyme" technique. I don't know who my other influences are, except for Rilke. Stories of the Old Testament and the lives of poets (Southwell, Heine, Rimbaud, Keats, Cummings, Crane) are important sources.

*　　*　　*

Despite the admiring remarks of distinguished poets and critics, John Logan has not been a popular poet in his native country, and the reasons are not hard to discover. Chiefly, of course, he early became known as a writer of religious verse of a particularly orthodox cast, replete with the conventional symbology of church ritual, and though he has more and more tended to break free both of the overt religious concerns and the metaphorical staples, it is only very recently that he has developed a style to which many of us can respond.

A more important factor in explaining Logan's relation to prospective readers of his verse has been the unfortunate misreading of the poetry by those who might have been expected to do better. Where even sensitive observers have seen nothing but orthodoxy in Logan's early poetry, a few have seen the radical ambiguity which so distinguishes Logan's approach to his materials. Too often the rather prosaic voice and straightforward presentation of sequential observations have been mistaken for ideological certitude and dully competent versification. Unnoticed have been the subtle exorcisms, the parody, the intuitive rejection of resolutions legitimized by a Catholicism that continues, whatever its failings, to hold Logan in its embrace. In fact, not until a 1968 study by Jerome Mazzaro was the relation between Logan's poetic artifacts and his thematic concerns successfully explored, to the extent that Logan's witty rhymes and absurd puns, for example, may be understood as essential to his verse, rather than as somehow frivolous posturings.

Logan's poetry evinces a remarkable quality of tenderness, of genuine love of creation, and the use of devices to undercut his sombre and touching evocations is a necessary element in his achievement of a modern voice. Occasionally, even in the most recent work, a quality of ingenuous exclamation and breathless wonderment intrudes, and one senses a wilful-generation of excitement that is only half-felt. The language, which has been called prosaic, is often richly ornamented, though he relies on metaphor only sparingly, and there is a distinct playfulness which regularly vies with the more reverential tones that dominate the verse. Similarly, the poems in Logan's third volume, *Spring of the Thief*, as well as the pieces that have lately appeared in various magazines, have been marked by a kind of erotic sensuality that has qualified and deepened the piety which rings in his utterance. This is no doubt related to Logan's quest for self-knowledge and the basically religious transcendence of self-love, so that the masturbatory reveries toward which so many of the better poems tend may be seen as part of a larger struggle, not as a manifestation of purely sexual despair.

Many of Logan's poems explore the spiritual and artistic lives of others, such as Rimbaud, Heine, and Keats, not to mention a host of religious figures, but the explorations are carried on in such a way that they implicate Logan's own problems at every turn. What fascinates Logan is the identity in certain men, especially artists, between scapegoat and priest, and it is this identity that he continually probes, searching out the sacramental qualities of a life in which too often the lovely and tender are obscured by the ugly.

—Robert Boyers

LOGUE, Christopher. British. Born in Portsmouth, Hampshire, 23 November 1926. Educated at Prior Park College, Bath; Portsmouth Grammar School. Served in the British Army, 1944–48. Lived in France, 1951–56. Contributor, *Private Eye*, London. Address: 18 Denbigh Close, London W. 11, England.

PUBLICATIONS

Verse

Wand and Quadrant. Paris, Olympia Press, 1953.
The Weekdream Sonnets. Paris, Jack Straw, 1955.
Devil, Maggot, and Son. Amsterdam, Stols, and Tunbridge Wells, Kent, Peter Russell, 1955.
First Testament. Rome, Botteghe Oscure, 1955.
She Sings, He Sings. Rome, Botteghe Oscure, 1957.
A Song for Kathleen. London, Villiers, 1958.
The Song of the Dead Soldier, To the Tune of McCafferty: One Killed in the Interests of Certain Tory Senators in Cyprus. London, Villiers, 1959.
Memoranda for Marchers. Privately printed, 1959.
Songs. London, Hutchinson, 1959; New York, McDowell Obolensky, 1960.
Songs from "The Lily-White Boys." London, Scorpion Press, 1960.
Logue's A.B.C. London, Scorpion Press, 1966.
I Shall Vote Labour. London, Turret, 1966.
The Words of Christopher Logue's Establishment Songs, Etcetera. London, Poet and Printer, 1966.
Selections from a Correspondence Between an Irishman and a Rat. London, Goliard Press, 1966.
Gone Ladies, music by Wallace Southam. London, Turret, 1968.
Rat, Oh Rat. Privately printed, 1968.
Hermes Flew to Olympus. Privately printed, 1968.
SL. Privately printed, 1969.
The Girls. Privately printed, 1969.
New Numbers. London, Cape, 1969; New York, Knopf, 1970.
For Talitha. London, Steam Press, 1971.
What. Richmond, Surrey, Keepsake Press, 1972.
Twelve Cards. London, Lorrimer, 1972.
Singles. London, John Roberts Press, 1973.
Mixed Rushes. London, John Roberts Press, 1974.
The Crocodile (for children). London, Cape, 1976.
Abecedary. London, Cape, 1977.
Red Bird: Love Poems. Guildford, Surrey, Circle Press, 1979.
Ode to the Dodo: Poems from 1953 to 1978. London, Cape, 1981.
War Music: An Account of Books 16 to 19 of Homer's Iliad. London, Cape, 1981.

Recordings: *Christopher Logue Reading His Own Poetry*, with Laurie Lee, Jupiter, 1960; *The Death of Patroclus*, Spoken Arts, 1963.

Plays

The Trial of Cob and Leach: A News Play (produced London, 1959).
The Lily-White Boys (lyrics only), book by Henry Cookson, music by Tony Kinsey and Bill LeSage (produced London, 1960).
Trials by Logue (Antigone and *Cob and Leach)* (produced London, 1960).

Friday, adaptation of a work by Hugo Klaus (produced London, 1971).   London, Davis Poynter, 1972.
War Music, music by Donald Fraser, adaptation of *The Iliad* (produced London, 1977).

Screenplay: *Savage Messiah*, 1972.

Television Play: *The End of Arthur's Marriage*, with Stanley Myers, 1965.

Novel

Lust (as Count Palmiro Vicarion).   Paris, Olympia Press, 1959.

Other

The Arrival of the Poet in the City: A Treatment for a Film. Amsterdam, Yellow Press, and London, Mandarin, 1963; revised edition, music by George Nicholson, Mainz, Germany, Schott, 1983.
Ratsmagic (for children).   London, Cape, and New York, Pantheon, 1976.
Puss-in-Boots Pop-Up (for children).   London, Cape, 1976; New York, Greenwillow, 1977.
The Magic Circus (for children).   London, Cape, and New York, Viking Press, 1979.
Bumper Book of True Stories.   London, Private Eye-Deutsch, 1980.

Editor, *Count Palmiro Vicarion's Book of Limericks*.   Paris, Olympia Press, 1959.
Editor, *Count Palmiro Vicarion's Book of Bawdy Ballads*.   Paris, Olympia Press, 1962.
Editor, *True Stories*.   London, New English Library, 1966.
Editor, *True Stories from "Private Eye."*   London, Deutsch, 1973.
Editor, *The Children's Book of Comic Verse*.   London, Batsford, 1979.
Editor, *London in Verse*.   London, Secker and Warburg, 1982.
Editor, *Sweet and Sour: An Anthology of Comic Verse*.   London, Batsford, 1983.
Editor, *The Oxford Book of Pseuds*.   London, Private Eye-Deutsch, 1983.

Translator, *The Man Who Told His Love: Twenty Poems Based on Pablo Neruda's "Los Cantos d'Amores."*   London, Scorpion Press, 1958.
Translator, *Patrocleia* (from Book XVI of Homer's *Iliad*). London, Scorpion Press, 1962; Ann Arbor, University of Michigan Press, 1963.
Translator, *Pax* (from Book XIX of Homer's *Iliad*).   London, Turret, 1967.

*

Theatrical Activities:
Actor: **Play**—First Player and Player King, in *Hamlet*, London, 1980; **Films**—*Dante's Inferno*, 1966; *The Peasants' Revolt*, 1966; *The Devils*, 1970; *Moonlighting*, 1982; **Television**—*The Gadfly*, 1977; *Bird of Prey*, 1982.

*   *   *

A powerful and original stylist, Christopher Logue is remarkable for the varied range of his talents. Aside from poetry, he has achieved fame as a playwright, and proved to be an effective actor in a number of film and television roles. During the 1960's he and Adrian Mitchell enjoyed something of a cult status as leaders of the poetry-reading movement, with its anti-Vietnam, "protest" associations. Like Mitchell, Logue holds radical opinions, but controls his anger to a greater degree within his poems. His bitter attacks on imperialism, capital punishment, and nuclear warfare are sheathed in a flawless, elegant verse often reminiscent of the Augustan age. Nor is he confined merely to political topics, showing himself equally adept as a social satirist, writer of comic children's verse, translator, and reteller of fairy tales. Logue's formidable gifts are evident from his earliest work in the 1950's. The descriptive landscapes and the song-like "Airs and Graces" of his first collection have a dream-vision quality exploited in later writings, while the charged sexuality of "Six Sonnets" reveals the poet as already an assured master of his craft. These poems display a marked awareness of poetry's origins in music and the spoken word.

Significantly, Logue's most consistently impressive collection is called *Songs*, and his Homeric retellings—themselves an interpretation of what was once oral poetry—have been adapted as a musical performance. *Songs* contains some of Logue's most enduring verses, their political message tempered by a poet's perception and distance. In "Song of the Dead Soldier" he attacks the idea of empires established by force, and in "Lullaby" the institution of capital punishment. "The Busker's Song" debunks the symbols of British imperial power as actors in a fairground sideshow, while poems like "Professor Tuholsky's Facts" and "Loyal to the King" ridicule mankind's delusions of grandeur, our vaunted battles and slaughters derided on a cosmic scale as the efforts of fleas on a ball of dung. Most memorable is "The Story of the Road," where in a skilfully matter-of-fact style Logue describes the attempt of downtrodden Third World peasants to build a neglected inland road in defiance of the authorities. *War Music*, his version of Books 16-19 of the *Iliad*, ranks with *Songs* as his finest achievement. It seems ironic that so anti-war a writer as Logue should so brilliantly capture the feeling of this ancient conflict, depicting with unforgettable skill the intrigues of gods and men, bringing home to the reader the shockingly brutal nature of hand-to-hand combat between Trojan and Greek.

Later collections show a change of emphasis, the poet's attention shifting during the 1960's from revolutionaries to pop stars and criminals, his verse reflecting the permissive and somewhat unreal atmosphere of the time. To one with such a sure grasp of style, there is always a dangerous tendency to appear glib, and certainly an element of slick facility creeps into satirical pieces like "Private Eye's True Stories" and "The Oxford Book of Pseuds," while in *The Arrival of the Poet in the City* Logue's surreal treatment of everyday London transformed into nightmare seems deliberately to provoke the reader with its account of "forbidden" sexual and sadistic acts. All the same, to accuse Logue of triviality in his later work is less than the truth. Rather, he accurately portrays a world intent on trivialising itself through its own mass media: "Twilight in autumn. Late birds shake their wings. / Terrorists laugh among the chimneytops. / Yard rises through a skylight. Crack. One drops. / Voices complain about the state of things." His eye remains keen, the strength and balance of his verse if anything more pronounced. The variety of his writing continues to impress, from the comic verse of *The Crocodile* or the psychedelic-Lewis Carroll vision of "The Isles of Jessamy", to the fragmented interior monologues and detailed imagery of *The Girls*, where the characters' inner thoughts alternate with passages of inspired description: "Leaves mute the weir. Its waters sound / like cola seething in a paper cup." Whether recounting the gradual corruption of a rock idol,

the downfall of affluent criminals, or producing the witty capsule masterpieces of *Abecedary* and "Singles," Logue's ability is
undeniable. In "Urbanal," his bitter lament for a tree felled by his
neighbour contains all the old anger in its neatly measured lines,
while the wry wit of his tribute to Betjeman admits that sometimes one must accept the world on its own terms: "Now—for
£5 a line ('At maximum eight,') / true poet of beauties undone, /
forgive me for saying no more than, 'You're great!' / as I pick up
the money and run."

—Geoff Sadler

LONGLEY, Michael. Irish. Born in Belfast, Northern Ire-
land, 27 July 1939. Educated at the Royal Belfast Academical
Institution, 1951-58; Trinity College, Dublin, B.A. (honours) in
classics 1963. Married to Edna Broderick; two daughters and
one son. Assistant Master, Avoca School, Blackrock, 1962-63,
Belfast High School and Erith Secondary School, 1963-64, and
Royal Belfast Academical Institution, 1964-69. Since 1970,
Director for Literature and the Traditional Arts, Arts Council of
Northern Ireland, Belfast. Recipient: Eric Gregory Award, 1965.
Address: 32 Osborne Gardens, Malone, Belfast 9, Northern
Ireland.

PUBLICATIONS

Verse

Ten Poems. Belfast, Festival, 1965.
Room to Rhyme, with Seamus Heaney and David Hammond.
 Belfast, Arts Council of Northern Ireland, 1968.
Secret Marriages: Nine Short Poems. Manchester, Phoenix
 Pamphlet Poets Press, 1968.
Three Regional Voices, with Barry Tebb and Iain Crichton
 Smith. London, Poet and Printer, 1968.
No Continuing City: Poems 1963-1968. London, Macmillan,
 and Chester Springs, Pennsylvania, Dufour, 1969.
Lares. London, Poet and Printer, 1972.
An Exploded View: Poems 1968-1972. London, Gollancz,
 1973.
Fishing in the Sky: Love Poems. London, Poet and Printer,
 1975.
Penguin Modern Poets 26, with Dannie Abse and D.J. Enright.
 London, Penguin, 1975.
Man Lying on a Wall: Poems 1972-1975. London, Gollancz,
 1976.
The Echo Gate: Poems 1975-1978. London, Secker and War-
 burg, 1979.
Selected Poems 1963-1980. Winston-Salem, North Carolina,
 Wake Forest University Press, 1980.
Poems 1963-1983. Edinburgh, Salamander Press, 1985.

Other

Editor, *Causeway: The Arts in Ulster.* Belfast, Arts Council of
 Northern Ireland, and Dublin, Gill and Macmillan, 1971.
Editor, *Under the Moon, Over the Stars: Young People's Writing from Ulster.* Belfast, Arts Council of Northern Ireland,
 1971.

*   *   *

Michael Longley is one of several interesting Irish poets who
made their debut during the 1960's. His first collection, *No
Continuing City,* was already quite mature, although a number
of the poems dated from Longley's undergraduate years. His
second collection, *An Exploded View,* showed he had acquired
greater technical assurance and had further humanized and
extended his thematic range.

Longley has consistently maintained a careful and disciplined
attitude towards his craft whether writing free verse or using
rhyme and metre. He has successfully accommodated contemporary idiom within a wide variety of traditional forms, ranging
from *terza rima* and sonnet to octo-syllabic eight-line stanzas;
and some of the earlier poems suggest that this skill owes much
to a profound study of the metaphysical poets. Without having
assimilated John Donne, Longley could hardly have written as
he has of moths (in "Epithalamion"):

> Who hazard all to be
> Where we, the only two it seems,
> Inhabit so delightfully
>
> Wings spread wide for balance where he trod,
> Her feathers full of water and her neck
> Under the water like a bar of light.

Longley's deep sympathy with the animal world is self-evident.
The variety of creatures in his poems is so large that there is a
feeling at times of having wandered into a nature reserve. It is
with a kindly eye that Longley looks on animals. Sometimes they
suggest the working of elemental forces; thus the badger "manages the earth with his paws." But the red in tooth and claw finds
no place in this poet's vision of nature and his animals are never
put to use as images of cruelty or menace.

In the earlier poems Longley made effective use of certain
resonant words, such as "brainstorm," "histories," and "anthem,"
but tended to overexploit them. With increasing maturity his
technique has become more finely honed and he no longer finds
it necessary to resort to such props. At the same time his ability
to suggest the mysteries which underlie the appearance of life has
been retained. "Casualty," a poem about a decaying sheep, has
this kind of awareness in spite of the absence of the earlier
poeticism:

> For the ribs began to scatter
> The wool to move outward
> As though hunger still worked there
>
> As though something that had followed
> Fox and crow was desperate for
> A last morsel and was
> Other than the wind or rain.

Reaction to the troubles in Northern Ireland has given rise to
some of Longley's most compassionate poems. One of these
links the delayed effects on his father of wounds sustained in the
Great War with the murders in Belfast of three British soldiers
and a bus conductor. Given such an environment it is not surprising that Longley should sometimes convey an impression of
déracinement but he has shown no sign of rejecting the fractured
and psychically scarred society to which he is heir as so many
Irish writers before him have done. On the contrary he has made
a point of claiming Ireland as his country "though today / *Timor
mortis conturbat me*." Longley's awareness of his Irish identity is

indeed, like the standing stone of a later poem, firmly set to help the poet

> To record the distances
> Between islands of sunlight
> And, as hub of the breezes,
> To administer the scene.

—Rivers Carew

LORDE, Audre (Geraldin). American. Born in New York City, 18 February 1934. Educated at Hunter College, New York, B.A. 1959; Columbia University, New York, M.L.S. 1961. Married Edwin A. Rollins in 1962 (divorced, 1970); one daughter and one son. Staff member, Mount Vernon Public Library, New York, 1961-63; Instructor, Town School, New York, 1966-68; Poet-in-Residence, Tougaloo College, Mississippi, 1968; Instructor, City College of New York, 1968-70, and Lehman College, New York, 1969-70; Lecturer, 1970-71, Associate Professor, 1972-78, and Professor of English, 1978-81, John Jay College of Criminal Justice, New York. Since 1981, Professor of English, Hunter College. Poetry Editor, *Chrysalis*, San Diego, California; Advisory Editor, *Black Box*, Washington, D.C.; Contributing Editor, *Black Scholar*, San Francisco. Recipient: National Endowment for the Arts grant, 1968; Creative Artists Public Service grant, 1972, 1976; Broadside Poets award, 1975. Address: c/o Crossing Press, P.O. Box 640, Trumansburg, New York 14886, U.S.A.

PUBLICATIONS

Verse

The First Cities. New York, Poets Press, 1968.
Cables to Rage. Detroit, Broadside Press, and London, Paul Breman, 1970.
From a Land Where Other People Live. Detroit, Broadside Press, 1973.
New York Head Shop and Museum. Detroit, Broadside Press, 1975.
Between Our Selves. San Francisco, Eidolon, 1976.
Coal. New York, Norton, 1976.
The Black Unicorn. New York, Norton, 1978.
Chosen Poems—Old and New. New York, Norton, 1982.

Other

Uses of the Erotic: The Erotic as Power. New York, Out and Out, 1978.
The Cancer Journals. Argyle, New York, Spinsters Ink, 1980.
Zami: A New Spelling of My Name. Watertown, Massachusetts, Persephone, 1982.
Sister Outsider: Essays and Speeches. Trumansburg, New York, Crossing Press, 1984.

*   *   *

"But I wear my nights as I wear my life / and my dying / absolute and unforgiven." It is with lines such as these that Audre Lorde carves from the complex, multifaceted nature of her own existence—she is Black, feminist, mother, lesbian—

poems of stunning originality, honesty, and power. Through them she seems both to define and clarify the boundaries of her own life.

From the rage and disillusionment which characterize her first volume of poems, "We have no passions left to love the spring / who had suffered autumn as we did, alone," she has come to find even the most negative of human experiences useful: "everything can be used / except what is wasteful / (you will need / to remember this when you are accused of destruction.)" Thus, her gift to her children is not a protective, idyllic world; rather, "I submit them / loving them above all others save myself / to the fire to the rage to the ritual scarifications / to be tried as new steel is tried." As for herself, "I have not been able to touch the destruction / within me. / But unless I learn to use / the difference between poetry and rhetoric / my power too will run corrupt as poisonous mold / or lie limp and useless as an unconnected wire."

The discovery that power and strength can be forged from destruction is neither intuitive nor fanciful. For Lorde it is the result of a life lived in the grip of ancient torments. In poems which tend more and more to recall her own childhood, the poet continues to grapple with the spectre of a mother whose lightness of skin and obsessive desire to be white "had bleached her face of everything / but very private furies," and whose aspirations for her daughter caused her to "try to beat me whiter every day." For the poet, the resultant conflict held both racial and sexual implications: "Who shall I curse that I grew up / believing in my mother's face / or that I lived in fear of the potent darkness / that wore my father's shape." In song, "Ballad from a Childhood," and nightmare, "Sequelae," the past is revisited, the ritual of exorcism painfully effected.

While confronting the past, however, Lorde continues to engage those issues and situations which define her present reality. In poems like "The Day They Eulogized Mahalia," "The American Cancer Society," and "Monkeyman," she candidly assesses the debilitating social, economic, and psychological impact of white racism on Blacks. But she is equally aware of the contribution which Blacks make to their own victimization: "We forgot to water the plantain shoots / when our houses were full of borrowed meat / and our stomachs with the gift of strangers." And, because she is a feminist, she challenges an uncritical acceptance of the idea of Black Power. "I do not believe / our wants have made all our lies / holy," for "Under the sun on the shores of Elmina / a black man sold the woman who carried / my grandmother in her belly." Intra-racial betrayal, male of female, makes necessary a separate struggle for power, *within* the race.

It is the drive for power, for Black female power, which informs the most original and effective of Lorde's recent poetry. In "Scar," she acknowledges this "masculine" element in her own nature: "Donald de Freeze I never knew you so well / as in the eyes of my own mirror." Later, she dreams "of a big black woman with jewels / in her eyes / ...her head in a golden helmet / ...her name is Colossa." And in the poem "Meet," a stunning evocation of sensual love which begins "woman when we met on the solstice / high over halfway between your world and mine," the poet compares her own lovemaking to mating between unfettered jungle animals: "You shall get young as I lick your stomach / hot and at rest before we move off again."

If a fusion of the distinctive elements of Audre Lorde's identity occurs at all, it occurs poetically, in those poems in which she employs aspects of the mythology and history of West Africa, embracing the Dahomean Amazons and the powerful yet maternal goddesses, Seboulisa and Yemanjá. In poems of haunting beauty, the poet successfully transcends limitations of time, place, and race, giving to the idea of "woman" a mythic, primal significance: "I have been woman / for a long time / beware my smile...I am / woman / and not white."

—Saundra Towns

LOWBURY, Edward (Joseph Lister).   British.   Born in London, 6 December 1913. Educated at St. Paul's School, London, 1927-33; University College, Oxford (Newdigate Prize, 1934, Matthew Arnold Memorial Prize, 1937), 1933-37, B.A. (honours) 1936, B.M., B.Ch. 1939; London Hospital, University of London, M.A. 1940, D.M. 1957. Specialist in Pathology, Royal Army Medical Corps, 1943-47. Married Alison Young, daughter of the poet Andrew Young, in 1954; three daughters. Bacteriologist, 1946-49, and Member, Medical Research Council Scientific Staff, Birmingham Accident Hospital; Consultant Adviser in Bacteriology, Birmingham Regional Hospital Board, and Honorary Director, Hospital Infection Research Laboratory, Birmingham, 1960-79. Editor, *Equator* magazine, Nairobi, Kenya, 1945-46. Visited the United States as a World Health Organization Consultant in 1965; John Keats Memorial Lecturer, Guy's Hospital, London, 1973; Visiting Professor, University of Aston, Birmingham, 1979. Recipient: University of Birmingham Research Fellowship, 1957. D.Sc.: University of Aston, Birmingham, 1977; LL.D.: University of Birmingham, 1980. Fellow, Royal College of Pathologists, Royal College of Physicians, 1977, and Royal College of Surgeons, 1978. Fellow, Royal Society of Literature, 1974. O.B.E. (Officer, Order of the British Empire), 1979. Address: 79 Vernon Road, Birmingham B18 9SQ, England.

PUBLICATIONS

Verse

Fire: A Symphonic Ode.   Oxford, Blackwell, 1934.
Crossing the Line.   London, Hutchinson, 1946.
Metamorphoses.   Privately printed, 1955.
Time for Sale.   London, Chatto and Windus-Hogarth Press, 1961.
New Poems.   Richmond, Surrey, Keepsake Press, 1965.
Daylight Astronomy.   London, Chatto and Windus-Hogarth Press, and Middletown, Connecticut, Wesleyan University Press, 1968.
Figures of Eight.   Richmond, Surrey, Keepsake Press, 1969.
Green Magic (for children).   London, Chatto and Windus, 1972.
Two Confessions.   Richmond, Surrey, Keepsake Press, 1973.
The Night Watchman.   London, Chatto and Windus-Hogarth Press, 1974.
Poetry and Paradox: An Essay, with Nineteen Relevant Poems.   Richmond, Surrey, Keepsake Press, 1976.
Troika, with John Press and Michael Riviere.   Stoke Ferry, Norfolk, Daedalus Press, 1977.
Selected Poems.   Aberystwyth, Celtion Press, 1978.
The Ring.   Birmingham, Pardoe, 1979.
A Letter from Masada.   Richmond, Surrey, Keepsake Press, 1982.

Recording: *The Poet Speaks 2,* Argo.

Other

Facing North (miscellany), with Terence Heywood.   London, Mitre Press, 1960.
Thomas Campion: Poet, Composer, Physician, with Timothy Salter and Alison Young.   London, Chatto and Windus, and New York, Barnes and Noble, 1970.
Drug Resistance in Antimicrobial Therapy.   Springfield, Illinois, Thomas, 1974.

Editor, with others, *Control of Hospital Infection: A Practical Handbook.*   London, Chapman and Hall, 1975.
Editor, *Widening Circles: Five Black Country Poets.*   Stafford, West Midland Arts, 1976.
Editor, *Night Ride and Sunrise: An Anthology of New Poems.*   Aberystwyth, Celtion Press, 1978.
Editor, with Alison Young, *The Poetical Works of Andrew Young.*   London, Secker and Warburg, 1985.

*

Manuscript Collections: University of Birmingham Library; State University of New York Library, Buffalo.

Critical Study: "Edward Lowbury" by John Press, in *Southern Review* (Baton Rouge, Louisiana), Spring 1970.

Edward Lowbury comments:

Poetry is an obsessional activity through which, at intervals in my medical life, I have been able to work off accumulated tension; it is, for me, an exploration, through words, of various experiences, and in particular of painfully or pleasurably exciting or disturbing or conflicting experiences—love; hardship and loss; the attritions of time; childhood and age; nature and the unknown; experiences in my medical work. Situations that cause laughter as well as those which cause emotional responses seem to me suitable material for poetry. In the poem I discover verbal, visual and metrical equivalents to represent the conflicts and ambiguities of the world about which I write. When the components shape themselves into structures (i.e. poems) with an inner tension, with what I judge to be the correct balance of thought and feeling, of harmony and discord, and when the structures give me—and others—a simultaneous feeling of surprise and inevitability, I feel I have found whatever it was I was looking for in my "exploration." I usually take many wrong turnings before I find (if I ever do find) the right one; I think I can recognise when I have struck the right path and the place where I should stop but I realize that neither the writer nor any individual critic can make categorical judgements.

*   *   *

The poetry of Edward Lowbury demonstrates that there is still a place for the competent neo-Georgian who has understood and purged himself of the vices of the original Georgian school. He had a fine master in his late and great father-in-law, Andrew Young. He has shown no development, but has worked hard to record his observations sensitively and in a well-handled verse—his work on Thomas Campion has served him in good stead here. Such a poem as "The Collector" shows him at his best: too over-dependent on Young, certainly, to achieve a really individual voice—but there is the minimum of irrelevant chatter, and the poet means what he says. He collects bluebells, then other kinds of flowers—but discovers that he can never get enough, so that he ends:

A lifetime brought this new collector's itch:
In a world of flowers, names, necessities—
To see how many I could do without:
And at last the distant shout
"Come home" finds me exulting in a wealth
Of unpossessions—all of it, perhaps,
A practice-run for doing without myself.

This is his most successful manner. In love poetry, or less precisely observed nature poetry, he is more awkward; nor do his attempts at the colloquial come off, as the opening of "Astrology" aptly demonstrates: "So it's true, all that nonsense/About the stars controlling destiny:/True, anyway, for migrant birds!..." But he is at all times a modest and unstrident poet, whose quiet achievement outstrips that of many of his better known contemporaries.

—Martin Seymour-Smith

LUCIE-SMITH, (John) Edward (McKenzie). British. Born in Kingston, Jamaica, 27 February 1933. Educated at King's School, Canterbury; Merton College, Oxford, B.A. 1954. Education Officer, Royal Air Force, 1954-56. Free-lance journalist. Co-Founder, Turret Books, London, 1965. Recipient: Rhys Memorial Prize, 1962; Arts Council Triennial Poetry Prize, 1962. Fellow, Royal Society of Literature. Agent: Deborah Rogers Ltd., 49 Blenheim Crescent, London, W11 2EF, England.

PUBLICATIONS

Verse

(Poems). Oxford, Fantasy Press, 1954.
A Tropical Childhood and Other Poems. London and New York, Oxford University Press, 1961.
Penguin Modern Poets 6, with Jack Clemo and George MacBeth. London, Penguin, 1964.
Confessions and Histories. London and New York, Oxford University Press, 1964.
Fir-Tree Song. London, Turret, 1965.
Jazz for the N.U.F. London, Turret, 1965.
A Game of French and English. London, Turret, 1965.
Three Experiments. London, Turret, 1965.
Gallipoli—Fifty Years After. London, Turret, 1966.
Cloud Sun Fountain Statue. Cologne, Hansjörg Mayer, 1966.
Silence, music by Wallace Southam. London, Turret, 1967.
"Heureux Qui, Comme Ulysse..." London, Turret, 1967.
Borrowed Emblems. London, Turret, 1967.
Towards Silence. London, Oxford University Press, 1968.
Teeth and Bones. London, Pebble Press, 1968.
Six Kinds of Creature. London, Turret, 1968.
Snow Poems. London, Turret, 1969.
Egyptian Ode. Stoke Ferry, Norfolk, Daedalus Press, 1969.
Six More Beasts. London, Turret, 1970.
Lovers. Frensham, Surrey, Sceptre Press, 1970.
The Rhino. London, Steam Press, 1971.
A Girl Surveyed. London, Hanover Gallery, 1971.
The Yak, The Polar Bear, The Dodo, The Goldfish, The Dinosaur, The Parrot (posters). London, Turret, 1971.
Two Poems of Night. London, Turret, 1972.
The Rabbit. London, Turret, 1973.

The Well-Wishers. London and New York, Oxford University Press, 1974.
Seven Colours. Cambridge, Rampant Lions Press, 1974.
Inscriptions/Inscripciones. Mexico City, Ainle Press, 1975.
Beasts with Bad Morals. London, Leinster Fine Books, 1984.

Novel

The Dark Pageant. London, Blond and Briggs, 1977.

Other

Mystery in the Universe: Notes on an Interview with Allen Ginsberg. London, Turret, 1965.
Op Art, edited by Duncan Taylor. London, BBC, 1966.
What Is a Painting? London, Macdonald, 1966.
Thinking about Art: Critical Essays. London, Calder and Boyars, 1968.
A Beginner's Guide to Auctions (as Peter Kershaw). London, Rapp and Whiting, 1968.
Movements in Art since 1945. London, Thames and Hudson, 1969; revised edition, 1975, 1984; as Late Modern: The Visual Arts since 1945, New York, Praeger, 1969; revised edition, 1976.
A Concise History of French Painting. London, Thames and Hudson, and New York, Praeger, 1971.
Eroticism in Western Art. London, Thames and Hudson, 1972.
Symbolist Art. London, Thames and Hudson, and New York, Praeger, 1972.
Movements in Modern Art, with Donald Carroll. New York, Horizon Press, 1973.
The First London Catalogue: All the Appurtenances of a Civilized, Amusing, and Comfortable Life. London, Paddington Press, and New York, Two Continents, 1974.
World of the Makers: Today's Master Craftsmen and Craftswomen. London, Paddington Press, and New York, Two Continents, 1975.
The Waking Dream: Fantasy and the Surreal in Graphic Art 1450-1900, with Aline Jacquiot. London, Thames and Hudson, and New York, Knopf, 1975.
The Invented Eye: Masterpieces of Photography 1839-1914. London, Paddington Press, and New York, Two Continents, 1975.
The Burnt Child: An Autobiography. London, Gollancz, 1975.
Joan of Arc. London, Allen Lane, 1976; New York, Norton, 1977.
How the Rich Lived, and Work and Struggle: The Painter as Witness 1870-1914, with Celestine Dars. London and New York, Paddington Press, 2 vols., 1976-77.
Henri Fantin-Latour. Oxford, Phaidon, and New York, Rizzoli, 1977.
Art Today: From Abstract Expressionism to Superrealism. Oxford, Phaidon, and New York, Morrow, 1977; revised edition, Phaidon, 1983.
Toulouse-Lautrec. Oxford, Phaidon, 1977; New York, Dutton, 1978; revised edition, Phaidon, 1983.
Outcasts of the Sea: Pirates and Piracy. London and New York, Paddington Press, 1978.
A Concise History of French Painting. London, Thames and Hudson, and New York, Oxford University Press, 1978.
Super-Realism. Oxford, Phaidon, 1979.
Furniture: A Concise History. London, Thames and Hudson, and New York, Oxford University Press, 1979.
Cultural Calendar of the Twentieth Century. Oxford, Phaidon, 1979.

Art in the Seventies. Oxford, Phaidon, and Ithaca, New York, Cornell University Press, 1980.

The Story of Craft: A History of the Craftsman's Role. Oxford, Phaidon, and Ithaca, New York, Cornell University Press, 1981.

The Art of Caricature. London, Orbis, and Ithaca, New York, Cornell University Press, 1981.

The Body: Images of the Nude. London, Thames and Hudson, 1981.

The Sculpture of Helaine Blumenfeld. London, Sinclair Browne, 1982.

Bertie and the Big Red Ball (for children). London, Murray-Gallery Five, 1982.

A History of Industrial Design. Oxford, Phaidon, and New York, Van Nostrand, 1983.

Art Terms: An Illustrated Dictionary. London and New York, Thames and Hudson, 1984.

Editor, *Rubens.* London, Spring, 1961.

Editor, *Raphael.* London, Batchworth Press, 1961.

Editor, with Philip Hobsbaum, *A Group Anthology.* London, Oxford University Press, 1963.

Editor, *The Penguin Book of Elizabethan Verse.* London, Penguin, 1965.

Editor, *The Liverpool Scene.* London, Rapp and Carroll, and New York, Doubleday, 1967.

Editor, *A Choice of Browning's Verse.* London, Faber, 1967.

Editor, *The Penguin Book of Satirical Verse.* London, Penguin, 1967.

Editor, *Holding Your Eight Hands: A Book of Science Fiction Verse.* New York, Doubleday, 1969; London, Rapp and Whiting, 1970.

Editor, with Patricia White, *Art in Britain 1969-70.* London, Dent, 1970.

Editor, *British Poetry since 1945.* London, Penguin, 1970; revised edition, 1984.

Editor, with Simon Watson-Taylor, *French Poetry Today: A Bi-Lingual Anthology.* London, Rapp and Whiting-Deutsch, 1971.

Editor, *Primer of Experimental Poetry 1870-1922.* London, Rapp and Whiting-Deutsch, 1971.

Editor, *A Garland from the Greek: Poems from the Greek Anthology.* London, Trigram Press, 1971.

Editor, *Masterpieces from the Pompidou Centre.* London, Thames and Hudson, 1983.

Translator, *Manet,* by Robert Rey. Milan, Uffici Press, 1962.

Translator, *Jonah: Selected Poems of Jean-Paul de Dadelsen.* London, Rapp and Carroll, 1967.

Translator, *Five Great Odes,* by Paul Claudel. London, Rapp and Whiting, 1967; Chester Springs, Pennsylvania, Dufour, 1970.

Translator, *The Muses,* by Paul Claudel. London, Turret, 1967.

*

Manuscript Collections: Humanities Research Center, University of Texas, Austin; Pennsylvania State University, University Park.

Edward Lucie-Smith comments:

My activities, though various, seem to revolve about poetry and the modern arts in general. I hate the term "poet." I'm simply a man who tries to react honestly to the world.

Since I was one of the founder-members of "The Group," and for some years chairman of its discussions, I'm in that sense a "Group" poet. Nowadays I can't think of anyone who writes much like me.

I think my development as a poet could be described roughly as follows: I began in the wake of the Movement, among a group of undergraduate poets at Oxford which included Anthony Thwaite, George MacBeth, Adrian Mitchell and Geoffrey Hill. I was then a poet of tight conventional forms and my chief subject was childhood experience. Under the influence of the sessions of "The Group," I began to write longer poems, often dramatic monologues, which were greatly influenced by Browning. Poems of this sort appear in my second volume, *Confessions and Histories.* At this period I gradually became dissatisfied with conventional verse forms and especially with their lack of real flexibility. I began to look for forms which would give: (*a*) greater colloquialism, (*b*) greater simplicity, and (*c*) greater concision. The results of these experiments can be seen in my third book, *Towards Silence,* and I have continued them in my more recent work. The metrical principle in most of my recent poetry is twofold—a strict syllabic "ground," and a melody of strong and light stresses. I use the syllabic pattern to syncopate the metre I have chosen which is usually mismatched to it, e.g. dactyls and a seven- or eleven-syllable line. The effect is, I think, very like that of Greek or Latin poetry, without strictly copying Greek or Latin forms. The influences are various: Catullus, the Elizabethan experiments with classical metre and especially Campion, Rochester (for his colloquial directness), French medieval poetry, and Pound. I am very concerned to preserve strict prose-order of words. A common criticism of my recent work is that it is too "thin"—not complex enough. My translators, on the other hand, tend to complain of simplicity which conceals difficulty.

I am interested in extending the scope of poetry—in writing poster-poems and poems to be set to music, for example.

My themes are, I think, commonly erotic (poems about love), historical and aesthetic (poems about artists and works of art, etc.), and occasionally religious.

*   *   *

Edward Lucie-Smith's poetry has ranged over the years from the neatly turned and rhymed "Movement" verses of his Fantasy Press pamphlet of 1954 to the experimentation and freedom of syllabics in, for example, his collection, *Towards Silence,* published in 1968. Together with this variety and development goes an impression of a conscious artistry—not only in individual poems, but in the compilation of the collections themselves. The poems in *Towards Silence* gain from being read as a collection, though each poem stands in its own right. Then there is the influence of Lucie-Smith's knowledge of and occupation with the visual arts. The carefully juxtaposed visual images are often starkly clear, and the poems themselves have frequently been prompted by paintings or sculpture: "An unstrung bow. The white, slack/Body collapsing. Mourners/Like mountains/Pieta."

The danger with such poetry can be that the artistry too finely applied tends to exclude feeling; but in the best of Lucie-Smith's poetry this is not so. In early personal poems about his boyhood, such as "A Tropical Childhood" or "The Lesson," the feeling is to be clearly felt: "I cried for knowledge which was bitterer/Than any grief. For there and then I knew/That grief has uses." In the group of poems about artists in the collection *Confessions and Histories,* for example, the popular "Caravaggio Dying" and the, to my mind, much better "Soliloquy in the Dark," he succeeds in expressing an empathy not only with the situation he takes as his subject matter, but with the feelings of the characters involved:

—how I used to stumble
From framè to frame and rap upon the glass
And scratch the canvas with my old man's nails,
Tears smarting useless eyes with salt and gum.
Flat is not round. And dankness is not colour.

In more recent poems, while using much freer forms, the earlier note of personal feeling comes through strongly:

Don't wonder what it was
that filled the space between
thinking and thinking.
        Gone.
My day is like a staircase
with one step missing.

It was the collection *Towards Silence* which signalled a movement into a more markedly direct simplicity of statement and form, though the implications and overtones may be far from being so, as in that near perfect poem "Silence" which rounds off the collection: "Hear/Your own noisy machine, which/Is moving towards silence." From the same period comes the remarkable translation of Paul Claudel's *Five Great Odes* in which Lucie-Smith captures the quality and feelings of this high, near-baroque poetry. To set this translation beside the simple directness of his recent poetry is to illustrate the versatility of Edward Lucie-Smith and the range of his accomplishment.

—John Cotton

MacADAMS, Lewis (Perry, Jr.). American. Born in San Angelo, Texas, 12 October 1944. Educated at Princeton University, New Jersey, B.A. 1966; State University of New York, Buffalo, M.A. 1968. Married Phoebe Russell in 1967 (divorced); two sons. Worked as switchman on Southern Pacific Railroad; Director, Bolinas Community Public Utility District, 1973-75, and San Francisco State University Poetry Center, 1975-78. Recipient: Poets Foundation Award, 1967; Committee on Poetry grant, 1977. Address: c/o Proteus Publishing, 9 West 57th Street, New York, New York 10019, U.S.A.

PUBLICATIONS

Verse

City Money. Oxford, Burning Water Press, 1966.
Water Charms. San Francisco, Dariel Press, 1968.
The Poetry Room. New York, Harper, 1970.
Dance as Individual Body-Power. Canton, New York, Institute of Further Studies, 1972.
Now Let Us Eat of This Pollen and Place Some on Our Heads, For We Are to Eat of It. New York, Harper, 1973.
The Population Explodes. Storrs, University of Connecticut Library, 1973.
News from Niman Farm. Bolinas, California, Tombouctou, 1976.
Live at the Church. New York, Kulchur, 1977.

Other

A Bolinas Report: Reportage and Exhortation. San Francisco, Zone Press, 1971.
Tilth: Interviews. Bolinas, California, Bolinas Future Studies Center, 1972.
The Grateful Dead. New York, Proteus, 1983.

Editor, with others, *Where the Girls Are: A Guide to Eastern Women's Colleges.* New York, Dial Press, 1966.

*

Critical Study: review by John Koethe, in *Poetry* (Chicago), April 1972.

Lewis MacAdams comments:
    I would like to introduce myself to you as the work of a poet that derides masks. It's that the wind sings through me, and there is no personality there—anywhere. "Speech" is the state of human things, and the words of the poet telescope elemental space and fire into geometry, which is the dance of sexual joy. It is incredible to be listed in the middle of a huge book linked with thousands of humans only because we all write in the various forms of English, so I would like to say Hello to Bob Marley in Jamaica, to Haile Selassie, to Chinua Achebe, and to Kwesi Brew. I am the words of an average man trained to composition and honed by consciousness and gravity to song. And alot of meat's gone down the pike before. And now, here is a poem by me and Tom Clark:

100 Poets in "The Rolling Stone"

    such a smile, like having you near
    and so many other poets I
    yet never shall my song omit
    to sigh and moan, more fit for Ovid
    than Shakespeare, for David Bowie
    than the Troggs, or Mike "Eggs" Benedict.

    We shall not be mooed at gracefully
    this afternoon, nor shall we either feel
    a hard-on. One inch deeper in shit.
    Well, at least it's my shit,
    you think. It's
    Ocean Lee's shit,
    justly entitled Cupid's Hill.

    I'd embrace those struggling rocks
    with John and Ed and so many a
    happy face. Wal kick my ass.
    The neck, in which strange graces lurk
    has eyes, and looks up into my face.
    And I realized I was in a body
    that would not die.

*   *   *

It is characteristic of Lewis MacAdams's poetry, like that of surrealist poetry in general, that metaphors are neither sustained nor exhaustive. The world of experience is too busy a place; no one sense of it is sufficient. Instead, there is a lavishness of images. Some are startling, totalizing: "Her hand on my chin/turning my head around/like cut flowers." Others are more yielding and assuring, such as the closing of "Sonnet": "we will drift/under trees after the rain in dry clothes, and our eyes." He is capable of a dazzling array, all made to cohere by a dynamic personality. Many of the images, flashing as they do, take his own advice: "To outlive time, live through it,/faster than ever before."

Some of MacAdams's word montages defy the absurd ("Like a mongoose the east and west/stalk eternity"), others revel in it (he revels, to reveal). Some are disquieting, such as "The Pyramids" haunted by a murderess named Candy, the "widow-maker," who "waits for the white dot on your lung to show./She is waiting in the white dress at your window"—the rhyme sealing the sense of doom. Most often there is the affirmative: "The most spectacular/paradiso cowboy hitch-hike through the mountains/through the fir trees and pine, through the flush blue sky." His poems luxuriate in such images or end in a sweep of metaphor: "Nothing is working, I'm dropping out of history, I'm/Mephistopheles annexed, I'm a pie being throwed." Dialect, humor, whatever serves to expand the multiplicity of being—MacAdams is a poet of total consciousness, advancing from the west Texas plains like his early hero Kerouac's Dan Moriarty, "mad to live, mad to talk, mad to be saved, desirous of everything at the same time." His poems are never passively descriptive. Even the longest passages of pure description explode into celebration:

Moon gone. Cold gone. Sandpipers
criss-cross the tidal pools below soft Venus light
on your breast most purely womanly form revealed
through a loose boy's shirt in a sleeping bag I roll toward
to heat up before daylight sun blasts and man stands
   alone with just
fifty-five centavos for an orange crush grande and no coy,
sexual, pacific darkness. I love you! I marry you! Speech
   good!

He is a poet of unmediated experience, wherever it can be found, whether in a public circumstance or the most intimate and domestic. In the superb "Raw Honey," after an encounter with some bees, he writes:

        Give me a song to sing. Give me focus and legend,
and following their whirr outside I see unchallenged gold
in the waters of Bolinas Bay
and the slight south wind surrounding
their departure brings me morning's second whiff of
   coffee
followed closely by your palm on my cheek and your
   voice
aching softly asks would I like a piece of fresh baked
   bread and butter?
With a little honey?

Such life-affirming tenderness rocks us from within.

Since MacAdams started living in California, his poems have grown larger and less implacably surreal, although his is still a poetry of evocation. It is characterized by a seemingly endless resourcefulness. The Population Explodes, a long celebration written for friends back in Buffalo, is as exuberant and uplifting as anything by Whitman or Ginsberg. It differs from MacAdams's earlier poetry by its continuous flow and movement away from disparate images, but sacrificing none of their jarring vividness—with marvelous puns ("the saxophones ring") and the poet himself as "mailman-angel" proffering "mantic semaphores," insisting "that life must be praised raucously in the best ways." He celebrates not just brotherhood among persons or friends, but the widest, most inclusive of creation's possibilities as befitting the new age. In such a vast throbbing ecosystem, life appears very familiar, sexy, and divine: "life stands revealed totally in

majestic black/underpants coming out of the bathroom with a towel round her head/and wings on her heels." The poet concludes by offering the knowledge that "A breath itself is a gift/from a leaf. And the recipient chest sings Wow." There is not a single drop in voltage between MacAdams's "Wow" and Whitman's "Body Electric" as MacAdams leads us through the next time-lock and into a huge but knowable cosmic room, called, after the title of his second collection, the Poetry Room.

—George F. Butterick

MacBETH, George (Mann). Scottish. Born in Shotts, Lanarkshire, 19 January 1932. Educated at King Edward VII School, Sheffield; New College, Oxford, B.A. (honours) 1955. Married 1) Elizabeth Browell Robson in 1955 (marriage dissolved, 1975); 2) the writer Lisa St. Aubin de Téran in 1982, one son. Producer, Overseas Talks Department, 1957, and Talks Department, 1958, and Editor, Poet's Voice, 1958-65, New Comment, 1959-64, and Poetry Now, 1965-76, BBC, London. Editor, Fantasy Poets series, Fantasy Press, Oxford, 1952-54. Recipient: Faber Memorial Award, 1964; Cholmondeley Award, 1977. Lives in Norfolk. Agent: Anthony Sheil Associates, 43 Doughty Street, London WC1N 2LF, England.

PUBLICATIONS

Verse

A Form of Words. Oxford, Fantasy Press, 1954.
Lecture to the Trainees. Oxford, Fantasy Press, 1962.
The Broken Places. Lowestoft, Suffolk, Scorpion Press, 1963; New York, Walker, 1968.
Penguin Modern Poets 6, with Jack Clemo and Edward Lucie-Smith. London, Penguin, 1964.
A Doomsday Book: Poems and Poem-Games. Lowestoft, Suffolk, Scorpion Press, 1965.
The Twelve Hotels. London, Turret, 1965.
Missile Commander. London, Turret, 1965.
The Calf. London, Turret, 1965.
The Humming Birds: A Monodrama. London, Turret, 1966.
The Castle. Privately printed, 1966.
The Screens. London, Turret, 1967.
The Colour of Blood. London, Macmillan, and New York, Atheneum, 1967.
The Night of Stones. London, Macmillan, 1968; New York, Atheneum, 1969.
A War Quartet. London, Macmillan, 1969.
A Death. Frensham, Surrey, Sceptre Press, 1969.
Zoo's Who. Privately printed, 1969.
The Burning Cone. London, Macmillan, 1970.
The Bamboo Nightingale. Frensham, Surrey, Sceptre Press, 1970.
Poems. Frensham, Surrey, Sceptre Press, 1970.
The Hiroshima Dream. London, Academy, 1970.
Two Poems. Fresham, Surrey, Sceptre Press, 1970.
A Prayer, Against Revenge. Rushden, Northamptonshire, Sceptre Press, 1971.
The Orlando Poems. London, Macmillan, 1971.
Collected Poems 1958-1970. London, Macmillan, 1971.
A Farewell. Rushden, Northamptonshire, Sceptre Press, 1972.

Lusus: A Verse Lecture.   London, Fuller d'Arch Smith, 1972.
A Litany.   Rushden, Northamptonshire, Sceptre Press, 1972.
Shrapnel.   London, Macmillan, 1973.
Prayers.   Solihull, Warwickshire, Aquila, 1973.
The Vision.   Rushden, Northamptonshire, Sceptre Press, 1973.
A Poet's Year.   London, Gollancz, 1973.
Shrapnel, and A Poet's Year.   New York, Atheneum, 1974.
Elegy for the Gas Dowsers.   Knotting, Bedfordshire, Sceptre Press, 1974.
In the Hours Waiting for the Blood to Come.   London, Gollancz, 1975.
The Journey to the Island.   Knotting, Bedfordshire, Sceptre Press, 1975.
Last Night.   Knotting, Bedfordshire, Sceptre Press, 1976.
Buying a Heart.   London, J. Jay, and New York, Atheneum, 1978.
The Saddled Man.   Richmond, Surrey, Keepsake Press, 1978.
Poem for Breathing.   Knotting, Bedfordshire, Sceptre Press, 1979.
Typing a Novel about the War.   Knotting, Bedfordshire, Sceptre Press, 1980.
Poems of Love and Death.   London, Secker and Warburg, and New York, Atheneum, 1980.
Poems from Oby.   London, Secker and Warburg, 1982; New York, Atheneum, 1983.
The Long Darkness.   London, Secker and Warburg, 1983; New York, Atheneum, 1984.

Plays

The Doomsday Show (produced London, 1964).   Published in *New English Dramatists 14*, London, Penguin, 1970.
The Scene-Machine, music by Anthony Gilbert (produced Kassel, Germany, 1971; London, 1972).   Mainz, Germany, Schott, 1971.

Novels

The Transformation.   London, Gollancz, 1975.
The Samurai.   New York, Harcourt Brace, 1975; London, Quartet, 1976.
The Survivor.   London, Quartet, 1977; New York, Harcourt Brace, 1978.
The Seven Witches.   London, W.H. Allen, and New York, Harcourt Brace, 1978; as *Cadbury and the Seven Witches*, London, New English Library, 1981.
The Born Losers.   London, New English Library, 1981.
A Kind of Treason.   London, Hodder and Stoughton, 1981; as *The Katana*, New York, Simon and Schuster, 1982.
Anna's Book.   London, Cape, 1983; New York, Holt Rinehart, 1984.
The Lion of Pescara.   London, Cape, 1984.

Other

Noah's Journey (for children).   London, Macmillan, and New York, Viking Press, 1966.
Jonah and the Lord (for children).   London, Macmillan, 1969; New York, Holt Rinehart, 1970.
My Scotland: Fragments of a State of Mind.   London, Macmillan, 1973.
The Rectory Mice (for children).   London, Hutchinson, 1982.

Editor, *The Penguin Book of Sick Verse.*   London, Penguin, 1963.

Editor, *The Penguin Book of Animal Verse.*   London, Penguin, 1965.
Editor, *Poetry 1900-1965: An Anthology.*   London, Longman-Faber, 1967; revised edition, 1979.
Editor, *The Penguin Book of Victorian Verse: A Critical Anthology.*   London, Penguin, 1969.
Editor, *The Falling Splendour: Poems of Alfred, Lord Tennyson.*   London, Macmillan, 1970.
Editor, with Martin Booth, *The Book of Cats.*   London, Secker and Warburg, 1976; New York, Morrow, 1977.
Editor, *Poetry for Today.*   London, Longman, 1983.

*

Manuscript Collections: University of California, Los Angeles; State University of New York, Buffalo.

Critical Studies: *The New Poets: American and British Poetry since World War II* by M.L. Rosenthal, New York and London, Oxford University Press, 1967; "The Poetry of George MacBeth" by D.M. Black, in *Scottish International* (Edinburgh), August 1968; Roger Garfitt, in *British Poetry since 1960*, edited by Michael Schmidt and Grevel Lindop, Oxford, Carcanet Press, 1972; *Travelling Through the Senses: A Critical Study of the Poetry of George MacBeth* by Martin Booth, Portree, Isle of Skye, Aquila, 1984.

*   *   *

George MacBeth is the most inventive poet of his generation in Britain. His fluency with ideas is accompanied by an equally pronounced skill in versification. He has been very influential, and although he is eclectic in style it is already possible to point to passages in other poets' work which show his influence. He disclaims the title of an intellectual, but he has a seminal intelligence which is perhaps the strongest in British poetry since Auden. Like Auden, he is a popular poet: even his most recondite pieces are written for the general public. Often he overestimates the public's willingness to work at a poem and consequently he can be obscure. But every poem is well planned—he is not hermetic and does not subscribe to a closed aesthetic order or a professional poets club in the manner of Robert Graves. He is a very prolific writer and publishes a lot in pamphlets and limited editions and his poems are often seen in magazines.

MacBeth's first book, *A Form of Words*, is now a collector's piece. These intellectual shavings from the later Caroline poets and from Empson were almost parodies, but revealed for the first time his playfulness with words. His second book, *The Broken Places*, is still, in many ways, his strongest. His preoccupation with violence and cruelty, which has been much remarked on, is present in this book in poems such as "Report to the Director," "The Disciple," "Drop," and "The Son," but so in other poems is a classically sustained note of elegy and a sympathetic talent for autobiography. It should be stressed that the caricature of him as a poet obsessed with the gamiest forms of nastiness is a simplification amounting to a calumny. *The Broken Places* also contains some of the first of MacBeth's dandified interpretations of the past. He has celebrated authors who are men of action like Hemingway and D'Annunzio and he has a natural sympathy for the larger-than-life artists of the late nineteenth century. One of the most original poems in *The Broken Places* is "The Spider's Nest," an ingenious monologue spoken by Eugene Lee-Hamilton, the crippled English poet who lived in Florence. Fin-de-siegle enthusiasms have grown on him until the diction and rhythms of some of his recent poems have acquired a drugged and purple solemnity which is not his best style.

A Doomsday Book is a collection of poems in honour of Homo Ludens, a figure MacBeth, like Auden, places very high in the Pantheon of fallen man. The tone of MacBeth's macabre jokes, such as "Fin-du-Globe" (an apocalyptic card-game poem) and "The Ski Murders," is equivocal. He has a love of picture-stories and games with rules and has used them in poems to take the portentousness out of death and violence. He is not frivolous but appears frequently as a player: his finest work is as detailed and energetic as a medieval Triumph of Death. Both *The Colour of Blood* and *The Night of Stones* show him continuing to explore his major themes but also experimenting with techniques of the avant-garde. MacBeth's originality as a poet lies in the use he makes of the hundreds of styles available to the modern poet. He is not a dedicated innovator and after producing a suitably outrageous experimental poem, he will often write another in a traditional mode. His realisations of Chinese poems in *The Colour of Blood* are hilarious bits of chinoiserie and show him ready to use concrete poetry and sound poetry for his own purposes. In his copious output there are many remarkable poems about animals and a number of successful ones for children, of which "Noah's Journey" is the most considerable. "At Crufts" and "Fourteen Ways of Touching the Peter" from *The Night of Stones* are vignettes in syllabics of pedigree dogs and his own cat. Here is part of his description of the Chow: "your / tail / over-curled / as if attempting / to open / yourself / like a tin / of pilchards...."

MacBeth's copiousness continued unchecked throughout the first part of the 1970's, resulting in such forays into his chosen worlds as *A War Quartet*, where four scenes from the Second World War, including the Axis viewpoint (U boats and Stalingrad), were shaped into dramatic monologues, *My Scotland*, a wryly poetic collection of pensées on his natal land, rather like poisoned shortbread in tartan wrappers, and *Lusus*, a highly original verse essay on poetic metre. The publication of his *Collected Poems* in 1971 may be seen retrospectively as a watershed in MacBeth's artistic career. Much was omitted from this attempt at a canon, though he reprinted excellent uncollected poems such as "The Crab-Apple Crisis" and "Amelia's Will." Soon after this he left his job as a BBC Radio Producer partly to follow a new career as a novelist. It is not the business of this brief essay to try to assess his novelistic output: it will suffice to say that he believes that the erotic need not be unbeautiful and that the extravagant may yet be house-trained. The most successful of his several novels is a recent one, *Anna's Book*, based on a Swedish attempt to traverse the North Pole by balloon in the early years of this century. It is, however, the series of "Cadbury" novels, openly erotic fantasies, which has brought him public success as a writer of prose.

From the middle of the 1970's onwards, MacBeth's poetry has shown a marked shift away from the gamey and extravagant forms once so favoured by him towards the more formal side of his craft. This progress has been gradual, so that *In the Hours Waiting for the Blood to Come* and *Buying a Heart* are still possessed of a ludic quirkiness which often flowers into types of arcane beauty. In the later 1970's MacBeth went to live in Norfolk on the Broads in an old rectory, and the books which have resulted from his rural life are much more relaxed and almost serene. He has moved house again—this time nearer the Wash—and we may expect his forthcoming work to continue the country-calendar mode which marks *Poems from Oby* and *The Long Darkness*. In these books strict shapes and formal versification do not serve a classical and marmoreal gravitas as once they did for him, but are devoted to everyday matters of domestic living and the small-scale genocides of animal and insect life. But, as *Poems of Love and Death* reveals, MacBeth

remains one of the few British poets who tackles important subjects on a large scale.

—Peter Porter

———————

MacCAIG, Norman (Alexander). Scottish. Born in Edinburgh, 14 November 1910. Educated at Royal High School, Edinburgh; Edinburgh University, M.A. (honours) in classics 1932. Married Isabel Munro in 1940; one son and one daughter. Schoolteacher, 1934-67, and Headmaster, 1969-70, Edinburgh; Fellow in Creative Writing, Edinburgh University, 1967-69; Lecturer in English Studies, 1970-72, and Reader in Poetry, 1972-77, University of Stirling. Recipient: Scottish Arts Council Award, 1954, 1966, 1970, 1971, 1978, 1980, 1984; Society of Authors travelling scholarship, 1964, prize, 1967; Heinemann Award, 1967; Cholmondeley Award, 1975. D. Univ.: University of Stirling, 1981; D.Litt.: Edinburgh University, 1983. Associate, Royal Scottish Academy; Fellow, Royal Society of Edinburgh; Fellow, Royal Society of Literature, 1965. O.B.E. (Officer, Order of the British Empire), 1979. Address: 7 Leamington Terrace, Edinburgh EH10 4JW, Scotland.

PUBLICATIONS

Verse

Far Cry. London, Routledge, 1943.
The Inward Eye. London, Routledge, 1946.
Riding Lights. London, Hogarth Press, 1955; New York, Macmillan, 1956.
The Sinai Sort. London, Hogarth Press, and New York, Macmillan, 1957.
A Common Grace. London, Chatto and Windus-Hogarth Press, 1960.
A Round of Applause. London, Chatto and Windus-Hogarth Press, 1962.
Measures. London, Chatto and Windus, 1965.
Surroundings. London, Chatto and Windus-Hogarth Press, 1966.
Rings on a Tree. London, Chatto and Windus-Hogarth Press, 1968.
A Man in My Position. London, Chatto and Windus-Hogarth Press, 1969.
Midnights. London, Poem-of-the-Month Club, 1970.
Three Manuscript Poems. Exeter, Devon, Rougemont Press, 1970.
Selected Poems. London, Hogarth Press, 1971.
Penguin Modern Poets 21, with George Mackay Brown and Iain Crichton Smith. London, Penguin, 1972.
The White Bird. London, Chatto and Windus, 1973.
The World's Room. London, Chatto and Windus, 1974.
Three Poems. Stirling, Stirling University, 1975.
Nothing Too Much and Other Poems. Stirling, Stirling University, 1976.
Tree of Strings. London, Chatto and Windus-Hogarth Press, 1977.
Inchnadamph and Other Poems. Stirling, Stirling University Press Room, 1978.
Old Maps and New: Selected Poems. London, Chatto and Windus-Hogarth Press, 1978.

The Equal Skies. London, Chatto and Windus-Hogarth Press, 1980.
A World of Difference. London, Chatto and Windus, 1983.

Other

Editor, *Honour'd Shade: An Anthology of New Scottish Poetry to Mark the Bicentenary of the Birth of Robert Burns.* Edinburgh, Chambers, 1959.
Editor, with Alexander Scott, *Contemporary Scottish Verse 1959-1969.* London, Calder and Boyars, 1970.

*

Critical Studies: in *Akros 7* (Preston, Lancashire), 1968; *"Unemphatic Marvels": A Study of Norman MacCaig's Poetry* by Erik Frykman, Gothenburg, Sweden, Gothenburg Studies in English, 1977.

* * *

Norman MacCaig began his poetic career as one of the most apocalyptic of all the White Horseman's Scottish followers with the two collections *Far Cry* and *The Inward Eye.* Like most of the movement's writers, his verse lunged about in a climate of uncontrolled Romanticism.

I brought you elephants and volcano tops
and a eucalyptus tree on a coral island.
I had them in baskets. You looked with surprise
and went away to pick weeds out of the garden....

Nine years elapsed before MacCaig's next book, *Riding Lights,* appeared; with it the real poet emerged, his imagery now disciplined and sensuously relevant. The book explores his perhaps initally Donne-inspired thematic preoccupation, the relationship of the seeing eye to the world of appearances:

Straws like tame lightnings lie about the grass
And hang zigzag on hedges. Green as glass
The water in the horse-trough shines.
Nine ducks go wobbling by in two straight lines....

Self under self, a pile of selves I stand
Threaded on time, and with metaphysic hand
Lift the farm like a lid and see
Farm within farm, and in centre, me.

For the next decade or so, MacCaig concentrated on exploring, through the physical geography of his two worlds of Edinburgh and the West Highlands, the endlessly variable relationship of the observer to the observed, enriching and often surprising the perceptions of his readers in the doing.

By the mid-1960's, there were some who felt that MacCaig had become merely repetitive, playing variants on his intellect with a limited number of themes (a criticism that overlooks the sheerly enjoyable quality of so much of the contents of each succeeding volume in the 1950's and early 1960's). With *Surroundings* and *Rings on a Tree,* however, he confounded his critics. Visits to Italy and America opened up new reaches and possibilities. The structure of his verse forms loosened, the variety of his themes increased, a tone of accepting sadness became more apparent and in poems like "Assisi" and "Visiting Hour" the metaphysical "royal me" of his New Apocalypse 'prentice days (never wholly tamed, though long since trained to an original and observant

maturity) moved over to allow emotional room for wider compassion.

The poetry of his later years, though still nerved by his metaphysical preoccupation, has lost none of its delicate accuracy of seeing, its rock-sure handling of language. The imagery, for the most part, has become more fundamental to the direction of his thought, stripped to the bareness of necessity and now only occasionally relaxing into the sensuous ornamentation that regularly graced so many of his middle-period poems. Meanwhile, the poet has noticeably sharpened his wit on the edge of his own wryness, as in "Gone Are the Days" (*The World's Room*):

Impossible to call a lamb a lambkin
or say eftsoons or spell you ladye.
My shining armour bleeds when it's scratched;
I blow the nose that's part of my visor....
So don't expect me, lady with no e,
To look at a lamb and feel lambkin
or give me a down look because I bought
my greaves and cuisses at Marks and Spencers.

Pishtushery's out....

Sometimes in the later work, his metaphor of speculation is not always quite strong enough to support a particular poem, and one is left with a slightly uncomfortable sense of cleverness, a thing constructed for its own sake (a danger to which metaphysicians of every sort constantly lay themselves open). But there has not yet been a MacCaig volume without a number of new poems outstanding even when measured against his own lengthening achievement. MacCaig's territories both of the physical country and of experience, though now creatively fairly fully charted, still seem capable of yielding surprises.

In his increasing communal concern, particularly for the way of life of the people of his beloved Sutherlandshire, MacCaig may perhaps be seen as a kind of Scottish counterpart to R. S. Thomas, though with a metaphysical rather than a Christian bent of tolerance. Certainly, as Thomas has made the harsh enduring of the Welsh small farm tradition comprehensible to the rest of the English-speaking world, so MacCaig, with an alert freshness of the imagination that belies the Scottish metaphysical tradition from which (in part at least) he springs, has illumined an aspect of mind that has played a major part in the shaping of the Scottish character. Since the death of MacDiarmid in 1978, the mantle of Scotland's *eminence grise* has fallen upon MacCaig. Yet his contribution to poetry in English written during the second half of the 20th century is as enjoyably individual as it is richly distinguished.

—Maurice Lindsay

—————

MacEWEN, Gwendolyn (Margaret). Canadian. Born in Toronto, Ontario, 1 September 1941. Educated in public and secondary schools. Married 1) Milton Acorn, *q.v.*; 2) Nikos Tsingos in 1972. Full-time writer; Writer-in-Residence, University of Western Ontario, London, 1984-85. Recipient: CBC Prize, 1965; Governor-General's Award, 1970; Canada Council grant, 1973, 1977, 1981; A.J.M. Smith Award, 1973; Du Maurier Gold and Silver awards, 1983. Lives in Toronto. Address: Writers Union of Canada, 24 Ryerson Avenue, Toronto, Ontario M5T 2P3, Canada.

PUBLICATIONS

Verse

Selah; The Drunken Clock. Toronto, Aleph Press, 1961.
The Rising Fire. Toronto, Contact Press, 1963.
A Breakfast for Barbarians. Toronto, Ryerson Press, 1966.
The Shadow-Maker. Toronto, Macmillan, 1969.
The Armies of the Moon. Toronto, Macmillan, 1972.
Magic Animals: Selected Poems, Old and New. Toronto, Macmillan, 1975.
The Fire-Eaters. Ottawa, Oberon Press, 1976.
Trojan Women (includes play and translations from Yannis Ritsos). Toronto, Exile, 1981.
The T.E. Lawrence Poems. Oakville, Ontario, Mosaic Press, 1982.
Earthlight 1968-1982: Selected Poetry. Toronto, General, 1982.

Recording: *Open Secrets,* CBC, 1972.

Plays

Terror and Erebus (broadcast, 1965). Published in *Tamarack Review* (Toronto), October 1974.
The Trojan Women, adaptation of a play by Euripides (produced Toronto, 1978). Toronto, Playwrights, 1979.

Radio Plays: *Terror and Erebus,* 1965; *Tesla,* 1966; *The World of Neshiah,* 1967; *The Last Night of James Pike,* 1976.

Novels

Julian the Magician. Toronto, Macmillan, and New York, Corinth, 1963.
King of Egypt, King of Dreams. Toronto, Macmillan, 1972.

Short Stories

Noman. Ottawa, Oberon Press, 1972.

Other

Mermaids and Ikons: A Greek Summer. Toronto, Anansi, 1978.
The Chocolate Moose (for children). Toronto, NC Press, 1981.
The Honey Drum (for children). Oakville, Ontario, Mosaic Press, 1983.

*

Manuscript Collection: University of Toronto.

Critical Studies: "A Complex Music" by George Bowering, in *Canadian Literature 21* (Vancouver), 1964; *Butterfly on Rock* by Doug Jones, Toronto, University of Toronto Press, 1970; "MacEwen's Muse," in *Canadian Literature 45* (Vancouver), 1970, *Survival,* Toronto, Anansi, 1972, and *Second Words,* Toronto, Anansi, 1982, Boston, Beacon Press, 1984, all by Margaret Atwood; "The Secret of Alchemy," in *Open Letter* (Toronto), Spring 1973, and *From Here to There,* Erin, Ontario, Press Porcépic, 1974, both by Frank Davey; "A Broken Bundle of Mirrors" by Gordon Johnson, in *Canadian Forum* (Toronto), January 1983; *Invocations: The Poetry and Prose of Gwendolyn MacEwen* by Jan Bartley, Vancouver, University of British Columbia Press, 1983.

Gwendolyn MacEwen comments:

I write in order to make sense of the chaotic nature of experience—and also to create a bridge between the inner world of the *psyche* and the "outer" world of things. For me, language has enormous, almost magical power, and I tend to regard poetry in much the same way as the ancients regarded the chants or hymns used in holy festivals—as a means of invoking the mysterious forces which move the world and shape our destinies.

I write to communicate joy, mystery, passion...not the joy that naively exists without knowledge of pain, but that joy which arises out of and conquers pain. I want to construct a myth.

*   *   *

"Gwendolyn MacEwen is preoccupied with time and its multiple meanings, with the ambivalences of existence, with the archetypal patterns that emerge and re-emerge from ancient times to now," as George Woodcock wrote in his entry devoted to the poet in the *Supplement to the Oxford Companion to Canadian History and Literature* (1973). This may be so, yet the explanation seems heavy beside the achievement, which is light, graceful, imaginative, and refreshingly free of pretension.

The quest for a leader, or saviour, or cultural hero, has taken MacEwen through two novels and a collection of short stories, all essentially poetic. *Julian the magician* creates an imaginary alchemist out of wholecloth. With *King of Egypt, King of Dreams,* she finds her mythic man in the person of Ikhnaton, the heretic-pharaoh of Ancient Egypt, and this permits her to present the vision in the form of historical fiction. Perhaps the most successful of the prose works is *Noman,* in which the poet's fancy is free to make wide connections without the need to create a credible personality for her mysterious "Noman." The elusive figure, a kind of Jean Sans Terre, "became whatever he encountered."

If *Noman* is poetry written in the form of prose, MacEwen's books of verse are very much poetry. From *The Rising Fire* (1963) to *The Armies of the Moon* (1972), her poems have grown more self-contained and her vision of the magical properties of everyday things has grown clearer. Like a mediaeval alchemist, she turns base experiences into rare epiphanies. Coupled with the imaginative insights there is a *fey* quality to her writing which, playful and elusive, may be found in her description, say, of a cat hiding behind its own shadow, or her lines "there are so many places for places to hide," or her view that the moon is sending Morse Code messages to the earth. And in "The Vacuum Cleaner Dream" she imagines herself an angelic char "vacuuming the universe." It is only slightly upsetting when she finds among the debris "the sleeping body of my love."

A sense of the magic and wonderful movement of MacEwen's work can be felt in the final stanza of "The Discovery," from *The Shadow-Maker*:

> When you see the land naked, look again
> (burn your maps, that is not what I mean),
> I mean the moment when it seems most plain
> is the moment when you must begin again.

—John Robert Colombo

MACKIE, Alastair (Webster). Scottish. Born in Aberdeen, 10 August 1925. Educated at Skene Square School, 1930-37; Robert Gordon's College, Aberdeen, 1937-43; University of

Aberdeen, 1946-50, M.A. (honours) in English 1950. Served in the Royal Air Force, 1943, and the Royal Navy, 1944-46. Married Elizabeth Law in 1951; two children. English teacher, Stromness Academy, Orkney, 1951-59. Since 1959, English teacher, Waid Academy, Anstruther, Fife. Recipient: Saltire Prize, 1963; Scottish Arts Council bursary, 1976. Address: 13 St. Adrian's Place, Anstruther, Fife, Scotland.

PUBLICATIONS

Verse

Soundings. Preston, Lancashire, Akros, 1966.
To Duncan Glen. Preston, Lancashire, Akros, 1971.
Clytach. Preston, Lancashire, Akros, 1972.
At the Heich Kirk-Yaird: A Hielant Sequence. Preston, Lancashire, Akros, 1974.

Other

Editor, Four Gates of Lothian and Other Poems, by Forbes Macgregor. Privately printed, 1979.

*

Critical Studies: introduction to Contemporary Scottish Verse 1959-1969 edited by Norman MacCaig and Alexander Scott, London, Calder and Boyars, 1970, and articles in Glasgow Review 1, Summer 1972, and The MacDiarmid Makars 1923-1972, Preston, Lancashire, Akros, 1972, both by Scott; Whither Scotland? edited by Duncan Glen, London, Gollancz, 1971; by Robert Garioch in Lines Review 42-43 (Edinburgh), 1972; "The Progress of Scots" by J. Herdman, in Akros 20 (Preston, Lancashire), 1972; J.A.K. Annand and Donald Campbell, in Akros 21 (Preston, Lancashire), 1973; Two North-East Makars: Alexander Scott and Alastair Mackie: A Study of Their Scots Poetry by Leonard Mason, Preston, Lancashire, Akros, 1975; "The Poetry of Alastair Mackie" by George Bruce, in Akros 33 (Preston, Lancashire), April 1977.

Alastair Mackie comments:
   My work is directed towards developing the limits of Scots as a vehicle for poetry in the contemporary setting as I am placed in regard to it. I continue the work of MacDiarmid and attempt to annex areas where his influence has not extended. For example, I have written a space sequence in Scots called "Captus Cupidine Coeli." I work for a more extended canon of Scots in order to give Scots poetry bulk and variety. I am more attracted to English translations of European poets—Amichai, Holub, Herbert—than to any contemporary English poetry.

*   *   *

   The publication of Alastair Mackie's collection of poems, Clytach (barbarous words) was a matter of consequence to the continuing tradition of poetry in Scots. The book is yet another vindication of the claim Hugh MacDiarmid made 50 years previously to the effect that poetry in the Scots tongue could still contribute apprehensions and perceptions relevant to contemporary life which could not be conveyed in English. In his previous collection, Soundings, Mackie's poems in English showed terseness and temper. In his "Notes on 'The Truce' by Primo Levi" he writes:

Auschwitz in due time
exported its surplus

Afterwards, the truce
when the soiled ex-objects

took to trains and began
their picaresque novels.

This tight-lipped speech has a secure base in the Aberdeenshire dialect which was Alastair Mackie's birthright, though the style witnesses to other influences. His poems in Scots, however, have a rich texture and an intimate responsiveness to his subjects, as well as an ironic turn of phrase that is art and part of his Scots idiom. The wide range of the poet's interests is evident from the titles of the poems in Clytach. These include: "The Cosmonaut Hero," "Binary Sets," "Orpheus and Eurydice," "Lines from Mallarmé," "Leopardi on the Hill," "Scots Pegasus," and "Still-Life: Cézanne." Just how appropriate his Scots is to this last subject is clear even from a few phrases. He describes the table on which the apples are set: "The white claith wid aye jist / cowp doun like a lynn aneth the aipples' wecht" [the white cloth would always just tumble down like a waterfall beneath the apples' weight]. He again refers to the apples in the phrase "Yon was mason's work." To re-enact in words the sense of durability and solidity—as if it were the weight of the world that was being presented—requires a language that has retained physical characteristics. One of the best poems that Mackie has written, "Mongul Quine" (Mongol Girl), presents the child with a blunt directness that draws one up sharply. Mackie writes—"Her blond baa-heid wags [Her blond ball-head wags]/frae side to side"—yet the poem ends gently and mysteriously with the words: "Ayont the hert-brak her een / are set for ever on an unkent airt" [Beyond the heartbreak her eyes are set forever on an unknown place].

   Though the Scots may initially daunt readers unacquainted with it, the centrality of Mackie's interest and comments makes a study of the work of this writer very desirable for all interested in the developments in contemporary poetry.

—George Bruce

MACLEAN, Alasdair. Scottish. Born in Glasgow, Lanarkshire, 16 March 1926. Recipient: Cholmondeley Award 1974; Heinemann Award, 1974. Address: Sanna, Kilchoan, Ardnamurchan, Argyllshire, Scotland.

PUBLICATIONS

Verse

From the Wilderness. London, Gollancz, 1973; New York, Harper, 1975.
Waking the Dead. London, Gollancz, 1976.

Other

Night Falls on Ardnamurchan. London, Gollancz, 1984.

*   *   *

The attempt to come to grips with the fundamental questions about life with which serious literature ought to concern itself need not of itself relate to the physical location of the writer. Alasdair Maclean left university to work a croft near Ardnamurchan, in Argyll. *From the Wilderness* did not appear before the public until he was into his forties, although something of his quality could be seen from anthologised poems in the annual *Scottish Poetry* and others. He is therefore a late starter, at any rate so far as publication is concerned. All to the good, since it means that for the most part he wants to say things, not merely to gyrate like some youthful virtuoso for the sake of attracting fashionable attention. He also has an assured and personal voice.

He tells his reader bluntly what to expect from him:

> I leave the foothills of the images
> and climb. What I pursue's not means but ends.
> You may come, if you've a mind to travelling.
> Meet me at the point where the language bends.

At his best, Maclean writes with a hard, direct economy, drawing his imagery and the strength of his thought from the way of life he loves and with which he is familiar. For instance, there is the countryman's unsentimental approach to matters of life and death, focussed into "Hen Dying":

> The other hens have cast her out.
> They batter her with their beaks
> Whenever they come across her.
> Most of them are her daughters.
> Hens are inhuman.

His poems "Rams," using the same terse short-sentence style, builds up a powerful apprehension of nature's sexual prodigality, and mindless directorial force, a fact which the ingenuity of *homo sapiens* often contrives for comfort to fudge:

> I found a ram dead once.
> It was trapped by the forefeet
> in the dark waters of a peatbog,
> drowned before help could arrive
> by the sheer weight of its skull.
> Maiden ewes were grazing near it,
> immune to its clangerous lust.
> It knelt on the bank, hunched over its own image
> its great head buried in the great head facing it.
> Its horns, going forward in the old way,
> had battered through at last to the other side.

Not a word, not a rhythm is false there; and Maclean has many poems with this quality in his first collection. There is also some harsh satire apparently arising, though not always admitting such origin, out of the unconfessed awareness of the Gael that his way of life and his culture are now peripheral, and that, rant as he may against the urban-dwelling Lowlander, the Gael himself has been his own worst enemy. Not all of these outbursts are entirely plausible, as in "Eagles":

> An eagle of that breed once, for a joke,
> picked up a stunted Highlander
> and flew him south, witless from the journey
> but fertile still,
> Hence your race of Lowlands Scots.

Inevitably, as in every collection, there are some bookfiller pieces in which there is evident the metaphysical influence of the later, and poetically drier, Norman MacCaig; such a poem is "Sea and Sky," its feyly sentimental conclusion so out of keeping with the firmness of this poet's best texture and direct-sounding voice. Fanciful trifling of that sort is far below the level of a poet who can ring fierce, rough honesty out of the stoney fields of Ardnamurchan, and the hard life their isolation demands. To me, Maclean is certainly the most interesting Scottish poet to make his appearance for at least a couple of decades.

—Maurice Lindsay

MAC LOW, Jackson. American. Born in Chicago, Illinois, 12 September 1922. Educated at the University of Chicago, 1939-43, A.A. 1941; Brooklyn College, New York, 1955-58, A.B. (cum laude) in Greek 1958. Formerly married to the painter Iris Lezak; two children. Free-lance music teacher, English teacher, translator, and editor, 1950-66; reference book editor, Funk and Wagnalls, 1957-58, 1961-62, and Unicorn Books, 1958-59; copy editor, Alfred A. Knopf, 1965-66, all in New York. Member of the editorial staff, and Poetry Editor, 1950-54, *Why?*, later *Resistance*, a pacifist-anarchist magazine. Instructor, American Language Institute, New York University, 1966-73. Poetry Editor, *WIN* magazine, New York, 1966-75. Recipient: Creative Artists Public Service grant, 1973, 1976; P.E.N. grant, 1974; National Endowment for the Arts fellowship, 1979. Address: 42 North Moore Street, New York, New York 10013, U.S.A.

PUBLICATIONS

Verse

The Pronouns: A Collection of 40 Dances—for the Dancers—6 February—22 March 1964. New York, Jackson Mac Low, 1964; London, Tetrad Press, 1970.
August Light Poems. New York, Eshleman, 1967.
22 Light Poems. Los Angeles, Black Sparrow Press, 1968.
23rd Light Poem: For Larry Eigner. London, Tetrad Press, 1969.
Stanzas for Iris Lezak. New York, Something Else Press, 1970.
4 Trains, 4-5 December 1964. Providence, Rhode Island, Burning Deck, 1974.
36th Light Poem: In Memoriam Buster Keaton. London, Permanent Press, 1975.
21 Matched Asymmetries. London, Aloes, 1978.
A Dozen Douzains for Eve Rosenthal. Toronto, Gronk, 1978.
Phone. New York, Printed Editions, 1979.
Asymmetries 1-260. New York, Printed Editions, 1980.
Antic Quatrains. Minneapolis, Bookslinger, 1980.
From Pearl Harbor Day to FDR's Birthday. College Park, Maryland, Sun and Moon, 1982.
"Is That Wool Hat My Hat?" Milwaukee, Membrane Press, 1983.

Recordings: *A Reading of Primitive and Archaic Poems*, with others, Broadside; *From a Shaman's Notebook*, with others, Broadside.

Plays

The Marrying Maiden: A Play of Changes, music by John Cage
(produced New York, 1960).
Verdurous Sanguinaria (produced New York, 1961).   Baton
Rouge, Louisiana, Southern University, 1967.
Thanks: A Simultaneity for People (produced Wiesbaden,
1962).
Letters for Iris, Numbers for Silence (produced Wiesbaden,
1962).
A Piece for Sari Dienes (produced Wiesbaden, 1962).
Thanks II (produced Paris, 1962).
The Twin Plays: Port-au-Prince, and Adams County, Illinois
(produced New York, 1963).   New York, Mac Low and Bloe-
dow, 1963.
Questions and Answers: A Topical Play (produced New York,
1963).   New York, Mac Low and Bloedow, 1963.
Asymmetries No. 408, 410, 485 (produced New York, 1965).
Asymmetries, Gathas and Sounds from Everywhere (produced
New York, 1966).
A Vocabulary for Carl Fernbach-Flarsheim (produced New
York, 1977).

Composer: incidental music for *The Age of Anxiety* by W.H.
Auden, produced New York, 1954; for *The Heroes* by John
Ashbery, produced New York, 1955.

*

Theatrical Activities:
Actor: **Plays**—in *Tonight We Improvise* by Pirandello, New
York, 1959, and other plays.

Jackson Mac Low comments:
I consider myself a composer: of poetry, music, and theatre
works.
I do not think that I belong to any particular school of poetry,
but my work, especially that of 1954-80, is closely related to that
of such composers as John Cage, Morton Feldman, Earle
Brown, Christian Wolff, and La Monte Young, and it has close
affinities with the work of such "concrete" poets as Emmett
Williams.
While my earliest work (1937-40) uses mostly free verse and
experimental forms, the poems between 1940 and 1954 tend to
alternate between traditional metrical forms (and variations on
them) and experimental forms, most of which are varieties of
free verse. However, from 1954, the poems, plays, and simultaneities incorporate methods, processes, and devices from modern music, including the use of chance operations in composition
and/or performance, silences ranging in duration from breath
pauses to several minutes, and various degrees of improvisation
by performers. Many of the works are "simultaneities"—works
performed by several speakers and/or producers of musical
sounds and noises at once. These range from completely instrumental pieces (e.g., "Chamber Music for Barney Childs," 1963;
"Winds/Instruments," 1980), through works combining speech
and other sounds (e.g., *Stanzas for Iris Lezak* as simultaneity,
1960), to ones involving only speech (e.g., "Peaks and Lamas,"
1959). Other features include indeterminacy (the quality of a
work which is in many ways different at every performance) and
various degrees of "syntacticalness," ranging from structures
that are essentially strings of unrelated words to ones that are
partially or fully syntactical in the ordinary sense of the word.
Works after 1960 use various proportions of chance and choice

in composition and performance. Some performance poems
(e.g., "Velikovsky Dice-Song," 1968; "A Vocabulary for Annie
Brigitte Gilles Tardos," 1979) incorporate multiple slide projections or films.
After November 1981 most of my poems and prose works
have been written directly (without use of chance operations,or
similar systems) although some chance operations have been
employed in composing performance works. Performers' choices usually figure largely in performances of the latter. I have
also written and recorded four radio works—three for West-
deutscher Rundfunk, Cologne (1981, 1983, and 1984) and one
for a production group in New York (1984).

*   *   *

Jackson Mac Low's multifarious activities as an artist are all
directed toward the exploration of limits and boundaries: the
boundary between poetry and music, poetry and drama, even
poetry and dance; or, taken differently, the limits of the ego, of
will, of meaning, of significant order. Although he has written in
traditional metrical forms and continues to write in an uninhibited variety of free verse which he calls "spontaneous expression," his most characteristic work is an investigation of indeterminacy, chance, and improvisation. His language frequently
breaks down to the phonemic level and becomes pure sound. Its
meaning derives directly from its structure rather than—like
traditional poetry—from its semantic content. In a world in
which all meaning appears to become increasingly statistical, the
evidence of Mac Low's poetry is of central importance.
The sources of Mac Low's work are diverse. He was educated
as a neo-Aristotelian at the University of Chicago, and he
remains, in a sense, a classical formalist. He is, however, also a
self-proclaimed anarchist and, like John Cage, he has been
heavily influenced by Buddhist thought. His practice embodies
these ideas in microcosm with remarkable consistency by creating works, as he says, "wherein both other human beings & their
environments & the world 'in general' (as represented by such
objectively hazardous means as random digits) are all able to act
within the general framework & set of 'rules' given by the poet
'the maker of plots or fables' as Aristotle insists—not necessarily
of everything that takes place within that framework!"
At its simplest Mac Low's theory produces work like "The
Phone Poems," a suite of randomly-generated variations on one
of his spontaneous poems. Mac Low, however, is primarily a
performance poet, and many of his most characteristic pieces—
the gathas and other similar pieces written on graph paper, for
example—are not well published. ("5th Gatha" in *America: a
Prophecy*, edited by Jerome Rothenberg and George Quasha,
1973, is one of the most widely available examples of these
works.) Typically, in the grid poems, he randomly selects words
or phrases from some vocabulary source and arranges them on
the grid by predetermined rules. In performance, this "score"
becomes the basis for rule-governed improvisation. Although
the rules vary from piece to piece, Mac Low always insists that it
is an exercise in listening: the performers are asked to give
careful attention to the overall form as it develops and to try to
contribute to the dynamics of the whole. The performance, in
other words, becomes an exploration of group psychology and
social order.
In *22 Light Poems*, which is perhaps Mac Low's most beautifully conceived book, the central device is a more or less randomly prepared chart which is keyed to playing cards. "1st Light
Poem" is purely a result of random selections from the chart.
Others admit "coincidental" input from the environment in
which the poem is written (a radio, for example), allow concrete
events to stand in place of poems, or freely mix his own spon-

taneous expression with random material. In one of the light poems written since the publication of the book—there are now thirty-six or more—he allows his numerous typing errors to stand. Despite the indeterminacy, however, *22 Light Poems*, as well as imaginative realizations of the dances in *The Pronouns*, withstand rigorous formal analysis. Order, given an opportunity, thrives.

Mac Low's work adduces cogent evidence that the classic western attitudes toward meaning derive from categorical distinctions which result alternatively in radical isolation of consciousness and ruthless exploitation of the external world. The act of poem as Mac Low conceives it, rather than isolating the poet in his vision, opens free and useful intercourse between the poet and the external world.

—Don Byrd

MACNAB, Roy (Martin).   South African.   Born in Durban, 17 September 1923. Educated at Hilton College, Natal; Jesus College, Oxford, M.A. Naval Officer, 1942-45. Married to Rachel Mary Heron-Maxwell; one son and one daughter. Cultural Attaché, South African High Commission, London, 1955-59; Counsellor for Cultural and Press Affairs, South African Embassy, Paris, 1959-67; Director, South Africa Foundation, London, 1968-84. Fellow, Royal Society of Arts (UK). Address: c/o Travellers Club, London S.W.1, England.

PUBLICATIONS

Verse

Testament of a South African.   London, Fortune Press, 1947.
The Man of Grass and Other Poems.   London, St. Catherine Press, 1960.
Winged Quagga, with *Reassembling World*, by Douglas Reid Skinner.   Cape Town, David Philip, 1981.

Other

South and Central Africa.   New York, McGraw Hill, 1954.
Journey into Yesterday: South African Milestones in Europe. Cape Town, H. Timmins, and London, Bailey Brothers and Swinfen, 1962.
The Youngest Literary Language: The Story of Afrikaans.   Johannesburg, South African Broadcasting Corporation, 1973.
The French Colonel: Villebois-Mareuil and the Boers 1899-1900.   Cape Town and London, Oxford University Press, 1975.
The English-Speaking South Africans.   Johannesburg, South African Broadcasting Corporation, 1975.
The Story of South Africa House.   Johannesburg, Jonathan Ball, 1983.

Editor, with Martin Starkie, *Oxford Poetry 1947.*   Oxford, Blackwell, 1947.
Editor, with Charles Gulston, *South African Poetry: A New Anthology.*   London, Collins, 1948.
Editor, *Towards the Sun: A Miscellany of South Africa.*   London, Collins, 1950.
Editor, *Poets in South Africa: An Anthology.*   Cape Town, Maskew Miller, 1958.

*

Manuscript Collection: Thomas Pringle Collection, Rhodes University, Grahamstown.

Critical Studies: by Anthony Delius, in *Books Abroad* (Norman, Oklahoma), Summer 1955; Guy Butler, in *Listener* (London), 24 May 1956; William Plomer, in *London Magazine*, February 1957; *A Critical Survey of South African Poetry in English*, by G.M. Miller and Howard Sergeant, Cape Town, Balkema, 1957; *South African Poetry*, Pretoria, University of South Africa, 1966.

*   *   *

Roy Macnab's first book of poetry strikes the reader as a very sincere attempt to convey the poet's thoughts and feelings, but unfortunately the result is somewhat obscured by his struggle with words, a struggle which he seems to have been aware of himself in "The Word":

> Said he, the word is a faithless flirt,
> Not a lover to your art,
> Deceiving with a warm coquetry
> Your dreamfilled youth
> A spidery dilettante, fondling
> Your silver web of thought.

Half-hidden behind this veil of words one senses a very genuine feeling for nature, a deep compassion for the less fortunate among his fellow men and a natural tenderness which finds its best expression in the poem "To a Child." In the poem "The Sick Room" this compassion rises to an impotent fury which unfortunately spoils the poetry and thus proves the truism that genuine involvement does not guarantee genuine poetry.

Although the poems cover a variety of subjects, one experience seems to overshadow all other events in the author's life—his active participation in the Second World War. This experience left him with a feeling of restless discontent and, like the soldiers of Erich Remarque's books he is constantly searching for a meaning or a purpose in his present life that is noble enough to merit the sacrifices of the war that made it possible, and he is inevitably disappointed. His heroes come back from the War "Battered but unbroken in the time of test," and this is what they find (in "From Turning Tomorrow's Pages"):

> Reluctantly turning tomorrow's pages
> Where no new sensation is stored,
> Only the inevitable dullness of Friday's wages
> And further occasion for being bored.

Even those soldiers who died on the battlefield are not allowed to rest in peace, and Macnab is haunted by the knowledge that consequent ages may change their attitude to his heroes. This feeling he expresses in one of his most successful poems, "El-Alamein Revisited":

> Six feet is no depth for tragic men
> Said the wind and the wind never ceases
> To pile up high the soft grey tombs,
> And move them where it pleases....

In his disgust with urban life and its tedium Macnab turns to the pioneers, the settlers, the seekers of gold, for it is in these people that he finds the spirit of exploration that so obviously appeals to him.

—Kirsten Holst Petersen

MACPHERSON, (Jean) Jay. Canadian. Born in London, England, 13 June 1931; emigrated to Canada in 1940. Educated at Carleton University, Ottawa, B.A. 1951; University College, London, 1951-52; University of Toronto, M.A. 1955, Ph.D. 1964. Since 1957, Member of the Department of English, currently Professor, Victoria College, University of Toronto. Recipient: *Contemporary Verse* prize, 1949; Levinson Prize (*Poetry*, Chicago), 1957; President's Medal, University of Western Ontario, 1957; Governor-General's Award, 1958. Address: Victoria College, University of Toronto, Toronto M5S 1K7 Canada.

PUBLICATIONS

Verse

Nineteen Poems. Deyá, Mallorca, Seizin Press, 1952.
O Earth Return. Toronto, Emblem, 1954.
The Boatman. Toronto, Oxford University Press, 1957.
Welcoming Disaster: Poems 1970-1974. Toronto, Saannes, 1974.
Poems Twice Told (includes *The Boatman* and *Welcoming Disaster*). Toronto, Oxford University Press, 1981; New York, Oxford University Press, 1982.

Other

The Four Ages of Man: The Classical Myths (textbook). Toronto, Macmillan, and New York, St. Martin's Press, 1962.
Pratt's Romantic Mythology: The Witches' Brew (lecture). St. John's, Newfoundland, Memorial University, 1972.
The Spirit of Solitude: Conventions and Continuities in Late Romance. New Haven, Connecticut, Yale University Press, 1982.

Editor, *New Poems*, by Dorothy Livesay. Toronto, Emblem, 1955.

*

Critical Studies: by Kildare Dobbs, in *Canadian Forum* (Toronto), xxxvii, 438; "Poetry" by Northrop Frye, in "Letters in Canada: 1957," in *University of Toronto Quarterly*, xxvii; "The Third Eye" by James Reaney, in *Canadian Literature 3* (Vancouver); Milton Wilson, in *Fiddlehead 34* (Fredericton, New Brunswick); Munro Beattie, in *Literary History of Canada*, Toronto, University of Toronto Press, 1965; "Poetry" by Michael Gnarowski, in "Letters in Canada: 1974," in *University of Toronto Quarterly*, xliv; *Second Words: Selected Critical Prose* by Margaret Atwood, Toronto, Anansi, 1982, Boston, Beacon Press, 1984.

*   *   *

Jay Macpherson's *The Boatman* has been reprinted five times since its first publication in 1957, and has been accepted with enthusiasm by academic critics as well as the general public. The book is a subtly organised suite of lyrics, elegiac, pastoral, epigrammatic, and symbolist, which utilises the traditional forms of quatrain and couplet with great metrical virtuosity and a remarkable flair for the presentation of serious philosophical and, indeed, religious themes in verse that is sometimes beautifully lyrical and sometimes comic in the tradition of Lear or Gilbert or the nursery rhymes—and sometimes both at once.

The book has as its unifying theme the transmutation of time-bound physical reality into the eternal and the spiritual through the magical intermediary of man's imagination. Symbol and myth are the instruments, and the drama of man's fall and redemption is worked out in terms derived from the Bible, Milton, Blake, and such modern poets and scholars as Robert Graves and Northrop Frye. Among the protagonists whose fables supply the seeds of the mystical drama unifying the book are Noah, Leviathan, Sheba, Mary of Egypt, Eurynome, Merlin, Helen, and such symbolic figures as The Plowman, The Fisherman, The Shepherd, and the Angels. One of the reasons for the success of these poems is that they take the reader into the world of childhood's faith in the unquestionable truth of fairy tale and legend. The elegance and grace of the writing and the authority with which wit and a sense of comedy are conveyed in verse that is both timeless and contemporary give the book an appeal also to the most sophisticated of readers.

—A.J.M. Smith

MacSWEENEY, Barry. British. Born in Newcastle upon Tyne, Northumberland, 17 July 1948. Educated at Rutherford Grammar School; Harlow Technical College, 1966-67. Married Elaine Randell in 1972. Formerly, free-lance journalist, Director, Blacksuede Boot Press, and Editor, with Elaine Randell, *Harvest* and *The Blacksuede Boot*, Barnet, Hertfordshire. Recipient: *Stand* prize, 1967; Arts Council grant, 1971. Address: c/o Pig Press, 7 Cross View Terrace, Melville's Cross, Durham DH1 4JY, England.

PUBLICATIONS

Verse

Poems 1965-1968: The Boy from the Green Cabaret Tells of His Mother. Hastings, Sussex, The English Intelligencer, 1967; New York, McKay, 1969.
The Last Bud. Newcastle upon Tyne, Blacksuede Boot Press, 1969.
Joint Effort, with Peter Bland. Barnet, Hertfordshire, Blacksuede Boot Press, 1970.
Flames on the Beach at Viareggio. Barnet, Hertfordshire, Blacksuede Boot Press, 1970.
Our Mutual Scarlet Boulevard. London, Fulcrum Press, 1971.
Just 22 and Don't Mind Dyin': The Official Biography of Jim Morrison, Rock Idol. London, Curiously Strong, 1971.
Brother Wolf. London, Turret, 1972.
5 Odes. London, Transgravity Advertiser, 1972.
Dance Steps. London, Joe DiMaggio Press, 1972.
Fog Eye. London, Ted Cavanagh, 1973.
6 Odes. London, Ted Cavanagh, 1973.
Pelt Feather Log. London, Grosseteste Press, 1975.
Black Torch. London, New London Pride, 1978.

Odes.   London, Trigram Press, 1979.
Blackbird: Elegy for William Gordon Calvert, Being Book Two of Black Torch.   Durham, Pig Press, 1980.

Other

Elegy for January: An Essay Commemorating the Bi-Centenary of Chatterton's Death.   London, Menard Press, 1970.

*

Barry MacSweeney comments:

   Influenced by Shelley, Pound, Blake, Rimbaud; try to reach into the gap between the "real" and the Vita Nuova of the Ideal; the air between the poet and his "dark ideals," some political poetry; lyrical, romantic; Newcastle and Northumberland are a great influence, the hard and sometimes vaporous geography of the fells and valleys. Music is also an influence: Berlioz, Bartok, Vivaldi, Debussy. Also helped revive the poem as the spoken medium; doing many readings. Hard, industrial landscapes of childhood and youth, reflected in the poems, lucid and tensile words like steel or coal; then, softer words reflecting the hills and streams where I go fishing and shooting.

*   *   *

   The diversification of British poetry in the 1960's meant that attention was frequently focused on poets operating from, or at least with their roots in, the provinces. Liverpool was a breeding ground for the so-called "pop" poets, but an equally lively—and in many ways more fertile—scene developed in and around Newcastle. Barry MacSweeney was an important member of the Newcastle poetry community, and time has proved that he is one of the most talented of the various poets who survived the initial wave of group enthusiasm and went on to establish themselves as individuals.

   MacSweeney's early work, as represented in *The Boy from the Green Cabaret Tells of His Mother*, has a strong sense of the geography of his locality, and there are frequent references to its physical appearance. But, more important, the rhythm of the poems, and their structure, seem to be shaped by the twin influences of the city and the country. It would be wrong to call MacSweeney a purely urban poet because, like many provincials, he's obviously aware of often being on the edge of the moors or close to the coast. The land, and the sea, spill into his poems, balancing them, and keeping them from becoming merely bright exercises in urban playfulness.

   As time passed MacSweeney altered his area of operation, both in physical terms (he left Newcastle in the 1960's) and in terms of what his work dealt with. He began to produce poems (see *Our Mutual Scarlet Boulevard*) which, in his own words, "had to do with dreams; either sleep, fantasy, or the luxurious influence of various hallucinogens." Although perhaps a worthwhile experiment, and certainly displaying skill in construction, the poems lacked the directness and concern of the earlier work, and one wondered if MacSweeney had lost his way in a fashionable maze. But he soon demonstrated that the experience was something he had learned from, rather than being changed by it, and *Brother Wolf* proved he was still his own man. It had a tautness that seemingly came from a desire to discard the unnecessary, and was rich in form and content.

   More recent work has continued to revolve around his major interests. *Black Torch* is a long poem-sequence built on the events of a 19th-century miners' strike in the North East, but it also brings in the poet's connection with the area, its traditions, and its landscapes, as well as referring to 20th-century problems

facing an idealist in an imperfect world. It is an ambitious work, and although flawed, has much to recommend it. *Odes* goes off in another direction, and is almost mystical at times with Mac-Sweeney seemingly concerned to milk words for the meaning deriving from their rhythm and sound rather than their dictionary definitions. Not all of the pieces work, but at their best they are provokingly mysterious and some lines linger in the mind as if to tease with their play on the subconscious.

   The dual role that MacSweeney continues to perform—and his two sides can, and do, intertwine—assures one that he still has much to offer. A semi-surreal view of real events may yet be his major achievement, and the prospect of him bringing it to fruition is an exciting one. He is still a relatively young poet, and yet has built up a fairly impressive body of work in which technical skill is always in evidence. If he continues to blend confidence and imagination he should eventually have a sustained and vigorous bibliography to his credit.

—Jim Burns

MADGE, Charles (Henry).   British.   Born in Johannesburg, South Africa, 10 October 1912. Educated at Winchester College; Magdalene College, Cambridge. Married 1) Kathleen Raine, *q.v.* (marriage dissolved), one son and one daughter; 2) Inez Pearn (died, 1976), one son and one daughter; 3) Evelyn Brown (died, 1984). Reporter, *Daily Mirror*, London, 1935-36; founded Mass-Observation, 1937; Staff Member, National Institute of Economic and Social Research, 1940-42; Research Staff, Policy and Economic Planning, 1943; Director, Pilot Press, London, 1944; Social Development Officer, Stevenage, 1947-50; Professor of Sociology, University of Birmingham, 1950-70. Member, United Nations Technical Assistance Mission, Thailand, 1953-54, India, 1957-58, Southeast Asia, 1959-60; Leader, Mission to Ghana, United Nations Economic Commission for Africa, 1963. Address: 28 Lynmouth Road, London N2 9LS, England.

Publications

Verse

The Disappearing Castle.   London, Faber, 1937.
The Father Found.   London, Faber, 1941.

Other

Mass-Observation, with T. Harrisson.   London, Muller, 1937.
War-Time Pattern of Saving and Spending.   Cambridge, University Press, and New York, Macmillan, 1943.
Industry after the War: Who Is Going to Run It?, with Donald Tyerman.   London, Pilot Press, 1943.
Village Communities in North East Thailand.   New York, U.N. Technical Assistance Programme, 1955.
Survey Before Development in Thai Villages.   New York, U.N. Secretariat, 1957.
Village Meeting Places: A Pilot Inquiry.   Delhi, Indian Ministry of Information, 1958.
Evaluation and the Technical Assistance Expert: An Operational Analysis.   Paris, UNESCO, 1961.
Society in the Mind: Elements of Social Eidos.   London, Faber, and New York, Free Press of Glencoe, 1964.

Art Students Observed, with Barbara Weinberger. London, Faber, 1973.
Inner City Poverty in Paris and London, with Peter Willmott. London, Routledge, 1981.

Editor, with others, *May the Twelfth: Mass Observation Day-Surveys 1937, by over 200 Observers*. London, Faber, 1937.
Editor, with T. Harrisson, *First Year's Work, 1937-38, by Mass Observation*. London, Lindsay Drummond, 1938. \
Editor, with T. Harrisson, *Britain, by Mass Observation*. London, Penguin, and New York, Famous Books, 1938.
Editor, with T. Harrisson, *War Begins at Home, by Mass Observation*. London, Chatto and Windus, 1940.
Editor, *Pilot Guide to the General Election*. London, Pilot Press, 1945.
Editor, *Pilot Papers: Social Essays and Documents, 1945-47*. London, Pilot Press, 1947.

*   *   *

Charles Madge, who was educated at Winchester and Cambridge (where he came under the influence of William Empson), is an intellectual poet, which may to some extent explain why his poetry has never received the attention it deserves. His earliest poems, collected in *The Disappearing Castle*, demonstrate his readiness to try out new ideas and techniques in his search for an effective medium of communication. If they display many of the weaknesses of the experimentalist, such as ambiguous statements, imprecise images, occasional striving after effects, and surrealistic word-play almost for its own sake, they also hint at his potentialities and reveal an original turn of mind. "Solar Creation," "In Conjunction," "Fortune," and the sequence entitled "Delusions" are among the best of these poems. Like many other poets of the thirties, Madge was concerned with social conditions and "the strain of being man upright in the flat world," but even in these early pieces there is little evidence of the over-simplified analysis of the situation such as those proffered by the Auden-Spender group with whom he has been identified. He had closer affinities with the *Twentieth Century Verse* group of poets, led by Julian Symons, whose theory that the poet ought to be "the perfect mass-observer" was probably derived from Madge's contribution to the development of Mass Observation as a valid instrument of social research.

Madge's second volume, *The Father Found*, marks a distinct advance in technical proficiency. The romantic landscapes, the verbal tricks and ambiguities, have all been discarded, and the poems are written in a controlled and compact language, of which psychological concepts and accurate scientific references form an integral part, against a localised background of filling-stations, factories, traffic, theodolites, airwaves and television. Such poems as "Binocular Vision," "Drinking Bolton," and "Through the Periscope" indicate the change that had taken place and show a new objectivity in Madge's approach to his chosen themes. If the language presents any difficulties, they arise from the intractable nature of the material he is working upon and his highly individual way of looking at things. As he observes in "Philosophical Poem": "This window by a curious trick can see/Workaday things and a white rising planet."

Charles Madge has succeeded in translating his philosophical beliefs into action in the sociological sphere, so that his theories have been tested by experience; direct activity in the sociological field in its turn has assisted his creative work by keeping him in close touch with reality; while the dual nature of his vision has enabled him to perform "the curious trick" by which he establishes the connection between "workaday things" and the "white rising planet." It can, therefore, be argued that his best poetry has social value.

This is confirmed by the later and, as yet, uncollected pieces such as "Visions of Camden Town," "In the Lens of Observation," "For an Altar," the sequence "Poem by Stages," and the long poem entitled "The Storming of the Brain," which can best be described as a poetic treatment, in allegorical form acceptable at several levels, of the conflict between detached intellectualism and the unruly and unpredictable forces of life. With "The Storming of the Brain" before us it is possible not only to ascertain the progress Madge has made, but also to trace the direction in which he seems to be moving. First it was necessary to effect a reconciliation between his romantic impulses and his trained scientific methods, and then his intellectual beliefs had to be related to his idealistic concern for humanity in such a way as to maintain his artistic integrity and yet provide a basis for positive action.

In "The Storming of the Brain" Madge lays emphasis upon the need for the integration of society as distinct from the prevailing tendency towards division into armed ideological camps, and indicates what seems to him to be the only practical way in which unity of purpose can be achieved.

—Howard Sergeant

MAGEE, Wes. British. Born in Greenock, Renfrew, 20 July 1939. Educated at Ilford County High School, Essex, 1951-56; Goldsmiths' College, University of London, 1964-67, teachers certificate. Served in the British Army Intelligence Corps, 1960-62. Married Janet Parkhouse in 1969; one son and one daughter. Worked as a bank clerk in the 1950's; Headmaster, Blackthorn Junior School, Welwyn Garden City, Hertfordshire, 1978; Headteacher, Brough County Primary School, North Humberside, 1981. Editor, *Prism* magazine, London, 1964-67. Recipient: Leeds University New Poets award, 1973. Address: S/Bank, Low Street, Sancton, near York, England.

PUBLICATIONS

Verse

Postcard from a Long Way Off. Portrush, County Antrim, Ulsterman, 1969.
The Radish. Frensham, Surrey, Sceptre Press, 1970.
Urban Gorilla. Leeds, School of English Press, 1972.
Proust in a Crowded Store. Rushden, Northamptonshire, Sceptre Press, 1974.
No Man's Land. Richmond, Surrey, Keepsake Press, 1976.
Creature of the Bay: A Set of Poems. Kingston upon Thames, Surrey, Court Poetry Press, 1977.
Headland Graffiti. Knotting, Bedfordshire, Sceptre Press, 1978.
No Surrender. Liverpool, Headland, 1978.
The Dream Spectres. Nottingham, Byron Press, 1978.
No Man's Land (collection). Belfast, Blackstaff Press, 1978.
Aberllefenni: At the Slate Quarry. Bristol, Xenia Press, 1979.
Wrecks. Bristol, Xenia Press, 1980.
Poems for a Course, with John Cotton. Hitchin, Hertfordshire, Priapus, 1980.
The Football Replays. Higham Ferrers, Northamptonshire, Greylag Press, 1980.

A Dark Age. Belfast, Blackstaff Press, 1982.

Play

The Real Spirit of Christmas (for children; produced Welwyn
Garden City, Hertfordshire, 1978). London, French, 1978.

Other (for children)

Reptile Rhymes. Bristol, Xenia Press, 1977.
Oliver, The Daring Birdman. London, Longman, 1978.
The Space Beasts. Maidstone, Kent Library Service, 1979.

Editor, *All the Day Through.* London, Evans, 1982.

*   *   *

In Wes Magee's first major collection, *Urban Gorilla,* the
poems are taken from personal experience and written in a clear,
down-to-earth manner which somehow combines a colloquial
diction with a strikingly fresh use of image and metaphor in a
style which is unique to Magee. In the poem entitled "Maybe I'd
Do Well in Tibet" he looks at other poets' ways of life and
reaches his own conclusion:

> I'm plainly
> for the poet keeping his cool in the city,
> being steady in the isolation
> of his mortgaged box,
> a monk without privilege or position,
> solitary in his cell,
> above the yelping and the traffic snarl.

Magee, then, is definitely an urban poet, concerned with
events and situations to be found in everyday life and especially
those which make their impact upon him in his role as teacher. In
this collection there are several poems featuring incidents at
school. In "Today's Lesson: An Observation" a group of
teachers on a refresher course visit a show school "learning that
what's good for smaller fry is/fine for us, and how to make the
educated/guess when things go wrong." "The Bell Sequence"
features a teacher watching children in the playground. Another
poem deals with basic training during National Service. There
are a couple of poems about football, though one of these is a
metaphorical account of the reaction of young poets against the
prominence given to Establishment figures. Throughout all
these poems there are compassion, a wry sense of irony, and an
insight into the human situation, though it cannot be said that
any clear philosophy emerges.

Two pamphlet collections, *The Dream Spectres* and *No Surrender,* together with some later poems, were incorporated in his
second volume, *No Man's Land.* Although the diction employed
in this volume is still that of everyday speech, there is greater
control of form and in some of the poems, particularly those
describing farm life, the language is muscular and gritty, reminiscent of Ted Hughes in his animal poems, though not in any
way derivative:

> Urban-soft I feel anguish for the runt
> in each litter, the weakling hanging back
> while the familial toughs fight for pig-meal
> or a swift guzzle at the sow's milk bar.
> Here, in this harsh Irish outhouse, the runts
> surrender. They stand with ears ripped to rags
> and tails snapped to stumps by the pink nasties,
> butts for the *angst* rife in the squalid pens.

> "Better dead, than fed," my boss cracks, and rakes
> his blackthorn stick up and down the sow's spine.

Occasionally, this concentration upon language appropriate
to the theme leads him into some awkward combinations and
over-ripe alliteration—"Then squelched slow.... Strode to the
stone-strewn summit." The range of subject is extended in this
second volume, too, and a number of highly imaginative poems,
though taking some trivial incident as starting-point, penetrate
beneath the surface of the material to provide strange insights, as
in "Biography of the Skull," "Yorick in a Junk Shop," "The
Skull's Will," "Woman from the Kingdom of Pain," and "Threshold." Magee has a rare gift for fresh and sometimes startling
simile and metaphor—"the day was grey as school socks," "sky-
larks topple like early birdmen," a ridge is "undulating as a
boxer's nose," air is "lemon-juice sharp," night "blindfolds the
houses," skin like a "frost-bitten potato," and night gathering
"like black-suited men at a country funeral." Poems such as
"Woman from the Kingdom of Pain," "Snaps," and "No Surrender" show this unusually talented poet at his best. So far he
seems to have been testing the ground and developing an individual style, trying out different themes and ideas and modes of
expression, but there can be little doubt of his enormous
potentiality.

—Howard Sergeant

MAHAPATRA, Jayanta. Indian. Born in Cuttack, Orissa,
22 October 1928. Educated at Stewart European School, Cuttack, 1933-41; Ravenshaw College, Cuttack, B.Sc. (honours)
1946; Patna University, M.Sc. (honours) in physics 1949. Married Jyotsna Rani Das in 1951; one son. Sub-editor, *Eastern
Times,* Cuttack, 1949; Lecturer in Physics, Ravenshaw College,
1950-58, G.M. College, Sambalpur, 1958-61 and 1962-65,
Regional Engineering College, Rourkela, 1961-62, and B.J.B.
College, Bhubaneswar, 1965-69, all in Orissa; Reader in Physics,
F.M. College, Balasore, 1969-70, and Ravenshaw College, 1970-
81. Since 1981, Reader in Physics, Shailabala Women's College,
Cuttack. Visiting Writer, University of Iowa, Iowa City, 1976-
77, and in Australia, 1978, and Japan, 1980; Visiting Fellow,
Shivaji University, Kolhapur, 1983. Associate Editor, *Gray
Book,* Cuttack, 1972-73; Guest Editor, *South and West,* Fort
Smith, Arkansas, 1973. Since 1979, Editor, *Chandrabhaga,* Cut-
tack. Recipient: Jacob Glatstein Memorial Award (*Poetry,* Chi-
cago), 1975; National Academy of Letters award, 1981. Address:
Tinkonia Bagicha, Cuttack 753 001, Orissa, India.

Publications

Verse

Close the Sky, Ten by Ten. Calcutta, Dialogue, 1971.
Svayamvara and Other Poems. Calcutta, Writers Workshop,
1971.
A Rain of Rites. Athens, University of Georgia Press, 1976.
A Father's Hours. Calcutta, United Writers, 1976.
Waiting. New Delhi, Samkaleen, 1979.
The False Start. Bombay, Clearing House, 1980.
Relationship. Greenfield, New York, Greenfield Review Press,
1980.
Life Signs. New Delhi, Oxford University Press, 1983.

Other

Tales from Fakirmohan (for children).   Cuttack, Orissa, Students' Store, 1969.
True Tales of Travel and Adventure (for children).   Cuttack, Orissa, Students' Store, 1969.

Translator, *Countermeasures: Poems*, by Soubhagya Kumar Misra.   Calcutta, Dialogue, 1973.
Translator, *Wings of the Past: Poems*, by Jadunath Das Mohapatra.   Calcutta, Rajasree, 1976.
Translator, *Song of Kubja and Other Poems*, by Sitakant Mahapatra.   New Delhi, Samkaleen, 1981.

*

Critical Studies: by K. Ayyappa Paniker, in *Osmania Journal of English Studies* (Hyderabad), vol. 13, no. 1, 1977; "Crisis of Belief" by Frank Allen, in *Parnassus* (New York), Spring-Summer 1981; "Jayanta Mahapatra: A Poetry of Decreation" by Meena Alexander, in *Journal of Commonwealth Literature* (Oxford), vol. 18, no. 1, 1983; "Vision of a Reconciliator" by Gary Corseri, in *Fiction, Literature, and the Arts Review* (Brookline, Massachusetts), Spring 1983.

*   *   *

Many of Jayanta Mahapatra's poems are hermetic and refer obliquely to unspecified desires, guilts, memories which haunt that "inner world of his own making—a world spaced by his own life, of secret allusions, of desire and agony, of a constantly changing alignment between dream and reality" to which Mahapatra refers in "The Inaudible Resonance in English Poetry in India" (*Literary Criterion*, XV, 1, 1980). It is the creation of an inner world, evolving in complexity and richness from poem to poem, volume to volume, that makes Mahapatra a postmodernist constructing his own realm of silence, solitude, memory, and desire, while remaining haunted by the Indian environment, with its rituals and myths, from which he feels separated by his Christian upbringing, scepticism, and scientific education.

He early developed a unique style in which multiplicity of significances, dislocated, often baffling syntax, and disruption of grammar are held together rather by rich patterns of imagery and sound than by any clarity of argument or narrative. In the poem "Love" in *Close the Sky, Ten by Ten*, we are warned: "leave thought alone/to find the meaning/...it will not turn/to/a sentence." The title *Close the Sky, Ten by Ten* comes from "Sanctuary," a statement of withdrawal into the self (possibly from extra-marital pleasures): "now i close the sky/with a square ten by ten." The obscurity results from a complexity of themes presented obliquely within short lyrics built from contrasts, contradictory statements and other techniques that tend to oppose or deconstruct what at first appears to be claimed.

Mahapatra first pulled his fragmented themes together into a more unified vision in *A Rain of Rites*, where meditation on the local landscape is a starting place for the articulation of emotions felt at the edge of awareness. In such poems as "Dawn," "Village" "Old Palaces," and "Samsāra" the imagination acknowledges the external world, then decreates it, finding a possible alternative reality within the self passively awaiting illumination and renewal. Some poems, such as "The Whorehouse in a Calcutta Street," reveal a new interest in social content, while others, such as "Indian Summer Poem," obliquely allude to traditional Indian symbols and myths. The volume is unified by its recurrence of themes and images and by a constancy of tone and mood, with the rain, sky, dawn, river, flowers, roots, shadows, stones, trees, sun becoming symbols in the poet's quest for significance: "What is there in ceremony, in a ritual's deeply hidden meaning?/The familiar words are roots, and out of place."

His titles seem part of a continuing private autobiography—*Waiting, The False Start, Relationship, Life Signs*. The evolving body of poetry alludes to false starts, hopes, disillusionments, anxieties, and contradictions as Mahapatra gropes "from poem to poem for the key to human understanding." While the lyrics are rich in the atmosphere of the Indian landscape, its legends, and the historical past of Orissa, their main concern is what Mahapatra has called "the essentiality of his being." He often returns to the problem of what he is, the truth of what he sees and feels, and his sense of being distinct from the traditional India of his surroundings. In "Waiting" he contrasts the "deadened dust," "soiled three-year-old children," and "luckless widows shuffling up and down/the fractured temple steps" with his observation of them: "You hardly know the vision isolates you," "Every day I see them debase themselves/and am afraid, understanding nothing."

Relationship is a 12-part dream epic, a psychic quest into the poet's roots as represented by the past and symbolism of Orissa. It is an attempt to go beyond the self, to give classical poetic status to the locality, while unburdening the sense of guilt that results from the poet's alienation from the culture in which he lives: "I know I can never come alive/if I refuse to consecrate at the altar of my origins."

In *Life Signs* Mahapatra's vision is his main theme: "the song that reaches our ears is just our own"; "It is the silence which says the world is not ours"; "So we drag meanings/from what we see"; "Or is it only desire, hoping to resume its inner light." The magnificent "The Lost Children of America" is as much about the poet's own relationship to India as about those foreigners drawn to the myths of his country. While it is easy to become impatient with his mannerisms, obscurity, private symbols, and long, incantatory lines, Mahapatra has developed the unique vision, style, and poetic mode of a major writer.

—Bruce King

MAHON, Derek.   British.   Born in Belfast, Northern Ireland, 23 November 1941. Educated at Belfast Institute; Trinity College, Dublin, B.A. 1965. Married Doreen Douglas in 1972; two children. English teacher, Belfast High School, 1967-68, and Language Centre of Ireland, Dublin, 1968-70; Writer-in-Residence, University of East Anglia, Norwich, 1975, Emerson College, Boston, 1976-77, and New University of Ulster, Coleraine, 1977-79. Co-Editor, *Atlantis*, Dublin, 1970-74; has been drama critic of *The Listener* and features editor of *Vogue*, both London. Recipient: Eric Gregory Award, 1965; Arts Council bursary, 1981. Agent: Deborah Rogers Ltd., 49 Blenheim Crescent, London W11 2EF, England.

PUBLICATIONS

Verse

Twelve Poems.   Belfast, Festival, 1965.
Design for a Grecian Urn.   Cambridge, Massachusetts, Erato, 1967.

Night-Crossing. London, Oxford University Press, 1968.
Ecclesiastes. Manchester, Phoenix Pamphlet Poets Press, 1970.
Beyond Howth Head. Dublin, Dolmen Press, 1970.
Lives. London, Oxford University Press, 1972.
The Man Who Built His City in Snow. London, Poem-of-the-Month Club, 1972.
The Snow Party. London and New York, Oxford University Press, 1975.
Light Music. Belfast, Ulsterman, 1977.
In Their Element: A Selection of Poems, with Seamus Heaney. Belfast, Arts Council of Northern Ireland, 1977.
The Sea in Winter. Dublin, Gallery, and Old Deerfield, Massachusetts, Deerfield Press, 1979.
Poems 1962-1978. London, Oxford University Press, 1979.
Courtyards in Delft. Dublin, Gallery, 1981.
The Hunt by Night. Oxford, Oxford University Press, 1982; Winston-Salem, North Carolina, Wake Forest University Press, 1983.
A Kensington Notebook. London, Anvil Press Poetry, 1984.

Plays

High Time, adaptation of a play by Molière (produced 1984).

Radio features on Brian Moore, 1975, J.G. Farrell, 1980, Olivia Manning, 1981, John Montague, 1982, and Robert Lowell, 1984.

Television Adaptations: *Shadows on Our Skin*, 1980, and *How Many Miles to Babylon?*, 1981, both by Jennifer Johnston; *First Love*, by Turgenev, 1982; *The Demon Lover*, by Elizabeth Bowen, 1983; *A Moment of Love*, by Brian Moore, 1984; *The Cry*, with Chris Menaul, by John Montague, 1984.

Other

Editor, *Modern Irish Poetry*. London, Sphere, 1972.

Translator, *The Chimeras*, by Nerval. Dublin, Gallery, 1982.

*   *   *

What one initially notices in the poetry of Derek Mahon is a strong sense of place. Some of his best poems appear, on first reading, to be topographical. They have titles such as "Day Trip to Donegal," "April on Toronto Island," and "Teaching in Belfast." Like the others, the locale in this last is created with intense specificity: "the cries of children,/ screaming of bells, the rattle of milk bottles,/ Footfall echoes of jails and hospitals...." But the scene is created primarily to facilitate an escape: "This is the moment my fantasy begins/ And I drive with a generous lady, long since lost,/ Against the traffic to the glittering west...."

In poem after poem, local properties are assiduously assembled. "A Garage in Co. Cork" has "Building materials, fruit boxes, scrap iron,/ Dust-laden shrubs and coils of rusty wire...." But always, clearly signalled, is the possibility of release—in this instance: "Beyond, a swoop of mountain where you heard,/ Disconsolate in haze, a single blackbird...."

This idea of an individual gesture dissolving the present clutter is, again, highly characteristic of Mahon. In the dawn, after the late-night hubbub described in "Rock Music," he hears "a single bird/ Drown with a whistle that residual roar...." A similar signal suggests the positive quality Mahon finds in the work of a distinguished predecessor. "At Carrowdore Churchyard" is an elegy on Louis MacNeice: "Maguire, I believe, suggested a blackbird/ And over your grave a phrase from Euripides...."

The quality Mahon admires in MacNeice is typified in his own work by a characteristic so insistent as to justify employing the term "poetic touchstone":

From the pneumonia of the ditch, from the ague
Of the blind poet and the bombed-out town you bring
The all-clear to the empty holes of spring;
Rinsing the choked mud, keeping the colours new.

Detritus, both urban and rural, is associated with death in an occluding physical form. Set against this is a sense of release evoked in a series of images suggesting an individual form of *claritas*. In "Consolations of Philosophy" a few of the dead, immured in rotten boards and broken urns, "remember with delight/ The dust gyrating in a shaft of light...."

A similar contrast, between detritus and release, is seen in "A Refusal to Mourn." An old man's house—"Cinders moved in the grate,/ And a warm briar gurgled"—is set against his deliverance, not to a graveyard, but to the oblivion conferred by the seasons: "In time the astringent rain/ Of those parts will clean/ The words from his gravestone...." The imprisoned masses referred to in "A Disused Shed in Co. Wexford" wait for "light meter and relaxed itinerary." The exiled proprietor in "The Chinese Restaurant in Portrush" sees "the light/ Of heaven upon the mountains of Donegal." "The Poet in Residence" describes Corbière as a fugitive in a ruined convent, "Masonry pitted with such gaping holes/ There was no knowing which one was the door." Much of the poem consists of a letter to Corbière's lover which is written and torn up. The words of Corbière escape, as he cannot: "The little bits of white/ Looked, in the mist, like gulls in flight."

These touchstones all involve a sense of release and deploy a vocabulary which is characteristic: "the *glittering* west," "a *swoop* of mountains," "the all-*clear*," " a shaft of *light*," "*clean*/ The words," "the *light* of heaven," and this last, "gulls in *flight*." The examples could be multiplied, but the drift is clear, subsumed in the poem called, punningly, "Light Music": "A land of cumulus/ seen from above/ is the life to come...." This, in its turn, relates to Mahon's observation in "A Garage in Co. Cork": "We might be anywhere—in the Dordogne,/ Iquitos, Bethlehem...."

The places that abound in Mahon's poetry seem to be created as a means of providing the launching-pad for a release of the spirit. The sense of place and of occlusion assert themselves simultaneously, only to be dissolved into *claritas*. This is a poetry that represents a decisive adaptation of Auden and MacNeice, Mahon's two acknowledged masters. It may well in the end form an oeuvre fit to stand beside theirs in literary history.

—Philip Hobsbaum

MAJOR, Clarence. American. Born in Atlanta, Georgia, 31 December 1936. Educated at the Art Institute, Chicago (James Nelson Raymond Scholar), 1952-54; Armed Forces Institute, 1955-56; New School for Social Research, New York, 1972. Served in the United States Air Force, 1955-57. Married Joyce Sparrow in 1958 (divorced 1964). Research analyst, Simulmatics, New York, 1967. Taught in the Harlem Education Program Writers Workshop, New York, 1967, and the Teachers and Writers Collaborative, New York, 1967-72; Member of the Faculty, Sarah Lawrence College, Bronxville, New York, after 1972. Currently, Member of the Faculty, University of Colorado, Boulder. Editor, *Coercion Review*, Chicago, 1958-60; Associate Editor, *Anagogic and Paideumic Review*, and *Proof*, Chicago, 1961-63, *Caw!*, 1967-68, *Journal of Black Poetry*, 1967-70, and *Dues*, 1972-73. Recipient: National Endowment for the Arts grant, 1970; New York Cultural Foundation grant, 1971. Agent: Howard Moorepark, 444 East 82nd Street, New York, New York 10028, U.S.A.

PUBLICATIONS

Verse

The Fires That Burn in Heaven. Privately printed, 1954.
Love Poems of a Black Man. Omaha, Nebraska, Coercion Press, 1965.
Human Juices. Omaha, Nebraska, Coercion Press, 1965.
Swallow the Lake. Middletown, Connecticut, Wesleyan University Press, 1970.
Symptoms and Madness. New York, Corinth, 1971.
Private Line. London, Paul Breman, 1971.
The Cotton Club: New Poems. Detroit, Broadside Press, 1972.
The Syncopated Cakewalk. New York, Barlenmir House, 1974.

Novels

All-Night Visitors. New York, Olympia Press, 1969.
NO. New York, Emerson Hall, 1973.
Reflex and Bone Structure. New York, Fiction Collective, 1975.
Emergency Exit. New York, Fiction Collective, 1979.

Other

Dictionary of Afro-American Slang. New York, International, 1970; as *Black Slang: A Dictionary of Afro-American Talk*, London, Routledge, 1971.
The Dark and Feeling: Black American Writers and Their Work. New York, Third Press, 1974.
The Other Side of the Wall. San Francisco, Black Scholar Press, 1982.

Editor, *Writers Workshop Anthology.* New York, Harlem Education Project, 1967.
Editor, *Man Is Like a Child: An Anthology of Creative Writing by Students.* New York, Macomb's Junior High School, 1968.
Editor, *The New Black Poetry.* New York, International, 1969.

*

Bibliography: "Clarence Major: A Checklist of Criticism" by Joe Weixlmann, in *Obsidian* (Fredonia, New York), iv, 2, 1978; "Toward a Primary Bibliography of Clarence Major" by Joe Weixlmann and Clarence Major, in *Black American Literature Forum* (Terre Haute, Indiana), Summer 1979.

Critical Studies: in *New York Times*, 7 April 1969; *Quarterly Journal of Speech* (New York), April 1971; *Saturday Review* (New York), 3 April 1971; *Chicago Sun-Times*, 28 April 1971; *Poetry* (Chicago), August 1971; *Virginia Quarterly Review* (Charlottesville), Winter 1971; *New York Times Book Review*, 1 July 1973; *Interviews with Black Writers*, edited by John O'Brien, New York, Liveright, 1973.

Clarence Major comments:

I am trying to break through the artificial effects of language. I'm also trying to break down the artificial distinctions between poetry and fiction.

*   *   *

In an epigraph to his novel *Reflex and Bone Structure* Clarence Major announces that the book "is an extension of, not a duplication of reality. The characters and events are happening for the first time." The statement equally well describes the poetry in which Major's deliberate opacity discourages our attempt to track his language as references to an empirical world. Even when reading verse we expect words readily to demonstrate a correspondence to outside things or events, because our linguistic competency develops through the code of usage. Like other post-Modern writers, however, Major uses language as a newly constructed code.

His poems are cast subjectively as dramas of feelings, sometimes in conflict, other times their complexities resolved by time. Always, though, the dynamic comes from a logic of emotional knowledge that, more often than not, conceals the subject— what the poem is about. Such verse holds that the structures of feeling have been shaped uniquely, and it follows that the patterns of expression must be intrinsic to poetic execution. In "Overbreak" he writes

> there is a remarkable verb of
> things
> here: a remarkable sensation of
> infected spirits feeling
> & pushing bravely like nurtured waves in
> the machines of
> the sensation, the tremor of water as it
> surrounds the heart beat

The absence of conventional punctuation makes "Overbreak" an uninterrupted utterance intensely felt; yet, the original stimulus has been absorbed into abstractions, the currency of mental constructions that nevertheless stop short of concept.

Major's code regularly employs eccentric punctuation and unusual typographical arrangement so that the poems must be seen as well as heard. Clotted lines, such as "O supreme sledgehammer of reposing verbal stacks of/nouns verbs adjectives charming," insist upon the primary sensation of words as sounds. These eccentricities, and others, then reinforce the premise implied by such fused syntax as in this passage from "The Design":

> I am tired of the
> apartment is dull a place but it comes
> to this each
> item you left, a few belongings....

If conventional syntax asserts the dominance of rational order, then this disruption argues the existence of an "extension of reality," its integrity requiring designation of a new, arbitrary system of signs.

Because it stakes all on the tone conveyed by a linguistic code we can never entirely decipher, Major's verse risks obscurity. But, of course, the risk is well taken. The discontinuities between his verse and the patterns of conventional usage become an experiment in poetics as well as poems.

—John M. Reilly

MALOUF, David. Australian. Born in Brisbane, Queensland, 20 March 1934. Educated at Brisbane Grammar School, 1947-50; University of Queensland, Brisbane, 1951-54, B.A. (honours) in English 1954. Lecturer, University of Sydney, 1968-77. Recipient: Australian Literature Society Gold Medal, 1974, 1983; Grace Leven Prize, 1975; James Cook Award, 1975; Australia Council Fellowship, 1978; New South Wales Premier's Prize, for fiction, 1979; Melbourne *Age* Book of the Year Award, 1982. Agent: Curtis Brown (Australia) Pty. Ltd., 86 William Street, Paddington, New South Wales 2021; or, Curtis Brown, 162-168 Regent Street, London W1R 5TA, England. Address: 242 Kingsford Smith Drive, Hamilton, Brisbane, Queensland 4007, Australia.

PUBLICATIONS

Verse

Four Poets, with others. Melbourne, Cheshire, 1962.
Bicycle and Other Poems. Brisbane, University of Queensland Press, 1970; as *The Year of the Foxes and Other Poems*, New York, Braziller, 1979.
Neighbours in a Thicket. Brisbane, University of Queensland Press, 1974.
Poems 1975-76. Sydney, Prism, 1976.
Selected Poems. Sydney, Angus and Robertson, 1980.
Wild Lemons. Sydney, Angus and Robertson, 1980.
First Things Last. Brisbane, University of Queensland Press, 1980; London, Chatto and Windus, 1981.

Novels

Johnno. Brisbane, University of Queensland Press, 1975; New York, Braziller, 1978.
An Imaginary Life. New York, Braziller, and London, Chatto and Windus, 1978.
Child's Play, with Eustace and the Prowler. London, Chatto and Windus, 1982; as *Child's Play, The Bread of Time to Come: Two Novellas*, New York, Braziller, 1982.
Fly Away Peter. London, Chatto and Windus, 1982.
Harland's Half Acre. London, Chatto and Windus, and New York, Knopf, 1984.

Short Stories

Antipodes. London, Chatto and Windus, 1985.

Other

New Currents in Australian Writing, with Katharine Brisbane and R.F. Brissenden. Sydney and London, Angus and Robertson, 1978.

Editor, with others, *We Took Their Orders and Are Dead: An Anti-War Anthology.* Sydney, Ure Smith, 1971.
Editor, *Gesture of a Hand* (anthology of Australian poetry). Artarmon, New South Wales, Holt Rinehart, 1975.

*

Manuscript Collections: University of Queensland, Brisbane; Australian National University Library, Canberra.

Critical Studies: interviews in *Commonwealth 4* (Rodez, France), 1979-80, *Meanjin 39* (Melbourne), and *Australian Literary Studies* (Hobart, Tasmania), October 1982; "David Malouf as Humane Allegorist" by James Tulip, in *Southerly* (Sydney), 1981; "David Malouf and the Language of Exile" by Peter Bishop, in *Australian Literary Studies* (Hobart, Tasmania), October 1982.

David Malouf comments:

I like to think of poetry as work done at a place of concordance: where the past and future meet in visible present, where change is celebrated but continuity established, where the actual is open to the fabulous, where the individual stands as the point of connection between a single life and the totality of things. Language also belongs to two worlds: the world of "communication" and of our mysterious naming to ourselves of what surrounds us. Standing as it does at this crossing-point between adjacent, and perhaps rival, zones, it seems like an ideal vehicle for the "passages" I have in mind. Poems are acts of reconciliation.

*   *   *

Although relatively unprolific as a poet, David Malouf has attained a high degree of achievement in what he has published. He first appeared, as one of a Brisbane-based group of new poets in *Four Poets*, and in that selection already laid out many of his ongoing preoccupations: childhood incidents and resonances (expressed with considerable delight in small, concrete detail); a cosmopolitan familiarity with European history and culture as something intrinsic to his vision; and a sharp, ironic view of contemporary man's social and political milieu—most deftly expressed in "Epitaph for a Monster of Our Times", about Adolf Eichmann:

> an organization man
> *par excellence*, whom we
> need only convict at last
> of gross efficiency.

Bicycle and Other Poems followed after a long period of apparent silence and it immediately placed Malouf in the forefront of his generation. It confirmed the mature, ironic yet sympathetic view of life and events, but added a capacity to blend elements of quiet fantasy with more subterranean urgencies of wonder, loss, and the precariousness of living. The Brisbane poems in this volume have the extraordinary richness of observation and sensuous focus that characterise his first novel, *Johnno*, but the book is perhaps most notable for its wide-ranging resources of reference—something pursued even further in his next collection, *Neighbors in a Thicket*. In this book, though it contains some striking poems of childhood recall (the perspective, now, is richer, and darker), Malouf explores a strong vein of cultural and personal association, a sort of cross-hatching of reflective (and reflexive) emblems of recall. These are essentially meditative poems, poems of exploration rather than arrival, and their starting point is always a fine awareness of the past as being something as immediate and contemporaneous as the present. This capacity to respond to time laterally rather than chronologically makes Malouf unique among Australian poets in that it enables him to transcend issues of cultural identity and assertion, issues that have been of dominant concern in so much Australian writing. Malouf's sense of region is intense and sharply visual. He is thus the most European, yet one of the most regional, of contemporary Australian poets.
Poems 1975-76 can be seen as a lyrical interlude in Malouf's output. It is a short book, dominated by two love sequences of unusual resonance, mainly through their recognition that it is through the *word* that all avenues of perception may be opened

up. Malouf's exploration of language is here heightened by an overtly celebrative intent. In his poems published since this book, elements of pure invention have increasingly concerned the poet, often achieving a sense of almost breathtaking virtuosity. David Malouf's second novel, *An Imaginary Life*, which is virtually a prose poem of great lyric power, has achieved international acclaim since it was first published in New York. His first American collection, *The Year of the Foxes* though it is essentially a reprint of *Bicycle and Other Poems*, is a further sign of international recognition of this most elegant and cosmopolitan of Australian poets.

—Thomas W. Shapcott

MANDEL, Eli(as Wolf). Canadian. Born in Estevan, Saskatchewan, 3 December 1922. Educated at the University of Saskatchewan, Saskatoon, B.A. 1949, M.A. 1950; University of Toronto, Ph.D. 1957. Served in Europe in the Army medical Corps during World War II. Married Ann Mandel in 1967; three children. Instructor, University of Toronto, 1952-53; Assistant Professor, 1953, and Associate Professor of English, 1955-57, Collège Militaire Royal de Saint-Jean, Quebec; Associate Professor, 1957-63, and Professor of English 1964-65, University of Alberta, Edmonton. Associate Professor, 1965-66, and since 1967, Professor of English and Humanities, York University, Downsview, Ontario. Writer-in-Residence, University of Regina, Saskatchewan, 1978-79; Visiting Professor, University of Victoria, British Columbia, 1979-80. Recipient: President's Medal, University of Western Ontario, 1963; Centennial Medal, 1967; Governor-General's Award, 1968; Canada Council Award, 1971, 1974, 1977; Ontario Arts Council Award, 1973, 1976, 1977, 1979, 1980; Queen's Silver Jubilee Medal, 1977. Fellow, Royal Society of Canada, 1982. Address: Department of English, York University, 4700 Keele Street, Downsview, Ontario M3J 1P3, Canada.

PUBLICATIONS

Verse

Trio, with Gael Turnbull and Phyllis Webb. Toronto, Contact Press, 1954.
Fuseli Poems, Toronto, Contact Press, 1960.
Black and Secret Man. Toronto, Ryerson Press, 1964.
An Idiot Joy. Edmonton, Alberta, Hurtig, 1967.
Crusoe: Poems Selected and New. Toronto, Anansi, 1973.
Stony Plain. Erin, Ontario, Press Porcépic, 1973.
Out of Place. Erin, Ontario, Press Porcépic, 1977.
Mary Midnight. Toronto, Coach House Press, 1979.
Dreaming Backwards: Selected Poetry 1954-1981. Toronto, General, 1981.

Recording: *Eli Mandel*, Ontario Institute for Studies in Education, 1971.

Other

Criticism: The Silent-Speaking Words. Toronto, CBC, 1966.
Irving Layton. Toronto, Forum House, 1969.
Another Time (essays). Erin, Ontario, Press Porcépic, 1977.

Teaching Poetry, with Phyllis B. Schwartz. Vancouver, CommCept, 1979.
Life Sentence: Poems and Journals 1976-1980. Victoria, British Columbia, Press Porcépic, 1981.
The Poetry of Irving Layton. Toronto, Coles, 1981.

Editor, with Jean-Guy Pilon, *Poetry 62*. Toronto, Ryerson Press, 1961.
Editor, *Five Modern Canadian Poets*. Toronto, Holt Rinehart, 1970.
Editor, with Desmond Maxwell, *English Poems of the Twentieth Century*. Toronto, Macmillan, 1971.
Editor, *Contexts of Canadian Criticism*. Chicago, University of Chicago Press, 1971.
Editor, *Poets of Contemporary Canada 1960-1970*. Toronto, McClelland and Stewart, 1972.
Editor, *Eight More Canadian Poets*. Toronto, Holt Rinehart, 1972.
Editor, *The Poems of Irving Layton*. Toronto, McClelland and Stewart, 1977.

*

Manuscript Collection: University of Manitoba, Winnipeg.

Critical Studies: "Eli Mandel, Poet of the Prairies" by Michael Higgins, in *Chelsea Journal 4* (Saskatoon, Saskatchewan), no. 1, 1978; "Eli Mandel's Investigations" by David Staines, in *Book Forum 4* (Rhinecliff, New York), no. 1, 1978; "Poet as Critic as Prairie Poet" by Peter Stevens, in *Essays on Canadian Writing 18-19* (Downsview, Ontario), 1980; Andrew Suknaski, in *Brick 14* (Ilderton, Ontario), 1981; "Inside Out" by Kenneth Sherman, in *Waves 10* (Toronto), no. 4, 1982.

*   *   *

"I am a fable looking for a plot," Eli Mandel wrote in "Aesop" in *Black and Secret Man*. "Actually, I am an unwritten tale." The search for the tale to tell has taken Eli Mandel from Greek mythology and Old Testament fable to modern Freudian and Jungian theories of human motivation. What has remained constant—from his "Minotaur Poems" in *Trio*, where his work appeared with that of Phyllis Webb and Gael Turnbull, to his more recent books—is his feeling for tortured imagery, his sense of the grotesque, his urbane tone of irony, and his language which is by turns dramatic and melodramatic.

It might be argued that Eli Mandel is an academic poet in the best sense of that term. He is interested in the mythopoeic theories of Northrop Frye, and sees in the act of criticism itself (especially in his radio talks published as *The Silent Speaking Words*) an inevitable counterpoint to the practice of poetry. When he edited *Poetry 62* with Jean-Guy Pilon, he isolated the imaginative and dramatic strains in Canadian poetry. To all his writing, he brings a heightened sense of the immediacy of the imaginative act, which owes something to the writing of William Blake.

His first book, *Fuseli Poems*, is full of fragmentation and a concern for anthropology and myth. Writing about "The Anarchist-Poets" in *Black and Secret Man*, he advises the reader to "step carefully through this rubble of words. / Can you really say which wrecks were once poems, / which weapons?" In "The Burning Man" from *An Idiot Joy*, he stresses the anarchic quality of the poetic imagination: "I'm a walking crime wave." His poem "In the 57th Century of Our Lord" begins, "Semitic and secret I plan new evasions, / survival, the tribal rite."

Eli Mandel's imagery, often full of literary allusions, is usually bold and arresting. The hermetic and the heroic battle it out within his poems—Orpheus and Hercules united in one man. He ends "Pictures in an Institution" with the following lines:

> Notice: there will be no further communication
> lectures are cancelled
> all students are expelled
> the reading of poetry is declared a public crime.

—John Robert Colombo

MANHIRE, Bill (William Manhire). New Zealander. Born in Invercargill, 27 December 1946. Educated at Otago Boys High School; University of Otago, Dunedin, B.A. 1967, M.A. (honours) 1968, M.Litt. 1970; University College, London, 1970-73, M.Phil. 1973. Married Barbara McLeod in 1970; one daughter and one son. Lecturer, 1973-78, and since 1978, Senior Lecturer in English, Victoria University, Wellington. Editor, Amphedesma Press, Dunedin, 1971-75; General Editor, New Zealand Stories series, Victoria University Press. Recipient: New Zealand Book Award, 1978; Nuffield Fellowship, 1980. Address: Department of English, Victoria University of Wellington, Private Bag, Wellington 1, New Zealand.

PUBLICATIONS

Verse

Malady. Dunedin, Amphedesma Press, 1970.
The Elaboration. Wellington, Square and Circle, 1972.
Song Cycle. Wellington, Sound-Movement Theatre, 1975.
How to Take Off Your Clothes at the Picnic. Wellington, Wai-te-ata Press, 1977.
Dawn/Water. Eastbourne, New Zealand, Hawk Press, 1979.
Good Looks. Auckland, Auckland University Press-Oxford University Press, 1982.
Locating the Beloved and Other Stories. Wellington, Single Title Press, 1983.
Zoetropes: Poems 1972-82. Sydney and Wellington, Allen and Unwin-Port Nicholson Press, 1984.

Other

Editor, *New Zealand Universities Arts Festival Yearbook 1969.* Dunedin, Arts Festival Committee, 1969.
Editor, *N.Z. Listener Short Stories 1-2.* Wellington, Methuen, 2 vols., 1977-78.
Editor, with Marion McLeod, *Some Other Country: New Zealand s Best Short Stories.* Wellington, Unwin, 1984.

*

Critical Studies: "Pavlova and Wrists: The Poetry of Bill Manhire" by Peter Crisp, in *Islands 24* (Auckland), November 1978; "The Poetry of Bill Manhire" by Hugh Lander, in *Landfall* (Christchurch), September 1983.

*   *   *

Poems choose to give expression to conditions of writing. Poems are strategies for discovery, but do not habitually "articu-late solutions to the business of living." The poems are arbitrary facts, not only of the life of whoever writes them but of the lives of those who read them. They arise out of some situation which is in some way true; they are elaborations of whatever the truth of that situation is and in being elaborated they move away from any condition of raw truth towards a condition as fictions. A poem is like a snap shot which may be effected by a camera, insofar as the artifact (the poem) is to be identified with the creative process from which the fiction-fact emerges, "a snap, as it were, at the right moment, in the awareness that the disposition of such moments is not in any sense within the control of the artist." The productive process may be fostered by inducing a state "which borders on narcolepsy, where it seems possible to relax into some generous relationship with words," a state not likely to last more than a few moments which carries with it the consequence that any poem so produced is likely to be quite short.

Bill Manhire's poems are often delightful, but also often cryptic. The statement above may be taken as an account of how they are produced, or were formerly produced. It is compounded from two statements by Manhire, one published in 1972 (in *The Elaboration*) and the other in 1973 (in *The Young New Zealand Poets*). If we take it at all seriously, Manhire was paying tribute to the usefulness of what was once called inspiration, although in the way in which he writes of the poem's arrival he seems to be urging something more like automatic writing. That may be, at the outset, but the poems which arrive before us have fairly obviously been well worked over. They may retain something of the dream about them (which accounts for part of their strange appeal), something of a sense of a showing forth so that their truth "is in some way true," presenting the reader with a tantalising puzzle element which is likely to serve in getting the reader's interest, in which case the poem as "arbitrary fact" meets the condition the poet argues for: of the poem more as an interaction process than as something relatively autonomous.

A qualification was put in earlier that perhaps Manhire's poems were formerly produced in this fashion implying that they may not now be so. Some recent pieces suggest that a good deal more contriving, fictionalising, is being employed. Since Manhire is not at all prolific, it is likely to be some time before this may be properly known. At present, the fictionalising is admitted, whatever weight is given to the spontaneous, the involuntary, part. Looking back, one may be inclined to wonder about the voluntary and the involuntary, the *ordonné* and the *dieudonné* of which Valéry spoke, and their respective contributions. In a poem such as "The Cinema" the dream factor may be registered, but one recognises as well that this is remarkably of a piece with some of Louis Simpson's poems. Elsewhere one is reminded of Robert Bly, and indeed of Bly's expressed attitudes, just as one is reminded of poets of other languages than English.

Whatever the debts, Manhire is distinctive in the considerable economy of his means, the precise control of his *The Elaboration* pieces, the more expansive (but still far from indulgent) longer-lined and richer textured poems of *How to Take Off Your Clothes at the Picnic*, or the more diverse and discursive of more recent poems. In either severe constraint or in relaxation of this, he is eminently lyrical, eminently given to celebration, to being playful in poems of love or domesticity, and extraordinarily adept at provoking the reader. Sentiment and intelligence are complementary, like fact and fiction, and as interchangeable.

—Kendrick Smithyman

MANIFOLD, John (Streeter). Australian. Born in Melbourne, Victoria, 21 April 1915. Educated at Geelong Grammar School, Victoria; Jesus College, Cambridge, 1934-37, B.A. (honours) in modern languages 1937. Served with the Intelligence Corps, 1940-46: Captain. Married the singer Katharine Hopwood in 1940 (died, 1969); one son and one daughter. President, Brisbane Realist Writers Group, 1956-66; President, Fellowship of Australian Writers, Queensland Branch, 1959; Commonwealth Literary Fund Lecturer at the universities of New England, Queensland, and South Australia. Currently, Vice-President, National Council of Realist Writers' Groups, and Poetry Editor, *The Realist.* Editor, Bandicoot Ballads series in the 1950's. Toured China in 1963 as a guest of the Association for Cultural Relations with Foreign Countries; toured the U.S.S.R. in 1963 as a guest of the Union of Soviet Writers; Delegate, International Writers' Meeting, Berlin, 1965. Agent: David Higham Associates Ltd., 5-8 Lower John Street, London W1R 4HA, England. Address: c/o University of Queensland Press, P.O. Box 42, St. Lucia, Queensland 4067, Australia.

PUBLICATIONS

Verse

The Death of Ned Kelly and Other Ballads. London, Favil Press, 1941.
Trident, with Hubert Nicholson and David Martin. London, Fore, 1944.
Selected Verse. New York, Day, 1946; London, Dobson, 1948.
Nightmares and Sunhorses. Melbourne, Overland, 1961.
Op. 8: Poems 1961-69. Queensland, Queensland University Press, 1970.
Broadsheets. Privately printed, 1973.
Six Sonnets on Human Ecology. Privately printed, 1974.
Collected Verse. Brisbane, University of Queensland Press, 1978.

Other

The Amorous Flute: An Unprofessional Handbook for Recorder Players and All Amateurs of Music. London, Workers Music Association, 1948.
The Music in English Drama from Shakespeare to Purcell. London, Barrie and Rockliff, 1956.
The Violin, The Banjo and the Bones: An Essay on the Instruments of Bush Music. Ferntree Gully, Victoria, Ram's Skull Press, 1957.
Who Wrote the Ballads? Notes on Australian Folksong. Sydney, Australasian Book Society, 1964.
The Changing Face of Realism. Brisbane, Communist Arts Group, 1971.

Editor, *Three Pieces from the Plaine and Easie Introduction to Musick 1597,* by Thomas Morley. London, Schott, 1948.
Editor, with Walter Bergmann, *Petite Suite for Two Descant Recorders and Piano.* London, Schott, 1948.
Editor, *The Queensland Centenary Pocket Songbook.* Sydney, Edwards and Shaw, 1959.
Editor, *The Penguin Australian Songbook.* Melbourne, Penguin, 1964.

*

Critical Study: *J.S. Manifold: An Introduction to the Man and His Work* by Rodney Hall, Brisbane, University of Queensland Press, 1978.

John Manifold comments:
My verse is old-fashioned. It is about women, horses, soldiers, revolutionists, landscapes, myths, and history. A lot of it is narrative. I enjoy wrestling with the strict forms—the apparently artless ballad being just as strict a form in its way as the apparently artful sonnet or limerick. I learnt from "Banjo" Paterson, Heredia, Heine, Aragon, and more recently Brecht, to strive for clarity, brevity, balance and impersonality.
Melius est quod reprehendent nos grammatici quam non intelligant populi (Saint Augustine).

*   *   *

John Manifold's *Selected Verse* was well received upon publication both in England and the United States. It centered around a brilliantly cool yet ardent sonnet series that was directly derived from the work of Auden. Manifold was able to bring his own heritage—wealthy pioneer ancestry, brilliant Cambridge career, conversion to Communism—unobtrusively but ingratiatingly into these poems, giving them a lightness and cultivatedness that were disarming and unexpected in Australian poetry of the late 1940's. Returning to Australia, Manifold retired to a small village outside Brisbane and, with his wife, taught local children how to make, and perform upon, antique musical instruments—recorders, lutes, citterns. His poetry became influenced by his own attempts to revive and reanimate early Australian bush-ballad traditions, the results of which were not very convincingly shown in his next collection, *Nightmares and Sunhorses.* Manifold has published a number of volumes on Elizabethan and Jacobean music, as well as Australian folksong. His most important recent work, however, is the verse collection *Op.8,* which includes a number of recent sonnets that recapture the wit and poise of his earlier work, as well as other work that remains admirable and unashamedly elegant. (Elegant in sensibility, not affectation.) John Manifold has been a personal influence on a number of Australian poets, from David Campbell to Rodney Hall. His writing perhaps captures only part of the man's complex and individual personality. But in itself that remains something of a nectar to be savoured and remembered.

—Thomas W. Shapcott

MANN, Chris(topher Michael Zithulele). South African. Born in Port Elizabeth, 6 April 1948. Educated at the University of the Witwatersrand, Johannesburg, B.A. 1970; Oxford University (Rhodes Scholar; Newdigate Prize, 1973); University of London, M.A. 1975. Married Julia G. St. John Skeen in 1982. Teacher, Baring High School, Swaziland, 1976-78; Lecturer, Rhodes University, Grahamstown, 1979-81. Since 1982, Director, Valley Trust, near Durban. Recipient: Olive Schreiner Prize, 1983. Agent: David Philip Publishers Pty. Ltd., Box 408, Claremont, Cape Province, 7735. Address: Box 33, Botha's Hill Natal 3660, South Africa.

PUBLICATIONS

Verse

First Poems. Johannesburg, Bateleur Press, 1977.
New Shades. Cape Town, David Philip, 1982.

Play

The Sand Labyrinth (produced Grahamstown, 1980).

Other

Editor, with Guy Butler, *A New Book of South African Verse in English*. Cape Town, Oxford University Press, 1979; Oxford, Oxford University Press, 1980.

*   *   *

Chris Mann's *First Poems* exhibited many of the faults common to a début volume: mawkish naivety ("Kneeling in moonlight, / with all your kissable crinkles"—in a poem titled "Darkness, Ivory, and Clay"!); uncertainty of touch and tone (particularly evident in tacked-on and contrived conclusions to poems that deserved better—as in "Summer Evening at the Kowie," with its bizarrely irrelevant close: "as the foam begins to gleam, / paddle between the devil / and the deep, receptive sea"); self-conscious poeticisms and unconscious echoes ("the well-doved day"; "halfway to heaven on a reapripe day"; "Two women on a beach at evening, / who murmur of this and that"). Yet despite its very uneven quality, there is much of interest in Mann's first collection—not least, its exuberant variety of styles and modes, ranging from ballad-stanzas adapted to a South African voice and setting ("Bennie and Anna," based on Hood's "Ben Battle") to social satire (in which the targets are disappointingly predictable); and from the alliterative "View from the Edge" (an exercise in the style of Swinburne) to the formal lyricism of "Words of the Overseas Missionary." There are some promising "Poems of Place," and Mann is clearly interested in the oral potential of verse: one section comprises "Poems to Be Said Aloud." Few of the "Love Poems" are altogether successful: a notable exception is the brief but finely realized "A Few Initial Words":

> What is there
> to say
> when the girl
> who walks ahead of you
> turns,
> and knee-deep
> in a sea of green barley
> opens out her arms?

New Shades, Mann's second volume, is a much more assured and rounded achievement. Themes and modes attempted in the preceding volume recur, but are more sparingly indulged and more subtly developed, as in the ballad-rhythms of "To Lucky with His Guitar":

> So here's Lucky, Coolhand Lucky the Tall;
> Sunday afternoon, easing into town;
> hasn't a word (drifting over New Street);
> nothing to tell us (tapping the pavement);
> but Coolhand riffs; zig-zag bass; stringshine chords.

Evocations of persons and places in this volume are more thoughtful in tone, more substantial in content: examples are "Nightscapes" and "The Pupil and Teacher's Reunion," in which the self-conscious awkwardness experienced on such occasions is sympathetically explored, rather than cleverly hit off:

> We grope onwards (retired Matrons, famous
> tries and expulsions, nicknames and googlies)

trudging upstream like anxious sangomas
for bonds, for kinships which eddy and shift
like shapes in the water but will not show.

The use of "sangomas" (from the Zulu, meaning "a diviner") in that stanza points to Mann's increasing use of words and phrases from indigenous languages, beside the more pointed "South Africanisms" of his colloquial poems.

New Shades is characterized also by a larger proportion of "poems for performance": these may be more effective in presentation (or with musical accompaniment) than they appear to be in print. Although Mann on occasion lapses into pseudo-profundities (as in "Bush and Sky") and mere imitation (the Laurentian note is unmistakable in "Napes"), his second volume is a distinct advance on the first. It remains to be seen whether he can discipline and channel his talents toward the attainment of a more truly individual voice and style.

—E. Pereira

MARLATT, Daphne (née Buckle). Australian. Born in Melbourne, Victoria, 11 July 1942. Educated at the University of British Columbia, Vancouver, B.A. 1964; Indiana University, Bloomington, M.A. 1968. Married Alan Marlatt (divorced); one son. Instructor in English, Capilano College, North Vancouver, 1968, 1973-76. Poetry Editor, *Capilano Review*, Vancouver, 1973-76; Editor, with Paul de Barros, *Periodics*, Vancouver, 1977-81. Recipient: Canada Council grant, 1969, 1973. Address: c/o Turnstone Press, Suite 603, 99 King Street, Winnipeg, Manitoba R3B 1H7, Canada.

PUBLICATIONS

Verse

Frames of a Story. Toronto, Ryerson Press, 1968.
Leaf Leaf/s. Los Angeles, Black Sparrow Press, 1969.
(Poems). Kyoto, Origin, 1970.
Vancouver Poems. Toronto, Coach House Press, 1972.
Steveston. Vancouver, Talonbooks, 1974.
Our Lives. Carrboro, North Carolina, Truck Press, 1975; revised edition, Lantzville, British Columbia, Oolichan, 1979.
Here and There. Lantzville, British Columbia, Island, 1981.
How Hug a Stone. Winnipeg, Turnstone Press, 1983.

Novel

Zócalo. Toronto, Coach House Press, 1977.

Other

Rings (miscellany). Toronto, York Street Commune, 1971.
Selected Writing: Net Work, edited by Fred Wah. Vancouver, Talonbooks, 1980.
What Matters: Writing 1968-1970. Toronto, Coach House Press, 1980.

Editor, *Steveston Recollected: A Japanese-Canadian History*. Victoria, Provincial Archives of British Columbia, 1975.

*   *   *

In "Musing with Mothertongue" (in *Tessera*) Daphne Marlatt notes that "language is first of all for us a body of sound." It is this sense of poetry (and, indeed, all language) as sound that gives Marlatt's work its characteristic rhythms and which explains, as well, the other quality which marks the writing: its meticulous attention to detail and form. The images which Marlatt selects are, in themselves, exact renderings of the environment she is describing, but their appropriateness extends beyond the mimetic; they fragment and rejoin to form impressions governed by the sounds they make in combination. These new relationships of word elements and phrases, sometimes created by spontaneous association and sometimes by carefully crafted quibbles or punctuation, create in the poems—and even in the prose criticism—a series of new and deeper meanings as the writing progresses. It is as process, then, that the poems must be read and, in fact, that the whole body of Marlatt's work to date should be seen.

The early poems in *Frames* establish Marlatt's desire for an escape into a literary process which will free her two protagonists from the framing influence of their grandmother's strict past, even as it frees Marlatt from the framing strictures of traditional literary expression. To some extent the dilemma is autobiographical in that Marlatt is the child of colonial British parents (a background she later explores in "In the month of hungry ghosts"), and was ending a relationship at the time of writing. More important, the struggle of the two girls to see themselves and each other through new frames, to create a world out of their own perceptions, becomes the central aim of the poems since. The two girls—each an extension of one aspect of Marlatt's own struggle toward commitment and self—do not succeed in finding freedom; nor does Marlatt find her independent voice.

In *Leaf Leaf/s*, however, Marlatt begins to assemble experience from the disparate images around her and to create poetry from the sounds these images evoke in words. The curious amalgam of visual and aural images which mark her writing from this point forms a series of complex photographs which simultaneously present a picture, its sounds, the effect of the image on the perceiver, and the resonance of that perception in the reader's ear. These four sets of stimuli for every impression, each one independent but all necessary for the total effect, force a process in reading which renders the poetry not only amazingly precise, but experiential. One does not observe the world Marlatt reports, but enters it and, in fact, creates it with her.

Her vision has been called "phenomenological" by Douglas Barbour, Robert Lecker, and others, and certainly by the time she writes the *Steveston* poems it is clear that her universe has become one of sense perceptions. It is important, however, to observe the role of sound as one of these sensations, in itself a separate aspect of the world and an equal building block with other influences in which the poet finds herself immersed. This composite universe does not follow sequential conscious intellectual analysis in her groupings of phenomena; yet, in the relationship of sound to meaning, and of personal experience to poetic moment, a strict relationship of cause and effect emerges.

It is not, however, a linear construct. Marlatt seeks in a central metaphor of birth for an explanation of the writing impulse and a feminine vision of causality. Indeed, in *Rings* the entrances of the husband into the private world of mother and child mark a shift from a soft and creative language to one of more complex, but less felt ideas, and of direct connections. The experiences which fill Marlatt's world become more and more fragments of feminine process: blood, water, a letting go, mouths as sucking. Again, in *Tessera* she suggests "like the mother's body, language is larger than us and carries us along with it. It bears us, it births us, insofar as we bear with it."

A growing feminist bias develops in the work since *How Hug a Stone*, although, in retrospect, one can see in the earliest poems the clear roots of the poet's identification with language as an extension of the female body and the process of writing as linked to the processes of female sexuality. The rhythms of the new erotic poems pick up the recurring images of rivers and flowing water to become menstrual and orgasmic; the birth of children becomes the birth of a new, female syntax; the harmony of all sensa becomes the harmony of two women's bodies in the act of love. The sounds become more gentle as they are freed of what Marlatt calls "terms for dominance tied up with male experience," such as those she employs in the angry sociological statements of *Steveston*. But they retain their astonishing clarity, and the precise patterns they form create the multiple and overlapping impressions which are the core of Marlatt's poetry.

—S.R. Gilbert

MARSHALL, Jack.   American.   Born in Brooklyn, New York, 25 February 1937. Educated at Lafayette High School, Brooklyn. Married Kathleen Fraser, *q.v.*, in 1961 (divorced, 1970), one son. Shipping clerk, salesman, farmhand, steel mill hand, deck hand; copywriter, J.C. Penney, New York; longshoreman, San Francisco. Taught in poetry workshops at the University of Iowa, Iowa City, 1969-71, California Western College, San Diego, 1972-74, San Francisco State University, 1975, and United States International University, San Diego. Recipient: Bay Area Book Reviewers award, 1984. Address: 1056 Treat Avenue, San Francisco, California 94110, U.S.A.

PUBLICATIONS

Verse

The Darkest Continent.   New York, For Now Press, 1967.
Bearings.   New York, Harper, 1969.
Floats.   Iowa City, Cedar Creek Press, 1971.
Surviving in America, with Anselm Hollo and Sam Hamod.   Iowa City, Cedar Creek Press, 1972.
Bits of Thirst.   Iowa City, Cedar Creek Press, 1972.
Bits of Thirst and Other Poems and Translations.   Berkeley, California, Blue Wind Press, 1976.
Arriving on the Playing Fields of Paradise.   Santa Cruz, California, Jazz Press, 1983.

Other

Editor, with Howard Roberts, *Instant Blues: Funky Style*, by Harley James.   North Hollywood, Playback, 1973.

*

Jack Marshall comments:
My poems are playful investigations and perceptions of possible alternate realities. I write them because no one else does. I write them with as much economy as I can; music and metaphor being the compression-chamber of the senses.

*   *   *

In his early book, *Bearings*, Jack Marshall impresses one as a poet with considerable energy and talent who cannot always harness them successfully; often the poem gets the upper hand, its forceful rhetoric becoming mannered, unclear, or somewhat rambling. Marshall has a talent for stately speech and a rich vocabulary, packing his lines with strong sounds and closely-bunched movements of imagery and thought. The problem is that often his lines are *too* dense; they become crabbed, straining the reader's attention, or else they get caught up in following associations of emotion and image that draw away from the poem's main thrust.

When his poems succeed, some of the qualities apparent in the poorer poems make the successes impressive ones—density of sound and sense, dramatic tone, specificity, variety of vocabulary and image. A great number of his best poems (like "Setting Out" and "On the President's State Visit to Mexico") make an extensive use of syntactical parallelism, a device which at once accommodates his forceful rhetoric, producing a kind of persistent thrust, and also provides a simple structure which tends to prevent excessive convolution or rambling courses of association.

It isn't apparent whether or not the poems are arranged chronologically, but there seems to be a considerable improvement in the poems of the third and fourth sections over those in the first and second, and a more personal and relaxed tone enters the book in poems like "Walking Across Brooklyn Bridge" and "For Kathleen, Gone on a Brief Journey." It should be added that in poems which have appeared in various places since his first book Marshall has assumed a new, freer style which allows him to make a series of non-rational associations without cramping the poem or seeming to get lost in it.

—Lawrence Russ

MARTY, Sid. Canadian. Born in South Shields, County Durham, England, 20 June 1944; raised in southern Alberta. Educated at Mount Royal Junior College, Calgary, 1963-65; Sir George Williams University, Montreal, B.A. 1967, B.A. (honours) 1969. Married Myrna Clarke Jamison in 1968; two sons. Worked as park warden in national parks in Yoho, 1966-68, Jasper, 1970-72, Prince Albert, 1972-73, and Banff, 1973-78. Since 1978, full-time writer. Recipient: Canadian Authors Association prize, 1978; Alberta Government grant, 1978. Address: Box 22, Lundbreck, Alberta TOK 1HO, Canada.

PUBLICATIONS

Verse

Headwaters. Toronto, McClelland and Stewart, 1973.
Tumbleweed Harvest. Wood Mountain, Saskatchewan, Sundog Press, 1973.
Nobody Danced with Miss Rodeo. Toronto, McClelland and Stewart, 1981.

Other

Men for the Mountains (on park wardens). Toronto, McClelland and Stewart, 1978; New York, Vanguard Press, 1979.

A Grand and Fabulous Notion (on national parks). Toronto, NC Press, 1984.

*

Critical Studies: by M. Travis Lane, in *Fiddlehead* (Fredericton, New Brunswick), Winter 1973 and Winter 1981; William French, in *Toronto Globe and Mail*, 26 January 1974; Lorne Hicks, in *Canadian Forum* (Toronto), May 1974; Marty Gervais in *Windsor Star* (Ontario), 4 April 1981.

*   *   *

Sid Marty is one of the younger poets who emerged in Canada during the 1970's with a remarkable sense of closeness to the geo-historical environment. Before that period, the general tendency of Canadian poets had been either to avoid the wilderness as a poetic terrain, or else to follow in literary terms the example of the pioneers who tried to tame the wilderness because they feared it. Typical of such literary taming was the way in which poets like Charles G.D. Roberts and Archibald Lampman tried to express the uniqueness of the Canadian terrain in forms the Romantics had devised to project a European experience; even poets as late as A.J.M. Smith evoked the wild lands in formalist patterns that had little relation to the experience of having inhabited them. Northrop Frye's concept of Canada as a "garrison society," embattled against the threatening natural world, was certainly a reasonably accurate projection of the attitudes found in Canadian poetry until the present generation.

It was really poets like Al Purdy and John Newlove, coming to maturity in the late 1950's, and wandering over the country, hitchhiking and taking jobs that linked them into the life of remote places, who began to develop a poetry related directly to experience of the land as wilderness and to the life-style that implied an acceptance of the natural world as it is rather than as a source of raw materials to be exploited.

Among the poets most influenced—or perhaps most liberated—in a positive way by the example of Purdy and Newlove is Sid Marty, perhaps the first convincingly successful poet of the Rocky Mountains, and successful because he has sought, not to confront the mountains, to objectify them, but rather to see them as a presence in whose face to live. One of the poems in Sid Marty's first book, *Headwaters*, is entitled "Each Mountain," and begins: "Each mountain/its own country/in the way a country/must be/A state of mind." Another poem, this time about encounters with the denizens of the mountains rather than with the mountains themselves, is entitled "Three Bears," and ends:

> But I am reminded
> I am not at home
> Here where I live
> only at hazard
>
> There is a darkness
> along the bright petals

Between them, these fragments bound a territory of the mind that Sid Marty had made peculiarly his own. The geography of the land extends the geography of the mind, and in the very act of extension is takes us perhaps not into alien territory, but into country where we are exposed beyond the benefit of certainty.

Sid Marty's poems have a telling directness when they describe the incidents of his life as a park warden in the Rockies, drawing the reader close to the mountain face, to the guarded encounters with nature personified as grumpy grizzlies, to the companionship that grows up between men and their horses, to the ambiguous relationships between human mind and animal mind created by the coyote's cleverness:

> Coyote keeps his real name secret
> so no one gets that handle to beat him with...
> Returning in other pelts, he walks
> over the graves of pious men
> looking for secret vices
>
> Goes on living, closer to the town
> each year, until he winds up
> feeding in the alleys of night
> a jump away from the bush or prairie
>
> Full of pride, he makes up melodies
> to multiply his saga, a skilled ventriloquist
> moving in from all directions at once.

Sid Marty's is a poetry of episode transmuting into myth, very directly bedded in personal experience, and combining a laconic verbal tone with vividly experienced imagery. It is a poetry of sharp observation, and hence a true nature poetry, and also of tight and compelling narrative.

—George Woodcock

MASSINGHAM, Harold (William).   British.   Born in Mexborough, Yorkshire, 25 October 1932. Educated at Mexborough Grammar School, 1943-51; Manchester University, 1951-54, B.A. in English 1954. Married Patricia Audrey Moran in 1958; three sons and one daughter. School teacher, Manchester Education Committee, 1955-70. Since 1971, Tutor, Extra-mural Department, University of Manchester. Co-Founder, *Manchester University Poetry*, 1953. Recipient: Cheltenham Festival Guinness Prize, 1962; Arts Council award, 1965; Cholmondeley award, 1968. Address: 30 Spring Bridge Road, Manchester M16 8PW, England.

PUBLICATIONS

Verse

Black Bull Guarding Apples.   London, Longman, 1965.
Creation.   Oxford, Sycamore Press, 1968.
The Magician: A Poem Sequence.   Manchester, Phoenix Pamphlet Poets Press, 1969.
Storm.   Frensham, Surrey, Sceptre Press, 1970.
Snow-Dream.   Rushden, Northamptonshire, Sceptre Press, 1971.
The Pennine Way.   London, BBC, 1971.
Frost-Gods.   London, Macmillan, 1971.
Doomsday.   London, Poem-of-the-Month Club, 1972.

Other

Mate in Two (chess problems).   Manchester, P.C. Woolley, 1976.

Editor, *Poetry Workshop.*   Manchester, University of Manchester Extramural Department, 3 vols., 1973-76.

---

*

Critical Studies: by Alan Ross, in *London Magazine*, August 1965; "A Yorkshireman" by Douglas Phillips, in *Western Mail* (Cardiff), November 1965; "Northern World 1" by Patrick Henry, in *Phoenix 10* (Manchester), July 1973.

Harold Massingham comments:
   As a poet, and apart from certain lyrics and fanciful poems for children, my main concern is to re-live, explore and re-present native experience in concrete terms. Some poems embody natural forces, birth-dreams and animal-nightmares; some relate to the North of England, especially a Yorkshire childhood; others celebrate persons and occasionally treat of domestic issues. The tendency is to create sensuous, physical, elemental impressions in a thick texture of tight phrasing and concrete imagery: most of which imagery has its genesis in my early life. I am indebted to Keats for the earliest impulse to use my own verbal resources (see also *London Magazine* ix, 1); Laurie Lee and Dylan Thomas were later fugitive influences; and for many years my main stylistic influence has been Anglo-Saxon verse, in its ruggedness, deliberate alliterations and seemingly irregular (pre-iambic) rhythms. I have translated a great deal of it, usually as "free versions." Non-literary inspirations have been van Gogh and Beethoven. I have no orthodox political or religious affiliations, but certain pantheistic sympathies and a preoccupation with self-expression and with the genesis and individuality of things.

*   *   *

Harold Massingham was born in 1932 in Mexborough, Yorkshire, the son of a collier, and spent the first twenty years of his life there. The poems of his first book of verse, *Black Bull Guarding Apples*, are very much those of a Northerner ("The air nips, blonds, it is eye-living light./North-born, I could do worse than house in it"). It is concerned with the history and climate of Northern England and the "separateness" of animals (bull, rat, lizard, spider, frog, jackdaw). The language is terse, the description compact and imaginative (of the rat: "He was filthy silk"). People are represented by a snuff addict, a war veteran, his children, his mining father. Half-rhymes are usual. Significantly, there are versions of the Anglo-Saxon "The Seafarer" and "The Wanderer."
   Frost-Gods also celebrates "Northness." Most of these poems are unrhymed; the writing is both more sophisticated and more fanciful ("tree-rain/Fell like isaac-newton apples"). Animals are still represented: a swan, an Alsatian, a cow ("this suede Empress"). There are translations of thirteen Anglo-Saxon riddles and three longer Anglo-Saxon poems. One poem describes the old and the poor in a cafeteria, another ("Winter in Wensleydale") is a very typical poem of landscape and season. These are two of the most successful, and illustrate the two main manifestations of Massingham's talent. There are also two nightmare poems: one childish ("Flitter-Rats"), one adult ("Nightmare of Blazing Vultures"). These are not so successful; nor is his children's verse, some of which appeared in *The Magician*. He is a poet who writes best about animals, natural objects, ordinary people. When he has his eye on these, his poems benefit. Humour, satire, political intention, are entirely absent. This is an art of straightforward projection, making the reader see what the poet sees, with very little variation of theme or tone.

—Gavin Ewart

MATCHETT, William H(enry). American. Born in Chicago, Illinois, 5 March 1923. Educated at Westtown School, Pennsylvania; Swarthmore College, Pennsylvania, B.A. (highest honors) 1949; Harvard University, Cambridge, Massachusetts, M.A. 1950, Ph.D. 1957. Conscientious Objector: Civilian Public Service, 1943-46. Married Judith Wright in 1949; two sons and one daughter. Teaching Fellow, Harvard University, 1953-54; Instructor, 1954-56, Assistant Professor, 1956-60, Associate Professor, 1960-66, and Professor of English, 1966-82, now Emeritus, University of Washington, Seattle. Editor, *Modern Language Quarterly*, Seattle, 1963-82. Since 1961, Member of the Editorial Board, *Poetry Northwest*, Seattle. Recipient: *Furioso* prize, 1952; Washington State Governor's Award, 1982. Address: Department of English, GN-30, University of Washington, Seattle, Washington 98195, U.S.A.

PUBLICATIONS

Verse

Water Ouzel and Other Poems. Boston, Houghton Mifflin, 1955.
Fireweed and Other Poems. Cranberry Isles, Maine, Tidal Press, 1980.

Other

Poetry: From Statement to Meaning, with Jerome Beaty. New York, Oxford University Press, 1965.
The Phoenix and the Turtle: Shakespeare's Poem and Chester's "Loues Martyr." The Hague, Mouton, 1965.

Editor, *The Life and Death of King John,* by William Shakespeare. New York, New American Library, 1966.

*

William H. Matchett comments:
    No doubt the best of my poetry tends to move from closely observed natural images to small affirmations achieved through the implications of understatements, but there is a fairly wide range of subjects, forms, and approaches.

*   *   *

    Subdued, civil, and marked by an easy grace, William H. Matchett's poems have found favor in several reprintings. Long before Ecology became the fashionable cry, he praised the fragile lives of wild birds, now become extinct, or nearly so, by the wanton hand of predatory man. His sensitive descriptions of nature are based on acute observation and conveyed through personification and perky humor, but they often close in pessimism. "Hang on to the end!" he urges the Ivory Bill, "You still may thrive/The Fates of us all are linked." He places little trust, however, in "the human pest," concluding there may be room for delicate wildfowl when man is extinct. Viewing man against man in war, he despairs, "lacking the strength to put the world in order." In other topographical poems, casual, conversational sketches preface philosophical meditations on nature as a source of grace and "second sight." Dry reflection follows the vivid portraiture of "Old Inn on the Eastern Shore," but finally gives way to mockery. The impression of nature is short-lived, "insight will fade"; the student soon considers himself "no sinner," and "Will go in to bathe before dinner."
    This penchant for the didactic is more pronounced in compact

rimed lyrics on a simple wedding, a Quaker funeral, Spring, and September, where aphorisms and moral tags render the scenes curiously bloodless. More spirited are the several internal monologues by personages caught in dramatic moments. Bloodthirsty and self-righteous, Mather, scourge of witches, rants to his angry God. Surrounded by dust and dry earth, Kruger waits placidly for death. The selfish patriarch remembers the powers of youth; imperious still in strengthless old age, he is aware of the symbolism of a flower but oblivious to the granddaughter who brings it. The visiting poet slyly avoids, then confronts, his imperceptive admirers—and the vision of his younger, better self. In "Packing a Photograph from Firenze" Matchett's several themes and methods join. Leaving an old house soon to be replaced by a modern jungle of structural steel, a home for statisticians who "doodle death with indelible ink," he marks the end of a life cycle and reaffirms the values of crooked lines, dirty fingers, fertile minds, living things.

—Joseph Parisi

———————

MATHIAS, Roland (Glyn). British (Welsh). Born near Talybont-on-Usk, Breconshire, 4 September 1915. Educated at Caterham School; Jesus College, Oxford (Meyricke Exhibitioner, 1934; Honorary Scholar, 1936), B.A. (honours) in modern history 1936, B.Litt. 1939, M.A. 1944. Married Mary (Molly) Hawes in 1944; three children. Senior History Master, Cowley School, St. Helens, Lancashire, 1938-41; Resident Master, Blue Coat School, Reading, Berkshire, 1941-45; Senior History Master, St. Clement Danes Grammar School, London, 1946-48; Headmaster, Pembroke Dock (later Pembroke) Grammar School, Wales, 1948-58, Herbert Strutt School, Belper, Derbyshire, 1958-64, and King Edward's Five Ways School, Birmingham, 1964-69. Since 1969, full-time writer. Schoolmaster-Fellow, Balliol College, Oxford, 1961, and University College, Swansea, 1967; part-time extra-mural lecturer, University College, Cardiff, 1970-77; Visiting Lecturer, University of Rennes, France, 1970, University of Brest, France, 1970, and University of Alabama, Birmingham, 1971. Editor, *The Anglo-Welsh Review*, 1961-76. Chairman, English Section, Yr Academi Gymreig, 1975-78; Chairman, Literature Committee, Welsh Arts Council, 1976-79. Recipient: Welsh Arts Council bursary, 1968, award, 1969, and prize, 1972, 1980. Address: Deffrobani, 5 Maescelyn, Brecon, Powys LD3 7NL, Wales.

PUBLICATIONS

Verse

Days Enduring and Other Poems. Ilfracombe, Devon, Stockwell, 1943.
Break in Harvest and Other Poems. London, Routledge, 1946.
The Roses of Tretower. Pembroke Dock, Dock Leaves Press, 1952.
The Flooded Valley. London, Putnam, 1960.
Absalom in the Tree and Other Poems. Llandybie, Dyfed, Gomer, 1971.
Snipe's Castle. Llandysul, Dyfed, Gomer, 1979.
Burning Brambles: Selected Poems 1944-1979. Llandysul, Dyfed, Gomer, 1983.

Short Stories

The Eleven Men of Eppynt and Other Stories. Pembroke
Dock, Dock Leaves Press, 1956.

Other

*Whitsun Riot: An Account of a Commotion Amongst Catholics
in Herefordshire and Monmouthshire in 1605.* Cambridge,
Bowes, 1963.
Vernon Watkins. Cardiff, University of Wales Press, 1974.
The Hollowed-Out Elder Stalk: John Cowper Powys as Poet.
London, Enitharmon Press, 1979.

Editor, with Sam Adams, *The Shining Pyramid and Other
Stories by Welsh Authors.* Llandysul, Dyfed, Gomer, 1970.
Editor, *David Jones: Eight Essays on His Work as Writer and
Artist.* Llandysul, Dyfed, Gomer, 1976.
Editor, with Sam Adams, *The Collected Short Stories of
Geraint Goodwin.* Tenby, H.G. Walters, 1976.
Editor, with Raymond Garlick, *Anglo-Welsh Poetry 1480-
1980.* Bridgend, Glamorgan, Poetry Wales Press, 1984.

*

Critical Study: "The Poetry of Roland Mathias" by Jeremy
Hooker, in *Poetry Wales* (Llandybie), Summer 1971.

Roland Mathias comments:

In my earlier poetry the sense of "place" was very strong....
Even love poems used the "place" or "history" symbol.

Of recent years the process has changed. The secret "place" is
always Wales, but since my return to it physically there has been
a blurring of the remembered image by the present reality. In
consequence I have become slightly more personal in my poetry,
in an overt sense, but there are more people about, more predicaments than mine. I think of history still, of my stock, my
parents, family love, and my own insufficiency in the line of
descent. For me the old Noncomformist sense of guilt is not
inhibiting and useless: it gives me a particular vision of the
present through the past, a measurement. Out of it I can write.

I would add, however, that I continue to find significance in
the parochial and believe that poetry is often weakened and
diluted by being devoted to situations in which the element of the
personal is small. My vision begins with Wales and the rest of the
world merely adheres to it.

*   *   *

Roland Mathias was born in 1915 at Talybont-on-Usk in
Breconshire, a border county which is still largely rural in character. Although he has spent much of his adult life in Pembrokeshire and England, this borderland of his birth, where "Nightin-
gales struggle with thorn-trees for the gate of Wales" and where
Welsh and English have rubbed shoulders for hundreds of years,
remains an important part of his personal landscape. He has
written that in his earlier poetry "the sense of 'place' was very
strong...it was always of tremendous importance to me to know
exactly *where* I was and what mood the place engendered in me.
People might help to form that mood but the moment of ignition
was always (or almost always) produced by solitude, the particular place and the history of men in that place."

In all his writing his appreciation of landscape is profoundly
enriched by his sense of history and his concern for truth. He has
no time for loose rhetoric or the easy attitude. His poetry pre-

sents a consistent view of the world expressed in a tough and
concentrated verse of considerable individuality.

Alliteration is a powerful unifying device and with its help he
often creates a rhythmic undertow which tugs against the surface
flow. His images are concrete, hardly ever merely pictorial, but
suggestive of layers of meaning beneath the obvious. His poetry
is not always easy, but it is always rewarding.

—John Stuart Williams

MATTHEWS, William (Proctor). American. Born in Cincinnati, Ohio, 11 November 1942. Educated at Yale University,
New Haven, Connecticut, B.A. 1965; University of North Carolina, Chapel Hill, M.A. 1966. Married Marie Harris in 1963
(divorced, 1974); two sons. Instructor in English, Wells College,
Aurora, New York, 1968-69; Assistant Professor, Cornell University, Ithaca, New York, 1969-74, and University of Colorado,
Boulder, 1974-77; Associate Professor, and Director of Creative
Writing, University of Washington, Seattle, 1978-83. Since
1983, Visiting Professor, University of Houston, and Brooklyn
College of City University of New York. Visiting Lecturer, Uni-
versity of Iowa, and Poetry Editor, *Iowa Review*, Iowa City,
1976-77. Member of the Editorial Board, Wesleyan University
Press, 1969-74; Member, 1976-79, and Chairman, 1978-79,
Literature Panel, National Endowment for the Arts. Since 1966,
Co-Founding Editor, Lillabulero Press, and *Lillabulero*, Aurora,
New York. Recipient: National Endowment for the Arts Fellow-
ship, 1974, 1984; Guggenheim Fellowship, 1980. Address: 523
West 121st Street, New York, New York 10027, U.S.A.

PUBLICATIONS

Verse

Broken Syllables. Aurora, New York, Lillabulero Press, 1969.
Ruining the New Road. New York, Random House, 1970.
The Cloud. Boston, Barn Dream Press, 1971.
The Moon. Baltimore, Penyeach Press, 1971.
Poems for Tennessee, with Robert Bly and William Stafford.
Martin, Tennessee Poetry Press, 1971.
Sleek for the Long Flight: New Poems. New York, Random
House, 1972.
Without a Mouth. Norfolk, Virginia, Penyeach Press, 1972.
The Secret Life. Rochester, New York, Valley Press, 1972.
An Oar in the Old Water. San Francisco, Stone Press, 1973.
Sticks and Stones. Milwaukee, Pentagram Press, 1975.
Rising and Falling. Boston, Little Brown, 1979.
Flood. Boston, Little Brown, 1982.
A Happy Childhood. Boston, Little Brown, 1984.

Other

Translator, with Mary Feeney, *Removed from Time*, by Jean
Follain. Tannersville, New York, Tideline Press, 1977.
Translator, with Mary Feeney, *A World Rich in Anniversaries:
Prose Poems*, by Jean Follain. Iowa City, Grilled Flowers
Press, 1979.

*

Critical Studies: in *Tennessee Poetry Journal* (Martin), Spring 1970; interview in *Ohio Review* (Athens), Spring 1972.

William Matthews comments:

My poems hope to speak for themselves. Much of their speech would be silence. Just as an architect uses walls to organize space, I use the words of a poem to organize silences. In those silences, the echoes, reverberations, assents, denials and secrets of my poems occur. These mute events are closely linked to the silences and strange landscapes in the natural world. That natural world, to an American, is large, often melodramatic, and strange—even in the most settled regions, where I have spent most of my life. My poems aren't self-consciously or programmatically American, but it matters—for all my travels—that I have lived here so long, in certain places, with certain people.

The language in my poems is the language one would love if he had grown up loving much British poetry and much American speech. I have grown to love American poetry and what I have heard of British (and Canadian) speech, but the memories of childhood are intense ones, indelible it seems. Of course it is all mixed, in moil, when I write. But I know from listening to what I have written that I love in language those moments which blur the distinctions between "formal" and "street" language. I distrust such categories, so I blur them often. I love best those poems which seem just to have emerged from a thicket of silence and intense emotion.

*   *   *

William Matthews's Romanticism, filtered through Roethke and the Spanish surrealists, is manifest in the candor and vividness of his first collection, *Ruining the New Road*, published in 1970. Introducing himself as "a journalist/who can't believe in objectivity," Matthews uses deep image and free verse to explore such themes as loneliness and desire, pain, transfiguration, and political wrong. As in several of his early collections, love ("life's best work") offers security, and nature supplies much of the imagery.

Displaced, like the "elk come too far south," which must run "through snowy fields/on melting legs," the young Matthews seeks integrality through location. Wanting the response of his beloved and of all things, he recognizes that "We're sewn into each other/like money in a miser's coat" and imagines a kind of amnesty: "Don't cry. Your wounds are/beautiful if you'll love mine." He sees discomfort as a quality common to all Americans: his final answer to his title "Why We Are Truly a Nation" is

> Because grief unites us,
> like the locked antlers of moose
> who die on their knees in pairs.

Out of pain ("heaving under you/like frost ruining the new road") might come keener awareness and repose, if not transformation. The final section of poems in *Ruining the New Road* imagines fundamental change: dying, one is an old plank absorbing water until "you split along the grain"; flesh falls off "like the glad lover's underwear"; grapes rot to readiness. The invisible parts of a fogbound lake challenge the poet to "let go," and he vows to "curse the lies I have lived by."

By the later 1970's, in the poems of *Rising and Falling*, Matthews's exuberant belief in the truth of the image has been tempered. Declaring his study to be "the scripture of matter,/our long narcosis of parting," he focuses on process and consequence. While some topics are predictable—aging, death, ero-

sion, and remembrance—he articulates some memorable implications of mortality. In "Old Records" a friend immediately tapes records in order not to have to wear them out by playing them, a paradox that prompts Matthews to observe, "We're like a fire/and save things from ourselves." An old woman who as a girl urged, "Daddy drive faster," is now "stunned by the speed of her life" ("Opening Her Jewel Box"). Things pass, Matthews says, "the way the links of a fugue become/one another's strict abandonments."

Instead of vaguely defined mysticism or "the subconscious," Matthews regards time, the news, and family as the connectives among people. "The stories grow crooked inside/you," he says in "Strange Knees"; "In memory," he explains in "A Roadside near Ithaca," "you can carry/by constant revision/some loved thing...." Now the poetic effort is not so much a trusting in startling images as it is a diving for meaning, or, as "Living among the Dead" has it, a search through the drawers of the furniture of the dead.

"Information keeps our senses linked," he says in "Snow Falling Through Fog." Indeed, in these poems, in which Matthews is most interested in the changes of perception over time, he has turned to stanzas, narrative, and explanation. And the mystery of life seems no less than before. "Nurse Sharks" vividly depicts the risks of knowing the depths. The second section of "Taking the Train Home" is a virtuoso handling of images to recreate the boyhood dream of ease and plenty. Sobered, accustomed to living singly, keenly aware of the body's ineptness as well as its pleasures, Matthews can now be consoled by probing, even though it does not always result in knowledge. "...So we go," he smiles in "Outer Space," "stupid ideas//for feet."

From the start of his career, Matthews's talent for imagery has produced striking lines like "You're going to shave a stranger/backwards every morning" and "you can hear the suburbs coming/on their elbows," from *Sleek for the Long Flight*. "Bystanders," a long poem in *Flood* about a fatal auto accident on an icy hill, shows he can still turn out memorable narratives. But Matthews will have to guard against excess. *Sleek for the Long Flight* is already badly dated by an overreliance on the mannerisms of the deep imagists, and *Flood* is marred by repetitive imagery, trite conceptions, and thematic confusion. One hopes that Matthews's subsequent books will regain the balance between perceiver and perceived of *Rising and Falling*.

—Jay S. Paul

MATTHIAS, John (Edward). American. Born in Columbus, Ohio, 5 September 1941. Educated at Ohio State University, Columbus, 1959-63, B.A. 1963; Stanford University, California, 1963-65, M.A. 1966; University of London (Fulbright Fellow), 1966-67. Married Diana Adams in 1967; two children. Assistant Professor, 1967-73, Associate Professor, 1973-80, and since 1980, Professor of English, University of Notre Dame, Indiana. Visiting Professor, Clare Hall, Cambridge, 1976-77, Skidmore College, Saratoga Springs, New York, Summer 1978, and University of Chicago, Spring 1980. Recipient: Columbia University Translation Center Award, 1979; Ingram-Merrill Foundation Award, 1984. Address: Department of English, University of Notre Dame, Notre Dame, Indiana 46556, U.S.A.

PUBLICATIONS

Verse

Other Poems. Ann Arbor, Michigan, Cat's Pajamas Press,
1971.
Bucyrus. Chicago, Swallow Press, 1971.
Herman's Poems. Rushden, Northamptonshire, Sceptre Press,
1973.
Turns. Chicago, Swallow Press, and London, Anvil Press Poet-
ry, 1975.
*Double Derivation, Association and Cliché: From the Great
Tournament Roll of Westminster.* Chicago, Wine Press,
1975.
Two Poems. Knotting, Bedfordshire, Sceptre Press, 1976.
Crossing. Chicago, Swallow Press, and London, Anvil Press
Poetry, 1979.
Rostropovich at Aldeburgh. Knotting, Bedfordshire, Sceptre
Press, 1979.
Bathory and Lermontov. Ahus, Sweden, Kalejdoskop, 1980.
Northern Summer. Athens, Swallow Press-Ohio University
Press, and London, Anvil Press Poetry, 1984.

Other

Editor, *23 Modern British Poets.* Chicago, Swallow Press,
1971.
Editor, *Five American Poets.* Manchester, Carcanet, 1979.
Editor, *Introducing David Jones.* London, Faber, 1980.
Editor and Translator, with Göran Printz-Påhlson, *Contemporary Swedish Poetry.* Chicago, Swallow Press, and London, Anvil Press Poetry, 1980.

Translator, with Göran Printz-Påhlson, *Rainmaker,* by Jan
Östergren. Athens, Ohio University Press, 1983.

*

Critical Studies: "John Matthias: Crossing" by William Sylvester, in *Credences* (Buffalo), Spring 1981; "The Poetry of John
Matthias: Between the Castle and the Mine" by Vincent Sherry,
in *Salmagundi* (Saratoga Springs, New York), Fall 1984.

John Matthias comments:
    It is probably best not to say very much about one's own work.
The background to mine includes a brief, early, but intense
period of study with John Berryman and three years at Stanford
University in the middle 1960's when I first became acquainted
with a group of poets—all at that time students of Yvor
Winters—whose work is now well known: Robert Hass, John
Peck, Robert Pinsky, and James McMichael. I still feel a considerable affinity with these four poets. In the late 1960's, I began
spending long periods of time in England. The pre-history,
history, and geography of East Anglia have been crucial for my
writing, both as background and foreground, during more than
15 years. More recently, the direction of my work has been
shaped by a short but very significant period of time spent in
Fife, Scotland, and by several years of collaboration with Göran
Printz-Påhlson translating contemporary Swedish poetry.
Though I am an American poet, most of what seems to me my
best work has been written in Britain, often about British subjects. Stylistically, I consider myself an eclectic and would
defend eclecticism. Like Robert Duncan, I can say that much of
my work is derivative without feeling unhappy about it. I, too,
would often be glad to "emulate, imitate, reconstrue, approxi-

mate." My deepest and in some ways contradictory enthusiasms
among English language poets of our century are for Pound,
David Jones, early Auden, and Geoffrey Hill. This is not so
much a question of influence as a matter of gratitude and awe.

*   *   *

    The essential oddity and eccentricity of John Matthias's sen-
sibility, and of his always interesting and inventive poetry, can be
most easily suggested by pointing out that he is clearly influenced by two odd and eccentric poets who are also quite exceptionally different from each other, John Berryman and David
Jones, on both of whom Matthias has written excellent critical
essays. From the former, he takes a proud, performing—
perhaps even self-regarding—poetic self, and a readiness to be
painfully personal; and from the latter he takes a penetrating
interest in the recovery of a history and a tradition from a
particular landscape (in Matthias primarily the Fen country)
and a magpie hoarding of out-of-the-way information and anecdote, which form the kernel of a number of ruminative poems.
The combination of the American and the British influence
seems a necessary one for Matthias who, American by birth, has
strong British connections and family, and has lived in both
countries: the relationship between the two is signalled in the
title of one of his books, *Crossing.*
    It is probably clear that any poet who feels himself capable of
absorbing and assimilating two such potently individual voices
must have himself a strong poetic personality and constitution;
and this is, indeed, the case with Matthias, who rarely actually
sounds like Berryman or Jones, but profitably turns their influence in his own work into an original kind of linguistic playfulness and daring. Through a number of very different kinds of
poem, Matthias manages to establish and maintain a recognisable voice of his own: high-pitched and excitable; sometimes
showily displaying its range of cultural reference (but usually
with a genuinely Berrymanic kind of urgency and enthusiasm
which save it from the merely boastful); but undermined, often,
by a distinct sadness, a profound sense of the transience of
earthly delights—whether those of history and culture, or those
of the personal life, those of the world, or those of the flesh.
    It is extremely difficult to quote from Matthias's work, since
many of his best poems are lengthy sequences which explore a
particular theme, and worry at a particular set of circumstances,
or historical occasion, with an expansive experimental or
exploratory breadth and energy. Music is obviously important
to him: composers and musical pieces are mentioned quite frequently in the poems; and some of the separate parts of his
sequences have a kind of musical inter-relatedness. Matthias
actually speaks about the activity of writing these poems as
"assembling certain kinds of structure." "Turns: Towards a Provisional Aesthetic and a Discipline," for instance—the poem
which gives its name to his second volume, *Turns*—runs an
elaborate descant on the extraordinary "theme" of its opening
part, a "translation" into Middle English of the opening sentences of *Jude the Obscure.* This zany toying and tinkering with
different epochs and cultures is one of the essential signatures of
Matthias: it is apparent in many of his most innovative
sequences—"The Stefan Batory Poems," for instance, and "The
Mihail Lermontov Poems."
    Personally, I like most, however, those long reflective poems,
often addressed to friends or to members of his family, in which
important personal memories or sensations are evoked and set in
their larger contexts of the public and political worlds. In some
of these poems, the America of the 1960's, and especially the
experience of Vietnam, is given an exceptionally vivid poetic
presence. These immediacies and realities earth a poetry which

is, perhaps, sometimes in danger of over-elaboration and over-sophistication, ripe for parody. But usually the extraordinarily recondite learning and allusiveness—complete with considerable annotation—function as genuine elements of style and vision, and not as mere parade or decoration. Some of the excitement of reading Matthias comes from being kept on one's toes; but it is when the sophistication is firmly at the service of human emotion that his work gains its most remarkable effects. This is undoubtedly the case in one of his finest poems, "Epilogue from a New Home: For Toby Barkan," which is an apology to the wife of a dead friend for not being able to write an elegy. In apologising, of course, a marvellous elegy does get written. This is its final stanza:

> Oh, I remember you that day: the terror in .
>   your face, the irony and love. And I remember
> What you wanted me to do. That ancient charge: to
>   read whatever evidence in lives or lies appears,
> In stones or bells—transform, transfigure then whatever
>   comedy, catastrophe or crime, and thus
> Return the earth, thus redeem the time. And this:
>   to leave it all alone (unspoken always: look, I have
> This moment and this place): *Cum on, cum on my owyn*
>   *swet chyld; goo we hom and take owr rest...*
> *Sing we to the oldest harpe, and playe...* Old friend,
>   old debt: I'm welcoming at last your presence now.
> I'm but half oriented here. I'm digging down.

—Neil Corcoran

MAYER, Gerda (Kamilla, née Stein). British. Born in Carlsbad, Czechoslovakia, 9 June 1927; emigrated to Britain in 1939; became citizen in 1949. Educated at schools in Czechoslovakia and England, 1933-44; Bedford College, London, 1960-63, B.A. 1963. Married Adolf Mayer in 1949. Worked on farms in Worcestershire and Surrey, 1945-46; office worker in London, 1946-52. Address: 12 Margaret Avenue, London E4 7NP, England.

PUBLICATIONS

Verse

Oddments. Privately printed, 1970.
Gerda Mayer's Library Folder. Kettering, Northamptonshire, All-In, 1972.
Treble Poets 2, with Florence Elon and Daniel Halpern. London, Chatto and Windus, 1975.
The Knockabout Show (for children). London, Chatto and Windus, 1978.
Monkey on the Analyst's Couch. Sunderland, Ceolfrith Press, 1980.
The Candy-Floss Tree (for children), with Norman Nicholson and Frank Flynn. Oxford, Oxford University Press, 1984.

Other

Editor, *Poet Tree Centaur: A Walthamstow Group Anthology.* London, Oddments, 1973.

*

Gerda Mayer comments:

I use a fair amount of humour; even the serious poems sometimes contain an element of verbal clowning. Some of the poems begin seriously and end in a joke, and vice versa. This, together with the fact that I have written quite a number of flimsy whimsies, tends to obscure the more painful messages. Conversely, I have known people to overlook the humour altogether. Perhaps my verse is like those trick-pictures that contain two images, of which it is possible to perceive only one at a time.

*   *   *

Gerda Mayer's poems have that direct simplicity of approach that gives them an air of timelessness, something of the atmosphere of the folk tales which will address God or the universe as if it was as casual as speaking over the fence to your next door neighbour. I don't know if this has anything to with Mayer's Czechoslovakian origins and memories, but I suspect it has, and the fact is there, her poems are like that. "Save the world God, save your creatures save us for a rainy day." Even when she is taking on current subjects and concerns such as the environment the same approach comes to the fore and the "Consumer" assumes a fabulosity:

> The Great Consumer
> crops the ground bare
> where are the flowers?
> where the sweet parsnips?

It is the same quality which enables her to invest the everyday with the surreal clarity of dreams:

> The waiter licks the tablecloth clean
> he licks clean the plates the glasses the
> flowers his tongue
> moves between the prongs of the forks

It is a superb talent and it is Mayer's own, and it makes her a fine creator of poems for young people. Poems which, like all the best poems for young people, are not written down to them, but are a natural extension of the rest of her work, with the same sharp humour and directness of approach:

> In childhood I took it for granted
> that Adam and Eve were Jews:
> though implied rather than stated
> it was Good News.

Mayer's collection *Monkey on the Analyst's Couch* confirms her place alongside those other poets of a sharp-eyed sparkling wit such as Stevie Smith. But at the back of Mayer's poetry is a depth of dark experience which makes her balanced and wry view of the world the more remarkable and worthy of our attention.

Eminently readable and deceptively simple, Gerda Mayer's poetry is penetrating stuff. It should be read with care, as readers can suddenly find themselves falling unexpectedly into great wells of meaning and emotion.

—John Cotton

MAYNE, Seymour. Canadian. Born in Montreal, Quebec, 18 May 1944. Educated at McGill University, Montreal (Chester Macnaghten Prize, 1962), B.A. (honours) 1965; University of British Columbia, Vancouver, M.A. 1966, Ph.D. 1972. Lecturer, Jewish Institute, Montreal, 1964, and University of British Columbia, 1972. Assistant Professor 1973-78, and since 1978, Associate Professor of English, University of Ottawa. Visiting Professor, Hebrew University of Jerusalem, 1979-80, 1983-84, and Concordia University, Montreal, 1982-83. Co-Editor, *Cataract*, Montreal, 1961-62; Poetry Editor, *Forge*, Montreal, 1961-62; Editor, *The Page*, 1962-63, and *Catapult*, Montreal, 1964; Managing Editor, Very Stone House, Vancouver, 1966-69; Poetry Editor, *Ingluvin*, 1970-71, and Managing Editor, Ingluvin Publications, 1970-73, Montreal; Editor, *Jewish Dialog*, Toronto, 1974-81, and *Stoney Monday*, Ottawa, 1978. Since 1982, Contributing Editor, *Viewpoints*, Montreal. Recipient: Canada Council Bursary, 1969, and grant, 1973, 1977; Segal Prize, 1974. Address: Department of English, University of Ottawa, Ottawa K1N 6N5, Canada.

PUBLICATIONS

Verse

That Monocycle the Moon. Privately printed, 1964.
Tiptoeing on the Mount. Montreal, McGill, 1965; revised edition, Montreal, Catapult, 1965.
From the Portals of Mouseholes. Vancouver, Very Stone House, 1966.
I Am Still the Boy. Vancouver, Western Press, 1967.
Ticklish Ticlicorice. Vancouver, Very Stone House, 1969.
The Gigolo Teaspoon. Vancouver, Very Stone House, 1969.
Earseed. Vancouver, Very Stone House, 1969.
Anewd. Vancouver, Very Stone House, 1969.
Mutetations. Vancouver, Very Stone House, 1969.
Manimals (includes prose). Vancouver, Very Stone House, 1969.
Mouth. Kingston, Ontario, Quarry Press, 1970.
For Stems of Light. Vernon, British Columbia, Very Stone House, 1971; revised edition, Ottawa, Valley, 1974.
Face. Burnaby, British Columbia, Blackfish, 1971.
Name. Erin, Ontario, Press Porcépic, 1975; revised edition, Oakville, Ontario, Mosaic Press, 1976.
Diasporas. Oakville, Ontario, Mosaic Press, 1977.
Begging. Oakville, Ontario, Mosaic Press, 1977.
Racoon. Ottawa, Valley, 1979.
Abel and Cain. Jerusalem, Sifrei HaEmek, 1980.
The Impossible Promised Land: Poems New and Selected. Oakville, Ontario, Mosaic Press, 1980.
Seven Poems. Toronto, League of Canadian Poets, 1983.
Neighbour Praying. Jerusalem, Sifrei HaEmek, 1984.

Other

Editor, with Patrick Lane, *Collected Poems of Red Lane.* Vancouver, Very Stone House, 1968.
Editor, with Victor Coleman, *Poetry of Canada.* Buffalo, Intrepid Press, 1969.
Editor, with Dorothy Livesay, *Forty Women Poets of Canada.* Montreal, Ingluvin, 1971.
Editor, *Engagements: The Prose of Irving Layton.* Toronto, McClelland and Stewart, 1972.
Editor, *Cutting the Keys.* Ottawa, University of Ottawa, 1975.
Editor, *Splices.* Ottawa, University of Ottawa, 1975.

Editor, *The A.M. Klein Symposium.* Ottawa, University of Ottawa, 1975.
Editor, *Choice Parts.* Ottawa, University of Ottawa, 1976.
Editor, *Irving Layton: The Poet and His Critics.* Toronto, McGraw Hill Ryerson, 1978.
Editor, and translator with Rivka Augenfeld, *Generations: Selected Poems,* by Rachel Korn. Oakville, Ontario, Mosaic Press, 1982.

Translator, with Catherine Leach, *Genealogy of Instruments,* by Jerzy Harasymowicz. Oakville, Ontario, Mosaic Press, 1974.
Translator, *Burnt Pearls: Ghetto Poems of Abraham Sutzkever.* Oakville, Ontario, Mosaic Press, 1982.

*

Critical Studies: by Peter Stevens, in *Canadian Forum* (Toronto), March 1968; "Other Vancouverites" by A.W. Purdy, in *Canadian Literature 35* (Vancouver), Winter 1968; "New Poetry of the East" by Tom Marshall, in *New: American and Canadian Poetry 15* (Trumansburg, New York), April-May 1971; Greg Gatenby, in *English Quarterly* (Waterloo, Ontario), Winter 1975-76; Aviva Layton, in *Quill and Quire* (Toronto), December 1978; Kenneth Sherman, in *Canadian Literature 80* (Vancouver), Spring 1979; Mervin Butovsky, in *Jewish Book Annual,* New York, Jewish Book Council, 1982; Anita Norich, in *Shdemot 18* (Tel Aviv), 1982; John Oughton, in *Books in Canada* (Toronto), March 1982; Bert Almon, in *Choice* (Middletown, Connecticut), July-August 1982; Michael Thorpe, in *Canadian Literature 95* (Vancouver), Winter 1982.

Seymour Mayne comments:

What I have to say about poetry is written into the poems and titles of my books. I have learned from the early study of Biblic poetry and Hebraic liturgy and prayer. More immediately I wish to acknowledge the Montreal poets whose work and example taught me much.

*   *   *

As an editor of several little magazines; as a founder of two private presses named Very Stone House and Ingluvin Press; as a broadcaster of radio documentaries on literary subjects; as the compiler of the prose writings of Irving Layton; and as many other things as well, Seymour Mayne has made a name for himself in the world of Canadian poetry.

But reputations of this sort are ephemeral and double-edged. Perhaps what he will be known for in the future is his own poetry which has been appearing since the 1960's and attracting increased interest of late. He has not been an experimental poet (his concrete work has the sense of *déjà vu*) but he has been persistent. His central publication is *Mouth,* a full-length collection of miscellaneous poems, some of which chart the relationship of the various bodily orifices and, in a Freudian fashion, find a link between or among them. As he writes in "Fang of Light": "and make the mouth/one vibrating hoop/of his whole/orificial self." The mood and image are there, but the language, especially the diction, is mixed and not always specific or emotional.

There are various contradictory themes in embryo—or in suspension—in Mayne's poetry, and these include: human desire as against bodily guilt; human transcendence as against whimsical reasonableness or ironic insight. Perhaps it is through a Jewish reconciliation of these opposites that Mayne's poetry will pass. The necessary drive is there, for the poet writes in "You Don't Scream":

Tear yourself away.
Bleed, if you must.
A fever will rise in your eyes
and burn like a need.

—John Robert Colombo

McAULEY, James J(ohn). Irish. Born in Dublin, 8 January 1936. Educated at Clongowes Wood College, 1948-53; University College, Dublin, 1960-62, B.A. 1962; University of Arkansas, Fayetteville, 1966-68, M.F.A. 1971. Married 1) Joan McNally in 1958 (divorced, 1968), three children; 2) Almut R. Nierentz, 1968, two children; 3) Deirdre O'Sullivan in 1982. Journalist, Electricity Supply Board, Dublin, 1954-66; Lecturer, Municipal Gallery of Modern Art, Dublin, 1965-66; Graduate Assistant, University of Arkansas, 1966-68; Assistant Professor and Director of the Creative Writing Program, Lycoming College, Williamsport, Pennsylvania, 1968-70. Assistant Professor, 1970-73, Associate Professor, 1973-78, and since 1978, Professor of English, Eastern Washington State University, Cheney. Art critic, *Kilkenny Magazine*, Dublin, 1960-66; Associate Editor, *Poetry Ireland*, Dublin, 1962-66; arts consultant, *Hibernia National Review*, Dublin, 1964-66; book reviewer, *Irish Times*, Dublin, 1964-66; reporter, *North West Arkansas Times*, Fayetteville, 1967. Since 1978, Editor, Dolmen Press, Dublin. Recipient: National Endowment for the Arts grant, 1972. Agent: Lordly and Dame Inc., 51 Church Street, Boston, Massachusetts 02116. Address: Department of English, Eastern Washington State University, Cheney, Washington, 99004, U.S.A.

PUBLICATIONS

Verse

Observations. Blackrock, Ireland, Mount Salus Press, 1960.
A New Address. Dublin, Dolmen Press, London, Oxford University Press, and Chester Springs, Pennsylvania, Dufour, 1965.
Draft Balance Sheet: Poems 1963-1969. Dublin, Dolmen Press, London, Oxford University Press, and Chester Springs, Pennsylvania, Dufour, 1970.
Home and Away. Privately printed, 1974.
After the Blizzard. Columbia, University of Missouri Press, 1975.
The Exile's Recurring Nightmare. San Francisco, Aisling Press, 1975.
Recital: Poems 1975-1980. Portlaoise, County Laoighis, Dolmen Press, 1982.
The Exile's Book of Hours. Lewiston, Idaho, Confluence Press, 1982.

Play

The Revolution (produced Dublin, 1966).

*

Critical Studies: review in *Hibernia* (Dublin), 1970; *Choice*, edited by Michael Hartnett and Desmond Egan, Dublin, Goldsmith Press, 1970, revised edition, 1979.

James J. McAuley comments:

My first book, *Observations*, consists of 16 confessional lyrics; very young poems, imitative, private. *A New Address* is the offspring of my two-year love affair with *Roget's Thesaurus*: poems reulting from my preoccupation with words, their sounds and associations. *Draft Balance Sheet* resulted from my two-year study of Poetry and Poetics under James Whitehead at Arkansas. *After the Blizzard* is a collection of love-poems, satires, narratives, and monologs. *The Revolution* is a satire on Easter, 1916, and its end result, the modern Irish state. *Recital* is a collection of varied work over five years. *The Exile's Books of Hours* follows the pattern of the medieval prayer-books.

*   *   *

James J. McAuley's poetry has changed very considerably, perhaps not altogether convincingly, since this move from Ireland to America. His newer, distinctly American tone, hardly seems natural to him—although the themes of his poems are clearly ones of his natural choice. Unlike such a poet as John Montague, who has also been closely associated with America, McAuley seems half-inclined to drop his "Irishry," which may in his case be a mistake. (Denise Levertov did turn from an English neo-Georgian into a modernist American—but she married an American and became an American citizen.) Easily the best of McAuley's poetry is his sharp and telling satire on things Irish; this is of course a special prerogative of Irish writers from (to give the remark a characteristically paradoxical Irish air) the Englishman Swift onwards; but McAuley does it well, and lends a dimension of his own to his criticism of Ireland, which is not genial. Other poetry, though composed with great care, tends to be over-literary, falsely fastidious, a shade over-graceful. But the good taste and the intelligence are certainly present: this stanza from "Stella" (dating from the early 1960's) demonstrates both his defects and his virtues:

The swan pierced by an arrow lies
Immortal on sharp stars
Above the bowed head ringing with the tones,
Vibrations, plangent chords of love.
About him, night sounds:
A leaf touching his shoulder
Whispered, descended, dying
At his feet.

—Martin Seymour-Smith

McCLURE, Michael (Thomas). American. Born in Marysville, Kansas, 20 October 1932. Educated at Wichita State University, Kansas, 1951-53; University of Arizona, Tucson, 1953-54; San Francisco State University, B.A. 1955. Married Joanna Kinniston in 1954; one daughter. Assistant Professor, 1962-77, and since 1977, Associate Professor, California College of Arts and Crafts, Oakland. Playwright-in-Residence, American Conservatory Theatre, San Francisco, 1975; Associate Fellow, Pierson College, Yale University, New Haven, Connecticut, 1982. Editor, with James Harmon, *Ark II/Moby I*, San Francisco, 1957. Recipient: National Endowment for the Arts grant 1967, 1974; Guggenheim Fellowship, 1973; Magic Theatre Alfred

Jarry Award, 1973; Rockefeller Fellowship, for drama, 1975; Obie Award, for drama, 1978. Agent: Helen Merrill, 337 West 22nd Street, New York, New York 10011. Address: 264 Downey Street, San Francisco, California 94117, U.S.A.

PUBLICATIONS

Verse

Passage.   Big Sur, California, Jonathan Williams, 1956.
Peyote Poem.   San Francisco, Wallace Berman, 1958.
For Artaud.   New York, Totem Press, 1959.
Hymns to St. Geryon and Other Poems.   San Francisco, Auerhahn Press, 1959.
The New Book: A Book of Torture.   New York, Grove Press, 1961.
Dark Brown.   San Francisco, Auerhahn Press, 1961.
Two for Bruce Conner.   San Francisco, Oyez, 1964.
Ghost Tantras.   Privately printed, 1964.
Double Murder! Vahroooooooohr!   Los Angeles, Wallace Berman, 1964.
Love Lion, Lioness.   Privately printed, 1964.
13 Mad Sonnets.   Milan, East 128, 1964.
Poisoned Wheat.   Privately printed, 1965.
Unto Caesar.   San Francisco, Dave Haselwood, 1965.
Mandalas.   San Francisco, Dave Haselwood, 1965.
Dream Table.   San Francisco, Dave Haselwood, 1966.
Love Lion Book.   San Francisco, Four Seasons, 1966.
Hail Thee Who Play: A Poem.   Los Angeles, Black Sparrow Press, 1968; revised edition, Berkeley, California, Sand Dollar, 1974.
Muscled Apple Swift.   Topanga, California, Love Press, 1968.
Plane Pomes.   New York, Phoenix Book Shop, 1969.
Oh Christ God Love Cry of Love Stifled Furred Wall Smoking Burning.   San Francisco, Auerhahn Press, 1969 (?).
The Sermons of Jean Harlow and the Curses of Billy the Kid.   San Francisco, Four Seasons, 1969.
The Surge: A Poem.   Columbus, Ohio, Frontier Press, 1969.
Hymns to St. Geryon, and Dark Brown.   London, Cape Goliard Press, 1969; San Francisco, Grey Fox Press, 1980.
Lion Fight.   New York, Pierrepont Press, 1969.
Star.   New York, Grove Press, 1971.
99 Theses.   Lawrence, Kansas, Tansy Press, 1972.
The Book of Joanna.   Berkeley, California, Sand Dollar, 1973.
Transfiguration.   Cambridge, Massachusetts, Pomegranate Press, 1973.
Rare Angel (writ with raven's blood).   Los Angeles, Black Sparrow Press, 1974.
September Blackberries.   New York, New Directions, 1974.
Solstice Blossom.   Berkeley, California, Arif Press, 1974.
Fleas 189-195.   New York, Aloes, 1974.
A Fist Full (1956-1957).   Los Angeles, Black Sparrow Press, 1974.
On Organism.   Buffalo, Institute of Further Studies, 1974.
Jaguar Skies.   New York, New Directions, 1975.
Man of Moderation: Two Poems.   New York, Hallman, 1975.
Flea 100.   New York, Hallman, 1975.
Antechamber.   Berkeley, California, Poythress Press, 1977.
Antechamber and Other Poems.   New York, New Directions, 1978.
Fragments of Perseus.   New York, Jordan Davies, 1978.
Letters.   New York, Jordan Davies, 1978.
The Book of Benjamin, with Wesley B. Tanner.   Berkeley, California, Arif, 1982.

Fragments of Perseus (collection).   New York, New Directions, 1983.

Plays

The Feast (produced San Francisco, 1960).   Included in *The Mammals,* 1972.
Pillow (produced New York, 1961).   Included in *The Mammals,* 1972.
The Growl, in *Four in Hand* (produced Berkeley, California, 1970; *The Growl* produced New York, 1976).   Published in *Evergreen Review* (New York), April-May 1964.
The Blossom; or, Billy the Kid (produced New York, 1964).   Milwaukee, Great Lakes Books, 1967.
The Beard (produced San Francisco, 1965; New York, 1967; London, 1968).   Privately printed, 1965; revised version, New York, Grove Press, 1967.
The Shell (produced San Francisco, 1970; London, 1975).   London, Cape Goliard Press, 1968; in *Gargoyle Cartoons,* 1971.
The Cherub (produced Berkeley, California, 1969).   Los Angeles, Black Sparrow Press, 1970.
The Charbroiled Chinchilla: The Pansy, The Meatball, Spider Rabbit (produced Berkeley, California, 1969).   Included in *Gargoyle Cartoons,* 1971.
Little Odes, Poems, and a Play, The Raptors.   Los Angeles, Black Sparrow Press, 1969.
The Brutal Brontosaurus: Spider Rabbit, The Meatball, The Shell, Apple Glove, The Authentic Radio Life of Bruce Conner and Snoutburbler (produced San Francisco, 1970; *The Meatball* and *Spider Rabbit* produced London, 1971, New York, 1976; *The Authentic Radio Life of Bruce Conner and Snoutburbler* produced London, 1975).   Included in *Gargoyle Cartoons,* 1971.
The Pansy (produced London, 1972).   Included in *Gargoyle Cartoons,* 1971.
Gargoyle Cartoons (includes *The Shell, The Pansy, The Meatball, The Bow, Spider Rabbit, Apple Glove, The Sail, The Dear, The Authentic Radio Life of Bruce Conner and Snoutburbler, The Feather, The Cherub*).   New York, Delacorte Press, 1971.
Polymorphous Pirates: The Pussy, The Button, The Feather (produced Berkeley, California, 1972).   *The Feather* included in *Gargoyle Cartoons,* 1971.
The Mammals (includes *The Blossom, The Feast, Pillow*).   San Francisco, Cranium Press, 1972.
The Grabbing of the Fairy (produced Los Angeles, 1973).   St. Paul, Minnesota, Truck Press, 1978.
The Pussy, The Button, and Chekhov's Grandmother; or, The Sugar Wolves (produced New York, 1973).
Gorf (produced San Francisco, 1974).   New York, New Directions, 1976.
The Derby (produced Los Angeles, 1974; New York, 1981).
General Gorgeous (produced San Francisco, 1975; Edinburgh, 1976).   New York, Dramatists Play Service, 1982.
Two Plays.   Privately printed, 1975.
Sunny-Side Up (includes *The Pink Helmet* and *The Masked Choir*) (produced Los Angeles, 1976).   *The Pink Helmet* included in *Two Plays,* 1975; *The Masked Choir* published in *Performing Arts Journal* (New York), August 1976.
Minnie Mouse and the Tap-Dancing Buddha (produced San Francisco, 1978).   Included in *Two Plays,* 1975.
Two for the Tricentennial (includes *The Pink Helmet* and *The Grabbing of the Fairy*) (produced San Francisco, 1976).
Range War (produced San Francisco, 1976).
Goethe: Ein Fragment (produced San Francisco, 1977).   Pub-

lished in *West Coast Plays 2* (Berkeley, California), Spring 1978.
Josephine the Mouse Singer, adaptation of a story by Kafka (produced New York, 1978). New York, New Directions, 1980.
The Red Snake (produced San Francisco, 1979).
The Mirror (produced Los Angeles, 1979).
Coyote in Chains (produced San Francisco, 1980).
The Beard, and Vktms: Two Plays. New York, Grove Press, 1984.

Radio Play: *Music Peace*, 1974.

Television Play: *The Maze* (documentary), 1967.

Novels

The Mad Cub. New York, Bantam, 1970.
The Adept. New York, Delacorte Press, 1971.

Other

Meat Science Essays. San Francisco, City Lights, 1963; revised edition, San Francisco, Dave Haselwood, 1967.
Freewheelin' Frank, Secretary of the Angels, as Told to Michael McClure by Frank Reynolds. New York, Grove Press, 1967.
Scratching the Beat Surface. Berkeley, California, North Point Press, 1982.

Editor, with David Meltzer and Lawrence Ferlinghetti, *Journal for the Protection of All Beings 1* and *3*. San Francisco, City Lights, 2 vols., 1961-69.

*

Bibliography: *A Catalogue of Works by Michael McClure, 1956-1965* by Marshall Clements, New York, Phoenix Book Shop, 1965.

Manuscript Collection: Simon Fraser University, Burnaby, British Columbia.

Critical Studies: "This Is Geryon," in *Times Literary Supplement* (London), 25 March 1965; interview in *San Francisco Poets* edited by David Meltzer, New York, Bantam, 1971; "Michael McClure Symposium" in *Margins 18* (Milwaukee), 1975.

Theatrical Activities
Actor: **Films**—*Beyond the Law*, 1968; *Maidstone*, 1970.

*   *   *

In *A Catalogue of Works by Michael McClure, 1956-1965* Marshall Clements lists translations into French, German, Spanish, Italian. More than 20 years ago, people recognized Michael McClure's high seriousness. His purpose was not to *épater le bourgeois* but rather to present—without any moralizing—*épatement* itself as a process. Postcards, pictures, plays, poems break through "the preconception of poem and stanzas"—as in the 1959 picture of a horse's head, and above it a horse with the words "Fuck Death." In "Double Murder! VAHROOOOM!" Jack Ruby shoots Oswald. At the zoo, McClure recorded the lion's roar and his own "beast language" from *Ghost Tantras*. His play *The Beard* has actors take roles

about real people, Jean Harlow and Billy the Kid, who had become actors in roles of history.

In one play, *The Cherub*, a bed is an actor—snores, wakes up, speaks, has a missile count-down while Jesus and Camus "are at it again upstairs." The explosive exuberance leads to a sweetly innocent and still moving conclusion: a naked man and a naked woman repeat "good morning" to each other. A movie of clouds becomes a cluster of grapes. They repeat "yes" to each other. The light flares up and dies out, a leaves a cluster of grapes.

The force of the play comes from the interwoven "topologies of reality," as McClure phrases it in a preface to his poetry, *Rare Angel*. The meanings of "topology" cluster around *topos*, place, and *logos*, word. A word finds place, "gives birth to itself from the substrate by writing out muscular and body sensations which are the source of thought." His sense of the body-cave, cave-body, the body with open pores, open to the world, and an open system appears in most of his works, and in particular in *Meat Science*. He involves the reader by typographical disjunctions and a vertical tracking down the page. Sometimes the typography seems to shape the voice:

LET'S STOP! LET'S STOP
THIS ENDLESS MURDER BY POLITICS!
LET
US
DO WHAT
WE CAN TO STOP
so very much useless pain!

A highly varied length of line ventilates an otherwise strict sestina (*Antechambers*). Sometimes capitals seem to draw attention to a *discordia concors*:

LITTLE ODE

for Joanna

AND DEATH SHALL HAVE NO TERROR WHEN LOVE
MAY BALANCE THEE, MADONNA, IN MY HEART.
I shall die with the wrinkled lines
around thy eyes upon my shield
of consciousness,
I confess
I worship thee
and all material things.

Rose petals falling!

The secret loves of wolves!

Deer mice trembling in the snow!

Turquoise set in worn and darkended silver!

This poem for Joanna McClure—herself a poet—seems to echo his early sonnets and villanelles in tone and affinity, but the motion remains his own, as in his well-established volumes such as *September Blackberries* or *Jaguar Skies*. All of his poems *move*. Logos also implies "order," "sequence." E-motion is from *emovere*.

The motion of perception is at least as important as the particulars of what is perceived.

One reads in his recent *The Daily Vision* on page 9: "COMING/BACK/THROUGH/THE/SKY"; on page 18: "COMING/BACK/THROUGH/THE/SKY:/COMING/BACK/WITH/OBSESSIONS;/COMING BACK THROUGH

THE SKY"; on page 23: "COMING/BACK/THROUGH/ THE/SKY/TO THE SUBSTRATE"; on page 30 "THE HOP OF A SILVERFISH//THE AWKWARD HOP OF A SIL- VERFISH/is perfect!"; on page 31: "COMING/BACK/ THROUGH/THE/SKY,/THE/AWKWARD/HOP/OF/A/ SILVERFISH/IS/PERFECT." The disparate elements meet, or separate, in the kinetics of perception. The typography and the words create a "flicker of interacting," the effects of will and of luck: the visual image of the conclusion of "The Cherub," a cluster of grapes, has an analogous statement in *The Daily Vision*: "WE ARE GRAPES/We are/aggregates/in bunches./ BLACK GRAPES."

A quotation attributed to Piaget is singularly relevant to McClure's writing: "it is precisely when the subject is most self- centered that he knows himself the least, and it is to the extent that he discovers himself that he places himself in the universe." Early and late, the poems are open to each other, a body of poetry, like the body, an open system, a single poem-play, or as an aggregate, like great lovers, the poems are ever about us, their great warm bulk fills the air.

—William Sylvester

McDONALD, Roger. Australian. Born in Young, New South Wales, 23 June 1941. Educated at the University of Sydney, 1959-62, B.A. 1962. Married Rhyll McMaster in 1967; three children. School teacher, Murrumburrah and Wellington, New South Wales, 1963-64; Producer, Educational Radio and Televi- sion, Brisbane, Queensland, and Hobart, Tasmania, 1964-69; Editor, University of Queensland Press, Brisbane, 1969-76. Since 1977, free-lance writer. Delegate, Hari Sastra National Litera- ture Conference, Sabah, Malaysia, 1973. Recipient: Australia Council Fellowship, 1977-79, 1981-82; *The Age* award, 1979; South Australia Government prize, 1980; Canada-Australia prize, 1981. Address: c/o University of Queensland Press, P.O. Box 42, St. Lucia, Queensland 4067, Australia.

PUBLICATIONS

Verse

Citizens of Mist. Brisbane, University of Queensland Press, 1968.
Airship. Brisbane, University of Queensland Press, 1975.

Novels

1915. Brisbane, University of Queensland Press, 1979; New York, Braziller, 1980; London, Faber, 1982.
Slipstream. Brisbane, University of Queensland Press, and London, Faber, 1982; Boston, Little Brown, 1983.

Other

Editor, *The First Paperback Poets Anthology*. Brisbane, Uni- versity of Queensland Press, 1974.

*

Manuscript Collection: National Library of Australia, Canberra.

Roger McDonald comments:

I would like to think that an introspective strain in my poetry is made acceptable, even interesting, by firmly physical writing. I find abstractions impossible to approach without the armour of careful description. I like to find things said in precise and evocative ways in the work of other writers, and hope that the qualities I prefer can be found in my own work, including the novels I have now turned to writing.

*   *   *

Reading Roger McDonald's poetry one is struck by his fasci- nation with the past, with extracting details from past happen- ings and making them unique to the present. This is in fact a poetry of moments. Almost cinematically the action is seen to stop—and the frozen frame examined. But seldom does he con- clude the poem by, as it were, setting the film in motion again; more often he slightly recasts the details and leaves it at that. It is as if he is saying: Now, at this unrepeatable point of time, I'm going to declare all I have shown you to be a mere collage of appearances whose independent and contemporary meanings already assert themselves, a leap ahead of any attempt I might make at interpretation.

The poem "Two Summers in Moravia" is a clear example of this. In the first summer (looking back to wartime),

This was a day
when little happened
though inch by inch everything changed.
A load of hay narrowly crossed the bridge,
the boy caught a fish underneath in shade,
and ducks quarrelled in the reeds

and in the second summer, the present-time of the poem, he records an almost unchanged scene but, like positive to negative, simple details seem unaccountably reversed; there is a brooding feeling, a threat, the suggestion that some other dimension moves within them.

In another recent poem, "The Hollow Thesaurus," a similar process is applied to language itself, so that here McDonald is writing about his medium as a means of demonstrating his use of it:

Names for everything I touch
were hatched in bibles, in poems cupped by madmen
on rocky hills, by marks on sheets of stone,
by humped and sticky lines in printed books.

Lexicographers burned their stringy eyeballs black
for the sake of my knowing. Instinctive generations
hammered their victories, threaded a chain,
and lowered their strung-up wisdom in a twist
of molecules. But with me in mind
their time was wasted.

When the bloodred, pewter, sickle, sick or meloned moon
swells from nowhere,
the chatter of vast informative print
spills varied as milk. Nothing prepares me
even for common arrivals like this.

Look. The moon comes up. Behind certain trees are bats
that wrench skyward like black sticks.
Light falls thinly on grass, from moon and open door.
This has not happened before.

These recent poems are markedly more original in concept than those in his first book, *Citizens of Mist*, where, although he sustained his interest in gradual decay (whether the doomed politeness of Victorian gentility or flies buzzing about a carcass) by setting it within a context of collapse on a massive scale, the implications remained narrow. There was a tendency for the universal to be cramped by the particular, where now the particular is its point of release.

He is a careful, thoughtful writer. His output is not large but his position in Australian literature is assured. Compact and intelligent, this is a poetry that is never quirky or flashy. Its limitation is that it might be thought too even, too neat, too safe.

Roger McDonald is also a book editor of distinction and is having an important influence on the directions being taken in poetry and prose in Australia today.

—Rodney Hall

McFADDEN, David. Canadian. Born in Hamilton, Ontario, 11 October 1940. Night proofreader, 1962-70, and reporter, 1970-76, Hamilton *Spectator*; free-lance journalist and editor, 1976-79; Writer-in-Residence, Simon Fraser University, Burnaby, British Columbia, 1978; Instructor in Writing, David Thompson University Centre, Nelson, British Columbia, 1979-82; taught creative writing, Victoria Park and Don Mills schools, Toronto, 1982-83; Writer-in-Residence, University of Western Ontario, London, 1983-84. Founding Editor, *Mountain Magazine*, Hamilton, 1960-63, and *Writing Magazine*, Nelson, British Columbia, 1979-82; Member of Editorial Board, *Swift Current*, 1983-84; Contributing Editor, *Quill and Quire*, Toronto, 1983-84. Recipient: Canada Council bursary, 1968, and Fellowship, 1976, 1982; Mickey Award, 1975; Nebula Award, 1977; Canadian Broadcasting Corporation prize, 1979; National Magazine Award, 1981, 1982. Address: 204-66 Spadina Road, Toronto, Ontario M5R 2T4, Canada.

PUBLICATIONS

Verse

The Poem Poem. Toronto, Weed/Flower Press, 1967.
The Saladmaker: A Humility Cycle. Montreal, Imago, 1968; revised edition, Montreal, Cross Country, 1977.
Letters from the Earth to the Earth. Toronto, Coach House Press, 1968.
Poems Worth Knowing. Toronto, Coach House Press, 1971.
Intense Pleasure. Toronto, McClelland and Stewart, 1972.
The Ova Yogas. Toronto, Weed/Flower Press, 1972.
A Knight in Dried Plums. Toronto, McClelland and Stewart, 1975.
The Poet's Progress. Toronto, Coach House Press, 1977.
On the Road Again. Toronto, McClelland and Stewart, 1978.
I Don't Know. Montreal, Véhicule Press, 1978.
A New Romance. Montreal, Cross Country Press, 1979.
My Body Was Eaten by Dogs: Selected Poems, edited by George Bowering. Toronto, McClelland and Stewart, and Flushing, New York, Cross Country, 1981.
Country of the Open Heart. Edmonton, Longspoon Press, 1982.
A Pair of Baby Lambs. Toronto, Front Press, 1983.
The Art of Darkness. Toronto, McClelland and Stewart, 1984.

Plays

The Collected World of David McFadden (produced Hamilton, Ontario, 1977).
Nirvana at Twilight (produced Toronto, 1982).
At the Corner of King and Kenilworth (produced Toronto, 1983).

Novels

The Great Canadian Sonnet. Toronto, Coach House Press, 1970.
A Trip Around Lake Huron. Toronto, Coach House Press, 1980.
A Trip Around Lake Erie. Toronto, Coach House Press, 1981.

Short Stories

Three Stories and Ten Poems. Toronto, Prototype, 1982.
Animal Spirits: Stories to Live By. Toronto, Coach House Press, 1983.

*   *   *

"I'm particularly pleased to inhabit the same world as McFadden," wrote Al Purdy when he read the manuscript of *Intense Pleasure*, "even if he's crazy as a bedbug." Although David McFadden—a poet and newspaperman who lives and writes in Hamilton, Ontario, a community not celebrated for its artists—has been publishing short collections of his poems and Richard Brautigan-like prose since 1967, it was not until 1972, with the appearance of *Intense Pleasure*, that McFadden's work reached a wide public and the nature of his singular talent became clear.

McFadden is not as "crazy as a bedbug," for he is as "crazy as a fox—and as witty and often as irrelevant as Dick Gregory and any number of stand-up comedians who specialize in witty one-liners and put-downs and one-upmanships. Many of his poems are nightclub routines with fast lines like: "He knew he was pregnant," "I'm addicted to toothpicks," "Now I'm middle-aged I want to be an alligator." The poems are amusing, lively and light, and often exhausted on a single reading.

In the poem "Ova Yoga," McFadden writes, "Inside every chicken is a human being trying to get out," and inside McFadden there is another poet beginning to be heard. This is the observer of modern society beset—but not swallowed up by—the incongruities and irrationalities of the contemporary world. This is the poet who in one poem presents a midget's-eye view of the world, who in another discovers Adolf Hitler living in Hamilton and arranges an interview. This is the poet who is attracted to the pop and kitsch characteristics of Canadian advertising: "This is Bruce Marsh speaking / for Kraft Foods in Canada."

On first reading one might mistake this McFadden for the stand-up comedian. But the emerging poet is one who like Apollinaire seeks to celebrate "the heroic of the everyday," who tries to grant a modicum of immortality to such things as "three Motorcycles parked diagonally at the curb / in front of 111 Brucedale Avenue." One looks at the Liverpudlian poets for something approximating McFadden's tone; but to long-dead but always-resurrectible Dadaists and Surrealists for McFadden's sense of the nostalgia of the evanescent. Thus David McFadden is the prophet of the ephemeral present.

—John Robert Colombo

McFADDEN, Roy. Born in Belfast, Northern Ireland, 14 November 1921. Educated at Regent House School, Newtownards, County Down; Queen's University, Belfast. Co-Editor, *Ulster Voices*, 1941-42, *Rann: An Ulster Quarterly of Poetry*, 1948-53, and *Irish Voices*, 1953, all in Belfast. Address: 13 Shrewsbury Gardens, Belfast 9, Northern Ireland.

PUBLICATIONS

Verse

A Poem: Russian Summer. Dublin, Gayfield Press, 1942.
Three New Poets, with Alex Comfort and Ian Serraillier. Billericay, Essex, Grey Walls Press, 1942.
Swords and Ploughshares. London, Routledge, 1943.
Flowers for a Lady. London, Routledge, 1945.
The Heart's Townland. London, Routledge, 1947.
Elegy for the Dead of The Princess Victoria. Lisburn, County Antrim, Lisnagarvey Press, 1952.
The Garryowen. London, Chatto and Windus, 1971.
Verifications. Belfast, Blackstaff Press, 1977.
A Watching Brief. Belfast, Blackstaff Press, 1979.
The Selected Roy McFadden, edited by John Boyd. Belfast, Blackstaff Press, 1983.

*

Critical Studies: in *Rann 20* (Belfast); Michael Longley, in *Causeway: The Arts in Ulster*, Belfast, Arts Council of Northern Ireland, 1971; *Northern Voices* by Terence Brown, Dublin, Gill and Macmillan, 1975.

*   *   *

Few of the usual anthologies reprinted Roy McFadden. Their editors all too often copied each other's selections in preference to seeking out authentic poets not previously anthologized. McFadden published his powerful first collection during the Second World War, but it seems to have been lost among more metropolitan ventures. Yet *Swords and Ploughshares* deserves a place beside other work that has lasted. Certainly the title of the book is appropriate for the first appearance of a war poet.

What may have gone against McFadden is that the vision of war he presented was distinctively Irish. This led him, among other matters, to a rehandling of the ballad form in one of his most impressive early poems, "An Irish Peasant Woman Summons Her Absent Children"—"Call them home where there is light / And still a candle and a prayer...." However, equally potent as an influence was Yeats, and for a long time this proved counter-productive. The vibrant oratory of the older poet was, in many ways, inimical to McFadden's Northern temperament. One result of this was what seemed to be a struggle in McFadden's verse, between inherent character and acquired style.

McFadden's second and third books, perhaps because of this struggle, show something of a romantic instability in tone. Indeed, after *The Heart's Townland*, he published no major collection for 24 years. That did not help his reputation during a period when his contemporaries were, for the most part, building on their early successes. In this interval, however, his *Elegy for the Dead of the "Princess Victoria"* came out in a limited edition. This, while it could do little for its author on the public stage, revealed to an intimate group of admirers a compassionate scope that augured well for the years ahead.

The bitter circumstances of Ulster have decreed that McFadden remain a war poet. However, his developing ability to write directly of domestic circumstance has enabled a human face to emerge from behind the Yeatsian rhetoric. *The Garryowen* has, as a collection, an unforced authority lacking in the earlier books. Its sequence "Family Album" is especially poignant. A sense of time passing, illustrated by vignettes of children, is carried forward into a sequel, *Verifications*, with equally effective evocations of children growing up.

The latest verse has a distinct narrative voice: disillusioned but never cynical. *A Watching Brief*, perhaps the best collection yet, is unified by its running theme, that of a lawyer going through the forms and ceremonies in a lawless city. Here McFadden's knowledge and experience as a working solicitor give him a hand on pulses that Yeats, for all his sublimity, never touched. The key poem has, almost defiantly, a Yeatsian title, "The Law Courts Revisited." Nevertheless, the poem itself is substantially and sardonically McFadden:

> The side courts closed, Queen's Bench and Chancery—
> Counsel gone
> Back to the burrow of their library,
> Litigants home
> To chew the frayed ends of the argument,
> Cleaners' time
> To mop and scour the day's sufficiency
> Of crumpled claim and counterclaim,
> Stubbed out or smouldering plea....

This inwardness with the law seems to have led McFadden into a remarkable renewal of tactics in a recent sequence based on the life and works of Dickens. Here McFadden, for all his Irishness, shows himself able to penetrate into the psyche of this most metropolitan of all novelists:

> His clients were
> Characters with impediments,
> Eccentrically
> Knotted and private; yet obliged,
> Language's litigants,
> To remonstrate. He covertly
> Ran to the stairhead, dusted the office chair....

This detached and ironic tone is characteristic of McFadden's latest phase. One need have no hesitation in describing this as one of the most authentic voices to be heard in our time. By purging his verse of oratory, McFadden has gained eloquence. He speaks of the pity of war, and his tones echo well beyond his native province. By remaining in Northern Ireland Roy McFadden has, paradoxically enough, come to stand at stage centre.

—Philip Hobsbaum

McGOUGH, Roger. British. Born in Liverpool, Lancashire, 9 November 1937. Educated at St. Mary's College, Crosby, Lancashire; Hull University, Yorkshire, B.A. in French and geography 1957, Cert. Ed. 1960. Married Thelma Monaghan in 1970 (marriage dissolved, 1980); two sons. School teacher, Liverpool, 1960-64; Lecturer, Liverpool College of Art, 1969-70; Poetry Fellow, University of Loughborough, Leicestershire, 1973-75. Formerly, member of the performing group The Scaffold. Free-lance writer and performer. Recipient: *Signal* award, for children's verse, 1984. Agent: A.D. Peters, 10 Buckingham Street, London WC2N 6BU, England.

PUBLICATIONS

Verse

The Mersey Sound: Penguin Modern Poets 10, with Adrian Henri and Brian Patten. London, Penguin, 1967; revised edition, 1974, 1983.
Frinck, A Life in the Day of, and Summer with Monika: Poems (novel and verse). London, Joseph, and New York, Ballantine, 1967.
Watchwords. London, Cape, 1969.
After the Merrymaking. London, Cape, 1971.
Out of Sequence. London, Turret, 1973.
Gig. London, Cape, 1973.
Sporting Relations. London, Eyre Methuen, 1974.
In the Glassroom. London, Cape, 1976.
Summer with Monika, revised edition. London, Deutsch, 1978.
Holiday on Death Row. London, Cape, 1979.
Unlucky for Some. London, Bernard Stone, 1980.
Waving at Trains. London, Cape, 1982.
New Volume, with Adrian Henri and Brian Patten. London, Penguin, 1983.
Crocodile Puddles. London, Pyramid, 1984.

Recordings: *The Incredible New Liverpool Scene*, CBS, 1967; *McGough McGear*, Parlophone; *"Scaffold" Live at Queen Elizabeth Hall*, Parlophone; *"Scaffold" L. The P.*, Parlophone; *Grimms*, Island; *Fresh Liver*, Island; *Sleepers*, DJM; *McGough/Patten*, Argo; *Summer with Monika*, Island, 1978; *Gifted Wreckage*, with Brian Patten and Adrian Henri, Talking Tape, 1984.

Plays

Birds, Marriages and Deaths, with others (produced London, 1964).
The Chauffeur-Driven Rolls (produced Liverpool, 1966).
The Commission (produced Liverpool, 1967).
The Puny Little Life Show (produced London, 1969). Published in *Open Space Plays*, edited by Charles Marowitz, London, Penguin, 1974.
Zones (produced Edinburgh, 1969).
Stuff (produced London, 1970).
P.C. Plod (produced London, 1971).
Wordplay (produced London, 1975).
Summer with Monika, music by Andy Roberts (produced London, 1978).
Watchwords (produced Nottingham, 1979).
Like Father, Like Son, Like (produced Nottingham, 1980).
Lifeswappers (produced Edinburgh and London, 1980).
All the Trimmings, music by Peter Brewis (produced London, 1980).
Golden Nights and Golden Days (produced on tour, 1980).
Behind the Lines (revue), with Brian Patten (produced London, 1982).
The Mouthtrap, with Brian Patten (produced Edinburgh and London, 1982).

Radio Plays: *Gruff—A TV Commercial*, 1977; *Walking the Dog*, 1981.

Television Plays: *The Lifeswappers*, 1976; *Kurt, B.P. Mungo, and Me*, 1983.

Other (for children)

Mr. Noselighter. London, G. Whizzard, 1976.
You Tell Me, with Michael Rosen. London, Kestrel, 1979.
The Great Smile Robbery. London, Kestrel, 1982.
Sky in the Pie. London, Kestrel, 1983.

Editor, *Strictly Private: An Anthology of Poetry*. London, Kestrel, 1981.

*

Manuscript Collection: University of Hull.

*   *   *

More than his fellow Liverpool poets, Roger McGough remains as much a performer as a writer. From his collaborations with Henri and Patten, through brief pop stardom with the Scaffold and beyond, the performance element is present in virtually all his poems, with their echoes of circus, pantomime, and old-time music hall. The wit and verbal mastery that are his principal gifts find straightforward expression in a style whose apparent simplicity often hides the skill behind it. This ability enables him to write equally well for children and adults, without condescending or altering his style. *Sky in the Pie*, for instance, shows the same quirky humour and sly wordplay that distinguish the adult collections, not only in the surreal title-poem, but in the more down-to-earth "Snowman" and "Pantomime Poem," which portrays an important source of inspiration. Of the Liverpool trio, McGough is the natural comic, the bulk of his work written in humorous vein, while Henri and Patten supply only the occasional laugh. This is not to suggest that he is not a serious artist, merely that his writing tends rather to amusement than bitter anger. Polemics from him are few and far between, usually made from a humanitarian rather than a political standpoint. The anti-war "A Square Dance," where the poet addresses the doomed troops like the "caller" at a hoe-down, and the anti-racist "I'm Dreaming of a White Smethwick" ("May your days be merry and bright / And may all your citizens be white") are typical examples.

McGough's main concern is with the flaws and frailties of human nature, the joys and vicissitudes of love. Humour allows him to regard these with a wry detachment, aided by his ability to make the real seem strange: "for in the morning / when a policeman / disguised as the sun / creeps into your room / and your mother / disguised as birds / calls from the trees / you will put on a dress of guilt / and shoes with broken high ideals." With McGough the actual blurs into the world of dream with inanimate objects taking on human characteristics while people metamorphose into pets or programmed robots. The horror he introduces is of a semi-comic kind that one finds in certain types of fairy story, or on the pantomime stage. "The Scarecrow" and the man-eating pigs of "The Lake" belong to this genre.

All the same, McGough's involvement with the human race is real enough, and at times his laughter is tinged with sympathy and compassion. "Head Injury" portrays the nightmare world of the damaged victim ("I feel a colour coming, mottled, mainly black") by one who has clearly taken the trouble to live inside his mind. More touching is the poignant scene in "The Identification" where a distraught father, faced with the charred body of his son, struggles to explain why the boy was carrying cigarettes when forbidden to smoke. In such moments as these, McGough's matter-of-fact delivery and avoidance of sentimentality bring home the meaning of the tragedy of those concerned. Poems like

"The Identification" are proof of a talent which in McGough's case is often overlooked.

Human tragedy apart, there are few subjects on which McGough cannot raise a smile. He makes frequent jibes at poetry itself, in works like "I Don't Like the Poems" or "Take a Poem, Miss Smith," where various stock clichés are dictated by the bored poet to his all-too-compliant secretary. His ability to laugh at himself has never been in question, from the amused resignation of "Aren't We All" to his later tongue-in-cheek assessment of McGough the rock star: "I was somebody then (the one on the right / with glasses singing Lily the Pink)." His penchant for punning and wordplay re-emerges in "Nottingham," where he rejects the thought of seducing an Eng. Lit. student, not wishing to be "laid / alongside our literary heritage / allocated my place in her / golden treasury of flesh." Guilty at all times of "poetic licentiousness," McGough sees his poetry as a subversive act, a flying in the face of tradition and the canons of respectable taste: "May they (your poems) break and enter, assault and batter / and loiter in the mind with intent.../ may they bush-whack bandwagons / then take to the hills / may they break new wind...."

McGough's seriousness is real, if not always immediately apparent. His insights are keen, his touch deft and assured, never unduly laboured. These light-fingered but winning ways will continue to draw readers to him, whatever the fluctuations of poetic fashion in the 1980's.

—Geoff Sadler

McGRATH, Thomas M. American. Born near Sheldon, North Dakota, 20 November 1916. Educated at Sheldon public schools; University of North Dakota, Grand Forks, B.A. in English 1939 (Phi Beta Kapa); Louisiana State University, Baton Rouge, M.A. in English 1940; New College, Oxford (Rhodes Scholar), 1947-48. Served in the United States Army Air Force, 1943-46. Married Eugenia Juanopoulos in 1960; one son. English Instructor, Colby College, Waterville, Maine, 1940-41; Assistant Professor, Los Angeles State College, 1950-54, and C. W. Post College, Long Island, New York, 1960-61; Associate Professor, North Dakota State University, Fargo, 1962-67. Since 1969, Associate Professor of English, Moorhead State College, Minnesota. Formerly, film writer; Editor, *California Quarterly*, Davis. Since 1960, Founding Editor, with Eugenia McGrath, *Crazy Horse*, Fargo. Recipient: Swallow Book Award, 1955; Amy Lowell traveling scholarship, 1965; Guggenheim Fellowship, 1967; National Endowment for the Arts grant, 1974; Bush Foundation Fellowship, 1976, 1981. D.Litt.: University of North Dakota, 1981. Address: 615 South 11th Street, Moorhead, Minnesota 56560, U.S.A.

PUBLICATIONS

Verse

First Manifesto. Baton Rouge, Louisiana, Swallow, 1940.
Three Young Poets, with William Peterson and James Franklin Lewis, edited by Alan Swallow. Prairie City, Illinois, Decker Press, 1942.
The Dialectics of Love. Prairie City, Illinois, Decker Press, 1944.
To Walk a Crooked Mile. New York, Swallow, 1947.

Longshot O'Leary's Garland of Practical Poesie. New York, International, 1949.
Witness to the Times. Privately printed, 1954.
Figures from a Double World. Denver, Swallow, 1955.
Letter to an Imaginary Friend. Denver, Swallow, 1962.
New and Selected Poems. Denver, Swallow, 1962.
Letter to an Imaginary Friend, Parts I and II. Chicago, Swallow Press, 1970.
The Movie at the End of the World: Collected Poems. Chicago, Swallow Press, 1973.
Voyages to the Inland Sea III, with others, edited by John Judson. La Crosse, University of Wisconsin Center for Contemporary Poetry, 1973.
Voices from Beyond the Wall. Moorhead, Minnesota, Territorial Press, 1974.
A Sound of One Hand. St. Peter, Minnesota, Minnesota Writers' Publishing House, 1975.
Letters to Tomasito. Minneapolis, Holy Cow, 1977.
Open Songs: Sixty Short Poems. Mt. Carroll, Illinois, Uzzano Press, 1977.
Trinc: Praises II. Port Townsend, Washington, Copper Canyon Press, 1979.
Waiting for the Angel. Menomonie, Wisconsin, Uzzano Press, 1979.
Passages Toward the Dark. Port Townsend, Washington, Copper Canyon Press, 1982.
Echoes Inside the Labyrinth. New York, Thunder's Mouth Press, 1983.

Novel

The Gates of Ivory, The Gates of Horn. New York, Mainstream, 1957.

Other (for children)

About Clouds. Los Angeles, Melmont, 1959.
The Beautiful Things. New York, Vanguard Press, 1960.

*

Manuscript Collections: University of North Dakota, Grand Forks; North Dakota State University, Fargo; Moorhead State University, Minnesota.

Critical Studies: by Tom Bond, in *Measure 2* (Boston), 1958; Charles Potts, in *Small Press Review* (Paradise, California), 1974; "Thomas M. McGrath Issue" of *North Dakota Quarterly* (Grand Forks), Summer 1983.

Thomas McGrath comments:
Some of the work is a restructuring of traditional forms; some of it is open and "free." I have written a lot of short haiku-like poems and I'm now working on what may turn out to be the longest poem in America. I think the poems are quite personal in idiom, often "autobiographical" and politically revolutionary.

*   *   *

Like John Gardner in fiction or Sam Shepard in drama, Thomas McGrath is above all an American artist, whose work reflects the idioms and images of contemporary national life. His two dominant moods are private reminiscence, often meditation on a rural landscape, and public denunciation, often invective at an urban landscape. McGrath is the chronicler of both "the little lost towns...towns of the dark people: a depot, a beer joint, a small / Fistful of lights flung east as the red-ball train goes past," and of "the rattle of voting machines / In the Las Vegas of the national politic." These lines from his finest work to date, the long poem *Letter to an Imaginary Friend*, suggest the remarkable range of theme and tone typical of McGrath at his best.

In his book *Goatfoot Milktongue Twinbird* the poet Donald Hall judges McGrath the best poet of public denunciation and invective in America today, surpassing both Ginsberg and Bly. McGrath's invective arises from the political idealism that informs all his verse, and often appears as satirical contrasts between homely rural images and mechanical urban ones:

    And these but the stammering simulacra of the Rand
      Corpse wise men—
    Scientists who have lost the good of the intellect,
      mechanico-humanoids
    Antiseptically manufactured by the Faustian homunculus
      process.
    And how they dream in their gelded towers these
      demi-men!
    (Singing of overkill, kriegspiel, singing of blindfold chess—
      Sort of ainaleckshul rasslin matches to sharpen their
      fantasies
    Like a scout knife.)
                Necrophiles.
                        Money protectors.

The plastic urban world of machine-men is a world of ludicrous fantasies of power, but those fantasies are dangerous, even deadly: McGrath derides the death of intellect and conscience in modern technological America, even as he fears the consequent destruction it deals out to the weak or exploited. Loss is a recurrent motif, national loss of mind, loss of health, loss of compassion, loss of destiny, loss of tradition or anchoring past.

    Windless city built on decaying granite, loose ends
    Without end or beginning and nothing to tie to, city down
      hill
    From the high mania of our nineteenth century destiny—
      what's loose
    Rolls there, what's square slides, anything not tied down
    Flies in...
             kind of petrified shitstorm.   Retractable
    Swimming pools.
               Cancer Farms.
                        Whale dung

    At the bottom of the American night refugees tourists
      elastic
    Watches...

McGrath excels at this sort of national panorama, the poet's catalogue of a decaying society manifesting its putrescence in images of death and madness. "The citizens wrapped like mummies in their coats with poisoned sleep, / The dreamers, crazed, in their thousands, nailed to a tree of wine...." There is rage in this loss, and sorrow over the devastation.

In a more private vein, McGrath likes to fashion personal reminiscences into "pseudo-autobiography," as he calls *Letter to an Imaginary Friend* (from which all quotations here are taken). Then the mood is calmer, the tone more positive, sometimes serene, the humor amused but never ironic, the landscape often the cold north woods.

    So, worked together. Fed the wood to the saw
    That had more gaps than teeth. Sweated, and froze

    In the dead-still days, as clear as glass, with the biting
    Acetylene of the cold cutting in through the daylight,
    And the badman trees snapping out of the dusk
    Their icy pistols. So, worked, the peddlars pack of us.

Work is a source of peace and pleasure, from the Dakota woods to northern mountains and farms: "the vagrant farms of the north: Montana, Saskatchewan, / With the farmers still on them, merrily plowing away."

McGrath's verse shares points of similarity with that of many modern American poets, from Frost to Ginsberg, yet his voice is distinctly personal. He shares Frost's acute sense of nature and Ginsberg's rage, but blends those almost polar qualities into a single viewpoint capable of rare range and intensity.

                              —Jan Hokenson

McGUCKIAN, Medbh (née McCaughan). Irish. Born in Belfast, Northern Ireland, 12 August 1950. Educated at Dominican Convent, Fortwilliam Park, Belfast, 1961-68; Queen's University, Belfast, 1968-74, B.A. 1972, M.A. in English and Dip.Ed. 1974. Married John McGuckian in 1977; two sons. Since 1975, English teacher, St. Patrick's College, Knock, Belfast. Recipient: Eric Gregory Award, 1980; Rooney Prize, 1982; Arts Council award, 1982; Alice Hunt Bartlett Award, 1983. Lives in Belfast. Address: c/o Oxford University Press, Walton Street, Oxford OX2 6DP, England.

PUBLICATIONS

Verse

Single Ladies: Sixteen Poems. Budleigh Salterton, Devon, Interim Press, 1980.
Portrait of Joanna. Belfast, Honest Ulsterman Press, 1980.
Trio Poetry, with Damian Gorman and Douglas Marshall. Belfast, Blackstaff Press, 1981.
The Flower Master. Oxford and New York, Oxford University Press, 1982.
The Greenhouse. Oxford, Steane, 1983(?).
Venus and the Rain. Oxford and New York, Oxford University Press, 1984.

                           *

Medbh McGuckian comments:
    I don't really feel "established" enough to be of interest to the "general reader." My "work" is usually regarded as esoteric or exotic, but that is only because its territory is the feminine subconscious, or semi-conscious, which many men will or do not recognise and many women will or can not admit. My poems do not seek to chart "real" experience but to tap the sensual realms of dream or daydream for their spiritual value, which enhances and makes bearable the real. Through suffering, emotion, illness, people achieve order, art, strength. I believe wholly in the beauty and power of language, the music of words, the intensity of images to shadow-paint the inner life of the soul. I believe life is a journey upwards, beyond, inwards, a ripening process. As the body wearies the spirit is born. My themes are as old as the hills and out of date—love, nature, the seasons, children—but I hope

what is new is the voice binding them all, sophisticating itself into something eventually simple.

                        *   *   *

It is already a commonplace to criticise Medbh McGuckian's poetry for obscurity, lack of focus, and a plethora of images. It was ever thus: the Irish, like the Scots and the Welsh, have long experienced and understood the tyranny of English lucidity, which seeks to control the very ways in which it is permissible to create meaning. McGuckian's poetry recognises that one mode of resistance is obliquity, the refusal to be bullied into proprietorial, "acceptable" meaning. The same conflict lies behind such diverse works as Robert Graves's "Welsh Incident" and Heaney's *North*. Being Irish and being female combine to place McGuckian at a double remove from the dominant powers. She responds with a power of her own, a power born of awareness, for she has anticipated her (English) critics: in *Venus and the Rain* she declares "This oblique trance is my natural/Way of speaking." And she can expose the connections between language and domination, in lines like "my longer and longer sentences/Prove me wholly female," where what at first appears to be submissiveness and self-mockery turns out to subvert the reader's hasty assumptions.

Her poems revel in their imaginative and elaborate qualities. It is not just a matter of dense imagery and difficult metaphor. Meaning is constantly deferred; sometimes, by a careful twist, the meaning is placed out of reach *after* the reader thinks he has grasped it. Even her syntax questions the ways of dominance, for her long accretive sentences deny us the easy passage which can come only when one clause is ruthlessly subordinated to another.

Yet all this is achieved with most elegant wit, for the challenges to the unself-aware custodians of power and meaning are delivered implicitly, even in disguise. Sometimes the disguise is of a person innocent of most things beyond domesticity, certainly eschewing polemic or overtly political language, apparently engaged only in "a little ladylike sewing." But her domestic subjects are saved from cosiness by placing them near bold images of desire and sexuality. Woven like a sampler, *The Flower Master* is a deliberately florid book, structured with innumerable flower images. Likewise *Venus and the Rain* is conceived as a coherent whole, an attempt to map out a distinctively female mythology and erotics. There are many other signs of her talent, such as her ability to be extravagant and careful, modest, and ambitious at the same time, or the way in which the "I" enters and leaves even her earliest poems (in *Single Ladies*) with complete naturalness and assurance of tone.

These poems call forth from the reader a patient, slow approach, willingly given after one begins to understand her aims. The contract between poem and reader is like that between lovers, with the poem rejecting whatever smacks of brusque violation. Secretive, these poems nevertheless yield up a charge of authentic emotion each time. Sexual approach or rejection, indeed, is their paradigm for the approach to meaning:

Yours is the readership
Of the rough places where I make
My sweet refusals of you, your
Natural violence.

There is, of course, a risk inherent in subversive obliquity. Not the risk that a certain readership will be baffled, but that the impulse to translate everything into something else can lead to involutions which divert one from one's own purposes, as she is aware when she writes of "my tenable/Emotions largely playing with themselves." In its blending of the native and the exotic, and

in its strivings with language, Medbh McGuckian's talent sometimes suggests the Yeats of *Crossways* and *The Rose*. Perhaps she may have to become content with less before she can achieve more. But the prospect is exciting.

                                                        —R.J.C. Watt

                        _____

McHUGH, Heather. American. Born in California, 20 August 1948. Educated at Radcliffe College, Cambridge, Massachusetts, 1965-69, B.A.; Denver University, M.A. 1972. Married in 1968 (divorced). Visiting Lecturer, Antioch College, Yellow Springs, Ohio, 1971-72; Poet-in-Residence, Stephens College, Columbia, Missouri, 1974-76; Assistant, then Associate Professor of English, State University of New York, Binghamton, 1976-84. Since 1984, Milliman Writer-in-Residence, University of Washington, Seattle. Visiting Professor, Warren Wilson College, Swannanoa, North Carolina, 1980-85, Columbia University, New York, 1980 and 1981, and University of California, Irvine, 1982. Member, Board of Directors, Associated Writing Programs, 1981-83, and Literature Panel, National Endowment for the Arts, 1983-86. Recipient: Academy of American Poets prize, 1972; MacDowell Colony fellowship, 1973, 1974, 1976; National Endowment for the Arts grant, 1974, 1981; Houghton Mifflin New Poetry Series award, 1977; Creative Artists Public Service grant, 1980; Rockefeller Foundation Bellagio Residency, 1984. Address: 220 Water Street, Eastport, Maine 04631, U.S.A.

PUBLICATIONS

Verse

Dangers.   Boston, Houghton Mifflin, 1977.
A World of Difference.   Boston, Houghton Mifflin, 1981.

Other

Translator, *D'après tout: Poems*, by Jean Follain.   Princeton, New Jersey, Princeton University Press, 1981.

                                        *

Heather McHugh comments:
    I write in resistance to language. Commonplaces plague us; yet I care for what we have in common. In music I love the improvised embellishment in connection with the laws of the repeated line; they need each other. But I'm a bad follower, and English means to pull me down some humdrum paths (suddenly you find yourself at some colonial garden or moral vantage point; and as the kid said to his father, 15 minutes into his first plane-ride: "When do we start getting smaller?"). I love the surprise of human being and of moment—each (like the others) unlike anyone, despite all the misters and Mondays of our smaller callings.

                        *   *   *

Heather McHugh took Browning's line "Our interest's on the dangerous edge of things" as the epigraph of her first book, *Dangers*, poems in which she contrives to "drive/together argument and matter till you know/not what the matter is but how it shouts." Even though she sounds solitary and defiant, choosing "the artifice of hate," through which "the face//refuses to shine," she is conscious of connections with family and lovers, and interested in knowing and thus sustaining such ties. "Life is the mother/with murder in her eye"; nonetheless, McHugh wants to see and connect: "Give me strength,/lost gods," she prays in "Adenosene Triphosphate," "for the looking/glass, the glass/ that scars and heals."

"The sweetness/is of paradox," she says, and her poems are violent with contrast and contradiction. In the nine small dramas of singleness and interaction that comprise the book's middle section, "Public Places," the characters are always endangered, and equally persistent. Whether one is drinking by herself in a YWCA room and vowing independence, curling away in the quilt-like comfort of an asylum, or dining with a lover in a sunny inn, there is always the "mob" within the person, the "peasant love/of trouble." McHugh makes us see what the young mother discovers at the end of "Park": "It's only human,/and was never mine to lose, this/nature I thought I was rid of."

Concentrating on "unmediated life," McHugh nearly always succeeds in showing life to be frightening—and still worth living. Her people risk themselves in bearing children, in farming, in loving. The coast, where water can threaten, is her favorite vehicle to show that, even though life comprises "little/gross and no net/worth," "you know you can't/live anywhere else." Hardly shying from threat, she feels that "A body is seduced by damages" and declares, "I'd rather honor/in the flesh than hide/disaster's sprawl of substance...."

McHugh's interest in *A World of Difference* is less in the social than the spiritual. She assigns herself responsibility for comprehending. On one hand, she rejects the contemporary ethic that "one-of-a-kind [is] a lie." On the other, she repudiates confessionalism, caricaturing such writers as "gunning/their electrics, going/I I I I I," and insists the "vision isn't insight,/buried at last in the first/person's eye."

She accepts the phenomenal world as actual (see, for instance, "Message at Sunset for Bishop Berkeley"). But it is a world in which "the form of life/is a motion" and "color is the frequency and not the object." In such a context, human importance is dubious. Take the lovers in "When the Future Is Black," who regard themselves as a presence "designed to keep//the past and future from forever/meeting." Although we like to insist that "we make/a world of difference," McHugh craves selfless transcendence. Unlike those who would name—i.e. possess—God and try to "read/themselves into his will" (note the pun), she wants to forget "all names//for worship" and "our history of longing" and be God's "great blue breath,/his ghost and only song."

A formidable task, presumptuous perhaps, even inviting madness—but she maintains vigilance, scouring even her language of misleading and distracting meaning. "Always I have to resist/the language I have/to love," she says in "Like," expressing her simultaneous skepticism of and reliance upon words. But unlike the discursive, sometimes pedantic poems of *Dangers*, which are frequently rhymed and metrical, the spareness and eccentricity of *A World of Difference* produce a remarkable clarity for the reader. "Intensive Care" and "Language Lesson, 1976" are both notable in this way. In the latter, for instance, after seeming to satirize sayings like "hold the relish" (meaning "forget" it) and "love" (meaning, in tennis, "nothing"), McHugh abruptly turns the final third of the poem into a powerful love lyric:

> I'm saying go so far
> the customs are told,
>
> make nothing without words

and let me be
the one you never hold.

In such cases—and there are plenty in *A World of Difference*—McHugh's poems float nearly free of reference, and like some of the poems of Jean Follain, which McHugh has translated, assume the disquieting applicability of fable.

—Jay S. Paul

McKEOWN, Tom (Thomas Shanks McKeown). American. Born in Evanston, Illinois, 29 September 1937. Educated at the University of Michigan, Ann Arbor, 1957-62, A.B. 1961, A.M. 1962. Instructor, Alpena College, Michigan, 1962-64, and Wisconsin State University, Oshkosh, 1964-68; Poet-in-Residence, Stephens College, Columbia, Missouri, 1968-74, and University of Wisconsin, Stevens Point, 1976-81. Recipient: Hopwood Award, University of Michigan, 1968; Wurlitzer Foundation grant, 1972, 1975; Yaddo grant, 1973, 1975. Address: 3100 Ellis, No. 23, Stevens Point, Wisconsin 54481, U.S.A.

PUBLICATIONS

Verse

Alewife Summer. Albuquerque, New Mexico, Road Runner Press, 1967.
Last Thoughts. Madison, Wisconsin, Abraxas Press, 1969.
The Winds of the Calendar. Albuquerque, New Mexico, Road Runner Press, 1969.
Drunk All Afternoon. Madison, Wisconsin, Abraxas Press, 1969.
The Milk of the Wolf. Columbia, Missouri, Asari Press, 1970.
The Cloud Keeper. Dublin, Seafront Press, 1972.
The House of Water. Fredonia, New York, Basilisk Press, 1974.
The Luminous Revolver. Fremont, Michigan, Sumac Press, 1974.
Driving to New Mexico. Santa Fe, New Mexico, Sunstone Press, 1974.
Certain Minutes. Stevens Point, Wisconsin, Scopcraeft Press, 1978.

*

Critical Studies: "Contemporary Poetic Statements," in *Road Apple Review* (Oshkosh, Wisconsin), 1971; in *December Magazine* (Western Springs, Illinois), December 1971; in *Back Door* (Poquoson, Virginia), 1971; in *New Voices in American Poetry: An Anthology*, edited by David Allan Evans, Cambridge, Massachusetts, Winthrop, 1973.

Tom McKeown comments:
Have several unfinished novels but I have little interest in them now. Poetry is my full-time obsession.
I lean toward the surreal in poetry. Like experimentation rather than the tired, heavy academic stuff.
Write in free verse almost entirely. No major themes really other than the usual ones: love, death, separation, alienation, war, etc. I am mainly concerned with the *dream* and poetic

possibilities that arise out of the *dream*. This is the area of the surreal where a non-sequitur progression of images or image clusters are drawn from the unconscious mind. The surreal deals with the landscapes of dreams and thus there are infinite possibilities for new and startling creations. Always there is a possibility for a *satori* or sudden illumination. Have been influenced perhaps by Neruda, Breton and Trakl.

Recently, my poems have been reaching more toward the mystical and supernatural.

*   *   *

Tom McKeown is a poet who is able to be both concrete and surreal in his poetry. He admits the influence on his verse of such Spanish and Latin American poets as Lorca and Neruda; like Neruda, his surrealism has a strong grip on the natural landscape in which McKeown lives. Like other young American poets such as Greg Kuzma, McKeown manages a synthesis of the concrete and the surreal, the traditions of English nature poetry and Spanish and French surrealism. McKeown is one of the most promising exponents of this approach. He also sees the poet as a shaman in a poem from *Drunk All Afternoon* called "The Buffalo, Our Sacred Beast":

> I am running with them
> through the streets, drunk
> on buffalo milk and nourished
> by dung.
> I carry a flag with a buffalo on it
> and on my staff I spin a human skull.

In an essay he contributed to *Their Place in the Heat*, McKeown notes that he is attracted to both the nature/mythic/archetypal approach and the surreal approach as well in his writing. The former approach is evident in the poem quoted above, in which McKeown sees himself as a medicine man leading the buffalo back to trample the civilization that crushed them. Another poem (in a three poet issue of the *Road Apple Review*), "Aztec Dream," also evokes ancient rites, again involving human sacrifice: "a thin dagger parts the softness of air/of youth of flesh giving over all happy/silence to the carved gods of stone...." McKeown is, however, basically a compassionate poet; even in the first poem, he half apologizes to the human victims for the well-merited revenge of the buffalo, and one of his strongest groups of poems is a small collection of four elegies, *Last Thoughts*, which contains one of the strongest denunciations of the Viet Nam War, all the stronger for bringing it home in "Body En Route":

> A twenty year old boy
> is en route home. Killed
> in Viet Nam. En route home
> to the funeral parlor.
> Home. En route to Oshkosh.
> Twenty below zero. Heavy snow.
> He is riding home to be lifted
> from the baggage car
> of the Chicago-Northwestern.
> Quietly and smoothly
> he will be driven home
> through the frozen luminous streets.
> Nothing stirs in the gray houses.
> Silence from his metal box.

> The park is without voices.
> The wind blows a terrible darkness.

—Duane Ackerson

McNEIL, Florence. Canadian. Born in Vancouver, British Columbia, 8 May 1940. Educated at the University of British Columbia, Vancouver, B.A. 1961, M.A. 1965. Married David McNeal in 1973. Instructor, Western Washington State College (now University), Bellingham, 1965-68; Assistant Professor, University of Calgary, Alberta, 1968-73, and University of British Columbia, 1973-76. Since 1976, full-time writer. Recipient: Macmillan of Canada Prize, 1965; Canada Council award, 1976, 1978, 1980, 1982; Canadian National Magazine Award, 1979. Address: 20 Georgia Wynd, Delta, British Columbia V4M 1A5, Canada.

PUBLICATIONS

Verse

A Silent Green Sky.   Vancouver, Klanak Press, 1965.
Walhachin.   Fredericton, New Brunswick, Fiddlehead, 1972.
The Rim of the Park.   Port Clements, British Columbia, Sono Nis Press, 1972.
Emily.   Toronto, Clarke Irwin, 1975.
Ghost Towns.   Toronto, McClelland and Stewart, 1975.
A Balancing Act   Toronto, McClelland and Stewart, 1979.
The Overlanders.   Saskatoon, Thistledown Press, 1982.
Barkerville.   Saskatoon, Thistledown Press, 1984.

Play

Radio Play: *Barkerville: A Play for Voices*, 1980.

Other

When Is a Poem: Creative Ideas for Teaching Poetry Collected from Canadian Poets.   Toronto, League of Canadian Poets, 1980.
Miss P and Me (for children).   Toronto, Clarke Irwin, 1982; New York, Harper, 1984.
All Kinds of Magic (for children).   Vancouver, Douglas and McIntyre, 1984.

Editor, *Here Is a Poem*.   Toronto, League of Canadian Poets, 1983.

*

Critical Studies: in *Canadian Literature* (Vancouver), Autumn 1977; *CV 2* (Winnipeg), Autumn 1982.

Florence McNeil comments:
I'm interested in visual imagery and contrasts. Therefore my poetry is often about art and visual imagery, and my imagery is mainly visual. I'm also intrigued by history and the passing of time—how things remain the same and yet are different, how the past not only informs but also judges us, and how we are haunted by images of the past and the distant. I like to write about the

family, an important historical link or connection to me; I come from Hebridean Scots, newly emigrated in the 1920's bringing with them the Gaelic language and a romantic, ironic, self-effacing world view. They have crept into many of my poems—the sense of continuity with the past, with the ties of an extended family, and with a culture in many ways at odds with the North American culture provides much of my material. I am also interested in linked, connected poems—*Emily*, *Walhachin*, and *Barkerville* are all a series of connected poems. *The Overlanders* is a long poem, based on an historical event. I am interested in the narrative, perhaps because I heard so many tales and legends as a child, but in transforming the narrative into something that speaks to us today, creating a universal situation, set of emotions. I use irony and wit in my poetry—to underline contrasts between reality and unreality. I've always been interested in the differences: representation of the thing and the thing itself and the various shades of truth in what is perceived. Perhaps it comes down to trying to unentangle reality and illusion and ponder the unanswerable question—is there any way to know. In my poetry I try to go below the surface of things, if not to know, at least to make peace with the entanglement of fact and fiction.

*   *   *

Although Florence McNeil cannot be identified with any specific group, she is, like many other Canadian poets, a graduate of a university creative writing program and in dedicating *A Balancing Act* thanks Earle Birney "for his help and encouragement in the beginning." As well, she has a Canadian interest in the long documentary poem or linked series of poems based on historical material about a person, tribe, place, or event. In her first book, *Walhachin*, she chose a settler's "imagined monologue" to tell the story of Walhachin, a town by the Thompson River in the British Columbian dry belt. After initial prosperity, the town returned to sagebrush and wilderness after World War I killed many of its men and a disastrous rainstorm destroyed irrigation flumes. (The fascination with extinct communities is echoed in the title of another book, *Ghost Towns*.) Monologue also unifies the poems in *Emily*, based on the life and work of the great English-born West Coast painter Emily Carr (1871-1945), who is able to "find a leaf large as the coast." In her most recent book, *Barkerville*, she draws on the gold rush days of an 1860's boom-town in the Cariboo country of northeastern British Columbia. Illustrated with period photographs, the book uses the metaphor of a stage-set to exhibit a frenetic cast of riches-seeking adventurers. Reinforcing the theatrical motif are poems and prose poems about the Barkerville Dramatic Society, Martin "the World-Renowned Wonder-Creating Magician," concerts and minstrel performances, dancehall girls. The effect is of a photograph album filled with vivid snapshots, and the focal figure Billy Barker, the hard-drinking Cornish sailor who struck gold but died penniless in 1894: "someone mentioned that he almost made it into the twentieth century."

The documentary impulse also extends to poems which illustrate scenes from McNeil's own life, particularly in *The Rim of the Park*. In her most substantial work, *Ghost Towns*, she returns to her childhood, as well as to "Old Movies," "Montgolfier's Balloon," "Lilienthal's Glider," the channel crossing of Louis Bleriot. Even when the personal "I" intervenes she is the onlooker. In "The Extra," perhaps her best poem, she says, "I am half a Roman spectator/at the cardboard coliseum" and asks:

> is there a place (beyond the corner of the screen)
> to utilize

> my enduring inability
> to be completed?

Although sometimes at the expense of the imagistic incisiveness that marked poems like "At a Poetry Convention" ("The moon shone with transparent purpose/cutting through the lean quarrels of ice"), in recent work McNeil has moved toward more fluid diction and increased openness of form. The sense of historical wonder remains.

—Fraser Sutherland

McNEILL, Anthony. Jamaican. Born in St. Andrew, 17 December 1941. Educated at Excelsior College, 1952; St. George's College, 1953-59; Nassau Community College, 1964-65; Johns Hopkins University, Baltimore, 1970-71, M.A. 1971; University of Massachusetts, Amherst, M.A. 1976. Married Olive Samuel in 1970; one child. Civil service clerk, Port Maria and Kingston, 1960-64; journalist, The Gleaner Company, Kingston, 1965-66; scriptwriter, JIS radio, St. Andrew, 1966-68; trainee manager, Jamaica Playboy Club-Hotel, 1968-69; Assistant to Editor, *Jamaica Journal*, Kingston, 1970; Teaching Assistant, University of Massachusetts, 1971-75; Assistant Director (Publications), Institute of Jamaica, Kingston; columnist, *The Gleaner*, 1981-82; Lecturer, Excelsior Community College, Kingston, 1982-83. Recipient: Jamaica Festival prize, 1966, 1971; Silver Musgrave Medal, 1972. Address: c/o L. Wint, Linstead P.O., Jamaica, West Indies.

PUBLICATIONS

Verse

Hello Ungod. Baltimore, Peacewood Press, 1971.
Reel from "The Life-Movie." Mona, Jamaica, Savacou, 1975.
Credences at The Altar of Cloud. Kingston, Institute of Jamaica, 1979.

Other

Editor, with Neville Dawes, *The Caribbean Poem: An Anthology of 50 Caribbean Voices.* Kingston, Institute of Jamaica, 1976.

*

Critical Studies: "An Extreme Vision" by Mervyn Morris, in *Sunday Gleaner* (Kingston), 28 January 1973; Wayne Brown, in *Jamaica Journal* (Kingston), March-June 1973.

Anthony McNeill comments:
My poems are struck sorrow-lanterns.

*   *   *

Anthony McNeill is the first and most accomplished poet to appear out of the "now" generation of the anglophone Caribbean. McNeill is "new" in the sense that coming to maturity in the late sixties, he is past the rhetorical colonial assertions and dramatic nationalist self-doubts of the *entre des guerres* writing which gave us Carter, Roach and the early Derek Walcott. He is very much into his own "thing." That thing is "now" in that it deals with clairol and speed, and is very much concerned with splitting, suicide and animal / identity. But there is nothing gratuitously "today" about these energies and work. Here is a poet of patient, scrupulous craftsmanship, concerned with rhythm, cadence, form and the fissionable, rather than fashionable qualities of his word. His most definitive collection to date is *Reel from "The Life-Movie."* It contains 30 poems, 18 of which appear in his earlier 20-poem *Hello Ungod*. The two together give a fair idea of McNeill's thematic interests and poetic development. He begins (setting/style) as a "lyrical" "Nature" poet ("Cliff-Walking"): "and this cliff / where swallows confirm / the sooncome of rain, / of long evenings adrift / from your meaning again and again." But this is not traditional "Nature" where metaphors come to rest in contemplation of superordinate glories. Note the "*adrift* / from your meaning" in that last line of the poem which just before said "and my eyes ride / upward, oaring me back / to *loneliness*" (my italics). It is this modern / urban problem and paradox, the concern of anglophone poetry from Auden through Lowell to Plath, that quickly comes to dominate his page. The sense of interior loneliness so pervades McNeill's poetry, in fact, that even physical love ("Mummy +," "Dermis") is vitiated by it, until the persona / victim loses his hold of self and becomes "other": as in the zoo-poem "Rimbaud Jingle," for example:

> When you trip
> on my skin of sickness, bruised blue,
>
> I'll slip from my cage and into
> the pure life of lions. I'm death-
> sick of being two...

which leads to a frighteningly clear and "cool" contemplation of the anti-solutions: suicide ("Who'll See He Dive?") and / or the use of hallucinogens ("The Lady Accepts the Needle Again"):

> The lady slips
> out to her loveliness
> lost irrevocably lost The Lady cries out
> for ships The Lady cries out for Paris...
>
> The Lady gets sexy & rings
> a towering eunuch into her hell

But what makes McNeill an important new voice is his comprehensive perception of this agony: the result of interior loneliness is not just personal freak, but social impasse ("Reel," "American Leader") and cultural, perhaps even cosmic catastrophe ("Hello Ungod," "Black Space"). All the post-Dostoevsky archetypes gather in his poetry, suffering from the death of God: the mad clown, the schizophrenic, the ape, Aunt Angel, The Lady, Godot, Dracula, and the dread ikons from McNeill's own formative experience of the Kingston ghetto: Brother Joe, Saint Ras, and Don Drummond, the sacred trombone-man. All these walk through a broken shadowed wordscape "whose irradiant stop is light"; whose "true country" is "Both doubt and light."

It is from this double (paradoxical, sometimes schizoid) vision that McNeill's remarkable sensibility expresses itself. But his development contains its own perils. More and more the light of his poetry seems to radiate not from the sun, no matter how distant, but from an agnostic space lit only by the flicker of a (life)-*movie*, so that the poet finds himself locked into the "ponderous ingot / that weights down the base of / his / box," until only a dark solar doubt (unseen ungod) is left: "At twenty-nine

guru / I'm still unprepared; / one day I will shatter / / yank loose in the wind / as a man stuck together with pins. / When the god comes, I'll tell him *the perfect flamingo he gifted is gone*" ("Flamingo"; my italics). But this, surely, with one so seriously embattled with his own talent, can only be a temporary or apparent illumination. McNeill's "solutions" over the next few years will be one of the major achievements in our literature.

—Edward Kamau Brathwaite

McPHERSON, Sandra. American. Born in San Jose, California, 2 August 1943. Educated at Westmont College, Santa Barbara, California, 1961-63; San Jose State College, B.A. in English 1965; University of Washington, Seattle, 1965-66. Married Henry Carlile in 1966; one daughter. Technical writer, Honeywell Inc., Seattle, 1966. Member of the faculty, Writers Workshop, University of Iowa, Iowa City, 1974-76, 1978-80. Since 1981, member of the faculty, Pacific Northwest College of Art Oregon Writers' Workshop, Portland. Poetry Editor, *Antioch Review*, Yellow Springs, Ohio, 1979-81. Recipient: Helen Bullis Prize (*Poetry Northwest*), 1968; Bess Hokin Prize, 1972, and Oscar Blumenthal Prize, 1975 (*Poetry*, Chicago); Ingram Merrill grant, 1972, 1984; Poetry Society of America Emily Dickinson Prize, 1973; National Endowment for the Arts grant, 1974, 1980; Guggenheim Fellowship, 1976. Address: 7349 S.E. 30th Avenue, Portland, Oregon 97202, U.S.A.

PUBLICATIONS

Verse

Elegies for the Hot Season. Bloomington, University of Indiana Press, 1970.
Radiation. New York, Ecco Press, 1973.
The Year of Our Birth. New York, Ecco Press, 1978.
Sensing. San Francisco, Meadow Press, 1980.
Patron Happiness. New York, Ecco Press, 1983.
Pheasant Flower. Missoula, Montana, Owl Creek Press, 1985.

*   *   *

"Centerfold Reflected in a Jet Window" is the title of a beautiful short poem in Sandra McPherson's *The Year of Our Birth.* This is its first stanza:

> There is someone naked flying alongside the airplane.
> The man in the seat in front of me is trying to hold her.
> But she reflects, she is below zero, would freeze the
> skin off his tongue.

Her characteristic elevation of the prosaic—a traveler staring at photographs in *Playboy*— and gracefully, almost routinely oblique angles of vision are by now, after three collections, hallmarks. What perception gives us—or, when she is reaching for it, what can be wrested from perceptions—is never seen to be strange, but taken and investigated on faith.

The danger in this strategy—it can be sometimes faux-naif—is usually overcome without visible struggle. At her best, which is how she writes, she rivals Elizabeth Bishop in her ability to domesticate the strange and make the ordinary marvelous. The surface of the sea is "crumpled brine." A coconut bobs in water "like a bucket of oak or a light wodden dory," and its hair is like a baby's hair. "Grapefruit's white energetic light / befits it as a morning dish." Sometimes such passages work overtime. "Orange peels in her skillet like lions in the dark / blackened, witching an aroma through the ancient rooms." The conspiracy of "witching" and "ancient" alludes to more significance than the lines can use or justify; but the orange peels curling up like blackened lions are unforgettable, especially and justly in the dark.

She seems, for all her exact quirkiness of vision, so thoroughly a realist who believes that attention to material detail will produce the immaterial significances for which her poems strive—that she can only fail to invoke the world by slackened technique or reticence. Slackened technique is almost unknown to her. Sometimes her poems about love, marriage, and friendship grow opaque from a central reticence about what her angles of vision are variations on. The problem is often that the reticences are incomplete, and need either wholly to erase the traces of an actual biographical subject, or give the poem more use of it. Sections of "Studies of the Imaginary," all traceable to the actual, as I read them, work—and sometimes don't work—this way.

And yet how small my cavils are, given the lustrous, strange body of work she's produced already. "Perception" and "faith," I wrote earlier, suggesting two poles by which we describe the blurred and fascinating continuum of experience. Sandra McPherson has given us, already, indelible evidence about the ways we live by that blur:

> Because I have turned my head for years
> in order to see the bittern
> I won't mind not finding
> what I am looking for
> as long as I know it could be there,
> the cover is right,
> it would be natural.

—William Matthews

McWHIRTER, George. Canadian. Born in Belfast, Northern Ireland, 26 September 1939. Educated at Grosvenor High School, Belfast, 1951-57; Queen's University, Belfast, 1957-62, B.A. 1961; University of British Columbia, Vancouver (Macmillan Prize), 1968-70, B.A. 1970. Married Angela Coid in 1963; one daughter and one son. Assistant Master, Kilkeel Secondary School, Northern Ireland, 1962-64, and Bangor Grammar School, Northern Ireland, 1964-65; English Teacher, University of Barcelona, Spain, 1965-66, and Alberni Secondary School, Port Alberni, British Columbia, 1966-68. Since 1970, Professor, and since 1983, Head of Creative Writing, University of British Columbia. Associate Editor, 1970-73, Editor, 1978, and since 1979, Advisory Editor, *Prism International*, Vancouver; Editor, *Words from the Inside*, Kingston, Ontario, 1973. Recipient: Canada Council grant, 1969, 1975; Commonwealth Poetry Prize, 1972. Address: 4637 West 13th Avenue, Vancouver, British Columbia V6R 2V6, Canada.

PUBLICATIONS

Verse

Catalan Poems. Ottawa, Oberon Press, 1971.

Columbuscade. Vancouver, Hoffer, 1974.
Bloodlight for Malachi McNair. San Francisco, Kanchenjunga, 1974.
Twenty-Five. Fredericton, New Brunswick, Fiddlehead, 1975.
Queen of the Sea. Ottawa, Oberon Press, 1976.
The Island Man. Ottawa, Oberon Press, 1981.
Fire Before Dark. Ottawa, Oberon Press, 1983.

Novel

Paula Lake. Ottawa, Oberon Press, 1984.

Short Stories

Bodyworks. Ottawa, Oberon Press, 1974.
God's Eye. Ottawa, Oberon Press, 1981.
Coming to Grips with Lucy. Ottawa, Oberon Press, 1982.

*

George McWhirter comments:

My work to date has been preoccupied with people and substance: people as consumers of substance and at the same time as those consumed by substance. He who eats will in turn be eaten. Such was the base of *Catalan Poems*. The family, man, woman, and child, one flesh, one substance was the central dramatic vehicle for this. *Columbuscade* uses the idea of Columbus to deal with the impossibility of escape from the flesh in terms of space: we can jump no farther than ourselves. Even if there was a new world, few would embark; the superscription of the book runs, "All are chosen for the crew, but few embark fearing a new world." This is the fundamental dilemma in *Queen of the Sea* which is set in the Belfast shipyards. Recenlty, I've come to regard things and substance as part of the infinite imagination of light. The unknown is the point of disembarkation, the intellect provides place names as we pass, the real rudder in the rear of the head is the intuition. The main thing that poetry does for me is turn ideas or intimations into the properties of the five senses; this is what life itself does for us. Poetry, in short, is life.

*   *   *

George McWhirter has been accused of producing "deftly crafted anachronisms—still, cold and timeless to the point of utter irrelevance." But the same critic, a Canadian, acknowledged the poet's skill, describing *Catalan Poems* as "a collection of exquisitely sculptured impersonal lyrics." The barrier between poet and reader in this case appears to have derived from the fact that McWhirter's poems were not set in Canada and did not present a Canadian point of view.

To an outsider the virtues of the book are more apparent. The skill is certainly present: there are vividly memorable images such as these lines about a man plucking and eating grapes from a bunch: "Seconds drop *pip* into a dish. / Time plants a sprig of green bone / In the empty glass." The style is impressionistic, highly visual, and admittedly somewhat detached. It would be unfair, though, to dismiss this collection as impersonal or irrelevant. It is not confessional, first-person poetry; but there are sharply-observed portraits of people—market-women, a prostitute, a soldier, and in particular the aging, anxious but undauntedly swaggering Eduardo with his long-suffering wife; and insights into the uneasy commitments and compromises of the Catholic faith (far from irrelevant when one remembers that the poet comes from Belfast). Here and elsewhere we are free to draw our own parallels. George McWhirter's world is not a comfortable one, but we cannot ignore his picture of it.

—Fleur Adcock

MEAD, Matthew. British. Born in Buckinghamshire, 12 September 1924. Served in the British Army, 1942-47, including three years in India, Ceylon and Singapore. Married to Ruth Adrian. Editor, *Satis* magazine, Edinburgh, 1960-62. Has lived in Germany since 1962, currently in Bad Godesberg. Address: c/o Anvil Press Poetry, 69 King George Street, London SE10 8PX, England.

PUBLICATIONS

Verse

A Poem in Nine Parts. Worcester, Migrant Press, 1960.
Identities. Worcester, Migrant Press, 1964.
Kleinigkeiten. Newcastle upon Tyne, Satis, 1966.
Identities and Other Poems. London, Rapp and Carroll, 1967.
The Administration of Things. London, Anvil Press Poetry, 1970.
Penguin Modern Poets 16, with Harry Guest and Jack Beeching. London, Penguin, 1970.
In the Eyes of the People. Edinburgh, Satis, 1973.
Minusland. Edinburgh, Satis, 1977.
The Midday Muse. London, Anvil Press Poetry, 1979.

Other

Translator, with Ruth Mead, *Shadow Land: Selected Poems of Johannes Bobrowski*. London, Carroll, 1966; revised edition, London, Rapp and Whiting, 1967.
Translator, with Ruth Mead, *Generation*, by Heinz Winfried Sabais. Ednburgh, Satis, 1967.
Translator, with Ruth Mead and others, *O the Chimneys*, by Nelly Sachs. New York, Farrar Straus, 1967; as *Selected Poems of Nelly Sachs*, London, Cape, 1968.
Translator, with Ruth Mead, *Generation and Other Poems*, by Heinz Winfried Sabais. London, Anvil Press Poetry, 1968.
Translator, with Ruth Mead, *Amfortiade and Other Poems*, by Max Hölzer. Edinburgh, Satis, 1968.
Translator, with Ruth Mead, *Horst Bienek*. Santa Barbara, California, Unicorn Press, 1969.
Translator, with Ruth Mead, *Elisabeth Borchers*. Santa Barbara, California, Unicorn Press, 1969.
Translator, with Ruth Mead and Michael Hamburger, *The Seeker and Other Poems*, by Nelly Sachs. New York, Farrar Straus, 1970.
Translator, with Ruth Mead, *Selected Poems*, by Johannes Bobrowski and Horst Bienek. London, Penguin, 1971.
Translator, with Ruth Mead, *Mitteilungen / Communications*, by Heinz Winfried Sabais. Darmstadt, Roether, 1971.
Translator, with Ruth Mead, *Socialist Elegy*, by Heinz Winfried Sabais. Darmstadt, Roether, 1975.
Translator, with Ruth Mead, *From the Rivers*, by Johannes Bobrowski. London, Anvil Press Poetry, 1975.
Translator, with Ruth Mead, *The Tightrope Walker*, by Christa Reinig. Edinburgh, Satis, 1981.

Translator, with Ruth Mead, *The People and the Stones*, by Heinz Winfried Sabais. London, Anvil Press Poetry, 1983.
Translator, with Ruth Mead, *The Raven*, by Gunter Bruno Fuchs. Edinburgh, Satis, 1984.
Translator, with Ruth Mead, *Shadow Lands*, by Johannes Bobrowski. London, Anvil Press Poetry, 1984.

*

Critical Studies: by Christopher Middleton, in *London Magazine*, 1964, and in *Neue Deutsche Literatur* (Berlin), February 1965; by A. Kingsley Weatherhead, in *The British Dissonance*, Columbia, University of Missouri Press, 1983.

*   *   *

Matthew Mead has been spoken of as a modernist, a social critic, a poet who is proletarian and unacademic. On the contrary, his qualities are those of literary accomplishment. He can turn an epigram or a ballade as well as anyone writing today. The reader may feel his way through deliberately fragmented *hommages* to Ezra Pound or Robert Creeley to light upon such finely tooled verses as

> Bodies are rolled from bed to scuffed slippers
> and day stiff-jointed; in sense repetition;
> in spring one more spring; the figure
> in a worn carpet traced with a dull eye.
>
> And the house old, the wind's sound, each ache
> lent art and length, given due weight
> the dragging footfall. For this are we bent
> and gnarled and wrinkled—to cross the room....

It is not that Mead is an escapist; his translations of Bobrowski, done in collaboration with his wife, would assure us of that. Rather he is a Poundian in a sense deeper than that of technical allegiance: an aesthete distressed by the blood and chaos of totalitarian Europe. The poem quoted, "To Redistort a Weltanschauung," comes from his retropective collection, *Identities*. Here is an extract from his more recent *The Administration of Things*:

> What she herself believes
> No man alive conceives
>
> We tell the lawful tale
> (All fictions else must fail)
>
> And loyal beyond the lie
> Nor daring to deny
>
> That what we have she gave
> We make of what we have
>
> Lending it length and art
> Embellishing each part
>
> A faith to ravage noon
> With phases of the moon....

It is clear that writing such as this resembles nothing so much as the more Elizabethan lyrics of Donne—"But come bad chance / And we join to it our strength / And we teach it art and length / Itself o'er us to advance..."—or the more lapidary verse of Marvell—"Caesar's head at last / Did through his laurels blast /

...And if we must speak true / Much to the man is due..." At present, in Mead's original work, there is a gap between subject and presentation. Those who have followed his work with interest all these years must hope that he will turn this characteristic hiatus to dramatic use. Or, if not that, then they must wish him to find a range of subject matter suited to the cool detachment of his technique.

—Philip Hobsbaum

MEHROTRA, Arvind Krishna. Indian. Born in Lahore, Pakistan, 16 April 1947. Educated at the University of Allahabad, Uttar Pradesh, 1964-66, B.A. 1966; University of Bombay, 1966-68, M.A. 1968. Married Vandana Jain in 1969; one son. Lecturer in English, 1968-77, and since 1978, Reader in English, University of Allahabad. Visiting Writer, University of Iowa, Iowa City, 1971-73; Lecturer in English, University of Hyderabad, India, 1977-78. Editor, *damn you / a magazine of the arts*, Allahabad, 1965-68; Founder, Ezra-Fakir Press, Bombay, 1966. Recipient: Homi Bhabha Fellowship, 1981. Address: Department of English Studies, University of Allahabad, Allahabad 211 002, Uttar Pradesh, India.

PUBLICATIONS

Verse

Bharatmata: A Prayer. Bombay, Ezra Fakir Press, 1966.
Woodcuts on Paper. London, Gallery Number Ten, 1967.
Pomes / Poemes / Poemas. Baroda, India, Vrischik, 1971.
Nine Enclosures. Bombay, Clearing House, 1976.
Distance in Statute Miles. Bombay, Clearing House, 1982.
Middle Earth. New Delhi, Oxford University Press, 1984.

Other

Translator, *Three Poems*, by Bogomil Gjuzel. Allahabad and Iowa City, Ezra Fakir Press, 1973.

*

Critical Studies: "Image as an Immoderate Drug" by N.R. Shastri, in *Osmania Journal of English Studies 13* (Hyderabad), 1, 1977; "A Wonderland of Riddles and Fantasies" by Bibhu Padhi, in *Toronto South Asian Review 2*, no. 2, 1983.

*   *   *

Arvind Krishna Mehrotra has said that a poem comprises "games, riddles and accidents...and the poet creates as many accidents as he can." Mehrotra is probably the best-known Indian writer of surrealist English verse today, using some of the characteristic techniques of surrealist writing, such as an uninhibited dependence on chance or accident in composition; the collocation of unusual words and phrases; the yoking together of heterogeneous objects and situations and contexts; broken syntax; the ascription of unusual characteristics to familiar objects; the exaltation of the dream state. The general aim is to transform the reader's consciousness and to change his conception of reality. Mehrotra has cited Breton's fist *Manifesto* (1924) as one of the influences on his work. Breton defined surrealism as "pure psychic automatism by which it is intended to express either verbally or in writing, the true function of thought. Thought dictated in the absense of all control exerted by reason and outside all aesthetic or moral control." These aims were of course later modified, and not all of Mehrotra's poetry fits in the surrealist category. For instance, poems such as "Songs of the Ganga" (*Nine Enclosures*) are relatively "straightforward" works in which experimentation is held down to the minimum. Another, perhaps better-known, poem which is more characteristic and not particularly difficult is "The Sale" in which the language of salesmanship is exploited to suggest the sell-out of the world and its impending conversion to a wasteland. It would be misleading, however, to suggest that Mehrotra's poetry is "about" this or that, about something external to itself. The poems are "enclosures" whose aim is to capture the reader within themselves. Their principal means are the haunting poetic rhythm and the disturbing image:

> The widow next door
> Lives off her trained
> Parrot.
> It reads the future
> And tells you when
> To avoid it.
> At night
> She dances in the streets
> And fills the air
> With abuse.
> The decorated general
> Is alone
> In his tent;
> The pyres burn
> Like new volcanoes.

While the second strophe reads like a summary of first World War poetry, the first one reads rather like a joke, a story, a song. Children enjoy it as it is, and don't ask for its meaning. The world of the child and the world of the grown-ups are juxtaposed, and the meaning arises from this juxtaposition.

Poetry such as Mehrotra's is international, and it is not much bothered with the question of "Indianness" which is such a persistent concern of some of his Indian contemporaries. His poetry is difficult, and "chancy." But the chances quite often come off. His latest poems, however, seem to be written in a non-European mode with only a touch of the surrealistic technique:

> Summer is at hand.
> New leaves fill the branches
> With sunlight, a red and green kite
> Bends into the wind. It is two bits
> Of thin paper joined
> In the middle. It opens the sky.
> I have three small rooms and a terrace
> Where I sit out and read Han Shan
> To my new-born son, or make
> That kite. My possessions are few.
> I'll stay here.

Poems such as these raise no questions, debate no issues, wave no flags. Peaceful in themselves, they are the cause of peace also in their readers.

—S. Nagarajan

MEINKE, Peter. American. Born in Brooklyn, New York, 29 December 1932. Educated at Hamilton College, Clinton, New York, A.B. 1955; University of Michigan, Ann Arbor, M.A. 1961; University of Minnesota, Minneapolis, Ph.D. in English 1965. Served in the United States Army, 1955-57. Married Jeanne Clark in 1957; two daughters and two sons. English teacher, Mountain Lakes High School, New Jersey, 1958-60; Assistant Professor of English, 1961-66, and Poet-in-Residence, 1973, Hamline University, St. Paul, Minnesota. Assistant Professor, 1966-68, Associate Professor, 1968-72, and since 1972, Professor of Literature and Director of the Writing Workshop, Florida Presbyterian College, later named Eckerd College, St. Petersburg, Florida. Visiting Professor, University of Sussex, Brighton, Summer 1969; Director, AMFC French Program, University of Neuchâtel, Switzerland, 1971-72; Fulbright Lecturer, University of Warsaw, 1978-79; Poet-in-Residence, Hamilton College, Winter 1981; Jenny Moore Lecturer, George Washington University, Washington, D.C., 1981-82. Recipient: National Endowment for the Arts Fellowship, 1974; Poetry Society of America Gustav Davidson Award, 1976, and Lucille Medwick Prize, 1984; Emily Clark Balch Prize (*Virginia Quarterly Review*), for fiction, 1982; O. Henry Award, for fiction, 1983; PEN award, for fiction, 1984. Address: 147 Wildwood Lane S.E., St. Petersburg, Florida 33705, U.S.A.

PUBLICATIONS

Verse

Lines from Neuchâtel. Gulfport, Florida, Konglomerati Press, 1974.
The Night Train, and The Golden Bird. Pittsburgh, University of Pittsburgh Press, 1977.
The Rat Poems; or, Rats Live on No Evil Star. Cleveland, Bits Press, 1978.
Trying to Surprise God. Pittsburgh, University of Pittsburgh Press, 1981.

Other

Howard Nemerov. Minneapolis, University of Minnesota Press, 1968.
The Legend of Larry the Lizard (for children). Richmond, John Knox Press, 1968.
Very Seldom Animals (for children). St. Petersburg, Florida, Possum Press, 1969.

*

Manuscript Collection: University of Florida, Gainesville.

Critical Studies: "Speaking to Us All" by Philip Jason, in *Poet Lore* (Boston), 1982; "Trying to Surprise God" by Eric Nelson, in *Mickle St. Review* (Philadelphia), 1983.

Peter Meinke comments:
My poems and stories have to stand on their own and I have little to say about them. I am a slow writer in both genres and try to write as clearly as possible—I am seldom "surreal" though occasionally my dreams enter my writing in strange ways. I'm interested in the formal problems of sounding contemporary in traditional forms. I don't know what I would do if I didn't write—I've never tried it.

*   *   *

Peter Meinke's *The Night Train, and The Golden Bird* contains a variety of poems, both lyric and comic, free-form and formal, yet all embued with this poet's seriousness and hard-headedness, an unmistakable tone which the reader discovers in the very first poem, a title poem, "The Night Train." In Meinke's train, the passengers are suicides on the way to nowhere, and their misery and futility is embodied in the rhythm of the train:

> their fingers drum the drumroll of their wake
> on train compartment windows, when they take
> their lives it is the right place
> this closed anonymous world inside a train
> a nothing sort of place; for god's sake
> get on with it: there's nothing much at stake

Notice the rhymes here: wake, take, sake, stake. By breaking his lines where he does, by the repetitive rhymes, and by reducing punctuation to a minimum, Meinke has created a powerful and evocative poem.
What Meinke does in "The Night Train" is similar to what he does in most of his work. He seems to let the poem dictate its own form, to let the lines break where they must and punctuate themselves. What gives his poems power is this ability to risk lines like these, in the grimly comic, "Vegetables:"

> Disemboweled peas
>
> slide into tumbrils, dizzy
> with air, beets bleed on the
> sinkboard, celery wilts with its heart
> in our hands.

At the same time, his poems are highly controlled and show a firm understanding of conventional prosody. The second title poem, "The Golden Bird," is a villanelle, and here is a moving anti-war poem, "The Monkey's Paw," that demonstrates Meinke's lyric gifts as well as his concern and his anger:

> When the war is over the bones of the lonely dead
> will knit and rise from ricefield and foxfield
> like sea-things seeking the sea, and will head
> toward their homes in Hanoi or Seattle
> clogging the seaways, the airways, the highways
> climbing the cliffs and trampling the clover
> heading toward Helen, Hsueh-ying, or Mary
> when the war is over

Measures like these make Peter Meinke a rare poet in our time, one who hears music where there is mostly din, a poet to keep our eyes on.

—Cynthia Day

—————

MELTZER, David. American. Born in Rochester, New York, 17 February 1937. Educated at public schools in Brooklyn and Los Angeles; Los Angeles City College, 1955-56; University of California, Los Angeles, 1956-57. Married Christina Meyer in 1958; three daughters and one son. Manager, Discovery Bookshop, San Francisco, 1959-67; Editor, *Maya*, Mill Valley, California, 1966-71; teacher, Urban School, San Francisco, 1975-76.

Since 1970, Editor, *Tree* magazine and Tree Books, Bolinas, later Berkeley, California. Composer, musician, and singer: performed with Serpent Power and David and Tina, 1970-72. Recipient: Council of Literary Magazines grant, 1972, 1981; National Endowment for the Arts grant, 1974, for publishing, 1975. Address: Box 9005, Berkeley, California 94709, U.S.A.

PUBLICATIONS

Verse

Poems, with Donald Schenker. Privately printed, 1957.
Ragas. San Francisco, Discovery, 1959.
The Clown. Larkspur, California, Semina, 1960.
Station. Privately printed, 1964.
The Blackest Rose. Berkeley, California, Oyez, 1964.
Oyez! Berkeley, California, Oyez, 1965.
The Process. Berkeley, California, Oyez, 1965.
In Hope I Offer a Fire Wheel. Berkeley, California, Oyez, 1965.
The Dark Continent. Berkeley, California, Oyez, 1967.
Nature Poem. Santa Barbara, California, Unicorn Press, 1967.
Santamaya, with Jack Shoemaker. San Francisco, Maya, 1968.
Round the Poem Box: Rustic and Domestic Home Movies for Stan and Jane Brakhage. Los Angeles, Black Sparrow Press, 1969.
Yesod. London, Trigram Press, 1969.
From Eden Book. San Francisco, Cranium Press, 1969.
Abulafia Song. Santa Barbara, California, Unicorn Press, 1969.
Greenspeech. Goleta, California, Christopher, 1970.
Luna. Los Angeles, Black Sparrow Press, 1970.
Letters and Numbers. Berkeley, California, Oyez, 1970.
Bronx Lil/Head of Lillin S.A.C. Santa Barbara, California, Capra Press, 1970.
32 Beams of Light. Santa Barbara, California, Capra Press, 1970.
Knots. Bolinas, California, Tree, 1971.
Bark: A Polemic. Santa Barbara, California, Capra Press, 1973.
Hero/Lil. Los Angeles, Black Sparrow Press, 1973.
Tens: Selected Poems 1961-1971, edited by Kenneth Rexroth. New York, Herder, 1973.
The Eyes, The Blood. San Francisco, Mudra, 1973.
French Broom. Berkeley, California, Oyez, 1973.
Blue Rags. Berkeley, California, Oyez, 1974.
Harps. Berkeley, California, Oyez, 1975.
Six. Santa Barbara, California, Black Sparrow Press, 1976.
Bolero. Berkeley, California, Oyez, 1976.
The Art, The Veil. Milwaukee, Membrane Press, 1981.
The Name: Selected Poetry 1973-1983. Santa Barbara, California, Black Sparrow Press, 1983.

Recordings: *Serpent Power*, Vanguard, 1972; *Poet Song*, Vanguard, 1974; *David Meltzer Reading*, Membrane, 1981; *Nurse*, S-Tapes, 1982.

Novels

Orf. North Hollywood, Essex House, 1968.
The Agency. North Hollywood, Essex House, 1968.
The Agent. North Hollywood, Essex House, 1968.
How Many Blocks in the Pile? North Hollywood, Essex House, 1968.
Lovely. North Hollywood, Essex House, 1969.
Healer. North Hollywood, Essex House, 1969.
Out. North Hollywood, Essex House, 1969.
Glue Factory. North Hollywood, Essex House, 1969.
The Martyr. North Hollywood, Essex House, 1969.
Star. North Hollywood, Brandon House, 1970.

Other

We All Have Something to Say to Each Other: Being an Essay Entitled "Patchen" and Four Poems. San Francisco, Auerhahn Press, 1962.
Introduction to the Outsiders (essay on Beat Poetry). Fort Lauderdale, Florida, Rodale, 1962.
Bazascope Mother (essay on Robert Alexander). Los Angeles, Drekfesser Press, 1964.
Journal of the Birth. Berkeley, California, Oyez, 1967.
Isla Vista Notes: Fragmentary, Apocalyptic, Didactic Contradictions. Santa Barbara, California, Christopher, 1970.
Abra (for children). Berkeley, California, Hipparchia Press, 1976.
Two-way Mirror: A Poetry Note-book. Berkeley, California, Oyez, 1977.

Editor, with Lawrence Ferlinghetti and Michael McClure, *Journal for the Protection of All Beings 1* and *3*. San Francisco, City Lights, 2 vols., 1961-69.
Editor, *The San Francisco Poets*. New York, Ballantine, 1971; revised edition, as *Golden Gate*, San Francisco, Wingbow Press, 1976.
Editor, *Birth: An Anthology*. New York, Ballantine, 1973.
Editor, *The Secret Garden: An Anthology in the Kabbalah*. New York, Seabury Press, 1976.
Editor, *The Path of the Names*, by Abraham Abulafia. Berkeley, California, Tree, and London, Trigram Press, 1976.
Editor, *Birth: An Anthology of Ancient Texts, Songs, Prayers, and Stories*. San Francisco, North Point Press, 1981.
Editor, *Death* (anthology). Berkeley, North Point Press, 1984.

Translator, with Allen Say, *Morning Glories*, by Shiga Naoya. Berkeley, California, Oyez, 1975.

*

Manuscript Collections: Washington University, St. Louis; University of Indiana, Bloomington; University of California, Los Angeles.

Critical Studies: *David Meltzer: A Sketch from Memory and Descriptive Checklist*, Berkeley, California, Oyez, 1965, and *6 Poets of the San Francisco Renaissance*, Fresno, California, Giligia Press, 1967, both by David Kherdian; in *Vort* (Berkeley), 1979.

*   *   *

David Meltzer's poetry is well-known as the presence of a second volume of selected poems (*The Name*, 1984) indicates. In the introduction, he tells us that his first poem was at age 11, a "trance-mission." He has indeed had a long career. He was first made known, as he gratefully acknowledges, by the efforts of Kenneth Rexroth. Some of Meltzer's affiliations are indicated by his *Golden Gate Interviews* with Rexroth, Everson, Ferlinghetti, Welch, McClure—one of the few collections of interviews where the interviewer is also interesting. For example, Lew

Welch mentioned that he had learned how fast he could run when he was a boy beset by other boys. Meltzer then asked: "How did you become interested in language? For instance, you talk about your speed, being able to move..when did you realize that language was a way of moving too?" and Lew Welch responded: "That's a well-put question." He also appeared in the historically important *Floating Bear* edited by Diane di Prima and Amiri Baraka (then LeRoi Jones). Meltzer's roots are with the San Francisco poets, but he found that language was a way of moving in space and time.

One can scarcely sum up his poetry: he has "home movies" and "Rustic and Domestic Home Movies for Stan and Jane Brakhage." He has "translated" a Chinese rice paper notebook containing his scrawls into poems for Jack and Ruth Hirschman. He has notes for a poem to H.P. Lovecraft and he admonishes us that "the gods exhort us to understand the form of light." He seems to phrase the question for us: "Who is it in there./ Wiring these poems" (*Blue Rags*). (Period. No question mark. "Questions are Remarks," Wallace Stevens wrote.) But there is no obvious answer. It is not necessarily true that "The Jew in me is the ghost of me/ hiding under a stairway" (*The Dark Continent*) because his poetry also has a wide range of Hebraic lore, as if we were threatened by having a Golem's shapeless mass:

> Without Neshamah (light of God)
> the Golem's intelligence was small.
> Also lacking the other two intelligences:
> *Chochmah* (Wisdom) & *Bina* (Judgement)

His poetry coheres by consistent ways of feeling rather than by conceptually calibrated systems.

> Others balance by
> Kneeling to pray.
> I allow them their poem
>
> This is mine.
> A patchwork poem
> Pathwork.

Patchwork—pathwork. Fragmentation provides opportunity: one perceives through fragments, and finds unexpected connections, as for example in "Lamentation for Lee Harvey Oswald": "the moment they long to see,/ the shattered skull, the blood/ We are all spies." In an epigraph from the Zohar to his book *Yesod* the 22 fragments, the 22 letters of the Hebrew alphabet, make perception possible, as the ten words (presumably the Sephiroth, the names of God) make analogies possible. (Yesod, basis, was perceived by Pico della Mirandola as analogous to the sphere of Luna.)

He has an energizing range of scholarly material. His anthologies *Birth* and *Death* collect ancient and modern myths, stories texts sayings from South America, New Zealand, India, over the world, through time. In *Birth* the ten pages of sources and checklist seem to be culled from much larger lists, because they are consistently interesting and important.

His own mythmaking can put an amusing tone to serious purpose, as for example in his work *Bark* (a particular favorite among younger poets):

> Dog didn't know he was a dog and climbed a tree, hung from a branch with his tail, swinging back and forth, singing a song that sounded like it came out of a tenor saxophone.
> "Dogs don't do such things," a master said, passing by the tree.

He put dog in his place and give him a name and a collar and trained him with rolled up newspaper never to sing again.

He can also be more immediate, and with less parable:

IT'S SIMPLE

> It's simple.
> One morning
> Wake up ready
> For new work
> Pet the dog,
> Dog's not there
> Rise and shine.
> Sun's not there.
> Take a deep breath
> No air
> Look for the sun.
> No sun.
>
> It's simple
> Wake up one morning
> Ready for new work
> & the animals are on strike
> With the air, the sea the
> Earth quit us
> Casts us off
> Like a sickness in the firey core.

A temporary restng place for his poetry ("the end/ Not the end") can be taken in his concluding words for the 1984 selected poems:

> each word the word creating
> protecting life in lights of song or silence
> all else goes against it
>
>
> A period.
> A pause floats in space.
> An end, not an end.

—William Sylvester

MEREDITH, William (Morris, Jr.). American. Born in New York City, 9 January 1919. Educated at Lenox School, Massachusetts; Princeton University, New Jersey (Woodrow Wilson Fellow, 1946-47), B.A. (magna cum laude) 1940. Served in the United States Army Air Force, 1941-42, and in the United States Naval Reserve, 1942-46, 1952-54: Lieutenant Commander. Copyboy and reporter, *The New York Times*, 1940-41; Resident Fellow in Creative Writing, Princeton University, 1947-48, 1949-50, 1965-66; Assistant Professor of English, University of Hawaii, Honolulu, 1950-51; Member of the Department, 1955, Professor of English, 1965-83, Connecticut College, New London. Taught at Bread Loaf Writers Conference, Vermont, summers 1958-62. Opera critic, *Hudson Review*, New York, 1955-56. Member, Connecticut Commission on the Arts, 1963-65; Director of the Humanities, Upward Bound Program, 1964-68; Poetry Consultant, Library of Congress, Washington, D.C.,

1978-80. Recipient: Yale Series of Younger Poets Award, 1943; Harriet Monroe Memorial Prize, 1944, and Oscar Blumenthal Prize, 1953 (*Poetry*, Chicago); Rockefeller grant, for criticism, 1948, for poetry, 1968; *Hudson Review* fellowship, 1956; American Academy grant, 1958; Ford Fellowship, for drama, 1960; Loines Award, 1966; Van Wyck Brooks Award, 1971; National Endowment for the Arts grant, 1972, fellowship, 1984; Guggenheim Fellowship, 1975; Vaptsarov Prize (Bulgaria), 1979. Member, American Academy; Chancellor, Academy of American Poets. Address: 3024 Porter Street NW, Apt. 104, Washington, D.C. 20008, U.S.A.

PUBLICATIONS

Verse

Love Letter from an Impossible Land.   New Haven, Connecticut, Yale University Press, 1944.
Ships and Other Figures.   Princeton, New Jersey, Princeton University Press, 1948.
The Open Sea and Other Poems.   New York, Knopf, 1958.
The Wreck of the Thresher and Other Poems.   New York, Knopf, 1964.
Winter Verse.   Privately printed, 1964.
Earth Walk: New and Selected Poems.   New York, Knopf, 1970.
Hazard, The Painter.   New York, Knopf, 1975.
The Cheer.   New York, Knopf, 1980.

Recording: *Selected Poems*, Watershed, 1977.

Play

The Bottle Imp (libretto), adaptation of the story by Robert Louis Stevenson, music by Peter Whiton (produced Wilton, Connecticut, 1958).

Other

Reasons for Poetry, and The Reason for Criticism (lectures). Washington, D.C., Library of Congress, 1982.

Editor, *Shelley.*   New York, Dell, 1962.
Editor, *University and College Poetry Prizes, 1960-66, in Memory of Mrs. Fanny Fay Wood.*   New York, Academy of American Poets, 1966.
Editor, with Mackie L. Jarrell, *Eighteenth Century Minor Poets.* New York, Dell, 1968.

Translator, *Alcools: Poems 1878-1913,* by Apollinaire.   New York, Doubleday, 1964.

*

Manuscript Collection: Middlebury College, Vermont.

Critical Study: *Three Contemporary Poets of New England* by Guy Rotella, Boston, Twayne, 1983.

*   *   *

Introducing William Meredith's *Love Letter from an Impossible Land*, Archibald MacLeish observed that this poet's "instincts are sound" ("He seems to know, without poisoning himself in the process, which fruits are healthful and which fruits

are not"). The consistencies in his subsequent volumes have proved MacLeish's prediction true. Although his meters have loosened in recent books, Meredith remains a formal poet who achieves imaginative participation in his subjects by creating them at an aesthetic distance. Poise and understanding are sought and revealed in the subjection of the facts of experience to an imaginative yet rational order. If the experience in a Meredith poem begins as a brute fact or raw emotion, it is transmuted into a shapelier, more civil and more intelligible image of itself. His work renders emotional force into forms. In a period when many poets sacrifice convention and form for force and immediacy, the risks in this aesthetic are evident. Yet the reader responsive to the legitimate demands such poetry makes will find among the resulting poems those which acknowledge the forces which engendered them. In his elegy to the sailors lost in a sunken submarine (the title poem from *The Wreck of the Thresher*) Meredith writes:

Why can't our dreams be content with the terrible facts?
The only animal cursed with responsible sleep.
We trace disaster always to our own acts.
I met a monstrous self trapped in the black deep:
All these years, he smiled, *I've drilled at sea*
For this crush of water. Then he saved only me.

Confronting the inexplicable tragedy of meaningless death, Meredith characteristically concludes, "Whether we give assent to this or rage/ Is a question of temperament and does not matter."

This poem reflects two of his abiding concerns, the threat of death and the loneliness of the sea, already enunciated in the last ten poems of his first book. Service as a naval aviator in two Pacific wars has marked out for Meredith a part of his *donnée*: images of oceanic space, the lonely sky, distant islands seen from vast heights, the unknown destinies of men in wartime, and the responses of an American to Oriental cultures (Japan, Korea, Hawaii) recur in his poems. Characteristically, he deals with such themes pictorially, fixing his images as though in a painting, imposing upon them the designs imagination discovers and the forms and meters appropriated by a scrupulously sensitive ear. His instinct is to render such design; in "Rus in Urbe" (from *The Open Sea*) he chooses "In a city garden an espalliered tree," not nature unadorned but nature shaped by human skill and imagination. Yet in a later poem, "Roots" (from *The Wreck of the Thresher*), a dialogue narrative in the mode of Frost, he discovers in nature itself the pattern which in "Rus in Urbe" imagination had to wrest by altering the shapes of trees.

The new poems in *Earth Walk: New and Selected Poems* use a conversational, colloquial style, as in "Walter Jenks' Bath": "These are my legs. I don't have to tell them, legs,/ Move up or down or which leg." With like informality of diction Meredith explores dreams, probes memory, creates characters, and, as in the title poem, makes his wry statement about being himself at a time when almost everyone else is preoccupied by somebody else's moon walk. The formality of this recent work is less a matter of surface and detail (such as regular stanza, rhythm, rhyme) than formerly, but the design of the experience is quietly interiorized in each poem. His tone is modest rather than boisterous, his range deceptively larger than the voice whose speech provides the style.

Hazard, The Painter is a series of 16 poems dramatizing the life not only of the artist of its title but, by inference, of his time. For two years Hazard has been at work on a painting of a falling parachutist, "the human figure dangling safe...full of half-remembered instruction/ but falling, and safe." Hazard "is in charge of morale in a morbid time"—the time of Nixon's election, when the "nation has bitterly misspoken itself." He measures his own modest gift against the greatness of Titian and Renoir, and reflects on his relationships to his wife, children, friends, and the earth. The tone of these poems is at once intimate and slightly distanced by third-person narration; the effect of the suite is that of a novel in verse, a whole life economically suggested by these glimpses. Its theme is no less than the artist's responsibility in a time when "more of each day is dark": "Gnawed by a vision of rightness/that no one else seems to see,/what can a man do/but bear witness." This is Meredith's finest book thus far.

Meredith has also published a complete translation of *Alcools* by Apollinaire, a poet whose intuitive mode of apprehending experience would seem quite different from his own. In his poem "For Guillaume Apollinaire," Meredith writes, "But these poems—/How quickly the strangeness would pass from things if it were not for them." The same may be said of his own best work.

—Daniel Hoffman

MERRILL, James (Ingram). American. Born in New York City, 3 March 1926. Educated at Lawrenceville School; Amherst College, Massachusetts, B.A. 1947. Served in the United States Army, 1944-45. Recipient: Oscar Blumenthal Prize, 1947, Levinson Prize, 1949, Harriet Monroe Prize, 1951, Eunice Tietjens Memorial Prize, 1958, and Morton Dauwen Zabel Prize, 1966 (*Poetry*, Chicago); National Book Award, 1967, 1979; Bollingen Prize, 1973; Pulitzer Prize, 1977; Los Angeles *Times* award, 1983; National Book Critics Circle Award, 1984. Member, American Academy, 1971. Address: 107 Water Street, Stonington, Connecticut 06378, U.S.A.

PUBLICATIONS

Verse

Jim's Book: A Collection of Poems and Short Stories. Privately printed, 1942.
The Black Swan and Other Poems. Athens, Icaros, 1946.
First Poems. New York, Knopf, 1951.
Short Stories. Pawlet, Vermont, Banyan Press, 1954.
A Birthday Cake for David. Pawlet, Vermont, Banyan Press, 1955.
The Country of a Thousand Years of Peace and Other Poems. New York, Knopf, 1959; revised edition, New York, Atheneum, 1970.
Selected Poems. London, Chatto and Windus-Hogarth Press, 1961.
Water Street. New York, Atheneum, 1962.
The Thousand and Second Night. Athens, Christos Christou Press, 1963.
Violent Pastoral. Privately printed, 1965.
Nights and Days. New York, Atheneum, and London, Chatto and Windus-Hogarth Press, 1966.
The Fire Screen. New York, Atheneum, 1969; London, Chatto and Windus, 1970.
Two Poems. London, Chatto and Windus, 1972.
Braving the Elements. New York, Atheneum, 1972; London, Chatto and Windus, 1973.
Yannina. New York, Phoenix Book Shop, 1973.

The Yellow Pages: 59 Poems. Cambridge, Massachusetts, Temple Bar Bookshop, 1974.
Divine Comedies. New York, Atheneum, 1976; London, Oxford University Press, 1977.
Metamorphosis of 741. Pawlet, Vermont, Banyan Press, 1977.
Mirabell: Books of Number. New York, Atheneum, 1978; London, Oxford University Press, 1979.
Ideas, etc. New York, Jordan Davies, 1980.
Scripts for the Pageant. New York, Atheneum, 1980.
The Changing Light at Sandover. New York, Atheneum, 1982.
Marbled Paper. Salem, Oregon, Seluzicki, 1982.
Santorini: Stopping the Leak. Worcester, Massachusetts, Metacom Press, 1982.
From the First Nine: Poems 1947-1976. New York, Atheneum, 1982.
Souvenirs. New York, Nadja, 1984.
Bronze. New York, Nadja, 1984.
Late Settings. New York, Atheneum, 1985.

Plays

The Bait (produced New York, 1953). Published in *Artists' Theatre: Four Plays*, edited by Herbert Machiz, New York, Grove Press, 1960.
The Immortal Husband (produced New York, 1955). Published in *Playbook: Plays for a New Theatre*, New York, New Directions, 1956.

Novels

The Seraglio. New York, Knopf, 1957; London, Chatto and Windus, 1958.
The (Diblos) Notebook. New York, Atheneum, and London, Chatto and Windus, 1965.

*

Bibliography: by Jack W.C. Hagstrom and George Bixby, in *American Book Collector* (New York), November-December 1983.

Manuscript Collection: Washington University, St. Louis.

Critical Studies: interview, in *Contemporary Literature* (Madison, Wisconsin), ix, 1, 1968; *Alone with America* by Richard Howard, New York, Atheneum, 1969, London, Thames and Hudson, 1970, revised edition, Atheneum, 1980; interview, in *Saturday Review of the Arts* (New York), December 1972; "Feux d'Artifice" by Stephen Yenser in *Poetry* (Chicago), June 1973; Richard Saez, in *Parnassus* (New York), 1974; *James Merrill: Essays in Criticism* edited by David Lehman and Charles Berger, Ithaca, New York, Cornell University Press, 1983; *James Merrill: An Introduction to the Poetry* by Judith Moffett, New York, Columbia University Press, 1984; interview, in *Writers at Work 6* edited by George Plimpton, New York, Viking Press, 1984, London, Secker and Warburg, 1985.

*   *   *

James Merrill's books of poems are like the rings of a tree: each extends beyond the content, expression, outlook, and craft of the previous work. Merrill has patiently, even doggedly, pursued his craft, giving each poem, however short or terse or ephemeral, a certain lapidary sheen and hardness. Merrill's complete output of verse, fiction, and plays is notable as an absorption with technique and difficulty. This would have assured Merrill a place in poetry as one of our better minor lyricists, one of our perfectionists, had it not been for the sudden turnaround of his two recent books, *Divine Comedies* and *Mirabell: Books of Number*. Suddenly Merrill has become our grand inquisitor, a poet of metaphysical humor and daring who blithely invents spirits of the Ouija board to confess to us the history of space, the chemical future of man, the heavenly wars at the dawn of being, the whereabouts of old geniuses now reincarnated as scientists and technicians. The whole madcap experiment wobbles and shuffles forward into a sort of greatness—sustained by Merrill's nonchalantly argumentative nature.

His earliest poems are turgid with rime, metric tricks, stuffy diction. Merrill came onto the literary scene during the vogue of revived metaphysical poetry, a verse wrought with high polish and formal orthodoxy. Such is the poetry of his first major book, *The Country of a Thousand Years of Peace*, with its elegant persona, his widely cultivated tastes, his voice of leisured travel and gracious living—the poetry, in gist, of an American aristocrat. *Water Street* maintains this elegant discourse on the vicissitudes of life, love, travel, the perennially chilly rooms and beds of his daily life.

But with *The Fire Screen* we get a new perspective on the persona with his life in Greece, where the warm sun, the old culture, the intimacy of life provoke a deeper self-awareness. Instead of the isolated, inward existence of New England, the speaker is thrust into a more primal and assertive culture where his passions and convictions are awakened. There are also poems of return to the northeastern United States, with lyrics of resignation and quiet regrets. In the American edition is the endless verse narrative "The Summer People," with its heavy-handed irony; Robert Lowell said more about the vacation culture in his one page poem "Skunk Hour." *Braving the Elements* is both freer in its forms and more open and intimate in its voice. Instead of the choppy quality of his earlier, tightly-wrought lines, there is now a smooth, conversational rhythm in his three- or four-line stanza structures. "Days of 1935," "18 West 11th Street," which laments the death of young anti-war radicals, "Days of 1971" are open, intimate revelations of the poet's feelings.

Merrill's progress is toward a balance between rigid formalism and the open poem, where craft would continue to discipline the choice and assembly of language but where the content would be free to take its own course. That balance is reached in the long sequence "The Book of Ephraim" included in *Divine Comedies*. The twenty-six alphabetically ordered parts are interwoven through a leisurely plot where the poet and his lover communicate with the spirit of Ephraim through the Ouija board, whose insight and wit make life seem a mere instant in a vast spiritual universe. In discovering this broader realm, Merrill is dazzling as a conversational poet. Ephraim's reckless honesty about the other side enables the speaker to unravel a complex plot of lives and afterlives, including his own father's, in a humorous, novel-like progression of poems. The verse never impedes the narrative; it enhances it with its exuberance of puns, amazing condensations of ideas and observations, feats of beautiful lyric sound.

The success of this sequence makes clear Merrill's earlier difficulties with orthodox convention: his verve and spontaneity of imagination, his life as a contemporary, were too straitened by the demands of closed forms of verse. Merrill has seized upon the cut-and-paste, leaping perceptual technique of recent poets without relinquishing his metrical skill and eloquence. With *Mirabell: Books of Number*, what might have seemed a fresh new idea in "Ephraim" has become the second step of an important long sequence, a poem capable of making effective summary of the ideational renaissance that has flourished all century long. Merrill's wit is of a class with Auden's, who features prominently in this book—his disciplined diction moves gracefully through difficult formulations without sagging into prose. Through *Mirabell* and work to come, we have a romance in the making—a grasp of what man now becomes after a century of redefinition.

—Paul Christensen

———

MERWIN, W(illiam) S(tanley). American. Born in New York City, 30 September 1927. Educated at Princeton University, New Jersey, A.B. in English 1947. Tutor in France and Portugal, 1949, and to Robert Graves's son in Mallorca, 1950; free-lance translator, London, 1951-54; Playwright-in-Residence, Poet's Theatre, Cambridge, Massachusetts, 1956-57; Poetry Editor, *The Nation*, New York, 1962; Associate, Théâtre de la Cité, Lyons, France, 1964-65. Recipient: Yale Series of Younger Poets Award, 1952; *Kenyon Review* fellowship, 1954; American Academy grant, 1957; Arts Council of Great Britain bursary, 1957; Rabinowitz Research Fellowship, 1961; Bess Hokin Prize, 1962, and Harriet Monroe Memorial Prize, 1967 (*Poetry*, Chicago); Ford grant, 1964; Chapelbrook Award, 1966; P.E.N. Translation Prize, 1969; Rockefeller grant, 1969; Pulitzer Prize, 1971; Academy of American Poets Fellowship, 1973; Shelley Memorial Award, 1974; National Endowment for the Arts grant, 1978; Bollingen prize, 1979. Member, American Academy. Address: c/o Atheneum Publishers, 597 Fifth Avenue, New York, New York 10017, U.S.A.

PUBLICATIONS

Verse

A Mask for Janus. New Haven, Connecticut, Yale University Press, 1952.
The Dancing Bears. New Haven, Connecticut, Yale University Press, 1954.
Green with Beasts. London, Hart Davis, and New York, Knopf, 1956.
The Drunk in the Furnace. New York, Macmillan, and London, Hart Davis, 1960.
The Moving Target. New York, Atheneum, 1963; London, Hart Davis, 1967.
The Lice. New York, Atheneum, 1967; London, Hart Davis, 1969.
Three Poems. New York, Phoenix Book Shop, 1968.
Animae. San Francisco, Kayak, 1969.
The Carrier of Ladders. New York, Atheneum, 1970.
Signs: A Poem. Iowa City, Stone Wall Press, 1971.
Writings to an Unfinished Accompaniment. New York, Atheneum, 1974.
The First Four Books of Poems. New York, Atheneum, 1975.
Three Poems. Honolulu, Petronium Press, 1975.
The Compass Flower. New York, Atheneum, 1977.
Feathers from the Hill. Iowa City, Windhover Press, 1978.
Finding the Islands. Berkeley, California, North Point Press, 1982.
Opening the Hand. New York, Atheneum, 1983.

Plays

Darkling Child, with Dido Milroy (produced 1956).
Favor Island (produced Cambridge, Massachusetts, 1957).
Eufemia, adaptation of the play by Lope de Rueda, in *Tulane Drama Review* (New Orleans), December 1958.
The Gilded West (produced Coventry, England, 1961).
Turcaret, adaptation of the play by Alain Lesage, in *The Classic Theatre*, edited by Eric Bentley, New York, Doubleday, 1961.
The False Confession, adaptation of a play by Marivaux (produced New York, 1963). Published in *The Classic Theatre*, edited by Eric Bentley, New York, Doubleday, 1961.
Yerma, adaptation of the play by García Lorca (produced New York, 1966).
Iphigenia at Aulis, with George E. Dimock, Jr., adaptation of a play by Euripides (produced Princeton, New Jersey, 1982). New York, Oxford University Press, 1982.

Other

A New Right Arm (essay). Oshkosh, Wisconsin, Road Runner Press, n.d.
Selected Translations 1948-1968. New York, Atheneum, 1968.
The Miner's Pale Children. New York, Atheneum, 1970.
Houses and Travellers. New York, Atheneum, 1977.
Selected Translations 1968-1978. New York, Atheneum, 1979.
Unframed Original: Recollections. New York, Atheneum, 1982.

Editor, *West Wind: Supplement of American Poetry*. London, Poetry Book Society, 1961.

Translator, *The Poem of the Cid*. New York, New American Library, and London, Dent, 1959.
Translator, *The Satires of Persius*. Bloomington, Indiana University Press, 1961; London, Anvil Press Poetry, 1981.
Translator, *Some Spanish Ballads*. London, Abelard Schuman, 1961; as *Spanish Ballads*, New York, Doubleday, 1961.
Translator, *The Life of Lazarillo de Tormes: His Fortunes and Adversities*. New York, Doubleday, 1962.
Translator, *The Song of Roland*, in *Medieval Epics*. New York, Modern Library, 1963; published separately, New York, Random House, 1970.
Translator, *Transparence of the World: Poems of Jean Follain*. New York, Atheneum, 1969.
Translator, *Products of the Perfected Civilization: Selected Writings*, by Sebastian Chamfort. New York, Macmillan, 1969.
Translator, *Voices: Selected Writings of Antonio Porchia*. Chicago, Follett, 1969.
Translator, *Twenty Love Poems and A Song of Despair*, by Pablo Neruda. London, Cape, 1969.
Translator, with others, *Selected Poems: A Bilingual Edition*, by Pablo Neruda, edited by Nathaniel Tarn. London, Cape, 1969; New York, Delacorte Press, 1972.
Translator, *Chinese Figures: Second Series*. Mount Horeb, Wisconsin, Perishable Press, 1971.
Translator, *Japanese Figures*. Santa Barbara, California, Unicorn Press, 1971.
Translator, *Asian Figures*. New York, Atheneum, 1973.
Translator, with Clarence Brown, *Selected Poems of Osip Mandelstam*. London, Oxford University Press, 1973; New York, Atheneum, 1974.
Translator, *Vertical Poems*, by Roberto Juarroz. Santa Cruz, California, Kayak, 1977.

Translator, with J. Moussaieff Masson, *Sanskrit Love Poetry*. New York, Columbia University Press, 1977; as *The Peacock's Egg: Love Poems from Ancient India*, Berkeley, California, North Point Press, 1981.
Translator, *Four French Plays*. New York, Atheneum, 1984.
Translator, *From the Spanish Morning*. New York, Atheneum, 1984.

*

Bibliography: "Seven Princeton Poets," in *Princeton Library Chronicle* (Princeton, New Jersey), Autumn 1963.

Critical Studies: "W.S. Merwin Issue" of *Hollins Critic* (Hollins College, Virginia), June 1968; "W.S. Merwin and the Nothing That Is" by Anthony Libby, in *Contemporary Literature 16* (Madison, Wisconsin), 1973; "The Continuities of W.S. Merwin" by Jarrold Ramsey, in *Massachusetts Review 14* (Amherst), 1973.

*   *   *

I imagine the writing of a poem, in whatever mode, still betrays the existence of hope, which is why poetry is more and more chary of the conscious mind in our age.

The mystery of man's condition, like the mystery of the word, is like the sea—which fills W.S. Merwin's poetry—with its attendant whales, birds, moon, tides, rocks, and bells; this is a poetry filled with silences and distances, doors and dreams. The early works were sometimes remarkable in their lyrical ease—i.e., "Song of Marvels," "Song of Three Smiles," "Song of the New Fool." Others, more formal and elegant, were long and elaborate narratives based upon folk tales and myth, where story and character were of secondary importance to the poet's questions, much like Wallace Stevens's, about reality and art. In "East of the Sun and West of the Moon," an elaborate, 500-line poem of 39 13-line stanzas in iambic pentameter, Merwin adapts a Norse fairy tale, itself an adaptation of Apuleius's Cupid and Psyche legend. But the story remains mere decoration, a frame within which he contemplates the relationship of art and imagination to reality. "All magic is but metaphor," he writes, with the following: "All metaphor...is magic." Then, speculating on the perfection of art and eternity over the flux of this world, his character ponders: "Why should I/complain of such inflexible content,/ Presume to shudder at such serenity,/ Who walk in some ancestral fantasy." Like Yeats's Oisin, Merwin's persona is drawn to this world and would "ride a while the mortal air."

Perhaps his numerous and remarkable translations (Porchia, Neruda, Follain, Char, Guillén, *The Song of Roland*, *The Poem of the Cid*) have stimulated or reinforced his own experiments with meter and form (from Yeats's and Stevens's Symbolism to Neruda's Surrealism and Follain's linguistic innovations). Nevertheless, by the mid-1960's, Merwin had honed the form we most often associate with him: the spare and sometimes epigrammatic line, simple language, and the absence of allusion, myth, rhyme, and punctuation. His focus had turned in great part to the articulation of the "desert of the unknown"—the Absurd, Nothingness, Silence, as in "Daybreak": "The future woke me with its silence/ I join the procession/ An open doorway/ Speaks for me/ Again." This world of the unknown, always benignly indifferent to man, beckons the poet, in his infinite imagination, for articulation; the poet begs for comprehension and consolation.

Merwin has been associated with the tradition of contemporary poets known as the oracular poets, and if his surrealistic style has been compared to that of Roethke, Bly, Wright, Dickey, Plath, Olson, and even Lowell, his apocalyptic vision is entirely his own. Death for Merwin is not an entrance into harmony with the universe; rather it is an entrance into nothingness; in an impressive blending of form and content, Merwin's muted voice and conspicuous absence of punctuation reflect his very quest and felt experience: "I know nothing/learn of me," he writes; "I taught them nothing. Everywhere/The eyes are returning under the stones. And over/My dry bones they built their churches, like wells" ("The Saint of the Uplands"). Like Beckett, a master in the spare articulation of "Nothing," Merwin writes: "It is when I assert to nothing that I assert to all."

Merwin's attraction to nothingness, and the knowledge which that inspires, is often associated with water, also associated with sleep, night, and even erotic experience, as in "Sailor Ashore": "the waters are/Under the earth. Now to run from them./It is their tides you feel heaving under you,/Sucking you down, when you close your eyes with women." Such knowledge, which all men aspire to and only a few can articulate in their own limited terms, becomes their statement of personal tragedy. Of the informed sailor, in "The Shipwreck," he writes "...this sea, it was/Blind, yes, as they had said, and treacherous—/They had used their own traits to character it—but without/Accident in its wildness, in its rage,/Utterly and from the beginning without/Error. And to some it seemed the waves/Grew gentle, spared them, while they died of that knowledge."

At times the poet cries out for revelation: "Oh objects come and talk with us while you can." But, perhaps more frequently, he feels paralyzed and in an intolerable pain of spiritual emptiness. Sometimes nature is forbidding and frightening: "The whole night is alive with hands./Is aflame with palms and offerings/...in mid-winter...empty gloves."

Merwin concretizes the benign indifference of the universe in his many plants and animals, which have the knowledge he seeks. In "Noah's Raven" the raven turns away from Noah and says: "Why should I have returned?/My knowledge would not fit into theirs [man's]." Again recalling Wordsworth's imagery, he describes his isolation in the face of an enlightened nature: "You would think the fields were something/To me, so long I stare out, looking/For their shapes or shadows through the matted gleam, seeing/Neither what is nor what was, but the flat light rising."

When the poet achieves revelation, his vision is one of "blindness," his condition that of a stone; perhaps man is ultimately "invisible, invisible, invisible," an alien in "silence," "trying to read what the five polars are writing/On the void" ("A Scene in May"). In an utter calm of despair, he writes: "Not that heaven does not exist but/That it exists without us./...Everything that does not need you is real" ("The Widow").

Given a world of cosmic indifference, one would hope for comfort in the world of men. Merwin's most bitter poems treat man's brutality to man. Of family relationships he writes: "tell me anything more/Of every kinship than its madness..." ("Uncle Hess"). Man has ruined his environment and he has destroyed nature: "Men think they are better than grass" ("The River of Bees"). But nature will avenge men who "made up their minds to be everywhere because why not/everywhere was theirs because they thought so" ("The Last One"). Man has also created a ludicrous, albeit murderous, political world. In several poems Merwin writes of contemporary atrocities in Asia as a pattern throughout history as well as his own personal act: "I/all that/has become of them/clearly all is lost." The political liberal mocks himself in "I Live Up Here": "...a little bit to the left/And I go down only/For the accidents." American society encourages its own collapse in "Unfinished Book of Kings." Merwin's despair for America's future resounds in "News of the Assassins":

"An empty window has overtaken me/After the bees comes the smell of cigars/In the lobby of darkness."

The most recent *Opening the Hand* is an exquisite collection of poems that trace the poet's childhood experiences, especially with his father, and his awakening to the world of change and time, abundance and mystery. The volume expresses Merwin's reconciliation to the facts of silence and isolation and his celebration of the occasional knowledge that all things touch and are touched by every other thing.

The opening poem, "The Waters," is a beautiful evocation of the moment of finality, of what he elsewhere calls Nothingness, and it is written in a spirit of exaltation and epiphany reminiscent of Yeats's "Byzantium." The music of the lines, also reminiscent of Frost, and the purity of his language reinforce a deeply felt affirmation toward the balance of all things: "I was the whole summer remembering/more than I knew/as though anything could stand still/in the waters/there were lights that turned and appeared to wait/and I went toward them looking/sounds carry in water but not/what I called so far/sun and moon shone into/the moving water/and after many days/joys and griefs I had not thought were mine/woke in this body's altering dream/knowing where they were/faces that would never die returned/toward our light through mortal waters."

The poet will persist in his search for revelation and the poetry that communicates, as he has said in some well-known lines: "It has taken me this long/to know what I cannot say/...that my words are the garments of what I shall never be/like the tucked sleeve of a one-armed boy."

—Lois Gordon

MEZEY, Robert. American. Born in Philadelphia, Pennsylvania, 28 February 1935. Educated at Kenyon College, Gambier, Ohio, 1951-53; University of Iowa, Iowa City, 1956-60, B.A. 1959; Stanford University, California (Poetry Fellow, 1961), 1960-61. Served in the United States Army, 1953-55; discharged as subversive. Married Ollie Simpson in 1963; two daughters and one son. Worked as probation officer, psychology technician, social worker, and advertising copywriter; Instructor, Western Reserve University, Cleveland, 1963-64, and Franklin and Marshall College, Lancaster, Pennsylvania, 1965-66; Assistant Professor, Fresno State University, California, 1967-68; Associate Professor, University of Utah, Salt Lake City, 1973-76. Since 1976, Professor of English and Poet-in-Residence, Pomona College, Claremont, California. Poetry Editor, *Trans Pacific*, Yellow Springs, Ohio, 1968-74. Recipient: Lamont Poetry Selection Award, 1960; Ingram Merrill Foundation Fellowship, 1973; Guggenheim Fellowship, 1977; American Academy award, 1983. Address: Department of English, Pomona College, Claremont, California 91711, U.S.A.

PUBLICATIONS

Verse

Berg Goodman Mezey. Philadelphia, New Ventures Press, 1957.
The Wandering Jew. Mount Vernon, Iowa, Hillside Press, 1960.
The Lovemaker. Iowa City, Cummington Press, 1961.

White Blossoms.   Iowa City, Cummington Press, 1965.
Favors.   Privately printed, 1968.
The Book of Dying.   Santa Cruz, California, Kayak, 1970.
The Door Standing Open: New and Selected Poems 1954-1969.   Boston, Houghton Mifflin, and London, Oxford University Press, 1970.
Last Words: For John Lawrence Simpson, 1896-1969.   West Branch, Iowa, Cummington Press, 1970.
Couplets.   Kalamazoo, Michigan, Westigan Press, 1976.
Small Song.   Grand Rapids, Michigan, Humble Hills Press, 1979.

Other

Selected Translations.   Kalamazoo, Michigan, Westigan Press, 1981.

Editor, with Stephen Berg, *Naked Poetry: Recent American Poetry in Open Forms.*   Indianapolis, Bobbs Merrill, 1969; *The New Naked Poetry,* 1976.
Editor and Translator, *Poems from the Hebrew.*   New York, Crowell, 1973.

Translator, *The Mercy of Sorrow,* by Uri Zvi Greenberg.   Philadelphia, Three People Press, 1965.

*

Critical Study: by Ralph J. Mills, Jr., in *American Poetry Review* (Philadelphia), Fall 1974.

Robert Mezey comments:
  There are many schools of poetry; I don't feel allegiance to any. Of my contemporaries, I especially admire Donald Justice and Philip Larkin.
  My poems are largely mysterious to me—I have no desire to analyze them. I have written love poems, poems of outrage at daily universal fraud and cruelty, expressions of gratitude to mountains and trees, jokes, messages, enigmas, obscenities. My theme is mortality and life everlasting. Influences: Catullus, Po Chu-i, Herbert (both George and Zbigniew), Ecclesiastes, Blake, Clare, Loren Eiseley, Cabeza de Vaca, Sam Cooke, Kenneth Rexroth, Issa, Archilocus, John Fowles, and a dog named Nina.

*   *   *

  Robert Mezey is a metaphysical poet not because like Donne he ransacks scholastic philosophy for images, but because like Hamlet and all true metaphysicians he is given to asking unanswerable questions about himself and the world. He is not, however, a "philosophical poet." A great weight of passion accumulates behind his studied reserve and what finally emerges over the dam is intensely felt, tightly controlled poetry.
  Early in his career, Robert Mezey came under the influence of the formalist critic and poet Yvor Winters, and *The Lovemaker,* Mezey's early book, betrays this influence clearly. Of Winters and his own subsequent development he writes wryly in a note appended to a group of his poems in *Naked Poetry,* an anthology of American poems in open forms edited by himself and Stephen Berg:

  When I was quite young I came under unhealthy influences—Yvor Winters, for example, and America, and my mother, though not in that order. Yvor Winters was easy to exorcise; all I had to do was meet him. My

mother and America are another story and why tell it in prose?
  One in Iowa City a friend said, "Why do your write in rhyme and meter? Your poetry is nothing like your life." "What do we know of another's life," I thought, but I had nothing to say. I no longer write in rhyme and meter, and still my life is not much like my poetry. At least, I don't think so. It is possible I'm not a poet at all. But I am a man, a Piscean, and unhappy, and therefore I make up poems.

  Robert Mezey is a poet all right and an important one, but there is no doubt that a kind of passionate melancholy underlies most of his poetry. Yeats said "Out of our quarrel with the world we make rhetoric; out of the quarrel with ourselves, poetry"; Mezey is never rhetorical, but his quarrel really seems to be with the nature of things. He avoids the Hardian rhetoric against the universe through the adroit use of images which supply objective correlatives for his own moods. In "There," for example, microcosm (the poet) and macrocosm (the world) seem to fuse together:

> It is deep summer. Far out
> at sea the young squalls darken
> and roll, plunging northward,
> threatening everything. I see
> the Atlantic moving in slow
> contemplative fury
> against the rocks, the frozen
> headlands, and the towns sunk deep
> in a blind northern light. Here,
> far inland, in the mountains
> of Mexico, it is raining
> hard, battering the soft mouths
> of flowers. I am sullen, dumb,
> ungovernable. I taste myself
> and I taste those winds, uprisings
> of salt and ice, of great trees
> brought down, of houses and cries
> lost in the storm; and what breaks
> on that black shore breaks in me.

  The tone here is perhaps more Byronic than usual in his poems, where urban images have their place along with natural ones. But the poem does show quite clearly his strategy for making turbid and passionate feelings objective through the use of corresponding images from the natural world.
  Mezey thinks of himself as having abandoned traditional meter and rhyme. His and Berg's anthology is exclusively concerned with poems in what he calls "open form." Yet as one reads over the poem just quoted one becomes aware that a great measure of the force of the poem is owing to the tightly controlled rhythms employed. No line in the poem contains more than four stresses or less than three, a close approach to "regular" meter; yet these fluctuations in line length do much to suggest the fluctuating pressures of the storm and the sea. One senses too that such powerful rhythmic control had to be exerted to keep the poem from exploding all over the page. And the control over raw emotion manifests itself mainly through the poet's handling of rhythm.
  Mezey obviously values clarity in a writer. Three things, I think, account for the unfailing clarity of these passionate poems. Two have already been mentioned, sharp clear images, many of which turn out to be objective correlatives, rhythmic control, and frequent, unobtrusive, but effective employment of articulatory symbolism: the forced miming by the organs of

speech of the very action or object being described. To illustrate,
I quote from another of his poems about autumn, "Touch It."
This is the second stanza:

> Past the thinning orchard the fields
> are on fire. A mountain of smoke
> climbs the desolate wind, and at its roots
> fire is eating dead grass with many small teeth.

The very shaping of the words in the final line here enforces upon
the reader a sort of *chewing* action. Or again, in "There"—"it is
raining / hard, battering the soft mouths / of flowers"—simply
shaping the words pantomimes the effect the words describe.

These three factors, and perhaps many more that have
escaped me, but at least these three, make possible shaping the
raw emotion of these poems toward the extraordinary clarity
they achieve.

—E. L. Mayo

MICHIE, James. British. Born in London in 1927. Educated
at Trinity College, Oxford. Worked as an editor and lecturer.
Currently, Director, The Bodley Head, publishers, London.
Address: The Bodley Head, 9 Bow Street, London WC2E 7AL,
England.

PUBLICATIONS

Verse

Possible Laughter. London, Hart Davis, 1959.
New and Selected Poems. London, Chatto and Windus, 1983.

Other

Editor, with Kingsley Amis, *Oxford Poetry 1949.* Oxford,
 Blackwell, 1949.
Editor, *The Bodley Head Book of Longer Short Stories.* Lon-
 don, Bodley Head, 1974; as *The Book of Longer Short Sto-
 ries,* New York, Stein and Day, 1975.
Editor, with P. J. Kavanagh, *The Oxford Book of Short Poems.*
 Oxford, Oxford University Press, 1985.

Translator, *The Odes of Horace.* New York, Orion, 1963;
 London, Hart Davis, 1964.
Translator, *The Poems of Catullus: A Bilingual Edition.* Lon-
 don, Hart Davis, and New York, Random House, 1969.
Translator, *The Epigrams of Martial.* London, Hart Davis
 MacGibbon, and New York, Random House, 1973.
Translator, *Selected Fables,* by La Fontaine. London, Allen
 Lane, and New York, Viking Press, 1979.
Translator, with Colin Leach, *The Helen of Euripides.* Lon-
 don and New York, Oxford University Press, 1981.

*   *   *

James Michie is better known as a translator, probably, than
as an original poet, which is hardly surprising considering the wit
and energy of his versions of Horace, Catullus and Martial.

These translations are not "modern" in the usual sense—they
have nothing in common, for example, with the free renderings
and "homages" of Pound or Lowell—but are cast in the neo-
classical tradition of Pope and Dryden in which the order of
English rhyme and meter offers a kind of substitute satisfaction
for the unrenderable richness of Latin. Thus Catullus' celebrated
"Odi et amo. Quare id faciam, fortasse requiris? / Nescio, sed
fieri sentio at excrucior" becomes, in Michie's version,

> I hate and love. If you ask me to explain
>   The contradiction,
> I can't, but I can feel it, and the pain
>   Is crucifixion.

Michie's own poetry thus far is collected in one slender
volume—very slender indeed, with 32 poems, few of which are
longer than a page. They reflect some of the qualities of the Latin
verse which Michie has translated, the economy, the sophistication and particularly the good natured cynicism about human
nature. The chief English influence seems to have been the light
(but serious) black doggerel of Auden during the 'thirties, with
its popular ballad forms and quick, surprisingly imagery. In
"Quiet, Child," for example, Michie observes

> Glumly we chew on with murder
>   Long past the appetite of hate.
> Nothing but their shadows' outlines
>   Left, like grease-stains on a plate,
> People leaning over bridges
>   Quietly evaporate.
>
> And big as a telephone directory
>   His bomber's casualty list,
> Gloved, the pilot leaves behind him,
>   Represented by a mist,
> Individuals who were furious,
>   But no longer now exist.

The poems vary considerably in theme and metrical form, from
the Betjeman-like "Park Concert" to the more troubled, individual voice of "Nightmare" and "At Any Rate," with their darker
observations about human cruelty and helplessness. Time is the
enemy, with its subtle erosions:

> The hours, pretending they do not know how to combine,
> Walk up as charming freebooters, unarmed, disclaiming
> Allegiance to that remote and iron-grey battle-line.

Fidelity is weak. The lovers may

> hold like amulets
> Precious hands, or go linking
> Arms, but no one gets
> Cleanly through without slinking.
> Quite innocent,
> Moving to kiss, although they hadn't meant
> It, they'll find themselves archly winking.

The prevailing tone of Michie's verse, however, is neither brutal
nor tragic but much more in the spirit of the wise man in "The
End of the Sage" who dies

> "Much wiser and much dafter,
> Now that I quite agree
> To become dead,
> I achieve a witticism,

And I see at last," he said,
"Hazy like foothills possible laughter."

—Elmer Borklund

MIDDLETON, (John) Christopher.   British.   Born in Truro,
Cornwall, 10 June 1926. Educated at Felsted School, Essex;
Merton College, Oxford, B.A. 1951, D.Phil. 1954. Served in the
Royal Air Force, 1944-48. Lecturer in English, Zurich University, 1952-55; Senior Lecturer in German, King's College, University of London. Since 1966, Professor of Germanic Languages and Literature, University of Texas, Austin. Recipient:
Geoffrey Faber Memorial Prize, 1964; Guggenheim Fellowship,
1974; DAAD Kunstlerprogramm fellowship, Berlin, 1975, 1978;
National Endowment for the Arts fellowship, 1980. Address:
Department of German, University of Texas, Austin, Texas
78712, U.S.A.

PUBLICATIONS

Verse

Poems.   London, Fortune Press, 1944.
Nocturne in Eden: Poems.   London, Fortune Press, 1945.
The Vision of the Drowned Man.   Ditchling, Sussex, Ditchling
Press, 1950(?).
Torse 3: Poems 1949-1961.   London, Longman, and New
York, Harcourt Brace, 1962.
Penguin Modern Poets 4, with David Holbrook and David
Wevill.   London, Penguin, 1963.
Nonsequences: Selfpoems.   London, Longman, 1965; New
York, Norton, 1966.
Our Flowers and Nice Bones.   London, Fulcrum Press, 1969.
Die Taschenelefant: Satire.   Berlin, Neue Rabenpresse, 1969.
The Fossil Fish: 15 Micropoems.   Providence, Rhode Island,
Burning Deck, 1970.
Briefcase History: 9 Poems.   Providence, Rhode Island, Burning Deck, 1972.
Fractions for Another Telemachus.   Knotting, Bedfordshire,
Sceptre Press, 1974.
Wildhorse.   Knotting, Bedfordshire, Sceptre Press, 1975.
The Lonely Suppers of W. V. Balloon.   Cheadle, Cheshire,
Carcanet, and Boston, Godine, 1975.
Razzmatazz.   Austin, Texas, W. Thomas Taylor, 1976.
Eight Elementary Inventions.   Knotting, Bedfordshire, Sceptre
Press, 1977.
Pataxanadu and Other Prose.   Manchester, Carcanet, 1977.
Carminalenia.   Manchester, Carcanet, 1980.
Woden Dog.   Providence, Rhode Island, Burning Deck, 1982.
111 Poems.   Manchester, Carcanet, 1983.
Serpentine (prose).   London, Oasis, 1984.

Play

The Metropolitans (libretto), music by Hans Vogt.   Kassel,
Alkor, 1964.

Other

Bolshevism in Art and Other Expository Writings.   Manchester, Carcanet, 1978.

The Troubled Sleep of America: 40 Collages.   Austin, Texas,
Laguna Gloria Art Museum, 1982.
The Pursuit of the Kingfisher: Essays.   Manchester, Carcanet,
1983.

Editor and Translator, with Michael Hamburger, *Modern German Poetry 1910-1960: An Anthology with Verse Translations.*   London, MacGibbon and Kee, and New York, Grove
Press, 1962.
Editor and Translator, with William Burford, *The Poet's Vocation: Selections from the Letters of Hölderlin, Rimbaud, and
Hart Crane.*   Austin, University of Texas Press, 1967.
Editor, *German Writing Today.*   London, Penguin, 1967.
Editor, *Selected Poems*, by Georg Trakl.   London, Cape, 1968.
Editor, and Translator with others, *Goethe: Selected Poems.*
Cambridge, Massachusetts, Suhrkamp-Insel, and London,
Calder, 1983.
Editor, and Translator with others, *The Figure on the Boundary
Line: Selected Prose*, by Christoph Meckel.   Manchester,
Carcanet, 1983.

Translator, *The Walk and Other Stories*, by Robert Walser.
London, Calder, 1957.
Translator, with others, *Primal Vision*, by Gottfried Benn.
New York, New Directions, 1960.
Translator, with others, *Poems and Verse Plays*, by Hugo von
Hofmannsthal.   New York, Pantheon, 1961.
Translator, with Michael Hamburger, *Selected Poems*, by Günter Grass.   London, Secker and Warburg, and New York,
Harcourt Brace, 1966.
Translator, *Jakob von Gunten*, by Robert Walser.   Austin,
University of Texas Press, 1969.
Translator, *Selected Letters*, by Friedrich Nietzsche.   Chicago,
University of Chicago Press, 1969.
Translator, with Michael Hamburger, *Poems*, by Günter Grass.
London, Penguin, 1969; as *Selected Poems*, 1980.
Translator, *The Quest for Christa T.*, by Christa Wolf.   New
York, Farrar Straus, 1970; London, Hutchinson, 1971.
Translator, with Michael Hamburger, *Selected Poems*, by Paul
Celan.   London, Penguin, 1972.
Translator, *Selected Poems*, by Friedrich Hölderlin and Eduard
Mörike.   Chicago, University of Chicago Press, 1972.
Translator, *Inmarypraise*, by Günter Grass.   New York, Harcourt Brace, 1974.
Translator, *Kafka's Other Trial: The Letters to Felice*, by Elias
Canetti.   New York, Schocken, 1974; London, Penguin,
1978.
Translator, with Michael Hamburger, *In the Egg and Other
Poems*, by Günter Grass.   New York, Harcourt Brace, 1977;
London, Secker and Warburg, 1978.
Translator, with others, *Selected Stories*, by Robert Walser.
Manchester, Carcanet, and New York, Farrar Straus, 1982.
Translator, *The Spectacle at the Tower*, by Gerd Hofmann.
New York, Fromm, 1985.

*

Critical Study: "Shapes in Imaginary Space" by Philip Crick, in
Ninth Decade 2, 1983.

*   *   *

In an interview in *The London Magazine* in 1964 Christopher
Middleton criticised his English contemporaries for a parochialism of form and content which cut them off from the great
heritage of European Modernism. The latter, he argued, had "at

most points connected...a strong sense of social revolution, a catastrophic view of history," with an "interest in the radical remaking of techniques." Both in his translations, primarily from the German, and in his own poetry, Middleton has tried to keep open this connection. Middleton's "catastrophic view of history" leads him continually to those moments at which personal crisis interlocks with social crisis. Thus, in "The Arrest of Pastor Paul Schneider," the pastor is dragged reluctantly from a nightmare of arrest to its actuality; in "January 1919" history rips the "holed head" of the murdered German revolutionary Liebknecht out of context, to display it "bleeding across a heap of progressive magazines"; in "The Historian," Procopius, official historian to the tyrant Justinian, is snatched from the desk where he writes his secret exposé of the regime just as he realizes that the only authentic opposition is in deeds not words. The interrupted sentence which closes the poem reveals the fragility of men amidst a history they cannot control, the witness always potentially a victim ("The thought still bothers me, that, instead of writing, I might have changed the"). Many of Middleton's poems turn Hitler's and Stalin's death camps into universal symbols of 20th-century history, uprooting men from their own proper lives to a dream of deportation and massacre, whether the "figures torn from a fog," "feeding on garbage in the camp near Voronezh" of "Pavlovic Variations," or the "eclipsed / Future[s]" slid into the ovens at Treblinka ("Idiocy of Rural Life"). But terror lurks not only in the major events of a public history. Middleton's poetry detects the threat of extinction in more mundane, trivial situations. A pair of gloves left on the floor of a a lavatory (so that, "it seems, you'd think, smothering a giggle, / someone has been sucked down the john") can summon up a terrifying vision of disappeared persons. Middleton's poetry repeatedly evokes, in his own words, "A really live sense of what it is like to live in a society where the direction of life has fallen into the hands of malevolent or ignorant functionaries, where all human values seem to be threatened by inhuman organization." Poems such as "Octobers" and "Autobiography" record how this menace inserts itself into the most idyllic and private experiences. But "History...isn't the past at all, it is the multitudinous new life saturating the present," and "the little significant things" which it is the poet's duty to "unravel" ("Glaucus") contain promise as well as threat, renewal as well as destruction. This is perhaps why so many of Middleton's poems are concerned with children, the inheritors for whom history, the future, is always open, though it may again and again be suppressed, as for "Fania, ten / at the turn of the century" in "The Pogroms in Sebastopol," or for "Pavel's child" who "came to pieces in my hands," dug out of the snow of the camps ("Pavlovic Variations"), or for those napalmed Vietnamese children in "Mérindol Interior" whose photographed agony intrudes into the poet's comfortable middle-class world.

At its best, there are a hardness, a tautness, a lack of false colour and sentimentality to Middleton's language which argue an ascetic's imagination; yet, at the same time, his poetry is passionately involved in the world—"odd as it is to care" (as he says in one poem) "anyhow for things / their mass & contour / & all beginnings." His world is substantial, yet curiously abstract; figured, and yet not personalized. He writes often in the third or second person, and even when he appears himself attention is nearly always focussed on what's out there rather than on subjective response. This classical yet human distance is maintained by a deliberate employment of that "defamiliarization" technique described by the Russian Formalist Viktor Shklovsky (whom Middleton acknowledges on several occasions). The disjunctions, dislocations and unexpected collocations of his language, the experimental diversity of structure and theme, and a movement between extremes of abstrusity and explicitness, using the very opacity of his language to concentrate our gaze as if for the first time on familiar object and event, all enable Middleton to pursue that "defining of enigmas" which is for him the poetic vocation, exposing us to "the strangeness of being alive,...the strangeness of living things outside oneself."

In "Oystercatchers," for example, the unexpected verb discloses a world strangely detached from man ("rocks in the bay below / Retrieved their shadows"); while "Wire Spring" turns the pun of the title into a sinister vision by reviving dead metaphors ("The first clock said: it is time we killed. / The second clock said: it is time we told"). "The simplest model for such poems is not the linguistic 'statement' but the question," Middleton notes on the dust-jacket of *The Lonely Suppers*; and, indeed, all his poetry is hermeneutic, interrogative, quizzical, questioning reality with a sceptical and informed eye, and perpetually reminding us that language is not an innocent carrier of meaning but itself a force for good or ill that pre-empts all our seeing. It is this which accounts for the range of Middleton's experiments with the resources of language, whether concrete or "found" poems, cut-ups and grafts, or such pieces as "Computer's Karl Marx" which, starting with a joke (a history of revolution written by a computer that has only the letters of the words "production relations" to play with) goes on to show how the limits of our language are the limits of our world. It is perhaps finally in this ludic sense of the ludicrous, derived from Dada and Surrealism, coupled with a quite un-English seriousness, that Middleton justifies his claim to the European inheritance.

—Stan Smith

MILES, Josephine (Louise). American. Born in Chicago, Illinois, 11 June 1911. Educated at the University of California, Los Angeles, A.B. 1932 (Phi Beta Kappa); University of California, Berkeley, M.A. 1934, Ph.D. 1938. Since 1940, Member of the English Department, since 1952, Professor of English, and since 1973, University Professor, University of California, Berkeley. Recipient: Shelley Memorial Award, 1936; Phelan Award, 1937; American Association of University Women fellowship, 1939; Guggenheim Fellowship, 1948; American Academy grant, 1956; Oscar Blumenthal Prize (*Poetry*, Chicago), 1959; American Council of Learned Societies Fellowship, 1965; National Endowment for the Arts grant, 1967, Fellowship, 1980; James Russell Lowell Prize, 1975; Academy of American Poets Award, 1978; Fred Cody Memorial Award, 1984; Lenore Marshall Prize, 1984. D.Litt.: Mills College, Oakland, California, 1965. Fellow, American Academy; American Academy of Arts and Sciences. Address: 2275 Virginia Street, Berkeley, California 94709, U.S.A.

PUBLICATIONS

Verse

Lines at Intersection. New York, Macmillan, 1939.
Poems on Several Occasions. New York, New Directions, 1941.
Local Measures. New York, Reynal, 1946.
After This Sea. San Francisco, Book Club of California, 1947.
Prefabrications. Bloomington, Indiana University Press, 1955.
Poems 1930-1960. Bloomington, Indiana University Press, 1960.

Civil Poems. Berkeley, California, Oyez, 1966.
Bent. Santa Barbara, California, Unicorn Press, 1967.
Kinds of Affection. Middletown, Connecticut, Wesleyan University Press, 1967.
Fields of Learning. Berkeley, California, Oyez, 1968.
Saving the Bay. San Francisco, Open Space, 1969.
American Poems. Berkeley, California, Cloud Marauder Press, 1970.
To All Appearances: New and Selected Poems. Urbana, University of Illinois Press, 1974.
Coming to Terms. Urbana, University of Illinois Press, 1979.
Collected Poems 1930-1983. Urbana, University of Illinois Press, 1983.

Recording: *Today's Poets 2*, with others, Folkways, 1968.

Play

House and Home (produced Berkeley, California, 1960). Published in *First Stage* (Lafayette, Indiana), Fall 1965.

Other

Wordsworth and the Vocabulary of Emotion. Berkeley, University of California Press, 1942.
Pathetic Fallacy in the 19th Century: A Study of the Changing Relation Between Object and Emotion. Berkeley, University of California Press, 1942.
The Vocabulary of Poetry: Three Studies. Berkeley, University of California Press, 1946.
The Continuity of Poetic Language: Studies in English Poetry from the 1540's to the 1940's. Berkeley, University of California Press, 1951.
  1. *The Primary Language of Poetry in the 1640's.* Berkeley, University of California Press, 1948.
  2. *The Primary Language of Poetry in the 1740's and 1840's.* Berkeley, University of California Press, 1950.
  3. *The Primary Language of Poetry in the 1940's.* Berkeley, University of California Press, 1951.
Eras and Modes in English Poetry. Berkeley, University of California Press, 1957; revised edition, 1964.
Renaissance, Eighteenth-Century, and Modern Language in English Poetry: A Tabular View. Berkeley, University of California Press, 1960.
Ralph Waldo Emerson. Minneapolis, University of Minnesota Press, 1964.
Style and Proportion: The Language of Prose and Poetry. Boston, Little Brown, 1967.
Poetry and Change: Donne, Milton, Wordsworth, and the Equilibrium of the Present. Berkeley, University of California Press, 1974.
Working Out Ideas: Predication and Other Uses of Language. Berkeley, University of California, 1979.

Editor, with Mark Schorer and Gordon McKenzie, *Criticism: The Foundations of Modern Literary Judgment.* New York, Harcourt Brace, 1948; revised edition, 1958.
Editor, with others, *Idea and Experiment.* Berkeley, University of California Press, 1950.
Editor, *The Poem: A Critical Anthology.* Englewood Cliffs, New Jersey, Prentice Hall, 1959; revised edition as *The Ways of the Poem*, 1961, 1973.
Editor, *Classic Essays in English.* Boston, Little Brown, 1961; revised edition, 1965.
Editor, *Berkeley Street Poems, May 1969.* Berkeley, California, Other Ways, 1969.

Translator, with others, *Modern Hindi Poetry.* Bloomington, Indiana University Press, 1965.

*

Manuscript Collections: State University of New York, Buffalo; Washington University, St. Louis; Bancroft Poetry Archive, University of California, Berkeley.

Critical Studies: "Distance and Surfaces" by Robert Beloof, in *Prairie Schooner* (Lincoln, Nebraska), Winter 1958-59; in *Voyages* (Washington, D.C.), Fall 1968; "The Habits of the Poet" by Denis Donoghue, in *Times Literary Supplement* (London), 25 April 1975; "By the Fingers, by the Patterns, by the Issues: A Celebration of Josephine Miles" (includes essays by Eve Sedgwick, Diane Wakoski, and Rory Holseher), in *Epoch* (Ithaca, New York), Fall-Winter 1982.

Josephine Miles comments:
  Interest in poetry of spoken thought, of meditation, of literally making sense of ideas. Main themes, human doubt and amazement. A strong beat of meaning playing against the beat of pattern. Some critics say "western," but I am not aware of this.

*   *   *

  Josephine Miles shares, with William Carlos Williams and his followers, credit for exalting "the American idiom" into the standard language of poetry—a feat surrounded by risk, by the danger of being charged with flatness and being forsaken by all but the most sensitive of critics. Her achievement is that she has successfully laid aside her academic powers (she is one of the land's best scholars) in order to paint with a great gentleness—and sense of their fragility and evanescence—the landscapes of the American scene—its speech, jazz, billboards, comics and assassinations, and those dark streets of towns where three creeks meet. She has raised these materials into a high form of poetry, and her insights in poems provide an enlightening commentary on American life. In clearing her vision of scholarship, in renouncing sophistication and working exclusively with native materials, Miles offers, essentially, the *persona* of a Willa Cather schoolmarm discoursing gently on the wisdom she has acquired from the prairies and a few rides in tin cars. Even when confessing her scholarship ("Bad quartos were my first love") she remains matter of fact. Her skill is in rendering the quotidian stillness of an American street; and she avoids exoticism, even in her treatment of "Bombay" and "Tehachapi South." She is most at home rendering the sadness, the matter-of-factness, the every-evening miracle, of the moon rising over the lumber yard, and perhaps a whiskey bottle; the rendering is pure, strikes life's tonic note of recognition. Her work is at once primitive and sophisticated, like that of Chekhov and Williams. It must be said too that an undercurrent of sharp physical pain runs through her poems. She has always eschewed self-pity, and refers matter-of-factly (in "Doll") to the early onset of a disabling, life-long illness:

> Later Miss Babcox the sitter,
> After many repetitive card games,
> Said, We must talk about bad things.
> Let me tell you
> Some of the bad things I have known in my life.
> She did not ask me mine, I could not have told her.

Her balanced calm directs her narratives, ever in the American idiom, "carefully awkward," as Randall Jarrell said of her. Alfred Corn has written of her taste for "imbalances and 'off' constructions...the effective askew."

Miles writes with a deep sense of history, with a mixture of verve and despair. Her elegy for John Kennedy is a lament for the loss of real quality in American life. She grieves the assertion of mediocrity through violence, as if power drifts away from those of character, into the hands of the insensitive. With the metaphor of Daniel Boone's bear-shooting, Miles transforms a national event into a myth. One feels that her poem did a better job of accounting for that event than did the many volumes of the Warren Report. And in "Witness" she wrote eloquently of the sad Vietnam era:

> Gassed going between classes
> Students said little,
> Huddled their books and ran.
> As helicopter crews waved down low at them
> They were silent,
> Yelled and were silent.

She saw clearly that the war and those who were asked to consent to it were not separated by an ironically named Pacific Ocean. As her works of subtle idiom and close observation of scene may depend heavily on the common experience of her readers, it is possibly this larger sense of national tragedy— communicated in many poems—that will appeal for many years to readers all over the world who turn to poetry to understand what is happening in a culture so bewildering as the American. Miles has always struggled with the passion of a sociologist and the devoted labors of an anthropologist as well as the powers of her formidable talent, beautifully represented in her *Collected Poems*.

—David Ray

MILLER, Vassar (Morrison).   American.   Born in Houston, Texas, 19 July 1924. Educated at the University of Houston, B.S. 1947, M.A. 1952. Instructor in Creative Writing, St. John's School, 1975-76. Address: 1615 Vassar Street, Houston, Texas 77006, U.S.A.

PUBLICATIONS

Verse

Adam's Footprint.   New Orleans, New Orleans Poetry Journal, 1956.
Wage War on Silence: A Book of Poems.   Middletown, Connecticut, Wesleyan University Press, 1960.
My Bones Being Wiser.   Middletown, Connecticut, Wesleyan University Press, 1963.
Onions and Roses.   Middletown, Connecticut, Wesleyan University Press, 1968.
If I Could Sleep Deeply Enough.   New York, Liveright, 1974.
Small Change.   Houston, Wings Press, 1977.
Approaching Nada.   Houston, Wings Press, 1977.
Selected and New Poems.   Austin, Texas, Latitudes Press, 1982.

Struggling to Swim on Concrete.   New Orleans, New Orleans Poetry Press, 1984.

*

Vassar Miller comments:
   Traditional lyrics, but also free verse and syllabic. Religious themes, though also more humanistic of late.

*   *   *

The value of Vassar Miller's poetry is measured in the bittersweet humor that emerges from the contrast she creates between the ideal civilization of God and the saints and her quotidian, dog-eared, and colloquial hemisphere of loveless and lonely selves as expressed in one of her earliest poems, "Adam's Footprint":

> How could a tree be so unclean?
> Nobody knows but Augustine.
> He nuzzled pears for dam-sin's dugs—
> And I scrunched roly-poly bugs.

The humor in these lines is achieved not only in the self-effacing comparison between the poet and the saint, but in the active, nearly slap-stick, power of the verbs. Miller is a master at choosing the word that is wound one spiral too tight. In doing so her typically sparse poems achieve a tension that is barely contained within the poems' staid and traditional forms. What have been considered Miller's best poems are those with religious themes, but of these the ones which excel are those which have a glib spirit created by this tension that for too long has been the undervalued hallmark of Miller's talent.

That Miller is a poet of technique rather than theme is exemplified in the range of subjects she addresses in her more recent poems. Her standard religious theme has been reduced to being one of many themes wherein death and dying are the most prevalent. In these new poems, she enunciates her private concerns with specificity and drama. In "Senility" an "old mind" is addressed as a "broken turtle half out of its shell," a metaphor that is further developed into being the embodiment of the poet's deteriorating creative abilities:

> No, your final curiousness
> has got you in trouble
> snooping among the Last Things,
> has taken you far too far,
> wriggling along, stupid joke,
> too slow with the punch line

One of Miller's enduring interests is the art of poetry and the status of the poet. That death is frightening because with it ends the ability to create is not a surprising sentiment from a poet who has assumed that immortality is the reward for writing verse:

> Every poet knows
> what the saint knows
>
> that every new day is
> to retake the frontier of one's name.

Miller is indeed a poet of the inner self. With the exception of religious figures, the few characters that appear in her poems are alluded to without names and are valued only for the ways they

have affected her private world. Nevertheless, her personal musings are so unabashedly honest that it seems that her poems are
populated with the voices of a humane civilization.

—Susan Kaplan

MILLWARD, Eric. British. Born in Longnor, Staffordshire,
12 March 1935. Educated at Longnor Church of England
School, 1941-46; Buxton College 1946-54. Married 1) Anne
Craig in 1961, two sons; 2) Rosemary Anne Wood in 1975.
Address: 4 King's Road, Horsham, Sussex, England.

PUBLICATIONS

Verse

A Child in the Park. Walton-on-Thames, Surrey, Outposts,
1969.
Dead Letters. Liskeard, Cornwall, Peterloo Poets, 1978.

*

Eric Millward comments:

It is my intention to write good, readable, comprehensible
poems about the things/people I find important/happy/sad/
helpless/beautiful/ugly/kind/cruel. I have to admit that things
sad/helpless/ugly/cruel seem at present to predominate.

I have willingly written poems since the age of 14. I hope my
work has shown some improvement. I do not think I know what
poetry is: I just know I like it—or some of it. I often find myself
apologising for the (apparent) transparency of my poems; but I
feel that this may be the fault of those poets who seem to feel that
density implies depth! Anyway, I have my own favourite poets—
not all of whom are of the upper echelon. Yet.

*   *   *

The work of Eric Millward has appeared in magazines and
anthologies for more than a decade now. Yet it has never
achieved permanence between the covers of a hard-back volume.
However, of many uncollected poets, he is one whose poems
deserve collection.

Eric Millward relates to a tradition deriving from Clare,
Hardy, Edward Thomas, and Edmund Blunden. But he is not,
any more than these earlier poets, simply pastoral. His themes
are various, as instanced by the titles of his better poems: "Children with Hands," "Spastic," "Cows," "The Girl's Confession,"
"The Widow's Bird," "Mrs. Monk," "When His Wife Died,"
"Sudden Rain," "A Short Life," "The Cat Returns," "A Winter
Wedding," and—two very impressive pieces—"Freeing a Bird"
and "A Child in the Park." These two are essentially religious
poems.

The plot of "Freeing a Bird" unfolds itself decisively to build
up the sense that the sparrow falls into our hands as we ourselves
fall into the hands of God. The point is not insisted upon, but,
when caught at length, the sparrow is "a sheeted bundle" and it is
thrown out into the night "like crumbs." What comes out clearly
is the alienation between one species and another, and the sense
that there is a similar lack of contact between man and his
maker—"And we, who might perhaps presume to teach,/Should

count the missions we initiate/That end in failure to communicate."

"A Child in the Park" is a poem of the same kind. It is a
meditative lyric on a large scale, couched in traditional but
highly expressive metres. Like the previous poem, it recounts a
story with a strongly allegorical bent.

> It may be some perverse desire
> For pain that lets me watch my child
> Wander away in the terrible park
> Towards a distant target, called
> By a half-heard, compelling bark
> To cuddle some ungainly cur....

The child, of course, loses his perspective and finds himself
alone. Naturally, the father obeys his instinct to run after the
child and soothe his fears. But the allegory becomes marked if we
mentally capitalize the protagonists, for the final stanzas are a
reproach from the mortal Child to the heavenly Father:

> Meanwhile we wandering children move
> Within our park, unheld by hands,
> Some finding peace which grows from trust
> In power that loves and understands;
> Some, loving children, doubting, must
> Concede the power, question the love.

To call Eric Millward a religious poet seems reasonable
enough, but the statement must be qualified. This is, for all its
formal certainty, a poetry allied to the cries like dead letters sent
by the poets of a line that constitutes a key English tradition. In
the 20th century this tradition has been carried on by Walter de
la Mare, Andrew Young, Norman Cameron, and Joan Barton.
It does not seem too much to claim for Eric Millward a place
among these distinguished poets.

But his most recent work has taken on a harder, more satiric,
tone. We take civilisation to the natives, he tells us, and are soon
"exchanging gifts and bacteria." A quirky little poem says that,
without your thumbs, you've "got a fight on your hands." A
parody of a hymn snarls out "God moves in a mysterious way/
His duties to ignore." But none of this seems quite sharp enough.
Millward is a charitable rather than a mordant poet. He resorts
to attack, possibly, because he lacks a myth to defend. Perhaps,
like so many 20th-century poets in this eclectic last quarter,
Millward is seeking a fiction outside his personal experience.
With his technique and fine ear for verse, he will be a poet to be
reckoned with if he finds one.

—Philip Hobsbaum

MILNE, (Charles) Ewart. Irish. Born in Dublin, 25 May
1903. Educated at Pembroke Street National School, Sandymount, 1909-10; Nun's Cross School, Rathnew, County Wicklow, 1910-15; Christ Church Cathedral Grammar School, Dublin, 1915-19. Married 1) Kathleen Ida Bradner in 1927 (divorced,
1945), one son; 2) Thelma Dobson in 1948 (died, 1964), two sons.
Merchant seaman, 1920-35; then journalist: book reviewer, *Irish
Times*, Dublin; staff member, *Ireland Today*, Dublin; co-
founder, with Leslie Daiken, *Irish Front* (later, *Irish Democrat*),
1936; and book reviewer, *Irish Press*, Dublin, 1968-70; farmer in
Suffolk, 1946-62. Address: 46 De Parys Avenue, Bedford MK40
2TP, England.

PUBLICATIONS

Verse

Forty North, Fifty West. Dublin, Gayfield Press, 1938.
Letter from Ireland. Dublin, Gayfield Press, 1940.
Listen Mangan. Dublin, At the Sign of the Three Candles, 1941.
Jubilo. London, Muller, 1944.
Boding Day. London, Muller, 1947.
Diamond Cut Diamond: Selected Poems. London, Lane, 1950.
Elegy for a Lost Submarine. Burnham on Crouch, Essex, Plow Poems, 1951.
Galion: A Poem. Dublin, Dolmen Press, 1953.
Life Arboreal. Tunbridge Wells, Kent, Pound Press, 1953.
Once More to Tourney: A Book of Ballads and Light Verse, Serious, Gay, and Grisly. London, Linden Press, 1958.
A Garland for the Green. London, Hutchinson, 1962.
Time Stopped: A Poem Sequence with Prose Intermissions. London, Plow Poems, 1967.
Drift of Pinions. Portree, Isle of Skye, Aquila, 1976.
Cantata under Orion. Portree, Isle of Skye, Aquila, 1976.
Deus Est Qui Regit Omnia. Mornington, County Meath, St. Beuno's, 1980.
Spring Offering. Portree, Isle of Skye, Aquila, 1981.
The Folded Leaf. Portree, Isle of Skye, Aquila, 1983.

*

Manuscript Collection: State University of New York, Buffalo.

Critical Studies: "Self Portrait" by the author, in *Poetry Ireland* (Dublin), April 1949; "The Poetry of Ewart Milne" by Peter Russell, in *Chantecleer* (London) i, 3, 1953; "The Poetry of Ewart Milne" by Lawrence Lipton, in *Poetry* (Chicago), September 1955; *A Poet's War: British Poets in the Spanish Civil War* by Hugh Ford, Philadelphia, University of Pennsylvania Press, 1965; "Recent Poetry" by Terry Eagleton, in *Stand* (Newcastle upon Tyne), 1967; Penelope Palmer, in *Agenda* (London), 1968; *The Outsiders: Poets of Contemporary Ireland* by Frank Kersnowski, Fort Worth, Texas Christian University Press, 1975; "Ewart Milne Issue" of *Prospice 14* (Portree, Isle of Skye), 1983; Paul Ravenscroft, in *Iron 42* (Cullercoats, Tyne and Wear), 1983.

Ewart Milne comments:

My poetry is about people, places, things, events, happenings, and non-happenings. It is not simply about the poet and his words and wordcraft. It is about my relationship to the world, and to the other world, to life and death (which, together, seem to make up one whole identity), with what to do with my life and how to do it, with the past and present of man as I learn about it and about him. All the assurance I have is the certain knowledge that I am in good company, in the mainstream of poets and poetry in English, from Thomas Wyatt to Milton, Blake, and Hardy, even though I am not in the mainstream of much of the poetry being written at present, which seems to me to be the heretical poetry of the eye rather than the ear, as also the poetry of the inward-turning poet seeking only himself and to examine himself. But when I have said that, I find it is a contradiction because the volume I have completed, in the seventy-sixth year of my life, and which I have called *The Folded Leaf*, is almost entirely made up of pieces about my boyhood in the early years of the twentieth century, spent in Dublin and Wicklow. Still, the book is peopled with relatives, friends, and others. And anyway, if I contradict myself, as Whitman said, I contradict myself. So what?

*   *   *

Ewart Milne began to write in the late 1930's when the new poets were concerned with political and social problems. He has published a dozen volumes, widely ranging in their themes and varied in their moods. He spent some years in the British Merchant Navy, became a teacher, was for some time an ambulance driver in the Spanish Civil War. Of his experiences at sea he has written little except for the moving "Elegy for a Lost Submarine," and an effective allegory, "The Waterside Poem":

> Shanghaied aboard
> We signed on later because we must.
> In a smelly cabin among charts and paraffin
> We signed on for the round trip:
> Where we were bound for had been left blank.
>
> And a hard going we had of it.
> You were below then, in the stokehold, while I
> Swung overside in a bosun's chair
> Was repainting the ship's name on the rusty bow.
> Her name was, as I remember, the steamship Earth.

He has written a number of moving poems, however, about the tragic events which he witnessed in Spain. He has experimented in diverse metrical forms but usually writes in free verse. His opinions are Leftist, but he avoids purely political themes and concentrates on social conditions in Ireland and elsewhere.

A Garland for the Green was inspired by his return to his native country and is romantic in its mood. In contrast, two successive volumes, *Letter from Ireland* and *Listen Mangan*, are satiric in mood. His style is direct and, by disciplined selection, can, at its best, be evocative, as in "Tinker's Moon":

> A potato patch to thin on the way, a hen to kill,
> And hunger again: and sleep again:
> And a moonlight flit while the salmon leaps
> From a smouldering spot by the riverside;
> The tinker's children take their chance, and bide.

Once More to Tourney is, as the subtitle indicates, a book of light verse, gay and grisly by turn. In an introduction to this volume, J.M. Cohen notes that the poet has a voice of his own and belongs to no school: "His poems are as easy to read as nursery-rhymes, and as tough as a saloon-bar argument."

Milne's 1967 volume *Time Stopped* is a long dramatic poem in a variety of measures, mostly rhymed, deeply tragic in its mood. Written in the first person, it describes how a poet discovers from the letters after her death that his wife had been unfaithful to him with a friend of his. By the use of deliberate plain statement, the tragic mood is set:

> In nineteen sixty-four the United States Medical Council
> Decreed that cigarette smoking constituted a health hazard
> And could cause death from lung cancer; in that year
> In that summer in that September when you died

The bitterness and disillusion expressed in the poem will remind readers of *Modern Love*, that cycle of irregular sonnets by George Meredith. Even in its despairing mood, the poem is guarded by its own discipline:

I sat by her bedside and watched her die
And the hopeless and defeated one   that was I
The helpless one the condemned one   that was I
Left over   left to live on   mercilessly
Left with the fallen bricks of my house of poetry.

—Austin Clarke

MINHINNICK, Robert. British. Born in Neath, Glamorgan, Wales, 12 August 1952. Educated at Bridgend Grammar School; University College, Cardiff, 1978-82, B.A. 1981, M.A. 1982. Married Margaret Minhinnick in 1977; one daughter. Has worked as clerk, postman, salvage worker, and teacher. Recipient: Eric Gregory Award, 1980; Welsh Arts Council award, 1980, 1984. Address: 11 Park Avenue, Porthcawl, Mid-Glamorgan, Wales.

PUBLICATIONS

Verse

A Thread in the Maze. Swansea, Christopher Davies, 1978.
Native Ground. Swansea, Triskele, 1979.
Life Sentences. Bridgend, Glamorgan, Poetry Wales Press, 1983.

*

Robert Minhinnick comments:
  My poems are simply the statement of a man declaring an interest. They examine the process of living, while hopefullly contributing to it.

*   *   *

  A sense of place, and a sense of the past, are the closely inter-related twin themes predominant in the work of Robert Minhinnick; and from these he patiently evolves his own mythology "on native ground." In "The Strata" excavations evoke the activity of another Welsh poet, working here six centuries earlier, and prompt the impulse "To fashion with blunt words my own design." The "rooky archaelogist" of "The Midden," "history's black/Sediment...under [his] nails," likewise digs for the past in quest of a shared genealogy. Everywhere Minhinnick apprehends the presence of "time's hidden strata": in the wave-battered Atlantic promontory of Sker, and the primeval agelessness of rock and turbulent water which "seems to fall out of a fierce past" in "The Force"; in the "medieval" cries of owl and nightjar, and the ghosts which haunt ruined places—abandoned quarry, locomotive yard, or even garage.
  The potent spell of the past persists in the poet's own life too. Recapturing the feel and flavour of his early experience with sensuous precision, he works the seam of boyhood memory as profitably as did Seamus Heaney in his early work. The pungency of ivy—authentic "odour of childhood"—recalls the atmosphere of that vanished world: of flight from the gamekeeper and his dogs, "fright hot as nettlerash," or stealing unripe fruit from the orchard and "The sour exhilaration of that sin"; hide-and-seek in the graveyard among "the dead in their dormitory," the savagery of the ritual village pig-killing, the sharp grief of loss in "After a Friendship." Especially memorable and mov-

ing are several affectionately detailed cameos of his grandfather in poems like the fine "Native Ground" and "Ways of Learning," in "Drinks after the Funeral" and "Grandfather in the Garden," seeds "like ammunition in his hands."
  Minhinnick's relish for human personality emerges from his various portraits drawn from both rural and industrial South Wales, which he knows with equal intimacy. "That axe-wielding man," Reilly the gardener, and estate workers sitting among freshly sawn logs stacked "Like new loaves, the smell as sweet," keep company with the ganger whose "sweat bursts from his skin like tar-blisters," and the tough mother of "hard-skinned miners/ Kicking a pig's bladder on the coal-slip." Poems like "Old Ships," "Salvage," and "Profile in Iron" vigorously delineate the Cardiff dock-workers for whom "the dialect/Of iron is more powerful than psalms." The loneliness of the beery racing man with a genuine love of horses is observed with sympathetic perception as well as visual vividness; so, too, are his bemused drinking companions—"pub-fixtures" like "gargoyles carved from the bar's stained wood."
  That simile serves to illustrate the impact of Minhinnick's imagery, which is as strikingly individual in his observation of nature as of people: in his lovingly meticulous scrutiny of plants in "Herbals," of grasshopper and dragonfly, or of "the strange night turbulence of eels.../ Inscribing circles on tar-black water." He watches "a crown of foam winking/Like beer-froth" on the sea, or wheeling swifts "swastika the sky"; the winter constellations' "archipelagoes of light", and shadow "Stamping bone-coloured frosts/And grass as stiff as canvas."
  Robert Minhinnick handles language with a controlled economy which at the same time conveys the impression of powerful energy in leash. This blend of technical assurance with an imaginative intensity bred of his self-confessed "violent need to praise," make him one of the most interesting and accomplished younger poets writing in Wales today.

—Margaret Willy

MITCHELL, Adrian. British. Born in London, 24 October 1932. Educated at Dauntsey's School, Wiltshire; Christ Church, Oxford (Editor, *Isis* magazine, 1954-55), 1952-55. Served in the British Army, 1951-52. Reporter, *Oxford Mail,* 1955-57, and *Evening Standard,* London, 1957-59; columnist and reviewer, *Daily Mail, Woman's Mirror, The Sun, The Sunday Times, Peace News, The Black Dwarf,* and *The Guardian,* all in London. Instructor, University of Iowa, Iowa City, 1963-64; Granada Fellow in the Arts, University of Lancaster, 1967-69; Fellow, Wesleyan University Center for the Humanities, Middletown, Connecticut, 1971-72; Resident Writer, Sherman Theatre, Cardiff, 1974-75; Visiting Writer, Billericay Comprehensive School, Essex, 1978-80; Judith E. Wilson Fellow, Cambridge University, 1980-81; Resident Writer, Unicorn Theatre for Children, London, 1982-83. Recipient: Eric Gregory Award, 1961; P.E.N. Translation Prize, 1966; Tokyo Festival Television Film Award, 1971. Agent: Fraser and Dunlop Scripts Ltd., 91 Regent Street, London W1R 8RU, England.

PUBLICATIONS

Verse

(Poems). Oxford, Fantasy Press, 1955.

Poems. London, Cape, 1964.

Peace Is Milk. London, Peace News, 1966.

Out Loud. London, Cape Goliard Press, and New York, Grossman, 1968; revised edition, as *The Annotated Out Loud,* London, Writers and Readers, 1976.

Ride the Nightmare: Verse and Prose. London, Cape, 1971.

Cease-Fire. London, Medical Aid Committee for Vietnam, 1973.

Penguin Modern Poets 22, with John Fuller and Peter Levi. London, Penguin, 1973.

The Apeman Cometh. London, Cape, 1975.

For Beauty Douglas: Collected Poems 1953-1979. London, Allison and Busby, 1982.

Nothingmas Day (for children). London, Allison and Busby, 1983.

On the Beach at Cambridge. London, Allison and Busby, 1984.

Recording: *Poems,* with Stevie Smith, Argo, 1974.

Plays

The Ledge (libretto), music by Richard Rodney Bennett (produced London, 1961).

The Persecution and Assassination of Jean-Paul Marat as Performed by the Inmates of the Asylum of Charenton under the Direction of the Marquis de Sade, adaptation of the play by Peter Weiss (produced London, 1964; New York, 1965). London, Calder, 1965; New York, Atheneum, 1966.

The Magic Flute, adaptation of the libretto by Schikaneder and Giesecke, music by Mozart (produced London, 1966).

US, with others (produced London, 1966). Published as *US: The Book of the Royal Shakespeare Production US/ Vietnam /US/Experiment/Politics...,* London, Calder and Boyars, 1968; as *Tell Me Lies,* Indianapolis, Bobbs Merrill, 1968.

The Criminals, adaptation of a play by José Triana (produced London, 1967; New York, 1970).

Tyger: A Celebration of the Life and Work of William Blake, music by Mike Westbrook (produced London, 1971). London, Cape, 1971.

Tamburlane the Mad Hen (for children; produced Devon, 1971).

Man Friday, music by Mike Westbrook (televised, 1972; produced London, 1973). Included in *Man Friday, and Mind Your Head,* 1974.

Mind Your Head, music by Andy Roberts (produced Liverpool, 1973; London, 1974). Included in *Man Friday, and Mind Your Head,* 1974.

The Inspector General, adaptation of a play by Gogol (produced Nottingham, 1974).

Man Friday, and Mind Your Head. London, Eyre Methuen, 1974.

A Seventh Man, music by Dave Brown, adaptation of the book by John Berger and Jean Mohr (produced London, 1976).

White Suit Blues, music by Mike Westbrook, adaptation of works by Mark Twain (produced Nottingham and London, 1977).

Houdini: A Circus-Opera, music by Peter Schat (produced Amsterdam, 1977; Aspen, Colorado, 1980). Amsterdam, Clowns, 1977(?).

Uppendown Mooney (produced Welwyn Garden City, Hertfordshire, 1978).

The White Deer (for children), adaptation of the story by James Thurber (produced London, 1978).

Hoagy, Bix, and Wolfgang Beethoven Bunkhaus (produced London, 1979; Indianapolis, 1980).

The Mayor of Zalamea; or, The Best Garrotting Ever Done, adaptation of a play by Calderón (produced London, 1981). Edinburgh, Salamander Press, 1981.

Mowgli's Jungle, adaptation of *The Jungle Book* by Kipling (pantomime; produced Manchester, 1981).

You Must Believe All This (for children), adaptation of "Holiday Romance" by Dickens, music by Nick Bicat and Andrew Dickson (televised, 1981). London, Thames Television-Methuen, 1981.

The Wild Animal Song Contest (for children; produced London, 1982).

Life's a Dream, with John Barton, adaptation of a play by Calderón (produced London, 1984).

The Great Theatre of the World, adaptation of a play by Calderón (produced Oxford, 1984).

Screenplays: *Marat/Sade,* 1966; *Tell Me Lies* (lyrics only), 1968; *The Body* (commentary), 1969; *Man Friday,* 1976; *The Tragedy of King Real,* 1983.

Radio Play: *The Island* (libretto), music by William Russo, 1963.

Television Plays: *Animals Can't Laugh,* 1961; *Alive and Kicking,* 1971; *William Blake* (documentary), 1971; *Man Friday,* 1972; *Somebody Down There Is Crying,* 1974; *Daft As a Brush,* 1975; *The Fine Art of Bubble Blowing,* 1975; *Silver Giant, Wooden Dwarf,* 1975; *Glad Day,* 1979; *You Must Believe All This,* 1981; *Juno and Avos,* from libretto by Andrei Voznesensky, music by Alexei Rybnikov, 1983.

Initiated and helped write student shows: *Bradford Walk,* Bradford College of Art; *The Hotpot Saga, The Neurovision Song Contest,* and *Lash Me to the Mast,* University of Lancaster; *Move Over Jehovah,* National Association of Mental Health; *Poetry Circus,* Wesleyan University; *Mass Media Mash* and *Mud Fair,* Dartington College of the Arts, 1976 and 1977.

Novels

If You See Me Comin'. London, Cape, 1962; New York, Macmillan, 1963.

The Bodyguard. London, Cape, 1970; New York, Doubleday, 1971.

Wartime. London, Cape, 1973.

Man Friday. London, Futura, 1975.

Other

Naked In Cheltenham (miscellany). Cheltenham, Gastoday, 1978.

Editor, with Richard Selig, *Oxford Poetry 1955.* Oxford, Fantasy Press, 1955.

Editor, *Jump, My Brothers, Jump: Poems from Prison,* by Tim Daly. London, Freedom Press, 1970.

Translator, with Joan Jara, *Victor Jara: His Life and Songs.* London, Hamish Hamilton, 1976.

*

Theatrical Activities:
Actor: **Play**—*C'mon Everybody,* London, 1984.

Adrian Mitchell comments:

My mind and imagination and my life have been altered by many things and many people. Other people's poetry has been among my most important experiences and I don't just mean great poetry. Politically speaking, it was poetry as much as anything else which pushed me first in the direction of left-wing political action (in which I include committee work, demonstrating, envelope-addressing as well as poetry). To cite some of the poets who have educated and influenced me: Wilfred Owen, Walt Whitman, Kenneth Patchen, Alex Comfort, Brecht, Beckett, John Arden, Allen Ginsberg and most of all, William Blake. (But I've been influenced by hundreds of others, most of all by my close friends and my family and a teacher called Michael Bell.) I'm sometimes called a committed poet. So's your old man. There are many poets who because they turn their back on politics, believe they are somehow not engaged. But their indifference or their silence contributes towards the status quo. And the status quo demands, at different periods, exploitation, starvation, poverty, mass-murder, torture, vile prisons, the stunting of children's imaginations and—in some part of the world during every day of my lifetime—war. When the revolution comes, I expect some poetry to make some contribution toward it—every revolution so far has had its own songs and poems. That contribution towards changing the world may be very small, but the smallest contribution helps when it's a matter of changing the world. (I don't think that poets should sit down and say: I've got to write a political poem.) But I think a poet, like any other human being, should recognise that the world is mostly controlled by political forces and should become politically active. And if a poet attempts to live his politics, his poems will become politically active too.

*   *   *

Commitment is the key to the writings of Adrian Mitchell, his poems a series of revolutionary acts. To those who object that his work suffers from its involvement with such causes as nuclear disarmament and the Vietnam war, Mitchell argues that poets also hold opinions, and that detachment is itself commitment of a negative kind. Ultimately, he implies, one cannot be neutral about injustice. His work goes beyond party labels, attacking class privilege, property, Western capitalism, Stalinism, even "civilization" when this is used as a cover for genocide: "The brand name for a tribe of killer apes/Is civilization." In his play *Man Friday* the white liberal world-view personified by Crusoe is challenged and ridiculed but the alternative lifestyle of Friday's tribe, whose supposed barbarism is shown as equally valid and far less likely to lead to war. Mitchell savages most establishment concepts in his poems and dramas, drawing on elements of broadsheet and tract, radio and television comedy, parodies, pop songs, and pantomime. A spiritual precursor of the Liverpool poets, he helped to found the poetry reading boom, with its cult of "protest" and rebellion. Audience participation is of prime importance to him, and at times he appears to reject the finished work of art as an end in itself, hewing closer to the "primitive" view, where the process of creation in performance is what matters most. Many of his poems seem produced for special occasions, valid only while they are being read. For all that, his lineage is traditional enough, with definite echoes of the 1930's W.H. Auden. Mitchell's work shares the same tight structure, the verbal and rhyming felicity, the ability to utilise popular song forms. "Sorry Bout That" and "C'mon Everybody" have more than a little Auden in them: "Truth is a diamond/A diamond is hard/You don't exist/Without a Barclaycard."

His spiritual ancestor is William Blake, whose revolutionary and anti-authoritarian stance is shown in all the younger poet's work. In *Tyger* and the TV play *Glad Day* Mitchell renders tribute to Blake with "celebrations" that blend propaganda and satire with slapstick comedy, *Tyger* allowing for audience involvement. Many of Mitchell's poems echo the Blake of the *Songs* in style and content, while in the dramas he is quoted directly.

Mitchell's rage is that of one who cares, a man angered at the sight of human suffering. In "We Call Them Subnormal Children" and "Old Age Report" he champions abandoned young and downtrodden old alike ("The hell with retiring/Let them advance"). A constant opponent of nuclear weapons and the power of money, he attacks the religion that builds churches instead of homes for the poor, the society that condemns a woman for letting her child starve, but turns a blind eye to starving millions abroad. He is also aware of subtler tyrannies, the cultural colonialism presented in "The Castaways or Vote for Caliban," where after the relentless "civilizing" of a desert island, the one uncorrupted character walks: "Past the Prospero Souvenir Shop/Past the Robert Louis Stevenson Movie Studios/Past the Daniel Defoe Motel" and finally: "opened her eyes wide/To the usual incredible sunset." His hatred of politicians is fierce and unremitting, given full rein in "Statesman Stomp" and "Ode to Enoch Powell." Critics, in "Private Transport," receive equally short shrift.

At his worst—usually his most long-winded—Mitchell is coarse, self-indulgent and trivial. Nowadays some of his targets seem dated, and with few exceptions his anti-Vietnam war writings no longer have the same relevance. His anger, though, stems from an excess rather than a lack of feeling, his gentler side revealed in "Celia Celia" and the poem for his daughter, "Beatrix Is Three." A master of memorable one-liners ("I play golf so I exist"), Mitchell is at his best when most concentrated. His finest work is to be found in his plays, and the shorter, structured poems, notable "Briefing" and "The Dust." The latter, his most impressive indictment of nuclear war, brings home the horror by the restraint of its language: "When the bombs fell, she was sitting with her man,/Straight and white in the family pew/While in her the bud of a child grew/The city crumbled, the deaths began."

This is the poetry of Mitchell that seems destined to survive, not merely readings, but the judgment of future generations.

—Geoff Sadler

MITCHELL, David (John).   New Zealander.   Born in Wellington, 10 January 1940. Educated at Wellington College, 1953-57; Wellington Teachers College and Victoria University, Wellington, 1958-59. Married Elsebeth Nielsen in 1963 (divorced, 1976); one daughter. Recipient: Katherine Mansfield-Menton Fellowship, 1975. Address: c/o R.K.S. ART, 41a Victoria Street West, Auckland, New Zealand.

PUBLICATIONS

Verse

The Orange Grove.   Auckland, Poets Cooperative, 1969.
Pipe Dreams in Ponsonby.   Auckland, Association of Oriental Syndics, 1972.

*

Critical Study: "He Sing fr You" by C.K. Stead, in *Islands* (Auckland), Spring 1972.

*   *   *

The physical appearance of David Mitchell's poetry—spacing, setting, punctuation, part-phonetic spelling, etc.—places it at once in the general current that flows out of the work of the Americans Pound, W.C. Williams and Charles Olson. A Mitchell poem is not sequential in any obvious sense except that some things follow others. There is neither logic nor narrative. Each poem is a succession of images, juxtaposition, associations, dissociations, around a central subject or idea. The writing picks out and heightens each phrase, even each word, which is a note of music before it is a sign pointing to anything beyond itself. At their best (and Mitchell is a talented poet whose public readings are especially effective in bringing out the best in his work) the poems are lyrical, nostalgic, wry, generous in feeling and confident in tone. Where they fail it is a failure of denotation. Words used too exclusively for their musical qualities and secondary resonances begin to look under-employed, suggesting the transient brightness of a pop culture rather than the basic stuff which alone endures changes of taste. But Mitchell has also a fine ear for the music latent in the roughest vernacular speech, and this, together with his sense of humour, is likely to keep his poetry concrete and to strengthen its fibre as he goes on writing. Mitchell is a genuine stylist on a literary scene that has been most remarkable for hacking fence posts out of kauri logs, and as such he is surely welcome.

—C.K. Stead

The Way to Write, with John Fairfax. London, Elm Tree, and New York, St. Martin's Press, 1981.

*   *   *

John Moat's work exhibits a Yeatsian smoothness, which, while moving more interestingly towards the rhythms of speech, still stays close to Yeats's special brand of rhetoric for its effects:

> I inherited the garden towards dawn
> And keep it with a very moderate art;
> Though this may prosper now a child is born
> To simplify complexities of heart:
>
> The toil is simple while the love is one;
> Two kids would tear a toiling soul apart.
> For charity I work a routine spell
> As premium to save my brat from hell.

Moat does better than "routine spells" in some of the sequence entitled "The Overtures"—notable Overture 37, a love poem where the strong sense of his wife's identity prevents him from drifting off into self-enchantment with what he has to say about it, and words are used for other than musical purposes. He is, on the evidence of this single book, a Romantic who needs plenty of room to transcend his own rather limited idea of what a poem can be. Some longer poems—"Winter Passage," "Stages of Solar Eclipse"—show a possible way forward.

—Robert Nye

MOAT, John. British. Born in Mussoorie, India, 11 September 1936. Educated at Exeter College, Oxford. Married; two children. Co-Founder, The Arvon Foundation. Currently, freelance writer. Lives in North Devon. Agent: A.D. Peters, 10 Buckingham Street, London WC2N 6BU, England.

PUBLICATIONS

Verse

Sixpence per Annum: 12 Poems. Newbury, Berkshire, Phoenix Press, 1966.
Thunder of Grass. London, Barrie and Rockliff-Cresset Press, 1970.
The Ballad of the Leat. Gillingham, Kent, ARC, 1973.
Fiesta, and The Fox Reviews His Prophecy. London, Enitharmon Press, 1980.
Skeleton Key. Newbury, Berkshire, Phoenix Press, 1982.

Novels

Heorot. London, Barrie and Rockliff-Cresset Press, 1968.
The Tugen and the Toot. London, Barrie and Jenkins, 1973.
Mai's Wedding. London, Collins, 1983.

Other

A Standard of Verse. Newbury, Berkshire, Phoenix Press, 1969.
Bartonwood (for children). London, Chatto and Windus, 1978.

MOFFETT, Judith. American. Born in Louisville, Kentucky, 30 August 1942. Educated at Hanover College, Indiana, 1960-64, B.A. (cum laude) 1964; Colorado State University, Fort Collins, 1964-66, M.A. in English 1966; University of Pennsylvania, Philadelphia, 1969-71, M.A. 1970, Ph.D. in American civilization 1971. Fulbright Lecturer, University of Lund, Sweden, 1967-68; Assistant Professor, Behrend College, Pennsylvania State University, Erie, 1971-75; Visiting Lecturer, Program in Creative Writing, University of Iowa, Iowa City, 1977-78. Visiting Lecturer, 1978-79, and since 1979, Assistant Professor of English, University of Pennsylvania. Recipient: Fulbright grant, 1967, 1973; American Philosophical Society grant, 1973; Swedish Institute grant, 1973, 1976, 1983; Nathhorst Foundation (Sweden) grant, 1973; Eunice Tietjens Memorial Prize, 1973, and Levinson Prize, 1976 (*Poetry*, Chicago); Borestone Mountain Poetry Award, 1976; Ingram Merrill grant, 1977, 1980; Columbia University Translation Prize, 1978; Bread Loaf Writers Conference Tennessee Williams Fellowship, 1978; Swedish Academy translation prize, 1982; National Endowment for the Humanities translation fellowship, 1983; National Endowment for the Arts fellowship, 1984. Address: 608 Meadowvale Lane, Media, Pennsylvania 19063, U.S.A.

PUBLICATIONS

Verse

Keeping Time. Baton Rouge, Louisiana State University Press, 1976.

Whinny Moor Crossing. Princeton, New Jersey, Princeton University Press, 1984.

Other

James Merrill: An Introduction to the Poetry. New York, Columbia University Press, 1984.

Translator, *Gentleman, Single, Refined, and Selected Poems 1937-1959* (bilingual edition), by Hjalmar Gullberg. Baton Rouge, Louisiana State University Press, 1979.

*

Judith Moffett comments:

As a child I was given no guidance or encouragement about poetry, but I was born into a family of Southern Baptists and heard the King James Bible read and quoted more or less daily throughout my early life, and it seems to me now that those Biblical cadences still underlie the way I hear and use language. By the age of ten or eleven I had discovered Kipling's *Jungle Books* in the library and memorized the small poems introducing each story ("Now Chil the Kite brings home the night/That Mang the Bat set free...") with the purest pleasure; later I happened upon, and was entranced by, Vachel Lindsay's "Ghosts of the Buffaloes"; still later it was Stephen Vincent Benét's *John Brown's Body.* With each discovery came the urge to imitate; and that was how I started trying to write poems. From the beginning, sound was valued more than sense: galloping tetrameters were what I responded to, and therefore what I tried to write. I marvel now at my best students' intuitive understanding of what poetic *language* is and does, since I grew up depending almost entirely on the surge or quietness of forms to make language into poetry.

Having come thus far on my own, I stalled for a while in graduate school. Then, in graduate school I had the tremendous luck to be James Merrill's student for half a semester, and the experience of his poetry at that time had the force of a revelation; it quite literally changed my life. Merrill showed me, by his example, how to move ahead. I could see in his work the effects I cared about most in poetry (beauty, metrical skill, narrative) cranked up to a height tremendously beyond my own reach, yet as it were on the same extension ladder: though we cared, and wrote, about quite different things, somehow the listening and controlling *ear* was much the same.

Because of this ear, at variance with the sensibilities of all but a handful of my own generation of poets, I learned only slowly and with difficulty to appreciate and then to write free verse, and still find formal verse more satisfactory in a fundamental way for much of what I want to say.

Eventually I seemed to use poetry more and more often to tell a story; even short lyric stanzas add up, like beads on a string, and carry a narrative line. I have found also that nearly every poem I finished has what a friend has called a "ruminative" quality—that is seems appropriate to think things over in a poem—which may explain why, unlike many writers, I've never felt out of place in Academe. I have consciously worked to become more restrained in emotional expression, to imply and suggest instead of serving up great shovelsful of feelings, and also to fight clear of my earlier experiments at compressing by way of linguistic density, and have had fair success. I've also consciously tried to be briefer, but at that have done far less well. In early middle life, I have settled most happily into the longish local-color narrative-cum-philosophical-exploration on the one hand, and the unabashedly formal lyric on the other, with various other odes and styles thrown in from time to time. In the impulse to this I recognize a reassertion of my early, much loved, influences; but—as far as I can tell—it has caused me (*pace* Harold Bloom) no anxiety. The family resemblance gives me pleasure, but what I have had to say and do is different.

Most recently, I've been trying to teach myself to write science fiction.

*   *   *

Few poets in her generation would undertake the stylistic balances Judith Moffett attempts: an urbane, ethical, and ultimately social tone for which the recent model is Auden and the ultimate model Horace; a range of rhyme and stanza patterns that calls attention to her considerable technical skills, her master in this respect being James Merrill; and an affection for meditative tone and autobiographical subject matter that links her to the most interesting poets of her generation. These lines from a sonnet sequence, "Now or Never," in which the woman speaker, childless in her mid-thirties, is considering if she will ever have children, are characteristic.

They gave me in my kindergarten year
What seemed irrelevant, an Old Maid deck.
Gems, wrinkled skin, strange glasses on a stick,
Long gloves, pressed lips, and horrible orange hair,
No child, no husband ever to be hers,
That gaunt crone wasn't anything like me!
I got her meaning fast: *ignominy*
Is being single in a game of pairs.

The benign contest between discursion and formal tension is her favorite effect, a moral as well as technical balance. She distrusts the bardic; and the merely personal, or even the very personal unconstrained by formal considerations chosen before the poem, can be self-serving. She has the learning and literary range to strike such poise; she's a Ph.D., has written an excellent book on Merrill's work, and has translated from contemporary Swedish poetry.

Her poems err sometimes towards chattiness ("I always liked even upchucky babies"). And her ability to find poetry in daily life can lead her with cries of delight to the obvious ("Now whatever I glimpse qualifies the vast"). But she is willing to risk these lapses to arrive at lines like these from "Bending The Twig," a poem about a girl who passes through puberty earlier than her peers. It builds on topics we have seldom heard discussed without smirking or melodrama, though it builds, too, on smirking and melodrama, not despising what we cling to.

Looking older than one's age required,
it dismayed me to learn, a decorum
appropriate not to the real but to the apparent.

This intelligent, skillful and deceptively full-hearted poet is one of the most interesting and quietly ambitious of her generation; what she'll be able to make out of her auspicious beginnings may well be of real importance to us.

—William Matthews

MOKASHI-PUNEKAR, Shankar. Indian. Born in Dharwar, Mysore State, 8 May 1928. Educated at K.E.B.'s High School, Dharwar; K.E.B.'s Art College; University of Bombay,

B.A. 1948; Karnatak College, Dharwar, M.A. 1953, Ph.D. 1965. Married Girija Radha Shankar in 1948; five children. Assistant Lecturer in English, Lingaraj College, Belgaum, 1954-56, and Kishinchand Chellaram College, Bombay, 1956-61; Lecturer, 1961-69, and Assistant Professor of English, 1969-70, Indian Institute of Technology, Bombay; Reader in English, Karnatak University, Mysore, 1970-80. Since 1980, Professor of English, Institute of Kannada Studies, University of Mysore. Editor, *Jayakarnatak*, 1950-51; music critic, *The Times of India*, Bombay, 1965-70, 1978-80. Recipient: Mysore University award, 1970; Sahitya Academy award, 1979; Sudha award, for novel, 1982. Address: Institute of Kannada Studies, University of Mysore, Manasa Gangotri, Mysore 570 006, India.

PUBLICATIONS

Verse

Ganakeli (Riot of Song), with Govind Manekal and K.D. Kurtakoti. N.p., Rasika Mandira, 1947.
The Captive. Bombay, Popular Prakashan, 1965.
The Pretender. Calcutta, Writers Workshop, 1967.
An Epistle to Professor David McCutchion. Calcutta, Writers Workshop, 1970.
Maviya Mooru Mukhagalu (Three Faces of Maya). Alleppey, Kerala State, Prakashan, 1970.

Other

Gangawwa Gangamai (Mother Ganges and River Ganges). N.p., Manohar Granthamala, 1958.
The Later Phase in the Development of W.B. Yeats: A Study in the Stream of Yeats's Later Thought and Creativity. Dharwar, Karnatak University, 1966; Folcroft, Pennsylvania, Folcroft Editions, 1977.
P. Lal: An Appreciation. Calcutta, Writers Workshop, 1968.
Indo-Anglian Creed and Allied Essays. Calcutta, Writers Workshop, 1972.
Interpretations of the Later Poems of W.B. Yeats. Dharwar, Karnatak University, 1973.
Vinayaka Krishna Gokak. Mysore, Institute of Kannada Studies, 1974.
Paschatya Vimarsheya Itihasa (History of Western Criticism). Bangalore, Bangalore University, 1976.
Theoretical and Practical Studies in Indo-English Literature. Dharwar, Karnatak University, 1978.
Sahitya Mattu Abhiruchi. Mysore, Mitra Prakashan, 1982.

Editor, with others, *Indian Studies in American Fiction.* Dharwar and New Delhi, Karnatak University-Macmillan, 1974.
Editor, with M.K. Naik, *Perspectives on Indian Drama in English.* Madras, Oxford University Press, 1977.

Translator, *Ritusamharam: The Cycle of Seasons*, by Kalidasa. Bombay, Sigma, 1966.

Other books in Kannada: *Sri Bendre*, 1962; *Natanarayani*, 1982.

*

Shankar Mokashi-Punekar comments:

I am a poet cursed with a wide diversification of ability and consequent sapping of single-minded energy. I stand for proto-classical values; these involve me in controversies wherein I sometimes use verse for illustration, sometimes for mounting an attack; by and large, I am a lyricist with a high content of ratiocinative passion.

I wish to be a cosmopolitan Hindu in both theme and style, but I love to use—and wherever possible fuse—the terminology and imagery of Christian theology to express my Hindu inspiration. I am confident of selling my ideas in a decade or so.

As a lyricist, I wish not to repeat or practise any single form as a demonstration of having evolved a manner. I want each poem to be faithful to its kind. Within its kind, I try to achieve the fullest possible expression and rhythm. Unfortunately, I find that English does not have certain kinds of inspiration, and if it had them once, it has now evolved social manners which make them sound false or repellent or outmoded—ethical inspiration, bardic self-confidence, clear-cut distinction between friend and enemy (blurred by the Liberal credo), for instance. Nazism made nationalism odious to the English ear, but I cannot help being a nationalist; am I to pare myself to fit into contemporary English stereotypes? Certainly not. I prefer to remain halted, outlandish, even incommunicative; as a compensation, I try to pack my poems with thought and imagery valuable in themselves and hope for the best. I am confident of my prosody and brook no criticism on that score. The turn of my idiom has raised some controversy, but my non-British thought is bound to militate against the culture-created idiom of English. In my opinion, poetry pre-exists single poems, and no single poem can have finality. It is an index and a good reader alone can drown the shortcomings of a poem in the poetry he can perceive. Our love makes things complete, said Yeats.

*   *   *

In India most of the successful poets in English come from a certain socio-economic background in the urban areas where the exposure to the English language is the most intense. In such company Shankar Mokashi-Punekar stands out as a unique and solitary voice. He is different from the others both in his attitude to the English language and in his response to life. He is a critic as well as a poet, and his two activites are not unconnected. In his criticism he puts forward entirely original and thought-provoking ideas, often taking unfashionable stands. For example, in 1967 he wrote a serious and cogent critical article on the poetry of Sarojini Naidu, when no one who read or wrote English poetry in India regarded her to be anything more than a facile versifier. He even justified her archaisms and poetic inversions on the ground that the mere existence of these devices cannot disqualify a poem from critical consideration. He does not hesitate to use such devices in his own poetry.

Mokashi-Punekar's poetry reflects what in his monograph on the poetry of P. Lal he calls "a new philosophy of English." This apparently consists of an attempt to be free from the associations that English words have for people in English-speaking countries, and a refusal to be blindly guided by the poetic standards set by someone else in another country. In his poetry this results in an occasional oddity of syntax and diction which is sometimes his strength and occasionally his weakness. His poems vary from witty epigrams, whimsical ballads and sonnets to dramatic monologues, sketches combining prose and poetry, and long poems of philosophic reflections. The general impression is that of a poet whose imagination is verbal and cerebral rather than visual. His poems are often interspersed with literary and academic references, but his most memorable poem, "The Pioneers-II," is remarkably free of these.

Apart from being a critic and a poet in English Mokashi-Punekar is also a translator. His translation from Sanskrit poetry has a deliberate quaintness achieved through the use of rhyme, inversions and outmoded words such as "lass" and "affrighted." One may question the validity of such usage in a modern translation, but Mokashi-Punekar tranlates, as he does everything else, with such total conviction in matters of principle that no one can take his work casually.

—Meenakshi Mukherjee

MOLE, John. British. Born in Taunton, Somerset, 12 October 1941. Educated at King's School, Bruton, Somerset; Magdalene College, Cambridge, 1961-64, B.A. (honours) in English 1964, M.A. Married Mary Norman in 1968; two sons. English Teacher, Haberdashers' Aske's School, Elstree, Hertfordshire, 1964-73; Chairman of the English Department, Verulam School, Hertfordshire, 1973-81. Since 1984, Chairman of the English Department, St. Albans School. Exchange Teacher, Riverdale Country School, New York, 1969-70. Presenter, *Poetry Now* and *Time for Verse*, BBC Radio; regular poetry reviewer, *Encounter*, London. Editor, with Peter Scupham, Cellar Press, and Mandeville Press, both in Hitchin, Hertfordshire. Recipient: Eric Gregory Award, 1970. Address: 11 Hill Street, St. Albans, Hertfordshire AL3 4QS, England.

PUBLICATIONS

Verse

A Feather for Memory. London, Outposts, 1961.
The Instruments. Manchester, Phoenix Pamphlet Poets Press, 1970.
Something about Love. Oxford, Sycamore Press, 1972.
The Love Horse. Manchester, E.J. Morten, 1974.
Landscapes. Berkhamsted, Hertfordshire, Priapus, 1975.
A Partial Light. London, Dent, 1975.
The Mortal Room. Berkhamsted, Hertfordshire, Priapus, 1977.
The Tales of Rover. Hitchin, Hertfordshire, Mandeville Press, 1977.
Our Ship. London, Secker and Warburg, 1977.
On the Set. Richmond, Surrey, Keepsake Press, 1978.
From the House Opposite. London, Secker and Warburg, 1979.
Once There Were Dragons (for children), with Mary Norman. London, Deutsch, 1979.
Christmas Past, with Peter Scupham. Hitchin, Hertfordshire, Mandeville Press, 1981.
Feeding the Lake. London, Secker and Warburg, 1981.
Christmas Games, with Peter Scupham. Hitchin, Hertfordshire, Mandeville Press, 1983.
In and Out of the Apple. London, Secker and Warburg, 1984.

Other

Understanding Children Writing, with others. London, Penguin, 1973.

Editor, with Anthony Thwaite, *Poetry 1945 to 1980*. London, Longman, 1983.

*

Manuscript Collection: State University of New York, Buffalo.

John Mole comments:

Apart from the routine essays, I didn't write much at school except for deeply purple prose in our true-blue magazine. I preferred novels, and, as for poetry, I was more concerned to know about it than to read it; I was, at least, aware that there was something intellectually distinguished about claiming an interest in *modern* poetry—anyone could read novels, but I went on reading them. Then, one Sunday in 1960, I picked up the "Review" section of the *Observer* and noticed a front page spread of poems by Robert Graves called "Symptoms of Love." I began reading, casually, became disconcertingly excited, and by the time I had finished the sequence I knew that I wanted to write poetry. Robert Graves wasn't an unfamiliar name to me; after all, he wrote novels—but what was this? So off I went and fashioned lapidary love poems with titles like "Prodigal Daughter," "Bard in Exile" etc. (see my first pamphlet in the Outposts series). I sent them to Graves who was, at that time, Professor of Poetry at Oxford and he said kind things; he even rewrote the closing lines of one of them in order to tighten up the syntax. It was important to get the shape right; mere feeling, as a later Oxford professor remarked, was too easy. I was hooked. Swinburne had blessed the baby Graves while he was still in his pram, and now Graves had corrected my syntax. The lineage was apparent.

I find poetry hard to talk about except in terms of my shifting enthusiasm for different poets and my permanent concern for patterning and craftsmanship. I enjoy what W.H. Auden calls "hanging around language" and there's usually some verbal sport going on in my most overtly "serious" poems whether it be counting syllables or manipulating couplets. I don't believe that counting and manipulating, mathematical or geometric though they may sound, squeeze out feeling; I think they squeeze it *in*. In general, I hope that the best of my work may be memorable and capable of moving my readers. Anything else to be said about it must be said by others if they will.

*   *   *

There are special qualities about John Mole's poetry, one of which is wit; the other is more difficult to define. This latter has its roots in what we might call old-fashioned virtues, not that these virtues have disappeared or are not prized today. They have something about being straightforwardly on-the-right-side as was, say, Sherlock Holmes or Miss Marple, plus a touch of the undemonstrative courage of a Biggles without the bigotry. If I use fictional examples it is because they help to fix the date and ethos that much more clearly. I suspect the word we are looking for is wholesome, as John Mole puts it, "Unique and wholesome as a loaf of bread" ("A Sunday Painter").

This could suggest a sort of cosy safeness which might be off-putting, but even in his sequence of poems about Victorian "Penny Toys," praised for its lightness of touch, the poems are not as safe as all that. Far from it. While Jack-in-the-Box may be reassuringly faithful and true, he still "wants you," and there are the rumblings of time's winged chariot and the shadows of the necessary end are cast long across the nursery: "With a hey do diddle my cat Brown/The time has come to put him down."

Then there is the wit. Wit is not a word that figures much in recent critical writing, because, perhaps, it expresses a quality of sharpness of intellect that does not occur much in recent poetry. Yet it is a word which springs to mind when discussing Mole's work. This is not just because Mole has written humorous poetry, *vide* his longish jazz poems and the delightful adaptations of Robert Desnos's "Chantefables," where the pleasure they give is derived from the display of technical high jinks, as in "The Owls":

Mother owls make beau-
tiful mothers, a few
might brew more nourishing mouse stew
than they do,
but most of them muddle through

It is because the mind behind and the intellectual pressure driving all Mole's work is what distinguishes it, the poems impinging on us through the impetus of their logical progression. In the poems contained in his recent collections *From the House Opposite* and *In and Out of the Apple* we find more and more the wit and the humour progressing towards penetrating observations of the human situation. The justly celebrated "The Tales of Rover" is a case in point, and even a seemingly light poem, "Bestial Homilies" ends: "Be warned by Nature not to let things go—/The animals prepare to say: We told you so"—and a certain menace shows through the jokey surface.

Often the seemingly straightforwardly and clearly defined everyday scenes possess a disturbingly Magritte-like quality of mystery: "The rain of course/still falls as it should/which is not on them" ("The Mirror"). "Depths" would seem to me a key poem to John Mole's work. It is a poem which deals directly with what is basic to the theme of his serious work, and a poem which states prophetically:

Such a depth
Is fearful, nothing moves
But thoughts of what may start there
Even at this moment
Coming up.

—John Cotton

MONTAGUE, John (Patrick). Irish. Born in Brooklyn, New York, 28 February 1929. Educated at St. Patrick's College, Armagh; University College, Dublin, B.A. in English and history 1949, M.A. 1952; Yale University, New Haven, Connecticut (Fulbright Scholar), 1953-54; University of Iowa, Iowa City, M.F.A. 1955. Married 1) Madeleine de Brauer in 1956 (divorced, 1972); 2) Evelyn Robson in 1973, two daughters. Film critic, Dublin *Standard*, 1949-52; worked for Irish Tourist Board, 1956-59; Paris correspondent, *Irish Times*, 1961-64; taught at the Poetry Workshop, University of California, Berkeley, Spring 1964 and 1965, University College, Dublin, Spring and Summer 1967, and Spring 1968, and the Experimental University of Vincennes. Currently, Lecturer in Poetry, University College, Cork. Recipient: May Morton Memorial Award, 1960; Arts Council of Northern Ireland grant, 1970; Irish American Cultural Institute prize, 1976; Marten Toonder award, 1977; Alice Hunt Bartlett Memorial award, 1979; Guggenheim Fellowship, 1979. Member, Irish Academy of Letters. Agent: A.D. Peters, 10 Buckingham Street, London WC2N 6BU, England. Address: Department of English, University College, Cork, Ireland.

PUBLICATIONS

Verse

Forms of Exile. Dublin, Dolmen Press, 1958.
The Old People. Dublin, Dolmen Press, 1960.

Poisoned Lands and Other Poems. London, MacGibbon and Kee, 1961; Chester Springs, Pennsylvania, Dufour, 1963.
Six Irish Poets, with others, edited by Robin Skelton. London, Oxford University Press, 1962.
All Legendary Obstacles. Dublin, Dolmen Press, 1966.
A Chosen Light. London, MacGibbon and Kee, 1967; Chicago, Swallow Press, 1969.
The Rough Field. Dublin, Dolmen Press, and London, Oxford University Press, 1972; Winston-Salem, North Carolina, Wake Forest University Press, 1979.
Patriotic Suite. Dublin, Dolmen Press, 1966.
Home Again. Belfast, Festival, 1967.
Hymn to the New Omagh Road. Dublin, Dolmen Press, 1968.
The Bread God: A Lecture, with Illustrations in Verse. Dublin, Dolmen Press, 1968.
A New Siege. Dublin, Dolmen Press, 1969.
The Planter and the Gael, with John Hewitt. Belfast, Arts Council of Northern Ireland, 1970.
Tides. Dublin, Dolmen Press, 1970; Chicago, Swallow Press, 1971.
Small Secrets. London, Poem-of-the-Month Club, 1972.
The Cave of Night. Cork, Golden Stone Press, 1974.
O'Riada's Farewell. Cork, Golden Stone Press, 1975.
A Slow Dance. Dublin, Dolmen Press, and Winston-Salem, North Carolina, Wake Forest University Press, 1975.
The Great Cloak. Dublin, Dolmen Press, London, Oxford University Press, and Winston-Salem, North Carolina, Wake Forest University Press, 1978.
The Leap. Dublin, Gallery, and Old Deerfield, Massachusetts, Deerfield Press, 1979.
Selected Poems. Dublin, Dolmen Press, Oxford, Oxford University Press, and Winston-Salem, North Carolina, Wake Forest University Press, 1982.
The Dead Kingdom. Dublin, Dolmen Press, Oxford, Oxford University Press, and Winston-Salem, North Carolina, Wake Forest University Press, 1984.

Recording: *The Northern Muse,* with Seamus Heaney, Claddagh, 1968.

Play

The Rough Field (produced London, 1973).

Short Stories

Death of a Chieftain and Other Stories. London, MacGibbon and Kee, 1964; Chester Springs, Pennsylvania, Dufour, 1967.

Other

Editor, *The Dolmen Miscellany of Irish Writing.* Dublin, Dolmen Press, 1962.
Editor, with Liam Miller, *A Tribute to Austin Clarke on His Seventieth Birthday, 9 May 1966.* Dublin, Dolmen Press, and Chester Springs, Pennsylvania, Dufour, 1966.
Editor, *The Faber Book of Irish Verse.* London, Faber, 1974; as *The Book of Irish Verse,* New York, Macmillan, 1977.

Translator, *A Fair House: Versions of Irish Poetry.* Dublin, Cuala Press, 1973.
Translator, with Evelyn Robson, *November,* by André Frénaud. Cork, Golden Stone Press, 1977.

*

Critical Studies: *The New Poetry* by M.L. Rosenthal, New York and London, Oxford University Press, 1967, and *The Modern Poetic Sequence* by Rosenthal and Sally M. Gall, New York and Oxford, Oxford University Press, 1983; by John MacInerney, in *Hibernia* (Dublin), 15 December 1972; D.S. Maxwell, in *Critical Quarterly* (London), Summer 1973; Derek Mahon, in *Malahat Review* (Victoria, British Columbia), July 1973; Thomas Dillon Redshaw, in *Studies* (Dublin), Spring 1974; *John Montague* by Frank Kersnowski, Lewisburg, Pennsylvania, Bucknell University Press, 1975; "John Montague, Seamus Heaney, and the Irish Past" by Graham Martin, in *The Present* (New Pelican Guide to English Literature) edited by Boris Ford, London, Penguin, 1983.

John Montague comments:

I am usually classed as an Irish poet and that is true insofar as I am deeply involved with the landscape and people of Ireland, particularly Ulster. In Gaelic poetry, Ireland appears both as a maiden and a hag, a sort of national muse, and her hold is still strong, especially now that her distinctive culture is being submerged. But underneath these tribal preoccupations beats a more personal struggle, the effort to affirm lovingly, to salvage some order, in the face of death and change. The technique is a blend of post-modern (Williams and Pound) and old Gaelic poetry, which could also be regarded as an aspect of nationality, for an Irish poet (following Joyce, Yeats, Beckett) has a better chance of being international than an English writer. But my effort to understand as much of the modern world as possible serves only to illuminate the destruction of that small area from which I initially came, and that theme in turn is only part of the larger one of continually threatened love. All of us are uprooted now, subject to the seismic waves of the late twentieth century; we must warn and warm ourselves against a new ice age.

*　　*　　*

There is something tight-lipped about John Montague's poetry, revealed even in the terse titles of his volumes and the repeated use of a short, abrupt line, where enjambment projects the reader into sudden peripeties and reversals, and the shifts of pace and meaning have the effect of a clipped, curt rebuff. Yet, within these constraints, the poetry can flower into an unexpected, lyric generosity. Not many poets, for example, could carry off successfully the Anglo-Saxon bluntness of "Love, A Greeting" (*Tides*):

> a lifetime's
> struggle to exchange
> with the strange
> thing inhabiting
> a woman—
> 　　　　face,
> breasts, buttocks,
> the honey sac
> of the cunt....

It's the puritanical tautness of his speech that can bring off such large gestures. Constriction is Montague's native ground, as "Home Again" admits. Narrowness runs as a theme through his work, an expression of that bare past and "bleak economic future" shared, as he has written, by all such peripheral and remote areas of Europe as Ulster, Brittany, the Highlands. It's this which marks him out clearly as one of the "Ulster school" of poets, despite the casual displacement of his Brooklyn birth. The

"Narrow huckster streets" of Belfast, "All this dour, despoiled inheritance," together with the heritage of sectarian hatred, in "a culture where constraint is all," have a precise, economic origin: "narrow fields wrought such division." The "Rough Field" which gives the title to one of his major collections is not just a translation of the Gaelic name for his native village, but—in the words of an Afghan proverb which provides his epigraph—the summary of an historical destiny: "I had never known sorrow,/ Now it is a field I have inherited, and I till it." This in turn, in "The Bread God," he sees reproduced in "the lean parish of my art." Deracination is a major theme for Montague, from his first volume, *Forms of Exile*, through to his latest collection, ostensibly of love lyrics, *The Great Cloak*.

"A Lost Tradition," in *The Rough Field*, laments the physical expropriation that goes with the loss of the Gaelic, which no amount of "school Irish" can compensate for: "The whole landscape a manuscript/ We had lost the skill to read,/ A part of our past disinherited." And the whole volume explores the consequences of this uprooting, spanning several hundred years of Irish history, while always relating the public events to the particular lives of individual men and families, including his own forebears. "A Grafted Tongue" sees the linguistic loss not just as a metaphor for this larger dispossession, but its key event: "To grow/a second tongue, as/harsh a humiliation/as twice to be born." "Lament for the O'Neills" and "Stele for a Northern Republican" indicate that the loss is one which lies close to the heart of both communities in the North. The latter poem unsentimentally, but with bitterness, acknowledges his own father's "right to choose a Brooklyn slum/rather than a half-life in this/by-passed and dying place."

In *A Slow Dance* Montague moves away from history into the shadowier realms of Celtic myth to explain the current violence of the North, resurrecting that ancient "Black widow goddess" whose "love-making/is like a skirmish" and who wears "a harvest necklace of heads." The move brings with it a loss of precisely that kind of acute historical particularity which distinguishes his best verse, but it remains nevertheless an impressive volume. The "slow dance" of the title unites human and elemental cycles, pagan and Christian Ireland in a ritual return to origins, where fertility and massacre are intimately linked. But it is, finally, the "sad awkward/dance of pain" of all the living upon the graves of all the dead, and its most moving sequence, perhaps, is the intense and personal elegy for his close friend, the composer O'Riada, who died in 1971.

The love poems of *The Great Cloak* return to the lucid, melodic airs of *Tides* and *A Chosen Light*, but the atmosphere has been darkened by the intervening, public violence, which now finds its correlative in personal life. These poems are as much concerned with loss, jealousy, marital breakdown and its humiliations and shames, as with the lyric celebration of love—"that always strange moment/when the clothes peel away/(bark from an unknown tree)" ("Do Not Disturb"). The violence spoken of as inseparable from love in such a fine early poem as "The Same Gesture" (*Tides*) is now felt more urgently, and as a greater threat. Only briefly, in the sequence of poems which explore the consciousness of the estranged wife, is any connection explicitly acknowledged between personal disintegration and the larger violence of the North ("She Writes"). But, throughout, Montague is groping towards a new understanding of the interdependence of the personal and the political, and their common roots in a harsh and souring history. Such a quest can bring him desperately close to the unspeakable, to silence, shamefaced and appalled, as "No Music" recognizes:

> To tear up old love by the roots,
> To trample on past affections:

There is no music for so harsh a song.

The Dead Kingdom charts a journey north, along "minor roads of memory" from Cork to Fermanagh, summoned by his mother's death to traverse a landscape dense with personal, historic and mythic associations. The volume itself is a "dead kingdom," preserving in print "things that are gone," sardonically accepting its own ultimate disappearance, like the library of Alexander before it, and more recent "substantial things/hustled oblivion," down the naw of Spenser's "goddess Mutability,/dark lady of Process,/our devouring Queen." When individuals die, a unique "world of sense & memory" vanishes with them. Races and nations alike are "locked/in their dream of history," subjective realms as "fragile/as a wild bird's wing," bulldozer and butterfly alike ephemeral forms. Even the archaeological relics of ancient Ireland are now torn up by the mechanized peat-cutters that destroy the bog wholescale. Yet, as "A Flowering Absence" suggests, the poet's own childhood experience of exile and fostering compels him to fill that emptiness, urged by a "terrible thirst" for knowledge and love "to learn something of that time/Of confusion, poverty, absence." Thus the journey upstream to the source, which is also, as the last poem, "Back," indicates, a journey to his own death. "There is no permanence," an epigraph from *The Book of Gilgamesh* tells us. But another speaks of the need to discover the "Source of lost knowledge," and, in the penultimate poem, it is the impulse to name which provides those "frail rope-ladders/across fuming oblivion" which offer "A new love, a new/litany of place names," and allow the poet to return home, to "a flowering presence."

—Stan Smith

MOORE, Nicholas. British. Born in Cambridge, 16 November 1918; son of the philosopher G.E. Moore. Educated at Dragon School, Oxford; Leighton Park School, Reading; Trinity College, Cambridge, B.A. Married 1) Priscilla Patience Craig (marriage dissolved), one daughter; 2) Shirley Putnam in 1953 (died, 1982), one son and one daughter (deceased). Editor, *Seven*, 1938-40, and *New Poetry*, 1944-45; Editorial Assistant, Editions Poetry London. Has held jobs in horticulture, and written horticultural journalism. Recipient: Patrons Prize (*Contemporary Poetry*, Baltimore), 1945; Harriet Monroe Memorial Prize (*Poetry*, Chicago), 1947; Barbara Campion Award, 1980. Address: 89 Oakdene Road, St. Mary Cray, Kent BR5 2AL, England.

PUBLICATIONS

Verse

A Wish in Season: Poems. London, Fortune Press, 1941.
The Island and the Cattle. London, Fortune Press, 1941.
A Book for Priscilla. Cambridge, Epsilon Pamphlets, 1941.
Buzzing Around with a Bee and Other Poems. London, Editions Poetry London, 1941.
The Cabaret, The Dancer, The Gentleman. London, Fortune Press, 1942.
The Glass Tower: Poems 1936-43. London, Editions Poetry London, 1944.
Three Poems, with Fred Marnau and Wrey Gardiner. London, Grey Walls Press, 1944.

Thirty-five Anonymous Odes. London, Fortune Press, 1944.
The War of the Little Jersey Cows: Poems by Guy Kelly. London, Fortune Press, 1945.
Recollections of the Gala: Selected Poems, 1943-1948. London, Editions Poetry London, 1950.
Identity. London, Cadenza Press, 1969.
Resolution and Identity. London, Covent Garden Press, 1970.
Spleen: Thirty-One Versions of Baudelaire's "Je Suis Comme le Roi." London, Blacksuede Boot Press, 1973.

Other

Henry Miller. Wigginton, Hertfordshire, The Opus Press, 1943; Folcroft, Pennsylvania, Folcroft Editions, 1969.
The Tall Bearded Iris. London, Collingridge, and New York, Transatlantic Arts, 1956.

Editor, with John Bayliss and Douglas Newton, *The Fortune Anthology.* London, Fortune Press, 1942.
Editor, *The P L Book of Modern American Short Stories.* London, Editions Poetry London, 1945.
Editor, with Douglas Newton, *Atlantic Anthology.* London, Fortune Press, 1945.

*

Critical Studies: "The Glass Tower" by Kenneth Gee, in *The New English Weekly* (London), 10 May 1945; G.W. Stonier, in *The New Statesman* (London), 1945; "The Poetry of Nicholas Moore" by G.S. Fraser, in *Poetry Quarterly 9* (London), 1947; Preface by Kenneth Rexroth to *New British Poets*, New York, New Directions, 1949; "Nicholas Moore: A Problem Poet" by Margaret Crosland, in *Poetry Quarterly 14* (London), Spring 1952.

Nicholas Moore comments:

Writing in *The Spectator* on January 8th, 1943, Sheila Shannon wrote, in a review of "Some New Poets" as follows: "But too many of the poets under review here write poems as the result of their education; too few of them use any but a single sense at a time in conjunction with the mind. It was with delight and relief that, after much reading, I came across Nicholas Moore's poem in *Poetry Folios*. It is poetry written by a man functioning in all his senses and having a mind and an imagination equal to the tasks of conception and construction. Moore has sensibility; he has great sense of enjoyment; he can be witty and gentle; he can also be silly and trivial, which is the result of an unusual and refreshing exuberance."

Whether I deserve this or not, of course, I don't know, but it does represent, in part at least, what I would like to be true.

So, too, with "In much of Moore's writing there is a sense of justice, a morality that refuses to have anything to do with any morality bespoken by rulers or bewildered crowds," or, "but Mr. Moore is really a reflective poet, his best poems take their shape and movement from his thought, and grow with it; in the later poems in this book, his consciousness has a greater range, and the words of the poems bring to life other words and ideas that are not on the page but are discovered in reading. He is a civilized poet who has much to say, and to say well, against the evils of his civilization.... He can also write with some faith and hope which one feels to be real," from Kenneth Gee; and G.W. Stonier's "the intricacy of workmanship makes one want to reject one meaning for another more intricate; or we turn the poem over feelingly like a scarab," and "I should like to emphasize Mr. Moore's accomplishment in these various phases. Nevertheless, the poems which appeal most are those in which vividness of phrase is matched by vividness of idea.... It comes naturally to him to see sharply and form patterns, and an epigrammatic gaiety is one of the surprises of his talent."

Some of these comments might seem to be mutually exclusive; but that, really, is the point. Victoria Sackville-West in another review (of *Three Poems*) described me as "slightly surrealist." At that time, I thought this a silly comment, but now on reflection I'm not sure that most of the poems of mine I like best myself are not "slightly surrealist."

I do not consider myself a romantic—though I have written some romantic poems—"Ode to Sexual Beauty" and "The Aquatic Stag" for instance—because that seemed appropriate to the particular theme, or particular time and place. In its early days I was associated with The New Apocalypse movement, and contributed to *The White Horseman*. But once it started calling itself—or was it Herbert Read who called it?—The New Romanticism, I was out of sympathy. My own personal tastes—in poetry—were more for the Southern group of writers in America, particularly Ransom and John Peale Bishop, and for the Metaphysicals (Donne, Herbert, Vaughan), and the Elizabethans: Shakespeare, of course; Marlowe; Webster; and especially Ralegh and Fulke Greville.

In other words, I believed—and do believe—in a poetry of greater universality and width of range than any narrow categorising can encompass.

*   *   *

In the 1940's Nicholas Moore was well known as a talented and prolific poet, whose work appeared frequently in little magazines and anthologies. He published several collections, of which the most substantial were *The Glass Tower* and *Recollections of the Gala*. But after the appearance of the latter volume Moore appeared to stop writing completely, and this silence was broken only in the late sixties, when he once more began to contribute verse to literary reviews.

Nicholas Moore's origins in the late 1930's are evident in the prevalent influence of Auden, and particularly of Auden's songs and light verse. Moore picked up and carried on Auden's talent for the mellifluous but slightly cerebral lyric. Other influences were Blake, notably the "Songs of Innocence and Experience," and, most interestingly, Wallace Stevens. Moore read and admired Stevens many years before he became a prominent and even fashionable poet; indeed, Stevens was almost wholly unknown in England in the 1940's, when Moore was paying him the tribute of deliberate imitation in a poem such as "Ideas of Disorder at Torquay." From Stevens Moore acquired a flowing music and a deliberate rhetoric that stiffened the colloquial thirties manner and the throwaway wit. Moore's poems of the early forties were sometimes excessively fluent, with a suggestion of more manner than matter. But *Recollections of the Gala* is a very accomplished collection which represents Moore's poetry at its best, variously fantastic, sardonic and lyrical. His most recent work is as adroit and witty as ever; particularly in *Spleen*, a set of 31 versions of a famous Baudelaire poem, which provides a series of dazzling variations on a theme.

—Bernard Bergonzi

MORAES, Dom(inic Frank).   British.   Born in Bombay, India, 19 July 1938; son of the journalist and writer Frank Moraes.

Educated at Jesus College, Oxford (Editor, *Gemini*, 1958-60), B.A. in English 1959, M.A. Served as Honorary Colonel with the United States Army in Vietnam, 1971-73. Married 1) Judith St. John in 1963 (marriage dissolved), one son; 2) Leela Naidu in 1969. Journalist, and scriptwriter and director, BBC and ITV; roving reporter, *New York Times Sunday Magazine*, 1968-71; Managing Editor, *Asia Magazine*, Hong Kong, 1971-73; Chief Literary Consultant, United Nations Fund for Populations, 1973-77. Recipient: Hawthornden Prize, 1958; Lamont Poetry Selection Prize, 1960; Overseas Press Citation (USA), 1972. Lives in Bombay. Agent: Curtis Brown, 162-168 Regent Street, London W1R 5TA, England.

PUBLICATIONS

Verse

A Beginning.   London, Parton Press, 1957.
Poems.   London, Eyre and Spottiswoode, 1960.
Penguin Modern Poets 2, with Kingsley Amis and Peter Porter. London, Penguin, 1962.
John Nobody.   London, Eyre and Spottiswoode, 1965.
Poems 1955-1965.   New York, Macmillan, 1966.
Bedlam Etcetera.   London, Turret, 1966.
Absences.   New Delhi, Sterling, 1983.

Other

Green Is the Grass (on cricket).   Bombay, Asia Publishing House, 1951.
Gone Away: An Indian Journal.   London, Heinemann, and Boston, Little Brown, 1960.
My Son's Father: An Autobiography.   London, Secker and Warburg, 1968; as *My Son's Father: A Poet's Autobiography*, New York, Macmillan, 1969.
The Tempest Within: An Account of East Pakistan.   New York, Barnes and Noble, 1971.
From East and West: A Collection of Essays.   New Delhi, Vikas, 1971.
A Matter of People.   London, Deutsch, and New York, Praeger, 1974.
The Open Eyes: A Journey Through Karnataka.   Bangalore, Government of Karnataka, 1976.
Mrs. Gandhi.   London, Cape, 1980; as *Indira Gandhi*, Boston, Little Brown, 1980.
Bombay.   New York, Time Life, 1980.

Editor, *Voices for Life: Reflections on the Human Condition*. New York, Praeger, 1975.

Translator, *The Brass Serpent*, by T. Carmi.   London, Deutsch, 1964; Athens, Ohio University Press, 1965.

*

Manuscript Collections: University of Texas, Austin; State University of New York, Buffalo; University of Arizona, Tucson.

Critical Study: *The Poetry of Encounter: Three Indo-Anglian Poets* by Emmanuel Narendra Lall, New Delhi, Sterling, 1983.

*   *   *

Among Indian poets writing in English today perhaps the best-known is Dom Moraes. It is true that neither in his themes nor in his imagery, neither in the landscape of his poetry nor in his references and allusions is there anything distinctively Indian; but this does not matter much since "Indianness," whatever it may be, is not a poetic virtue *per se*. Moraes's first book of poems, *A Beginning*, published when he was only 19, won the Hawthornden Prize and brought him immediate fame; he was the first non-English poet to win it.

What distinguishes Moraes among Indian poets is his powerful organic sensibility, a very skilful use of words in metrical and verse-patterns, a striking imagery and an authentic personal experience. His difficulty at the moment seems to be that he has not as yet found any convincingly felt solution of his personal problems. This is a difficulty which is almost inevitable in the early poetry of a young poet who is honest, sincere and individual. As a result of this difficulty, however, the style of some of his poems tends to overweigh "the idea." For example, in "Vivisection" (*John Nobody*) the "virgin" (modern version) betrays her own deepest instincts and kills the "unicorn" (original version). The sustained imagery of the poem does not breathe any new life into the commonplace conclusion. Similarly in "The General" (*John Nobody*) the poet speaks of the dilemma of living in a world of horror and violence in which the attitude of neither "the anchorite" nor "the clown" is appropriate—both of them are killed—and there seems to be no permanent escape from contingent becoming into pure being; the elaborate set-up of the story of these poems is hardly justified by the fairly simple conclusions and emotional dilemmas of the poet's situation. The machinery (myths, references, allusions, etc.) is quite often excessive for the jobs that the poet plans. The poet does not always achieve creative mastery of his personal experience. We get to know that he is deeply "troubled" and is searching for solutions. There is an intimation that he accepts life and love and the necessity of struggle against the evil in oneself. Considering the gifts of the poet, it is reasonable to expect that this intimation will obtain convincing poetic realization in due course of time.

Not all the poems, however, suffer from this incompleteness. There are many poems in which the aim and scope of the poet are "impersonal" and these succeed very well. Such for instance are "Figures in the Landscape" (*A Beginning*), "Kanheri Caves" (*A Beginning*) and "Melancholy Prince (*John Nobody*). In "Figures in the Landscape" the poet re-interprets the story of the Pied Piper to suggest the trustfulness and innocence of the children and the Piper's betrayal—of which he is aware—of that trust. The poem on the Kanheri Caves recreates in clear sharp detail the poetic impression of the caves and makes skilful use of the scientific hypothesis of evolution and Keats's reference to "stout Cortez" to intimate the cyclic nature of life and civilization; the poem is also an excellent illustration of Moraes's command of word-music. "Melancholy Prince" may not say anything fresh or original about *Hamlet*—hard task to do so—but it conveys admirably the tragedy of Ophelia and the peculiar atmosphere of the play. It is in these comparatively "public" poems that Moraes has greater variety of interest and success to offer than in his purely "personal" poems. He has been deeply concerned of late with public issues such as racial segregation in England, and we may expect him to modulate what he has himself recognized as "a small whimper" and attempt a larger mode without losing his individuality of response and style.

—S. Nagarajan

———————

MORGAN, Edwin (George). Scottish. Born in Glasgow, 27 April 1920. Educated at Rutherglen Academy; Glasgow High School; Glasgow University, 1937-40, 1946-47, M.A. 1947. Served in the Royal Army Medical Corps, 1940-46. Assistant Lecturer, 1947-50, Lecturer, 1950-65, Senior Lecturer, 1965-71, Reader, 1971-75, and Titular Professor in English, 1975-80, Glasgow University. Recipient: Cholmondeley Award, 1968; Scottish Arts Council award, 1969, 1973, 1975, 1977, 1978, 1983; Hungarian P.E.N. Memorial Medal, 1972. O.B.E. (Officer, Order of the British Empire), 1982. Address: 19 Whittingehame Court, Glasgow G12 OBG, Scotland.

PUBLICATIONS

Verse

The Vision of Cathkin Braes. Glasgow, Maclellan, 1952.
The Cape of Good Hope. Tunbridge Wells, Kent, Peter Russell, 1955.
Starryveldt. Frauenfeld, Switzerland, Gomringer Press, 1965.
Scotch Mist. Cleveland, Renegade Press, 1965.
Sealwear. Glasgow, Gold Seal Press, 1966.
Emergent Poems. Stuttgart, Hansjörg Mayer, 1967.
The Second Life. Edinburgh, Edinburgh University Press, 1968.
Gnomes. Preston, Lancashire, Akros, 1968.
Proverbfolder. Corsham, Wiltshire, Openings Press, 1969.
Penguin Modern Poets 15, with Alan Bold and Edward Kamau Brathwaite. London, Penguin, 1969.
The Horseman's Word: A Sequence of Concrete Poems. Preston, Lancashire, Akros, 1970.
Twelve Songs. West Linton, Peeblesshire, Castlelaw Press, 1970.
The Dolphin's Song. Leeds, School of English Press, 1971.
Glasgow Sonnets. West Linton, Peeblesshire, Castlelaw Press, 1972.
Instamatic Poems. London, Ian McKelvie, 1972.
The Whittrick: A Poem in Eight Dialogues. Preston, Lancashire, Akros, 1973.
From Glasgow to Saturn. Cheadle, Cheshire, Carcanet, and Chester Springs, Pennsylvania, Dufour, 1973.
The New Divan. Manchester, Carcanet, 1977.
Colour Poems. Glasgow, Third Eye Centre, 1978.
Star Gate: Science Fiction Poems. Glasgow, Third Eye Centre, 1979.
Poems of Thirty Years. Manchester, Carcanet, 1982.
Grafts/Takes. Glasgow, Mariscat Press, 1983.
4 Glasgow Subway Poems. Glasgow, National Book League, 1983.
Sonnets from Scotland. Glasgow, Mariscat Press, 1984.

Plays

The Apple-Tree: A Medieval Dutch Play (produced Edinburgh, 1982). Glasgow, Third Eye Centre, 1982.
Master Peter Pathelin, adaptation of a medieval French farce. Glasgow, Third Eye Centre, 1983.

Opera librettos: *The Charcoal-Burner*, 1969; *Valentine*, 1976; *Columba*, 1976; *Spell*, 1979.

Other

Essays. Cheadle, Cheshire, Carcanet, 1975.
Rites of Passage: Translations. Manchester, Carcanet, 1975.
Hugh MacDiarmid. London, Longman, 1976.

East European Poets.   Milton Keynes, Buckinghamshire, Open University Press, 1976.
Provenance and Problematics of "Sublime and Alarming Images" in Poetry.   London, British Academy, 1977.
Edwin Morgan: An Interview, with Marshall Walker.   Preston, Lancashire, Akros, 1977.

Editor, *Collins Albatross Book of Longer Poems: English and American Poetry from the Fourteenth Century to the Present Day.*   London, Collins, 1963.
Editor, with George Bruce and Maurice Lindsay, *Scottish Poetry One* to *Six.*   Edinburgh, Edinburgh University Press, 1966-72.
Editor, *New English Dramatists 14.*   London, Penguin, 1970.
Editor, *Scottish Satirical Verse: An Anthology.*   Manchester, Carcanet, 1980.

Translator, *Beowulf.*   Aldington, Kent, Hand and Flower Press, 1952; Berkeley, University of California Press, 1962.
Translator, *Poems from Eugenio Montale.*   Reading, Berkshire, University of Reading School of Art, 1959.
Translator, *Sovpoems: Brecht, Neruda, Pasternak, Tsvetayeva, Mayakovsky, Martynov, Yevtushenko.*   Worcester, Migrant Press, 1961.
Translator, with David Wevill, *Sándor Weöres and Ferenc Juhász: Selected Poems.*   London, Penguin, 1970.
Translator, *Wi the Haill Voice: Poems by Mayakovsky.*   Oxford, Carcanet, 1972.
Translator, *Fifty Renascence Love-Poems,* edited by Ian Fletcher.   Reading, Berkshire, Whiteknights Press, 1975.
Translator, *Selected Poems,* by Platen.   West Linton, Peeblesshire, Castlelaw Press, 1978.

*

Bibliography: *Edwin Morgan: A Selected Bibliography 1950-1980* by Hamish Whyte, Glasgow, Mitchell Library, 1980.

Manuscript Collections: Glasgow University Library; Mitchell Library, Glasgow; National Library of Scotland, Edinburgh.

Critical Studies: by Tom Buchan, in *Scottish International* (Edinburgh), August 1968; "Scottish Poets: Edwin Morgan and Iain Crichton Smith" by Robin Fulton, in *Stand* (Newcastle upon Tyne), x, 4, 1969; *Worlds: Seven Modern Poets,* London, Penguin, 1974; *Contemporary Scottish Poetry* by Robin Fulton, Edinburgh, M. Macdonald, 1974; J.A.M. Rillie, in *Lines Review* (Edinburgh), March 1976; *An Introduction to Fifty Modern British Poets* by Michael Schmidt, London, Pan, 1979, as *A Reader's Guide to Fifty Modern British Poets,* London, Heinemann, 1979, New York, Barnes and Noble, 1982; "The Poetry of Edwin Morgan: Translator of Reality" by Robin Hamilton, in *Akros* (Nottingham), April 1980; *Science and Psychodrama: The Poetry of Edwin Morgan and David Black* by Robin Hamilton, Frome, Somerset, Bran's Head, 1982.

*   *   *

"It seems this is a world of change..."—the extra-terrestrial narrator of "Memories of Earth" speaks also for Edwin Morgan, who aims to reflect a world "continually changing and changing fast" in poems of notable variety. Yet in his first collection, *The Vision of Cathkin Braes,* some persistent features of his work are already apparent. His sense of the comic shows in the title poem,

in which a wildly unlikely group—including Salome, John Knox, Mungo Park, and Lauren Bacall—end up dancing together. Linguistic playfulness, where words dance together, is already established in "Verses for a Christmas Card," whose wordweldings ("endyir starnacht," "brookrims hoartrack") look back through Joyce and Hopkins to the Anglo-Saxon poets.

Significantly, some translations from the Anglo-Saxon were included in *Dies Irae,* a collection intended to complement *The Vision of Cathkin Braes,* although unpublished until 1982. The loneliness of individuals in alien environments, and the destruction of cities, are themes of these poems which recur in "Dies Irae" itself, in the distinctly nuclear apocalypses offered by "Stanzas of the Jeopardy," and in many later poems. But recurrent, too, in Morgan's poems is their expression of hopefulness, of faith in humankind's ability to fight on, to continue exploring.

Still missing, except in glimpses, was a sense of the everyday, contemporary world in its many aspects. Morgan has suggested that *The Cape of Good Hope* dealt with, but did not resolve "the dilemma of the...solitary creator and his...involvement with humanity." The resolution began with the "Glasgow poems," started around 1962/63, and appearing in *The Second Life* (1968). They may record moments of pure observation ("Linoleum Chocolate"), or events of more personal involvement ("In the Snack-bar"); they may be celebratory ("Trio"), partly comic ("The Starlings in George Square"), or verging on nightmare, as in "The Suspect," with its several voices, or "Glasgow Green": "Cut the scene./Here there's no crying for help,/it must be acted out, again, again."

Closely related is a series of love poems, adumbrated in the title poem and beginning, perhaps, in "The Unspoken." They share a simplicity of language with the "Glasgow poems"; they move from joy to sadness to something more sombre. But most distinctively new in *The Second Life,* and in *Emergent Poems* and *Gnomes,* is the group of concrete and related poems. One aim of concrete poetry, simultaneity, is attained in the single line of "Siesta of a Hungarian Snake," while other possibilities are explored in "The Chaffinch Map of Scotland" with its strongly kinetic effect, and the playful permutations of "The Computer's First Christmas Card." Related, but more serious, are the variations in "Opening the Cage" on John Cage's "I have nothing to say and I am saying it and that is poetry," including, for instance, "It is and I am and I have poetry saying say that to nothing." Such work is not, as has been suggested "necessarily slight," as "Message Clear," one of the "emergent poems," shows, whose last line,

i am the resurrection and the life

gradually emerges from the statements which can be extracted from it, like

```
i am  he   r            e
i am       re     n     t
```

Morgan's belief that poets today should be more concerned with science and technology, especially space-exploration, is confirmed by several poems. Yet "In Sobieski's Shield," with its Beckettian ending, "...its's hard/to go let's go," and "From the Domain of Arnheim," stressing courage, are as close to those Anglo-Saxon poems as to SF.
Instamatic Poems presents life not through direct observation but through events, often bizarre or macabre, culled from newspapers. They are written in a deadpan style of apparent objectivity, reminiscent of Robbe-Grillet's *Instantanés,* but often with a sharp, if barely stated, comment. The poems in the supplemen-

tary collection *Takes* have a more relaxed, more overtly author-ial tone, and humour outweighs horror.

From Glasgow to Saturn is as wide-ranging as the title sug-gests. Morgan has stated that many of his poems are really dramatic monologues. Here they include attempts "to get *every-thing* speaking," whether an animal, in the rather Hughesian "Hyena," an object ("The Apple's Song"), or the (perhaps) myth-ical ("The Loch Ness Monster's Song," a memorable sound-poem). Playfulness ("Itinerary" and many more) and apocalypse ("Last Message") find many forms; love-poems express estrange-ment and loss; one poem, such as "London," may move from memories, dreams, and collage to direct observation and com-ment; and the powerful concluding group approaches its Glas-gow themes through the phantasmagoric, direct and satiric.

This diversity is forwarded by *The New Divan* and *Star Gate* where, for instance, clichés and proverbs are dreadfully multi-plied in "The Clone Poem," Dunbar is updated in "A Good Year for Death," and "emergent" poems become divergent in "Lévi-Strauss at the Lie-Detector," where "any classification is super-ior to chaos" yields "any class fic tion is superior chaos." With Morgan, travel in space or time tends to return us to the present, so that "Memories of Earth" finally celebrates "ordinary forti-tude." And *The New Divan*, a sequence of 100 short poems dedicated to the Persian poet Hafiz, relates both to *his* world and to the Middle East of Morgan's war-service.

There are moments in this sequence which may remind us of Stevens. And indeed, Morgan has consistently shown (and acknowledged) an involved awareness of the American modern-ist tradition from Whitman through Williams, Olson, Creeley, and Ginsberg to Ashbery. Yet his work is unlike that of any similarly aware English poet. Undoubtedly his Scottishness has provided another tradition, that of Dunbar, Burns, and MacDiarmid. And he has supplemented this by looking abroad, in his considerable work as a translator, to such different talents as Mayakovsky, Michaux, Gomringer, and Montale.

His versatility continues to be manifest in his recent work. In *Grafts/Takes* the "Grafts," Morgan explains, "are based on fragments from abandoned poems by Michael Schmidt," but it would be futile to ask which bits are Schmidt's for they are undetectable. The "Sonnets from Scotland" (as yet uncollected) alternate between comic invention ("Outward Bound") and apo-calyptic vision ("The Target"), and Scotland is seen often in some remote past or desolate future. Morgan is not, ever, a re-assuring poet.

—Geoffrey Soar

MORGAN, (George) Frederick. American. Born in New York City, 25 April 1922. Educated at St. Bernard's School, New York, 1927-35; St. Paul's School, Concord, New Hampshire, 1935-39; Princeton University, New Jersey, 1939-43, A.B. 1943. Served in the United States Army Tank Destroyer Corps, 1943-45: Staff Sergeant. Married 1) Constance Canfield in 1942 (divorced), six children (two deceased); 2) Rose Fillmore in 1957 (divorced); 3) Paula Deitz in 1969. Founder, with Joseph Ben-nett and William Arrowsmith, and since 1947, Editor, *The Hud-son Review*, New York. Since 1974, Chairman of the Advisory Council, Department of Romance Languages and Literatures, Princeton University. Address: c/o The Hudson Review, 684 Park Avenue, New York, New York 10021, U.S.A.

PUBLICATIONS

Verse

A Book of Change. New York, Scribner, 1972.
Poems of the Two Worlds. Urbana, University of Illinois Press, 1977.
Death Mother and Other Poems. Urbana, University of Illi-nois Press, 1979.
The River. New York, Nadja, 1980.
Refractions (translations). Omaha, Abattoir, 1981.
Northbook. Urbana, University of Illinois Press, 1982.
Eleven Poems. New York, Nadja, 1983.

Other

The Tarot of Cornelius Agrippa. Sand Lake, New York, Sagarin Press, 1978.

Editor, *The Hudson Review Anthology.* New York, Random House, 1961.
Editor, *The Modern Image: Outstanding Stories from "The Hudson Review."* New York, Norton, 1965.

Translator, *Seven Poems*, by Mallarmé. New York, Chris-topher Wilmarth, 1981.

*

Critical Studies: "The Shocks of Normality" by Laurence Lieb-erman, in *Yale Review* (New Haven, Connecticut), Spring 1974; "The Poetry of Frederick Morgan" by Hayden Carruth, in *New Republic* (Washington, D.C.), 15 May 1976; "Poet's View" by Thomas Lask, in *New York Times*, 15 April 1977; Chad Walsh, in *Washington Post*, 22 May 1977; "Recent American Poetry" by Andrew Waterman, in *PN Review 8* (Manchester), 1978; interview in *New England Review* (Hanover, New Hampshire), Spring 1979; "Frederick Morgan's 'Tarot' " by Sydney Lea, in *Southern Review* (Baton Rouge, Louisiana), Autumn 1979; *Harvard Guide to Contemporary American Writing* edited by Daniel Hoffman, Cambridge, Massachusetts, Harvard Univer-sity Press, 1979; "To Articulate Sweet Sounds Together" by Alfred Corn, in *Washington Post Book World*, 2 March 1980; James Finn Cotter, in *America* (New York), 22 March 1980; "Mother of Pain, Mother of Beauty" by David Sanders, in *Tar River Poetry* (Greenville, North Carolina), Spring 1980; "Poems of Imagination and Fancy" by Richard Tillinghast, in *Sewanee Review* (Tennessee), Summer 1980; "Three Poets in Mid-Career" by Dana Gioia, in *Southern Review* (Baton Rouge, Louisiana), Summer 1981; G.E. Murray, in *Chicago Sun-Times*, 4 July 1982; in *The Reaper 6* (Evansville, Indiana), Autumn 1982.

*   *   *

Of the various strains in Frederick Morgan's poetry, two predominate: the legendary-fabulous and the celebratory-con-solatory. In addition, he has a number of fanciful and whimsical poems, personal poems in various modes—nostalgic memories, grateful love songs to his wife, companionable conversations with children—and thoughtful poems that explore the natural world and man's place in it.

In its purest form, the legendary-fabulous is the mode of *The Tarot of Cornelius Agrippa*, a set of 22 little fables of rogues, sorceresses, magicians, kings, queens, princesses, and other animate and inanimate denizens of fairyland and the Tarot pack.

The fables are cast as prose poems, but in very loose rhythms and the unsophisticated language of children's stories. Indeed, Morgan's images for the imaginative and religious projections of adult sensibility often have the simplicity and naivety of a child's vision:

> Child, you will die; but between that breath and this—
> now at this moment, unless you put her off—
> eternity outspreads her glittering fields
> where animals play and rivers dance in the sun:
> mostly invisible to the time-bent mind....

The 21st poem of *A Book of Change*, from which these lines are taken, is in what I am calling the celebratory-consolatory mode. Morgan is engaged in such poems with deep emotional and spiritual issues—here the paradise within, informed by the "glowing, sacred center." Further, he is committed to *sharing* his insights into life, death, love, time, a spiritualized natural world, eternity, and God in the commendable hope that such insights will help us with our perplexities and sorrows. Given his personal losses, he might well say with Walt Whitman, "I am the man, I suffer'd, I was there," and with D.H. Lawrence, "Look! We have come through!"

Many of these poems, however, seem to be conceived less as art than as communication—ways of sharing joys and sorrows, of stating opinions and attitudes, of asserting faith, hope, and charity (or sexual love). An instructive comparison could be made, for example, between the glittering generalities of the passage just quoted and the poetically charged specifics of the analogous section in William Carlos Williams's "Asphodel, That Greeny Flower"—the opening of the "Coda," in which Williams meditates strenuously on the "huge gap/between the flash/and the thunderstroke." Of course Morgan can't be faulted for not being Williams. It's just that, given the worth of the enterprise, one hopes for more of the poetic development manifested between his first and second books.

One cluster in particular in *Poems of the Two Worlds* has a spare clarity and evocativeness that demonstrate Morgan's mastery of his medium: "The Old Days," "The Priest," "Hideyoshi," and "Maitreya." "Hideyoshi," certainly one of Morgan's best poems, performs the unusual feat of making believable a character in whom love of violence and love of beauty are integrated in the interests of justice and spiritual wholeness. On the one hand, the Japanese warrior-hero of the poem cuts his enemy to pieces; on the other, he makes a flower arrangement out of emblems of war:

> So he took a bucket, and his horse's bit
> (which he hung by one ring from the bucket-handle)
> and rigged them into a flower-holder,
>
> then with his bloody sword
> cut wild blossoms and grasses
> and in an hour's silence
> composed a subtle and delicate combination...
>
> Those whom he had conquered
> he now must judge:
> he wished a mind clean-purged
> of violence and ardor.

The effect is rather as if one of Yeats's bitter and violent men who "longed" for "sweetness...night and day" ("Ancestral Houses") had somehow, on Morgan's page, completed himself.

—Sally M. Gall

MORGAN, (Colin) Pete(r).   British.   Born in Leigh, Lancashire, 7 June 1939. Educated at Normanton School, Buxton, Derbyshire, 1950-57. Served in the British Army Infantry, 1958-63. Married Kate Smith in 1965; one daughter and one son. Free-lance writer: creative writing appointments for Northern Arts, and at Loughborough University, 1975-77; also a television writer. Member of Literature Panel of Yorkshire Arts, 1973-76, and Northern Arts. Recipient: Scottish Arts Council bursary, 1969; Arts Council of Great Britain award, 1973. Agent: David Higham Associates, 5-8 Lower John Street, London W1R 4HA. Address: c/o Secker and Warburg Ltd., 54 Poland Street, London W1V 3DF, England.

PUBLICATIONS

Verse

A Big Hat or What?   Edinburgh, Kevin Press, 1968.
Loss of Two Anchors.   Edinburgh, Kevin Press, 1970.
Poems for Shortie.   Solihull, Warwickshire, Aquila, 1973.
The Grey Mare Being the Better Steed.   London, Secker and Warburg, 1973.
I See You on My Arm.   Todmorden, Lancashire, ARC, 1975.
Ring Song.   Gulfport, Florida, Konglomerati, 1977.
The Poet's Deaths.   Manchester, North West Arts, 1977.
Alpha Beta.   Ilkley, Yorkshire, Scolar Press, 1979.
The Spring Collection.   London, Secker and Warburg, 1979.
One Greek Alphabet.   Sunderland, Ceolfrith, 1980.
Reporting Back.   Leamington, Warwickshire, Other Branch, 1983.
A Winter Visitor.   London, Secker and Warburg, 1984.
The Pete Morgan Poetry Pack.   Ilkley, Yorkshire, Proem, 1984.

Plays

Still the Same Old Harry (produced Edinburgh, 1972).
All the Voices Going Away (produced Ilkley, Yorkshire, 1979).

Screenplay (documentary): *Gardens by the Sea,* 1973.

Television Documentaries: *Coming On Strong* series, 1974; *Here Comes Everybody* series, 1975; *Between the Heather and the Sea,* 1982; *A Voyage Between Two Seas,* 1983.

Other

Editor, *C'mon Everybody: Poetry of the Dance.*   London, Corgi, 1969.

*   *   *

The first words in Pete Morgan's Introduction to his anthology, *Poetry of the Dance*, are: "Plato said it—'The dance is god-like in itself. It is a gift from heaven.'" These words also describe Pete Morgan's poetry at its best. As his poems bound along, or dance, with effortless ease, and as they present their innocent pictures of knights, stallions, "the bull with the rumpus horn," my Moll and partner Joe, the impression is of something given, not made. His poems seem to be immediately original without any special seeking after difference, yet their origins are evident. They begin in the world of nursery rhymes. Nursery rhymes have a known audience which they captivate. Equally Pete Morgan poems have an audience or rather many audiences which respond to his excellent readings. Some of the poems are

well suited for ballad-style music settings. Yet despite the immediacy of communication and surface simplicity of the poems,
beneath is a psychological curiosity and a sharpness of perception which reveal the poet has not sold out his intelligence.
"The White Stallion" begins:

> There was that horse
> that I found then
> my white one
> big tall and lean as
> and mean as hell

The supple movement, the momentary halt in the penultimate
line, and the unexpected drive of the last line, is the work of a
craftsman who has learned from, amongst others, Auden,
though the last poems of Yeats have also been caught in Morgan's ear to his advantage. More significant perhaps is the use he
makes of the commonplace "mean as hell." He rejoices in the
lively vernacular phrase. There is so much delight in his first
book, *A Big Hat or What?*, in such poems as "My Moll and
Partner Joe," "Whoops! I nearly smiled again," "Elegy for
Arthur Prance," and "My enemies have sweet voices," that the
subtle tones and undertones may not be regarded.

By the mid-1970's, a different poet, taking off directly from his
physical environment, emerges, culminating in the singular
appreciation of the life about him of "A Winter Visitor." The
high style has been replaced by a reflective, conversational voice:
"The first thin snow of winter/ Settles our differences/ And that's
what's good about it." This is the norm in which Morgan takes
account of Robin Hood Bay, its history, some geology, a few of
its people, and happenings such as the birth of a calf:

> There's nothing giving! At her rump
> The folds of skin are bloody, raw.
> Her calf, still pinioned in that trap,
> Sticks out a thick tongue, clears a snout
>
> That sniffs and learns the smell of May.
> Already ancient though not born
> The brown eyes—wide intelligent—
> Look into mine for something more
>
> Than I can ever give to him.
> Then like a curded milk he comes—
> A slabby from a bottle' neck
> Shuddering across the floor.

Despite the absorption into the intimate sensations of the birth,
Morgan can still suggest the more detached, professional character of Shillah:

> I start the engine, drive away,
> Bucking on the ruts of earth,
> From Shillah picking petty faults
> With what looked marvellous to me.

There is a scrupulous honesty in Morgan's dealing with the facts.
The continuity of nature is projected against the precariousness
of human life: "We need to know just where we stand, what
odds/ Are stacked against us by which gods." Ultimately respect
and affection for the natural world, and for its people, including
his son, whom he teaches not to bring down the conkers from the
chestnut tree with sticks but to wait for a "garnering and gathering," and then:

> From that ripe minute when they fell

> Into my son's good sight and he
> Comes singing home
> From gentle harvesting.

This is an impressive achievement, and a very taking one.

—George Bruce

MORGAN, Robert. British. Born in Glamorgan, Wales, 17
April 1921. Educated at Fircroft College, Birmingham, 1949-51;
Bognor Regis College of Education, Sussex, 1951-53, Dip.Ed.
1953; Southampton University, 1969-70, Advanced Diploma in
Special Education. Married Jean Elizabeth Morgan in 1953; two
daughters. Coal miner in South Wales, 1936-48; teacher in pri-
mary schools, 1951-64; Head of Remedial Department, Cow-
plain Secondary School, 1964-74; Advisor in Special Education,
Hampshire Education Authority, 1974-81. Since 1981, full-time
writer. Painter for many years: individual shows—Plestor Gallery,
Selborne, Wiltshire, 1966; Mermaid Theatre, London, 1967;
Winchester Art Gallery, 1972; Hiscock Gallery, Portsmouth,
1976; Surrey University, 1978; Southampton University, 1979.
Formerly, Art Organizer for Welsh Artists Workshop, Cardiff.
Address: 72 Anmore Avenue, Denmead, Portsmouth, Hamp-
shire PO7 6NT, England.

PUBLICATIONS

Verse

*The Night's Prison: Poems, and Rainbow Valley: A Play for
    Broadcasting.* London, Hart Davis, 1967.
Poems and Extracts. Exeter, Exeter University Press, 1968.
For Lofthouse. Richmond, Surrey, Keepsake Press, 1973.
On the Banks of the Cynon. Todmorden, Lancashire, Arc,
    1974.
The Storm. Llandybie, Dyfed, Christopher Davies, 1974.
The Pass. Portsmouth, Indigo, 1976.
Impressions. London, Davis Poynter, 1981.
Poems and Drawings. Portsmouth, Indigo, 1984.

Plays

Rainbow Valley (broadcast, 1967). Included in *The Night's
    Prison*, 1967.
The Master Miners (produced Cardiff, 1971). Published in
    Anglo-Welsh Review 47 (Pembroke Dock, Wales), 1971.
Fragments of a Dream (produced Cardiff, 1971). Published in
    Anglo-Welsh Review 54 (Pembroke Dock, Wales), 1972.
Voices in the Dark. Todmorden, Lancashire, Arc, 1976.

Radio Plays: *Rainbow Valley*, 1967; *The Master Miners*, 1972.

Other

My Lamp Still Burns. Llandysul, Dyfed, Gomer, 1981.

*

Bibliography: exhibition catalogue, Winchester, Southern Arts
Association, 1972.

Critical Studies: by M.H.G. Norman, in *Anglo-Welsh Review 40* (Pembroke Dock, Wales), 1969; Preface to exhibition catalogue, Winchester, Southern Arts Association, 1972.

Robert Morgan comments:

I was born in the Cynon Valley, South Wales, a deep, narrow valley with a polluted river, railway sidings and terraced cottages perched on the mountainside. There were seven coal-mines within sight from the cottage where I lived.

My father worked as a coal miner for over 50 years. His father and grandfather had also been coal miners, so it seemed natural that I should become a miner. To me, at 14, the mine was an Aladdin's cave with fairy lights. I began work down the mine a few days after I left school and I stayed a miner until the age of 26.

Those 12 years in the earth's hive, working like a mole in the dark left their marks, some of which can never be erased. There are memories of pit life I cherish, and some I try to forget.

I wrote when I was a miner, not poems, but short stories, some of which were published when I was still a miner. I began writing poems several years after I left the mine, and I must have written over a hundred and fifty poems connected with mines and miners. In such poems I recalled the experiences of the lamplit mine where I worked. I wrote of the dangers, the comradeship, the tragedy of accidents, terraced cottages and derelict mines on a spoiled landscape.

I have been involved in the teaching of children with learning difficulties and I have dipped into this experience for poems. I now live in a Hampshire village where I am absorbing the countryside's landscape of trees, wild flowers, animal and bird life, and these things are also influencing my work.

I suppose I could be labelled an autobiographical poet, as I write directly from my personal experiences, and as I am not able to shed completely my early experiences as a miner I still write the occasional mining poem.

*   *   *

With his collection *The Night's Prison*, Robert Morgan produced a fine document about the South Wales coalfields. He was a miner for 12 years and wrote out of real experience, unlike some other Anglo-Welsh poets who lived in the mining areas but never went down a pit. No other poet since the late Idris Davies has written quite so vivid and bitter a tract about life in the depressed valleys. Morgan sums up much of the essence of his work in these lines:

> I know there are bright places
> Under the brow of the hill slag
> But it was in the shadows I
> Wandered where the truth was thickest.

He has been criticised for returning endlessly to the "oblique, remembered streets" and the "stale shadows / of burning hills," but perhaps such repetition is inevitable, given the limitations of the subject-matter. Also, being very much *inside* the experience, he tends to rush to emotional climaxes, anxious to *move* the reader, to make him share his own harsh memories. The fatal shadow of Dylan Thomas falls on these lines, too: "He lies in his city room in the bandage / of dark clinging to runaway years / of green time in the mist of memories."

But, despite the occasional uneven, untidy lapses, the clichéd symbols and repetitive vocabulary ("buckled hands," "musical silence," and "silica" often recur), Morgan's poems are usually forceful and, indeed, informative in the best sense when he concentrates on tight description (reminding us that he is also a talented painter and sculptor):

> We are charmed by thin mice
> Eating crumbs and blind
> Flies dancing in the lamp's
> Cold light and we are always
> Curious of the black, squeezed
> Roads behind cross-sticks where
> Our grandfathers worked as boys.

Among his fully effective poems are "Gomer," "Farewell on a Wet Day," and "Blood Donor," which are chiselled and steely, far superior to some of his looser, hastier constructions. One of his most anthologised pieces is "The Carpenter," which is not about Wales at all and so escapes from the pull of inheritance and Morgan's customary burning necessity to remain faithful to his past and to his dead comrades. This is a fine poem, and so, too, is his long broadcast play *Rainbow Valley*, where he has room to spread himself, as it were, capturing all the simple emotion and the stark tragedy through individual voices naming their own fears and memories.

One still cannot say whether his mining past, which he has already looted and ransacked, will continue to sustain Robert Morgan's work, though he has written an excellent poem, "Maladjusted Boys," and others stemming from his experience as a compassionate teacher of backward children. The mining seam could be worked out, and he may have to look elsewhere for nourishment to avoid becoming trapped and sealed within a monotonous theme. Even the bleak but dignified history of the Welsh pits cannot bear too much repeating, and Morgan has already achieved much by leaving a small monument to them in his poetry. His vitality, faith, honesty and sincerity are unquestioned, and the possible extension of his range may be hinted at in these, his own words:

> The background is overgrown with dreams
> And the horizon fades into smooth tips
> Sprinkled with the blood of coal.
> But the weight of time strengthens
> The corner stones of my heritage.

—John Tripp

MOSS, Howard. American. Born in New York City, 22 January 1922. Educated at the University of Michigan, Ann Arbor, 1939-40; University of Wisconsin, Madison, 1940-43, B.A. 1943; Harvard University, Cambridge, Massachusetts, 1944; Columbia University, New York, 1946. Book reviewer, *Time*, New York, 1944; Instructor in English, Vassar College, Poughkeepsie, New York, 1944-46. Since 1948, Poetry Editor, *The New Yorker*. Taught at Washington University, St. Louis, 1972, Barnard College, New York, 1976, Columbia University, New York, 1977, 1981, University of California, Irvine, 1979, and University of Houston, 1980. Recipient: Jeannette Sewell Davis Award (*Poetry*, Chicago), 1944; American Academy award, 1968; Ingram Merrill Foundation grant, 1972; National Book Award, 1972; Brandeis University Creative Arts Award, 1983; National Endowment for the Arts award, 1984. Member, American Academy. Address: 27 West 10th Street, New York, New York 10011, U.S.A.

PUBLICATIONS

Verse

The Wound and the Weather. New York, Reynal, 1946.
The Toy Fair. New York, Scribner, 1954.
A Swimmer in the Air. New York, Scribner, 1957.
A Winter Come, A Summer Gone: Poems 1946-1960. New York, Scribner, 1960.
Finding Them Lost and Other Poems. New York, Scribner, and London, Macmillan, 1965.
Second Nature. New York, Atheneum, 1968.
Selected Poems. New York, Atheneum, 1971.
Chekhov. New York, Albondocani Press, 1972.
Travel. A Window. New York, Albondocani Press, 1973.
Buried City. New York, Atheneum, 1975.
A Swim Off the Rocks: Light Verse. New York, Atheneum, 1976.
Tigers and Other Lilies (for children). New York, Atheneum, 1977.
Notes from the Castle. New York, Atheneum, 1979.
Rules of Sleep. New York, Atheneum, 1984.

Plays

The Folding Green (produced Cambridge, Massachusetts, 1954; New York, 1964). Included in *Two Plays*, 1980.
The Oedipus Mah-Jongg Scandal (produced New York, 1968).
The Palace at 4 A.M. (produced East Hampton, New York, 1972). Included in *Two Plays*, 1980.
Two Plays: The Palace at 4 A.M., and The Folding Green. New York, Sheep Meadow Press, 1980.

Other

The Magic Lantern of Marcel Proust. New York, Macmillan, 1962; London, Faber, 1963.
Writing Against Time: Critical Essays and Reviews. New York, Morrow, 1969.
Instant Lives (satire). New York, Saturday Review Press, 1974.
Whatever Is Moving (essays). Boston, Little Brown, 1981.

Editor, *Keats.* New York, Dell, 1952.
Editor, *The Nonsense Books of Edward Lear.* New York, New American Library, 1964.
Editor, *The Poet's Story.* New York, Macmillan, 1973; London, Collier Macmillan, 1974.
Editor, *New York: Poems.* New York, Avon, 1980.

Translator, *The Cemetery by the Sea,* by Paul Valéry. New York, Auralia Press, 1985.

*

Manuscript Collections: Syracuse University Library, New York; Lilly Library, University of Indiana, Bloomington.

Critical Studies: *Alone with America* by Richard Howard, New York, Atheneum, 1969, London, Thames and Hudson, 1970, revised edition, Atheneum, 1980; "Recent Poetry: Exiles and Disinterments" by Laurence Lieberman, in *Yale Review* (New Haven, Connecticut), Autumn 1971; "A Gathering of Poets" by Richard Shramm, in *Western Humanities Review* (Salt Lake City), Autumn 1972.

*   *   *

Howard Moss has had a rich career not only as a poet but as literary critic, playwright, and editor. As poetry editor of *The New Yorker* since 1948, he has been a quiet and eloquent resource for poets whom he has helped, and for that reason, perhaps, his advocacy of his own poetry has not been so passionate and replete with concrete service as his devotion to the careers of those he has admired and sponsored, e.g., Elizabeth Bishop and Richard Wilbur. Partly as a consequence of this role, his own talent has been often underrated. Yet he has with consistent productivity—rivalled only by poets like A.R. Ammons and Robert Penn Warren—turned out volume after volume and has dutifully and with impressive scholarship written criticism on both Marcel Proust and contemporary poets. He has edited books and written plays that have been well-received in production. He is, in short, an American man-of-letters in a sense largely missing from our literary culture. Without people like Howard Moss we could, indeed, have no literary culture. One might, in a given decade, quarrel with his tastes, but few would fail to come to a respect for the ardor and maturity reflected in that taste.

As poet and editor Moss, has often surprised the public with new work or talent expressed in a manner indicative of new breakthroughs in his values and definitions of the major goals of poetry. A good example would be his sudden advocacy of the work of Paul Blackburn some 20 years ago at a time when Blackburn was neglected. Moss gave Blackburn's career a new pride and incentive, and helped him reach a wide audience. In his own poems Moss has often surprised those who might have typecast him as an urban poet. Since he has often written occasional and humorous verse, those readers who might have expected *only* satire or occasional verse were surprised when his own poems came up to the standards of W.H. Auden and Elizabeth Bishop. Yet what I value most in his work is not the technical virtuosity, often apparent, but the relaxed and confident discursiveness in poems like "The Restaurant Window," where art hides art and observations are richly shared, offhand and intimate:

> A time-lapse camera might do it justice,
> This street outside the restaurant window,
> Feeling hurrying by one side
> And thought on the other.
> Gradually night sponges up vision,
> A moment so made up of other moments
> No one can tell one famous variation
> From another. Soom they will become the theme.
> It is then that the power of form is felt
> (Could it have been, all along, the subject matter?)
> Connecting everything, the ginkgo's gesture
> And the ginkgo, even permitting
> The streetlamp turning on every evening
> Its one small circle of illumination....

Such poems have obviously influenced poets like John Ashbery and James Merrill. Thus the almost communal generosity of Moss as poet and editor is doubly beneficial. His line "Love is the only place we live," is also an assertion of unconditional love for great poetry—whether it is one's own or another's.

Howard Moss has written many poems that catch the tonalities of particular places and seasons. His elegies are memorable, e.g., "September Elegy":

> The dead undo our sleep so they can rest.
>   Their August vanishes: the beachy dreams
>   Of sea grass, naked limbs, the stuttering wave...

Yet contra-indicated bodies move
On space...the summer sprays, the water birds
   Depart, but some things never disappear,

The faces of the dead: one drowned, one hurled,
   Drunk, through a subway window to be smashed
Against an iron post, one burned to ash
   In Key West, Florida, and one whose heart,
Clogged up, destroyed the finest wit of all.
   The world of pain is one great hospital.

Profoundly visual and musical, Moss understands the vital role of art and fantasy, and yet often expresses anxiety about disillusionment: "And thus we might arrive at the Impossible: / That place where there is nothing left to see" ("Movies for the Home"). In a statement included in Engle and Langland's *Poet's Choice*, discussing the creation of "Going to Sleep in the Country," Moss speaks of the pleasure of a poem that seemed to arrive "without struggle, apparently without forethought, as if it has been waiting in the wings." The poem was "a kind of reward, as if the struggle and labor of other poems had paid off in this almost effortless one, as if a great deal of conscious training had finally been put to use without my having to do much more than transcribe what the past had stored up."

—David Ray

MOSS, Stanley. American. Born in New York City, 21 June 1935. Educated at Trinity College, Hartford, Connecticut, B.A.; Yale University, New Haven, Connecticut, M.A. Served in the United States Navy: Purple Heart. Married 1) Anna Maria Vandellos Nicholson in 1953 (divorced, 1960); 2) Jane Zech in 1967. Since 1959, President, Stanley Moss & Co., art dealers, New York; since 1977, Publisher, Sheep Meadow Press, New York. Formerly, Poetry Editor, *New American Review*, New York. Recipient: Rockefeller grant, 1967. Address: Sheep Meadow Press, 2 West 67th Street, New York, New York, 10023, U.S.A.

PUBLICATIONS

Verse

The Wrong Angel. New York, Macmillan, 1966.
The Wrong Angel (augmented edition). London, Anvil Press Poetry, 1969.
Skull of Adam. New York, Horizon Press, and London, Anvil Press Poetry, 1979.

*   *   *

Skull of Adam, Stanley Moss's second volume of poems, has solidified a fine reputation that he earned with seperate poems in such outlets as *The Times Literary Supplement*, *The New Yorker*, *The New Republic*, *Encounter*, and *The Nation*, and especially with the publication of his first collection, *The Wrong Angel*. That earlier collection reflected his capacity to imbue a moment—biblical, present, any moment—with an exquisite sense of immediacy, often with an ironic ominousness. Thus, for example, even as he watched his father, Moss observed: "Death hooks over the corners of his lips. / The wrong angel takes over

the lesson." The trait was reflected powerfully in "Another Reply for Pompey," a perversion of the traditional tale of Pompey's respect for hospitality when he refused his captain permission to cut a ship from its mooring to send his sleeping guests, Caesar, Antony, and Lepidus, to oblivion. In the Moss version, which was tinged with characteristic tough humor, Pompey began with modest enough malevolence by ordering the cutting of the mooring. As his sense of decency was further diminished, in what Moss made a powerful account of becalmed ambition whipped up by a rising gale, Pompey even troubled to have the throats of his guests cut—an act which, by that stage, he was able to rationalize without much difficulty.

Moss has always looked at the world with both love and the sadness of dismay—a combination that arouses in him a great sense of responsibility. Those simultaneously and paradoxically held emotions of his have grown more intense in *Skull of Adam*, though Moss still often manages to keep the trace of smile on his lips when he expresses them. He goes around carrying "the law under...[his] arm like bread" ("Kangaroo"), reading it aloud with warmth, power, good nature whether he is writing whimsically about excrement or seriously about his being the ghost of his father. Perhaps the simple lines from "Prayer for Zero Mostel (1915-1977)" best resound with Moss's view: "If you love life / you simply can't believe / how bad it is." He walks his audience along the brink between the undeniable and the love.

—Alan R. Shucard

MOTION, Andrew. British. Born in London, 20 October 1952. Educated at Radley College, 1965-70; University College, Oxford, B.A. 1975. Editor, *Poetry Review*, London, 1980-82. Since 1982, Poetry Editor, Chatto and Windus, publishers, London. Recipient: Eric Gregory Award, 1978; Cholmondeley Award, 1979; Arvon-*Observer* prize, 1981; John Llewelyn Rhys prize, 1984. Agent: Pat Kavanagh, A.D. Peters, 10 Buckingham Street, London WC2N 6BU. Address: Chatto and Windus, 40 William IV Street, London WC2N 4DF, England.

PUBLICATIONS

Verse

Goodnestone: A Sequence. London, Workshop Press, 1972.
Inland. Burford, Oxfordshire, Cygnet Press, 1976.
The Pleasure Steamers. Manchester, Carcanet, 1978.
Independence. Edinburgh, Salamander Press, 1981.
Secret Narratives. Edinburgh, Salamander Press, 1983.
Dangerous Play: Poems 1974-1984. Edinburgh, Salamander Press, 1984.

Other

The Poetry of Edward Thomas. London, Routledge, 1980.
Philip Larkin. London, Methuen, 1982.

Editor, with Blake Morrison, *The Penguin Book of Contemporary British Poetry.* London, Penguin, 1982.

*   *   *

Andrew Motion is one of a group of younger contemporary English poets whose work reveals a fascination with "narrative"—with, that is, the potential effectiveness of refracting some kind of story or plot through an essentially lyric form, or sequence. His first volume, *The Pleasure Steamers*, contained one such lengthy sequence, "Inland," which, in the character of a fenland villager of the early 17th century, told the story of the introduction of enclosures from the point of view of someone dispossessed by them. The main effort of the sequence is to point up the fragility and brittleness of the personal life when set against its controlling context in the public world:

> Tomorrow, high tides will press
> our future from us
> back into emptiness;
> so now, unpin your hair,
> open your dress.

This becomes a characteristic procedure in Motion's work: effects of pathos are created by the attempt at some kind of interiority of empathy with the sufferings of fictionalised characters drawn usually from episodes of English history: the 17th century fen country, the Second World War, the end of the British Empire in India.

In selecting such episodes for his material, Motion—who has written a critical book on Edward Thomas—reveals himself as a quintessentially "English" poet: the word "England" echoes through some of his work. In one poem, it is an England which "turns out of the sun"; and the very powerful sense of loss in Motion's work is intimately responsive to the experience of a nation, or a class, undergoing the anxieties and uncertainties of post-imperial and post-colonial withdrawal. This sense of loss also derives, however, from the tragic experience of Motion's own adolescence, when his mother had a riding accident and suffered a coma which lasted until her death ten years later. This grim circumstance recurs in a number of different forms in Motion's work, and particularly in the third section of *The Pleasure Steamers*, where the effects of pathos are in complete consonance with those of "Inland":

> Whatever time might bring,
> all my journeys take me
> back to this dazzling dark:
> I watch my shadow ahead
> plane across open fields,
> out of my reach for ever,
> but setting towards your bed
> to find itself waiting there.

The "narratives" in Motion's poems, then, take their particular edge of unease from the way their predominant emotions act as some kind of filter or mask for the poet's own. Their obliquities and *lacunae*—features remarked on by a number of reviewers—avoid direct statement and leave a large part of the act of interpretation open to the reader. Half way, perhaps, between personal lyric and dramatic monologue, such poems as "The Letters," "Resident at the Club," and the superbly complicated and inclusive "Independence" (whose narrator is a retired Anglo-Indian widower, whose wife has died in childbirth) return again and again to images of loss, abandonment, and estrangement and to a fundamental preoccupation with the final human loss, death, and its human response, grief. The poem "Open Secrets," which opens his recent volume, *Secret Narratives*, explores Motion's own self-consciousness about these procedures, in a way that suggests how some further intensification of his own narrative strategies will be the future development of his work:

> He was never
> myself, this boy, but I know if I tell you his story
> you'll think we are one and the same: both of us hiding
> in fictions which say what we cannot admit to ourselves.

—Neil Corcoran

MTSHALI, (Mbuyiseni) Oswald. Name formerly Oswald Joseph Mtshali. South African. Born in Vryheid, Natal, 17 January 1940. Educated at Queen of the Angels Primary School and Inkamana High School, Vryheid; Columbia University, New York, M.A. in creative writing, M.Ed.; currently doctoral candidate, Rhodes University, Grahamstown. Married to Dinah Mtshali; four children. Driver for an engineering firm, 1963-65; after 1965, messenger and general delivery man for a Johannesburg investment company. Currently, Deputy Headmaster, Pace Commercial College, Jabulani, Soweto. Columnist, *Rand Daily Mail*, Johannesburg, 1972. Address: 5803 Zone 5, Pimville 1808, Soweto, South Africa.

PUBLICATIONS

Verse

Sounds of a Cowhide Drum. Johannesburg, Renoster, 1971; London, Oxford University Press, and New York, Third Press, 1972.
Fireflames. Pietermaritzburg, Natal, Shuter and Shooter, 1980; Westport, Connecticut, Lawrence Hill, 1983.

Play

Money Makes Madness, with Barney Simon and others, music by M. Davashe and others, adaptation of *Volpone* by Ben Jonson (produced Johannesburg, 1972).

*

Bibliography: *Oswald Mbuyiseni Mtshali, South African Poet: An Annotated Bibliography* by Gillian Goldstein, Johannesburg, University of the Witwatersrand Department of Bibliography, 1974.

Oswald Mtshali comments:

I am neither a Romantic nor a Traditionalist. Maybe I am a socially involved poet of South Africa as Charles Dickens was a socially involved novelist of England.

I consider Lorca, Allen Ginsberg and Yevtushenko as some of the poets I admire. I draw my themes from my life as I live and experience it. I write in the free verse form because it allows me more freedom in expression without the restriction of metre and rhyme. I depict the life of humanity as a whole as reflected in my environment, Mofolo Village; my community, Soweto; my society, Johannesburg; my country, South Africa. As an aspirant black poet in South Africa, I have no model poet on whom to base my style.

* * *

Oswald Mtshali's *Sounds of a Cowhide Drum* sold over 10,000 copies in South Africa in less than a year. Most of his poems deal with racial tensions. Some, as he says, punch "wildly at the immense powers," but many more successfully control narrative, imagery and the details of linguistic connotation in witty, anecdotal sketches of individuals under pressure or of bitterly ludicrous social injustices. More interestingly still, some longer poems, such as "Snowfall on Mount Frere," achieve a mode of emblematic narration (not unlike the Irish *aisling*) in which political pressure is recast in terms of the natural landscape of the oppressed country. Mtshali's ability to control larger structures, together with his acute visual memory, exploited in vivid analogies—"A newly-born calf / is like oven-baked bread / steaming under a cellophane cover" or "The skin was pale and taut / like a glove on a doctor's hand"—could lead to developments in his work that will make him not only a man with an urgent and well-spoken message, but a poet with a unique voice of international validity.

—Anne Cluysenaar

MULDOON, Paul. Irish. Born in County Armagh, Northern Ireland, 20 June 1951. Educated at St. Patrick's College, Armagh; Queen's University, Belfast. Radio producer, BBC Northern Ireland. Lives in Northern Ireland. Recipient: Eric Gregory Award, 1972; Geoffrey Faber Memorial Prize, 1982. Address: c/o Faber and Faber Ltd., 3 Queen Square, London WC1N 3AU, England.

PUBLICATIONS

Verse

Knowing My Place. Belfast, Ulsterman, 1971.
New Weather. London, Faber, 1973.
Spirit of Dawn. Belfast, Ulsterman, 1975.
Mules. London, Faber, 1977.
Names and Addresses. Belfast, Ulsterman, 1978.
Why Brownlee Left. London, Faber, 1980.
Immram. Dublin, Gallery Press, 1980.
Quoof. London, Faber, 1983.

Other

Editor, *The Scrake of Dawn: Poems by Young People from Northern Ireland*. Belfast, Blackstaff Press, 1979.

*   *   *

Paul Muldoon achieved maturity early in life. What is now a rare pamphlet, engagingly entitled *Knowing My Place*, was issued when the author was twenty. Even then, we were listening to a true professional:

> Starlings bring their acquired rococo
> To the flat greys of the city.
> Every evening they line the high buildings,
> Emphasise eaves and window ledges
> With their actual gift for chiaroscuro....

That is just the first stanza of a poem called "Belfast," never reprinted. The inner lines are almost free of scansion, yet there is still the suggestion of a lilting pentametric structure. The stanza

itself is secured as a whole by the pararhyme, "rococo" / "chiaroscuro," linking the first and last lines. One might also notice the way in which the pictorial metaphor—"flat greys" / "line" / "emphasise"—makes for exactitude without succumbing to lushness. In little, we see here a confidence of technique which lays the foundation for better-known poems.

The first major collection, *New Weather*, came out when Muldoon was just 22 years old. It was plain that here was a highly accomplished poet. Yet there was a central paradox in his work even then that has persisted until now. The most careful artistry is used to communicate distance, apartness, departure. *New Weather* portrays love, for instance, in terms of fragmentation. In "Wind and Tree" Muldoon writes:

> One tree will take
> Another in her arms and hold.
>
> Their branches that are grinding
> Madly together and together,
>
> It is not real fire.
> They are breaking each other....

He himself voices a wish to be a single tree, going nowhere. This is characteristic. Elsewhere he identifies with the hedgehog, the goldfish, a lamb stillborn—"better dead than dyed...."

The second collection, *Mules*, brings events up against the reader more immediately than tended to be the case in the first book. "A tree would give its neighbour the elbow/And both look the other way...." This change of emphasis is perhaps induced by the disaffections of Northern Ireland, where Muldoon has always lived. In the guise of the Mexican revolutionary Pancho Villa, advising a young poet, he says "There's more to living in this country/Than stars and horses, pigs and trees...." One would guess as much from the poems in *Mules*. Even so, nobody would call Muldoon a political writer, and some of his triumphs are those of formalism. The mule's afterbirth—"Trailed like some fine, silk parachute,/That we would know from what heights it fell...."

The third collection, *Why Brownlee Left*, is an astonishingly good book in spite of the fact that the protagonists of various poems are seen in characteristic attitudes of melancholia and isolation. The successful lover in "Bran" remembers his past: "He weeps for the boy on the small farm/Who takes an oatmeal Labrador/In his arms,/Who knows all there is of rapture." There the poem ends, tautly and precisely. The assonance of "Labrador"/"rapture" betokens a faultless ear. Consider, too, the patterning of "The Boundary Commission":

> Today he remarked how a shower of rain
>
> Had stopped so cleanly across Golightly's lane
> It might have been a wall of glass
> That had toppled over. He stood there, for ages,
> To wonder which side, if any, he should be on.

The poem, as ever, ends with a satisfying click. It is not just a technical matter; nevertheless, the poem engages, so to speak, while the persona remains aloof.

In *Quoof*, the fourth collection, this disparity between persona and technique is an order of being. The characteristic attitude is a kind of spiritual apartheid:

> An hotel room in New York City
> with a girl who spoke hardly any English,
> my hand on her breast

like the smouldering one-off spoor of the yeti
or some other shy beast
that has yet to enter the language.

With all this apartness, the patterning is close. Notice the way in which the "yet to" of the last line picks up the "yeti" of two lines before. This is intimacy of a sort in spite of the persona remaining aloof from anything he touches. How can so elegant a sensibility enter the arena of communication without foundering under its own bewilderment? Yet Muldoon has effected such an entry and has survived as one of the true originals of our time. He was 32 years of age when he published *Quoof*. Already he is an Old Master.

—Philip Hobsbaum

MURPHY, Richard. Irish. Born in County Mayo, 6 August 1927. Educated at Canterbury Cathedral Choir School (Cathedral Chorister, 1940); King's School, Canterbury (Milner Scholar), 1941-42; Wellington College, Berkshire, 1943-44; Magdalen College, Oxford, 1945-48, M.A. 1948; the Sorbonne, Paris, 1954-55. Married Patricia Avis in 1955 (divorced, 1959); one daughter. Director, English School, Canea, Crete, 1953-54; Writer-in-Residence, University of Virginia, Charlottesville, 1965; Visiting Fellow, Reading University, Berkshire, 1968; Compton Lecturer in Poetry, University of Hull, Yorkshire, 1969; O'Connor Professor of Literature, Colgate University, Hamilton, New York, 1971; Visiting Professor of Poetry, Bard College, Annandale-on-Hudson, New York, 1972, 1974, Princeton University, New Jersey, 1974-75, University of Iowa, Iowa City, 1976-77, Syracuse University, New York, 1977-78, Catholic University, Washington, D.C., 1984, and Pacific Lutheran University, Tacoma, Washington, 1985. Recipient: AE Memorial Award, 1951; Guinness Award, 1962; Arts Council of Great Britain bursary, 1967, award, 1976; Marten Toonder Award, 1980; American-Irish Foundation award, 1983. Fellow, Royal Society of Literature (UK), 1968. Member, Aosdana. Address: Knockbrack, Glenalua Road, Killiney, County Dublin, Ireland.

PUBLICATIONS

Verse

The Archaeology of Love. Dublin, Dolmen Press, 1955.
Sailing to an Island. Privately printed, 1955.
The Woman of the House: An Elegy. Dublin, Dolmen Press, 1959.
Three Irish Poets, with John Montague and Thomas Kinsella. Dublin, Dolmen Press, 1961.
The Last Galway Hooker. Dublin, Dolmen Press, 1961.
Six Irish Poets, with others, edited by Robin Skelton. London and New York, Oxford University Press, 1962.
Sailing to an Island (collection). London, Faber, 1963; New York, Chilmark Press, 1964.
Penguin Modern Poets 7, with Jon Silkin and Nathaniel Tarn. London, Penguin, 1966.
The Battle of Aughrim and The God Who Eats Corn. London, Faber, and New York, Knopf, 1968.
High Island: New and Selected Poems. London, Faber, 1974; New York, Harper, 1975.
Selected Poems. London, Faber, 1979.

The Price of Stone. London, Faber, 1985.

Recording: *The Battle of Aughrim,* Claddagh, 1969.

*

Critical Studies: *Richard Murphy, Poet of Two Traditions: Interdisciplinary Studies* (includes bibliography by May Fitzgerald), edited by Maurice Harmon, Dublin, Wolfhound Press, 1978.

*   *   *

Richard Murphy's poems have, from the earliest collections, been written in a variety of modes and have been set in contrasting landscapes. Poems on Paris and Crete, on a painting by Mantegna, and on Biblical and classical themes, appear in *The Archaeology of Love.* They are technically proficient, but lack full emotional commitment. The strongest poems, and perhaps the most characteristic, are those in which Murphy adopts a Yeatsian, aristocratic stance and writes of the decay of great houses and of the auction of property: "alone I come,/ To bid for damp etchings,/ My great-aunt's chair." He sees himself in the role of conserver and restorer: "I have grown to restore/ From dust each room." He is nostalgic about the passing of the older, more graceful way of life represented by the Protestant ascendancy in Ireland, but his attitude was evolving by the time he published *Sailing to an Island.* He accepts the burden of his family's past, and his responsibility towards what survives of it. In powerful narrative poems, "The Last Galway Hooker" and "The Cleggan Disaster," the past is now that of the place itself, and not merely that part of it created by the Protestant settlers. In "The Last Galway Hooker" Murphy describes the construction, previous owners, and subsequent history of "a strong, safe, fishing and cargo boat" which he has bought and proposes to renew: "So I chose to renew her, to rebuild, to prolong/ For a while the spliced yards of yesterday."

Among those "spliced yards" are the long narratives from oral tradition which Murphy has transformed into "The Cleggan Disaster" and, on a smaller scale, "Pat Cloherty's Version of *The Maisie.*" Part of the fascination of these poems is formal: Murphy is one of the very few contemporaries who have used narrative verse techniques. They also give a valuable picture of the changing way of life of the fishing villages and rural farmers. Murphy's tone is too astringent to say his attitude is nostalgic, but there is a streak of romantic primitivism in his work. In the past 15 years one sees it steadily give way to a more ironic stance. His reconstruction of the battle of Aughrim, performed by the BBC in 1968, is as harsh in its treatment of vain Catholic generals as of savage Protestant soldiery. The Irish commander Luttrell, who "sold his country to preserve his class," becomes a type of the traitor. There is a new variety of verse forms in "The Battle of Aughrim," and a new density of language. What is perhaps most striking is Murphy's conviction that "the past is happening today." When he writes of an Irish Protestant landowner in the 1820's in "Droit de Seigneur," and of white settlers in Africa in our own time (in "The God Who Eats Corn"), he finds the same mentality. His own family are far from typical representatives of the Protestant mind, though they share the legacy sufficiently to make Murphy's meditations on his family reach out to a larger historical experience. The strong vein of radical irony in Murphy has not been fully recognized: it helped him replace the proud facade of Yeatsian disdain in his early verse with a view of the world more truly humane.

Murphy's recent work is divided between the landscape of the island off County Galway where he lives, and scenes remembered from his childhood in Ceylon. They show his growing power of description:

> When the great bull withdraws his rod, it glows
> Like a carnelian candle set in jade.
> The cow ripples ashore to feed her calf;
> While an old rival, eyeing the deed with hate,
> Swims to attack the tired triumphant god.

The "High Island" poems show Murphy consciously seeking a richer texture of metaphor and syntax. They also reveal a new openness to personal feelings. He is breaking new ground in "Sunup," in particular. It is a hauntingly moving love poem.

—Eric Homberger

MURRAY, Les(lie) A(llan). Australian. Born in Nabaic, New South Wales, 17 October 1938. Educated at Taree High School; University of Sydney (Co-Editor, *Arna* and *Hermes*; Literary Editor, *Honi Soit*), 1957-60, 1962. Served in the Royal Australian Naval Reserve, 1960-61. Married Valerie Gina Maria Morelli in 1962; three sons and two daughters. Translator, Australian National University, Canberra, 1963-67. Co-Editor, *Poetry Australia*, Sydney, 1974-80. Writer-in-Residence at universities of New England, Armidale, New South Wales, Stirling, Newcastle upon Tyne, Copenhagen, and New South Wales, Kensington; Scottish-Australian Writers Exchange fellow, 1981. Recipient: Grace Leven Prize, 1965, 1980; Australian Commonwealth Literary Fund Fellowship, 1968, 1971; Cook Bi-Centenary Prize, 1970; Literature Board Senior Fellowships, 1973-79, 1981-84; National Book Council Award, 1975; C.J. Dennis Memorial Prize, 1977. Address: 27 Edgar Street, Chatswood, New South Wales 2067, Australia.

PUBLICATIONS

Verse

The Ilex Tree, with Geoffrey Lehmann. Canberra, Australian National University Press, 1965.
The Weatherboard Cathedral. Sydney, Angus and Robertson, 1969.
Poems Against Economics. Sydney and London, Angus and Robertson, 1972.
Lunch and Counter Lunch. Sydney, Angus and Robertson, 1974.
Selected Poems: The Vernacular Republic. Sydney, Angus and Robertson, 1976.
Ethnic Radio. Sydney, Angus and Robertson, 1979.
The Boys Who Stole the Funeral. Sydney, Angus and Robertson, 1979.
The Vernacular Republic: Poems 1961-1981. Sydney, Angus and Robertson, Edinburgh, Canongate, and New York, Persea, 1982.
Equanimities. Copenhagen, Razorback Press, 1982.
The People's Otherworld. Sydney and London, Angus and Robertson, 1983.

Other

The Peasant Mandarin: Prose Pieces. Brisbane, University of Queensland Press, 1978.
Persistence in Folly. Sydney, Angus and Robertson, 1984.
The Australian Seasons, photographs by Peter Solness. Sydney, Angus and Robertson, 1985.

Translator, *An Introduction to the Principles of Phonological Description*, by Trubetzkoy The Hague, Nijhoff, 1968.

*

Manuscript Collection: National Library of Australia, Canberra.

Critical Studies: "The Poetry of Les A. Murray" by Dianne Ailwood, in *Southerly* (Surrey Hills, New South Wales), no. 3, 1971; "An Interview with Les A. Murray," in *Quadrant* (Sydney), December 1976, and "Garlands of Ilex," in *Poetry Australia* (Sydney), May 1979, both by Robert Gray; "Evading the Modernities: The Poetry of Les A. Murray" by Gary Catalano, in *Meanjin* (Melbourne), May 1977; *Study Notes on the Poetry of Les A. Murray* by Penelope Nelson, Melbourne, Methuen, 1978; Ken Goodwin, in *Australian Poems in Perspective*, Brisbane, University of Queensland Press, 1979; "Country Poetry and Town Poetry: A Debate with Les Murray" by Peter Porter, in *Australian Literary Studies* (Hobart, Tasmania), May 1979; "The Frequent Image of Farms: A Profile of Les Murray" by Graham Kinross-Smith, in *Westerly* (Nedlands, Western Australia), September 1980; "Les Murray's Watershed" by C.J. Koch, in *Quadrant* (Sydney), September 1980; "The Common Dish and the Uncommon Poet" by John Barnie, in *Kunapipi* (Aarhus, Denmark), no. 1, 1982.

*   *   *

Les A. Murray is the poet of his generation who is most clearly indicated for celebrity and for inclusion on lists of tertiary-level-course set books. His work, as the *Selected Poems: The Vernacular Republic* made clear, combines extraordinary force of personality in the views of expression, and a masterful confrontation with—you could say a masterful dancing among—large and difficult subjects.

Early poems in the uncharacteristically-named first book he shared with his friend Geoffrey Lehmann, mostly treat of country places and customs—an abiding preoccupation. The exception is the much-anthologized "The Burning Truck," a sustained seemingly-long run of 36 lines about the truck and the fearfully delighted onlookers.

The later books have been named so as to emphasize Murray's local and partisan temper and his uncompromising allegiances. These can be explored in the book of critical essays and reviews, *The Peasant Mandarin*. The poems present a wide range of reflections on man's interactions with nature, firmly localized—Murray of all Australian poets has most strongly celebrated the small-farming districts, particularly his own Northern Rivers (of New South Wales) with its dairy industry. This interest first culminates in a magnificent sequence, "Walking to the Cattle Place," in *Poems Against Economics*. In many different forms, quirkily ranging from Sanskrit derivations to ideas of God, from bullock-jumping in Australia to the salutation of a Xhosa tribesman, the poems encounter, discuss, play with man's age-old role as cattleherder. But there are discussions of other creations of man: the Lee Enfield rifle ("SMLE"), Law and Order ("The Police: Seven Voices") and Learning ("Sidere Mens Eadem Mutato," a reminiscence and discussion in nine unrhymed sonnets, based on Murray's university experience). Groaningly funny is "Vindaloo in Merthyr Tydfil," and not-merely-funny, "Folklore."

David Malouf, in a careful discussion ("Subjects Found and Taken Up" in *Poetry Australia*) of *Lunch and Counter Lunch*, began by calling Murray "perhaps the most naturally gifted poet of his generation"; remarked on his "almost unlimited" verbal inventiveness, the freshness and originality of his insights, and his wit and humour—and then stated his uneasiness at Murray's need for a debating stance. He felt the earlier subject-matter had been worked through and new material must be found "fully expressive" of Murray's gifts.

What has come is the astonishing adaptation in English of the aboriginal Song-Cycle. "The Buledelah-Taree Holiday Song Cycle" has thirteen long-lined sections that look Whitmanesque on the page but are distinctive; there is some rhythmical affinity with Robinson Jeffers, but Murray's lines are end-stopped. The poems celebrate the country-bred city-dweller's yearly return with his family to his childhood district, camping and picnicking, fishing, observing how things are the same or are changed. It is, then, a continuation of Murray's earlier interest, and its finest articulation. But the enterprise and skill—and scholarly scruple, for Murray is a polyglot who has worked as a translator—involved in using the Song-Cycle also points to a newly-urgent interest in the racial mix in Australia, first strongly signalled in "Jószef" in *Lunch and Counter Lunch*. This is carried into poems relating to Celtic origins and also celebrating the arrival of his wife's family in Australia.

Murray's verse novel, *The Boys Who Stole the Funeral*, has a plot characteristically expressive of principled rebellion, and Murray's need to put a case, in his own person or not. The hero's encounter in the bush with two mentors—one white and one black—is an interesting variation of a motif used by Xavier Herbert in his 1938 novel *Capricornia*. But Murray's energy in reaching towards sufficiently subtle and final-sounding truths and principles is all his own.

Murray's influence was widely felt during the 1970's through his editorship of *Poetry Australia*, the best-playing poetry quarterly in the country. Editing now for Angus and Robertson, he is in a position to influence what poetry is published. An indefatigable traveller, he is a vivid and dogmatic presence at conferences. His sometimes reactionary but thought-out and complex opinions will continue to win him the polemic responses he apparently needs to release his most gamesome and profound writing.

—Judith Rodriguez

MURRAY, Rona. Canadian. Born in London, England, 10 February 1924. Educated at Queen Margaret's School, Duncan, British Columbia, 1933-41; Mills College, Oakland, California, 1941-44; Victoria College, British Columbia, 1960-61, B.A. 1961; University of British Columbia, Vancouver, 1963-65, M.A. 1965; University of Kent, Canterbury, Ph.D. 1972. Married 1) Ernest Haddon in 1944, two sons and one daughter; 2) Walter Dexter in 1972. Special Instructor, University of Victoria, 1961-62; Head of English Department, Rockland School, Victoria, 1962-63; teaching assistant/lecturer, University of British Columbia, 1963-66; Associate Lecturer, Selkirk College, Castlegar, British Columbia, 1968-74; Instructor, Douglas College, Surrey, British Columbia, 1974-76; Visiting Lecturer in Creative Writing, 1977-79, and in English, 1981-83, University of Victoria. Recipient: British Columbia Centennial One-Act Play Award, 1958; Macmillan of Canada Award, 1964; Norma Epstein Award, 1965; Canada Council grant, 1976, 1979; Pat Lowther Award, 1982. Agent: Felicity Bryan, Curtis Brown, 162-168 Regent Street, London W1R 5TA, England. Address: 3825 Duke Road, R.R.1, Victoria, British Columbia V8X 3W9, Canada.

PUBLICATIONS

Verse

The Enchanted Adder. Vancouver, Klanak Press, 1965.
The Power of the Dog and Other Poems. Victoria, British Columbia, Morriss, 1968.
Ootischenie. Fredericton, New Brunswick, Fiddlehead, 1974.
Selected Poems. Delta, British Columbia, Sono Nis Press, 1974.
From an Autumn Journal. Toronto, League of Canadian Poets, 1980.
Journey. Victoria, British Columbia, Sono Nis Press, 1981.
Adam and Eve in Middle Age. Victoria, British Columbia, Sono Nis Press, 1984.

Plays

Blue Ducks' Feather and Eagledown (produced Vancouver, 1958).
One, Two, Three Alary (produced Castlegar, British Columbia, 1970; Seattle, 1983).
Creatures (produced Seattle, 1980). Published in *Event 7* (New Westminster, British Columbia), no. 2, n.d.

Other

Editor, with Walter Dexter, *The Art of Earth: An Anthology.* Victoria, British Columbia, Sono Nis Press, 1979.

*

Rona Murray comments:

In my poetry I attempt to record subjective, personal experience through concrete detail and, generally, through the manner in which the material is spaced on the page rather than through traditional forms, although recently I have been returning to the latter. There appear to be two distinct demands from which it grows: the first to form order, as I see it, out of chaos; the second to record certain ecstatic, usually numinous occurrences. The poems are literal rather than symbolic, and I have been astonished at critics who have ascribed symbolic meanings to my reality. My last book has a political, feminist basis, although I hope it moves beyond this to a universal statement on the varying attitudes, in our culture, between the male and female. I consider poetry a "given" aesthetic form, realized in a state of excitement, with ease, and then subjected to the writer's critical judgement. Therefore, it appears to be most successful if the poet masters his techniques and then trusts to the mercy of inspiration. I believe that it originates in the subconscious, or in the right side of the brain, or in Yeats's *Spiritus Mundi*, and that all the scribe can do is to wait for its emergence when it chooses to manifest itself. Forced poetry appears to me to be inevitably boring. Perhaps for this reason I am now concentrating on fiction: one can be a professional fiction writer, but not a professional poet except in so far as one teaches, or writes about, the craft: not in its practice. Presently I have a collection of short fiction under consideration with a publishing house and am working on a novel.

*   *   *

It is impossible to read very many of Rona Murray's poems without encountering the word "white." The word may appear as a noun or as an adjective but it is always used symbolically. What it symbolizes is hard to say. Most of the poems in her *Selected Poems* have numbers rather than titles. The first poem begins, "I have been into the halls of the dead," and it ends:

> I have been into the halls of the dead;
> the old man said I wore white,
> and white makes the woman invulnerable,
> he said.

The colour white has always been symbolic of purity and innocence, but it may also be symbolic of cold and frigidity. The eighth poem goes further:

> The whiteness   the birches
> grasp me   closer
> than   can
> any lover or   friend

From these extracts it may be sensed that Murray's poems are somewhat abstract. Yet what they may lack in specific meaning or setting, they more than make up in the insistence on meaning. They require that the reader grant them a significance, otherwise the odd references—to angels, the Old King, Lazarus, summer solstice, the Tarot, the I Ching—pass by unnoticed.

"The Beach," one of the few poems with a setting, contrasts the "daughter...looking lonely for shells" with the shore-scene around her: "waves poured onto lava fists," "lidless eyes of crabs," "killer whales gouging chuncks of flesh," "a sea of blood," etc. Clearly the intent is to contrast the innocence of childhood with the experience of the natural world. This is the intent of the sequence called "Ootischenie" after the village in the Interior of British Columbia founded by Doukhobors. In these poems there is a "seductive whiteness" but also a strong sense of the continuity of generations being disrupted.

Murray's concerns are perhaps most clearly expressed in her later volumes, *Journey* and *Adam and Eve in Middle Life*. In the first book, poems like "Homing" express the notion of the journey and the return being somehow identical: "the circle is arcing/ round to its start." Utterances are "core/caw/cry of self." Travellers are in search of a "changeless place" in the poem "Moving through Japanese Gardens." Suitably for poems written in search of stasis, the texts are symmetrically centred on the page:

Freighted/naked

even

so

In her last book she may have had her own writing in mind when she noted: "I explore / five-finger exercises. / No more." But her poems, her probings, her attempts to find stasis in a changing world, do more than that. They are journeys and returns to find the significances of "white."

—John Robert Colombo

MUSGRAVE, Susan. Canadian. Born in Santa Cruz, California, 12 March 1951. Writer-in-Residence, University of Waterloo, Ontario, 1983-85. Recipient: Canada Council grant 1970, 1973, and bursary, 1972. Address: 2407 Tryon Road, R.R. 3, Sidney, British Columbia V8L 3X9, Canada.

PUBLICATIONS

Verse

Songs of the Sea-Witch. Vancouver, Sono Nis Press, 1970.
Skuld. Frensham, Surrey, Sceptre Press, 1971.
Birthstone. Frensham, Surrey, Sceptre Press, 1972.
Entrance of the Celebrant. Toronto, Macmillan, and London, Fuller d'Arch Smith, 1972.
Equinox. Rushden, Northamptonshire, Sceptre Press, 1973.
Kung. Rushden, Northamptonshire, Sceptre Press, 1973.
Grave-Dirt and Selected Strawberries. Toronto, Macmillan, 1973.
Gullband Thought Measles Was a Happy Ending (for children). Vancouver, J.J. Douglas, 1974.
Against. Rushden, Northamptonshire, Sceptre Press, 1974.
Two Poems. Knotting, Bedfordshire, Sceptre Press, 1975.
The Impstone. Toronto, McClelland and Stewart, 1976; London, J. Jay, 1977.
Kiskatinaw Songs, with Seán Virgo. Victoria, Pharos Press, 1977.
Selected Strawberries and Other Poems. Victoria, Sono Nis Press, 1977.
For Charlie Beaulieu.... Knotting, Bedfordshire, Sceptre Press, 1977.
Two Poems for the Blue Moon. Knotting, Bedfordshire, Sceptre Press, 1977.
Becky Swan's Book. Erin, Ontario, Porcupine's Quill, 1977.
A Man to Marry, A Man to Bury. Toronto, McClelland and Stewart, 1979.
Conversation During the Omelette aux Fines Herbes. Knotting, Bedfordshire, Sceptre Press, 1979.
Taboo Man. N.p., Celia Duthie, 1981.
Tarts and Muggers: Poems New and Selected. Toronto, McClelland and Stewart, 1982.
The Plane Put Down in Sacramento. Vancouver, Hoffer, 1982.
I do not know if things that happen can be said to come to pass or only happen. Vancouver, Hoffer, 1982.

Plays

Gullband (produced Toronto, 1976).

Novels

The Charcoal Burners. Toronto, McClelland and Stewart, 1980.
Hag Head (for children). Toronto, Clarke Irwin, 1980.

*

Manuscript Collection: McMaster University, Hamilton, Ontario.

Critical Study: "The White Goddess: Poetry of Susan Musgrave" by Rosemary Sullivan, in *Contemporary Verse 2,* 1975.

*   *   *

In my review of Susan Musgrave's poetry in the 1975 *Contemporary Poets* I misjudged her. Her obsessive, poignant treatment of death, insanity, and blood reminded me of Sylvia Plath's poetry in *Ariel* and I unwisely voiced my fear that Musgrave might meet the same end as Plath.

The feminist stances of the two poets were similar; so were their attitudes towards men, lesbianism, and sex. Musgrave's imitation of Plath's "Daddy" and "Lady Lazarus" in her poem "Exposure" was unmistakable. She was the celebrant of death, "the spilled child," and all she looked at was transformed into death. In "The Opened Grave," she placed herself at the "edge of things." Her poems of witchcraft read like strange and deeply disturbing myths of blood rites and sexuality, pervaded with violence. The inhabitants of her witch kingdoms resembled those in Gustave Doré's illustrations—beetles, white moths, and figures with bloated heads angling out of hunched shoulders and shrivelled torsos, shaking their gnarled hands, leering at their prey. Lines from "Finding Love" were chilling:

> From my bed I could hear
> the ripe wound open, the thick sea
> pouring in. I told you, then,
> the first lie I had in my heart;
> the carcass of a dull animal
> slipped between our sights.

Her poem "MacKenzie River, North" was imbued with terror.

What I failed to recognize was that although her range was limited in her two collections, *Songs of the Sea-Witch* and *Entrance of the Celebrant*, and her themes were obsessive and derivative, her sense of the bizarre and her ability to evoke the mood of bewitched kingdoms could serve her well in an entirely different vein of poetry. In the earlier collections, she used these gifts to evoke strange, disturbing worlds fraught with psychological significance. In the third section of *Grave-Dirt and Selected Strawberries* she transforms them to create a high-spirited, bawdy, and wonderfully affectionate pastiche of poems and prose in celebration of the strawberry. Gleefully, Musgrave parodies herself and writes in the best eighteenth-century traditions of comedy. In her fanciful history, the strawberry is her picaresque hero. His origins are traced, his baptism marked, his emergence in the writings of others is duly recorded, and all the facts about him that every strawberry lover would like to know are catalogued. In her "character study" of the strawberry, Musgrave feigns an anthropological tone and hilariously records the harvest customs of the strawberry, its method of reproduction, its behaviour in captivity, its sense of fellowship. To satisfy her audience's appetite for books of homespun truths and extraordinary feats, she pens her hero's proverbs and "the Guinness Book of Strawberries." "A Child's Garden of Strawberries" and "Strawberry at Colonus" place her hero in the literary context he deserves. The collection is giddy, witty, and full of good fun. It could not be more unlike her other poetry.

Her other volumes, from *Equinox* through *The Impstone*, reflect continued growth in the kind of poetry that won her acclaim. "Memorial to a Lover" (*Two Poems*) imitates Plath. "The Firstborn" (*Two Poems*), *Kung, Against, For Charlie Beaulieu...., Two Poems for the Blue Moon*, and *Equinox* show further workings on her poetry of Indian lore and witchcraft. The moon poems, like the "Kiskatinaw Songs" (*Grave-Dirt and Selected Strawberries*), experiment with rhythms from songs, chants, and ballads and turn the hackneyed lyrics and rhythms into a new music. Poems like "The Firstborn" and *Equinox* represent Musgrave's best handling of the world of nightmare and demons where dark rituals are enacted between the self and its demon other. What I look for now is more poetry in the comic vein discovered in "Selected Strawberries" or in the raucous vein of the pulsing, erotic, simple, and primitive Indian songs in the "Kiskatinaw Songs" celebrating the cunt and the phallus.

—Carol Simpson Stern

NANDY, Pritish. Indian. Born in Bhagalpur, Bihar, 15 January 1947. Educated at La Martiniere, Calcutta; Presidency College, Calcutta. Married Rina Mumtaz in 1966 (divorced), two children. Since 1968, Editor, *Dialogue Calcutta*, later *Dialogue India*; since 1969, Public Relations Manager, Guest Keen Williams Ltd., Calcutta. Address: Dialogue Publications, 5 Pearl Road, Calcutta 700 017, India.

PUBLICATIONS

Verse

Of Gods and Olives: 21 Poems. Calcutta, Writers Workshop, 1967.
I Hand You in Turn My Nebbuk Wreath: Early Poems. Calcutta, Dialogue, 1968.
On Either Side of Arrogance. Calcutta, Writers Workshop, 1968.
Rites for a Plebeian Statue: An Experiment in Verse Drama. Calcutta, Writers Workshop, 1969.
From the Outer Bank of the Brahmaputra. New York, New Rivers Press, 1969.
Masks to Be Interpreted as Messages. Calcutta, Dialogue, 1970.
Madness Is the Second Stroke. Calcutta, Dialogue, 1972.
The Poetry of Pritish Nandy. Calcutta, Oxford University Press, 1973.
Dhritarashtra Downtown: Zero. Calcutta, Dialogue, 1974.
Riding the Midnight River: Selected Poems. New Delhi, Arnold Heinemann, 1975.
Lonesong Street. Calcutta, Poets Press, 1975.
Songs of Mirabei. New Delhi, Arnold Heinemann, 1975.
A Stranger Called I. Calcutta, Poets Press, 1976.
In Secret Anarchy. Calcutta, United Writers, 1976.
Nowhere Man. New Delhi, Arnold Heinemann, 1978.
Anywhere Is Another Place. New Delhi, Arnold Heinemann, 1979.
Tonight This Savage Rite: The Love Poetry of Kamala Das and Pritish Nandy. New Delhi, Arnold-Heinemann, 1979.
The Rainbow Last Night. New Delhi, Arnold Heinemann, 1981.
Some Friends. New Delhi, Arnold Heinemann, 1983.

Other

Editor, *Indian Poetry in English 1947-1972.* Calcutta, Oxford University Press, 1972.
Editor, *Modern Indian Poetry.* New Delhi, Arnold Heinemann, 1974; London, Heinemann, 1976.
Editor, *Bengali Poetry Today.* East Lansing, Michigan State University Press, 1974.
Editor, *Strangertime: An Anthology of Indian Poetry in English.* New Delhi, Hind, 1977.

Editor, *The Vikas Book of Modern Indian Love Stories* [*Poetry*]. New Delhi, Vikas, 2 vols., 1979.

Transcreator, *The Complete Poems of Samar Sen*. Calcutta, Writers Workshop, 1970.

Editor and translator of several other volumes.

*

Critical Studies: *The Poetry of Pritish Nandy*, Calcutta, Writers Workshop, 1969, and "Workpoints for a Study of Pritish Nandy's 'In Transit, Mind Seeks' " in *Banasthali Vidyapith Magazine*, 1969, both by Satyabrata Pal; *Pritish Nandy* by Subharanjan Dasgupta, New Delhi, Arnold Heinemann, 1975.

Pritish Nandy comments:
  Trying to achieve an entirely new breakthrough in form and evolve a new language to characterise Indian writing in English. Feel that creative writing in English by Indians is generally imitative in both form and approach. What is required is a new language that will be characteristic and structurally powerful, with a logic of its own. It is this Indian English that must be worked out and that is what I am trying to do. Also trying to discover/build a tradition for Indo-Anglian poetry: the fusion of a modern language with the myths and symbols we have. Indian writers in English till now have ignored this quest for a tradition, which I consider vital for a living poetry. Finally: a personal quest—a secular, politically-involved poet has his own peculiar problems.

*   *   *

  Pritish Nandy's early poems are often in short-line free verse; others form typographical pictures, or use Cummings-style spacing. He sceptically mingles Indian, classic, and Christian imagery, with gentle irony towards gods who "have aged and are not aware," or Christ who "came third in the contest/with death/ and wrote a poem on the cross." Nandy indeed pities those who have to live with him—he "shreds their magic faith into a million assumptions." He is equally skeptical about such rationalists as the recluse found dead: "having read too much of/Salinger/he had checkmated himself in one/man chess." Indeed, "To understand by cataloguing is like/splitting hairs on a bald head."
  Perhaps this is why he thinks English poetry stopped at Auden (American "never began"); he most frequently alludes to Spanish-language poets, notably Lorca. His own effort is to combine, and symbolize: "What you cannot explain in terms of symbols is lost forever like blind totems and ruins in an old man's face." For words are only "masks to be interpreted in terms of messages."
  He was long preoccupied with the frustrations of penetrating to realities, or saying anything meaningful if one did; he praised a friend for seeking "a new level of communication" and so compacted his own images as to make very sur-real sense: "your eyes bled like a violet tiger/as I watched the winds strangle/ whispers of the apocalypse." But certain themes are clear: death, loneliness, suffering—and the mitigations of love, sex, friendship.
  In *Masks to Be Interpreted as Messages* he changed to short statements in rhythmic prose, and in his best-known poem, "Calcutta, If You Must Exile Me," states in brutally direct style the cruelties which revolt him. Next year, the Bangla Desh horrors jolted him into plain, moving statements of sympathy with all victims of hate: in India, Vietnam, or Colombia "the marauders changed their name but the sufferers each time were the same." At times he despairs—"blood is a country you and I have loved in vain"—but he no longer thinks of leaving: "Dark city I shall not disown you again." And though he writes for those who cannot read the language he uses, "my voice is the voice of my people, for I speak of their loves and ambitions and secret shames."
  Later, he found consolation in translating Tagore's last poems, a "devastating confrontation with death"; the message, of "haunting simplicity," is that "death is but a new birth of the spirit into the great unknown." Modern Indian poetry, he says, draws "strength from the bedrock of our tradition," yet is "violent, anguished, brutally contemporary." His own certainly is.

—George McElroy

NATHAN, Leonard (Edward). American. Born in Los Angeles, California, 8 November 1924. Educated at Georgia Institute of Technology, Atlanta, 1943; University of California, Los Angeles, 1946-47; University of California, Berkeley, B.A. (summa cum laude) 1950, M.A. 1952, Ph.D. in English 1961. Served in the United States Army during World War II. Married Carol Nash in 1949; one son and two daughters. Instructor, Modesto Junior College, California, 1954-60. Since 1960, Member of the Department of Rhetoric, Chairman of the Department, 1969-72, and currently Professor of Rhetoric, University of California, Berkeley. Recipient: Phelan Award, 1959; Longview Award, 1961; American Institute of Independent Studies Fellowship, 1966; University of California Creative Awards Fellowship, 1967; American Academy award, 1971; Guggenheim Fellowship, 1976. Address: 40 Beverly Road, Kensington, California 94707, U.S.A.

PUBLICATIONS

Verse

Western Reaches. San Jose, California, Talisman Press, 1958.
The Glad and Sorry Seasons. New York, Random House, 1963.
The Matchmaker's Lament and Other Astonishments. Northampton, Massachusetts, Gehenna Press, 1967.
The Day the Perfect Speakers Left. Middletown, Connecticut, Wesleyan University Press, 1969.
Flight Plan. Berkeley, California, Cedar Hill Press, 1971.
Without Wishing. Berkeley, California, Thorp Springs Press, 1973.
Coup and Other Poems. Lincoln, Nebraska, Windflower Press, 1975.
Returning Your Call. Princeton, New Jersey, Princeton University Press, 1975.
The Likeness: Poems Out of India. Berkeley, California, Thorp Springs Press, 1975.
The Teachings of Grandfather Fox. Ithaca, New York, Ithaca House, 1976.
Lost Distance. Madison, Wisconsin, Chowder, 1978.
Dear Blood. Pittsburgh, University of Pittsburgh Press, 1980.
Holding Patterns. Pittsburgh, University of Pittsburgh Press, 1982.

Other

The Tragic Drama of William Butler Yeats: Figures in a Dance.
New York, Columbia University Press, 1965.

Editor, *Talisman Anthology.* Georgetown, California, Talisman Press, 1963.

Translator, with others, *Modern Hindi Poetry.* Bloomington, Indiana University Press, 1965.

Translator, *First Person, Second Person*, by Ageyeya. Berkeley, California, Center for South and Southeast Asia Studies, 1971.

Translator, *The Transport of Love: The Meghaduta of Kalidasa.* Berkeley, University of California Press, 1976.

Translator, *Grace and Mercy in Her Wild Hair: Selected Poems to the Mother Goddess*, by Ramprasad Sen. Boulder, Colorado, Great Eastern, 1982.

Translator, with James Larson, *Songs of Something Else: Selected Poems*, by Gunnar Ekelöf. Princeton, New Jersey, Princeton University Press, 1982.

*

Manuscript Collection: Syracuse University Library, New York.

Critical Studies: in *Shenandoah* (Lexington, Virginia), Autumn 1969; *Malahat Review* (Victoria), October 1969; *Quarterly Journal of Speech* (New York), Winter 1970; *Poetry* (Chicago), January 1971; *Ohio Review* (Athens), Spring-Summer 1976; *Advocate* (Los Angeles), 16 June 1976; *Southern Humanities Review* (Auburn, Alabama), Fall 1976; *Small Press Review* (Paradise, California), March 1977; *Prairie Schooner* (Lincoln, Nebraska), Fall 1980; *Northwest Review* (Eugene, Oregon), no. 3, 1981; *New Letters* (Kansas City), Summer 1981; *Hudson Review* (New York), Fall 1982; *Chowder Review* (Quincy, Massachusetts), Summer 1983; *Salmagundi* (Saratoga Springs, New York), Fall 1983.

Leonard Nathan comments:

Nathan's poetry over the years has moved steadily toward the development of a voice that might give human conversation the form to make it memorable. He returns again and again to certain subjects: the difficult redemption possible in human relations; the pathos and courage of human purpose set adrift in an inhuman universe; and the sudden illumination that can transform experience into a meaning so intense that the only term for it is supernatural.

*   *   *

In his review of *The Glad and Sorry Seasons* for *Poetry*, John Woods quite rightly observed that Leonard Nathan has a "preference for statements of revelation" and that his demands on metaphor are relatively minor. Nathan convinces by conclusive statement, seldom by narrative or emotional persuasion. Although he inclines towards declarative and reductionist poetry, his lines are not so concentrated as, say, W.S. Merwin's, nor has he Merwin's power to startle and amaze through revelation. Leonard Nathan employs a steady iambic meter, with frequent variation in end rhymes. His lines seldom fail; they are refined, restrained, and well polished.

The dominant tonality of *The Glad and Sorry Seasons* is autumnal. The poet is middle-aged and wise, detached and reflective:

I sweeten by the minute, bodying •
The spirit of my seed; hear how I sing
Inside my skin—that's blood, that growing sound,
The psalm of mellowing....

The following lines from "First Girl," while perhaps uncharacteristic of Nathan's lyrics, reveal the intensity he is capable of:

As she bent, I woke, and felt a pull like water
And saw above her head a foreign blue,
And nothing was homely, even my heavy body,
And what I had never learned I always knew.

This snow queen, resplendent in frosted radiance, has transformed the poet and "crystallized the wildest flux of nature." But the time of ecstasy is past and "too long ago for second thoughts."

The Day the Perfect Speakers Left seems to bemoan the disintegration of high culture and humanistic values. Several poems strike a pose reminiscent of Ezra Pound's "Hugh Selwyn Mauberley," in its condemnation of our "botched civilization," our "old bitch gone in the teeth." In Nathan's "The Crisis" a shadowy figure, a Greek or Jew, has come "To see his children's children, how they escaped/His law, his love, his unpronounceable name." The title poem of this volume confirms the notion and may remind one of Arnold's "Dover Beach." The birds have assembled for what the poet fears is final migration:

And leave-taking was another,
Sadder version of dusk we were attending,
And as though a whole age were going out,
Its head covered, and going out with it
A purpose including stars and stones.

More recently, *Returning Your Call* is less derivative in style and subject than his earlier books. His voice is more direct, less given to cleverness and wit than previously. There are fine single achievements, such as "Audit" and "Breathing Exercises." In the latter poem the poet cries, in fear and urgency, "For God's sake, keep breathing." There is in this book more sense of tension, near disaster, and struggle against loss. "Breathing Exercises" also tells us, "inside Leonard/Nathan is a little spirit." While hardly confessional, his poetry now seems willing to grapple more intensely with tougher topics. We hear a voice struggling to regain contact with itself, and with close friends. There is also a suggestion Nathan recognizes the cleverness and restraint of his verse: "someday I'm going to speak/in my own voice ...you'll have to cover my mouth with your free hand..." This is precisely what is missing from Nathan's poetry: a strong, direct, and unfettered voice.

In general, the consistently polished flow of his lines is both remarkable and lamentable; one soon craves roughness in line and subject. It is Nathan's very control of his material that keeps most of his poems, while always of craft, from becoming poems of authority. By his own construct ("Mao for nightmare, Mozart for slippers") we need to hear more of Nathan's nightmares, less about his slippers.

—John R. Cooley

NEMEROV, Howard (Stanley). American. Born in New York City, 1 March 1920. Educated at Fieldston School, New York, graduated 1937; Harvard University, Cambridge, Massachusetts (Bowdoin Prize, 1940), A.B. 1941. Served in the Royal Canadian Air Force and the United States Air Force, 1941-45: First Lieutenant. Married Margaret Russell in 1944; three sons. Instructor in English, Hamilton College, Clinton; New York, 1946-48; Member of the Literature Faculty, Bennington College, Vermont, 1948-66; Professor of English, Brandeis University, Waltham, Massachusetts, 1966-69. Hurst Professor of English, 1969-76, and since 1976, Edward Mallinckrodt Distinguished University Professor, Washington University, St. Louis. Visiting Lecturer, University of Minnesota, Minneapolis, 1958-59; Writer-in-Residence, Hollins College, Virginia, 1962-64; Consultant in Poetry, Library of Congress, Washington, D.C., 1963-64. Associate Editor, *Furioso*, Madison, Connecticut, later Northfield, Minnesota, 1946-51. Recipient: *Kenyon Review* Fellowship, 1955; Oscar Blumenthal Prize, 1958, Harriet Monroe Memorial Prize, 1959, Frank O'Hara Prize, 1971, and Levinson Prize, 1975 (*Poetry*, Chicago); *Virginia Quarterly Review* Short Story Award, 1958; American Academy grant, 1961; New England Poetry Club Golden Rose, 1962; Brandeis University Creative Arts Award, 1962; National Endowment for the Arts grant, 1966; Theodore Roethke Award, 1968; Guggenheim Fellowship, 1968; St. Botolph's Club Prize, 1968; Academy of American Poets Fellowship, 1970; Pulitzer Prize, 1978; National Book Award, 1978; Bollingen Prize, 1981. D.L.: Lawrence University, Appleton, Wisconsin, 1964; Tufts University, Medford, Massachusetts, 1969; Washington and Lee University, Lexington, Virginia, 1976; University of Vermont, Burlington, 1977; Cleveland State University; Hamilton College, Clinton, New York; McKendree College, Lebanon, Illinois. Fellow, American Academy of Arts and Sciences, 1966; Member, American Academy, 1976; Chancellor, Academy of American Poets, 1977. Address: Department of English, Washington University, St. Louis, Missouri 63130, U.S.A.

PUBLICATIONS

Verse

The Image and the Law. New York, Holt, 1947.
Guide to the Ruins. New York, Random House, 1950.
The Salt Garden. Boston, Little Brown, 1955.
Small Moment. Los Angeles, Ward Ritchie Press, 1957.
Mirrors and Windows. Chicago, University of Chicago Press, 1958.
New and Selected Poems. Chicago, University of Chicago Press, 1960.
The Next Room of the Dream: Poems and Two Plays. Chicago, University of Chicago Press, 1962.
Five American Poets, with others, edited by Ted Hughes and Thom Gunn. London, Faber, 1963.
Departure of the Ships. Cambridge, Massachusetts, Lowell House, 1966.
The Blue Swallows. Chicago, University of Chicago Press, 1967.
A Sequence of Seven. Roanoke, Virginia, Tinker Press, 1967.
The Winter Lightning: Selected Poems. London, Rapp and Whiting, 1968.
The Painter Dreaming in the Scholar's House. New York, Phoenix Book Shop, 1968.
Gnomes and Occasions. Chicago, University of Chicago Press, 1972.

The Western Approaches: Poems 1973-1975. Chicago, University of Chicago Press, 1975.
The Collected Poems of Howard Nemerov. Chicago, University of Chicago Press, 1977.
By Al Lebowitz's Pool. New York, Nadja, 1979.
Sentences. Chicago, University of Chicago Press, 1980.
Inside the Onion. Chicago, University of Chicago Press, 1984.

Play

Endor. New York, Abingdon, 1962.

Novels

The Melodramatists. New York, Random House, 1949.
Federigo; or, The Power of Love. Boston, Little Brown, 1954.
The Homecoming Game. New York, Simon and Schuster, and London, Gollancz, 1957.

Short Stories

A Commodity of Dreams and Other Stories. New York, Simon and Schuster, 1959; London, Secker and Warburg, 1960.
Stories, Fables and Other Diversions. Boston, Godine, 1971.

Other

Poetry and Fiction: Essays. New Brunswick, New Jersey, Rutgers University Press, 1963.
Journal of the Fictive Life. New Brunswick, New Jersey, Rutgers University Press, 1965.
Reflexions on Poetry and Poetics. New Brunswick, New Jersey, Rutgers University Press, 1972.
Figures of Thought: Speculations on the Meaning of Poetry and Other Essays. Boston, Godine, 1978.
New and Selected Essays. Carbondale, Southern Illinois University Press, 1985.

Editor, *Longfellow.* New York, Dell, 1959.
Editor, *Poets on Poetry.* New York, Basic Books, 1966.

*

Bibliography: *Elizabeth Bishop and Howard Nemerov: A Reference Guide* by Diana E. Wyllie, Boston, Hall, 1983.

Manuscript Collection: Olin Library, Washington University, St. Louis.

Critical Studies: *Howard Nemerov* by Peter Meinke, Minneapolis, University of Minnesota Press, 1968; *The Critical Reception of Howard Nemerov: A Selection of Essays and a Bibliography* edited by Bowie Duncan, Metuchen, New Jersey, Scarecrow Press, 1971; *The Shield of Perseus* by Julia Bartholomay, Gainesville, University of Florida Press, 1972; *The Stillness in Moving Things: The World of Howard Nemerov* by William Mills, Memphis, Memphis State University Press, 1975; "The Signature of Things" by Mary Kinzie, in *Parnassus* (New York), Fall-Winter 1977; *Howard Nemerov* by Ross Labrie, Boston, Twayne, 1980.

*   *   *

Not content merely to record images and instances, Howard Nemerov is a poet of the intelligence. From his verse dramas,

"Endor" and "Cain," to the succinct scale of his epigrams, he is by choice a discursive poet. His poems are "fictions" in the commonest usage of that term, and his driving impulse is to make sense of the enigma of the world as given. To this task he brings language and rhythms which are both formal and natural, and a temperament at once stoical and ironical.

Nemerov is willing to accept the paradox that, while the pains and immediacies of the world need no human capacity for their invention, yet (from "Creation of Anguish"):

> Whatever sleeping in the world awakes,
> We are the ones who to become ourselves
> Awaken it, we are the ones who reach
> Forever further, where the forest and the sky
> And the incessantly restless sea invite
> The voice that tells them fables of themselves

These lines adequately illustrate the characteristic texture of Nemerov's poetry, and his sense that the world is simultaneously a physical complex and a construct of consciousness. The gap between these two is the space in which his imagination works, the autonomy of things and yet their vulnerability to our attentions (as in "The Distance They Keep"):

> Let them stay
> Pieces of the world we're not responsible for,
> Who can be killed by cleverness and hate,
> But, being shy enough, may yet survive our love.

Yet an important Nemerov theme is the nature and significance of art—the reflexive connection between, say, thumbprints and sanderlings—on which his finest meditation is the sequence "The Painter Dreaming in the Scholar's House."

Three phases of Nemerov's life are usually taken to be of note: an urban childhood, war service in Europe, and then a long period of living in the country during which he has become progressively more deeply conscious of nature. From this last vantage point he has been positioned to respond trenchantly to the misplaced urbanities of metropolitan life and to depressing social and political realities.

"The Goose Fish," an early and often anthologised poem, serves to illustrate a number of things: first, a typical clarity of form and statement, concerning which Nemerov seems to have learned importantly from Auden; second, a characteristic stance of objectivity and detachment (though not complete impersonality; it has been said of Nemerov that he is a realist with a romantic sensibility); and third, a belief in the traditional means of poetry, such as full rhyme and a well-established and sustained metrical pattern. This last is not so much conservatism as a freedom from being fashion-bound, for Nemerov once said that "The poet must be allowed to choose any way he thinks he needs." What lifts Nemerov's work at its best above banality is another quality traditional to fine poetry, a sense of mystery, the touch of wayward imagination.

Both in poetry and criticism, Nemerov has spoken out against the slackness widely perpetrated under the guise of "free form," but he has spoken also against "the rigid domination of the past over present and future," his sense of which can only have been deepened by his wartime experience in Europe. His war poems, especially immediately after the war, express a sense of anticlimax or, as one poem concludes: "It does not seem that anything was lost." Reinforced by his measured iambic rhythms, this is varied at times by quasi-surrealist imagery ("They say the war is over. But water still/Comes bloody from the taps"). War seems to have fully awakened in him the sense that life itself is both banal and dangerous, though the greatest danger is resignation,

to which is preferred, as the texture of many poems conveys, a stoic continuance (see, for example, "Life Cycle of the Common Man").

A temperament given to stoical scepticism, reinforced by the war, is applied to the society in which the poet finds himself. This is adumbrated most concentratedly in a section of *The Blue Swallows*, "The Great Society," a society which is "Fueled by super-pep high octane money/And lubricated with hypocrisy," while its "steering gear is newsprint powered by/Expediency."

From the city and the war, Nemerov came "an amateur" to nature, and this is explored in one of his finest poems, "The Salt Garden." The garden near the shore has been reclaimed from the ocean, and the protagonist contrasts his puniness with a great sea-roving gull who:

> Had come, brutal, mysterious,
> To teach the tenant gardener,
> Green fellow of this paradise,
> Where his salt dream lies.

The poem's verbal ambiguities show Nemerov's strong side. Finally, the short poem "Trees" serves to show the strengths and limitations of Nemerov's fundamentally rational sense of poetry. Admiring the giant trees, which "stand for the constant presence of process," he observes:

> Poems or people are rarely so lovely,
> And even when they have great qualities
> They tend to tell you rather than exemplify....

—Charles Doyle

NEWLOVE, John (Herbert). Canadian. Born in Regina, Saskatchewan, 13 June 1938. Married Susan Mary Phillips in 1966; two step-children. Formerly, Senior Editor, McClelland and Stewart Ltd., publishers, Toronto. Writer-in-Residence, Concordia University, Montreal, 1974-75, University of Western Ontario, London, 1975-76, University of Toronto, 1976-77, Regina Public Library, 1979-80, and David Thompson University Centre, Nelson, British Columbia, 1982-83. Recipient: Koerner Foundation grant, 1964; Canada Council grant, 1965, 1967, 1977, 1983; Governor-General's Award, 1973; Saskatchewan Writers' Guild Founders' Award, 1984. Address: c/o McClelland and Stewart Ltd., 25 Hollinger Road, Toronto, Ontario M4B 3G2, Canada.

PUBLICATIONS

Verse

Grave Sirs. Vancouver, Robert Reid, 1962.
Elephants, Mothers and Others. Vancouver, Periwinkle Press, 1963.
Moving In Alone. Toronto, Contact Press, 1965.
Notebook Pages. Toronto, Charles Pachter, 1966.
Four Poems. Platteville, Wisconsin, It, 1967.
What They Say. Toronto, Weed/Flower Press, 1967.
Black Night Window. Toronto, McClelland and Stewart, 1968.
The Cave. Toronto, McClelland and Stewart, 1970.

7 Disasters, 3 Theses, and Welcome Home. Click. Vancouver, Very Stone House, 1971.
Lies. Toronto, McClelland and Stewart, 1972.
The Fat Man: Selected Poems 1962-1972. Toronto, McClelland and Stewart, 1977.
Dreams Surround Us: Fiction and Poetry, with John Metcalf. Delta, Ontario, Bastard Press, 1977.
The Green Plain. Lantzville, British Columbia, Oolichan, 1981.

Other

Editor, *Dream Crâters,* by Joe Rosenblatt. Erin, Ontario, Press Porcépic, 1974.
Editor, *The Collected Poems of Earle Birney.* Toronto, McClelland and Stewart, 2 vols., 1975.
Editor, *Canadian Poetry: The Modern Era.* Toronto, McClelland and Stewart, 1977.
Editor, *The Collected Poems of F. R. Scott.* Toronto, McClelland and Stewart, 1981.

*

Bibliography: "An Annotated Bibliography of Works by and about John Newlove" by Robert A. Lecker, in *Essays on Canadian Writing* (Downsview, Ontario), Spring 1975.

Manuscript Collections: University of Toronto Library; Humanities Research Center, University of Texas, Austin.

Critical Studies: "How Do I Get Out of Here: The Poetry of John Newlove" by Margaret Atwood, Spring 1973, and "Something in Which to Believe for Once: The Poetry of John Newlove" by Jan Bartley, Fall 1974, both in *Open Letter* (Toronto).

John Newlove comments:
    If I had a personal statement to make on my own work, it would consist of the fifth part of Wallace Stevens's "Thirteen Ways of Looking at a Blackbird."

*   *   *

    John Newlove has moved from an initial stage of matter-of-fact, personal recollection through a middle phase of essentially negative vision and a conscious edging towards marginal projectivism, to a latter condition in which there has been a noticeable darkening of his horizons coupled with a new intellectual toughness, and a more studied method in his technique.
    In the early poems the most consistent locus is that of a series of private observations, and the tone—understandably personal and not infrequently nostalgic—is honest and outspoken. The correlatives are of youthful experiences; the remembered journey; the sense and sensation of simply being alive. A sombre shift takes place with *Moving In Alone* and with *What They Say* where death, isolation and the pointlessness and ugliness of existence become the hallmarks of much of what Newlove has to say. There is also a sense of a kind of desperate activity; movement; travel in the tumbleweed moods of the hitch-hiker which suggests rootlessness and a worrisome escape.
    Disengagement and the poet's alienation continue to dominate *Black Night Window,* Newlove's most ambitious collection, and stamp him with the mark of small "e" existentialism. He continues to be autobiographical although his perspective transcends the purely subjective, and his imagination grapples effec-

tively with abstraction and succeeds in striking a balance between his own vision, the ideas of poetry, and the larger consciousness of collective man.
    Newlove's marginal projectivism stems from the technical bias of the Canadian West Coast *TISH*-movement with which the poet has links. His early style has a laconic, forthright quality with later development into relative complexities of jigsaw structuring of concrete, immediate and precise images.

—Michael Gnarowski

———————

NICHOL, Barrie Phillip (bpNichol). Canadian. Born in Vancouver, British Columbia, 30 September 1944. Attended the University of British Columbia, Vancouver. Formerly taught grade school. Co-Editor, *Ganglia* magazine and Ganglia Press, 1965-72, and *grOnk* magazine, Toronto. Recipient: four Canada Council grants; Governor-General's Award, 1971. Address: 98 Admiral Road, Toronto, Ontario M5R 2L6, Canada.

PUBLICATIONS

Verse

Cycles Etc. Cleveland, 7 Flowers Press, 1965.
Scraptures: 2nd Sequence. Toronto, Ganglia Press, 1965.
Strange Grey Town, with David Aylward. Toronto, Ganglia Press, 1966.
Tonto or. Toronto, Ganglia Press, 1966.
Calendar. Woodchester, Gloucestershire, Openings Press, 1966.
Scraptures: 3rd Sequence. Toronto, Ganglia Press, 1966.
Scraptures: 4th Sequence. Niagara Falls, New York, Press Today Niagara, 1966.
Fodder Folder. Toronto, Ganglia Press, 1966.
Portrait of David. Toronto, Ganglia Press, 1966.
A Vision in the U of T Stacks. Toronto, Ganglia Press, 1966.
A Little Poem for Yur Fingertips. Toronto, Ganglia Press, 1966.
Langwedge. Toronto, Ganglia Press, 1966.
Alaphbit. Toronto, Ganglia Press, 1966.
Stan's Ikon. Toronto, Ganglia Press, 1966.
The Birth of O. Toronto, Ganglia Press, 1966.
The Chocolate Poem. Toronto, privately printed, 1966.
Letters Home. Toronto, Coach House Press, 1966.
Scraptures: 9th Sequence. Toronto, Ganglia Press, 1967.
Last Poem with You in Mind. Toronto, Ganglia Press, 1967.
Konfessions of an Elizabethan Fan Dancer. London, Writers Forum, 1967; revised edition, Toronto, Weed/Flower Press, 1973.
bp (includes *Journeying and The Returns, Letters Home,* and a recording, *Borders*). Toronto, Coach House Press, 1967.
Scraptures: 10th Sequence. Toronto, Ganglia Press, 1967.
Scraptures: Sequence 11. Toronto, Fleye Press, 1967.
Ruth. Toronto, Fleye Press, 1967.
The Year of the Frog: A Study of the Frog from the Scraptures: Ninth Sequence. Toronto, Ganglia Press, 1967.
Cold Mountain. Toronto, Ganglia Press, 1967.
Ballads of the Restless Are. Sacramento, California, Runcible Spoon Press, 1968.
Dada Lama: A Sound Sequence in Six Parts. London, Cavan McCarthy, 1968.

D.A. Dead.   Toronto, grOnk, 1968.
Kon 66 and 67.   Toronto, grOnk, 1968.
The Complete Works.   Toronto, Ganglia Press, 1968.
Sail.   Toronto, Ganglia Press, 1969.
A New Calendar.   Toronto, Ganglia Press, 1969.
Astronomical Observations July 1969.   Toronto, Ganglia Press, 1969.
Third Fragment from a Poem Continually in the Process of Being Written.   Toronto, Ganglia Press, 1969.
Beast.   Sackville, New Brunswick, Mount Allison University, 1969.
Postcard.   Toronto, Coach House Press, 1969.
Lament.   Toronto, Ganglia Press, and London, Writers Forum, 1970.
Grease Ball Comics.   Toronto, Ganglia Press, 2 vols., 1970-72.
A Condensed History of Nothing.   Toronto, Ganglia Press, 1970.
Still Water.   Vancouver, Talonbooks, 1970.
Beach Head.   Sacramento, California, Runcible Spoon Press, 1970.
MONO tones.   Vancouver, Talonbooks, 1971.
ABC: The Aleph Beth Book.   Ottawa, Oberon Press, 1971.
The Other Side of the Room: Poems 1966-69.   Toronto, Weed/Flower Press, 1971.
Parallel Texts, with Steve McCaffery.   Toronto, Anonbeyond, 2 vols., 1971.
The Captain Poetry Poems.   Vancouver, blewointmentpress, 1971.
The Adventures of Milt the Morph in Colour, with Barbara Caruso.   Toronto, Seripress, 1972.
Collbrations, with Steve McCaffery.   Toronto, Ganglia Press, 1972.
The Martyrology.   Toronto, Coach House Press, 3 vols., 1972-82.
Scraptures: Basic Sequences.   Toronto, Massassauga, 1973.
Love: A Book of Remembrances.   Vancouver, Talonbooks, 1974.
Alephunit.   Toronto, Seripress, 1974.
Unit of Four.   Toronto, Seripress, 1974.
H: An Excursion, with Barbara Caruso.   Toronto, Seripress, 1976.
A Draft of Book IV of The Martyrology.   Privately printed, 1976.
Scraptures: 2nd Sequences: Alternate Takes.   Vancouver, BC Monthly, 1977.
From "In Lakeland."   Toronto, grOnk, 1978.
Alphhabet Ilphabet.   Toronto, Seripress, 1978.
White Sound: A Variation.   Toronto, grOnk, 1978.
Mollie Darling.   Toronto, Ganglia Press, 1978.
From My Window.   Toronto, Seripress, 1978.
In England Now That Spring, with Steve McCaffery.   Toronto, Aya Press, 1979.
A Christmas Vision in the Voice of St. Nicholas.   Privately printed, 1979.
The Martyrology Book V Chain B.   Toronto, CHP Manuscript Editions, 1979.
Absolute Statement for My Mother.   Toronto, Seripress, 1979.
Door to Oz.   Toronto, Seripress, 1979.
Love Affair.   Toronto, Seripress, 1979.
Movies.   Toronto, Seripress, 1979.
Doors: To Oz and Other Landscapes.   Toronto, grOnk, 1979.
As Elected: Selected Writings 1962-1979.   Vancouver, Talonbooks, 1980.
Familiar.   Privately printed, 1980.
Sharp Facts: Selections from TTA 26.   Milwaukee, Membrane Press, 1980.

A Bouquet as Thanks.   Privately printed, 1980.
Briefly.   Lantzville, British Columbia, Island, 1981.
Hour 18.   Privately printed, 1981.
The Frog's Obsession with the Fly.   Toronto, Curvd H&Z, 1981.
Digging Up the Pas T.   Privately printed, 1981.
Of Lines: Some Drawings.   Toronto, Underwhich, 1981.
Continental Trance.   Lantzville, British Columbia, Oolichan, 1982.
The Martyrology Book V Chain 10.   Toronto, Curvd H&Z, 1982.
A Draft of Inchoate Road.   Privately printed, 1982; revised edition, 1982.
Window, Constantly Broken: Selections from TTA 26.   Toronto, grOnk, 1982.
Novel.   Toronto, Curvd H&Z, 1982.
A B.C. Childhood, with Brian Dedora.   Toronto, grOnk, 1982.
The Grammar Trilogy.   Burnaby, British Columbia, Simon Fraser University, 1982.
The Frog Variations.   Toronto, Curvd H&Z, 1982.
Tales of the Myth Collector: The Teaching of Arress Kinken.   Privately printed, 1982.
Three Drafts.   Toronto, Music Gallery, 1982.
Ruins of C.   Toronto, Curvd H&Z, 1983.
Song for Saint Ein.   Vancouver, Slug Press, 1983.
New H Blues.   Toronto, Curvd H&Z, 1983.
Haiku (for David A).   Toronto, Curvd H&Z, 1983.
Hologram 4.   Toronto, Curvd H&Z, 1983.
Transformational Unit.   Privately printed, 1983.
Ghosts 2.   Toronto, grOnk, 1983.
Wall.   Toronto, Ganglia Press, 1983.
Possibilities of the Poem.   Toronto, Curvd H&Z, 1984.
Cycle?   Toronto, Curvd H&Z, 1984.
Theory 1—4.   Toronto, Curvd H&Z, 1984.
Continuum.   Toronto, Underwhich, 1984.

Recording: *Motherlove,* Allied, 1968.

Plays

Radio Play: *Little Boy Lost Meets Mother Tongue,* 1969.

Television Writing: for *Fragglerock.*

Other plays: *The Brown Book,* 1978; *Group,* with Nelles Van Loon, 1980; *Tracks,* with Mary Barton and Philip Schaus, 1983.

Novels

Two Novels (Andy and *For Jesus Lunatick).*   Toronto, Coach House Press, 1969; revised edition, 1971.
Still: 1982 Three Day Novel Contest Winner.   Vancouver, Arsenal Pulp Press, 1983.

Short Stories

Nights on Prose Mountain.   Toronto, grOnk, 1969.
The True Eventual Story of Billy the Kid.   Toronto, Weed/Flower Press, 1970.
Craft Dinner: Stories and Texts 1966-1976.   Toronto, Aya Press, 1978.

Other

Journal.   Toronto, Coach House Press, 1978.
Translating Translating Apollinaire.   Milwaukee, Membrane

Press, 1979.

Extreme Positions. Edmonton, Longspoon Press, 1981.

Moosequakes and Other Disasters (for children). Windsor, Ontario, Black Moss Press, 1981.

The Man Who Loved His Knees (for children). Windsor, Ontario, Black Moss Press, 1983.

Once: A Lullaby (for children). Windsor, Ontario, Black Moss Press, 1983.

To the End of the Block (for children). Windsor, Ontario, Black Moss Press, 1984.

Editor, *The Cosmic Chef: An Evening of Concrete.* Ottawa, Oberon Press, 1970.

Editor, with Jiri Valoch, *The Pipe: Recent Czech Concrete Poetry.* Toronto, Coach House Press, 1973.

Editor, with Steve McCaffery, *The Story so Four.* Toronto, Coach House Press, 1976.

Editor, with Steve McCaffery, *Sound Poetry: A Catalogue.* Toronto, Underwhich, 1978.

Editor, *The Arches: Selected Poems,* by Frank Davey. Vancouver, Talonbooks, 1980.

Editor, with Steve McCaffery, *Canadian 'Pataphysics.* Toronto, Underwhich, 1981.

*

Manuscript Collection: Simon Fraser University Library, Burnaby, British Columbia.

Critical Studies: *bp Nichol: What History Teaches* (includes bibliography) by Stephen Scobie, Vancouver, Talonbooks, 1984.

bpNichol comments:

(1970) primarily i consider myself to be serving an apprenticeship in language, hopefully to find ways out of the self-imposed trap it has evolved into.

i suppose if i have a general theme it's the language trap and that runs thru the centre of everything i do. in this regard Bill Bissett first pointed the direction with a poem called "They Found th Wagon Cat in Human Body." hence style is disregarded in favor of reproduction of actual states of mind in order to follow these states thru the particular traps they become in search of possible exits. hence for me there is no discrepancy to pass back and forth between trad poetry, concrete poetry, sound poetry, film, comic strips, the novel or what have you in order to reproduce the muse that musses up my own brain.

as large influences i would like to note Chester Gould's *Dick Tracy,* Walt Kelly's *Pogo,* & Winsor McKay's *Dream's of a Rarebit Fiend & Little Nemo in Slumberland.* In addition the poetry of Olson and Creeley, e.e. cummings, gertrude stein & james joyce, rube goldberg, & the children's books by Dr. Seuss.

*　　*　　*

bpNichol is internationally known as the Canadian concrete poet, a role bestowed on him by that self-conscious international movement.

Konfessions of an Elizabethan Fan Dancer consists of typewriter poems, visual poetry dependent on the identical size of typewriter letters. "The Return of the Repressed," reminiscent of a genetic chart, evolves in time:

```
                     Q
OOOOOOOOOⵔOOOOOQOOOO
OOOOOOOOOⵔOOOOOQOOOOO
OOOOOOOOOⵔOOOOOQOOOO
```

```
QQQQQQQQQQQQQQQQQQQQQQQQQ
QQQQQQQQQQQQQQQQQQQQQQQQQ
QQQQQQQQQQQQQQQQQQQQQQQQQ
QQQQQQQQQQQQQQQQQQQQQQQQQ
```

The progenitor is replaced by his sons. Nichol uses the more extravagant Press-On Type for "tight imagistic" effects, not meant as pictures, he says, but as "syllabic and sub-syllabic messages to who care to listen." In "Window," Nichol paints with letters the aural and emotional complex suggested by a window; "imagism" seems to be an appropriate analogue. *Still Water* is a box of poems on cards, cleanly printed in sans-serif type. Many are funny, like this rap at high coo: "2 leaves touch/ bad poems are written." Others are one-liners using onomatopoetic permutations: "beyond a bee yawned abbey on debby honda beyond." Although one-line poems are in vogue, their creators seem defensive, probably because scale in poetry and in painting has grown larger through this century, more heroic, more inclusive.

In any case, there is nothing new or unusual about Nichol's concrete poetry. In his book on Canadian literature, Northrop Frye concluded that the country's literary energy had been absorbed in meeting a standard, a self-defeating enterprise because real standards can only be established, not met. Canadian writing, according to Frye, is academic in the pejorative sense, an imitation of a prescribed model, second rate in conception, not merely execution.

The poetry which is loosely called concrete, however, is self-investigative. Richard Kostelanetz, a theoretician of the movement, compares it to minimalism. Like minimal artists, concrete poets will restrict themselves to the means of making statements. Nichol writes a poem on mortality which consists of rhyme: "FLOWERS/(hours)." The Toronto Research Group, in which Nichol is prominent, investigates translation and narrative in an imaginative rather than critical context. The very process of imitation seems to have freed Nichol from that malaise.

The Martyrology, a three-volume large-scale work, is certainly readable. It's about a bunch of saints he made up. Saint Ranglehold, for instance, is the patron of the sea, and he gives lovers a hard time on their Petrarchan voyages; were there such things as "the good" and "the bad" saints, Nichol asks, where would we place him?

a ship in perilous storm
the lover doth compare his state to

often he loses
　　　　　　　　　　　(sinking out of view)

dedications change as frequently as the moon

riding the white waves
patterns seem strangely familiar

ruler of the ships & sea
saint ranglehold guides lovers with a flaccid hand

snickers knowingly
as they flounder on dry land

Saint Reat, like Charles Olson, had difficulty breathing and, as a wanderer in search of breath, he is the patron saint of poetry. Saint Orm, a loser, gets kicked Kafka-style around a circus. Nichol has a special devotion to Saint Orm. These saints are neither Eastern nor Christian but very tough. It takes a Dick Tracy or Emma Peel to handle them.

random brain stranded in the station

sam & dick & emma peel
oh how the real world gets lost in you

the loose ends shrivel

           & are gone

faces denote the places growing song

The Martyrology is a creation myth. The saints once lived in the clouds. Saint And was the first to leave. Orm followed, expecting rain. Saint Iff had a terrible time, landing in the desert and dying near water. Only Saint Rike and the lady of past nights stayed behind, and their tale is curious indeed. But so are the other tales.

—Michael André

NICHOLSON, Norman (Cornthwaite). British. Born in Millom, Cumberland, 8 January 1914. Educated at local schools. Married Yvonne Gardner in 1956 (died, 1982). Frequent public lecturer. Recipient: Heinemann Award, 1945; Cholmondeley Award, 1967; Northern Arts Association grant, 1969; Society of Authors award, 1972; Arts Council bursary, 1977; Queen's Gold Medal for Poetry, 1977. M.A.: Manchester University, 1959; Open University, 1975; D.Litt.: University of Liverpool, 1980; University of Lancashire, 1984. Honorary Fellow, Manchester Polytechnic, 1979. Fellow, Royal Society of Literature, 1945. O.B.E. (Officer, Order of the British Empire), 1981. Address: 14 St. George's Terrace, Millom, Cumbria LA18 4DB, England.

PUBLICATIONS

Verse

Selected Poems, with J.C. Hall and Keith Douglas. London, John Bale and Staples, 1943.
Five Rivers. London, Faber, 1944; New York, Dutton, 1945.
Rock Face. London, Faber, 1948.
The Pot Geranium. London, Faber, 1954.
Selected Poems. London, Faber, 1966.
No Star on the Way Back: Ballads and Carols. Manchester, Manchester Institute of Contemporary Arts, 1967.
A Local Habitation. London, Faber, 1972.
Hard of Hearing. London, Poem-of-the-Month Club, 1974.
Cloud on Black Combe. Hitchin, Hertfordshire, Cellar Press, 1975.
Stitch and Stone: A Cumbrian Landscape. Sunderland, Ceolfrith, Press, 1975.
The Shadow on Black Combe. Ashington, Northumberland, MidNAG, 1978.
Sea to the West. London, Faber, 1981.
Selected Poems 1940-1982. London, Faber, 1982.

Recording: *Poems,* with Tony Connor, Argo, 1974.

Plays

The Old Man of the Mountains (produced London, 1945). London, Faber, 1946; revised edition, 1950.

Prophesy to the Wind: A Play in Four Scenes and a Prologue (produced London, 1949). London, Faber, 1950.
A Match for the Devil (produced Edinburgh, 1953). London, Faber, 1955.
Birth by Drowning (produced Mirfield, Yorkshire, 1959). London, Faber, 1960.

Television Play: *No Star on the Way Back,* 1963.

Novels

The Fire of the Lord. London, Nicholson and Watson, 1944; New York, Dutton, 1946.
The Green Shore. London, Nicholson and Watson, 1947.

Other

Man and Literature. London, S.C.M. Press, 1943.
Cumberland and Westmorland. London, Hale, 1949.
H.G. Wells. London, Barker, and Denver, Swallow, 1950.
William Cowper. London, Lehmann, 1951.
The Lakers: The Adventures of the First Tourists. London, Hale, 1955.
Provincial Pleasures. London, Hale, 1959.
William Cowper. London, Longman, 1960.
Portrait of the Lakes. London, Hale, 1963; revised edition, as *The Lakes,* 1977.
Enjoying It All (BBC talks). London, Waltham Forest Books, 1964.
Greater Lakeland. London, Hale, 1969.
Wednesday Early Closing (autobiography). London, Faber, 1975.
The Candy-Floss Tree (for children), with Gerda Mayer and Frank Flynn. Oxford, Oxford University Press, 1984.

Editor, *An Anthology of Religious Verse Designed for the Times.* London, Penguin, 1942.
Editor, *Wordsworth: An Introduction and Selection.* London, Phoenix, and New York, Dent, 1949.
Editor, *Poems,* by William Cowper. London, Grey Walls Press, 1951.
Editor, *A Choice of Cowper's Verse.* London, Faber, 1975.
Editor, *The Lake District: An Anthology.* London, Hale, 1977.

*

Manuscript Collections: National Collection of Poetry Manuscripts, London; Northern Arts Manuscript Collection, Newcastle upon Tyne.

Critical Studies: *Christian Themes in Contemporary Poets* by Kathleen Morgan, London, S.C.M. Press, 1965; *Norman Nicholson* by Philip Gardner, New York, Twayne, 1973; "Still Living at Home: Norman Nicholson at Seventy" by Matt Simpson, in *London Magazine,* July 1984; *Between Comets: For Norman Nicholson at 70* (includes bibliography), edited by William Scammell, Durham, Taxus Press, 1985.

Norman Nicholson comments:
(1970) The most obvious characteristic of my poetry is the fact that I draw by far the greater amount of my imagery from my own immediate environment—i.e., from the fells, dales, farms, sea-shore and estuaries of the English Lake District, and from the houses, streets, blast furnaces, mines, etc. of the small industrial town of Millom where I still live in the house where I was

born. But, though the topographical element is prominent in my earlier verse, I do not think of myself primarily as a local poet. On the contrary, I feel that, through drawing on my knowledge of the place and the people where and among whom I have spent all my life, I am able to say what I want to say about man in relation to his physical environment and about human society, man in relation to man. In particular, I believe that in a small, somewhat isolated town like Millom, the problems of society, the dwelling-together of people different types, ages and class, and the pattern of the repetition and variation shown from generation to generation, can be seen on a scale small enough for the mind to grasp it whole.

(1974) After the publication of *The Pot Geranium*, I wrote very little poetry for about ten years, but then began writing again and produced the poems collected together under the title of *A Local Habitation*, which was The Poetry Book Society's Autumn Choice for 1972. This work is, on the whole, more direct, more colloquial in tone, and, though I am as concerned as ever with the problem of environment, the new poems deal more with people than with places, and in particular with the people of Millom, with my family and other memories of childhood and youth.

(1985) During the last ten years, with the complete closing down and demolition of both the ironworks and the iron ore mines, Millom has ceased to be an industrial town. As a "working model" of an industrial society situated close to the wild countryside of Cumberland, it now exists only in the past and in my memory. In my more recent poetry, and especially in *Sea to the West*, though I still write occasionally of the town's and my own past, I have turned, to some extent, to the elementary natural world out of which the town sprang in the first place, the world of rocks, becks, shingle, sand, and sea. The result is not so much "descriptive poetry" as poetry which tries to relate human life to its basic physical grounding and to place it within the time-scale of the slow changes of the natural world.

*   *   *

The insights and imagery of Norman Nicholson's work are rooted deep in the soil of his native Cumbria. Having lived for more than seventy years in his birthplace—a distinction surely to be claimed by few poets today—he writes of the "local habitation" and its people with the intimacy bred of long knowledge. He has witnessed with sadness the process of change in the life of his small community: the mine where his grandfather was foreman now "Drowned under stagnant waters, chimneys felled and uprooted,/ Slagbanks ploughed down." His poems on the closing, and later dismantling, of Millom ironworks, memorably elegize a whole age pensioned off when "they shovelled my childhood/ On to a rubbish heap." "The Bloody Cranesbill" crystallizes the same regret, on finding the remembered, fragile flower still stubbornly surviving on the site of the derelict mine once so active. With its demolition he sees the town's purpose subside; and in a prophetic moment, envisages the "known tight streets, the hunched chapels," once hacked from the dynamited combe of "Millom Old Quarry," themselves swept back there and "The quick turf push a green tarpaulin over/ All that was mortal in five thousand lives."

Nicholson's awareness of impermanence extends to larger perspectives of change when he contemplates the ceaseless, centuries-old reshaping of the earth's contours by "the wild weather of time." Many poems communicate his preoccupation with the flux of elemental energy: observed not only in rivers, tides, and seasons, but in the movement of the glacier, the fluidity of rocks which in the interplay of cloud and mist, sun and rain, "disintegrate, dissolve...waste daily away."

His sense of a living past contained within the present pervades Nicholson's explorations of more personal experience. Many varied incidents surface, with mingled humour and pathos, from the landscape of memory: such as the Christmas of his mother's death, so vigorously yet poignantly recaptured in "Comprehending It Not." His grandmother, uprooted in youth from rural to industrial poverty, springs to energetic life in this and several other poems which acknowledge the strength of family ties. "Cornthwaite" celebrates the poet's debt to the patient labour of distant ancestors cultivating unpromising land, as he too now prepares "To hack out once again my inherited thwaite/ And sow my peck of poems, not much of a crop."

The wry, self-mocking modesty is characteristic. As sharply precise in detail as his portraits of people are those of particular places: Cumbrian rivers, including Duddon, with its affectionately chronicled Wordsworthian echoes; the mines so atmospherically evoked in "Egremont" and "Cleator Moor"; or towns like Whitehaven and his beloved native Millom. Yet Nicholson is seldom merely descriptive, or in any narrow sense a "regional" poet confined to his local scene. Keenly as he savours the prosaic familiar surface of his home town—inn and institute, garage and grocer's, kite-flying boys and the temperance brass band—he is never unaware of a deeper underlying reality: "Beneath the stone, the idea of a stone,/ Beneath the idea, the love."

Through this habit of metaphysical speculation, parables are repeatedly perceived in the ordinary occurrences and apparent commonplaces of daily life. The toffee-eating small boy of "Rising Five," so proud of his age, provides a chilling parallel with the human propensity for wishing life away. In "The New Cemetery" the jubilation of working horses put out to grass anticipates his own release, "unblinkered and at last delivered/ Of a lifetime's/ Load of parcels." In another prospect of death, "Sea to the West," the images of dark and dazzle have something of Herbert's spiritual quality—still more vividly recalled in the metaphor of the soul's seasons in "St. Luke's Summer." The cosmic inclusiveness of its vision makes "The Pot Geranium" perhaps Nicholson's most powerfully memorable poem. Like Donne's lovers, his urban flower encompasses within one small room the vastness of the universe: "Contains the pattern, the prod and pulse of life,/ Complete as the Nile or the Niger."

Vigorously colloquial in diction, with a gift for the homely image—lake "bright as sixpence," tide "Unwrapping like a roll of oilcloth"—and apt, arresting analogy, Norman Nicholson universalizes the particular to illustrate and illumine profounder perceptions. Many earlier poems were on biblical subjects and explicitly Christian in thought. Although his emphasis has more recently shifted to meditation on dissolution and renewal in "the earth's/ Fluid overcoat," an essentially religious view of life has prevailed throughout Nicholson's work. "Nobbut God" is the pervasive presence, whether in the hollow quarry or the stone hewn from it to make "the built splendour/ We call a cathedral."

—Margaret Willy

NIMS, John Frederick. American. Born in Muskegon, Michigan, 20 November 1913. Educated at De Paul University, Chicago; University of Notre Dame, Indiana, A.B. 1937, M.A. 1939; University of Chicago, Ph.D. in comparative literature 1945. Married Bonnie Larkin in 1947; four children. Taught at the University of Notre Dame, 1939-45, 1946-58; University of Toronto, 1945-46; Visiting Fulbright Professor of American

Literature, Bocconi University, Milan, 1952-53, and University of Florence, 1953-54; Visiting Professor of American Studies, University of Madrid, 1958-60 (Smith-Mundt grant). Professor of English, University of Illinois, Urbana, 1961-65, and since 1973, Chicago Circle. Visiting Professor, Harvard University, Cambridge, Massachusetts, 1964, 1968-69, 1974, Bread Loaf School of English, Vermont, 1965-69, University of Florida, Gainesville, 1973-76, Williams College, Williamstown, Massachusetts, 1975, College of Charleston, South Carolina, 1981, and University of Chicago, Spring 1982. Associate Editor, 1945-48, Guest Editor, 1960-61, and Editor, 1978-84, *Poetry*, Chicago. Recipient: Harriet Monroe Memorial Prize, 1942, Guarantors Prize, 1943, and Levinson Prize, 1944 (*Poetry*, Chicago); National Endowment for the Arts grant, 1967; American Academy grant, 1968; Brandeis University Creative Arts Award, 1974; Academy of American Poets Fellowship, 1982. Address: Department of English, University of Illinois, Box 4348, Chicago, Illinois 60680, U.S.A.

PUBLICATIONS

Verse

Five Young American Poets: Third Series, with others.   New York, New Directions, 1944.
The Iron Pastoral.   New York, Sloane, 1947.
A Fountain in Kentucky and Other Poems.   New York, Sloane, 1950.
Knowledge of the Evening: Poems 1950-1960.   New Brunswick, New Jersey, Rutgers University Press, 1960.
Of Flesh and Bone.   New Brunswick, New Jersey, Rutgers University Press, 1967.
The Kiss: A Jambalaya.   Boston, Houghton Mifflin, 1982.
Selected Poems.   Chicago, University of Chicago Press, 1982.

Other

Western Wind: An Introduction to Poetry.   New York, Random House, 1974; revised edition, 1983.

Editor, with others, *The Poem Itself.*   New York, Holt, 1960.
Editor, *Ovid's Metamorphoses: The Arthur Golding Translation.*   New York, Macmillan, 1965.
Editor, *Love's Cruelty*, by James Shirley.   New York, Garland, 1980.
Editor, *The Harper Anthology of Poetry.*   New York, Harper, 1981.

Translator, *The Poems of St. John of the Cross.*   New York, Grove Press, 1959; revised edition, 1968; Chicago, University of Chicago Press, 1979.
Translator, *Andromache*, in *Euripides III* of *The Complete Greek Tragedies.*   Chicago, University of Chicago Press, 1959.
Translator, *Sappho to Valéry: Poems.*   New Brunswick, New Jersey, Rutgers University Press, 1971; revised edition, Princeton, New Jersey, Princeton University Press, 1980.

*

Critical Studies: *Babel to Byzantium* by James Dickey, New York, Farrar Straus, 1968; "A Higher Fidelity" by Brewster Ghiselin, in *Sewanee Review* (Tennessee), Spring 1973.

*   *   *

John Frederick Nims is a poet known since the 1940's for poems in classical meters, poems with beauty that partakes of the rococo or of art nouveau; many of the poems have the quality of the wrought-iron facades on Louis Sullivan buildings in Chicago, the city most associated with Nims. His poems could also be compared to carved, antique furniture or to cut-glass. The concern is ever with the ornate, the well-wrought, the carved, etched, and finely honed. The lines are musical and intense, and he is fond of working with ancient metrics, giving his work a hammered and occasionally labored quality. He is quite the opposite of a poet whose first thoughts are held sacred; his aesthetic is quite counter to that of free verse. He does not play without a net.

This reader's favorites (and they have been so for many years) are "The Young Ionia" (elegiac, romantic, and classical), "The Lover" (mordantly ironic, influenced perhaps by John Crowe Ransom), and "The Evergreen" (a memorable elegy for his young son).

> *Under the snow, what lies?*
>   Treasure the hemlock covers—
> Skysail of frost, and riding in
>   Starlight keen and steep.
> *But the boy below?* What's here is
>   Gear in a sea-chest only.
> Stowed for a season, then
>   Pleasure-bound on the deep.

Nims includes, in his *Selected Poems*, sequences of Shakespearean sonnets, "Foto-Sonnets" (five scenes from a vacation trip), and "The Masque of Blackness" (an elegy for the lost son): "Though past and future's gone, some Now remains./ No mountain blazing candid, no, not one—/ They picked up pebbles and these argued stone." A few of Nims's poems ("Dollar Bill," "Penny Arcade," "Magazine Stand," and "The Genuine Ellis") reflect the kind of 1940's passion for pop-culture and public visitations that one sees in Karl Shapiro's poems; other passages seem to anticipate or share the stage with Lowell, as "The Indolent Day":

> Having all day no wisdom weighed or spoken,
> A sheepish no-good I lie alone,
> My veins a-humming still like violin strings,
> A fife or froggy bassoon in every bone.

Nims is certainly an urban poet, and one whose work reflects his Catholicism, more mystical than ritual. Dudley Fitts said of his poems that "in their moral passion lies their peculiar strength." Nims has been criticized for excessive imagery, for thrusting upon the reader more than he or she can, perhaps, handle (but who is qualified to make such a judgement?), and for rigidity of form ("technical acuity"). His strong sense of contrast between the mourned classical world (of cities lost to time and vulgarity) and the contemporary scene is haunting. In "A Fountain in Kentucky" a paint-flaked cast-iron fountain on a town square becomes a symbol of mythic power neglected but intact. Nims has translated work from several languages, and more than capably; these too are endued with classicism and mysticism as well as a deep love of form. "All the poems I had ever known throbbed with a physical rhythm, had what is called *form*," Nims has written. "Form is what I thought poems came into the world with, as plants and animals do."

Subtlety and elegiac feeling are likely to be this poet's legacy.

In "Human Kind Cannot Bear Very Much Reality" a sense of disaster averted by care hovers near:

> Hence tricks of dimension on us soft as kisses;
> Vagueness of towns seen from a little way;
> Tact of the hillside oak, giant that presses
> Mild on the eye, a feather of grey.

In the next stanza disaster bears down:

> Hence the world rushing down fast from the plane.
> In ten seconds Gulliver's toy, its human places
> Amusing and trim: no room for the cripple's grin at the pane,
> The men swinging jagged beerbottles, blood on their faces.

The last stanza addresses the tragic errors and disasters of romantic love or lust run wild: domesticity and the bourgeois are protective virtues.

> Hence too the fortunate limits of love,
> Indifference, tedium, pride. Else, carefree and tall,
> What man on the lunch-hour street freely could move,
> So dumbfounded in love with the plain least girl of all?

Clearly the subtle and understated image is meant to convey a great deal. Elsewhere the poet endorsed "racy verve—quirks and oddities—rugged English gusto." Nims doesn't mind making the reader work. But such an opting for classicism may not always have served Nims as an editor. As editor of *Poetry* he was, perhaps, not always open to work that represented other schools or sensibilities. "Words are suggested as much by rhythm as by the argument," Nims has stated, "...the form of the poem exists before the ideas. Since form determines subject...." These remarks were made in reference to his book of translations from nine languages (and these translations are often inspired), but they are deeply held and pervasive convictions; such views might not have led Nims to much sympathy with poets who work from other resources. Nims paid a price, no doubt, as editors often do, for his views and his aesthetic convictions; the role is a no-win position, certainly for one whose own work is his foremost responsibility. Having resigned the editorship of *Poetry*, Nims can presumably return to his more important work.

Nims's poetry will long be remembered, for it is powerful enough to transcend and survive the parochialism of aesthetic arguments and the politics of publishing fashions, as well as divergences of views on vital world issues, conflicts that have polarized poetry as well as other areas of our lives.

—David Ray

NORRIS, Leslie. Welsh. Born in Merthyr Tydfil, Glamorgan, 21 May 1921. Educated at Cyfthfa Castle School, 1931-38; City of Coventry College, 1947-48; University of Southampton (Ralph Morley Prize, 1958), 1955-58, Dip.Ed., M.Phil., 1958. Served in the Royal Air Force, 1940-42. Married Catherine Mary Morgan in 1948. Teacher, Grass Royal School, Yeovil, Somerset, 1948-52; Deputy Head, Southdown School, Bath, 1952-55; Head Teacher, Aldingbourne School, Chichester, 1956-58; Principal Lecturer in Degree Studies, College of Education, Bognor Regis, Sussex, 1958-73; Visiting Lecturer, University of Washington, Seattle, 1973, 1980; Resident Poet, Eton College, 1977; Arts Council Writing Fellow, West Sussex Institute of Higher Education, 1979-80; Professor of English, Brigham Young University, Provo, Utah, 1983, 1984, 1985. Recipient: Welsh Arts Council award, 1967, 1968, and prize, 1978; Alice Hunt Bartlett Prize, 1970; Cholmondeley Prize, 1978; David Higham Prize, for fiction, 1978; Katherine Mansfield award, 1981. Agent: Charles Schlessiger, Brandt and Brandt, 1501 Broadway, New York, New York 10036, U.S.A. Address: Plas Nant, Northfields Lane, Aldingbourne, Chichester, Sussex PO2O 6UH, England.

PUBLICATIONS

Verse

Tongue of Beauty. London, Favil Press, 1941.
Poems. London, Falcon Press, 1946.
The Ballad of Billy Rose. Leeds, Northern House, 1964.
The Loud Winter. Cardiff, Triskel Press, 1967.
Finding Gold. London, Chatto and Windus, 1967.
Curlew. St. Brelade, Jersey, Armstrong, 1969.
Ransoms. London, Chatto and Windus, 1970.
His Last Autumn. Rushden, Northamptonshire, Sceptre Press, 1972.
Mountains, Polecats, Pheasants and Other Elegies. London, Chatto and Windus, 1973.
Stone and Fern. Winchester, Southern Arts Association, 1973.
At the Publishers'. Berkhamsted, Hertfordshire, Priapus, 1976.
Ravenna Bridge. Knotting, Bedfordshire, Sceptre Press, 1977.
Islands Off Maine. Cranberry Isles, Maine, Tidal Press, 1977.
Merlin and the Snake's Egg. New York, Viking Press, 1978.
Hyperion. Knotting, Bedfordshire, Sceptre Press, 1979.
Water Voices. London, Chatto and Windus—Hogarth Press, 1980.
Walking the White Fields: Poems 1967-1980. Boston, Little Brown, 1980.

Recording: *Poems*, with Dannie Abse, Argo, 1974.

Short Stories

Sliding: Short Stories. New York, Scribner, 1976; London, Dent, 1978.

Other

Glyn Jones. Cardiff, University of Wales Press, 1973.

Editor, *Vernon Watkins, 1906-1967.* London, Faber, 1970.
Editor, *Andrew Young: Remembrance and Homage.* Cranberry Isles, Maine, Tidal Press, 1978.
Editor, *The Mabinogion*, translated by Lady Charlotte Guest. London, Folio Society, 1980.

*

Manuscript Collection: National Library of Wales, Aberystwyth.

Critical Studies: by Sam Adams, in *Poetry Wales* (Cardiff), 1972; R. Jenkins, in *Anglo-Welsh Review* (Pembroke Dock), 1972; Ted Walker, in *Priapus* (Berkhamsted, Hertfordshire), 1972; Norman Rosenfeld, in *Tar River Poetry* (Greenville, North Carolina), 1983.

Leslie Norris comments:

My poetry is an attempt to recreate, not to describe. The birds or animals or people or buildings or trees existing in my poems, must exist root branch claw skin and stone. The texture of my words must be made of feathers or bones bark or whatever, the lines must move with real muscle. I think I am a Jungian poet, bringing up the images from some unknown source. The poems come unbidden, and my task is to recognise them; often I am well towards the end of a poem before I know what it is "about." But afterwards I work with unremitting labor to make sure of the poem's clarity, to make its surface perfect. I think my poems ought to be like onions; the golden outer skin flawless, the weight surprisingly heavy, solid, much more than you'd expect; then when the outer skin is peeled, there is moist, pearly inner layer of meaning, then another and another.

Somewhere in the process you might begin to weep.

*   *   *

Leslie Norris's birth at Wern Farm, just outside Merthyr Tydfil, Wales's Klondike of the 19th century, and his subsequent residence in southern England together provide the cultural tension that, after a long silence, generated his poetry again in the 1960's and made it something quite different from the early work in *Tongue of Beauty*. The gap is bridged, of course, by Norris's fascination with and power over words, but the Merthyr to which he could never go back (which was, in the spirit of his youth and that of other writers his seniors, quite dead) was the source of many elegies, in *Finding Gold* in particular, which were an expression both of the irrecoverability of his own youth and of a more general irrecoverability ("And yes, those boys are gone"). It was not that he could not return to Wales—he did that, first with holidays in Cardiganshire and then by the purchase of his cottage "Wthan"—but what this did was to make it possible to approach the Welsh heritage in a way which would have been strange to the Merthyr-bound man: it also linked and contrasted the peaceful rurality of Sussex with the more wayward and half-tamed spirit of the countryside round Llandysul. Leslie Norris was always, perhaps, a man of the country and his great achievement, visible more and more in later books like *Mountains, Polecats, Pheasants*, has been to use the simple, physical stimuli of a rural world to make poems which are no more than occasionally recondite and are always couched in a language which accommodates images in the most natural manner possible and gives continuous pleasure. His syntax is rarely distorted or difficult. What he has evolved is that most difficult thing to master and obtain, a style which in its limpidity, clarity and latent force carries the simple, the anecdotal, even the common, experience and gives it an unexpected memorability. Nor is this quality confined to his poetry, for which he received the Cholmondeley Prize in 1978; the ecstatic reception of his volume of short stories, *Sliding* (he was awarded both the David Higham Prize and a Welsh Arts Council Prize for this), was the recognition of an achievement very similar. Like Edward Thomas and, to a lesser extent, Andrew Young, he can conjure common observation into his own idiosyncratic mode. His recourse, even in later books, to boyhood memories of the boxing ring or the collier's care for birds or dogs—or, more piercingly, to recollection of a classmate killed at Aberfan—provides the variety that makes his countryman's perception the more poignant. Leslie Norris is that rare poet who has made his work accessible without cheapening the experience of the poem or blunting its delicacy. In this sense he is an ambassador for poetry at the court of the general public in a generation that sorely needs one.

—Roland Mathias

NORSE, Harold. American. Born Harold George Rosen in New York City, 6 July 1916. Educated at Brooklyn College, B.A. 1938; New York University, M.A. 1951. Worked as sheet metal worker, dancer, proof-reader, 1941-44; Instructor in English, Cooper Union, New York, 1949-52, Lion School of English, Rome, 1956-57, and U.S. Information Service School, Naples, 1958; part-time teacher, San Jose State University, California, 1973-75. Founding Editor, *Bastard Angel*, San Francisco. Recipient: Borestone Mountain Poetry Award, 1968; National Endowment for the Arts Fellowship, 1974; De Young Museum grant, 1974. Address: 157 Albion Street, San Francisco, California 94110, U.S.A.

PUBLICATIONS

Verse

The Undersea Mountain. Denver, Swallow, 1953.
The Dancing Beasts. New York, Macmillan, 1962.
Ole. Bensenville, Illinois, Open Skull, 1966.
Karma Circuit: 20 Poems and a Preface. London, Nothing Doing in London, 1967; San Francisco, Panjandrum Press, 1974.
Christmas on Earth. N.p., Minkoff Rare Editions, 1968.
Penguin Modern Poets 13, with Charles Bukowski and Philip Lamantia. London, Penguin, 1969.
Hotel Nirvana: Selected Poems 1953-1973. San Francisco, City Lights, 1974.
I See America Daily. San Francisco, Mother's Hen, 1974.
Carnivorous Saint: Gay Poems 1941-1976. San Francisco, Gay Sunshine Press, 1977.
Mysteries of Magritte. San Diego, Atticus Press, 1984.

Novel

Beat Hotel. Augsburg, Maro, 1975; San Diego, Atticus Press, 1983.

Other

Translator, *The Roman Sonnets of G.G. Belli*. Highlands, North Carolina, Jargon, 1960.

*

Manuscript Collection: Lilly Library, Indiana University, Bloomington.

Critical Studies: *Bomb Culture* by Jeff Nuttall, London, MacGibbon and Kee, 1968, New York, Delacorte Press, 1969; *Orpheus Unacclaimed: A Study of the Poetry of Harold Norse* by John A. Wood, Fayetteville, University of Arkansas unpublished thesis, 1969; "Hotel of the Carnivorous Heart: The Norse Saga Rediscovered" by Paul Grillo, in *NorthEast Rising Sun 2*, no. 6-7, 1977; in *Isthmus 6* (San Francisco), 1977; Nanos Valaoritis, in *Surréalisme 2*, Paris, Savelli, 1977; "An American Catullus" by W.I. Scobie, in *The Advocate* (Los Angeles), 19 October 1977; *The Great American Poetry Bake-Off* by Robert Peters, Metuchen, New Jersey, Scarecrow Press, 1979.

Harold Norse comments:

Using the American vulgate, I generally tend to record experience through a spontaneous, heart-centered, autobiographical poetry for readers, not specialists. Via a rather surrealistic approach that attempts to capture the complexity of living by means of an anagogical imagery of the absurd, contradictory and tragi-comic, I try to present the passions, feelings, and events of my own life and time, often centered in the erotic tradition of Greco-Roman poetry, secular and profane. I see the function of my poetry as a voicing of the sub-strata of the passional life, in both senses of strong emotion and suffering. I don't know whether I've chosen this or been chosen for it, as I've always written in this way—and God help the poor reader!

*   *   *

Harold Norse has suffered from a number of disadvantages, as far as making a poetic reputation is concerned. An expatriate and a slow starter, he does not seem to have sought, and certainly has not managed to find, a regular market for his work. He was a protégé, like Ginsberg, of William Carlos Williams, and his mature poems are related to the Beats, yet retain a sufficient stylistic distance to prevent him from being swept up into the Beat movement as a whole, and borne along on its current of energy.

It must also be admitted that he is an uneven writer. His first book, which he now seems to have rejected almost totally, is *The Undersea Mountain*, published in 1953. The prevailing influence is that of Hart Crane. These lines, from a poem called "The Tankers," are exactly in the manner of Crane's *The Bridge*:

> The gunmount flashes, flashing metal grey
> also the opaque aft, as down the harbor
> estuary under steam towards turquoise streams
> she plies.
>   And dagger-eyed the gull veers overhead.

Norse next surfaces, seven years later, with a remarkable book of translations—from the sonnets in Roman dialect of G.G. Belli. What these seem to have enabled him to do was to relate his feeling for American vernacular to his feeling for Europe. Belli, with his baroque use of an exuberantly popular diction, was the liberating influence Norse needed.

His more recent poems, couched in the ranging free-verse which is now an accepted American idiom, tend to vary in quality according to the amount of information, and the kind of information, he manages to pack in to them. Quite a few people do the drug poem, and the tantric poem, rather better than Norse. His speciality, if only he would realise it, is of a more traditional kind—he charts the meetings of the Old World and the New with a kind of exuberant delicacy. His best essay in this manner is the appropriately titled "Classic Frieze in a Garage," which takes an idiom which is basically the one Pound forged for *The Cantos* and uses it in a personal, and, to me, extremely seductive way:

> perfect! & how strange! garage
>   swallows sarcophagus!
> mechanic calmly spraying
>   paint on a
>   fender
> observed in turn by lapith & centaur!

—Edward Lucie-Smith

NOTLEY, Alice. American. Born in Bisbee, Arizona, 8 November 1945. Educated at Barnard College, New York, B.A. 1967; University of Iowa, Iowa City, M.F.A. 1969. Married the writer Ted Berrigan in 1972 (died, 1983); two sons. Recipient: National Endowment for the Arts grant, 1980; Poetry Center Award, 1981; G.E. Foundation Award, 1983. Address: 101 St. Marks Place, 12A, New York, New York 10009, U.S.A.

PUBLICATIONS

Verse

165 Meeting House Lane.   New York, "C" Press, 1971.
Phoebe Light.   Bolinas, California, Big Sky, 1973.
Incidentals in the Day World.   New York, Angel Hair, 1973.
For Frank O'Hara's Birthday.   Cambridge, Street Editions, 1976.
Alice Ordered Me to Be Made: Poems 1975.   Chicago, Yellow Press, 1976.
A Diamond Necklace.   New York, Frontward, 1977.
Songs for the Unborn Second Baby.   Lenox, Massachusetts, United Artists, 1979.
When I Was Alive.   New York, Vehicle, 1980.
Waltzing Matilda.   New York, Kulchur, 1981.
How Spring Comes.   West Branch, Iowa, Toothpaste Press, 1981.
Three Zero, Turning Thirty, with Andrei Codrescu, edited by Keith and Jeff Wright.   New York, Hard Press, 1982.
Sorrento.   Los Angeles, Sherwood Press, 1984.
Margaret and Dusty.   West Branch, Iowa, Coffee House, 1985.

Other

Doctor Williams' Heiresses: A Lecture.   Berkeley, California, Tuumba Press, 1980.
Tell Me Again (autobiography).   Santa Barbara, California, Am Here, 1981.

*   *   *

Alice Notley is an American poet whose expression has been shaped by a conscious indebtedness to the legacy of William Carlos Williams. Regarding herself as one of "Doctor Williams' Heiresses," Notley has realized that "you could use him to sound entirely new if you were a woman. It was all about this woman business. I thought we didn't need to read women—I mean find the hidden in the woodwork ones—so much as find the poems among whatever sex that made you feel free to say whatever you liked. Williams makes you feel that you can say anything, including your own anything."

In most of her published work to date, "your own anything" for Notley has centered around her life with her late husband, the poet Ted Berrigan, and their children in New York City's lower East Side. Her poetry reflects her intelligence, humor, and commitment to her craft, and it is perhaps strongest when she is expressing her remarkable sensitivity to the nuances of human relationships. Rather than insist on her own emotional independence as an emancipated woman in the fashion of her New York contemporaries Anne Waldman and Diane Wakoski, Notley stresses the bonds between people, savoring with great refinement the closeness and communication that result from shared feelings. With delicacy and simple wonder she describes the miracle of physical possession in "Song," from the collection *When I Was Alive*:

Who shall have my fair lord
Who but I who but I who but Alice
By the black window
Softly in November
Who but I who but I who but Alice

In more complex poems like "Sonnet" (from *A Diamond Necklace*) she brilliantly explores the components of a long marriage between two famous people, the comedy team of George Burns and Gracie Allen:

The late Gracie Allen was a very lucid comedienne,
Especially in the way that lucid means shining and bright.
What her husband George Burns called her illogical logic
Made a halo around our syntax and ourselves as we laughed.

George Burns most often was her artful inconspicuous straight-
man.
He could move people about stage, construct skits and scenes,
write
And gather jokes. They were married as long as ordinary magic
Would allow, thirty-eight years, until Gracie Allen's death.

In her fifties Gracie Allen developed a heart condition.
She would call George Burns when her heart felt funny and
fluttered.
He'd give her a pill and they'd hold each other till the palpitation
Stopped—just a few minutes, many times and pills. As magic
fills
Then fulfilled must leave a space, one day Gracie Allen's
heart fluttered
And hurt and stopped. George Burns said unbelievingly to the
doctor,
"But I still have some of the pills."

Notley responds to a broad spectrum of American culture, and her experiments with poetic forms and free verse owe as much to Gertrude Stein, Frank O'Hara, and Ted Berrigan as they do to William Carlos Williams. Like them, she believes that she is writing primarily to express her own personal tone of voice, which is her music and her breath. She understands Williams's concept of the variable foot to mean "the dominance of tone of voice over other considerations.... I break my lines where I do, as I'm being as various as my voice should be in our intimacy." She feels her speech sounds as the voice of "the new wife, & the new mother" in her own time, but her intent is to make a poem, rather than present a platform of social reform: "I'm not all that interested in being a woman, it's just a practical problem that you deal with when you write poems. You do have to deal with the problem of who you are so that you can be a person talking."

Describing herself as an "imperfect medium," Notley insists on her own limitations as a poet. She often deliberately deflates what she senses as her own pretensions, as in "The Prophet," a long poem from the collection *How Spring Comes*, that ends with the lines "You must never/ Stop making jokes. You are not great you are life." When this tone of self-depreciation is absent, however, and she concentrates on presenting her keen perceptions of her subject, her work has considerably more substance. Despite her loyalty to Williams, it would appear from the evidence of her poetry that her reflections—like Emily Dickinson's—are as sharp as her observations: Notley should trust them more, along with her heart.

—Ann Charters

* * *

NOTT, Kathleen (Cecilia). British. Born in London. Educated at Mary Datchelor School, London; King's College, London; Somerville College, Oxford, B.A. (honours) in philosophy, politics, and economics. Married Christopher Bailey in 1929 (marriage dissolved, 1960). Worked in Army Education and with Air Raid Precautions in World War II. President, Progressive League, London, 1958-60. Since 1960, Editor, *P.E.N. International*, London. President, International P.E.N., English Centre, 1974-75. Recipient: Arts Council bursary, 1968. Fellow, Royal Society of Literature, 1977. Address: 5 Limpsfield Avenue, Thornton Heath, Surrey CR4 6BG, England.

PUBLICATIONS

Verse

Landscapes and Departures. London, Editions Poetry London, 1947.
Poems from the North. Aldington, Kent, Hand and Flower Press, 1956.
Creatures and Emblems. London, Routledge, 1960.
Elegies and Other Poems. Richmond, Surrey, Keepsake Press, 1981.

Novels

Mile End. London, Hogarth Press, 1938.
The Dry Deluge. London, Hogarth Press, 1947.
Private Fires. London, Heinemann, 1961.
An Elderly Retired Man. London, Faber, 1963.

Other

The Emperor's Clothes: An Attack on the Dogmatic Orthodoxy of T.S. Eliot, Graham Greene, Dorothy Sayers, C.S. Lewis and Others. London, Heinemann, and Bloomington, University of Indiana Press, 1954.
A Clean Well-Lighted Place: A Private View of Sweden. London, Heinemann, 1960.
Objections to Humanism, with others. London, Hodder and Stoughton, 1963.
A Soul in the Quad. London, Routledge, 1969.
Philosophy and Human Nature. London, Hodder and Stoughton, 1970.
The Good Want Power: An Essay in the Psychological Possibilities of Liberalism. London, Cape, and New York, Basic Books, 1977.

Editor, with C. Day Lewis and Thomas Blackburn, *New Poems 1957.* London, Joseph, 1957.

Translator, *Northwesterly Gale*, by Lucien Chauvet. London, Hutchinson, 1947.
Translator, *Son of Stalin*, by Riccardo Bacchelli. London, Secker and Warburg, 1956.
Translator, *The Fire of Milan*, by Riccardo Bacchelli. London, Secker and Warburg, 1958.

*

Kathleen Nott comments:
I am primarily a poet, but I had a philosophical training and I am very much concerned with ethics and aesthetics. *A Soul in the Quad* took over five years to write and is a largish book

describing in an autobiographical and intellectual-social setting what I conceive the relations of poetry and philosophy to be.

I regard poetry as a special language and an existential one. It is the language of beings of rather peculiar physiological and psychological organization. It works out as the most favourable selection and balance of the colours, implications, weights, stresses and relations of words—most favourable, that is, to project a highly authentic personal vision (which may be of a momentary kind). Hence rhythmical and musical sense strikes me as paramount.

*   *   *

As a philosopher Kathleen Nott is a humanist but also a respectful opponent of logical positivism and the "scientism" of Karl Popper. Her position is in fact a remarkably original and interesting one, and it is in her poetry that we find it most subtly and yet explicitly stated. For, like Valéry, she believes in the formulative power of music (in the Valérian sense of that preconceived rhythm that "visits" a poet before he is consciously aware of its content or significance). Thus rhythm is an important aspect of her work: she seldom works within strictly conventional forms, but her line is elegantly formed and controlled. This is also the strongest feature of her work—its weaknesses are unconfident or blurred diction, and an apparent inability to do justice to her initial impulse. Thus "Absolute Zero" begins promisingly:

> There are no tall engines standing in the polar North
> or none that is ready for use. They are all
> sheeted and hooded with the snow: who could discern them
> among faceless pines
> and blinded firs?

But this vision gradually peters out into a confusion of metaphors, only to recover itself at the end of the poem: the result is unintentionally elliptical. There seems little explanation for the wrenched diction ("and at last to be seen of eyes...") that characterizes the middle section of the poem. Fortunately this does not always happen: "Nature's Betrayal," about Wordsworth and nature, is in a tighter form, and there is more control of meaning and metaphor as well as of rhythm. At her best Kathleen Nott is an interesting philosophical poet whose thinking, in this form, deserves more attention than it has been given.

—Martin Seymour-Smith

NUTTALL, Jeff. British. Born in Clitheroe, Lancashire, 8 July 1933. Educated at Hereford School of Art, graduated 1951; Bath Academy of Art, graduated 1953. Served in the Royal Army Education Corps. Married Jane Louch in 1954 (divorced, 1979). Taught in the art departments of several secondary schools; Lecturer in Foundation Studies, Bradford College of Art, Yorkshire, 1968-70; Lecturer in Fine Art, Leeds College of Art, 1970-80; Artist-in-Residence, Deakin University, Geelong, Victoria, 1984. Editor, *My Own Mag*, 1964-67; Co-Founder, The People Show, theatre group, 1967-71, and worked as performance artist until 1975; Poetry Critic, *The Guardian*, London, 1979-81; has exhibited paintings, sculptures, and constructions. Address: 392 Halifax Road, Todmorden, Lancashire, England.

PUBLICATIONS

Verse

The Limbless Virtuoso, with Keith Musgrove.   London, Writers Forum, 1963.
Songs Sacred and Secular.   Privately printed, 1964.
Poems I Want to Forget.   London, Turret, 1965.
Pieces of Poetry.   London, Writers Forum, 1965.
Isabel.   London, Turret, 1967.
Journals.   Brighton, Sussex, Unicorn Bookshop, 1968.
Penguin Modern Poets 12, with Alan Jackson and William Wantling.   London, Penguin, 1968.
Love Poems.   Brighton, Sussex, Unicorn Bookshop, 1969.
Selected Poems.   London, Horizon, 1970.
Poems 1962-69.   London, Fulcrum Press, 1970.
Sun Barbs.   Hayes, Middlesex, Poet and Peasant, 1976.
Objects.   London, Trigram Press, 1976.
Grape Notes, Apple Music.   Bradford, Rivelin Press, 1980.

Plays

Barrow Boys (produced Bradford, Yorkshire, 1972).
Kosher (produced Bradford, Yorkshire, 1972).

Fiction

Come Back Sweet Prince: A Novelette.   London, Writers Forum, 1966.
The Case of Isabel and the Bleeding Foetus.   London, Turret, 1967.
Mr. Watkins Got Drunk and Had to Be Carried Home.   London, Writers Forum, 1968.
Oscar Christ and the Immaculate Conception.   London, Writers Forum, 1968.
Pig.   London, Fulcrum Press, 1969.
Snipe's Spinster.   London, Calder and Boyars, 1974.
The Foxes' Lair.   London, Aloes, 1974.
The House Party.   Toronto, Basilike, 1975.
The Anatomy of My Father's Corpse.   Toronto, Basilike, 1975.
The Gold Hole.   London, Quartet, 1978.
What Happened to Jackson.   London, Aloes, 1978.
The Patriarchs: An Early Summer Landscape.   London, Bean and Aloes Arc, 1978.
Muscle.   Bradford, Rivelin Press, 1983.

Other

Bomb Culture.   London, MacGibbon and Kee, 1968; New York, Delacorte Press, 1969.
Man/Not Man.   Llanfynydd, Unicorn Bookshop, 1975.
Common Factors, Vulgar Factions, with Rodick Carmichael.   London, Routledge, 1977.
King Twist: A Portrait of Frank Randle.   London, Routledge, 1978.
Performance Art: Memoirs and Scripts.   London, Calder, and New York, Riverrun, 2 vols., 1980.

Editor, *25: Writing from Leeds Polytechnic.*   Leeds, Art and Design Press, 1971.

*

Jeff Nuttall comments:

I make a line out of a rhythmic figure. The previous figure

suggests the subsequent one. The rhythmic figures owe much to Parker's saxophone phrasing.

I look to my obsessions to provide me with syllables to fill out the necessary figure.

I am hardly at all concerned with direct verbal/syntactical "meaning." Silly to call my verse "obscure" unless you're short sighted.

*   *   *

Jeff Nuttall's writing is founded on the realisation that the world changed for ever at Hiroshima. Severing us from our future, stranding us with only our sensations, the bomb puts us in the same position as the Dadaists of 1916, aware that logic and rationality will no longer serve and that absurd practices are appropriate for art. One strand in his work is thus minimalist, concrete poetry; but another is a generous, sprawling effort to celebrate human vitality in a hurry "during these last days of the species."

"Make love not war." Nuttall takes the slogan seriously. Wallowing in the life of the body, turning "the taps that run sensations" full on, he uses scatology and "obscenity" as his weapons against the "grey evangelists," the puritans, the bomb-makers: the true obscenity is theirs. But in *Bomb Culture* he writes of a mid-1960's event he helped organise: "Its unrelieved obscenity was neither dynamic nor bawdy. It was headachy, oppressive. You came out and the world was dimmer." It is a risk his poetry is often prepared to take. With enemies like Nuttall, puritanism may gain friends. His verse depicts people as metonyms of their anatomical parts, tortured by pleasure, fragmented and reduced to a concrete physicality which is, curiously, the very language of the empiricists, "MC² initiates," whom he condemns. In fact his scatology is therapy for himself as much as for his audience: in *Man/Not Man* he writes of his "mother's untold terror of shit" and how she instilled the same fear in him. He energetically exorcises that fear by the repetitions which reduce the power of language to shock.

"Make love not war": but the sexuality in his verse is usually violent. Intuitively he perceives that sexuality and politics are closely related. "Impotence," its meaning poised between the two realms, is a favourite word. Life itself is reaffirmed by "orgy and violence": "the knives are out,/The blades are keen in miracle." Throughout his work, symptom and cure, cause and effect are elided. So are pleasure and disgust, delight and horror: "Brutal Baby Stabbing: somehow a weeping relief." Often complicit with what he attacks, he is also honest enough to admit it: "All/Our blistered protest was perverse praise, loving recognition."

A garrulous Ginsberg but also a terse Dadaist, a lover of anarchic violence but a fearer of nuclear destruction, Nuttall is richly confused and self-contradictory in ways which are central to his time. Choosing an aim or a destination is problematic: "The Intercity Eitherway Arrows don't indicate whichaway." There remains a manifesto for a way of living from moment to moment, where everything is done "just/For topsy-turvy fun."

His later verse, in which the cheerfully rampant id drives him less furiously, begins to notice that there are one or two things outside himself, such as people and objects. If he is too hearty and beery at times, he makes up for it by amused tolerance and a capacity for self-mockery. His new West Yorkshire domesticity in *Objects* and *Sun Barbs* is no apostasy, for it is the times which have changed more than he. The prophet of the 1960's becomes a Falstaff outside the pub, waiting for the No. 64 bus to Huddersfield: if he hasn't drowned in the pub, "I shall drown in her./I want to drown in her." Still master of the delicate compliment ("My love is a rat with slanted incisors"), he is left contemplating

"the alimentary canal from Halifax to Burnley." Like the best surrealism, his is firmly grounded in the real. He has always had the courage to challenge the self-interested lie that the way things are is given and immutable, the "must-be-cos-it-says-so":

> Reality is looking again
> Summon spittle.

—R.J.C. Watt

NYE, Robert. British. Born in London, 15 March 1939. Educated at Dormans Land, Sussex; Hamlet Court, Westcliff, Essex; Southend High School. Married 1) Judith Pratt in 1959 (divorced, 1967), three sons; 2) Aileen Campbell in 1968, one daughter, one stepdaughter, and one stepson. Free-lance writer. Since 1967, Poetry Editor, *The Scotsman*; since 1971, Poetry Critic, *The Times*. Writer-in-Residence, University of Edinburgh, 1976-77. Recipient: Eric Gregory Award, 1963; Scottish Arts Council bursary, 1970, 1973, and publication award, 1970, 1976; James Kennaway Memorial Award, 1970; *Guardian* Fiction Prize, 1976; Hawthornden Prize, 1977. Fellow, Royal Society of Literature, 1977. Agent: Anthony Sheil Associates, 2-3 Morwell Street, London WC1B 3AR, England; or, Wallace and Sheil Inc., 177 East 70th Street, New York, New York 10021, U.S.A.

PUBLICATIONS

Verse

Juvenilia 1.   Northwood, Middlesex, Scorpion Press, 1961.
Juvenilia 2.   Lowestoft, Suffolk, Scorpion Press, 1963.
Darker Ends.   London, Calder and Boyars, and New York, Hill and Wang, 1969.
Agnus Dei.   Rushden, Northamptonshire, Sceptre Press, 1973.
Two Prayers.   Richmond, Surrey, Keepsake Press, 1974.
Five Dreams.   Rushden, Northamptonshire, Sceptre Press, 1974.
Divisions on a Ground.   Manchester, Carcanet, 1976.

Plays

Sawney Bean, with Bill Watson (produced Edinburgh, 1969; London, 1972; New York, 1982).   London, Calder and Boyars, 1970.
Sisters (broadcast, 1969; produced Edinburgh, 1973).   Included in *Penthesilea, Fugue, and Sisters*, 1976.
Penthesilea, adaptation of a play by Heinrich von Kleist (broadcast, 1971; produced London, 1983).   Included in *Penthesilea, Fugue, and Sisters*, 1976.
The Seven Deadly Sins: A Mask, music by James Douglas (produced Stirling, 1973).   Rushden, Northamptonshire, Omphalos Press, 1974.
Mr. Poe (produced Edinburgh and London, 1974).
Penthesilea, Fugue, and Sisters.   London, Calder and Boyars, 1976.

Radio Plays: *Sisters*, 1969; *A Bloody Stupit Hole*, 1970; *Reynolds, Reynolds*, 1971; *Penthesilea*, 1971; *The Devil's Jig*, with Humphrey Searle, from a work by Thomas Mann, 1980.

Novels

Doubtfire. London, Calder and Boyars, and New York, Hill and Wang, 1968.
Falstaff. London, Hamish Hamilton, and Boston, Little Brown, 1976.
Merlin. London, Hamish Hamilton, 1978; New York, Putnam, 1979.
Faust. London, Hamish Hamilton, 1980; New York, Putnam, 1981.
The Voyage of the Destiny. London, Hamish Hamilton, and New York, Putnam, 1982.

Short Stories

Tales I Told My Mother. London, Calder and Boyars, 1969; New York, Hill and Wang, 1970.
Penguin Modern Stories 6, with others. London, Penguin, 1970.
The Facts of Life and Other Fictions. London, Hamish Hamilton, 1983.

Other (for children)

Taliesin. London, Faber, 1966; New York, Hill and Wang, 1967.
March Has Horse's Ears. London, Faber, 1966; New York, Hill and Wang, 1967.
Bee Hunter: Adventures of Beowulf. London, Faber, 1968; as *Beowulf: A New Telling*, New York, Hill and Wang, 1968; as *Beowulf, The Bee Hunter*, Faber, 1972.
Wishing Gold. London, Macmillan, 1970; New York, Hill and Wang, 1971.
Poor Pumpkin. London, Macmillan, 1971; as *The Mathematical Princess and Other Stories*, New York, Hill and Wang, 1972.
Cricket: Three Stories. Indianapolis, Bobbs Merrill, 1975; as *Once upon Three Times*, London, Benn, 1978.
Out of the World and Back Again. London, Collins, 1977; as *Out of This World and Back Again*, Indianapolis, Bobbs Merrill, 1978.
The Bird of the Golden Land. London, Hamish Hamilton, 1980.
Harry Pay the Pirate. London, Hamish Hamilton, 1981.
Three Tales. London, Hamish Hamilton, 1983.

Other

Editor, *A Choice of Sir Walter Ralegh's Verse*. London, Faber, 1972.
Editor, *William Barnes: A Selection of His Poems*. Oxford, Carcanet Press, 1972.
Editor, *A Choice of Swinburne's Verse*. London, Faber, 1973.
Editor, *The Faber Book of Sonnets*. London, Faber, 1976; as *A Book of Sonnets*, New York, Oxford University Press, 1976.
Editor, *The English Sermon 1750-1850*. Manchester, Carcanet, 1976.

*

Manuscript Collections: University of Texas, Austin; National Library of Scotland, Edinburgh; University of Edinburgh.

Critical Studies: by A. Alvarez, in *The Observer* (London), 1961, 1963; Martin Seymour-Smith, in *The Scotsman* (Edinburgh),

1963; in *Times Literary Supplement* (London), 1963; *British Book News* (London), February 1970.

*   *   *

The career of Robert Nye has been a peculiar one. He began with some éclat, publishing poems in *The London Magazine* and *Delta* when he was only 16 years of age. One of these lyrics, "Other Times," is almost his best. It appears, somewhat revised, in a definitive collection, *Darker Ends*:

> Midsummer's liquid evenings linger even
> And melt the wind in autumn, when bonfires
> Burn books and bones, and lend us foreign faces.
> At such a heart's November I might wish
> For summer's heir to come, with his cruel kiss
> Sealing the promises we could not keep.

One may feel that there are a few too many possessives here—"midsummer's," "heart's," "summer's." And yet the poem is purged in diction from its earlier version in *Juvenilia 1*:

> Midsummer's liquid evenings linger even
> And leave four hours of autumn bonfires—
> Terre Gaste of your sleevelessness; imp and scraps,
> The oily rags, old bike spokes, bones and cans
> And executed dolls forstitched and lax
> Folding pink little arms precipitant to ash.

This, in its turn, was altered from the first published version, in *Delta*, Autumn 1956, where we have "a tragedy of autumn bonfires/Raw with a gardener's rubbish, flesh and scraps...." The older, more austere Nye appears to have spent the intervening years weeding through several of his teenage pastures. There is no doubt that some fine Gravesian lyrics are the result. What he has done with "Other Times," he has also done with "Kingfisher," "I've Got Sixpence," and "At Last." In this final draft, Nye appears to have found his poetic feet in a rhythm not all that way after Andrew Young:

> Dear, if one day my empty heart,
> Under your cheek, forgets to start
> Its life-long argument with my head—
> Do not rejoice that I am dead
> And need a colder, harder bed,
> But say: "At last he's found the art
> To hold his tongue and lose his heart."

Clearly Nye has risen on the stepping-stones of his former romantic selves to finer things. After the baroque ambitions of his earlier years, he has emerged as a poet of wit, epigram, distinction.

The poems in his most recent volume of verse, *Divisions on a Ground*, are at their best when most purged and spare. Nye achieves some poignant effects not so much through words in themselves but by telling combination of words: "The least disgust betrays the heart's persistence./You kiss the snowscape on the windowpane;/I watch your breath shrink from it, a warm fleck/In freckled glass" ("At the Window"). It is all there: the identification of warmth, life, the capacity to feel disgust at death—a capacity which overcomes the merely aesthetic appreciation which led the girl to kiss the windowpane in the first place. Or again, consider "All Hallows" from the same sequence:

> Once as a child I saw the willows
> Across the river at All Hallows,

Each one distinct although six miles away.
What brought them close and brings them now again
Sharp to the mind's eye like an icon of it?
An orthodox theology of tears.

The poet compares the sharpness of youthful eyesight with the acuity of adult memory honed by a life's experience. It is as austere and telling as a haiku translated by Bosley or Thwaite, or a Catullan lyric.

Perhaps Nye's verse, as distinct from his prose, will never "please the million"—or even the thousand. His themes tend towards what is commonly thought of as literary. But it is safe to say that there is no poet writing whose next volume is awaited with more interest.

—Philip Hobsbaum

OAKES, Philip (Barlow). British. Born in Burslem, Staffordshire, 31 January 1928. Educated at Royal School, Wolverhampton; Darwen Grammar School. Married to Stella Fleming; one son and two daughters. Reporter, Sly's Court Reporting Service, 1945-46, 1949-55; reporter and columnist ("The World I Watch"), *Daily Express*, London, 1955-56; columnist and literary editor, *Truth*, London, 1955-56; film critic, *Evening Standard*, London, 1956-58; television scriptwriter, Granada and BBC, London, 1958-62; film critic, *Sunday Telegraph*, London, 1963-65; assistant editor, *Sunday Times Magazine*, London, 1965-67; arts columnist, *Sunday Times*, London, 1965-80. Agent: Elaine Greene Ltd., 31 Newington Green, London N16 9PU, England.

PUBLICATIONS

Verse

Unlucky Jonah: Twenty Poems. Reading, Berkshire, University of Reading School of Art, 1954.
In the Affirmative. London, Deutsch, 1968.
Notes by the Provincial Governor. London, Poem-of-the-Month Club, 1972.
Married/Singular. London, Deutsch, 1973.
Selected Poems. London, Deutsch, 1982.

Play

Screenplay: *The Punch and Judy Man* with Tony Hancock, 1962.

Novels

Exactly What We Want. London, Joseph, 1962.
The God Botherers. London, Deutsch, 1969; as *Miracles: Genuine Cases Contact Box 340*, New York, Day, 1971.
Experiment at Proto. London, Deutsch, and New York, Coward McCann, 1973.
A Cast of Thousands. London, Gollancz, 1976.

Other

Tony Hancock. London, Woburn Press, 1975.

From Middle England: A Memory of the Thirties. London, Deutsch, 1980; New York, St. Martin's Press, 1983.
Dwellers All in Time and Space: A Memory of the 1940's. London, Deutsch, 1982; New York, St. Martin's Press, 1984.
At the Jazz Band Ball: A Memory of the 1950's. London, Deutsch, 1983.

Editor, *The Entertainers.* London, Woburn Press, 1975.
Editor, *The Film Addict's Archive.* London, Elm Tree, 1977.

*

Manuscript Collection: State University of New York, Buffalo.

Philip Oakes comments:
I consider myself an all-round writer, subject at any time to the demands of poetry. Although I was corralled with the Movement poets in the 1950's and still share their concern for form and discipline, the labelling was, I think, a critical-cum-political convenience and no longer applies.

I write about the need for domestic order and the impulse to resist it; also about love and eccentrics I rather admire. These are non-conformist heroes who harm no-one—a retired soldier who hunted unicorns, a sea-captain who sailed to meet mermaids, the fattest man in England and a sad recluse who lived in fear of falling into a pit. Poets whose influence I recognise include Donne, Graves, Auden, and Philip Larkin. Also I suspect, many writers and composers of Hymns Ancient & Modern. Here beginneth the first ballad....

*   *   *

Despite a comparatively slender output, and the competing pressures of journalism and novel-writing, Philip Oakes remains one of the best of the generation of English poets who emerged in the 1950's, and were loosely grouped under the label of the "Movement." His early poems provided social and moral comments in tight, clipped forms in the characteristic manner of the Movement; but Oakes was less severely formal and intellectual than some of his contemporaries. A mild but authentic vein of lyricism lies not far below the cool, conversational surface. Indeed, there is a basic human warmth, recalling Thomas Hardy, at the heart of Oakes' practice as a poet. In his work of the sixties and seventies, collected in *In the Affirmative* and *Married/Singular*, he has written of personal and domestic themes, in direct language and unfussily formal verse. At times, admittedly, the low key descriptions are merely flat, and the metre occasionally falters. But Oakes' successes are more frequent—notably in his admirable evocations of the pieties and crises of modern family life.

—Bernard Bergonzi

O'GORMAN, Ned (Edward Charles O'Gorman.) American. Born in New York City, 26 September 1929. Educated at St. Michael's College, Vermont, A.B.; Columbia University, New York, M.A. Has one son. Taught at Brooklyn College, New York; New School for Social Research, New York; Manhattan College, New York; Editor, *Jubilee* magazine, New York, 1962-65; State Department American Studies Specialist in Chile, Argentina, and Brazil, 1965. Since 1966, Headmaster, Children's

Storefront School, New York. Recipient: Guggenheim Fellowship, 1956, 1962; Lamont Poetry Selection Award, 1958; Rockefeller Fellowship, 1972, 1977; Rothko Chapel Truth and Freedom Award, 1981. D.Litt.: St. Michael's College. Agent: Peter Matson, 264 Fifth Avenue, New York, New York 10001. Address: 2 Lincoln Square, New York, New York 10023, U.S.A.

PUBLICATIONS

Verse

The Night of the Hammer. New York, Harcourt Brace, 1959.
Adam Before His Mirror. New York, Harcourt Brace, 1961.
The Buzzard and the Peacock. New York, Harcourt Brace, 1964.
The Harvesters' Vase. New York, Harcourt Brace, 1968.
The Flag the Hawk Flies. New York, Knopf, 1972.
How to Put Out a Fire. New York, Eakins, 1984.

Other

The Storefront: A Community of Children on Madison Avenue and 129th Street. New York, Harper, 1970.
The Blue Butterfly (for children). New York, Harper, 1971.
The Wilderness and the Laurel Tree: A Guide to Parents and Teachers on the Observation of Children. New York, Harper, 1972.
The Children Are Dying. New York, New American Library, 1978.

Editor, *Prophetic Voices: Essays and Words in Revolution.* New York, Random House, 1969.
Editor, *Perfected Crystal, Terrible Steel: An Unconventional Source Book of Spiritual Readings in Prose and Poetry.* New York, Seabury Press, 1981.

*

Manuscript Collection: Immaculata College, Malvern, Pennsylvania.

*   *   *

Ned O'Gorman's poems hope that, in the collision of metaphysical and metaphorical opposites, theme and meaning will arise. Compressed and "lush," there are a mystery and lyric extravagance to the poems which, when most successful, provoke a lasting dreamlike quality.

Images repeat exotic light, birds, water, colors, honey, holy oils, vegetables, seeds, centers and sun, in a luxuriant usage of—oftentimes—a pentameter. There are many examples. The result can be overwhelming. At other times O'Gorman's poems have the impact of an abstract painting of planes and trajectories ("What Three?" and "Written on the Occasion in Cairo...").

The conflicts underlying the poems are intelligent, abstract, controlled, metaphysical. The reader is attracted by the beauty of composition in many poems; real chaos is only mentioned here, but it is of a different world. O'Gorman's best poems address themselves seriously to *things*, making a concrete frame of reference available in direct statement: "The Donkey who is in the field/in this increasing fall is/tall as a hedge of wild rose." Imagery when solely the representative of concept at least must not seem so, unless it is allegory. The poet must have a personal stake

in the poem and must risk it as O'Gorman does in his finest efforts, such as "The Graveyard," "In Honor of the Mother of God," "The Aunt," and "To the Memory of Lydia Hoffman." When this expenditure is not made we sense, with a reviewer of *The Flag the Hawk Flies,* that the "imagery touches on nothing real," that the poet merely "names." Or perhaps it is true that in the contemporary world a vision of horror—as in "War"— strikes us as natural and credible while O'Gorman's visions of beauty seem extravagant. This is tragic, yet the poet must take account of the fact or risk a failure—no matter of great beauty.

—Joseph Wilson

———————

O'GRADY, Desmond (James Bernard). Irish. Born in Limerick, 27 August 1935. Educated at St. Michael's Primary School, Limerick; Sacred Heart College, Limerick; Cistercian College, Roscrea, County Tipperary; National University of Ireland, Dublin, 1954-56; Harvard University, Cambridge, Massachusetts, Ph.D. in Celtic studies. Has four children. Taught at Berlitz School in Paris; Cambridge Institute and British Institute, Rome; St. George's English School, Rome; English Language School, Rome; Roxbury Latin School, West Roxbury, Massachusetts; Harvard University; Overseas School of Rome; American University, Cairo; University of Alexandria, Egypt. Member, Aosdana; Academy of Irish Letters. Address: c/o Gallery Press, 19 Oakdown Road, Dublin 14, Ireland.

PUBLICATIONS

Verse

Chords and Orchestrations. Limerick, Echo Press, 1956.
Reilly. London, Phoenix Press, 1961.
Professor Kelleher and the Charles River. Cambridge, Massachusetts, Carthage Press, 1964.
Separazione. Rome, Rapporti Europei, 1965.
The Dark Edge of Europe. London, MacGibbon and Kee, 1967.
The Dying Gaul. London, MacGibbon and Kee, 1968.
Hellas. Dublin, New Writers Press, 1971.
Separations. Dublin, Goldsmith Press, 1973.
Stations. Cairo, American University in Cairo Press, 1976.
Sing Me Creation. Dublin, Gallery Press, 1977.
His Skaldcrane's Nest. Dublin, Gallery Press, 1979.
The Headgear of the Tribe. Dublin, Gallery Press, 1979.
These Fields in Springtime. Dublin, Gallery Press-Deerfield Press, 1984.
The Wandering Celt. Dublin, Gallery Press, 1984.

Other

Translator, *Off Licence: Translations from Irish, Italian and Armenian Poetry.* Dublin, Dolmen Press, 1968.
Translator, *The Gododdin,* from the Welsh of Aneirin. Dublin, Dolmen Press, 1977.
Translator, *A Limerick Rake: Versions from the Irish.* Dublin, Gallery Press, 1978.
Translator, *Grecian Glances.* Cambridge, Massachusetts, Inkling Press, 1981.

*

Desmond O'Grady comments:

My early work dealt with the experience of growing up on the west coast of Ireland, with the leaving of that place for the cities of the Continent and America and the need to connect my life there with the one I had left. My later work deals with the theme of "the journey" and the theme that emerges from that, "separation"; separation from people, places, things.

My middle work, the long poem *The Dying Gaul*, was an attempt at making a self portrait of what it is to be a Celt. It is this "persona" that journeys and is "separated" in my later work. He is a "wandering Celt" who records his wanderings and experiences and attempts to connect what was left with what is found.

The Prologue of my volume *Sing Me Creation* gives an attempt at condensing my purpose:

> Who saw everything to the ends
> of the land began
> at the end of a primary road.
> Who saw the mysteries, knew
> secret things, went a long
> journey and found the whole story
> cut in stone.
> His purpose: praise, search,
> his appointed pain, and the countries
> of the world that housed
> his image. Weary,
> worn out with his labours,
> he returned and told
> what he's seen and learned
> to help kill the winter.

There is also a great deal of translation from the languages of others under the general title *The Unauthorised Version*. These were done principally to learn the methods of those poets, classical and modern, whose work I admire, the better to extend my own range and at the same time to make their work available to young Irish poets who may not have heard of them or cannot read them in the original in the hope that I might make some contribution to the revitalisation of verse being written in Ireland by the young.

*   *   *

Desmond O'Grady spent some years in Paris but has taught in Rome and elsewhere since 1965. In his second collection, *Reilly*, he uses as a satirical *persona* a bohemian young man and describes amusingly his reckless adventures in Dublin:

> tables and chairs cleared of books and belongings,
> the firegrate stuffed with stale fish-and-chips
> and a dry whiskey bottle.
> Finger-rubbed into the windowpane dust:
> *Reilly Rotted Here.*

The Dark Edge of Europe is a selection from O'Grady's previous work. Many of his poems evoke Paris and Italy, and the imagery in them is contemporary in its unexpectedness, as in "Girl and Widow on a Sea Park Bench":

> In this park by the sea, marvellous
> As marble, under the fronded green of the palms,
> The sun strafing
> The stones with flat tracers of light, water like mercury

> Tinnular out of the fountain.
> You come to me out of the gold stained day like a word.

O'Grady spent his early years in Limerick and many of his poems are inspired by his return visits, as in "Homecoming":

> The familiar pull of the slow train
> trundling after a sinking sun on shadowed fields.
> White light splicing the broad span of the sky.
> Evening deepens grass, the breeze,
> like purple smoke, ruffles its surface.
> Straight into herring-dark skies the great cathedral spire
> is sheer Gothic.

Like Joyce and other Irish writers, O'Grady expresses in compressed lines the effect of Puritanic education:

> Unwinking eyes of saints and hushed confession queue—
> For one loud nervous boot
> Of frightened heart,
> I felt the Churcheyed, fidget fear of schooltied youth.

Sometimes he objectifies his early experiences as in his depiction of an old man, who turns "for the safest healer/To a clean and bandaged silence of the heart."

—Austin Clarke

———

OKAI, John. Ghanaian. Born in Ghana. Educated at the Gorky Literary Institute, Moscow, M.A. (Litt.) 1967; University of Ghana, Accra; University of London, M.Phil. Lived in the U.S.S.R., 1961-67. Currently, Lecturer in Russian, University of Ghana, Legon. Recipient: Royal Society of Arts Fellowship, 1968. Address: Department of Modern Languages, University of Ghana, P.O. Box 25, Legon, Ghana.

PUBLICATIONS

Verse

Flowerfall. London, Writers Forum, 1969.
The Oath of Fontomfrom and Other Poems. New York, Simon and Schuster, 1971.
Lorgorligi Logarithms and Other Poems. Tema, Ghana Publishing, 1974.

*   *   *

The use of musical rhythms in poetry is nothing unusual, but few contemporary writers make so great a use of the musical heritage of their culture as does John Okai. The sounds of the talking drums of Ghana figure strongly in his poems and the titles of most of them, such as "Fugue for Fireflies" and "Okponglo Concerto" bear witness of the musical bent of his work. The repetition and alliterative forms which are a part of traditional verse are brought by Okai into the English language, producing effects which are often close to hypnotic, as in "Modzawe" where the line "Let human beings be human beings again" is repeated six times and Okai refers to traditional drums, allowing the musicality of their names to shape his lines:

Descend O God! descend O God!
To the echo-wail-boom and music of
The Dodonpo and the Odono
And the festive Bintim Obonu...

His Ghanaian background is not the only source Okai draws from, however. Having studied in England, America and Russia, Okai can refer as familiarly to apple trees as to palms and his poems often contain catalogues of people and places reflecting this catholic experience:

the swallow
    and the bougainvillea...
modigliani's woman with a necklace...
leonardo da vinci's mona lisa
the parrot
    and the bougainvillea...
shostakovich's leningrad symphony...
dvorak's new world symphony (part two)...
the sparrow
    and the bougainvillea
frank lloyd wright's falling water...
ya-na's palace at wa in ghana...

If there is a fault in Okai's work, it may be that some of his lines take on a singsong quality, seeming to sacrifice sense in favor of sound, for Okai can be more alliterative in his writing than was Old English verse. His "Sunset Sonata" is filled with such lines as:

Still stand stubborn
    To stones that strangle the dawn,
Still stand stubborn
    To stones that maim the morn,
Still stand stubborn
    To stones that assail the sun...

and because of this some critics attempt to dismiss Okai easily, not seeing that even in his most highly alliterative passages there is still meaning.

It cannot be denied that Okai's work is assertive and, especially when read aloud, charged with vitality. His recent work has been a great influence in enlivening the poetry scene in Ghana and the directions in which his poems move take advantage of a rich and, in English, relatively unexplored patrimony.

—Joseph Bruchac

PUBLICATIONS

Verse

Poetry from Africa, with others, edited by Howard Sergeant. Oxford, Pergamon Press, 1968.
The Fisherman's Invocation. London, Heinemann, 1978.

Novel

The Voice. London, Deutsch, 1964; New York, Africana, 1970.

*

Critical Study: *Mother Is Gold: A Study of West African Literature* by Adrian A. Roscoe, London, Cambridge University Press, 1971.

*   *   *

One of the most gifted, and certainly the least literary, of the African poets is Gabriel Okara. Okara has proved to be what can only be described as a "natural," in that he is highly original in both outlook and expression, and appears to have learned his craft without being influenced unduly by the stylistic mannerisms of any other poet. This, however, has not been without considerable effort on his part. "In order to capture the vivid images of African speech," he observed in an article (printed in *Transition*), "I had to eschew the habit of expressing my thoughts first in English. It was difficult at first, but I had to learn." That he has been successful in capturing the African scene, the African colour and excitement, and the changing African moods, is evidenced by such poems as "The Mystic Drum," "Were I to Choose," "Adhiambo," and "Piano and Drums."

There is, in fact, almost a mystical quality about his work which seems to spring from his racial inheritance, his instincts and sensitivity rather than from his intellect, and he exhibits a curious power when he draws upon the great oral traditions to release this nervous energy, as in "The Mystic Drum." In "Adhiambo" he tries to define his feelings on the subject: "Maybe I'm a medicine man/hearing talking saps/seeing behind trees," and in "Piano and Drums," he writes of the jungle drums "telegraphing the mystic rhythm, urgent, raw like bleeding flesh." In other poems which will probably make more impact upon non-African readers he is practical and down to earth, extremely perceptive in his judgements, and almost analytical in his approach, as in "Once Upon a Time"—"There was a time indeed/they used to shake hands with their hearts"—and "You Laughed and Laughed and Laughed" where the ancient world of Africa merges with the modern world.

—Howard Sergeant

OKARA, Gabriel (Imomotimi Gbaingbain). Nigerian. Born in Bumodi, Ijaw District, Rivers State, Western Nigeria, 21 April 1921. Educated at the Government College, Umuahia; trained as a bookbinder; studied journalism at Northwestern University, Evanston, Illinois, 1956. Principal Information Officer, Eastern Regional Government, Enugu, until 1967; Biafran Information Officer, Nigerian Civil War, 1967-69. Since 1972, Director of the Rivers State Publishing House, Port Harcourt. Recipient: Nigerian Festival of the Arts award, 1953; Commonwealth Poetry Prize, 1979. Address: c/o Heinemann Educational Books Ltd., 22 Bedford Square, London WC1B 3HH, England.

OLIVER, Mary (Jane). American. Born in Maple Heights, Ohio, 10 September 1935. Educated at Ohio State University, Columbus, 1955-56; Vassar College, Poughkeepsie, New York, 1956-57. Chairman of the Writing Department, Fine Arts Work Center, Provincetown, Massachusetts, 1972-73; Mather Visiting Professor, Case Western Reserve University, Cleveland, 1980,

1982. Recipient: Poetry Society of America prize, 1962, Shelley Memorial Award, 1970, and Alice Fay di Castagnola Award, 1973; National Endowment for the Arts fellowship, 1972; Guggenheim fellowship, 1980; American Academy award, 1983; Pulitzer Prize, 1984. Agent: Molly Malone Cook Literary Agency, Box 338, Provincetown, Massachusetts 02657, U.S.A.

PUBLICATIONS

Verse

No Voyage and Other Poems.   London, Dent, 1963; revised edition, Boston, Houghton Mifflin, 1965.
The River Styx, Ohio, and Other Poems.   New York, Harcourt Brace, 1972.
The Night Traveler.   Cleveland, Bits Press, 1978.
Twelve Moons.   Boston, Little Brown, 1978.
Sleeping in the Forest.   Athens, Ohio Review Chapbook, 1979.
American Primitive.   Boston, Little Brown, 1983.

*   *   *

life's winners are not the rapacious but the patient:
what triumphs and takes new territory

has learned to lie for centuries in the shadows
like the shadows of the rocks.

Mary Oliver did not lie in the shadows for centuries before receiving her Pulitzer Prize for poetry in 1984. However, she has been a very quiet, modest poet, whose work reflects a pastoral life lived (first in Ohio, then in Provincetown) with plants and animals far more than with human beings. Her early work was reviewed by both Philip Booth and Joyce Carol Oates as being influenced by Robert Frost, and like Frost her first book, *No Voyage and Other Poems*, was published in England.

Like Frost, also she has migrated to a home in New England, whose landscape dominates the poetry in both *Twelve Moons* and *American Primitive*. She is also like her mentor in being anything but the "primitive" that her work guilefully suggests. In fact, if one thinks of a tradition in American letters created by Thoreau—the man who talked about the value of independence, self-subsistence, and a life connected with the land while in fact, as Leon Edel points out, living in a cabin close enough to his mother's house to enable him to go there every day for home-baked cookies and other things he didn't care to provide for himself—then we can see Oliver as part of that tradition. Her poems enrich the fantasy-life of Americans who read the L.L. Bean catalogues, dress for hunting, hiking, and the outdoor life, while in fact not ever facing the hardships which are part of that life.

Reading Mary Oliver's poetry gives that same wonderful vicarious satisfaction. Her knowledge of plants and animals is so rich that no one could question its authenticity. But it is presented, not in realistic, but beautiful images; (speaking of raccoons) "walking,/silvery, slumberous,/each a sharp set of teeth,/each a grey dreamer"; (speaking of hibernating snakes) "and their eyes are like jewels—/and asleep, though they cannot close.//And in each mouth the forked tongue,/sensitive as an angel's ear"; (about being in a swamp) "I feel/not so much wet as/painted and glittered/with the fat grassy/mires, the rich/and succulent marrows/of earth"; (about egrets)

Even half-asleep they had
such faith in the world

that had made them—
tilting through the water,
unruffled, sure,
by the laws
of their faith not logic,
they opened their wings
softly and stepped
over every dark thing.

so that one never experiences fear, pain, frustration, being out of control, all the miseries that we urbanized creatures usually feel in the wilderness. Oliver's poetry gives each reader the illusion that the natural world is graspable, controllable, beautiful. In addition, the reader feels that he *is* facing truth, reality, all the struggles that he knows are out there.

This vision of gentleness and possibility, that the natural world *is* obtainable and belongs to anyone who simply opens his eyes, comes from Thoreau, through Frost, and is one which not a lot of other contemporary poets have really grappled with. (Perhaps Maxine Kumin would be another example of a poet who works in this mode.) However, Oliver's poems have been compared by Robert DeMott to Roethke and Kinnell, saying that all three poets are "sensitive to visitations by the 'dark things' of the wood." But if Oliver writes of "dark things" they are friendly, benevolent dark things. Even her vision of death is gentle, pastoral, and haunting, rather than fearful and violent. What all the critics seem to be pointing out is that there is alive today in American poetry a strain of writing which glorifies man's natural relationship to animals, plants, and the non-human world. It seems to be a necessary vision, one where beauty and simplicity, achieved through a non-violent portrait of nature's eco-systems, could replace nuclear holocaust. Mary Oliver writes this vision clearly, persuasively, and with natural elegance.

—Diane Wakoski

<hr>

OLSON, Elder (James).   American.   Born in Chicago, Illinois, 9 March 1909. Educated at the University of Chicago, B.A. 1934 (Phi Beta Kappa), M.A. 1935, Ph.D. 1938. Married 1) Ann Elizabeth Jones in 1937 (divorced, 1948), one daughter and one son; 2) Geraldine Louise Hays in 1948, two daughters. Instructor, Armour Institute of Technology, Chicago, 1935-42. Assistant Professor, 1942-48, Associate Professor, 1948-53, Professor of English from 1954, and Distinguished Service Professor, 1971-77, University of Chicago; now emeritus. Rockefeller Visiting Professor, University of Frankfurt, 1948, and University of the Philippines, Quezon City, 1966-67; Visiting Professor, University of Puerto Rico, Rio Piedras, 1952-53; Powell Professor of Philosophy, 1955, Visiting Professor of Literary Criticism, 1958-59, Fellow, School of Letters, 1961, and Patten Lecturer, 1964, University of Indiana, Bloomington. Recipient: Witter Bynner Award, 1927; Guarantors Prize, 1931, and Eunice Tietjens Memorial Prize, 1953 (*Poetry*, Chicago); Poetry Society of America Chap-Book Award, 1955; Academy of American Poets Award, 1956; Longview Foundation Award, 1958; Balch Award (*Virginia Quarterly Review*), 1965; Quantrell Award, University of Chicago, 1966. Address: 1501 Los Alamos Avenue, Albuquerque, New Mexico 87104, U.S.A.

PUBLICATIONS

Verse

Thing of Sorrow.   New York, Macmillan, 1934.
The Cock of Heaven.   New York, Macmillan, 1940.
The Scarecrow Christ and Other Poems.   New York, Noonday Press, 1954.
Plays and Poems 1948-58.   Chicago, University of Chicago Press, 1958.
Collected Poems.   Chicago, University of Chicago Press, 1963.
Olson's Penny Arcade.   Chicago, University of Chicago Press, 1975.
Last Poems.   Chicago, University of Chicago Press, 1984.

Plays

A Crack in the Universe, in *First Stage* (Lafayette, Indiana), Spring 1962.
The Abstract Universe: A Comedy of Masks, in *First Stage* (Lafayette, Indiana), Summer 1963.

Other

General Prosody, Rhythmic, Metric, Harmonics.   Chicago, University of Chicago Press, 1938.
Critics and Criticism, with others.   Chicago, University of Chicago Press, 1952.
The Poetry of Dylan Thomas.   Chicago, University of Chicago Press, 1954.
Tragedy and the Theory of Drama.   Detroit, Wayne State University Press, 1961.
The Theory of Comedy.   Bloomington, Indiana University Press, 1968.
On Value Judgments in the Arts and Other Essays.   Chicago, University of Chicago Press, 1976.

Editor, *American Lyric Poems: From Colonial Days to the Present.*   New York, Appleton Century Crofts, 1963.
Editor, *Aristotle's "Poetics" and English Literature: A Collection of Critical Essays.*   Chicago, University of Chicago Press, 1965.
Editor, *Major Voices: 20 British and American Poets.*   New York, McGraw Hill, 1973.

*

Critical Study: *Elder Olson* by Thomas E. Lucas, New York, Twayne, 1972.

*   *   *

The early poems from *Thing of Sorrow* which now make up Part I of Elder Olson's *Collected Poems* are elegiac, deliberately understated and restrained in their expression of some lasting preoccupations: the beauties of this earth, despite our disappointments ("The Tale"); the relationship between the artist's personal sorrows and his work ("Wishes for His Poem"); and, most important by far, the compensations available to a mind able at least to contemplate its losses and vulnerability. Thus Olson writes (in "To Man") that, whatever our limitations:

> —Bird, beast, flower, and star
> Are of no thing but thought,
> Since if mind wills, they are,
> Or if mind wills, are not.

> The Rose surviving Time
> Is patterned in your brain;
> Without such paradigm
> No rose had ever been....

> Be comforted at length,
> Be brave; till you are free,
> Accept this frailty
> That tenders you this strength.

Nevertheless any possible acceptance is more than overshadowed by the awareness of loss, particularly the passing of love:

> It is that love goes in the end.
> It is that of all this amazement and pain,
> The bright harm, the royal woe,
> The brilliant wound and the stain,
> Naught shall remain
> To emblazon one rose-leaf,
> To illumine a prism of snow
> or a rainbow's crystal, to
> Incline the course of wind
> A gull's-wing's width, to bend
> The worn sea to a grave:

> ...And the mind knows this well;
> But the heart breaks if it believes.

The tones remain muted throughout, nearly feminine in Olson's preference for short lines and delicate, internal sound patterns. The influences attractive to a young poet starting out in the 1930's are not what one might expect—Eliot, Yeats and Pound—but rather, it seems, Léonie Adams and Louise Bogan.

The poems which stand as Part II of the *Collected Poems* suffer by being torn from the context of *The Cock of Heaven,* a long philosophical sequence which Olson has described as "an epitome of human history...the destruction of the world, and the causes of both destruction and creation...[and] the universal catastrophe." Devised in terms of expert imitations of the whole range of voices at work in English poetry (and not only English poetry at that), from the Anglo Saxon through T.S. Eliot, these eighty-seven pieces, now radically diminished to twenty-five, create an uncertain focus and effect. The despairing tones of *Thing of Sorrow* are still present, rendered more forcefully (man is a poor talking animal "possessed by angels and impelled by fiends"), but Olson now seems haunted by the possible revelations behind Christian symbols. The opening "text" asserts: "it is manifest that Man is eternally damned...And I consider that to save this world God Himself must needs be born into it; and even then even He can but make it worthy to be destroyed." The relationship between Christian doctrine and Olson's apparently naturalistic view of life is not easy to define, but perhaps the poet's own statement, in the tender "Nocturnal for His Children," comes close. After surveying various theories of divinity and the divine plan he concludes:

> My children, I cannot tell
> Which of these is right.
> I never heard God's voice,
> To me no angels descend.
> All I know is my soul
> Which is, like this night sky,
> Far more dark than bright,
> Yet in that dark waste
> While I watch out its night
> All strives from dark to light:

Not knowing false from true,
I yet know good from bad;
I cannot think my God
Worse than myself: I
Demand a nobler faith.

The finest later poems are varied in the best sense of the term. There are the familiar elegiac strains ("For the Demolition of a Theater"), the same concern for the Christian symbols of death and mortality ("Crucifix") and, increasingly, a new display of informal humor and relaxed good nature ("Exhibition of Modern Art," "Directions to the Armourer," "Able, Baker, Charlie, Et Al.," and the superb "Childe Roland, Etc." and "Entertainment for a Traveller"). When Olson treats his most serious themes with quick, metaphorical wit the results are memorable (as in "The Last Entries in the Journal," which may well be his best poem to date). The good will of generous acceptance now dominates almost entirely:

I praise the weaknesses
That make us fellows;
Fine faults, that keep us kin....

To that implacable Angel, the stern Scribe
Of heaven or of our consciences, I wish
Short memory, bad ink, a sputtering pen:

Our faults, our common faults, have kept us kin.

With *Tragedy and the Theory of Drama* and *The Theory of Comedy*, Elder Olson has established himself as an indispensable critic. The poery is much less widely known, which is a great pity, considering its seriousness and technical brilliance. But then one of Olson's virtues as a critic and a poet is that he has never been in a hurry. What he has done is likely to last.

—Elmer Borklund

OLSON, Toby (Merle Theodore Olson). American. Born in Berwyn, Illinois, 17 August 1937. Educated at Occidental College, Los Angeles, 1962-64, B.A. 1964; Long Island University, Brooklyn, New York, 1964-66, M.A. 1966. Served as a surgical technician in the United States Navy, 1957-61. Married 1) Ann Yeomans in 1963 (divorced, 1965); 2) Miriam Meltzer in 1966. Associate Director, Aspen Writers Workshop, Colorado, 1964-67; Assistant Professor, Long Island University, 1966-74; Member of the Faculty, New School for Social Research, New York, 1967-75. Assistant Professor, 1975-79, and since 1981, Associate Professor and Director of Creative Writing, Temple University, Philadelphia. Poet-in-Residence, State University of New York, Cortland, 1972, and Friends Seminary, New York, 1974-75. Recipient: Creative Artists Public Service grant, 1975; P.E.N. Faulkner Award, for fiction, 1983. Address: 329 South Juniper Street, Philadelphia, Pennsylvania 19107, U.S.A.

PUBLICATIONS

Verse

The Brand: A Five-Part Poem. Mount Horeb, Wisconsin, Perishable Press, 1969.

Worms into Nails. Mount Horeb, Wisconsin, Perishable Press, 1969.
The Hawk-Foot Poems. Madison, Wisconsin, Abraxas Press, 1969.
Maps. Mount Horeb, Wisconsin, Perishable Press, 1969.
Pig/s Book. New York, Doctor Generosity Press, 1970.
Cold House. Mount Horeb, Wisconsin, Perishable Press, 1970.
Poems. Mount Horeb, Wisconsin, Perishable Press, 1970 (?).
Tools. New York, Doctor Generosity Press, 1971.
Shooting Pigeons. Mount Horeb, Wisconsin, Perishable Press, 1971.
Vectors. Milwaukee, Ziggurat-Membrane Press, 1972.
Home (broadsheet). Chicago, Wine Press, 1972.
Fishing. Mount Horeb, Wisconsin, Perishable Press, 1973.
The Wrestlers and Other Poems. New York, Barlenmir House, 1974.
City. Milwaukee, Membrane Press, 1974.
A Kind of Psychology. Milwaukee, Lionhead, 1974.
Changing Appearance: Poems 1965-70. Milwaukee, Membrane Press, 1975.
A Moral Proposition. New York, Aviator Press, 1975.
Priorities. Milwaukee, Lionhead, 1975.
Seeds. Milwaukee, Membrane Press, 1975.
Standard-4. New York, Aviator Press, 1975.
Home. Milwaukee, Membrane Press, 1976.
Three and One. Mount Horeb, Wisconsin, Perishable Press, 1976.
Doctor Miriam: Five Poems by Her Admiring Husband. Mount Horeb, Wisconsin, Perishable Press, 1977.
Aesthetics. Milwaukee, Perishable Press, 1978.
The Florence Poems. London, Permanent Press, 1978.
Birdsongs: Eleven New Poems. Milwaukee, Perishable Press, 1980.
Two Standards. Madison, Wisconsin, Salient Seedling Press, 1982.
Still/Quiet. Madison, Wisconsin, Landlocked Press, 1982.
We Are the Fire: A Selection of Poems. New York, New Directions, 1984.

Novels

The Life of Jesus. New York, New Directions, 1976.
Seaview. New York, New Directions, 1982; London, Boyars, 1985.

Other

Editor, *Margins 1976.* Milwaukee, Margins Press, 1976.

*

Critical Study: by Robert Vas Dias, in *Poetry Information* (London), Winter 1976-77.

Toby Olson comments:

I remember receiving the impression in school that poetry was a kind of crossword/jigsaw puzzle; the student was helped to figure out meanings and fittings, and in the end he could say he "understood" the poem. Often the result didn't seem worth the effort that got him to it. School talk seldom moved beyond puzzle solving to the possibilities of appreciation. Though this kind of attitude may still prevail, I am no longer able to think of poetry, that which I write and read and value, in this puzzle solving way.

For me poetry is no less than good talk about important things, and this good talk has as its end the telling and presentation of truth. I would like it if my poems were able to fix important talk, make it in some way permanent. I would like it if when my poems were difficult it was because the things I was trying to talk about were difficult things to say; there should be no other reason for them being hard to understand.

My poems are not often very difficult in the puzzle sense of it. I am not much interested in metaphor as comparison, symbolism, or myth; I am very interested in finding structures of good talk that can then become the fixed structures of particular poems. I feel that there is enough in the world around me and what it can recall to me from my own past to make any poem. I trust that the experience of the human tribe is enough in each of us so that if I speak out of attention and with care I'll be heard by those who can give a little time for listening.

I suppose, then, that I feel that my poetry intends to be always both autobiographical and communal, that it is through writing about what I can see, hear, and feel that I can best touch the nature that I believe is common in all of us.

*   *   *

The title of Toby Olson's first major collection, *Changing Appearance: Poems 1965-1970*, should alert the reader to this poet's preoccupation with those scenes of persons and objects immediately and literally given to him. In this preoccupation, Olson is heir to an attitude of attention, to a certain tone—ironic, but not unsympathetic—of attention, and for a certain number of such scenes that may be identified with the work of the late Paul Blackburn (1926-71) and through Blackburn to the "no ideas but in things" aspect of William Carlos Williams and, less directly, to the imagist phase of Ezra Pound. This is not an inconsiderable inheritance. Technically, it involves the sure handling of speech rhythms in varying line lengths and stanza formations, the reporting of exactly what is before one's eyes—with a predilection for the urban, the unelevated, the unsublime—and with an equal predilection for all the ironies revealed by that reporting. And like Blackburn and Williams, their heir Olson is also the writer of forthright, unconventional love poems.

Yet this inheritance, like any other, has its limitations. Its special appeal is that of the sharply focused but spontaneous snap-shot: in a few words evocative images are constructed and entire scenes laid out. The snapshot or, to use a phrase from Blackburn, out-the-window poem is limited by its very focus to the personal, the local. It has no horizon and its emphasis on brevity allows for little if any complexity of perception or sustained development of perception. Olson deals with the inherent limitations of his approach in a number of ways. In the early poetry of *Changing Appearance*, he most often uses thematic grouping, e.g., the poems of the "Pig/s Book" section all involve the pig in relation with other animals. Later, he turns to the series. And, in a published note on this mode of organization, Olson has commented that he did so because it allows for the clarity of the individual poem and for "the a-rational quality of the poems' genesis extended over a period of time." The most impressive treatment of series in Olson's work can be found in *Home*, a long poem of 36 parts that successfully enlarges upon its title's theme which would at first appear the very embodiment of the restricted personal/local, and in *Aesthetics*, which seeks not simply a larger space, but a constantly expanding and complex subject matter as well. As the opening lines of this latter book declare: "*Paint what you see*/is already a philosophical problem:/a blood-spot on the eye's membrane/absent in the still-life." In another book of the same year, *The Florence Poems*, Olson returns to thematic grouping for an entire volume. This

time the theme is the early death of a friend. Beginning with reflections at "Graveside," each poem of the group remembers past incidents of shared experience and, in the book's progression, leads toward the final commending "into the perfect/community of our isolate lives." Olson's combination here of detailed, unsentimental recollection with mythic elements such as the trickster figure and Indian whale legends along with the constant spiritual notion of "our secret names" is both masterful and moving.

Again like Williams, Olson has also published prose fiction. His *The Life of Jesus* is experimental in its style and in its depiction of the Christ resulting from that style. Interweaving occasional pages of verse with prose narrative, which resembles Robbe-Grillet's spikey emphasis upon the physically particular—though Olson's use of imagery clearly distinguishes him from the French writer—the novel follows the general outline of the Biblical story. Where it differs is a matter of additional—not necessarily contradictory—detail. Olson's Christ, for instance, has a pet dog named Hound who sits in the chair of Elijah at the last supper and who, after his own martyrdom, rejoins his resurrected master in a cloud bank heaven worthy of Tiepolo. Thus we know not simply more, but quite different things about the Christ in Olson's fictional biography. One of the major differences is the degree to which the Christ is made to speak in his own voice. The effect, inasmuch as what Olson's Christ says must diverge from the Biblical, is startling. It would be wrong, however, to consider the novel a challenge to Christian belief. It is more an investigation into the Christ story as it came to be reconstructed in the mind of a young boy at Catholic school listening to the stories of Irish nuns. The novel is both that reconstructed story and its investigation. This unique fiction, along with the poetry of *Home* and *The Florence Poems*, is Toby Olson's most significant work to date.

—John Taggart

ONDAATJE, (Philip) Michael. Canadian. Born in Colombo, Ceylon, 12 September 1943. Educated at St. Thomas' College, Colombo; Dulwich College, London; Bishop's University, Lennoxville, Quebec, 1962-64; University of Toronto, B.A. 1965; Queen's University, Kingston, Ontario, M.A. 1967. Married Betty Kimbark in 1963; one daughter and one son. Taught at the University of Western Ontario, London, 1967-71. Since 1971, Member of the Department of English, currently Professor, Glendon College, York University, Toronto. Editor, *Mongrel Broadsides*. Recipient: Ralph Gustafson Award, 1965; Epstein Award, 1966; E.J. Pratt Medal, 1966; President's Medal, University of Western Ontario, 1967; Canada Council grant, 1968, 1977; Governor-General's Award, 1971, 1980; Canada-Australia prize, 1980. Address: Department of English, Glendon College, York University, Toronto, Ontario M4N 3M6, Canada.

PUBLICATIONS

Verse

The Dainty Monsters. Toronto, Coach House Press, 1967.
The Man with Seven Toes. Toronto, Coach House Press, 1969.
The Collected Works of Billy the Kid: Left Handed Poems.

Toronto, Anansi, 1970; New York, Norton, 1974; London, Boyars, 1981.

Rat Jelly. Toronto, Coach House Press, 1973.

Elimination Dance. Ilderton, Ontario, Nairn Coldstream, 1978; revised edition, Ilderton, Brick, 1980.

There's a Trick with a Knife I'm Learning to Do: Poems 1963-1978. Toronto, McClelland and Stewart, and New York, Norton, 1979; as *Rat Jelly and Other Poems 1963-1978,* London, Boyars, 1980.

Secular Love. Toronto, Coach House Press, 1984; New York, Norton, 1985.

Play

The Collected Works of Billy the Kid (produced Stratford, Ontario, 1973; New York, 1974; London, 1984).

Novel

Coming Through Slaughter. Toronto, Anansi, 1976; New York, Norton, 1977; London, Boyars, 1979.

Other

Leonard Cohen. Toronto, McClelland and Stewart, 1970.
Claude Glass. Toronto, Coach House Press, 1979.
Tin Roof. Lantzville, British Columbia, Island, 1982.
Running in the Family. Toronto, McClelland and Stewart, and New York, Norton, 1982; London, Gollancz, 1983.

Editor, *The Broken Ark* (animal verse). Toronto, Oberon Press, 1971; revised edition, as *A Book of Beasts,* 1979.
Editor, *Personal Fictions: Stories by Munro, Wiebe, Thomas, and Blaise.* Toronto, Oxford University Press, 1977.
Editor, *The Long Poem Anthology.* Toronto, Coach House Press, 1979.

*

Theatrical Activities:
Director: **Films**—*Sons of Captain Poetry,* 1971; *Carry on Crime and Punishment,* 1972; *Royal Canadian Hounds,* 1973; *The Clinton Special,* 1974.

*   *   *

Michael Ondaatje's first book of poems, *The Dainty Monsters,* elicits prophecy. Its poems forecast the possibility that their successors will be poems of the first intensity. Ondaatje was included among the group that a year previously was heralded as the "New Wave" poets. There was nothing much new about this group. The poetry largely derived from the William Carlos Williams/Black Mountain school; eventually from that great re-animator Ezra Pound. The method has been persistent elsewhere for years. What was inadvertently refreshing was the presence of three or four Canadian poets whose practice indicated a choice counter to the standard derivation. Ondaatje was one of these.

His shaping of language was formal and musical; his content was balanced. Departing from the prevailing lack of metrical challenge to dispersed rhythm, aware of verbal sound inherent in the meaning, unaffianced to the egocentric confessional, Ondaatje engages attention. His shapings of a poem do not leak either salt tears or sawdust or inarticulations or empty spaces. The first essential is here: sheer love of language. Otherwise he can be what he wants to be: metaphysician, sociologist, domestic or saint.

His area is dainty monsters. That is satisfyingly contemporary enough. His universal monsters live in Toronto:

When snows have melted
how dull to find just grass and dog shit.
Why not polemic bones of centaurs
—remnants of a Toronto bullet,
punishment for eating gladioli.

Why not? It is good to have his centaurs back, his sows like chinless duchesses on spread thighs watching "the sun/finger-snapping out the dying summer." He doesn't want hippopotami barred from public swimming pools. He is equally aware that "Deep in the fields/behind stiff dirt fern/nature breeds the unnatural." You can look but you better not touch, a title of one of his poems tell us:

We must build new myths
to wind up the world,
provoke new christs
with our beautiful women.

He is on a mythopoeic voyage from Lilith in Eden, "pivoting on the horn/of corrupted unicorns," to modern man on his cold mountain, moving "with fast passion from necessity," and, mutilated, drowning "in the beautiful dark orgasm of his mouth."

He shows evidence of having that rarest of all elements, presently almost destroyed by the tearings of metal and the dark idiocy of its manufacturers: comic perspective and rescuing wit high on poetry and hospitals:

Three floors down
my appendix
swims in a jar
O world, I shall be buried all over Ontario.

—Ralph Gustafson

OPPENHEIMER, Joel (Lester). American. Born in Yonkers, New York, 18 February 1930. Educated in Yonkers public schools; Cornell University, Ithaca, New York, 1947-48; University of Chicago, 1948-49; Black Mountain College, North Carolina, 1950-53. Married 1) Rena Furlong in 1952 (divorced, 1960), two sons; 2) Helen Bukberg in 1966 (divorced, 1977), three children. Worked in advertising typography, 1953-66; Director of the Poetry Project, St. Mark's Church-in-the-Bowery, 1967-69, and Teachers and Writers Collaborative, 1969-70, both New York; columnist, *Village Voice,* New York, 1969-84; formerly, Editor, *Kulchur,* New York. Since 1969, free-lance journalist, and poetry consultant, Bobbs Merrill, publishers, Indianapolis. Adjunct Associate Professor and Poet-in-Residence: City College, New York, 1969-81; Visiting Poet, St. Andrews Presbyterian College, Laurinburg, North Carolina, winters 1977-82; Gannett Distinguished Visiting Professor in the Humanities, Rochester Institute of Technology, New York, 1984-85. Since 1982, Associate Professor of Communications and Poet-in-Residence, New England College, Henniker, New Hampshire. Recipient: Creative Artists Public Service grant, 1971; National Endowment for the Arts fellowship, 1980. Address: Department of Communication, New England College, Henniker, New Hampshire 03242, U.S.A.

PUBLICATIONS

Verse

Four Poems to Spring. Privately printed, 1951.
The Dancer. Highlands, North Carolina, Jargon, 1952.
The Dutiful Son. Highlands, North Carolina, Jargon, 1957.
The Love Bit and Other Poems. New York, Totem, 1962.
A Treatise. New York, Brownstone Press, 1966.
Sirventes on a Sad Occurrence. Mount Horeb, Wisconsin, Perishable Press, 1967.
In Time: Poems 1962-1968. Indianapolis, Bobbs Merrill, 1969.
On Occasion: Some Births, Deaths, Weddings, Birthdays, and Other Events. Indianapolis, Bobbs Merrill, 1974.
The Woman Poems. Indianapolis, Bobbs Merrill, 1975.
Acts. Mount Horeb, Wisconsin, Perishable Press, 1976.
Advance Token to Boardwalk. New York, Smyrna Press, 1978.
On the Giving of the Tallis. Privately printed, 1979.
Names, Dates, and Places. Laurinburg, North Carolina, St. Andrews Press, 1979.
Just Friends/ Friends and Lovers: Poems 1959-1962. Highlands, North Carolina, Jargon, 1980.
Houses. Buffalo, White Pine Press, 1981.
At Fifty. Laurinburg, North Carolina, St. Andrews Press, 1982.
Poetry, The Ecology of the Soul. Buffalo, White Pine Press, 1983.
New Spaces. Santa Barbara, California, Black Sparrow Press, 1985.

Plays

The Great American Desert (produced New York, 1961). New York, Grove Press, 1965.
Miss Right (produced New York, 1962).
Like a Hill (produced New York, 1963).

Short Stories

Pan's Eyes. Amherst, Massachusetts, Mulch Press, 1974.

Other

The Wrong Season (on baseball). Indianapolis, Bobbs Merrill, 1973.
Marilyn Lives! New York, Delilah, 1981.

*

Bibliography: *Joel Oppenheimer: A Checklist* by George F. Butterick, Storrs, University of Connecticut Library, 1975.

Manuscript Collection: Wilbur Cross Library, University of Connecticut, Storrs.

Critical Studies: by Gilbert Sorrentino, in *Kulchur* (New York), Spring 1963; Robert Sward, in *Poetry* (Chicago), August 1963; *A Quick Graph* by Robert Creeley, San Francisco, Four Seasons, 1970; Hayden Carruth, in *Hudson Review* (New York), Summer 1974; George F. Butterick, in *American Poets since World War II* edited by Donald J. Greiner, Detroit, Gale, 1980; T. Leverett Smith, Jr., in *St. Andrews Review* (Laurinburg, North Carolina), Spring-Summer 1980; "Simply Survival: David Budbill and Joel Oppenheimer" by David W. Landrey, in *Cre-* dences (Buffalo), Fall-Winter 1981-82; Donald Phelps, in *The Word and Beyond*, New York, The Smith, 1982.

Joel Oppenheimer comments:
The poems depend on the real and are motivated by the occasion. They start from the particular and the personal and, hopefully, move out and on to the outside world.

*   *   *

Joel Oppenheimer was actually a student at that mythical institution, Black Mountain College, and he calls Olson, Creeley, and Ginsberg his "teachers and makers" ("The Excuse" from *In Time*), but in fact his real teacher and maker-mentor has been William Carlos Williams, and he shares an interest in what might be called the occasional poem with his contemporaries, Paul Blackburn and Frank O'Hara. His poems are constructed of talk, the most effective being poems like "Sirventes on a Sad Occurrence" which describes an old lady in a tenement in New York who could not control her bowels and shamed herself and her daughter on the stairs to their apartment. Oppenheimer is best when he is, as in this poem, describing the occasions of everyday occurrences, and uttering his compassion and sympathy with the life of humble people.

Oppenheimer's writing style is typified by hip jargon used by New York artists, Olson-style punctuation, and a continuous line which is punctuated with line-breaks that give the voice pauses where the syntax affords none. His long monologues are personal meditations on everyday occasions such as his wife's breasts or a ball game in the park or going to work, but use those occasions or subjects to spin off into a meditation on how good the world is in spite of everything. The banal style of writing/ talking of the poems actually serves as a foil to disarm the reader and suddenly allow him to see that perhaps one kind of poem *is* the simple occasion of being human and appreciating that fact.

The poems are quiet and patient, like an old teacher, waiting for the reader to stop and look at his own life with as much tenderness as Oppenheimer looks at his. At times, the poems have an insidious internal rhyming structure which will pun on old poems or songs or sayings. Poems like "The Cop Out" illustrate this sense of a poem's music which he shares with Blackburn and Creeley. Oppenheimer is a master of the everyday; one feels that the poems ask us all to live intelligently and above all with some mercy for others. They are proper poems for a time in which every educated man writes poems and uses the act of writing and the poem itself to help with his own enlightenment. The actual modesty of the poems underneath the seeming self-aggrandizement of whole poems about the trivia of existence is touching and compelling for its humane reminder of how important each of us thinks his life is and yet how each of us knows, underneath, how little any of us counts for in the larger view.

—Diane Wakoski

ORMOND, John. Welsh. Born in Dunvant, near Swansea, Glamorgan, 3 April 1923. Educated at Swansea Grammar School, 1935-41; University College of Swansea, 1941-45, B.A. 1945. Married Glenys Roderick in 1946; three children. Staff writer, *Picture Post*, London, 1945-49; Sub-Editor, *South Wales Evening Post*, Swansea, 1949-55; BBC Television news assistant,

Cardiff, 1955-57. Since 1957, BBC documentary film-maker, Cardiff. Recipient: Welsh Arts Council prize, 1970, 1974, bursary, 1973; Cholmondeley Award, 1975. Agent: Oxford University Press, Walton Street, Oxford OX2 6DP, England. Address: 15 Conway Road, Cardiff, Wales.

PUBLICATIONS

Verse

Indications, with James Kirkup and John Bayliss. London, Grey Walls Press, 1942.
Requiem and Celebration. Llandybie, Dyfed, Christopher Davies, 1969.
Corgi Modern Poets in Focus 5, with others, edited by Dannie Abse. London, Corgi 1971.
Definition of a Waterfall. London, Oxford University Press, 1973.
Penguin Modern Poets 27, with Emyr Humphreys and John Tripp. London, Penguin, 1979.

Recording: *Poets of Wales*, with Raymond Garlick, Argo.

Other

Graham Sutherland, O.M.: A Memorial Address. Cardiff, National Museum of Wales, 1981.
In Place of Empty Heaven: The Poetry of Wallace Stevens (lecture). Swansea, University College of Swansea, 1983.

Documentary Films include: *Under a Bright Heaven* (on Vernon Watkins), 1966; *A Bronze Mask* (on Dylan Thomas), 1968; *The Fragile Universe* (on Alun Lewis), 1969; *R.S. Thomas: Priest and Poet*, 1971; *The Land Remembers*, 1972; *A Day Eleven Years Long*, 1974; *The Life and Death of Picture Post*, 1977; *Fortissimo Jones*, 1978; *Graham Sutherland in Wales*, 1978; *A Land Against the Light*, 1978; *The Colliers' Crusade*, 1979.

*

Critical Studies: by Leslie Norris, in *Poetry Wales* (Cardiff), Winter 1969; Robert Shaw, in *Poetry* (Chicago), November 1970; introduction by Dannie Abse to *Corgi Modern Poets in Focus 5*, 1971; "The Poetry of John Ormond" by Randal Jenkins, in *Poetry Wales* (Cardiff), Summer 1972; "The Accessible Song: A Study of John Ormond's Recent Poetry" by Jeremy Hooker, in *Anglo-Welsh Review* (Tenby), Spring 1974; "The Anglo-Welsh Poet John Ormond" by Michael J. Collins, in *World Literature Today* (Norman, Oklahoma), Autumn 1977.

*   *   *

John Ormond, like his compatriot Leslie Norris, is a poet who came to prominence in the 1970's, in his sixth decade, after a lengthy silence. His *Definition of a Waterfall* contained the best of his work from the earlier collection *Requiem and Celebration*, which had appeared in Wales a few years before, together with some newer poems. The collection was reportedly snapped up by O.U.P. within days of its manuscript's arrival. The reasons are clear: here is a mature man delivering a book of mature writing, almost unheralded.

Ormond's credentials could not have been more sound. He had been schooled in the professionalism, the excitement of being a reporter for the magazine *Picture Post* in its heyday; he had won acclaim for his work in directing television film por-

traits of Vernon Watkins, Alun Lewis, Dylan Thomas, and R.S. Thomas. His success as a journalist and film-director fused sound and image in poems such as "Cathedral Builders":

> Saw naves sprout arches, clerestories soar,
> Cursed the loud fancy glaziers for their luck,
> Somehow escaped the plague, got rheumatism,
> Decided it was time to give it up,
>
> To leave the spire to others; stood in the crowd
> Well back from the vestments at the consecration,
> Envied the fat bishop his warm boots,
> Cocked up a squint eye and said, "I bloody did that."

Ormond is as acutely aware of community values and social injustices as one would expect from a man who grew up in industrial South Wales through the late 1920's and 1930's. It is the way in which he expresses such feelings while extending the possibilities of conventional "Welsh character" poetry in a piece such as "My Grandfather and His Apple-Tree" that distinguishes him:

> But in the time that I remember him
> (his wife had long since died, I never saw her)
> The sour half took over. Every single apple
> Grew—across twenty Augusts—bitter as wormwood.
> He'd sit under the box-tree, his pink gums
> (Between the white moustache and goatee beard)
> Grinding thin slices that his jack-knife cut,
> Sucking for sweetness vainly. It had gone,
> Gone. I heard him mutter
> Quiet Welsh oaths as he spat the gall-juice
> Into the seeding onion-bed, watched him toss
> The big core into the spreading nettles.

There's a sadness in the anger; life scars the man and the poet's conclusion carries implicit understanding and compassion as well as anger and criticism. The poem rises above labels such as "Anglo-Welsh." Of course Ormond's poetry is rooted in the South Wales community and landscape but upon these roots his best work grows to a wider significance.

His inclusion, with John Tripp and Emyr Humphreys, in the last of the Penguin Modern Poets series brings together some of those poems from the 1973 collection and later work. Though there is a mannered, overwrought style evident in some of the recent work—"Boundaries," "Captive Unicorn"—the best of this new work is very good indeed—"Message in a Bottle," "An Ending," and the superb "Landscape in Dyfed":

> And, at the water's edge,
> A struck havoc of trees clutches the interim season,
> The given roots bare, seeming to feed on the wind;
>
> And in their limbs what compass of sun
> Is contained, what sealed apparitions of summer,
> What transfixed ambulations. If you could cut
> Right to the heart and uncouple the innermost rings
> beyond those nerves you would see the structure of air.

John Ormond is constructing a body of work that may never be large, but is humane and visionary at once. Here is a poet dedicated to his craft, writing steadily and with profundity. One awaits another collection in the certainty that the writing will engage the reader at the deepest levels of experience.

—Tony Curtis

ORMSBY, Frank. Irish. Born in Enniskillen, County Fermanagh, Northern Ireland, 30 October 1947. Educated at Queen's University, Belfast, 1966-71, B.A. 1970, M.A. 1971. Married Mary Elizabeth McCaffrey in 1968; two children. Since 1969, Editor, *Honest Ulsterman* magazine, Belfast; since 1971, Teacher of English, Royal Belfast Academical Institution. Recipient: Eric Gregory Award, 1974. Address: 70 Eglantine Avenue, Belfast BT9 6DY, Northern Ireland.

PUBLICATIONS

Verse

Ripe for Company. Belfast, Ulsterman, 1971.
Business as Usual. Belfast, Ulsterman, 1973.
A Store of Candles. London, Oxford University Press, 1977.
Being Walked by a Dog. Belfast, Ulsterman, 1978.

Other

Editor, *Poets from the North of Ireland.* Belfast, Blackstaff Press, 1979.

*   *   *

Like several of his Northern Ireland contemporaries, Frank Ormsby cultivates the seeing eye. One cannot help but admire the precision of phrase that defines a neighbour in terms of his childless yard; that finds delight in an old tyre turned into a circular flowerbed; or that—even if only momentarily—sees, in "The Barracks," the official garnishing of a police-station in terms of an ordinary garden:

> The woman tending flowers bends her head,
> At work on the lupins. Elsewhere the beds
> Are weeded. Turned-up soil darkens the edge
> Of lawn and plastered wall. The chipped hedge
> At the rear might be suburban.

Ormsby is at work on the lupins, and on the Massage Parlour, the Police Museum, and the Air-Raid Shelter. He is industrious in his attempts to compose a Landscape with Figures, and not only in the poem of that name:

> What haunts me is a farmhouse among trees
> Seen from a bus window, a girl
> With a suitcase climbing a long hill
> And a woman waiting.

At first it seems as though the poems exist for the things seen. And certainly Ormsby has a determined faithfulness to his subjects that almost entails a rejection of elegance and what used to be called verbal magic. The individual poems yield up their attractions reluctantly. However, a personality emerges from the composite: certainly dour, but also tender; grimly honest, but refreshingly so. At times Ormsby can be quite moving, as in "In Memoriam":

> Father, I'm forgetting you. Mind struggles
> With the smudge of ten years, that shadow loitering
> Off-focus. Squat as a tumulus, you've gone
> To ground.

Moving, too, are poems about his mother and about marriage;

and the insight in these poems does much to mitigate what might otherwise seem an occasional gaucherie.

Ormsby certainly has the prose virtues, especially clarity and particularity, but these are qualities of poetry, also. The writer is his own best critic when he takes the title of his major collection from a phrase in a poem called "Under the Stairs." Under the stairs he finds the usual jumble of a life's progress—the shaft of a broom, a tyre, assorted nails. But he also finds that which, however modestly, can illumine the jumble: "a store of candles for when the light fails."

—Philip Hobsbaum

ORR, Gregory (Simpson). American. Born in Albany, New York, 3 February 1947. Educated at Hamilton College, Clinton, New York, 1964-66; Antioch College, Yellow Springs, Ohio, 1966-69, B.A. 1969; Columbia University, New York, 1969-72, M.F.A. 1972. Married Trisha Winer in 1973; one daughter. Junior Fellow, University of Michigan, Ann Arbor, 1972-75. Assistant Professor, 1975-80, and since 1980, Associate Professor of English, University of Virginia, Charlottesville. Visiting Writer, University of Hawaii, Manoa, Fall 1982. Since 1976, Poetry Consultant, *Virginia Quarterly Review*, Charlottesville. Recipient: YM-YWHA Discovery Award, 1970; Academy of American Poets prize, 1970; Bread Loaf Writers Conference *Transatlantic Review* award, 1976; Guggenheim Fellowship, 1977; National Endowment for the Arts fellowship, 1978; Fulbright grant, 1983. Address: Department of English, University of Virginia, Charlottesville, Virginia 22903, U.S.A.

PUBLICATIONS

Verse

Burning the Empty Nests. New York, Harper, 1973.
Gathering the Bones Together. New York, Harper, 1975.
Salt Wings. Charlottesville, Virginia, Poetry East, 1980.
The Red House. New York, Harper, 1980.

Other

Stanley Kunitz: An Introduction to the Poetry. New York, Columbia University Press, 1985.

*

Critical Studies: "Transparency and Prophecy" by Greg Kohl, in *American Poetry Review 4* (Philadelphia), no. 4, 1975; "Silence, Surrealism, and Allegory" by Alan Williamson, in *Kayak 40* (Santa Cruz, California), November 1975; "On Gregory Orr" by Hank Lazer, in *Iowa Review* (Iowa City), Winter 1981; "Falling and Returning: The Poetry of Gregory Orr" by David Wyatt, in *Pequod 15* (New York), 1983.

*   *   *

> At twelve, I killed a brother by accident,
> my mother died soon after: my whole life

I sensed as a lugged burden
of the invisible and unforgiving dead.

—from "On the Lawn at Ira's"

In his poetry Gregory Orr shares the lugged burden of his haunted past. Throughout his work themes reappear: how to deal with deep loss and guilt, how to find solace in nature, how to make connections with family and friends. As the title of his second volume suggests, Orr's art as well as his life is a process of "gathering the bones together" to make himself whole again. As he walks "toward [us] on this bridge/of poems: a thousand/-paper coffins/laid end to end," we can appreciate the immense suffering he had endured, and his pains become ours. His work, though, never seems cloying or self-pitying; instead, it is the heartfelt testament of a man wrestling with himself.

Reading through his work, we see Orr come to grips with his technique as well as with his past. Much of *Burning the Empty Nests* suffers from the poet trying too hard. Too many images are packed in too small a space, and the result is often needless obscurity. But the volume closes with a remarkable sequence of poems, an unfolding parable about "the stone and the wound." Here Orr is content to use primarily just these two images in poem after poem, and they gain a depth and density because of it:

A Courting Poem

The wound sought out the stone, because
it was tired of living alone and formless
like a cloud in a cave.

But the stone feared the wound,
sensing that it was not like other things
that were there and then gone.
The stone needed the wound, but still

the silence would never be the same again,
because of the hum of blood in its veins.
The long walks after the first snowfall
would be different: now there would be footprints.

Orr's next two volumes merge crisp images and clear narrative to produce lean and powerful works, as in "The Waterfall," part of his "Domestic Life" sequence:

Failing to hold on to things,
a man can become
a waterfall. His friends
stare, silent and aghast,
as he disappears
over the cliff, carrying
off his books, his wife,
all his furniture.

However, Orr's work shows him increasingly able to hold onto things. He is now even capable of celebrating the commonplace, as in "Work Gloves" or "Indian Summer" from *The Red House*. In "On the Lawn at Ira's" Orr says to a friend, "you never/let the early hurt be felt and so/it governs you; I now admit I'm mostly/happy, even feel blessed among so many friends." By allowing his own early hurt to be felt in his poems, Orr has become able to govern it. Perhaps he has even become able to move beyond it. In the final poem of *The Red House*, "A Last Address to My Ghosts," Orr says farewell to those guides from the past who "accompanied me so far/and with such ambiguous/fidelity." With this valediction, Orr hints he and his work will be moving to

new ground. With his now sure-handed style, Orr offers us much to look forward to.

—Dennis Lynch

———————

ORTIZ, Simon J. American Indian (Acoma Pueblo). Born in Albuquerque, New Mexico, 27 May 1941. Educated at Fort Lewis College, Durango, Colorado, 1962-63; University of New Mexico, Albuquerque, 1966-68; University of Iowa, Iowa City (International Writing Fellow), 1968-69. Served in the United States Army. Married Marlene Foster; three children. Public relations consultant, Rough Rock Demonstration School, Arizona, 1969-70, and National Indian Youth Council, Albuquerque, 1970-73; taught at San Diego State University, California, 1974, Institute of American Arts, Sante Fe, New Mexico, 1974, Navajo Community College, Tsaile, Arizona, summers 1975-77, College of Marin, Kentfield, California, 1976-79, and University of New Mexico, 1979-81. Since 1982, Consultant Editor, Pueblo of Acoma Press. Editor, *Quetzal*, Chinle, Arizona, 1970-73. Recipient: National Endowment for the Arts grant, 1969, 1982. Address: 308 Sesame S.W., Albuquerque, New Mexico 87105, U.S.A.

PUBLICATIONS

Verse

Naked in the Wind. Pembroke, North Carolina, Quetzal Vhio Press, 1970.
Going for the Rain. New York, Harper, 1976.
A Good Journey. Berkeley, California, Turtle Island Press, 1977.
Song, Poetry, Language. Tsaile, Arizona, Navajo Community College Press, 1978.
From Sand Creek: Rising in This Heart Which Is Our America. New York, Thunder's Mouth Press, 1981.
A Poem Is a Journey. Bourbanais, Illinois, Pternandon Press, 1981.

Short Stories

Howbah Indians. Tucson, Blue Moon Press, 1978.
Fightin': New and Collected Stories. New York, Thunder's Mouth Press, 1983.

Other

The People Shall Continue (for children). San Francisco, Children's Press, 1977.
Fightback: For the Sake of the People, For the Sake of the Land. Albuquerque, University of New Mexico Native American Studies, 1980.
Blue and Red (for children). Acoma, New Mexico, Pueblo of Acoma Press, 1982.
The Importance of Childhood. Acoma, New Mexico, Pueblo of Acoma Press, 1982.

Editor, with Rudolfo A. Anaya, *A Ceremony of Brotherhood 1680-1980.* Albuquerque, Academic, 1981.
Editor, *Earth Power Coming.* Tsiale, Arizona, Navajo Community College Press, 1983.

Editor, *These Hearts, These Poems*. Acoma, New Mexico, Pueblo of Acoma Press, 1984.

*

Critical Studies: by Willard Gingerich, in *Fiction International* (San Diego, California), 1983; "Common Walls: The Poetry of Simon Ortiz" by Kenneth Lincoln, in *The Colphin 9* (Aarhus, Denmark), 1984.

Simon J. Ortiz comments:

My writing, mostly using the tradition of Native American oral narrative, is a stand within the storm that is America. The wind will change; there will be calm.

*   *   *

The poetry of Simon J. Ortiz is a powerful and moving record of a native American who is an alien in his own land. In "A Designated National Park," he writes, "This morning,/I have to buy a permit to get back home." The Preface to *A Good Journey*, the most important collection of his work, is an excerpt from an interview. Ortiz is asked: "Why do you write? Whom do you write for?" His reply: "Because Indians always tell a story. The only way to continue is to tell a story and that's what Coyote says...Your children will not survive unless you tell something about them—how they were born, how they came to this certain place, how they continue."

In "Notes for My Child," he does tell his daughter how she was born, and, in the context of his other work—in which his native tradition asserts itself most tellingly in the ritualization of significant events—it is a bemused but good-humored account of an encounter with the impersonality of a hospital. Many of his poems also are about coming to certain places. His sense of place is always precise. Even when he is in relatively unfamiliar territory, he is able to locate himself in the human geography. Above all, however, these are poems of continuance. Ortiz has a confidence that things do go on, a confidence which no Euroamerican, I expect, has ever been able to feel, and this assurance informs all of his work.

The fundamental strata of *A Good Journey* are story-telling and prayer. Even in the poems which deal with the confusion, ugliness, and impersonality of modern American life—as in "Burning River—the memory of the timeless rituals serves as an orientation. In some ways, of course, the original sources are as lost to him as they are to other Americans: "The prayers of my native selfhood," he writes, "have been strangled in my throat." Some of the more self-conscious "traditional" poems, such as "Telling about Coyote," in which Coyote is "the existential man, Dostoevsky Coyote," suffer from the paradox inherent in any attempt to restore a lost tradition: it is of course the *lack* of self-consciousness which makes the tradition most attractive. In poems like "Earth and Rain, The Plants and Sun," "Canyon de Chelly," "Apache Love," "Vision Shadows," and "When It Was Taking Place," Ortiz gives us some of the most complete articulations to be found in English of that consciousness which swells in proximity with the eternity which ritual makes manifest.

Ortiz should *not* be read as a specimen native American or an anthropological curiosity. He is, above all, an American poet and a very good one. Neither his loss of orientation in the Los Angeles airport nor his obvious enthusiasm for the variety and drama of American geography are uniquely native American. Lines such as these might be envied by any poet: "And the immensity of the place/settles upon me without weight./I knew that we were near/one of the certain places/that is the center of the center."

—Don Byrd

O'SULLIVAN, Vincent (Gerard). New Zealander. Born in Auckland, 28 September 1937. Educated at University of Auckland, M.A. 1959; Lincoln College, Oxford, B.Litt. 1962. Married. Formerly, Lecturer, Victoria University, Wellington, and Reader, Waikato University, Hamilton; Visiting Fellow, Yale University, New Haven, Connecticut, 1976; Writer-in-Residence, Victoria University, 1981, University of Tasmania, Hobart, 1982, and Deakin University, Geelong, Victoria, 1982; Playwright-in-Residence, Downstage Theatre, Wellington, 1983. Editor, *Comment*, Wellington, 1963-66; Literary Editor, *New Zealand Listener*, Wellington, 1978-79. Recipient: Commonwealth Scholarship, 1960; Macmillan Brown Prize, 1961; Jessie MacKay Award, 1965; Farmers Poetry Prize, 1967, 1971; Fulbright award, 1976; Wattie Book Award, 1979; New Zealand Book Award, 1981. Address: c/o John McIndoe Ltd., 51 Crawford Street, P.O. Box 694, Dunedin, New Zealand.

PUBLICATIONS

Verse

Our Burning Time. Wellington, Prometheus, 1965.
Revenants. Wellington, Prometheus, 1969.
Bearings. Wellington and London, Oxford University Press, 1973.
From the Indian Funeral. Dunedin, McIndoe, 1976.
Butcher & Co. Wellington, Oxford University Press, 1976; London, Oxford University Press, 1978.
Brother Jonathan, Brother Kafka. Wellington and Oxford, Oxford University Press, 1980.
The Rose Ballroom and Other Poems. Dunedin, McIndoe, 1982.
The Butcher Papers. Auckland, Oxford University Press, 1982.

Play

Shuriken. Wellington, Victoria University Press, 1984.

Novel

Miracle: A Romance. Dunedin, McIndoe, 1976.

Short Stories

The Boy, The Bridge, The River. Dunedin, McIndoe, 1978.
Dandy Edison for Lunch and Other Stories. Dunedin, McIndoe, 1981.

Other

New Zealand Poetry in the Sixties. Wellington, Department of Education, 1973.
Katherine Mansfield's New Zealand. Melbourne, Lloyd O'Neal, 1974; London, Muller, 1975.

James K. Baxter. Wellington, Oxford University Press, 1976; London, Oxford University Press, 1977.

Editor, *An Anthology of Twentieth-Century New Zealand Poetry.* London, Oxford University Press, 1970; revised edition, Wellington and London, Oxford University Press, 1976.

Editor, *New Zealand Short Stories 3.* Wellington, Oxford University Press, 1975; London, Oxford University Press, 1976.

Editor, *The Aloe, with Prelude,* by Katherine Mansfield. Wellington, Port Nicholson Press, 1982; Manchester, Carcanet, and Atlantic Highlands, New Jersey, Humanities Press, 1983.

Editor, with M.P. Jackson, *New Zealand Writing since 1945.* Auckland, Oxford University Press, 1983.

Editor, with Margaret Scott, *The Collected Letters of Katherine Mansfield 1: 1903-1917.* Oxford and New York, Oxford University Press, 1984.

*   *   *

Despite the sheer gusto and figurative invention of his verse, Vincent O'Sullivan suffers on two counts from being a New Zealand academic. "New Zealand" in his own words (from his preface to a selection of New Zealand poetry) means burdened with the "cultural penalty" of dissociation from Europe and searching for self-definition. "Academic" means knowing all the skills in theory. O'Sullivan argues that this gap between uninformed heart or reality and over-informed head or technique can be bridged in two ways: by the "rigorous liberty" allowed by the exiled condition, and by the adaptation of old forms which is itself construction. O'Sullivan's occasional achievements by either avenue are memorable; more often his poems fall into the wasteland between original autobiographical experience and borrowed or highly-wrought belle-lettrism.

The clearest example of O'Sullivan's original success is his re-working of Greek myth: using the common facts themselves for a striking image (Helen "who once had a town to read by"); dramatising the characters' experience (Ulysses—"Lip me to silence then, true Penelope"); or twisting the story (the labyrinth is now within Theseus). At the other extreme is his beautiful lyric gift in reporting private experience, usually love ("You, your own leaven, knead perpetual myth"). When tied closely to a dramatic setting, as in "Island Bay," the result is a perfect harmony of form and feeling. In this poem, the poet recalls a love affair as he watches the red bus which carried him to their assignation, resolving to forget it all:

> But if the seventh, sacred wave rides higher by an inch...
> or the sky lightens, so much as with a match
> struck by some walker half a mile off...
> then all's unsaid. Reason walks the plank.
> We wait for a bus to drive out of the sea.

Too often, though, the objective correlative to the poet's emotion or imagery is insufficiently evoked, resulting in obscurity or rhetorical indulgence. The long sonnet sequence on the French engraver Charles Meryon tries to dramatise just this problem, the dangerous divorce of imagination from reality. Here reality is Meryon's vision of Paris, and his New Zealand experience abandoned—"Akaroa, the south, lay a hulk, a boyish error." Yet as O'Sullivan ably shows through his own art, New Zealand was the real, "in the way a hawk/over these hills can switch a sky to metal/for the stilled prey." The allegorical meaning is clear: O'Sullivan must begin with himself, "the swan of the body" and not the seductive artifice of Yeats's embroidered coat: "Skin and bones are verbs,/and there's our crown."

Masterly as O'Sullivan's gift is for the right image, the dramatic moment, and the colloquial expression, unfortunately he rarely employs it. In the earlier poetry he is seduced by elegance: "The girl I'd talk of, she goes decked in this"; "Limbs, Lady, Are Like Islands" goes a ponderous title; we find words like "uniquest" and "unvintageable." In later work the problem is uninspired exposition, a feeling of forced writing, often redeemed only by a clever final line (a poem about archery ends, "and when you close your eyes the bird-like drift of it," or a poem about a mad neighbour boarding a bus—"the doors shut behind her like palace sluts"). Even the title sequence from *Butcher & Co.,* featuring a Crow-like butcher who "grizzles" his knife on the stone, swamps his vulgar vitality with calculated images ("death, that perfect hinge") and awkward metaphysics ("Power Sticks Says B. As the Fan Flings"). Brute Butcher reads the *Odyssey,* instead of (as Bloom) being it.

Because of the gaudy juxtaposition of myth and reality in Central American life, and because it is essentially a report on experience, *From the Indian Funeral* is remarkably successful. Here O'Sullivan does give himself to his environment rather than to literature ("I am sick of the smooth ending"). As a New Zealander "facing the world without myth," he borrows everyday imagery to recreate the American's world ("your next meal as planned for as a vacation"), and Aztec imagery to imply the poverty of his own (the tourists dine by a statue of an Aztec "whose god ate time").

When O'Sullivan simply assumes his undeniable skill at adapting other myths and symbols, then, and like his mentor Yeats "lies down in the foul rag and bone shop of the heart" to take the "rigorous liberty" of communicating his own experience—then his words "are out and hunting." So far, and too often, his poetry has been impenetrably private, philosophically abstruse, or forgettably occasional—like his girls in *Revenants* who have merely "bartered talk."

O'Sullivan has lately concentrated on fiction and drama. His most recent volumes of poetry are *The Butcher Papers,* which refines the character of Butcher in a series of telegraphic playlets and monologues ("*the 20th Century, sport, that's the age of the Meat Man*") that finally prove tedious in their elliptical philosophising; and *The Rose Ballroom,* poems which expand in more congenial terms the poet's epistemological and metaphysical bent. Anchoring himself to the everyday, O'Sullivan transforms moments like a tramp drinking from a fountain or the Maori name of a river ("we have a fiction that we live by: it is the river") into philosophical paradigms.

—David Dowling

OWENS, Rochelle. Pseudonym for Rochelle Bass. American. Born in Brooklyn, New York, 2 April 1936. Educated at Lafayette High School, Brooklyn, graduated 1953. Married George Economou, *q.v.,* in 1962. Worked as clerk, typist, telephone operator. Founding Member, New York Theatre Strategy. Visiting Lecturer, University of California, San Diego, 1982; Adjunct Professor, and host of radio program "The Writer's Mind," University of Oklahoma, Norman, 1984. Recipient: Rockefeller grant, 1965, 1975; Ford grant, 1965; Creative Artists Public Service grant, 1966, 1973; Yale University Drama School Fellowship, 1968; Obie Award, for drama, 1968, 1971, 1982; Guggenheim Fellowship, 1971; National Endowment for the Arts grant, 1974; Villager Award, 1982. Agent: Fifi Oscard

Associates, 19 West 44th Street, New York, New York 10036.
Address: 1401 Magnolia, Norman, Oklahoma 73069, U.S.A.

PUBLICATIONS

Verse

Not Be Essence That Cannot Be. New York, Trobar Press, 1961.
Four Young Lady Poets, with others, edited by LeRoi Jones. New York, Totem, 1962.
Salt and Core. Los Angeles, Black Sparrow Press, 1968.
I Am the Babe of Joseph Stalin's Daughter. New York, Kulchur, 1972.
Poems from Joe's Garage. Providence, Rhode Island, Burning Deck, 1973.
The Joe 82 Creation Poems. Los Angeles, Black Sparrow Press, 1974.
The Joe Chronicles 2. Santa Barbara, California, Black Sparrow Press, 1979.
Shemuel. St. Paul, Minnesota, New Rivers Press, 1979.
French Light. Norman, Oklahoma Press with the Flexible Voice, 1984.

Recordings: *A Reading of Primitive and Archaic Poetry,* with others, Broadside; *From a Shaman's Notebook,* with others, Broadside; *The Karl Marx Play,* Kilmarnock, 1975; *Totally Corrupt,* Giorno, 1976; *Black Box 17,* Watershed Foundation, 1979; *Sweet Potatoes,* EarPlay.

Plays

Futz (produced Minneapolis, 1965; New York, Edinburgh and London, 1967). New York, Hawk's Well Press, 1961; revised version in *Futz and What Came After,* 1968; in *New Short Plays 2,* London, Methuen, 1969.
The String Game (produced New York, 1965). Included in *Futz and What Came After,* 1968.
Istanboul (produced New York, 1965; London, 1982). Included in *Futz and What Came After,* 1968.
Homo (produced Stockholm and New York, 1966; London, 1969). Included in *Futz and What Came After,* 1968.
Beclch (produced Philadelphia and New York, 1968). Included in *Futz and What Came After,* 1968.
Futz and What Came After (includes *Beclch, Homo, The String Game, Istanboul*). New York, Random House, 1968.
The Karl Marx Play, music by Galt MacDermot, lyrics by Rochelle Owens (produced New York, 1973). Included in *The Karl Marx Play and Others,* 1974.
The Karl Marx Play and Others (includes *Kontraption, He Wants Shih!, Farmer's Almanac, Coconut Folksinger, O.K. Certaldo*). New York, Dutton, 1974.
He Wants Shih! (produced New York, 1975). Included in *The Karl Marx Play and Others,* 1974.
Kontraption (produced New York, 1978). Included in *The Karl Marx Play and Others,* 1974.
Emma Instigated Me, in *Performance Arts Journal 1* (New York), Spring 1976.
The Widow, and The Colonel, in *The Best Short Plays 1977,* edited by Stanley Richards. Philadelphia, Chilton, 1977.
Mountain Rites, in *The Best Short Plays 1978,* edited by Stanley Richards. Philadelphia, Chilton, 1978.
Chucky's Hunch (produced New York, 1981).
Who Do You Want, Peire Vidal? (produced New York, 1982).

Screenplay: *Futz* (additional dialogue), 1969.

Short Stories

The Girl on the Garage Wall. Mexico City, El Corno Emplumado, 1962.
The Obscenities of Reva Cigarnik. Mexico City, El Corno Emplumado, 1963.

Other

Editor, *Spontaneous Combustion: Eight New American Plays.* New York, Winter House, 1972.

*

Manuscript Collections: Mugar Memorial Library, Boston University; University of California, Davis; University of Oklahoma, Norman; Lincoln Center Library of the Performing Arts, New York.

Critical Studies: in *World 29* (New York), April 1974; "Rochelle Owens Symposium," in *Margins 24-26* (Milwaukee), 1975; *Contemporary Authors Autobiography Series,* Detroit, Gale, 1985.

Rochelle Owens comments:

I know that the only tradition that interests me as a writer is the tradition of breaking away from the fixed and familiar patterns to living new structures and the creation of new forms, with all its risks and manifold facets.

* * *

Rochelle Owens is better known as a playwright than as a poet, but perusal of her poems shows them to be close to her theatrical imagination and an essential stimulus to it. In poetry (as distinct from poetic drama) she can concentrate her energies exclusively on verbal invention, coining words, splitting them, splashing them disjunctively on the page, disrupting grammar and free-associating with maximum tonal contrast:

O IF I FORGET THEE O ZION
LET AMERICA'S BALLS RUST

In her collection *I Am the Babe of Joseph Stalin's Daughter* both her verbal incandescence and dramatic proclivities emerge. As in her play *Futz,* she fearlessly explores the psychic realities of deviant personae. The Deebler Woman poems and "Bernard Fruchtman in Town & Country" create voices speaking fragments of plays. "The Voluminous Agony of Karl Marx" plainly grew into *The Karl Marx Play,* in which Marx, a modern Hebrew prophet cries out to Yahweh, as Job did, to relieve his boils so he can sit down and "write the book."

Owens, herself Jewish and married to a Greek, relishes Old Testament themes and the Mediterranean arena of contrast between Jew and Christian, Turk and Greek, which metaphorically extends to other conflicts—black *vs.* white, male *vs.* female, always juxtaposing ancient and traditional faith and language with contemporary slang and secular thought. A more recent work, *The Joe 82 Creation Poems,* is a sequence of over a hundred poems titled for the gut-creative act which inspires graffiti on the New York subways. Although its subtitle is "a theater piece," this sequence nevertheless has strongly biblical and epic qualities. In the voices of a primal couple, Wild-Man and Wild-Woman, Owens redesigns the myths of creation in terms of the immediate creativity of every mind confronting its own experience. It is an ambitious task, with impressive results. Still an innovator, this poet is enlarging her originality of thought and exuberance of language to create a new vision of the world which rests on the old virtues of praise and joy:

O World (Yes)
Thy feet   are graced with everything!

—Jane Augustine

OXLEY, William. British. Born in Manchester, Lancashire, 29 April 1939. Educated at College of Commerce, Manchester; qualified as Chartered Accountant. Married Patricia Holmes in 1963; two daughters. Office boy, Salford, Lancashire, 1955-57; articled clerk, Manchester, 1957-64; chartered accountant, Deloitte and Company, London, 1964-68, and Lazard Brothers, London, 1968-76. Since 1976, free-lance writer. Editor or Co-Editor, *New Headland*, 1969-74, *Laissez Faire*, 1971-75, *Orbis*, 1972-74, *Littack*, 1972-76, *Village Review*, 1973-74, *Poetry Newsletter*, 1976-78, *Littack Supplement*, 1976-80, *Lapis Lazuli*, 1977-78. Since 1984, review editor, *Acumen*. Member, Royal Institute of Philosophy, 1982-83. Address: 6 The Mount, Furzeham, Brixham, South Devon TQ5 8QY, England.

PUBLICATIONS

Verse

The Dark Structures. London, Mitre Press, 1967.
New Workings. Privately printed, 1969.
Passages from Time: Poems from a Life. Epping, Essex, Ember Press, 1971.
The Icon Poems. Epping, Essex, Ember Press, 1972.
Opera Vetera. Privately printed, 1973.
Mirrors of the Sea. London, Quarto Press, 1973.
Fightings (as Jason Hardy). Epping, Essex, Ember Press, 1974.
Eve Free. Knotting, Bedfordshire, Sceptre Press, 1975.
The Mundane Shell. Egglescliffe, Cleveland, Uldale House, 1975.
Superficies. Breakish, Isle of Skye, Aquila, 1976.
Wind. Leicester, Cog Press, 1976.
The Exile. Egglescliffe, Cleveland, Uldale House, 1979.
The Notebook of Hephaestus and Other Poems. Kinross, Lomond Press, 1981.
The Vitalist Reader: A Selection of the Poetry of Anthony L. Johnson, William Oxley, and Peter Russell, edited by James Hogg. Salzburg, University of Salzburg, 1982.
A Map of Time. Salzburg, University of Salzburg, 1984.
The Triviad and Other Satires. Salzburg, University of Salzburg, 1984.

Other

Sixteen Days in Autumn (travel). Privately printed, 1972.
Three in Campagna. Privately printed, 1973.
Synopthegms of a Prophet. Brixham, Devon, Ember Press, 1981.
The Idea and Its Imminence. Salzburg, University of Salzburg, 1982.

Of Human Consciousness. Salzburg, University of Salzburg, 1982.
The Cauldron of Inspiration. Salzburg, University of Salzburg, 1983.

Translator, *Poems of a Black Orpheus,* by Léopold S. Senghor. London, Menard Press, 1981.
Translator, *Ndesse,* by Léopold S. Senghor. London, Menard Press, 1981.

*

Bibliography: *William Oxley: A Bibliography* by James Hogg, Salzburg, University of Salzburg, 1984.

Critical Studies: "Poet in Profile: William Oxley" by Mike Shields, in *The Writer* (Aylesbury, Buckinghamshire), April 1975; "Littack: On the Attack" by Derek Stanford, in *The Statesman* (Karachi), 12 and 19 April 1975; "Through Littack to Vitalism" by V. Fenech, in *Bulletin and Times of Malta,* 1976; *William Oxley: A Survey of His Poetry and Philosophy* by P.H., Salzburg, University of Salzburg, 1984; *The Vitalist Seminar* edited by James Hogg, Salzburg, University of Salzburg, 1984.

William Oxley comments:

Towards the end of the 1960's I began to take an active interest in contemporary poetry. I found it a time of great confusion and in retrospect can see that much of that confusion rubbed-off on me. I was most pained not just by the apparent absence of standards but also by the very real attack on all standards that was everywhere being made. Against this I reacted strongly whilst, at the same time, endeavouring a rational analysis of the situation as far as it affected the current poetry scene. Naturally, in such chaotic circumstances, my reaction, insofar as it took printed form, tended to be something of an over-reaction as well as philosophically confusing in itself.

For some time—as a consequence of my analysis of the then poetry scene—I had one basic aim, which was to contribute something towards bringing about a change in the prevailing climate of poetry and poetics in the United Kingdom. A movement away from what I considered to be the dry academic poetry on offer in certain more conservative quarters, and away from the formless morass of undisciplined experimentalism and gimmickry on offer in more populist and radical quarters. Towards this end the magazine *Littack* was founded in 1972 with the aim of working out in open forum a new poetics. A more vital poetry was sought by a number of poets who have since become loosely known at the Vitalist Poets.

In 1976 *Littack* was replaced by *The Littack Supplement* which endeavoured to concentrate upon widening the definition of "a vitalist poetry" through a less polemical and more thoughtful series of editorials, as well as by the careful reviewing of a wide range of poetry books and pamphlets. Also, to emphasise the importance of freeing poetry from its chains of prose literalness/ and formlessness, I sought to encourage in *The Littack Supplement* the printing of poems which inclined towards imaginative and symbolic values couched in lyrical, or at least rhythmical, forms, rather than either the purely literal and superficial descriptions of experience, or the pseudo-innovatory poetry that, by and large, still predominated.

Even with the passing of *The Littack Supplement* in 1980, my hope remains the same: to see the re-vitalisation of the true tradition of poetry (which works through a multi-dimensional and analogical use of language, rather than by a one-dimensional prose discourse) giving a poetry of sufficient breadth of concern as to be variously described as "a poetry of the whole mind" and "a poetry of cosmic concern." It is a hope that I have observed slowly but surely being realised in several quarters over the last few years.

One question, however, continues to rear its head, despite the half decade which has elapsed since the cessation of the whole *Littack* venture, and that is as to the exact nature of "a vitalist poem." Most of all has this arisen because of the mistaken assumption made by several critics that a vitalist poem must always be characterised by "aggressivity" and "strong language." This is not so. For while it is true to say that the inner integrity of any poem depends upon its possessing a certain vitality, like an electric circuit, and while some poems, like some human beings, may be said to possess more vitality than others, the tone and voice of the poet—even his verbal gestures—do not determine that vitality. What determines the vitality of a poem is the particular conjunction of feeling and thought. If feeling and thought are successfully married in a given verbal pattern (which pattern they largely determine) then the whole will possess a certain vitality. A vitality which, in turn, reflects the natural vitality of whatever is the poem's particular subject. But neither an active disposition, nor a reflective disposition, nor a strong nor a weak personality on the part of the poet, guarantees vitality to any particular poem. For as Keats rightly observed the "negative capability" of the poet is the most crucial factor of all in poetic creativity. It is the life-giving or life-imparting gift of the poet. It does not matter whether a poem be classified as personal or public, epic or sonnet, cooked or raw—or any way other described—a poem must develop a life of its own, generate its own vitality, in order to live. So any good poem—no matter what its tone, mood, or subject—is a vitalist poem. Finally, it is my own view that a certain philosophical blood transfusion is needed from time to time for good poetry to be written, and for this reason I hold that a truly vitalist poem says something of significance about the human condition.

*   *   *

William Oxley has been publishing poetry since 1967, and began writing seriously some three years before that. In the years since then his poetry has broadened greatly in vision and achievement and his development has been marked by an increasing clarity of purpose. His earliest poems, with a few exceptions, are heavily influenced by early modernism, by the example of Eliot and Pound. Yet Oxley never appears fully happy in the idiom, for all the undoubted competence of many of the poems. His own sense of this is evident in the "Apologia" to his *Opera Vetera*, a collection (or at least a selection) of poems written between 1964 and 1969. There he writes that "during the latter half of 1972 I called a halt deliberately to what has, since 1964/65 been a very prolific period of versifying. In short, I vowed poetic celibacy. I did this because I felt I was simply not developing poetically in any consistent way; indeed, I wasn't even sure if I was developing at all." The period of celibacy was the beginning of a conscious redirecting of his poetical activity, the beginning of a new kind of commitment.

This commitment has been evidenced in a number of ways. On the one hand he has produced some prose works remarkable for their independence and honesty of thought, and for what they betoken of a determination to analyse the very bases of creative activity, as perceived and experienced by Oxley himself. *Of Human Consciousness* and *The Idea and Its Imminence* are philosophical works which are, in the best and highest sense, the work of an amateur; they are, that is to say, the product of love, and they are free from the debilitations of most contemporary philosophical jargon. In the same way, *The Cauldron of Inspira-*

tion, though it has unmistakable weaknesses, constitutes an exciting and perceptive account of poetry and its importance which would be well beyond most "academic" critics. This far-reaching reflection upon the fundamentals of his thought and his craft was accompanied by his campaigning editorship of the periodical *Littack*. Here there was elucidated his concept of "Vitalist" poetry, not a conception reducible to easy formulae but a stimulating consideration of the limitations of much contemporary verse and an attempt to indicate possible ways forward.

In terms of his own poetic productions, all this activity has borne fruit in a quantity of work radically different from, and superior to, his earlier work. He has, with some courage, pursued the creation of a language and idiom for a kind of philosophical and discursive poetry which has long been out of fashion. A series of long poems—e.g., *The Exile, The Mundane Shell, The Rose on the Tree of Time, A Map of Time*—have tackled very large ideas in forms and manners of some considerable interest and individuality. These are works of great understanding, and often of considerable beauty, and deserve to be better known. Given the prevailing poetic climate they might be termed experimental poems, and, like most experiments, they have their moments of failure. Taken as a whole, however, they constitute a valuable extension and development of that "tradition" represented by the longer poems of MacDiarmid and Russell. His shorter poems are perhaps less fully individual, though many are very attractive—his love lyrics, for example (the series "To Lily," "Lily Inviolate," and "My Lily"), or his intense poems of place and landscape, such as "The Lane," "Green Lanes," "Wheat," and "Paradise." His satirical works, both in epigram and in mock-heroic (e.g., *The Triviad*), are less successful: stridency too often replaces precise judgement. In the considerable body of his best work, however, William Oxley has displayed poetic intelligence and metaphysical understanding of a high order. There is every reason to hope that his poetic development will continue for a long time yet.

—Glyn Pursglove

PACK, Robert. American. Born in New York City, 29 May 1929. Educated at Dartmouth College, Hanover, New Hampshire, B.A. 1951; Columbia University, New York, M.A. 1953. Married 1) Isabelle Miller in 1950; 2) Patricia Powell in 1961, two sons and one daughter. Taught at Barnard College, New York, 1957-64, and Poetry Workshop of the New School for Social Research, New York. Since 1970, Abernathy Professor, Middlebury College, and since 1973, Director, Bread Loaf Writers Conference, Vermont. Editor, *Discovery*, New York. Recipient: Fulbright Fellowship, 1956; American Academy grant, 1957; Borestone Mountain Poetry Award, 1964; National Endowment for the Arts grant, 1968. Address: Middlebury College, Middlebury, Vermont 05742, U.S.A.

PUBLICATIONS

Verse

The Irony of Joy. New York, Scribner, 1955.
A Stranger's Privilege. Hessle, Yorkshire, Asphodel, and New York, Macmillan, 1959.

Guarded by Women. New York, Random House, 1963.
Selected Poems. London, Chatto and Windus, 1964.
Home from the Cemetery. New Brunswick, New Jersey, Rutgers University Press, 1969.
Nothing But Light. New Brunswick, New Jersey, Rutgers University Press, 1972.
Keeping Watch. New Brunswick, New Jersey, Rutgers University Press, 1976.
Waking to My Name: New and Selected Poems. Baltimore, Johns Hopkins University Press, 1980.
Faces in a Single Tree: A Cycle of Monologues. Boston, Godine, 1984.

Other

Wallace Stevens: An Approach to His Poetry and Thought. New Brunswick, New Jersey, Rutgers University Press, 1958.
The Forgotten Secret (for children). New York, Macmillan, 1959.
Then What Did You Do? (for children). New York, Macmillan, 1961.
How to Catch a Crocodile (for children). New York, Knopf, 1964.

Editor, with Donald Hall and Louis Simpson, *The New Poets of England and America.* New York, Meridian, 1957; London, New English Library, 1974; *Second Selection,* Meridian, 1962.
Editor and Translator, with Marjorie Lelach, *Mozart's Librettos.* Cleveland, World, 1961.
Editor, with Tom Driver, *Poems of Doubt and Belief: An Anthology of Modern Religious Poetry.* New York, Macmillan, 1964.
Editor, with Marcus Klein, *Literature for Composition on the Theme of Innocence and Experience.* Boston, Little Brown, 1966.
Editor, with Marcus Klein, *Short Stories: Classic, Modern, Contemporary.* Boston, Little Brown, 1967.
Editor, *Selected Letters,* by Keats. New York, New American Library, 1974.

*

Critical Study: "Fresh Flowers for the Urn: Reassessing Robert Pack" by Paul Mariani, in *Massachusetts Review* (Amherst), Winter 1982.

*   *   *

Robert Pack's poetry asserts man's connection to all levels of creation. "Grieving on a Grand Scale," a representative work, ranges from the imagined death of a lover, through speculations on the inevitable demise of the entire scale of nature, to the impending fate of the persona. Though the poem resolves "..to mourn softly, without hope of resurrection," the final lines comfort with the image of an unknowing yet elegiac universe: "...young deer/ Do not move—their loose watery lips/ Slide over their gums with a sound like weeping." Pack avoids sentimentality by acknowledging both human involvement in "the crooked weasel's crooked chase" ("Canoe Ride"), and the horror, however stylized, of the cycle of existence: "...lace/ Of mouse bones in owl feces" ("The Black Ant"). That carnage defines and fuses with human beauty implies frightening questions. Poems like "Descending" interpret the terror implicit in the universe as the real cost of exclusion from paradise, but generally Pack, while negating traditional answers, substitutes openness to the wonders of creation, whatever its origin: "...above, no missing God/ I miss; high satisfying sky though, and below,/ Chrysanthemums in garb of gaiety" ("Raking Leaves"). The key image of delight is the family; "Breakfast Cherries" celebrates the richness of ephemeral family moments. In "Everything Is Possible," the expectant father achieves the illusion of godhead, while the husband in "Were It Not" sees daily life as a recapitulation of paradise. Though children "redeem all sorrow," such redemption never completely calms latent anxiety. "The Mountain Ash Tree" with its equivocally symbolic berries is Pack's most complex version of man's precarious optimism; despite the ominous appearance and bitter taste of the fruit, its unraveled meanings force the reader to share the final affirmation: "I am still alive."

Because of the relatedness of all elements in the universe, man can revert to the "hermit crab" comfort of "shell" and "tentacles" ("My House"), or aspire to a level where "only his thought remains—/melodious and luminous..." ("Venus"). Such diversity parallels man's inevitable transcending of generational limits as he enacts several family roles simultaneously. A son, struggling to distinguish mother from wife and himself from his dead father, invokes the father's return and, ironically, a renewal of the whole process: "Dreaming, I seek your skeleton below;/ I dig the worms and find your embryo" ("Father"). The strongest dramatization of this theme is "The Boat," in which the speaker, with deadpan earnestness, accepts both the fusion and separateness of roles: "I dressed my father in his little clothes,/ Blue sailor suit, brass buttons on his coat./ He asked me where the running water goes./ ...He told me where all the running water goes./ And dressed me gently in my little clothes." Here the strict *terza rima* with its subtle variations of phrasing perfectly embodies the theme of freedom within the ambiguous comfort of family cycles.

If the family generates order, however unstable, sexual love generates the family. Pack's love poems, stressing man's connections to all natural phenomena, produce some striking images: "and if I nibbled your ear,/ an elephant, trumpeting its charge,/ would thunder through the forest/ of your veins at large" ("A Modest Boast at Meridian"). Though long poems like "Home from the Cemetery" and "The Last Will and Testament of Art Evergreen" understandably lack such sustained intensity, they reveal Pack's characteristic command of symbolic image and tactful control of the overall pattern, in both works Pack's obsessive equation of acceptance of death with acceptance of life.

While Pack can shock with passages of bitter comedy or can sustain an ironic voice throughout a poem, he fails at social satire in works like "Routine" (wisely excised from the selected poems Pack wishes to preserve in *Waking to My Name*). And the recent literary satire "Advice to Poets" overworks its emphasis on the artist's necessarily sexual relation to the Muse; "stroke her caesura." Pack is wittiest in "Wilt Thou Condemn Me?" which teases with 15 stanzas on the ambiguous virtues of irony: "The man who needs to meet death/ with a final laugh, better/ have nerves of irony.... There were no differences/ that day to day could not be/ ironied out between them."

Such amplification through repetition is almost a stylistic signature for Pack, especially in the varying of verb forms: "I grow by choosing what I choose to know" ("Song to Myself"). Pack's special contribution, among a variety of sestinas, villanelles, and freer forms, is a moral nursery rhyme in which a convincingly guileless speaker agonizes, with inevitable repetition, towards a solution that both repels and involves the reader: "I shot an otter because I had a gun" leads through six stanzas only to "He shot an otter because he had a gun" ("The Shooting"). *Waking to My Name* documents Pack's consistently high level of achievement for over 25 years, both in his new poems and in those earlier works, sometimes revised, that he wishes in his canon. The same strong voice worries over generational links and celebrates man's connection to the natural world; the same formal control polishes and refines. Pack's recent work, if its skill no longer surprises, more than compensates through the sound of this strong, nuanced voice.

—Burton Kendle

PADGETT, Ron. American. Born in Tulsa, Oklahoma, 17 June 1942. Educated at Columbia University, New York (Boar's Head Poetry Prize and George E. Woodberry Award, 1964), A.B. 1964; Fulbright Fellow, Paris, 1965-66. Married; one son. Since 1968, has taught poetry workshops at St. Mark's-in-the-Bowery, New York, and poetry writing in New York public schools. Associate Editor, *Paris Review*, 1968-70; Founding Editor, Full Court Press, 1973. Since 1981, Director of Publications, Teachers and Writers Collaborative, New York. Recipient: Gotham Book Mart prize, 1964; Poets Foundation grant, 1965, 1968; Columbia University Translation Center Award, 1976; National Endowment for the Arts fellowship, 1983. Address: 342 East 13th Street, New York, New York 10003, U.S.A.

PUBLICATIONS

Verse

In Advance of the Broken Arm. New York, "C" Press, 1964.
Sky. London, Goliard Press, 1966.
Bean Spasms: Poems and Prose, with Ted Berrigan. New York, Kulchur, 1967.
Tone Arm. Brightlingsea, Essex, Once Press, 1967.
100,000 Fleeing Hilda, with Joe Brainard. New York, Boke, 1967.
Bun, with Tom Clark. New York, Angel Hair, 1968.
Some Thing, with Ted Berrigan and Joe Brainard. Privately printed, n.d.
Great Balls of Fire. New York, Holt Rinehart, 1969.
Sweet Pea. New York, Aloe, 1971.
Sufferin' Succotash, with Joe Brainard, with *Kiss My Ass,* by Michael Brownstein. New York, Boke, 1971.
Poetry Collection. Penfield, New York, Strange Faeces Press, 1971.
Back in Boston Again, with Ted Berrigan and Tom Clark. Philadelphia, Telegraph, 1972.
Oo La La, with Jim Dine. London, Petersburg Press, 1973.
Crazy Compositions. Bolinas, California, Big Sky, 1974.
Toujours l'Amour. New York, Sun Press, 1976.
Arrive by Pullman. Paris, Generations, 1978.
Tulsa Kid. Calais, Vermont, Z Press, 1980.
Triangles in the Afternoon. New York, Sun Press, 1980.
How to Be a Woodpecker. West Branch, Iowa, Toothpaste Press, 1983.

Plays

Seventeen: Collected Plays, with Ted Berrigan. New York, "C" Press, 1965.
Chrononhotonothologos, with Johnny Stanton, adaptation of the play by Henry Carey. New York, Boke, 1971.

Novel

Antlers in the Treetops, with Tom Veitch. Toronto, Coach House Press, 1973.

Short Stories

2/2 Stories for Andy Warhol. New York, "C" Press, 1965.

Other

The Adventures of Mr. and Mrs. Jim and Ron, with Jim Dine. London, Cape Goliard Press, and New York, Grossman, 1970.

Editor, with David Shapiro, *An Anthology of New York Poets.* New York, Random House, 1970.
Editor, with Bill Zavatsky, *The Whole Word Catalogue 2.* New York, McGraw Hill, 1977.

Translator, *The Poet Assassinated,* by Guillaume Apollinaire. New York, Holt Rinehart, 1968; augmented edition, as *The Poet Assassinated and Other Stories,* Berkeley, California, North Point Press, 1984.
Translator, *Dialogues with Marcel Duchamp,* by Pierre Cabanne. New York, Viking Press, 1970; London, Thames and Hudson, 1971.
Translator, with David Ball, *Rldasedlrad les Dlcmhypbdf,* by Valéry Larbaud. New York, Boke, 1973.
Translator, with Bill Zavatsky, *The Poems of A.O. Barnabooth,* by Valéry Larbaud. Tokyo, Mushinsha, 1974.
Translator, *Kodak,* by Blaise Cendrars. New York, Boke, 1976.

*

Critical Study: "The New American Poetry" by Jonathan Cott, in *The New American Arts,* New York, Horizon Press, 1966.

*   *   *

Deeply influenced by modern painting and its techniques, Ron Padgett modulates poems beyond traditional limits. In "Wonderful Things," for example, his diction varies from the language of formal elegy ("Anne, who are dead...") to that of insanity ("Seriously, I have this mental (smuh!) illness..."). Then, taking a new direction, he wraps the whole poem, retroactively, in the disarmingly ingenuous diction of a master storyteller ("and that's what I want to do/tell you wonderful things").

A native world surfaces in this poetry: mysterious appearances, holes in the sky, falling clouds, ghosts, secret notes, funny animals, elves:

DECEMBER

I will sleep
in my little cup.

At its purest, its effect is wonder: "A child draws a man and the earth/is covered with snow." Padgett's power comes from this voice. When it speaks directly, it is the clearest voice of a child in modern poetry. When it speaks indirectly, the irony is clear.

Behind his irony, Padgett grows full of Dada ("What modern poetry needs/is a good beating"), ready to parody anything established ("When I see birches/I think of nothing...One could do worse than see birches"). Like the Dadaists, he can pit Art against Life with ease:

> Let's take a string quartet
> Playing one of Beethoven's compositions
> We may explain it as the scratching
> Of a horse's hair against a cat's gut
> Or we may explain it as the mind
> Of a genius soaring up to an infinite
> Horse's hair scratching against an infinite cat's gut.

The dilemma Padgett especially enjoys is that of the man who climbs after a ball of gold in the sky, actually gets it, but then doesn't know what to do with it:

> And...the way Madison Avenue really
> Does go to Heaven
> And then turns around and comes back, disappointed.

In his own search for values, Padgett is deeply affected by Surrealism's black humor, unmistakable imagery, and its antipathy towards the merely rational. Intellectual history, Padgett writes,

> Is now only an imitation of itself
> Like a car
> Driving towards itself in the rain
> Only to be photographed from behind
> As we all eventually are...
> Breaking the visible chains of logic.

Whether he is, like a wise fool, proclaiming "Socrates was a mute, this is generally not known/But understood at some hilarious fork/For a few years! oh," or, like a child full of belief, stretching his hand into a painting to pick up one chocolate from a box, "Breaking the visible chains of logic" is what Padgett is about.

—Edward B. Germain

PAGE, Geoff(rey Donald). Australian. Born in Grafton, New South Wales, 7 July 1940. Educated at the Armidale School, 1952-57; University of New England, Armidale, New South Wales, 1958-62. National military service, 1959. Married Carolyn Anne Page in 1959; one son. English and history teacher, Canberra high schools, 1964-74. Since 1974, Senior English Teacher, Narrabundah College, Canberra. Recipient: Australian Literature Board grant, 1975, 1983. Address: 8 Morehead Street, Curtin, A.C.T. 2605, Australia.

PUBLICATIONS

Verse

Two Poets, with Philip Roberts. Brisbane, University of Queensland Press, 1971.
Smalltown Memorials. Brisbane, University of Queensland Press, 1975.
Collecting the Weather. Brisbane, Makar Press, 1978.

Cassandra Paddocks. Sydney, Angus and Robertson, 1980.
Clairvoyant in Autumn. Sydney, Angus and Robertson, 1983.

Plays

Radio Plays: *The Line of Least Resistance*, 1976; *The Life and Death of James Lionel Michael*, 1982.

Novel

Benton's Conviction. Sydney, Angus and Robertson, 1985.

Other

Using "The First Paperback Poets Anthology". Brisbane, University of Queensland Press, 1974.

Editor, *Shadows from the Wire: Poems and Photographs of Australians in the Great War.* Ringwood, Victoria, Penguin, 1983.

*   *   *

Geoff Page emerged later than some of his contemporaries as a poet of importance in Australia. He is under-represented in anthologies, but has produced a body of honestly felt and moving work which is impressive in its totality.

His work is characteristic for its clarity and succinctness of image, as in these lines from "Flying over the Western Districts":

> Down
> through five clear miles of air
>
> the patterns of our tenure
> lie strange across the ground.

or in these lines from "Prowlers":

> A floorboard sprung
> will bring a groan
> vaguely down the hall.
>
> Angles of furniture
> hold them strangely.
> Books along a shelf give out
>
> their varying degrees of light
> as, guiltless yet,
> they slip away—

The accuracy and deceptive plainness of his imagery derives from William Carlos Williams. But this combines in Page's work with a very Australian concern for landscape, history, and narrative. He is perhaps the most typically Australian poet of his generation, without being in any way nationalistic in his work. His deliberately dry and low-key delivery and the celebration of survival in poems such as "Grit" which praises

> the country women
> of my mother's generation...
> that hard abundance year by year
> mapped in a single word

may be seen by some, particularly outsiders, as archetypally Australian. This is to simplify Australians, and Page, himself no simplifier, would see himself and other Australians in more complex terms.

In poem after poem he is concerned with wastage and lost opportunities, as in these lines from "Break-up":

> Once, quite near the end,
> we showered together.
> While the soap
> clung round your nipples
> and the water slid
> down either back,
> my body
> committed
> yours
> to memory.

Or in his poems about World War I, or the death of his grandmother, or "Aubade." Memories of making love conclude on this note: "we listen to the world/fill up with light/and with our losses." Page's determinedly negative stance and his painstaking understatement cumulatively spell out a passionate rhetoric of loss. He is not unaware of the decorative and filmic aspects of his subject-matter. So in "Daguerrotype Tennis" he writes:

> The roller's hauled
> one unaware last time
> and left,
> the game postponed.

This self-awareness includes a wry, implicit humour. Occasionally there are overtly humorous poems such as "In Dante's Hell," which deals with the Australian obsession of discussing vintages.

—Geoffrey Lehmann

PAGE, P(atricia) K(athleen). Canadian. Born in Swanage, Dorset, England, 23 November 1916; emigrated to Canada in 1919. Educated at St. Hilda's School for Girls, Calgary, Alberta; Art Students League, and Pratt Institute, New York. Married William Arthur Irwin in 1950; three step-children. Formerly, sales clerk and radio actress, Saint John, New Brunswick; filing clerk and historical researcher, Montreal; script writer, National Film Board, Ottawa, 1946-50. Painter, as P.K. Irwin: individual shows—Picture Loan Society, Toronto, 1960; Galeria de Arte Moderna, Mexico City, 1962; Art Gallery of Greater Victoria, British Columbia, 1965. Recipient: Bertram Warr Award (*Contemporary Verse*), 1940; Oscar Blumenthal Award (*Poetry*, Chicago), 1944; Governor-General's Award, 1955. Officer of the Order of Canada, 1977. Address: 3260 Exeter Road, Victoria, British Columbia, Canada.

PUBLICATIONS

Verse

Unit of Five, with others, edited by Ronald Hambleton. Toronto, Ryerson Press, 1944.
As Ten as Twenty. Toronto, Ryerson Press, 1946.
The Metal and the Flower. Toronto, McClelland and Stewart, 1954.

Cry Ararat! Poems New and Selected. Toronto, McClelland and Stewart, 1967.
Poems, Selected and New. Toronto, Anansi, 1974.
Five Poems. Toronto, League of Canadian Poets, 1980.
Evening Dance of the Grey Flies. Toronto, Oxford University Press, 1981; New York, Oxford University Press, 1982.

Novel

The Sun and the Moon (as Judith Cape). Toronto, Macmillan, and New York, Creative Age Press, 1944.

Short Stories

The Sun and the Moon, and Other Fictions. Toronto, Anansi, 1973.

Other

Editor, *To Say the Least: Canadian Poets from A to Z*. Erin, Ontario, Press Porcépic, 1979.

*

Bibliography: "The Poetry of P.K. Page: A Checklist" by Michele Preston, in *West Coast Review* (Burnaby, British Columbia), January 1979.

Manuscript Collection: Canadian Archives, Ottawa.

Critical Studies: by Daryl Hine, in *Poetry* (Chicago), 1968; "Traveller, Conjuror, Journeyman" by the author, in *Canadian Literature* (Vancouver), Autumn 1970; *The Bush Garden* by Northrop Frye, Toronto, Anansi, 1971; "The Poetry of P.K. Page" by A.J.M. Smith, in *Canadian Literature* (Vancouver), Autumn 1971; "P.K. Page: The Chameleon and the Centre" by Constance Rooke, in *Malahat Review* (Victoria), January 1978; "A Size Larger Than Seeing: The Poetry of P.K. Page" by Rosemary Sullivan, in *Canadian Literature* (Vancouver); "Retrospect and Prospect: P.K. Page" by Jean Mallinson, in *West Coast Review* (Burnaby, British Columbia), January 1979.

*   *   *

P.K. Page is an artist of many aspects; she has written a romance (*The Sun and the Moon*), short stories, essays on the writer's role; under her married name of P.K. Irwin she is a painter and print-maker of repute. The various arts she practices interact, and her poetry is distinguished by the strongly visual aspect of the white and green country of the imagination that extends before the mind's eye as one reads. There are times when her poetry works like a painting.

Page began to publish in the early 1940's when her first poems appeared in *Preview*, one of the most influential Canadian magazines of modern poetry. In 1944, with four other poets, she contributed a group of poems to *Unit of Five*, and two years later published her first independent book, *As Ten as Twenty*, which showed a strong awareness of British avant garde trends of the 1930's and an appropriate social radicalism. Since then her publication has been limited by a rigorous and highly self-critical selectivity. In 1954 she published *The Metal and the Flower* and in 1967 *Cry Ararat*, which included a number of poems from her earlier books. In 1974 appeared *Poems, Selected and New*, a "definitive" collection which is in fact incomplete, since it contains only 85 poems, and misses out some of the most interesting pieces in the earlier collections. Her most recent book, *Evening*

Dance of the Grey Flies, consists entirely of recent uncollected poems.

Page's early verse tended to be largely inspired by the need for social protest, though even in her first book there are visionary poems that create luminous worlds of their own, like the haunting "Stories of Snow," in which legend and dream and childhood memories are mingled in what A.J.M. Smith once called "a crystal clairvoyance." She soon moved from the generalities of social radicalism to an empathetic recreation of individual plights—those of the lonely or of people whom circumstances have made seem contemptible. In poems like "The Stenographers" she treats such situations with a tense combination of satire and compassion.

> In the felt of the morning the calico-minded
> sufficiently starched, insert papers, hit keys,
> efficient and sure as their adding machines;
> yet they weep in the vault, they are taut as net curtains
> stretched upon frames. In their eyes I have seen
> the pin men of madness in marathon trim
> race round the track of the stadium pupil.

From the inner landscapes—the quasi-biographies—of such poems Page moved in the 1960's, after almost a decade of silence, towards a quasi-mystical seeing out of the self towards images—such as Captain Cook's Glasshouse Mountains in Australia and Mount Ararat—that suggest a way of liberation from the alienated, prisoned self.

> The bird in the thicket with his whistle
> the crystal lizard in the grass
> the star and shell
> tassel and bell
> of wild flowers blowing where we pass,
> this flora-fauna flotsam, pick and touch,
> requires the focus of the total I.
>
> A single leaf can block a mountainside;
> all Ararat be conjured by a leaf.

These are poems in which the visual evokes the visionary, and this shift is not unconnected with Page's concentration at this period on painting and drawing, a conjunction of the arts which she evokes with marvellous economy in the six lines of "Bark Drawing": "(an alphabet the eye/lifts from the air/as if by ear/two senses/threaded through/a knuckle bone)".

There is a formal development in Page's recent verse which seems to parallel her philosophic turning towards the mystical traditions of Sufism. In one of the poems of *Cry Ararat*, "After Rain," she asks that "the whole may toll/its meaning shine/clear of the myriad images that still—/do what I will—encumber its pure line." And a progressive purification of the line is evident, especially in the more recent poems of *Evening Dance of the Grey Flies*. In her earlier poems the line was long and flowing, with a kind of full eloquence. In later poems there is still a fluidity, but it is more controlled, sparser yet ever-moving, and combined with a metaphysical intent.that shifts direction from the inward dream images of the earlier poems to images drawn from the natural world that seem to offer a way of liberation to the self.

The poems in *Evening Dance of the Grey Flies* carry this quality into a kind of Delphic utterance, almost a possession by the vision. Though these poems are perhaps more sharply and intensely visual than ever in their sensuous evocation of colour and space, their imagery takes us magically beyond any ordinary seeing into a realm of visionary apprehension in which the normal world seems, to be shaken like a vast kaleidoscope and revealed in unexpected and luminous relationships where the ordinary becomes transfigured and translucent, as in "Finches Feeding":

> They fall like feathered cones from the tree above,
> *sumi* the painted grass where the birdseed is,
> skirl like a boiling pot
> or a shallow within a river—
> a bar of gravel breaking the water up.
>
> Having said that, what have I said?
> Not much.
>
> Neither my delight nor the length of my watching is conveyed
> and nothing profound recorded, yet these birds
> as I observe them
> stir such feelings up—
> such yearnings for weightlessness, for hollow bones,
> rapider heartbeat, east/west eyes
> and such wonder—seemingly half-remembered—as they rise
> spontaneously into air, like feathered cones.

—George Woodcock

PALMER, Michael. American. Born in New York City, 11 May 1943. Educated at Harvard University, Cambridge, Massachusetts, 1961-68, B.A. in French 1965, M.A. in comparative literature 1967. Married Cathy Simon in 1972; one daughter. Editor, *Joglars* magazine, Providence, Rhode Island, 1964-66; Contributing Editor, *Sulfur* magazine, Los Angeles. Recipient: National Endowment for the Arts Fellowship, 1975. Address: 265 Jersey Street, San Francisco, California 94114, U.S.A.

PUBLICATIONS

Verse

Plan of the City of O. Boston, Barn Dream Press, 1971.
Blake's Newton. Los Angeles, Black Sparrow Press, 1972.
C's Songs. Berkeley, California, Sand Dollar, 1973.
Six Poems. Los Angeles, Black Sparrow Press, 1973.
The Circular Gates. Los Angeles, Black Sparrow Press, 1974.
Without Music. Santa Barbara, California, Black Sparrow Press, 1977.
Alogon. Berkeley, California, Tuumba Press, 1980.
Notes for Echo Lake. Berkeley, California, North Point Press, 1981.
First Figure. Berkeley, California, North Point Press, 1984.

Plays

Radio Plays: *Idem 1-4*, 1979.

Dance Scenarios (collaborations with Margaret Jenkins Dance Company): *Interferences*, 1975; *Equal Time*, 1976; *Video Songs*, 1976; *About the Space in Between*, 1977; *No One But Whitington*, 1978; *Red, Yellow, Blue*, 1978; *Straight Words*, 1980; *Versions by Turns*, 1980; *Cortland Set*, 1982; *First Figure*, 1984.

Other

Editor, *Code of Signals: Recent Writings in Poetics.*   Berkeley, California, North Atlantic, 1983.

Translator, with Geoffrey Young, *Relativity of Spring: 13 Poems,* by Vicente Huidobro.   Berkeley, California, Sand Dollar, 1976.

Translator, *Jonah Who Will Be 25 in the Year 2000* (screenplay), by Alain Tanner and John Berger.   Berkeley, California, North Atlantic, 1983.

*

Critical Studies: by Michael Davidson, in *Caterpillar 20* (Sherman Oaks, California), 1973; Steve McCaffery, in *Open Letter* (Toronto), Fall 1975, April 1978, and Fall 1978; David Chaloner, in *Poetry Information* (London), Summer 1976; William Corbett, in *L=A=N=G=U=A=G=E 2* (New York), 1978; Martin Dodman, in *Montemora 5* (New York), June 1979; George Lakoff, in *Poetics Journal 2* (Berkeley, California), 1982; Alan Soldofsky, in *Ironwood 19* (Tucson), 1982.

*   *   *

It has long been a dogma of poetic criticism that a poem cannot be paraphrased. But, of course, most poems can, and it is frequently useful, especially when the reader is making first acquaintance with a work. The poetry of Michael Palmer *cannot* be paraphrased. Its meaning is strictly a function of the complex interrelations of specific linguistic details.

A typical poem—"On the Way to Language," for example—is a linguistic environment in which poetic particles, phonemes, rhythms, rhymes, images, bits and pieces of "found" language, perform a complex dance. The present example shares its title with a translation of one of Heidegger's philosophic treatises. The reader must assume that this is no accident: it is clear that Palmer is a reader of modern philosophy. Having made this somewhat arcane connection (it is not one of Heidegger's better known works), however, one by no means has a key to the poem. In fact, the information seems to lead nowhere. The poem takes the form of answers and questions, upsetting normal expectations of order, and although it suggests certain Heideggerian themes, it is non-committal. The poem closes when the abstract title produces an image of a concrete "way": "the valley of desire/crossed by the bridge/of frequent sighs," but, in context, this is really another enigma rather than a resolution.

The theme of Palmer's work—to the extent that it may be said to have such—is a Heideggerian or, perhaps more to the point, Wittgensteinian, astonishment at the existence of phenomena. We are presented with a world and a language which is endlessly fascinating. It is possible to trace local connections, follow this or that line of thought to its frequently absurd conclusion, but there is no closure except the confrontation with the inexplicable and irreducible stuff of language and the world.

It is demanding poetry. Its ideal reader is one who can combine intense concentration with willingness to play—in all senses of the word—to play as a child and also, perhaps more importantly, to play as a musician. Despite the fact that his most interesting volume is entitled *Without Music,* all of his work is best read in the spirit of a musician studying a score, trying different tempos, different phrasings, and so forth.

Palmer is involved in an exploration of possibilities in language which have been largely disregarded. He takes a passage from Géza Róheim's *Magic and Schizophrenia* as the epigraph to *Without Music,* and he also names Louis Wolfson's *Le Schizo*

et les Langues as one of his important sources. We are beginning to learn that traditional syntax and traditional forms of poetic organization are merely labor-saving devices which allow a vague, careless attention access to language. When such simple strategies are exposed, however, and attention is brought to bear without reservation, it begins to discover possibilities for the production of meaning far more powerful than those we have previously known. Only one of the unexpected turns in this situation is that we learn the schizophrenic's bewilderment is a result of wandering unaided into this difficult and exciting realm of experience.

Michael Palmer is perhaps the only one of his generation to have established himself without question as an important poet.

—Don Byrd

———————

PARKINSON, Thomas (Francis).   American.   Born in San Francisco, California, 24 February 1920. Educated at the University of California, Berkeley, A.B. (summa cum laude) 1945, M.A. 1946, Ph.D. in English 1948. Served in the United States Army Air Force, 1943. Married Ariel Reynolds in 1948. Assistant Professor, 1948-53, Associate Professor, 1953-60, Professor of English since 1960, and special assistant to the Chancellor, 1979-81, University of California, Berkeley. Visiting Assistant Professor, Wesleyan University, Middletown, Connecticut, 1951-52; Fulbright Professor, University of Bordeaux, 1953-54, University of Frankfurt, 1954, University of Nice and University of Grenoble, 1965-66, and University of Rome, 1970; Visiting Professor, University of Washington, Seattle, 1968, Oxford University, 1969, and York University, 1970. Recipient: Guggenheim Fellowship, 1957; American Philosophical Society travel grant, 1957, 1968; Institute of Creative Art Fellowship, 1963. Honorary Fellow, St. Peter's College, Oxford, 1969-70. Address: 1001 Cragmont, Berkeley, California 94708, U.S.A.

PUBLICATIONS

Verse

Men, Women, Vines.   Berkeley, California, Ark Press, 1959.
Thanatos: Earth Poems.   Berkeley, California, Oyez, 1965; revised edition, 1976.
Protect the Earth (includes essays).   San Francisco, City Lights, 1970.
Homage to Jack Spicer and Other Poems: Poems 1965-1969.   Berkeley, California, Ark Press, 1970.
Canters, Chiefly Concerning John Wayne and His Horse and Many Incredibilities.   Berkeley, California, Thorp Springs Press, 1978.
From the Grand Chartreuse.   Berkeley, California, Oyez, 1980.
Collected Poems.   Berkeley, California, Oyez, 1980.

Play

What the Blind Man Saw; or, Twenty-Five Years of the Endless War.   Berkeley, California, Thorp Springs Press, 1974.

Other

W.B. Yeats, Self-Critic: A Study of His Early Verse.   Berkeley,

University of California Press, and London, Cambridge University Press, 1951.
W.B. Yeats: The Later Poetry. Berkeley, University of California Press, and London, Cambridge University Press, 1964.

Editor, *A Casebook on the Beat.* New York, Crowell, 1961.
Editor, *Masterworks of Prose.* Indianapolis, Bobbs Merrill, 1962.
Editor, *Robert Lowell: A Collection of Critical Essays.* Englewood Cliffs, New Jersey, Prentice Hall, 1968.
Editor, *Hart Crane and Yvor Winters: Their Literary Correspondence.* Berkeley, University of California Press, 1978.

*

Thomas Parkinson comments:
My poetry is primarily meditative poetry written in various forms but moving increasingly toward a formal free verse that makes use of all the devices of historical poetry in English, not excluding rhyme. My main concerns are the relation of man to nature, of history to wilderness, and of death to love.

*   *   *

From his position on the Berkeley campus Thomas Parkinson has witnessed first-hand the free speech movement, war resistance and protest, and the student strikes which have been so prominently focused there. His poetry and essays traverse an astonishingly wide range from public, often political, topics to events personal and confessional. Parkinson has himself escaped death by inches, has seen death close at hand, and shows painful awareness of the infinite varieties of dying. His poetry reveals a continual amazement over the very process and flux of life, the cruel ecology of organisms, the fragility, and the mystery of it all. It is like being at the beach at low tide, watching the squirting, crawling, opening abundance of life until you can absorb no more, "And the entire planet screams in the mind, an interminable/feeding, and swelling and expiring."

Parkinson's *Protect the Earth* contains short environmental and political essays and a long poem, "Litany for the American People," which records his outrage over inhuman governmental actions. The book is based on Parkinson's conviction that "so long as human beings go on building up levels of tolerance against the abominable, the abominable will grow." It records his deep concern for the quality of human life and his rages against human arrogance and environmental insensitivity. Parkinson sees himself as a Franciscan; he is also a poet ecologist in sympathy if not in league with Barry Commoner and Paul Ehrlich.

The poetry of *Homage to Jack Spicer* and *Thanatos: Earth Poems* is considerably more personal. The eight "Spicer" poems span eighteen years of close friendship with Spicer, between 1947 and 1965. There is also the pain of watching Spicer, also a writer, tear and drink himself dead. "He was a battered radio/in the city dump, connections busted, batteries shot...," dead at forty. Parkinson also refers to his "Dry Season" during this period. He is shot in his office by a "poor lunatic" who believes he is a Communist. His student assistant is killed and sixty pieces of bird shot hit Parkinson in the face and jaw. "My wound/throbs and my wired jaw/Aches." It is a time when "clocks fail, hearts/stumble," poison and violence surround him yet he can affirm "violence only creates more violence." Still, for Parkinson "surviving's not enough," he seeks not merely law and order but inner order, and the "expression of an inner psychological har-

mony." *Thanatos* presents both a series of "Soliloquies for the Dead," the dying, and a further search, through solitude, for the inner order he craves. He recognizes in life:

> A spark ongoing, and in the ever-branching
>   heavens of the night
> A life-tree bearing on and on.

With the *Thanatos* poems Parkinson's lines are less tightly imagistic, more expansive and more memorable, as seen in "Death as Solitude":

> Moon passes and sun sets, whatever is holy rests
> In the rising susurrah. From their quiet, ecstasy.
> And the sanctified earth turns and turns.

—John R. Cooley

PARTHASARATHY, R(ajagopal). Indian. Born in Tirupparaiturai, near Tiruchchirappalli, Tamil Nadu, 20 August 1934. Educated at Don Bosco High School, Bombay, 1944-51; Siddharth College, Bombay University, 1957-59, M.A. in English 1959; Leeds University, Yorkshire (British Council Scholar), 1963-64, postgraduate diploma in English studies 1964. Married Shobhan Koppikar in 1969; two sons. Lecturer in English, Ismail Yusuf College, Bombay, 1959-62, and Mithibai College, Bombay, 1962-63, 1964-65; Lecturer in English Language Teaching, British Council, Bombay, 1965-66; Assistant Professor of English, Presidency College, Madras, 1966-67; Lecturer in English, South Indian Education Society College, Bombay, 1967-71. Regional Editor, Madras, 1971-78, and since 1978, Editor, New Delhi, Oxford University Press. Member of the International Writing Program, University of Iowa, Iowa City, 1978-79. Since 1978, Member of the Advisory Board for English, National Academy of Letters, New Delhi. Recipient: Ulka Poetry Prize (*Poetry India*), 1966. Address: Oxford University Press, 2/11 Ansari Road, Daryaganj, Box 7035, New Delhi 110 002, India.

PUBLICATIONS

Verse

Rough Passage. New Delhi, Oxford University Press, 1977.

Other

Editor, with J.J. Healy, *Poetry from Leeds.* Calcutta, Writers Workshop, 1968.
Editor, *Ten Twentieth-Century Indian Poets.* New Delhi, Oxford University Press, 1976.

*

Critical Studies: "Two Indian Poets" by William Walsh, in *Literary Criterion 11* (Mysore), Winter 1974; "The Last Refinement of Speech" by M. Sivaramakrishna, in *Literary Criterion 12* (Mysore), 2-3, 1976; "R. Parthasarathy: Images of a Poet" by Roger Iredale, in *Tenor 1* (Hyderabad), July 1978; "The Parthasarathy Passage: An Interview" by Ayyappa Paniker, in *Tenor 2*

(Hyderabad), January 1979; "The Achievement of R. Parthasarathy" by Brijraj Singh, in *Chandrabhaga 2* (Cuttack), Winter
1979.

R. Parthasarathy comments:

One of the problems that the Indian poet writing in English
faces is the problem of trying to relate himself meaningfully to a
living tradition. The poet who writes only in English is unable to
relate himself to any specific tradition. He cannot relate himself,
for instance, to the tradition of English verse, nor can he relate
himself to a tradition of verse in any one of the Indian languages.

From the beginning I saw my task as one of acclimatizing the
English language to an indigenous tradition. In fact the tenor of
Rough Passage is explicit: to initiate a dialogue between myself
and my Tamil past. "Homecoming," in particular, tries to derive
its sustenance from grafting itself on to whatever I find usable in
the Tamil tradition. I was eventually able to nativize in English
something that had eluded me over the years—the flavour, the
essence of Tamil mores.

I am aware of the hiatus between the soil of the language I use
and my own roots. Even though I am Tamil-speaking and yet
write in English, there is the overwhelming difficulty of using
images in a linguistic tradition that is quite other than my own. I
believe that an Indian poet who thinks long and hard enough on
his own use of language, even if it is English, sooner or later will,
through the English language, try to come to terms with himself
as an Indian, with his Indian past and present, and that the
language will become acclimatized to the Indian environment.
Further, if the poet has access to an Indian language, though he
may not find himself writing in it, he can gradually try to appropriate that language's tradition. This would mean reconciling
ourselves to Tamil English verse, Kannada English verse, Marathi English verse, and so on—all segments of a pan-Indian mosaic that we recognize as the literatures of India. When that
happens, the severed head, Indian English verse, will no longer
"choke to speak another tongue."

Perhaps *Rough Passage*, as it is now, points to a future poem
in Tamil.

*   *   *

Rough Passage, R. Parthasarathy's only book of verse so far,
is a collection of the poems that he had been writing for twenty
years. In the preface he says that the poems should be really read
as one poem, an autobiographical poem in fact. The initiating
experience of the poem is the tension felt by the poet concerning
his cultural identity—Tamil-born, but passionately in love with
English and English literature. (In retrospect, the love has
seemed to him a "whoring after English gods.") Parthasarathy's
dilemma has been felt by many, if not all, Indian writers in
English: how can an Indian poet or writer in general be himself,
be an Indian, in a language which is not his or that of his
community or of his tradition? The first part of the poem "Exile"
poses the problem; the second part resolves the problem in a way
by opening a dialogue with the poet's Tamil past. The individual
poems, written in three-line stanzas of varying length, form
sections in these three parts. While it cannot be claimed that the
sections succeed each other in inevitable order, the argument is
developed clearly and cogently enough. Parthasarathy has tried
to overcome the difficulties that the English language creates for
him as a medium of perception and expression by trying to write
in images that help the direct apprehension of experience. The
sentences are packed—sometimes over-packed—with images
that appeal to more than one sense at a time. The problem cannot

of course be solved entirely in this way because the images are in
English words. Parthasarathy has therefore tried to do what he
says Ramanujan has notably succeeded in doing: to convey in
English "what is locked up in another linguistic tradition."
(Parthasarathy could have cited the much earlier example of
Raja Rao in fiction.) He has tried to give us poems that sound
like renderings in contemporary tone and idiom of a Tamil
original: to adapt a phrase from the poem, to give us a "coloured
English" poem. The example that he cites is the third section of
"Homecoming":

And so it eventually happened—
a family reunion not heard of
since grandfather died in '59—in March

this year. Cousins arrived in Tiruchchanur
in overcrowded private buses,
the dust of unlettered years

clouding instant recognition.
Later, each one pulled,
sitting cross-legged on the steps

of the choultry, familiar coconuts
out of the fire
of rice-and-pickle afternoons.

Sundari, who had squirrelled up and down
forbidden tamarind trees in her long skirt
every morning with me,

stood there, that day, forty years taller,
her three daughters floating
like safe planets near her.

In spite of the poet's claim, it is a moot point whether we can
instantly recognize this as an un-English poem in English dress
as we do when we chance upon an English haiku or a Pound
translation, or even a prose passage from Raja Rao's *Kanthap-
ura*. The Tamil that Parthasarathy favours is, however, not
contemporary Tamil, which he denounces as a flea-ridden carcass. Of this cultural degeneration the fate of the river Vaigai
near Madurai, once capital of a great Tamil empire, is symbolic.
Emperors and poets once slept in her arms, says the poet. Now
people use the water to clean themselves.

Parthasarathy is aware that the problem of cultural rootless-
ness, or rather, of roots that have become desiccated, is not
solved by writing Tamil-English poems. As T.S. Eliot realized in
After Strange Gods, tradition is much more than literary tradition. Unfortunately Parthasarathy's conception of tradition is
not very promising. After exhorting himself to "turn inward," he
writes: "Scrape the bottom of your past./ Ransack the cupboard/
for skeletons of your Brahmin childhood." Between people who
think of tradition as a river whose waters can be used for cleaning
themselves and those who think of it as a skeleton in the cupboard which they can rattle, the difference is not very great. At
the moment it looks as though Parthasarathy has reached a dead
end. In a poem published after *Rough Passage* but intended to
form part of it, he writes:

I've rolled my fate
into a paper ball and tossed it
out of the window. I can now walk
to the end of the marriage
on my knees for my unspeaking sons.

But children can revive or nurture a tradition only if their parents have made it part of their upbringing.

—S. Nagarajan

PARVIN, Betty (née Ledsam). British. Born in Cardiff, Glamorgan, 10 October 1916. Educated at Heathfield House Convent School, 1927-33; extramural classes, University of Nottingham and University of Leicester. Married D.F. McKenzie Parvin in 1941; one son. Secretary in the Civil Service, 1940-43. Secretary, 1966-71, Vice-President, 1973-79, and since 1980, President, Nottingham Poetry Society. Reviewer, *Outposts*, London. Recipient: Lake Aske Memorial Award, 1968, 1971, 1980; Manifold Century scholarship, 1968; Scottish Open Poetry Competition prize, 1980; South Wales Miners Eisteddfod prize, 1983. Address: Bamboo, Bunny Hill Top, Costock, near Loughborough, Leicestershire LE12 6UX, England.

PUBLICATIONS

Verse

A Stone My Star. London, Outposts, 1961.
The Bird with the Luck: Twelve Poems. Nottingham, Byron Press, 1968.
Sketchbook from Mercia. London, Manifold, 1968.
Sarnia's Gift. Loughborough, Leicestershire, Griffin Press, 1972.
A Birch Tree with Finches: Poem-Pictures for Bird Lovers. Nottingham, Nottingham Poetry Society, 1974.
Country Matters: Poem-Pictures. Nottingham, Em-press, 1979.
The Book of Daniel. Nottingham, Em-press, 1980.
Prospect Poems. Nottingham, Em-press, 1981.

Other

Editor, *Poetry Nottingham 1970.* Nottingham, Nottingham Poetry Society, 1970.

*

Manuscript Collection: Nottingham Central Library.

Critical Study: introduction by G.S. Fraser to *The Bird with the Luck*, 1968.

Betty Parvin comments:
    When G.S. Fraser read some of my first poems in the early sixties he remarked: "You have a Parnassian gift. Don't let it go!" From that time I ceased to denigrate its Palgravian roots or to attempt consciously to change my style. Poets I have learned to revere since force-fed schooldays have contemporized my work without my conscious manipulation, but still when the rhyme would chime, I permit it. Not unnaturally, many of these poets have similar roots: Hardy, Edward and R.S. Thomas, Larkin, Day Lewis, Wilbur, Fraser; some of the younger "moderns."
    My theme is whatever warms me emotionally; I am past the time of powerful bias, unless it be for the beautiful—that which, some would persuade us, has never existed.

Inclusion in textbooks and anthologies has resulted in calls upon me to read and talk about my poems in schools, etc.—a valuable contact with my "public," one which I enjoy.

*   *   *

Betty Parvin is more widely known and respected among readers of poetry than her small booklets would appear to indicate, for her work has been published in a number of magazines and anthologies and has been translated into Portuguese and Byelorussian. There is nothing that might be regarded as pretentious in her poetry and no attempt is made at intellectual hair-splitting, though her poems are informed by a cool intelligence and control of language that do not give way to sentimentality or egotism. She concentrates largely upon her own everyday experiences—memories of youth and childhood, encounters with people, family connections, places she has visited or lived in, or moods "caught on the wing at play in timeless Wales." An ivy-wreathed gateway or a gothic window is enough to stimulate her creative imagination. Yet it would be a mistake to regard her as a domestic poet. She has such an individual way of looking at things, whether it is the absurb gait of a magpie or gulls searching for food in the "green harbour muck," and of placing them in some kind of perspective, that the reader is subtly brought into contact with fundamentals, the paradox and underlying reality of life itself. In such poems as "Gulls Aground," "Welsh Cottagers," and "Mothering," Betty Parvin is to be seen at her best.

—Howard Sergeant

PASTAN, Linda (née Olenik). American. Born in New York City, 27 May 1932. Educated at the Fieldston School, New York; Radcliffe College, Cambridge, Massachusetts, B.A. 1954; Simmons College, Boston, M.L.S. 1955; Brandeis University, Waltham, Massachusetts, M.A. 1957. Married Ira Pastan in 1953; two sons and one daughter. Recipient: Swallow Press New Poetry Series Award, 1972; National Endowment for the Arts grant, 1972; Bread Loaf Writers Conference John Atherton Fellowship, 1974; Alice Fay di Castagnola Award, 1977. Agent: Jean V. Naggar Literary Agency, 336 East 73rd Street, New York, New York 10021. Address: 11710 Beall Mountain Road, Potomac, Maryland 20854, U.S.A.

PUBLICATIONS

Verse

A Perfect Circle of Sun. Chicago, Swallow Press, 1971.
On the Way to the Zoo. Washington, D.C., Dryad Press, 1975.
Aspects of Eve. New York, Liveright, 1975.
The Five Stages of Grief. New York, Norton, 1978.
Selected Poems. London, Murray, 1979.
Setting the Table. Washington, D.C., Dryad Press, 1980.
Waiting for My Life. New York, Norton, 1981.
PM/AM: New and Selected Poems. New York, Norton, 1982.

*   *   *

Linda Pastan sees herself as Eve—one of the fallen, not the temptress. The bathers in "At Woods Hole" "learn nothing, lying/on sand hot and pliant as each other's flesh." Trapped in sensuality, they may appreciate beauty, but that is part of the cosmic deception: "waves seem to bring the water in forever/ even as the tide moves surely out." Like Poe, she is conscious of the limits of the human mind, and the impossibility of exceeding them. In "The Last Train" she imagines a boy fascinated with disappearing buffalo, another with the vanishing long-distance passenger train, and concludes that we all "follow sleep as well as we are able/along disintegrating paths of vapor, /high above the dreamlike shapes of clouds."

But she seems more willing to abide by the limits of consciousness than Poe. Her effort has been to clarify this humanness. In "Distances," she images the frustration of being apart:

> Straight and cold as railroad track
> I lie in my old roadbed
> measuring distances—
> waiting for you to pass
> over me once again,
> on your way somewhere else.

In "At the Gynecologist's" her "body so carefully/contrived for pain" "gallop[s] towards death/with flowers of ether in my hair." Acutely aware of her mortality, she does *try* to escape it. In "Williamsburg" she seeks the authenticity of history only to have the spell broken when "a Woolworth pencil" falls from the basketmaker's pocket. She senses "what wildness/is left" in "Bicentennial Winter," and though she is tempted to skate the frozen Potomac, she does not partake of that "dangerous/freedom." She finds violence instead of beauty in "Evening at Bird Island": "under my rocking floor/fish swallow other fish,/feeding/like bad dreams/under the surfaces of sleep." The problem is that the human necessarily prevades everything: "There is a figure in every landscape."

While Pastan's vision has been clear and consistent throughout her books—and her language lucid and intelligent—*The Five Stages of Grief* is the most effective arraying of responses. There is *denial*, when life is made up largely of the familiar and even deaths "wait like domestic animals" "patient and loving" ("After"). And *anger*, when she'd just as soon "everything happen/off-stage" and let her stay "with the scenery" ("Exeunt Omnes"). The stage of *bargaining* produces minimal consolations: "We must learn/the cold lessons/the dinosaurs learned:/to freeze magnified/in someone else's history;/to leave our bones behind" ("Ice Age"). In *depression* even the sun, as her husband's grandmother talks of the Florida weather, seems like a "huge stone/rolled against the door of death/to hold it shut" ("It Is Still Winter Here"). Finally, there is *acceptance*, when the sun is "warm amnesia" and a woman and her griefs sing back and forth ("Old Woman"). But *acceptance*, though "its name is in lights," proves unattainable: as the title poem states "Grief is a circular staircase." Thus, what might have been linear turns out to be confining, and Pastan must remain a seeker of "the pure/center of light/within the dark circle/of...demons" ("It Is Raining on the House of Anne Frank").

—Jay S. Paul

PATERSON, Alistair (Ian Hughes). New Zealander. Born in Nelson, 28 February 1929. Educated at Nelson College, 1943-47; Christchurch Teachers College, 1948-49, diploma 1949; Victoria University College, Wellington, 1951-52, B.A. 1953; New Zealand Armed Services Command and Staff College, Whenuapai, 1969; University of Auckland, Dip.Ed. 1972. Married Karen Hope Edwards in 1954 (divorced, 1978); three daughters and two sons. Teacher, Auckland Point School, Nelson, 1950, and Taita North School, Wellington, 1953; Instructor Officer, rising to rank of Lieutenant Commander, Royal New Zealand Navy, 1954-74; Dean of General Studies, New Zealand Police Department, 1974-78. Since 1978, Education Officer, New Zealand Education Department. Consultant, American Institute of Police Science, 1977-78. Editor, *Mate*, 1973-77, and *Climate*, 1978-81, both Auckland. Since 1982, Editor, *Pilgrims*, Dunedin. Recipient: Fulbright Fellowship, 1977; Reid Memorial Award (University of Auckland), 1981. Agent: Stephen Higginson, P.O. Box 5101, Dunedin. Address: P.O. Box 9612, Newmarket, Auckland, New Zealand.

PUBLICATIONS

Verse

Caves in the Hills: Selected Poems. Christchurch, Pegasus Press, 1965.
Birds Flying. Christchurch, Pegasus Press, 1973.
Cities and Strangers. Dunedin, Caveman Press, 1976.
The Toledo Room: A Poem for Voices. Dunedin, Pilgrims South Press, 1978.
Qu'appelle. Dunedin, Pilgrims South Press, 1982.
Incantations for Warriors. Dunedin, Pilgrims South Press, 1984.

Other

The New Poetry. Dunedin, Pilgrims South Press, 1982.

Editor, *15 Contemporary New Zealand Poets.* Dunedin, Pilgrims South Press, 1980; New York, Grove Press, 1982.
Editor, with James Laughlin, *New Directions 46* (New Zealand issue). New York, New Directions, 1983.

*

Alistair Paterson comments:

After commencing in the traditional New Zealand lyric/pastoral mode, I moved into a study of recent American verse—a study that has resulted in the development of a style and technique based on "open" form as expounded by Pound, Creeley, and Olson. This development has led to poems of the longer form (about 400 lines) as typified by *The Toledo Room*. As an editor and reviewer I have concentrated on the encouragement of postmodern writing in open forms and (hopefully) the extension of this type of writing into the work of other New Zealand poets.

*   *   *

Alistair Paterson's first book, *Caves in the Hills*, was very much the conventional collection of the post-war years—thirty or so pieces more or less well-made on a variety of subjects in a variety of forms, fairly impersonal, "modern" in tone and language (no Romantic poeticizing), each poem a discrete item. There was the feeling of a man looking around for subjects on which poems might be written. But there was one item which stood apart. The sequence called "The Metropolis" is an early Paterson attempt (not altogether successful) at what has lately become characteristic of his work. The language, one feels, is struggling to gain ascendancy over the statement the poem is making, so that reference, meaning, the poem's "subject," will be only one element in a total poetic structure.

In his second and third books, *Birds Flying* and *Cities and Strangers*, we can see Paterson experimenting, reaching out for freer forms. His subject remains on the whole what it was for the Wellington poets of the 1950's—a rather gloomy realism about domestic, urban, and suburban life, and about human relationships. Again in the best of these poems, however, there is an attempt to make the movement of language, the flow of syntax and grammar, more than direct statement or imagery, carry the feelings that spring from the occasion or event which is the subject. This is a distinct advance from the mode in which Paterson began, where poets too often seemed to feel they could do the fiction writer's job in a few dozen lines, summing up a human action (and particularly human failure) in smart, well-organized images and phrases. Paterson has found his way out of that mode, it seems, by a close study of the post-Modernist American poets. From their work he has acquired his interest in open form and sequences.

The Toledo Room combines Paterson's characteristic subject with his developing interest in open form. It is a dramatic work in which a number of characters speak, none of them clearly identified. They seem to talk about their lives, their love affairs, their failures, the political climate. They are concerned about, and caught up in, the roles their circumstances impose. But the adopting of roles, the assuming of masks, is the game of life itself; and the whole vision, though perhaps negative, is also wry, amused, and is gathered into a music—the structure of the poem itself—which has beauty. This is Paterson writing at his best.

    Summer
    & the sounds of summer—
            we should all be accustomed to it
            but the sun throws down such heat
    it seems like dying (or death)
    fading, falling into silence
            seizing the albatross in its flight.
    Outwards we follow the horizon
            the sweep of the bay
               inwards translate
    what's seen and said into another language
             into some kind of script
    words, phrases, pages with footnotes:
            Marsden's weather-worn cross
    in that far country above lonely water.

                              —C.K. Stead

PATTEN, Brian. British. Born in Liverpool, Lancashire, 7 February 1946. Educated at Sefton Park Secondary School, Liverpool. Formerly, reporter, *Bootle Times*, and editor, *Underdog*, both Liverpool. Recipient: Eric Gregory Award, 1967; Arts Council grant, 1969. Agent: Anthony Sheil Associates Ltd., 2-3 Morwell Street, London WC1B 3AR. Address: c/o Allen and Unwin Ltd., 40 Museum Street, London WC1A 1LU, England.

PUBLICATIONS

Verse

Portraits. Privately printed, 1962.

The Mersey Sound: Penguin Modern Poets 10, with Adrian Henri and Roger McGough. London, Penguin, 1967; revised edition, 1974, 1983.
Little Johnny's Confession. London, Allen and Unwin, 1967; New York, Hill and Wang, 1968.
Atomic Adam. London, Fulham Gallery, 1967.
Notes to the Hurrying Man: Poems Winter '66-Summer '68. London, Allen and Unwin, and New York, Hill and Wang, 1969.
The Homecoming. London, Turret, 1969.
The Irrelevant Song. Frensham, Surrey, Sceptre Press, 1970.
Little Johnny's Foolish Invention: A Poem (bilingual edition), translated by Robert Sanesi. Milan, M'Arte, 1970.
Walking Out: The Early Poems of Brian Patten. Leicester, Transican, 1970.
At Four O'Clock in the Morning. Frensham, Surrey, Sceptre Press, 1971.
The Irrelevant Song and Other Poems. London, Allen and Unwin, 1971; revised edition, 1975.
When You Wake Tomorrow. London, Turret, 1971.
And Sometimes It Happens. London, Steam Press, 1972.
The Eminent Professors and the Nature of Poetry as Enacted Out by Members of the Poetry Seminar One Rainy Evening. London, Poem-of-the-Month Club, 1972.
Double Image, with Michael Baldwin and John Fairfax. London, Longman, 1972.
The Unreliable Nightingale. London, Rota, 1973.
Vanishing Trick. London, Allen and Unwin, 1976.
Grave Gossip. London, Allen and Unwin, 1979.
Love Poems. London, Allen and Unwin, 1981.
New Volume, with Adrian Henri and Roger McGough. London, Penguin, 1983.

Recordings: *Selections from Little Johnny's Confession and Notes to the Hurrying Man and New Poems*, Caedmon, 1969; *Vanishing Trick*, Tangent, 1976; *The Sly Cormorant*, Argo, 1977; *Gifted Wreckage*, with Roger McGough and Adrian Henri, Talking Tape, 1984.

Plays

The Pig and the Junkle (produced Nottingham, 1975; London, 1977).
The Sly Cormorant (produced London, 1977).
The Ghosts of Riddle Me Heights (produced Birmingham, 1980).
Behind the Lines (revue), with Roger McGough (produced London, 1982).
The Mouthtrap, with Roger McGough (produced Edinburgh and London, 1982).

Radio Plays: *The Hypnotic Island*, 1977; *Blind Love*, 1983.

Television Plays: *The Man Who Hated Children*, 1978; *Mr. Moon's Last Case*, from his own story, 1983.

Other (for children)

The Elephant and the Flower: Almost-Fables. London, Allen and Unwin, 1970.
Jumping Mouse. London, Allen and Unwin, 1972.
Manchild. London, Covent Garden Press, 1973.
Two Stories. London, Covent Garden Press, 1973.
Mr. Moon's Last Case. London, Allen and Unwin, 1975; New York, Scribner, 1976.
Emma's Doll. London, Allen and Unwin, 1976.

The Sly Cormorant and the Fishes: New Adaptations into Poetry of the Aesop Fables. London, Kestrel, 1977.
Gargling with Jelly. London, Viking Kestrel, 1985.

Other

Editor, with Pat Krett, *The House That Jack Built: Poems for Shelter.* London, Allen and Unwin, 1973.
Editor, *Clare's Countryside: Natural History Poetry and Prose,* by John Clare. London, Heinemann, 1981.
Editor, *Gangsters, Ghosts, and Dragonflies: A Book of Story Poems.* London, Allen and Unwin, 1981.

*   *   *

Outwardly the most serious of the "Liverpool" poets, Brian Patten creates work notable for its romanticism. Love figures largely throughout his work, with recurrent images of seduction and its aftermath—the sleep of sated lovers, cast-off dresses, the sadness of parting. Another feature, akin to the poets of an earlier century, is his fondness for quiet contemplation away from the hustle of urban life, moments of solitude in deserted woods, or under the rain. His precocious ability is evident in the poems he wrote in the 1960's, where Patten's youth is betrayed by a number of schoolboy reminiscences and parallels. "Little Johnny's Confession," for all its acid wit, suggests an author himself not long out of school, while the worldly assurance of "Party Piece" fails to convince entirely. In "Where Are You Now, Batman?" the lament for the heroes of a vanished childhood displays a real, and recent, nostalgia. These poems demonstrate the writer's potential, and indicate the decisions he has already reached on the nature and purpose of his chosen form. "Interruption at the Opera House" and the more self-indulgent "Prosepoem Towards a Definition of Itself" reveal his view of poetry as a natural, and subversive, act, at once a gift to the masses—"the rightful owners of the song"—and a rejection of the cultured elite who regard it as their property. Wary of critics, suspicious of intellectual analysis, Patten in "A Literary Gathering" tells of his unease among the dissectors, and his relief when once outside he is free of "the need/To explain away any song."

A writer with a penchant for the hardness and clarity of the fairy tale, Patten has produced several books for children, one of them a retelling of Aesop's fables. Ironically, much of his adult poetry is less accessible than that of Henri or McGough, the style dense and compact, with abrupt changes, short intense lines, and potent images—"our love like a whale from its deepest ocean rises"—which sometimes threaten to overwhelm the rest of the poem. Rejecting the carefully packaged sentiments and elegant observations of conventional poetry, Patten demands a means of expression that reflects the harshness of reality: "I want to give you something/that bleeds as it leaves my hand/and enters yours,/something that by its rawness,/that by its bleeding/demands to be called real." Despite the frequent complexity of his utterances, he finds inspiration from the commonest sources. Patten hears celestial music as a girl sings in the bathroom, offers his beloved a blade of grass in lieu of a poem, even finds a small dragon in his woodshed. At his best, he compels the reader's acceptance, piercing a thicket of sentences with rare and startling visions. Occasionally he can become tedious, his words chosen merely for effect and twisted out of their meanings, a tendency not helped by variations—"jubilance," "neglection," "dulled"—which often don't work. All the same his voice remains striking and original, not least when he recalls those times of love and parting so central to his poetry: "I was thinking of our future/and of what we would do together,/and where we would go and

how,/when night came/burying me bit by bit,/and you entered the room trembling and solemn-faced,/on time for once."

—Geoff Sadler

———————

PATTERSON, Raymond R(ichard). American. Born in New York City, 14 December 1929. Educated at Lincoln University, Pennsylvania, 1947-51, A.B. 1951; New York University, 1954-56, M.A. 1956. Served in the United States Army, 1951-53. Married Boydie Alice Cooke in 1957; one child. Children's supervisor, Youth House for Boys, New York, 1956-58; Instructor in English, Benedict College, Columbia, South Carolina, 1958-59; English teacher in New York City public schools, 1959-68. Since 1968, Lecturer in English, City College of the City University of New York. Recipient: Borestone Mountain award, 1950; National Endowment for the Arts grant, 1969; Creative Artists Public Service grant, 1977. Address: 2 Lee Court, Merrick, New York 11566, U.S.A.

PUBLICATIONS

Verse

Twenty-Six Ways of Looking at a Black Man and Other Poems. New York, Award Books, and London, Tandem, 1969.
For K.L. Buffalo, White Pine Press, 1980.
Elemental Blues. Merrick, New York, Cross-Cultural Communications, 1983.

*

Critical Studies: by Aaron Kramer, in *Freedomways* (New York), 1970; Eugene B. Redmond, in *Drumvoices,* New York, Anchor Press, 1976.

Raymond R. Patterson comments:

For me writing poetry is an exploration of the possibilities of experience; a poem written is a poem dis-covered, providing useful knowledge about the territory we travel through.

*   *   *

Contemporary Black poetry is rooted in the special upheaval that gripped the United States during the 1950's and 1960's, when, in a last ditch push for full integration, Black people—North and South—took to the streets. The result of their effort was the recognition, by some, that the country would cede nothing through protest. From that political truth grew the Black Power Movement. Its cultural arm, the Black Arts Movement, views all art as a weapon in the struggle for Black liberation. In this context, the aim of Black literature is the total evaluation of the ideas and images by which Blacks have traditionally defined themselves.

Poet Raymond R. Patterson reflects the influence of all these forces. The result has been a body of poetry that is seminal in its explorations of black life. Concerned more with the psychological than the physical, Patterson is the poet-chronicler, capturing in verse the revolution in Black thought that created the 1960's. "Come into my black hands./Touch me. Feels the grip/And cramp of angry circumstance...." From the crucial admission of individual rage—a rage given force and articulation in real life by

Malcolm X—the poet moves on to attack the various ploys used by Blacks to navigate the American holocaust: "Black boys push carts in alligator shoes," while aspiring integrationists "...carry the word in Brooks Brothers suits," and the tiny elite, while fully convinced of its infallibility, are "Thinking, sometimes.../ Someone lied. Sometimes thinking suicide." But all is illusion and self-deception, insists the poet; beneath the carefully controlled masks, "There is enough/Grief-/Energy in/The Blackness/Of the whitest Negro/To incinerate/America."

Incineration is the key to "Riot Rimes U.S.A.," the eighty-five poem sequence that is Patterson's most popular work. The poems are humorous and ironic by turn, in their first person depictions of the Harlem riot of 1965. From the poet's perspective, that event was the high point of the African experience in America: "My mama hadn't said one word/To my daddy for two whole years./But after the riots, she was so happy/She was crying tears.../Nothing suits a family like a big strong male."

—Saundra Towns

PAULIN, Tom. British. Born in Leeds, Yorkshire, 25 January 1949. Recipient: Eric Gregory Award, 1976; Somerset Maugham Award, 1978; Geoffrey Faber Memorial Prize, 1982. Address: c/o Faber and Faber Ltd., 3 Queen Square, London WC1N 3AU, England.

PUBLICATIONS

Verse

Theoretical Locations. Belfast, Ulsterman, 1975.
A State of Justice. London, Faber, 1977.
Personal Column. Belfast, Ulsterman, 1978.
The Strange Museum. London, Faber, 1980.
The Book of Juniper. Newcastle upon Tyne, Bloodaxe, 1981.
Liberty Tree. London, Faber, 1983.

Play

The Riot Act (produced Belfast, 1984).

Other

Thomas Hardy: The Poetry of Perception. London, Macmillan, and Totowa, New Jersey, Rowman and Littlefield, 1975.
Ireland and the English Crisis. Newcastle upon Tyne, Bloodaxe, 1985.

Editor, with Peter Messent, *Henry James: Selected Tales.* London, Dent, 1982.

*   *   *

Tom Paulin is one of that group of poets from the North of Ireland who, following John Montague, Seamus Heaney, Michael Longley, and Derek Mahon, have made such a great impact on contemporary British writing. Paulin is an intellectual and academic as well as a poet; and, in his case, the poetry seems part of a large endeavour of situating and describing the crisis in the North—as much in critical and political essays as in poetry—in a way calculated to confront *blasé* or unconcernedly prejudiced

English attitudes. The characteristic tone of his poetry is, as a result, the opposite of ingratiating: dour, tight-lipped, and fricative in his first two books; more relaxed, oblique, and dialectically slippery in his third, *Liberty Tree*: but, throughout, determined to clear a space for itself, to muscle in, to intrude.

The essential procedure of much of the earlier work—on which, perhaps, the major influence is Auden—is to discover, in nature and in earlier historical epochs, particularly revolutionary and post-revolutionary Russia, metaphors or analogous anecdotes for his own sense of "history." The poetry works through probing various oppositions and confrontations with a fine analytical passion: "stillness" and "history"; poetry and political fact; "formal elegance" and the vindictive god who "scatters/ bodies everywhere and has broken the city." These confrontations, it is plain, are essentially those of Paulin's own nature: the poetry longs, sometimes in a virtually dandified way, for a release from the necessity of public conscience, but feels guilt about that longing, and must labour to recover a sense of responsibility and urgency. In the earlier work, Paulin is at his best with a kind of Marvellian compaction of an insistent personal lyric cadence with a clear-eyed, unsentimental public concern which weighs the difficulties a poem has in assuming a position, and goes ahead:

> Special constables train their
> machine guns on council flats;
> water cannon, fire, darkness.
> The clocks are bleeding now on
> public buildings. Their mottoes,
> emblems of failure, tell us:

> *What the wrong gods established
> no one can ever save.*

In the third book, Paulin's language—under the sway now of Yeats, perhaps, and Pound—undergoes an astonishing and unpredictable transformation. He writes in much looser, freer, sometimes very thin forms, and employs Ulster dialect as a major element in his lexicon of "English" possibilities. Such words as "neapish," "fremd," "glubbed," "biffy," and "sleakit" pepper many of the poems. This is clearly the result of Paulin's desire to invigorate what he regards as moribund in "standard" English usage; but it does present difficulties—in poems which already have difficulties enough—for a reader unfamiliar with the dialect: annotation would be a great help. The dialect words, however, are only one aspect of a new delighted sensuousness of apprehension. In some of these poems, Paulin has created a kind of writing *sui generis*, in which he anatomises the futility of the present stasis in the North with a grim disgust (in the excellent "Desertmartin," for instance) and measures, imaginatively, the possibilities of an eventual resolution of the conflict.

Several critics have criticised the politics of these poems as Utopian; and certainly it is difficult to see that the more prophetic of them could be in any way a valuable contribution to realistic debate. But their surely justified poetic strategy is to withhold definition or resolution and to open instead into the allusive, the suggestive, the metaphoric, and the emblematic. The best of them—and, in my opinion, one of the best poems written in English in recent times—is the lengthy sequence, "The Book of Juniper." The poem allegorises the juniper plant, which "wills its own survival" in desolate places, in a series of religious, natural, historical, and culinary evocations. This richly inventive poem culminates in a vision of Northern and Southern armies of juniper-carriers meeting to form

that sweet
equal republic
where the juniper
talks to the oak,
the thistle,
the bandaged elm,
and the jolly jolly chestnut.

This is a Utopian politics, perhaps; but the urgent sweetness of its imagined release is a measure, too, of its desperation. Tom Paulin is one of the poets in whom the most important matter of contemporary British politics is finding its most appropriate poetic voice.

—Neil Corcoran

PECK, John (Frederick). American. Born in Pittsburgh, Pennsylvania, 13 January 1941. Educated at Allegheny College, Meadville, Pennsylvania, A.B. 1962; Stanford University, California, Ph.D. in English 1973. Married Ellen Margaret McKee in 1963 (divorced); one daughter. Instructor in English, 1968-70, and Visiting Lecturer, 1972-75, Princeton University, New Jersey. Assistant Professor, 1977-79, and Professor of English, 1980-82, Mount Holyoke College, South Hadley, Massachusetts. Recipient: American Academy award, 1975; American Academy in Rome Fellowship, 1978; Guggenheim Fellowship, 1981. Address: Beustweg 3 Z.42, 8032 Zurich, Switzerland.

PUBLICATIONS

Verse

Shagbark. Indianapolis, Bobbs Merrill, 1972.
The Broken Blockhouse Wall. Boston, Godine, 1978; Manchester, Carcanet, 1979.

*

Critical Studies: in *Trying to Explain* by Donald Davie, Ann Arbor, University of Michigan Press, 1979, Manchester, Carcanet, 1980; James Powell, in *Occident* (Berkeley, California), 1980.

*   *   *

John Peck's *Shagbark* has rightly been called the most brilliant first book of poetry since *Harmonium*. Difficult, encoded, it is yet recognizable at once as original and ambitious, and its 43 poems are inscribed in a language as various as it is precise. The originality is, in part, a result of its insistently revealed ancestry, tracings that comprise the heartwood of this autobiography whose main metaphor is the organic growth of a tree. If Peck's first father has been Ezra Pound, the subject of his doctoral thesis and modernist perfector of the hieratic moment which Peck will flamboyantly inherit and make his own, other forebears are Browning, Hardy, H.D., Yeats, and Blake. Peck's erudition is enormous, as is the range of his reference. Painters—Cole, Van Gogh, Kollwitz—the anatomist, Vesalius, and philosophers such as Leibniz and Kierkegaard are passionately addressed and re-imagined. Like Leibniz, the poet searches for unity in diversity; like Kierkegaard, he invents against the pull of

dread and terror. I would guess that the great Polish teacher and poet, Czeslaw Milosz, is present here too for Peck shares and practices his interest in the way things begin and then endure and change through time. In Peck's most beautiful and ambitious poem, "March Elegies," the centerpiece of his second volume, *The Broken Blockhouse Wall*, he writes:

Circling, a man may
        retell the story
Lived by another because neither
        Is in that way free.

That expressed tension between past and present, father and son, the passing on of fictions, describes Peck's whole poetic succinctly and refers, too, to the duty, felt with chivalric ardor, of being true to a chosen other. A poet becomes himself through mimesis and breaking free.

Peck's strategics for creating a self are manifest in the structure of *Shagbark*. The first section is nearly claustrophobic, for the poet is alone in nature, beset by dreams, inventing routes of escape from solitude. An imagery of doors, sills, thresholds underlines the desire for growth and new entrances. Human presences are distant or dreamed. In section II poems are addressed to relatives, teachers, friends; their stories listened to and re-told. In "Reliquary" the poet listens to a Polish exile who has landed in his Pennsylvania hometown "trace/The history of those things he wished to share,/Tokens obscure with other time and place." The expanded awareness of time and place leads Peck to those moments of break-through which are at once groves or circles of light, psychic transition from one state to another and, synonymously, the origins of poetry itself. In a Browningesque monolog, "The Factor Remembers His Lady," we have:

And when I asked her what plan
She would follow were she to lose her way, then

She said her father once learned from his father
An oath in runes for entry into the core

Of their old wood; and learned the path leading there
And learned the look of that hid place, forever.

Peck's tracings backwards have a Jungian thrust and his poems move ambitiously toward the recreation of both a personal and a racial unconscious—disclosed.

The greatest adventure of the book is undertaken in the poems in section III. Each of these incontestably superb poems is based on the art or account of another artist; the geography covered extends from the English village of "Ringers" to the Holland of Vesalius to ancient China—a Poundian destination—where two handscrolls are minutely observed. He enters them and, like the spectators of old, adds his own scrupulously rendered reactions and thoughts to them. Coming to the end of Chang Tse-tuan's famous scroll of the Festival at the River, he ruminates on what is "picturable/but not pictured." These studies prepare him not only for his role as poet but as a human being continuously willing himself to grow by the highest moral and aesthetic standards. Finally, in section IV, like Ulysses returning home to Ithaka, Peck breaks through into a present which has been there throughout the journey but is only at this point representable; he meets, as if for the first time, the Penelope whose "sweater on the couch" now seems rich and an object allowable in his poems. A modern epic has been achieved. A poet has come to being.

In *A Broken Blockhouse Wall* Peck returns to the obdurate landscapes of his Pennsylvania childhood and the imagery of rock, mine, river, barge, freight. Again, the clear and the blurred, the hard and the yielding, wind and land underwrite the dialectic Peck finds everywhere. In that return is also a new freedom to ride out the drift of analogies, a riding that describes his odd genius. In "March Elegies" Peck relives moments from family history and dazzles with language that moves from the "beshatted drawers" of a civil war immigrant to the high dreams of mythological heroes. A perfect example of Peck's method, his humor, his fascination with the energy and power of poetry, and his delight in curiosity and chance is transparent in "Letting Up." It begins with reflections and an ordinary walk through his neighborhood and moves him back to a moment in the Civil War:

> When the gray infantry broke through at Shiloh
> They found campfires, skillets over them cooking,
> Sunday breakfasts laid out, and swirls of steam still
>   Coming off coffee.
>
> Communion that seems an end, fleeting, factive,
> Must begin somewhere. They stopped, ate and drank,
>   snooped
> Through tents and read letters from girls. And they
>   were Lost to the advance.

Peck's most recent poems, published in *Salmagundi*, strike me as peculiarly difficult and repetitive. One hopes and predicts that these are the beginning of a new breakthrough.

—Joan Hutton Landis

PERRY, Grace. Australian. Born in Melbourne, Victoria, 27 January 1926. Educated at Sydney University, M.B., B.S. 1951, qualified as a physician. Married Harry Kronenberg in 1951; two daughters and one son. Has held several pediatric positions; currently in general medical practice. Editor, *Poetry Magazine*, Sydney, 1962-64. Since 1963, Writing School and Festival Director, and since 1964, Proprietor, South Head Press, and Editor, *Poetry Australia*, Sydney. Recipient: Australian Council Fellowship, 1973, and grant, 1980. Address: South Head Press, The Market Place, Berrima, New South Wales 2577, Australia.

PUBLICATIONS

Verse

I Am the Songs You Sing and Other Poems. Sydney, Consolidated Press, 1944.
Red Scarf. Sydney, Edwards and Shaw, 1964.
Frozen Section. Sydney, Edwards and Shaw, 1967.
Two Houses: Poems 66-69. Sydney, South Head Press, 1969.
Black Swans at Berrima. Sydney, South Head Press, 1972.
Berrima Winter. Sydney, South Head Press, 1974.
Journal of a Surgeon's Wife and Other Poems. Sydney, South Head Press, 1976.
Snow in Summer. Sydney, South Head Press, 1980.

Play

Last Bride at Longsleep, with John Millett. Sydney, South Head Press, 1981.

*

Manuscript Collection: Mitchell Library, Sydney.

Critical Studies: by James Libdroth, in *Spirit* (South Orange, New Jersey), Spring 1970; James Tulip, in *Southerly* (Sydney), no. 2, 1973; J.E. Chamberlin, in *Hudson Review* (New York), Summer 1973; Fred Holzknect, in *Makar* (Brisbane), 1973; Elaine Lindsay, in *The Australian* (Sydney), 1976.

*   *   *

Grace Perry has been a central figure in Australian poetry since the mid-1960's. Largely this has come from her role in founding and editing the journal *Poetry Australia*, which has become in the course of its 70 issues a focal point for poets of all ranges and interests. In the 1960's and early 1970's she established her position with immense energy—writing six books of verse, organising poetry conferences, publishing other poets at South Head Press and running a busy medical practice. More recently she has chosen to live almost in seclusion in the New South Wales country town of Berrima, where as well as recouping her imaginative energies she has developed an interest in grazing and stud cattle.

Her poetry has always been, until recently, the alter ego of her life. As distinct from the frenetic life style she has followed, her poems step into a deep passivity, almost a trance, a high-toned incantation of an inward reflective self. She has ranged over many subjects.

Red Scarf begins with a sequence "Where the Wind Moves" which is characteristic of the strong personal force in Grace Perry's writing that never quite becomes a personal presence but is more a mood, suffused and deep-pitched. A romantic yearning finds itself in a world which cannot satisfy its longings, and the poetry disciplines itself in the gestures it can make. Poems to do with her medical experience appear in *Red Scarf*, and become a major element in her next book *Frozen Section*. The medical world of the operating theatre takes on a ritualistic quality in Grace Perry's poems. But she does not stay fixed in this intense, a-personal mode for long. Her poetry in *Frozen Section* shows her reaching out to random and occasional studies of Australian experience. The "Parramatta Gaol, 1966" sequence foreshadows something of the quality and interests of her more recent Berrima world.

The old sandstone buildings of colonial Berrima appeal to her feel for history, georgraphy, gardens and houses. Her lines have opened up towards images of sensation; there is less irony in the garden world she lives in beside the Wingecarribee; her passivities are no longer a retreat but a resource:

> Black birds in pairs under rock ledges
>   tremble wings
>   carve up red scum
> towards midstream cloud islands in clear water
> to name them
>   is to anchor them
>   between willow and willow
> long wings fan smoke
> over mounds softened by sundown
> fiery mouths
>   swallow valley and valley
> sucked down
>   the slow surge
>   around
>   above

the water lifting underneath
                        spread out
the wake unbroken
               arrows shore to shore

There is in lines such as these a subjective reading of the Australian country environment which is leading Grace Perry to make her own personal mythology from her life and the world round about her. In *Black Swans at Berrima, Berrima Winter*, and *Journal of a Surgeon's Wife* this process of her inner life has refined and liberated itself in several ways.

Often she seems to thrive off negations of negations: a double negative pattern of denying some impossibly romantic idea is her way into and through many a poem. But her most recent and as yet unpublished verse is a confrontation with pain and loss of love in ways that will surely be compared with those of Anne Sexton and Sylvia Plath. Her poetry of inwardness has been an unusual feature of the Australian poetic scene in the last dozen years. Now it seems that her world is re-emerging into drama.

—James Tulip

PESKETT, William. British. Born 12 May 1952. Educated at the Royal Belfast Academical Institution; Christ's College, Cambridge, degree in zoology. Married to Naomi Peskett. Has worked as journalist and biology teacher. Recipient: Eric Gregory Award, 1976. Address: 47 Ryfold Road, London, S.W. 19, England.

PUBLICATIONS

Verse

Cleaning Stables. Belfast, Ulsterman, 1974.
The Nightowl's Dissection. London, Secker and Warburg, 1975.
A Killing in the Grove. Belfast, Ulsterman, 1977.
A More Suitable Terrain. Belfast, Ulsterman, 1978.
Survivors. London, Secker and Warburg, 1980.

         *   *   *

A training in zoology, reinforced by years of teaching science, has afforded William Peskett a pabulum denied to most contemporary poets. He writes about the nightowl, crayfish, ant, and moth, and does so without the urge to gloss or prettify. In "Moths" he says:

The female moth is like the male.
When you crush it,
it doesn't bleed—
it sprinkles your hands with talcum.

Peskett sees Man as having aggrandized his position in the universe at the expense of his fellow-beings. He compares his posturings unfavourably with the silent practicality of vegetables, and is glad that Darwin established a new cage at the zoo for *Homo sapiens*. Several times over he shows the human being violating the dignity of other species. In "The Nightowl's Examination," for instance, he says:

I take every cell from him
and every molecule
from each of these

and examine them.
I take everything. He gives
me nothing in return.

The pressure of Peskett's subject matter compels his verse into a certain stripped economy. What has been quoted so far looks less like illustration excerpted from larger works than independent epigram or even haiku. This is a quality of style, especially in the earlier poems. Peskett advocates appreciation as distinct from analysis, but finds himself having to bow before the precocity of youth. As expressed in the poem "My Child," the attitude comes out thus: "my child / will slowly select a summer / and apply it firmly / to the spring."

That is a crisp way of indicating growth and disillusion. However, such crispness goes along with some negative qualities. Peskett's poems as wholes tend towards the prosaic. One misses the verbal roll and rise found in his elder contemporaries from Ulster, especially Seamus Heaney and Derek Mahon. This lack would not be so noticeable if the epigrams already quoted were in existence by themselves. But once they are read in context, as part of the poems from which they were culled, they look like precepts embedded in a tissue of explication. There is an account of Belfast courageously proceeding with business as usual that, for all its formal layout, is little better than prose—"Across the road a bar / might be open as usual, / its lounge blown out / and fenced on the pavement / as a book is pulled from the shelf...." This is not saved by the book metaphor. It would need more rhythmic shape and linguistic zest to be lifted out of the merely circumstantial. Yet the epigrammatic conclusion of the poem has that *ictus* that the poem as a whole lacks: "A man says you can cut / the tongue from an ox / but never take the shine / from its eye." Given a definitive title, that could be a poem standing, self-explanatory, on its own.

The point is, perhaps, more true of the earlier verse than of the later. There is more warmth in Peskett's second book. He wants to leave the world to the kingfisher, the blackbird, the kestrel—"these beautiful casualties," as he describes them. The elusiveness of feline identity fascinates him, and the loss of dignity even in the demise of a mouse—"the little shame of urine."

With such attention to detail, the next book really ought to be called *The Fall of a Sparrow*. Though more purged and dry than that of Lawrence, Peskett's vision resembles in some degree Rupert Birkin pondering in *Women in Love*: "a world empty of people, just uninterrupted grass, and a hare sitting up." Epigrammatically—as ever, when at his best—Peskett phrases his version of this feeling in "Coypu":

Slowly the coypu peels a view
from the ecstatical level of the river.
The banks fall
to the landscape's climax.

—Philip Hobsbaum

PETERS, Lenrie (Leopold Wilfred). Gambian. Born in Bathurst (now Banjul), 1 September 1932. Educated at Trinity College, Cambridge, B.A.; University College Hospital, London, M.B., B. Chir. Surgical Registrar, Northampton General Hospital, England, 1966-69; surgeon, Victoria Hospital, Gambia, 1969-72. Since 1972, surgeon in private practice, Banjul. Fellow, Royal College of Surgeons. Address: Westfield Clinic, P.O. Box 142, Banjul, Gambia.

PUBLICATIONS

Verse

Poems. Ibadan, Nigeria, Mbari, 1964.
Satellites. London, Heinemann, 1967.
Katchikali. London, Heinemann, 1971.
Selected Poetry. London, Heinemann, 1981.

Novel

The Second Round. London, Heinemann, 1965.

*

Manuscript Collection: School of Oriental and African Studies, London.

Critical Studies: *New West African Literature* edited by Kolawole Ogungbesan, London, Heinemann, 1979; *Understanding African Poetry* by K.L. Goodwin, London, Heinemann, 1982.

*   *   *

Two biographical influences stand out in the poetry of Lenrie Peters. The first is that he is a surgeon and the second is that he has been considerably influenced by an adulthood spent outside Africa. Surgery is the source of many of his most effective images and themes. No poem demonstrates this more effectively than "Sounds of the Ocean" which frequently resorts to the image of a surgeon groping in the body of a patient to represent the precarious search and exploration for limited objectives through which man eventually achieves self realisation and the peace that this brings: "Hand fumbling with bowel / Or wringing out the brain / Reaches no further than / The moment allows." The end of the poem holds out the hope that this fumbling search will produce results: "But there will be for each / Who seeks with dedication / a solitary triumph of peace." The guarded optimism of "Sounds of the Ocean" is a recurrent note in Peters's poetry which never seeks, however, to conceal the agony, the uncertainty, and the loneliness of the search that leads to self realisation.

The second biographical fact—Peters's African birth and his subsequent physical alienation from Africa—comes out in many ways. He is continually remembering Africa and realises in poetry the physical return to it which was long delayed. It is significant that his only novel so far, *The Second Round,* is based on the experiences of a doctor returning to his home after many years of study abroad. The impression one gets is of the poet continually balancing the alternatives in his mind—a felt duty to Africa and a duty to himself which dictates continued residence in Europe. These poetic returns abound in his poetry: "I shall return / When daylight saunters on / When evening shadows the berry / And fiery night the sun." Like others of Peters's poems, however, this is not just a simple return to a country; there is the implication of a return to a basic state of nature which requires an elimination of outward trappings; the return is in fact a spiritual rather than a physical return. Other "Homecoming" poems show a similar meaningful ambiguity. Peters's vicarious returns are thus symbolically significant.

In spite of his sojourn abroad, the poet is concerned with the fate of Africa. The consequences of independence, the broken promises, the petty tyrannies are all reflected in the long poem "In the Beginning," where Peters exploits his talent for broken pieces of suggestive dialogue to picture the relationship between the ordinary voter and his new rulers:

"But excuse me, Sir;
We're free.
Why do we have to beg?"
Industrial development
Dams, factories, the lot—
change the face of the Continent.
"I see
But my children—
beg pardon Sir,
will they go to school?"
Later!
"Will thay have food to eat
and clothes to wear?"
Later I tell you!
"Beg pardon Sir;
a house like yours?"
Put this man in jail.

The concern for the common man in the hands of authority is treated in contexts other than the African:

Every time they shut the gates
And hang up notices
On steel plates
That love-making is forbidden
After eight

This has more of the background of Hyde Park than of Freetown's Victoria Park as has his "Song" which pictures prostitutes "selling old boot / On wet pavements."

Peters has succeeded in making a harmony of his two backgrounds and he uses each without self-consciousness. The range of his interests is very wide. Very few African poets would write a eulogy of Winston Churchill, whom Peters seems genuinely to have admired. The explosion of the Chinese bomb is similarly the unlikely subject of another poem. The result of all this is that Peters is an unlocalised poet, whose concern is ultimately for the general human predicament.

—Eldred D. Jones

———————

PETERSEN, Donald. American. Born in Minneapolis, Minnesota, 11 November 1928. Educated at the Sorbonne, Paris, 1948-49; Carleton College, Northfield, Minnesota, B.A. 1950; Indiana University, Bloomington; University of Iowa, Iowa City, M.F.A. 1952. Married Jeanine Ahrens in 1952; three sons and one daughter. Taught at the University of Iowa, 1954-56. Since 1956, Member of the English Department, and currently, Professor of English, State University of New York, Oneonta. Assistant Editor, *Western Review,* Iowa City, 1950-55. Address: Department of English, State University of New York, Oneonta, New York 13820, U.S.A.

PUBLICATIONS

Verse

The Spectral Boy.   Middletown, Connecticut, Wesleyan University Press, 1964.

* * *

Donald Petersen is a formalist, an elegist, and a pastoral poet whose works are rooted in his small town (rural America) and big city (Paris) experiences. Despite the fact that he studied under such poets as Robert Lowell, Karl Shapiro, Paul Engle, and John Berryman, he regards himself as neither a literary nor an academic poet.

His work is pervaded by a haunting nostalgia for things of value which lends genuine feeling to his lines without becoming mournful:

> Home is a place of resurrections. Fears
> I ran away from, sorrows that I fled,
> Come back to haunt me now from other years.
> Two neighbors I remember best are dead.

Petersen states, "My memory plays a large role in making a poem. A poem of mine is often an amalgam of old and new verse, and its subject matter is often concerned with memory. It is also likely to be, in unlikely terms, a religious poem." Central to his poetry are attempts to experience renewal or to effect regeneration through relationships to time, to nature, to religion, and between individuals. The range of these relationships is frequently evinced through "the terrifying extremes" of hot and cold and their possible harmony:

> Then summer slid beneath her cold inversion
> With sunny slopes and crowded canopies,
>   But we were happy.
>
> Fell winter without tears that when they freeze
> Can pierce the summer-keeping heart and be
>   Forever dripping.
>
> Desire these days, my dear, that we may be
> Two ever-shifting dunes of fine white snow,
>   Made one completely.

Petersen further describes himself as one of the few remaining poets who writes in complete sentences. But his poetry is rigidly formed, a characteristic which he accounts for because he is dealing with very "slippery" content.

—Charles L. James

PETRIE, Paul (James).   American.   Born in Detroit, Michigan, 1 July 1928. Educated at Wayne State University, Detroit, 1946-51, B.A. 1950, M.A. 1951; University of Iowa, Iowa City, Ph.D. 1957. Served in the United States Army, 1951-53. Married Sylvia Spencer in 1954; two daughters and one son. Instructor, 1959-62, Assistant Professor, 1962-66, Associate Professor, 1966-69, and since 1969, Professor of English, University of Rhode Island, Providence. Address: 66 Dendron Road, Peace Dale, Rhode Island 02879, U.S.A.

PUBLICATIONS

Verse

Confessions of a Non-Conformist.   Mount Vernon, Iowa, Hillside Press, 1963.
The Race with Time and the Devil.   Francestown, New Hampshire, Golden Quill Press, 1965.
The Leader: For Martin Luther King, Jr.   Providence, Rhode Island, Hellcoal Press, 1968.
From under the Hill of Night: Poems.   Nashville, Tennessee, Vanderbilt University Press, 1969.
The Idol.   Kingston, Rhode Island, Biscuit City Press, 1973.
The Academy of Goodbye.   Hanover, New Hampshire, University Press of New England, 1974.
Light from the Furnace Rising.   Providence, Rhode Island, Copper Beech Press, 1978.
Time Songs.   Kingston, Rhode Island, Biscuit City Press, 1979.
Not Seeing Is Believing.   LaCrosse, Wisconsin, Juniper Press, 1983.
Strange Gravity: Songs, Physical and Metaphysical.   Cranberry Isles, Maine, Tidal Press, 1984.

*

Paul Petrie comments:

My whole approach to poetry, both thematic and technical, is governed by a hatred of dogmatic theorizing, and since the twentieth century represents the very apotheosis of theorizing, a paradise for half-baked creeds and counter-creeds, I find myself in a "school" of one. If there is any critical notion which I find appealing, it is Keats' idea of Negative Capability, but even that has its limitations. In short I believe that there is nothing that cannot be said in poetry and that there is no limitation on the way it can or should be said. A poem need not be "new" or "old," in "free verse" or "meter," "understated" or "overstated"—all that it must be is a good poem.

As for my own work, I would describe it as lyrical, relatively emotional, dramatic in its inclusion of opposites with a stronger current of movement than is common in verse today, and perhaps an over-indulgence in the doctrine of statement through images. My major strenghts are rhythm and organization; my major weaknesses are a lack of exact detail and firm diction. I have a personal notion of the poem as an act of praise (be it positive or negative in theme and tone), and I tend to regard poetry as a semi-religious vocation, but I do not demand that others share these attitudes and I can think of excellent poems which would stretch these terms to the breaking point. The poems will remain; the theory will go.

* * *

Paul Petrie is well known to students of contemporary American poetry. For two decades his poems have appeared in a wide variety of literary journals, magazines, and in several volumes. A sense of death-in-life and our fragile mortality seems to be the exclusive concern of the books. Haunted by death in his dreams and plagued by it in his waking life, Petrie, in an intense and passionate creative act, transforms his fear and dread into art. As *The Race with Time and the Devil* suggests, such an act is not an easy or an unambiguous triumph. His best poems are alive with the sense of a real person's struggle to achieve an elemental relationship with and understanding of the natural cycles of life and death.

There is a clear movement toward concentration, sharpness and mastery of medium. *Confessions of a Non-Conformist* is an adequate work, though not particularly original. *The Race with Time and the Devil* is a marked improvement and contains a number of fine poems, especially the five poem sequence "Pictures of Departure," "The Last Words of Frederick II," "Chain," "The Church of San Antonio De La Florida," "Morning Psalm," and "In Defense of Colds." *From under the Hill of Night* deserves the most praise. Poems such as "Under the Hill of Night," "The Party," "Mark Twain," "Kindertoten," and "Notes of a Would-Be Traveler," are excellent. In them, Petrie has achieved fully his desire to articulate his organic sense of his world.

—Richard Damashek

PETTY W(illiam) H(enry). British. Born in Bradford, Yorkshire, 7 September 1921. Educated at Bradford Grammar School, 1931-40; Peterhouse, Cambridge, B.A. 1946, M.A. 1950; University of London, B.Sc. 1953. Served in the Royal Artillery, 1941-45. Married Margaret Bastow in 1948; two daughters and one son. Administrator and teacher in London and Yorkshire, 1946-64. Deputy Education Officer, 1964-73, and County Education Officer, 1973-84, Kent County Council. President, Society of Education Officers, 1980-81; Chairman, County Education Officers Society, 1982-83. Recipient: Cheltenham Festival Prize, 1968; Camden Festival Prize, 1970; Greenwood Prize, 1978; Lake Aske Memorial Award, 1980. D.Litt.: University of Kent, Canterbury, 1983. C.B.E. (Commander, Order of the British Empire), 1981. Address: Godfrey House, Hollingbourne, near Maidstone, Kent ME17 1TX, England.

PUBLICATIONS

Verse

No Bold Comfort. London, Outposts, 1957.
Conquest and Other Poems. London, Outposts, 1967.

*

Critical Studies: in the *Times Literary Supplement* (London), July 1957; by Vernon Scannell, in *Outposts* (London), Summer 1957; in *Poetry Review* (London), Winter 1958; in the *Times Educational Supplement* (London), July 1967.

W.H. Petty comments:

An experience—intellectual, emotional, visual—itself informs me when I should write a poem. The process of writing always reveals connections, often subtle connections, with other experiences of which I had not been conscious before beginning to write the poem. The process of writing also indicates the techniques, such as rhythm, rhyme and word and line patterns—or, at times, the deliberate avoidance of these—which appear to be the most effective means of expression. I never "force" a poem: I never pre-determine a technique. This means that the poems I write are comparatively few in number—which seems to me advantageous in the circumstances of today.

*   *   *

Although only two booklets of W. H. Petty's work have been published, his poems have appeared in a wide range of magazines and anthologies, and he has been awarded prizes in the Cheltenham Festival of Literature and the Camden Festival of Music and the Arts. *No Bold Comfort* is a collection of 20 lyrics, mostly descriptive of scenes or events which seem to have been thrust upon the poet's attention—"Futility in Cagnes," "Nightmare in Bruges," "Skinningrove Steel-Works," etc.—rather than having been selected as subjects to illustrate a central theme, though there are also a few reflective poems about life in general or personal experience in particular which reveal the poet's philosophy.

Even in his earliest poems, Petty exhibited a fastidious concern for language and form, but undoubtedly the most noticeable feature of his modest style was the capacity to evoke a scene or recreate an atmosphere by means of striking visual imagery. In poem after poem one comes across such phrases as "the town's white angularities and the morning tables bright as tight fruit," "the village fat with snow," and "the rough kidney cobbles of the Pennine streets"; and occasionally a masterly use of monosyllables to achieve the desired effect, as in "Market";

So the high sun brings all things here to pattern
Even the fat cattle amiably
Ambling between the buxom-windowed shops
To curt death.

Conquest is a long poem in which the poet reviews his past from childhood to the present, touching upon life in Bradford and Cambridge, and holidays at home and abroad, in the belief that "to contemplate our past is to savour / Mastery, for the past only exists / when the spool of memory is turned / By one's self." W. H. Petty turns the spool to considerable purpose here.

—Howard Sergeant

PICKARD, Tom. British. Born in Newcastle upon Tyne, Northumberland, in 1946. Educated in Newcastle secondary schools; Ruskin College, Oxford, 1977-78. Married 1) Constance Davison, one son and one daughter; 2) Joanna Voit, one son. Worked for a seed merchant, construction company, and wine merchant, 1962-64; served an apprenticeship to Basil Bunting; Co-Founder and manager, Morden Tower Book Room, 1963-72, and Ultima Thule Bookshop, 1969-73, Newcastle; C. Day Lewis Fellow, Rutherford Comprehensive School, London, 1976-77; Creative Writing Fellow, University of Warwick, Coventry, 1978-79. Recipient: Northern Arts Award, 1965; Arts Council grant, 1969, 1973. Agent: Judy Daish Associates, 83 Eastbourne Mews, London, W2 6LQ, England.

PUBLICATIONS

Verse

High on the Walls. London, Fulcrum Press, 1967; New York, Horizon Press, 1968.
New Human Unisphere. Newcastle upon Tyne, Ultima Thule, 1969.

An Armpit of Lice.   London, Fulcrum Press, 1970.
The Order of Chance.   London, Fulcrum Press, 1971.
Dancing under Fire.   Philadelphia, Middle Earth, 1973.
Hero Dust: New and Selected Poems.   London, Allison and
   Busby, 1979.
O.K. Tree!   Durham, Pig Press, 1980.
Domestic Art.   Vancouver, Slug Press, 1981.
In Search of "Ingenuous."   Vancouver, 1981.

Plays

Radio Documentary: *The Jarrow March*, 1976.

Television Scripts: *Squire*, 1974; *The Dragon Story*, 1983.

Short Stories

Guttersnipe.   San Francisco, City Lights, 1972.

Other

Serving My Time to a Trade.   Orono, Maine, Paideuma, 1980.
Jarrow March, with Joanna Voit.   London, Allison and Busby,
   and New York, Schocken, 1982.

                              *

Bibliography: in *Poetry Information 18* (London), 1978.

Manuscript Collections: Northern Arts, Newcastle upon Tyne;
State University of New York, Buffalo.

Critical Studies: "Tom Pickard," in *Lip 1* (Philadelphia), 1972,
and in *Poetry Information 18* (London), 1978, both by Eric
Mottram; "Pick's Progress" by Richard Caddell, in *Literary
Review 6* (London), 1979; "Hero Dust" by Kenneth Cox, in
Montemora 7 (New York), 1980.

Tom Pickard comments:
   Instead of a personal statement I send this poem which says all
I want to say about writing poetry, at this moment.

                 in search of "ingenuous"

                 opening a dictionary
                 between inflict
                 and inhuman

                 my eye falls
                 on a flower
                 placed there
                 and preserved
                 by you

                 seeing
                 it informs
                 my heart
                 infolds

                              *

                 between idolize
                 and I.L.O.
                 a violet
                 whose moth petals
                 hover on

                 ignotum per ignotius

                 explanation
                 obscures the object

              *   *   *

         "ad rather be skint than an industrial cog"

   A commitment, apparently against all the odds for a working-
class Newcastle school-leaver, to poetry, and a refusal to accept
the menial life allocated to him lay behind the achievement of
Tom Pickard's first book, *High on the Walls*. His "horror of
being limited" helped him to an early awareness of modern
American writing, fostered by contact with Dorn, Creeley, and
others. The spareness of such lyrics as "City Summer" certainly
has affinities with Williams and these later poets, yet Pickard
sought to remain true to his own area and language and
working-class experience. His work is permeated by a sense of
Northumbrian locality, whether a countryside still close to
Thomas Bewick's ("The Game Bird"), the industrial heritage of
"Stowell Street Corporation Yard," or the settings of his prose-
work *Guttersnipe*. The human consequences of that heritage are
set out in "Birthplace—Bronchitis"—"The old men cannot walk
up banks / without leaving brown cockles on the path"—and
local speech is strongly used in such poems as "Rape" and
"Scrap." Complementary are lyrics of sexual love and involvement ("To Puberty," "The Bodies Are Touching") and the experience of parenthood ("The Bairn").
   In his Preface to *High on the Walls*, Basil Bunting (whose
work Pickard had helped to rescue from neglect and who in turn
offered encouragement and continued advice) praised Pickard's
"skill to keep the line compact and musical" and hoped he would
learn "to sing with a longer breath." This can be related to the
problem of evolving forms to embody a range of themes from the
most personal to the social and political. A subtle merging is
already apparent in as brief a poem as "Factory"—"fingers of a
hand / that whisper softly / at my napes hair / / smoke blowing /
in the winds of engines." But *The Order of Chance* begins with a
poem that marks a new move forward. An angry lament for
generations of such men as his father, "The Devil's Destroying
Angel Exploded" is dedicated to John Martin, and has something of the Northumbrian painter's sombre vision, while referring insistently to the present:

                    no colour
                 but dancing black
                 producers of heat
                 confused in the cold
                    moon full above the dole

   As Eric Mottram (his most perceptive and informed critic) has
stressed, mythic and folk elements were becoming important in
Pickard's work, nourished by his reading in Jung, his own
dreams, and direct knowledge of local folk rituals. Such elements are notably present in "New Body," with its magical
transformations—"As you felt my bear's claw / I was a snake / /
As you stroked my cat's fur / I was a fish." The volume ends with
the prose-sequence "Warmth," but before that comes part of a
long poem bearing the title "Magpie."
   That poem became the substantial and complex "Dancing
under Fire," exploring, through varying forms, the possibilities
of energy—in, for instance, a move from stone as defensive wall
or the oppressiveness of "city concrete" to stone used construc-

tively, to walls dissolved by love, and "stone stances" which "one fixed gaze / burns into life"; or the sequence from plant (in the now separate poem "The Order of Chance") to coal to fire. The past, the mythic, and the personal alternate and merge. A row of street lamps is "...a dragon coiled / in the valley" which is also sexual love and the flames of industrial fires, energy whose exploitation can be damaging (both socially and personally) or revivifying. A sequence of individual transformation, re-iterating the word "dissolve," precedes the evocation of the shell-shock victim, Marta, whose "lack of words makes us suppose so much," counter-balanced in turn by "a voice from someone's telly"—which offers only "shadows / of the real event."

The final stress is on love, on active acknowledgement—"father you built the lines I travel on"—and the assertion, perhaps central to Pickard's work, "what is chosen / remains." A group of "Snake Poems" continues the dragon-fire-energy theme, in dreamlike, often violent visions of family relationships still rooted, as in "Gateshead," in actuality. A family is more directly seen in the TV play, *Squire*, while the poems interspersed in his radio documentary, *The Jarrow March*, stress the human warmth, the solidarity of parents and children, in that political action by "Family men / hunger dancers".

"Hero Dust," Pickard's next long poem, opposes to a blues-style prophecy of "bad news" a synthesis, in 28 numbered but formally differing verses, of some recurrent themes, from industrial desolation—"moss mottled with oil / and slime"—through the possibilities of chance, especially those of love, action, the entwinement of pain and joy, and a fierce energy—"my fury flames furnaces"—to end in lostness and betrayal counterbalanced by the quoted words: "I have saved the bird in my breast." The transforming potential of love is again suggested in "Ballad" and "City Garden," while such poems as "Rat Palace" (with the unanswered "how can we help each other?") and "My Radio" ("interprets the past / manages the present") detail, with an enhanced Europe-wide awareness, the evils of political control. Yet against these, he can set his own practice as a writer—"my pen insists it knows best and wants to manage its own affairs / / my pen demands complete autonomy." The last words of the playful, vivid "Recipe," although referring to the hazards of cookery, also express the spirit of much of his work: "fight back."

—Geoffrey Soar

PIERCY, Marge. American. Born in Detroit, Michigan, 31 March 1936. Educated at the University of Michigan, Ann Arbor (Hopwood Award, 1956, 1957), A.B. 1957; Northwestern University, Evanston, Illinois, M.A. 1958. Instructor, Indiana University, Gary, 1960-62; Poet-in-Residence, University of Kansas, Lawrence, 1971; Visiting Lecturer, Thomas Jefferson College, Grand Valley State Colleges, Allendale, Michigan, 1975; staff member, Fine Arts Work Center, Provincetown, Massachusetts, 1976-77; Writer-in-Residence, College of the Holy Cross, Worcester, Massachusetts, 1976; held Butler Chair of Letters, State University of New York, Buffalo, 1977. Recipient: Borestone Mountain Award, 1968, 1974; National Endowment for the Arts grant, 1977. Agent: Lois Wallace, Wallace and Sheil Agency, 177 East 70th Street, New York, New York 10021. Address: Box 943, Wellfleet, Massachusetts 02667, U.S.A.

PUBLICATIONS

Verse

Breaking Camp. Middletown, Connecticut, Wesleyan University Press, 1968.
Hard Loving. Middletown, Connecticut, Wesleyan University Press, 1969..
A Work of Artifice. Detroit, Red Hanrahan Press, 1970.
4-Telling, with others. Trumansburg, New York, Crossing Press, 1971.
When the Drought Broke. Santa Barbara, California, Unicorn Press, 1971.
To Be of Use. New York, Doubleday, 1973.
Living in the Open. New York, Knopf, 1976.
The Twelve-Spoked Wheel Flashing. New York, Knopf, 1978.
The Moon Is Always Female. New York, Knopf, 1980.
Circles on the Water: Selected Poems. New York, Knopf, 1982.
Stone, Paper, Knife. New York, Knopf, and London, Pandora Press, 1983.

Recordings: *Laying Down the Tower*, Black Box, 1973; *Reading and Thoughts*, Everett Edwards, 1976; *At the Core*, Watershed, 1978.

Play

The Last White Class: A Play about Neighborhood Terror, with Ira Wood (produced Northampton, Massachusetts, 1978). Trumansburg, New York, Crossing Press, 1980.

Novels

Going Down Fast. New York, Simon and Schuster, 1969.
Dance the Eagle to Sleep. New York, Doubleday, 1970; London, W.H. Allen, 1971.
Small Changes. New York, Doubleday, 1973.
Woman on the Edge of Time. New York, Knopf, 1976; London, Women's Press, 1979.
The High Cost of Living. New York, Harper, 1978; London, Women's Press, 1979.
Vida. New York, Summit, and London, Women's Press, 1980.
Braided Lives. New York, Summit, and London, Allen Lane, 1982.
Fly Away Home. New York, Summit, and London, Chatto and Windus, 1984.

Other

The Grand Coolie Damn. Boston, New England Free Press, 1970.
Parti-Colored Blocks for a Quilt. Ann Arbor, University of Michigan Press, 1982.

*

Marge Piercy comments:
I have always worked to try to make my poems accessible and meaningful to an audience. That does not mean that the poem is necessarily simple; it is as complicated as it needs to be. A poem can speak through rich and complex imagery as long as it is emotionally coherent. I also write a type of poem with little or no ornament, just as I also work in long line, short lines, and lines that hover around iambic tetrameter or pentameter. In making the arrangement of sounds and silences that the notation of a

poem on the page is supposed to create in the air or in the reader's mind, I am working in measures drawn from American speech and American prosody. However, my influences are various, ancient as well as modern, and international.

I imagine that I speak for a constituency, living and dead, and that I give utterance to energy, experience, insight, words flowing from many lives as well as my own. In truth I don't make much distinction between the sources inside and outside. What I mean by being of use is not that the poems function as agitprop or that they are didactic, although some of them are. I have no more hesitation than Pope or Hesiod did to write in that mode as well as many others. What I mean is simply that readers will find poems that speak to and for them, take those poems into their lives and say them to each other and put them up on the kitchen or bathroom or bedroom wall and remember bits of them in stressful or quiet times. That the poems may give voice to something in the experience of our lives has been my intention. For women especially to find ourselves spoken for in art gives dignity to our pain, our anger, our lust, our losses. We can hear what we hope for and what we fear, in the small release of cadenced utterance.

*   *   *

Now, in the mid-1980's, Marge Piercy is well-known for her numerous novels and volumes of poetry and for her commitment to feminism. Her early writings in the 1960's introduced the major theme she has explored ever since: the complex interface between personal relationships and political forces. During that period her allegiances shifted away from general political activism, whose sexist underpinnings she exposed in a much-anthologized essay, "The Grand Coolie Damn," to commitment to the women's movement as the most potent force for social change in the world today.

As in much revolutionary thought, anger frequently supplies motivation, tone, and content of Piercy's poems, but anger mitigated by intelligence and a gift for apt and striking metaphor. But through the 1970's increasingly a new element emerged in her life and her writing: earned affluence. The poverty and struggle of her youth receded. Her novels sold well, and her many poetry readings and lectures on college campuses made her popular. From her travels she returned gratefully to her semi-rural life on Cape Cod. Many poems in *Living in the Open* and *The Twelve-Spoked Wheel Flashing* spring from the locale of her country farm. They are rich lush poems full of appreciation for foods—lettuce, raspberries, tomatoes—and domestic accoutrements, expressing her wish to live congruent with the seasons and "live my life whole, / round, integral as the earth spinning."

A major strength of Piercy in her poems of the late 1970's and early 1980's consists in her ability to apply images out of her robust and early experience to illuminate psychological situations. Such charged language and intensified metaphor are seen in "The Greater Grand Rapids Lover":

> How the strange
> minds twine and glitter and swing
> looped like words in a hammock.
> How the strange minds joining stand
> charmed snakes glittering
> to dance their knowledge

Her 1980 collection, *The Moon Is Always Female*, is energized by a new love in her life and by her deepening study of an identification with women. In its final sequence, "The Lunar Cycle," she connects the 13 lunar months with stages of her own

life—a new variant of her seasonal motif—and subtitles each poem with the Celtic name for the "moonth." She begins with her birth month, Saille (Aries, the first month of the zodiacal calendar), and sets out these stages in terms of many ancient pagan objects, rituals, and myths associating the moon with femaleness. The sequence ends with a coda celebrating the full moon as the vision of full womanhood, but the poem just before it, "Crescent moon like a canoe," completes a personal circle for Piercy by evoking in moving detail her mother's life. The month Fearn was the last month of the mother's pregnancy before the daughter's birth, and as the poet describes the woman from whom she had to part to be herself, she calls her mother her muse, thus uniting her passions for poetry, feminism, and contact with earth, linking these back to the female life-cycle. The poem ends powerfully:

> My muse, your voice on the phone wavers with tears.
> The life you gave me burns its acetylene
> of buried anger, unused talents, rotted wishes,
> the compost of discontent, flaring into words
> strong for other women under your waning.

Stone, Paper, Knife continues and augments earlier themes. Poems of love and orgasm are punctuated by poems of hate and betrayal; celebrations of the beautiful natural world are interspersed among jeremiads against political evils, the anger not always under control. In the best of these, however, mythological reference softens excess polemic. Sometimes her satire is funny, as in "For the Furies," a poem of savagely humorous curses on men in power which ends seriously with a sense of interconnections among women:

> fates, gorgons, furies, expanding to muses,
> contracting into the round moon. Justice
> of the many is wishes, the slow connection
> weaving like a net, a strong net
> woven of dreams and cursing, to catch sharks.

In the final section of this book, and especially in the title poem, "Stone, paper, knife," Piercy expands her positive vision of interconnection with everyone living. She is quiet in tone, philosophical, sharing responsibility for the planet. The materials of the old children's game—stone, paper, rock—are transformed into theological building blocks, *logos*, and the breath of the Holy Spirit:

> We must begin with the stone of mass
> resistance, and pile stone on stone on stone,
> begin cranking out whirlwinds of paper,
>
> the word that embodies before any body
> can rise to dance on the wind, and the sword
> of action that cuts through. We must shine
> with hope, stained glass windows that shape
> light into icons...

This largeness of mind and spirit carries her into wider and subtler spheres. Her passion is not diminished as compassion increases, and this poetry of commitment contains both. It is good work.

—Jane Augustine

PILLIN, William. American. Born in Alexandrowsk, Russia, 3 December 1910. Educated at Lewis Institute, Chicago; Northwestern University, Evanston, Illinois; University of Chicago. Married Polia Pillin in 1934; one son. Since 1948, self-employed artist-potter. Recipient: Jeannette Sewell Davis Award (*Poetry*, Chicago), 1937. Address: 4913 Melrose Avenue, Los Angeles, California 90029, U.S.A.

PUBLICATIONS

Verse

Poems. Prairie City, Illinois, Decker Press, 1939.
Theory of Silence. Los Angeles, George Yamada, 1949.
Dance Without Shoes. Francestown, New Hampshire, Golden Quill Press, 1956.
Passage after Midnight. San Francisco, Inferno Press, 1958.
Pavanne for a Fading Memory. Denver, Swallow, 1963.
Everything Falling. Santa Cruz, California, Kayak, 1971.
The Abandoned Music Room. Santa Cruz, California, Kayak, 1975.

*

Critical Studies: by James Dickey, in *Poetry* (Chicago), May 1959; Felix Anselm, in *Prairie Schooner* (Lincoln, Nebraska), Winter 1959-60; introduction by Robert Bly to *Everything Falling*, 1971; Stewart Granger, in *Northwest Review* (Eugene, Oregon), Spring 1972; "William Pillin: A Certain Music" by Charles Fishman, in *Literary Review* (Madison, New Jersey), Spring 1978; "Resisting Nothingness: Discovering William Pillin" by Gregory Orafealea, in *Gargoyle* (Washington, D.C.), Spring 1984; "To the End of Time and Beyond" by Jascha Kessler, in *Madrona*, Spring 1984.

William Pillin comments:

Earlier poems in strict classical forms, later poems depending largely on cadence and free of rhyme. Characteristic subjects: I identify myself with the great mass of ordinary people, not necessarily in an ideological sense, but in terms of needs, aspirations, attitudes. My moonlight shines in a backyard, not on a formal garden, and I observe the stars from a kitchen window. General influences are poets who emphasize imagery and the surreal: Neruda, Vallejo, Lorca, etc., and poets whose emphasis is social, like Brecht.

Felix Anselm in his *Prairie Schooner* review wrote the following: "His world is characterized by a hopeless nostalgia...a gentle and affectionate appreciation of the small things of daily living that issue touches of warmth and beauty." If his estimate is correct, I have been successful in my literary intentions.

*   *   *

William Pillin's poetry shows evidence of more resources than results. He often draws his subject matter from his immigrant background: the Eastern European culture, pulverized by the urban pressures of twentieth-century Los Angeles, is alternately celebrated for its other-worldliness and lamented in its imminent evaporation. But the rhetoric we hear most often resounds with self-conscious nostalgia: "To you I say a farewell daily." The poet, too haunted by memories to speak with unchecked force, leaves behind a language of enervated regret, a prosaic numbering that ends by numbing the sense still further:

My nights are haunted by footsteps
on the wind. The sky, the trees
are kisses of memory on my forehead.

The lack of incisive presentation of sensory images, and the blurring of metaphors by abstraction, prevent Pillin's joy its fullest rendering. He presents his description of the poem as "at best / a black bordered / post-card of grief," but the border is drawn without sufficient care, and it threatens to take over the entire space of the poem. His irony might be tenser, his wit more agile, but too often the syntax of exposition turns stanzas into what Edmund Wilson called "shredded prose."

Besides this nostalgic poetry of the Jewish immigrant, Pillin attempts several love poems, and poems on aesthetic subjects, the latter usually in praise of some artist. This sort of subject matter is rendered more successfully, and emotions are clearer and more forceful. He wishes his daughter's piano playing will "continue somewhat green / and ignorantly sweet." His kiln grins "like a pot-bellied devil / licking with a glowing tongue / opaline on stone jars." But when he strives for a larger scope, the inflated language goes limp, exemplified by the poem on Isadora Duncan, which begins: "Hallucinatory, like theatrical twilight, is her passage." The weak passive construction and the alliterating, but over-obvious, adjective are unfortunately his characteristic weaknesses. When we are told that the city contains "nudities on streetcorners / instigating youths to bacchanalian cakewalks," we are told too much and allowed to see too little. Pillin's poetry displays more emotion than skill, and while that limits it, it marks it as unusual, for he never descends to the merely glib, though he seldom sings his distress into rapture.

—Charles Molesworth

_____

PILLING, Christopher (Robert). British. Born in Birmingham, Warwickshire, 20 April 1936. Educated at King Edward's School, Birmingham, 1947-54; University of Leeds, Yorkshire, 1954-57, B.A. (honours) 1957; Institute of French Studies, La Rochelle, France, 1955; Loughborough College, University of Nottingham, 1958-59, Cert.Ed. 1959. Married Sylvia Pilling in 1960; one son and two daughters. Assistant in English, Ecole Normale, Moulins, France, 1957-58; French teacher, Wirral Grammar School, Cheshire, 1959-61, King Edward's Grammar School, Birmingham, 1961-62, and Ackworth School, Pontefract, Yorkshire, 1962-71, 1972-73; Head of Modern Languages, Knottingley High School, Yorkshire, 1973-78; Tutor in English, University of Newcastle upon Tyne Department of Adult Education, 1978-80. Since 1980, Head of French, Keswick School, Cumbria. Reviewer, *Times Literary Supplement*, London, 1973-74. Recipient: Arts Council grant, 1971, 1977; Kate Collingwood Award, 1983. Address: 25 High Hill, Keswick, Cumbria CA12 5NY, England.

PUBLICATIONS

Verse

Snakes and Girls. Leeds, University of Leeds School of English Press, 1970.
Fifteen Poems. Leeds, University of Leeds School of English Press, 1970.

In All the Spaces on All the Lines. Manchester, Phoenix Pamphlet Poets Press, 1971.
Wren and Owl. Leeds, University of Leeds School of English Press, 1971.
Andrée's Bloom and the Anemones. Rushden, Northamptonshire, Sceptre Press, 1973.
Light Leaves. Hitchin, Hertfordshire, Cellar Press, 1975.
War Photographer since the Age of 14. Hitchin, Hertfordshire, Starwheel Press, 1983.

*

Critical Study: by Julian MacKenney, in *Poetry and Audience* (Leeds), 1 May 1970.

*   *   *

In All the Spaces on All the Lines and *Snakes and Girls* show Christopher Pilling bringing out, at his best, the subjective depths of everyday domestic moments by forming around them multiple concrete and abstract analogies, as in "Sunscape," "Old Celtic Cocoon," and "Partial Ellipse" (all in *Snakes and Girls*). The opening of the third of these illustrates how concretely observant this poetic evocation can be:

> My wife's wedding ring is no longer
> Circular:
>
> A gold curve
> Is all I see on a hand-coloured
>
> Background.
> One does not think the world is
>
> Round.

More discursive poems tend to be less fully achieved, but do suggest Pilling's developing intellectual grasp of his life-loving orientation:

> The world is not so sinister, such dark.
> The left-handed is another turn of truth.
> The poet needs an ambidextrous strain.
> The words must not go to the ends of the earth.
> Hammer them to the gallows of a poem
> And let them cry of a spirit they have denied.

Though not poetically successful, "Crow Answers by Flight" takes on Ted Hughes's poem intelligently, and one senses that the younger poet has a more than lyrical basis for future work.

—Anne Cluysenaar

PINSKY, Robert (Neal). American. Born in Long Branch, New Jersey, 20 October 1940. Educated at Rutgers University, New Brunswick, New Jersey, B.A. 1962; Stanford University, California (Woodrow Wilson, Stegner, and Fulbright fellow), M.A., Ph.D. 1966. Married Ellen Bailey in 1961; three daughters. Assistant Professor of Humanities, University of Chicago, 1967-68; Professor of English, Wellesley College, Massachusetts, 1968-80. Since 1980, Professor of English, University of California, Berkeley. Visiting Lecturer, Harvard University,

Cambridge, Massachusetts, 1979-80; Hurst Professor, Washington University, St. Louis, 1981. Since 1978, Poetry Editor, *New Republic*, Washington, D.C. Recipient: Massachusetts Council on the Arts grant, 1974; Oscar Blumenthal Prize (*Poetry*, Chicago), 1978; American Academy award, 1980; Saxifrage Prize, 1980; Guggenheim Fellowship, 1980. Address: Department of English, University of California, Berkeley, California 94720, U.S.A.

PUBLICATIONS

Verse

Sadness And Happiness. Princeton, New Jersey, Princeton University Press, 1975.
An Explanation of America. Princeton, New Jersey, Princeton University Press, and Manchester, Carcanet, 1979.
Five American Poets, with others. Manchester, Carcanet, 1979.
History of My Heart. New York, Ecco Press, 1984.

Other

Landor's Poetry. Chicago, University of Chicago Press, 1968.
The Situation of Poetry: Contemporary Poetry and Its Traditions. Princeton, New Jersey, Princeton University Press, 1976.

Translator, with Robert Hass, *The Separate Notebooks,* by Czeslaw Milosz. New York, Ecco Press, 1984.

*

Manuscript Collection: Regenstein Library, University of Chicago.

Critical Studies: by Hugh Kenner, in *Los Angeles Times,* 11 February 1976; Robert van Hallberg, in *Chicago Review,* Spring 1976; William Pritchard, in *Times Literary Supplement* (London), 11 June 1976; Louis Martz, in *Yale Review* (New Haven, Connecticut), Autumn 1976.

*   *   *

To begin at the edge, "'Wonder' is an inclusive name for our most significant feelings in response to nature, an abrupt and non-referential awe...Wonder is non-referential in the sense that as a feeling it seems unrelated, by cause or analogy, to the rest of life," writes Robert Pinsky in *The Situation of Poetry,* a critical work which attempts to situate modern poetry in an historical context. Yet in his first book of poetry, *Sadness And Happiness,* life and the response to life are woven together by the varieties of wonder. The incommensurability between a cause and its effects, between the fact seen and the feelings born there, grows into poetry:

> Someone is reading the way a rare child reads,
>
> A kind of changeling reading for the love of reading,
> For love and for the course of something leading
>
> Her child's intelligent soul through its inflection.

"Library Scene," composed in couplets of flowing meter and delicate rhyme (that quoted is the single true rhyme, which forms the center of a variety of imperfect ones) turns concisely about the still figure, deftly giving it motion.

Wonder, however, is an inclusive response, and in Pinsky's longer poems, the discursive techniques predominate: digressions, lists, and the free association of images and feelings lead us remorsefully but remorselessly through the inflections of our inadequate terms for feelings ("Sadness And Happiness"):

> That they have no earthly measure
> is well known—the surprise is
> how often it becomes impossible
> to tell one from the other in memory:
>
> the sadness of past failures, the strangely
> happy—doubtless corrupt—
> fondling of them. Crude, empty
> though the terms are, they do
>
> organize life.

Such poems resist short quotation, but there is a hint of the poem's shape in the dashes, commas, and colons of this one. With these punctuational road signs, Pinsky navigates the bumpy borders which lie between sadness and happiness, crossing and recrossing from one territory to the other.

The shorter poems of *Sadness And Happiness*, such as "Library Scene," have an estimable clarity, precision, and grace, but Pinsky is evidently bending his energies toward longer forms. "Essay on Psychiatrists," 17 pages long, quotes from a journalistic variety of sources, including comic strips (*Rex Morgan, M.D.*, of course), *The Bacchae*, and Walter Savage Landor (the subject of Pinsky's first critical work, *Landor's Poetry*). "Essay on Psychiatrists" again takes up the inadequate terms we have for circumscribing experience—"sanity," "genius," or "madness"—but arrives at a conclusion that seems to strain for a larger field:

> —goods
> and money in their contingency and spiritual
>
> Grace evoke the way we are all psychiatrists,
> All fumbling at so many millions of miles
> Per minute and so many dollars per hour
>
> Through the exploding or collapsing spaces
> Between stars, saying what we can.

Pinsky's current work in progress—"An Explanation of America"—has perhaps found a category large enough for his particular form of speech. In the three sections published so far, the musical theme-and-variation form evident in earlier poems has been applied rigorously, and the resulting work is as clear and as faceted as crystal. The question of limiting terms is being approached from its other side: properly linked and joined, such terms can be used to enclose a territory from without. While remaining highly personal and responsive, Robert Pinsky's poetry seems to be growing ever more inclusive.

—Walter Bode

PITCHFORD, Kenneth (Samuel). American. Born in Moorhead, Minnesota, 24 January 1931. Educated at the Uni-

versity of Minnesota, Minneapolis, B.A. (summa cum laude) 1952; Magdalen College, Oxford (Fulbright Fellow), 1956-57; New York University (Penfield Fellow, 1957), M.A. 1959. Served in the United States Army, 1953-55: Sergeant. Married Robin Morgan in 1952; one child. Member of the Department of English, New York University, 1958-62; Writer-in-Residence, Yaddo, Saratoga Springs, New York, Summer 1958; taught at the Poetry Workshop, New School for Social Research, New York, 1960; Associate Editor *The New International Yearbook*, New York, 1960-66. Currently, free-lance editor, New York. Recipient: Borestone Mountain Award, 1964. Address: c/o Purchase Press, P.O. Box 5, Harrison, New York 10528, U.S.A.

PUBLICATIONS

Verse

The Blizzard Ape. New York, Scribner, 1958.
A Suite of Angels and Other Poems. Chapel Hill, University of North Carolina Press, 1967.
Color Photos of the Atrocities. Boston, Little Brown, 1973.

Other

Translator, *The Sonnets to Orpheus*, by Rilke. Harrison, New York, Purchase Press, 1981.

*

Kenneth Pitchford comments:

I consider myself a writer. My medium, then, is language. Any form that can be composed of words is of interest to me. Alongside the poems I write, I have also written plays, stories, a novel, essays, etc.

I began writing poetry to express the inexpressible sensation of being alive—before I knew that a formal discipline called poetry existed. In college, I achieved the mastery of traditional forms of poetry under superb taskmasters, but while my first book of poems reflects these acquired skills, I feel that my own poetic bent has always lain elsewhere. My second book of poems shows the attempt to put "schooling" behind me and seize my own sense of poetry more directly. My third book begins to show me a configuration that is uniquely my own.

This "growing into myself" is also reflected in the progression of subject matter that has preoccupied me. Previous to the first book, my work was an uncontrolled outcry about the despair and ignorance that was the lot of a working-class youngster— and the sources of beauty open to such a one. In the first book, written during the McCarthyist Fifties, I had not become so domesticated that this subject matter was totally obscured. But with the second book, several strands come together: the exploration and laying to rest of a tortuous psychological journey from suicide and sexual conflict toward intimations of personal liberation; and a growing refusal to accept the amount of general suffering required to maintain the present shape of society. In the new poems, the commitment is totally to political revolution and a struggle to imagine what social liberation would be like. I find myself embittered now about the years of "training" I underwent in the 1950's—training designed to transform intransigence into passivity and to drive wedges between thought and action, literary values and human needs, taste and utility. I see the whole literary endeavor as presently pursued to be the stutterings of a dying culture. The attempt to tell some part of the truth will be considered propaganda; the urgent outcry will be considered vulgar; the abandonment of outworn forms and assumptions will be seen as inartistic. Yet the revolutionary poet, in trying to re-create himself, will take all these risks, will attempt to fuse thought and action, value and need, and in so doing, perhaps, build a new language strong enough to be of help in the growing worldwide struggle for human liberation from want, greed and domination. Whether the new world that emerges will want to remember such writing is really unimportant. Venceremos!

*   *   *

...I might have made some greater difference than I did
(though never enough, never mind total)
but all my poems were trying to curry favor
with the *Kenyon Review* and other extinct areas of
    sensibility
when there was this rage in me that only now has
    exploded into the
realization that my right to be sensitive, to love the art
    of any suffering
people, was taken from me by their calling me
faggot faggot faggot—and that all I have to do to reclaim
    that right
is to realize how faggot is my salvation, whatever they
    called Chopin.

—"I've Never Been to Majorca"

Kenneth Pitchford's festering rage is well concealed in *The Blizzard Ape*. The poems are chiselled and carefully wrought: many are written as lyrics to be set to music and use the ballad form and colloquial idiom to sing jauntily of the barmaid propositioned by a customer in Tony's Hashhouse, or to sing the "Young Buck's Sunday Blues" when he discovers that his hell raisin' woman has left him to seek comfort with a preacher "full as brimstone, cash, and hell." Others evoke fleeting moods and meditate upon the difficulty of making a poem speak and the loss experienced when the poem is perfected; finally, a very few, "A Bride's Song," "Still-Life from a Packing Plant," and "The Solipsist at Midnight," strike the macabre note later sustained in many of the poems on conjury and others in *A Suite of Angels*. The spectre of death that chills the lovers' kiss in "A Bride's Song," and the still-life image of the cow slaughtered in the kill room where "...red-aproned men have come, / affixed the cable to bruise the senseless neck, replaced the hooks through the achilles tendons, hoisted the body upwards, set casters / in the grooves of the shiny rail above them, to send it wheeling down rows of skinners and cutters" brutally hint at the rage mounting in the poet as he confronts the butchery and violence in society and in himself which have done their best to slay his gentler, more delicate instincts.

In *A Suite of Angels* a number of the poems continue to rework Greek myths and write in an objective voice designed to win favor from the *Kenyon Review*, but most begin to speak in the first person confessional voice, and begin to dredge up the painful memories from the past and recreate the nightmares of his present marriage. Many express the ambivalence Pitchford feels towards himself as a man and towards women as they have been defined in their traditional roles. The scene of the bull slaughtered repeats itself; the male is transformed into a Wer-Man, turned into this creature by his lust for men but held prisoner by women who demand to feed his blood hunger. The poems speak of moments in childhood when he heard the muffled, scuffling sounds of his father wringing the necks of mallards which his sister later cleaned; when he heard his sister talking of wanting to take her mother's place in her father's bed;

when he decried his father's crime of denying him love. Finally, in "Nightmares," his nightmares and those of his wife war upon the two of them: he haunted by his role as Wer-Man, male supremacist, sucking his wife's blood because long ago he was denied his other love; she struggling with spectres of nazi doctors with their scalpels, come to sterilize, rape, or otherwise mutilate her. He becomes the nazi doctors; she the Wer-man's mistress: both trace their nightmares to the wrongs done them by their parents and by an evolutionary history that made the male the dominant species; both briefly overcome the fiendish tortures of sleep when their love finally unites them.

But *Color Photos of the Atrocities* allows no such easy solution to the anti-gender struggle. Pitchford's rage has burst; he has found his cause. Although the reader may find the poems too wordy, the cant of revolution, egalitarianism, racism, sexism, gay liberationism, and militant feminism too much a part of the nostalgia of the 1960's, Pitchford believes he must abandon his old controls and struggle painfully to make explicit the plight of the effeminist married to Robin Morgan (authoress of *The Monster* and a radical feminist herself) who wants to come to terms with his feelings for her, their son, Blake, his lover, Michael, and the future movement which now consumes him. In this volume, all atrocities, Auschwitz, the holocaust, the Attica prison riots, and the mass killings of Brazil's Indians, are one to Pitchford: all bespeak the brutality and violence which has defined The Man, the white straight male, whom Pitchford now identifies with the Establishment, the Kennedys, Rockefellers, and all the moguls. The faggot is their prisoner who awaits a revolution in which, as Pitchford declares, "he will risk his whole self or die." But the enemy is also the faggot himself who cannot entirely get rid of the violence in him that has always made him oppressor, and who cannot survive if the force he believes in, the liberated woman, is to have her way. For she, in Pitchford's poems, must become the real heroine of the revolution and pull the trigger that kills him. Pitchford dreams of a time:

...when there is no more religion or family or
    male domination
    or money or property or mine or yours or
    forced obedience
...when women are free
    not only to shape their own lives
    but to realize a vision of liberation
    that will shape the lives of all of us
...when men are able
    to hug and kiss babies not for show,
    but able to care for them in every sense
    and for each other
...when I'm no longer called queer
    for wishing my father had held me
        with a love like that,
    for loving still any rare stray
    glimmer of tenderness in a man....

—"The Flaming Faggots"

But the poetry sees this as a dream; and the reality he wrestles with is one in which suicide or murder seem the more necessary outcomes. At their best, these poems candidly capture the joy of fatherhood, the delight derived from simple domestic moments, and the dizzying pleasure found in music. At their worst, they are too insistent, propagandistic, repetitive, and voguish.

—Carol Simpson Stern

PITTER, Ruth. British. Born in Ilford, Essex, 7 November 1897. Educated at Coborn School for Girls, East London. War Office clerk, 1916-18. Painter for Walberswick Peasant Pottery Company, Suffolk, 1918-30, and from 1930, Partner, Deane and Forester, London. Now retired. Recipient: Hawthornden Prize, 1937; Heinemann Award, 1954; Queen's Gold Medal for Poetry, 1955. Companion of Literature, 1974. C.B.E. (Commander, Order of the British Empire), 1979. Address: The Hawthorns, Chilton Road, Long Crendon, Aylesbury, Buckinghamshire, England.

PUBLICATIONS

Verse

First Poems. London, Cecil Palmer, 1920.
First and Second Poems 1912-1925. London, Sheed and Ward, 1927; New York, Doubleday, 1930.
Persephone in Hades. Privately printed, 1931.
A Mad Lady's Garland. London, Cresset Press, 1934; New York, Macmillan, 1935.
A Trophy of Arms: Poems 1926-1935. London, Cresset Press, and New York, Macmillan, 1936.
The Spirit Watches. London, Cresset Press, 1939; New York, Macmillan, 1940.
The Rude Potato. London, Cresset Press, 1941.
Poem. Southampton, Shirley Press, 1943.
The Bridge: Poems 1939-1944. London, Cresset Press, 1945; New York, Macmillan, 1946.
Pitter on Cats. London, Cresset Press, 1947.
Urania (selections). London, Cresset Press, 1950.
The Ermine: Poems 1942-1952. London, Cresset Press, 1953.
Still by Choice. London, Cresset Press, 1966.
Poems 1926-1966. London, Barrie and Rockliff-Cresset Press, 1968; as *Collected Poems,* New York, Macmillan, 1969.
End of Drought. London, Barrie and Jenkins, 1975.

*

Critical Study: preface by the author to *Poems 1926-1966,* 1968.

Ruth Pitter comments:

I am not even a professional writer, just a poet; the occupations of my life other than this have been simply to gain a subsistence, and I have mostly worked with my hands.

I look at life, and listen inside myself, and try to express what I feel mostly in the wellworn forms of our tradition. From infancy I have intently observed nature (including people), fascinated chiefly by the mysteries of things.

*   *   *

In a literary period of revolution, reflecting that of Western society, the poetry of Ruth Pitter stands as an isolated monument, untouched by the changes, both technical and moral, around it. She says in the Foreword to her *Collected Poems* that "I have been trying to write poetry since 1903, when I was about five; but I produced little that I now think worth keeping until about the age of thirty." That is a long, and humble apprenticeship. The humility comes from an ever closer dedication to Christian Faith, of an almost Traherne-like individuality and isolation. The persistence comes from a character obstinate, assured and humorous. As she also says, "I have had strange thoughts at times about comedy." They not only emerge in much of her verse. They also play a part in securing her in her assurance of

her own idiom as a craftsman in that verse, by making her self-critical without at the same time freezing her muse into sterility. Seriousness, a necessary ingredient of poetry, can be damaged, even crippled, by self-laughter.

Since 1920 Miss Pitter has practised her art, obstinately personal, rather as a goldsmith at his bench. She uses words as that precious metal, manipulating it into verbal shapes of recognised modes: the sonnet, the *terza rima,* the couplet and blank verse. In all those shapes it is lucid, simple. Its vowels echo round the halls of the English Pantheon, where Milton has entoned and Spenser sung. But it is a music on its own, self-taught, self-tuned. It is poetry, not merely verse.

That must by why, in the early 1940's, Hilaire Belloc spoke to me about her one day at lunch, saying that he had written an introduction to a book of poems by a young woman of remarkable skill and intellectual and spiritual force. She has persisted since then, singing her own song. It is mainly a *Magnificat,* in praise of life as she has encountered it, close up and through the sharp eye of an intense curiosity. She has not dissipated her literary vitality on professional writing, such as literary journalism, nor, as far as I know, on prose work of any kind. She has been solely a poet, and has made her living at work wholly apart from this major activity which, to be secure in its achievement, demands as much fidelity and patience as marriage. Hers has been a monophilic art, sustained, as I have said, by bouts of extraneous humour, as when she writes verse about cats and gardening, amusing relaxations from the demands of her more devout work.

That work is based upon religious faith, not dogmatic but metaphysical and exalted. It is astonishingly beautiful, and clothed in sensuous phrases and images. Like the swallows (she calls them "freemasons of the air"), in a poem which is a masterpiece, she is one of those "Spirits who can sleep on high / And hold their marriage in the sky." That is an example of close observation of the goings-on of nature, and of the imaginative power to translate such earthy traffic into terms of spiritual symbolism.

This process occupies most of her work. Again and again, she sets out demurely, almost cataloguing something she has noticed in her daily round and common task, then suddenly it is turned round, irradiated, and made to reveal a divine significance. Thus, in a poem called "The Apple Tree," she says:

A dear and blessed thing to see,
The lovely laden apple-tree.
I sit me down his boughs below,
The cold and tortuous musings go;
I from the lowest branches take
Four apples for my childhood's sake.

Somehow, that takes us back to Genesis and the Garden of Eden, and the springtime of the mind. Note, too, how the obsolete device of inversion, so much frowned on today, adds to the effect of total return to the garden of prime innocence.

Much more could be said about her work: its simplicity, its quiet self-assurance; but its source and strength can be summed up in her short lyric "For Sleep or Death":

Cure me with quietness,
Bless me with peace;
Comfort my heaviness,
Stay me with ease.
Stillness in solitude
Send down like dew;
Mine armour of fortitude
Piece and make new;

That when I rise again
I may shine bright
As the sky after rain,
Day after night.

—Richard Church

———————

PLANZ, Allen. American. Born in New York City, 2 January 1937. Educated at New York University, M.A. 1961. Served in United States Army, 1960-61. Married to Doris Sommers; one child. Formerly taught at Hunter College, New York, University of North Carolina, Chapel Hill, and Queens College, New York; Lecturer, Chapman College, Montauk, New York, 1973-74. Poetry Editor, *The Nation*, New York, 1969-70. Currently, self-employed fisherman. Recipient: New York Poetry Center Younger Poets prize, 1963; Swallow Press New Poetry Series Award, 1969; Creative Artists Public Service grant, 1975. Address: c/o Living Poets Press, 139 Seventh Avenue, Brooklyn, New York 11217, U.S.A.

PUBLICATIONS

Verse

Poor White and Other Poems. Lanham, Maryland, Goosetree Press, 1964.
Heir to Anger. New York, Lower East Press, 1965.
Studsong. New York, Lower East Press, 1968.
A Night for Rioting. Chicago, Swallow Press, 1969.
Wild Craft. New York, Living Poets Press, 1975.

Other

American Wilderness. San Francisco, Sierra Club, 1970.

*

Allen Planz comments:
   Recently, I've come to think of my best work as discovery—discovering again the ancient relations between man and earth, man and man, man and woman, the excess of joy and terror and splendor which in rediscovery becomes celebration, toward which each poem strives, praising earth and the people on it.

*   *   *

In *A Night for Rioting*, Allen Planz combines visions of urban and rural deterioration. The process of decay, due to technology and industry, occurs wherever modern man locates himself. The disintegration caused by an increasingly object-oriented culture ("gentlemen delivered to chrome by a caress") has radiated outward from the cities to poison the land as well.
   In Planz's poetry, speed is both subject and essence to style. Automobiles signify the quest for masculinity and the rapidly accelerating pace of life. However exhilarating it may be, velocity without positive direction is meaningless and destructive ("sons wild / on curves who met their manhood on a wall"). A country that worships power, speed and violence is more than a bit frightening, and Planz concedes this ("if ever I get the courage / to have a son") while capturing the culture:

I put on a uniform & laid down my life

& thereafter lived in dread of it,
thru fear & violence
becoming quite American.

As a resistance poet, he speaks out against the threatening array of anti-life forces—the dollar, the dictator, and the diplomat ("admen felt for their sex in watchpockets"). The land that remains unoccupied (place and state of mind) is where the revolutionary takes hold ("now as a man, dizzy still with gravity / and hard loving, I name my upland rapture"). The land is real:

...nothing but the land survives,
for only the land lasts, outlasting
citizen, city, empire.

The revolt starts with one man ("having found a rifle / a good thing to lie by") in the natural world, a guerilla who recognizes the need to reverse ongoing destructive processes and the cost of the effort ("My heart, my land, it is the courage to starve to death / I work to give or to get").
   In *Wild Craft*, Planz continues his revolution of one. Charting his own course, traveling unknown waters, he sings of his craft as fisherman and captain. The poems, imagery-laden, convey with clarity the savagery and terrible beauty of the sea-world which calls to him. The opening poem ("Offshore") begins: "I go to sea, before dawn, wondering / what else wanders these waters in the dark." Here especially change and growth are possible, positive, and necessary. "Offshore" concludes:

alone in this stillness
knowing we change
and affirming
for out to sea we change
and change ourselves
forever.

In "Sharks" the speaker changes from a mindless killer to a perceiver who shares life's unity: "The darkness is one dance/ one life, one love."
   Planz, amphibian-like, returns to the land and his urban dwelling-place. As in his earlier book, cities pollute the bodies, warp the minds, and stifle the spirits of their inhabitants. The city poems present the senseless violence (physical and psychological), the oppressive claustrophobia and routine, and the waiting to die which characterize so many of the people. Yet, despite the muggers, perverts, and junkies, here are family and friends; Planz concedes in the last poem ("The Tidefall Wilderness"), "I carry in my side / a green unease / gotten where I swept over a reef / into a glade where a girl showed me my need of peoples." In this poem, too, the poet states "The sea itself is survival"—and survival, land or sea, is what *Wild Craft* is ultimately about.

—Carl Lindner

———————

PLUMLY, Stanley (Ross). American. Born in Barnesville, Ohio, 23 May 1939. Educated at Wilmington College, Ohio, B.A. 1961; Ohio University, Athens, M.A. 1968. Married Hope Plumly in 1974. Visiting Poet, Louisiana State University, Baton

Rouge, 1968-70; Ohio University, 1970-73; University of Iowa, Iowa City, 1974-76; Princeton University, New Jersey, 1976-78; Columbia University, New York, 1977-79; University of Michigan, Ann Arbor, Spring 1979. Since 1979, Professor of English, University of Houston. Poetry Editor, *Ohio Review*, Athens, 1970-75, and *Iowa Review*, Iowa City, 1976-78. Recipient: Delmore Schwartz Memorial Award, 1973; Guggenheim grant, 1973; National Endowment for the Arts grant, 1977, 1984. Address: Department of English, University of Houston, Houston, Texas 77004, U.S.A.

PUBLICATIONS

Verse

In the Outer Dark.   Baton Rouge, Louisiana State University Press, 1970.
Giraffe.   Baton Rouge, Louisiana State University Press, 1973.
How the Plains Indians Got Horses.   Crete, Nebraska, Best Cellar Press, 1975.
Out-of-the-Body Travel.   New York, Ecco Press, 1977.
Summer Celestial.   New York, Ecco Press, 1983.

*

Manuscript Collection: State University of New York, Buffalo.

Critical Studies: "Stanley Plumly and the Mind of Summer" by Edward Hirsch, in *Crazyhorse* (Little Rock, Arkansas), Fall 1983; "Out Beyond Rhetoric" by David Young, in *Field* (Oberlin, Ohio), Spring 1984; "Matthews on Plumly" by William Matthews, in *Ohio Review* (Athens), Fall 1984.

Stanley Plumly comments:

I see my poems as attempts to make something whole of the disparate and difficult parts of my experience. In that sense they are fictions—that which is made of other materials.

*   *   *

Stanley Plumly says, "I believe in a poetry of protagonist-antagonist relationship, in which the energy, the tension...is the result of what happens between the two....Which means that for me a poem is a problem of the trinity, father-son-ghost." The ghost is created by the friction of father and son; it is the poem's content, born mainly through metaphor. Thus, he argues that "[b]ringing the disparate into immediate and intimate relation ...is the hope I have for my poems. My father in the ground is a unifying principle." Plumly's *artful* use of "ground" in this apparently discursive observation is characteristically manifold.

In the Outer Dark is constructed of primal polarities, some more abstract than others. But no abstraction is simply disembodied, no object locked in specificity. Central are light-darkness, motion-stillness, speech-silence, water-stone, father-son. Sun, wind, and tongue flesh out the first three parts; consciousness and humanized Christian allusion generalize the others. The metaphors conveying these tensions are "moving toward one center," "still inside me," a prior "source," an "embryo," a "womb," an original (not this outer) dark. Moreover, they are so compact that the polarities and our senses of them, as though synesthetic, seem interchangeable: "The body tunes to a single sense...." So, just as "stillness" may be sensed both aurally and kinesthetically, the speaker listens with his hands and "warms" not the cold but "the dark."

For Plumly the antagonist and protagonist may despair, but

not the poem's content. It can celebrate, "art [being] first of all a moral act." It is hard to say if this book is finest in darkness, light, or shadow, but Plumly chooses man's inevitable position and in "Between Flesh and What Follows" he arranges the first and penultimate lines so as to say "The Dark that lies...And the Light that lies." Any poem's true content is shadow.

Animal titles designate the three parts of *Giraffe*. Plumly perceives and identifies with an incipience of flight in each creature, especially as it is conceived at night or in dream. They are, then, emblems of the poet's awakening to transcendence. "Walking Out" makes the point more humanly clear: "I would be silence. Even the sleeves / of my best coat would not know me." These various, still unrealized, leavetakings are, however, not only initiated by a poem about loneliness ("Since England Is an Island") but lead back to another on that same subject ("One of Us").

While the father continues to provide tension, conflict between the desires for death and the transformation of life is equally basic. But the poems of darkness and extinction neither dull the volume's celebratory edge nor fail in themselves to honor struggle (as in the lovely, elegiac "Jarrell") and survival (as in "Dreamsong"). Though never evasive about Jarrell's lifelong flirtation with easing himself out of life, Plumly regards him as a man who, even imaginatively, doubted his own seriousness, and ultimately as "a man walking out of himself on a road at dawn" with "the dark piled up behind." Before rising and walking the water, the persona of "Dreamsong" says, "I wanted to die. / I wanted the whole / day."

Perhaps the key to the collection is in "One Line of Light," the geographical background of which is flood country:

> I think of my house as a ship
> lit up like a birthday.
> I walk around inside it
> with the page of a poem—
> the day's log,
> the night's psalm.
> The dark is my ocean.
> I know the water's rising
> in the next town.

In "Jarrell" that poet is himself "the page of his poem filling up" (a masterstroke of ambiguity and metonymy). In "Walking Out" and "Heron," "flight" or its "mockery" are *imagined* "at the edge of water."

"The Wish to Be a Red Indian," a bit of Katka provided as postscript to *Giraffe*, is equally preface to *Out-of-the-Body Travel*. It involves naturalness and creature identification as conditions of pure motion and the dissolution of fetters. When the speaker says, "We lie in that other darkness, ourselves," he is, among other things, considering the truth of lives not our own. Getting out of ourselves is at once impossible and imperative. These poems realize the poet's experience only as a portion of the lives, deaths and painful self-divisions of others, particularly the members of his family. Two poems entitled "Anothering" are about the mother's transcendence through her progeny but in conjunction with the sad vacancy the child's "out-of-the-body travel" leaves in its wake. But death is the principal battleground for transcendence. Recurrently, as in the last two poems, Plumly discovers perpetuity and new life in identification with the dead, especially the father, both as person and archetype:

> Whatever two we were, we become
> one falling body, one breath.
>
> And whosoever be reborn in sons

so shall they be also reborn....
And you, my anonymous father,
be with me when I wake.

The title poem, devoid of all artiness, is perfectly apt. His "raw, red cheek / pressed against the cheek of the [violin's] wood," the father elevates his merely "sad relatives" with that mournful music Yeats knew and made through "Lapis Lazuli."

Plumly's subtle prosody continues in *Summer Celestial*, the key word being "witness." His focus shifts more strongly to the maternal nurture of youth and the natural, especially botanical, wonders of his early life in Ohio.

—David M. Heaton

POMEROY, Ralph. American. Born in Evanston, Illinois, 12 October 1926. Educated at the Art Institute, Chicago; University of Illinois, Urbana; University of Chicago, B.A. 1949. Magazine editor, lecturer, and free-lance writer: Associate Editor, *Art News*, New York, 1965-70; New York Correspondent, 1966-71, and San Francisco Correspondent, 1973, *Art and Artists*, London; Contributing Editor, *Arts* magazine, New York 1982-83; Co-Editor, *A Just God* magazine, 1983-84; Visiting Lecturer, Machaelis College of Art, Cape Town, 1973; Assistant Professor of Comparative Literature, San Francisco State University, 1971-74; Visiting Lecturer, Winchester School of Art, and Lecturer, Cardiff College of Art, 1971; Visiting Lecturer on Painting, New York School of Interior Design, 1983-84. Also a painter and exhibition curator. Recipient: Yaddo Fellowship, 1955; MacDowell Colony Fellowship, 1967; Centrum Foundation Fellowship, 1984. Address: 115 West 71st Street, Apartment 3-A, New York, New York 10023, U.S.A.

PUBLICATIONS

Verse

Book of Poems. Winnetka, Illinois, New Press, 1948.
Stills and Movies. San Francisco, Gesture, 1961.
The Canaries as They Are. Washington, D.C., Charioteer Press, 1965.
In the Financial District. New York, Macmillan, 1968.

Other

Stamos. New York, Abrams, 1974.
The Ice Cream Connection: All You'd Love to Know about Ice Cream. New York and London, Paddington Press, 1975.
First Things First: A Connoisseur's Companion to Breakfast. New York and London, Paddington Press, 1977.

*   *   *

The writer, painter, and art critic Ralph Pomeroy has introduced a new, idiomatic voice to American poetry. But at the same time, he has expressed, in his personal way, traditional artistic themes. In particular, he is concerned with art and its relative stability; with the contrasting transience of human experience; and with the American artist as transient and outsider. Technically his signature characteristic, a function perhaps of his emphasis upon the visual, is the bringing to the foreground of

the implied dramatic situations which, like negatives, underlie all lyric poetry.

His concern with the allied disciplines of poetry and painting is directly represented in poems clearly connected with artists whom he associates with his own creative world: the writers Marianne Moore, Katherine Anne Porter, Pasternak, Glenway Wescott, Giuseppe di Lampedusa; the painters Edward Hopper, Seurat, Matisse. Set against the seeming permanence of their work, however, is Pomeroy's concern with the paradoxically constant mutability sovereign in everyday life itself. Love ("Confession"), death ("Between Here and Illinois"), the seasonal cycle ("Life of an Apple"), day and night ("Morning in Tarragona"), present familiar aspects of change.

But it is his celebrations of locations, arrivals and departures, implied motionlessness and movement, which are especially significant as expressions of impermanence. Specific examples of this version of what might be called the American picaresque, with the artist as outsider or traveller, include the New York poem, "In the Financial District," "2 P.M. Going Westward on the Chicago, Burlington & Quincy," and such poems of expatriate experience as "The Concerts" and "Visiting, Tiberton Court, near Gloucester." But the most significant of these poems, and the finest example of his lyric dramatic method, is "Corner." The speaker loiters uneasily in what could be a Hopper urban landscape, and, watching him, "The Cop slumps alertly on his motorcycle" until the scene's precarious balance is broken by an explosion of movement.

Finally, in "Sentry Seurat," Pomeroy perhaps best suggests the way in which his own sporadic, "autobiographical" poems operate. Commenting on the painter's pointillist style, he observes: "Later, accused of poetry, he rejoined, 'I apply my method.' / (Dots so set down that distance blinds and binds them.)" When Pomeroy's individual poems, quiet highlights of life's events, are considered with the proper distancing, they too combine to conjure a whole and detailed story.

—Gaynor F. Bradish

PORTER, Peter (Neville Frederick). Australian. Born in Brisbane, Queensland, 16 February 1929. Educated at the Church of England Grammar School, Brisbane; Toowoomba Grammar School. Married Jannice Henry in 1961 (died, 1974); two daughters. Journalist in Brisbane; came to England in 1951; worked as clerk and bookseller, and as advertising writer for 10 years. Since 1968, free-lance writer. Compton Lecturer in Poetry, University of Hull, Yorkshire, 1970-71; Visiting Lecturer in English, University of Reading, Berkshire, Autumn 1972, University of Sydney, 1975, and University of New England, Armidale, New South Wales, 1977; Writer-in-Residence, Melbourne University, 1983. Recipient: Cholmondeley Award, 1976; Society of Authors travelling scholarship, 1980; Duff Cooper Prize, 1984. D.Litt.: Melbourne University. Address: 42 Cleveland Square, London W.2, England.

PUBLICATIONS

Verse

Once Bitten, Twice Bitten. London, Scorpion Press, 1961.
Penguin Modern Poets 2, with Kingsley Amis and Dom Moraes. London, Penguin, 1962.

Poems Ancient and Modern. Lowestoft, Suffolk, Scorpion Press, and New York, Walker, 1964.

Words Without Music. Oxford, Sycamore Press, 1968.

Solemn Adultery at Breakfast Creek: An Australian Ballad, music by Michael Jessett. Richmond, Surrey, Keepsake Press, 1968.

A Porter Folio: New Poems. Lowestoft, Suffolk, Scorpion Press, 1969.

The Last of England. London and New York, Oxford University Press, 1970.

Epigrams by Martial. London, Poem-of-the-Month Club, 1971.

After Martial. London, Oxford University Press, 1972.

Preaching to the Converted. London, Oxford University Press, 1972.

Jonah, illustrated by Arthur Boyd. London, Secker and Warburg, 1973.

A Share of the Market. Belfast, Ulsterman, 1973.

Peter Porter Reads from His Own Work (includes recording). Brisbane, University of Queensland Press, 1974.

The Lady and the Unicorn, illustrated by Arthur Boyd. London, Secker and Warburg, 1975.

Living in a Calm Country. London, Oxford University Press, 1975.

Les Très Riches Heures. Richmond, Surrey, Keepsake Press, 1978.

The Cost of Seriousness. London, Oxford University Press, 1978.

English Subtitles. Oxford and New York, Oxford University Press, 1981.

The Animal Programme. London, Anvil Press Poetry, 1982.

Collected Poems. Oxford, Oxford University Press, 1983.

Fast Forward. Oxford, Oxford University Press, 1984.

Narcissus, illustrated by Arthur Boyd. London, Secker and Warburg, 1984.

The Run of Your Father's Library. London, Albion Press, 1984.

Plays

Radio Plays: *The Siege of Munster,* 1971; *The Children's Crusade,* 1973; *All He Brought Back from the Dream,* 1978.

Other

Roloff Beny in Italy, with Anthony Thwaite. London, Thames and Hudson, and New York, Harper, 1974.

The Shape of Poetry and the Shape of Music. Hobart, University of Tasmania, 1980.

Sydney. New York and London, Time Life, 1980.

Editor, *New Poems, 1971-72.* London, Hutchinson, 1972.

Editor, *A Choice of Pope's Verse.* London, Faber, 1972.

Editor, with Anthony Thwaite, *The English Poets: From Chaucer to Edward Thomas.* London, Secker and Warburg, 1974.

Editor, with Charles Osborne, *New Poetry 1.* London, Arts Council, 1975.

Editor, *Poetry Supplement.* London, Poetry Book Society, 1980.

Editor, *Thomas Hardy.* London, Weidenfeld and Nicolson, 1981.

Editor, with Howard Sergeant, *The Gregory Awards Anthology 1980.* London, Secker and Warburg, 1981.

Editor, *The Faber Book of Modern Verse,* 4th edition. London, Faber, 1982.

*

Manuscript Collections: Lockwood Memorial Library, State University of New York, Buffalo; University of Indiana, Bloomington; British Library, London; University of Reading, Berkshire; Australian National Library, Canberra.

Critical Studies: by Clive James, in *The Review 24* (Oxford); Roger Garfitt, in *British Poetry since 1960* edited by Michael Schmidt and Grevel Lindop, Oxford, Carcanet, 1972.

*   *   *

Peter Porter is one of the most substantial and various talents among the English poets of the middle generation; the quality of his achievement has been amply confirmed by the appearance of his *Collected Poems.* An expatriate Australian who does not intend to return to the country of his birth (see "Sidney Cove, 1788" in *Poems Ancient and Modern* and "Recipe" in *A Porter Folio* for examples of his ironic and mistrusting attitude towards it), he casts a scathing and rueful eye on contemporary English civilisation; and yet is inescapably held by it. The loyalty is not only an aversion to an Australia where, he felt, writing in the *TLS* in 1971, "nobody has any natural talent and the Great Supervisor fails me over a whole range of Anglo-Saxon virtues." It is a positive adoption of England, and indeed Europe. It is a respect for, and a comfort in the sense of, "the continuity of the living and the dead which I find in England":

> Sailing away from ourselves, we feel
> The gently tug of water at the quay—
> Language of the liberal dead speaks
> From the soil at Highgate, tears
> Show a great water table is intact.
> You cannott leave England, it turns
> A planet majestically in the mind.

To this point of affirmation, which is nevertheless much qualified by a brooding, increasing sense of the presence of death in his more recent poetry, he has moved through a series of volumes which have been unerring in their recording of the follies of mankind in general with a satire that is grave, sometimes brutal and always acutely observant. He has a considerable flair for a kind of bitter, epigrammatic wit and for elaborately entertaining fantasy (for example, "Fair Go for Anglo-Saxons" in *A Porter Folio*). If there is scarcely any lyric ease or relaxation in his writing, it is not all impassioned seriousness: he can often be extremely funny, sometimes in a sad self-deprecating vein but more often in a way which exorcises the facts of aging and death with mordant, pertinacious satire (in *Preaching to the Converted,* "Sex and the Over Forties" and "Affair of the Heart" show this side of his talent).

The strong positive element in Porter's poetry is there in his celebration of the high points of European culture (particularly in the field of music). The great artist survives death, remains a living presence in the sonatas of a Scarlatti or the portraits of a Giotto. But the lines on Giotto's portrait of Dante display the ambivalence out of which springs much of Porter's most arresting and absorbing verse:

> I've eaten in a restaurant named for you
> and seen your posthumous life-mask. You tell us
> we never get home but are buried in eternal exile.

Art is enduring, but death is even more enduring than art; and life is, at best, a kind of exile from any imaginable happiness or reassurance. These themes are continued right up to the present, in Porter's two 1980's volumes, *English Subtitles* and *Fast Forward*.

Both the satirical tone and the affirmations are echoed in Porter's two collaborations with the Australian artist Arthur Boyd on illustrated poem sequences. Porter essays modern readings of the two legends ("I don't like what's happening in Nineveh, /...it's all parks and permissiveness and lying about"). But these are much more comfortably and unobtrusively accommodated in the exquisitely illustrated *The Lady and the Unicorn* than in *Jonah*, where the modern references seem forced and where it would be charitable to describe Boyd's drawings as merely appalling.

The poems on personal themes, sometimes deriving from dreams (he describes his dreams as a kind of private cinema) or centred on his own personal life-patterns against a garish urban background, are, as a result, largely wry, angry, and self-reproaching; though the emotions are never simple. His love poetry presents that emotion as a tarnished thing, pitiable and unsuccessful, unsuited for treatment in a sensuous or delicate style:

> What I want is a particular body,
> The further particulars being obscene
> By definition. The obscenity is really me,
> Mad, wanting mad possession: what else can mad mean?

His entire style is formal and compressed, with moments of measured solemnity and some successful excursions into the grand manner. There is an air of highly intelligent, witty, intensely committed yet immensely zestful conversation about it; though he is rarely colloquial. Yet Porter has achieved an impressive expansion of range, through the medium of his "version" of the great Roman satirist, in his volume *After Martial*. Porter both updates Martial, making his satires pointful in a modern age of high, permissive living and egotistic pretentiousness, and preserves the spirit of the original. Otherwise, great formal artists of the past and present—Bach, Shakespeare, Laclos, Hardy, Stravinsky—remain his principal admirations; though a ranging, lively and formidable intellect draws him equally to Marston, Christopher Smart, Schopenhauer, Rilke, Mahler, Auden. There is considerable brilliance, and obvious relish, in his employment of the great as mentors, and in a sense, companions, in a life-situation out of which it is difficult to make final sense or derive any ultimate hope.

But the governing emotion in Porter's poetry is a fierce moral emphasis, suggesting that at least something may be wrested from the human predicament if we confront and understand the inadequacy and impermanence of life itself. All this gains an added poignancy in *The Cost of Seriousness*, where poems about England, Australia, and the arts of literature, music and painting form a "frame" around a group of deeply moving poems occasioned by the tragic death of the poet's wife in December 1974. Writing elsewhere about this book, Porter describes its main concern as "the inability of art (poetry in this instance) to alter human circumstances or alleviate human distress." Yet the best poems here, as critics have generally acknowledged, show a new lucidity and power in the handling of the traditional major themes of poetry—love, war, death.

The most recent book, *Fast Forward*—which has followed quickly after the *Collected Poems*—is a work of increased complexity, showing traces of new influences such as the American poet John Ashbery. The images and references come to the reader at an even faster pace, as if Porter believes that civilization in the nuclear age may be speeding to its own destruction. The history of our race is moving "fast-forward, / the tape so

stretched it might at any second / snap to oblivion." But the most moving poems here are another set of what are, in effect, elegies—for his wife, his father, and even for a beloved family animal: "Clipboard," "Venetian Incident," "Where We Came In," and "Dis Manibus." And in a notably vivid poem about Italy, "The Cats of Campagnatico," he experiences—rare for him—"a sudden vision of belonging." It is momentary only, among friends in an Italian landscape made beautiful by civilized use—

> between the fur of the cat
> And the cement of extinction, there are only
> Cypress moments lingering and the long tray of the sky.

But this transient experience seems imperishable in the assured eloquence of the poem.

—Alan Brownjohn

POULIN, A(lfred A.), Jr. American. Born in Lisbon, Maine, 14 March 1938. Educated at St. Francis College, Biddeford, Maine, B.A. 1960; Loyola University, Chicago, M.A. 1962; University of Iowa, Iowa City, M.F.A. 1968; State University of New York, Buffalo, 1975. Married Basilike H. Parkas in 1966; one daughter. Assistant Professor of English, 1962-64, 1968-71, and Chairman of the Division of Humanities, 1968-71, St. Francis College; Lecturer in English, University of Maryland European Division, Heidelberg, 1965, and University of New Hampshire, Durham, 1965-66. Since 1971, Member of the Department of English, Director of the Writer's Forum, 1972-75, and currently Professor and Faculty Exchange Scholar, State University of New York, Brockport. Visiting Fulbright Lecturer, universities of Athens and Thessaloniki, 1980. Since 1972, Editor at Large, *American Poetry Review*, Philadelphia; since 1976, Founding Editor, BOA Editions, Brockport, New York; since 1978, Founding Executive Director, New York State Literary Center, Rochester. Recipient: National Endowment for the Arts Fellowship, 1974, grant, 1982; Columbia University Translation Award, 1976. Address: 92 Park Avenue, Brockport, New York 14420, U.S.A.

PUBLICATIONS

Verse

In Advent. New York, Dutton, 1972.
Catawba: Omens, Prayers, and Songs. Port Townsend, Washington, Graywolf Press, 1977.
The Widow's Taboo: Poems after the Catawba. Tokyo, Mushinsha, 1977.
The Nameless Garden. Athens, Ohio, Croissant, 1978.
The Slaughter of Pigs. Athens, Ohio Review, 1981.
Makers and Lovers. Houston, Ford Brown, 1984.

Other

Editor, with David A. DeTurk, *The American Folk Scene: Dimensions of the Folksong Revival.* New York, Dell, 1967.
Editor, *Contemporary American Poetry.* Boston, Houghton Mifflin, 1971, 4th edition, 1985.

Editor, *A Ballet for the Ear: Interviews, Essays, and Reviews*, by
John Logan. Ann Arbor, University of Michigan Press,
1983.

Translator, *Duino Elegies and The Sonnets to Orpheus*, by
Rainer Maria Rilke. Boston, Houghton Mifflin, 1977.
Translator, *Saltimbanques: Prose Poems*, by Rainer Maria Rilke.
Port Townsend, Washington, Graywolf Press, 1978.
Translator, *The Roses and The Windows*, by Rainer Maria
Rilke. Port Townsend, Washington, Graywolf Press, 1979.
Translator, *Poems*, by Anne Hébert. Princeton, New Jersey,
Quarterly Review of Literature, 1980.
Translator, *The Astonishment of Origins*, by Rainer Maria Rilke.
Port Townsend, Washington, Graywolf Press, 1982.
Translator, *Orchards: A Sequence of French Poems*, by Rainer
Maria Rilke. Port Townsend, Washington, Graywolf Press,
1982.
Translator, *The Migration of Powers*, by Rainer Maria Rilke.
Port Townsend, Washington, Graywolf Press, 1985.

*

A. Poulin, Jr., comments:

Although I've become increasingly intent on incorporating
many of the more traditional qualities of poetry in my work—
urgency, passion, intensity and richness of language, variations
on formal and organic forms, music—I write from no predetermined or circumscribed aesthetic formula. Rather, I hope
that each successful poem will be its own incarnate statement of
poetics.

My subjects continue to shift from my French-Canadian,
Roman-Catholic experience as a child and adolescent in a small
rural town in Maine to my present diurnal experiences as a
mature lover, husband, father, artist, and intellectual. (For the
artist and intellectual, ideas are as tangible and sensual as sex,
lobster, and gin.) Whether dealing with reverie or with more
immediate existential reality, I work for ways to give my subjects
viable images of themselves that will redeem them, not only from
the indifferent deterioration of objective entropy but also from
the more pernicious deterioration of too common human desperation. I categorically deny the role of the poet as any kind of
priest or shaman. But, at a time when the work of some poets is
praised for being rooted in no recognizable reality, I hope my
poems will continue to be rooted in the most fundamental of
reality that can be recognized by readers who know and feel what
the quality and consequences of our remembered and daily lives
is and can be.

Meanwhile, I am long-convinced that translation is poetry's
natural sister-art—and not the poor, adopted step-sister it's still
considered to be in some circles. Only poets can translate poetry;
only poets know the extent to which the translation of poetry can
be as creatively rewarding as the writing of poetry. Given the
proper combination of craft and humility, at one level translation is a bid to be an original contribution to our native poetic
tradition. When successful, that's just what it is.

*   *   *

A. Poulin, Jr., is perhaps best known for his work editing
Contemporary American Poetry, as fine an anthology of its
subject as one will find. In an essay in that book Poulin states
that politics, sex, and religion are three of the major concerns to
which today's poets address themselves. As his own volumes of
poetry reveal, these are certainly the concerns of Poulin himself.

The American political scene of the Vietnam era produced
many protest poems, but, unfortunately, most of these were
written with too much topicality and too little art. But Poulin's
"Famine: 1970" is a poem that merits many rereadings, and it is a
work that will be relevant whenever any society at any time
becomes a moral wasteland:

> The cry of frogs rings the island, rings,
> bullets ricocheting off raw steel. Spring.
> Tonight the full moon rises pure, precise,
> and deadly cold. Everything will freeze.
>
> Trees petrify, their first and fragile
> leaves the clatter of slate chips. In
> the garden sharp white shoots are glowing
> bones of young men rising in revenge.
>
> Buds on bushes fall and shatter, empty
> eggs and skulls of a generation turned
> to salt. Our eyes turn and, marble, shine.
> Our hands and feet root into veins of lead.
>
> Our mouths already fill with sand.
> And beyond the moonlight, in the dark dawn
> will never break, we can hear the long and
> eager moan of boulders as they mate and spawn.

Like this poem, Poulin's other poetry is filled with fearful
forebodings. For example, in "Script Prospectus," addressed to
his wife, the poet says, "any / day some stranger, relative, or /
friend will kill me. Or you will." A paranoic fear of his own death
and the loss of loved ones stalks the poet throughout *In Advent*.
Fortunately, there are moments of happiness, as in the closing
section of the remarkable "Buddha and the Pirates," another
poem to the poet's wife, who he fears has been unfaithful:

> Morning sails into our bed-
> room, the splintered
> ghost of a Venetian ship.
> You aren't here. I find
> you in the sunlight
> of the alcove. Once more,
> across the ocean of my
> deepest nightmare, you've
> come back, our baby at your
> breast. Love, my Buddha,
> you are always here.

Love is, indeed, Poulin's Buddha. In his poetry love and
religion are inseparably united. In the poem "In Advent," for
instance, the birth of Poulin's baby is linked to the birth of
Christ. Poulin's poems find in the worship of loved ones a faith
that enables the poet to live in a savage world.

A very different world is found in *Catawba*, a thin volume in
which Poulin successfully recreates the voice of the Catawba
Indians. These poems awaken in us a reverence for a culture
based on the most elemental human values. In this volume we
listen to Indians pray to insects, teach simple virtues to their
children, prescribe folk remedies, and even retell moments of
creation, as in "Hummingbird": "the hummingbird was made by
a man / he took a dandelion turned to seed / he held it in his hand
and blew on it / yes and a hummingbird flew off / that man was
very smart." And so were the Catawba Indians, a tribe that
Poulin feels has much to teach us.

In his poems about the politics, sex, and religion of our day,
and in his poems about the customs and beliefs of a lost culture,
Poulin has sought clues to help him survive in this world. These
clues have in turn led to a continual process of self-discovery. As

Poulin says in "Totem," "I am arriving to myself." Though he is a poet fully aware of the worst horrors of our times, he is also a poet fully aware of our highest potentials. As such, A. Poulin, Jr., is one of the most hopeful poets currently at work.

—Dennis Lynch

POWELL, Craig. Australian. Born in Wollongong, New South Wales, 16 November 1940. Educated at Sydney Boys' High School; Sydney University, M.B., B.S. 1964; New South Wales Institute of Psychiatry, 1969-70; Toronto Institute of Psychoanalysis, 1977-81. Married Janet Dawson in 1965; one daughter and one son. Resident Medical Officer, Royal Prince Alfred Hospital, 1965, and Western Suburbs Hospital, Sydney, 1966; Psychiatrist, Parramatta Psychiatric Centre, Sydney, 1968-72, Brandon Mental Health Centre, Manitoba, 1972-75, and London Psychiatric Hospital, Ontario, 1976-82. Since 1983, Visiting Medical Officer, Westmead Hospital Department of Psychiatry, Sydney; also psychiatrist in private practice. Recipient: *Poetry Magazine* Award, 1964; Commonwealth Literary Fund grant, 1966, 1968, 1972; Henry Lawson Festival Award, 1969; Canada Council grant, 1977; Mattara Prize, 1983. Address: 24 Minga Street, Ryde, New South Wales 2112, Australia.

PUBLICATIONS

Verse

A Different Kind of Breathing. Sydney, South Head Press, 1966.
I Learn by Going. Sydney, South Head Press, 1968.
A Country Without Exiles. Sydney, South Head Press, 1972.
Selected Poems 1963-1977. London, Ontario, Killaly Press, 1977.
Rehearsal for Dancers. Winnipeg, Turnstone Press, 1978.
A Face in Your Hands. Sydney, South Head Press, 1984.

*

Manuscript Collection: Mitchell Library, Sydney.

Critical Studies: "Gauging Honesty, Engaging Voice" by William H. New, in *Poetry Australia 49* (Sydney), 1973; "The Freedom of a New Landscape" by David Heaton, in *Poetry Australia 73* (Sydney), 1980.

Craig Powell comments:
    I was a musician for many years before I began writing poetry. While my work is less formal than it used to be, the musical element remains crucial. My poems are written as a witness to the sustaining, and disdaining, inward spirit; and to the mortal human body which, if it cannot rise beyond its own existence, can at least fall slowly dancing.

*   *   *

Just as Melbourne University, in the late 1950's, produced a group of lively poets who forced readers to reconsider available currency, so Sydney University in the early 1960's produced three poets who were to epitomise the counter-claim of a revived Vitalist tradition. These were Geoffrey Lehmann, Les A. Mur-

ray, and Craig Powell. Of the three, Powell has been least concerned with expounding large scale Life Views. Indeed, his most characteristic verse has been confined within the limitations of the sonnet and the triolet forms.

As a medical practitioner, Craig Powell has openly expressed an admiration of the American poet-medico Merrill Moore, who was reputed to have filing cabinets of sonnets stored away. Powell has never achieved, however, the relaxed assurance of Merrill Moore. His work is essentially dramatic, a performance. For this reason, he is most successful in poems that deal with themes of violence or conflict. Undoubtedly his best work is in the group of hospital and psychiatric poems in his third volume, or in the openly rhetorical "In Memory of Hans Mueller," possibly one of the most effective poems written in Australia on the Vietnam theme. In poems of a personal or lyric tone, one senses an underlying discomfort, with the result that the gestures often fail to convince. Craig Powell is still a young and developing writer. His best work has an admirable vigour and punch—and a formal control—that promise considerable scope for growth and development.

—Thomas W. Shapcott

POWELL, Neil. British. Born in London, 11 February 1948. Educated at Sevenoaks School, Kent, 1959-66; University of Warwick, Coventry, 1966-71, B.A. in English and American literature 1969, M.Phil. in English 1975. Teacher of English, Kimbolton School, Huntingdon, 1971-74. Since 1974, Teacher of English, St. Christopher School, Letchworth, Hertfordshire. Recipient: Eric Gregory Award, 1969. Address: 18 Church Street, Baldock, Hertfordshire SG7 5AE, England.

PUBLICATIONS

Verse

At Little Gidding. Rushden, Northamptonshire, Sceptre Press, 1974.
Afternoon Dawn. Hitchin, Hertfordshire, Cellar Press, 1975.
Suffolk Poems. Hitchin, Hertfordshire, Mandeville Press, 1975.
Four Letters. Sundridge, Kent, Letter Press, 1976.
A Mandeville Troika, with Peter Scupham and George Szirtes. Hitchin, Hertfordshire, Mandeville Press, 1977.
At the Edge. Manchester, Carcanet, and Chester Springs, Pennsylvania, Dufour, 1977.
Out of Time. Hitchin, Hertfordshire, Mandeville Press, 1979.
A Season of Calm Weather. Manchester, Carcanet, 1982.

Other

A Commentary on Henry V. Petersfield, Hampshire, Studytapes, 1973.
Carpenters of Light: Some Contemporary British Poetry. Manchester, Carcanet, 1979; New York, Barnes and Noble, 1980.

*

Critical Study: "A Slight Angle" by the author, in *Critical Quarterly* (Manchester), Summer 1982.

Neil Powell comments:

Poetry is a craft on bad days, an art on rare good ones: I started writing poems (and gave up trying to write novels) because I liked making these things out of words—the things being sonnets or villanelles or anything which offered the challenge and discipline of form. I remain fascinated by the oddly liberating possibilities of formal poems, though I increasingly venture out towards more obvious poetic freedoms. Either because I like patient craftsmanship, or because I'm lazy, or because I enjoy writing prose too, my poetic output is unprolific: half-a-dozen poems a year, perhaps, though it can vary enormously. I'm not unduly depressed if I haven't written a poem for months nor unduly surprised if I suddenly write several in a week.

Poems are a mysterious way of pickling experience: I'm aware that my most personal pieces are likely to operate on at least two levels—one, allusive and encoded, addressed to the private reader; the other universalising without fully disclosing the poem's intimate origin. With luck, the two levels enrich each other. But many of my poems are—no less personally—about places: I've been called a "topographical poet," and I like the doubly down-to-earth implications of the phrase. For me, the sense of place is often the most potent way into the occasion of the poem; and one doesn't, after all, need to be a Martian to send postcards home.

*   *   *

Neil Powell's collection, *At the Edge*, carries as epigraph a verse by Donald Davie: "The purest hue, let only the light be sufficient / Turns colour"; the book itself is a conscious attempt to form a poetic in accordance with the precept. A firm admiration for the controlled force found in the work of Davie and Thom Gunn has led him to a consciousness that to write poetry is to exercise the intelligence, as well as the heart, and that the disciplines of a severe formalism are those most likely to prove fruitful:

> The poem's flow—the rock pools or the bends,
> Metre or syntax, shaping its slow progress—
>
> Becomes a formal fountain as we turn
> Our private art to public artifice.

The exact and exacting patterns, accurate rhyme-schemes, and clear stanzaic forms of the poems are deployed to hold up to the light episodes of time past and time present: inside these crystals the past and the present become each other, and their relationship is celebrated with a restrained, intelligent affection and a consciousness that ends and beginnings are artful mimics of each other:

> The years are misting over. I recall
> Something I didn't say a dream ago,
> Return abruptly to the reading class.
> The weeping condensation on a window
> Becomes the image of another day,
> A conversation in a different place
> Minutely glimpsed, and very far away.

In these handy-dandyings of personal time Powell makes an easy, rueful use of a conjuror's personal box of props: a golden world gathers its tarnish to the accompaniment of a bric-a-brac of talk, drink, jazz, and old sunlight. More subtle and striking deeper home come the meditations on time in collusion with place. The poems show a wariness of dramatic effects and grand gestures, at their happiest with the undemonstrative and hidden landscapes of East Anglia. The poet is freqently found in the role of eavesdropper, watcher, revenant, alert for the chance disclosure of some part of the secret compact which place and time have made: a compact itself under threat.

> Trespasser? Tenant? Neither will win, the sea insists,
>   in the vanished places—Dunwich, Walberswick—
> where lanes scrawl to the margin of a torn-off coastline
>   whose history is written by the tide.

Always beyond the local familiarities and the boundaries, the edges and lines formed by masons and poets, lie worlds evading circumscription. Some of Powell's most impressive poems move out towards enigmatic and uncharted areas of sea, dizzying weathers, oblivion. Roads lead endlessly and nightmarishly on

> Until "The North" proclaims a giant sign,
> As if the north were somewhere you could reach
> By following a disembodied line
> Which joins nowhere to nowhere, each to each,
>
> And work to home. Or will it merely end
> In featureless space, an orange void stretching
> On each side of the road, round the next bend,
> With distant amber lamps, the planets, gleaming?

The stance taken by the poet at this stage of his career is one of some ambivalence: the game is played neither at home nor away, but often in some temporary ground we may provisionally call either. Metaphor is used sparingly; Powell prefers an accurate and evocative use of detail held in place by an intellectual scaffolding. This can lead to a rather dry philosophical tone and a preponderance of abstraction in the weaker poems. His more recent work shows a relaxed and sparer style emerging, however, which promises to bring a suppler tension to his forms:

> I walk through the silent town. A breeze is blowing
> Snuffed-out candles from horse-chestnut trees,
> The unknown is on the air, and I am knowing
> Something I cannot recognise, unless
>
> It is a distant prospect of the future, showing
> All that is and all that will come to be,
> As blossoms of the past are going, going.

—Peter Scupham

PRINCE, F(rank) T(empleton). British. Born in Kimberley, Cape Province, South Africa, 13 September 1912. Educated at Christian Brothers' College, Kimberley; Balliol College, Oxford; Princeton University, New Jersey, 1935-36; Study Groups Department, Chatham House, 1937-40. Served in the Intelligence Corps, 1940-46. Married Pauline Elizabeth Bush in 1943; two children. Member of the English Department, from 1946, and Professor of English, 1957-74, University of Southampton. Visiting Fellow, All Souls College, Oxford, 1968-69; Clark Lecturer, Cambridge University, 1972-73; Professor of English, University of the West Indies, Jamaica, 1975-78; Visiting Professor / Writer, Brandeis University, Waltham, Massachusetts, 1978-80, Amherst College, Massachusetts, 1979, Washington University, St. Louis, 1980-81, Sana'a University, North Yemen,

1981-83, and Hollins College, Virginia, Spring 1984. Recipient: American Academy E.M. Forster Award, 1982. D.Litt.: University of Southampton, 1981; D.Univ.: University of York, 1982. Address: 32 Brookvale Road, Southampton, Hampshire S02 1QR, England.

PUBLICATIONS

Verse

Poems.   London, Faber, and New York, New Directions, 1938.
Soldiers Bathing and Other Poems.   London, Fortune Press, 1954.
The Stolen Heart.   San Francisco, Press of the Morning Sun, 1957.
The Doors of Stone: Poems 1938-1962.   London, Hart Davis, 1963.
Memoirs in Oxford.   London, Fulcrum Press, 1970.
Penguin Modern Poets 20, with John Heath-Stubbs and Stephen Spender.   London, Penguin, 1971.
Drypoints of the Hasidim.   London, Menard Press, 1975.
Afterword on Rupert Brooke.   London, Menard Press, 1976.
Collected Poems.   London, Anvil Press Poetry-Menard Press, and New York, Sheep Meadow Press, 1979.
The Yüan Chên Variations.   New York, Sheep Meadow Press, 1981.
Later On.   London, Anvil Press Poetry, 1983.

Other

The Italian Element in Milton's Verse.   Oxford, Clarendon Press, 1954.
In Defence of English (lecture).   Southampton, University of Southampton Press, 1959.
William Shakespeare: The Poems.   London, Longman, 1963.

Editor, *Samson Agonistes,* by Milton.   London, Oxford University Press, 1957.
Editor, *The Poems,* by Shakespeare.   London, Methuen, and Cambridge, Massachusetts, Harvard University Press, 1960.
Edior, *Paradise Lost, Books I and II,* by Milton.   London, Oxford University Press, 1962.
Editor, *Comus and Other Poems,* by Milton.   London, Oxford University Press, 1968.

Translator, *Sir Thomas Wyatt,* by Sergio Baldi.   London, Longman, 1961.

*

Critical Study: *F.T. Prince: A Study of His Poetry* by Alka Nigam, Salzburg, University of Salzburg, 1983.

*   *   *

For half a century, F.T. Prince has stood fast among the tides of fashion. His verse is leisurely, eloquent, syntactically elaborate. It suggests the spaciousness of a bygone age:

> A beautiful girl said something in your praise.
> And either because in a hundred ways
> I had heard of her great worth and had no doubt
> To find her lovelier than I thought
> And found her also cleverer....

"To a Friend on His Marriage" relates to modern classics such as the Yeats of "Her Praise" and "No Second Troy" and, more remotely, the Auden of "A Bride in the 30's." Prince's poem does not, however, merely derive from these. Rather, what we have here is a remarkable absorption of sources. That is to say, the eloquence of Prince is an achievement in its own right.

Though his mode may seem essentially that of the meditative lyric, Prince has turned it to account in several ambitious monologues. Leonardo da Vinci informs his patron

> You should understand that I have plotted,
> Being in command of all the ordinary engines
> Of defence and offence and fifteen buildings
> Less others less complete: complete, some are courts of
>   serene stone....

In a tone not dissimilar, Michelangelo surveys his old age; elegiacally, but with a certain detachment:

> And there is always
> Some victor and some vanquished, always the fierce
>   substance
> And the divine idea, a drunkenness
> Of high desire and thought, or a stern sadness....

This, in its turn, relates to the resigned stance imputed to Edmund Burke:

> in both worlds
> There is now this fistulous sore that runs
> Into a thousand sinuosities; and the wound now
> Opens the red west, gains new ground....

These voices have a family resemblance. They share a deliberated vocabulary and slowness of movement. The tone is essentially that of such meditative lyrics as "The Babiaantje," "The Question," and "To a Friend on His Marriage" itself. It would seem that the oeuvre of Prince adds up to a respectable contribution to modern literature by a scholar-poet.

However, this characterization of Prince is not complete. He has, as most academics have not, his classic. It is a poem that lives in the mind rather than in the study. "Soldiers Bathing" is one of the few great poems of the Second World War—the only one, perhaps, that could justly be said to stand beside the classics of the First World War. It is a remarkable fact that the techniques deployed in Prince's other poems do duty here: the slow-moving line, the distilled concept, the imagery refracted through recollection of great art. Yet the total effect is, unlike the Leonardo and Michelangelo poems, urgent and poignant:

> The sea at evening moves across the sand.
> Under a reddening sky I watch the freedom of a band
> Of soldiers who belong to me. Stripped bare
> For bathing in the sea, they shout and run in the warm
>   air;
> Their flesh worn by the trade of war, revives
> And my mind towards the meaning of it strives....

The plot is direct and moving. Soldiers stripped of the accoutrements of war show themselves thereby at once released and vulnerable. Such a datum need not come a poet's way once in a lifetime. The poem superbly combines story-line with archetype. Further, there is a highly characteristic vision here. We are aware of a detached persona considering all this: not Leonardo, not Michelangelo, but certainly someone not unlike Prince's presentation of those firgures—erudite, distanced, eloquent. The persona is a kind of ideal aesthete:

> Because to love is frightening we prefer
> The freedom of our crimes. Yet, as I drink the dusky air,
> I feel a strange delight that fills me full,
> Strange gratitude, as if evil itself were beautiful,
> And kiss the wound in thought, while in the west
> I watch a streak of red that might have issued from
>   Christ's breast.

F.T. Prince is unlikely to thank his critics for setting "Soldiers Bathing" far above the rest of his work, intelligent and informed though that work is. Notwithstanding, it will be the specialist who analyses "The Old Age of Michelangelo" and who will go on to peruse Prince's autumnal works: thoughtful studies of the communal life of the Hasidim, of Rupert Brooke at Cambridge, of the love life of Laurence Sterne. Those who are not aware of caring especially for poetry may, on the other hand, find that they know "Soldiers Bathing" off by heart.

—Philip Hobsbaum

PROKOSCH, Frederic. American. Born in Madison, Wisconsin, 17 May 1908. Educated at Haverford College, Pennsylvania, 1922-25, M.A. 1926; Yale University, New Haven, Connecticut, 1930-31, Ph.D. 1933; King's College, Cambridge, 1935-37, M.A. 1937. Instructor in English, Yale University, 1932-34, and New York University, 1936-37; Printer, of modern poetry, in Bryn Mawr, Pennsylvania, Cambridge, Florence, Venice, and Lisbon, 1933-40; Cultural Attaché, American Legation, Stockholm, 1943-45; Visiting Lecturer, University of Rome, 1950-51. Squash-Racquets Champion of France, 1933-39, and of Sweden, 1944. Recipient: Guggenheim Fellowship, 1937; Harper Prize, 1937; Harriet Monroe Memorial Prize (*Poetry*, Chicago), 1941; Fulbright Fellowship, 1951; National Endowment for the Arts grant, 1977; Prix Médicis, 1984. Address: "Ma Trouvaille," Plan de Grasse, Alpes Maritimes, France.

PUBLICATIONS

Verse

Three Mysteries. New Haven, Connecticut, privately printed, 1932.
Three Sorrows. New Haven, Connecticut, privately printed, 1932.
Three Deaths. New Haven, Connecticut, privately printed, 1932.
Three Images. New Haven, Connecticut, privately printed, 1932.
The Voyage. Bryn Mawr, Pennsylvania, privately printed, 1933.
The Dolls. Bryn Mawr, Pennsylvania, privately printed, 1933.
The Grotto. Bryn Mawr, Pennsylvania, privately printed, 1933.
The Enemies. Bryn Mawr, Pennsylvania, privately printed, 1933.
The Survivors. Bryn Mawr, Pennsylvania, privately printed, 1934.

Going Southward. Bryn Mawr, Pennsylvania, privately printed, 1935.
The Red Sea. Cambridge, privately printed, 1935.
Andromeda. Cambridge, privately printed, 1935.
The Assassins. Cambridge, privately printed, 1936.
The Assassins (collection). New York, Harper, and London, Chatto and Windus, 1936.
The Sacred Wood. Cambridge, privately printed, 1936.
The Carnival. New York, Harper, and London, Chatto and Windus, 1938.
Death at Sea. New York, Harper, and London, Chatto and Windus, 1940.
Sunburned Ulysses. Lisbon, privately printed, 1941.
Among the Caves. Lisbon, privately printed, 1941.
Song. New York, privately printed, 1941.
Song. Stockholm, privately printed, 1943.
Fable. New York, privately printed, 1944.
Chosen Poems. London, Chatto and Windus, 1944; New York, Doubleday, 1947.
The Flamingoes. Rome, privately printed, 1948.
Snow Song. Paris, privately printed, 1949.
Boat Song. Venice, privately printed, 1950.
Wood Song. Florence, privately printed, 1951.
Phantom Song. Naples, privately printed, 1952.
Banquet Song. Barcelona, privately printed, 1953.
Temple Song. Stuttgart, privately printed, 1954.
Fire Song. Zurich, privately printed, 1955.
Island Song. Hong Kong, privately printed, 1956.
Jungle Song. Bangkok, privately printed, 1957.
The Death Ship. Singapore, privately printed, 1958.
The Ghost City. Antwerp, privately printed, 1959.
The Mirror. Vienna, privately printed, 1960.

Novels

The Asiatics. New York, Harper, and London, Chatto and Windus, 1935.
The Seven Who Fled. New York, Harper, and London, Chatto and Wndus, 1937.
Night of the Poor. New York, Harper, and London, Chatto and Windus, 1939.
The Skies of Europe. Ne York, Harper, 1941; London, Chatto and Windus, 1942.
The Conspirators. New York, Harper, and London, Chatto and Windus, 1943.
Age of Thunder. New York, Harper, and London, Chatto and Windus, 1945.
The Idols of the Cave. New York, Doubleday, 1946; London, Chatto and Windus, 1947.
Storm and Echo. New York, Doubleday, 1948; London, Faber, 1949.
Nine Days to Mukalla. New York, Viking Press, and London, Secker and Warburg, 1953.
A Tale for Midnight. Boston, Little Brown, 1955; London, Secker and Warburg, 1956.
A Ballad of Love. New York, Farrar Straus, 1960; London, Secker and Warburg, 1961.
The Seven Sisters. New York, Farrar Straus, 1962; London, Secker and Warburg, 1963.
The Dark Dancer. New York, Farrar Straus, 1964; London, W.H. Allen, 1965.
The Wreck of the Cassandra. New York, Farrar Straus, and London, W.H. Allen, 1966.
The Missolonghi Manuscript. New York, Farrar Straus, and London, W.H. Allen, 1968.

America, My Wilderness.   New York, Farrar Straus, and London, W.H. Allen, 1971.

Other

Voices: A Memoir.   New York, Farrar Straus, and London, Faber, 1983.

Translator, *Some Poems of Friedrich Höolderlin.*   New York, New Directions, 1943; London, Grey Walls Press, 1947.
Translator, *Love Sonnets of Louise Labé.*   New York, New Directions, 1947; London, Grey Walls Press, 1948.
Translator, *The Medea of Euripides.*   New York, Dial Press, 1949.

*

Manuscript Collection: University of Texas, Austin.

Critical Study: *Frederic Prokosch* by Radcliffe Squires, New York, Twayne, 1964.

Frederic Prokosch comments:

(1974) A poet is ill-advised to make a "personal statement," i.e., a *credo.* He cannot possibly do justice to himself in this manner. It will sound stitled, coy pompous, irrelevant, even false. As I meditate on the question of why my poetry is totally unlike all other contemporary poetry, I feel puzzled; but I conclude that my conception of a poem is not the current one. To use a poem as a "confessional," a "protest," or a manifesto, a self-analysis or in any way as a self-indulgence, seems to me to abuse and degrade the true function of poetry. A poem should aim for the perfection, the timeless and impersonal "stillness" of a Chinese vase. I think of Yeats and Rilke; I think of Catullus, Goethe and Hölderlin. The present is not an age for poetry, needless to say. The timeless, impersonal stillness is drowned in an orgy of howls and moans, not to mention vituperations, indignations, and masturbations.

(1980) Still, I feel that there is a change in the air. Auden heralded the change, and it was also signaled by Dylan Thomas (though in both cases there was a sharp deterioration in their final phases). I mean this: that certain limits are eventually reached in the purely exploratory. Exploration per se is refreshing and liberating, to be sure, but it becomes a cul-de-sac if it isn't continually nourished by new passions, new experiences, new aperçus. It imposes in the end an artificial strain on the poet, the painter, the novelist. But I detect a new freshness creeping into the atmosphere, a liberation from dogma, a rejection of doctrine, and a subtler, more delicate spirit of affirmation.

*   *   *

Frederic Prokosch made his reputation with three volumes, *The Assassins, The Carnival,* and *The Death at Sea,* published just before or at the beginning of the second World War. His poetry impressed T.S. Eliot and Edwin Muir, and it shows the evidence of influences, particularly those of Eliot himself and Yeats, which it was impossible for any ripening talent to avoid at that period. His work has, however, an undoubted poetic individuality. In the first place it is elaborate, sumptuous, formal, musical, characteristically checking the usual long gliding line with a shorter, sharper turn. In the second, there is something of an older, a more traditional and European, manner in the poet's calm assumption of a public poem, in his treatment of the grand, impressive theme, in the formal clarity of his diction and his intricately rhyming patterns. Not that he isn't clearly, highly

sensitive to the strains of his own violent times. He is intensely moved by the combination in reality of style and disaster, by the blend, for example, in "The Country House" of platonic, shadowed lawns, cool airs, instinctive poise, and howling conflagration, or in "Molière" of the suppressed presence in an intricately spun civilisation, with its lucid laws of reason, its learning and perception, of Othello's howl and Dido's unforgettable cave. He is much preoccupied with Yeats's rough beast, and he is conscious beneath the mask of civilisation of the hooked, retaliating nightmare and the horrible disorderly whirlpool. The particular attractiveness of the poetry comes from its joining a cool and cultivated surface to a nightmare vision of inward and inevitable fatality. In Frederic Prokosch's reading of life, the clipped and ordered park, the salon, the formal avenue he so much appreciates and so finely evokes, are "rosy with the approaching glow and spectacle of Hell."

—William Walsh

———————

PRYNNE, J(eremy) H(alward).   British.   Born in England, 24 June 1936. University Lecturer in English, and Librarian, Gonville and Caius College, Cambridge. Address: Gonville and Caius College, Cambridge CB2 1TA, England.

Publications

Verse

Force of Circumstance and Other Poems.   London, Routledge, 1962.
Kitchen Poems.   London, Cape Goliard Press, and New York, Grossman, 1968.
Day Light Songs.   Pampisford, Cambridgeshire, R. Books, 1968.
Aristeas.   London, Ferry Press, 1968.
The White Stones.   Lincoln, Grosseteste Press, 1969.
Fire Lizard.   Barnet, Hertfordshire, Blacksuede Boot Press, 1970.
Brass.   London, Ferry Press, 1971.
Into the Day.   Privately printed, 1972.
A Night Square.   London, Albion Village Press, 1973.
Wound Response.   Cambridge, Street Editions, 1974.
High Pink on Chrome.   Privately printed, 1975.
News of Warring Clans.   London, Trigram Press, 1977.
Down Where Changed.   London, Ferry Press, 1979.
Poems.   Edinburgh, Agneau 2, 1982.
The Oval Window.   Privately printed, 1983.

*   *   *

Apart from his first and—as it were—apprentice collection, *Force of Circumstance,* J.H. Prynne's poetry has subsequently maintained an utterly singular development, paying no regard whatsoever to the recognized currency of contemporary English verse. This singularity is created and sustained through an intense but usually indirect reference to entire ranges of previous literatures and the writing of other cultures—American, European, Middle and even Far Eastern. Prynne's poetry is to a high degree intellectually complex, and it has consistently made minimum concessions to the reader's conventional expectations. A continuous effect encountered in the close reading of his texts is the experience of being thrown back upon all of one's interpretative resources, and often enough of being chastened by the limitations of one's knowledge. In this way the reader finds that s/he has to construct a meaning which can only be fragmentary, and beyond this a beguiling lure remains, indicating that there is much more still to be known, in terms of the formal beauty and the ethical purchase which the lines offer and withdraw. This is to say that Prynne's poetry requires its reader continuously to consider how any meaning is derived at any point during the process of interpretation, and further, that whatever meaning is temporarily entertained, be then subject to rigorous question. To read Prynne is to undergo an education.

How do we actually keep up with our dangerous and complex times? How does anyone avoid giving up the relentless effort of understanding, so as not to collapse into resentment or some hopeless form of nostalgia for a safely distant past? A good deal of contemporary poetry might be said to be broken in these ways, in that it is not of the moment, but is archaic or even (terrible fate) old fashioned; Prynne's writing, however, can be considered within the terms of many utterly pressing, absolutely current debates. References to economic pressure or to arguments within the life sciences are intrinsic to many of his poems, and the central strategy of putting into question the nature of our meanings is itself a procedure which has a good deal in common with the more interesting forms of "deconstruction," so called. His poems examine the economic structures of need, and the place which human values such as trust, hope, or the experience of damage may occupy within them; again, these concerns have real parallels within Marxist debates. His strategic use of such specialized vocabularies, more usually thought of as exclusively "scientific," attempts to propose an ethical regimen from the complexities of what are conventionally taken to be technical knowledges.

Prynne's poems are not *only* severe; their intransigence often rises to effects of sharp beauty, a kind of cool aesthetic which draws on imagery of ice, tundra, human extremity, and (to steal an adjective, itself beautiful, from *Into the Day*) "madrigalian" formal perfection. The angular, austere delights of these poems are themselves a virtue; but it is exactly this concentration upon what is crystalline which creates the faceted resources of the texts' meanings.

From where may a view be taken, from which point may all the information be totalized, in the system of our society where all the systems interpenetrate to a degree which is virtually physiological, as complex as a body? Do we *need* a view from which to take proper heed of all the variables? What would such a vantage be, when we are implicated by way of terror, harm, disgust, and even joy, with all the operations of this infinitely complex world, where no one language can hope to cover all options, but each language is pervaded by the values of the others? From *The Oval Window*:

> Think now
> or pay now and think later, the levels
> of control nesting presume a reason
> to cut back only and keep mum.

In Prynne's poetry large-scale economic movements and closely detailed aspects of medical physiology are read into one another, so that the subject—our self— is caught within the defining structures of social force, and biological necessity; between these parameters the conduct of our ethical and emotional lives (themselves mutually implicated) is explored:

> So: from now on too, or soon lost,

the voice you hear is your own
revoked, on a relative cyclical downturn
imaged in latent narrow-angle glaucoma.

By virtue of this plangent scope, the poem may again have become the most conscious point of its time, and this won't by any means make it the most restful locus.

—Nigel Wheale

PRYS-JONES, A(rthur) G(lyn). British (Welsh). Born in Denbigh, North Wales, 7 March 1888. Educated at Llandovery College, Carmarthenshire; Jesus College, Oxford (History Scholar), B.A. (honours) 1912, M.A. 1912. Married Elizabeth Jane Gibbon (died, 1976); two children. Grammar school teacher in Macclesfield and Walsall; Assistant Master, Dulwich College, London, 1916-19; Inspector of Schools, Wales; Staff Inspector, Secondary Education, Wales, 1919-49. Secretary, Welsh Committee, Festival of Britain, 1950-52; Co-Founder and former Chairman, Cardiff Little Theatre; former Chairman, Cardiff Literary Society. Currently, Vice-President, Cardiff Writers Circle; President, English Section, Welsh Academy. O.B.E. (Officer, Order of the British Empire), 1949. Addess: 50 Coombe Lane West, Kingston-upon-Thames, Surrey KT2 7BY, England.

PUBLICATIONS

Verse

Poems of Wales. Oxford, Blackwell, 1923.
Green Places: Poems of Wales. Aberystwyth, Gwasg Aberystwyth, 1948.
A Little Nonsense. Cowbridge, Glamorgan, Eastgate Press, 1954.
High Heritage: Poems of Wales. Llandybie, Dyfed, Christopher Davies, 1969.
Valedictory Verses. Llandysul, Dyfed, Gomer, 1978.

Other

Gerald of Wales: His "Itinerary" Through Wales and His "Description" of the Country and Its People. London, Harrap, 1955.
The Story of Carmarthenshire. Llandybie, Dyfed, Christopher Davies, 2 vols., 1959-72.

Editor, *Welsh Poets: A Representative Selection in English from Contemporary Writers.* London, Erskine Macdonald, 1917.
Co-Editor, *They Look at Wales.* Cardiff, University of Wales Press, 1946.
Editor, *The Fountain of Life: Prose and Verse from the Authorized Version of the Bible.* London, Pan Books, 1949; Boston, Beacon Press, 1950.
Co-Editor, *The National Songs of Wales.* London, Boosey and Hawkes, 1959.

*

A. G. Prys-Jones comments:
(1970) My themes are almost entirely concerned with the past

history, traditions, personalities and scenery of Wales: and my approach is essentially simple, lyrical and romantic. I aim at making my poems pass the test of being read or declaimed aloud, and thus suitable for individual or choral speech. A number have been set to music and published as songs. If I have succeeded at all, it is in this direction, and also in having interpreted the past of Wales, more especially for its young people. In my writing I often use some of the simpler metrical and alliterative devices of Welsh poetry.

*   *   *

Most of the veteran A. G. Prys-Jones's poems in his volume *High Heritage* (1969) appeared in *Poems of Wales* (1923) and *Green Places* (1948). He himself has modestly suggested that *High Heritage* is intended as an anthology of verse-speaking in schools, and certainly it is a book eminently suitable for this purpose. He has brought into modern English verse something of the visual imagery shaped by his native Welsh tongue. Technically adept, he has a very delicate sense of rhythm, as shown in "Spring Comes to Glamorgan," and a refined gift for the original image:

> And how the ragged mendicants of mist
> In shifty garb rise up from stealthy lairs
> Thrusting their shapeless hands about your face.

Prys-Jones's style is unfashionable nowadays, but he manages to project the Georgian manner into the turbulent present or past, maintaining a regular rhyme-scheme and a firm stanza-structure. Thus, his well-known, rollicking "Henry Morgan's March on Panama":

> Twelve hundred famished buccaneers,
> Bitten, blistered and bled,
> A sweltering mob, accursed and flayed
> By the fierce sun overhead:
> Twelve hundred starving scarecrows
> With hardly a crust to eat,
> And only sips from festering pools
> In that grim, monstrous heat.

This has been called "Chestertonian heroic verse in the style of the twenties," and such a strict structure does tend to limit the intention that certain poems are supposed to fulfil. Soaked in history, most of his work involves celebration or nostalgia, reflecting the formal Georgian mode, which could be so exquisite and yet so fustian. He has no time for jagged irregularity, being interested only in building and holding a consistent form. In this he has long reached a mastery, and it is a pity that the stock phrases of "modern" criticism are not equipped to cope with skilled structures like Prys-Jones's even if his content now appears to be somewhat obsolete. He has a high command of language, splendidly shaped, and many moments of rare beauty which could make a welcome return in our own gloomy time— such as this musical glimpse of a historic Wales: "The tides of evening pass, deep-drenched with rose / And all the perfumes of the summer night."

—John Tripp

———————

PURCELL, Sally (Anne Jane).   British.   Born 1 December 1944. Educated at Lady Margaret Hall, Oxford (Countess of Warwick prize, 1965), B.A. 1966, M.A. 1970. Recipient: Arts Council award, 1971. Address: c/o Anvil Press Poetry, 69 King George Street, London SE10 8PX, England.

PUBLICATIONS

Verse

The Devil's Dancing Hour.   London, Anvil Press Poetry, 1968.
The Holly Queen.   London, Anvil Poetry Press, 1972.
(Poems).   Berkhamsted, Hertfordshire, Priapus, 1976.
Dark of Day.   London, Anvil Press Poetry, 1977.
By the Clear Fountain.   Bath, Mammon Press, 1980.

Other

Editor, with Libby Purves, *The Happy Unicorns: The Poetry of the Under-25's.*   London, Sidgwick and Jackson, 1971.
Editor, *George Peele.*   Oxford, Carcanet, 1972.
Editor and Translator, *Monarchs and the Muse: Poems by Monarchs and Princes of England, Scotland, and Wales.*   Oxford, Carcanet, 1972.
Editor, *The Poems of Charles of Orleans.*   Cheadle, Cheshire, Carcanet, 1973.
Editor, *The Early Italian Poets,* translated by D.G. Rossetti. London, Anvil Press Poetry, and Berkeley, University of California Press, 1981.

Translator, *Provençal Poems.*   Oxford, Carcanet, 1969.
Translator, *The Exile of James Joyce,* by Hélène Cixous.   New York, David Lewis, 1972; London, Calder, 1976.
Translator, *Amorgos,* by Nikos Gatsos.   Hay-on-Wye, Powys, Other Poetry Editions, 1980.
Translator, *Literature in the Vernacular,* by Dante.   Manchester, Carcanet, 1981.

*

Sally Purcell comments:
I was brought up as a classicist, and I believe in courtesy, craftsmanship and honesty.

*   *   *

Sally Purcell read Medieval French at Lady Margaret Hall, Oxford, and she has published a volume of translations from the troubadour poetry of Provence. Her researches and studies clearly coloured her early poetry both in its content and texture. Many of these poems, in the form of dramatic lyrics, explored the mysteries and characters of classical and medieval legends. Their very titles were indicative of their nature: "Bale Fires on the Dark Moor," "Loquitur Arthurus," "Tarot XII." The settings too, were in keeping: misty shires, a drowned winter world, a petrified chalcedony forest or a ring of standing stones. What gave these poems their special quality was Sally Purcell's imaginative insight into that twilight world of superstition, replete with "prodigies and signs of doom" and especially her ability to pinpoint the accompanying physical sensations of such a world:

> Queen Proserpina walks
> through late autumn:
> the glowing fruits of ice
> that she holds

covers the dying sun, & chills
all ripeness to the bone

The best way to describe the texture of the verse is as that of an intellectual sensuality where the precise syntax both knits the poems together and leads the reader into them, while the involvement of the physical senses creates the necessary suspension of disbelief. Thus in "Baroque Episode" Sally Purcell is able to engage the reader in an imagined world where,

Mingling blood for love's token
He hopes to symbolise affection's depth
Achieve the untenable equation
That added selves make one.

It is a world where self-delusion is rife, and in "Oxford, Early Michaelmas Term" she draws a modern parallel where "hypnotised by hearsay, by skilful propaganda—the aesthetes flower gently."

In her more recent poetry Sally Purcell has used these skills to invest landscapes and places with a curiously threatening purpose, as if each embodied their own myths, giving them a past and a future existing collaterally, a sense of unreleased powers locked in stone or hill:

Castellan of a strong headland, forever
Build, renew defences out of silt and rock
Against the shifting meadows of olive or turquoise light;
Here only detail and haste are known—
Further out, the historian or another sees
In Time the laborious perfect.

All the time there smoulders in the background a dark sensuality waiting to entrap the unwary and the pretentious:

the muse medusa caresses her body,
glories in her flesh firmness,
smiles at the promises they assume
who believe in her advances.

It is a poetry of forebodings and warnings, as much against its own tenebrous embraces as any other.

—John Cotton

PURDY, Al(fred Wellington). Canadian. Born in Wooller, Ontario, 30 December 1918. Educated at Dufferin Public School, Trenton, Ontario; Albert College, Belleville, Ontario; Trenton Collegiate Institute, Ontario. Served in the Royal Canadian Air Force during World War II. Married Eurithe Parkhurst in 1941; one son. Has held numerous jobs; taught at Simon Fraser University, Burnaby, British Columbia, Spring 1970; Poet-in-Residence, Loyola College, Montreal, 1973, University of Manitoba, Winnipeg, 1975-76, and University of Western Ontario, London, 1977-78. Recipient: Canada Council Fellowship, 1960, 1965, 1968, 1971, award, 1973, and grant, 1974, 1977; President's Medal, University of Western Ontario, 1964; Governor-General's Award, 1966; A.J.M. Smith Prize, 1974; Jubilee Medal, 1978. Address: Rural Route 1, Ameliasburgh, Ontario K0K 1A0, Canada.

PUBLICATIONS

Verse

The Enchanted Echo. Vancouver, Clarke and Stuart, 1944.
Pressed on Sand. Toronto, Ryerson Press, 1955.
Emu, Remember! Fredericton, University of New Brunswick, 1956.
The Crafte So Longe to Lerne. Toronto, Ryerson Press, 1959.
Poems for All the Annettes. Toronto, Contact Press, 1962.
The Old Woman and the Mayflowers. Ottawa, Blue R, 1962.
The Blur in Between: Poems 1960-61. Toronto, Emblem, 1962.
The Cariboo Horses. Toronto, McClelland and Stewart, 1965.
North of Summer: Poems from Baffin Land. Toronto, McClelland and Stewart, 1967.
Poems for All the Annettes (selected poems). Toronto, Anansi, 1968.
Wild Grape Wine. Toronto, McClelland and Stewart, 1968.
Spring Song. Fredericton, New Brunswick, Fiddlehead, 1968.
The Winemaker's Beat-étude. Willowdale, Ontario, Fiddlehead, 1968.
Interruption. Willowdale, Ontario, Fiddlehead, n.d.
Love in a Burning Building. Toronto, McClelland and Stewart, 1970.
Five Modern Canadian Poets, with others, edited by Eli Mandel. Toronto, Holt Rinehart, 1970.
The Quest for Ouzo. Trenton, Ontario, M. Kerrigan Almey, 1970.
Selected Poems. Toronto, McClelland and Stewart, 1972.
Hiroshima Poems. Trumansburg, New York, Crossing Press, 1972.
On the Bearpaw Sea. Burnaby, British Columbia, Blackfish Press, 1972.
Sex and Death. Toronto, McClelland and Stewart, 1973.
Scott Hutcheson's Boat. Prince George, British Columbia, Caledonia, 1973.
In Search of Owen Roblin. Toronto, McClelland and Stewart, 1974.
Sundance at Dusk. Toronto, McClelland and Stewart, 1976.
The Poems of Al Purdy. Toronto, McClelland and Stewart, 1976.
At Marsport Drugstore. Sutton West, Ontario, Paget Press, 1977.
A Handful of Earth. Coatsworth, Ontario, Black Moss Press, 1977.
No Second Spring. Coatsworth, Ontario, Black Moss Press, 1977.
Moths in the Iron Curtain. Cleveland, Black Rabbit, 1977.
Being Alive: Poems 1958-78. Toronto, McClelland and Stewart, 1978.
The Stone Bird. Toronto, McClelland and Stewart, 1981.
Piling Blood. Toronto, McClelland and Stewart, 1984.

Recording: *Al Purdy,* Ontario Institute for Studies in Education, 1971.

Other

No Other Country. Toronto, McClelland and Stewart, 1977.

Editor, *The New Romans: Candid Canadian Opinions of the United States.* Edmonton, Alberta, Hurtig, and New York, St. Martin's Press, 1968.
Editor, *Fifteen Winds: A Selection of Modern Canadian Poems.* Toronto, Ryerson Press, 1969.

Editor, *I've Tasted My Blood: Poems 1956-1968*, by Milton
  Acorn.   Toronto, Ryerson Press, 1969.
Editor, *Storm Warning: The New Canadian Poets*.   Toronto,
  McClelland and Stewart, 1971; *Storm Warning 2*, 1976.
Editor, *Wood Mountain Poems*, by Andrew Suknaski.   To-
  ronto, Macmillan, 1976.
Editor, *Into a Blue Morning: Poems Selected and New 1968-
  1981*, by C.H. Gervais.   Toronto, Hounslow Press, 1982.

*

Bibliography: by Marianne Micros, in *The Annotated Bibliography of Canada's Major Authors 2*, edited by Robert Lecker
and Jack David, Downsview, Ontario, ECW Press, 1980.

Manuscript Collections: University of Saskatoon; Queen's University, Kingston, Ontario.

Critical Studies: "In the Raw: The Poetry of A.W. Purdy" by
Peter Stevens, in *Canadian Literature* (Vancouver), Spring 1966;
interview with Gary Geddes, in *Canadian Literature* (Vancouver), 1969; *Al Purdy* by George Bowering, Toronto, Copp
Clark, 1970; *Harsh and Lovely Land* by Tom Marshall, Vancouver, University of British Columbia Press, 1979.

Al Purdy comments:

(1970) Themes? Sex and death (which last naturally includes life). Subjects? Anything that appeals to me. Form? Pretty irregular, but generally with rhythm running somewhere, sometimes off rhymes and assonance. Influences? Very many, including the usual big names (Pound, Eliot, Yeats); also César Vallejo, Neruda, Superveille, Charles Bukowski, Robinson Jeffers, etc., etc. Style? I have some strong prejudices against schools of any kind, including most particularly the Creeley-Olson Black Mountain bunch and their imitators. I do not dismiss these people and believe it is possible to learn much from them, but only IF one remains oneself, something most of them apparently find difficult. I believe that when a poet fixes on one style or method he severely limits his present and future development. By the same token I dislike the traditional forms. But I use rhyme, metre and (occasionally) standard forms when a poem seems to call for it. Rules tend to be exclusive of anything outside their own strictures: I think most traditional poets would agree with this, but go right on using traditional metre and rhymes—poets like prime ministers are all against war and on the side of truth and justice.

Perhaps I should say that: I began to write nearly 40 years ago, influenced at that time by people whom I don't appreciate very much now. For instance, I like some of G.K. Chesterton's poems, and his influence no doubt remains with me but is, I think, difficult to discern in what I write today. At one time iambic metrics were so deeply implanted in my mind that it took me years of not-trying to break out of iambics to finally break out of iambics. I suppose other people's styles were apparent in my stuff until publication of *Poems for All the Annettes* in '62, and this book (and *Blur in Between*, also published '62 but earlier poems than *Annettes*) is the transitional period between what I was and am and change into. I have a fixation about change, which can also be regarded as a self-conscious weakness as well as a strength. And yet I wrote a poem in Athens, Greece, in January, 1969 ("The Time of Your Life"), which is probably the best I've ever written: at least I think so now.

*   *   *

Al Purdy is one of the most prolific of Canadian poets, with more than 20 books to his credit, and also one of the most consistently interesting. He has been publishing poetry for a generation and writing it longer. Yet, though his first volume, *The Enchanted Echo*, appeared in 1944, it was only during the mid-1960's, already well into middle age, that he emerged as one of Canada's leading poets, vigorous in statement, energetic in travelling the land to read his poetry and travelling the world to gather experience. He is a writer "for whom the visible world exists" palpably and directly, and the impressions gathered in travel have always played a recognizable role in shaping both the content and the mood of a great deal of his poetry. But the heart of Purdy's world, the place which gave its name to so many of his poems and appears as the symbolic omphalos of his imaginative world, is Roblin Lake where he lives, near Ameliasburgh in the heart of Loyalist Ontario, whose traditions, transmitted in the lives of his farmer forebears, have stirred the emotions inspiring many of his best poems, such as "My Grandfather's Country":

But the hill-red has no such violence of endings
the woods are alive
and gentle as well as cruel
unlike sand and sea
and if I must give my heart to anything
it will be here in the red glow
where failed farms sink back into earth
the clearings join and fences no longer divide
where the running animals gather their bodies together
and pour themselves upward
into the tips of falling leaves
with mindless faith that presumes a future.

Purdy's lack of an academic background, unusual in the Canadian literary world, has been an advantage to him in many ways, leading him to wander far and freely, to work at many callings and to bring to his writing a wide down-to-earth experience. On the technical side it has liberated him from formal disciplines and has enabled him to work at his own pace, apart from the literary fashions that sweep North American campuses, and taking what he wanted where he wanted, from Williams, from Auden and Thomas, from Pratt and Birney and Layton; by such means he has progressed from the traditional lyricism of *The Enchanted Echo* to the open forms and personal voice of mid-period books like *The Cariboo Horses* and *Wild Grape Wine* and of recent books like *The Stone Bird* and *Piling Blood*. What has struck one about Purdy's verse since the later 1950's is its intense oral impact. It is free verse in the truest form: fluent, untrammeled by conventions, yet possessing rhythmic and grammatical forms that distinguish it from statement in prose.

Purdy's verse is always near to experience; the poem emerges from life and the concept from the poem. Pieces about his wanderings in Canada, like those in *Cariboo Horses*, or abroad, like those in *Hiroshima Poems*, often seem to have served Purdy as a journal, so close is the interval between conception and creation, so immediate the response to experience. This does at times lead to unevenness in tone and quality, which Purdy controls to an extent by weeding out much of a voluminous production.

The Crafte So Longe to Lerne is the volume in which Purdy's special character as a poet first detaches itself from his original derivativeness, in the opening of forms and in the thematic evolution of a type of poetry that is really a philosophic continuum where the here-and-now, immediately perceived, becomes the Blakean grain wherein, if not the world, at least universal values are reflected. Purdy himself regards a later volume, *For All the Annettes*, as the point where "other people's styles" ceased to be apparent in his work. Certainly by the time he won the Governor-General's Award with *Cariboo Horses*, he was writing at the top of his individual form, having developed a long-lined and colloquially free manner, as well as an ability to be intellectually direct without sacrificing the suggestive dimensions of poetic imagery. Purdy has drawn freely on the funds of miscellaneous knowledge that a generalizing and autodidactic mind accumulates; yet, though densely allusive, he is never obscure. Often his poems show a remarkable ability to bring images drawn from great sweeps of time and space into a meaningful relationship with what he sees before him in the everyday contemporary setting. A fine example is "In the Caves," the concluding poem of *Being Alive*. Purdy imagines the creative passion of a palaeolithic artist and by implication relates it to the poet's modern agony:

> And I do not know why
> whether because I cannot hunt with the others
> and they laugh
> or because the things I have done are useless
> as I may be useless
> but there is something I must follow
> into myself to find
> outside myself in the mammoth
> beyond the scorn of my people
> who are still my people
> my own pain and theirs
> joining the shriek that does not end
> that is inside me now

Such poetry traps with an extraordinary appearance of spontaneity the roving speculations of a highly original mind.

Being Alive includes most of Purdy's best poems up to the late 1970's and perhaps shows his work in its greatest variety. Yet there are a strength and a technical mastery in his two recent volumes, *The Stone Bird* and *Piling Blood*, that place him securely among the major Canadian poets. Thematically, these books do not mark a radical change; Purdy is still fascinated with human character and human destiny, still writing with humour and compassion. But it is with a power and even a radiance of peculiar intensity that he now projects a haunting message of the rejuvenative power of the natural world and of the strange glory of that petty creature, man:

> Look down on me
> spirit of everyplace
> guardian beyond the edge of chaos
> I may be a slight reminder
> of a small tribe that occurred to you
> when you were thinking of something else
> even tho I am of little importance
> and conversely of great importance
> I am waiting here
> until the dark velvet curtains
> are drawn and the scrap of darkness
> I clutched in one hand
> has changed to light

—George Woodcock

PYBUS, Rodney. British. Born in Newcastle upon Tyne, Northumberland, 5 June 1938. Educated at Rossall School, Lancashire, 1951-56; Gonville and Caius College, Cambridge (exhibitioner), 1957-60, B.A. 1960, M.A. 1965. Married Ella Johnson, in 1961; two sons. Teacher, Aiglon College, Switzerland, 1960-61, and Firfield Road Boys School, Newcastle, 1961-62; journalist, Newcastle *Journal*, 1962-64; writer and producer, Tyne Tees Television, Newcastle, 1964-76; Tutor in the Adult Education Poetry Workshop, University of Newcastle, 1974-76; Lecturer in English, Macquarie University, Sydney, 1976-79; Literature Officer, Northern Arts, Cumbria, 1979-81; Tutor, University of Liverpool Department of Extension Studies, 1981-82. Since 1982, full-time writer. Australian Poetry Editor, *Stand*, Newcastle, 1976-78. Recipient: Alice Hunt Bartlett Prize, 1973; Arts Council Fellowship, 1982. Address: 21 Plough Lane, Sudbury, Suffolk CO10 6AU, England.

PUBLICATIONS

Verse

In Memoriam Milena. London, Chatto and Windus, 1973.
Bridging Loans and Other Poems. London, Chatto and Windus, 1976.
At the Stone Junction. Newcastle upon Tyne, Northern House, 1978.
The Loveless Letters. London, Chatto and Windus, 1981.
Wall, with others, edited by Noel Connor. Brampton, Cumbria, LYC Press, 1981.
Talitha Cumi, with David Constantine. Newcastle upon Tyne, Bloodaxe, 1983.

Other

Editor, with William Scammell, *Adam's Dream: Poems from Cumbria and Lakeland*. Ambleside, Cumbria Literature, 1981.

*

Manuscript Collection: Literary and Philosophical Library, Newcastle upon Tyne.

Rodney Pybus comments:

Different historical periods and characters often give me a means of focussing on the present: through such "impersonations" I have tried to dramatise and deepen the resonance of my writing. The figures I use have all lived at times of great social upheaval. What they salvaged they did by a combination of intelligence and scepticism, and I have tried to express my debt to such exemplary humans. Obviously I do not see the use of a historical perspective as an evasion of the stresses and pressures of the present. I hope some of my concern for the relationship between language and moral, emotional, and political matters can be discerned in the language of my poems: the word and the world are inextricable. Another preoccupation is the exploration of places both urban and rural, mainly in the North-East of England where my roots lie deepest, but also, more recently, in Australia—self-exploration of a kind, and all varieties of location and dislocation.

I prefer compression to expansiveness, craft to *faux-naif* spontaneity, the "cooked" to the "raw." I think I have learned more about possibilities of poetry in the second half of the 20th century from European and British poets than American. I believe that a poet's concern for and use of language have never been more important then they are now, in the great age of double-think, new-speak, talk-back, and audio-visual hocus pocus. I try to make the words I write communicate something of that belief; sometimes, I think, they do.

*   *   *

Many of the most successful of Rodney Pybus's poems are those which confront the extremes of contrast between the world of possibilities and the horror man has made of it: "Strange to think/The same language, the same letters/written by Hitler and Heine." This he manages via historical personae, sometimes ancient: Petronius or Procopius; sometimes more recent: Milena Jesenská, the friend of Kafka, or Yevgeny Zamyatin. The parallels between Nero's Rome and Hitler's Germany are telling, and the way of coping with them, enduring them, are similar. The adoption of either a carapace of stoicism or an urbane disdain is nevertheless vulnerable for sooner or later life's acid will dissolve it or the jack boot smash it. Yet the spirit, manifest in an often oblique dignity, remains untouched: "I am the conscience that runs out."

This is not a cry of despair, but a restatement of human dignity in its refusal to flinch from the truth. The language, too, especially in those poems set in ancient Rome or Constantinople, underlines this. The modern colloquialisms not only bring the situations into relation with the twentieth century, but are an expression of the sardonic intelligence which protects the mind from the horrors it encounters:

> I despair, Caius, I despair!
> Everything is in the hands
> of that trigger-happy
> paranoid lecher—
> except me, thank heaven!

The poems in which the subject is external nature: "Foxes," "Stoop," "Greenfinch" are sharply observed and often hold the reader by means of startling images ("Greenfinch"):

>   Wound-up
> by hunger or habit, it jerks
> its food out in a parody
> of famine—broad bill
> bashing into nuts,
> then filching slivers
> between the strings
> as if they sizzled—
>
> cocking its head
> like that of a tiny
> galvanised parrot.

The violence of "bashing," "sizzled," "galvanised," forces the reader's attention. But good as they are, these poems have the air of exercises in that others have treated these subjects, and as well, before. It is when Rodney Pybus explores the emotional world of the survival of individual values in a situation where such values have collapsed, or achieves an empathy with the exceptional, as in his poem on Samuel Palmer, "Summer's Lease," that he is his own man and writes poems that only he could have written.

—John Cotton

RAINE, Craig (Anthony).   British.   Born in Bishop Auckland, County Durham, 3 December 1944. Educated at Barnard Castle School; Exeter College, Oxford, 1963-68, B.A. in English 1966, B. Phil. 1968. Married Ann Pasternak Slater in 1972; one daughter and one son. Lecturer, Exeter College, 1971-72, Lincoln College, 1974-75, and Christ Church, 1976-79, Oxford. Since 1981, Poetry Editor, Faber and Faber, London. Books Editor, *New Review*, London 1977-78; Editor, *Quarto*, London, 1979-80; Poetry Editor, *New Statesman*, London, 1981. Recipient: Cheltenham Literary Festival Prize, 1977, 1978; Prudence Farmer Award, 1978; Cholmondeley Award, 1983. Address: c/o Faber and Faber, 3 Queen Square, London WC1N 3AU, England.

PUBLICATIONS

Verse

The Onion, Memory.   London, Oxford University Press, 1978.
A Martian Sends a Postcard Home.   London, Oxford University Press, 1979.
A Journey to Greece.   Oxford, Sycamore Press, 1979.
A Free Translation.   Edinburgh, Salamander Press, 1981.
Rich.   London, Faber, 1984.

Play

Radio Documentary: *James Joyce: A Touch of the Artist*, 1982.

*   *   *

Craig Raine, who is usually considered the leading light in a group of poets who have come to be known collectively, after the title of Raine's second book, as the "Martians," is an immensely *clever* poet. His poems have always been exciting verbal performances, elaborate structures of proliferating metaphor, in which an immense web of inter-relationship is spun. A butcher "stands/smoking a pencil like Isambard Kingdom Brunel"; a baker "smiles like a modest quattrocento Christ"; a college quad is "cobbled like a blackberry." A vacuum cleaner is a cow; falling bricks decline a Latin pronoun ("hic, haec, hoc"); houses in North Oxford are troops on parade; a market is a book; a breast is a blister; a marquee is "Gulliver's grimy white shirt"; and—the title of one poem—"Two Circuses Equal One Cricket Match." And so on, through poems that contort and gyrate through a great acrobatics of perception.

The performance is extremely self-conscious in its desire to revise received opinion about the world. The poem that gave its title to the "Martians," "A Martian Sends a Postcard Home," takes this perceptual revision to one extreme, when it imagines how the most familiar and domesticated elements of our lives might seem to an alien from Outer Space:

> Rain is when the earth is television.
> It has the property of making colours darker.
>
> Model T is a room with the lock inside—
> a key is turned to free the world
>
> for movement, so quick there is a film
> to watch for anything missed.
>
> But time is tied to the wrist
> or kept in a box, ticking with impatience.
>
> In homes, a haunted apparatus sleeps,
> that snores when you pick it up.

If the ghost cries, they carry it
to their lips and soothe it to sleep

with sounds. And yet, they wake it up
deliberately, by tickling with a finger.

This is entirely characteristic of Raine in its delighted, self-entranced ingenuity, and also in the way it seems to crave some more innocent, cleansed version of the world to be at home in. Some of the poems in this vein become, perhaps, over-ingenious, and invite a certain element of self-congratulation in the reader who unravels them. It might also be said of some of his work what has been said of John Donne—a poet for whom Raine clearly has the profoundest respect—that once you have mastered it, there is little else you can do with it.

However, it is apparent in Raine's third book, *Rich*, that he is well aware of these possible objections to some of his procedures, and intends to go on from the more obvious Martian mannerisms into further linguistic inventions and explorations. He writes poems in forms of dialect, in pidgin English, and in "translationese." But this ingenuity—which is delightfully clever and inventive in itself—is now more clearly in the service of apprehensible emotional and moral meanings: the dandyish element of the earlier work is completely eradicated. He writes, in *Rich*, a marvellously responsive poetry of childhood—not least in the long and extraordinary prose memoir about his extraordinary father, "A Silver Plate." He writes superb poems about bereavement, political terror, and the odd universe inhabited by the mentally disordered. And—an element always present in his work, but not always so successfully—he writes a richly tender erotic poetry. In the volume's title poem, Raine imagines Nature as a bountiful woman who must be wooed with words by the poet. At one point in the poem, she is imagined "transforming the world / like the eye in love," when in flood. Raine's own vision, at its best, operates, erotically, on the world in a similar way. His delighted, sensuous evocations of ordinary human cicumstances have a genuinely transforming reverence and tenderness—as when, for instance, he conjures up the mental world inhabited by his small daughter in a way that sets it in parallel with the remoteness from us of the civilisation of the Incas:

> How she comes, a serious face
> from every corner of the garden,
> cupping a secret
> she wants me to see,
> as if she had somehow
>
> invented the wheel. O Inca.

—Neil Corcoran

RAINE, Kathleen (Jessie). British. Born in London, 14 June 1908. Educated at County High School, Ilford; Girton College, Cambridge, M.A. in natural sciences 1929. Married 1) the writer Hugh Sykes Davies (divorced); 2) Charles Madge, *q.v.* (marriage dissolved), one daughter and one son. Research Fellow, Girton College, Cambridge, 1955-61; Andrew Mellon Lecturer, National Gallery of Art, Washington, D.C., 1962. Since 1981, Co-Editor, *Temenos*. Recipient: Harriet Monroe Memorial Prize, 1952, and Oscar Blumenthal Prize, 1961 (*Poetry*, Chicago); Arts Council award, 1953; Chapelbrook Award; Cholmondeley Award, 1970;

Smith Literary Award, 1972; Foreign Book Prize (France), for non-fiction, 1979. D. Litt.: Leicester University, 1974; Durham University, 1979. Address: 47 Paultons Square, London SW3 5DT, England.

PUBLICATIONS

Verse

Stone and Flower: Poems 1935-43. London, Nicholson and Watson, 1943.
Living in Time: Poems. London, Editions Poetry London, 1946.
The Pythoness and Other Poems. London, Hamish Hamilton, 1949; New York, Farrar Straus, 1952.
Selected Poems. New York, Weekend Press, 1952.
The Year One. London, Hamish Hamilton, 1952; New York, Farrar Straus, 1953.
The Collected Poems of Kathleen Raine. London, Hamish Hamilton, 1956; New York, Random House, 1957.
Christmas 1960: An Acrostic. Privately printed, 1960.
The Hollow Hill and Other Poems 1960-1964. London, Hamish Hamilton, 1965.
Six Dreams and Other Poems. London, Enitharmon Press, 1968.
Ninfa Revisited. London, Enitharmon Press, 1968.
Pergamon Poets 4: Kathleen Raine and Vernon Watkins, edited by Evan Owen. Oxford, Pergamon Press, 1968.
A Question of Poetry. Crediton, Devon, Gilbertson, 1969.
Penguin Modern Poets 17, with David Gascoyne and W.S. Graham. London, Penguin, 1970.
The Lost Country. Dublin, Dolmen Press, and London, Hamish Hamilton, 1971.
Three Poems Written in Ireland. London, Poem-of-the-Month Club, 1973.
On a Deserted Shore. Dublin, Dolmen Press and London, Hamish Hamilton, 1973.
The Oval Portrait and Other Poems. London, Enitharmon Press-London, Hamish Hamilton, 1977.
Fifteen Short Poems. London, Enitharmon Press, 1978.
The Oracle in the Heart and Other Poems 1975-1978. Dublin, Dolmen Press, and London, Allen and Unwin, 1980.
Collected Poems 1935-1980. London, Allen and Unwin, 1981.

Other

William Blake. London, Longman, 1951; revised edition, 1965, 1969.
Coleridge. London, Longman, 1953.
Poetry in Relation to Traditional Wisdom. London, Guild of Pastoral Psychology, 1958.
Blake and England (lecture). Cambridge, W. Heffer, 1960.
Defending Ancient Springs (essays). London and New York, Oxford University Press, 1967.
The Written Word. London, Enitharmon Press, 1967.
Blake and Tradition. Princeton, New Jersey, Princeton University Press, 1968; London, Routledge, 1969; abridged edition, as *Blake and Antiquity,* 1974.
William Blake. London, Thames and Hudson, 1971.
Faces of Day and Night (autobiography). London, Enitharmon Press, 1972.
Yeats, The Tarot and the Golden Dawn. Dublin, Dolmen Press, 1972; New York, Humanities Press, 1973; revised edition, Dolmen Press, 1976.

Hopkins, Nature, and Human Nature (lecture). London, Hopkins Society, 1972.

Autobiography:

1. *Farewell Happy Fields.* London, Hamish Hamilton, 1973; New York, Braziller, 1977.
2. *The Land Unknown.* London, Hamish Hamilton, and New York, Braziller, 1975.
3. *The Lion's Mouth.* London, Hamish Hamilton, 1977; New York, Braziller, 1978.

Death-in-Life and Life-in-Death (lecture). Dublin, Dolmen Press, 1974.

David Jones: Solitary Perfectionist. Ipswich, Golgonooza Press, 1974.

A Place, A State, drawings by Julia Trevelyan. London, Enitharmon Press, 1974.

The Inner Journey of the Poet. Ipswich, Golgonooza Press, 1976.

Berkeley, Blake, and the New Age (lecture). Ipswich, Golgonooza Press, 1977.

From Blake to "A Vision." Dublin, Dolmen Press, 1978.

David Jones and the Actually Loved and Known. Ipswich, Golgonooza Press, 1978.

Blake and the New Age. London, Allen and Unwin, 1979.

Cecil Collins, Painter of Paradise. Ipswich, Golgonooza Press, 1979.

"What Is Man?" Ipswich, Golgonooza Press, 1980.

The Human Face of God: William Blake and the Book of Job. London, Thames and Hudson, 1982.

The Inner Journey of the Poet and Other Papers, edited by Brian Keeble. London, Allen and Unwin, and New York, Braziller, 1982.

Yeats to Initiate: Essays on Certain Themes in the Writings of W.B. Yeats. Dublin, Dolmen Press, 1984; London, Allen and Unwin, 1985.

Editor, with Max-Pol Fouchet, *Aspects de Littérature Anglaise, 1918-1945.* Paris, Fontaine, 1947.

Editor, *Letters of Samuel Taylor Coleridge.* London, Grey Walls Press, 1950.

Editor, *Selected Poems and Prose of Coleridge.* London, Penguin, 1957.

Editor, with George Mills Harper, *Thomas Taylor the Platonist: Selected Writings.* Princeton, New Jersey, Princeton University Press, and London, Routledge, 1969.

Editor, *A Choice of Blake's Verse.* London, Faber, 1974.

Editor, *Shelley.* London, Penguin, 1974.

Translator, *Talk of the Devil*, by Dénis de Rougemont. London, Eyre and Spottiswoode, 1945.

Translator, *Existentialism*, by Paul Foulquié. London, Dobson, 1948.

Translator, *Cousin Bette*, by Balzac. London, Hamish Hamilton, 1948.

Translator, *Lost Illusions*, by Balzac. London, Lehmann, 1951.

Translator, with R.M. Nadal, *Life's a Dream* by Calderón. London, Hamish Hamilton, 1968; New York, Theatre Arts, 1969.

*

Manuscript Collections: British Library, London; University of Texas, Austin; University of California, Irvine.

Critical Study: *Kathleen Raine* by Ralph J. Mills Jr., Grand Rapids, Michigan, Eerdmans, 1967.

Kathleen Raine comments:

I began as a poet of spontaneous inspirations, drawing greatly on nature and fortified by my more precise biological studies. Though I was born in London, my poetic roots were in wild Northumberland where I lived as a child. Most of my poems have been written in Cumberland or Scotland, some in Italy, Greece or France, but very few in London, where I at present live.

I have studied the symbolic language of Blake, Shelley, Yeats, Coleridge, and other poets of the "Romantic" tradition; who employ that language of analogy inseparable from the Perennial Philosophy (of which Christianity is our own cultural branch) which regards man as a spiritual and immortal being. Increasingly, in an atheist society, the meaning of words and the symbolic implications of traditional poetry become changed or lost. And this makes it difficult, if not impossible, for a poet of my kind to be anthologized with writers committed to another view of the nature of things. I have much sympathy for the young generation now reacting against materialist culture; but I am too firmly rooted in the civilization of the past to speak their language. *Temenos* is an attempt to re-affirm values which we regard as essential if the arts are to recover from their present decline, which we attribute to the loss of the imaginative vision— the sacred dimension—in an increasingly secular society.

*   *   *

The young poets who caught the widest public attention in the 1930's were a group of Oxford poets, W.H. Auden, C. Day Lewis, Stephen Spender, and Louis MacNeice. A group of Cambridge poets of the same generation, Kathleen Raine, William Empson, Ronald Bottrall, and Miss Raine's second husband, Charles Madge, attracted on the whole less public attention. It was not that they were less politically engaged—two good Cambridge poets, John Cornford and Julian Bell, died in the Spanish Civil War; it was, perhaps, that there was a greater austerity in the Cambridge tradition. Miss Raine studied the natural sciences, not literature, at Cambridge, and an exactness of natural observation (very notable in her first volume, *Stone and Flower*, beautifully illustrated by Barbara Hepworth) is one of the main qualities of her poetry. Another is a beautifully natural and graceful lyric movement, and a third is what might be called a transparency of diction. She has never attempted wit poetry, or the poetry of personal self-analysis, "confessional" poetry: in gathering together her *Collected Poems* she said in her preface that she had at first excluded all poems of "mere human emotion" but, persuaded by a friend that this was a too grandly austere statement—might not Chaucer and Shakespeare be described as poets of "mere human emotion"?—she substituted for that phrase the phrase "the transient." Miss Raine thinks of herself as a poet in a Platonic or neo-Platonic tradition that has included Spenser, Milton, Blake, Shelley and Yeats in its members among the poets of the greater English tradition. The combination of the approach of a trained botanist and geologist with neo-Platonic mysticism may seem strange, but a link could be found in Miss Raine's interest in abstract art, in the sculptures of Barbara Hepworth and the drawings of Ben Nicholson. Both these artists might be thought of as seeking in outward nature archetypal forms, or Platonic ideas, as might another English artist whom Miss Raine greatly admires, Henry Moore. Such artists and the older poets whom she has praised in her book of essays *Defending Ancient Springs* might be thought of as Miss Raine's deepest sources. She has little sympathy with most contemporary poetry, feeling that even her old Cambridge friend, William Empson, is in his poetry and prose her spiritual antagonist. Poetry is only true poetry for her if it utters in traditional language the truths of the perennial philosophy, of ancient wisdom, of ancient revelation. Working on Blake over many years of patient scholarship, she has been concerned with the Blake who created a mythology and a cosmology, not with the Blake who spoke of "the lineaments of gratified desire." It follows that, though her poetry has always been admired by sound judges, some have found it thin and unearthly, speaking too much for what Yeats called soul, not enough for what Yeats called self, not enough for "the fury and the more of human veins." Her lyrical sweetness, the beauty of the voice that is heard in the poems, is praised, but the vision itself found abstract or schematic. Carefully reading and listening with the inner ear will tell another story. Only a very proud and passionate woman would wage such a stern war, through all her work, against human pride and passion. These are the poems of a sybil, perhaps, of a rapt visionary, but not of a saint.

—G.S. Fraser

RAKOSI, Carl. American. Born in Berlin, Germany, 6 November 1903. Educated at the University of Wisconsin, Madison, B.A. 1924, M.A. 1926; University of Pennsylvania, Philadelphia, M.S.W., 1940; University of Chicago; University of Texas, Austin. Married Leah Jaffe in 1939; one daughter and one son. Instructor, University of Texas, 1928-29; social worker, Chicago, New York, New Orleans, Brooklyn, St. Louis, and Cleveland, 1932-45; Executive Director, Jewish Family and Children's Service, Minneapolis 1945-68; Writer-in-Residence, University of Wisconsin, 1969-70, and Michigan State University, East Lansing, 1974. In private practice of psychotherapy, Minneapolis, 1955-71. Recipient: National Endowment for the Arts award, 1969, fellowship, 1972, 1978. Address: 128 Irving Street, San Francisco, California 94122, U.S.A.

PUBLICATIONS

Verse

Selected Poems. New York, New Directions, 1941.
Two Poems. New York, Modern Editions Press, 1942.
Amulet. New York, New Directions, 1967.
Ere-VOICE. New York, New Directions, 1971.
Ex Cranium, Night. Los Angeles, Black Sparrow Press, 1975.
My Experiences in Parnassus. Santa Barbara, California, Black Sparrow Press, 1977.
Droles de Journal. West Branch, Iowa, Toothpaste Press, 1981.
History. London, Oasis, 1981.
Spiritus I. Durham, Pig Press, 1983.

Other

Collected Prose. Orono, Maine, National Poetry Foundation, 1984.

*

Manuscript Collections: University of Wisconsin, Madison; Harvard University, Cambridge, Massachusetts.

Critical Studies: "The Objectivist Poet: Interviews with Oppen,

Rakosi, Reznikoff, and Zukofsky," in *Contemporary Literature* (Madison, Wisconsin) x, 2, and "The Poetry of Carl Rakosi," in *Iowa Review* (Iowa City), ii, 1, both by L.S. Dembo.

Carl Rakosi comments:
I am identified with the Objectivists but it is questionable whether the term has meaning any more.

*   *   *

Carl Rakosi was a member of a group of poets in the thirties who called themselves "The Objectivists." Louis Zukofsky, Charles Reznikoff, and George Oppen were other poets identified with this group. Rakosi and Oppen both went unpublished for many years between the thirties and the present time, either writing secretly or not writing at all, as they were both involved with active social protest against the oppression of the laboring classes and, as is usually the case, when active politics reign in a man's life, he has no place for the more meditative art of poetry.

Now as older men, they have both begun to write and publish prolifically. Rakosi, who led his life as a social worker in the Midwest, still concerns his poems with pithy practical comments on life and its injustices. Ironically, however, his best poems are pastoral observations of the natural world, often with tiny comments such as those you might find in early Japanese or Chinese poetry.

Rakosi's poetry is short and spritely and not at all meditative, though seemingly made up of conclusions about the meaning of the world. It feels like the language of a man who has been active all of his life and now has comments about everything he has experienced, slightly wry and not at all uncritical, though delivered with friendliness. As a poet, he is a sort of gadfly, not taking on any epic subjects (perhaps even having wry words about such subjects), but stinging and buzzing about everything, a reminder that to live intelligently is never to relax or to leave unnoticed any slightly foolish thing—the poet as commentator on all of life.

—Diane Wakoski

RAMANUJAN, A(ttipat) K(rishnaswami). Indian. Born in Mysore, Karnataka, 16 March 1929. Educated at the University of Mysore, B.A. 1949, M.A. in English 1950; Deccan College, Yeravada, Poona, diplomas 1958 and 1959; Indiana University, Bloomington (Fulbright and Smith-Mundt fellowships, 1959), Ph.D. in linguistics 1963. Married Molly Daniels in 1962; one daughter and one son. Teacher in India, 1950-58. Research Associate in Tamil, 1961, Assistant Professor, 1962-65, Associate Professor, 1966-68, since 1968, Professor of Dravidian Studies and Linguistics, departments of Linguistics and South Asian Languages, and since 1972, Professor, Committee on Social Thought, University of Chicago. Visiting Professor, University of Wisconsin, Madison, 1965, 1971, University of California, Berkeley, 1967, 1973, University of Michigan, Ann Arbor, 1970, and Carleton College, Northfield, Minnesota, 1978. Recipient: American Institute of Indian Studies Fellowship, 1963; Indiana School of Letters Fellowship, 1963; Tamil Writers' Association Award, 1969; American Council of Learned Societies Fellowship, 1973; National Endowment for the Arts grant, 1977, 1982; MacArthur Foundation Award, 1983; Padma Sri, Government of India, 1976. Address: 5629 South Dorchester Avenue, Chicago, Illinois 60637, U.S.A.

PUBLICATIONS

Verse

The Striders. London and New York, Oxford University Press, 1966.
No Lotus in the Navel (in Kannada). Dharwar, Manohar Granthamala, 1969.
Relations. London, Oxford University Press, 1972.
Selected Poems. New Delhi and London, Oxford University Press, 1976.
And Other Poems (in Kannada) Dharwar, 1977.

Novel

Mattobbana Atmacaritre (in Kannada). Dharwar, Granthamala, 1978.

Other

Proverbs (in Kannada). Dharwar, Karnatak University, 1955.
The Literature of India, with others. Chicago, University of Chicago Press, 1974.

Translator, *Fifteen Poems from a Classical Tamil Anthology.* Calcutta, Writers Workshop, 1965.
Translator, *The Yellow Fish* (into Kannada), by Molly Ramanujan. Dharwar, Manohar Granthamala, 1966.
Translator, *The Interior Landscape: Love Poems from a Classical Tamil Anthology.* Bloomington, Indiana University Press, 1967; London, Owen, 1970.
Translator, *Speaking of Siva.* London, Penguin, 1973.
Translator, *Samskara,* by U.R. Anantha Murthy. New Delhi, Oxford University Press, 1976.
Translator, *Hymns for the Drowning: Poems for Visnu by Nammalvar.* Princeton, New Jersey, Princeton University Press, 1981.
Translator, *Poems of Love and War: From the Eight Anthologies and the Ten Songs of Classical Tamil.* New York, Columbia University Press, 1984.

*

Critical Studies: in *Poetry Book Society Bulletin* (London), April 1966; *Ten Twentieth-Century Indian Poets* edited by R. Parthasarathy, New Delhi, Oxford University Press, 1976; *The Poetry of Encounter: Three Indo-Anglian Poets* by Emmanuel Narendra Lall, New Delhi, Sterling, 1983.

* * *

A.K. Ramanujan achieved recognition when his first book, *The Striders,* was recommended by the Poetry Society of London. He is a South Indian, and has been living in the U.S.A. for many years now, teaching linguistics and Dravidian studies at the University of Chicago. This biographical information is relevant in reading his poems which are mostly poems of memory, quite often nostalgic. They have their origin in an emotion arising from the Indian experience which is recollected in an American environment—not always in a mood of tranquillity. Many of the poems are based on the cultural predicament of a person who has been brought up in a very traditional culture, but who is now living in a very different culture. One of the best poems in *The Striders* which exemplifies these remarks is "Conventions of Despair." The poem opens with the description of a modern hell whose representative figure is the Marginal Man,

culturally and linguistically displaced and unsettled, perhaps permanently. But the hell to which the poet feels he is consigned is the Hindu hell of traditional description in which he must "translate and turn/till I blister and roast/for certain lives to come, 'eye-deep'/in those Boiling crates of Oil." This is the punishment for loving a prohibited person. In this Hindu hell he will be condemned to witness the tortures of the beloved person also. But the worst of his punishments comes from the modern hell. It consists in catching a glimpse of a grandchild "bare/her teenage flesh to the pimps/of ideal Tomorrow's crowfoot eyes/and the theory of a peacock-feathered future." The poet finally chooses to live in the present, content with continuous existence. He prefers the archaic despair of Hindu thought which sees human life as a continuous cycle of birth, death and rebirth. The cycle, it is believed, has always existed. Ramanujan, significantly, does not say anything about the complementary belief that we can end this cycle if we so will.

Five years after *The Striders* appeared *Relations.* The poetic impulse and the theme are the same—announced in the epigraph poem which is a beautiful rendering of a classical Tamil poem. (Perhaps Ramanujan's real forte is translation.) The ambiguous nature of the freedom away from home is brought out most satisfactorily in the images:

> Like a hunted deer
> on the wide white
> salt land,
>   a flayed hide
>   turned inside out,
> one may run,
> escape.
>   But living
> among relations
> binds the feet.

The sense of loss is most often connected with mother. "My cold parchment tongue licks bark/in the mouth when I see her four/still sensible fingers slowly flex/to pick a grain of rice from the kitchen floor" ("Of Mothers, among others things"). The metaphors in the first two lines emphasise the rough, bitter taste of the memory, and the last two lines provide an irresistible "objective correlative" of the emotion. Every poet who communicates principally in images—as Ramanujan does—takes chances, but fortunately most of the chances that Ramanujan takes come off. If there is any cause for dissatisfaction with these poems, it is that many of them are intellectually somewhat thin, though there are numerous exceptions. For example, "A River" in *The Striders* where the images comment obliquely on the blind imitation of past models; or "History" in *Relations* which may be read as an illustration of Eliot's "historical sense" on the plane of personal relations. One no doubt misses a sense of an unfolding pattern in the total experience of these poems, but this lack may disappear as the poet masters his past and learns to assimilate the present. As he himself says: "After the lightning/strikes the tree/and takes all the leaves,/an amnesiac may break into hives/...but recognize nothing present/to his concave eye groping only/for mother and absences."

Technically, Ramanujan is a very interesting poet. His sense of rhythm, his manipulation of syntax, his ability to use ordinary words in extraordinary ways, exploiting fully their semantic potentialities, his run-ons, even his line alignments, above all, his tone, all make his poems a very rewarding experience.

—S. Nagarajan

RAMSEY, Paul. American. Born in Atlanta, Georgia, 26 November 1924. Educated at the University of Chattanooga, Tennessee; University of North Carolina, Chapel Hill, B.A., M.A.; University of Minnesota, Minneapolis, Ph.D. 1956. Served in the United States Navy during World War II. Married to Bets Ramsey; four children. Taught at the University of Alabama, Tuscaloosa, 1948-50, 1953-57; Elmira College, New York, 1957-62; Raymond College, Stockton, California, 1962-64; University of the South, Sewanee, Tennessee, 1964-66. Professor of English, 1966-70, since 1966, Poet-in-Residence, and since 1970, Alumni Distinguished Service Professor, University of Tennessee, Chattanooga. Recipient: Folger Library Senior Fellowship, 1967; English-Speaking Union prize, 1976. Address: Department of English, University of Tennessee, 615 McCallie Avenue, Chattanooga, Tennessee 37402, U.S.A.

PUBLICATIONS

Verse

Triptych, with Sy Kahn and Jane Taylor. Stockton, California, Raymond College Press, 1964.
In an Ordinary Place. Raleigh, North Carolina, Southern Poetry Review Press, 1965.
A Window for New York. San Francisco, Two Windows Press, 1968.
The Doors. Martin, Tennessee Poetry Press, 1968.
The Answerers. San Francisco, Two Windows Press, 1970.
No Running on the Boardwalk. Athens, University of Georgia Press, 1975.
Antiphon: An Introit for Christmas, music by Alec Wyton. Carol Springs, Illinois, Agape Press, 1975.
Eve, Singing. Easthampton, Massachusetts, Pennyroyal Press, 1976.

Other

The Lively and the Just: An Argument for Propriety. University, University of Alabama Press, 1962.
The Art of John Dryden. Lexington, University of Kentucky Press, 1969.
The Fickle Glass: A Study of Shakespeare's Sonnets. New York, AMS Press, 1979.

*

Critical Studies: review in *Virginia Quarterly Review* (Charlottesville), 1968; by Scott Bates, in *Times* (Chattanooga, Tennessee), 13 July 1975; Charles Israel, in *Sandlapper* (Columbia, South Carolina), October 1975; Claire Hahn, in *Commonweal* (New York), 22 October 1976.

Paul Ramsey comments:

My poetry is varied, ambitious, exploratory, traditional. For some years I wrote only traditional forms, mostly accentual-syllabics. Since then I have worked in traditional forms, forms I have invented, free verse, combinings of free verse with traditional forms or methods. Valid poetry should enliven and sustain rhythm, touch on and at times enter mystery, offer understanding. My chief and underlying themes are Christian, as is manifest in my long poems "The Flight of the Heart," *A Window for New York*, "The Naming of Adam," a Christianity which permits and includes, for instance, nature's bounty and strangeness, ethical reality, the turns and crowds of events, love's cele-

brations and complaints, and images that recur: doors, windows, mists, rocks, the sea, the cross.

*   *   *

Paul Ramsey in his best work often combines the virtues of men whose work he has studied carefully: John Dryden, Allen Tate, and Yvor Winters. The combination may at first seem strange. Yet Dryden is godfather to our critical wars and poetical age; and Tate and Winters were not so far apart as poets as their critical squabbles suggested. Aiming for compression, some of Ramsey's early poems were so tightly packed that they seemed more cryptic than epigrammatic. The quatrain "Art" is an often cited example ("Art is act/ Betrayed by passion and by artifact/ Till images encounter their repose"). Aiming at a general loosening of the poetic line and at a more conversational vocabulary in a fashionable manner, some of his later poems (and the whole book *The Doors*) have become diffuse, sketchy, even lacking in content. Yet superb lines appear in both the tight early poems ("Art" ends: "The mind must learn to suffer what it knows") and the diffuse later experiments ("The Doors" sequence ends with the line "Blood loosens the rust of the keys"); and in all the poems, one finds subtle metrical skill as well as intellectual integrity and grace. Ramsey's profound Christian humanitarian outlook gives moving substance to many of his poems, and informs others with moral strength and character. This habit of mind evidences itself in such poems as the apology to Wordsworth, an apology for having taught that man's poems badly; and to the assertion in the challenging and important critical work *The Lively and the Just*, that of the English Odes examined in the book Wordsworth's Intimations Ode is the greatest. Such a remark, coming from a Dryden scholar and a student of the so-called "New Criticism" is a measure of rigorous intellectual integrity.

No poet writes great poems all the time; nor even good poems. One must, I think, pass over such experiments as *The Doors* and most of Ramsey's "occasional" poems, as one would any other poet's. Then one finds a solid body of work. He has written at least one major poem, "Address to Satan," 14 iambic pentameter lines in two stanzas riming a-a-b-b-c-c-c, and beginning "Now curl about your wisdom and be still,/ Old serpent-tooth." In addition he had written some very fine poems, "Forest" and "Even Umpires Wager with Pascal" among them. The poems of a man of such skill and integrity will survive, past fads and fashions. The man who wrote such poems as "Address to Satan" and "Forest" is still composing. His lively verbal imagination will, knock wood, give us more good poems.

—James Korges

RANDALL, Dudley (Felker). American. Born in Washington, D.C., 14 January 1914. Educated at Eastern High School, Detroit; Wayne State University, Detroit, A.B. 1949; University of Michigan, Ann Arbor, M.A.L.S. 1951. Served in the United States Army Signal Corps, 1943-46. Married 1) Ruby Hands in 1935 (marriage dissolved), one daughter; 2) Mildred Pinckney in 1942 (marriage dissolved); 3) Vivian Spencer in 1957. Worked for Ford Motor Company, Dearborn, 1932-37; Post Office carrier and clerk, Detroit, 1937-51; Librarian, Lincoln University, Jefferson City, Missouri, 1951-54, Morgan State College, Baltimore, 1954-56, and Wayne County Federated Library System,

Detroit, 1956-69. Since 1969, Librarian and Poet-in-Residence, University of Detroit. Founding Publisher, Broadside Press, Detroit. Visited Paris, Prague and the U.S.S.R. with a delegation of black artists, 1966. Recipient: Wayne State University Tompkins Award, for fiction and poetry, 1962, for poetry, 1966; Kuumba Award, 1973. Address: Broadside Press, 74 Glendale Avenue, Highland Park, Michigan 48203, U.S.A.

PUBLICATIONS

Verse

Ballad of Birmingham.   Detroit, Broadside Press, 1965.
Dressed All in Pink.   Detroit, Broadside Press, 1965.
Booker T. and W.E.B.   Detroit, Broadside Press, 1966.
Poem, Counterpoem, with Margaret Danner.   Detroit, Broadside Press, 1966.
Cities Burning.   Detroit, Broadside Press, 1968.
On Getting a Natural.   Detroit, Broadside Press, 1969.
Love You.   London, Paul Breman, 1971.
More to Remember: Poems of Four Decades.   Chicago, Third World Press, 1971.
Green Apples.   Detroit, Broadside Press, 1972.
After the Killing.   Chicago, Third World Press, 1973.
A Litany of Friends: Poems Selected and New.   Detroit, Lotus Press, 1981.

Other

A Capsule Course in Black Poetry Writing, with others.   Detroit, Broadside Press, 1975.
Broadside Memories: Poets I Have Known.   Detroit, Broadside Press, 1975.

Editor, with Margaret G. Burroughs, *For Malcolm: Poems on the Life and the Death of Malcolm X.*   Detroit, Broadside Press, 1967.
Editor, *Black Poetry: A Supplement to Anthologies Which Exclude Black Poets.*   Detroit, Broadside Press, 1969.
Editor, *The Black Poets: A New Anthology.*   New York, Bantam, 1971.

                                *

Dudley Randall comments:
   Writes poetry of the Negro. Formal, reflective, with occasional humor.

                    *   *   *

   Dudley Randall's verse eases its audience into a pleased approval of the poet's viewpoint. Take, for example, what must be his most famous piece, "Booker T. and W.E.B." References to the doctrines of the famous black leaders in this imagined dialogue seem even-handed, each speaker uses in-group language in a manner appropriate to his personality, and the dispute quite appropriately has no logical resolution within the poem. On the other hand, Randall's heavy end-rhymes develop qualitative contrasts as Washington admonishes "...do not grouse,/But work, and save, and buy a house" and DuBois responds that Washington should "try his little plan,/But as for me, I'll be a man." Upon second thought auditors may feel there is less than

justice in this mock dialogue in which just one participant gets mocked, but it has been a delight.
   Randall generates such verse between the poles of a wit modulated by the rhythms of popular idiom and a strong ethical concern. Frequently he works as a satirist invoking the integrity of discipline and good sense to censure those who sanctify getting high ("Hail, Dionysos"), indulge themselves in fashionable introspection ("Analysands"), or parade as "stone" revolutionaries ("Abu"). The satiric structure, as often as not, builds upon enumeration as in "F.B.I. Memo" where the perfect spy is equipped with beard, Afro, tiki, dashiki, Swahili, and the cry "Kill the Honkies"; and deceptive simplicity is the background for wit, as in "Black Poet, White Critic" where Randall blandly records the critic's advice to write on universal themes symbolized by a white unicorn: "A *white* unicorn?"
   Wit, the popular idiom, and an ethical concern are good for more than satire, however. The metaphoric identification of black speech with the Southern land in "Laughter in the Slums" lyrically images a soul world as vividly as Jean Toomer ever did, while "Roses and Revolutions" conveys a prophecy in a striking metaphysical image.
   We owe much to Dudley Randall, for his devotion to art that delights and instructs led him to found the very important Broadside Press, first publisher of a number of the new black American poets. Appropriately, though, the epitome of his entire project, as poet and publisher of poets, is to be found in his own verse. Try his beautiful elegy "Langston Blues." It's all there: wit, popular form, and feeling that defies objective description. It's perfect.

                                                    —John M. Reilly

                         ————————

RANDALL, Julia.   American. Born in Baltimore, Maryland, 15 June 1923. Educated at Bryn Mawr School, Baltimore; Bennington College, Vermont, A.B. 1945; Johns Hopkins University, Baltimore, M.A. 1950. Biology laboratory technician, Harvard University, Cambridge, Massachusetts, 1946-48; Instructor, Johns Hopkins University, 1949-52, and University of Maryland overseas extension, Paris, 1952-53; Library Assistant, Goucher College, Towson, Maryland, 1954-56; Instructor, Peabody Conservatory, Baltimore, 1956-59; Instructor, then Assistant Professor, Towson State College, Baltimore, 1958-62. Assistant Professor, 1962-66, and since 1966, Associate Professor of English, Hollins College, Virginia. Recipient: *Sewanee Review* Fellowship, 1957; National Endowment for the Arts grant, 1966, 1982; American Academy grant, 1968. Address: Hartley Mill Road, Glen Arm, Maryland 21057, U.S.A.

PUBLICATIONS

Verse

The Solstice Tree.   Baltimore, Contemporary Poetry, 1952.
Mimic August.   Baltimore, Contemporary Poetry, 1960.
4 Poems.   Hollins College, Virginia, Tinker Press, 1964.
The Puritan Carpenter.   Chapel Hill, University of North Carolina Press, 1965.
Adam's Dream.   Hollins College, Virginia, Tinker Press, 1966.
Adam's Dream: Poems.   New York, Knopf, 1969.
The Farewells.   Chicago, Elpenor Press, 1981.

*

Critical Study: "The Double Dream of Julia Randall" by Mary Kinzie, in *Hollins Critic* (Virginia), February 1983.

Julia Randall comments:

It seems to me quite beyond the call of duty, modesty, or even common sense to answer questions about one's own verse. Influences? The usual ones for our time: Eliot, Yeats, Rilke, Stevens, Thomas; behind them Hopkins, Wordsworth, Dickinson, the great ambiguous ghost of Milton, and the lesser ghosts of hymn- and ballad-makers. Also, very importantly, musicians, painters, naturalists, novelists, philosophers, and prophets. My subjects are drawn about equally from nature (especially the Maryland- Virginia countryside) and from the arts, which is to say about half my poems are literal and half imaginary. They are personal or local, rather than dramatic or topical. My forms are frequently traditional quatrains, but tend now toward something larger or looser with either sustained or irregular use of slant rhyme. I belong to no school that I know of. I try to achieve at least an articulation of the questions that particular experience seems to pose: how do we attach ourselves to or separate ourselves from each other, or from time? how do we know? where or to whom do we most belong? how do we mean? I try to write complete poems, sensible to the eye and ear as well as to the mind.

*   *   *

The poems of Julia Randall are tough and compressed, with a complexity that demands much of the reader, hard lines in the traditional sense, taut and metaphysical; but they are also lyrical and musically beautiful, written in a language that sings even as it tightens into knots of fused word and idea. The poems are highly allusive and are often witty in the fullest sense; language leaps to imagination and words contort themselves for the mind's delight. They are highly charged entities in which the arcane and archaic are alloyed with metaphysical passion into an active communion with the colloquial and the immediate. The days of her poems are precise and detailed, often carefully dated, but they open out, forward and back, into thought, memory and belief, into what can best be termed imaginative meditation—the mind fully at work in the harmonies (and disharmonies) of the present, not analyzing and organizing it but rather experiencing it down to the very bone.

Her earlier poems were more self-consciously aesthetic, almost hermetic at times, but even in them, she wrote from a commitment to the immediacy of experience, to learning from the inside out. For example, in the poem "Inscape I" from her first book, *The Solstice Tree*:

You

that curl the blind hand over the breast,
sing for a sign, sign for a feast,

fasten the blade, explore the vein,
learn the familiar blood.

Her later poems have become more openly personal, less artificially wrought, while losing none of the compressed intensity of the early poems. She addresses the world and her "masters" (Stevens and Rilke, Wordsworth, Lawrence, Woolf and Yeats); she invokes them, plant and poet, stone and artist, demanding of them and of herself "what we see clear, but clumsily half-tell." What she sees is the world of bone and blood and words, but also the power of being itself, beyond and through them all:

I walked by the stream. The hay was loud
with bugs escaping; they know
what danger is. I too
feared once the many-bladed mower.
Once, but not now.

—R.H.W. Dillard

RANDALL, Margaret.   Born in New York City, 6 December 1936. Educated at the University of New Mexico, Albuquerque, 1954-55. Married 1) Sam Jacobs in 1955 (divorced, 1958); 2) Sergio Mondragon in 1962 (marriage dissolved, 1967); lived with Robert Cohen, 1968-75, and with Antonio Castro, 1976-79; married Floyce Alexander in 1984; four children. Assistant to Director, Spanish Refugee Aid, New York, 1960-61; Editor, *El Corno Emplumado*, Mexico City, 1962-69; Editor, Cuban Book Institute, Havana, 1969-75; self-employed writer and photographer, 1976-80; Publicist, Nicaraguan Ministry of Culture, Managua, 1981-82; staff member, Foreign Press Center, Managua, 1983; Instructor, University of New Mexico, 1984-85. Recipient: American Academy grant, 1960; Carnegie Fund grant, 1960. Address: 51 Cedar Hill Road NE, Albuquerque, New Mexico 87122, U.S.A.

PUBLICATIONS

Verse

Giant of Tears and Other Poems.   New York, Tejon Press, 1959.
Ecstasy Is a Number.   New York, Gutman Foundation, 1961.
Poems of the Glass.   Cleveland, Renegade Press, 1964.
Small Sounds from the Bass Fiddle.   Albuquerque, New Mexico, Duende Press, 1964.
October.   Mexico City, El Corno Emplumado, 1965.
25 Stages of My Spine.   New Rochelle, New York, Elizabeth Press, 1967.
Water I Slip Into at Night.   Privately printed, 1967.
So Many Rooms Has a House But One Roof.   Nyack, New York, New Rivers Press, 1968.
Getting Rid of Blue Plastic: Poems Old and New, edited by Pritish Nandy.   Calcutta, Dialogue, 1968.
Part of the Solution.   New York, New Directions, 1972.
Day's Coming!   Privately printed, 1973.
With Our Hands.   Vancouver, New Star, 1974.
All My Used Parts, Shackles, Fuel, Tenderness, and Stars.   Privately printed, 1976.
We.   New York, Smyrna Press, 1978.
Carlota.   Vancouver, New Star, 1978.

Other

Los Hippies.   Mexico City, Siglo XXI, 1968.
Cuban Woman Now.   Toronto, Canadian Women's Educational Press, 1974.
La Situación de la Mujer.   Lima, Centro de Estudios de Participación Popular, 1974.

Spirit of the People: Vietnamese Women Two Years from the Geneva Accords. Vancouver, New Star, 1975.
Inside the Nicaraguan Revolution: The Story of Doris Tijerino. Vancouver, New Star, 1978.
No se Puede Hacer la Revolución sin Nosotras. Havana, Casa de las Américas, 1978.
El Pueblo no Sólo es Testigo: La Historia de Dominga. Rio Piedras, Puerto Rico, Huracán, 1979.
Sueños y Realidades de un Guajiricantor. Mexico City, Siglo XXI, 1979.
Women in Cuba: Twenty Years Later. New York, Smyrna Press, 1981.
Sandino's Daughters: Testimonies of Nicaraguan Women in Struggle. Vancouver, New Star, and London, Zed, 1981.
Testimonios. San José, Costa Rica, Alforja Centro de Estudios de Participación Popular, 1983.
Christians in the Nicaraguan Revolution. Vancouver, New Star, 1984.
Risking a Somersault in the Air: Conversations with Nicaraguan Writers. San Francisco, Solidarity, 1984.

Editor, *Las Mujeres.* Mexico City, Siglo XXI, 1970.
Editor, *This Great People Has Said "Enough!" and Has Begun to Move: Poems from the Struggle in Latin America.* San Francisco, People's Press, 1972.

Translator, *Let's Go!,* by Otto-René Castillo. London, Cape Goliard Press, 1970; Willimantic, Connecticut, Curbstone Press, 1984.
Translator, *These Living Songs: Fifteen New Cuban Poets.* Fort Collins, Colorado State Review Press, 1978.
Translator, *Breaking the Silences* (Cuban women poets). Vancouver, Pulp Press, 1981.
Translator, *Carlos, Dawn Is No Longer Beyond Our Reach,* by Romas Borge. Vancouver, Pulp Press, 1984.

                                              *

Manuscript Collection: New York University Library.

Critical Study: "The Sense of the Risk in the Coming Together" by Alvin Greenberg, in *Minnesota Review* 6 (St. Paul), no. 2, 1966.

Margaret Randall comments:

The poem is vital to me, as a life experience. In recent years I have become involved, as well, in photography. That, oral history, and the poem are linked to one another in my expression. Women's creativity is particularly important to me.

                         *   *   *

The strength of Margaret Randall's poetry comes from its position on the immediate edges of experience: experience fresh and untempered whatever its quality (loving or violent), and brought forth directly as an offering of the poet's own self. She has been consistently a poet whose major concern is to confront whatever happens—however new and however great the risks—prepared to grow, as artist and person, from that encounter, always seeking to "create a new language for this, a new place." The dangers of such an approach are great—that the experience will be too raw, too unformulated, to become meaningful, or that, particularly in areas of political or social concern, failure to find the new words may cause one to fall back on sloganizing—but the values, as she shows, are well worth the risk: giving a sense of the immediacy of the poet living through a significant

encounter (with self, dreams, other people, events, new places), discovering herself in the midst of that encounter, and opening up to the reader the potential for a similar discovery.

Thus her poems deal, for the most part, with, as she says in "Everyone Comes to a Lighted House," "people moving together" and with her own emergence, as detailed in "Eyes," through such encounters to new vision: "The dream went on but I woke up./The bus is full my stop's coming up everyone has new eyes." The brief prose pieces included in her 1972 book *Part of the Solution* present in greater detail encounters comparable to those which take place in the poems; they are not actually stories but meetings, generally bizarre and traumatic, in which the poet confronts, or has forced upon her, experiences which call her entire sense of self, society, or relationships into question. Again, as in all her work—and in the movement of her life as well—what is pre-eminent is the sense of risk, and of risk as potential for the new, for learning and growth, as in "So Many Rooms Has a House But One Roof":

> One side a surface where the hole forms, opens,
> to persist means look through
> or change
> as water runs over the found object.

One changes, she indicates, not by becoming something different but by self-discovery, even in the act of writing; the encounters around which her writing centers become the potential for creativity in both her life and her poetry, and the odds which she describes Fidel risking in the mountains become as well her own sense of challenge and possibility, as she concludes in "Both Dreams": "in forests we'll conquer because we have to."

                                              —Alvin Greenberg

                         ―――――――――

RAWORTH, Tom (Thomas Moore Raworth). British. Born in Bexleyheath, Kent, 19 July 1938. Educated at St. Joseph's Academy, London, 1949-54; University of Essex, Colchester, 1967-71, M.A. 1971. Owner and Publisher, Matrix Press, and Editor, *Outburst,* London, 1959-64; Founding Editor, with Barry Hall, Goliard Press, London, 1965-67; Poet-in-Residence or Lecturer, University of Essex, 1969-70, Bowling Green State University, Ohio, 1972-73, Northeastern Illinois University, Chicago, 1973-74, University of Texas, Austin, 1974-75, and King's College, Cambridge, 1977-78. Recipient: Alice Hunt Bartlett Prize, 1969; Arts Council grant, 1970, 1972; Cholmondeley Award, 1972. Address: c/o T.A. Raworth, 8 Avondale Road, Welling, Kent, England.

PUBLICATIONS

Verse

Weapon Man. London, Goliard Press, 1965.
Continuation. London, Goliard Press, 1966.
The Relation Ship. London, Goliard Press, 1967; New York, Grossman, 1969.
Haiku, with John Esam and Anselm Hollo. London, Trigram Press, 1968.
The Big Green Day. London, Trigram Press, 1968.
Lion, Lion. London, Trigram Press, 1970.

Moving. London, Cape Goliard Press, and New York, Grossman, 1971.
Penguin Modern Poets 19, with John Ashbery and Lee Harwood. London, Penguin, 1971.
Pleasant Butter. Northampton, Massachusetts, Sand Project Press, 1972.
Tracking. Bowling Green, Ohio, Doones Press, 1972.
Time Being, with Asa Benveniste and Ray DiPalma. London, Blue Chair, 1972.
Here. Privately printed, 1973.
An Interesting Picture of Ohio. Privately printed, 1973.
Back to Nature. London, Joe DiMaggio Press, 1973.
Act. London, Trigram Press, 1973.
Ace. London, Cape Goliard Press, 1974; Berkeley, California, Figures, 1977.
Bolivia: Another End of Ace. London, Secret, 1974.
Cloister. Northampton, Massachusetts, Sand Project Press, 1975.
That More Simple Natural Time Tone Distortion. Storrs, University of Connecticut Library, 1975.
Common Sense. Healdsburg, California, Zephyrus Image, 1976.
The Mask. Berkeley, California, Poltroon Press, 1976.
Sky Tails. Cambridge, Lobby Press, 1978.
Four Door Guide. Cambridge, Street Editions, 1979.
Nicht Wahr, Rosie? Berkeley, California, Poltroon Press, 1979.
Writing. Berkeley, California, Figures, 1982.
Lèvre de Poche. Durham, North Carolina, Bull City Press, 1983.
Heavy Light. London, Actual Size, 1984.
Tottering State: New and Selected Poems 1963-1983. Berkeley, California, Figures, 1984.
Tractor Parts. Peterborough, Cambridgeshire, Spectacular Diseases, 1984.

Recording: *Little Trace Remains of Emmett Miller*, Stream Records, 1969.

Play

Screenplay: *A Plague on Both Your Houses*, 1966.

Other

The Minicab War (parodies), with Anselm Hollo and Gregory Corso. London, Matrix Press, 1961.
Betrayal. London, Trigram Press, 1967.
A Serial Biography. London, Fulcrum Press, 1969; Berkeley, California, Turtle Island, 1977.
Sic Him Oltorf! San Francisco, Zephyrus Image, 1974.
Logbook. Berkeley, California, Poltroon Press, 1977.
Cancer. Berkeley, California, Turtle Island, 1979.

Translator, with Valarie Raworth, *From the Hungarian.* Privately printed, 1973.

*

Manuscript Collections: Wilbur Cross Library, University of Connecticut, Storrs; John Barrell Collection, King's College, Cambridge.

Critical Studies: by Jeff Nuttall, in *Poetry Information 9-10* (London), 1974; Geoffrey Ward, in *Perfect Bound* (Cambridge), Winter 1976-77; John Barrell, in *Granta* (Cambridge), Autumn 1977; Rod Mengham, in *L=A=N=G=U=A=G=E 6* (New York), December 1978; *The British Dissonance* by A. Kingsley Weatherhead, Columbia, University of Missouri Press, 1983; William Corbett, in *Poetics Journal 2* (Berkeley, California), 1983; Colin MacCabe, in *Times Literary Supplement* (London), December 1983.

*   *   *

In Tom Raworth's poetry, there is a reluctance to sort, and so distort, language from experience. It is an agreement the poet has with himself, to let things stand, to accept the persistent fall of experience. His lines are a succession of phrases and images that are principally autonomous, non-referential statements. These are flicks of the mind's eye, pure cinematics, seemingly promiscuous because the pattern may be on too large a scale or too subliminal for usual acts of perception. The problem is briefly explored in *Tracking:* "the connections (or connectives) no/longer work—so how to build the long/poem everyone is straining for? (the/synopsis is enough for a quick mind now/(result of film?.)..." The associations are not ideas or feelings, but patterns of mind meeting events, recorded not so much for sake of discovery but to document how words and experience might occur with a minimum of willed intervention.

Randomness is his faith. It is in part a response to media explosion, a revolt against data bombardment. He is distrustful of the world that words circumscribe and, in order to be free of the rule of language manipulation, is driven beyond cohesion and clarity as values—"Until finally writing becomes the only thing that's not a petroleum by-product, or a neat capsule available without prescription." He resists the exploitations of the conscious mind, and is aware of the long tradition of such resistance (a dinghy hauled behind in *Logbook* is named "Automatic Writing"). His procedure and form are increasingly that of the notebook, and are summarized in three quick lines from a series of such jottings published as *Pleasant Butter*: "random gives/faster flicker/to draw from." Already in *The Relation Ship*, there is a poem with the title "Notebook," along with others of a similar activity, notably "Six Days," a "documentary" written while staying briefly in Paris, on loose sheets afterwards pieced together, the scraps of each day; while in *Moving*, the sequence "Antlers" has only dates and times for titles.

An important clue to Raworth's compositional technique can be found in the prose *A Serial Biography*, which grew out of letters to Edward Dorn (serial in the sense of produced in instalments, but hardly an orderly sequence). There, the narrator tells of writing a book with a friend while working for a pharmaceuticals firm. Each would type out a chapter a day on memo paper, exchanging them through the internal mails. In one section, which he himself is not satisfied with, the narrator pulls the sheet from the typewriter and adds in pencil: "Imagine slightly to the left of this paragraph." (Similarly, in "Wedding Day" in *The Relation Ship*, the poet writes, "i/inhabit a place just to the left of that phrase.") That is, the writing is deliberately off-centered, oblique, out of focus—the way a painter might squint or step back and cover an eye to gain a fresh approach to a painting stale or stubborn.

There are startling juxtapositions and a troubling elliptical quality to Raworth's work, but his deliberate amassing of inert material, non-organic, desensitized data, is not surrealism. Surrealism makes a crooked sense. Moreover, its images are dream-vivid and their junctures evident. Here, there is a ribbon flatness. Language is cut off from anything other than its own momentum (nor is it self-generative, with puns and allusions). One knows from poems such as "The Others," "Morning," "Got Me," or

"Shoes," that the poet is capable of humor, sarcasm, wit, even envy and despair. It is evident he actively chooses discontinuity, or, more precisely, allows it and the silences in between. The "buzz," he calls it—a blank honesty. He allows his personality to remain deliberately flat, withdrawn, so the words may be cast in deeper shadows. The result is what Dorn, in writing about Raworth, calls "the experience of apparently inconsequential *detail* shorn of manner." Ultimately, it is a poetry characteristic not of indecision but immense tolerance and patience toward the human condition, a careful lowering of the threshold through which coherence must pass.

—George F. Butterick

———————

RAY, David. American. Born in Sapulpa, Oklahoma, 20 May 1932. Educated at the University of Chicago, B.A. 1952, M.A. 1957. Married Judy Morrish in 1970; three daughters and one son. Member of the Faculty, Wright Junior College, Chicago, 1957-58, Northern Illinois University, DeKalb, 1958-60, and Cornell University, Ithaca, New York, 1960-64; Assistant Professor of Literature and Humanities, Reed College, Portland, Oregon, 1964-66; Lecturer in English, University of Iowa, Iowa City, 1969-71. Since 1971, Professor of English, University of Missouri, Kansas City. Visiting Professor, Syracuse University, New York, 1978-79, and University of Rajasthan, India, 1981-82. Editor, *Chicago Review*, 1956-57; Associate Editor, *Epoch*, Ithaca, New York, 1960-64. Since 1971, Editor, *New Letters*, Kansas City, Missouri. Recipient: *New Republic* Young Writers Award, 1958; Bread Loaf Writers Conference Robert Frost Fellowship, 1964; Woursell Foundation and University of Vienna fellowship, 1966; Coordinating Council of Literary Magazines fellowship, 1979; William Carlos Williams award, 1979; National Endowment for the Arts fellowship, 1983; Sotheby's Arvon prize, 1983; P.E.N. fiction award, 1983, 1984. Address: Department of English, University of Missouri, Kansas City, Missouri 64110, U.S.A.

PUBLICATIONS

Verse

X-Rays.   Ithaca, New York, Cornell University Press, 1965.
Dragging the Main and Other Poems.   Ithaca, New York, Cornell University Press, 1968.
A Hill in Oklahoma.   Shawnee Mission, Kansas, Bkmk Press, 1973.
Gathering Firewood: New Poems and Selected.   Middletown, Connecticut, Wesleyan University Press, 1974.
Enough of Flying: Poems Inspired by the Ghazals of Ghalib. Calcutta, Writers Workshop, 1977.
The Tramp's Cup.   Kirksville, Missouri, Chariton Review Press, 1978.
Five Missouri Poets, with others, edited by Jim Barnes.   Kirksville, Missouri, Chariton Review Press, 1979.
The Farm in Calabria and Other Poems, edited by Morty Sklar. Iowa City, Spirit That Moves, 1980.
The Touched Life: Poems Selected and New.   Metuchen, New Jersey, Scarecrow Press, 1982.
On Wednesday I Cleaned Out My Wallet.   San Francisco, Pancake Press, 1984.

Short Stories

The Mulberries of Mingo.   Austin, Texas, Cold Mountain Press, 1978.

Other

Editor, *The Chicago Review Anthology*.   Chicago, University of Chicago Press, and London, Cambridge University Press, 1959.
Editor, *From the Hungarian Revolution: A Collection of Poems*.   Ithaca, New York, Cornell University Press, 1966.
Editor, with Robert Bly, *A Poetry Reading Against the Vietnam War*.   Madison, Minnesota, American Writers Against the Vietnam War, 1966.
Editor, with Robert M. Farnsworth, *Richard Wright: Impressions and Perspectives*.   Ann Arbor, University of Michigan Press, 1973.
Editor, with Judy Ray, *New Asian Writing*.   Calcutta, Writers Workshop, 1979.
Editor, with Jack Salzman, *The Jack Conroy Reader*.   New York, Burt Franklin, 1980.
Editor, *From A to Z: 200 Contemporary American Poets*. Athens, Swallow Press—Ohio University Press, 1981.
Editor, *Collected Poems*, by E.L. Mayo.   Athens, Ohio University Press, 1981.
Editor, with Amritjit Singh, *India: An Anthology of Contemporary Writing*.   Athens, Ohio University Press, 1983.
Editor, *New Letters Reader 1* and *2*.   Athens, Swallow Press—Ohio University Press, 2 vols., 1984.

Translator, *Not Far from the River* (from the Prakrit).   Jaipur, India, Prakrit Society, 1984.

*

David Ray comments:

I like comparisons that have been made of my poems to X-rays or to found objects, as my poems are attempts to render verbal equivalents of what happens inside me or in persons or things I have found in the world and which have given me and sometimes them a different context through my finding them.

*   *   *

David Ray's poems are rooted in personal experience—those that have befallen him or persons he knows—and in place—his childhood homes, his hometown, various American cities and countrysides, foreign shores. At their best, and much of Ray's work to date is excellent, his poems reveal their maker's deep understanding of the subject at hand while, simultaneously, offering the reader an elegance of expression. Never is his work heavy-handed or fey, but always honest, whether he is zeroing in on memories of his childhood or on his socio-political concerns. Speaking to his son in "At the Washing of My Son," Ray remembers aloud when he first saw the boy, focusing on a topic most fathers would find difficult, if not impossible, to approach—the Oedipal situation—with such sharpness and candor that one is momentarily awe-struck: "You were / Covered with your mother's blood, and I saw / That navel where you and I were joined to her."

Ray displays a lyrical intensity that is enthralling. A boy's terror over growing old is revealed in the second of "Two Farm Scenes:"

Oh why does he fear his grandfather
Grey in the startling sun, beyond silken curls?
Only that that man might bother
To stoop and tell him how years flee,
Delicate and skittish as his pale pony.

The wonderful contrast of the "grandfather / Grey in the startling sun" with the "silken curls" of corn tassels, a youthful and
sexual image, shows Ray's craft at its most effective. It may also
be observed in "The Paseo in Irun," in which "the *novia* / and the
novio"

                    ...stroll along
    once more   nothing
    gets accomplished   except
    what is seen   on a face

or in "At the Train Station in Pamplona," in which lovers break
up. The woman leaves on a train, although she would "still / die
for" her man's love: "When she settles herself by the window /
she is already broadcasting to other / men the message of her
helplessness."

Ray's poems reverberate with detail. Some are of a private,
lyrical nature. In "This Life" the narrator bemoans his lack of
sons and his abundance of daughters and asks, "Who knew I
would bear such a bounty of daughters / girls of slippers and
wheat / girls of roses and sighs...." Other details in his work are
decidedly public in nature, evoking a particular time and place.
In a poem such as "Deathlace," these include: "pink stucco,"
"Standard Oil," "dinosaur balloons," "Highway 66," and "Dodge,
Ford, Pontiac, Studebaker."

Many of Ray's poems offer poignant, even brutal, views of
rural or small-town life. The "I" in one of the strongest of these,
"Dragging the Main," finally speaks with the girl with whom he
is infatuated and whom he has been following "round and round
the / City blocks" all night:

She said it wasn't love stinging my face
But only the pure cars of America that
Were dragging the main, looking for fools
Who want to hold even the lights of Main
Street, and the sweetness of a face.

But urban life doesn't escape Ray's eye. In poems such as "A
Midnight Diner by Edward Hopper," "Skid Row," and "To
Queen Elizabeth," the loneliness of city-dwellers is revealed.

While most of Ray's work is personal, even private, there is a
public side to him: a strong social concern that rarely sinks into
the pedantic or propagandistic. Whether addressing issues of
international importance or those rampant only in the United
States, his public poetry is as deeply felt and intelligent as his
more private work. In "Some Notes on Vietnam," for instance,
his bitterness over U.S. involvement in Vietnam is concisely,
powerfully stated: "What have they brought to the streets / of
Saigon except smog / and for the kids lessons on how to suck?"
Yet, his social consciousness does not exclude the possibility of,
even the need for, humor in dealing with the social ills of our day.
"The Indians near Red Lake," told from a Native American's
point of view, reveals, humorously at times, the absurdity of
white chauvinism:

When the white man comes
he comes to see a grave,
to look at the little house
over the grave, to ask
how the dead can eat the food

placed there
and always we give him the same answer
"The same way, white man,
your dead can smell your flowers."

—Jim Elledge

REANEY, James (Crerar). Canadian. Born in South East-
hope, Ontario, 1 September 1926. Educated at Elmhurst Public
School, Easthope Township, Perth County; Stratford High
School; University College, Toronto (Epstein Award, 1948),
B.A. 1948, M.A. 1949, Ph.D. in English 1958. Married Colleen
Thibaudeau in 1951; two sons (one deceased) and one daughter.
Member of the English Department, University of Manitoba,
Winnipeg, 1949-60. Since 1960, Professor of English, Middlesex
College, University of Western Ontario, London. Founding Edi-
tor, *Alphabet* magazine, London, 1960-1971. Active in little
theatre groups in Winnipeg and London. Recipient: Governor-
General's Award, for verse, 1950, 1959, for drama, 1963; Presi-
dent's Medal, University of Western Ontario, 1955, 1958;
Chalmers Award, for drama, 1975, 1976. D.Litt.: Carleton Uni-
versity, Ottawa, 1975. Fellow, Royal Society of Canada: Member,
Order of Canada. Agent: Sybil Hutchinson, Apartment 409,
Ramsden Place, 50 Hillsboro Avenue, Toronto, Ontario M5R
1S8, Canada.

PUBLICATIONS

Verse

The Red Heart.   Toronto, McClelland and Stewart, 1949.
A Suit of Nettles.   Toronto, Macmillan, 1958.
Twelve Letters to a Small Town.   Toronto, Ryerson Press,
1962.
The Dance of Death at London, Ontario.   London, Ontario,
Alphabet, 1963.
Poems, edited by Germaine Warkentin.   Toronto, New Press,
1972.
Selected Shorter [and *Longer*] *Poems,* edited by Germaine
Warkentin.   Erin, Ontario, Press Porcépic, 2 vols., 1975-76.
Imprecations: The Art of Cursing Revived.   Windsor, Ontario,
Black Moss Press, 1984.

Plays

Night-Blooming Cereus (broadcast, 1959; produced Toronto,
1960). Included in *The Killdeer and Other Plays,* 1962.
The Killdeer (produced Toronto, 1960; Glasgow, 1965). Included
in *The Killdeer and Other Plays,* 1962; revised version (pro-
duced Vancouver, 1970), in *Masks of Childhood,* 1972.
One-Man Masque (produced Toronto, 1960).   Included in *The
Killdeer and Other Plays,* 1962.
The Easter Egg (produced Hamilton, Ontario, 1962).   Included
in *Masks of Childhood,* 1972.
The Killdeer and Other Plays (includes *Sun and Moon, One-
Man Masque, Night-Blooming Cereus*).   Toronto, Macmil-
lan, 1962.
Sun and Moon (produced Winnipeg, 1971).   Included in *The
Killdeer and Other Plays,* 1962.
Names and Nicknames (produced Winnipeg, 1963).   Roway-
ton, Connecticut, New Plays for Children, 1969.

Apple Butter (puppet play; also director: produced London, Ontario, 1965). Included in *Apple Butter and Other Plays,* 1973.

Let's Make a Carol: A Play with Music for Children, music by Alfred Kunz. Waterloo, Ontario, Waterloo Music, 1965.

Listen to the Wind (produced London, Ontario, 1965). Vancouver, Talonbooks, 1972.

Colours in the Dark (for children; produced Stratford, Ontario, 1967). Vancouver and Toronto, Talonbooks-Macmillan, 1970.

Ignoramus (for children; produced Toronto, 1967). Included in *Apple Butter and Other Plays,* 1973.

Geography Match (for children; produced London, 1967). Included in *Apple Butter and Other Plays,* 1973.

Three Desks (produced Calgary, 1967). Included in *Masks of Childhood,* 1972.

Masque, with Ron Cameron (produced Toronto, 1972). Toronto, Simon and Pierre, 1974.

Masks of Childhood (includes *The Killdeer, Three Desks, The Easter Egg*), edited by Brian Parker. Toronto, New Press, 1972.

All the Bees and All the Keys, music by John Beckwith (for children; produced Toronto, 1972). Erin, Ontario, Press Porcépic, 1976.

Apple Butter and Other Plays for Children (includes *Names and Nicknames, Ignoramus, Geography Match*). Vancouver, Talonbooks, 1973.

The Donnellys: A Trilogy:
  1. *Sticks and Stones* (produced Toronto, 1973). Erin, Press Porcépic, 1975.
  2. *St. Nicholas Hotel* (produced Toronto, 1974). Erin, Ontario, Press Porcépic, 1976.
  3. *Handcuffs* (produced Toronto, 1975). Erin, Ontario, Press Porcépic, 1976.

Baldoon, with C.H. Gervais (produced Toronto, 1975). Erin, Ontario, Porcupine's Quill, 1976.

The Dismissal; or, Twisted Beards and Tangled Whiskers (produced Toronto, 1977). Erin, Ontario, Press Porcépic, 1979.

Wacousta! adaptation of the novel by John Richardson (produced Toronto, 1978). Erin, Ontario, Press Porcépic, 1979.

King Whistle! (produced Stratford, Ontario, 1979). Published in *Brick 8* (Ilderton, Ontario), Winter 1980.

Gyroscope (produced Toronto, 1981). Toronto, Playwrights Canada, 1983.

The Shivaree (opera), music by John Beckwith (produced Toronto, 1982).

The Canadian Brothers (produced Calgary, Alberta, 1983). Published in *Major Plays of the Canadian Theatre 1983-1984,* edited by Richard Perkyns. Toronto, Irwin, 1984.

Radio Play: *Night-Blooming Cereus,* 1959.

Other

The Boy with an "R" in His Hand (for children). Toronto, Macmillan, 1965.

14 Barrels from Sea to Sea. Erin, Ontario, Press Porcépic, 1977.

*

Critical Studies: *James Reaney* by Alvin A. Lee, New York, Twayne, 1968; *James Reaney* by Ross G. Woodman, Toronto, McClelland and Stewart, 1971; *James Reaney* by J. Stewart Reaney, Agincourt, Ontario, Gage, 1977.

Theatrical Activities:
Director: **Plays**—*One-Man Masque and Night-Blooming Cereus,* Toronto, 1960; *Apple Butter,* London, Ontario, 1965.
Actor: **Plays**—In *One-Man Masque and Night-Blooming Cereus,* Toronto, 1960.

James Reaney comments:

My poetry can probably best be summed up in three words: What I've tried to do and what I keep trying to do is Listen to the Wind, see Colours in the Dark.

*   *   *

One of the most original and imaginative poets in Canada, James Reaney has published only a small body of work in the past two decades, but it is poetry with a powerful consistency and concentration of mind. His plays have added to the body of his work, and so has his critical writing and editorial direction of the magazine *Alphabet,* which he founded and edited for ten years.

Alphabet, following the critical theories of Northrop Frye, under whom Reaney once studied, is concerned with "the iconography of the imagination," and successive issues have developed specific mythopoeic themes in poetry, prose, and the fine arts. Reaney as editor sometimes took up characteristic positions critical of science and of rationalism, but his own poetry is both wider and deeper (more personally focused) than these ideas would suggest. It is as a poet that he makes his strongest impact, and his imagination seems to be ordered by deep inner necessity rather than by any special theory or criticism.

His first book, *The Red Heart,* already contains the essential elements of his view of life. It offers dazzling and provocative leaps of fantasy, free-wheeling satire, and wild surrealist wit. But there are also deeply serious poems which set the tone for the book and for Reaney's later work.

These poems deal with death, with the universal stage of nature marked by change and destined for ultimate extinction, and with the mystery of the perishable individual heart and mind. Against this backdrop, the world of human concerns withers into insignificance, and thus provides the subject for Reaney's brilliant secular satires.

Further, in the context of death and human folly, the poetry reveals a powerful attachment to childhood memories and emotions. Against the world of childhood, the adult world becomes polarized as its opposite, the scene of triviality and horror.

Reaney's second book, *A Suit of Nettles,* is a complex satire, purportedly directed at Canadian life in Ontario Province, but really concerned with life generally, under the guise of an animal allegory. The poem is a metrical *tour-de-force* in imitation of Spencer's *Shepheardes Calender.* Language is used with a good deal of archaizing arbitrariness and artificial word-placing, but the whole effect is one of great skill and virtuousity in satirical handling. The themes of the earlier book are formalized into what is now clearly a unifying vision, and in technical skill the whole is a professional execution of a full and unified work.

The nature of this vision is thoroughly traditional and recognizably Christian. The *contemptus mundi* is fully explored in the farm and goose allegory; and the complementary theme of eternal order is only touched on here and there. In all his work so far, the Christian resolution appears in only two crucial passages, one at the close of *The Dance of Death,* and the other toward the end of *A Suit of Nettles,* in the November section.

A Suit of Nettles is Reaney's most ambitious and satisfying book. The collections published since are minor developments of his central themes. *Twelve Letters to a Small Town* is written in the style of mock infantilism; it explores the world of childhood in the satirical secular dimension. *The Dance of Death at London, Ontario* is an imitation of the late medieval genre, continuing the same satire on a more general social canvas.

—Louis Dudek

REDGROVE, Peter (William). British. Born in Kingston, Surrey, 2 January 1932. Educated at Taunton School; Queens' College, Cambridge. Married 1) Barbara Redgrove (marriage dissolved), two sons and one daughter; 2) Penelope Shuttle, *q.v.*, one daughter. Scientific journalist and editor, 1954-61; Visiting Poet, State University of New York, Buffalo, 1961-62; Gregory Fellow in Poetry, Leeds University, 1963-65; Poet-in-Residence, Falmouth School of Art, Cornwall, 1966-83. O'Connor Professor, Colgate University, Hamilton, New York, 1974-75. Recipient: Fullbright Fellowship, 1961; Arts Council grant, 1969, 1970, 1973, 1977, 1982; *Guardian* Prize, for fiction, 1973; Prudence Farmer Award, 1977; Imperial Tobacco Award, for radio play, 1978; Giles Cooper Award, for radio play, 1981; Italia Prize, for radio play, 1982. Fellow, Royal Society of literature, 1982. Lives in Falmouth, Cornwall. Agent: David Higham Associates, 5-8 Lower John Street, London W1R 4HA, England.

PUBLICATIONS

Verse

The Collector and Other Poems. London, Routledge, 1960.
The Nature of Cold Weather and Other Poems. London, Routledge, 1961.
At the White Monument and Other Poems. London, Routledge, 1963.
The Force and Other Poems. London, Routledge, 1966.
The God-Trap. London, Turret, 1966.
The Old White Man. London, Poet and Printer, 1968.
Penguin Modern Poets 11, with D.M. Black and D.M. Thomas. London, Penguin, 1968.
Works in Progress MDMLXVIII. London, Poet and Printer, 1968.
The Mother, The Daughter and the Sighing Bridge. Oxford, Sycamore Press, 1970.
The Shirt, The Skull and the Grape. Frensham, Surrey, Sceptre Press, 1970.
Love's Journeys. Cardiff, Second Aeon, 1971.
The Bedside Clock. Oxford, Sycamore Press, 1971.
Love's Journeys: A Selection. Crediton, Devon, Gilbertson, 1971.
Dr. Faust's Sea-Spiral Spirit and Other Poems. London, Routledge, 1972.
Two Poems. Rushden, Northamptonshire, Sceptre Press, 1972.
The Hermaphrodite Album, with Penelope Shuttle. London, Fuller d'Arch Smith, 1973.
Sons of My Skin: Selected Poems 1954-1974, edited by Marie Peel. London, Routledge, 1975.
Aesculapian Notes. Knotting, Bedfordshire, Sceptre Press, 1975.
Skull Event. Knotting, Bedfordshire, Sceptre Press, 1977.
Ten Poems. London, Words Press, 1977.

The Fortifiers, The Vitrifiers, and the Witches. Knotting, Bedfordshire, Sceptre Press, 1977.
From Every Chink of the Ark and Other New Poems. London, Routledge, 1977.
Happiness. Berkhamsted, Hertfordshire, Priapus Press, 1978.
The White, Night-Flying Moths Called "Souls." Knotting, Bedfordshire, Sceptre Press, 1978.
The Weddings at Nether Powers and Other New Poems. London, Routledge, 1979.
The First Earthquake. Knotting, Bedfordshire, Martin Booth, 1980.
The Apple-Broadcast and Other New Poems. London, Routledge, 1981.
The Working of Water. Durham, Taxus Press, 1984.
A Man Named East and Other New Poems. London, Routledge, 1985.

Plays

The Sermon: A Prose Poem (broadcast, 1964). London, Poet and Printer, 1966.
Three Pieces for Voices. London, Poet and Printer, 1972.
In the Country of the Skin (broadcast, 1973). Rushden, Northamptonshire, Sceptre Press, 1973.
Miss Carstairs Dressed for Blooding and Other Plays. London, Boyars, 1977.
The God of Glass (broadcast, 1977). London, Routledge, 1979.
The Hypnotist (produced Plymouth, 1978).
Martyr of the Hives (broadcast, 1980). Published in *Best Radio Plays of 1980,* London, Eyre Methuen, 1981.

Radio Plays: *The White Monument,* 1963; *The Sermon,* 1964; *The Anniversary,* 1964; *In the Country of the Skin,* 1973; *The Holy Sinner,* from a novel by Thomas Mann, 1975; *Dance the Putrefact,* music by Anthony Smith-Masters, 1975; *The God of Glass,* 1977; *Martyr of the Hives,* 1980; *Florent and the Tuxedo Millions,* 1982; *The Sin-Doctor,* 1983; *Dracula in White,* 1984; *The Scientists of the Strange,* 1984.

Television Play: *Jack Be Nimble,* 1980.

Novels

In the Country of the Skin. Rushden, Northamptonshire, Sceptre Press, 1972.
The Terrors of Dr. Treviles, with Penelope Shuttle. London, Routledge, 1974.
The Glass Cottage: A Nautical Romance, with Penelope Shuttle. London, Routledge, 1976.
The God of Glass. London, Routledge, 1979.
The Sleep of the Great Hypnotist. London, Routledge, 1979.
The Beekeepers. London, Routledge, 1980.
The Facilitators; or, Mr. Hole-in-the-Day. London, Routledge, 1982.

Other

The Wise Wound: Menstruation and Everywoman, with Penelope Shuttle. London, Gollancz, 1978; as *The Wise Wound: Eve's Curse and Everywoman,* New York, Marek, 1979.

Editor, *Poet's Playground 1963.* Leeds, Schools Sports Association, 1963.
Editor, *Universities Poetry 7.* Keele, Universities Poetry Management Committee, 1965.

Editor, with John Fuller and Harold Pinter, *New Poems 1967*. London, Hutchinson, 1968.
Editor, with Jon Silkin, *New Poetry 5*. London, Hutchinson, 1979.
Editor, *Cornwall in Verse*. London, Secker and Warburg, 1982.

*

Manuscript Collections: Humanities Research Center, University of Texas, Austin; Brotherton Library, University of Leeds.

Critical Studies: "Groupings" by Roger Garfitt, in *British Poetry since 1960* edited by Michael Schmidt and Grevel Lindop, Oxford, Carcanet, 1972; "Peter Redgrove" by Marie Peel, in *Books and Bookmen* (London), April 1973; "Ways of Booming" by Douglas Dunn, in *Encounter* (London), September 1975; interview with Jed Rasula and Mike Erwin, in *Hudson Review* (New York), Autumn 1975; "The Voice of the Green Man" by Anne Stevenson, in *Times Literary Supplement* (London), 18 November 1977; *Tradition and Experiment in English Poetry* by Philip Hobsbaum, London, Macmillan, and Totowa, New Jersey, Rowman and Littlefield, 1979; "Peter Redgrove Issue" of *Poetry Review* (London), September 1981; "Not Mad or Bad" by George Szirtes, in *Quarto* (London), January-February 1982; "Summer Cobwebs" by Peter Bland, in *London Magazine*, February 1982; interview with Michelene Wandor, in *On Gender and Writing*, London, Pandora Press, 1983; interview with Philip Fried in *Manhattan Review*, Summer 1983.

* * *

"The most ordinary people have the most extraordinary dreams, and in them have a capacity for understanding and adaptation far beyond their waking lives," Peter Redgrove wrote in a recent review (*Guardian*, 12 April 1979). "Why do we so taboo the dream life when it is so plainly a continuum with the waking creative imagination?"

This continuum has always been a preoccupation of Redgrove's work, and most of his recent poetry has had the free associations, the astonishing, surreal proliferation of details, and the magical transformations of plot and image which we associate with dream. But even in his early poems, Redgrove was concerned to explore that tabooed interface where the ordinary domesticated ego feels both appalled and exhilarated by the sweeping energies of an exuberant and amoral instinctual world. The house, invaded by apparently alien forces which turn out to be an essential part of its being, is a frequent symbol of this process. In the fine poem "Old House," the richly kinetic verbs and boisterous syntax record such an invasion with ambiguous enthusiasm. The man, trying to sleep, but afraid of it (as in so many of these early poems), seems at first to be threatened by a dark, deathly force, suffocating in the debris of the past. But it's not the past but the future which terrifies, as the last line of each stanza indicates, speaking of a child not yet born, and his dread of bringing it into such a world. Only with the reassurance of the last stanza, which reduces his terror to a "silly agony" as his wife turns in her sleep and calls to him, does he learn "what children were to make a home for." In poem after poem this theme is repeated, in "Expectant Father" and "Foundation," for example, or "Bedtime Story for My Son," which turns, in the end, into a story aimed at reassuring the father as much as the child. The house seems to be haunted by the voice of a small boy. It becomes clear, finally, that the ghost is not the past, but the future pressing into existence: the voice comes "From just underneath both our skins," and the poem concludes, like so

many of these early ones, on a carefully prepared note of discovery, educating man and wife into love, procreation and time, which carries, as its obverse, a grasping of the supersession latent in all fulfilment. It is the tension, in these early poems, between domesticity, responsibility, the worried, paternal ego in the hard-earned house, and the spawning, heady but anarchic powers of the instinct, which makes for their success. The emotional strain of keeping the spiritual house in order gives the poems a linguistic resolution and vigour and a sense of contained energies. But the strain also breeds those nagging, fretful ghosts that haunt the early works, lurking in corners, unused rooms and (in "Corposant") a mouldy larder. In "Ghosts," the realization to which the poem works in its last lines is that the terrace is haunted after ten years of marriage, not by anything external, but by the "bold lovers" themselves, wth their "hints of wrinkles./Crows-feet and shadows," haunted. "Like many places with rough mirrors now./By estrangement, if the daylight's strong."

Later poems are more at ease, into a flamboyant and vertiginous whirl of language and imagery, to communicate their sense of the vibrant energies of the natural world. "Lazarus and the Sea," in Redgrove's first volume, presages this development, initiating that theme of Orphic descent which is at times to overwhelm his poetry. Lazarus, dredged "Back to my old problems and to the family" out of "the tide of my death," is resentful of his saviour, feeling uprooted as if by some hostile judgment which charges him "with unfitness for this holy simplicity." An antinomian desire for return to such "holy simplicity" lies behind much of the later poetry. In *The Weddings at Nether Powers*, as the title suggests, the theme is still strong. In "Pleasing the Black Vicar" Redgrove here speaks of wanting "to accept/The presence beyond the altar, beyond appearances," a wish that also lies behind the macabre yet strangely translucent parable of the Emperor who wishes to be flayed in "The Son of My Skin" (*Pieces for Voices*). A note to *Weddings* tells us that "the poems descend, and return with something not thought or felt before." In a sense, this is not just a descent into the unconscious of nature, into dream and the lost continent of the carnal body; it is also a descent in the unconscious language, which has always for Redgrove been corporeal, tangible, fleshly. In his poems we pass, as in "The House in the Acorn," through a series of opening and beckoning doors, losing ourselves in a more and more mysterious world where dimension and proportion are lost, a world where, as in "Dr. Faust's Sea-Spiral Spirit," "The roses have learnt to thunder" and "The plain pinafores alert themselves / And are a hive of angry spots," passing though the ritual mysteries of language as we pass through the metamorphoses of a nature where all is flux and entropy, creation and decreation, decomposition and renewal. In "The Case" Redgrove offers a line which sums up this double process, of discovery and return, where all changes and all remains the same: "It was like a door opening on a door of flowers that opened on flowers that were opening." In "Power" he tells us "We rose out of magma where power put his finger,/ And the lines show." In "The Force" a mill-wheel which produces electricity from a mountain beck becomes a symbol of the relation of consciousness to its unconscious sources: "It trembles with stored storms/That pulse across the rim to us, as light."

In the *Apple-Broadcast* electricity and water are again linked. Water is the Heraclitean flux that "makes her way, accustomed,/ Into all places." In poem after poem it assumes a multitude of forms, travelling along the food chain and infusing the cells of animal and plant and human being alike, in an electrochemical transfer of energies. The "apple broadcast" of the title is revealed in "Dream Kit" by a pun which blooms into literalness. TVs and radio sets are "Materialising cabinets" in which a reality in flux is made manifest: "The whole/Earth's atmosphere is a pond/Of trembling waves." But the TV is only an artificial dreaming-kit compared with the dreaming mind "that pushes its tumbler/Into the river that flows/Under the skin." From the opening poem of the volume, with it wineglass left out on the patio overflowing with thunderwater greedily gulped down by the poet, through to the title poem, which closes the volume, the poet is a divine, for whom "Water is everywhere, and I think with it,/And remember with it" ("From the Life of a Dowser"), translating its broadcasts into speech-acts and poems and his own life. Thus he propagates (again in a double sense) that message inscribed in the DNA of the genetic code, in which, as in "The Eye of Dr. Horus," the child is always the apple of the parent's eye, and from its eye in turn "the next life peers," reminding him of his own supplanting, so that "I can see that I am passing through/And withering as her gaze grows." Yet Redgrove refuses to be thrown by this sense of supersession, delighting rather in its reassurance of renewal.

Poems such as "The Idea of Entropy at Maenporth Beach," in which a girl in a white dress renews herself by a baptismal immersion in "the fat, juicy, incredibly tart muck" of the beach, and studies such as "*The Wise Wound*, about menstruation, insist on recovering the rejected, the spurned and tacky origins of our being, restoring an image of the human as a living process of ingustation, excretion, sheddings, and growth, like the nature which is all flux and exhalation, wind, water, spore, and, in the title of one poem, "Nothing but Poking." Redgrove pursues this vision with a missionary zeal, even insisting, in the review cited above, "that the Special Theory of Relativity originated in a wet dream of the young Albert Einstein, in which he was riding through the universe astride a beam of light.... Whether you think the story beautiful or ugly, possible or not, will depend on your knowledge of the true ways of the imagination."

—Stan Smith

REED, Henry. British. Born in Birmingham, Warwickshire, 22 February 1914. Educated at King Edward VI School, Birmingham; University of Birmingham (Robertson Scholar, 1934), B.A. (honours) in language and literature 1934, M.A. 1936. Served in the British Army, 1941-42. Teacher and free-lance journalist, 1937-41; with Foreign Office Naval Intelligence, London, 1942-45. Since 1945, broadcaster, journalist, and radio writer. Visiting Professor, 1964 and 1967, and Assistant Professor of English, 1965-66, University of Washington, Seattle. Recipient: Italia Prize, for radio play, 1953; Pye award, 1979. Address: c/o Jonathan Cape Ltd., 30 Bedford Square, London WC1B 3EL, England.

PUBLICATIONS

Verse

A Map of Verona. London, Cape, 1946; New York, Reynal, 1947.
Lessons of the War. New York, Chilmark Press, 1970.

Plays

Moby Dick: A Play for Radio from Herman Melville's Novel (broadcast, 1947). London, Cape, 1947.

The Queen and the Rebels, adaptation of a play by Ugo Betti (broadcast, 1954; produced London, 1955). Included in *Three Plays,* 1956.
The Burnt Flower-Bed, adaptation of a play by Ugo Betti (produced London, 1955; New York, 1974). Included in *Three Plays,* 1956.
Summertime, adaptation of a play by Ugo Betti (produced London, 1955). Included in *Three Plays,* 1956.
Island of Goats, adaptation of a play by Ugo Betti (produced New York, 1955). Published as *Crime on Goat Island,* London, French, 1960; San Francisco, Chandler, 1961.
Three Plays (includes *The Queen and the Rebels, The Burnt Flower-Bed, Summertime,* adaptations of plays by Ugo Betti). London, Gollancz, 1956; New York, Grove Press, 1958.
Corruption in the Palace of Justice, adaptation of a play by Ugo Betti (broadcast, 1958; produced New York, 1963).
The Advertisement, adaptation of a play by Natalia Ginzburg (produced London, 1968; New York, 1974). London, Faber, 1969.
The Streets of Pompeii and Other Plays for Radio (includes *Leopardi: The Unblest, The Monument; The Great Desire I Had; Return to Naples; Vincenzo*). London, BBC, 1971.
Hilda Tablet and Others: Four Pieces for Radio (includes *A Very Great Man Indeed; The Private Life of Hilda Tablet; A Hedge, Backwards; The Primal Scene, As It Were...*). London, BBC, 1971.

Radio Plays (selection): *Noises On,* 1946, expanded version as *Noises—Nasty and Nice,* 1947; *Moby Dick,* from the novel by Melville, 1947; *Pytheas,* 1947; *Leopardi: The Unblest, and The Monument,* 1949-50; *A By-Election in the Nineties,* 1951; *The Dynasts,* from the poem by Hardy, 1951; *Malatesta,* from a play by Henry de Montherlant, 1952; *The Streets of Pompeii,* 1952; *The Great Desire I Had,* 1952; *Return to Naples,* 1953; *All for the Best,* from a play by Pirandello, 1953; *A Very Great Man Indeed,* 1953; *The Private Life of Hilda Tablet,* 1954; *Hamlet, or, The Consequences of Filial Piety,* from a work by Jules Laforgue, 1954; *The Battle of the Masks,* from a work by Virginio Puecher, 1954; *The Queen and the Rebels,* from a play by Ugo Betti, 1954; *Emily Butter,* 1954; *Holiday Land,* from a play by Betti, 1955; *Vincenzo,* 1955; *A Hedge, Backwards,* 1956; *Don Juan in Love,* from a work by Samy Fayad, 1956; *Alarica,* from a play by Jacques Audiberti, 1956; *Irene,* from a play by Betti, 1957; *Corruption in the Palace of Justice,* from a play by Betti, 1958; *The Primal Scene, As It Were...,* 1958; *The Auction Sale,* 1958; *The Island Land Where the King Is a Child,* from a play by Montherlant, 1959; *One Flesh,* from a work by Silvio Giovaninetti, 1959; *Not a Drum Was Heard,* 1959; *Musique Discrète,* with Donald Swann, 1959; *The House on the Water,* from a play by Betti, 1961; *A Hospital Case,* from a work by Dino Buzzati, 1961; *The America Prize,* from a work by Buzzati, 1964; *Zone 36,* from a work by Buzzati, 1965; *Summer,* from a work by Romain Weingarten, 1969; *The Two Mrs. Morlis,* from a play by Pirandello, 1971; *The Strawberry Ice,* from a play by Natalia Ginzburg, 1973; *Room for August,* from a play by Pirandello, 1974; *Like the Leaves,* from a play by Giuseppe Giacosa, 1976; *The Wig,* from a play by Ginzburg, 1976; *Duologue,* from a play by Ginzburg, 1977; *The Soul Has Its Rights,* from a play by Giacosa, 1977; *Sorrows of Love,* from a play by Giacosa, 1978; *I Married You for Fun,* from a play by Ginzburg, 1980.

Other

The Novel since 1939. London, Longman, 1946.

Translator, *Perdu and His Father*, by Paride Rombi.   London,
  Hart Davis, 1954.
Translator, *Larger Than Life*, by Dino Buzzati.   London,
  Secker and Warburg, 1962.
Translator, *Eugénie Grandet*, by Balzac.   New York, New
  American Library, 1964.

*   *   *

Henry Reed, although he has published only one collection of
poems, *A Map of Verona*, is a much underrated writer. He is
better known for the highly amusing dramatic pieces he has
written for radio than for his poems.

A Map of Verona divides itself fairly simply into four
sections—poems written about the last World War, personal
poems, dramatic monologues, and a sequence entitled "Tintagel." Reed is also a comic poet, and he is certainly the only
writer of importance who has (in "Chard Whitlow") parodied
T.S. Eliot with complete success. This too must be taken into
account.

Henry Reed is a poet with a fine ear, a strongly disciplined
sense of form, and passionate feelings. The personal poems,
which will be considered first, are all the more effective because
emotion is never allowed to get out of hand; Reed always
eschews chaos. The title poem of his book is a good example of
all his finest qualities. Here are its first two stanzas:

  The flutes are warm: in to-morrow's cave the music
  Trembles and forms inside the musician's mind,
  The lights begin, and the shifting lights in the causeways
  Are discerned through the dusk, and the rolling river
    behind

  And in what hour of beauty, in what good arms,
  Shall I those regions and that city attain
  From whence my dreams and slightest movements rise?
  And what good Arms shall take them away again?

Here is nostalgia without a trace of sentimentality. Every
word is carefully chosen and placed. All this can be found in
other personal poems where, by sheer artistry, the poet can
communicate and, at the same time, keep the distance which all
very good poems of human feeling must have if they are not to
fall into bathos or formlessness.

"Morning," "The Return," "Outside and In," and "The Door
and the Window" all fall into this group of personal poems. The
last named has the beautiful opening stanza:

  My love, you are timely come, let me lie by your heart,
  For waking in the dark this morning, I woke to that
    mystery,
  Which we can all wake to, at some dark time or another:
  Waking to find the room not as I thought it was,
  But the window further away, and the door in another
    direction.

The sensibility which informs such poems as these is evident in a
rather different way in the poems about the Army written during
the 1939 war. *Here*, Reed displays irony as well as observation.
There is a section entitled "Lessons of the War" which is composed of three parts, "Naming of Parts," "Judging Distances,"
and "Unarmed Combat." In the first of these poems, the training
of soldiers and the arrival of Spring are most dexterously and
tellingly blended. The second stanza runs:

  This is the lower sling swivel. And this

  Is the upper sling swivel, whose use you will see
  When you are given your slings. And this is the piling
    swivel,
  Which in your case you have not got. The branches
  Hold in the gardens their silent eloquent gestures,
    Which in our case we have not got.

All the futility of war is rendered in these lines. Nature goes on
while men train in order to kill their enemy across the English
Channel. The last lines of "Naming of Parts" complete what is, in
its own very individual way, a most remarkable poem about war:
"and the almond-blossom/Silent in all the gardens and the bees
going backwards and forwards,/For to-day we have naming of
parts."

Henry Reed always writes with a skill which conceals itself.
This becomes more and more clear in the sequence called "The
Desert" (also much concerned with war) and "Tintagel." In the
latter, this poet's descriptive gifts are shown at their most
intense. Part One, "Tristram" contains these lines:

  The ruin leads your thoughts
  Past the moment of darkness when silence fell over the
    hall,
  And the only sound rising was the sound of frightened
    breathing...
  To the perpetually recurring story,
  The doorway open, either in the soft green weather,
  The gulls seen over the purple-threaded sea, the cliffs,
  Or open in mist....

"Tintagel" also demonstrates Reed's ability to enter into the
characters of others, which we find in the two monologues,
"Chrysothemis" and "Philoctetes." In these poems, his highly-
developed dramatic gift is clearly evident, especially in the matter of dialogue. Reed really brings Philoctetes to life in lines such
as the following:

  To my companions become unbearable,
  I was put on this island. But the story
  As you have heard it is with time distorted,
  And passion and pity have done their best for it...
  ...They seized me and forced me ashore,
  And wept.

The poet is completely identified with Philoctetes and his plight.

Finally we must glance at "Chard Whitlow (Mr. Eliot's Sunday Evening Postscript)," Henry Reed's brilliant parody of the
T.S. Eliot of *Four Quartets*. Here we have just two passages
from what is not a long piece:

  Seasons return, and to-day I am fifty-five
  And this time last year I was fifty-four,
  And this time next year I shall be sixty-two.

            I think you will find this put,
  Far better than I could ever hope to express it,
  In the words of Kharma: "It is, we believe,
  Idle to hope that the simple stirrup-pump
  Can extinguish hell."

This is true parody, both uproariously funny and shrewdly
ironic. Eliot's tone is perfectly caught, and Reed's mockery is not
unkind but illustrates the ownership of a fine ear and a mastery
of language.

Why such a good poet has written so little poetry is strange.
The BBC has a way of inadvertently making its poet-employees

either "dry-up" altogether or else produce a poem only now and then (Terence Tiller is another case in point). But Henry Reed has written a handful of poems that may well last; these are probably the war poems. His command over verse-forms and language is flawless. Perhaps, in old age, he will return to poetry again. It would be a loss to English literature if he did not.

—Elizabeth Jennings

REED, Ishmael (Scott). American. Born in Chattanooga, Tennessee, 22 February 1938. Educated at the University of Buffalo, New York, 1956-60. Married 1) Priscilla Rose (divorced), one daughter; 2) Carla Blank. Co-Founder of the *East Village Other*, New York, and *Advance*, Newark, New Jersey, 1965. Since 1971, Chairman and President of Yardbird Publishing Company, and since 1973, Director, Reed Cannon and Johnson Communications, both Berkeley, California. Guest lecturer, University of California, Berkeley, 1968, 1969, 1974, 1976; Lecturer, University of Washington, Seattle, 1969-70; Visiting Professor, Yale University, New Haven, Connecticut, Fall 1979. President, Before Columbus Foundation. Recipient: National Endowment for the Arts grant, 1974; Rosenthal Foundation Award, 1975; Guggenheim Fellowship, 1975; American Academy Award, 1975; Michaux Award, 1978. Address: c/o Reed and Young's Quilt, 2140 Shattuck Avenue, Room 311, Berkeley, California 94704, U.S.A.

PUBLICATIONS

Verse

Catechism of d neoamerican hoodoo church. London, Paul Breman, 1970.
Conjure: Selected Poems 1963-1970. Amherst, University of Massachusetts Press, 1972.
Chattanooga. New York, Random House, 1973.
A Secretary to the Spirits. New York, NOK, 1978.

Novels

The Free-Lance Pallbearers. New York, Doubleday, 1967; London, MacGibbon and Kee, 1968.
Yellow Back Radio Broke-Down. New York, Doubleday, 1969; London, Allison and Busby, 1971.
Mumbo-Jumbo. New York, Doubleday, 1972.
The Last Days of Louisiana Red. New York, Random House, 1974.
Flight to Canada. New York, Random House, 1976.
The Terrible Twos. New York, St. Martin's Press—Marek, 1982.

Other

The Rise, Fall, and...? of Adam Clayton Powell (as Emmett Coleman), with others. New York, Bee-Line, 1967.
Shrovetide in Old New Orleans (essays). New York, Doubleday, 1978.
God Made Alaska for the Indians. New York, Garland, 1982.

Editor, *19 Necromancers from Now.* New York, Doubleday, 1970.

Editor, *Yardbird Reader* (annual). Berkeley, California, Yardbird, 5 vols., 1971-77.
Editor, with Al Young, *Yardbird Lives!* New York, Grove Press, 1978.
Editor, *Calafia: The California Poetry.* Berkeley, California, Yardbird, 1979.
Editor, *Quilt 2-3.* Berkeley, California, Reed and Young's Quilt, 2 vols., 1981-82.

*

Bibliography: "Mapping Out the Gumbo Works: An Ishmael Reed Bibliography" by Joe Weixlmann, Robert Fikes, Jr., and Ishmael Reed, in *Black American Literature Forum* (Terre Haute, Indiana), Spring 1978.

Ishmael Reed comments:
Themes—personal, magic, race, politics; no particular verse form.

* * *

Ishmael Reed is a satirist who today is primarily a novelist, but like many other Black American writers he started his literary career writing poetry. *Conjure* is his first collection of poetry and although it was not published until 1972 it is made up of renderings dating back to 1963—four years before his first novel.

Many of these poems foreshadow the subjects of his novels and point up the fact that his more recent preoccupations are the result of thinking over an extended period of time. For example, in his introduction to *19 Necromancers from Now*, Reed writes that because "Black writers have in the past written sonnets, iambic pentameter, ballads, [and] every possible Western gentleman's form," they have sacrificed their own originality. He further says that "Sometimes I feel that the condition of the Afro-American writer in this country is so strange that one has to go to the supernatural for an analogy." It is from this feeling that Reed has developed the view that the Black artist should function as a "conjuror" who employs "Neo-HooDoo" as a means of freeing his fellow victims from the psychic attack of his oppressors.

Ishmael Reed's poems are not unique either in their intent or their responsibility but they are poignant earlier examples of the dynamic wit and unabashed approach which he demonstrates in his novels. It is scathing, uncompromising satire, but he is always in full control. A typical example of his thematic focus on the incompatibility of Western civilization and the cultures of Africa and Asia is illustrated in this excerpt from "Badman of the Guest Professor":

> its not my fault dat yr tradition
> was knocked off wop style & let in
> d alley w/pricks in its mouth. i
> read abt it in d papers but it was no
> skin off my nose
> wasnt me who opened d gates & allowed
> d rustlers to slip thru unnoticed. u
> ought to do something about yr security or
> mend yr fences partner

and again in his prosey dictum from "The Ghost of Birmingham," a poem for which he feels impelled to apologize because it "shows the influence of people I studied in college":

> There has never been in history another culture as the
> Western civilization—a culture which has practiced the

belief
that the physical and social environment of man is subject
to
rational manipulation and that history is subject to the
will and
action of man; whereas central to the traditional cultures
of
the rivals of Western civilization, those of Africa and
Asia, is a
belief that it is environment dominates man.

Reed's works are certainly controversial among both Black and White critics, but he wouldn't have it any other way.

—Charles L. James

REEVE, F(ranklin) D(olier). American. Born in Philadelphia, Pennsylvania, 18 September 1928. Educated at Princeton University, New Jersey, A.B. 1950; Columbia University, New York, A.M. 1952, Ph.D. 1958. Married Helen Schmidinger in 1956; five children, including the actor Christopher Reeve. Taught at Columbia University, 1952-61. Associate Professor and Chairman of the Russian Department, 1962-64, Professor of Russian, 1964-66, and since 1968, Adjunct Professor of Letters, Wesleyan University, Middletown, Connecticut. Visiting Professor, Oxford University, 1964. Since 1972, Visiting Lecturer in English, and Fellow of Saybrook College, Yale University, New Haven, Connecticut. Member of the Governing Board, and Vice-President, Poetry Society, 1980-84; editor, *The Poetry Review*, New York. Recipient: Ford Fellowship, 1955; American Council of Learned Societies Fellowship, 1961; Ingram-Merrill Foundation award, 1961; American Academy grant, 1970; Rockefeller Fellowship, 1976. Lives in Vermont. Address: College of Letters, Wesleyan University, Middletown, Connecticut 06457, U.S.A.

PUBLICATIONS

Verse

The Stone Island. Middletown, Connecticut, Salamander Press, 1964.
Six Poems. Middletown, Connecticut, Salamander Press, 1964.
In the Silent Stones. New York, Morrow, 1968.
The Blue Cat. New York, Farrar Straus, 1972.
Angling. Colorado Springs, Press at Colorado College, 1984.

Play

The Three-Sided Cube (produced New London, Connecticut, 1972).

Novels

The Red Machines. New York, Morrow, 1968.
Just over the Border. New York, Morrow, 1969.
The Brother. New York, Farrar Straus, 1971; Henley-on-Thames, Oxfordshire, Ellis, 1975.
White Colors. New York, Farrar Straus, 1973; Henley-on-Thames, Oxfordshire, Ellis, 1974.

Other

Aleksandr Blok: Between Image and Idea. New York, Columbia University Press, 1962.
Robert Frost in Russia. Boston, Little Brown, 1964.
On Some Scientific Concepts in Russian Poetry at the Turn of the Century. Middletown, Connecticut, Wesleyan University Center for Advanced Studies, 1966.
The Russian Novel. New York, McGraw Hill, 1966; London, Muller, 1967.

Editor and Translator, *Five Short Novels of Turgenev.* New York, Bantam, 1961.
Editor and Translator, *An Anthology of Russian Plays.* New York, Random House, 2 vols., 1961-63; as *Nineteenth-* (and *Twentieth-*) *Century Russian Plays,* New York, Norton, 2 vols., 1973.
Editor and Translator, *Great Soviet Short Stories.* New York, Dell, 1963.
Editor and Translator, *Contemporary Russian Drama.* New York, Pegasus, 1968.
Editor and Translator, *Nobel Lecture by Alexander Solzhenitsyn.* New York, Farrar Straus, 1972.

*

F.D. Reeve comments:
The play between the surface—things as seen—and the depths—the moral interpretations of things—is the life of poetry. Traditions supply the concepts, the forms, which we train ourselves to use to catch the experience of change. A poem's landscape delights the mind's eye by moving forward and back out of the present, transfixing change in tensions among words, ferrying between what is outside and the fictions in the imagination. The substance of poetry is metaphor, at times given in colloquial language and images from casual life, at times given in strict verse patterns and difficult images of implication. The mask of the poet—philosopher, songster, clown, apostle—expresses his personality, dances before the reader until the reader picks up a new consciousness.

*   *   *

F.D. Reeve's first collection, *In the Silent Stones,* is mostly rhymed and metrical—jingling anapests or more flexible iambics. A sign of uncertainty is the frequency with which elaborate stanza forms are undertaken only to be modified. Devices often seem tricks of the trade rather than expressive means: "I head for the heart of a girl / on the soft white breast of the world." But the wit can be amusing, even when it merely decorates a banal observation: "The conversation seesaws on the rim of a teacup. / Highwire ladies drop to save a faux pas..." ("Summer Circus"). One is aware of echoes—of the "Movement" ("Chinese Poem"), of Lowell ("The Plaque...for My Classmates Killed in Korea"), of Stevens ("A Tangram").

The Blue Cat shows more rhythmic subtlety and less ostentation (though a line like "That shallop symmetry burst from the hawse of her father" is hardly unforced). The imagery continues to be uneven, varying from the witty-elusive—"Like ribs around my body this armillary sphere / cages the fancy with old bars new Marco Polos must unbend" ("Hands")—to the merely flashy—"her hair / swinging like ten pendulums in love" ("The Blue Cat's Daughter"). Outstanding in the book, however, is a sequence of fourteen poems on the life of Thoreau which often achieves a moving intensity in evoking the New England moral climate. As Reeve gives himself to Thoreau we hear the voice of a man with more on his mind than self-display:

> Immoral slave who pleads a moral cause,
> bankrupt in Heaven and on earth a stone,
> man sets his course against the natural laws,
> plotting the steps to seize the beautiful

> but coming, after all, to his own wet bones.

—Seamus Cooney

REID, Alastair. British. Born in Whithorn, Wigtonshire, Scotland, 22 March 1926. Educated at the University of St. Andrews, Scotland, M.A. (honours) 1949. Served in the Royal Navy, 1943-46. Has one son. Taught at Sarah Lawrence College, Bronxville, New York, 1950-55; Fellow in Writing, Columbia University, New York, 1966; Visiting Professor of Latin American Studies, Antioch College, Yellow Springs, Ohio, 1969-70, Oxford University and St. Andrews University, 1972-73, Colorado College, Colorado Springs, 1977, 1978, Yale University, New Haven, Connecticut, 1979, and Dartmouth College, Hanover, New Hampshire, 1979. Since 1959, Staff Writer and Correspondent, *The New Yorker*. Gave lecture tours for the Association of American Colleges, 1966, 1969. Recipient: Guggenheim Fellowship, 1957, 1958; Scottish Arts Council award, 1979. Lives in New York and Spain. Address: c/o The New Yorker, 25 West 43rd Street, New York, New York 10036, U.S.A.

PUBLICATIONS

Verse

To Lighten My House. Scarsdale, New York, Morgan and Morgan, 1953.
Oddments Inklings Omens Moments. Boston, Little Brown, 1959; London, Dent, 1961.
Corgi Modern Poets in Focus 3, with others, edited by Dannie Abse. London, Corgi, 1971.
Weathering: Poems and Translations. Edinburgh, Canongate, and New York, Dutton, 1978.

Other

I Will Tell You of a Town (for children). Boston, Houghton Mifflin, 1956; London, Hutchinson, 1957.
Fairwater (for children). Boston, Houghton Mifflin, 1957.
A Balloon for a Blunderbuss (for children). New York, Harper, 1957.
Allth (for children). Boston, Houghton Mifflin, 1958.
Ounce Dice Trice (for children). Boston, Little Brown, 1958; London, Dent, 1961.
The Millionaires, with Bob Gill. New York, Simon and Schuster, 1959.
Supposing (for children). Boston, Little Brown, 1960; London, Sidgwick and Jackson, 1973.
Passwords: Places, Poems, Preoccupations. Boston, Little Brown, 1963; London, Weidenfeld and Nicolson, 1965.
To Be Alive! (for children). New York, Macmillan, 1966.

Mother Goose in Spanish, with Anthony Kerrigan. New York, Crowell, 1967.
Uncle Timothy's Traviata (for children). New York, Delacorte Press, 1967.
La Isla Azul (for children). Barcelona, Editorial Lumen, 1973.

Editor, with Emir Rodriguez Monegal, *Borges: A Reader*. New York, Dutton, 1981.

Translator, with others, *Ficciones*, by Jorge Luis Borges. New York, Grove Press, and London, Weidenfeld and Nicolson, 1965.
Translator, *We Are Many*, by Pablo Neruda. London, Cape Goliard Press, 1967; New York, Grossman, 1968.
Translator, with Anthony Kerrigan, *Jorge Luis Borges: A Personal Anthology*. New York, Grove Press, 1967; London, Cape, 1968.
Translator, with Ben Belitt, *A New Decade: Poems 1958-67*, by Pablo Neruda. New York, Grove Press, 1969.
Translator, with others, *Selected Poems: A Bilingual Edition*, by Pablo Neruda, edited by Nathaniel Tarn. London, Cape, 1970; New York, Delacorte Press, 1972.
Translator, *Extravagaria*, by Pablo Neruda. London, Cape, 1972; New York, Farrar Straus, 1974.
Translator, with others, *Selected Poems*, by Jorge Luis Borges. New York, Delacorte Press, and London, Penguin, 1972.
Translator, *Sunday Sunday*, by Mario Vargas Llosa. Indianapolis, Bobbs Merrill, 1973.
Translator, *Fully Empowered*, by Pablo Neruda. New York, Farrar Straus, 1975; London, Souvenir Press, 1976.
Translator, *The Gold of the Tigers*, by Jorge Luis Borges. New York, Dutton, 1977; with *The Book of Sand*, London, Allen Lane, 1979.
Translator, *Don't Ask Me How the Time Goes By: Poems 1964-1968*, by José Emilio Pacheco. New York, Columbia University Press, 1978.
Translator, *Isla Negra: A Notebook*, by Pablo Neruda. New York, Farrar Straus, 1981; London, Souvenir Press, 1982.
Translator, with Andrew Hurley, *Legacies: Selected Poems*, by Herberto Padilla. New York, Farrar Straus, 1982.

*

Manuscript Collections: State University of New York, Buffalo; National Library of Scotland, Edinburgh.

*   *   *

Alastair Reid's most recent collection of poems, *Weathering*, which includes a generous selection from his previous books, makes more evident, by a shift of focus, his distinctive contribution to literature. In *Oddments Inklings Omens Moments* a playful interest in words and in such subject matter as mirrors, magic, ghosts, cats, frogs, children, and games gives such immediate pleasure, that his deeper, underlying human concerns may be overlooked. The concern was there in the earlier poems. In "Cat-Faith" Reid's gratitude for the existence of a creature secure in its individuality, beautifully adapted for survival in a hazardous life, is at bottom a confirmation of an ultimate virtue in life itself. His valuation found explicit expression in: "Amazement is the thing./Not love, but the astonishment of loving." This affirmation is made in the recognition and acceptance for the law that "The garden is not ours." We are tenants in "Mediterranean":

The rent is paid in breath
and so we freely give
the apple tree beneath
our unpossessive love.

It is the writer's "unpossessive love" which allows him to accept the variety of life as it presents itself, and it is his fascination by words, which gives his poems their rare music as in "The Rain in Spain": "Faces press to windows./Strangers moon and booze./Innkeepers doze." The poet's technique draws the ordinary scene intimately and delicately as in "Me to You": "Tell me about the snowfalls/at night, and tell me how we'd sit in firelight/hearing dogs huff in sleep."

Affection, and generally tenderness, is written into the individual thing observed, and we are made aware of its transient nature, but unlike the more characteristic contemporary poet, there is no sense of threat to identity. Consequently there is an absence of tension or drama in the verse. If this is a limitation one should not conclude that this poetry, just in its observation and openness to impression, has been easily achieved. The more recent poetry shows reasons for his confidence and sense of wholeness. In "The Spiral" he writes:

the rooted self in me
maps out its true country.
And, as my father found
his own small weathered island,
so will I come to ground

—George Bruce

REID, Christopher. British. Born in Hong Kong, 13 May 1949. Educated at Tonbridge School, Kent, 1962-67; Exeter College, Oxford, 1968-71, B.A. (honours), 1971. Married Lucinda Catherine Gane in 1979. Recipient: Eric Gregory Award, 1978; Somerset Maugham Award, 1980; Hawthornden Prize, 1981. Address: 5/7 Camden Park Road, London N.W.1, England.

PUBLICATIONS

Verse

Arcadia. London and New York, Oxford University Press, 1979.
Pea Soup. Oxford and New York, Oxford University Press, 1982.

*   *   *

Christopher Reid is frequently associated with Craig Raine as one of the "Martian" school of poets, whose work is characterised, above all, by an extravagant or exuberant use of visual simile and metaphor, in an attempt to make the familiar (frequently the domestic) seem, in fact, the theatre of the richly exotic and strange. "Douanier Rousseau had no need to travel /to paint the jungles of his paradise," Reid says in one of his poems; and, referring often in his work to a wide variety of painters (notably Vuillard, Vermeer, Brueghel and Matisse), he shares with Rousseau a certain intense sharpness and immediacy of childlike vision:

Welcome to our peaceable kingdom,
where baby lies down with the tiger-rug

and bumblebees roll over like puppies
inside foxglove-bells....

Like some of the other writers loosely associated as Martians, Reid can occasionally seem to produce poems that are little more than collections of special effects. I particularly like the tankards in a London pub which, "pot-bellied, on hooks,/are lords of the air and as free/as a flight of sitting-room ducks," where the joke of the rhyme is in affectionately sympathetic consonance with the deflating hyperbole of the simile. And I like too the amazing conceits of "Baldanders," where a series of similes for a weight-lifter culminates like this:

Glazed, like a mantelpiece frog,
he strains to become

the World Champion (somebody, answer it!)
Human Telephone.

But Reid has more profound, and larger, preoccupations in his work than the mere elaboration of such visual inter-relationships, his "playground of impromptu metaphors," beguiling as this often is. The delighted apprehensions of his work are given their particular edge by an insistent pressure, from just outside, of everything that is not delight. What he calls "art's oddness and justness" is a different kind of ritual to cope with, above all, the pressure of mortality, now that the consolations of religion are no longer operable.

Many of Reid's poems do actually elaborate some kind of religious imagery, making—as it were—newly domestic sacraments out of the secular; and others, like the excellent "Magnum Opus" and "Charnel," consider, quite a way after Larkin's "Church Going," the emptied meanings of a Christian cathedral and graveyard. Similarly, when visiting Japan, Reid is drawn to the traditional stamping-grounds of the sacred in "a world/lacking all reciprocity." The conclusion of one of these poems, "Itsukushima," addresses a very secular prayer to very secular objects, but suggests, nevertheless, the impulse everywhere apparent in Reid to coax some kind of benediction out of the necessary and contingent circumstances of ordinary life: "Green seaweed wraiths, a beer-can, drunk,/are tugged by the tide...You Nothings, bless/me in my next-to-nothingness!" Christopher Reid's delight is never light-headed; it knows the nothingness it has to work hard not to be. Like his own eponymous "Ambassador," visiting a planet inhabited by children's toys, Reid too no doubt adheres

to the maxim, that through a studious
reading of chaos we may
arrive at the grammar of civilisation.

—Neil Corcoran

RICH, Adrienne (Cecile). American. Born in Baltimore, Maryland, 16 May 1929. Educated at Roland Park Country School, Baltimore, 1938-47; Radcliffe College, Cambridge, Massachusetts, A.B. (cum laude) 1951 (Phi Beta Kappa). Married Alfred H. Conrad in 1953 (died, 1970); three sons. Lived in the Netherlands, 1961-62. Taught at the YM—YWHA Poetry Center Workshop, New York, 1966-67; Visiting Poet, Swarthmore College, Pennsylvania, 1966-68; Adjunct Professor, Graduate Writing Division, Columbia University, New York, 1967-69; Lecturer, 1968-70, Instructor, 1970-71, Assistant Professor of English, 1971-72, and Professor, 1974, City College of New York; Fannie Hurst Visiting Professor, Brandeis University, Waltham, Massachusetts, 1972-73; Professor of English, Douglass College, New Brunswick, New Jersey, 1976-78. Since 1981, A.D. White Professor-at-Large, Cornell University, Ithaca, New York. Recipient: Yale Series of Younger Poets award, 1951; Guggenheim Fellowship, 1952, 1961; Ridgely Torrence Memorial Award, 1955; American Academy award, 1960; Amy Lowell Traveling Scholarship, 1962; Bollingen Foundation grant, for translation, 1962; Bess Hokin Prize, 1963, and Eunice Tietjens Memorial Prize, 1968 (*Poetry*, Chicago); National Translation Center grant, 1968; National Endowment for the Arts grant, 1969; Shelley Memorial Award, 1971; Ingram Merrill Foundation grant, 1973; National Book Award, 1974; Donnelly Fellowship, Bryn Mawr College, Pennsylvania, 1975; Fund for Human Dignity Award, 1981. D.Litt.: Wheaton College, Norton, Massachusetts, 1967; Smith College, Northampton, Massachusetts, 1979. Address: c/o W.W. Norton Inc., 500 Fifth Avenue, New York, New York 10110, U.S.A.

PUBLICATIONS

Verse

A Change of World.   New Haven, Connecticut, Yale University Press, 1951.
(Poems).   Oxford, Fantasy Press, 1952.
The Diamond Cutters and Other Poems.   New York, Harper, 1955.
The Knight, after Rilke.   Privately printed, 1957.
Snapshots of a Daughter-in-Law: Poems 1954-1962.   New York, Harper, 1963; London, Chatto and Windus, 1970.
Necessities of Life: Poems 1962-65.   New York, Norton, 1966.
Focus.   Privately printed, 1966.
Selected Poems.   London, Chatto and Windus, 1967.
Leaflets: Poems 1965-1968.   New York, Norton, 1969; London, Chatto and Windus, 1972.
The Will to Change: Poems 1968-1970.   New York, Norton, 1971; London, Chatto and Windus, 1973.
Diving into the Wreck: Poems 1971-1972.   New York, Norton, 1973.
Poems Selected and New 1950-1974.   New York, Norton, 1975.
Twenty-One Love Poems.   Emeryville, California, Effie's Press, 1976.
The Dream of a Common Language: Poems 1974-1977.   New York, Norton, 1978.
A Wild Patience Has Taken Me This Far: Poems 1978-1981.   New York, Norton, 1981.
Sources.   Woodside, California, Heyeck, 1983.
The Fact of a Doorframe: Poems Selected and New 1950-1984.   New York, Norton, 1984.

Recordings: *Today's Poets 4*, with others, Folkways; *Adrienne Rich Reading at Stanford*, Stanford, 1973; *A Sign I Was Not Alone*, with others, Out and Out, 1978.

Plays

Ariadne.   Baltimore, Furst, 1939.
Not I, But Death.   Baltimore, Furst, 1941.

Other

Of Woman Born: Motherhood as Experience and Institution.   New York, Norton, 1976; London, Virago, 1977.
Women and Honor: Some Notes on Lying.   Pittsburgh, Motheroot, 1977; London, Onlywomen Press, 1979.
On Lies, Secrets, and Silence: Selected Prose 1966-1978.   New York, Norton, 1979; London, Virago, 1980.
Compulsory Heterosexuality and Lesbian Existence.   London, Onlywomen Press, 1981; Denver, Antelope Press, 1982.

*

Critical Studies: "Voice of the Survivor: The Poetry of Adrienne Rich" by Willard Spiegelman, in *Southwest Review* (Dallas), Autumn 1975; *Adrienne Rich's Poetry* edited by Barbara Charlesworth Gelpi and Albert Gelpi, New York, Norton, 1975; *American Triptych: Anne Bradstreet, Emily Dickinson, Adrienne Rich* by Wendy Martin, Chapel Hill, University of North Carolina Press, 1984.

*   *   *

Adrienne Rich's first volume, *A Change of World*, reflects the poet's early interest in intellectual clarity and formal control. Somewhat derivative of Auden and Yeats, it questions traditional values, her contemporary world. Among several love poems in the volume Rich introduces two themes that will become synonymous with her mature work: time ("Storm Warnings") and the woman's plight. In "An Unsaid Word," she dictates the difficult lesson all women must learn—patience and accommodation to the usually estranged man: "She who has power to call her man/ From that estranged intensity/ Where his mind forages alone,/ Yet keeps her peace and leaves him free,/ And when his thoughts to her return/ Stands where he left her, still his own/ Knows this the hardest thing to learn."

The same resignation fills *The Diamond Cutters and Other Poems*: "We had to take the world as it was given," but the poems emphasize the isolation and loneliness of the woman who must "always...live in other people's houses" ("The Middle-Aged"). *Snapshots of a Daughter-in-Law* brings forth a new voice, looser forms, and sharper themes. The title poem, within a historical, mythic, and literary framework, describes the woman's lot wherein "our blight has been our sinecure." Attacking the fashionable feminine mystique, she describes the housewife's daily chores as funereal preparations: "Soon we'll be off, I'll pack us into parcels/ stuff us in barrels, shroud us in newspapers, / pausing to Marvel at old bargain sales" ("Passing On"). Woman is the product of an alien male society, perversely dependent upon men for sustenance, isolated from other women in "solitary confinement," filled with self-hatred and longings for self-expression. In such a world, where "time is male," the waste of creative energy is profound; suffocated or turned inward it becomes hysteria or guilt, ultimately depression or suicide: "A thinking woman sleeps with monsters/ The beak that grabs her, she becomes." One source of this remains clear, and in "A Marriage in the 'Sixties," Rich portrays: "Two strangers, thrust for life upon a rock, /...two minds, two messages," and she asks: "Will nothing ever be the same,/ even our quarrels take a different key,/ our dreams exhume new metaphors?"

Rich embraces the personal and historical past now as something to be confronted and clarified ("From Morning Glory"). She longs to change the world, and the door to change exists; "poised, trembling and unsatisfied," the poet stands "before an unlocked door"; yet, she warns, "The door itself/makes no promises./It is only a door" ("Prospective Immigrants Please Note").

In *Necessities of Life* Rich again cries out against the woman's desperate plight. She focuses now upon both erotic experience and her solitariness in nature—in order to regain contact with her body, as well as a childlike, even womblike security. To her lover she says: "Sometimes at night/you are my mother:/...and I crawl against you, fighting/for shelter, making you/my cave" ("Like This Together").

In *Leaflets*, in even more colloquial language, her political rage surfaces. As poet and woman, Rich calls out for sisterhood, a new politics, a new language: "I wanted to choose words that even you would have been changed by." In "On Edges" Rich's resistance is active:

> I'd rather
> taste blood, yours or mine, flowing
> from a sudden slash, than cut all day
> with blunt scissors on dotted lines
> like the teacher told.

The Will to Change develops these themes, especially the problem of using "oppressor's language" ("The Burning of Paper Instead of Children"): "We are bound on the wheel of an endless conversation." "I had pledged myself to try any/instrument that came my way" ("Shooting Script"). Perhaps poetry and erotic sexuality might connect the mind back to feeling: "When will we lie clear headed in our flesh again." "The moment when a feeling enters the body/is political." Then Rich, "in the prime of life" declares her position: "I am bombarded yet.../I am an instrument in the shape/of a woman trying to translate pulsations/into images for the relief of the body/and the reconstruction of the mind" ("Planetarium").

Rich comments that she is a feminist because she feels "endangered, psychically and physically, by this society, and because we have come to an edge of history when men—in so far as they are embodiments of the patriarchal idea—have become dangerous to children and other living things, themselves included." In *Diving into the Wreck* she commits herself to a full-fledged descent into the rubble of sexual-political warfare. In some of the poems she admits, more directly than ever, her hatred of men and her conditioned responses as girl, wife, and mother ("Dialogue"):

> I do not know
> if sex is an illusion
>
> I do not know
> who I was when I did those things
> or who I said I was
> or whether I willed to feel
> what I had read about
> or who in fact was there with me
> Or whether I knew, even then
> that there was doubt about these things.

To her male adversary she says: "I hate you./I hate the mask you wear, your eyes/Assuming a depth/they do not possess"; and she admits: "The only real love I have ever felt/was for children and other women./Everything else was lust, pity,/self-hatred, pity, lust/This is a woman's confession." "Phenomenology of Anger," is a militantly feminist poem in which Rich rages against repressed human energy, which in men finds its outlet in war and murder ("The prince of air and darkness/computing body counts, masturbating/in the factory/of facts"), in women, in

"Madness, Suicide. Death." The ills of patriarchy can be abolished only through sisterhood, through nurturing.

"The Stranger" goes beyond sexual warfare. Indeed a prisoner of language, Rich portrays herself as the androgyne, both the male and female, whose loving and nurturing would be restorative: "I am the androgyne/I am the living mind you fail to describe/in your dead language." "Diving into the Wreck" amplifies this:

> And I am here, the mermaid whose dark hair
> streams black, the merman in his armored body
> We circle silently
> about the wreck
> we dive into the hold.
> I am she: I am he
> whose drowned face sleeps with open eyes.

—Lois Gordon

RIDING, Laura. American. Born Laura Reichenthal in New York City, 16 January 1901; adopted the surname Riding in 1926. Educated at Girls' High School, Brooklyn; Cornell University, Ithaca, New York. Married 1) Louis Gottschalk in 1920 (divorced, 1925); 2) Schuyler B. Jackson in 1941 (died, 1968). Associated with the Fugitive group of poets; lived in Europe, 1926-39: with Robert Graves established the Seizin Press, 1928, and *Epilogue* magazine, 1935. Recipient: Fugitive prize, 1925; Mark Rothko Appreciation award, 1971; Guggenheim Fellowship, 1973; National Endowment for the Arts Fellowship, 1979. Address: Box 35, Wabasso, Florida 32970, U.S.A.

PUBLICATIONS

Verse

The Close Chaplet (as Laura Riding Gottschalk). London, Hogarth Press, and New York, Adelphi, 1926.
Voltaire: A Biographical Fantasy (as Laura Riding Gottschalk). London, Hogarth Press, 1927; Folcroft, Pennsylvania, Folcroft Editions, 1969.
Love As Love, Death As Death. London, Seizin Press, 1928.
Poems: A Joking Word. London, Cape, 1930.
Twenty Poems Less Paris, Hours Press, 1930.
Though Gently. Deyá, Mallorca, Seizin Press, 1930.
Laura and Francisca. Deyá, Mallorca, Seizin Press, 1931.
The Life of the Dead (in French and English), illustrated by John Aldridge. London, Barker, 1933.
The First Leaf. Deyá, Mallorca, Seizin Press, 1933.
Poet: A Lying Word. London, Barker, 1933.
Americans. Los Angeles, Primavera, 1934.
The Second Leaf. Deyá, Mallorca, Seizin Press, 1935.
Collected Poems. London, Cassell, and New York, Random House, 1938.
Selected Poems: In Five Sets. London, Faber, 1970; New York, Norton, 1973.
The Poems of Laura Riding. Manchester, Carcanet, and New York, Persea, 1980.

Novels

No Decency Left (as Barbara Rich, with Robert Graves). London, Cape, 1932.

14A, with George Ellidge. London, Barker, 1934.
Convalescent Conversations (as Madeleine Vara). Deyá, Mallorca, Seizin Press, and London, Constable, 1936.
A Trojan Ending. Deyá, Mallorca, Seizin Press, London, Constable, and New York, Random House, 1937.

Short Stories

Experts Are Puzzled. London, Cape, 1930.
Progress of Stories. Deyá, Mallorca, Seizin Press, and London, Constable, 1936; Freeport, New York, Books for Libraries, 1971; revised edition, New York, Dial Press, and Manchester, Carcanet, 1982.
Lives of Wives. London, Cassell, and New York, Random House, 1939.

Other

A Survey of Modernist Poetry, with Robert Graves. London, Heinemann, 1927; New York, Doubleday, 1928.
A Pamphlet Against Anthologies, with Robert Graves. London, Cape, 1928; as *Against Anthologies*, New York, Doubleday, 1928.
Contemporaries and Snobs. London, Cape, 1928.
Anarchism Is Not Enough. London, Cape, and New York, Doubleday, 1928.
Four Unposted Letters to Catherine. Paris, Hours Press, 1930.
Pictures. London, 1933.
Len Lye and the Problem of Popular Films. London, Seizin Press, 1938.
The Covenant of Literal Morality. London, Seizin Press, 1938.
The Telling. London, Athlone Press, 1972; New York, Harper, 1973.
From the Chapter "Truth" in "Rational Meaning: A New Foundation for the Definition of Words" (Not Yet Published), with Schuyler B. Jackson. Berkhamsted, Hertfordshire, Priapus, 1975.
It Has Taken Long (selected writings), in "Riding Issue" of *Chelsea 35* (New York), 1976.
Description of Life. New York, Targ, 1980.

Editor, *Everybody's Letters*. London, Barker, 1933.
Editor, *Epilogue 1-3*. Deyá, Mallorca, Seizin Press, and London, Constable, 3 vols., 1935-37.
Editor, *The World and Ourselves: Letters about the World Situation from 65 People of Different Professions and Pursuits*. London, Chatto and Windus, 1938.

Translator (as Laura Riding Gottschalk), *Anatole France at Home*, by Marcel Le Goff. New York, Adelphi, 1926.
Translator, with Robert Graves, *Almost Forgotten Germany*, by Georg Schwarz. Deyá, Mallorca, Seizin Press, London, Constable, and New York, Random House, 1936.

*

Bibliography: by Alan Clark, in *Chelsea 35* (New York), 1976.

Critical Study: *Laura Riding's Pursuit of Truth* by Joyce Piell Wexler, Athens, Ohio University Press, 1979.

Laura (Riding) Jackson comments:
My first book of poems was published as by Laura Riding Gottschalk, this surname being mine by an early marriage which terminated in divorce. Thereafter my name, authorial and personal, was Laura Riding, until 1941, when I married Schuyler B. Jackson, American poet and critical writer; my authorial name became then Laura (Riding) Jackson, with "Laura Riding" used for republication of work so signed. After the publication of my *Collected Poems* (1938), and my return to the U.S.A. in 1939—I had been long abroad—I renounced poetry, for reasons of principle. I now permit the republication of my poems if a statement on this renunciation accompanies them.

In my high-school years I received extraordinarily good language-education. At Cornell University I was also very fortunate in teachers (in languages, literature, history). I left before completing my undergraduate career, living then, as a young professor's wife, in the sphere of two other universities, doing some studying, and continuing the writing of poems, become important to me at Cornell—and publishing some in magazines. At the close of 1925, after a period of uncertainty, I went abroad to live. I had found my American fellow-poets more concerned with making individualistic play upon the composition-habitudes of poetic tradition than with what concerned me: how to strike a personal accent in poetry that would be at once an authentic truth-impulsion, of universal force; I saw them as combining something less than complete poetic seriousness with something less than complete personal seriousness. In the English and cross-Atlantic literary atmosphere, there was, instead of crowding individualism, a loose assemblage of unsure positions, occupied with a varying show of modernistic daring; I had there solitariness in which to probe the reality of poetry as a spiritual, not merely literary, inheritance.

In my pursuits abroad, which, besides poetry, included criticism, story-writing, activity in printing and publishing ventures, the editing of a literary-critical miscellany, I became increasingly aware of the prime dependence of worth, in everything formed of words, on observance of the linguistic integrities. I conceived of a work that would help to dissipate the confusion existing in the knowledge of word-meanings—where, I believed, all probity of word must start. This project did not take deep root until after I returned to America. My husband joined me in it, bringing to it poetic experience and linguistic learning and a moral sense of language of his own, and strong-heartedness for facing difficulties, of which there were many, within and outside the task. The resultant book was far advanced when he died, in 1968. I am trying to complete it.

[Asked if she considers herself primarily a poet, Laura (Riding) Jackson says:] Up to 1940 I considered myself centrally a poet, with every other writing activity coming under a government of values (a unity of values prerequisite for truth) that I conceived of as centrally poetic. This moral and spiritual emphasis on poetry I took to be practically justified by the linguistic urgency in poetry towards rightness of word; poetry seemed where the verbal maximum could be one with and the same as the truth-maximum. When, after long-sustained faith in this seeming poetic potential, and pressing of the linguistic possibilities of poetic utterance towards further and further limits, I comprehended that poetry had no provision in it for ultimate practical attainment of that rightness of work that *is* truth, but led on ever only to a temporizing less-than-truth (the lack eked out with illusions of truth produced by physical word-effects), I *stopped*. I stopped—but I went on to search for the way to that rightness of word that is truth, and as the natural yield of words cultivated for truth's sake, not as the product of an *art* of words....And in so doing I did not, renouncing poetry, transfer allegiance to some other form of literary procedure. I intensified my application to the problem of the knowledge of the meanings of words, and, for the rest, dedicated myself to the saying of what I might be able to say with a more far-reaching trueness of word than I had attained in any special literary climate, poetic or otherwise.

[Asked if she identifies herself with a particular school of poetry, she explains:] I have never belonged to any "school" of poetry—though the values I defined for the poetic use of words, which were nothing other than the values of language treated only as a verbal discipline but one on which the intellectual integrity and total spiritual worth of poems depended, became associated in people's minds as a school of my instituting. (Thus W.B. Yeats, in a letter: "I wrote today to Laura Riding...that her school was too thoughtful, reasonable, truthful, that poets were good liars....") All I did was to endeavor to make poetic goodness—the goodness of the "good" poem—comprehensive enough for the good poem to be no mere performance on the stage of a tradition, but something *literally* good, having so much reality as language that it fulfilled the function of language of authenticating the reality of the experiences of human consciousness (this function still only very imperfectly fulfilled in human speaking and writing, on the whole). This amounted to making the linguistic conscience the monitor of poetic goodness.

I had no models, in my particular approach to the question of what "good" is in poetry, no collaborators: the approach was, simply, a unique kind of seriousness directed upon poetry. I lessoned poets with whom I had association, in this work of literal poetic goodness. Though all took away something, and in one case at least the something was massive, none gave much thought to the depths of general principle from which this "higher" literalism, this new poetic gospel of linguistic probity, came—their interest, and therefore their gains, did not exceed the literary. Many poets outside personal range, known and unknown to me, have taken away something variedly, from the linguistic atmosphere of my poems, with superficial results—appearances of new linguistic distinction, and verbal sophistication, not backed by internal events of new experience in terms of principle, the travel within to new places in thought. In the case of one poet never more than a stranger to me, every abstractable manner of tone, diction, rhythmic movement, of mine was worked into the technique of this other—with not mere period-consequences. An application of my method of textual testing of poetic substance to a certain poem, in a book in which I was a collaborator, became the starting point from which a particular poet drew out the line of a critical career; and the resultant diffusion of the idea of such a method caused it to have further part in poetry-criticism developments, in further separation from its background-thought, as the mark of the "new" (for a time). Thus was it with me as to influences, being of a "school," or generating a "school": I have no influences on myself to record, or membership in any school. (In the early twenties I was made an honorary member of the group of Southern poets that called itself "The Fugitives." But I had no programmatic association with them. The membership was a tribute to my work.) My influence on others, directly and remotely, has been extensive and wasted. I think the reason of this is in the moral condition of poets; they have taken on the morals of their time which are not good enough for a thorough concern with goodness, poetic or otherwise.

*   *   *

In an early poem, "As Well As Any Other," Laura Riding asks: "But for familiar sense what need can be/Of my most singular device or me...." The "singular device" became more and more recognizable as a virtue of dedication in the development of the whole of her work: criticism, stories, editorial and collaborative writings, as well as the poems, and then the later post-poetic rebeginning in a new closeness to words themselves

as "secreting in their meanings a natural eloquence of truth" (a recent comment of hers). Her purposes were and are supra-individual: she is bent upon locating the yet unfound in thought, saying the yet unsaid "For All Our Sakes" (the title of another early poem). Her work implies necessary reorientations of values and positions: it tends to test the minds of its readers and critics.

To turn to Laura Riding's poetry is to turn to her thought also. She warns: "The nicest thought is only gossip/If merchandized into plain language and sold/For so much understanding to the minute..." ("The Talking World"). Some of the poems will be found immediately lucid. Others, the kind to which the long-celebrated difficulty is attributed, will make one stop—not just "stop and think" but stop and read. If this necessity is "difficulty," it is associated with the virtues of the poems, and contributory to a happy consequence in the immediate freshness they have on each return to them. The language has precision, but also litheness of expression-movement; it is language alive and at work. Because there is a right way in, and no other way, one may feel puzzled or dazzled until it is found. A poem of hers is a process; one must travel with it, and, if one does, one "understands" because the process develops and defines itself. This approach is outlined as a reading-method in *A Survey of Modernist Poetry* (pp. 138-49), with reference to "The Rugged Black of Anger."

The strong quality of personal voice and presence permeating Laura Riding's poems can induce the idea that they are full of private references, while her never-absent governing sense of the universal context of all particular contexts can suggest the label "abstract." These two tendencies are interlocked, function as a unity, and so demand integration in the readers' minds: no poem-subject of hers is so general that there is not an immediate personal bearing, but its large force will be lost if realistic private identifications are sought for. When she writes, for instance, of "the tragedy of selfhood/And self-haunting," the case is (she avers) not a narrative of personal tragedy but of the approach to knowledge of the human necessity of graduation from the self as tragic. Thus her sensibility of personal crisis as an aspect of a total human event of crisis makes itself felt, as it pulsates through the *Collected Poems*, within an ever-widening emphasis upon the universal context: "The lone defiance blossoms failure,/But risk of all by all beguiles/Fate's wreckage into similar smiles" ("Doom in Bloom").

Much of her thought has a quality of inexorability: "The mercy of truth—it is to be truth." Her poetic standard was for the perfect: the rightness stipulated was "for always"; she meant real survival, minds on the side of permanence, as in "Autobiography of the Present":

> Whole is by breaking and by mending.
> The body is a day of ruin,
> The mind, a moment of repair.
> A day is not a day of mind
> Until all lifetime is repaired despair...

Death, in her poetic—and general—sense of the nature of things, is, as she has recently put it, "the reality of the necessity of an end, for that which has a limit. But the coming to a term of the limited is not mere predestined nullification: the mark of the end is a mark of rightness, and so death has, thus, aspects of significance and character which spell the perfect and the true, not mortality and loss." The mental perspective in which she views death can be found in depiction both stern and touched with happy wit ("There Is Much at Work"):

> Exchange the multiplied bewilderment
> For a single presentation of fact by fairness;

And the revelation will be instantaneous.
We shall all die quickly.

Her controls of the solemn and the large themes, the report of
their reality as belonging intimately to the human experience,
are everywhere firm. But not only is severity of definition and
vision tempered with tenderness: the culminating words are
often of a profoundly tender cheer, as in the transcendent "The
Flowering Urn," where the fond supersedes the grim:

> ...Will rise the same peace that held
> Before fertility's lie awoke
> The virgin sleep of Mother All:
> The same but for the way in flowering
> It speaks of fruits that could not be.

("Mother All" comes with characteristic cleanness. She uses
such figures with serious ontological intent, not for purposes of
mythological rhetoric.)

There is an essence of simplicity in these poems. Their many
questions are approaches to answers. "What knows in me?/Is it
only something inside/That I can't see?" comes from the beginning, and "What were we, then,/Before the being of ourselves
began?" from the end, of the *Collected Poems* progression, while
almost at its centre "As Many Questions As Answers" reveals the
implicity unity of the process. This spirit of simplicity brings the
problem of knowledge within the intelligence's intimate range; it
informs not only Laura Riding's poems but also such propositions of hers as "we experience reality to the degree to which we
are at once a question about reality and its answer" (*Epilogue
III*, 1937). She has not been afraid to let her intelligence press its
points with the insistence of a child-like refusal to settle for
no-answer. She pictures the alternative to this mental mode in
rather passionate assault ("Unread Pages"):

> Too orthodox maturity
> For such heresy of child-remaining—
> On these the dusty blight of books descends,
> Weird, pundit babyhoods
> Whose blinking vision stammers out the past
> like a big-lettered foetus-future.

The internal simplicity of her poetic offering, the unity of its
motivations and attitudes—so much missed when readers do not
read *into* it, but content (or discontent) themselves with surface
impressions of "difficulty" or "obscurity"—can provide a key to
her ultimate renouncing of poetry. One might say that she
moved from an initial belief that the answers we must find with
our right questions could be found in poetry by its implicit
invitation to (its demand of) truthfulness of word—never, for
her, an obscure intellectualized or sentimentally spiritualized
ideal, but a literal objective—to an ultimate feeling that poetry
itself limits achievement in the unclosable gap between the verbal realms of question and answer. Her preface to the *Collected
Poems* of 1938 is a soaring and persuasive defence of poetry; that
to her *Selected Poems* of 1970 tells how she has "devoutly
renounced allegiance to poetry as a profession and faith in it as
institution." To turn from one preface to the other is to feel one's
loose world of poetry and prose, ordinary and literary language,
tightening into tensions that suggest the labour of opening up
that "other language-path" that has been Mrs. Jackson's commitment since 1940.

—Alan Clark

RIDLER, Anne (Barbara, née Bradby). British. Born in
Rugby, Warwickshire, 30 July 1912. Educated at Downe House
School; King's College, London, diploma in journalism 1932.
Married Vivian Ridler in 1938; two sons and two daughters.
Member of editorial department, Faber and Faber, publishers,
London, 1935-40. Recipient: Oscar Blumenthal Prize, 1954, and
Union League Civic and Arts Foundation Prize, 1955 (*Poetry*,
Chicago). Address: 14 Stanley Road, Oxford OX4 1QZ, England.

PUBLICATIONS

Verse

Poems. London, Oxford University Press, 1939.
A Dream Observed and Other Poems. London, Editions Poe-
try London, 1941.
The Nine Bright Shiners. London, Faber, 1943.
The Golden Bird and Other Poems. London, Faber, 1951.
A Matter of Life and Death. London, Faber, 1959.
Selected Poems. New York, Macmillan, 1961.
Some Time After and Other Poems. London, Faber, 1972.
Italian Prospect: Six Poems. Oxford, Perpetua Press, 1976.
Dies Natalis. Oxford, Perpetua Press, 1980.

Plays

Cain (produced Letchworth, Hertfordshire, 1943; London,
1944). London, Editions Poetry London, 1943.
The Shadow Factory: A Nativity Play (produced London,
1945). London, Faber, 1946.
Henry Bly (produced London, 1947). Included in *Henry Bly
and Other Plays*, 1950.
Henry Bly and Other Plays (includes *The Mask* and *The Missing
Bridegroom*). London, Faber, 1950.
The Mask, and The Missing Bridegroom (produced London,
1951). Included in *Henry Bly and Other Plays*, 1950.
The Trial of Thomas Cranmer, music by Bryan Kelly (produced
Oxford, 1956). London, Faber, 1956.
The Departure, music by Elizabeth Maconchy (produced Lon-
don, 1961). Included in *Some Time After and Other Poems*,
1972.
Who Is My Neighbour? (produced Leeds, 1961). Included in
Who Is My Neighbour? and How Bitter the Bread, 1963.
Who Is My Neighbour? and How Bitter the Bread. London,
Faber, 1963.
The Jesse Tree: A Masque in Verse, music by Elizabeth
Maconchy (produced Dorchester, Oxfordshire, 1970). Lon-
don, Lyrebird Press, 1972.
Rosinda, translation of the libretto by Faustini, music by Cavalli
(produced Oxford, 1973; London, 1975).
Orfeo, translation of the libretto by Striggio, music by Monte-
verdi (produced Oxford, 1975; London, 1981). London,
Faber, 1975; revised edition, 1981.
Eritrea, translation of the libretto by Faustini, music by Cavalli
(produced Wexford, Ireland, 1975). London, Oxford University Press, 1975.
The King of the Golden River, music by Elizabeth Maconchy
(produced Oxford, 1975).
The Return of Ulysses, translation of the libretto by Badoaro,
music by Monteverdi (produced London, 1978).
The Lambton Worm, music by Robert Sherlaw Johnson (produced Oxford, 1978). London, Oxford University Press,
1979.
Orontea, translation of the libretto by Cicognini, music by Cesti
(produced London, 1979).

Agrippina, translation of the libretto by Grimani, music by Handel (produced London, 1982).
La Calisto, translation of the libretto by Faustini, music by Cavalli (produced London, 1984).

Other

Olive Willis and Downe House: An Adventure in Education. London, Murray, 1967.

Editor, *Shakespeare Criticism 1919-1935.* London and New York, Oxford University Press, 1936.
Editor, *A Little Book of Modern Verse.* London, Faber, 1941.
Editor, *Time Passes and Other Poems,* by Walter de la Mare. London, Faber, 1942.
Editor, *Best Ghost Stories.* London, Faber, 1945.
Editor, *The Faber Book of Modern Verse,* revised edition. London, Faber, 1951.
Editor, *The Image of the City and Other Essays,* by Charles Williams. London, Oxford University Press, 1958.
Editor, *Selected Writings,* by Charles Williams. London, Oxford University Press, 1961.
Editor, *Shakespeare Criticism 1935-1960.* London and New York, Oxford University Press, 1963.
Editor, *Poems and Some Letters,* by James Thomson. London, Centaur Press, and Urbana, University of Illinois Press, 1963.
Editor, *Thomas Traherne: Poems, Centuries, and Three Thanksgivings.* London, Oxford University Press, 1966.
Editor, with Christopher Bradby, *Best Stories of Church and Clergy.* London, Faber, 1966.
Editor, *Selected Poems of George Darley.* London, Merrion Press, 1979.
Editor, *The Poems of William Austin.* Oxford, Perpetua Press, 1984.

*

Critical Study: *The Christian Tradition in Modern British Verse Drama* by William V. Spanos, New Brunswick, New Jersey, Rutgers University Press, 1967.

*   *   *

Anne Ridler's poems demonstrate a triumph (minor, but still perfectly valid) of intelligence and skill in dealing with quiet, domestic themes and "occasional" subjects: meditations on married love, observations and celebrations of children, recordings of places and pictures. They are characteristically low-toned, but a distinct and not at all tepid personality comes through, with a strong sense of loyalty, the need for roots, and an awareness of the divine transfiguring the commonplace.

The quality of the best earlier poems (such as "At Parting" and "For a Child Expected" in *The Nine Bright Shiners*) lies partly in their assured rhythmical sense, traditional and yet not slavishly so, and partly in the transparent sweetness of their diction:

Since we through war a while must part
Sweetheart, and learn to lose
Daily use
Of all that satisfied our heart:
Lay up those secrets and those powers
Wherewith you pleased and cherished me these two years.

It is a note not often heard in contemporary English poetry; the saccharine flavour of women's magazine verse is quite different. Anne Ridler has herself said that she has learned from Wyatt, and Eliot seems to have been a liberating and beneficial modern influence; but her proper poetic ancestry seems to lie in the 17th century, in Herbert. In "Deus Absconditus" (from *The Golden Bird*), Eliot and Herbert both seem somewhere in the background, but not obtrusively so:

Here he is endured, here he is adored.
And anywhere. Yet it is a long pursuit,
Carrying the junk and treasure of an ancient creed,
To a love who keeps his faith by seeming mute
And deaf, and dead indeed.

Ridler's most ambitious work has been in partly or wholly dramatic form (e.g., *Cain, The Shadow Factory, The Trial of Thomas Cranmer,* the Christmas broadcasts and the title-poem from *The Golden Bird*), but none of these is wholly satisfactory. Much the best of the longer poems is "A Matter of Life and Death," which gave its title to her 1959 volume. This is a two-voiced meditation, of mother and child, on a birth:

I did not see the iris move,
I did not feel the unfurling of my love...

I have seen the light of day,
Was it sight or taste or smell?
What I have been, who can tell?
What I shall be, who can say?

Anne Ridler is not at all a prolific poet, and her slimness of output, together with her lack of any self-assertiveness, seems unjustly to have made her work much less noticed than it should be.

—Anthony Thwaite

_____

ROBERTS, Philip (Davies). Canadian. Born in Magog, Quebec, 9 October 1938. Educated at Acadia University, Wolfville, Nova Scotia, B.A. 1959; Jesus College, Oxford (Rhodes Scholar), B.A. 1962, M.A. 1966; University of Sydney, B.Mus. 1979. Married Carol Lynn Berney in 1978 (divorced, 1984); two daughters. English teacher, British Institute, Madrid, 1962; sub-editor, Reuters news agency, London, 1963-66; public relations consultant, Peters Bishop and Partners, London, 1966-67; Lecturer, 1967-74, and Senior Lecturer in English, 1974-79, University of Sydney. Since 1980, self-employed writer. Founding Editor, Island Press, Sydney, 1970-79; Poetry Editor, Sydney *Morning Herald,* 1970-74. Agent: Jüri Gabriel, 16 Roseneath Road, London SW11 6AH, England. Address: P.O. Box 262, Wolfville, Nova Scotia B0P 1X0, Canada.

PUBLICATIONS

Verse

Just Passing Through. Ladysmith, Quebec, Ladysmith Press, 1969.
Two Poets, with Geoff Page. Brisbane, University of Queensland Press, 1971.

Crux.   Sydney, Island Press, 1973.
Will's Dream.   Brisbane, University of Queensland Press, 1975.
Selected Poems.   Sydney, Island Press, 1978.

Other

Editor, *The Inside Eye: A Study in Pictures of Oxford College Life*, photographs by Jüri Gabriel.   Abingdon, Berkshire, Abbey Press, 1961.
Editor, with J.C. and P.M. Bright, *Models of English Style* (textbook).   Sydney, Science Press, 1971.

*

Manuscript Collection: National Library of Australia, Canberra.

Critical Study: "Breaking the Tribal Bounds" by Peter Porter, in *Times Literary Supplement* (London), 9 April 1976.

Philip Roberts comments:

My first real poems came in 1961 when I was living in Oxford, though I had been playing with words for several years before that. They were triggered off, I remember, by the idiom of three lines in the first section of Robert Lowell's "Quaker Graveyard in Nantucket"—just a glance at them seemed to reveal a whole new range of possibilities. I showed some of my new poems to Robert Graves (who was then Professor of Poetry at Oxford) and received not only his blessings but also a great deal of critical support during the next three or four years. Graves read more or less every poem I wrote during this time, and gave detailed written criticism to most of them. That such a prolific poet and writer was able to find time for this is a kindness I shall never forget.

Although my work was first published in establishment publications, I did not have a book of poetry published until I had moved to Australia. Consequently, my work has been better known there than anywhere else, though I am now a Canadian resident. The poetry comes when it wants to, and I don't generally think about it at other times. I have not much interest in other poets or their work, though I was initially influenced by Frost, Graves, Cavafy, and Seferis (the latter two in translation).

I am sad that poetry reaches so few readers. Academics have latched onto poetry as their own special preserve, and in doing so have had to exalt discursive, allusive, and referentially complex poetry above all else. The fact that few academics possess the musicality to be able to read the simplest lyric aloud with any competence does not appear to worry them or in any way diminish their authority as arbiters of poetic taste. I also regret that I never seem to have lived in any one country long enough to have felt part of any national literary community. (Perhaps this is not altogether a bad thing—one is at least granted privacy in which to write.)

My view of poetry very much accords with the structuralist-semiotic views of Yury Lotman's *Analysis of the Poetic Text*, for me one of the great explicatory revelations of the past decade.

*   *   *

Philip Roberts has had a restless career—Canadian by birth and upbringing, Australian by virtue of twelve years' residence and his literary contribution there, several years a resident of the United States. He has always spread his light, publishing in English, Canadian, U.S., and Australian periodicals. As befits

his life, the writing is condensed, sophisticated and cosmopolitan.

Already in *Just Passing Through* locations and personal experience are submitted to an exigent craftsmanship. Roberts's initial equipment includes an almost precious eloquence and an interest in precise manoeuvre such as the time-reveals of "Time Study," the dramatic riddling of "Summer Night," the cunning casualness with which metaphors are assembled in "Testing Song," and the humorous decorum of carnality in "Hungry Horse Café." Again in "Single Eye," a preoccupation with life's ambivalence and risks begets delicate, typically short-lined lyrics such as "Conversation" and "Master Peter's Puppet Show," model constructions such as "Now I Shall Reveal Everything," and some aptly-tuned jokes.

Roberts's peculiar combination of daring articulateness, unexpected detail, and subtle feeling emerge in "Tiny Tim Faces Death":

> I want to ask the funeral man
> to pack me on my side
> curled up in flannelette
> pyjamas. He'll say
> the coffin would look like a sump:
> my friends would all know I was scared.
>
> What if I proved the Hittites
> or Abyssinians did it—what then?
> Could the world accept me
> like a rollmop after all?
> the giant earth nestle round
> with black unending love?

Crux, handset by the author, notably includes a little satire ("That'd Be Good"), several neat jests ("Genres," "Peppermills," "Amen"), and a fine reflection on the relation of the original artist to followers ("Rescuers"): "Stop here and wait for them?/And what kind of comfort could they bring?/that stone-eyed mob, still groping the dark,/admiring the bones of your last-year's fire!" Something of a departure is the openness of the three-page account of five cases of derangement in "Neuro Ward," where Roberts's control elicits keen and unqualified compassion. The book ends with accomplished translations of seven Anglo-Saxon elegies. The personal and dramatic dimension of these pieces perhaps led on to *Will's Dream*, a tour de force consisting of 113 poems, mostly short. They recount and comment upon the relations between Willoughby, Big Mary, Blake, and Pymbal, though a larger cast is evoked. The rich achievement of this book, acclaimed especially by Robert Adamson in a review in *The Australian* (31 January 1976), surprised only those whose earlier reading had missed Roberts's quality.

Never a band-wagon poet, Roberts showed editorial stringency in compiling his attractive *Selected Poems*—55 pieces. He set a useful example of modesty for other poets more inclined to include than cull. The selection shows a development towards plainer language and finer shades of wit.

Roberts is something of a Horatian. His command is surest in short poems; the refined cool is his vein; his skills are too polished to be popular, and yet a close reading does not suggest limited interest or resources. It is worth noting that he is a flautist and keyboard-player; the musical surety of his lines never falters. He has had influence on Australian publishing, as the discriminating typesetter and editor of Island Press. He has published several significant poets and ten anthologies of Australian poetry, *Poet's Choice*. For a distinctive stylist he has been astonishingly receptive to a wide range of work, and by careful invitation has easily eclipsed in interest the later Angus and Robertson anthologies. In the 1970's, *Poet's Choice* became the principle showcase of current Australian poetry.

—Judith Rodriguez

ROBINSON, Roland (Edward). British. Born in Balbriggan, Ireland, 14 June 1912. Educated in secondary schools. Member, Kirsova Ballet, 1944-47. Ballet critic, 1956-66, and currently, book reviewer, *Sydney Morning Herald*. Editor, *Poetry Magazine*, Sydney. President, Poetry Society of Australia. Recipient: Grace Leven Award, 1952; Commonwealth Literary Fellowship, 1954; Australian Council for the Arts grant, 1973; Australian Book Council Award, for non-fiction, 1974. Order of Australia. Address: 10 Old Main Road, Belmont North, New South Wales 2280, Australia.

PUBLICATIONS

Verse

Beyond the Grass-Tree Spears: Verse. Adelaide, Jindyworobak, 1944.
Language of the Sand: Poems. Sydney, Lyre Bird, 1948.
Tumult of the Swans. Sydney, Edwards and Shaw, 1953.
Deep Well. Sydney, Edwards and Shaw, 1962.
Grendel. Brisbane, Jacaranda Press, 1967.
Selected Poems. Sydney, Angus and Robertson, 1971.
Selected Poems. Armidale, New South Wales, Kardaordir Press, 1984.

Play

Television Play: *The Ballad of the Aborigines,* 1972.

Short Stories

Black-Feller, White-Feller. Sydney, Angus and Robertson, 1958.

Other

Legend and Dreaming: Legends of the Dream-Time of the Australian Aborigines. Sydney, Edwards and Shaw, 1952.
The Feathered Serpent: The Mythological Genesis and Recreative Ritual of the Aboriginal Tribes of the Northern Territory of Australia. Sydney, Edwards and Shaw, 1956.
The Man Who Sold His Dreaming. Sydney, Currawong, 1965.
Aboriginal Myths and Legends. Melbourne, Sun, 1966.
The Australian Aboriginal in Colour, photographs by Douglas Baglin. Sydney, Reed, 1968.
The Drift of Things: An Autobiography 1914-1952. Melbourne, Macmillan, 1973.
The Shift of Sands: An Autobiography 1952-1962. Melbourne, Macmillan, 1976.
A Letter to Joan: An Autobiography 1962-1973. Melbourne, Macmillan, 1978.

Editor, *Wandjina: Children of the Dreamtime: Aboriginal Myths and Legends.* Brisbane, Jacaranda Press, 1968.

*

Critical Study: by Evan Jones, in *The Literature of Australia* edited by Geoffrey Dutton, Melbourne, Penguin, 1964; revised edition, 1976.

Roland Robinson comments:
[I belong to the] Jindyworobak school—devoted to poetry with distinctive Australian environment.
Themes are Australia, its fauna and flora, its inhabitants, Aboriginal and European. Latest theme is involvement in Mankind in its modern environment of cities, industry, etc.
A poem should have the texture and character of its subject. I detest abstract cerebral verse. A poem's sound should argue of its sense. A poem's form should be sculptural. A poet should bring all his senses alive on the page: sight, hearing, taste, smell. A poem's rhythm should express its emotion. A poem should agonize to find its own unique form whether it be a Shakespearean sonnet or the Twenty-third Psalm. Prescribed form is meaningless.
Influences are Edward Thomas, Anglo-Saxon Poetry, Ted Hughes, R.S. Thomas.

*   *   *

Something of a legend in his own lifetime, Roland Robinson has become a familiar figure reading (brilliantly) his own poems in lecture halls and schools across Australia, his shock of white hair flowing and, latterly, a white wolfhound in attendance. His own career has been colourful enough, ranging from jackeroo to ballet critic for the *Sydney Morning Herald* to greenkeeper of a municipal golf links. He was largely instrumental in organizing a writer's cooperative publishing venture (the Lyre Bird Writers series) around 1950 and has, in the early 1970's, revived this series in order to publish the work of younger poets. With this background of activity and variety, it is perhaps surprising that Roland Robinson's own poetry remained for so long centrally concerned with a very private search through the desert and bird-and-animal landscape of outback Australia, a lyrical and often delicate Wanderer's voyage of discovery and communion. The many short lyrics published in magazines and even books over some twenty years were collected and arranged in the volume *Deep Well* in a way that showed them to be, not merely occasional campfire nature pieces, but components of a definite search and expression of centrally understood vision. *Deep Well* remains the centre of Roland Robinson's achievement, and must be regarded as expressing something close to the very core of that poetic reawakening that began in Australia during the Second World War years, a reawakening that for the first time directed Australians unselfconsciously to their own landscape, and with a language at last equipped to approach it. It is interesting that of the two poets most occupied with this task one, Douglas Stewart, was a New Zealander; the other, Roland Robinson, was born in Ireland. Roland Robinson will be remembered for naming, for us, points of a journey both private and universal.

—Thomas W. Shapcott

ROCHE, Paul. British. Born in India, 25 September 1928. Educated at Gregorian University, Rome, Ph.B., Ph.L. 1949. Married to Clarissa Tanner; five children. Instructor, Smith

College, Northampton, Massachusetts, 1957-59; Poet-in-Residence, California Institute of the Arts, Valencia, 1972-74, Emory and Henry College, Emory, Virginia, Spring 1980, and Notre Dame University, Indiana, Autumn 1980. Recipient: Bollingen Foundation Fellowship, 1958; Alice Fay di Castagnola Award, 1965; Alice Hunt Bartlett Prize, 1966; Vogelstein Foundation Fellowship, 1978. Agent: Bryan Hunt, 5 Devonshire Street, London W.1, England.

PUBLICATIONS

Verse

The Rank Obstinacy of Things: A Selection of Poems. New York, Sheed and Ward, 1962.
22 November 1963 (The Catharsis of Anguish). London, Adam, 1965.
Ode to the Dissolution of Mortality. New York, Madison Avenue Church Press, 1966.
All Things Considered. London, Duckworth, 1966; New York, Weybright and Talley, 1968.
To Tell the Truth. London, Duckworth, 1967.
Te Deum for J. Alfred Prufrock. New York, Madison Avenue Church Press, 1967.
Lament for Erica: A Poem. Bembridge, Isle of Wight, Yellowsands Press, 1971.
Enigma Variations and.... Gloucester, Thornhill Press, 1974.
The Kiss. Richmond, Surrey, Keepsake Press, 1974.

Recording: *Death at Fun City,* Mercury, 1972.

Plays

Medea, adaptation of the play by Euripides (produced New York, 1978). Included in *Three Plays of Euripides,* 1974.
Oedipus the King, Oedipus at Colonus, and *Antigone,* adaptations of plays by Sophocles (produced New York, 1980).

Screenplay: *Oedipus the King,* 1967.

Novels

O Pale Galilean. London, Harvill Press, 1954.
Vessel of Dishonour. London, Sheed and Ward, 1962; New York, New American Library, 1963.

Other

The Rat and the Convent Dove and Other Tales and Fables (for children). Aldington, Kent, Hand and Flower Press, 1952.
New Tales from Aesop for Reading Aloud. Notre Dame, Indiana, University of Notre Dame Press, and London, Honeyglen, 1982.
With Duncan Grant in Southern Turkey. London, Honeyglen, 1982.

Translator, *The Oedipus Plays of Sophocles.* New York, New American Library, 1958.
Translator, *The Orestes Plays of Aeschylus.* New York, New American Library, 1963.
Translator, *Prometheus Bound,* by Aeschylus. New York, New American Library, 1964.
Translator, *The Love Songs of Sappho.* New York, New American Library, 1966.
Translator, *3 Plays of Plautus.* New York, New American

Library, 1968.
Translator, *Philoctetes, lines 676-729,* by Sophocles. Bembridge, Isle of Wight, Yellowsands Press, 1971.
Translator, with others, *The Living Mirror: Five Young Poets from Leningrad.* London, Gollancz, and New York, Doubleday, 1972.
Translator, *Three Plays of Euripides: Alcestis, Medea, The Bacchae.* New York, Norton, 1974.

*

Critical Studies: by John Engels, in *Minnesota Review* (St. Paul), 1963; Patricia deJoux, in *The Times* (London), 5 January 1968; John Moffitt, in *America* (New York), May 1968.

Paul Roche comments:

(1970) There is always a "sufficient reason" even for the worst of happenings, and it is always sufficiently human. I say in my work: "Father forgive them for they know not what they do: and forgive *me*." Poetry is awareness heightened to the point of love. It is a way of apprehending the intensity of being. I try to re-create experience more intensely, reduce it to a luminous whole, render intuitive the meaning and metaphysics of the universe—and so feed myself and others the kernel of being. My greatest influences have been the Bible (Authorised or Douay), Shakespeare, Hopkins, Eliot, Aeschylus, Sophocles, Euripides and Sappho.

(1974) For me poetry is an incantation of exact experience that seizes the mind and the heart; it is the orchestration of language towards maximum perception; it is condensed verbal impact....Poetry and art are the unique channels through which knowledge is humanised: enters the blood-stream, is made part of ourselves. Although I write my poems to please myself (to purge myself), I am fully aware of using myself as the exemplar for all human beings, and so ultimately I write for humanity. However embedded in the particular consciousness (even confessional) of a poet his poem is, for me it is only successsful if it reaches universality. Which is to say, if anyone (or almost anyone....some people are just too bovine to bother with) picking up that poem is wounded, is hit, is illuminated, and can say: "This is about me. Or it may not exactly be about me, but I now know what it is like to be that person."

*   *   *

Although born in India and educated in England and at the Gregorian University in Rome, where he graduated in philosophy, Paul Roche has lived in the United States, West Indies and Mexico in addition to his own country. As a result of an outlook that has never been confined by national boundaries, he has never been unduly influenced by localised coteries, though profiting from them all, and his poetry is equally enjoyed in Britain and America. His skill as a translator had been fully exploited in his own creative writing so that even what he describes as "mere verse" has a liveliness and command of language lacking in the work of many other poets. Whether he writes about events or personal relationships, draws upon his impressive knowledge of mythology or religion, or makes use of private experience as a starting-point for reflection upon the nature of things and the behavior of his fellows, he has a flair for spotlighting major issues in a playfully ironic and often humorous vein, whilst getting to grips with reality. One of his methods is to approach the metaphysical through the physical, and he has written a whole series of poems about such inanimate objects as "The Brick," "The Spent Matchstick," "The Hairbrush," and "The Nail-Scissors."

His "Act of Love" still remains one of the most satisfactory poems ever written on such an intimate and delicate subject, and his "Paradigm of Love" is a remarkable example of wordplay used in a valid and effective manner:

> Does love live
> Only
> As a mirror lives
> And give
> So much back
> Only
> As a mirror gives
> Which gazes
> Only
> With what gazing gave
> And gives
> By gazing back
> *That* only?

In *To Tell the Truth* Roche continued his somewhat hit-or-miss exploration of the significance of experience in a variety of styles, encompassing the satirical "Spring Song of the Petroleum Board Meeting," the amusing commentary on Eliot's poetry, "Te Deum for J. Alfred Prufrock," the lyrical "Her Love Longs for Tears," and a poem of protest entitled "The Lobotomy":

> Oh God! The explosion that shook me up so,
> That series of small deadly jolts
> Dislocating me for one whole dessicated year,
> And the sinister cutting away of something I didn't know...
> How I wish I had gone on a real war,
> had been shredded with shrapnel
> Or lost half my head.

Enigma Variations and ... is uneven, too. Everything is thrown into the pot—word-play, literary games, light verse, satire, paradox ("The hollow in the bowl/Present by its absence"), lyrics, lively sketches, serious comment—as if to illustrate the title, yet here and there insights seep through:

> Everyone is walking with an inner space
> Everyone is moving with an inner time
> Everyone is growing with an inner change
> Everyone is being with an inner pace
> Walking, moving, growing, being
> Within, beside, beyond, behind
> From and to and in and through
> Everyone is growing
> Everyone is going
> Everyone is coming, coming, coming
> Everyone is...
> Becoming.

Death at Fun City, a long satirical poem concerned with what man is making of his own environment, shows the poet working towards greater freedom in his choice of form.

—Howard Sergeant

B.D.S. 1960. Married Patricia Woods in 1959; three daughters and one son. Currently a dentist in private practice. Editor, radio poetry programme, New Zealand Broadcasting Corporation, 1968-69, 1973-74. Address: 25 Tweed Street, Dunedin, New Zealand.

PUBLICATIONS

Verse

The Eye Corrects: Poems 1955-1965. Auckland, Blackwood and Janet Paul, 1967.

Other

Allen Curnow. Wellington, Oxford University Press, 1980; Oxford, Oxford University Press, 1981.

Editor, *Home Ground*, by Charles Brasch. Christchurch, Caxton Press, 1974.
Editor, *Collected Poems*, by Charles Brasch. Wellington, Oxford University Press, 1984.

*   *   *

No critic or anthologist has yet done justice to Alan Roddick's poetry, perhaps because it has only its merits as poetry to recommend it. The subject matter is not in itself arresting, the manner is not in any obvious sense innovatory, and Roddick has lacked the advantage (in terms of publicity) gained by poets who start their careers belonging to a movement. He has had to make his way on his own.

Precision, particularly, hardness of outline, descriptive exactness, flexibility of form, wit—these are some of the qualities of Roddick's poetry. The run of the lines commonly matches the action of the subject; the poem is beautifully shaped to the event it describes. He is fond of paradoxes—particularly the paradoxes of mirrors, which (like poems) reflect and yet are not the world. Time, memory, love, the responsibilities and discoveries of parenthood—if his subjects are commonplaces they are also eternal. They are seen in the suburban and domestic setting in which they have been experienced, seen good-humouredly, without Larkinish distaste, but with no room for decorative sentiment either.

The other side of Roddick's poetic merits may be a caution that will not chance its arm. In one poem ("A Patient") he has ventured into unusual territory, making poetry of his day-to-day experience as a dentist. In a recent verse-letter he has experimented technically with a form borrowed from the Russian of Pushkin. Otherwise he has remained within narrow bounds. But Roddick has the kind of literary intelligence and tact that knows you cannot extend yourself stylistically by acts of will. It must be something that happens to the whole man. In the meantime he remains a rare example among New Zealand poets of a perfect miniaturist.

—C.K. Stead

RODDICK, Alan. New Zealander. Born in Belfast, Northern Ireland, 22 July 1937. Educated at Auckland Grammar School; University of Auckland; University of Otago, Dunedin,

RODEFER, Stephen. American. Born in Bellaire, Ohio, 20 November 1940. Educated at Rossall School, Fleetwood, Lancashire, 1958-59; Amherst College, Massachusetts, 1959-63,

B.A. 1963; State University of New York, Buffalo (Faculty Fellow), 1963-67, M.A. 1972. Married Penny Kaplan in 1962; three sons. Research Assistant, 1965-66, and Instructor in English, 1966-67, State University of New York, Buffalo; Assistant Professor of English and Co-Director of the Creative Writing Program, University of New Mexico, Albuquerque, 1967-71; Editor, *Fervent Valley*, Placitas, New Mexico, 1972-75; Poetry Specialist, Berkeley Unified School District, California, 1976-80; Lecturer, San Francisco State University Center for Experimental and Interdisciplinary Arts, 1981-84; Visiting Lecturer in Creative Writing, University of California, San Diego, 1984-85. Address: 6434 Raymond Street, Oakland, California 94609, U.S.A.

PUBLICATIONS

Verse

The Knife. Toronto, Island Press, 1965.
One or Two Love Poems from the White World. San Francisco, Pick Pocket, 1976.
The Bell Clerk's Tears Keep Flowing. Berkeley, California, Figures, 1978.
Plane Debris. Berkeley, California, Tuumba, 1981.
Four Lectures. Berkeley, California, Figures, 1982.
Oriflamme Day, with Benjamin Friedlander. Oakland, California, Jimmy's House of Knowledge, 1984.

Plays

A & C, in *Hills 9* (San Francisco), Spring 1983.
Tennyson (produced San Francisco, 1983).

Other

Translator, *After Lucretius*. Storrs, University of Connecticut Press, 1973.
Translator (as Jean Calais), *Villon*. Placitas, New Mexico, Duende Press, 1976.
Translator, *Safety*. San Francisco, Miam, 1977.
Translator, *Orpheus*, by Rilke. San Francisco, Little Press in Tuscany Alley, 1981.

*

Critical Studies: by Tom Mandel, in *San Francisco Review of Books*, February 1977; John Jacob, in *Booklist* (Chicago), 15 October 1977; Gloria Frym, in *San Francisco Review of Books*, May 1978; George F. Butterick and Don Byrd, in *Sulfur 8* (Los Angeles), 1983; Anselm Hollo, in *Poetry Project Newsletter* (New York), April 1983; Jed Rasula, in *Poetics Journal* (Berkeley, California), May 1983; Tom Clark, in *San Francisco Chronicle*, 19 October 1983; Imre Salusinszky, in *Times Literary Supplement* (London), 9 December 1983.

Stephen Rodefer comments:
My writing is an addition to English literature and an improvement of my Life.
If I hear it, I write it down. If I like seeing it, I keep it.
This will all get decided later. We're just the bodies, whose only purpose is to keep working.

*   *   *

The poems in Stephen Rodefer's first collection, *The Knife*, satisfy us by their domestic wit ("for Christ's sake/there are crumbs/in our bed/the size of sandwiches"). They make use of Cummings à la Creeley syncopations and enjambments along with brevity, couplets for structure, wryness, and advantageous breath-lengths. One poem, about eating an ear of corn, seeks to embody (and in part parody) Creeley's "Form is never more than an extension of content," a popular song on everybody's radio those days. Despite the threat (which never materializes) of its title, the volume is mostly coups d'oeil, though proving Rodefer is capable of closely held precisions, tight ironies, comic understatement, and—no matter how concealed or twisted from—sentiment. His best early poems, however, were never collected. "I Make Out Henry Moore" and "The Commotion" are notable for their management of time, both perceptual and narrative, and lead to other fine poems, such as "Characters of a Foreign Letter," in the manner of Frank O'Hara and the conversational, casual, interchangeable quality of time in *Lunch Poems*, which had just been published.

After this, the poetry takes on another language and another tone, the inconclusive rhetoric of the lesser New York poets (although written while the poet was living first in Albuquerque, then Oakland). The poems in *The Bell Clerk's Tears Keep Flowing* (a line from Elvis Presley's "Heartbreak Hotel") are dominated by the world of the quick take, the elusive glamour and superficial accomplishment of the urban style, where either the humor is not bitter enough or the thrust not deep enough. It is a language of approximation and acquisition that would be decorous if sustained—"a storm of unexpected destiny," "a history of resilient feeling," "a proceeding of great endurance," "a figure of spectacular concoction." Poems like "Samson and Delilah," despite an occasional brilliance of image, are overlong, rambling, compulsive. Most are addressed to a nameless, ambisexual "you," with the "I" or "me" just as vague. Some are surprisingly undisguised repetitions of O'Hara, "Accolade" is one of the more accomplished in this mode, but perhaps the best example, and the best poem in the volume, is "Friends of the Hopi," beginning "Living alone is not so bad actually./If you can get by sleeping alone/It's quite possible....," taking us through one such possible day, and concluding:

> Living alone you soon learn
> to cultivate the *least* of it.
>
> And think of how you can get by
> With avocados and a lot of tonic,
> A friend of the Hopi,
> Washing your dishes in a tea cup.

No matter the delights of such poems, Rodefer's special contribution lies in his "translations" or derivations from the classics—to date, the Greek Anthology and Villon. His renderings of Villon are completely street-wise, without any pumped-up slang or dusted-off argot—with a running commentary any media personality would love to have the advantage of. The notes below each of the poems are what add genius to the clearly established talent, so that the entire volume, in addition to being faithful in spirit to the text of Villon, is a happy invention, all Rodefer's own. His workings from the Greek Anthology which followed, published under the title *Safety*, are equally remarkable for their beguiling simplicity. He lifts the originals live from the page and transforms them without hesitation into classic American. Here is his reactivization of the traditional complaint against devastation by beauty: "Your eyes are like lips./No one in the sunlight/comes even near your shadow.//The navy,/The marines,/The air force,/You kill them all." Such poems are not translations, they are revitalizations. It is in this form that Rodefer also makes known his unique voice—charmingly oblique and irreplaceable.

—George F. Butterick

RODGERS, Carolyn M(arie). American. Born in Chicago, Illinois, in the 1940's. Educated at the University of Illinois, Urbana, 1960-61; Roosevelt University, Chicago, 1961-65. Y.M.C.A. social worker, Chicago, 1965; Lecturer in Afro-American Literature, Columbia College, Chicago, 1968, University of Washington, Seattle, 1970, and Indiana University, Bloomington, Summer 1973; Writer-in-Residence, Albany State College, Georgia, 1971, and Malcolm X College, Chicago, 1972. Formerly, Mid-West Editor, *Black Dialogue*, New York. Recipient: Conrad Kent Rivers Award, 1968; National Endowment for the Arts grant, 1969. Address: 12750 South Sangamon, Chicago, Illinois 60643, U.S.A.

PUBLICATIONS

Verse

Paper Soul. Chicago, Third World Press, 1968.
Two Love Raps. Chicago, Third World Press, 1969.
Songs of a Blackbird. Chicago, Third World Press, 1969.
Now Ain't That Love. Detroit, Broadside Press, 1969.
For H.W. Fuller. Detroit, Broadside Press, 1970.
Long Rap/Commonly Known as a Poetic Essay. Detroit, Broadside Press, 1971.
How I Got Ovah: New and Selected Poems. New York, Doubleday, 1975.
The Heart as Ever Green. New York, Doubleday, 1978.
Translation. Chicago, Eden Press, 1980.
Eden and Other Poems. Chicago, Eden Press, 1983.

Novel

A Little Lower Than Angels. Chicago, Eden Press, 1984.

*

Carolyn M. Rodgers comments:
I seek to tell the truth. To explore the human condition, the world's condition. To illuminate the ordinary, the forgotten, the overlooked, to show that the specific me is often the general you and us. To exemplify God working in man and the consequences of man defying and denying God, not only in himself but in the universe. I seek to write simply, so that a child might understand; and to write simply profoundly, so that the educated, the intellectual may enjoy and find mental food, find delight, the Light, and truth. What is written by me is written through me as well. That is to say I am an instrument. An inkpen of God's.

*   *   *

Carolyn M. Rodgers's poetry is a poetry of naming. What is to be named is how the personal and the political are interwoven in

our behavior, in our dreams, in our daily ideologies. The difficulty for the namer, Rodgers would have us see, is in showing how the strands come together—in making one voice represent the many threads that compose the single psyche within culture: "I've had tangled feelings lately..../there are several of me and/all of us fight to show up at the same time" ("Breakthrough"). In the course of her work, Rodgers speaks as a militant for black unity, as a lover, as a daughter, as a devout Christian, as a self-conscious artist. These personae, both complementary and contradictory, constitute a powerful image of black womanhood fighting to define itself against the power and privilege of the white world.

Given the dynamics of racial oppression, the plurality of Rodgers's voice is perhaps less remarkable than the fact of the voice *per se.* In "The Quality of Change" the poet refers to a muted past that reaches into the present:

> we have spent the years
> talking in profuse & varied
> silences to people
> who have erected walls for themselves
> to hear through.

Her poems, especially the early works, are efforts to break the silences, to break down the walls. The reader must hear the harshness of life in the streets of Chicago ("U Name This One"):

> where pee wee cut lonnell fuh fuckin wid
> his sistuh and blood baptized the street
> at least twice ev'ry week and judy got
> kicked outa grammar school fuh bein pregnant
> and died tryin to ungrow the seed

Those things that have been hidden, hushed, or repressed in black culture must be recognized and understood, as are the forms of "high" white culture (in "To the White Critics"):

> my baby's tears are a three-act play, a sonnet, a novel,
> a volume of poems.
> my baby's laugh is the point and view,
> a philosophical expression of
> oppression and survival

The self that challenges the oppressor also challenges itself, and Rodgers's work makes clear the complications that arise from trying to be free of damaging constraints. Many of her most personal poems address the problem that what is wrong usually comes packaged with what is right—a slavish sexuality may be the most honest ("Now Ain't That Love?"); the least visible revolutionary strategy may be the most effective ("For H.W. Fuller"); material possessions may provide an intensely necessary pleasure ("Things"). The poems about her mother, e.g., "It Is Deep," illustrate the contradictions of maternal gifts: this woman who

> thinks that I am under the influence of
>   **communists**
> when I talk about Black as anything
> other than something ugly

is also

>   very obviously,
> a sturdy Black bridge that I
> crossed over, on

In Carolyn Rodgers's aesthetic, the challenge to the poet is to give form to the "consistent incongruity" ("Breakthrough") that characterizes her life. The measure of her success is our understanding that the incongruity is ours.

—Janis Butler Holm

RODITI, Edouard (Herbert). American. Born in Paris, France, 6 June 1910. Educated at Elstree School, Hertfordshire; Charterhouse, Godalming, Surrey; Balliol College, Oxford, 1927-28; University of Chicago, B.A. 1939; University of California, Berkeley. Art Critic, *L'Arche*, Paris, and since 1975, *Pictures on Exhibit*, New York; Co-Editor, *Das Lot*, Berlin, 1947-49; Contributing Editor, *Antaeus*, New York, *European Judaism*, Amsterdam, *The Expatriate Review*, Staten Island, New York, *Shantih*, Brooklyn, *Arts in Society*, Madison, Wisconsin, *Conjunctions*, New York, and *Frank*, Paris. Recipient: Gulbenkian Foundation grant, 1969; American Academy Marjorie Peabody Waite Award, 1982. Address: 142 Boulevard Massena, No. 1070, Paris 75013, France.

PUBLICATIONS

Verse

Poems for F. Privately printed, 1935.
Prison Within Prison: Three Elegies on Hebrew Themes. Prairie City, Illinois, Decker Press, 1941.
Pieces of Three, with Paul Goodman and Meyer Liben. Harington, New Jersey, 5x8 Press, 1942.
Poems 1928-1948. New York, New Directions, 1949.
New Hieroglyphic Tales: Prose Poems. San Francisco, Kayak, 1968.
Emperor of Midnight. Los Angeles, Black Sparrow Press, 1974.
In a Lost World. Santa Barbara, California, Black Sparrow Press, 1978.
Thrice Chosen. Santa Barbara, California, Black Sparrow Press, 1981.
New Old and New Testaments (prose poems). New York, Red Ozier Press, 1983.
Etre un Autre: Poems in French. Privately printed, 1983.

Short Stories

The Delights of Turkey: Twenty Tales. New York, New Directions, 1977.
The Temptations of a Saint. Rancho Santa Fe, California, Ettan Press, 1980.

Other

Oscar Wilde. New York, New Directions, 1947.
Dialogues on Art. London, Secker and Warburg, 1960; New York, Horizon Press, 1961.
Joachim Karsch. Berlin, Mann, 1960.
Chagall, Ernst, Miro: Propos sur l'Art. Paris, Editions Sedimo, n.d.
Selbstanalyse eines Sammlers. Cologne, Galerie der Spiegel, 1960.
Ida Kerkovius. Constance, Simon und Koch, n.d.
De L'Homosexualité. Paris, Editions Sedimo, 1962.

Magellan of the Pacific. London, Faber, 1972; New York, McGraw Hill, 1973.
The Disorderly Poet and Other Essays. Santa Barbara, California, Capra Press, 1975.
Meetings with Conrad. Los Angeles, Press of the Pegacycle Lady, 1977.
More Dialogues on Art. Santa Barbara, California, Ross Erikson, 1983.

Editor, *Mein Lieblingsmord*, by Ambrose Bierce. Frankfurt am Main, Insel, 1963.

Translator, *Selected Works*, by Peter Takal. New York, International University Press, 1945.
Translator, *Young Cherry Trees Secured Against Hares*, by André Breton. New York, View, and London, Zwemmer, 1946.
Translator, *The Pillar of Salt*, by Albert Memmi. London, Elek, 1956.
Translator, *The Essence of Jewish Art*, by Ernest Namenyi. New York and London, Yoseloff, 1960.
Translator, *Memed, My Hawk*, by Yashar Kemal. London, Harvill Press, and New York, Pantheon, 1961.
Translator, *Toros y Toreros*, by Pablo Picasso. London, Thames and Hudson, 1961.
Translator, *Art Nouveau*, by Robert Schmutzler. London, Thames and Hudson, 1964.
Translator, *Genesis Rejuvenated*, by Carlos Suares. London, Menard Press, 1973.
Translator, *The Wandering Fool*, by Yunus Emre. Tiburon Belvedere, California, Cadmus, 1984.

*

Manuscript Collection: Special Collections, University of California at Los Angeles Library.

Critical Studies: by Alvin Rosenfeld, in *Judaism* (New York), Spring 1969; Sidney Rosenfeld, in *Books Abroad* (Norman, Oklahoma), Summer 1972.

Edouard Roditi comments:
   Originally a Surrealist, I have sought to broaden the scope of Surrealist poetry so that it can include elegiac, didactic or metaphysical poetry in addition to more strictly lyrical poetry.
   My major themes are those that have inspired a great number of poets of the past, ranging from Horace to Baudelaire and T.S. Eliot; in my devotional poetry, however, I have always remained within a strictly Jewish tradition. The American poet and philosopher Paul Goodman has compared me, as an elegiac poet, to Rilke and also to Eliot. I suppose I remain too philosophical a poet to have an important following, as my very critical approach to the philosophical themes that I handle excludes any surprising innovations of style or of thought that would not, in my opinion, withstand the tests of time.
   I feel that my work now illustrates a very clear and positive evolution in the course of which I have achieved, as a poet, almost all that I had proposed to achieve. I do not feel the need to add much more to what I have already written, though much of my poetry of recent years remains unpublished, partly because I may wish to correct it before publication.

*   *   *

   Edouard Roditi is two poets, both evolved from that exhausted

European romanticism he grew up with that appears in his earliest, adolescent poems:

> The sky oppresses me, its vault
> Of stone-grey clouds has kept my mind
> Imprisoned in sepulchral gloom...

The conventional Roditi, encouraged and goaded by Eliot, began and remains elegiac, in cadence typically iambic, often end-rimed, becoming over the years slightly more lyrical, more rhythmically varied, enjambing more: a poetry of loss, loneliness, moral outrage, nearly always with an echo of literature in the lines:

> Lady, there being nothing more to say
> About your beauty that has not been said
> By other men about their other loves...

The other mature Roditi is surrealist. In 1927 he began drawing upon correspondences between the world of surrealism and the world of his anterior temporal lobe seizures, seizures characterized by deeply rhythmic intense hallucinations of unusually vivid colors and symbolic forms, rather than by convulsions and unconsciousness. Encouraged by Desnos, and the Paris surrealists, Roditi recorded and organized a mythic, metamorphic land beyond nightmares—for its images do not invade consciousness, rather the other way around; consciousness seems to invade the dream, opening its shifting symbols to daylight exploration. These are the "vision mantras," as Roditi labeled them in 1928, finally collected in *New Hieroglyphic Tales* (1968), 40 years after the first were written. A remarkable poetry, especially in the light of many more recent, often less ambitious or successful surrealist experiments. As in his conventional poetry, the tone is elegiac, but the images come as startlingly clear as dreams:

> And she gazed into the green eyes, her own eyes, and
> lay down on the black slab of the sea. And as the
> last woman's steel body stiffened, brittle relic
> exposed upon the black marble altar of a dead
>   planet,
> out of her mouth rose a star: the last star.

At Oxford University that same year, Roditi wrote the first manifesto of surrealism in English, "The New Reality," which was generally ignored. So were his 1930's experiments in black humor and the surrealist absurd. (Some of these are included in his more recent Black Sparrow volume.) In spite of this initial neglect, the surrealist Roditi has obscured the accomplishments of the conventional poet. As reality has come to seem more and more surreal itself, Roditi's conception has become more meaningful. "I accept reality as if I were a found object of an ambiguous nature," Roditi has written. "Those [interpretations of it] that I choose remain, of course, the ones which reveal most clearly my sense of being personally threatened by...an alien and hostile force."

—Edward B. Germain

RODRIGUEZ, Judith (née Green). Australian. Born in Perth, Western Australia, 13 February 1936. Educated at Brisbane Girls' Grammar School, 1950-53; University of Queensland, Brisbane, 1954-57, B.A. 1958; Girton College, Cambridge, 1960-62, M.A. 1965; University of London, Cert. Ed. 1968. Married 1) Fabio Rodriguez in 1964, three daughters and one son; 2) Thomas W. Shapcott, *q.v.*, in 1982. Resident teacher, Fairholme Presbyterian Girls' College, Toowoomba, 1958; Lecturer, University of Queensland Department of External Studies, 1959-60; Lecturer in English, Philippa Fawcett College of Education, London, 1962-63, and University of the West Indies, Kingston, Jamaica, 1963-65; Lecturer, St. Giles School of English, London, 1965-66, and St. Mary's College of Education, Twickenham, Middlesex, 1966-68; Lecturer, 1969-76, and Senior Lecturer, 1976-85, La Trobe University, Melbourne. Writer-in-Residence, University of Western Australia, Perth, Summer 1978. Poetry Editor, *Meanjin*, Melbourne, 1979-82. Artist and illustrator: one-woman shows in Melbourne, Brisbane, and Adelaide. Recipient: Australia Council fellowship, 1974, 1978, 1983; South Australian Government prize, 1978; Artlook Victorian prize, 1979; P.E.N. Stuyvesant Prize, 1981. Address: 62 Cremorne Road, Cremorne, New South Wales 2060, Australia.

PUBLICATIONS

Verse

Four Poets (as Judith Green), with others. Melbourne, Cheshire, 1962.
Nu-Plastik Fanfare Red and Other Poems. Brisbane, University of Queensland Press, 1973.
Broadsheet Number Twenty-Three. Canberra, Open Door Press, 1976.
Water Life. Brisbane, University of Queensland Press, 1976.
Shadow on Glass. Canberra, Open Door Press, 1978.
3 Poems. Melbourne, Old Metropolitan Meat Market, 1979.
Angels. Melbourne, Old Metropolitan Meat Market, 1979.
Arapede. Melbourne, Old Metropolitan Meat Market, 1979.
Mudcrab at Gambaro's. St. Lucia, University of Queensland Press, 1980.
Witch Heart. Melbourne, Sisters, 1982.
Mrs. Noah and the Minoan Queen, with others, edited by Rodriguez. Melbourne, Sisters, 1983.

Other

Editor, *Mrs. Noah and the Minoan Queen.* Melbourne, Sisters, 1983.

*

Manuscript Collection: Fryer Research Library, University of Queensland, Brisbane.

Critical Studies: "More Wow than Flutter" by Les A. Murray, in *Quadrant* (Sydney), October 1976; "Bolder Vision than Superintrospection" by P. Neilsen, in *The Age* (Melbourne), 12 March 1977; "Sea Change" by C. Treloar, in *Twenty-Four Hours* (Sydney), August 1977; interviews in *Women and Writing: Into the Eighties,* . Clayton, Victoria, Monash University, 1980, *Uomini e Libri 97* (Milan), January-February 1984, and *Bagdala* (Novi Sad, Yugoslavia), 1984; "Restless, domestic..." by Chris Wallace-Crabbe, in *Australian Book Review* (Melbourne), December 1980; "A Positive Poetic" by Jennifer Strauss, in *Australian Book Review* (Melbourne), April 1983.

Judith Rodriguez comments:

I write poetry to live more fully, strange seeing that the act—or attitude?—of writing leaves less time for living.

So far I've learned my living by teaching. Teaching-and-research has a loving, jealous, difficult relationship with writing. So do the media. Over-eager foster-parents, necessary furtherers?

Maybe in an attempt to bust straight through to audience, I've been working with singer Robyn Archer, doing lyrics for stage-plays; and on libretti, one for composer Mary Mageau. The partnership's the thing, really; beyond that looms the theatrical agent's manoeuvring....

My first close critic was the poet John Manifold. As a student I admired everyone in turn; perhaps most intensely, Brennan and Mallarmé; lastingly, Herbert, George Eliot...what is the use of lists? Lorca, Borges, Cortázar would be there too.

Recent interest: employment.

*   *   *

Judith Rodriguez first attracted attention (under her maiden name Judith Green) in 1962 as one of the contributors to *Four Poets*, a volume that presented the early work of four young writers with Brisbane affiliations and, in effect, announced the emergence of a new force in Australian poetry—a force that was to be tagged, over a decade later, "the Queensland Octopus," indicative of a sort of energy that was less regional than adaptive. Each of the original "Four Poets" (Rodriguez, David Malouf, Rodney Hall, Don Maynard) came to occupy important editorial positions—and in States other than Queensland, so often regarded as the "Deep South" of Australian culture.

Rodriguez, in her first poems, displayed a vigorous manipulation of language (barely kept in check by the formal lyricism of the time) to serve the ends of immediacy and directness of expression. There is the sense of a new writer still seeking a style and a voice, though the uneven "Essay on M.K." comes closest to pushing the author into a genuine self-exploration. It was not until a long period in Europe and Jamaica and an uneventful return to Australia that her second volume, *Nu-Plastik Fanfare Red*, was published. The increase in command and in certainty of direction is immediately clear in poems such as "Sojourners at Phoenix":

They are here, Svetlana, as they were there.
Men. Difficult to love. Difficult not to.

Slavers strung out in harness, iron-galled;
smiths of ideals, lining up at the anvil for thrashing.

Stalin, that fathered five-year plans and prisons.
And an architect of together. You can't say fairer.

And when you left, Svetlana, and when you left
with nothing ahead but maybe

glimmer in the jaws of the escape hatch
you could not perhaps slip through whole....

Her poetry had become imbued with a warm female sharpness—precisely observed moments and objects and responses, place rather than time, people through things, humanity through attitudes. Her tone had become clipped, never sloppy; her poems as tight-packed as a larder full of preserves. She has found a way with language to contain her wide experience and range of interests.

Her next book, *Water Life*, was illustrated (or rather, complemented) with the author's own vigorous and sensuous lino-

cuts and awarded a major literary award. Rodriguez's femininity is never embittered, though the exploration of her womanness has been increasingly fruitful for her writing and her development—and has led to moments of painful honesty. *Water Life* summed up not only stages in the poet's own intellectual and emotional development, but that of a generation of women, and in ways directed to growth and celebrative instincts rather than rejection and self immolation. A more recent, small, collection, *Shadow on Glass*, refines the characteristic Rodriguez energy to an almost clenched lyricism. It could be said that the lyrical mode has always exercised this poet's mind; but only in her most recent work has the combination of song-flow and mind-stress fully cohered, and even then, fitfully. She is in many ways the most exciting and explorative of the "Brisbane Octopus" generation, her work providing the sense of an intellect—and a female strength—in course of liberation and growth. In any terms, her achievement and challenging way with language are already apparent.

—Thomas W. Shapcott

ROOK, (William) Alan. British. Born in Ruddington, Nottinghamshire, 31 October 1909. Educated at Uppingham School, Rutland; Oxford University, 1936-39, B.A. (honours) in English 1939. Served in the Royal Artillery, 1939-44: Major. Since 1947, Managing Director, Skinner Rook and Chambers Ltd., wine merchants. Fellow, Royal Society of Literature. O.B.E. (Officer, Order of the British Empire), 1980. Address: Stragglethorpe Hall, Lincoln, England.

PUBLICATIONS

Verse

Songs from a Cherry Tree. Oxford, Halls, 1938.
Soldiers, This Solitude. London, Routledge, 1942.
These Are My Comrades: Poems. London, Routledge, 1943.
We Who Are Fortunate. London, Routledge, 1945.

Other

Not as a Refuge (literary criticism). London, Lindsey Drummond, 1948.
Diary of an English Vineyard. London, Wine and Spirit Publications, 1972.

Editor, with A. W. Sandford, *Oxford Poetry 1936.* Oxford, Blackwell, 1936.

*   *   *

Alan Rook was one of the most prolific poets of World War II, but he fell silent immediately the war ended. The coincidence is surely a little too pat? Reading Rook's poems now, forty years after they were written, one sees that they were precisely adapted to the taste of their time, and in many ways antagonistic to that of ours. The diction has a lush fullness which appealed to the war-time taste for the romantic; and in his first volume—the bulk of it, incidentally, written before war broke out—there are in uneasy juxtaposition to this romanticism, distinct echoes of the work Auden was doing in the late thirties.

Yet this volume also contains at least one poem of real interest—Robin Skelton rightly chose it for his representative anthology, *Poetry of the Forties*. This poem is "Dunkirk Pier," and it is one of the few English attempts to sum up the experience of defeat—a muted, but still genuine echo of the kind of poetry Aragon wrote in *Les Yeux d'Elsa*:

> Deeply across the waves of our darkness fear,
> like the silent octopus, feeling, groping, clear
> as a star's reflection, nervous and cold as a bird,
> tells us that pain, tells us that death is near.

What is still about Rook's poems is that they encapsulate a mood, a way of feeling otherwise out of reach. The poetic means are often imperfect, but the interest lies in the meeting of the individual and the time—just as it does with much of the poetry of the First World War.

—Edward Lucie-Smith

ROOT, William Pitt. American. Born in Austin, Minnesota, 28 December 1941. Educated at the University of Washington, Seattle, B.A. 1964; University of North Carolina, Greensboro, M.F.A. 1967. Married Judy Bechtold in 1965 (divorced, 1970); one daughter. Instructor, Slippery Rock State College, Pennsylvania, 1967; Assistant Professor of English, Michigan State University, East Lansing, 1967-68; Stegner Creative Writing Fellow, Stanford University, California, 1968-69; Visiting Lecturer or Writer, Mid-Peninsula Free University, 1969-70, Amherst College, Massachusetts, 1971, Wichita State University, Kansas, 1977, University of Southwestern Louisiana, Lafayette, 1977, and University of Montana, Missoula, 1978, 1980-81. Since 1971, active in poets-in-schools programs in several states. Recipient: Academy of American Poets university prize, 1966; Rockefeller grant, 1969; Guggenheim grant, 1970; National Endowment for the Arts grant, 1973; Bicentennial Exchange Fellowship, 1978. Address: c/o Atheneum Publishers, 597 Fifth Avenue, New York, New York 10017, U.S.A.

PUBLICATIONS

Verse

The Storm and Other Poems. New York, Atheneum, 1969.
Striking the Dark Air for Music. New York, Atheneum, 1973.
The Port of Galveston. Galveston, Texas, Galveston Arts Center, 1974.
A Journey South. Port Townsend, Washington, Graywolf Press, 1977.
7 Mendocino Songs. Portland, Oregon, Mississippi Mud Press, 1977.
Coot and Other Characters: Poems New and Familiar. Lewiston, Idaho, Confluence Press, 1977.
Fireclock. Boston, 4 Zoas Press, 1979.
Reasons for Going It on Foot. New York, Atheneum, 1981.
In the World's Common Grasses. Santa Cruz, California, Moving Parts, 1981.

Plays

Films (with Ray Rice): *Song of the Woman and the Butterflyman*, 1975; *7 for a Magician*, 1976; *Faces*, 1981.

Other

Editor, *What a World, What a World! Poetry by Young People in Galveston Schools.* Galveston, Texas, Pipedream Press, 1974.

*

Manuscript Collection: University of North Carolina Library, Greensboro.

Critical Studies: by Benjamin DeMott, in *New York Times Book Review*, 10 December 1967; "Notes on Current Books," in *Virginia Quarterly* (Charlottesville), August 1969; "The Storm" by Robin Skelton, in *Malahat Review* (Victoria, British Columbia), October 1969; "Striking the Dark Air for Music" by Paul Nelson, in *Carleton Miscellany* (Northfield, Minnesota), September 1974; "An Ultimate Magician: Notes on the Work of William Pitt Root" by Floyd Skloot, in *Chowder Review* (Wallaston, Massachusetts), Winter 1978.

William Pitt Root comments:

As a counter to the proliferation of much instant poetry, I regard with respect the efforts of such men as Bly and Merwin in America or Hughes in England, who, with others, bring into English the works of writers from other cultures where the conditions for the development of the human spirit are still more trying, more essentially demanding.

Regarding my own work, I hope it reflects something of the qualities I admire most in Roethke (whose primordial consciousness is inimitable), Frost (who forged memorable work out of an inconsolable solitude), Williams (whose love of animation in people and nature was inexhaustible), García Lorca (whose passions were essential, unsummoned), Whitman, Blake, Neruda, Lawrence, and Jeffers (who share the impulse to accomplish the mythic common bond out of the apparently commonplace)—these are men who in opening to their own experience can extend us as well. These poets are makers, not designers, and what they make is self being freed of ego, first defining, then transcending those limits. In America, now, the most exciting groundwork for such growth is being established by the waking generations of women who dare to explore their own frontiers. I should add I mean those who travel by foot, to distinguish between them and those who travel by bandwagon. No frontier has ever been approached by bandwagon.

*   *   *

William Pitt Root's latest book, *Reasons for Going It on Foot*, is so animated with the beauty and mysteries of wildlife one is convinced that Root's earlier obsession with the dead and the dying has been dismissed for being only part of the story. In *Striking the Dark Air for Music* Root exposes a vision of death as being the mean conclusion to a short and troublesome life.

> I saw the crippled trees
> crumple into colors, shedding
> their brilliant disease of leaves
> that left the branches dead.

If life must be celebrated, it must be noted that life is mostly menacing. In "A Start" the poet recognizes spring while holding his young daughter's "flowersmeary hands." Then he feels "the green blades cocked/in dry wood/drive free." The word "cocked" serves to undermine the poem's theme of new life with the hint that it arrives armed and dangerous. Root's latest work, however, nearly abandons these earlier worries with poems that celebrate life and the living. Everywhere in the book, the living are awake with action. In one poem, slugs are making love, in another it's the spiders who are amorous. Throughout the book, the images of birds dancing, of men and women "diving like seals," of hands as "quick fish" appear as the sparkling rewards of the book's quest expressed in its title poem:

> ...I may identify
> myself as a stranger
>
> eager to know
> the ways of those
>
> I beg my life from
> as I pass.

The desire is to be filled with the happenings of others' lives, to be as conspicuously alive as the "Slugs Amorous in the Air," not to feel empty and alone after the "white birds like spirits gathered for a ceremonial/dance.../and drew their long yellow legs onto the commotion of/their wings" and were gone.

Though Root's theme has changed, his style hasn't. Root's snap-to-it diction and no-frills syntax remain. And though he was already the unsung master of personification, Root's skill in this area has become even more sophisticated since he now more readily compounds metaphor with sound as exemplified in the contrast between the earlier line, "The sun heats and robs me," and the more recent and musical line, "a single horse/stood beneath the single singing tree."

What has not changed is Root's continuing experimentation with the poem's form. *Reasons for Going It on Foot*, like his earlier books, exhibits a variety of stanza patterns that range from the couplet, to the quatrain, to stanzas with unjustified margins, to stanzas justified like prose. Root's versatile use of form is one of his enduring traits as a craftsman; his ability to evoke the pains of life and the lushness of nature in thrifty images is his enduring trait as a poet.

—Susan Kaplan

ROSENBLATT, Joe (Joseph Rosenblatt). Canadian. Born in Toronto, Ontario, 26 December 1933. Educated at Central Technical School, and George Brown College, Toronto. Married Faye Smith in 1970; one son. Worked as laborer, factory worker, plumber's mate, gravedigger, and civil servant until 1958; worked for Canadian Pacific Railway, 1958-65. Since 1969, Editor, *Jewish Dialog* magazine, Toronto. Writer-in-Residence, University of Western Ontario, London, 1978-80. Artist: individual show of drawings, Gadatsy Gallery. Recipient: Canada Council grant, 1966, 1968, 1973; Governor-General's Award, 1976. Address: Jewish Dialog, 60 St. Clair West, Toronto, Ontario, Canada.

PUBLICATIONS

Verse

Voyage of the Mood. Don Mills, Ontario, Heinrich Heine Press, 1963.
The LSD Leacock. Toronto, Coach House Press, 1966.
Winter of the Luna Moth. Toronto, Anansi, 1968.
Greenbaum. Toronto, Coach House Press, 1971.
The Bumblebee Dithyramb. Erin, Ontario, Press Porcépic, 1972.
Blind Photographer: Poems and Sketches. Erin, Ontario, Press Porcépic, 1973.
Dream Craters, edited by John Newlove. Erin, Ontario, Press Porcépic, 1974.
Virgins and Vampires. Toronto, McClelland and Stewart, 1975.
Top Soil. Erin, Ontario, Press Porcépic, 1976.
Loosely Tied Hands: An Experiment in Punk. Windsor, Ontario, Black Moss Press, 1978.
Snake Oil. Toronto, Exile, 1978.
The Sleeping Lady. Toronto, Exile, 1979.
Brides of the Stream. Lantzville, British Columbia, Oolichan, 1983.

Recording: *Joe Rosenblatt,* High Barnet, 1971.

Short Story

Tommy Fry and the Ant Colony. Windsor, Ontario, Black Moss Press, 1979.

Other

Doctor Anaconda's Solar Fun Club: A Book of Drawings. Erin, Ontario, Press Porcépic, 1977.

*

Manuscript Collections: Public Archives of Canada, Ottawa; University of Toronto.

Joe Rosenblatt comments:

My own verse and prose-poems basically attack the human condition and society with its crass materialism and phony value-structure.

My poetry is traditional and influenced by American poets such as Hart Crane and Robert Frost. My poems are concerned with the Moloch or Mammon monster of society and the insatiable appetite of the creature. The monster finds its expression in my animal poems.

For example, in my bat poems the psyche of man is found in this terrestrial animal of darkness. Therefore my kinship is with Swift and misanthropes. My super hero is Ambrose Bierce. In nearly all my poems the quest of man is spiritual cannibalism—soul theft and the protein of money—I use the traditional devices of poetry in my work such as rhyme, assonance and metric extension.

*   *   *

Joe Rosenblatt "is a poet of the small presses," but he is, nevertheless, well-known in Canada. At times he has seemed, superficially, more interested in the world of plants, insects and animals than that of human beings; but this is more an aspect of his fascination with the unusual, the rare, and the minute than a lack of sympathy with the race of men. He has said, "I only deal with the bizarre," but adds that his newer poems are "more directly confessional poems, written without the intervention of imagery or my old animal disguises." Lately, he has been drawing as well as writing poems, and in the drawings images of grotesque, and curiously human, though debased, animals and reptiles abound. He has had exhibitions of his drawings in several Toronto galleries and his 1973 book (*Blind Photographer*) might more properly be called a book of drawings illustrated by poems than the opposite. He has said that "drawings are the lazy man's way to writing anti-poems, poems without intellectualizing and verbalizing." It is typical of Rosenblatt to hint that he is not much interested in thoughtful technique; in fact, in both poems and drawings, he is always meticulously careful of detail. His interest in "insect and plant sexuality" is extraordinary and Norman Snider has said rightly that "Rosenblatt is a miniaturist in his sensibility, his poems are minute and exquisite observations of the tiny phenomena of nature." It only remains to add that, in the real meaning of the word, wit is the prime mark of his work.

—John Newlove

ROSENTHAL, M(acha) L(ouis). American. Born in Washington, D.C., 14 March 1917. Educated at the University of Chicago, B.A. 1937 (Phi Beta Kappa), M.A. 1938; New York University, Ph.D. 1949. Married Victoria Himmelstein in 1939; two sons and one daughter. Instructor, Michigan State University, East Lansing, 1939-45. Since 1945, Member of the English Department, since 1961, Professor of English, and Director of the Poetics Institute, 1977-79, New York University. United States Cultural Exchange Program Visiting Specialist in Germany, 1961, Pakistan, 1965, Poland, Romania, and Bulgaria, 1966, and Italy and France, 1980; Visiting Professor, University of Pennsylvania, Philadelphia, 1974; Visiting Poet, Israel, 1974, and Yugoslavia, 1980; Distinguished Scholar, People's Republic of China, 1982; Visiting Professor, University of Zurich, 1984. Poetry Editor, *The Nation*, New York, 1956-61, *The Humanist*, Buffalo, 1970-78, and *Present Tense*, New York, since 1973. Recipient: American Council of Learned Societies Fellowship, 1942, 1950; Guggenheim Fellowship, 1960, 1964; *Explicator* Award, for criticism, 1984. Agent: Fox Chase Agency, 419 East 57th Street, New York, New York 10022. Address: 17 Bayard Lane, Suffern, New York 10901, U.S.A.

PUBLICATIONS

Verse

Blue Boy on Skates. New York and London, Oxford University Press, 1964.
Beyond Power: New Poems. New York and London, Oxford University Press, 1969.
The View from the Peacock's Tail. New York and London, Oxford University Press, 1972.
She: A Sequence of Poems. Brockport, New York, Boa, 1977.
Poems 1964-1980. New York, Oxford University Press, 1981.

Other

Effective Reading: Methods and Models, with W. C. Hummel

and V. E. Leichty. Boston, Houghton Mifflin, 1944.
Exploring Poetry, with A.J.M. Smith. New York, Macmillan, 1955; revised edition, 1973.
A Primer of Ezra Pound. New York, Macmillan, 1960.
The Modern Poets: A Critical Introduction. New York and London, Oxford University Press, 1960.
The New Poets: American and British Poetry since World War II. New York and London, Oxford University Press, 1967.
Randall Jarrell. Minneapolis, University of Minnesota Press, 1972.
Poetry and the Common Life. New York and London, Oxford University Press, 1974.
Sailing into the Unknown: Yeats, Pound, and Eliot. New York and London, Oxford University Press, 1978.
The Modern Poetic Sequence: The Genius of Modern Poetry, with Sally M. Gall. New York and Oxford, Oxford University Press, 1983.

Editor, with Thomas H. Jameson, *A Selection of Verse.* Paterson, New Jersey, Littlefield, 1952.
Editor, with Gerald D. Sanders and John Herbert Nelson, *Chief Modern Poets of Britain and America.* New York, Macmillan, 1962; revised edition, 1970.
Editor, *Selected Poems and Two Plays of W.B. Yeats.* New York, Macmillan, 1962; revised edition, 1973.
Editor, *The William Carlos Williams Reader.* New York, New Directions, 1966; London, MacGibbon and Kee, 1967.
Editor, *The New Modern Poetry: An Anthology of British and American Poetry since World War II.* New York, Macmillan, 1967; revised edition, New York, Oxford University Press, 1969.
Editor, *100 Postwar Poems: British and American.* New York, Macmillan, 1968.

Translator, *The Adventures of Pinocchio: Tale of a Puppet,* by C. Collodi. New York, Lothrop, 1983.

*

Critical Studies: "In Spite of Solitude" by Stuart Holroyd, in *John O'London's,* 2 March 1961; "Judgements and Interpretations" by Thomas Lask, in *New York Times,* 25 April 1967; "The Lyre in the Larger Pattern" by Robert D. Spector, in *Saturday Review* (New York), 10 June 1967; "Voices of Victims" by Robie Macauley in *New York Times Book Review,* 10 September 1967; Thomas Lask, in *New York Times,* 29 August 1969; "Sensibilities" by William Heyen, in *Poetry* (Chicago), March 1970; "Wild with the Morning: The Poetry of M.L. Rosenthal" by Sally M. Gall, in *Modern Poetry Studies* (Buffalo), Autumn 1977; "The Poetry of M.L. Rosenthal" by Emile Capouya, in *The Nation* (New York), 1 and 22 October 1977 and 21 January 1978; "Lyrical Readings" by Robert Langbaum, in *New York Times Book Review,* 2 April 1978; "The Many-Sidedness of Modernism" by Theodore Weiss, in *Times Literary Supplement* (London), 1 February 1980; "Modernism, Yeats, and Eliot" by James Ulney, in *Sewanee Review* (Tennessee), Spring 1983; "Taking a New Look at the Poet-Critic" by James Schevill, in *East Side Monthly* (Providence, Rhode Island), May 1983; "Poetize or Bust" by Hugh Kenner, in *Harper's* (New York), September 1983; "From a Common Bed of Feeling" by Seamus Heaney, in *New York Times Book Review,* 20 November 1983.

*   *   *

With the publication of five volumes of poetry since 1964, the distinguished critic and teacher M.L. Rosenthal has emerged as a genuinely important poet in his own right. Rosenthal is capable of considerable variety in tone and form, and this flexibility provides suitable expressive parallels to the breadth of his subject matter. The tone of individual poems varies, for example, from the playfulness of "Jim Dandy," and the sardonic and transforming wit of "Love in the Luncheonette," to the controlled grief of "I Strike a Match....," and the poems range in form from the disciplined lyricism of "Visiting Yeats's Tower" to more open forms with deceptively relaxed conversational rhythms. In addition, certain poems explore within the framework of a single work the relationships between prose and verse themselves.

Rosenthal's subject matter is drawn from deeply felt personal experience; from Biblical allusions; from literary references to such diverse figures as, among others, Keats, Pasternak, Rilke, Hart Crane, and Mayakovsky; and occasionally from political and historical events. But the triumph of individual poems lies in Rosenthal's ability to place in new and contemporary perspective some of the great and traditional themes: love and death, youth and age; innocence and experience; the identity of man.

The key perhaps to this diversity of style and content is Rosenthal's inclusive and paradoxical concept of the poet himself: in his own case a combination of "a 'tragic view of life' *and* an optimistic 'nature.'" Throughout his work one is aware of the pained intensity of a deeply compassionate man who observes the contradictory behavior of those "Sentimental scorpions," human beings, and who yearns nevertheless—as "Seniority, or It Stands to Reason" indicates—for ultimate metaphors of reconciliation:

> These autumn leaves, with their gold or crimson sheen,
> could hardly recommend the fresh young green
> spring leaves for mature responsibilities.
> You need *experience* to capture sun for trees.

—Gaynor F. Bradish

ROSS, Alan. British. Born in Calcutta, India, 6 May 1922. Educated at Haileybury; St. John's College, Oxford. Served in the Royal Naval Volunteer Reserve, 1942-47. Married Jennifer Fry in 1949; one son. Staff member, British Council, 1947-50; staff member, *The Observer*, London, 1950-71. Since 1961, Editor, *London Magazine*; since 1965, Managing Director, London Magazine Editions, formerly Alan Ross Publishers, London. Recipient: Atlantic-Rockefeller Award, 1946. Fellow, Royal Society of Literature, 1971. C.B.E. (Commander, Order of the British Empire), 1982. Address: 4 Elm Park Lane, London S.W.3, England.

PUBLICATIONS

Verse

Summer Thunder. Oxford, Blackwell, 1941.
The Derelict Day: Poems in Germany. London, Lehmann, 1947.
Something of the Sea: Poems 1942-1952. London, Verschoyle, 1954; Boston, Houghton Mifflin, 1955.
To Whom It May Concern: Poems 1952-57. London, Hamish Hamilton, 1958.
African Negatives. London, Eyre and Spottiswoode, 1962.

North from Sicily: Poems in Italy 1961-64. London, Eyre and Spottiswoode, 1965.
Poems 1942-67. London, Eyre and Spottiswoode, 1967.
A Calcutta Grandmother. London, Poem-of-the-Month Club, 1971.
Tropical Ice. London, Covent Garden Press, 1972.
The Taj Express: Poems 1967-1973. London, London Magazine Editions, 1973.
Open Sea. London, London Magazine Editions, 1975.
Death Valley. London, London Magazine Editions, 1980.

Other

Time Was Away: A Notebook in Corsica. London, Lehmann, 1948.
The Forties: A Period Piece. London, Weidenfeld and Nicolson, 1950.
The Gulf of Pleasure (travel). London, Weidenfeld and Nicolson, 1951.
Poetry 1945-50. London, Longman, 1951.
The Bandit on the Billiard Table: A Journey Through Sardinia. London, Verschoyle, 1954; revised edition, as *South to Sardinia*, London, Hamish Hamilton, 1960.
Australia 55: A Journal of the M.C.C. Tour (cricket). London, Joseph, 1955.
Cape Summer, and The Australians in England. London, Hamish Hamilton, 1957.
The Onion Man (for children). London, Hamish Hamilton, 1959.
Danger on Glass Island (for children). London, Hamish Hamilton, 1960.
Through the Caribbean: The M.C.C. Tour of the West Indies 1959-1960 (cricket). London, Hamish Hamilton, 1960.
Australia 63 (cricket). London, Eyre and Spottiswoode, 1963.
The West Indies at Lord's (cricket). London, Eyre and Spottiswoode, 1963.
The Wreck of Moni (for children). London, Alan Ross, 1965.
A Castle in Sicily (for children). London, Alan Ross, 1966.
Colours of War: War Art 1939-45. London, Cape, 1983.
Ranji, Prince of Cricketers. London, Collins, 1983.

Editor, *Selected Poems of John Gay*. London, Grey Walls Press, 1950.
Editor, with Jennifer Ross, *Borrowed Time: Short Stories*, by F. Scott Fitzgerald. London, Grey Walls Press, 1951.
Editor, *Abroad: Travel Stories*. London, Faber, 1957.
Editor, *The Cricketer's Companion*. London, Eyre and Spottiswoode, 1960; revised edition, London, Eyre Methuen, 1979.
Editor, *Poetry Supplement*. London, Poetry Book Society, 1963.
Editor, *London Magazine Stories 1-11*. London, London Magazine Editions, 1964-79.
Editor, *Leaving School*. London, London Magazine Editions, 1966.
Editor, *Living in London*. London, London Magazine Editions, 1974.
Editor, *Selected Poems*, by Lawrence Durrell. London, Faber, 1977.
Editor, *New Stories 7*. London, Hutchinson, 1982.
Editor, *The Turf*. Oxford, Oxford University Press, 1982.
Editor, *Selections from The Tatler and Spectator*. London, Penguin, 1982.

Translator, *Undersea Adventure*, by Philippe Diolé. New York, Messner, 1953.

Translator, *Sacred Forest*, by Pierre Gaisseau. London, Wei-
denfeld and Nicolson, 1954.
Translator, *Death Is My Trade*, by Robert Merle. London,
Verschoyle, 1954.
Translator, *Seas of Sicily*, by Philippe Diolé. London, Sidg-
wick and Jackson, 1955; as *Gates of the Sea*, New York,
Messner, 1955.

*

Manuscript Collection: Arts Council of Great Britain, London.

*   *   *

Alan Ross began as what is vaguely called a war poet. He was
in Germany during the early part of the Occupation, and his
subjects were German gun sites and military hospitals, day and
night in Hamburg, Lüneburg Heath, the dark night of the soul
that as he saw it was closing on Germany. The subjects were
grim, but the poet's spirit did not fully reflect them; his awareness of the sensuous world was too strong. "Lüneburg," for
instance, has a refrain: "The courtroom holds the afternoon in
chains." The idea is to convey that Germany too is in chains, but
the verse that follows might reflect a peaceful life in Oxford:
"October settles on water and weeping willows./Under stone
bridges, leaves like boats/ Drift golden...."
Many years later, when preparing his collected poems, Ross
changed many of these early pieces in a remarkable way, stiffening them, making exact what had been vague. "Sengwarden"
originally began and ended: "At Sengwarden the silence is the
space in the heart." (As a young poet Ross had a weakness for
this kind of romantic and not very meaningful statement.) This
line has been dropped, and the revised poem begins:

> Something (but what) could be made of this.
> Two U-boat officers turning to piss
> In swastika shapes against a wall.

These revised early poems which bear only the relationship of
mood to their originals are certainly among his best work. In
general he shows a love of colour and gaiety that sometimes
declines to mere prettinesss. He has written about cricket at
Brighton and the World Cup, the Grand Canal and mine dances
in Johannesburg, the Autostrada del Sole and the Finchley
Road. He records the scene very vividly, but too often seems
content just to do that without looking beneath or outside it.
"Beyond the window the tyre-coloured road deflates/ Like a tube
at night" his poem about the Finchley Road begins. One appreciates the ingenious aptness of the image, but it is expressive only
upon a superficial level. Sometimes a general moral is drawn in
the last verse, in an attempt to add meaningfulness to a poem
which is really no more than a record of observations.
Perhaps Ross was unlucky in the period at which he began
writing. His natural tendency to romantic excess was encouraged by the War and by the poets most in favour at the time. In
the 1930's or the 1950's his tendency to see everything in terms of
brightly coloured pictures would have been controlled, and this
in fact he has tried to do himself. The poems he wrote in Africa
between 1958 and 1960 offer pictures just as clear as those in
earlier work but some of them, like "Rock Paintings," "Sometime Never" and "Such Matters as Rape" go a good deal further
by expressing some involvement with the scenes described.
These, and the rewritten early poems, suggest a possible new line
of development in the next decade.

—Julian Symons

ROTHENBERG, Jerome (Dennis).   American.   Born in New
York City, 11 December 1931. Educated in New York public
schools, 1937-48; City College of New York, B.A. 1952; University of Michigan, Ann Arbor, M.A. 1953. Served in the United
States Army in Germany, 1954-55. Married Diane Brodatz in
1952; one son. Instructor, City College of New York, 1959-60;
Lecturer in English, Mannes College of Music, New York, 1961-
70; Regents Professor, University of California, San Diego,
1971; Visiting Lecturer in Anthropology, New School for Social
Research, New York, 1971-72; Visiting Professor, University of
Wisconsin, Milwaukee, 1974-75, San Diego State University,
1976-77, University of California, San Diego, 1977-79 and 1980-
84, University of California, Riverside, 1980, and University of
Oklahoma, Norman, 1985; Distinguished Aerol Arnold Chair in
English, University of Southern California, Los Angeles, 1983.
Founding publisher, Hawk's Well Press, New York, 1958-65;
Editor or Co-Editor, *Poems from the Floating World*, 1960-64,
Some/Thing, 1965-69, and *Alcheringa*, 1970-76, all New York,
and *New Wilderness Letter*, since 1976; Contributing Editor,
Stony Brook, Stony Brook, New York, *Change International*,
Paris, *Dialectical Anthropology*, Amsterdam, and *Sulfur*, Pas-
adena, California. Recipient: Longview Foundation Award,
1961; Wenner-Gren Foundation grant, 1969; Guggenheim grant,
1974; National Endowment for the Arts grant, 1976; Before
Columbus Foundation award, 1982. Address: c/o New Directions, 80 Eighth Avenue, New York, New York 10011, U.S.A.

PUBLICATIONS

Verse

White Sun, Black Sun.   New York, Hawk's Well Press, 1960.
The Seven Hells of the Jigoku Zoshi.   New York, Trobar, 1962.
Sightings I-IX, with *Lunes* by Robert Kelly.   New York,
Hawk's Well Press, 1964.
The Gorky Poems (bilingual edition).   Mexico City, El Corno
Emplumado, 1966.
Between: Poems 1960-1963.   London, Fulcrum Press, 1967.
Conversations.   Los Angeles, Black Sparrow Press, 1968.
Poems 1964-1967.   Los Angeles, Black Sparrow Press, 1968.
Offering Flowers, with Ian Tyson.   London, Circle Press, 1968.
Sightings I-IX & Red Easy a Color.   London, Circle Press,
1968.
Poland/1931.   Santa Barbara, California, Unicorn Press, 1969.
The Directions, with Tom Phillips.   London, Tetrad Press,
1969.
Polish Anecdotes.   Santa Barbara, California, Unicorn Press,
1970.
Poems for the Game of Silence 1960-1970.   New York, Dial
Press, 1971.
A Book of Testimony.   Bolinas, California, Tree, 1971.
Net of Moon, Net of Sun.   Santa Barbara, California, Unicorn
Press, 1971.
A Valentine No a Valedictory for Gertrude Stein.   London,
Judith Walker, 1972.
Seneca Journal I: A Poem of Beavers.   Madison, Wisconsin,
Perishable Press, 1973.
Three Friendly Warnings, with Ian Tyson.   London, Tetrad
Press, 1973.
Esther K. Comes to America, 1931.   Greensboro, North Carol-
ina, Unicorn Press, 1974.
The Cards.   Los Angeles, Black Sparrow Press, 1974.
Poland/1931 (complete edition).   New York, New Directions,
1974.
The Pike and the Pearl.   Berkeley, California, Tree, 1975.

Seneca Journal: Midwinter, with Philip Sultz. St. Louis, Singing Bone Press, 1975.

A Poem to Celebrate the Spring and Diane Rothenberg's Birthday. Madison, Wisconsin, Perishable Press, 1975.

Book of Palaces: The Gatekeepers. Boston, Pomegranate Press, 1975.

I Was Going Through the Smoke, with Ian Tyson. London, Tetrad Press, 1975.

Rain Events. Milwaukee, Membrane Press, 1975.

The Notebooks. Milwaukee, Membrane Press, 1976.

A Vision of the Chariot in Heaven. Boston, Hundred Flowers Book Shop, 1976.

Narratives and Realtheater Pieces, with Ian Tyson. Bretenoux, France, Braad, 1977.

Seneca Journal: The Serpent, with Philip Sultz. St. Louis, Singing Bone Press, 1978.

A Seneca Journal (complete edition). New York, New Directions, 1978.

Songs for the Society of the Mystic Animals, with Ian Tyson. London, Tetrad Press, 1979.

B*R*M*Tz*V*H. Madison, Wisconsin, Perishable Press, 1979.

Abulafia's Circles. Milwaukee, Membrane Press, 1979.

Letters and Numbers. Madison, Wisconsin, Salient Seedling Press, 1979.

Vienna Blood and Other Poems. New York, New Directions, 1980.

For E.W.: Two Sonnets. London, Spot Press, 1981.

Imaginal Geography 9: The Bishop. San Diego, Atticus Press, 1982.

A History of Dada as My Muse. London, Spot Press, 1982.

Altar Pieces. Barrytown, New York, Station Hill Press, 1982.

That Dada Strain. New York, New Directions, 1983.

15 Flower World Variations, with Harold Cohen. Milwaukee, Membrane Press, 1984.

Recordings: *Origins and Meanings*, Folkways, 1968; *From a Shaman's Notebook*, Folkways, 1968; *Horse Songs and Other Soundings*, S-Press, 1975; *6 Horse Songs for 4 Voices*, New Wilderness, 1978; *Jerome Rothenberg Reads Poland/1931*, New Fire, 1979.

Plays

The Deputy, adaptation of a play by Rolf Hochhuth (produced New York, 1964). New York, French, 1965.

Radio Play: *Das Hörspiel des Bibers*, 1984 (Germany).

Other

Pre-Faces and Other Writings. New York, New Directions, 1981.

Editor and Translator, *New Young German Poets*. San Francisco, City Lights, 1959.

Editor, *Ritual: A Book of Primitive Rites and Events* (anthology). New York, Something Else Press, 1966.

Editor, *Technicians of the Sacred: A Range of Poetries from Africa, America, Asia and Oceania*. New York, Doubleday, 1968; revised edition, Berkeley, University of California Press, 1985.

Editor, *Shaking the Pumpkin: Traditional Poetry of the Indian North Americas*. New York, Doubleday, 1972.

Editor, with George Quasha, *America a Prophecy: A New Reading of American Poetry from Pre-Columbian Times to the Present*. New York, Random House, 1973.

Editor, *Revolution of the Word: A New Gathering of American Avant Garde Poetry 1914-1945*. New York, Seabury Press, 1974.

Editor, with Michel Benamou, *Ethnopoetics: A First International Symposium*. Boston, Alcheringa, 1976.

Editor, with Harris Lenowitz and Charles Doria, *A Big Jewish Book: Poems and Other Visions of the Jews from Tribal Times to the Present*. New York, Doubleday, 1978.

Editor, with Diane Rothenberg, *Symposium of the Whole: A Range of Discourse Toward an Ethnopoetics*. Berkeley, University of California Press, 1983.

Translator, *The Flight of Quetzalcoatl*, from a Spanish prose version of the original Aztec by Angel Maria Garibay. Brighton, Sussex, Unicorn Bookshop, 1967.

Translator, with Michael Hamburger and the author, *Poems for People Who Don't Read Poems*, by Hans Magnus Enzensberger. New York, Atheneum, and London, Secker and Warburg, 1968; as *Poems*, London, Penguin, 1968.

Translator, *The Book of Hours and Constellations*, by Eugen Gomringer. New York, Something Else Press, 1968.

Translator, *The 17 Horse Songs of Frank Mitchell, Nos. X-XIII*. London, Tetrad Press, 1969.

Translator, with Harris Lenowitz, *Gematria 27*. Milwaukee, Membrane Press, 1977.

*

Manuscript Collection: Archive for New Poetry, University of California, San Diego.

Critical Studies: "20th Century Music" by Diane Wakoski, in *Parnassus* (New York), Fall-Winter 1972; *Preferences* edited by Richard Howard, New York, Viking Press, 1974; *Boundary 2* (Binghamton, New York), April 1975; *Vort 7* (Bloomington, Indiana), 1975; review by Victor Turner, in *Boundary 2* (Binghamton, New York), Winter 1978; "In the Beginning Was Aleph" by Jonathan Cott, in *New York Times Book Review*, 23 April 1978; "Uniting History in a 'Biological Fellowhood'" by Paula Gunn Allen, in *Contact II* (New York), Fall 1978; *The Old Poetics and the New* by Richard Kostelanetz, Ann Arbor, University of Michigan Press, 1981; Thomas Meyer, in *American Book Review* (New York), September-October 1981; George F. Butterick, in *Sulfur 4* (Pasadena, California), 1982; David Toolan, in *Commonweal* (New York), 4 November 1983; *Interpreting the Indian: Twentieth Century Poets and the Native American* by Michael Castro, Albuquerque, University of New Mexico Press, 1983.

Jerome Rothenberg comments:

I think of myself as making poems that other poets haven't provided for me & for the existence of which I feel a deep need.

I look for new forms & possibilities, but also for ways of presenting in my own language the oldest possibilities of poetry going back to the primitive & archaic cultures that have been opening up to us over the last hundred years.

I believe that everything is now possible in poetry, & that our earlier "western" attempts at closed definitions represent a failure of perception we no longer have to endure.

I have recently been translating American Indian poetry (including the "meaningless" syllables, word distortions & music) & have been exploring ancestral sources of my own in the world of Jewish mystics, thieves & madmen.

My personal manifesto reads: 1) I will change your mind; 2)

any means (= methods) to that end; 3) to oppose the "devourers"=bureaucrats, systemmakers, priests, etc. (W. Blake); 4) "& if thou wdst understand that wch is me, know this: all that I have sd I have uttered playfully—& I was by no means ashamed of it" (J.C. to his disciples, The Acts of St. John).

*   *   *

There is a bit of tradition in American letters which shows that some of our best writers must go abroad to find their true recognition. Europeans were touting Walt Whitman for his revolutionary and refreshing manner of writing himself into his poems while Americans were still hemming and hawing. Poe had to be translated by Baudelaire, and today Charles Bukowski finds his greatest audience in France. Jerome Rothenberg also is understood in Europe better than he is here, partly because his digging into the intellectual roots of poetry through his study of oral tradition looks less sound and more avant garde to American academics, many of whom are still trying to find a straight line from the English Romantics to American verse.

What has become apparent in recent years is the immense intellectual energy which has gone into Rothenberg's poetry and, even more, his aesthetic explorations and writings. Anthologies "edited" by Rothenberg are not merely collections of books full of poems. Each one is an exercise in studying the possibilities of poetry. Not only his selections, but his editorial writing and essays continue to show us how superficial our readings and definitions of poetry have become. In this sense he is part of that great movement in letters created by Pound and carried on by Olson, to search for the real connections in art and history, life and language, beyond the formal and narrow ones.

Rothenberg's recent work has been evolving round a personal mythology which includes his sense of himself as an American Jew, born in Brooklyn in 1931 of East European ancestors, but also as an inheritor of the Native American traditions which he has come to revere and feel part of by study, and adoption into one of the tribes of the Seneca. In That Dada Strain he acknowledges other origins and resonances, in particular a use of the Dadaist's sense of 20th-century language collapsing in on itself and needing to be reconstructed by all who wish to make language meaningful.

In Vienna Blood he concluded the book with a tour de force, "Abulafia's Circles," an homage to Tristan Tzara, founder of the Dada movement. It is poem written for performance, as well as a ritual presentation of all of Rothenberg's own secret ideas about poetry, and after reading it (or preferably, hearing him perform it) one must be overwhelmed by the wideness of the spectrum of possibilities Rothenberg takes into the poem. He uses incantation. He uses catalogues. He uses historical perspective and narrative devices for presenting that perspective. He uses both surrealist and realist imagery. He uses ritual, song, and even analytical discussion. All these techniques are for showing the complexity of any identity once we consider all its possible origins.

Rothenberg's first collection of poems, White Sun, Black Sun, gave little indication of the rich intellectual feast which was to follow. The poems are vivid, small imagistic works, some of which like the title poem were deeply influenced by Blake's Songs of Innocence, but all held a surrealist promise of uncovering the dream world and the world of the unconscious, rather than an intellectual journey. Perhaps one of the things wrong with contemporary civilization (certainly Olson thought so) is that we do split up the mind and the heart and the body. However, what Rothenberg has obviously been searching for in the 25 years which have ensued since White Sun, Black Sun is a means of using language to express our whole existence. For him, the psyche through image, especially dream image, was a door to enter this whole space. But his researches have carried him to an astonishingly vivid set of possibilities for poetry and language. Like the good scholar-poet that he is, Rothenberg takes all his researches personally, and continually finds ways of fitting what he thinks about into the realm of feeling and poetry.

He begins Vienna Blood with the poem "The Structural Study of Myth":

> the thief became the rabbi
> in that old story
> others would say he was his father
> all along the way the moon
> reflected in the water
> is the water
> maybe the master gonnif come to earth
> old Trickster brother Jesus
> didn't us Jews tell stories of his magic
> "because we are like him"
> the Crow Indian had said about Coyote
> hitting the nail at last

It is not just condensation which Rothenberg has achieved in this poem so successfully. It is that Whitmanian attempt to understand all of civilization through one's own personal myths, reduced skillfully into possibilities for everyone. Perhaps Rothenberg is the first 20th-century Everyman poet, one who can teach us all the possibilities of ourselves.

—Diane Wakoski

ROWBOTHAM, David (Harold). Australian. Born in Toowoomba, Queensland, 27 August 1924. Educated at Toowoomba Grammar School; University of Sydney (Lawson Prize, 1949); University of Queensland, Brisbane (Ford Medal, 1948), B.A. Served in the Royal Australian Air Force, Southwest Pacific, 1942-45. Married Ethel Jessie Matthews in 1952; two daughters. Editorial staff member, The Australian Encyclopedia, 1950-51; columnist, Toowoomba Chronicle, 1952-55; broadcaster, Australian Broadcasting Commission National Book Review Panel, 1957-63. Literary and theatre critic, 1955-64, chief book reviewer, 1964-69, Arts Editor, 1969-80, and since 1980, Literary Editor, Brisbane Courier-Mail. Commonwealth Literary Fund Lecturer, University of Queensland, 1956, 1964, and University of New England, Armidale, New South Wales, 1961; Senior Tutor in English, University of Queensland, 1965-69. Advisory Editor, Poetry Magazine, Sydney. Since 1964, Council Member, Australian Society of Authors. Recipient: Sydney Morning Herald Competition prize, 1949; Grace Leven Prize, 1964; Xavier Society Award, 1966; Australian Commonwealth Literary Fund travel grant, 1972; Australia Council grant, 1974. Address: 28 Percival Terrace, Holland Park, Brisbane, Queensland 4121, Australia.

PUBLICATIONS

Verse

Ploughman and Poet.   Sydney, Lyre Bird Writers, 1954.
Inland.   Sydney, Angus and Robertson, 1958.

All the Room. Brisbane, Jacaranda Press, 1964.
Bungalow and Hurricane: New Poems. Sydney, Angus and Robertson, 1967.
The Makers of the Ark. Sydney, Angus and Robertson, 1970.
The Pen of Feathers. Sydney, Angus and Robertson, 1971.
Selected Poems. Brisbane, University of Queensland Press, 1975.
Maydays. Brisbane, University of Queensland Press, 1980.

Novel

The Man in the Jungle. Sydney and London, Angus and Robertson, 1964.

Short Stories

Town and City: Tales and Sketches. Sydney, Angus and Robertson, 1956.

Other

Brisbane. Sydney, University of Sydney, 1964.

Editor, *Queensland Writing.* Brisbane, Fellowship of Australian Writers, 1957.

*

Manuscript Collection: Australian National Library, Canberra.

Critical Studies: *Australian Literature* by Cecil Hadcraft, London, Heinemann, 1960; *Creative Writing in Australia* by John K. Ewers, Melbourne, Georgian House, 1966; *Focus on David Rowbotham* by John Strugnell, Brisbane, University of Queensland Press, 1969; "Some Recent Australian Poetry" by Ronald Dunlop, in *Poetry Australia* (Sydney), 1972; "Australian Poetry" by Vernon Young, in *Parnassus 7* (New York) no. 1, 1978; *Modern Australian Poetry 1920-1970* by Herbert C. Jaffa, Detroit, Gale, 1979; David Malouf, in *Australian Literary Studies 10* (Brisbane), no.3, 1982.

David Rowbotham comments:

In reading my work backwards (for the purposes of making a selection), I have found my beginnings true to subsequent ends. I have been concerned with being and words. I have not been engaged with furnishing values and fighting causes, only with seeing and speaking as myself in the issue called life, and wherever time has taken me. All that a poet has to do is: merely to be. This can still be a task when so many of us have made the most natural things the hardest of all. A common review observation about my early work (in the 1950's)—"landscape is not enough"—has never been enough, for me, in terms of a really human view. No element of one's self—in my case it was landscape—should be disowned by the self though others depreciate or dismiss it. I would only regret, not disown, poems unworthy as poems of their (my) origins. Neither should a writer working in the element of nature disown what has not been admitted or discerned: his element of man. I acknowledge—as a guidance to my earlier work done among my Australian home-countryside, and to my later work done (say) within the sense of surrounding larger worlds—that man and landscape (outer? inner?) can not be separated, and that it never occurred to me whether or not they could be. I also acknowledge that poetry is a passion before it is anything else; I have been concerned with a language for living. We are farmers of ourselves, said Donne; and I would not mind if the whole of my work, from poems

about ploughmen to poems about men in space and about wars, emigration, and travel, were seen and summed up in the light of that remark.

*   *   *

David Rowbotham began writing and publishing after World War II as a young follower of the *Bulletin* school of nature poets in Australia, a school that encouraged Australian writers to look more closely at and reaffirm their own regional identity and meaning. Such a coming to terms with Australian landscape was important at that time, but it threatened our poetry with an ever expanding wash of minor bird and billabong versification. David Rowbotham wrote a number of very delicate lyrics in his first book, *Ploughman and Poet,* but his second collection, *Inland,* though it contained probably his most anthologised— and one of his best—poems, "Mullabinda," did not really prepare his readers for the change in direction, to a more introverted and personal poetry, that was first displayed in the volume *All the Room.*

From this point on, Rowbotham's poetry has struggled its way doggedly, and with considerable effort, into areas of response and experience far removed from the gentle sunny Darling Downs countryside of the earlier books. It is a measure of Rowbotham's integrity that he has not paid easy court to current fashionable styles and mannerisms, even when they have been shown to be amenable to the sort of personal self-exploration he has been struggling to realize. At its worst, then, his later work, in *Makers of the Ark* and *The Pen of Feathers,* is marred by a residue of quatrain-making habits not fully explored or justified. At its best, the recent poetry counterpoints a conservative vocabulary and rhythm with an intensely felt response to the poet's own discoveries and concerns, which have been thought through with an almost painful honesty to their own relevance in Rowbotham's poetic search. David Rowbotham is becoming one of the significant loners in Australian poetry.

—Thomas W. Shapcott

ROWLAND, J(ohn) R(ussell). Australian. Born in Armidale, New South Wales, 10 February 1925. Educated at Cranbrook School; University of Sydney, B.A. 1945. Married Moira Armstrong in 1956; one son and two daughters. Member of the Department of Foreign Affairs: Canberra, 1944, 1949-52, 1959-65; Moscow, 1946-48; London, 1948-49, 1957-59; Saigon, 1952-55; Washington, D.C., 1955-57; Ambassador to the U.S.S.R., 1965-68; High Commissioner to Malaysia, 1969-72; Ambassador to Austria, Czechoslovakia, and Hungary, 1973-75; Deputy Secretary, Canberra, 1975-78; Ambassador to France, 1978-82. Visiting Fellow, Australian National University, Canberra, 1982-83. Officer, Order of Australia, 1981. Address: 15 Grey Street, Deakin, A.C.T. 2600, Australia.

PUBLICATIONS

Verse

The Feast of Ancestors. Sydney, Angus and Robertson, 1965.
Snow. Sydney, Angus and Robertson, 1971.

Times and Places: Poems of Locality.   Canberra, Brindabella
 Press, 1975.
The Clock Inside.   Sydney and London, Angus and Robertson,
 1979.

*

J.R. Rowland comments:
   Very much a spare-time poet; primarily a diplomat—
unfortunately. Lyric verse; poems usually not longer than thirty
lines; strongly visual; mostly personal in theme rather than social
or philosophical.

*   *   *

   The settings of J.R. Rowland's poems reflect the fact that he
has lived in many varied and various parts of the world. Yet
whether it be the Australian desert, winter in Moscow, a hotel
room in Cairo or Southeast Asia, it is always possible for him in
just a few lines to create a landscape and an atmosphere. What
helps him so much to achieve this effect is his eye for the tiny but
important detail and his gift for the unusual, apt, and fresh
image, simile or metaphor.
   We are always aware that this is a man with a quiet, dry sense
of humour, a man able to laugh at human foibles and pretensions but at the same time questioning his right to do so, realising
how easy it is to be "the slick observer." There is a cavalier touch
to his verse, the touch of a man who is concerned but who knows
that there is nothing worse than taking oneself too seriously.
   Much of his verse is personal, concerned with what he himself
has described as domesticities. These deal with the wife, children, and ordinary everyday events of family life. To all of these
incidents he gives a depth and singularity and if his family
holiday by the sea seems a little dull to us he reminds us ("At
Noosa") that

> Lara and Zhivago
> Had no children, nor is laundry mentioned
> By Lawrence in a similar situation
>   With Frieda in the cottage at Thirroul:
> It makes a certain difference to the tone.
> Exaltation needs to be alone

   His special plea is for originality, for men of vision. Against
the dull, monotonous routine of suburbia where "admirals pick
tomatoes/In their back garden," he sets the Australian continent. This for him is a "half-unearthly country," a land of
mystery, a visionary landscape, "a cure for habit," For Rowland
the East has the same ability to stir the imagination, both have a
"promise/Of strangeness and discovery." There is a celebration
not only of the Australian landscape but of the people enveloped
by it, of "the natural human pulse/Of Country living." With
horror the poet looks at the trends of urban Australia and
suggests (in "The Hotel Namatjira") that

> To find some essence ours, that is the land's,
> True to its nature, fitted to its ends,
> Direct, attuned and native, we return
>
> To men and buildings of the primary age.

—Anna Rutherford

ROWSE, A(lfred) L(eslie).   British.   Born in St Austell,
Cornwall, 4 December 1903. Educated at Christ Church, Oxford
(Douglas Jerrold Scholar), M.A. in English literature 1929.
Fellow, All Souls College, Oxford, 1925-74, now Emeritus. Pres-
ident of the English Association, 1952-53; Millar Visiting Pro-
fessor, University of Illinois, Urbana, 1952-53; Raleigh Lecturer,
British Academy, 1957; Trevelyan Lecturer, Cambridge Univer-
sity, 1958; Visiting Professor, University of Wisconsin, Madison, 1959-60; Research Associate, Huntington Library, San
Marino, California, 1962-69; Beatty Memorial Lecturer, McGill
University, Montreal, 1963. Recipient: Royal Society of Literature Benson Medal, 1982. D.Litt.: Oxford University, 1952;
University of Exeter, 1960; D.C.L: University of New Brunswick, Fredericton, 1960. Fellow, British Academy, 1958; Fellow,
Royal Society of Literature. Agent: Andre Hewson, 45-47 Clerkenwell Green, London EC1R 0HT, England; or, Curtis Brown,
575 Madison Avenue, New York, New York 10022, U.S.A.
Address: Trenarren House, St. Austell, Cornwall, England.

PUBLICATIONS

Verse

Poems of a Decade 1931-1941.   London, Faber, 1941.
Poems Chiefly Cornish.   London, Faber, 1944.
Poems of Deliverance.   London, Faber, 1946.
Poems Partly American.   London, Faber, 1959.
Poems of Cornwall and America.   London, Faber, 1967.
Strange Encounter.   London, Cape, 1972.
The Road to Oxford.   London, Cape, 1978.
A Life: Collected Poems.   Edinburgh, Blackwood, 1981.

Short Stories

West Country Stories.   London, Macmillan, 1945; New York,
 Macmillan, 1947.
Cornish Stories.   London, Macmillan, 1967.
Night at the Carn.   London, Kimber, 1984.

Other

On History: A Study of Present Tendencies.   London, Paul
 Trench Trubner, 1927; as *Science and History: A New View of
 History,* New York, Norton, 1928.
Politics and the Younger Generation.   London, Faber, 1931.
The Question of the House of Lords.   London, Hogarth Press,
 1934.
Queen Elizabeth and Her Subjects, with G.B. Harrison.   Lon-
 don, Allen and Unwin, 1935.
Mr. Keynes and the Labour Movement.   London, Macmillan,
 1936.
Sir Richard Grenville of the Revenge: An Elizabethan Hero.
 London, Cape, and Boston, Houghton Mifflin, 1937.
Tudor Cornwall: Portrait of a Society.   London, Cape, 1941;
 revised edition, London, Macmillan, and New York, Scribner,
 1969.
A Cornish Childhood: Autobiography of a Cornishman.   Lon-
 don, Cape, 1942; New York, Macmillan, 1947.
The Spirit of English History.   London, Longman, 1943; New
 York, Oxford University Press, 1945.
The English Spirit: Essays in History and Literature.   London,
 Macmillan, 1944; revised edition, 1966; New York, Funk and
 Wagnalls, 1967.
The Use of History.   London, English Universities Press, 1946;

New York, Macmillan, 1948; revised edition, English Universities Press, and New York, Collier, 1963.

The End of an Epoch: Reflections on Contemporary History. London, Macmillan, 1947.

The England of Elizabeth: The Structure of Society. London, Macmillan, 1950; New York, Macmillan, 1951.

The English Past: Evocations of Persons and Places. London, Macmillan, 1951; New York, Macmillan, 1952; revised edition, as *Times, Persons, Places: Essays in Literature,* New York, Macmillan, 1965.

A New Elizabethan Age? London, Oxford University Press, 1952.

History of France, by Lucien Romier (translated and completed). London, Macmillan, and New York, St. Martin's Press, 1953.

An Elizabethan Garland. London, Macmillan, and New York, St. Martin's Press, 1953.

The Expansion of Elizabethan England. London, Macmillan, and New York, St. Martin's Press, 1955.

The Churchills: The Story of a Family. London, Macmillan, and New York, Harper, 2 vols., 1956-58

The Elizabethans and America. London, Macmillan, and New York, Harper, 1959.

St. Austell: Church, Town, Parish. St. Austell, Cornwall, H.E. Warne, 1960.

All Souls and Appeasement: A Contribution to Contemporary History. London, Macmillan, 1961; as *Appeasement: A Study in Political Decline 1933-1939,* New York, Norton, 1961.

Ralegh and the Throckmortons. London, Macmillan, 1962; as *Sir Walter Ralegh, His Family and Private Life,* New York, Harper, 1962.

William Shakespeare: A Biography. London, Macmillan, and New York, Harper, 1963.

Christopher Marlowe: A Biography. London, Macmillan, 1964; as *Christopher Marlowe: His Life and Work,* New York, Harper, 1965.

A Cornishman at Oxford: The Education of a Cornishman.- London, Cape, 1965.

Shakespeare's Southampton: Patron of Virginia. London, *A Cornishman at Oxford: The Education of a Cornishman.* London, Cape, 1965.

Shakespeare's Southampton: Patron of Virginia. London, Macmillan, and New York, Harper, 1965.

Bosworth Field and the Wars of the Roses. London, Macmillan, 1966; as *Bosworth Field: From Medieval to Tudor England,* New York, Doubleday, 1966.

The Contribution of Cornwall and Cornishmen to Britain. Newton Abbot, Devon, Seale-Hayne Agricultural College, 1969.

The Elizabethan Renaissance:
1. *The Life of the Society.* London, Macmillan, 1971; New York, Scribner, 1972.
2. *The Cultural Achievement.* London, Macmillan, and New York, Scribner, 1972.

The Tower of London in the History of the Nation. London, Weidenfeld and Nicolson, and New York, Putnam, 1972.

The Abbey in the History of the Nation, in *Westminster Abbey.* London, Weidenfeld and Nicolson, 1972.

Shakespeare the Man. London, Macmillan, 1973.

Windsor Castle in the History of the Nation. London, Weidenfeld and Nicolson, and New York, Putnam, 1974.

Simon Forman: Sex and Society in Shakespeare's Age. London, Weidenfeld and Nicolson, 1974; New York, Scribner, 1975; as *The Case Books of Simon Forman,* London, Pan, 1976.

Peter, The White Cat of Trenarren. London, Joseph, 1974.

Robert Stephen Hawker, A Belated Medieval, with Cornish Ballads and Other Poems. St. Germans, Cornwall, Elephant Press, 1975.

Discoveries and Reviews: From Renaissance to Restoration. London, Macmillan, and New York, Barnes and Noble, 1975.

Jonathan Swift, Major Prophet. London, Thames and Hudson, 1975; New York, Scribner, 1976.

Oxford in the History of the Nation. London, Weidenfeld and Nicolson, and New York, Putnam, 1975.

Brown Buck: A Californian Fantasy (for children). London, Joseph, 1976.

A Cornishman Abroad. London, Cape, 1976.

Matthew Arnold, Poet and Prophet. London, Thames and Hudson, 1976.

Homosexuals in History: A Study of Ambivalence in Society, Literature, and the Arts. London, Weidenfeld and Nicolson, and New York, Macmillan, 1977.

Milton the Puritan. London, Macmillan, 1977.

Shakespeare the Elizabethan. London, Weidenfeld and Nicolson, and New York, Putnam, 1977.

Heritage of Britain. London, Artus, and New York, Putnam, 1977.

The Byrons and Trevanions. London, Weidenfeld and Nicolson, 1978; New York, St. Martin's Press, 1979.

Chalky Jenkins: A Little Cat Lost. London, Weidenfeld and Nicolson, 1978.

Tommer, The Black Farm-Cat. London, Weidenfeld and Nicolson, 1978.

Three Cornish Cats (omnibus). London, Weidenfeld and Nicolson, 1979.

A Man of the Thirties. London, Weidenfeld and Nicolson, 1979.

Portraits and Views, Literary and Historical. London, Macmillan, and New York, Barnes and Noble, 1979.

The Story of Britain. London, Treasure, and New York, Putnam, 1979.

The Illustrated History of Britain. New York, Crown, 1979.

Memories of Men and Women. London, Eyre Methuen, 1980.

Shakespeare's Globe: His Intellectual and Moral Outlook. London, Weidenfeld and Nicolson, 1981; as *What Shakespeare Read—and Thought,* New York, Coward McCann, 1981.

Eminent Elizabethans. London, Macmillan, and Athens, University of Georgia Press, 1983.

Shakespeare's Characters: A Complete Guide. London, Methuen, 1984.

Prefaces to Shakespeare's Plays. London, Orbis, 1984.

Shakespeare's Self-Portrait. London, Macmillan, and Washington, D.C., University Press of America, 1984.

Glimpses of the Great. London, Methuen, 1985.

Editor, with M.I. Henderson, *Essays in Cornish History,* by Charles Henderson. London, Oxford University Press, 1935.

Editor, *The West in English History.* London, Hodder and Stoughton, 1949.

Editor, *Shakespeare's Sonnets.* London, Macmillan, and New York, Harper, 1964; revised edition, as *Shakespeare's Sonnets: The Problems Solved,* Macmillan and Harper, 1973.

Editor, *A Cornish Anthology.* London, Macmillan, 1968.

Editor, *The Two Chiefs of Dunboy: A Story of 18th Century Ireland,* by J.A. Froude. London, Chatto and Windus, 1969.

Editor, with John Betjeman, *Victorian and Edwardian Cornwall from Old Photographs.* London, Batsford, 1974.

Editor, *The Poems of Shakespeare's Dark Lady*. London, Cape, 1978.

Editor, *The Annotated Shakespeare*. London, Orbis, and New York, Potter, 3 vols., 1978.

Editor, *A Man of Singular Virtue, Being a Life of Sir Thomas More*, by William Roper. London, Folio Society, 1980.

Editor, *Contemporary Shakespeare Series*. London, University Press of America-Eurospan, 1984—.

*

A.L. Rowse comments:

A Celt, growing up in Cornwall, I was early influenced by the Irish poets, especially Yeats. At Oxford I discovered the poetry of T.S. Eliot, whose work, help, and friendship became the most fruitful and enduring affiliation in my career of writing. He first published my work in prose as well as verse, and recognizably wrote the blurbs for the first three volumes of my poems. In my early verse I was particularly interested in exploring the emotion of fear, and—naturally, owing to long years of illness—in expressing the heightened sensitivity, the extra-sensory experiences that went with it. Wartime brought renewed health, a more varied and outgoing response, some reconciliation with life, which I always found difficult. Hence the strain of bitterness, an iron element, that runs all through my work, disgust with human foolery, *contemptus mundi*, though not in a religious sense, any more than with Yeats. (Swift and Hardy much influenced my outlook from youth on.)

As a Celt I have an extra-sensitivity to atmosphere and have given it expression all along, chiefly in relation to Cornwall, but also in Oxford and America. (Very few British poets have been inspired to write about America.) Places speak to me rather than people and are apt to mean more to me. My inner life, from which the poetry springs, has been withdrawn—my outer life has gone into history and politics. But the inner life has always meant more, and by keeping it apart I have kept a flow of inspiration going, where some of my more publicized contemporaries have dried up. One should never be self-conscious about the springs of art. I don't mind the price of not having my poetry noticed— rather a joke really—since it enables me to continue to write. (The joke is on the critics: the combined work in prose and verse, history and literature, is evidently too much for them at present, though they should see that there is a rare literary phenomenon to be investigated.)

A self-contained life, withdrawn from the public eye, a solipsistic outlook, is best for an artist in the hideous contemporary world, so discouraging to real poetry (other than journalistic)— what Yeats described as "this filthy modern tide." He held fast to "his ghostly solitude" as I do. So, I have held by Yeats, early and late, with no more compassion for fools than he or Swift had.

I find traditional verse forms sufficient for what I have to say. Earlier I was attracted by disjoined couplets in rhyme and half-rhyme, like Wilfred Owen, another Celt. Neither blank verse nor free verse has been altogether blank or free with me: each has had a good deal of unobtrusive decoration, internal as well as end-rhymes, and much alliteration (instinctive, the unconscious mark of the poet). Eliot liked (as well as published) my poetry and used to say that I should give myself more to it; but I was afraid of losing inspiration if I forced myself and *worked* at it: I prefer to trust to the creative urges of the unconscious. However, before I die I should like to write one long narrative poem on a Cornish theme. (1985: I at last succeeded in writing one that I had in mind for thirty years: "Duporth," published in my *Collected Poems*, 1981.)

Perhaps I have given to history—and wasted on politics— something of what should have gone to poetry.

*   *   *

Readers and admirers of A.L. Rowse's autobiographical books have on the whole failed to follow the history of his personality into the field of his poetry, which continues to reveal one of the most complex, sometimes irritating, always sensitive and interesting personalities of our time. His earlier collections (*Poems Chiefly Cornish* or *Poems of a Decade*) chronicle his love-hate relationship with Cornwall, and through the subsequent volumes his landscape poems continue to be remarkably vivid. But the personal note continues, too, and grows stronger. Sometimes it is recognisably the tone in which Dr. Rowse conducts his public altercations: "The Cornish crowd/Into the compartment, chattering/As ever with platitudinous vacuity"; but, more rewardingly, it is dark, melancholy, inward-turned: "A public man, scarred with injuries,/Seared by sad experience, without illusion/Or any hope, dedicated to despair." But then there is the note of simple pleasure, in such traditionally pure verses as "How Many Miles to Mylor" and "Child's Verses for Winter." Dr. Rowse's poetry shows almost as many faces as his prose (he is historian, literary critic, editor, biographer, short-story writer). Sturdily in traditional forms, it opens out his personality—as it should—more fully than his critics have understood, and it is much undervalued.

—Derek Parker

RUDOLF, Anthony. British. Born in London, 6 September 1942. Educated at City of London School, 1953-60; British Institute, Paris, 1961; Trinity College, Cambridge, 1961-64, B.A. in modern languages and social anthropology 1964. Has one son and one daughter. Junior executive, British Travel Association, London and Chicago, 1964-66; English and French teacher, 1967-68; worked in bookshops, London, 1969-71; London editor, *Stand* magazine, Newcastle upon Tyne, 1969-72; Literary Editor, 1970-72, and Managing Editor, 1972-75, *European Judaism*, London; Advisory Editor, *Modern Poetry in Translation*, London, 1973-83, Heimler Foundation Publications, London, 1974-76, and *Jewish Quarterly*, London 1975-82. Since 1969, Co-Founder and Editor, Menard Press, London. Address: 8 The Oaks, Woodside Avenue, London N12 8AR, England.

PUBLICATIONS

Verse

The Manifold Circle. Oxford, Carcanet, 1971.
The Same River Twice. Manchester, Carcanet, 1976.
After the Dream: Poems 1964-1979. St. Louis, Cauldron Press, 1980.

Plays

The Soup Complex, adaptation of a play by Ana Novac. Newcastle upon Tyne, Northumberland, Stand, 1972.
The Storm: The Tragedy of Sinai, adaptation of a play by Eugene Heimler. London, Menard Press, 1976.

Other

Editor, with Richard Burns, *An Octave for Octavio Paz*. Farnham, Surrey, Sceptre Press—Menard Press, 1972.

Editor, *Poems from Shakespeare IV*. London, Globe Playhouse Trust, 1976.

Editor, with Howard Schwartz, *Voices Within the Ark: The Modern Jewish Poets*. New York, Avon, 1980.

Translator, *Selected Poems*, by Yves Bonnefoy. London, Cape, 1968; New York, Grossman, 1969.

Translator, *Two Poems from Veines*, by Jean-Paul Guibbert. Rushden, Northamptonshire, Sceptre Press, 1972.

Translator, *Tyorkin, and The Stovemakers: Poetry and Prose of Alexander Tvardovsky*. Cheadle, Cheshire, Carcanet, 1974.

Translator, *Relative Creatures: Victorian Women in Society and the Novel 1837-1867*, by Françoise Basch. London, Allen Lane, 1974.

Translator, with Peter Jay and Petru Popescu, *Boxes, Stairs, and Whistle Time: Poems*, by Popescu. Knotting, Bedfordshire, Omphalos Press, 1975.

Translator, with Daniel Weissbort, *The War Is Over: Selected Poems*, by Evgeny Vinokurov. Cheadle, Cheshire, Carcanet, 1976.

Translator, *A Share of Ink*, by Edmond Jabès. London, Menard Press, 1979.

*

Critical Study: review by George Mackay Brown, in *The Scotsman* (Edinburgh), 21 January 1977.

Anthony Rudolf comments:

After the Dream is the "definitive" collection of my short poems, since it *re-works*, to my relative satisfaction, the two early collections.

*   *   *

The Same River Twice is Anthony Rudolf's first full-length collection of poetry and serves as a fine guide to the range of his abilities and concerns. Known primarily as an editor and publisher and for his excellent translations from the French and Russian—notably works by Edmond Jabès, Yves Bonnefoy, Alexander Tvardovsky, Evgeny Vinokurov—Rudolf's poems are imbued with international flavor and reference. Poems to Karl Kraus, Kafka, Balthus, Paul Celan, Chagall, Edward Hopper display linked yet diverse elements in his book.

Rudolf appears to write two basic forms of poem: one is closed, i.e., the hermetic or philosophical poem usually written in a terse dense language; the other is what I'd call the open poem, i.e., poems more immediately detailed, with more warmth in the language, and whose usual subject matters are domestic realities and travel. His closed poems often resemble the effect of implosion, a deliberate collapse of language, a process of most intense condensing. The influence of Jabès and other French poets seems present in these works and neutralizes Rudolf's voice. Whereas the open poems have a much greater measure of music in the language and I find them very attractive to read.

What is clear in the poems is Rudolf's desire to create poems of substance and, as is traditional with the "first book," his failures are as significant as his triumphs. Many of the poems are homages to literary teachers like Celan, Cafavy, and Borges, others are homages to his Jewish heritage and yearnings. The variety of forms and voices is not that extreme that one can't appreciate the potential intrinsic in this collection. It will be interesting to see

how Rudolf is able to clarify his focus in future collections and add to the power and purpose of his art.

—David Meltzer

———————

RUMENS, Carol. British. Born in London, 10 December 1944. Educated at Coloma Convent Grammar School, Croydon, Surrey, 1955-63; Bedford College, University of London, 1964-66. Married David Rumens in 1965; two children. Publicity assistant, 1974-77, and advertising copywriter, 1977-81, London; Poetry Editor, *Quarto*, London, 1981-82. Since 1982, Poetry Editor, *Literary Review*, London. Creative Writing Fellow, Kent University, Canterbury, 1983-85. Regular book reviewer, *The Observer*, London. Recipient: Alice Hunt Bartlett Award, 1982; Arts Council award, 1982; Cholmondeley Award, 1984. Fellow, Royal Society of Literature, 1984. Agent: Deborah Rogers, 49 Blenheim Crescent, London W11 2EF. Address: c/o Chatto and Windus, 40 William IV Street, London WC2N 4DF, England.

PUBLICATIONS

Verse

Strange Girl in Bright Colours.   London, Quartet, 1973.
A Necklace of Mirrors.   Belfast, Ulsterman, 1978.
Unplayed Music.   London, Secker and Warburg, 1981.
Scenes from the Gingerbread House.   Newcastle upon Tyne, Bloodaxe, 1982.
Star Whisper.   London, Secker and Warburg, 1983.
Direct Dialing.   London, Chatto and Windus, 1985.

Other

Jean Rhys: A Critical Study.   London, Macmillan, 1985.

Editor, *Making for the Open: The Chatto Book of Post-Feminist Poetry 1964-1984*.   London, Chatto and Windus, 1985.

*   *   *

Carol Rumens wrote in a Poetry Book Society Bulletin on the occasion of the publication of her first collection *Unplayed Music*: "Experiencing things imaginatively as an alternative for dealing with 'real' occurrences is, I suppose, an activity especially familiar to anyone who writes." As "real" is in quotation marks we can assume a particular meaning, which I take to be "directly experienced," because it is possible (indeed it is the strength of Rumens's poetry that she does this so well) to experience imaginatively occurrences which, while not direct to the poet, were direct occurrences to others. These, while not unreal, have to be apprehended by the poet imaginatively. She goes on to say in another P.B.S. Bulletin: "I do not belong to that school of thought which says in the face of extreme horror, suffered by others, one should be silent. On the contrary I believe that all the forces of imagination should be employed to speak of their suffering."

I labour this point because some of the most telling of her recent poems have been concerned with the sufferings, horrors, persecutions, and exiles during and deriving from the history of Europe in the first half of this century, subjects which many of those who lived through that period have deliberately avoided as being too immediate in their enormity and their emotional charge for what they felt would be an adequate response. That Rumens's "distance" from these events allows her to experience them imaginatively, and that her use of this particular aspect of the intelligence is such that the empathy she achieves in a poem such as *Outside Osweicin* is stunning, is a source of the power of her work.

This daring of Rumens in taking on subjects of such over-whelming impact is a recent development. Most of the poems in her first collection and her more recent *Star Whisper* display an acute observation and an ability to touch the emotional nerves underlying the domestic and the personal. Then there is the technical accomplishment which in itself is no small contribution to the quality of her poetry. This quality is best illustrated by quoting what is as near a perfect poem as I have encountered in recent years, "The Last Day of March":

> The elms are darkened by rain
> On the small, park-sized hills
> Sigh the ruined daffodils
> As if they shared my refrain
> —That when I leave here, I lose
> All reason to see you again.
>
> What's finishing was so small,
> I never mentioned it.
> My time, like yours, was full,
> And I would have blushed to admit
> How shallow the rest could seem;
> How so little could be all.

Carol Rumens's poetry to date offers achievements which leave us in anticipation of her work to come.

—John Cotton

———

RUSSELL, (Irwin) Peter. British. Born in Bristol, 16 September 1921. Served in the British Army, 1939-46. Married; two sons and two daughters. Owner, Pound Press, 1951-56, Grosvenor Bookshop, 1951-58, and Gallery Bookshop, London, 1959-63; lived in Venice from 1964. Poet-in-Residence, University of Victoria, British Columbia, 1975-76, and Purdue University, Lafayette, Indiana, 1976-77; Teaching Fellow, Imperial Iranian Academy of Philosophy, Tehran, 1977-79. Editor, *Nine* magazine, 1949-58. Address: c/o Anvil Press Poetry, 69 King George Street, London SE10 8PX, England.

PUBLICATIONS

Verse

Picnic to the Moon. Privately printed, 1944.
Omens and Elegies. Aldington, Kent, Hand and Flower Press, 1951.
Descent: A Poem Sequence. Privately printed, 1952.

Three Elegies of Quintilius. Tunbridge Wells, Kent, Pound Press, 1954.
The Spirit and the Body: An Orphic Poem. Privately printed, 1956.
Images of Desire. London, Gallery Bookshop, 1962.
Dreamland and Drunkenness. London, Gallery Bookshop, 1963.
Complaints to Circe. Privately printed, 1963.
Visions and Ruins: An Existentialist Poem. Aylesford, Kent, Saint Albert's Press, 1964.
Agamemnon in Hades. Aylesford, Kent, Saint Albert's Press, 1965.
The Golden Chain: Lyrical Poems 1964-1969. Privately printed, 1970.
Paysages Légendaires. London, Enitharmon Press, 1971.
The Elegies of Quintilius. London, Anvil Press Poetry, 1975.
Acts of Recognition: Four Visionary Poems. Ipswich, Suffolk, Golgonooza Press, 1978.
Theories. Tehran, Crescent Moon Press, 1978.
The Vitalist Reader: A Selection of the Poetry of Anthony L. Johnson, William Oxley, and Peter Russell, edited by James Hogg. Salzburg, University of Salzburg, 1982.
All for the Wolves: Selected Poems 1947-1975, edited by Peter Jay. London, Anvil Press Poetry, and Redding Ridge, Connecticut, Black Swan, 1984.

Other

Epigrammata: Malice Aforethought, or; The Tumour in the Brain. Salzburg, University of Salzburg, 1981.
Elemental Discourses. Salzburg, University of Salzburg, 1982.

Editor, *Ezra Pound: A Collection of Essays...to be Presented to Ezra Pound on His Sixty-Fifth Birthday.* London, Peter Nevill, 1950; as *An Examination of Ezra Pound,* New York, New Directions, 1950.
Editor, *Money Pamphlets by £.* London, Peter Russell, 6 vols., 1950-51.
Editor, with Khushwant Singh, *A Note...on G.V. Desani's "All about H. Hatterr" and "Hali."* London and Amsterdam, Szeben, 1952.
Editor, *ABC of Economics,* by Ezra Pound. Tunbridge Wells, Kent, Pound Press, 1953.

Translator, *Landscapes,* by Camillo Pennati (bilingual edition). Richmond, Surrey, Keepsake Press, 1964.

*

Critical Studies: *A Servant of the Muse: A Garland for Peter Russell on His Sixtieth Birthday,* Salzburg, University of Salzburg, 1981, and *The Salzburg Peter Russell Seminar 1981-82,* University of Salzburg, 1982, both edited by James Hogg.

*   *   *

For me, Peter Russell is the major neglected talent of our time—the author of the finest book of purely "English" lyrics (*The Golden Chain*) of the last twenty years; the author of a gigantic, mostly unpublished epic poem, *Ephemeron,* running to some two thousand pages; the author of *Paysages Légendaires,* a book impregnated with great wisdom and that music the Celts call the "cael moer" or the "great music." In Peter Russell, we are dealing with not just the Poundian theory of the multilingual poet of the future (and Russell was Pound's greatest disciple), but with the realization of such a poet as fact. The sheer magnitude of the job of investigating the innumerable works produced by Russell since *Picnic to the Moon* in 1944 is not a sufficient excuse for not trying. Still less is it an excuse for the wanton neglect of a poet of whom such a figure as Hugh MacDiarmid has written: "Peter Russell is, in my opinion, a writer who has so far received nothing like due recognition...no one in Great Britain today has rendered anything like the disinterested, many-sided and sustained service to Poetry"—the latter comment referring to Russell's work as editor of *Nine* and as publisher of so many of today's established figures long before they were known.

Of *Paysages Légendaires*, Hugh McKinley's phrase "tribute open-eyed, yet illuminate, of life entire" is remarkably apposite. This is how the poem opens:

Palladian villas and the changing seasons

An old man digging in the shade

The gold sun varnishes
The small viridian of the elms
And gilds the hidden cadmium of the glades.

In fact, its way of expression throughout is best described as an open-eyed style.

So, too, it is a rare book of unimpeachable seriousness and poetic wisdom. Perhaps the most interesting feature of *Paysages Légendaires* (and the explanation of its style) is the absence of a close or particularly tense (or over-tense) verbal and syntactical density, which induces an unusual clarity in the verse. And this goes a long way towards compensating for the major disadvantage of a modern sequential but non-narrative long poem, namely, the breaks in continuity which so trouble the average reader. It is a poem that reads well.

The sheer intelligence of the poem commands respect; but what matters is that one feels it is an extraordinarily "aware" poem—a poem aware of, and in touch with the main-stream of human thought. This awareness of the "now" is undoubtedly achieved by a profound knowledge of the "then" and exemplifies what is, perhaps, the poem's central preoccupation:

It will take time to build again,
To build the soul's tall house,
The tower of the wandering self
Foursquare beneath the moon.

Many people, myself among them, think that poetry—the "real" of the thing, the heart's meat of the matter—is the line, or lines of words that are necklace-perfect. Something that glitters with ineffable quality, wisdom, beauty, LIFE—a kind of instant revelation in words, the discovery, as Russell puts it, that "Every natural effect has a spiritual cause/(That which is above, is below)." Indeed, if poetry is the unshakable line, memorable phrase—then Peter Russell is probably the greatest English poet now writing.

Myth is the stuff of thought one might say and *Paysages Légendaires* is a "thoughtful poem." There is little concrete description, and, where there is, the object tends towards the emblematic and metaphorical. There is, however, one short passage where the descriptive element is uppermost:

Sweet bones are growing in the earthly night

Slow maturations in the endless dark
Of subterranean galleries, telluric force
That broods whole centuries upon a single grain

That crumbles or coagulates.

One gets a sense of the tremendousness of life, its continual working; the key word is "broods"—it reveals brilliantly the meaning behind the description, the life within.

Apart from the practical problem of the range of this poet's work, there is one other problem, which is only a "problem" in the framework of present day poetry's dusty picture. This derives from the fact that the more one reads Russell's poetry, the more one realises that it demands imagination. In poem after poem, one finds the feeling transcending the flat detail of experience. So, too, there is a copious knowledge displayed of life both past and present, and there is that true linguistic metamorphosis at times, which provides a permanent frame—be it only a single good line—in which the present is held up before our eyes to be seen in infinite terms. Therefore, parodying Pound, these poems must "go to the imaginative" if they are to be understood, and to the serious if they are to be loved.

—William Oxley

RUTSALA, Vern. American. Born in McCall, Idaho, 5 February 1934. Educated at Reed College, Portland, Oregon, B.A. 1956; University of Iowa, Iowa City, M.F.A. 1960. Served in the United States Army, 1956-58. Married Joan Colby in 1957; three children. Since 1961, member of the English Department, currently Professor, Lewis and Clark College, Portland, Oregon. Visiting Professor, University of Minnesota, Minneapolis, 1968-69; Bowling Green State University, Ohio, 1970. Editor, *December* magazine, Western Springs, Illinois, 1959-62. Recipient: National Endowment for the Arts grant, 1974, 1979; Northwest Poets Prize, 1975; Guggenheim Fellowship, 1982. Address: Department of English, Lewis and Clark College, Portland, Oregon, 97219, U.S.A.

PUBLICATIONS

Verse

The Window. Middletown, Connecticut, Wesleyan University Press, 1964.
Small Songs: A Sequence of Poems. Iowa City, Stone Wall Press, 1969.
The Harmful State. Lincoln, Nebraska, Best Cellar Press, 1971.
Laments. New York, New Rivers Press, 1975.
The Journey Begins. Athens, University of Georgia Press, 1976.
Paragraphs. Middletown, Connecticut, Wesleyan University Press, 1978.
The New Life. Portland, Oregon, Trask House, 1978.
Walking Home from the Icehouse. Pittsburgh, Carnegie Mellon University Press, 1981.

Other

Editor, *British Poetry 1972.* Phoenix, Arizona, Baleen Press, 1972.

*

Critical Study: by Norman Friedman, in *Chicago Review*, June 1967.

Vern Rutsala comments:

(1980) Many of the poems in *The Window* are centered in and around houses—often houses in some worn suburb—and are concerned with what might be seen in such an area. The central image of the window is appropiate, then, and the poems reflect both what can be observed and what happens within. More recent work follows this pattern though its focus is usually much more inward. Though the rhythms I use are relatively free, I often like to make use of regular stanza forms. My themes are not unusual—the common obsessions of poets: how does one live? why is the world as it is? *Paragraphs*, a collection of prose poems, explores directions that differ a good deal from my earlier work. *Laments* and *The Journey Begins* have continued my concern with contemporary life while also beginning to explore the past and our relationship to it. *The New Life* focuses rather directly on Western America. It is part of a longer work called *Walking Home from the Icehouse*.

*   *   *

Vern Rutsala has one the keenest poetic responses to contemporary middle-class society since Cummings, Auden, the earlier Karl Shapiro, and some of Louis Simpson. His special achievement in *The Window* is to have made the furniture of everyday bourgeois life in America available to the uses of serious poetry. He is thus somewhat like one of the better Pop artists, such as Edward Kienholz, who makes assemblages out of found objects—the chassis of an old car, for example—and, with a few skillfully-constructed wire figures, can confront us with ourselves as we fumble erotically in the back seat with our dates in a doomed search for pleasure and joy ("Lovers in Summer").

But there is here not merely a familiar world of skate keys, wagons, bicycles ("Sunday"); there is also a commanding vision which governs the shaping of that world. He hears the glacier knocking in the cupboard and the rumble of violence and despair hidden within our domestic walls. Rutsala deals card after card, building up unbearably to a remorseless climax, until not a corner is left for us to hide in, nothing is spared—not a toothbrush, family album, mantlepiece clock, visit from relatives, souvenir ashtray, flushing of the toliet, garden hose—nothing escapes his illumination of things so ordinary we have forgotten them, so close we haven't really seen them, revealing what we thought we already knew but never quite understood.

Each aspect of our lives, each object of our mundane environment, is a badge of the numb but terrible disparity between life's possibilities and the horror of diminishment we are all suffering from. A bathroom mirror is a symbol of the abyss, which is not so much the inevitable loss of childhood as the crushing emptiness of spirit characteristic of living in an imperialistic, commercial, and technological civilization ("Gilbert and Market"). In such a society, even childhood is no Eden, and children are not spared ("Playground").

"Nightfall" is one of the most moving poems in the book:

> Night settles like a damp cloth
> over the houses. The houses that are shut,
> that show no wear. Lawns
> are patrolled by plywood flamingoes
> or shrubbery clipped from magazines.

The poem develops to reveal our compulsive housecleaning, sports pages, basement workshops, repairing skills, dinner, dishes in the kitchen sink, bills, two cars, committee meetings, unused telephone appointment pads—and our desperate and suicidal children. Then, as the time for sleep comes, some of us lie awake in the glow of a cigarette, obsessed by disappointment and heartbreak. And the poem concludes, perfectly:

> Dawn lies coiled in clocks.
> There are no conclusions here. The dark is there.
> Cigarettes burn down and are ground out
> in souvenir ashtrays from vacations by the sea.

The Window does, however, suffer from an overly-even stylistic tone, as well as from a certain distance placed between its persona and the world he sees so clearly. But these flaws are on their way to being redeemed in Rutsala's subsequent work. Although *Small Songs*, a sequence of invitations by common household objects, is a rather minor effort and seems really to lack development, *Laments*, his next full volume, marks an advance in depth and variety. Decorated with etchings by James Burgess of fruits, plants, and nuts which seem more like grotesque lobsters, this book, as its title indicates, is still fascinated by the party-is-over mood, by loss, by what to make of a diminished thing. And yet the speaker moves more into the foreground, thus providing that sense of involvement lacking in *The Window*, and the situations, imagery, and rhythms are more consciously diversified, thus mitigating that threat of monotony. Nevertheless, the feeling of exasperation, even exhaustion, remains much the same, and Rutsala's grasp of its significance, or even of other possible moods, awaits further insight.

The Journey Begins and *Paragraphs* signal a shift out of that impasse. In the former volume he proclaims, as usual, that "Here we practice the cottage/industry of the banal; here we/probe the mysteries of the commonplace" ("Like the Poets of Ancient China"), but something else is beginning to happen: "we must nurse/the deadness from the air/so we may breathe" ("Unlocking the Door"). Those mysteries are beginning to yield up a significance ("Beginning"):

> The past gone,
> an instant, drained like stream
> water full of clarity, light,
> ice, the flavor of mountains
> that gave you only one thing:
> a wetness on your lips, taste.

Such unaccustomed freshness of taste enables the poet at last to touch, in *Paragraphs*, the springs of neurosis itself and find the mirror—even the cause—of all that desolation in society. His sense of the abyss, in other words, becomes internalized. The pieces in this book are brief prose poems but are also related, as he says, "to the fable, the aphorism, the maxim, the character, and the joke." Many are effectively epigrammatic and eminently quotable, but we must limit ourselves to a single characteristic example, entitled "Demon":

> No matter how you shuffle your traits—making diligence and order turn up regularly—he is always there, waiting. In fact, the harder you try to hide him the more often he breaks into your nights like a party-crashing drunk spilling drinks, upending tables, yelling obscenities at ancient maidens. The trick, you see, is to admit him calmly, see that he is really you—not a double, but *you*, not some actor or black sheep but simply you. He fits your skin; take him places, feed him smoked oysters and good bourbon, let him dance any time he wants to, let him sing. If you fail to do this he will kill himself.

Having found the demon, we must acknowledge him, enable him, or we are doomed to the impasse, and we would do well to follow Rutsala in his tormented progress, extending his forms as he deepens his vision.

—Norman Friedman

SAIL, Lawrence (Richard). British. Born in London, 29 October 1942. Educated at Sherborne School, Dorset, 1956-61; St. John's College, Oxford, 1961-64, B.A. in French and German 1964. Married Teresa Luke in 1965 (divorced, 1981); one son and one daughter. Administration Officer, Greater London Council, 1965-66; Head of Modern Languages, Lenana School, Nairobi, 1966-70; part-time teacher, Millfield School, Somerset, 1973-74; teacher, 1976-80, and visiting writer, 1980-81, Blundells School, Devon. Since 1982, teacher, Exeter School, Devon. Since 1980, Editor, *South West Review*, Exeter. Address: The Lodge, Puddington, near Tiverton, Devon, England.

PUBLICATIONS

Verse

Opposite Views. London, Dent, 1974.
The Drowned River. Hitchin, Hertfordshire, Mandeville Press, 1978.
The Kingdom of Atlas. London, Secker and Warburg, 1980.

Play

Radio Play: *Death of an Echo*, 1980.

Other

Children in Hospital, with Teresa Sail. Gloucester, Thornhill Press, 1976.

*

Lawrence Sail comments:
   The poetic statement of intent which most appeals to me is that suggested by Auden in his poem in memory of Yeats: "In the prison of his days / Teach the free man how to praise." That praise is, as with every writer, contained within and expressed through particular interests and obsessions—such as the relationship of fact and history to dream and hope, as we grow older, the constant challenge of experience to meaning, fragmentation to order. However various the occasions of poems, I find recurrent references in certain landscapes and in particular in the sea. Most of my poems have a strong and often traditional sense of form and structure.

*   *   *

> Do it once more. Lob the stone
> you have just chosen—a layered chip
> of Siena cathedral, green and whitish,
> pummelled by pressures greater than Gothic—

and see it slither, mix to the mile-long
shelf of the foreshore.

—"On Porlock Beach"

A typical Lawrence Sail stanza. Verses seem to rise like the tide or a wave, and then fall or subside. The next stanza is another "breath" start; the tone of subdued elegance pervades poem after poem. Sail certainly crafts and constructs his work with precision. While his language appears robust, the rise/fall rhythm tends to lull the reader.

Sail examines the natural world—we read about roses climbing, autumn closures, beech trees. Only occasionally do people intrude on these pastorals. The careful approach is everywhere evident, as is a sense of genuine concern for the world and its minor inhabitants. Sail offers a variety of forms—stanzas can be three, four, five lines or more; line lengths vary pleasingly—yet still that similar rhythm whatever the shape of the poem on the page, as in "Wild Buddleia":

> One gust released them
> to shed the purple perfume
> on facades, city traffic:
> Imperial messengers, bearing
> prophylactic annunciations.

Ted Hughes is a ghostly figure behind some of the work. The occasional move into taut, tough language is followed by Sail's sense of cathedral calm. He is the considered poet, intent and watching, just now and then finding a subject worthy of his attention. Like Larkin, he is careful with his output, niggardly as regards quantity. The reader invariably nods with satisfaction at the end of a Lawrence Sail poem; everything is in its place, the artefact is complete, but there is less than sufficient to satisfy the hunger for greater sustenance.

—Wes Magee

ST. JOHN, Bruce (Carlisle). Barbadian. Born in Barbados, West Indies, 24 December 1923. Educated at St. Giles' Boys' School, Combermere Secondary School, and Harrison College, 1929-42; Loughborough College, Leicestershire, England, 1945-47, External B.A. (University of London), 1953; Royal Conservatory of Music, Toronto, 1956; University of Toronto, 1962-64, M.A. in Spanish 1964. Married Ruby Marjorie Skeete in 1959 (divorced, 1981); one daughter and one son. Assistant Master, St. Giles' Boys' School, 1942-44, and Combermere School, 1944-64; Lecturer, 1964-75, and since 1976, Senior Lecturer in Spanish, University of the West Indies, Bridgetown, Barbados. Member, National Council for Arts and Culture, Barbados. Recipient: Yaddo grant, 1972, 1976, 1978; Yoruba Foundation prize, 1973. Address: P.O. Box 64, Bridgetown, Barbados, West Indies.

PUBLICATIONS

Verse

The Foetus Pains. Bridgetown, EP, 1972.
The Foetus Pleasures. Bridgetown, EP, 1972.

Bruce St. John at Kairi House. Port of Spain, Kairi, 1974; revised edition, 1975.
Joyce and Eros and Varia. Bridgetown, Yoruba Press, 1976.
Bumbatuk 1. Bridgetown, Cedar Press, 1982.

Play

The Vests (produced Bridgetown, 1977; Manchester, 1980).

Other

Por el Mar de las Antillas: A Spanish Course for Caribbean Secondary Schools. London, Nelson, 1978.

Editor, with Beverley A. Steele, *Tim Tim Tales: Children's Stories from Grenada, West Indies.* St. George's, Grenada, University of West Indies Extra Mural Department, 1976.
Editor, with others, *Aftermath: An Anthology.* Greenfield Center, New York, Greenfield Review Press, 1977.
Editor, *Caribanthology 1.* Bridgetown, Cedar Press, 1981.

*

Critical Studies: "The Poetry of Bruce St. John" by Michael Gitkes, in *Tapia* (Port of Spain), 15 June 1975; "Sex and Class in the Poetry of Bruce St. John" by Elaine Fido, in *Tapia* (Port of Spain), 24 August 1975; "If Barbados Could Speak" by Robert L. Morris, in *Manjak 9* and *10* (Bridgetown), 1975; introduction by Christopher David, to *Bruce St. John at Kairi House,* 1975.

Bruce St. John comments:

In my poetry in Barbadian dialect I try to express viewpoints on Barbadian human situations, in the natural language of Barbadians as they actually speak it—according to my knowledge of the Barbadian dialect lexicon, and its structure of thought and speech. Each poem is tested and re-tested in sound before, during, and after its composition. The views expressed are not always my own; they are *our* views, as Barbadians.

In my poetry in English I tend to express my own views, in Barbadian speech rhythms, and in an English which is my own, in that I choose and position words in order to say effectively what I want to say. In short, I strive to develop a language of my own in order to express *my* self. In my English poems I give fully the whole range of my experience and draw on my exposure to other cultures. I restrict this range somewhat in my dialect poems.

*   *   *

Although there has been "dialect" in Caribbean poetry "from the beginning," as it were, when plantocratic poets and poetasters attempted to reproduce the "broken lingo" of their black servant/slaves; and although Louise Bennett had been writing and reciting exclusively in "dialect verse" since the early 1940's, there was still, as late as the mid-1960's, a passionate debate as to whether patois could be seriously used as the language of poetry. Edward Brathwaite's *Rights of Passage* (1967) appeared finally to settle the matter, but it was not until the poets of the 1970's, above all, Bruce St. John, a former concert singer, physical education instructor, and (presently) lecturer in Spanish at the University of the West Indies, that *nation-language,* conceived of and used as alternative rather than "bad" or "bongo" grammar, came into its own—especially with the large increasingly culturally conscious audiences; to such a degree, that it is practically unthinkable today for any "serious" Caribbean poet not to include at least some kind of nation-language in his work; and

moving closer and closer stylistically to the kaiso and reggae singers who of course have always assumed *native* to be the norm and atom. The miracle of nation-language, at its poetic perfect, is that it not only reproduces the language of the people, but it reaches and re-echoes their inner vibration and bone; so that not only word, but psyche and sense become involved: the "nation" poet expressing as he should, the total culture of his subject: word, soul, and body-language.

St. John's first "discovery" (though Bennett always used it, since it is natural to the form and culture) is the dialogue or dramatic monologue. But what St. John adds is a sense of superstructure: the dialogue becomes a litany which in itself becomes a commentary on the Bajan personality; and the language is itself intensified, not only through the intensified form, but through the expression of contemporary politico-moral issues, juxtaposed against traditional norms expressed through proverb and riddle, as in "Bajan Litany":

> Follow pattern kill Cadogan. *Yes, Lord.*
> America got black power? *O Lord.*
> We got black power. *Yes, Lord.*
> Wuh sweeten goat mout bun 'e tail... *O Lord.*
> Jamaica got industry? *O Lord.*
> We got industry. *Yes Lord.*
> Jamaica got bauxite? (Silence)
> (Louder) Jamaica got bauxite?... *Yes, Lord.*
> De higher monkey go, de more he show 'e tail.

From here St. John was able to tackle "traditional" subjects such as kite flying, cricket, sea-bathing, the "other woman," and more "modern" issues such as the ambiguities of post-colonial politics, and (constantly) the whole vexed question of Bajan education (contrasted with the more native *studyation*); and said in a way that we are able to see/hear them for the first time as it were, from inside, through the persona of "Archie." Archie/St. John are aware that education and the language man uses are intimately connected, and that the respect for this connection says more about one's cultural authenticity than any politician or pedagogue ever could ("Bajan Language"):

> Evah language got a rhythm but Bajan
> Lick guitar drum an banjo stiff wid blows
> Imag'ry purty an sweet like a rose
> Limey try fuh muck up we poor nation
> But Bajan save we life so here we goes...

St. John is as Bajan as Miss Lou is Jamaican as Paul Keens-Douglas is Trinidadian: and yet they transcend territorial boundaries to capture and express the spirit of the Caribbean. It is in this new/ancient tradition that the future of Caribbean poetry lies: the word-seers, the sound-poets. But the body of their poetry will have to be constantly enriched (as is being done) with the emerging underground resources of culture itself.

—Edward Kamau Brathwaite

———————

SANCHEZ, Sonia. American. Born in Birmingham, Alabama, 9 September 1934. Educated at New York University; Hunter College, New York, B.A. 1955. Married Etheridge Knight, *q.v.* (divorced); three children. Staff member, Downtown Community School, 1965-67, and Mission Rebels in

Action, 1968-69, San Francisco; Instructor, San Francisco State College, 1967-69; Lecturer in Black Literature, University of Pittsburgh, 1969-70, Rutgers University, New Brunswick, New Jersey, 1970-71, Manhattan Community College, New York, 1971-73, and Amherst College, Massachusetts, 1972-73. Since 1977, Associate Professor of English, Temple University, Philadelphia. Recipient: PEN award, 1969; American Academy grant, 1970. Ph.D. in Fine Arts: Wilberforce University, Ohio. Address: Department of English, Temple University, Broad and Montgomery, Philadelphia, Pennsylvania 19041, U.S.A.

PUBLICATIONS

Verse

Homecoming. Detroit, Broadside Press, 1969.
WE a BaddDDD People. Detroit, Broadside Press, 1970.
Liberation Poem. Detroit, Broadside Press, 1970.
It's a New Day: Poems for Young Brothas and Sistuhs. Detroit, Broadside Press, 1971.
Ima Talken bout The Nation of Islam. Astoria, New York, Truth Del., 1971(?).
Love Poems. New York, Third Press, 1973.
A Blues Book for Blue Black Magical Women. Detroit, Broadside Press, 1974.
I've Been a Woman: New and Selected Poems. Sausalito, California, Black Scholar Press, 1979.
Homegirls and Handgrenades. New York, Thunder's Mouth Press, 1984.

Recordings: *Homecoming,* Broadside Voices; *We a BaddDDD People,* Broadside Voices; *A Sun Woman for All Seasons,* Folkways, 1971; *Sonia Sanchez and Robert Bly,* Black Box.

Plays

The Bronx Is Next (produced New York, 1970). Published in *The Drama Review* (New York), Summer 1968.
Sister Son/ji (produced Evanston, Illinois, 1971). Published in *New Plays from the Black Theatre,* edited by Ed Bullins, New York, Bantam, 1969.
Dirty Hearts '72, in *Break Out! In Search of New Theatrical Environments,* edited by James Schevill. Chicago, Swallow Press, 1973.
Uh, Uh: But How Do It Free Us?, in *The New Lafayette Theatre Presents,* edited by Ed Bullins. New York, Doubleday, 1974.
I'm Black When I'm Singing, I'm Blue When I Ain't (produced Atlanta, 1982).

Short Stories

A Sound Investment. Chicago, Third World Press, 1979.

Other

The Adventures of Fathead, Smallhead, and Squarehead (for children). New York, Third Press, 1973.

Editor, *Three Hundred Sixty Degrees of Blackness Comin' at You.* New York, 5X, 1972.
Editor, *We Be Word Sorcerers: 25 Stories by Black Americans.* New York, Bantam, 1973.

*

Critical Studies: "Sonia Sanchez and Her Work" by S. Clarke, in *Black World* (Chicago), June 1971; "The Poetry of Three Revolutionists: Don L. Lee, Sonia Sanchez, and Nikki Giovanni" by R. Roderick Palmer, in *CLA Journal* (Baltimore), September 1971; "Sonia Sanchez Creates Poetry for the Stage" by Barbara Walker, in *Black Creation* (New York), Fall 1973; "Notes on the 1974 Black Literary Scene" by George Kent, in *Phylon* (Atlanta), June 1974; *Black Women Writers at Work* edited by Claudia Tate, New York, Continuum, 1983; *Black Women Writers (1950-1980)* edited by Mari Evans, New York, Doubleday, 1984.

* * *

A leading poet of the Black Arts Movement, Sonia Sanchez continues to write for political, economic, and social purposes, seeing no necessary dichotomy of cause-oriented utilitarian writing and art. Believing that Afro-Americans are now expressing thoughts that previous generations were afraid to utter, she sees the times as propitious and urgent for black artistic militancy. "I write because I must," she declares, and "if you write from a black experience, you're writing from a universal experience as well." Although much of her poetry is principally directed to black people and she is popular among them, contrary to popular misconception, Sanchez also has a sizeable white following, especially among those that she characterizes as "progressive" whites.

In an early poem she writes, "white people / ain't rt bout nothing," and she chastises blacks who would adopt whites' values and life styles. She does not allow herself to be victimized by negative white forces: "this is a fool's world / pain is an idiot's ailment / for the wise man knows / how to reconnoiter pain / and make it colloquial." Blacks who "have come to / believe that we are / not" must, as she does, "inhale the ancient black breath." So she teaches that blacks must know their enemies, accept themselves, demonstrate ethnic pride and unity, be moral, act communally, and be about the serious business of intelligent and courageous self-direction. In delivering such messages, much of her poetry is direct, uncompromising, demanding, militant, even abrasive; yet it is not without tenderness, a quality openly evident in her poems for children and in her love poems—notably those dealing with love among blacks and man-woman love.

As her collected works show, Sanchez's poetry has not been static in substance and technique. *Homecoming* is a young poet's grappling with conceptions of self, others, and the world. *We a BaddDDD People* stresses black strength and self-love, identification of human and institutional enemies of black people, "we"-ness in place of the personal and subjective "I." *It's a New Day* "poems for young brothas and sistuhs," warns of dangers, points out the necessity for unity, wholeness of spirit, cleanness of purpose and actions. Having by this time joined the Nation of Islam, Sanchez in *Love Poems* tones down her language as she explores the dynamics of healthy and healthful relationships among black people. The poet's still evolving technical style is apparent in *A Blues Book for Blue Black Magical Women,* an autobiographical, perhaps confessional, volume. Addressed to "Queens of the Universe" and divided into sections "Past," "Present," "Rebirth," and "Future," it is not an anthology or collection; it is, rather, thematically unified poetry that ironically and satirically echoes subtly T.S. Eliot's *The Waste Land,* a key difference being that Eliot is pessimistic and Sanchez is determinedly optimistic. *I've Been a Woman* is a gathering of new and selected poems. In the continuum of her poetry, Sanchez has moved from a declamatory to a declarative style, from exhorter to persuader.

The figurative language that Sanchez employs tends to be imagistic, metaphorical, and ironical. Many of her allusive constructs depend upon intellectual and emotive recognition by Afro-Americans, a recognition often predicated upon what critic Stephen Henderson would call the reader's/hearer's ethnic "Saturation." For example, in an ironic image reversal, she writes about patriarchal poet Sterling Brown as "griot of the wind / glorifying red gums smiling tom-tom teeth," and in a poem about singer Billie Holiday she writes, "speak yo / strange / fruit amid these / stones."

As to structure, Sanchez usually fits form to substance. Her poems are "modern" in their spatial configurations. Occasionally she uses the sonnet form. She composes haiku and tanka poems, and although they follow line and syllable conventions, they tend in substance to be statements rather than suggestive evocations of fleeting experiences.

Critical assessments of Sanchez the poet vary. It is not unusual for academic and "establishment" critics who rely upon traditional, received criteria to pay only passing attention to her work. Women critics tend to regard her poetry very favorably. Sanchez indicates that early in her career, and before her "rediscovery" by Afro-American critics, women critics began paying serious attention to her poetry. Afro-American critics and literary academicians generally consider Sonia Sanchez to be an unusually talented and significant poet.

—Theodore R. Hudson

SANDERS, (James) Ed(ward). American. Born in Kansas City, Missouri, 17 August 1939. Educated at the University of Missouri, Columbia, 1957-58; New York University, B.A. in classics 1963. Married Miriam Kittell in 1961; three children. Editor and Publisher, *Fuck You: A Magazine of the Arts*, and *Dick*, both New York; organizer and lead singer of The Fugs, a literary-political rock group. Professor, Free University of New York, after 1965; Owner, Peace Eye Bookstore, New York. Recipient: National Endowment for the Arts grant, 1966, 1969. Address: c/o Station Hill Press, Station Hill Road, Barrytown, New York 12507, U.S.A.

PUBLICATIONS

Verse

Poem from Jail. San Francisco, City Lights, 1963.
King Lord—Queen Freak. Cleveland, Renegade Press, 1964.
The Toe-Queen: Poems. New York, Fuck You Press, 1964.
Banana: An Anthology of Banana-Erotic Poems. New York, Fuck You Press, 1965.
The Complete Sex Poems of Ed Sanders. New York, Fug-Press, 1965.
Peace Eye. Buffalo, Frontier Press, 1965; revised edition, Cleveland, Frontier Press, 1967.
Fuck God in the Ass. New York, Fuck You Press, 1967.
Shards of God. New York, Grove Press, 1971.
Egyptian Hieroglyphics. Canton, New York, Institute of Further Studies, 1973.
Investigative Poetry. San Francisco, City Lights, 1976.
20,000 A.D. Plainfield, Vermont, North Atlantic, 1976.

Love and the Falling Iron. Bolinas, California, Yanagi, 1977.
The Cutting Stone. Santa Barbara, California, Am Here-Immediate Editions, 1981.
The Z-D Generation. Barrytown, New York, Station Hill Press, 1981.

Novel

Fame and Love in New York. Berkeley, California, Turtle Island Foundation, 1980.

Short Stories

Tales of Beatnik Glory. New York, Stonehill, 1975.

Other

The Family: The Story of Charles Manson's Dune Buggy Attack Battalion. New York, Dutton, 1971; London, Hart Davis, 1972.
Vote!, with Abbie Hoffman and Jerry Rubin. New York, Warner, 1972.

Editor, *Poems for Marilyn.* New York, Fuck You Press, 1962.
Editor, *Bugger: An Anthology of Buttockry.* New York, Fuck You Press, 1964.
Editor, *Despair: Poems to Come Down By.* New York, FU Press, 1964.
Editor, with Ken Weaver and Betsy Klein, *The Fugs' Song Book!* New York, Peace Eye Bookshop, 1965.
Editor, *The Party.* Woodstock, New York, Poetry Crime and Culture Press, 1980.

*

Manuscript Collection: University of Connecticut Library, Storrs.

*   *   *

In Ed Sanders's poetry the raw energy of a 1960's-style peace march, a rock concert, and an orgy impels a fine intelligence. Many of his poems can be read as political protest; some might be read, by a reader intent upon it, as pornography. The best of his work in *Peace Eye* and *20,000 A.D.*—probably the two most interesting books—however, should be read as representing a perhaps unexpected turn in the tradition of Pound and Olson.

"Ed Sanders' language," Charles Olson writes, "advances in a direction of production which probably isn't even guessed at." His language is always near the breaking point, always at the verge of howl and groans. Rude, slangy, obscene, blasphemous, it violates any remaining verbal taboos. At the same time, however, it frequently spills over into Greek, Egyptian hieroglyphs, and glyph-like drawings, giving the impression that one language, or even language itself, cannot contain Sanders's, to use one of his terms, "Endless Gush" (which, it should be noted, is a translation of Anaximander's central term, *tò ápeiron*). Especially when he recites it himself, one has a sense in his language of an archaic power. At its best, however, it is more than that: we begin to sense the relationship between "the holy" and "the accursed" as it is recorded in the etymology of "sacred." The closing section of "The Fugs," "Hymn to the Vagina of Mercy," like "Arise Garland Flame" and "Holy Was Demeter Walking the Corn Furrow," are, as it were, songs from a satyr play.

Sanders's poetry is truly outrageous: that is its beauty. It is a test of Blake's proverbs of Hell. Read at length, it loses its shock value and tends to become tedious, but it is not intended for that kind of consumption. His poems are performance pieces for an athletic performer like Sanders himself, who was the lead singer with a rock group for several years.

The most recent turn in Sanders's work can also be seen as an outgrowth of the Pound-Olson tradition. They propose poetry as a gathering of significant information. Sanders characteristically pushes any possibility to its literal limits. We must be, Olson says, "cooked / and ruled by information." Sanders's response to this demand is what he call "investigative poetry." *The Family*, his careful, objective, and thorough report on the Charles Manson case, was his first investigative poem, or at least the idea of investigative poetry derived from his experience of writing that book. Manson was a sign that something had gone seriously wrong with the political movements of the 1960's. The message of investigative poetry—though it stretches traditional definitions of poetry perhaps even beyond the breaking point— is that no political movement can be effective without complete information. It is an attempt to find a fulcrum for political power at precisely the point where governments are most vulnerable: in gathering, organizing, and effectively communicating knowledge. In the manifesto "To the Z-D Generation," he writes, "Never hesitate to open up a case file even upon the bloodiest of beasts or plots! We will see the day of relentless pursuit of data! Interrogate the Abyss."

In "The Karen Silkwood Cantata," first performed on 20 May 1979, Sanders combined performance with the results of investigation.

—Don Byrd

SANDY, Stephen. American. Born in Minneapolis, Minnesota, 2 August 1934. Educated at Yale University, New Haven, Connecticut, A.B. 1955; Harvard University, Cambridge, Massachusetts (Dexter Fellow, 1961), M.A. 1958, Ph.D. in English 1963. Served in the United States Army, 1955-57. Married Virginia Scoville in 1969; two children. Instructor in English, Harvard University, 1963-67; Fulbright Lecturer, University of Tokyo, 1967-68; Visiting Assistant Professor of English, Brown University, Providence, Rhode Island, 1968-69; Visiting Lecturer, University of Rhode Island, Kingston, 1969. Member of the Literature Faculty, 1969-74, and since 1975, Professor of English, Bennington College, Vermont. Director of poetry workshops at Chautauqua Institution, New York, 1975, 1977, Johnson State College, Vermont, 1976, 1977, Bennington College, 1978-80, and Wesleyan University, Middletown, Connecticut, 1981. Recipient: Academy of American Poets award, 1955; *Harvard Monthly* prize, 1961; Huber Foundation fellowship, 1973; Vermont Council on the Arts fellowship, 1974. Phi Beta Kappa Poet, Brown University, 1969. Address: Box 524, North Bennington, Vermont 05257, U.S.A.

PUBLICATIONS

Verse

Caroms. Groton, Massachusetts, Groton School Press, 1960.
Mary Baldwin. Privately printed, 1962.
The Destruction of Bulfinch's House. Cambridge, Massachusetts, Identity Press, 1963.
The Norway Spruce. Milford, New Hampshire, Ferguson Press, 1964.

Wild Ducks. Milford, New Hampshire, Ferguson Press, 1965.
Stresses in the Peaceable Kingdom. Boston, Houghton Mifflin, 1967.
Home Again, Looking Around. Milford, New Hampshire, Ferguson Press, 1968.
Spring Clear. Pascoag, Rhode Island, Delmo Press, 1969.
LVIII: To Caelius (version of poem by Catullus). Tokyo, Voyagers' Press, 1969.
Japanese Room. Providence, Rhode Island, Hellcoal Press, 1969.
A Dissolve, music by Richard Wilson. New York, Schirmer, 1970.
Light in the Spring Poplars, music by Richard Wilson. New York, Schirmer, 1970.
Jerome. North Bennington, Vermont, Grel Press, 1971.
Roofs. Boston, Houghton Mifflin, 1971.
Soaking, music by Richard Wilson. New York, Schirmer, 1971.
Elegy, music by Richard Wilson. New York, Schirmer, 1972.
Phrases, Fields, Kanda (6 P.M.). North Bennington, Vermont, Grel Press, 1972.
Can, music by Richard Wilson. New York, Fischer, 1973.
One Section from "Revolutions." San Francisco, Grabhorn Hoyem, 1973.
The Difficulty. Providence, Rhode Island, Burning Deck, 1975.
Landscapes. White Creek, New York, White Creek, 1975.
From "Freestone." Binghamton, New York, Bellevue Press, 1975.
The Austin Tower. San Francisco, Empty Elevator Shaft, 1975.
Freestone: Sections 25 and 26. Binghamton, New York, Bellevue Press, 1977.
End of the Picaro. Pawlet, Vermont, Banyan Press, 1977.
Arch (card). Binghamton, New York, Bellevue Press, 1977.
The Hawthorne Effect. Lawrence, Kansas, Tansy Press, 1980.
After the Hunt. Brattleboro, Vermont, Moonsquilt Press, 1982.
Chapter and Verse. Brattleboro, Vermont, Moonsquilt Press, 1982.
Flight of Steps. Binghamton, New York, Bellevue Press, 1982.
Riding to Greylock. New York, Knopf, 1983.

Play

Hieronymo: An Antiphonal Cantata, music by Henry Brant. New York, MCA Music, 1973.

Other

The Raveling of the Novel: Studies in Romantic Fiction from Walpole to Scott. New York, Arno Press, 1980.

*

Manuscript Collection: Houghton Library, Harvard University, Cambridge, Massachusetts.

Critical Studies: "Like the Bones of Dreams" by Heather Ross Miller, in *American Scholar* (Washington, D.C.), Autumn 1967; Vernon Young, in *Hudson Review* (New York), Winter 1971-72; Richard Howard, in *American Poetry Review* (Philadelphia), May-June 1973; "The Difficulty" by Dick Higgins, in *Margins 24-26* (Milwaukee), 1975; Kate Lewis, in *Harvard Advocate* (Cambridge, Massachusetts), June 1983; "Witnesses and Seers" by Terence Diggory, in *Salmagundi* (Saratoga Springs, New

York), Fall 1983; "Stafford, Sandy, and Willard" by Jerome Mazzaro, in *Michigan Quarterly Review* (Ann Arbor), Summer 1984.

*   *   *

The Difficulty, The Austin Tower, and *End of the Picaro* reflect a growing maturation in Stephen Sandy's art. The themes and events that preoccupied his earlier poetry are still in evidence, but his concern with social issues that haunted the 1960's in America—the war in Viet Nam, the plight of the Indian, man's assault upon his environment—has been replaced with a concern for more fundamental philosophical questions and a more studied interest in art's ability to resolve some of them.

In *Stresses in the Peaceable Kingdom* Sandy treated the theme of loss and employed a style which combined conversational ease with clarity of diction and penetrating powers of observation. The poems were a series of epiphanies which compelled the reader to see vividly the objects or moments Sandy recalled. Loss of innocence, or past traditions, or old historical landmarks were treated, sometimes nostalgically, more often with good humor, occasionally with painful irony. In "Destruction of Bulfinch's House," he rendered an old mansion which had declined into a tenement in a mood reminiscent of Eliot's "Preludes"; in "Can" he transformed a can into "a bent tin soldier," jobless, knocking about, grinning through jagged teeth; in "Home from the Range" he turned the familiar folksong refrain into the lament of a soldier returning from a firing range where he had partially lost his hearing.

In *Roofs,* Sandy presented a series of poems tracing his journey from New England to Japan and back again. He reflected upon the paradoxes inherent in modern Japanese life and in his reaction to it. This volume contains his bitterest poems of social protest. His elegy, "Charley," was an intensely personal response to the death of his friend killed in the demilitarized zone. He discovered technical devices to render visually in his poetry the disparities that he wrote about. He preserved tension and a sense of space by actually separating the print on the page with large spaces. His skill as an artist was more certain in this volume: he captured the stylized figures of Japan's past; his verbal plays were less ostentatious and self-conscious than before; the world he depicted was more complex.

In *The Difficulty* and *End of the Picaro* Sandy traces the mental journey of his speaker. In *The Difficulty,* comprised of six parts, Sandy monochromatically muses about himself (or a thinly disguised extension of himself; the persona in all his poems is highly autobiographical) and an other. The other is a collector, a man who cares who he is, where he has come from, and wants to know the identity of the things he collects, who made them, when, and where. Sandy worries; meanings escape him. Petulantly and pseudocryptically, he retorts to the other: "When you grow up/nothing/is personal." Sandy fights the impulse to order, but later, sensing the continuity between himself and others, the past and present, he submits to the undertow that pulls him, ironically, towards style. The rage for order conquers in this sequence of poems.

End of the Picaro continues the quest that is prefigured in *The Difficulty.* Less colloquial than *The Difficulty,* returning to the vein of rich imagistic renderings of moments and objects so frequently present in *Stresses in the Peaceable Kingdom, End of the Picaro* wrestles explicitly with the problem of perspective, the poet's relationship to his personal and historical pasts, and his need to trace the journey of his literary counterpart and double, the Picaro, whose history is often episodic, and whose future this poet must fashion if Sandy is to know himself and mouth his "banal testimony." The poem closes on a celebratory note, with the poet back on the vagabond's road, having understood that the past and the past remembered are not the same, and that possibilities known to him in the present can be discovered in the past, transforming it into the future. The conclusion mingles Sandy's two styles, the one slangy, monosyllabic, and modern, the other richly lyrical, decasyllabic, and descriptive, and invents a new rhythm and style for his verse. Perhaps his next volume will offer what he calls "the simple testament," the base line that he and all men reach for.

—Carol Simpson Stern

SANER, Reg(inald Anthony).   American.   Born in Jacksonville, Illinois, 30 December 1931. Educated at St. Norbert College, West De Pere, Wisconsin, B.A. 1952; University of Illinois, Urbana, M.A. 1956, Ph.D. in English 1962. Served in the United States Army Infantry, 1952-53: Lieutenant; Bronze Star. Married Anne Costigan in 1958; two sons. Free-lance photographer, Illinois, 1953-54; photographer and writer, Montgomery Publishing Company, Los Angeles and San Francisco, 1956. Assistant Instructor, 1956-60, Instructor, 1961-62, Assistant Professor, 1962-67, Associate Professor, 1967-72, and since 1972, Professor of English, University of Colorado, Boulder. Recipient: Fulbright scholarship, 1961; Borestone Mountain Poetry Award, 1972; Academy of American Poets Walt Whitman Award, 1975; National Endowment for the Arts Fellowship, 1976; Creede Repertory Theatre prize, 1981; University of Colorado Distinguished Research Scholarship, 1983; Colorado Governor's award, 1983. Address: 1925 Vassar Drive, Boulder, Colorado 80303, U.S.A.

PUBLICATIONS

Verse

Climbing into the Roots.   New York, Harper, 1976.
So This Is the Map.   New York, Random House, 1981.
Essay on Air.   Athens, Ohio Review Books, 1984.

*

Critical Studies: interviews in *Gumbo Review* (Fort Collins, Colorado), Spring 1977, *Aspen Anthology* (Colorado), Fall 1978, and *Ohio Review 32* (Athens), 1984.

Reg Saner comments:
   Living among rocks, clouds, and trees in Colorado, I tend to get my most immediate impulses from them. Nature poetry; always a crossroads where earth and air intersect. My feel for things and men is temporal. Man on the edge, the dangerous edge of things fascinates me. I look into ways our address defines us, because I believe what we are will always be where.
   Being an atheist, I write poetry that is perhaps naturally religious, though mountain environment, by its potential hostility, staggers anyone's complacent sentimentalizing. Being a Catholic atheist, I have a sense of man that is historical. Wherever I look, either among Anasazi Indian ruins of Chaco Canyon or into the brickwork lining Brunelleschi's cupola over the Duomo of Florence, I hear people saying, "We were." The sound is of mayflies hitting ice.

*   *   *

Poems about mountains have a tendency to diminish into what Reg Saner calls "pure calendar art," but even as he acknowledges this risk Saner shows how to avoid the traps in *Climbing into the Roots*. By making the mountains his "chosen place" Saner has staked out a claim that will long bear his mark, even if he eventually abandons it for some other territory. For Saner's concern is less with the grandeur of the mountains than with the perspective they allow—"this difficult magnificence/ where we are most our own." In these poems he climbs into a cleaner, purer air where—feet planted firmly on rock—he can look out to look in, just as he has climbed *up* to get *into* the roots:

> Under the rosy foreskin of dawn,
> turned for a parting glance, I leave
> and take all I can. The mountain's huge
> bite of glacial cirque
> hovers, a small glass square
> pressed to the shape of a tent,
> with, still slightly warm,
>
> a sleep print. All summer I'll come
> and go, eating spaces like these
> to make sure.
> My death must be a simply enormous death.

Throughout Saner's poems one feels an embracing sense of place, a blend of the physical and the spiritual, but even more impressive is the enlarged time frame within which this place—the American Rocky Mountains—is so finely realized. In a manner that is reminiscent of Loren Eiseley's powerful essays, Saner makes these poems compellingly human—"staring up between, guessing/how huge a dark we're in"—but the intelligence that is guessing here is quite aware that the mountains on which he stands evolved from an earlier geological state, and further that they are now posed "under gravity's big guns" ready to wear or crash down to become the sand of the desert below. The tension such an awareness creates prevents any of these poems from being still lifes, even though they are largely unpeopled. It also establishes a rich context for Saner to confront in concrete ways a range of issues prehistoric and historic, physical and metaphysical.

Not all of Saner's poems are set in the mountains, of course, nor are all of them flawless successes. At times, his usually brilliant metaphors overreach themselves, the tensions of the poems become too explicit, and the imaginative leaps become forces ("At ponds/whose tundra edges seem rich/I put my hand on Miss America's muff"). There are also some poems in this 1975 Walt Whitman Award-winning collection (especially "One War Is All Wars," "Flag," and "Smiling at 180") that appear to contribute little if anything to the otherwise unified trajectory of the book. Saner is not usually his best in small situations, and when he moves away from the mountains his poems sometimes seem to lose vital energy and become more self-consciously rhetorical. Fortunately, such breaks are few.

One of the qualities that distinguishes *Climbing into the Roots* is that so much of it appears to be the product of mature, intelligent listening. Saner accepts the rhythms operating on the mountains ("timing/our talk to the tent's nylon whip and crackle" or—as he puts it in another poem—"To make talk, we listen"), and he channels his energy into confronting the experience and resisting facile interpretations:

> Like a silence coming out of the stones,
> the universe flying at terrible speeds

further into itself.
If it is not here it is nowhere.
The stillness where all words are kept.

In an age where the hard-sell has become commonplace, it is a rare pleasure to find such fertile listening in so many excellent poems. And it is clearly one of the reasons why the best of Reg Saner's work has a lasting quality. He has listened with sensitivity to enrich and enlarge, rather than exploit, his experience, and thus he can now take us closer to "the place that we know/must always/be part of the distance."

—Stanley W. Lindberg

———————

SAROYAN, Aram. American. Born in New York City, 25 September 1943; son of the writer William Saroyan. Educated at Trinity High School, New York; University of Chicago; New York University; Columbia University, New York. Married Gailyn McClanahan in 1968; two daughters and one son. Founding Editor, *Lines*, 1964-65, and Publisher, Lines Books, New York. Recipient: National Endowment for the Arts grant, 1966, 1968. Lives in Ridgefield, Connecticut. Agent: Erica Spellman, William Morris Agency, 1350 Avenue of the Americas, New York, New York 10019, U.S.A.

PUBLICATIONS

Verse

Poems, with Jenni Caldwell and Richard Kolmar.   New York, Acadia Press, 1963.
In.   Eugene, Oregon, Bear Press, 1964.
Top.   New York, Lines, 1965.
Works.   New York, Lines, 1966.
Sled Hill Voices.   London, Goliard Press, 1966.
(Poems).   Cambridge, Massachusetts, Lines, 1967.
Coffee Coffee.   New York, 0 to 9, 1967.
© 1968.   New York, Kulchur, 1968.
(Poems).   New York, Random House, 1968.
Pages.   New York, Random House, 1969.
Words and Photographs.   Chicago, Big Table, 1970.
The Beatles.   Cambridge, Massachusetts, Barn Dream Press, 1970.
5 Mini-Books.   Privately printed, 1971.
The Rest.   Philadelphia, Telegraph, 1971.
Cloth: An Electric Novel.   Chicago, Big Table, 1971.
Six Little Poems, with Victor Bockris.   N.p., Unicorn Books, 1972.
Poems.   Philadelphia, Telegraph, 1972.
By Air Mail, with Victor Bockris.   London, Strange Faeces Press, 1972.
San Francisco, with Andrei Codrescu.   Privately printed, 1972.
The Bolinas Book.   Lancaster, Massachusetts, Other, 1974.
O My Generation and Other Poems.   Bolinas, California, Blackberry, 1976.

Novel

The Street: An Autobiographical Novel.   Lenox, Massachusetts, Bookstore Press, 1975.

Other

Marijuana and Me. Privately printed, 1974.
Genesis Angels: The Saga of Lew Welch and the Beat Generation. New York, Morrow, 1979.
Last Rites: The Death of William Saroyan as Chronicled by His Son. New York, Morrow, 1982.
William Saroyan. New York, Harcourt Brace, 1983.
Trio: Gloria Vanderbilt, Carol Matthau, Oona Chaplin. New York, Simon and Schuster, 1985.

*

Manuscript Collections: Special Collections, University of California, Los Angeles; University of Connecticut, Storrs; Mugar Memorial Library, Boston University.

Aram Saroyan comments:
(1970) I write on a typewriter, almost never in hand (I can hardly handwrite, I tend to draw words), and my machine—an obsolete red-top Royal Portable—is the biggest influence on my work. This red hood holds the mood, keeps my eye happy. The typeface is a standard pica; it if were another style I'd write (subtly) different poems. And when a ribbon gets dull my poems I'm sure change.—1966.

ELECTRIC POETRY

By electric I mean instantaneous—without any reading process at all; and therefore continuous—as the Present is—without beginning, middle, or end.—1968.
(1974) Having spent the past five years largely organizing my previous work and seeing most of it into print, I now find myself writing again, but with a new orientation.
Although I regard my work as a concrete poet, and my later work with the book form itself (*Words and Photographs, Cloth, 5 Mini-Books,* and *The Beatles*) as valid, I feel I have explored this direction as thoroughly as I am able, and hence I am no longer personally interested in it. My new writing, which began with my settling in Bolinas, California, in August 1972, is primarily a return to and an extension of my earlier work as a poet (*Poems*) in which I wrote about my life as honestly as I could, employing conventional syntax. I feel I made a breakthrough in this mode with a poem called "Lines for My Autobiography," written over a period of three days in Bolinas; and seemingly on the momentum of this work have followed three books (the third currently in the writing)—*Lines for My Autobiography, Friendly Persuasion,* and *Poetry in Motion.* With the second of these books, I began composing poems in hand.
(1980) My current project is a book called Families, in which I juxtapose a photographic portrait of a family on each right hand page with excerpts from a taped interview with that family on each left hand page. The structure of this book seems to me to harken back to *Words and Photographs,* but the content is more mainstream America, reflecting my changes in relation to the culture in the past decade, most fundamentally the change of becoming a family man myself. The next project I have in mind is writing a screenplay of my novel *The Street.*
(1985) I am completing a book called *Trio,* which might be characterized as a non-fiction novel. The emphasis in narrative, as opposed to that in journalism, seems to me to lie in presenting perception itself as subject matter, moment by moment. Color, the weather, and minute details of physiological and emotional response seem to me to be the unique province of fiction, whatever its guise. I find that the third person, in this kind of writing,

provides an infinitely freer range of possibility than the first person. I have come full circle now with my autobiographical writing of the past decade. I no longer am intrigued by "I" per se, but more with "he" or "she."

*   *   *

Aram Saroyan's first published poetry, written during the 1960's, established him as an experimental poet whose chief interest was concrete and "minimal" poetry. These poems, skillful as they are, do not often extend beyond a kind of poster-like play with words and the letters of the alphabet. They become objects instantly perceived, and thus fuel for lengthy contemplation for readers so inclined. Such a poem is the untitled one-word "crickets" repeated for 37 or 42 lines, depending on which anthology you find it in. I suppose the length of this poem depends on size of the page, and perhaps Saroyan would accept the notion that a two-line version is likewise complete if printed on a shallow page:

crickets
crickets

The concept may well be an isolation of the components of conscious thought, and in a poem like the one just quoted, repetition and the word itself mimes its subject, and the ubiquitous nature of the crickets' song. A favorite of mine is his "My arms are warm" printed directly over his name; many of the letters used for the statement are those in "Aram Saroyan." Saroyan writes that his "concrete/minimal work now seems to have a lot to do with the strange 'time' the Sixties was for most of us. The one-word poem has *no* time in it, it can be read instantly—and this seemed to me 'perfect' for a while. Now I'm interested less in perfection and more in 'time'—I like lines, sentences, stanzas...."
Saroyan's 1972 book, *Poems,* which he says contains his earliest poems, exemplifies his current interest in the more "traditional" forms, heavily influenced, as ever, by the "New York School," where nothing is too mundane for a place in the poem. Even Saroyan's "traditional" poems are uncommonly spare: here is all of "Almost Midnight":

I type & think & look at the painting of Poe & out
the window there's the top of my head, to the left
and behind me, is the bookcase.

At times this perfected attention captures completely the glimmer of city life, and it is in poems like these that Saroyan's work most distinctly justifies the glorification of the ordinary:

This morning I ate (bacon
& eggs) and
tied my tie
in a hurry
when I went outside
gilt was flashing
in the sidewalk
and the street
sounded like a movie

—Geof Hewitt

SARTON, (Eleanor) May. American. Born in Wondelgem, Belgium, 3 May 1912, daughter of the historian of science George Sarton; emigrated to the United States in 1916; naturalized, 1924. Educated at the Institut Belge de Culture Française, Brussels, 1924-25; Shady Hill School and the High and Latin School, both in Cambridge, Massachusetts. Apprentice, then Member, and Director of the Apprentice Group, Eva Le Gallienne's Civic Repertory Theatre, New York, 1930-33; Founder and Director, Apprentice Theatre, New York, and Associated Actors Inc., Hartford, Connecticut, 1933-36. Taught creative writing and choral speech, Stuart School, Boston, 1937-40. Documentary scriptwriter, Office of War Information, 1944-45. Poet-in-Residence, Southern Illinois University, Carbondale, Summer 1945; Briggs-Copeland Instructor in English Composition, Harvard University, Cambridge, Massachusetts, 1950-53; Lecturer, Bread Loaf Writers Conference, Middlebury, Vermont, 1951-52, and Boulder Writers Conference, Colorado, 1953-54; Phi Beta Kappa Visiting Scholar, 1959-60; Danforth Lecturer, 1960-61; Lecturer in Creative Writing, Wellesley College, Massachusetts, 1960-63; Poet-in-Residence, Lindenwood College, St. Charles, Missouri, 1964, 1965; Visiting Lecturer, Agnes Scott College, Decatur, Georgia, Spring 1972. Recipient: New England Poetry Club Golden Rose, 1945; Bland Memorial Prize, 1945 (*Poetry*, Chicago); American Poetry Society Reynolds Prize, 1953; Bryn Mawr College Lucy Martin Donnelly Fellowship, 1953; Guggenheim Fellowship, 1954; Johns Hopkins University Poetry Festival Award, 1961; National Endowment for the Arts grant, 1966; Sarah Josepha Hale Award, 1972; College of St. Catherine Alexandrine Medal, 1975. Litt.D.: Russell Sage College, Troy, New York, 1958; New England College, Henniker, New Hampshire, 1971; Bates College, Lewiston, Maine, 1974; Colby College, Waterville, Maine, 1974; Clark University, Worcester, Massachusetts, 1975; University of New Hampshire, Durham, 1976; King School of the Ministry, Berkeley, California, 1976; Nasson College, Springvale, Maine, 1980; University of Maine, Orono, 1981; Bowdoin College, Brunswick, Maine, 1983. Fellow, American Academy of Arts and Sciences. Agent: Russell and Volkening Inc., 551 Fifth Avenue, New York, New York 10017. Address: Box 99, York, Maine 03909, U.S.A.

PUBLICATIONS

Verse

Encounter in April. Boston, Houghton Mifflin, 1937.
Inner Landscape. Boston, Houghton Mifflin, 1939; with a selection from *Encounter in April,* London, Cresset Press, 1939.
The Lion and the Rose. New York, Rinehart, 1948.
The Leaves of the Tree. Mount Vernon, Iowa, Cornell College, 1950.
Land of Silence and Other Poems. New York, Rinehart, 1953.
In Time like Air. New York, Rinehart, 1957.
Cloud, Stone, Sun, Vine: Poems, Selected and New. New York, Norton, 1961.
A Private Mythology: New Poems. New York, Norton, 1966.
As Does New Hampshire and Other Poems. Peterborough, New Hampshire, Richard R. Smith, 1967.
A Grain of Mustard Seed: New Poems. New York, Norton, 1971.
A Durable Fire: New Poems. New York, Norton, 1972.
Collected Poems 1930-1973. New York, Norton, 1974.

Selected Poems, edited by Serena Sue Hilsinger and Lois Brynes. New York, Norton, 1978.
Halfway to Silence: New Poems. New York, Norton, 1980.
Letters from Maine: New Poems. New York, Norton, 1984.

Plays

The Underground River. New York, Play Club, 1947.

Screenplays (documentaries): *Valley of the Tennessee,* 1945; *A Better Tomorrow,* with Irving Jacoby, 1945; *The Hymn of the Nation,* 1946.

Novels

The Single Hound. Boston, Houghton Mifflin, and London, Cresset Press, 1938.
The Bridge of Years. New York, Doubleday, 1946.
Shadow of a Man. New York, Rinehart, 1950; London, Cresset Press, 1952.
A Shower of Summer Days. New York, Rinehart, 1952; London, Hutchinson, 1954.
Faithful Are the Wounds. New York, Rinehart, and London, Gollancz, 1955.
The Birth of a Grandfather. New York, Rinehart, 1957; London, Gollancz, 1958.
The Small Room. New York, Norton, 1961; London, Gollancz, 1962.
Joanna and Ulysses. New York, Norton, 1963; London, Murray, 1964.
Mrs. Stevens Hears the Mermaids Singing. New York, Norton, 1965; London, Peter Owen, 1966.
Miss Pickthorn and Mr. Hare: A Fable. New York, Norton, 1966; London, Dent, 1968.
Kinds of Love. New York, Norton, 1970.
As We Are Now. New York, Norton, 1973; London, Gollancz, 1974.
Crucial Conversations. New York, Norton, 1975; London, Gollancz, 1976.
A Reckoning. New York, Norton, 1978; London, Gollancz, 1980.
Anger. New York, Norton, 1982.

Other

The Fur Person: The Story of a Cat. New York, Rinehart, 1957; London, Muller, 1958.
I Knew a Phoenix: Sketches for an Autobiography. New York, Holt Rinehart, 1959; London, Owen, 1963.
Plant Dreaming Deep (autobiography). New York, Norton, 1968.
The Poet and the Donkey (for children). New York, Norton, 1969.
Journal of a Solitude. New York, Norton, 1973.
Punch's Secret (for children). New York, Harper, 1974.
A World of Light: Portraits and Celebrations. New York, Norton, 1976.
A Walk Through the Woods (for children). New York, Harper, 1976.
The House by the Sea: A Journal. New York, Norton, 1977; London, Prior, 1978.
Recovering: A Journal 1978-1979. New York, Norton, 1980.
Writings on Writing. Orono, Maine, Puckerbrush Press, 1980.
At Seventy: A Journal. New York, Norton, 1984.

Bibliography: *May Sarton: A Bibliography* by Lenora P. Blouin, Metuchen, New Jersey, Scarecrow Press, 1978.

Manuscript Collections: Berg Collection, New York Public Library; Houghton Library, Harvard University, Cambridge, Massachusetts; Amherst College, Massachusetts (letters); Westbrook College, Maine.

Critical Studies: *May Sarton* by Agnes Sibley, New York, Twayne, 1972; "Home to a Place of Exile: The *Collected Poems* of May Sarton" by Henry Taylor, in *Hollins Critic* (Hollins College, Virginia), June 1974; *May Sarton: Woman and Poet* edited by Constance Hunting, Orono, Maine, National Poetry Foundation, 1982; interview with Karen Saum, in *Paris Review*, October 1983.

*   *   *

Bare of nuance and ambiguity, May Sarton's verse is often indistinguishable from ordinary prose. Within her limits, her earnest and bookish sensibility has for fifty years reassured readers about the joys and even the anguishes of love, and the dedication necessary to generate art from everyday life, often at the expense of love and other relationships; beginning with *The Lion and the Rose*, many poems have soothingly transcribed the response of an aroused conscience to the horrors of war, and the deep, but curable, guilt of our racism. Her first volume articulates a view of the universe that supports many later poems on the relations between art and nature, between the artist and his work: "Objects and people/exist within this world/only if they can find their places/in a pattern" ("Portraits of One Person— As by Chirico"). Sometimes Sarton more concisely and effectively stylizes nature: "...the Japanese look of sleet/When it slants back the way the wind blows" ("To the Weary"), a perception that still charms many years later in *A Private Mythology*: "How Japanese the rain looked/In Cambridge" ("A Child's Japan"). As early as *The Land of Silence*, Sarton reveals an occasional skill at capturing natural detail: "As shadows made a river of the road" ("Evening Journey"). Unfortunately, she failed to develop this strength until her later volumes. Many poems celebrate specific works of art, from the early "Portraits of the Artist," which praises both the evocative and organizational power of van Cleve's self-portrait, to "Dutch Interior," which 35 years later analyzes de Hooch's skill at suggesting both the psychology and formal function of the woman in the painting. Avoiding undue modesty, Sarton places an equally high value on her own efforts: "A Letter to James Stephens" prays to transform the "Quick-burning fire of youth" to "...that bush of flame/That...contained the angel who could speak God's name...." Sometimes this intense dedication collides with a familiar metaphor: "Imagine a moment when student and teacher/(Long after the day and the lesson are over)/Will soar together to the pure immortal air/And find Yeats, Hopkins, Eliot waiting there" (Poet in Residence").

Nor are Sarton's perpetual love poems convincing, whether the youthful ecstasies of *Encounter in April* or the paeans to love at 60 of *A Durable Fire*. The lover/antagonist achieves neither credible humanity nor symbolic force as an ultra-human principle in an allegory. Since Sarton consistently uses the Shakespearean sonnet, but has difficulties with the final couplet, the poems never reach the resolution implicit in the form. Infrequently in the first volume, the final lines embody a sensuousness that suggests a real relationship and the metrical skill to dramatize it: "Now let us rest. Now let me lay my hand/In yours—like a smooth stone on the smooth sand" ("Sonnet 15"). Too often, however, the couplets strive for Millay's flippancy or Drayton's wit, but stumble: "I am come home to you, for at the end,/I find I cannot live without you, friend" ("Sonnet 14"). Even the competent "Autumn Sonnets," in *A Durable Fire* suffer from Sarton's predilection for familiar abstraction and rhetoric: "Truth is, her daily battle is with death,/Back to the wall and fighting for her breath" ("Sonnet 6").

For all her insistence on strict form an her occasional success with slant rhymes, Sarton is best with free verse. *A Private Mythology*, her strongest volume, succeeds with short poems on Japan, perhaps suggested by haiku, which concentrate image and eliminate the superfluous moral addenda flawing much of her work: "We regretted the rain/Until we saw the mists/Floating the mountains/On their dragon-tails" ("On the Way to Lake Chuzen-ji"). Other poems in the collection display a previously-concealed humor and some assurance with conventional forms, especially in "A Late Mowing," in which vivid images vivify the traditional comfort of the eternality of the natural cycle; "A sky flung down to earth as daisies" returns reassuringly in the final stanza: "While overhead your dazzling daisy skies/Flower in the cold, bright mowing that will keep." The success of *A Private Mythology* suggested that Sarton's eclecticism and moral earnestness had found an authentic voice, but other recent volumes are less encouraging. *A Durable Fire* keeps her signature vocative command to a minimum; but "Elegy (for Louise Bogan)" embarrasses not only with Sarton's familiar rhetorical question, but also with a general failure of taste and technique: "Louise, Louise, why did you have to go/In this hard time of wind and shrouding snow[?]" And *A Grain of Mustard Seed* makes a series of awkward pronouncements on American outrages of the 1960's. Depite these flaws and a continuing fondness for stereotyped treatment of abstract themes in abstract language, Sarton's verse has at least transcended the Henleyesque bravado of *Inner Landscape* and has apparently won an audience in a dozen published volumes. Sarton's greatest problem has always been a tendency toward excessive length and repetition in individual works and a willingness to publish everything. Even the *Collected Poems* stops short of the restlessness necessary to eliminate the inferior. However, Sarton has produced enough competent, low-keyed verse to support her credo (expressed in "Second Thoughts on the Abstract Gardens of Japan"):

> Unbuttoned ego, I have staked
> My life on controlled native powers;
> My garden, so untamed, still has not lacked
> Its hard-won flowers.

—Burton Kendle

SAVORY, Teo. American. Born in Hong Kong. Educated privately in Hong Kong; at the Royal College of Music, London, and Conservatoire, Paris; studied with Harry Plunket Greene. Married the writer Alan Brilliant in 1958. Producer, American National Theatre and Academy, New York. Since 1966, Editor-in-Chief, Unicorn Press and *Unicorn Journal*, Santa Barbara, California, later Greensboro, North Carolina. Recipient: National Endowment for the Arts grant, 1969, 1979. Address: Unicorn Press, P.O. Box 3307, Greensboro, North Carolina 27402, U.S.A.

PUBLICATIONS

Verse

Traveler's Palm: A Poetry Sequence. Santa Barbara, California, Unicorn Press, 1967.
The House Wrecker. Santa Barbara, California, Unicorn Press, 1967.
A Christmas Message Received During a Car Ride. Aptos, California, Grace Hoper Press, 1967.
Snow Vole: A Poetry Sequence. Santa Barbara, California, Unicorn Press, 1968.
Transitions. Santa Barbara, California, Unicorn Press, 1973.
Dragons of Mist and Torrent. Greensboro, North Carolina, Unicorn Press, 1974.

Novels

The Landscape of Dreams. New York, Braziller, 1960.
The Single Secret. New York, Braziller, and London, Gollancz, 1961.
A Penny for the Guy. London, Gollancz, 1963; as *A Penny for His Pocket,* Philadelphia, Lippincott, 1964.
To a High Place. Santa Barbara, California, Unicorn Press, 1971.
Stonecrop: The Country I Remember. Greensboro, North Carolina, Unicorn Press, 1977.
A Childhood. Greensboro, North Carolina, Unicorn Press, 1978.
To Raise a Rainbow. Greensboro, North Carolina, Unicorn Press, 1980.

Short Stories

A Clutch of Fables. Greensboro, North Carolina, Unicorn Press, 1976.

Other

Translator, *Corbière, Supervielle, Prévert, Jammes, Michaux, Guillevic, Queneau, Eich.* Santa Barbara, California, Unicorn Press, 8 vols., 1967-71.
Translator, *Selected Poems of Guillevic.* London, Penguin, 1974.
Translator, *Zen Poems,* by Nhat Hanh. Greensboro, North Carolina, Unicorn Press, 1974.
Translator, *Euclidians,* by Guillevic. Greensboro, North Carolina, Unicorn Press, 1975.
Translator, *Liberté,* by Paul Éluard. Greensboro, North Carolina, Unicorn Press, 1977.
Translator, *Words for All Seasons: Selected Poems of Jacques Prévert.* Greensboro, North Carolina, Unicorn Press, 1979.

* * *

Teo Savory could be a contemporary version of Colette. She has starred on the stage, and produced books of a high quality—verse, verse translation, and novels.

In her fiction, strong plot line and engaging dialogue are her trademarks. Her poetry seems less economical. The vividness of such a novel as *To a High Place* could effectively be tranferred to the poetry. Similarly, her translations seem close to the mark, but I would like to see her make the same imaginative leaps she uses in her prose.

The Unicorn Press and *Unicorn Journal,* both of which she founded in 1966, have produced a striking number of original books and translations.

—Glenna Luschei

———————

SCANNELL, Vernon. British. Born in Spilsby, Lincolnshire, 23 January 1922. Educated at Queen's Park School, Aylesbury, Buckinghamshire; University of Leeds, Yorkshire, 1946-47. Served in the Gordon Highlanders, 1941-45. Married Josephine Higson in 1954; five children. Formerly, amateur and professional boxer; teacher of English, Hazelwood School, Limpsfield, Surrey, 1955-62. Freelance writer and broadcaster since 1962. Resident Poet, village of Berinsfield, Oxfordshire, 1978; Visiting Poet, Shrewsbury School, Shropshire, 1978-79, and King's School, Canterbury, 1979. Recipient: Heinemann Award, 1961; Arts Council grant, 1967, 1970; Cholmondeley Award, 1974; Southern Arts Writers Fellowship, 1975. Fellow, Royal Society of Literature, 1960. Granted Civil List pension, 1981. Address: 51 North Street, Otley, West Yorkshire LS21 1AH, England.

PUBLICATIONS

Verse

Graves and Resurrections. London, Fortune Press, 1948.
A Mortal Pitch. London, Villiers, 1957.
The Masks of Love. London, Putnam, 1960.
A Sense of Danger. London, Putnam, 1962.
Walking Wounded. London, Eyre and Spottiswoode, 1965.
Epithets of War: Poems 1965-1969. London, Eyre and Spottiswoode, 1969.
Mastering the Craft. Oxford, Pergamon Press, 1970.
Selected Poems. London, Allison and Busby, 1971.
Company of Women. Frensham, Surrey, Sceptre Press, 1971.
Corgi Modern Poets in Focus 4, with others, edited by Jeremy Robson. London, Corgi, 1971.
Incident at West Bay. Richmond, Surrey, Keepsake Press, 1972.
The Winter Man: New Poems. London, Allison and Busby, 1973.
Meeting in Manchester. Rushden, Northamptonshire, Sceptre Press, 1974.
The Loving Game. London, Robson, 1975.
An Ilkley Quintet. Privately printed, 1975(?).
A Morden Tower Reading 1, with Alexis Lykiard. Newcastle upon Tyne, Morden Tower, 1976.
New and Collected Poems 1950-1980. London, Robson, 1980.
Winterlude. London, Robson, 1982.

Plays

Radio Plays: *A Man's Game,* 1962; *A Door with One Eye,* 1963; *The Cancelling Dark,* music by Christopher Whelen, 1965.

Novels

The Fight. London, Peter Nevill, 1953.
The Wound and the Scar. London, Peter Nevill, 1953.
The Big Chance. London, Long, 1960.

The Shadowed Place.   London, Long, 1961.
The Face of the Enemy.   London, Putnam, 1961.
The Dividing Night.   London, Putnam, 1962.
The Big Time.   London, Longman, 1965.
Ring of Truth.   London, Robson, 1983.

Other

Edward Thomas.   London, Longman, 1963.
The Dangerous Ones (for children).   Oxford, Pergamon Press, 1970.
The Tiger and the Rose: An Autobiography.   London, Hamish Hamilton, 1971.
The Apple-Raid and Other Poems (for children).   London, Chatto and Windus, 1974.
Three Poets, Two Children, with Dannie Abse and Leonard Clark, edited by Desmond Badham-Thornhill.   Gloucester, Thornhill Press, 1975.
Not Without Glory: Poets of the Second World War.   London, Woburn Press, 1976.
A Proper Gentleman.   London, Robson, 1977.
A Lonely Game (for children).   Exeter, Wheaton, 1979.
Catch the Light (for children), with Gregory Harrison and Laurence Smith.   Oxford, Oxford University Press, 1982; New York, Oxford University Press, 1983.
How to Enjoy Poetry.   Loughton, Essex, Piatkus, 1983.
How to Enjoy Novels.   London, Piatkus, 1984.

Editor, with Patricia Beer and Ted Hughes, *New Poems 1962.*   London, Hutchinson, 1962.

*

Manuscript Collection: British Library, London.

Vernon Scannell comments:
    Major themes: violence, the experience of war, the "sense of danger" which is part of the climate of our times; these are contrasted with poems of a more private nature which affirm the continuity and indestructibility of the creative spirit. Some verse satire; the work is traditional, very direct and firmly rooted in recognizable human experience.

*   *   *

    Vernon Scannell's poems began to appear in the magazines in the late 1940's but (despite the 1961 Heinemann Award for Literature, which was given to his book *The Masks of Love*) it was not until the publication of *A Sense of Danger* in 1962 that he showed his real talent as a skilful memorialist of the aspirations, daydreams, lust, disillusionments and ironies of a bruised, wry and incorrigible romantic. One supposes that it was for this romanticism that he was enlisted as a contributor to *Mavericks,* the anthology intended to be a counterblast to the suggested calm severities of *New Lines;* but in fact Scannell's poems in his later books (*A Sense of Danger* and *Walking Wounded*) have more in common with Philip Larkin than with anyone represented in *Mavericks.* The world of Scannell's incendiaries, suicides, psychopaths, adulterers—as well as telephone calls, pubs, insurance agents and radio interviews—is thoroughly mid-20th century urban, acutely and mordantly observed.
    Scannell's technical organisation of a poem is generally sound (he works easily and fluently within received forms), but his language is less sure—for example, in "The Fair":

The night sniffs rich at pungent spice,
Brandy snap and diesel oil:
The stars like scattered beads of rice
Sparsely fleck the sky's deep soil...

But this overheated metaphorical glow does not appear at all in the real successes of *A Sense of Danger,* such as "Dead Dog," "My Father's Face," "The Telephone Number," and "Hearthquake." Scannell's elegiac mood, well seen in the first two of these poems, is even better handled in *Walking Wounded,* best of all in "The Old Books" and the title-poem, which recreates a wartime memory of soldiers "Straggling the road like convicts loosely chained,/ Dragging at ankles exhaustion and despair."
    But the common concern of most of Scannell's poems is with something more immediate, the ordinary hurts of the ordinary world, the dark places and betrayals of everyday experience. Colloquial, easy, even winsome, the tone of voice is generally poised above a pessimism which is lightened with wit and even, sometimes, with coarseness. It has a brutal and unequivocal honesty:

What captivates and sells, and always will,
Is what we are: vain, snarled up, and sleazy.
No one is really interesting until
To love him has become no longer easy.

—Anthony Thwaite

———————

SCHEVILL, James (Erwin).   American.   Born in Berkeley, California, 10 June 1920. Educated at Harvard University, Cambridge, Massachusetts, B.S. 1942. Served in the United States Army, 1942-46. Married Margot Helmuth Blum in 1966; two daughters by an earlier marriage. Member of the Faculty, California College of Arts and Crafts, Oakland, 1950-59; Member of the Faculty, 1959-68, and Director of the Poetry Center, 1961-68, San Francisco State College. Since 1969, Professor of English, Brown University, Providence, Rhode Island. Recipient: National Theatre Competition prize, 1945; Dramatists Alliance Contest prize, 1948; Fund for the Advancement of Education Fellowship, 1953; Phelan prize, for biography, 1954, for play, 1958; Ford grant, for theatre, 1960; Rockefeller grant, 1964; William Carlos Williams Award (*Contact* magazine), 1965; Roadstead Foundation award, 1966; Rhode Island Governor's Award, 1975; Guggenheim Fellowship, 1981; McKnight Fellowship in Playwriting, 1984. Agent: Bertha Case, 345 West 58th Street, New York, New York 10019. Address: Department of English, Brown University, Providence, Rhode Island 02912, U.S.A.

PUBLICATIONS

Verse

Tensions.   San Francisco, Bern Porter, 1947.
The American Fantasies.   San Francisco, Bern Porter, 1951.
The Right to Greet.   San Francisco, Bern Porter, 1955.
Selected Poems 1945-1959.   San Francisco, Bern Porter, 1960.
Private Dooms and Public Destinations: Poems 1945-1962.   Denver, Swallow, 1962.
The Stalingrad Elegies.   Denver, Swallow, 1964.

Release. Providence, Rhode Island, Hellcoal Press, 1968.
Violence and Glory: Poems 1962-1968. Chicago, Swallow Press, 1969.
The Buddhist Car and Other Characters. Chicago, Swallow Press, 1973.
Pursuing Elegy: A Poem about Haiti. Providence, Rhode Island, Copper Beech Press, 1974.
The Mayan Poems. Providence, Rhode Island, Copper Beech Press, 1978.
Fire of Eyes: A Guatemalan Sequence. Providence, Rhode Island, Copper Beech Press, 1979.
The American Fantasies: Collected Poems 1945-1981. Athens, Swallow Press-Ohio University Press, 1983.

Recording: *Performance Poems,* Cambridge, 1984.

Plays

High Sinners, Low Angels, music by Schevill, arranged by Robert Commanday (produced San Francisco, 1953). San Francisco, Bern Porter, 1953.
The Bloody Tenet (produced Providence, Rhode Island, 1956; Shrewsbury, Shropshire, 1962). Included in *The Black President and Other Plays,* 1965.
The Cid, adaptation of the play by Corneille (broadcast, 1963). Published in *Classic Theatre Anthology,* edited by Eric Bentley, New York, Doubleday, 1961.
Voices of Mass and Capital A, music by Andrew Imbrie (produced San Francisco, 1962). New York, Friendship Press, 1962.
The Master (produced San Francisco, 1963). Included in *The Black President and Other Plays,* 1965.
American Power: The Space Fan and The Master (produced Minneapolis, 1964). Included in *The Black President and Other Plays,* 1965.
The Black President and Other Plays (includes *The Bloody Tenet* and *American Power: The Space Fan and The Master*). Denver, Swallow, 1965.
The Death of Anton Webern (produced Fish Creek, Wisconsin, 1966). Included in *Violence and Glory: Poems 1962-1968,* 1969.
This Is Not True, music by Paul McIntyre (produced Minneapolis, 1967).
The Pilots (produced Providence, Rhode Island, 1970).
Oppenheimer's Chair (produced Providence, Rhode Island, 1970).
Lovecraft's Follies (produced Providence, Rhode Island, 1970). Chicago, Swallow Press, 1971.
The Ushers (produced Providence, Rhode Island, 1971).
The American Fantasies (produced New York, 1972).
Emperor Norton Lives! (produced Salt Lake City, Utah, 1972; revised version, as *Emperor Norton,* music by Jerome Rosen, produced San Francisco, 1979).
Fay Wray Meets King Kong (produced Providence, Rhode Island, 1974). Published in *Wastepaper Theatre Anthology,* 1978.
Sunset and Evening Stance; or, Mr. Krapp's New Tapes (produced Providence, Rhode Island, 1974). Published in *Wastepaper Theatre Anthology,* 1978.
The Telephone Murderer (produced Providence, Rhode Island, 1975). Published in *Wastepaper Theatre Anthology,* 1978.
Cathedral of Ice (produced Providence, Rhode Island, 1975). Wood Hole, Massachusetts, Pourboire Press, 1975.
Naked in the Garden (produced Providence, Rhode Island, 1975).
Year after Year (produced Providence, Rhode Island, 1976).

Questioning Woman (produced Providence, Rhode Island, 1980).
Mean Man (produced Providence, Rhode Island, 1981).
Mean Man II (produced Providence, Rhode Island, 1982).
Edison's Dream (produced Providence, Rhode Island, 1982).
Cult of Youth (produced Minneapolis, 1984).

Radio Plays: *The Sound of a Soldier,* 1945; *The Death of a President,* 1945; *The Cid,* 1963 (Canada).

Novel

The Arena of Ants. Providence, Rhode Island, Copper Beech Press, 1977.

Other

Sherwood Anderson: His Life and Work. Denver, University of Denver Press, 1951.
The Roaring Market and the Silent Tomb (biographical study of the scientist and artist Bern Porter). Oakland, California, Abbey Press, 1956.

Editor, *Six Historians,* by Ferdinand Schevill. Chicago, University of Chicago Press, and London, Cambridge University Press, 1956.
Editor, *Break Out! In Search of New Theatrical Environments.* Chicago, Swallow Press, 1973.
Editor, *Wastepaper Theatre Anthology.* Providence, Rhode Island, Pourboire Press, 1978.

*

Manuscript Collection: John Hay Library, Brown University, Providence, Rhode Island.

Critical Studies: by Martin Robbins, in *Voyages* (Washington, D.C.), Winter 1970; unpublished thesis by Wanda Howard, University of Rhode Island, Kingston, 1981.

*   *   *

James Schevill, dramatist as well as poet, can make almost anything interesting: side by side in his large selected collection *Private Dooms and Public Destinations: Poems 1945-1962* there are pieces on the painter Seurat, the death of a cat, a meditation on trees, an Irish castle, a man working a hydraulic drill, and gambling in Las Vegas. It is perhaps inevitable that some of these subjects, and they are typical, move him more than others, and that his greatest thrust be reserved for the things that most matter to him (his wartime experiences as a coastguardsman, a scientist like Fabre), yet he is never trivial and poem after poem offers sharp responses and insights. He is, in short, a poet all the way, a somewhat rare species in our time, and has the vitality and the natural equipment to make so strenuous a poetic life possible: curiosity, sensitivity, wide learning and a truly impressive gift with language, reminding one at times of Dylan Thomas'. Here is the first stanza of "The Blue Jay" from the above mentioned collection:

Blue jay in the garden,
                    Cocky bastard!
Boor on stilts in your Cyrano plume
Where the purple wistaria hangs like grapes.

Go flirt in the boggy woods;
In the gardens of spring,
When the grosbeak sings from the song-struck tree,
What are you but a duenna to beauty,
The claptrap chaperon?

If it is true that reading the poet on such a variety of subjects, however unified the vision from piece to piece, can be a dizzying experience, his volume *The Stalingrad Elegies* offers something altogether different: it is a daring, deeply imaginative and altogether successful experiment, surely one of the most interesting books to come out of the mid-60's. Here the poet has found a theme—a licked German army trapped in the snows of Stalingrad and their attempts, for the most part puny, occasionally noble, to get their feelings into letters home—that taxes his talent to the full, and the talent shows itself to be formidable. One can read the book as one reads an exciting story, so carefully is the volume structured and variety assured—through the selection of sufficiently dissimilar types, through the choice of stanza patterns and meters. Here in one of the shortest poems a soldier writes his wife:

Bury your face in your hands
in order to forget;
You said that
in your last letter...
Two months of happiness
We had as man and wife,
Then I marched into
The dark nights of the east,
My hands slipping
from your body
As if it were only a dream of sex,
Not a marriage...I live
In a sense of space
And time so huge
That they devour
Every human face.
I can't even imagine your flesh
Any more; too cold...
You are the wife of death.

James Schevill, a poet of strong gifts and generous impulses, has created a durable body of work, some of it, as in *The Stalingrad Elegies*, of major order.

—Lucien Stryk

SCHMIDT, Michael (Norton). Mexican. Born in Mexico City, 2 March 1947. Educated at Christ's Hospital, Horsham, Sussex; Harvard University, Cambridge, Massachusetts, 1966-67; Wadham College, Oxford, B.A. in English 1970, M.A. 1977. Since 1969, Managing Director, Carcanet Press, Oxford, later Cheadle, Cheshire, and Manchester. Gulbenkian Fellow, University of Manchester, 1972-75. Since 1972, Fellow, Manchester Poetry Centre; since 1973, Co-Editor, *Poetry Nation*, later *PN Review*, Manchester. Address: Carcanet Press, 208 Corn Exchange Buildings, Manchester M4 3BQ, England.

PUBLICATIONS

Verse

Black Buildings. Oxford, Carcanet, 1969.
One Eye Mirror Cold. Oxford, Sycamore Press, 1970.
Bedlam and the Oakwood: Essays on Various Fictions. Oxford, Carcanet, 1970.
Desert of the Lions. Oxford, Carcanet, 1972.
It Was My Tree. London, Anvil Press Poetry, 1972.
My Brother Gloucester: New Poems. Manchester, Carcanet, 1976.
A Change of Affairs. London, Anvil Press Poetry, 1978.
Choosing a Guest: New and Selected Poems. London, Anvil Press Poetry, 1983.

Novel

The Colonist. London, Muller, 1980; as *Green Island*, New York, Vanguard Press, 1982.

Other

Editor, with Grevel Lindop, *British Poetry since 1960: A Critical Survey.* Oxford, Carcanet, 1972.
Editor, *Ten English Poets.* Manchester, Carcanet, 1976.
Editor, *The Avoidance of Literature: Collected Essays*, by C.H. Sisson. Manchester, Carcanet, 1978.
Editor, *An Introduction to Fifty British Poets 1300-1900.* London, Pan, 1979; as *A Reader's Guide to Fifty British Poets*, London, Heinemann, and New York, Barnes and Noble, 1980.
Editor, *An Introduction to Fifty Modern British Poets.* London, Pan, 1979; as *A Reader's Guide to Fifty Modern British Poets*, London, Heinemann, 1979; New York, Barnes and Noble, 1982.
Editor, with Peter Jones, *British Poetry since 1970: A Critical Survey.* Manchester, Carcanet, and New York, Persea, 1980.
Editor, *Eleven British Poets.* London, Methuen, 1980.
Editor, *Some Contemporary Poets of Britain and Ireland.* Manchester, Carcanet, 1983.

Translator, with Edward Kissam, *Flower and Song: Poems of the Aztec Peoples.* London, Anvil Press Poetry, 1977.

*   *   *

For a poet still early in his career, Michael Schmidt displays a formidable precocity. It is formidable because it is not showing off, not posturing, but has a confidence which seems to arise from the whole personality of the poet. Schmidt almost never writes poems of direct individual feeling, but he is not, on this account, ever devious or obscure; he never assaults us either with joy or grief, but he is never cold. He has read much and travelled much. From his travels much of the basic material of his work is drawn. It supplies him with imagery and description. Even in the early work of 1968 in *It Was My Tree*, sympathy for others is generalised and distanced by the utmost care in the use of language. Here, for example, are some lines from a poem called "Cancer":

...Find out
who is this discoloured
body always half-awake
to itself. A music

from the unrusting
instruments. How deep
the body drinks, customary
thirst, the frightened moon.

There is no lack either of compassion or powerful feeling here,
but it is checked by the immediacy of imagery. The same thing
happens in the last stanza of "For Pasternak":

Flowers have fallen on us
yellow like wings, fragrant
with the powder of the air; small petals
delicate as the sky. We have been
unable to hold them.

That last line is close to sadness, but grief is not allowed to
overflow.

In his booklet of 1969, Schmidt continued in much the same
vein. After that he brought out two full-scale volumes, *Bedlam
and the Oakwood* and *Desert of the Lions*. There are no violent
developments to be discerned in either of these volumes but
rather a surer grasp of Schmidt's early manner, a keener awareness of language and its potentialities for imagery and description. If he is to be faulted, then one can only do so by pointing
out the lack of any lyrical element in his poems and often an
unconscious unwillingness to confront the reader directly. The
appearance of concealment is at present only a minor blemish,
though there are moments when one longs for the poet to appear
fully himself, for the curtain to be raised. The following is an
example of what I mean, taken from "Nailed like Stoats":

Around you the suppliant
generosity to gifted invalids—
a lifetime of it. Critics were kept at bay.
Your correspondence was meticulously edited.

Echoes of other poets are hard to find in Schmidt's work but,
certainly in this poem, one can detect a small debt to early and
middle period Auden. *Bedlam and the Oakwood* is divided into
sections, and Part I is called "Biographies." Schmidt gives us
most vivid portraits of famous writers, as in "Jonathan Swift's
Body," "Samuel Johnson's Marriage" and "Hatching." In these
pieces the poet identifies himself completely with his chosen
characters and makes them truly alive. In another section, places
are also powerfully summoned up; one thinks particularly of
"Luncheon" and "Venice: A Letter to Robert Browning."

"Some Fictions," yet another section of *Bedlam and the Oakwood*, does show an inclination on the poet's part to reveal
himself in the round, but he is more willing to display his
thoughts than his feelings, an he is usually quick to move on to
other people or to characters from literature. This tendency is
evident in a poem called "Appendix": "This reading leaves me
seated,/in the gateway to some unlosable wisdom,/and here at
least I am no cynic." In these lines, and the following ones from
"Flown Eagle," Schmidt comes closest to setting aside his finely
chosen language and careful rhythms and telling us about
himself:

I have had to dispose of eagles, and the
things they seemed to touch: sky,
liner, and the deserted sea
which leaves me smaller territory.

Starting with such an accomplished though somewhat limited
technique together with so much external material to work
upon, Schmidt could hardly advance, in *Desert of the Lions*,

except by way of more personal revelation or a real lyric impulse.
The latter does not appear but, even if only unobtrusively, the
former fitfully does. Amid the scintillating and accurately conveyed settings we come upon such passages as the following: "I
follow you hunting with jar and trowel,/with gloves, this poison
tail" ("Scorpion"); "Speak cautiously before morning/of fishermen—the men/with nets, with hooks, with knives" and "I eaves-
drop on them/from our balcony..." ("Before Morning"); "We
can move near./We cannot touch this bird, stiff,/almost a sawdust dummy, but on fire" ("Reconciliation").

In such poems as these and "Funerals," "Hypothesis," the title
poem itself, and "Tourist Waking," this poet can be sensed.
Wherever he goes, he enters a new country, city, landscape, and
transforms them by the power of his sharp visual gift and his
control over form. For so young a man, all this, together with his
understanding of many different people, is quite exceptional.
Yet this very achievement makes it extremely hard to predict
where he can move next. A more varied feeling for movement
and sound would certainly be a definite advance, together with a
more intimate revelation of such an interesting personality. We
have the intellect; now we want more of the heart.

—Elizabeth Jennings

SCHMITZ, Dennis (Mathew). American. Born in Dubuque,
Iowa, 11 August 1937. Educated at Loras College, Dubuque,
B.A. 1959; University of Chicago, M.A. 1961. Married Loretta
D'Agostino in 1960; three daughters and two sons. Instructor in
English, Illinois Institute of Technology, Chicago, 1961-62, and
University of Wisconsin, Milwaukee, 1962-66. Assistant Profes-
sor, 1966-69, Associate Professor, 1969-74, and since 1974, Pro-
fessor of English, California State University, Sacramento.
Recipient: New York Poetry Center Discovery Award, 1968; Big
Table award, 1969; National Endowment for the Arts Fellow-
ship 1976; Guggenheim Fellowship, 1978. Address: Department
of English, California State University, 6000 Jay Street, Sacramento, California 95819, U.S.A.

PUBLICATIONS

Verse

We Weep for Our Strangeness. Chicago, Follett, 1969.
Double Exposures. Oberlin, Ohio, Triskelion Press, 1971.
Goodwill, Inc. New York, Ecco Press, 1976.
String. New York, Ecco Press, 1980.
Singing. New York, Ecco Press, 1985.

*   *   *

In the death-haunted poems in Dennis Schmitz's *We Weep for
Our Strangeness* a dying rabbit's intestines wind "like roads/
between the bones," a remembered farm "fed/on the blue hillsides," ants slide "their hills/wave on lipless wave/down the long
bay of grass."

Landscape endures, though in ceaseless modification by glacier, flood, burial, river, ants. Man seems "lost" here, in the
religious sense of the word. And indeed God is named often in
these poems, and appears still more frequently. In the book's last

poem, "The Rescue," three men are lost on a canoe trip. One of them—Peter!—is sick. Finally a small plane flies over:

> we signal
>
>> we are here, to those above
>> that we have suffered
>> the lonely ocean of green
>> life.

Has the plane spotted them? They can't be sure, but one of them says hopefully that help will come, someone will rescue them: "yes,/I said to Jack, yes he will."

Neither the religious echoes nor the emotional urgency of Schmitz's poems assumes a loud voice. His style is colloquial, his diction Midwestern. The conversational tone and sparse punctuation would make for swift, fluid poems, were not his lines consistently slowed—sometimes nearly broken down—by enjambment. Sometimes the result is needlessly knotty:

> %s are the signs. I remember
>> the birds broke up
> on the table. top. scratches
> like soft entrails we read sad
>> tidings if we are to believe
> examine the corners

and so on.

Such lapses are few. The three relaxed and fully achieved eclogues beginning the book are beyond the capabilities of most of his contemporaries. Among them he stands out for the authenticity of his vision, its thick obsession with death and its convincing religiosity:

> because you have loved your body closes its doors
> because you have eaten now the poor came.
> & your plate is clean as the skull of God.

—William Matthews

SCHROEDER, Andreas (Peter). Canadian. Born in Hoheneggelsen, Germany, 26 November 1946; came to Canada in 1951; naturalized, 1965. Educated at John Oliver High School, Vancouver; University of British Columbia, Vancouver, 1966-71, B.A. 1969, M.A. in creative writing and comparative literature 1972; University of Toronto, 1968. Married Sharon Elizabeth Brown in 1976; two daughters. Editorial Assistant, *Prism International*, Vancouver, 1968-69; critic, Vancouver *Province-Pacific Press*, 1968-73; Founding Editor, with J. Michael Yates, *Contemporary Literature in Translation*, Vancouver, 1968-81; Editor, *Poetry Canada*, Toronto, 1970-71; Editor MassAge Press, Maple Ridge, British Columbia, 1971-74; broadcaster, Canadian Broadcasting Corporation, Vancouver, 1971-74; taught at University of Victoria, British Columbia, 1975-77; Writer-in-Residence, University of Regina, Saskatchewan, 1980-81, and University of Winnipeg, 1983-84. Since 1971, Member of the Editorial Board, *Canadian Fiction* magazine, Prince George, British Columbia. Member of the Board of Directors, British Columbia Film Cooperative, 1970-71; Chairman, Writers' Union of Canada, 1976-77. Recipient: Canada Council grant, 1968, bursary, 1969, 1971, 1973, 1976, 1979; Woodward Memorial Award, for prose, 1969; National Film Board grant, 1970; Canadian Film Development grant, 1971; Koerner Foundation grant, 1974, 1975. Address: P.O. Box 3127, Mission City, British Columbia, V2V 4J3, Canada.

PUBLICATIONS

Verse

The Ozone Minotaur.   Vancouver, Sono Nis Press, 1969.
File of Uncertainties.   Vancouver, Sono Nis Press, 1971.
uniVerse, with David Frith.   Maple Ridge, British Columbia, MassAge Press, 1971.
Words Inside Out.   Maple Ridge, British Columbia, MassAge Press, 1984.

Plays

Screenplays: *The Plastic Mile*, 1969; *Immobile*, 1969; *The Pub*, 1970; *The Late Man*, 1972.

Radio Play: *The Theft*, 1983.

Novels

Toccata in D (micro-novel).   Lantzville, British Columbia, Oolichan, 1984.
Dust-Ship Glory.   Toronto, Sealbooks, 1985.

Short Stories

The Late Man.   Vancouver, Sono Nis Press, 1971.

Other

Shaking It Rough: A Prison Memoir.   Toronto, Doubleday, 1976; New York, Doubleday, 1977.
Compensation for Authors.   Regina, Saskatchewan Library Association, 1981.

Editor, with J. Michael Yates, *Contemporary Poetry of British Columbia.*   Vancouver, Sono Nis Press, 2 vols., 1970-72.
Editor, with Rudy Wiebe, *Stories from Pacific and Arctic Canada: A Selection.*   Toronto, Macmillan, 1974.

Translator, with Michael Bullock, *The Stage and Creative Arts.*   Greenwich, Connecticut, New York Graphic Society, 1969.
Translator, *Collected Stories of Ilse Aichinger.*   Vancouver, Sono Nis Press, 1974.

*

Critical Studies: "The Relevance of Surrealism with Some Canadian Perspectives" by Paul Green, in *Mosaic* (Winnipeg, Manitoba), Summer 1969; "The O-Zone and Other Places" by Alan Shucard, in *Canadian Literature 48* (Vancouver), Spring 1971; "Swarming of Poets" by George Woodcock, in *Canadian Literature 50* (Vancouver), Winter 1971; "A Certain Degree of Madness" by Patricia Morley, in *Ottawa Journal*, 13 May 1972.

Andreas Schroeder comments:

While I have always made considerable use of the surreal mode in both my poetry and prose, my more recent work varies greatly with respect to its surreality. The first book of verse which I published (*The Ozone Minotaur*) was a fairly orthodox example of the genre; the second (*File of Uncertainties*) was only occasionally characteristic of it. I find myself moving more and more toward that thin line where reality and surreality mesh, where a couple making love and a couple killing each other appear involved in identical acts. The result tends often to be cinematic, for which reason many of the stories have proven easily adaptable to film scripts. My poetry, too, makes increasing use of a more linear logic.

*   *   *

Andreas Schroeder, German-born though he emigrated in childhood, is unusually international among Canadian poets in his literary affiliations. It is impossible to consider him as a poet apart from his activities as editor of *Contemporary Literature in Translation*. His imaginative world is related to Kafka's and, equally, to that of Borges, and his poems have an intellectual complexity rare among young North American poets but relating him directly to the Modernist tradition. His first two books of verse, *The Ozone Minotaur* and *File of Uncertainties*, reveal a considerable development. The earlier poems are largely neo-surrealist in character, seeking to give verisimilitude to implausible but potent myths, such as "Introduction" in which "three men in tails" cross a cornfield to a creek:

> ...The man in the middle
> of the stream is stepping on the fish;
> he is intent. The fish swim through
> him and he walks through the fish.
> Notice that he is not surprised. The
> man on the other bank is sifting debris
> into a notebook; notice him. The man on
> the bank is now measuring the size of
> the sand grains.
> The man in the middle of the creek is
> walking on.
> He is stepping on the fish.

Schroeder's later poems, in *File of Uncertainties*, explore ambiguities of condition and consciousness like those exemplified in the man through whom the fish swim as he walks through them. The recognition of multiple consciousness, and the sense of being trapped in many selves, are in these later poems more explicit, more apprehensive, more convincing:

> Now, my constant fear:
> To stumble across my own remains
> when this snow melts.

—George Woodcock

SCHUYLER, James (Marcus). American. Born in Chicago, Illinois, 9 November 1923. Educated at Bethany College, West Virginia, 1941-43; University of Florence, 1947-48. Lived in Italy for several years; staff member, Museum of Modern Art, New York, 1955-61; critic, *Art News*, New York. Recipient: Longview Foundation award 1961; Frank O'Hara Prize (*Poetry*, Chicago), 1969; National Endowment for the Arts grant, 1969, 1972; American Academy award, 1977; Pulitzer Prize, 1981; Academy of American Poets fellowship, 1983. Agent: Maxine Groffsky, 2 Fifth Avenue, New York, New York 10011, U.S.A.

PUBLICATIONS

Verse

Salute. New York, Tiber Press, 1960.
May 24th or So. New York, Tibor de Nagy, 1966.
Freely Espousing. New York, Doubleday, 1969.
The Crystal Lithium. New York, Random House, 1972.
A Sun Cab. New York, Adventures in Poetry, 1972.
Penguin Modern Poets 24, with Kenneth Koch and Kenward Elmslie. London, Penguin, 1973.
Hymn to Life. New York, Random House, 1974.
Song. Syracuse, New York, Kermani Press, 1976.
The Fireproof Floors of Witley Court: English Songs and Dances. Newark, Vermont, Janus Press, 1976.
The Home Book: Prose and Poems 1951-1970, edited by Trevor Winkfield. Calais, Vermont, Z Press, 1977.
The Morning of the Poem. New York, Farrar Straus, and London, Faber, 1980.

Recording: *A Picnic Cantata*, music by Paul Bowles, Columbia, 1955.

Plays

Presenting Jane (produced Cambridge, Massachusetts, 1952).
Shopping and Waiting (produced Cambridge, Massachusetts, 1953).
Unpacking the Black Trunk, with Kenward Elmslie (produced New York, 1965).

Novels

Alfred and Guinevere. New York, Harcourt Brace, 1958.
A Nest of Ninnies, with John Ashbery. New York, Dutton, 1969.
What's for Dinner? Santa Barbara, California, Black Sparrow Press, 1978.

Other

Editor, with Charles North, *Broadway: A Poets and Painters Anthology.* New York, Swollen Magpie Press, 1979.

*   *   *

James Schuyler's is a poetry of perception, the recognition of shapes out of the indiscriminate sensory field. Reading him, there is a sense of focusing field glasses; always the sharper image results. We see what we had not thought possible before: "the clouds/hang in a traffic jam: summer/heads home." To be open-eyed is the goal, to go "out there," into the multifarious world, to be a "figure like an ex-/clamation point seen/through driving snow." In such a world, "Self-Pity is a Kind of Lying, Too," as the title of one of his poems has it—a poem organized similarly to many of his others, such as "Blizzard" or "Out There" itself, in which the scattered nature of experience is given, a catalogue of disparate phenomena, held in place like an assembly of restless lions by the trainer's commanding eye.

Schuyler's is one of the most accurately trained eyes of any poet writing in recent years, just as he is one of our finest nature poets (a surprising statement about a so-called "New York School" poet—except that such an observation should expose the limits inherent in any such designation). He is one of the sharpest observers of the lacework of nature. He writes with a paintbrush for pen, a great landscape artist and still-life perfectionist, encouraged by long association with painters. Moreover, he has an ear completely in tune with his eye. His observations are often told in short lines, where the rhythms can be modulated at will, effortlessly, so that all authority remains packed in the image. He is capable of an exceptional clarity of image, such as the unsurpassable compression at the end of "Light from Canada": "Above the wash/and bark of rumpled water, a gull/falls down the wind to dine/on fish that swim up to do same." The observation tells all, is an end in itself, the perfection of a perception when inextricable from the natural order. He writes in the idyll called "The Cenotaph" of the wind that "crumples the bay and stuffs it in a stone pocket." Always, the startling description. Likewise there is the quietest of natural observation in "Closed Gentian Distances," a painter's title: "Little fish stream/by, a river in water." His attitude of observation ("philosophy" may be too grand a word for Schuyler, who has never written of his "poetics" or revealed any ambitions in those terms) is summarized in the poem "December": "Californians need to do a thing to enjoy it./A smile may be loads! you don't have to undress everybody." It is a perspective by which small pleasures are made large.

There is colloquial ease in almost all his poems, the absence of the stiff and pretentious—but with a very formal awareness of pace and the structure of rhythm. In "A Sun Cab" the natural world is urban and hurries in appropriately dislocated syntax: "a train/sends up its/passing metal roll/through grills and gone/the more than daily Sunday...." As always in his work, the description is active, not the midriff-patting, self-contented passivity of a more easily satisfied talent. " 'The Elizabethans Called It Dying' " is a love poem, as much a tribute to love poems, in a manner exactly parallel to Frank O'Hara's "Having a Coke with You" and "Steps." In the more daring, haunted, tumultuous description of "Crocus Night" successive jagged images bloom in a final startling canvas ("then the moon goes crocus"). "Buried at Springs," written 11 years after O'Hara's death, is one of the finest elegies of our time. It combines heightened description (of the cemetery in the Southampton, New York, community known as Springs where O'Hara is buried) with a sense of abiding poignancy. Sentiment is not evaded, but neither is it heavily introduced; it surfaces in the natural order like the persistent stain of mortality itself.

"The Crystal Lithium," one of his most important poems, celebrates a panorama of contradictions. The theme is stated among shifting images as "that which is, which is beyond/ Happiness or love or mixed with them," i.e., "unchanging change," which is represented by the waters off Long Island, but in no passively descriptive terms. The poem ends in a dramatic rising in which the ocean presents itself as summation of all one needs to know: " 'Look,' the ocean said (it was tumbled, like our sheets), 'look in my eyes.' " (Always Schuyler's images are brought home to the familiar: "tumbled, like our sheets.") The poem is a tribute to experience, no matter how fluctuating and alternating that might be. Alternating is not the same as alienating. "The Crystal Lithium" is a clear-eyed description of the variegated world: not surrealistic mimicry of such, but a nobler acceptance of the divisions marbling all things.

Schuyler is determined to possess the natural world without a lapse into symbolism. Nature is not to be quarreled with, nor confused with human needs. The world is distinguishable among its parts as well as from the observing narrator. He has tried life and it fits; life matches art: "The red dog comes in out of the rain to enact the chromo, *The Hound on the Hearth*." Observing, sorting, seeking a pattern, seeking some control or controlling image, he writes "as though/the world were silk I could fold and

bring/with me in an Amelia Earheart Weekend Bag." And though we may be foredoomed, we will travel henceforth with a lilt.

—George F. Butterick

SCHWERNER, Armand. American. Born in Antwerp, Belgium, 11 May 1927. Educated at Cornell University, Ithaca, New York, 1945-47; University of Geneva, Switzerland, 1947-48; Columbia University, New York, B.S. 1950, M.A. 1964. Served in the United States Navy, 1945-46. Married Doloris Holmes in 1961 (divorced, 1978); two sons. Formerly, Instructor in English and French, Barnard School for Boys, Riverdale, New York; Instructor in English, Long Island University, New York, 1963-64. Instructor, 1964-66, Assistant Professor, 1966-69, Associate Professor, 1969-73, and since 1973, Professor of English, College of Staten Island, City University of New York. Recipient: National Endowment for the Arts grant, 1973, 1979; Creative Artists Public Service grant, 1973, 1975. Address: 30 Catlin Avenue, Staten Island, New York 10304, U.S.A.

PUBLICATIONS

Verse

The Lightfall. New York, Hawk's Well Press, 1963.
The Tablets I-VIII. West Branch, Iowa, Cummington Press, 1968.
(if personal). Los Angeles, Black Sparrow Press, 1968.
Seaweed. Los Angeles, Black Sparrow Press, 1969.
The Tablets I-XV. New York, Grossman, 1971.
Bacchae Sonnets 1-6. Omaha, Nebraska, Abattoir, 1974.
The Tablets XVI-XVIII. Deerfield, Massachusetts, Heron Press, 1976.
The Triumph of the Will. Mount Horeb, Wisconsin, Perishable Press, 1976.
This Practice: Tablet XIX and Other Poems. London, Permanent Press, 1976.
The Bacchae Sonnets 1-7. Baltimore, Pod, 1977.
The Work, The Joy, and the Triumph of the Will (includes translation of *Philoctetes* by Sophocles). New York, New Rivers Press, 1977.
Sounds of the River Naranjana and The Tablets I-XXIV. Barrytown, New York, Station Hill Press, 1984.

Recordings; *The Tablets I-XVIII*, S-Press, 1974; *Recent Poetry*; New Wilderness; *Philoctetes*, New Wilderness.

Other

Stendhal's "The Red and the Black": Notes and Criticism. New York, Study Master, 1963.
The Domesday Dictionary, with Donald M. Kaplan. New York, Simon and Schuster, 1963; London, Cape, 1964.
A Farewell to Arms: A Critical Commentary. New York, Study Master, 1963.
Billy Budd and Typee: Critical Commentary. New York, American R.D. M., 1964.
The Sound and the Fury: A Critical Commentary, with Jerome Neibrief. New York, American R.D. M., 1964.

John Steinbeck's "Of Mice and Men." New York, Monarch Press, 1965.
John Steinbeck's "The Red Pony" and "The Pearl." New York, Monarch Press, 1965.
André Gide's "The Immoralist," "Strait Is the Gate," and Other Works: A Critical Commentary. New York, Monarch Press, 1966.
Dos Passos' "U.S.A." and Other Works. New York, Monarch Press, 1966.
Albert Camus' "The Stranger": A Critical Commentary. New York, Monarch Press, 1970.

Translator, *Redspel: Eleven American Indian Adaptations.* Mount Horeb, Wisconsin, Perishable Press, 1974.

*

Critical Studies: "Son of the Cantos?" by Stanley Sultan, in *Chelsea* (New York), 1971; Allen Planz, in *The Nation* (New York), 19 June 1972; John Shawcross, in *American Poetry Review* (Philadelphia), March 1973; Diane Wakoski, in *Parnassus* (New York), Spring 1973; *Vort 8* (Bloomington, Indiana), 1975; Hugh Kenner, in *New York Times Book Review*, 12 February and 4 June 1978; Richard Kostelanetz, in *Performing Arts* (New York), Winter 1978; Burton Hatlen, in *Sagetrieb* (Orono, Maine), vol. 3, no. 1, 1984; Mark Weiss, in *Bluefish* (Southampton, New York), vol. 1, no. 2, 1984.

Armand Schwerner comments:

The (unidentifiable) voices of the *Tablets*, speaking through loss, celebration, primordial need for mensuration references, grief, ecstatic sexuality, psychotic and aphasic confusion, magical incantation, formal insult-modes, parental anxiety, lover's despair, eventuate in what seems to be a different voice, evident in *Tablet XXIV*, the final one in *Sounds of the River Naranjana* and *The Tablets I-XXIV*—the un-settled music of the voice alive in the sky-veins, the ores and the brilliant ground, profoundly at home in the bright unanchoring everywhere which is equally "the darkness every time for the first time," repeated nullifications of potentially separating concepts, process in which abstract and concrete share each other's attributes.

The syncretic ground of the *Tablets*, since the mid-1960's, the animistic, polytheistic and Buddhist matrices in the *Tablets*—the last most clearly informing *XXIV*—owe much to the needs and available choices in my own story, little to a predetermined paradigm. (The archaic pre-Christian antinomies of *kenosis* and *plerosis*, emptying and filling, characteristic of early Middle Eastern civilizations, served largely as a generalized and suggestive context.) My barely conscious but pronounced anxieties about my fatherhood informed some of the early, largely "animistic" *Tablets*; my increasing involvement in Tibetan, now Zen, Buddhist practice is present texture: interdependence, web of particulars, non-separation, transformation, emptiness. Since my understanding as it relates to these abstractions keeps changing from present to present, each poem is merely manifestation of, or rather, *is* "continuous practice," which as Dogen Zenji says, "is delight by virtue of continuous practice."

*   *   *

Armand Schwerner is a poet whose most significant work, a book-length poem called *The Tablets*, is a performance poem satirizing almost everything in the world, from the writing of poetry itself to elaborate rituals of translation scholarship to what making love is all about and even to what religion is. In this work the poems are presented as if they are fragments of ancient Icelandic poems written on tablets, and we are treated to every nonsensical reality which anyone who attempts to study ancient work is subjected to. The intention is humorous, comic, and sometimes even lyric—if one can think of making lyric out of mistake. But Schwerner carries that off too, and in the process leaves the reader thinking seriously about all his definitions of poetry.

> from nothing, from nothing, the stone beginning, tell me
>   my name,
> when I write letters and do accounts I am that other man
> and keep from trembling, o at the heart's root is not
>   cauldron but...
> come in come in come in says my pain
> run from the sun, wander around in me and profit, the
>   stars tell North
> but little else.
>   From nothing from nothing find me my name, say
> in some clear way if the end is sadness.

In retrospect, one begins to see this work of Schwerner's in the context of the poetry which came before and after it. Schwerner was a musician before he was a poet, seriously playing jazz clarinet for many years. In a love poem called "the pillow" he starts the poem with the line, "music first." But the problem of the 20th-century American poet who wants to make music first is that we no longer have a lyric poetry easily available to us. Unless we want to write songs and go the route of Bob Dylan and others, we must learn to find our music more diversely, certainly not first. If Schwerner wants "music first," he will constantly be at the mercy of all the new possibilities of poetry ranged against the limits of the old prosody. To me, this provides the reason why *The Tablets* is so crucial to Schwerner's work. He must first satirize the parody of music that scholars and translators have created out of the old poetic texts, then he must satirize the possibilities of poetry itself when it seems so impossible for poetry to fulfill what, to him, must seem like its primary function—to make music. Ironically, *The Tablets* create musical language over and over again, so that the final effect of the work *is* poetry (i.e., music) and not satire, parody, or even aesthetic discussion.

In the other title poem of his recent selected work, *Sounds of the River Naranjana and The Tablets I-XXIV*, Schwerner tries to structure the poem in sections corresponding to the alphabet, but while he starts with "a" he only gets to "r," and one feels again, as a reader, that Schwerner has asked poetry to be for him something he cannot sustain to extend to its natural conclusion.

> like the intermittent light in your delusion, you wander
> in the alien sounds of your names, listening
> for the river Naranjana....

Where is the music he wants to make, which must come first? It comes inevitably to him, as this final section of the poem becomes lyrical, musical, but he seems never to be able to accept this music, this poetry, as other than alien. Thus, when he is using the satiric structure of *The Tablets*, he does not have to justify this need for music. It is enough that it has left the world, and the result is this parody of poetry we find instead of the real thing. If by chance, he makes the music himself, then it comes without the ancient trappings of old prosody and ritual linguistic gestures.

For a poet whose vision of the world is as avant garde as Schwerner's obviously is, and as sophisticated linguistically, there cannot be a "music first" without the clunky, awkward trappings of academic poetry. Yet this longing is so clear in him and his work that it has taken the form of elaborate invention, and the making of a poem which totally transcends its original intention to satirize the realities of poetry. Only in the form of *The Tablets*, so far, has Schwerner been able to resolve the double-bind. One looks forward, with such a master of invention, to future solutions which please and astonish the reader as uniquely as *The Tablets* already have.

—Diane Wakoski

SCOTT, Alexander. British (Scottish). Born in Aberdeen, 28 November 1920. Educated at Aberdeen Academy, 1933-39; Aberdeen University, 1939-41, 1945-47, M.A. (honours) in English 1947. Served in the British Army, 1941-45: Military Cross, 1945. Married Catherine Goodall in 1944; two sons. Assistant Lecturer, Edinburgh University, 1947-48. Lecturer, 1948-63, Senior Lecturer, 1963-71, since 1971, Head of the Department and since 1976, Reader in Scottish Literature, Glasgow University. Editor, *Northeast Review*, 1945-46; *Scots Review*, 1950-51; *Saltire Review*, Edinburgh, 1954-57; General Editor, Scottish Library, Calder and Boyars, London, 1968-71, and Scottish Series, Routledge and Kegan Paul, London, 1972-75. Since 1968, Secretary, Universities Committee on Scottish Literature; since 1980, Editor, with Maurice Lindsay, *Scottish Review*. Recipient: Festival of Britain Award, for poetry, 1951, for verse drama, 1951; Arts Council Award, for drama, 1952; Scottish Community Drama Association Award, 1954; Scottish Arts Council Award, 1969. Address: 5 Doune Gardens, Glasgow G20 6DJ, Scotland.

PUBLICATIONS

Verse

The Latest in Elegies. Glasgow, Caledonian Press, 1949.
Selected Poems. Edinburgh, Oliver and Boyd, 1950.
Mouth Music: Poems and Diversions. Edinburgh, M. Macdonald, 1954.
Cantrips. Preston, Lancashire, Akros, 1968.
Greek Fire. Preston, Lancashire, Akros, 1971.
Double Agent: Poems in English and Scots. Preston, Lancashire, Akros, 1972.
Selected Poems 1943-1974. Preston, Lancashire, Akros, 1975.
Poems in Scots. Glasgow, Scotsown, 1978.

Plays

Prometheus 48 (produced Aberdeen, 1948). Aberdeen, S.R.C., 1948.
Untrue Thomas. Glasgow, Caledonian Press, 1952.
Right Royal (produced Glasgow, 1954).
Shetland Yarn. London, Evans, 1954.
Tam O'Shanter's Tryst (produced Glasgow, 1955).
The Last Time I Saw Paris. Edinburgh, Saltire Review, 1957.
Truth To Tell (produced Glasgow, 1958).

Other

Still Life: William Soutar 1898-1943. Edinburgh, Chambers, 1958.

The MacDiarmid Makars 1923-1972. Preston, Lancashire, Akros, 1972.

Editor, *Selected Poems of William Jeffrey.* Edinburgh, Serif, 1951.
Editor, *The Poems of Alexander Scott, 1530-1584.* Edinburgh, Oliver and Boyd, 1952.
Editor, *Diaries of a Dying Man*, by William Soutar. Edinburgh, Chambers, 1955.
Editor, with Norman MacCaig, *Contemporary Scottish Verse.* London, Calder and Boyars, 1970.
Editor, with Michael Grieve, *The Hugh MacDiarmid Anthology: Poems in Scots and English.* London, Routledge, 1972.
Editor, with Douglas Gifford, *Neil M. Gunn: The Man and the Writer.* Edinburgh, Blackwood, and New York, Barnes and Noble, 1973.
Editor, with Maurice Lindsay and Roderick Watson, *Scottish Poetry 7-9.* Glasgow, University of Glasgow Press, 1 vol., 1974; Manchester, Carcanet Press, 2 vols., 1975-76.
Editor, *Modern Scots Verse 1922-1977.* Preston, Lancashire, Akros, 1978.
Editor, *Scotch Passion: An Anthology of Scottish Erotic Poetry.* London, Hale, 1982.
Editor, with James Aitchison, *New Writing Scotland 2.* Aberdeen, Aberdeen University Press, 1984.
Editor, *Voices of Our Kind: Scottish Poetry 1920-1985.* Edinburgh, Harris, 1985.

*

Manuscript Collection: National Library of Scotland, Edinburgh.

Critical Studies: by Norman MacCaig, in *Akros 9* (Preston, Lancashire), 1969, and *Studies in Scottish Literature* (Columbia, South Carolina), 1978; George Bruce, in *Akros 19* (Preston, Lancashire), 1972; Lorn Macintyre, in *Akros 25* (Preston, Lancashire), 1974; David Buchan, in *Library Review* (Glasgow), 1975; *Two North-East Makars: Alexander Scott and Alastair Mackie: A Study of Their Scots Poetry* by Leonard Mason, Preston, Lancashire, Akros, 1975.

Alexander Scott comments:

I write in both English and Scots, the latter being my first speech. With me a poem begins itself, as it were, from a phrase which lashes into the mind unbidden and which may present itself in either English or Scots. Since the inception of any poem of mine is to that extent involuntary, I am not bothered, in any one case, by having to make a choice between the two languages. The choice is already made for me, by the initial words themselves, as they rise into the consciousness. Any other procedure, in my view, would be a falsehood so fundamental as to make a mockery of the poetic act.

*   *   *

Hugh MacDiarmid has said, with a typically Scottish finality, "We have no use for emotions, let alone sentiments, but are solely concerned with passions." If this is not true, regrettably, of all Scots, it is true of Alexander Scott, except that emotions do occasionally creep in—but not subversively, since a stiffening pith in the centre prevents them from deliquescing into sentimentality. He represents, in fact, more than any contemporary Scots poet other than MacDiarmid, those characteristic elements that define the Scots tradition and which are centred on a stubborn, passionate and sardonic realism that eschews the egotistical sublime, that deals with a remarkably high hand with what makes the substance of so much poetry—love, death, God, the Devil, etc.—and that robustly refuses to ignore the grit that forms the pearl, or even the grit. He also provides in himself a flat contradiction of the comical assumption that the Scots are dour, inarticulate and humourless and informs his work with the spirited gusto that makes, for example, Burns so heart-warming a writer.

Because these are his characteristic qualities, unsubtle sensibilities have been known to accuse him of a lack of sympathy, of brashness, of a brutal and unfeeling response to the tears of things. He can be shocking. But the hard directness of his statements (he is an Aberdonian and writes in granite) is infused with a real sympathy, a real tenderness, made triumphantly explicit in his love poems.

The bulk and the best of his poems are in Scots. Since this was his natural speech when he was young and since he has studied it in a scholarly, and responsive, way ever since, it is not surprising that he handles it with a lively naturalness that craftily exploits the wide range of expressive sounds that this almost too onomatopoeic language offers for use, or abuse. This Scots is muscular, athletic, with no fat on its bones, and is quite free from the pedantic antiquarianism that flaws the work of some other Scottish writers. And if his language is contemporary, so are his themes. He takes account of, but is not obsessed by, the past, either his own or his country's.

As for his poems in English, they could not have been written by anyone else. All the same, more of the author gets into the Scots poems—though in *Cantrips* there are some which offer evidence of a new thing in Scott's work, an exploration of looser forms which point forward to what may well be a new sort of achievement.

The plays not surprisingly share most of the characteristics of the poems, except that they mainly concern themselves with situations originally reasonable enough but roisterously developed according to the curious logic of farce. The life they have, and it is plenty, derives from Scott's comic invention, in plot and dialogue, and that healthy gusto which is so prominent a feature in all his work.

—Norman MacCaig

SCOTT, F(rancis) R(eginald). Canadian. Born in Quebec City, 1 August 1899. Educated at Quebec High School; Bishop's College, Lennoxville, Quebec, B.A. 1919; Magdalen College, Oxford (Rhodes Scholar), B.A. 1922, B.Litt. 1923; McGill University, Montreal, B.C.L. 1927, called to the Quebec Bar, 1927, Queen's Counsel, 1961. Married Marian Mildred Dale in 1928; one son. Teacher, Quebec High School, 1919; Bishop's College School, Lennoxville, 1920; Lower Canada College, Montreal, 1923. Assistant Professor of Federal and Constitutional Law, 1928-34, Professor of Civil Law, 1934-54, Macdonald Professor of Law, 1955-67, Dean of the Faculty of Law, 1961-64, and Visiting Professor, French Canada Studies Programme, 1967-69, McGill University. Visiting Lecturer, University of Toronto Law School, 1953-54, Michigan State University, East Lansing, 1957, and Dalhousie University Law School, Halifax, Nova Scotia, 1969-71; Writer-in-Residence, Concordia University, Montreal, 1979-80. National Chairman, C.C.F. Party, 1942-50; helped found New Democratic Party, 1960. U.N. Technical Assistant, Burma, 1952. Chairman, Canadian Writers Confer-

ence, 1955. Civil Liberties Counsel before the Supreme Court of Canada, 1956-64; Member, Royal Commission on Bilingualism and Biculturalism, 1963-71. Founding Editor, with A.J.M. Smith, *McGill Fortnightly Review*, Montreal, 1925-27; Editor, *Canada Mercury*, Montreal, 1928-29, *Canada Forum*, Toronto, 1936-39, and *Preview*, 1942-44, and *Northern Review*, 1945-47, both Montreal. Recipient: Guggenheim Fellowship, 1940; Guarantor's Prize (*Poetry*, Chicago), 1945; Royal Society of Canada Fellowship, 1947, and Lorne Pierce Medal, 1962; *Northern Review* Award, 1951; Banff Springs Festival Gold Medal, 1958; Quebec Government Prize, 1964; Canada Council Molson Award, 1965, grant, 1974, and translation prize, 1977; Governor-General's Award, for non-fiction, 1978, for poetry, 1982; Casgrain award, 1983. LL.D.: Dalhousie University, 1958; University of Manitoba, Winnipeg, 1961; Queen's University, Kingston, Ontario, 1964; University of British Columbia, Vancouver, 1965; Osgoode Hall Law School, Downsview, Ontario, 1966; McGill University, 1967; Laval University, Quebec, 1969; York University, Downsview, Ontario, 1976; Carleton University, Ottawa, 1977; Simon Fraser University, Burnaby, British Columbia, 1980; LL.B.: University of Saskatchewan, Saskatoon, 1965; D.Litt.: Sir George Williams University, Montreal, 1966; University of Toronto, 1969; D. ès Jur.: University of Montreal, 1966; D.C.L.: Bishop's University, Lennoxville, Quebec, 1970; Windsor University, Ontario, 1970. Fellow, Royal Society of Literature, 1947; Honorary Member, American Academy of Arts and Sciences, 1967; Corresponding Fellow, British Academy, 1978. Companion, Order of Canada, 1967. Address: 451 Clarke Avenue, Westmont, Quebec H3Y 3C5, Canada.

PUBLICATIONS

Verse

Overture. Toronto, Ryerson Press, 1945.
Events and Signals. Toronto, Ryerson Press, 1954.
The Eye of the Needle: Satires, Sorties, Sundries. Montreal, Contact Press, 1957.
Signature. Vancouver, Klanak Press, 1964.
Selected Poems. Toronto, Oxford University Press, 1966.
Trouvailles: Poems from Prose. Montreal, Delta Canada, 1967.
Poets Between the Wars, with others, edited by Milton T. Wilson. Toronto, McClelland and Stewart, 1967.
The Dance Is One. Toronto, McClelland and Stewart, 1973.
The Collected Poems, edited by John Newlove. Toronto, McClelland and Stewart, 1981.

Recording: *F.R. Scott,* Ontario Institute for Studies in Education, 1971.

Play

The Roncarelli Affair, with Mavor Moore (televised, 1974). Published in *The Play's the Thing: Four Original Television Dramas,* edited by Tony Gifford, Toronto, Macmillan, 1976.

Other

Admiralty Jurisdiction and Colonial Courts. Montreal, McGill University Press, 1929.
Succession Duties in the Province of Quebec (1892-1930), with W.F. Macklaier. Montreal, National Trust, 1930.
Canada and Socialism, with W.C. Wansbrough. Toronto, League for Social Reconstruction, 1934.

Social Reconstruction and the B.N.A. Act. Toronto, Nelson, 1934.

Labour Conditions in the Men's Clothing Industry, with H.M. Cassidy. Toronto, Nelson, 1935.

Canada and the Commonwealth. Toronto, Canadian Institution of International Affairs, 1938.

Canada To-day: A Study of Her National Interests and National Policy. Toronto, Oxford University Press, 1938.

Canada—One or Nine? Toronto, League for Social Reconstruction, 1938.

Recent Developments in New Zealand. Montreal, McGill University Press, 1939.

Canada and the United States, with David Lewis. Boston, World Peace Organization, 1941.

Make This "Your" Canada: A Review of C.C.F. History and Policy, with David Lewis. Toronto, Central Canada, 1943.

Co-operation for What? Canada and the British Commonwealth. New York, American Council, 1944.

Bibliography on Constitutional Law. Montreal, McGill University Press, 1948.

New Horizons for Socialism. Ottawa, Wordsworth House, 1951.

Technical Assistance and Economic Aid Through the United Nations. Toronto, University of Toronto Press, 1953.

The World War Against Poverty, with R.A. MacKay and A.E. Ritchie. Toronto, University of Toronto Press, 1953.

The World's Civil Service. New York, Carnegie Endowment for International Peace, 1954.

The Canadian Constitution and Human Rights (radio talks). Toronto, Canadian Broadcasting Corporation, 1959.

Civil Liberties and Canadian Federalism. Toronto, University of Toronto Press, 1959.

Dialogue sur la Traduction, with Anne Hébert. Montreal, Editions HMH, 1970.

Essays on the Constitution: Aspects of Canadian Law and Politics. Toronto, University of Toronto Press, 1977.

Editor, *Social Planning for Canada.* Toronto, 1935.

Editor, with Alexander Brady, *Canada after the War: Attitudes of Political, Social, and Economic Policies in Post-War Canada.* Toronto, Macmillan, 1944.

Editor, with A.J.M. Smith, *The Blasted Pine: An Anthology of Satire, Invective and Disrespectful Verse, Chiefly by Canadian Writers.* Toronto, Macmillan, 1957; revised edition, 1967.

Editor, with Michael Oliver, *Quebec States Her Case: Speeches and Articles from Quebec in the Years of Unrest.* Toronto, Macmillan, 1964.

Editor and Translator *Poems of French Canada.* Burnaby, British Columbia, Blackfish Press, 1977.

Translator, *St.-Denys Garneau and Anne Hébert.* Vancouver, Klanak Press, 1962; revised edition, 1978.

*

Bibliography: by Robert Still, in *The Annotated Bibliography of Canada's Major Authors 4* edited by Robert Lecker and Jack David, Downsview, Ontario, ECW Press, 1983.

Critical Studies: *Ten Canadian Poets* by Desmond Pacey, Toronto, Ryerson Press, 1958; *The Literary History of Canada* edited by Carl F. Klinck, Toronto, University of Toronto Press, 1965; "F.R. Scott and Some of His Poems" by A.J.M. Smith, in *Canadian Literature 31* (Vancouver), Winter 1967; *The McGill Movement: A.J.M. Smith, F.R. Scott, and Leo Kennedy* edited by Peter Stevens, Toronto, Ryerson Press, 1969; "The Road Back to Eden: The Poetry of F.R. Scott" by Stephen Scobie, in *Queen's Quarterly* (Kingston, Ontario), Autumn 1972; Clara Thomas, in *Our Nature—Our Voices: A Guidebook to English-Canadian Literature*, Toronto, New Press, 1972; *On F.R. Scott: Essays on His Contributions to Law, Literature, and Politics* edited by Sandra Djwa and R. St.J. Macdonald, Montreal, McGill-Queen's University Press, 1983.

F.R. Scott comments:

What is my personal conception of poetry? If I could define it, it would not be very different from my conception of life itself. The poet is a "maker"; the poetic potential underlies all living and all art, but comes to life in the poet through his special power to make something new and true with words. His tool is language, with which he explores the frontiers of the world inside and the world outside man. His method, and his revelations, are both unique, and can only flourish if he is free to pursue his vision wherever it may lead him.

*   *   *

F.R. Scott has been a kind of "double agent" who has succeeded in combining an active public life in politics and university teaching with the contemplative and yet very active and practical life of a poet. While still an undergraduate at McGill he helped to introduce the new poetry of the Eliot-Pound tradition into Canada, and for more than forty years he has been a leader of groups of younger poets and a stimulating force in the poetry scene. His own verse is divided into satirical poetry, a pungent form of social and political criticism, love poems ranging from the simple to the metaphysically or psychologically complex, and nature poems, which begin with simple examples of a northern imagism and develop into an elegance of style and a richness of allusion that suggest at times a Canadian Marvell.

"Lakeshore," the fine poem that stands at the beginning of *Selected Poems*, may be cited as an example. Written in a series of irregularly rhymed stanzas, it begins with the immediate and the personal—the poet standing by the "bevelled edge" of a lake in the air and the sunshine, then plunging into the breathless dark of the subaqueous world below. The senses stimulate the mind, and the theme of the poem becomes Man's history, which extends back into pre-history, before man developed lungs and ceased to be fish. With its unifying symbol of water as the source of life, the poem establishes a contact in awareness with biological history, stretching back to the primordial beginnings of life, and also (as we emerge again to the surface of the lake) with the earthbound now of "a crowded street." This poem is characteristic of Scott's mature non-satirical poetry. The themes and motives of much of his most completely articulated work are seen in it at their clearest and most direct. The fascination with water, as an element and as a symbol; the identification of the poet's self with Man and of the sensuous perceptive physical being with Mind; and the inescapable tendency to interchange the language and imagery of science (especially biology, geology, and psychology) with the language and imagery of religion are all seen in this poem as well as in a dozen other of Scott's more recent metaphysical lyrics and in the remarkable series of poems resulting from his travels in India, Burma, and the Far East.

Scott has managed, more successfully than most, to unify his public life of social responsibility with the private, perceptive and contemplative life of the poet. All his poems, from the gayest and lightest expressions of delight in life through his witty and sometimes savage satires to the metaphysical lyrics, are informed and qualified by a sense of responsibility and an inescapable sincerity, serious but never solemn.

—A.J.M. Smith

SCOTT, Tom. Scottish. Born in Glasgow, Lanarkshire, 6 June 1918. Educated at Hyndland Secondary School, Glasgow; Madras College, St. Andrews, Scotland; Edinburgh University, M.A., Ph.D. Served in the Royal Army Pay Corps, 1939-44. Married Heather Fretwell in 1963; one son and twin daughters. Recipient: Atlantic-Rockefeller Award, 1950; Carnegie Senior Fellowship and Scholarship; Arts Council Award, 1972. Address: Duddingston Park, Edinburgh 15, Scotland.

PUBLICATIONS

Verse

Seeven Poems o Maister Francis Villon. Tunbridge Wells, Kent, Peter Russell, 1953.
An Ode til New Jerusalem. Edinburgh, M. Macdonald, 1956.
The Ship and Ither Poems. London and New York, Oxford University Press, 1963.
At the Shrine o the Unkent Sodger: A Poem for Recitation. Preston, Lancashire, Akros, 1968.
Brand the Builder. London, Ember Press, 1975.
The Tree: An Animal Fable. Dunfermline, Fife, Borderline Press, 1977.

Other

A Possible Solution to the Scotch Question. Edinburgh, M. Macdonald, 1963.
Dunbar: A Critical Exposition of the Poems. Edinburgh, Oliver and Boyd, and New York, Barnes and Noble, 1966.
Tales of King Robert the Bruce (for children). Oxford, Pergamon Press, 1969.
Tales of Sir William Wallace, Guardian of Scotland. Edinburgh, Gordon Wright, 1981.

Editor, with John MacQueen, *The Oxford Book of Scottish Verse.* Oxford, Clarendon Press, 1966.
Editor, *Late Medieval Scots Poetry: A Selection from the Makars and Their Heirs down to 1610.* London, Heinemann, and New York, Barnes and Noble, 1967.
Editor, *The Penguin Book of Scottish Verse.* London, Penguin, 1970.

*

Critical Studies: "Tom Scott" by John Herdman, in *Akros 16* (Preston, Lancashire), April 1971; "Tom Scott Issue" of *Scotia Review* (Caithness), 1976.

Tom Scott comments:

After some years writing in English, to my own dissatisfaction, I found myself beginning to write in my native Scots, suppressed by my English education, in Sicily. Since that con-

version I have written mostly in that language, my own reworking of it, for verse, and in English for prose, until recently.

At the centre of my work is a vision of the Good Society. My poems mainly take two modes: visions of that society, and satires of existing society and its evils. Technically I have been influenced by Villon, Dunbar, and Lewis Grassic Gibbon, and stick close to traditional forms, in the main. I have recently revived the verse epistle for social criticism, owing perhaps something to Fergusson and Burns, but very much brought up to date. I am a Scottish nationalist and more concerned with the salvation of my nation than that of my own soul, believing that "he who saveth his soul shall lose it." I have a personal vision of Yeshua of Nazareth, but it accords little and quarrels much with orthodox religion. I am a writer, with no capacity for religion as such, being an observer rather than a man of action. My social vision is moral-aesthetic rather than scientific—old fashioned utopian socialism, I suppose.

*   *   *

Brand the Builder stands at the heart of Tom Scott's achievement. The language is a rich Scots vernacular, dignified by the formality of a verse that is sufficiently free to allow the direct speech of Brand to rise naturally out of it. In the strong affection of the poet, through the relaxed slow movement of the verse, which is also the pace of the man, Brand comes before the mind's eye, warm and living. The poem can contain without strain the ritual grace of Brand—"'Lord, for what we are about to receive/ Help us to be truly thankful—Aimen'"—and the racy vigorous image of the man dousing his face in water, to be followed by the conclusive last line: "The waater slorps frae his elbucks as he synds his phiz./ And this is aa the life he kens there is?" It is as if the poet stands aside to let the subject speak for itself, and this, according to a passage in *The Tree*, is the right stance for the poet. Significantly the solid character of the man is reflected in the character of the speech, a speech, which I regard as Tom Scott's most important inheritance, for it, along with other personal aspects, suggests a continuity of Scottish character, at this moment in history when that continuity might appear no longer to exist.

In terms of aspiration—Tom Scott's dedication to projecting the idea of the Good Society, and to warning the people of inevitable doom when a class-structured society sets money-making above all other ends—Brand is a small achievement. Nevertheless my observation of the rightness of the language in that poem relates to the problem of being in possession of an idiom and style that can be successfully applied to the major themes that are developed in *The Ship, At the Shrine o the Unkent Sodger,* and *The Tree.* Previous to writing *The Ship,* Scott had discovered that the major contribution to his literary identity came from the Scottish Makars of the later Middle Ages. MacDiarmid had already been at this source, but unlike him, Scott worked frequently within the modes of the period and with a language which acknowledged that Middle Scots might still help to create a living verse. The idiom of Tom Scott's translations, particularly in his *Seeven Poems o Maister Francis Villon,* which related to the period of the poems and to the present, was harmoniously right. There could hardly be a finer translation of "Mais où sont les neiges d'antan?" than "Ay, whaur are the snaws o langsyne?" It is warmer and stronger than "Where are the snows of yester year?" and without its feeling of manner, but when Scott employs a stanzaic form for original writing as in "Ithaka," "Fergus," and "A Prayer for the Fowk" (all from *The Ship and Ither Poems*), one is over-conscious of their Medieval reference. Even when the poet writes of the evils of his day—as in the lines

For the rackt by rates and rents and taxes,
Mulctict by insurancies,
For the spreit that nocht but drug relaxes,
Drunken dreams, fagged fantasies,
Let Your mercie, petie, peace
Circulate, no watered beer

—the controlled fluency and the antique spelling milks the verse of social concern.

For *The Ship*, an allegory on the consequences of the denial of the brotherhood of man based on the sinking of the *Titanic*, an idiom closer to Scots speech yet capable of rhetorical utterance was required, and achieved. The build and momentum of this long poem are impressive. The rhetoric carries the strong, sometimes impassioned, prophetic voice, to the extent of favouring the allegory at the expense of the tragic human tale, as in the substitution of comic archetypes for persons ("Mr and Mrs Warld-Steel were there/Sir James and Lady Banking and Finance"). Not that the less strident voice is unheard. An inventive, well observed passage detailing the reactions of passengers, has the lines: "A few/ Noticed some tell-tail detail telt nae tale—/ The matresses nae langer shoogled wi the Ship." Scott then has at his command a Scots capable of proselytising and of intimacy. In *At the Shrine o the Unkent Sodger* he exploits the larger voice, though, in this "poem for Recitation," the other is not lost.

When Tom Scott sets himself to embrace the subject of Evolution in English in what he calls "symphonic verse" in *The Tree*, which runs to 230 lines, the problem of recovering a valid idiom for his large purpose may be insoluble. From the outset he puts an apparently unreserved trust in an exhausted poetic diction. Whereas Scots, in certain circumstances, may still win acceptance for a romantic currency, the over-exploited English will not. References to the "Muses," "heart of mystery," and "mighty" even in a line with some evocation, such as "as may a mighty ship loom up through fog" put under suspicion the whole poem; and yet because of the poet's love for the subject, his detailed presentation of it, his deep affection for the great Scottish natural historian, D'Arcy Thompson—who is depicted in the poem—and his passionate concern about the issues he raises, the poem comes alive in passages. The poem is not the thing itself, as is *Brand the Builder*, but Tom Scott will go his own, independent way, and it would be hard to predict where next.

—George Bruce

SCOVELL, E(dith) J(oy). British. Born in Sheffield, Yorkshire, in 1907. Educated at Casterton School, Westmorland; Somerville College, Oxford, B.A. 1930. Married Charles Sutherland Elton in 1937; two children. Lives in Oxford. Address: c/o Secker and Warburg Ltd., 54 Poland Street, London W1V 3DF, England.

PUBLICATIONS

Verse

Shadows of Chrysanthemums and Other Poems. London, Routledge, 1944.
The Midsummer Meadow and Other Poems. London, Routledge, 1946.

The River Steamer and Other Poems. London, Cresset Press, 1956.
The Space Between. London, Secker and Warburg, 1982.

*   *   *

E.J. Scovell takes as her themes birth, motherhood, and the process of ageing. She sets these against the English countryside with its temperate birds, trees, and flowers. Hers is a quiet verse that, however, yields much to repeated frequentation. One of her qualities is to make a presence out of what a more superficial poet would see as a negative. She commends the pallor of the blooms in her poem "Mid-Winter Flowers." She expresses a preference for shadows over the palpable flowers that project them in "Shadows of Chrysanthemums":

Where the flowers lean to their shadows on the wall
The shadow flowers outshine them all,
Answering their wild lightness with a deeper tone
And clearer pattern than their own
(For they are like flames in sun, or saints in trance,
Almost invisible, dissolved in radiance)....

This sense of a world deeper than superficial description can reach is found in the many poems Scovell has devoted to small children. The apartness of the new-born baby is shown in "The First Year," a sequence that occurs in her first book. This is characteristic: in her second book, an acute sense of human frailty suffuses such a poem as "A Baby's Head":

The lamp shines on his innocent wild head again.
Only for a moment are you both flowers and men,
Your souls like souls of flowers wholly immanent;
Your soul a texture and your love a scent....

The brightness glimpsed here, in this and in other poems, is set off against a darkening world. The contrast is seen, for example, in "Leaves of Elm," a poem which recognizes the processes beneath the nostalgic landscape—the leaves "not blown to earth but loosed/ As though a hand opened and let them go...."

This is not, however, a negative vision. Even when the darkening world occurs in a poem actually called "The Dark World," there are compensating elements—"The young swans in their tender smoke-grey feathers/...Come docile with their parents still...." The swan is an image reiterated through Scovell's work. In the poem "The Swan's Feet" the creature is no airy phantasm:

Who is this whose feet
Close on the water,
Like muscled leaves darker than ivy
Blown back and curved by unwearying wind?
They, that thrust back the water,
Softly crumple now and close, stream in his wake....

The swan may seem, to a casual glance, built of light. In fact, it is propelled below the surface by muscled feet. This is a fitting metaphor to illustrate the mode of this poet who, as Eliot said of Andrew Marvell, deploys a tough reasonableness beneath the lyric grace.

It seemed as though Scovell had completed her cycle of work with the retrospective collection *The River Steamer* (1956). As well as reprinting some of the earlier verse, this book included more recent poems that touched upon new depths of speculation. There is a linking of nature's fruitfulness with human parturition in a poem about growing older, "After Midsummer"—"fruit is rounding on the lap of summer...." The title poem goes even further in design. It is an allegory of human life itself, couched in the poet's characteristically exploratory rhythms:

> Waiting for a spirit to trouble the water,
>
> Waiting for a spirit from beneath or over
> To trouble the surface of the river
> From which the hours like clouds reflected gaze
> White, and the daylight shines of all earth's days....

However, retrospective though this collection was, it did not signal a term to the poet's achievement. 26 years later, Scovell was to produce a volume as resonant as any of her three previous books. The poems have an autumnal poignancy, but they are more robust than they seem at first reading. "An Ordinary Autumn" makes friends with the necessity of dying—"I being old/(And that is common too) this year more dearly feel/The metaphor of autumn...." For all the air of valediction, there is no ebbing of power here. On the contrary, the title poem gives us a clue as to how we should read not only this latest book but the oeuvre as a whole. Not the imagery alone but what is behind the imagery forms the subject matter of this remarkable poet:

> Layer upon layer stretched, woven to all degrees
> Of part-transparency: the rose, knotted like lace
> To a star-pattern, thins between to stellar space.
> Though eyes before they learn level the galaxies,
> It is not the flowers' selves only, webbed in their skies of green
> It is depth they grant to sight; it is the space between.

Like all the poems that precede this, the final poem of the latest book, "The Space Between" shows E.J. Scovell to have a grasp of life in its deeper implications that puts her among the authoritative poets of the age. This is a poet to frequent in the same spirit as that in which we ponder the classics of our language.

—Philip Hobsbaum

SCULLY, James (Joseph).   American.   Born in New Haven, Connecticut, 23 February 1937. Educated at Southern Connecticut State College, New Haven, 1955-57; University of Connecticut, Storrs, B.A. 1959 (Phi Beta Kappa), Ph.D. 1964. Married Arlene Steeves in 1960; two children. Instructor, Rutgers University, New Brunswick, New Jersey, 1963-64; taught at Hartford Street Academy, Connecticut, 1968-69. Associate Professor, 1964-75, and since 1975 Professor of English, University of Connecticut. Visiting Associate Professor, University of Massachusetts, Amherst 1973. Recipient: Ingram Merrill Foundation Fellowship, 1962; Lamont Poetry Selection award, 1967; Contributors' prize (*Far Point*), 1969; Jennie Tane Award (*Massachusetts Review*), 1971; Guggenheim Fellowship, 1973; National Endowment for the Arts grant, 1976; Islands and Continents award, for translation, 1980. Address: 250 Lewiston Avenue, Willimantic, Connecticut 06226, U.S.A.

PUBLICATIONS

Verse

The Marches.   New York, Holt Rinehart, 1967.

Communications, with Grandin Conover.   Amherst, Massachusetts Review, 1970.
Avenue of the Americas.   Amherst, University of Massachusetts Press, 1971.
Santiago Poems.   Willimantic, Connecticut, Curbstone Press, 1975.
Scrap Book.   Willimantic, Connecticut, Ziesing Brothers, 1977.
May Day.   Corvallis, Oregon, Minnesota Review Press, 1980.
Apollo Helmet.   Willimantic, Connecticut, Curbstone Press, 1983.

Other

Editor, *Modern Poetics.*   New York, McGraw Hill, 1965; as *Modern Poets on Modern Poetry*, London, Collins, 1966.
Editor, and translator with Arlene Scully, *Poetry and Militancy in Latin America*, by Roque Dalton.   Willimantic, Connecticut, Curbstone Press, 1981.

Translator, with C. John Herington, *Prometheus Bound*, by Aeschylus.   New York and London, Oxford University Press, 1975.
Translator, with Maria A. Proser, *Quechua Peoples Poetry*, edited by Jesús Lara.   Willimantic, Connecticut, Curbstone Press, 1977.
Translator, with Maria A. Proser and Arlene Scully, *De Repente/All of a Sudden*, by Teresa de Jesús.   Willimantic, Connecticut, Curbstone Press, 1979.

*   *   *

The poems in James Scully's *The Marches* are meditative, dense as the persistence of the past in the present,

> as if,
> rockbound, this were the kingdom come,
>
> and the hunched fields were crystal-clear
> Jerusalem, and life was judged
> vibration in the summer air.

Connecticut, northern France, Lake Bled in Yugoslavia, Venice, Gibraltar, Lake Sunapee in New Hampshire—wherever, "you could almost hear/lost gods breathing in the earth." Another noise is time passing: "pink-pale clouds march/as far as the mind can reach, wilting,/central Jersey spread under like spilt milk."

Avenue of the Americas is a far less scattered book, focused by loss. A child is dead at six months, a brilliant and extravagant friend is dead, rapacious grief runs through the poems. Scully's language is less measured than before, more various—discursive, argumentative and lyrical all in the same few lines. Organizing themes are Edenic America, friendship and family, the failure of art to console and its power to instruct, the spiritual collapse of American political life in the 1960's. The rock-like past of *The Marches* is transmogrified by history, by evolution, and seems to be spending itself as fast as the present:

> Even the beautiful are too
>   heartsick for beauty,
> astronauts will never make it to the stars
> but burn up.

The book includes translations from Joseph Brodsky, whose political themes underscore Scully's own.
Occasionally so ambitious they fail of their own philosophical weight, Scully's newer poems have the urgency and personal risk

of letters to a beloved friend (and one group of poems in *Avenue of the Americas* was evidently written as such a series of letters). But the poems are not "confessional," nor does the poet set himself up in them as representative man. They move toward the wider life which is their persistent obsession by a manifest sense that language, perhaps more than history or evolution, is our shared life: "Maybe that's what poetry is, one of the species/ claiming grandeur./It's that helpless."

—William Matthews

SCUPHAM, (John) Peter. British. Born in Liverpool, Lancashire, 24 February 1933. Educated at The Perse, Cambridge, 1942-47; St. George's, Harpenden, 1947-51; Emmanuel College, Cambridge, 1954-57. Served in the Royal Army Ordnance Corps. Married Carola Braunholtz in 1957; one daughter and three sons. English teacher, Skegness Grammar School, Lincolnshire, 1957-61. Since 1961, Member of the English Department, St. Christopher School, Letchworth, Hertfordshire. Editor, with John Mole, Cellar Press, and since 1974, Owner, Mandeville Press, both in Hitchin, Hertfordshire. Address: 2 Taylor's Hill, Hitchin, Hertfordshire SG4 9AD, England.

PUBLICATIONS

Verse

The Small Containers. Stockport, Cheshire, Phoenix Pamphlet Poets Press, 1972.
The Snowing Globe. Manchester, E.J. Morten, 1972.
Children Dancing. Oxford, Sycamore Press, 1972.
The Nondescript. Stockport, Cheshire, Phoenix Pamphlet Poets Press, 1973.
The Gift: Love Poems. Richmond, Surrey, Keepsake Press, 1973.
Prehistories. London, Oxford University Press, 1975.
A Mandeville Troika, with Neil Powell and George Szirtes. Hitchin, Hertfordshire, Mandeville Press, 1977.
The Hinterland. London, Oxford University Press, 1977.
Megaliths and Water, drawings by Andy Christian. Brampton, LYC Museum, 1978.
Natura. Sidcot, Somerset, Gruffyground Press, and Iowa City, Windhover Press, 1978.
Summer Palaces. Oxford and New York, Oxford University Press, 1980.
Christmas Past, with John Mole. Hitchin, Hertfordshire, Mandeville Press, 1981.
Transformation Scenes: A Sequence of Five Poems. Hitchin, Hertfordshire, Red Gull Press, 1982.
Winter Quarters. Oxford, Oxford University Press, 1983.
Christmas Games, with John Mole. Hitchin, Hertfordshire, Mandeville Press, 1983.

*

Critical Studies: in *New Statesman* (London), 29 September 1972; by Michael Longley, in *Phoenix 9* (Stockport, Cheshire), Winter 1972; *Irish Times* (Dublin), 6 January 1973; *The Teacher* (London), 2 March 1973; *Encounter* (London), 18 May 1973; *Times Literary Supplement* (London), 23 May 1975 and 21

November 1977; "Lessons in Survival" (interview), in *PN Review* (Manchester), vol. 10, no. 5.

Peter Scupham comments:
I feel with Auden that poetry is a game of knowledge, and I enjoy the complexity of rules that make the game worth playing. I enjoy, and hope my work demonstrates, formalities, ironies, technical complexities, patterns, elegance. But since the game is a game of knowledge, I also hope my poems are *about* something, that they possess a strong sense of the reality of people and objects. The game should be played for someone or something else's sake; not for the poet's. I enjoy tightrope-walking, cadence, clarity, celebrations; I dislike the raw, the self-absorbed, the cosmic. The poets for whom I feel particular elective affinities would include James Reeves, Norman Cameron, Louis Mac-Neice, Richard Wilbur, John Crowe Ransom. I would like my best poems to unite the dance of beauty with the dance of death.

*   *   *

The subject matter of Peter Scupham's poetry reflects the wide ranging interests of an acute intelligence: archaeology in "Un Peu d'Histoire: Dordogne"; jazz in "Fats Waller"; children and family in "Small Pets," "Four Fish," and "Family Ties"; and so we could go on. The poetry itself is marked by a scrupulous care in the use of language and form which results in a precision of expression and feeling.

Scupham is keenly aware of our vulnerability, of that incidence of tragedy that lies close to the surface of even every day domestic life: "All this dark humus/ A soft compound of shared sufferings./The earth is knit together with absences" ("At Home"); and that is not without menace where in the nursery: "The small child tosses. It is not easy/To have wolves wished upon you./They wait patiently beside the bed" ("Wolves"). His preoccupation with our prehistory and the Earth's geological and historic past ties in here, for in Scupham's world the sense of a common bond between all humanity, past and present, is never far off; our concerns and fears are shared through the ages. It is a poetry of a committed conscience, deriving depth from a historical perspective where responsibility is everyman's. This is seen clearly in an impressive poem, "The Nondescript," which Scupham wrote for the Friends of the Earth, where the use of the first person in the poem manages to be strongly impersonal and yet all embracing: "I am plural. My interests are manifold/I see through many eyes. I am fabulous"—so that the poem manages to address the reader while involving him as a participant in its tragic consequences: "I have prepared a stone inheritance/It flourishes beneath my fertile tears."

Scupham's collection *The Hinterland* marks a movement towards more recent history, and the sonnet sequence which gives the collection its title has as its central theme the Great War of 1914-18. The dazzling technical feat of writing 15 sonnets linked by their first and last lines, the final sonnet composed of those lines, is such that it has beguiled critics from the quality of the work itself where the poet has infused his historical perspective with an emotional immediacy which is quite remarkable.

> Where blood and stone proclaim their unities
> Under the topsoil vagaries of green
> Works the slow justle of the small debris....

In his later collections, *Summer Palaces* and *Winter Quarters,* this trend is continued and there are splendidly direct and moving poems based on his father-in-law's First World War diaries and his own National Service. The latter's wry humour is conveyed in a series of dazzling conceits and metaphors. For while it is true that Scupham's poetry can be so loaded with meaning, overtones, and allusions that it reminds one of those great summer bees freighted with rich pollen, he has done the art some service in reminding us that technical excellence and true feeling are not inimical.

Indeed, his poetry recalls Jonathan Raban's concept of "The Society of the Poem," and once you have entered the world of a Scupham poem and accepted its perceptions and ethos all falls into place and the experience is profoundly enriching.

—John Cotton

SEIDEL, Frederick (Lewis). American. Born in St. Louis, Missouri, 19 February 1936. Educated at St. Louis Country Day School, 1948-53; Harvard University, Cambridge, Massachusetts, A.B. 1957. Married Phyllis Munro Ferguson in 1960 (divorced, 1969); one daughter and one son. Paris Editor, 1960-61, and since 1961, Advisory Editor, *Paris Review*, Paris and New York. Writer-in-Residence, Rutgers University, New Brunswick, New Jersey, 1964. Recipient: National Endowment for the Arts grant, 1968; *American Poetry Review* prize, 1979; Lamont Poetry Selection award, 1979; National Book Critics Circle award, 1981. Address: c/o Viking Press, 40 West 23rd Street, New York, New York 10010, U.S.A.

PUBLICATIONS

Verse

Final Solutions. New York, Random House, 1963.
Sunrise. New York, Viking Press, 1980.
Men and Women: New and Selected Poems. London, Chatto and Windus, 1984.

*   *   *

Past is ever present in Frederick Seidel's *Final Solutions*, as juxtaposed and overlapping time-frames trace the psychic travels of memorable souls. Uneasy, frightened, struggling, and tormented, personae reveal through internal monologues histories whose significance is both individual and universal. But, whether in painful resignation or in fitful turmoil, speakers' voices are modulated into meticulously wrought lines. The frequent contrast between the noisome details of suffering and the controlled tone of its expression results in powerful tension, agony heightened by an ominous placidity. "The Heart Attack," a remarkable evocation of ancient times, conveys eternal themes of lust, hurt, and regret in polished rimes; a long-departed mistress fills an old man's dreams with coy and spiteful recollections and gets a sort of revenge by her "presence" at the poem's dramatic close. The widower finds himself still held in the power of a wife who "killed/ Him in her dreams every day," a masochistic thrall perpetuated by his scolding grand-daughter. The retired Jewish analyst in "Daley Island" holds on, locked like the land in a sea of memory. Surrounded by the squalid artefacts of a Parisian spring, the soldier is drawn back by a half-remembered vision of idealism at Harvard and a desire for a girl with "Unmarriageable Minoan eyes,/ All intuition, delicately lidded."

Occasionally, the subtle, inferential handling of material gives way to an unfortunate bluntness. "Americans in Rome" proceeds by means of extended reveries and short dramatic scenes to show tenderness confronted by social realities, but leads to self-righteous pity for poor souls who "can give to piety/ Their ego, for amnesia," and ends in a crude critique of religious hypocrisy. In "The Beast Is in Chains," time-shifts operate once more, but in facile comparisons of wars (Napoleon's and the Allies') and in obvious commentary upon a fragile peace maintained by American flags in the City of Light. More successful is "A Year Abroad," in which the persona travels to and through modern Germany, with flashes of "Jewbaiting mothers" in Cologne, and further back still to the city of the Roman Varus, a journey made a parable of civilization versus freedom. In the final poem, "The Sickness," the poet gives a virtuoso display of his powers. Graphic scenes in Bellevue are pitted in ironic counterpoint against the world outside, where "others try life, try dope...join the Reserves,/ Or take the wife their life deserves." Following this unsettling prelude, the final mad fantasies of escape build to terrifying hallucinatory scenarios driven by crazy, relentless logic climaxing in breathless release. In lines such as these, Seidel answers his own question: "What/ Else is there but—to live—to care...?"

—Joseph Parisi

SEIDMAN, Hugh. American. Born in Brooklyn, New York, 1 August 1940. Educated at Massachusetts Institute of Technology, Cambridge, 1957-58; Polytechnic Institute of Brooklyn, 1958-61, B.A. 1961; University of Minnesota, Minneapolis, 1961-64, M.S. 1964; Columbia University, New York, 1967-69, M.F.A. 1969. Since 1976, member of the faculty, New School for Social Research, New York. Visiting Poet or Writer, Yale University, New Haven, Connecticut, 1971, 1973, City College of City University of New York, 1972-75, Wilkes College, Wilkes-Barre, Pennsylvania, 1975, Wichita State University, Kansas, 1978, New York State Poets-in-the-Schools, 1978-81, Washington College, Chestertown, Maryland, 1979, University of Wisconsin, Madison, 1981, and College of William and Mary, Williamsburg, Virginia, 1982. Recipient: Yale Series of Younger Poets Award, 1969; National Endowment for the Arts grant, 1970, and fellowship, 1972; Creative Artists Public Service grant, 1971; Yaddo fellowship, 1972, 1976; MacDowell Colony fellowship, 1974, 1976; *Writer's Digest* prize, 1982. Address: 463 West Street, New York, New York 10014, U.S.A.

PUBLICATIONS

Verse

Collecting Evidence. New Haven, Connecticut, Yale University Press, 1970.
Blood Lord. New York, Doubleday, 1974.
Throne/Falcon/Eye. New York, Random House, 1982.

Other

Co-Editor, *Westbeth Poets.* New York, Poetry New York, 1971.
Co-Editor, *Equal Time.* New York, Equal Time, 1982.

*

Critical Studies: reviews by Peter Davison, in *Atlantic* (New York), January 1971; Beth Bentley, in *Seattle Times*, 10 January 1971; Denis Donoghue, in *New York Review of Books*, 16 May 1971; Rochelle Ratner, in *East Village Other* (New York) 18 May 1971; Bill Zavatsky, in *New York Times Book Review*, 26 December 1971; Theodore Enslin, in *Occurrence 3* (Mechanicsburg, Pennsylvania), 1975; Gary Ross, in *Globe and Mail* (Toronto), 1 February 1975; John Koethe, in *Parnassus* (New York), Spring-Summer 1975; Joseph Parisi, in *Poetry* (Chicago), September 1975; Michael Heller, in *Granite* (Hanover, New Hampshire), Winter 1975-76; Marilyn Crabtree, in *Kansas City Star*, 27 February 1983; Richard Tillinghast, in *New York Times Book Review*, 2 May 1983; Paul Pines, in *American Book Review* (Newark, New Jersey), July-August and September-October 1984.

Hugh Seidman comments:

One gets up in the morning and goes to the typewriter. And one continues against whatever else.

It is pleasurable to make an object, in this case with words. As the desire to make something implies, coherence is a pressure. I like to think that there is some similarity between solving a problem in mathematics or physics, the two subjects of most of my academic training, and "solving" a poem. However, while a mathematical statement is finally only a relationship between abstract symbols relative to an axiomatic context, in the poem there is the possibility of saying something true, emotionally true. This is because our poems are smarter than we are no matter how we are ourselves struck into our own ignorance. Though truth may take a lifetime, since one's poems are never more than oneself.

At the risk of sounding ridiculous, I am interested in the ancient tasks of love, death, and rebirth. And in the ongoing tension and paradox of the private heart in the public world.

And this is the great excitement, the great adventure. Yet it is also the great risk, for one may fail utterly even if to others hardly a thing seems to be happening one way or the other. Which returns us to the fact that one gets up and still writes, even so, against all that one knows.

And all of this may not be so, yet it is.

*   *   *

Hugh Seidman's remarkable poems embody the disjunctive music of the present, a music of simultaneous dread and prophecy, of razor-like imagery and asperous beauty. In his first book of poems, *Collecting Evidence*, Seidman laid down for himself the mandate to write of: "each grief, each relief/each day and everyday/in consummate craft and artistry." In the following book, *Blood Lord* and now with *Throne/Falcon/Eye* the mandate seems to have been accomplished in a body of work of extraordinary originality and power.

The first thing to strike the reader of Seidman's poems is what marks them off from his contemporaries. For, unlike the bland horizontal mumbling of much current American poetry, Seidman's poems have a calligraphic jaggedness, a capacity to inscribe allusively, as they work down the page, large areas of emotion and complexity. From "Zero":

> The unbroken lake creaks
> but a rat snaps in the trap
> and thumb skin cracks and bleeds

> And once I jabbed a fish-hole
> and the black birds
> bud oddly on the trees in the furnace cold

> And the cloud rim is fire
> and the ice in space freezes harder
> and the astral TV flickers

The world registers on the poet not as a series of mediated images but as acutely sharp and painful arousals, calls to being of nearly inarticulate body and mind states, where: "...now I touch myself/like all dumb things at the ice-hole/who do not know why they know."

Central to Seidman's work is a vision of a world in which the cultural artifact, the iconic datum, whether it be high art or high tech or the pop spillage of the media, no longer shines in some exemplary light but instead exhibits with a fascinated horror the very price of its existence. Thus in "Agent Orange," touching on America's Vietnam experience, every "light has a dark/like the inhaled sun over gunships that stained jungles." The poem makes material that brooding nightmarish craziness of America where the astronaut can "leap like a boy with a robot's fervor" and "...the night of the high school prom begins/to glow/like a vast angel in a coma...."

In such poems, Seidman is both willing and able to draw on the resonances of the tradition, to play off the dancing syllables of the Metaphysicals, for example, not only for effect but for humor. His use of the traditional-sounding line often becomes an instrument of black comedy, of a childlike rhythmical analog, as in "Newton" from *Blood Lord*:

> Newton, praise Newton, his tree
> the apple is free...

> Nipple hairs tickle Newton's nose
> he feasts on cheese of toe, he cries
> Hosanna to the head

In "Couplets" from *Throne/Falcon/Eye*, a mock heroic poem of failed love which enjambs current politics, Fields (W.C.), and Fidel (Castro) into its meditations, we are told:

> The moral was too banal that we quarrelled
> like the mainland and the island...

> And below the stars I miss you in my bed
> Till the sun comes like a warhead

> Like love that flares to solitude
> beyond the evil and the good

Yet another dimension of Seidman's work, mysterious and enigmatic, is shown in the poems which allegorize the materials of Egyptian mythology, in particular Isis and the cult of the dead. These poems, even as they obliquely refer to the moral and existential dilemmas of the present, most nearly resemble a kind of pure poetry or the inverted symbology of a Nerval. They are at once gorgeous in tone and impenetrable as though structured in a kind of time warp or black hole where history and poetry are boiling at critical mass, as in these stunning lines from "Hymn":

> As all are commanded to yield like the mummy when the
>   dung beetle rolls the sun
> before all the befores of the trillion nights past night
>   and day
> though I knew that the broken receding mouth of the Sphinx

had nothing to add
of resurrection in the history of its grimace.

The ambitiousness of such poetry (with its wide range of
subjects: culture, parents, socio-political arenas) is matched by
Seidman's impeccable ear and craft. In his poems, one over-
hears, not only a formal cleanliness of language, but a reach for
larger intercommunicative ironies, for strategies by which the
poem can break with the solipsism of modern verse and enter
into meaningful dialogue with the world.

Such poetry is difficult and unsettling, for in a time of transposed and debased values, poetry, too, to touch the modern
reader, must be transposed. So the muse of the "Muse" is
invoked only to hail:

Ah, good-by!

Now you are like the ideal of a shadow
like the blank metals of the dark that long to be struck
into the coins of light

In such strikings, in its scale of poetic values and tones, Seidman's work incarnates a density of language and a corrosive
beauty found in few modern poets in English.

—Michael Heller

SERGEANT, (Herbert) Howard. British. Born in Hull,
Yorkshire, 6 May 1914. Educated at Hull Grammar School;
College of Commerce, Hull; Metropolitan College, St. Albans,
Hertfordshire, 1935-39; School of Accounting, London, 1939-
42. Married Jean Crabtree in 1954; one son and three daughters.
Accountant, 1935-39 and District Chief Accountant, 1939-41,
Broadcast Relay Services, Northern England; Travelling Accountant, British Air Ministry andd Ministry of Aircraft Production, 1941-49; Company Secretary and Chief Accountant,
Jordan and Sons, publishers, London, 1949-54, and E. Austin
and Sons, London, 1954-63; Lecturer in Accountancy, Economics, and English Literature, Norwood Technical College, London, 1963-65; Senior Lecturer in Accountancy, Wandsworth
Technical College, London, 1965-68; Senior Lecturer in Management Studies, 1969-72, and Head of the School of Management, 1972-78, Brooklands Technical College, Weybridge, Surrey. Creative Writing Fellow, Queen Mary's College, Basingstoke,
Hampshire, 1978-79. Since 1943, Founding Editor, *Outposts*
magazine and Outposts Publications, London and Walton-on-
Thames, Surrey. Recipient: Henry Shore award, 1979; Dorothy
Tutin award, 1980. M.B.E. (Member, Order of the British
Empire), 1978. Address: 72 Burwood Road, Walton-on-Thames,
Surrey KT12 4AL, England.

PUBLICATIONS

Verse

The Leavening Air. London, Fortune Press, 1946.
The Headlands. London, Putnam, 1953.
Selected Poems. London, Fuller D'Arch Smith, 1980.
Travelling Without a Valid Ticket. Bradford, Yorkshire, Rivelin
Press, 1982.

Other

The Cumberland Wordsworth. London, Williams and Nor-
gate, 1950.
Traditions in the Making of Modern Poetry. London, Britan-
nicus Liber, 1951.
A Critical Survey of South African Poetry in English, with G.M.
Miller. Cape Town, Balkema, 1957.

Editor, *For Those Who Are Alive: An Anthology of New Verse.*
London, Fortune Press, 1946.
Editor, *An Anthology of Contemporary Northern Poetry.*
London, Harrap, 1947.
Editor, *These Years: An Anthology of Contemporary Poetry.*
Leeds, Arnold, 1950.
Editor, with Robert Conquest and Michael Hamburger, *New
Poems 1953.* London, Joseph, 1953.
Editor, *A Selection of Poems,* by John Milton. London, Grey
Walls Press, 1953.
Editor, with Dannie Abse, *Mavericks.* London, Editions Poet-
ry and Poverty, 1957.
Editor, *Selected Poems,* by A.J. Bull. London, Outposts,
1966; revised edition, as *Collected Poems,* 1975.
Editor, *Commonwealth Poems of Today.* London, Murray,
1967.
Editor, *New Voices of the Commonwealth.* London, Evans,
1968.
Editor, with Jean Sergeant, *Poems from Hospital.* London,
Allen and Unwin, 1968.
Editor, *Poetry from Africa.* Oxford, Pergamon Press, 1968.
Editor, *Universities' Poetry 8.* Keele, Staffordshire, Universi-
ties Poetry Management Committee, 1968.
Editor, *Poetry from Australia.* Oxford, Pergamon Press,
1969.
Editor, *The Swinging Rainbow: Poems for the Young.* Lon-
don, Evans, 1969.
Editor, *Poetry from India.* Oxford, Pergamon Press, 1969.
Editor, *John Milton and William Wordsworth.* Oxford, Per-
gamon Press, 1970.
Editor, *Poetry of the 1940's.* London, Longman, 1970.
Editor, *Happy Landings* (for children). London, Evans, 1971.
Editor, *Evans Book of Children's Verse.* London, Evans, 1972;
as *The Two Continents Book of Children's Verse,* New York,
Two Continents, 1977.
Editor, *African Voices.* London, Evans, and New York, Law-
rence Hill, 1973; revised edition, Evans, 1978.
Editor, *For Today and Tomorrow.* London, Evans, 1974.
Editor, *New Poems 1976-77.* London, Hutchinson, 1976.
Editor, *Poetry South East 1.* Southborough, Kent, South East
Arts Association, 1976.
Editor, *Candles and Lamps.* Walton-on-Thames, Surrey,
Outposts, 1979.
Editor, *Poems from the Medical World.* Lancaster, MTP
Press, 1980.
Editor, *How Strong the Roots: Poems of Exile.* London,
Evans, 1981.
Editor, with Peter Porter, *The Gregory Awards Anthology
1980.* London, Secker and Warburg, 1981.
Editor, with Anthony Thwaite, *The Gregory Awards Anthology
1981-1982.* Manchester, Carcanet, 1982.
Editor, *Independent Voices 1-2: Public School Verse.* Walton-
on-Thames, Surrey, Outposts, 2 vols., 1983-84.
Editor, *A Package of Poems.* N.p., Nexus, 1984.
Editor, with John Fuller, *The Gregory Poets 1983-84.* Edin-
burgh, Salamander Press, 1984.

*

Critical Study: "The Poetry of Howard Sergeant" by Lionel Monteith, in *Poetry Quarterly* (London), Spring 1951.

* * *

Howard Sergeant's *Selected Poems* of 1980 collects together the best of his two early collections, *The Leavening Air* and *The Headlands*, both long out of print, with a few more recent pieces. The early poems are very much of their time—crafted lyrics, Romantic in that fierce "apocalyptic" way, as "Beach-Head":

O the waters I know will encompass my dead
    and drum them to folly, green tide after
tide to shore up their limbs in the warmth of my bed
    waves will deliver them and drive them to rafter
with ravens, tide-tongued in my head.

It was an era "bright with tongues" but its language has gone out of fashion, and the collection is interesting now primarily as a glimpse into the poetic heartland of Sergeant's more recent work. That phase of his work is announced by the typically self deprecating "Sampler" which puns on both the embroidery "apprentice piece" and serves as a craftsman's sampler of the poet's contemporary style. It seemed for many years that Mr. Sergeant's widely acclaimed work as editor of *Outposts* and as an anthologist had crowded out the inspiration of his own poetry. "Sampler" confirms that the craftsman has returned to his workshop and, beginning with such small scale but finely judged pieces, is preparing to tackle more substantial work:

Here where the kittiwakes idle
    on the coolest drills and checks,
the sun, sharp as a needle,
    sews ribbons round their necks,

And where the tweedy beaches
    are buttoned up with glass,
in long-armed feather stitches
    marries sand and marram grass.

In the five years since "Sampler" first appeared as a Mandeville Press poem-card in 1979 Howard Sergeant's work has been appearing regularly in journals and anthologies, and his sequence "Travelling Without a Valid Ticket" was published to considerable critical acclaim in 1982. With that sequence Sergeant's characteristic style in the later work is established—a generally light, witty, carefully crafted verse, subtly rhymed and delighting in puns which can deflect the reader from a seriousness of purpose that is sometimes only apparent when the poems are collected together. The sequence examines the relationship between the boy Howard Sergeant and his grandfather, a lifelong railwayman. The poet interweaves anecdote and the language of the locomotive shed and station timetable to draw a portrait of the old man that understands—without ever becoming portentous—the extent to which his job defined and shaped every aspect of his life. The opening poem is a good example of the tone, wit, and underlying gravitas which characterises Sergeant's recent work.

Assuming it a grave offence
to be caught travelling without a ticket
my grandfather's generation,
simple in their reverence
but certain of their destination,

set enormous store
by the massive family bible,
their trust in it implicit;
not merely as a guide
but as a kind of inter-tribal
Arrivals and Departures Board,
faithfully recording the score
in weddings, births, confirmations
and deaths, all formally certified
and offered up to the Lord,
in keeping with their proper stations.

Another sequence of poems around a common metaphor that has emerged among the later—so far uncollected—poems are to do with the idea of life viewed as a fairground-cum-circus ring. "Vanity Fair" establishes the metaphor: ostensibly another recollections-of-childhood poem, it opens out in the final stanza to suggest that the life of the fairground was a truer preparation for "real life" than the "familiar routines" of a provincial childhood

I meet these people
everywhere I go—the vendors at each cheapjack stall
the circus entertainers, knife throwers and clowns
escape artists and gamblers on the tricky wire—without
the razamatazz. Perhaps I never left the fairground
after all.

Poems like "Teenage Equestrian," "Trapeze Artist," "Magician," and "Double Knife-Throwing Act" are all portraits of characters from "the razamatazz," but are all, at another level, developing the deeper metaphor. And in "Crazy Love Poem for an Unseen Lady," a poem celebrating the return of his muse, Sergeant draws this self-portrait

I am dancing and juggling,
tossing my multi-coloured balls
in prismatic arcs that, falling,
break with light the surface of the sea.

That last image might well have been taken from an early poem—the sensibility and mastery of his craft that marked him out as one of the most promising poets of his generation is the same though the language has changed with the times. These late poems fulfil that promise; one hopes that they will soon be collected in a companion volume to the *Selected Poems* so that Howard Sergeant's achievement as *poet* as well as "poet maker" can be understood and paid due honour.

—Stewart Brown

SEYMOUR, A(rthur) J(ames). Guyanese. Born in Georgetown, British Guiana, now Guyana, 12 January 1914. Educated at Queen's College, Georgetown. Married Elma Bryce in 1937; three daughters and three sons. Assistant Chief Information Officer, 1943-54, and Chief Information Officer, British Guiana, 1954-62; Development Officer, Caribbean Organization, San Juan, Puerto Rico, 1962-64; public relations officer, Demerara Bauxite/Guyana Bauxite, Mackenzie, 1965-73; Director of Creative Writing, Institute of Creative Arts, Georgetown, 1973-79. Since 1973, Cultural Relations Adviser, Ministry of Culture,

Georgetown. Editor, *Kyk-over-Al*, Georgetown, 1945-61, and Miniature Poets series, 1945-61; Poetry Editor, *Kaie*, magazine of the National History and Arts Council, Guyana, 1965. Recipient: Golden Arrow of Achievement, Guyana, 1970. D.Litt.: University of the West Indies, Bridgetown, Barbados, 1983. Address: 23 North Road, Bourda, Georgetown, Guyana.

PUBLICATIONS

Verse

Verse. Georgetown, Daily Chronicle, 1937.
More Poems. Georgetown, Daily Chronicle, 1940.
Over Guiana Clouds. Georgetown, Demerara Standard, 1945.
Sun's in My Blood. Georgetown, Demerara Standard, 1945.
Six Songs. Privately printed, 1946.
Seven Poems. Privately printed, 1948.
We Do Not Presume to Come. Privately printed, 1948.
The Guiana Book. Georgetown, Argosy, 1948.
Leaves from the Tree. Georgetown, Miniature Poets, 1951.
Water and Blood: A Quincunx. Georgetown, Miniature Poets, 1952.
Three Voluntaries. Privately printed, 1953.
Variations on a Theme. Privately printed, 1961.
Selected Poems. Privately printed, 1965.
A Little Wind of Christmas. Privately printed, 1967.
Monologue. Privately printed, 1968.
Patterns. Privately printed, 1970.
I, Anancy. Privately printed, 1971.
Black Song. Privately printed, 1972.
Passport. Privately printed, 1972.
The Legend of Kaieteur. Georgetown, Carifesta, 1972.
Song to Man. Privately printed, 1973.
City of Memory. Privately printed, 1974.
A Bethlehem Alleluia. Privately printed, 1974.
Images Before Easter. Privately printed, 1974.
Italic. Privately printed, 1974.
Love Song. Privately printed, 1975.
Mirror. Privately printed, 1975.
A Song for Christmas. Privately printed, 1975.
Tomorrow Belongs to the People. Privately printed, 1975.
For Nicolas Guillen. Georgetown, Guyana Lithographic Company, 1976.
Georgetown General. Georgetown, National History and Arts Council, 1976.
Lament for Jacqueline Williams and Raymond Persaud. Privately printed, 1976.
My Resurrection Morning. Privately printed, 1976.
Shape of the Crystal. Privately printed, 1977.
Images of Majority: Collected Poems 1968-1978. Privately printed, 1978.
Religious Poems. Privately printed, 1980.
Lord of My Life. Privately printed, 1981.
Poems for Export Only. Privately printed, 1982.
70th Birthday Poems. Privately printed, 1984.

Short Stories

Nine Short Stories from "Kyk-over-Al." Privately printed, 1981.

Other

A Survey of West Indian Literature. Georgetown, Kyk-over-Al, 1950.

Caribbean Literature (radio talks). Privately printed, 1951.
Window on the Caribbean. Privately printed, 1952.
Edgar Mittelholzer: The Man and His Work. Georgetown, National History and Arts Council, 1968.
Introduction to Guyanese Writing. Georgetown, National History and Arts Council, 1971.
Looking at Poetry. Privately printed, 1974.
I Live in Georgetown. Privately printed, 1974.
Pilgrim Memories. Privately printed, 1974.
Growing Up in Guyana. Privately printed, 1976.
Family Impromptu. Privately printed, 1977.
Nine Caribbean Essays. Privately printed, 1977.
Cultural Policy in Guyana. Paris, Unesco, 1977.
The Making of Guyanese Literature. Privately printed, 1979.
A National Cultural Policy for the British Virgin Islands. Paris, Unesco, 1979.
What Is God Saying to Caribbean Man in His Poetry. Privately printed, 1981.
Studies in West Indian Poetry. Privately printed, 1981.
The Poetry of Frank A. Collymore. Privately printed, 1982.
The Poetry of Phyllis Shand Allfrey. Privately printed, 1982.
Thirty Years a Civil Servant. Privately printed, 1982.
Studies of Ten Guyanese Poems. Georgetown, Ministry of Education, 1982.
The Years in Puerto Rico and Mackenzie. Privately printed, 1983.

Editor, *The Kyk-over-Al Anthology of West Indian Poetry.* Georgetown, Kyk-over-Al, 1952; revised edition, 1957.
Editor, *Anthology of Guyanese Poetry.* Georgetown, Kyk-over-Al, 1954.
Editor, *Themes of Song.* Privately printed, 1959.
Editor, with Elma Seymour, *My Lovely Native Land.* London, Longman, 1971.
Editor, *New Writing in the Caribbean.* Georgetown, Government of Guyana, 1972.
Editor, *Independence Ten: Guyanese Writing 1966-1976.* Georgetown, Government of Guyana, 1977.
Editor, *A Treasury of Guyanese Poetry.* Privately printed, 1980.
Editor, *Dictionary of Guyanese Biography.* Privately printed, 1984.

*

Bibliography: *A.J. Seymour: A Bibliography* by Joan Christiani, Georgetown, Guyana, National Library, 1974.

Manuscript Collection: National Library, Georgetown.

Critical Studies: "A Study of the Poetry of A.J. Seymour" by Celeste Dolphin, in *New World Fortnightly* (Georgetown), 1965; *A.J. Seymour at 70* edited by Ian McDonald, privately printed, 1984.

A.J. Seymour comments:
I would feel that primarily I am a Love poet. I am strongly aware of political shifts in the Community climate in my own country and in the region. Historical personalities stimulate me, and myths and legends of the continent and archipelago also interest me.
I am very conscious of form in poetry—sonnets, terza rima, quatrains and rhyme generally. But everything is grist to the poetic mill and my present influences are W.B. Yeats, Borges, Neruda, and T.S. Eliot.

Like Frank Collymore, A.J. Seymour has not, over the years, only written poetry. He has also been concerned to encourage its writing by others. He edited the now defunct magazine, *Kyk-over-Al*, between 1945 and 1961, which, apart from a fair proportion of poems in its individual numbers, devoted three entire issues to anthologies. He produced a series, "The Miniature Poets," featuring the work of writers like Martin Carter, Cecil Herbert, and Phillip Sherlock; he conducted (and still conducts) writers workshops; and his weekly broadcast literary programmes did much to encourage an interest in the emerging Caribbean literature of the 1950's. He is also a critic, lecturer, and reader of considerable calibre. But above all, A.J. Seymour is a poet.

Three main themes emerge from this work: a feeling for heroes of history or literature, usually accompanied by a sense of violence and doom ("Caligula"):

> In killing, there must be a fierce, dark joy.
> —To stab a pulsing throat and see the blood
> Spurt angry purple from the quivering gash.
> Or choke life out with muscles tense and hard,
> And hammering temples, gloating at the sight
> Of thick veins swelling snake-like from the skin....

(or "Othello"): "The engine failing,/ The shattered peace,/ The athlete lost within his stride,/ The look over the edge of the abyss...." or a feeling for the continuity of Caribbean and Guyanese history, centred through the persona of an epic hero ("For Christopher Columbus"):

> He dreamed not that the ocean would bear ships
> Heavy with slaves in the holds, to spill their seed
> And fertilise new islands under whips
> ...dreamt not indeed
> Massive steel eagles would keep an anxious watch
> For strange and glittering fish where now was weed.

Seymour has also been concerned to weave a local past using Amerindian mythology—"Amalivaca," for instance, and "The Legend of Kaieteur." But these, with their over-emphatic singing pentameters are not as successful as the poems of the first group (the "literary" poems) where, as will be seen from the earlier quotations, he achieves real eloquence, or, as with "Diocletian," a certain sharpness of focus:

> I dream of Diocletian in his age
> Walking alone within his cabbage garden.
>
> A gaunt old man with power upon his face
> Straighter than furrows, and images of power
> Still moving in those deepest eagle eyes.

With these poems, in fact, we reach the paradox of Caribbean "colonial" poetry which tends, like the verse of Frank Collymore, to avoid "social reality"; or, as with Seymour's, to be most technically at home with the "literary." But Seymour is also a "transitional" poet, preparing the way, in "Tomorrow Belongs to the People," for writers like Martin Carter: "Ignorant/ Illegitimate/ Hungry sometimes,/ Living in tenement yards/ Dying in burial societies/ The people is a lumbering giant/ That holds history in his hand."

But it is in the third group of poems, those that disclose Seymour's personal perception of the living world and living love, that we find, perhaps, the most certain successes: "Time spirals upright this unflowing river/ This waterrise through the earth safely miracled/ This phallus from the deeps unbound and liquid,/ Reversal of the dying desert..." ("The Well"), and "Springtide":

> Nearly all women sleep when they are loved
>
> Maybe the body has to coil again
> From its full stretch, maybe the drowned brain
> Emerges from its Springtide into rest
> Maybe they bank their ectasy in dreams
> Against a future anguish and devaluation
>
> But as the unhurried stars wheel overhead
> Above a thousand million nests of love
> One or two women lie and think and glow.

—Edward Kamau Brathwaite

SEYMOUR-SMITH, Martin. British. Born in London, 24 April 1928. Educated at Highgate School, 1939-46; St. Edmund Hall, Oxford (Poetry Editor, *Isis*, 1950-51), 1948-51, B.A. (honours) 1951, M.A. Served in the British Army in the Near East, 1947-48: Sergeant. Married Janet de Glanville in 1952; two daughters. Tutor to Robert Graves's son, in Mallorca, 1951-54; school master, 1954-60. Since 1960, free-lance writer. Visiting Professor of English and Poet-in-Residence, University of Wisconsin Parkside, Kenosha, 1971-72. Editorial Assistant, *London Magazine*, 1955-56; Poetry Editor, *Truth*, London, 1955-57, and *The Scotsman*, Edinburgh, 1964-67; Literary Adviser, Hodder and Stoughton, publishers, London, 1963-65; General Editor, Gollancz Classics series, Victor Gollancz Ltd., London, 1967-69. Agent: Anthony Sheil Associates Ltd., 2-3 Morwell Street, London WC1B 3AR; or, Wallace and Sheil, 177 East 70th Street, New York, New York 10021, U.S.A. Address: 36 Holliers Hill, Bexhill-on-Sea, Sussex TN40 2DD, England.

PUBLICATIONS

Verse

Poems, with Rex Taylor and Terence Hards. Dorchester, Longman, 1952.
(Poems). Oxford, Fantasy Press, 1953.
All Devils Fading. Palma, Mallorca, Divers Press, 1954.
Tea with Miss Stockport: 24 Poems. London and New York, Abelard Schuman, 1963.
Reminiscences of Norma: Poems 1963-1970. London, Constable, 1971.

Other

Robert Graves. London, Longman, 1956; revised edition, 1965, 1970.
Bluff Your Way in Literature. London, Wolfe, 1966; New York, Cowles, 1968.
Fallen Women: A Sceptical Inquiry into the Treatment of Prostitutes, Their Clients, and Their Pimps in Literature. London, Nelson, 1969.
Poets Through Their Letters. London, Constable, and New York, Holt Rinehart, 1969.

Inside Poetry, with James Reeves. London, Heinemann, and
New York, Barnes and Noble, 1970.
Guide to Modern World Literature. London, Wolfe, 1973;
revised edition, London, Hodder and Stoughton, 4 vols.,
1975, London, Macmillan, 1 vol., 1984; as *Funk and Wagnalls Guide to Modern World Literature*, New York, Funk
and Wagnalls, 1973.
Sex and Society. London, Hodder and Stoughton, 1975.
Who's Who in Twentieth-Century Literature. London, Weidenfeld and Nicolson, 1976; New York, McGraw Hill, 1977.
An Introduction to Fifty European Novels. London, Pan,
1979; as *A Reader's Guide to Fifty European Novels*, London, Heinemann, and New York, Barnes and Noble, 1980.
The New Astrologer. London, Sidgwick and Jackson, 1981;
New York, Macmillan, 1983.
Robert Graves: His Life and Work. London, Hutchinson,
1982; New York, Holt Rinehart, 1983.

Editor, *Poetry from Oxford*. London, Fortune Press, 1953.
Editor, *Shakespeare's Sonnets*. London, Heinemann, 1963;
New York, Barnes and Noble, 1966.
Editor, *A Cupful of Tears: Sixteen Victorian Novelettes*. Lon-
don, Wolfe, 1965.
Editor, *Every Man in His Humour*, by Ben Jonson. London,
Benn, 1966; New York, Hill and Wang, 1968.
Editor, with James Reeves, *A New Canon of English Poetry*.
London, Heinemann, and New York, Barnes and Noble,
1967.
Editor, with James Reeves, *The Poems of Andrew Marvell*.
London, Heinemann, and New York, Barnes and Noble,
1969.
Editor, *Longer Elizabethan Poems*. London, Heinemann, and
New York, Barnes and Noble, 1970.
Editor, with James Reeves, *Selected Poems*, by Walt Whitman.
London, Heinemann, 1976.
Editor, *The English Sermon 1550-1650*. Cheadle, Cheshire,
Carcanet, 1976.
Editor, *The Mayor of Casterbridge*, by Thomas Hardy. Lon-
don, Penguin, 1978.
Editor, *Novels and Novelists: A Guide to the World of Fiction*.
London, Windward, and New York, St. Martin's Press, 1980.

*

Manuscript Collection: University of Texas, Austin.

Critical Study: "Poetry of Exactness" by Robert Nye, in *The
Scotsman* (Edinburgh), September 1963.

Martin Seymour-Smith comments:
(1970) My earlier poems tended to be "traditional" in form,
while the later ones are much freer—although they make full but
irregular use of rhyme. Browning seems to be a much more
persistent influence than until recently I would have liked to
acknowledge. I seem to write many poems about people: they
could be described, I suppose, as biographical poems. If I had to
sum up the kind of poem I should like to write (a hypothetical
question), I should probably say "something like Jacques Audiberti, but wholly anglicized and laced with plenty of native
humour." But I find answering questions like this damaging as I
write few poems and tend to conserve my energies for them. I like
a compact sort of poetry, and rely heavily on the non-
manufacturing side of myself in order to produce first drafts.
(1974) An introduction to my work as a poet for the general
reader would, I suppose, say that I am essentially a "phenomenological" poet but that I value coherence; that many people don't

seem to understand what I am about except when I am "being
funny"; that I never "submit" poems to anyone (except God), but
only send them when requested; that I find the general atmosphere of unread-poeticule-sucking-up-to-unread-poeticule irrelevant to what I am trying to do, since for any poet poetry is a
lonely business; that I would rather have, say, six (no, *ten*)
readers than a thousand carrion-fed unminds; that there are
contemporary poets whose poems I admire and to which I can
respond; that there is nothing left for me but to do exactly what I
have to do, in poetry, when I have to do it and in whatever way it
should be done; that I would rather be a poet than any kind of
dogmatist; that good grocerdom is undoubtedly more difficult
than good poetdom, but then in poetry the standards are considerably higher, too high.

*   *   *

Hart Crane once said: "Poetry, in so far as the metaphysics of
absolute knowledge extends, is simply the concrete evidence of
the experience of knowledge. It can give you a ratio of fact and
experience, and in this sense it is both perception and thing
perceived according as it approaches a significant articulation or
not."
Apart from a Fantasy Press pamphlet and an early book,
Poems, Martin Seymour-Smith has published only two collections, *Tea With Miss Stockport* and *Reminiscences of Norma*,
but the poems in these books which do not approach a significant articulation are few, for Seymour-Smith is nothing if not
fastidious—of language, and of the occasions when language
may permissibly aspire to poetry. Whether he is writing simply
about subtle thoughts and feelings, or with succinct irony at the
expense of his own sensitivity, his concern is the same: to "test"
the moment of self-knowledge by applying to it the resources of
an intelligent imagination. He is not a poet who finds questions
in his experience—in data "given" before the poem happens—
and then sets about providing himself, and us, with easy, knowing answers. Each poem is itself a questioning; when an answer is
offered it is usually tentative, an understatement of what has
been understood, and then that answer is often further qualified
by self-satire, as though the poet were mistrustful of where the
poem might take him, the satire being there to clarify his perception of his meaning. This makes for an intense and caustic poetry
of much exactness. See especially "The Northern Monster" in
the 1963 collection, and the thirteen poems which comprise
Section III of *Reminiscences of Norma*, and give that book its
title.

—Robert Nye

————————

SHAPCOTT, Thomas W(illiam). Australian. Born in Ipswich, Queensland, 21 March 1935. Educated at Ipswich Grammar School, 1949-50; University of Queensland, Brisbane, B.A.
in art 1968. Served in the National Service, 1953. Married 1)
Margaret Hodge in 1960, three daughters and one son; 2) Judith
Rodriguez, *q.v.*, in 1982. Clerk, H.S. Shapcott, Public Accountant, Ipswich, 1951-63; Partner, Shapcott and Shapcott, Accountant, Ipswich, 1963-72; Public Accountant, Sole Trader,
Ipswich, 1972-78. Since 1978, full-time writer. Since 1983, Director, Australia Council Literature Board, Sydney. Fellow, Australian Society of Accountants, 1970. Churchill Fellow (U.S.A.
and England), 1972. Member, Australian Arts Council Australian Literature Board, 1973. Recipient: Grace Leven Prize, 1962;

Sir Thomas White Memorial Prize, 1967; Sydney Myer Charity Trust Award, 1968, 1970; Canada-Australia prize, 1979. Address: 62 Cremorne Road, Cremorne, New South Wales 2060, Australia.

PUBLICATIONS

Verse

Time on Fire. Brisbane, Jacaranda Press, 1961.
Twelve Bagatelles. Adelaide, Australian Letters, 1962.
The Mankind Thing. Brisbane, Jacaranda Press, 1964.
Sonnets 1960-1963. Privately printed, 1964.
A Taste of Salt Water: Poems. Sydney, Angus and Robertson, 1967.
Inwards to the Sun. Brisbane, University of Queensland Press, 1969.
Fingers at Air: Experimental Poems 1969. Privately printed, 1969.
Begin with Walking. Brisbane, University of Queensland Press, 1972.
Interim Report. Privately printed, 1972.
Shabbytown Calendar. Brisbane, University of Queensland Press, 1975.
Seventh Avenue Poems. Sydney, Angus and Robertson, 1976.
Selected Poems. Brisbane, University of Queensland Press, 1979.
Turning Full Circle (prose poems). Sydney, Prism, 1979.
Stump and Grape and Bopple Nut (prose inventions). Brisbane, Bullion, 1981.
Welcome! St. Lucia, University of Queensland Press, 1983.

Play

The Seven Deadly Sins, music by Colin Brumby (produced Brisbane, 1970). Privately printed, 1970.

Novels

The Birthday Gift. St. Lucia, University of Queensland Press, 1982.
White Stag of Exile. Melbourne, Allen Lane, 1984.

Other

Focus on Charles Blackman (art monograph). Brisbane, University of Queensland Press, 1967.
Poetry as a Creative Learning Process. Kelvin Grove, Queensland, Kelvin Grove College of Advanced Education, 1978.
Flood Children (for children). Brisbane, Jacaranda Press, 1981.

Editor, with Rodney Hall, *New Impulses in Australian Poetry.* Brisbane, Univeristy of Queensland Press, 1968.
Editor, *Australian Poetry Now.* Melbourne, Sun, 1969.
Editor, *Poets on Record.* Brisbane, University of Queensland Press, 1970-73.
Editor, *Contemporary American and Australian Poetry.* Brisbane, University of Queensland Press, 1976.
Editor, *Consolidation: The Second Paperback Poets Anthology.* Brisbane, University of Queensland Press, 1982.

*

Manuscript Collections: Australian National Library, Canberra; Fryer Library, University of Queensland, Brisbane.

Critical Studies: by L. Clancy, in *Meanjin Quarterly* (Melbourne), 1967; Carl Harrison-Ford, in *Meanjin Quarterly* (Melbourne), 1972; interview in *Makar 11* (Brisbane), no. 3.

Thomas W. Shapcott comments:

(1980) When I first began writing and publishing poetry, in the 1950's, I was soaking myself eagerly in T.S. Eliot and Dylan Thomas, that decade's heroes, as well as discovering new worlds in the important Penguin anthologies of that period. When I had begun to be published I made contact with my own contemporaries and my Australian peers. I have always been interested in experimentation, in the challenge of form (closed forms, open forms), but in the 1950's experimental writing was unfashionable—and unpublishable. My early lyricism was more immediately accepted. In recent years I have been concerned with exploring ways of balancing essentially lyrical expression with the cadence of lyric speech.

I have always been interested in expressing a sense of region, whether it be the provincial backwaters of "Shabbytown" or "Seventh Avenue" mobility. But my essential concern has always been with issues of personality and belief: I once wrote "I believe poetry is a movement towards celebration. Art—Poetry—is to struggle toward the light, knowing the light burns all sight to blindness. We cannot outstare the sun, but it is not in our nature to endure the darkness. Thus all true poetry is in some way a form of experimentation, a groping outwards. Even the earth is moving, how can we stand still?" I still hold to that.

(1985) I still hold to that. Recent work in prose has been an attempt to integrate lyric form and tone with narrative and documentary techniques: it all becomes, in different ways, *evidence.*

*   *   *

In the development of the prolific Thomas W. Shapcott can be seen something of the history of Australian poetry since 1960. One major change, with which Shapcott was involved in his editorial and critical capacities, was the directing of attention to North America. With that re-alignment of allegiance went changes in the linguistic and formal nature of poetry, a transference of primacy from world to word, from the notion of the poem as recording, as when Shapcott says that his early poems "explored primarily responses to environment and a young man's apprehension of life," to the notion of the poem as an "invention," a word recurrent in Shapcott's later work.

The relatively early "Shadow of War" is eminently representative of Australian poetry as it had developed after 1940. It presents a world of solid and steady images, a rural world in which the intersection of landscape and human experience is effected by building the poem around a dramatic or narrative nexus. It is serious, with emotion contained by normative syntax and formal stanzaic structures, as when the evacuated boys watch their farmer-host turn away from the black cockatoos threatening his corn:

> We were too young to price the waste of a crop,
> or the shrug of that grim man, whose son was new dead
> in a battle out of reach. On the dead verandah
> we played at soldiers, khaki and black and red,
> and our cries were jeering birds on fire overhead.

In "Sestina with Refrain" (1976) we hear a very different voice, self-conscious about form, playing typographical games, fracturing syntax and narrative sequence as the speaker resists the "bruising" of his dead First War father:

and why me so long after War's so tired let it die
our century congeals with veterans all "War Babies" all
with obsessive yarns (horrible: back off) poolrooms are
    stuck
with them *me mate's jaw shot clean through and some-*
thing or other
gurgling there a voice faint & hoarse the call for water
what can you say remember it's over dad dead lie still

Nonetheless, in the 1975 collection *Shabbytown Calendar*, we can see reasons for speaking of "a range of underlying preoccupations" and one way of tracking Shapcott's continuity-in-progress is by the trees he has blazed en route. In early poems, generic trees are respectfully celebrated in grave, faintly mystical diction. But in 1965-70, when the historical poems emerge, not all their figures are as actual or admirable as "Macquarie as Father": among the historical inventions are tree-haters and tree-fellers like the convict who will "cut down every tree," because "Nobody told me trees watched,/connived, were not still,/were never still." And it is in the American "Central Park" poems that modernist trees appear, elements in a fragmented experience, to be composed by perception.

The mind-invented tree is not surprisingly present in "Casuarina Myth" from the so-called prose inventions of *Stump and Grape and Bopple Nut*, which, with a collection of prose poems and two novels, intervene between *Selected Poems* and *Welcome* (1983). Here, in "Ficus Benjaminii" the playfulness developed in the prose poems colours the irony whereby it is the remembered tree that language makes present in the poem, while the potplants literally confronting the peregrinatory poet are "only the rootless exile of its name." The poem's conclusion can be seen as a prelude to Shapcott's most recent work, *White Stag of Exile*, a summation, holding together in its mixed prose and verse form many of the thematic and formal elements persistent in his writing.

—Jennifer Strauss

* * *

SHAPIRO, David (Joel). American. Born in Newark, New Jersey, 2 January 1947. Educated at Columbia University, New York, B.A. (magna cum laude) 1968, Ph.D. 1973; Clare College, Cambridge (Kellett Fellow, 1968-70), B.A. (honours), 1970, M.A. 1974. Married Lindsay Stamm in 1970; one child. Instructor and Assistant Professor of English, Columbia University, 1972-81. Visiting Professor, Brooklyn College, 1979, and Princeton University, New Jersey, 1982-83. Since 1980, Writer-in-Residence, Cooper Union, New York, and William Paterson College, Wayne, New Jersey. Since 1963, a violinist with several orchestras, including the New Jersey Symphony and the American Symphony; since 1970, editorial associate, *Art News*, New York. Recipient: Gotham Book Mart award, 1962; Bread Loaf Writers Conference Robert Frost Fellowship, 1965; Ingram Merrill Foundation Fellowship, 1967; Book-of-the-Month Club Fellowship, 1968; Creative Artists Public Service grant, 1974; Morton Dauwen Zabel Award, 1977; National Endowment for the Arts grant, 1979, 1980. Address: 560 Riverside Drive, Apartment 16K, New York, New York 10027, U.S.A.

PUBLICATIONS

Verse

Poems. Privately printed, 1960.

A Second Winter. Privately printed, 1961.
When Will the Bluebird. Privately printed, 1962.
January: A Book of Poems. New York, Holt Rinehart, 1965.
Poems from Deal. New York, Dutton, 1969.
A Man Holding an Acoustic Panel. New York, Dutton, 1971.
The Dance of Things. New York, Lincoln Center, 1971.
The Page-Turner. New York, Liveright, 1973.
Lateness (single poem). New York, Nobodaddy Press, 1976.
Lateness (collection). Woodstock, New York, Overlook Press, 1978.
To an Idea. New York, Overlook Press, 1983.

Other

John Ashbery: An Introduction to the Poetry. New York, Columbia University Press, 1979.
Poets and Painters (exhibition catalog). Denver, Denver Art Museum, 1979.
Jim Dine: Painting What One Is. New York, Abrams, 1981.
Jasper Johns: Drawings 1954-1984. New York, Abrams, 1984.

Editor, with Ron Padgett, *An Anthology of New York Poets.* New York, Random House, 1970.

Translator, with Arthur A. Cohen, *The New Art of Color: The Writings of Robert and Sonia Delaunay.* New York, Viking Press, 1978.

Composer: incidental music for *The Scotty Dog* by Kenneth Koch, produced New York, 1967.

*

Manuscript Collection: Syracuse University Library, New York.

Critical Studies: in *New York Review of Books*, Christmas 1971; unpublished master's theses by Stephen Paul Miller, City University of New York, and Michael Simon, Brown University, Providence, Rhode Island, 1977.

Theatrical Activities:
Director: **Film**—*House* (*Blown Apart*), 1984.

David Shapiro comments:
Simone Weil said, "The Fool, taken literally, is speaking the truth." Often, in my favorite poets, paradoxia and "nonsense" achieve not so much the ambiguity analysed denotatively and connotatively by Mr. Empson, but a pointing to logos by its extreme absence. As early tribes were obsessed by shadows, convinced that an animal's shadow was part of the animal, so Stein, Carroll, Borges employ the techniques of "nonsense" because they are convinced, like me, that the poet's task is to subdue—in Rimbaud's terms—the formless. If the task of positivism was to expunge nonsense, the work of poetry is to use it. That is "the meaning of meaninglessness," to use nonsense and uncertainty and discontinuity as the central tone and abiding metaphor of our peculiar predicament.

* * *

David Shapiro is one of the most gifted members of what has come to be called the "New York School" of poetry, a loose confederation of talents inspired by the work of the late Frank O'Hara, John Ashbery, and Kenneth Koch.

Shapiro's poetry, although profoundly influenced by John Ashbery, whose sinuous intelligence and command of French poetic sources have stamped Shapiro's imagination, is nonetheless thoroughly original in the production of his imagery. The Shapiro image, nervous, agitated, associative in the psychoanalytic sense of eliciting connections from puns, sense confusions (both mystical and Rimbaudian), and fabulous and incredible synecdoches often leaves the reader gasping for meaning. However, there is throughout his work a hard rock of intelligence and arbitrariness and it is these which give assurance that his work will continue to explore and colonize the *terra incognita* between private worlds—childhood, music, love, suffering, madness—and the concerns of the reader. A very large talent, David Shapiro will surely, as *The Page-Turner* demonstrates, emerge as a major American poet.

—Arthur A. Cohen

SHAPIRO, Harvey. American. Born in Chicago, Illinois, 27 January 1924. Educated at Yale University, New Haven, Connecticut, B.A. 1947; Columbia University, New York, M.A. 1948. Served in the United States Army Air Force during World War II: Distinguished Flying Cross. Married Edna Lewis Kaufman in 1953; two sons. Instructor in English, Cornell University, Ithaca, New York, 1949-50, 1951-52; Creative Writing Fellow, Bard College, Annandale-on-Hudson, New York, 1950-51. Staff member, *Commentary*, New York, 1955-56, and *The New Yorker*, 1956-57. Assistant Editor, 1957-75, and since 1983 Deputy Editor, *New York Times Magazine*; Editor, *New York Times Book Review*, 1975-83. Recipient: YMHA Poetry Center award, 1952; Swallow Press award, 1954; Rockefeller grant, 1967. Address: 175 Clinton Street, Brooklyn, New York 11201, U.S.A.

PUBLICATIONS

Verse

The Eye. Denver, Swallow, 1953.
The Book and Other Poems. Cummington, Massachusetts, Cummington Press, 1955.
Mountain, Fire, Thornbush. Denver, Swallow, 1961.
Battle Report: Selected Poems. Middletown, Connecticut, Wesleyan University Press, 1966.
This World. Middletown, Connecticut, Wesleyan University Press, 1971.
Lauds. New York, Sun, 1975.
Lauds and Nightsounds. New York, Sun, 1978.
The Light Holds. Middletown, Connecticut, Wesleyan University Press, 1984.

*

Critical Studies: by David Ignatow, in *The Nation* (New York), 24 April 1967; "Rebels in the Kingdom" by Jascha Kessler, in *Midstream* (New York), April 1972.

Harvey Shapiro comments:
   My earlier work is marked by a preoccupation with Jewish (Hebraic) themes. In my later work I have followed mainly chassidic teachings. My later poems are free verse (earlier poems were more formal), anecdotal (based on autobiographical anec-

dotes), attempts to discover "The Way" (a way of right living). They have urban settings. But many have mystical (kabbalistic or chassidic or zen) underpinnings. Martin Buber has been an influence throughout.

*   *   *

Harvey Shapiro is among the few contemporary American poets who express a strong sense of gratitude toward life, an attitude of deep Hasidic awareness. And yet he is often a poet of despair and depression. Poetry is for him, clearly, a vehicle of redemption and understanding, as in "A Gift":

> She made him a gift of her touch,
> Softly turning the collar of his jacket down
> In the crowded elevator. To say,
> See, my spirit still hovers to protect.
>
> That he could prize such useless moments.
>
> Motorbikes break the night's silence.
> The President's face on the television screen.
> Green on my set. Words muffling perception.
> Everything keeps us from the truth, which
> Begins to have a religious presence.
> Why so many claim it, in the tail of the tiger
> Or elsewhere. No matter. When I find it,
> Being so rare, it is fiercer than whiskey.
> My eyes burn with happiness and I speak
> Collected into myself.

Shapiro is an urban poet, not only of New York City, his chief haunt and inspiration, but of many cities. He renders their anomie and despair, their loneliness, but he also bears witness to their bright miracles. His major poem, "A Jerusalem Notebook," states his aesthetic, honed on Hasidic and Zen awareness of small miracles in life:

> My way of being in the world:
> not perfect freedom or the pitch
> of madness, but that the particulars
> of my life become manifest
> to me walking these dark streets.

Shapiro clearly strives for simplicity; the scenes are familiar, and his presentation is as colloquial and straightforward as something from William Carlos Williams or Louis Simpson. Like theirs, his urgency seeks the underlying mystery; the poems are informed by an agonizing sense of purpose. A world busy with random chaos is a troubling challenge to the poet's quest for certainty—and Shapiro boldly confronts those terrors to which modern man is prey. Fortunately, some of the answers he finds are comforting:

> Whatever brought me here, to a new moon
> over Zion's hill, dark moon
> with the thin cusp silvered,
> help me believe in my happiness....

He finds too that happiness is not easy for philosophers:

> Illusions of my own ego causing destruction
> while outside the marvelous
> machinery of day has opened, light
> traffic on the road to the citadel.

Shapiro's poems share his search for love, his fight against depression, and his response to the bewildering assault of what we often term popular culture. His universe is richly inhabited, at times as crowded as an Expressionist nightmare, as in "Causing Anguish":

> That face
> is dead in my eyes, dead as an empty theater,
> which once meant festival, drinks
> on the house, erotic fantasy time,
> the Stones sending down
> clusters of bright balloons from the rafters
> of Madison Square Garden while
> the girl in front waved her ass
> and waved her ass.

Shapiro keeps trying to remember: "Rabbi Nachman's final message:/Gevalt! Do not despair!/There is no such thing as despair at all!/Shouted from the very depths of the heart" ("Learning"). Clearly, that's not easy, particularly since he is haunted by images of Holocaust and "an antique war drifting through my head." He served in the Air Force in World War II, and was awarded the Distinguished Flying Cross. The war is obviously an obsessive reference, as in "Memorial Day":

> no more real now
> than the Late Late Show.
> I don't even tell
> the stories any more. I don't
> remember what death
> was like. I can't even see
> the dead crewmen.
> Only enough memory left
> to feel the sun.

Surviving in the postwar period becomes a test of faith: "Forcing the spirit in New York/is the commonplace, we live/there as if we were in Jerusalem" ("A Jerusalem Notebook").

Shapiro sometimes shows us that he seeks the poem that might sum up a lifetime's search: "I play the role out. It is/not to tell the world/anything. What is it/the world would want to know?" ("City").

Harvey Shapiro is among our best contemporary poets, and he has also had an important career as an editor of *The New York Times Book Review*. In that post he has helped interpret our literary culture, and has unselfishly affirmed the careers of others.

—David Ray

SHAPIRO, Karl (Jay). American. Born in Baltimore, Maryland, 10 November 1913. Educated at the University of Virginia, Charlottesville, 1932-33; Johns Hopkins University, Baltimore, 1937-39; Pratt Library School, Baltimore, 1940. Served in the United States Army, 1941-45. Married 1) Evalyn Katz in 1945 (divorced, 1967), two daughters and one son; 2) Teri Kovach in 1967 (died, 1982). Associate Professor, Johns Hopkins University, 1947-50; Visiting Professor, University of Wisconsin, Madison, 1948, and Loyola University, Chicago, 1951-52; Visiting Professor, University of California, Berkeley and Davis, 1955-56, and University of Indiana, Bloomington,

1956-57; Professor of English, University of Nebraska, Lincoln, 1956-66, University of Illinois, Chicago Circle, 1966-68, and University of California, Davis, 1968-84. Editor, *Poetry*, Chicago, 1950-56, *Newberry Library Bulletin*, Chicago, 1953-55, and *Prairie Schooner*, Lincoln, Nebraska, 1956-66. Consultant in Poetry, 1946-47, and Whittall Lecturer, 1964, 1967, Library of Congress, Washington, D.C.; Lecturer, Salzburg Seminar in American Studies, 1952; State Department Lecturer, India, 1955; Elliston Lecturer, University of Cincinnati, 1959. Recipient: Jeannette Sewell Davis Prize, 1942, Levinson Prize, 1942, Eunice Tietjens Memorial Prize, 1961, and Oscar Blumenthal Prize, 1963 (*Poetry*, Chicago); *Contemporary Poetry* prize, 1943; American Academy grant, 1944; Guggenheim Fellowship, 1944, 1953; Pulitzer Prize, 1945; Shelley Memorial Award, 1946; Kenyon School of Letters Fellowship, 1956, 1957; Bollingen Prize, 1969. D.H.L.: Wayne State University, Detroit, 1960; D. Litt.: Bucknell University, Lewisburg, Pennsylvania, 1972. Fellow in American Letters, Library of Congress; Member, American Academy of Arts and Sciences, and American Academy, 1959. Address: 904 Radcliffe Drive, Davis, California 95616, U.S.A.

PUBLICATIONS

Verse

Poems. Privately printed, 1935.
Five Young American Poets, with others. New York, New Directions, 1941.
The Place of Love. Melbourne, Comment Press, 1942.
Person, Place and Thing. New York, Reynal, 1942; London, Secker and Warburg, 1944.
V-Letter and Other Poems. New York, Reynal, 1944; London, Secker and Warburg, 1945.
Essay on Rime. New York, Reynal, 1945; London, Secker and Warburg, 1947.
Trial of a Poet and Other Poems. New York, Reynal, 1947.
Poems 1940-1953. New York, Random House, 1953.
The House. Privately printed, 1957.
Poems of a Jew. New York, Random House, 1958.
The Bourgeois Poet. New York, Random House, 1964.
Selected Poems. New York, Random House, 1968.
There Was That Roman Poet Who Fell in Love at Fifty-Odd. Chicago, Madison Park Press, 1968.
White-Haired Lover. New York, Random House, 1968.
Auden (1907-1973). Davis, University of California Library Associates, 1974.
Adult Bookstore. New York, Random House, 1976.
Collected Poems 1940-1977. New York, Random House, 1978.
Love and War, Art and God. Winston-Salem, North Carolina, Stuart Wright, 1984.

Plays

The Tenor, with Ernst Lert, adaptation of a work by Wedekind, music by Hugo Weisgall (produced 1952). Bryn Mawr, Pennsylvania, Merion Music, 1957.
The Soldier's Tale, adaptation of libretto by C.F. Ramuz, music by Stravinsky (produced Chicago, 1968). Chicago, University of Chicago Department of Music, 1968.

Novel

Edsel. New York, Geis, 1971.

Other

English Prosody and Modern Poetry. Baltimore, Johns Hopkins Press, 1947.
A Bibliography of Modern Prosody. Baltimore, Johns Hopkins Press, 1948.
Poets at Work, with others, edited by Charles D. Abbott. New York, Harcourt Brace, 1948.
Beyond Criticism. Lincoln, University of Nebraska Press, 1953; as *A Primer for Poets*, 1965.
In Defense of Ignorance (essays). New York, Random House, 1960.
Start with the Sun: Studies in Cosmic Poetry, with James E. Miller, Jr., and Bernice Slote. Lincoln, University of Nebraska Press, 1960.
The Writer's Experience, with Ralph Ellison. Washington, D.C., Library of Congress, 1964.
A Prosody Handbook, with Robert Beum. New York, Harper, 1965.
Randall Jarrell. Washington, D.C., Library of Congress, 1967.
To Abolish Children and Other Essays. Chicago, Quadrangle, 1968.
The Poetry Wreck: Selected Essays 1950-1970. New York, Random House, 1975.

Editor, with Louis Untermeyer and Richard Wilbur, *Modern American and Modern British Poetry*, revised shorter edition. New York, Harcourt Brace, 1955.
Editor, *American Poetry.* New York, Crowell, 1960.
Editor, *Prose Keys to Modern Poetry.* New York, Harper, 1962.
Editor, *Tryne*, by Cynthia Bates, Steve Ellzey, and Bill Lynch. Privately printed, 1976.

*

Bibliography: *Karl Shapiro: A Descriptive Bibliography 1933-1977* by Lee Bartlett, New York, Garland, 1979.

Manuscript Collection: Library of Congress, Washington, D.C.

Critical Study: *Karl Shapiro* by Joseph Reino, Boston, Twayne, 1981.

*   *   *

The poetic career of Karl Shapiro is remarkable for its high accomplishment in various styles—all of them his own creations—and for its abrupt, unpredictable departures into new and fruitful territories. From *Person, Place and Thing*, published while he was still in the army, to the bold cycle of love poems, *White-Haired Lover*, his writing shows considerable range as well as changing interests and attitudes. His criticism, of which we can say little here, is perceptive, vigorous, and frequently outspoken; the opinions and judgments it expresses usually reflect the stylistic or other preoccupations of his poetry.

Much of Shapiro's earlier work, and that of his American contemporaries John Berryman, Delmore Schwartz, Muriel Rukeyser, Weldon Kees, and others, demonstrates a concern with the life and institutions of modern society. Like Auden, MacNeice, and Spender in England, whose influence they doubtless felt, these poets struggled towards individual styles that would embrace both personal intuition and public experience. No one is more successful in this achievement than Shapiro: the poetry of his first three books is polished, elegant, witty, conversational, but also marked by deep compassion and humanity quite evident in such poems as "Auto Wreck," "The Leg," and "Elegy for a Dead Soldier." A large number of pieces from the 1940's explore with surgical skill the ironies, hypocrisies, prejudices, and illusions of America and its institutions. "University" begins: "To hurt the Negro and avoid the Jew/Is the curriculum." In his poems about Hollywood he concentrates on its falsities, its manufactured dreams, but also wonders if it doesn't express something inherent in the nation:

> O can we understand it? Is it ours,
> A crude whim of a beginning people,
> A private orgy in a secluded spot?

And the poem "Necropolis" confronts the inequalities which persist between rich and poor even beyond the boundaries of death, reputedly the great equalizer.

In all of these poems Shapiro's voice and conscience are representative of humanity, take man's part before the spectacle and trials of modern existence; yet we find some poems—the sequence "Recapitulations" is an example—that reveal more closely his own life and private feelings. With *Trial of a Poet*, the first of several indications of change and experiment appears—in this instance, two prose poems which look forward to Shapiro's radical adoption of that form later for an entire book, *The Bourgeois Poet*. In addition, the new "Adam and Eve" sequence with which he opens his selected *Poems 1940-1953* announces a growing fascination with Jewish themes that leads directly on to his initial, unexpected departure from previous work in *Poems of a Jew*, a collection that includes both earlier and recent pieces and whose introduction is provocative; in it he attempts to identify a "Jewish consciousness" that is man "absolutely committed to the world" but also "essentially himself, beyond nationality, defenseless against the crushing impersonality of history." He cites Joyce's Leopold Bloom, "neither hero nor victim," as the best example of this "free modern Jew." Together with the controversial but enormously stimulating volume of critical essays, *In Defense of Ignorance* (the title and contents of which attack intellectualism and the New Criticism), published two years later, *Poems of a Jew* starts Shapiro off on a poetically rewarding quest for identity. If his criticism occasionally overstates matters, that is probably necessary in order to overthrow his allegiance to the literary prescriptions handed down by Eliot and the New Critics and to take up the support of such strong but too often neglected writers as Whitman, Lawrence, Henry Miller, and W.C. Williams.

The Bourgeois Poet, which follows after these first repudiations of artistic and intellectual convention, provides a complete breakthrough into novel, difficult areas of literary form. The prose poem, utilizing the prose paragraph, has a fine tradition in French literature but has seldom proved manageable in English. However, Shapiro's success is remarkable; the poems have a marvellous flexibility in mood, tone, and temper; they shift from the satirical to the lyric to the dreamlike or irrational with rhythmic facility and strength. This book belongs in a line of descent from Rimbaud, Joyce's *Ulysses*, Henry Miller, Céline, and Isaac Singer.

Shapiro's newest work does not simply try to repeat *The Bourgeois Poet*; he undertakes a certain artistic retrenchment in the love poems, though they profit immensely from his prose experiments and are themselves frank, intimate, tender, and moving—the latest instance of powerful exploratory imaginative gifts.

—Ralph J. Mills, Jr.

SHELTON, Richard. American. Born in Boise, Idaho, 24 June 1933. Educated at Harding College, Searcy, Arkansas, 1951-53; Abilene Christian College, Texas, B.A. in English 1958; University of Arizona, Tucson, M.A. 1960. Served in the United States Army, 1956-58. Married Lois Bruce in 1956; one son. Teacher, Lowell School, Bisbee, Arizona, 1958-60; Director, Ruth Stephan Poetry Center, Tucson, 1964-65. Instructor, 1960-64, Assistant Professor, 1969-73, Associate Professor, 1973-79, and since 1979, Professor of English, University of Arizona, Tucson. Recipient: International Poetry Forum United States award, 1970; Borestone Mountain award, 1972; National Endowment for the Arts fellowship, 1976. Address: Department of English, University of Arizona, Tucson, Arizona 85721, U.S.A.

PUBLICATIONS

Verse

Journal of Return. San Francisco, Kayak, 1969.
The Tattooed Desert. Pittsburgh, University of Pittsburgh Press, 1971.
The Heroes of Our Time. Lincoln, Nebraska, Best Cellar Press, 1972.
Of All the Dirty Words. Pittsburgh, University of Pittsburgh Press, 1972.
Calendar: A Cycle of Poems. Phoenix, Arizona, Baleen Press, 1972.
Among the Stones. Pittsburgh, Monument Press, 1973.
Chosen Place. Crete, Nebraska, Best Cellar Press, 1975.
You Can't Have Everything. Pittsburgh, University of Pittsburgh Press, 1975.
Desert Water. Pittsburgh, Monument Press, 1977.
The Bus to Veracruz. Pittsburgh, University of Pittsburgh Press, 1978.
Selected Poems 1969-1981. Pittsburgh, University of Pittsburgh Press, 1982.
A Kind of Glory. Port Townsend, Washington, Copper Canyon Press, 1982.

*

Critical Studies: in *Chicago Tribune Magazine*, 22 January 1970; *Prairie Schooner* (Lincoln, Nebraska), Summer 1972; *Poetry* (Chicago), July 1972, July 1973, and April 1978; *San Francisco Chronicle*, 27 May 1973; Dave Smith, in *Los Angeles Times*, 19 February 1978; Philip Allan Friedman, in *Gramercy Review* (New York), Summer 1979; *Rereadings* by Michael Hogan, Crete, Nebraska, Best Cellar Press, 1979; Victor Contoski, in *Western American Literature* (Logan, Utah), xiv, 1, 1979.

Richard Shelton comments:
I hope my work reflects something of the Sonora Desert, in which I have lived for more than 25 years.

*   *   *

At 25, Richard Shelton moved from Texas to southern Arizona (Tucson), where he has lived ever since, teaching literature courses at the University of Arizona and writing book after book of his perceptions and responses to the desert climate and terrain

he has called his "chosen place." Shelton is now an inveterate Southwesterner with deep, often spiritual affinity for the rocks and saguaro cactus of the desert, the mountains, the sea a hundred miles below him in the Gulf of California. These are his usual subjects in the many books he has written since his first publication, *Journal of Return.* The sea and desert are the extremes of his personal mythology; they frame the earth for him, an earth of silences, of ghostly night animals, of rocks that exchange brief whispers about the moon on nights of the long dry season. Tucson is ringed with mountains, the Tucson Mountains, Mt. Lemmon, Mica Mountain, and others, and they are a third dimension of nature for him, an urge of nature to thrust up into the sky, a dream of the rocks that lie scattered on the desert floor. The night sky is a brilliance of immense stars in Shelton's poems, under which dark, quiet, sometimes desperate lives are endured.

His verse technique consolidates some extreme tendencies of recent American poetry—the spiritual visions of nature to be found in Robinson Jeffers's and William Stafford's work together with Robert Lowell's painful self-excoriations; but the result for Shelton is often more discord and discontinuity than wholeness of vision. The desert remains for him an ambiguous metaphor—either it is a spiritual paradise or it is the hell of exiled human life. As a result, his poetry never leaps fully into one or the other possibility, but seems suspended between a potential vision of desert infinities and an obsession with his own life-long unhappiness and scepticism ("Mexico"):

> I never find what I am looking for
> and each time I return older
> with my ugliness intact
> but with the knowledge that if it isn't there
> in the darkness under Scorpio
> it isn't anywhere

He writes as though his own individuality will never quite hatch out to the larger realm of nature he longs to be part of.

This alone would be sufficiently interesting drama or poetry, but for Shelton it tends to sever his poetry from its intended depth and freedom. His canon has no perceptible growth or development of vision, but rather moves through cycles of restatement and reexamination of his dilemma. At his best, he can render the desert world with striking immediacy, particularly where he feels himself to be its interpreter and voice, as in "The Kingdom of the Moon":

> the moon commands the desert cold
> a word so harsh
> it splits the tongue
> of the true aloe
>
> the moon pulls stones
> to the surface
> and directs the ghosts
> of dry rivers in their paths
> toward the sea

And again, in "Burning":

> today the rain kept
> coming back as if it had
> nowhere else to go
>
> and each time
> the desert welcomed it

> the gates of the desert
> never rust but they open
> only to the voice of rain

Shelton's poetry must be judged-carefully—if it is at times didactic, sentimental, indeterminate, or merely repetitious of statement, these limitations are along the way of a large and beautiful intention: to capture a region and to impose upon it a human witness and contact of extraordinary thoroughness and sensitivity. Many of his poems will drop away in time, but what will remain of his canon will be durable lyrics that are essentially American in their effort to find spiritual jointure with the land.

—Paul Christensen

SHERWIN, Judith Johnson.   American.   Born in New York City, 3 October 1936. Educated at the Dalton Schools, New York, graduated 1954; Radcliffe College, Cambridge, Massachusetts, 1954-55; Barnard College, New York, B.A. (cum laude) 1958 (Phi Beta Kappa); Columbia University, New York (Woodrow Wilson Fellow, 1958), 1958-59. Married James T. Sherwin in 1955; three children. Promotion Manager, Arrow Press, New York, 1961; Instructor, Poetry Center, New York, 1976, 1978, 1981; Poet-in-Residence, Wake Forest University, Winston-Salem, North Carolina, 1980. Poet-in-Residence, 1980-81, and since 1981, Assistant Professor of English, State University of New York, Albany. President, 1975-78, and Chairman of the Executive Committee, 1979-80, Poetry Society of America. Recipient: Academy of American Poets prize, 1958; Yaddo fellowship, 1964; Poetry Society of America fellowship, 1964; Aspen Writers Workshop Rose Fellowship, 1967; Yale Series of Younger Poets Award, 1968; *St. Andrews Review* prize, 1975; *Playboy* award, for fiction, 1977; National Endowment for the Arts fellowship, 1981. Agent: Charlotte Sheedy Literary Agency, 145 West 86th Street, New York, New York 10024. Address: Department of English, State University of New York, Albany, New York 12203, U.S.A.

PUBLICATIONS

Verse

Uranium Poems.   New Haven, Connecticut, Yale University Press, 1969.
Impossible Buildings.   New York, Doubleday, 1973.
Waste: The Town Scold, Transparencies, Dead's Good Company.   Taftsville, Vermont, Countryman Press, 3 vols., 1977-79.
How the Dead Count.   New York, Norton, 1978.

Plays

Belisa's Love (produced New York, 1959).
En Avant, Coco (produced New York, 1961).
two untitled multimedia works (produced Brussels, 1971, 1972).
Waste (multimedia; produced London, 1972).

Short Stories

The Life of Riot.   New York, Atheneum, 1970.

*

Critical Studies: by Hayden Carruth, in *Harper's* (New York), June 1978, and *The Nation* (New York), January 1979; *Choice* (Middletown, Connecticut), July-August and December 1978; Rochelle Ratner, in *Soho Weekly News* (New York), 7 September 1978.

Judith Johnson Sherwin comments:

My poetry comes across in readings as drama or music more than as text. I enjoy reading with cool jazz or with quiet electronic music which provides spaces in the sound and between the sounds. Much of my poetry is meant to be sung or chanted or belted out in the shower.

All my life I have refused to let myself be limited to any theory of what poetry should be, either in form or in content. I write traditional sonnet sequences and I write surreal poems and sound poems. Every form, every technique is of equal interest; I should feel dissatisfied with my mind if there were any approach to poetry that did not excite me to see if I could go out and do likewise.

My writing, poetry, fiction and drama, is both feminist and political, but it is neither didactic nor hortatory. I write about my life as a woman and as a political animal because that's where my life is, those are the questions I have to face. However, I don't know the answers; any answer I examine is hypothesis, not conclusion.

I try to make a rough music, a dance of the mind, a calculus of the emotions, a driving beat of praise out of the pain and mystery that surround me and become me. My poems are meant to make your mind get up and shout.

*   *   *

Judith Johnson Sherwin's poems deal with the devastating effects of modern politics; they also constitute a weapon to defy it. Her style is characterized by incantatory repetitions and a skewed tense diction which strains the limits of conventional grammar and syntax. She often uses classic forms, sonnet and quatrain, updated with slant rhyme. Her similes and metaphors are extended and bizarre, drawn from the absurd artifacts of contemporary plastic culture but also reminiscent of the 17th-century metaphysical "conceit." Yet Sherwin's sensibility is ultra-modern, influenced by and reflective of jazz music, radio ads, and technological innovations.

Her style originated in her first book, *Uranium Poems*, where words pile up and hammer on each other without breath-break, a style suited to that book's theme and metaphor: uranium mining destroys the earth to procure ores to make bombs that destroy the world. There Sherwin also began to develop a theme which continues into her most recent work: various deaths permeate our lives, especially the death that haunts love and the bitter political deaths of our time—the murders by Eichmann, Marilyn Monroe's suicide. Love and human feeling are difficult to manifest in this destructive environment, but the poet is struggling to assert and maintain them.

In her second collection, *Impossible Buildings*, Sherwin is still hardheaded but her language and forms are less rough-hewn. In "Materials," a sequence of ten sonnets, each poems focusses on a natural substance, such as ice, wood, water, and each is made an elegant symbol for an aspect of sexual love. The prevailing theme there is larger than love, however, as the title poem makes clear. "Impossible buildings," as in M.C. Escher's drawings, are built by the artist's mind at its creative work: "the construction is/the information."

Her latest poems, in *How the Dead Count*, while often elegiac in tone (as in the long title poem) are also often angry and satiric. The stock-exchange mentality, Henry Kissinger, capitalist and technological abuses, all receive her contempt. Love comes back in this book too, as a freighted theme, a sometimes ebullient emotion but frequently bereft and sad in severance from the loved one, as in the section entitled "From Brussels." Grief shakes her and in "The Wake for Myself" induces a painful wittiness and word-play like John Donne's: "now soul, my soul, you lie so long apart/an entity, what was so long a part/and still i must retake you part by part/i search you with my study, and you fade." In this section extreme emotion leads to yet wilder metaphors—the yeti, dead yellowjackets, an acrobat's highwire, burned dinners, stereo records:

> one day the doorbell,
> striped eagles flapping their wings, rocketing
> care packages down (and i need them), they're
> mined, they go off,
> flash, sputter, burn out, but one...
> i grab, quick, tear, in it a record...
>   i dive
> onto it, drool all over it, crunch, gobble
> it down, ouch, the cut edges cut
> my throat

The pain of love rises out of conflict with, and seems to be the price of, the poet's life as an independent woman and artist. Yet this independence is also felt as an elemental source of power, not destructive to life. In "Three Power Dances" she creates the totem of herself:

> a great Female Bear
>   wide as a house   sings
> out of Her dark cave
>   under her fringed roots   sings
>   up from Her furred clutch   sings.

The emphasis is on female being over male doing: "I hold back your day/your death dance, your night of war/This is My Power dance."

The final assertion of this defiant yet profoundly compassionate sensibility comes in the title poem "How the Dead Count," an elegy for the young dead of the civil rights movement and the Vietnam war, which continues the theme of death intermingled with our lives. These deaths are terrifying but bring creative richness to birth in us. It is a cosmic theme which fully encompasses Sherwin's gift for song, and for intense, far-reaching comparisons as well as her love and commitment to the human creature:

> I will say: sweet are the bells...
> the ponderous gongs, the living breathing bells
> of the blood of the dead, the dead
> of the mouths of my city...
> as the dead count their words, as the dead count
> their wounds, as the dead count
> their lives in us, as the dead count
> continually, sweet singer say and
>   say
> as the dead count.

—Jane Augustine

SHUTTLE, Penelope (Diane). British. Born in Staines, Middlesex, 12 May 1947. Educated at Staines Grammar School, 1952-59; Matthew Arnold County Secondary School, 1959-65. Married to Peter Redgrove, *q.v.*; one daughter. Part-time shorthand typist, 1965-69. Recipient: Arts Council grant, 1969, 1972; Greenwood Poetry Prize, 1972; Eric Gregory Award, 1974. Lives in Falmouth, Cornwall. Agent: David Higham Associates Ltd., 5-8 Lower John Street, London W1R 4HA, England.

PUBLICATIONS

Verse

Nostalgia Neurosis. Aylesford, Kent, St. Albert's Press, 1968.
Branch. Rushden, Northamptonshire, Sceptre Press, 1971.
Midwinter Mandala. New Malden, Surrey, Headland, 1973.
The Hermaphrodite Album, with Peter Redgrove. London, Fuller D'Arch Smith, 1973.
Moon Meal. Rushden, Northamptonshire, Sceptre Press, 1973.
Autumn Piano and Other Poems. Liverpool, Rondo, 1974.
Photographs of Persephone. Feltham, Middlesex, Quarto Press, 1974.
The Songbook of the Snow and Other Poems. Ilkley, Yorkshire, Janus Press, 1974.
The Dream. Knotting, Bedfordshire, Sceptre Press, 1975.
Webs of Fire. London, Gallery Press, 1975.
Period. London, Words, 1976.
Four American Sketches. Knotting, Bedfordshire, Sceptre Press, 1976.
The Orchard Upstairs. Oxford, Oxford University Press, 1980; New York, Oxford University Press, 1981.
The Child-Stealer. Oxford, Oxford University Press, 1983.

Plays

Radio Plays: *The Girl Who Lost Her Glove*, 1975; *The Dauntless Girl*, 1978.

Novels

An Excusable Vengeance, in *New Writers 6.* London, Calder and Boyars, 1967.
All the Usual Hours of Sleeping. London, Calder and Boyars, 1969.
Wailing Monkey Embracing a Tree. London, Calder and Boyars, 1973.
The Terrors of Dr. Treviles, with Peter Redgrove. London, Routledge, 1974.
The Glass Cottage: A Nautical Romance, with Peter Redgrove. London, Routledge, 1976.
Jesusa. Falmouth, Cornwall, Granite Press, 1976.
Rainsplitter in the Zodiac Garden. London, Boyars, 1977; Nantucket, Massachusetts, Longship Press, 1978.
The Mirror of the Giant. London, Boyars, 1980.

Short Story

Prognostica. Knotting, Bedfordshire, Martin Booth, 1980.

Other

The Wise Wound: Menstruation and Everywoman, with Peter Redgrove. London, Gollancz, 1978; as *The Wise Wound: Eve's Curse and Everywoman*, New York, Marek, 1979.

*

Penelope Shuttle comments:

In my writing, I am concerned to present and investigate those significant experiences or channels of knowledge particular to the woman and not available directly to the man, the carnal knowledges of woman.

I am writing to repair the degradation of woman's experience, to delineate the cyclical shape of her being, and to chart the political response in the world to her vital powers.

Hers. Mine. Ours.

*   *   *

Although Penelope Shuttle is the author of some extraordinary novels, she is a poet who sometimes chooses to write poetry in prose, not a novelist who occasionally turns to poetry. For a long time her gift manifested itself in works of intense emotional obsession. Like her co-author and husband, Peter Redgrove, Shuttle dared, very young, to open her imagination to the forces of unconscious experience. In all her writing there is a surreal aspect, a commitment to exploring hidden regions of the psyche. This has led to a fascination with the "reality" of dream experience.

Shuttle's early, obsessional writing, however, can now be seen in relation to her mature development. Two collections of poetry have appeared since 1980, both of them remarkable achievements, both in matter and style. The thickly worded nightmares of her early work have given way to clear (moon-lit rather than sun-lit) landscapes of vivid impressions. In *The Orchard Upstairs* the imagery is directly connected with her experience of pregnancy and child-bearing. The most delicate poems, however, tell the truth "but tell it slant." The title poem, for instance, is typically symbolic.

Outside, the wind and the rain,
a darkness lurching against the threadbare house:
inside, the orchard upstairs

But I do not understand these fruits yet

A dichotomy is set up here between outside and inside, inhuman and human, destructive and creative...male and female, if you like, though Shuttle is careful not to forget that we need *two* genders to perform the creative miracle. Nevertheless, it is the woman who gives birth, who nourishes and stores away the "fruits." In so doing she suffers, not only physically, but through a loss of innocence:

A small speck or stain
on my heart,
it is my sadness for the lost room,
the pillaged house

The loss finds compensation in the gain of a child, the daughter whose presence haunts the poems of *The Child-Stealer*. Here child-bearing is still a theme, but it alternates with a second theme, that of child*hood*—her own and her daughter's. For Shuttle, childhood is the way back to innocence. The "child-stealer," then, is the witch, Lilith, stealer of unborn babies. Childhood is seen in a Blakean light, but Shuttle's taut language intercepts sentimentality.

In the boundless afternoon
the children are walking
with their gentle grammar on their lips.

From door to door
the little ones go, brightly tranquil,
repenting nothing.

How safe their journey,
their placid marching,
famous and simple voyage.

The poem might cloy if its language were less rigorous—or less ambiguous. We are not sure if these children are real living children, or possible unborn children, or dream children who never will be born. "The Children" convince us that innocence is possible by their "gentle grammar" and their impossibility. Shuttle's attitude throughout *The Child-Stealer* is religious, and uncompromisingly so. As she says in *Prayer*, she approaches the future (age, risk, death) as if she were rowing into winter water

the shore stretching back
into the sweetness of the past
as I embark across unfrozen waters.
I'm going somewhere unknown, untroubled,
mist rises from the kindly waters,
enfolds me in its secret placid linen.

Emily Dickinson might have used that image, but Emily Dickinson would not have anticipated precisely that "placid linen."

—Anne Stevenson

SILKIN, Jon. British. Born in London, 2 December 1930. Educated at Wycliffe and Dulwich colleges; University of Leeds (Gregory Fellow, 1958-60), B.A. (honours) in English 1962. Served in the Army Education Corps, 1948-50. Married to Lorna Tracy; three sons and one daughter (and one son deceased). Journalist, 1947; labourer, and teacher of English to foreign students, 1950-58. Formerly, Extramural Lecturer, University of Leeds, and University of Newcastle; Beck Visiting Lecturer of Writing, Denison University, Granville, Ohio; Visiting Lecturer, Writers Workshop, University of Iowa, Iowa City, 1968-69, Australian Arts Council and University of Sydney, 1974, and College of Idaho, Caldwell, 1978; Visiting Writer, Mishkenot Sha'ananim, Jerusalem, 1980; Bingham Visiting Professor, University of Louisville, 1981; Elliston Visiting Poet, University of Cincinnati, 1983. Since 1952, Founding Co-Editor, *Stand*, Newcastle upon Tyne; since 1964, Co-founding Editor, Northern House, publishers, Newcastle upon Tyne. Recipient: Northern Arts Award, 1965, 1984; Faber Memorial Prize, 1966; C. Day Lewis Fellowship, 1976. Address: 19 Haldane Terrace, Newcastle upon Tyne NE2 3AN, England.

PUBLICATIONS

Verse

The Portrait and Other Poems. Ilfracombe, Devon, Stockwell, 1950.
The Peaceable Kingdom. London, Chatto and Windus, 1954; New York, Yorick Books, 1969.

The Two Freedoms. London, Chatto and Windus, and New York, Macmillan, 1958.
The Re-ordering of the Stones. London, Chatto and Windus-Hogarth Press, 1961.
Flower Poems. Leeds, Northern House, 1964.
Nature with Man. London, Chatto and Windus-Hogarth Press, 1965.
Penguin Modern Poets 7, with Richard Murphy and Nathaniel Tarn. London, Penguin, 1966.
Poems New and Selected. London, Chatto and Windus, and Middletown, Connecticut, Wesleyan University Press, 1966.
Three Poems. Cambridge, Massachusetts, Pym Randall Press, 1969.
Killhope Wheel. Ashington, Northumberland, MidNAG, 1971.
Amana Grass. London, Chatto and Windus-Hogarth Press, and Middletown, Connecticut, Wesleyan University Press, 1971.
Air That Pricks Earth. Rushden, Northamptonshire, Sceptre Press, 1973.
The Principle of Water. Cheadle, Cheshire, Carcanet, 1974.
A "Jarapiri" Poem. Knotting, Bedfordshire, Sceptre Press, 1975.
The Little Time-Keeper. Ashington, Northumberland, and Manchester, MidNAG-Carcanet, 1976; New York, Norton, 1977.
Two Images of Continuing Trouble. Richmond, Surrey, Keepsake Press, 1976.
Jerusalem. Knotting, Bedfordshire, Sceptre Press, 1977.
Into Praising. Sunderland, Ceolfrith, 1978.
The Lapidary Poems. Knotting, Bedfordshire, Sceptre Press, 1979.
The Psalms with Their Spoils. London, Routledge, 1980.
Selected Poems. London, Routledge, 1980.
Autobiographical Stanzas. Durham, Taxus Press, 1984.
Footsteps on a Downcast Path. Bath, Mammon Press, 1984.

Other

Isaac Rosenberg, 1890-1918: A Catalogue of the Exhibition Held at Leeds University, May-June 1959, Together with the Text of Unpublished Material, with Maurice de Sausmarez. Leeds, University of Leeds, 1959.
Out of Battle: The Poetry of the Great War. London and New York, Oxford University Press, 1972.

Editor, with Anthony Cronin and Terence Tiller, *New Poems 1960.* London, Hutchinson, 1960.
Editor, *Living Voices: An Anthology of Contemporary Verse.* London, Vista, 1960.
Editor, *Poetry of the Committed Individual: A "Stand" Anthology of Poetry.* London, Gollancz-Penguin, 1973.
Editor, *The Penguin Book of First World War Poetry.* London, Allen Lane, 1979; revised edition, London, Penguin, 1981.
Editor, with Peter Redgrove, *New Poetry 5.* London, Hutchinson, 1979.
Editor, with Michael Blackburn and Lorna Tracy, *Stand One: An Anthology of Stand Magazine Short Stories.* London, Gollancz, 1984.
Editor, with Jon Glover, *The Penguin Book of First World War Prose.* London, Penguin, 1985.

Translator, *Against Parting,* by Nathan Zach. Newcastle upon Tyne, Northern House, 1968.

*

Manuscript Collections: British Library, London; Denison University, Granville, Ohio.

Critical Studies: "The Poetry of Jon Silkin" by Geoffrey Hill, in *Poetry and Audience 9* (Leeds), no. 12, 1962; *Iowa Review 1* (Iowa City), no. 1, 1969, "Stress in Silkin's Poetry and the Healing Emptiness of America," in *Contemporary Literature* (Madison, Wisconsin), Summer 1977, and *Double Lyric: Devisiveness and Communal Creativity in Recent English Poetry,* London, Routledge, 1980, all by Merle Brown; "Alone in a Mine of Reality: A Matrix in the Poetry of Jon Silkin" by Anne Cluysenaar, in *British Poetry since 1960* edited by Michael Schmidt and Grevel Lindop, Oxford, Carcanet, 1972, and *An Introduction to Fifty Modern British Poets,* London, Pan, 1979, as *A Reader's Guide to Fifty Modern British Poets,* London, Heinemann, 1979, New York, Barnes and Noble, 1982, by Schmidt; in *Times Literary Supplement* (London), 19 July 1974; in *The Tablet* (London), 10 August 1974; "The Hand That Erases" by Mark Abley, in *Oxford Literary Journal,* Spring 1977; "Reflections on Anglo-Jewish Poetry" by William Baker, in *Jewish Quarterly* (London), Autumn-Winter 1978-79; "Jon Silkin: The Voice in the Peaceable Kingdom" by Jon Glover, in *Bananas* (London), April 1980; "Jon Silkin Issue" (includes bibliography) of *Poetry Review* (London), June 1980.

Jon Silkin comments:

Most writers speak less interestingly of their own work, more openly and responsively about the work of those they admire or care for deeply. It is the difference between the desire to be meticulous about oneself, in a nicely judicious way, and the less pernickety response one affords another's work. Such self-introductory exculpations aren't likely to be productive, but they do at least show a degree of self-consciousness which ought to be the leavening to my faith in narrative, linear, Hebraic writing.

The narrative, we are told, is dead; and the writer's central act of faith is now directed towards imagism. Faith, of course, can do many things, but, for me at any rate, the lessons of imagism are to be *absorbed* and its effects used conjunctively with narrative. The dangers of sensuous art, an art committed to giving the sensuous adequate expression, are repetition, over-abundance and prolixity. These, I am sure, are my dangers, and narrative alone can't contain these productions. If imagism is impacted with narrative—or so I have believed—imagistic profile is given substance and value, and narrative is contained. More than contained, it is re-structured by the demands of imagism. Imagism continues to affect my work. I want to say what I have to say, once, and get out. The syntax must have an onwardness, and even when it's motionless, a moment, it must not be repetitious or anxious to produce an effect.

Yet having said these things, I am aware how much this is only half the story. It is the conscious application of one nexus of aspirations to a quite different psychology; thus my work is dual and in constant tension. That, too, must go for its thematic concerns. How does the Peaceable Kingdom make room for those creatures who do not want to belong to it, and would destroy it if it tried to bring them into its condition of love? That, approximately, is the impulsion of my concerns.

In his essay on Tolstoy's view of history, Isaiah Berlin quotes a fragment by the Greek poet Archilochus: "The fox knows many things, but the hedgehog knows one big thing." Berlin glosses this with: "Taken figuratively [the fragment divides] those, on one side, who relate everything to a single central vision...and, on the other side, those who pursue many ends, often unrelated, and even contradictory" (*The Hedgehog and the Fox*). I identify my work with the figure of the hedgehog as he is here typified, uneasy creature though he be; and I do this, not out of ambitiousness, but because I can write no other way. My first collection, *The Peaceable Kingdom*, re-enacts Isaiah's vision where "the wolf also shall dwell with the lamb, and the leopard shall lie down with the kid." My work has changed, but that root has never been torn up.

*   *   *

George Steiner in *Language and Silence* queried the relevance and value of poetry, asking whether we could really consider it a civilizing agent when the civilization that fashioned it also contrived the Holocaust. Jon Silkin, writing since 1950, assuming at times the voice of the Jew, at other the voice of the Northumbrian, attempts in his poetry to speak to the dilemma Steiner posed and write a poetry of "committed individuals." Describing his background as a "mixture of rationalist agnosticism and dilute Orthodox Judaism" (*The Little Time-Keeper*), and calling himself a poet who wants to mingle the techniques of Imagism with a discursive style that allows for moral commentary, Silkin has used his editorship of the Newcastle-based literary journal, *Stand*, to foster a poetry that speaks of responsibilities, of community, and moral probings and escapes the charge of excessive gentility that A. Alvarez levelled against the poets of The Movement.

Silkin's poetry is didactic in the sense urged by Matthew Arnold. Some of his poems express the regional voice of Northumbria and set the coal mines and the mist-enshrouded sheep pastures in their historical perspective. The poems in "Killhope Wheel" (*Amana Grass*; reprinted with one addition in *The Principle of Water*) commemorate the cast iron wheel that washed the ore in County Durham in 1860, and the miners bayoneted by soldiers in the strikes fought to bring relief to the workers from the wretched pay and whiggish policies of the mine owners. Other poems, beginning in *The Two Freedoms*, and becoming more overtly political in the recent volumes, *The Little Time-Keeper* and *Jerusalem*, speak of the Jewish problem, Silkin's own Jewishness, and Britain's expulsion of the Jews in 1190. Whether it is man's inhumanity to man enacted in the coal fields or the gas chambers, or his inhumanity to beasts or the humans he loves that Silkin writes of, he clings tenaciously to the hope that he can recover innocence. His lines in "Small hills among the fells" from "Killhope Wheel" are appropriate to many of his poems of social criticism: "I am trying to make again the feeling/ plants have, and each creature has, looked at,/demure, exultant...."

His early volume *The Peaceable Kingdom* introduced many of the themes later developed in Silkin's poetry: the majesty and innocence of animals, fear occasioned by knowledge of man's and nature's cruelty, man's struggle in darkness to love and to know himself, and man's bewilderment at a world too full of loss. As his verse has developed, Silkin has alternately practiced a lyrical poetry comparable in its simplicity to Blake's *Songs of Innocence and Experience* and an intricate, labyrinthian poetry, with wrenched syntax and obfuscating diction, which arduously struggles to express the contradictions inherent in love, and the triumph of the human spirit that somehow outlasts the degradations of the concentration camps. Two of Silkin's long narrative poems, "Amana Grass" and "The People," suffer from the flaws that mar Silkin's verse—convoluted syntax, overuse of ellipses, ponderous and lapidary building of similes and metaphors—but are worth the strain they put upon the reader. The dialogue is somewhat stilted in "Amana Grass" and the estrangement of the

lovers is too like that expressed in Frost's "The Hill Wife" or "Home Burial" while the comparison is unkind to Silkin. But in "The People" Silkin successfully narrates the slightly disguised autobiographical story that lies behind his most frequently praised poem, "Death of a Son," and enlarges its scope. He unfolds, largely through a series of dramatic monologues, the collective tragedy of his and his wife's love so sorely taxed by the birth of their brain-damaged son and the place of Stein, their neighbour and a victim of the concentration camps, in his anguishing experience. Stein becomes the agent to make "two unloving animals/find mercy's image: love." "The People" is probably Silkin's most ambitious poem to date, and next to "Death of a Son" it is his best. The characters, event, and language are unforgettable, and what difficulties there are that perplex the poem needlessly are easily overlooked.

In *The Little Time-Keeper* Silkin has returned to his simple style, with short poems, stanzaic divisions, and a heavy injection of social and political commentary. In this collection Silkin's fear deepens to embrace not only his personal fear of his own death and the death of those he loves, but a dread that an entropic view of the universe may indeed be scientifically and metaphysically correct. As Silkin matures, his poetry has become more certain, his moral concerns more timely, but also, perhaps, less subtle, and his subejcts more varied. At his best, he has written some of the most moving poems of the century.

—Carol Simpson Stern

SILKO, Leslie (Marmon). American. Born in 1948. Recipient: National Endowment for the Arts award, 1974. Address: c/o Seaver Books, 333 Central Park West, New York, New York 10025, U.S.A.

PUBLICATIONS

Verse

Laguna Woman. Greenfield Center, New York, Greenfield Review Press, 1974.

Novel

Ceremony. New York, Viking Press, 1977.

Other

Storyteller (includes short stories). New York, Seaver, 1981.

*

Critical Studies: *Leslie Marmon Silko* by Per Seyersted, Boise, Idaho, Boise State University, 1980; *Four American Indian Literary Masters* by Alan R. Veile, Norman, University of Oklahoma Press, 1982.

*   *   *

Although Leslie Silko's reputation rests upon her ability as a storyteller and her output of poems has been relatively small, her poems are a central part of her work as a writer and she often uses the forms of poetry even in the middle of such works of prose fiction as *Ceremony*. She makes little use of simile and metaphor in her verse. Image and narration are the key elements. Her autobiographical book, *Storyteller*, is a very interesting combination of old photographs, conventional short stories, and story-poems. (Silko herself denies that some of her poems are poems, seeing them instead as stories placed on the page with line-breaks which help to replicate more clearly the motion of a storytelling voice.)

Changing is an important theme in her work. "Bear Story" tells of how the bears can call people to them, make them become bears themselves. There are characters in Laguna and other southwestern Indian stories, the stories which she grew up with and which she always returns to, who are changers, who make others change and who can change themselves. Coyote is a prime example. The earthy, ironic humor in her poem "Toe'osh: A Laguna Coyote Story" has made it one of her most-often-quoted poems.

Silko is also a writer who celebrates the strength of women, and the title of her first book, *Laguna Woman*, underscores her identification with her sex. Whether it is Silko herself, the mythic Yellow Woman, or her own grandmother Marie Anaya Marmon, the women in Silko's poems are strong, independent, even wildly indomitable.

The world of Silko's poetry is very much shaped by a Native American consciousness. Born in Albuquerque, New Mexico, she was brought up at Laguna Pueblo among relatives whose roots went back many generations in traditional ways. Though regarded as one of the most "acculturated" of the pueblos, Laguna still possesses a strong sense of history and continuity. On the other hand, because Laguna adopted many western ways (and a number of whites, who married into the Pueblo, Silko's "great-grandpa Marmon" among them) it is not surprising that it has produced not only Silko, but several other significant writers whose concerns are those of the "half-breed," the person of mixed blood. Rather than viewing this heritage as a curse, Silko has used the western literary forms to move towards the strength of the Laguna earth and the stories of her family. These stories are both recent personal reminiscences and very old myths and, at times, the two blend. The boundary lines between the "real" world and the world of legends and between "today" and the ancient, though continuing past are very thin in all of her work. Indeed, her sense of time is not at all a European one. One feels in her poems that all things are very much interconnected. Her world is a world of both tremendous changes brought by western civilization and a lastingly strong natural environment (of which the Native American is part) in which everything is possessed of the power to *be* and *become*.

In such poems as "Where Mountain Lion Lay Down With Deer" we see this non-western sense of time. Things from past and present co-exist and change each other:

> I smell the wind for my ancestors
>   pale blue leaves
>   crushes wild mountain smell.
> Returning
>   up the gray stone cliff
>   where I descended
>   a thousand years ago
> Returning to faded black stone
> where mountain lion lay down with deer.

The image of the mountain lion and the deer may remind one of the Biblical lion and lamb, but the animals have different roles in this place, are charged with a different mythic power. When Silko says, later in the same poem,

> The old ones who remember me are gone
>   the old songs are all forgotten
> and the story of my birth.
> How I danced in snow-frost moonlight
>   distant stars to the end of the Earth...

her words are not a lament. They do not convey a sense of loss but rather a deep continuity which goes beyond conventional ideas of individual reality. Although a child of more than one culture, her voice clearly speaks for the Native American way—not a way which is gone, but one which continues beyond time, changing and unchanged.

—Joseph Bruchac

* * *

SILLITOE, Alan. British. Born in Nottingham, 4 March 1928. Educated in Nottingham schools until 1942. Served as a wireless operator in the Royal Air Force, 1946-49. Married Ruth Fainlight, *q.v.*, in 1959; one son and one daughter. Factory worker, 1942-45; air traffic control assistant, Langar Aerodrome, Nottinghamshire, 1945-46; lived in France and Spain, 1952-58. Recipient: Authors Club prize, 1958; Hawthornden Prize, for fiction, 1960. Fellow, Royal Geographical Society, 1975; Honorary Fellow, Manchester Polytechnic, 1977. Agent: Tessa Sayle Agency, 11 Jubilee Place, London SW3 3TE. Address: 21 The Street, Wittersham, Kent, England.

PUBLICATIONS

Verse

Without Beer or Bread.   London, Outposts, 1957.
The Rats and Other Poems.   London, W.H. Allen, 1960.
A Falling Out of Love and Other Poems.   London, W.H. Allen, 1964.
Love in the Environs of Voronezh and Other Poems.   London, Macmillan, 1968; New York, Doubleday, 1970.
Shaman and Other Poems.   London, Turret, 1968.
Poems, with Ted Hughes and Ruth Fainlight.   London, Rainbow Press, 1971.
Barbarians and Other Poems.   London, Turret, 1974.
Storm: New Poems.   London, W.H. Allen, 1974.
Day-Dream Communiqué.   Knotting, Bedfordshire, Sceptre Press, 1977.
From "Snow on the North Side of Lucifer."   Knotting, Bedfordshire, Sceptre Press, 1979.
Snow on the North Side of Lucifer.   London, W.H. Allen, 1979.
More Lucifer.   Knotting, Bedfordshire, Booth, 1980.
Sun Before Departure: Poems 1974-1982.   London, Granada, 1984.

Plays

The Ragman's Daughter (produced Felixstowe, Suffolk, 1966).
All Citizens Are Soldiers, with Ruth Fainlight, adaptation of a play by Lope de Vega (produced Stratford upon Avon and London, 1967).   London, Macmillan, and Chester Springs, Pennsylvania, Dufour, 1969.
The Slot Machine (as *This Foreign Field*, produced London, 1970).   Included in *Three Plays*, 1978.

Pit Strike (televised, 1977).   Included in *Three Plays*, 1978.
The Interview (produced London, 1978).   Included in *Three Plays*, 1978.
Three Plays (includes *The Slot Machine, Pit Strike, The Interview*).   London, W.H. Allen, 1978.

Screenplays: *Saturday Night and Sunday Morning*, 1960; *The Loneliness of the Long Distance Runner*, 1961; *The Ragman's Daughter*, 1974.

Television Play: *Pit Strike*, 1977.

Novels

Saturday Night and Sunday Morning.   London, W.H. Allen, 1958; New York, Knopf, 1959.
The General.   London, W.H. Allen, 1960; New York, Knopf, 1961; as *Counterpoint*, New York, Avon, 1968.
Key to the Door.   London, W.H. Allen, 1961; New York, Knopf, 1962.
The Death of William Posters.   London, W.H. Allen, and New York, Knopf, 1965.
A Tree on Fire.   London, Macmillan, 1967; New York, Doubleday, 1968.
A Start in Life.   London, W.H. Allen, 1970; New York, Scribner, 1971.
Travels in Nihilon.   London, W.H. Allen, 1971; New York, Scribner, 1972.
Raw Material.   London, W.H. Allen, 1972; New York, Scribner, 1973; revised edition, W.H. Allen, 1978.
The Flame of Life.   London, W.H. Allen, 1974.
The Widower's Son.   London, W.H. Allen, 1976; New York, Harper, 1977.
The Storyteller.   London, W.H. Allen, 1979; New York, Simon and Schuster, 1980.
Her Victory.   London, Granada, and New York, Watts, 1982.
The Lost Flying Boat.   London, Granada, 1983; Boston, Little Brown, 1984.
Down from the Hill.   London, Granada, 1984.

Short Stories

The Loneliness of the Long-Distance Runner.   London, W.H. Allen, 1959; New York, Knopf, 1960.
The Ragman's Daughter.   London, W.H. Allen, 1963; New York, Knopf, 1964.
A Sillitoe Selection, edited by Michael Marland.   London, Longman, 1968.
Guzman Go Home.   London, Macmillan, 1968; New York, Doubleday, 1969.
Men, Women, and Children.   London, W.H. Allen, 1973; New York, Scribner, 1974.
Down to the Bone (selection).   Exeter, Wheaton, 1976.
The Second Chance and Other Stories.   London, Cape, and New York, Simon and Schuster, 1981.

Other

Road to Volgograd (travel).   London, W.H. Allen, and New York, Knopf, 1964.
The City Adventures of Marmalade Jim (for children).   London, Macmillan, 1967; revised edition, London, Robson, 1977.
Mountains and Caverns: Selected Essays.   London, W.H. Allen, 1975.
Big John and the Stars (for children).   London, Robson, 1977.

The Incredible Fencing Fleas (for children).   London, Robson, 1978.
Marmalade Jim at the Farm (for children).   London, Robson, 1980.
The Saxon Shore Way: From Gravesend to Rye, photographs by Fay Godwin.   London, Hutchinson, 1983.
Marmalade Jim and the Fox (for children).   London, Robson, 1985.

Editor, *Poems for Shakespeare 7*.   London, Bear Gardens Museum and Arts Centre, 1979.

*

Critical Studies: *Alan Sillitoe* edited by Michael Marland, London, Times Authors Series, 1970; *Alan Sillitoe* by Allen Richard Penner, New York, Twayne, 1972; *Alan Sillitoe: A Critical Assessment* by Stanley S. Atherton, London, W.H. Allen, 1979.

Alan Sillitoe comments:

I use poetry to express emotions that can't be expressed in any other medium. At the same time it might be said that poetry expresses me, by activating emotions that would otherwise stay dormant. It is the industrial diamond of the creative drill-tip.

I am incapable of analysing my own poetry. When I first began to write I considered myself more a poet than a writer. However, novels and stories seem to have overtaken me—though I still am, and still consider myself to be, primarily a poet. A great deal of my "poetry" gets into my prose work, and it is often difficult to find a dividing line. If I have any aim in poetry it is to use images and language as a means of breaking through to new experience—that is to say, old experiences that have not been described before.

*   *   *

Alan Sillitoe is much better known as a novelist than he is as a poet, and one cannot help feeling that, in essence, this is the correct verdict. Yet it is also true to say that Sillitoe has not received credit for his poems. His first and most substantial collection, *The Rats*, was mostly written in the 1950's; and the poems in it reflect the boredom and impatience which many radical writers felt with the English society of that epoch. The "rats" of the title are the forces of conformity: "They are the government, these marsh-brained rats/Who give protection from outsider cats...." But, in addition to satires, the book also contains a number of tender love poems.

This impatience with society and the way it is going is just one of the characteristics which suggest a comparison with D.H. Lawrence. Lawrence, like Sillitoe, came from the working-class, from Nottingham, made his reputation as a novelist, and spent much time as an expatriate. Like Lawrence's, Sillitoe's poems have been consistently undervalued. More recent work, such as the poems in *Love in the Environs of Voronezh*, shows a marked increase in technical control, but also a continuing impatience with poetic convention—radical conventions as well as conservative ones. Sillitoe seems to write a poem because there is something which, as he sees it, needs to be said. The quality of the "saying" tends to vary a good deal from poem to poem, but one is always aware of the direct thrust of a powerful literary personality.

—Edward Lucie-Smith

SIMIC, Charles. American. Born in Belgrade, Yugoslavia, 9 May 1938; emigrated to the United States in 1954; naturalized, 1971. Educated at Oak Park High School, Illinois; University of Chicago, 1956-59; New York University, 1959-61, 1963-65, B.A. 1967. Served in the United States Army, 1961-63. Married Helen Dubin in 1964; one daughter and one son. Proofreader, Chicago *Sun-Times*; Member of the Department of English, California State College, Hayward, 1970-73. Since 1974, Associate Professor of English, University of New Hampshire, Durham. Editorial Assistant, *Aperture* magazine, New York, 1966-69. Recipient: PEN award, for translation, 1970, 1980; Guggenheim Fellowship, 1972; National Endowment for the Arts Fellowship, 1974, 1979; Edgar Allan Poe Award, 1975; American Academy award, 1976; Harriet Monroe Poetry Award, 1980; Poetry Society of America di Castignola Award, 1980; Ingram Merrill Fellowship, 1983; MacArthur Fellowship, 1984. Address: Department of English, University of New Hampshire, Durham, New Hampshire 03824, U.S.A.

PUBLICATIONS

Verse

What the Grass Says. San Francisco, Kayak, 1967.
Somewhere among Us a Stone Is Taking Notes. San Francisco, Kayak, 1969.
Dismantling the Silence. New York, Braziller, and London, Cape, 1971.
White. New York, New Rivers Press, 1972; revised edition, Durango, Colorado, Logbridge Rhodes, 1980.
Return to a Place Lit by a Glass of Milk. New York, Braziller, 1974.
Biography and a Lament: Poems 1961-1967. Hartford, Connecticut, Bartholomew's Cobble, 1976.
Charon's Cosmology. New York, Braziller, 1977.
Brooms: Selected Poems. Barry, Glamorgan, Edge Press, 1978.
School for Dark Thoughts. Pawlet, Vermont, Banyan Press, 1978.
Classic Ballroom Dances. New York, Braziller, 1980.
Shaving at Night. San Francisco, Meadow Press, 1982.
Austerities. New York, Braziller, 1982; London, Secker and Warburg, 1983.
Weather Forecast for Utopia and Vicinity: Poems 1967-1982. Barrytown, New York, Station Hill Press, 1983.

Other

Editor and Translator, with C.W. Truesdale, *Fire Gardens*, by Ivan V. Lalic. New York, New Rivers Press, 1970.
Editor and Translator, *Four Yugoslav Poets: Ivan V. Lalic, Brank Miljkovic, Milorad Pavic, Ljubomir Simovic.* New York, Lillabulero Press, 1970.
Editor and Translator, *The Little Box: Poems*, by Vasko Popa. Washington, D.C., Charioteer Press, 1970.
Editor, with Mark Strand, *Another Republic: 17 European and South American Writers.* New York, Ecco Press, 1976.
Editor and Translator, *Homage to the Lame Wolf: Selected Poems 1956-1975*, by Vasko Popa. Oberlin, Ohio, Oberlin College, 1979.

Translator, *Key to Dream According to Djordje.* Chicago, Elpenor, 1978.
Translator, with Peter Kastmiler, *Atlantis: Selected Poems of Slavko Mihalić.* Greenfield Center, New York, Greenfield Review Press, 1984.

*   *   *

Every so often American poetry exhausts its creative juices and requires new spiritual input for its rejuvenation. In the late 1960's verse was at such a stand-still and poets turned to read, translate, and absorb the ideas of a wide variety of South American and European poets, who offered them a language that mingled political distrust with dream logic and fantasy. The uneasy political and economic conditions of the 1970's made American poets eager to tap the energy of their counterparts. Mark Strand, Marvin Bell, W.S. Merwin, among others, distinguished themselves as translators of Spanish and French poetry and as poets of a new Symbolist era. Charles Simic is of their company, and his half-dozen books have now made him a major voice.

Simic's verse, composed in tightly worded quatrains and couplets, secretes a dark universe of haunting apparitions and animated common objects thriving beyond ordinary consciousness. The only allegory apparent here is a Symbolist one of catching the drift of one's dreams and dark interiors through distorted analogies to the waking world. The wonder of Simic is that however strange his vision of simple things, his grasp of the illogical is striking—the reader feels that somehow he has been there himself but never put to words his experience. Simic's declarations are deadpan; the syntax is as placid as a school teacher's geography lesson—even when the earth he describes (in "A Landscape with Crutches") becomes a Daliesque nightmare:

> I can't get any peace around here:
> The bread on its artificial limbs,
> A headless doll in a wheelchair,
> And my mother, mind you, using
> Two knives for crutches as she squats to pee.

But a makeshift vision assembles behind these brief lyrical configurations—a sense of imminent capture, of death behind every flash of life, of a pervasive whiteness suffusing everything with its sterility and lust for oblivion. He puts his persona into a lonely world of infinite emptiness where individuality shrinks to atomic size ("Euclid Avenue"):

> All my dark thoughts
> laid out
> in a straight line.
>
> An abstract street
> on which an equally abstract intelligence
> forever advances, doubting
> the sound of its own footsteps.

Simic's sense of modern political terror is all the more chilling for its mordant wit and nonchalance. His persona is often the unflappable nice guy before the monster apparitions of the dark. He has, in fact, something of Kafka's macabre fine touch and irony. Simic, born in Yugoslavia, has about him the sinister imagination that is characteristic of the Eastern European sensibility in literature—from its ghostly tales of Transylvania to the most recent Symbolist terrorism of contemporary Slavic poetry (of which Simic has been a prolific translator). And his lyric strikes deep into the American psyche—he not only brings to focus a deep horror of political tyranny and repression, he reminds us of our own tenuous freedoms.

The weakness of this kind of poetry is that it can use up its monochrome realm quickly. There are only so many chilling and intense metaphors for one's dreams and fears, and already Simic seems to be coming to the end of his subject. His early books mined out the worst, most terrifying memories and illusions of his Yugoslav childhood, whereas *Charon's Cosmology* seems less potent, even airy by comparison. The book may be transitional to a new subject, perhaps his American identity and his more immediate circumstances in academic life, which he already seems to be edging toward.

—Paul Christensen

SIMMONS, James (Stewart Alexander).   British.   Born in Londonderry, Northern Ireland, 14 February 1933. Educated at Foyle College, Londonderry; Campbell College, Belfast; Univerity of Leeds, Yorkshire, B.A. (honours) in English 1958. Married 1) Laura Stinson, four daughters and one son; 2) Imelda Poley, one daughter. Has taught at Friends School, Lisburn, Northern Ireland, Ahmadu Bello University, Zaria, Nigeria and New University of Ulster, Coleraine. Editor, *Poetry and Audience*, Leeds, 1957-58. Founder, *The Honest Ulsterman*, 1963, and The Poor Genius Record Company, 1976. Recipient: Eric Gregory Award, 1962; Cholmondeley Award, 1977. Address: 57 Taughey Road, Ballymoney, County Antrim, Northern Ireland.

PUBLICATIONS

Verse

Ballad of a Marriage.   Belfast, Festival, 1966.
Late But in Earnest.   London, Bodley Head, 1967.
Ten Poems.   Belfast, Festival, 1968.
In the Wilderness and Other Poems.   London, Bodley Head, 1969.
Songs for Derry, music by the author.   Belfast, Ulsterman, 1969.
No Ties.   Belfast, Ulsterman, 1970.
Energy to Burn.   London, Bodley Head, 1971.
No Land Is Waste, Dr. Eliot.   Richmond, Surrey, Keepsake Press, 1972.
The Long Summer Still to Come.   Belfast, Blackstaff Press, 1973.
West Strand Visions.   Belfast, Blackstaff Press, 1974.
Memorials of a Tour in Yorkshire.   Belfast, Ulsterman, 1975.
Judy Garland and the Cold War.   Belfast, Blackstaff Press, 1976.
The Selected James Simmons, edited by Edna Longley.   Belfast, Blackstaff Press, 1978.
Constantly Singing.   Belfast, Blackstaff Press, 1980.
From the Irish.   Belfast, Blackstaff Press, 1985.

Recordings: *City and Eastern*, Outlets; *Pubs*, BBC; *Love in the Post*, Poor Genius; *The Ballad of Claudy*, Poor Genius.

Play

Aikin Mata: The Lysistrata of Aristophanes, with T.W. Harrison.   Ibadan, Oxford University Press, 1966.

Other

Sean O'Casey.   London, Macmillan, 1983; New York, Grove Press, 1984.

Editor, with A.R. Mortimer, *Out on the Edge.*   Leeds, Leeds University, 1958.
Editor, *Ten Irish Poets: An Anthology.*   Cheadle, Cheshire, Carcanet, 1974.
Editor, *Soundings 3: Annual Anthology of New Irish Writing.*   Belfast, Blackstaff Press, 1975.

*

Manuscript Collections: University of Texas, Austin; New University of Ulster, Coleraine.

Critical Studies: interview with Robert Chapman, in *Confrontations* (New York), Spring 1975; Paul Durcan, in *Cork Examiner*, 3 July 1978; Alan Hollinghurst, in *Encounter* (London), February-March 1981.

James Simmons comments:
   I see myself in the mainstream of English poetry, following Shakespeare, as most of the poets I admire do, Blake, Hopkins, Hardy, Burns, Yeats, etc. Ewan MacColl reviving the old ballads opened up the possibility of better songs, and also a sense of serious writing, tragedy, being possible in a popular form. For all their self-indulgence the new song-writers (Dylan, Mitchell, Newman, etc.) have a sort of excitement that seems to be lacking in contemporary poetry. The new fashion for reading poetry aloud has turned out to be boring in most cases. Find myself getting curmudgeonly about "experiment," for it so often seems a way for bad poets to disguise their limitations. Don't feel much inclined to argue the toss anymore.

*   *   *

   James Simmons is a curiously vulnerable poet, despite his rumbustious style and the projected, even cultivated, persona of the good-humouredly lecherous boozer: "Our youth was gay but rough,/much drink and copulation./If that seems not enough/blame our miseducation." His rhymes thump steadily home giving the careless reader an impression of verbal insensitivity, and the humour is sometimes so robust that a superficial reading can leave one unaware of the quality of Simmons's sensibility, which may well account for the unfortunate reception given to his collections by certain reviewers. The poem "One of the Boys," from which the four lines quoted above are taken, can be seen as a joyfully iconoclastic romp: "the great careers all tricks,/ the fine arts all my arse,/ business and politics/a cruel farce." But the final lines get under the surface of this defensive philistinism, to point its emptiness and the subconscious awareness of its emptiness in its practitioners:

> Though fear of getting fired
> may ease, and work is hated
> less, we are tired, tired
> and incapacitated.
> On golf courses, in bars,
> crutched by the cash we earn,
> we think of nights in cars
> with energy to burn.

There is a sympathetic understanding here of a tragic sense of loss, which reminds me, obliquely, of the purport of that line in Philip Larkin's poem "Mr. Bleaney": "That how we live measures our own nature." And though "One of the Boys" is heavily rhymed, the rhymes can be seen to underpin the poem and as by no means intrusive. But while this poem succeeds, Simmons's style and stance are replete with the dangers of the sentimental "good-natured tart" variety, and it can involve a deal of casuistry as when in "The Wife-swappers" the poet attempts to equate (and therefore justify) a taste for lechery with an honest harmlessness.

It could be said, of course, that Donne, too, indulged in such sophistry; but he employed considerably more wit and subtlety, if that can be considered a defence. It all comes down to the fact, I suppose, that Simmons sees the poet as an entertainer and moralist, and while he never fails to entertain (no mean achievement) the entertainer sometimes elbows out the moralist. Yet, for the most part, not very far from the clowning and posturing surface of his more swashbuckling poems there is always a hint of *carpe diem* or an awareness of values missed: "Your dumbness on a walk/was better than my clown's talk./You showed me what you meant..." ("Goodbye Sally"). And at its best Simmons's poetry can express an understanding of and empathy with certain aspects of the human tragedy which are only considered minor because they occur with such frequency and are common to so many. Notice here, in "Antigone's Hour," how he moderates the often heavy beat of his poetry to a minor key as it were, so that the tragic element is, in fact, in the very ordinariness of what is often seen as an extraordinary situation:

> All risks are a tribute
> to the adventurous dead.
> Gathering fine small flowers
> was all they wanted said....
>
> No guards observed them
> acting the clown.
> Their own doubts what to do
> next let them down.

The very real strength of Simmons's poetry resides in his basic humanity, and his sympathy and preference for the human condition however fallible and whatever its faults, as in "Stephano Remembers": "We were distracted by too many things.../ the wine, the jokes, the music, fancy gowns/We were no good as murderers, we were clowns." The constant use of the "clown" as an archetype is a clue here.

—John Cotton

SIMPSON, Louis (Aston Marantz). American. Born in Jamaica, British West Indies, 27 March 1923. Educated at Munro College, Jamaica, 1933-40, Cambridge Higher Schools Certificate, 1939; Columbia University, New York, B.S. 1948, A.M. 1950, Ph.D. 1959. Served in the United States Army, 1943-45: Purple Heart and Bronze Star. Married 1) Jeanne Claire Rogers in 1949 (divorced, 1954), one son; 2) Dorothy Roochvarg in 1955 (divorced, 1979), one son and one daughter. Editor, Bobbs-Merrill Publishing Company, New York, 1950-55; Instructor, Columbia University, 1955-59; Professor of English, University of California, Berkeley, 1959-67. Since 1967, Professor of English, State University of New York, Stony Brook. Recipient: American Academy in Rome Fellowship, 1957; *Hudson Review* Fellowship, 1957; Edna St. Vincent Millay Award, 1960; Guggenheim Fellowship, 1962, 1970; American Council of Learned Societies grant, 1963; Pulitzer Prize, 1964; Columbia University Medal for Excellence, 1965; American Academy award, 1976; Institute of Jamaica Centenary Award, 1980; National Jewish Book Award, 1981. D.H.L.: Eastern Michigan University, Ypsilanti, 1977. Address: P.O. Box 91, Port Jefferson, New York 11777, U.S.A.

PUBLICATIONS

Verse

The Arrivistés: Poems 1940-1949. Privately printed, 1949.
Good News of Death and Other Poems. New York, Scribner, 1955.
A Dream of Governors. Middletown, Connecticut, Wesleyan University Press, 1959.
At the End of the Open Road. Middletown, Connecticut, Wesleyan University Press, 1963.
Five American Poets, with others, edited by Thom Gunn and Ted Hughes. London, Faber, 1963.
Selected Poems. New York, Harcourt Brace, 1965; London, Oxford University Press, 1966.
Adventures of the Letter I. London, Oxford University Press, and New York, Harper, 1971.
Tondelayo. Amherst, New York, Slow Loris Press, 1971.
The Mexican Woman. Cambridge, Massachusetts, Pomegranate Press, 1973.
The Invasion of Italy. Northampton, Massachusetts, Main Street, 1976.
Searching for the Ox: New Poems and a Preface. New York, Morrow, and London, Oxford University Press, 1976.
Armidale: Poems and a Prose Memoir. Brockport, New York, Boa, 1979.
Out of Season. Deerfield, Massachusetts, Deerfield Press, 1979.
Caviare at the Funeral. New York, Watts, 1980; Oxford, Oxford University Press, 1981.
The Best Hour of the Night. New Haven, Connecticut, Ticknor and Fields, 1983.
People Live Here: Selected Poems 1949-1983. Brockport, New York, Boa, 1983.

Recordings: *Louis Simpson Reads from His Own Works,* Carillon, 1961; *Today's Poets 1,* with others, Folkways, 1967.

Plays

The Father Out of the Machine: A Masque, in *Chicago Review,* Winter 1950.
Good News of Death, in *Hudson Review* (New York), Summer 1952.
Andromeda, in *Hudson Review* (New York), Winter 1956.
The Breasts of Tiresias, adaptation of the play by Apollinaire, in *Modern French Theatre,* edited by Michael Benedikt and George E. Wellwarth. New York, Dutton, 1964; as *Modern French Plays,* London, Faber, 1965.

Novel

Riverside Drive. New York, Atheneum, 1962.

Other

James Hogg: A Critical Study. Edinburgh, Oliver and Boyd, and New York, St. Martin's Press, 1962.
Air with Armed Men (autobiography). London, London Magazine Editions, 1972; as *North of Jamaica,* New York, Harper, 1972.

Three on the Tower: The Lives and Works of Ezra Pound, T.S. Eliot, and William Carlos Williams. New York, Morrow, 1975.

A Revolution in Taste: Studies of Dylan Thomas, Allen Ginsberg, Sylvia Plath, and Robert Lowell. New York, Macmillan, 1978; as *Studies of Dylan Thomas, Allen Ginsberg, Sylvia Plath, and Robert Lowell,* London, Macmillan, 1979.

A Company of Poets. Ann Arbor, University of Michigan Press, 1981.

Editor, with Donald Hall and Robert Pack, *The New Poets of England and America.* New York, Meridian, 1957; London, New English Library, 1974.

*

Bibliography: *Louis Simpson: A Reference Guide* by William H. Robertson, Boston, Hall, 1980.

Manuscript Collection: Library of Congress, Washington, D.C.

Critical Studies: "The Poetry of Louis Simpson" by C.B. Cox, in *Critical Quarterly 8* (Manchester), Spring 1966; "The Wesleyan Poets—II" by Norman Friedman, in *Chicago Review 19,* 1966; *Louis Simpson* by Ronald Moran, New York, Twayne, 1972, and *Four Poets and the Emotive Imagination* by Moran and George S. Lensing, Baton Rouge, Louisiana State University Press, 1976; "A Child of the World" by Dave Smith, in *American Poetry Review* (Philadelphia), January-February 1979.

Louis Simpson comments:

(1970) I have written about many subjects: war, love, American landscape and history. For several years I have been writing in free form. Influences: many poets, English and American—particularly Eliot and Whitman. I believe that poetry rises from the inner life of the poet and is expressed in original images and rhythms. Also, the language of poetry should be closely related to the language in which men actually think and speak.

(1980) My earliest published work was in traditional forms. At the end of the 1950's I began writing in irregular, unrhymed lines—I was attempting to write verse that would sound like speech. My subjects have frequently been taken from life and in many of my poems there is a narrative or dramatic element. I aim at transparency, to let the action, feeling, and idea come through with no interference. Writing well is like meditating, it requires rising above the merely personal.

*   *   *

Louis Simpson's *Selected Poems* contained portions from his previous volumes as well as a dozen "New Poems." The last two volumes alone, published only four years apart, revealed his remarkable growth. Dealing with war, love, history, the emptiness of modern life, the American in Europe, *A Dream of Governors* was knowing and intelligent but somewhat too formal, avoiding simultaneously the pressure of passion and the perspective of vision.

At the End of the Open Road, which received the Pulitzer Prize, was a very different matter entirely. Simpson found the key to the meaning and power of his themes. The development of the poem from the routine to the timeless, from situation to response, was no longer a matter of mere machinery but rather of vital shock. It is not simply that his style was getting more experimental, but more that his flexibility was a sign of growth

in the character and thought of the speaker, an openness to life whereby the poet risks being changed by what he experiences, and Simpson was on his way to becoming a major poet.

We have in this volume another group of poems about America, but they are much more penetrating than those in *Governors.* "In California," for example, begins: "Here I am, troubling the dream coast/With my New York face." And "In the Suburbs" begins: "There's no way out./You were born to waste your life." There are also three poems at the end inspired by Whitman, who was also hailed in "In California": Simpson knows that "The Open Road goes [now] to the used-car lot," and that, since the past keeps repeating itself, it cannot be cancelled out. And then, finally, that "At the end of the open road we come to ourselves." He had come a long way from the somewhat easy Sherwood-Andersonianism of "Hot Night on Water Street" and "The Boarder" from *Governors.* America's emptiness was now seen in its historical context, and thus the poet's satire has cause and direction.

Then there is a group of four wonderful love poems—"Summer Morning," "The Silent Lover," "Birch," and "The Sea and the Forest"—which are by far more meaningful and passionate than his earlier erotic lyrics. In the first named, for example, the speaker remembers having been with a girl in a intervening time, concluding: "So I have spoiled my chances. /For what? Sheer laziness,/The thrill of an assignation,/My life that I hold in secret." And finally, there is that remarkable piece called "American Poetry," a marvel of concise meaning, which I quote in full:

> Whatever it is, it must have
> A stomach that can digest
> Rubber, coal, uranium, moons, poems.
>
> Like the shark, it contains a shoe.
> It must swim for miles through the desert
> Uttering cries that are almost human.

Simpson had digested the indigestible and was now embarked on his long swim through the desert.

Thus we find him realizing, two years later, in "The Laurel Tree" from "New Poems": "I must be patient with shapes/Of automobile fenders and ketchup bottles./These things are the beginning/of things not visible to the naked eye." And, in the confrontation between the speaker and an unearthly visitor, in "Things," the latter tells him: "Things which to us in the pure state are mysteries,/Are your simplest articles of household use." To which the speaker replies: "I have suspected/The Mixmaster knows more than I do,/The air conditioner is the better poet."

The spirituality of the mundane is surely a Whitmanesque—not to say, Zen—theme, and Simpson returned in his next book, *Adventures of the Letter I,* to his obsession with America. In "Doubting," for example, he says: "I look on the negro as myself, I accuse myself/of sociopathic tendencies, I accuse my accusers." Here he has wittily captured the authentic Whitman mood and cadence—and then the feeling falls and he becomes depressed. But once more he must learn to be patient, he says, and "to breathe in, breathe out,/and to sit by the bed and watch."

Adventures was a marvelous and varied book, fulfilling all of his earlier promise and carrying it a stage further. It begins, for example, with a strange and fable-like section on Volhynia Province, where the poet creates an imaginary version of that part of Russia his mother came from. And there is a section called "Individuals," which contains a very effective narrative portrait, "Vandergast and the Girl," reminiscent in subject and tone of E.A. Robinson. In order to digest the trash of ordinary life, then, to see the light of meaning in the trivial, Simpson had to go into himself and learn to be patient indeed, trusting "in silence," and not believing "in ideas/unless they are unavoidable" ("An American Peasant").

And yet, in *Searching for the Ox*, Simpson's next book, that desert swim seems at moments to be floundering. There is an expected emphasis in his Preface to this volume upon the rendering of human experience and of the world we live in, but there is also a strange note, at its conclusion, when he recalls his former selves as they appear in some of these poems, of detachment: "But I have changed; I am different from the boy and the man I used to be.... These changes cry out for a life that does not change. The less we are at home in the world, the more we bear witness to that other life." Paying attention to his cue, we are not surprised to find that the style of this book is not simply clear, direct, the language of speech, but also that it is curiously level, limpid, even deliberately flat. And the recurring theme of homelessness, of feeling out of the world, becomes more intelligible, as when we read, for example, "When I look back at myself/it is like looking through a window/and seeing another person" ("The Springs at Gadara"), or again: "At dusk when the lamps go on/I have stayed outside and watched/the shadow-life of the interior,/feeling myself apart from it" (title poem). Passion and trust in silence and patience are alike at a low ebb, and one could only hope that the consequent shrinking of the ordinary would prove temporary and that this book represented a necessary stage toward reintegration.

Simpson's next two major collections of new poems, *Caviare at the Funeral* and *The Best Hour of the Night*, with one or two exceptions, do not answer to this hope. Although he continues to explore memories of his Jamaican childhood, his mother's tales of *her* childhood in Russia, and to puzzle over the mysteries of time and art, he nevertheless continues also to plumb the emptiness of the ordinary without transformation—and still in that dry, flat tone. It is not simply the emptiness of the lives of shop girls, soldiers on leave, cocktail waitresses, and of the gas stations, bars, hotels where they play out these lives—it is, of course, of suburban couples as well, their adulteries, and the shopping malls and restaurants where they play out *their* lives. And rarely does the speaker accuse himself, reserving for himself the role, rather, of wry observer.

One exception is "Armidale," a prose piece about a visit to Australia, and the four poems which accompany it, in *Caviare*. There is a vigor here, partly produced by the frontier-like milieu of the place, and partly by the moving effect of this milieu upon the speaker. The other exception is "Physical Universe," from *Best Hour*, which, although narrated in the third person, represents the speaker finding a Zen-like delight, once again, in the ordinary—a delight which he is, unfortunately, somewhat less likely to find in the lives of his neighbors. But perhaps it is, nevertheless, a good sign that reintegration is on the way.

—Norman Friedman

SIMPSON, R(onald) A(lbert). Australian. Born in Melbourne, Victoria, 1 February 1929. Educated at Royal Melbourne Institute of Technology, Associateship Diploma of Art; Melbourne Teachers' College, Primary Teachers' Certificate, 1951. Married to Pamela Simpson; two children. Lecturer in Art, 1968-71, and since 1972, Senior Lecturer, Chisholm Institute of Technology, Melbourne. Poetry Editor, *The Bulletin*,

Sydney, 1963-65. Since 1969, Poetry Editor, *The Age*, Melbourne. Recipient: Australian Arts Council travel grant, 1977. Address: 29 Omama Road, Murrumbeena, Melbourne, Victoria 3163, Australia.

PUBLICATIONS

Verse

The Walk along the Beach. Sydney, Edwards and Shaw, 1960.
This Real Pompeii. Brisbane, Jacaranda Press, 1964.
After the Assassination and Other Poems. Brisbane, Jacaranda Press, 1968.
Diver. Brisbane, University of Queensland Press, 1972.
Poems from Murrumbeena. Brisbane, University of Queensland Press, 1976.
The Forbidden City. Sydney, Edwards and Shaw, 1979.
Selected Poems. Brisbane, University of Queensland Press, 1981.

Other

Editor, *Poems from "The Age" 1967-79.* Melbourne, Hyland House, 1979.

*

Manuscript Collection: National Library of Australia, Canberra.

Critical Study: *The Literature of Australia* edited by Geoffrey Dutton, Melbourne, Penguin, 1976.

R.A. Simpson comments:

As a poet I use words in an effort to understand and clarify experiences. I get my main joy from poetry in the use of words; the struggle for clarification is the painful region. My early poetry was stiff and formal: I believe, and hope, that my recent work shows greater ease and freedom. My background as an art teacher contributed to my experiments in "concrete poetry," an area I no longer find interesting.

I do not see myself merely as an Australian poet, though there are obvious Australian attitudes in my poetry—and I have used Australian themes. Most present-day Australian poets would seriously believe that the best poetry being written today here and overseas reflects some kind of international style—a sense of the poet's responsibility to human beings in general. Australian poets feel part of the larger flow of ideas, even if they are not main contributors to the birth of ideas.

*   *   *

One of a group of Melbourne poets who came to prominence in the 1950's and to influence in the 1960's, R.A. Simpson has carefully maintained certain essential characteristics more consistently than have his fellow poets Vincent Buckley, Chris Wallace-Crabbe and Evan Jones, all of whom have modified their original formal regularity and slightly academic (or, at least, cloistered) affectations of irony and equipoise. Ron Simpson, in his first collection, *The Walk along the Beach*, quite firmly demonstrated a mind concerned with paring language down, with understatement, and with letting the image work with a minimum of encumbrances. The early poems were overtly concerned, however, often with the aftermath of guilt, heritage of a Catholic boyhood and subsequent loss of faith. Indeed, even through Simpson's more recent poetry, in *Diver*, the innate direction of mind is through channels of justification or expiation. Though there may be no God, for Simpson, there is still an implied Judgement.

The verse style that worries its way through these concerns is, still, strangely tight-lipped and reticent. At its weakest it seems hesitant, hardly daring to indulge even in connectives. At its best it is a strikingly taut and resonant instrument capable of playing upon (and preying upon) those central nervous gropings and ambivalences that our own speech can enmesh us in. The poetry of R.A. Simpson is not graceful or elegant. It is self-guarded, and keeps catching itself off guard. It remained outside current fashions, both in the 1960's and 1970's. Its essential honesty sustains it. It is a poetry one can return to many times, and always with a gain.

—Thomas W. Shapcott

SINCLAIR, Keith. New Zealander. Born in Auckland, 5 December 1922. Educated at Mount Albert Grammar School, Auckland; University of Auckland, B.A. 1945, M.A. 1946, Ph.D. 1954. Served in the New Zealand Army, 1941-44, and Navy, 1944-46. Married 1) Mary Land in 1947; four sons; 2) Raewyn Mary Dalzeil in 1976. Lecturer, 1947-59, Associate Professor, 1959-62, and since 1962, Professor of History, University of Auckland. Carnegie Visiting Fellow, Institute of Commonwealth Studies, London, 1954; Visiting Fellow, Australian National University, Canberra, 1967, and Cambridge University, 1968-69. Since 1967, Editor, *New Zealand Journal of History*, Auckland. Labour Party Parliamentary Candidate, 1969. Since 1974, Chairman, Authors' Lending Rights Advisory Committee; since 1982, Trustee, New Zealand National Library. Recipient: Walter Frewen Lord Prize for History, London, 1951; Ernest Scott Prize, for history, Melbourne, 1958, 1961; F.P. Wilson Prize for History, Wellington, 1966; Hubert Church Prose Award, 1966; Jessie Mackay Poetry Award, 1974; New Zealand Book Award, for non-fiction, 1977. Litt.D.: University of Auckland. C.B.E. (Commander, Order of the British Empire), 1983. Address: Department of History, University of Auckland, Private Bag, Auckland 1, New Zealand.

PUBLICATIONS

Verse

Songs for a Summer and Other Poems. Christchurch, Pegasus Press, 1952.
Strangers or Beasts. Christchurch, Caxton Press, 1954.
A Time to Embrace. Auckland, Paul's Book Arcade, 1963.
The Firewheel Tree. Auckland, Auckland University Press-Oxford University Press, 1973.

Other

The Maori Land League: An Examination into the Source of a New Zealand Myth. Auckland, University of Auckland, 1950.
Imperial Federation: A Study of New Zealand Policy and Opinion 1880-1914. London, Athlone Press, 1955.
The Origins of the Maori Wars. Wellington, New Zealand University Press, 1957; revised edition, 1961.

A History of New Zealand. London, Penguin, 1959; revised edition, Wellington and London, Oxford University Press, 1961; Penguin, 1970; London, Allen Lane, 1980.
Open Account: A History of the Bank of New South Wales in New Zealand, 1861-1961, with William F. Mandle. Wellington, Whitcombe and Tombs, 1961.
William Pember Reeves: New Zealand Fabian. Oxford, Clarendon Press, 1965.
The Liberal Government 1891-1912: First Steps Towards a Welfare State. Auckland, Heinemann, 1967.
Towards Independence. Auckland, Heinemann, 1976.
Walter Nash. Auckland, Auckland University Press, and New York and London, Oxford University Press, 1976.
The Reefs of Fire. Auckland, Heinemann, 1977.
Looking Back: A Photographic History of New Zealand, with Wendy Harrex. Wellington and New York, Oxford University Press, 1978; London, Oxford University Press, 1979.
History of the University of Auckland 1883-1983. Auckland, Auckland University Press, 1983.

Editor, *The Maori King*, by John Eldon Gorst. Auckland, Oxford University Press, 1959.
Editor, *Distance Looks Our Way: The Effects of Remoteness on New Zealand.* Auckland, University of Auckland, 1961.
Editor, with Robert Chapman, *Studies in a Small Democracy: Essays in Honour of Willis Airey.* Auckland, Paul's Book Arcade, and Sydney, Angus and Robertson, 1963.
Editor, *A Soldier's View of Empire: The Reminiscences of James Bodell 1831-1892.* London, Bodley Head, 1982.

*

Critical Study: *A Way of Saying: A Study of New Zealand Poetry* by Kendrick Smithyman, Auckland and London, Collins, 1965.

Keith Sinclair comments:

The main influence on my early verse of which I was conscious was John Donne; more recently, perhaps Yeats and Robert Graves. In general I have been influenced by contemporary New Zealand poets, especially James K. Baxter, in the early 1950's. My main subjects have been love of various sorts—of country, especially the coast, of children and family and women. I have thought that the intellect and feeling are inseparable in life and in poetry.

*   *   *

Three pointers toward changing sensibility: John Donne, Dylan Thomas, and Theodore Roethke. But pointers only of a way: to name names is not to describe, still less to define. From Donne's example Keith Sinclair learned, as he has said, to admire "a witty clarity, a clarity within which wits may find obscurity," although Sinclair is rarely obscure. From Thomas, an artifice, a rhetoric, which shows, say, in "The Sleeping Beauty" sequence, but he has not been as alive to metric—his own is idiosyncratic—as Thomas was, or as interested in the artifice of regulated patterns. For many years he respected, and still respects, Roethke whose practical bearing, whose homeliness, but most (probably) whose evident sense of pitch rather than tone may be thought at least partly to have persuaded Sinclair to that increased directness, that lowered pitch which have served his poems well in his maturity.

If these men helped shape a talent they did not do so totally. At his earliest, Sinclair's poems were his and no one else's; for those of later years the same is to be said. Poems like "Goat Island

Valley" and "Explaining Rain" (published in *Landfall* in 1967) clearly are mature expressions of what was present in a younger man's writing. The intelligence, the wit, the ebullience (not the exuberance) of his poems remains constant, producing a particular decorum which subsumes on the one hand what was once referred to as a fantastic element and, on the other, a sensuous if not sensual directness. The sensibility is not dissociated. The traditionalist and the contemporary man are one, with the family man, the Professor of History, the biographer, and the Labour Party candidate. If the latter emphasise the man of public conscience, of public obligation, the poems emphasise the man responsive to private conscience, of less advertised but not necessarily smaller or less significant pieties.

In 1973 Sinclair brought out another collection, *The Firewheel Tree*, but there has been no collection since then. (If in the 1970's the poet quietened, the historian was fully affirmed. Sinclair is probably the most adaptable of New Zealand historians, the most diverse in his professional skills that this country has seen, and the most productive.) Overall, the poems of *The Firewheel Tree* are more tightly constructed and in several ways more orthodox than may be said of his earlier work. There is less inclination to eccentric or flamboyant phrasings, to the *jeux d'esprit* in which he liked to indulge. Like so many others, he brought his poems closer to that condition of prose discourse which goes with directness of syntax and the subordination of assertive rhythms to the play and cross-play of cadences, guarding himself against the merely prosaic or the prose by recourse to a heightened diction which suits the lyrical celebrations which are often his occasion and by returning to that old device in English poetry, alliteration. The firewheel tree which affords his title signifies something which is exotic in an everyday situation. It refers to one of the *Embothrium* family of Chile and Australia, a tree which is striking in its flowering. The poem has something to do, as have others of the book, with Sinclair's second marriage, of a time when conscience and conventional pieties were exercised, when the lyrical and the sensual were borne in on him not merely as compelling awarenesses demanding to be celebrated but as powers which (in an old-fashioned metaphor) flowered exotically but were not simply lyrical or assuagingly sensual. The firewheel is the natural wheel of fire, yet also wheel of fortune. Man is "racked on a firewheel tree." Since 1973 Sinclair has published only a handful of occasional poems.

—Kendrick Smithyman

SISSON, C(harles) H(ubert). British. Born in Bristol, 22 April 1914. Educated at the University of Bristol, 1931-34, B.A. (honours) in philosophy and English literature 1934; University of Berlin and University of Freiburg, 1934-35; the Sorbonne, Paris, 1935-36. Served in the British Army Intelligence Corps in India, 1942-45. Married Nora Gilbertson in 1937; two daughters. Assistant Principal, 1936-42, Principal, 1945-53, Assistant Secretary, 1953-62, and Under Secretary, 1962-68, Ministry of Labour, London; Assistant Under Secretary of State, 1968-71, and Director of Occupational Safety and Health, 1971-73, Department of Employment, London. Co-Editor, *PN Review*, Manchester, 1976-83. Recipient: Senior Simon Research Fellowship, University of Manchester, 1956. D.Litt.: University of Bristol, 1980. Fellow, Royal Society of Literature, 1975. Agent: A.D. Peters, 10 Buckingham Street, London WC2N 6BU. Address: Moorfield Cottage, The Hill, Langport, Somerset TA10 9PU, England.

PUBLICATIONS

Verse

Versions and Perversions of Heine. London, Gaberbocchus, 1955.
Poems. Fairwarp, Sussex, Peter Russell, 1959.
Twenty-One Poems. Privately printed, 1960.
The London Zoo. London, Abelard Schuman, 1961.
Numbers. London, Methuen, 1965.
Catullus. London, MacGibbon and Kee, 1966; New York, Orion Press, 1967.
The Discarnation; or, How the Flesh Became Word and Dwelt among Us. Privately printed, 1967.
Metamorphoses. London, Methuen, 1968.
Roman Poems. Privately printed, 1968.
In the Trojan Ditch: Collected Poems and Selected Translations. Cheadle, Cheshire, Carcanet, 1974.
The Corridor. Hitchin, Hertfordshire, Mandeville Press, 1975.
Anchises. Manchester, Carcanet, 1976.
Exactions. Manchester, Carcanet, 1980.
Selected Poems. Manchester, Carcanet, 1981; Redding Ridge, Connecticut, Black Swan, 1982.
Collected Poems 1943-1983. Manchester, Carcanet, 1984.

Novels

An Asiatic Romance. London, Gaberbocchus, 1953.
Christopher Homm. London, Methuen, 1965.

Other

The Spirit of British Administration and Some European Comparisons. London, Faber, and New York, Praeger, 1959.
Art and Action. London, Methuen, 1965.
Essays. Privately printed, 1967.
English Poetry 1900-1950: An Assessment. London, Hart Davis, 1971.
The Case of Walter Bagehot. London, Faber, 1972.
David Hume. Edinburgh, Ramsay Head Press, 1976.
The Avoidance of Literature: Collected Essays, edited by Michael Schmidt. Manchester, Carcanet, 1978.
Anglican Essays. Manchester, Carcanet, 1983.

Editor, *A South African Album,* by David Wright. Cape Town, Philip, 1976.
Editor, *The English Sermon 1650-1750.* Manchester, Carcanet, 1976.
Editor, *Selected Poems,* by Jonathan Swift. Manchester, Carcanet, 1976.
Editor, *Jude the Obscure,* by Hardy. London, Penguin, 1978.
Editor, *Autobiographical and Other Papers,* by Philip Mairet. Manchester, Carcanet, 1981.
Editor, *The Rash Act,* by Ford Madox Ford. Manchester, Carcanet, 1982.
Editor, *Selected Poems,* by Christina Rossetti. Manchester, Carcanet, 1984.

Translator, *The Poetic Art: A Translation of Horace's Ars Poetica.* Cheadle, Cheshire, Carcanet, 1975.
Translator, *De Rerum Natura: The Poem on Nature,* by Laucretius. Manchester, Carcanet, 1976.
Translator, *Some Tales of La Fontaine.* Manchester, Carcanet, 1979.
Translator, *The Divine Comedy,* by Dante. Manchester, Carcanet, 1980; Chicago, Regnery, 1981.

Translator, *The Song of Roland*.   Manchester, Carcanet, 1983.
Translator, *The Regrets*, by Joachim Du Bellay.   Manchester,
   Carcanet, 1984.

                                    *

Critical Studies: by Martin Seymour-Smith, in *X* (London), ii, 3,
1961, in *Agenda* (London), Summer-Autumn 1970, and in
Guide to Modern World Literature, London, Wolfe, 1973;
Donald Davie, in *Listener* (London), 9 May 1974; Robert Nye,
in *Times Literary Supplement* (London), 29 November 1974;
David Wright, in *Agenda* (London), Autumn 1975; John Pil-
ling, in *Critical Quarterly* (Manchester), Spring 1979; "C.H.
Sisson Issue" of *PN Review* (Manchester), Spring 1984.

C.H. Sisson comments:
   My verse is about things that I am, at the moment of writing,
just beginning to understand. When I have understood them, or
have that impression, the subject has gone, and I have to find
another. Or stop. Generally, my resolution is to stop, but
another subject is found in time, and I begin again. I began by
stopping, so to speak, for having written some verse as an
adolescent, I gave up at twenty because I had a great respect for
poetry and did not think I could write it. The war and exile
produced a few hesitant verses, wrung from me, but I stopped
again without really having begun. A more productive start was
about 1950, when I was already on the declining side *del cammin
di nostra vita*; no wonder therefore that my themes have often
been age, decline and death, with the occasional desperate hopes
of the receding man. Naturally some facility has come with
practice, and the risk now is less from stopping than from going
on. One comes to understand too much, or to think one does.
   As to verse forms, whether they are what is called regular, or
not, it is a small matter: I have written in both kinds. What
matters is the rhythm, which is the identifying mark of the poem.
If that fails there is no need for a poem; better shut up.
   Influences: all one's interests bear, in unexpected ways, on
what one writes; still more, one's poetry may be prophetic of
interests one is about to have. The influence of other poets—
generally in youth—is deadly while it lasts. There is, however, a
deliberate, mature learning which is beneficial. For this purpose
I have found translations of the greatest value, with the Latins as
the great, though not the only, masters. What I aim at is to make
plain statements, and not more of them than I need. "It is in the
nature of man that puzzles me"; I should like to leave a few
recognizable—not novel—indications. The man that was the
same in Neolithic and in Roman times, as now, is of more
interest than the freak of circumstances. This truth lies at the
bottom of a well of rhythm.

                          *   *   *

   Two years before the publication of his collection *The London
Zoo* in 1961, C.H. Sisson had made his name with his *The Spirit
of British Administration*, the result of a comparative study of
public administration in several European countries. This book
was notable for its wit and the sharpness of the author's mind.
The same qualities are to be found in C.H. Sisson's poetry and
often the terrains overlap. Thus the long title poem of *The
London Zoo* gains point and edge from the author's own involvement in the world of the City and the administration that he
satirizes:

   And who am I, you ask, thus to belly-ache
   At my betters? I'll tell you, I am one of the same lot

   —Without lobsters and limousine, but, like the rest
   Expending my best energies on the second best.

   Much of Sisson's earlier poetry is uncomfortable in that it
looks at our pretensions and society with an unflinching and
critical eye. When it looks at our beliefs it can be just as disquiet-
ening as in "The Aeroplane" where below there are those who are
"gathered round the Easter cup" when "up here it is empty." This
poetry, while written from an uncompromisingly intellectual
standpoint, is by no means dispassionate, and can, as in the case
of what begins as a somewhat conventional satire on the cash-
nexus, explode violently into

   Suddenly you are in bed with a screeching tear-sheet
   This is money at last without her nightdress
   Clutching you against her fallen udders and sharp bones
   In an unscrupulous and deserved embrace.

   In later poems, however, this shrill voice has been muted and
the poems tend to be concerned with regret for times past and
age to come:

   I will act my senile part as the Furies desire
   Having discovered too late what I knew already:
   Nothing is new, nothing miraculous.
   The tree grows and flowers in order to fall

Is Sisson becoming sorry for himself? But we are reassured when
we read,

   One of a kind is the most anybody
   Can expect to be, and even that
   Is a presumption upon a classification
   Based upon reason which is wholly imaginary

and when the new muted Sisson gives us poems as splendid as
"This Morning":

   I do not know what the mist signifies
   When it comes, not swirling,
   Gathering itself like briony under my window

   The trees stand out of it,
   Wading, you might say,
   Have their dark tresses trailing in the water
   Which began the world.

Admirers of C.H. Sisson's poetry look forward to what else this
new vein will yield.

                                                    —John Cotton

                              _____

SITWELL, (Sir) Sacheverell; 6th baronet, 1969.   British.   Born
in Scarborough, Yorkshire, 15 November 1897; younger brother
of the poets Dame Edith and Sir Osbert Sitwell. Educated at
Eton College; Balliol College, Oxford. Served in the Grenadier
Guards during World War I. Married Georgia Doble in 1925
(died, 1980); two sons. Justice of the Peace, 1943; High Sheriff of
Northamptonshire, 1948-49. Freeman, City of Lima, Peru,
1960. Recipient: Royal Society of Literature Benson Medal,
1981. Companion of Honour, 1984. Address: Weston Hall,
Towcester, Northamptonshire, England.

PUBLICATIONS

Verse

The People's Palace. Oxford, Blackwell, 1918.
Doctor Donne and Gargantua: First Canto. London, Favil Press, 1921; Boston, Houghton Mifflin, 1930.
The Hundred and One Harlequins. London, Grant Richards, and New York, Boni and Liveright, 1922.
Doctor Donne and Gargantua: Canto the Second. London, Favil Press, 1923.
The Thirteenth Caesar and Other Poems. London, Grant Richards, 1924; New York, Doran, 1925.
Poor Young People, with Edith and Osbert Sitwell. London, The Fleuron, 1925.
Doctor Donne and Gargantua: Canto the Third. Privately printed, 1926.
Exalt the Eglantine and Other Poems. London, The Fleuron, 1926.
The Cyder Feast and Other Poems. London, Duckworth, and New York, Doran, 1927.
(Poems). London, Benn, 1928.
Two Poems, Ten Songs. London, Duckworth, 1929.
Doctor Donne and Gargantua: The First Six Cantos. London, Duckworth, and Boston, Houghton Mifflin, 1930.
Canons of Giant Art: Twenty Torsos in Heroic Landscapes. London, Faber, 1933.
Collected Poems. London, Duckworth, 1936.
Selected Poems. London, Duckworth, 1948; New York, AMS Press, 1980.
"Forty-Eight Poems," in *Poetry Review* (London), Summer 1967.
Tropicalia. Edinburgh, Ramsay Head Press, 1972.
To Henry Woodward. London, Covent Garden Press, 1972.
Agamemnon's Tomb. Edinburgh, Tragara Press, 1972.
Rosario d'Arabeschi; Baraka ("as the Moors call it") and Dionysia; Triptych of Poems; The Strawberry Feast; Ruralia; To E.S.; Variations upon Old Names of Hyacinths; Lily Poems; The Archipelago of Daffodils; A Charivari of Parrots; Flowering Cactus; Auricula Theatre; Lyra Varia; The House of the Presbyter; Nigritian; Summer Poems of 1962; Doctor Donne and Gargantua (Cantos Seven and Eight); Badinerie; An Indian Summer; Temple of Segesta; L'Amour au Théâtre Italien; Notebook on My New Poems; Notebook on Twenty Canons of Giant Art; A Note for Bibliophiles; Battles of the Centaurs; Les Troyens; Pastoral and Landscape with the Giant Orion; Nymphis et Fontibus and Nymphaeum; Serenade to a Sister; Placebo; Credo, or, An Affirmation; Two Themes Taken One at a Time; Harlequinade; Brother and Sister; Dodecameron; Diptycha Musica; The Octogenarian; Little Italy in London; Looking for the Gods of Light; The Rose-Pink Chapel; Scherzo di Capriccio; Scherzo di Fantasia; A Pair of Entr'actes for August Evenings; Nine Ballads, and Four More Lilies; Op. cit., et cetera; A Retrospect of Poems (1972-1979); Allotment or Assignment?; Catalysts in Collusion; Nocturnae Silvani Potenti. Privately printed, 1972-80.
An Indian Summer: 100 Recent Poems. London, Macmillan, 1982.

Plays

The Triumph of Neptune (ballet), music by Lord Berners. London, Chester, 1926.
All at Sea: A Social Tragedy in Three Acts for First-Class

Passengers Only, with Osbert Sitwell. London, Duckworth, 1927; New York, Doubleday, 1928.

Other

Southern Baroque Art: A Study of Painting, Architecture and Music in Italy and Spain of the 17th and 18th Centuries. London, Grant Richards, and New York, Knopf, 1924.
All Summer in a Day: An Autobiographical Fantasia. London, Duckworth, and New York, Doran, 1926.
German Baroque Art. London, Duckworth, 1927; New York, Doran, 1928.
A Book of Towers and Other Buildings of Southern Europe. London, Frederick Etchells and Hugh Macdonald, 1928.
The Gothick North: A Study of Mediaeval Life, Art, and Thought. Boston, Houghton Mifflin, 1929; London, Duckworth, 3 vols., 1929-30.
Beckford and Beckfordism: An Essay. London, Duckworth, 1930.
Far from My Home: Stories: Long and Short. London, Duckworth, 1931.
Spanish Baroque Art: With Buildings in Portugal, Mexico, and Other Colonies. London, Duckworth, 1931.
Mozart. New York, Appleton, and London, Davies, 1932.
Liszt. London, Faber, and Boston, Houghton Mifflin, 1934; revised edition, London, Cassell, 1955; New York, Philosophical Library, 1956.
Touching the Orient: Six Sketches. London, Duckworth, 1934; Folcroft, Pennsylvania, Folcroft Editions, 1976.
A Background for Domenico Scarlatti, 1685-1757; Written for His Two Hundred and Fiftieth Anniversary. London, Faber, 1935; Freeport, New York, Books for Libraries, 1970.
Dance of the Quick and the Dead: An Entertainment of the Imagination. London, Faber, 1936; Boston, Houghton Mifflin, 1937.
Conversation Pieces: A Survey of English Domestic Portraits and Their Painters. London, Batsford, 1936; New York, Scribner, 1937.
Narrative Pictures: A Survey of English Genre and Its Painters. London, Batsford, 1937; New York, Scribner, 1938.
La Vie Parisienne: A Tribute to Offenbach. London, Faber, 1937; Boston, Houghton Mifflin, 1938.
Roumanian Journey. London, Batsford, and New York, Scribner, 1938.
Edinburgh, with Francis Bamford. London, Faber, and Boston, Houghton Mifflin, 1938.
German Baroque Sculpture. London, Duckworth, 1938.
Trio: Dissertations on Some Aspects of English Genius, with Edith and Osbert Sitwell. London, Macmillan, 1938.
The Romantic Ballet in Lithographs of the Time, with Cyril W. Beaumont. London, Faber, 1938.
Old Fashioned Flowers. London, Country Life, and New York, Scribner, 1939.
Mauretania: Warrior, Man, and Woman. London, Duckworth, 1940.
Poltergeists: An Introduction and Examination Followed by Chosen Instances. London, Faber, 1940; New York, University Books, 1959.
Sacred and Profane Love. London, Faber, 1940.
Valse des Fleurs: A Day in St. Petersburg and a Ball at the Winter Palace in 1868. London, Faber, 1941.
Primitive Scenes and Festivals. London, Faber, 1942.
The Homing of the Winds and Other Passages in Prose. London, Faber, 1942.
Splendours and Miseries. London, Faber, 1943.
British Architects and Craftsmen: A Survey of Taste, Design,

and Style During Three Centuries 1600 to 1830.   London, Batsford, 1945; revised edition, 1947, 1949, 1960; New York, Scribner, 1946.

The Hunters and the Hunted.   London, Macmillan, 1947; New York, Macmillan, 1948.

The Netherlands: A Study of Some Aspects of Art, Costume and Social Life.   London, Batsford, 1948; revised edition, 1974; New York, Hastings House, 1974.

Morning, Noon and Night in London.   London, Macmillan, 1948.

Theatrical Figures in Porcelain: German 18th Century.   London, Curtain Press, 1949.

Spain.   London, Batsford, 1950; revised edition, 1951; New York, Hastings House, 1975.

Cupid and the Jacaranda.   London, Macmillan, 1952.

Truffle Hunt with Sacheverell Sitwell.   London, Hale, 1953.

Fine Bird Books 1700-1900, with Hanasyde Buchanan and James Fisher.   London, Collins, and New York, Van Nostrand, 1953.

Selected Works of Sacheverell Sitwell.   Indianapolis, Bobbs Merrill, 1953.

Portugal and Madeira.   London, Batsford, 1954.

Old Garden Roses: Part One, with James Russell.   London, Collins, 1955.

Selected Works of Sacheverell Sitwell.   London, Hale, 1955.

Denmark.   London, Batsford, and New York, Hastings House, 1956.

Great Flower Books 1700-1900: A Bibliographical Record of Two Centuries of Finely-illustrated Flower Books, with Wilfrid Blunt and Patrick M. Synge.   London, Collins, 1956.

Arabesque and Honeycomb.   London, Hale, 1957; New York, Random House, 1958.

Malta, photographs by Antony Armstrong-Jones.   London, Batsford, 1958.

Journey to the Ends of Time: Lost in the Dark Wood.   London, Cassell, and New York, Random House, 1959.

Bridge of the Brocade Sash: Travels and Observations in Japan.   London, Weidenfeld and Nicolson, 1959; Cleveland, World, 1960.

Austria, photographs by Toni Schneider.   London, Thames and Hudson, and New York, Viking Press, 1959.

Golden Wall and Mirador: From England to Peru.   London, Weidenfeld and Nicolson, and Cleveland, World, 1961.

The Red Chapels of Banteai Srei, and Temples in Cambodia, India, Siam and Nepal.   London, Weidenfeld and Nicolson, 1962; as *Great Temples of the East*, New York, Obolensky, 1963.

Monks, Nuns, and Monasteries.   London, Weidenfeld and Nicolson, and New York, Holt Rinehart, 1965.

Southern Baroque Revisited.   London, Weidenfeld and Nicolson, 1967.

Baroque and Rococo.   New York, Putnam, 1967.

Gothic Europe.   London, Weidenfeld and Nicolson, and New York, Holt Rinehart, 1969.

For Want of a Golden City (autobiography).   London, Thames and Hudson, and New York, Day, 1973.

Fugue: A Study of J.S. Bach's Organ Preludes and Fugues.   Privately printed, 1976.

Editor, *Great Houses of Europe*.   London, Weidenfeld and Nicolson, and New York, Putnam, 1961.

*

Bibliography: *A Bibliography of Edith, Osbert and Sacheverell Sitwell* by Richard Fifoot, London, Hart Davis, 1963; New York, Oxford University Press, 1964; revised edition, London, Hart Davis MacGibbon, 1976.

Critical Studies: *The Three Sitwells: A Biographical and Critical Study* by R.L. Mégroz, London, Richards Press, and New York, Doran, 1927; *A Nest of Tigers: Edith, Osbert, and Sacheverell Sitwell in Their Times* by John Lehmann, London, Macmillan, and Boston, Little Brown, 1968; *Sacheverell Sitwell: A Symposium* edited by Derek Parker, London, Rota, 1975; *Hand and Eye: An Anthology for Sacheverell Sitwell* edited by Geoffrey Elborn, Edinburgh, Tragara Press, 1977; *Façades: Edith, Osbert, and Sacheverell Sitwell* by John Pearson, London, Macmillan, 1978, as *The Sitwells: A Family's History*, New York, Harcourt Brace, 1980.

*   *   *

Born in 1897, Sir Sacheverell Sitwell was the youngest member of a brilliant family who, rejecting an assured status as members of the highest country gentry, flung themselves from early youth with dashing enthusiasm into the practice of the arts of prose and poetry and the appreciation of all the arts. They were, for a time, during the 1920's, brilliantly in fashion, and then suddenly out of it. Edith Sitwell attained her highest reputation during the Second World War with her bold, sweeping, and direct poems about the horrors of war and the strange mercies of God. Sir Osbert Sitwell, from whom Sir Sacheverell inherited the baronetcy, attained his highest reputation with his series of autobiographical writings, after the Second World War, in which he made his father, Sir George Reresay Sitwell, one of the greatest comic figures in European fiction. Sir Sacheverell, who has visited almost every country, and seen almost every important art-work in the world, never quite attained the fame of his elder brother and sister, though his almost Trollopeian or Jamesian output of books is larger than theirs, and his early autobiographical fantasia, *All Summer in a Day* (1926), is a masterpiece of poetic prose which neither of his siblings equalled. Between 1948 (when he published his *Selected Poems*, chosen from fifteen previous volumes) and 1972, he found no one willing to risk publishing more poems, though publishers rightly leap for his prose (his book about Japan made me resee, with fresh eyes, many things I thought I had already seen). Yet what I have seen of his poems since 1948—a large selection was printed in the *Poetry Review*, then edited by John Smith—seemed to me, retrospectively, to prove Sir Sacheverell's contention in a letter that he had been writing *better* poems, on the whole, since 1948. It was simply that Sitwells, first under Grigson and Leavis, and then under Robert Conquest and the "Movement," were out. The "movement," as such, is dead, and there is a growing tendency among young and serious poetic aestheticians, like Dr. Veronica Forrest-Thomson, to recognise that a poem is not a "slice of life," prose chunked up into clumsy verse, but a rational artifice, whose importance is much less in its outward reference to an "external world" which we know only through verbal conventions than in its inner play of interstresses of sound and sense. Poetry, in other words, is less a criticism of life than a criticism of *language*. When this new aesthetics prevails, as I think it will, Sir Sacheverell will have his due, and his siblings be restored to favour. People will no longer worry about the "meaning" but taste the crispness of

> The parrot's voice snaps out—
> No good to contradict—
> What he says he'll say again:
> Dry facts, dry biscuits

and the colour and lushness of

Let light like honey shine upon your skin:
When you're hot and like a comb of fire
Glide back into this shade,
Bend that heavy branch down with your hand upon its fruit,
Ripe cherries and a honeycomb must make my bread and wine.

—G.S. Fraser

_____

SKELTON, Robin. Canadian. Born in Easington, East
Yorkshire, England, 12 October 1925. Educated at Pocklington
Grammar School, near York, 1936-43; Christ's College, Cambridge, 1943-44; University of Leeds, 1947-51, B.A. (honours)
1950, M.A. in English 1951. Served in the Royal Air Force,
1944-47: Sergeant. Married Sylvia Mary Jarrett in 1957; one son
and two daughters. Assistant Lecturer, 1951-54, and Lecturer in
English, 1954-63, Manchester University. Associate Professor,
1963-66, since 1966, Professor of English, Director of the Creative Writing Program, 1967-73, and Chairman of the Department of Creative Writing, 1973-76, University of Victoria, British Columbia. Managing Director, Lotus Press, Hull, 1950-52;
examiner, National Universities Joint Matriculation Board,
1954-58, and Chairman of Examiners in English O Level, 1958-
60. Poetry reviewer, 1956-57, and drama reviewer, 1958-60,
Manchester *Guardian*; art reviewer, Victoria *Daily Times*, British Columbia, 1964-66. Founder member, Peterloo Group
(poets and painters), Manchester, 1957-60; founding secretary,
Manchester Institute of Contemporary Arts, 1960-62. Centennial Lecturer, University of Massachusetts, Amherst, 1962-63;
Visiting Professor, University of Michigan, Ann Arbor, 1967.
Editor, with John Peter, 1967-71, and sole editor, 1972-83, *Malahat Review*, Victoria; Editor-in-Chief, Sono Nis Press, Victo-
ria, 1976-83. Since 1972, Director, Pharos Press, Victoria. Collage maker: individual shows—Victoria, 1966, 1968, 1980. First
Vice-Chairman, 1981, and Chairman, 1982-83, Writers' Union
of Canada. Recipient: Canada Council grant, 1977. Fellow,
Royal Society of Literature, 1966. Address: Department of
Creative Writing, University of Victoria, Victoria, British
Columbia V8W 2Y2, Canada.

PUBLICATIONS

Verse

Patmos and Other Poems. London, Routledge, 1955.
Third Day Lucky. London and New York, Oxford University
    Press, 1958.
Begging the Dialect: Poems and Ballads. London and New
    York, Oxford University Press, 1960.
Two Ballads of the Muse. Cambridge, Rampant Lions Press,
    1960.
The Dark Window: Verses. London and New York, Oxford
    University Press, 1962.
A Valedictory Poem. Privately printed, 1963.
An Irish Gathering. Dublin, Dolmen Press, 1964.
A Ballad of Billy Barker. Privately printed, 1965.
Inscriptions. Victoria, Morriss, 1967.
Because of This and Other Poems. Manchester, Manchester
    Institute of Contemporary Arts, 1968.

The Hold of Our Hands: Eight Letters to Sylvia. Privately
    printed, 1968.
Selected Poems 1947-1967. Toronto, McClelland and Stew-
    art, and London, Oxford University Press, 1968.
Selected Verse (as Georges Zuk). San Francisco, Kayak, 1969.
Answers. London, Enitharmon Press, 1969.
An Irish Album. Dublin, Dolmen Press, 1969.
The Hunting Dark. London, Deutsch, 1971.
*Remembering Synge: A Poem in Homage for the Centenary of
    His Birth, 16 April 1871.* Dublin, Dolmen Press, 1971.
*A Different Mountain: Messages 1962-1970: Poems and Photo-
    graphs.* San Francisco, Kayak, 1971.
Private Speech: Messages 1962-1970. Vancouver, Sono Nis
    Press, 1971.
Three for Herself. Rushden, Northamptonshire, Sceptre Press,
    1972.
Musebook. Victoria, Pharos Press, 1972.
A Christmas Poem. Privately printed, 1972.
Country Songs. Rushden, Northamptonshire, Sceptre Press,
    1973.
Timelight. Toronto, McClelland and Stewart, and London,
    Heinemann, 1974.
Fifty Syllables for a Fiftieth Birthday. Privately printed, 1975.
The Underwear of the Unicorn (as Georges Zuk). Nanaimo,
    British Columbia, Oolichan, 1975.
Callsigns. Victoria, Sono Nis Press, 1976.
Because of Love. Toronto, McClelland and Stewart, 1977.
Three Poems. Knotting, Bedfordshire, Sceptre Press, 1977.
Landmarks. Victoria, Sono Nis Press, 1979.
The Collected Shorter Poems 1947-1977. Victoria, British
    Columbia, Sono Nis Press, 1981.
Limits. Erin, Ontario, Porcupine's Quill, 1981.
De Nihilo. Toronto, Aloysius Press, 1982.
Zuk. Erin, Ontario, Porcupine's Quill, 1982.
Wordsong. Victoria, British Columbia, Sono Nis Press, 1983.
The Man Who Sang His Sleep. Erin, Ontario, Porcupine's
    Quill, 1984.

Play

The Paper Cage. Lantzville, British Columbia, Oolichan,
    1982.

Other

John Ruskin: The Final Years. Manchester, John Rylands
    Library and Manchester University Press, 1955.
The Poetic Pattern. London, Routledge, 1956; Berkeley, Uni-
    versity of California Press, 1958.
Painters Talking: Michael Snow and Tony Connor Interviewed.
    Manchester, Peterloo Group, 1957.
Cavalier Poets. London, Longman, 1960.
Poetry. London, English Universities Press, 1963; New York,
    Dover, 1965.
The Writings of J.M. Synge. London, Thames and Hudson,
    1971.
The Practice of Poetry. London, Heinemann, and New York,
    Barnes and Noble, 1971.
J.M. Synge and His World. London, Thames and Hudson,
    1971.
J.M. Synge. Lewisburg, Pennsylvania, Bucknell University
    Press, 1972.
The Poet's Calling. London, Heinemann, and New York,
    Barnes and Noble, 1975.
Poetic Truth. London, Heinemann, and New York, Barnes
    and Noble, 1978.

Spellcraft. Toronto, McClelland and Stewart, and London, Routledge, 1978.

They Call It the Cariboo. Victoria, Sono Nis Press, 1979.

Hubert Siebner. Victoria, British Columbia, Sono Nis Press, 1979.

House of Dreams. Erin, Ontario, Porcupine's Quill, 1983.

Editor, *Leeds University Poetry 1949.* Leeds, Lotus Press, 1950.

Editor, with D. Metcalfe, *The Acadine Poets, Series I-III.* Hull, Yorkshire, Lotus Press, 1950.

Editor, *J.M. Synge: Translations.* Dublin, Dolmen Press, 1961.

Editor, *Four Plays and The Aran Islands,* by J.M. Synge. London and New York, Oxford University Press, 1962.

Editor, *Edward Thomas' Selected Poems.* London, Hutchinson, 1962.

Editor, *J.M. Synge: Collected Poems.* London, Oxford University Press, 1962.

Editor, *Six Irish Poets: Austin Clarke, Richard Kell, Thomas Kinsella, John Montague, Richard Murphy, Richard Weber.* London, Oxford University Press, 1962.

Editor, *Viewpoint: An Anthology of Poetry.* London, Hutchinson, 1962.

Editor, *Five Poets of the Pacific Northwest.* Seattle, University of Washington Press, 1964.

Editor, *Poetry of the Thirties.* London, Penguin, 1964.

Editor, *Selected Poems of Byron.* London, Heinemann, 1964; New York, Barnes and Noble, 1966.

Editor, *Collected Poems,* by David Gascoyne. London, Oxford University Press-Deutsch, 1965.

Editor, with David R. Clark, *The Irish Renaissance: A Gathering of Essays, Letters and Memoirs from the Massachusetts Review.* Dublin, Dolmen Press, and London, Oxford University Press, 1965.

Editor, with Ann Saddlemyer, *The World of W.B. Yeats: Essays in Perspective.* Seattle, University of Washington Press, 1965; revised edition, 1967.

Editor, *Poetry of the Forties.* London, Penguin, 1968.

Editor, *Riders to the Sea,* by J.M. Synge. Dublin, Dolmen Press, 1969.

Editor, *Introductions from an Island: A Selection of Student Writing.* Victoria, University of Victoria, 5 vols., 1969-74.

Editor, with Alan Clodd, *Collected Verse Translations,* by David Gascoyne. London, Oxford University Press-Deutsch, 1970.

Editor, *The Cavalier Poets.* London, Faber, and New York, Oxford University Press, 1970.

Editor, *Herbert Read: A Memorial Symposium.* London, Methuen, 1970.

Editor, *The Collected Plays of Jack B. Yeats.* London, Secker and Warburg, and Indianapolis, Bobbs Merrill, 1971.

Editor and Translator, *Two Hundred Poems from the Greek Anthology.* London, Methuen, and Seattle, University of Washington Press, 1971.

Editor, *Some Sonnets from "Laura in Death" after the Italian of Francesco Petrarch,* by J.M. Synge (bilingual edition). Dublin, Dolmen Press, 1971.

Editor, *Thirteen Irish Writers on Ireland.* Boston, Godine, 1973.

Editor, with William David Thomas, *A Gathering in Celebration of the Eightieth Birthday of Robert Graves.* Victoria, British Columbia, University of Victoria, 1975.

Editor, *Six Poets of British Columbia.* Victoria, British Columbia, Sono Nis Press, 1980.

*

Manuscript Collections: MacPherson Library, University of Victoria; University of Texas, Austin.

Robin Skelton comments:

I have been called a Muse Poet, a Lyrical Poet, a Confessional Poet, a Traditional Poet, and Innovative Poet, a Romantic Poet, a British Poet, an Irish Poet, and a Canadian Poet. I hope I am all these things and more. I relish most the compliment paid me by a very old lady, the mother of an eminent British poet, who said (to somebody else) of my work, "All human life is there!" I would like to think that this is the case. All my life I have tried to work in terms of Rabelais' dictum, "Everything that God allows to happen I allow to be written about." This has resulted in my finding myself using, and being used by, many different attitudes and emotions to an extent which makes it impossible for me to sum up a poetry which is, after all, my life and the life of those forces which have spoken through me. There is no point in listing my "masters" or the major "influences" upon my work, for I have learned something from almost every poet I have read from Homer to the present. I could perhaps suggest that the writings of Jung, to which I was introduced by Herbert Read, have been important to me for a quarter of a century, as also has been the Neo-Platonist Tradition from which he drew. I cannot stand back from my poetry and see it clearly, for, thank God, it is still in the writing; and therefore still changing its shape. Perhaps some critic other than I may detect connections between the poetry I have made and the authors I have edited or written about. Perhaps another critic may uncover a central theme or themes and disclose my "philosophy." I myself am in doubt. I can only respond to an editor's request for auctorial comment by parodying Archibald MacLeish's rightly famous line and saying "A poet should not mean, but be," and pray that I may continue to "be" a poet, by which I mean merely a man through whom poems continue to arrive.

*   *   *

Robin Skelton is English by birth, and it was in Britain that he published his first books of verse, before in 1963, in his crucial middle years, he moved to Canada where he has lived ever since. More than any other poet now working in Canada, he has remained a man of two worlds, European and North American. Since moving to Victoria, British Columbia, he has edited two anthologies of English verse (*Poetry of the Thirties* and *Poetry of the Forties*) and he has continued to write on the Irish renaissance and particularly on J.M. Synge, while a great deal of that background of early 20th-century Anglo-Irish literature has lingered since then in his own poems. He has also edited since 1967 an international literary journal—the *Malahat Review*—which is perhaps the only magazine wherein Canadian poetry competes on an egalitarian basis with the poetry of other traditions.

The effect of emigration on Skelton's own poetry has been to create a feeling of distance—rather than detachment—from significant experience: an inverted telescope view of situations and states of mind which one senses are in reality nearer to the poet than their magic realist aloofness at first suggests. Skelton's poetry from the beginning reflected the analytical and strongly structured frame of mind that dominates his excellent critical work on Ruskin and the Irish poets. He began in the Movement manner of the British 1950's, writing in a flat and almost audibly North country tone the deliberately unexciting verse which was favoured at that time in contrast to the emotional manner of the 1940's. Since then, however, his poetry has developed an individual style—reflective and, in the later poems especially, marked often by a stoic melancholy. Narrative, and especially the narrative of feelings—feelings prompted by memory and the sense of exile—is a mode that Skelton has particularly developed, in volumes like *The Hunting Dark* and *Because of Love*. At the same time, with a fine and continually experimental craftsmanship, he has written in a variety of lyric and satiric moods. More recently, in *Private Speech*, his verse turned towards the gnomic, and in his *Poems from the Greek Anthology* he explored the ambiguous borderland between translation and poetry.

Yet the reflective, quasi-autobiographical poem still shows Skelton at his best, and perhaps his finest work in this vein is contained in the poetic sequence, *Timelight*. In a sense this is Skelton's equivalent of Wordsworth's *Prelude*, a philosophical summing up of his life to date, but instead of being a structured discourse it takes the form of a series of discontinuous insights, sharp flashes of apprehension or, just as often, muted and elusive illuminations. As Skelton points out in his Preface, a prime clue to the whole venture is given in a single line of one of the poems: "Every travelling is of the soul." Yet the road the soul travels is often the way of the senses, and, as the poet says: "I am trapped/in memory's riot,/carried through/everything that/bones lay claim to." Some poems deal with places the poet has visited, but treat the mundane scene as a kind of translucent screen through which is seen a looming and ambiguous reality:

> it is the will of being's self
> that fills
> the crowding blossom
> with the gentle haze
> and asks the mountains
> for their certainties

Dramatic monologues discuss the problems of life and death. A Bestiary develops the animal symbolism of the world of gross existence through which the soul must pass. Memories of personal life, of dreams, of books are fused "to hint a whole/beyond the vagaries/of its parts." In such lines and in many other ways, *Timelight* and Skelton's other books show very clearly his links with the great modernists in whose shadow (or whose light according to one's viewpoint) he has always written, not only Eliot and Pound but also the later Yeats. Skelton, more than any poet I know, belongs not to one part but to the whole of the tradition of English poetry.

—George Woodcock

SKINNER, Knute (Rumsey). American. Born in St. Louis, Missouri, 25 April 1929. Educated at Culver-Stockton College, Canton, Missouri, 1947-49; University of Northern Colorado, Greeley, A.B. in speech and drama 1951; Middlebury College, Vermont, M.A. in English 1954; University of Iowa, Iowa City, Ph.D. in English 1958. Married 1) Jeanne Pratt in 1953 (divorced, 1954), one son; 2) Linda Kuhn in 1961 (divorced, 1977), two sons; 3) Edna Faye Kiel in 1978. English teacher, Boise High School, Idaho, 1951-54; Instructor in English, University of Iowa, 1960-61; Assistant Professor of English, Oklahoma College for Women, Chickasha, 1961-62. Part-time Lecturer, 1962-70, Associate Professor, 1971-73, and since 1973, Professor of English, Western Washington University, Bellingham. Poetry Editor, Southern Illinois University Press,

Carbondale, 1975-76. Since 1977, Co-Editor, *Bellingham Review*, and Editor and Publisher, Signpost Press, Bellingham. Recipient: Huntington Hartford Foundation Fellowship, 1961; National Endowment for the Arts grant, 1975. Address: 412 North State Street, Bellingham, Washington 98255, U.S.A.; or, Killaspuglonane, Lahinch, County Clare, Ireland (summer).

PUBLICATIONS

Verse

Stranger with a Watch. Francestown, New Hampshire, Golden Quill Press, 1965.
A Close Sky over Killaspuglonane. Dublin, Dolmen Press, 1968; St. Louis, Burton Press, 1975.
In Dinosaur Country. Greeley, Colorado, Pierian Press, 1969.
The Sorcerers: A Laotian Tale. Bellingham, Washington, Goliards Press, 1972.
Hearing of the Hard Times. South Thomaston, Maine, Northwoods Press, 1981.
The Flame Room. Tacoma, Washington, Folly Press, 1983.
Selected Poems. Portree, Isle of Skye, Aquila, 1985.

*

Manuscript Collection: Humanities Research Center, University of Texas, Austin.

Critical Studies: "From Ireland the American" by Gregory Fitz-Gerald, in *Ann Arbor Review* (Michigan), Summer 1968; by Thomas Churchill, in *Concerning Poetry* (Bellingham, Washington), Fall 1968; "Killaspuglonane" by Harry Chambers, in *Phoenix* (Manchester), Summer 1969; X.J. Kennedy, in *Concerning Poetry* (Bellingham, Washington), Fall 1969.

Knute Skinner comments:
I have attempted to embody (emphasis on body) love and death. In other poems I have analyzed character. In a few I have attempted to enter nature and have gone so far as to find spirit in a cow. I am no longer as interested in the distant and abstract as I am in my immediate surroundings. Some of my recent poems are set in Killaspuglonane, my adopted townland, and my most recent collection, *The Flame Room*, deals with friends and relatives. My influences are varied and usual. I began by writing rhymed stanzas and now write mostly free verse—though I still use rhyme, meter, syllabic or accentual if the poem asks for it.

* * *

Knute Skinner creates from remarkably disparate sources. His poems of love, death and isolation in *Stranger with a Watch* are powerfully underscored by a wry and acid humor which etches at the surface of experience to reveal inner situations and private struggles. He writes elegies for the living as well as the dead—mourns the mourners. In his constant interplay of mind and senses and in his perception of physical decay and time he recalls Hardy, Housman, and Yeats. Here is ironic laughter at twisted circumstance; here is understatement, word-play and a combination of metaphysical and sensual imagery; here is concern with madness, prophecy, and the stripping of poetic language to its bones and marrow. In form Skinner ranges widely and easily from lyric to epigram, from sonnet to ballad to free-style; but his vision is peculiarly his own. By his criticism he reveals how things are and thereby implies how they ought to be—how love should not be a commodity, how men should not journey alone, how formality and self-consciousness should not divert people from genuine feeling. Through his poems the reader catches glimpses of lost connections—of time, places, and people that are not what they were—and a sense of love's fragility and ineffability. In *A Close Sky over Killaspuglonane*, Skinner allies himself with his Irish heritage, reflecting the land, the people, and the traditions of Clare county. Here he writes most strongly out of a sense of place. *In Dinosaur Country* displays an exuberant sense of life through humor which can be gentle, whimsical and uproarious. Unflinchingly, Skinner reintroduces "gross" material into the life experience via poetry. He makes poems of "Blackheads," "Phlegm," "Urine," and presents "A Poem for the Class of 69" (in the concrete poetic style). His laughter is compelling and human, reminding the reader that nothing is ugly or alien unless he makes it so. ⸰

—Carl Lindner

SLAVITT, David (Rytman). American. Born in White Plains, New York, 23 March 1935. Educated at Phillips Academy, Andover, Massachusetts, graduated 1952; Yale University, New Haven, Connecticut, 1952-56, B.A. (magna cum laude) 1956; Columbia University, New York, M.A. 1957. Married 1) Lynn Meyer in 1956 (divorced, 1977), three children; 2) Janet Abrahm in 1978. Instructor, Georgia Institute of Technology, Atlanta, 1957-58; Associate Editor, *Newsweek* magazine, New York, 1958-65; Associate Professor of English, Temple University, Philadelphia, 1978-80. Address: 523 South 41st Street, Philadelphia, Pennsylvania 19104, U.S.A.

PUBLICATIONS

Verse

Suits for the Dead. New York, Scribner, 1961.
The Carnivore. Chapel Hill, University of North Carolina Press, 1965.
Day Sailing and Other Poems. Chapel Hill, University of North Carolina Press, 1969.
Child's Play. Baton Rouge, Louisiana State University Press, 1972.
Vital Signs: New and Selected Poems. New York, Doubleday, 1975.
Rounding the Horn. Baton Rouge, Louisiana State University Press, 1978.
Dozens: A Poem. Baton Rouge, Louisiana State University Press, 1981.
Big Nose. Baton Rouge, Louisiana State University Press, 1983.
The Walls of Thebes. Baton Rouge, Louisiana State University Press, 1985.

Play

The Cardinal Sins (produced New York, 1968).

Novels

Rochelle; or, Virtue Rewarded. London, Chapman and Hall, 1966; New York, Delacorte Press, 1967.

The Exhibitionist (as Henry Sutton). New York, Geis, 1967; London, Geis, 1968.
Feel Free. New York, Delacorte Press, 1968; London, Hodder and Stoughton, 1969.
The Voyeur (as Henry Sutton). New York, Geis, and London, Hodder and Stoughton, 1969.
Vector (as Henry Sutton). New York, Geis, 1970; London, Hodder and Stoughton, 1971.
Anagrams. London, Hodder and Stoughton, 1970; New York, Doubleday, 1971.
ABCD. New York, Doubleday, 1972; London, Hamish Hamilton, 1974.
The Liberated (as Henry Sutton). New York, Doubleday, 1973; London, W.H. Allen, 1974.
The Outer Mongolian. New York, Doubleday, 1973.
The Killing of the King. New York, Doubleday, and London, W.H. Allen, 1974.
King of Hearts. New York, Arbor House, 1976.
That Golden Woman (as Henry Lazarus). New York, Fawcett, 1976; London, Sphere, 1977.
The Sacrifice (as Henry Sutton). New York, Grosset and Dunlap, 1978; London, Sphere, 1980.
Jo Stern. New York, Harper, 1978.
The Idol (as David Benjamin). New York, Putnam, 1978.
The Proposal (as Henry Sutton). New York, Charter, 1980.
Cold Comfort. New York, Methuen, 1980.
Ringer. New York, Dutton, 1982; London, Severn House, 1983.
Alice at 80. New York, Doubleday, 1984; London, Severn House, 1985.
Secrets, with Bill Adler. New York, Doubleday, 1985.

Other

Understanding Social Life: An Introduction to Social Psychology, with Paul F. Secord and Carl W. Backman. New York, McGraw Hill, 1976.

Translator, *The Eclogues of Virgil.* New York, Doubleday, 1971.
Translator, *The Eclogues and the Georgics of Virgil.* New York, Doubleday, 1972.

*

Manuscript Collection: Beinecke Library, Yale University, New Haven, Connecticut.

Critical Study: interview in *The Writer's Voice* edited by George Garrett and John Graham, New York, Morrow, 1973.

*   *   *

In 1961, in the introduction to David Slavitt's first book of poems, John Hall Wheelock said that "one of the distinguishing characteristics of Mr. Slavitt's poetry is a severe restraint in the use of figurative language. It is the brilliance and clarity of his work, its brisk pace and taut resonance of line, its ironic and sardonic counterpoint, and, above all, its dramatic tensions, rather than any striking use of imagery or metaphor, that make it memorable." Slavitt's later books have borne out that description of his poetry, for he is a classicist—not one of the Eliot generation's neo-classicists who still depended so heavily on the "romantic image," but a genuine classicist, using reason and wit to order his experience, to explain it, to describe it rather than (like a romantic) to embody it or transcend it.

The voice of Slavitt's poetry is literally that of a man talking, an intelligent and urbane man, a man of wit and no little wisdom, speaking of life and more increasingly of death, often playfully, more often very seriously. His version of Virgil's *Eclogues* and *Georgics*, not strictly a translation of Virgil's poetic musings, but an application of Slavitt's own very striking voice and vision to those musings, is (not surprisingly) his finest book of poems, audacious, even arrogant, and brilliant throughout, a genuine translation of Virgil's approach to things into Slavitt's own well-honed modern classical idiom and a commentary on that approach as well.

As aware as any classical poet was of poetry as a self-conscious confidence trick, Slavitt is also aware of its real and necessary values. In this version of the eighth eclogue, he says:

> Madness—
> schizoid, of course—but it works, and you and I
> can read, hear, give ourselves up to the poem,
> and all our hurts too are healed, at least for a time.
> We're all like dogs. A bone, a sop, distracts,
> or the howl of another dog. We take it up,
> one or two at a time, and then whole packs,
> pouring out a grief we never felt
> or sharing a real grief with all the others,
> which becomes a public occasion, a communion,
> a kind of celebration, a kind of prayer.

David Slavitt masters the madness of that con game in his poems, and he speaks in a voice that is distinctive and immediately recognizable as his. In a romantic time, he has gone his own way, and it has proven to have been a way well worth the going.

—R.H.W. Dillard

SMITH, Dave (David Jeddie Smith). American. Born in Portsmouth, Virginia, 19 December 1942. Educated at the University of Virginia, Charlottesville, 1961-65, B.A. in English 1965; College of William and Mary, Williamsburg, Virginia, 1966; Southern Illinois University, Edwardsville, M.A. 1969; Ohio University, Athens, Ph.D. in English 1976. Served in the United States Air Force, 1969-72: Staff Sergeant. Married Deloras Mae Weaver in 1966; one son and two daughters. Teacher of English and French, and football coach, Poquoson High School, Virginia, 1965-67; part-time instructor, Christopher Newport College, Newport News, Virginia, 1970-72, Thomas Nelson, Community College, Hampton, Virginia, 1970-72, and College of William and Mary, 1971; Instructor, Western Michigan University, Kalamazoo, 1974-75; Assistant Professor, Cottey College, Nevada, Missouri, 1975-76; Assistant Professor, 1976-79, Director of the Creative Writing Program, 1976-80, and Associate Professor of English, 1979-81, University of Utah, Salt Lake City; Associate Professor of English, University of Florida, Gainesville, 1981. Since 1981, Professor of English, Virginia Commonwealth University, Richmond. Visiting Professor of English, State University of New York, Binghamton, 1980. Editor, *Sou'wester* magazine, Edwardsville, Illinois, 1967-68; Founding Editor, *Back Door* magazine, Poquoson, Virginia and Athens, Ohio, 1969-79; Poetry Editor, *Rocky Mountain Review*, Tempe, Arizona, 1978-80; columnist, *American Poetry Review*, Philadelphia, 1978-82. Recipient: *Kansas Quarterly* prize, 1975; Breadloaf Writers Conference John Atherton Fellowship, 1975;

Borestone Mountain award, 1976; National Endowment for the Arts Fellowship, 1976, 1981; *Southern Poetry Review* prize, 1977; American Academy award, 1979; *Portland Review* prize, 1979; Guggenheim Fellowship, 1982. Agent: Timothy Seldes, Russell and Volkening Inc., 50 West 29th Street, New York, New York 10001. Address: 1935 Stonehenge Drive, Richmond, Virginia 23225, U.S.A.

PUBLICATIONS

Verse

Bull Island. Poquoson, Virginia, Back Door Press, 1970.
Mean Rufus Throw Down. Fredonia, New York, Basilisk Press, 1973.
The Fisherman's Whore. Athens, Ohio University Press, 1974.
Drunks. Edwardsville, Illinois, Sou'wester, 1974.
Cumberland Station. Urbana, University of Illinois Press, 1976.
In Dark, Sudden with Light. Athens, Ohio, Croissant, 1977.
Goshawk, Antelope. Urbana, University of Illinois Press, 1979.
Dream Flights. Urbana, University of Illinois Press, 1981.
Blue Spruce. Syracuse, Tamarack, 1981.
Homage to Edgar Allan Poe. Baton Rouge, Louisiana State University Press, 1981.
In the House of the Judge. New York, Harper, 1983.
Gray Soldiers. Winston-Salem, North Carolina, Stuart Wright, 1983.

Novel

Onliness. Baton Rouge, Louisiana State University Press, 1981.

Short Stories

Southern Delights. Athens, Ohio, Croissant, 1984.

Other

Local Assays: On Contemporary American Poetry. Urbana, University of Illinois Press, 1985.

Editor, *The Pure Clear Word: Essays on the Poetry of James Wright.* Urbana, University of Illinois Press, 1982.

*

Critical Studies: by Robert DeMott, in *American Poets since World War II* edited by Donald J. Greiner, Detroit, Gale, 1980; "The Mind's Assertive Flow," in *New Yorker*, July 1980, and *Part of Nature, Part of Us*, Cambridge, Massachusetts, Harvard University Press, 1981, both by Helen Vendler; Alan Bold, in *Times Literary Supplement* (London), November 1981; *The Giver of Morning: On the Poetry of Dave Smith* (includes bibliography) edited by Bruce Weigl, Birmingham, Alabama, Thunder City Press, 1982; "Unfold the Fullness: Dave Smith's Poetry and Fiction" by Thom Swiss, in *Sewanee Review* (Tennessee), Summer 1983.

Dave Smith comments:

The poems I have written seem to me attempts, in their structure, to conflate the lyric and the narrative. I have wanted to find poetry in the prosaic and ordinary moments of our lives. I have wanted a language in the poem that was neither artificially poetic nor conversationally banal: a rough, but measurably cadenced music swelling out of and defining a minor narrative occasion. All this has rested and continues to rest on my assumption that poetry is about the individual spirit in crisis. Poetry is the knight doing psychic combat for us. It is the death-wrestler. I think it exists to give us pleasure in all the ways enumerated by Dr. Samuel Johnson: the pleasures of memory, of landscape, of diversion, of identity, of event, and of knowledge. But these pleasures are not smug self-congratulations. I think the poems which offer those particular delights are poems which reveal and reinforce the human bond, the human responsibility in this world. I would be pleased to believe my poems had such an effect on readers.

*   *   *

Dave Smith began by writing jealously and defiantly about "his" Virginia country, a peninsula surrounded by the Poquoson River and Chesapeake Bay, telling stories about tough, hard-working watermen and women. He wrote of it as if it were Troy, a place of elemental struggles and defeats. The man in "Hard Times, But Carrying On" has eyes, for example, "once blue and pure/as the Bay, but they too turned thick with gun trails of tasteless oil...":

> Even so
> he works his hole with craft
> eats fish for lunch at noon and dots
> it with a single swallow of rye, then
> drags back hard on the surging
> net....

The surface of the early poems is hard, tense, with the struggles occasioned not by political or spiritual forces, but by natural ones: wind, water, and sun. In "March Storm" and "Among the Oyster Boats at Plum Tree Cave" these forces are antagonists in a wild, passionate drama that leaves everyone exhausted, spent. In "Cumberland Station" the reader learns also why people, including Smith, leave the country behind with some relief.

In subsequent collections, a sequence called *Homage to Edgar Allan Poe* and another called *Men With/Without Women* exhibit quite different, but impressive powers of lyricism. "Waking Under Spruce With My Love," at the beginning of the series, says, for example,

> I can feel the sheet luff on my thighs, the emptiness
> cool and pleasant inside my body....
> I think this must be the silence that love always is....

This sequence of poems ends, fittingly, with "Wedding Song," a witty, clear-eyed tribute to the occasion that shows also the writer's strong sense of history and topography. In *Goshawk, Antelope*, Smith turned with equal vigor to the myths and perils of the Far West, Wyoming and Utah, where he moved in 1976.

In recent years, Smith turns from the tough regionalism of the early poems to a subtler, yet never careless language, with some indebtedness to Louis Simpson, to the narrative style of Robert Penn Warren, and more recently to James Wright in a poem appropriately entitled "Outside Martins Ferry, Ohio." The voice in these poems is, always, however, Smith's own, with a marvelous respect for place and for all that is best in contemporary language and song. Whatever he writes about takes on the look of Smith's territory, for he knows, as Flannery O'Connor would say, where he is *frum*.

—Michael True

SMITH, Iain Crichton. Gaelic name: Iain Mac A'Ghobhainn. British. Born on the Isle of Lewis, Outer Hebrides, Scotland, 1 January 1928. Educated at the University of Aberdeen, M.A. (honours) in English 1949. Served in the British Army Education Corps, 1950-52: Sergeant. Married. Secondary school teacher, Clydebank, 1952-55; teacher of English, Oban High School, 1955-77. Recipient: Scottish Arts Council award, 1966, 1968, 1974, 1977, and prize, 1968; BBC award, for television play, 1970; Book Council award, 1970; Silver Pen Award, 1971; Queen's Silver Jubilee Medal. LL.D.: Dundee University, 1983; D.Litt.: Glasgow University, 1984. Fellow, Royal Society of Literature. O.B.E. (Officer, Order of the British Empire), 1980. Address: Tigh na Fuaran, Taynuilt, Argyll PA35 1JW, Scotland.

PUBLICATIONS

Verse

The Long River. Edinburgh, M. Macdonald, 1955.
New Poets 1959, with Karen Gershon and Christopher Levenson. London, Eyre and Spottiswoode, 1959.
Deer on the High Hills: A Poem. Edinburgh, Giles Gordon, 1960.
Thistles and Roses. London, Eyre and Spottiswoode, 1961.
The Law and the Grace. London, Eyre and Spottiswoode, 1965.
Biobuill is Sanasan Reice (Bibles and Advertisements). Glasgow, Gairm, 1965.
Three Regional Voices, with Michael Longley and Barry Tebb. London, Poet and Printer, 1968.
At Helensburgh. Belfast, Festival, 1968.
From Bourgeois Land. London, Gollancz, 1969.
Selected Poems. London, Gollancz, and Chester Springs, Pennsylvania, Dufour, 1970.
Penguin Modern Poets 21, with George Mackay Brown and Norman MacCaig. London, Penguin, 1972.
Love Poems and Elegies. London, Gollancz, 1972.
Hamlet in Autumn. Edinburgh, M. Macdonald, 1972.
Rabhdan is rudan (Verses and Things). Glasgow, Gairm, 1973.
Eadar Fealla-dhà is Glaschu (Between Comedy and Glasgow). Glasgow, University of Glasgow Celtic Department, 1974.
Notebooks of Robinson Crusoe. London, Gollancz, 1974.
Orpheus and Other Poems. Preston, Lancashire, Akros, 1974.
Poems for Donalda. Belfast, Ulsterman, 1974.
The Permanent Island: Gaelic Poems, translated by the author. Edinburgh, M. Macdonald, 1975.
The Notebooks of Robinson Crusoe and Other Poems. London, Gollancz, 1975.
In the Middle—. London, Gollancz, 1977.
Selected Poems 1955-1980, edited by Robin Fulton. Edinburgh, M. Macdonald, 1982.
The Exiles. Manchester, Carcanet, 1984.
Selected Poems. Manchester, Carcanet, 1985.

Plays

An Coileach (The Cockerel; produced Glasgow, 1966). Glasgow, An Comunn Gaidhealach, 1966.
A 'Chuirt (The Trial; produced Glasgow, 1966). Glasgow, An Comunn Gaidhealach, 1966.
A Kind of Play (produced Mull, 1975).
Two by the Sea (produced Mull, 1975).
The Happily Married Couple (produced Mull, 1977).

Radio Play: *Goodman and Death Mahoney*, 1980.

Novels

Consider the Lilies. London, Gollancz, 1968; as *The Alien Light*, Boston, Houghton Mifflin, 1969.
The Last Summer. London, Gollancz, 1969.
My Last Duchess. London, Gollancz, 1971.
Goodbye, Mr. Dixon. London, Gollancz, 1974.
An t-Aonaran (The Hermit). Glasgow, University of Glasgow Celtic Department, 1976.
An End to Autumn. London, Gollancz, 1978.
On the Island. London, Gollancz, 1979.
A Field Full of Folk. London, Gollancz, 1982.
The Search. London, Gollancz, 1983.
The Tenement. London, Gollancz, 1985.

Short Stories

Burn is Aran (Bread and Water; includes verse). Glasgow, Gairm, 1960.
An Dubh is an Gorm (The Black and the Blue). Aberdeen, Aberdeen University, 1963.
Maighsirean is Ministearan (Schoolmasters and Ministers). Inverness, Club Leabhar, 1970.
Survival Without Error and Other Stories. London, Gollancz, 1970.
The Black and the Red. London, Gollancz, 1973.
An t-Adhar Ameireaganach (The American Sky). Inverness, Club Leabhar, 1973.
The Village. Inverness, Club Leabhar, 1976.
The Hermit and Other Stories. London, Gollancz, 1977.
Murdo and Other Stories. London, Gollancz, 1981.
Mr. Trill in Hades and Other Stories. London, Gollancz, 1984.

Other

The Golden Lyric: An Essay on the Poetry of Hugh MacDiarmid. Preston, Lancashire, Akros, 1967.
Iain Am Measg nan Reultan (Iain among the Stars; for children). Glasgow, Gairm, 1970.
River, River: Poems for Children. Edinburgh, M. Macdonald, 1978.
Na h-Ainmhidhean (The Animals; verse for children). Aberfeldy, Perthshire, Clo Chailleann, 1979.

Editor, *Scottish Highland Tales*. London, Ward Lock, 1982.

Translator, *Ben Dorain*, by Duncan Ban Macintyre. Preston, Lancashire, Akros, 1969.
Translator, *Poems to Eimhir*, by Sorley Maclean. London and Newcastle upon Tyne, Gollancz-Northern House, 1971.

*

Bibliography: in *Lines Review 29* (Edinburgh), 1969.

Critical Studies: interview in *Scottish International* (Edinburgh), 1971; *Contemporary Scottish Poetry* by Robin Fulton, Edinburgh, M. Macdonald, 1974; *Iain Crichton Smith*, Glasgow, National Book League, 1979; *Literature of the North* edited by David Hewitt and M.R.G. Spiller, Aberdeen, Aberdeen University Press, 1983; *New Edinburgh Review*, Summer 1984.

Iain Crichton Smith comments:

Interested in the conflict between discipline and freedom, as shown in the title *The Law and the Grace*. No particular sources, except that I admire Lowell's work.

*   *   *

Iain Crichton Smith's "The White Air of March," a long, elliptical poem in the manner of Pound's *Cantos* and Eliot's *Four Quartets*, opens on a characteristic note:

> This is the land God gave to Andy Stewart—we have our
>   inheritance.
> There shall be no ardour, there shall be indifference.
> There shall not be excellence, there shall be the average.
> We shall be the intrepid hunters of golf balls.

"Excellence! 'costing not less than everything' " has always been Crichton Smith's standard, and it is its conspicuous absence from his native country which stirs him, here and in such volumes as *From Bourgeois Land*, to indictment of a venal and hypocritical culture. "It is bitter," he observes, "to be an exile in one's own land" and "to write poems of exile/in a verse without honour or style." Yet, significantly, he is generous to honest incompetence like that of William McGonagall, whom he unexpectedly picks out as a "sign" of persistence, even wrongheadedly, at the highest things: "Endlessly you toil towards Balmoral/to the old lady knitting her slow empire." If the dream of the poem's close (in which "The dead bury their dead" and Scotland discovers, "In the white air of March/a new mind") is to be realized, her current "loss of passion, loss of power" has to be admitted, and the "impenetrable dullness" of a parochial culture overcome.

Should that ever happen, Iain Crichton Smith will have been one of its major agents. Staunchly Gaelic, writing fine poetry in that ancient language, he is nevertheless unequivocally in the mainstream of Modernism, like Hugh MacDiarmid and Basil Bunting, proving that a strong sense of regional loyalty is not inimical to the best spirit of cosmopolitanism. "Shall Gaelic Die?", which he has translated from his own Gaelic, is an aphoristic meditation on precisely this relationship, drawing on Wittgenstein and Saussure, among others, to build an impassioned argument for the survival of his native tongue, as one irreplaceable element in the "spectrum of beautiful languages" which constitute the human world and protect us from the dogmatic single vision of "The one-language descended like a church—like a blanket, like mist." But his concern for language is not an antiquarian's. The final section contrasts the "immutable, universal" absolute, Language, that unrusting gold which Midas found was deadly, to *speech*, the currency which, like "coins that are old and dirty, ...notes that are wrinkled like old faces," can "cop[e] with time." It is to the latter that he gives "allegiance, to these I owe honour, with sweetness." By turns aureate and colloquial, racy and refined with a grave and sober dignity, Crichton Smith's poetry explores the real texture of life and language in contemporary Scotland with an acute and unsentimental sensitivity. He can write of the clichés of "the Bed and Breakfast routine," of the "faded gentry" and shop girls "who holiday on pop and fish-and-chips" without the condescension of Eliot or Auden, but with a fusion of compassion and dispassionate observation which is peculiarly his own. While he brings a conscientious intellect to bear on the pharisaism of the Scottish gerontocracy, he has drawn sharp and sympathetic portraits of age.

Crichton Smith's poetry displays a democratic intellect which never stoops to a sentimental populism. Like his "Responsible Spinster" he always "inspect[s] justice through a queer air"; like his Kierkegaard, he is the "Forced theologian of the minimum place." In *Deer on the High Hills*, a fine sequence which recalls the lucid abstraction and sudden intellectual sensuousness of Wallace Stevens, he disposes of the pathetic fallacies by which we evade looking at the real world, concluding: "There is no metaphor. The stone is stony./The deer step out in isolated air./We move at random on an innocent journey."

In poem after poem he faces the fact of death; in his "World War One" sequence refusing the consolations of poetry and myth. "If You Are about to Die Now" returns to his fascination with the incomprehensible delusions of "great men," to speak of the insufficiency of language:

> If you are about to die now
> there is nothing I can write for you.
> History is silent about this.
> Even Napoleon, face huge as a plate,
> disguised the advance guard and said
> "Why they sent for my brother is because
> he, and not I, is in trouble."

His latest volume considers many modes of exile: Gaels forced by the clearances to find new homes in Canada or Australia; the Scots settler at 60 made a late wanderer by the transformation of Rhodesia to Zimbabwe; Bonny Prince Charlie in Italy; Prospero quitting his desert isle; the dead returning home from war or shipwreck to find their birthplace all changed; the poet himself knowing his native Lewis is now given over to holiday cottages, but believing, *in absentia*, that the true island remains, beneath appearances, "indifferent to the rumours and the stories/stony, persistent." In several poems, poetry itself becomes that authentic island, and, in "When My Poetry Making Has Failed," exile from its true tongue is the bitterest exile of all. Language in these poems is both home and exile at once, as for the Nazi war-criminal hiding in America, who has become "The Man Without a Name," cast into unmeaning, almost hoping to be found so that he can recover his true, guilty place in the human order. The whole theme of the volume is summed up in "Autumn": "It is true/that exile, parting, is our earthly lot." Yet it affirms, too, in the words of "The 'Ordinary' People" two other truths: "I begin to think there are no 'ordinary' people..../I believe that there is no such thing as tragedy."

Iain Crichton Smith has emerged as a poet of major stature. This latest volume, the Poetry Book Society Choice for 1984, on top of the new and substantial *Selected Poems*, makes it possible to see the contours of that achievement.

—Stan Smith

SMITH, John (Charles). British. Born in High Wycombe, Buckinghamshire, 5 April 1924. Educated at St. James's Elementary School, Gerrards Cross, Buckinghamshire. Director, 1946-58, and Managing Director, 1959-71, Christy and Moore Ltd., literary agents, London. Editor, *Poetry Review*, London, 1962-

65. Recipient: *Adam International* Prize, 1953. Address: 3 Adelaide Court, Palmeira Square, Hove, Sussex, England.

PUBLICATIONS

Verse

Gates of Beauty and Death (as C. Busby Smith). London, Fortune Press, 1948.
The Dark Side of Love. London, Hogarth Press, 1952.
The Birth of Venus. London, Hutchinson, 1954.
Excursus in Autumn. London, Hutchinson, 1958.
A Letter to Lao Tze. London, Hart Davis, 1961.
A Discreet Immorality. London, Hart Davis, 1965.
Five Songs of Resurrection. Privately printed, 1967.
Four Ritual Dances. Privately printed, 1968.
Entering Rooms. London, Chatto and Windus-Hogarth Press, 1973.
A Landscape of My Own: Selected Poems 1948-1982. London, Robson, 1982.
Songs for Simpletons. London, Robson, 1984.

Plays

The Mask of Glory (produced Gerrards Cross, Buckinghamshire, 1956.)
Mr. Smith's Apocalypse: A Jazz Cantata, music by Michael Garrick (produced Farnham, Surrey, 1969). London, Robbins Music, 1970.
The Stirring, music by Michael Garrick (produced Manchester, 1984).

Other

Jan le Witt: An Appreciation of His Work, with Herbert Read and Jean Cassou. London, Routledge, 1971.
The Broken Fiddlestick (for children). London, Longman, 1971.
The Early Bird and the Worm (for children). London, Burke, 1972.
The Arts Betrayed. London, Herbert Press, and New York, Universe, 1978.

Editor, with William Kean Seymour, *The Pattern of Poetry*. London, Burke, 1963.
Editor, *My Kind of Verse*. London, Burke, 1965; New York, Macmillan, 1968.
Editor, *Modern Love Poems*. London, Studio Vista, 1966.
Editor, with William Kean Seymour, *Happy Christmas*. Philadelphia, Westminster Press, and London, Burke, 1968.
Editor, *My Kind of Rhymes*. London, Burke, 1972.

*

John Smith comments:
As briefly as possible, I would describe my poetry as lyrical, metaphysical, formal, sardonic.

*   *   *

A certain civilised coolness at first seemed the main characteristic of John Smith's poetry. Admirers of *The Dark Side of Love*—and there were a considerable number—seemed to be looking, like the poet, back to the elegant verse-makers of the seventeenth century: "As any man/With any woman lies/Let him in sleep her lovely limbs discover...." Fortunately, the slightly overblown felicity of the early poems was controlled, in later collections, by a developing intelligence which in that early volume had informed the long "Conversations with the Moon." In subsequent books, while the language remains highly literate and elegant, unsophisticated in everything except its dexterity, the tone has become increasingly and more subtly esoteric; the allusions less romantically projected. Yet Smith has remained largely unnoticed by critics, unanthologised despite some eminently suitable pieces. This may be because he has declined to interest himself in various schools of poetry, has remained unassociated with any movement (except in his interesting experiments in writing verse for recital with jazz, which has resulted in some of the most successful pieces in that *genre*—again largely unnoticed, presumably because more serious than the Liverpool words-and-pop simplicities). Smith has steadfastly refused to be self-indulgent, preferring a private, though not difficult, wit to public clowning. His most recent verse has shown him as a valuable guide to contemporary social life, sometimes terrifying in its vision into psychiatric darkness, sometimes funny. He is perhaps the least recognised good poet writing in England at the moment.

—Derek Parker

SMITH, Ken(neth John). British. Born in Rudston, East Yorkshire, 4 December 1938. Educated at Hull and Knaresborough grammar schools; University of Leeds, Yorkshire, B.A. in English literature, 1963. Served in the Royal Air Force, 1958-60. Married Ann Minnis in 1960; two daughters and one son. Taught in an elementary school, Dewsbury, Yorkshire, 1963-64, and in a technical college, Batley, Yorkshire, 1964-65; Tutor, Exeter College of Art, Devon, 1965-69; Instructor in Creative Writing, Slippery Rock State College, Pennsylvania, 1969-72; Visiting Poet, Clark University, and College of the Holy Cross, both in Worcester, Massachusetts, 1972-73; Yorkshire Arts Fellow, Leeds University, 1976-78; Writer-in-Residence, Kingston Polytechnic, Surrey, 1979-81. Co-Editor, *Stand*, Newcastle upon Tyne, 1963-69; Editor, *South West Review*, Exeter, 1976-79. Recipient: Gregory Award, 1964; Arts Council bursary, 1975, 1978. Address: 78 Friars Road, London E6 1LL, England.

PUBLICATIONS

Verse

Eleven Poems. Leeds, Northern House, 1964.
The Pity. London, Cape, 1967.
Academic Board Poems. Harpford, Devon, Peeks Press, 1968.
A Selection of Poems. Gillingham, Kent, Arc, 1969.
Work, Distances. Chicago, Swallow Press, 1972.
The Wild Rose. Memphis, Stinktree, 1973.
Hawk Wolf. Knotting Bedfordshire, Sceptre Press, 1975.
Frontwards in a Backwards Movie. Todmorden, Lancashire, Arc, 1975.
Wasichi. London, Aloes, 1975.
Anus Mundi. Hardwick, Massachusetts, Four Zoas Press, 1976.
Henry the Navigator. Glen Ellyn, Illinois, Cat's Pajamas Press, 1976.

Blue's Rocket. Privately printed, 1976.
Tristan Crazy. Newcastle upon Tyne, Bloodaxe, 1978.
Tales of the Hunter. Boston, Night House, 1979.
Fox Running. London, Rolling Moss, 1980.
The Joined-Up Writing. Croydon, Surrey, X Press, 1980.
What I'm Doing Now (and for the Rose Lady) (30/4/80). London, Oasis, 1980.
Burned Books. Newcastle upon Tyne, Bloodaxe, 1981.
The Poet Reclining: Selected Poems 1962-1980. Newcastle upon Tyne, Bloodaxe, 1982.
Abel Baker Charlie Delta Epic: Sonnets. Newcastle upon Tyne, Bloodaxe, 1982.

*

Ken Smith comments:
Over the years my work has developed in response to the different environments in which I have arrived as much as to travel and the spaces between; mine are portable roots, some in Yorkshire, some in America, some in Devon, some now in London. Exeter, the city I most lived in, provided me with the figure of *The Wanderer* from the Anglo-Saxon *Exeter Book*; I have identified as much with him and his homelessness as with the irony of his poem having had in the cathedral library a home for the past 900 years. Writing is for me the act of discovering roots and pasts behind the present I find myself in, as if by some marvellous accident; I am located in the work I do and in the daily rediscovery of language, the magic liquid that connects me to all else. I live in that as much as anywhere. Devon also made available to me the ancient silences of Dartmoor, that marvellous museum of all that has happened to us: a museum I do not encourage anyone to visit. By Kestor, above Chagford, amongst the stoney leavings of the iron makers, is where I go whenever I have a decision to make, and there I feel the strongest root into the sullen past. On other days I am gregarious, and have moved recently closer and closer to dramatic expression. Community, environment, and all the minutiae of gesture and inflexion— these are all my concerns still.

Themes: environment (hence nature), domestic, human relations and human attitudes, the rural in conflict with the urban, our subjective world implanted in an indifferent objectivity. Usual verse forms—free, intuitively worked, organic. General sources—any—many accidental and incidental, but environment and history, the sense of being alive, etc. Literary sources— many and scattered, too many to mention but mostly twentieth-century.

Amongst other things, I want to express the way we live, and comment on it: the way we live in society, the way our environment is and we with it, how we form community—the minute ways in which the shapes of our lives are expressed in habits, gestures, buildings, our conscious and unconscious reactions to weather, landscape, each other—how we bind our lives down to the smallest detail distinguishing individual or community. So in this sense I am interested in custom, and in speech, and so in language, and so in process. The poem itself is a process more than a product of this interest. I want a language that enacts and makes living, that is living rather than merely representative: a language metaphoric in itself.

*   *   *

Ken Smith's early poems are harsh, almost cynical, though saved by a natural grace. He wants to shock the reader with his bold, clear-eyed realism. "I'm a non-nonsense person," these poems say repeatedly, and the sparse titles suggest the stark vision of the speaker: "Grass," "Dead Grass," "Facts," "Leaving." The title poem of his volume *The Pity* takes these lines from a statement by Mao Tse-Tung: "I cut my hands on the cords at the strangling post,/but no blood spilled from my veins;/instead of blood I watched and saw the pity run out of me." Other voices, other presences include Antonio Machado, Lorca, and the expressionist painters Max Ernst and Paul Klee, as well as memorable lines such as the following: "Do not forget the grass; that trodden softness/Could only be an innocence that insists, comes back,/season by growing season. It cannot stop itself."

Work, Distances, Smith's second collection, with the sound of an American voice, extends the subject matter and range of his work, with some exciting discoveries along the way: the Sioux Indians in Minnesota, the Amana colonies in Iowa, winters in Pennsylvania, loneliness in California. He takes in the landscape, the people, and the past with the careful eye of a cultural anthropologist, rediscovering the country for readers familiar with the scene. Yet these poems are personal, too, as if the expanse of country were part of an inner landscape, part of a vast loneliness that all people share. "In This Place," a poem that Smith omitted from his selected poems, has the strength of feeling, of intellect and conviction, that one associates with William Blake:

My hands pray to nothing.
I am the world of the little sand-grain
I allow nothing I am to be taken
    away.
I turn from the camera
Against what it takes from me.

But Smith's major achievement as a writer is *Fox Running*, an ambitious, varied, and fully realized "picaresque" poem, reminiscent, at times, of Prufrock and *The Waste Land*, in which Fox, a contemporary man-about-town, tells about his loves, his reading, writing, dreaming. He is Fox fearful, Fox alive and in motion, Fox laughing, and, in a powerful sequence, Fox contemplating a terrible end:

And I think: supposing it's now,
this night the voices all stop.
A flight of wild geese blips the radar
and all the technologies die.
Goodbye Newton Milton Socrates
Goodbye republics of raw nerve,
disputed borders of meaning.
Goodbye at last universe
thinking itself in our skulls.
Goodbye love. Woman I loved.

In this remarkable poem, and in several later, shorter ones, Ken Smith has caught the vitality and goodness of an ordinary man in this most disturbing and chaotic era. Such vitality suggests new directions for English poetry, building on the wit, energy, and strength of his verse. *The Poet Reclining: Selected Poems 1962-1980* gathers many of the best poems, with promises as well of important work still to come.

—Michael True

SMITH, Vivian (Brian). Australian. Born in Hobart, Tasmania, 3 June 1933. Educated at the University of Tasmania, Hobart, M.A. 1956; University of Sydney, Ph.D. 1971. Married Sybille Gottwald in 1960; two daughters and one son. Lecturer in French, University of Tasmania, 1955-67. Lecturer, 1967-74, Senior Lecturer, 1974-82, and since 1982, Reader in English, University of Sydney. Recipient: Grace Leven Prize, 1982. Address: 19 McLeod Street, Mosman, New South Wales 2088, Australia.

PUBLICATIONS

Verse

The Other Meaning.   Sydney, Edwards and Shaw, 1956.
An Island South.   Sydney, Angus and Robertson, 1967.
Familiar Places.   Sydney, Angus and Robertson, 1978.
Tide Country.   Sydney, Angus and Robertson, 1982.

Other

James McAuley.   Melbourne, Lansdowne Press, 1965; revised edition, 1970.
Les Vigé en Australie (for children).   Melbourne, Longman, 1967.
Vance Palmer.   Melbourne, Oxford University Press, 1971.
The Poetry of Robert Lowell.   Sydney, Sydney University Press, 1974.
Vance and Nettie Palmer.   New York, Twayne, 1975.
Tasmania and Australian Poetry.   Hobart, University of Tasmania, 1984.

Editor, *Australian Poetry 1969*.   Sydney, Angus and Robertson, 1969.
Editor, *Letters of Vance and Nettie Palmer 1915-1963*.   Canberra, National Library of Australia, 1977.
Editor, *Young St. Poets Anthology*.   Sydney, Wentworth, 1981.
Editor, with Peter Coleman and Lee Shrubb, *Quadrant: Twenty-Five Years*.   Brisbane, University of Queensland Press, 1982.

*

Manuscript Collection: Australian National Library, Canberra.

Critical Studies: "The Poetry of *The Other Meaning*" by Margaret Irvin, in *Poetry* (Sydney), February 1969; *Bread and Wine* by Kenneth Slessor, Sydney, Angus and Robertson, 1970; *Commonwealth Literature* by William Walsh, London, Oxford University Press, 1973; *A Map of Australian Verse* by James McAuley, Melbourne, Oxford University Press, 1976; "Two Poets" by Elaine Lindsay, in *Twenty-Four Hours* (Sydney), January 1979; *Modern Australian Poetry 1920-1970* by Herbert C. Jaffa, Detroit, Gale, 1979; "The Lyrical Poetry of Vivian Smith" by Elizabeth Perkins, in *Quadrant* (Sydney), 1982; "The Poetry of Vivian Smith" by Les A. Murray, in *Catholic Weekly* (Surrey Hills, New South Wales), January 1983.

Vivian Smith comments:
(1980) Within the context of Australian poetry I am, I suppose, something of a regionalist since most of my poems are about Hobart and Tasmania, though Sydney too has been one of the poles of my inspiration. I write in free and traditional forms, and my lyrics try to affirm both the sense of a personal inner world and the inescapable presence of the actual. There are two areas of influence in my work. The first is that of the Australian poets who most impressed me when I first started to write,

particularly Judith Wright and Kenneth Slessor with their focus on landscape and especially the sea, an inescapable element for a Tasmanian. The second is that of the French and German poets whose work I studied closely and lectured on for many years. Although I have lived in Sydney for the last 12 years, Tasmania, with its special qualities of light, vegetation, and landscape, is still the focal point of my work, and I have tried to capture something of its peculiar essence which is colonial, European-ised, astringent, secluded, peaceful, and wild. Hobart still seems to me more like a European town or city than any other place in Australia and the most beautiful of all the capital cities.

Looking back over my poems, I find that they are concerned with various attitudes of mind—how to go on living fully and humanly without dogma or theory, but without becoming a victim of unstructured experience. In other words, they are concerned with the nature and meaning of belief.

*   *   *

In the 1950's there appeared to be a blossoming of fresh young poetic talent, predominantly regional in origin, in Australia: David Rowbotham in Queensland, Randolph Stow in West Australia, and, in Tasmania, Christopher Koch and Vivian Smith. In his first volume, *The Other Meaning*, Smith showed a sensitive response to his environment. The "other meaning" which he sought was some aspect of the transient that gave it either definition or awareness.

In *An Island South*, the influence of the then-predominantly academic poets of dry wit in England and America is more apparent. Vivian Smith has published only occasional poems since that volume. His work has a reticence that sometimes underplays the deftness of observation and precision of control that give his best work a true luminosity. Though his themes have tended to remain persistently close to immediate response, Smith has appreciably hardened the texture of his poems to a gemlike precision. If he does not appear to have justified the early anticipations of his admirers, his work has grown in its own terms and with honesty and quiet dignity.

—Thomas W. Shapcott

SMITH, William Jay. American. Born in Winnfield, Louisiana, 22 April 1918. Educated at Blow School, St. Louis, 1924-31; Cleveland High School, 1931-35; Washington University, St. Louis, 1935-41, B.A. 1939, M.A. in French 1941; Institut de Touraine, Tours, France, 1938; Columbia University, New York, 1946-47; Wadham College, Oxford (Rhodes Scholar), 1947-48; University of Florence, 1948-50. Served as a Lieutenant in the United States Naval Reserve, 1941-45. Married 1) Barbara Howes, *q.v.*, in 1947 (divorced, 1965), two sons; 2) Sonja Haussmann in 1966, one stepson. Assistant in French, Washington University, 1939-41; Instructor in English and French, 1946-47, and Visiting Professor of Writing and Acting Chairman, Writing Division, 1973, 1974-75, Columbia University; Instructor in English, 1951, and Poet-in-Residence and Lecturer in English, 1959-64, 1966-67, Williams College, Williamstown, Massachusetts. Writer-in-Residence, 1965-66, Professor of English 1967-68 and 1970-80, and since 1980, Professor Emeritus, Hollins College, Virginia. Consultant in Poetry, 1968-70, and Honorary Consultant, 1970-76, Library of Congress, Washington, D.C.; Lecturer, Salzburg Seminar in American Studies, 1974. Poetry reviewer, *Harper's*, New York, 1961-64; editorial consultant, Grove Press,

New York, 1968-70. Democratic Member, Vermont House of Representatives, 1960-62. Recipient: Young Poets Prize, 1945, and Union League Civic and Arts Foundation Prize, 1964 (*Poetry*, Chicago); Alumni Citation, Washington University, 1963; Ford Fellowship, for drama, 1964; Henry Bellamann Major Award, 1970; Loines Award, 1972; National Endowment for the Arts grant, 1972, 1978; Gold Medal of Labor (Hungary), 1978; New England Poetry Club Golden Rose, 1979. D.Litt.: New England College, Henniker, New Hampshire, 1973. Member, American Academy, 1975. Agent: Marilyn Marlow, Curtis Brown, 575 Madison Avenue, New York, New York 10022. Address: 1675 York Avenue, Apartment 20-K, New York, New York 10028, U.S.A.

PUBLICATIONS

Verse

Poems. New York, Banyan Press, 1947.
Celebration at Dark. London, Hamish Hamilton, and New York, Farrar Straus, 1950.
Typewriter Birds. New York, Caliban Press, 1954.
The Bead Curtain: Calligrams. Privately printed, 1957.
Poems 1947-1957. Boston, Little Brown, 1957.
Two Poems. Pownal, Vermont, Mason Hill Press, 1959.
Prince Souvanna Phouma: An Exchange Between Richard Wilbur and William Jay Smith. Williamstown, Massachusetts, Chapel Press, 1963.
The Tin Can and Other Poems. New York, Delacorte Press, 1966.
New and Selected Poems. New York, Delacorte Press, 1970.
A Rose for Katherine Anne Porter. New York, Albondocani Press, 1970.
At Delphi: For Allen Tate on His Seventy-Fifth Birthday, 19 November 1974. Williamstown, Massachusetts, Chapel Press, 1974.
Venice in the Fog. Greensboro, North Carolina, Unicorn Press, 1975.
Verses on the Times, with Richard Wilbur. New York, Gutenberg Press, 1978.
Journey to the Dead Sea: A Poem. Omaha, Abattoir, 1979.
The Tall Poets. Winston-Salem, North Carolina, Palaemon Press, 1979.
The Traveler's Tree: New and Selected Poems. New York, Persea, 1980; Manchester, Carcanet, 1981.

Christmas Card Poems (with Barbara Howes): *Lachrymae Christi and In the Old Country*, 1948; *Poems: The Homecoming and The Piazza*, 1949; *Two French Poems: The Roses of Saadi and Five Minute Watercolor*, 1950—all privately printed.

Verse (for children)

Laughing Time. Boston, Little Brown, 1955; London, Faber, 1956.
Boy Blue's Book of Beasts. Boston, Little Brown, 1957.
Puptents and Pebbles: A Nonsense ABC. Boston, Little Brown, 1959; London, Faber, 1960.
Typewriter Town. New York, Dutton, 1960.
What Did I See? New York, Crowell Collier, 1962.
My Little Book of Big and Little (Little Dimity, Big Gumbo, Big and Little). Riverside, New Jersey, Rutledge, 3 vols., 1963.
Ho for a Hat! Boston, Little Brown, 1964.
If I Had a Boat. New York, Macmillan, 1966; Kingswood, Surrey, World's Work, 1967.

Mr. Smith and Other Nonsense.   New York, Delacorte Press, 1968.

Around My Room and Other Poems.   New York, Lancelot Press, 1969.

Grandmother Ostrich and Other Poems.   New York, Lancelot Press, 1969.

Play

The Straw Market, music by the author (produced Washington, D.C., 1965; New York, 1969).

Other

The Spectra Hoax (criticism).   Middletown, Connecticut, Wesleyan University Press, 1961.

Children and Poetry: A Selective Annotated Bibliography, with Virginia Haviland.   Washington, D.C., Library of Congress, 1969; revised edition, 1979.

Louise Bogan: A Woman's Words.   Washington, D.C., Library of Congress, 1972.

The Streaks of the Tulip: Selected Criticism.   New York, Delacorte Press, 1972.

Army Brat: A Memoir.   New York, Persea, 1980; London, Penguin, 1982.

Editor and Translator, *Selected Writings of Jules Laforgue.*   New York, Grove Press, 1956.

Editor, *Herrick.*   New York, Dell, 1962.

Editor, with Louise Bogan, *The Golden Journey: Poems for Young People.*   Chicago, Reilly and Lee, 1965; London, Evans, 1967.

Editor, *Poems from France* (for children).   New York, Crowell, 1967.

Editor, *Poems from Italy* (for children).   New York, Crowell, 1972.

Editor, *Light Verse and Satires,* by Witter Bynner.   New York, Farrar Straus, and London, Faber, 1978.

Editor, *A Green Place: Modern Poems* (for children).   New York, Delacorte Press, 1982.

Editor, with Emanuel Brasil, *Brazilian Poetry 1950-1980.*   Middletown, Connecticut, Wesleyan University Press, 1983; London, Harper, 1984.

Translator, *Scirroco,* by Romualdo Romano.   New York, Farrar Straus, 1951.

Translator, *Poems of a Multimillionaire,* by Valéry Larbaud.   New York, Bonaccio and Saul, 1955.

Translator, *Two Plays by Charles Bertin: Christopher Columbus and Don Juan.*   Minneapolis, University of Minnesota Press, 1970.

Translator, *Children of the Forest* (for children), by Elsa Beskow.   New York, Delacorte Press, 1970.

Translator, *The Pirate Book* (for children), by Lennart Hellsing.   New York, Delacorte Press, and London, Benn, 1972.

Translator, with Max Hayward, *The Telephone* (for children), by Kornei Chukovsky.   New York, Delacorte Press, 1977.

Translator, with Leif Sjöberg, *Agadir,* by Artur Lundkvist.   Pittsburgh, International Poetry Forum, 1979.

Translator, with Ingvar Schousboe, *The Pact: My Friendship with Isak Dinesen,* by Thorkild Bjørnvig.   Baton Rouge, Louisiana State University Press, 1983.

*

Manuscript Collection: Washington University, St. Louis.

Critical Studies: "William Jay Smith," in *Modern Verse in English, 1900-1950* edited by Lord David Cecil and Allen Tate, London, Eyre and Spottiswoode, and New York, Macmillan, 1958; "William Jay Smith" in *The Hollins Poets* edited by Louis D. Rubin, Charlottesville, University Press of Virginia, 1967; "The Lightness of William Jay Smith" by Dorothy Judd Hall, in *Southern Humanities Review* (Auburn, Alabama), Summer 1968; "A Poet Named Smith" by Jean G. Lawlor, in *Washington Post* (Washington, D.C.), 9 March 1969; "An Interview with William Jay Smith" by Elizavietta Ritchie, in *Voyages* (Washington, D.C.), Winter 1970; *Children's Literature in the Elementary School,* 3rd edition, by Charlotte S. Huck and Doris A. Young, New York, Holt Rinehart, 1976; *Children and Books,* 6th edition, by May Hill Arbuthnot, Zena Sutherland, and Dianne L. Monson, Chicago, Scott Foresman, 1981.

William Jay Smith comments:

I am a lyric poet, alert, I hope, as one of my fellow poets, Stanley Kunitz, has put it, "to the changing weathers of a landscape, to the motions of the mind, to the complications and surprises of the human comedy." I believe that poetry should communicate: it is, by its very nature, complex, but its complexity should not prevent its making an immediate impact on the reader. Great poetry must have resonance: it must resound with the mystery of the human psyche, and possess always its own distinct, identifiable, and haunting, music. My recent poems have been written in long unrhymed lines because the material with which I am dealing seems to lend itself to this form, which is often close to, but always different from, prose. I have always used a great variety of verse forms, especially in my poetry for children. I believe that poetry begins in childhood and that a poet who can remember his own childhood exactly can, and should, communicate to children.

*   *   *

William Jay Smith's first book, *Poems,* announced a poet of exotic subjects, high patina, and exquisite music, a combination suggestive of early Wallace Stevens. Such poems as "The Peacock of Java," "On the Islands Which Are Solomon's," and "Of Islands" transform a seascape of atolls which "brings, even/To the tree of heaven, heaven." Other poems, like "The Barber" and "The Closing of the Rodeo," initiate Smith's satirical rendering of the American commonplace, while "Cupidon" reflects his interest in incremental ballad form and fantasy. This early work seemed a very deft performance in the then-dominant metaphysical style, but Smith has always sounded a note of his own—his lightness, dexterity, elegance, and wit reflect not only the prevailing influence of Eliot, Tate, and Ransom, but also earlier poets who had influenced them.

During World War II, Smith served as a liaison officer aboard a Free French naval vessel, and he began his civilian career as a teacher of French literature at Columbia. He published a distinguished translation of Valéry Larbaud in 1955 and of Jules Laforgue in 1956. The qualities of formal versification, precarious poise, and wit in his early verse seem akin to those of Laforgue, the dreamwork suggestive of Larbaud. Further clues to his own verse are offered in Smith's two critical studies. *The Spectra Hoax* is an entertaining reconstruction of the successful leg-pull by Witter Bynner and Arthur Davidson Ficke, who not only concocted a fictitious school of poets in 1916-18, but, writing pseudonymously as its members, begat better poems than when using their own names and more conventional styles. The following year Smith's introduction to a selection of the poems of Robert Herrick described that poet as "a master of understatement [who] knows what to omit," "a perfect miniaturist; nothing is too small for him to notice or too great to reduce in size." These and other occasional essays are collected in *Streaks of the Tulip: Selected Criticism*.

His translations and studies of English, French, and American poets suggest the range and sources of Smith's fascination with satire, fantasy, and word-play, his comprehension of the true seriousness of successful light verse, and his devotion, until his most recent work, to brief lyrics, conventional forms, aesthetic distance from his subjects, and a burnished surface—as in his little poem "Tulip" which offers "Magnificence within a frame." Similar qualities animate his several books of verse for children; he has written, "I believe that poetry begins in childhood and that a poet who can remember his own childhod exactly can, and should, communicate to children." (One such communication, *Typewriter Town* [1960], anticipates by several years the vogue for concrete poetry among writers for adults.)

These qualities and Smith's characteristic lightness of touch are blended into an unmistakably American idiom in *Poems 1947-1957*, especially in "Letter," "Death of a Jazz Musician," and "American Primitive":

> Look at him there in his stovepipe hat,
> His high-top shoes, and his handsome collar;
> Only my Daddy could look like that,
> And I love my Daddy like he loves his Dollar.
> The screen door bangs, and it sounds so funny—
> There he is in a shower of gold;
> His pockets are stuffed with folding money,
> His lips are blue, and his hands feel cold.
>
> He hangs in the hall by his black cravat,
> The ladies faint, and the children holler:
> Only my Daddy could look like that,
> And I love my Daddy like he loves his dollar.

With *The Tin Can and Other Poems* and since, Smith, like most of the poets of his generation, moved on from the style he had mastered to a new, freer prosody, in which the dark side of experience is presented in a more unmediated way than in poems like "American Primitive" which had enclosed it in a play of wit and form:

> O dreadful night!...What train will come?...What tree is that?
>   ...a sycamore—the mottled bark stripped bare,
> Desolate in winter light against the track, and I continue on to
>   the mudflats
> By the roaring river where garbage, chicken coops, and houses
>   rush
>   by me on mud-crested waves,
> And at my feet are dead fish—catfish, gars—and there in a little
>   inlet
> Come on a deserted camp, the tin can in which the hoboes
>   brewed their
>   coffee stained bitter black
> As the cinders sweeping ahead under a milkweed-colored sky
>   along a
>   darkening track
>   And gaze into a slough's green stagnant foam,
>   and know that the way out is never back,
>   but down,
>   down...

> *What train will come*
> *to bear me back*
> *across so wide a town?*

At least one reviewer of *The Tin Can* suggested that the hitherto elegant Smith has succumbed to the prosier incantations of Allen Ginsberg. As with Ginsberg, this loose, rolling line makes possible the inclusion in Smith's work of many grubby realities which, like Herrick, he had earlier tended to omit or to transfigure. Smith's sensibility, however, has little in common with the Beat bard's; a likelier *point d'origine* for these recent poems is in the free verse and surreal observations of the contemporary by Valéry Larbaud. His long unrhymed line makes possible an amplitude of feeling as well as inclusiveness of subject, and in it Smith continues to explore both his descent into the inarticulate and the terrifying ("My voice goes out like a funicular over an abyss, and my hands hang at my sides, clenching the void;/My dreams are filled with bitter oranges and carrots, signifying calumny and sorrow") and his intimations of the unity of all things, as in "The Tin Can," a poem of withdrawal from the world and the resultant gift of vision to the spirit.

—Daniel Hoffman

SMITHER, Elizabeth (Edwina, née Harrington). New Zealander. Born in New Plymouth, 15 September 1941. Educated at New Plymouth Girls' High School, 1955-59; extra-mural studies at Victoria University, Wellington, and Massey University, Palmerston North, 1959-60; New Zealand Library School, Wellington, 1962. Married Michael Duncan Smither in 1963; one daughter and two sons. Library Assistant, 1959-62, Cataloguer, 1962-63, Children's Librarian, 1963-79, and since 1979, Relieving Librarian, New Plymouth Public Library. Recipient: New Zealand Literary Fund bursary, 1978; Auckland University Literary Fellow, 1984. Address: 19-A Mount View Place, New Plymouth, New Zealand.

PUBLICATIONS

Verse

Here Come the Clouds. Martinborough, Taylor, 1975.
You're Very Seductive William Carlos Williams. Dunedin, McIndoe, 1978.
Little Poems. New Plymouth, T.J. Mutch, 1979.
The Sarah Train (for children). Eastbourne, Hawk Press, 1980.
Casanova's Ankle. Auckland, Oxford University Press, 1981.
The Legend of Marcello Mastraoianni's Wife. Auckland, Auckland University Press-Oxford University Press, 1981.
Shakespeare Virgins. Auckland, Auckland University Press, 1983.

Novel

First Blood. London, Hodder and Stoughton, 1983.

Other

Tug Brother (for children). Auckland, Oxford University Press, 1983.

Editor, with David Hill, *The Seventies Connection*. Dunedin, McIndoe, 1980.

*

Critical Studies: "A Way of Understanding Ourselves" by Elizabeth Caffin, in *Landfall 118* (Christchurch), 1976; "Maurice Shadbolt Talks to Elizabeth Smither," in *Pilgrims 5* and *6* (Christchurch), 1978.

Elizabeth Smither comments:

Robert Lowell wrote me in a letter that my work showed "a strong fierce personality, finding words to wrap itself in." Overcome by reading his work for most of a year, I had impulsively written to him, enclosing as a poor sample my first collection. He went on to suggest that I tune my ear more finely, and the attempt to develop more musicality has been the concern of my latest work. I try to retain the direct emotional qualities for which sometimes characters are mouthpieces while being aware of the problem of the poem itself. An image for my work might be a canal in which the flowing water is the emotion and the banks and reflected poplars represent the absorbing strictures of craft. But there is air between the poplars and their reflections are light. For I think it is necessary to flow inside and within one's craft, like assembling out of bones the flesh and personality.

*   *   *

In something under ten years Elizabeth Smither has brought out five books of poems, and two of poems misleadingly suggested as "juveniles," along with some fiction. Wife of a well-known New Zealand painter and mother of three children, she began writing effectively when she was about thirty, fairly quickly found her voice (and a reputation), so she is substantially a poet without any juvenilia. She has done some travelling beyond New Zealand, where her home is not in one of the larger cities but in a provincial port, for long rather a Sleepy Hollow backed by a lush pastoral scene dominated by a spectacularly dead volcano, grounded in a long-term history of Maori settlement and a short-term history of European settlement but one with a notable passage to it of 19th-century colonial warfare. There is little recourse to that local history in Smither's poems although she has explored something of it in her prose and scarcely more to do with either landscape or seascape, or evident awareness of the transforming of Sleepy Hollow as the oil rigs on and offshore work away at their surroundings, the natural gas enterprises breed, the petrochemical plants riot over the paddocks. In neither earlier nor later books occurs much that may be confidently thought to come from family or immediate social experience. Some, from family; some, from friendships; much, from responding to literature, responding imaginatively. "Imagine this, now..." and she does. It is impressively a poetry of imagination. Where the poetry is of experience, it is likely to have some qualifying or mediating effect again from literature, or from a quiet Catholicism.

The poems are rarely long-lined, customarily shortish-lined pieces which probably will not reach half way down the page. They have a peculiarity in punctuation, of a kind which M.K. Joseph, another Catholic poet, used at one stage in his career. Syntax is disrupted in a modestly venturesome way which one may judge is aimed at evoking an illusion of immediacy, as of a slightly breathless utterance, whether the poet is assumed to be speaking in her own person or whether it is one or other of her personae, male or female, or a speaker whose sex is neither way assertive. The voice of the later poems is more likely to be a woman's (including the poems of *Casanova's Ankle*) and so too the viewpoint.

Sympathetic, empathetic, able to command that quick shrewd comment which delights the reader simply because it *is* so aptly shrewd or provocative, Smither's poems are not poems of wit in any usual sense any more than they are in a usual sense self-centred. She may be in them, but also distant from them. She may advertise that she attaches herself to Modernist modes as of Williams, Lowell, or Kinnell, but she is also distanced from those, not fully committed to them. To be more venturesome would become her.

She is a conservative Modernist. If you look at her evidenced Catholicism you see the Catholicism of family custom, plus an awareness of tradition—St. Teresa, St. Ignatius, St. Paul—and something latterday, Teilhard de Chardin, but not as latecome as Hans Küng. The poems of faith are poems of rapprochement, of subjective-objective or attachment-detachment, records of an impulse to reconcile at least two modes of tradition. She effects a reconciliation which complements by way of one particular universe of discourse the compromises apparent in her favoured strategies as a "maker."

The matter of playing off traditions is one thing. Recurring to compressed statement is another, in which calculated quizzical relating of tenor and vehicle in metaphor continues to result not so much in conveying a metaphoric statement as exciting a sense of incongruity without (as one might expect) a likely consequent nuance of comedy, yet increasingly more likely to dispose towards irony. Prosy reality re-imagined is heightened, disturbingly heightened even if Smither has from the start pinned and still usually pins her poetics on and over a firm basis of sentences which are quite sure how about how they stand in relation to expository prose. It is only when the sentences cumulate that the exposition becomes something other, a deceptive something other.

The heavy haulers pull their sometimes fantastically sculpted pieces of machinery to the industrial sites. Lights blaze from gantry and rig between sea and mountain. As Wallace Stevens did in Hartford, Elizabeth Smither sits to work with her back to the window.

—Kendrick Smithyman

SMITHYMAN, (William) Kendrick. New Zealander. Born in Te Kopuru, Auckland, 9 October 1922. Educated at Seddon Memorial Technical College; Auckland Teachers College; Auckland University College. Served in the New Zealand Artillery and the Royal New Zealand Air Force, 1941-45. Married 1) Mary Stanley in 1946 (died, 1980), three sons; 2) Margaret Edgcumbe in 1981. Primary school teacher, 1946-63. Since 1963, Senior Tutor, Department of English, University of Auckland. Visiting Fellow in Commonwealth Literature, University of Leeds, Yorkshire, 1969. Recipient: British Council grant, 1969; New Zealand Literary Fund grant, 1969; Jessie Mackay Award, 1969. Address: Department of English, University of Auckland, Private Bag, Auckland, New Zealand.

PUBLICATIONS

Verse

Seven Sonnets. Auckland, Pelorus Press, 1946.
The Blind Mountain and Other Poems. Christchurch, Caxton Press, 1950.

The Gay Trapeze. Wellington, Handcraft Press, 1955.
The Night Shift: Poems on Aspects of Love, with others. Wellington, Capricorn Press, 1957.
Inheritance. Auckland, Paul's Book Arcade, 1962.
Flying to Palmerston. Wellington, Oxford University Press, 1968.
Earthquake Weather. Auckland, Auckland University Press-Oxford University Press, 1972.
The Seal in the Dolphin Pool. Auckland, Auckland University Press-Oxford University Press, 1974.
Dwarf with a Billiard Cue. Auckland, Auckland University Press-Oxford University Press, 1978.
Stories about Wooden Keyboards. Auckland, Auckland University Press-Oxford University Press, 1984.

Other

A Way of Saying: A Study of New Zealand Poetry. Auckland and London, Collins, 1965.

Editor, *The Land of the Lost* (novel), by William Satchell. Auckland, Auckland University Press-Oxford University Press, 1971.

*

Critical Study: by MacD.P. Jackson, in *Thirteen Facets* edited by Ian Ward, Wellington, Government Printer, 1978.

*   *   *

Impersonal but idiosyncratic, colloquial in cadence but recondite in language and allusion, Kendrick Smithyman is one of the those poets who arrive at a distinctive style or way of saying "by being other than themselves in what they wrote." (Apparently a recipe for being a successful minor poet, the phrase is his own.) Collecting both from life and from the library, Smithyman is a hoarder of curious words and facts, a connoisseur of the arcane, an archaeologist of the "unimpressive shard carried home from a dig." However miniscule, the shards are for display, for he is by his own definition an academic poet, interested more in how he shows forth his finds than in any intrinsic significance they may be supposed to have. "Significance" in Smithyman's poems tends to be subtly undercut by irony.

Widely, and often strangely read, he uses his learning as raw material for slow and sinuous (*not* sensuous) meditation. He appears to revel in the timbre and texture of his own musings, but it has been observed that he is virtually "free of the tyranny of self." "Often enough," he once noted, "I wrote a poem because I proposed to myself some technical problem." Such a procedure is deliberate and controlled, though he has admitted that it does not always result in poems. Although he could never be charged with self-obsessed maunderings, he does occasionally meander into verbal self-indulgence.

His poems have been likened to epiphanies or emblems extended into meditations, usually oblique. In a perceptive review of *The Seal in the Dolphin Pool*, D.I.B. Smith compares him with the 17th-century emblem poets and their pursuit of the "divine hieroglyph" in the knowable universe (though the sceptic in Smithyman must have winced at that "divine"). Within limits, comparison may also be made with Charles Olson. Like him, Smithyman is a regionalist, a scribbler of intellectual and concrete jottings, and a dissenter from the anthropocentric version of the cosmos, perceiving man instead as part of a process much vaster than himself. Eliot, Ransom, Tate, and Lowell have been numbered among the influences on Smithyman's poetry, but he

seems closest in spirit to another American, Marianne Moore, the Modernist fabulist of curiosa. The affinity is most overtly evident in *Inheritance*, in such poems as "Zoo," "Porcupine Fish," and "Kemp's Passing."

Inheritance brought Smithyman's work into full focus. It and the ensuing collection *Flying to Palmerston* contains much of his most effective regionalist work, and it is instructive to compare, say, "Vignettes of the Maori Wars," "Demolishing the Farmhouse," or "Gathering the Toheroa" with poems on similar themes by James K. Baxter, Allen Curnow, or Denis Glover. Smithyman shares with Curnow an intellectual subtlety, but differs from him in always insistently striking the minor note, a tactic or condition of mind which is often enough very effective. A tightness of form established in the 1960's appears to have been relaxed with *The Seal in the Dolphin Pool* and subsequently. Sometimes language and syntax become "striated tissue/like surgical gauze." Sometimes the opening gambit of a poem reads like a clue to a crossword puzzle. The conundrum can become humdrum. Smithyman's major weakness is a tendency to lose (or not to gather) momentum before he has carried a poem through, so that, as one reviewer has it: "It is not the fish that is dead."

In fairness, it must be said that zest and quick-wittedness are more commonly characteristic. And besides, the reader is intended to dwell on the details, to appreciate the disparate items yoked with ironic allusiveness together, as in "Wanting," "Side Issue," and others. One poem, "Double Exposure," indicates importantly that Smithyman has come to see with eyes at once widely travelled and "wild colonial," the palimpsests of sophistication. With educated eyes and ears, he will chance upon "a tone/and an accidental, shape which exceeds/calculating," or upon "the lake, reserved to/its own logic," which "has no words. Needs none." Manifold ironies attend such circumstance, for he is full of words and (with the possible exception of Curnow) has the most "calculating" temperament of any New Zealand poet.

Apart from an intermittent tendency to play Polonius, Smithyman at his best is highly *readable*, provided the reading is not mere skimming but is genuine exploration. Simile, analogy, allusion—these and a teasing out of the possibilities of syntax are his means. Serious about his craft, he is modest about his aims or ends. His ultimate object, he has said, is to divert, to entertain, perhaps on a rare occasion to titivate (as in "The Man Who Wrote Short Stories" in *Dwarf with a Billiard Cue*). As often as not he prefers to invite us into the verbal maze, though once in a while to somewhere a little less kempt and deeper. A section of "Exchanging Cards" brings us to an appropriate summation point:

> I should like to send you a card
> showing the weir and a one way bridge
> five miles beyond Forest Headquarters almost
> where the logging road ends. After that, you're on
> your own, heading for the Tasman
> dazzled by unidentified bird cries.

—Charles Doyle

———

SNODGRASS, W(illiam) D(eWitt). American. Born in Wilkinsburg, Pennsylvania, 5 January 1926. Educated at Geneva College, Beaver Falls, Pennsylvania, 1943-44, 1946; State University of Iowa, Iowa City, 1946-55, B.A. 1949, M.A. 1951, M.F.A. 1953. Served in the United States Navy, 1944-46. Married 1) Lila Jean Hank in 1946 (divorced, 1953), one daughter; 2)

Janice Wilson in 1954 (divorced, 1966), one son; 3) Camille Rykowski in 1967 (divorced, 1978). Instructor in English, Cornell University, Ithaca, New York, 1955-57, University of Rochester, New York, 1957-58, and Wayne State University, Detroit, 1959-67; Professor of English and Speech, Syracuse University, New York 1968-77. Visiting Teacher, Morehead Writers Conference, Kentucky, Summer 1955, Antioch Writers Conference, Yellow Springs, Ohio, summers 1958-59, Narrative Poetry Workshop, State University of New York, Binghamton, 1977, Old Dominion University, Norfolk Virginia, 1978-79, and University of Delaware, Newark, 1979. Recipient: Ingram Merrill Foundation Award, 1958; *Hudson Review* Fellowship, 1958; Longview Award, 1959; Poetry Society of America Special Citation, 1960; Yaddo Resident Award, 1960, 1961, 1965, 1976, 1977; American Academy grant, 1960; Pulitzer Prize, 1960; Guinness Award (UK), 1961; Ford Fellowship, for drama, 1963; Miles Award, 1966; National Endowment for the Arts grant, 1966; Guggenheim Fellowship, 1972; Academy of American Poets Fellowship, 1973; Centennial Medal (Romania), 1977. Member, American Academy, 1972; Fellow, Academy of American Poets, 1973. Address: Department of English, University of Delaware, Newark, Delaware 19711, U.S.A.

PUBLICATIONS

Verse

Heart's Needle. New York, Knopf, 1959; Hessle, Yorkshire, Marvell Press, 1960.
After Experience: Poems and Translations. New York, Harper, and London, Oxford University Press, 1968.
Remains (as S.S. Gardons). Mount Horeb, Wisconsin, Perishable Press, 1970.
The Führer Bunker: A Cycle of Poems in Progress. Brockport, New York, BOA, 1977.
If Birds Build with Your Hair. New York, Nadja, 1979.
The Boy Made of Meat. Concord, New Hampshire, Ewert, 1983.
Magda Goebbels. Winston-Salem, North Carolina, Palaemon, 1983.
D.D. Byrde Callying Jennie Wrenn. Concord, New Hampshire, Ewert, 1984.

Play

The Führer Bunker (produced Norfolk, Virginia, 1980; New York, 1981).

Other

In Radical Pursuit: Critical Essays and Lectures. New York, Harper, 1975.

Editor, *Syracuse Poems 1969.* Syracuse, Syracuse University Department of English, 1969.

Translator, with Lore Segal, *Gallows Songs,* by Christian Morgenstern. Ann Arbor, University of Michigan Press, 1967.
Translator, *Six Troubadour Songs.* Providence, Rhode Island, Burning Deck, 1977.
Translator, *Traditional Hungarian Songs.* Baltimore, Seluzicki, 1978.
Translator, *Six Minnesinger Songs.* Providence, Rhode Island, Burning Deck, 1983.
Translator, *The Four Seasons.* New York, Targ, 1984.

*

Bibliography: *W.D. Snodgrass: A Bibliography* by William White, Detroit, Wayne State University Press, 1960.

Manuscript Collection: Lockwood Library, State University of New York, Buffalo.

Critical Study: *W.D. Snodgrass* by Paul L. Gaston, Boston, Twayne, 1978.

W.D. Snodgrass comments:
I am usually called a "confessional" poet or else an "academic" poet. Such terms seem to me not very helpful.
I first became known for poems of a very personal nature, especially those about losing a daughter in a divorce. Many of those early poems were in formal metres and had an "open" surface. All through my career, however, I have written both free verse and formal metres. At first, I published more of the formal work because it seemed more successful to me. Recently, my free (or apparently free) verse seems more successful so I publish more of it. My poems now are much less directly personal and often experiment with multiple voices or with musical devices. My work almost always goes very slowly and involves long periods of gestation and revision. This is not because I am particularly perfectionistic, but because it takes me so long to get through the conscious areas of beliefs and half-truths into the subrational areas where it may be possible to make a real discovery.

*   *   *

The publication of *Heart's Needle* and the award of the Pulitzer Prize for the volume gave W.D. Snodgrass almost immediate prominence as one of the better poets coming out of the 1950's. His work was compared to that of Jarrell and Lowell, both of whom had been his teachers, and from whom be obviously learned a great deal. Easy to peg as a personal, subjective poet who turned the pain and experience of his successive home lives into poems, Snodgrass continued to work painstakingly on poems though which he could objectify that life and transform it into art. Guilt-ridden, however, by the fact that he not only put his life on display, but the lives of his wives and children, he develops a taut style and rigidly controlled forms as if to say to the world "don't look at me, look at what I've been able to do with me, to make of me":

> Now I can earn a living
> By turning out elegant strophes.
> Your six-year teeth lie on my desk
> Like a soldier's trophies.

—he says to his daughter in "The First Leaf." The tone of this and most of his work in his first volumes is bitter ironic: Life's pain and grief cannot be indulged but must be acknowledged. Above all, motivation must be examined and grace and forgiveness granted wherever and whenever possible.
Even in the translations that make up part of *After Experience,* Snodgrass works with poems by Rilke, de Nerval, Rimbaud, Eichendorff, and others that elevate personal sorrow and pain through the medium of symbol to an objective, generalizable human experience. His search seems to be for a core of human weakness behind the guilt that makes possible the small, as well as the gross violations of human relationships.
Guilt and responsibility become the subjects of his recent volume *The Führer Bunker.* Here Snodgrass abandons his per-

sonal subjective poetry for the dramatic *tour de force* of the last days of Adolf Hitler, his senior officials, and his mistress Eva Braun. As if reacting to the charges of excessive concern for his own personal life and avoiding history, Snodgrass immerses himself in historical fact. So rooted in fact are the poems, that Snodgrass provides an afterword to certify what might otherwise be unbelievable, but which he claims he borrowed straight from historical record. The cycle of poems, yet in progress, is an effort to probe conscience and that elusive problem that Hannah Arendt tried to explore in *Eichmann in Jerusalem*: the banality of evil. How far he will take these poems and what he will do subsequently we will have to wait patiently to discover. In the meantime, this new direction is welcome as an indication of a new depth and range that adds another element to the appreciation of his work.

—Richard Damashek

SNYDER, Gary (Sherman). American. Born in San Francisco, California, 8 May 1930. Educated at Lincoln High School Portland, Oregon; Reed College, Portland, B.A. in anthropology 1951; Indiana University, Bloomington, 1951-52; University of California, Berkeley, 1953-56; studied Buddhism in Japan, 1956, 1959-64, 1965-68. Married 1) Alison Gass in 1950 (divorced, 1952); 2) Joanne Kyger, *q.v.*, in 1960 (divorced, 1965); 3) Masa Uehara in 1967, two sons. Seaman 1957-58; Lecturer in English, University of California, Berkeley, 1964-65. Recipient: Bess Hokin Prize, 1964, and Levinson Prize, 1968 (*Poetry*, Chicago); Bollingen grant, for Buddhist Studies, 1965; American Academy prize, 1966; Guggenheim Fellowship, 1968; Pulitzer Prize, 1975. Lives in California. Address: c/o New Directions, 80 Eighth Avenue, New York, New York 10011, U.S.A.

PUBLICATIONS

Verse

Riprap. Kyoto, Origin Press, 1959.
Myths and Texts. New York, Totem, 1960.
Hop, Skip, and Jump. Berkeley, California, Oyez, 1964.
Nanao Knows. San Francisco, Four Seasons, 1964.
The Firing. New York, R.L. Ross, 1964.
Across Lamarack Col. Privately printed, 1964.
Riprap, and Cold Mountain Poems. San Francisco, Four Seasons, 1965.
Six Sections from Mountains and Rivers Without End. San Francisco, Four Seasons, 1965; London, Fulcrum Press, 1968; augmented edition, Four Seasons, 1970.
Dear Mr. President. Privately printed, 1965.
Three Worlds, Three Realms, Six Roads. Marlboro, Vermont, Griffin Press, 1966.
A Range of Poems. London, Fulcrum Press, 1966.
The Back Country. London, Fulcrum Press, 1967; New York, New Directions, 1968.
The Blue Sky. New York, Phoenix Book Shop, 1969.
Sours of the Hills. New York, Portents, 1969.
Regarding Wave. Iowa City, Windhover Press, 1969; augmented edition, New York, New Directions, 1970; London, Fulcrum Press, 1971.
Anasazi. Santa Barbara, California, Yes Press, 1971.
Manzanita. Kent, Ohio, Kent State University Libraries, 1971.

Clear Cut. Detroit, Alternative Press, n.d.
Manzanita (collection). Bolinas, California, Four Seasons, 1972.
The Fudo Trilogy: Spell Against Demons, Smokey the Bear Sutra, The California Water Plan. Berkeley, California, Shaman Drum, 1973.
Turtle Island. New York, New Directions, 1974.
All in the Family. Davis, University of California Library, 1975.
True Night, illustrated by Bob Giorgio. Privately printed, 1980.
Axe Handles. Berkeley, California, North Point Press, 1983.

Recording: *Today's Poets 4,* with others, Folkways.

Other

Earth House Hold: Technical Notes and Queries to Fellow Dharma Revolutionaries. New York, New Directions, and London, Cape, 1969.
Four Changes. Privately printed, 1969.
On Bread and Poetry: A Panel Discussion, with Lew Welch and Philip Whalen. Bolinas, California, Grey Fox Press, 1977.
The Old Ways: Six Essays. San Francisco, City Lights, 1977.
He Who Hunted Birds in His Father's Village: The Dimensions of a Haida Myth. Bolinas, California, Grey Fox Press, 1979.
The Real Work: Interviews and Talks 1964-1979, edited by Scott McLean. New York, New Directions, 1980.
Passage Through India. Bolinas, California, Grey Fox Press, 1984.

Editor, with Gutetsu Kanetsuki, *The Wooden Fish: Basic Sutras and Gathas of Rinzai Zen.* Kyoto, First Zen Institute of America in Japan, 1961.

*

Bibliography: *Gary Snyder* by Katherine McNeill, New York, Phoenix, 1980.

Manuscript Collection: University of California, Davis.

Critical Studies: "Gary Snyder Issue" of *In Transit,* 1969; *Gary Snyder* by Bob Steuding, Boston, Twayne, 1976; *Gary Snyder* by Bert Almon, Boise, Idaho, Boise State University, 1979.

*   *   *

Thomas Parkinson (in *Southern Review,* July 1968) speaks of "the peculiar blending of Zen Buddhism with IWW political attitudes, Amerindian lore, and the mystique of the wilderness" in Gary Snyder's poetry, and later observes that his aim is "not to achieve harmony with nature but to create an inner human harmony that equals to the natural external harmony." Indeed, though Snyder writes about nature, he is far from the Romantic's idea of the Nature Poet. His valuing of the primitive tribe and its relation to the earth is not a sentiment but a call for action, and his beliefs are practically and explicitly worked out in both his poetry and his prose.

His literary antecedents are Ezra Pound and Kenneth Rexroth, but their influences were quickly absorbed. There is an echo of Pound's "River Merchant's Wife" in the first poem of Snyder's first book, "Mid August at Sourdough Mountain Lookout," but it is already fully Snyder's poem. It conveys an intense clarity of sensation and does so by statement, not by metaphor or symbols.

We are invited to test the statement against only the most available of human experiences, the knowledge of what it feels like to be up a mountain, for instance, or of what water tastes like. Snyder is not, indeed, interested in the unique experiences but in the shared or sharable experience, and this is why his poetry is so different from that of the "confessional" poets, even though like them he writes largely in the first person.

The shared experience is implicitly compared to an awakening—to wonder, to awareness, to sympathy. In another poem, from *The Back Country*, he recalls how, on a walking tour 15 years before, he and his first wife met a mountain lookout. It ends:

> I don't know where she is now;
> I never asked your name.
> In this burning, muddy, lying,
> blood-drenched world
> that quiet meeting in the mountains
> cool and gentle as the muzzles of
> three elk, helps keep me sane.

The image at the end is characteristic of Snyder at his best; precise, unrhetorical, and definitive. It resolves and cancels out the large generalities of the third and fourth lines quoted. In a sense the image is the whole poem. And this too is characteristic, for Snyder perceives and communicates largely through images.

They are not static images, however. There are few still-lifes in Snyder's poetry. His writing is full of things caught in motion: on the coast "mussels clamp to sea-boulders/Sucking the spring tides"; or a deer runs with "Stiff springy jumps down the snow-fields/Head held back, forefeet out,/Balls tight in a tough hair sack."

The structure of his poems varies anywhere from the traditionally shaped poem ending with a summation, like "Hop, Skip, and Jump," to the poem of thematic juxtaposition, like "Bubbs Creek Haircut." The second method is the more common in his early poems, where it is used with variety and inventiveness.

These poems (of the 1950's and the 1960's) are kept alive at every point by the rhythms and the language. The stressed and unstressed are sharply distinguishable and group easily into tight clear rhythmic units. The language is cool, firm, and exact, with no ambitions toward a grand style to intrude between him and his perceptions. Snyder records the world attentively, as an act of love, with all his senses open to it.

In his collections of the 1970's however, there has been a certain coarsening of the poetry. Snyder has become a public figure and—always a didactic poet—has evidently seen it as his duty to make himself more didactic. "I Went into the Maverick Bar" (*Turtle Island*) shows that his sharp observations and power of terse notation have never deserted him. In this poem he shows himself charmed afresh against his will, by "that short-haired joy and roughness" of middle America, but it all ends with a formula that crudely and moralistically dismisses the energy of his subject matter: "I came back to myself/to the real work." By simplifying experience thus he has done away with much of the vitality and flexibility of this poetry.

—Thom Gunn

SOLT, Mary Ellen (née Bottom). American. Born in Gilmore City, Iowa, 8 July 1920. Educated at Iowa State Teachers College (now University of Northern Iowa), Cedar Falls, B.A. 1941; University of Iowa, Iowa City, M.A. 1948; Indiana University, Bloomington, summers 1957, 1958. Married Leo Frank Solt in 1946; two daughters. English teacher, Dinsdale High School, 1941-42, Hubbard High School, 1942-44, and Estherville High School, 1944-46, all Iowa, and University High School, Iowa City, 1946-48, and Bentley School, New York, 1949-52. Assistant Professor, 1970-73, Associate Professor, 1973-80, and since 1980 Professor of Comparative Literature, Indiana University. Exchange Professor, Warsaw University, 1976-77. Recipient: *Folio* award, 1960. Address: Department of Comparative Literature, Indiana University, Bloomington, Indiana 47401, U.S.A.

PUBLICATIONS

Verse

Flowers in Concrete. Bloomington, Indiana University Department of Fine Arts, 1960.
A Trilogy of Rain. Urbana, Illinois, Finial Press, 1970.
Marriage. Urbana, Illinois, Finial Press, 1976.
The People-Mover. Reno, Nevada, West Coast Poetry Review, 1978.

Other

Editor, *Concrete Poetry: A World View.* Bloomington, Indiana University Press, 1968.

*

Manuscript Collection: Lilly Library, Indiana University, Bloomington.

Mary Ellen Solt comments:
Each poem presents a unique problem. What do I want to say? Express? What words in what kind of structure will offer the best solution? Sometimes the words arrange themselves in rhythmic lines because that is the best way to realize the poem object. Then again they group themselves as visual images or structures in relation to the space of the page. Such poetry is generally set apart from so-called normal poetry and labelled "concrete." To me concrete structures present simply the best way to say certain things, a further possibility for the lyric poem. Other things are better articulated in lines. But the ideographic constructs of concrete poetry must be readable as poems, not as purely typographical art.

*   *   *

Mary Ellen Solt is not only a concrete poet herself but also a well-known aesthetician of the "concrete poetry" movement. She stipulates that the definition of concrete poetry must be broad, covering visual, phonetic, kinetic, constructivist, and expressionist poems. She says, "The concrete poet seeks to relieve the poem of its century-old burden of ideas, symbolic reference, allusion and repetitious emotional content....the concrete poem communicates first and foremost its structure." Her own practice is rather classically mimetic and centrally located in the spectrum of what is labelled "concrete." In her collection *Flowers in Concrete*, she arranges the letters of flower-names in differing typefaces to suggest the natural shape of that flower—zinnia, geranium, forsythia. (She had the assistance of a typographer, John Dearstyne, after drawing the originals by hand.) Despite the disclaimer quoted above, her poem "Dogwood: Three Movements" has clear symbolic reference to the tree out of which Christ's cross was hewn, although the poem is primarily an evocation of the blossom's delicacy.

As with almost all concrete and visual poets, wit is a principal literary device with Solt. Her "Moonshot Sonnet" is a fine example. Her comment on it, in *Concrete Poetry: A World View*, reads: "Made by copying the scientists' symbols on the first photos of the moon in the *New York Times*: there were exactly fourteen 'lines' with five 'accents'...so the poem is both a spoof of old forms and a statement about the necessity for new."

Solt's 1968 poem (or poem-sequence) is very different from *Flowers in Concrete* both in form and theme. It could be called a "happening" or guerila theater, consisting of a set of ten posters reflecting the terrible events of that year: civil riots, the assassinations of King and Kennedy, Resurrection City and the presidential elections. They employ such concrete imagistic devices as the A in USA turned upside down to resemble a falling bomb, and punning on the "nix" in Nixon. This poem has been performed four times, most recently in 1970 with readers and slides of historical texts during the exhibition Expose Concrete Poetry at Indiana University.

Solt's extensive comments as editor of *Concrete Poetry: A World View* have served to explain and clarify this international movement to American readers, as well as to introduce multitudinous examples of this intermedial genre. Her own work indicates the range—from the pastoral lyric of flower-names to the poem-as-public-demonstration—which she herself has called for. It is to be expected that her present interest in semiotics will carry her in a new direction.

—Jane Augustine

SORRENTINO, Gilbert. American. Born in Brooklyn, New York, 27 April 1929. Educated in New York public schools; Brooklyn College, 1950-51, 1955-57. Served in the United States Army Medical Corps, 1951-53. Married 1) Elsene Wiessner (divorced); 2) Vivian Victoria Ortiz; two sons and one daughter. Re-insurance clerk, Fidelity and Casualty Company, New York, 1947-48; messenger, American Houses Inc., 1948-49; freight checker, Ace Assembly Agency, New York, 1954-56; packer, Bennett Brothers, New York, 1956-57; shipping room supervisor, Thermo-fax Sales, 1957-60. Editor, *Neon* magazine, 1956-60, and Grove Press, 1965-70, both New York; taught at Columbia University, New York, 1965; Aspen Writers Workshop, Colorado, 1967; Sarah Lawrence College, Bronxville, New York, 1971-72; New School for Social Research, New York, 1976-79. Since 1979, Edwin S. Quain Professor of Literature, University of Scranton, Pennsylvania. Recipient: Guggenheim Fellowship, for fiction, 1973; National Endowment for the Arts grant, 1974, 1978; Fels Award, 1975; Ariadne Foundation grant, 1975; Creative Artists Public Service grant, 1975; John Dos Passos Prize, 1981. Agent: Mel Berger, William Morris Agency, 1350 Avenue of the Americas, New York, New York 10019, U.S.A.

PUBLICATIONS

Verse

The Darkness Surrounds Us. Highlands, North Carolina, Jargon, 1960.

Black and White. New York, Totem, 1964.
The Perfect Fiction. New York, Norton, 1968.
Corrosive Sublimate. Los Angeles, Black Sparrow Press, 1971.
A Dozen Oranges. Santa Barbara, California, Black Sparrow Press, 1976.
White Sail. Santa Barbara, California, Black Sparrow Press, 1977.
The Orangery. Austin, University of Texas Press, 1978.
Selected Poems 1958-1980. Santa Barbara, California, Black Sparrow Press, 1981.

Play

Flawless Play Restored: The Masque of Fungo. Los Angeles, Black Sparrow Press, 1974.

Novels

The Sky Changes. New York, Hill and Wang, 1966.
Steelwork. New York, Pantheon, 1970.
Imaginative Qualities of Actual Things. New York, Pantheon, 1971.
Mulligan Stew. New York, Grove Press, 1979; London, Boyars, 1980.
Aberrations of Starlight. New York, Random House, 1980; London, Boyars, 1981.
Crystal Vision. Berkeley, California, North Point Press, 1981; London, Boyars, 1982.
Blue Pastoral. Berkeley, California, North Point Press, 1983; London, Boyars, 1984.

Short Story

Splendide-Hôtel. New York, New Directions, 1973.

Other

Something Said (essays). Berkeley, California, North Point Press, 1984.

Translator, *Sulpiciae Elegidia: Elegiacs of Sulpicia.* Mount Horeb, Wisconsin, Perishable Press, 1977.

*

Manuscript Collection: University of Delaware, Newark.

Critical Studies: in *Grosseteste Review* 6 (Pennsett, Staffordshire), 1-4, 1973; *Vort 6* (Silver Spring, Maryland), Fall 1974.

Gilbert Sorrentino comments:

I do not champion a "poetry of statement" and I despise narrative in verse. What I look for in my work is a verse dense in its particulars, but flexible in its total structure.

*   *   *

The concept that language must "inform" or carry messages is a concept abandoned by poets at least as far back as Rimbaud. I subscribe to this belief and distrust a poetry of narrative and "content," and, in so far as I have been able, I have attempted to make the language of my fiction function in the way that the language of my verse functions, i.e. *poetically*.

Gilbert Sorrentino's title *Corrosive Sublimate* provides a clue to his work. In the tradition of those who believe that poetry makes nothing happen, or that it should not mean but be, Sorrentino makes stark, non-metaphoric statements about the corrupt urban world, about his own personal pain, about the reality of death. Written in an open-ended way, usually signalled by his use of the single, open parenthesis, his work invites the reader simply to experience the poem; there is no morality, no vision, simply the thing itself (the "corrosive" reality). Sorrentino speaks of the photograph often, as if to say that this alone stops, or seems to stop, time, though, like the poem, it contains no "meaning." However, the eye, memory, and feeling transform the photo; so too, imagination tranforms language (the "sublimate"), which is dead until experienced: "The dead cannot be told anything so we revere them/The past is static. That is a photo./But mine—even the dead/sit up flaking in their graves—mine/is the heart/that fell apart/at the junction unremembered."

"Four Songs" treats questions of art and reality:

It's better not to think
that when the wind blows
in the white curtains
it's the real thing.

When the wind invisible
touches the curtains
stop it short as in
some photograph.

Some photograph show
the shape of the wind
the color is the white
color of the curtains.

Against the silence and
white wind and white curtains
imagine in a blank room
one perfect heart.

"The Handbook of Versification" concerns the reality of the word itself and the nonreferential nature of poetry:

One thought the recurring "image" in the poet's song an
instant of consciousness.
Clear, clear day, in sun, one's majority upon one, it
is seen to be simple obsession, and helpless,
The mind careening through the infinite spaces of itself
Snags on some plain word:
Through and between whose familiar letters the true
true image of what happened: of the blank world.

Nevertheless, many of Sorrentino's poems are photos, are glossies on this blank world, and his language is hard and clear, often New York vernacular, his subjects the surfaces of New York. Like the title of his novel *Steelwork*, his poems are scaffolds that only assert the forms of reality, the forms of New York. "I speak now, tell you a bright truth," writes the poet; "This is a bitter city"—one of violence, frustration, and empty dreams. Although Sorrentino may localize his dislikes—i.e., cults (the "moony people") and the mobile middle classes and intellectuals numb with anger and fear—he says of New York: "When you leave this town, you/Is just campin out." As he travels across America ("See America First"), he laments the poverty and unending violence and filth. Sorrentino would have us recover "certain portions of the heart," and heed the possibilities of a unique identity. In a sardonic fashion he warns: "Heed

the story of the man/who took the garbage out/and threw himself away" ("Beautiful Soup"). Of psychiatrists he asks: "Who's the character in the armchair/drinking cheap wine/...glum as hell"; of marriage he writes: "you get hurt, fierce...dear God." Sorrentino's New York is specific—he writes of El Bronx, Broadway, the Van Wyck Expressway—and his is a world peopled by Jung, Artaud, Stevens, Baudelaire, Apollinaire, Blackburn, Creeley, Dexter Gordon, Sarah Vaughan, Louis Armstrong, and Bunk Johnson.

Although some of his poems extend to specific survivors of American history—i.e., veterans, Indians, miners—his finest poems are the personal ones, those occasional moments of bittersweet nostalgia for the past and his own lost innocence. Bartering death's inevitability is the fecundity of memory. "Toward the End of Winter" concerns the poet's 38th birthday: he is "aware/of the birth of all time lost and buried." "Brought almost to tears/by the simple presence of myself in my own flesh, in the chair,/my familiar things around," he listens to a sentimental old song on the phonograph. As it arouses many associations, he sees "every act, each careful gesture/in tableau," and ultimately: "the singer enmeshed with the reality/of her voice in her own presence, of flesh.../there is no truth/but in dear event, shaken, sudden..../I miss everybody."

Many of these poems maintain an irony and self-mockery, along with the pain of lost innocence. Of "Marjorie" he says: "Now there must be/stretch marks beneath her fitted girdle" and muses "I had the very bud of her, beauty and clarity day clear"; he concludes: "God/all the things destroyed/since I last kissed her/on what bitter corner/in the Bronx." Awareness alone is redemptive; one must seek out of life "Some few moments/of bitter understanding," that "we were children/Of loveless worlds, or precisely, one world/and found that (or searched for that)/absolutely alone."

The new poems in *Selected Poems* include many of Sorrentino's flashy and flippant New York types, once again characterized by his bitter cynicism, puns, and local jargon—the man with "various patches on his tight tight pants," a former harlot from Perth Amboy whose "nights fell to their knees" as "Bibi stared into emptiness." For all of them, terror lurks in the trivial.

Sorrentino's basic assumption that the world means nothing but what it is ("Behind this world is nothing/This world reveals itself completely") also characterizes the new poems, and he takes to task Wordsworthian idealism. He will not write of daffodils but of daisies, and for his persona, the flowers, at best, will be nothing but boring; the spectator in nature, like anywhere else, remains isolated and afraid. "Daisies are just white," he writes, "nothing makes them change."

Despite the predominant cynicism of these tough and realistic poems, Sorrentino remains fascinated with the magic of things—not because they mean anything, but because they stir the imagination, the stuff of life itself: "The cucumber impaled upon the picket/Has no meaning whatsoever although it points" to an infinite number of associations many of which the poet suggests. He concludes that what he most admires are the "sets of data that makes a feast of lightning/occur...the bright and beautiful non-sequitur.../lurking mysterious but plain enormities hilarious/In their candor in their cruelty. Worlds of steel."

—Lois Gordon

SOTO, Gary. American. Born in Fresno, California, 12 April 1952. Educated at California State University, Fresno,

B.A. 1974; University of California, Irvine, M.F.A. 1976. Member of the Department of English, San Diego State University, California. Recipient: Academy of American Poets prize, 1975; *The Nation* award, 1975; Bess Hokin Prize (*Poetry*, Chicago), 1977; Guggenheim Fellowship, 1979. Address: c/o University of Pittsburgh Press, 127 North Bellefield Avenue, Pittsburgh, Pennsylvania 15260, U.S.A.

PUBLICATIONS

Verse

Entrance: Four Chicano Poets, with others, edited by Soto. Greenfield Center, New York, Greenfield Review Press, 1976.
The Elements of San Joaquin. Pittsburgh, University of Pittsburgh Press, 1977.
The Tale of Sunlight. Pittsburgh, University of Pittsburgh Press, 1978.
Father Is a Pillow Tied to a Broom. Pittsburgh, Slow Loris Press, 1980.
Where Sparrows Work Hard. Pittsburgh, University of Pittsburgh Press, 1981.
Black Hair. Pittsburgh, University of Pittsburgh Press, 1985.

Other

Editor, *Entrance: Four Chicano Poets.* Greenfield Center, New York, Greenfield Review Press, 1976.

*   *   *

Few poems are as closely linked to 20th-century agrarian reality as those of Gary Soto. Yet his subjects are not the familiar midwest farmers of Sandburg or the independent tillers of rocky soil found in Frost. Instead, Soto presents the worlds of Chicano workers whose lands are seldom their own and whose visions of America are those of ones looking up from the bottom, not out over wide expanses of possibility. It is somewhat ironic that a poet such as Soto, with the concerns of an existentialist Cesar Chavez, should find himself regularly published in *The New Yorker* and in beautiful volumes from a university press. However, despite their poverty, their despair and the ugliness of their surroundings, the world which his characters inhabit is one which is precisely visioned, full of a fierce love for life. Further, Soto's diction is classically spare, his images exact in creating this dangerous world where (in his poem "The Street" from *The Tale of Sunlight*):

> One could say a bottle
> That emptied like a cough
> Turned over, slashed at a face,
> And later a car tire.
>
> One could say the wound tears again
> Opening like an eye
> From a sleep
> That is never deep enough.
>
> The poor are unshuffled cards of leaves
> Reordered by wind, turned over on a wish
> To reveal their true suits.
> They never win.

With such clear similes, such technical virtuosity (which both gives the reader a distance from the experience and renders it

that much more achingly alive) it is, perhaps, less surprising that Soto's message of solidarity with some of the most wretched of the American earth should be found on upper-class coffee tables—and be carefully read.

There is an aggressive imagination in Soto, an imagination linked strongly to the most basic things of life, of the body. The first poem in *The Elements of San Joaquin*, sets a tone which Soto has followed throughout his work. It gives us the picture of a man who is overworked, locked in a seemingly hopeless existence, yet not a man who is without worth, not a man we cannot care about:

> On the road of factories
> Gray as the clouds
> That drifted
> Above them
> Leonard was among men
> Whose arms
> Were bracelets
> Of burns
> And whose families
> Were a pain
> They could not
> Shrug off....

Somehow that which is bitter in life becomes a richness, a resonance. The short lines and enumerated details draw our attention to each word and are characteristic of all his poetry and, I think, of his vision. The careful description, the exactness, the somatic nature of the simile are also characteristic of all of Soto's work, including his later autobiographical prose essays which read like poetry themselves.

At times Soto comes close to sentimentality, his unashamed love for people, for relatives, for the wounded and the wondering, coming too close to the surface, but he manages almost always to save himself from lapsing too far into overt pity by his control, by the distance which he keeps, a distance like that of the documentary filmmaker who allows the images and the lives of the people to shine through in a structure which lets them speak for themselves. In all his books thus far, Soto speaks with a concern reminiscent of the most political of the Latin American poets, yet still avoids the traps of rhetoric and overstatement which weaken many of the poems of such writers as Neruda. He also avoids appearing grandiose by concentrating—like an intense ray of sun that burns off a man's finger—his images on small incidents, on individuals rather than world-shaking events. These lines from his poem "The Space" are a sort of creed for Soto, though in the voice of a character he calls "Manuel Zaragoza," whose dramatic monologues give Soto even more distance to explore his favorite subject matter, the vision of the ordinary and oppressed:

> I say it is enough
> To be where the smells
> Of creatures
> Braid like rope
> And to know if
> The grasses' rustle
> Is only
> A lizard passing.

—Joseph Bruchac

SOUSTER, (Holmes) Raymond. Canadian. Born in Toronto, Ontario, 15 January 1921. Educated at University of Toronto schools; Humberside Collegiate Institute, Toronto. Served in the Royal Canadian Air Force, 1941-45. Married Rosalia Lena Geralde in 1947. Since 1939, staff member, and currently, Securities Custodian, Canadian Imperial Bank of Commerce, Toronto. Editor, *Direction*, Sydney, Nova Scotia, 1943-46; Co-Editor, *Contact*, Toronto, 1952-54; Editor, *Combustion*, Toronto, 1957-60. Chairman, League of Canadian Poets, 1968-72. Recipient: Governor-General's Award, 1964; President's Medal, University of Western Ontario, 1967; Centennial Medal, 1967; Silver Jubilee Medal, 1977. Address: 39 Baby Point Road, Toronto, Ontario M6S 2G2, Canada.

PUBLICATIONS

Verse

Unit of Five, with others, edited by Ronald Hambleton. Toronto, Ryerson Press, 1944.
When We Are Young. Montreal, First Statement Press, 1946.
Go to Sleep, World. Toronto, Ryerson Press, 1947.
City Hall Street. Toronto, Ryerson Press, 1951.
Cerberus, with Louis Dudek and Irving Layton. Toronto, Contact Press, 1952.
Shake Hands with the Hangman: Poems 1940-1952. Toronto, Contact Press, 1953.
A Dream That Is Dying. Toronto, Contact Press, 1954.
Walking Death. Toronto, Contact Press, 1954.
For What Time Slays. Privately printed, 1955.
Selected Poems, edited by Louis Dudek. Toronto, Contact Press, 1956.
Crêpe-Hanger's Carnival: Selected Poems 1955-58. Toronto, Contact Press, 1958.
Place of Meeting: Poems 1958-1960. Toronto, Gallery, 1962.
A Local Pride. Toronto, Contact Press, 1962.
12 New Poems. Lanham, Maryland, Goosetree Press, 1964.
The Colour of the Times: The Collected Poems of Raymond Souster. Toronto, Ryerson Press, 1964.
Ten Elephants on Yonge Street. Toronto, Ryerson Press, 1965.
As Is. Toronto, Oxford University Press, 1967.
Lost and Found: Uncollected Poems. Toronto, Clarke Irwin, 1968.
So Far So Good: Poems 1938-1968. Ottawa, Oberon Press, 1969.
The Years. Ottawa, Oberon Press, 1971.
Selected Poems, edited by Michael Macklem. Ottawa, Oberon Press, 1972.
Change-Up: New Poems. Ottawa, Oberon Press, 1974.
Double-Header. Ottawa, Oberon Press, and London, Dobson, 1975.
Rain-Check. Ottawa, Oberon Press, 1975; London, Dobson, 1976.
Extra Innings. Ottawa, Oberon Press, and London, Dobson, 1977.
Hanging In: New Poems. Ottawa, Oberon Press, 1979.
Collected Poems 1940-1983. Ottawa, Oberon Press, 5 vols., 1980-84.
Going the Distance. Ottawa, Oberon Press, 1983.
Jubilee of Death: The Raid on Dieppe. Ottawa, Oberon Press, 1984.
Queen City, photographs by Bill Brooks. Ottawa, Oberon Press, 1984.

Recording: *Raymond Souster*, Ontario Institute for Studies in Education, 1971.

Novels

The Winter of the Time (as Raymond Holmes). Toronto, Export, 1949.
On Target (as John Holmes). Toronto, Village Book Store Press, 1973; New York, New American Library, 1982.

Other

From Hell to Breakfast, with Douglas Alcorn. Toronto, Intruder Press, 1980.

Editor, *Poets 56: Ten Younger English-Canadians*. Toronto, Contact Press, 1956.
Editor, *Experiment: Poems 1923-1929*, by W.W.E. Ross. Toronto, Contact Press, 1958.
Editor, *New Wave Canada: The New Explosion in Canadian Poetry*. Toronto, Contact Press, 1966.
Editor, with John Robert Colombo, *Shapes and Sounds: Poems of W.W.E. Ross*. Toronto, Longman, 1968.
Editor, with Douglas Lochhead, *Made in Canada: New Poems of the Seventies*. Ottawa, Oberon Press, 1970.
Editor, with Richard Woollatt, *Generation Now* (textbook). Toronto, Longman, 1970.
Editor, with Douglas Lochhead, *100 Poems of Nineteenth Century Canada* (textbook). Toronto, Macmillan, 1973.
Editor, with Richard Woollatt, *Sights and Sounds* (textbook). Toronto, Macmillan, 1973.
Editor, with Richard Woollatt, *These Loved, These Hated Lands* (textbook). Toronto, Doubleday, 1975.
Editor, *Vapour and Blue: The Poetry of William Wilfred Campbell*. Sutton West, Ontario, Paget Press, 1978.
Editor, *Comfort of the Fields: The Best Known Poems of Archibald Lampman*. Sutton West, Ontario, Paget Press, 1979.
Editor, with Richard Woollatt, *Poems of a Snow-Eyed Country*. Don Mills, Ontario, Academic Press, 1979.

*

Bibliography: *Raymond Souster: A Descriptive Bibliography* by Bruce Whiteman, Ottawa, Oberon Press, 1984.

Manuscript Collection: Rare Book Room, University of Toronto Library.

Critical Studies: "Groundhog among the Stars" by Louis Dudek, in *Canadian Literature* (Vancouver), Autumn 1964; "To Souster with Vermont" by Hayden Carruth, in *Tamarack Review* (Toronto), Winter 1965; introduction by Michael Macklem to *Selected Poems*, 1972; *From There to Here*, Erin, Ontario, Press Porcépic, 1974, and *Louis Dudek and Raymond Souster*, Vancouver, Douglas and McIntyre, 1980, Seattle, University of Washington Press, 1981, both by Frank Davey.

Raymond Souster comments:
   Whoever I write to, I want to make the substance of the poems so immediate, so real, so clear, that the reader feels the same exhilaration—be it fear or joy—that I derived from the experience, object or mood that triggered the poem in the first place.... I like to think I'm "talking out" my poems rather than consciously dressing them up in the trappings of the academic school. For many years I held to the theory that all poetry must be written out of a sudden spontaneous impulse in which the

poet is unbearably moved to write down the words of that vision. Now I am more inclined to echo the view of Guiseppe Ungaretti when he says: "Between one flower gathered and the other given, the inexpressible Null."

*   *   *

The title of a book of poems by Raymond Souster is *As Is*. That is exactly the way the world is to be found in the work of Souster, as is, without idealistic impositions, without ideological distortion. The area of his approach and the locality it is centred upon can be pursued through any of his titles. He is after "The Colour of the Times" without sentimental illusions. "Shake Hands with the Hang-man," he tells us, realistically but without sombre destitution; life is "A Dream That Is Dying." Mortal but with comic integrity, we are engaged in a "Crêpe-Hanger's Carnival." His "Place of Meeting" is Toronto. No Canadian poet has exploited a Canadian city for more truth than Souster has Toronto. It is "A Local Pride" for him. But be careful. You may not have as much pride in your city as you think you have:

> The finger of Christ
> points straight from his pedestal
> on the Church of the Sailors
> down history-crawling streets
> to Joe Beef's, the oldest
> loudest tavern in town.

On its streets you are likely to meet a drunk on crutches, "Like this one now: this corpse/This living death coming toward you." Our urban world is not likely to turn out pretty—not if you have Souster's perspicacious eye and his peripatetic shoes. Harbouring all the compassion in the world, you are likely to be arrested for loitering. Move on and take refuge in computerization. Get cardboarded. It is the only safe way to escape the penalties of being human. Even so, you are likely to get punched:

> Wrap yourself well in that cheap coat that holds back
>   the wind like a sieve,
> you have a long way to go, the streets are dark, you
>   may have to walk all night before you can find
> another heart as lonely.

In this disillusioned stance, there is always the danger of becoming an inverted romantic. The bum is the hero. There is always the cynic's disease of blaming man for the cold glitter of the inimical stars. The city of Toronto is responsible for the acne on a girl's face. This is the shuffle dealt out by the freaked-out poets.

Souster does not whine. He knows we are all a little mad, that after our last beer the door opens on nothing, on darkness "into which we walk/dead drunk or chanting poetry/but upright, still with the living/my friend."He can apostrophize a drunken clock, a hollyhock, and birds

> which any moment
> may begin to sing!

> Who knows, my heart
> may beat again
> quick as the slap
> of the first skipping rope
> of spring.

Yonge Street is the ugliest main street of Toronto. Souster has ten grey elephants going up it, literally and metaphorically: "Ten grey eminences moving/with the daintiest of steps/and the great-est unconcern/up the canyon." His circus roller coaster takes off into the Empyrean.

Souster says: "I want to make the substance of the poem so immediate, so real, so clear, that the reader feels the same exhilaration—be it fear or joy—that I derived from the experience, object or mood that triggered the poem in the first place." He does. His life-work—so far, in the five volumes collecting it—is witness.

—Ralph Gustafson

SOYINKA, Wole (Akinwande Oluwole Soyinka). Nigerian. Born in Abeokuta, 13 July 1934. Educated at Government College, Ibadan; University of Leeds, Yorkshire, 1954-57, B.A. (honours) in English. Married; has children. Play reader, Royal Court Theatre, London, 1958-59; Research Fellow in Drama, University of Ibadan, 1960-61; Lecturer in English, University of Ife, 1962-63; Senior Lecturer in English, University of Lagos, 1964-67; Director of the School of Drama, University of Ibadan, 1969-72. Research Professor in Drama, 1972-75, and since 1975, Professor of Comparative Literature, University of Ife. Founding Director of the Orisun Theatre and the 1960 Masks theatre, Lagos and Ibadan. Political prisoner, Lagos and Kaduna, 1967-69. Recipient: Rockefeller grant, 1959; Dakar Arts Festival award, for drama, 1966; John Whiting award, for drama, 1966; Jock Campbell Award (*New Statesman*), for fiction, 1968. D.Litt: University of Leeds, 1973. Agent: Morton Leavy, Greenbaum Wolff and Ernst, 437 Madison Avenue, New York, New York 10022, U.S.A. Address: Department of Dramatic Arts, University of Ife, Ife-Ife, Nigeria.

Publications

Verse

Idanre and Other Poems. London, Methuen, 1967; New York, Hill and Wang, 1968.
Poems from Prison. London, Rex Collings, 1969.
A Shuttle in the Crypt. London, Eyre Methuen-Rex Collings, and New York, Hill and Wang, 1972.
Ogun Abibimañ. London, Rex Collings, 1976.

Plays

The Swamp Dwellers (produced London, 1958; New York, 1968). Included in *Three Plays*, 1963; *Five Plays*, 1964.
The Lion and the Jewel (produced Ibadan, 1959; London, 1966). London, Ibadan, and New York, Oxford University Press, 1963.
The Invention (produced London, 1959).
A Dance of the Forests (produced Lagos, 1960). London, Ibadan, and New York, Oxford University Press, 1963.
The Trials of Brother Jero (produced Ibadan, 1960; Cambridge, 1965; London, 1966; New York, 1967). Included in *Three Plays*, 1963; *Five Plays*, 1964.
Camwood on the Leaves (broadcast, 1960). London, Eyre Methuen, 1973; in *Camwood on the Leaves, and Before the Blackout*, 1974.
Three Plays: The Trials of Brother Jero, The Swamp Dwellers, The Strong Breed. Ibadan, Mbari, 1963.

The Strong Breed (produced Ibadan, 1964; London, 1966; New York, 1967).   Included in *Three Plays*, 1963; *Five Plays*, 1964.

Kongi's Harvest (produced Ibadan, 1964; New York, 1968). London, Ibadan, and New York, Oxford University Press, 1967.

Five Plays: A Dance of the Forests, The Lion and the Jewel, The Swamp Dwellers, The Trials of Brother Jero, The Strong Breed.   London, Ibadan, and New York, Oxford University Press, 1964.

Before the Blackout (produced Ibadan, 1964; Leeds, 1981). Ibadan, Orisun, 1971; in *Camwood on the Leaves, and Before the Blackout*, 1974.

The Republican (revue), with others (produced Lagos, 1964).

The Road (produced London, 1965).   London, Ibadan, and New York, Oxford University Press, 1965.

Madmen and Specialists (produced Waterford, Connecticut, and New York, 1970; revised version, produced Ibadan, 1971).   London, Methuen, 1971; New York, Hill and Wang, 1972.

The Jero Plays: The Trials of Brother Jero and Jero's Metamorphosis.   London, Eyre Methuen, 1973.

The Bacchae: A Communion Rite, adaptation of the play by Euripides (produced London, 1973).   London, Eyre Methuen, 1973; New York, Norton, 1974.

Collected Plays:
1. *A Dance of the Forests, The Swamp Dwellers, The Strong Breed, The Road, The Bacchae*.   London and New York, Oxford University Press, 1973.
2. *The Lion and the Jewel, Kongi's Harvest, The Trials of Brother Jero, Jero's Metamorphosis, Madmen and Specialists*.   London and New York, Oxford University Press, 1974.

Camwood on the Leaves, and Before the Blackout: Two Short Plays.   New York, Third Press, 1974; *Camwood on the Leaves* included in *Six Plays*, 1984.

Death and the King's Horseman (also director: produced Ife, 1976; Chicago, 1979).   London, Eyre Methuen, 1975; New York, Norton, 1976.

Opera Wonyosi, adaptation of a play by Brecht (produced Ife, 1977).   Bloomington, Indiana University Press, and London, Rex Collings, 1981.

Golden Accord (produced Louisville, 1980).

A Play of Giants.   London and New York, Methuen, 1984.

Six Plays (includes *The Trials of Brother Jero, Jero's Metamorphosis, Camwood on the Leaves, Death and the King's Horseman, Madmen and Specialists, Opera Wonyosi*).   London, Methuen, 1984.

Radio Plays: *Camwood on the Leaves*, 1960 (UK); *The Detainee*, 1965.

Television Plays: *Joshua: A Nigerian Portrait*, 1962 (Canada); *Culture in Transition*, 1963 (USA).

Novels

The Interpreters.   London, Deutsch, 1965; New York, Macmillan, 1970.

Season of Anomy.   London, Rex Collings, 1973; New York, Third Press, 1974.

Other

The Man Died: Prison Notes.   London, Eyre Methuen-Rex Collings, and New York, Harper, 1972.

In Person: Achebe, Awoonor, and Soyinka at the University of Washington.   Seattle, University of Washington African Studies Program, 1975.

Myth, Literature, and the African World.   London, Cambridge University Press, 1976.

Aké: The Years of Childhood (autobiography).   London, Rex Collings, 1981; New York, Random House, 1982.

Editor, *Poems of Black Africa*.   London, Secker and Warburg, 1974; New York, Hill and Wang, 1975.

Translator, *The Forest of a Thousand Daemons: A Hunter's Saga*, by D.O. Fagunwa.   London, Nelson, 1968; New York, Humanities Press, 1969.

*

Critical Studies: *Wole Soyinka* by Gerald Moore, London, Evans, and New York, Africana, 1971, revised edition, Evans, 1978; *The Writing of Wole Soyinka* by Eldred D. Jones, London, Heinemann, 1973, revised edition, 1983; *Three Nigerian Poets: A Critical Study of the Poetry of Soyinka, Clark, and Okigbo* by Nyong J. Udoeyop, Ibadan, Ibadan University Press, 1973; *Critical Perspectives on Wole Soyinka* edited by James Gibbs, Washington, D.C., Three Continents, 1980, London, Heinemann, 1981.

Theatrical Activities:
Director: **Plays**—by Brecht, Chekhov, Clark, Easmon, Eseoghene, Ogunyemi, Shakespeare, Synge, and his own works; *L'Espace et la Magie*, Paris, 1972; *The Biko Inquest* by Jon Blair and Norman Fenton, Ife, 1978, and New York, 1980.

Actor: **Plays**—Igwezu in *The Swamp Dwellers*, London, 1958; Obaneji and Forest Father in *A Dance of the Forests*, Lagos and Ibadan, 1960; Dauda Touray in *Dear Parent and Ogre* by R. Sarif Easmon, Ibadan, 1961; in *The Republican*, Lagos, 1964. **Film**—*Kongi's Harvest*, 1970; **Radio**—Konu in *The Detainee*, 1965.

*   *   *

Wole Soyinka's first volume of collected poems, *Idanre and Other Poems*, is a significant guide to the direction of the author's work. He first made his name as a writer of light satirical verse in poems like "Telephone Conversation," "The Immigrant," and "The Other Immigrant," all of which he has excluded from this collection. A pre-occupation with more sombre themes is represented by "Requiem" (also, and more surprisingly, excluded from the collected poems) where he explores the continuing but tenuous relationship between the dead and the living in a series of delicate images suggestive of barely perceptible contact; "You leave your faint depressions/Skim-flying still, on the still pond's surface./Where darkness crouches, egret wings/Your love is gossamer." This pre-occupation with death and beyond—particularly with death at speed on the road—is one of the features of his later poetry and drama. His poem "Death in Dawn" ends with the startled recognition by a victim of a car crash of his sudden translation: "Brother/Silenced in the startled hug of/Your invention—is this mocked grimace/This closed contortion—I?" Several pictures of this kind occur in Soyinka's prose, poetry, and drama. Indeed one of his impressive features is his consistency between genres and over the whole period of his writing.

In a magazine interview Soyinka spoke about the "personal intimacy which I have developed with a certain aspect of the road...it concerns the reality of death...." For him, death on the road is a kind of sacrifice to "progress," a notion which Soyinka treats with extreme scepticism. But sacrifice—self-sacrifice—martyrdom is another theme with which Soyinka has become increasingly concerned. Society often destroys its greatest benefactors; indeed it is ironically through the willingness of sensitive souls to suffer martyrdom if necessary that society advances. This is the central theme both of his play *The Strong Breed* and "The Dreamer," a poem based on the idea of the Crucifixion. The dreamer (like Eman in *The Strong Breed*) is martyred in his prime, but in the final stanza of the poem there is the suggestion that out of his bitter suffering arises a new and powerful growth:

> The burden bowed the boughs to earth
> A girdle for the sea
> And bitter pods gave voices birth
> A ring of stones
> And throes and thrones
> And incense on the sea.

This theme, that society needs these victims for its own salvation, is a very important one in Soyinka's writing. The captain in his play *A Dance of the Forests* is emasculated and sold into slavery for sticking to his principles—in this case a refusal to fight in a causeless war. There is evidence of Soyinka's growing concern with man's incorrigible urge for self-destruction through war. Nowhere is this better portrayed than in the long poem "Idanre" in which, using what has now become the dominant figure in his writing, Ogun, he pictures the god who, having been invited by men to fight on their behalf, is unable to distinguish friend from foe:

> He strides sweat encrusted
> Bristles on risen tendons
>
> Porcupine and barbed. Again he turns
> Into his men, butcher's axe
> Rises and sinks
>
>   Behind it, a guest no one
> Can recall.

The poet was forced to act out his poetic theme when, as a result of his abortive efforts to avert the Nigerian Civil War with a trip across the embattled frontiers— a typically Soyinkan gesture—he was arrested and detained by the Federal Military Government. The period of solitary confinement was the gestation period for the spate of writing which followed his release nearly two years later. The title of his volume *A Shuttle in the Crypt* (two of the poems had been smuggled out and separately published by Rex Collings as *Poems from Prison*), with its suggestion of confined energetic activity, symbolises both Soyinka's imprisoned state, an active mind frustrated by inactivity, as well as his refusal to accept mental defeat. His writings since his release, both prose and poetry, are characterized by a more activist message. In the prose of *The Man Died*: "These men are not merely evil, I thought. They are the mindlessness of evil made flesh. One should never stumble into their hands but seek the power to destroy them...To seek the power to destroy them is to fulfill a moral task." In the poetry of *A Shuttle in the Crypt*,

> Come, let us
> With the mangled kind
> Make pact, no less
> Against the lesser

> Leagues of death, and mutilations of the mind.
> Take justice
> In your hands who can
> Or dare.

"Flowers for My Land" (one of the two smuggled poems) from which that extract is taken does not really represent the mood of the entire collection which is more introspective—"a map of the course trodden by the mind," as Soyinka describes the collection in the Preface—but it does foreshadow the sharper edge of the other post-prison writings.

One African leader who dares to take justice in his hands is Samora Machel, President of Mozambique, who virtually declared war against the minority regime of Rhodesia, an act which inspired Soyinka's long poems *Ogun Abibimañ*, a celebration of Machel's symbolic act, and, in the pause before real and uncompromising battle is joined, a vision of the imminent war of liberation in which both parts of the continent—hitherto the separate territories of Shaka of the east and Ogun of the west—unite to overthrow the white tyranny: "Our histories meet, the forests merge/With the savannah.../and Ogun treads the earth of Shaka!" The poem sweeps along with a heady exhilaration, brushing aside all restraining considerations; it is too late for love, too late for reflection: "Can love outrace the random bullet/To possess the heart of black despair?/Remember Sharpville—not as aberration/Of the single hour, but years and generations." Will the war be won? Will the right weapons be found even after in a desperate search for them men have rifled "Our sacred groves to yield, in need, thighbones/Honed to drinking points...?" No one knows! Even those fighting on the side of right will be imperfect men; mistakes will be made; but there is no other way. As Soyinka asks with typically irreverent irony: "If man cannot, what god dare claim perfection?" Soyinka's ideas have not changed fundamentally; prison hardened the tone, but the poet remains the protagonist of freedom against tyranny, of the force of life against the forces of death.

Because Soyinka's work is an attempt to formulate a meaning out of the contradictory forces that govern human life and actions, Ogun, who unites these two qualities without separating them, is an apt symbol. The poet himself effects a similar fusion in his work between African and European influences. European dramatic and poetic conventions are fused with African conventions and ways of thought to produce an original type of poetry. He invokes the pantheon of Yoruba gods to forge a new ethic whose validity is not confined to Africa. He imbues English with a verve and an expansiveness which spring from the imagic nature of Yoruba speech. This is what makes Soyinka both an African and a world writer.

—Eldred D. Jones

SPACKS, Barry (Bernard). American. Born in Philadelphia, Pennsylvania, 21 February 1931. Educated at the University of Pennsylvania, Philadelphia, B.A. (honors) 1952; Indiana University, Bloomington, M.A. 1956; Pembroke College, Cambridge (Fulbright Scholar), 1956-57. Served in the United States Army Signal Corps, 1952-54. Married Patricia Meyer in 1955 (divorced, 1979); one daughter. Assistant Professor, University of Florida, Gainesville, 1957-59; Professor of English, Massachusetts Institute of Technology, Cambridge, 1960-83. Visiting Professor of English, University of Kentucky, Lexington, 1978-

79, and University of California, Berkeley, 1980, and Santa Barbara, 1980-85. Recipient: St. Botolph's award, 1971. Agent: Lynn Nesbit, International Creative Management, 40 West 57th Street, New York, New York 10019. Address: 1111 Bath Street, Santa Barbara, California 93101, U.S.A.

PUBLICATIONS

Verse

Twenty Poems. Santa Barbara, California, Sun Press, 1967.
The Company of Children. New York, Doubleday, 1969.
Something Human. New York, Harper's Magazine Press, 1972.
Teaching the Penguins to Fly. Boston, Godine, 1975.
Imagining a Unicorn. Athens, University of Georgia Press, 1978.
Spacks Street: New and Selected Poems. Baltimore, Johns Hopkins University Press, 1982.

Novels

The Sophomore. Englewood Cliffs, New Jersey, Prentice Hall, 1968; London, Collins, 1969.
Orphans. New York, Harper's Magazine Press, 1972.

*　　*　　*

Barry Spacks has been writing poetry for over 25 years. Yet he is not widely known, nor is he regarded as part of a school or movement. So far as I know he does not give readings; he does not publicize himself. But what he does do is write steadily and well, producing poems that are craftsmanlike, pleasant to read, genuine in feeling and tone. He writes on many subjects, many of them drawn from his life as a professor of English at M.I.T., but it is perhaps fair to say that his real subject is the life of the poet and his responsibilities and rights. Either directly stated or implied throughout his work are themes of the right of the poet to remain free, to say what he feels, to indulge himself in nostalgia, speculation, dream, fantasy, and metaphor. Spacks is a likeable writer—unpretentious is the word one is tempted to overuse in describing him—at home with himself and in love with his wife. His lyrics reveal an American poet-professor singing of the vagaries of the quotidian in a world which amuses, touches and delights him.

His subjects are as numerous as his poems: his boyhood, his daughter, famous writers he has seen in Boston (Berryman, Neruda, Borges), a student killed while hang-gliding, lustful thoughts in a laundromat, a Buster Keaton film. But he is particularly good at turning casual occasions into poems; he has the ability to take the small incident, the almost everyday occurrence, and turn it into a small and unpretentious but nevertheless satisfying poem. Grading papers late at night and mistaking the reflection of his light for someone else's, two friends cooking dinner, finding a design of leaves on the pavement, seeing his old professor drunk in a bar, landing at an airport, finding a Yiddish newspaper on the Riverside Line: such subjects furnish the basis for his meditative—perhaps ruminative is more accurate—lyrics. But this intellectual cud-chewing results in a very personal light verse, accomplished and sensitive in its handling of the stuff of everyday life.

Spacks has a good ear for language, and his poems are virtually without a false note; he loves the language and respects it. There is no rhetoric or bombast and little word play. The verse, often free verse but occasionally rhymed or in stanzas, is clean, "hard-edged," each word carefully chosen and placed. In his best poems one sees a delight and almost surprise in seeing things come together: what sometimes seems inconsequential at the outset suddenly resolves into a striking image or idea. In one of his best poems, "Like a Prism," the prism image comes to be an image of equality of opportunity; in "Teaching the Penguins to Fly" a whimsical idea becomes a wry comment on sixties-type notions of social liberation.

The images are often striking, with a whimsical or even surrealistic quality, such as the comparison of the sea to the "sound of 12,000 women scrubbing bloody chainmail," or these opening lines from "For a Pregnant Lady":

Doing my usual thing: vacuuming Death Valley;
　stitching up some weekday shrouds;
when all at once your nowhere-near-born child
gazes through my window, nose against the glass;

These lines would seem to follow the little ars poetica he outlines in "Wit and Whimsy":

Rule one: make precious
little sense.

Rule two: commit
no permanence.

Rule three: ignore
rule four.

But there is more to Spacks than mildly breaking the rules. In poems like "New Copley in the Gallery," "The Parent Birds," and "Malediction," he assembles some intricate machines that function smoothly. In his later work his subjects seem more topical, such as the ecological "Malediction," perhaps reflecting his fuller sense of his roles as father, poet, professor, citizen, and Bostonian. If these poems have little chance of changing the world or the direction of modern poetry (and I suspect their creator has no such hopes), they are nevertheless very accomplished, sensitive poems by someone the reader feels he would like to know and to be friends with.

—Donald Barlow Stauffer

SPARK, Muriel (Sarah, née Camberg). British. Born in Edinburgh. Educated at James Gillespie's School for Girls and Heriot Watt College, both Edinburgh. Married S.O. Spark in 1937 (divorced); one son. Worked in the Political Intelligence Department of the British Foreign Office during World War II. General Secretary of the Poetry Society, and Editor of the *Poetry Review*, London, 1947-49. Recipient: *The Observer* Story Prize, 1951; Italia Prize, for radio drama, 1962; Black Memorial prize, for fiction, 1966. D.Litt.: University of Strathclyde, Glasgow, 1971. Fellow, Royal Society of Literature, 1963; Honorary Member, American Academy, 1978. O.B.E. (Officer, Order of the British Empire), 1967. Lives in Rome. Address: c/o Macmillan London Ltd., 4 Little Essex Street, London WC2R 3LF, England.

PUBLICATIONS

Verse

Out of a Book (as Muriel Camberg). Leith, Midlothian, Millar and Burden, 1933(?).
The Fanfarlo and Other Verse. Aldington, Kent, Hand and Flower Press, 1952.
Collected Poems I. London, Macmillan, 1967; New York, Knopf, 1968.
Going Up to Sotheby's and Other Poems. London, Granada, 1982.

Plays

Doctors of Philosophy (produced London, 1962). London, Macmillan, 1963; New York, Knopf, 1966.

Radio Plays: *The Party Through the Wall*, 1957; *The Interview*, 1958; *The Dry River Bed*, 1959; *The Ballad of Peckham Rye*, 1960; *Danger Zone*, 1961.

Novels

The Comforters. London, Macmillan, and Philadelphia, Lippincott, 1957.
Robinson. London, Macmillan, and Philadelphia, Lippincott, 1958.
Memento Mori. London, Macmillan, and Philadelphia, Lippincott, 1959.
The Ballad of Peckham Rye. London, Macmillan, and Philadelphia, Lippincott, 1960.
The Bachelors. London, Macmillan, 1960; Philadelphia, Lippincott, 1961.
The Prime of Miss Jean Brodie. London, Macmillan, 1961; Philadelphia, Lippincott, 1962.
The Girls of Slender Means. London, Macmillan, and New York, Knopf, 1963.
The Mandelbaum Gate. London, Macmillan, and New York, Knopf, 1965.
The Public Image. London, Macmillan, and New York, Knopf, 1968.
The Driver's Seat. London, Macmillan, and New York, Knopf, 1970.
Not to Disturb. London, Macmillan, 1971; New York, Viking Press, 1972.
The Hothouse by the East River. London, Macmillan, and New York, Viking Press, 1973.
The Abbess of Crewe. London, Macmillan, and New York, Viking Press, 1974.
The Takeover. London, Macmillan, and New York, Viking Press, 1976.
Territorial Rights. London, Macmillan, and New York, Coward McCann, 1979.
Loitering with Intent. London, Bodley Head, and New York, Coward McCann, 1981.
The Only Problem. London, Bodley Head, and New York, Coward McCann, 1984.

Short Stories

The Go-Away Bird and Other Stories. London, Macmillan, 1958; Philadelphia, Lippincott, 1960.
Voices at Play (includes the radio plays *The Party Through the Wall, The Interview, The Dry River Bed, Danger Zone*). London, Macmillan, 1961; Philadelphia, Lippincott, 1962.

Collected Stories I. London, Macmillan, 1967; New York, Knopf, 1968.
Bang-Bang You're Dead and Other Stories. London, Granada, 1982.

Other

Child of Light: A Reassessment of Mary Wollstonecraft Shelley. London, Tower Bridge, 1951.
Emily Brontë: Her Life and Work, with Derek Stanford. London, Owen, 1953; New York, British Book Centre, 1960.
John Masefield. London, Nevill, 1953.
The Very Fine Clock (for children). New York, Knopf, 1968; London, Macmillan, 1969.

Editor, with Derek Stanford, *Tribute to Wordsworth.* London, Wingate, 1950.
Editor, *A Selection of Poems*, by Emily Brontë. London, Grey Walls Press, 1952.
Editor, with Derek Stanford, *My Best Mary: The Letters of Mary Shelley.* London, Wingate, 1953.
Editor, *The Brontë Letters.* London, Nevill, 1954; as *The Letters of the Brontës: A Selection*, Norman, University of Oklahoma Press, 1954.
Editor, with Derek Stanford, *Letters of John Henry Newman.* London, Owen, 1957.

*

Bibliography: *Iris Murdoch and Muriel Spark: A Bibliography* by Thomas T. Tominaga and Wilma Schneidermeyer, Metuchen, New Jersey, Scarecrow Press, 1976.

Critical Studies: *Muriel Spark: A Biographical and Critical Study* by Derek Stanford, Fontwell, Sussex, Centaur Press, 1963; *Muriel Spark* by Karl Malkoff, New York, Columbia University Press, 1968; *Muriel Spark* by Patricia Stubbs, London, Longman, 1973; *Muriel Spark* by Peter Kemp, London, Elek, 1974, New York, Barnes and Noble, 1975; *Muriel Spark* by Alan Massie, Edinburgh, Ramsay Head Press, 1979; *The Faith and Fiction of Muriel Spark* by Ruth Whittaker, London, Macmillan, 1982; *Muriel Spark* by Velma B. Richmond, New York, Ungar, 1983; *Comedy and the Woman Writer: Woolf, Spark, and Feminism* by Judy Little, Lincoln, University of Nebraska Press, 1983; *Muriel Spark: An Odd Capacity for Vision* by Alan Bold, London, Vision Press, and New York, Barnes and Noble, 1984.

*   *   *

"What's good enough for Archimedes/Ought to be good enough for me" ("Elementary"): Muriel Spark's verse mocks the inadequacy of scientific definition and rejoices in "An odd capacity for vision." Though "Against the transcendentalists" elevates "poets" over "visionaries" and hopes "...that if Byzantium/Should appear in Kensington/The city will fit the size/Of the perimeter of my eyes/And of the span of my hand," the poem paradoxically celebrates the miracle these limits create: "The flesh made word." And the Kensington that obsesses a number of other poems is "Kensington of dreadful night" ("The Pearl-Miners"), where the persona invokes "latent Christ" ("Elegy in a Kensington Churchyard"). Sometimes the miraculous becomes merely the talking steel chairs of familiar satire on human interchangeability with artifacts ("A Visit"). Conversely, the elegant colloquialism of "Fruitless Fable," a chronicle of Mr. Chiddicott's sudden enslavement by his "perfected tea-machine," raises the poem from mock-heroic moral fable ("Alas, the transience of bliss—") to genuine fantasy. Occasionally fantasy dramatizes obsession with "...my other/who sounds my superstition like a bagpipe" ("Intermittence"), or with "...the momentary name I gave/To a slight stir in a fictitious grave" ("Evelyn Cavallo").

Spark's most ambitious fusion of obsession with fantasy creates the "tremorous metropolis" of "The Ballad of the Fanfarlo," a hallucinatory "settlement of fever," in which vocal traffic lights and ether bowls seem as ordinary or extraordinary as everything else. This nightmare continuation of Baudelaire's prose satire traces the quest of the Romantic poet Samuel Cramer for his alter ego Manuela de Monteverde and the dancer Fanfarlo, but significantly changes the tone of the original. Baudelaire's Cramer ultimately edits a socialist journal and presumably no longer signs Manuela's name to "quelques folies romantiques," while Spark's hero, either true to his early vision or atoning for his defection, is willing to endure the horrors of "No-Man's Sanatorium" in his quest. Despite a generous epigraph from Baudelaire, the poem's atmosphere and stanza form suggest "The Ancient Mariner" and, at times, "Sir Patrick Spens" as filtered through Coleridge's "Dejection: An Ode": "The new moon like a pair of surgical forceps/With the old moon in her jaws." Only in such passages, when Spark defines Romantic art through parody, does the poem achieve the simultaneous recreation and mockery of Baudelaire toward which it aims.

Cramer is funnier in a brief appearance as a visiting journalist in "The Nativity," when he replies to rumors of mysterious happenings at the inn: "No good to me if it's local." "The Nativity," Spark's longest religious poem, precariously blends faith and fantasy in a portrait of bizarre wise men: "You with the nose on top of your head, smell out/The principalities of heaven for all of us." Riddling wit defines the limits of religious mystery in shorter works, "Conundrum," "Holy Water Rondel," and "Faith and Works" ("We are the truest saint alive/As near as two and two make five"). Even an apparently secular exercise like "The Rout," which fuses, in the manner of Marianne Moore, a news article about a battle between bees and wasps in a village church with a dispatch from Cromwell, reinforced by quotations from Lawrence and The Pocket Book of British Insects: The Honey Bee, produces not only the eloquent parody of "The murder of innumerable bees," but also an elegant questioning of man's relation to the rest of creation. Like Spark's seemingly casual treatment of religion, the moralizing is always implicit, offhand. However complex her tone, Spark's forms are generally traditional. The more controlled the verse, the more the strictness of the pattern causes a concentration in theme that becomes incantatory, as in "Edinburgh Villanelle":

> These eyes that saw the saturnine
>
> Waters no provident whim made wine
> Fail to infuriate the dull
> Heart of Midlothian, never mine.

—Burton Kendle

SPARSHOTT, Francis (Edward). Canadian. Born in Chatham, Kent, England, 19 May 1926; emigrated to Canada, 1950, naturalized, 1970. Educated at King's School, Rochester, Kent, 1934-43; Corpus Christi College, Oxford, 1943-44, 1947-50, B.A.

1950, M.A. 1950. Served in the British Army Intelligence Corps, 1944-47. Married Kathleen Elizabeth Vaughan in 1953; one daughter. Lecturer in Philosophy, University of Toronto, 1950-55. Lecturer in Classics, 1955-70, and Assistant Professor, 1955-62, Associate Professor, 1962-64, Professor, 1964-82, chairman of the Department of Philosophy, Victoria College, and since 1982, University Professor, University of Toronto. Visiting Professor, Northwestern University, Evanston, Illinois, 1958-59, University of Illinois, Urbana, 1966, and Sir George Williams University, Montreal, 1971. President, Canadian Philosophical Association, 1975-76, and League of Canadian Poets, 1977-79; President, American Society for Aesthetics, 1981-82. Recipient: President's Medal, University of Western Ontario, for poetry, 1959, for essay, 1962; American Council of Learned Societies Fellowship, 1961; Killan Fellowship, 1977; Canadian Broadcasting Corporation prize, 1981. Fellow, Royal Society of Canada, 1977. Address: 50 Crescentwood Road, Scarborough, Ontario M1N 1E4, Canada.

PUBLICATIONS

Verse

A Divided Voice. Toronto, Oxford University Press, 1965.
A Cardboard Garage. Toronto, Clarke Irwin, 1969.
The Naming of the Beasts. Windsor, Ontario, Black Moss, 1979.
The Rainy Hills. Privately printed, 1979.
New Fingers for Old Dikes. Toronto, League of Canadian Poets, 1981.
The Hanging Gardens of Etobicoke. Toronto, Childe Thursday, 1983.
The Cave of Trophonius. Ilderton, Ontario, Brick, 1983.

Other

An Enquiry into Goodness and Related Concepts, with Some Remarks on the Nature and Scope of Such Enquiries. Toronto, University of Toronto Press, and Chicago, University of Chicago Press, 1958.
The Structure of Aesthetics. Toronto, University of Toronto Press, and London, Routledge, 1963.
The Concept of Criticism. Oxford, Clarendon Press, 1967.
A Book by Cromwell Kent (humour). Scarborough, Ontario, Vanity Press, 1970.
Looking for Philosophy. Montreal, McGill-Queen's University Press, 1972.
The Theory of the Arts. Princeton, New Jersey, Princeton University Press, 1982.

*   *   *

It is a truism to say that there are really two Francis Sparshotts, the first the philosopher, the second the poet. But this is only a truism because the philosophic prose is rich in poetic insight and passion, and the poetry itself is not wanting in elegant clarity and donnish wit. Also common to both is the spirit of inquiry, for many of Sparshott's best poems turn on argumentation. "Argument with Dr. Williams" from *A Cardboard Garage* begins "But nothing depends/on your old wheel/ barrow." And "Rhetoric for a Divided Voice" from *A Divided Voice* has one voice making the following demand: "I challenge your world to atone/For my unmerited pain." The second voice responds, somewhat indignantly, and they finally conclude:

No. Here's the end of all out talk:
That I am I and you are you,
Though in your footsteps I must walk,
Though mine the eyes you must look through.

Mental and moral questioning seem at the core of Sparshott's work, so often do intellectual concerns and a formal use of language take precedence over emotional expression and lyrical flights of fancy.

—John Robert Colombo

———————

SPENDER, (Sir) Stephen (Harold). British. Born in London, 28 February 1909; son of the writer Harold Spender. Educated at University College School, London; University College, Oxford. Served as a fireman in the National Fire Service, 1941-44. Married 1) Agnes Marie Pearn in 1936; 2) Natasha Litvin in 1941; one son and one daughter. Editor, with Cyril Connolly, *Horizon* magazine, London, 1939-41; Co-Editor, 1953-66, and Corresponding Editor, 1966-67, *Encounter* magazine, London. Counsellor, Unesco Section of Letters, 1947. Elliston Lecturer, University of Cincinnati, 1953; Beckman Professor, University of California, Berkeley, 1959; Visiting Professor, Northwestern University, Evanston, Illinois, 1963; Clark Lecturer, Cambridge University, 1966; Visiting Professor, University of Connecticut, Storrs, 1968-70; Mellon Lecturer, Washington, D.C., 1968; Northcliffe Lecturer, London University, 1969; Visiting Lecturer, University of Florida, Gainesville, 1976, and Vanderbilt University, Nashville, Tennessee, 1979. Professor of English Literature, 1970-77, and since 1977 Professor Emeritus, University College, London. Since 1975, President, English Centre, P.E.N. Consultant in Poetry in English, Library of Congress, Washington, D.C., 1965-66. Fellow of the Institute of Advanced Studies, Wesleyan University, Middletown, Connecticut, 1967. Recipient: Queen's Gold Medal for Poetry, 1971. D.Litt.: University of Montpellier, France; Cornell University, Ithaca, New York; Loyola University, Chicago. Honorary Member, Phi Beta Kappa, and American Academy, 1969; Honorary Fellow, University College, Oxford, 1973. Fellow, and Companion of Literature, 1977, Royal Society of Literature. C.B.E. (Commander, Order of the British Empire), 1962. Knighted, 1983. Address: 15 Loudoun Road, London N.W. 8, England.

PUBLICATIONS

Verse

Nine Experiments by S.H.S., Being Poems Written at the Age of Eighteen. Privately printed, 1928.
Twenty Poems. Oxford, Blackwell, 1930.
Poems. London, Faber, 1933; revised edition, Faber, and New York, Random House, 1934.
Vienna. London, Faber, 1934; New York, Random House, 1935.
At Night. Privately printed, 1935.
The Still Centre. London, Faber, 1939.
Selected Poems. London, Faber, 1940.
Ruins and Visions. London, Faber, and New York, Random House, 1942.

Spiritual Exercises (To Cecil Day Lewis). Privately printed, 1943.
Poems of Dedication. London, Faber, 1946; New York, Random House, 1947.
Returning to Vienna 1947: Nine Sketches. Pawlet, Vermont, Banyan Press, 1947.
The Edge of Being. London, Faber, and New York, Random House, 1949.
Sirmione Peninsula. London, Faber, 1954.
Collected Poems 1928-1953. London, Faber, and New York, Random House, 1955.
I Sit at the Window. Baltimore, Linden Press, n.d.
Inscriptions. London, Poetry Book Society, 1958.
Selected Poems. New York, Random House, 1964; London, Faber, 1965.
The Generous Days: Ten Poems. Boston, Godine, 1969; augmented edition, as *The Generous Days*, London, Faber, and New York, Random House, 1971.
Descartes. London, Steam Press, 1970.
Art Student. London, Poem-of-the-Month Club, 1970.
Penguin Modern Poets 20, with John Heath-Stubbs and F.T. Prince. London, Penguin, 1971.
Recent Poems. London, Anvil Press Poetry, 1978.

Recordings: *Stephen Spender Reading His Own Poems*, Argo, 1958; *Stephen Spender Reading His Own Poems*, Caedmon.

Plays

Trial of a Judge (produced London, 1938). London, Faber, and New York, Random House, 1938.
Danton's Death, with Goronwy Rees, adaptation of a play by Georg Büchner (produced London, 1939). London, Faber, 1939; in *From the Modern Repertory*, edited by Eric Bentley, Bloomington, Indiana University Press, 1958.
To the Island (produced Oxford, 1951).
Mary Stuart, adaptation of the play by Schiller (produced New York, 1957; Edinburgh and London, 1958). London, Faber, 1959; New Haven, Connecticut, Ticknor and Fields, 1980.
Lulu, adaptation of the play by Frank Wedekind (produced New York, 1958).
Rasputin's End, music by Nicholas Nabokov. Milan, Ricordi, 1963.
Oedipus Trilogy, adaptations of plays by Sophocles (produced Oxford, 1983).

Novel

The Backward Son. London, Hogarth Press, 1940.

Short Stories

The Burning Cactus. London, Faber, and New York, Random House, 1936.
Engaged in Writing, and The Fool and the Princess. London, Hamish Hamilton, and New York, Farrar Straus, 1958.

Other

The Destructive Element: A Study of Modern Writers and Beliefs. London, Cape, 1935; Boston, Houghton Mifflin, 1936.
Forward from Liberalism. London, Gollancz, and New York, Random House, 1937.
The New Realism: A Discussion. London, Hogarth Press, 1939.

Life and the Poet. London, Secker and Warburg, 1942.

Jim Braidy: The Story of Britain's Firemen, with William Sansom and James Gordon. London, Drummond, 1943.

Citizens in War—and After. London, Harrap, 1945.

Botticelli. London, Faber, 1945; New York, Pitman, 1948.

European Witness (on Germany). London, Hamish Hamilton, and New York, Reynal, 1946.

Poetry since 1939. London and New York, Longman, 1946.

The God That Failed: Six Studies in Communism, edited by Richard H. Crossman. London, Hamish Hamilton, and New York, Harper, 1950.

World Within World: The Autobiography of Stephen Spender. London, Hamish Hamilton, and New York, Harcourt Press, 1951.

Europe in Photographs. London, Thames and Hudson, 1951;

Shelley. London, Longman, 1952.

Learning Laughter (on Israel). London, Weidenfeld and Nicolson, 1952; New York, Harcourt Brace, 1953.

The Creative Element: A Study of Vision, Despair, and Orthodoxy among Some Modern Writers. London, Hamish Hamilton, 1953.

The Making of a Poem (essays). London, Hamish Hamilton, 1955; New York, Norton, 1962.

The Imagination in the Modern World: Three Lectures. Washington, D.C., Library of Congress, 1962.

The Struggle of the Modern. London, Hamish Hamilton, and Berkeley, University of California Press, 1963.

Ghika: Paintings, Drawings, Sculpture, with Patrick Leigh Fermor. London, Lund Humphries, 1964; Boston, Boston Book and Art Shop, 1965.

The Magic Flute: Retold (for children). New York, Putnam, 1966.

Chaos and Control in Poetry (lecture). Washington, D.C., Library of Congress, 1966.

The Year of the Young Rebels. London, Weidenfeld and Nicolson, and New York, Random House, 1969.

W.H. Auden: A Memorial Address. Privately printed, 1973.

Love-Hate Relations: A Study of Anglo-American Sensibilities. London, Hamish Hamilton, and New York, Random House, 1974.

Eliot. London, Fontana, 1975; as *T.S. Eliot*, New York, Viking Press, 1976.

Cyril Connolly: A Memoir. Edinburgh, Tragara Press, 1978.

Henry Moore: Sculptures in Landscape, photographs by Geoffrey Shakerley. London, Studio Vista, 1978; New York, Potter, 1979.

The Thirties and After: Poetry, Politics, and People (1933-1975). London, Macmillan, and New York, Random House, 1978.

Venice, photographs by Fulvio Roiter. London, Thames and Hudson, and New York, Vendome Press, 1979.

America Observed, illustrated by Paul Hogarth. New York, Potter, 1979.

Letters to Christopher: Stephen Spender's Letters to Christopher Isherwood 1929-1939, with The Line of the Branch: Two Thirties Journals, edited by Lee Bartlett. Santa Barbara, California, Black Sparrow Press, 1980.

China Diary, illustrations and photographs by David Hockney. London, Thames and Hudson, 1982; New York, Abrams, 1983.

Editor, with Louis MacNeice, *Oxford Poetry 1929*. Oxford, Blackwell, 1929.

Editor, with Bernard Spencer, *Oxford Poetry 1930*. Oxford, Blackwell, 1930.

Editor, with John Lehmann and Christopher Isherwood, *New Writing, New Series 1-2*. London, Hogarth Press, 1938-39.

Editor, with John Lehmann, *Poems for Spain*. London, Hogarth Press, 1939.

Editor, *A Choice of English Romantic Poetry*. New York, Dial Press, 1947.

Editor, *Selected Poems*, by Walt Whitman. London, Grey Walls Press, 1950.

Editor, with Elizabeth Jennings and Dannie Abse, *New Poems 1956*. London, Joseph, 1956.

Editor, *Great Writings of Goethe*. New York, New American Library, 1958.

Editor, *Great German Short Stories*. New York, Dell, 1960.

Editor, with Donald Hall, *The Concise Encyclopedia of English and American Poets and Poetry*. London, Hutchinson, and New York, Hawthorn, 1963; revised edition, 1970.

Editor, with Irving Kristol and Melvin J. Lasky, *Encounters: An Anthology from the First Ten Years of "Encounter" Magazine*. London, Weidenfeld and Nicolson, and New York, Basic Books, 1963.

Editor, *The Poems of Percy Bysshe Shelley*. Cambridge, Limited Editions Club, 1971; New York, Heritage Press, 1974.

Editor, *Selected Poems*, by Abba Kovner and Nelly Sachs. London, Penguin, 1971.

Editor, *A Choice of Shelley's Verse*. London, Faber, 1971.

Editor, *D.H. Lawrence, Novelist, Poet, Prophet*. London, Weidenfeld and Nicolson, and New York, Harper, 1973.

Editor, *W.H. Auden: A Tribute*. London, Weidenfeld and Nicolson, and New York, Macmillan, 1975.

Translator, *Pastor Hall*, by Ernst Toller. London, Lane, 1939; with *Blind Man's Buff*, by Toller and Denis Johnston, New York, Random House, 1939.

Translator, with J.L. Gili, *Poems*, by García Lorca. London, Dolphin, and New York, Oxford University Press, 1939.

Translator, with J.B. Leishman, *Duino Elegies*, by Rainer Maria Rilke. London, Hogarth Press, and New York, Norton, 1939; revised edition, Hogarth Press, 1948, Norton, 1963.

Translator, with J.L. Gili, *Selected Poems*, by García Lorca. London, Hogarth Press, 1943.

Translator, with Frances Cornford, *Le dur Désir de Durer*, by Paul Éluard. Cobham, Surrey, Trianon Press, and Philadelphia, Grey Falcon Press, 1950.

Translator, *The Life of the Virgin Mary (Das Marien-Leben)* (bilingual edition), by Rainer Maria Rilke. London, Vision Press, and New York, Philosophical Library, 1951.

Translator, with Frances Fawcett, *Five Tragedies of Sex* (includes *Spring's Awakening, Earth-Spirit, Pandora's Box, Death and Devil, Castle Wetterstein*), by Frank Wedekind. London, Vision Press, and New York, Theatre Arts, 1952; abridged edition, as *The Lulu Plays and Other Sex Tragedies*, London, Calder and Boyars, 1972.

Translator, with Nikos Stangos, *Fourteen Poems*, by C.P. Cavafy. London, Editions Alecto, 1967.

*

Bibliography: *The Early Published Poems of Stephen Spender: A Chronology* by A.T. Tolley, Ottawa, Carleton University, 1967; *Stephen Spender: Works and Criticism: An Annotated Bibliography* by H.B. Kulkarni, New York, Garland, 1976.

Critical Studies: *Stephen Spender, Louis MacNeice, Cecil Day Lewis: A Critical Essay* by Derek Stanford, Grand Rapids, Michigan, Eerdmans, 1969; *Stephen Spender and the Thirties* by A. Kingsley Weatherhead, Lewisburg, Pennsylvania, Bucknell

University Press, 1975; *The "Angry Young Men" of the Thirties* by Elton E. Smith, Carbondale, Southern Illinois University Press, 1975; *Stephen Spender: A Study in Poetic Growth* by Surya Nath Pandey, Salzburg, University of Salzburg, and Atlantic Highlands, New Jersey, Humanities Press, 1982.

*   *   *

In *The Destructive Element* Stephen Spender described the difficulties of writing about contemporaries: "One is dealing in a literature of few accepted values. At best one can offer opinions ...at worst, bookmaking, or stockbroking." He goes on to consider a question vital to understanding his own work; he is interested in writers "faced by the destructive element, i.e., by the experience of an all-pervading Present, which is a world without belief." It is easily possible to regard Spender's poetry sympathetically as a near-traumatic reaction to "a void in the present," and much of his personal experience, e.g., his commitment and later disengagement involving communism, can be interpreted as a search for belief. Even the intensity of his well-known personal and literary loyalties (e.g., with Auden and Isherwood) and the value he has given to them in his autobiographies assume a new dimension in this light. Even in his journalism, his book on the Youth Aliyah effort to make homes for Jewish children in the Kibbutzim of Israel (*Learning Laughter*), his book based journals kept on a trip through Germany in 1945 (*European Witness*), his book on student unrest, a reader can discern a kind of seeking for belief; there is an element of wander-literature, even of Quixote—for Spender's faults are those of idealist generalizing, of a frequent, often irritating naivety.

His search for a metaphor in Berlin is perhaps illustrative: "At first Berlin seemed less damaged than I had expected, but as we approached the centre of the town it produced the same impression of desolation as all of the other large German towns...." A picture emerges, of a haunted palace—something out of Poe: "Charwomen responsible for the upkeep of the Chancellory, and still performing their tasks, concealed on their persons hammers with which they broke off fragments of the yellow marble top of this [Hitler's] desk as souvenirs in exchange for a few cigarettes." He concludes that "the Nazi and the Fascist leaders were often disappointed artists," somehow linking up the Nazi fate with "the gloom of Tennyson, the ennui of Baudelaire and the pessimism of Thomas Hardy." Spender carries away a piece of Hitler's desk. Commenting on its significance as an "unholy relic," he concludes that the Nazis taught us the necessity of choosing between good and evil.

Earlier, a friend had remarked on Spender's poems: "When you write in this way you are filled with social despair, and you have no religious or political beliefs whatever. Directly, out of a sense of conscience, you try to introduce a constructive idea into your writing, you fail." "All the same," Spender replies, "one must look for a constructive idea. If one has the sense of despair and of evil, then one must look for the sense of hope and of good with which to confront despair and evil."

It is perhaps this idealism, and the linking of abstraction with imagery (a Spender play concerns "the belief that man/can overthrow systems of injustice/and build systems of justice") that determine the final tone of a Spender poem.

> The secret of these hills was stone, and cottages
> Of that stone made,
> And crumbling roads
> That turned on sudden hidden villages

he writes in "The Pylons." But soon comes the intervention of politics, of the dark awareness:

> Now over these small hills they have built the concrete
> That trails black wire:
> Pylons, those pillars
> Bare like nude, giant girls that have no secret.

One thinks sometimes that Spender wanted to be the kind of poet George Orwell might have been: and appropriately, his best poems are perhaps those about the Spanish Civil War, in *The Still Centre* (especially "A Stop Watch and an Ordnance Map" and "Fall of a City"), though poems like "I Think Continually of Those Who Were Truly Great," "The Express," and "The Landscape near an Aerodrome" are justly famous. Certain lines of Spender's echo through the mind of anyone familiar with a modern anthology:

> Eye, gazelle, delicate wanderer,
> Drinker of horizon's fluid line;
> Ear that suspends on a chord
> The spirit drinking timelessness....

And who can forget the opening lines of "The Express"? "After the first powerful plain manifesto/The black statement of pistons, without more fuss/But gliding like a queen, she leaves the station" passing "gasworks and at last the heavy page/Of death, printed by gravestones in the cemetery." With the "jazzy madness" of the train we feel a growing confidence in the poet's power, his own confidence in his own as the train arrives at "Edinburgh or Rome."

Perhaps it is difficult to recapture a sense of relevance when it comes to remembering why Spender thought C. Day Lewis shouldn't be afraid of communists, or how Spender himself changed toward "the god that failed" but we can easily recall from some distance the way Spender has developed certain obsessive ideas about death and fame:

> For how shall we prove that we really exist
> Unless we hear, over and over,
> Our ego through the world persist
> With all the guns of the self-lover?

Through everything Spender has written has run the same idealism. And a reader can hear it as he speaks in *European Witness* of "a desire to see an International Review for Europe, on the very highest level, in which the best German writers were published side by side with English and French, and perhaps with Russian ones too." There everything was going to be "discussed very seriously and with equal frankness by thinkers of all nations, since they would be on a level which was human and not immediately controversial." Spender's final appeal to many readers is probably to an idealism they have themselves failed to keep alive.

—David Ray

SQUIRES, (James) Radcliffe. American. Born in Salt Lake City, Utah, 23 May 1917. Educated at the University of Utah, Salt Lake City, B.A. 1940; University of Chicago (John Billings Fiske Prize, 1946), A.M. 1945; Harvard University, Cambridge, Massachusetts, Ph.D. 1952. Served in the United States Naval Reserve, 1941-45: Lieutenant. Married Eileen Mulholland in 1945 (died, 1976). Instructor in English, Dartmouth College, Hanover, New Hampshire, 1946-48; Member of the Department of English, 1952-62, and Professor of English, 1963-81, University of Michigan, Ann Arbor. Fulbright Professor of American Culture, University of Salonika, Greece, 1959-60. Editor, *Chicago Review*, 1945-46, and *Michigan Quarterly Review*, Ann Arbor, 1971-77. Recipient: Young Poets prize (*Voices*), 1947. Address: c/o Department of English, University of Michigan, Ann Arbor, Michigan 48104, U.S.A.

PUBLICATIONS

Verse

Cornar. Philadelphia, Dorrance, 1940.
Where the Compass Spins. New York, Twayne, 1951.
Fingers of Hermes. Ann Arbor, University of Michigan Press, and London, Cresset Press, 1965.
The Light under Islands. Ann Arbor, University of Michigan Press, and London, Cresset Press, 1967.
Daedalus. Ann Arbor, Michigan, Generation Press, 1968.
Waiting in the Bone and Other Poems. Omaha, Abattoir, 1973.
The First Day Out from Troy. Omaha, Cummington Press, 1974.
Gardens of the World. Baton Rouge, Louisiana State University Press, 1981.
Journeys. Cold Spring Harbor, New York, Elysian Press, 1981.
The Envoy. Winston-Salem, North Carolina, Palaemon Press, 1983.

Other

The Loyalties of Robinson Jeffers. Ann Arbor, University of Michigan Press, and London, Oxford University Press, 1956.
The Major Themes of Robert Frost. Ann Arbor, University of Michigan Press, and London, Cresset Press, 1963.
Frederic Prokosch. New York, Twayne, 1964.
Allen Tate: A Literary Biography. Indianapolis, Bobbs Merrill, 1971.

Editor, *Allen Tate and His Work: Critical Evaluations*. Minneapolis, University of Minnesota Press, and London, Oxford University Press, 1972.

*

Manuscript Collections: State University of New York, Buffalo; Washington University, St. Louis.

Critical Studies: "In the Garden of Talos," in *Sewanee Review* (Tennessee), Fall 1975, and "The Gateless Garden," in *Western Humanities Review* (Salt Lake City), Autumn 1984, both by Brewster Ghiselin.

Radcliffe Squires comments:
I suppose that my major themes involve a belief I have that we have gotten too far out of Nature, we humans, ever to be able to think of it as home again. This has shaken our beliefs far more than the loss of religion has, so that it often seems to me that the only faith man is capable of today is one in which he tells himself that he cannot be good, but that at least he can be wicked, which is better than being nothing. Though this gloomy view haunts much of what I do, my poems owe more to a sense of place, mountains, the Mediterranean, than they do to any dogma.

Technically my verse tends to fall into blank verse with occasional or accidental rhyme. I am not a formalist, but I should feel sheepish to turn out a poem with less metrical discipline than iambics provide. Even so, if I should have to choose between meter and metaphor, I should take metaphor, for metaphor seems to me the essence of poetry, the poem within a poem. Luckily, poetry never insists on taking one thing or the other. I believe there are colorings in my verse that come from Thomas Hardy, Robinson Jeffers, T.S. Eliot, Wallace Stevens, W.H. Auden, and C.P. Cavafy. At any rate, I have admired these poets very deeply.

*   *   *

The quiet voice of Radcliffe Squires speaks through an extraordinary imagination. His poems are romantic in theme, yet metaphysical, heroic in scope, and yet delicate. It is as if the visionary élan of a Robinson Jeffers were grafted on to lyrical, narrative gifts of a Robert Frost.

Although all Squires' poems share common properties—wit, thought, and a philosophy of nature in which Man is a sacred, yet ruinous intrusion—they tend to fall into four distinct groups. His longer poems are parables drawn from mythology: Beowulf, Hercules, Daedalus. Squires uses these heroes as emblems of human creativity and self-discovery, often blurring the edge of his narrative with hermetic allusions. In his last three books, these long mythical poems are offset by shorter ones describing places, principally in Western America and Greece, by elegies and love poems, and by poems that might best be described as speculative.

It is in his speculative moods that Squires writes his most finished poems. In "Sunday in the Laboratory," the poet turns from an aquarium of newts "hardly less transparent than glass" to "The after-image of that human embryo/The size of a hand" whose "body is all the stupor of time."

Waiting in the Bone, anticipated by the earlier "Bone House," suggests that behind a prevailing sense of loss lies hope. Bones are the sources of life, of blood. "We shall come up from the bone now./We shall learn to weep again." Or, to quote the last line of "Self as an Eye," "A squint of tears can hold the sun."

Radcliffe Squires is an evocative poet, so good at his best that no one interested in poetry today should be ignorant of his work.

—Anne Stevenson

STAFFORD, William (Edgar). American. Born in Hutchinson, Kansas, 17 January 1914. Educated at the University of Kansas, Lawrence, B.A. 1937, M.A. 1947; University of Iowa, Iowa City, Ph.D. 1954. Conscientious Objector during World War II; active in Pacifist organizations, and since 1959 Member, Oregon Board, Fellowship of Reconciliation. Married Dorothy Hope Frantz in 1944; two daughters and two sons. Member of the English Department, 1948-54, 1957-60, and since 1960, Professor of English, Lewis and Clark College, Portland, Oregon. Assistant Professor of English, Manchester College, Indiana, 1955-56; Professor of English, San Jose State College, California, 1956-57. Consultant in Poetry, Library of Congress, Washington, D.C., 1970-71. United States Information Agency Lecturer in Egypt, Iran, Pakistan, India, Nepal, and Bangladesh, 1972. Recipient: Yaddo Foundation Fellowship, 1955; Oregon Centennial Prize, for poetry and for short story, 1959; Union League Civic and Arts Foundation Prize (*Poetry*, Chicago),

1959; National Book Award, 1963; Shelley Memorial Award, 1964; American Academy award, 1966, 1981; Guggenheim Fellowship, 1966; Melville Cane Award, 1974. D.Litt.: Ripon College, Wisconsin, 1965; Washington College, Chesterton, Maryland, 1981; L.H.D.: Linfield College, McMinnville, Oregon, 1970. Address: 1050 Sunningdale, Lake Oswego, Oregon 97034, U.S.A.

PUBLICATIONS

Verse

Poems. Portland, Oregon, Portland Art Museum, 1959 (?).
West of Your City. Los Gatos, California, Talisman Press, 1960.
Traveling Through the Dark. New York, Harper, 1962.
Five American Poets, with others, edited by Thom Gunn and Ted Hughes. London, Faber, 1963.
Five Poets of the Pacific Northwest, with others, edited by Robin Skelton. Seattle, University of Washington Press, 1964.
The Rescued Year. New York, Harper, 1966.
Eleven Untitled Poems. Mount Horeb, Wisconsin, Perishable Press, 1968.
Weather. Mount Horeb, Wisconsin, Perishable Press, 1969.
Allegiances. New York, Harper, 1970.
Temporary Facts. Athens, Ohio, Duane Schneider Press, 1970.
Poems for Tennessee, with Robert Bly and William Matthews. Martin, Tennessee Poetry Press, 1971.
Someday, Maybe. New York, Harper, 1973.
That Other Alone. Mount Horeb, Wisconsin, Perishable Press, 1973.
In the Clock of Reason. Victoria, British Columbia, Soft Press, 1973.
Going Places. Reno, Nevada, West Coast Poetry Review, 1974.
North by West, with John Haines, edited by Karen and John Sollid. Seattle, Spring Rain Press, 1975.
Late, Passing Prairie Farm. Northampton, Massachusetts, Main Street, 1976.
Braided Apart, with Kim Robert Stafford. Lewiston, Idaho, Confluence Press, 1976.
Stories That Could Be True: New and Collected Poems. New York, Harper, 1977.
The Design in the Oriole. N.p., Night Heron Press, 1977.
Two about Music. Knotting, Bedfordshire, Sceptre Press, 1978.
All about Light. Athens, Ohio, Croissant, 1978.
Passing a Crèche. Seattle, Sea Pen Press, 1978.
Tuft by Puff. Mount Horeb, Wisconsin, Perishable Press, 1978.
Around You, Your House; and A Catechism. Knotting, Bedfordshire, Sceptre Press, 1979.
The Quiet of the Land. New York, Nadja, 1979.
Absolution. Bedford, Martin Booth, 1980.
Things That Happen When There Aren't Any People. Brockport, New York, BOA, 1980.
Sometimes Like a Legend. Port Townsend, Washington, Copper Canyon Press, 1981.
A Glass Face in the Rain: New Poems. New York, Harper, 1982.
Roving Across Fields: A Conversation and Uncollected Poems 1942-1982, edited by Thom Tammaro. Daleville, Indiana, Barnwood Press, 1983.

Segues: A Correspondence in Poetry, with Marvin Bell. Boston, Godine, 1983.
Smoke's Way: Poems from Limited Editions (1968-1981). Port Townsend, Washington, Graywolf Press, 1983.
Listening Deep. Great Barrington, Massachusetts, Penmaen Press, 1984.
Stories, Storms, and Strangers. Rexburg, Idaho, Honeybrook Press, 1984.

Recording: *Today's Poets 2,* with others, Folkways, 1968.

Other

Down in My Heart (experience as a conscientious objector during World War II). Elgin, Illinois, Brethren, 1947.
Friends to This Ground: A Statement for Readers, Teachers, and Writers of Literature. Champaign, Illinois, National Council of Teachers of English, 1967.
Leftovers, A Care Package: Two Lectures. Washington, D.C., Library of Congress, 1973.
Writing the Australian Crawl: Views on the Writer's Vocation. Ann Arbor, University of Michigan Press, 1978.

Editor, with Frederick Candelaria, *The Voices of Prose.* New York, McGraw Hill, 1966.
Editor, *The Achievement of Brother Antoninus: A Comprehensive Selection of His Poems with a Critical Introduction.* Chicago, Scott Foresman, 1967.
Editor, with Robert H. Ross, *Poems and Perspectives.* Chicago, Scott Foresman, 1971.
Editor, with Clinton F. Larson, *Modern Poetry of Western America.* Provo, Utah, Brigham Young University Press, 1975.

*

Critical Studies: "William Stafford Issue" of *Northwest Review* (Eugene, Oregon), Spring 1974, and of *Modern Poetry Studies* (Buffalo, New York), Spring 1975; *Four Poets and the Emotive Imagination* by George S. Lensing and Ronald Moran, Baton Rouge, Louisiana State University Press, 1976; *The Mark to Turn: A Reading of William Stafford's Poetry* by Jonathan Holden, Lawrence, University Press of Kansas, 1976.

William Stafford comments:
My poetry seems to me direct and communicative, with some oddity and variety. It is usually not formal. It is much like talk, with some enhancement.
Often my poetry is discursive and reminiscent, or at least is that way at one level; it delivers a sense of place and event; it has narrative impulses. Forms are not usually much evident, though tendencies and patterns are occasionally flirted with. Thomas Hardy is my most congenial poetry landmark, but actually the voice I most consistently hear in my poetry is my mother's voice.

*   *   *

William Stafford seems a perfect blend of Americanisms—born in Kansas to a businessman and a teacher; a gentle, quiet religious youth; missionary work during the war (he was a conscientious objector); a private and meditative adulthood teaching at Lewis and Clark College in Oregon. It is a life that seems pinpointed at the center of American ideology—though Stafford goes his own way often enough to be called crusty. The drama of his poetry seems to turn on this very point—that he is at once all of us and yet his own vinegary individual, patriotic but wary of government, religious but without orthodoxy, modest and yet quick-witted, wise, at times even a visionary. Like Wordsworth, Stafford is rooted in the common world and his inspiration is to make it intense and brightly conscious. In poem after poem he catches the world nodding over the significant, the scant, the peripheral, and in a few spare lines raises minutiae to special attention: "A tumbleweed that was trying/all along through Texas, failed/and became a wraith one winter/in a fence beyond Las Vegas" ("Small Item"). Or this, "At noon in the desert a panting lizard/waited for history, its elbows tense, /watching the curve of a particular road/as if something might happen" ("At the Bomb Testing Site").

It is a verse that is so narrowly focused at times,that it seems the verse equivalent of column fillers. In a century aching from too much history, Stafford has spent his writing life squinting, at particulars, at leaf flutters and wind changes, bird calls in the solemn evening woods. His poetic is that everything matters, everything is delicately threaded together, that some spiritual basting has made life whole and as poet he daily makes discovery of this fact: "No touch can find that thread, it is too small./Sometimes we think we learn its course—/through evidence no court allows/a sneeze may glimpse us Paradise" ("Connections"). In other words, Stafford is an antidote to a nervous nation, a moment of utter and tranquil passivity before life, a voice so calm in its spiritual reserves that it lulls any reader into a dreamy curiosity about his own life and surroundings. His poetry is opposed to aggression, to acquisitiveness, to ends and results: "Deaf to process, alive only to ends,/such are the thinkers around me, the logical ones—/...I would sweep the watch face, narrowing angles,/catching at things left here that are ours" ("It Is the Time You Think").

But Stafford has written numerous volumes of verse on this slender poetic, collected in *Stories That Could Be True*, a size of canon contradictory to its modest intentions. The weakness of such quantity is that the trivial and particular cannot sustain an indefinite interest—and not all things under Stafford's pen connect to the spirit around them. Many poems are so flatly understated as to be wearying memories and jots, words of habit not of inspiration. In *Stories That Could Be True*, the tranquil stream of language sets off an unlikely response—a longing for something awful to happen just to quicken reality. Occasionally the poetry tracts real eventfulness and his language handles it well. One of his best and most difficult poems is "With My Crowbar Key," with its macabre loneliness and maniacal passion: "When I see my town over sights of a rifle,/and carved by light/ from the lowering sun,/then my old friends darken one by one."

In spite of sameness and occasional tedium, the competency of the verse is very high. Stafford has genius about him; there is in all this poetry his unique imprint, and numbers of poets have come to imitate his spiritual regionalism. The cold northwest winters, the silent desert, the long vigils at windows all shape themselves as a Stafford experience. When he writes "I could hear the wilderness listen," we believe him. Even his most sermonizing verse has about it some unquestionably honest purpose. In the long run, most of his poetry will fade, but a core of magical lyrics about our daily lives will remain and represent him.

Stafford continues to animate his universe with *trompe l'oeil* visions. *A Glass Face in the Rain* catches all sorts of sprites and lively flickers from the corner of his eyes. He is a bemused sage in these poems, and his simplifications of experience have pared his own existence down to very few essentials. His pleasures arise from mere walking, casual conversation, idle moments before a window.

A shadow hides in every stone.
When the sun goes down the shadow
crawls from inside its place; it reaches out.
When we walk by, one part of our step
touches alive the hidden self
awaiting nightfall to be real.

The woods are all that remain of paradise—but it still encloses the imaginary and real creatures that ancient myth once gave us. Stafford's tone is of a wanderer who limps along the margins of a sacred grove, cursed from entering it again, but whose belief in higher things is clear and firm. In fact, in this book, he makes peace with imminent death, indeed, seems almost to look forward to his end as though it posed some transformation into one of the things of his peripheral sight. Another world beckons in this book:

I know it is strange. And there's no measure
for this. The only connection we make
is like a twinge when sometimes they
      change
the beat in music, and we sprawl with it
and hear another world for a minute
that is almost there.

Younger poets have embraced his crisp, lean style of mysticism and copy him with enthusiasm. Among America's senior poets, he is one of the most loved and revered as he tirelessly rides the college circuits reading his poems and encouraging others with his unfailing faith in divine sight.

—Paul Christensen

STALLWORTHY, Jon (Howie). British. Born in London, 18 January 1935. Educated at Dragon School, Oxford, 1940-48; Rugby School, Warwickshire, 1948-53; Magdalen College, Oxford (Newdigate Prize, 1958), 1955-59, B.A. 1958, B.Litt. 1961. Served in the Oxfordshire and Buckinghamshire Light Infantry, Royal West African Frontier Force, 1953-55. Married Gillian Waldcock in 1960; one daughter and two sons. Editor, Oxford University Press, London, 1959-71, and Clarendon Press, Oxford, 1972-74; Deputy Academic Publisher, Oxford University Press, Oxford, 1974-77. Since 1977, John Wendell Anderson Professor of English, Cornell University, Ithaca, New York. Chatterton Lecturer, British Academy, 1970; Visiting Fellow, All Souls College, Oxford, 1971-72. Recipient: Duff Cooper Memorial Award, 1974; Smith Literary Award, for non-fiction, 1975; E.M. Forster Award, 1976. Fellow, Royal Society of Literature, 1971. Address: Long Farm, Elsfield Road, Old Marston, Oxford, England; or, 1456 Hanshaw Road, Ithaca, New York 14850, U.S.A.

PUBLICATIONS

Verse

The Earthly Paradise. Privately printed, 1958.
The Astronomy of Love. London, Oxford University Press, 1961.
Out of Bounds. London, Oxford University Press, 1963.
The Almond Tree. London, Turret, 1967.

A Day in the City. Exeter, Exeter Books, 1967.

Root and Branch. London, Chatto and Windus-Hogarth Press, and New York, Oxford University Press, 1969.

Positives. Dublin, Dolmen Press, 1969.

A Dinner of Herbs. Exeter, Rougemont Press, 1970.

Hand in Hand. London, Chatto and Windus-Hogarth Press, 1974.

The Apple Barrel: Selected Poems 1956-1963. London, Oxford University Press, 1974.

A Familiar Tree. London, Chatto and Windus-Oxford University Press, and New York, Oxford University Press, 1978.

Other

Between the Lines: Yeats's Poetry in the Making. Oxford, Clarendon Press, 1963.

Vision and Revision in Yeats's "Last Poems." Oxford, Clarendon Press, 1969.

Wilfred Owen. London, Chatto and Windus-Oxford University Press, 1974; New York, Oxford University Press, 1975.

Poets of the First World War. London, Oxford University Press, 1974.

Editor, *Yeats: Last Poems: A Casebook.* London, Macmillan, 1968; Nashville, Aurora, 1970.

Editor, with Seamus Heaney and Alan Brownjohn, *New Poems 1970-1971.* London, Hutchinson, 1971.

Editor, *The Penguin Book of Love Poetry.* London, Penguin, 1973; as *A Book of Love Poetry,* New York, Oxford University Press, 1974.

Editor, *The Complete Poems and Fragments,* by Wilfred Owen. London, Chatto and Windus-Oxford University Press, 1983; New York, Norton, 2 vols., 1984.

Editor, *The Oxford Book of War Poetry.* Oxford and New York, Oxford University Press, 1984.

Translator, with Jerzy Peterkiewicz, *Five Centuries of Polish Poetry,* revised edition. London, Oxford University Press, 1970.

Translator, with Peter France, *The Twelve and Other Poems,* by Alexander Blok. London, Eyre and Spottiswoode, and New York, Oxford University Press, 1970; as *Selected Poems,* London, Penguin, 1974.

Translator, with Peter France, *Selected Poems,* by Boris Pasternak. London, Allen Lane, and New York, Norton, 1983.

*

Critical Studies: "Playing with Words" by the author, in *Times Educational Supplement* (London), August 1976; Harry Marten, in *Contemporary Literature* (Madison, Wisconsin), Summer 1979.

Jon Stallworthy comments:

When a poet is asked to "make a statement" he should respond with a poem, but I am tongue-tied in police stations, so will echo Keats: "I am certain of nothing but the holiness of the heart's affection." The changing seasons of "the heart's affection" have prompted the best of the poems I have written since, at the age of seven, I set myself to learn how to make poems as a carpenter makes tables and chairs. I count myself a maker, and such other things as I have made with words—studies of Yeats "at work," translations of poems by Blok and Pasternak—have been made with one purpose in view; to learn how to make better poems. And what is a poem? When my daughter asked that question, I found my tongue:

A POEM IS

something that someone is saying
no louder, Pip, than my "goodnight"—
words with a tune, which outstaying
their speaker travel as far
as that amazing, vibrant light
from a long-extinguished star.

*   *   *

Jon Stallworthy is a quiet poet, a fastidious craftsman, whose talent did not reveal itself fully until the publication of his collection, *Root and Branch.* His earlier poems were carefully wrought, but lacked the individuality and style that are apparent in the looser but still controlled forms of *Root and Branch.*

The central poem in this collection is "The Almond Tree," which seeks to discover meaning in the agonizing event of the birth of a mongol son. Such poems are notoriously hard to write, and at the beginning this one achieves a rather high degree of success as it laconically describes the poet, unaware of disaster, driving to the hospital hoping for a son. Then it collapses into more contrived modes, ending with the bathetic "I have learnt that to live is to suffer,/to suffer is to live." Such a failure is, however, understandable: other more successful poems in the volume show that Stallworthy is capable of a more original brand of compassion when he writes less painfully near to the event. "A Poem about Poems about Vietnam" memorably attacks the glib ease of the "protest" poets; those killed in the conflict "whisper in their sleep/louder from underground than all/the mikes that were hung upon your lips/when you were at the Albert Hall." But one of Stallworthy's themes is compassion, concern for suffering, and in "Bread" he illustrates how concern can be meaningful; as he eats the bread for his breakfast he remembers

stick limbs and hunger-blown
bellies; the aftermath
of drought, flood flotsam, cyclone

fodder. And sawdust crams my mouth.

That is an admirable and convincing record of how anguish at that suffering from which one is removed by circumstances can be more than a mere emotion. Now that he has eschewed traditional formal strictness, Stallworthy seems to write better and more imaginatively. Sometimes the exquisiteness for which he strives seems to be dwarfed by the largeness of his subject—as in "War Song of the Embattled Finns 1939"; increasingly, however, the care of his writing and his almost imagistic talent for description match up to his subjects.

—Martin Seymour-Smith

STANFORD, Ann. American. Born in La Habra, California, 25 November 1916. Educated at Stanford University, California (Phelan Fellowship, 1938), B.A. 1938 (Phi Beta Kappa); University of California, Los Angeles, M.A. in journalism 1958, M.A. in English 1961, Ph.D. in English and American literature 1962. Married Ronald Arthur White in 1942; three daughters and one son. Executive secretary, 1957-58, Instructor in Journalism, 1958-59, and poetry workshop instructor, 1960-61, University of California, Los Angeles. Assistant Professor, 1962-66,

Associate Professor, 1966-68, and since 1968, Professor of English, San Fernando Valley State College, later California State University, Northridge. Poetry reviewer, Los Angeles *Times*, 1958-68; Editor, *Uclan Review*, Los Angeles, 1961-64; Co-Founding Editor, California State University Renaissance Editions; Member, Editorial Board, *Early American Literature*, Amherst, Massachusetts, 1971-73. Recipient: Yaddo Fellowship, 1957, 1967; Borestone Mountain Award, 1960; National Endowment for the Arts grant, 1967, 1974; Shelley Memorial Award, 1969; American Academy Award, 1972; Alice Fay di Castagnola Award, 1976. Address: 9550 Oak Pass Road, Beverly Hills, California 90220, U.S.A.

PUBLICATIONS

Verse

In Narrow Bound. Gunnison, Colorado, Swallow, 1943.
The White Bird. Denver, Swallow, 1949.
The Weathercock. San Jose, California, Talisman Press, 1956.
Magellan: A Poem to Be Read by Several Voices. San Jose, California, Talisman Press, 1958.
The Weathercock (collection). New York, Viking Press, 1966.
The Descent. New York, Viking Press, 1970.
Climbing Up to Light. Los Angeles, Magpie Press, 1973.
In Mediterranean Air. New York, Viking Press, 1977.

Other

Anne Bradstreet, The Worldly Puritan: An Introduction to Her Poetry. New York, Burt Franklin, 1974.

Editor, *The Women Poets in English: An Anthology.* New York, McGraw Hill, 1972.
Editor, with Pattie Cowell, *Critical Essays on Anne Bradstreet.* Boston, Hall, 1983.

Translator, *The Bhagavad Gita: A New Verse Translation.* New York, Herder, 1970.

*

Critical Study: *Dives and Descents: Thematic Strategies in the Poetry of Adrienne Rich and Ann Stanford* by Polly Naoshire Chenoy, unpublished dissertation, Salt Lake City, University of Utah, 1975.

Ann Stanford comments:

I try to set down the inner experiences of human beings, especially their relationships to time and the world. The expression is by means of imagery drawn from the visible, especially the natural, scene. The verse forms vary from traditional metrical verse to free verse in long or short cadences.

*   *   *

Ann Stanford's poetry thrives in the realm of reverie, bordered by nightmare, "beset by spirits," whose voices reveal the world as a "sifting down of shadows." Objects, often classified, are seldom sharply defined; human actions, attended by larger forces, turn either febrile or hollow. Whatever comforts are presented bob along in a welter of surrender: though "sleepy and warm," in "Night Rain," she falls back to sleep where she can say, "I dream of the great horned owl/Snatching birds like plums out of trees." Inside the "black ball of [her] mind," she

protects the "one white thought," but it's unclear whether this is a node of joy or concentrated pain. Imagine the extreme situations of Sylvia Plath done over into the sensibility of H.D. and you have some of this poetry's texture: she invokes the "blessed dark that turns across the day" as an opening force.

Her method reveals through abstraction, and though she wants to "descend from ideal to actual touch," her motions are often upward. Upon descent, however, she discovers the "earth with all its destinies," and promise and threat take the shape of an unknown future buried in an immutable plan:

> The noun
> Is what is feared; to name the sly
> Commotion of the blood which runs
> Unplanned as leaves to their own ways.

Filled with earth and sky, kernel and shell, this poetry presents assured and limited returns—its horrors are all in the coming and going—but it lacks instantaneous images where accuracy might break open into ecstasy. A poetry of general nouns and basic verbs, its lyricism rides along on stores of emotion: "From the center of our body/Come the bright flowers." The main accomplishment here derives from a quiet honesty; it offers the sureness of craft and the surprises of self-possession. Her victories originate in her willingness to ignore the odds and keep watch at night. She shuns, to advantage, the ordinary and domestic subjects, but hasn't perhaps the complete frenzy to fathom the Blakean excesses; her language is her own, but she is too satisfied with it to complete her experiments. "Caught between never and now," she makes all she can of her patience and her predicament, and her ways are sufficiently beautiful.

—Charles Molesworth

STARBUCK, George (Edwin). American. Born in Columbus, Ohio, 15 June 1931. Educated at the California Institute of Technology, Pasadena, 1947-49; University of California, Berkeley, 1950-51; University of Chicago, 1954-57; Harvard University, Cambridge, Massachusetts, 1957-58. Served in the United States Army, 1952-54. Married 1) Janice King in 1955 (divorced, 1961); 2) Judith Luraschi in 1962 (divorced, 1968); 3) Kathryn Salyer in 1968; five children. Fiction Editor, Houghton Mifflin Company, Boston, 1958-61. Member of the English Department, State University of New York, Buffalo, 1963-64; Associate Professor, 1964-67, and Director, Writers Workshop, 1967-70, University of Iowa, Iowa City. Since 1971, Professor of English, Boston University. Recipient: Yale Series of Younger Poets Award, 1960; American Academy in Rome Fellowship, 1961, 1962, and award, 1983; Guggenheim Fellowship, 1961; Ingram Merrill Fellowship; Lenore Marshall Prize, 1983. Address: Department of English, Boston University, Boston, Massachusetts 02215, U.S.A.

PUBLICATIONS

Verse

Bone Thoughts. New Haven, Connecticut, Yale University Press, 1960.
White Paper: Poems. Boston, Little Brown, 1966.
Three Sonnets. Iowa City, Windhover Press, n.d.

Elegy in a Country Church Yard. Boston, Pym Randall Press, 1975.

Desperate Measures. Boston, Godine, 1978.

Talkin' B.A. Blues: The Life and a Couple of Deaths of Ed Teashack; or, How I Discovered B.U., Met God, and Became an International Figure. Boston, Pym Randall Press, 1980.

The Argot Merchant Disaster: Poems New and Selected. Boston, Little Brown, and London, Secker and Warburg, 1982.

Recordings: *George Starbuck*, Carillon, 1960; *Election Day*, Watershed, 1981.

*

George Starbuck comments:

I have the American academic's common interest in common speech. Do I exchange gossip and advice with a set of peers? No. Am I proud of that? No.

Characterize my poems? In subject, obsessed by wars, religions, beautiful weird Americans, beautiful weird American talk. In impulse, utterly frivolous and formal. Put it this way: One of my poems is a 156-line acrostic in dactylic monometer, heavily alliterated. No poet in his right mind would attempt such a thing. Audiences tell me its one of my most fluent and forceful and serious poems. What am I to do? For me, the long way around, through formalisms, word-games, outrageous conceits (the worst of what we mean by "wit") is the only road to truth. No other road *takes* me. Put it another way: Rather than chisel away at the rock of language, hoping to leave the world an Easter present of great stone Truths, I dump the rock, a piece at a time, into acid. The acid is brute, arbitrary, simple: this it eats, this it rejects. But find the right acid, and suddenly the rock will, of itself, yield up a whole shaped world—a world I *could not have known* was there. Lovely complexity of fact, of the pre-existence. Fossils, yes. How do you bring them to light? Not by regarding the language as bland *medium* for your own exquisite machinations. Not by chiseling at it. By genuine *experiment* on it—the putterer's destructive prank. Some writers' lives are a search for the philosopher's stone. My search is for *aqua regia.* Not *aqua fortis.*

None of your lesser "acid." Against marble, rhyme. Shakespeare had the idea. Rhyme, pun, palindrome—whatever may do violence *enough* to the shapes we think we have already given Truth. Put it yet another: *Conscious* slavery to the language. The only alternatives are unconscious slavery, or the sainthood of the wholly silent. And if the slave still merely grumbles and wisecracks under his breath, if he shies from the full fervor of insurrection, at least he will know whose fault and choice it is.

Affinities? My great admirations are for Frost, Auden, Hopkins, Dylan Thomas, Merwin, Plath—all lovers of the spoken English sentence, all but the first two fascinated with both the syntax and the metaphysics of metaphor. But who to *lump* me with? Wilbur? Dugan? Hecht? Hollander? A lesser, drearier catalog of names? How does a poet know? James Wright never glommed onto an ounce of Frost's tone or sense or way with American speech, until after he thought he had broken with Frost as a model.

Important experiences? Majoring in mathematics at CalTech. Studying the standard textbooks of 1950: Brooks and Warren, O. Williams' anthologies. More recently, winning a long legal battle for free speech in the State University of New York, and in the process realizing that maybe I had never, myself, hazarded in public a truly difficult, unpopular, or dangerous truth. (See "truth" again. I love to bandy bad words.)

*   *   *

As well as any contemporary American poet's , George Starbuck's poems illustrate Robert Penn Warren's observation that poetry is the mathematics of literature. Educated in math at Cal Tech, Starbuck is always counting as he writes. "Get me in ten-man tandem with them poets of the olden time," he crows in "Sunday Brunch in the Boston Restoration," "pillaging the quotidian, parceling it up into rhyme." If he is guilty of "whimsy," as he confesses in "Tuolomne," he uses his craft (like his "mother the rewrite expert" in "Dedication") to avoid commonplaces, truisms, and whatever other high-sounding sentiments "you would expect to find floating around/in the hot air looking for a place to settle."

A matter of intelligence rather than mechanics or anxiety, numbers for Starbuck lead to pleasure and truth. Frivolity, wrenching forms, and outrageous wit permit him to speak convincingly to the world's horrors. He dramatizes police brutality in "The Deposition," a sonnet in irregular lines. "I Dreamt I Went Shooting Fish in My Bare Chest," besides taking a swipe at the old Maidenform Bra commercial ("I dreamt I....in my Maidenform Bra"), employs 12-line stanzas of tetrameter, trimeter, and dimeter to harangue against Ian Fleming's machismo.

Reviewing Starbuck's quarter century of published verse, one must appreciate the consistency with which the intricacies of language solidify the poems. And one senses Starbuck's growing confidence. During the 1950's his lines are shorter, more restrained, his treatment of subjects more descriptive. Later, actuality gives rise to fancies, and the lines surge across the page. The confidence necessary for this unfettering is voiced at the end of "Tuolomne," his "apology" to God for the shortcomings of his writing career:

> I mean why not? I know the wind I seek
> To flee from seven days an average week.
> If everything it says to me is Greek,
> And everything it means to me is All,
> And all I care about is the unknown,
> Who is to say I'm loco if I fall
> Into a little singsong of my own....

Talkin' B.A. Blues, Starbuck's book-length satire of higher education, epitomizes his recent free-wheeling manner. Reminiscent of the folk tradition of Woody Guthrie, Bob Dylan, and Sterling A. Brown's "The Last Ride of Wild Bill" (the numbers runner) and Slim Greer poems, Starbuck's poem stars Ed Teashack, "an antiquark" "in cast-off jeans," "the cosmological counterploy/To all that jive an' all that jargon," who "shows us every year/with a dead guitar an' a bridge too far bit/into by the strings." In language as supercharged as Norman Mailer's in *Why Are We in Vietnam?* Starbuck confronts Teashack with hippies, demonstrators, small-time administration types, a liberal campus chaplain, and "Long John Silver" (modeled upon John Silber, controversial president of Boston University). The wonder of the poem is two-fold: the extravagance of the situations (Teashack is killed robbing a bank and returned to earth as a college student, for instance) and the fearlessness of the language. When Teashack questions the meaning of Silver's being carried in a chair as construction equipment repossesses the campus, Starbuck, with what may be a record number of modifiers, has the fawning Trustee trot out

> one o' them gut-wrenchin'
> Instant-Academy-Award-mention
> Ear-twistin' an teeth-clinchin'

Goodbye-cartilage-hello-piles
Hurts-me-more-than-it-hurts-you cam-pain *smiles.*

Starbuck's vision has unfolded as he has become easy with improvising upon actuality. "The world *is* too much for us," he concludes in "Magnificat in Transit from the Toledo Airport," "wait and see!" "The right-now/Flutters its huge prosthetics at us" ("Sign"). Whimsy and stupefying reality collide in "The Spell Against Spelling," "The Great Dam Disaster a Ballad," and "Sonnet in the Shape of a Potted Christmas Tree." In "The Universe Is Closed and Has REMs," considering the outcome of creation, he muses, "If having a trick thumb can tip the odds,/Why us-the-klutz? Why not cephalopods?" The irrepressible delight underneath such play gets articulated after he has thought about nuclear holocaust: "Dumb, then, for the merely not-yet-dead of us/To love the thing that kills us. But I do." He gives his love of the "beautiful...various...new" its most exhilarated expression in the long lines, exotic detail, and ingenious rhyming of the seventh section of "Sunday Brunch in the Boston Restoration."

This exhilaration—this singing for all he's worth in the face of the crass and inhumane—has apparently struck Starbuck as an essential modality for our time. "Wonderful," he quips at the end of "The Universe Is Closed and Has REMs,"

> we just graduate from Isis
> And Kali and Jehovah and all that
> And start to see how hugely where-we're-at
> Exceeds the psychedelic pipedreams of it,
> And whammo.
>   Tell the whole shebang I love it,
> And buck the odds, and hope, and give it my
> Borrowed scratched-up happy hello-goodbye.

With hindsight, we can see that Starbuck's subjects are commanded by their era, so some age; but the voice persists, and the wit, the mind. Already his best poems seem distinguished because of the flamboyance, the penetration of his intelligence.

—Jay S. Paul

STEAD, C(hristian) K(arlson). New Zealander. Born in Auckland, 17 October 1932. Educated at Mount Albert Grammar School; Auckland University, B.A. 1954, M.A. (honours) 1955; Bristol University (Michael Hiatt Baker Scholar), Ph.D. 1961. Married Kathleen Elizabeth Roberts in 1955; two daughters and one son. Lecturer in English, University of New England, New South Wales, 1956-57. Lecturer, 1959-61, Senior Lecturer, 1962-64, Associate Professor, 1964-68, and since 1969, Professor of English, Auckland University. Chairman, New Zealand Literary Fund, 1973-75. Recipient: Poetry Awards Incorporated prize (U.S.A.), 1955; Readers Award (*Landfall*), 1959; Katherine Mansfield Award, for fiction and for essay, 1961, and Fellowship, 1972; Nuffield Travelling Fellowship, 1965; Jessie Mackay Poetry Award, 1973; New Zealand Book Award, 1976. Litt.D.: Auckland University, 1982. Address: 37 Tohunga Crescent, Parnell, Auckland 1, New Zealand.

PUBLICATIONS

Verse

Whether the Will Is Free: Poems 1954-62.   Auckland, Paul's Book Arcade, 1964.
Crossing the Bar.   Auckland, Auckland University Press-Oxford University Press, 1972.
Quesada: Poems 1972-1974.   Auckland, The Shed, 1975.
Walking Westward.   Auckland, The Shed, 1979.
Geographies.   Auckland, Auckland University Press-Oxford University Press, 1982.
Poems of a Decade.   Dunedin, Pilgrims South Press, 1983.
Paris.   Auckland, Auckland University Press-Oxford University Press, 1984.

Novels

Smith's Dream.   Auckland, Longman Paul, 1971.
All Visitors Ashore.   London, Harvill Press, 1984.

Short Stories

Five for the Symbol.   Auckland, Longman Paul, 1981.

Other

The New Poetic: Yeats to Eliot.   London, Hutchinson, 1964; New York, Harper, 1966.
In the Glass Case: Essays on New Zealand Literature.   Auckland, Auckland University Press-Oxford University Press, 1981.

Editor, *New Zealand Short Stories: Second Series.*   London, Oxford University Press, 1966.
Editor, *Measure for Measure: A Casebook.*   London, Macmillan, 1971.
Editor, *The Letters and Journals of Katherine Mansfield: A Selection.*   London, Allen Lane, 1977.
Editor, *Collected Stories,* by Maurice Duggan.   Auckland, Auckland University Press-Oxford University Press, 1981.

*

Critical Studies: by Roy Fuller, in *London Magazine,* July 1964; James Bertram, in *Islands 2* (Christchurch), 1972; Peter Crisp, in *New Argot* (Auckland), 1975; Rob Jackaman, in *Landfall 114* (Christchurch), 1975; Ken Arvidson, in *Journal of New Zealand Literature 1,* 1983; interview with Michael Harlow, in *Landfall 132* (Christchurch), 1983.

C.K. Stead comments:
I am always troubled that I can't write more poems than I do, that although I am a fairly conscientious and hard-working person, the Muse will not warm to these virtues, in fact, seems bored by them. I don't take the view that poets who write more than I do are less demanding of themselves; that "more means worse." I envy their fluency and still hope one day to learn the trick.

Reviewers tell me (with an emphasis that varies, of course, from approval to disapproval) that my poems are disciplined. This seems to suggest labour, conscious effort, self-control—all the qualities that go (for example) into my critical prose. But for me the discipline by which poems are achieved is quite different and still something I don't properly understand. I have to step out of the world in which I fill various roles (critic, professor, committee member, family man, etc.) and in which the clock rules. I have to sink back into myself to a point where all the trappings, all the things that are accidental, are lost. Then what is dredged up will sometimes seem worth polishing and putting on display.

Although I have on one occasion worked a poem into being through literally hundreds of drafts (an experience which was itself a kind of "possession," and not at all pleasant) it is usually true for me that hard labour doesn't help, and that Keats's dictum holds: "if poetry come not as naturally as the leaves to the tree it might as well not come at all." To be in that rare state where poetry comes naturally is for me the greatest felicity. I am always afraid that it will never happen again.

I am a self-regarding younger son. My natural tone is secure but not definitive. I am a liberal, fitted neither for moralising nor for command. But when I am able to dig deep enough, discover another self who (though not very likable) is perhaps the best of the poet in me. I conceive of this person as German, romantic, authoritarian, detached yet full of passion, above all a musician. To learn that a poet I admire (Yeats, for instance, or the New Zealander, James K. Baxter) could not sing in tune shocks me almost to disbelief.

When I write poetry I very often have in mind the image of a place; and whatever the subject or "approach" of the poem, that image will carry through into the final form. But I also have the feeling that if a poem is merely personal it may be trivial; and I often catch myself, in the process of writing, nudging the personal vision towards some kind of general or public utterance.

In my earlier poems influences are clearly apparent but I don't think I am much influenced any longer by other poets. For better or worse, I seem to have found my own form. Though I still write occasionally in formal stanzas, more often I find myself writing a cluster of short pieces, all springing out of one mood, one experience, one preoccupation,' which together make up the poem. I like to write with as little punctuation as possible, accommodating line-lengths and syntax to one another in a free-flowing verse-sentence in which words echo one another and the pauses and runs of sound parallel the sense.

To be invited to write about oneself is, of course, a trap. What can a poet say about his own work except that he does the best he can and that he hopes someone else will enjoy it?

                              *   *   *

In 1965 C.K. Stead named Truth, Generosity, and Delight as the qualities which he would like his poems to manifest, although in such a way that the three would not readily be separable. His idea of Truth, of "responses to occasions" and of fidelity to experience which cannot presume to think itself total but may justly be selective, wants to be more than simply honest. His poems should be true as long as they recognize that poetry serves "Art before Principle, because Art serves the world which Principle admonishes."

Stead later qualified this view. The importance of Principle increased, intensified, under the influence of more resolute political commitment prompted by Vietnam, to inform poems (Stead refers to the poems of the first section of his *Crossing the Bar*) with a troubled and indignant or outraged sense of the inhumanity of men, the irresponsible reductiveness of those for whom responsibility was properly their occupation. The poems are inclined to be shortlined, declarative, direct. Their tensions are of patently different orders from those of *Whether the Will Is Free* and in the matter of tension as such as well as in such ploys as regarding Washington as a latecome Rome he may be reflecting one whom he did not name as an influence in his 1970

statement for the first edition of *Contemporary Poets*. That is, Allen Tate.

Stead's poems of protest are naturally enough concerned with intimations of the consequences of power politics, particularly the denial of identity and individual right. "Anonymous" or "anonymity" are words which his reader has to register. Vexatious questioning of identity is old hat but a continuous business. It is also to be affirmed as a matter of Principle, but as principle is affirmed through the means of the art. The second qualification to Stead's 1965 view may be traced in an article on James K. Baxter's later poems, the *Jerusalem Sonnets*. In Baxter's sonnets Stead found an eminent value, "their creation of a personality...a heightened sense of life." He went on to talk about "the world fresh to our awakening senses."

Increasingly Stead's poetry has moved to the cultivation of personality, to assert a heightened sense of life threatened by the devious contrivings of men of affairs and the unpredictability of everyday accident (a smashed car, a neck broken while swimming), and fresh awakenings to the possibilities of whatever part of the world in which his poems find their scenes, which are now very varied indeed. The scenes, the occasions, and Stead's technical resources along with them are at this date astonishingly varied. In the 1950's he was accomplished, resourceful, but fairly conservative. His "Pictures in a Gallery Undersea" which put to work his expertise in the New Poetic, is an accomplished suite which readers have seen as a tribute to Eliot but which Stead himself regards as more of a tribute to Pound. The success of "Pictures" made him more confident. He extended his range, in forms, in tonalities, in personae. He produced more poems than before and while not as prolific, say, as Baxter, the indications are that his output is still increasing and likely to continue that way. He has enhanced the facts, the Truth, of his poems by splendidly marrying the occasions, his feelings (which may be rich and complex) and his formidable intelligence and delighting ingenuities.

When Professor Stead wrote about John Mulgan (in *Islands*) he subtitled his article "A Question of Identity." The first part of that article is about Stead identifying with places known to John Mulgan when young, and how Mulgan became part of the making of Stead. In that same issue Stead published a set of poems under the title "Scoria" which in parts connect with or overlap with scenes of Mulgan's childhood. Literature in a place, or the placing of literature as part of the process of identifying and finding identity, is an apparent impulse. Throughout his career he has returned to enquire into and effectively to reorganise his own past. "Only what lies behind" he said years ago "falls into shape." "Scoria" seeks out shapes of childhood, events of childhood, stories of its places, and along with these makes an unprecedented (for Stead) use of early New Zealand writers. It is a sustained exercise in recovery and discovery, in which again part of the discovery is finding appropriate forms, and one remembers Allen Tate once more, saying "The form is the meaning."

Discovery of appropriate forms has continued as an occupation, particularly in exploring "Open Form" (on which see his essay "From Wystan to Carlos—Modern and Modernism in Recent New Zealand Poetry" in *In The Glass Case*). At one time his poetry could be seen shifting from comment on experience to being direct experience, culminating in his Open Form works which conform to the principles he expounded in 1979, but nonetheless he proposed to his reader that what was to be directly experienced was necessarily varied in its kinds, both in kinds of directness and kinds of experience (as he transmitted it) was concerned. His complex reality came to encompass an active sense of the mythological in a usual way of understanding that word, giving a fresh vitality to Truth, Generosity, and Delight;

and to encompass as well a sense of what was open to mythologising, such as a cultivated man might have as response to the material and immaterial facts of being in Paris. This he has done in the ten-part sequence *Paris*.

The *Paris* sequence is not Open Form. The poems of the sequence are regulated about lines and sentences which have not entirely forgotten about pentameters and hexametrics. Liberty is not license, discourse not readily digressive, spontaneity a something less than what it wants to pass for. At the centre is a regulating intelligence, cunning about the poems' craft. When we look back to the otherwise persuasive sets—"Yes T.S." and "The Clodian Songbook," say, of *Geographics*—we may not so much see as properly hear that acute and rightly self-conscious judgmental talent listening-and-speaking at work, making and remaking mythologies, constructing and deconstructing what we had thought were "facts." His voice is asserted again and again whatever the recourse to playing with the poem which is visible on the page. His world continues to be fresh, freshly presented, to our awakened senses.

—Kendrick Smithyman

STEPANCHEV, Stephen. American. Born in Mokrin, Yugoslavia, 30 January 1915; emigrated to the United States, 1922; naturalized, 1938. Educated at the University of Chicago, A.B. 1937 (Phi Beta Kappa), M.A. 1938; New York University Ph.D. 1950. Served as a Lieutenant in the United States Army, 1941-45: Bronze Star. Instructor in English, Purdue University, Lafayette, Indiana, 1938-41; New York University, 1946-47, 1948-49. Member of the English Department, 1949-64, and since 1964, Professor of English, Queens College, Flushing, New York. Fulbright Professor of American Literature, University of Copenhagen, Spring 1957. Recipient: Society of Midland Authors Prize (*Poetry*, Chicago), 1937; National Endowment for the Arts grant, 1968. Address: Department of English, Queens College, Flushing, New York 11367, U.S.A.

PUBLICATIONS

Verse

Three Priests in April. Baltimore, Contemporary Poetry, 1956.
Spring in the Harbor. Flushing, New York, Amity Press, 1967.
Vietnam. Los Angeles, Black Sparrow Press, 1968.
A Man Running in the Rain. Los Angeles, Black Sparrow Press, 1969.
The Mind. Los Angeles, Black Sparrow Press, 1972.
The Mad Bomber. Los Angeles, Black Sparrow Press, 1972.
Mining the Darkness. Los Angeles, Black Sparrow Press, 1975.
Medusa and Others. Los Angeles, Black Sparrow Press, 1975.
The Dove in the Acacia (bilingual edition, translation by Rasa Popov). Vrsac, Yugoslavia, KOV, 1977.
What I Own. Santa Barbara, California, Black Sparrow Press, 1978.

Other

American Poetry since 1945: A Critical Survey. New York, Harper, 1965.

*   *   *

A New York poet-professor, Stephen Stepanchev writes lucid, urbane poems which depict dream- or city-scapes, remember parents or childhood, recount quarrels with a lover, or observe a fellow-victim of life with sympathy. Mostly they're first-person poems and usually the speaker is a wry detached observer: "The telephone squatted all day/ In the equilibrium of indifference./ No one called that wrong number,/ Me, poking among dead men's words" ("A Visit"). The poems rely for their energy on a rapid montage of images, rendered in a succession of simple declarative sentences without much rhythmic intensity (like much current image-centered poetry, they might well be translations). The images are usually clever, seldom memorable. "November withdraws like a junkie," he writes, or "I was of two minds, like traffic," or "I live in the rice paddies of my desperation": one registers the effect, admires the invention, and passes on unmoved. Sometimes one cannot even admire: "Yesterday I poured gasoline all over myself/ And flamed like a monk/ To move you" seems both lurid and unpleasantly exploitative. Still, the general effect is an agreeable one, well represented by the following complete poem from *The Mad Bomber*, called "In the Gallery":

> Repetition makes a garden,
> But these roses are, clearly, unemployed.
> Nature does so much better than this painter
> I am expected to admire. My attention
> Wanders to a gallery guest whose hair
> Is a lair of lights, whose face dreams
> Like a wheat field, and whose eyes glisten
> With tears induced by her contact lenses.
> I mix her in my martini and drink
> Her down at the window overlooking the East
> River, where the moon is breaking up in shivers.

—Seamus Cooney

STEPHENS, Alan (Archer). American. Born in Greeley, Colorado, 19 December 1925. Educated at the University of Colorado, Boulder, 1946-48; University of Denver, Colorado, A.B., M.A. 1950; Stanford University, California; University of Missouri, Columbia, Ph.D. 1954. Served in the United States Army Air Force, 1943-45. Married Frances Jones in 1948; three sons. Assistant Professor of English, Arizona State University, Tempe, 1954-58. Assistant Professor, 1959-63, Associate Professor, 1963-67, and since 1967, Professor of English, University of California, Santa Barbara. Recipient: Swallow Press New Poetry Series Award, 1957. Address: Department of English, University of California, Santa Barbara, California 93106, U.S.A.

PUBLICATIONS

Verse

The Sum. Denver, Swallow, 1958.
Between Matter and Principle. Denver, Swallow, 1963.
The Heat Lightning. Brunswick, Maine, Bowdoin College Museum of Art, 1967.
Tree Meditation and Others. Chicago, Swallow Press, 1970.

White River Poems. Chicago, Swallow Press, 1975.
In Plain Air: Poems 1958-1980. Chicago, Swallow Press, 1982.

Other

Editor, *Selected Poems,* by Barnabe Googe. Denver, Swallow, 1961.

*

Alan Stephens comments:

(1970)I caught my share of the academic influenzas of the late '40's and early '50's. As for style, themes, and all that: I used to write like this:

Heavily from the shadeless plain to the river
The bull slants down and bends his head to draw
Bright water in, that goes unbroken ever.

But now I write like this—

—suppose that the words came in
the way a flight of blackbirds
I once watched entered a tree
in the winter twilight:
finding places for themselves
quickly along the bare branches
they settled into their singing
for the time.

*   *   *

Alan Stephens is a nature poet. Up to this time, his main interest has been to render nature faithfully, but as a realization of a meditative response which answers to the sensibility in natural objects. He seeks an effect similar to that of Wordsworth's early "Influence of Natural Objects." Stephens has remarked about his own poems that they are "descriptive meditations rather than meditative descriptions...." To this end he wishes his poetry naked, the form invariably open, the expression spare. His utterances are, however, either clipped directions, like a dramatist's for the settling of scenes, or discursive meanderings, too often simple only for being denuded of figurative speech. Hence, from "A Breath," a stanza of this sort:

A quiet, cool, spring morning—
the sun up, and its light
crossing things without emphasis,
merely bringing out the pale colors.

Of course, the limitations of this manner are sometimes quite successfully accommodated to a larger context, as in "Home Rock."

While society and socially conscious or sophisticated speech are almost entirely absent from Stephens' quiet poetry, his work is effective in those instances where domestic man is projected against a natural backdrop. In such cases, he usually works with a motif of black and white, of darkness and tenuously comforting light. Meditating on the omnivorous incursion of dark space even into his own beard, the speaker of "To Fran" achieves this minimal consolation:

it must be we belong in it—at once remotely
and intimately; the way a sheepherder's fire at night
    belongs
in the distance on a desert upland.

And returning from the moonlit night and "the black shadow of the house," the speaker of "Sounds" reports that: "I go back in, and hunch over/ The familiar hiss of my pencil tip/ Racing across the lighted page."

—David M. Heaton

———————

STEPHENS, Meic. Welsh. Born in Treforest, Pontypridd, Glamorgan, 23 July 1938. Educated at University College of Wales, Aberystwyth and Bangor, B.A. (honours) in French; University of Rennes, France, Diplôme de Langue et de Littérature Française. Married Ruth Wynn Meredith in 1965; three daughters and one son. French Master, Ebbw Vale Grammar School, 1962-66; Director, Triskel Press, Merthyr Tydfil, Glamorgan, 1962-67. Founding Editor, *Poetry Wales,* Llandybie, 1965-73; Staff Journalist, *Western Mail,* Cardiff, 1966-67. Since 1967, Assistant Director, then Literature Director, Welsh Arts Council; Co-Editor, Writers of Wales series. Address: 9 Museum Place, Cardiff CF1 3NX, Wales.

PUBLICATIONS

Verse

Triad: Thirty-Three Poems, with Peter Gruffydd and Harri Webb. Merthyr Tydfil, Glamorgan, Triskel Press, 1963.
Exiles All. Swansea, Christopher Davies, 1973.

Other

Linguistic Minorities in Western Europe. Llandysul, Dyfed, Gomer, 1976.

Editor, with John Stuart Williams, *The Lilting House: An Anthology of Anglo-Welsh Poetry, 1917-1967.* London, Dent, and Llandybie, Dyfed, Christopher Davies, 1969.
Editor, *Artists in Wales.* Llandysul, Dyfed, Gomer, 3 vols., 1971-77.
Editor, *The Welsh Language Today.* Llandysul, Dyfed, Gomer, 1973.
Editor, *A Reader's Guide to Wales: A Selected Bibliography.* London, National Book League, 1973.
Editor, with Peter Finch, *Green Horse: An Anthology by Young Poets of Wales.* Swansea, Christopher Davies, 1978.
Editor, *The Arts in Wales 1950-75.* Cardiff, Welsh Arts Council, 1979.
Editor, *The Curate of Clyro: Extracts from the Diary of Francis Kilvert.* Newtown, Gregynog Press, 1983.
Editor, *The Oxford Companion to the Literature of Wales.* Oxford, Oxford University Press, 1985.

*   *   *

Meic Stephens has been primarily concerned in recent years with the problem of explaining, through his poetry, the predicament of many of his compatriots in Wales who feel themselves to be "exiled," emotionally and intellectually, from their proper Welsh heritage. Brought up English-speaking and learning Welsh as an adult, he is well aware of this condition—not only in his own country but elsewhere in Europe. His deep-rooted social commitment is made vivid by the convincing detail embedded in his "nationalist" poems and those to do with memories of a dwindling valley community. He has also done much as an editor of commendable severity, and as a small publisher, for writers of talent and promise.

His own poems are extremely well-made; he writes sparingly and produces perhaps three or four a year. He is a meticulous craftsman, even if some of his images tend to be a trifle thread-bare, tired, and banal, coming perilously near cliché. One of his best, in my view, is a sonnet about Christmas 1968 when the major Welsh-language poet, Gwenallt Jones, died, with his fragment of prayer for his daughters:

> may they belong
> to Wales as he did, cherishing most of all
> his faith, his language and his living song.

Predictions are dangerous, but one feels that Stephens's mark in the future, providing he develops at the pace he has been keeping, could well be made as a continuous explorer of this "spiritual homelessness" among a large segment of his people. A stoic, not easily given to rose-tinted illusion, he possesses the necessary credentials and could bring the right unsentimental and unromantic approach to the task.

—John Tripp

STERN, Gerald. American. Born in Pittsburgh, Pennsylvania, 22 February 1925. Educated at the University of Pittsburgh, B.A. 1947; Columbia University, New York, M.A. 1949. Served in the United States Army Air Corps. Married Patricia Miller in 1952; one daughter and one son. Instructor, Temple University, Philadelphia, 1957-63; Professor, Indiana University of Pennsylvania, Indiana, 1963-67. Since 1968, Professor, Somerset County College, Somerville, New Jersey. Visiting Poet, Sarah Lawrence College, Bronxville, New York, 1977; Visiting Professor, University of Pittsburgh, 1978. Since 1973, Consultant in Literature, Pennsylvania Arts Council, Harrisburg. Recipient: National Endowment for the Arts grant, 1976; Lamont Poetry Selection Award, 1977. Address: Somerset County College, Box 3300, Somerville, New Jersey 08876, U.S.A.

PUBLICATIONS

Verse

The Naming of Beasts and Other Poems. West Branch, Iowa, Cummington Press, 1973.
Rejoicings. Fredericton, New Brunswick, Fiddlehead, 1973.
Lucky Life. Boston, Houghton Mifflin, 1977.
The Red Coal. Boston, Houghton Mifflin, 1981.
Paradise Poems. New York, Random House, 1984.

*

Gerald Stern comments:

(1980)If I could choose one poem of mine to explain my stance, or my artistic position, it would be "The One Thing in Life," which appears in *Lucky Life*. In this poem I stake out a place for myself, so to speak, that was overlooked or ignored or

disdained, a place no-one else wanted. I mean this in a psychological and metaphorical and philosophical sense. The poem is short, so I'll quote it:

> Wherever I go now I lie down on my own bed of straw
> and bury my face in my own pillow.
> I can stop in any city I want to
> and pull the stiff blanket up to my chin.
> It's easy now, walking up a flight of carpeted stairs
> and down a hall past the painted fire doors.
> It's easy bumping my knees on a rickety table
> and bending down to a tiny sink.
> There is a sweetness buried in my mind;
> there is water with a small cave behind it;
> there's a mouth speaking Greek.
> It is what I keep to myself; what I return to;
> the one thing that no one else wanted.

When I think about the place "no-one else wanted," I think of an abandoned or despised area; I think of weeds, a ruin, a desert; but I think of these things not as remote in time or place from that which is familiar and cherished and valuable—our civilization—but as things which lie just under the surface and just out of eyesight; and I think especially of the dynamic and ironic interpenetration of the two. Thus, my poetry is concerned a great deal with opposites, city—country, present—past, civilization—savagery, powerful—weak, well-known—obscure, and it often dualistic in nature, though it is not informed, in any formal sense, by a philosophical or religious principle of dualism. (I clearly favor the "weaker" of the two, but I have affection for both.) Ultimately the "abandoned place" is a state of mind, or an energy-state, or condition, that is within me and I merely am reaching out for "examples" to approximate this state.

Another aspect of the poetry is that of rebirth or regeneration. A great many of my poems are concerned with rebirth and I find that the spring season, the time of rebirth, and those holidays and celebrations, religious and otherwise, that relate to rebirth are important in my poems: "God of Rain, God of Water" and "The Sensitive Knife" from *Lucky Life* and "In Kovalchick's Garden" and "The Blessed" from *Rejoicings*.

I have been living for the last ten years on the Delaware River, near Easton, Pennsylvania, less than two hours away from Philadelphia or New York City. I find myself spending a lot of time in the city, and writing about it, as well as in the country, and I find that the relationship of these two is an embodiment of my underlying myth, so that I am living my life symbolically even as I live it literally. Thus when I write of the literal I am simultaneously writing "symbolically," and the language, which is precise and descriptive, takes on overtones and layers. Several critics, confused by my exact and literal observations (insofar as what I was describing was not common knowledge), mistakenly described me as a surrealist poet.

I find, especially recently, that I am moved a great deal by Jewish mysticism and Chasidism, but I am not unaware that these are parts of huge historical systems that involve commitments and obligations and that I am in a sense "tasting" from the banquet of Judaism those delicacies that suit me. I do believe, though, that even if I don't practice the ritual, I realize, whether I mention him specifically or not, the lot of the Jew in history, and embody him, and his spirit, in my poems.

I have discovered that my poetry is prized because it comes so much to life orally and I have discovered that I am a success as a "reader." I put it this way because I did not start off intending my poems to be part of the "oral revolution" of recent American poetry. I believe my poems stand by themselves on the page, but I am delighted, also, to find how well they work "out loud."

I'm not sure who my precursors are, who has influenced me the most. I am delighted to live in an age without masters.

*   *   *

Gerald Stern's deeply felt poetry is written in the "confessional" mode, practiced by such other contemporary poets as Ginsberg and Ferlinghetti, and in company with them he continues the American romantic tradition of Walt Whitman with its emphasis upon the writer himself as contemporary everyman and its celebration of place. But Stern uses his narrative and emotional self-portraiture to create a uniquely detailed central figure or speaker, and his America is rendered with Biblical intensity and a Judaic sense of time and loss.

Van Gogh, "Against the Whirling Lines,/Small and powerful in the hands of the Blue God" ("Self-Portrait"), becomes a vivid counterpart figure for Stern himself as wanderer and artist. But as Stern travels in his own personal landscape the journeys are usually return journeys and the place visited effaced by time. "Straus Park," with its specific references, is an especially vivid example:

If you know about the Babylonian Jews
coming back to their stone houses in Jerusalem...
then you must know how I felt when I saw Stanley's
    Cafeteria
boarded up and the sale sign out.

"On the Island," "Four Sad Poems on the Delaware," and "County Line Road" present similar time metaphors in rural settings, and Stern brings both the rural and urban aspects of his world together in "One Foot in the River": "Going to New York I carry the river in my head/and match it with the flow on 72nd Street and the flow on Broadway."

Like Whitman and the poets of the "Beat Generation," Stern makes considerable use of repetition for rhetorical effect. But the repetitions work in other ways as well. In the central poem "Lucky Life" they emphasize an ironic optimism and the importance of a survival without illusion, but a survival enhanced by tradition and by the recurring rituals of everyday life. The return journeys are, of course, repetitions also. And the final lines of "Let Me Please Look into My Window" seem to summarize Stern's view of all such wanderings: "Let me wake up happy, let me know where I am, let me lie still,/as we turn left, as we cross the water, as we leave the light."

—Gaynor F. Bradish

———————

STEVENS, Peter. Canadian. Born in Manchester, Lancashire, England, 17 November 1927. Educated at Burnage High School, Manchester; Nottingham University, B.A. (honours) in English, Cert.Ed. 1951; McMaster University, Hamilton, Ontario, 1963-64, M.A. 1963; University of Saskatchewan, Saskatoon, Ph.D. 1968. Married June Sidebotham in 1957; two daughters and one son. Schoolteacher in England, 1951-57; Chairman of the Department of English, Hillfield College, Hamilton, Ontario, 1957-64; Lecturer, Extension Division, McMaster University, 1961-64; Assistant Professor of English, University of Saskatchewan, 1964-69, Associate Professor, 1969-73, and since 1973, Professor of English, University of Windsor, Ontario. Poetry Editor, *Canadian Forum*, Toronto, 1968-73; Director and Editor, Sesame Press, Windsor, 1974-81;

Since 1973, jazz columnist, Windsor *Star*. Recipient: Canada Council award, 1969. Address: Department of English, University of Windsor, Windsor, Ontario N9B 3P4, Canada.

PUBLICATIONS

Verse

Plain Geometry. Toronto, Ganglia Press, 1968.
Nothing But Spoons. Montreal, Delta Canada, 1969.
A Few Myths. Vancouver, Talonbooks, 1971.
Breadcrusts and Glass. Fredericton, New Brunswick, Fiddlehead, 1972.
Family Feelings and Other Poems. Guelph, Ontario, Alive Press, 1974.
Momentary Stay. London, Ontario, Killaly Press, 1974.
And the Dying Sky Like Blood: A Bethune Collage for Several Voices. Ottawa, Borealis Press, 1974.
The Bogman Pavese Tactics. Fredericton, New Brunswick, Fiddlehead, 1977.
And All That Jazz. Toronto, League of Canadian Poets, 1980.
Coming Back. Windsor, Ontario, Sesame Press, 1981.
Revenge of the Mistresses. Windsor, Ontario, Black Moss Press, 1981.

Other

Modern English-Canadian Poetry: A Guide to Information Sources. Detroit, Gale, 1978.

Editor, *The McGill Movement: A.J.M. Smith, F.R. Scott, and Leo Kennedy*. Toronto, Ryerson Press, 1969.
Editor, with J.L. Granatstein, *Forum: Canadian Life and Letters 1920-1970: Selections from "The Canadian Forum."* Toronto, University of Toronto Press, 1972.
Editor, *The First Day of Spring: Stories and Other Prose*, by Raymond Knister. Toronto, University of Toronto Press, 1976.

*

Manuscript Collection: University of Saskatchewan, Saskatoon.

Peter Stevens comments:
I deal with the local landscape and places: the prairie, its place in my own personal and family life, its past, its geologic history, its "mythology." I write usually in free verse paragraphs and have experimented with some concrete forms: a method of using anagrams I call Anagrammatics. General influences are simply Canada and being Canadian—Canadian writers I admire and whose work has probably made an impression on mine are Al Purdy and Earle Birney. I admire the technical facility of Auden and early Ezra Pound. I have paid attention to the North American-ness of W.C. Williams, particularly as it emerges in a Canadian manner in the poetry of W.W.E. Ross and Raymond Souster.

*   *   *

Peter Stevens is a poet who reflects the immigrant experience. Coming to Canada from Britain, he brought a poetic sensibility influenced by the low-toned writing of the English 1950's. That sensibility has since been modified by Canadian experience, and the result is a manner that is undramatic, deliberately uncolourful, but — rather like an early spring landscape in the Prairies

where Stevens spent much of his time in Canada—slowly revealing subtleties of perception and tone, pleasing gradations in the
range of grey and brown. Generally speaking, there is little
metaphorical or adjectival colour in Stevens's poems; the images
are meant to speak dryly for themselves, as in the opening lines
of "Fuschia":

> blood drops belled
> hanging in hedges
> above the bay curved
> under cliffs I remember
> an island in my past...

or in "Seeing Is Seeing Is Believing in Poetry":

> A stalker lurches across the snow.
> His shadow stretches inhuman long
> across snow's glistening crust of ice.
>
> A rabbit sits stark still, then spurts away
> to black trees, dark lines blacker on the white,
> as this dense shadow slides into his eye.
>
> All I see is rabbit flashing into shadows
> away from stealthy shadow: no comment.
> The eye does not speak, it does not think....

The poems I have quoted come from *Breadcrusts and Glass*, one
of the best of Stevens' several small books. They show his sharp,
thoughtful perception of the natural world; other poems show
him equally sharply aware of the anomalies and frustrations of
the plastic life, and here emerges an ironic, almost acerbic view
of the self, and, at times, a curious questioning consciousness of
literature as pretension.

—George Woodcock

STEVENSON, Anne (Katherine).   American.   Born in Cambridge, England, 3 January 1933. Educated at University High
School, Ann Arbor, Michigan, 1947-50; University of Michigan,
Ann Arbor (Hopwood Award, 1951, 1952, 1954), B.A. 1954 (Phi
Beta Kappa), M.A. 1962; Radcliffe Institute, Cambridge, Massachusetts, 1970-71. Married 1) R.L. Hitchcock in 1955 (divorced), one daughter; 2) Mark Elvin in 1962 (divorced), two sons;
3) Michael Farley. School Teacher, Lillesden School, Hawk-
hurst, Kent, 1955-56, Westminster School, Georgia, 1959-60,
and Cambridge School of Weston, Massachusetts, 1961-62;
Advertising Manager, A.&C. Black, publishers, London, 1956-
57; Tutor, Extra-Mural Studies, University of Glasgow, 1970-
73; Counsellor, Open University, Paisley, Renfrew, 1972-73;
Writing Fellow, University of Dundee, 1973-75. Fellow, Lady
Margaret Hall, Oxford, 1975-77; Writer-in-Residence, Bul-
mershe College, Reading, Berkshire, 1977-78. Co-Founder, with
Michael Farley and Alan Halsey, Poetry Bookshop, Hay-on-
Wye, Powys, 1979. Northern Arts Literary Fellow, Newcastle
and Durham, 1981-82 and 1984-85. Since 1978, Co-Editor,
Other Poetry, Leicester, Mid-Day Publications, Oxford, and
Other Poetry Editions. Member of the Literature Panel, Arts
Council, 1983-85. Recipient: Scottish Arts Council bursary,
1973; Southern Arts bursary, 1978; Welsh Arts Council bursary,
1981. Fellow, Royal Society of Literature, 1978. Address: 30
Logan Street, Langley Park, Durham DH7 9YN, England.

PUBLICATIONS

Verse

Living in America.   Ann Arbor, Michigan, Generation Press,
1965.
Reversals.   Middletown, Connecticut, Wesleyan University
Press, 1969.
Correspondences: A Family History in Letters.   Middletown,
Connecticut, Wesleyan University Press, and London, Oxford
University Press, 1974.
Travelling Behind Glass: Selected Poems 1963-1973.   London,
Oxford University Press, 1974.
A Morden Tower Reading 3.   Newcastle upon Tyne, Morden
Tower, 1977.
Cliff Walk.   Richmond, Surrey, Keepsake Press, 1977.
Enough of Green.   London, Oxford University Press, 1977.
Sonnets for Five Seasons.   Hereford, Five Seasons Press, 1979.
Minute by Glass Minute.   Oxford, Oxford University Press,
1982.
Making Poetry.   Oxford, Pisces Press, 1983.
A Legacy.   Durham, Taxus Press, 1983.
Black Grate Poems.   Oxford, Inky Parrot Press, 1984.
The Fiction-Makers.   Oxford, Oxford University Press, 1985.

Plays

Radio Plays: *Correspondences*, 1975; *Child of Adam*, 1976.

Other

Elizabeth Bishop.   New York, Twayne, 1966.

*

Critical Studies: by Dorothy Donnelly, in *Michigan Quarterly
Review* (Ann Arbor), Fall 1966 and April 1971; Jay Parini, in
Lines Review 50 (Edinburgh), September 1974, and in *Plough-
shares* (Cambridge), Autumn 1978.

Anne Stevenson comments:
Each of my books, I think, represents a stage in a quest. In the
1960's, like many people, I was questioning the assumptions I'd
grown up with: what was good, what was evil, what was love,
what was responsibility, by what freedom of will could I choose
my life? In *Correspondences* I became aware of the differing
voices of my own American contradictions. These led to the near
nihilism of the poems of *Enough of Green* (1977). In 1980, when
I lived in the Wye valley on the Welsh border, it occurred to me
one could with equal integrity answer "yes" to the religious
question as "no." If you did, it made all the difference between
despairing and loving. So the poems of *Minute by Glass Minute*
explored a tentative belief in belief. In the event, I wrote the
poems of *The Fiction-Makers*—not religious poems, but poems
which suppose that the act of imagination is a religious act, an
act of faith. This is not to say that poems can be written without
an acute consciousness of language. But my feeling is now that
faith in language also has to be faith in meaning. Or you could
put it that poetry is one way of rationally communicating the
reality of the a-rational.

*   *   *

"We were the very landscape/We walked through," Anne
Stevenson wrote in her first volume, *Living in America*. The
correspondence of physical and moral landscapes has recurred

throughout her work, whether the "Landscape without regrets" of the Sierra Nevada (*Reversals*), the modest frugality of Cambridge and the Fens, or, more recently, the isolation and asperity of the North-East coast of Scotland, which is the setting for most of the poems in *Enough of Green*. "Living in America" describes a continent that threatens its residents, its two shores "hurrying towards each other" while "Desperately the inhabitants hoped to be saved in the middle,/Pray to the mountains and deserts to keep them apart." "The Suburb" gives human face to this fear— a sullen and domesticated defeatism that says "Better/to lie still and let the babies run through me"; while "The Women" quietly records a similar suppression, in its picture of "Women, waiting, waiting for their husbands,/sit[ting] among dahlias all the afternoons,/while quiet processional seasons drift and subside at their doors like dunes."

But much of Anne Stevenson's poetry has been a revolt against this tyranny of environment over self. *Correspondences*, a "Family History in Letters," traces 150 years in the life of the Chandler family on both sides of the Atlantic. In the last letter of the volume, the fictitious poetess Kay Boyd writes to her father, from London, of her flight from the United States: "'Nowhere is safe.'/It is a poem I can't continue./It is America I can't contain." Flight here involves refusing "the tug back" of "allegiance to innocence which is not there," deliberately leaving it unclear whether it is innocence or allegiance which is lacking. The "correspondences" of the title are in one sense those between the unsustainable poetic project and the unimaginable magnitude of America. But in the letters themselves new correspondences emerge, as successive generations live through corresponding dilemmas, flights, returns, sometimes unwittingly using the same language to describe their plights. Thus Kay's sister, Eden, writes to her of a recurring nightmare after their mother's death, asking her to come home, in words which echo their ancestor Reuben Chandler, a prodigal son writing to his father, a Vermont minister, in 1832, of his own wish to return. Kay's desire to "make amends for what was not said," not just in her own relationship with her parents but through all the fraught generations of her family, to "Do justice to the living, to the dead," likewise recalls that earlier father, writing to his errant daughter, mourning, in Yorkshire, a husband lost at sea. Preferring, in her father's words, "the precarious apartments of the world/to the safer premises of the spirit," his daughter nevertheless chooses a fall from grace that brings a profounder suffering than he, in his naive self-righteousness, can ever know. Kay Boyd, having the last word in the book, makes it clear that this is a price worth paying.

Travelling Behind Glass attempted to justify this peripatetic living as a conscious moral choice. The title poem toys with residence, imagining "A heart at grass" among the "predictable greens" of an accepted landscape, but opts instead for "the paranoid howl of the/highway," where the "carapace" of the car becomes a symbol of the free-wheeling will that prefers even the risk of madness to domesticity. The theme of renunciation is reiterated in *Enough of Green*. This volume makes it clear that it is precisely the green world of the senses ("love grown rank as seeding grass") which has to be renounced, in favour of the steely, ascetic discipline of an art which has replaced the Christian God as task-master. There is in all Anne Stevenson's poetry an extremist's desire for the sterility and outrage of the puritan's scalpel. What makes the Scottish landscape so attractive is its sense of life as stress and erosion, an attrition which uncovers the essential contours of a mind and a place.

There is a certain relentlessness of imagination, a dogged, insistent quality, to Anne Stevenson's poetry; but it is protected from the stridency of those "intense shrill/ladies and gaunt, fanatical burnt out old women" whose fate she clearly fears in "Coming Back to Cambridge" and elsewhere by both an elegiac sadness and a sly, wicked wit. The former is revealed in those poems which speak of love as the "remorseless joy of dereliction" ("Ragwort"), a song made out of deprivation and loss; the latter in a poem such as "Theme with Variations," with its cool worldliness.

Minute by Glass Minute uses landscape as the embodiment of contrary impulses. The sequence at its heart, "Green Mountain, Black Mountain" contrasts the cold green mountains of Vermont where she spent childhood with the "lusher Black Mountains of South Wales (rich in history and myth, but new to me)" of more recent residence. In part an elegy for her American parents, it speculates on the dialectical tension of Old and New Worlds, puritan and hedonistic impulses, a landscape threaded with history compared with one still apparently inviolate. "Threads", as a trope which links meaning, handwriting, stitching, and affiliation, threads through the sequence, raising questions about that larger impulse to establish connections, stitch together significances, which pervades the volume. The landscapes of this volume are damp, bedrizzled, misted, and even summer is "steamy" with wet. Weather gets in the way of an eye that wants simplicity and transparency of meanings. In one poem she charges Blake with romantic obfuscation: "How dare you inflict imagination on us!/What halo does the world deserve?" But she also recognizes her own incompetence before a world that refuses meanings, where "Even my cat knows more about death than I do". She is driven to quiet fury by the inadequacy of words, unable to paint "the mudness of mud" or the "cloudness of clouds". But this poem, "If I Could Paint Essences", sums up the antitheses of her vision, admitting that just as she arrives at the "true sightness of seeing" she unexpectedly wants to play on "cellos of metaphor", "And in such imaginings I lose sight of sight". Whatever else might be said, it is certainly true that Stevenson does not, in *Minute by Glass Minute*, lose sight either of words or things. Her most powerful volume yet, it suggests a talent that is still growing in exploring the world and its own imaginative possibilities.

—Stan Smith

STEWART, Douglas (Alexander). Australian. Born in Eltham, New Zealand, 6 May 1913. Educated at New Plymouth Boys High School, New Zealand; Victoria University College, New Zealand. Married Margaret Coen in 1946; one daughter. Literary Editor, *The Bulletin*, Sydney, 1940-61; Literary Adviser, Angus and Robertson Ltd., publishers, Sydney, 1961-72. Recipient: Jessie Mackay Poetry Award, 1941; Prior Memorial Award, for drama, 1945; Grace Leven Prize, 1968; Encyclopaedia Britannica Award, 1968; Wilke Award, for non-fiction, 1975; Con Wiekhart Award, for non-fiction, 1984. O.B.E. (Officer, Order of the British Empire), 1960; Officer, Order of Canada, 1979. Agent: Curtis Brown (Australia) Pty Ltd., 86 William Street, Paddington, New South Wales 2021. Address: 2 Banool Avenue, St. Ives, New South Wales 2075, Australia.

PUBLICATIONS

Verse

Green Lions. Auckland, Whitcombe and Tombs, 1937.
The White Cry. London, Dent, 1939.

Elegy for an Airman. Sydney, Frank C. Johnson, 1940.

Sonnets to the Unknown Soldier. Sydney and London, Angus and Robertson, 1941.

The Dosser in Springtime. Sydney and London, Angus and Robertson, 1946.

Glencoe. Sydney and London, Angus and Robertson, 1947.

Sun Orchids and Other Poems. Sydney and London, Angus and Robertson, 1952.

The Birdsville Track and Other Poems. Sydney and London, Angus and Robertson, 1955.

Rutherford and Other Poems. Sydney and London, Angus and Robertson, 1962.

The Garden of Ships: A Poem. Sydney, Wentworth Press, 1962.

(Poems), selected and introduced by the author. Sydney, Angus and Robertson, 1963.

Collected Poems 1936-1967. Sydney and London, Angus and Robertson, 1967.

Selected Poems. Sydney, Angus and Robertson, 1973.

Plays

Ned Kelly (produced Sydney, 1944; London, 1977). Sydney and London, Angus and Robertson, 1943.

The Fire on the Snow and The Golden Lover: Two Plays for Radio. Sydney and London, Angus and Robertson, 1944.

Shipwreck (produced Sydney, 1948). Sydney, Shepherd Press, 1947.

Four Plays (includes *The Fire on the Snow, The Golden Lover, Ned Kelly, Shipwreck*). Sydney and London, Angus and Robertson, 1958.

Fisher's Ghost: An Historical Comedy (produced Sydney, 1961). Sydney, Wentworth Press, 1960.

Screenplay: *The Back of Beyond,* with others, 1954.

Radio Plays: *The Fire on the Snow,* 1941; *The Golden Lover,* 1943; *The Earthquake Shakes the Land,* 1944.

Short Stories

A Girl with Red Hair and Other Stories. Sydney and London, Angus and Robertson, 1944.

Other

The Flesh and the Spirit: An Outlook on Literature. Sydney and London, Angus and Robertson, 1948.

The Seven Rivers. Sydney, Angus and Robertson, 1966; selection, as *Fishing Around the Monaro,* Canberra, Australian National University Press, 1978.

The Broad Stream: Aspects of Australian Literature. Sydney, Angus and Robertson, 1975.

Norman Lindsay: A Personal Record. Melbourne, Nelson, 1975.

A Man of Sydney: An Appreciation of Kenneth Slessor. Melbourne, Nelson, 1977.

Writers of the Bulletin (lectures). Sydney, Australian Broadcasting Commission, 1977.

Springtime in Taranaki: An Autobiography of Youth. Sydney, Hale and Iremonger, and Auckland, Hodder and Stoughton, 1984.

Editor, *Coast to Coast: Australian Stories.* Sydney, Angus and Robertson, 1945.

Editor, with Nancy Keesing, *Australian Bush Ballads.* Sydney, Angus and Robertson, 1955.

Editor, with Nancy Keesing, *Old Bush Songs and Rhymes of Colonial Times, Enlarged and Revised from the Collection of A.B. Paterson.* Sydney, Angus and Robertson, 1957.

Editor, *Voyager Poems.* Brisbane, Jacaranda Press, 1960.

Editor, *The Book of Bellerive,* by Joseph Tischler. Brisbane, Jacaranda Press, 1961.

Editor, *(Poems),* by A.D. Hope. Sydney, Angus and Robertson, 1963.

Editor, *Modern Australian Verse: Poetry in Australia II.* Sydney, Angus and Robertson, 1964; Berkeley, University of California Press, 1965.

Editor, *Selected Poems,* by Hugh McCrae. Sydney, Angus and Robertson, 1966.

Editor, *Short Stories of Australia: The Lawson Tradition.* Sydney, Angus and Robertson, 1967.

Editor, with Nancy Keesing, *The Pacific Book of Bush Ballads.* Sydney, Angus and Robertson, 1967; as *Favourite Bush Ballads,* 1977.

Editor, with Nancy Keesing, *Bush Songs, Ballads, and Other Verse.* Penrith, New South Wales, Discovery Press, 1968.

Editor, with Beatrice Davis, *Best Australian Short Stories.* Hawthorne, Victoria, Lloyd O'Neil, 1971.

Editor, *The Wide Brown Land: A New Selection of Australian Verse.* Sydney, Pacific, 1971.

Editor, *Norman Lindsay Gallery and Museum, Springwood: A Guide.* Observatory Hill, New South Wales, National Trust of Australia, 1975.

Editor, *Norman Lindsay's Cats.* Melbourne, Macmillan, 1975.

Editor, *Australia Fair: Poems and Paintings.* Sydney, Ure Smith, 1976.

*

Manuscript Collection: National Library, Canberra.

Critical Studies: *Douglas Stewart* by Nancy Keesing, Sydney, Oxford University Press, 1965; *Douglas Stewart* by Clement Semmler, New York, Twayne, 1975.

*   *   *

For just over 20 years (1940 to 1961) Douglas Stewart was literary editor of the Sydney weekly, *The Bulletin,* and in that period he was largely—indeed, centrally—influential in bringing about what can now be clearly seen as the first great school of Australian regional poetry—a school that recognized Robert D. FitzGerald as its elder figure, and encouraged the talents of virtually every notable Australian poet of the period (the significant exception being A.D. Hope). Douglas Stewart, a prolific writer himself, played not only a central editorial role, but a creative one as well. His critical attitudes were more ambiguously decisive: he was an ardent follower of Norman Lindsay's "vitalist" philosophy, which favoured hedonistic energy and a sort of Classical Romp—and rejected entirely the taint of "modernity." In positive terms, Stewart translated this into a code for a sensible concreteness of expression; negatively, it led him to a suspicion of experimentation and a hostility towards many European (and American) developments. In the 1940's the discovery of an intense identification with the Australian environment (heightened by the war years) was strongly encouraged by Stewart's insistence on the concrete and the direct. He pared down much of the mushy pseudo-poetic affectation that still lingered in much local verse. By the 1950's cultural isolation was becoming less possible, and Stewart's own later work is an attempt to come to terms with forces and issues outside the finally restricting field of regional lyricism.

Douglas Stewart was born in New Zealand, and his first volume, *Green Lions*, is entirely devoted to explorations of that countryside. *The White Cry* clarifies Stewart's essentially lyrical voice, but it is in the two early wartime books, *Elegy for an Airman* and *Sonnets to the Unknown Soldier*, that a sudden energising force is revealed. The sonnets were criticized at the time (and later) because "they did not rhyme," and were written in a period of patriotic and emotional stress that did lead to tub-thumping; but they were written, also, with a quite new element of laconic perception:

> You see that fellow with the grin, one eye on the girls,
> The other on the pub, his uniform shabby already?
> Well, don't let him hear us, but he's the Unknown Soldier,
> They just let him out, they say he lives for ever.
> They put him away with flowers and flags and forget him.
> But he always comes when they want him. He does the
>   fighting.

Not until Bruce Dawe, two decades later, is the sense of Australian vernacular speech so precisely captured and made integral to the poem's expression.

Experiments with ballad and song form in *The Dosser in Springtime* led to important modifications in Stewart's style and prepared the way for his mature lyric achievement in *Sun Orchids* and *The Birdsville Track*. Yet despite the still exhilarating successes in these volumes, there is also a sense of a somewhat self-constricting talent, trivializing, not intensifying. It is for this reason that *Rutherford* both surprises and impresses. A long poem based on the heroic, exploring, and enduring aspect of man (in the Lindsay "vitalist" tradition), its subject is the New Zealand physicist. Although novel at the time (poems about scientists were still rare), it accords well with Stewart's own positive theories: "Mostly too busy to think—too busy thinking. But thinking was doing." It is an almost unconscious irony that what is possibly the finest poem of Norman Lindsay's most ardent disciple should deal with Science, that Modernist windmill of all windmills.

Douglas Stewart contributed four impressive verse plays to the Australian repertoire, in a period when it was thought this was a form that could be revived. The subsequent discovery of new, essentially poetic forms of drama (by Ionesco, Beckett, Pinter, many others) has placed Stewart's verse dramas, like those of Fry, Duncan, and their contemporaries, on a shelf of disregard. Yet *The Fire on the Snow* and *The Golden Lover*—at least in print—combine a warm lyricism with movement and dramatic impetus. It is possible to imagine a time when their enduring qualities will be rediscovered.

Since the publication of *Collected Poems* in 1967 Stewart has virtually retired himself from the poetic scene in Australia. Two generations, or waves, of writers have subsequently arrived and declared (sometimes stridently) their place on the map. His silence is, I think, regrettable. If he had in some way restricted his poetic horizons, he had certainly staked out a sizeable portion of his world and his culture for himself. It is ground still capable of yielding up a wealth of invention.

—Thomas W. Shapcott

STEWART, Harold (Frederick). Australian. Born in Sydney, New South Wales, 14 December 1916. Has lived in Japan since 1966. Recipient: Australia Council Fellowship, 1978. Address: No. 501, Keifuku Daini Manshon, Shugakuin, Sakyo-ku, Kyoto 606, Japan.

PUBLICATIONS

Verse

The Darkening Ecliptic (as Ern Malley, with James McAuley). Melbourne, Reed and Harris, 1944; as *Poems*, Melbourne, Lansdowne Press, 1961.
Phoenix Wings: Poems 1940-6. Sydney and London, Angus and Robertson, 1948.
Orpheus and Other Poems. Sydney, Angus and Robertson, 1956.
The Exiled Immortal: A Song Cycle. Canberra, Brindabella Press, 1980.
By the Old Walls of Kyoto: A Year's Cycle of Landscape Poems with Prose Commentaries. Tokyo and New York, Weatherhill, 1981.

Other

Translator, *A Net of Fireflies: Japanese Haiku and Haiku Paintings.* Tokyo and Rutland, Vermont, Tuttle, 1960.
Translator, *A Chime of Windbells: A Year of Japanese Haiku.* Tokyo and Rutland, Vermont, Tuttle, 1969.
Translator, with Bando Shojun, *Tannisho: Passages Deploring Deviations of Faith.* Kyoto, Eastern Buddhist Press, 1980.

*

Critical Studies: "Poet's Progress," in *Hemisphere* (Canberra), December 1973, "Ern Malley's Other Half," in *Quadrant* (Sydney), August 1977, and "A Candle in the Sunrise," in *Eastern Buddhist 14* (Kyoto), no. 2, 1981, all by Dorothy Green; "A Pilgrim's Progress in Japan" by Ronald Dunlop, in *Southerly* (Sydney), 1983.

Harold Stewart comments:

Poetry founded on Tradition is to me not only a way of life but a spiritual method, a kind of Yoga, both mantric and bhaktic, yoking the poet by means of work with the Word. The poet, in turn, has a ministerial function, mediating between the Muse and the reader, and it is his duty to praise and express his gratitude for the inspiration which he receives from above. As a follower of Tradition, I am opposed to "modernism" of every kind in art and thought. My aim is not to be contemporary, but timeless.

Although some of my earlier work treated European themes, since about 1950 I have concentrated entirely on giving poetic expression to certain of the Traditional Doctrines of the Far East, especially those of Buddhism, Taoism and Hinduism. During the past century, Oriental scholarship has opened up the vast treasure houses of the metaphysical, religious and artistic traditions of Asia; yet these have remained largely unexplored by Western poets.

I have devoted the past 45 years to their study, drawing poetic inspiration from these rich resources and endeavouring to acclimatize English poetry to these old but newly rediscovered regions of the spirit, both by direct translation and by original composition. At first I drank from the fountainheads, India and China; but since coming to live in Japan in 1966, I have turned to a more personal expression of religious devotion, to the Pure Land School of Buddhism, Jodo Shinshu, as well as attempting to capture some of the natural and cultural atmosphere of Kyoto and its environs.

My poetic methods have always been strictly Traditional, using the regular metres of English verse, often with rhyme, and a modern English diction of a slightly heightened tone, but striving always for greater clarity and simplicity in expressing sometimes difficult and unfamiliar subjects.

I think that I can fairly claim the discovery of two new principles of stanza formation: the inverted stanza, in which the order of rhymes is inverted from the previous one, the two stanzas alternating in various patterns; and the variation stanza, in which each new stanza is formed by a different permutation of a fixed number of rhymes. I have also invented a new sonnet-form.

*   *   *

In his sensitive study of James McAuley's poem "Prometheus" in *Workshop* ii, 1, Harold Stewart praises McAuley for using a method which is obviously his own. Stewart writes, "It is only through the myth that reality can be presented in the round: the superficially realist work can give only a one-sided and distorted projection." McAuley's method consists in the presentation of a myth, and at the same time of incorporating into that presentation what the poet himself has called "interpretative words and phrases." In his poem "The Myths" Stewart expresses the same idea in a more poetic form:

> Myths are a never-empty urn
> Of meaning: poets thence in turn
> Pour out the symbols that presage
> The rise or ruin of their age.

Stewart draws his material not only from European myth but also from the myths of Buddhism and Taoism, and thus endeavours to give his poetry a universal timeless appeal: "My aim is not to be contemporary, but timeless."

Mr. Stewart seems to be struggling along with Plato, the Christian Saints and Eastern gurus to overcome his earthly desires, his burden of flesh, in order to be liberated into pure spirit and a feeling of oneness with nature. When he achieves this in "The Annunciation," for example, the poet savours the rare moment of illumination and insight: "Rarely is flesh from purpose thus untied / It is as though my aching blood were still."

The struggle to obtain this spiritual freedom is the subject of the main body of the poetry, including a very personal interpretation of the myth of Orpheus and Eurydice. Through this personal use of the myths the poet casts new light on his subjects and in turn enriches our understanding of the myths.

—Kirsten Holst Petersen

STOW, (Julian) Randolph. Australian. Born in Geraldton, Western Australia, 28 November 1935. Educated at Guildford Grammar School, Western Australia; University of Western Australia, Nedlands, B.A. 1956. Formerly, anthropological assistant, working in Northwest Australia and Papua New Guinea. Taught at the University of Adelaide, 1957; Lecturer in English Literature, University of Leeds, Yorkshire, 1962, and University of Western Australia, 1963-64; Lecturer in English and Commonwealth Literature, University of Leeds, 1968-69.

Recipient: Australian Literature Society Gold Medal, 1957, 1958; Miles Franklin Award, for novel, 1959; Commonwealth Fund Harkness Travelling Fellowship, 1964-66; Britannica-Australia Award, 1966; Grace Leven Prize, 1970; Australia Council grant, 1973; Patrick White Prize, 1979. Agent: c/o Richard Scott Simon Ltd., 32 College Cross, London N1 1PR, England.

PUBLICATIONS

Verse

Act One.   London, Macdonald, 1957.
Outrider: Poems 1956-1962.   London, Macdonald, 1962.
A Counterfeit Silence: Selected Poems.   Sydney and London, Angus and Robertson, 1969.
Poetry from Australia: Pergamon Poets 6, with Judith Wright and William Hart-Smith, edited by Howard Sergeant.   Oxford, Pergamon Press, 1969.

Recording: *Poets on Record 11*, University of Queensland, 1974.

Plays

Eight Songs for a Mad King, music by Peter Maxwell Davies. London, Boosey and Hawkes, 1969.
Miss Donnithorne's Maggot, music by Peter Maxwell Davies (produced 1974).   London, Boosey and Hawkes, 1977.

Novels

A Haunted Land.   London, Macdonald, 1956; New York, Macmillan, 1957.
The Bystander.   London, Macdonald, 1957.
To the Islands.   London, Macdonald, 1958; Boston, Little Brown, 1959; revised edition, Sydney, Angus and Robertson, 1981; London, Secker and Warburg, and New York, Taplinger, 1982.
Tourmaline.   London, Macdonald, 1963; New York, Taplinger, 1981.
The Merry-Go-Round in the Sea.   London, Macdonald, 1965; New York, Morrow, 1966.
Visitants.   London, Secker and Warburg, 1979; New York, Taplinger, 1981.
The Girl Green as Elderflower.   London, Secker and Warburg, and New York, Viking Press, 1980.
The Suburbs of Hell.   London, Secker and Warburg, and New York, Taplinger, 1984.

Other

Midnite: The Story of a Wild Colonial Boy (for children). Melbourne, Cheshire, and London, Macdonald, 1967; Englewood Cliffs, New Jersey, Prentice Hall, 1968.

Editor, *Australian Poetry 1964.*   Sydney, Angus and Robertson, 1964.

*

Bibliography: *Randolph Stow: A Bibliography* by P.A. O'Brien, Adelaide, Libraries Board of South Australia, 1968; " A Randolph Stow Bibliography" by Rose Marie Beston, in *Literary Half-Yearly* (Mysore), July 1975.

Manuscript Collection: National Library of Australia, Canberra.

Critical Studies: "Raw Material" by the author, in *Westerly* (Nedlands, Western Australia), 1961; "The Quest for Permanence" by Geoffrey Dutton, in *Journal of Commonwealth Literature* (Leeds, Yorkshire), September 1965; "Outsider Looking Out" by W.H. New, in *Critique 9* (Minneapolis), 1, 1967; "Waste Places, Dry Souls" by Jennifer Wightman in *Meanjin* (Melbourne), June 1969; "Voyager from Eden" by Brandon Conron, in *Ariel (Canada)* (Calgary, Alberta), October 1970; "The Family Background and Literary Career of Randolph Stow," July 1975, and "The Poetry of Randolph Stow," 1977, both by John B. Beston, in *Literary Half-Yearly* (Mysore); *Randolph Stow* by Ray Willbanks, Boston, Twayne, 1978; *Randolph Stow* by Anthony J. Hassall, Brisbane, University of Queensland Press, 1985.

*   *   *

Randolph Stow's already considerable poetic reputation both overseas and in Australia rests on a comparatively small amount of published poetry. However, he is also a novelist who has written in both genres concurrently and the worlds and visions of his novels and of his poetry are interwoven. A discussion of his poetry should not forget these links and it is relevant to note the title of his selected poetry—*A Counterfeit Silence* on whose title page he quotes Thornton Wilder (*The Bridge of San Luis Rey*): "Even speech was for them a debased form of silence; how much more futile is poetry, which is a debased form of speech."

Stow's youthful poetry displayed technical mastery. He often contained great passion in graceful and ingenious traditional forms and frequently wrote a ballad-like verse which he has continued to use and to develop from time to time. Many of his early poems were autobiographical and displayed a sometimes almost oppressive awareness of the physical features of his Western Australian childhood and of its people expressed in lively and telling images: "...living where the sun/rolled on the land like a horse in a cloud of dust."

A series of Sydney Nolan's paintings decorate Stow's second book, *Outrider*. After this publication the term "surrealist" was heard of his work, wrongly I think. He has not, in that volume or later, abandoned effects and forms of great simplicity. Poems like "Ruins of the City of Hay" are many-sided, intricately stratified and dreamlike, but actual experience is their base. One may need a key to perceive the reality and logic but nothing in them is over or beyond reality, or beyond wit and irony ("Ruins of the City of Hay"):

> But the wind of the world descended on lovely Petra
> and the spires of the towers and the statues and belfries
>   fell.
> The bones of my brothers broke in the breaking columns.
> The bones of my sisters, clasping their broken children,
> cracked on the hearthstones, under the rooftrees of hay.
> I alone mourn in the temples, by broken altars
> bowered in black nightshade and mauve salvation-jane.

Stow has an acute, and acutely Australian, sense of dynasty. He is close in time and in imagination to his forebears who explored, possessed, named and tamed territories: "I am the country's station; all else is fever. / Did we ride knee to knee down canyons, or did I dream it!" ("Strange Fruit"). This dynastic vision is clearest and most open in "Stations," a suite for three voices and three generations. A man, woman and youth speak for each generation, brilliantly evoking the history of a place and family; the whole concludes with this affirmative couplet spoken by the woman: "Across the uncleared hills of the nameless country/I write in blood my blood's abiding name." In "Thailand Railway" a dying Australian prisoner of war thinks of "children on horseback, hordes of my own coutnry," rejects the utterance of "some warning or some charge, some testament" to enjoin: "think of the childless dead and be our sons."

Stow's poetry is international by virtue of his wide reading, his allusiveness in sound, rhythm and sense but unmistakably national as to its imagery, viewpoint and frequent use of Australian idiom.

—Nancy Keesing

———————

STRAND, Mark. American. Born in Summerside, Prince Edward Island, Canada, 11 April 1934; came to the United States in 1938. Educated at Antioch College, Yellow Springs, Ohio, B.A. 1957; Yale University, New Haven, Connecticut (Cook Prize and Bergin Prize, 1959), B.F.A. 1959; University of Florence (Fulbright Fellow), 1960-61; University of Iowa, Iowa City, M.A. 1962. Married 1) Antonia Ratensky in 1961 (divorced, 1973), one daughter; 2) Julia Rumsey Garretson in 1976. Instructor, University of Iowa, 1962-65; Fulbright Lecturer, University of Brazil, Rio de Janeiro, 1965-66; Assistant Professor, Mount Holyoke College, South Hadley, Massachusetts, 1967; Visiting Professor, University of Washington, Seattle, 1968, 1970; Adjunct Associate Professor, Columbia University, New York, 1969-72; Visiting Professor, Yale University, 1969; Associate Professor, Brooklyn College, New York, 1970-72; Bain-Swiggett Lecturer, Princeton University, New Jersey, 1973; Hurst Professor, Brandeis University, Waltham, Massachusetts, 1974-75; Visiting Professor, University of Virginia, Charlottesville, 1976 and 1978, California State University, Fresno, 1977, University of California, Irvine, 1978, Wesleyan University, Middletown, Connecticut, 1979, Harvard University, Cambridge, Massachusetts, 1980. Since 1981, Visiting Professor, University of Utah, Salt Lake City. Recipient: Ingram Merrill Foundation Fellowship, 1966; National Endowment for the Arts grant, 1967, 1977; Rockfeller award, 1968; Guggenheim Fellowship, 1974; Edgar Allan Poe Award, 1974; American Academy award, 1975; Academy of American Poets Fellowship, 1979. Member, American Academy. Address: 1408 Yale Avenue, Salt Lake City, Utah 84105, U.S.A.

PUBLICATIONS

Verse

Sleeping with One Eye Open. Iowa City, Stone Wall Press, 1964.
Reasons for Moving. New York, Atheneum, 1968.
Darker: Poems. New York, Atheneum, 1970.
The Story of Our Lives. New York, Atheneum, 1973.
The Sergeantville Notebook. Providence, Rhode Island, Burning Deck, 1973.
Elegy for My Father. Iowa City, Windhover Press, 1973.
The Late Hour. New York, Atheneum, 1978.
Selected Poems. New York, Atheneum, 1980.

Short Stories

Mr. and Mrs. Baby and Other Stories. New York, Knopf, 1985.

Other

The Monument.   New York, Ecco Press, 1978.
The Planet of Lost Things (for children).   New York, Potter, 1982.
The Night Book (for children).   New York, Potter, 1985.

Editor, *The Contemporary American Poets: American Poetry since 1940.*   Cleveland, World, 1969.
Editor, *New Poetry of Mexico.*   New York, Dutton, 1970; London, Secker and Warburg, 1972.
Editor and Translator, *The Owl's Insomnia: Selected Poems of Rafael Alberti.*   New York, Atheneum, 1973.
Editor and Translator, *Souvenir of the Ancient World: Selected Poems of Carlos Drummond de Andrade.*   New York, Antaeus, 1976.
Editor, with Charles Simic, *Another Republic: 17 European and South American Writers.*   New York, Ecco Press, 1976.
Editor, *Art of the Real: Nine American Figurative Painters.* New York, Potter, 1983; London, Aurum Press, 1984.

Translator, *18 Poems from the Quechua.*   Cambridge, Massachusetts, Halty Ferguson, 1971.
Translator, *Texas,* by Jorge Luis Borges.   Austin, University of Texas Humanities Research Center, 1975.

*

Manuscript Collection: Lilly Library, University of Indiana, Bloomington.

Critical Studies: "Mark Strand: *Darker*" by James Crenner, in *Seneca Review* (Geneva, New York), April 1971; "A Conversation with Mark Strand," in *Ohio Review* (Athens), Winter 1972; "Dark and Radiant Peripheries: Mark Strand and A.R. Ammons" by Harold Bloom, in *Southern Review* (Baton Rouge, Louisiana), Winter 1972; "Beginnings and Endings" by Robert McKlitsch, in *Literary Review* (Rutherford, New Jersey), Spring 1978; David Kirby, in *Times Literary Supplement* (London), 15 September 1978.

*   *   *

For a number of years one has had the pleasure of admiring the work of Mark Strand. He is one of the finest, most controlled of lyric poets, and his poems, written with an impeccable and seemingly effortless technique, have become increasingly fascinating. They are fascinating as superbly finished poetry. They are fascinating as well for the artistic strategies they employ, and, despite his own completely distinct voice, fascinating for the other writers and artists they do not echo but evoke. The quintessential Strand at its purest can be found in the concluding "poem" of "Seven Poems" (*Darker*):

> I have a key
> so I open the door and walk in.
> It is dark and I walk in.
> It is darker and I walk in.

Spare, windblown, stripped of everything non-essential. The utter simplicity of action and language, the repetitions, the subtle alternations in sentence structure, and especially the shift to the comparative, "darker," and the placings of the "I" work to wondrous and mysterious effect. The voice is unmistakably Mark Strand and no one else, and thematically he has always

had the "key" to darkness. Yet these repetitions, the simple denotative words tricked into unexpected connotations, the darkness, he shares with Beckett.

Strand's own lines apply to the kind of indirection displayed in the above example of his poetry: "Later, he could learn to say what he meant/without actually saying it" (*The Story of Our Lives*). The four lines are a touchstone to other important aspects of Strand's poetry as well. The symmetry of the last two lines shows an exquisite sense of balance, and precarious balances between dichotomies, opposites, and contradictions, such as absence/presence, dark/light, life/death, night/day, indoor/outdoor, are basic to this technique. The contraries like the vocabulary are simple, but they are artfully arranged, re-arranged, and varied to create patterns of meaning and complication. An example central to man and artist is "I empty myself of my life and my life remains" ("The Remains," *Darker*). And since the Romantic beguilement with it, which has accounted for so much then and since, the subject-object dichotomy has provided the "magic" caesura that allows the contraries to merge, reverse themselves. Across that same willing caesura and pliable "and," as it were, is the work of Beckett and Pinter also written and "reality," as in Strand, so brilliantly undermined.

This undermining or transformation of the landscape of "reality" by these three writers in order to create the private worlds which state their enigmatic "truths" or "meanings" is accomplished in addition by the suppression of narrative fact and dramatic situation, usually defined in plays, implicit in lyric poetry. The entire volume of *The Story of Our Lives*, with its deliberate allusion to story-telling, makes use of this method. Like Beckett, like Pinter, Strand manipulates here and elsewhere narrative time and the sequence of events, beginning and ending, and deliberately excludes needed information. Beckett is a virtuoso with ends and beginnings, and Pinter tells *Betrayed* backward. Here Strand begins with "Elegy for My Father," the end of one of the stories, moves to a poem called "To Begin," and ends the final poem "The Untelling" with "He sat and began to write."

In withholding information Beckett is of course the master. The identity of Godot is but the most famous instance, and Pinter by the same device, as well as by rearranging what details of plot there are, turns what would be ordinary melodramas into intriguing, deliberately unsolved mysteries. As Deeley says in *Old Times*, "It's the castors that make all this possible." The telling, not telling, or retelling of stories, central to *Old Times*, is explored extensively by Strand. The opening "Elegy," with its ambiguous and intensifying "refrain" "Nothing could stop you," is one kind of story. "To Begin" recounts the true beginning, the struggle to write. "The Room" is an ambiguous dramatic situation which recalls in its oblique angle of vision Robbe-Grillet's *Jealousy* and his screenplay for Resnais's *Last Year in Marienbad*. The surface story is presented and dismissed in "The Story of Our Lives." "Inside the Story" follows, and the volume is climaxed by the brilliant construction and deconstruction of a narrative in "The Untelling." Here an account of a memory is told four times. Each time its telling is not right, and at the close the fifth attempt is about to commence. The story itself in its four variations is haunting and surreal, as these lines suggest:

> *Although I have tried to return, I have always*
> *ended here, where I am now. The lake*
> *still exists, and so does the lawn, though the people*
> *who slept there that afternoon have not been seen since.*

Here many parallels come to mind. Among them are the strangely shifting landscapes of Seurat, the novels of John Hawkes, the theater work of Robert Wilson and Pinter's screenplay for *The Go-Between*.

Yet for Mark Strand, this poet of darkness, perhaps "like a ghost in sunlight,/ barely visible," the words are at the outset; it is the words that are important. After all, in the beginning was the Word.

—Gaynor F. Bradish

STRYK, Lucien. American. Born in Chicago, Illinois, 7 April 1924. Educated at Indiana University, Bloomington, B.A. 1948; University of Maryland, College Park, M.F.S. 1950; University of London; the Sorbonne, Paris, M.F.S.; University of Iowa, Iowa City, M.F.A. 1956. Served in the United States Army, 1943-45. Married; two children. Since 1958, Member of the English Department, and currently Professor of English, Northern Illinois University, DeKalb. Visiting Lecturer, Niigata University, Japan, 1956-58, and Yamaguchi University, Japan, 1962-63; Fulbright Lecturer, Iran, 1961-62. Recipient: Grove Press Fellowship, 1970; Yale University Asia Society grant, 1961; Ford Foundation Faculty Fellowship, University of Chicago, 1963; Isaac Rosenbaum Award (*Voices*), 1964; Swallow Press award, 1965; National Translation grant, 1969; National Endowment for the Arts award, 1974; Rockefeller Fellowship, 1983. Address: Department of English, Northern Illinois University, DeKalb, Illinois 60115, U.S.A.

PUBLICATIONS

Verse

Taproot. Oxford, Fantasy Press, 1953.
The Trespasser. Oxford, Fantasy Press, 1956.
Notes for a Guidebook. Denver, Swallow, 1965.
The Pit and Other Poems. Chicago, Swallow Press, 1969.
Awakening. Chicago, Swallow Press, 1973.
Selected Poems. Chicago, Swallow Press, 1976.
The Duckpond. London, J. Jay, 1978.
Collected Poems 1953-1983. Athens, Swallow Press-Ohio University Press, 1984.

Other

Encounter with Zen: Writings on Poetry and Zen. Athens, Swallow Press-Ohio University Press, 1981.

Editor and Translator, with Takashi Ikemoto, *Zen: Poems, Prayers, Sermons, Anecdotes, Interviews.* New York, Doubleday, 1965.
Editor, *Heartland: Poets of the Midwest.* DeKalb, Northern Illinois University Press, 1967; *Heartland 2*, 1975.
Editor, *World of the Buddha: A Reader.* New York, Doubleday, 1968.
Editor and Translator, with Takashi Ikemoto, *Afterimages: Zen Poems of Shinkichi Takahashi.* Chicago, Swallow Press, and London, Alan Ross, 1970.
Editor, and Translator with Takashi Ikemoto, *The Penguin Book of Zen Poetry.* Chicago, Swallow Press, and London, Allen Lane, 1977.
Editor, *Prairie Voices: A Collection of Illinois Poets.* Peoria, Illinois, Spoon River Poetry Press, 1980.

Translator, with Takashi Ikemoto, *Zen Poems of China and Japan: The Crane's Bill.* New York, Doubleday, 1973.
Translator, with Takashi Ikemoto, *Twelve Death Poems of the Chinese Zen Masters.* Providence, Rhode Island, Hellcoal Press, 1973.
Translator, *Three Zen Poems after Shinkichi Takahashi.* Knotting, Bedfordshire, Sceptre Press, 1976.
Co-Translator, *Haiku of the Japanese Masters.* Derry, Pennsylvania, Rook Press, 1977.
Co-Translator, *The Duckweed Way: Haiku of Issa.* Derry, Pennsylvania, Rook Press, 1977.

*

Manuscript Collection: Mugar Memorial Library, Boston University.

Lucien Stryk comments:

I consider myself primarily a poet with a strong interest in Oriental philosophy. Some critics have associated me with other poets and "schools" but, frankly, I like to think of myself as an "independent."

I don't think a grown-up poet can do much about the content of his verse: he either has or hasn't worthy concerns, he is either small or large-minded, and such things as his politics and social attitudes generally get into this verse, one way or another. My chief concern as a poet is to *make* something, something firmly enough crafted to assure its life for longer than one hurried reading. How to get this done is the main study of my life. I suppose that what some critics have called my economy of statement has to a certain degree been influenced by my work as a translator of Zen poetry, but I'm far from certain about that.

Anyhow, I try for a firm line and, most important of all, image and/ or metaphor without which, so far as I'm concerned, there cannot be poetry. Whatever else he is—and he had better be much more—the poet is an active finely-tuned sensorium, his eye working perfectly with his ear, and his fingers touching delicately. When the poet *is* that, and when his theme is worthy, he *may* produce a good poem. Yet the making of a good poem is never less than a mystery, and no poet would really want it to be anything less, however much he despairs.

*   *   *

For two decades, from *Taproot* (1953) to *Awakening* (1973), war haunted Lucien Stryk's poetry. War has been the bone beneath the smile, the human constant against which love, loyalty, reverence, and all other qualities or notions of higher being must survive as best they can. This is a deep and complex awareness in Stryk, and is grounded in the poet's own memories: "memories [that] converge to form a shaft of pain" ("The Stack among the Ruins"). Generated by "the gibbet and the gas chamber," by the bombing of a Red Cross ship, by "the screaming victims thrown/ From out the burning hospital/ Into the burning town," the early poem "Song" from *The Trespasser* indicates just how pervasive these memories are. "Song" ends:

> The withered trees are in bloom again,
>   The earth is ripe and warm,
> But now we watch the lecher worm
>   That stains the vestal bud
> And like a fighter in the sun
>   The acrobatic bird.

We can see here the extent to which his song and vision have been colored. The mind that contemplates even the spring carries with it and always will the horrors of the past. From here on, Stryk, metaphorically speaking, will project into the body of every bird the propensities of the warplane. In "Summer," from *Awakening*, the poet's neighbor

> scowls up at my maple, rake
> clogged and trembling,
> as its seeds spin down—
>
> not angels, moths, but paratroopers
> carried by the wind,
> planting barricades along his eaves.

However this is read, whatever irony is directed against the sensibility that obsessively reads nature in martial terms, what is clear is that the poet understands this predilection and its origins only too well. Poem after poem will tell us that he had his fill of that life at war, that repulsive anti-life. At the same time, I think, Stryk would agree that the whole of life somehow has to be gotten into each poem.

Stryk's poems are the embodiment of an evolution that carries him along from the despair of the early work to the more balanced and hopeful strains of the later. *Taproot* and *The Trespasser* name the experiences that will temper the life's work. War becomes known, in part, through the occasional realization of love, its divine opposite. In "For Helen" from the former volume Stryk declares

> I know that all
> True lovers and their words but serve
> A love more tender than their own. Our
> Child, the pollened wind, the swirl of
> Homing birds proclaim its power.

In *Notes for a Guidebook*, the poet's selves become students, wanderers, tourists, beachcombers. The presences of the poems visit for a first time or return to familiar places and wonder how best to live in such a world of flux and seeming contradiction. This volume seems occasionally to labor for ultimate truth and morality, for something to hold to once and for all. *Notes*, I believe, represents a tense and crucial period in the poet's life. In *The Pit and Other Poems*, Stryk comes to grips with the function and worth of his life's work, "this house / of paper" as he terms it. The recognition of this book is that the poem must change, that life is motion, that systems are at once fluid and rotted in a divine One, that if there is no final way to resolve pain and loss and death forever, a man can still come to an ease, can become, as Whitman said, a "cosmos." In "Memo to the Builder" of his house, Stryk directs: "Build me a home / The living day can enter, not a tomb." The title poem, filled with horrifying images of a pit of bodies, ends: "Ask anyone who / Saw it: nobody won that war." This represents a resolution for the poet, an insistence that, although war is a human fact and constant, its acceptance is wrong and a man could and should publish it for what it is and also, at the same time, properly distance himself from it. As he says in "Zen: The Rocks of Sesshu," "The weed also has the desire / To make clean, / Make pure, there against the rock."

As it is in *Notes*, in *The Pit* the same desire for a spiritual calm is apparent. What is new with this book, and what deepens and matures in *Awakening*, is a dimension of peace in the face of what were previously almost debilitating conflicts and fears. "Ask anyone who / Saw it: nobody won that war"—in its

straightforwardness, in its staunchness, this is a note of celebration that prefigures the grace and wisdom of Stryk's most recent work.

—William Heyen

STUART, Dabney. American. Born in Richmond, Virginia, 4 November 1937. Educated at Davidson College, North Carolina, 1956-60, A.B. 1960; Harvard University, Cambridge, Massachusetts (Summer Poetry Prize, 1962), A.M. 1962. Married to Sandra Westcott (second marriage); one daughter and two sons. Instructor in English, College of William and Mary, Williamsburg, Virginia, 1961-65. Instructor, 1965-66, Assistant Professor, 1966-69, Associate Professor, 1969-74, and since 1974, Professor of English, Washington and Lee University, Lexington, Virginia. Visiting Professor, Middlebury College, Vermont, 1968-69, and Ohio University, Athens, Spring 1975; resident poet, Trinity College, Hartford, Connecticut, 1978; Visiting Lecturer, University of Virginia, Charlottesville, 1981, 1982-83. Poetry Editor, *Shenandoah*, Lexington, 1966-76. Recipient: Poetry Society of America Dylan Thomas Prize, 1965; National Endowment for the Arts grant, 1969, and fellowship 1974, 1982; Borestone Mountain award, 1969, 1974, 1977; Virginia Governor's Award, 1979. Address: Department of English, Washington and Lee University, Lexington, Virginia 24450, U.S.A.

PUBLICATIONS

Verse

The Diving Bell. New York, Knopf, 1966.
A Particular Place. New York, Knopf, 1969.
Corgi Modern Poets in Focus 3, with others, edited by Dannie Abse. London, Corgi, 1971.
The Other Hand. Baton Rouge, Louisiana State University Press, 1974.
Friends of Yours, Friends of Mine. Richmond, Virginia, Rainmaker Press, 1975.
Round and Round: A Triptych. Baton Rouge, Louisiana State University Press, 1977.
Rockbridge Poems. Emory, Virginia, Iron Mountain Press, 1981.
Common Ground. Baton Rouge, Louisiana State University Press, 1982.

Other

Nabokov: The Dimensions of Parody. Baton Rouge, Louisiana State University Press, 1978.

*

Manuscript Collection: Virginia Commonwealth University, Richmond.

Critical Studies: by X.J. Kennedy, in *Shenandoah* (Lexington, Virginia), Autumn 1966; John Unterecker, in *Shenandoah* (Lexington, Virginia), Autumn 1969; Dannie Abse, in *Corgi Modern Poets in Focus 3*, 1971; by the author, in *Contemporary Poetry in America*, edited by Miller Williams, New York, Random House, 1973; D.E. Richardson, in *Southern Review* (Baton

Rouge, Louisiana), Autumn 1976; Stephen Dobyns, in *Washington Post Book World*, 7 November 1982; Fred Chappell, in *Roanoke Times* (Virginia), 27 March 1983; "Ghostlier Demarcations, Keener Sounds" by Barbara Fialkowski, in *Poets in the South* (Tampa, Florida), Fall 1984.

Dabney Stuart comments:

My work has vacillated formally between traditional English forms (the sonnet in *The Diving Bell*, ballads in *Round and Round*) and so-called "free" (i.e., associative, non-metrical) verse (the whole of *The Other Hand*). I have been consistently involved with certain themes, themselves less fragmented and wandering than my voice: son/father and father/son, levels of consciousness, the unforeseen and ubiquitous past, the aloof self-regard of women, the illusion of solidity and perspective, death and punning.

*   *   *

Dabney Stuart has received impressive tributes for his skill, his intelligence, and his veracity to experience. In his first book, *The Diving Bell*, he revealed himself as a master of the well-made poem. His command of language and his confident handling of relatively traditional forms are combined there with a gentle candour which enables many of the poems to transcend the category of Lowellesque confessional verse into which they run the risk of falling. There is nothing trite about his contribution to this genre. For example, in a poem for the small daughter whom he seldom sees he speaks of her as a conjuror: "Your voice a wand, you called the olives grapes," but adds later:

Yet, deserting your role,
You called me by my name—
I'd rather
Have been that metaphor, your father.

Here language is both image and instrument.

His second book makes a necessary advance into more adventurous territory. It includes, in fact, a number of poems about places, contemplative in tone, dwelling on stone and water, air and stillness. But it explores also deeper regions of symbol and myth, psychic landscapes, in forms which owe little to tradition.

There is always a danger that this kind of poem may not come off. A few here, even in Stuart's accomplished hands, fail. About those which do not it is, in a sense, impossible to make final judgments: their success depends very much on the range of experience and the type of attention which the reader brings to them, and on the reverberations they cause in his mind. Many of the poems in this book have a haunting resonance which gives more with every reading.

—Fleur Adcock

SUKNASKI, Andrew, Jr. Canadian. Born in Wood Mountain, Saskatchewan, 30 July 1942. Educated at the Ambassador School, Wood Mountain; L.V. Rogers High School, Nelson, British Columbia; Kootenay School of Art, Nelson, 1961-62, 1966-67, diploma in fine arts 1967; University of Victoria, British Columbia, 1964-65; Montreal Museum of Fine Arts School of Art and Design, 1965; Notre Dame University, Nelson, 1966-67; University of British Columbia, Vancouver, 1967-68; Simon Fraser University, Burnaby, British Columbia, 1968-69. Editor, *Elfin Plot*, 1968-74, and *Sundog*, 1973-76, and Deodar Shadow Press, 1970-71, Anak Press, 1971-76, and Sundog Press, 1973-78, all Wood Mountain. Since 1982, Editor, *Three Legged Coyote*, Wood Mountain. Writer-in-Residence, St. John's College, University of Manitoba, Winnipeg, 1977-78. Recipient: Canada Council grant, 1971, 1972, 1973, 1976, 1978, 1980, 1982; Canadian Authors Association prize, 1978; Saskatchewan Culture and Youth grant, 1981. Address: Wood Mountain, Saskatchewan S0H 4L0, Canada.

PUBLICATIONS

Verse

The Shadow of Eden Once.   Wood Mountain, Deodar Shadow Press, 1970.
Circles.   Wood Mountain, Deodar Shadow Press, 1970.
In Mind ov Xrossroads ov Mythologies.   Wood Mountain, Anak Press, 1971.
Rose Way in the East.   Toronto, Ganglia Press, 1972.
Old Mill.   Vancouver, Blewointmentpress, 1972.
The Nightwatchman.   Wood Mountain, Anak Press, 1972.
The Zen Pilgrimage.   Wood Mountain, Anak Press, 1972.
Y th Evolution into Ruenz.   Wood Mountain, Anak Press, 1972.
Four Parts Sand: Concrete Poems, with others.   Ottawa, Oberon Press, 1972.
Wood Mountain Poems.   Wood Mountain, Anak Press, 1973; expanded edition, edited by Al Purdy, Toronto, Macmillan, 1976.
Suicide Notes, Book One.   Wood Mountain, Sundog Press, 1973.
Phillip Well.   Prince George, British Columbia, College of New Caledonia, 1973.
These Fragments I've Gathered for Ezra.   Edinburg, Texas, Funch Press, 1973.
Leaving.   Seven Person, Alberta, Repository Press, 1974.
On First Looking Down from Lion's Gate Bridge.   Wood Mountain, Anak Press, 1974; revised edition, Windsor, Ontario, Black Moss Press, 1976.
Blind Man's House.   Wood Mountain, Anak Press, 1974.
Leaving Wood Mountain.   Wood Mountain, Sundog Press, 1975.
Writing on Stone: Poemdrawings 1966-1976.   Wood Mountain, Anak Press, 1976.
Octomi.   Saskatoon, Thistledown Press, 1976.
Almighty Voice.   Toronto, Dreadnaught Press, 1977.
Moses Beauchamp.   Winnipeg, Turnstone Press, 1978.
The Ghosts Call You Poor.   Toronto, Macmillan, 1978.
Two for Father, with George Morrissette.   Wood Mountain, Sundog Press, 1978.
East of Myloona.   Saskatoon, Thistledown Press, 1979.
In the Name of Narid: New Poems.   Erin, Ontario, Porcupine's Quill, 1981.
Montage for an Interstellar Cry.   Winnipeg, Turnstone Press, 1982.
The Land They Gave Away: Selected and New Poems.   Edmonton, NeWest Press, 1982.
Silk Trail.   Toronto, Blewointmentpress, 1984.

Play

Don'tcha Know the North Wind and You in My Hair, with others (produced Saskatoon, 1978).

Other

Translator, *The Shadow of Sound*, by Andrei Voznesensky. Prince George, British Columbia, College of New Caledonia, 1975.

*

Critical Studies: "Writing along the Road to Wood Mountain," in *Another Time* by Eli Mandel, Erin, Ontario, Press Porcépic, 1977; "Shadows of Our Ancestors" by Harvey Spak, and "Ghostly Voices" by Stephen Scobie, both in *Ne West ReView* (Edmonton), October 1978; Kristjana Gunnars, in *Arts Manitoba* (Winnipeg), Fall 1983.

Andrew Suknaski, Jr., comments:

(1980) 1. Concerns: the meaning of home and a vaguely divided guilt; guilt for what happened to the Indian, his land taken, imprisoned on his reserve; and guilt because to feel this guilt is a betrayal of what you ethnically are, the son of a homesteader and his wife who must be rightfully honoured in one's mythology

2. Origins: mythic mainsprings—the meaning of self: *self* your place of birth, *self* the proximity of the buried to the living of that place, *self* in *home...being* your *dreamtime* (tribal history, the ancestral way of life—that place where you leave going beyond to become faceless...mind and heart telescoped, forever yearning to return...*home*)

3. Naming the Lost: in the western prairie labyrinth where the poet as art casualty must retie the severed threads: guilt, betrayal, and populist myth on the margins of the dreaming utopia that victimizes one *naming the lost* to arrest niggling visions of where the Godly becomes monstrous, where reality becomes myth...as Leslie Fiedler warns, where myth often victimizes the innocent as one's humanity is shortchanged by the tickettaker at the circus gate—that point of entry to our nightmares and *otherness*

(1985) 4. *Definition of West: Divining for West*/part II of CELESTIAL MECHANICS/life fragment in progress...drift of word, humanity and myth from Sanskrit *Narayan*, "Man-Path," to *Amurru* "Westerners"—mountain Amorites west from Akkad and Sumer; drift of etymon anchoring mythic west and mariners...from Islamic trade secret in name of Al-Gharb, "The West," *edge of the known world* to become Phoenician *Algarve* guarded by Pillars of Hercules; from *Ne Plus Ultra* to *Plus Ultra*..."More Beyond"/dream *...there is a beyond...perhaps another place and NorthWest Passage*; the search, the beginning in journies beyond and back home by water...binary home/old and new...the New West...from dream of ancient vestal virgins illuminating heart of the old city to counterfeit dream of new vestal virgins—the brokers of Wall Street...West no longer a simple definition but a lifelong project and projection along the map of word and flesh.

*   *   *

"If Canada ever needed an argument in defence of the regional writer, Andrew Suknaski is it," wrote a reviewer of this poet who has taken the Canadian Prairies as his province. Suknaski, of Polish-Ukrainian parentage, was born on a farm outside the village of Wood Mountain, in southwestern Saskatchewan. He lives there and writes about his background and that of the prairies: Indians, East European settlers, Mounties, Americans. Reading *Wood Mountain Poems*, one is aware that, in this region, if space has expanded time has contracted, so that the past is ever-present, but Toronto and Vancouver are light years

distant. The poems in *The Ghosts Call You Poor* take the form of jottings, rambling letters, documentations, etc., but they are all concerned with what sociologists call "marginalized people." The Indians and Métis are pre-eminently among these, as he shows in "Dreaming of the Northwest Passage":

> the native showed us the way
> the native drew the first map on sand and earth
> the northern esquimaux drew in snow
> and did with small shale cairns
> what contour lines do
> to indicate mountains
> for scottish and british explorers
>
> the indian showed us the way to the heart
> of the prairie
> and distant mountains

There is more rhetoric than drama in his poetry, more feeling for great masses of people than for individuals, more a sense of summing up a patchwork past than of signaling a new society or a significant future. Only in one of his lesser-known books, *Leaving*, does Suknaski write about his travels throughout Europe and the East. The poems there have a bright quality lacking in the prairie poems.

—John Robert Colombo

———

SUMMERS, Hollis (Spurgeon, Jr.). American. Born in Eminence, Kentucky, 21 June 1916. Educated at Georgetown College, Kentucky, A.B. 1937; Bread Loaf School of English, Middlebury College, Vermont, M.A. 1943; University of Iowa, Iowa City, Ph.D. 1949. Married Laura Vimont Clarke in 1943; two sons. Taught at Holmes High School, Covington, Kentucky, 1937-44; Professor of English, Georgetown College, 1945-49, and the University of Kentucky, Lexington, 1949-59. Professor, 1959-63, and since 1964, Distinguished Professor of English, Ohio University, Athens. Adviser, Ford Foundation Conference on Writers in America, 1958; Lecturer, Arts Program, Association of American Colleges, 1958-63; Danforth Lecturer, 1963-66, 1971; Fulbright Lecturer, University of Canterbury, Christchurch, New Zealand, 1978. Recipient: Fund for the Advancement of Education grant, 1951; *Saturday Review* Poetry Award, 1957; Colleges of Arts and Sciences Award, 1958; National Endowment for the Arts Fellowship, 1974, grant, 1975. LL.D.: Georgetown College, 1965. Address: 181 North Congress Street, Athens, Ohio 45701, U.S.A.

PUBLICATIONS

Verse

The Walks near Athens.   New York, Harper, 1959.
Someone Else: Sixteen Poems about Other Children (for children).   Philadelphia, Lippincott, 1962.
Seven Occasions.   New Brunswick, New Jersey, Rutgers University Press, 1965.
The Peddler and Other Domestic Matters.   New Brunswick, New Jersey, Rutgers University Press, 1967.
Sit Opposite Each Other.   New Brunswick, New Jersey, Rutgers University Press, 1970.

Start from Home. New Brunswick, New Jersey, Rutgers University Press, 1972.
Occupant, Please Forward. New Brunswick, New Jersey, Rutgers University Press, 1976.
Dinosaurs. Athens, Ohio, Rosetta Press, 1978.

Play

A Note to Myself: A Thanksgiving Play. Chicago, Dramatic Publishing Company, 1946.

Novels

City Limit. Boston, Houghton Mifflin, 1948.
Brighten the Corner. New York, Doubleday, 1952.
Teach You a Lesson (as Jim Hollis, with James Rourke). New York, Harper, 1955; London, Foulsham, 1956.
The Weather of February. New York, Harper, 1957.
The Day after Sunday. New York, Harper, 1968.
The Garden. New York, Harper, 1972.

Short Stories

How They Chose the Dead. Baton Rouge, Louisiana State University Press, 1973.
Standing Room. Baton Rouge, Louisiana State University Press, 1984.

Other

Editor, *Kentucky Story: A Collection of Short Stories.* Lexington, University of Kentucky Press, 1954.
Editor, with Edgar Whan, *Literature: An Introduction.* New York, McGraw Hill, 1960.
Editor, *Discussions of the Short Story.* Boston, Heath, 1963.

*

Manuscript Collections: University of Kentucky, Lexington; Ohio University Library, Athens.

Critical Study: by Carol C. Harter, in *American Novelists since World War II*, 2nd series, edited by James E. Kibler, Jr., Detroit, Gale, 1980.

Hollis Summers comments:
 Could these words serve, some of them, as a statement of faith?

A poem is moving down a summer street,
Darkly, unsure, yet pretending
That assumption is a name for fact;

Pretending even street and season,
It walks with carefully balanced faith to meet
A space for turning, to bring
The eyes, even if blinded for the act,
To look back,
  To ask the reason
For the movement:
  Darkness again, perhaps, or
Darkness barred with slanted light from an opened door.

 —from "A Poem Is Moving Down a Summer Street"
 in *The Walks near Athens*

You can tell almost all in a poem.
Tears, semen, and bowel movements
Come precisely with fairly simple aids:
Color and consistency charts
Stapled to the wish to show and shout.

I also wish to show and shout,
Look at me, look here, look out
From where you read, considering the poems I need.
I'm sorry I have been reared
Believing poems that said, "Look there."

A poem is room enough to skin a cat in;
A poem is shaking a stick at a cat;
A poem is skinning a cat more ways than one.

 —from "For Three Specific Friends"
 in *The Peddler and Other Domestic Matters*

*   *   *

 Since *The Walks near Athens*, Hollis Summers's poetry has been characterized by an ease of expression, an effortlessness that balances his classical elegance with rhythms so casual that they seem spontaneous. The beginning lines of "On Looking at Television's Late Movies," for example, move so surely that they seem almost offhand:

John Keats sank into nothingness
Over a star or the song of a bird
Or a vase or marbles, or even the sea
In which he assumed his name was writ.

The lines turn their corners perfectly, as the poem begins to turn on its ironies. Summers's labor has always been to understand the assumptions that we consider facts, and to write clearly about them. This poem ends: "In the water where Keats wrote I have read / Permanence. I am glad he is dead."
 Here and throughout Summers's poetry, romantic notions of beauty (perhaps the most important word in his work) are turned mercilessly on the spit of experience. Faiths built on notions of meaning or permanence are held in the light for what they are. We sing, Summers concludes in the title poem of *Seven Occasions*, "for no final reason." "Song to Be Attached" from *The Peddler and Other Domestic Matters* might serve as a metaphor for his unrelenting vision. Three stanzas tell us to "Decorate the carcass / Thread with amethyst," to "Deck the bowels with ruby." But the poem concludes:

Braise in precious ointment
Drench it if you will
Decorate the carcass
It is a carcass still.

It is not easy to say these things. In "Song for a Dead Lady" from *Sit Opposite Each Other*, Summers tells us that "it is good she is dead... / But I had to live a long time / To say this song." Summers is one of America's finest, most underrated poets. Volume after volume has clarified a voice and a vision that will come to engage us as among the most memorable of our time.

 —William Heyen

SWARD, Robert S. American; Canadian Landed Immigrant. Born in Chicago, Illinois, 23 June 1933. Educated at Von Steuben High School, Chicago; San Diego Junior College, California, 1951; University of Illinois, Urbana, 1953-56, B.A. (honors) 1956 (Phi Beta Kappa); Bread Loaf School of English, Middlebury, Vermont, summers 1956-58; University of Iowa, Iowa City, M.A. 1958; University of Bristol (Fulbright Fellow), 1960-61. Served in the United States Navy in Korea, 1951-53. Married Diane Kaldes (second wife) in 1960 (divorced, 1969), two daughters and one son; married Judith Essenson in 1969 (divorced, 1972); married Irina Schestakowich in 1975, one daughter and one son. Research Fellow, 1956-58, and Poet-in-Residence, Spring 1967, University of Iowa; Lecturer in English, Connecticut College, New London, 1958-59; Writer-in-Residence, Cornell University, Ithaca, New York, 1962-64, Aspen Writers' Conference, Colorado, Summer 1967, and University of Victoria, British Columbia, 1969-73. Founding Editor, Soft Press, 1970-77, and Editor, Hancock House Editions, 1976-79, both in Victoria. Since 1979, free-lance writer: book reviewer, Toronto Star, and broadcaster, CBC Radio. Recipient: Dylan Thomas Award, 1958; Yaddo Fellowship, summers, 1959-69; MacDowell Colony Fellowship, summers, 1959-72; Guggenheim Fellowship, 1966; Canada Council grant, 1973, 1981, 1982, 1983; Ontario Arts Council grant, 1982, 1983, 1984. Address: 3 Wyandot Avenue, Toronto Island, Toronto, Ontario M5J 2E6; or, c/o Writers Union of Canada, 24 Ryerson Avenue, Toronto, Ontario M5T 2P3, Canada.

PUBLICATIONS

Verse

Advertisements. Chicago, Odyssey, 1958.
Uncle Dog and Other Poems. London, Putnam, 1962.
Kissing the Dancer and Other Poems. Ithaca, New York, Cornell University Press, 1964.
Thousand-Year-Old Fiancée and Other Poems. Ithaca, New York, Cornell University Press, 1965.
In Mexico and Other Poems. London, Ambit, 1966.
Horgbortom Stringbottom, I Am Yours, You Are History. Chicago, Swallow Press, 1970.
Quorum, with *Noah*, by Charles Doyle. Victoria, Soft Press, 1970.
Songs from The Jurassic Shales. Victoria, Soft Press, 1970.
Hannah's Cartoon. Victoria, Soft Press, 1970.
Gift. Victoria, Soft Press, 1970.
Raspberry (as Dr. Soft). Victoria, Soft Press, 1971.
Risk. Victoria, Soft Press, 1971.
Letter to a Straw Hat. Victoria, Soft Press, 1974.
Five Iowa Poems. Iowa City, Stone Wall Press, 1975.
Honey Bear on Lasqueti Island, B.C. Victoria, Soft Press, 1978.
Six Poems. Toronto, League of Canadian Poets, 1980.
Twelve Poems. Toronto, Island House, 1982.
Poems New and Selected (1957-1983). Toronto, Aya Press, 1983.
Movies: Left to Right. London, South Western Ontario Poetry Publications, 1983.
The Three Roberts: Premier Performance, with Robert Priest and Robert Zend. Toronto, HMS Press, 1984.

Recording: *Thousand-Year-Old Fiancée and Other Poems*, Aural.

Novel

The Jurassic Shales. Toronto, Coach House Press, 1975.

Other

The Toronto Islands: An Illustrated History. Toronto, Dreadnaught, 1983.

Editor, with Tim Groves and Mario Martinelli, *Vancouver Island Poems.* Victoria, Soft Press, 1973.
Editor, *Cheers for Muktananda.* Victoria, Soft Press, 1976.

*

Bibliography: by John Gill, in *New: American and Canadian Poetry* (Trumansburg, New York), 1973.

Manuscript Collections: Washington University Library, St. Louis; National Library of Canada, Ottawa; University of Victoria.

Critical Studies: "The Voices Have Range" by John Malcolm Brinnin, in *New York Times Book Review*, 25 October 1964; introduction by William Meredith to *Kissing the Dancer and Other Poems*, 1964; *A Controversy of Poets* edited by Paris Leary and Robert Kelly, New York, Doubleday, 1965; "A Poetry Chronicle" by Constance Urdang, in *Poetry* (Chicago), 17 February 1972; introduction by Earle Birney to *Poems New and Selected (1957-1983)*, 1983.

*   *   *

A striking feature of Robert Sward's poetry is its range: he is a master of unique observation, gifted with emotional recall, capable of goofy humor as well as experiments in disdain, and properly turned off by war and the diplomatic posture of his native America. Sward's "Statement of Poetics"—a poem that appeared in *New: American & Canadian Poetry 20*—may indicate his attitudes accurately enough, though it may also indicate his disdain for unanswerable poetic questions. He is outrageous as often as not, seeming capable of walking on words halfway between double exposures of put-on and truth:

> Talk
> people talking, getting that
> into one's poetry that
> is my poetics. Love
> hate lies laughing stealings
> self-confession self-destruction
> get them all get
> them all into writing.
> No one has to
> read them. No one
> has to publish them.
> I am more and
> more for unpublished poetry.

Sward's delight with language is evident in all his poetry, and the reader senses a healthy dose of play at work in every poem. He revels in the power of the final word, which he uses with delight against the innocent as well as those who have crossed him. He writes in "Mothers-In-Law" (both of whom he lost through divorce) that the first of them "required, upon departure,/The services of three gentlemen with shoehorns/To get her back into her large black/Studebaker." The reader experiences vicarious pleasure imagining the lady in question thumbing through Robert's book. It may be play of an adolescent nature, but how grand to have a poet awaken the childishness within us.

Indeed, if we accept spontaneity as a primary quality of childhood, Sward's childishness is virtually unequalled. The poetry that results is sometimes half-baked, but so direct of statement that we feel, unquestionably, the poet's complete, warty presence: I'll take this kind of unguarded, risky stuff anyday in preference to the urbane, sophisticated verse of poets (half his age!) who write within only a limited range of highly selected posturings. Sward is willing to let his reader hate him; yet he, himself, escapes the pit of self-hatred. At times, his spontaneity works against him, as in the polemic "In Mexico," where after describing his opposition to American war policies, he concludes: "What a country!/ For even/ Your stupidity,/ The Charm/ Of Your/ Tastelessness,/ Vitality,/ Greed// America, get out/of Vietnam,/ The Dominican Republic,/ Africa, Europe/ Southeast Asia// Has begun to smell/ Has begun to smell/ I would say/ Like the Pentagon,/ Like senility/ Like death." I believe poems written without deference to academic standards should rise above such standards, not be vulnerable to the kind of bitchy complaint that says the subjects "stupidity" and "charm" are not capable of their verbs, and the abstract image is not even linguistically interesting, unless Sward intends a different subject. In any case, spontaneity in this instance results in dull rhetoric.

For each of his few failed risks, Sward has many poems that win against the odds; his only form, the integrity of his voice. The language is tight, the words comprehensible, and he can move up off the page, out of the words, like a man coming into sunlight. I admire his fullness, and will end with excerpts from two distinctly different poems, "San Cristobal" and "Risk":

> Pine cones, aspen,
> Starlight, the light
> World one way, then another
> The light rising,
> The light drawn up into stars
>
> Voice is light,
> The world is light
> The stars, their hands
> Striking through

It's a calculated risk, whatever you do.
    A man has cancer of the rectum. You
    take out his rectum and
maybe he dies of heart failure.
Or he's fine and goes on for 20 years.

—Geof Hewitt

SWEETMAN, David. British. Born in Northumberland, in 1943. Educated at the University of Durham; University of East Africa. Worked for the British Council for 8 years, mainly in Africa. Currently, Arts Producer, BBC Television, London. Address: c/o Faber and Faber Ltd., 3 Queen Square, London WC1N 3AU, England.

PUBLICATIONS

Verse

Looking into the Deep End. London, Faber, 1981.

Other (for children)

Queen Nzinga. London, Longman, 1971.
Picasso. London, Wayland, 1973.
Captain Scott. London, Wayland, 1974.
The Borgias. Hove, Sussex, Wayland, 1976.
Patrice Lumumba. London, Longman, 1978.
Spies and Spying. Hove, Sussex, Wayland, 1978.
The Amulet. London, Longman, 1980.
The Moyo Kids. London, Longman, 1980.
Skyjack over Africa. London, Longman, 1980.
Bishop Crowther. London, Longman, 1981.
Women Leaders in African History. London, Heinemann, 1984.

*   *   *

In a *New Statesman* article published in the late 1970's, James Fenton recognised a way of writing that opened up experience as if it were new and strange, perceived for the first time. David Sweetman's work seemed, when *Looking into the Deep End* appeared in 1981, an important and impressive addition to this kind of what Fenton had called "Martian" writing. Metaphors sparkle conceitedly—an African nipple, for example, "black as a missionary's biretta" or one moving train seen from another "Noisy as a factory...[projecting] its out of frame film show."

But two things distinguished Sweetman from the other Martians. One was his continual closeness to extremity, and the other was an interest in the grimmest of contemporary events. It was as though Sylvia Plath had survived to the 1980's, her terrible gift for self-examination turned to one for gazing at the ugliest parts of humankind's games with itself. For Sweetman, a B52 bomber resembles a flasher's flyzip, and the starving child is, horribly, "pregnant with hunger."

Someone in our time had to write a poem about atomic catastrophe. Sweetman's piece is typical of the best of his work. It begins with a beguiling gentleness in a Japanese potter's studio, with the poet showing off considerable technical gifts. Note the lulling assonances and alliterations:

> Teabowl and vase, tray and ewer
> stacked in the studio like shapes
> fragmented from a landscape...

and the perverse rightness of the image of the "melting hands" "drawn...from the grey slip." Even though the shapes are fragmented and the clay "strangled," nothing prepares us for the coloured horror of the bombs that hit Hiroshima and "stripes Kenji the cold white/ and midnight blue of a mackerel's belly...."

As well as beginnings and holocausts, in "The Art of Pottery 1945," "Burning a Baby," and "0900 hrs23/10/4004 BC" Sweetman also "contemplates the menace of the ordinary." Like people in an Ian McEwan short story, Sweetman's common or garden characters progress inexorably towards a final horror: drowning, castration, madness. Repetition often points up the surreal ghastliness: "always failing, failing, failing," for instance; and so do the continuation marks...that became a cliché of the Martian school, giving it a passing, dotty resemblance to the novels of John Wyndham.

Sweetman's first book will be read and re-read as a pyrotechnical piece of evidence of the fragrant decadence of modernism. Fragrant, as I've shown; modernistic in the yoking together of utterly different modes of speech; but decadent, finally, in its air of having not quite enough to say about the horrors it contemplates in the language its time fortuitously gives it.

—Fred Sedgwick

SWENSON, May. American. Born in Logan, Utah, 28 May 1919. Educated at Utah State University, Logan, B.A. 1939. Editor, New Directions, publishers, New York, 1959-66. Poet-in-Residence, Purdue University, Lafayette, Indiana, 1966-67; University of North Carolina, Greensboro, 1968-69 and 1975; Lethbridge University, Alberta, 1970, and University of California, Riverside, 1973; Hurst Professor, Washington University, St. Louis, Spring 1981. Recipient: Rockefeller Fellowship, 1955, 1967; Bread Loaf Writers' Conference Robert Frost Fellowship, 1957; Guggenheim Fellowship, 1959; William Rose Benét Prize, 1959; Longview Foundation Award, 1959; Amy Lowell Traveling Fellowship, 1960; American Academy Award, 1960; Ford Fellowship, for drama, 1964; Brandeis University Creative Arts Award, 1966; Utah State University Distinguished Service Gold Medal, 1967; Lucy Martin Donnelly Fellowship, Bryn Mawr College, 1968; Shelley Memorial Award, 1968; National Endowment for the Arts grant, 1974; Academy of American Poets Fellowship, 1979; Bollingen Prize, 1981. Member, American Academy; Chancellor, Academy of American Poets, 1980. Address: 73 The Boulevard, Sea Cliff, New York 11579, U.S.A.

PUBLICATIONS

Verse

Another Animal. New York, Scribner, 1954.
A Cage of Spines. New York, Holt Rinehart, 1958.
To Mix with Time: New and Selected Poems. New York, Scribner, 1963.
Poems to Solve (for children). New York, Scribner, 1966.
Half Sun, Half Sleep: New Poems. New York, Scribner, 1967.
Iconographs. New York, Scribner, 1970.
More Poems to Solve (for children). New York, Scribner, 1971.
New and Selected Things Taking Place. Boston, Little Brown, 1978.

Recordings: *Today's Poets 2*, with others, Folkways, 1968; *The Poetry and Voice of May Swenson*, Caedmon, 1976.

Play

The Floor (produced New York, 1966). Published in *First Stage* (West Lafayette, Indiana), vi, 2, 1967.

Other

The Contemporary Poet as Artist and Critic. Boston, Little Brown, 1964.
The Guess and Spell Coloring Book (for children). New York, Scribner, 1976.

Translator, with Leif Sjöberg, *Windows and Stones: Selected Poems*, by Tomas Tranströmer. Pittsburgh, University of Pittsburgh Press, 1972.

*

Manuscript Collections: Rare Book Room, Washington University Library, St. Louis; Lockwood Library, State University of New York, Buffalo.

Critical Studies: "The Poetry of May Swenson" by Betty Miller Davis, in *Prairie Schooner* (Lincoln, Nebraska), Winter 1960; "About May Swenson" by John Hall Wheelock, in *Wilson Library Bulletin* (New York), January 1962; "One Knows by Seeing" by Richard Moore, in *The Nation* (New York), 10 August 1963; "Turned Back to the Wild by Love" by Richard Howard, in *Tri-Quarterly* (Evanston, Illinois), 1966; "A Ball with Language" by Karl Shapiro, in *New York Times Book Review*, 7 May 1967; "The Art of Perceiving" by Ann Stanford, in *Southern Review* (Baton Rouge, Louisiana), January 1969; "May Swenson" by Alicia Ostriker, in *American Poetry Review* (Philadelphia), March 1978; interview with Karla Hammond, in *Parnassus* (New York), Fall-Winter 1978; "Perpetual Worlds Taking Place" by Dave Smith, in *Poetry* (Chicago), February 1980.

May Swenson comments:

I devise my own forms. My themes are from the organic, the inorganic, and the psychological world. I sometimes tend to create a typographical or iconographic frame for my poems *after* the text is complete.

*   *   *

May Swenson is extremely deft and inventive with sounds and shapes in language. And with that, she is reckless, an attempter of oddities. A juggler and acrobat, she has performed so consistently that her poems find their way into many well known magazines, such as *Harper's*, *The Atlantic*, and *The New Yorker*.

Her agile language has brought fame. Another quality has saved her from the hovering envy of competing writers: she forces her talent into metaphysical attempts and into the service of causes that have solid appeal.

To hear her read to an audience is to become aware of what she has yoked together. Her voice is intense, not at ease—at work. And her surprising, fountaining lines go steadily into their blend of brilliance and integrity. It is the combination that distinguishes her.

She is from the West—Utah. But she has made New York City into her place. An example, an emblem for the foregoing characterizations, is her poem "On Seeing Rocks Cropping Out of a Hill in Central Park" (*Half Sun, Half Sleep*):

Boisterous water arrested, these rocks
are water's body in death.Transparent

water falling without stop makes a wall,
the frenzied soul of rock its white breath.

Dark water's inflated wave, harsh spray
is ghost of a boulder and cave's

marble, agitated drapery. Stillness
water screams for, flying forth,

the body of death. Rock dreams
soul's motion, its hard birth.

—William Stafford

SYMONS, Julian (Gustave). British. Born in London, 30
May 1912. Educated in various state schools. Married Kathleen
Clark in 1941; one son and one daughter (deceased). Has worked
as a shorthand typist, secretary for an engineering company, and
advertising copywriter. Founding Editor, *Twentieth Century
Verse*, London, 1937-39; Reviewer, Manchester *Evening News*,
1947-56; Editor, Penguin Mystery Series, 1974-77. Since 1958,
reviewer for the *Sunday Times*, London. Visiting Professor,
Amherst College, Massachusetts, 1975-76. ·Co-Founder, 1953,
and Chairman, 1958-59, Crime Writers Association; Chairman,
Committee of Management, Society of Authors, 1969-71;
Member of the Council, Westfield College, University of London, 1972-75. Since 1976, President, Detection Club. Recipient
(for fiction): Crime Writers Association Award, 1957, 1966;
Mystery Writers of America Edgar Allan Poe Award, 1961,
1973, and Grand Master Award, 1982; Swedish Academy of
Detection Grand Master Diploma, 1977. Fellow, Royal Society
of Literature, 1975. Agent: Curtis Brown, 162-168 Regent
Street, London W1R 5TA. Address Groton House, 330 Dover
Road, Walmer, Deal, Kent CT14 7NX, England.

PUBLICATIONS

Verse

Confusions about X.   London, Fortune Press, 1939.
The Second Man.   London, Routledge, 1943.
A Reflection on Auden.   London, Poem-of-the-Month Club,
   1973.
The Object of an Affair and Other Poems.   Edinburgh, Tragara
   Press, 1974.
Seven Poems for Sarah.   Edinburgh, Tragara Press, 1979.

Plays

Radio Plays: *Affection Unlimited*, 1968; *Night Ride to Dover*,
1969.

Television Plays: *I Can't Bear Violence*, 1963; *Miranda and a
Salesman*, 1963; *The Witnesses*, 1964; *The Finishing Touch*,
1965; *Curtains for Sheila*, 1965; *Tigers of Subtopia*, 1968; *The
Pretenders*, 1970; *Whatever's Peter Playing At*, 1974.

Novels

The Immaterial Murder Case.   London, Gollancz, 1945; New
   York, Macmillan, 1957.
A Man Called Jones.   London, Gollancz, 1947.
Bland Beginning.   London, Gollancz, and New York, Harper,
   1949.
The Thirty-First of February.   London, Gollancz, and New
   York, Harper, 1950.
The Broken Penny.   London, Gollancz, and New York, Harper,
   1953.
The Narrowing Circle.   London, Gollancz, and New York,
   Harper, 1954.

The Paper Chase.   London, Collins, 1956; as *Bogue's Fortune*,
   New York, Harper, 1957.
The Colour of Murder.   London, Collins, and New York,
   Harper, 1957.
The Gigantic Shadow.   London, Collins, 1958; as *The Pipe
   Dream*, New York, Harper, 1959.
The Progress of a Crime.   London, Collins, and New York,
   Harper, 1960.
The Killing of Francie Lake.   London, Collins, 1962; as *The
   Plain Man*, New York, Harper, 1962.
The End of Solomon Grundy.   London, Collins, and New
   York, Harper, 1964.
The Belting Inheritance.   London, Collins, and New York,
   Harper, 1965.
The Man Who Killed Himself.   London, Collins, and New
   York, Harper, 1967.
The Man Whose Dreams Came True.   London, Collins, 1968;
   New York, Harper, 1969.
The Man Who Lost His Wife.   London, Collins, 1970; New
   York, Harper, 1971.
The Players and the Game.   London, Collins, and New York,
   Harper, 1972.
The Plot Against Roger Rider.   London, Collins, and New
   York, Harper, 1973.
A Three-Pipe Problem.   London, Collins, and New York,
   Harper, 1975.
The Blackheath Poisonings.   London, Collins, and New York,
   Harper, 1978.
Sweet Adelaide.   London, Collins, and New York, Harper,
   1980.
The Detling Murders.   London, Macmillan, 1982; as *The
   Detling Secret*, New York, Viking Press, 1983.
The Name of Annabel Lee.   London, Macmillan, and New
   York, Viking Press, 1983.

Short Stories

Murder! Murder!   London, Fontana, 1961.
Francis Quarles Investigates.   London, Panther, 1965.
*Ellery Queen Presents Julian Symons' How to Trap a Crook and
   Twelve Other Mysteries.*   New York, Davis, 1977.
The Great Detectives: Seven Original Investigations.   London,
   Orbis, and New York, Abrams, 1981.
The Tigers of Subtopia and Other Stories.   London, Macmil-
   lan, 1982; New York, Viking Press, 1983.

Other

A.J.A. Symons: His Life and Speculations.   London, Eyre and
   Spottiswoode, 1950.
Charles Dickens.   London, Barker, and New York, Roy, 1951.
Thomas Carlyle: The Life and Ideas of a Prophet.   London,
   Gollancz, and New York, Oxford University Press, 1952.
Horatio Bottomley.   London, Cresset Press, 1955.
The General Strike: A Historical Portrait.   London, Cresset
   Press, 1957.
The Thirties: A Dream Revolved.   London, Cresset Press,
   1960; revised edition, London, Faber, 1975.
A Reasonable Doubt: Some Criminal Cases Re-examined.
   London, Cresset Press, 1960.
The Detective Story in Britain.   London, Longman, 1962.
Buller's Campaign.   London, Cresset Press, 1963.
England's Pride: The Story of the Gordon Relief Expedition.
   London, Hamish Hamilton, 1965.
Crime and Detection: An Illustrated History from 1840.   Lon-

don, Studio Vista, 1966; as *A Pictorial History of Crime*, New York, Crown, 1966.

Critical Occasions. London, Hamish Hamilton, 1966.

Bloody Murder. London, Faber, 1972; as *Mortal Consequences*, New York, Harper, 1972; revised edition, as *Bloody Murder*, London and New York, Viking Press, 1985.

Between the Wars: Britain in Photographs. London, Batsford, 1972.

Notes from Another Country. London, London Magazine Editions, 1972.

The Tell-Tale Heart: The Life and Works of Edgar Allan Poe. London, Faber, and New York, Harper, 1978.

Conan Doyle: Portrait of an Artist. London, G. Whizzard, 1979.

The Modern Crime Story. Edinburgh, Tragara Press, 1980.

Critical Observations. London, Faber, and New Haven, Connecticut, Ticknor and Fields, 1981.

Tom Adams' Agatha Christie Cover Story (paintings by Tom Adams). Limpsfield, Surrey, Dragon's World, 1981; as *Agatha Christie: The Art of Her Crimes*, New York, Everest House, 1982.

Crime and Detection Quiz. London, Weidenfeld and Nicolson, 1983.

Dashiell Hammett. New York, Harcourt Brace, 1985.

Editor, *An Anthology of War Poetry.* London, Penguin, 1942.

Editor, *Selected Writings of Samuel Johnson.* London, Grey Walls Press, 1949.

Editor, *Selected Works, Reminiscences and Letters*, by Thomas Carlyle. London, Hart Davis, 1956; Cambridge, Massachusetts, Harvard University Press, 1957.

Editor, *Essays and Biographies*, by A.J.A. Symons. London, Cassell, 1969.

Editor, *The Woman in White*, by Wilkie Collins. London, Penguin, 1974.

Editor, *The Angry 30's.* London, Eyre Methuen, 1976.

Editor, *Selected Tales*, by Poe. London and New York, Oxford University Press, 1976.

Editor, *Verdict of Thirteen: A Detection Club Anthology.* London, Faber, and New York, Harper, 1979.

Editor, *The Complete Sherlock Holmes*, by Arthur Conan Doyle. London, Secker and Warburg, and New York, Abrams, 1981.

Editor, *New Poetry 9.* London, Hutchinson, 1983.

Editor, *Classic Crime Omnibus.* London, Penguin, 1984.

*

Manuscript Collection: Humanities Research Center, University of Texas, Austin.

Critical Study: in *Auden and After: The Liberation of Poetry 1930-1941* by Francis Scarfe, London, Routledge, 1942.

*   *   *

Julian Symons's career as a poet was fairly brief (he has only just begun to write poems again) and attracted less notice than his valuable work as editor of *Twentieth Century Verse*, historian, novelist, and critic. But his books of 1939 and 1943 have a great deal more than historical interest. Of his contemporaries, Symons seems temperamentally most akin to Roy Fuller and Alun Lewis. He shared their preference for precise, formal versification; he, too, disliked the emotional excesses of the Apocalyptic poets. And, like Fuller and Lewis, Symons was a man of the left and was young enough for the war, not the depression, to have been the formative influence on his work.

He was not interested in the topical or propagandistic possibilities of verse. Rather, Symons elaborates a view of society which has metaphysical as well as political overtones. In his work the "political" merges with the epistemological to question the meaning of reality and our purchase upon it. He is, like Louis MacNeice, a sharp critic of the bourgeois tendency to evade problems and to live on "islands." But being himself bourgeois, Symons is every bit as quick to identify within himself the lingering romanticism, compromises, and opportunism which he dislikes. His argument is, to a considerable extent, with himself, though set against a backdrop of "dramatic truces" and newspapers which announce war.

His work gives at times a rich feeling of observed life, of the joys of the ordinary universe: "The twopenny bookstall bargains, the automaton wireless,/ The complete sets of dead magazines, the held hand/ In the cinema, the smackable bouncing blonde." At his best, in the excellent "Clapham Common" in *The Second Man*, Symons demonstrates considerable power of psychological insight, and effective use of symbols. But far too often his struggles are with epistemological uncertainty: "What seems/ To be real is unreal." In another poem a precise description of a pub is followed by "This moment exists and is real." When in "Whitsun 1940" he writes "Our compensation is the sense of touch,/ Convincing tyros that the real is real," the effect is to deepen the confusion. He does not possess a truly philosophic mind, and in the end one regrets that he did not leave metaphysics to the metaphysicians and write more persistently about that "real" world around him. There was, as well, a political dimension to his impasse:

If I could give power to
My burning thoughts! This ink turn acid and the pen
Become a gun: pointed against the murderers,
The corrupt class, the scum
Of a top-heavy civilisation:
If I could extinguish the voice that says
Man can endure corruption and be happy.

But such reflections are not quite poetry. His best work appears in *The Second Man*, in poems like "Clapham Common" in which there is complex, exploratory openness to subjective experience and memory. Symons's work gives us a distinct sense of the conflict between the subjective traditions of lyric poetry, and the political conscience in an age of crisis: "for me the spring advances and the unlimited/ Areas of conflict remain outside, the problems of action/ And honesty are still unreconciled." It may be that the decision to give up writing poetry came out of an excessively strong respect for its integral wholeness, a wholeness which the divided consciousness can seldom locate.

—Eric Homberger

SZIRTES, George. British. Born in Budapest, Hungary, 29 November 1948. Educated at Kingsbury County Grammar School, 1960-68; Harrow School of Art, 1968-69; Leeds College of Art, 1969-72, B.A. in fine art 1972; Goldsmiths' College, London, 1972-73. Married Clarissa Upchurch in 1970; one son and one daughter. Part-time teacher in colleges and schools, 1973-75; Head of Art, Hitchin Girls School, Hertfordshire, 1975-81. Since 1981, Head of Art, St. Christopher School,

Letchworth, Hertfordshire. Proprietor, Starwheel Press, Hitchin. Recipient: Faber Memorial Prize, 1980; Arts Council grant, 1983. Fellow, Royal Society of Literature, 1982. Address: 20 Old Park Road, Hitchin, Hertfordshire SG5 2JR, England.

PUBLICATIONS

Verse

Poems. Leeds, Perkin, 1972.
The Iron Clouds. Hitchin, Hertfordshire, Dodman Press, 1975.
Visitors. Hitchin, Hertfordshire, Mandeville Press, 1976.
An Illustrated Alphabet. Hitchin, Hertfordshire, Mandeville Press, 1977.
A Mandeville Troika, with Neil Powell and Peter Scupham. Hitchin, Hertfordshire, Mandeville Press, 1977.
At the Sink. London, Keepsake Press, 1978.
Silver Age. Hitchin, Hertfordshire, Dodman Press, 1978.
The Slant Door. London, Secker and Warburg, 1979.
Sermon on a Ship. Hitchin, Hertfordshire, Dodman Press, 1980.
Homage to Cheval. Berkhamsted, Hertfordshire, Priapus, 1980.
November and May. London, Secker and Warburg, 1981.
The Kissing Place. Hitchin, Hertfordshire, Starwheel Press, 1982.
Short Wave. London, Secker and Warburg, 1983.

Other

Editor, *A Starwheel Portfolio, The Transparent Room, Strict Seasons, Spring Offensive, Cloud Station, States of Undress* (verse and etching portfolios). Hitchin, Hertfordshire, Starwheel Press, 6 vols., 1978-84.

*

Critical Studies: reviews by Peter Porter, in *The Observer* (London), 19 August 1979, 22 January 1984; Christopher Hope, in *London Magazine*, March 1980; William Palmer, in *Poetry Review* (London), December 1981; Carol Rumens, in *Quarto* (London), February 1982; Ian Bamforth, in *Edinburgh Review*, Spring 1982; Tim Dooley, in *Times Literary Supplement* (London), 13 January 1984; Michael Hulse, in *Literary Review* (London), January 1984.

George Szirtes comments:

I think that at whatever point the reader picks up my poetry he will find a conflict between two states of mind. The first is delighted by the possibility of happiness, the second lives in apprehension of disaster. The early poems in *The Slant Door* often used pictures as starting points in order to freeze events on the edge of some drama. Elsewhere they took apparently domestic circumstances and set them in a wider, wilder context. Nearly always the subject matter was (and is) human and intimate. The characters in the poems tend to inhabit rooms of flats in cities rather than natural scenery. Often though, the reader will find another reality behind the surfaces presented. The sensuous surfaces (and many people have commented on the intensely visual nature of my imagery) often provide the delight or happiness, the world below is often a cause of terror.

In "The Birdsnesters," for example, a poem from my second book, three ordinary enough shepherds set out to find the new Christ whose birth has been foretold them in a vision which they do not fully trust. They stop by a colony of pigeons and spend the night killing them in a brilliantly lit tableau. This has the force of a religious experience but it results in the shepherds giving up their quest. The unresolved balance between beauty and terror is set here in a narrative context. The book *November and May* has its share of hauntings. However, I tend to rebel against the solemnity of horror, through humour. In *Short Wave* the tragedies witnessed by the artist in "Goya's Chamber of Horrors" are accompanied by a teasing of Goya himself for his tendency to dramatise both himself and the horror he deals in. The title of the book refers to my Hungarian background and to the world of the European imagination.

I am at present an "English" poet whose first language was not English. I think this can sometimes lead to misunderstanding. Whatever comfort or tenderness there is in my poetry is snatched comfort, snatched tenderness. The English language is now my language, but England is my second home. My sympathies are with Europe broadly, and with England and Hungary specifically.

I don't think I am a difficult poet particularly in the later poems. I enjoy formal devices of metre and rhyme and I try to keep my diction as clear as the subject allows. I am not a "university" poet but, I hope, an intelligent one, and a human one in whom ideas, things, affections as well as delights and fears can meet without hysteria on one side or cosiness on the other. Writing the poems is a delicate balancing act: it's nice sometimes to dance along the tightrope and make a few extravagant gestures. I like the idea of poetry as a dangerous, true, and memorable entertainment.

*   *   *

His early training as a student of Fine Art has helped shape George Szirtes's poetry in ways more subtle than are usually appreciated by literary assessors unused to drawing accurate parallels and distinctions between the two arts. Szirtes is not conspicuously a visual poet, one who sees the surface of the world with a painter's eye and whose descriptions of it are therefore more detailed. Interestingly, his career as a poet has coincided with the rise to prominence of the "Martian" school of poetry, but he has not been attracted to this "cartouche" way of celebrating visual likenesses. He has, indeed, a good eye, but it is the shape made by thought and the composed structure of language he has stressed in his poems. A poem may be invented almost as if it were being planned on squared-up paper, and it is one of Szirtes's strengths that his poetry recognizes that since words are symbols, ideas are just as much true gifts to the poet as scenes and objects.

Szirtes's Hungarian origins (he came to England at the age of eight with his parents in 1956) may have given him a wider range of sympathies (Surrealism, perhaps, and a fondness for fables and folk legends), but a deeply rooted English tradition lies behind much of his work. While a student at Leeds he came under the influence of the late Martin Bell, a poet of great erudition and a brilliant translator from the French. From Bell, and later from his own reading and involvement in English literature, Szirtes took a central path—the vision of the English mystic including the Caroline Poets, Smart, Blake, and Samuel Palmer. Much of his verse is set indoors, in the lush wonderland of the domestic hearth, full of voices, furniture, bric-à-brac, and the remembrance of dreams. His first book, *The Slant Door*, is lulled by a dreamy resonance which occasionally overpowers the syntax and structure of the verse. Its Surrealist tone is never obtrusive, though it can be surprising, as in "The Bird Cage, 1851," where a genre scene of a girl stooping to kiss and pout at a caged bird in a conservatory becomes an image of immanent menace:

> The glass is vibrant with its rainbows; flowerpots
> Perched sullenly on the rough sill glow brick-red.
> The bird's small feet are sharp and her beak cuts
> The pouted fruitage of the lady's head.

November and May and *Short Wave* show how strongly Szirtes's talent has developed. His latest poems add a dramatic force to the richness of their language, and he is now master of traditional forms, stanzas, regular metres, etc., as well as freer tropes. He has a fine and corrosive wit and rather unexpectedly produces many excellent parodies and satires. Examples are "The Cosmo Guide to Culture," "Homage to the Postman Cheval," and "Slow Tango for Six Horses."

It is difficult to place Szirtes in the league of today's poets, as can be seen from his exclusion from such a taste-setting anthology as Morrison's and Motion's *Penguin Book of Contemporary British Poetry*. Serious readers, however, have reason to believe that Szirtes's talent is one of the strongest of all. Few poets in Britain under the age of forty have achieved as much, and none suggests a richer garnering in the future.

—Peter Porter

TAGLIABUE, John. American. Born in Cantu, Como, Italy, 1 July 1923. Educated at Columbia University, New York, B.A. 1944 (Phi Beta Kappa), M.A. in art and literature 1945, 1947-48; University of Florence, Italy (Fulbright Scholar), 1950-52. Married Grace Ten Eyck in 1946; two daughters. Lecturer in American Poetry, American University of Beirut, Lebanon, 1945-46, and Washington State College, Pullman, 1946-47; Assistant Professor of American Literature, Alfred University, New York, 1948-50; Fulbright Lecturer in American Poetry, University of Pisa, Italy, 1950-52, Tokyo University, Japan, 1958-60, and Fudan University, Shanghai, China, 1984. Member of the English Department, 1953-58, Associate Professor, 1960-71, and since 1971, Professor of English, Bates College, Lewiston, Maine. Formerly, Poet-in-Residence, Bennett College, Greensboro, North Carolina, International Institute of Madrid, Spain, University of Rio Grande do Norte, Natal, Brazil, and Anatolia College, Thessalonika, Greece. Recipient: Bates College grant, 1969. Address: 12 Abbott Street, Lewiston, Maine, 04240, U.S.A.

PUBLICATIONS

Verse

Poems. New York, Harper, 1959.
A Japanese Journal. San Francisco, Kayak, 1966.
The Buddha Uproar. San Francisco, Kayak, 1967.
The Doorless Door. Tokyo, Mushinsha Press, 1970.
Every Minute a Ritual. Lewiston, Maine, Grace Tagliabue, 1973.
The Great Day: Poems 1962-1983. Plainfield, Indiana, Alembic Press, 1984.

Plays

Mario in the Land of the Unicorn [the Green Queen] (puppet plays), in *Carolina Quarterly* (Chapel Hill, North Carolina), Spring and Summer, 1964.

Other puppet plays produced and published.

*

Manuscript Collection: George Arents Research Library, Syracuse University, New York.

John Tagliabue comments:

(1970) Poetry is all a matter of design, play, ritual, decorations, symbolism, and like our life it is always changing. I have been writing poems for many years and my moods and styles have changed—sometimes as I see new places, new people, get new suggestions—and yet something which at the moment I can't say in prose doesn't seem to change. I like poems and dances to help make us realize many festivals, all kinds of holidays.

(1985) Often and there are thousands of them, written in many moods, in many centuries, in many religions and love affairs, the poems speak, sing, dance, celebrate for themselves-and-others. I must let it go at that now. The many Travel Journals that I've been keeping might help; they are related to the USA and Italy, Spain, France, England, Greece, Turkey, Yugoslavia, Lebanon, Syria, Mexico, Guatemala, Brazil, Peru, Japan, Nepal, India, People's Republic of China, and some other places.

*   *   *

John Tagliabue is an unashamedly happy poet, content—too—to be an inexorably minor one. In an age of what Robert Graves once called "posterity-conscious heavyweights" this is no bad thing; but one has to add that many of Tagliabue's poems, charming though they are, are almost too insubstantial to make their presence felt at all. They tend to blow away before one has finished reading them: "Mountain/of Chinese noodles,/heaven for a poor man." This is too obvious, too matter-of-fact, to achieve the true quality of the kind of miniaturist Japanese poetry that has so entranced and influenced this author. Many attempts, of course, have been made to carry over this quality into English verse, and very few of them have succeeded. It is perhaps unfortunate that Tagliabue has confined so much of his poetic intention to the effort. When he becomes more thoughtful he is not only enchanted by life (which is the chief, and attractive, feature of his verse as a whole) but also enchanting, as in "Friendship"

> Sleep sat next to me
> Like a man on the subway.
> Sleep said, Write a poem.
> I said, You are a poem.
> Sleep was my friend.
> Always between places
> we are closing our eyes
> and growing. We are
> always going towards
> each other or poetry.
> Sleep said, Have I written you?
> You said, I am sleepy.

—Martin Seymour-Smith

TARN, Nathaniel. American. Born in Paris, France, 30 June 1928. Educated at Cambridge University, B.A. (honours) 1948, M.A. 1952; the Sorbonne and Ecole des Hautes Etudes, Paris, Cert. C.F.R.E.; University of Chicago, M.A. 1952, Ph.D. 1957; London School of Economics; School of Oriental and African Studies, University of London. Divorced: two children; married Janet Rodney in 1981. Has worked as an anthropologist in Guatemala, Alaska, and Burma. Formerly, Member of the Faculty, University of Chicago, and University of London; Visiting Professor, State University of New York, Buffalo, and Princeton University, New Jersey, 1969-70. Since 1970, Professor of Comparative Literature, Rutgers University, New Brunswick, New Jersey. Visiting Professor, University of Pennsylvania, Philadelphia, 1976, and Jilin University, China, 1982. General Editor, Cape Editions, and director, Cape Goliard Limited, publishers, London, 1967-69. Recipient: Guinness Prize, 1963; Commonwealth of Pennsylvania Fellowship, 1984. Address: 96 New Street, New Hope, Pennsylvania 18938, U.S.A.

PUBLICATIONS

Verse

Old Savage/Young City. London, Cape, 1964; New York, Random House, 1965.
Penguin Modern Poets 7, with Richard Murphy and Jon Silkin. London, Penguin, 1966.
Where Babylon Ends. London, Cape Goliard Press, and New York, Grossman, 1968.
The Beautiful Contradictions. London, Cape Goliard Press, 1969; New York, Random House, 1970.
October: A Sequence of Ten Poems Followed by Requiem Pro Duabus Filiis Israel. London, Trigram Press, 1969.
The Silence. Milan, M'Arte, 1970.
A Nowhere for Vallejo: Choices, October. New York, Random House, 1971; London, Cape, 1972.
Lyrics for the Bride of God: Section: The Artemision. Santa Barbara, California, Tree, 1973.
The Persephones. Santa Barbara, California, Tree, 1974.
Lyrics for the Bride of God. New York, New Directions, and London, Cape, 1975.
Narrative of This Fall. Los Angeles, Black Sparrow Press, 1975.
The House of Leaves. Santa Barbara, California, Black Sparrow Press, 1976.
From Alashka: The Ground of Our Great Admiration of Nature, with Janet Rodney. London, Permanent Press, 1977.
The Microcosm. Milwaukee, Membrane Press, 1977.
Birdscapes, with Seaside. Santa Barbara, California, Black Sparrow Press, 1978.
The Forest, with Janet Rodney. Mount Horeb, Wisconsin, Perishable Press, 1978.
Atitlan/Alashka: New and Selected Poems, with Janet Rodney. Boulder, Colorado, Brillig Works Press, 1979.
The Land Songs. Plymouth, Blue Guitar, 1981.
Weekends in Mexico. London, Oxus Press, 1982.
The Desert Mothers. Grenada, Mississippi, Salt Works Press, 1984.
At the Western Gates. Santa Fe, Tooth of Time Press, 1984.

Other

Editor and Translator with others, *Con Cuba: An Anthology of Cuban Poetry of the Last Sixty Years.* London, Cape Goliard Press, and New York, Grossman, 1969.

Editor and Translator with others, *Selected Poems: A Bilingual Edition,* by Pablo Neruda. London, Cape, 1970; New York, Delacorte Press, 1972.

Translator, *The Heights of Macchu Picchu,* by Pablo Neruda. London, Cape, 1966; New York, Farrar Straus, 1967.
Translator, *Stelae,* by Victor Segalen. Santa Barbara, California, Unicorn Press, 1969.

*

Critical Studies: in *Le Belle Contradizzioni,* Milan, Munt Press, 1973; "Nathaniel Tarn Symposium" in *Boundary 2* (Binghamton, New York), Fall 1975; "The House of Leaves" by A. Kingsley Weatherhead, in *Credences 4* (Kent, Ohio), 1977; Ted Enslin and Rochelle Ratner, in *American Book Review 2* (New York), no. 5, 1980; *Translating Neruda* by John Felstiner, Stanford, California, Stanford University Press, 1980; "America as Desired: Nathaniel Tarn's Poetry of the Outsider as Insider" by Doris Sommer, in *American Poetry 1* (Albuquerque), no. 4, 1984.

Nathaniel Tarn comments:

Poetry for me is the discovery of a sound which arises out of unimpeded listening. The sound, once recognized, can assume a number of voices; my life-history happens to have given me no convincing English of my own. I have always been fascinated by the interplay between restricted and elaborated codes, between common parlances and formal rhetorics. Form is usually allowed to grow out of content, though I am aware of moving towards more and more open form as I discover that there is less and less that *cannot* be discussed in poetry. In the early work my anthropological experience prompted me to speak out of various personae associated with *Old Savage*; an old, wise Amerindian or Melanesian, aware of what our culture has done to his, forgiving, sad at his own destruction principally because it mirrors the destruction of the whole natural earth. Dropping anthropology as a profession has enabled me to speak as an anthropologist and add the dialectic of observer and observed to the previous one-dimensional picture. As a result, politics have become a major factor in recent work such as *The Beautiful Contradictions*. This complex material is offset by simple lyrical-erotic sequences such as occur in *October*. The aim is to work towards more and more satisfactory resolutions of the tension between simplicity and complexity.

We may be living at a time when only the exasperation of contradictions is possible for the artist; synthesis is closed to him because of the intolerable weight of new information he must shoulder each day. In this situation, poetry is more than ever a discipline, the means whereby a poet not only discovers, but literally creates, himself out of the total flux. Silence is more than poetry's complement: it is that which poetry must sink back into the moment it ceases to perform this function. It follows that poetry for poetry's sake—decoration *et al.*—is intolerable.

Translation is (i) a duty within the Republic of Letters; (ii) a way of allowing various voices to speak; (iii) a means of letting air into the stale bed of English letters. Editorial activity is an extension of translation, not only from languages but from disciplines. *Transformation* is a key concept, linking early allegiances to Surrealism with present interests in Structuralism.

*   *   *

I remember on the shores of the most beautiful lake in the world
whose name in its own language means abundance of waters

as if the volcanoes surrounding it had broken open the
    earth
there in the village of Saint James of Compostela one cold
    night
not the cereus-scented summer nights in which a voice I
    never traced
sang those heartbreaking serenades to no one known
a visiting couple gave birth in the market place
the father gnawing the cord like a rat to free the child
and before leaving in the morning they were given the
    freedom of the place

I mean the child was given

A child of nowhere, Nathaniel Tarn has been given, and has
given himself, a freedom of place that is rare among contemporary poets. Anglo-French by birth, a dual citizen, his childhood
was bilingual, and he was educated on both sides of the Channel.
In the 1950's and 1960's he had a short career as a (self-described)
"25th-rate" French surrealist poet, and a more successful run as
an up-and-coming young English poet: an associate of the literary group called "The Group," and editor of the extraordinary
Cape Editions. Furthermore, he was an anthropologist, a student of Lévi-Strauss and Griaule in Paris and Redfield in Chicago, writing monographs on the Atitlan region of Guatemala.
And he was a Buddhist scholar, author of, among other writings,
a book on the monastic politics of Burma. In 1970 Tarn followed
his literary affinities and moved to the United States where, at the
moment—always subject to sudden metamorphosis—he is an
American poet and citizen, a professor of comparative literature,
and a Mayanist. As an anthropologist he continues to write on
Guatemala, and as a Buddhist scholar he is involved with the
Tibetan diaspora.

This range of Tarn's is mirrored, in his four major book-length
poems, in a poetry of place where the place is always changing
(The Beautiful Contradictions); a love poetry where the object of
desire undergoes countless transformations (Lyrics for the Bride
of God); and a deeply personal poetry which the poet allows to
be spoken by others (A Nowhere for Vallejo, which is a collage of
lines and invented lines by the Peruvian poet, in Spanish and
English translation, mingled with the voice of "Tarn"; and
Alashka, written with Janet Rodney, and perhaps the century's
only collaborative poem which does not identify the individual
contributions). Moreover the poetry has, in the poet's words,
frequent "unconscious thrusts, sudden irruptions into the body
of the work, almost like spirit-cult possessions," where the poet
speaks in other voices, and sometimes other languages.

What holds it together is Tarn's ecstatic vision, his continuing
enthusiasm for the stuff of the world. It is a poetry whose native
tongue is myth, and it rolls out in long lines of sacred hymns that
oscillate between the demotic and the hieratic (heir to Smart and
Blake, to Whitman and the Neruda of The Heights of Macchu
Picchu, which he translated) and sequences of short poems, small
linked bursts of sharp image and speech, which tie Tarn to
Williams and contemporary practitioners like Snyder and Kelly.

Since the death of Kenneth Rexroth, he is the major celebrant
of heterosexual love in the language. His combination of ingenious metaphor and sexual exuberance has not been heard in
English since the 17th century. (Indeed, much of Tarn's American work may be read as an epic elaboration of Donne's erotic
geography of the "new found land.") Like Rexroth, he is the
author of travel narratives that restore the adjective "readable"
to poetry. And, like Rexroth and MacDiarmid, his poetry
encompasses Eastern philosophy, world myth, revolutionary
politics, and precise descriptions of the natural world. His poems
have more birds than Clare's.

Not an exile, longing for the abandoned home, but a nomad,
longing for the idea of home: it is the American condition, and
the Jewish condition. Tarn, both American and Jewish, has
declared that sparagmos ("the falling to pieces/the tearing to
pieces/of the world as body") is "the inescapable theme of our
time." (And he can, at times, be as indignant as Pound at the
destroyers of culture and of the wilderness.) His poetry, along
with that of few others these days, sets course for a mythical
unity: the hierosgamos, marriage of earth and sky, when history
will be forever in the present tense, somewhere will be everywhere, and the author everyone:

            ...that the branch may break
    that the long voyage may end for the planet
    and the furthest point of death be returned from
    the separation into dead and live
    summer and winter, and only green be seen above ground
                that he might go home

                                                —Eliot Weinberger

---

TATE, James (Vincent). American. Born in Kansas City,
Missouri, 8 December 1943. Educated at the University of Missouri, Kansas City, 1963-64; Kansas State College, Pittsburg,
B.A. 1965; University of Iowa, Iowa City, M.F.A. 1967. Visiting
Lecturer, University of Iowa, 1965-67, and University of Cali-
fornia, Berkeley, 1967-68; Assistant Professor, Columbia University, New York, 1969-71, and Emerson College, Boston, 1970-
71. Since 1971, Member of the English Department, University
of Massachusetts, Amherst. Since 1967, Poetry Editor, Dickinson Review, North Dakota. Currently, Associate Editor, Pym
Randall Press, Cambridge, Massachusetts, and Barn Dream
Press; Consultant, Coordinating Council of Literary Magazines.
Recipient: Yale Series of Younger Poets Award, 1966; National
Endowment for the Arts grant, 1968, 1969; American Academy
award, 1974; Guggenheim Fellowship, 1976. Address: Department of English, University of Massachusetts, Amherst, Massachusetts 01002, U.S.A.

PUBLICATIONS

Verse

Cages. Iowa City, Shepherds Press, 1966.
The Destination. Cambridge, Massachusetts, Pym Randall
    Press, 1967.
The Lost Pilot. New Haven, Connecticut, Yale University
    Press, 1967.
The Torches. Santa Barbara, California, Unicorn Press, 1968;
    revised edition, 1971.
Notes of Woe. Iowa City, Stone Wall Press, 1968.
Mystics in Chicago. Santa Barbara, California, Unicorn Press,
    1968.
Camping in the Valley. Chicago, Madison Park Press, 1968.
Row with Your Hair. San Francisco, Kayak, 1969.
Is There Anything. Fremont, Michigan, Sumac Press, 1969.
Shepherds of the Mist. Los Angeles, Black Sparrow Press,
    1969.
The Oblivion Ha-Ha. Boston, Little Brown, 1970.
Amnesia People. Girard, Kansas, Little Balkans, 1970.

Deaf Girl Playing.   Cambridge, Massachusetts, Pym Randall Press, 1970.
Are You Ready Mary Baker Eddy?, with Bill Knott.   San Francisco, Cloud Marauder Press, 1970.
The Immortals.   Santa Barbara, California, Unicorn Press, 1970.
Wrong Songs.   Cambridge, Massachusetts, Halty Ferguson, 1970.
Hints to Pilgrims.   Cambridge, Massachusetts, Halty Ferguson, 1971; revised edition, Amherst, University of Massachusetts Press, 1982.
Nobody Goes to Visit the Insane Anymore.   Santa Barbara, California, Unicorn Press, 1971.
Absences: New Poems.   Boston, Little Brown, 1972.
Apology for Eating Geoffrey Movius' Hyacinth.   Santa Barbara, California, Unicorn Press, 1972.
Viper Jazz.   Middletown, Connecticut, Wesleyan University Press, 1976.
Riven Doggeries.   New York, Ecco Press, 1979.
The Land of Little Sticks.   Worcester, Massachusetts, Metacom Press, 1982.
Constant Defender.   New York, Ecco Press, 1983.

Novel

Lucky Darryl, with Bill Knott.   New York, Release Press, 1977.

Short Stories

Hottentot Ossuary.   Cambridge, Massachusetts, Temple Bar Bookshop, 1974.

                                              *

Manuscript Collection: Humanities Research Center, University of Texas, Austin.

James Tate comments:
     I am in the tradition of the Impurists: Whitman, Williams, Neruda.... I am trying to combine words in such a way as to lend a new life, a new hope, to that which is lifeless and hopeless. If the vision in the poems is occasionally black, it is so in order to see more clearly the fabric of which that blackness is made, and thereby understand the source. If the source is understood, there is the possibility of correcting it.
     In my poems it seems one of the recurring themes must be the agony of communication itself: despair and hatred are born out of this failure to communicate. The poem is man's noblest effort because it is utterly useless.
     I use the image as a kind of drill to penetrate the veils of illusion we complacently call the Real World, the world of shadows through which we move so confidently. I want to split that world and release the energy of a higher reality. There is nothing I won't do because I see a new possibility each day.

                          *   *   *

     In 1967, then 23 years old, James Tate won the Yale Series of Young Poets award for his first book, *The Lost Pilot.* The bored world of contemporary American poetry was jolted: one so young doesn't often gain such recognition, and the foreword by Dudley Fitts said Tate "sounds...like no one I have ever read— utterly confident, with an effortless elegance of control, both in diction and in composition, that would be rare in a poet of any age and that is particularly impressive in a first book."

More than most of his peers, Tate understands the magic of language itself as distinguished from language that seeks to share the magic of ideas. *The Lost Pilot* bore out the claims of the foreword, but in spite of all the fine use of language, only a few of the poems take on enough substance to stick. Those which most closely reveal Tate retain the elegance, and subtance shadows charm. The poet's imagination, like a circus, offers both a fun house and the house of horrors. The title poem, an elegy to his father (1922-1944), addresses conceptions of "father" and stereotypes of astronauts, as well as a cosmological question involving worlds. It is a poem that stretches for, and attains, true importance.
     Within two years of *The Lost Pilot*, Tate had another dozen collections in print or accepted for publication (surely a record of sorts), and the critics began to make their claims and demands. Maybe if he could write good poems younger than anyone else, he could also get wisdom sooner. At an age when many writers benefit from neglect, Tate was busy with public readings and what must have been a gratifying if insatiable demand for his new poems.
     Most amazing of all this is how gracefully Tate rode it out. He seemed to enjoy himself, and to be aware of the position he was in. At the same time, there were poems like "The Hermit" whose final, second quatrain casts a shadow on what we consider to be required sociability: "From the mountainside,/I watch their fallen faces/rise, and scarcely believe/the luck I have had." A question surfaces: how much of grace is just plain tact? What wear is done to the soul in the name of manners?
     Enough of claims and demands. Tate has already written some extraordinary poems; he has an energy of language that may well demand over-production, imagination flooding and sometimes drowning sensibility. The resulting poems can be heavily imagistic, flashy, and confusing, like the two-line "Flushing & Swarming": "She dreamed of excreting white plankton/then woke with a hiccup of white hatchets." The poem seems to center on the idea of white excrement; the difference between dream and reality, however, is not this impossible color, but the substance. Who "she" is, why she would have such a strange experience, and of what importance it all is, Tate charateristically neglects to mention.
     Tate's more recent work has taken a fascinating turn towards the depth suggested by "The Lost Pilot," where the imagination is trained on credible events, however zany. Here are the opening lines of "Apology for Eating Geoffrey Movius' Hyacinth":

> It has come to this,
> a life of uncalculated passion
> for the barely wriggling throb
> of the invisible tube of force
> that manufactures a laugh
> for smothering pentagons,
> fructifying useless poems,
> and salvaging broken-hearted penguins.

It may be Tate's concept that the laugh can smother a pentagon, his idea of "useless poems" that fortify an attitude of unchecked absurdity.
     When he abandons this stance, to write openly of himself and those people he loves, he demonstrates the self-awareness that balances him between redemption and the curse of prodigal attention ("The Blue Canyon"):

> To be something different like a brussels sprout
> it's as if we were ants so far away
> made of charcoal made of dust,
> good enough to erase and coming down

if I had not grown up dissolving into
the swan the way they think of me.

To retain this balance requires the abundance of grace which he
alone so naturally has.

—Geof Hewitt

TAYLOR, Andrew (McDonald).   Australian.   Born in Warr-
nambool, Victoria, 19 March 1940. Educated at Scotch College,
Melbourne, graduated 1957; University of Melbourne, 1958-61,
B.A. (honours) 1961, M.A. 1971. Married 1) Jill Burriss in 1964
(divorced, 1978), one son; 2) Beate Josephi, one daughter. Tutor,
1962-63, and Lockie Fellow, 1966-68, University of Melbourne;
teacher, British Institute, Rome, 1964-65; American Council of
Learned Societies Fellow, State University of New York, Buffalo, 1970-71. Lecturer, 1971-74, and since 1975, Senior Lecturer
in English, University of Adelaide. Address: Department of English, University of Adelaide, Adelaide, South Australia 5001,
Australia.

PUBLICATIONS

Verse

The Cool Change.   Brisbane, University of Queensland Press,
   1971.
Ice Fishing.   Brisbane, University of Queensland Press, 1973.
The Invention of Fire.   Brisbane, University of Queensland
   Press, 1976.
The Cat's Chin and Ears: A Bestiary.   Sydney, Angus and
   Robertson, 1976.
Parabolas: Prose Poems.   Brisbane, Makar Press, 1976.
The Crystal Absences, The Trout.   Sydney, Island Press, 1978.
Selected Poems 1960-1980.   Brisbane, University of Queens-
   land Press, 1982.

Other

Editor, *Byron: Selected Poems.*   Melbourne, Cassell, 1971.
Editor, with Ian Reid, *Number Two Friendly Street.*   Adelaide,
   Adelaide University Union Press, 1978.

*

Manuscript Collection: National Library of Australia, Canberra.

Andrew Taylor comments:
   (1980) Looking back across them, I find that my poems are
about the ordinary things of life: they grow out of such things as
happiness, a response to the weather, and the more traumatic
occurrences that a normal life is prey to: breakup of a marriage,
separation from a child, a new being in love, travel, etc. The
larger historical dramas and the political scenarios aren't for me.
   On the other hand, I don't see my poetry as particularly
domestic. I try to convey the way the mundane particulars of my
life, because they're so pressing to me, conform to larger patterns
that express common experience and give it importance. As a
result my poems are an attempt at finding the myth within which
we live. (Lévi-Strauss suggests that the number of myths is small,

but the forms they take almost infinite.) My poems are thus the
result of a lot of listening to what's within me.
   I've tried to make colloquial speech say what it rarely says in
talk. This has meant moving away from the more formal phrasing and cadences of my first book towards a plainer speech that
says more interesting things. This has also meant a move toward
longer poems—toward multiples though, rather than narratives.
   I suppose you could say I'm a city poet rather than a rural or a
nature poet, even though the country and the sea are an inexhaustible source of images for me. It's in cities that, for me
anyway, most life is lived. I find that in Australia it's still possible
to live in a city without totally losing touch with the country.
   (1985) Supplement: since writing the above I have travelled
extensively and am continuing to do so. This has inevitably had
some effect on my poetry, although I have tried to maintain its
Australian quality.

*   *   *

   Andrew Taylor was one of the principal Australian participants at a 1979 poetry seminar, at Macquarie University,
entitled, "The American Model." His paper on early influences
showed he is one of the several Australian poets aged about 40
for whom the surprises in the formative reading of their teens
and twenties came from United States poets, and who have
shown this influence in an increasing freedom with verse forms,
and an increasing openness to personally-associative progressions within the poem. Taylor has absorbed these lessons the
more readily because, from the very beginning of his published
poetry, his has been an emotionally interpreted world.
   The early poems are remarkable for the poet's alertness. They
are copiously detailed, in their rendering of places and of moods.
The forms are solid and richly-worked—long stanzas, discursive
chunks of 20 lines or more, often the three-beat Eliot line.
There's openness in a willing use of rhyme, which rarely comes
into tyrannical prominence. The academic emerges in a well-
bred air of being always informed, but Taylor's real business is
listening for the personal suggestiveness that living gives to
things. Accordingly, his voice is never raised; the tone is intimate. The tenderness of his love poems is distinctive—as in "the
fur coat." His second book deliberately explores the breaking-up
of form. In its five parts, the last three referring to a stay in the
United States, there are several sequences of short numbered
segments. Although the poems derive their clearest human
appeal from crises in relationships—the death of a father, a love
affair—Taylor keeps his world rich with things and weathers and
is liable at any moment to let a gentle, rather introverted humour
play among them.
   Perhaps his most tonally ambitious work is the Cathedral
section of *The Invention of Fire,* a celebration of continuing life
in love and art. The sequence works very differently from the
"Beyond Silence" assemblages of tiny poems, which have
attracted much notice. The nine Cathedral poems have wide
literary and historical reference, tend to lyrical but intense conclusions, and only (it seems) by lack of vigilance and sudden
pressure allow a nakedly personal cry to emerge:

> The whole roof
> bursts into earth
> at the (careful
> of skin cancer you say)
> touch of summer
>
> villages have burnt like banknotes
> for the profit of sunburn lotion

& you've taken our son away

in the vault's wreckage
small pieces of sky
glitter.

The latest book is a sustained love-discourse written over two months. *The Crystal Absences, The Trout* is particularly fluid, a continuous, eager, and intimate communication of memories—notes on present happenings and emotions—and the straining towards a reunion. It is extraordinarily difficult to represent it by quotation. Here the laboured solidity of Taylor's early manner has quite gone, his quick attentiveness has achieved a form suitably mobile. The play of moods is not trivial, and a Protean short line and Taylor's optimism and unaffectedness keep even intense perceptions from weighing and slowing the poem:

a life in the world
        a barefoot
and sure walk over stones
the *feel* of a place we know
because it's now thoroughly ours
thus thoroughly other
and can never be known
                ourselves
at home in that mystery
                Parsifal's
divine stupidity
        a shaman's
trust in flight
        a man's
and a woman's trust in each other
a child's confidence in love.

It will be interesting to see whether Taylor continues within the tonal limits his writing has so far mostly accepted.

—Judith Rodriguez

THOMAS, D(onald) M(ichael). British. Born in Redruth, Cornwall, 27 January 1935. Educated at Redruth Grammar School; University High School, Melbourne; New College, Oxford, B.A. (honours) in English, 1958, M.A. Served in the British Army (national service), 1953-54. Has two sons and one daughter. Teacher, Teignmouth Grammar School, Devon, 1959-63; Senior Lecturer in English, Hereford College of Education, 1964-78. Visiting Lecturer in English, Hamline University, St. Paul, Minnesota, 1967; Creative Writing Teacher, American University, Washington, D.C., 1982. Recipient: Richard Hillary Memorial Prize, 1960; Cholmondeley Award, 1978; *Guardian*—Gollancz Fantasy Novel prize, 1979; Los Angeles *Times* prize, for fiction, 1981; Silver Pen Award, 1982. Address: 10 Greyfriars Avenue, Hereford HR4 OBE, England.

PUBLICATIONS

Verse

Personal and Possessive. London, Outposts, 1964.
Penguin Modern Poets 11, with D.M. Black and Peter Redgrove. London, Penguin, 1968.

Two Voices. London, Cape Goliard Press, and New York, Grossman, 1968.
The Lover's Horoscope: Kinetic Poem. Laramie, Wyoming, Purple Sage, 1970.
Logan Stone. London, Cape Goliard Press, and New York, Grossman, 1971.
The Shaft. Gillingham, Kent, Arc, 1973.
Lilith-Prints. Cardiff, Second Aeon, 1974.
Symphony in Moscow. Richmond, Surrey, Keepsake Press, 1974.
Love and Other Deaths. London, Elek, 1975.
The Rock. Knotting, Bedfordshire, Sceptre Press, 1975.
Orpheus in Hell. Knotting, Bedfordshire, Sceptre Press 1977.
The Honeymoon Voyage. London, Secker and Warburg, 1978.
Dreaming in Bronze. London, Secker and Warburg, 1981.
Selected Poems. London, Secker and Warburg, and New York, Viking Press, 1983.
News from the Front, with Sylvia Kantaris. Todmorden, Lancashire, Arc, 1983.

Plays

Radio Plays: *You Will Hear Thunder*, 1981; *Boris Godunov*, from play by Pushkin, 1984.

Novels

The Flute-Player. London, Gollancz, and New York, Dutton, 1979.
Birthstone. London, Gollancz, 1980.
The White Hotel. London, Gollancz, and New York, Viking Press, 1981.
Ararat. London, Gollancz, and New York, Viking Press, 1983.
Swallow. London, Gollancz, and New York, Viking Press, 1984.

Other

The Devil and the Floral Dance (for children). London, Robson, 1978.

Editor, *The Granite Kingdom: Poems of Cornwall.* Truro, Cornwall, Barton, 1970.
Editor, *Poetry in Crosslight.* London, Longman, 1975.
Editor, *Songs from the Earth: Selected Poems of John Harris, Cornish Miner 1820-84.* Padstow, Cornwall, Lodenek Press, 1977.

Translator, *Requiem, and Poem Without a Hero*, by Anna Akhmatova. London, Elek, and Athens, Ohio University Press, 1979.
Translator, *Way of All the Earth*, by Anna Akhmatova. London, Secker and Warburg, and Athens, Ohio University Press, 1979.
Translator, *Invisible Threads*, by Evtushenko. New York, Macmillan, 1981.
Translator, *The Bronze Horseman and Other Poems*, by Pushkin. London, Secker and Warburg, and New York, Viking Press, 1982.
Translator, *A Dove in Santiago*, by Evtushenko. London, Secker and Warburg, 1982; New York, Viking Press, 1983.
Translator, *You Will Hear Thunder*, by Anna Akhmatova. London, Secker and Warburg, 1985.

*

D.M. Thomas comments:

(1974) My poetry does not move far from love and death. Early poems (see *Penguin Modern Poets 11*) use science fiction themes as images of desire and separation. More recently, my most obsessive themes have been sexuality, family deaths and a search for lost roots.

*   *   *

To follow the work of D.M. Thomas from his first Outpost booklet, *Personal and Possessive*, through to his latest collection, *Dreaming in Bronze*, is to encounter an impressive development and variety. The early erotic poetry gives way to the series of science fiction poems which established his reputation, and then moves on to a poetry of a more subtle and tender exploration of relationships and emotions. He is a poet who keeps his readers on the alert, never quite knowing what to expect next. In *The Honeymoon Voyage* we find robust reworkings of Brazilian and Japanese myths together with poems which hark back to his family and roots in Cornwall. One is reminded of Fernando Pessoa, the Portuguese poet who invented three other poets to write in modes other than his own, for Thomas could well do the same if he was so minded.

Yet for all Thomas's versatility there is a common factor in his work. Thomas is essentially a narrative poet. He is more than that, of course, but he can maintain a narrative flow and thrust which carry the reader along. It is this which gives his science-fiction poems their strength, and in this he reminds us of the Victorian narrative poets and especially Browning in such SF monologues as "Tithonus," "Cygnus," and "Hera's Spring." They are, in addition, remarkably atmospheric poems, not only in their exotic settings, but in the depth of feeling they convey of desire and separation: "Believe me, dear, thought it will seem strange/to you, I have wept too for all these/things you mention" ("Hera's Spring").

Yet even in his shorter poems it is the narrative thread, however tenuous, which holds them together and helps to give them unity and coherence. It is the same narrative skill which finds him adapting style, language, and rhythm to match the characters and situations he depicts. For Thomas is a fine craftsman and his style, while often deceptively unobtrusive, is clearly adapted and related to his subject matter. A case in point is "Under Carn Brea," a series of Cornish portraits ranging from the ribald Mona—"Groaned, bumped and thumped and showed how far/Snapped suspenders sank back in the fat./'I'n it shameful!' Whooped her anguish"—to the gentle depths of the understanding of Perry who was to become a near recluse on the death of her husband: "It would have been a shocking waste of life/But it was Perry's self, and nothing else." This is true also of his prose: witness the superb pastiche of Sigmund Freud's style in *The White Hotel*.

In *Dreaming in Bronze* we find a strongly personal element emerging so that even in his historical reconstructions Thomas's own memories and experiences intrude and merge to construct his own highly charged and sensual fables. The dangers of an emotionally erotic self-indulgence are inherent in this and can be observed in such poems as "Big Deaths, Little Deaths." But it is this element of risk which makes D.M. Thomas one of the more exciting poets writing today. At his best his talent for a creative empathy and selective use of detail succeeds in evoking the complex of emotions which underlie the situations of which he writes.

—John Cotton

THOMAS, R(onald) S(tuart). Welsh. Born in Cardiff, Glamorgan, 29 March 1913. Educated at County School, Holyhead; University College, Bangor; St. Michael's College, Llandaff; University of Wales, Cardiff, B.A. in classics 1935. Married Mildred Eldridge in 1940; one son. Ordained Deacon, 1937, Priest, 1937: Curate of Chirk, Denbigh, 1936-40; Curate of Hanmer, Flintshire, 1940-42; Rector of Manafon, Montgomery, 1942-54; Vicar of St. Michael's, Eglwysfach, Denbigh, 1954-67, and of St. Hywyn, Aberdaron, with St. Mary, Bodferin, 1967-78; Rector of Rhiw, with Llanfaelrhys, 1972-78. Recipient: Heinemann Award, 1955; Queen's Gold Medal for Poetry, 1964; Welsh Arts Council award, 1968, 1976; Cholmondeley Award, 1978. Address: Sarn-y-Plas, Y Rhiw, Pwllheli, Gwynedd, Wales.

PUBLICATIONS

Verse

The Stones of the Field. Carmarthen, Druid Press, 1946.
An Acre of Land. Newtown, Montgomeryshire Printing Company, 1952.
The Minister. Newtown, Montgomeryshire Printing Company, 1953.
Song at the Year's Turning: Poems 1942-1954. London, Hart Davis, 1955.
Poetry for Supper. London, Hart Davis, 1958; Chester Springs, Pennsylvania, Dufour, 1961.
Judgement Day. London, Poetry Book Society, 1960.
Tares. London, Hart Davis, and Chester Springs, Pennsylvania, Dufour, 1961.
Penguin Modern Poets 1, with Lawrence Durrell and Elizabeth Jennings. London, Penguin, 1962.
The Bread of Truth. London, Hart Davis, and Chester Springs, Pennsylvania, Dufour, 1963.
Pietà. London, Hart Davis, 1966.
Not That He Brought Flowers. London, Hart Davis, 1968.
Pergamon Poets 1, with Roy Fuller, edited by Evan Owen. Oxford, Pergamon Press, 1968.
Postcard: Song. N.p., Fishpaste, 1968.
The Mountains. New York, Chilmark Press, 1968.
H'm: Poems. London, Macmillan, and New York, St. Martin's Press, 1972.
Selected Poems 1946-1968. London, Hart Davis MacGibbon, 1973; New York, St. Martin's Press, 1974,
What Is a Welshman? Llandybie, Dyfed, Christopher Davies, 1974.
Laboratories of the Spirit. London, Macmillan, 1975; Boston, Godine, 1976.
The Way of It. Sunderland, Ceolfrith Press, 1977.
Frequencies. London, Macmillan, 1978.
Between Here and Now. London, Macmillan, 1981.
Poet's Meeting. Stratford-upon-Avon, Celandine, 1983.
Later Poems: A Selection. London, Macmillan, 1983.

Other

Words and the Poet (lecture). Cardiff, University of Wales Press, 1964.
Young and Old (for children). London, Chatto and Windus, 1972.
Selected Prose, edited by Sandra Anstey. Bridgend, Glamorgan, Poetry Wales Press, 1983; Chester Springs, Pennsylvania, Dufour, 1984.

Editor, *The Batsford Book of Country Verse.* London, Batsford, 1961.
Editor, *The Penguin Book of Religious Verse.* London, Penguin, 1963.
Editor, *Selected Poems*, by Edward Thomas. London, Faber, 1964.
Editor, *A Choice of George Herbert's Verse.* London, Faber, 1967.
Editor, *A Choice of Wordsworth's Verse.* London, Faber, 1971.

*

Critical Studies: in *Welsh Anvil* (Llandybie), 1949, 1952; *Critical Quarterly* (Manchester), ii, 4, 1960; *A Review of English Literature* (Leeds), iii, 4, 1960; in *Anglo-Welsh Review* (Pembroke Dock, Wales), xiii, 31, 1963; *R.S. Thomas* by R. George Thomas, London, Longman, 1964; "R.S. Thomas Issue" of *Poetry Wales* (Llandybie), Winter 1972; *R.S. Thomas* by William Moelwyn Merchant, Cardiff, University of Wales Press, and Mystic, Connecticut, Verry, 1979; *Yeats, Eliot, and R.S. Thomas: Riding the Echo* by A.E. Dyson, London, Macmillan, 1981; *Critical Writings on R.S. Thomas* edited by Sandra Anstey, Bridgend, Glamorgan, Poetry Wales Press, 1982.

*   *   *

R.S. Thomas's calling is pastoral in a double sense, as a minister in the Welsh hill-country concerned with the spiritual salvation of his parishioners, and as a poet preoccupied with their figurative redemption in verse. This is pastoral poetry with a sour edge to it, set in a bleak, eroded landscape—"The marginal land where flesh meets spirit/Only on Sundays and the days between/Are mortgaged to grasping soil." Thomas is aware of the parochiality of this world, where "the hedge defines/The mind's limits," and he knows that, lost in "the dark wood" of such life, the search for "the path/To the bright mansions" expresses not so much a religious need as the desperation of minds denied all hope of earthly consolation. His response is both forthright and yet strangely equivocal. In *The Minister*, a dramatic verse narrative for radio, he explores the inadequate Protestantism of ministers such as Morgan, "Condemned to wither and starve in the cramped cell/Of thought their fathers made them," courageous but callow absolutists unable to comprehend "the soul's/Terrible impotence in a warm world," finally defeated by the "sly/Infirmities" of their flock. Poetry, for Thomas, in its large, forgiving gestures, recovers the love "our science has disinfected"—the last refuge of charity in a secularized world. Yet at the same time, poetry sets a rigorous standard. In "Reservoirs," for example, Thomas sees the material causes of Wales' decline, and "the English/Scavenging among the remains/Of our culture." But he is not content to rest there. As the real reservoir is a source of sustenance to English towns at the expense of drowned Welsh villages, so the "serenity" of Welsh landscape and culture has become "a pose/For strangers, a watercolour's appeal/To the mass" only with Welsh complicity, and "the poem's/Harsher conditions" here become a reproach to the compromises and hypocrisies for which, throughout his poems, he castigates his fellow-countrymen.

Thomas's peasants—Walter Llywarch, Job Davies, or Iago Prytherch ("Just an ordinary man of the bald Welsh hills/Who pens a few sheep in a gap of cloud")—transcend their particularity primarily because of his own unease with them. Prytherch for example reveals "something frightening in the vacancy of his mind" which shocks "the refined,/But affected, sense with...stark naturalness," and it is precisely this which makes him a "proto-

type" of human endurance. In "The Face" the memory of a man ploughing on the bare hillside becomes a symbol of that "long wrestling with the angel/Of no name" which is not just theological despair but the hard economic facts of life, which outlast the changing "tenancies of the fields." But Thomas is here aware of the extent to which he *is* creating a symbol in "the mind's gallery." He recognizes, too, without sentimentality, the dereliction, depletion, and shabbiness of this fallen world, seeing, in "Funeral," the grudges and the gossip, the "incidence of pious catarrh/At the grave's edge," and acknowledging, in "Welsh Landscape," the "sham ghosts" of an "impotent people," "Worrying the carcase of an old song." For all his passionate Welshness he knows that, in the end, there is only one Kingdom, and a mere accident of nature endowed him with "the absurd label/Of birth, of race hanging askew/About my shoulders" ("Welsh Testament"). In "Here" he writes of the self as a tree, fixed now, but looking back from its topmost branches to the "footprints that led up to me," finally opting (because he must) to "stay here with my hurt." Staying "in the place I happened to be" is for Thomas the true calling: an acknowledgment of fallenness which allows the soul to struggle against contingency. "In Church" catches the poet/minister searching for God in an empty church, no sound in the darkness except that "of a man/Breathing, testing his faith/On emptiness, nailing his questions/One by one to an untenanted cross." Like those other castaways "Clinging to their doomed farms" ("Those Others") he finds belief in the very moment of doubt, "Trying to understand" why, even when there were so many places to be born, "This was the cramped womb/At last took me in/From the void of unbeing." It is a measure of the quiet sophistication of Thomas's faith, as of his poetry, that the phrase "took me in" can live with its dangerous ambiguities. Like "Taliesin 1952," the poet, "Knowing the body's sweetness, the mind's treason," can still affirm, in his desperate faith, "a new world, risen,/Stubborn with beauty, out of the heart's need."

—Stan Smith

THWAITE, Anthony (Simon).** British. Born in Chester, Cheshire, 23 June 1930. Educated in Leeds; Sheffield; the United States, 1940-44; at Kingswood School, Bath; Christ Church, Oxford, B.A. (honours) 1955, M.A. 1959. Military Service, 1949-51. Married Ann Harrop (i.e., the writer Ann Thwaite) in 1955; four daughters. Visiting Lecturer in English Literature, Tokyo University, Japan, 1955-57; radio producer, BBC, London, 1957-62; Literary Editor, *The Listener*, London, 1962-65; Assistant Professor of English, University of Libya, Benghazi, 1965-67; Literary Editor, *New Statesman*, London, 1968-72; Visiting Professor, University of Kuwait, 1974. Since 1973, Co-Editor, *Encounter*, London. Recipient: Richard Hillary Memorial Prize, 1967; Henfield Writing Fellowship, University of East Anglia, Norwich, Summer 1972; Cholmondeley Award, 1983. Fellow, Royal Society of Literature, 1978. Address: The Mill House, Low Tharston, Norfolk NR15 2YN, England.

PUBLICATIONS

Verse

(Poems). Oxford, Fantasy Press, 1953.
Home Truths. Hessle, Yorkshire, Marvell Press, 1957.

The Owl in the Tree: Poems. London, Oxford University Press, 1963.

The Stones of Emptiness: Poems 1963-66. London, Oxford University Press, 1967.

Penguin Modern Poets 18, with A. Alvarez and Roy Fuller. London, Penguin, 1970.

Points. London, Turret, 1972.

Inscriptions: Poems 1967-72. London, Oxford University Press, 1973.

Jack. Hitchin, Hertfordshire, Cellar Press, 1973.

New Confessions. London, Oxford University Press, 1974.

A Portion for Foxes. London, Oxford University Press, 1977.

Victorian Voices. Oxford and New York, Oxford University Press, 1980.

Telling Tales. Sidcot, Somerset, Gruffyground Press, 1983.

Poems 1953-1983. London, Secker and Warburg, 1984.

Other

Essays on Contemporary English Poetry: Hopkins to the Present Day. Tokyo, Kenkyusha, 1957; revised edition, as *Contemporary English Poetry: An Introduction*, London, Heinemann, 1959; Chester Springs, Pennsylvania, Dufour, 1961.

Japan in Colour, photographs by Roloff Beny. London, Thames and Hudson, and New York, McGraw Hill, 1967.

The Deserts of Hesperides: An Experience of Libya. London, Secker and Warburg, and New York, Roy, 1969.

Poetry Today 1960-1973. London, Longman, 1973; revised edition, as *Poetry Today: A Critical Guide to British Poetry 1960-1984*, 1985.

Roloff Beny in Italy, with Peter Porter. London, Thames and Hudson, and New York, Harper, 1974.

Beyond the Inhabited World: Roman Britain (for children). London, Deutsch, 1976; New York, Seabury Press, 1977.

Twentieth-Century English Poetry. London, Heinemann, and New York, Barnes and Noble, 1978.

Odyssey: Mirror of the Mediterranean, photographs by Roloff Beny. London, Thames and Hudson, and New York, Harper, 1981.

Editor, with Hilary Corke and William Plomer, *New Poems 1961*. London, Hutchinson, 1961.

Editor, and Translator with Geoffrey Bownas, *The Penguin Book of Japanese Verse*. London, Penguin, 1964.

Editor, with Peter Porter, *The English Poets: From Chaucer to Edward Thomas*. London, Secker and Warburg, 1974.

Editor, *Poems for Shakespeare 3*. London, Globe Playhouse, 1974.

Editor, with Fleur Adcock, *New Poetry 4*. London, Hutchinson, 1978.

Editor, *Larkin at Sixty*. London, Faber, 1982.

Editor, with Howard Sergeant, *The Gregory Awards Anthology 1981-1982*. Manchester, Carcanet, 1982.

Editor, with John Mole, *Poetry 1945 to 1980*. London, Longman, 1983.

Editor, *Six Centuries of Verse*. London, Thames TV-Methuen, 1984.

*

Manuscript Collection: Brynmor Jones Library, University of Hull.

*   *   *

Paradox confronts the reader in the work of Anthony Thwaite.

A man with strong domestic ties, yet impelled to uproot himself in search of new horizons. A creature of habit, but resenting it, inwardly longing for a change of scene. A modern poet, with a deep and abiding sense of the past. A formal, austere artist, troubled by a lurking unease. An inveterate collector, who admits to the futility of life. Thwaite sets down his contradictions with dispassionate honesty, blending them into a body of work striking in its range and conviction, at once urbane and challenging.

Collecting is the most obvious of his traits, described and mulled over in several poems. Wherever Thwaite goes, he takes "luggage" with him, as "Personal Effects" testifies ("an affluent magpie in a nest that creaks/With impedimenta"). In "The Antiquarian" he asks himself the reason for this compulsive hoarding, and finds no definite answer. Further reading suggests that in fact these random collections of objects serve him as evidence of the physical world, and more subtly as talismans, proofs, and reminders of past ages. By them, history is made a continuum, where the endless cycle of man's rise, brief glory, and inevitable fall are mirrored in a pattern of centuries. This linking of past and present in one unbroken sequence enables Thwaite to unite them in "The Letters of Synesius," the laconic epistles of the 4th-century bishop interwoven with the poet's current asides, barbarian invaders given modern parallels as tourists and oil tycoons. This ability to project himself into a figure from the past surfaces again in *Victorian Voices*, a series of monologues by factual and fictitious personalities of the age. Thwaite excels in these portraits, whether presenting the children's author drawing homilies from nature, the doomed rebellion of a novelist's wife, or the engaging roguery of the anonymous Irish beggar. *Victorian Voices* is possibly the most sustained of Thwaite's collections, and undeniably impressive, but one hesitates to call it his best. A certain sameness of tone denies it that range and diversity characteristic of the poet's finest work.

Thwaite is fascinated by history and its message, decoded from the archaeological fragments he assembles. Burrowing in the ruins of Jamestown, eyeing the crumbling cliff-edges of Dunwich, he finds proof of mankind's fragility, the slow wearing away of all things under the pressure of time. The images reappear in "The Stones of Emptiness," the desert boulders of the title-poem that emphasize the wilderness ("They define the void. They assert/How vast the distance are, featureless, bare..."). "Dust" is seen as the one unalterable substance, the common denominator to which everything must be reduced. Musing on the customs of Japanese and North Africans, juxtaposing in his mind the Roman and Axis armies who fought vainly over the same stretch of desert, Thwaite's lines pulse with images of death—buzzards above Cyrene, scraps of uniform and skulls among the thorns. To the passing tourist, the Arab street vendor may—at a price—supply meaning of a kind ("for fifty piastres I give you a past to belong to"), but for the poet this is no answer. Closer to home, he clings to the security he has, the treasured litany of objects in "At the Ironmonger's," the welcome respite of domesticity outlined in "The Simple Life." Nothing, though, remains stable for long. Thwaite's daughter, once defined in earlier poems, in "Called For" is growing away from him to womanhood, loved yet distant. Change leads inexorably to death and dissolution, the dark menace of which underlies his calmest thoughts. His poetry is a shield against it, the elegant, ordered syllables warring with its terrifying illogic. Still, it breaks through. A caring, compassionate man, troubled by slaughtered cows or captured minnows, Thwaite reads from them his and mankind's fate ("as if creation's prodigal act/Shrank to this empty jam-jar at the end"). In "The Unnamable" and "By the Sluice" Thwaite reveals the nature of his fear, in two of the most intensely charged of all his poems, the latter in particular bringing home the shock of foreseen mortality: "What have I hidden here, or let go, lost,/ With less to come than's gone, and so much gone?/ Under the gate the river slams its door."

—Geoff Sadler

TILLER, Terence (Rogers). British. Born in Truro, Cornwall, 19 September 1916. Educated at Latymer Upper School, Hammersmith, London; Jesus College, Cambridge (Chancellor's Medal, 1936), B.A. (honours) in history 1937, M.A. 1940. Married Doreen Hugh Watson in 1945; two daughters. Research Scholar and Director of Studies, 1937-39, and University Lecturer in Medieval History, 1939, Cambridge University; Lecturer in English History and Literature, Fuad I University, Cairo, Egypt, 1939-46. Radio writer and producer, Features Department, 1946-65, and Drama Department, 1965-76, BBC, London. Recipient: Cholmondeley Award, 1980. Lives in Roehampton, London. Address: c/o Chatto and Windus Ltd., 40-42 William IV Street, London WC2N 4DF, England.

PUBLICATIONS

Verse

Poems. London, Hogarth Press, 1941.
The Inward Animal. London, Hogarth Press, 1943.
Unarm, Eros. London, Hogarth Press, 1947.
Reading a Medal and Other Poems. London, Hogarth Press, 1957.
Notes for a Myth and Other Poems. London, Hogarth Press—Chatto and Windus, 1968.
That Singing Mesh and Other Poems. London, Hogarth Press—Chatto and Windus, 1979.

Plays

The Death of Adam (produced Edinburgh, 1950).
The Vision of Piers Plowman, adaptation of the poem by Langland (broadcast, 1980). London, BBC Publications, 1981.

Radio Writings: hundreds of features and plays, including the following plays: *The Wakefield Shepherds' Play* and *Play of Noah,* 1947-48; *The Death of a Friend,* 1949; *The Cornish Cycle of Mystery Plays,* 1949-62; *Lilith,* 1950; *The Tower of Hunger,* 1952; *The Parlement of Foules,* from the work by Chaucer, 1958; *Final Meeting,* 1966; *The Carde of Fancie,* from the work by Robert Greene, 1966; *The Diversions of Hawthornden,* 1967; *The Assembly of Ladies,* 1968; *Zeus the Barnstormer,* 1969; *After Ten Years,* from a work by C.S. Lewis, 1969; *The Flower and the Leaf,* 1970; *The Batchelar's Banquet,* from a work by Thomas Dekker, 1971; *Four of a Kind,* from a work by Verlaine, 1975; *Madame Aubin,* from a work by Verlaine, 1976; *The Defence,* from the novel by Nabokov, 1979; *The Vision of Piers Plowman,* from the poem by Langland, 1980; *The Romance of the Rose,* from the poem by Chaucer, 1982; *Ladies Lost and Found,* from the poems *The Book of the Duchess* and *The House of Fame* by Chaucer, 1984.

Other

Editor, with others, *Personal Landscape: An Anthology of Exile.*

London, Editions Poetry London, 1945.
Editor, with Anthony Cronin and Jon Silkin, *New Poems 1960.* London, Hutchinson, 1960.
Editor and Translator, *Confessio Amantis (The Lover's Shrift),* by John Gower. London, Penguin, 1963.
Editor and Co-Translator, *The Inferno,* by Dante. London, BBC, 1966; New York, Schocken, 1967.
Editor, *Chess Treasury of the Air.* London, Penguin, 1966.

*

Terence Tiller comments:

I am a poet only in so far as my other interests and occupations are *coloured* by my being a poet. Of course I look at history, novels, music, radio, etc., *differently* because of that. But I don't, and can't, and would never have been able to, earn my living as a poet.

I have been called, and am willing to call myself, "a modern metaphysical." Certainly, I have been more influenced by the "metaphysicals" than by any other poets except Dante and Rilke. Minor, sometimes transient, influences, include obvious names like Hopkins, Eliot, early-to-middle Auden. Most of *them* would/ would have disown/disowned me! As far as verse-form is concerned, I tend almost exclusively towards the "traditional," while allowing myself such "license" as I need for specific purposes. I feel strongly that regular prosody is a "springboard" that a poet abandons at his own risk. (Always provided that he can cope with it! Whatever else I am or am not, I am a *technician* in verse.)

Themes? Almost entirely a-political as far as poetry is concerned—except that poetry and politics involve morality, and I am fairly committed *there* (though not with any "party" or "sectarian" affiliation). I would claim to be a polymath, and to attempt poems as a kind of syncretism of the emotions, speculations, and symbolic coincidences, that arise out of my physical and mental experience.

*   *   *

Terence Tiller's first volume, *Poems,* is immature, but foreshadows certain positive qualities of his later work: the ability, for example, to control complex verse patterns, accomplished rhetoric and an impressive, if cold, heraldic use of imagery. *The Inward Animal* reflects Tiller's experiences as a civilian in the Middle East of the war years, where he was associated with the "Personal Landscape" group: Lawrence Durrell, Bernard Spencer, and Robin Fedden. Flanked by two poems, "Eclogue for a Dying House" and "The Birth of Christ," which attempt in social and religious modes respectively to generalise the pattern of war, exile and single strangeness, the volume's theme in Tiller's own words is to explore the impact of that strangeness which "must have shaken, and perhaps destroyed, many a customary self. There will have been a shocked and defensive rebellion; reconciliation must follow; the birth of some mutual thing in which the old and the new, the self and the alien, are combined after war.... The birth of something at once myself, the new self and 'Egypt' is the 'inward animal.' " Such a dialectic makes the volume sound somewhat more schematised than it actually is, but underlines the fact that Tiller has always applied stratagems in his work and has never minimised the importance of pure craft. Rilke and the Metaphysicals are presences in *The Inward Animal.* Tiller preferred (until his most recent work) assonance to rhyme, using rhyming only when he wished to enact finality. The poems are strongest where they rise from some observed scene or persons, least sensuous when "Egypt" is missing from the record, even if one allows some dramatic cogency in the ordering of individual poems. Once or twice it becomes difficult to distinguish the "metaphysical" idiom from highly accomplished *New Statesman* competition verse:

> The silence that I break was more profound,
> and purer sound
> —as being absent is a kind
> of closer bridal in the mind.

It is difficult to see what purpose this allusiveness achieves. The impact of such poems as "Bathers," "Sphinx," "The Convalescent Party," and "Egyptian Dancer" (interesting to compare with Bernard Spencer's "Egyptian Dancer at Subra": these gifted poets seem on occasion to have tackled topics in collusion) is immediate—and lasting. Another feature of *Inward Animal* is a happy sensuousness that counterpoints the heraldic coldness, arrived at by dense and witty use of figure, perhaps more *concettist* than metaphysical, though Tiller rarely suppresses the tenor of his metaphors. *Inward Animal* abounds with felicities: "the flags that slap his plunging knee,/and the cold stocking of the stream" ("Bathers"), or "and the soft lath of woman bears/a heaven's agonising weight" ("The Incubus"). "Europa," the second of four folk songs, wittily reads a locomotive and its shed as a modern version of a fertility myth and demonstrates Tiller's virtuosity.

Unarm, Eros is perhaps Tiller's finest collection. The bold sensuousness, the wit and enigma of the surface work together. It is difficult to isolate particular triumphs, but perhaps "Perfumes," "Roman Portraits," "Hospital" (compare Spencer's "In a Foreign Hospital"), "Beggar," an example of strict, compassionate observation, and "Image in a Lilac Tree" incise themselves most sharply. *Reading a Medal* contains individual poems as striking as any Tiller has written, but a general impression persists of pressure diffused, lyricism of less intensity, puzzles not altogether worth solving and the impression is more strongly marked in *Notes for a Myth*. Tiller is reported to have remarked that "mere experience is a distraction" (doubtless he meant something more subtle) but one can barely avoid applying this somewhat ironically to his later work, where the tensions, the concrete situations that underlay *The Inward Animal* and *Unarm, Eros* have been gravely attenuated. The poems have tended to become longer, to retreat further into pattern and myth. The social commentator who kept such good company with the introvert has disappeared. But Tiller's poetry has already asserted its own lingering resonances. He remains something of a poet's poet and must always appeal to those who respond to the mystery of the vocation.

—Ian Fletcher

TILLINGHAST, Richard. American. Born in Memphis, Tennessee, 25 November 1940. Educated at the University of the South, Sewanee, Tennessee (Assistant Editor, *Sewanee Review*), A.B. 1962; Harvard University, Cambridge, Massachusetts (Woodrow Wilson Fellow), A.M. 1968, Ph.D. 1970. Assistant Professor of English, University of California, Berkeley, 1968-73; Instructor, San Quentin Prison College Program, 1975-78; Visiting Assistant Professor, University of the South, 1979-80; Briggs-Copeland Lecturer, Harvard University, 1980-83. Since 1983, Professor of English, and Co-Director of the M.F.A. Program, University of Michigan, Ann Arbor. Address: 1317 Granger Avenue, Ann Arbor, Michigan 48104, U.S.A.

PUBLICATIONS

Verse

The Keeper. Cambridge, Massachusetts, Pym Randall Press, 1968.
Sleep Watch. Middletown, Connecticut, Wesleyan University Press, 1969.
The Knife and Other Poems. Middletown, Connecticut, Wesleyan University Press, 1980.
Sewanee in Ruins. Sewanee, Tennessee, University Press, 1981.
Our Flag Was Still There. Middletown, Connecticut, Wesleyan University Press, 1984.

*

Critical Studies: "Five Sleepers" by Robert Watson, in *Poetry* (Chicago), March 1970; "The Future of Confession" by Alan Williams, in *Shenandoah* (Lexington, Virginia), Summer 1970; "At the First Doorway of the Lost Life" by James Atlas, in *Chicago Review*, Autumn 1970; Bruce Bennett, in *New York Times Book Review*, 10 May 1981; Jay Parini, in *Quest*, September 1981; Alan Williamson, in *Parnassus* (New York), Winter 1981; "Reflections on *The Knife*" by Andrea Blaugrund, in *Harvard Advocate* (Cambridge, Massachusetts), December 1981; Paul Breslin, in *New York Times Book Review*, 22 July 1982; Wyatt Prunty, in *Southern Review* (Baton Rouge, Louisiana), Fall 1984.

Richard Tillinghast comments:

I see poetry as a kind of invocation of the spiritual realities inherent in things—the hidden and mysterious significance of colours, sounds, smells, textures. It is something like the speech of animals and plants, if they could speak. As an early, oral, non-rational art, unashamedly archaic in its origins, poetry still carries some of the magic of the early days of the human race. At its best it is consistent with the grace, naturalness, solidity, charm, thrill, and sense of necessity that are found in the earliest human accomplishments: hunting, fire-building, cooking, cultivation of the soil, fishing, and weaving. To mention poetry in the same breath with these things must also remind one of the practice, skill, and expertise that are necessary for the accomplishment of good writing.

*   *   *

Richard Tillinghast's *Sleep Watch* amazed its readers with a startling, ingenious way of seeing things. Here is an animal describing God's bungling of Creation: "Later on when he saw that things had gone wrong/...it rested him to look at us/And I found I could love him in his weakness/as I never could before/the beauty left his face...." Here is "Waking on the Train": "after the commuters/cigars windows being jerked open/your body begins to know it hasn't slept/It thinks of all the parts of itself/that would touch a bed...."

Many of Tillinghast's poems touch on that dream-like area of consciousness between waking and sleeping. Everything real is in doubt, and that may be desirable. "Is everything sliding?" he asks in a poem called "Everything Is Going to Be All Right" and answers himself, "Nothing/to worry about—/Getting lost means sliding in all directions."

The present American fashions in poetry—eastern mysticism, Nature worship, confession—hover dangerously about Tillinghast's work, but they are kept at bay by his delicate obliqueness plus a hawk's eye for metaphor. "I put the cap back onto the pen/the way a court reunites a/ mother and child." "I am alert at once/and think of the cat/coasting on its muscles...."

One of the best poems in *Sleep Watch* is about rising from a childhood illness and confronting the world of health. The poet senses an undefined disappointment in his parents; he has not given them cause to mourn: "For them I am closing the door to the place/where the dead children are stored/where the pets have gone to heaven."

A certain self-consciousness has led Tillinghast to develop his own style. He uses spaces where one would normally expect punctuation, allowing his poem to lie on the page between breathing intervals, like directions for speech. Self-consciousness and sensitivity: there is an abundance of this. It will be interesting to see where Tillinghast goes after having given us this brilliant tour of his complex psyche.

—Anne Stevenson

TOMLINSON, (Alfred) Charles. British. Born in Stoke-on-Trent, Staffordshire, 8 January 1927. Educated at Longton High School; Queens' College, Cambridge, B.A. 1948, M.A.; Royal Holloway and Bedford colleges, University of London, M.A. 1955. Married Brenda Raybould in 1948; two daughters. Lecturer, 1957-68, Reader, 1968-82, and since 1982, Professor of English, University of Bristol. Visiting Professor, 1962-63, and Witter Bynner Lecturer, 1976, University of New Mexico, Albuquerque; O'Connor Professor of Literature, Colgate University, Hamilton, New York, 1967-68; Visiting Professor, Princeton University, New Jersey, 1981; Southey Lecturer, University of Bristol, 1982; Clark Lecturer, Cambridge University, 1982; Kenneth Allott Lecturer, University of Liverpool, 1983. Artist: Individual Shows—Oxford University Press, London, 1972, Clare College, Cambridge, 1975, and Arts Council tour, 1978. Recipient: Bess Hokin Prize, 1956, Levinson Prize, 1960, Oscar Blumenthal Prize, 1960, Union League Civic and Arts Foundation Prize, 1961, Inez Boulton Prize, 1964, and Frank O'Hara Prize, 1968 (*Poetry*, Chicago); University of New Mexico D.H. Lawrence Fellowship, 1963; National Translation Center grant, 1968; Institute of International Education Fellowship, 1968; Cholmondeley Award, 1979. D.Litt.: University of Keele, Straffordshire, 1981; Colgate University, 1981. Fellow, Royal Society of Literature, 1974. Honorary Fellow, Queens' College, Cambridge, 1974. Address: Brook Cottage, Ozleworth Bottom, Wotton-under-Edge, Gloucestershire GL12 7QB, England.

PUBLICATIONS

Verse

Relations and Contraries. Aldington, Kent, Hand and Flower Press, 1951.
The Necklace. Oxford, Fantasy Press, 1955; revised edition, London, Oxford University Press, 1966.
Solo for a Glass Harmonica. San Francisco, Poems in Folio, 1957.
Seeing Is Believing. New York, McDowell Obolensky, 1958; London, Oxford University Press, 1960.
A Peopled Landscape. London, Oxford University Press, 1963.
Poems: A Selection, with Tony Connor and Austin Clarke. London and New York, Oxford University Press, 1964.

American Scenes and Other Poems. London, Oxford University Press, 1966.
The Matachines. Cerillos, New Mexico, San Marcos Press, 1968.
To Be Engraved on the Skull of a Cormorant. London, Unaccompanied Serpent, 1968.
Penguin Modern Poets 14, with Alan Brownjohn and Michael Hamburger. London, Penguin, 1969.
The Way of a World. London, Oxford University Press, 1969.
America West Southwest. Cerillos, New Mexico, San Marcos Press, 1969.
Renga, with others. Paris, Gallimard, 1970; translated by the author, New York, Braziller, 1972; London, Penguin, 1979.
Words and Images. London, Covent Garden Press, 1972.
Written on Water. London, Oxford University Press, 1972.
The Way In and Other Poems. London, Oxford University Press, 1974.
The Shaft. London, Oxford University Press, 1974.
Selected Poems 1951-1974. London, Oxford University Press, 1978.
Oppositions: Debate with Mallarmé for Octavio Paz. Santa Barbara, California, Unicorn Press, n.d.
Stone Speech. Ashington, Northumberland, MidNAG, n.d.
On Water. Ashington, Northumberland, MidNAG, n.d.
The Flood. Oxford and New York, Oxford University Press, 1981.
Airborn/Hijos del Air, with Octavio Paz. London, Anvil Press Poetry, 1981.
Notes from New York and Other Poems. Oxford, Oxford University Press, 1984.

Other

The Poem as Initiation. Hamilton, New York, Colgate University Press, 1967.
In Black and White (graphics). Cheadle, Cheshire, Carcanet, 1976.
Some American: A Personal Record. Berkeley, University of California Press, 1981.
Isaac Rosenberg of Bristol (lecture). Bristol, Bristol Historical Association, 1982.
Poetry and Metamorphosis (lectures). Cambridge and New York, Cambridge University Press, 1983.
The Sense of the Past: Three Twentieth-Century Poet (lecture). Liverpool, Liverpool University Press, 1983.
Translations. Oxford, Oxford University Press, 1983.

Editor, *Marianne Moore: A Collection of Critical Essays.* Englewood Cliffs, New Jersey, Prentice Hall, 1969.
Editor, *William Carlos Williams: Critical Anthology.* London, Penguin, 1972.
Editor, *Selected Poems,* by William Carlos Williams. London, Penguin, 1976.
Editor and Translator, *Selected Poems,* by Octavio Paz. London, Penguin, 1979.
Editor, *The Oxford Book of Verse in English Translation.* Oxford, Oxford University Press, 1980.

Translator, *Versions from Fyodor Tyutchev, 1803-1873.* London, xford University Press, 1960.
Translator, with Henry Gifford, *Castilian Ilexes: Versions from Antonio Machado.* London, Oxford University Press, 1963.
Translator, with Henry Gifford, *Ten Versions from Trilce,* by César Vallejo. Cerillos, New Mexico, San Marcos Press, 1970.

*

Manuscript Collections: British Library, London; State University of New York, Buffalo.

Critical Studies: "Negotiation: American Scenes and Other Poems," in *Essays in Criticism* (Oxford), July 1967, and "Philip Larkin and Charles Tomlinson: Realism and Art," in *The Present Age* edited by Boris Ford, London, Penguin, 1983, both by Michael Kirkham; "The Poetry of Charles Tomlinson," in *Agenda 9* (London), 1970, and "Charles Tomlinson," in *Twentieth Century Poetry*, Milton Keynes, Buckinghamshire, Open University Press, 1976, both by Michael Edwards; Calvin Bedient, in *Eight Contemporary Poets*, London and New York, Oxford University Press, 1974; Michael Schmidt, in *PN Review 5* (Manchester), no. 1, 1977; interview with Alan Ross, in *London Magazine*, January 1981.

Charles Tomlinson comments:

My theme is relationship. The hardness of crystals, the facets of cut glass; but also the shifting of light, energizing weather which is the result of the combination of sun and frost—these are the images for a certain mental climate, components for the moral landscape of my poetry in general. One critic has described that climate as Augustan. But it is an Augustanism that has felt the impact of French poetry—Baudelaire to Valéry—and of modern American poetry. A phenomenological poetry, with roots in Wordsworth and in Ruskin, is what I take myself to be writing. Translation has been an accompanying discipline and so have drawing and painting.

*   *   *

A rootedness in things, an intelligence of eye and ear, have informed Charles Tomlinson's poetry from the beginning. What Donald Davie wrote in his introduction to *The Necklace* (1955) applies with probably greater force to his most recent poetry: "The world of these poems is a public one, open to any man who has kept clean and in order his nervous sensitivity to the impact of shape and mass and colour, odour, texture, and timbre. The poems appeal outside of themselves only to the world perpetually bodied against our senses. They improve that world. Once we have read them, it appears to us renovated and refreshed, its colours more delicate and clear, its masses more momentous, its sounds and odours sharper, more distinct."

Tomlinson is also a visual artist and there is a quality of *seeing*, a beauty derived from a minute observation of particular things, in his finest work. His words exactly fit his objects, whereas bad poetry erects a barrier between our perceptions and external reality. Allied to this is a lack of rhetoric, and a stillness, perhaps exemplifed best in "Farewell to Van Gogh."

But Charles Tomlinson's work has not remained static. In *American Scenes*, there is a quality of *sound* which reinforces and vitalizes what was at times in the early work mere precision of visual description. These poems exemplify Louis Zukofsky's statement: "To see is to inform all speech." The best of these poems grow out of "solitary, sharpened perception" (to quote one of them) in desert places, or the heart of Winter:

Between the graves, you find
a beheaded pigeon, the blood and grain
trailed from its bitten crop, as alien to all
the day's pallor as the raw
wounds of the earth, turned above
a fresh solitary burial.

In the "American Scenes" section of this book, it is the desolation of ghost towns ("Speak of the life that uselessness has unconstrained"), and of the desert that produced some of the most solid and lucid poetry published in England in the sixties. In many of these poems also there is a concern for people. This is particularly present in "Death in the Desert," in memory of an old Hopi doll-maker.

Good poets often discover poets that they are particularly suited to translate and Tomlinson is no exception. His collaboration with Henry Gifford in versions of the Spanish poet Antonio Machado, *Castilian Ilexes*, has enriched English poetry, added a new dimension, and this is the one justification for the translation of poetry. A love of people also permeates these poems. One of the most moving, "Lament of the Virtues and Verses on Account of the Death of Don Guido," is an elegy which has, at the same time, a lightness, hilaritas, that could not have come out of England. It is a creative achievement to have brought this across so that the poem has become part of the English tradition:

The here
and the there,
cavalier,
show in your withered face,
confess the infinite:
the nothingness.
Oh the thin cheeks
yellow
and the eyelids, wax,
and the delicate skull
on the bed's pillow!

In *The Way of a World* and *Written on Water* Tomlinson continues to define his perceptions of people, landscape, air and water. In "Clouds," from the former collection, he has almost overcome the immense difficulties involved in finding adequate words for such intangibles, though here, of course, Shakespeare has excelled him. At times, in Tomlinson's later poetry, there is an over-complexity of language—the vocabulary and sentence structure have the effect of distancing the reader from the subject matter of the poems. But there are several powerful poems in both *The Way of a World* and *Written on Water*, e.g., "The Apparition."

Charles Tomlinson's finest poems are rhythmic units of beauty. They fix moments of heightened perception, of sound and sight, in permanent words. I think particularly here of "The Well," in the Mexican section of *American Scenes*. It is a complete, perfectly balanced statement (consequently it is impossible to substantiate what I am saying by a quotation) while being a complex pattern of things felt with roots extending at the same instant into many areas of experience both past and present.

—William Cookson

TONKS, Rosemary (D. Boswell). British. Born in London. Married. Has lived in West Africa and Pakistan. Poetry Reviewer, BBC European Service.

PUBLICATIONS

Verse

Notes on Cafés and Bedrooms. London, Putnam, 1963.

Iliad of Broken Sentences.   London, Bodley Head, 1967.

Novels

Opium Fogs.   London, Putnam, 1963.
Emir.   London, Adam, 1963.
The Bloater.   London, Bodley Head, 1968.
Businessmen as Lovers.   London, Bodley Head, 1969; as *Love among the Operators,* Boston, Gambit, 1970.
The Way Out of Berkeley Square.   London, Bodley Head, 1970; Boston, Gambit, 1971.
The Halt During the Chase.   London, Bodley Head, 1972; New York, Harper, 1973.

Other

On Wooden Wings: The Adventures of Webster (juvenile). London, Murray, 1948.
The Wild Sea Goose (juvenile).   London, Murray, 1951.

*

Rosemary Tonks comments:

(1970) I have developed a visionary modern lyric, and, for it, an idiom in which I can write lyrically, colloquially, and dramatically. My subject is city life—with its sofas, hotel corridors, cinemas, underworlds, cardboard suitcases, self-willed buses, banknotes, soapy bathrooms, newspaper-filled parks; and its anguish, its enraged excitement, its great lonely joys.

*   *   *

The extravagant ego of Rosemary Tonks's vivacious, heady poetry is a compound of violent opposites, of roles held together not only by a flamboyant imagination but also by a sense of the flagrant contradictions of the city in which that imagination has its origins. Whatever the aspect displayed—street arab, lover, gambler, "gutter lord," dressing-gowned dreamer, or thief—the poet remains the mirror of the city, its gentle lover, tenderly exposing its most painful truths, diamond cutting diamond, until the violence of the city's reaction transforms him suddenly into its tormentor, a blood-stained matador: "the diamond smells blood and gores/The poet in the ribs in self-defence" ("Poet and Iceberg").

Tonks's cities are always cosmopolitan, whether they be London, Paris, Rome, or Istanbul; each has its own flavour, but all are blended together in the experience of a self-acknowledged transient, a bedouin, an inhabitant of hotel corridors. The poet sees the whole city, "the whole/Imperial rubbish heap of wastrels, scullions,/Houris, fauns and bedouin" ("Bedroom in an Old City"); but frames her vision in her own chosen perspective of decadence and decay: "I had/My lodgings in that quarter of the city/Like a cat's ear full of cankered passages" ("Gutter Lord"). Romantically, she revels in squalor glamourised with a Baudelairean exoticism. The oriental imagery of "Gutter Lord" transforms the green slime underfoot: "Like dungeon floors which/Cobras have lubricated/Your time was kept in shiny yawns."

The "Auroras, icy champagnes" of "Escape" can't be savoured by the city palate until they are processed in the city's foul kitchens: "Your soul knows half the flavour/Lies underfoot in dirty flagstones." Poetry, sex, drugs, and alcohol are not the means to transcend the city's foulness but images of its intoxicating ferments. "Bedouin of the London Morning" acknowledges "My (half-erotic) convulsion of loathing/For the night"; the poet leaning against "The Sash Window" forlornly "Eats again

the reek" of a glass she knows she should shatter; "Orpheus in Soho" makes his own hell, deliberately looking for his Eurydice in dingy flesh-markets where she could never be: "there is so little risk of finding her/In Europe's old blue Kasbah, and he knows it."

The poetry lives through a perpetual nostalgia for a stormy adolescence, contrasting black, infernal moods with sudden gushes of refreshing scents ("Oath"); similarly, in "Bedroom in an Old City," squalor has as its focus the sleeping face of "a London minx of seventeen," "a life so young, secret and clean." "Adolescent" fuses the images of adolescent and bohemian, and explores further the nature of adolescence, which it sees as a refusal to be formed, an insistence on staying on the fringes, which produces the feverishly throbbing pulse of "real" life. The delinquent has an original place in history, set apart from all those who accept the uniform of convention. Not only the professionals—gloved surgeon and thief—but also the gloved dandy in his fastidious detachment, the Baudelairean *flâneur*, are spurned for the vandal's attack:

You, who would tame with toolbag or certificate
My shudder...as the east
Drinks diamonds, and the world's born blazing underfoot!
Surgeon and robber learn their touch in the great city,
But I am after heavenly spoil, and it is
As a gloveless trespasser that I desire supremacy.

It's hard to know sometimes what the poet intends us to make of her self-indulgent bohemianism. The masculine personae of some of her poems indicates a certain desire to keep the role at a distance. The self-deprecating title of "April and the Ideas-Merchant" undercuts the self-congratulation of a text which informs us that: "Poets are only at work/...When they live, dream, *bleed*—within an inch of giving in to art"; in "On the Advantage of Being Ill-treated by the World" an imaginative sense of humour deflates all Romantic pretension. Elsewhere, there is evidence of a commitment to the posture alarming in its intensity—not only to the reader, but to the role-player herself. The poetry confesses: "I have been young too long, and in a dressing-gown/My private modern life has gone to waste." Between the lines, "A Few Sentences Away," lurks a sense of the real vacancy which no amount of violent attitudinising can disguise:

Let me *hide*, well away from a past that dreams
Like that. Away from streets that taste of blood and sugar
When the glowing month smashes itself against the hedges
In the dark.

—Jennifer Birkett

TRANTER, John (Ernest).   Australian. Born in Cooma, New South Wales, 29 April 1943. Educated at Moruya Intermediate High School; Hurlstone Agricultural High School, graduated 1960; Sydney University, B.A. 1970. Married Lynette Maree in 1968; one daughter and one son. Asian Editor, Angus and Robertson, publishers, Singapore, 1971-73; radio producer, Australian Broadcasting Commission, Sydney and Brisbane, 1974-77. Recipient: Australia Council Fellowship, 1974, 1978, 1979, 1980, 1982, 1984. Address: 74 Corunna Road, Stanmore, New South Wales 2048, Australia.

PUBLICATIONS

Verse

Parallax and Other Poems.   Sydney, South Head Press, 1970.
Red Movie and Other Poems.   Sydney, Angus and Robertson,
   1972.
The Blast Area.   Brisbane, Makar Press, 1974.
The Alphabet Murders: Notes from a Work in Progress.   Syd-
   ney, Angus and Robertson, 1976.
Crying in Early Infancy: One Hundred Sonnets.   Brisbane,
   Makar Press, 1977.
Selected Poems.   Sydney, Hale and Iremonger, 1982.

Plays

The Man on the Landing (produced Sydney, 1967?).

Radio Plays and Scripts: *Looking for Hunter,* 1974; *Le Morte
d'Arthur,* from the work by Thomas Malory, 1974; *Knight-
Prisoner: The Life of Sir Thomas Malory,* 1974; *Sideshow People,* 1976; *The Poetry of Frank O'Hara,* 1976(?).

Other

Editor, *The New Australian Poetry.*   Brisbane, Makar Press,
   1979.

*

Manuscript Collection: Australian National Library, Canberra.

Critical Studies: "Opening a Murder List" by Alan Gould, in
Nation Review (Melbourne), 4-10 June 1976; "Poems That Go
Angst in the Night" by Martin Duwell, in *The Australian* (Syd-
ney), 11-12 September 1982.

John Tranter comments:
   Australian reviewers have called my work complex, technically assured, cynical, humourless, humorous, too concerned
with avant-garde ideas, conservative, and experimental. Though
I like a poem to be moving, I dislike gush; though I admire wit
and skill, I like to have a good time.

*   *   *

   In 1968 John Tranter achieved publication of a substantial
collection of poems, *Parallax,* through the slightly devious
means of a special issue of the magazine *Poetry Australia.* It was
one way of side-stepping the Commonwealth Literary Fund
(then the major funding body), which had refused support for
this manuscript. It is always easy, in retrospect, to illustrate the
insensitivity of any offical patronising (and funding) body; but,
in the instance of Tranter, it seems extraordinary. *Parallax,*
re-read a decade later, almost bends backwards to present a
conservative front—though with integrity. Its direction, though,
is clearly towards an absorption of the then recently available
American experiments in formal innovation and what has been
termed "Drug culture." *Parallax* remains a reprimand to
orthodox conservatism; the elements that spoke compromise
can now be seen as the least creatively helpful for the young poet,
the elements that pointed towards innovation and genuine
growth were, in fact, modified by the existing cultural climate
but their freshness remains stimulating.
   It was in 1972, and with the publication of his volume *Red
Movie,* that Tranter spelled out the real dimension of his innova-

tive talent. The early poems had shown an eclectic voracity for
stimuli—from Bly to Slessor, from Ginsberg to Beaver—but *Red
Movie* made eclecticism a virtue. *Red Movie* (and especially the
title poem) remains a pivotal experiment in language—in making
language rub against itself, in making it rub against a culture, a
commerce, an environment. Although its surface mimics (perhaps even mocks) current American preoccupations with surreal
and telescopic forms, its essential laconicism is peculiarly Australian. It was succeeded by a follow-up series of poems, some of
them successful, some blatant (and provocative) in their failure,
but Tranter's latest collection, *Crying in Early Infancy,* became,
for the late 1970's, what *Red Movie* was for the first half of the
decade: the quintessential statement. It is sub-titled (significantly
enough) "one hundred sonnets." The renewal of interest in older
forms is part of late-1970's culture, though the deeply ironic
undertones are particularly Australian—and personal. These
"sonnets" are indeed classic in their combination of "sounding
against each other" and sounding upon the admass culture of this
generation. Nothing in Australian writing quite precedes their
constructive use of negative force associations to build up,
finally, a resonance of deep vulnerability. Tranter has, in *Crying
in Early Infancy,* brought what is perhaps the most intelligent
verbal equipment of his generation to a point of creative
breakthrough—and of challenge. The challenge is enormous,
partly because the alternatives now presented to Tranter are so
sharp; his tone of wry mockery may become dangerously brittle;
his cautious exploration of the self self-defeating. He is, essentially, a City poet, thoroughly urban in his preoccupations. No
other poet of his generation is so well equipped to define whole
areas of poetic territory as Tranter; and, possibly, no other so
sharply aware of the risks.

—Thomas W. Shapcott

———————

TREMAYNE, Sydney (Durward).   Scottish.   Born in Ayr, 15
March 1912. Educated at Ayr Academy, 1917-27. Served as a
fireman in London during World War II. Married 1) Lily Hanson in 1931 (marriage dissolved), two sons; 2) Constance Lipop
in 1946. Journalist, *Yorkshire Evening News,* Leeds, 1929, and
for newspapers in Harrogate, Selby, Northampton, Sunderland,
and Newcastle upon Tyne, 1929-38. Staff member, 1938, Chief
Sub-Editor, 1939-48, Leader Writer, 1948-54, and Special Writer, 1969-74, *Daily Mirror,* London. Leader Writer, *Daily
Herald,* 1954-64, and *The Sun,* London, 1964-69. Recipient:
Scottish Arts Council Award, 1970. Address: Peterburn, Gair-
loch, Ross-shire, Scotland.

PUBLICATIONS

Verse

For Whom There Is No Spring.   London, Pendulum Press,
   1946.
Time and the Wind.   London, Collins, 1948.
The Hardest Freedom.   London, Collins, 1951.
The Rock and the Bird.   London, Allen and Unwin, 1955.
The Swans of Berwick.   London, Chatto and Windus-Hogarth
   Press, 1962.
The Turning Sky.   London, Hart Davis, 1969.
Selected and New Poems.   London, Chatto and Windus, 1973.

*

Manuscript Collection: National Library of Scotland, Edinburgh.

Critical Studies: by Austin Clarke, in *Irish Times* (Dublin), 10 December 1955; George Bruce, in *Akros* (Preston, Lancashire), August 1978.

Sydney Tremayne comments:

I have written verse since the age of eleven but did not publish until the Second World War. My poems have arisen out of the need to clarify experience and from pleasure in language. All are written to be heard. I hope, simply, that they speak for themselves.

* * *

Sydney Tremayne at the beginning of his practice as a poet used largely the language of romantic poetry. He never rejected it, nor did he develop an interest in new verse techniques, yet thanks to his genuineness, his literary discrimination, and an ability to recognize those subjects that have a special meaning for him, his poems have a winning freshness and frequently authority. He has a robust and immediate response to the animals that he sees—as it were—at his door, as in "Earth Spirits":

> The world of the young hare
> Is hairy as his milky mother's teat
> Who suckles him and rolls him off his feet,
> Licks him with rapid care,
> Then leaves him with a leap to his own care
> Among forget-me-nots to sit and stare.

He has the genuineness to take this poem no further, but in his poem, "The Fox," he begins with a glimpse of the animal: "Out of the corner of his yellow eye/Glanced round his shoulder. Seeing nothing there/Skirted the tall dry biscuit coloured grass...." He then associates the image with a person, "One who was brave and frightened, fugitive,/Fox coloured hair." The poem ends: "Swiftly comes/The verbal thought how many years she's dead./The fox has slipped away in the dark wood." He has achieved a poise whereby he can use natural imagery (without ever falling for the discredited pathetic fallacy) as a means of disclosing the delicately balanced, sometimes threatened, always isolated life of man in a natural environment. The disclosure is tactfully and tenderly made in "Outposts in Winter": "We two adrift in winter share with birds/Confinement in the dark, that comes,/Silence banked upon silence, stranding words." This poem, from *The Turning Sky*, shows an increasing freedom of movement between fact and idea, a recognition that even the conditioning natural world becomes words in poetry. This flexibility, when applied to the details of the environment, which has been the material of his better poems, has given a new depth to some of the most recent poems, as in "Wanting News":

> Waiting for words to fall into the box
> And ice to drop from hedges, wanting news,
> Missing your voice, cold stillness, builds unease:
> The eye looks round for movement, like a fox.

Some of Sydney Tremayne's poems have been referred to as water colour painting. It is true that some have the merit and limitation of that art. The better poems rebut the allegation. It would seem that after sixty he is in a position to take further the developments of his later poems.

—George Bruce

TRIPP, John. Welsh. Born in Bargoed, Glamorgan, 22 July 1927. Educated at Whitchurch Senior School, Cardiff; Morley College, London, diploma in moral philosophy, 1963. Served in the Royal Army Pay Corps, 1945-48: Sergeant. BBC news researcher and Sub-Editor, London, 1951-58; press officer, Indonesian Embassy, London, 1958-67; information officer, Central Office of Information, London, 1967-69. Literary Editor, *Planet*, Llangeitho Tregaron, 1971-79. Since 1969, free-lance writer, Cardiff. Member, English Language Section, Welsh Academy of Letters. Recipient: Welsh Arts Council bursary, 1969, 1972. Address: 2 Heol Penyfai, Whitchurch, Cardiff CF4 1SB, Wales.

PUBLICATIONS

Verse

Diesel to Yesterday. Cardiff, Triskel Press, 1966.
The Loss of Ancestry. Llandybie, Dyfed, Christopher Davies, 1969.
The Province of Belief. Llandybie, Dyfed, Christopher Davies, 1971.
Bute Park and Other Poems. Cardiff, Second Aeon, 1972.
The Inheritance File. Cardiff, Second Aeon, 1973.
Collected Poems 1958-1978. Swansea, Christopher Davies, 1978.
Penguin Modern Poets 27, with John Ormond and Emyr Humphreys. London, Penguin, 1979.
For King and Country. Swansea, Swansea Poetry Workshop, 1980.
The Road from Los Alamos. Swansea, Element Five, 1982.
Passing Through. Bridgend, Glamorgan, Poetry Wales Press, 1984.

Play

Radio Play: *The Seed of Dismemberment*, 1972.

Short Stories

The Thinskin Award. Barry, Glamorgan, Edge Press, 1978.
Last Day in England. Port Talbot, Glamorgan, Alun, 1979.

*

Manuscript Collections: National Library of Wales, Aberystwyth; Education Authority, Clwyd.

Critical Studies: by Sam Adams, in *Poetry Wales* (Cardiff), 1969; Roland Mathias, in *Anglo-Welsh Review* (Pembroke Dock, Wales), 1970; Charles Elliott, in *Anglo-Welsh Review* (Pembroke Dock, Wales), 1972; "Poetry in Wales" by Glyn Jones, in *British Poetry since 1960: A Critical Survey* edited by Michael Schmidt and Grevel Lindop, Oxford, Carcanet, 1972; Richard Poole, in *Poetry Wales* (Cardiff), Spring 1979; Jeremy Hooker, in *Anglo-Welsh Review 65* (Pembroke Dock, Wales), 1979.

John Tripp comments:

The major themes in my work have to do with Wales, its history and people, from the viewpoint of one who is extremely conscious of his roots. I have tried to create a small document about my country, its harsh past, its difficult present, and its chances for the future — including the preservation of the Welsh language. This subject-matter has often been framed within a tight, terse verse-form which has been described as "tough and steely." (There have also been many references to my wryness, dryness, irony and "gallows humor.") But one has tried to keep a cold eye and a warm heart on the raw material—which is often recalcitrant — to find a union of reason and emotion in pulling away from the sentimental nostalgia and discursive rhetoric of much of the poetry common to the overstating Celt. Our problem has always been one of economy.

I suppose I am still a modern who reeks of the museum, caught between two cultures, and well aware of a vacuum of disinheritance. To my published work has recently been added a series of elegies on other writers, and in my latest collection I cover a wider range of subject-matter.

*   *   *

Most of John Tripp's writing is set in Wales. Like many poets, he is thin in generalization, better in sharp particulars:

Snow mucks to slush, the yellow
streaks of dog piss on the lovewalk,
thin layered frost on their crud
at the trees' base...

Too much of his work consists of praise of the Welsh and denunciation of the English. The insight missing in his simply nationalistic poems comes out when he speaks, not of the Welsh, but of individual Welshmen—Lloyd George, Aneurin Bevan, Jack Jones, and, best of all, R. Williams Parry, whom, in a sustained analogy, he represents as "The Bard of Winter":

He was a careful little man
who looked more like a bank manager
than a bard: chalk-striped
suit, waistcoat, hornrimmed spectacles,
and horror behind the eyes.
In the woods and fields of Gwynedd
he was frightened when he saw the fear
of wood-pigeon, wild fowl, hare and fox...

He was buried on a January day
too cold to lift its head—
a day of honest weather he might have liked
and fitting for a true poet...
On the hillside at Bethesda
under the snow his wild companions
nestle for shelter.

The language never catches fire, but, equally, Mr. Tripp seems never at a loss for a subject. He gets a good deal of humour and observation, too, into these wry professions of a middle-aged Welshman. It may well be, however, that for all his toughness and irony, Mr. Tripp is insufficiently interested in the craft of verse to make the best of his talent. On the other hand, a novel or a collection of stories from his pen would be interesting to read.

—Philip Hobsbaum

TRYPANIS, Constantine (Athanasius).   Greek.   Born in Chios, 22 January 1909. Educated at Chios Classical Gymnasium, 1920-26; University of Athens, M.A. 1931, D.Phil. 1939; University of Berlin, 1932-34; University of Munich, 1935-37; Oxford University, M.A. 1946. Served in the Greek Army, 1940-41: Sub-Lieutenant. Married Alice Macri in 1942; one daughter. Lecturer in Classics, University of Athens, 1939-47. Bywater and Sotheby Professor of Byzantine and Modern Greek Language and Literature, and Fellow, Exeter College, Oxford, 1947-69; since 1969, Emeritus Fellow; University Professor of Classics, University of Chicago, 1968-74, now Emeritus. Visiting Professor, Hunter College, New York, 1963, Harvard University, Cambridge, Massachusetts, 1963-64, University of Chicago, 1965-66, University of Cape Town, 1969, and University of Vienna, 1971. Greek Minister of Culture and Science, 1974-77. Member, Institute for Advanced Study, Princeton, New Jersey, 1959-60. Recipient: Academy of Athens Koraes Prize, 1933; Heinemann Award, 1960; Herder Prize, 1983. D.Litt.: Oxford University, 1970; D.H.L.: MacMurray College, Jacksonville, Illinois, 1974; Assumption College, Worcester, Massachusetts, 1977. Fellow, Royal Society of Literature, 1958; Member, 1974, and Secretary General, since 1981, Academy of Athens; Member, Medieval Academy of America; Honorary Fellow, British Academy, 1978; Archon Megas Hieromnemon, Oecumenical Patriarchate. Address: 3 Georgiou Nikolaou Kefisia, Athens, Greece.

PUBLICATIONS

Verse

Pedasus: Twenty-Four Poems.   Reading, Berkshire, University of Reading School of Art, 1955.
The Stones of Troy.   London, Faber, 1957.
The Cocks of Hades.   London, Faber, 1958.
Grooves in the Wind (The Stones of Troy and The Cocks of Hades).   New York, Chilmark Press, 1964.
Pompeian Dog.   London, Faber, 1964; New York, Chilmark Press, 1965.
The Elegies of a Glass Adonis.   New York, Chilmark Press, 1967.
The Glass Adonis.   London, Faber, 1972; New York, Chilmark Press, 1973.

Plays

Antigone, adaptation of the play by Sophocles (broadcast, 1958; produced London, 1984).

Radio Plays (UK): Oedipus King, 1955; Oedipus at Colonus, 1958; Antigone, 1958; Persians, 1958; Electra, 1959; The Oresteia, 1959.

Other

Eric Arthur Barber 1888-1965.   London, Oxford University Press, 1967.
Greek Poetry: From Homer to Seferis.   London, Faber, and Chicago, University of Chicago Press, 1981.

Editor, Alexandrian Poetry.   Athens, Garouphalias, 1943.
Editor, Medieval and Modern Greek Poetry: An Anthology.   Oxford, Clarendon Press, 1951.
Editor and Translator, Callimachus: Aetia, Iambi, Lyric Poems, Hecale, Minor Epic and Elegiac Poems, Fragments of Epi-

grams of Uncertain Location. London, Heinemann, and Cambridge, Massachusetts, Harvard University Press, 1958.

Editor, with Paul Maas, Sancti Romani Melodi Cantica. Oxford, Clarendon Press, 2 vols., 1963-70.

Editor, Fourteen Early Byzantine Cantica. Vienna, Academy of Austria, 1968.

Editor, The Penguin Book of Greek Verse. London, Penguin, 1970.

Editor, The Homeric Epics. Warminster, Wiltshire, Aris and Phillips, 1977.

*

Manuscript Collection: Library of the State University of New York, Buffalo.

Critical Studies: by W.H. Auden, in Encounter (London), 1956; Pamela Beattie, in Orbis (Bakewell, Derbyshire), 1976.

Constantine Trypanis comments:

Themes come from the Greek world — ancient, medieval, and modern. Both traditional forms and free verse have been used. Classical Greek poetry and the poetry of Yeats have influenced me.

*   *   *

Born on the island of Chios, Constantine Trypanis had an English nanny and spoke fluent and correct English from his childhood. For many years he was Professor of Byzantine and Medieval Greek at Oxford, and, in the 1950's particularly, was noted for his kindness and sympathy to young poets — it was a flowering period for poets in Oxford — and began, in middle age, to write poems himself, modestly asking for advice from poets much younger than himself. He uses in poetry his marvellous knowledge of Greek history and literature and his special sense of the pathos of the periods of Greece in the Hellenistic, Rome-dominated period and after the conquest of Constantinople by the Ottoman Turks. In his sense of the fragility and irony of a great tradition in decline he resembles the great modern Alexandrian poet, Kavafis or Cavafy, and Auden, who adored Cavafy, greeted one of Trypanis's earlier volumes with delight (and Auden, like Eliot, tended rather studiously to avoid reviewing his contemporaries). Trypanis's longest and most distinguished poem, The Glass Adonis, is a study of a great culture in the stage of vitrification. He writes a formal but not in the least stiff English, rather like the English of the other Greek who chose English for his medium, the late Demetrios Capetanakis. His poems are learned and allusive but full of profound and simple pathos in the emotions they express.

—G.S. Fraser

TURCO, Lewis (Putnam). American. Born in Buffalo, New York, 2 May 1934. Educated at Suffield Academy, Connecticut, 1947-49; Meriden High School, Connecticut, 1949-52; University of Connecticut, Storrs, 1956-59, B.A. 1959; University of Iowa, Iowa City, 1959-60, 1962, M.A. 1962. Served in the United States Navy, 1952-56. Married Jean Cate Houdlette in 1956; one son and one daughter. Editorial Assistant, University of Iowa

Writers Workshop, 1959-60; Instructor, 1960-64, and Poetry Center Founding Director, 1961-64, Cleveland State University; Assistant Professor, Hillsdale College, Michigan, 1964-65. Assistant Professor, 1965-68, Associate Professor, 1968-71, since 1969, Director of the Writing Arts Program, and since 1971, Professor of English, State University of New York, Oswego. Visiting Professor of English, State University of New York, Potsdam, 1968-69. Bingham Poet-in-Residence, University of Louisville, 1982. Recipient: Yaddo grant, 1959, 1977; Academy of American Poets prize, 1960; Bread Loaf Writers Fellowship, 1961; Helen Bullis Prize (Poetry Northwest), 1972; National Endowment for the Arts-P.E.N. prize, for fiction, 1983. Agent: Arthur Orrmont, Author Aid Associates, 340 East 52nd Street, New York, New York 10022; or, Lordly and Dame, 51 Church Street, Boston, Massachusetts 02116. Address: c/o Mathom Press Enterprises, P.O. Box 362, Oswego, New York 13126, U.S.A.

PUBLICATIONS

Verse

Day after History. Arlington, Virginia, Samisdat, 1956.

First Poems. Francestown, New Hampshire, Golden Quill Press, 1960.

The Sketches of Lewis Turco and Livevil: A Mask. Cleveland, American Weave Press, 1962.

Awaken, Bells Falling: Poems 1959-1967. Columbia, University of Missouri Press, 1968.

The Inhabitant. Northampton, Massachusetts, Despa Press, 1970.

Pocoangelini: A Fantography and Other Poems. Northampton, Massachusetts, Despa Press, 1971.

The Weed Garden. Orangeburg, South Carolina, Peaceweed Press, 1973.

Courses in Lambents (as Wesli Court). Oswego, New York, Mathom, 1977.

A Cage of Creatures. Potsdam, New York, Banjo Press, 1978.

Seasons of the Blood. Rochester, New York, Mammoth Press, 1980.

American Still Lifes. Oswego, New York, Mathom, 1981.

The Compleat Melancholick. St. Paul, Bieler Press, 1984.

Broadsides, cards, etc.: At Yule, 1958; O Well, 1963; Pocoangelini 8, 1965; The Burning Bush, 1966; Image Tinged with No Color, 1966; School Drawing, 1966; My Country Wife, 1966; Nativity, 1967; The Children and the Unicorn, 1968; The Glass Nest, 1968; Burning the News, 1968; The Sign, 1970; A Carol for Melora's First Xmas, 1971; The Magi, 1972; Nursery Rime, 1973; The Fences, 1973; The Pond, 1974; The Vista, 1975; The House, 1976; The Habitation, 1978; Albums, 1979; The Covered Bridge, 1979; Prothalamion, 1980; Millpond, 1981; The Summons, 1981; Winter, 1982; Lineage, 1983; Company, 1983.

Plays

Dreams of Stone and Sun (produced Storrs, Connecticut, 1959). Published in Theatre Journal (Oswego, New York), Fall 1971.

The Elections Last Fall (produced Oswego, New York, 1969). Published in Polemic 6 (Cleveland), 1961.

Ballet Scenario: While the Spider Slept, 1965.

Other

The Book of Forms: A Handbook of Poetics.   New York,
Dutton, 1968.
The Literature of New York (bibliography).   Oneonta, New
York State English Council, 1970.
Creative Writing in Poetry.   Albany, State University of New
York, 1970.
Poetry: An Introduction Through Writing.   Reston, Virginia,
Reston Publishing Company, 1973.
Freshman Composition and Literature.   Saratoga Springs,
New York, Empire State College, 1973.
Murgatroyd and Mabel (for children; as Wesli Court).   Os-
wego, New York, Mathom, 1978.

Editor, *The Spiritual Autobiography of Luigi Turco*.   Ann
Arbor, Michigan, University Microfilms Books, 1969.

*

Bibliography: "Lewis Turco: A Bibliography of His Works and
of Criticism of Them," in *F.W. Crumb Memorial Library Bibliographies*, Potsdam, State University of New York, 1972.

Manuscript Collection: Wilbur Cross Library, University of
Connecticut, Storrs.

Critical Studies: "The Formalism of Lewis Turco" by Hyatt H.
Waggoner, in *Concerning Poetry* (Bellingham, Washington),
Fall 1969; "The Progress of Lewis Turco" by William Heyen, in
Modern Poetry Studies (Buffalo), v. 2, 1976; "Sympathetic
Magic" by the author, in *American Poets in 1976* edited by
William Heyen, Indianapolis, Bobbs Merrill, 1976; introduction
by H.R. Coursen to *American Still Lifes*, 1981; interview with
Donald Masterson, in *Cream City Review* (Milwaukee), 1983;
Mary Doll, in *Dictionary of Literary Biography Yearbook 1984*
edited by Mary Bruccoli and Jean W. Ross, Detroit, Gale, 1985.

Lewis Turco comments:

I consider that poetry is the genre of language art, as distinguished from fiction, which is the genre of written narrative;
drama, the genre of theatrical narrative; and essay, the genre of
written argument or exposition. Thus, the poet concentrates
upon language as substance, in much the same manner as ceram-
icists concentrate on clay as shape or dancers on the body as
motion. The poet may use any and all language techniques that
are available to other writers, but the purpose for which he uses
these techniques is secondary to the shaping of language. Like
writers in any of the other genres, the poet may use either of two
modes — prose, which is unmetered language, or verse, which is
metered language. Any of the genres may be written in either of
the modes; that is to say, there may be prose or verse fiction,
prose or verse drama; prose or verse essay; prose or verse poetry.
These distinctions between *genre* and *mode*, it seems to me,
ought to be obvious, but that people continue to confuse the two
is evident in the often-asked question, "What is the difference
between prose and poetry?" There is only one logical answer:
"Prose is a mode, and poetry is a genre."

It is my intention as a writer to know as much as I possibly can
about all the genres, and about both the modes, so that I may
write whatever I please, however I please, shaping the language
as well as I am capable of doing for any purposes I wish. I am not
interested in *a* style, I am interested in *all* styles; not in one form,
but in every form. I do not care to inhabit a conceptual or artistic
prison by limiting myself to techniques agonists approve for

some reason of theory or manifesto of poetics. I will throw
nothing away before I discover what I may do with it.

But these are pragmatics and rationalities. All worthwhile
writing has its emotions as well, its imponderables, and I tried to
address these in a dedicatory poem in my 1968 collection, written
on lines from Joel Sloman's "Argonauts":

> If it is true that
> "the sea worm is a decorated flute
>   that pipes in the most ancient mode"—
>   and if it is true, too, that
>   the salt content of mammalian blood
>   is exactly equivalent
> to the salinity of the oceans
> at the time life emerged onto the land;
>
>   and if it is true
>   that man is the only mammal with a
>   capacity for song, well, then,
>   that explains why the baroque
>   worm swims in our veins, piping, and why
>   we dance to his measure inch by
> equivocal inch. And it explains why
> this song, even as it explains nothing.

*   *   *

Since the beginning of his career, Lewis Turco has been cited
by many as his generation's practitioner par excellence of formal
verse, that bugaboo of contemporary American poetry, a distinction that, from some, is an honor, while an insult from others.
Regardless, it is misleading. Turco's work is not a compendium
of exercises in poetical technique. In fact, his vision—here dark
and brooding, there deceptively light, even witty—has led him
into almost as many camps of American poetry as exist.

Turco's poetry falls into two divisions. The more obviously
formal is found in his first two collections. Their less successful
work is overly flat and prosaic, as in "Narcissus to His Fleshly
Shade"—

> I want her to be what I need
> her to be, *i.e.*, a mirror for my
> want. There is no man but owns his own soul.
>   His lack lies in the catalyst.
> Surmise it or not, what she cannot know
>   is what image she replaces

—or is too repetitive, which dulls the image, as in the opening
sentence of "The Old Professor and the Sphinx," "It is a dry
word in a dry book / drying out my ear."

Yet, a great deal from this period is very strong. The Audenesque "An Immigrant Ballad" wonderfully contrasts the profane and the sacred: "The girl was pleased: she'd saved a soul / (O
light a stogie with a coal)." "A Tale of Rivers and a Boy," which
begins,

> Long once ago in our town was a boy
> moon blue grass sparse as August's thirsty bones
> who down to rivers ran to sense them flow
> between all acorns grown as tall as high...

is at once fairy-tale-like and syntactically innovative. A richness
of sound is obvious in "My Country Wife:"

> My country wife bends to rinse. Her skirt is
>   unwrinkled. Its print of flowers rounds

out her womb like the rug of violets
    that mounds or dimples the chapel
burying ground. She would be grotesque where
    hydrants irrigate gutters.

In his second period, Turco's formalism is supplanted by a mild experimentalism. *The Inhabitant*, whose poems are allegorical, is comprised of alternating prose poems and lyrics with short lines. Often in the lyrics, punctuation is missing and syntax skewed. Throughout, the poet persistently narrows his vision, aiming in each prose poem at the larger picture, then focusing in each lyric on a smaller, but no less important, specific aspect of the prose poem. The prose pieces are engaging and melodic, as in "The Guestroom:"

> There is a room where an old man lies dreaming
> of worms. In the moments of his eyes all
> the world is buried: its fables and laces
> are spread like tablecloths for his sons
> to walk on.

Yet, Turco's strength here, as in each of his collections, lies in his lyrics. In "The Looking-Glass," the companion to "The Guestroom," he zeroes in on an eye perceiving itself:

>   ...there lying in
>   its circle
>
>   of smooth things the
>   eye preens
>
>   in its own vision
>   before it
>
>   rakes the wind again
>   and rises
>
>   into the sun the
>   fierce air.

Since *The Inhabitant*, Turco has published volumes in a variety of styles, from a collection based, for the most part, on the Tarot, to the dramatic monologs of "Bordello." His "Pocoangelini" sequence has a folk-tale flavor. "The Sketches" is a sequence of over two dozen poems which has some of Turco's most contemporary diction: "scram on home or I'll bop your nose" ("Gene") and "...have a Milky Way; / look, they've been in the Frigidaire" ("Mrs. Martino the Candy Store Lady"), for example.

However, in *American Still Lifes*, Turco's most exaggerated change takes place. Nature becomes his chief concern and metaphor. No longer are individuals important—except for the one in these poems who perceives nature. A haiku-like quality characterizes them: "Wind calls over the lake; / snow rises to the voice of air / falling and falling" ("Snow Moon"). Even when the poems are about objects associated with people, such as "The Tavern" or "The Meetinghouse," the absence of human being is strongly felt, and often not completely understood.

—Jim Elledge

TURNBULL, Gael (Lundin). British. Born in Edinburgh, 7 April 1928. Married; three chldren. Medical practioner; cur-

rently in private practice. Editor, with Mike Shayne, *Migrant* magazine, Worcester, and Ventura, California, 1959-60. Address: 25 Church Walk, Ulverston, Cumbria LA12 7EN, England.

PUBLICATIONS

Verse

Trio, with Eli Mandel and Phyllis Webb. Toronto, Contact Press, 1954.
The Knot in the Wood and Fifteen Other Poems. London, Revision Press, 1955.
Bjarni Spike-Helgi's Son and Other Poems. Ashland, Massachusetts, Origin Press, 1956.
A Libation. Privately printed, 1957.
With Hey, Ho.... Birmingham, Migrant Press, 1961.
To You, I Write. Birmingham, Migrant Press, 1963.
A Very Particular Hill. Edinburgh, Wild Hawthorn Press, 1963.
Twenty Words, Twenty Days: A Sketchbook and a Morula. Birmingham, Migrant Press, 1966.
Walls. Privately printed, 1967.
Briefly. Nottingham, Tarasque Press, 1967.
A Trampoline: Poems 1952-1964. London, Cape Goliard Press, 1968.
I, Maksoud. Exeter, University of Exeter, 1969.
Scantlings: Poems 1964-1969. London, Cape Goliard Press, 1970.
Finger Cymbals. Edinburgh, Satis, 1972.
A Sea Story. Saffron Walden, Essex, Byways, 1973(?).
A Random Sapling. Newcastle upon Tyne, Pig Press, 1974.
Residues: Down the Sluice of Time. Pensnett, Staffordshire, Grosseteste, 1976.
Thronging the Heart. Belper, Derbyshire, Aggie Weston's, 1976.
If a Glance Could Be Enough. Edinburgh, Satis, 1978.
The Small Change. Malvern, Worcestershire, Migrant Press, 1980.
Rain in Wales. Edinburgh, Satis, 1981.
Nine Intersections. Twickenham, Middlesex, Circle Press, 1982.
A Gathering of Poems 1950-1980. London, Anvil Press Poetry, 1983.
From the Language of the Heart. Glasgow, Mariscat Press, 1983.
Traces. Twickenham, Middlesex, Circle Press, 1983.
Circus. Malvern, Worcestershire, Peacock Press, 1984.

Other

Translator, with Jean Beaupré, (*Poems*), by Paul-Marie Lapointe and others. Privately printed, 1955.
Translator, with Jean Beaupré and Jill Iles, *Twelve Poems*, by Jean Follain. Nailsworth, Gloucestershire, Moschatel Press, 1983.

*

Critical Study: "Gael Turnbull's Poetry" by Kenneth Cox, in *Scripsci* (Melbourne), June 1984.

*   *   *

Gael Turnbull was born in Scotland and now lives in Cumbria where he practices medicine. During his apprenticeship both as a physician and as a poet, however, he lived in North America where his early poems were published in, among other journals, *Black Mountain Review*. Until he returned to Britain in 1964, there was some confusion about whether he ought properly to be regarded as a Canadian, an American, or a British poet, and, evidently, at one point Donald Allen considered publishing a selection of Turnbull's poems (at Robert Duncan's suggestion) in his important anthology, *The New American Poetry*. Though Turnbull readily acknowledges his debt to poets like Duncan, Robert Creeley, Charles Olson, and Denise Levertov, he ought not to be looked upon as a kind of minor British Black Mountaineer. English poets like Basil Bunting, Roy Fisher, and Matthew Mead have also been important to his development and, in the end, the character of his best work turns out to be personal and quite unique.

The danger for Turnbull is minimalism, and he is at his best when he is not attempting to refine and purify his writing down to the quintessential five or six four-syllable lines (or less) in the manner of Cid Corman, the early Creeley, or Ian Hamilton Finlay. For me, his strongest poem to date is a long piece in *A Trampoline* called "Twenty Words/Twenty Days" which ends: "and I remember an Edinburgh room and one saying,/when I asked what he'd done that day, how much—/I tore/it up...I wisnae pure enough when I wrote...I wisnae/pure enough...." The poem, in fact, is marvellously *impure*. A word is chosen by a random method and each day's journal-like entry is constructed around it in a language as relaxed and supple as good prose but which has, in spite of its casual appearance on the page (it is broken up into units by dashes and ellipses), the concentration one expects from poetry. Rhythmatically, it is very engaging: the rhythms of contemporary speech are handled as effectively as they are in William Carlos Williams. The poem is richly anecdoctal. Turnbull responds to his responsibilities as a doctor and citizen, to his private experience as a husband and father, and to his memories and desires as a poet and as a man. The twenty days happened to be November 17th to December 6th, 1963, and while November 22nd was the date of John Kennedy's assassination, and while that event figures centrally enough, it is just as important for the final effect of the poem that on November 20th Turnbull prevented a child from choking during a tonsillectomy and "had pleasure in [his] skill" or that on December 2nd he woke up unexpectedly remembering a girl he had met years before "out walking in the Appalachians." The poem is a moving human document. One can say of it, as Turnbull writes elsewhere: "The phrases are apt/The scene is not unusual/The joy is in the attention."

Turnbull's work after *A Trampoline* is gathered in a second volume, *Scantlings*. The note on the title is important: "Of limited or prescribed dimension; a portion, an alloted quantity; a builder's or carpenter's measuring rod; in a building, the small beams or pieces of wood; in archery, the distance from a mark, within which a shot is not regarded as a miss." The most ambitious poem in the new book is "A Word," a piece in some ways related to "Twenty Words/Twenty Days" but which, I feel, suffers from its minimalist and concretist affinities. Any of one hundred and twelve phrases are meant to be interchangable in such a way that they may relate to any of twenty-eight nouns. The printed version, we are told in a note, "is no less final than any other." For example, the first four lines of the printed version, "a word/against silence/a love/impelled to be uttered," could also be "a love/against silence/a word/impelled to be uttered." And so on through all the permutations.

—John Matthias

TUWHARE, Hone.   New Zealand Maori.   Born in Kaikohe, 21 October 1922. Educated at Campbell's Kindergarten, Victoria Park; Kaikohe Primary School; Avondale Primary School; Mangere Central Primary School; Beresford Street School, Auckland; Seddon Memorial Technical College, Auckland, 1939-41; Otahuhu Technical College, 1941. Served in the Maori Battalion, 1945, and the New Zealand Second Divisional Cavalry, 1945-47. Married Jean Tuwhare in 1949; three sons. Formerly, Member, Wellington Boilermakers Union; Amalgamated Society of Railway Servants; Wellington Public Service Association; Freezing Workers Union; Wellington Tramway Workers Union; and District Executive, Communist Party of New Zealand; President, Te Manhoe Local, New Zealand Workers Union, 1962-64. Since 1964, Member, Auckland Boilermakers Union. President, Birkdale Maori Cultural Committee, Auckland, 1966-68; Councillor, Borough of Birkenhead, Auckland, 1968-70; Organizer of the Maori Artists and Writers Conference, Te Kaha, 1973. Recipient: Internal Affairs Department travel grant, 1956; New Zealand Award for Achievement, 1965; Robert Burns Centennial Fellowship, University of Otago, 1969. Address: c/o John McIndoe Ltd., 51 Crawford Street, P.O. Box 694, Dunedin, New Zealand.

PUBLICATIONS

Verse

No Ordinary Sun.   Auckland, Blackwood and Janet Paul, 1964.
Come Rain Hail.   Dunedin, University of Otago Bibliography Room, 1970.
Sapwood and Milk.   Dunedin, Caveman Press, 1972.
Something Nothing.   Dunedin, Caveman Press, 1973.
Making a Fist of It (includes stories).   Dunedin, Jackstraw Press, 1978.
Selected Poems.   Dunedin, McIndoe, 1980.
Year of the Dog.   Dunedin, McIndoe, 1982.

Recording: *Wind Song and Rain*, Kiwi, 1975.

*

Critical Study: by M.P. Jackson, in *Landfall 74* (Christchurch), June 1965.

Hone Tuwhare comments:
Strongly influenced by translated works of Mayakovsky, Mao Tse-tung, García Lorca, Louis Aragon, Pablo Neruda and Shakespeare, and R.A.K. Mason of New Zealand, together with a close study of *Nga Moteatea me nga harikari o te Iwi Maori*: a collection of untranslated Maori songs. Also, the Old Testament.

*   *   *

Hone Tuwhare is the first Maori to achieve a reputation for poetry written in English. The fact that he is a Maori and that elements of his native culture find their way into the work has meant that he has attracted wider attention than is the case with most New Zealand poets. In addition, Tuwhare is an attractive personality who reads his poetry well in public and is frequently in demand and on tour. His work is already studied widely in schools and his books go on being reprinted.

His early work (appearing, however, when Tuwhare was already in his early forties) was lyrical, with a strongly aural quality, full of assonance and half-rhyme within a tightly written free-verse form. In the natural scene trees, mountains, rivers, sun, wind, rain, were addressed directly, "personified." The universe was animate. This was a Maori quality, yet it was also "literary" (even artificial), and there was a sense sometimes of confusion between the two. The weaker poems could descend into whimsy; or they might at times remind the reader of the faded 19th-century langauge into which Maori poetry was customarily translated by early scholars. And Tuwhare was often more effective when he spoke directly and plainly than when he sought after images and conceits. "Tree let your arms fall/raise them not sharply in supplication/to the bright enhaloed cloud" is weaker, being more literary, than the directness (especially in the second and third lines) of "o voiceless land, let me echo your desolation./ The mana of my house has fled,/the marae is but a paddock of thistle." ("Mana" means pride/prestige; and "marae" is the meeting ground of the tribe. Both words are entirely familiar to European New Zealanders.)

Distinct from the predominant lyricism of the early work there is a strong, personal, anecdotal style, humorous, generous in feeling, colloquial in language, and this has come to predominate in Tuwhare's later books. Some reviewers have regretted the change, but it seems clear the gains outweigh any losses.

Some subjects suit Tuwhare better than others in that they get the best, the most authentic, out of him linguistically; and this is especially so of poems dealing with the countryside and with occasions that take him back to his own family. Into such poems he works a physical quality of experience which all New Zealanders recognize but which few of European race can translate so directly into words: "I bend/my back. Ankle deep in water how reassuring/to hear the knock and rattle of cockle in the/flax kit as I strain black sand away." Tuwhare is particularly good in poems dealing with bereavement, exploiting the Maori custom in which the corpse is addressed by the mourner and kinship is claimed. There is something of Maori oratory in the direct speech of all his work; and his humour is a unifying quality, making the reader feel a consistent personality running through the poems. Tone of voice is an intangible element which often makes the difference between success and failure in poetry and there is in Tuwhare's tone at its best a distinct combination of qualities, at once informal, colloquial New Zealand English, but with a decorum recognizably Maori:

> Eat the gifts of the sea raw. That's basic.
> Wrap yourself around some of it. Now take this cluster
> of mussels for example:
>
> I prise a couple loose, and with one in each palm see,
> I clap my hands and crack their hairy heads together
> Then I go *shlup*, and spit the broken bits out after.

Read in Tuwhare's rich, breathy voice, such poems become admirable performing scripts.

—C.K. Stead

UPDIKE, John (Hoyer). American. Born in Shillington, Pennsylvania, 18 March 1932. Educated in Shillington public schools; Harvard University, Cambridge, Massachusetts, A.B. (summa cum laude) 1954; Ruskin School of Drawing and Fine Arts, Oxford, 1954-55. Married 1) Mary Pennington in 1953 (marriage dissolved), two daughters and two sons; 2) Martha

Bernhard in 1977. Staff reporter, *New Yorker*, 1955-57. Recipient: Guggenheim Fellowship, 1959; Rosenthal Award, for fiction, 1960; National Book Award for fiction, 1964; O. Henry Award, for fiction, 1966; Foreign Book Prize (France), 1966; New England Poetry Club Golden Rose, 1979; MacDowell Medal, 1981; Pulitzer Prize, for fiction, 1982; American Book Award, for fiction, 1982; National Book Critics Circle Award, for fiction, 1982, for criticism, 1984; Union League Club Abraham Lincoln Award, 1982; National Arts Club Medal of Honor, 1984. Member, American Academy, 1976. Address: 675 Hale Street, Beverly Farms, Massachusetts 01915, U.S.A.

PUBLICATIONS

Verse

The Carpentered Hen and Other Tame Creatures. New York, Harper, 1958; as *Hoping for a Hoopoe*, London, Gollancz, 1959.
Telephone Poles and Other Poems. New York, Knopf, and London, Deutsch, 1963.
Verse. New York, Fawcett, 1965.
Dog's Death. Cambridge, Massachusetts, Lowell House, 1965.
The Angels. Pensacola, Florida, King and Queen Press, 1968.
Bath after Sailing. Monroe, Connecticut, Pendulum Press, 1968.
Midpoint and Other Poems. New York, Knopf, and London, Deutsch, 1969.
Seventy Poems. London, Penguin, 1972.
Six Poems. New York, Aloe, 1973.
Query. New York, Albondocani Press, 1974.
Cunts (Upon Receiving the Swingers Life Club Membership Solicitation). New York, Hallman, 1974.
Tossing and Turning. New York, Knopf, and London, Deutsch, 1977.
Sixteen Sonnets. Cambridge, Massachusetts, Halty Ferguson, 1979.
An Oddly Lovely Day Alone. Richmond, Virginia, Waves Press, 1979.
Five Poems. Cleveland, Bits Press, 1980.
Facing Nature. New York, Knopf, and London, Deutsch, 1985.

Plays

Three Texts from Early Ipswich: A Pageant. Ipswich, Massacusetts, 17th Century Day Committee, 1968.
Buchanan Dying. New York, Knopf, and London, Deutsch, 1974.

Novels

The Poorhouse Fair. New York, Knopf, and London, Gollancz, 1959.
Rabbit, Run. New York, Knopf, 1960; London, Deutsch, 1961.
The Centaur. New York, Knopf, and London, Deutsch, 1963.
Of the Farm. New York, Knopf, 1965.
Couples. New York, Knopf, and London, Deutsch, 1968.
Rabbit Redux. New York, Knopf, 1971; London, Deutsch, 1972.
A Month of Sundays. New York, Knopf, and London, Deutsch, 1975.
Marry Me: A Romance. New York, Knopf, 1976; London, Deutsch, 1977.

The Coup. New York, Knopf, 1978; London, Deutsch, 1979.
Rabbit Is Rich. New York, Knopf, 1981; London, Deutsch, 1982.
The Witches of Eastwick. New York, Knopf, and London, Deutsch, 1984.

Short Stories

The Same Door. New York, Knopf, 1959; London, Deutsch, 1962.
Pigeon Feathers and Other Stories. New York, Knopf, and London, Deutsch, 1962.
Olinger Stories: A Selection. New York, Knopf, 1964.
The Music School. New York, Knopf, 1966; London, Deutsch, 1967.
Penguin Modern Stories 2, with others. London, Penguin, 1969.
Bech: A Book. New York, Knopf, and London, Deutsch, 1970.
The Indian. Marvin, South Dakota, Blue Cloud Abbey, 1971.
Museums and Women and Other Stories. New York, Knopf, 1972; London, Deutsch, 1973.
Warm Wine: An Idyll. New York, Albondocani Press, 1973.
Couples: A Short Story. Cambridge, Massachusetts, Halty Ferguson, 1976.
Too Far to Go: The Maples Stories. New York, Fawcett, 1979; as *Your Lover Just Called: Stories of Joan and Richard Maple*, London, Penguin, 1980.
Problems and Other Stories. New York, Knopf, 1979; London, Deutsch, 1980.
Three Illuminations in the Life of an American Author. New York, Targ, 1979.
The Chaste Planet. Worcester, Massachusetts, Metacom Press, 1980.
The Beloved. Northridge, California, Lord John Press, 1982.
Bech Is Back. New York, Knopf, 1982; London, Deutsch, 1983.

Other

The Magic Flute (for children), with Warren Chappell. New York, Knopf, 1962.
The Ring (for children), with Warren Chappell. New York, Knopf, 1964.
Assorted Prose. New York, Knopf, and London, Deutsch, 1965.
A Child's Calendar. New York, Knopf, 1965.
On Meeting Authors. Newburyport, Massachusetts, Wickford Press, 1968.
Bottom's Dream: Adapted from William Shakespeare's "A Midsummer Night's Dream" (for children). New York, Knopf, 1969.
A Good Place. New York, Aloe, 1973.
Picked-Up Pieces. New York, Knopf, 1975; London, Deutsch, 1976.
Hub Fans Bid Kid Adieu. Northridge, California, Lord John Press, 1977.
Ego and Art in Walt Whitman. New York, Targ, 1978.
Talk from the Fifties. Northridge, California, Lord John Press, 1979.
People One Knows: Interviews with Insufficiently Famous Americans. Northridge, California, Lord John Press, 1980.
Hawthorne's Creed. New York, Targ, 1981.
Hugging the Shore: Essays and Criticism. New York, Knopf, 1983; London, Deutsch, 1984.

Editor, *Pens and Needles*, by David Levine. Boston, Gambit, 1970.
Editor, with Shannon Ravenel, *The Best American Short Stories 1984.* Boston, Houghton, Mifflin, 1984; as *The Year's Best American Short Stories*, London, Severn House, 1985.

*

Bibliography: *John Updike: A Bibliography* by C. Clarke Taylor, Kent, Ohio, Kent State University Press, 1968; *An Annotated Bibliography of John Updike Criticism 1967-1973, and a Checklist of His Works* by Michael A. Olivas, New York, Garland, 1975; *John Updike: A Comprehensive Bibliography with Selected Annotations* by Elizabeth A. Gearhart, Norwood, Pennsylvania, Norwood Editions, 1978.

Manuscript Collection: Harvard University, Cambridge, Massachusetts.

Critical Studies (selection): interviews in *Life* (New York), 4 November 1966, *Paris Review*, Winter 1968, and *New York Times Book Review*, 10 April 1977; *John Updike* by Charles T. Samuels, Minneapolis, University of Minnesota Press, 1969; *John Updike* by Robert Detweiler, New York, Twayne, 1972; *John Updike: A Collection of Critical Essays* edited by David Thorburn and Howard Eiland, Englewood Cliffs, New Jersey, Prentice Hall, 1979; *John Updike* by Suzanne H. Uphaus, New York, Ungar, 1980; *The Other John Updike: Poems/Short Stories/Prose/Play* by Donald J. Greiner, Athens, Ohio University Press, 1981; *Critical Essays on John Updike* edited by William R. Macnaughton, Boston, Hall, 1982.

John Updike comments:
(1970) I began as a writer of light verse, and have tried to carry over into my serious or lyric verse something of the strictness and liveliness of the lesser form. My extensive prose writing has consumed much of the energy that might have gone into my development as a poet, though my long poem, "Midpoint," is an attempt to catch up.
(1985) In my most recent collection, *Facing Nature*, I am proudest of the sonnets and the seven linked "odes" to natural processes.

*   *   *

The verse of John Updike is not as accomplished as his prose fiction. Specimens of it collected in *Hoping for a Hoopoe* and *Telephone Poles* do not require to be read, however, in that spirit of indulgence usually exended to novelists who have lost their way in poems. He is invariably neat, his wit is well-dressed, and he has a lively interest in form. The better of his verses look like superior exercises in the art of cheering oneself up by playing with words:

> Many-maned scud-thumper, tub
> of male whales, maker of worn wood, shrub-
> ruster, sky-mocker, rave!
> portly pusher of waves, wind-slave.

These four lines, which comprise a complete poem entitled "Winter Ocean," show the verse-making Updike's merits, and his strict limitations. Sophistication seizes upon a lyrical impulse and throttles it with style. It is as though G.M. Hopkins had settled for a job concocting elegant clues for crosswords puzzles, or one of the Anglo-Saxon riddlers had been washed up on the staff of *The New Yorker*.

Updike is not always so slight—the title piece in the volume *Midpoint and Other Poems* shows him in a more serious or at any rate energetic mood.

—Robert Nye

URDANG, Constance (Henriette).   American.   Born in New York City, 26 December 1922. Educated at Fieldston School; Smith College, Northampton, Massachusetts, A.B. 1943; University of Iowa, Iowa City, M.F.A. 1956. Military Intelligence Analyst, United States Department of the Army, Washington, D.C., 1944-46. Married Donald Finkel, *q.v.*, in 1956; two daughters and one son. Copy Editor, Bellas Hess Inc., publishers, New York, 1947-51; Editor, P.F. Collier and Son, publishers, New York, 1952-54. Co-ordinator, Writers Program, Washington University, St. Louis, 1977-84. Recipient: *Carleton Miscellany* Centennial Award, 1967; National Endowment for the Arts grant, 1976; Delmore Schwartz Memorial Award, 1981. Agent: Anne Borchardt, Georges Borchardt Inc., 136 East 57th Street, New York, New York 10022. Address: 6943 Columbia Place, St. Louis, Missouri 63130, U.S.A.

PUBLICATIONS

Verse

Charades and Celebrations.   New York, October House, 1965.
The Picnic in the Cemetery.   New York, Braziller, 1975.
The Lone Woman and Others.   Pittsburgh, University of Pittsburgh Press, 1980.
Only the World.   Pittsburgh, University of Pittsburgh Press, 1983.

Novel

Natural History.   New York, Harper, 1969.

Other

Editor, with Paul Engle, *Prize Stories '57.*   New York, Doubleday, 1957.
Editor, with Paul Engle and Curtis Harnack, *Prize Stories '59.*   New York, Doubleday, 1959.
Editor, *The Random House Vest Pocket Dictionary of Famous People.*   New York, Random House, 1962.

*

Manuscript Collection: Washington University, St. Louis.

*   *   *

Constance Urdang's first volume of poems, *Charades and Celebrations*, revealed a poet fully in command of poetic craft and concerned with exploring two major themes: what it means to be a woman, expressed through myths and metaphors of the moon, and what the arbitrary accidents of life altogether might mean, expressed through a collage technique of free-associative juxtapositions. In the introduction to her next volume of poems,

The Picnic in the Cemetery, Richard Howard said: "It is still a celebration, the new Constance Urdang poem—the picnic in the cemetery is a feast aware of the dead...." Her more recent poems are indeed new in their strength and wisdom, the language never tentative yet not overdone, the duellist's perfectly executed sword-stroke. Her themes have developed in breadth and depth; pain, loneliness, betrayal, old age, sickness, and death are the human condition but are seen by Urdang through the particulars of the lives of women.

To look unflinchingly at death is the motif of *The Picnic in the Cemetery*. As the title indicates, our whole life exists among monuments to the dead, which no one wants to acknowledge—old ladies sitting on park benches wait for "the big Oldsmobile"—death. "Woman in the Attic" (the mind) sits among "mouse bones like antique lace":

> *triste* souvenirs
> messages from the spirit world
>
> I write with my finger on the window pane
> "If only there were some adventure other than death."

Death takes many forms, especially for women—in "The Girl" and "Becoming a Woman," the deaths of childishness and conventionality come with taking on the difficulties of adulthood. Alienation of love means death in the three "Adultery" poems; "Childless Woman" and "Abortion" deal with painful experiences unique to women, ambiguously linking death and birth. In "Walking Around" the bagwoman evidently finds means to resist death, but only true mystics, like "The Woman with Three Eyes," can see beyond death by transcending the injury, loneliness, and fear that are the lot of the world's elderly and poor.

Implicit in these poems is the landscape of unfeeling unseeing America, a landscape made explicit in "Midamerica," a funny, half-barbed diatribe which suggests that, as in New Madrid, Missouri, in the 1800's, the great earthquake which destroys America will rise from here. All her themes unite in "The Players and the Game": life in America, life altogether, is a game of Monopoly in which both capitalism and hope are failing, and the players who bulk largest in this scene are women. The volume concludes with the poem "Instead of History":

> Instead of history
> revolution lives
> in the daughter of rape...
>
> in the sour potato
> from which the old woman makes soup

The first section of Urdang's 1980 volume, *The Lone Woman and Others*, celebrates the "feme sole" and other unpopular, unenticing types of women—witch, menopausal woman, old maid, runaway girls—without pitying or romanticizing them. The poems of section two create objective correlatives from domestic existence, the house itself and objects—umbrellas, kites—which show the roots of cosmic events in the unremarkable mundane: assassinations begin in "the assassination-kitchen." In section three a series of prose poems ends with the sequence "Reinventing America," which casts a doleful yet humorous glance at the America of beauty parlors, vanished hats, mothers as "always secondary" and students "studying western civilization": "Now they are inventing gunpowder, and the printing/press. See what is printed: ETAOIN SHRDLU." This satire has bite but is not wholly unaffectionate; finally, on a boat that goes to look at whales, the poet is inspired to offer praise and biblical hope:

O great whales, sisters, you warm-blooded islands in
   the
bitter sea....I would scatter a blessing on the waters for
you, a blessing on the salt cold water that surrounds
America, from which life springs.

Only the World, Urdang's 1983 collection, takes its title from
the epigraph by Martin Buber: "There is no world of appearances, there is only the world." Thus in this volume, as in section
four of *The Lone Woman and Others*, landscapes—Mexico,
Chicago, Brazil, the Ozarks, the suburbs, indoors, outdoors—
are real and simply themselves, and exploratory travel among
them the fundamental activity of the human body and mind.
Going out and returning as contradictory yet primal impulses
are explored in "Coming Home," "Ways of Returning," "Aesthetics of Escape," and "The Wish to Settle Down," which
concludes that the only resting place is "the final one."
   Language is the one transcendent element in this landscape. In
Roses and Bricks the poet notes that the Spanish conquistadors
called all flowers in Mexico roses, as "they followed the long
dream of treasure.../Whereas in another language/The self takes
many forms"—lily, fern, wandering Jew. This naming creates
life, she asserts, "And I understand why/The Mexicans have a
dozen words for *brick*." Thus she sees, in her final poem of this
volume that "the world is full of poets" because words are, after
all, available to everyone and those who use them are using the
building-blocks—the bricks—of the world. Poetry, said T.S.
Eliot, should not be "poetic"; it should try to point beyond itself.
Constance Urdang's poems point beyond themselves to a powerful and generous vision of the real, language's utmost accomplishment. They are excellent.

                                                   —Jane Augustine

---

VALENTINE, Jean.   American.   Born in Chicago, Illinois,
27 April 1934. Educated at Milton Academy, 1949-52; Radcliffe
College, Cambridge, Massachusetts, 1952-56, B.A. (cum laude)
1956. Married James Chace in 1957 (divorced, 1968); two
daughters. Poetry workshop teacher, Swarthmore College,
Pennsylvania, 1968-70, Barnard College, New York, 1968, 1970,
Yale University, New Haven, Connecticut, 1970, 1973-74, Hunt-
er College, New York, 1970-75; Member of the Faculty, Sarah
Lawrence College, Bronxville, New York, after 1974. Currently,
Member of the Department of Writing, Columbia University,
New York. Recipient: Yale Series of Younger Poets Award,
1965; National Endowment for the Arts grant, 1972; Guggen-
heim Fellowship, 1976. Address: Department of Writing,
Columbia University, New York, New York 10027, U.S.A.

PUBLICATIONS

Verse

Dream Barker and Other Poems.   New Haven, Connecticut,
   Yale University Press, 1965.
Pilgrims.   New York, Farrar Straus, 1969.
Ordinary Things.   New York, Farrar Straus, 1974.
Turn.   Oberlin, Ohio, Pocket Pal Press, 1977.
The Messenger.   New York, Farrar Straus, 1979.

                              *

Manuscript Collection: Lamont Library, Harvard University,
Cambridge, Massachusetts.

                    *   *   *

   From her first volume, *Dream Barker*, Jean Valentine's
poems have translated dreams into living experience. Now in the
later volumes, *Ordinary Things* and *The Messenger*, she almost
reverses this process to show life as veiled and inconclusive,
suggestive rather than definitive, dream-like. The elliptical yet
lucid craft of these late poems is unobtrusive while serving the
poet's vision of experience as only imperfectly graspable. The
poems ride lightly on the waves of thought, more textures than
statements, soft as some woven fabric which incorporates rough
knots and bright ribbons in a matrix of pale yarn. Whereas the
early poems of *Dream Barker* referred openly to events such as
first love, wedding, childbirth, parenthood, the later poems are
mistier and more private in their reference. Valentine is very
careful not to make any over-statement or premature conclusion
that might mar the sense of the importance of emotional atmosphere over external incident. But despite the oblique approach,
the poems do not ignore cruel realities nor evade the pain of
existence. She writes of the loss of love, separations, a child's
death, war. Her sensitivity to these sufferings is projected
through images of the physical body, heartbeat, arms and legs
moving, ribs, hands, faces smiling or somber, against a muted
background of gross American culture, radios, graffiti, police.
Her delicacy makes her incline to withdraw from this coarseness
and brutality, but her honesty will not allow her to blink them
away or to consider them more "real" than her own thoughts
which transform the harsh exterior landscape into an austere but
habitable room within.
   Valentine's reluctance to refer to her more recent personal life
in overt ways has evidently contributed to her interest in translation, since in that mode she can speak through another poet's
voice, identifying with the other's experience but leaving the
reader to decide the extent of affinity between the two. The
volume *Ordinary Things* includes a translation of the Dutch
poet Huub Oosterhuis's "Twenty Days' Journey," a moving
meditation on the the death of someone the poet has deeply
loved. One can infer that Valentine was attracted to this poem
for the dream-nightmare quality of grief which completely consumes, yet is simply and delicately expressed: "my body turns to
mist but still stays alive,/an eye that will not close." The final
section is also a dream:

              I rang for days at the door
              a long talk going on and on
              through me like a wire

              I crawled to the roof
              where you were
              when I got there you were gone

   This expression of immediacy and physicality, as well as the
sense of love enduring beyond personal absence or presence is a
mirror of Valentine's own long poem "Fidelities," in which she is
reading a letter from a lover. As she reads, her room becomes his,
the park is both present and remembered and becomes another
field in which both are walking:

   We walked back up the field to the house.
   Your room there. This white room. Books, paper, letters.

Stamps. The telephone. Our lives
We're always choosing our lives.

Yet, reticent as she is, in her latest poems Valentine comes to a well-won affirmation, celebration even, of things as they are, with this lover, present or afar, and with the world:

Here, sitting up late, with a friend
listening, talking, touching her hand, his hand
I touch your hand. No one
says anything much. No one leaves anyone.

Her world is now softened and subdued, bounded by solitude, memories, and letters, peaceful days providing perspective on her life. Friendship is the chief motif of *The Messenger*; she befriends in memory her parents and old acquaintances, cradles and resolves her feelings for them. The poems are sometimes titled merely with a date, and often quote the words of others in a gently free-associative style, usually fragmented in structure, which is faithful to flickering thought ("March 21st"):

to drift   allowing
forgetting my name   my life

the salt of our hands
touching

changing:
over and over: ...

the play of the breath of the world
they   he   she   you

Jean Valentine has created a gentle loving world through her meditation on the raw and painful events of everyday life. She has thus become a modern rarity: a poet without bitterness, self-pity or self-aggrandizement.

—Jane Augustine

VAN DUYN, Mona (Jane). American. Born in Waterloo, Iowa, 9 May 1921. Educated at the University of Northern Iowa, Cedar Falls, B.A. 1942; University of Iowa, Iowa City, M.A. 1943. Married Jarvis Thurston in 1943. Instructor in English, University of Iowa, 1944-46, and University of Louisville, Kentucky, 1946-50; Lecturer in English, Washington University, St. Louis, 1950-67; Lecturer, Salzburg Seminar in American Studies, 1973. Poetry Consultant, Olin Library Modern Literature Collection, Washington University. Editor, with Jarvis Thurston, *Perspective: A Quarterly of Literature*, St. Louis, 1947-67. Recipient: Eunice Tietjens Memorial Prize, 1956, and Harriet Monroe Memorial Prize, 1968 (*Poetry*, Chicago); Helen Bullis Prize (*Poetry Northwest*), 1964; National Endowment for the Arts grant, 1966; Borestone Mountain Poetry prize, 1968; Hart Crane Memorial Award, 1968; Bollingen Prize, 1971; National Book Award, 1971; Guggenheim Fellowship, 1972; Loines Award, 1976; Academy of American Poets Fellowship, 1981; Cornell College Sandburg Prize, 1982. D.Litt.: Washington University, 1971; Cornell College, Mt. Vernon, Iowa, 1972. Member, American Academy, 1983. Address: 7505 Teasdale Avenue, St. Louis, Missouri 63130, U.S.A.

PUBLICATIONS

Verse

Valentines to the Wide World.   Iowa City, Cummington Press, 1959.
A Time of Bees.   Chapel Hill, University of North Carolina Press, 1964.
To See, To Take.   New York, Atheneum, 1970.
Bedtime Stories.   Champaign, Illinois, Ceres Press, 1972.
Merciful Disguises: Poems Published and Unpublished.   New York, Atheneum, 1973.
Letters from a Father and Other Poems.   New York, Atheneum, 1982.

*

Manuscript Collection: Olin Library, Washington University, St. Louis.

*   *   *

The awarding of the Bollingen Prize in 1971 to Mona Van Duyn brought long overdue general recognition to this excellent poet, whose insight, humor, and technical skill deserve to find a larger audience. "The wintry work of living, our flawed art" is her principal theme. Her poetic craft emanates from, in fact is identical with, the conscious intelligence which everyone has and uses to shape random everyday happenstance into meaningful experience. Mind itself then is her subject-matter. "The world blooms and we all bend and bring/from ground and sea and mind its handsome harvests." Poetry-making therefore becomes a metaphor for activities of living minds. "Join us with charity," she says in "To My Godson, On His Christening," "whose deeds, like the little poet's metaphors,/are good only in brave approximations,/who design, in walled-up workrooms, beautiful doors." In "Three Valentines to the Wide World," she calls the beauty of the world "merciless and intemperate" and suggests that against "that rage" we must "pit love and art, which are compassionate." The tension in Van Duyn's poems rises from two dualisms; the world seen as cruel but lovely, a "brilliant wasting," and the technical exposition of strict forms (often long-lined slant-rhymed quatrains) with prose-like statements, themselves varying from Yeatsian elegance to plain midwestern colloquialism.
Her mind is therefore both the wood and the chisel which cuts into it. She ranges wide and deep. She can be philosophical, ironic, elegiac, penetratingly personal. She lives in and looks at domestic life in suburbia, where she finds that experience is as murderous as on battlefields, highways, and ghetto streets, the terrain of masculinist poets. But she sees as clearly as they, perhaps more clearly, the terror of living. To save and strengthen love is her major concern, which leads her to investigate the mind's attitudes toward love. Sometimes she is gently hopeful—"love is that lovely play/that makes and keeps us." Sometimes she is disillusioned, as in "What I Want to Say":

What do you think love is, anyway?
I'll tell you, a harrowing...
To say I love you is a humiliation...
It is the absolute narrowing of possibilities,
and everyone, down to the last man,
dreads it.

But Van Duyn's fullest exploration of love's permutations comes in the poems about marriage scattered throughout her work from early to late. In one section of "Toward a Definition of Marriage," the marital relationship is typically described in literary terms:

> It is closest to picaresque, but essentially artless...
> How could its structure be more than improvising,
> when it never ends, but line after line plod on...
> But it's known by heart now; it rounded the steeliest shape
> to shapeliness, it was so loving an exercise.

Because of this parallelism between life and poetry, overt literary reference is frequent in Van Duyn, notably to Christopher Smart and Yeats's "Leda and the Swan." The richest expression of this parallelism, however, occurs in "An Essay on Criticism," in which the poet adapts the genre and heroic couplet form of Pope's 18th-century poem to develop her own full-fledged philosophical discourse on the interrelationships of love and the making of poems. As the poem begins, the poet is in the kitchen about to open a package of dried onion soup when a young woman poet friend rushes in to describe her love affair: "I've learned what love is—how love is like a poem—/how it 'makes nothing happen,' how it 'lies in the valley of its saying.' " The analogy is built up and sustained through many references to well-known theories of poetry until the human acts of loving and creating poetry become identical in the moment in which the beloved, the reader of poetry, meets the lover, the poet: "two humans, artless and similar—/a likeness proved out of difference—and, enlightened in its sunshine,/he sees they've been caring about each other the whole time." Then the poem switches back to the kitchen and the onion soup. The poet is in tears, but onion juice didn't cause them:

> but poetry didn't cause them either. The pain, that tear-jerk, was life, asserting its primacy in a well-timed rebuke,

and the assertion is valid. A poem can stay formally seated till its person-to-person call, centuries later, is completed...

> But these tears, I remind, well and fall in a room without a clock. Out of action they come, into action they intend to hurry back.

So the poet concludes that her tears have a "rhetoric" which says: "We must move in time, time moves, we must care right away!/ Less beautifully patient than a poem, one might call them an essay." "Essay," punning on "attempt" as well as "literary form," is a considerable understatement of Mona Van Duyn's complex achievement. Her astonishing and moving work has come out of her loyalty to the unfashionable stringencies of tight forms both in life and art. These have been true and sufficient means to promulgate a lifelong delight and torment in her love-affair with the world.

—Jane Augustine

VARMA, Monika. Indian. Born in Allahabad, Uttar Pradesh, 5 August 1916. Educated privately. Married Brigadier K.K. Varma in 1938; two sons. Delegate, All India Poets Meet, June 1973. Recipient: *Caravan* magazine prize, 1956, 1958; *Illustrated Weekly of India* prize, for short story, 1970; Urmilla Kanoria Creative Arts Fund award, 1976. Address: c/o Mr. Sanjaya Varma, B 88 Sarvodaya Enclave, New Delhi 100 017, India.

PUBLICATIONS

Verse

Dragonflies Draw Flame. Calcutta, Writers Workshop, 1962.
Gita Govinda and Other Poems. Calcutta, Writers Workshop, 1966.
Green Leaves and Gold. Calcutta, Writers Workshop, 1970.
Quartered Questions and Queries. Calcutta, Writers Workshop, 1971.
Past Imperative: A Collection of Poems 1953-1964. Calcutta, Writers Workshop, 1972.
Across the Vast Spaces. Calcutta, United Writers, 1975.
Alakananda. Calcutta, Writers Workshop, 1976.

Other

Facing Four: A Critique of Four Indo-Anglian Women Poets. Calcutta, Writers Workshop, 1974.
Lord Krishna, Love Incarnate. New Delhi, Vikas, 1978.

Translator, *A Bunch of Poems,* by Rabindranath Tagore. Calcutta, Writers Workshop, 1966.
Transcreator, *The Gita Govinda of Jayadeva.* Calcutta, Writers Workshop, 1968.
Transcreator, *Pather Panchali,* by Bibhuti Bhusan Banerjee. Calcutta, Writers Workshop, 3 vols., 1973.

*

Manuscript Collection: Bangalore University Library, Mysore.

Critical Studies: "Some Poets of the Writers Workshop" by Amalendu Bose, in *Critical Essays on Indian Writings in English,* Dharwar, Karnatak University, 1968; "An Exchange Between Monika Varma and Amalendu Bose," in *Miscellany 30* (Calcutta), December 1968; S.C. Saha, in *Thought* (Delhi), June 1969; "Women Poets from Writers Workshop," in *Deccan Herald Magazine,* May 1972; *Insights* by P.K. Saha, Calcutta, Writers Workshop, 1972; "Thought Process and Imagery in Monika Varma's Poetry" by Syed Ameer Uddin, in *Commonwealth Quarterly* (Mysore), December 1978; *Essays on Commonwealth Literature* by K.C. Lahiri, Howrah, Goutam Ghosal, 1984.

Monika Varma comments:

The two important points to remember in any understanding of my poetical works are that the metaphors are totally Indian, and the idioms are based on classical Indian philosophy.

Nobody writing English can be said to be devoid of influences of past poets. And Dylan Thomas is the Poet of all poets. But in my case, I think, I can say that a kind of transmutation has taken place in the crucible of Indian thinking.

The stress on "Indian" is obvious on reading all the references to birds, flowers, beasts, in the Nature poems. If the Lake Poets were influenced by their environment, my environment has also had a profound effect on me.

Besides being an Indian, I am a Bengali. The Bengali race is always sensitive to its surroundings. This fact shows up in all Bengali poetic writing and can be seen from my translations of the Tagore poems and finally, in the perfect prose statement of Bibhuti Bhusan Banerjee's *Pather Panchali*. The Bengali poets who have had a profound influence on me are Jibanananda Das and Ajit Dutta. Unfortunately the latter's works have never been translated and there isn't a really good translation of all Jibana-nanda Das's works.

My philosophical outlook and poetic statements are based on Indian philosophy but if any Western influence has to be sought it is Gerard Manley Hopkins. Though today my philosophical thinking is totally Indian, I have been greatly influenced by the New Testament and the Christ's Life as such, His parables, words, and the words of early Christian mystic saints.

Dr. S. Radhakrishnan's works, his comparative notes on the Western, Indian, and Islamic Sufi saints would also cover the metaphysical aspect of my poetry.

In fact, to understand and appreciate my works, the importance of the metaphysical aspect must be taken into consideration the whole time. Without this realization the subtleties are lost. The simplest statements have a depth of meaning.

It has not been a conscious effort, and it is only on analysis that I find that the metaphysical idiom is the most vital aspect in content. Even in style this is important.

I have, over and over again, in my poems talked about "Words." This love of words is a love of rhythm and music. At one time I was a dedicated student of Western classical music and it was the pure music of Bach that always appealed most to me. Therefore the rules of music, the idioms and phrases of the theory of music have walked into my verse.

The rhythm of words was originally learnt by a love of Swin-burne's use of words and their toccata rhythm.

And, finally, a deep religious love for my land permeates my poetry.

*   *   *

There must be something in the exclusive use of the English language in the context of present-day India that eventually gives a number of poets a vague sense of limitation. There is no other explanation why so many of the more significant poets who started off by writing only in English have later taken up translation from an Indian language into English as a simultaneous activity. Outstanding examples are A.K. Ramanujan, P. Lal, Mokashi-Punekar, Gauri Deshpande, Suniti Namjoshi, and Paul Jacob.

Monika Varma is another such poet who finds a creative challenge in translation. She has published several volumes of original poems and her shorter lyrics have a remarkable capacity of vividly crystallizing a fleeting image or a passing thought, but to me her most impressive and sustained achievement so far is her English rendering of the work of a 12th-century Sanskrit poet, Jayadeva. Jayadeva's *Gita Govinda* is on the surface a long love poem full of beautiful erotic images, but it has a symbolic and mystic undertone that gives the poem a universal significance. Monika Varma successfully conveys the mythic structure and the sensuous texture in contemporary English without doing violence to the spirit of the original. There is a sense of total devotion and enjoyment in this translation that recreates the *bhakti* quality of medieval *vaishnavic* literature.

Monika Varma's own imaginative world is vivid with birds and trees and glow-worms that are not just objects in nature, but personally felt experiences. Grass is not just green but:

> Grass is in my mouth, my throat,
> grass is on my tongue, my taste,
> grass is my love, my touch.
> The scent of grass: green,
> it is my life, my breath.

Here is a mature sensibility, sensitive to touch, to colour, to the seasons, and to the magic of the sound of words. On the whole

her work has a width of vision and a rootedness quite different in flavour from the academic sophistication of the "alienated" urban poets.

—Meenakshi Mukherjee

VAS DIAS, Robert (Leonard Michael). American. Born in London, England, 19 January 1931. Educated at Grinnell College, Iowa, B.A. 1953; Columbia University, New York, 1959-61. Served in the United States Army, 1953-55. Married Susan McClintock in 1961; one son. Assistant Editor, Prentice Hall, publishers, New York, 1955-56; Staff Editor, Allyn and Bacon, publishers, Boston, 1956-57; free-lance editor, 1957-65; Instructor in English, Long Island University, Brooklyn, New York, 1964-66; Instructor, American Language Institute, New York University, 1966-71; Tutor and Poet-in-Residence, Thomas Jefferson College, Grand Valley State College, Allendale, Michigan, 1971-74; Lecturer, Antioch International Writing Program, London, 1977-81. Since 1981, Lecturer, University of Maryland European Division. Director, Aspen Writers Workshop, Colorado, 1964-67; Director of the National Poetry Centre, and General Secretary, Poetry Society, London, 1975-78. Associate Editor, *Sumac*, Fremont, Michigan, 1970-72, and *Mulch*, Amherst, Massachusetts, 1973-74; Editor, *Atlantic Review*, London, 1978-80. Since 1972, Publisher, Permanent Press, London and New York. Recipient: Creative Artists Public Service grant, 1975; C. Day Lewis Fellowship, 1980. Address: 52 Cascade Avenue, London N.10, England.

PUBLICATIONS

Verse

Ribbed Vision. Privately printed, 1963.
The Counted. New York, Caterpillar, 1967.
The Life of Parts; or, Thanking You for the Book on Building Birdfeeders. Mount Horeb, Wisconsin, Perishable Press, 1972.
Speech Acts and Happenings. Indianapolis, Bobbs Merrill, 1972.
Making Faces. London, Joe DiMaggio Press, 1975.
Ode. Omaha, Abattoir, 1977.
Poems Beginning: "The World." London, Oasis, 1979.

Other

Editor, *Inside Outer Space: New Poems of the Space Age.* New York, Doubleday, 1970.

*

Manuscript Collection: University of Virginia, Charlottesville.

Critical Studies: by Linda Wagner, in *Red Cedar Review* (East Lansing, Michigan), 1973; Toby Olson, in *Margins 28-30* (Milwaukee), 1976; Lee Harwood, in *Poetry Information 15* (London), 1976.

Robert Vas Dias comments:
Though born in England, I grew up and lived in the USA for

34 years, and a large proportion of my work has been published there. I've now been living in London for the past decade, so one could say I'm thoroughly mid-Atlantic, whatever that means. I have never considered myself a member of a school or group, but I do recognize affinities of approach between my work and that of the Black Mountain poets, the American Objectivists, and certain poets living or who used to live in New York. My poems reflect the congruences and incongruities of my daily life, and therefore they often express the tension between a conscious and an instinctual apperception. I like the way the literal particular, the expositional, the familiar, can shade into the numinous. The language is as I find it.

*   *   *

Robert Vas Dias writes a poetry of crisp understatement, often in segments arranged unexpectedly. He has long expressed a mock-serious view of the world, a world much like that of William Carlos Williams, David Ignatow, and Paul Blackburn in that its images are those of winter birds, children, junkyards, movies, trees, boats. The substance of Vas Dias's poetry is the commonplace; the stance is, often, the stoic; but the real métier of the poetry—and, one suspects, of the poet's philosophy—is the play within the language and the structure.

Although W.H. Auden defined a poet as one who loved to play with words, the affinities between Vas Dias's recent verbal constructs and the writing of Gertrude Stein are more noticeable. In *Making Faces* Vas Dias creates high-jinks of word repetition and association, shifting meaning jumping to sprung meaning, all caught within a heavily rhythmic context. The title poem, with its play on *face* ("defaced with the face I face"), introduces a collection in which nearly every poem moves from a root noun (which is also used as verb) to unlikely extensions, clichés, compounds, and misreadings—as variant as the single face in the process of "making faces." The comic use of the contemporary poet's "identity theme," which has dominated American poetry for 20 years, is refreshing. What is impressive is Vas Dias's ability to achieve thematic coherence through what looks to be only word play. Some of the strongest poems are "Poem Starting with Words Written on a Postcard" (using *state* and forms of *to be*; the opening line is "I miss you because I am in another state"), "The Gift of Snakes" (here the word play leads to darker associations in theme), and the funny sexual "Poem of Places and Tongues."

In his earlier collection, *Speech Acts and Happenings*, Vas Dias wrote a more conventional poetry, satisfying his need for invention through creating various speakers. While there are some poems in his later work about other personae, tapping his ability to re-create the idioms of characters he has conceived, most of the later poems express the Vas Dias sense of language and theme—in some ways, this later work is less virtuoso and closer to the poet himself. We see his deep sense of loss over Paul Blackburn's death; his feeling of displacement—at least temporarily—as he returns to his childhood home of England; his melancholy, tempered with tranquility, in winter. We come to know his friends and his fears. But the process of knowing the persona in the poems is not arduous or tiresome; it is lively, interesting, and convincing.

Other recent poems and collections evince this same kind of preoccupation with the sense of play in language, and the poet's responsibility to name. "Time Exposure" gives the reader glimpses of the poet persona as he moves back into moments of his past, but always near the threatening, alluring water. Earth and flight are juxtaposed as other constants in this search for self. The chapbook *Ode* is a prose-poem montage expressing loss, suiting the definition of "ode" to the content of the poem. Heavily emotional, inventive in its mixed forms, the poem sequence juxtaposes guide-book explanations of the losses of cultural landmarks with the poet's often oblique poem-commentaries: "Blackfriars Convent had been washed away by 1754" appears just before "left window in the row/of windows left/in the wall standing/lights behind me quick/as the vandal sun runs/behind the winter/wall of trees." Effective as a sound and image poem, the verse also repeats words and designs used in other poems within the sequence. Again, the reader must be impressed with the spare control. *Poems Beginning: "The World"* is just that, a group of many poems which have to do with the ponderous themes the phrase suggests. Again, Vas Dias's shifting rhythms and generally taut voice, coupled with his sense of play, make the collection effective. When he writes, "we're afloat but hardly," the reader shares the grimace, not a lament. Whether Vas Dias is writing his way through the world or making faces, his poems are striking examples of the poet creating his own world through his own sense of language; and that, after all, is what poets and poems have been about since the beginning. It did, after all, start with the word.

—Linda W. Wagner

VIERECK, Peter (Robert Edwin).   American.   Born in New York City, 5 August 1916. Educated at Horace Mann School for Boys, New York; Harvard University, Cambridge, Massachusetts, B.S. (summa cum laude) 1937 (Phi Beta Kappa), M.A. 1939, Ph.D. 1942; Christ Church, Oxford (Henry Fellow), 1937-38. Served in the United States Army, 1943-45, and Instructor in History, United States Army University, Florence, Italy, 1945. Married 1) Anya de Markov in 1945 (divorced, 1970), one son and one daughter; 2) Betty Martin Falkenberg in 1972. Teaching Assistant, 1941-42, Instructor in German, and Tutor in History and Literature, 1946-47, Harvard University; Assistant Professor of History, 1947-48, and Visiting Professor of Russian History, 1948-49, Smith College, Northampton, Massachusetts. Associate Professor, 1948-55, Professor of History, 1955-65, Alumnae Foundation Chair of Interpretive Studies, 1965-79, and since 1979, William R. Kenan, Jr., Chair of History, Mount Holyoke College, South Hadley, Massachusetts. Visiting Lecturer in American Culture, Oxford University, 1953; Whittall Lecturer in Poetry, Library of Congress, Washington, D.C., 1954, 1963, 1979; Fulbright Lecturer, University of Florence, 1955; Elliston Lecturer, University of Cincinnati, Ohio, 1956; Visiting Professor, University of California, Berkeley, 1957, 1964, and City College of New York, 1964; State Department Cultural Exchange Lecturer in the U.S.S.R., 1961; Visiting Scholar, American Academy in Rome, 1977-78. Poetry Workshop Director, New York Writers Conference, 1965-67. Recipient: Eunice Tietjens Prize (*Poetry*, Chicago), 1948; Guggenheim Fellowship, 1948; Pulitzer Prize, 1949; Rockefeller grant, 1958; Horace Mann School Award, 1958; Twentieth Century Fund Scholarship, 1962; National Endowment for the Arts Fellowship, 1969; Sadin Prize (*New York Quarterly*), 1977; Columbia University Translation Center prize, 1978; Artists Foundation Fellowship, 1978. L.H.D.: Olivet College, Michigan, 1959. Address: 12 Silver Street, South Hadley, Massachusetts 01075, U.S.A.

PUBLICATIONS

Verse

Terror and Decorum: Poems 1940-1948.   New York, Scribner, 1948.
Strike Through the Mask! New Lyrical Poems.   New York, Scribner, 1950.
The First Morning: New Poems.   New York, Scribner, 1952.
The Persimmon Tree: New Pastoral and Lyric Poems.   New York, Scribner, 1956.
New and Selected Poems 1932-1967.   Indianapolis, Bobbs Merrill, 1967.

Play

The Tree Witch (produced Cambridge, Massachusetts, 1961). Published as *The Tree Witch: A Poem and a Play (First of All a Poem),* New York, Scribner, 1961.

Other

Metapolitics: From the Romantics to Hitler.   New York, Knopf, 1941; revised edition, as *Metapolitics: The Roots of the Nazi Mind,* New York, Putnam, 1961; revised edition, Baton Rouge, Louisiana State University Press, 1979.
Conservatism Revisited: The Revolt Against Revolt, 1815-1949.   New York, Scribner, 1949; London, Lehmann, 1950.
Shame and Glory of the Intellectuals: Babbitt Jr. vs. the Rediscovery of Values.   Boston, Beacon Press, 1953; revised edition, New York, Putnam, 1965.
Dream and Responsibility: Four Test Cases of the Tension Between Poetry and Society.   Washington, D.C., University Press of Washington, 1953.
The Unadjusted Man: A New Hero for Americans: Reflections on the Distinction Between Conforming and Conserving.   Boston, Beacon Press, 1956; revised edition, New York, Putnam, 1962.
Conservatism: From John Adams to Churchill.   Princeton, New Jersey, Van Nostrand, 1956.
Inner Liberty: The Stubborn Grit in the Machine (lecture). Wallingford, Pennsylvania, Pendle Hill Pamphlets, 1957.
Conservatism Revisited and the New Conservatism: What Went Wrong?   New York, Macmillan, 1962; revised edition, Baton Rouge, Louisiana State University Press, 1980.

*

Critical Study: *Peter Viereck* by Marie Henault, New York, Twayne, 1969.

*   *   *

A nervous daring informs the characteristic verse of Peter Viereck. Occasionally, the cleverness overreaches itself, when strained sound effects trivialize the image of Nazi evil "Hiking in shorts through tyranny's Tyrols" ("Crass Times Redeemed by Dignity of Souls"). But Viereck's gambles generally win; his sound patterns can create the illusion of a new etymology: "...Aeneas on the boat from Troy/Before harps cooled the arson into art" ("Lot's Wife"). This bravado works best in his epic treatment of "Kilroy," and in "To a Sinister Potato," where echoes of "Ode on a Grecian Urn" heighten the bizarre grandeur of the parody: "O vast earth-apple, waiting to be fried,/Of all life's starers the most many-eyed,/What furtive purpose hatched you long ago/In Indiana or in Idaho?" The zest animating these poems from *Terror and Decorum* not only suits his frequent comic rhymes, or his bastardized Spenserian language in "Ballad of the Jollie Gleeman," but also supports the tender, frightening "Six Theological Cradle Songs," which use nursery jingles and childhood games to dramatize the terror implicit in mortality. Sometimes, Viereck concentrates his frenzy to achieve the gnomic wit of the elegy for Hart Crane, whose exotic polysyllables he elsewhere imitates: "...and he found/New York was the clerks his daddy hired/Plus gin plus sea; then Hart felt tired,/Drank both and drowned" ("Look, Hart, That Horse You Ride Is Wood").

Though the later volumes provide less outrageous fun than the first, they offer greater control of ambitious themes. The straightforward comic verse falters, as in "Full Cycle," a series of parodies of new critics and modern poets, including Viereck himself. But Viereck develops an impressive group of poems with extraordinary personae: "To My Isis" wittily yet accurately summarizes Viereck's range from "Whatever shimmers...birch or trout" to "...Mud I also mimic: Let salivating wart-hogs gambol by,/Preening their bristles. All gross masks I'll try/But hairy spiders. These I still can't stomach." His most striking impersonations are of trees; an oak threatens a willow: "Your chance of passing next week's Woodlore Test/Is—bear it oakly—not the best./You know the price! The beaver foreman claims/He needs just one more truck to mend his dams" ("The Slacker Need Not Apologize"). Then an ironic "stage-direction" states: "beavers in over-alls drag away storm-felled oak" (Viereck's frequent sub-title notes and epigraphs suggest a nervous, though charming editor, eager to help, but unwilling to compromise the integrity of his text). The willow survives: "Mere echo (-strummer?), mad (-or wild with truth?),/But contours of the winds lured far too far,/I'm left behind when even God flies south/(If 'God' means all climate I ignore)." The dashes, questions, and parentheses heighten the struggling uncertainty already outlined by the dialectic format of the poem. Here, or in a Goethe/Crane debate in "Decorum and Terror," Viereck dramatizes viewpoints limited and belligerent that fuse for the reader into a compassionate accepting overview. Viereck's show-off rhymes: "Courtier's prance/Otto Kahn's," and play on "k" sounds ("barrack/Weimaric/Pyrrhic/wreck" are the rhymes in one quatrain) make both speakers less than Olympian and prepare for the triumphant final rhyme of "Viereck," which asserts the poet's fusion of decorous form and Romantic terror that are the antagonists of the poem.

Viereck's tree poems, while obviously allegories of particular human attitudes, are equally exciting as delicate versions of non-human psyche. After reading "The Slacker Apologizes," it is impossible to deny that a "crass young weed" would boast:

> Last night my stamen
> Could hear her pistil sigh...
> ...
> My pollen's shy
> Deep nuzzling tells her: weeds must love or die.

Despite his skill in these poems and his flair for dialogue, both elegant and colloquial, Viereck disappoints with *The Tree Witch,* a morality play in verse which places man between the force of nature symbolized by a dryad and the force of technology and conformity symbolized by the Furies (disguised as maiden aunts). Viereck's fondness for dialectic and his familiar satiric targets produce episodes more repetitious than cumulative in their dramatic force, though there are some lovely lyrics, some amusing moments and, occasionally, an explosion of pithy magic: "Lively is not alive; a funeral pyre/Is snugger than a hearth a little while."

Viereck's exaltation of unromanticized nature is a constant in his work, finding strongest expression in "The Autumn Instant: "I am your sky; look up; my clouds are altars/To worship you with desecrating rain." Because of this frightening context in which nature and man exist, many Viereck poems praise the precarious splendor of the moment, often the moment of August ripeness, with Keatsian intensity, and "Sing the bewildered honor of the flesh" ("Some Lives in Three Parts"). Though his recent work has received insufficient acclaim, *New and Selected Poems* develops this obsessive theme with seemingly artless intensity—the fine sequence "Five Walks on the Edge" makes the Massachusetts coast an inevitable and powerful emblem fusing man's psychological, metaphysical and aesthetic limits; Viereck's characteristic formal control gives resonance and assurance to nervous uncertainties:

> World, world, what wreath from soil so thin?
> The roots replenish till the time
> They don't replenish. Many times
> The warmth is gaining. All the time
> The loss is gaining anyhow.

—Burton Kendle

VILLA, José Garcia. Filipino. Born in Manila, Philippines, 5 August 1908. Educated at the University of the Philippines, Manila, 1926-29; University of New Mexico, Albuquerque, A.B. 1933; Columbia University, New York. Associate Editor, New Directions, publishers, New York, 1949-51; Director, City College of New York Poetry Workshop, 1952-63; taught at the University of the Philippines, Quezon City, 1960, and Far Eastern University, Manila, 1960-61; Professor of Poetry, New School for Social Research, New York, 1964-73. From 1968, Member of the Philippine Consular Service, at the Philippine Embassy, Washington, D.C., and the Philippine Mission to the United Nations, New York; now retired. Since 1981, Editor, *Bravo: The Poet's Magazine*, New York. Recipient: American Academy grant, 1942; Guggenheim Fellowship, 1942; Bollingen fellowship, 1951; Shelley Memorial Award, 1959; Philippine Republic Cultural Heritage Award, 1962, and National Artist; Rockefeller Fellowship, 1963. Litt.D.: Far Eastern University, Manila, 1959; L.H.D.: University of the Philippines, 1973. Address: 780 Greenwich Street, New York, New York 10014, U.S.A.

PUBLICATIONS

Verse

Many Voices. Manila, Philippine Book Guild, 1939.
Poems by Doveglion. Manila, Philippine Writers' League, 1941.
Have Come, Am Here. New York, Viking Press, 1942.
Volume Two. New York, New Directions, 1949.
Selected Poems and New. New York, McDowell Obolensky, 1958.
Poems in Praise of Love. Manila, A.S. Florentino, 1962.
Poems 55: The Best Poems of José Garcia Villa as Chosen by Himself. Manila, A.S. Florentino, 1962.
Appassionata. New York, King and Cowen, 1979.

Short Stories

Footnote to Youth: Tales of the Philippines and Others. New York, Scribner, 1933.
Selected Stories. Manila, A.S. Florentino, 1962.

Other

The Portable Villa. Manila, A.S. Florentino, 1962.
The Essential Villa. Manila, A.S. Florentino, 1965.

Editor, *Philippine Short Stories.* Manila, Philippine Free Press, 1929.
Editor, *A Celebration for Edith Sitwell.* New York, New Directions, 1948.
Editor, *A Doveglion Book of Philippine Poetry.* Manila, Katha, 1962; revised edition, as *The New Doveglion Book of Philippine Poetry*, Manila, Caliraya Foundation, 1975.

*   *   *

José Garcia Villa is one of the most distinguished contributions of the Philippines to world poetry in English. One of greater versatility and range and more productivity has surpassed him to become a major poet, and a few others are fast catching up with him, two or three hoping to better his feat. *Poems 55* (1962) contains what Villa has chosen as his best poems. But it is *Selected Poems and New* (1958) that will enable him to retain a place in the front ranks of Philippine poetry in English.

Villa started as a writer of short stories, then shifted to poetry and art, and over the last several years, so we are told, he has been at work on a theory or philosophy of poetics. But during the last few years nothing definite about the evolution or progress of his poetics has emanated from his direction. In 1976 this writer tried to seek him out three times in his known hideouts in New York City, but to no avail. Villa is now in the evening of life, now past his 77th year, and would do well to come out with his vaunted multi-volume masterpiece. It might be said that even if the work should fall short of the work of a master, so long as it is the product of his best efforts, and added to his previous achievement, Villa could still attain the rank of a major writer.

Villa is still remembered by his countrymen as an eccentric non-conformist, even a militant rebel. Early in his college career, he was suspended for one year by the University of the Philippines for authoring a poem, published in the local press, that was deemed obscene by the college authorities. He was to be readmitted after one year if he publicly apologized to his teachers and promised not to repeat the same offense. He did not accept the conditions for his readmission. Instead he went to the United States and enrolled in the University of New Mexico, where he took an A.B. degree in 1933 and then went on to Columbia University for further studies. Thirty years later the University of Philippines extended to him an appointment as Professorial lecturer in English, and even later conferred on him the honorary degree of Doctor of Humane Letters.

Villa's main achievement in poetry has been in experimentation; he has produced a number of poems considered original by critics native to the English language. Not having been born to English, he nevertheless has assiduously studied the language and has acquired a peculiar knowledge of it. This has enabled him to express himself in English with a high degree of originality which sometimes contains flushes of revelation. Some of his poems have been described as among the finest in the English language.

Villa has been concerned mainly with the individual human being, largely in his erotic and spiritual relations. He has been largely unconcerned, even in his prose fiction, with man as a social being, as a member of a larger community, with problems more complex and more difficult of solution. The possibility therefore is that the novelty of much of his poetry, particularly those verses exuding unalloyed narcissism, will wear off and his significance as a poet may decline. In fact, in the Philippines, although he is widely respected for the reputation which he has acquired among a number of foreign critics, Villa is not seriously regarded as a poet of significant achievement by the more thoughtful students of humane letters.

—Leopoldo Y. Yabes

WADDINGTON, Miriam (née Dworkin). Canadian. Born in Winnipeg, Manitoba, 23 December 1917. Educated at Machray School, Winnipeg; Lisgar Institute, Ottawa; University of Toronto, B.A. 1939, Diploma in Social Work 1942, M.A. 1968; University of Pennsylvania, Philadelphia, M.S.W. 1945. Married Patrick Donald Waddington in 1939 (divorced, 1965), two sons. Caseworker, Jewish Family Service, Toronto, 1942-44, 1957-60, and Philadelphia Child Guidance Clinic, 1944-45; Assistant Director, Jewish Child Service, Montreal, 1945-46; Lecturer and Supervisor, McGill School of Social Work, Montreal, 1946-49; caseworker, Montreal Children's Hospital Speech Clinic, 1950-52, and John Howard Society, 1955-57; supervisor, North York Family Service, 1960-62. Since 1964, Member of the English Department, and since 1973, Professor of Literature, York University, Toronto. Recipient: Canada Council Fellowship, 1962, 1968, 1971, 1979. D.Litt.: Lakehead University, Thunder Bay, Ontario, 1975. Address: 32 Yewfield Crescent, Don Mills, Ontario M3B 2Y6, Canada.

PUBLICATIONS

Verse

Green World. Montreal, First Statement Press, 1945.
The Second Silence. Toronto, Ryerson Press, 1955.
The Season's Lovers. Toronto, Ryerson Press, 1958.
The Glass Trumpet. Toronto, Oxford University Press, 1966.
Call Them Canadians. Ottawa, Queen's Printers and National Film Board, 1968.
Say Yes. Toronto, Oxford University Press, 1969.
Dream Telescope. London, Anvil Press Poetry, 1972.
Driving Home: Poems New and Selected. Toronto, Oxford University Press, 1972; London, Anvil Press Poetry, 1973.
The Price of Gold. Toronto, Oxford University Press, 1976.
Mister Never. Winnipeg, Turnstone Press, 1978.
The Visitants. Toronto, Oxford University Press, 1981; New York, Oxford University Press, 1982.

Plays

Radio Documentaries: *Chekov*, 1958; *Poe*, 1962.

Short Stories

Summer at Lonely Beach: Selected Short Stories. Oakville, Ontario, Mosaic Press, 1982.

Other

A.M. Klein. Toronto, Copp Clark, 1970.
The Function of Folklore in the Poetry of A.M. Klein (lecture). St. John's, Newfoundland, Memorial University, 1983.

Editor, *Essays, Poems, Controversies*, by John Sutherland. Toronto, McClelland and Stewart, 1973.
Editor, *The Collected Poems of A.M. Klein.* Toronto, McGraw Hill Ryerson, and New York, McGraw Hill, 1974.

*

Bibliography: "Miriam Waddington: A Checklist 1936-1975" by Laurence R. Ricou, in *Essays on Canadian Writing* (Toronto), Fall 1978.

Manuscript Collection: Public Archives of Canada, Ottawa.

Critical Studies: "The Lyric Craft of Miriam Waddington" by Ian Sowton, in *Dalhousie Review* (Halifax, Nova Scotia), Summer 1958; "Into My Green World: The Poetry of Miriam Waddington" by Laurence R. Ricou, in *Essays on Canadian Writing* (Toronto), Fall 1978; *Twelve Voices* by Jon Pearce, Ottawa, Borealis Press, 1980; *Miriam Waddington* by Cathy Matyas, Toronto, Dundurn Press, 1982.

Miriam Waddington comments:

About my poetry: the key to it is the language. My Canadian English takes its cue from the prairies where I was born and conceals more than it reveals. Some concealments: the social, mythic, and linguistic reverberations of the Yiddish and Russian cultures of my childhood, plus the austerity and Scottish accents of my early teachers.

*   *   *

"Your poems fuse the flesh and the dream," wrote Anaïs Nin of the poetry of Miriam Waddington, who must be one of the finest lyric poets of the day. Of her books to date, the first three are full of images of changing seasons, green worlds, alfresco silences, lovers meeting and parting, flowers galore; the later ones branch out more from her native Manitoba to Canada as a country, and beyond, with evocative trips to Russia, Poland, Israel, and Germany. Common to both phases of her work are characteristic assertions of human worth and warmth, gentle imperatives, and a self-deprecating wit. Her imagery is intelligent without being intellectual, yet apt and derived from personal observation, as when she describes children playing hockey as being "stiff as flowers."

When *Driving Home: Poems New and Selected* appeared in 1972, it became apparent that hers was an essentially lyrical gift, for she sings of what is and finds in the world of desire the point of meeting of what was and what could have been. Hers is a poetry of acceptance rather than of search, for the important thing is to realize the values we have rather than those that we had or hope to have. While other poets were bemoaning the lack of a useable past or vainly engineering the future, she wrote in "Canadians":

> We look
> like a geography but
> just scratch us
> and we bleed
> history.

In other poems she describes bittersweet experiences with the directness of a folk tale and an awareness of modern psychology, for "in my mind/summer never ended." Her playfulness and relationship to the writers of Europe can be seen in the last lines of a characteristic poems, "Sad Winter":

> Dear Nelly Sachs,
> dear Nathalie Sarraute,
> isn't there anything
> you can teach me
> about how to write
> better in Canada?

—John Robert Colombo

WAGONER, David (Russell). American. Born in Massillon, Ohio, 5 June 1926. Educated at Pennsylvania State University, University Park, B.A. 1947; Indiana University, Bloomington, M.A. in English 1949. Served in the United States Navy, 1944-46. Married Patricia Parrott in 1961. Instructor, DePauw University, Greencastle, Indiana, 1949-50, and Pennsylvania State University, 1950-54. Assistant Professor, 1954-57, Associate Professor, 1958-66, and since 1966, Professor of English, University of Washington, Seattle. Elliston Lecturer, University of Cincinnati, 1968; Editor, Princeton University Press Contemporary Poetry Series, 1977-81. Since 1966, Editor, *Poetry Northwest*, Seattle. Recipient: Guggenheim Fellowship, 1956; Ford Fellowship, for drama, 1964; American Academy grant, 1967; Morton Dauwen Zabel Prize, 1967, Oscar Blumenthal Prize, 1974, Eunice Tietjens Memorial Prize, 1977, and English-Speaking Union Prize, 1980 (*Poetry*, Chicago); National Endowment for the Arts grant, 1969; Fels prize, 1975; Sherwood Anderson Award, 1980. Chancellor, Academy of American Poets, 1978. Address: 1918-144th SE, Mill Creek, Washington 98102, U.S.A.

PUBLICATIONS

Verse

Dry Sun, Dry Wind. Bloomington, Indiana University Press, 1953.
A Place to Stand. Bloomington, Indiana University Press, 1958.
Poems. Portland, Oregon, Portland Art Museum, 1959.
The Nesting Ground. Bloomington, Indiana University Press, 1963.
Five Poets of the Pacific Northwest, with others, edited by Robin Skelton. Seattle, University of Washington Press, 1964.
Staying Alive. Bloomington, Indiana University Press, 1966.
New and Selected Poems. Bloomington, Indiana University Press, 1969.
Working Against Time. London, Rapp and Whiting, 1970.
Riverbed. Bloomington, Indiana University Press, 1972.
Sleeping in the Woods. Bloomington, Indiana University Press, 1974.
A Guide to Dungeness Spit. Port Townsend, Washington, Graywolf Press, 1975.
Travelling Light. Port Townsend, Washington, Graywolf Press, 1976.

Collected Poems 1956-1976. Bloomington, Indiana University Press, 1976.
Who Shall Be the Sun? Poems Based on the Lore, Legends, and Myths of Northwest Coast and Plateau Indians. Bloomington, Indiana University Press, 1978.
In Broken Country. Boston, Little Brown, 1979.
Landfall. Boston, Little Brown, 1981.
First Light. Boston, Little Brown, 1984.

Plays

An Eye for an Eye for an Eye (produced Seattle, 1973).

Screenplay: *The Escape Artist*, 1981.

Novels

The Man in the Middle. New York, Harcourt Brace, 1954; London, Gollancz, 1955.
Money, Money, Money. New York, Harcourt Brace, 1955.
Rock. New York, Viking Press, 1958.
The Escape Artist. New York, Farrar Straus, and London, Gollancz, 1965.
Baby, Come On Inside. New York, Farrar Straus, 1968.
Where Is My Wandering Boy Tonight? New York, Farrar Straus, 1970.
The Road to Many a Wonder. New York, Farrar Straus, 1974.
Tracker. Boston, Little Brown, 1975.
Whole Hog. Boston, Little Brown, 1976.
The Hanging Garden. Boston, Little Brown, 1980; London, Hale, 1982.

Other

Editor, *Straw for the Fire: From the Notebooks of Theodore Roethke 1943-1963.* New York, Doubleday, 1972.

*

Manuscript Collections: Olin Library, Washington University, St. Louis; University of Washington, Seattle.

Critical Studies: "The Poetry of David Wagoner" by Robert Boyers, in *Kenyon Review* (Gambier, Ohio), 1970; "An Interview with David Wagoner," in *Crazy Horse 12* (Marshall, Minnesota), 1972; " A Conversation with David Wagoner," in *Yes* (Avoca, New York), iv, 1, 1973; "On David Wagoner," in *Salmagundi* (Saratoga Springs, New York), Spring-Summer 1973, and "Pelting Dark Windows," in *Parnassus* (New York), Spring-Summer 1977, both by Sanford Pinsker.

David Wagoner comments:
I have an affinity for the dramatic lyric, in tones ranging from the loud and satiric through the quiet and conversational.

*   *   *

While it is true that Theodore Roethke, his undergraduate teacher at Pennsylvania State University, was instrumental in bringing David Wagoner to the Pacific Northwest, one could argue that he would have found his way there anyway. After spending his formative years in Whiting, Indiana, that industrial suburb of Chicago which is hard to surpass for disfigured earth, Dantesque fire, polluted water and air, Wagoner has understandably found his place to stand near one of the few regions in

America which still has some unspoiled wilderness and some unspoiled people, American Indians.

Wagoner is surely one of America's most prolific and versatile writers. Not only has he published many volumes of poetry—his *Collected Poems* comes to nearly 300 pages—but he has also produced ten substantial novels. The novelist's feeling for detail enriches the poetry, not only in such mythical narrative poems as "The Return of Icarus," "The Labors of Thor," and "Beauty and the Beast," but also in dramatic and lyric poems. His versatility is patent. His themes are important ones: survival, anger at those who violate the natural world, a Chaucerian delight in human oddity. He manages tones from gaiety to meditative seriousness. He is rarely solemn.

Wagoner has been publishing poetry for nearly three decades. After his first two volumes—nothing from the first and little from the second appears in *Collected Poems*—Wagoner moved beyond the influence of Roethke and Edgar Lee Masters to find his own forms. They include the mock instruction manuals best exemplified by "Advice to the Orchestra," "The Singing Lesson," "Staying Alive," "Sleeping in the Woods," and "Meeting a Bear"; elegies far from Theocritus such as the mordant "For a Forest Clear-cut by the Weyerhaeuser Company"; and, most recently, mythic poems based on American Indian materials.

"Staying Alive" is one of the best American poems since World War II, a profoundly sensible set of instructions to one lost in the woods which is also valuable to anyone anywhere who is interested in staying alive. "Sleeping in the Woods" goes on from "Staying Alive" to show us Wagoner achieving his peculiar harmony with the natural world. The poem opens,

> Not having found your way out of the woods, begin
> Looking for somewhere to bed down at nightfall
> Though you have nothing
> But parts of yourself to lie on....

In "Talking to Barr Creek" Wagoner succeeds at what Matthew Arnold failed to do in "A Summer Night." He realistically aspires to a harmony with nature not beyond human possibility. At the end of the poem the speaker prays:

> Grant me your endless, ungrudging impulse
> Forward, the lavishness of your light movements,
> Your constant inconstancy....
> Your sudden stillness....
> Teach me your spirit, going yet staying, being
> Born, vanishing, enduring.

For a man so attuned to the wild natural world where still live American Indians, it seems almost a matter of course that recent work should include a whole book prompted by Indian myths. The final two stanzas of the title poem of *Who Shall Be the Sun?* gives an idea of Wagoner's sensitive, respectful handling of Indian lore:

> The People said, "We shall have no sun at all!"
> But Snake whispered, "I have dreamed I was the sun."
> Raven, Hawk, and Coyote mocked him by torchlight:
> "You cannot scream or howl! You cannot run or fly!
> You cannot burn, dazzle or blacken the earth!
> How can you be the sun?" "By dreaming," Snake whispered.
> He rose then out of the rich night.
> He coiled in a ball, low in the sky.
> Slowly he shed the Red Skin of Dawn,
> The Skin of the Blue Noontime, the Skin of Gold,
> And last the Skin of Darkness, and the People
> Slept in their lodges, safe, till he coiled again.

T.S. Eliot wrote of Tennyson that "he has three qualities which are seldom found in the greatest poets: abundance, variety, and complete competence." Those qualities are also impressively evident in the poetry of David Wagoner.

—James K. Robinson

WAIN, John (Barrington). British. Born in Stoke-on-Trent, Staffordshire, 14 March 1925. Educated at the High School, Newcastle-under-Lyme, Staffordshire; St. John's College, Oxford, B.A. 1946, Fereday Fellow, 1946-49, M.A. 1950. Married 1) Marianne Urmston in 1947 (marriage dissolved, 1956); 2) Eirian James in 1960; three sons. Lecturer in English, University of Reading, Berkshire, 1947-55; Professor of Poetry, Oxford University, 1973-78. Churchill Visiting Professor, University of Bristol, 1967; Visiting Professor, Centre Universitaire Expérimentale, Vincennes, France, 1969. First Holder, Fellowship in Creative Arts, 1971-72, and since 1973, Supernumerary Fellow, Brasenose College, Oxford. Recipient: Maugham Award, 1958; Heinemann Award, 1975, and Black Memorial Award, 1975, both for non-fiction; Whitbread Award, for fiction, 1982. Fellow, Royal Society of Literature, 1960; resigned, 1961. C.B.E. (Commander, Order of the British Empire), 1984. Lives in Oxford. Address: c/o Macmillan and Company Ltd., 4 Little Essex Street, London WC2R 3LF, England.

PUBLICATIONS

Verse

Mixed Feelings: Nineteen Poems. Reading, Berkshire, Reading University School of Art, 1951.
A Word Carved on a Sill. London, Routledge, and New York, St. Martin's Press, 1956.
A Song about Major Eatherly. Iowa City, Qara Press, 1961.
Weep Before God. London, Macmillan, and New York, St. Martin's Press, 1961.
Wildtrack: A Poem. London, Macmillan, and New York, Viking Press, 1965.
Letters to Five Artists. London, Macmillan, 1969; New York, Viking Press, 1970.
The Shape of Feng. London, Covent Garden Press, 1972.
Feng. London, Macmillan, and New York, Viking Press, 1975.
Poems for the Zodiac (12 booklets), illustrated by Brenda Stones. London, Pisces Press, 1980.
Thinking about Mr. Person. Beckenham, Kent, Chimaera Press, 1980.
Poems 1949-1979. London, Macmillan, 1981.
Twofold. Frome, Somerset, Bran's Head, 1981.

Plays

Harry in the Night: An Optimistic Comedy (produced Stoke-on-Trent, 1975).

Radio Plays: *You Wouldn't Remember,* 1978; *A Winter in the Hills,* from his own novel, 1981; *Frank,* 1982.

Television Play: *Young Shoulders,* with Robert Smith, from the novel by Wain, 1984.

Novels

Hurry on Down. London, Secker and Warburg, 1953; as *Born in Captivity*, New York, Knopf, 1954.
Living in the Present. London, Secker and Warburg, 1955; New York, Putnam, 1960.
The Contenders. London, Macmillan, and New York, St. Martin's Press, 1958.
A Travelling Woman. London, Macmillan, and New York, St. Martin's Press, 1959.
Strike the Father Dead. London, Macmillan, and New York, St. Martin's Press, 1962.
The Young Visitors. London, Macmillan, and New York, Viking Press, 1965.
The Smaller Sky. London, Macmillan, 1967.
A Winter in the Hills. London, Macmillan, and New York, Viking Press, 1970.
The Pardoner's Tale. London, Macmillan, 1978; New York, Viking Press, 1979.
Young Shoulders. London, Macmillan, 1982; as *The Free Zone Starts Here*, New York, Delacorte Press, 1984.

Short Stories

Nuncle and Other Stories. London, Macmillan, 1960; New York, St. Martin's Press, 1961.
Death of the Hind Legs and Other Stories. London, Macmillan, and New York, Viking Press, 1966.
The Life Guard. London, Macmillan, 1971; New York, Viking Press, 1972.
King Caliban and Other Stories. London, Macmillan, 1978.

Other

Preliminary Essays. London, Macmillan, and New York, St. Martin's Press, 1957.
Gerard Manley Hopkins: An Idiom of Desperation. London, Oxford University Press, 1959.
Sprightly Running: Part of an Autobiography. London, Macmillan, 1962; New York, St. Martin's Press, 1963.
Essays on Literature and Ideas. London, Macmillan, and New York, St. Martin's Press, 1963.
The Living World of Shakespeare: A Playgoer's Guide. London, Macmillan, and New York, St. Martin's Press, 1964; revised edition, 1979.
Arnold Bennett. New York, Columbia University Press, 1967.
A House for the Truth: Critical Essays. London, Macmillan, 1972; New York, Viking Press, 1973.
Samuel Johnson. London, Macmillan, 1974; New York, Viking Press, 1975; revised edition, Macmillan, 1980.
A John Wain Selection, edited by Geoffrey Halson. London, Longman, 1977.
Professing Poetry. London, Macmillan, 1977; New York, Viking Press, 1978.
Lizzie's Floating Shop (for children). London, Bodley Head, 1981.
Samuel Johnson 1709-84, with K.K. Yung. London, Herbert Press, 1984.

Editor, *Contemporary Reviews of Romantic Poetry*. London, Harrap, and New York, Barnes and Noble, 1953.
Editor, *Interpretations: Essays on Twelve English Poems*. London, Routledge, 1955; New York, Hillary House, 1957.
Editor, *International Literary Annual*. London, Calder, and New York, Criterion, 2 vols., 1959-60.
Editor, *Fanny Burney's Diary*. London, Folio Society, 1960.

Editor, *Anthology of Modern Poetry*. London, Hutchinson, 1963.
Editor, *Pope*. New York, Dell, 1963.
Editor, *Selected Shorter Poems of Thomas Hardy*. London, Macmillan, and New York, St. Martin's Press, 1966; revised edition, 1975.
Editor, *The Dynasts*, by Thomas Hardy. London, Macmillan, and New York, St. Martin's Press, 1966.
Editor, *Selected Shorter Stories of Thomas Hardy*. London, Macmillan, and New York, St. Martin's Press, 1966.
Editor, *Shakespeare: Macbeth: A Casebook*. London, Macmillan, 1968.
Editor, *Shakespeare: Othello: A Casebook*. London, Macmillan, 1971.
Editor, *Johnson as Critic*. London, Routledge, 1973.
Editor, *Lives of the English Poets: A Selection*, by Samuel Johnson. London, Dent, and New York, Dutton, 1975.
Editor, *Johnson on Johnson: A Selection of the Personal and Autobiographical Writings of Samuel Johnson*. London, Dent, and New York, Dutton, 1976.
Editor, *The Poetry of Thomas Hardy: A New Selection*. London, Macmillan, 1977.
Editor, *An Edmund Wilson Celebration*. Oxford, Phaidon Press, 1978; as *Edmund Wilson: The Man and His Work*, New York, New York University Press, 1978.
Editor, *Personal Choice: A Poetry Anthology*. Newton Abbot, Devon, David and Charles, 1978.
Editor, *Anthology of Contemporary Poetry: Post-War to the Present*. London, Hutchinson, 1979.
Editor, *Everyman's Book of English Verse*. London, Dent, 1981.
Editor, *The Private Memoirs and Confessions of a Justified Sinner*, by James Hogg. London, Penguin, 1983.

Translator, *The Seafarer*. Warwick, Greville Press, 1980.

*

Bibliography: *John Braine and John Wain: A Reference Guide* by Dale Salwak. Boston, Hall, 1980.

Manuscript Collection: Edinburgh University Library.

Critical Studies: "John Wain et le Magie de l'Individu" by Françoise Barrière, in *Le Monde* (Paris), 8 August 1970; "John Wain: Révolte et Neutralité" by Pierre Yvard, in *Études Anglaises 23* (Paris), October-December 1970; "The New Puritanism, The New Academism, The New..." by the author, in *A House for the Truth*, 1972.

John Wain comments:
As a writer of fiction, I see myself as being in the tradition of the realistic novel—credible characters, everyday settings, and on the whole outward-looking rather than introspective. In poetry I welcome the freedom to get right outside these boundaries if I want to—to go back into remote history (*Feng*) or to be very personal and write directly about my own experience. Poetry, to me, is essentially wide-ranging, which is why I have trained myself to write it over a wide stylistic range and in many forms, popular and "free."

*   *   *

Perhaps better known as a novelist, short-story writer, and critic, John Wain contributed to Robert Conquest's influential anthology of the mid-1950's, *New Lines*; and his poems in this selection alone uncompromisingly defined his distrust of glib emotionalism and the "poetic" gesture. Yet the apparent toughness of his determined anti-romanticism, and a note of conscious cleverness sometimes reminiscent of the early Auden, were superficially deceptive. Wain's refusal to write orthodox nature poetry, or indulge in the rant of conventional patriotism for "this mildewed island," rejects an easy emotive tone for the "sterner choice" of recording without embellishment a "love that I can never speak by rote." His attitude towards the love relationship, although resolutely unsentimentalized, also communicates authentic depth of feeling in pieces like "Poem in Words of One Syllable," "On Reading Love Poetry in the Dentist's Waiting Room," and "Don't Let's Spoil It All, I Thought We Were Going to Be Such Good Friends." A self-evident initial taste for novel, attention-arresting subjects and titles is most strikingly illustrated by the wittily original "Poem Feigned to Have Been Written by an Electronic Brain." Its technical inventiveness, culminating in the explosive stutter of the furiously frustrated machine, conveys a wholly serious statement about the nature of poetry. It is, in fact, not emotion but its cheapening by florid rhetorical diction and the distortions of sentimental poeticism which Wain has strenuously rejected. "When It Comes," a lament written under the shadow of the mushroom cloud for those unfulfilled at the "burning instant" of the world's annihilation, is the more poignantly telling for the strict control of its form.

In his aspiration to "strip our stale speech clean," Wain has shown an Augustan admiration for restraint and the imposition of order upon emotion. Indeed in *Mixed Feelings* and *A Word Carved on a Sill* he seemed in danger of becoming imprisoned by the restriction of his favourite Empsonian verse-forms, terza rima and villanelle. This gave much of his earlier work, for all its aphoristic wit, a certain monotony and air of the accomplished intellectual exercise. Yet the effectiveness of these tight verbal disciplines may be seen in the delectable "Gentleman Aged Five Before the Mirror," which has the same insight and impact as "Villanelle: For Harpo Marx": "In your fake world of frantic gag and pose/We see our real despair come striding near./The clown may speak what silent Hamlet knows."

In *Weep Before God* the threatened stranglehold of neat three-line stanzas was successfully broken to achieve a far greater metrical versatility. The exuberantly varied rhythms of "Boisterous Poem about Poetry" are as uninhibited as its expression of faith in the poet's vocation in an age of "empty clangour" and "wilderness of craving silences." In personal poems like "Time Was," "Anniversary," "To a Friend in Trouble," and the moving love-lyrics "Apology for Understatement" and "Anecdote of 2 a.m.," emotion has become unashamedly explicit. Wain returns to the theme of completeness in "Wise Men, All Questioning Done," a poem as quietly yet powerfully memorable as the fine "This above All Is Precious and Remarkable." Aspects of contemporary violence and individual responsibility are explored in the portrait of the hunted Gestapo man in "On the Death of a Murderer"; and in the long, technically adventurous "A Song about Major Eatherly," which voices a conviction that the later penitence of the pilot who dropped the atom bomb on Nagasaki "will not take away our guilt."

Wain's recent work has developed in more experimental directions. His addresses in *Letters to Five Artists* to two poets, a painter, a sculptor, and a musician, ranging widely in time and place but unified by recurring reference to key figures like Ovid and Villon, attempt as he says to examine "some of the complex truth about man and his situation." This freely allusive blend of personal, philosophical, and historical is a natural extension of the dominant theme is his long poem *Wildtrack*: the interplay of

past and present, public and private, of—again to quote his own words—the "inward-looking Night-self and outward-looking Day-self that together constitute the human personality." *Feng*, based on an early version of the Hamlet myth, is a sequence of 17 dramatic monologues in a flexible diversity of verse-patterns interwoven with prose passages. Its analysis of hallucinated fanaticism, focusing on the figure of the usurper-uncle fettered and finally destroyed by the power he has seized, has a sharp relevance for the present century.

--Margaret Willy

WAINWRIGHT, Jeffrey. British. Born in Stoke-on-Trent, Staffordshire, 19 February 1944. Educated at Florence County Primary Junior School; Longton High School, 1955-62; University of Leeds, B.A. 1965, M.A. 1967. Married Judith Batt in 1967; one son and one daughter. Lecturer in American Literature, University College of Wales, Aberystwyth, 1967-72. Since 1973, Lecturer, then Senior Lecturer in English, Manchester Polytechnic. Visiting Instructor, Long Island University, New York, 1970-71. Address: 11 Hesketh Avenue, Didsbury, Manchester M2O 8QN, England.

PUBLICATIONS

Verse

The Important Man. Newcastle upon Tyne, Northern House, 1970.
Heart's Desire. Manchester, Carcanet, 1978.
Selected Poems. Manchester, Carcanet, 1985.

Play

The Mystery of the Charity of Joan of Arc, adaptation of a work by Charles Péguy (produced Stratford upon Avon, 1984).

*

Critical Study: introduction by the author to *Heart's Desire* in *Poetry Book Society Bulletin* (London), Spring 1978.

*   *   *

"History, which is Eternal Life, is what/We need to celebrate." From his early poems on the battles of Waterloo and Jutland in *The Important Man* to "Thomas Müntzer" in *Heart's Desire,* Jeffrey Wainwright has been drawn to historical subjects. He treats them in a language sparse and plain enough to be easily underestimated. But Wainwright is a poet of vision. His poems show that social reality is everywhere a construct, made by human beings and therefore capable of being changed by them; and his unusual gift is in writing of the particular human activity or transaction in a way which reveals the larger power relations and social constructions which inform what is apparently personal. Without depending on rhetorical or analytical language he can show that questions of "politics," class, wealth, or power are not optional extras to understanding, nor simply the province of the committed, but are implicit in all that we do. It follows that the psychology of our actions, even our theology, is all of a piece with its politics, and Wainwright is as interested in states of mind, emotion, and beliefs as in material action.

Müntzer, the 16th-century Protestant reformer and leader in the Peasant War, is the subject of Wainwright's longest poem. Reviled as a madman and liar for daring to propose that "God made/ All men free with his own blood shed," Müntzer's vision is inseparable from his struggle for justice. The poem conveys the power of his exultant faith: inspired by God's "promised rainbow" at the battle of Frankenhausen, he says, "I thought I could catch their bullets in my hands." Vision and courage like his is the precondition of social justice, but it is not the sufficient means, for what it confronts in the poem is the material power of those who monopolise wealth and learning: you *can't* catch bullets. Wainwright is not afraid to show the heroic visionary as sometimes ridiculous, self-punishing, and self-indulgent—perhaps necessarily so. The pursuit of Paradise on Earth is both idealism and action, both hopeful and terrible: as another poem, "Before Battle," puts it, "We wade so deep in our desire for good."

The title-sequence in *Heart's Desire* treats the same themes in more personal terms. Poems of love and grief show how we may "escape ourselves alone": love is the first move beyond self. "Heart's desire" is almost an oxymoron, in which the most inward and personal are yoked to what points out beyond the self, for our desires must be formed and chosen. In forming them we may actually have to fight "our dealing hearts and flying brain." These limpid lyrics are carefully woven out of the repetitions of a few nouns—desire, dream, heart, light—which, like all the most common and familiar words in the language, bear the most complex charges of meaning.

Wainwright's spare language suggests utterance wrung from silence. It suggests human beings reduced to vulnerable simplicity and truthfulness by the pressure of immediate and particular circumstances, driven to speech by the need to become conscious of their situations. His socialism, too, is the stronger for its near-reticence, its being allowed to emerge in the reader's own construction of the poem's juxtaposed images.

—R.J.C. Watt

WAKOSKI, Diane. American. Born in Whittier, California, 3 August 1937. Educated at the University of California, Berkeley, B.A. in English 1960. Married 1) S. Shepard Sherbell in 1965 (divorced); 2) Michael Watterlond in 1973 (divorced, 1975); 3) Robert J. Turney in 1982. Clerk, British Book Centre, New York, 1960-63; English teacher, Junior High School 22, New York, 1963-66; Lecturer, New School for Social Research, New York, 1969; Poet-in-Residence, California Institute of Technology, Pasadena, Spring 1972, University of Virginia, Charlottesville, autumns 1972-73, Willamette University, Salem, Oregon, Spring 1974, University of California, Irvine, Fall 1974, Hollins College, Virginia, 1974, Lake Forest College, Illinois, 1974, Colorado College, Colorado Springs, 1974, Macalester College, St. Paul, 1975, Michigan State University, East Lansing, Spring 1975, University of Wisconsin, Madison, Fall 1975, Whitman College, Walla Walla, Washington, Fall 1976, University of Washington, Seattle, Spring-Summer 1977, University of Hawaii, Honolulu, Fall 1978, and Emory University, Atlanta 1980-81. Since 1976, Writer-in-Residence, Michigan State University. United States Information Agency lecturer, Romania, Hungary, and Yugoslavia, 1976. Recipient: Bread Loaf Writers Conference Robert Frost Fellowship, 1966; Cassandra Foundation Award, 1970; New York State Council on the Arts grant, 1971; Guggenheim grant, 1972; National Endowment for the Arts grant, 1973; Fulbright Fellowship, 1984. Address: 607 Division, East Lansing, Michigan 48823, U.S.A.

PUBLICATIONS

Verse

Coins and Coffins. New York, Hawk's Well Press, 1962.
Four Young Lady Poets, with others, edited by LeRoi Jones. New York, Totem-Corinth, 1962.
Dream Sheet. New York, Software Press, 1965.
Discrepancies and Apparitions. New York, Doubleday, 1966.
The George Washington Poems. New York, Riverrun Press, 1967.
Greed Parts One and Two. Los Angeles, Black Sparrow Press, 1968.
The Diamond Merchant. Cambridge, Massachusetts, Sans Souci Press, 1968.
Inside the Blood Factory. New York, Doubleday, 1968.
A Play and Two Poems, with Robert Kelly and Ron Loewinsohn. Los Angeles, Black Sparrow Press, 1968.
Thanking My Mother for Piano Lessons. Mount Horeb, Wisconsin, Perishable Press, 1969.
Greed Parts 3 and 4. Los Angeles, Black Sparrow Press, 1969.
The Moon Has a Complicated Geography. Palo Alto, California, Odda Tala Press, 1969.
The Magellanic Clouds. Los Angeles, Black Sparrow Press, 1970.
Greed Parts 5-7. Los Angeles, Black Sparrow Press, 1970.
The Lament of the Lady Bank Dick. Cambridge, Massachusetts, Sans Souci Press, 1970.
Love, You Big Fat Snail. San Francisco, Tenth Muse, 1970.
Black Dream Ditty for Billy "The Kid" Seen in Dr. Generosity's Bar Recruiting for Hell's Angels and Black Mafia. Los Angeles, Black Sparrow Press, 1970.
Exorcism. Boston, My Dukes, 1971.
This Water Baby: For Tony. Santa Barbara, California, Unicorn Press, 1971.
On Barbara's Shore. Los Angeles, Black Sparrow Press, 1971.
The Motorcycle Betrayal Poems. New York, Simon and Schuster, 1971.
The Pumpkin Pie, Or Reassurances Are Always False, Tho We Love Them. Only Physics Counts. Los Angeles, Black Sparrow Press, 1972.
The Purple Finch Song. Mount Horeb, Wisconsin, Perishable Press, 1972.
Sometimes a Poet Will Hijack the Moon. Providence, Rhode Island, Burning Deck, 1972.
Smudging. Los Angeles, Black Sparrow Press, 1972.
The Owl and the Snake: A Fable. Mount Horeb, Wisconsin, Perishable Press, 1973.
Greed Parts 8, 9, 11. Los Angeles, Black Sparrow Press, 1973.
Dancing on the Grave of a Son of a Bitch. Los Angeles, Black Sparrow Press, 1973.
Winter Sequences. Los Angeles, Black Sparrow Press, 1973.
Trilogy: Coins and Coffins, Discrepancies and Apparitions, The George Washington Poems. New York, Doubleday, 1974.
Looking for the King of Spain. Los Angeles, Black Sparrow Press, 1974.
The Wandering Tatler. Mount Horeb, Wisconsin, Perishable Press, 1974.
Abalone. Los Angeles, Black Sparrow Press, 1974.

Virtuoso Literature for Two and Four Hands. New York, Doubleday, 1975.

The Fable of the Lion and the Scorpion. Milwaukee, Pentagram Press, 1975.

Waiting for the King of Spain. Santa Barbara, California, Black Sparrow Press, 1976.

The Laguna Contract of Diane Wakoski. Madison, Wisconsin, Crepuscular Press, 1976.

George Washington's Camp Cups. Madison, Wisconsin, Red Ozier Press, 1976.

The Last Poem, with *Tough Company*, by Charles Bukowski. Santa Barbara, California, Black Sparrow Press, 1976.

The Ring. Santa Barbara, California, Black Sparrow Press, 1977.

Overnight Projects with Wood. Madison, Wisconsin, Red Ozier Press, 1977.

Spending Christmas with the Man from Receiving at Sears. Santa Barbara, California, Black Sparrow Press, 1977.

The Man Who Shook Hands. New York, Doubleday, 1978.

Pachelbel's Canon. Santa Barbara, California, Black Sparrow Press, 1978.

Trophies. Santa Barbara, California, Black Sparrow Press, 1979.

Cap of Darkness, Including Looking for the King of Spain and Pachelbel's Canon. Santa Barbara, California, Black Sparrow Press, 1980.

Making a Sacher Torte. Mount Horeb, Wisconsin, Perishable Press, 1981.

Saturn's Rings. New York, Targ, 1982.

The Lady Who Drove Me to the Airport. Worcester, Massachusetts, Metacom Press, 1982.

Divers. N.p., Barbarian Press, 1982.

The Magician's Feastletters. Santa Barbara, California, Black Sparrow Press, 1982.

Looking for Beethoven in Las Vegas. New York, Red Ozier Press, 1983.

The Collected Greed: Parts 1-13. Santa Barbara, California, Black Sparrow Press, 1984.

Other

Form Is an Extension of Content. Los Angeles, Black Sparrow Press, 1972.

Creating a Personal Mythology. Los Angeles, Black Sparrow Press, 1975.

Variations on a Theme. Santa Barbara, California, Black Sparrow Press, 1976.

Toward a New Poetry. Ann Arbor, University of Michigan Press, 1980.

*

Manuscript Collection: University of Arizona Library, Tucson.

Critical Study: "A Terrible War: A Conversation with Diane Wakoski" by Philip Gerber and Robert Gemmett, in *Far Point 4* (Winnipeg), Spring-Summer 1970.

Diane Wakoski comments:

I think of myself as a narrative poet, a poet creating both a personal narrative and a personal mythology. I write long poems, and emotional ones. My themes are loss, imprecise perception, justice, truth, the duality of the world, and the possibilities of magic, transformation, and the creation of beauty out of ugliness. My language is dramatic, oral, and as American as I can make it, with the appropriate plain surfaces and rich vocabulary. I am impatient with stupidity, bureaucracy, and organizations. Poetry, for me, is the supreme art of the individual using a huge magnificent range of language to show how special and different and wonderful his perceptions are. With verve and finesse. With discursive precision. And with utter contempt for pettiness of imagination or spirit.

*   *   *

One of America's most important and controversial contemporary poets, Diane Wakoski is also one of the most prolific, having published 14 collections of new poems since 1962. Early appraisals of her work as a product of her association with the "deep image" poets of New York, and later efforts to discount it as "confessional," or angry or self-pitying, have all proved inadequate or unjust characterizations of her indefatigable imagination. In fact, like Wallace Stevens (one of her favorite poets), she has made the imagination itself the real subject of her work. In her efforts to show us how the mind may work to acknowledge or create beauty in virtually any situation, she has found the story-teller's narration as useful as the image, and the actor's use of masks and roles as telling as the *cri de coeur*. The self in this body of work has become an instrument to awaken the imaginative consciousness of others. Paradoxically, this intellectual poet, who makes no secret of her love for classical music or her wide-ranging knowledge of nature and cultures, is also a "popular" poet. In great demand for readings, she is warmly received by large audiences, not because she "spills her guts" (to use Anne Sexton's famous phrase), but because her digressive style allows so many points of entry into the webs of thought and feeling she creates.

Wakoski's best works have always engaged the most enduring problems of the relationship between ourselves and other human beings, nature, or the ideas we use to order our lives. "Justice Is Reason Enough," the much anthologized poem about the suicide of an imagined brother, is a case in point. Another is "The Ice Eagle" from her best-known and most surrealist book, *Inside the Blood Factory*; it concerns the relationship of women to a national symbol of power. A third and later example, "Looking for the Bald Eagles in Wisconsin," focuses on the poet's sense of responsibility toward vanishing forms of nature. *The Collected Greed* brings together poems that have appeared in chapbooks since 1968, showing both the continuity of Wakoski's poetic interests and the seriousness of her effort to develop an "esthetique du mal"—a poetic stance capable of dealing authentically with life's uglier aspects. In this stance lies her distinction. She has created an idiosyncratic form that allows her to be discursive or imagistic, factual or mythical, mundane or visionary, and to shift from one of these levels to another without losing her audience, relying primarily on common language and ordinary rhythms of speech.

Wakoski has been a mythological poet from the beginning. Her well-known poems confronting "the man's world" in the person of George Washington, and her more singular creation of a fantasy figure called the "King of Spain" are only the most obvious manifestations of a pervasive tendency to see ordinary experience in mythic terms. Perhaps her most impressive achievement as a mythmaker has been to imagine a female self who is equal to the challenges of contemporary life. Although her poems are still filled with people, she takes increasing pleasure in nature: in the lady slipper which she loves now "more than jewels or gold or men," or in the mushroom's inky "cap of darkness" (a phrase she has also used to refer to her invisible Athena-like helmet for combatting the ghost of greed). Although she remains painfully aware of imperfections—her own as well as the culture's—her recent collection, *The Magician's Feastletters*, is really a celebration of the adequacy of the poet's imagination.

Wakoski's talent, courage, conscience, breadth of vision, and insight into human weakness seem likely to make this ambitious, coherent *oeuvre* one of the hallmarks of our time.

—Estella Lauter

WALCOTT, Derek (Alton). British. Born in Castries, St. Lucia, West Indies, 23 January 1930. Educated at St. Mary's College, St. Lucia; University of the West Indies, Kingston, Jamaica, B.A. 1953. Married 1) Fay Moston in 1954 (divorced, 1959); 2) Margaret Ruth Maillard in 1962; three children. Taught at St. Mary's College and Jamaica College. Formerly, feature writer, *Public Opinion*, Kingston, and *Trinidad Guardian*, Port-of-Spain. Since 1959, Founding Director, Trinidad Theatre Workshop. Recipient: Rockefeller Fellowship, for drama, 1957; Guinness Award, 1961; Royal Society of Literature Heinemann Award, 1966, 1983; Cholmondeley Award, 1969; Order of the Humming Bird, Trinidad and Tobago, 1969; Obie Award, for drama, 1971; Jock Campbell Award (*New Statesman*), 1974; Welsh Arts Council International Writers Prize, 1980; MacArthur Fellowship, 1981. Address: 165 Duke of Edinburgh Avenue, Diego Martin, Trinidad.

PUBLICATIONS

Verse

25 Poems. Port-of-Spain, Trinidad, Guardian Commercial Printery, 1948.
Epitaph for the Young: XII Cantos. Bridgetown, Barbados Advocate, 1949.
Poems. Kingston, Jamaica, City Printery, 1951.
In a Green Night: Poems 1948-1960. London, Cape, 1962.
Selected Poems. New York, Farrar Straus, 1964.
The Castaway and Other Poems. London, Cape, 1965.
The Gulf and Other Poems. London, Cape, 1969; as *The Gulf*, New York, Farrar Straus, 1970.
Another Life. New York, Farrar Straus, and London, Cape, 1973.
Sea Grapes. London, Cape, and New York, Farrar Straus, 1976.
Selected Poems, edited by O.R. Dathorne. London, Heinemann, 1977.
The Star-Apple Kingdom. New York, Farrar Straus, 1979; London, Cape, 1980.
Selected Poetry, edited by Wayne Brown. London, Heinemann, 1980.
The Fortunate Traveller. New York, Farrar Straus, 1981; London, Faber, 1982.
Midsummer. New York, Farrar Straus, 1983; London, Faber, 1984.

Plays

Henri Christophe: A Chronicle (produced St. Lucia, 1950; London, 1951). Bridgetown, Barbados Advocate, 1950.
Henri Dernier: A Play for Radio Production. Bridgetown, Barbados Advocate, 1951.

The Sea at Dauphin (produced Trinidad, 1954; London, 1960; New York, 1978). Mona, University College of the West Indies Extra-Mural Department, 1954; in *Dream on Monkey Mountain and Other Plays*, 1971.
Ione: A Play with Music (produced Trinidad, 1957). Mona, University College of the West Indies Extra-Mural Department, 1954.
Drums and Colours (produced Trinidad, 1958). Published in *Caribbean Quarterly* (Kingston), vii, 1 and 2, 1961.
Ti-Jean and His Brothers (produced Port-of-Spain, Trinidad, 1958; New York, 1972). Included in *Dream on Monkey Mountain and Other Plays*, 1971.
Malcochon; or, Six in the Rain (produced St. Lucia, 1959; as *Six in the Rain*, produced London, 1960; as *Malcochon*, produced New York, 1969). Included in *Dream on Monkey Mountain and Other Plays*, 1971.
Dream on Monkey Mountain (produced Toronto, 1967; Waterford, Connecticut, 1968; New York, 1971). Included in *Dream on Monkey Mountain and Other Plays*, 1971.
In a Fine Castle (produced Jamaica, 1970; Trinidad, 1971; Los Angeles, 1972).
Dream on Monkey Mountain and Other Plays (includes *Ti-Jean and His Brothers, Malcochon, The Sea at Dauphin*, and the essay "What the Twilight Says"). New York, Farrar Straus, 1971; London, Cape, 1972.
The Charlatan, music by Galt MacDermot (produced Los Angeles, 1974).
The Joker of Seville, adaptation of a play by Tirso de Molina (produced Port-of-Spain, 1974). Included in *The Joker of Seville, and O Babylon!*, 1978.
O Babylon! (produced Port-of-Spain, 1976). Included in *The Joker of Seville, and O Babylon!*, 1978.
The Joker of Seville, and O Babylon! New York, Farrar Straus, 1978; London, Cape, 1979.
Remembrance (produced New York, 1978; London, 1980). Included in *Remembrance, and Pantomime*, 1980.
Pantomime (broadcast, 1979; produced London, 1979; Washington, D.C., 1981). Included in *Remembrance, and Pantomime*, 1980.
Remembrance, and Pantomime. London, Faber, and New York, Farrar Straus, 1980.
The Isle Is Full of Noises (produced Hartford, Connecticut, 1982).
Beef, No Chicken (produced New Haven, Connecticut, 1982). Included in *Three Plays*, 1985.
Three Plays (includes *The Last Carnival; Beef, No Chicken; A Branch of the Blue Nile*). New York, Farrar Straus, 1985.

Radio Play: *Pantomime*, 1979 (UK).

*

Bibliography: *Derek Walcott: A Bibliography of Published Poems...1944-1979* by Irma E. Goldstraw, St. Augustine, Trinidad, University of the West Indies, 1979.

Critical Studies: *Derek Walcott: Memory as Vision* by Edward Baugh, London, Longman, 1978; *Derek Walcott: Poet of the Islands* by Ned Thomas, Cardiff, Welsh Arts Council, 1980; *Derek Walcott* by Robert D. Hamner, Boston, Twayne, 1981.

*   *   *

In a period distinguished by a surprising number of striking, brilliant poets, even if their range is often limited, it has long been a common concern that today's poetry has not gained the deserved wider and more general audience poetry has so frequently achieved in the past. But of the poets now before us, Derek Walcott may have the opportunity to create such an opening. In addition, while passionately opposed to oppression and colonialism, and deeply aware of the cultural isolation of his Caribbean origins, he has by a personal alchemy found the gold and silver of language and place and more than anyone else fired them into a new tradition of West Indian poetry in general English, as in "North and South":

> Now at the rising of Venus...
>   ...I accept my function
> as a colonial upstart at the end of an empire,
> a single, circling, homeless satellite...
> It's good that everything's gone, except their language.

And of course, there is the commanding achievement, the excellence of the poetry itself. He is clearly a major figure, and attention should now be paid to these emerging and defining strokes of his accomplishment.

There are several reasons for Walcott's current and potential success in gaining attention. The most important is a crucial technical breakthrough he may have provided. In his finest poems—they are too numerous to mention here, but most of the poems in *The Star-Apple Kingdom* and *The Fortunate Traveller* must be included—he has deftly managed to negotiate a new arrangement between the surface complexity of modernism, which too often dissipates in depth, and the decepive clarity of much poetry of the past, the lyrics of *In Memoriam*, for example, where the surface although easily understood, quickly recedes like that of a pool into mystery and contradiction. The star-apple, and the title poem of *The Star-Apple Kingdom*, in one of their dimensions become metaphors for the method. The fruit, indigenous to the Caribbean islands and their heritage, is easily recognized, but when cut open, probed, or analyzed as it were with a knife, reveals its hidden design within.

Walcott's relative accessibility, despite the genuine complexity of his poetry, is also due to the common touch he has learned as a dramatist. His plays, written in West Indian or Creole English, constitute a kind of dramatic poetry that communicates sufficiently and quickly with the varied and immediate audience drama requires. Among Walcott's allegiances, although many, is certainly the literature of Renaissance England. As he remarks ironically in *The Fortunate Traveller*, its title a reversal of Nashe's 1594 novel *The Unfortunate Traveler*, "What was my field? Late sixteenth century." Of course during this period Shakespeare, Marlowe, and others practised simultaneously lyric, dramatic, and narrative poetry to rather spectacular advantage. Without his own common touch and poetic versatility Shakespeare's seemingly direct, but aristocratic and difficult sonnets probably would not have been possible. Walcott's experience with drama also heightens the pressure in his poetry and expands his skill in fashioning the implied dramatic situations common to lyric poetry. Other factors that have contributed to Walcott's growing reputation, although not central, are important in the current quest for a wider readership for recent poetry. These include his well-known teaching at Harvard, Columbia, and Boston University; his MacArthur grant; his media attention; and his dual residency in, south, Trinidad, and his adopted Boston, north.

In making new use of the language that is not gone, the younger Walcott came under the influence of many poets, some accepted and some rejected. But poets always begin this way. There is Keats with his Spenser, Shakespeare, and all the others. And in trying to establish an American tradition, nascent American literature did the same from Anne Bradstreet and the English metaphysicals to Cooper and Scott. Surely the trip north in *The Fortunate Traveller* recognizes the parallels of the task, both literary and historial. But since *Another Life*, and in so many earlier poems as well, the new voice has clearly declared itself. The symbolic locus for the mature Walcott tradition, written in a voice with increasing authority and unmistakably his own, is a rather shabby hotel and pool outside Port of Prince, Trinidad. It seems to have become Walcott's Caribbean reference point and deliberately contradicts the glamorous tourist image of the islands he rejected at the very outset of his career. It is a place for transients of all times and places. Here Ovid, an impoverished tourist in a frayed robe, comes to visit, and from its perspective double exposures, brilliantly common in his poetry, routinely occur. In the South section of *The Fortunate Traveller* the Aegean and the Caribbean, with their islands, merge and evoke the Trojan War; "The Cove" recalls the "Legend of Yseult"; "A sepia lagoon" links an abandoned Navy base "to dim Pacific surf." If Walcott *should* choose to look into that particular pool ("Entering a glass/ I surface quickly now"), unlike the "Narcissi, brooding on boards," his own visage, outline intact, would quickly merge in the depths with figures from the past and times long ago.

The poetic image has always been the indispensable requirement of great lyric poetry, and here Walcott is not outshone by any contemporary poet. The required sea-change is remarkable. His images range from the grand to the most colloquial, and there are seldom problems of modulation or adjustment. In this sense, his imagery parallels his occasional use of Caribbean English in his most exalted poems, such as "The Schooner Flight" from *The Star-Apple Kingdom*. Occasionally they become over-freighted with the possibility of implications, but usually they have the necessary, precarious balance between the concrete and the connotative. Imagery is his principal vehicle for his journeys, even when they are partly literal as in *The Fortunate Traveller*. There in "Upstate" he explains/ parodies locomotion: "A knife blade of cold air keeps prying/ the bus window open." "The spring country/ won't be shut out," nor will simile and metaphor. The mode of transportation suddenly changes. His imagery can be both direct and apparently simple, or ecstatic and highly-wrought. There are the final lines of the "envoi" of "The Hotel Normandie Pool," remarkable for their dramatic simplicity: "Dusk. The trees blacken like the pool's umbrellas./ Dusk. Suspension of every image and its voice." Then there is the rising net image in the opening stanza of "The Season of Phantasmal Peace": "the net rising soundless as night, the birds' cries soundless...." Walcott's achievement parallels what García Lorca achieved in his brief career for Spanish poetry in the 1920's and 1930's.

Like Lorca, too, Walcott is a genuine romantic, and like the English Romantics of the late 18th and early 19th centuries, he has a Coleridgean sense of organic form and a sure metrical instinct. He is not, in his words, "a free verse nightingale." This sense of form, again as in the case of the great romantics, expands from individual poems to larger concepts. There is what has been called his *Prelude*, *Another Life*, which parallels the development of man and artist. There are the lyric cross-references of *The Star-Apple Kingdom*. There is the virtuoso use of Nashe's novel in *The Fortunate Traveller*. The former is about a young man who goes from England to Italy. Walcott's collection is about an older man who goes north. As Walcott correctly perceives, both learn through the experience of journey. They are complementary works of picaresque brilliance, and in *Fortunate* the word is partly ambiguous, the seeming reversals fascinating.

There are, of course, reservations to be made about the work of almost any writer. Here passion occasionally breaks into sentimentality, and deeply felt themes can when repeated too often become monotonous. But do Seamus Heaney, Derek Walcott, James Merrill, and John Ashbery really have any genuine peers in the very first rank of poets writing in English? Only a few. And Walcott's own line from "Shabine Leaves the Republic" surely applies to himself: "I had no nation now but the imagination."

—Gaynor F. Bradish

WALDMAN, Anne (Lesley). American. Born in Millville, New Jersey, 2 April 1945. Educated at Bennington College, Vermont, B.A. in English 1966. Married Reed Eyre Bye in 1980; one son. Assistant Director, 1966-68, and Director, 1968-78, St. Mark's Church-in-the-Bowery Poetry Project, New York. Since 1974, Founding Co-Director, with Allen Ginsberg, Jack Kerouac School of Poetics, Naropa Institute, Boulder, Colorado. Editor, *The World*, *Angel Hair* and Angel Hair Books, and Full Court Press, all New York, and *Rocky Ledge*, Boulder. Recipient: Dylan Thomas Award, 1967; Cultural Artists grant, 1976; National Endowment for the Arts grant, 1979. Agent: Lynn Lynn, Hyacinth Girls Music, 799 Broadway, Suite 325 D3, New York, New York 10003. Address: Naropa Institute, 1111 Pearl Street, Boulder, Colorado 80302, U.S.A.

PUBLICATIONS

Verse

On the Wing. New York, Boke, 1967.
Giant Night. New York, Angel Hair, 1968.
O My Life! New York, Angel Hair, 1969.
Baby Breakdown. Indianapolis, Bobbs Merrill, 1970.
Up Through the Years. New York, Angel Hair, 1970.
Giant Night: Selected Poems. New York, Corinth, 1970.
Icy Rose. New York, Angel Hair, 1971.
No Hassles. New York, Kulchur, 1971.
Memorial Day, with Ted Berrigan. New York, Poetry Project, 1971.
Holy City. Privately printed, 1971.
Goodies from Anne Waldman. London, Strange Faeces Press, 1971.
Light and Shadow. Privately printed, 1972.
The West Indies Poems. New York, Boke, 1972.
Spin Off. Bolinas, California, Big Sky, 1972.
Self Portrait, with Joe Brainard. New York, Siamese Banana Press, 1973.
Life Notes: Selected Poems. Indianapolis, Bobbs Merrill, 1973.
The Contemplative Life. Detroit, Alternative Press, n.d.
Fast Speaking Woman. Detroit, Red Hanrahan Press, 1974.
Fast Speaking Woman and Other Chants. San Francisco, City Lights, 1975; revised edition, 1978.
Sun the Blond Out. Berkeley, California, Arif, 1975.
Journals and Dreams. New York, Stonehill, 1976.
Shaman. Boston, Munich, 1977.
4 Travels, with Reed Bye. New York, Sayonara, 1978.
To a Young Poet. Boston, White Raven, 1979.
Countries. West Branch, Iowa, Toothpaste Press, 1980.
Cabin. Calais, Vermont, Z Press, 1982.

First Baby Poems. Boulder, Colorado, Rocky Ledge, 1982; augmented edition, New York, Hyacinth Girls, 1983.
Make-Up on Empty Space. West Branch, Iowa, Toothpaste Press, 1984.

Recordings: *John Giorno and Anne Waldman*, Giorno, 1978; *Fast Speaking Woman*, S Press Tapes; *Uh-Oh Plutonium!*, Hyacinth Girls, 1982.

Other

Editor, *The World Anthology: Poems from the St. Mark's Poetry Project*, and *Another World*. Indianapolis, Bobbs Merrill, 1969-71.
Editor, with Marilyn Webb, *Talking Poetics from Naropa Institute*. Boulder, Colorado, Shambala, 2 vols., 1978-79.

*

Critical Studies: by Alicia Ostriker, in *Partisan Review* (New Brunswick, New Jersey), Spring-Summer 1971, and *Parnassus* (New York), Fall-Winter, 1974; Gerard Malanga, in *Poetry* (Chicago), January 1974; Richard Morris, in *Margins* (Milwaukee, Wisconsin), October-November 1974; Aram Saroyan, in *New York Times Book Review*, April 1976; *The Beats: Literary Bohemians in Postwar America* edited by Ann Charters, Detroit, Gale, 2 vols., 1983.

*   *   *

"Poetry should be a joy...a pleasure.... The whole thing of the suffering poet...it's so unnecessary. You can get so intense that you can't produce. There's work to be done." Whatever else it may or may not do, Anne Waldman's poetry keeps this promise. Most often her poems find their inspiration and shape in an implicitly celebratory display of the diverse pleasures of things— life in New York, world-travel, sex and friendships, even her own fantasies and dreams. The high-spiritedness, rich humor, and eager openness that sustain her work derive less from the idealism than from the affluence of the 1960's. But then, she can't help it if she's lucky. What matters is that she improves upon her luck, for the imaginative persuasiveness of her best poems recalls Whitman's insight that "the most affluent man is he that confronts all the shows he sees by equivalents out of the stronger wealth of himself." Poetry, for Waldman, justifies itself as the show of life, and the pleasures it offers are inherent in the process whereby the impulses of life are released into living forms.

And if she dismisses the "suffering poet" it is almost always in the spirit of one for whom suffering can properly show itself only indirectly, as the elusive and finally unappeasable passion that both nourishes and chastens the poet's creative play: "There is work to be done." Nowhere is this element in her work more crucial than in her best-known work, "Fast Speaking Woman," which goes like this, with very little variation of pattern, for nearly 600 lines:

> I'm a witch woman
> I'm a beggar woman
> I'm a shade woman
> I'm a shadow woman
> I'm a leaf woman
> I'm a leaping woman

This remarkable piece could never hold our attention for 6 lines, let alone 600, were it not for its creative recklessness, at once desperate and playful. This is a matter, chiefly, of Waldman's splendidly uninhibited aesthetic opportunism, so that each line seems generated by some under-played excess of the matter and movement of preceding ones. The imaginative power of the poem inheres in the immediacy of its language yet remains apart, its freshness not just unharmed but actually enriched by any show it has made.

"Fast Speaking Woman" is something of a tour de force, but even in its extremity it is characteristic of the aims and methods of Waldman's work. She is committed to the classic American mode of "open-form" or "projective" verse, though, despite the idiomatic pungency and speed of her language, the music of her poetry is closer to that of song than of speech. This is especially true of the "chants" in *Fast Speaking Woman*, but even her less regular pieces, the best of which, I think, are in *Baby Breakdown* ("I Am Not a Woman" and "Conversational Poem") and, especially, *Journals and Dreams* ("Blues Cadet," "Mirror Meditation," "My Lady," and "When the World Was Steady"), strike the ear not as speech but as snatches of song stitched into even more various musical patterns—a variousness in music which answers to and resolves a rich contradictoriness of feeling and perception.

From its beginnings the open-form tradition has rested on some form of belief in the correspondence between inner and outer worlds, but one must go back to Whitman to find precedent for Waldman's astonishingly unstudied practical faith that discoveries of self are revelations of a world, and vice versa. The epigraph to "Fast Speaking Woman" is "I is other," and what counts in her work is less the tenacity than the nonchalance of her exploration of the truth of this. She neither apologizes for her egotism nor worries about her otherness. Coming from any poet this is exhilarating, but coming from a woman it is truly revolutionary. The word "woman" appears in nearly every line of "Fast Speaking Woman," yet it receives little rhythmic or semantic stress: it is treated simply as the natural point of departure and return for each excursus of self, as if nothing better could or need be imagined than to create a world in terms of a woman's acts of self-realization. The form of this poem gives the game away more unmistakably than others, but it is far from the only one to play that game with extraordinary inventiveness and grace.

—John Hinchey

WALKER, Margaret (Abigail). American. Born in Birmingham, Alabama, 7 July 1915. Educated at Northwestern University, Evanston, Illinois, B.A. 1935; University of Iowa, Iowa City, M.A. 1940, Ph.D. 1965; Yale University, New Haven, Connecticut (Ford Fellow), 1954. Married Firnist James Alexander in 1943; two sons and two daughters. Has worked as social worker, reporter, and magazine editor; taught at Livingstone College, Salisbury, North Carolina, 1941-42, 1945-46, and West Virginia State College, Institute, 1942-43. Since 1949, Professor of English, and since 1968, Director of the Institute for the Study of the History, Life and Culture of Black Peoples, Jackson State College, Mississippi. Recipient: Yale Series of Younger Poets Award, 1942; Rosenwald Fellowship, 1944; Houghton Mifflin Literary Fellowship, for fiction, 1966; Fulbright Fellowship, 1971; National Endowment for the Arts grant, 1972. D.Litt: Northwestern University, 1974; Rust College, Holly Springs, Mississippi, 1974; D.F.A.: Denison University, Granville, Ohio, 1974; D.H.L.: Morgan State University, Baltimore, 1976. Address: 2205 Guynes Street, Jackson, Mississippi 39213, U.S.A.

PUBLICATIONS

Verse

For My People. New Haven, Connecticut, Yale University Press, 1942.
Ballad of the Free. Detroit, Broadside Press, 1966.
Prophets for a New Day. Detroit, Broadside Press, 1970.
October Journey. Detroit, Broadside Press, 1973.

Recording: *The Poetry of Margaret Walker*, Folkways, 1975.

Novels

Come Down from Yonder Mountain. Toronto, Longman, 1962.
Jubilee. Boston, Houghton Mifflin, 1966.

Other

How I Wrote "Jubilee." Chicago, Third World Press, 1972.
A Poetic Equation: Conversations Between Margaret Walker and Nikki Giovanni. Washington, D.C., Howard University Press, 1974.
The Daemonic Genius of Richard Wright. Washington, D.C., Howard University Press, 1982.

*   *   *

Margaret Walker's reputation as a poet rests mainly upon *For My People*, which in 1942 won the Yale Series of Younger Poets competition. These race-conscious poems, because of their prescient militancy, strength, and celebration of Black identity, purposes, and traditions, are admired by the current generation of young Afro-American poets and poetry readers.

This volume contains three groupings of poems, each demonstrating the author's creative resourcefulness and technical control. The first grouping is written in Miss Walker's rather distinctive experimental reverse-indented, paragraph-style stanzas. Some of the lines have sentence syntax, as in "Lineage"; some of the stanzas are clause structured, as in the title poem; some of the stanzas are paragraph structured, as in "Dark Blood." All show to advantage her skill in poetry-as-statement. Characteristically, each stanza in a poem is a catalog of images and evocative statements, and each stanza is an increment toward the poem's climax, point, or resolution. The second grouping is lively ballads and narratives informed by Negro folk characters, lore, and traditions. The language is infused with the idioms, cadences, and intonations of Negro oral traditions. The third grouping is sonnet variations, often informed too by what the author has seen, learned, and felt as a Negro American.

Margaret Walker's poetry since *For My People* mainly deals with current subjects, people, and events of significance to Afro-Americans. These later poems continue to be insightful, compassionate, and sincere; increasingly they have become utilitarian. Her imagery continues to be precise and graphic, perhaps more realistic and less romanticized than in her earlier work, and her language continues to be plain and direct. Her use of free verse techniques has increased.

—Theodore R. Hudson

WALKER, Ted (Edward Joseph Walker). British. Born in Lancing, Sussex, 28 November 1934. Educated at Steyning Grammar School; St. John's College, Cambridge, B.A. (honours) in modern languages 1956. Served in the Royal Naval Volunteer Reserve. Married Lorna Benfell in 1956; two daughters and two sons. Head of the French Department, Southall Grammar School, Middlesex, 1958-61; Head of the Modern Languages Department, Bognor Regis School, Sussex, 1961-63; Assistant Spanish Master, Chichester High School, Sussex, 1963-64. Since 1971, Poet-in-Residence, New England College, Arundel, Sussex. Founder with John Cotton and Editor since 1962, *Priapus*, Berkhamsted, Hertfordshire. Recipient: Eric Gregory Award, 1964; Cholmondeley Award, 1966; Alice Hunt Bartlett Prize, 1968; Arts Council travel grant, 1978; PEN Ackerley prize, for autobiography, 1983. Fellow, Royal Society of Literature. Agent: David Higham Associates Ltd., 5-8 Lower John Street, London W1R 4HA. Address: Argyll House, The Square, Eastergate, Chichester, Sussex, England.

PUBLICATIONS

Verse

Those Other Growths.   Leeds, Northern House, 1964.
Fox on a Barn Door: Poems 1963-4.   London, Cape, 1965; New York, Braziller, 1966.
The Solitaries: Poems 1964-5.   London, Cape, and New York, Braziller, 1967.
The Night Bathers: Poems 1966-8.   London, Cape, 1970.
Gloves to the Hangman: Poems 1969-72.   London, Cape, 1972.
Burning the Ivy: Poems 1973-77.   London, Cape, 1978.

Plays

Radio Scripts: *The Final Miracle*, 1979; *The Third Person*, 1980; *The Trotliners*, 1981; *A Hill in Southern England*, 1982; *Before Crufts*, 1983; *A Portrait of William Plomer*, 1983.

Television Plays: *Big Jim and the Figaro Club*, 1980; *The Gaffer*, 1983; *A Family Man*, 1984.

Other

The Lion's Cavalcade (for children).   London, Cape, 1980.
The High Path (autobiography).   London, Routledge, 1982.

*

Manuscript Collection: Lockwood Memorial Library, State University of New York, Buffalo.

Ted Walker comments:
   My poetry seems to deal with loneliness and isolation. Since I live in the country, my imagery tends to be rural and even regional. My territory is Sussex and the Sussex coast.

*   *   *

   Much of Ted Walker's poetry is in the great tradition of English nature poetry. It is a tradition which stretches in modern times from Wordsworth to Ted Hughes. In Walker's case it is a poetry which, while one of close and accurate detail, looks beyond external nature to where parallels are observed and implications relating to the human condition are drawn: "regret/the vacant seemliness/by which we live. For which we lost/that proper, vital gift of waste" ("Crocuses"). The territory of Walker's poetry is the seashore with its inlets and breakwaters, the isolated lonely areas of the English countryside and the creatures that inhabit them. The parallel drawn is that of the ultimate solitude of the human soul when confronting the universe in which it finds itself, and where man finds himself unsatisfied and incomplete in contrast to the aptness and completeness of the rest of the animal kingdom in relation to its environment. It is where man looks both within himself and out towards "that God I won't believe in" for something beyond his immediate experience to meet the spiritual loneliness which is reflected in the isolation of the situations depicted in the poem. It is not without significance that the title of Ted Walker's second collection was *The Solitaries*.

   In his third collection, *The Night Bathers*, there is a shift of emphasis. The same qualities of precise observation and craftsmanship are there; but the poet grows older and the past begins to haunt the present to the point where it enriches it and gives it depth of meaning. The title poem explores the poet's relationship with his son as a reflection of that between himself and his own father:

> when he was young to understand
> why, momently out of the night
> and purposeful beyond the reach
> of all his worry, I had swum
> deep into banks of sea-fret
> too far to have to answer him.

   There is, too, a clearly observable growth in Walker's technical mastery which allows him to relax his earlier tight control and use a language closer to the colloquial. This development was to continue in his collection *Gloves to the Hangman*, where in poems such as "Letter to Barbados" there is an ease of expression which gives the poem an immediacy of reception without any diminution of strength: "Dear far-off brother. Thank you for yours,/And for the gift you send of little shells."

   His latest collection, *Burning the Ivy*, finds Walker using this skill to write poetry of a more directly personal dimension, the personae are being abandoned and a more vulnerable area of feeling and emotion is being expressed, often tellingly so as in the elegy for William Plomer, "After the Funeral," and the poem for Paul Coltman on his retirement, "For His Old English Master." One feels we are getting nearer to the truth of things here, than in the earlier assaults on the universal plan, splendid as they were.

—John Cotton

———————

WALLACE-CRABBE, Chris(topher Keith). Australian. Born in Richmond, Victoria, 6 May 1934. Educated at Scotch College; University of Melbourne, Victoria, B.A. 1956; M.A. (Lockie Fellow) 1964; Yale University, New Haven, Connecticut (Harkness Fellow), 1965-67. Married; two children. Since 1968, Senior Lecturer in English, University of Melbourne. Visiting Fellow, University of Exeter, Devon, 1973; Visiting Senior Fellow, Linacre College, Oxford, 1983-84. Address: 121 Victoria Street, Fitzroy, Victoria 3065, Australia.

PUBLICATIONS

Verse

No Glass Houses. Melbourne, Ravenswood Press, 1956.
The Music of Division. Sydney, Angus and Robertson, 1959.
Eight Metropolitan Poems. Adelaide, Australian Letters, 1962.
In Light and Darkness. Sydney, Angus and Robertson, 1964.
The Rebel General. Sydney, Angus and Robertson, 1967.
Where the Wind Came. Sydney, Angus and Robertson, 1971.
Selected Poems 1955-1972. Sydney, Angus and Robertson, 1973.
Act in the Noon. Melbourne, Cotswold Press, 1974.
The Shapes of Gallipoli. Melbourne, Cotswold Press, 1975.
The Foundations of Joy. Sydney, Angus and Robertson, 1976.
The Emotions Are Not Skilled Workers. Sydney, Angus and Robertson, 1979; London, Angus and Robertson, 1980.
The Amorous Cannibal and Other Poems. Oxford, Oxford University Press, 1985.

Recording: *Chris Wallace-Crabbe Reads from His Own Work,* University of Queensland Press, 1973.

Novel

Splinters. Adelaide, Rigby, 1981.

Other

Melbourne or the Bush: Essays on Australian Literature and Society. Sydney, Angus and Robertson, 1973.
Toil and Spin: Two Directions in Modern Poetry. Melbourne, Hutchinson, 1979.
Three Absences in Australian Writing. Townsville, Queensland, Foundation for Australian Literature Studies, 1983.

Editor, *Six Voices: Contemporary Australian Poets.* Sydney, Angus and Robertson, 1963; Westport, Connecticut, Greenwood Press, 1979.
Editor, *The Australian Nationalists.* Melbourne, Oxford University Press, 1971.
Editor, *Australian Poetry 71.* Sydney, Angus and Robertson, 1971.
Editor, *The Golden Apples of the Sun: Twentieth Century Australian Poetry.* Melbourne, Melbourne University Press, 1980.

*

Critical Studies: "A Modest Radiance" by E.A.M. Colman, in *Westerly* (Nedlands, Western Australia), 1969; "To Move in Light: The Poetry of Chris Wallace-Crabbe" by Peter Steele, in *Meanjin* (Melbourne), 1970; "Transition and Advance" by James Tulip, in *Southerly* (Sydney), 1972.

Chris Wallace-Crabbe comments:

My early poetry explored the nature of social order and of intellectual coherence in a world in which religious sanctions seemed irrelevant; my concern at this stage was to make poetic structures which testified to the strength which was inherent in human reason and (hopefully) to humorous resilience as a way of meeting the contradictions of experience. Later, finding my early poetry rather too stiff, rigorous and explicit, I came to seek more supple rhythms and more autonomous images—a poetry which was more fully charged with the physical world. And a poetry which questioned the English language.

Over the past few years I have increasingly been trying to come to terms with violence: political, personal and intrapersonal. I am interested in the paradox that we tend most profoundly to worship vitality for its own sake, while we are bound at the same time to deplore such vitality as manifests itself in the form of violence. Poetry, like other constructive activities, issues from forces that are potentially destructive. The self, when it is most vital, is not reducible to a moral agent. These are the central concerns which I have been trying to dramatize in my recent poems. At the same time, inevitably, my poetry has been growing less formal, less architecturally shaped, and more sinuous, more shifting, more various in its effects and directions. Psychomachia concerns me greatly, especially in its lyrical forms.

My current attitude to poetry is best summed up in A. D. Hope's haunting line, "What questions are there that we fail to ask?" That, and my sense that the language I use subverts itself, but not nearly so fast as it subverts me. My latest poems, family romances of mental structure, play out despairing comedies with words that keep falling away. How, but with wit, can one survive as "the gene's blind way of making another gene"? And another lyric answers, "Ah, that would be telling/Just as he always does."

*　　*　　*

Chris Wallace-Crabbe's volume of poems *The Music of Division* confirmed the promise indicated by the appearance of his work in Australian literary journals since the early 1950's. His first work was unusual in an Australian context in that it avoided the over-indulgence and exuberance normally associated with a young writer. *The Music of Division* exhibited a coolness and a quality of apparent detachment that looked forward to the early 1960's, rather than back to the more romantic 1950's of Australian poetry. In the first volume, the most notable poems are based upon observation of political forces, particularly as they implicate individual personalties in the tension between "public" and "private" responses. This preoccupation is developed and expanded in the later books, *In Light and Darkness* and *The Rebel General*, and is perhaps taken to its furthest stretch in the prize-winning long poem "Blood Is the Water," included in the volume *Where the Wind Came*.

Such a continuous preoccupation with and development of the themes of power and political motivation has, interestingly enough, led Wallace-Crabbe away from the earlier detachment to an increasing relaxation and a sense of full humanness in his writing. He himself has written, "After stoical-formalist beginnings, I seek a poetry of Romantic fullness and humanity. I want to see how far lyrical, Dionysian impulses can be released and expressed without loss of intelligence." His *Selected Poems*, published in his fortieth year, would seem to mark a significant watershed in his work. It is worth noting that this volume commences with a series of "Meditations" which imply that he is reaching out in new directions, perhaps more fully exploring the vein of lyricism that has glittered tantalisingly throughout the volumes that preceded it and are abridged into it. The almost ruthless severity of the abridgement still indicates, however, that Chris Wallace-Crabbe exercises a powerful and severe intelligence in the organisation of his compositions. At this point in his development he is certainly one of the leaders of his generation of Australian poets.

—Thomas W. Shapcott

WALSH, Chad. American. Born in South Boston, Virginia, 10 May 1914. Educated at Marion Junior College, Virginia, 1934-36; University of Virginia, Charlottesville, 1936-38, A.B. in French 1938 (Phi Beta Kappa); University of Michigan, Ann Arbor (Hopwood Award, for drama, 1939), 1938-43, A.M. in French 1939, Ph.D. in English 1943. Married Eva May Tuttle in 1938; four daughters. Teaching Fellow, University of Michigan 1942-43; Research Analyst, United States Army Signal Corps, Arlington, Virginia, 1943-45. Member of the faculty from 1946, Professor of English, 1952-77, and Writer-in-Residence, 1969-77, Beloit College, Wisconsin. Fulbright Lecturer, Turku, Finland, 1957-58, and Rome, 1962; Visiting Professor, Wellesley College, Massachusetts, 1958-59, Juniata College, Huntingdon, Pennsylvania, 1977-78, Roanoke College, Salem, Virginia, 1979, and Abo Akademi, Finland, 1982. Ordained Priest, Episcopal Church, 1949. Founder, with Robert Glaber, *Beloit Poetry Journal*, 1950. Recipient: Catholic Poetry Society Spirit Gold Medal, 1964; Society of Midland Authors Award, 1965, 1970; Yaddo Fellowship, 1966, 1970; Banta Award, 1982. D.H.L.: Rockford College, Illinois, 1963; St. Norbert College, West De Pere, Wisconsin, 1972. Address: Meadowbrook C-1, Joy Drive, South Burlington, Vermont 05401, U.S.A.

PUBLICATIONS

Verse

The Factual Dark. Prairie City, Illinois, Decker Press, 1949.
Eden Two-Way. New York, Harper, 1954.
The Psalm of Christ: Forty Poems on the Tweny-Second Palm. Philadelphia, Westminster Press, 1963.
The Unknowing Dance. New York and London, Abelard Schuman, 1964.
The End of Nature: Poems. Chicago, Swallow Press, 1969.
Hang Me Up My Begging Bowl. Chicago, Swallow Press, 1981.

Novel

The Rough Years. New York, Morehouse Barlow, 1960.

Other

Stop Looking and Listen: An Invitation to the Christian Life. New York, Harper, 1947; London, SCM Press, 1948.
C.S. Lewis: Apostle to the Skeptics. New York, Macmillan 1949.
Early Christmas of the 21st Century. New York, Harper, 1950.
I Chose the Episcopal Church. Greenwich, Connecticut, Seabury Press, 1953.
Campus Gods on Trial. New York, Macmillan, 1953; revised edition, 1962.
Knock and Enter. New York, Morehouse Gorham, 1953; London, Faith Press, 1959.
Faith and Behavior: Christian Answers to Moral Problems, with Eric Montizambert. New York, Morehouse Gorham, 1954.
Nellie and Her Flying Crocodile (for children). New York, Harper, 1956.
Behold the Glory (meditations). New York, Harper, 1956.
God at Large. New York, Seabury Press, 1960.
The Personality of Jesus. New York, Know Your Bible, 1961.
Why Go to Church?, with Eva Walsh. New York, Association Press, 1962.
Doors into Poetry (textbook). Englewood Cliffs, New Jersey, Prentice Hall, 1962.

From Utopia to Nightmare. New York, Harper, and London, Bles, 1962.
The Story of Job. New York, Doubleday, 1963.
Twice Ten: An Introduction to Poetry, with Eva Walsh. New York, Wiley, 1976.
The Literary Legacy of C.S. Lewis. New York, Harcourt Brace, and London, Sheldon Press, 1979.
A Rich Feast: Encountering the Bible from Genesis to Revelation. New York, Harper, 1981.

Editor, *Today's Poets: American and British Poetry since the 1930's*. New York, Scribner, 1965.
Editor, *Garlands for Christmas: A Selection of Poetry*. New York, Macmillan, 1965.
Editor, *The Honey and the Gall: Poems of Married Life*. New York, Macmillan, 1967.
Editor, *The Visionary Christian: 131 Readings from C.S. Lewis*. New York, Macmillan, 1981.

*

Manuscript Collections: Lockwood Memorial Library, State University of New York, Buffalo; Beloit College Library, Wisconsin; Newberry Library, Chicago.

Critical Study: Introduction by Carl Bode, to *The Unknowing Dance*, 1964.

Chad Walsh comments:

(1974) As a boy, I had a strong quasi-pantheistic, quasi-scientific interest in nature. I roamed the fields and woods, did lanscape paintings (as photographic as my ability would permit), daydreamed of being a forester or landscape architect. My interest in poetry began at about the age of ten. Two things triggered it. One was that my eldest brother, who had introduced me to the magic of language by reading Dickens aloud, became briefly interested in poetry. We memorized snatches of Shakespeare's sonnets and of Keats, and strode up and down the country lane near our home, reciting. About the same time my teacher, Miss Louis Johnston, told the students that each should write a poem about autumn. I recall only the ending of mine—"The leaves are falling fast,/ Many of the birds are missing,/ But cats will stay to the last." Anyway, she praised it, and from that time on I found myself writing poetry.

I have published over twenty books in all, six of them poetry—and these are the books closest to my heart. I find it hard to "label" my poetry—I have experienced the influence, along the way, of diverse poets—Catullus, Villon, Dante, Shakespeare and minor Elizabethan poets, Donne, Keats, Baudelaire, Heine, Hopkins, Yeats, Frost, Eliot, Auden, etc., even Housman, and Kipling. I suppose the two poets whose influence is most evident in my work are Frost and Auden.

I earn my living mainly as a college professor, with some moderate income from writing and from poetry readings and lectures that I give on campuses. I am also an Episcopal priest, but a part-time one, helping on weekends at the local church. This three-fold role sometimes suggests to people that I must lead a schizophrenic or polyphrenic life; if I do I am not aware of it.

Perhaps the most frequent theme in my verse is the dialogue between human and divine love. So far as subject-matter is concerned, many of my poems fall into categories: love, religion, nature, geographical impressions, social commentary, etc. I am always experimenting in various forms and tend to swing back and forth between relatively free verse and very complicated forms. I have invented a number of forms and used them extensively—such as the "quintina," the "circular sonnet," and the "rima quinta triplicata." In the last few years I have experimented a great deal with composing poetry directly on the tape recorder, so as to get as free and flowing a quality as possible. I want to experiment with devising a kind of poetic drama in which a number of voices (some perhaps taped) could be used; it would be a unified program of maybe 50 minutes duration. I think public poetry readings are evolving in this direction, and through them a thoroughly modern kind of verse drama may emerge.

I suppose I can best describe what I ideally want to be as a poet by saying that it seems to me the two best American poets of recent times are the late Theodore Roethke and the living Robert Lowell. I'd like to have Roethke's heart and Lowell's head, to write poetry that somehow combines their strengths; in short, I'd like to be both Apollonian and Dionysian as Yeats was. Others must decide how close I come to this.

(1980) At the moment my main poetic project is a book-length sequence of Petrarchan sonnets on the relation of human and divine love. I find that the sonnet form still "works" so long as I rough it up with half-rhymes and metrical variations.

*   *   *

At the expense of inviting argument I maintain that Chad Walsh is the finest religious poet writing in America today. He has taken a noble but gnarled tradition, has reaffirmed its statement of love, has widened its technical range, and has brought it home to a growing if still sparse audience.

By now he has produced half a dozen volumes of verse. They all celebrate a God who is to be beloved rather than venerated and a humankind which is to be comprehended but never condemned. The writing in these volumes has benefited from the constant refining of Chad Walsh's sensibility. It is a sensibility with at least two levels. One is a response to the variegated worlds in which he moves that has been sharpened instead of being dulled by the passage of time. The other, more practical, more humane, is a comradely awareness of the way his work will look to others; for him his readers are really important. This sense of comradeship has resulted in his experimenting with varied modes and stances, in order to move closer to his readers as well as to help the flow of his poetry. Reacting at one point in his career against a preoccupation with form which led him to devise a circular sonnet, so called, and a quintina, he turned, as he has reported, to the tape recorder and simply said his poetry as it came to him. On the other hand, he remarks in his latest book that he found two-thirds of his taped poetry "still uninteresting even after revision" and so discarded it.

Not surprisingly, his best book is his latest, *Hang Me Up My Begging Bowl*. However, the two prior ones, *The Unknowing Dance* and *The End of Nature*, also contain some memorable poetry. Among the lyrics in them which affect me most are his stately ode "The Destruction by Fire of the Beloit College Chapel"; his urbanely metaphysical "Ode on a Plastic Stapes," in which he meditates on man's replacement for a God-given bone in the poet's inner ear; his "Nuptial Hymn," addressed to an uneasy young bridegroom on the bridal night; and one of many invocations to his wife, "We Were So Busy Being Young." In these two volumes his most enduring poems relate man to God or man to woman; his least permanent originate as reflections about his travels abroad.

Those travels disappear in *Hang Me Up My Begging Bowl*. The poems in this volume are frequently infused by love tinctured with humor; they have the tang of youth. And they are both matter-of-fact and visionary. For example: the opening stanza of "Terrestrial Love":

For everything under the sun, a time, a reason.
Coffee and toast at breakfast,
Christ's body for my dinner once a week,
Cocktails or wine at 5:00 o'clock,
And the dark sweetness of your body when in season.

In the most compelling poetry the matter-of-fact turns into the transcendental but never at the expense of excess. In the poem "Ascension" the poet floats far above the auto wreck which has just killed him; yet, as he rises, he does not look up at the heavenly face of God but down at the Great Lakes glistening under a rain like "five petals of a flower."

Two notable poems in this book deal with fellow poets. The first is addressed to Robert Hayden, a distinguished Black poet and classmate of Chad Walsh's. Although they have been warm friends since college days, Black and white racists are struggling to split them apart. The lyric limns the everyday details of the friendship which Chad Walsh urges be maintained till death— and beyond. "I think we could sleep in peace/Side by side," he concludes. The second poem is a bold one indeed, for it is a eulogy of Auden modeled on Auden's masterly eulogy of Yeats. I myself believe it succeeds.

Chad Walsh remains his own poet, remembering the reader but composing the poetry he considers he should compose. In present-day America no form except the epic is less fashionable than the sonnet sequence. No subject is less fashionable than the love of God. Nevertheless, he is at work preparing a book-length sequence of Petrarchan sonnets about the relation of divine love to human.

—Carl Bode

WARNER, Francis (Robert Le Plastrier). British. Born in Bishopthorpe, Yorkshire, 21 October 1937. Educated at Christ's Hospital, 1947-54; London College of Music, 1954-55; County Technical College, Guildford, Surrey, 1955-56; St. Catharine's College, Cambridge (Music Scholar), 1956-59, B.A., M.A. Married 1) Mary Hall in 1958 (divorced, 1972), two daughters; 2) Penelope Anne Davis in 1983. Supervisor, St. Catharine's College, 1959-65; extramural tutor, Cambridge University, 1963-65. Since 1965, Fellow and Tutor in English Literature, St. Peter's College, Oxford. Founder, Pilgrim's Way Players, touring company, 1954, Cambridge University Elgar Centenary Choir and Orchestra, 1957, and the Samuel Beckett Theatre, Oxford, 1967. Assistant Director, Yeats International Summer School, Sligo, Ireland, 1961-67; a Director, James Joyce Symposium, Dublin, 1967, and the James Joyce Foundation, Tulsa, Oklahoma. Recipient: Messing International Award, 1972. Agent: M.L.R., 200 Fulham Road, London SW10 9PN. Address: St. Peter's College, Oxford OX1 2DL, England.

PUBLICATIONS

Verse

Perennia. Cambridge, Golden Head Press, 1962.
Early Poems. London, Fortune Press, 1964.
Experimental Sonnets. London, Fortune Press, 1965.
Madrigals. London, Fortune Press, 1967.
The Poetry of Francis Warner. Boston, Pilgrim Press, 1970.

Meeting Ends.   Rushden, Northamptonshire, Sceptre Press, 1973.
Lucca Quartet.   Knotting, Bedfordshire, Omphalos Press, 1975.
Morning Vespers.   Knotting, Bedfordshire, Martin Booth, 1980.
Spring Harvest.   Drayton, Somerset, Martin Booth, 1981.
Epithalamium.   Drayton, Somerset, Martin Booth, 1984.
Collected Poems 1960-1984.   Gerrards Cross, Buckinghamshire, Smythe, 1985.

Plays

Maquettes (also director: produced Oxford, 1970; London, 1972).   Oxford, Oxford Theatre Texts, 1972.
Lying Figures (also director: produced Oxford, 1971; London, 1972).   Oxford, Oxford Theatre Texts, 1972.
Meeting Ends (also director: produced Edinburgh, 1973; London, 1974).   Cheadle, Cheshire, Oxford Theatre Texts, 1974.
Killing Time (also director: produced Edinburgh, 1974).   Cheadle, Cheshire, Oxford Theatre Texts, 1976.
A Conception of Love (produced Oxford, 1978).   Gerrards Cross, Buckinghamshire, Smythe, 1978.
Light Shadows (produced Cantebury, 1979).   Gerrards Cross, Buckinghamshire, Smythe, 1980.
Moving Reflections (produced Edinburgh, 1982).   Gerrards Cross, Buckinghamshire, Smythe, 1983.

Other

Editor, *Eleven Poems*, by Edmund Blunden.   Cambridge, Golden Head Press, 1965.
Editor, *Garland: A Little Anthology of Poetry and Engravings.*   Cambridge, Golden Head Press, 1968.
Editor, *Studies in the Arts: Proceedings of the St. Peter's College Literary Society.*   Oxford, Blackwell, 1968; New York, Barnes and Noble, 1969.

*

Manuscript Collections: St. Louis University Library; University Library, Cambridge.

Critical Studies: *Francis Warner, Poet and Dramatist* edited by Tom Prentki, Knotting, Bedfordshire, Sceptre Press, 1977; *Francis Warner and Tradition: An Introduction to the Plays* by Glyn Pursglove, Gerrards Cross, Buckinghamshire, Smythe, 1981.

Theatrical Activities:
Director: **Plays**—several of his own plays.

Actor: **Plays**—in *Lessness* by Samuel Beckett, Oxford, 1982, and other plays.

*   *   *

The Poetry of Francis Warner* was compiled from several previous books and "represents those poems written in the decade 1960-69, with which the...poet chooses to be associated, on which he stakes his reputation."
The formal tradition of English poetry is very much alive in Mr. Warner's work. There are ten "Experimental Sonnets" which, while they do not sustain the exact form, do maintain the spirit of the Shakespearian sonnet. The elegy "Plainsong" is written mostly in blank verse, and "A Legend's Carol" in eleven stanzas of matched lines artfully arranged with both end and internal rhymes. Scarcely any of the "Lyrical and Meditative Poems" fail to fall into a pattern of rhythm, rhyme, or form. There are songs, lyrics, ballads, and even an aubade and a calypso ballad. "Perennia" is composed in Spenserian stanzas except for Perennia's song which, quite aptly, is written in the rhyme and meter of Swinburne's "Hymn to Proserpine."
What of the wine that Mr. Warner pours into these familiar forms? The "Sonnets" are deeply introspective; "The dark offstage preoccupies my mind," the poet says, and, indeed, the thread of mutability stitches them together. "Plainsong" seeks and finds a resolution for the final change of death in the constant renewal of life, but "A Legend's Carol" undercuts this somewhat by seeing in the archetypal birth of Mary's Son, the simultaneous death of Pan. "Lyrical and Meditative Poems" are Mr. Warner at his best; they are too finely diverse to tarnish with a generalization, but the poet seems to have accepted the urgings of "Venus and the Poet": "Come, leave mutability,/Lie me down beneath this tree"—love does provide both the ecstatic and only practical answer to the inevitability of change. The long poem "Perennia" says this, too, in telling a lovely dream-myth.
Hoping to introduce a poet to new followers often results in an earnest over-simplifying of his work. Mr. Warner is a poet who should be read, not read about; only then can one experience the incarnation he has achieved by mating word with form.

—Norman T. Gates

────────────

WARNER, Rex (Ernest).   British. Born in Birmingham, Warwickshire, 9 March 1905. Educated at St. George's School, Harpenden, Hertfordshire; Wadham College, Oxford (open classical scholar), B.A. (honours) in classics and English literature 1928. Served in the Home Guard, London, 1942-45. Married 1) Frances Chamier Grove in 1929, two sons and one daughter; 2) Barbara Lady Rothschild in 1949, one daughter; 3) remarried Frances Chamier Grove in 1966. Schoolmaster in Egypt and England, 1928-45; worked for the Control Commission in Berlin, 1945, 1947; Director, British Institute, Athens, 1945-47; Tallman Professor, Bowdoin College, Brunswick, Maine, 1962-63; Professor of English, University of Connecticut, Storrs, 1963-74. Recipient: Black Memorial Prize, for fiction, 1961. D. Litt.: Rider College, Trenton, New Jersey, 1968. Honorary Fellow, Wadham College, 1973. Commander, Royal Order of the Phoenix, Greece, 1963. Address: Anchor House, St. Leonard's Lane, Wallingford, Oxfordshire, England.

PUBLICATIONS

Verse

Poems.   London, Boriswood, 1937; New York, Knopf, 1938; revised edition, as *Poems and Contradictions*, London, Lane, 1945.

Plays

Screenplays (documentaries): *World With End*, 1953; *The Immortal Land*, 1958.

Novels

The Wild Goose Chase.   London, Boriswood, and New York,

Knopf, 1937.

The Professor. London, Boriswood, 1938; New York, Knopf, 1939.

The Aerodrome. London, Lane, 1941; Philadelphia, Lippincott, 1946.

Why Was I Killed? A Dramatic Dialogue. London, Lane, 1943; as *Return of the Traveller*, Philadelphia, Lippincott, 1944.

Men of Stones: A Melodrama. London, Lane, 1949; Philadelphia, Lippincott, 1950.

Escapade: A Tale of Average. London, Lane, 1953.

The Young Caesar. London, Collins, and Boston, Little Brown, 1958.

Imperial Caesar. London, Collins, and Boston, Little Brown, 1960.

Pericles the Athenian. London, Collins, and Boston, Little Brown, 1963.

The Converts. London, Bodley Head, and Boston, Little Brown, 1967.

Other

The Kite (for children). Oxford, Blackwell, 1936; revised edition, London, Hamish Hamilton, 1963.

English Public Schools. London, Collins, 1945.

The Cult of Power: Essays. London, Lane, 1946; Philadelphia, Lippincott, 1947.

John Milton. London, Parrish, 1949; New York, Chanticleer Press, 1950.

Views of Attica and Its Surroundings. London, Lehmann, 1950.

E.M. Forster. London, Longman, 1950.

Men and Gods. London, MacGibbon and Kee, 1950; New York, Farrar Straus, 1951.

Ashes to Ashes: A Post-Mortem on the 1950-51 Tests, with Lyle Blair. London, MacGibbon and Kee, 1951.

Greeks and Trojans. London, MacGibbon and Kee, 1951.

Eternal Greece, photographs by Martin Hurlimann. London, Thames and Hudson, and New York, Viking Press, 1953.

The Vengeance of the Gods. London, MacGibbon and Kee, 1954.

Athens. London, Thames and Hudson, and New York, Studio, 1956.

The Greek Philosophers. New York, New American Library, 1958.

Look at Birds (for children). London, Hamish Hamilton, 1962.

The Stories of the Greeks. New York, Farrar Straus, 1967.

Athens at War: Retold from the History of the Peloponnesian War of Thucydides. London, Bodley Head, 1970; New York, Dutton, 1971.

Men of Athens: The Story of Fifth Century Athens. London, Bodley Head, and New York, Viking Press, 1972.

Editor, with Laurie Lee and Christopher Hassall, *New Poems 1954.* London, Joseph, 1954.

Editor, *Look Up at the Skies! Poems and Prose*, by Gerard Manley Hopkins. London, Bodley Head, 1972.

Translator, *The Medea of Euripides.* London, Lane, 1944; New York, Chanticleer Press, 1949.

Translator, *Prometheus Bound*, by Aeschylus. London, Lane, 1947; New York, Chanticleer Press, 1949.

Translator, *The Persian Expedition*, by Xenophon. London, Penguin, 1949.

Translator, *Hippolytus*, by Euripides. London, Lane, 1949; New York, Chanticleer Press, 1950.

Translator, *Helen*, by Euripides. London, Lane, 1951.

Translator, *The Peloponnesian War*, by Thucydides. London, Penguin, 1954.

Translator, *The Fall of the Roman Republic: Marius, Sulla, Crassus, Pompey, Caesar, Cicero: Six Lives*, by Plutarch. London, Penguin, 1958; revised edition, 1972.

Translator, *Poems of George Seferis.* London, Bodley Head, 1960; Boston, Godine, 1979.

Translator, *War Commentaries of Caesar.* New York, New American Library, 1960.

Translator, *Confessions of St. Augustine.* New York, New American Library, 1963.

Translator, with .Th. D. Frangopoulos, *On the Greek Style: Selected Essays in Poetry and Hellenism*, by George Seferis. Boston, Little Brown, 1966.

Translator, *A History of My Times*, by Xenophon. London, Penguin, 1966.

Translator, *Moral Essays*, by Plutarch. London, Penguin, 1971.

*

Manuscript Collection: University of Connecticut, Storrs.

Critical Studies: *Rex Warner, Writer* by A.L. McLeod, Sydney, Wentworth Press, 1960, and *The Achievement of Rex Warner* (includes bibliography) edited by McLeod, Wentworth Press, 1965.

*   *   *

Rex Warner's poetry celebrates the force of nature, symbolized usually by birds, either powerful, often ugly—"smothering an airpuff with heave of shoulder" ("Egyptian Kite")—or graceful—"easy on the flying twig's trapeze" ("Longtailed Tit"). In their plenitude and behavior, they reflect the immanent plan shaping the universe ("Mallard"):

> designed so deftly that all air is advantage
> till, with few flaps, orderly as they left earth,
> alighting among curlew they pad on mud.

Frequently human beings submit their emotions to benevolent or tyrannical phenomena that manifest this same control: "to be awed by mountains, & feel the stars friendly" ("Sonnet"). Even in the political poems deleted from his revised edition, *Poems and Contradictions*, Warner plays on the agricultural implications of the Soviet emblem and attributes impending revolution to the working of this natural power: "For blight in the meadows, and for our master builders/let sickle be a staggerer and hammer heavy" ("Sonnet"). Thus, Warner dramatizes political change as the eruption of seasonal forces in the individual and society: "Come, then, companions, this is the Spring of blood,/heart's heyday, movement of masses, beginning of blood" ("Sonnet").

Warner can create images startling yet ultimately appropriate: "These bottle-washer trees that give no shade" ("Palm Trees"). However, too often, even in the ambitious sonnet sequence "Contradictions," he depends on words like "love" and "lust" and "birth" and "seed" in contexts which fail to sustain the pulsating effect toward which this language aspires. This attempt, reinforced by elaborate sound and metrical patterns, to recreate the elemental surges of existence, ironically seems more literary than primeval: "All mud & mould shudders with life today;/birth bursts by flooding, bloodless without pain" ("Spring

Song"). Sometimes, however, Warner masters complex effects of rhythm and alliteration: "Plover, with under the tail pine-red, dead leafwealth in down displayed" ("Lapwing"); but these long lines, whether derived from Hopkins or the fourteenth-century alliterative revival, seem divorced from a living tradition and incapable of generating a new one.

Though Warner has published no verse for almost thirty years, except for his translations of George Seferis and classical dramatists, the promise of his best poetry has contributed to the distinguished style he has continuously polished in a stream of novels and translations of classical prose. His learning and eclecticism provide even minor verse with graceful echoes: the Virgilian "shores of leaning light" give resonance to "Spring Song," and the Audenesque "when kneecaps won't loose leg" enlivens the otherwise rhetorical promise of utopia in "Chorus." Besides this ability to evoke a whole range of other authors and traditions, Warner's real, though undeveloped, strengths lie in the compassionate wit of "Epithalamion and Hymn"—"Let moon and sun approve the fun/that Church and State allow"—and in the epigrammatic concentration of "Sonnet XV": "sinking I see the certain fire and say: 'There are the useful stars, & here am I!' "

—Burton Kendle

WARREN, Robert Penn. American. Born in Guthrie, Kentucky, 24 April 1905. Educated at Guthrie High School; Vanderbilt University, Nashville, Tennessee, B.A. (summa cum laude) 1925; University of California, Berkeley, M.A. 1927; Yale University, New Haven, Connecticut, 1927-28; Oxford University (Rhodes Scholar), B.Litt. 1930. Married 1) Emma Brescia in 1930 (divorced, 1950); 2) the writer Eleanor Clark in 1952, one son and one daughter. Assistant Professor, Southwestern College, Memphis, Tennessee, 1930-31, and Vanderbilt University, 1931-34; Assistant and Associate Professor, Louisiana State University, Baton Rouge, 1934-42; Professor of English, University of Minnesota, Minneapolis, 1942-50. Professor of Playwriting, 1950-56, Professor of English, 1962-73, and since 1973, Professor Emeritus, Yale University. Member of the Fugitive Group of poets: Co-Founding Editor, *The Fugitive*, Nashville, 1923-25. Founding Editor, *Southern Review*, Baton Rouge, Louisiana, 1935-42; Advisory Editor, *Kenyon Review*, Gambier, Ohio, 1942-63. Consultant in Poetry, Library of Congress, Washington, D.C., 1944-45; Jefferson Lecturer, National Endowment for the Humanities, 1974. Recipient: Caroline Sinkler Award, 1936, 1937, 1938; Levinson Prize, 1936, Union League Civic and Arts Foundation Prize, 1953, and Harriet Monroe Prize, 1976 (*Poetry*, Chicago); Houghton Mifflin Literary Fellowship, 1939; Guggenheim Fellowship, 1939, 1947; Shelley Memorial Award, 1943; Pulitzer Prize, for fiction, 1947, for poetry, 1958, 1979; Robert Meltzer Award, Screen Writers Guild, 1949; Foreign Book Prize (France), 1950; Sidney Hillman Prize, 1957; Edna St. Vincent Millay Memorial Prize, 1958; National Book Award, 1958; New York *Herald-Tribune* Van Doren Award, 1965; Bollingen Prize, 1967; National Endowment for the Arts grant, 1968, and lectureship, 1974; Henry A. Bellaman Prize, 1970; Van Wyck Brooks Award, 1970; National Medal for Literature, 1970; Emerson-Thoreau Medal, 1975; Copernicus Award, 1976; Presidential Medal of Freedom, 1980; Common Wealth Award, 1981; MacArthur Fellowship, 1981; Brandeis University Creative Arts Award, 1983. D.Litt.: University of Louisville, Kentucky, 1949; Kenyon College, Gambier,

Ohio, 1952; Colby College, Waterville, Maine, 1956; University of Kentucky, Lexington, 1957; Swarthmore College, Pennsylvania, 1959; Yale University, 1960; Fairfield University, Connecticut, 1969; Wesleyan University, Middletown, Connecticut, 1970; Harvard University, Cambridge, Massachusetts, 1973; Southwestern College, 1974; University of the South, Sewanee, Tennessee, 1974; Monmouth College, Illinois, 1979; New York University, 1983; Oxford University, 1983; LL.D.: Bridgeport University, Connecticut, 1965; University of New Haven, Connecticut, 1974; Johns Hopkins University, Baltimore, 1977. Member, American Academy, and American Academy of Arts and Sciences; Chancellor, Academy of American Poets, 1972. Address: 2495 Redding Road, Fairfield, Connecticut 06430, U.S.A.

PUBLICATIONS

Verse

Thirty-Six Poems.   New York, Alcestis Press, 1936.
Eleven Poems on the Same Theme.   New York, New Directions, 1942.
Selected Poems 1923-1943.   New York, Harcourt Brace, 1944; London, Fortune Press, 1952.
Brother to Dragons: A Tale in Verse and Voices.   New York, Random House, 1953; London, Eyre and Spottiswoode, 1954; revised edition, Random House, 1979.
To a Little Girl, One Year Old, in a Ruined Fortress.   Privately printed, 1956.
Promises: Poems 1954-1956.   New York, Random House, 1957; London, Eyre and Spottiswoode, 1959.
You, Emperors, and Others: Poems 1957-1960.   New York, Random House, 1960.
Selected Poems: New and Old 1923-1966.   New York, Random House, 1966.
Incarnations: Poems 1966-1968.   New York, Random House, 1968; London, W.H. Allen, 1970.
Audubon: A Vision.   New York, Random House, 1969.
Or Else: Poem/Poems 1968-1974.   New York, Random House, 1974.
Selected Poems 1923-1975.   New York, Random House, and London, Secker and Warburg, 1977.
Now and Then: Poems 1976-1978.   New York, Random House, 1978.
Two Poems.   Winston-Salem, North Carolina, Palaemon Press, 1979.
Being Here: Poetry 1977-1980.   New York, Random House, and London, Secker and Warburg, 1980.
Rumor Verified: Poems 1979-1980.   New York, Random House, and London, Secker and Warburg, 1981.
Chief Joseph of the Nez Perce.   New York, Random House, and London, Secker and Warburg, 1983.
New and Selected Poems 1925-1985.   New York, Random House, 1985.

Recordings: *Robert Penn Warren Reads from His Own Works,* CMS, 1975; *Robert Penn Warren Reads Selected Poems,* Caedmon, 1980.

Plays

Proud Flesh (in verse, produced Minneapolis, 1947; revised [prose] version, produced New York, 1947).
All the King's Men, adaptation of his own novel (as *Willie Stark: His Rise and Fall,* produced Dallas, 1958; as *All the King's*

Men, produced New York, 1959). New York, Random House, 1960.

Novels

Night Rider. Boston, Houghton Mifflin, 1939; London, Eyre and Spottiswoode, 1940.
At Heaven's Gate. New York, Harcourt Brace 1943; London, Eyre and Spottiswoode, 1946.
All the King's Men. New York, Harcourt Brace, 1946; London, Eyre and Spottiswoode, 1948.
World Enough and Time: A Romantic Novel. New York, Random House, 1950; London, Eyre and Spottiswoode, 1951.
Band of Angels. New York, Random House, 1955; London, Eyre and Spottiswoode, 1956.
The Cave. New York, Random House, and London, Eyre and Spottiswoode, 1959.
Wilderness: A Tale of the Civil War. New York, Random House, 1961; London, Eyre and Spottiswoode, 1962.
Flood: A Romance of Our Time. New York, Random House, and London, Collins, 1964.
Meet Me in the Green Glen. New York, Random House, 1971; London, Secker and Warburg, 1972.
A Place to Come To. New York, Random House, and London, Secker and Warburg, 1977.

Short Stories

Blackberry Winter. Cummington, Massachusetts, Cummington Press, 1946.
The Circus in the Attic and Other Stories. New York, Harcourt Brace, 1948; London, Eyre and Spottiswoode, 1952.

Other

John Brown: The Making of a Martyr. New York, Payson and Clarke, 1929.
I'll Take My Stand: The South and the Agrarian Tradition, with others. New York, Harper, 1930.
Understanding Poetry: An Anthology for College Students, with Cleanth Brooks. New York, Holt, 1938; revised edition, 1950, Holt Rinehart, 1960, 1976.
Understanding Fiction, with Cleanth Brooks. New York, Crofts, 1943; revised edition, Appleton Century Crofts, 1959; Englewood Cliffs, New Jersey, Prentice Hall, 1979; abridged edition, as *The Scope of Fiction,* 1960.
A Poem of Pure Imagination: An Experiment in Reading, in *The Rime of the Ancient Mariner,* by Samuel Taylor Coleridge. New York, Reynal, 1946.
Modern Rhetoric: With Readings, with Cleanth Brooks. New York, Harcourt Brace, 1949; revised edition, 1958, 1970, 1979.
Fundamentals of Good Writing: A Handbook of Modern Rhetoric, with Cleanth Brooks. New York, Harcourt Brace, 1950; London, Dobson, 1952.
Segregation: The Inner Conflict in the South. New York, Random House, 1956; London, Eyre and Spottiswoode, 1957.
Selected Essays. New York, Random House, 1958; London, Eyre and Spottiswoode, 1964.
Remember the Alamo! (for children). New York, Random House, 1958; as *How Texas Won Her Freedom,* San Jacinto, Texas, San Jacinto Museum of History, 1959.
The Gods of Mount Olympus (for children). New York, Random House, 1959; London, Muller, 1962.
The Legacy of the Civil War: Meditations on the Centennial. New York, Random House, 1961.
Who Speaks for the Negro? New York, Random House, 1965.

A Plea in Mitigation: Modern Poetry and the End of an Era (lecture). Macon, Georgia, Wesleyan College, 1966.
Homage to Theodore Dreiser. New York, Random House, 1971.
John Greenleaf Whittier's Poetry: An Appraisal and a Selection. Minneapolis, University of Minnesota Press, 1971.
A Conversation with Robert Penn Warren, edited by Frank Gado. Schenectady, New York, The Idol, 1972.
Democracy and Poetry (lecture). Cambridge, Massachusetts, Harvard University Press, 1975.
Robert Penn Warren Talking: Interviews 1950-1978, edited by Floyd C. Watkins and John T. Hiers. New York, Random House, 1980.
Jefferson Davis Gets His Citizenship Back. Lexington, University Press of Kentucky, 1980.

Editor, with Cleanth Brooks and John Thibaut Purser, *An Approach to Literature: A Collection of Prose and Verse with Analyses and Discussions.* Baton Rouge, Louisiana State University Press, 1936; revised edition, New York, Crofts, 1939, Appleton Century Crofts, 1952; Englewood Cliffs, New Jersey, Prentice Hall, 1975.
Editor, *A Southern Harvest: Short Stories by Southern Writers.* Boston, Houghton Mifflin, 1937.
Editor, with Cleanth Brooks, *An Anthology of Stories from the Southern Review.* Baton Rouge, Louisiana State University Press, 1953.
Editor, with Albert Erskine, *Short Story Masterpieces.* New York, Dell, 1954.
Editor, with Albert Erskine, *Six Centuries of Great Poetry.* New York, Dell, 1955.
Editor, with Albert Erskine, *A New Southern Harvest.* New York, Bantam, 1957.
Editor, with Allen Tate, *Selected Poems,* by Denis Devlin. New York, Holt Rinehart, 1963.
Editor, *Faulkner: A Collection of Critical Essays.* Englewood Cliffs, New Jersey, Prentice Hall, 1966.
Editor, with Robert Lowell and Peter Taylor, *Randall Jarrell 1914-1965.* New York, Farrar Straus, 1967.
Editor, *Selected Poems of Herman Melville.* New York, Random House, 1970.
Editor and part author, with Cleanth Brooks and R.W.B. Lewis, *American Literature: The Makers and the Making.* New York, St. Martin's Press, 2 vols., 1973.
Editor, *Katherine Anne Porter: A Collection of Critical Essays.* Englewood Cliffs, New Jersey, Prentice Hall, 1979.

*

Bibliography: *Robert Penn Warren: A Reference Guide* by Neil Nakadate, Boston, Hall, 1977; *Robert Penn Warren: A Descriptive Bibliography 1922-79* by James A. Grimshaw, Jr., Charlottesville, University Press of Virginia, 1981.

Manuscript Collection: Beinecke Library, Yale University, New Haven, Connecticut.

Critical Studies (selection): *Modern Poetry and the Tradition* by Cleanth Brooks, Chapel Hill, University of North Carolina Press, 1939, London, Editions Poetry London, 1948; *Robert Penn Warren* (in German) by Klaus Poenicke, Heidelberg, Winter, 1959; *The Fugitive Group* by Louise Cowan, Baton Rouge, Louisiana State University Press, 1959; *Fugitives' Reunion* edited by Rob Roy Purdy, Nashville, Tennessee, Vanderbilt University Press, 1959; *Robert Penn Warren: The Dark and Bloody Ground* by Leonard Casper, Seattle, University of

Washington Press, 1960; *The Faraway Country* by Louis D. Rubin, Jr., Seattle, University of Washington Press, 1963; *The Hidden God* by Cleanth Brooks, New Haven, Connecticut, Yale University Press, 1963; *Robert Penn Warren* by Charles H. Bohner, New York, Twayne, 1964, revised edition, 1981; *Robert Penn Warren* by Paul West, Minneapolis, University of Minnesota Press, 1964, London, Oxford University Press, 1965; *Robert Penn Warren: A Collection of Critical Essays* edited by John Lewis Longley, Jr., New York, New York University Press, 1965; *The Burden of Time* by John Lincoln Stewart, Princeton, New Jersey, Princeton University Press, 1965; *A Colder Fire: The Poetry of Robert Penn Warren*, Lexington, University of Kentucky Press, 1965, and *The Poetic Vision of Robert Penn Warren*, University Press of Kentucky, 1977 both by Victor H. Strandberg; *Robert Penn Warren: A Vision Earned* by Marshall Walker, Edinburgh, Harris, and New York, Barnes and Noble, 1979; *Robert Penn Warren: A Collection of Critical Essays* edited by Richard Gray, Englewood Cliffs, New Jersey, Prentice Hall, 1980; *Critical Essays on Robert Penn Warren* edited by William B. Clark, Boston, Twayne, 1981; *Robert Penn Warren: Critical Perspectives* edited by Neil Nakadate, Lexington, University Press of Kentucky, 1981; *The Achievement of Robert Penn Warren* by James H. Justus, Baton Rouge, Louisiana State University Press, 1981; *Then and Now: The Personal Past in the Poetry of Robert Penn Warren* by Floyd C. Watkins, Lexington, University Press of Kentucky, 1982; *Homage to Robert Penn Warren* edited by Frank Graziano, Durango, Colorado, Logbridge Rhodes, 1982; *Robert Penn Warren* by Katherine Snipes, New York, Ungar, 1983; *A Southern Renascence Man: Views of Robert Penn Warren* edited by Walter B. Edgar, Baton Rouge, Louisiana State University Press, 1984.

*   *   *

So much acclaim has been given his novels, critical studies and social comment, that it is well to emphasize that Robert Penn Warren is incontestably one of the most distinguished poets now writing. His poems are the meditations of a ghost-haunted philosopher, a man who can remember an agrarian way of life with families closely knit and rooted to the land, a man who has come as far from such pastoral simplicities as has his country and his region. A native of Kentucky, Warren grew up among a taletelling, ballad-singing, proudly individualistic people. The American South has always had a distinctive regional culture and Warren had the fortune to begin writing as a member of its most influential literary party. Attending Vanderbilt University (1921-25), he studied with John Crowe Ransom and soon joined the Fugitive Movement along with Allen Tate, Donald Davidson, Stark Young, and others. These poets and critics wrote in the hope that the agrarian culture of the South could be preserved against the encroachments of industrial and mercantile values (see *I'll Take My Stand*, 1930). These social attitudes were reflected in their aesthetic, which embodied the values of a presumed stable and hieratic society; a devotion to classical literature; the influence of metaphysical poetry; and the conception of verse as public discourse, formal in diction, traditional in meter, impersonal in tone. These qualities appear, e.g., in the last stanza of Warren's early poem, "Problem of Knowledge":

> The rodent tooth has etched the bone,
> Beech bole is blackened by the fire:
> Was it a sandal smote the troughed stone?
> We rest, lapped in the arrogant chastity of our desire.

The problem of knowledge has been Warren's continuing concern, but of all the Fugitives he was to move farthest from this

conservative social and aesthetic position. After his *Selected Poems 1923-1943*, he published no lyrical verse until *Promises: Poems 1954-1956*, which embodied a style and an aesthetic markedly different from his Fugitive period. In the years since, he has remained true to this later style which he has put to increasingly adventurous uses.

A paradigm of Warren's lasting concerns is found in the poem "Original Sin: A Short Story," a short poem telling a long story indeed of the inescapability of man's knowledge of his fallen state. Its title suggests two permanent aspects of Warren's sensibility, his concern with the dark side of human nature and his commitment to narrative in a period when many poets have eschewed story for symbol, image, ideogram, or other non-discursive devices. These commitments are fully explored and dramatized in Warren's verse novel, *Brother to Dragons*. Here the narrative arises from the historical context most significant to a Southern man of letters. The story, based upon an actual set of events, involves the murderous Oedipal fixation of Lilburn Lewis, a nephew of Thomas Jefferson, whose motives are masked by self-righteousness and by his self-binding idealization of his mother's memory. The character of Lewis is dismaying to Jefferson, whose Augustan faith in human nature allowed no place for such irrationality and violence in one of his own blood, or in any man. Jefferson's idealism proves to be an abstraction which, like the nephew's insane self-righteousness, blinds its possessor to the truth of human nature. As the crime which Lewis commits is the wanton murder of his slave, the narrative poem thus involves also the special guilt of the old South, which Jefferson lamented but could neither assuage nor prevent. Warren's tale is in the Gothic vein (the same murder had been used by Poe as the plot of his verse drama *Politian*), but this is Gothicism deepened by moral responsibility and philosophical questing. The "dragon" of the title is the monster within man.

The brooding violence and terror that striate *Brother to Dragons* characterize Warren's later poetry also. With some poets one recalls lines or stanzas; with Warren it is often characters and actions which persist in the reader's memory: the folktale story of "The Ballad of Billy Potts," the terror and pity of "School Lesson Based on Word of the Tragic Death of Entire Gillum Family," the haunted sievings of time past in "Ballad of a Sweet Dream of Peace." In Warren's poems since *Promises* the narrative element is often subordinated to a brooding metaphysical contemplation of the event, the event itself sometimes not disclosed until the reader is well on into the long, looping sequences in which the poems are arranged. There is also a change in the metrical structure, the stressed meters and regular stanzas now replaced by broken rhythms; clusters of lines arranged in patterns the feelings compel, rather than in those a design proposes; and a beautifully controlled playing-off of speech against the silences of white space, of eye-breaks against the continuity of the brooding, solitary voice.

Selected Poems: New and Old 1923-1966 places the latest work first. The opening poem begins, "The stars are only a backdrop for/the human condition"; this line and a half introduce the two most frequent images in the recent verse: the vast impersonal grandeur of the stars, and the human condition, particularly the remembrance of that inexplicable affront, death. There are elegiac series of poems on the deaths of a boyhood companion ("Ballad: Between the Boxcars, 1923"), and of an old man ("Chain Saw at Dawn in Vermont," "Fall Comes in Back-Country Vermont"); a neighbor's remembered suicide ("The Day Dr. Knox Did It"); the death of the poet's father, his mother, his family's old Negro servant ("Mortmain," "Tale of Time"), as well as the imagined deaths of a Confederate and a Union soldier ("Two Studies in Idealism"). The brooding effort to re-experience, to understand, to explain, to endure these losses is counterpointed by images of stars, space, the diminution of the human scale when seen from an airplane—as in "Homage to Emerson, on Night Flight to New York," in which the poet tests but cannot accept the comforting transcendentalism of the philosopher who "had forgiven God everything," though he admits that "At 38,000 feet Emerson/Is dead right."

Later in the same poem he writes:

Now let us cross that black cement which so resembles the arctic ice of
Our recollections. There is the city, the sky
Glows, glows above it, there must be

A way by which the process of living can become Truth.

Let us move toward the city. Do you think you could tell me
What constitutes the human bond?

It is this "human bond," as well as how "the process of living can become Truth," which Warren is concerned to know, to experience, to celebrate. In *Audubon: A Vision*, a sequence of seven poems, Warren freely dramatizes an episode from an entry in the journal of the explorer-ornithologist. Audubon becomes a symbol of the artist in the New World, experiencing the grandeur and beauty of the natural environment and the meanness and violence of human life on the frontier. The tale is thematically similar to that in the earlier "The Ballad of Billy Potts," an encounter with greed, lust, and murder. The language of this long poem is so translucent that the reader is aware not of its diction but of the sensibility which records and responds to the action. "I did not know what was happening in my heart," writes the Audubon of the poem, but the reader knows that he has endured a confrontation with the darkest passions of human nature and has questioned the meaning of human existence; the poem concludes:

> Tell me a story.
>
> In this century, and moment, of mania,
> Tell me a story.
>
> Make it a story of great distances, and starlight.
>
> The name of the story will be Time,
> But you must not pronounce its name.
>
> Tell me a story of deep delight.

Intrinsic with Warren's transfiguration of tragedy into "deep delight" are his celebrations of the senses and the human bonds of love. Warren's loyalties are deep and passionate, loyalties to a way of life he can define and pursue despite the difficulties of the divided soul and the contemporary "century, and moment, of mania." The accomplishment and range of his poetry, as well as the dramatic use of an agrarian sensibility to measure the imperfections of the human lot, suggest that Warren is one of the few living poets comparable to Robert Frost.

—Daniel Hoffman

WARSH, Lewis. American. Born in New York City, 9 November 1944. Educated at the City College of New York,

B.A. 1966, M.A. 1975. Married Bernadette Mayer in 1975; two daughters and one son. Teacher, St. Marks Church-in-the-Bowery Poetry Project, New York, 1973-75, Naropa Institute, Boulder, Colorado, 1978, and New England College, Henniker, New Hampshire, 1979-80. Editor, *Angel Hair* and Angel Hair Books, New York, 1966-77, and *Boston Eagle*, 1972-74. Since 1977, Editor, *United Artists* and United Artists Books, New York. Recipient: National Endowment for the Arts grant, 1966, 1979; Poets Foundation Award, 1972; Creative Artists Public Service grant, 1978; Coordinating Council of Literary Magazines award, 1981. Address: 172 East 4th Street, New York, New York 10009, U.S.A.

PUBLICATIONS

Verse

The Suicide Rates. Eugene, Oregon, Toad Press, 1967.
Highjacking. New York, Boke, 1968.
Moving Through Air. New York, Angel Hair, 1968.
Chicago, with Tom Clark. New York, Angel Hair, 1969.
Two Poems. Windsor, Ontario, Orange Bear Reader, 1971.
Dreaming as One. New York, Corinth, 1971.
Long Distance. London, Ferry Press, 1971.
Today. New York, Adventures in Poetry, 1974.
Immediate Surrounding. Lancaster, Massachusetts, Other, 1974.
Blue Heaven. New York, Kulchur, 1978.
Hives. New York, United Artists, 1979.
Methods of Birth Control. College Park, Maryland, Sun and Moon, 1983.

Novel

Agnes and Sally. New York, Fiction Collective, 1984.

Other

Part of My History. Toronto, Coach House Press, 1972.
The Maharajah's Son (autobiography). New York, Angel Hair, 1977.

Translator, *Night of Loveless Nights*, by Robert Desnos. New York, Ant's Forefoot, 1973.

*

Manuscript Collection: New York University Library.

*   *   *

In the last line of "Brothers Levernoch," Lewis Warsh writes, "People who are discontented shock me." The voice which speaks in his poems is always—at least nearly—content. Although the poems are personal, or seem to be, they are not "confessional" in the usual sense of the term. Warsh is the calm and detached observer. Immediate autobiography, things remembered from long ago, newspaper reports, accounts of his family—all enter on equal footing. The commonest events assert themselves as worthy of complete and careful attention. The writing itself is almost colorless. There is nothing flashy or stylish. The careless reader will miss the mastery.

Warsh seldom commits a generalization. The largest collection of his work in recent years, *Blue Heaven* (presumably from the song), opens with a poem about the pleasures and dangers of thinking:

> Thoughts make men strangers
> and create great moments of urgency,
> as well as nervousness, when a thought
> moves you to wake up and light a cigarette
> and lie back on pillow, content
> in thinking, in playing the thought through,
> that's the only way for it to die!

To the extent he thinks in his poetry, Warsh is willing to let his thought have this quality, as one of the media, along with perception, of existence. The danger of thought is that it can become so absorbing that one misses other important things—the cigarette, the pillow. After a certain point, he is willing to let everything go to its proper death. In "Single File," he writes, "All my poems/no center/everything scattered/many voices trailing off/empty illusions/of emotions and thoughts/incredible pipe dreams/disappearing/beneath waves." Too many poets this would be cause for despair; to Warsh it is merely the way things are.

Inside these limits, in which irony is raised to a total sense of the world, he is capable of immense variety. He does not play endless variations on two or three successful themes or forms. He can be epigrammatic or tightly imagistic, but he is also effective in looser, anecdotal poems. He has written some strong prose poems and some of his poems seem to cry out for a musical setting: "At times like this/we leave our fears behind and enter/a world/where what we see/doesn't exist, where words/dance out along the curb/like playful cubs/and the heart sings on/—to High Heavens—regardless."

There are no poems which can be called typical—a remarkable fact in a poet who might best be called a formalist. Though he does not work in conventional forms, his poems turn again and again on the recognition of formal connections. This can be seen perhaps most clearly in a poem like "Footnote," which is an exploration of the formal relationship between the Percy Shelley-Harriet Westbrook-Thomas Hogg circle and the Friedrich Nietzsche-Lou Salome-Paul Ree circle. An awareness of relationships of this *kind*, on both the most minute and on the grandest scales, generates the energy of his poetry. It is one of the truest kinds of intelligence, and the pleasure of reading Warsh's work is that he generously makes his intelligence available.

—Don Byrd

WATERMAN, Andrew (John). British. Born in London, 28 May 1940. Educated at Trinity School, Croydon, 1951-57; University of Leicester, 1963-66, B.A. (honours) in English 1966; Worcester College, Oxford, 1966-68. Married Angela Marilyn Hannah Eagle in 1982 (second marriage); one son. Lecturer, 1968-78, and since 1978, Senior Lecturer in English, University of Ulster, Coleraine. Recipient: Cholmondeley Award, 1977; Arvon Foundation prize, 1981. Address: 15 Hazelbank Road, Coleraine, County Londonderry, Northern Ireland.

PUBLICATIONS

Verse

Last Fruit. Hitchin, Hertfordshire, Mandeville Press, 1974.

Living Room. London, Marvell Press, 1974.
From the Other Country. Manchester, Carcanet, 1977.
Over the Wall. Manchester, Carcanet, 1980.
Out for the Elements. Manchester, Carcanet, 1981.

Other

Editor, *The Poetry of Chess.* London, Anvil Press Poetry, 1981.

*

Critical Studies: "Mature Students: Peter Scupham and Andrew Waterman," in *British Poetry since 1970* edited by Peter Jones and Michael Schmidt, Manchester, Carcanet, and New York, Persea, 1980, and "Waterman and the Elements," in *Helix 17* (Ivanhoe, Australia), 1984, both by Neil Powell.

Andrew Waterman comments:

Some of one's poems are personal and autobiographical, others range into themes or times remote from one's immediate life and circumstances. From my own point of view, however, all I write feels finally "of a piece," however disparate the superficial materials. England, where I grew up and which I frequently revisit, and Ireland, where I have lived and worked since 1968, both supply my poetry with settings and subject material. I find a poem begins with a sort of fermenting in one's mind of some detail or occasion, perhaps in itself trivial, anything from a view across a field or supermarket to a scrap of conversation or personal incident or encounter, until a pressure evolves so that one feels nagged to get out pencil and paper and start jotting, crossing out, trying again; and only the labour of working itself discovers what, if anything, is there that can be won into poetry. One tries to intuit the right rhythm and shape, pick up imaginative glints as one works. The process is comparable not to working from a blueprint, but to starting with material like a sculptor with a mass of stone, and a sense of a harmonious finished statue which might, with luck, be conjured from this material. At the start one is not sure of the exact form of the finished work—only that it is possible. At the end, the rubble one has chipped away litters one's draft sheets, and the poem is "finished," a contraption of words which floats free of one, with luck embodying a pattern of feelings and perceptions that will speak to and please other people, an imaginative world that imaginations can inhabit.

*   *   *

Andrew Waterman's poetry has a sharp awareness of the typical and the commonplace, particularly when he is quoting and inventing the direct speech of others. In his own voice the same colloquial language often holds people at a distance, reducing them to types: "an old dear yammering," "Annes, Pams, Joyces." Such long perspectives have their use, for they enable him to take in big sweeps of history and social change, and the wider the view the more convincing he becomes. When dealing with particular issues, such as the peasant fixities being swept away by the television and computer society, Waterman strikes familiar attitudes reminiscent of Leavis, in a tone like Larkin's. But when more ambitious he can be powerfully discursive and subtly symbolical at the same time, as in "Playing Through Old Games of Chess" in *Over the Wall*, where a hundred years of change are counterpointed against chess games, and history is shown as the product of a complex logic of interlocking choices. In *From the Other Country*, his first book-length collection, the articulate stops just short of the prolix, and he is prepared to tolerate the occasional flaccid phrase (an aeroplane is a "hushed cylinder of steel") for the sake of broad and bold effects.

Outspoken in both his criticism and his liking of "stunted" Northern Ireland, he claims the privileges of both insider and outsider, "among, not of, all this." He can have it both ways, not just in allegiance to place and culture but also to class, occupation, and friends. In many poems about the tangled wastes of love, selfishness, and cross-purposes, he writes of emotion indulged but also mistrusted ("fatuities of poignancy"), or combines the wistful with the ruthless: "growth is a process perpetually/of abandonment, amputation." He evokes a well-dramatised instability here, several feeling and thinking sensibilities inhabiting the same self, generated by a language which veers abruptly between the racy and the poetically heightened. He is closer to American confessional verse than many of his British contemporaries will go, and his personal poems include some of his greatest successes as well as failures.

The inanimate world in Waterman has a life of its own, "furniture settling ton by ton into fitted carpets." Lines suggesting the autonomy of nature are often used to show up the human world, for the charm of the non-human is that it promises meaning but seldom grants it, unlike his acquaintances "touting problems, all queueing for further transfusions." Poems in *Over the Wall* thrive energetically on unashamed rage at the nuisance value of friends whose "dingy mouths keep working" and who "terribly foul/your bed," or of more predictable targets like the "write-off in residence" and the "Hairy Scrotum School" of poets. But Waterman is now a master of form, wittily controlling stanzas which though elaborate have naturalness of rhythm and freedom of movement.

The title poem of *Out for the Elements* marks Waterman's full poetic maturity. In a stanza form based loosely on the sonnet he sustains for 1500 lines an intelligent discursive meditation in a manner which stands comparison with Auden's *Letter to Lord Byron.* In this spacious and immensely readable poem there is for the first time room for his various subjects—social observation, Northern Ireland, autobiography—happily to coexist, held together by a mellower and more flexible tone than before. Without posturing now, he can keep "faith with the bruised common heart." Waterman has tapped a rich vein, and recent uncollected poems suggest there is more to come.

—R.J.C. Watt

WATSON, Robert (Winthrop). American. Born in Passaic, New Jersey, 26 December 1925. Educated at Williams College, Williamstown, Massachusetts, B.A. 1946; University of Zurich (Swiss-American Exchange Fellow), 1946-47; Johns Hopkins University, Baltimore, M.A. 1950, Ph.D. in English 1955. Served in the United States Naval Reserve, 1943-45. Married Elizabeth Ann Rean in 1952; one son and one daughter. Instructor, Williams College, 1947-48, 1952-53, and Johns Hopkins University, 1950-52. Member of the Faculty since 1953, and since 1965, Professor of English, University of North Carolina, Greensboro. Visiting Poet, California State University, Northridge, 1968-69. Recipient: *American Scholar* Prize, 1961; National Endowment for the Arts grant, 1974; American Academy award, 1977. Address: 9-D Fountain Manor Drive, Greensboro, North Carolina 27403, U.S.A.

PUBLICATIONS

Verse

A Paper Horse. New York, Atheneum, 1962.
Advantages of Dark. New York, Atheneum, 1966.
Christmas in Las Vegas. New York, Atheneum, 1971.
Watson on the Beach. Greensboro, North Carolina, SB Press, 1972.
Selected Poems. New York, Atheneum, 1974.
Island of Bones. Greensboro, North Carolina, Unicorn Press, 1977.
Night Blooming Cactus. New York, Atheneum, 1980.

Play

A Plot in the Palace, in *First Stage* (Lafayette, Indiana), 1964.

Novels

Three Sides of the Mirror. New York, Putnam, 1966.
Lily Lang. New York, St. Martin's Press, 1977.

Other

Editor, with Gibbons Ruark, *The Greensboro Reader.* Chapel Hill, University of North Carolina Press, 1964.

*

Critical Studies: by Thomas Lask in *New York Times,* 11 December 1971; Grover Smith, in *Above Ground Review* (Arden, North Carolina), Winter 1971; Sister Bernetta Quinn, in *Georgia Review* (Athens), Fall 1977; James Finn Cotter, in *Hudson Review* (New York), Summer 1981.

Robert Watson comments:

I am primarily a poet, but in my spare time I also enjoy writing fiction and drama. Though I have written some criticism and reviews, I write informative prose only at the point of a gun.

With few exceptions the statements made by poets in our time about their work seem pretentious, silly, boring or all three at once. Theories get much attention, more than the poems from which they come; no theories for me. And if I try to detail characteristics of my poetry, then I am writing my obituary. In vague terms I try to make my work as musical (in the poetic sense), alive, and intimate as I can, and try to get in the way people feel about their lives and their world. I do dramatic, lyric and narrative poems in a wide variety of forms, most of my own invention. What doesn't seem to fit poems I put in prose fiction.

*   *   *

Robert Watson's poetry is energetic and economical, splendidly suited to the difficult art of creating characters in verse. Watson's first volume, *A Paper Horse,* established these facts with far more authority and consistency than is usual in first collections; the book demonstrates a mastery of staccato compression in a variety of formal approaches ranging from free verse to strict rhyme and meter. Most of the poems are soliloquies, spoken by a variety of characters particularly qualified to speak of the loss of youth, freedom, or love. The surface bleakness of the characters' lives is mitigated by Watson's compassion for them, and by his strong and distinctive style.

Advantages of Dark does not reveal much stylistic development, but it extends the range of starting points for Watson's poetry. In addition to a few soliloquies, there are a number of satires of contemporary life, some of which portray with harrowing humor the willful recalcitrance of everyday inanimate objects. The book also contains an ambitious long poem, "The City of Passaic," which evokes, through the lives of a few of its inhabitants, the life of the city where Watson was born. "Line for a President" also deserves mention as one of the very few convincing and genuine American poems on the assassination of President Kennedy.

Christmas in Las Vegas is something of a return to the bleakness of *A Paper Horse*. In his accustomed style, which suddenly appears to have been developed for just this purpose, Watson explores the brittle brilliance of modern urban life, in which people are almost indistinguishable from the machines they have become enslaved by. The somber tones of this collection, paradoxically deepened by the relentless presence of artificial light, are more profound than any Watson has struck before.

—Henry Taylor

WATSON, Roderick (Bruce). Scottish. Born in Aberdeen, 12 May 1943. Educated at Aberdeen Grammar School, 1955-61; Aberdeen University, 1961-65. M.A. in English 1965; Peterhouse, Cambridge (Lucy Jack Scholar), 1966-69, Ph.D. 1971. Married Celia Hall Mackie in 1966; one son and one daughter. Lecturer in English, University of Victoria, British Columbia, 1965-66. Since 1971, Lecturer in English, University of Stirling. Recipient: Scottish Arts Council bursary, 1970. Address: 19 Millar Place, Stirling FK8 1XD, Scotland.

PUBLICATIONS

Verse

28 Poems, with James Rankin.   Aberdeen, Aberdeen University Poetry Society, 1964.
Poems.   Preston, Lancashire, Akros, 1970.
Trio: New Poets from Edinburgh, with Valerie Simmons and Paul Mills, edited by Robin Fulton.   New York, New Rivers Press, 1971.
True History on the Walls.   Edinburgh, M. Macdonald, 1976.

Other

Hugh MacDiarmid.   Milton Keynes, Buckinghamshire, Open University, 1976.
The Penguin Book of the Bicycle, with Martin Gray.   London, Allen Lane, 1978.
The Literature of Scotland.   New York, Schocken, and London, Macmillan, 1985.

Editor, with Alexander Scott and Norman Lindsay, *Scottish Poetry Seven* [to *Nine*].   Glasgow, Glasgow University Press, 1 vol., 1974; Manchester, Carcanet, 2 vols., 1975-76.
Editor, with Angus Ogilvy and George Sutherland, *Birds: An Anthology of New Poems.*   Stirling, Stirling Gallery, 1978.
Editor, with Angus Ogilvy and George Sutherland, *Stones.*   Stirling, Stirling Gallery, 1980.

*

Manuscript Collection: National Library of Scotland, Edinburgh.

Critical Studies: by Philip Hobsbaum, in *Lines Review 42-43* (Edinburgh), September 1972-February 1973; Donald Campbell, in *Akros 8* (Preston, Lancashire), March 1973; David Hewitt, in *Aberdeen University Review*, xliv, 3, 1973; *Contemporary Scottish Poetry* by Robin Fulton, Edinburgh, M. Macdonald, 1974; R. Calder, in *Lines Review 61* (Edinburgh), June 1977.

Roderick Watson comments:

The poem begins in the collision which happens when you say things by means of other things. But I am also concerned to preserve the integrity of these "other things." The images, experiences, and histories which one collects must be themselves too, and not merely the source material for striking metaphors. The long line I use has been a great help in this. So I prefer an angular resistance in the language of poetry, a certain opacity, and a conclusion which retains some of the tension of the poem, rather than one which resolves it with a final epigrammatic flourish.

In the past I have identified this understanding with my origins in the Northeast of Scotland. I'm sure that this is true, but recently I have been thinking that it is not the whole story either. I don't know what the rest is yet. *True History* focussed on newsclippings, graffitti, or other marks on stone as the characteristic signs we leave behind us. My more recent poems are involved with the less tangible realm of recorded voices, or snatches of music and radio echoes on the airwaves—all realigned to become a form of memory and elegy.

*   *   *

Introducing the poems of Roderick Watson in *Trio: New Poets from Edinburgh*, Robin Fulton singled out three characteristic features of his work up to that date (1971): "a treatment of family history alongside the wider history of the century; an ability to localise and focus these wider movements; and the use of a long line and a full paragraph through which his verse can deliberate." The last word is well chosen. Punctuated by gaps which require the reader to stop and mark his words, Watson's twelve poems in that book have a slow, recollecting speech-rhythm that suits his preoccupation with stones, bones, cave paintings, the track of time. There is a kind of archaeology at the back of his imagination, typically active in "3 Stones," which contrasts a stone used as a weapon, a stone used for grinding corn, and a stone on which a message has been cut:

> Leave wax and pigment   and ink the stone itself
> —a beginner's exercise in lithography.
> The printing shows old scars   lines   seams
> a play of forces on matter   collected and recorded.
> Time accumulates thus   and in quarries   mines
> heart shafts   the deep places   it is true history
> written on the walls.   This is a picture of it.
> (And the track of ions too   in a cloud chamber).

Watson did post-graduate work on MacDiarmid, and the experience seems to have inspired him to try to write the kind of poetry MacDiarmid wants—"words coming from a mind / Which has experienced the sifted layers on layers / Of human lives." The result is occasionally clotted and repetitious, but full of possibilities for the future.

—Robert Nye

WAYMAN, Tom (Thomas Ethan Wayman). Canadian. Born in Hawkesbury, Ontario, 13 August 1945. Educated at the University of British Columbia, Vancouver, 1962-66, B.A. 1966; University of California, Irvine, 1966-68, M.F.A. 1968. Instructor in English, Colorado State University, Fort Collins, 1968-69; worked at construction, demolition, and factory jobs, and as a teacher's aide, 1969-75; Writer-in-Residence, University of Windsor, Ontario, 1975-76; Assistant Professor of English, Wayne State University, Detroit, 1976-77; Writer-in-Residence, University of Alberta, Edmonton, 1978-79; Faculty Member, David Thompson University Centre School of Writing, Nelson, British Columbia, 1980-82; Writer-in-Residence, Simon Fraser University, Burnaby, British Columbia, Spring 1983; Instructor, Kwantlen College, Surrey, British Columbia, Fall 1983. Since 1984, Faculty Member, Kootenay School of Writing, Vancouver. Recipient: Helen Bullis Prize (*Poetry Northwest*) 1972; Borestone Mountain Poetry Award, 1972, 1973, 1974, 1976; Canadian Authors Association prize, 1974; Canada Council Senior Grant, 1975, 1977; A.J.M. Smith Prize, Michigan State University, 1976; U.S. Bicentennial Award, 1976. Address: 2796 East 27th Avenue, Vancouver, British Columbia V5R 1N5, Canada.

PUBLICATIONS

Verse

Mindscapes, with others, edited by Ann Wall. Toronto, Anansi, 1971.
Waiting for Wayman. Toronto, McClelland and Stewart, 1973.
For and Against the Moon: Blues, Yells, and Chuckles. Toronto, Macmillan, 1974.
Money and Rain: Tom Wayman Live! Toronto, Macmillan, 1975.
Routines. Seattle, Black Eye Press, 1976.
Transport. Toronto, Dreadnaught Press, 1976.
Kitchener/Chicago/Saskatoon. Windsor, Ontario, Flat Singles Press, 1977.
Free Time: Industrial Poems. Toronto, Macmillan, 1977.
A Planet Mostly Sea: Two Poems. Winnipeg, Turnstone Press, 1979.
Introducing Tom Wayman: Selected Poems 1973-1980. Princeton, New Jersey, Ontario Review Press, 1980.
Living on the Ground: Tom Wayman Country. Toronto, McClelland and Stewart, 1980.
The Nobel Prize Acceptance Speech: New and Selected Poems. Saskatoon, Thistledown Press, 1981.
Counting the Hours: City Poems. Toronto, McClelland and Stewart, 1983.

Other

Inside Job: Essays on the New Work Writing. Madeira Park, British Columbia, Harbour, 1983.

Editor, *Beaton Abbot's Got the Contract: An Anthology of Working Poems.* Edmonton, NeWest Press, 1974.
Editor, *A Government Job at Last: An Anthology of Working Poems, Mainly Canadian.* Vancouver, MacLeod, 1976.
Editor, *Going for Coffee: Poetry on the Job.* Madeira Park, British Columbia, Harbour, 1981.

*

Critical Studies: "Tom Wayman: An Introduction" by Paul Delany, in *Little Magazine* (New York), Winter 1975-76; "Way Out with Wayman: The Engaged Voice" by Marlowe Anderson, in *CV 2* (Winnipeg), January 1976.

Tom Wayman comments:

What I want to do with my poems, and with the poems by others that I try to encourage and collect, is to bring into Canadian literature a poetry of everyday life based on what I consider to be the central experience of everyday life—work. By "work" I mean what people do for a living, whether paid or unpaid, blue- or white-collar. To me this experience is central because I believe the work we do affects every other aspect of our lives, including our loves, deaths, appreciations of nature, and all other topics considered to be "poetic." This work poetry, which I feel must originate from first-hand experience to be of any value, is "not poetic" in the sense that it is not romantic, not concerned with an imaginary past or an imaginary future. It is concerned with the present. And so I like to think that this kind of writing gives readers a chance to interact with these poems—a chance they don't have when they are dealing with some poet's or fiction writer's imaginary world. The present is something people know about themselves, and therefore they are not threatened or put off by it. If they don't like what is said about it they can stand up and tell you; such poetry in this way has some potential of becoming an art with an audience.

*   *   *

Tom Wayman is one of the few Canadian political poets, and it is perhaps to his advantage—as a poet—that his politics is somewhat distanced from the present Canadian scene. It is the politics of the North American 1960's, when Wayman was personally involved in the radical student movement in California and later, as he said, lived "by hustle, construction labouring, unemployment insurance, and welfare." It is a politics with its own kind of realism, accepting defeat without disillusionment, and having—at least in the imagination—its own imperatives of action, as suggested in Wayman's early and moving poem, "The Dream of the Guerillas": "And night quiet/after the dream./Street lights burn on./The slogans are calm on dim walls. The clock,/the clock says: now/the guerillas are coming and you must go with them."

Wayman's radicalism is mingled with a great deal of nostalgia; he looks to the lost causes of the past as well as the losing causes of the present. He has actually been a member of the moribund IWW, and he ends a recent poem, on the continuity of submerged libertarian ideals ("The Ghosts of the Anarchists Speak of George Woodcock"), with a Spanish anarchist saying:

Still, we don't win.   So now what happened here
must be written down.   Not that anybody could list
all the arguments, the wind, the food,
the sweat and thinking and fighting
that led us to try this and try that,
to be successful here and fail there.   But we need
true words that tell what we did

so compactly, so magnificently
they are like a seed you can hold in your hand
and see in it all the intricate beauty
of the strong dark flowers that will come.

Tom Wayman first emerged out of publication in poetry magazines when a group of his poems was printed (with work by three other writers) in *Mindscapes*. The volumes he has published since then, such as *Waiting for Wayman*, *For and Against the Moon: Blues, Yells, and Chuckles*, and *Money and Rain: Tom Wayman Live!*, have projected—as their titles suggest—not only a resolutely minoritarian political attitude, but also a highly idiosyncratic personality. There is indeed a great element of the dramatic in Wayman's poetic method; a comic persona named Wayman faces the world as a kind of Schweikian guerilla, and in this role dominates a whole series of poems that are devoted to exposing the enormities of the world against which the poet clumsily and futilely but relentlessly fights.

But underlying the comedy, and expressed in other poems with a good deal of sincere pathos, is a recognition of the misery and pain which are undergone by the economically and politically oppressed, who represent the greater part of the world's population, a recognition that does not give way to despair, but no longer rises high in the heavens of hope, and no longer sees self-sacrifice as an imperative: "I no longer believe my pain/will help another human being."

But there are times also when Wayman abandons both comedy and pathos and writes with a pure and tender lyricism in which the persona dwindles to a reflective eye, and the voice sings quietly. An example is another recent poem, "Herself, Walking"; in the first two verses the poet imagines the woman walking in June through the pine forest, in winter through the snow; the final verse reads:

> And what is she doing
> at her kitchen table
> on a stormy morning,
> lights on since eight,
> the rain drumming
> on the house roof,
> the woods and the dock
> soaked with it,
> while she
> sitting at her table
> working
> meanwhile goes walking
> on the rain-swept rocks
> by the turbulent,
> difficult sea?

Wayman is vigorous, Protean in fancy, and more self-critical than most poets of his highly productive kind. Facility is his temptation, but so far it has rarely led him away from true feeling and he is likely to develop in power as his verse becomes less consciously political.

—George Woodcock

WEBB, Harri.   Welsh.   Born in Swansea, Glamorgan, 7 September 1920. Educated at Glanmôr Secondary School, Swansea; Magdalen College, Oxford. Former librarian in Dowlais

and Mountain Ash, Glamorgan. Recipient: Welsh Arts Council prize, 1970. Address: 2 Rose Row, Cwmbach, Aberdare, Glamorgan, Wales.

<small>PUBLICATIONS</small>

Verse

Triad: Thirty-Three Poems, with Peter Gruffydd and Meic Stephens.   Merthyr Tydfil, Triskel Press, 1963.
The Green Desert.   Llandysul, Dyfed, Gomer, 1969.
A Crown for Branwen.   Llandysul, Dyfed, Gomer, 1973.
Rampage and Revel.   Llandysul, Dyfed, Gomer, 1977.
Poems and Points.   Llandysul, Dyfed, Gomer, 1983.

Play

Television Play: *He'll Never Play for Wales*, 1980.

Other

Dic Penderyn and the Merthyr Rising of 1831.   Swansea, Gwasg Penderyn, 1956.
Our National Anthem: Some Observations on "Hen wlad fy nhadau."   Merthyr Tydfil, Triskel Press, 1964.
Tales from Wales (for children).   London, Granada, 1983.

*   *   *

Most of Harri Webb's poetry deals directly with some aspect of Wales: its landscape, culture, language, history, or national identity. In his collections *The Green Desert* and *A Crown for Branwen* his passionate concern for, and commitment to, the nationalist cause is total and remarkable. He possesses the well-known Welsh "lovely gift of the gab." His poems reveal his delight in language and his flowing facility, his wit and wide references (few Anglo-Welsh poets are as erudite about their country), his technical versatility ranging from simple folk verses to the most sophisticated forms, and a gift for the memorable phrase, as in the lyrical and delicate "Carmarthen Coast":

> In the steep hayfields, in the deep lanes
> Where the primroses linger till autumn
> And the white trefoils star the hedgerow grass,
> Where all the flowers bloom at once and forever,
> You are near, but may not cross, the frontier of time.
> Sweet heifers graze the saltings,
> The tide laps at the roots of elder and thorn,
> But the ferryman does not come to the ruined bellhouse.

Webb is also a popular balladist, pamphleteer, political journalist, and former Plaid Cymru candidate, and this background is shown in the considerable variety of approach and technique which characterises his work. There are many deeply-felt, nostalgic, sometimes bitter responses to what he sees as the tragedy of modern Wales, and odd political squibs like his famous "Ode to the Severn Bridge": "Two lands at last connected/Across the waters wide/And all the tolls collected/On the English side." But the whiplash satire, clever parody, and biting mockery in his work are amply balanced by such powerful, profound and moving poems as "The Stone Face," a dramatic evocation of historical heroes in which he refers to "the special Welsh tone of voice/Half banter, half blind fervour" and which develops with urgency and authority. Nowhere is his love of Wales and the serious side of his talent seen more clearly than in this very fine poem.

Harri Webb's occasional rhetorical discursiveness, and the obligation he feels to preach his cause, have been viewed by some cool critics as inhibiting his poetic intelligence. But his range of moods, forms, and styles, his sheer inventiveness and genial, high-spirited humour have placed him, through the last ten years, in the upper ranks of Anglo-Welsh bards. He is, in a real sense, a "poet of the people."

The simple sincerity, for example, of "Heat Wave," his address to an eminent long-dead Catholic Welshman exiled in Rome, commands the utmost respect:

>   Will I,
> An Anglican atheist writing in the wrong language, exile,
> In the way of my century, here at home, earn something
> Of the understanding I feel for you, when future men,
> If there are any, read my dreams?

> —John Tripp

WEBB, Phyllis. Canadian. Born in Victoria, British Columbia, 8 April 1927. Educated at the University of British Columbia, Vancouver, B.A. 1949; McGill University, Montreal, 1953. Secretary, Montreal, 1956; staff member, University of British Columbia, Vancouver, 1961-64; Program Organizer, 1964-67, and Executive Producer, 1967-69, Canadian Broadcasting Corporation, Toronto; has taught at the University of British Columbia, Banff Centre, Alberta, and University of Alberta, 1980-81; now Lecturer, Creative Writing Department, University of Victoria, British Columbia. Recipient: Canadian Government Overseas Award, 1957; Canada Council bursary, 1963, and award, 1969, 1981; Governor-General's Award, 1983. Address: P.O. Box 11, Fulford Harbour, British Columbia V0S 1C0, Canada.

PUBLICATIONS

Verse

Trio, with Gael Turnbull and Eli Mandel. Toronto, Contact Press, 1954.
Even Your Right Eye. Toronto, McClelland and Stewart, 1956.
The Sea Is Also a Garden. Toronto, Ryerson Press, 1962.
Naked Poems. Vancouver, Periwinkle Press, 1965.
Selected Poems 1954-1965, edited by John Hulcoop. Vancouver, Talonbooks, 1971.
Wilson's Bowl. Toronto, Coach House Press, 1980.
Sunday Water: Thirteen Anti Ghazals. Lantzville, British Columbia, Island, 1982.
The Vision Tree: Selected Poems, edited by Sharon Thesen. Vancouver, Talonbooks, 1982.
Water and Light: Ghazals and Anti Ghazals. Toronto, Coach House Press, 1985.

Other

Talking. Montreal, Quadrant, 1982.

*

Manuscript Collection: National Library of Canada, Ottawa.

Critical Studies: "The Structure of Loss" by Helen Sonthoff, in *Canadian Literature* (Vancouver), Summer 1961; "Phyllis Webb and the Priestess of Motion" in *Canadian Literature* (Vancouver), Spring 1967, and introduction to *Selected Poems 1954-1965*, 1971, both by John Hulcoop; introduction by Sharon Thesen to *The Vision Tree*, 1982.

*   *   *

Phyllis Webb is a poet of austere dedication whose relatively few finely crafted poems have slowly compelled the attention of readers.

Her first poems appeared at the beginning of the 1950's in Alan Crawley's historic little magazine, *Contemporary Verse*. Since then her publication has always been sparse; there has seemed a reluctance in all her decisions to release a poem into print or speech, and her works when they appear have been honed down to an extraordinary intellectual spareness. Her first volume—*Trio*—she shared with two poets remarkably unlike herself, Gael Turnbull and Eli Mandel. Her first individual volume, *Even Your Right Eye*, appeared in 1956, and while *The Sea Is Also a Garden* and the sparse *Naked Poems* were issued close together in the early 1960's, her *Selected Poems* of 1971 included nothing published after 1965, and it was followed by a long gap before her next collection. *Wilson's Bowl*, appeared in 1980, to be followed in 1982 by *Sunday Water: Thirteen Anti-Ghazals* and *The Vision Tree: Selected Poems*, which includes a few poems written since *Wilson's Bowl*. These most recent books have finally established Webb among Canada's leading poets. Northrop Frye described *Wilson's Bowl* as a "landmark in Canadian poetry," and *The Vision Tree* won her the establishment recognition of a Governor-General's Award. She continues to write in reclusion, to polish, and, very often, to discard. *The Vision Tree*, her nearest thing to a "collected poems," represents the work of more than 30 years in a mere 154 pages.

For Webb, growing maturity as a poet meant in fact for many years a growing withdrawal: a narrowing of the circle of the creative self in keeping with the somewhat solipsistic character of much of her verse. More than 20 years ago she said that "The public and the person are inevitably/one and the same self." But while this may have been true of the Webb who in her early twenties campaigned as a socialist parliamentary candidate, it was not true for many years of the poet who became concerned with personal emotions, the loneliness of living, the knife edge paths on which we painfully dance our way to death. Art she has seen as a "remedy"—no more; as "a patched, matched protection for Because."

The result was perhaps foreshadowed in an early poem, "Is Our Distress":

>   This our inheritance
>   is our distress
>   born of the weight of eons
>   it skeletons our flesh,
>   bearing us on
>   we wear it
>   though it bares us.

The philosophic pessimism—on unguarded moments breaking down into self-pity — which these lines suggest, has tended to control the development of thought in Webb's poems, the devolution away from the elaborate and the assured, which led her towards the simplified life view of anarchists like Kropotkin, the view that the less one demands of existence, the less one has to defend. One of "Some Final Questions," a section of *Naked Poems*, reads:

> *Now, you are sitting doubled up in pain.*
> *What's that for?*
>
> doubled up I feel
> small like these poems
> the area of attack
> is diminished

The *Naked Poems* are indeed reductive in terms of verse as well as life. They were preluded by a significant piece in *The Sea Is also a Garden*, "Poetics Against an Angel of Death", in which she says:

> Last night I thought I would not wake again
> but now with this June morning I run ragged to elude
> The Great Iambic Pentameter
> who is the Hound of Heaven in our stress
> because I want to die
> writing Haiku
> or, better,
> long lines, clean and syllabic as knotted bamboo. Yes!

And indeed her poems did at this point become quasi-Haikus, small, simple, as packed with meaning as stone artifacts, and punctuated by periods of stubborn silence. These "naked poems," austerely beautiful as weathered bones, are crucial to her career. She emerged in the later poems of *Wilson's Bowl* and in their successors into what is in fact a structure of "long lines, clean and syllabic as knotted bamboo." The poems of this last period are no longer minimalist. They expand not only formally into complex patterns of sound, but also in thought, in what Webb herself has called "the dance of the intellect in the syllables," and there is a return, on another apolitical level, to the humane considerations of her earliest phase, as she weaves the problems of self and other into pieces like her "Kropotkin Poems":

> *The Memoirs of a Revolutionist* before me, things fall
> together now. Pine needles, arbutus bark, the tide
> comes in, path to the beach lights with sun-fall.
> Highest joys? The simple profundity of a deadman works
> at my style. I am impoverished. He the White Christ.
> Not a case of identification. Easier to see myself
> in the white cat asleep on the bed. Exile. I live
> alone. I have a phone. I shall go to Russia. One
> more day run round and the 'good masterpiece of work'
> does not come. I scribble. I approach some distant dream.
> I wait for moonlight reflecting on the night sea. I can
> wait. We shall see.

Phyllis Webb, more than most other poets, has forced herself to know the limitations of her talent, and in this way has learnt its full powers.

—George Woodcock

WEDDE, Ian. New Zealander. Born in Blenheim, 17 October 1946. Educated at the University of Auckland, M.A. (honours)

1968. Married Rosemary Beauchamp in 1967; three sons. Formerly, forester, factory worker, gardener, and postman. British Council teacher, Jordan, 1969-70; poetry reviewer, *London Magazine*, 1970-71; broadcasting editor, New Zealand Broadcasting Corporation, 1972; Writer-in-Residence, Victoria University, Wellington, 1984. Currently, art critic, Wellington *Evening Post*. Recipient: Robert Burns Fellowship, University of Otago, 1972; Arts Council bursary, 1974, and travel award, 1983; New Zealand Book Award, for fiction, 1977, and for verse, 1978. Address: 118-A Maidavale Road, Roseneath, Wellington, New Zealand.

PUBLICATIONS

Verse

Homage to Matisse. London, Amphedesma Press, 1971.
Made Over. Auckland, Stephen Chan, 1974.
Earthly: Sonnets for Carlos. Akaroa, New Zealand, Amphedesma Press, 1975.
Pathway to the Sea. Christchurch, Hawk Press, 1975.
Don't Listen. Christchurch, Hawk Press, 1977.
Spells for Coming Out. Auckland, Auckland University Press, 1977.
Castaly and Other Poems. Auckland, Auckland University Press-Oxford University Press, 1980; Oxford, Oxford University Press, 1981.
Tales of Gotham City. Auckland, Auckland University Press-Oxford University Press, 1984.
Georgicon. Wellington, Victoria University Press, 1984.

Plays

Eyeball Eyeball (produced Packakariki, 1983).
Double or Quit: The Life and Times of Percy Topliss (produced on tour, England, 1984).

Radio Plays: *Stations*, music by Jack Body, 1969; *Pukeko*, music by John Rimmer, 1972.

Novel

Dick Seddon's Great Dive. Auckland, Islands, 1976.

Short Stories

The Shirt Factory and Other Stories. Wellington, Price Milburn, 1981.

Other

Translator, with Fawwas Tuqan, *Selected Poems*, by Mahmud Darwish. Cheadle, Cheshire, Carcanet, 1974.

*

Ian Wedde comments:
    Poems are ways out of solipsis, not necessarily the poet's. If the poems are any good, then he in writing & readers in reading are transported. Poems are not mirrors but creations, where "creations" is understood as a kind of present participle. I am myself sceptical about the "perfectibility" of people—I think they change to remain the same. For this reason, & because of what I've said above about poetry, & because poetry is not discrete but a function of people, I am not interested in poems as objects,

potentially perfectible, but as processes which involve us. Naturally, the ways in which they do this are not unimportant. But the notion that poems "order" the world interests me only insofar as they may be said to do this by bringing us, through the intercourse in which they involve us, to cognition of varieties of the world's DISorder. This disorder, after all, can be every bit as shapely as the most exquisite *poème bien fait*, so called. My own impulse in writing poems is to inquire rather than describe. At the same time I am attracted by the idea of a *forma formans*, a shape or the ghost of a shape which as Yves Bonnefoy has pointed out in his notes on translating Yeats, can determine the as yet uncertain "content" of which it becomes, reciprocally, an aspect. Mathematics can show us an exact principle of symmetry shared by one of the very oldest creatures, the nautilus, by a Greek temple, by innumerable supermarkets. With luck, poetry can offer us a similarly continuous and vital perspective.

*   *   *

Ian Wedde is one of a group of younger New Zealand poets who are graduates in English from the University of Auckland and who have been influenced by the American Modernist tradition as it flows from Pound, early Eliot, and William Carlos Williams through Charles Olson, Robert Duncan, and Robert Creeley. This is a major shift of emphasis in New Zealand poetry, and probably most readers would concede Wedde's place as the leading exponent. At the same time, unlike some of his contemporaries, Wedde does not seem trapped inside a narrow and restrictive mode. He experiments freely. Most often he lets the feeling determine the shape of the poem; but in an unusual departure he has written a sequence of "sonnets" in which there is no rhyme, there is a free flow of idea and image, the predominance of the speaking voice is maintained (all of this in common with Robert Lowell's sonnets), but all is contained within a tight syllabic count, 10 syllables to the line, yet no line permitted to fall into the old iambic beat.

Wedde has spent some time travelling outside New Zealand, and his experiences in Italy and the Middle East, particularly in Jordan, provided the occasion for a number of striking poems; in this connexion his translation (in collaboration with Fawwas Tuqan) of the poems of Mahmud Darwish should be mentioned.

Wedde is consistently at the centre of his own poetry, creating himself (it might be said) as he goes. He is sensitive, voluble, full of energy. There is always the sense that more is being registered than can be mastered, more felt than finds expression—and this is the right sort of imbalance for the production of poetry. His poems may sometimes seem over-charged, producing a hectic, even agitating effect; but this is preferable to a smooth parnassian surface, and inevitable in poems which aim to be highly active and to involve the reader in their activity. Wedde's poems are "open" not merely in finding their forms as they go, but in being deliberately less than complete statements. The reader is invited in—his imagination is engaged to do that part of the work which the poet leaves for him. This, I think, is what Wedde means when he writes (in an anthology of younger New Zealand poets): "The reduction of quests and discoveries to their essentials makes them more charismatic, more dependent upon the mysterious triggers which we all share to greater or lesser extent, which can propel us violently or as though in a dream into previously unknown or unimagined or misunderstood territories and times." The judgment involved in such a strategy has to be very exact.

Wedde's temperament is affirmative. He is expansive, rhapsodic, apostrophising, ecstatic, which means he is in more or less constant occupation of that area where a fine line divides the celebratory from the effusive and sentimental. In this, it should be said, he is with Keats—and with Keats on dangerous ground. High spirits anywhere can be as offensive to the mean in heart as to the genuinely oppressed, and New Zealand being on the whole a dour, repressive society, Wedde is likely to run into critical trouble. But if that affirmative energy is the quality that makes him vulnerable it is also his greatest strength—the source of the continual vitality and sense of freshness in his language, or (as Arnold said of Keats) that "indescribable *gusto* in the voice":

> & what's better to do than celebrate
> the fact? Look
>   the dark bloom's left your eyes
> spring's ripe   the horizon the blue sky
> the air pours towards you   the bean flower's sweet
> again   that fucking ferryman grates
> his rowlocks in mid channel again   high
> clouds are spinning like tops again & I
> couldn't ever have enough of all that
>
> & you again & again & again:
> waking, quickening, travelling through one
> world after another   through all the weird
> stations of the earthly paradise named
> for one impossible diamond-backed dream
> or another, as though no one else cared

Ian Wedde has added considerably to the range of New Zealand poetry. To imagine the scene without him is to imagine it seriously depleted.

—C.K. Stead

WEISS, Theodore (Russell). American. Born in Reading, Pennsylvania, 16 December 1916. Educated at Muhlenberg College, Allentown, Pennsylvania, B.A. 1938; Columbia University, New York, M.A. 1940. Married Renée Karol in 1941. Instructor in English, University of Maryland, College Park, 1941, University of North Carolina, Chapel Hill, 1942-44, and Yale University, New Haven, Connecticut, 1944-47; Assistant Professor, 1947-52, Associate Professor, 1952-55, and Professor of English, 1955-66, Bard College, Annandale-on-Hudson, New York; Lecturer, New School for Social Research, New York, 1955-56; Visiting Professor of Poetry, Massachusetts Institute of Technology, Cambridge, 1961-62; Lecturer, New York City Young Men's Hebrew Association, 1965-67. Poet-in-Residence, 1966-67, Professor of English and Creative Writing, 1968-77, and since 1977, Paton Professor, Princeton University, New Jersey. Hurst Professor, Washington University, St. Louis, 1977. Since 1943, Founding Editor, *Quarterly Review of Literature*. Member, Wesleyan University Press Poetry Board, 1963-68; General Editor, Princeton University Press Contemporary Poets series, 1975-78. Since 1964, Honorary Fellow, Ezra Stiles College, Yale University. Recipient: Ford Fellowship, 1953; Wallace Stevens Award, 1956; National Endowment for the Arts grant, 1967, 1969; Ingram Merrill Foundation grant, 1974; Brandeis University Creative Arts Award, 1977. D.Litt.: Muhlenberg College, 1968; Bard College, 1973. Address: 26 Haslet Avenue, Princeton, New Jersey 08540, U.S.A.

PUBLICATIONS

Verse

The Catch.   New York, Twayne, 1951.
Outlanders.   New York, Macmillan, 1960.
Gunsight: A Poem.   New York, New York University Press, 1962.
The Medium.   New York, Macmillan, 1965.
The Last Day and the First.   New York, Macmillan, 1968.
The World Before Us: Poems 1950-1970.   New York, Macmillan, 1970.
Fireweeds.   New York, Macmillan, 1976.
Views and Spectacles: Selected Poems.   London, Chatto and Windus, 1978.
The Aerialist.   Princeton, New Jersey, Pilgrim Press, 1978.
Views and Spectacles: New and Selected Shorter Poems.   New York, Macmillan, 1979.
Recoveries: A Poem.   New York, Macmillan, and London, Collier Macmillan, 1982.
A Slow Fuse: New Poems.   New York, Macmillan, 1984.

Recording: *Theodore Weiss Reads from His Own Work,* CMS, 1975.

Other

Gerard Manley Hopkins, Realist on Parnassus.   Privately printed, 1940.
The Breath of Clowns and Kings: A Study of Shakespeare.   New York, Atheneum, and London, Chatto and Windus, 1971.
The Man from Porlock: Engagements 1944-1981.   Princeton, New Jersey, Princeton University Press, 1982.
Toward a Classical Modernity and a Modern Classicism.   Portree, Isle of Skye, Aquila, 1982.

Editor, *Selections from the Note-books of Gerard Manley Hopkins.*   New York, New Directions, 1945.
Editor, with Renée Weiss, *Contemporary Poetry.*   Princeton, New Jersey, Princeton University Press, 1975.

*

Manuscript Collection: Princeton University Library, New Jersey.

Critical Studies: by Harry Berger, in *The Fat Abbot* (New Haven, Connecticut), Summer-Fall 1961; Richard Howard, in *Alone with America,* New York, Atheneum, 1969, London, Thames and Hudson, 1970, revised edition, Atheneum, 1980, and in *Perspective* (St. Louis), 1969; interview, with Colette Inez, in *First Person Singular* edited by Joyce Carol Oates, Princeton, New Jersey, Ontario Review Press, 1983.

*   *   *

Theodore Weiss is a formidable figure. For 40 years he has edited *The Quarterly Review of Literature.* His book *The Breath of Clowns and Kings* is probably the best study of Shakespeare's early work that we have. *The Man from Porlock,* a recent collection of essays, offers unexpected insights into such 20th-century writers as Wallace Stevens, Ezra Pound, Yvor Winters, and Philip Larkin. The approach here is not dissimilar in some respects to that of C.S. Lewis, a comparison that Weiss might

welcome. Biography, intentionality, personal recollection—these all perform functions which the New Critics of yesteryear would have fulfilled through verbal analysis.

However, Weiss's techniques succeed because the prose in which they are deployed is easy and unforced. One is always conscious of a personal voice. Indeed, Weiss's criticism is so well written that it seems to spill over into his poetry. One could, in fact, say that much of his poetry is itself a kind of criticism. It is unfailingly literary, preoccupied with art and artistic effect, and powered by a highly evident interest in language. Weiss brought out his first book at an age unusually mature for a poet. Perhaps because of this, it is an especially attactive venture. It opens with a poem, "The Hook," commemorating a young sculptress—"the woman who at last—/'I do not use live models'—sculptured fish...."

There is a lyrical energy in that poem which is characteristic of Weiss's work taken as a whole. Run-on lines and composite words are typical, almost a matter of mannerism. They testify that one of Weiss's poetic ancestors is Gerard Manley Hopkins. The use of short lines and stepped verse betoken William Carlos Williams to be another. Like this latter poet, Weiss aspires after the long poem. However, also like Williams, Weiss has more gift for energy of phrase than for construction. The result is that the mind is often dazzled by local rhetoric while failing to grasp the larger works as entities. This is especially true of the ambitious poem, *Gunsight,* which fills a volume of 55 pages. On the back cover of this volume there is an apt description of the poem within. "[*Gunsight*] is a narrative-dramatic psychological fantasy that records the sensations and memories of a wounded soldier as he undergoes surgery." This comment gives us a good idea of the subject-matter. But it also suggests dispersion—"narrative-dramatic psychological fantasy" seems to indicate a fairly mixed genre. At no point is a situation located with the degree of precision we find, for instance, in Robert Lowell's *Life Studies* or in Galway Kinnell's "The Avenue Bearing the Initial of Christ into the New World." Rather, there is a kind of lyric haze: detail that never quite coalesces into scene or setting—"You zigzag like a furled-out, wind-flopt moth./The breakers, toppled, hurl you onto roaring/rocks...." *Gunsight* is, like its progenitor, Williams's *Paterson,* best read as a series of interconnected lyrics rather than as a single poem with a unifying tendency and a plot.

Weiss scores especially when his scholarship intersects with what seems to be a natural disposition towards elegy and regret. "Two for Heinrich Bleucher" from his collection of 1965 recalls a friend and colleague—"one, apart, till now squinting through the fumes...." This poem is ratified in the most recent collection at the time of writing, *A Slow Fuse.* It is, perhaps, the most distinguished book of verse Weiss has issued since *The Catch.* Blücher, as the name is now spelt, is commemorated once more, along with Hannah Arendt, in possibly the most sustained verse its author has so far accomplished:

> At once I'm in a living
> room, its windows flung wide open
> to the sky, as if, someone unfolding
> a letter—
>   pressed inside its leaves
> a tiny, faded flower, mountain laurel,
> what is left of one particular morning—
> morning, atop this autumn afternoon,
> its blazoning forth;
>   gusts rousing
> out of trees and braided with day's ric-
> ochet from mountains hulked behind,
> a couple dally, once more fledglings

nestled like the larks that towered round
them, rue-and-laurel-interwoven wreath....

This is a symphony of recollection and evocation. The tribute is so splendid as to compel belief in the quality of the couple thus invoked. Here, the wide-ranging scholarship and empathy with the dead conjoin. The transitions have the inevitability we would expect of so practised an editor; the pattern of sound in the verse has a richness and variety that suggests, in no merely derivative sense, the major Romantics. This volume, together with *The Catch*, would have been enough to set Theodore Weiss in the forefront of contemporary poets. With the oeuvre of the intervening 30 years, including the opulent contribution of the criticism, Weiss is certain, when future scholars come to review our literature, to appear a key to the age.

—Philip Hobsbaum

WEISSBORT, Daniel. British. Born in London, 1 May 1935. Educated at St. Paul's School, London, 1948-52; Queens' College, Cambridge, 1953-56, B.A. (honours) 1956, M.A. Married Jill Anderson in 1961 (divorced, 1979), two daughters and one son. Director, Albion Knitwear, London, 1957-61. Advisory Director, Poetry International, London, 1970-73; Director, Carcanet Press, Oxford, later Cheadle, Cheshire, and Manchester, 1972-80. Since 1964, Co-Founding Editor, with Ted Hughes, *Modern Poetry in Translation*, London. Visiting Professor of Comparative Literature, 1974-75, since 1975, Director of Translation Workshop, and since 1980, Professor of English and Comparative Literature, University of Iowa, Iowa City. Member of the Poetry Society General Council, London, 1972-74. Since 1982, Member of the Executive Board, American Literary Translators Association. Recipient: Arts Council bursary, for translation, 1971, 1972; University of Iowa Writing Fellowship, 1973; Glatstein Memorial Prize (*Poetry*, Chicago), 1978; National Endowment for the Arts Translation Fellowship, 1981. Agent: John Johnson, 45-47 Clerkenwell Green, London EC1R 0HT, England. Address: Department of English, University of Iowa, Iowa City, Iowa 52242, U.S.A.

PUBLICATIONS

Verse

The Leaseholder. Oxford, Carcanet, 1971.
In an Emergency. Oxford, Carcanet, 1972.
Soundings. Manchester, Carcanet, 1977.

Other

Editor and Translator, *Natalya Gorbanevskaya: Poems, Trial, Prison.* Oxford, Carcanet, 1972.
Editor and Translator, *Post-War Russian Poetry.* London, Penguin, 1974.
Editor and Translator, with John Glad, *Russian Poetry: The Modern Period.* Iowa City, University of Iowa Press, 1978.

Translator, *The Soviet People and Their Society*, by Pierre Sorlin. London, Pall Mall Press, and New York, Praeger, 1968.

Translator, *Guerillas in Latin America: The Technique of the Counter-State*, by Luis Mercier Vega. London, Pall Mall Press, and New York, Praeger, 1969.
Translator, *Scrolls: Selected Poems of Nikolai Zabolotsky.* London, Cape, 1971.
Translator, *A History of the People's Democracies: Eastern Europe since Stalin*, by François Fetjö. London, Pall Mall Press, 1971.
Translator, *The Rare and Extraordinary History of Holy Russia*, by Gustave Doré. London, Alcove Press, 1972.
Translator, *Nose! Nose? No-se! and Other Plays*, by Andrei Amalriki. New York, Harcourt Brace, 1973.
Translator, with Anthony Rudolf, *The War Is Over: Selected Poems*, by Evgeny Vinokurov. Cheadle, Cheshire, Carcanet, 1976.
Translator, *From the Night and Other Poems*, by Lev Mak. Ann Arbor, Michigan, Ardis, 1978.
Translator, *Ivan the Terrible and Ivan the Fool*, by Yevgeny Yevtushenko. London, Gollancz, 1979.
Translator, *Missing Person*, by Patrick Modiano. London, Cape, 1980.
Translator, *The World about Us*, by Claude Simon. Princeton, New Jersey, Ontario Review Press, 1983.

*   *   *

Daniel Weissbort's is the poetry of unease, depicting as it does the struggles of one whose attempts at an orderly routine are continually threatened by the chaos of life. A prolific editor and translator of Russian literature, he himself often resembles a character out of Goncharov or Dostoevsky, with his gloomy drinking bouts, low self-esteem, and the forebodings that dog his brief moments of happiness. Guilt and loss are themes that recur constantly in his work, love itself seen as fragile and elusive, not entirely to be trusted. Even in the ecstasies of physical passion, Weissbort is still painfully aware that he remains separate and apart: "With each caress I lose you more/ —pleasure's no guarantee at all—." Writing serves him as an escape, an unreal ordering of experience in which—unlike life—he feels at home. Initiated into love and its pain, Weissbort looks back ruefully to his unattached innocence, and finds himself writing comfortably in the beloved's absence. Safety of this kind, though, cannot endure. Relationships, responsibilities break in upon him, disrupting his illusory calm, and the poems he describes as "fantasies of growing up."

As presented in his poetry, Weissbort strikes one as being somehow less than complete, a perennial child seeking to be indulged and reassured. Helplessly he scans the unmistakable signs of age, reminders of his impotence and failure. Instinct draws him backward to the past in his quest for salvation. He recalls a moment's closeness with his child, searches vainly for security in memories of his father's respectable business—once so hated, now seized on with desperate hope. His thoughts turn to friends now dead, unable to join him in a night of drunken well-being. Again and again, he is forced to admit his powerlessness in the face of life, and passions over which he has no control: "Love is not healing me/ And I'm not doing much for myself either."

Still, he handles his unease with a certain amount of detachment, viewing the catalogue of failures from a distance. Though there are hints of self-pity in his writing, he never sinks to mawkishness. Flickers of gallows humour light the sad procession of his life as portrayed in his writings, as the above quotation indicates. This, too, is in keeping with his interest in the Russian literature he translates, where often the most doomladen philosophy is pierced by the driest of jokes. Bitter smiles rather than belly-laughs are Weissbort's stock in trade, when they appear at all, but the reader is wary of accepting the poet's low estimate of himself completely. After all, he writes about it so well that one suspects a greater degree of self-knowledge than he would have us believe. The final image, though, has to be that of the ordered man caught in the stream of day-to-day living, fighting vainly to get out. Life and love are dangerous, Weissbort is saying, and like most of us he's not too sure how they ought to be handled. In "Return," confronted by wife and children after a long absence, he finds himself as incapable of giving reassurance as he is of being reassured: "The children are growing up,/but they still look to me./They look for routes to me,/between each other,/to me. Their eyes search and plan./Ineffectually I float my arms about them,/touching here a shoulder, there a head."

—Geoff Sadler

WELCH, James.   American.   Born in Browning, Montana, in 1940. Educated at the University of Montana, Missoula, B.A.; Northern Montana College, Harve. Recipient: National Endowment for the Arts grant, 1969. Address: Roseacres Farm, Route 6, Missoula, Montana 59801, U.S.A.

PUBLICATIONS

Verse

Riding the Earthboy 40.   Cleveland, World, 1971; revised edition, New York, Harper, 1975.

Novels

Winter in the Blood.   New York, Harper, 1974; London, Bantam, 1975.
The Death of Jim Loney.   New York, Harper, 1979; London, Gollancz, 1980.

*

Critical Studies: *Four American Indian Literary Masters* by Alan R. Velie, Norman, University of Oklahoma Press, 1982; *James Welch* by Peter Wild, Boise, Idaho, Boise State University, 1983.

*   *   *

James Welch is a young poet whose Native American background helps shape his first volume of poetry, *Riding the Earthboy 40*, a book which is one of the strongest first volumes of poetry published in the United States in recent years. As is the case with such other fine young American Indian writers as Simon Ortiz, Leslie Silko, Duane Niatum, and Ray Youngbear, Welch brings to his writing a deep consciousness of the earth which makes his poems exciting and alive, full of depth and mystery. This consciousness, mingled with a sense of loss, makes for some of the most powerful moments in his poems, as in the last lines of "Thanksgiving at Snake Butte":

On top, our horses broke, loped through

a small stand of stunted pine, then jolted
to a nervous walk. Before us lay
the smooth stones of our ancestors, the fish,
the lizard, snake and bent-kneed

bowman—etched by something crude,
by a wandering race, driven by their names
for time: its winds, its rain, its snow
and the cold moon tugging at the crude figures
in this, the season of their loss.

Welch's poems frequently revolve around contemporary Indian experience, but without the sentimental overlay which too many bad non-Indian poets have brought to their writings about Native Americans. The images in Welch's poems are like the Northwest winds of a Montana winter, hard, crystal-cold and powerful as in "Christmas Comes to Moccasin Flat": "Christmas comes like this: Wise men/unhurried, candles bought on credit (poor price/for calves), warriors face down in wine sleep./Winds cheat to pull heat from smoke...," or in "Going to Remake This World":

From my window, I see bundled Doris Horseman,
black in the blowing snow, her raving son,
Horace, too busy counting flakes to hide his face.
He doesn't know. He kicks my dog
and glares at me, too dumb to thank the men
who keep him on relief and his mama drunk...

His poem "The Man from Washington" is already a minor classic with its picture of a Bureau of Indian Affairs bureaucrat—"a slouching dwarf with rainwater eyes..." who promises

that life would go on as usual,
that treaties would be signed, and everyone—
man, woman and child—would be innoculated
against a world in which we had no part,
a world of money, promise and disease.

With irony and honesty, James Welch has approached being an Indian and being a poet in contemporary America and come out of it with poems which are always memorable and, in some cases, close to great. It seems certain that he will continue to be a vital force in American writing, not just as an Indian or a poet, but as both.

—Joseph Bruchac

WELLS, Robert.   British.   Born in Oxford in 1947. Address: c/o Carcanet Press, 208 Corn Exchange Buildings, Manchester M4 3BQ, England.

PUBLICATIONS

Verse

Shade Mariners, with Dick Davis and Clive Wilmer.   Cambridge, Gregory Spiro, 1970.
The Winter's Task.   Manchester, Carcanet, 1977.

Other

Translator, *The Georgics*, by Virgil. Manchester, Carcanet, 1982.

*   *   *

First published in company with Dick Davis and Clive Wilmer in *Shade Mariners* (a booklet with an unintentionally leaden introduction by Tony Tanner), Robert Wells could never be called an over-prolific poet. A selection of his work has been included in two anthologies edited by Michael Schmidt—*Ten English Poets* (1976) and *Some Contemporary Poets of Britain and Ireland* (1983)—and we have one book of poems: *The Winter's Task*. Nor is Wells set on dazzling the reader with any youthful display of a showy brilliance quite within his technical range.

Instead we find in his too few poems a quiet yet confident ability to render a variety of feeling in words with precision and clarity. Wells is a poet who feels no need to adopt a persona in order to make poems. He is a man whose attention is focused on a landscape or place outside himself who renders the place as itself while simultaneously remaining aware of his own sensations in relation to it. As in "At the Back of His Mind":

> He had forgotten the solitude, the touch
> Of air on skin, water in the thirsty mouth.
> This was the memory that remained with him,
> Grass, earth, branches and flame melting together,
> Of the steep hillside where he had laboured once.

Perhaps similarly the early "The Wind Blows" succinctly expresses the small particulars of a sunny landscape through a subtle and delicate rhythm:

> The wind blows. Winds blow the
> Hill green and grey. Olives
> Are alive with light. Fat grow the
> Grapes green-misted with a mist that lives.

Wells is the contemplative artist. If this appears to set him apart from many of the more active inventors of a contemporary idiom, it also allows him a nonetheless distinctly recognisable style of his own; unforced and natural in tone. As in "Shape of Air":

> It has lighted on you, this shape of air.
> I don't want you to know that it is there:
> Not yours or mine, as by the gate you stand
> That divides the mountain from the worked land

His modest stylishness always remains true to a feeling for words and rhythms. His poems are often laconic; at times almost lapidary in their brevity. One such, "Not Like the Fields" quoted here in full, adopts an understatement which expresses an unruly emotion and two types of nature indirectly:

> His nature was mild like the fields.
> It was the soft turf under his tread,
> The alteration of weather.
>
> But desire was in his nature too
> And that was not like the fields.

If these poems have antecedents then Edward Thomas has to be named. In fact Wells is one of a line of English poets who never strain for effects, rhetorical or otherwise, and without whom we would be without some of our most authentic talents of the last forty years: Norman Cameron, James Reeves, Philip Larkin among them.

The rigour of epigram mixed with a meditative sensibility make Wells's poems all his own. He is a poet who takes us into his confidence and who is not afraid to appear at first sight vulnerable, at second curiously impersonal at times. As in his recent uncollected poem "For Pasolini" which is about the passing of time and the endurance, or otherwise, of human effort:

> Vecchio ragazzo di Casarsa, dear protagonist,
> Where shall we find the like of your intelligence?
> The hunters who come here on Sunday with their dogs and guns
> Are not enough to keep the forest paths open.
> Two years untrodden, and bramble will cover the track,
> The broom lean across.

In 1982 appeared Wells's translation of *The Georgics* of Virgil. In his introduction Wells supplies us, quite unintentionally, with an insight into his own passionate delight in both Virgil and what poetry can do in the world:

> Virgil's clarity is not a clarity of surface—it has not that
> sharpness of edge and line that Ezra Pound has taught us
> to look for. To read Virgil is like looking down through
> very clear water; one is barely conscious of the surface,
> but the objects on the riverbed are made to shine. Bathed
> in his sensibility the world has a subdued brightness, like
> pebbles under water, all their colours enlivened. I have
> tried to render something of this.

We should not overlook Wells's work in the crowded world of contemporary poetry if we set any store by Thomas Hardy's phrase defining poetry as "closeness of phrase to vision," which is precisely what Wells aims for, and at times achieves.

—Jonathan Barker

WEVILL, David (Anthony). Canadian. Born in Yokohama, Japan, 15 March 1935. Educated at Trinity College School, Port Hope, Ontario; Fisher Park High School, Ottawa; Caius College, Cambridge, B.A. 1957. Married Assia Gutman in 1960. Lecturer in English, University of Mandalay, Burma, 1958-60; Fellow, National Translation Center, Austin, Texas, after 1968. Currently, Member of the Department of English, University of Texas, Austin. Recipient: Eric Gregory award, 1963; Richard Hillary Memorial Prize, 1965; Arts Council Triennial Prize, 1965, and bursary, 1965, 1966 (Great Britain). Address: c/o Curbstone Publishing, P.O. Box 7445, University of Texas Station, Austin, Texas 78712, U.S.A.

PUBLICATIONS

Verse

Penguin Modern Poets 4, with David Holbrook and Christopher Middleton. London, Penguin, 1963.
Birth of a Shark. London, Macmillan, and New York, St. Martin's Press, 1964.

A Christ of the Ice-Floes. London, Macmillan, and New York, St. Martin's Press, 1966.
Firebreak. London, Macmillan, 1971.
Where the Arrow Falls. London, Macmillan, 1973; New York, St. Martin's Press, 1974.

Other

Casual Ties. Austin, Texas, Curbstone, 1983.

Translator, *Selected Poems of Terence Juhasz*. London, Penguin, 1969.

*

Critical Study: "David Wevill's *A Christ of the Ice-Floes*: Vision of the Elemental World" by Anthony Saroop, in *Pluck 1* (Edmonton, Alberta), 1967.

David Wevill comments:

I have tried to create complete poems, not just passing observations. So far I think I have succeeded only in a few poems. I do not know what direction a poem will take until it is finished: the theme therefore is unconscious. I have been much taken with Spanish poetry: Lorca, Neruda, Machado, Paz. They have a terseness which I admire and am only just, perhaps, starting to achieve. I do not use any particular verse form: the poem takes its own form. I can't point to any particular influences; these have been many—as much, say, from prose and painting as from other poetry. Landscape is in my poetry not as "nature" but in the North American or Spanish sense, as something "out there."

*   *   *

David Wevill's poetry is one of intense personal responses intellectualized to a high degree and of essentially religious stances conveyed in the language of organic and frequently violent imagery. A Canadian poet in his origins—and in the occasional reference—he is almost characteristically un-Canadian in his tone in that sense of fatalistic ennui which distinguishes certain of his works. If there are discernible affinities in his poems then these lie with contemporary British poetry and it is as a British poet that one tends to see him.

The common denominators of *Birth of a Shark* are visceral and metamorphic, with a great deal of concentration on a concern which can be best described as that of "life process." Wevill is most impressive in his ability to bring a sophisticated method to the pulpy and primal matter which heaves convincingly and metabolically in his poems:

The sun seeps into and through your bones.
Flushing the clotted soil,
Tapping bacteria, mites, and the locked
Purses of beetles. And you, fiery and whole

Are pure waste matter, aged to a diamond's strength;
Your will and body, stone and root....

A Christ of the Ice-Floes shows an extension of earlier interests and a firming of the intellectual posture which makes for the clipped and acerbic quality of Wevill's statement. A religious dimension associates itself with some of the poems as the poet engages in an elaborate and, at times, vicarious ritual of self-discovery which ranges through the metaphor of substitute lives; the experience of travel and geography; and an understanding fundamental to Wevill that life is cyclical and our knowledge of it regenerative: "I hold my ancestry in my hand.../ The death of my limbs/ Must mean the nucleus is still alive./ The afterlife at its roots searching for you...."

Technically, there is little departure from tried and true norms in Wevill's poems and his style is marked by a conventional sureness and an all-too-respectable limitation of experiment; yet he manages a discreet vividness and an authority and conviction in his statement which more than repay the reader.

—Michael Gnarowski

WHALEN, Philip (Glenn). American. Born in Portland, Oregon, 20 October 1923. Educated at Reed College, Portland, B.A. in literature and languages 1951. Served in the United States Army Air Force, 1943-46. Lecturer and teacher: ordained as Zen Buddhist priest, 1973; Shuso (Acting Head Monk), Zen Mountain Center, 1975. Lecturer, San Francisco Zen Center and Zen Mountain Center, Tassajara Springs, California. Recipient: Poets Foundation award, 1962; Ratcliff award, 1964; American Academy grant, 1965; Commission on Poetry grant, 1968, 1970, 1971. Address: c/o Four Seasons Foundation, P.O. Box 31190, San Francisco, California 94131, U.S.A.

PUBLICATIONS

Verse

Three Satires. Privately printed, 1951.
Self-Portrait, from Another Direction. San Francisco, Auerhahn Press, 1959.
Like I Say. New York, Totem-Corinth, 1960.
Memoirs of an Interglacial Age. San Francisco, Auerhahn Press, 1960.
Hymnus ad Patrem Sinensis. San Francisco, Four Seasons, 1963.
Monday in the Evening: 21 VIII 61. Milan, East 128, 1963.
Three Mornings. San Francisco, Four Seasons, 1964.
Goddess. Privately printed, 1964.
Every Day. Eugene, Oregon, Coyote, 1965.
Dear Mr. President. Privately printed, 1965.
Highgrade: Doodles, Poems. Eugene, Oregon, Coyote, 1966.
The Education Continues Along. Eugene, Oregon, Toad Press, 1967.
T/O. San Francisco, Dave Haselwood, 1967.
On Bear's Head: Selected Poems. New York, Harcourt Brace, 1969.
Severance Pay: Poems 1967-1969. San Francisco, Four Seasons, 1970.
Scenes of Life at the Capital. Bolinas, California, Grey Fox Press, 1971.
The Kindness of Strangers: Poems 1969-1974. Bolinas, California, Four Seasons, 1975.
Decompressions: Selected Poems. Bolinas, California, Grey Fox Press, 1977.
Enough Said: Fluctuat nec Mergitur: Poems 1974-1979. San Francisco, Grey Fox Press, 1980.
Heavy Breathing. San Francisco, Four Seasons, 1983.

Novels

You Didn't Even Try. San Francisco, Coyote, 1967.
Imaginary Speeches for a Brazen Head. Los Angeles, Black Sparrow Press, 1972.

Other

The Invention of the Letter: A Beastly Morality (for children). New York, Carp and Whitefish Press, 1967.
Prolegomena to a Study of the Universe. Berkeley, California, Poltroon Press, 1976.
On Bread and Poetry: A Panel Discussion, with Lew Welch and Gary Snyder. Bolinas, California, Grey Fox Press, 1977.
Off the Wall: Interviews with Philip Whalen, edited by Donald Allen. Bolinas, California, Four Seasons, 1978.
The Diamond Noodle. Berkeley, California, Poltroon Press, 1979.

*

Critical Study: "Whalen Issue" of *Intransit* (Eugene, Oregon), 1967.

Philip Whalen comments:

I try to write in colloquial American speech, but I often fail because many of the subjects I'm interested in—Buddhism, Chinese and Japanese literature and painting and architecture, formal symphonic music, the history of science, historiography, archaeology—aren't much discussed by my fellow Americans. I try to do the best I can. I began studying English poetry at an early age and I continue to work at it.

*   *   *

Many contemporary American poets, including Allen Ginsberg, W.S. Merwin, Gary Snyder, and Lucien Stryk, have been deeply affected by Zen, but none so much as Philip Whalen, who lives in a Zen commune in California. Whalen turned to Zen rather late in life, but when he did he committed himself completely. Now, with shaved head and saffron robes, Whalen is a unique figure on the poetic scene.

But Whalen has always been different from everyone else, and has felt proud of it. In an early poem, "Further Notice," he proclaims "I shall be myself—/ Free, a genius, an embarrassment/ Like the Indian, the buffalo/ Like Yellowstone National Park." In his early writings, however, Whalen's sense of his singularity often led to feelings of alienation and even, in his frequent references to his "own gross shape," to self-loathing. It also led to producing some exceedingly shrill political verse.

Whalen's Zen awakening changed his approach. Though still believing, as he states in his fine "Birthday Poem," "The world is wicked by definition; my job is to stay aware of it," Whalen now uses methods of expression and poetic subjects which are more subtle. In his preface to *Decompressions* Whalen remarks, "I have a hunch that if I write a really good poem today about the weather, about a flower or any apparently 'irrelevant'...subject, that the revolution will be hastened considerably more than if I composed a pamphlet attacking the government and the capitalist system." Thus, instead of overt political statements, his later work offers insights gained by and expressed in the traditional Zen manner, as in his arresting poem " 'Never Apologize, Never Explain' ":

A pair of strange new birds in the maple tree
Peer through the windows,
Mother and father visiting me:
    "You are unmarried,
    No child begot
    Now we are birds, now you've
        forgotten us
    Although in dreams we visit you
        in human shape"

They speak Homer's language
Sing like Aeschylus

The life a poet: less than 2/3rds of a second

In "Science and Language" Whalen writes, "It is impossible to write in English about Japanese/ Persons, places and things," but his own work, in poems like "Eamd," belies this. Nevertheless, his subject matter is most frequently American, and usually centered on "the ruined city/ San Francisco." What is perhaps most remarkable about his work is the contrast made between its Zen sensibility and its contemporary American setting, a society in which, as "In the Night" says, we "fall upward/ Into a fake superiority."

Zen offers Whalen a genuine superiority. It is a discipline that requires much of a man and of a writer, and it is one which makes one constantly aware of one's own shortcomings. Nevertheless, in Zen, as in the poetic imagination, there always exists the potential for human perfection. This is all captured succinctly in "For Kai Snyder":

7:V:60 (an interesting *lapsus calami*)
A few minutes ago I tried a somersault; couldn't do it
I was afraid and I couldn't remember how.
I fell over on one shoulder,
Rolled about and nearly went over backwards
And finally hurt my chest.
What kind of psychomotor *malebolge* had I got into...
"This is old age, &c."

After thinking it all over
Imagining how it might be done
I performed three forward somersaults, 7:V:70
Aged 46 years 6 months and 37 days.

—Dennis Lynch

WHIGHAM, Peter (George). British. Born in Oxford, 6 March 1925. Married Jean Scratton in 1950. Formerly, gardener, schoolmaster, and repertory actor. Since 1966, free-lance university lecturer in verse translation, currently in the Department of Comparative Literature, University of California, Berkeley. Address: c/o Anvil Press Poetry, 69 King George Street, London SE10 8PX, England.

PUBLICATIONS

Verse

Clear Lake Comes from Enjoyment, with Denis Goacher. London, Spearman, 1959.

The Marriage Rite, with Denis Goacher. Ditchling, Sussex, Ditchling Press, 1960.
The Ingathering of Love. Santa Barbara, California, Work in Progress, 1967.
The Blue Winged Bee: Love Poems of the VIth Dalai Lama; The Ingathering of Love. London, Anvil Press Poetry, 1969.
Astapovo; or, What We Are to Do. London, Anvil Press Poetry, 1970.
The Crystal Mountain. Berkeley, California, Sand Dollar, 1971.
Langue d'Oeil. Los Angeles, Press of the Pegacycle Lady, 1971.
Things Common, Properly: Selected Poems 1942-1982. London, Anvil Press Poetry, and Redding Ridge, Connecticut, Black Swan, 1984.

Other

Editor, with Denis Goacher, *Women of Trachis*, by Ezra Pound. London, Spearman, 1956.
Editor, *The Music of the Troubadours*. Santa Barbara, California, Ross Erikson, 1979.

Translator, with Mary de Rachewiltz, *The Detail and the Design*, by Umberto Mastroianni. Bologna, Segnacolo, 1963.
Translator, *Black Eros*, by Boris de Rachewiltz. London, Allen and Unwin, and New York, Lyle Stuart, 1964.
Translator, *Introduction to African Art*, by Boris de Rachewiltz. New York, New American Library, 1965; London, John Murray, 1966.
Translator, *The Poems of Catullus*. London, Penguin, 1966; revised edition, Penguin, and Berkeley, University of California Press, 1969.
Translator, with Peter Jay, *The Poems of Meleager*. London, Anvil Press Poetry, 1975; Berkeley, University of California Press, 1976.
Translator, *Letter to Juvenal: 101 Epigrams from Martial*. London, Anvil Press Poetry, 1985.

*   *   *

Peter Whigham's poetry deserves to be better known. He is one of the few English poets of his generation to be firmly rooted in the modernist tradition and has produced a considerable amount of interesting and varied writing as well as a number of important translations. A few of his early poems are more likely to survive than any produced by poets associated with "The Movement" or "The Group." "The Orchard Is Not Cut Down" is short enough to quote in full:

> The orchard is gone. A space, con-
>   ventionally like Passchendaele,
>   linearly framed by black rail-
> ings, rises to a wide field on
> which, inert, the milk-brown cows sun
>   themselves and where the bush mail-
> van and the bus brightly curtail,
> on the road sudden as a gun
> the field,—the vanished grove.
>
>   No dream
>   of priest or king can empower mind
>   to seize the blossom on the wind;
> only, in passing, I have seen

> swan leaning on confused swan
> fall inwards like a folding fan.

Whigham is probably best known as the author of the Penguin Catullus, and to have produced the liveliest English version of this poet is no mean achievement. Cyril Connolly defined its quality when he wrote: "I feel that he has really lived these poems; he brings back his translations as something that actually happened to him, like Noah's dove with the olive, and this enables him to bring the longer poems to life, in some cases for the first time."

The Blue Winged Bee is Whigham's finest collection of original poetry—most impressive is a long poem, *The Ingathering of Love*. This is difficult to quote from adequately as it creates its effect by the slow accumulation of images. Here are a few lines to give a glimpse of its quality:

> All day the willow weeps by the summerhouse.
> Bits of grass, the detritus of summer, lie on the floor;
> the birds are muted
>   appeased by nest-building & egg laying:
> a plane fades like mild thunder and
> the sun, an atmosphere, pervades the grey sky.

Astapovo is, I think, less successful. He seems here to have lost his own voice in a harsh stridency foreign to his earlier writing. This perhaps presents an example of the bad influence certain kinds of American poetry can exert on an English poet.

—William Cookson

———————

WHISTLER, (Alan Charles) Laurence. British. Born in Eltham, Kent, 21 January 1912; younger brother of the artist Rex Whistler. Educated at Stowe School; Balliol College, Oxford (Chancellor's Essay Prize, 1934), B.A. 1934. Served in the Rifle Brigade, 1939-45: Captain, 1942. Married 1) Jill Furse in 1939 (died, 1944), one son and one daughter; 2) Theresa Furse in 1950, one son and one daughter. Glass engraver: goblets in point engraving, and church windows and panels at Sherborne Abbey; Moreton, Dorset; Checkendon, Oxfordshire; Ilton, Somerset; Eastbury, Berkshire; Guards Chapel, London; Ashmansworth, Berkshire; Steep, Hampshire; Stowe, Buckinghamshire; St. Hugh's College, Oxford; Hannington, Hampshire; Yalding, Kent; Thornham Parva, Suffolk; Salisbury Cathedral; exhibitions—Agnews, London, 1969; Marble Hill, Twickenham, 1972; Corning Museum, New York, 1974; Ashmolean Museum, Oxford, 1976. First President, Guild of Glass Engravers, 1975-80. Recipient: King's Gold Medal for Poetry, 1935; Rockefeller-Atlantic Award, 1945. Honorary Fellow, Balliol College, Oxford, 1974. O.B.E. (Officer, Order of the British Empire), 1955; C.B.E. (Commander, Order of the British Empire), 1973. Fellow, Royal Society of Literature, 1960. Address: The Old Manor, Alton Barnes, Marlborough, Wiltshire SN8 4LB, England.

PUBLICATIONS

Verse

Children of Hertha and Other Poems. Oxford, Holywell Press, 1929.

Proletaria, en avant! A Poem of Socialism. Oxford, Alden Press, 1932.
Armed October and Other Poems. London, Cobden Sanderson, 1932.
Four Walls. London, Heinemann, 1934; New York, Macmillan, 1935.
The Emperor Heart. London, Heinemann, 1936; New York, Macmillan, 1937.
In Time of Suspense. London, Heinemann, 1940.
The Burning-Glass. Privately printed, 1941.
Ode to the Sun and Other Poems. London, Heinemann, 1942.
Who Live in Unity. London, Heinemann, 1944.
¡OHO! Certain Two-Faced Individuals Now Exposed by the Bodley Head, with Rex Whistler. London, Lane, 1946.
The World's Room: The Collected Poems of Laurence Whistler. London, Heinemann, 1949.
The View from This Window. London, Hart Davis, 1956.
Audible Silence. London, Hart Davis, 1961.
Fingal's Cave: A Poem. Birmingham, F.E. Pardoe, 1963.
To Celebrate Her Living. London, Hart Davis, 1967.
On Llangynidr Bridge. Cambridge, Golden Head Press, 1968.
For Example: Ten Sonnets in Sequence to a New Pattern. Birmingham, F.E. Pardoe, 1969.
Way: Two Affirmations, in Glass and Verse. Cambridge, Golden Head Press, 1969.
A Bridge on the Usk. Birmingham, Pardoe, 1976.
AHA: Verses to Reversible Faces by Rex Whistler. London, Murray, 1978; Boston, Houghton Mifflin, 1979.

Other

Sir John Vanbrugh, Architect and Dramatist 1664-1726. London, Cobden Sanderson, 1938; New York, Macmillan, 1939.
Jill Furse: Her Nature and Her Poems 1915-1944. London, Chiswick Press, 1945.
The Masque of Christmas, with *Christmas His Masque,* by Ben Jonson. London, Curtain Press, 1947.
The English Festivals. London, Heinemann, 1947.
Rex Whistler 1905-1944: His Life and His Drawings. London, Art and Technics, 1948; New York, Pellegrini and Cudahy, 1949.
The Engraved Glass of Laurence Whistler. Hitchin, Hertfordshire, Cupid Press, 1952.
Rex Whistler: The Königsmark Drawings. London, Richards Press, 1952.
The Kissing Bough: A Christmas Custom Described. London, Heinemann, 1953.
The Imagination of Vanbrugh and His Fellow Artists. London, Art and Technics-Batsford, 1954.
Stowe: A Guide to the Gardens. London, Country Life, 1956; revised edition, with Michael Gibbon and George Clarke, Buckingham, Hillier, 1968.
Engraved Glass 1952-1958. London, Hart Davis, 1959.
The Work of Rex Whistler, with Ronald Fuller. London, Batsford, 1960.
The Initials in the Heart (autobiography). London, Hart Davis, and Boston, Houghton Mifflin, 1964.
Pictures on Glass. Ipswich, Cupid Press, 1972.
The Image on the Glass. London, Murray, 1975.
Scenes and Signs on Glass. Ipswich, Cupid Press, 1985.

Editor, *Selected Poems of John Keats.* London, Grey Walls Press, 1950.

*   *   *

Laurence Whistler has gained a double reputation, as a poet and as an engraver on glass, whose work in both media is characterised by technical skill, elegance, and lyrical sensibility. His notes on "Fore-Rhyme" and on "A Woven Sonnet" reveal his preoccupation with poetic form and with the possibilities of extending traditional formal patterns in the interests of greater exactness and imaginative power.

Most of his early work, for all its easy grace, is little more than accomplished verse-writing. The death of his beloved first wife, Jill Furse, gave him a powerful poetic theme which preoccupied him over a long period. Indeed, many of his poems, continually revised, may be regarded as parts of one long elegiac poem, which appears to have assumed its final shape in *To Celebrate Her Living,* a volume related to his prose work, *The Initials in the Heart.* The tone is varied, ranging from lyrical tenderness to sombre reflection, and the movement of the verse sometimes recalls the subtle yet direct mode of utterance perfected by the English Metaphysical poets:

> She whom I loved—she whom I love
> Years deep in abject death—who was,
> Who will be that to which I move
> In this or any world...

Apart from this sequence, Laurence Whistler's work includes a number of poems which are likely to survive when the verse of flashier and inferior talents is forgotten. The range and quality of his art are reflected in such poems as "The Guest," "A Form of Epitaph," and "A Portrait in the Guards," an elegy on his brother Rex.

—John Press

WHITE, Ivan. British. Born in Seven Kings, Essex, 23 May 1929. Divorced; two children. Educated at the University of York; University of Manchester. Tutor-Organiser, Workmen's Educational Association, in Lancashire and Cumbria. Recipient: Guinness Prize, 1964. Address: Park Cottage, Tanpits Lane, Burton, Camforth, Lancashire, England.

PUBLICATIONS

Verse

Cry Wolf: A Poem of Urgency. London, Hephaestus Circle, 1962.
Crow's Fall. London, Cape Goliard Press, and New York, Grossman, 1969.
Removal of an Exhibition. London, Writers and Readers, 1976.

*   *   *

Ivan White is an intellectual—one may even say metaphysical—poet, of sensitivity, seriousness, modesty, sensibility and feeling. His poetry is only occasionally banal ("...I thought of Keats and Dylan Thomas,/How suspect their respective loves became in death./The one for a woman unmoved,/the other for humanity") and it is significant that when he is, he is also, usually, inaccurate (Fanny Brawne was not "unmoved"); but this comes from an uncharacteristically long, prosaic and rank bad "conversation" poem called "The Suspect Love." His best piece is the title piece from *Crow's Fall*, about a bird striking the stained-glass window of a buttress and killing itself:

> Falling into like black it scraped
> Mortar from arms that were flesh stripped.
>
> As earth broke over its slight head
> The beak point rasped against fluted
>
> Rock poised towards the impetus
> Of its feathered dive....
>
> They replaced the glass....
> ...an act of half truth,
>
> Deep from which stress drove the dark bird
> Like a maxim that somehow strayed
>
> From its claw holes or grip on life
> That slipped, leaving no trace nor grief.

This may have been influenced or prompted by reading Ted Hughes; but it contains more thought, less hideously gratuitious violence, than anything by Hughes. Unfortunately White has written few other poems as effective: his chief fault seems to be an inability to discover a personal rhythm: too many of his poems are spoiled because they read like prose chopped arbitrarily into lines.

—Martin Seymour-Smith

WHITE, Kenneth. British. Born in Glasgow, Lanarkshire, 28 April 1936. Educated at the University of Glasgow, M.A. (honours) in French and German 1959; University of Munich; University of Paris. Married to Marie-Claude Charlut. Lecturer in English, the Sorbonne, Paris, 1962-63, and Faculty of Letters, Pau, France, 1967-68; Lecturer in French, University of Glasgow, 1963-67. Lecturer in English, Institut Charles V, 1969-83, and since 1983, Professor of 20th-Century Poetics, the Sorbonne, University of Paris. Founder, *Jargon Papers*, Glasgow, *Feuillage*, Pau, and *The Feathered Egg*, Paris. Recipient: Prix Médicis Etranger, 1983. Address: Gwenved, Chemin du Goaquer, 22560 Trebeurden, France.

PUBLICATIONS

Verse

Wild Coal. Paris, Club des Etudiants d'Anglais, 1963.
En Toute Candeur (includes essays). Paris, Mercure de France, 1964.
The Cold Wind of Dawn. London, Cape, 1966.
The Most Difficult Area. London, Cape Goliard Press, and New York, Grossman, 1968.
A Walk along the Shore. Guildford, Surrey, Circle Press, 1977.
Mahamudra (bilingual edition). Paris, Mercure de France, 1979.
Ode fragmentée à la Bretagne. Bordeaux, William Blake, 1980.

Le Grand Rivage (bilingual edition). Paris, Nouveau Commerce, 1980.
Scènes d'un monde flottant (bilingual edition). Paris, Grasset, 1983.
Terre de diamant (bilingual edition). Paris, Grasset, 1983.

Fiction

Letters from Gourgounel. London, Cape, 1966.
Les Limbes incandescents. Paris, Denoël, 1976.
Dérives. Paris, Nadeau, 1978.
L'Écosse avec Kenneth White. Paris, Flammarion, 1980.
Le Visage du vent d'est. Paris, Presses d'Aujourd'hui, 1980.
La Route bleue. Paris, Grasset, 1983.

Other

The Tribal Dharma: An Essay on the Work of Gary Snyder. Dyfed, Unicorn, 1975.
The Life-Technique of John Cowper Powys. Swansea, Galloping Dog Press, 1978.
Segalen: Théorie et pratique du voyage. Paris, Eibel, 1979.
La Figure du dehors. Paris, Grasset, 1982.

Translator, *Selected Poems*, by André Breton. London, Cape Goliard Press, 1969.
Translator, *Ode to Charles Fourier*, by André Breton. London, Cape Goliard Press, 1969.

*

Manuscript Collection: National Library of Scotland, Edinburgh.

Critical Studies: *The Truth of Poetry* by Michael Hamburger, London, Weidenfeld and Nicolson, 1969, New York, Harcourt Brace, 1970; by Hans ten Berge, in *Raster* (Amsterdam), Autumn 1970; Robert Bréchon, in *Critique* (Paris), April 1979.

Kenneth White comments:

(1980) I can call myself a poet providing the word be adequately defined. I like Elie Faure's description: "The poet is he who never ceases to have confidence precisely because he does not attach himself to any port...but pursues...a form that flies through the tempest and is lost unceasingly in the eternal becoming."

The theme of my poetry (and prose) is the way to the complete and utter realisation of myself (which I see as the real and central content of art, without which it degenerates into a collection of more or less formally or psychologically interesting comments or objects). With a play on words and with the knowledge that "whiteness" is the synthesis of all colours, I tend, for the moment, to call this "complete realisation of myself"—"whiteness," and to translate moments of unity by terms indicative of whiteness. My aim, beyond the temporary realisations of "whiteness," is to ground this idea, this myth (as programme), to situate the ecstasy extensively, and find, discover, create a "white world."

In more philosophical terms, I see myself living in a world of separation and scission, and my aim, my desire is to move beyond this world of separation into unity. I find the theme in Hegel, who speaks of the early Greek world as "an immaculate world unadulterated by any scission." While the Hegelian synthesis, however, is purely intellectual, ideal, my aim is concrete realisation.

In this direction, I have been influenced, or confirmed, by Whitman, and Nietzsche (critique of present civilization, affirmation of life, will to self-realisation). Both of these, also, mean the end of a certain Western culture and, as I see it, an opening to the East (which can help us to discover a deeper West, create, in the West, a civilisation more existentially alive, more integrated, rather than merely mechanically active and essentially incoherent).

It's in the East that I find the terms and the vocabulary (and examples) more consonant with my search. In *L'Esprit Synthetique de la Chine*, Liou Kia-Hway speaks of the aim of Eastern life-thought (as contrasted with the radical dualism and abstraction of the West) as "a concrete totality which suffers no separation," penetrating beyond the dualisms into the "ground of being."

The way I see myself travelling towards this ground-realisation is the *sunyavada*, which Linnart Mäll, in his *Terminologia Indica*, translates as "The Zero Way"—"a quite original way of thought, so original it seems impossible to compare it with anything else."

My travelling on this way I express through poems (and prose), the poems, in general, expressing more intense moments of concentration, the prose recounting the travelling, attempting a synthesis of information, interspersed with moments of higher unity. The poems are characterised perhaps by intuitive rhythm, inner form, simplicity (i.e. a highly organised complexity, without elaboration) and a recurrent iconography (gulls and recent convergent image of the Rosy Gull), which makes for a characteristic "world." They are meant to satisfy demands, desires such as Bashō expresses: "There are many who write verse, but few who keep to the rules of the heart," understanding "heart" here not sentimentally, but as a psychosensual/intellectual synthesis, the poem itself being such a synthesis, uniting a content of ontological significance with an aesthetic of delight. "Before a poet can write haiku," writes Otsuji, and the same goes for poems in general as I understand them, "he must find a unity within his life which must come from the effort to discover his true self."

How far do I think I've travelled on my way? After passing through "the most difficult area," I'd say, with Paul Klee, "a little nearer to the heart of creation than is normal but still too far away."

*   *   *

If we except the more ecstatic passages, *Letters from Gourgounel* contains some of Kenneth White's most achieved writing to date in the sense that in the prose of that book we see his language engaging with substantial, particular experience more fully than has been the general rule in his poetry. It is not simply that much of his earlier poetry was too content with routine romantic gestures and unsubstantiated claims ("the deep-down poetry I trade my life for"..."I speak in knowledge to all men/the great things and the beautiful I bring"). It is rather that in his poetry he has set himself the difficult task of exploring those areas of experience where emptiness and silence may be sensed not in terms of negation but in terms of a more positive approach to a sense of immanence and revelation. Thus we have references to such phenomena as "this light that is/the limit of austerity/and makes words blind"; statements like "at the limits of saying/the soul flies to the mouth/and the poem is born"; and poems such as "In the Emptiness" which assert, in the emptiness, an experience of "reality right to the bone."

The general difficulty, then, is to reconcile the mystic's pull towards wordlessness and the poet's ineradicable dependence on words. In particular, the poetry's frequent resort to assertion, to statements *about* experience, may be characterised both by abstractions and by a lack of clear focus upon such concrete details as are mentioned. To what extent White is going to solve such a problem, in a manner germane to his sensibility, remains to be seen. But there are several poems (e.g. "Extraordinary Moment," "Sesshu") which do seem to indicate a possibility: these have clearly learned from oriental models, and their strength is that their focus on particulars is sharp and their implications are clear without being overspelt.

—Robin Fulton

WHITEHEAD, James. American. Born in St. Louis, Missouri, 15 March 1936. Educated at Central High School, Jackson, Mississippi; Vanderbilt University, Nashville, Tennessee, B.A. in philosophy 1959, M.A. in English 1960; University of Iowa, Iowa City, M.F.A. 1965. Married to Gen Graeber; seven children. Member of the Faculty, Millsaps College, Jackson, Mississippi, 1960-63. Currently, Professor of English, University of Arkansas, Fayetteville. Recipient: Bread Loaf Writers Conference Robert Frost Fellowship, 1967; Guggenheim grant, 1972. Address: Department of English, University of Arkansas, Fayetteville, Arkansas 72701, U.S.A.

PUBLICATIONS

Verse

Domains. Baton Rouge, Louisiana State University Press, 1966.
Local Men. Urbana, University of Illinois Press, 1979.

Novel

Joiner. New York, Knopf, 1971.

*   *   *

A strong sense of place and personality dominates James Whitehead's writing. In both his books of poems, *Domains* and *Local Men*, and in his novel, *Joiner*, real people live in real houses. The novel contains flowerings of the earlier poems, indicating the depth to which Whitehead's vision is rooted in the rich earth of the places and people he has known.

The concrete imagery in Whitehead's poems often suggests Frost. Not a cold fire-under-ice Frost, but a passionate poet who sings the breaks and bayous of the South as Frost sang the field and west-running brooks of New England. Which is not to say that Whitehead is a nature poet; his river raises "floaters," drowned people, "Bringing a stern sight to all of us/ In the country where only the deaths of the aged were clear." His places are always peopled, and his poems make us believe that there *was* a Dallas Tanksley, a Mary Fletcher, and a dead baby brother.

Whitehead is a witty poet ("Walking Around," "For Gen") with a fine feel for irony ("Desertions," "He Remembers How He Didn't Understand What Lieutenant Dawson Meant"), but his best poetry is imbrued with a passionate sense of life and its evanescence. He is torn between the domains of the crusading spirit and of the lusting flesh, but in his loveliest lines they become one kingdom. At the end of "Domains," the title poem of his first book, he prays for the strength to see that he is "...not fit/To serve at once/Two dying bodies with equal wit." But in his best poems he does just that.

—Norman T. Gates

WHITMAN, Ruth (née Bashein). American. Born in New York City, 28 May 1922. Educated at Radcliffe College, Cambridge, Massachusetts, B.A. (magna cum laude) 1944 (Phi Beta Kappa), M.A. 1947. Married 1) Cedric Whitman in 1941, two daughters; 2) Firman Houghton in 1959, one son; 3) Morton Sacks in 1966. Editorial Assistant, 1941-42, and Educational Editor, 1944-45, Houghton Mifflin Company, publishers, Boston; Editor, Harvard University Press, 1945-60; Poetry Editor, *Audience* Cambridge, Massachusetts, 1958-63. Director, Cambridge Center for Adult Education Poetry Workshop, 1964-68; Scholar in Poetry, Radcliffe Institute, 1968-70, and since 1970, Instructor in Poetry, Radcliffe College. Director of the Massachusetts Schools Poetry Writing Program, 1971-74. Since 1974, Founding President, Poets Who Teach, Inc. Poet-in-Residence, Hampden-Sydney College, Virginia, 1974, Trinity College, Hartford, Connecticut, 1975, University of Denver, 1976, College of the Holy Cross, Worcester, Massachusetts, 1978, Massachusetts Institute of Technology, Cambridge, 1979, University of Massachusetts, Amherst, 1980, and Centre College, Danville, Kentucky, 1980; Kentucky Arts Commission writer, 1981; Fulbright Writer-in-Residence, Jerusalem, 1984-85. Recipient: MacDowell Colony Fellowship, 1962, 1964, 1972-74, 1979, 1982; Poetry Society of America Reynolds Lyric Award, 1962, Alice Fay di Castagnola Award, 1968, Reedy Award, 1974, Ford Award, 1975, and Masefield Award, 1976; Tane Award (*Massachusetts Review*), 1964; National Foundation for Jewish Culture grant, 1968, 1969; Jewish Book Council of America Kovner Award, 1969; Chanin Award, for translation, 1972; National Endowment for the Arts grant, 1974; Tananbaum Foundation grant, 1979, 1980; Rhode Island State Council on the Arts grant, 1981. Address: 40 Tuckerman Avenue, Middletown, Rhode Island 02840, U.S.A.

PUBLICATIONS

Verse

Blood and Milk Poems. New York, Clarke and Way, 1963.
The Marriage Wig and Other Poems. New York, Harcourt Brace, 1968.
The Passion of Lizzie Borden: New and Selected Poems. New York, October House, 1973.
Tamsen Donner: A Woman's Journey. Cambridge, Massachusetts, Alice James, 1977.
Permanent Address: New Poems 1973-1980. Cambridge, Massachusetts, Alice James, 1980.

Other

Becoming a Poet: Source, Process, Practice. Boston, The Writer, 1982.

Editor and Translator, *An Anthology of Modern Yiddish Poetry.* New York, October House, 1966.

Editor, *Poemmaking: Poets in Classrooms.* Cambridge, Massachusetts Council of Teachers of English, 1975.

Translator, with others, *Selected Poems,* by Alain Bosquet. New York, New Directions, 1963.
Translator, *Selected Poems,* by Jacob Glatstein. New York, October House, 1972.

*

Ruth Whitman comments:

(1985) In writing poetry my purpose has changed from celebrating my own cycle of experience to bearing witness to the experience of other men and women. I believe such poetry teaches us how to live, how to cope with loss and disaster, how to survive. It asserts the value of the individual in an apocalyptic world. I work continually at the craft of poetry, often with the analogy of musical forms in my mind. I want my poems to sing. I also want them to communicate the meaning and reality of our lives.

*   *   *

Ruth Whitman is pre-eminently the poet of magic or ephiphanal moments. She seems to spy out cracks in the great unknown, and then, as if to capture them before they close, dashes words on a page to hold them. These quicksilver moments shimmer on the page as if held in a state of dynamic tension, an uneasy status between word and page, finally constrained by carefully crafted form that allows them to resonate in our minds. From the beginning, these moments tend to be personal, subjective, and strongly formal. Throughout her poetry there is a concern for the discovery of herself through her heritage. Jewish to the core, she explores that heritage in a variety of poems ("The Old Man's Mistress," "The Lost Steps," "Tuoro Synagogue," "Yom Kippur: Fasting"). Her second volume, *The Marriage Wig and Other Poems,* is a fuller examination of this theme of being Jewish and Ruth Whitman. The volume takes us deeper into the past as a dimension of the present.

Although brilliant moments are primarily the substance of Whitman's work, she strains after another realm of being. From time to time she seems to be haunted by ghosts or voices from other women. The two that have attracted Whitman's attention are Lizzie Borden (from the volume *The Passion of Lizzie Borden*) and Tamsen Donner (from the single volume *Tamsen Donner: A Woman's Journey*). Both women become vehicles for expressing profound insight into the psychology and situation of women. Borden is depicted as the victim of a cruel, repressive life that turns inward and perverts passion and the need for self-realization into murderous behavior. The act of killing her parents becomes a moment of creation and fulfillment. Donner is a kind of counterpart: for her the total devotion to her husband and children, even her decision to remain with her dying husband, is not a sacrifice but a fulfillment. Both 19th century women become counterparts for the poet herself as she searches for the proper role and mode of self-actualization in a new world where freedom to achieve self-fulfillment comes into continual conflict with deeply embedded psychological, historical, and traditional societal and religious restraints. Yet, the poet celebrates freedom. In poem after poem, she explores moments of unfettered desire, lavishly choreographed against a backdrop of exotic seas and sunlit shores, as in "the moon over the sea," and "Sachuest Point." In these poems Whitman reaches a level of precision, of craft molded with exquisite passion, that few of her contemporaries can match. Her two most recent volumes,

Tamsen Donner and *Permanent Address: New Poems 1973-1980*, have provided us with two more brilliant contributions to contemporary poetry and leave us in a state of happy anticipation of what Ruth Whitman might do next.

—Richard Damashek

WHITTEMORE, (Edward) Reed (II). American. Born in New Haven, Connecticut, 11 September 1919. Educated at Yale University, New Haven, A.B. 1941; Princeton University, New Jersey, 1945-46. Served in the United States Army Air Force, 1941-45: Captain. Married Helen Lundeen in 1952; two daughters and two sons. Member of the Department of English, 1947-62, Chairman of the Department, 1962-64, and Professor of English, 1962-67, Carleton College, Northfield, Minnesota; Bain-Swiggett Lecturer, Princeton University, 1967-68. Since 1968, Professor of English, University of Maryland, College Park, now Emeritus. Editor, *Furioso*, 1939-53, and *Carleton Miscellany*, 1960-64, both in Northfield, Minnesota. Literary Editor, *New Republic*, Washington, D.C., 1969-73. Consultant in Poetry, 1964-65, and Interim Consultant, 1984-85, Library of Congress, Washington, D.C. Recipient: Emily Clark Balch Prize (*Virginia Quarterly Review*), 1962; National Endowment for the Arts grant, 1968; American Academy Award of Merit, 1970. Litt.D.: Carleton College, 1971. Address: 4326 Albion Road, College Park, Maryland 20740, U.S.A.

PUBLICATIONS

Verse

Heroes and Heroines. New York, Reynal, 1946.
An American Takes a Walk and Other Poems. Minneapolis, University of Minnesota Press, 1956.
The Self-Made Man and Other Poems. New York, Macmillan, 1959.
The Boy from Iowa: Poems and Essays. New York, Macmillan, 1962.
Return, Alpheus: A Poem for the Literary Elders of Phi Beta Kappa. Williamsburg, Virginia, King and Queen Press, 1965.
Poems, New and Selected. Minneapolis, University of Minnesota Press, 1967.
50 Poems 50. Minneapolis, University of Minnesota Press, 1970.
The Mother's Breast and the Father's House. Boston, Houghton Mifflin, 1974.
The Feel of Rock: Poems of Three Decades. Washington, D.C., Dryad Press, 1982.

Other

Little Magazines. Minneapolis, University of Minnesota Press, 1963.
The Fascination of the Abomination: Poems, Stories, and Essays. New York, Macmillan, 1963.
Ways of Misunderstanding Poetry. Washington, D.C., Library of Congress, 1965.
From Zero to the Absolute: Essays. New York, Crown, 1967.
William Carlos Williams: Poet from Jersey. Boston, Houghton Mifflin, 1975.

The Poet as Journalist: Life at the New Republic. Washington, D.C., New Republic, 1976.

Editor, *Browning.* New York, Dell, 1960.

*   *   *

Reed Whittemore was among the first poets of his generation to make full use of the graceful and natural rhythms of William Carlos Williams's poetry. And in his editorship of *Furioso* and the *Carleton Miscellany*, as well as in his career as teacher and biographer, Whittemore has influenced the course of American language over the past thirty years. For one poem in particular, he deserves a permanent place in American poetry, the first and among the most powerful discussions of the idiocy and waywardness of the nuclear age. That memorable lyric, "Lines Composed upon Reading an Announcement by Civil Defense Authorities Recommending That I Build a Bomb Shelter in My Backyard," concludes on this sensible note:

> But I'll not, no not do it, not go back
> And lie there in that dark under the weight
> Of all that earth on that old door for my state.
> I know too much to think now that if I creep
> From the grown-up's house to the child's house I'll keep.

The Self-Made Man, Whittemore's longest poem, with echoes of Stevens's "The Comedian as the Letter C," extends the range of his ironic vision. It treats the Emersonian ideal with both mockery and tragic insight, as when the hero asks, "Where in my chatter, where in my banter/Where, where in this impious figure before you/Is God's wrath?" Among the New England worthies satirized in the poem is Mary Baker Eddy, in this memorable refrain, from Section VI:

> Mary Baker of New Hampshire,
> Mary Baker of New Hampshire.
> I speak it twice; the rhythm stamps her
> Simple Mary of New Hampshire.

Although capable of the clearest observation, as in "The Party," about children's seriousness at play, Whittemore turned away from more complex emotions, and many of his poems after about 1960 can only be regarded with disappointment, as if there were some failure of nerve or energy.

A terrible darkness broods among those light, Horatian satires about cultural conferences and New York sophisticates, but inevitably the speaker refuses to face the deeper implications of his ironic view. Why were all those obvious opportunities ignored, one wonders, as in "Dead Walk" for example, or "The Storing of Soul"? Beside the fully realized humor of the early poems, one must set the frequently moving but inadequately rendered sadness of the later ones. Only occasionally is that sureness and grace evident again, and Whittemore's admirers rightfully hope for more consistently structured verses, like the following from "The Feel of Rock":

> My father went broke on a shaded street.
> My mother drank there.
> My brothers removed themselves; they were complete.
> I kept my room and slicked down my hair....
> I did not know until grown how alone,
> In bed in a dark room,
> One could be, one had been, little father clone.

—Michael True

WIENERS, John (Joseph). American. Born in Boston, Massachusetts, 6 January 1934. Educated at Boston College, A.B. in English 1954; Black Mountain College, North Carolina, 1955-56; State University of New York, Buffalo (Teaching Fellow), 1965-67. Library clerk, Lamont Library, Harvard University, Cambridge, Massachusetts, 1955-57; actor and stage manager, Poets Theatre, Cambridge, 1956; assistant bookkeeper, 8th Street Bookshop, New York, 1962-63; Subscriptions Editor, Jordan Marsh Company, Boston, 1963-65; class leader, Beacon Hill Free School, Boston, 1973. Co-Founding Editor, *Measure*, Boston. Recipient: Poets Foundation grant, 1961; New Hope Foundation Award, 1963; National Endowment for the Arts grant, 1966, 1968; American Academy award, 1968; Committee on Poetry grant, 1970, 1971, 1972. Address: c/o Raymond Foye Editions, Chelsea Hotel, 222 West 23rd Street, No. 807, New York, New York 10011, U.S.A.

PUBLICATIONS

Verse

The Hotel Wentley Poems. San Francisco, Auerhahn Press, 1958; revised edition, San Francisco, Dave Haselwood, 1965.
Ace of Pentacles. New York, Carr, 1964.
You Talk of Going But Don't Even Have a Suitcase. Spoleto, Italy, Spoleto Festival, 1965.
Chinoiserie. San Francisco, Dave Haselwood, 1965.
Hart Crane, Harry Crosby, I See You Going over the Edge. Detroit, Artists' Workshop Press, 1966.
Pressed Wafer. Buffalo, Gallery Upstairs Press, 1967.
King Solomon's Magnetic Quiz. Pleasant Valley, New York, Kriya Press, 1967.
Long Distance. Mount Horeb, Wisconsin, Perishable Press, 1968.
Selected Poems. London, Cape, 1968.
L'Abysse. New York, Minkoff, 1968.
On Looking in the Mirror. New York, Brownstone Press, 1968.
Unhired. Mount Horeb, Wisconsin, Perishable Press, 1968.
A Letter to Charles Olson. New York, Charters, 1968.
Idyll. Santa Barbara, California, Unicorn Press, 1968.
To Do. Stony Brook, New York, Stony Brook Poetics Foundation, 1968.
Asylum Poems. New York, Angel Hair, 1969.
Invitation. Santa Barbara, California, Unicorn Press, 1970.
Youth. New York, Phoenix Book Shop, 1970.
Nerves. London, Cape Goliard Press, and New York, Grossman, 1970.
Larders. Cambridge, Massachusetts, Restau Press, 1970.
Reading in Bed. San Francisco, White Rabbit Press, 1970.
First Poem after Silence since Thanksgiving. San Francisco, Butterfly, 1970.
Selected Poems. London, Cape, and New York, Grossman, 1972.
Playboy. Boston, Good Gay Poets, 1972.
We Were There! New York, Athanor, 1973.
God Is the Organ of Novelty. Cambridge, Massachusetts, Pomegranate Press, 1973.
Yes, Youth Are Marching On Against the World. Philadelphia, Middle Earth Bookstore, 1973.
Behind the State Capitol; or, Cincinnati Pike. Boston, Good Gay Poets, 1975.
Collected Poems 1958-1984. Santa Barbara, California, Black Sparrow Press, 1985.

Plays

Still-Life (produced New York, 1961).
Of Asphodel, in Hell's Despite (produced New York, 1963). New York, Judson Poet's Theatre, n.d.
Anklesox and Five Shoelaces (produced New York, 1966).

Television Documentary: *The Spirit of Romance*, with Robert Duncan, 1965.

Other

A Memory of Black Mountain College. Cambridge, Massachusetts Institute of Technology Press, 1969.
Woman. Canton, New York, Institute of Further Studies, 1972.
The Lanterns Along the Wall. Buffalo, Other Publications, 1972.
Hotels. New York, Angel Hair, 1974.

*

Bibliography: "John Wieners: A Checklist" by George F. Butterick, in *Athanor 3* (Clarkson, New York), Summer-Fall 1973.

Critical Studies: by Denise Levertov, in *Poetry* (Chicago), February 1965; Robert Duncan, in *The Nation* (New York), 31 May 1965; Lewis Warsh, in *Boston Phoenix*, January 1973; interview, in *Gay Sunshine* (San Francisco), March 1973.

John Wieners comments:

(1970) My themes are heartfelt ones of youth and manly desire. Their subjects are despair, frustration, ideal satisfaction, with Biblical and classical referential echoes. Their forms are declarative, orderly and true, without invention. General sources are Edna St. Vincent Millay, United States prose writers of the twentieth century, lyricists in the Greek anthology. Homer; Sappho; Horace; Virgilius; the songs of Geoffrey Chaucer, and subsequent strains of the English tradition. Characteristic stylistic devices are the direct address of German lieder, Near Eastern intimacy and Chinese abbreviation.

(1974) Poetry since 16 has been an obsession, every day, every minute, hearkening to the form of poetry, its practitioners and personables continue to remain fixed as divinities equal to those of the French novelists since 1945 or the Pléiades of court presentation. I have kept the sun and myself upon a balcony bent under its power to lead my attainment towards magnitudinous worldly success and ultimately the presentation towards one person of its worth. For what would it matter if I could not be of use or of importance to this possible derelict in the world's eyes, but to my heart, husband-god, king-emperor. And yet not that. Simply a poor person in need of myself.

Along its possession blossoms many rewards, leisure, conversation, books, friends, entertainment for the ultimate collected editions to merit his devotion.

*   *   *

Perhaps the most appealing thing about John Wieners's poems is the vulnerability which they express. He has produced some of the most poignant lyrics of their kind ever. His dominant theme is dolor, loss of love and rapture. His is a poetry of feeling rather than will, small chapels for devotion. He is preoccupied with glamour and unattainable desire, yet is saved from self-pity by service to a poetry larger than even his despair: "It is eternal audience/and my feet hardend, my heart/blackend, nodding and/bowing before it." He avoids triteness by the almost perfect timing, the exquisite phrasing. His best poems are relieved from sentimentality by precarious rhyme, perilous syntax, dramatic poise. He is capable of the most precise syncopations: "Yet so tenuous, so fine/this thing is, I am/sitting on the hard bed...." The casual lines only heighten the authenticity of his voice. The despair is so matter-of-fact, not only do we ache for the pity of it, but we believe that to be overcome by such despair is inevitable for the poet. That is the awe which is awful. It is a single tone played repeatedly, like Housman. Weiners is easily the torch singer he once said he wished he could be. No one has sung so convincingly of the haunted underside of life save Billie Holiday, his heroine, or perhaps Edith Piaf, whose fragility his resembles. How out of the sordid and decadent he is able to raise the purest strains is his specialization and accomplishment. We remain before his poems as the poet does his image of himself—"all morning/long./With my hand over my mouth."

Along with *The Hotel Wentley Poems*, Wieners's finest collection remains *Ace of Pentacles*. There are some excellent poems in *Nerves*, a few otherwise uncollected ones in *Selected Poems*, and fewer still in the most recent *Behind the State Capitol*, a collection of "cinema decoupages; verses, abbreviated prose insights," that takes its title from the poet's residence below Beacon Hill in Boston, behind the state capitol building. Wieners has not been his own best representative, as *Selected Poems* too often attests. Not only did he leave out some of his finest poems — "Long Nook," "A Poem for Trapped Things," "Moon Poems," "Not Complete Enough," "My Mother," "The Meadow Where All Things Grow," "Hart Crane, Harry Crosby," "Billie"—but many of those included have been revised, and not always with success. Whether through loss of confidence or false notions of improvement, in almost every case the alterations are for the poorer, usually a misguided effort to attain a more "poetic" effect, most often through the elimination of articles and copulas or the compression of openly whispered lines into more regular stanzas—but in effect eliminating the spoken directness and accuracy of the original. For example, the poet adds the title "153 Avenue C" (on New York's Lower East Side, where the poem was written) to previously untitled lines, but takes away their perfectly understated horror by removing the copulas of natural speech. Other changes are simply strange if not inept, and they are endemic throughout the volume; while in *Behind the State Capitol*, produced from copy apparently prepared by the poet himself, typing eccentricities have been allowed to stand, contributing nothing but confusion. The poet has forsaken his own genius and the stark simplicity of the original statements, so forthright they cannot be doubted or denied. He has lost the touch which enabled him to revise so successfully "A Poem for Painters" (if one compares the original version with that in the 1958 *Hotel Wentley Poems*), which contains his most famous lines and the summarization of his consistent theme:

> My poems contain no
> wilde beestes, no
> lady of the lake, music
> of the spheres, or organ chants.
>
> Only the score of a man's
> struggle to stay with
> what is his own, what
> lies within him to do.

He has continued loyal to his "voices," those to whom *Ace of Pentacles* was dedicated; only now, youth gone, there are more of them, crowding about, incessant, obscuring the flame. The clear, elegant voice and lyric perfection of the early poems has been lost to the multiple personalities, and the consequence is warring diction, abuse of rhyme, and linguistic excess. The *dérèglement* Rimbaud prepared us for has occurred.

—George F. Butterick

WILBUR, Richard (Purdy). American. Born in New York City, 1 March 1921. Educated at Amherst College, Massachusetts, B.A. 1942; Harvard University, Cambridge, Massachusetts, M.A. 1947. Served in the United States Army, 1943-45: Sergeant. Married Charlotte Ward in 1942; one daughter and three sons. Member of the Society of Fellows, 1947-50, and Assistant Professor of English, 1950-54, Harvard University; Associate Professor of English, Wellesley College, Massachusetts, 1955-57; Professor of English, Wesleyan University, Middletown, Connecticut, 1957-77. Since 1977, Writer-in-Residence, Smith College, Northampton, Massachusetts. General Editor, Laurel Poets series, Dell Publishing Company, New York. State Department Cultural Exchange Representative to the U.S.S.R., 1961. Recipient: Harriet Monroe Memorial Prize, 1948, and Oscar Blumenthal Prize, 1950 (*Poetry*, Chicago); Guggenheim Fellowship, 1952, 1963; American Academy in Rome Fellowship, 1954; Pulitzer Prize, 1957; National Book Award, 1957; Edna St. Vincent Millay Memorial Award, 1957; Ford Fellowship, for drama, 1960; Melville Cane Award, 1962; Bollingen Prize, for translation, 1963, and for verse, 1971; Sarah Josepha Hale Award, 1968; Brandeis University Creative Arts Award, 1970; Prix Henri Desfeuilles, 1971; Shelley Memorial Award, 1973; Harriet Monroe Award, 1978; P.E.N. Translation Award, 1983; Drama Desk Award, 1983. L.H.D.: Lawrence College, Appleton, Wisconsin, 1960; Washington University, St. Louis, 1964; Williams College, Williamstown, Massachusetts, 1975; University of Rochester, New York, 1976; Carnegie Mellon University, 1980; D.Litt.: Amherst College, 1967; Clark University, Worcester, Massachusetts, 1970; American International College, Springfield, Massachusetts, 1974; Marquette University, Milwaukee, 1977; Wesleyan University, 1977; Lake Forest College, Illinois, 1982. Member, American Academy of Arts and Sciences: President, 1974-77, and Chancellor, 1977-78, 1981, American Academy of Arts and Letters; Chancellor, Academy of American Poets; Chevalier, Order National des Palmes Académiques, 1983. Agent: Curtis Brown, 575 Madison Avenue, New York, New York 10022. Address: Dodwell Road, Cummington, Massachusetts 01026, U.S.A.

PUBLICATIONS

Verse

The Beautiful Changes and Other Poems. New York, Reynal, 1947.
Ceremony and Other Poems. New York, Harcourt Brace, 1950.
Things of This World. New York, Harcourt Brace, 1956; one section reprinted as *Digging to China*, New York, Doubleday, 1970.
Poems 1943-1956. London, Faber, 1957.
Advice to a Prophet and Other Poems. New York, Harcourt Brace, 1961; London, Faber, 1962.

The Poems of Richard Wilbur. New York, Harcourt Brace, 1963.

The Pelican from a Bestiary of 1120. Privately printed, 1963.

Prince Souvanna Phouma: An Exchange Between Richard Wilbur and William Jay Smith. Williamstown, Massachusetts, Chapel Press, 1963.

Complaint. New York, Phoenix Book Shop, 1968.

Walking to Sleep: New Poems and Translations. New York, Harcourt Brace, 1969; London, Faber, 1971.

Seed Leaves: Homage to R.F. Boston, Godine, 1974.

The Mind-Reader: New Poems. New York, Harcourt Brace, 1976; London, Faber, 1977.

Verses on the Times, with William Jay Smith. New York, Gutenberg Press, 1978.

Seven Poems. Ohamah, Abattoir, 1981.

Recordings: *Poems*, Spoken Arts, 1959; *Richard Wilbur Reading His Poetry*, Caedmon, 1972.

Plays

The Misanthrope, adaptation of the play by Molière (produced Cambridge, Massachusetts, 1955; New York, 1956). New York, Harcourt Brace, 1955; London, Faber, 1958; revised version, music by Margaret Pine (produced New York, 1977).

Candide (lyrics only, with others), book by Lillian Hellman, music by Leonard Bernstein, adaptation of the novel by Voltaire (produced New York, 1956; London, 1959). New York, Random House, 1957.

Tartuffe, adaptation of the play by Molière (produced Milwaukee, Wisconsin, 1964; New York, 1965). New York, Harcourt Brace, 1963; London, Faber, 1964.

School for Wives, adaptation of a play by Molière (produced New York, 1971). New York, Harcourt Brace, 1971.

The Learned Ladies, adaptation of a play by Molière (produced Williamstown, Massachusetts, 1977; London, 1981). New York, Harcourt Brace, 1978.

Andromache, adaptation of the play by Racine. New York, Harcourt Brace, 1982.

Other

Emily Dickinson: Three Views, with Louise Bogan and Archibald MacLeish. Amherst, Massachusetts, Amherst College Press, 1960.

Loudmouse (for children). London, Crowell Collier, and New York, Collier Macmillan, 1963.

Opposites (for children), drawings by the author. New York, Harcourt Brace, 1973.

Responses: Prose Pieces 1953-1976. New York, Harcourt Brace, 1976.

The Whale and Other Uncollected Translations. Brockport, New York, BOA, 1982.

On My Own Work. Portree, Isle of Skye, Aquila, 1983.

Editor, with Louis Untermeyer and Karl Shapiro, *Modern American and Modern British Poetry*, revised shorter edition. New York, Harcourt Brace, 1955.

Editor, *A Bestiary* (anthology). New York, Pantheon, 1955.

Editor, *Complete Poems of Poe*. New York, Dell, 1959.

Editor, with Alfred B. Harbage, *Poems of Shakespeare*. London, Penguin, 1966; revised edition, as *The Narrative Poems, and Poems of Doubtful Authenticity*, 1974.

Editor, *Selected Poems*, by Witter Bynner. New York, Farrar Straus, and London, Faber, 1978.

Translator, *The Funeral of Bobo*, by Joseph Brodsky. Ann Arbor, Michigan, Ardis, 1974.

*

Bibliography: *Richard Wilbur: A Bibliographical Checklist* by John P. Field, Kent, Ohio, Kent State University Press, 1971.

Manuscript Collections: Amherst College, Massachusetts; Lockwood Memorial Library, State University of New York, Buffalo.

Critical Studies: *Richard Wilbur* by Donald L. Hill, New York, Twayne, 1967; *Richard Wilbur* by Paul F. Cummins, Grand Rapids, Michigan, Eerdmans, 1971; "On Richard Wilbur" by William Heyen, Summer 1973, "Verse Translation and Richard Wilbur" by Raymond Oliver, Spring 1975, and "Richard Wilbur: The Quarrel with Poe" by Bruce F. Michelson, Spring 1978, all in *Southern Review* (Baton Rouge, Louisiana); "The Motions of the Mind" by Anthony Hecht, in *Times Literary Supplement* (London), 20 May 1977; "The Cheshire Smile: On Richard Wilbur" by Mary Kinzie, in *American Poetry Review* (Philadelphia), May-June 1977; "Richard Wilbur's World" by Robert B. Shaw, in *Parnassus* (New York), Spring-Summer 1977; "Reconsideration: The Poetry of Richard Wilbur" by Frank McConnell, in *New Republic* (Washington, D.C.), 29 July 1978; *Richard Wilbur's Creation* edited by Wendy Salinger, Ann Arbor, University of Michigan Press, 1983.

Richard Wilbur comments:

Poetry, for me, is an exasperating and clarifying play with certain images and themes which I cannot escape and prefer not to state here in prose. As the title of my selected prose (*Responses*) would suggest, I have generally written criticism on invitation, but also out of an appreciative involvement with the subject. My translations also have largely come about through a sense of affinity—a desire to put whatever knacks I may have at the service of some admired original.

*   *   *

In his 1966 essay "Poetry and Happiness" Richard Wilbur offers the measure by which poetry should be judged: "When the sensibility is sufficient to the expression of the world, and when the world, in turn, is answerable to the poet's mind and heart, then the poet is happy and can make his reader so." In *The Mind-Reader* he disregards the criticism that his poetry wants passion, that its subjects, although nicely perceived in all their inherent paradoxes, lack significance, and that his voice and sensibility are too academic. He continues to strike that difficult balance between solipsism and scientific objectivity upon which his best poetry depends. Wilbur's poem "Cottage Street, 1953" (*The Mind-Reader*) answers the critic that holds that the play of the mind upon an object has become unfashionable—that only the noisy iconoclasm of the Beats, or the naked outpourings of psyche in the Confessional Poets can excite emotions proper to poetry. It also implicitly sustains Wilbur's belief that even in this day a baroque fountain, or a Delacroix painting, or a boy-grown man asking forgiveness of his dead dog are as significant subjects for verse as man's passions or private confession.

"Cottage Street, 1953" recalls a gathering in the Cambridge kitchen of Wilbur's mother-in-law, Mrs. Ward, shortly after Sylvia Plath's unsuccessful suicide attempt. In an atmosphere of strain, the good-hearted Mrs. Ward, Plath's mother, and Wilbur awkwardly struggle to cheer up Sylvia. Wilbur concludes his poem affirming the love of Edna Ward over the denial of Sylvia Plath:

> And Edna Ward shall die in fifteen years,
> After her eight-and-eighty summers of
> Such grace and courage as permit no tears,
> The thin hand reaching out, the last word love,
>
> Outwitting Sylvia, who condemned to live,
> Shall study for a decade, as she must,
> To state at last her brilliant negative
> In poems free and helpless and unjust.

Wilbur's poems acknowledge pain. His early poems protesting World War II and the more recent occasional poems on the Vietnam War decry war's disorder. The complex and infinitely rich "Castles and Distances" brilliantly knits blood and love together:

> Oh, it is hunters alone
> Regret the beastly pain, it is they who love the foe
> That quarries out their force, and every arrow
> Is feathered soft with wishes to atone;
> Even the surest sword in sorrow
> Bleeds for its spoiling blow.

Some of the lines in this poem makes us feel the "harpoon's hurt," the piteous eyes of the "hounded stag," the seeming wantonness of slaughter, but others recast this pain, not softening, but altering it, reminding us that pain is there, but also joy. Neither can be eliminated; experience will not allow the simple, albeit brilliant denial of Sylvia Plath.

To complain that Wilbur is "shy," or "restrained," or "too charitable" is to misunderstand the intent of his poems which is not to distort, but rightly to see the tensions which inform our sense of the world, to set isolated moments in a perspective. Wilbur's is a world of balanced discord.

In "Poetry and Happiness" Wilbur also acknowledged his debt to John Crowe Ransom and defended his choice to write stanzaically formal verse, full of practiced metrical irregularities which set forth contrapuntally thesis and antithesis and reach a resolution appropriately ironic to suit the disordered world mirrored in the poems. He did detect that his poetry over the years had grown plainer and less precocious, less the jaunty verbal technics of a poet-juggler, and he observed that his manner had moved slightly away from the ironic meditative lyric of "Caserta Gardens" and "A Baroque Wall-Fountain in the Villa Sciarra" to the dramatic poem employing two distinct voices, "Two Voices in a Meadow." He saw the common theme of his poetry as having to do with "the proper relation between the tangible world and the intuitions of the spirit."

The poems in *Walking to Sleep* and *The Mind-Reader* continue to evolve in the direction Wilbur described while remaining constant to his theme and sensibility. Most often Wilbur is fascinated by movement and perspective and manipulates language to create a highly kinesthetic poetry. In "Grace" he wrote of the pause and the leap saying "And Nijinsky hadn't the words to make the laws/ For learning to loiter in air; he merely said,/ 'I merely leap and pause.'" Wilbur's poetry searches for the words Nijinsky lacked. Often Wilbur develops his poems by arresting the reader's eye and taking it through a minute study of the object—be it from nature, history, legend, or his personal past—which the poem contemplates. As he unfolds the object to the seer, he uses a language of such studied movement and rest that we delight at the variety of ways in which a thing can move and

marvel at the final figure of the poem which balances the conflicting motions. Poems such as "Lightness," "The Juggler," and "On the Marginal Way" typify this method.

Thinking about the relationship between ideas and poetry, Wilbur wrote: "what poetry does with ideas is redeem them from abstraction and submerge them in sensibility." "Love Calls Us to the Things of This World" discovered the corporeal in the spiritual. "The Eye" and "The Fourth of July" in *The Mind-Reader* continue to make ideas live. Wilbur's diction in *The Mind-Reader* remains academic, but he experiments more with a colloquial speech. "Piccola Commedia" can be seen to have descended from "A Black November Turkey" (*Poems, 1943-1956*). Wilbur still demurs in his poems from speaking directly of his life, his personal poems speak obliquely; he still relies on humor and the fanciful to distance himself. "The Writer" shows excellently how Wilbur depicts a private and family moment with affection, light humor, and candor. The longer, blank-verse poems "In Limbo" and the title poem "The Mind-Reader" along with "Walking to Sleep" depart from most of Wilbur's verse in their length and sustained characterization of himself, but their concern with perspective, irony, minute detail, and a speech of varied kinds immediately relates them thematically and tonally to the body of Wilbur's writing.

—Carol Simpson Stern

WILD, Peter. American. Born in Northampton, Massachusetts, 25 April 1940. Educated at the University of Arizona, Tucson, 1958-62, 1965-67, B.A. 1962, M.A. 1967; University of California, Irvine, 1967-69, M.F.A. 1969. Married 1) Sylvia Ortiz in 1966; 2) Rosemary Harrold in 1981. Assistant Professor of English, Sul Ross State University, Alpine, Texas, 1969-71. Assistant Professor, 1971-73, Associate Professor, 1973-79, and since 1979, Professor of English, University of Arizona. Since 1974, Contributing Editor, *High Country News*, Lander, Wyoming; since 1983, Consulting Editor, *Diversions*. Recipient: *Writer's Digest* Prize, 1964; Hart Crane and Alice Crane Williams Memorial Fund grant, 1969; *Ark River Review* prize, 1972; Ohio State University President's Prize, 1982. Address: 1547 East Lester, Tucson, Arizona, 85719, U.S.A.

PUBLICATIONS

Verse

The Good Fox. Glassboro, New Jersey, Goodly, 1967.
Sonnets. San Francisco, Cranium Press, 1967.
The Afternoon in Dismay. Cincinnati, Art Association of Cincinnati, 1968.
Mica Mountain Poems. Ithaca, New York, Lillabulero Press, 1968.
Joining Up and Other Poems. Sacramento, California, Runcible Spoon, 1968.
Mad Night with Sunflowers. Sacramento, California, Runcible Spoon, 1968.
Love Poems. Northwood Narrows, New Hampshire, Lillabulero Press, 1969.
Three Nights in the Chiricahuas. Madison, Wisconsin, Abraxas Press, 1969.
Poems. Portland, Oregon, Prensa de Lagar, 1969.
Fat Man Poems. Belmont, Massachusetts, Hellric, 1970.

Terms and Renewals. San Francisco, Two Windows Press, 1970.
Grace. Pennington, New Jersey, Stone Press, 1971.
Dilemma. Poquoson, Virginia, Back Door Press, 1971.
Wild's Magical Book of Cranial Effusions. New York, New Rivers Press, 1971.
Peligros. Ithaca, New York, Ithaca House, 1972.
New and Selected Poems. New York, New Rivers Press, 1973.
Cochise. New York, Doubleday, 1973.
The Cloning. New York, Doubleday, 1974.
Tumacacori. Berkeley, California, Two Windows Press, 1974.
Health. Berkeley, California, Two Windows Press, 1974.
Chihuahua. New York, Doubleday, 1976.
The Island Hunter. Tannersville, New York, Tideline Press, 1976.
Pioneers. Tannersville, New York, Tideline Press, 1976.
The Cavalryman. Tannersville, New York, Tideline Press, 1976.
House Fires. Santa Cruz, California, Greenhouse Review Press, 1977.
Gold Mines. Iola, Wisconsin, Wolfsong Press, 1978.
Barn Fires. Point Reyes, California, Floating Island, 1978.
Zuni Butte. Bisbee, Arizona, San Pedro Press, 1978.
The Lost Tribe. Iola, Wisconsin, Wolfsong Press, 1979.
Jeanne d'Arc: A Collection of New Poems. Memphis, St. Luke's Press, 1980.
Rainbow. Des Moines, Iowa, Blue Buildings Press, 1980.
Wilderness. St. Paul, Minnesota, New Rivers Press, 1980.
Heretics. Madison, Wisconsin, Ghost Pony Press, 1981.
Bitterroots. Tucson, Blue Moon Press, 1982.
The Light on Little Mormon Lake. Point Reyes, California, Floating Island, 1983.
The Peaceable Kingdom. Rochester, New York, Adler Press, 1983.
Getting Ready for a Date. Madison, Wisconsin, Abraxas Press, 1984.

Other

Pioneer Conservationists of Western [and *Eastern*] *America.* Missoula, Montana, Mountain Press, 2 vols., 1979-83.
Enos Mills. Boise, Idaho, Boise State University, 1979.
Clarence King. Boise, Idaho, Boise State University, 1981.
James Welch. Boise, Idaho, Boise State University, 1983.
Barry Lopez. Boise, Idaho, Boise State University, 1984.

Editor, with Frank Graziano, *New Poetry of the American West.* Durango, Colorado, Logbridge Rhodes, 1982.

*

Critical Studies: "Eight Chapbooks," in *The Dragonfly* (Pocatello, Idaho), Fall and Winter 1970; "Keeping Us Mad" by B. Salchert, in *Wisconsin Review* (Oshkosh), Spring 1972; "Lillabulero's Pamphlets," in *Greenfield Review* (Greenfield Center, New York), June 1972; "Mud Men, Mud Women" by Robert Peters, in *Margins* (Milwaukee, Wisconsin), October-November 1974; "Peter Wild: Ways of Promise" by Philip Allan Friedman, in *Gramercy Review* (Los Angeles), Summer 1978; interview, in *Blue Moon News* (Tucson), 1980.

Peter Wild comments:
   Both figuratively and in reality I have always felt a necessity to spend a great deal of time in the open, in the outdoors. Hence, the deterioration of the natural environment, overpopulation and the erosion of man's cultural diversity are conditions of great concern to me. Furthermore, due to a strong sense of place, as a resident of the American Southwest, a region of the Anglo, Mexican and American Indian, I often hold conflicting sympathies and allegiances. This is not to imply that I consider myself either a "nature poet" or a regional poet—a poet must write for all men—but in general it may be of help for a reader to remember that the above concerns and circumstances of my life undoubtedly underlie and temper much of my writing.

*   *   *

   In 1973, Peter Wild published a new and selected poems, at the age of 33 and after publishing his poetry for only 6 years. Why this premature act? Of course, this was partly because of a strong interest in Wild's poetry and a very successful debut into the world of writing. William Matthews wrote in the introduction to the book about Wild's poems that "the effect is of a baroque telegram, or the wildest photo caption you'll ever read". Wild's poems were realistic enough to use vivid details, as in this short poem ("Talking with the Cook When the First Man Comes to Coffee"):

> In the sky
> gauze patches
> soak over our wounds
> that drip sparks,
> flying in a second to the horizon.
>
> we dig our needle
> heels in against it, our spurs
> founder in the dust
> up to our knees, the calf
> gone mad on his white
> intestine of a rope.
>
> until the first hand
> closes around the cup,
> a scar covered with hair
> and the light shines out
>   from the tips of our boots.

But each poem also revealed a sense of the inner world of magic, the unconscious, the dream world. It was a kind of surrealism very attractive to readers and critics from many different backgrounds. In a poem called "Last Night Emily Dickinson," Wild fuses our dream world, a kind of comic book image of a literary figure and the natural world. Goats are watching this phenomena:

> Last night Emily Dickinson
>   flew over my house
> on a fried chicken liver,
>   mushy grass hair
>   unloosed
> and her apron tucked up
>   under her white knees.
> ...
> she shot
>   over the dark margin of the trees
> like a comet
>   bound to explode:
> and in the pale light of it
>   I saw their bloodless faces
> white like the heads of tapeworms

              turn in a even sweep
                 to watch her go

           we set our teeth
                but the explosion
                    never came
           so we went back to bed;
           there were only grease spots
           on the window panes
           in the imminent darkness
                    like a butterfly
                       my heart tore
                          in two.

I quote portions of this poem at length because it shows the Peter Wild who is a magic realist, a poet writing in and out of the real world, with a normal expected psychological dimension juxtaposed against the distortion of both reality and fantasy.

   However, since that time Wild has been evolving into a very very different poet. One who is a genuine surrealist, working beyond the attractive vision of snakes as dragons, then dragon kites, men whose sense of the real world is so strong that their boots glow in the morning air, or a fast-food Emily Dickinson, leaving more grease than good taste in the pop-consumer's life. This turning away from easy (though brilliant and attractive) writing has lost Wild many of his earlier readers. His poems now demand a very different facility from readers, and never grant the jig-saw puzzle satisfaction that his earlier work did. In his most recent book of poems, *Peaceable Kingdom*, there is a poem which seems to address this very issue, for surely Wild, like many poets whose work has grown and changed so that it is scarcely recognizable to his early readers, must be plagued with people wanting him to remain the same. In "Favors" he begins, "The moon wants to talk to me/but I have nothing to say to him./Is he a bill collector scratching at the door,/telephoning late at night?" The poem goes on to describe the pesky bill collector following him and he begins to see the bill collector in different disguises and other identities. He concludes the poem,

                    Or at last
           recognize him, the scrannel St. Bernard
           who lives in the basement of the abandoned Mormon
                church
           coming out to tip over our garbage cans, feed there.
           "Ethel," I shout from the back porch, "get me
           my shotgun, the one with birdshot in it,"
                    and blast him away
           a balloon losing its air with first and final voice,
           doing the whole neighborhood a favor.

   What, I think, has happened to Wild over the years is that his political sense of conscience (he is a member of the Sierra Club and quite involved with environmental issues) has invaded his more orderly and aesthetic surrealism from the past, giving his vision a new complexity, one that brooks nothing simple and easy. He begins a poem called "Babylon" with the lines, "The poor would love to live here/in this garage of sparkling white-wash,/your storage room." It is one of many poems which do not make easy constructs or present witty comments on life. These poems, even more than John Ashbery's, often seem to start in one place and end without any logical connections. Psychological connections, either. Perhaps the latter is the greatest change to be seen in Wild's work, that he no longer makes an attempt to gratify the reader psychologically. This is a risky step the poet has taken, but one the reader who wants more than delightful images must be very gratified to observe. Perhaps

publishing a premature *New and Selected Poems* at such an early age, then, was a gesture of commitment on his part to leave behind an old vision, not one he would renounce but one he wishes to move forward from? One he wishes his readers to leave behind, as pleasant history, while we look at the new and dangerous future ahead of us.

                                                    —Diane Wakoski

————————

WILLARD, Nancy. American. Born in Ann Arbor, Michigan, 26 June 1936. Educated at the University of Michigan, Ann Arbor (five Hopwood awards), B.A. 1958, Ph.D. in English 1963; Stanford University, California (Woodrow Wilson Fellow), M.A. 1960. Married to Eric Lindbloom; one son. Currently, part-time lecturer in English, Vassar College, Poughkeepsie, New York. Staff member, Broad Loaf Writers Conference, Vermont. Recipient: Devins Memorial Award, 1967; O. Henry Award, for short story, 1970; National Endowment for the Arts grant, 1976; Creative Artists Public Service award; American Library Association Newbery Medal, for children's book, 1982. Agent: Jean V. Naggar, 336 East 73rd Street, New York, New York 10021. Address: 133 College Avenue, Poughkeepsie, New York 12603, U.S.A.

PUBLICATIONS

Verse

In His Country. Ann Arbor, Michigan, Generation, 1966.
Skin of Grace. Columbia, University of Missouri Press, 1967.
A New Herball. Baltimore, Ferdinand Roten Galleries, 1968.
Nineteen Masks for the Naked Poet. Santa Cruz, California, Kayak, 1971.
Carpenter of the Sun. New York, Liveright, 1974.
Household Tales of Moon and Water. New York, Harcourt Brace, 1982.

Verse (for children)

The Merry History of a Christmas Pie, With a Delicious Description of a Christmas Soup. New York, Putnam, 1974.
All on a May Morning. New York, Putnam, 1975.
A Visit to William Blake's Inn: Poems for Innocent and Experienced Travelers. New York, Harcourt Brace, 1981; London, Methuen, 1982.

Novel

Things Invisible to See. New York, Knopf, 1985.

Short Stories

The Lively Anatomy of God. New York, Eakins Press, 1968.
Childhood of the Magician. New York, Liveright, 1973.
Angel in the Parlor: Five Stories and Eight Essays. New York, Harcourt Brace, 1983.

Fiction (for children)

Sailing to Cythera and Other Anatole Stories. New York, Harcourt Brace, 1974.

The Snow Rabbit. New York, Putnam, 1975.
Shoes Without Leather. New York, Putnam, 1976.
The Well-Mannered Balloon. New York, Harcourt Brace, 1976.
Strangers' Bread. New York, Harcourt Brace, 1977.
Simple Pictures Are Best. New York, Harcourt Brace, 1977; London, Collins, 1978.
The Highest Hit. New York, Harcourt Brace, 1978.
Papa's Panda. New York, Harcourt Brace, 1979.
The Island of the Grass King: The Further Adventures of Anatole. New York, Harcourt Brace, 1979.
The Marzipan Moon. New York, Harcourt Brace, 1981.
Uncle Terrible: More Adventures of Anatole. New York, Harcourt Brace, 1982.
The Nightgown of the Sullen Moon. New York, Harcourt Brace, 1983.

Other

Testimony of the Invisible Man: William Carlos Williams, Francis Ponge, Rainer Maria Rilke, Pablo Neruda. Columbia, University of Missouri Press, 1970.

*

Manuscript Collection (children's books): Kerlan Collection, University of Minnesota, Minneapolis.

*   *   *

As if by magic, Nancy Willard transforms the ordinary into the mythic. Like the poet's radio in the sequence "19 Masks for the Naked Poet," she "warms to her subjects,/allows for all points of view." Her mythological poet is asked to teach others how "to walk/naked as a new planet"; and as "His old skin unravels,/he knits it into a new song." Spiritual rebirth and purity of vision abound in Willard's poetry for both adults and children.

In "How to Stuff a Pepper," which appears in both her major collections, *Carpenter of the Sun* and *Household Tales of Moon and Water*, the cook gives the recipe for Willard's poetics. The secret is to approach and behold the luminous by entering into the commonplace:

> Slash open the sleeve
> as if you were cutting a paper lantern,
> and enter a moon, spilled like a melon,
> a fever of pearls,
> a conversation of glaciers.
> It is a temple built to the worship
> of morning light.

In poems about plants and flowers such as Indian pipe, moss, canna lily, fern, mushroom, tulip, strawberry, and, most notably, the pumpkin, her imagination casts a spell and she takes the reader on a journey into realms of mystery.

In "A Humane Society," also included in both major collections, she further reveals the dimensions of her animate universe: "I need a simple room papered with voices." A domestic poet *par excellence* who, because she has a fine ear for manifold voices, can stay at home and yet carry the reader into the marvelous, Willard wittily argues that a world in which animals are excluded is in no way "humane." It is no accident that her young son, the carpenter who repairs the sun, provides the drama in a number of the aptly titled "household tales." With him, the poet re-enters and repossesses the worlds of sun and moon, of fable and fairy tale. Her devotion to learning and rediscovery is announced at the end of "Night Light": "It is time to turn on the moon./It is time to live by a different light."

Like the poet in "19 Masks," Willard has indeed learned to speak "in proverbs to delight the young." Her enthusiasm for the poetry of William Blake comes as no surprise. The epigraph she uses from *The Marriage of Heaven and Hell* for "19 Masks" becomes, in the Newbery Medal-winning *A Visit to William Blake's Inn*, the whole of the concluding "Blake's Advice to Travelers": "He whose face gives no light/will never become a star." Echoing her mythic poet, Willard's Blake says, "We'll start on our journey as children." In this dazzling cycle Willard's versatility, virtuosity, and vision convince us that her powers as a poet are growing and that her star will rise as she continues the journey.

—Norbert Krapf

———

WILLIAMS, C(harles) K(enneth). American. Born in Newark, New Jersey, 4 November 1936. Educated at Bucknell University, Lewisburg, Pennsylvania; University of Pennsylvania, Philadelphia, 1955-59, B.A. 1959. Married 1) Sarah Jones in 1965; 2) Catherine Mauger in 1975; one daughter and one son. Since 1972, Contributing Editor, *American Poetry Review*, Philadelphia. Visiting Professor, Franklin and Marshall College, Lancaster, Pennsylvania, 1977, and University of California, Irvine, 1978. Recipient: Guggenheim Fellowship, 1974. Address: c/o Burning Deck, 71 Elmgrove Avenue, Providence, Rhode Island 02906, U.S.A.

PUBLICATIONS

Verse

A Day for Anne Frank. Philadelphia, Falcon Press, 1968.
Lies. Boston, Houghton Mifflin, 1969.
I Am the Bitter Name. Boston, Houghton Mifflin, 1972.
The Sensuous President. New York, New Rivers Press, 1972.
With Ignorance. Boston, Houghton Mifflin, 1977.
The Lark, The Thrush, The Starling. Providence, Rhode Island, Burning Deck, 1983.
Tar. New York, Random House, 1983.

Other

Translator, with Gregory W. Dickerson, *Women of Trachis*, by Sophocles. New York, Oxford University Press, 1978; London, Oxford University Press, 1979.

*

Critical Studies: by Richard Howard in *Kenyon Review* (Gambier, Ohio), Summer 1970, and in *American Poetry Review* (Philadelphia), November 1972; L.E. Sissman, in *Boston Sun-Globe*, 18 July 1972; Morris Dickstein, in *Parnassus* (New York), Fall 1972, and in *New York Times*, 10 July 1977; Stanley Plumly, in *American Poetry Review* (Philadelphia), January 1978; Dave Smith, in *Western Humanities Review* (Salt Lake City), Autumn 1978.

* * *

"I am uncertain about just about everything—the use of poetry, the form of it," C.K. Williams said, but judging from his early poems, one would never guess that he was uncertain about anything. The tone is swift, almost brittle in its sureness. There Williams, like Thomas Hardy and Stephen Crane before him, shakes his fist in the face of God or god, saying,

> your lists of victims dear
> god like rows of sharp little teeth
> have made me crazy look
> I have crushed by poor balls
> for you I have kissed the blank
> pages drank the pissy chalice
> water and thrown up

Such poems in *Lies* and *I Am the Bitter Name* are concerned principally with desperate, abandoned, but patient souls. Both books end with long poems about specific victims. "Come sit with me here/kiss me; my heart too is wounded/with forgiveness," the speaker says to the young girl, in "The Day for Anne Frank." And "In the Heart of the Beast—May 1970—Cambodia, Kent State, Jackson State," a person tired of forgiving asks:

> this is fresh meat right mr nixon
> this is even sweeter than mickey schwerner
> or fred hampton right?
> even more tender than the cherokee nation or
> guatemala or greece

In an era of death, Williams tells "just what is," "remembering iwo jima remembering the bulge seoul my lai."

Heavy "political" messages are unusual, nonetheless, among poems that belong to the moral or even theological order. An exchange between two Old Testament figures, for example, provided the title for the second book: "Abraham said to him, 'Art thou, indeed, he that is called Death?' He answered, and said 'I am the Bitter Name!'"

In the later volumes, *With Ignorance* and *Tar*, Williams moves in new directions, experimenting with a long, almost casual line and a different voice. The characteristic attitude is suggested by this line in "The Gas Station": "I'm just trying, I think, to keep my head as empty as I/can for as long as I can." In listening to the peculiar sounds, the discordant and violent voices of the present, Williams seems called upon to think things through anew. In such poems, one is aware of that uncertainty mentioned earlier, and Williams's commitment to take nothing for granted. Their vitality indicates also that American language is again on the move.

Carolyn Kizer has called C.K. Williams "the most exciting poet alive." In his promise of things to come, one recognizes the truth of such a statement and looks forward to new poems with the authority and sureness of the older ones.

—Michael True

WILLIAMS, Emmett. American. Born in Greenville, South Carolina, 4 April 1925. Educated at Kenyon College, Gambier, Ohio, B.A. 1949; University of Paris. Served in the United States Army, 1943-46. Married 1) Laura Powell MacCarteney in 1949, two daughters and one son; 2) Ann Noël Stevenson in 1970, one son. Lived in Europe, 1949-66: assistant to the ethnologist Paul Radin; associated with the Darmstadt group of concrete poets; Founding Member of the Domaine Poetique, Paris; European Coordinator of the Fluxus group. Editor, Something Else Press, New York, 1966-70. Artist-in-Residence, Fairleigh Dickinson University, Madison, New Jersey, 1968, and University of Kentucky, Lexington, 1969; Professor of Critical Studies, California Institute of the Arts, Valencia, 1970-72; Visiting Professor of Art, Nova Scotia College of Art and Design, Halifax, 1972-74; Visiting Artist, Mount Holyoke College, South Hadley, Massachusetts, 1975-77; Visiting Lecturer, Carpenter Center for the Visual Arts, Harvard University, Cambridge, Massachusetts, 1977-80; Artist-in-Residence, Berliner Künstler Programm, 1980. Since 1981, Artist-in-Residence and Guest Professor, Hochschule der Künste, Berlin, and Hochschule für bildender Künste, Hamburg. Recipient: National Endowment for the Arts fellowship, 1979. Address: c/o DAAD, Berliner Künstler Programm, Steinplatz 2, D-1000 Berlin 12, West Germany.

PUBLICATIONS

Verse

Konkretionen. Darmstadt, Germany, Material, 1958.
13 Variations on 6 Words by Gertrude Stein (1958). Cologne, Galerie der Spiegel, 1965.
Rotapoems. Stuttgart, Hansjörg Mayer, 1966.
The Last French-Fried Potato and Other Poems. New York, Something Else Press, 1967.
Sweethearts. Stuttgart, Hansjörg Mayer, 1967; New York, Something Else Press, 1968.
The Book of Thorn and Eth. Stuttgart, Hansjörg Mayer, 1968.
The Boy and the Bird. Stuttgart, Hansjörg Mayer, and New York, Wittenborn, 1968; new edition, illustrated by the author, Stuttgart and London, Hansjörg Mayer, 1979.
A Valentine for Noël. Stuttgart, Hansjörg Mayer, 1973.
Selected Shorter Poems 1950-1970. Stuttgart, Hansjörg Mayer, 1974; New York, New Directions, 1975.
The Voyage. Stuttgart, Hanjörg Mayer, 1975.
Faustzeichnungen, illustrated by the author. Berlin, Rainer, 1983.
A Little Night Book, illustrated by Keith Godard. New York, Works, 1983.

Plays

Ja, Es war noch da (produced Darmstadt, Germany, 1960). Published in *Nota 4* (Munich), 1960; as *Yes It Was Still There* (produced New York, 1965).
A Cellar Song for 5 Voices (produced New York, 1961).
4-Directional Song of Doubt for 5 Voices (produced Wiesbaden, Germany, 1962).
The Ultimate Poem (produced Arras, France, 1964).

Other

Six Variations upon a Spoerri Landscape: A Suite of Lithographs. Halifax, Nova Scotia College of Art and Design Lithography Workshop, 1973.
Zodiac (lithographs). Tokyo, Gallery Birthday Star, 1974.
Schemes and Variations (autobiographical essays and illustrations). Berlin, Nationalgalerie, and Stuttgart and London, Hansjörg Mayer, 1981.
Holdup (photodrama), with Keith Godard. New York, Works, 1981.

Chicken Feet, Duck Limbs, and Dada Handshakes. Vancouver, Western Front, 1984.

Editor, *Poésie et cetera américaine.* Paris, Biennale, 1963.
Editor, *An Anthology of Concrete Poetry.* New York, Something Else Press, 1967.
Editor, *Store Days,* by Claes Oldenburg. New York, Something Else Press, 1967.
Editor, "Language Happenings," in *Open Poetry: Four Anthologies of Expanded Poems.* New York, Simon and Schuster, 1973.

Translator, *An Anecdoted Topography of Chance...,* by Daniel Spoerri. New York, Something Else Press, 1966.
Translator, *The Mythological Travels of a Modern Sir John Mandeville...,* by Daniel Spoerri. New York, Something Else Press, 1970.
Translator, *Mythology and Meatballs: A Greek Island Diary-Cookbook,* by Daniel Spoerri. Berkeley, California, Aris, 1982.

*

Bibliography: in *Schemes and Variations,* 1981.

Manuscript Collections: Sohm Archive, Staatsgalerie, Stuttgart; Sackner Archive, Miami.

*   *   *

Emmett Williams's name is better known than his poetry, and one reason for this discrepancy is that he edited *An Anthology of Concrete Poetry,* which has outsold its competitors (including an anthology of mine), while most of his poetry remains unpublished, particularly in his native country. Unlike other American writers of his generation, Williams became closely involved, back in the 1950's, with the European intermedia avant-garde, epitomized by the "Darmstadt Circle," in which he figured prominently. By the sixties, he was an initiator of Fluxus, an international post-Dada, mixed-means movement which won considerable attention at the time (but has so far escaped most historians of contemporary art and literature). Thus, his writing reflects, to an unusual degree, the experimental tradition in the non-literary arts. He echoed not Dylan Thomas but Kurt Schwitters, for instance, in his early "performance poems," to use the term that refers to poems whose most appropriate form is not the printed page but live performance.

It was Williams's good fortune to learn, back in the 1950's, that English-language poetry could be composed in radically alternative ways—different not only from the academic poetry of that time but also from the declamatory expressionism of, say, Allen Ginsberg. Instead, Williams pioneered the art of "concrete poetry," in which the poet eschews conventional syntax (and related devices) to organize language in other ways. Rather than "free form" (whatever that might be), Williams favored such severe constraints as repetition, permutation, and linguistic minimalism. His masterpiece, the book-length *Sweethearts,* consists of one word (the title) whose eleven letters are visually distributed over 150 or so sequentially expressive pages, the work as a whole relating the evolution of a man-woman relationship. Like Williams's other work, *Sweethearts* is extremely witty; and like much else in experimental writing, it must be seen (and read) for its magic to be believed.

—Richard Kostelanetz

WILLIAMS, (David) Gwyn. British (Welsh). Born in Port Talbot, Glamorgan, 24 August 1904. Educated at Port Talbot Grammar School; University College of Wales, Aberystwyth, B.A. 1925; Jesus College, Oxford, M.A. 1944. Married twice; three sons and two daughters. Schoolteacher in Egypt, 1927-35; Lecturer in English Literature, Cairo University, 1935-42; Assistant Professor of English, Alexandria University, 1942-51; free-lance writer, 1951-56, and since 1969; Professor of English, University of Libya, Benghazi, 1956-61; Professor of English Literature, Istanbul University, 1961-69. Recipient: Welsh Arts Council Prize, 1977. Agent: Curtis Brown, 162-168 Regent Street, London W1R 5TA, England. Address: 40 Queen Street, Aberystwyth, Dyfed SY23 1PU, Wales.

PUBLICATIONS

Verse

Inns of Love: Selected Poems. Llandybie, Dyfed, Christopher Davies, 1970.
Foundation Stock. Llandysul, Dyfed, Gomer, 1974.
Choose Your Stranger. Poet Talbot, Glamorgan, Alun, 1979.
Y ddefod goll (The Lost Rite). Port Talbot, Glamorgan, Alun, 1980.

Novels

This Way to Lethe. London, Faber, 1962.
The Avocet. Swansea, Christopher Davies, 1970.
Two Sketches of Womanhood. Swansea, Christopher Davies, 1975.
Y cloc tywod (The Sand Clock). Talybont, Y Lolfa, 1984.

Other

An Introduction to Welsh Poetry from the Beginning to the Sixteenth Century. London, Faber, and Philadelphia, Dufour and Saifer, 1953.
Green Mountain: An Informal Guide to Cyrenaica and Jebel Akhdar. London, Faber, 1963.
Turkey: A Traveller's Guide and History. London, Faber, 1967.
Eastern Turkey. London, Faber, 1972.
Twrci a'i Phobl. Cardiff, Gwasg y Dref Wen, 1975.
To Look for a Word: Collected Translations from Welsh Poetry. Llandysul, Dyfed, Gomer, 1976.
The Land Remembers: A View of Wales. London, Faber, 1977.
An Introduction to Welsh Literature. Cardiff, University of Wales Press, 1978.
ABC of (D)GW: A Kind of Autobiography. Llandysul, Dyfed, Gomer, 1980.
Person and Persona: Studies in Shakespeare. Cardiff, University of Wales Press, 1981.

Editor, *Presenting Welsh Poetry: An Anthology of Welsh Verse in Translation and of English Verse by Welsh Poets.* London, Faber, 1959.
Editor, *Troelus a Chresyd.* Llandysul, Dyfed, Gomer, 1976.

Translator, *The Rent That's Due to Love.* London, Editions Poetry London, 1950.
Translator, *Against Women.* London, Golden Cockerel Press, 1953.

Translator, *The Burning Tree: Poems from the First Thousand Years of Welsh Verse.* London, Faber, 1956; revised edition, as *Welsh Poems: Sixth Century to 1600,* 1973; Berkeley, University of California Press, 1974.

Translator, *In Defence of Woman: A Welsh Poem,* by William Cynwal. London, Golden Cockerel Press, 1960.

*

Manuscript Collection: National Library of Wales, Aberystwyth.

Critical Study: *The Cost of Strangeness* by Anthony Conran, Llandysul, Dyfed, Gomer, 1982.

Gwyn Williams comments:

I have long thought that I wrote a poem when an experience or a thought occurred, usually in Wales or around the eastern end of the Mediterranean, which called for a poem to express it, and that it then broke away from me to an independent life, unless it stayed as an object on my mental mantel-shelf, to be taken down sometimes and dusted. A long poem, "Charlemagne in Constantinople," 1970, orbited away quite quickly, bearing several bees from my bonnet. But I publish because the act of communication is part of the creation. One is not a poet unless one is accepted as a poet. Publication is a channel for the poet's urge to induce some order into the apparently absurd universe, to place himself in partial relationship with the universe about him. He may thus help his reader towards a similar integration. A social function. In recent years I have written rather more in Welsh than in English, sometimes allowing an impulse to develop collaterally in both languages. Technically I have learnt most from translating Welsh poetry I like into English verse. (For my ideas on the nature and practice of poetry see "Letter to a Grandson," *Poetry Wales,* Autumn 1980.)

*   *   *

Gwyn Williams has won a high reputation as a translator of Welsh poetry. He has also written a fine travel book, *Turkey,* among many other volumes. He has travelled widely, and spent much of his working life teaching literature at universities in the Near East.

His selected poems, *Inns of Love,* shows how the better verse translators also happen to be good poets in their own right. Like Pound's, the output of Professor Williams may be seen at its best when working through other literatures, as if he needs a framework of translation to keep his intellect and imagination at full stretch. He uses the past, and masterpieces in other languages, as a sort of combined filter for his own peculiar vision.

The most ambitious poem in this spendidly entertaining collection is "Charlemagne in Constantinople," which occupies almost half the book. It is a long narrative work about Charlemagne's legendary encounter with Hu Gadarn in Byzantium, based on the medieval Welsh version of the story in the 14th-century *Red Book of Hergest.* A highly individual treatment, one of its most intriguing features is the daring manner in which Williams employs an obtrusive 20th-century narrator—eloquent, flamboyant, witty, ironic—who marshals his characters, comments, draws parallels to their actions, juxtaposes past and present, legend and contemporary reality, and surveys the European and Eastern scenes of the story through the centuries. This produces a certain shock effect which might bring howls of protest from purists, but the method largely succeeds with the verve of its conversational style:

> Byzantium is the separate city, the ultimate Cokayne
> or the golden point of departure into decline;
> vision of a viable order or retreat into
> a fabricated region of potency; the landing
> on the Moon or the two-gun man doing
> his best with Eskimo Nell. As a ticket of entry you present
> bones, Mary's milk, the pill, the plunging neckline,
> the sports car, the space rocket or a glossy work on cooking.

This concluding passage, with a vigorous and almost vulgar tone, justifies itself by the way in which it clarifies Williams's interpretation of his source, not treating it as a "museum piece gathering scholarly dust but as a living work of art." Looking deeply into the distant past becomes a way of understanding the present.

In another poem, "City under Snow," a fairly conventional subject evokes a fresh response:

> Mosques into snow-palaces; banks, bagnios,
> party headquarters and apartment blocks
> acquire an innocence; L.S. Lowry figures
> lean into flocked air;
>
> spittle, pigeon-dung, dogshit and broken
> glass, the layer of soot all iced over and
> a new fall powders the cleaned crotches
> of cobbled alleys.

Generally, *Inns of Love* and the later poems are the work of a writer for whom places remain important as nodal points where lines usually thought of as time, sensory impression, tradition, and a view of life intersect. And so the places in which he has lived and worked—Egypt, Libya, Turkey, and now Wales—are more than a background: they form an integral part of the experience which is the poem. Entry into the nature of a place eliminates the illusion of time and throws "hooks into the self," as Williams would put it.

The accomplishment of Gwyn Williams as a valuable verse-translator is considerable, and few more erudite and cultivated men have emerged from Wales—an academic who is yet very much involved in living and the future of his own country. He has recently made a separate, if less permanent, reputation on television as an articulate guide to the long history and archaeology of Wales.

—John Tripp

WILLIAMS, Hugo (Mordaunt). British. Born in Windsor, Berkshire, 20 February 1942; son of the actor and playwright Hugh Williams. Educated at Eton College, 1955-60. Married Hermine Demoriane in 1965; one daughter. Staff writer, *Telegraph Magazine,* London, 1965; Assistant Editor, *London Magazine,* 1966-70; Henfield Fellow, University of East Anglia, Norwich, 1981. Currently, television critic and poetry editor, *New Statesman,* London. Recipient: Eric Gregory Award, 1966; Arts Council bursary, 1966; Cholmondeley Award, 1971; Faber Memorial Prize, 1980. Address: 3 Raleigh Street, London N.1, England.

PUBLICATIONS

Verse

Symptoms of Loss. London and New York, Oxford University Press, 1965.
Poems. London, The Review, 1969.
Sugar Daddy. London and New York, Oxford University Press, 1970.
Cherry Blossom. London, Poem-of-the-Month Club, 1972.
Some Sweet Day. London and New York, Oxford University Press, 1975.
Love-Life. London, Whizzard Press, 1979.

Recording: *British Poets of Our Times*, with Adrian Henri, Argo.

Other

All the Time in the World (travel). London, Alan Ross, 1966; Philadelphia, Chilton, 1968.
No Particular Place to Go (travel). London, Cape, 1981.

Editor, *"London Magazine" Poems, 1961-1966*. London, Alan Ross, 1966.

*   *   *

Hugo Williams has been one of those poets—Colin Falck and David Harsent are others—most closely associated with the magazines *The Review* and *The New Review*. The poems particularly admired by Ian Hamilton, the editor of these journals and a central presence in the criticism of contemporary English poetry, have several immediately recognisable characteristics. They are almost always short, sometimes very short indeed; their subject matter is almost always domestic, amatory, familial, concerned with the minutiae of personal relationships; they almost always attempt a tight-lipped, tough-minded, very "English" stance in relation to the emotions they describe; and yet their characteristic cadences are, nevertheless, almost always plangent, melancholy, nostalgic. For a poetry that makes claims to speak with honesty about the casual exigencies of modern living, this poetry can sometimes sound disconcertingly close to the wan debilitation of the *fin-de-siècle*.

Williams himself provides ample opportunity for making these generalisations and strictures, and for adding those of inconsequentiality and an almost adolescent self-absorption and sentimentality. This, for instance, is a poem called "Once More with Feeling" in its entirety:

> My voice breaks
> And I know it must be time
> To pour out my heart to you again.
>
> Believe me,
> I would like to make you cry
> This once,
> But you smile encouragingly,
> Prepared to understand.

This is a message that I cannot be alone in wishing Williams had addressed in an envelope, and then forgotten about, rather than thinking it worthy of preservation in a published book. And his own disarming admissions—"Don't tell me, I know/I'm mumbling to myself again," he says in "The Ribbon"—which are

presumably intended to charm us out of hostility, should not be allowed to do so.

But there is a more interesting side to Williams; and this is largely a matter of his ability to make the very ordinary and prosaic seem suddenly extraordinary and resonantly mysterious by verbalising odd, tangential perceptions, sometimes in an ambiguously wayward syntax. This is "Holidays":

> We spread our things on the sand
> In front of the hotel
> And sit for hours on end
> Like merchants under parasols
> Our thoughts following the steamers
> In convoy across the bay
> While far away
> Our holidays look back at us in surprise
> From fishing boats and fairs
> Or wherever they were going then
> In their seaweed head-dresses.

Like the holidays here, the end of this singular sentence looks back at its beginning in surprise, wondering how it had ever started out there, or ended up here. Whether we read "they" in the penultimate line as referring to "holidays" or "fishing boats and fairs," or, somehow, to both, the effect of the really very strange statement being made is to set the whole poem in front of a kind of distorting mirror, performing crazily acrobatic feats with its facial muscles. And—a feeling reinforced by the ghostly presence of J. Alfred Prufrock in the final line—the poem is distinctly disturbing, like a sudden gust of sand on an otherwise peaceful beach.

This note echoes sufficiently in Williams to provide sustenance in thin volumes that would otherwise seem a little too precious, surrounding the undoubted delicacy of their perceptions with so much white space. The best of Williams—as in the early poem "The Butcher"—is a depth of unease that goes a long way beyond the wry, bemused, or ironical poses he is often too readily content with:

> I think he knows about my life. How we prefer
> To eat in when it's cold. How someone
>
> With a foreign accent can only cook veal.
> He writes the price on the grease-proof packet
>
> And hands it to me courteously. His smile
> Is the official seal on my marriage.

—Neil Corcoran

_____

WILLIAMS, John Stuart. British (Welsh). Born in Mountain Ash, Glamorgan, 13 August 1920. Educated at Mountain Ash County School; University College, Cardiff, B.A. (honours) in English literature, M.A. Married Sheelagh Williams in 1948; two sons. Formerly, English Master, Whitchurch Grammar School, Glamorgan, and Head of the Department of English and Drama, City of Cardiff College of Education; Head of Department of Communications, South Glamorgan Institute of Higher Education, Cardiff, from 1977, now retired. Member of the Welsh Arts Council Literature Committee, 1973-77. Composer. Member, English Section, Welsh Academy (Yr Academi

Gymreig). Recipient: Welsh Arts Council prize, 1971. Address: 52 Dan-y-Coed Road, Cyncoed, Cardiff CF4 6HE, Wales.

PUBLICATIONS

Verse

Last Fall. London, Outposts, 1962.
Green Rain. Llandybie, Dyfed, Christopher Davies, 1967.
Dic Penderyn and Other Poems. Llandysul, Dyfed, Gomer, 1970.
Banna Strand: Poems 1970-74. Llandysul, Dyfed, Gomer, 1975.

Other

Editor, with Richard Milner, *Dragons and Daffodils.* Llandybie, Dyfed, Christopher Davies, 1960.
Editor, with Meic Stephens, *The Lilting House: An Anthology of Anglo-Welsh Poetry 1917-1967.* Llandybie, Dyfed, Christopher Davies, and London, Dent, 1969.
Editor, *Poems '69.* Llandysul, Dyfed, Gomer, 1969.

*

Manuscript Collection: National Library of Wales, Aberystwyth.

Critical Studies: in *Outposts* (London), Winter 1967; introduction by Roland Mathias, to *Green Rain*, 1967; *An Introduction to Anglo-Welsh Literature* by Raymond Garlick, Cardiff, University of Wales Press, 1970, revised edition, 1972; Alun Rees, in *Poetry Wales* (Cardiff), Winter 1976.

John Stuart Williams comments:

I was born and brought up in a sceptically anglicised mining community which had few problems about its identity; it was stubbornly Welsh, and had small faith in easy solutions. It was a place of sharp contrasts: the open hill was a short step from the coalpits in the centre of town and we were often reminded of death by the colliery hooter signalling an accident underground. A sense of the ambiguity of reality has remained with me and much of my work is an attempt to establish footholds in place and time from which to explore this and the obliquity of our personal and national myths. "Banna Strand," first published in *Decal Poetry Review* is a recent example:

> In my raincoat pocket, a faded carnet de bal;
> the stillness of mist, a girl on horseback
> frightened by something other than the sea,
> watching, waiting;
> such a pretty little beach...
> Is it my business what they do,
> what answers may come with sudden gardens?
> I am not Control,
> Hoofs in the shallows,
> fear in shadows coursing along the wet sand,
> the sharp fountains of sprayed light...
> What do you see through your Ross?
> A misleading group, windblown hair
> falsely suggesting private warmth.
> Everything is coded, graffiti on old stone,
> on Banna strand or beside the midland sea.

After writing this I was disconcerted to find that Banna strand was where Casement had landed in Ireland for the last fatal time.

It would be easy and misleading to isolate literary influences, as my first lessons in rhythm came from music and the cinema. From the first I learned that rhythm is more subtle than traditional metric easily allows, and from the second I first learned about montage and the inter-relation of images, something later confirmed in conversations with the late John Grierson. The reading came later. The natural order of words is important to me even when I write in more obviously traditional forms, for it is against this pattern that I try to work my variations. This sometimes misfires, for what is natural to me, a valleys Welshman, may be different from what seems so to others. The danger inherent in my subject-matter is compounded in this way. One man's *déjà vu* is, in any case, sometimes another's boredom. But this is a risk I have to take:

> Listening to silence,
> I praise both light and darkness.

*   *   *

John Stuart Williams's premier achievement is a long dramatic poem, "Dic Penderyn," originally written for radio, which won a Welsh Arts Council prize in 1971. It is the story of the Merthyr Riots of 1831, the conflict between the workers and ironmasters, the violence and reprisals, and the struggle of men for free and decent lives. Dic Penderyn himself was the figure at the centre of the trouble: he wounded a Highlander (one of the troops brought in to quell the riots) and was later hanged at Cardiff. In this impressive poem, Penderyn focuses most of the emotion, as he did in real life among the oppressed ironworkers. (There are also four narrators who impersonate characters in the story, plus several lyrics for a folksinger.) Williams's treatment is what might be termed poetic documentary—accurate, clear, and ordered, with the dramatic tension mounting effectively to its climax. The poetry contributes sinewy and colourful language to the sweep of events, linking images of blood, metal, fire, and nature:

> And the fierce summer leaps in
> With torchlight red on broken glass.
> The throbbing pulse grows louder,
> Until the whole town drowns
> In the blind heat of a dull drum.

Williams's individual poems are usually short, neat impressionistic pieces, resembling attractive snapshots, with titles like "Gironde," "River Walk," or "Beach at Ifracombe." One criticism levelled at him is that these rather "gnomic" poems briefly interest and entertain, but are essentially inconsequential. Apart from "Dic Penderyn," Williams's craft may be a modest one, but it is also a true one, honestly attained. There is a place in literature, as in painting, for the miniature water-colour, even though the heavy guns of contemporary criticism would have us believe otherwise. This particular, largely unsentimental Welsh miniaturist has a good deal to offer in the way of fresh observation and disinterested understanding. He can often breathe life into the oldest stock scenes and the most ordinary, banal moments.

—John Tripp

WILLIAMS, Jonathan (Chamberlain). American. Born in Asheville, North Carolina, 8 March 1929. Educated at St. Albans School, Washington, D.C., 1941-47; Princeton University, New Jersey, 1947-49; Atelier 17, New York, 1949-50; Institute of Design, Chicago, 1951; Black Mountain College, North Carolina, 1951-56. Conscientious Objector: served in the United States Army Medical Corps, 1952-53. Since 1951, Executive Director, The Jargon Society, Inc., publishers, Highlands, North Carolina. Scholar-in-Residence, Aspen Institute, Colorado, 1962, 1967-68, and Maryland Institute College of Art, Baltimore, 1968-69; Poet-in-Residence, University of Kansas, Lawrence, 1971, and University of Delaware, Newark, 1977. Since 1980, Curator, Jargon Society Archive, State University of New York, Buffalo. Photographer: individual show—Southeastern Center for Contemporary Art, Winston-Salem, North Carolina, 1981. Recipient: Guggenheim Fellowship, 1957; Longview Foundation grant, 1960; National Endowment for the Arts grant, 1968, 1969, 1970, 1973, 1977, 1978; Coordinating Council of Little Magazines award, 1974; Carey-Thomas award, for publishing, 1977. D.H.L.: Maryland Institute College of Art, 1969. Address: Highlands, North Carolina 28741, U.S.A.; or, Corn Close, Dentdale, Sedbergh, Cumbria, England.

PUBLICATIONS

Verse

Garbage Litters the Iron Face of the Sun's Child. San Francisco, Jargon, 1951.
Red Gray. Black Mountain, North Carolina, Jargon, 1952.
Four Stoppages. Stuttgart, Jargon, 1953.
Lord! Lord! Lord! Highlands, North Carolina, Jargon, 1959.
The Empire Finals at Verona. Highlands, North Carolina, Jargon, 1960.
Amen Huzza Selah. Black Mountain, North Carolina, Jargon, 1960.
Elegies and Celebrations. Highlands, North Carolina, Jargon, 1962.
In England's Green & (A Garland and a Clyster). San Francisco, Auerhahn Press, 1962.
Emblems for the Little Dells and Nooks and Corners of Paradise. London, Jargon, 1962.
The Macon County North Carolina Meshuga Sound Society, Jonathan Williams, Musical Director, Presents: Lullabies, Twisters, Gibbers, Drags (à la manière de M. Louis Moreau Gottschalk, late of the City of New Orleans). London, Jargon, 1963.
Petite Concrete Concrete Suite. Detroit, Fenian Head Centre Press, 1965.
Twelve Jargonelles from the Herbalist's Notebook. Bloomington, Indiana University Design Department, 1965.
Ten Jargonelles from the Herbalist's Notebook. Urbana, University of Illinois Design Department, 1966.
Four Jargonelles from the Herbalist's Notebook. Cambridge, Massachusetts, Lowell, 1966.
Paean to Dvorak, Deemer, and McClure. San Francisco, Dave Haselwood, 1966.
Affilati Attrezzi Per I Giardini di Catullo (bilingual edition). Milan, Lerici Editore, 1966.
Mahler Becomes Politics, Beisbol. London, Marlborough Gallery, 1967.
50! Epiphytes, -taphs, -tomes, -grams, -thets! 50! London, Poet and Printer, 1967.
A French 75! San Francisco, Dave Haselwood, 1967.
Polycotyledonous Poems. Stuttgart, Hansjörg Mayer, 1967.

The Lucidities: Sixteen in Visionary Company. London, Turret, 1967.
Eight Jargonelles from the Herbalist's Notebook. Bloomington, Indiana University Design Department, 1967.
LTGD. Bloomington, Indiana University Design Department, 1967.
Les Six Pak. Aspen, Colorado, Aspen Institute, 1967.
Sharp Tools for Catullan Gardens. Bloomington, Indiana University Fine Arts Department, 1968.
Ripostes. Stuttgart, Domberger, 1969.
An Ear in Bartram's Tree: Selected Poems 1957-67. Chapel Hill, University of North Carolina Press, 1969.
On Arriving at the Same Age as Jack Benny. Urbana, Illinois, Finial Press, 1969.
Mahler. London, Cape Goliard Press, 1969.
Six Rusticated, Wall-Eyed Poems. Baltimore, Maryland Institute Press, 1969.
The New Architectural Monuments of Baltimore City. Baltimore, Maryland Institute Press, 1970.
The Apocryphal Oracular Yeah-Sayings of Mae West. Baltimore, Maryland Institute Press, 1970.
Strung Out with Elgar on a Hill. Urbana, Illinois, Finial Press, 1971.
Blues and Roots, Rue and Bluets: A Garland for the Appalachians. New York, Grossman, 1971.
The Loco Logodaedalist in Situ: Selected Poems 1968-70. London, Cape Goliard Press, 1971; New York, Grossman, 1972.
Epitaph, with Thomas Meyer. Privately printed, 1972.
Fruits Confits, with Thomas Meyer. Privately printed, 1972.
Adventures with a Twelve-Inch Pianist Beyond the Blue Horizon. N.p., DBA, 1973.
Who Is Little Enis? Highlands, North Carolina, Jargon, 1974.
Five from Up t'Dale. Kendal, Cumbria, Finial Press, 1974.
Pairidaeza. Dentdale, Cumbria, Jargon, 1975.
Hasidic Exclamation on Stevie Smith's Poem "Not Waving But Drowning." Storrs, University of Connecticut Library, 1975.
My Quaker-Atheist Friend. London, Philip Bryden, 1975.
Gists from a Presidential Report on Hardcornponeography. Highlands, North Carolina, Jargon, 1975.
A Wee Tot for Catullus. Nailsworth, Gloucestershire, Moschatel Press, 1975.
A Celestial Centennial Reverie for Charles Edward Ives. N.p., DBA, 1975.
Imaginary Postcards. London, Trigram Press, 1975.
gAy BC's. Champaign, Illinois, Finial Press, 1976.
In the Field at the Solstice. Champaign, Illinois, Finial Press, 1976.
Untinears and Antennae for Maurice Ravel. St. Paul, Truck Press, 1977.
An Omen for Stevie Smith. New Haven, Connecticut, Yale University Sterling Library, 1977.
A Blue Ridge Weather Prophet. Frankfort, Kentucky, Gnomon Press, 1977.
Super-Duper Zuppa Inglese. Belper, Derbyshire, Aggie Weston's, 1977.
A Blue Ridge Weather Prophet Makes Twelve Stitches in Time on the Twelfth Day of Christmas. Frankfort, Kentucky, Gnomon Press, 1977.
A Hairy Coat near Yanwath Yat. Rocky Mount, North Carolina Wesleyan College, 1978.
Elite/Elate Poems: Poems 1971-1975. Highlands, North Carolina, Jargon, 1979.
Shankum Naggum. Rocky Mount, North Carolina Wesleyan College Friends of the Library, 1979.
The Delian Seasons. N.p., Topia Press, 1979.
St. Swithin's Swivet. Guildford, Surrey, Circle Press, 1979.

Glees, Swarthy Monotonies, Rince Cochon, and Chozzerai for Simon. N.p., DBA, 1979.
Homage Umbrage Quibble and Chicane. N.p., DBA, 1980.
Get Hot or Get Out: A Selection of Poems 1957-1981. Metuchen, New Jersey, Scarecrow Press, 1982.

Other

Lines about Hills above Lakes. Fort Lauderdale, Florida, Roman, 1964.
Descant on Rawthey's Madrigal: Conversations with Basil Bunting. Lexington, Kentucky, Gnomon Press, 1968.
The Appalachian Photographs of Doris Ulmann. Highlands, North Carolina, Jargon, 1971.
Clarence John Laughlin: The Personal Eye. New York, Aperture, 1973.
The Family Album of Lucybelle Crater. Highlands, North Carolina, Jargon, 1974.
T. Ben Williams. Highlands, North Carolina, Jargon, 1974.
How What? Collages, Texts, Photographs. Dublin, Georgia, Mole Press, 1975.
Portrait Photographs. Frankfort, Kentucky, Gnomon Press, and London, Coracle, 1979.
Jonathan Williams: A Poet Collects (exhibition catalog). Winston-Salem, North Carolina, Southeastern Center for Contemporary Art, 1981.
The Magpie's Bagpipe (essays). Berkeley, California, North Point Press, 1982.

Editor, *Edward Dahlberg: A Tribute.* New York, David Lewis, 1970.
Editor, *Epitaphs for Lorine: 33 Poets Celebrate Lorine Niedecker.* Highlands, North Carolina, Jargon, 1973.
Editor, *The Sleep of Reason,* by Lyle Bonge. Highlands, North Carolina, Jargon, 1974.
Editor, *Madeira and Toasts for Basil Bunting's 75th Birthday.* Highlands, North Carolina, Jargon, 1977.
Editor, *I Shall Save One Land Unvisited: Eleven Southern Photographers.* Frankfort, Kentucky, Gnomon Press, 1978.

*

Manuscript Collections: Jargon Society Archive, University of North Carolina, Chapel Hill, and State University of New York, Buffalo.

Critical Studies: introduction by Guy Davenport to *An Ear in Bartram's Tree: Selected Poems 1957-67,* 1969; "The Sound of Our Speaking" by Robert Morgan, in *The Nation* (New York), 6 September 1971; Herbert Leibowitz, in *New York Times Book Review,* 21 November 1971; Raymond Gardner, in *The Guardian* (London), 3 July 1972; in *Vort 4* (Silver Spring, Maryland), 1973; *Fiftieth Birthday Celebration for Jonathan Williams* edited by Jonathan Greene, Frankfort, Kentucky, Truck-Gnomon Press, 1979.

Jonathan Williams comments:

I am primarily a poet, but since we do not live for ourselves alone I have always assumed (since 1951) that the publishing of my poetic enthusiasms was part of the job. And the reading of poems aloud to audiences—which I have done approximately 850 times from Vancouver to Wien.

I have been called a Black Mountain Poet, a Beat Poet, a Southern-Poetry-Today Poet, a Light Poet, an Informalist Poet, a Formalist Poet, a Concrete Poet, a Found-Object Poet, a Relentlessly and Tiresomely Avant-garde Poet. To my knowledge all I am is a poet, like anyone else, I write as I can.

The masters of delectation and precision are my mentors: Blake, Marvell, Buson, Archilochos, Martial, Catullus, Dickinson, Ono no Komachi, Basho, and Whitman. From more immediate times: Pound, William Carlos Williams, Robinson Jeffers, Kenneth Patchen, Kenneth Rexroth, Charles Olson, Ian Hamilton Finlay, Stevie Smith, Basil Bunting, J.V. Cunningham...I use all the devices I know, all the tricks in Orpheus's black bag—if it is possible to move rocks and trees, it is just possible to keep ice from forming in other human hearts. Poems are passionate things to give courage to those who respond to their messages. I write for those who long for the saving grace of the language. I never write for Laodiceans. The gentle reader and I are going to go round and round. Richard of St. Victor teaches us that in art and in life there are more things to love than we could possibly have imagined. *Odi et amo,* said Catullus. I want Catullus in the poems, and Willie Mays and Thomas Jefferson and Charles Ives and Apollo and hill farmers and people who talk trash. The language is airy, earthy, Regency, witty, offensive, etc.—whatever it needs to be. This is your friendly Local, Ecological Logodaedalist talking.

*   *   *

Like most folk remedies, Jonathan Williams's poems have a little vinegar in them. They can either be celebratory (as witness his many epitaphs) or meant to increase circulation by chaffing. He recognizes that poems can be jokes, in their compression and timing, and that timing can have a greater effectiveness than sincerity or moral indignation. God is Pun. No ear bends our own closer to the intricacies of words, the multiplicity of play possible in a word, than Williams's. More a lodestone than semi-precious, he's got a nose for irony, and finds it everywhere in the world around him.

He is a public-spirited private man, who keeps gravestones swept clean and foibles clear of hypocrisy. Since sexuality is one of the most abused of our notions, it gets a good deal of Williams's attention. A man of judgment, he honors and condemns. He's an incessant observer, constantly contrasting *haute monde* with down home. He knows the *moeurs* of his people; he sizes up a culture in a flash:

> come on,
> Gene
>
> the
> Boogers
> got
>
> Lummy Jean Licklighter
>
> in an attic
> over near Viper!

For Williams, the first American poem might have been the one carved by Daniel Boone on a tree after he killed his first bear, unless it was the one on the tree at Roanoke Colony—wherever people have invested in words, whatever they have trusted to the permanence of letters. His is a poetry of use, whether as cenotaph or whammy-diddle, such as that whittled by his acquaintance Sam Ward. I hear America singing: "o the Smokies are ok but me/I go for Theosophy,/higher things, Hindu-type philosophy,/none of this licker and sex...." Wherever there is man there are sneezes, scratching, and foibles.

In terms of recent literature, he's a Ben Franklin, another active man in the world, or else why "Aunt Creasy, On Work": "shucks/I make the livin/uncle/just makes the livin worthwhile"? And not just American or Appalachian, either. This, from Bessie from the Hebrides:

> well then, what do you do
> with all the steel wool
> you steal?
>
> well then,
> I'm knittin'
> a kettle!

Oh, he can get to scowling and scolding when he wants to ("Cobwebbery"), but it's a modest enough goal he's after: "The poet, as ever, has little to offer but the veracity of his ears and eyes, in the hope he has kept them sharp and affectionate." Yet neighborhoods, universities, cities, may rise or fall on such a principle.

His is a primitivism combined with a nobility of outlook and refined exactitude. He is rarely introspective; all that searching, one senses, goes on *before* he discovers the poem. He and Twain would have conversed famously. He is rarely descriptive, seldom prescriptive, but unusually perceptive. Is he a Luddite? Was Samuel Johnson? There seems to be a forgiving quality before any hauteur has a chance to take hold. He is one of the few poets about whom it could be said, he has never bored a reader. That's because it can be said there isn't anything he doesn't find interesting. Inertia doesn't stand a chance. Pick up, shake, sniff, squint at, and put back exactly where he's found it, or slightly atilt in a new light. He handles every word, every name, to see if it rattles, to find if it reverberates with primary or secondary meanings.

He has been the Ideal Reader for about fifty of our best writers and musicians and photographers, including Bunting, Dahlberg, Olson, W.C. Williams, Mingus, Meatyard, Siskind, it's no wonder he's got fifty "cosmic" readers in return, who are loyal to him like initiates of a cargo cult. Perhaps loyalty more than any other value besides wit is what he commands. What sort of man sets out to be an epigrammist for our times? One who insists on the last word, a man fearful of his own oblivion, an upholder of the value of friendship, a thrifty man cleansed of cynicism. Heaven knows, it requires as much energy to chisel an inscription as to let loose a heart.

—George F. Butterick

WILLIAMS, Miller. American. Born in Hoxie, Arkansas, 8 April 1930. Educated at Arkansas State College, Conway, B.S. in biology 1951; University of Arkansas, Fayetteville, M.S. in zoology 1952. Married 1) Lucille Day in 1951 (divorced); 2) Rebecca Jordan Hall in 1969; two daughters and one son. Taught biology at McNeese State College, Lake Charles, Louisiana, and Millsaps College, Jackson, Mississippi; Instructor, 1962-63, and Assistant Professor of English, 1964-66, Louisiana State University, Baton Rouge; Associate Professor of English, Loyola University, New Orleans, 1966-70; Fulbright Professor of American Studies, National University of Mexico, 1970. Associate Professor, 1971-73, since 1973, Professor of English and since 1978, Chairman of the Comparative Literature Program, University of Arkansas. Visiting Professor, University of Chile, Santiago, 1964. Poetry Editor, Louisiana State University Press, 1966-68; Editor, *New Orleans Review*, 1967-70; Contributing Editor, *Translation Review*, Richardson, Texas, 1978-81. Since 1980, Director, University of Arkansas Press. President, American Literary Translators Association, 1979-81. Recipient: Henry Bellaman Award, 1957; Bread Loaf Writers Conference Fellowship, 1961; Amy Lowell Traveling Scholarship, 1963; Arts Fund Award, 1973; American Academy in Rome Fellowship, 1976. Address: Department of English, University of Arkansas, Fayetteville, Arkansas 72701, U.S.A.

PUBLICATIONS

Verse

A Circle of Stone. Baton Rouge, Louisiana State University Press, 1964.
Recital (bilingual edition). Valparaiso, Chile, Ediciones Océano, 1964.
So Long at the Fair. New York, Dutton, 1968.
The Only World There Is. New York, Dutton, 1971.
Halfway From Hoxie: New and Selected Poems. New York, Dutton, 1973.
Why God Permits Evil: New Poems. Baton Rouge, Louisiana State University Press, 1977.
Distractions. Baton Rouge, Louisiana State University Press, 1981.
The Boys on Their Bony Mules. Baton Rouge, Louisiana State University Press, 1983.

Other

19 Poetas de Hoy en los EEUU. Valparaiso, Chile, United States Information Agency, 1966.
The Poetry of John Crowe Ransom. New Brunswick, New Jersey, Rutgers University Press, 1972.
Railroad: Trains and Train People in American Culture, with James A. McPherson. New York, Random House, 1976.
Patterns of Poetry. Baton Rouge, Louisiana State University Press, 1984.

Editor, with John William Corrington, *Southern Writing in the Sixties: Fiction* and *Poetry.* Baton Rouge, Louisiana State University Press, 2 vols., 1966-67.
Editor, *Chile: An Anthology of New Writing.* Kent, Ohio, Kent State University Press, 1968.
Editor, *The Achievement of John Ciardi: A Comprehensive Selection of His Poems with a Critical Introduction.* Chicago, Scott Foresman, 1969.
Editor, *Contemporary Poetry in America.* New York, Random House, 1973.
Editor, with John Ciardi, *How Does a Poem Mean?,* revised edition. Boston, Houghton Mifflin, 1975.
Editor, *A Roman Collection: Stories, Poems, and Other Good Pieces by the Writing Residents of the American Academy in Rome.* Columbia, University of Missouri Press, 1980.
Editor, *Ozark, Ozark: A Hillside Reader.* Columbia, University of Missouri Press, 1981.

Translator, *Poems and Antipoems,* by Nicanor Parra. New York, New Directions, 1967; London, Cape, 1968.
Translator, *Emergency Poems,* by Nicanor Parra. New York, New Directions, 1972; London, Boyars, 1977.
Translator, *Sonnets of Giuseppe Belli.* Baton Rouge, Louisiana State University Press, 1981.

*

Manuscript Collection: Special Collections, University of Arkansas Library, Fayetteville.

Critical Study: "About Miller Williams" by James Whitehead, in *Dickinson Review* (North Dakota), Spring 1973.

Miller Williams comments:

I'm not sure that one ought to discuss one's poetry in public; it seems somehow not quite decent, and besides, almost anyone will have a better perspective on a body of poems than the poet. It may mean something if I say that I distrust the Romantic Vision and dislike the Classical. Beyond this, the poems are there to be read, for what they have to say and how they say it.

*   *   *

Miller Williams is a poet of the American small town, its streets and neighborhoods, its bus stations and shabby factories. Simple logic reveals, however, that a town ultimately takes its character from the character of its people. Williams has learned this lesson early, and learned it well, for a strength throughout his career has been his adeptness at portraiture. In the introduction to Williams's first book of poems, *A Circle of Stone*, Howard Nemerov links him to the character-portrait tradition of Edgar Lee Masters, and one may as well add to that tradition those of Edwin Arlington Robinson and John Crowe Ransom. Where Williams is most successful at these portraits, he achieves a balance between the subtle irony of Masters or Ransom and the more blatant irony of Robinson. "On the Death of a Middle Aged Man," perhaps Williams's best-known early poem, strikes such a balance.

A reader learns quickly of the character's unambiguous feeling toward his unambiguous name:

Beverly
who wished his mother wanting a girl again
had called him something at best ambiguous
like Francis or Marion

Williams achieves subtle irony, though, in giving ambiguity a large role in the poem, in the question, for example, of whether the sexual encounters of Beverly's sweetheart, Helen, really "counted" since they were with her older brother and her minister. Ambiguity enriches the poem, too, in Williams's statement that Beverly "went for eleven years to the Packard plant/and bent to Helen who punched the proper holes/how many bodies." This bending to connotes both a romantic gesture, bowing, and a sexual one, bending toward or bending over someone in the act of love-making. Williams retains this ambiguity, in his *New and Selected Poems*, when he changes "bent to" to "turn for," the act of turning suggestive again both of a romantic gesture and a sexual one, as in "turning a trick."

Williams's work calls to mind—in addition to Masters, Robinson, and Ransom—such Latin American surrealists as Nicanor Parra, whose poems Williams translated and published as *Emergency Poems*. Taking ideas and images to their zany extremes seems a surrealist method for which Williams has a flair. "I Got Out of the House for the First Time," "Toast to Floyd Collins," and "And Then," all new poems in his *New and Selected Poems*, use repetition to create a sense of lost equilibrium and absurdity. "And Then" conveying a more serious tone than the first two:

Your toothbrush won't remember your mouth
Your shoes won't remember your feet

Your wife one good morning
will remember your weight
will feel unfaithful
thowing the toothbrush away
dropping the shoes in the Salvation Army box
will set your picture in the living room

someone wearing a coat you would not have worn
will ask was that your husband
she will say yes

Williams's stylistic range encompasses an ornate but energetic formalism, a flat prosaic free verse, and a more sharply hewn free verse. In "Leaving New York in the Penn Central to Metuchen" (*Halfway to Hoxie*), Williams uses alliteration in his rhymed couplets to such a degree that it might be called over-used if the lines did not evoke so well the motion of a subway train: "Go buck, go hiss and the bright balled works/tremble and turn. Go clank and the car jerks."

More than a handful of poems, however, leave behind rhythm when they leave behind rhyme. "Lying," from *Distractions*, lacks a vitality which a stronger sense of music would give it. The casualness of the lines does approach the mood of someone passing time, but one cannot help but feel that the language itself lacks energy:

Standing beside a library in Brooklyn
I wait for my ride to come. I turn some pages.
A man puts his foot on a fire hydrant
and bends to tie his shoe. I see a gun.

Yet Williams can, as "And Then" illustrated above, shape his free verse to musical ends, avoiding the prosaic and giving that free verse an almost incantatory power.

Two of Williams's finest poems, both from *Distractions*, depart from his typical sardonic tone. In "Rebecca, for Whom Nothing Has Been Written Page after Page," Williams addresses a granddaughter and tries to explain that, despite his esteem for language, language cannot do justice to a description of her. This theme is not new. Yet Williams's tone succeeds in establishing an intimacy rare in his own work and a degree of intimacy rare in the work of many other poets. After acknowledging the serviceability of language, Williams writes elegiacally of its limitations:

What phrase explains, what simile can guess
a daughter's daughter? We half know who you are,
moment by moment, remembering what you were
as you grow past, becoming by quick revisions
an image in the door.

The sardonic tone is gone, too, in "Evening: A Studio in Rome," and while it would be hard to prove a cause-and-effect relation, this change in tone seems to allow Williams to write movingly of a city just as he can write movingly of small towns. This meditative poem, in contrast to some of his others, is more luxurious, more willing to take its time in fleshing out the moment:

The window here is hung in the west wall.
It lays on the opposite wall a square of light.
Sliced by the lopsided slats of the broken blind,
the light hangs like a painting. Now, and now,
the shadow of a swallow shoots across it.

One recognizes Williams's deftness with alliteration, here the "sw" in "swallow" breaking up nicely the "sh" in "shadow" and in "shoots." What is new, however, is the acute perception of the swallow's shadow on the wall: "Now, and now." Such a patience also provides the poet with his final passage, a passage which seems to indicate that Miller Williams's good poems are getting better:

> This minute Rome is dark
> as only Rome is dark, as if somebody
> could go out reaching toward it, and find no Rome.

—Martin McGovern

WILMER, Clive. British. Born in Harrogate, Yorkshire, 10 February 1945. Educated at King's College, Cambridge, B.A. 1967, M.A. in English 1971. Married Diane Redmond in 1971; one daughter and one son. Teacher of English as a foreign language, Cambridge and Italy; also free-lance university teacher and journalist. Recipient: Arts Council grant, 1979. Agent: Frances Kelly, 9 King Edward Mansions, 629 Fulham Road, London SW6. Address: 96 Mawson Road, Cambridge CB1 2EA, England.

PUBLICATIONS

Verse

Shade Mariners, with Dick Davis and Robert Wells. Cambridge, Gregory Spiro, 1970.
The Dwelling-Place. Manchester, Carcanet, 1977.
Devotions. Manchester, Carcanet, 1982.

Other

Editor, *The Occasions of Poetry: Essays in Criticism and Autobiography*, by Thom Gunn. London, Faber, and New York, Farrar Straus, 1982.

Translator, with George Gömöri, *Forced March: Selected Poems*, by Miklós Radnóti. Manchester, Carcanet, 1979.

*

Critical Studies: by John Mole, in *Times Literary Supplement* (London), 13 January 1978; Peter Gilbert in *Jewish Quarterly* (London), Summer-Autumn 1980; Donald Davie in *London Review of Books*, 19 August 1982; Martin Dodsworth, in *The Guardian* (London), 19 August 1982; Thom Gunn, in *PN Review 30* (Manchester), vol. ix, no. 4; Tim Dooley, in *Times Literary Supplement* (London), 7 January 1983.

Clive Wilmer comments:
   My work is formal—usually in a traditional way, but by no means always so. Form is a matter of artifice and therefore derives from our human sense of order. Language is a means of communicating to others the meaning our experience has for us. Poetry is language at its most intense and most formal. It is something which stands aside from the current of everyday life in an attempt to understand. Behind what I write I always feel a kind of dialogue going on—between art and nature, between the

flux of undifferentiated matter and the human need for meaning and permanence.

*   *   *

Clive Wilmer's poetry is largely traditional, often unfashionable, and, given what it attempts, remarkably successful. Without embarrassment Wilmer can reword a story from *Ivanhoe*, write of chivalry, honour, and Renaissance courtesy as if they still lived, and use foursquare hymn stanzas without slipping into protective irony or parody. And he can usually do these things without making his reader cringe. Yet he is not an anachronism nor a purveyor of nostalgia: he has his own kind of involvement with the present, and even has some lessons for those with more up-to-date assumptions.
   Wilmer's first strength is as an elegist and epitaphist. His preoccupation is not with death but with the dead and their relation to the living, and less with the dead themselves than with their works, their legacy which forms the preconditions of our own entry into meaning. Fascinated by the lapidary force of inscriptions, Wilmer writes verse as strikingly unegotistical, as empty of the posturing lyric "I," as a powerful tombstone inscription. He is not ashamed to praise and admire greatly, to celebrate virtues and achievements, and can do so without gush because celebration for him does not entail the suspension of rationality and judgment. In his introduction to Thom Gunn's critical essays, Wilmer quotes Gunn on Yvor Winters: "The conveying [of experience] has little meaning without the evaluation." Wilmer admires both, as poets of "contained energy"; for him as for Gunn, Hardy, W.C. Williams, and Ben Jonson, all poetry is occasional and the true poet is "true to his occasions," more interested in the world than in himself. We are apparently back in a world of stable certainties and moral virtues, and with a poetry which acknowledges the charm and moving power of abstract as well as concrete language. Wilmer is a Christian who can put his trust in "a simple, disembodied word, the truth," but if that seems far too unproblematic at this end of the century, the word "disembodied" there suggests the losses, as well as the satisfactions, of abstract certainty and faith.
   In his critical writing Wilmer has defended the use of archaisms in poetry. Sometimes his own language seems worn smooth, over-familiar, or merely imitative of (say) 18th-century effects. But more often his poetry demonstrates the validity of his perception that the conventional epithet can be more painful, more pathos-laden, than the sharp new phrase. Meaning, after all, is a matter of employing conventional signs. Wilmer is more modern than he appears. His "devotional" poetry, more interested in the text than its writer, finds a way out of the traps of expressionism. In both his volumes poem after poem shows people rapt out of themselves by becoming absorbed in some work or pursuit: a boy staring at the riches of the sea-bed, a bird-watcher patiently awaiting his prey's return, becoming "less than himself and more." Likewise to the intelligent Christian the play of difference is no decentring nightmare but another perception of Babel, for in the world we all inhabit language is "shattered into vagrant syllables" and we can only dream of a world where "the sense / Of things woud be the things themselves and words / Would gem the melismatic harmony / Rarely, articulating it." He is well aware of the circuitous approach of language to truth and meaning, or of human to divine.
   The middle section of *Devotions* shows Wilmer is no traditionalist merely for the sake of being so, for here he sets aside his taut traditional stanzas and metrics and experiments with counterpoising half-lines by weight.
   Wilmer's best work has dignity, emotional force, elegance, and even grandeur. The poems avoid sonority or self-satisfaction

by admitting into themselves all the forces which would destroy their scheme of values—desolation, terror, malignity, slaughter—and then fending them off, thus conveying the precious fragility of what they seek to create: "A clearing, where love grows, and rests."

—R.J.C. Watt

WILSON, Keith. American. Born in Clovis, New Mexico, 26 December 1927. Educated at the United States Naval Academy, Annapolis, Maryland, B.S. 1950; University of New Mexico, Albuquerque, M.A. 1956. Served in the United States Navy, 1950-54: Lieutenant. Married Heloise Brigham in 1958; four daughters and one son. Instructor, University of Nevada, Reno, 1956-57; technical writer, Sandia Corporation, Albuquerque, 1958-60; Instructor, University of Arizona, Tucson, 1960-65. Since 1965, Professor of English and Poet-in-Residence, New Mexico State University, Las Cruces. Fulbright Professor, University of Cluj, Romania, 1974-75. Recipient: University of New Mexico D.H. Lawrence Fellowship, 1972; P.E.N. American Center grant, 1972; Westhafer Award, 1972; National Endowment for the Arts grant, 1974. Address: 1500 South Locust, Las Cruces, New Mexico, 88001, U.S.A.

PUBLICATIONS

Verse

Sketches for a New Mexico Hill Town. Concord, Massachusetts, Wine Press, 1966.
The Old Car and Other Blackpoems. Sacramento, California, Grande Ronde Press, 1968.
II Sequences. Portland, Oregon, Wine Press, 1968.
Graves Registry and Other Poems. New York, Grove Press, 1969.
Psalms for Various Voices. Las Cruces, New Mexico, Tolar Creek Syndicate, 1969.
Homestead. San Francisco, Kayak, 1970.
The Old Man and Others: Some Faces for America. Las Cruces, New Mexico State University Press, 1970.
The Shadow of Our Bones. Portland, Oregon, Trask House, 1971.
Rocks. Oshkosh, Wisconsin, Road Runner Press, 1971.
MidWatch: Graves Registry Part IV and V. Fremont, Michigan, Sumac Press, 1972.
Song of Thantog. New York, Athanor, 1972.
Thantog: Songs of a Jaguar Priest. Dennis, Massachusetts, Salt-Works Press, 1977.
While Dancing Feet Shatter the Earth. Logan, Utah State University Press, 1978.
The Streets of San Miguel. Tucson, Arizona, Maguey Press, 1978.
Desert Cenote. Fort Kent, Maine, Great Raven Press, 1978.
The Shaman Deer. Dennis, Massachusetts, Salt-Works Press, 1978.
Retablos. Albuquerque, San Marcos Press, 1980.
Stone Roses: Poems from Transylvania. Logan, Utah State University Press, 1983.

*

Critical Studies: by William Winthrop, in *New Mexican* (Santa Fe), 25 August 1968; in *San Marcos Review* (Albuquerque), February 1978.

Keith Wilson comments:
I hold with (or to) a number of concepts of the New American Poetry.
Three major areas of concern: (1) New Mexico Southwest, (2) the Sea, (3) Emotional Geography. I often use methods derived, in part at least, from Charles Olson's Projective Verse—he, Robert Duncan and Robert Creeley have been large influences on me, as have both William Carlos Williams and—from childhood—Robert Burns.

*   *   *

Keith Wilson's poetry is informed by a strong sense of history: both the sometimes violent history before his time in his own Southwest, and his own personal experience with violence as a naval officer during the Korean War. A collection central to the first of these preoccupations, tracing both his personal and historical awareness of the Southwest, is his fine book, *Homestead; Graves Registry* traces the Korean War experience, and *MidWatch* (or *Graves Registry*, Parts IV and V) extends his meditations on his war experience and man's attraction to violence through the Vietnam War. These poems face up to the most unpleasant aspects of human existence, and contain powerful images: fountains of flesh rising from bombings, faces blown away by a single bullet, a man who shoots a pregnant sow and feasts on her piglets. Wilson's poetry gains additional force from his willingness to strive toward an affirmation, and, beyond this, a way toward some better life, in the face of the horrendous evidence of past human history. As he says toward the end of *MidWatch*:

> Ghosts walk, here in the memory
> I have lived a thousand lives or more,
> so have you, and you, and you, but our brains
> are recent ones, we live in the ruins of castles
> and forget we built them.

It is this sense of our own complicity, whether through repetition or reincarnation, in past history, that makes his preoccupation with his own ancestral past and New Mexico's roots in the past valuable; it is not merely nostalgia, but rather a desire to learn from the past how to avoid bumping into it again in the future, how to let the new brain rise from the ruins of the old: "It was the purpose of these poems to show/the glories of war, sadnesses of peace./Replace them both."

These poems are ultimately heartening; Wilson brings a compassion rather than self righteous anger to human follies, a forgiveness that may help us to forgive ourselves. Perhaps even violence is better than nothingness, he reminds us in "Sidewinder," than not being able to relate to one another at all:

> I let him pass,
> bearing him no enmity—how
> quickly he is gone. We'll never
> be friends and he can't eat
> me. We're no use to each other.

—Duane Ackerson

WINGFIELD, Sheila (Claude). British. Born in Hampshire, 23 May 1906. Educated at Roedean School, Brighton, Sussex. Married the Honourable M. Wingfield, later Viscount Powerscourt, in 1932 (died, 1973); one daughter and two sons. Lives in Switzerland. Address: c/o Rawlinson and Hunter, 1 Hanover Square, London W1A 4SR, England.

PUBLICATIONS

Verse

Poems. London, Cresset Press, 1938.
Beat Drum, Beat Heart. London, Cresset Press, 1946.
A Cloud Across the Sun. London, Cresset Press, 1949.
A Kite's Dinner: Poems 1938-1954. London, Cresset Press, 1954.
The Leaves Darken. London, Weidenfeld and Nicolson, 1964.
Her Storms: Selected Poems 1938-1977. Dublin, Dolmen Press, and London, Calder, 1977.
Admissions: Poems 1974-1977. Dublin, Dolmen Press, and London, Calder, 1977.
Collected Poems 1938-1982. London, Enitharmon Press, and New York, Hill and Wang, 1983.

Other

Real People (autobiography). London, Cresset Press, 1952.
Sun Too Fast (as Sheila Powerscourt). London, Bles, 1974.

*

Manuscript Collection: Houghton Library, Harvard University, Cambridge, Massachusetts.

Critical Studies: by Monk Gibbon, in *Poetry Review* (London), 1949; prefaces by G.S. Fraser to *Her Storms*, 1977, and *Collected Poems*, 1983.

Sheila Wingfield comments:

My determination to be a poet was formed in the nursery. But my passion for poetry was an affair that had to conducted in a hole-and-corner way. In youth, parental disapproval forced the study of literature to be a hidden occupation; later a marital ban on meeting literary personalities was even stronger. Also, private and public commitments swallowed up most of my time. So it was impossible for me to get to know other practitioners of my generation or younger writers. Hence my unhappy ignorance about what was being done or hatched by contemporaries; I read them, but usually long after various "movements" had been established.

Though it grieved me to miss what I thought of as vital and fertilising contacts, this privacy may have been good for my work. In such an intellectual vacuum, I had to be myself.

Technically, I have tried to give each poem its own form, smell, rhythm and logic. And to employ as large a vocabulary as possible. Also to use the impact of consonants to gain certain effects.

As for subject-matter—the Irish and English countryside and country ways in general are so deeply rooted in me that I fancy much of this blows through my work. History, archaeology, folklore and the superb economy of the classical Greeks are other influences. These tendencies come together in forming my poetic outlook. This can be stated simply. What is personally felt must be fused with what is being, and has been, felt by *others*. But always in terms of the factual. Nothing woolly or disembo-

died will do. The same goes for events (which are in fact emotions suffered throughout history and in many lands). Personal dislike for amorphous description is shown by the 2,000-line poem, *Beat Drum, Beat Heart*, which compares men at war with women in love, and men at peace with women out of love, and is in fact a lengthy psychological-philosophical piece without one word in it that experts use. Or so I hope. It attempts to sweep over many cultures, histories, and legends. But invariably in terms of known or perhaps only suspected feelings, expressed in a way that makes such feelings recognisable by a great variety of human beings.

* * *

Sheila Wingfield's first book, *Poems*, contained work that was praised by Yeats and Walter de la Mare, and her later collections *A Cloud Across the Sun*, *A Kite's Dinner*, and *The Leaves Darken* have all had their admirers. Yet her verse as a whole remains little known, and she is hardly ever represented in anthologies. This seems unfair, since despite some faults of poetic diction ("No longer, Muse, no longer shall I wait"), her poems are technically well-accomplished and sometimes memorable. The sections "Women in Love" and "Women at Peace" from her long poem *Beat Drum, Beat Heart* contain what is perhaps the best of her work, and it is observable that in them she writes rather more personally than is her usual custom, with a result that the rhythms are more natural and various. Elizabeth Jennings has drawn attention to her other virtues: "At her best she has a sense of the heraldic, the emblematic which can produce glittering lines. One should not forget either Miss Wingfield's detailed observation of natural objects. She never goes wrong when she writes about the countryside or about animals."

—Robert Nye

WITHEFORD, Hubert. New Zealander. Born in Wellington, 18 March 1921. Educated at Wellesley College, Wellington; Victoria University, Wellington, M.A. in history 1943. Married Noel Brooke Anderson in 1941; one son. Staff member, New Zealand Prime Minister's Office, 1939-45, and New Zealand War History Branch, 1945-53. Staff member, 1954-67, Head of Overseas Section, 1968-78, and Director, Reference Division, 1978-81, Central Office of Information, London. Recipient: New Zealand Award of Achievement, 1963. Address: 88 Roxborough Road, Harrow, Middlesex, England.

PUBLICATIONS

Verse

Shadow of the Flame: Poems 1942-47. Auckland, Pelorus Press, 1949.
The Falcon Mask. Christchurch, Pegasus Press, 1951.
The Lightning Makes a Difference. Auckland, Paul's Book Arcade, and London, Brookside Press, 1962.
A Native, Perhaps Beautiful. Christchurch, Caxton Press, 1967.
A Possible Order. London, Ravine Press, 1980.

*

Critical Study: by C.K. Stead, in *Landfall* (Christchurch), December 1968.

*   *   *

Hubert Witheford has carved a small niche for himself in New Zealand poetry not so much by the often too amorphous content of his poetry as by what a critic called his "singular precision in his continual whittling of language." Where he begins with something to say, an "idea," it seems, he tends to fail: such a poem as "Elegy in Orongoringo Valley," though gracefully written, seems too manufactured—as in its final stanza:

> Here and in exile and in lost anguish
> He found no frenzy to win him this wanton—
> In his full failure glistens the wild bush
> Too long remembered, too long forgotten.

This rather slack and artificial use of language contrasts strongly with such lines as:

> Each year my heart becomes more dry.

> Through nerveless fingers life like me
> In slow storm runs to the ground;
> Not distance nor insentience provides
> Cuirass against that mild fatality.

This is both subtle and precise, and the irony of "mild" is nicely and honestly placed. Witheford, however, is on the whole at his best in freer forms, where his rhythms are more confident and he does not feel obliged to be "poetical" in order to fit himself into a preconceived mould. Thus "Barbarossa" is one of his most adventurous and original poems, in which he uses rhyme as and when he wishes, and to good effect:

> ...I sit down
> A stop to stories of the deaths of kings.
> I watch the telegraph
> Poles. A great hand plucks the strings.

—Martin Seymour-Smith

WOODCOCK, George. Canadian. Born in Winnipeg, Manitoba, 8 May 1912. Educated at Sir William Borlase's School, Marlow, Buckinghamshire; Morley College, London. Married Ingeborg Linzer in 1949. Clerk, Great Western Railway, London, 1929-40; Editor, *Now*, London, 1940-47; free-lance writer, 1947-54; Lecturer, University of Washington, Seattle, 1954-55; Lecturer, 1956-57, Assistant Professor, 1958-61, Associate Professor of English, 1961-63, and Lecturer in Asian Studies, 1966-67, University of British Columbia, Vancouver. Editorial Adviser, Porcupine Press, London, 1946-48, and Canadian Broadcasting Corporation *Anthology* programme, 1955-61; Advisory Editor, *Tamarack Review*, Toronto, 1956-60; Editor, *Canadian Literature*, Vancouver, 1959-77; Contributing Editor *Arts Magazine*, New York, 1962-64. Since 1954, Contributing Editor, *Dissent*, New York. Recipient: Guggenheim Fellowship, 1951; Canadian Government Overseas Fellowship, 1957; Canada Council travel grant, 1961, 1963, 1965, 1968, Killam Fellowship, 1970, Molson Prize, 1972, and Senior Arts grant, 1974; Governor-General's Award, for non-fiction, 1967; Canadian Centennial Medal, 1967; University of British Columbia Medal, for biography, 1972, 1976. LL.D.: University of Victoria, British Columbia, 1967; University of Winnipeg, 1975; D.Litt.: Sir George Williams University, Montreal, 1970; University of Ottawa, 1974; University of British Columbia, 1977. Fellow, Royal Society of Canada, 1968 (resigned), and Royal Geographical Society, 1971. Address: 6429 McCleery Street, Vancouver, British Columbia V6N 1G5, Canada.

PUBLICATIONS

Verse

Six Poems.   London, Lahr, 1938.
Ballad of an Orphan Hand.   London, Lahr, 1939.
The White Island.   London, Fortune Press, 1940.
Solstice.   London, Blue Moon Press, n.d.
The Centre Cannot Hold.   London, Routledge, 1943.
Imagine the South.   Pasadena, California, Untide Press, 1947.
Selected Poems.   Toronto, Clarke Irwin, 1967.
Notes on Visitations: Poems 1936-1975.   Toronto, Anansi, 1975.
Anima; or, Swann Grown Old: A Cycle of Poems.   Coatsworth, Ontario, Black Moss Press, 1977.
The Kestrel and Other Poems of Past and Present.   Sunderland, Ceolfrith Press, 1978.
The Mountain Road.   Fredericton, New Brunswick, Fiddlehead, 1980.
Collected Poems.   Victoria, British Columbia, Sono Nis Press, 1983.

Plays

Maskerman (broadcast, 1960).   Published in *Prism* (Vancouver), Winter 1961.
The Benefactor (broadcast, 1963).   Lantzville, Ontario, Oolichan, 1982.
Gabriel Dumont and the Northwest Rebellion (as *Six Dry Cakes for the Hunted*, broadcast, 1975).   Toronto, Playwrights Co-op, 1976.
Two Plays (includes *The Island of Demons* and *Six Dry Cakes for the Hunted*).   Vancouver, Talonbooks, 1977.

Radio Plays: *Maskerman*, 1960; *The Island of Demons*, 1962; *The Benefactor*, 1963; *The Empire of Shadows*, 1964; *The Floor of the Night*, 1965; *The Brideship*, music by Robert Turner, 1967; *Six Dry Cakes for the Hunted*, 1975.

Other

New Life to the Land: Anarchist Proposals for Agriculture.   London, Freedom Press, 1942.
Railways and Society.   London, Freedom Press, 1943.
Anarchy or Chaos.   London, Freedom Press, 1944.
Homes or Hovels: The Housing Problem and Its Solution.   London, Freedom Press, 1944.
Anarchism and Morality.   London, Freedom Press, 1945.
What Is Anarchism?   London, Freedom Press, 1945.
William Godwin: A Biographical Study.   London, Porcupine Press, and New York, Irving Ravin, 1946.
The Basis of Communal Living.   London, Freedom Press, 1947.

The Incomparable Aphra.   London, Boardman, 1948.
The Writer and Politics: Essays.   London, Procupine Press, 1948.
The Paradox of Oscar Wilde.   London, Boardman, and New York, Macmillan, 1950.
British Poetry Today (lecture).   Vancouver, University of British Columbia, 1950.
The Anarchist Prince: A Biographical Study of Peter Kropotkin, with Ivan Avakumovic.   London, Boardman, 1950.
Ravens and Prophets: An Account of Journeys in British Columbia, Alberta and Southern Alaska.   London, Wingate, 1952.
Pierre-Joseph Proudhon: A Biography.   New York, Macmillan, and London, Routledge, 1956.
To the City of the Dead: An Account of Travels in Mexico.   London, Faber, 1957.
Incas and Other Men: Travels in the Andes.   London, Faber, 1959.
Anarchism: A History of Libertarian Ideas and Movements.   Cleveland, Meridian, 1962; London, Penguin, 1963.
Faces of India: A Travel Narrative.   London, Faber, 1964.
Civil Disobedience.   Toronto, Canadian Broadcasting Corporation, 1966.
The Greeks in India.   London, Faber, 1966.
Asia, Gods and Cities: Aden to Tokyo.   London, Faber, 1966.
The Crystal Spirit: A Study of George Orwell.   Boston, Little Brown, 1966; London, Cape, 1967.
Kerala: A Portrait of the Malabar Coast.   London, Faber, 1967.
The Doukhobors, with Ivan Avakumovic.   Toronto and New York, Oxford University Press, and London, Faber, 1968.
The British in the Far East.   London, Weidenfeld and Nicolson, and New York, Atheneum, 1969.
Hugh MacLennan.   Toronto, Copp Clark, 1969.
Henry Walter Bates: Naturalist of the Amazons.   London, Faber, and New York, Barnes and Noble, 1969.
Odysseus Ever Returning: Essays on Canadian Writers and Writing.   Toronto, McClelland and Stewart, 1970.
The Hudson's Bay Company.   New York, Crowell Collier, 1970.
Canada and the Canadians.   Toronto, Oxford University Press, London, Faber, and Harrisburg, Pennsylvania, Stackpole, 1970; revised edition, Toronto, Macmillan, and Faber, 1973.
Mordecai Richler.   Toronto, McClelland and Stewart, 1970.
Into Tibet: The Early British Explorers.   London, Faber, and New York, Barnes and Noble, 1971.
Gandhi. New York, Viking Press, 1971; London, Fontana, 1972.
Dawn and the Darkest Hour: A Study of Aldous Huxley.   London, Faber, and New York, Viking Press, 1972.
Herbert Read: The Stream and the Source.   London, Faber, 1972.
The Rejection of Politics and Other Essays.   Toronto, New Press, 1972.
Who Killed the British Empire?   London, Cape, and New York, Quadrangle, 1974.
Amor de Cosmos, Journalist and Reformer.   Toronto, Oxford University Press, 1975.
Gabriel Dumont: The Métis Chief and His Lost World.   Edmonton, Hurtig, 1975.
South Sea Journey.   Toronto, Fitzhenry and Whiteside, and London, Faber, 1976.
Canadian Poets 1960-1973: A List.   Ottawa, Golden Dog Press, 1976.
Peoples of the Coast: The Indians of the Pacific Northwest.   Edmonton, Hurtig, and Bloomington, Indiana University Press, 1977.

Gabriel Dumont (for children).   Don Mills, Ontario, Fitzhenry and Whiteside, 1978.
Thomas Merton, Monk and Poet: A Critical Study.   Vancouver, Douglas and McIntyre, Edinburgh, Canongate, and New York, Farrar Straus, 1978.
Faces from History.   Edmonton, Hurtig, 1978.
The Canadians.   Don Mills, Ontario, Fitzhenry and Whiteside, 1979; Cambridge, Massachusetts, Harvard University Press, and London, Athlone Press, 1980.
100 Great Canadians.   Edmonton, Hurtig, 1980.
A Picture History of British Columbia.   Edmonton, Hurtig, 1980.
The World of Canadian Writing: Critiques and Recollections.   Vancouver, Douglas and McIntrye, 1980.
The George Woodcock Reader, edited by Douglas Fetherling.   Ottawa, Deneau and Greenberg, 1980.
Taking It to the Letter.   Montreal, Quadrant, 1981.
Confederation Betrayed: The Case Against Trudeau's Canada.   Madeira Park, British Columbia, Harbour, 1981.
Ivan Eyre.   Don Mills, Ontario, Fitzhenry and Whiteside, 1981.
British Columbia: A Celebration, with J.A. Kraulis.   Edmonton, Hurtig, 1983.
Letter to the Past (autobiography).   Don Mills, Ontario, Fitzhenry and Whiteside, 1983.

Editor, *A Hundred Years of Revolution: 1848 and After.*   London, Porcupine Press, 1948; New York, Haskell House, 1974.
Editor, *The Letters of Charles Lamb.*   London, Grey Walls Press, 1950.
Editor, *A Choice of Critics.*   Toronto, Oxford University Press, 1966.
Editor, *Variations on the Human Theme.*   Toronto, Ryerson Press, 1966.
Editor, *The Egoist*, by Meredith.   London, Penguin, 1968.
Editor, *The Sixties: Writers and Writing of the Decade.*   Vancouver, University of British Columbia Press, 1969.
Editor, *A Tale of Two Cities*, by Dickens.   London, Penguin, 1970; New York, Greenwich House, 1982.
Editor, *Malcolm Lowry: The Man and His Work.*   Vancouver, University of British Columbia Press, 1971.
Editor, *Wyndham Lewis in Canada.*   Vancouver, University of British Columbia Press, 1971.
Editor, *Typee: A Peep at Polynesian Life*, by Herman Melville.   London, Penguin, 1972.
Editor, *Poets and Critics: Essays from "Canadian Literature" 1966-1974.*   Toronto, Oxford University Press, 1974.
Editor, *Colony and Confederation: Early Canadian Poets and Their Background.*   Vancouver, University of British Columbia Press, 1974.
Editor, *The Canadian Novel in the Twentieth Century: Essays from "Canadian Literature."*   Toronto, McClelland and Stewart, 1975.
Editor, *The Anarchist Reader.*   Hassocks, Sussex, Harvester Press, and Atlantic Highlands, New Jersey, Humanities Press, 1977.
Editor, *The Return of the Native*, by Hardy.   London, Penguin, 1979.

*

Critical Studies: *George Woodcock* by Peter Hughes, Toronto, McClelland and Stewart, 1974; *From Here to There* by Frank Davey, Erin, Ontario, Press Porcépic, 1974; *A Political Art: Essays and Images in Honour of George Woodcock* edited by

W.H. New, Vancouver, University of British Columbia Press, 1978.

George Woodcock comments:
In the 1960's I was more concerned with dramatic verse than other types of poetry. Recently I have returned to lyric poetry.

I think that, whatever he may spout about his verse, almost every poet has long lost sight of everything except the work as it stands and is not even the best man to talk about its more multiple meanings. I have often found that readers have found true things in my poems of which I have been at first unaware.

*   *   *

One critic noted that George Woodcock has written more books than most people have read. Over the years the distinguished author of travel books, biographies, and literary criticism has evolved a prose style which is readable and durable if somewhat unremarkable. Perhaps the same may be said of his poetical style.

If Woodcock's style is unremarkable, the range of subjects presented is worthy of note. There are 185 poems in the *Collected Poems*. The poet writes in a foreword that this volume is "in some way nearer to an autobiography than it is to an ordinary collection of verse." The poems give thoughtful expression to the poet's experiences in London from the 1920's to the 1940's, his reactions to the Second World War, his fine feeling for the landscape and legends of British Columbia where he settled in 1949.

It is possible to trace in his poetical development a movement from formal verse to free verse, yet the principal considerations remain constant. There is a strong sense of place and of the seasons of the year. For all its autobiographical flavour, one learns little about the author, for the poems are public utterances rather than private griefs. There is a recognition of the need for inspiration. "Notes on Visitations" begins:

> Sometimes
> when I am alone
> the music strikes
> and I sing
> with confidence and ease

Woodcock's confidence is nowhere better shown than in his "Ballad for W.H. Auden" which ends with these stanzas:

> If your Anglican God has received you
>   As Auden or Wystan or Dear,
> I know that all is accepted
>   Without irony, without fear,
>
> As the fog drains off the mountains
>   And the air blows wet with sleet,
> Walking ghostly out one evening,
>   Walking down Granville Street.

Occasionally sentimentality or triteness intrude, as in the poem "On Completing a Life of Dumont" which argues that the poet-biographer may have little in common with the Métis general he wrote about but "that freedom is a word our hearts both sing."

Few books published in the last decade are as well thought out as Woodcock's *Collected Poems*. The contents are arranged in eleven thematic sections, non-chronologically, with each poem carefully dated. These are characteristics one has grown to expect from Woodcock, care and consideration. The volume is dedicated to Roy Fuller and Julian Symons, "Poets, Contemporaries and Friends." The three gentlemen share the same year of birth. That, too, is the kind of detail one appreciates in Woodcock.

—John Robert Colombo

———

WOODS, John (Warren). American. Born in Martinsville, Indiana, 12 July 1926. Educated at Indiana University, Bloomington, B.S. 1949, M.A. 1955; University of Iowa, Iowa City. Served in the United States Air Force. Married Emily Newbury in 1951; two sons. Assistant Professor, 1955-60, Associate Professor, 1961-64, and since 1965, Professor of English, Western Michigan University, Kalamazoo. Visiting Professor of English, University of California, Irvine, 1967-68. Recipient: Bread Loaf Writers Conference Robert Frost Fellowship, 1962; Yaddo Fellowship, 1963, 1964; Theodore Roethke Prize (*Poetry Northwest*), 1968; National Endowment for the Arts grant, 1969, and Fellowship, 1982. Address: Department of English, Western Michigan University, Kalamazoo, Michigan 49008, U.S.A.

PUBLICATIONS

Verse

The Deaths at Paragon, Indiana. Bloomington, Indiana University Press, 1955.
On the Morning of Color. Bloomington, Indiana University Press, 1961.
The Cutting Edge. Bloomington, Indiana University Press, 1966.
Keeping Out of Trouble. Bloomington, Indiana University Press, 1968.
Turning to Look Back: Poems 1955-1970. Bloomington, Indiana University Press, 1972.
The Knees of Widows. Kalamazoo, Michigan, Westigan Review Press, 1972.
Voyages to the Inland Sea II: Essays and Poems, with Felix Pollack and James Hearst, edited by John Judson. La Crosse, University of Wisconsin Center for Contemporary Poetry, 1972.
Alcohol. Grand Rapids, Michigan, Pilot Press, 1973.
A Bone Flicker. La Crosse, Wisconsin, Juniper, 1973.
Striking the Earth. Bloomington, Indiana University Press, 1976.
Thirty Years on the Force. La Crosse, Wisconsin, Juniper, 1977.
The Night of the Game. Bloomington, Indiana, Raintree Press, 1982.
The Valley of Minor Animals. Port Townsend, Washington, Dragon Gate, 1982.
The Salt Stone: Selected Poems. Port Townsend, Washington, Dragon Gate, 1984.

*

Critical Studies: by Richard Hugo, in *Northwest Review* (Eugene, Oregon), 1967; David Etter, in *Chicago Review*, Winter 1972.

John Woods comments:
All that is important about my poetry to the general reader lies

in the poetry itself. If, Dear General Reader, we might sit down together over a bottle, we might begin a friendship, an enemyship, a love affair, whatever. Until then, the great whirling mass of particulars that make up You, and I, can only meet at the interface of my poems.

*   *   *

John Woods, a master of contemporary idiom, sets his poems in the 20th-century midwest. Through three generations of Indiana farm folk, "between the two wars of father and son," he expresses human hopes and anxieties with an exceptional poetic sense of place and of time. Grandfather's recollection of genealogy is vague, yet certain:

> I don't know where we came from.
> So many graves stay open too long,
> so many girls lie back tonight
> trying to be secret rivers in the limestone.

Woods has discovered a language needing no support of learned notes for characters who "think back along their bones." Generations die back into the Indiana corn knowing, instinctively, that Adonis is violently stoned red before regeneration. Wood chooses apt items for his own totem:

> I shaped a man, my totem animal,
> from branches, murky soil, and pasture dung...
> From a bird stoned red beneath an elm,
> I took a wing for tongue.

Woods, indeed, takes a wing for tongue. His language is lively, his imagery precise, and his rhythms range from the conversational tempo of the elegiac poems on life before death to a swift tumble of images in his wry, humorous asides on life's perplexities.

Turning to Look Back and *The Salt Stone* represent his poetic range amply. His first group in both collections, "The Deaths at Paragon," gathers elegiac poems on generation and death. Sophisticated love poems, both lithe and muscular, follow in "In Time of Apples." Poems of social commentary are gathered in "Red Telephones"; and formal lyrics, including a fine sestina, in "Barley Tongues."

Dave Etter, writing in the *Chicago Review* (1972), declares Woods, "the best poet writing in America today." James Wright (in *Westigan Review*, Final Issue, 1983) says, "John Woods is one of the best poets we have." Lewis Turco (in "The Year in Poetry," *DLB Yearbook*, 1983) echoes Wright, and adds, "It's time he was considered for some of the major prizes."

—Edward Callan

WRIGHT, Charles (Penzel, Jr.). American. Born in Pickwick Dam, Tennessee, 25 August 1935. Educated at Davidson College, North Carolina, 1953-57, B.A. 1957; University of Iowa, Iowa City, 1961-63, M.F.A. 1963; University of Rome (Fulbright Fellow), 1963-65. Served in the United States Army Intelligence Corps, 1957-61: Captain. Married Holly McIntire in 1969; one son. Member of the English Department, University of California, Irvine, 1966-83. Since 1983, Professor of English, University of Virginia, Charlottesville. Fulbright Lecturer, University of Padua, 1968-69; Visiting Lecturer, University of Iowa, 1974-75, Princeton University, New Jersey, 1978, and Columbia Univer-

sity, New York, 1978. Recipient: Eunice Tietjens Award (*Poetry*, Chicago), 1969; National Endowment for the Arts grant, 1974; Guggenheim Fellowship, 1975; Poetry Society of America Melville Cane Award, 1976; Academy of American Poets Edgar Allan Poe Award, 1976; American Academy grant, 1977; P.E.N. Translation Prize, 1979; Ingram Merrill Fellowship, 1980; American Book Award, 1983. Address: 940 Locust Avenue, Charlottesville, Virginia 22901, U.S.A.

PUBLICATIONS

Verse

The Voyage. Iowa City, Patrician Press, 1963.
6 Poems. London, Freed, 1965.
The Dream Animal. Toronto, Anansi, 1968.
Private Madrigals. Madison, Wisconsin, Abraxas Press, 1969.
The Grave of the Right Hand. Middletown, Connecticut, Wesleyan University Press, 1970.
The Venice Notebook. Boston, Barn Dream Press, 1971.
Backwater. Santa Ana, California, Golem Press, 1973.
Hard Freight. Middletown, Connecticut, Wesleyan University Press, 1973.
Bloodlines. Middletown, Connecticut, Wesleyan University Press, 1975.
Colophons. Iowa City, Windhover Press, 1977.
China Trace. Middletown, Connecticut, Wesleyan University Press, 1977.
Wright: A Profile. Iowa City, Grilled Flowers Press, 1979.
Dead Color. Salem, Oregon, Seluzicki, 1980.
The Southern Cross. New York, Random House, 1981.
Country Music: Selected Early Poems. Middletown, Connecticut, Wesleyan University Press, 1982.
The Other Side of the River. New York, Random House, 1984.

Other

Translator, *The Storm and Other Poems*, by Eugenio Montale. Oberlin, Ohio, Oberlin College, 1978.
Translator, *Orphic Songs.* Oberlin, Ohio, Oberlin College, 1984.

*

Critical Studies: interview, in *Field 17* (Oberlin, Ohio), Fall 1977; by Helen Vendler, in *New Yorker*, 29 October 1979; interview, in *Poetry West* (Salt Lake City), Summer 1981; Calvin Bedient, in *Parnassus* (New York), Summer 1982; George F. Butterick, in *Dictionary of Literary Biography Yearbook 1982* edited by Richard Ziegfeld, Detroit, Gale, 1983.

*   *   *

Charles Wright has cited Pound and Montale (whose *Bufera e altro* he has recently—and brilliantly—translated) as his chief influences, but the poet who is perhaps his most immediate model is the remarkable German visionary Georg Trakl. Here is the beginning of Trakl's "Abendland": "Mond, als träte ein Totes/Aus blauer Höhle,/Und es fallen der Blüten/Viele über den Felsenpfad" (Moon, as if a dead thing/Stepped out of a blue cave,/And many blossoms fall/Across the rocky path). Compare the first stanza of Wright's "Clear Night":

> Clear night, thumb-top of a moon, a back-lit sky.
> Moon-fingers lay down their same routine

On the side deck and the threshold, the white keys
    and the black keys.
Bird hush and bird song. A cassia flower falls.

Or this, from "Stone Canyon Nocturne": "The moon, like a dead heart, cold and unstartable, hangs by a thread / At the earth's edge, / Unfaithful at last, splotching the ferns and the pink shrubs." And, in a poem appropriately called "Thinking of Georg Trakl," there is an interesting echo of the "blue cave" of "Abendland": "Lips part in the bleached willows. / Finger by finger, above Orion, God's blue hand unfolds."

Wright's poetry is less feverish, less emotional than Trakl's, but he shares the German poet's ability to shift imperceptibly and with seeming ease from the real to the surreal, from the concrete, observable object to something strange and imaginary. Here is a poem called "California Twilight":

Late evening, July, and no one at home.
In the green lungs of the willow, fly-worms and lightning
    bugs
Blood-spot the whips and wings. Blue

Asters become electric against the hedge.
What was it I had in mind?
The last whirr of a skateboard dwindles down Oak Street
    hill.

Slowly a leaf unlocks itself from a branch.
Slowly the furred hands of the dead flutter up from their
    caves.
A little pinkish flame is snuffed in my mouth.

The poem begins matter-of-factly by establishing the scene, but that scene remains oddly undeveloped and unresolved. It is neither the backdrop for a specific dramatic incident nor the occasion for autobiographical rumination. The concrete precision here is not that of Imagism; rather, the particulars of the poet's experience are filtered through the veil of dream. Thus the poem moves from observable natural phenomena—the branches of the willow, seen at twilight, which remind the poet of "green lungs," and the "Blue / Asters" which "become electric against the hedge"—to a silence in which the mind invents its own fictions: "Slowly the furred hands of the dead flutter up from their caves." In the wake of this momentary vision of death, "A little pinkish flame is snuffed in my mouth": it is as if the light in the poet's heart is suddenly extinguished. He experiences a sense of deprivation, of diminution—a faint chill. Yet there is nothing personal in his sense of loss; it is simply part of the ongoing process of nature, a ritual to be experienced again and again in the normal course of things.

The tension between normalcy and mystery is reflected in the poem's sound structure: three tercets evenly arranged on the page, whose lines are characterized by densely woven alliteration and assonance. Thus "green lungs of the willow" is phonemically echoed by "lightning bugs" and the *fu* of "furred hands" reappears in "flutter" and then, chiastically, in "snuffed." Wright has said that he always counts syllables and stresses and that "All my lines are extensions of seven-syllable lines, or contradictions." So, in "California Twilight," lines 3 and 5 have seven syllables, whereas the climactic eighth line doubles that length. Against such symmetries, Wright creates complex stress patterns, no two lines quite the same and no predominantly rising or falling rhythm. What look like neat stanza-containers thus have unpredictable configurations.

Such intensely perceptual poetry takes great risks. Sometimes the effect doesn't quite come off. Take the second poem in the "Tattoos" sequence in *Bloodlines*:

The pin oak has found new meat,
The linkworm a bone to pick.
Lolling its head, slicking its blue tongue,
The nightflower blooms on its one stem....

Of this, Wright himself has said with rare candor: "Nightflower is a metaphor. The death flower, and one wishes one had not said it three years later." The self-conscious metaphor, that is to say, is at odds with the sense of wonder the poet wishes to convey. A similar problem is created when a poem is made to yield an abstract formulation as in these pieces from "Skins": "Alone with the owl and the night crawler / Where all is a true turning, and all is growth," or "That milky message of breath on cold mornings—/ That what you take in is seldom what you let out."

But in *China Trace*, still, I think, his best book, such moralizing is rare. Rather, these short "Chinese" lyrics embody the mystery of being. Consider the exquisite "Spider Crystal Ascension," in which man is passive while the white spider, drifting "on his web / through the night sky...Looks down, waiting for us to ascend." Implausibly, "At dawn, he is still there, invisible, short of breath, mending his net." But how can the "I" know this if the spider is invisible? Because the insect remains at the very edge of consciousness, a nagging presence whose memory can produce a startling metamorphosis: "All morning we look for the white face to rise from the lake like a tiny star. / And when it does, we lie back in our watery hair and rock." This is the Rimbaldian "On me pense"—a poetry of muted but intense animism.

—Marjorie Perloff

WRIGHT, David (John Murray). British. Born in Johannesburg, South Africa, 23 February 1920. Educated at St. John's Preparatory School, Johannesburg, 1927; Northampton School for the Deaf, 1934-39; Oriel College, Oxford, 1939-42, B.A. 1942. Married Phillipa Reid in 1951. Staff member, *Sunday Times*, London, 1942-47; Editor, with Tristram Hull, *Nimbus*, London, 1955-56; Editor, with Patrick Swift, *X* magazine, London, 1959-62. Recipient: Rockefeller-Atlantic Award, 1950; Guinness Award, 1958, 1960; Gregory Fellowship, University of Leeds, 1965-67. Fellow, Royal Society of Literature, 1967. Agent: A.D. Peters Ltd., 10 Buckingham Street, London WC2N 6BU. Address: Bongate Mill House, Appleby in Westmorland, Cumbria CA16 6UR, England.

PUBLICATIONS

Verse

Poems. London, Editions Poetry London, 1949.
Moral Stories. St. Ives, Cornwall, Latin Press, 1952.
Moral Stories. London, Verschoyle, 1954.
Monologue of a Deaf Man. London, Deutsch, 1958.
Adam at Evening. London, Hodder and Stoughton, 1965.
Poems. Leeds, Leeds University, 1966.
Nerve Ends. London, Hodder and Stoughton, 1969.
Corgi Modern Poets in Focus 1, with others, edited by Dannie Abse. London, Corgi, 1971.

A South African Album, edited by C.H. Sisson. Cape Town,
Philip, 1976.
A View of the North. Ashington, Northumberland, and Man-
chester, MidNAG—Carcanet, 1976.
To the Gods the Shades: New and Collected Poems. Manches-
ter, Carcanet, 1976.
Metrical Observations. Manchester, Carcanet, 1980.
Selected Poems. Johannesburg, Donker, 1980.

Other

Roy Campbell. London, Longman, 1961.
Algarve, with Patrick Swift. London, Barrie and Rockliff,
1965; revised edition, Barrie and Jenkins, 1971.
Minho and North Portugal: A Portrait and a Guide, with Patrick
Swift. London, Barrie and Rockliff, 1968.
Deafness: A Personal Account. London, Allen Lane, and New
York, Stein and Day, 1969.
Lisbon: A Portrait and a Guide, with Patrick Swift. London,
Barrie and Jenkins, 1971.

Editor, with John Heath-Stubbs, *The Forsaken Garden: An
Anthology of Poetry 1824-1909*. London, Lehmann, 1950.
Editor, with John Heath-Stubbs, *The Faber Book of Twentieth
Century Verse: An Anthology of Verse in Britain 1900-
1950*. London, Faber, 1953; revised edition, 1965, 1975.
Editor, *South African Stories*. London, Faber, 1960.
Editor, *Seven Victorian Poets*. London, Heinemann, 1964;
New York, Barnes and Noble, 1966.
Editor, *The Mid-Century: English Poetry 1940-60*. London,
Penguin, 1965.
Editor, *Longer Contemporary Poems*. London, Penguin, 1966.
Editor, *The Penguin Book of English Romantic Verse*. Lon-
don, Penguin, 1968.
Editor, *Recollections of the Lakes and the Lake Poets*, by Tho-
mas De Quincey. London, Penguin, 1970.
Editor, *Records of Shelley, Byron, and the Author*, by Edward
Trelawny. London, Penguin, 1973.
Editor, *The Penguin Book of Everyday Verse: Social and Doc-
umentary Poetry 1250-1916*. London, Allen Lane, 1976.
Editor, *Under the Greenwood Tree*, by Hardy. London, Pen-
guin, 1978.
Editor, *Selected Poems*, by Hardy. London, Penguin, 1978.
Editor, *Selected Poems and Prose*, by Edward Thomas. Lon-
don, Penguin, 1981.

Translator, *Beowulf*. London, Penguin, 1957.
Translator, *The Canterbury Tales*, by Geoffrey Chaucer. London,
Barrie and Rockliff, 1964; New York, Random House, 1965.

*

Manuscript Collections: Arts North, Newcastle upon Tyne;
Rhodes University, Grahamstown, South Africa.

Critical Studies: by Dannie Abse, in *Corgi Modern Poets in
Focus 1*, 1971; *Guide to Modern World Literature* by Martin
Seymour-Smith, London, Wolfe, 1973; Richard Poole, in *Poetry
Wales* (Cardiff), Spring 1977; Anthony Cronin, in *Aquarius 10*
(London), 1978; *The Avoidance of Literature* by C.H. Sisson,
Manchester, Carcanet, 1978; "David Wright at Sixty," in *P.N.
Review 14* (Manchester), Summer 1980.

David Wright comments:
    Love, death, liberty, and what we are all here for,

Whether the date is November twenty-three or doomsday,
Discussions of this kind, they somehow manage to ignore:
Theirs is a message of purest frivolity.

Affirming the unprovable, they have nothing to say
But that the fine point of existence, the instant's span
Between the void before and the void after, is really
Valid (and what is the use of knowing this?). Again,

They do not say anything but by analogy.

*   *   *

Two features emerge very clearly from a reading of David
Wright's poetry: the way in which deafness (the result of scarlet
fever, at the age of seven) has impinged on his work; and the way
in which South Africa, the country of his birth, has remained a
force in his writing, despite the fact that he left the country at 13
and has been fully absorbed in the literary life of London for
almost half a century. Although he could describe himself, in
1950, as one "Born in a dominion to which he hoped not to go
back/Since predisposed to imagine white possibly black," his
relationship with South Africa (which he revisited within a year
of writing the above) has remained ambivalent. Return visits
were primarily for his mother's sake—she continued to live for
many years in Orange Grove, Johannesburg, where he was
born—but the ironic acknowledgment contained in the following lines (on his departure for England in 1937, after a lengthy
school vacation) has proved prophetic: "I wave from the deck of
the Union-Castle liner,/ And an exile waves from the quay./ Why
do we love the places we were born in?" The dilemma is posited,
but there is no trauma, no wrenching of roots, for unlike Plomer,
Wright maintained his links with South Africa: his two worlds
are in apposition, not opposition, and he can identify himself
with one as fully as with the other. The circumstances of his life
and education had a great deal to do with this; subsequently his
own sense of vocation as a poet and the discipline he exercised in
shaping his career as well as his art, contributed to the achievement of a voice at once poised and objective—the "metrical
observer" of his 1980 volume—yet deeply humane and vulnerably self-aware.
    The need to overcome his disability and assert his sense of
"self" accounts, on the one hand, for the prevalence in Wright's
oeuvre of the "autobiographical" poem and, on the other, for the
quick and sympathetic way he responds to affliction in others—
particularly birds and animals. Examples of the former range
from the "Funeral Oration" he composed at thirty—a self-
deprecatory exercise in a mode popular among poets of the
1930's—and "Monologue of a Deaf Man" to the poignant brevity of:

Abstracted by silence from the age of seven,
Deafened and penned by as black calamity
As twice to be born, I cannot without pity
Contemplate myself as an infant;

Or fail to speak of silence as a priestess
Calling to serve in the temple of a skull
Her innocent choice. It is barely possible
Not to be affected by such a distress.

Less directly personal is his recognition, in "Encounter," of the
ways in which the half-world of the handicapped can, at least
momentarily, expand to a new fulness.
    As observer, Wright can be sharply ironic, as in "For Roy
Campbell":

My countryman, the poet, wears a Stetson;
He can count his enemies, but not his friends.
A retired soldier living in Kensington,
Who limps along the Church Street to the Swan.

In subsequent stanzas, however, the Campbell who is here mock-ingly saluted as an anachronism emerges as a still-potent figure, inhabiting a world of elemental forces and legendary forms—and compelling our admiration:

Horses and bulls, the sable and impala,
Thunder between his fingers; as they run,
He hears another thunder in the sun,
Time and the sea about Tristan da Cunha.

Wright is frequently the celebrant of persons and places. The limitations of deafness may well have directed him to the verse epistle or conversational poem, in which former friendships are recalled, or new sensations shared with an actual or imagined auditor; his "Zennor Revisited," "Notes on a Visit," and other poetic journals serve similar purpose. Then, too, the many dedi-catory verses and tributes are evidence of the value Wright attaches to friendship, as well as his need to define—and perhaps refine—his response to others (and this includes writers and artists of the past). Some of his finest poems are evocations of scene or place: the Lake District is a favourite haunt, but Regent's Park can prove equally fascinating; and more often than not his attention is directed to the past (with its richness of association), viewed from the perspective of the here and now. The "Peripatetic Letter to Isabella Fey" (dated November 1973) characteristically veers between the mundane reality of London and the Transvaal (where past and present are strikingly juxta-posed, and from which he had recently returned); five years later the same dualism is posited in "A Letter from Westmorland," to the same correspondent:

The only news I have to tell
Is the quotidian miracle,
The commonplace continuous.
I look out of my window; note
Uninvolved and a spectator,
That elder trees are puddled white
With new bloom of another year.
Now is midsummer; heavy June
Leaves hang where snow of April hung.
The scene is where I would belong
But do not, any more than there
Do I belong, where I was born.

The narrative mode appeals strongly to Wright and he has successfully employed it, notably in "Kleomedes." He is, how-ever, essentially a lyric poet, gifted with a sure touch and an unobtrusive rhythmic technique. In a 1980 interview, Wright remarked that the present emphasis on socially "committed" writing—the idea that the writer and his work belong to the community—is misplaced: "I think you can have an artist express a completely personal vision, what he himself sees (it's no use trying to express what you think other people will see—just say what you yourself see) and it will belong to others." His best work attests to the validity of that belief.

—E. Pereira

WRIGHT, Judith (Arundell). Australian. Born in Armidale, New South Wales, 31 May 1915. Educated at New South Wales Correspondence School; New England Girls School, Armidale; University of Sydney. Married J.P. McKinney (died, 1966); one daughter. Secretary and clerk, 1938-42; administrative clerk, University of Queensland, Brisbane, 1945-48. Commonwealth Literary Fund Lecturer, Australia, 1949, 1962. Since 1967, Honours Tutor in English, University of Queensland. Member, Australia Council, 1973-74. Recipient: Grace Leven Prize, 1950, 1972; Commonwealth Literary Fund Fellowship, 1964; Austra-lia—Britannica Award, 1964; Australian Academy of the Humanities Fellowship, 1970; Australian National University Creative Arts Fellowship, 1974; Senior Writers Fellowship, 1977; Fellowship of Australian Writers Robert Frost Memorial Award, 1977. D.Litt.: University of Queensland, 1962; Univer-sity of New England, Armidale, 1963; Sydney University, 1977; Monash University, Clayton, Victoria, 1977; Australian National University, Canberra, 1981. Address: "Edge," Half Moon Wild-life District, Mongarlowe, New South Wales 2622, Australia.

PUBLICATIONS

Verse

The Moving Image. Melbourne, Meanjin Press, 1946.
Woman to Man. Sydney, Angus and Robertson, 1949.
The Gateway. Sydney, Angus and Robertson, 1953.
The Two Fires. Sydney, Angus and Robertson, 1955.
Australian Bird Poems. Adelaide, Australian Letters, 1961.
Birds: Poems. Sydney, Angus and Robertson, 1962.
(Poems), selected and introduced by the author. Sydney, Angus and Robertson, 1963.
Five Senses: Selected Poems. Sydney, Angus and Robertson, 1963.
City Sunrise. Brisbane, Shapcott Press, 1964.
The Other Half. Sydney, Angus and Robertson, 1966.
Poetry from Australia: Pergamon Poets 6, with Randolph Stow and William Hart-Smith, edited by Howard Sergeant. Ox-ford, Pergamon Press, 1969.
Collected Poems 1942-1970. Sydney, Angus and Robertson, 1971.
Alive: Poems 1971-72. Sydney, Angus and Robertson, 1973.
Fourth Quarter and Other Poems. Sydney, Angus and Robert-son, 1976; London, Angus and Robertson, 1977.
The Double Tree: Selected Poems 1942-1976. Boston, Houghton Mifflin, 1978.

Recording: *Judith Wright Reads from Her Own Work,* Univer-sity of Queensland Press, 1973.

Short Stories

The Nature of Love. Melbourne, Sun, 1966.

Other

Australian Poetry (lecture). Armidale, New South Wales, University of New England, 1955 (?).
King of the Dingoes (for children). Melbourne, Oxford Uni-versity Press, 1958; London, Angus and Robertson, 1959.
The Generations of Men. Melbourne, Oxford University Press, 1959.
The Day the Mountains Played (for children). Brisbane, Jaca-randa Press, 1960; London, Angus and Robertson, 1963.

Range the Mountains High (for children).   Melbourne, Lansdowne Press, and London, Angus and Robertson, 1962; revised edition, Lansdowne Press, 1971.

Country Towns (for children).   Melbourne, Oxford University Press, 1963; London, Oxford University Press, 1964.

Charles Harpur.   Melbourne, Lansdowne Press, 1963; revised edition, Melbourne and London, Oxford University Press, 1977.

Shaw Neilson (biography and selected verse).   Sydney, Angus and Robertson, 1963.

Preoccupations in Australian Poetry.   Melbourne and London, Oxford University Press, 1965.

The River and the Road (for children).   Melbourne, Lansdowne Press, 1966; London, Angus and Robertson, 1967; revised edition, Lansdowne Press, 1971.

Henry Lawson.   Melbourne, London, and New York, Oxford University Press, 1967.

Conservation as an Emerging Concept.   Sydney, Australian Conservation Foundation, 1970.

Because I Was Invited (essays).   Melbourne, Oxford University Press, 1975; London, Oxford University Press, 1976.

Charles Harpur.   Melbourne and London, Oxford University Press, 1977.

The Cry for the Dead.   Melbourne, London, and New York, Oxford University Press, 1981.

Editor, *Australian Poetry 1948.*   Sydney, Angus and Robertson, 1949.

Editor, *A Book of Australian Verse.*   Melbourne and London, Oxford University Press, 1956; revised edition, 1968.

Editor, *New Land, New Language: An Anthology of Australian Verse.*   Melbourne and London, Oxford University Press, 1957.

Editor, with A.K. Thomson, *The Poet's Pen.*   Brisbane, Jacaranda Press, 1965.

Editor, with Val Vallis, *Witnesses of Spring: Unpublished Poems*, by Shaw Neilson.   Sydney, Angus and Robertson, 1970.

Editor, with others, *Report of the National Estate.*   Canberra, Government Publishing Service, 1974.

Editor, with others, *Reef, Rainforest, Mangroves, Man.*   Cairns, Wildlife Preservation Society of Queensland, 1980.

*

Bibliography: *Judith Wright: A Bibliography*, Adelaide, Libraries Board of South Australia, 1968; *Judith Wright* by Shirley Walker, Melbourne, Oxford University Press, 1981.

Critical Studies: *Focus on Judith Wright* by W.N. Scott, Brisbane, University of Queensland Press, 1967; *Critical Essays on Judith Wright* edited by A.K. Thomson, Brisbane, Jacaranda Press, 1968; *Judith Wright* by A.D. Hope, Melbourne, Oxford University Press, 1975; *Judith Wright: An Appreciation* edited by N. Simms, Hamilton, New Zealand, Outrigger Press, 1976; *The Poetry of Judith Wright: A Search for Unity* by Shirley Walker, Melbourne, Arnold, 1980.

Judith Wright comments:

The background of my work lies in my main life concerns, as an Australian whose family on both sides were early comers to a country which was one of the last to be settled by the whites, and were from the beginning farmers and pastoralists. Brought up in a landscape once of extraordinary beauty, but despised by its settlers because of its unfamiliarity, I have I suppose been trying to expiate a deep sense of guilt over what we have done to the country, to its first inhabitants of all kinds, and are still and increasingly doing. This is one aspect of the sources of my work. I have never for long been an urban-dweller, and the images I use and also my methods no doubt reflect my ties to the landscape I live in. I tend to use "traditional"—i.e., biological—rhythms more than free or new forms, which I see as better adapted to urban living and urban tensions and problems.

Another strong influence on my work has been my relationship with my husband whose philosophical investigation of the sources and development of Western thought I shared in till his death. As a woman poet, the biological aspect of feminine experience has naturally been of importance in my work also. I expect my poetry is of a kind which no urban technological society will produce again, but I have tried to remain faithful to my own experience and outlook rather than engage in experimental verse for which it does not fit me.

*   *   *

"Poetry ought not to be thought of as a discipline, but as a kind of praise....Poetry is a means of regaining faith in man...a way of finding a difficult balance: relating inner and outer...our reality is in relation": these gleanings from Judith Wright's prolific, weighty essays provide a helpful gloss on the total achievement of perhaps the world's, certainly Australia's, greatest living woman poet.

Although traditional in form and predominantly lyrical, Wright's poems are acutely modern in recording an attempt to find peace in a godless world: to find a saving balance between "what I think and what I see," the romantic vision and polluted environment, Platonic certainties and Heraclitean flux, philosophical order and body's pulse. In her essays on the Australian artist, dropped out of Europe into "a pocket of silence and space," Wright records her own primal awareness of an alien, fallen world; her landscape is a waste land of bones, rock, fire, and flood, haunted by the Aborigine and swagman. Wright's solution to this sense of alienation, like that of the Australian poets she admires, is metaphysical (Kendall, Baylebridge, Brennan) or romantic (Harpur, above all Nielson and his "folly of Spring").

The latter impulse Wright expressed most notably in *Woman to Man*, a volume centring on the experience of childbirth ("O move in me, my darling"), and in those poems spread throughout her work and addressed to her philosopher husband or to her daughter. In "The Curtain" Wright watches her returned, grown daughter as she sleeps: "So grown you looked, in the same unaltered room,/so much of your childhood you were already forgetting,/while I remembered." But even in these poems there is the metaphysical distrust of instinctive sentiment; the pregnant woman winces at "The blind head butting at the dark,/the blaze of light along the blade./Oh hold me, for I am afraid." The virgin in "Naked Girl and Mirror" is really a vessel for the spirit which reluctantly makes peace with the transitory and soon to be corrupted body.

In Wright's other most famous poem, "Bullocky," an Australian workman is given mythic dimension when he is likened to Moses. This is typical of the poet's constant intellectual effort to retrieve her subject—often herself—from the "wheel of life" in order to praise it, believe in it, or simply get into some balanced relationship. The poetic act is often the image for this retrieval, whether in relation to trees ("When the last leaf and bird go/Let my thoughts stand like trees here") or birds ("He met me like a word/I needed—pity? love?—the rainbow-bird"). Her middle period contains an excessive number of poems about poetry, and culminates in the lurid yet strangely compelling vision of the

Montreal Poetry Conference, where poets burn ignored in high-rise windows, their words falling like "unacceptable holy ghosts."

Wright's central concern is, indeed, language. From her first volume ("Words are rubbed smooth and faceless as old coins"), Wright has laboured with the world's command, "interpret me in god-made words." In lesser poems she capitulates to the rhetorical solution of "love," but her best poetry captures the drama of words struggling to comprehend the world. Although she believes strongly in the poet as social commentator ("No panic, and no heroics,/the market's steady" is the satirical advice to a young poet), the humanity in Wright's modification of her early approval of Stevens in "The Unnecessary Angel"—"Sing with one reserve;/Silence might be best"—points to the distinctive quality of her poetry, which A.D. Hope defined as "nobility." There is even nobility in the slightness of her latest volumes, her awareness of her waning powers of balance and the increasing incomprehensibility of the modern world: "I've cultivated stability/by keeping my horizons straight./Now of a sudden we're crossing/very mountainous country."

Wright has warned that a critic must take account of a poet's context, what he was "trying to do" and the "play of feeling" which a poem crystallises. I have suggested that she tries to balance opposites, the unwieldy paradoxes of our existence (look at the dualities in her titles—*Woman to Man, The Other Half, The Two Fires, Fourth Quarter*); her "play of feeling" is the exhilarating sense of momentary achievement. One couplet epitomises these essential aspects of her large and varied oeuvre about the relationship of man to earth:

> On her dark breast we spring like points of light
> and set her language on the map of night.

> —David Dowling

WRIGHT, Kit. British. Born in Kent in 1944. Educated at Berkhamsted School, Hertfordshire; New College, Oxford. Taught in a comprehensive school, London; Lecturer in English, Brock University, St. Catharines, Ontario, for 3 years. Education Secretary, Poetry Society, London, 1970-75. Fellow-Commoner in Creative Arts, Trinity College, Cambridge, 1977-79. Recipient: Geoffrey Faber Memorial Prize, 1978; Poetry Society Alice Hunt Bartlett Prize, 1978; Arts Council bursary, 1985. Address: c/o Viking Kestrel, 536 King's Road, London SW10 0DA, England.

PUBLICATIONS

Verse

Treble Poets 1, with Stephen Miller and Elizabeth Maslen. London, Chatto and Windus, 1974.
The Bear Looked over the Mountain. London, Salamander Imprint, 1977.
Bump-Starting the Hearse. London, Hutchinson, 1983.
From the Day Room. Liverpool, Windows Press, 1983.

Other (for children)

Arthur's Father [*Granny, Sister, Uncle*]. London, Methuen, 4 vols., 1978.
Rabbiting On and Other Poems. London, Fontana, 1978.

Hot Dog and Other Poems. London, Kestrel, 1981.
Professor Potts Meets the Animals of Africa. London, Watts, 1981.

Editor, *Soundings: A Selection of Poems for Speaking Aloud*. London, Heinemann, 1975.
Editor, *Poems for 9-Year-Olds and Under*. London, Kestrel, 1984.
Editor, *Poems for Over 10-Year-Olds*. London, Viking Kestrel, 1984.

*   *   *

Rumour has it that Kit Wright writes lyrics for musical reviews and the like, and I can well believe it. Many of his poems have that breezily rhythmical, easily rhyming quality which shouts out for a catchy tune. Sometimes he even provides a chorus or two:

> She's got
> Red boots on, she's got
> Red boots on,
> Kicking up the winter
> Till the winter is gone.

What is certain is that there is more to it than that, and if Wright's rhythms and rhymes have literary forebears then one must be Auden—the echoes are there:

> Coming out of nowhere,
> Into nowhere sped,
> Blind as time, my darling,
> Blind nothing in its head.

What are Wright's own are his wit, his insights into our urban life, and the refreshing contemporaneity of his language which does not eschew transatlantic overtones, while making sure they are the genuine article and not the language that never was of the popular entertainer.

> I light the last one from the pack. Outside
> An evening of wind and rain drivels and blusters
> Against my sidestreet window.

Add to all this Kit Wright's sense of fun and you get sudden glimpses of a world which, however bizarre, is never far from the world we know, sometimes brittly bright, as in "Humpty's Fatalism"—"I was a tough old egg/Philip Marlow/hanging in/sunny side up"—at other times getting its effects by contrasting the language used and the theme it expresses—"I was thinking about her all the way from Troy/(I slipped town when the Greek Horse showed)"—but never far off pushing at the nerve of real feeling, as in "Elizabeth" or "What were you going to say?":

> What were you going to say
> On the path above the sea
> When we stared down at the bay
> And suddenly
> The film of the bright day
> Snapped at the end of a reel.

It is certainly this facility, together with his lively inventiveness which makes his collections of verse for young people so deservedly popular.

This has become more apparent in his second collection, *Bump-Starting the Hearse*. There are, of course, the wildly and hilariously scurrilous pieces such as "Underneath the Archers": "Everyone's on about Walter's willy/Down at The Bull tonight." But alongside are poems such as "The Day Room," about a mental hospital, and "The Specialist":

> Imagine you dreamed this
> stone-cold dream
> and woke and the whole cold
> thing were true

which induce those shudders which used to be described as "some one walking over your grave."

A "light verse master" is how Peter Porter has described Kit Wright, and so he is. But while his poetry amuses and entertains, it also disturbs, making us look at the commonplace with fresh insight and sharpness of feeling even when it is at its most self-deprecating.

—John Cotton

YATES, J. Michael. Canadian. Born in Fulton, Missouri, United States, 10 April 1938. Educated at Westminster College, Fulton; University of Kansas City, Missouri (Poetry Prize, 1960), B.A. 1960, M.A. 1961; University of Michigan, Ann Arbor (Hopwood Award, for poetry, 1964, for drama, 1964), 1962-64. Married Ann West in 1970. Promotional Director, Public Radio Corporation, Houston, 1961-62; Teaching Fellow, University of Michigan, 1962-63; taught at Ohio University, Athens, 1964-65, University of Alaska, Fairbanks, 1965-66; Assistant Professor, 1966-69, and Associate Professor of English, 1969-71, University of British Columbia, Vancouver; taught at University of Arkansas, Fayetteville, Fall 1972, and University of Texas, Dallas, 1976-77. Editor-in-Chief, 1966-67, and Poetry Editor, 1966-71, *Prism International*, and Member of the Editorial Board, Prism International Press, Mission, British Columbia, 1966-71; Founding Editor, with Andreas Schroeder, *Contemporary Literature in Translation*, Vancouver, 1968-81; Member of the Editorial Board, *Mundus Artium*, Athens, Ohio; General Editor, *Campus Canada*; Head of Special Projects Division, University of British Columbia Press, 1977-78. Since 1971, President, Sono Nis Press, Vancouver, later Victoria, British Columbia; since 1978, sales representative, Mitchell Press. Recipient: International Broadcasting Award, 1961, 1962; Canada Council grant, 1968, 1969, 1971, and Senior Arts Award, 1972, 1974. Address: c/o Sono Nis Press, 1745 Blanshard Street, Victoria, British Columbia V8W 2J8, Canada.

PUBLICATIONS

Verse

Spiral of Mirrors. Francestown, New Hampshire, Golden Quill Press, 1967.
Hunt in an Unmapped Interior and Other Poems. Francestown, New Hampshire, Golden Quill Press, 1967.
Canticle for Electronic Music. Victoria, British Columbia, Charles Morriss, 1967.
Parallax, with Bob Flick. Victoria, British Columbia, Charles Morriss, 1968.
The Great Bear Lake Meditations. Ottawa, Oberon Press, 1970.

Nothing Speaks for the Blue Moraines: New and Selected Poems. Vancouver, Sono Nis Press, 1973.
Breath of the Snow Leopard. Vancouver, Sono Nis Press, 1974.
The Qualicum Physics. San Francisco, Kanchenjunga Press, 1975.
Esox Nobilior non Esox Lucius. Fredericton, New Brunswick, Fiddlehead, 1978.
Fugue Brancusi. Victoria, British Columbia, Sono Nis Press, 1983.
The Queen Charlotte Islands Meditations. Moonbeam, Ontario, Penumbra Press, 1983.

Plays

Subjunction (produced Fairbanks, Alaska, 1965).
Night Freight (broadcast, 1968; produced Toronto, 1972). Toronto, Playwrights, 1972.
The Abstract Beast: New Fiction and Drama (includes the plays *The Abstract Beast, The Border, The Broadcaster, The Calling, The Panel, Smokestack in the Desert, Theatre of War*). Vancouver, Sono Nis Press, 1971.
Quarks (includes *The Net, Search for the Tse-Tse Fly; The Calling*). Toronto, Playwrights, 1975.

Screenplay: *The Grand Edit,* 1966.

Radio Plays: *The Broadcaster,* 1968; *Theatre of War,* 1968; *The Calling,* 1968; *Night Freight,* 1968; *The Panel,* 1969; *The Abstract Beast,* 1969; *Smokestack in the Desert,* 1970; *Poet in an Arctic Landscape,* 1970; *The Border,* 1971; *Realia,* 1975; *The Net,* 1975; *Search for the Tse-Tse Fly,* 1975; *Sinking of the North West Passage,* 1975; *The Secret of State,* 1976.

Short Stories

Man in the Glass Octopus. Vancouver, Sono Nis Press, 1968.
Fazes in Elsewhen: New and Selected Fiction. Vancouver, Intermedia Press, 1977.

Other

Editor, with Andreas Schroeder, *Contemporary Poetry of British Columbia.* Vancouver, Sono Nis Press, 2 vols., 1970-72.
Editor, with Charles Lillard, *Volvox: Poetry from the Unofficial Languages of Canada in English Translation.* Vancouver, Sono Nis Press, 1971.
Editor, *Contemporary Fiction of British Columbia.* Vancouver, Sono Nis Press, 1971.

*

J. Michael Yates comments:

1. For me, an image is one of an infinite number of entrances into an arena where something ineffable is going on. If the thing I'm after were statable, probably it would be better said in expository prose. The issues most often taken up by good poetry usually require use of the silences between and behind words. For this mode of communication, metaphor, indirection are the best engines.

2. With each piece, I attempt to cause a structure, a system, of images whose parts belong dissonantly to a whole whose meaning cannot be stated. I mean Stravinsky's dissonance. In the *Poetics of Music,* he suggests that dissonance is only a transitional element; consonance must be achieved one way or another—either in the instrumentation or in the ear of the lis-

tener. The latter is my way—to give the reader the "thing" I'm talking about, frame by frame, and ask him to project it inside him in the manner that most entertains him. Different and isolate as each of us is, it seems the only honesty.

3. Ideally, fifteen readers will make fifteen very different (and fifteen equally justifiable) poems from a piece I have written. As I'm different from you at any moment, I differ from myself through successive moments—even the most familiar things change with changes in the coordinates of consciousness and time, I couldn't possibly recreate the coordinates of consciousness that produced a given piece and thereby tell you what it means.

4. Ideally, a reader would come to a poem relaxed, with open consciousness, no preconceptions nor suspicions that the poem is a locked door and someone somewhere—probably the treacherous bastard author—is hiding the key. The parts of a poem which persist inside a reader arrive there via personal correspondences. Exterior interpretations remain merely exterior. Belief in one's own associations is difficult, very difficult. But only those will translate the poem from "mine" to "yours."

5. Ideally, one would read a poem as if he were the first reader in history to read a poem—and as if no one on earth were reading a poem at that moment. Impossible. Necessary.

6. Ideally, I write as if no one has ever written a poem. As if no one is writing now. Ridiculous. Imperative.

7. "Understanding" is a sweet, vague Renaissance dream which never came true. According to me, poems are not to be understood, but responded to. Understanding promises universal truth. Naive. I'm a rare user and no pusher at all of either reality or its ism. I don't assume a "representative universe." As if one could come to an "understanding" about such things.

*   *   *

An overview of the work of J. Michael Yates is complicated by the diversity of forms in which he writes and by his marked experimentation, self-education, and maturation as a writer. This apologia notwithstanding, there are themes and images common to all Yates's output, from the early poems to the plays of *The Abstract Beast*. And common to all his work, too, is a certain self-consciousness, arising partly from the experimentation, but largely from a self-image of the "young man as Artist," an image which matures as surely as does his technique. In fact, there is a connection between these two observations, for Yates's self-image is not a pose, but, rather, a preoccupation with the notion that the ideas of the writer are his whole world and reality. This Lockean fascination with a state of being in which the mind becomes a substitute for the existent is seen perhaps most clearly in *Man in the Glass Octopus* but is prefigured in the early poems of *Hunt in an Unmapped Interior* (whose title suggests it) and continues into the endless series of lenses viewing lenses of the *Parallax* poems. It also prompts the recurrent images of animals eating animals, cameras filming cameras, and mirrors mirroring mirrors with which the poems are filled. As well, it explains the persona of the author/narrator as Adam naming Creation, which D.G. Jones has cited as a major theme of all Canadian writing and which in Yates's poems (notably *The Great Bear Lake Meditations*), is extended until the mind of Adam becomes the Mind of God, Itself an insubstantial mirror of Yates's own consciousness. And finally, it is embodied in the name of Yates's press, at once an *impressa* and a complication: Sono Nis—"the I is not."

Each of these concerns is introduced in *Hunt in an Unmapped Interior*, a collection of poems strongly reminiscent of Wallace Stevens, in which the short pieces are deft and incisive, the longer poems ruminative. *Canticle for Electronic Music* is disappoint-

ing after this auspicious first collection; again Yates has difficulty in sustaining the longer poem. *Great Bear Lake Meditations* is a more mature work, in which the Adam persona is accepted and in which Yates's love of words becomes congruent with his myth—if the poet's only reality is imaginative, then words become symbols of nothing other than aspects of his imagination. In *Parallax*, Yates gropes toward but fails to quite reach a further refinement in which if "words are better than talk...[then] silence [is] better than words." The poems attempt the visual, building upon camera imagery. But to create a "silent" poem without words is ultimately to produce a blank page and these poems, however compelling, are "at the verge of total desire that ends in the half-act."

In *The Abstract Beast*, Yates looks to other forms and modifies his poems into the prose they have always approached and into highly successful short radio plays (which would be less successful on stage). Perhaps realizing after *Man in the Glass Octopus* that the end-point of his self-preoccupation would be self-nihilism, Yates has tempered his myth; while it is still obvious it is less obsessive. The result is a collection that with the exception of some unfortunately reprinted early pieces is as inventive as it is exciting. What thinness does arise in the stories and the sometimes disturbing inconclusiveness of the plays is most likely the result of another shift in development and hopefully will not continue into later work. Much more will be heard of J. Michael Yates.

—S.R. Gilbert

_____

YAU, John. American. Born in 1950. Address: c/o Holt Rinehart and Winston, 521 Fifth Avenue, New York, New York 10175, U.S.A.

PUBLICATIONS

Verse

Crossing Canal Street. Binghamton, New York, Bellevue Press, 1976.
Sometimes. New York, Sheep Meadow Press, 1979.
The Sleepless Night of Eugene Delacroix. New York, Release Press, 1980.
Broken Off by the Music. Providence, Rhode Island, Burning Deck, 1981.
Corpse and Mirror. New York, Holt Rinehart, 1983.

*   *   *

It is said the palace was modeled on a dream, but even what the
    king remembers of his dream is not necessarily the dream
    itself.
Will this space between the pages of sleep and the writing
    of day
always exist? I do not know. I might never know. I am only
    a guard—
a fixture that moves like the polished hands of a clock.

John Yau, like Garret Hongo, is a young American poet whose first collection of poems (following four chapbooks from small presses) was published in 1983. Like Hongo, he works with his combined Oriental heritage and a sense of himself as an American, both aesthetically and culturally. Consequently, strong in this work is a sense of the doubleness of things, which must come out of the double heritage, and gives him a kind of contemporary vision which, while occurring to him naturally, is intellectually appealing to all of us who feel that the nature of materialistic reality and the reality of the dream-life or unconscious are two very different things. Writing, then, becomes a bridge for many of us to connect the two. In "Two Kinds of Song" Yau assigns himself the role of guard in the dream palace, whose function "like the polished hands of a clock" places him in time, though without knowledge.

Contemporary thinkers are all interested in the relationship of time to being and some definitions of consciousness. Yau, in *Corpse and Mirror*, tries to extend those definitions. In "Two Kinds of Language," near the close of the book ("Two Kinds of Song" appears near the beginning), a prose poem in two sections, he extends this sense of being in time without knowledge. One section describes hearing parents speaking in Chinese by a son who does not understand but who thinks he might understand. The second section describes driving in a car in North Carolina, listening to the radio, feeling as if one is a child, juxtaposing this with a sentence about there being another room in which a language which the hearer cannot understand is being spoken. In both sections of the poem, the speaker is in a sound environment which is natural to him, but of which he only experiences partial understanding. There is no sense of frustration or even mystery, but rather an acceptance that the world is one where, even though one feels comfortable, reality can only be partially known and related to. And even the knowing in both sections of the poem is only the sense of barely understanding, or partially understanding, or thinking that perhaps one understands. Yau posits a world where there are no absolutes—even the doubleness is only the double image of mirror image, one image reversed—but in the context of time, we have the certainty of the clock. Time is certain. Knowing is not.

Yau uses his visual sense of the world well, and his lyrical sense of love perhaps comes through traditions of Chinese poetry. But it is his probing of our impressions of time and space and consciousness that gives his work its greatest power. In "Third Variation On Corpse and Mirror" he gives us once again the world of doubles.

> I crossed the street
> but not before
> noticing the knife
> poised along the moment's
> throat, ready to divide
> its destination into
> two further choices.
> In the yard beside me
> two dogs played catch
> with someone's head,
> while a hand waved good-bye
> to the body it once carried.

Life and death here are the doubles, along with the head (the life of the mind) and the hand (the life of material, practical reality). "Choices," he calls them, but nowhere does he indicate how this choice is made. But perhaps he tries to answer this question in the many poems which show the exchange of this double reality, that one side is only the mirror image of the other. In "Three Poems for Li Shng-yin" (moving from the polar double to the magical number, three), the first poem is

> When she left she took everything—her hair
> Was a dream filled with colors gone by noon.

> Yet, if nothing can be retrieved, I am still pulled
> Toward this woman, who is still asleep, locked
> Away in another life; her hair
> Piled up like red peonies at noon.

Does he give us an anwer here? That knowing *is* the physical filled with the metaphysical, that neither exists without the other?

Yau's poems present a vivid combination of the body and the mind, just as they come out of a unique fusion of the Oriental and Occidental cultures.

—Diane Wakoski

YOUNG, Al(bert James). American. Born in Ocean Springs, Mississippi, 31 May 1939. Educated at the University of Michigan, Ann Arbor (Co-Editor, *Generation* magazine), 1957-61; Stanford University, California (Wallace E. Stegner Creative Writing Fellow), 1966-67; University of California, Berkeley, A.B. in Spanish 1969. Married Arline June Belch in 1963; one son. Free-lance musician, 1958-64; disc jockey, KJAZ-FM, Alameda, California, 1961-65; Instructor and Linguistic Consultant, San Francisco Neighborhood Youth Corps Writing Workshop, 1968-69; Writing Instructor, San Francisco Museum of Art Teenage Workshop, 1968-69; Jones Lecturer in Creative Writing, Stanford University, 1969-74; screenwriter, Laser Films, New York, 1972, Stigwood Corporation, London and New York, 1972, Verdon Productions, Hollywood, 1976, First Artists Ltd., Burbank, California, 1976-77, and Universal, Hollywood, 1979; Writer-in-Residence, University of Washington, Seattle, 1981-82. Since 1979, Director, Associated Writing Programs. Founding Editor, *Loveletter*, San Francisco, 1966-68. Since 1972, Co-Editor, *Yardbird Reader*, Berkeley, California; Contributing Editor, since 1972, *Changes*, New York, and since 1973, *Umoja*, New Mexico; since 1981, Co-Editor and Co-Publisher, *Quilt*, Berkeley. Recipient: National Endowment for the Arts grant, 1968, 1969, 1974; San Francisco Foundation Joseph Henry Jackson Award, 1969; Guggenheim Fellowship, 1974; Pushcart prize, 1980; Before Columbus Foundation award, 1982. Agent: Lynn Nesbitt, International Creative Management, 40 West 57th Street, New York, New York 10019. Address: 514 Bryant Street, Palo Alto, California 94301, U.S.A.

PUBLICATIONS

Verse

Dancing. New York, Corinth, 1969.
The Song Turning Back into Itself. New York, Holt Rinehart, 1971.
Some Recent Fiction. San Francisco, San Francisco Book Company, 1974.
Geography of the Near Past. New York, Holt Rinehart, 1976.
The Blues Don't Change: New and Selected Poems. Baton Rouge, Louisiana State University Press, 1982.

Plays

Screenplays: *Nigger*, 1972; *Sparkle*, 1972.

Novels

Snakes. New York, Holt Rinehart, 1970; London, Sidgwick and Jackson, 1971.
Who Is Angelina? New York, Holt Rinehart, 1975; London, Sidgwick and Jackson, 1978.
Sitting Pretty. New York, Holt Rinehart, 1976.
Ask Me Now. New York, McGraw Hill, and London, Sidgwick and Jackson, 1980.

Other

Bodies and Soul: Musical Memoirs. Berkeley, California, Creative Arts, 1981.
Kinds of Blue: Musical Memoirs. Berkeley, California, Creative Arts, 1984.

Editor, with Ishmael Reed, *Yardbird Lives!* New York, Grove Press, 1978.

*

Bibliography: in *New Black Voices,* edited by Abraham Chapman, New York, New American Library, 1972.

Critical Studies: "Reader's Report" by Martin Levin, in *New York Times Book Review,* 17 May 1970; "Growing Up Black" by L.E. Sissman, in *The New Yorker,* 11 July 1970; "Jazzed Up," in the *Times Literary Supplement* (London), 30 July 1971.

Al Young comments:
    I see my poetry as being essentially autobiographical in subject matter and detail, characterized by a marked personal and lyrical mysticism as well as a concern with social and spiritual problems of contemporary man in a technological environment that grows hourly more impersonal and unreal. My favorite themes are those of love, the infinite changeability of the world as well as its eternal changelessness, and the kind of meaning (both private and universal) that flowers out of everyday life. My influences in general have been Black culture and popular speech (Southern rural and urban U.S.) and music in particular (jazz, Afro-American folk and popular music, the music of Charles Mingus and John Coltrane which defies categorization, Caribbean music of both English- and Spanish-speaking peoples); American Indian poetry and song; Hindu philosophy. Some poets I admire and have consciously learned from: Li Po, Nicolás Guillén; Rabindranath Tagore, the poetry of the *Bible,* Federico García Lorca, Kenneth Patchen, Blaise Cendrars, early T.S. Eliot, Rimbaud, Brecht, LeRoi Jones, Mayakovsky, Denise Levertov, Léopold Senghor, Kenneth Rexroth, Cervantes, Diane Wakoski and Nicanor Parra.
    Besides being as necessary as food, water, air, sunlight and sleep—poetry is my way of celebrating Spirit, in all of its infinite forms (charted and uncharted) as the central unifying force in Creation.

*   *   *

    Al Young's 1976 book of verse, *Geography of the Near Past,* contains five poems satirically representing "art as a hustle." Purporting to be dictations by O.O. Gabugah, "a militant advocate of the oral tradition," the poems are full of posturing and the rhetoric of racial politics. Technically facile, they ridicule not the literary method of poets like Gabugah, but their dedication to the notion of art as weapon. Nothing could be further from the practice of Young himself who calls poetry a

magic wafer you take
into your mouth
&
swallow for dear life

    To Al Young poetry is a means "to swim against/world current/knowing it to be as much a dream/as it is drama on the highest stage." The trick is to know that "Each universe is only/an ever-shifting sea/in the surfacing eyes of former fish." Inevitably, then, poetry for Young takes an autobiographical subject, seeking authenticity in the flux of process.
    A first step occurs in poems of controlled focus where accidental details of ordinary life gain meaning by association. The sequence of a day's ordinary events becomes a love letter in "Dear Arl," and in "A Dance for Li Po" bringing home groceries stimulates reflection on the variety of good places the poet has been over the years. The continuity of associative time converts memory into the principle of a fluid reality in "The Song Turning Back into Itself." Here the images of circling in time and space lead into statement of the power of song to create new versions of love, and loneliness, while also organizing past experience of those states. There is, too, the sense, shared with musicians, of the capacity of art to generate identity through expression of a lyrical mysticism. Appropriately the sequence concludes with a jazz inspired fly-away song in which the poet soars over rooftops.
    As though for the time being his aesthetic needs no further statement, Young's poems in *Geography of the Near Past* return to detailing the small incident, so that he can plumb it for significance. A series of poems on the cities of Manhattan, Boston, Providence, Detroit, and Denver relate moments of intense feeling; the verse renounces commentary or explication in favor of a recreation of a moment's mood. The moments are brief, the mood without ambiguity, but there is no mistaking the effect. It is that of poetry performing its ancient function of discovery.

—John M. Reilly

———————

YOUNG, David (Pollock). American. Born in Davenport, Iowa, 14 December 1936. Educated at Carleton College, Northfield, Minnesota, B.A. 1958; Yale University, New Haven, Connecticut, M.A. 1959, Ph.D. 1965. Married Chloe Hamilton in 1963; two children. Instructor, 1961-65, Assistant Professor, 1965-68, Associate Professor, 1969-73, and since 1973, Professor of English, Oberlin College, Ohio. Since 1969, Editor, *Field: Contemporary Poetry and Poetics,* Oberlin. Co-Owner, Triskelion Press, Oberlin. Recipient: Tane Award (*Massachusetts Review*), 1965; National Endowment for the Arts grant, 1967, and Fellowship, 1981; International Poetry Forum United States Award, 1968; Guggenheim Fellowship, 1978. Address: 220 Shipherd Circle, Oberlin, Ohio 44074, U.S.A.

PUBLICATIONS

Verse

Sweating Out the Winter. Pittsburgh, University of Pittsburgh Press, 1969.
Thoughts of Chairman Mao. Oberlin, Ohio, Triskelion Press, 1970.
Boxcars. New York, Ecco Press, 1974.

Work Lights: Thirty-Two Prose Poems.   Cleveland, Cleveland
   State Poetry Center, 1977.
The Names of a Hare in English.   Pittsburgh, University of
   Pittsburgh Press, 1979.

Other

*Something of Great Constancy: The Art of "A Midsummer
   Night's Dream."*   New Haven, Connecticut, Yale University
   Press, 1966.
The Heart's Forest: A Study of Shakespeare's Pastoral Plays.
   New Haven, Connecticut, Yale University Press, 1972.

Editor, *Twentieth Century Interpretations of "Henry IV, Part
   Two": A Collection of Critical Essays.*   Englewood Cliffs,
   New Jersey, Prentice Hall, 1968.
Editor, with Stuart Friebert, *A Field Guide to Contemporary
   Poetry and Poetics.*   New York, Longman, 1980.
Editor, with Stuart Friebert, *Longman's Anthology of Poe-
   try.*   New York, Longman, 1982.
Editor, with Keith Hollaman, *Magical Realist Fiction.*   New
   York, Longman, 1984.

Translator, *Six Poems from Wang Wei.*   Oberlin, Ohio, Tris-
   kelion Press, 1969.
Translator, *Magic Strings: Nine Poems from Li Ho.*   Oberlin,
   Ohio, Pocket Pal Press, 1976.
Translator, *Duino Elgies,* by Rilke.   New York, Norton, 1978.
Translator, *Wang Wei, Li Po, Tu Fu, Li Ho: Four T'ang Poets.*
   Oberlin, Ohio, Oberlin College, 1980.
Translator, with Stuart Friebert and David Walker, *Valuable
   Nail: Selected Poems,* by Günter Eich.   Oberlin, Ohio, Ober-
   lin College, 1981.
Translator, with Dana Hábova, *Interferon; or, On Theater,* by
   Miroslav Holub.   Oberlin, Ohio, Oberlin College, 1982.

*

David Young comments:
   My collections of poetry, I find, tend to be more and more
unified by recurrent figures and themes. Since I depend very
much on what is called "inspiration" in writing my poetry, it is
gratifying to be able to shape the materials presented to me in
that fashion into larger wholes that benefit from mirroring and
echoing. The newest collection, *Foraging* (due in February
1986), is filled with images of mushrooms (and mushroom-
hunting, a hobby of mine) and ghosts. Both of these leading
motifs relate to the way the imagination reuses and recycles what
is lost, decayed, or difficult to accept.

*   *   *

   David Young's poetry has a strong sense of the American
Midwest where he was born and now teaches; it is a poetry of flat
land dreaming of quiet transformations, unsatisfied but calm:
"All to the south the dazed, hot landscape lies,/ Under its piled
thunderheads,/ Dreaming of love and survival."
   His poetry reminds one of the work of another Midwestern
poet, William Stafford, in that it has a controlled skilfulness
which makes itself unobtrusive. There is an essential modesty to
their work. And, like Stafford, Young has a quality of faithfulness, of commitment to his own problematic existence; he does
not, as so many Americans do, attempt to change his life by
merely changing place, by running to New York or California.
He faces the emptiness and solitude the land presents to him:

A lonely country?...
...What's this but
Acceptable solitude? And who'd
Trade it for any multitude?

   Young's work is that of a man whose edges are gently blurring,
who reaches quietly for something just outside of the room he
lives in—a twilight poetry in which past and present, desire and
"reality," lose their hard outlines, gliding in and out of one
another.
   Two of the most prominent influences on Young's writing are
apparent in his excellent imitations of Stevens ("Putting It
Mildly") and of Robert Bly ("Oh Salmon-colored Edsel"), but he
is not confined by any particular mode. His poems are sometimes
humorous, often witty, and on some occasions even employ
rhyme or meter. The mainstream of Young's poetry, though, is
apparent in his "The Small-Town Poets," a fine poem which
seems a self-portrait of sorts. The small plane which appears
there, as it does in many of his poems, is an apt emblem for his
poetic imagination, looping easily, observing things from a certain height with nostalgia and delight, wit and good will.

—Lawrence Russ

———————

YOUNG, Ian (George).   British; Canadian Landed Immigrant.
Born in London, 5 January 1945. Educated at Beal Grammar
School, Ilford, Essex; Malvern Collegiate Institute, Toronto;
Victoria College, University of Toronto, 1964-67, 1970. Since
1969, Director, Catalyst Press, Scarborough, Ontario. Press
Secretary, 1969-71, and Chairman, 1972-73, University of Toronto
Homophile Association. Recipient: Canada Council grant, 1969,
1974, 1976, 1977, bursary, 1972. Address: 315 Blantyre Avenue,
Scarborough, Ontario M1N 2S6, Canada.

PUBLICATIONS

Verse

White Garland: 9 Poems for Richard.   Scarborough, Ontario,
   Cyclops, 1969.
Year of the Quiet Sun.   Toronto, Anansi, 1969.
Double Exposure.   Trumansburg, New York, New Books,
   1970; revised edition, Trumansburg, Crossing Press, 1974.
Cool Fire, with Richard Phelan.   Scarborough, Ontario, Cata-
   lyst, 1970.
Lions in the Stream, with Richard Phelan.   Scarborough,
   Ontario, Catalyst, 1971.
Some Green Moths.   Scarborough, Ontario, Catalyst, 1972.
Autumn Angels.   Toronto, Village Book Store, 1973.
Yuletide Story.   Scarborough, Ontario, Catalyst, 1973.
Don.   Scarborough, Ontario, Catalyst, 1973.
Invisible Words.   Toronto, Missing Link Press, 1974.
Alamo.   Toronto, Dreadnaught Press, 1976.
Common-or-Garden Gods.   Scarborough, Ontario, Catalyst,
   1976.
Whatever Turns You On in the New Year.   Scarborough, Ontar-
   io, Catalyst, 1976.
Schwule Poesie.   Hunfeld, Germany, Aschenbach, 1978.

Other

The Male Homosexual in Literature: A Bibliography. Metuchen, New Jersey, Scarecrow Press, 1975; revised edition, 1982.

Editor, *The Male Muse: A Gay Anthology.* Trumansburg, New York, Crossing Press, 1973.
Editor, *On the Line: New Gay Fiction.* Trumansburg, New York, Crossing Press, 1981.
Editor, *The Son of the Male Muse: New Gay Poetry.* Trumansburg, New York, Crossing Press, 1984.

Translator, *Curieux d'Amour,* by Count Jacques d'Adelsward Ferson. London, Timothy d'Arch Smith, 1970.

*

Critical Studies: "The Younger Toronto Poets Add Up to Just One" by Andreas Schroeder, in *Vancouver Province,* 7 February 1969; by Debbie Young, in *The Carleton* (Ottawa), 6 February 1970; Bob Bossin, in *The Varsity* (Toronto), 6 February 1970; introduction by John Gill, to *Double Exposure,* 1970; Robert Peters, in *Gay Sunshine* (San Francisco) January-February 1973; "Ian Young's Verse Delights" by Jim Eggeling, in *The Advocate* (Los Angeles), 25 April 1973; "The Poetry of Ian Young" by Robert Hawkes, in *Margins* (Milwaukee), March 1976; "Gay in Not So Jocund Company" by Pier Giorgio di Cicco, in *Books in Canada* (Toronto), May 1976; "Telegraphic Images" by Andrew Bifrost, in *Dodeca 15* (New York), 1976.

*   *   *

Ian Young is the Strato of contemporary poetry. Most recently he has published *The Male Muse,* an anthology of contemporary gay poetry that is the *Mousa Paidike* of is time. That there is a doctrinaire cast to Young's introduction to the anthology—"the growing impetus of the homophile/gay liberation movement"—is indicative of the weaknesses in that anthology, which nonetheless contains some very fine work by some surprising authors.

It is indicative too of a more general flaw in Young's own work—the tendency for obsession to override poetry. Only occasionally does one think of Cavafy—or better, Durrell's poem on Cavafy—the ironic distance and the tough-minded disdain for what Sir Thomas Browne called "the foolishest act that a man ever commits in his life."

But such disdain for the foolishness of the flesh is not fashionable at the moment, certainly not in Canadian poetry where a great deal of over-compensating for the 19th century is still in full voice. And one has, in fairness, to point to a fine descriptive ability and a delicious sensuality in Young's work:

> How I wanted him
> when he came
> into the room
> with a new blue kerchief
>
> when he knotted it
> round his neck
> like a noose of sky

But there is sometimes a sense of strain in his work—the necessary touches of fashionable surrealism or the laboured deference to haiku and the cults of karma and *om.* Here more than anywhere one feels the absence of a restraining versification

where emotion might be recollected in a tranquility productive of better poetry. The "punk's hands" that he fears and celebrates are a paradigm of that wrestle in poetry with which more often he needs to engage. For there is no doubt of his ability who is, in his own words, "hunter/hunted/and long sharp knife."

—D.D.C. Chambers

ZEND, Robert. Canadian. Address: c/o Exile Editions, 69 Sullivan Street, Toronto, Ontario M5T 1C2, Canada.

PUBLICATIONS

Verse

From Zero to One, translated by the author and John Robert Colombo. Vancouver, Sono Nis Press, 1973.
Arbormundi. Vancouver, Blewointment Press, 1982.
Beyond Labels, translated by the author and John Robert Colombo. Toronto, Hounslow Press, 1982.
Nicolette. Toronto, Exile, 1983.
OAB. Toronto, Exile, 2 vols., 1983.
The Three Roberts: Premier Performance, with Robert Priest and Robert Sward. Toronto, HMS Press, 1984.

Other

Editor, *Ariel and Caliban: Selected Poems,* by Peter Singer. Toronto, Aya Press, 1981.

*   *   *

Robert Zend is a member of a gifted generation of Hungarian *émigrés* to Canada that includes the poet George Faludy and the poet-journalist George Jonas. He is a metaphysician of minutiae, and the blurbs for and dedication to *From Zero to One* trace artistic affiliations and affinities. The filmmaker Norman McLaren calls him a "wry geometer"; Marcel Marceau (who also did the book's jacket and frontispiece drawings) says that Zend is "a mime with words"; and the pianist Glenn Gould refers to "cynically witty, abrasively hedonistic, hesitantly compassionate, furtively God-seeking poems." The book is dedicated to the cartoonist Saul Steinberg and to Réne Magritte, and takes its title from a comment by the Hungarian philosopher Frederic Karinthy that "the way from Zero to One is longer than from One to a Hundred-thousand-million...it is about as long as the way from life to death."

Fond of wordplay but using conventional syntax, Zend offers us parables, proverbs, epigrams, and narrative longer poems, thereby running the usual risks: lameness in the shorter forms, rhetorical windiness in the longer. Sometimes, too, the poems seem flashy, merely tossed off for effect. But at their best the mind at work in them reminds one of such acerbic ironists as Blaise Cendrars and Karl Kraus. In "The Most Beautiful Things" Zend leans toward Zen: "...the beautiful roses of the universe/bloom on the invisible/stems of space." This poem obviously bears some relation to a later one, "Nothing," with the latter's virtuoso improvisions on the concept:

Naturally, you think I said nothing in this poem.
But I said something. Not everything.
Nothing is everything. Everything is just something.

Beyond Labels, which collects poems from 1962 to 1982, begins with a statement Zend made at a writers' congress: totalitarian governments "begin simplifying and polarizing the labelling of people," adding that Karinthy, for example, "wasn't willing to accept any label, either for himself or for others." Neither will Zend, it seems. In fact, the exile's dilemma of suspension between two countries or states of being actually fuels his work, as in "My City":

Budapest is my homeland.
Toronto is my home.

In Toronto I am nostalgic for Budapest.
In Budapest I am nostalgic for Toronto.

Everywhere else I am nostalgic for nostalgia.

In recent years, there have been two developments in Zend's work. Since 1965 he has been writing increasingly in English (earlier work was translated with John Robert Colombo's able assistance). He also has become interested in visual modes—typographical *jeux d'esprit* or concrete poems—two forms of which he calls "Ditto Poems" and "Drop Poems." The latter come with a title and one line, the line formed by letters dropped from the title, e.g.:

MAR AR T   HATC
     G   E   T   HER

It's possible that in exploring such new techniques, Zend is deliberately or unconsciously seeking a visual meta-language that transcends and is intelligible in both Hungarian and English.

—Fraser Sutherland

ZIMMER, Paul. American. Born in Canton, Ohio, 18 September 1934. Educated at Kent State University, Kent, Ohio, 1952-53, 1956-59, B.A. 1968. Married Suzanne Koklauner in 1959; one daughter and one son. Macy's book department manager, San Francisco, 1961-63; Manager, San Francisco News Company, 1963-65; Manager, UCLA Bookstore, Los Angeles, 1965-67; Poet-in-Residence, Chico State College, California, Spring 1971; Associate Director, University of Pittsburgh Press, and Editor, Pitt Poetry series, 1967-78; Director, University of Georgia Press, Athens, 1978-84. Since 1984, Director, University of Iowa Press, Iowa City. Recipient: Borestone Mountain Award, 1971; National Endowment for the Arts grant, 1974; Helen Bullis Memorial Award (*Poetry Northwest*), 1975. Address: 204 Lexington, Iowa City, Iowa 52242, U.S.A.

PUBLICATIONS

Verse

A Seed on the Wind. Privately printed, 1960.
The Ribs of Death. New York, October House, 1967.

The Republic of Many Voices. New York, October House, 1969.
The Zimmer Poems. Washington, D.C., Dryad Press, 1976.
With Wanda: Town and Country Poems. Washington, D.C., Dryad Press, 1980.
The Ancient Wars. Pittsburgh, Slow Loris Press, 1981.
Earthbound Zimmer. Milton, Massachusetts, Chowder, 1983.
Family Reunion: Selected and New Poems. Pittsburgh, University of Pittsburgh Press, 1983.
The American Zimmer. Athens, Georgia, Night Owl Press, 1984.

*

Critical Studies: by Hayden Carruth, in *Hudson Review* (New York), Summer 1968; Robert Boyers, in *Partisan Review* (New Brunswick, New Jersey), 1969; James Den Boer, in *Voyages* (Washington, D.C.), Spring 1970; the author, in *American Poets in 1976* edited by William Heyen, Indianapolis, Bobbs Merrill, 1976, and in *Gravida* (New York), 1979; *Zimmer as Poet, Poet as Zimmer* edited by Jan Susina, Birmingham, Alabama, Thunder City Press, n.d.

Paul Zimmer comments:

In working on the arrangement of my selected poems, I began to recognize certain themes that are dominant in my work and that the various personae of my poems speak in (I hope) meaningful ways to each other. Thus I determined not to arrange the poems in the chronological order of their composition, but to orchestrate them around these main movements which roughly follow the span of my life. I am no longer a "young poet" (never really was!). My life responsibilities have increased significantly. It is interesting for me to realize how this affects my work as a poet. I find myself harder to please, but more rewarded when I feel I have accomplished something. I am still sustained and renewed by careful rereadings of poets like Yeats, Wyatt, Whitman, Dante, Browning, Shakespeare, Chaucer, Skelton, Clare, Frost, Roethke, Dickinson, Wright, and many others.

*   *   *

Paul Zimmer is a protean poet whose personae are not so much depicted as created; we witness poet and subjects in process of becoming. A vivid verbal imagination projects the common, lonely, unwanted, neurotic, merely eccentric, and truly mad people of these poems into the elements which surround them and are soon to reclaim them in death, while inanimate objects assume the habits and attributes of human life. Zimmer makes the stock-in-trade of synaesthesia and personification his own by force of an original, often startling point-of-view: "One Vision./Mine." *The Ribs of Death* not only shows this individual stamp on a wide variety of material but also demonstrates a poetic development. A deft, almost eighteenth-century irony characterizes the first poems. Lord Fluting dreams of an illusory America "where the buffalo turn/Broadside to the hunting horns," but discovers the horrors of a primitive country, and asks "Where are the teepees filled with gold?" The Colonies are infected with the sins and superstitions of the Old World; the "great new land" seemed "too full of sun/For ancient shadows," yet the darkness has become so deep that witches are needed to fill "the belly of some flame." The malaise lingers on, but in turning to more recent times, Zimmer becomes more personal in tone, particularly when speaking of his life and art. The once-Catholic poet is "projected into shapes," his province now catholic enough to gather the buckskinned pioneer, the football player, the oil driller, and the witty Handel with the dying Keats and seafaring Conrad under the title of Poet. He can portray death in the placid invalid and eager consumptive and read it in the quick demise of a snapping wave-tip and in the dullness of a blighted apple.

In *The Republic of Many Voices*, he aims again at a variety of subjects, linked now with a connecting theme of rebirth, and death and with a self-conscious tone. But what was magical in the earlier volume tends to lose its charm through repetition. From his still-skewed angle of vision, people fascinate not as personalities so much as curiosities; after the first half-dozen and despite the variation, would-be originals give off a superficial glint, like other objects of a mechanical process. Alonzo is a snowflake, Rollo bears the ocean, Fritz strangles on the world, Carlos becomes the mountain he climbs. Invested with attributes of nature, certain personae have the power of fantastic hybrids. Gus's "guts ache with elm blight" as he "shaves his dewy chin of all its pixie moss." In the "Mordecai" poems Zimmer works several character transformations upon a Black man, but with typically liberal guilt calls the portraiture mere "egghead prattling." Enlarging his self-portrait, he presents telling sketches of home and school, marred, though, with sentimentality and adolescent peevishness (one poem wreaks vengeance upon an old teaching "nun"). Scenes of youthful adventure, close-calls, and lucky accidents shine more vividly, evoking crucial moments of emerging poetic insight. Though lines sometimes get clotted with botanical metaphors, tenderness and good humor infuse his tales of adolescent sexuality and love. "I know I sing the bird," he notes, "And bloom the flower myself."

In *The Zimmer Poems*, he continues his song of himself. However, despite the egotism implied by the title, this book is not an exercise in hybris but humility. Examining past failures, as well as future fears, the poet seems to have come to terms with the personae of earlier poems and, perhaps more important, with his imperfect former self (or selves). One measure of this reconciliation is the warmth and good humor with which he considers the intimidations, inadequacies, and unfulfilled desires of youth and manhood. He projects himself into the decrepitudes of old age, the decay of alcoholism, and the inevitability of death, but the fact that he can confront his fears is itself a sign of new strength. Sharing his aching memories as well as his fears, we can accept that it is not simple narcissism when he says: "I am so much, mean so much." Through these revelatory, touching lines we can also agree with the poet: "Zimmer does not mean./ He is."

—Joseph Parisi

ZINNES, HARRIET (née Fich). American   Born in Hyde Park, Massachusetts. Educated at Hunter College, New York, B.A. 1939; Brooklyn College, New York, M.A. 1944; New York University, Ph.D. 1953. Married Irving Zinnes in 1943; one daughter and one son. Editor, Raritan Arsenal Publications Division, Metuchen, New Jersey, 1942-43; Associate Editor, *Harper's Bazaar*, New York, 1944-46; Tutor, Hunter College, 1946-49, Assistant Professor, 1949-53, Associate Professor, 1962-78, and since 1978, Professor of English, Queens College, City University of New York. Director, Poetry and Fiction Workshop, University of Oklahoma, Norman, 1959-60; Lecturer, Rutgers University, New Brunswick, New Jersey, 1960-62; art and literary critic, *Weekly Tribune*, Geneva, Switzerland, 1968-69; Visiting Professor of American Literature, University of Geneva, Spring 1970. Editorial staff member, *Pictures on*

Exhibit, New York, 1971-81. Poetry Coordinator, Great Neck Library, Long Island, New York. Recipient: MacDowell Fellowship, 1972, 1973, 1974, 1977; Virginia Center for the Creative Arts Fellowship, 1975, 1976, 1981, 1982; Yaddo Fellowship, 1978, 1981; American Council of Learned Societies grant, 1978. Address: Department of English, Queens College, Flushing, New York 11367, U.S.A.

PUBLICATIONS

Verse

Waiting and Other Poems.   Lanham, Maryland, Goosetree Press, 1964.
An Eye for an I.   New York, Folder, 1966.
I Wanted to See Something Flying.   New York, Folder, 1976.
Entropisms.   Arlington, Virginia, Gallimaufry, 1978.
Book of Ten.   Binghamton, New York, Bellevue Press, 1979.

Other

Editor, *Ezra Pound and the Visual Arts.*   New York, New Directions, 1980.

*

Manuscript Collections: Lockwood Memorial Library, State University of New York, Buffalo; Sweet Briar College Library, Virginia.

Critical Studies: by Robert Hazel, in *Masterplots: 1966 Annual* edited by Frank N. Magill, New York, Salem Press, 1967; *Booklist* (Chicago), 15 July 1978; *Choice* (Middletown, Connecticut), September 1978; Marianne Hauser, in *American Book Review* (New York), November-December 1980; *Critical Survey of Short Fiction 1981* edited by Frank Magill, Englewood Cliffs, New Jersey, Salem Press, 1981.

Harriet Zinnes comments:

In my earlier work Ezra Pound was my chief influence—principally through his emphasis on a new music discovered through a spare and rigorous poetic line. Robert Bly was my second significant influence, but my newer work emphasizes what was always true, my hard, ironical approach to a reality that is as much surreal as real. I am finding more and more that I am writing narrative poems (I am also writing short fiction) but narratives where more is omitted than related, and where characters involved may or may not be present. Dramatic tension is characteristic of my work (whether or not there is a story line) as in my prose poems where there are strange, sudden juxtapositions. But it is through language that I hope to achieve that tension, through its seductive music, its syntax and meanings, that can be chopped up, destroyed, denied, changed, or affirmed. I want my poems to declare the complexity of experience, its surprises, for to me a poem is the consequence of a deep realization that what is, is not; that what seems likely to arrive, will never; that what is least expected, will be. Jacques Prévert's work that I have translated fascinates me, therefore. He makes his language, through his puns, his ironic gestures, his linguistic games, demonstrate the complexities, absurdities, barbarities of a world that he loves: "*Dans ma maison qui n'est pas ma maison tu viendras.*" *Voilà*: what is, is not, and yet, "*tu viendras.*"

*   *   *

Harriet Zinnes's poetry invites analogies to modern painting and sculpture. Many of her poems are verbal collages, collections of "found objects" (verse equivalents of Duchamp's "ready-mades"), the significance of whose juxtaposition depends, at least in part, upon the ingenuity of the reader. In the four-part "Electronic Music" she bows and points to Rauschenberg, splicing together the tapes and other electronic communications gear with the debris of a technological society. Others of her poetic constructs display the irony, wit, and seeming innocence of a Miro sculpture, where, again, the relevance of the configuration lies in the eye of the imaginative beholder. She notes: "(Nothing is far-fetched/that the mind seizes upon.)" She makes Dadaist games of the jumble of life. The persona exclaims: "What an antic traffic jam I am." Playful typography figures in "MEn" and "and the fruit," while drawings supplement other poems, for "Words are not enough/(as any poet knows)." Despite her considerable skill, she harbors a lingering distrust for the lexicon; she is dissatisfied with words "utilized until meaningless." After the first echo, "That word remembered/is death/a verbal corpse."

Nonetheless, she is seldom at a loss for the precise terms to fashion a spare and telling line, particularly when writing of city life. The urban child is engrossed in a gutter pool before his yardless house. In the dark the persona views sparrows and ducks with affection and annoyance. A green leaf pushes its way into an artist's "acrylic garden." The twittering air conditioners in "Cityscape" must do for murmuring sea waves, and the stone birds on the mantlepiece have to stand in for living sea gulls. She captures the city-dweller at his classic recreation, the cocktail party, where one guest beckons: "Come find me as I whisper to my enemies." Another, insecure in the company of such sophisticates, lets her masks fall and asks in anguish: "Is it I?" Zinnes also catches the rhythms of conversation in several segments of "Entropisms," a long prose poem made partly of snippets that seem cut from intellectual-artistic soirées, New York style. Along with the snatches of wit and aphorism, she lets mingle fragments both banal and arch. (She even allows Buckminster Fuller to parody himself.) Again as in *An Eye for an I*, she depicts existential moments; her selected short scenes and speeches jostle one another or make curious associations. "All things are not equal. Two substances and two other substances make all kinds of things." Let another "Entropism" serve as partial index to her art: "Hour after hour a fledgling word in space. Silence surrounds embodies sings *only when the word cuts it*."

—Joseph Parisi

APPENDIX

APPENDIX

BAXTER, James K(eir). New Zealander. Born in Dunedin, 29 June 1926. Educated at Quaker schools in New Zealand and England; Otago University, Dunedin; Victoria University, Wellington, B.A. 1952. Married Jacqueline Sturm in 1948; two children. Worked as a labourer, journalist and school-teacher. Editor, *Numbers* magazine, Wellington, 1954-60. Spent 5 months in India studying school publications, 1958. Started commune in Jerusalem (a Maori community on the Wanganui River), 1969. Recipient: Jessie Mackay Award, 1951, 1959, 1967, 1971; Unesco grant, 1958; Robert Burns Fellowship, University of Otago, 1966, 1967; Hubert Church Prose Award, 1972. *Died 22 October 1972.*

PUBLICATIONS

Verse

Beyond the Palisade. Christchurch, Caxton Press, 1944.
Blow, Wind of Fruitfulness. Christchurch, Caxton Press, 1948.
Hart Crane. Christchurch, Catspaw Press, 1948.
Charm for Hilary. Christchurch, Catspaw Press, 1949.
Rapunzel: A Fantasia for Six Voices. Privately printed, 1952(?).
Poems Unpleasant, with Louis Johnson and Anton Vogt. Christchurch, Pegasus Press, 1952.
The Fallen House. Christchurch, Caxton Press, 1953.
Lament for Barney Flanagan. Privately printed, 1954.
Traveller's Litany. Wellington, Handcraft Press, 1955.
The Night Shift: Poems on Aspects of Love, with others. Wellington, Capricorn Press, 1957.
The Iron Breadboard: Studies in New Zealand Writing (verse parodies). Wellington, Mermaid Press, 1957.
In Fires of No Return: Selected Poems. London and New York, Oxford University Press, 1958.
Chosen Poems 1958. Bombay, Konkan Institute of Arts and Sciences, 1958.
Ballad of Calvary Street. Privately printed, 1960.
Howrah Bridge and Other Poems. London and New York, Oxford University Press, 1961.
A Selection of Poetry. Wellington, Poetry Magazine, 1964.
A Bucket of Blood for a Dollar. Christchurch, John Summers, 1965.
Pig Island Letters. London and New York, Oxford University Press, 1966.
A Small Ode on Mixed Flatting. Christchurch, Caxton Press, 1967.
The Lion Skin. Dunedin, Otago University Bibliography Room, 1967.
A Death Song for M. Mouldybroke. Christchurch, John Summers, 1968.
The Rock Woman: Selected Poems. London and New York, Oxford University Press, 1969.
Ballad of the Stonegut Sugar Works. Privately printed, 1969.
Jerusalem Sonnets: Poems for Colin Durning. Dunedin, University of Otago Bibliography Room, 1970.
The Junkies and the Fuzz. Wellington, Wai-te-ata Press, 1970.
Jerusalem Blues (2). Wellington, Bottle Press, 1971.
Jerusalem Daybook. Wellington, Price Milburn, 1972.
Autumn Testament: Poetry and Prose Journal. Wellington, Price Milburn, 1972.
Four God Songs. Kanori, Futuna Press, 1972.
Stonegut Sugar Works, The Junkies and the Fuzz, Ode to Auckland, and Other Poems. Dunedin, Caveman Press, 1972.
Letter to Peter Olds. Dunedin, Caveman Press, 1972.
Runes. London and New York, Oxford University Press, 1973.
Two Obscene Poems. Wellington, Mary Martin, 1973(?).

The Tree House and Other Poems for Children. Wellington, Price Milburn, 1974.
The Labyrinth: Some Uncollected Poems 1944-1972. Wellington and New York, Oxford University Press, 1974; London, Oxford University Press, 1975.
The Holy Life and Death of Concrete Grady: Various Uncollected and Unpublished Poems, edited by J.E. Weir. London, Oxford University Press, 1976.
The Bone Chanter: Unpublished Poems 1945-1972, edited by J.E. Weir. Wellington, London, and New York, Oxford University Press, 1976.
Collected Poems, edited by J.E. Weir. Wellington and London, Oxford University Press, 1980.
Selected Poems, edited by J.E. Weir. Auckland and Oxford, Oxford University Press, 1982.

Recording: *Lament for Barney Flanagan and Other Poems,* Price Milburn-Bowmar, 1973.

Plays

Jack Winter's Dream (broadcast, 1958). Included in *Two Plays,* 1959.
The Wide Open Cage (produced Wellington, 1959; New York, 1962). Included in *Two Plays,* 1959.
Two Plays: The Wide Open Cage and Jack Winter's Dream. Hastings, Capricorn Press, 1959.
Three Women and the Sea (produced 1961).
The World Is? (produced Dunedin, 1961?).
The Spots of the Leopard (produced New York, 1963; Wellington, 1967).
The Band Rotunda (produced Dunedin, 1967). Included in *The Devil and Mr. Mulcahy, The Band Rotunda,* 1971.
The Cross, The Woman, The Axe and the Mirror (produced Dunedin, 1967). Published in *Landfall 29* (Christchurch), 1975.
The First Wife (produced Dunedin, 1967?).
The Hero (produced Dunedin, 1967?).
The Sore-Footed Man, based on *Philoctetes* by Euripides (produced Dunedin, 1967). Included in *The Sore-Footed Man, The Temptations of Oedipus,* 1971.
The Bureaucrat (produced Dunedin, 1967).
The Devil and Mr. Mulcahy (produced Dunedin, 1967). Included in *The Devil and Mr. Mulcahy, The Band Rotunda,* 1971.
Mr. O'Dwyer's Dancing Party (produced Dunedin, 1968).
The Runaway Wife (produced Dunedin, 1968).
The Starlight in Your Eyes (produced Dunedin, 1968).
The Day That Flanagan Died (produced Dunedin, 1969).
The Temptations of Oedipus (produced Dunedin, 1970). Included in *The Sore-Footed Man, The Temptations of Oedipus,* 1971.
The Devil and Mr. Mulcahy, The Band Rotunda. Auckland, Heinemann, 1971.
The Sore-Footed Man, The Temptations of Oedipus. Auckland, Heinemann, 1971.

Radio Plays: *Jack Winter's Dream,* 1958; *The Silver Plate: An Eclogue in Honour of Samuel Beckett,* 1961; *Mr. Brandywine Chooses a Gravestone,* 1967.

Other

Recent Trends in New Zealand Poetry. Christchurch, Caxton Press, 1951.

The Fire and the Anvil: Notes on Modern Poetry. Wellington, New Zealand University Press, 1955; revised edition, New York, Cambridge University Press, 1960.

Oil. Wellington, School Publications, 1957.

The Coaster. Wellington, School Publications, 1959.

The Trawler. Wellington, Government Printing, 1961.

New Zealand in Colour, photographs by Kenneth and Jean Bigwood. Wellington, Reed, 1961; London, Thames and Hudson, and Belmont, Massachusetts, Wellington Books, 1962.

The Old Earth Closet: A Tribute to Regional Poetry. Wellington, Wai-te-ata Press, 1965.

Aspects of Poetry in New Zealand. Christchurch, Caxton Press, 1967.

The Man on the Horse (lectures). Dunedin, University of Otago, and London, Oxford University Press, 1967.

The Flowering Cross (essays). Dunedin, New Zealand Tablet, 1969.

The Six Faces of Love: Lenten Lectures. Wellington, Futuna Press, 1972.

A Walking Stick for an Old Man. Wellington, CMW Print, 1972.

Notes on the Country I Live In, with Tim Shadbolt, photographs by Ans Westra. Wellington, Alister Taylor, 1972.

Thoughts about the Holy Spirit. Kanori, Futuna Press, 1973.

James K. Baxter as Critic: A Selection from His Literary Criticism, edited by Frank McKay. Auckland, Heinemann, 1978.

*

Bibliography: *A Preliminary Bibliography of Works by and Works about James K. Baxter* by J.E. Weir and Barbara A. Lyon, Christchurch, University of Canterbury, 1979.

Manuscript Collection: Hocken Library, University of Otago, Dunedin.

Critical Studies: *The Poetry of James K. Baxter* by J.E. Weir, Wellington, Oxford University Press, 1970; *James K. Baxter 1926-1972: A Memorial Volume,* Wellington, Alister Taylor, 1972; *James K. Baxter* by Charles Doyle, Boston, Twayne, 1976; *James K. Baxter* by Vincent O'Sullivan, Wellington, Oxford University Press, 1976, London, Oxford University Press, 1977.

* * *

At his best one of the finest English-language poets of the past 40 years, James K. Baxter is the one New Zealand poet of undeniable international reputation. Although he died in his mid-forties, his literary career lasted for over 30 years. Its fruits were many volumes of poems, a handful of plays, four separate works of literary commentary or criticism, a considerable number of essays on religious topics, and a small amount of fiction (he was a fine exponent of the parable).

With *Beyond the Palisade,* published when he was 18, Baxter at once became a figure of note, both as a poet and a maverick bohemian. As he wrote later:

> In Calvin's town
> At seventeen I thought I might see
> Not fire but water rise
>
> From the shelves of surf beyond St Clair
> to clang the dry bell. Gripping

> A pillow wife in bed
> I did my convict drill,
> And when I made a mother of the keg
> The town split open like an owl's egg....

Within a few years and with the publication of *Blow, Wind of Fruitfulness* he, and his demons, already occupied a central position in the New Zealand literary scene, so that his booklet, *Recent Trends in New Zealand Poetry,* a beautifully condensed commentary, was from the first accepted as authoritative.

When in the late 1940's Baxter moved north to Wellington he began his long friendship and collaboration with Louis Johnson. They became the focus of a "romantic" element in New Zealand writing, which centred on Wellington for the next dozen years or so. The group around them acted as a catalyst and as counter-energy to their predecessors, the poets of the 1930's, and to the nationalism of Allen Curnow. Part of this activity was the characteristically erratic periodical *Numbers,* which Johnson and Baxter edited with Charles Doyle (and, latterly, others), and which was the only alternative to the few "establishment" periodicals, such as *Landfall.*

In books which ranged from makeshift to brilliant, Baxter throughout the 1950's produced a prolific variety of poems, plays, short stories, and criticism. He made no effort to establish a reputation outside New Zealand and, apart from a boyhood year in England, travelled abroad only once, on a UNESCO award to India and Japan in 1958. But by the late 1950's he was being published by the London branch of Oxford University Press and by 1967 they had issued the three titles which, except for the very last phase, are the core of his achievement—*In Fires of No Return, Howrah Bridge and Other Poems,* and *Pig Island Letters.* Substantial parts of the first two collections had been printed earlier by a distinguished New Zealand publisher, the Caxton Press.

These three books, and especially the first and last, show clearly why Baxter more than once has been said to have a touch of genius. It is manifest in such poems as "The Cave," "Rocket Show," "Lament for Barney Flanagan," and the sequence of "Pig Island Letters." The characteristic tone is caught in a moving early poem, "The Bay":

> So now I remember the bay, and the little spiders
> On driftwood, so poisonous and quick.
> The carved cliffs and the great outcrying surf
> With currents round the rocks and the birds rising.
> A thousand times an hour is torn across
> And burned for the sake of going on living.
> But I remember the bay that never was
> And stand like stone, and cannot turn away.

One important turning point in Baxter's life was his conversion to Roman Catholicism in 1958. Another was the award of a Burns Fellowship, which enabled him to return to the University of Otago, where he had been a student twenty years earlier, for the 1966 university year. He remained for two years, did a large amount of writing, and established in particular a virtually new career as a playwright. Equally important, he took up Catholic catechetical work and this led directly into the final rich phase of his career.

Besides the plays, the Dunedin years produced two important critical-autobiographical pieces, *The Man on the Horse* and *Aspects of Poetry in New Zealand,* but the period of catechetical work in the city led to writing which has been reckoned Baxter's most important. In 1967 he went into solitude for some months at Hiruharama (Jerusalem), on the Wanganui River. Later at this tiny religious settlement he founded a commune for troubled youths and social drop-outs and he was also the moving spirit in setting up doss-houses in both Auckland and Wellington.

These ventures took much of his energy, but this was also the time of a further remarkable shift in the development of his poetry, especially in the so-called Jerusalem writings, *Jerusalem Sonnets*, *Jerusalem Daybook*, and *Autumn Testament*. He achieved a very personal "sonnet" form, in fluid pentameter couplets and, particularly in *Jerusalem Daybook*, made most effective use of an amalgam of prose and verse.

New Zealand has in the past 50 years at times had a remarkably strong poetry. If today it is in its weakest phase since the 1920's, this is partly due to Baxter's early death in 1972. Baxter's poems have a natural incandescence, which owes something to his being exposed to the finest poetry from early childhood, but which also comes from a sense of the human universe based on religion. New Zealand, at least until very recently, has been a relatively successful social welfare state, secular in spirit. Baxter, notably, brought to it the example of a strong religious consciousness. His legacy to his country is a double one: a substantial amount of first-rate writing, especially poems, and the example of a man impelled to carry the spiritual life as far as it can go.

—Charles Doyle

BERRYMAN, John. American. Born John Allyn Smith, in McAlester, Oklahoma, 25 October 1914; took step-father's name, 1926. Educated at schools in Oklahoma, Florida, and New York City; South Kent School, Connecticut, 1928-32; Columbia University, New York (Rensselaer Prize, 1935), 1932-36, A.B. 1936 (Phi Beta Kappa); Clare College, Cambridge (Kellett Fellow, 1936-37; Oldham Shakespeare Scholar, 1937), 1937-38, B.A. 1938. Married 1) Eileen Patricia Mulligan in 1942 (divorced, 1956); 2) Elizabeth Ann Levine in 1956 (divorced, 1959), one son; 3) Kathleen Donahue in 1961, two daughters. Instructor in English, Wayne State University, Detroit, 1939-40, and Harvard University, Cambridge, Massachusetts, 1940-43; Instructor in English, 1943, Associate in Creative Writing, 1946-47, Resident Fellow, 1948-49, and Hodder Fellow, 1950-51, Princeton University, New Jersey; Lecturer in English, University of Washington, Seattle, 1950; Elliston Professor of Poetry, University of Cincinnati, 1952; taught creative writing, University of Iowa, Iowa City, 1954; Assistant Professor, 1955-56, Associate Professor, 1957-62, Professor, 1962-72, and Regents' Professor of Humanities, 1969-72, University of Minnesota, Minneapolis. U.S. Information Service Lecturer, India, 1957; Visiting Professor, University of California, Berkeley, 1960, and Brown University, Providence, Rhode Island, 1962-63. Poetry Editor, *Nation*, New York, 1939. Recipient: Rockefeller Fellowship, 1944-46, 1956; *Kenyon Review*-Doubleday award, for short story, 1945; Guarantors Prize, 1949, and Levinson Prize, 1950 (*Poetry*, Chicago); Shelley Memorial Award, 1949; Guggenheim Fellowship, 1952, 1966; Harriet Monroe Award, 1957; *Partisan Review* fellowship, 1957; Brandeis University Creative Arts Award, 1959; Ingram Merrill Foundation grant, 1964; Loines Award, 1964; Pulitzer Prize, 1965; Academy of American Poets fellowship, 1967; National Endowment for the Arts award, 1967, and senior fellowship, 1971; Emily Clark Balch Prize (*Virginia Quarterly Review*), 1968; Bollingen Prize, 1969; National Book Award, 1969. D.Let.: Drake University, Des Moines, Iowa, 1971. Member, American Academy; American Academy of Arts and Sciences; Academy of American Poets. *Died (suicide) 7 January 1972.*

PUBLICATIONS

Verse

Five Young American Poets, with others. New York, New Directions, 1940.
Poems. New York, New Directions, 1942.
Two Poems. Privately printed, 1942.
The Dispossessed. New York, Sloane, 1948.
Homage to Mistress Bradstreet. New York, Farrar Straus, 1956; as *Homage to Mistress Bradstreet and Other Poems*, London, Faber, 1959.
His Thought Made Pockets & the Plane Buckt. Pawlet, Vermont, Claude Fredericks, 1958.
77 Dream Songs. New York, Farrar Straus, and London, Faber, 1964.
Two Dream Songs. Privately printed, 1965.
Berryman's Sonnets. New York, Farrar Straus, 1967; London, Faber, 1968.
Short Poems. New York, Farrar Straus, 1967.
I Have Moved to Dublin.... Dublin, Graduates Club, 1967.
His Toy, His Dream, His Rest: 308 Dream Songs. New York, Farrar Straus, 1968; London, Faber, 1969.
The Dream Songs. New York, Farrar Straus, 1969.
Two Dream Songs. Privately printed, 1969.
Two Poems. Privately printed, 1970.
Love and Fame. New York, Farrar Straus, 1970; London, Faber, 1971; revised edition, Farrar Straus, 1972.
Delusions, Etc. New York, Farrar Straus, and London, Faber, 1972.
Selected Poems 1938-1968. London, Faber, 1972.
Henry's Fate and Other Poems 1967-1972, edited by John Haffenden. New York, Farrar Straus, 1977; London, Faber, 1978.

Novel

Recovery. New York, Farrar Straus, and London, Faber, 1973.

Other

Stephen Crane (biography). New York, Sloane, 1950; London, Methuen, 1951.
The Freedom of the Poet (miscellany). New York, Farrar Straus, and London, Faber, 1976.
One Answer to a Question. Portree, Isle of Skye, Aquila, 1981.
Stephen Crane: The Red Badge of Courage. Portree, Isle of Skye, Aquila, 1981.

Editor, with Ralph Ross and Allen Tate, *The Arts of Reading* (anthology). New York, Crowell, 1960.
Editor, *The Unfortunate Traveller; or, The Life of Jack Wilton*, by Thomas Nashe. London, Putnam, 1960.

*

Bibliography: *John Berryman: A Checklist* by Richard J. Kelly, Metuchen, New Jersey, Scarecrow Press, 1972; *John Berryman: A Descriptive Bibliography* by Ernest C. Stefanik, Jr., Pittsburgh, University of Pittsburgh Press, 1974; *John Berryman: A Reference Guide* by Gary Q. Arpin, Boston, Hall, 1976.

Manuscript Collection: University of Minnesota, Minneapolis.

Critical Studies: *John Berryman* by William J. Martz, Minneapolis, University of Minnesota Press, and London, Oxford University Press, 1969; *John Berryman* by James M. Linebarger, New York, Twayne, 1974; *A Tumult for John Berryman: A Homage* edited by Marguerite Harris, Takoma Park, Maryland, Dryad Press, 1976; *The Poetry of John Berryman* by Gary Q. Arpin, Port Washington, New York, Kennikat Press, 1977; *John Berryman: An Introduction to the Poetry* by Joel Conarroe, New York, Columbia University Press, 1977; *John Berryman: A Critical Commentary*, New York, New York University Press, and London, Macmillan, 1980, and *The Life of John Berryman*, London, Routledge, 1982, both by John Haffenden; *Poets in Their Youth* by Eileen Simpson, New York, Random House, and London, Faber, 1982.

*   *   *

From the appearance of his "Twenty Poems" in the anthology *Five Young American Poets*, John Berryman was immediately recognized at the forefront of his talented generation, a group of poets including Robert Lowell, Delmore Schwartz, and Randall Jarrell. Most of Berryman's early poems and those in several subsequent volumes are reprinted in his *Short Poems*, but this part of his *oeuvre*—which might well represent another poet's life work—has been quite overshadowed by his three long sequences: *Homage to Mistress Bradstreet*, two volumes of his "dream songs," and *Berryman's Sonnets* (published in 1967 but written in the 1940's). In a period when most poets attempting works of magnitude have followed the examples of Yeats, Pound, and Eliot and abandoned commitment to a single strophic form, Berryman wrote long, intricate works in regular (though sometimes variably repeated) stanzas. The imposition of a formal order upon his wildly conflicting emotions and wide-ranging materials is among Berryman's most impressive accomplishments.

The *Sonnets* are strictly Petrarchan, the convention revived in a fashion both traditional and contemporary. This is the psychological analysis of a love affair, the purpose for which the sonnet form was first devised. Berryman's syncopated, frank, and quirky diction stamps these sonnets as his own. *Homage* successfully enacts an extended metaphysical conceit, that "Mistress Bradstreet," the Puritan poetess, is both the mistress, across the dead centuries, of the contemporary poet, and his alter ego. Like all of Berryman's work this poem is psychologically intense and complex; the voice begins as his own, then merges into Anne Bradstreet's: the verse is crabb'd, allusive to details in her work, life, and readings. The tangible sense of her spiritual searchings and straitened self-fulfilment striates the knotty music of Berryman's lines. His participation in her life becomes a means of his imaginative discovery of America.

The complex texture, the intensity of vision, the willed idiosyncrasy of syntax and the confected diction of *Homage* all prefigure the verse in *77 Dream Songs* and *His Toy, His Dream, His Rest*. These later books comprise a single work in 385 sections, each arranged in three six-line stanzas, the lines varying greatly in length and stress, the stanzas in rhyme pattern. Here the conceit of "dream songs" gives the poet warrant for nondiscursive syntax and for the manipulation of several projected voices. One is a white man in black-face who speaks the dialect of the Negro in a minstrel show and is named Henry, or Pussy-cat. He is heard in meditation or in colloquy with a friend who calls him Mr. Bones. At other times we hear the poet's more normative voice.

These strategies—simple in conception, intricate in effect—make possible the exploration of, seemingly, any and every subject, a man's whole life and dream-life poured through his varied voices. The scope of the work suggests comparison to *The Cantos*, the differences as revealing as the parallels. Where Pound rooted his work in his historical imagination, Berryman reflects the inward self-preoccupation of a later generation whose sensibility reflects psychoanalytic experience. This is the generation which found Robert Lowell's *Life Studies* the key to its sufferings. Lowell, in that book rejecting history, myth and rhetoric, followed W.C. Williams in achieving the simple syntax of and immediacy of unpremeditated speech; but Berryman, who sometimes writes with analogous clarity, achieves his effects by counterpointing his several voices, natural, colloquial, literary, grand-mannered, demotic. Yet his dream songs share with *Life Studies* their confessional tone and air of uninhibited self-revelation. What comes through as a result of the complexity of tone and texture is a very uneven yet compelling image of modern man suffering, exulting, catching himself exulting and putting himself down, taking wry delight in the knowledge of his own small pleasures and larger failures. The reader is required to bear with many dry patches, much incoherence, and he is obliged to learn a new language in order to let Berryman's dreamer, its sole speaker, converse with him:

> Henry sats in de plane & was gay.
> Careful Henry nothing said aloud
> but where a Virgin out of cloud
> to her Mountain dropt in light,
> his thought made pockets & the plane buckt.
> "Parm me, lady." "Orright."

The willed colloquiality produces comic effects. Elsewhere the tone is tender, wry, fierce, anguished. The minstrel master of demotic syntax is a persona of the same sensibility who swiped a memorable title, *His Toy, His Dream, His Rest*, from three compositions in *The Fitzwilliam Virginal Book* by Giles Farnaby (c.1560-1600?). Berryman's archness, his wildly comic alternations between the emotionally freer, more libidinous lifestyle of his white-man-in-black-face and the self that can't escape the strictures of the external world; the primitive energy of his playfulness with language; and perhaps above all the sense of subversion against the rigidities of society given by the willed dream-life in which Berryman's voices mock and undermine and lash out against the pieties of the world they and he can manage to live in only, or best, in dreams: these effects of the dream songs on the reader make his long poem memorable. Its idiosyncrasies seem determined by its time; its delights may well prove to be lasting.

After *Dream Songs* Berryman published two further books of verse, *Love and Fame* and, posthumously, *Delusions, Etc.* In these his style underwent yet a further transformation; abandoning the involutions, elisions, and intensities of *Dream Songs*, he abandoned also the melange of voices and the 18-line verse unit; in their place, now writing in irregularly rhythmic quatrains, came a self-exploitative, determinedly prosaic style, as the poet re-imagined his student days at Columbia and Cambridge universities in the first of these books, and addressed Beethoven, Frost, and other great predecessors in the second. Both contain sequences of religious themes, as Berryman continued to search for his lost faith. Another posthumous work was his novel, *Recovery*, also autobiographical, an account of his struggle with alcoholism.

Berryman's *oeuvre* reflects his life-long effort to find or fuse a style equal to the terrible psychological pressures of his themes of self-revelation and self-discovery. It seems probable that *Homage to Mistress Bradstreet* and *Dream Songs* will be found the most enduring of his works; *Homage* is surely the best unified of his longer poems, though there are structural patterns and thematic continuities and refrains secreted in *Dream Songs* which, when identified, make that long series seem less a random miscellany, more an artistic construct. In any case its structure, based on the accumulation of discrete poems with violent changes of diction, tone, and persona, like Robert Lowell's *Notebook*, represents in its flux and exacerbation the fate of the long poem in America during the latter part of the present century.

—Daniel Hoffman

BLACKBURN, Paul. American. Born in St. Albans, Vermont, 24 November 1926. Educated at New York University; University of Wisconsin, Madison, B.A. 1950; University of Toulouse, France (Fulbright Fellow), 1954-55. Served in the United States Army, 1945-47. Married 1) Winifred Grey McCarthy in 1954 (divorced, 1963); 2) Sara Golden in 1963 (divorced, 1967); 3) Joan D. Miller in 1968, one son. Lecturer, University of Toulouse, 1955-56; Assistant Editor, Funk and Wagnalls *New International Yearbook*, New York, 1959-62; Poetry Editor, *The Nation*, New York, 1962; Associate Editor, *World Scope Encyclopedia Yearbook*, 1963-65; Poet-in-Residence, 1965, and Lecturer in Poetry, 1966-67, Aspen Writers' Workshop, Colorado; Poet-in-Residence and Lecturer in English, City College of New York, 1966-69; Assistant Professor of English, State University of New York, Cortland, 1970-71. Recipient: Guggenheim Fellowship, 1967. *Died 13 December 1971.*

PUBLICATIONS

Verse

The Dissolving Fabric. Palma, Mallorca, Divers-Press, 1955.
Brooklyn-Manhattan Transit: A Bouquet for Flatbush. New York, Totem, 1960.
The Nets. New York, Trobar Press, 1961.
Sing-Song. New York, Caterpillar, 1966.
Sixteen Sloppy Haiku and a Lyric for Robert Reardon. Cleveland, 400 Rabbit Press, 1966.
The Reardon Poems. Madison, Wisconsin, Perishable Press, 1967.
The Cities. New York, Grove Press, 1967.
In, On, or About the Premises, Being a Small Book of Poems. New York, Grossman, and London, Cape Goliard Press, 1968.
Two New Poems. Mount Horeb, Wisconsin, Perishable Press, 1969.
Three Dreams and an Old Poem, edited by Allen De Loach. Buffalo, University Press at Buffalo, 1970.
Gin: Four Journal Pieces. Mount Horeb, Wisconsin, Perishable Press, 1970.
The Assassination of President McKinley. Mount Horeb, Wisconsin, Perishable Press, 1970.
The Journals: Blue Mounds Entries. Mount Horeb, Wisconsin, Perishable Press, 1971.
Early Selected y Mas: Poems 1949-1966. Los Angeles, Black Sparrow Press, 1972.
Halfway Down the Coast: Poems and Snapshots. Northampton, Massachusetts, Mulch Press, 1975.

The Journals, edited by Robert Kelly. Los Angeles, Black Sparrow Press, 1975.
By Ear. New York, # Magazine, 1978.
Against the Silences. London, Permanent Press, 1980.
The Selection of Heaven. Mount Horeb, Wisconsin, Perishable Press, 1980.
The Collected Poems, edited by Edith Jarolim. New York, Persea, 1984.

Recording: *Poems for Peace,* Portents-Folkways, 1966.

Other

Translator, *Proensa: From the Provençal.* Palma, Mallorca, Divers Press, 1953.
Translator, *Poem of the Cid.* New York, American RDM Corporation, 1966.
Translator, *End of the Game and Other Stories,* by Julio Cortázar. New York, Pantheon, 1967; London, Collins, 1968; as *Blow-up and Other Stories,* New York, Collier, 1968.
Translator, *Hunk of Skin,* by Pablo Picasso. San Francisco, City Lights, 1968.
Translator, *Cronopios and Famas,* by Julio Cortázar. New York, Pantheon, 1969; London, Boyars, 1978.
Translator, *Peire Vidal.* New York, Mulch Press, 1972.
Translator, *The Treasure of the Muleteer and Other Spanish Tales,* by Antonio Jiménez-Landi. New York, Doubleday, 1974.
Translator, *Guillem de Poitou: His Eleven Extant Poems.* Mount Horeb, Wisconsin, Perishable Press, 1976.
Translator, *Proensa: An Anthology of Troubadour Poetry,* edited by George Economou. Berkeley, University of California Press, 1978.
Translator, *Lorca/Blackburn: Poems of Federico García Lorca.* San Francisco, Momo's Press, 1979.

*

Bibliography: *Paul Blackburn: A Checklist* by Kathleen Woodward, San Diego, University of California Archive for New Poetry, 1980.

Manuscript Collection: University of California Archive for New Poetry, San Diego.

Critical Studies: "Blackburn Issue" of *Sixpack 7-8* (London), Spring-Summer 1974.

*   *   *

The poetry of Paul Blackburn suffered an erratic publishing history during his lifetime, in part due to his seeming reluctance to put his work forward in widely accessible form. This diffidence is in remarkable contrast to the sense of confidence one feels in his handling of diverse material in the poems, the respect and admiration for his work by his contemporaries, his support and encouragement of younger poets and editors, and his active and early participation in the poetry-reading phenomenon in America beginning in the late 1950's. Blackburn published only one major collection during his lifetime, *The Cities*, which, together with a much smaller collection, *In, On, or About the Premises*, gave the general reader access to his work. However, even *The Cities* included less than half of his output between the early 1950's and 1966 and thus gave only a partial idea of the poetry of that period. Even now, there still remains a large body of uncollected and in many cases unpublished poems. By comparison, the literary translations he did to support himself achieved considerable success during his lifetime.

The impossibility of seeing Blackburn's work whole was reflected by critical comment which fastened on only the more immediate features of his work. He was identified as "a poet of the streets" who had a fine ear for slang and colloquial speech rhythms, as a writer of occasional poems, a celebrator of *machismo*, a poet who relied on the visual elements in grouping blocks of material on the page, who was self-deprecatory, ironical, sharply observant, nostalgic, a compulsive list-maker. His later poetry, *The Journals* in particular, was thought by some to take open-form poetry to an extreme of inconclusiveness, to lack "finish."

In fact, *The Journals* represents the culmination—as it unfortunately happened—of a poetic towards which Blackburn had been consistently working. In a 1960 radio interview he said: "Put a person in varied landscapes or cityscapes and he is surrounded by life—you find out a lot about the quality of the city or the country and the quality of the person. This is very valid material for poetry. What else is there? The man in what surrounds him. That he loves or hates or just hears and sees." In the earliest published poems, the concern is to present "the man in what surrounds him" by interweaving specific observations, images, acts, within a carefully delineated frame; this frame may be consciously literary, as in the poem "Two Greeks" (1949), which employs the pastoral tradition of the shepherd's complaint to his unresponsive lover. The earlier work is more consciously crafted, more lyrical, and the poem is more "closed" than the later work; that is, it is structured in a linear fashion, with a tightly unified progression of images leading to a definite closure which both depends upon and binds together the previous images. Though he did not completely abandon the closed form—see the later poem "At the Well," in *Three Dreams and an Old Poem*—his interest lay in the use of seemingly random observations and associations to achieve a different kind of unity: an organic relation among the elements, based on Charles Olson's open-field theories ("one perception...instanter, on another"). An outstanding example of this kind of poem is "Pre-Lenten Gestures," which is constructed of a series of observations, associations, and allusions which occur within a firmly located setting (a bakery-restaurant). Though seemingly casual in conception, every element in the poem is structurally and thematically tied together, but one is not conscious, as in the early work, of an ordering, "literary" sensibility.

In most of Blackburn's poetry, an overwhelming feeling of isolation is present, reinforced by his emphasis on the objects which reveal place and determine the effect; with few exceptions, even women are treated as erotic or aesthetic objects. He is the detached observer and recorder of the passing scene in a city street, a subway car, restaurant, ale-house. But in a very real sense, Blackburn's writing is a means to establish contact with the world of the living, for whom the urban state is a defining condition. He is very much *in* the world, and his love for it is reflected by his refusal to make it over in his image. The world is as he finds it: just as American painters of the 1960's recognised in the mass-produced artifact the paradigm of modern life, so Blackburn found in the alienated inhabitants of the city and their random rubbish the possibility of identification, affirmation, and, finally, communion ("Meditation on the BMT"):

        1 coffee can without a lid
        1 empty pint of White Star, the label
                faded by rain
        1 empty beer-can
        2 empty Schenley bottles

        1 empty condom, seen from
        1 nearly empty train...

            My eyes
    enter poor backyards, backyards
            O I love you,

    backyards, I make you my own, and you
    my barren, littered embankments, now that you
    've a bit of fire to warm & cleanse you, be
    grateful that men still tend you, still will
            rake your strange leaves
    your strange leavings.

While Blackburn's poetry is quintessentially a poetry of place, he nevertheless uses places to locate the self in a particular time and circumstance, as in "How to Get Up Off It": "in some forgotten way/we carry the masks of places all our lives,/a kind of fate." The places in Blackburn's life are France, where he went originally as a Fulbright scholar at the University of Toulouse to study the Provençal manuscripts for the *Proensa* translations; Spain—in particular, Catalonia—; and New York City "which was most his home and center"; *The Journals* also contain poems from his trips to Puerto Rico, the Colorado Rockies, the West Coast, and his place of last residence, upper New York State. But in assembling his larger collections, Blackburn did not organise them according to geographical correspondences but, rather, as he once defined it with respect to *The Cities*, according to the wish to balance the rhythms of different sorts of poems: the concrete, object-determined poems, the love poems, and the "idea" poems. The aim was not simply to alternate them, but to set up rhythms, as in jazz solos and riffs, which would help prevent the reader from getting bogged down in an extended run of the same kind of poem. It is Blackburn's emphasis on the poem (as well as the book) as a musical structure, in short, his sense of rhythm in both its discrete and larger aspects, that has been recognised as one of his outstanding strengths as a poet, and in which he had few peers. The accuracy (never slack) with which he reproduced colloquial speech, his skilled use of repetition, the effortless but disciplined variation of tone, line stress, line division, and stanza breaks, the ability to absorb and functionally to use diverse material and tonal values within a single poem: these are characteristics of a master craftsman.

It is evident that in his approach to his art Blackburn owed much to Pound, William Carlos Williams, Olson, Robert Creeley, the Objectivist poets Louis Zukofsky and Charles Reznikoff, and the troubadours (he had worked on the Provençal translations for twenty years, from the time in 1949-50 when Pound first convinced him that the troubadours needed contemporary American-English versions, until his death). But just as, if not more important, is his reliance on everyday American-English speech patterns and their "notation" in breath units that act as "scores" for oral presentation. This poetic coincided with, or was a direct outgrowth of, the movement to restore the communal experience of poetry which provoked the poetry-reading phenomenon of the 1950's.

The Journals, the work of Blackburn's last five years, can be regarded as "A Poem of a Life," as Zukofsky described "*A*," rather than as a collection of individual poems. No other contemporary poet has expressed in his work such a coterminous statement between the life and the art as has Blackburn; he literally did make a poetry of daily existence. *The Journals* shows, as his previous poetry shows, that he used information, data, detailed observation, to discover connections between habits, chores, ablutions (with which *The Journals* abound)—in a word, the commonplaceness of everyday existence—and a transcendent plane of existence in which an image recurs, in which the numinous inhabits a place or object, and with which other people are intimately associated. The "minute particulars" make the place his own, define him, make intense and specific the time he lived through and the space he inhabited. The significance of Blackburn's innovation is that the process subsumes both the work and the working out, the poem and the making of the poem. *The Journals* are extraordinary compositions of subtlety and range which permit us to follow the journeyings of a man, a poet, who made attention to his craft and art a way of life.

—Robert Vas Dias

GARRIGUE, Jean. American. Born in Evansville, Indiana, 8 December 1914. Educated at the University of Chicago, B.A. 1937; University of Iowa, Iowa City, M.F.A. 1943. Edited a weekly newspaper for the U.S.O. during World War II. Instructor, Bard College, Annandale-on-Hudson, New York, 1951-52, Queens College, Flushing, New York, 1952-53, New School for Social Research, New York, 1955-56, and University of Connecticut, Storrs, 1960-61; Lecturer in Poetry, Smith College, Northampton, Massachusetts, 1965-66; Poet-in-Residence, University of Washington, Seattle, 1970. Poetry Editor, *New Leader*, New York, 1965-72. Scholar, Radcliffe Institute for Independent Study, Cambridge, Massachusetts, 1968-70. Recipient: Rockefeller grant, 1954, 1966; Union League Civic and Arts Foundation prize (*Poetry*, Chicago), 1956; *Hudson Review* Fellowship, 1957; Longview Award, 1958; Guggenheim grant, 1960; American Academy grant, 1961; Lowell Mason Palmer Award, 1961; Emily Clark Balch Prize (*Virginia Quarterly Review*), 1966; Melville Cane Award, 1968. *Died 27 December 1972.*

PUBLICATIONS

Verse

Five Young American Poets, with others. New York, New Directions, 1944.
The Ego and the Centaur. New York, New Directions, 1947.
The Monument Rose. New York, Noonday Press, 1953.
A Water Walk by Villa d'Este. New York, St. Martin's Press, 1959; London, Macmillan, 1960.
Country Without Maps. New York, Macmillan, 1964.
New and Selected Poems. New York, Macmillan, 1967.
Studies for an Actress and Other Poems. New York, Macmillan, 1973.

Short Stories

The Animal Hotel. New York, Eakins Press, 1966.
Chartres and Prose Poems. New York, Eakins Press, 1971.

Other

Marianne Moore. Minneapolis, University of Minnesota Press, 1965; London, Oxford University Press, 1966.

Editor, *Translations by American Poets.* Athens, Ohio University Press, 1970.

Editor, *Love's Aspects: The World's Great Love Poems.* New York, Doubleday, 1975.

*

Critical Study: *Ex Libris Jean Garrigue*, Saratoga Springs, New York, Skidmore College Library, 1975.

*   *   *

The best summation of Jean Garrigue's idea of poetry is found in the first lines of "Catch What You Can":

The thing to do is try for that sweet skin
One gets by staying deep inside a thing.
The image that I have is that of fruit—
The stone within the plum or some such pith
As keeps the slender sphere both firm and sound.

Throughout her career Garrigue attempted to get deep inside the things she wrote about. The result was poems of exquisite (and at times excessive) delicacy about such subjects as music, nature, travel, and, most especially, love. Her work requires patient and sympathetic readers, for her poems have little narrative interest, almost no topical references, and little humor. But at its best her work offers compassionate and minutely detailed pictures of the world about her, and shows us the sweet skin of fine poetry.

Garrigue progressed much in her career and learned from her mistakes. Her early poems suffer from an uncontrolled intensity, as these lines from "Forest" show:

There are short-stemmed forests so close to the ground
You would pity a dog lost there in the spore-budding
Blackness where the sun has never struck down.
There are dying ferns that glow like a gold mine
And weeds and sumac extend the Sodom of color.
Among the divisions of stone and the fissures of branch
Lurk the abashed resentments of the ego.
Do not say this is pleasurable!

One admires Garrigue's image-making ability here, but one also feels that the last two lines are much too blatant. Elsewhere in her early poems Garrigue's rich, lyric phrasings at times unaccountably give way to patches of flatness, as in these lines from the otherwise fine piece "False Country of the Zoo": "Another runner, the emu, is even better/at kicking. Oh the coarse chicken feet/Of this bird reputed a fossil!"

In her final volumes, starting with *A Water Walk by Villa d'Este*, Garrigue developed a firmer, surer poetic voice. Discarding the tortuously ornate wordings of some of her early poems, Garrigue produced works of powerful directness. She had experimented with prose poems and, though these were not very successful, Garrigue did begin to use in her other poems rhythms and words closer to that of everyday speech. Her finest volume is *Country Without Maps*. There are some wonderful evocations of cities in this book in such poems as "Amsterdam Letter" and "New York: Summertime" and "What Tender Bough." But the best poem in this book, and the longest (about 500 lines) Garrigue ever attempted is "Pays Perdu." Here for once narrative plays an important part as the poet recounts a long walk she took in the mountains of Provence. On this trip, which has allegorical, almost epic, undertones, the narrator finds herself lost and by chance meets a remarkable couple living in almost complete isolation in this "country without maps." This is a poem which takes us into uncharted areas of psyche; this had always been Garrigue's aim as a writer, but here she was able, as she was not earlier, to perform this feat with great subtlety and understatement.

Garrigue's final poems before her death show that she was continuing to move forward, experimenting with ballads and even, in "Written in London after a Protest Parade," tackling a contemporary political issue. "Any messages, messages, any word?" asks this poem three times. The first time it is a prosaic inquiry; the third, a question of deep implications. In between Garrigue produced a poem which movingly showed her deep love for all life. It was in her later poems, such as this one, with their simplified, more vigorous style, that Garrigue was at her best.

—Dennis Lynch

JARRELL, Randall. American. Born in Nashville, Tennessee, 6 May 1914. Educated at Vanderbilt University, Nashville, B.S. in psychology 1936 (Phi Beta Kappa), M.A. in English 1939. Served as a celestial navigation tower operator in the United States Army Air Corps, 1942-46. Married Mary Eloise von Schrader in 1952. Instructor in English, Kenyon College, Gambier, Ohio, 1937-39, University of Texas, Austin, 1939-42, and Sarah Lawrence College, Bronxville, New York, 1946-47; Associate Professor, 1947-58, and Professor of English, 1958-65, Women's College of the University of North Carolina (later University of North Carolina at Greensboro). Lecturer, Salzburg Seminar in American Civilization, 1948; Visiting Fellow in Creative Writing, Princeton University, New Jersey, 1951-52; Fellow, Indiana School of Letters, Bloomington, Summer 1952; Visiting Professor of English, University of Illinois, Urbana, 1953; Elliston Lecturer, University of Cincinnati, Ohio, 1958. Acting Literary Editor, *The Nation*, New York, 1946-47; poetry critic, *Partisan Review*, New Brunswick, New Jersey, 1949-53, and *Yale Review*, New Haven, Connecticut, 1955-57; Member of the Editorial Board, *American Scholar*, Washington, D.C., 1957-65. Consultant in Poetry, Library of Congress, Washington, D.C., 1956-58. Recipient: *Southern Review* Prize, 1936; Jeannette Sewell Davis Prize, 1943, Levinson Prize, 1948, and Oscar Blumenthal Prize, 1951 (*Poetry*, Chicago); J.P. Bishop Memorial Literary Prize (*Sewanee Review*), 1946; Guggenheim Fellowship, 1946; American Academy grant, 1951; National Book Award, 1961; Oliver Max Gardner Award, University of North Carolina, 1962; American Association of University Women Award, 1964; Ingram Merrill Award, 1965. D.H.L.: Bard College, Annandale-on-Hudson, New York, 1962. Member, American Academy; Chancellor, Academy of American Poets, 1965. *Died 14 October 1965.*

PUBLICATIONS

Verse

Five Young American Poets, with others. New York, New Directions, 1940.
Blood for a Stranger. New York, Harcourt Brace, 1942.
Little Friend, Little Friend. New York, Dial Press, 1945.
Losses. New York, Harcourt Brace, 1948.
The Seven-League Crutches. New York, Harcourt Brace, 1951.

Selected Poems. New York, Knopf, 1955; London, Faber, 1956.
Uncollected Poems. Privately printed, 1958.
The Woman at the Washington Zoo: Poems and Translations. New York, Atheneum, 1960.
Selected Poems. New York, Atheneum, 1964.
The Lost World: New Poems. New York, Macmillan, 1965; London, Eyre and Spottiswoode, 1966.
The Complete Poems. New York, Farrar Straus, 1969; London, Faber, 1971.
The Achievement of Randall Jarrell: A Comprehensive Selection of His Poems with a Critical Introduction, by Frederick J. Hoffman. Chicago, Scott Foresman, 1970.
Jerome: The Biography of a Poem. New York, Grossman, 1971.

Recording: *Randall Jarrell Reads and Discusses His Poems Against War*, Caedmon, 1972.

Play

The Three Sisters, adaptation of a play by Chekhov (produced New York, 1964; London, 1965). New York, Macmillan, 1969.

Novel

Pictures from an Institution: A Comedy. New York, Knopf, and London, Faber, 1954.

Other (for children)

The Rabbit Catcher and Other Fairy Tales of Ludwig Bechstein. New York, Macmillan, and London, Macmillan, 1962.
The Golden Bird and Other Fairy Tales by the Brothers Grimm. New York, Macmillan, and London, Macmillan 1962.
The Gingerbread Rabbit. New York, Macmillan, and London, Collier Macmillan, 1964.
The Bat-Poet. New York, Macmillan, 1964; London, Kestrel, 1977.
The Animal Family. New York, Pantheon, 1965; London, Hart Davis, 1967.
Snow-White and the Seven Dwarfs: A Tale from the Brothers Grimm. New York, Farrar Straus, 1972; London, Kestrel, 1974.
The Juniper Tree and Other Tales from Grimm, with Lore Segal. New York, Farrar Straus, 1973; London, Bodley Head, 1974.
Fly by Night. New York, Farrar Straus, 1976; London, Bodley Head, 1977.
A Bat is Born. New York, Doubleday, 1978.
The Fisherman and His Wife. New York, Farrar Straus, 1980.

Other

Poetry and the Age. New York, Knopf, 1953; London, Faber, 1955.
Poets, Critics, and Readers (address). Charlottesville, University Press of Virginia, 1959.
A Sad Heart at the Supermarket: Essays and Fables. New York, Atheneum, 1962; London, Eyre and Spottiswoode, 1965.
The Third Book of Criticism. New York, Farrar Straus, 1969; London, Faber, 1975.
Kipling, Auden, & Co.: Essays and Reviews 1935-1964. New York, Farrar Straus, 1980; Manchester, Carcanet, 1981.

Randall Jarrell's Letters: An Autobiographical and Literary Selection, edited by Mary Jarrell. Boston, Houghton Mifflin, 1985.

Editor, *The Anchor Book of Stories*. New York, Doubleday, 1958.
Editor, *The Best Short Stories of Rudyard Kipling*. New York, Hanover House, 1961; as *In the Vernacular: The English in India* and *The English in England*, New York, Doubleday, 2 vols., 1963.
Editor, *Six Russian Short Novels*. New York, Doubleday, 1963.

Translator, with Moses Hadas, *The Ghetto and the Jews of Rome*, by Ferdinand Gregorovius. New York, Schocken, 1948.
Translator, *Goethe's Faust, Part One*. New York, Farrar Straus, 1976; London, Faber, 1978.

*

Bibliography: *Randall Jarrell: A Bibliography* by Charles M. Adams, Chapel Hill, University of North Carolina Press, and London, Oxford University Press, 1958, supplement in *Analects I* (Greensboro, North Carolina), Spring 1961; "A Checklist of Criticism on Randall Jarrell 1941-70" by D.J. Gilliken, in *Bulletin of the New York Public Library*, April 1971.

Manuscript Collections: Walter Clinton Jackson Library, University of North Carolina, Chapel Hill; Berg Collection, New York Public Library.

Critical Studies: *Randall Jarrell 1914-1965* edited by Robert Lowell, Peter Taylor, and Robert Penn Warren, New York, Farrar Straus, 1967; *The Poetry of Randall Jarrell* by Suzanne Ferguson, Baton Rouge, Louisiana State University Press, 1971, and *Critical Essays on Randall Jarrell* edited by Ferguson, Boston, Hall, 1983; *Randall Jarrell* by M.L. Rosenthal, Minneapolis, University of Minnesota Press, 1972; *Randall Jarrell* by Bernetta Quinn, Boston, Twayne, 1981.

*   *   *

The sustained richness of Randall Jarrell's *Selected Poems* and of his last collection, *The Lost World*, tends to obscure the fact that despite his early technical sophistication, he matured slowly as a poet. The posthumous *Complete Poems* now includes all the verse (some dating from 1934) which Jarrell himself had wisely omitted from the 1955 selection—poems which suffer badly from Auden's influence and are further weakened, as Delmore Schwartz once observed, by a "thinness and abstractness of texture and reference." The poems in *Little Friend, Little Friend*, however, especially the frequently anthologized war pieces, are completely Jarrell's own and in retrospect explain his initially cryptic remark that all good poets are essentially war poets.

In a 1951 poem, "The Face," Jarrell's aging Princess (the Marschallin of Strauss and von Hofmannsthal) looks into her mirror and thinks:

> This is what happens to everyone.
> At first you get bigger, you know more,
> Then something goes wrong.
> You are, and you say: I am—
> And you were...I've been too long.

I know there's no saying no,
But just the same you say it, No.
I'll point to myself and say: I'm not like this.
I'm the same as always inside.
—And even that's not so.

I thought: If nothing happens...
And nothing happened.
Here I am.
                    But it's not *right*.
If just living can do this,
Living is more dangerous than anything:

It is terrible to be alive.

The theme, stated here with untypical directness, is repeated with infinitely subtle variations in some of Jarrell's most moving later poems, "Seele im Raum," "Next Day," and "The Lost Children," and is in fact never more than just below the immediate surface of his best verse. The war which all men fight—and inevitably lose—is the war with time and an indifferent universe. Thinking sadly about a maimed veteran Jarrell asks:

How can I care about you much, or pick you out
From all the others other people loved
And sent away to die for them! You are a ticket
Someone bought and lost on, a stray animal:
You have lost even the right to be condemned.
I see you looking helplessly about, in histories,
Bewildered with your terrible companions, Pain
And Death and Empire: what have you understood, to die?
Were you worth, soldier, all that people said
To be spent so willingly? Surely your one theory, to live,
Is nonsense to the practice of the centuries.

But of course Jarrell does care, intensely. The speaker in "The Survivor among Graves" realizes that everyone faces the same hopeless struggle:

> The haunters and the haunted, among graves
> Mirror each other sightlessly; in soundless
> Supplication, a last unheard
> Unison, reach to each other: *Say again,*
> Say the voices, *say again*
> *That life is—what it is not;*
> *That, somewhere, there is—something, something;*
> *That we are waiting; that we are waiting.*

"What life is not" is fulfillment, the sense of a justifying purpose for human life and suffering. The child of "90 North" reaches his fabled North Pole only to find:

Here at the actual pole of my existence,
Where all that I have done is meaningless,
Where I die or live by accident alone—

Where, living or dying, I am still alone;
. . . .
I see at last that all the knowledge

I wrung from darkness—that the darkness flung me—
Is worthless as ignorance; nothing comes from nothing,
The darkness from the darkness. Pain comes from the darkness
And we call it wisdom. It is pain.

It is poems such as these that confirm Robert Lowell's observation that with all his dazzling gifts, Jarrell was "the most heart-breaking English poet of his generation."

Just as the soldier serves as a basic metaphor for Jarrell, so too does the child, learning by his losses (and through his encounters with the *märchen*, those symbolic fairy tales for which Jarrell had an almost obsessive fascination), and the sensitive adult as well, experiencing great works of the imagination, whether in music, the visual arts, or literature. The import of the true work, as Jarrell states repeatedly throughout his poetry and criticism, is that of Rilke's archaic torso of Apollo: *you must change your life*—you must grow, that is, into a new, more intense consciousness of being. Yet the imperative to change leads to the tragic paradox at the center of Jarrell's work. We change, by the pressure of experience, knowledge and increasing sensitivity, but there is no goal to achieve, no transcendence, no escape, finally, from a world in which it is "terrible to be alive." There is only stoicism, such consolation as knowing the worst can bring, and the compassionate realization that others too must suffer. Life is made bearable—perhaps bearable—by such knowledge and sympathy and in Jarrell's own case by the miraculous recapturing of childhood happiness. "I reach out to it empty handed," Jarrell wrote at the end, and:

> my hand comes back empty,
> And yet emptiness is traded for its emptiness,
> I have found that Lost World in the Lost and Found
> Columns whose grey illegible advertisements
> My soul has memorized world after world:
> LOST—NOTHING. STRAYED FROM NOWHERE. NO
> REWARD.
> I hold in my own hands, in happiness,
> Nothing: the nothing for which there's no reward.

The lost world of childhood no longer exists, is "nothing" now; and yet through memory (and by the art of fixing memory in the poem), the poet can hold his nothing in his hands, "in happiness." There is no reward beyond this: memory and art carry their own fulfillment for the poet and for his perceptive readers, who have lived vicariously through the superlative imaginative recreations which Jarrell presents in this final volume.

No brief thematic identification of Jarrell's concerns can begin to do justice to the embodied beauty of the poems themselves. Sweeping judgments are as dangerous as they are vulnerable, but among the poets who followed after the first great generation of modern American poets, Eliot, Stevens, Frost, and Pound, Jarrell may well be the most gifted and eloquent. His poetry is frequently demanding in its subtleties, but is difficult, finally, in the same sense that Jarrell had in mind when he observed that some of Frost's best poems are "hard to understand, but easy to love."

—Elmer Borklund

LOWELL, Robert (Traill Spence, Jr.). American. Born in Boston, Massachusetts, 1 March 1917. Educated at schools in Washington, D.C., and Philadelphia; Brimmer School, Boston; Rivers School; St. Mark's School, Southboro, Massachusetts, 1930-35; Harvard University, Cambridge, Massachusetts, 1935-37; Kenyon College, Gambier, Ohio, 1938-40, A.B. (summa cum laude) 1940 (Phi Beta Kappa); Louisiana State University, Baton Rouge, 1940-41. Conscientious objector during World War II: served prison sentence, 1943-44. Married 1) the writer Jean Stafford, in 1940 (divorced, 1948); 2) the writer Elizabeth Hardwick in 1949 (divorced, 1972), one daughter; 3) the writer Caroline Blackwood in 1972, one son. Editorial Assistant, Sheed and Ward, publishers, New York, 1941-42; taught at the University of Iowa, Iowa City, 1950, 1953, and Kenyon School of Letters, Gambier, Ohio, 1950, 1953; lived in Europe, 1950-52; taught at Salzburg Seminar on American Studies, 1952, University of Cincinnati, 1954, Boston University, 1956, Harvard University, 1958, 1963-70, 1975, 1977, and New School for Social Research, New York, 1961-62; Professor of Literature, University of Essex, Wivenhoe, Colchester, 1970-72. Consultant in Poetry, Library of Congress, Washington, D.C., 1947-48; Visiting Fellow, All Souls College, Oxford, 1970. Recipient: Pulitzer Prize, 1947; American Academy grant, 1947; Guggenheim Fellowship, 1947, 1974; Harriet Monroe Poetry Award, 1952; Guinness prize, 1959; National Book Award, 1960; Ford grant, 1960, for drama, 1964; Bollingen Poetry Translation Award, 1962; New England Poetry Club Golden Rose, 1964; Obie Award, for drama, 1965; Sarah Josepha Hale Award, 1966; Copernicus Award, 1974; National Medal for Literature, 1977. Member, American Academy. *Died 12 September 1977.*

PUBLICATIONS

Verse

Land of Unlikeness. Cummington, Massachusetts, Cummington Press, 1944.
Lord Weary's Castle. New York, Harcourt Brace, 1946.
Poems 1938-1949. London, Faber, 1950.
The Mills of the Kavanaughs. New York, Harcourt Brace, 1951.
Life Studies. London, Faber, 1959; augmented edition, New York, Farrar Straus, 1959; Faber, 1968.
Imitations. New York, Farrar Straus, 1961; London, Faber, 1962.
For the Union Dead. New York, Farrar Straus, 1964; London, Faber, 1965.
Selected Poems. London, Faber, 1965.
The Achievement of Robert Lowell: A Comprehensive Selection of His Poems with a Critical Introduction, edited by William J. Martz. Chicago, Scott Foresman, 1966.
Near the Ocean. New York, Farrar Straus, and London, Faber, 1967.
The Voyage and Other Versions of Poems by Baudelaire. New York, Farrar Straus, and London, Faber, 1968.
Notebook 1967-1968. New York, Farrar Straus, 1969; augmented edition, as *Notebook,* London, Faber, and Farrar Straus, 1970.
The Dolphin. London, Faber, and New York, Farrar Straus, 1973.
For Lizzie and Harriet. London, Faber, and New York, Farrar Straus, 1973.
History. London, Faber, and New York, Farrar Straus, 1973.
Poems: A Selection, edited by Jonathan Raban. London, Faber, 1974.
Selected Poems. New York, Farrar Straus, 1976; revised edition, 1977.
Day by Day. New York, Farrar Straus, 1977; London, Faber, 1978.

Recording: *Robert Lowell: A Reading,* Caedmon, 1978.

Plays

Phaedra, adaptation of the play by Racine (produced London,
1961). Included in *Phaedra and Figaro*, New York, Farrar
Straus, 1961; as *Phaedra*, London, Faber, 1963.
The Old Glory (*Benito Cereno* and *My Kinsman, Major Moli-
neux*)(produced New York, 1964; *Benito Cereno* produced
London, 1967). New York, Farrar Straus, 1964; expanded
version, including *Endecott and the Red Cross* (produced
New York, 1968), London, Faber, 1966; Farrar Straus, 1968.
Prometheus Bound, adaptation of a play by Aeschylus (pro-
duced New Haven, Connecticut, 1967; London, 1971). New
York, Farrar Straus, 1969; London, Faber, 1970.
The Oresteia of Aeschylus. New York, Farrar Straus, 1978;
London, Faber, 1979.

Other

Editor, with Peter Taylor and Robert Penn Warren, *Randall
Jarrell 1914-1965*. New York, Farrar Straus, 1967.

Translator, *Poesie*, by Montale. Bologna, Lanterna, 1960.

*

Bibliography: *Robert Lowell: A Reference Guide* by Steven
Gould Axelrod and Helen Doese, Boston, Hall, 1982.

Manuscript Collection: Houghton Library, Harvard University,
Cambridge, Massachusetts.

Critical Studies: *Robert Lowell: The First Twenty Years* by
Hugh B. Staples, New York, Farrar Straus, and London, Faber,
1962; *The Poetic Themes of Robert Lowell* by Jerome Mazzaro,
Ann Arbor, University of Michigan Press, 1965, and *Profile of
Robert Lowell* edited by Mazzaro, Columbus, Ohio, Merrill,
1971; *Robert Lowell: A Collection of Critical Essays* edited by
Thomas Parkinson, Englewood Cliffs, New Jersey, Prentice
Hall, 1968; *Robert Lowell* by Richard J. Fein, New York,
Twayne, 1970, revised edition, 1979; *The Autobiographical
Myth of Robert Lowell* by Phillip Cooper, Chapel Hill, Univer-
sity of North Carolina Press, 1970; *The Public Poetry of Robert
Lowell* by Patrick Cosgrave, London, Gollancz, 1970, New
York, Taplinger, 1972; *Robert Lowell: A Portrait of the Artist in
His Time* edited by Michael London and Robert Boyers, New
York, David Lewis, 1970; *Robert Lowell* by Jay Martin, Min-
neapolis, University of Minnesota Press, 1970; *Critics on Robert
Lowell* edited by Jonathan Price, Coral Gables, University of
Miami Press, 1972, London, Allen and Unwin, 1974; *The Poetic
Art of Robert Lowell* by Marjorie G. Perloff, Ithaca, New York,
Cornell University Press, 1973; *The Poetry of Robert Lowell* by
Vivian Smith, Sydney, Sydney University Press, 1974; *Robert
Lowell* by John Crick, Edinburgh, Oliver and Boyd, 1974; *Pity
the Monsters: The Political Vision of Robert Lowell* by Alan
Williamson, New Haven, Connecticut, Yale University Press,
1974; *Circle to Circle: The Poetry of Robert Lowell* by Stephen
Yenser, Berkeley, University of California Press, 1975; *Robert
Lowell: Life and Art* by Steven Gould Axelrod, Princeton, New
Jersey, Princeton University Press, 1978; *American Aristocracy:
The Lives and Times of James Russell, Amy, and Robert Lowell*
by C. David Heymann, New York, Dodd Mead, 1980; *Robert
Lowell* by Burton Raffel, New York, Ungar, 1981; *Robert
Lowell: A Biography* by Ian Hamilton, New York, Random
House, 1982, London, Faber, 1983; *Robert Lowell: Nihilist as
Hero* by Vereen M. Bell, Cambridge, Massachusetts, Harvard
University Press, 1983; *Robert Lowell: An Introduction to the
Poetry* by Mark Rudman, New York, Columbia University
Press, 1983.

Robert Lowell commented:
(1970) I belong to no "school" of poetry, but various living or
once-living poets have fascinated me—W.C. Williams, Pound,
Tate, Ransom, Eliot, and Yeats. And many, many others,
though perhaps I've tried to be a chameleon in vain.
   A critical statement on my own verse? I know about my verse,
I have been looking at it for a long time since I first started to
write and revise. But this question must not be answered. One
must only analyse oneself with great seriousness, or casually and
intuitively. All these things you inquire about are subjects for the
professors, their subjects, their inventions. I suppose these things
have value, but go against the intellect. I don't like to read such
pieces, see a writer I understand laid on the surgeon's table, see
what was comprehensible made dull.

*   *   *

   Robert Lowell's career plots the middle decades of the century,
an era in which America consolidated its empire and leapt to the
status of world power. After these ends were achieved, however,
there followed the accelerated disintegration of the European
heritage in America as technological and economic reorganiza-
tion tended to devaluate the past. Caught in this transition were
Lowell and other poets who believed deeply in the humanistic
values and traditions of Europe, and who had a morbid distrust
of the forces that seemed to be sweeping them away.
   Hence Lowell's own life was his primary subject—the persona
he projects must be seen as the late, possibly a final flowering of
the New England spirit, with its deep attachment to Europe and
its own American values of individuality and self-reliance. The
political, economic, and cultural changes of the mid-century
increasingly isolated Lowell, until even his personal disasters
and pains became metaphors of the torment of historic change.
Later in his canon, Lowell remembers other writers and friends,
most of them now dead, as a last generation of true literacy, and
that he now faced the cultural void alone.
   Lowell began by embracing the strict literary conservatism of
the southern Fugitive poets (themselves staunchly against indus-
trialization) and wrote a book under their influence, *Land of
Unlikeness*, of brittle and cluttered verse in traditional forms.
"He was obsessed with his Augustinian idea of the modern world
as a 'land of unlikeness' (*regio dissimilitudinis*)," Steven Axelrod
observed, "a land in which human beings have lost their likeness
to God and therefore have become alienated from themselves as
well." Two years later, Lowell explored this theme more deeply
in *Lord Weary's Castle*, but with more grace and flexibility. The
poems are sombre expressions of post-World War II disillusionment and religious outrage: "war has taught me to revere/
The rulers of this darkness," he declared in one poem. Lowell
received the Pulitzer Prize for *Lord Weary's Castle*, but there
followed a long and difficult period of writing that resulted in
The Mills of the Kavanaughs, entirely made of dramatic monologues weighted with tedious detail and long, circuitous
meditations.
   Eight years later Lowell issued his masterpiece, *Life Studies*,
which combines self-analysis with myth and history in a limpidly
pure and imagistic language. Depths of agony and despair are
illuminated with candid analysis and lifted beyond personal
torment by a mind saturated with historical analogues. By wit
and charm the voice urges upon us dreadful images of a life torn
by disaster and alienation but without pathos or self-pitying.
Throughout there is the persona caught reading and writing in a

hell of domestic terrors—an image of the imperishable will and conscience. The verse is a balance of openness and measured diction achieved from careful study of William Carlos Williams. This freer style carried over to *For the Union Dead* with equal success—which sustains the attention to discord, private and public, and the suffering but resilient self.

Lowell chafed against his image as doleful confessionalist and returned to a stricter, more formalized verse in his series of *Notebooks*, later reordered as *History*, which he intended as his long poem. It too makes art from life but without the varied rhythms and forms of his earlier works. The fourteen-line segments become an unwieldy and monotonous pace for the immense length of this journal of ancient and current history. Lowell had lost the immediacy of felt life in this verse and became a mere chronicler instead. It too continues the theme of a lost culture and a dying past. A final work, *Day by Day*, returns to the conversational rhythm of *Life Studies* and is sombre in mood. The poet acknowledges the coming end of his own life at sixty years of age, and is elegiac on the deaths of many other poets.

Lowell is credited with having created confessional poetry—a verse that specializes in self-scrutiny and personal suffering in the mode of dramatic monologue. But the confessional impetus is only a small part of Lowell's purpose—in essence, he found his own life to be the instance of broadly shared feelings and so plundered and explored himself as a means of poetry. Many poets were influenced by his style, but few could catch the unique tonality and interest of a typical Lowell poem. Most imitators lost the Lowell ambience either by being mundanely thorough in their confessions or by shrilly exceeding him with tales of horror. The secret of Lowell is that he fully understood his moment in American history and reacted passionately to his times—creating therein both the integrity and the value of his self-analyzing poetry.

—Paul Christensen

O'HARA, Frank (Francis Russell O'Hara). American. Born in Baltimore, Maryland, 27 June 1926. Educated privately in piano and musical composition, 1933-43; at New England Conservatory of Music, Boston, 1946-50; Harvard University, Cambridge, Massachusetts, 1946-50, A.B. in English 1950; University of Michigan, Ann Arbor (Hopwood Award, 1951), M.A. 1951. Served in the United States Navy, 1944-46. Staff member, 1951-54, Fellowship Curator, 1955-64, Associate Curator, 1965, and Curator of the International Program, 1966, Museum of Modern Art, New York. Editorial Associate, *Art News* magazine, New York, 1954-56; Art Editor, *Kulchur Magazine*, New York, 1962-64. Recipient: Ford Fellowship, for drama, 1956. *Died 25 July 1966.*

PUBLICATIONS

Verse

A City Winter and Other Poems. New York, Tibor de Nagy, 1952.
Oranges. New York, Tibor de Nagy, 1953.
Meditations in an Emergency. Palma, Mallorca, M. Alcover, 1956; New York, Grove Press, and London, Calder, 1957.

Hartigan and Rivers with O'Hara: An Exhibition of Pictures, with Poems. New York, Tibor de Nagy, 1959.
Second Avenue. New York, Totem-Corinth, and London, Centaur Press, 1960.
Odes. New York, Tiber, 1960.
Featuring Frank O'Hara. Buffalo, New York, Audit/Poetry, 1964.
Lunch Poems. San Francisco, City Lights, 1964.
Love Poems: Tentative Title. New York, Tibor de Nagy, 1965.
In Memory of My Feelings: A Selection of Poems, edited by Bill Berkson. New York, Museum of Modern Art, 1967.
Two Pieces. London, Long Hair, 1969.
Odes. New York, Poets Press, 1969.
The Collected Poems of Frank O'Hara, edited by Donald Allen. New York, Knopf, 1971.
Belgrade, November 19, 1963. New York, Adventures in Poetry, n.d.
Selected Poems, edited by Donald Allen. New York, Knopf, 1974.
Hymns of St. Bridget, with Bill Berkson. New York, Adventures in Poetry, 1974.
Early Poems 1946-1951, edited by Donald Allen. Bolinas, California, Grey Fox Press, 1976.
Poems Retrieved 1951-1966, edited by Donald Allen. Bolinas, California, Grey Fox Press, 1977.

Plays

Try! Try! (produced Cambridge, Massachusetts, 1951; revised version, New York, 1952). Published in *Artists' Theatre*, edited by Herbert Machiz, New York, Grove Press, 1960.
Change Your Bedding (produced Cambridge, Massachusetts, 1951).
Love's Labor: An Eclogue (produced New York, 1960). New York, American Theater for Poets, 1964.
Awake in Spain (produced New York, 1960; London, 1982). New York, American Theater for Poets, 1960.
The General Returns from One Place to Another (produced New York, 1964; London, 1982). Published in *Eight Plays from Off-Off Broadway*, edited by Nick Orzel and Michael Smith, Indianapolis, Bobbs Merrill, 1966.
Surprising J.A., with Larry Rivers, in *Tracks 1*, November 1974.
Selected Plays. New York, Full Court Press, 1978.
Kenneth Koch: A Tragedy, with Larry Rivers (produced London, 1982).

Screenplay: *The Last Clean Shirt*.

Other

Jackson Pollock. New York, Braziller, 1959.
Standing Still and Walking in New York, edited by Donald Allen. Bolinas, California, Grey Fox Press, 1975.
Art Chronicles 1954-1966. New York, Braziller, 1975.
Early Writings, edited by Donald Allen. Bolinas, California, Grey Fox Press, 1977.

Editor, *Robert Motherwell: A Catalogue with Selections from the Artist's Writings.* New York, Museum of Modern Art, 1966.

*

Bibliography: *Frank O'Hara: A Comprehensive Bibliography* by Alexander Smith, Jr., New York, Garland, 1980.

Manuscript Collection: University of Connecticut Library, Storrs.

Critical Studies: *Frank O'Hara, Poet among Painters* by Marjorie G. Perloff, New York, Braziller, 1977; *Frank O'Hara* by Alan Feldman, Boston, Twayne, 1979.

Theatrical Activities:

Actor: **Play**—*Desire Caught by the Tail* by Pablo Picasso, New York, 1952.

*　　*　　*

F.S.C. Northrop speaks in *The Logic of the Sciences and the Humanities* of the value of relentlessly generalizing a given verifiable scientific theory. This extends, as he himself might point out, to the humanities, where the weakness of a particular aesthetic may be seen by the relentless attempt to hypostasize it. In much of so-called "New York School" work, the relentless derivatives of American surrealism, "abstract expressionism," pop, or what label you will, show weaknesses of an art without the transcendental term; an art low, repetitive, solipsistic. But in the great original, Frank O'Hara, one sees the intense first case, with all its multifoliate strengths. While the few verse plays seem merely vapid verse descendants of the early Auden-and-Isherwood collaborations, or the Auden of "The Orators," the poetry of O'Hara speaks to us as a sensuous analogue of Lorca.

If the weakness of the "hardboiled empiricist," in Northrop's scheme, is that of the impressionist, fresh but lacking in the theoretical or moral component, then the charge of "frivolity," often hurled at O'Hara, can be understood. O'Hara's way out of a mere "abstract impressionism" was to be converted early to a Pasternakian sense of "the revolutionary city." While the "pure facts" of his "I Do This—I Do That" poems are now everyone's ineffable birthright, O'Hara's mature strength lies in this continuous affirmation of liberty and possible liberations. His personalism, randomnesses, spontaneities, hermeticisms, etc., must be interpreted as Dr. Meyer Schapiro interpreted the paintings of Pollock: efforts in a hypocritical age to maintain an integrity despite manufactured vocabularies.

In some of the poems of Allen Ginsberg—a friend of O'Hara's—there is adumbrated a romantic love of "experience and travel" and O'Hara's connection to this was in his love for the purely inductive methods of empiricism. He was, in this sense, as Kenneth Koch pointed out years ago, the most competent poet to convey New York City in its pure factuality. If he has seemed a revolutionary poet without a revolution, he made of this lack a central and abiding metaphor.

Very early he mastered and modulated academic dictions into something tessellated, vivid, everyday. The early "To the Harbormaster," recited at his funeral by John Ashbery, remains one of the finest examples of his coherent laments. His later, discontinuous streams might seem the work of a mind unable to sustain a vehicle or tenor, but this early exemplum proves that he could.

His discontinuities were selected audaciously to break down false, glib, "silver" continuities (see in the by-now infamous Hall-Pack anthology of the 1950's) with a reliance on neo-Georgianism, neo-Yeatsism, "neo, neo, neo." O'Hara's disjunction was a betrayal of the norm, releasing the usual emotions of such a betrayal. Psychologism, naturalism, verismo, too, are betrayed, as they are in his flat, parodistic plays (one is reminded, too, of Koch's farces).

Where the political poems of the Latin American surrealists often seem purple and mismanaged, O'Hara was able to synthesize private and public dimensions through a *collagiste* method

analogous to Robert Rauschenberg's. Influenced by Neruda, he is capable of the rhapsodical manner allied to a drab and touching quality of newspaperese.

While never as flat and plain as the prose parodies of John Ashbery, it is O'Hara's *collagiste* flatness, in juxtaposition to his glamours, camps, and *potestas* or bravura passages, which distinguish him from the Latin Americans of his generation—the witty prose of Borges being the exception here. While James Wright and Robert Bly were influenced by the Chinese poets of the Tang period, Rilke, Trakl, and the Latin American surrealists, O'Hara seemed best able to digest and enucleate all such influences but with no connotatively encrusted diction. And his parodies are explicit and sharp.

Behind his images of whimsy, his Firbankian modes, behind his nostalgias and manners, behind the "Chaucerian cheerfulness" that Vendler has evaluated, lies O'Hara's peculiarly revolutionary hedonism, shared by Koch, and which, in the love poems (see *Love Poems: Tentative Title*) result in poems of exquisite empathies in a time of crisis. The Keatsian obsession with pleasure is fundamental, but an elementary other is addressed, a Buberian need for a real "you" is resolved, and the poems seem as convincing as overheard telephone conversations. In his long "Ode to Michael Goldberg's Birth and Other Births," with its closing crescendo "and he shall be the wings of an extraordinary liberty," one notes a sustained mode of examining one's self as an "other," as in the self-lacerating monologues of Ashbery. These sustained, self-lacerating, prose-ridden odes seem exemplary syntheses.

For many poets of his so-called "New York School" the problem lay in the aestheticization of the universe. This problem, comparable to the eroticization of the ego, with its concomitant dessications and addictions, was not a problem for O'Hara, who did not give in to a regressive narcissism. He found a proper relationship to things, and he speaks of this rapport in his great Mayakovskian "A True Account of Talking to the Sun at Fire Island." As with his friend LeRoi Jones, cultural psychopathology was adequately summoned, abused, and/or countermanded. His adequate vision of the city was not one of mere Whitmanesque joys; even in *Second Avenue*, the city is also an incubus, a spectre, like the cyst which grew larger than the host. In many poets influenced by O'Hara, the city and the facts of urbanity loom more solidly than the poets themselves. But this was not O'Hara's problem, though he is seen too often as thoughtless and exponentially dandified.

His poetry is filled with his resentments, and his rights to those resentments. While his coterie may have glamorized false collaborations (see the *Locus Solus* issue on Collaboration, edited by Koch) in direct ratio to its truer lack of relations, the best work of O'Hara is of a non-imperialistic ego, never engulfed or engulfing. If his work seems capricious, it reminds us that, as Whitehead said, "exactness is a fake."

—David Shapiro

OLSON, Charles (John). American. Born in Worcester, Massachusetts, 27 December 1910. Educated at Wesleyan University, Middletown, Connecticut, B.A. 1932, M.A. 1933; Yale University, New Haven, Connecticut; Harvard University, Cambridge, Massachusetts. Taught at Clark University, Worcester, and Harvard University, 1936-39; Instructor and Rector, Black Mountain College, North Carolina, 1951-56; taught at

State University of New York, Buffalo, 1963-65, and University of Connecticut, Storrs, 1969. Recipient: Guggenheim grant (twice); Wenner-Gren Foundation grant, 1952; Oscar Blumenthal Prize (*Poetry*, Chicago), 1965; American Academy grant, 1966, 1968. *Died 10 January 1970.*

PUBLICATIONS

Verse

Corrado Cagli March 31 Through April 19 1947. New York, Knoedler, 1947.
Y & X. Washington, D.C., Black Sun Press, 1948.
Letter for Melville 1951. Privately printed, 1951.
This. Black Mountain, North Carolina, Black Mountain College Graphics Workshop, 1952.
In Cold Hell, in Thicket. Palma, Mallorca, Divers Press, 1953; San Francisco, Four Seasons, 1967.
The Maximus Poems 1-10. Stuttgart, Jonathan Williams, 1953.
Ferrini and Others, with others. Berlin, Gerhardt, 1955.
Anecdotes of the Late War. Highlands, North Carolina, Jargon, 1955.
The Maximus Poems 11-22. Stuttgart, Jonathan Williams, 1956.
O'Ryan 2 4 6 8 10. San Francisco, White Rabbit Press, 1958; expanded edition as *O'Ryan 12345678910,* 1965.
The Maximus Poems. New York, Jargon-Corinth, and London, Centaur Press, 1960.
The Distances. New York, Grove Press, 1960.
Maximus, From Dogtown I. San Francisco, Auerhahn Press, 1961.
Signature to Petition on Ten Pound Island Asked of Me by Mr. Vincent Ferrini. San Francisco, Oyez, 1964.
West. London, Goliard Press, 1966.
Charles Olson Reading at Berkeley, edited by Zoe Brown. San Francisco, Coyote, 1966.
Before Your Very Eyes!, with others. London, Cape Goliard Press, 1967.
The Maximus Poems, IV, V, VI. London, Cape Goliard Press, and New York, Grossman, 1968.
Reading about My World. Buffalo, Institute of Further Studies, 1968.
Added to Making a Republic. Buffalo, Institute of Further Studies, 1968.
Clear Shifting Water. Buffalo, Institute of Further Studies, 1968.
That There Was a Woman in Gloucester, Massachusetts. Buffalo, Institute of Further Studies, 1968.
Wholly Absorbed into My Own Conduits. Buffalo, Institute of Further Studies, 1968.
Causal Mythology. San Francisco, Four Seasons, 1969.
Archaeologist of Morning: The Collected Poems Outside the Maximus Series. London, Cape Goliard Press, and New York, Grossman, 1970.
Maximus, to Himself. San Francisco, Spanish Main Press, 1970.
New Man and Woman. Privately printed, 1970.
May 20, 1959. Middletown, Connecticut, Wesleyan University, 1970.
The Maximus Poems, Volume Three, edited by Charles Boer and George F. Butterick. New York, Grossman, 1975.
The Horses of the Sea. Santa Barbara, California, Black Sparrow Press, 1976.
Some Early Poems. Iowa City, Windhover Press, 1978.

Spearmint and Rosemary. Berkeley, California, Turtle Island, 1979.
The Maximus Poems, edited by George F. Butterick. Berkeley, University of California Press, 1983.

Recording: *Charles Olson Reads from Maximus Poems,* Folkways, 1975.

Plays

The Fiery Hunt and Other Plays. Bolinas, California, Four Seasons, 1977.

Short Story

Stocking Cap: A Story. San Francisco, Four Seasons, 1966.

Other

Call Me Ishmael: A Study of Melville. New York, Reynal, 1947; London, Cape, 1967.
Apollonius of Tyana: A Dance, with Some Words, for Two Actors. Black Mountain, North Carolina, Black Mountain College, 1951.
Mayan Letters, edited by Robert Creeley. Palma, Mallorca, Divers Press, 1953; London, Cape, and New York, Grossman, 1968.
Projective Verse. New York, Totem, 1959.
A Bibliography on America for Ed Dorn. San Francisco, Four Seasons, 1964.
Human Universe and Other Essays, edited by Donald Allen. San Francisco, Auerhahn Press, 1965.
Proprioception. San Francisco, Four Seasons, 1965.
Selected Writings, edited by Robert Creeley. New York, New Directions, 1966.
Pleistocene Man: Letters from Charles Olson to John Clarke during October, 1965. Buffalo, Institute of Further Studies, 1968.
Letters for "Origin" 1950-1956, edited by Albert Glover. London, Cape Goliard Press, 1969; New York, Grossman, 1970.
The Special View of History, edited by Ann Charters. Berkeley, California, Oyez, 1970.
Poetry and Truth: The Beloit Lectures and Poems, edited by George F. Butterick. San Francisco, Four Seasons, 1971.
Additional Prose: A Bibliography on America, Proprioception, and Other Notes and Essays, edited by George F. Butterick. Bolinas, California, Four Seasons, 1974.
The Post Office: A Memoir of His Father. Bolinas, California, Grey Fox Press, 1974.
In Adullam's Lair (lecture). Provincetown, Massachusetts, To the Lighthouse Press, 1975.
Charles Olson in Connecticut: Last Lectures as Heard by John Cech, Oliver Ford, Peter Rittner. Iowa City, Windhover Press, 1975.
Charles Olson and Ezra Pound: An Encounter at St. Elizabeths, edited by Catherine Seelye. New York, Grossman, 1975.
Muthologos: The Collected Lectures and Interviews of Charles Olson, edited by George F. Butterick. Bolinas, California, Four Seasons, 2 vols., 1976-79.
Olson/Den Boer: A Letter. Santa Barbara, California, Christopher's, 1979.
D.H. Lawrence and the High Temptation of the Mind. Santa Barbara, California, Black Sparrow Press, 1980.
Charles Olson and Robert Creeley: The Complete Correspondence, edited by George F. Butterick. Santa Barbara, California, Black Sparrow Press, 5 vols., 1980-83.

*

Bibliography: *A Bibliography of Works by Charles Olson* by George F. Butterick and Albert Glover, New York, Phoenix Book Shop, 1967.

Manuscript Collections: University of Connecticut, Storrs; University of Texas, Austin.

Critical Studies: *What I See in the Maximus Poems* by Ed Dorn, Ventura, California, and Worcester, Migrant Press, 1960; *Olson/Melville: A Study in Affinity*, San Francisco, Oyez, 1968, and *Charles Olson: The Special View of History*, San Francisco, Oyez, 1970, both by Ann Charters; "Charles Olson Issues" of *Boundary* (Binghamton, New York), Fall 1973 and Winter 1974; *Charles Olson in Connecticut* by Charles Boer, Chicago, Swallow Press, 1975; *A Guide to the Maximus Poems of Charles Olson* by George F. Butterick, Berkeley, University of California Press, 1978; *Olson's Push: "Origin," Black Mountain, and Recent American Poetry* by Sherman Paul, Baton Rouge, Louisiana State University Press, 1978; *Charles Olson: Call Him Ishmael* by Paul Christensen, Austin, University of Texas Press, 1978; *Charles Olson: The Scholar's Art* by Robert von Hallberg, Cambridge, Massachusetts, Harvard University Press, 1978; *Charles Olson's Maximus* by Don Byrd, Urbana, University of Illinois Press, 1980; *To Let Words Swim into the Soul: An Anniversary Tribute to the Art of Charles Olson* by Gavin Selerie, London, Binnacle Press, 1980; *Charles Olson and Edward Dahlberg: A Portrait of a Friendship* by John Cech, Victoria, British Columbia, English Literary Studies, 1982; *The Poetry of Charles Olson: A Primer* by Thomas F. Merrill, Newark, University of Delaware Press, 1982.

*   *   *

Because Charles Olson has been considered the mentor of an entire school of poets—that growing out of the extremely interesting Black Mountain College group in the early Fifties—his readers have been as interested in knowing his doctrines as his poems. A typical (and reductive) summary of Olson's essay on Projective Verse is a claim by former Oxford Professor of Poetry Roy Fuller that Olson's Essay "conveniently contains its recipes and claims," chiefly "a number of exhortations to write good verse.... A poem is to concentrate on the syllable rather than, e.g., on metre and rhyme. The line must be kept from slowness, deadness, by being suspicious of description, of adjectives, of similes. The individual breath gives language its force, the force of speech, and in so far as the logical conventions of syntax hamper this force they must, in projective verse, go. The typewriter, because of its precision with spacing, is the personal and instantaneous recorder of the poet's work: with it he can indicate exactly the breath, the pauses, the suspension—even of syllables—and the juxtaposition—even of parts of phrases—he intends." Fuller then comments on Olson's sentimentality, perhaps failing to realize that sentimentality and dead seriousness often look alike. In his major work, *The Maximus Poems*, Olson not only demonstrated his theories, "found his measure," but also constructed a suitable vehicle for quite varied poems, both of his personal experience and of his reactions to the city of Gloucester, Massachusetts "where fishing continues/and my heart lies." Whether his poem's parallels and indebtedness to Pound's *Cantos* and Williams's *Paterson* really matters, I can't say; to me the poem justifies itself in individual songs:

that which will last,
that! o my people, where shall you find it, how, where, where

shall you listen
when all is become billboards, when, all, even silence, is
    spray-gunned?
when even our bird, my roofs,
cannot be heard
when even you, when sound itself is neoned in?

Olson's domestic poems of everyday life are intense, whether he is cussing out the Melville society (his *Call Me Ishmael* is an important book, especially in tracing Melville's sources in Shakespeare), or commenting on his household:

Or the plumbing,
that it doesn't work, this I like, have even used paper clips
as well as string to hold the ball up And flush it
with my hand
But that the car doesn't, that no moving thing moves
without that song I'd void my ear of, the musickracket
of all ownership....

But Olson harks "back to an older polis,/who has this tie to a time when the port" was involved in a fabulous history. To me, these lines about John Smith and Miles Standish, about what fourteen men required as food and supplies in the winter of 1624/25, these asides on "the nature of the cargo" are not so interesting as the present, when Olson observes:

love was
Or ought to be,
like an orange tree!
(The way they do grow
in that ex-sea soil,
in that pumice dust only a fowl
can scratch a living from).

His pictures achieve the vividness of a Hiroshige, or of netsuke:

They should raise a monument
to a fisherman crouched down
behind a hogshead, protecting
his dried fish.

Many of Olson's disciples prefer to concentrate on the philosophy in his work, and on his fairly systematic and interesting ideas, delivered in reaction to the classics, to Sumerians and Mayans, expounded in letters that have become a literature in themselves; they would be unhappy to find him characterized as a master of sketches, glimpses. But to me his best poems are humorous and domestic, rather than scholarly; his best work can be read without footnotes. Many who worship Olson, whose integrity as teacher and artist has inspired them, have perhaps overlooked his lines: "There is a limit/to what a car/will do." In concentrating on his seriousness they overlook the maker of netsuke; they neglect to admire the lightness, the humor, of the artist they've overlooked by turning him into a sage. This is, after all, the man who ate his own polishing cloth:

Trouble
with the car. And for a buck
they gave me
what I found myself
eating! A polishing
cloth. And I went right on
eating it, it was that good.
And thick, color
orange & black, with a map—the billowing dress

the big girl wears
every so often.

In the time since his death, Olson has been more than ever venerated as a poet who inspired and taught such students as Robert Creeley and Hilda Morley, who continue to acknowledge his importance for their work. Many poets, including this one, felt a genuine grief for the loss of Charles Olson, and some of us much resented the vulgarity of the picture published in *The Antioch Review* of Charles Olson in his casket. A better memorial is in the work of his students and followers, in whom his words are "modified in the guts of the living."

—David Ray

PLATH, Sylvia. American. Born in Boston, Massachusetts, 27 October 1932. Educated at schools in Wellesley, Massachusetts; Smith College, Northampton, Massachusetts (Glasscock Prize, 1955), B.A. (summa cum laude) in English 1955 (Phi Beta Kappa); Newnham College, Cambridge (Fulbright Scholar), 1955-57, M.A. 1957. Married Ted Hughes, *q.v.*, in 1956 (separated, 1962); one daughter and one son. Guest Editor, *Mademoiselle* magazine, New York, Summer 1953. Instructor in English, Smith College, 1957-58. Moved to England in 1959. Recipient: Bess Hokin Award (*Poetry*, Chicago), 1957; Yaddo Fellowship, 1959; Cheltenham Festival award, 1961; Saxon Fellowship, 1961. *Died (suicide) 11 February 1963.*

PUBLICATIONS

Verse

A Winter Ship (published anonymously). Edinburgh, Tragara Press, 1960.
The Colossus. London, Heinemann, 1960; New York, Knopf, 1962.
Ariel, edited by Ted and Olwyn Hughes. London, Faber, 1965; New York, Harper, 1966.
Uncollected Poems. London, Turret, 1965.
Wreath for a Bridal. Frensham, Surrey, Sceptre Press, 1970.
Million Dollar Month. Frensham, Surrey, Sceptre Press, 1971.
Fiesta Melons. Exeter, Rougemont Press, 1971.
Crossing the Water, edited by Ted Hughes. London, Faber, and New York, Harper, 1971.
Crystal Gazer. London, Rainbow Press, 1971.
Lyonnesse: Hitherto Uncollected Poems. London, Rainbow Press, 1971.
Winter Trees, edited by Ted Hughes. London, Faber, 1971; New York, Harper, 1972.
Child. Exeter, Rougemont Press, 1971.
Pursuit. London, Rainbow Press, 1973.
Two Poems. Knotting, Bedfordshire, Sceptre Press, 1980.
Two Uncollected Poems. London, Anvil Press Poetry, 1980.
The Collected Poems, edited by Ted Hughes. London, Faber, and New York, Harper, 1981.
Selected Poems, edited by Ted Hughes. London, Faber, 1985.

Recordings: *The Poet Speaks 5,* Argo, 1965; *Sylvia Plath Reading Her Poetry,* Caedmon, 1977.

Play

Three Women: A Monologue for Three Voices (broadcast, 1962; produced New York and London, 1973). London, Turret, 1968.

Radio Play: *Three Women,* 1962 (UK).

Novel

The Bell Jar (as Victoria Lucas). London, Heinemann, 1963; as Sylvia Plath, London, Faber, 1966; with drawings, New York, Harper, 1971.

Other

Letters Home: Correspondence 1950-1963, edited by Aurelia Schober Plath. New York, Harper, 1975; London, Faber, 1976.
The Bed Book (for children). New York, Harper, and London, Faber, 1976.
Sylvia Plath: A Dramatic Portrait (miscellany), edited by Barry Kyle. London, Faber, 1976.
Johnny Panic and the Bible of Dreams, and Other Prose Writings, edited by Ted Hughes. London, Faber, 1977; augmented edition, Faber, and New York, Harper, 1979.
The Journals of Sylvia Plath, edited by Ted Hughes and Frances McCullough. New York, Dial Press, 1982.

Editor, *American Poetry Now: A Selection of the Best Poems by Modern American Writers.* London, Oxford University Press, 1961.

*

Bibliography: *A Chronological Checklist of the Periodical Publications of Sylvia Plath* by Eric Homberger, Exeter, University of Exeter American Arts Documentation Centre, 1970; *Sylvia Plath and Anne Sexton: A Reference Guide* by Cameron Northouse and Thomas P. Walsh, Boston, Hall, 1974; *Sylvia Plath: A Bibliography* by Gary Lane and Maria Stevens, Metuchen, New Jersey, Scarecrow Press, 1978.

Critical Studies: *The Art of Sylvia Plath: A Symposium* edited by Charles Newman, Bloomington, Indiana University Press, and London, Faber, 1970; *The Poetry of Sylvia Plath: A Study of Themes* by Ingrid Melander, Stockholm, Almqvist & Wiksell, 1972; *A Closer Look at "Ariel": A Memory of Sylvia Plath* by Nancy Hunter Steiner, New York, Harper's Magazine Press, 1973, London, Faber, 1974; *Sylvia Plath: Her Life and Works* by Eileen M. Aird, Edinburgh, Oliver and Boyd, and New York, Barnes and Noble, 1973; *Sylvia Plath: Method and Madness* by Edward Butscher, New York, Seabury Press, 1976, and *Sylvia Plath: The Woman and Her Work* edited by Butscher, New York, Dodd Mead, 1977, London, Owen, 1979; *Sylvia Plath: Poetry and Existence* by David Holbrook, London, Athlone Press, 1976; *Chapters in Mythology: The Poetry of Sylvia Plath* by Judith Kroll, New York, Harper, 1976; *Sylvia Plath* by Caroline King Barnard, Boston, Twayne, 1978; *Sylvia Plath and Ted Hughes* by Margaret Dickie Uroff, Urbana, University of Illinois Press, 1979; *Sylvia Plath: New Views on the Poetry* edited by Gary Lane, Baltimore, Johns Hopkins University Press, 1979; *Sylvia Plath: The Poetry of Limitation* by Jon Rosenblatt, Chapel Hill, University of North Carolina Press, 1979; *Protean Poetics: The Poetry of Sylvia Plath* by Mary Lynn Broe, Columbia, University of Missouri Press, 1980; *Plath's Incarnations:*

Woman and Creative Process by Lynda K. Bundtzen, Ann Arbor, University of Michigan Press, 1983; *Ariel Ascending: Writings about Sylvia Plath* edited by Paul Alexander, New York, Harper, 1985.

*   *   *

Collected Poems chronologically groups all the poetry Sylvia Plath wrote from 1956 until her suicide in 1963 and includes an appendix of selected pre-1956 juvenilia. This arrangement by temporal sequence—confounded in formerly published selections of her work—focuses attention on stylistic development and thematic elaboration rather than on interpretations of Plath's life or her psychopathology. She herself said, "I think my poems immediately come out of the sensuous and emotional experiences I have but...I believe that one should be able to control and manipulate experiences, even the most terrifying ...with an informed and intelligent mind...I believe it [personal experience] should be relevant and relevant to the larger things, the bigger things such as Hiroshima and Dachau and so on."

Plath is not consistent in her ability "to control and manipulate experiences" and make them "relevant to the larger things." Some of her poems ("A Secret" and "The Fearful," for example) are too encapsulated in private detail and too dominated by images that are never clarified to be understood without biographical knowledge. She is not really interested, however, in describing her life-events and, in most of her poems, the experiences that gave rise to them are effectively generalised into a wider context than autobiography can afford. In poems such as "The Applicant," "Daddy," "The Jailer," and "Purdah" resentment against husband and father is extended to marriage and men in general and "Lady Lazarus," opening quite casually with, "I have done it again./One year in every ten/I manage it—," interweaves comments on the speaker's suicide attempts with allusions to Nazism and the persecution of the Jews in a way that succeeds in linking private pain with general human suffering.

Plath went through a succession of styles in her literary career. The pre-1956 poems, in which metaphors are used primarily to over-state and diction is constrained and formal, vary traditional verse-forms and imitate poets as diverse as John Crowe Ransom, Wallace Stevens, Robert Lowell, and Dylan Thomas. The technical elements of poetry, such as assonance, alliteration, and rhyme, are displayed with mastery in *The Colossus* but tend to dominate and restrict the subject matter of the poems so that the style appears too controlled and the content too emotionally distanced. The later poetry moves from traditional to more open poetic forms and from formal to more colloquial diction and congruent speech-rhythms. Personal experience is re-ordered through sequences of images and ideas that give the poems in *Ariel* and *Winter Trees* an urgency and immediacy that are lacking in *The Colossus*. Single metaphors by which earlier poems are "organised" give way to multiple metaphors that indicate successive and transient associations of thoughts and feelings. The extraordinary technical control and the intensity and power of the language in the emergent dramatic mode form the distinctive voice of Plath's most successful poems and sup-·port the assertion made by A. Alvarez that, "The *real* poems began in 1960."

Thematically, from the earliest poems to the latest, the world is represented either as menacing or as senseless and the pervading mood is one of fear and depression. There is a sense of alienation from reality—or even from being—and there are problems in identifying with personal history and the physical body. Oppression from other people, nature, and cosmic forces devastates self-identity.

In the early poems birth is a "cosmic accident" and death "the final grotesque joke" ("Dirge for a Joker"—juvenilia). "Fear/Of total neutrality" is mitigated by the miraculous possibility of "patch[ing] together a content/Of sorts" ("Black Rook in Rainy Weather") and death itself, as it "shatters the fabulous stars and makes us real" ("Tale of a Tub"), comes to be perceived as a form of validation. The struggle with external forces is placed in a context of "perilous poles that freeze us in/a cross of contradiction" ("Metamorphoses of the Moon"—juvenilia), a polarisation reflected in ambivalent attitudes to death, the family, and the natural world. At one moment husband and child, "smiling out of the family photo," are hurtful and intrusive, "little smiling hooks" that catch at the skin ("Tulips") while, at another, the child is the only certainty, "the one/Solid the spaces lean on" ("Nick and the Candlestick").

The struggle for a sense of being and the conflicting longing for and fear of death are Plath's major preoccupations and the recurrent theme of disintegration in her poetry reflects a fascination with self-renewal rather than with negation. Her attempts to bring the dead back to life in *The Colossus* emphasise the desire for rebirth and an assimilation of the past. The images used in the poems suggest that something eternal of the dead person always remains and that death is not total annihilation. "The old myth of origins/Unimaginable" survives in "Full Fathom Five" and the death-wish ("Father, this thick air is murderous./I would breathe water") suggests a need to re-order personal history rather than a desire for oblivion. In the stone imagery of "The Colossus," the dead father, although removed from feeling and thought ("I shall never get you put together entirely"), can still afford shelter from the external world ("Nights, I squat in the cornucopia/Of your left ear, out of the wind") and, in the poem entitled "The Stones," renewal *is* achieved and a positive identity can be held: "The vase, reconstructed, houses/The elusive rose."

Self-identity is repeatedly lost, however, and attempts to bring the dead to life fail, intensifying the conflict between death as an obliterating force and death as renewal. Fears that were projected onto the natural world—"the weight/Of stones and hill of stones could break/Her down to mere quartz grit" ("Hardcastle Crags")—can no longer be opposed by an omnipotent and protecting parent. The dead are perceived as tyrannous, the dead father as "Not God but a swastika" ("Daddy"), and God himself as "O You who eat/People like light rays" ("Brasilia")—the ultimate destructive power. There is greater identification with the external world of nature: rocks that were harsh and unresponsive to human suffering are now seen as "fingers, knuckled and rheumatic,/Cramped on nothing" ("Finisterre"). Eventually, external/internal distinctions are lost altogether. In the devastating, compelling ride into the sun in "Ariel" the leap from image to image fuses horse and rider:

> And now I
> Foam to wheat, a glitter of seas.
> The child's cry
>
> Melts in the wall.
> And I
> Am the arrow,
>
> The dew that flies
> Suicidal, at one with the drive
> Into the red
>
> Eye, the cauldron of morning.

The polarities of attitude are never reconciled and a sense of failure and exhaustion underlies many of the last poems: "Dead egg, I lie/Whole/On a whole world I cannot touch..." ("Paralytic"). The poetry itself, however, does not fail and, as a symbolic quest for transformation, reveals Sylvia Plath as a poet of enormous resonance.

—B.T. Kugler

ROETHKE, Theodore (Huebner). American. Born in Saginaw, Michigan, 25 May 1908. Educated at John Moore School, 1913-21, and Arthur Hill High School, 1921-25, Saginaw; University of Michigan, Ann Arbor, 1925-29, B.A. 1929 (Phi Beta Kappa), M.A. 1936; Harvard University, Cambridge, Massachusetts, 1930-31. Married Beatrice O'Connell in 1953. Instructor in English, 1931-35, Director of Public Relations, 1934, and varsity tennis coach, 1934-35, Lafayette College, Easton, Pennsylvania; Instructor in English, Michigan State College, East Lansing, Fall 1935; Instructor, 1936-40, Assistant Professor, 1940-43, and Associate Professor of English Composition, 1947, Pennsylvania State University, University Park; Instructor, Bennington College, Vermont, 1943-46; Associate Professor, 1947-48, Professor of English, 1948-62, and Honorary Poet-in-Residence, 1962-63, University of Washington, Seattle. Recipient: Yaddo fellowship, 1945; Guggenheim grant, 1945, 1950; Eunice Tietjens Memorial Prize, 1947, and Levinson Prize, 1951 (*Poetry*, Chicago); American Academy grant, 1952; Fund for the Advancement of Education Fellowship, 1952; Ford grant, 1952, 1959; Pulitzer Prize, 1954; Fulbright Fellowship, 1955; Borestone Mountain Award, 1958; National Book Award, 1959, 1965; Bollingen Prize, 1959; Poetry Society of America Prize, 1962; Shelley Memorial Award, 1962. D.H.L.: University of Michigan, 1962. *Died 1 August 1963.*

PUBLICATIONS

Verse

Open House. New York, Knopf, 1941.
The Lost Son and Other Poems. New York, Doubleday, 1948; London, Lehmann, 1949.
Praise to the End! New York, Doubleday, 1951.
The Waking: Poems 1933-1953. New York, Doubleday, 1953.
Words for the Wind: The Collected Verse of Theodore Roethke. London, Secker and Warburg, 1957; New York, Doubleday, 1958.
The Exorcism. San Francisco, Mallette Dean, 1957.
Sequence, Sometimes Metaphysical. Iowa City, Stone Wall Press, 1963.
The Far Field. New York, Doubleday, 1964; London, Faber, 1965.
Two Poems. Privately printed, 1965.
The Achievement of Theodore Roethke: A Comprehensive Selection of His Poems, with a Critical Introduction, edited by William J. Martz. Chicago, Scott Foresman, 1966.
The Collected Poems. New York, Doubleday, 1966; London, Faber, 1968.
Selected Poems, edited by Beatrice Roethke. London, Faber, 1969.

Recordings: *Words for the Wind,* Folkways; *The Light and Serious Side of Theodore Roethke,* Folkways; *Theodore Roethke Reading His Poetry,* Caedmon, 1972.

Other

I Am! Says the Lamb (for children). New York, Doubleday, 1961.
Party at the Zoo (for children). New York, Crowell Collier, 1963.
On the Poet and His Craft: Selected Prose of Theodore Roethke, edited by Ralph J. Mills, Jr. Seattle, University of Washington Press, 1965.
Selected Letters, edited by Ralph J. Mills, Jr. Seattle, University of Washington Press, 1968; London, Faber, 1970.
Straw for the Fire: From the Notebooks of Theodore Roethke 1943-1963, edited by David Wagoner. New York, Doubleday, 1972.
Dirty Dinky and Other Creatures: Poems for Children, edited by Beatrice Roethke and Stephen Lushington. New York, Doubleday, 1973.

*

Bibliography: *Theodore Roethke: A Bibliography* by James R. McLeod, Kent, Ohio, Kent State University Press, 1973; *Theodore Roethke's Career: An Annotated Bibliography* by Keith R. Moul, Boston, Hall, 1977.

Manuscript Collection: University of Washington, Seattle.

Critical Studies: *Theodore Roethke* by Ralph J. Mills, Jr., Minneapolis, University of Minnesota Press, and London, Oxford University Press, 1963; *Theodore Roethke: Essays on His Poetry* by Arnold S. Stein, Seattle, University of Washington Press, 1965; *Theodore Roethke: An Introduction to the Poetry* by Karl Malkoff, New York, Columbia University Press, 1966; *The Glass House: The Life of Theodore Roethke* by Allan Seager, New York, McGraw Hill, 1968; *Profile of Theodore Roethke* edited by William Heyen, Columbus, Ohio, Merrill, 1971; *The Wild Prayer of Longing: Poetry and the Sacred* by Nathan A. Scott, New Haven, Connecticut, Yale University Press, 1971; *A Concordance to the Poems of Theodore Roethke* by Gary Lane, Metuchen, New Jersey, Scarecrow Press, 1972; *Theodore Roethke's Dynamic Vision* by Richard Allen Blessing, Bloomington, Indiana University Press, 1974; *Theodore Roethke: The Garden Master* by Rosemary Sullivan, Seattle, University of Washington Press, 1975; *The Echoing Wood of Theodore Roethke* by Jenijoy La Belle, Princeton, New Jersey, Princeton University Press, 1976;*"The Edge Is What I Have": Theodore Roethke and After* by Harry Williams, Lewisburg, Pennsylvania, Bucknell University Press, 1976; *Theodore Roethke: An American Romantic* by Jay Parini, Amherst, University of Massachusetts Press, 1979; *Theodore Roethke: Poetry of the Earth, Poet of the Spirit* by Lynn Ross-Bryant, Port Washington, New York, Kennikat Press, 1981; *Theodore Roethke* by George Wolff, Boston, Twayne, 1981; *Theodore Roethke: The Poetics of Wonder* by Norman Chaney, Lanham, Maryland, University Press of America, 1982; *Theodore Roethke: The Journey from I to Otherwise* by Neal Bowers, Columbia, University of Missouri Press, 1983.

* * *

Theodore Roethke was one of the most original of the postwar American poets. He was a nature poet, with all the particular concatenation of themes and images that word implies. His poetic ancestors, as he was fond of calling them, were the visionary poets: Blake, Wordworth, Clare, Smart, and their American counterparts, Whitman, Emerson — poets who find in the metamorphic world of nature a direct language of being. But Roethke's vision of nature was eccentric. His great poetry begins in the private world of the greenhouses of his childhood. His father had been a florist in Michigan, owning what were at one time the largest greenhouses in the state. This was the kind of world that could shape a poet's imagination, since the greenhouse came to be a microcosmic image; in fact a universe, complete, exhaustive, with its own eschatology of heaven and hell, a moist artificial womb of growth. When Roethke reclaimed this world, his attention was riveted on growth, on the wilful tenacious struggle of plants into being in a drive against death: "I can hear, underground, that sucking and sobbing,/In my veins, in my bones I feel it"; in effect, in this artificial cell of forced growth, he sought to explore the essentially creative impulse compelling life. Later his natural realm would extend to swamps and boglands, those perfect mirrors of the turbulent psyche; to snails, slugs, snakes and frogs, the "small shapes, willow-shy" which in his work represent the extremity of instinctual life alien to the human condition. What overwhelms in this instinctive world is Roethke's capacity for empathic response, his ability to place himself within the life he contemplated in order to coincide with it, to achieve an experience of identity. There is something child-like, or better, primitive and animistic in his celebration of the intuitive capacity of the imagination which endears him to all readers. Yet as Stanley Kunitz remarked, Roethke could not be content with simply naming the things he loved, he was driven to converting them to symbols, that painful ritual.

He came into his own as a poet with the greenhouse sequence written between 1942 and 1946 when he discovered how to use the slimy world of botanic growth as an imagistic focus to embody private suffering and disorder. *The Lost Son* sequence, one of his greatest achievements as a poet, followed. These are dark poems of suffering and mental disorder composed in a surrealistic language which attempts to reproduce the psychic shorthand of the unconscious. They describe an interior journey into complete and terrifying self-absorption. Throughout his life Roethke suffered from periodic experiences of mental breakdown which he symbolized as the condition of the lost son. His private relationship to his father, who died when he was fifteen, became the model for his sense of an existential state of loss, one of those transformations that are the key to great art. What may have been a struggle for personal identity became a human struggle for spiritual identity: "a struggle out of the slime...a slow spiritual progress."

Roethke's regressive exploration of psychic extremity was very sophisticated, often indebted to Jung through Maud Bodkin, so that the concepts of collective unconscious, rebirth, integration, are essential to his poems. Through his harrowing experiences he became convinced of an *a priori* principle of being beyond intellect—a still center or soul, not an objective reality but a goal in an on-going process of spiritual ascent. In his later poems, which are almost neo-Elizabethan in their formal elegance, he is deeply interested in mysticism, that area of psychic experience so puzzling and yet so vital to modern sensibility. Yet there is no mystical piety in his work. The idea of soul is an emotional hypothesis built out of the sheerest force of will, an act of faith which had to be constantly renewed. In the end, he is a poet of life, of celebration: "Now I adore my life/With the Bird, the abiding Leaf, ...For Love, for Love's sake." One is drawn to the words of James Dickey for a final assessment of Roethke's work: "There is no poetry anywhere that is so valuably conscious of the human body ... no poetry that can place the body in an *environment*—wind, seascape, greenhouse, forest, desert, mountainside, among animals or insects or stones—so vividly and

evocatively, waking unheard-of exchanges between the place and human responsiveness at its most creative. He more than any other is a poet of pure being."

—Rosemary Sullivan

SEXTON, Anne (née Harvey). American. Born in Newton, Massachusetts, 9 November 1928. Educated at Garland Junior College, Boston; Radcliffe Institute, Cambridge, Massachusetts (Scholar), 1961-63. Married Alfred M. Sexton in 1948 (divorced, 1974); two daughters. Fashion model, Boston, 1950-51. Taught at Wayland High School, Massachusetts, 1967-68; Lecturer, 1970-71, and Professor of Creative Writing, 1972-74, Boston University. Crawshaw Professor of Literature, Colgate University, Hamilton, New York, 1972. Recipient: Bread Loaf Writers Conference Robert Frost Fellowship, 1959; Levinson Prize (*Poetry*, Chicago), 1962; American Academy Traveling Fellowship, 1963; Ford grant, 1964; Shelley Memorial Award, 1967; Pulitzer Prize, 1967; Guggenheim Fellowship, 1969. Litt.D.: Tufts University, Medford, Massachusetts, 1970; Regis College, Weston, Massachusetts, 1971; Fairfield University, Connecticut, 1971. Fellow, Royal Society of Literature. *Died (suicide) 4 October 1974.*

PUBLICATIONS

Verse

To Bedlam and Part Way Back. Boston, Houghton Mifflin, 1960.
All My Pretty Ones. Boston, Houghton Mifflin, 1962.
Selected Poems. London, Oxford University Press, 1964.
Live or Die. Boston, Houghton Mifflin, 1966; London, Oxford University Press, 1967.
Poems, with Douglas Livingstone and Thomas Kinsella. London and New York, Oxford University Press, 1968.
Love Poems. Boston, Houghton Mifflin, and London, Oxford University Press, 1969.
Transformations. Boston, Houghton Mifflin, 1971; London, Oxford University Press, 1972.
The Book of Folly. Boston, Houghton Mifflin, 1972; London, Chatto and Windus, 1974.
O Ye Tongues. London, Rainbow Press, 1973.
The Death Notebooks. Boston, Houghton Mifflin, 1974; London, Chatto and Windus, 1975.
The Awful Rowing Toward God. Boston, Houghton Mifflin, 1975; London, Chatto and Windus, 1977.
The Heart of Anne Sexton's Poetry, edited by Linda Gray Sexton and Lois Ames. Boston, Houghton Mifflin, 1977.
Words for Dr. Y.: Uncollected Poems with Three Stories, edited by Linda Gray Sexton. Boston, Houghton Mifflin, 1978.
The Complete Poems. Boston, Houghton Mifflin, 1981.

Play

45 Mercy Street (produced New York, 1969). Edited by Linda Gray Sexton, Boston, Houghton Mifflin, 1976; London, Secker and Warburg, 1977.

Other

Eggs of Things (for children), with Maxine Kumin. New York, Putnam, 1963.
More Eggs of Things (for children), with Maxine Kumin. New York, Putnam, 1964.
Joey and the Birthday Present (for children), with Maxine Kumin. New York, McGraw Hill, 1971.
The Wizard's Tears (for children), with Maxine Kumin. New York, McGraw Hill, 1975.
Anne Sexton: A Self-Portrait in Letters, edited by Linda Gray Sexton and Lois Ames. Boston, Houghton Mifflin, 1977.

*

Bibliography: Sylvia Plath and Anne Sexton: A Reference Guide by Cameron Northouse and Thomas P. Walsh, Boston, Hall, 1974.

Critical Studies: "Les Belles Dames sans Merci" by Geoffrey H. Hartman, in Kenyon Review (Gambier, Ohio), Autumn 1960; "The Hungry Sheep Looks Up" by Neil Meyers, in Minnesota Review (Minneapolis), Fall 1960; "A Return to Reality" by Cecil Hemley, in Hudson Review (New York), Winter 1962-63; "Seven Voices" by M. L. Rosenthal, in Reporter (New York), 3 January 1963; "Interview with Anne Sexton" by Patricia Marx, in Hudson Review (New York), Winter 1965; Contemporary American Poetry by Ralph J. Mills, Jr., New York, Random House, 1965; "In Spite of Artifice" by Hayden Carruth, in Hudson Review (New York), Winter 1966-67; "O Jellow Eye" by Philip Legler, in Poetry (Chicago), May 1967; "Achievement of Anne Sexton" by Robert Boyers, in Salmagundi (Saratoga Springs, New York), Spring 1967; interview with Barbara Kevles, in Paris Review, Spring 1971; Anne Sexton: The Artist and Her Critics edited by J.D. McClatchy, Bloomington, Indiana University Press, 1978.

Anne Sexton commented:

(1970) It is said that I am part of the so-called "confessional school." I prefer to think of myself as an imagist who deals with reality and its hard facts.

I write stories about life as I see it. As one critic put it I am "metaphor-mad." I work happily within strict forms that differ poem by poem or in what I call loose poems. Each time I look for the voice of the poem and each time it is a different one. I have been influenced by Rilke, Rimbaud, Kafka, Neruda. My themes deal with life and death; insanity, daughterhood, motherhood and love. My poems are intensely physical.

*   *   *

By the time of her death in 1974, Anne Sexton had won a wide and attentive audience, ranging from Robert Lowell to young students of poetry at universities in England and America. Her work began in the mode of what is often called the "confessional school," inaugurated by Lowell's Life Studies (1959) and including Lowell, Sexton, Plath, Berryman, and others. Each of their works might be entitled "A Study of My Life," especially Sexton's poems: the lyricist's self-portrait, drawn in concrete details of personal life rendered as metaphor. Initially, on the American poetry scene of the late 1950's, the metaphors were familiar fare—"the beach waits like an altar./ We are lying on a cloth of sand" ("The Kite")—only to become increasingly hallucinatory—"as I lay in a chloral cave of drugs" ("Angles of the Love Affair No.2")—and even grotesque—"myself, Ms. Dog" ("Is It True?")—then at the last the Sexton metaphor diffuses into verse parable.

Through changing styles, her canon is remarkably uniform in its themes. From changing perspectives, and with different possibilities of resolution, she asks herself the same questions, querying the nature and sources of emotional pain, the value of the effort to survive such pain, the existence of God.

Roughly, her work falls into three stages: first, the beginnings, in To Bedlam and Part Way Back and All My Pretty Ones, her record of madness, of estrangement and reunion as daughter and as mother, of willed faith in healers and in nature's seasonal healings; second, the chastened and more spare, less celebratory and more caustic verse culminating in Live or Die, which many readers consider her finest collection; third, darker in many ways but ultimately more hopeful still, the last period bridging The Book of Folly and The Awful Rowing Toward God, works rooted in nightmare and grotesques, but culminating in the resilient poet's entrance into Heaven, where God challenges her to a poker match and beats her royal flush with his wild card, in "lucky love." As in much of Sexton's work, one can hear in that phrase both faith and dread, because both are always present in her verse, in varying and often indeterminate emphasis.

Confused metaphorical structures and mannerisms typical of the period mar her early work. But as Sexton began tempering the excessively personal references in the late 1960's and to explore archetypal images derived mostly from psychiatry and Christianity ("the fire woman," "the leather men," the witch, the bird, the sea-breast), while tapping into her own bedrock of New England folklore and superstitions, she found rich sources of cynical wonder and figures for its articulation. Her early distress at the lack of human mutual understanding, and her compassion for the mad and the healers alike, cedes (in the Vietnam War years) to disgust with the limitations of human action, and Love Poems celebrates limited pleasure and joy shared in respite from all else. But no joy remains unalloyed, mostly because Sexton is her parents' daughter, suffering their suffering, and her own daughter's mother, suffering the same love and the same estrangement—but this time mysteriously responsible for it.

Love is prized, but no emotion can be definitive because the poet is haunted by its sources and its extensions, all finally unknowable, all ultimately God in the late work. The poetry of the early 1970's seems at first to have a more casual tone, since the language is more colloquial, the style more elliptic, the world of childhood memories more inviting; but the old questions are still there, indeed more intense and haunting than ever: grief of self and of humankind without God, loneliness with the "dead heart" of the too tried and trying, frail joy at brief perceptions of physical beauty or of "useful objects," fear of "EVIL." Finally in The Awful Rowing Toward God EVIL finds a counterweight in her certainty—perhaps not of God himself, but of her own perfected articulation of faith in God, an expression sought a lifetime.

She began capitalizing EVIL in the early 1970's, and there is surely more than an echo of Baudelaire in her "After Auschwitz" ("And death looks on with a casual eye/and scratches his anus"), and in other poems of this period. It is certain that she deliberately echoes Rimbaud and the Kafka of Parables and Paradoxes. Through all the allusions, EVIL means primarily the pained ignorance that is everywhere, that seeps out of telephone coin boxes, even out of useful objects unexpectedly, out of the invisible sources of things. The immediate effects of EVIL are treble: first, the sub-human actions of people and oneself in brutality, deceit, ignorance of self, as well as the pain one feels at such failings of the (basically Romantic) standard; second, the esthetic incapacity of the poet, in poems about dead eyeless bees no longer swarming; third, the unstable "I," The woman who cannot keep a covenant, saying, "Evil is maybe lying to God./ Or better, lying to love" ("Is It True?").

Unlike the poetry of the mentors she invokes, Sexton's verse is primarily emotional, scornful of ideas, grounded upon a rich store of metaphors for emotional pain, amid a nagging hope in God. "To be without God is to be a snake/who wants to swallow an elephant" ("The Play"), she concludes, affirming the impossibility even as she affirms the desire. Such metaphors for human ignorance and aspiration, along with figures for Mother and Daughter, Lover and Sea, distinguish her haunted verse.

—Jan Hokenson

SPICER, Jack (John Lester Spicer). American. Born in Hollywood, California, 30 January 1925. Educated at the University of Redlands, California, 1943-44; University of California, Berkeley, B.A. 1947, M.A. 1950. Taught at the University of Minnesota, Minneapolis, 1950-52, University of California, Berkeley, 1952-53, California School of Fine Arts, 1953-55; editor and curator in the Rare Book Room, Boston Public Library, 1955-56; taught at San Francisco State College, 1957; assistant on Linguistic Geography to David Reed, Berkeley, 1957-65. Co-Founder, Six Gallery, San Francisco, 1953, Founder, White Rabbit Press, San Francisco, 1957, and the magazines *J*, *M*, and *Open Space*. Died 17 August 1965.

PUBLICATIONS

Verse

After Lorca. San Francisco, White Rabbit Press, 1957; London, Aloes, n.d.
Homage to Creeley. Privately printed, 1959.
Billy the Kid. Stinson Beach, California, Enkidu Surrogate, 1959.
The Heads of the Town Up to the Aether. San Francisco, Auerhahn, 1962.
Lament for the Makers. Oakland, California, White Rabbit Press, 1962; London, Aloes, 1971.
The Holy Grail. San Francisco, White Rabbit Press, 1964.
Language. San Francisco, White Rabbit Press, 1965.
The Redwood Forest. San Francisco, White Rabbit Press, 1965.
Book of Magazine Verse. San Francisco, White Rabbit Press, 1966.
The Day Five Thousand Fish Died in the Charles River. Pleasant Valley, New York, Kriya Press, 1967.
A Book of Music. San Francisco, White Rabbit Press, 1969.
Indian Summer: Minneapolis 1950. New York, Samuel Charters, 1970.
The Red Wheelbarrow. Berkeley, California, Arif Press, 1971.
The Ballad of the Dead Woodcutter. Berkeley, California, Arif Press, 1972.
Some Things from Jack. Verona, Plain Wrapper Press, 1972.
Fifteen False Propositions about God. San Francisco, Man-Root, 1974.
Admonitions. New York, Adventures in Poetry, 1974; Portree, Isle of Skye, Aquila, 1981.
Berkeley in a Time of Plague. Berkeley, California, Arif Press, 1974.
An Ode and Arcadia, with Robert Duncan. Berkeley, California, Ark Press, 1974.
A Lost Poem. Verona, Plain Wrapper Press, 1974.

The Collected Books of Jack Spicer, edited by Robin Blaser. Los Angeles, Black Sparrow Press, 1975.
There Is an Inner Nervousness in Virgins. Eureka, California, Spotted Pig Press, 1975(?).
One Night Stand and Other Poems, edited by Donald Allen. San Francisco, Grey Fox Press, 1981.

Plays

Pentheus and the Dancers, in *Caterpillar 12* (Sherman Oaks, California), July 1970.

Other

Dear Ferlinghetti/Dear Jack: The Spicer-Ferlinghetti Correspondence. San Francisco, White Rabbit Press, 1962(?).

*

Bibliography: "A Checklist of the Published Writings of Jack Spicer" by Sanford Dorbin, in *California Librarian* (Sacramento), October 1970.

Manuscript Collection: Simon Fraser University Library, Burnaby, British Columbia.

Critical Studies: "Spicer/Blaser Issue" of *Caterpillar 12* (Sherman Oaks, California), July 1970; "Spicer Issue" of *Boundary 2* (Binghamton, New York), Fall 1977.

*   *   *

Jack Spicer's poetry is so totally engaged with his poetics that the two often serve as complementary (or contending) voices within any given poem. For this reason, the poems appear to be arguments with themselves, opaque to a casual reading and at the same time possessed of an arch and playful wit. Their coherence depends upon the intensity of this argument, extended through a series of short poems and gathered into small books or "serial poems." Each single poem depends upon the others in the series to advance or revise what has gone before so that things appear to be constantly in motion. The tone of debate provides the primary mood in Spicer's work, the poet struggling with forces beyond him which threaten to inhabit the work. In this drama of poetic contentions, these forces (or "ghosts," as Spicer points out) might be rhetoric, ethical statement, authorial intention, or the canons of taste represented by official academic and scholarly opinion. Spicer wants the poem to come to him in the form of cryptic message or occult code rather emanate from his own will to form. The poet, then, is not an inspired or possessed artificer but rather a "radio" (to use his favorite image) through whom the poem broadcasts.

Although Spicer refused to define his poetics separate from the poems themselves, he provided a useful statement about his method of dictation in "Vancouver Lectures" (*Caterpillar 12*) describing poetry as "spiritual method" and the central poetic act as "emptying yourself as a vessel," rather than finding equivalences for subjective experience. For Spicer the poem which is engaged with the *play* of meaning (puns, anagrams, jokes, semantic doublings) is one which operates in the largest domain of meaning—that is, where ideas and experiences have a multifarious existence. In this sense Spicer respects the so-called "innocent" poetry of nursery rhymes and the slightly more intentionalized nonsense of Lewis Carroll and Edward Lear.

Paradoxically, this desire for a playful sliding of meaning provides a more accurate translation of the world. In one of the letters addressed to García Lorca in *After Lorca*, Spicer makes the following distinction:

> I would like to make poems out of real objects. The lemon to be a lemon that the reader could cut or squeeze or taste—a real lemon like a newspaper in a collage is a real newspaper. I would like the moon in my poems to be a real moon, one which could be suddenly covered with a cloud that has nothing to do with the poem—a moon utterly independent of images. The imagination pictures the real. I would like to point to the real, disclose it, to make a poem that has no sound in it but the pointing of a finger.

The fault with most modern poetry, Spicer feels, is that it searches for a more exact objective correlative or image—a "picture" of the real. Spicer wants a poetry which "corresponds" with the world, not by imitating it but by being an activity within it. Unlike Baudelaire's formulation of correspondences, Spicer's poetry is not directed toward a super-sensual effect of mystic apprehension; it is concerned with the world in all of its accidental and unanticipated occasions, frightening and sublime at the same time.

The volatile atmosphere of San Francisco during the 1950's and 1960's provided a fertile ground for such a poetics. In the bars and coffee houses of North Beach, the new poetry appeared to Spicer as the gospel of a heretical sect or Gnostic enclave. Spicer sat at the central table of bars like The Place or Gino/Carlo's and held a kind of court in which the university English Department and east coast publishing firms could be regarded as the Pope's army and the new poetry emerging from San Francisco's "Beat" movement functioned as the secret (and spirited) language of Catharist adepts. With Robert Duncan and Robin Blaser, Spicer charged the air with his sense of a literary renaissance on the west coast, one not bound by official proclamations or manifestos but constantly engaged in poetry's problematic nature.

—Michael Davidson

WRIGHT, James (Arlington). American. Born in Martins Ferry, Ohio, 13 December 1927. Educated at Kenyon College, Gambier, Ohio, B.A. 1952; University of Washington, Seattle, M.A. 1954, Ph.D. 1959. Married Edith Anne Runk; two sons from previous marriage. Taught at the University of Minnesota, Minneapolis, 1957-64, Macalaster College, St. Paul, Minnesota, 1963-65, and Hunter College, New York, 1966-80. Recipient: Fulbright Scholarship, 1952; Eunice Tietjens Memorial Prize, 1955, and Oscar Blumenthal Prize, 1968 (*Poetry*, Chicago); Yale Series of Younger Poets award, 1957; American Academy grant, 1959; Guggenheim Fellowship, 1964, 1978; Brandeis University Creative Arts Award, 1970; Academy of American Poets Fellowship, 1971; Melville Cane Award, 1972; Pulitzer Prize, 1972. Member, American Academy, 1974. *Died 25 March 1980.*

PUBLICATIONS

Verse

The Green Wall. New Haven, Connecticut, Yale University Press, 1957.

Saint Judas. Middletown, Connecticut, Wesleyan University Press, 1959.
The Lion's Tail and Eyes: Poems Written Out of Laziness and Silence, with Robert Bly and William Duffy. Madison, Minnesota, Sixties Press, 1962.
The Branch Will Not Break. Middletown, Connecticut, Wesleyan University Press, and London, Longman, 1963.
Shall We Gather at the River. Middletown, Connecticut, Wesleyan University Press, 1968; London, Rapp and Whiting, 1969.
Collected Poems. Middletown, Connecticut, Wesleyan University Press, 1971.
Two Citizens. New York, Farrar Straus, 1974.
Moments of the Italian Summer. Washington, D.C., Dryad Press, 1976.
Old Booksellers and Other Poems. Melbourne, Cotswold Press, 1976.
To a Blossoming Pear Tree. New York, Farrar Straus, 1977; London, Faber, 1979.
The Journey. Concord, New Hampshire, Ewert, 1981.
This Journey. New York, Random House, 1982.
The Temple in Nimes. Worcester, Massachusetts, Metacom Press, 1982.

Recordings: *Today's Poets 3,* with others, Folkways; *The Poetry and Voice of James Wright,* Caedmon, 1977.

Other

The Summers of James and Annie Wright. New York, Sheep Meadow Press, 1980.
Collected Prose, edited by Anne Wright. Ann Arbor, University of Michigan Press, 1982.

Editor and Translator, *Poems,* by Hesse. New York, Farrar Straus, 1970; London, Cape, 1971.

Translator, with Robert Bly, *Twenty Poems of Georg Trakl.* Madison, Minnesota, Sixties Press, 1961.
Translator, with Robert Bly and John Knoepfle, *Twenty Poems of César Vallejo.* Madison, Minnesota, Sixties Press, 1962.
Translator, *The Rider on the White Horse,* by Theodor Storm. New York, New American Library, 1964.
Translator, with Robert Bly, *Twenty Poems of Pablo Neruda.* Madison, Minnesota, Sixties Press, and London, Rapp and Whiting, 1968.

*

Bibliography: "James Wright: A Checklist" by Belle M. McMaster, in *Bulletin of Bibliography 31* (Boston), 1974.

Critical Studies: by Robert Coles, in *American Poetry Review* (Philadelphia), 1974; *Four Poets and the Emotive Imagination* by George S. Lensing and Ronald Moran, Baton Rouge, Louisiana State University Press, 1976; "Wright Issue" of *Ironwood 10* (Tucson), 1977; *The Pure Clear Word: Essays on the Poetry of James Wright* edited by Dave Smith, Urbana, University of Illinois Press, 1982.

James Wright commented:
(1970) I have written about the things I am deeply concerned with—crickets outside my window, cold and hungry old men, ghosts in the twilight, horses in a field, a red-haired child in her mother's arms, a feeling of desolation in the fall, some cities I've known.

I try and say how I love my country and how I despise the way it is treated. I try and speak of the beauty and again of the ugliness in the lives of the poor and neglected.

I have changed the way I've written, when it seemed appropriate, and continue to do so.

*   *   *

James Wright's *Collected Poems* contains most of *The Green Wall* and all of *Saint Judas, The Branch Will Not Break*, and *Shall We Gather at the River*, plus some translations and 33 new poems. This impressive volume, although it covered only 14 years of the poet's career, revealed a genuine experimenter, a poet who could, like Yeats, consciously transform himself. Thus we could already speak of Wright's "phases," discerning three distinct stages of development: the early rich and formal poems of the first two books, the spare and "deep-image" work of *Branch*, and the loose and pain-filled later poems. For these stages also suggested a strange and tragic curve of emotional development: Wright's concern for human suffering, which was never absent from his earlier work and which seemed to have been temporarily balanced by the bright joy of so much of *Branch*, now reappeared as an obsession without let or hindrance or (often) control in an avalanche of anguish and despair in *River* and "New Poems."

The Green Wall and *Saint Judas* are written largely in regular stanzas and literary language. The first is lush with the Dylan Thomas-like ecstacy of a young poet discovering his medium and his powerful sensibility, and is notable for its hallucinatory sense of the seasons and their montagistic overlappings. *Saint Judas* is somewhat reminiscent, however, in its more rugged subjects and feelings, of Hardy, Robinson, Masters, and Frost. It deals in a stark and compassionate way with love and loss and death in the lives of a dramatic cast of characters. Then there is a sequence of love poems treating painfully but movingly the loss and sorrow of a love that is failing. Finally there is a section concerned with crime and violence, the innocent and the guilty—as, for example, in the Caryl Chessman and George Doty poems. Here is more than a merely abstract humanitarianism, for Wright sees no absolute difference between the murderer and the rest of us, that the executioner is only doing coldly what his victim did out of madness or passion or grief.

No longer using conventional diction, regular stanzas, and straightforward structures, *Branch* is given to open and direct lines, poems of varying length, and easy and natural language. Wright built his poems, in haiku fashion, on hard images which are juxtaposed in shocking combinations of experience, leaving the connections and transitions to be inferred by the reader. There is correspondingly a tendency to shift from the external dramatic world inward to the subjective. "Autumn Begins in Martins Ferry, Ohio," for example, although still in the objective mode of the preceding volume, implies universes of suppressed violence within as it portrays the erotic frustration of the parents of high-school football players, and concludes: "Therefore, /Their sons grow suicidally beautiful/At the beginning of October,/And gallop terribly against each other's bodies." Others, such as "Lying on a Hammock at William Dufy's Farm," "Fear Is What Quickens Me," "Today I Was So Happy, So I Made This Poem," and "A Blessing" must also be mentioned.

The emotional—and sometimes artistic—descent, however, is dizzying as we come to *River* and the "New Poems." For unrelieved wretchedness, these pieces must be unmatched in contemporary poetry and suggest that Wright was returning, after the brief high of *Branch*, to some old and unresolved fundamental despair. Surely the name of this volume itself pictures the Dead gathering by the Styx, and some of the titles are all-too-indicative

of its contents and mood: "In Terror of Hospital Bills," "The Poor Washed Up by Chicago Winter," "Old Age Compensation," "Listening to the Mourners." But it is not until the "New Poems" that we actually touch, in "A Secret Gratitude," what one hoped would be the bottom of this agony. There is a strange desperation here, and in "Many of Our Waters," which did, however, presage Wright's transition to phase four:

All this beautiful time I've been slicking into my own words
The beautiful language of my friends.
I have to use my own, now.
That's why this scattering poem sounds the way it does.

He was ready for another transformation, and he seems bewildered: "The kind of poetry I want to write is/The poetry of a grown man." I do not think, though, that the poetry of a grown man is found by writing poorly and then by acknowledging that one is writing poorly. Irony and self-awareness, even anti-poetry, require more than that.

Two Citizens, Moments of the Italian Summer (14 prose pieces), and *To a Blossoming Pear Tree* (containing work from *Moments*), however, indeed represented a new stage. To be sure, there remained a certain looseness, ingenuousness, and that trick of turning back to comment on what he has just written, but gone are the bitterness, hopelessness, and self-indulgence. What we have here, in fact, is a growing sense of complexity concealed within a surface of deceptive simplicity. Resolutely sticking now to his own plain Ohioan speech, as he proclaims, he speaks out openly of his and his wife's travels through France and Italy, of his boyhood in Martins Ferry, of his love, of nature and her creatures, and yet he does something strange at the same time. One of my favorites, "Well, What Are You Going to Do?" (from *Citizens*), tells of his boyhood experience of assisting their cow to give birth to Marian, his calf. At first he feels helpless, not knowing what to do "about the problem/Of beautiful women." Finally, at the moment of birth itself, he helps Marian come out, and he concludes:

I don't know that I belonged
In that beautiful place. But
What are you going to do? Be kind? Kill?
Die?

The ordinary has been somehow transformed into an erotic hallucination, a wondering apotheosis of universalized excitement.

And he unpretentiously effects such transformation in poem after poem. I could wish away some of the repeated "by Gods," "sweet leaping Jesuses," "son of a bitches," "lifes," "dies," "beautifuls," "loves," "wings," and so on, but these are a small price to pay for such honest and human intensity. When all is said and done, Wright was a genuinely passionate/compassionate poet who did not withhold or spare himself, and his best work makes him one of the most interesting and valuable poets of his generation in America.

James Wright died in 1980 at the age of 53, and it is with infinite regret that I undertake the task here of rounding off his earthly career. It seems appropriate, moreover, to indulge in a personal memory to bring out what I feel. It was during the late 1950's, when he came to give a reading at the campus where I was then teaching, and it was the only time we ever met. Despite the fact that he was the visiting celebrity, what I most remember were his kind comments on a poem I myself had just published in the campus literary magazine, and I intend this anecdote to illustrate his selflessness rather then my egotism. Was there ever a man and poet who so combined such sweet gentleness with the intensity of such Keatsian negative capability?

I see the same qualities in his next and last major collection, *This Journey*, containing somewhat over 70 pieces, which he completed just before his death. He continues to write about his childhood in Martins Ferry, his adult travels in France and Italy, and about his profound responsiveness to nature—recurring images of wind, rain, stone, and ligh abound, as well as of birds, lizards, spiders, fish, flowers, fields, and trees. And he does so primarily in his lucidly deep free-verse style, although there are a number of prose poems and a few rhymed and metered pieces. What has changed, however, is that he has come well past the terrible despair of *River*, and even of the uncertainties of style in his more hopeful phase, and has reintegrated his ability passionately to transform the commonplace with a calm assurance and consistency that belie the approach of a too-early death.

There is much to cherish here—too much to comment on in this brief space. My favorites are "May Morning," "The Journey," "Greetings in New York City," "In Memory of Mayor Richard Daley," and "On Having My Pocket Picked in Rome." The first is one of the most exciting pieces I have read in a long time, a relatively brief prose poem picturing winter hanging on along the Mediterranean during the approach of spring, and concluding: "One olive tree below Grottaglie welcomes the winter into noontime shade, and talks as softly as Pythagoras. Be still, be patient, I can hear him say, cradling in his arms the wounded head, letting the sunlight touch the savage face."

A fitting close to this account of James Wright is the conclusion of "The Journey," in which the speaker sits beside a spider web he finds among the dust-blown Tuscan hills, noticing how the spider frees herself somehow of the dust accumulating on her web, and reflecting:

> The secret
> Of this journey is to let the wind
> Blow its dust all over your body,
> To let it go on blowing, to step lightly, lightly
> All the way through your ruins, and not to lose
> Any sleep over the dead, who surely
> Will bury their own, don't worry.

—Norman Friedman

ZUKOFSKY, Louis. American. Born in New York City, 23 January 1904. Educated at Columbia University, New York, M.A. 1924. Married Celia Thaew in 1939; one son. Taught at the University of Wisconsin, Madison, 1930-31; Colgate University, Hamilton, New York, 1947; Polytechnic Institute of Brooklyn, New York, 1947-66. Recipient: Longview Foundation Award, 1961; Union League Civic and Arts Foundation Prize, 1964, and Oscar Blumenthal Prize, 1966 (*Poetry*, Chicago); National Endowment for the Arts grant, 1966, 1968; American Academy award, 1976. *Died 12 May 1978.*

PUBLICATIONS

Verse

First Half of "A"-9. Privately printed, 1940.
55 Poems. Prairie City, Illinois, Decker Press, 1941.
Anew. Prairie City, Illinois, Decker Press, 1946.

Some Time: Short Poems. Stuttgart, Germany, Jonathan Williams, 1956.
Barely and Widely. New York, Celia Zukofsky, 1958.
"A" 1-12. Ashland, North Carolina, Origin Press, 1959; London, Cape, 1966.
16 Once Published. Edinburgh, Wild Hawthorn Press, 1962.
I's Pronounced "Eyes." New York, Trobar Press, 1963.
After I's. Pittsburgh, Boxwood Press, 1964.
Found Objects 1962-1926. Georgetown, Kentucky, H.B. Chapin, 1964.
An Unearthing: A Poem. Privately printed, 1965.
Iyyob. London, Turret, 1965.
I Sent Thee Late. Privately printed, 1965.
Finally a Valentine. Stroud, Gloucestershire, Piccolo Press, 1965.
"A" Libretto. Privately printed, 1965.
All: The Collected Short Poems 1923-1958 and 1956-1964. New York, Norton, 2 vols., 1965-66; London, Cape, 2 vols., 1966-67; Norton, 1 vol., 1971.
"A"-9. Cologne, Hansjörg Mayer, 1966.
"A"-14. London, Turret, 1967.
"A" 13-21. London, Cape, and New York, Doubleday, 1969.
The Gas Age: A Poem. Newcastle upon Tyne, Ultima Thule, 1969.
Initial. New York, Phoenix Book Shop, 1970.
"A"-24. New York, Grossman, 1972.
"A"-22 and 23. New York, Viking Press, 1975; London, Trigram Press, 1978.
"A" (complete version). Berkeley, University of California Press, 1978.
80 Flowers. Lunenburg, Vermont, Stinehour Press, 1978.

Plays

Arise, Arise. New York, Grossman, 1973.

Short Stories

It Was. New York, Origin Press, 1961.
Little: A Fragment for Careenagers. Los Angeles, Black Sparrow Press, 1967; complete version, New York, Grossman, 1970.
Ferdinand, Including It Was. London, Cape, and New York, Grossman, 1968.

Other

Le Style Apollinaire. Paris, Les Presses Modernes, 1934.
5 Statements for Poetry. San Francisco, San Francisco State College, 1958.
Bottom: On Shakespeare. Austin, Texas, Ark Press, 1963.
Prepositions: The Collected Critical Essays of Louis Zukofsky. London, Rapp and Carroll, 1967; New York, Horizon Press, 1968; revised edition, Berkeley, University of California Press, 1981.
Autobiography. New York, Grossman, 1970.

Editor, *An "Objectivists" Anthology.* Le Beausset, France, To Publishers, 1932.
Editor, *A Test of Poetry.* New York, Objectivist Press, 1948; London, Routledge, 1952.

Translator, *Albert Einstein,* by Anton Reiser. New York, Boni, 1930.
Translator, with Celia Zukofsky, *Catullus: Fragmenta,* music by Paul Zukofsky. London, Turret, 1969.

Translator, with Celia Zukofsky, *Catullus*. London, Cape Goliard Press, and New York, Grossman, 1969.

Bibliography: *A Bibliography of Louis Zukofsky*, Los Angeles, Black Sparrow Press, 1969, and "Year by Year Bibliography of Louis Zukofsky," in *Paideuma 7* (Orono, Maine), Winter 1978, both by Celia Zukofsky; *A Catalogue of the Louis Zukofsky Manuscript Collection* edited by Marcella Booth, Austin, University of Texas Humanities Research Center, 1975.

Critical Studies: *At: Bottom* by Cid Corman, Bloomington, Indiana, Caterpillar, 1966; Guy Davenport, in *Agenda* (London), Autumn-Winter 1970; "Zukofsky Issue" of *Grosseteste Review* (Lincoln, England), Winter 1970, and of *Maps 5*, 1974; Kenneth Cox, in *Agenda* (London), Autumn-Winter 1971; Peter Quartermain, in *Open Letter Second Series* (Toronto), Fall 1973; article, in *Journal of English Literary History*, Spring 1978, and *Zukofsky's "A": An Introduction*, Berkeley, University of California Press, 1983, both by Barry Ahearn; *Louis Zukofsky, Man and Poet* edited by Carroll F. Terrell, Orono, University of Maine Press, 1979.

*   *   *

Perfected in 1978, after fifty years of insight, Louis Zukofsky's *"A"* indirectly assesses his other writings, exemplifies his "objectivist" theory (with which William Carlos Williams, Charles Reznikoff, and others were associated in the 1930's) and by a blending of lyric and epigrammatic qualities achieves an enduring, epic scope.

The 24 sections (A-1 to A-24) are followed by an index so that the poem begins on page 1 with "A/Round of fiddles playing Bach," and ends on page 826 (sic) with the word "Zion." The letter "z" is also in the last line of A23, a section which announces the "music, thought, drama, story, poem," the simultaneous voices which quote his previous works, and (set to music of Handel) form a collage, 240 pages long, a complex coda. The index also begins with the letter (or word) "A" and includes the instances when "an" and "the" appear, words he usually suppresses in his search for concentration. Names of public significance are in the index, so that one can be reassured that "Henry R." of the text is indeed Henry Rago of *Poetry* magazine, and that "Ludwig" is Wittgenstein. Essentially the index stresses the main concerns of the poem. The words most frequently found in the poem are man, eye, and day; and, next to these three, body, child, face, hand, heart, home, love, and sun.

"A" is "one song" with "many voices" ranging from the "lower limit, speech," to "upper limit song." Through collages, quotations, and puns ("Better a fiddler than a geiger" reminds us that Geige is "fiddle" in German), the individual perception of public history is frivolously, seriously interwoven with his private history for public perception—his son Paul, and his wife Celia: "Blessed/Ardent/Celia, unhurt/Happy" also announces BACH, that the fiddles are playing.

The poem provides occasions for delight in patterns, a naive delight in counting, as well as what is counted. The 24 A's are twenty-four hours, but A-12 is "twelve years." A-9 consists of two sets of sonnets, five sonnets in each set followed by a concluding five-line stanza. The terminal words of the first set are also the terminal words of the second set, with some surprising variations ("into," "thin to").

These dispersive elements cluster around a central theory, far too complex for a summary. His theory involves motion, the motion of physical sounds, of letters, the movement of the mind toward abstraction, the motion of light as it is brought to a focus. His interest is in the act of focusing, rather than what is focused upon. "The image is not the sole object of knowledge," for there is the "image of a voice." He uses "object" in the sense of *objectif*, a lens. Indeed, he believes "it is possible in imagination to divorce speech of all graphic elements" (A-24).

The "objectivist" then is not a photographer. The tendency to manifest motion itself rather than what is moving becomes associated with extraordinary concentration. When we read for example, in A-21, "See here splendent stellar candid/sign forever....," we find it almost easier to go back to the Plautus he is translating for an "explanation": "ita sum ut videtis, splendens stella cándida...." But the words *sum ut*, "I am as," are precisely the sort that Zukofsky suppresses. His concentrated passages may seem "difficult" if one wishes to elucidate them conceptually, but the effect is immediate: "Late later and much later/surge sea erupts boiling molten/lava island from ice, land." One may or may not agree that, conceptually, the lines present "a surge within the sea erupts into boiling water, owing to the lava pouring down from an island, from ice, and land, from Iceland," but the immediate effect is a distillation of feeling. The search for conceptual connections will move away from the poem, but those motions too are part of his poetry, which often curves back upon itself: "An unforeseen delight a round/beginning ardent; to end blest..." from A-23 echoes many earlier passages of "blest, ardent Celia," Bach, and a round of fiddles.

Zukofsky is capable of extraordinary wit, as in some of his poems collected in *All*, or in *Ferdinand*, and there is a delightful coruscation at the periphery of "A"; yet the central impulse is the immediacy of experience—man, eye, day:

> what hurries? why hurry? wit's
> but the fog, the literal senses
> senses move in light's song
> modesty cannot force, blind call
> its own, nor self-effaced fled
>
> to woods perpend without pride
> stone into lotus.

One exercises one's wit in running the index from A to Z, but the light's song emerges at the end of A-24 "What is it, I wonder that makes thee so loved?" a quotation from A-20 which includes a list of works for Paul, an evocation of a "sound akin to mosaic": "Each writer writes/one long work whose beat he cannot/entirely be aware of." The entire corpus of Zukofsky's poetry moves to a beat that is hard to define. He himself has come as close as anybody to describing it: "Thus one modernizes/His lute.../The melody! the rest is accessory."

—William Sylvester

TITLE
INDEX

The following list includes the titles of all books listed in the Verse section of the entries in the book, including the appendix. The name(s) in parenthesis is meant to direct the reader to the appropriate entry where full publication information is given. Following the list of titles is a list of writers volumes of whose poetry have been translated by entrants. Full information is given in the Translator section of the entries.

A (Zukofsky, appendix), from 1940
ABC (Nichol), 1971
ABC/Wan Do Tree (Cobbing), 1978
ABC's (C. Ford), 1940
Abalone (Wakoski), 1974
Abandoned Music Room (Pillin), 1975
Abandoned Sofa (Doyle), 1971
Abecedary (Logue), 1977
Abel and Cain (Mayne), 1980
Abel Baker Charlie Delta Epic (K. Smith), 1982
Aberllefenni (Magee), 1979
Able Was I Ere I Saw Elba (Hoffman), 1977
Abominable Temper (Curnow), 1973
Abortion (Heyen), 1979
About Time (Kavanagh), 1970
About Time (Kearns), 1974
About Women (Creeley), 1966
Abracadabra (Colombo), 1967
Abraham's Knife (Garrett), 1961
Absalom in the Tree (Mathias), 1971
Absences (Moraes), 1983
Absences (Tate), 1972
Absolute Statement for My Mother (Nichol), 1979
Absolution (Stafford), 1980
Abulafia Song (Meltzer), 1969
Abulafia's Circles (Rothenberg), 1979
Academic Board Poems (K. Smith), 1968
Academy of Goodbye (Petrie), 1974
Accidental Center (Heller), 1972
Ace (Raworth), 1974
Ace of Pentacles (Wieners), 1964
Achievement of Memory (H. Guest), 1974
Achilles' Song (Duncan), 1969
Acid Test (Geddes),.1981
Acre of Land (R. Thomas), 1952
Across Countries of Anywhere (P. Hanson), 1971
Across Lamarack Col (Snyder), 1964
Across the Vast Spaces (Varma), 1975
Act (Raworth), 1973
Act in the Noon (Wallace-Crabbe), 1974
Act of Recognition (Russell), 1978
Act One (Stow), 1957
Acts (Oppenheimer), 1976
Acts in Oxford (Finch), 1959
Adam and Eve in Middle Age (R. Murray), 1984
Adam and the Sacred Nine (T. Hughes), 1979
Adam at Evening (D. Wright), 1965
Adam Before His Mirror (O'Gorman), 1961
Adam Unparadised (Bottrall), 1954
Adamnan (Hirschman), 1972
Adam's Dream (J. Randall), 1966
Adam's Footprint (Miller), 1956
Added to Making a Republic (C. Olson, appendix), 1968
Addictions (Enright), 1962
Adequate Earth (Finkel), 1972
Adharca Broic (Hartnett), 1978
Adieu à Charlot (Ferlinghetti), 1978
Adjacent Columns (Buchanan), 1984
Administration of Things (Mead), 1970

Admissions (Wingfield), 1977
Admonitions (Spicer, appendix), 1974
Adrienne's Blessing (Gatenby), 1976
Adrift on the Star Brow of Taliesin (Fairfax), 1975
Adult Bookstore (K. Shapiro), 1976
Advance Token to Boardwalk (Oppenheimer), 1978
Advancing Day (Lindsay), 1940
Advantanges of Dark (Robert Watson), 1966
Adventures of Milt the Morph (Nichol), 1972
Adventures of the Letter I (L. Simpson), 1971
Adventures with a Twelve-Inch Pianist Beyond the Blue Horizon (Jonathan Williams), 1973
Advertisements (Sward), 1958
Advice from a Mother (Graves), 1970
Advice to a Prophet (Wilbur), 1961
Aegis (Corman), 1984
Aerialist (Weiss), 1978
Aesculapian Notes (Redgrove), 1975
Aesopic (Hecht), 1967
Aesthetics (T. Olson), 1978
Affair of Culture (Knoepfle), 1969
Affilati Attrezzi Per I Giardini di Catullo (Jonathan Williams), 1966
Africa, Paris, Greece (Bukowski), 1975
Africa We Knew (Currey), 1973
African Boog (A. Fisher), 1983
African Negatives (Ross), 1962
African Panorama (Brew), 1981
Afrikan Revolution (Baraka), 1973
After Dark (Harsent), 1973
After Every Green Thing (Abse), 1949
After Experience (Snodgrass), 1968
After Gray Days (Knoepfle), 1970
After I's (Zukofsky, appendix), 1964
After Lorca (Spicer, appendix), 1957
After Martial (Porter), 1972
After Summer (Heaney), 1978
After the Ark (Jennings), 1978
After the Assassination (R. Simpson), 1968
After the Blizzard (McAuley), 1975
After the Cries of the Birds (Ferlinghetti), 1967
After the Dream (Rudolf), 1980
After the Hunt (Sandy), 1982
After the Killing (D. Randall), 1973
After the Merrymaking (McGough), 1971
After the Russian (Finlay), 1969
After the War (Antin), 1973
After This Sea (Miles), 1947
Afterlife (Levis), 1977
Afternoon Dawn (N. Powell), 1975
Afternoon in Dismay (Wild), 1968
Afterword on Rupert Brooke (Prince), 1976
Against (Musgrave), 1974
Against a League of Liars (Acorn), 1960
Against a Setting Sun (Bottrall), 1984
Against Perspective (Cogswell), 1977
Against the Blues (Aubert), 1972
Against the Circle (Ghiselin), 1946
Against the Cruel Frost (Holbrook), 1963
Against the Silences (Blackburn, appendix), 1980

NOTES
ON
ADVISERS
AND
CONTRIBUTORS

ACKERSON, Duane. Free-lance writer. Author of several verse pamphlets, including *UA Flight to Chicago*, 1971, *Inventory*, 1971, *Old Movie House*, 1972, *Weathering*, 1974, and *The Eggplant*, 1977, and of fiction in magazines and anthologies. Editor of anthologies of poetry, and former editor of the magazine *Dragonfly*. **Essays:** Russell Edson; Geof Hewitt; Robert Huff; David Jaffin; John Knoepfle; James Koller; Tom McKeown; Keith Wilson.

ADCOCK, Fleur. See her own entry. **Essays:** Basil Dowling; George McWhirter; Dabney Stuart.

AITCHISON, James. Free-lance writer and critic. Author of two collections of poetry—*Sounds Before Sleep*, 1971, and *Spheres*, 1975. Co-editor of *New Writing Scotland 1-2*. **Essay:** Maurice Lindsay.

ALCOCK, Peter. Senior Lecturer in English, Massey University, Palmerston North, New Zealand; Associate Editor of *World Literature Written in English*. Member of the Executive Committee, Association for Commonwealth Literature and Language, 1968-77. **Essay:** Alistair Campbell.

ALLEN, Donald. Associated with Grove Press, 1950-70; Editor, with Barney Rosset, of *The Evergreen Review*, 1957-59, and West Coast Editor, 1960-70; Owner, Grey Fox Press, Bolinas, California. Editor or translator of works by Lorca, Ionesco, Olson, Lew Welch, Kerouac, Dorn, Creeley, Ginsberg, and Frank O'Hara, and editor of the anthologies *The New American Poetry 1945-60*, 1960, *New American Story*, 1965, *New Writing in the U.S.A.*, 1967, and *Poetics of the New American Poetry*, 1973.

ANDRÉ, Michael. Executive Director of Unmuzzled Ox Books and magazine, New York. Author of 4 books of poetry—*Get Serious, My Regrets, Studying the Ground for Holes*, and *Letters Home*—and of *The Poets' Encyclopedia* and articles in *Art News*. **Essays:** Bill Bissett; Robin Blaser; Michael Brownstein; Paul Carroll; Gene Fowler; Barrie Phillip Nichol.

ASTLE, David. Principal Lecturer in Communication Studies, Sheffield City Polytechnic. **Essay:** Roy Fuller.

AUGUSTINE, Jane. Adjunct Assistant Professor of English, Pratt Institute, Brooklyn and Member of the Faculty, New School for Social Research, New York. Author of *Lit by the Earth's Dark Blood*, 1977, fiction in the anthology *Solo*, 1977, and poetry for little magazines. Member, Feminist Writers Guild. **Essays:** Marilyn Hacker; Richard Kostelanetz; Rochelle Owens; Marge Piercy; Judith Johnson Sherwin; Mary Ellen Solt; Constance Urdang; Jean Valentine; Mona Van Duyn.

BAKER, Houston A., Jr. Greenfield Professor of English, University of Pennsylvania, Philadelphia. Has taught at Yale University, New Haven, Connecticut, and the University of Virginia, Charlottesville. Author of *Long Black Song: Essays in Black American Literature and Culture*, 1972, *Singers of Daybreak: Studies in Black American Literature*, 1974, *A Many-Colored Coat of Dreams: The Poetry of Countée Cullen*, 1974, *The Journey Back: Issues in Black Literature and Criticism*, 1980, *Blues, Ideology, and Afro-American Literature*, 1984, and a book of verse, *No Matter Where You Travel You Still Be Black*, 1979. Editor of *Black Literature in America*, 1971, *Twentieth-Century Interpretations of "Native Son,"* 1972, and *English Literature: Opening Up the Canon* (with Leslie A. Fiedler), 1981. **Essay:** James A. Emanuel.

BARKER, Jonathan. Poetry Librarian, Arts Council Poetry Library, London. Author of articles and reviews in *Agenda, PN*

Review, Times Literary Supplement, and other journals. Editor of *The Arts Council Poetry Library Catalogue*, 6th edition, 1981, and *Selected Poems of W.H. Davies*, 1985. **Essays:** Alistair Elliot; Donald Justice; Robert Wells.

BEAVER, Bruce. See his own entry. **Essays:** Geoffrey Dutton; Geoffrey Lehmann.

BERGONZI, Bernard. Professor of English, University of Warwick, Coventry. Author of *Descartes and the Animals*, 1954; *The Early H.G. Wells*, 1961; *Heroes' Twilight*, 1965; *The Situation of the Novel*, 1970; *T.S. Eliot*, 1972; *Gerard Manley Hopkins*, 1977; *Reading the Thirties*, 1978; *Years: Sixteen Poems*, 1979; *The Roman Persuasion* (novel), 1981. **Essays:** Robert Conquest; Malcolm Cowley; Gavin Ewart; Colin Falck; David Gascoyne; Geoffrey Grigson; John Holloway; Richard Kell; Nicholas Moore; Philip Oakes.

BERTRAM, James. Emeritus Professor of English, Victoria University of Wellington; General Editor of *New Zealand Writers and Their Work* series. Editor of *Phoenix*, 1932; associated with the founding of *Landfall*, 1946. Author of several books on China, and of *Charles Brasch*, 1976. Editor of *New Zealand Letters of Thomas Arnold the Younger*, 1966; contributor to *Student Guide to English Poetry*, 1969. **Essay:** Ruth Dallas.

BIRKETT, Jennifer. Lecturer in French, University of Dundee, Scotland. Author of *The Body and the Dream: French Erotic Fiction 1464-1900*, 1983, and forthcoming studies of the French Decadence, and sexuality, politics, and fiction in the French Revolution. **Essays:** Anne Cluysenaar; Elaine Feinstein; Rosemary Tonks.

BIRNEY, Earle. See his own entry.

BLOOM, Harold. Professor of Humanities, Yale University, New Haven, Connecticut. Author of several books on Blake and the Romantics; his most recent books are *The Anxiety of Influence*, 1973; *A Map of Misreading*, 1975; *Kabbalah and Criticism*, 1975; *Poetry and Repression*, 1976; *Wallace Stevens: The Poems of Our Climate*, 1977; *Agon: Towards a Theory of Revisionism*, 1981; *The Breaking of the Vessels*, 1982; and the novel *The Flight to Lucifer*, 1979. Editor of several anthologies and of works by Ruskin, Shelley, Pater, and Coleridge. **Essay:** John Hollander.

BODE, Carl. Professor of American Literature and American Studies, University of Maryland, College Park. Author of three books of verse (most recently *Practical Magic*, 1980), and of several books on American civilization, including *Antebellum Culture*, 1970, *Mencken*, 1973, and *Maryland: A Bicentennial History*, 1978. Editor of works by Thoreau, Emerson, and Mencken, and of *The Young Rebel in American Literature*, 1959, and *Ralph Waldo Emerson*, 1968. **Essay:** Chad Walsh.

BODE, Walter. Assistant Editor, Viking Press, New York. Editor of *Audition Pieces: Monologues for Student Actors*. **Essays:** Richard Emil Braun; Irving Feldman; Daniel Halpern; Robert Hass; Robert Pinsky.

BORKLUND, Elmer. Associate Professor of English, Pennsylvania State University, University Park. Former Associate Editor of *Chicago Review*. Author of *Contemporary Literary Critics*, 1977 (2nd edition, 1982), and of articles for *Modern Philology, Commentary, New York Herald-Tribune Book Week*, and *Journal of General Education*. **Essays:** Randall Jarrell (appendix); James Michie; Elder Olson.

BOSTIC, Corrine E. Part-time faculty member, Quinsigamond Community College, Worcester, Massachusetts; Radio Broadcaster, WTAG and WICN-FM. Author of *Requiem for Bluesville* (verse), 1970, *The Horns of Freedom* (play), 1971, and *Blacks* (essay), 1972. Editor of *Message in Black*, 1971. **Essays:** Victor Hernández Cruz; Calvin C. Hernton.

BOYERS, Robert. Professor of English, Skidmore College, Saratoga Springs, New York; Editor of *Salmagundi* magazine. Author of *Excursions: Selected Literary Essays*, 1976, *Lionel Trilling: Negative Capability and the Wisdom of Avoidance*, 1977, *F.R. Leavis: Judgment and the Discipline of Thought*, 1978, and *R.P. Blackmur*, 1981. Editor of *Robert Lowell: The Poet in His Time* (with Michael London), 1969, *Contemporary Poetry in America*, 1975, *The Salmagundi Reader* (with Peggy Boyers), 1983, and several collections of articles. **Essays:** Alan Dugan; John Logan.

BRADISH, Gaynor F. Adjunct Associate Professor, Union College, Schenectady, New York. Author of the introduction to Arthur Kopit's *Oh Dad, Poor Dad...*, 1960. Director of *Asylum* by Kopit, New York, 1963, and of many plays for drama workshops and university groups. **Essays:** Kay Boyle; John Ciardi; Ralph Pomeroy; M.L. Rosenthal; Gerald Stern; Mark Strand; Derek Walcott.

BRATHWAITE, Edward Kamau. See his own entry. **Essays:** George Campbell; Martin Carter; Wilson Harris; Anthony McNeill; Bruce St. John; A.J. Seymour.

BROWN, Lloyd W. Member of the Department of Comparative Literature, University of Southern California, Los Angeles. Author of *Women Writers in Black Africa*, 1981, and *West Indian Poetry*, 1984. Editor of *The Black Writer in Africa and the Americas*, 1973. **Essay:** Edward Kamau Brathwaite.

BROWN, Stewart. Free-lance writer. Author of *Room Service*, 1977, and *Specimens*, 1979 (both poetry). Editor of *Caribbean Poetry Now*, 1984. **Essay:** Howard Sergeant.

BROWNJOHN, Alan. See his own entry. **Essays:** Ian Hamilton; Peter Porter.

BRUCE, George. See his own entry. **Essays:** Alan Bold; Tom Buchan; Stewart Conn; Robin Fulton; Duncan Glen; Alastair Mackie; Pete Morgan; Alastair Reid; Tom Scott; Sydney Tremayne.

BRUCHAC, Joseph. Editor of *Greenfield Review*, Greenfield Center, New York. Author of several collections of poetry (most recently *Translator's Son*, 1980, and *Remembering the Dawn*, 1983), three novels (most recently *No Telephone to Heaven*, 1983), and two books for children. Editor of many collections of writing, including *Songs from This Earth on Turtle's Back: Poetry by American Indian Writers*, 1983, and *Breaking Silence: An Anthology of Contemporary Asian American Poets*, 1984. **Essays:** Chinua Achebe; Dennis Brutus; Syl Cheyney-Coker; Michael Echeruo; Lyn Lifshin; Taban lo Liyong; John Okai; Leslie Silko; Gary Soto; James Welch.

BURNS, Jim. See his own entry. **Essays:** Ray Bremser; Michael Horovitz; Barry MacSweeney.

BUTTERICK, George F. Curator of Literary Archives and Lecturer in English, University of Connecticut, Storrs. Author of *A Guide to the Maximus Poems of Charles Olson*, 1978, and three books of poetry. Editor of *The Postmoderns: The New American Poetry Revised*, 1982, and of works by Vincent Ferrini and by Charles Olson, including his correspondence with Robert Creeley, 5 vols., 1980-83. **Essays:** Amiri Baraka; Joanne Kyger; Lewis Mac-

Adams; Tom Raworth; Stephen Rodefer; James Schuyler; John Wieners; Jonathan Williams.

BYRD, Don. Member of the Department of English, State University of New York, Albany. Author of *Aesop's Garden* (verse), 1976, *Charles Olson's Maximus*, 1980, and criticism in journals. **Essays:** William Bronk; Michael Davidson; Allen Ginsberg; Kenneth Irby; Jackson Mac Low; Simon J. Ortiz; Michael Palmer; Ed Sanders; Lewis Warsh.

CALLAN, Edward. Distinguished University Professor, Emeritus, Western Michigan University, Kalamazoo. Author of *Yeats on Yeats*, 1981, *Alan Paton*, revised edition 1982, and *Auden: A Carnival of Intellect*, 1983, and other books and articles. **Essay:** John Woods.

CAREW, Rivers. Deputy Chief Sub-Editor, Radio Telefís Eireann, Dublin. Editor of *Dublin Magazine*, 1964-69. Author of *Figures Out of Mist* (with Timothy Brownlow), 1966, and of verse in *The Penguin Book of Irish Verse*, 1970, and in periodicals. **Essays:** Monk Gibbon; Michael Longley.

CARRUTH, Hayden. See his own entry. **Essays:** Carol Bergé; Arthur Gregor; Kenneth Koch; James Laughlin.

CHAMBERS, D.D.C. Associate Professor of English, Trinity College, Toronto. **Essays:** Leonard Cohen; John Robert Colombo; David Helwig; Ian Young.

CHARTERS, Ann. Professor of English, University of Connecticut, Storrs. Author of two books on Charles Olson, *Nobody: The Story of Bert Williams*, 1970, *Kerouac: A Biography*, 1973, a bibliography of Kerouac, *I Love: The Story of Vladimir Mayakovsky and Lili Brik* (with Samuel Charters), 1979, and a study of ragtime. Editor of *The Beats: Literary Bohemians in Postwar America*, 2 vols., 1983. **Essay:** Alice Notley.

CHARTERS, Samuel. Poet, critic, and music historian. His most recent books are *From a Swedish Notebook* (verse), *Some Poems/ Poets* (critical studies), *Robert Johnson: A Life, The Songs, The Legacy of the Blues, I Love: The Story of Vladimir Mayakovsky and Lili Brik* (with Ann Charters), 1979, *The Roots of the Blues*, 1980, and *Of Those Who Died*, 1980. **Essays:** James Broughton; Larry Eigner; Philip Lamantia.

CHRISTENSEN, Paul. Assistant Professor of Modern Literature, Texas A. & M. University, College Station. Author of several books of poetry and of *Charles Olson: Call Him Ishmael*, 1978. **Essays:** Helen Adam; Bill Berkson; Charles Bernstein; Robert Bly; Robert Creeley; Albert Goldbarth; Lyn Hejinian; Robert Lowell (appendix); James Merrill; Richard Shelton; Charles Simic; William Stafford.

CHURCH, Richard. Poet, novelist, and critic. His most recent books were *Prince Albert* (novel), 1963, *The Burning Bush* (verse), 1967, and *The Wonder of Words*, 1970. Died 1972. **Essay:** Ruth Pitter.

CLARK, Alan. Deputy Librarian, Royal Society Library, London; has conducted poetry courses at Braziers Park Adult College, Ipsden, Oxfordshire. Author of an essay on Laura Riding in *Stand* and of a checklist of Laura Riding's publications in *Chelsea*, 1976. **Essay:** Laura Riding.

CLARKE, Austin. Poet, playwright, and literary critic. His *Collected Poems* edited by Liam Miller were published in 1974. Died,

1974. **Essays:** Pearse Hutchinson; Ewart Milne; Desmond O'Grady.

CLUYSENAAR, Anne. See her own entry. **Essays:** Roy Fisher; Oswald Mtshali; Christopher Pilling.

COHEN, Arthur A. Founding President, Ex Libris rare books, New York; former General Manager, Viking Press, New York. Author of four novels (most recently *An Admirable Woman*, 1983), several studies of comparative religion and of Judaism, and books on Osip Mandelstam and Robert and Sonia Delaunay. Editor of many collections of essays on religion and social questions. **Essay:** David Shapiro.

COLOMBO, John Robert. See his own entry. **Essays:** Margaret Atwood; George Bowering; Elizabeth Brewster; Fred Cogswell; Frank Davey; Ronald Everson; Greg Gatenby; Gary Geddes; Don Gutteridge; Daryl Hine; Lionel Kearns; Dennis Lee; Douglas LePan; Gwendolyn MacEwen; Eli Mandel; Seymour Mayne; David McFadden; Rona Murray; Francis Sparshott; Andrew Suknaski, Jr.; Miriam Waddington; George Woodcock.

COOKSON, William. Author of *A Guide to the Cantos of Ezra Pound*, 1984. Editor of *Agenda*, London. **Essays:** Anne Beresford; Peter Dale; Charles Tomlinson; Peter Whigham.

COOLEY, John R. Associate Professor of English, Western Michigan University, Kalamazoo. Author of articles on Hardy, Welty, Stephen Crane, Hemingway, and O'Neill. **Essays:** Hayden Carruth; Norman Dubie; George Economou; Leonard Nathan; Thomas Parkinson.

COONEY, Seamus. Associate Professor of English, Western Michigan University, Kalamazoo; Editor of *Sparrow* magazine. Author of articles on Byron, Scott, Lawrence, Binyon, and Austin Clarke. Editor of *By the Well of Living and Seeing: New and Selected Poems* by Charles Reznikoff. **Essays:** David Bromige; Cid Corman; Theodore Enslin; Jonathan Greene; Jack Hirschman; Larry Levis; Ron Loewinsohn; F.D. Reeve; Stephen Stepanchev.

CORCORAN, Neil. Member of the Department of English, University of Sheffield. Author of *The Song of Deeds: A Study of "The Anathemata" of David Jones*, 1982, and of reviews in *PN Review* and *Times Literary Supplement.* **Essays:** George Mackay Brown; James Fenton; Thom Gunn; Tony Harrison; Geoffrey Hill; Michael Hofmann; A.D. Hope; Peter Levi; John Matthias; Andrew Motion; Tom Paulin; Craig Raine; Christopher Reid; Hugo Williams.

COTTON, John. See his own entry. **Essays:** Alan Brownjohn; Jim Burns; Roger Garfitt; David Holbrook; Glyn Hughes; James Kirkup; Edward Lucie-Smith; Gerda Mayer; John Mole; Sally Purcell; Rodney Pybus; Carol Rumens; Peter Scupham; James Simmons; C.H. Sisson; D.M. Thomas; Ted Walker; Kit Wright.

CRAIG, Patricia. Free-lance writer and reviewer. Author of three books on popular literature with Mary Cadogan—*You're a Brick, Angela!*, 1976, *Women and Children First*, 1978, and *The Lady Investigates*, 1981. **Essay:** Fleur Adcock.

CURTIS, Tony. Senior Lecturer in English, Polytechnic of Wales, Cardiff; Founding Editor of Edge Press. Author of several books of verse (most recently *Preparations*, 1980, and *Letting Go*, 1983), *Out of the Dark Wood* (fiction and essays), 1977, a book for children, and articles in *Anglo-Welsh Review*, *Poetry Wales*, and other journals. Editor of anthologies of Welsh verse and of *The Art of Seamus Heaney*, 1982. **Essays:** Gillian Clarke; Raymond Garlick; Jeremy Hooker; John Ormond.

DAMASHEK, Richard. Member of the Department of Literature, Sangamon State University, Springfield, Illinois. Author of articles on Randall Jarrell and Ingmar Bergman, and reviews in *Books Abroad* and other periodicals. **Essays:** Philip Booth; R.H.W. Dillard; Laurence Lieberman; Paul Petrie; W.D. Snodgrass; Ruth Whitman.

DAVIDSON, Michael. See his own entry. **Essay:** Jack Spicer (appendix).

DAY, Cynthia. Free-lance writer, Syracuse, New York. Work published in *Ironwood*, *Literary Review*, and *En Passant.* **Essays:** David Budbill; Amy Clampitt; Stephen Dobyns; Peter Meinke.

DILLARD, R.H.W. See his own entry. **Essays:** Diane Ackerman; John Engels; Brendan Galvin; George Garrett; Julia Randall; David Slavitt.

DOEPKE, Dale. Free-lance writer; author of essays on 19th-century American literature. **Essay:** Jane Cooper.

DORSINVILLE, Max. Associate Professor of English, McGill University, Montreal. Author of *Caliban Without Prospero: An Essay on Quebec and Black Literature*, 1974, and articles in *PMLA, Canadian Literature*, and *Livres et Auteurs Québecois.* **Essay:** Joan Finnigan.

DOUGHERTY, David C. Professor of English, Loyola College, Baltimore. Author of articles on Robinson Jeffers, James Wright, Saul Bellow, Raymond Chandler, John Updike, and Walker Percy, and of reviews in the Baltimore *Sunday Sun.* **Essay:** Galway Kinnell.

DOWLING, David. Senior Lecturer in English, Massey University, Palmerston North, New Zealand; Editor of the quarterly *Landfall*, and theatre reviewer. Author of *Introducing Bruce Mason*, 1983, *Bloomsbury Aesthetics and the Novels of Forster and Woolf*, 1984, and articles on Mansfield, Woolf, and commonwealth poetry. Editor of *Novelists on Novelists*, 1983. **Essays:** Charles Doyle; Lauris Edmond; Vincent O'Sullivan; Judith Wright.

DOYLE, Charles. See his own entry. **Essays:** James K. Baxter (appendix); Robert Duncan; Howard Nemerov; Kendrick Smithyman.

DUDEK, Louis. See his own entry. **Essays:** D.G. Jones; James Reaney.

ELLEDGE, Jim. Assistant Editor, *Poetry*, Chicago; Member of the Department of English, University of Illinois, Chicago Circle. Author of *James Dickey: A Bibliography, Weldon Kees: A Critical Introduction*, and poetry and criticism in *Poetry, Studies in Short Fiction, American Poetry, Sou'wester, Madison Review*, and other journals. **Essays:** James Bertolino; Tony Connor; Ronald Johnson; David Ray; Lewis Turco.

EMANUEL, James A. See his own entry.

EWART, Gavin. See his own entry. **Essay:** Harold Massingham.

FLETCHER, Ian. See his own entry. **Essay:** Terence Tiller.

FRASER, G.S. Reader in Modern English Literature, University of Leicester, 1964-79. Author of several books of verse (collected as *Poems*, 1981); travel books; critical studies of Yeats, Dylan Thomas, Pound, Durrell, and Pope; and of *The Modern Writer and His World*,

1953, *Vision and Rhetoric*, 1959, *Metre, Rhythm and Free Verse*, 1970, and *A Stranger and Afraid: The Autobiography of an Intellectual*, 1983. Editor of works by Keith Douglas and Robert Burns, and of verse anthologies. Died 1980. **Essays:** Samuel Beckett; Lawrence Durrell; Kathleen Raine; Sacheverell Sitwell; Constantine Trypanis.

FRIEDMAN, Norman. Professor of English, Queens College, City University of New York. Author of *E.E. Cummings: The Art of His Poetry*, 1960, *Poetry: An Introduction to Its Form and Art* (with C.A. McLaughlin), 1961, *Logic, Rhetoric, Style* (with McLaughlin), 1963, *E.E. Cummings: The Growth of a Writer*, 1964, *Form and Meaning in Fiction*, 1975, and *The Magic Badge* (poems), 1985. Editor of *E.E. Cummings: A Collection of Critical Essays*, 1972. **Essays:** Kenneth Burke; Robert Francis; Richard Howard; Barbara Howes; Vern Rutsala; Louis Simpson; James Wright (appendix).

FULTON, Robin. See his own entry. **Essay:** Kenneth White.

GALL, Sally M. Free-lance writer; has taught at New York University, and Drew University, Madison, New Jersey. Author of *The Modern Poetic Sequence* (with M.L. Rosenthal), 1983, and articles on Rosenthal, Ramon Guthrie, and Sylvia Plath in *Modern Poetry Studies* and *American Poetry Review*. Editor of *Maximum Security Ward and Other Poems* by Ramon Guthrie, 1984. **Essays:** J.V. Cunningham; Frederick Morgan.

GATES, Norman T. Emeritus Professor of English, Rider College, Trenton, New Jersey. Author of *The Poetry of Richard Aldington*, 1974, and *A Checklist of the Letters of Richard Aldington*, 1977. **Essays:** Francis Warner; James Whitehead.

GERMAIN, Edward B. Instructor in English, Phillips Academy, Andover, Massachusetts. Editor of *Flag of Ecstasy: Selected Poems of Charles Henri Ford*, 1972, *Shadows of the Sun: The Diaries of Harry Crosby*, 1977, and *English and American Surrealist Poetry*, 1977. **Essays:** Robert Dana; Charles Henri Ford; Donald Hall; Lee Harwood; Ron Padgett; Edouard Roditi.

GILBERT, S.R. Professor of Drama and Canadian Literature, Capilano College, North Vancouver; Drama Editor of *Capilano Review*. Author of *A Glass Darkly* (play), 1972, "A Bibliography of British Columbia Studies" in *Communique*, 1973, and articles on Canadian literature and drama in *Canadian Drama, Canadian Theatre Review*, and other journals. **Essays:** Phyllis Gotlieb; Daphne Marlatt; J. Michael Yates.

GIOIA, Dana. Free-lance writer, Hastings-on-Hudson, New York. **Essay:** Ted Kooser.

GNAROWSKI, Michael. Professor of English, Carleton University, Ottawa. Author of two books of verse and several bibliographies and checklists of Canadian literature. Editor of works by Goldsmith, Archibald Lampman, Raymond Knister, Leonard Cohen, and Louis Joseph Quesnel, and of *The Making of Modern Poetry in Canada* (with Louis Dudek), 1967. **Essays:** Milton Acorn; Douglas Barbour; Henry Beissel; Dorothy Livesay; John Newlove; David Wevill.

GORDON, Lois. Chairman and Professor of English and Comparative Literature, Fairleigh Dickinson University, Teaneck, New Jersey. Author of *Stratagems to Uncover Nakedness: The Dramas of Harold Pinter*, 1969, *Donald Barthelme*, 1981, *Robert Coover: The Fictionmaking Universe*, 1983, the forthcoming *Portrait of America 1920-1980* (with Alan Gordon), and articles on Eberhart, Jarrell, Faulkner, T.S. Eliot, Philip Roth, Beckett, Arthur Miller, and

others. **Essays:** Donald Davie; Richard Eberhart; W.S. Merwin; Adrienne Rich; Gilbert Sorrentino.

GREENBERG, Alvin. Professor of English, Macalester College, St. Paul, Minnesota. Author of several volumes of verse, the most recent being *In/Direction*, 1978, two novels, *Going Nowhere*, 1971, and *The Invention of the West*, 1976, and short stories (most recently *The Man in the Cardboard Mask*, 1985). **Essay:** Margaret Randall.

GUNN, Thom. See his own entry. **Essay:** Gary Snyder.

GUSTAFSON, Ralph. See his own entry. **Essays:** Louis Dudek; Robert Finch; Michael Ondaatje; Raymond Souster.

HALL, Donald. See his own entry.

HALL, Rodney. See his own entry. **Essay:** Roger McDonald.

HALPERN, Daniel. See his own entry.

HARNETT, Ruth. Lecturer in English, Rhodes University, Grahamstown, South Africa. **Essay:** Guy Butler.

HEATON, David M. Associate Professor of Comparative Literature, and Chairman of the Comparative Literature Program, Ohio University, Athens. Verse, verse translations, and articles on Ted Hughes and Alan Sillitoe published in periodicals. **Essays:** Jon Anderson; Ben Belitt; Marvin Bell; Stanley Plumly; Alan Stephens.

HELLER, Michael. See his own entry. **Essay:** Hugh Seidman.

HEWITT, Geof. See his own entry. **Essays:** Léonie Adams; Peter Davison; George Hitchcock; Bill Knott; Aram Saroyan; Robert Sward; James Tate.

HEYEN, William. See his own entry. **Essays:** Lucien Stryk; Hollis Summers.

HILL, Douglas. Literary Editor of *Tribune*, London. Author of several works of non-fiction, fiction for children, and poetry in periodicals and anthologies. Editor of *Tribune 40*, 1977, and of collections of fantasy writing. **Essay:** Bernard Kops.

HINCHEY, John. Member of the Department of English, Swarthmore College, Pennsylvania. **Essay:** Anne Waldman.

HOBSBAUM, Philip. See his own entry. **Essays:** Francis Berry; Keith Bosley; Stanley Cook; Jeni Couzyn; U.A. Fanthorpe; Zulfikar Ghose; Christopher Levenson; Derek Mahon; Roy McFadden; Matthew Mead; Eric Millward; Paul Muldoon; Robert Nye; Frank Ormsby; William Peskett; F.T. Prince; E.J. Scovell; John Tripp; Theodore Weiss.

HOFFMAN, Daniel. See his own entry. **Essays:** A.R. Ammons; John Berryman (appendix); William Meredith; William Jay Smith; Robert Penn Warren.

HOKENSON, Jan. Associate Professor of Languages and Linguistics, Florida Atlantic University, Boca Raton. Author of articles on Beckett, Céline, and Proust, in *James Joyce Quarterly, L'Esprit Créateur, Far-Western Forum*, and *Samuel Beckett: An Anthology of Criticism* edited by Ruby Cohn, 1975. **Essays:** Thomas McGrath; Anne Sexton (appendix).

HOLM, Janis Butler. Assistant Professor of English, Ohio University, Athens. Author of a number of articles on cultural perceptions of women. **Essay:** Carolyn M. Rodgers.

HOMBERGER, Eric. Lecturer, School of English and American Studies, University of East Anglia, Norwich. Author of *The Art of the Real: Poetry in England and America since 1939*, 1977, and co-author of *The Novel and the Second World War*, 1983. Editor, *The Cambridge Mind* (with others), 1970, and *Ezra Pound: The Critical Heritage*, 1972. **Essays:** Richard Murphy; Julian Symons.

HUDSON, Theodore R. Graduate Professor of English, Howard University, Washington, D.C. Author of *A LeRoi Jones (Amiri Baraka) Bibliography*, 1971, *From LeRoi Jones to Amiri Baraka: The Literary Works*, 1973, and numerous articles. **Essays:** Lucille Clifton; Don L. Lee; Sonia Sanchez; Margaret Walker.

JAMES, Charles L. Associate Professor of English, Swarthmore College, Pennsylvania. Author of *The Black Writer in America* (bibliography), 1969. Editor of *From the Roots: Short Stories by Black Americans*, 1970. **Essays:** Gwendolyn Brooks; Michael S. Harper; Etheridge Knight; Donald Petersen; Ishmael Reed.

JENNINGS, Elizabeth. See her own entry. **Essays:** Henry Reed; Michael Schmidt.

JONES, Eldred D. Professor of English, Fourah Bay College, University of Sierra Leone, Freetown. Author of *Othello's Countrymen: The Africans in English Renaissance Drama*, 1955, and *The Writing of Wole Soyinka*, 1973 (revised 1982). Editor of the annual *African Literature Today*, and with Clifford N. Fyle, of *A Krio-English Dictionary*, 1980. **Essays:** Lenrie Peters; Wole Soyinka.

KAPLAN, Susan. Ph.D. candidate, University of Houston. **Essays:** Vassar Miller; William Pitt Root.

KEESING, Nancy. Writer, critic, and editor. Chairman of the Literature Board of the Australia Council, 1974-77. Author of verse (most recently *Hails and Farewells*, 1977), memoirs (*Garden Island People*, 1975), biography (*John Lang*, 1979), critical studies of Douglas Stewart and Elsie Carew, and books for children. Editor of several anthologies of Australian songs and ballads, and of *Gold Fever*, 1967, and *Shalom: Australian Jewish Short Stories*, 1978. **Essay:** Randolph Stow.

KENDLE, Burton. Professor of English, Roosevelt University, Chicago. Author of articles on D.H. Lawrence, John Cheever, William March, Tennessee Williams, and others. **Essays:** David Gill; Sandra Hochman; Robert Pack; May Sarton; Muriel Spark; Peter Viereck; Rex Warner.

KENNELLY, Brendan. See his own entry. **Essay:** Michael Hartnett.

KING, Bruce. Albert Johnston Professor of Literature, University of North Alabama, Florence. Author of books on Dryden, Marvell, Fielding, Shaw, Ibsen, 17th-century literature, and *The New English Literatures: Cultural Nationalism in a Changing World*, 1980. Editor of collections of essays on Dryden, African literature, and West Indian literature. **Essay:** Jayanta Mahapatra.

KINSELLA, Thomas. See his own entry.

KORGES, James. Free-lance writer. Editor of *Critique: Studies in Modern Fiction*, 1962-70. Author of *Erskine Caldwell*, 1969. Died 1975. **Essays:** Howard Baker; Edgar Bowers; Paul Ramsey.

KOSTELANETZ, Richard. See his own entry. **Essays:** Clark Coolidge; Emmett Williams.

KRAPF, Norbert. Professor of English, C.W. Post College, Long Island University, Greenvale, New York. Author of several collections of poetry (most recently *Lines Drawn from Dürer*, 1981, *Heartwood*, 1983, and *Circus Songs*, 1984), and of fiction, translations, and articles in journals. **Essays:** William Heyen; Nancy Willard.

KUGLER, B.T. Senior Clinical Psychologist, Harper House Children's Service, Hertfordshire. Author of articles in *British Journal of Psychiatry, Psychiatry Research*, and other journals and collections. **Essays:** John Fuller; David Harsent; Sylvia Plath (appendix).

LANDIS, Joan Hutton. Member of the Faculty, Curtis Institute of Music, Philadelphia. Author of poetry in *New York Times Book of Verse, Transatlantic Review*, and *Quadrille*, essays on contemporary poets in *Salmagundi* and *Midway*, and articles on Shakespeare in *Modern Language Studies* and *Hamlet Studies*. **Essay:** John Peck.

LAUTER, Estella. Associate Professor of Humanistic Studies, University of Wisconsin, Green Bay. Author of *Women as Mythmakers: Poetry and Art by Twentieth-Century Women*, 1984. **Essay:** Diane Wakoski.

LEHMANN, Geoffrey. See his own entry. **Essays:** Robert Gray; Kevin Hart; Geoff Page.

LINDBERG, Stanley W. Editor of *The Georgia Review* and Professor of English, University of Georgia, Athens. Author of *The Annotated McGuffey*, 1976, and *Van Nostrand's Plain English Handbook*, 1980. **Essays:** R.A.D. Ford; Reg Saner.

LINDNER, Carl. Member of the Humanistic Studies Division, University of Wisconsin-Parkside, Kenosha. **Essays:** Michael Anania; Philip Dacey; Edward Field; Allen Planz; Knute Skinner.

LINDSAY, Maurice. See his own entry. **Essays:** George Bruce; Valerie Gillies; Norman MacCaig; Alasdair Maclean.

LUCIE-SMITH, Edward. See his own entry. **Essays:** Barry Cole; Hamish Henderson; Harold Norse; Alan Rook; Alan Sillitoe.

LUSCHEI, Glenna. Associated with the Solo Press and the Cosmep Women's Committee, San Luis Obispo. Author of *Back into My Body: Poems*, 1974. **Essay:** Teo Savory.

LYNCH, Dennis. Instructor with the Great Books Foundation, Chicago. Author of articles on William Stafford and other American writers in *Modern Poetry Studies, New Republic, American Poetry Review*, and other periodicals. **Essays:** Richard Brautigan; Lawrence Ferlinghetti; Donald Finkel; Jean Garrigue (appendix); Jim Harrison; X.J. Kennedy; Gregory Orr; A. Poulin, Jr.; Philip Whalen.

MacCAIG, Norman. See his own entry. **Essays:** Laurie Lee; Alexander Scott.

MACNAB, Roy. See his own entry. **Essays:** R.N. Currey; Anthony Delius.

MAGEE, Wes. See his own entry. **Essays:** John Cotton; John Fairfax; Lawrence Sail.

MATHIAS, Roland. See his own entry. **Essays:** Dannie Abse; Glyn Jones; Leslie Norris.

MATTHEWS, William. See his own entry. **Essays:** Coleman Barks; Gary Gildner; Jorie Graham; Kenneth O. Hanson; Sandra McPherson; Judith Moffett; Dennis Schmitz; James Scully.

MATTHIAS, John. See his own entry. **Essay:** Gael Turnbull.

MAYO, E.L. Professor of English, Drake University, Des Moines, Iowa, 1947-75. Author of four books of poetry and *Collected Poems* edited by David Ray, 1981. Died. **Essays:** Anselm Hollo; Robert Mezey.

McELROY, George. Lecturer at Indiana University Northwest, Gary. Author of textbooks and regular reviews in *Opera News.* **Essays:** D.K. Das; Pritish Nandy.

McGOVERN, Martin. Doctoral Fellow in the Creative Writing Program, University of Houston. Author of poetry in *Poetry, North American Review,* and other journals, and of criticism in *Sewanee Review, Chicago Review,* and *Montana Review.* **Essays:** John Haines; Miller Williams.

MELTZER, David. See his own entry. **Essays:** Asa Benveniste; John Brandi; Diane di Prima; Lenore Kandel; Anthony Rudolf.

MILLS, Ralph J., Jr. Professor of English, University of Illinois at Chicago Circle. Author of books on Theodore Roethke, Richard Eberhart, Edith Sitwell, and Kathleen Raine, and of *Contemporary American Poetry,* 1965, *Creation's Very Self,* 1969, and *Cry of the Human: Essays on Contemporary American Poetry,* 1975, and several books of poetry (most recently *Living with Distance,* 1979, *With No Answer,* 1980, and *March Light,* 1982). Editor of Roethke's prose and letters and of works by David Ignatow. **Essays:** Stephen Berg; Karl Shapiro.

MIOLA, Robert. Associate Professor of English, Loyola College, Baltimore. **Essays:** Charles Edward Eaton; Anthony Hecht; Philip Levine.

MOKASHI-PUNEKAR, Shankar. See his own entry. **Essay:** P. Lal.

MOLE, John. See his own entry. **Essay:** Patric Dickinson.

MOLESWORTH, Charles. Professor of English, Queens College, City University of New York. Author of *The Fierce Embrace: A Study of Contemporary American Poetry,* 1979, and *Words to That Effect* (poetry), 1981. **Essays:** William Dickey; William Pillin; Ann Stanford.

MONTAGUE, John. See his own entry. **Essays:** John Hewitt; Thomas Kinsella; Carolyn Kizer.

MORGAN, Edwin. See his own entry. **Essays:** David Black; Ian Hamilton Finlay; W.S. Graham; Dom Sylvester Houédard; Tom Leonard; Liz Lochhead.

MORRISON, Blake. Deputy Literary Editor, *The Observer,* London. Author of *The Movement: English Poetry and Fiction of the 1950's,* 1980, *Seamus Heaney,* 1982, *Dark Glasses* (poetry), 1984, and poetry in *Poetry Introduction 5,* 1982. Editor, with Andrew Motion, of *The Penguin Book of Contemporary British Poetry,* 1982.

MUKHERJEE, Meenakshi. Reader in English, University of Hyderabad, India. Author of *The Twice-Born Fiction* (on the Anglo-Indian novel), 1971. Editor of anthologies of fiction and criticism. Translator of *The Virgin Fish of Babughat* by Lokenath Bhattacharya, 1975, *The Cheese Doll* by Tagore, 1980, and of Bengali poetry into English. **Essays:** Paul Jacob; Shankar Mokashi-Punekar; Monika Varma.

NAGARAJAN, S. Professor of English, University of Hyderabad, India. **Essays:** Nissim Ezekiel; Arvind Krishna Mehrotra; Dom Moraes; R. Parthasarathy; A.K. Ramanujan.

NELSON, Rudolph L. Assistant Professor of English, State University of New York, Albany. **Essay:** Edwin Honig.

NEWLOVE, John. See his own entry. **Essay:** Joe Rosenblatt.

NYE, Robert. See his own entry. **Essays:** Anthony Howell; John Moat; Martin Seymour-Smith; John Updike; Roderick Watson; Sheila Wingfield.

OXLEY, William. See his own entry. **Essays:** Dick Davis; John Heath-Stubbs; Peter Russell.

PARIS, Jerry. Member of the Department of English, State University of New York, Albany. **Essays:** Judson Crews; Judson Jerome.

PARISI, Joseph. Associate Editor of *Poetry* magazine, Chicago. Editor (with Daryl Hine) of *The "Poetry" Anthology 1912-1977,* 1978. **Essays:** Charles Boer; William Burford; Alfred Corn; Louis Coxe; Josephine Jacobsen; William H. Matchett; Frederick Seidel; Paul Zimmer; Harriet Zinnes.

PARKER, Derek. Author of many books, including *The Fall of Phaeton* (poetry), 1954, *Byron and His World,* 1968, *John Donne and His World,* 1974, and works on astrology, the chorus girl, and popular entertainers. Editor of anthologies of poetry and fiction. Registrar of the Royal Literary Fund, and Chairman of the Management Committee of the Society of Authors. Former Editor, *Poetry Review,* London. **Essays:** Alex Comfort; Christopher Fry; John Lehmann; A.L. Rowse; John Smith.

PAUL, Jay S. Associate Professor of English, Christopher Newport College, Newport News, Virginia. Author of poetry, fiction, essays, and reviews in periodicals. **Essays:** Bob Dylan; Nikki Giovanni; William Matthews; Heather McHugh; Linda Pastan; George Starbuck.

PEREIRA, E. Professor of English, University of South Africa, Pretoria. Author of radio broadcasts, and articles in journals, encyclopedias, and *The Dictionary of South African Biography.* Editor of the anthologies *The Poet's Circle, Contemporary South African Plays,* and *Tellers of Tales, Singers of Songs,* and co-editor of *Companion to South African English Literature,* a collected edition of Thomas Pringle, and Pauline Smith's miscellaneous prose writings. President of the English Academy of Southern Africa, 1981-83. **Essays:** Perseus Adams; Chris Mann; David Wright.

PERLOFF, Marjorie. Florence R. Scott Professor of English, University of Southern California, Los Angeles. Author of *Rhyme and Meaning in the Poetry of Yeats,* 1970, *The Poetic Art of Robert Lowell,* 1973, *Frank O'Hara: Poet among Painters,* 1977, *The Other Tradition: Towards a Postmodern Poetry,* 1980, *George Oppen, Man and Poet,* 1981, *The Poetics of Indeterminancy,* 1982, and an article on Frank O'Hara and John Ashbery in *Yearbook of English Studies,* 1978. **Essays:** David Antin; John Ashbery; Kathleen Fraser; Charles Wright.

PETERSEN, Kirsten Holst. Member of the Commonwealth Literature Division, University of Aarhus, Denmark; reviewer for *Danida.* Author of *A Critical View on John Pepper Clark's Selected Poems,* 1981. Editor of *Enigma of Values* (with Anna Rutherford), 1975. **Essays:** John Pepper Clark; Roy Macnab; Harold Stewart.

PLOMER, William. Novelist, short story writer, and poet. His most recent books were *Celebrations* (verse), 1972, and *The Autobiography*, 1975; *Electric Delights* (selections), edited by Rupert Hart-Davis, was published in 1978. Died 1973.

PORTER, Peter. See his own entry. **Essays:** George MacBeth; George Szirtes.

PRESS, John. Former British Council Officer; retired 1980. Author of three books of poetry and several critical works, including *Rule and Energy*, 1963, *A Map of Modern English Verse*, 1969, *The Lengthening Shadows*, 1971, *John Betjeman*, 1974, *Poets of World War I*, 1983, and *Poets of World War II*, 1984. **Essays:** J.C. Hall; Laurence Whistler.

PURSGLOVE, Glyn. Lecturer in English, University College, Swansea. Author of *Francis Warner and Tradition: An Introduction to the Plays*, 1981. Editor and translator of a forthcoming bilingual anthology of poetry from Renaissance Ferrara. **Essays:** Ronald Bottrall; Kenward Elmslie; Robert Kelly; Brendan Kennelly; William Oxley.

RAVENSCROFT, Arthur. Senior Lecturer in English Literature, University of Leeds. Author of *Chinua Achebe*, 1969 (revised 1977), *Nigerian Writers and the African Past*, 1978, and co-author of *A Guide to 20th-Century English, Irish and Commonwealth Literature*, 1983. Translator, with C.K. Johnman, of *Journal of Jan Van Riebeeck*, vol. 3, 1958. Founding Editor of *Journal of Commonwealth Literature*, 1965-79.

RAY, David. See his own entry. **Essays:** James Dickey; Ed Dorn; Patricia Goedicke; Josephine Miles; Howard Moss; John Frederick Nims; Charles Olson (appendix); Harvey Shapiro; Stephen Spender.

REILLY, John M. Professor of English, State University of New York at Albany. Author of bibliographical essays on Black Literature in *American Literary Scholarship* and of articles on Afro-American writers and popular literature. Editor of *Twentieth-Century Interpretations of "Invisible Man,"* 1970, *Richard Wright: The Critical Reception*, 1978, the reference book *Twentieth-Century Crime and Mystery Writers*, 1980 (2nd edition 1985), and *Afro-American Literature* (with Robert B. Stepto), 1982. **Essays:** Alvin Aubert; Clarence Major; Dudley Randall; Al Young.

RICKARDS, Colin. Press correspondent in Latin America and the Caribbean for 12 years; now with Caribnews, London. Author of *Caribbean Power*, 1963, and *The Man from Devil's Island*, 1968, and several books about the American West. **Essay:** Louise Bennett.

ROBINSON, James K. Professor of English, University of Cincinnati. Editor of *The Mayor of Casterbridge* by Hardy and of several anthologies. **Essays:** Wendell Berry; Tess Gallagher; Louise Glück; David Wagoner.

RODDICK, Alan. See his own entry. **Essays:** Sam Hunt; Kevin Ireland.

RODRIGUEZ, Judith. See her own entry. **Essays:** John Blight; Vincent Buckley; Dorothy Hewett; Les A. Murray; Philip Roberts; Andrew Taylor.

RUSS, Lawrence. Free-lance writer; verse published in magazines and anthologies. **Essays:** Milton Kessler; Lou Lipsitz; Jack Marshall; David Young.

RUTHERFORD, Anna. Head of the Commonwealth Literature Division, University of Aarhus, Denmark; Editor of *Kunapipi*, and Chairman of the European branch of the Commonwealth Literature and Language Association. Editor of *Commonwealth Short Stories* (with Donald Hannah), 1971, *Commonwealth* (essays), 1972, and *Enigma of Values* (with Kirsten Holst Petersen), 1975. **Essay:** J.R. Rowland.

SADLER, Geoff. Free-lance writer of western and plantation novels, as Jeff Sadler and Geoffrey Sadler. **Essays:** Gavin Bantock; Kevin Crossley-Holland; Ruth Fainlight; Karen Gershon; Adrian Henri; Brian Jones; Christopher Logue; Roger McGough; Adrian Mitchell; Brian Patten; Anthony Thwaite; Daniel Weissbort.

SAFFIOTI, Carol Lee. Associate Professor of English, University of Wisconsin-Parkside, Kenosha. **Essay:** Sterling A. Brown.

SCHMIDT, Michael. See his own entry.

SCHROEDER, Andreas. See his own entry. **Essay:** Michael Bullock.

SCOTT, Alexander. See his own entry. **Essays:** Donald Campbell; Alan Jackson.

SCUPHAM, Peter. See his own entry. **Essays:** Freda Downie; Neil Powell.

SEDGWICK, Fred. Headmaster, Downing Primary School, Ipswich, Essex. Author of several books of poetry, most recently *From Another Part of the Island*, 1981, and *A Garland for William Cowper*, 1984. **Essays:** Douglas Dunn; David Sweetman.

SERGEANT, Howard. See his own entry. **Essays:** Kofi Awoonor; Taner Baybars; Martin Booth; Kwesi Brew; Edwin Brock; Jack Clemo; Marcus Cumberlege; John Figueroa; Robert Gittings; Bryn Griffiths; Harry Guest; Keith Harrison; Philip Hobsbaum; Geoffrey Holloway; Jenny Joseph; Douglas Livingstone; Charles Madge; Wes Magee; Gabriel Okara; Betty Parvin; W.H. Petty; Paul Roche.

SEYMOUR-SMITH, Martin. See his own entry. **Essays:** John Malcolm Brinnin; George Buchanan; Federico Espino; Robert Fitzgerald; Ian Fletcher; Denis Goacher; Robert Graves; Charles Higham; Andrew Hoyem; Alejandrino G. Hufana; Peter Jay; P.J. Kavanagh; Edward Lowbury; James J. McAuley; Kathleen Nott; Jon Stallworthy; John Tagliabue; Ivan White; Hubert Witheford.

SHAPCOTT, Thomas W. See his own entry. **Essays:** Robert Adamson; Bruce Dawe; Rosemary Dobson; Rodney Hall; Evan Jones; David Malouf; John Manifold; Craig Powell; Roland Robinson; Judith Rodriguez; David Rowbotham; R.A. Simpson; Vivian Smith; Douglas Stewart; John Tranter; Chris Wallace-Crabbe.

SHAPIRO, David. See his own entry. **Essay:** Frank O'Hara (appendix).

SHARMA, J.N. Professor of English, University of Jodhpur, India. **Essays:** Sam Cornish; Kamala Das.

SHEPPARD, Robert. Author of two books of poetry—*The Frightened Summer*, 1981, and *Returns*, 1985—and of reviews in *PN Review* and other periodicals. Co-Editor of *Rock Drill*. **Essay:** Bob Cobbing.

SHERMAN, William David. Free-lance writer and teacher. Author of several books of poetry (most recently *Heart Attack and*

Spanish Songs in Mandaine, 1981, and *The Time the A's Went West*, 1982), two books on film, a screenplay, and articles and reviews in many journals. **Essay:** Allen Fisher.

SHUCARD, Alan R. Associate Professor of English, University of Wisconsin-Parkside, Kenosha. Author of three books of poetry and a study of Countee Cullen. **Essays:** Mari Evans; Stanley Moss.

SILKIN, Jon. See his own entry. **Essay:** Michael Hamburger.

SMITH, A.J.M. Late Professor of English, Michigan State University, East Lansing. Author of 6 books of poetry (the most recent was *The Classic Shade: Selected Poems*, 1978), and books on Robert Bridges, E.J. Pratt, and Canadian literature. Editor of many general collections of poetry and of specialised collections of Canadian writing. Died 1980. **Essays:** Margaret Avison; Ralph Gustafson; Irving Layton; Jay Macpherson; F.R. Scott.

SMITH, Stan. Senior Lecturer in English, University of Dundee, Scotland. Author of *A Sadly Contracted Hero: The Comic Self in Post-War American Fiction*, 1981, *Inviolable Voice: History and Twentieth-Century Poetry*, 1982, the introduction to *20th-Century Poetry*, 1983, essays in collections and journals, and forthcoming studies of Auden and of the origins of modernism. **Essays:** Basil Bunting; Seamus Heaney; Ted Hughes; Christopher Middleton; John Montague; Peter Redgrove; Iain Crichton Smith; Anne Stevenson; R.S. Thomas.

SMITHYMAN, Kendrick. See his own entry. **Essays:** Louis Johnson; Bill Manhire; Keith Sinclair; Elizabeth Smither; C.K. Stead.

SOAR, Geoffrey. Assistant Librarian, University College Library, London. **Essays:** Edwin Morgan; Tom Pickard.

SQUIRES, Radcliffe. See his own entry. **Essay:** Brewster Ghiselin.

STAFFORD, William. See his own entry. **Essays:** William Everson; May Swenson.

STAUFFER, Donald Barlow. Associate Professor of English, State University of New York, Albany. Author of several articles on Poe, and *A Short History of American Poetry*, 1974. **Essays:** Stanley Burnshaw; Gregory Corso; Barry Spacks.

STEAD, C.K. See his own entry. **Essays:** Allen Curnow; Janet Frame; David Mitchell; Alistair Paterson; Alan Roddick; Hone Tuwhare; Ian Wedde.

STEELE, Timothy. Free-lance writer, currently a Guggenheim Fellow. Author of one collection of poetry—*Uncertainties and Rest*, 1979—and three chapbooks (most recently *On Harmony*, 1984). **Essay:** Charles Gullans.

STERN, Carol Simpson. Professor, Department of Performance Studies, Northwestern University, Evanston, Illinois. Member of the advisory board, *Literature in Performance*, research consultant and contributor, *English Literature in Transition*, and theatre and book reviewer for *Victorian Studies* and Chicago *Sun-Times*. **Essays:** A. Alvarez; Peter Everwine; Pauline Hanson; Erica Jong; Susan Musgrave; Kenneth Pitchford; Stephen Sandy; Jon Silkin; Richard Wilbur.

STEVENS, Joan. Professor of English, Victoria University, Wellington, New Zealand; now retired. Author of *The New Zealand Novel 1860-1965*, 1966, *New Zealand Short Stories: A Survey*, 1968, and articles on the Brontës, Thackeray, and Dickens. Editor of works by Sir John Logan Campbell, Edward Wakefield, George Chamier, and Mary Taylor. **Essay:** Ruth Gilbert.

STEVENSON, Anne. See her own entry. **Essays:** Penelope Shuttle; Radcliffe Squires; Richard Tillinghast.

STEWART, Douglas. See his own entry. **Essay:** Robert D. Fitz-Gerald.

STRAUSS, Jennifer. Senior Lecturer in English, Monash University, Clayton, Victoria. **Essays:** John Forbes; Gwen Harwood; Thomas W. Shapcott.

STRYK, Lucien. See his own entry. **Essay:** James Schevill.

SULLIVAN, Rosemary. Associate Professor of English, University of Toronto. Author of *Theodore Roethke: The Garden Master*, 1975, and of articles on Roethke, Samuel Beckett, Robert Lowell, Margaret Atwood, and P.K. Page. **Essays:** Patrick Lane; Theodore Roethke (appendix).

SUTHERLAND, Fraser. Free-lance writer; Managing Editor of *Books in Canada*, Toronto. Author of several books, including *The Style of Innocence: A Study of Hemingway and Callaghan*, 1972, *Madwomen* (poetry), 1978, and *John Glassco: An Essay and Bibliography*, 1984, and of fiction, poetry, and criticism in journals and anthologies. **Essays:** Marilyn Bowering; Robert Bringhurst; Florence NcNeil; Robert Zend.

SYLVESTER, William. Professor of English and Comparative Literature, State University of New York, Buffalo. Author of *Honky in the Woodpile*, 1982, *Dig the Flower Children*, 1983, *Listen to the Ice*, 1984, and criticism in *Sagetrieb* and *Credences*. **Essays:** Maya Angelou; Andrew Crozier; Daniel Hoffman; Michael McClure; David Meltzer; Louis Zukofsky (appendix).

SYMONS, Julian. See his own entry. **Essay:** Alan Ross.

TAGGART, John. Member of the Department of English, Shippensburg State College, Pennsylvania; Editor of *Maps* poetry magazine. Author of 5 books of poetry and articles on William Bronk and Louis Zukofsky. **Essay:** Toby Olson.

TATE, Allen. Poet, novelist, and literary critic. Collections of his work include *Collected Poems*, 1977, *The Fathers and Other Fiction*, 1976, *Collected Essays*, 1959, and *Memoirs and Opinions*, 1975. Died 1979.

TAYLOR, Henry. Professor of Literature, American University, Washington, D.C. Author of three books of verse—*The Horse Show at Midnight*, 1966, *Breakings*, 1971, and *Afternoon of Pocket Billiards*, 1975—and *Poetry: Points of Departure* (textbook), 1974, and *Desperado*, 1979. Editor of *The Water of Light: A Miscellany in Honor of Brewster Ghiselin*, 1976. Co-translator of *The Children of Herakles* by Euripides, 1981. **Essays:** Samuel Hazo; Robert Watson.

TAYLOR, Myron. Associate Professor of English, State University of New York, Albany. Author of articles on Shakespeare in *The Christian Scholar, Studies in English*, and *Shakespeare Quarterly*. **Essay:** Daniel Berrigan.

TERRY, Arthur. Professor of Literature, University of Essex,

Colchester. Author of *Catalan Literature*, 1972, and a study of Antonio Machado. Editor of *An Anthology of Spanish Poetry 1500-1700*, 2 vols., 1965-68, and *Selected Poems of Ausias March*, 1976. **Essay:** Laurence Lerner.

THWAITE, Anthony. See his own entry. **Essays:** Kingsley Amis; George Barker; Patricia Beer; Charles Causley; Philip Larkin; Anne Ridler; Vernon Scannell.

TOWNS, Saundra. Lecturer in English, Bernard Baruch College, City University of New York. Author of essays and reviews in *The Nation, Black Books Bulletin, Black World, Black Position*, and other periodicals. **Essays:** June Jordan; Keorapetse Kgositsile; Audre Lorde; Raymond R. Patterson.

TRIPP, John. See his own entry. **Essays:** Anthony Conran; Robert Morgan; A.G. Prys-Jones; Meic Stephens; Harri Webb; Gwyn Williams; John Stuart Williams.

TRUE, Michael. Professor of English, Assumption College, Worcester, Massachusetts. Author of *Worcester Poets*, 1972, *Poets in the Schools: A Handbook*, 1976, *Homemade Social Justice*, 1982, and articles on Karl Shapiro and other writers in *Contemporary Literary Criticism, American Writers, Commonweal, New Republic*, and other periodicals. **Essays:** Stephen Dunn; Barbara Guest; David Ignatow; Maxine Kumin; Stanley Kunitz; John L'Heureux; Dave Smith; Ken Smith; Reed Whittemore; C.K. Williams.

TULIP, James. Associate Professor of English, Sydney University. **Essay:** Grace Perry.

VAS DIAS, Robert. See his own entry. **Essays:** John Ash; Paul Blackburn (appendix); Michael Heller.

VENKATACHARI, K. Professor of English, Andhra Pradesh Open University, Hyderabad, India. **Essays:** Arun Kolatkar; Shiv K. Kumar.

WAGNER, Linda W. Professor of English, Michigan State University, East Lansing; Editor of *Centennial Review*. Author of *The Poems* (1964) and *Prose* (1970) *of William Carlos Williams, Denise Levertov*, 1967, *Hemingway and Faulkner: Inventors, Masters*, 1975, *Introducing Poems*, 1976, *John Dos Passos*, 1979, and *Ellen Glasgow: Beyond Convention*, 1982. Editor of *Critical Essays on Sylvia Plath*, 1984. **Essays:** Carolyn Forché; Robert Vas Dias.

WAKOSKI, Diane. See her own entry. **Essays:** Charles Bukowski; Clayton Eshleman; Denise Levertov; Mary Oliver; Joel Oppenheimer; Carl Rakosi; Jerome Rothenberg; Armand Schwerner; Peter Wild; John Yau.

WALSH, William. Professor of Commonwealth Literature, Chairman of the School of English, and Acting Vice-Chancellor, University of Leeds; now retired. Author of *Use of Imagination*, 1958, *A Human Idiom*, 1964, *A Manifold Voice*, 1970, and books on R.K. Narayan, V.S. Naipaul, D.J. Enright, Patrick White, F.R. Leavis, Coleridge, and Keats. **Essays:** A.L. Hendriks; George Johnston; Frederic Prokosch.

WATT, R.J.C. Lecturer in English, University of Dundee, Scotland. **Essays:** Henry Graham; Medbh McGuckian; Jeff Nuttall; Jeffrey Wainwright; Andrew Waterman; Clive Wilmer.

WEINBERGER, Eliot. Free-lance poet and translator; Editor of the poetry journal *Montemora*, New York. Most recently translator and editor of *Selected Poems* by Octavio Paz and *Seven Nights* by Jorge Luis Borges; editor of the forthcoming *Random House Book of 20th-Century Spanish Poetry*. **Essays:** Jonathan Griffin; Nathaniel Tarn.

WHEALE, Nigel. Member of the Faculty, Cambridgeshire College of Arts and Technology. Author of reviews in *Times Literary Supplement, Poetry Review*, and *JEGP*, poetry in *Grosseteste Review*, and a forthcoming collection of poetry. **Essay:** J.H. Prynne.

WILLIAMS, John Stuart. See his own entry. **Essay:** Roland Mathias.

WILLY, Margaret. Lecturer for the British Council, and at the City Literary Institute and Morley College, London. Author of two books of poetry (*The Invisible Sun*, 1946, and *Every Star a Tongue*, 1951), and several critical books, including studies of Chaucer, Traherne, Fielding, Browning, Crashaw, Vaughan, Emily Brontë, and English diarists. Editor of two anthologies and of plays by Goldsmith. **Essays:** D.J. Enright; Phoebe Hesketh; Elizabeth Jennings; Robert Minhinnick; Norman Nicholson; John Wain.

WILSON, Joseph. Lecturer in Creative Writing, Anna Maria College, Paxton, Massachusetts. Verse published in little magazines. **Essays:** Michael Dennis Browne; Paul Engle; Joseph Langland; Ned O'Gorman.

WOODCOCK, George. See his own entry. **Essays:** Earle Birney; Eldon Grier; Sid Marty; P.K. Page; Al Purdy; Andreas Schroeder; Robin Skelton; Peter Stevens; Tom Wayman; Phyllis Webb.

WRIGHT, Judith. See her own entry. **Essay:** William Hart-Smith.

YABES, Leopoldo Y. Professor Emeritus of Literature and Philippine Studies, University of the Philippines, Quezon City. Author of more than 20 books and numerous essays and articles; books include *The University and the Fear of Ideas*, 1956, *Philippine Literature in English*, 1958, *The Filipino Struggle for Intellectual Freedom*, 1959, *Jose Rizal on His Centenary*, 1963, *The Ordeal of a Man of Academe*, 1967, and *Graduate Education at the University of the Philippines*, 1975. Editor of many books, most recently *Philippine Short Stories*, 2 vols., 1975-81. Former Editor of *Philippine Social Sciences and Humanities Review*. **Essays:** Ricaredo Demetillo; José Garcia Villa.

YOUNG, Steven. Member of the Department of English, Pomona College, Claremont, California; theatre director and actor. Has made or collaborated on several art books, including *1″ : 1,000,000* (with Mowry Baden), *Fifty Postcard Views*, and *Twelve Images* (with Jan Raithel). **Essays:** Michael Benedikt; Tom Clark.

611639 I T
6-6-89
St James.